# RANDOM HOUSE
# WORD
# MENU™

RANDOM HOUSE

# WORD MENU

™

BY STEPHEN GLAZIER

RANDOM HOUSE, NEW YORK
1992

Copyright © 1992 by The Estate of Stephen Glazier

All rights reserved under International and Pan-American Copyright
Conventions. Published in the United States by Random House,
Inc., New York, and simultaneously in Canada by Random House
of Canada Limited, Toronto.

LIBRARY OF CONGRESS CATALOGING–IN-PUBLICATION DATA

Glazier, Stephen.
        Random House word menu / by Stephen Glazier.
            p.   cm.
        Includes index.
        ISBN 0-679-40030-3
        1. English language—Glossaries, vocabularies, etc.   2. English
    language—Synonyms and antonyms.   3. English language—
    Terms and phrases.   4. Vocabulary.   I. Title.   II. Title: Word
    menu.
    PE1680.G58   1992                                    92-13539
                                                              CIP

Manufactured in the United States of America

FIRST EDITION

In memory of my father, Bill Glazier,
and for Anna, *sine qua nihil*.

# Brief Table of Contents

# ACKNOWLEDGMENTS

Hundreds of people have contributed in many different ways to the creation of the *Random House Word Menu*. Without three in particular, the book might never have been completed. These three are Karen Pedersen, Heide Lange, and Bob Costello.

Karen Pedersen served as my right hand, associate, and collaborator in the early stages of creating the structure and gathering the list of words. She did her conscientious and professional best for deferred payments at well under her regular fee and well below the value of her work.

Heide Lange, my agent at Sanford J. Greenburger, was the finest and most devoted agent an author could hope to have and never lost faith in me. She orchestrated the business aspects brilliantly from beginning to end and stood beside me as an agent and as a friend, providing me the moral and emotional support that I needed.

Bob Costello, as Editor-in-Chief of the Random House Dictionaries, was the first professional lexicographer to recognize my work as valuable and unique. He had the foresight and the courage to place his authority behind it.

For the past twenty years, two very special friends have worked with me in all areas of my writing, providing invaluable encouragement at all times. They are my closest friend and brother, Jeff Spurrier, who listened to all my complaints and ravings and always responded with generosity out of the goodness of his spirit; and Angus Cameron, my mentor in publishing, who worked with me through not one but two ten-year projects and instilled in me the belief that, no matter how audacious, I could do anything I set out to do.

I am grateful to B.J. Markel, my colleague at the Disney Channel magazine, who suggested that the list of words I had been keeping for many years might be useful to other writers and students. For the first time, I realized that these lists, which had always been a private writer's tool for me, might be compiled in a systematic way and made available commercially.

My dear friend Jack Siler (the Colossus of Bouzigues) helped me create the original proposal and develop the initial list of categories. Don Erik Franzen, my attorney in Los Angeles, devised a mechanism through which investors could acquire a portion of the book and other spinoff products. These investors included Dr. Jack Zoldan; Alex Carlin; my mother, Harriet Glazier; Florence Nixon; Mort Olshan; and Mark Wallner.

In the late summer of 1986, Karen and I were deep at work, creating a structure by studying old classification systems and arranging 3 x 5 cards in a fluid and contemporary hierarchy while also developing individual lists. I also hired outside research assistants to take over certain special categories. First and foremost of these contributors was Michael Rich, generator of the original lists for Chemistry, Biology, and Medicine. Several others who deserve special mention are Barry Koffler, Georg Zappler, Terence Mulry, and Roger Packard.

My thanks also go to Phil Friedman, who introduced me to the distinguished lexicographer Walter Glanze. Walter lent his considerable reputation and intellectual support to this project. Peter Skolnik, my first agent at Sanford J. Greenburger, was another early supporter, as was Jim Landis.

I must also thank Mike Weiner and his staff: Karen Atkinson, Jonathan Sacks, Paul Wetehnall, Mark Momuth, Mike Reidlinger, Fran Knight, Kathy Schaeffer, and Caroline Hodgkins. They encouraged me greatly in the development of the hierarchical system.

The entire staff of the Reference and Electronic Publishing Division at Random House deserve my gratitude, particularly my editors, Sol Steinmetz and Enid Pearsons. I feel privileged to have worked with them. Charles Levine and Jack Hornor gave unstintingly of their time and efforts, as did the rest of the staff, especially Catherine Fowler, Charlotte Mayerson, Pat Ehresmann, Joyce O'Connor, Naomi Osnos, Alice Kovac Somoroff, Chris Mohr, Lani Mysak, Barbara Burke, Terry Chisholm, Gus Panagakis, and Maria Padilla.

I would also like to thank my friend and publisher, Michael Mellin, whose enthusiasm and creativity were a constant inspiration. It was he who guided the *Random House Word Menu* through its final year of publication.

In the summer of 1991, I deposited the final version of the 3000-page manuscript at Random House. I then left for a vacation in Mexico, where I became ill. My friends Clifford Irving and Maureen Earle literally saved my life and sent me back to New York, where Dr. Richard Bergland, Chief of Neurosurgery at Beth Israel Medical Center, diagnosed and treated me with skill and compassion. I wish to thank the Higher Power, who enabled me to recognize the need for a book such as this in the world, provided the inspiration to see how to fill that need, and sustained my will over the years it took to bring the conception of the book to its fully realized form.

And finally, I come to my beloved Anna—my muse, editor, co-conspirator, gadfly, and, ultimately, wife—who stood by me every difficult step of the way, offering support, feedback, editorial guidance, and love—*sine qua nihil*.

Stephen Glazier
New York
1991

# STAFF AND CONSULTANTS

Conceived and Created by Stephen Glazier in Association with Karen Pedersen

*Editors:* Sol Steinmetz, Enid Pearsons

*Managing Editor:* Mia McCroskey

*General Editors:* Carol Braham, Robert B. Costello, Joyce O'Connor

*Contributing Editors:* Barry Koffler (Life Sciences), Penny Marienthal, Terence Mulry (Religion), Roger Packard (Chemistry), Michael Rich (Medicine), Roberta Rubin-Dorsky, Georg Zappler (Life Sciences)

*Copy Editors:* James Gullickson, Judy Johnson, Felice Levy, Linda Massie, Jesse T Sheidlower, Alice Kovac Somoroff

*Production Director:* Patricia W. Ehresmann

*Design Director:* Naomi Osnos

*Designer:* Robert Bull Design

*Publisher:* Michael Mellin

*Associate Publishers:* Catherine Fowler, John L. Hornor III

## CONSULTANTS

Lisa Andreini (Photography)
Karen Atkinson (Computers)
Harriet Balkind (Advertising)
Paula Biran (Classical Music)
David Black (Publishing)
Christopher Blunden (Law)
Michael Bunyaner (Securities)
Angus Cameron (Fishing/Hunting/Firearms)
Carl P. Carrigan (Theater)
Dan Del Col (Advertising)
Stephen Donaldson (Prison/Eastern Religions)
Wayne Dynes (Homosexuality)
Peter R. Feuche (Theater)
Andrew Field (Real Estate)
Gary Fleisher (Medicine)
Carl Giordano (Sports)
Donald Goldstein (Economics)
Sharon Goldstein (Linguistics/Grammar/Phonetics)
Jeff Grambs (Weapons/Military)
Lee Greathouse (Telecommunications)
Elizabeth Greenberg (Theater)
Ruth Gross (Psychology)
Joan Keener (Ballet)
Verly Klinkenborg (Literature)
Denise Marika (Sculpture)
Bob Merlis (Rock Era Dances)
Joyce O'Connor (Fashion)

Joan Pancoe (New Age)
Jan Paradise (Medicine)
Enid Pearsons (Computers)
David Peters (Graphic Design)
Alison Postman (Hair Styles)
Bruce Postman (Cinema)
Charles Pye (Taxation/Accounting)
James Rader (Birds/Prefixes and Suffixes)
Anna Raviv (Theater)
Jon Resier (Anatomy)
Kurt Richards (Aircraft)
Deane Rink (Physics)
Jon Rubin (Popular Music)
Carol Sacks (Geology)
Roger Scorcio (Building Materials/Structural Components)
Simon Sheridan (Tools and Hardware)
Martin Smith (Television)
Zachary Smith (Basketball)
Alice Kovac Somoroff (Geography)
Jeff Spurrier (Journalism)
Ann Summa (Photography)
Emanuel Thorne (Mathematics)
Richard Van Dorn (Electricity and Electronics)
William Van Dorn (Ships and Boats)
Antoinette White (Ballet)
Wendell Williams (Automobiles)

# PREFACE

The explosion of knowledge and information in the second half of the twentieth century has been the catalyst of enormous social and technological changes. Since language is an ever-evolving reflection of these changes, lexicons too should reflect them. Yet the most recent classification system for language is Roget's thesaurus, published in 1852.

Not only has the English language evolved to keep pace with new technology and cultural growth, but the way we think has changed as well. Our approach to work and learning in the high-speed age of the computer cannot always accommodate the more patient, intellectual approach of the past. There are times when we want our information quickly, in bite-size chunks, and times when we cannot afford the luxury of searching through disparate sources to find the information we need. The average person today is forced to be a narrow specialist, with only a smattering of knowledge about other subjects, which are often difficult and unfamiliar. Making sense of our complex existence is a daunting task.

In keeping with this task, the *Random House Word Menu®*, conceived and created by the late Stephen Glazier (see Biography of the Author) and produced over a period of eight years, presents an entirely new classification system for language and information. Its goal is to help bring the expanding, multilayered world of the late twentieth century into clearer focus by creating a framework for ordering the mass of information that is constantly bombarding us. This framework is in the form of a structure that allows users to find information with ease in any of hundreds of different subjects and areas of interest.

A hierarchical structure is familiar to most users of the standard thesaurus: it goes from the general to the specific, from the idea or subject to particular words, from the whole to the parts. But whereas the structure of the standard thesaurus is based on philosophical categories such as "Abstract Relations," "Space," "Matter," and "Volition," the structure of this book (outlined in the Table of Contents) is built on natural, contemporary categories and logical relations among not just concepts, but things. Thus the seven major classes in our structure are everyday subjects: Nature, Science and Technology, Domestic Life, Institutions, Arts and Leisure, Language, and The Human Condition. Nature as a class is further divided into three subclasses: The Human Body, Living Things, and The Earth. The Earth, in turn, is broken down into five categories: Geology; Geography; Minerals, Metals, and Rocks; Landscapes and Seascapes; and Weather and Natural Phenomena. Each of these categories is then divided into subcatecories, such as (under Landscapes and Seascapes) Hills, Hollows, and Valleys; Plains and Marshes; Woods and Brush; Inland Waterways and Lakes; and Coastal Land, Islands, and the Sea.

Another important difference between this book and the standard thesaurus is that while the latter deals with common synonyms and antonyms, this book is concerned with *words related by subject*, i.e., with the vocabulary or terminology of hundreds of different areas of knowledge or activity. While we include under certain categories (as Character and Behavior or Common Expressions) numerous synonyms and antonyms, these are subordinate to the purpose of this book, which is to provide information about words in a manner that is not found in any standard thesaurus or dictionary.

Thus, for example, this book contains much information that is usually found in encyclopedias and almanacs, such as the Nations of the World, each with its capital, area in square miles, population number, language, major religion, and currency; the names and descriptions of all the Christian denominations and sects; major world cities; States of the United States; annual national and religious holidays; military ranks; names and functions of government departments; list of common abbreviations; and so on.

Finally, this work differs from the standard thesaurus because it discriminates among its entries with far greater precision, offering definitions of the words it identifies.

The author did not intend this work to replace the usual thesaurus or dictionary. Like a dictionary, it includes thousands of definitions, but it is not a general dictionary. The *Random House Word Menu* is quite different from either a dictionary or a thesaurus, and it is precisely this unique quality that makes it so useful as a companion to these standard references.

The book is designed to be a language tool as well as a creativity tool. As a language tool, it serves the functions of: a reverse dictionary, for finding a word when one knows only the meaning or definition; a thesaurus of related terms, organized by category or subject matter and with entries defined as in dictionary; a collection of diverse glossaries, for learning the terminology of an unfamiliar field or for learning to use technical terms correctly.

As a creativity tool, the book's logical structure and word associations can assist in brainstorming, aid in preliminary research, help overcome creative blocks or memory lapses, and provide a source of words for enlivening everything one writes. We hope that users will also browse through the pages to expand their knowledge and vocabulary as well as for entertainment.

Stephen Glazier created this book as a reference tool for busy writers like himself. All the organizing and defining of terms is done for them. The internal logic and easy associations of the classification system allow them to know instantly where to look for an unknown word in one of the nearly 800 categories and subcategories. The range of subjects, the concise, telegraphic definitions, and the contemporary format offer not only a resource for serious writers but a natural way to build vocabulary, help to solve crossword puzzles or to win at word games, or add vigor and variety to any piece of writing.

The author chose the title carefully, to reflect the idea of a detailed list of items, or minutiae, married to the computer-age concept of a menu: a list of options available to the user. The *Random House Word Menu*'s lists provide a schematic that opens up the English language in a way never before realized. Its single and overriding purpose is to help the writer or speaker find the *mot juste*—the indispensable word that the occasion calls for, no matter how arcane or specialized its references.

All difficult or technical terms, as well as most slang and informal terms, are defined in this book. In order to insure the accuracy and clarity of the definitions, the author availed himself of consultants in many fields, with whom he reviewed not only the pertinent definitions but also the selection of entries for each subject or category. Definitions were thus updated and sharpened, relationships between entries clarified, and obsolete terms replaced with current ones.

In every field, close attention was paid to the most recent advances and developments, especially as reflected in changes and innovations in terminology. The category Biology, for example, includes the Five Kingdoms now used to classify organisms, and the subcategory Viruses is further divided into Bacteriophages, Plant Viruses, and Animal Viruses. The user is urged to examine the classification system in the Table of Contents, for an understanding of the various divisions and subdivisions will make the book's contents more familiar and accessible.

This book extends a lexicographic tradition for which Stephen Glazier had profound respect. He hoped to create a work that would become part of that tradition, that would complement its predecessors by providing a new tool for improving the accuracy and clarity with which we can explore and exploit the incredible range of the English language. He wanted to give us new ways of discovering language and new ways to increase our expressive powers. We who worked closely with Stephen, and came to admire and respect him for his intense dedication, regard this book as a fitting memorial to his indomitable spirit. We believe it is an important contribution to English lexicography, deserving far-reaching recognition and widespread use.

The Editors

# Biography of the Author

Stephen Glazier was born in 1947 in Washington, D.C. A gifted child, he learned to read and write at an early age, encouraged by parents who read to him from the English classics. When he was five years old, the family moved to California. Inspired by family trips to the Shakespeare festival in Ashland, Oregon, Stephen began writing plays at the age of seven on such subjects as the Trojan War, the Three Musketeers, and English royal history. He skipped several grades in elementary school and later attended high school in Exeter, New Hampshire, and La Jolla, California. During his senior year in La Jolla, he was both managing editor of the school paper and a reporter for a local weekly, *La Jolla Journal*. After graduation in 1965 he was admitted to Harvard University, his father's alma mater.

Although he did well at Harvard, after a year he decided to follow his La Jolla classmates, most of whom had enrolled at the University of California at Berkeley. This was then the center of the Free Speech movement and a mecca for the radical young. At Berkeley, Stephen majored in theater, wrote plays, marched in the streets, and became involved with the music scene in the Bay area. He graduated from Berkeley in 1969 and the following year toured Great Britain and the Continent. While in London, he began writing a novel, a sprawling saga of three different families, which he called *Patches*. It was while working on this novel, part of which was set in the 1800s, that he started going through a recently acquired unabridged dictionary, making lists of words, mostly clothing and housing terms, to use in the historical sections of the novel.

The word list expanded as did the novel, which by 1977 had grown to 1400 pages. To make ends meet while writing, Glazier taught English as a second language and spent three months every winter doing income tax work for various accounting firms. In 1978 he found a literary agent and began working at once on the first draft of a new historical novel, *The Lost Provinces*. This book was published in 1981 to excellent reviews, and a year later was optioned for a movie. The producer who optioned it invited Glazier to write the screenplay, which resulted in a new career in Los Angeles as a screenwriter, copywriter, and editor.

In 1982 Glazier became associate editor of the Disney Channel magazine, where he wrote descriptions of shows and on-air programming material. Meanwhile his lists of words continued to grow. One day in 1984 he showed the lists of colors and of verbs of motion to a fellow copywriter at the Disney Channel. His colleague asked to see more of the lists and suggested to Glazier that his personal writer's tool might benefit other writers.

This prospect led Glazier to develop a more systematic and comprehensive approach to his word collection. Recognizing that he was dissatisfied with the existing methods of classifying words and information, he made a study of the classification systems used by Melvil Dewey (of the Dewey library catalog system), the Library of Congress, and Peter Mark Roget, back to Francis Bacon and the trivium and quadrivium of the Middle Ages. The system he finally developed combined a traditional approach to the division of knowledge with a contemporary hierarchical structure influenced by the computer age. Glazier believed this to be a compelling marriage of classic and modern intellectual elements.

During the next two years he divided his time between a new job synopsizing science fiction stories for the story department of Steven Spielberg's Amazing Stories, working on the draft of a new historical novel, *The Caliph's Cup,* and organizing his lists of words on a 64K CPM computer.

By 1985 the basic format and nucleus of what was to become the present book had been worked out, and Glazier's agent had begun submitting proposals for the book to publishing houses. After several rounds of submissions, one publisher accepted it and Glazier set out to create the large book of words he envisioned. He began to hire a staff of research assistants and solicited investors for the project. Within a year he was able to raise the funds he needed. Much of the money went to pay for consultants in the many fields covered in the book. Glazier himself consulted over four hundred books for glossary words and verification of usages.

Two years of work produced a 2000-page manuscript, which was too long for the publisher. A new round of submissions began while Glazier continued working on the book. Finally, in 1989, a 2500-page manuscript was submitted to Random House, and a year later this firm bought the book rights to what is now the *Random House Word Menu*. Glazier was jubilant, for this was the house he had always hoped would publish his book.

During the following two years Glazier became almost a fixture in the Random House Reference Department. He was a charming, personable man, filled with energy and creativity. No amount of work seemed to faze him. He was indefatigable. He could spend hours researching a single fact, for nothing but the truth would satisfy him. He was welcomed at Random House as a colleague and friend, having earned the affection and esteem of the Reference Department staff.

In the fall of 1991, after putting the finishing touches on the now 3000-page manuscript, Glazier set out for a well-deserved vacation in Mexico. Some weeks later friends and relatives received alarming news that he was seriously ill and was returning to New York City for hospital tests and treatment. The tests showed that he had a malignant brain tumor. After surgery and extensive radiation therapy, Stephen seemed to be doing better. Though physically debilitated, his mind was alert and his personality as warm and outgoing as always. His will to live and work was evident. He had lengthy discussions with his editors and publisher over plans for this book. Always by his side was his beloved wife, the actress Anna Raviv, whom he had met in 1985. He seemed happy and at peace. Early in 1992, his condition suddenly worsened. Stephen died on January 20, 1992. He was forty-four years old.

The *Random House Word Menu®* organizes the English language by subject matter. Subject categories are listed in the Table of Contents. The categories are arranged in a logical structure that runs from the general—Nature, or Arts and Leisure—to the specific—the Reproductive System, or Stringed Instruments. The lowest level of the structure contains nearly 800 individual lists, each with 50 to 200 defined terms.

The logical structure and its word associations are designed to make it easy to find the group of words one is seeking. In technical and institutional areas this logic is virtually absolute—*Parts of Ships, Sails, and Equipment* must lie within *Ships and Boats,* which must lie within *Transportation,* which must lie within *Science and Technology.* In nonconcrete areas like *Language, Cognition,* or *Faith,* users will quickly become familiar with the structure so that they can locate *Judgment and Criticism,* or *Magic and the Occult,* or *Exclamations,* or *Verbs of Motion.*

Thus, to find a verb that describes disagreement or opposition, turn first to the category *Judgment and Criticism,* where you will find the subcategory *Opposition, Disagreement, and Attack.* There you can compare definitions and choose from among such terms as "niggle," "nitpick," "quibble," "repudiate," and "take issue with." If these do not seem strong enough, move on to the next subcategory: *Blame, Censure, Ridicule, and Contempt.*

Or to find the difference between a davenport, a divan, an ottoman, and a settee (perhaps you need the word to describe a room in a story, or you plan to talk to a furniture salesperson), turn to the subcategory *Chairs and Sofas* in the list of *Furnishings* under *The Home* in the general class *Domestic Life.*

If you want to know the names of the moons of Jupiter, go to *Celestial Bodies* (in *Astronomy and Space Science*) to find the Galilean moons Callisto, Europa, Ganymede, and Io.

Or, if you can't remember the word for "a close-fitting academic cap with flat, square top and tassel," look under *Hats* (in the category *Hats, Headgear, and Hairpieces*) to find the word "mortarboard."

The reverse-dictionary function can also be useful in solving crossword puzzles, where the clue is a definition and leads to the appropriate subject. For example, a five-letter word beginning with *k* for "a short, curved sword with a broad blade used in India" would lead you to the list of *Blades, Clubs, and Projectiles* under the category *Weapons and Armaments,* where you would find the word "kukri."

Conversely, if you know the word and wish to learn its spelling, definition, or part of speech, look up the word in the Index at the back of the book. Or, if you don't know the word but do know a synonym or related word, look up the latter in the Index. Parts, chapters, and categories are also listed in the Index, in boldface. The Index leads you directly to the page where the word you are looking for is listed.

Another quick way to find information in the book is by checking the Guide Words above the black line at the top of each page. The Guide Words indicate in distinctive type faces the chapter number and subclass, the category, and the subcategory appearing on the page. For example:

**5. TECHNOLOGY**
COMPUTERS
SOFTWARE, LANGUAGES, AND PROGRAMMING

Most words listed under a category have concise definitions, except where they form a long list defined by its heading, as the list of *Pet Names* under the category *Terms of Endearment and Respect* or the list under *Meats and Cuts of Meat.*

Many entry words are followed by italicized labels that describe the level of usage of a word. The commonest of these restrictive labels are *Slang* and *Informal.* These labels are often very specific, as, for example, *Vulgar Slang, Yiddish Derogatory Slang.* Labels serve to warn you that using the labeled word in formal contexts may be inappropriate. Trademarks are indicated by the italicized label *Trademark* before the definition.

Though this book includes definitions, it is clearly not intended to replace a standard dictionary. Pronunciations of words, etymologies, and usage notes are not included in this book, and users should consult a standard college-level dictionary, such as the *Random House Webster's College Dictionary,* to obtain this and other more detailed lexical information.

Again, unlike a standard dictionary, this book does not provide all the meanings of a word in one place. Instead, each meaning or usage of a word appears as a separate entry in the appropriate place in the structure. For example, the word "mole" appears in eight places: *Animals; Chemistry; Medical Problems; Machinery; Ships and Boats; Foods; International Relations; and Strategy, Intrigue, and Deception.*

Definitions of the same word appearing under different categories (for example, *Trinity,* appearing under two categories) may differ in wording in order to focus on the distinctive use of the word in each category.

All listed words, defined and undefined, are arranged in alphabetical order. Example: *solar, solar corona, solar eclipse, solar flare, solar nebula, solar wind, solstice.*

With few exceptions, nouns and noun phrases are listed without a part-of-speech label. Verbs, adjectives, and adverbs are given an abbreviated part-of-speech label after the entry word. The labels appear in italics within parentheses, thus: (*vb*) for verbs, (*adj*) for adjectives, (*adv*) for adverbs. Defined entries whose headings indicate exclusive verbal use (e.g., *Eating Verbs*) do not show the (*vb*) part-of-speech label.

Derivatives of words, as those ending in *-ed, -ing, -ly, -ness,* and *-ation,* are usually not listed separately from the base word. We thus enter "abjure" but not abjuration, "indict" but not indictment, "relative" but not relatively, "paradox" but not paradoxical or paradoxically.

To show the network of relationships among subject categories, a list of "See also" cross references to related subjects is given at the beginning of each category. Thus, below the heading of the category *Kinship and Family Relations,* you will find cross references to the categories *Marriage and Divorce, Parents and Children, Anthropology,* and *Sociology.*

The following abbreviations occur in the book:

| | | |
|------|---|-----------|
| adj | = | adjective |
| adv | = | adverb |
| arch. | = | archaic |
| Brit. | = | British |
| c. | = | century |
| etc. | = | et cetera |
| esp. | = | especially |
| lit. | = | literally |
| n | = | noun |
| opp. | = | opposite |
| orig. | = | originally |
| pl. | = | plural |
| sing. | = | singular |
| usu. | = | usually |
| vb | = | verb |

The best way to become familiar with this book is to use it, especially as a quick reference for certain types of information: a list of the world's currencies (Chapter 12 - THE ECONOMY, *Finance, World Currencies*); or a list of medical prefixes and suffixes (Chapter 4 - THE SCIENCES, *Medicine, Prefixes and Suffixes*); or a list of cyclical events (Chapter 3 - THE EARTH, *Weather and Natural Phenomena, Forecasting and Meteorology/Cyclical Events*).

Or you might use the book to find a Latin, French, or other synonym for an English word (Chapter 21 - FOREIGN EXPRESSIONS); or to find a particular job title (Chapter 12 - THE ECONOMY, *Occupations and Job Titles*) or a list of titles and ranks (Chapter 11 - SOCIAL ORDER, *Titles of Rank*); or to find the correct name of a particular tool (Chapter 5 - TECHNOLOGY, *Tools and Hardware, Common Tools and Tool Types*).

You can find all of these and many other types of information by any of the three routes described above: the Table of Contents, the Guide Words, or the Index. Before long you will find this volume to be a useful and indispensable reference book.

# TABLE OF CONTENTS

RANDOM HOUSE

# WORD MENU™

# NATURE

# CHAPTER 1

# The Human Body

# ANATOMY

Head and Neck
Eyes
Ears
Mouth and Teeth
Trunk
Limbs and Extremities
Brain and Central Nervous System
Heart, Circulatory, and Lymphatic System
Digestive and Excretory System
Respiratory System
Endocrine System and Glands
Reproductive System
Skeleton
Muscles
Tissue, Fiber, and Integumentary System

**SEE ALSO**: Chap. 1: Medical Problems; Health, Fitness, and Enhancement; Physical Appearance; Chap. 2: Biology; Chap. 4: Medicine; Chap. 8: Parents and Children; Chap. 24: Death

## HEAD AND NECK

**Adam's apple** projection of thyroid cartilage in front of throat; thyroid cartilage

**adenoids** growths of lymphoid tissue in upper pharynx at rear of throat

**beak** *Slang*. nose

**bean** *Slang*. head

**bridge** bony portion of nose where it joins brow

**brow** forehead

**buccal cavity** hollow formed by mouth containing tongue, teeth, and salivary glands

**cheek** side of face below eye, between nose and ear

**cheekbone** outer portion of eye's bony orbit, reaching across upper cheek

**chin** portion of face below lower lip at projection of lower jaw

**coconut** *Slang*. head, skull

**cranial cavity** hollow formed by skull, containing brain

**cranium** bone enclosing brain; skull excluding lower jaw

**epiglottis** flap of cartilage covering windpipe to prevent swallowed food from entering lungs

**esophagus** tube through which food passes from pharynx to stomach

**face** front of head beneath hairline, including eyes, nose, mouth, and chin

**forehead** flat front of face between eyebrows and hairline

**gourd** *Slang*. head

**hair** fine, threadlike growth, esp. covering top of skull

**head** bony topmost portion of body, containing brain and sense organs

**jaw** hinged bones that frame mouth, open and close it, and hold teeth

**kisser** *Slang*. face

**larynx** muscles and cartilage at upper end of trachea holding vocal cords

**lip** either of two fleshy folds that form opening of mouth, used in speech

**mandible** bone of lower jaw

**mastoid process** projection of skull behind ear

**maxilla** bone of upper jaw

**mouth** opening framed by lips through which food enters body; speech organ

**mug** *Slang*. face

**muzzle** *Slang*. projecting portion of face, esp. nose

**nape** back of neck

**nares** nostrils, nasal openings

**nasal cavity** hollow containing sinuses and interior of nose

**neck** top of spinal column between skull and shoulders, connecting head to trunk

**noggin** *Slang*. head

**noodle** *Slang*. head

**nose** narrow, projecting part of face between mouth and eyes with two openings for passage of air into body; organ of smell

**nostril** one of two external openings of nose; one of the nares

**occiput** back portion of skull

**orbital cavity** bony hollow containing eyeball

**pate** top of head

**pharynx** top of alimentary canal leading from mouth and nose to larynx and esophagus

**philtrum** vertical groove on surface of upper lip, below septum of nose

**proboscis** snoutlike nose

**puss** *Slang*. face

**scalp** skin across top and rear of skull, usu. covered with hair

**schnozz** *Slang*. nose

**scruff** back of neck

**sebum** oily secretion of sebaceous glands that keeps hair and scalp soft and waterproof

**septum** dividing wall or membrane, esp. between nostrils of nose

**sinus** hollow air cavity beneath skull connected to nostrils

**skull** bones that cover brain and frame face

**snoot** *Slang*. nose

**snout** *Slang*. nose

**temple** flattened surface on either side of forehead in front of ear

**throat** interior passageway through neck from chin to collarbone

**thyroid cartilage** Adam's apple

**tongue** movable muscular part of floor of mouth, used in talking, tasting, and eating

**tonsil** either of two masses of lymphoid tissue lying on each side of throat at rear of mouth

**trachea** main tube carrying air from larynx to two bronchi entering lungs

**vocal cords** the lower of two pairs of mucous membrane folds in laryngeal cavity that vibrate to produce speech sounds

**voice box** larynx

**windpipe** trachea

# EYES

**aqueous humor**  jellylike fluid that fills eye chamber in front of lens

**baby blues**  *Slang.* eyes

**blind spot**  point where optic nerve joins retina that is insensitive to light

**blinkers**  *Slang.* eyes

**bony orbit**  framework of bones surrounding eye socket

**choroid coat**  pigmented membrane that is continuous with iris and that nourishes retina and absorbs scattered light

**ciliary body**  smooth muscle and its connection to suspensory ligament of lens

**conjunctiva**  protective layer of mucous membrane lining inner surface of eyelid over cornea

**cornea**  transparent covering over iris that produces refraction needed to focus image on retina

**epicanthic fold**  epicanthus

**epicanthus**  long fold of skin on upper eyelid; epicanthic fold

**eye**  receptor of light and organ of sight

**eyeball**  globe of the eye containing nervous tissue stimulated by light

**eyebrow**  ridge over eye socket with hair growing on it

**eyelash**  fringe of hair growing on edge of eyelid

**eyelid**  protective lid of skin and muscle that closes over eye

**eye socket**  hollow of bone in face holding eyeball; orbital cavity

**fovea centralis**  small depression at back of retina that is point of sharpest vision

**iris**  colored circular muscle in front of eye that controls amount of light entering eye

**lens**  transparent, biconvex element between iris and vitreous humor that focuses light rays on retina

**optic nerve**  nerve that sends sight impulses from eye to brain

**orbital cavity**  bony hollow containing eyeball

**peepers**  *Slang.* eyes

**pupil**  round contractile aperture in iris of eye

**retina**  inner layer of eye wall composed of nervous tissue stimulated by light to send impulses to brain

**sclera**  tough, white, fibrous membrane forming protective outer wall of eyeball except area of cornea

**twenty-twenty**  *(adj)* having normal visual acuity

**vitreous humor**  jellylike material that fills eyeball and forms its shape

# EARS

**auditory nerve**  either of pair of cranial nerves, consisting of sensory fibers that conduct impulses from ear to brain

**auricle**  pinna

**cerumen**  ear wax; yellow, waxlike secretion of external ear

**cochlea**  spiral tube in inner ear filled with liquid that senses loudness and pitch and sends nerve impulses to brain

**concha**  shell-like structure of external ear

**ear**  organ of hearing and equilibrium consisting of outer, middle, and inner ears

**ear canal**  bony cavity from eardrum to opening of external ear

**eardrum**  thin, vibrating membrane over middle ear; tympanic membrane

**ear wax**  cerumen

**Eustachian tube**  canal from middle ear to pharynx

**helix**  curved fold along rim of external ear

**incus**  anvil-shaped ossicle of middle ear

**inner ear**  receptor for sound and sense organ of balance

**labyrinth**  system of tubes and hollows in inner ear

**lobe**  fleshy lower tip of outer ear

**malleus**  hammerlike outermost ossicle of middle ear

**middle ear**  part of ear with eardrum and bony adjacent cavity; tympanum

**organ of Corti**  part of ear in cochlea that hears sounds

**ossicle**  small bone in middle ear that passes vibrations from eardrum to oval window: incus, malleus, or stapes

**outer ear**  short, protective tube leading to eardrum

**oval window**  thin membrane that passes vibrations from middle ear to labyrinth of inner ear

**pinna**  structure of skin and cartilage fixed to head forming visible portion of outer ear; auricle

**saccule**  smaller of two saclike cavities in labyrinth

**semicircular canal**  one of three curved tubular canals in labyrinth of ear, serving to maintain equilibrium

**stapes**  stirrup-shaped innermost ossicle of middle ear

**tragus**  nublike prominence at front of external opening of ear

**tympanic membrane**  eardrum

**tympanum**  middle ear

**utricle**  larger of two saclike cavities in labyrinth

**vestibule**  hollow forming approach to inner ear

# MOUTH AND TEETH

**alveolus**  socket within jawbone in which roots of teeth are set

**bicuspid**  premolar tooth with two-pointed crown

**buccal cavity**  hollow formed by mouth containing tongue, teeth, and salivary glands

**canine**  sharp, pointed tooth behind incisor

**cementum**  thin bony tissue covering roots of tooth

**choppers**  *Slang.* teeth

**crown**  enameled portion of tooth above gum line

**cusp**  pointed projection on crown of tooth

**cuspid**  canine tooth with single-pointed crown

**dentine**  hard, bonelike substance forming main part of tooth

**enamel**  hard substance forming outer cover of tooth

**fangs**  *Slang.* teeth, esp. cuspids

**gingiva**  gum

**grinders**  *Slang.* teeth, esp. molars

**gum**  soft tissue portion of jaw enveloping bases of teeth; gingiva

**incisor**  tooth with cutting edge at front of mouth

**ivories**  *Slang.* teeth

**lips**  two fleshy folds that form opening of mouth

**molar**  flat-surfaced grinding tooth at rear of mouth

**mouth**  opening through which food enters body, also used in forming speech sounds

**neck**  narrowed portion of tooth between crown and root

**occlusion**  fitting together of teeth of lower jaw with teeth of upper jaw

**overbite** occlusion in which upper incisor teeth overlap lower ones

**palate** roof of mouth, separating it from nasal cavity

**pearly whites** *Slang.* teeth

**periodontal membrane** fibrous connective tissue between cementum of tooth and alveolus

**premolar** bicuspid tooth in front of molar

**pulp** soft tissue at center of tooth containing nerves and blood vessels

**rictus** opening of the mouth

**root** part of tooth embedded in and attached to gum

**saliva** mucus-containing liquid secreted by glands in mouth to lubricate passage of food through alimentary canal

**soft palate** posterior, muscular portion of palate; velum

**taste bud** receptor of taste on surface of tongue that responds to bitter, sweet, sour, or salt

**tongue** movable fleshy part of floor of mouth with sense receptors and small glands that assists in talking and eating

**tooth** hard, usu. sharp, bony structure in mouth for biting food

**trap** *Slang.* mouth

**underbite** occlusion in which lower incisor teeth overlap upper ones

**uvula** pendent fleshy lobe in middle posterior of palate

**velum** soft palate

**wisdom tooth** third molar at rear of mouth

**yap** *Slang.* mouth

## TRUNK

**abdomen** part of body lying between thorax and pelvis and containing digestive organs; belly

**abdominal cavity** hollow within abdomen containing digestive organs

**appendix** narrow, blind tube three inches long in lower right part of abdomen; vermiform appendix

**back** rear part of body from neck to base of spine

**backbone** spinal column

**belly** midriff; abdomen

**bellybutton** *Informal.* navel

**bosom** breast, esp. female

**breadbasket** *Slang.* stomach

**breast** front upper portion of chest; either of two milk-secreting glands in upper chest of female; corresponding undeveloped gland in male

**breastbone** sternum

**buttocks** rear of hip forming fleshy seat for body; *Slang:* arse, ass, backside, behind, bippy, booty, bottom, bum, buns, butt, can, cheeks, derrière, duff, fanny, gluteus maximus, heinie, hind end, keister, patootie, posterior, prat, rear, rear end, rump, seat, stern, tail, tokus, tush

**chest** part of body enclosed by ribs and sternum

**clavicle** bone linking sternum and scapula; collarbone

**coccyx** end of spinal column beyond sacrum that represents vestigial tail

**collarbone** clavicle

**crotch** point where legs fork from base of trunk

**dorsal** (*adj*) on or near the backside

**groin** juncture of lower abdomen and inner thigh

**hipbone** either of two bones forming sides of pelvis

**ilium** broad upper portion of hipbone

**ischium** lower portion of hipbone

**loin** region on either side of spinal column between hip and ribs

**love handles** *Slang.* rolls of fat around midriff

**midriff** front of torso between abdomen and chest

**navel** small scar, usu. depression, in middle of abdomen where umbilical cord was attached to fetus

**nipple** small protuberance of breast where milk duct discharges in female; teat

**paunch** flabby midriff

**pectoral girdle** arch formed by scapulae and clavicles

**pelvic cavity** bony hollow formed by pelvic girdle

**pelvic girdle** arch formed by ilium, ischium, and pubis

**pelvis** basin-shaped skeletal structure formed by pelvic girdle and adjoining bones of spine

**pericardial cavity** thin, membranous sac enclosing heart

**perineum** area between anus and male scrotum or edge of vulva in female

**pleural cavity** thin, membranous lining of chest cavity that encloses lungs

**potbelly** flabby midriff

**pubis** part of hipbone forming front of pelvis

**rib** paired curved bones protecting entire viscera, ten fixed and two floating

**sacrum** compound bone forming back of pelvis

**scapula** large triangular bone lying in each dorsal lateral part of thorax; shoulder blade

**shoulder blade** scapula

**solar plexus** nerve complex at pit of stomach

**spare tire** *Informal.* roll of fat around midriff

**spinal column** series of joined vertebrae forming axial support for skeleton and carrying nerves; backbone; spine

**spine** spinal column

**sternum** flat bone of upper chest connecting ribs to shoulder girdle; breastbone

**teat** nipple

**thoracic cavity** hollow in trunk containing heart and lungs

**thorax** part of body between neck and abdomen, containing thoracic cavity

**torso** trunk containing organs

**trunk** central portion of body apart from head, arms, and legs

**tummy** *Informal.* stomach

**umbilicus** navel

**ventral** (*adj*) abdominal; located on lower front surface of trunk, opposite back

**vermiform appendix** appendix

**viscera** organs in thoracic and abdominal cavities, including heart, lungs, stomach, liver, and kidneys

## LIMBS AND EXTREMITIES

**ankle** joint between foot and leg

**annulary** ring finger, esp. on left hand

**arm** upper limb between shoulder and wrist

**armpit** axilla

**axilla** hollow under shoulder where arm joins trunk; armpit; underarm

**ball** rounded portion at front of bottom of foot, behind the toes

**biceps** lateral muscle along inside of upper arm

**big toe** largest toe, on inner edge of foot

**calf** fleshy hind part of leg below knee

**carpus** wrist, esp. bones of wrist

**crazy bone** *Slang.* elbow

**crook** inside bend of elbow or knee

**cuticle** hardened epidermis that accumulates at base of fingernail

**digit** finger or toe

**dogs** *Slang.* feet

**dukes** *Slang.* hands, fists

**elbow** hinge joint at mid-arm

**extremity** limb, esp. hand or foot

**femur** proximal bone of upper leg; thighbone

**fibula** outer, smaller bone between knee and ankle

**fin** *Slang.* arm

**finger** any of five terminating digits of upper forelimb: thumb, index finger, middle finger, ring finger, little finger

**fist** hand clenched with fingers curled inward

**flapper** *Slang.* arm

**foot** terminal part of leg upon which person stands

**footsies** *Slang.* feet

**forearm** half of arm between elbow and wrist; forelimb

**funny bone** *Slang.* elbow

**gams** *Slang.* legs

**hamstring** long muscle down back of thigh

**hand** grasping extremity, with fingers, at end of arm

**haunch** hip, hindquarter

**heel** rear portion of foot below ankle

**hip** region on each side of lower part of trunk, formed by pelvis and upper femur

**hollow** pit beneath shoulder

**hoof** *Slang.* foot

**index finger** finger closest to thumb

**instep** arched middle portion of foot

**knee** joint where upper and lower leg meet

**knuckle** protuberance at joint of finger, esp. large joint at middle of finger

**leg** lower limb used to walk and support body

**limb** arm or leg

**little finger** smallest finger, furthest from thumb; pinkie

**middle finger** second finger from thumb, usu. longest finger

**mitt** *Slang.* hand

**paw** *Slang.* hand

**pinkie** *Informal.* little finger

**pins** *Slang.* legs

**pups** *Slang.* feet

**ring finger** third finger from thumb, next to little finger, traditionally finger on which engagement ring or wedding band is worn

**shank** part of leg between knee and ankle

**shinbone** tibia

**shoulder** joint that connects arm to upper trunk

**soupbone** *Slang.* arm

**sticks** *Slang.* legs, esp. thin ones

**stumps** *Slang.* legs, esp. thick ones

**tarsus** ankle, esp. bones of ankle

**thigh** segment of lower limb from hip to knee

**thighbone** femur

**thumb** short, thick digit of hand nearest wrist, in opposition to other fingers

**tibia** long, inner bone of leg between knee and ankle; shinbone

**toe** one of five terminal digits of foot

**tootsies** *Slang.* feet

**triceps** lateral muscle along back of upper arm

**ulna** bone on little finger side of forearm

**underarm** axilla

**upper arm** portion of arm between elbow and shoulder

**wheels** *Slang.* legs

**wing** *Slang.* arm

**wrist** ball-and-socket joint between hand and lower arm

# BRAIN AND CENTRAL NERVOUS SYSTEM

**alpha wave** long, slow brain wave of relaxation

**axon** long, threadlike part of neuron that conducts impulses away from cell body

**beta wave** short, fast brain wave of activity

**brain** seat of nervous system controlling neural coordination and thought

**central nervous system** CNS; portion of nervous system comprising brain and spinal cord

**cerebellum** part of brain that regulates coordination of voluntary muscle movement

**cerebral cortex** gray matter covering forebrain

**cerebral hemisphere** either of the rounded halves of the cerebrum

**cerebrospinal fluid** liquid that fills space in middle of spine and cavities in brain

**cerebrum** left and right hemispheres at front of brain that send and receive stimuli to and from voluntary muscles, perceive sensory input, and control memory and thought

**CNS** *central nervous system*

**corpus callosum** mass of nerve fibers connecting two hemispheres of cerebrum

**cortex** outer layer of gray matter covering most of brain; pallium

**dendrite** short, branching, threadlike part of neuron that carries impulses to cell body

**frontal lobe** anterior portion of each cerebral hemisphere

**ganglion** solid mass of neural cell bodies that serves as relay center for impulses

**gray matter** nervous tissue forming inner part of spinal cord and outer part of brain

**hypothalamus** basal part of third ventricle beneath thalamus that regulates pituitary gland, body temperature, and sleep

**impulse** traveling wave of excitation that sends message through neuron

**limbic system** ringlike section in midline of brain, concerned with emotions and memory

**medulla** part of brain joined to spinal cord that controls sense organs, respiration, and cardiac muscle

**meninges** *sing.* meninx; three membranes covering spinal cord and brain

**meninx** one of three meninges

**motor** (*adj*) designating nerve that stimulates muscle or organ to move or act

**myelin** protective sheath around peripheral nerve fibers

**neocortex** outer layer of brain, center of intellect and imagination

**nerve** bundle of neurons supported by connective tissue, conveying impulses of sensation or motion

**nervous system** nerve tissue that coordinates all activities and receives all sensory stimuli, consisting of brain, spinal cord, axons, dendrites, and synapses, and composed of the following major nerves:

**brachial nerve** nerve in upper arm
**cervical nerve** nerve in neck and shoulder
**coccygeal nerve** nerve at base of spine
**digital nerve** nerve in fingers
**femoral nerve** nerve in thigh
**intercostal nerve** nerve between ribs
**lumbar nerve** nerve in groin
**mandibular nerve** nerve in lower jaw
**maxillary nerve** nerve in jaw
**median nerve** nerve in middle of arm
**ophthalmic nerve** nerve in eye
**peroneal nerve** nerve in lower leg near fibula
**radial nerve** nerve around lower arm
**sacral nerve** nerve from spinal cord in sacrum
**sciatic nerve** nerve running down spinal cord and back of each thigh
**thoracic nerve** nerve in thorax
**tibial nerve** nerve in lower leg near tibia
**ulnar nerve** nerve in forearm and elbow

**neuron** single cell consisting of axon and dendrites in system of nerves that conducts impulses
**node of Ranvier** recurring gap at intervals in myelin sheath along nerve axon
**occipital lobe** most posterior portion of each cerebral hemisphere
**olfactory lobe** anterior portion of each cerebral hemisphere, responsible for sense of smell
**pallium** cortex
**parietal lobe** middle portion of each cerebral hemisphere
**pons** band of nerve fibers through which impulses pass between various parts of brain
**sciatic nerve** largest nerve in body, running down spinal cord and back of each thigh
**sense organs** eyes, ears, nose, and taste buds, the organs containing nervous tissue that responds to particular external stimuli
**sensory receptors** sense organs and other tissue that respond to external stimuli, recording temperature and sensations such as pain and heat
**spinal column** series of jointed vertebrae forming axial support for skeleton and carrying nerves
**spinal cord** cylindrical mass of nervous tissue running through spinal column
**synapse** meeting place of axons and dendrites along which impulse travels from neuron to neuron
**temporal lobe** lateral portion of each cerebral hemisphere, in front of occipital lobe
**thalamus** lower anterior portion of brain above pituitary gland that acts as main relay center for impulses to cerebrum
**ventricle** any of four cavities within brain filled with cerebrospinal fluid

## HEART AND CIRCULATORY AND LYMPHATIC SYSTEMS

**agglutination** sticking together of red blood cells
**aorta** main artery leaving heart

**arteriole** small artery with walls of smooth muscle that controls blood supply to capillaries
**artery** blood vessel conducting blood from heart to tissue
**atrium** auricle
**auricle** upper chamber in heart that receives blood from veins; atrium
**blood** liquid of circulatory system containing dissolved digestive products and conveying oxygen to tissue: plasma, red and white blood cells, and platelets
**bloodstream** flow of blood through circulatory system
**blood vessel** artery, vein, or capillary
**capillary** very small blood vessel with thin, permeable walls
**capillary network** arrangement of branching capillaries in tissue
**cardiac muscle** muscle in walls of heart with action that is automatic, regular, and faster than that of involuntary muscle
**carotid artery** one of two principal arteries on either side of neck that conveys blood from aorta to head
**circulatory system** network of vessels through which blood is pumped by heart
**clot** network of fibrin fibers that trap red blood cells and platelets to form solid mass
**coronary artery** either of two arteries that originate in aorta and supply heart with blood
**corpuscle** free-floating blood or lymph cell
**diastole** stage of relaxation in action of heart muscle
**erythrocyte** red blood cell
**fibrin** insoluble protein that forms fibers in blood clotting
**heart** hollow organ with muscular walls that pumps blood through circulatory system
**heartbeat** pulsation of heart, including one complete systole and diastole
**hematic** (*adj*) of, pertaining to, or contained in blood
**hemoglobin** oxygen-carrying substance in red blood cells which gives them red color
**homeostasis** state of maintaining constant blood composition
**leukocyte** white blood cell
**lymph** colorless fluid that bathes body cells and contains lymphocytes
**lymphatic system** system of small vessels by which lymph is circulated through body
**lymph node** small organ that produces lymphocytes to filter foreign bodies and bacteria from lymph
**lymphocyte** white blood cell of the immune system that attacks foreign substances directly or by producing antibodies
**pericardial cavity** thin, membranous sac enclosing heart
**phagocyte** white blood cell that defends against bacterial attack and digests tissue debris
**plasma** clear, colorless liquid left after blood cells are taken out of blood
**platelet** minute disk of cytoplasm formed in bone marrow that assists in blood clotting; thrombocyte
**portal system** veins that conduct blood from one capillary network to another
**pulmonary artery** artery that conveys blood from right ventricle of heart to lungs
**pulmonary vein** vein that conveys blood from lungs to left auricle of heart
**pump** *Slang*. heart

**red blood cell** elastic blood cell formed in bone marrow and containing hemoglobin; erythrocyte

**Rhesus factor** antigen present on surface of red blood cells of most people; Rh positive blood

**serum** liquid obtained from clotted blood; form of plasma

**spleen** organ that produces lymphocytes and stores red blood cells

**systole** stage of contraction in action of heart muscle

**thrombin** enzyme in blood serum that promotes production of fibrin

**thrombocyte** platelet

**ticker** *Slang.* heart

**vascular system** circulatory and lymphatic systems of vessels for conducting blood and lymph through body

**vein** blood vessel conducting blood from tissue back to heart

**vena cava** main vein entering auricle of heart with blood from upper and lower parts of body

**ventricle** lower chamber in heart that receives blood from auricle and pumps it back through circulatory system

**white blood cell** phagocyte or lymphocyte blood cell without coloring material that fights bacteria in body; leukocyte

## DIGESTIVE AND EXCRETORY SYSTEM

**alimentary canal** long tube, running from mouth to anus, for digestion and absorption of food

**anus** excretory opening at end of alimentary canal

**ascending colon** portion of colon rising from cecum

**bladder** urinary bladder

**bowel** any of divisions of intestine; gut

**cecum** small bag at start of large intestine

**colon** main absorptive part of large intestine, running from cecum to rectum

**defecation** act of passing feces from rectum out through anus

**descending colon** portion of colon leading to rectum

**digestive system** organs causing chemical decomposition of food into substances that body can absorb or excrete

**duodenum** part of small intestine joined to stomach, with ducts leading to liver and pancreas

**enzyme** complex protein substance produced by cells to catalyze metabolic processes such as digestion

**esophagus** long muscular tube from pharynx down neck to stomach

**excrement** waste products discharged from body

**excretion** discharge of waste products from body

**feces** remains of undigested food excreted from bowels through anus

**gastric juice** liquid secretion produced by walls of stomach to aid digestion

**gastrointestinal tract** portion of alimentary canal from esophagus to rectum

**gullet** esophagus; throat

**gut** portion of alimentary canal between pylorus and anus; bowel; intestine

**ileum** last division of small intestine, opening into large intestine

**intestine** part of alimentary canal between stomach and anus for absorption of food into body

**jejunum** middle portion of small intestine between ileum and duodenum

**kishkes** *Slang.* intestines

**large intestine** broad tube with muscular walls, consisting of colon and rectum, that absorbs water, leaving feces

**peristalsis** wavelike muscle movement in alimentary canal that pushes contents along

**pylorus** opening between stomach and duodenum

**rectum** storage area for feces in last part of large intestine, ending with anus

**sigmoid flexure** curving final portion of colon that ends in rectum

**small intestine** long tube between stomach and large intestine where absorption and digestion of food occur

**sphincter** annular muscle that closes and opens rectum

**stomach** baglike part of alimentary canal below esophagus with muscular walls that mix food with gastric juice

**transverse colon** portion of colon running from ascending colon to descending colon

**ureter** tube leading from kidney to urinary bladder

**urethra** tube from urinary bladder to outside of body for discharge of urine; in males, also used to discharge sperm through penis

**urinary bladder** baglike structure for storing urine prior to its discharge from body; bladder

**urinary tract** system of tubes that conducts urine from kidney through ureter, urinary bladder, and urethra

**urine** liquid containing dissolved urea and salts, discharged by kidney to bladder and through urethra out of body

**villus** small, fingerlike structure growing out of mucous membrane of small intestine that absorbs and carries off food material

## RESPIRATORY SYSTEM

**alveolus** tiny, blind-ended cavity in lung that receives carbon dioxide from blood and gives back oxygen

**bronchiole** small air passageway in lung; division of bronchus

**bronchus** tube leading from trachea to each lung

**cilium** hairlike fringe on walls of trachea and bronchus that flaps to drive dust from lungs back up to mouth

**diaphragm** cup-shaped muscle between thorax and abdomen that flattens when air is drawn into lungs

**exhalation** process of pushing air out of lungs; expiration

**expiration** exhalation

**inhalation** process of taking air into lungs; inspiration

**inspiration** inhalation

**intercostal muscle** muscle between two ribs that contracts when air is inhaled

**lung** either of two organs for breathing that takes carbon dioxide from blood and returns oxygen to it

**pleura** membranous, baglike outer covering of lung

**pleural cavity** thin, membranous sac that lines chest cavity and contains lungs

**respiration** process by which oxygen is conveyed to tissues and carbon dioxide is given off in exchange

**respiratory system** organs involved in exchange of carbon dioxide and oxygen between body and environment: nose and mouth, pharynx, larynx, trachea, bronchi, and lungs

**sputum** saliva ejected from respiratory passages

**trachea** tube leading from mouth and nose down throat to lungs for in-and-out passage of air

# ENDOCRINE SYSTEM AND GLANDS

**adrenal gland** either of two endocrine glands lying above the kidney; suprarenal gland

**adrenalin** epinephrine

**apocrine** (*adj*) designating glands in which part of secreting cell goes into secretion, as in mammary gland

**bile** green, alkaline liquid produced by liver that forms emulsion with fat to assist enzyme action

**bile duct** tube that conducts bile from liver to duodenum

**duct** short pipe through which secretions leave gland

**eccrine** (*adj*) designating glands that secrete externally, as certain sweat glands

**endocrine gland** any gland that secretes a hormone into the bloodstream

**epinephrine** hormone secreted by adrenal glands that increases heartbeat, sends blood to brain and muscles, increases perspiration, and enlarges eye pupil; adrenalin

**exocrine gland** any gland that discharges a secretion through an opening on epithelial surface

**follicle** small cavity or gland

**gallbladder** small vessel near liver for bile storage

**gland** organ that selectively removes materials from blood, chemically alters them, and secretes them for further use in body or discharges them from body

**glandular system** system of organs that produce secretions

**holocrine** (*adj*) designating glands in which cells disintegrate entirely to form secretion, as in sebaceous glands

**hormone** organic substance, such as insulin, prolactin, adrenalin, estrogen, or testosterone, produced by endocrine glands and carried by bloodstream to produce a metabolic effect

**islets of Langerhans** insulin-producing cells in pancreas

**kidney** either of a pair of bean-shaped glands in upper abdominal cavity that control amount of water in blood, maintain homeostasis, and excrete waste water as urine

**lacrimal gland** either of two tear-secreting glands located at top of eye

**lactation** production of milk in mammary glands

**liver** large gland that secretes bile and stores glycogen

**mammary gland** either of two milk-producing glands on female upper chest

**melatonin** hormone secreted by pineal gland, important in regulating biological rhythms

**merocrine** (*adj*) designating glands in which secreting cells remain intact, as in sweat glands

**ovary** female reproductive gland that produces ova

**pancreas** gland that produces digestive juice and insulin

**pancreatic juice** digestive juice secreted by pancreas and passed to duodenum

**parathyroid gland** one of four small glands on or near thyroid

**parotid gland** largest salivary gland, located below each ear

**pineal body** small endocrine gland in brain that secretes melatonin

**pituitary gland** endocrine gland beneath floor of brain that controls action of all other endocrine glands

**prostate gland** muscular gland surrounding male urethra at base of bladder

**renal** (*adj*) designating artery supplying blood to kidneys

**salivary glands** three pairs of glands in mouth that secrete saliva: parotid, sublingual, submaxillary

**sebaceous gland** gland in dermis, opening onto hair root, that produces oily sebum

**sublingual gland** one of a pair of salivary glands located below the tongue

**submaxillary gland** one of a pair of salivary glands located on each side of and below the lower jaw

**suprarenal gland** adrenal gland

**sweat gland** small, coiled, tubular gland in subcutaneous tissue that regulates body temperature by secretion of perspiration through duct and out pores in skin

**testis** male reproductive gland that produces sperm

**thymus** gland in neck that produces lymphocytes and becomes vestigial after puberty

**thyroid gland** endocrine gland that controls rate of metabolism and growth and production of body heat

**urea** soluble organic compound formed from ammonia in liver

# REPRODUCTIVE SYSTEM

**afterbirth** placenta and fetal membranes

**cervix** short, narrow tube leading from uterus to vagina

**clitoris** small, sensitive organ at anterior part of vulva

**embryo** developing human in womb during first eight weeks after conception

**epididymis** long tube that receives and stores sperm

**fallopian tube** tube that conducts ovum from ovary to uterus

**fetus** embryo that has appearance of fully developed offspring; also, *esp. Brit.* foetus

**gamete** reproductive cell with chromosomes in nucleus: male spermatozoon, female ovum

**genitals** external reproductive organs, male or female

**glans** head of penis or clitoris

**gonad** reproductive gland that produces gametes: male testis, female ovary

**labia** folds at margin of vulva, majora and minora

**menstruation** periodic discharge of blood, secretions, and tissue due to shedding of uterine lining when ovum is not fertilized

**mons veneris** rounded eminence of fatty tissue on female pubic region

**ovary** female reproductive gland that produces ova

**ovum** female gamete or unfertilized egg cell

**penis** erectile male organ with many blood vessels, through which sperm passes for internal fertilization of ova, also used for urination

**placenta** vascular organ that surrounds fetus and unites it with uterus for nutrition

**reproductive system** organs and structures concerned with production of gametes and conception of new individuals of a given species

**scrotum** external pouch containing male testes

**seminal vesicle** either of two glands on each side of male bladder that add nutrients to sperm passing through vas deferens

**smegma** cheesy secretion by sebaceous glands at genitalia

**spermatozoon** male gamete with flagellum that allows it to swim toward female gamete; sperm

**testicle** male gonad; baglike structure that produces sperm

**testis** male reproductive gland that produces sperm; testicle

**umbilical cord** cord connecting fetus with placenta

**urethra** tube in males used to discharge sperm through penis

**uterus** muscular hollow organ in female in which embryo and fetus develop; womb

**vagina** canal leading from cervix to outside of body in female that receives sperm and acts as birth passage

**vas deferens** long tube that passes sperm from testes to urethra

**vulva** external portion of female genital organs

**womb** uterus

## SKELETON

**backbone** spinal column

**ball-and-socket joint** round end of one bone that fits into hollow of another, allowing movement in any direction

**bone** hard, largely calcareous substance of skeleton

**boss** round, knoblike protuberance on bone

**cartilage** tough, elastic, whitish tissue that forms skeleton of embryo, most of which later turns to bone

**flex** (*vb*) bend joint so angle between two bones becomes smaller

**gliding joint** joint where surface of one bone moves over surface of another

**Haversian canal** small tube in bones containing nerves and blood vessels

**hinge joint** joint such as knee or elbow, in which round end of one bone turns on flat surface of another in one direction only

**joint** structure that joins two bones so they can move together

**ligament** strong band of fiber that holds bones of joint . together

**marrow** soft, fatty material that forms inside of bone

**ossification** hardening of cartilage into bone

**process** bony outgrowth on larger structure

**skeleton** hard internal structure that supports organs and tissue, composed of the following major bones:

> **acetabulum** hip socket
> **calcaneus** heel bone
> **carpus** wrist bones
> **clavicle** collarbone
> **coccyx** base of spine
> **coxa** hip joint
> **cranium** skull bone
> **femur** upper leg bone
> **fibula** lower leg bone
> **frontal** front of cranium
> **gladiolus** sternum, breastbone
> **humerus** upper arm bone
> **ilium** upper portion of hipbone
> **ischium** lower portion of hipbone
> **lacrimal** forehead
> **lumbar vertebrae** five vertebrae of middle back
> **mandible** lower jawbone
> **manubrium** upper breastbone
> **mastoid** bone behind ear
> **maxilla** upper jawbone
> **metacarpus** bone in fingers
> **metatarsus** bone in toes

> **nasal** nose bone
> **occipital** back of cranium
> **orbit** eye socket
> **parietal** top of cranium
> **patella** knee bone
> **pelvis** bone forming pelvic cavity
> **phalanges** bones at ends of toes and fingers
> **pubis** groin bone
> **radius** lower arm bone
> **ribs** twenty-four curved bones around chest cavity
> **sacral vertebrae** five vertebrae of lower back
> **sacroiliac** joint between sacrum and ilium
> **sacrum** bone forming back of pelvis
> **scapula** shoulder blade
> **skull** bones covering brain
> **sphenoid** base of skull
> **sternum** breastbone
> **tarsus** foot bone
> **temporal** side of cranium
> **thoracic vertebrae** twelve vertebrae of upper back
> **tibia** shinbone
> **ulna** bone in forearm
> **vertebrae** thirty-three bony segments of spinal column
> **xiphoid process** point of lower breastbone
> **zygomatic** cheek bone

**spinal column** series of joined vertebrae forming axial support for skeleton and carrying nerves; backbone; spine; vertebral column

**spine** spinal column

**tailbone** coccyx

**torus** rounded projection on bone

**vertebra** hollow bone with large central mass and fingerlike pieces of bone standing out from core

**vertebral column** spinal column

## MUSCLES

**abductor** muscle that moves from median axis of body

**adductor** muscle that pulls toward median axis of body

**constrictor** muscle that contracts cavity or opening or compresses organ

**coordination** muscles acting together to produce same effect

**erector** muscle that erects body or body parts

**involuntary muscle** muscle tissue in sheets around hollow organs that contracts slowly without conscious control

**muscle** tissue consisting of long cells with power to contract, causing all movements of body parts

**muscular system** system of muscles that cause all bodily movements, composed of the following major muscles:

> **abdominal** stomach muscle
> **biceps** muscle at front of upper arm
> **deltoid** shoulder muscle
> **erector** lower back muscle
> **extensor** forearm muscle
> **fascia lata** hip muscle
> **flexor** forearm muscle
> **gastrocnemius** calf muscle
> **gluteus** buttocks muscle
> **hamstring** muscle at back of thigh
> **latissimus dorsi** back muscle
> **oblique** muscle at side of torso
> **pectoral** upper chest muscle

**quadriceps** muscle at front of thigh
**rectus abdominis** long muscle in abdomen
**rectus femoris** long muscle in front of thigh
**rotator cuff** muscle in shoulder under deltoid
**sartorius** muscle across front of thigh
**soleus** muscle down back of lower leg to foot
**sternocleidomastoid** neck muscle
**trapezius** upper back muscle
**triceps** muscle at back of upper arm

**reflex** simple behavior in which nerve stimulus causes set response in muscle
**tendon** band of connective tissue that attaches muscle to bone
**tensor** muscle that stretches a body part, making it tight
**voluntary muscle** long muscle able to contract rapidly that moves bones of joints in locomotion by conscious control

## TISSUE, FIBER, AND INTEGUMENTARY SYSTEM

**adipose** (*adj*) designating fat in connective tissue
**cartilage** tough, elastic, whitish tissue around bones or through muscles; embryonic skeleton that turns to bone
**connective tissue** fibrous tissue that provides support for other tissue or organs
**cuticle** epidermis, esp. hardened outer layer of skin
**dermis** inside layer of skin cells, providing elastic strength
**epidermis** outside layer of cells
**epithelium** tissue that forms surface or outside of organism, such as skin, or covers inside of tubes and cavities
**fascia** thin layer of connective tissue around and between muscles or organs
**fat** ester of glycerol and fatty acid; tissue of cells expanded with greasy or oily matter
**fiber** strong, threadlike structure of protein
**hair** fine, threadlike growth from skin, concentrated on head, in armpits, and above genitals
**hair follicle** small cavity in epidermis from which hair develops
**horny layer** tough, protective outer layer of epidermis
**integumentary system** any of various kinds of tissue covering body or enclosing organs
**irritability** ability to respond to stimuli, characteristic of all living tissue
**ligament** strong band of fiber holding bones of joint together
**lobe** portion of an organ separated by fissures
**marrow** soft, fatty material that forms inside of bone
**matrix** solid material made by cells and secreted around them
**melanin** insoluble pigment that gives dark color to skin and hair
**melanocyte** cell that produces melanin in skin and hair
**membrane** thin, pliable sheet of tissue that forms covering or lining
**mucous membrane** lubricating membrane lining organ or internal surface such as alimentary or respiratory canal
**mucus** sticky, lubricating liquid secreted by some membranes
**nail** thin, horny plate covering end of top of finger or toe

**organ** body part with definite structure and particular function
**skin** outer covering, containing dermis and epidermis
**soft tissue** muscle, fat, or tissue not part of skeleton or organ
**subcutaneous** (*adj*) designating tissue situated just beneath epithelium
**synovial capsule** baglike membrane in joint filled with sticky lubricating liquid
**system** all organs and tissues concerned with particular function of organism
**tendon** band of connective tissue that attaches muscle to bone
**tissue** mass of cells and intercellular material which performs specific function in organism
**vessel** tube for conducting fluids within organism

# MEDICAL PROBLEMS

Diseases and Infestations
Afflictions and Conditions
Defects and Disabilities
Injuries and Accidents
Signs and Symptoms
Diagnostic Terminology

**SEE ALSO**: Chap. 1: Anatomy; Health, Fitness, and Enhancement; Chap. 2: Biology; Chap. 4: Medicine

## DISEASES AND INFESTATIONS

**acquired immune deficiency syndrome** AIDS
**Addison's disease** condition marked by weakness, low blood pressure, and dark pigmentation due to inadequate hormone secretion by adrenal glands
**adenitis** regional inflammation of gland or lymph node
**adenocarcinoma** malignant epithelial tumor in glandular pattern
**agranulocytosis** acute illness caused by chemicals or drug reaction in which certain white blood cells disappear, causing rapid, massive infection
**ague** malaria; general malaise marked by fever
**AIDS** acquired immune deficiency syndrome; severe weakening or destruction of body's immune system by human immunodeficiency virus, allowing opportunistic diseases and infections to attack, spread by direct contact of body fluids such as blood or semen: SIDA
**AIDS-related complex** ARC; chronic enlargement of lymph nodes and persistent fever caused by AIDS virus
**ailment** physical disorder or chronic disease
**Alzheimer's disease** progressive, untreatable dementia and brain degeneration in elderly
**amebiasis** infection with or disease caused by amebas
**amebic dysentery** severe dysentery caused by protozoan amebas
**amyotrophic lateral sclerosis** progressive loss of muscle bulk and control due to nerve disease; Lou Gehrig's disease

**anthrax** acute infectious livestock disease, transmitted to humans by contact, causing pneumonia or skin ulcerations

**aplastic anemia** anemia due to failure of bone marrow to produce sufficient leukocytes and blood platelets

**apoplexy** stroke

**appendicitis** acute inflammation of vermiform appendix that requires surgical removal

**ARC** AIDS-related complex

**arteriosclerosis** deposit of cholesterol on artery walls; hardening of the arteries

**arthritis** inflammation of joints

**asbestosis** lung disease caused by inhalation of asbestos fibers, sometimes leading to lung cancer

**atheroma** degeneration of artery walls due to fatty plaques and scar tissue; common form of arteriosclerosis; atherosclerosis

**atherosclerosis** atheroma

**autoimmune disease** disorder that permits destruction of tissue by body's own antibodies

**bacterial endocarditis** inflammation of lining of heart cavity and valves due to bacterial infection

**basal cell carcinoma** common, usu. curable, slow-growing malignant tumor on skin

**beriberi** often fatal nutritional disorder due to vitamin $B_1$ deficiency

**bilirubinemia** excess bile pigment in blood that causes jaundice

**Black Death** bubonic plague

**black lung** slow-developing respiratory disease due to regular inhalation of coal dust or asbestos; miner's lung; pneumoconiosis

**blackwater fever** rare complication of malaria, with massive destruction of red blood cells, that causes hemoglobin in urine

**blastomycosis** infectious, potentially fatal lung disease that can spread to skin, caused by fungus

**blepharitis** inflammation, scaling, and crusting of eyelids

**botulism** serious toxin-produced bacterial food poisoning

**Bright's disease** nephritis

**bronchitis** inflammation of walls of bronchi in lungs due to virus or bacteria, causing coughing and production of sputum

**brown lung** occupational disease due to inhalation of cotton dust; byssinosis

**brucellosis** bacterial infection causing remittent fever

**bubonic plague** often fatal bacterial epidemic disease transmitted to humans by rat fleas, with painful swelling of lymph nodes; Black Death

**byssinosis** brown lung

**cancer** malignant tumor anywhere in body due to uncontrolled cell division, causing disruption of metabolism and invasion and destruction of neighboring tissue

**candidiasis** yeastlike fungus infection in mouth and moist areas of body; thrush

**carbuncle** staphylococcus infection of skin that causes boils with multiple drainage channels

**carcinoma** cancer in epithelium lining skin or internal organs

**cardiac arrest** cessation of heart pumping, due esp. to fibrillation, that results in rapid brain damage or death

**cardiac stenosis** abnormal narrowing of heart valve

**cardiomyopathy** chronic viral, congenital, or other disorder that affects heart muscle and causes heart failure, arrhythmias, or embolisms

**carditis** inflammation of heart

**caries** decay and crumbling of tooth or bone; dental cavity

**cat-scratch disease** viral infection causing fever and swelling of lymph glands, due to scratch of cat

**cellulitis** inflammation of connective tissue due to bacterial infection

**cerebrospinal fever** bacterial meningitis; spotted fever

**cerebrovascular accident** sudden and severe attack of cerebrovascular disease; stroke

**cerebrovascular disease** disorder of blood vessels in brain due to atheroma or hypertension, causing cerebral hemorrhage or thrombosis and cerebrovascular accident

**cervicitis** inflammation of cervix

**chickenpox** mild, highly infectious viral disease primarily in children with itchy rash of red pimples, blisters, and pustules; varicella

**childbed fever** puerperal fever

**chlamydia** sexually transmitted, viruslike microorganism causing conjunctivitis, urethritis, and cervicitis

**cholera** acute bacterial infection of small intestine causing massive diarrhea, often leading to dehydration

**chorea** neurological disease of the basal ganglia that causes jerky, involuntary movements and distorted posture of shoulders, hips, and face; St. Vitus's dance

**chronic fatigue syndrome** persistent, extreme exhaustion and weakness due to unknown causes

**cirrhosis** progressive liver condition from various causes, esp. alcoholism or hepatitis, in which cells die and the liver turns tawny and knobby

**clap** *Vulgar slang.* gonorrhea

**coccidioidomycosis** fungal infection characterized by cough, fever, and abscesses under the skin, often disappearing spontaneously but can be fatal

**cold** contagious respiratory infection that causes inflammation of mucous membrane and nasal discharge; common cold

**colitis** any inflammation of colon, causing diarrhea and lower abdominal pain

**collagen diseases** various diseases characterized by changes in makeup of connective tissue: lupus, rheumatic fever, rheumatoid arthritis, and scleroderma

**common cold** cold

**congestive heart failure** inability of heart to adequately supply blood to body tissue, often due to weakening of cardiac muscle, causing body swelling and shortness of breath

**conjunctivitis** inflammation of mucous membrane covering front of eye, often with discharge of pus; pinkeye

**consumption** any disease that causes wasting of tissues, esp. pulmonary tuberculosis

**contact dermatitis** skin inflammation produced by contact with some substance that causes redness, swelling, and often itching

**coronary** coronary heart disease; heart attack

**coronary heart disease** serious condition affecting coronary artery

**coronary infarction** myocardial infarction

**coronary occlusion** coronary thrombosis

**coronary thrombosis** formation of a blood clot in coronary artery that obstructs blood flow to heart and causes coronary infarction, usu. due to atherosclerosis; coronary occlusion

**coryza** catarrhal inflammation of mucous membrane in nose

**cowpox** viral infection of cow's udder, transmitted to humans by direct contact, causing mild version of symptoms similar to smallpox

**crab louse** crablike louse that infests pubic regions, transmitted by sexual contact

**crib death** sudden infant death syndrome

**Crohn's disease** condition marked by chronic inflammation and thickening of alimentary tract

**croup** inflammation and obstruction of larynx in young children due to viral respiratory infections, characterized by harsh cough

**cryptococcosis** severe fungal infection, usu. in men of middle age, that affects central nervous system and brain membranes

**Cushing's disease** syndrome due to excess corticosteroid hormone, causing weight gain, excess body hair, and high blood pressure

**cystic fibrosis** hereditary disease of exocrine glands that produces respiratory infections, malabsorption, and sweat with high salt content

**cystitis** often infectious inflammation of urinary bladder that causes frequent painful passage of urine

**deficiency disease** any disease, such as beriberi, caused by nutritional deficiency

**dengue** viral disease transmitted by mosquitoes in the tropics, causing fever, severe pain in back and joints, rash, and sore throat

**dermatitis** skin inflammation

**diabetes** diabetes mellitus

**diabetes insipidus** rare deficiency of pituitary hormone that causes constant thirst and excessive urination

**diabetes mellitus** common deficiency, possibly inherited, of the pancreatic hormone insulin, causing disorder in carbohydrate metabolism and inability to properly utilize sugars; diabetes

**diphtheria** acute, highly contagious bacterial infection of the throat that can cause death from respiratory obstruction or carditis

**disease** physical disorder with specific physiological cause and recognizable signs and symptoms

**diverticulitis** colonic diverticulosis with inflammation

**diverticulosis** condition characterized by existence of diverticular sacs at weak points in walls of alimentary tract, esp. intestine

**dracontiasis** infestation from contaminated drinking water of tropical parasitic guinea worm beneath skin, causing large blisters on extremities

**droplet infection** disease spread by droplets expelled by sneezing or coughing

**duodenal ulcer** ulcer in lining of duodenum caused by excess stomach acid

**dysentery** infection of intestinal tract that causes severe diarrhea mixed with blood and mucus

**dystrophy** organ or muscle disorder caused by insufficient nourishment or hereditary disorder

**elephantiasis** gross enlargement of legs or other body parts due to obstructed lymph drainage, caused by parasitic worm transmitted by mosquitoes

**emphysema** air in tissues; pulmonary disorder, characterized by increase in size of air sacs due to destruction of their walls, causing shortness of breath

**encephalitis** viral or bacterial inflammation of brain, also caused by infection or allergic reaction; sleeping sickness

**endocarditis** inflammation and damage to heart cavity lining due to bacterial infection or rheumatic fever

**enteritis** viral or bacterial inflammation of small intestine, causing diarrhea

**epilepsy** one of various brain disorders that cause recurrent, sudden convulsive attacks

**Epstein-Barr syndrome** infectious mononucleosis caused by herpeslike virus; glandular fever

**erysipelas** skin infection from streptococcus bacteria that causes inflammation, swelling, and fever

**fibroma** usu. benign tumor composed mainly of fibrous or connective tissue

**fibrosarcoma** malignant tumor of connective tissue, esp. in legs

**filariasis** disorder that affects lymphatic system, caused by parasite

**flu** influenza

**food poisoning** digestive system disorder, usu. from the consumption of bacteria or bacterial toxins in food, causing vomiting, diarrhea, nausea, and fever

**frambesia** yaws

**functional disorder** condition for which no physical cause can be found

**fungus** simple parasitic organism that can infect humans and cause disease

**gastric ulcer** stomach ulcer caused by action of acid on stomach lining

**gastritis** inflammation of stomach lining from an ingested substance, infection, or chronic irritation

**gastroenteritis** inflammation of stomach and intestine, due to virus, bacteria, or food poisoning, that causes vomiting

**genital herpes** infection of genital area by herpes simplex virus

**German measles** rubella

**gingivitis** inflammation of gums, sometimes with bleeding

**glandular fever** Epstein-Barr syndrome; mononucleosis

**glaucoma** abnormally high fluid pressure in the eye, often leading to loss of vision

**glioma** cancer of nerve tissue

**glomerulonephritis** potentially fatal streptococcal infection of kidney

**gonorrhea** sexually transmitted bacterial disease that affects mucous membranes in genital tract, pharynx, or rectum

**gout** accumulation of excess uric acid in bloodstream and joints that causes joint destruction, kidney stones, and arthritis

**grand mal** generalized epileptic seizure with flexion and extension of extremities and loss of consciousness

**Graves' disease** disease characterized by enlarged thyroid and increased basal metabolism, due to excessive thyroid secretion

**grippe** influenza

**Hansen's disease** leprosy, caused by aerobic bacteria Hansen's bacilli

**heart attack** myocardial infarction

**heart failure** inadequate pumping of heart ventricle due to coronary thrombosis, hypertension, or arrhythmia; congestive heart failure

**hepatitis** inflammation of liver, due to virus transmitted by food or drink (infectious hepatitis) or blood on needle or in transfusion (serum hepatitis), causing fever and jaundice

**herpes** herpes simplex; small viral blisters on skin

**herpes simplex** virus in herpes family; nonvenereal blisters on mucous membrane that can cause conjunctivitis, vaginal inflammation, or cold sores; herpes

**herpes zoster** virus in herpes family characterized by vesicles, often with severe pain along distribution of nerve; shingles

**histoplasmosis** fungal infection of lymph nodes, usu. caused by inhalation

**HIV** *human immunodeficiency virus*

**Hodgkin's disease** condition marked by malignancy in lymphatic tissue that causes enlarged lymph nodes, fever, and profuse sweating

**hookworm** infestation of small intestine by parasitic hookworm that penetrates skin and causes diarrhea, debility, and sometimes anemia

**human immunodeficiency virus** HIV; virus that causes AIDS

**Huntington's chorea** hereditary chorea with progressive dementia due to widespread degeneration of neurons throughout brain

**hydrophobia** rabies

**hypernephroma** malignant tumor in kidney cells

**hyperthyroidism** overactivity of thyroid gland that causes rapid heartbeat, sweating, tremors, weight loss, and anxiety

**hypoglycemia** glucose deficiency in bloodstream that causes weakness, confusion, and sweating, often in patients with diabetes mellitus who take an insulin overdose

**hypothyroidism** subnormal thyroid gland activity that can lead to cretinism if present at birth

**icthyosis** hereditary skin disease causing flaking of skin in large scales

**ileitis** inflammation of ileum in small intestine

**illness** disease or condition that causes poor health

**impetigo** contagious skin infection from streptococcal or staphylococcal bacteria, esp. in children, causing crusty yellow blisters

**infantile paralysis** poliomyelitis

**infectious disease** disease caused by a microorganism or parasite and usu. passed by direct human contact; communicable or contagious disease

**infestation** invasion of body by animal parasites

**influenza** highly contagious viral infection of respiratory system, transmitted by coughing or sneezing, that causes headache, fever, general aches and pains; flu; grippe

**kala-azar** chronic, often fatal disease transmitted by sandfly in which liver and spleen become enlarged

**Kaposi's sarcoma** KS; cancer of skin characterized by multiple purplish lesions on face and extremities, often associated with AIDS and usu. fatal

**keratitis** inflammation of cornea of eye due to infection or outside agent

**KS** Kaposi's sarcoma

**kwashiorkor** malnutrition due to protein deficiency in diet, esp. in children ages one to three

**laryngitis** inflammation of larynx and vocal cords, due to bacterial or viral infection, causing coughing, husky voice, or complete voice loss

**Lassa fever** highly contagious viral disease that produces wide range of symptoms affecting most parts of body and leading to death

**legionnaires' disease** bacterial lung infection that causes malaise, fever, chest pain, and coughing

**leprosy** chronic contagious tropical disease caused by Hansen's bacilli that results in lumps and patches on skin, thickening of nerves and skin, numbness, and paralysis; Hansen's disease

**leptospirosis** bacterial infection passed by contact with infected rats, causing fever, muscle pain, and jaundice

**leukemia** overproduction of abnormal white blood cells by bone marrow and other blood-forming organs, usu. causing fatal systemic malignancy

**lockjaw** tetanus

**Lou Gehrig's disease** amyotrophic lateral sclerosis

**louse** small, wingless insect that is an external parasite

**lung cancer** malignancy in epithelium of air passages or lung, esp. due to smoke or other outside agents

**lupus** any of several chronic skin diseases, esp. lupus erythematosus

**lupus erythematosus** chronic inflammation of connective tissue that causes red scaly rash on face, arthritis, and organ damage

**lupus vulgaris** rare tuberculous skin infection

**Lyme disease** spirochetal infection transmitted by a tiny tick that causes skin rash, headache, fever, and sometimes arthritis and heart damage

**lymphoma** malignant tumor of lymph nodes that is not Hodgkin's disease

**malady** disease or illness

**malaria** infection caused by parasitic protozoa in red blood cells, transmitted by mosquito in tropics and subtropics, causing fever, sweating, and anemia

**mastitis** inflammation of breasts due to bacterial infection, often through damaged nipples

**measles** highly infectious viral epidemic disease, mainly in children, that causes high fever and elevated pink rash; rubeola

**melanoma** malignant tumor of melanin-forming cells, esp. in skin

**Ménière's syndrome** disease of labyrinth of inner ear, causing deafness and vertigo

**meningitis** inflammation of membranes lining skull and vertebral canal, due to viral or bacterial infection, causing fever, intense headache, muscular rigidity, and sometimes convulsion, delirium, or death; spinal meningitis

**mesothelioma** tumor of pleural epithelium, often due to exposure to asbestos dust

**miliaria** inflammatory skin disease characterized by formation of vesicles or papules about sweat glands; prickly heat

**Minamata disease** form of mercury poisoning found in Japan that causes numbness, impaired speech and hearing, and lack of coordination

**miner's lung** black lung

**mononucleosis** infectious disease that manifests a high number of monocytes in blood, enlarged lymph nodes, prolonged fever, appetite loss, and malaise, esp. in young adults; glandular disease caused by Epstein-Barr virus; glandular fever

**MS** multiple sclerosis

**multiple sclerosis** MS; chronic nervous system disease with recurrent symptoms of unsteady gait, shaky limb movements, rapid involuntary eye movements, and speech defects

**mumps** viral infection that causes fever and swelling of parotid salivary glands, esp. among children

**muscular dystrophy** inherited muscle disease marked by degeneration of muscle fiber

**myasthenia gravis** muscular weakness that has its onset with repetitive activity and leads to paralysis

**mycosis** fungus infection

**myeloma** malignancy of bone marrow

**myocardial infarction** death of portion of heart muscle due to interrupted blood supply; heart attack; coronary infarction

**myocarditis** acute or chronic inflammation of heart muscle

**nephritis** inflammation of kidney; Bright's disease

**neuritis** inflammation of nerves; neuropathy

**neurodermatitis** localized skin disease with itching and thickening of skin

**neurofibromatosis** congenital disease that causes growth on fibrous nerve coverings of benign tumors that may become malignant

**neuropathy** neuritis

**orchitis** inflammation of testis that causes pain, redness, and swelling of scrotum, usu. due to infection such as mumps

**organic disorder** disorder associated with physiological changes in structure of organ or tissue

**osteoarthritis** joint cartilage disease that causes pain and impaired joint function and occurs in later life, due to overuse of joint or as a complication of rheumatoid arthritis

**osteomyelitis** inflammation of bone marrow and adjacent bone, mostly from infection, esp. after compound fractures where marrow is exposed

**osteoporosis** loss of bony matrix that causes brittle bones, due to injury, infection, or old age

**otitis** inflammation of ear, due to viral or bacterial infection, causing severe pain and high fever

**otosclerosis** disease of bone surrounding inner ear, causing impaired hearing

**pancreatitis** inflammation of pancreas with sudden, severe pain

**paratyphoid fever** bacterial infectious disease, caused by nontyphoidal salmonella and spread by poor sanitation, marked by diarrhea, fever, and pink rash on chest

**parkinsonism** Parkinson's disease

**Parkinson's disease** neurological disorder of late middle age characterized by tremor, rigidity, and little spontaneous movement; parkinsonism

**pediculosis** infestation of body and/or scalp by lice, causing itching and sometimes bacterial infection with weeping lesions

**pellagra** B-vitamin nutritional deficiency that causes scaly dermatitis, diarrhea, and depression

**peptic ulcer** breach in lining of digestive tract due to excess acid, occurring in esophagus, stomach, or duodenum

**pericarditis** acute or chronic inflammation of sac surrounding heart, due to viral infection, uremia, or cancer, often causing fever, chest pain, and fluid accumulation

**periodontal disease** disease of gums, mouth lining, and bony structures supporting teeth, caused by plaque; pyorrhea

**peritonitis** inflammation of abdominal cavity membrane, often due to bacteria spread in bloodstream or perforation or rupture of abdominal organ, causing pain, swelling, fever, and shock

**pernicious anemia** autoimmune disease, due to vitamin $B_{12}$ deficiency, that can affect nervous system

**pertussis** whooping cough

**pestilence** severe contagious or infectious epidemic disease

**petit mal** lesser epileptic seizure characterized by brief spells of sleepiness or unconsciousness

**pharyngitis** inflammation of pharynx that causes sore throat or tonsillitis

**phlebitis** inflammation of vein wall, esp. in legs as complication of varicose veins, causing extreme tenderness

**pinkeye** conjunctivitis

**plague** acute epidemic bacterial disease of rats, transmitted to humans by rat fleas, causing severe headache, fever, enlarged lymph nodes, and delirium, usu. fatal

**pleurisy** inflammation of pleura that cover lungs, usu. due to pneumonia or other lung disease, causing painful breathing

**pneumoconiosis** black lung

**pneumonia** inflammation or infection of lungs in which air sacs fill with pus, causing coughing and chest pain

**pneumonic plague** plague bacterium in lungs, usu. fatal

**podagra** gout of foot, esp. big toe

**polio** poliomyelitis

**poliomyelitis** infectious viral disease of central nervous system, formerly epidemic, causing stiffness and sometimes paralysis of muscles, esp. respiratory system muscles; infantile paralysis; polio

**prickly heat** miliaria

**prostatitis** inflammation of prostate gland, due to bacterial infection, sometimes causing urinary obstruction

**psychosomatic illness** disease caused at least in part by emotional state

**puerperal fever** blood poisoning in mother shortly after childbirth due to infection of womb lining or vagina; childbed fever

**pyorrhea** periodontal disease

**Q fever** typhuslike, systemic disease caused by microorganism, transmitted to humans from ruminants through raw milk

**quinsy** pus-discharging inflammation of tonsils

**rabies** acute viral infection of central nervous system, transmitted by bite of infected mammal, causing fever, excitation, painful spasms of throat muscles, paralysis, and death; hydrophobia

**radiation sickness** acute disease caused by exposure to radioactive emissions, causing nausea, vomiting, diarrhea, bleeding, hair loss, and death

**relapsing fever** infectious bacterial disease transmitted by tick and lice bites, causing fever, headache, and muscle pain that lapse and then recur

**reticulosis** abnormal malignant overgrowth of cells of lymphatic glands or immune system

**Reye's syndrome** acute disorder primarily in children after viral infections such as chickenpox or influenza, associated with aspirin use, causing brain swelling and affecting organs

**rheumatic fever** delayed complication of upper respiratory streptococcus infection, esp. in young, characterized by fever, arthritis of joints, chorea, carditis, and erythematosus rash

**rheumatic heart disease** scarring and chronic heart inflammation from progressive state of rheumatic fever

**rheumatism** any disorder causing aches and pains in muscles or joints

**rheumatoid arthritis** common form of arthritis that affects extremities, digits, and hips

**rickets** malformation of unhardened bones in children due to vitamin D deficiency

**Rocky Mountain spotted fever** disease caused by rickettsial microorganism, transmitted to humans by dogs and wood ticks, characterized by fever, muscle pain, and profuse red rash

**roseola** rubella

**rubella** highly contagious viral infection, primarily in children, causing enlarged lymph nodes in neck and pink rash; German measles; roseola

**rubeola** measles

**salmonella poisoning** food poisoning caused by aerobic intestinal bacteria

**sandfly fever** influenzalike viral fever transmitted by bite of sandfly in Mediterranean area

**sarcoma** tumor of connective tissue

**scabies** skin infection from infestation of mites that causes severe itching, esp. around groin, nipples, and between fingers

**scarlatina** scarlet fever

**scarlet fever** highly contagious childhood disease caused by streptococcus bacteria, characterized by sore throat and widespread rash; scarlatina

**schistosomiasis** intestinal disease in tropics, due to infestation of blood flukes, that causes anemia, diarrhea, dysentery, and cirrhosis; snail fever

**scleroderma** thickening and hardening of tissues beneath skin, causing rigidity of skin

**scrofula** tuberculosis of lymph nodes in neck

**scurvy** vitamin C deficiency from absence of fresh fruit and vegetables in diet that causes swollen, bleeding gums, subcutaneous bleeding, and death when prolonged

**seborrheic dermatitis** skin eruption due to excess secretion of sebum, common on face at puberty

**serum hepatitis** liver inflammation that causes fever and jaundice, transmitted by infected hypodermic needle or blood transfusion

**sexually transmitted disease** STD; modern term for venereal disease

**shingles** herpes zoster

**sickle cell anemia** hereditary blood disease that mainly affects blacks, in which abnormal hemoglobin distorts blood cells and causes anemia

**sickness** disease, illness; condition of poor health caused by disease

**SIDA** common name for AIDS outside United States, based on Spanish *síndrome inmuno-deficiencia adquirido* or French *syndrome immuno-déficitaire acquis*

**SIDS** sudden infant death syndrome

**silicosis** chronic lung disease caused by prolonged exposure to silica dust

**sinusitis** inflammation or infection of sinus sacs behind and around nose, causing headache and discharge through nose

**sleeping sickness** condition characterized by presence in blood of parasite from bite of African tsetse fly, causing lethargy, drowsiness, and pain in limbs and joints; encephalitis

**smallpox** acute viral infection that causes high fever and a scarring rash of blisters, usu. fatal, now eradicated by vaccine; variola

**snail fever** schistosomiasis

**social disease** *Informal.* venereal disease

**somatogenic psychosomatic disorder** disease caused by lowering of immunity to pathogens, due to stress

**spinal meningitis** meningitis

**spotted fever** type of bacterial meningitis; cerebrospinal fever

**STD** sexually transmitted disease

**strep throat** infection of throat by streptococcus bacteria

**stroke** sudden weakness or paralysis, usu. on one side of body, due to interruption of blood flow to brain caused by thrombosis, embolus, or hemorrhage; apoplexy; cerebrovascular accident

**St. Vitus's dance** chorea

**sty** acute bacterial infection of gland at base of eyelash

**sudden infant death syndrome** SIDS; death of baby in its bed due to undetermined cause; crib death

**Sydenham's chorea** chorea that affects children, associated with rheumatic fever

**syphilis** bacterial sexually transmitted disease that causes a chancre in acute stage and may lead to blindness or paralysis in chronic stage and insanity in advanced stage

**tabes dorsalis** syphilis of spinal cord and its appendages, sometimes leading to paralysis

**tapeworm** parasitic flatworm that lives in human intestine

**TB** tuberculosis

**teratoma** tumor composed of tissues not normally found at site, esp. in testis or ovary

**tetanus** acute bacterial infection of contaminated wound with release of toxin that affects central nervous system and causes muscle spasms and rigidity, convulsions, and extreme pain; lockjaw

**thrombophlebitis** inflammation of a vein and formation of blood clot that adheres to its wall

**thrush** whitish spots and ulcers on mouth due to parasite, esp. in children; candidiasis

**tonsillitis** inflammation of tonsils, due to bacterial or viral infection, causing sore throat and fever

**Tourette's syndrome** neurological disorder characterized by excessive, sudden, violent movements and convulsive noises and thoughts

**toxicosis** any disease caused by toxic effect of a substance

**toxoplasmosis** infection of lymph nodes caused by protozoan that can cause blindness and mental retardation in newborn when transmitted to fetus, often acquired from cats

**trachoma** chronic, contagious, rickettsial conjunctivitis, often causing blindness

**trench mouth** respiratory infection caused by bacteria, producing ulcers on mucous membrane of mouth and throat

**trichinosis** intestinal infestation by worm larvae from undercooked meat that causes diarrhea, nausea, and pain in limbs

**trypanosomiasis** any of various debilitating, parasitic diseases transmitted by flies, including sleeping sickness

**tuberculosis**  TB; infectious bacterial disease characterized by formation of nodular lesions in tissue, esp. lungs and lymph nodes, causing coughing, fever, night sweats, and spitting of blood

**tularemia**  disease transmitted to humans from rabbits by deer flies or direct contamination, characterized by infection with ulcers, fever, aches, and enlarged lymph nodes

**typhoid fever**  bacterial infection of digestive system, transmitted through contaminated food or water, that causes high fever, red rash on stomach, chills, sweating, and sometimes intestinal hemorrhage

**typhus**  one of various infections caused by parasitic rickettsiae that results in high fever, severe headache, widespread rash, and delirium

**ulcerative colitis**  inflammation and ulceration of colon and rectum

**urethritis**  inflammation of urethra, esp. among males, due to bacterial or viral infection or obstruction

**vaginitis**  irritation of vagina, due to inflammation or infection, causing burning pain and discharge

**varicella**  chickenpox

**variola**  smallpox

**VD**  *venereal disease*

**venereal disease**  VD; any infectious disease transmitted by sexual contact, now usu. called sexually transmitted disease; social disease

**whooping cough**  acute contagious bacterial infection of mucous membrane lining air passages, esp. in children, causing fever and paroxysmal cough with bleeding from mouth and nose; pertussis

**xanthoma**  skin condition characterized by raised patches on eyelids, neck, or back, related to liver disease

**yaws**  tropical infectious disease caused by spirochete in skin, marked by fever, pain, small crusty tumors, and lesions; frambesia

**yellow fever**  infectious viral disease of tropics, transmitted by mosquitoes, causing liver and kidney degeneration with reduced urine flow, jaundice, and death

## Afflictions and Conditions

**acidosis**  excess acidity in blood, due to kidney malfunction or diabetes

**acne**  inflammation of sebaceous glands in skin, esp. on face during adolescence

**addiction**  state of physical or psychological dependence due to habitual consumption of habit-forming substance; dependence

**aeroembolism**  compressed air sickness

**affliction**  painful or debilitating condition, esp. a chronic one

**airsickness**  motion sickness during air flight

**alcoholism**  addiction to alcoholic liquor

**alkalosis**  condition in which blood becomes too alkaline, due to acid loss from vomiting, kidney malfunction, or ingestion of alkalis

**allergy**  hypersensitivity to particular substance or antigen, such as pollens, furs, feathers, mold, dust, drugs, dyes, cosmetics, or foods, causing characteristic symptoms when encountered, ingested, or inhaled

**alopecia**  absence of hair from area where it normally grows, esp. progressive hair loss in men; baldness

**altitude sickness**  respiratory illness from lack of oxygen and reduced atmospheric pressure at high altitudes that causes nausea and exhaustion

**amaurosis**  partial or complete blindness

**amblyopia**  poor sight not caused by intrinsic eye disease

**amenorrhea**  absence or cessation of menstruation due to congenital defect, hormonal deficiency, hypothalamus disorder, or emotional problem

**amnesia**  total or partial memory loss due to disease, injury, or trauma

**anaphylaxis**  acute, allergic reaction to substance to which person has been previously sensitized, resulting in faintness, palpitations, loss of color, difficulty in breathing, and shock

**anemia**  reduced hemoglobin in blood, causing fatigue, breathlessness, and pallor

**anorexia nervosa**  extreme loss of appetite, esp. in adolescent females, causing severe weight loss and starvation

**anoxia**  condition in which body tissues receive inadequate oxygen

**anxiety disorder**  physiological symptoms caused by anxiety neurosis

**asthma**  paroxysmal attacks of bronchial spasms that cause difficulty in breathing, often hereditary; bronchial asthma

**astigmatism**  distortion of visual images due to failure of retina to focus light

**athlete's foot**  contagious fungal infection of skin between toes; tinea

**atopy**  allergic reaction, esp. one separate from point of contact with antigen, such as eczema on skin due to swallowed substance

**autism**  severe psychiatric disorder of childhood that causes inability to speak or form abstract concepts and withdrawal from reality

**backache**  chronic and persistent or recurrent pain in lower back or shoulders, usu. due to tension or injury

**bacteremia**  blood poisoning

**baldness**  alopecia

**Barlow's syndrome**  congenital heart murmur due to defective mitral valve, causing susceptibility to bacterial infection

**bedwetting**  enuresis

**Bell's palsy**  paralysis of muscles on one side of face and inability to close eye, sometimes with loss of taste and excess sensitivity to noise

**bends**  compressed air sickness

**binge-purge syndrome**  bulimia

**blood poisoning**  prolonged invasion of bloodstream by pathogenic bacteria due to infectious disease or skin lesions; bacteremia; septicemia; toxemia

**boil**  tender, inflamed, pustulant area of skin, usu. due to staphylococcus infection; furuncle

**bronchial asthma**  asthma

**bulimia**  usu. psychogenic syndrome of overeating followed by vomiting, also caused by hypothalamus lesion; binge-purge syndrome

**bunion**  swelling of joint between big toe and first metatarsal

**bursitis**  inflammation of small fibrous sacs lined with synovial membrane, due to injury or infection, characterized by pain and stiffness in joints

**caisson disease**  compressed air sickness

**calcinosis**  abnormal deposit of calcium salts in tissue

**cancrum**  ulceration of lip or mouth; canker

**canker**  cancrum

**carpal tunnel syndrome**  compression of median nerve entering palm of hand that causes pain and numbing in middle and index fingers

**carsickness** motion sickness in automobile

**catalepsy** maintenance of abnormal postures or physical attitudes, esp. in catatonia

**cataplexy** recurrent, sudden collapses without loss of consciousness

**cataract** opacity of eye lens that causes blurred vision, esp. in elderly

**catatonia** syndrome of motor abnormalities, usu. stupor and catalepsy, due to mental condition

**celiac disease** hereditary intestinal disorder involving intolerance to wheat and rye

**chapping** sore roughening or cracking of skin from overexposure to elements

**cholelithiasis** presence of gallstones

**claudication** cramping pain from inadequate blood supply to muscle

**compressed air sickness** formation of nitrogen bubbles in bloodstream after experiencing high pressure at great ocean depths or high altitudes, characterized by pain and blockage of circulation; aeroembolism; bends; caisson disease; decompression sickness

**condition** state of ill health, esp. recurrent or chronic, caused by illness, injury, or heredity

**convergence insufficiency** difficulty in focusing eyes upon a nearby point or object

**corn** area of hard or thickened skin on or between toes

**cyst** any of various abnormal, liquid-filled sacs lined with epithelium, due to blocked duct, tumor, or congenital problem

**dandruff** small flakes of dead skin on scalp; scurf

**decompression sickness** compressed air sickness

**dehydration** deficiency or loss of water in body tissues marked by thirst, nausea, and exhaustion

**delirium** acute mental disorder due to organic brain disease, causing hallucinations, disorientation, and extreme excitation

**delirium tremens** dt's; psychosis due to alcoholic withdrawal, causing tremors, anxiety, sweating, and vivid hallucinations

**dependence** physical or psychological compulsion to consume certain drugs; addiction

**diaper rash** painful, reddened, raw area of skin around anus, buttocks, and genitals due to irritant stools, urine-soaked diapers, or candidiasis infection

**diplegia** paralysis involving both sides of body, esp. legs

**disorder** malfunction of normal metabolic or physiological process or part

**dropsy** former term for edema

**dysmenorrhea** painful, difficult menstruation

**ectopic pregnancy** state in which fertilized egg implants at site other than uterus

**eczema** superficial inflammation of skin characterized by itching, red rash, and scaling, due to various causes

**edema** excessive accumulation of fluid in tissues; dropsy

**enuresis** involuntary urination, esp. at night, usu. functional in nature; bedwetting

**fibrosis** thickening and scarring of connective tissue due to injury or inflammation

**furuncle** boil

**gallstone** hard mass of bile pigments, cholesterol, and calcium salts in gallbladder that causes pain or passes into and obstructs bile duct

**gangrene** decay and death of body tissue due to insufficient or absent blood supply, caused by disease or injury

**goiter** swollen neck due to enlarged thyroid gland

**hangnail** sliver of cuticle separated along edge of fingernail

**hay fever** common, usu. seasonal allergy to plant pollen that causes sneezing, runny nose, and watery eyes

**heat exhaustion** heat prostration

**heat prostration** fatigue and collapse from low blood pressure due to loss of body fluids after prolonged exposure to heat; heat exhaustion

**heatstroke** increased body temperature and eventual loss of consciousness without sweating, due to failure of body's heat regulating mechanism after prolonged exposure to heat; sunstroke

**hemophilia** hereditary deficiency of one blood coagulant that causes slowness in clotting and prolonged or spontaneous bleeding

**hemorrhoids** enlarged veins in anus walls, esp. due to prolonged constipation or diarrhea, characterized by fissure, painful swelling, and bleeding; piles

**hives** round, red itching wheals up to several inches across on skin, caused by acute or chronic allergic reaction; urticaria

**housemaid's knee** fluid-filled swelling of bursa in front of kneecap, often caused by prolonged kneeling

**hydrocephalus** excess of cerebrospinal fluid in brain ventricles that causes enlargement of head in children and pressure and drowsiness in adults

**hyperinsulinism** overproduction of insulin, due to glandular disturbances or poor nutrition, producing symptoms of hypoglycemia

**incontinence** involuntary passage or leakage of urine

**ingrown toenail** condition in which toenail grows into surrounding tissue

**intestinal obstruction** blockage that prevents passage of feces through intestine, due to hernia, tumor, or inflammation, causing pain and sometimes vomiting

**irritable bowel syndrome** recurrent chronic abdominal pain with constipation and/or diarrhea caused by abnormal contractions of colon muscles; spastic colon

**jet lag** disruption of biological and psychological rhythms by lengthy jet travel, causing mood alterations, sleep disturbance, and stress

**kidney stone** hard, pebblelike mass in kidney that causes pain and blood in urine; nephrolithiasis; renal calculus

**lentigo** liver spot

**liver spot** brown, roundish flat spot on skin that results from excess melanin, usu. in elderly; lentigo

**malnutrition** insufficient food consumption to satisfy bodily needs over prolonged period

**menorrhagia** excessive or prolonged menstrual bleeding

**migraine** recurrent, intense headache, often accompanied by blurred vision and vomiting, caused by contraction and dilation of arteries in brain

**mole** flat or raised area of brown pigment in skin

**motion sickness** nausea, vomiting, dizziness, and headache caused by motion

**myxedema** dry, firm, waxy swelling of skin and subcutaneous tissue, also characterized by labored speech and blunted senses

**narcolepsy** extreme tendency to fall asleep in quiet circumstances or during monotonous activities

**nephrolithiasis** presence of kidney stones

**nephrosis** syndrome characterized by edema, excess albumin in urine, and cholesterol in blood

**obesity** accumulation of excess fat, esp. in subcutaneous tissues, usu. due to overeating or nutritional imbalance

**pica** abnormal craving for unnatural foods due to nutritional deficiencies

**piles** hemorrhoids

**plantar wart** deep wart on sole of foot

**pneumonitis** inflammation of walls of air sacs in lungs due to virus or unknown causes

**premature birth** birth of baby before full term of pregnancy

**priapism** persistent erection of penis due to blood clottage

**psilosis** falling out of hair; sprue

**psoriasis** condition characterized by chronic, itchy, scaly silvery patches of skin, esp. on elbows, forearms, knees, and scalp, of unknown cause but sometimes due to anxiety

**pulmonary embolism** obstruction by blood clot of artery that conveys blood from heart to lungs

**Raynaud's disease** disorder, esp. in women, in which spasms of arteries to extremities cause fingertips and toes to turn pale, blue, and numb

**renal calculus** kidney stone

**retinitis pigmentosa** hereditary condition that causes progressive degeneration of retina of eye

**ringworm** highly contagious fungal infection of skin, esp. scalp and feet or under beard

**rosacea** chronic acne characterized by red, pustular lesions about nose, cheeks, and forehead

**sciatica** condition marked by pain down back of thigh, due to disintegration of intervertebral disk, accompanied by numbness and stiff back

**sclerosis** hardening of tissue after inflammation due to scarring, esp. in spinal cord or brain, causing progressive paralysis

**scurf** dandruff

**seasickness** motion sickness on ship or boat

**sebaceous cyst** cyst in oil-secreting gland of skin, filled with sebum; wen

**seborrhea** excessive secretion by sebaceous glands in face, esp. at puberty

**septicemia** tissue destruction by disease-causing bacteria or toxins absorbed from bloodstream; blood poisoning

**spastic colon** irritable bowel syndrome

**spondylosis** degeneration of intervertebral disks in backbone, causing pain and restricting movement

**sprue** deficient absorption of food due to intestinal disease that causes diarrhea, anemia, and inflamed tongue; psilosis

**stretch marks** whitish streaks, usu. on abdomen or thighs, due to short-term stretching of skin, as during pregnancy

**sunstroke** heatstroke

**surfer's knot** fluid-filled swelling of bursa in front of kneecap due to prolonged kneeling on surfboard

**tendonitis** inflammation of bands of connective tissue that join muscle to bones and joints, due to physical trauma or hereditary disease

**tennis elbow** painful inflammation of tendon on outer side of elbow due to overuse

**thalassemia** genetic, anemic condition characterized by deficiency of hemoglobin in blood

**thrombocytosis** condition marked by increase in number of platelets in blood

**thromboembolism** condition in which blood clot forms at one point in circulation, dislodges, and moves to another point

**thrombosis** formation of clots in blood, potentially causing obstruction of blood vessels

**tinea** athlete's foot

**tolerance** lessening of normal response to drug or other substance taken over a prolonged period, requiring increased dosages for normal reaction

**toxemia** blood poisoning caused by toxins formed by bacteria at site of infection

**tubal pregnancy** pregnancy in which fertilized egg implants in fallopian tube

**ulcer** open, inflamed, nonhealing sore in skin or mucous membrane, esp. in lining of alimentary canal

**urticaria** hives

**varicose veins** bulging, distended, sometimes painful veins in legs, rectum, or scrotum due to obstruction of blood flow

**vegetative state** severe brain damage and deep, persistent coma that cannot be reversed, necessitating maintenance of life functions by machines

**verruca** wart

**vertigo** feeling that one's surroundings are in motion, esp. spinning or tilting, due to disease of inner ear or vestibular nerve

**wart** small, hard, benign growth in skin, caused by virus; verucca

**wen** sebaceous cyst

**withdrawal** syndrome of sweating, vomiting, and tremors at cessation of consumption of substance to which one is addicted

## DEFECTS AND DISABILITIES

**abnormality** physical malformation or dysfunction

**achondroplasia** hereditary defect in bone and cartilage of limbs, which fail to grow to normal size; form of dwarfism

**acromegaly** abnormal growth of face, hands, and feet due to excessive pituitary production of growth hormone

**agnosia** associational brain disorder that prevents correct interpretation of sensations despite functioning sense organs

**albinism** inherited deficiency of pigment in skin, hair, and eyes

**alexia** acquired inability to read due to brain disease

**amaurosis** partial or complete blindness

**amputation** loss or removal of a limb or part of a limb

**anencephaly** partial or complete absence of bones of skull and large portions of brain, causing death in infants

**aphasia** speech and language comprehension disorder due to disease in left half of brain

**birth defect** disability or physical deformity present at birth, either inherited or acquired, that stems from problems during fetal period; congenital defect

**birthmark** skin blemish present at birth, often diminishing in size over time; nevus

**blindness** inability or marked reduction in ability to see, due to disease, injury, or birth defect

**blue baby** infant with congenital malformation of heart in which deoxygenated blood is pumped through body, producing bluish color in skin and lips

**bowleg** abnormal outcurving of legs that creates gap between knees

**bucktooth** extreme overbite of teeth of upper jaw over lower jaw

**cauliflower ear** enlarged and permanently deformed ear due to injury or repeated blows

**central hearing loss** hearing loss due to damage to auditory nerve between inner ear and brain or to brain's hearing center

**cerebral palsy** abnormal development of brain, usu. due to birth defect, that causes weakness and lack of limb coordination

**clawfoot** foot with excessively high arch and instep, usu. due to neuromuscular disease

**clawhand** extension of fingers at joint to hand, giving clawlike appearance, due to injury or leprosy

**cleft palate** fissure in midline of palate that did not properly fuse in embryonic stage

**clubfoot** birth defect in which foot is twisted downward and inward so sole cannot be placed flat on ground; talipes

**color blindness** any of various inherited conditions causing confusion of one or more colors; daltonism

**conductive hearing loss** hearing loss caused by block to passage of sound vibrations through outer or middle ear

**congenital defect** birth defect

**cretinism** congenital dwarfism, mental retardation, and coarseness of skin due to lack of thyroid hormone

**crippling** birth defect, disease, or injury that severely inhibits movement of limbs, esp. ability to walk

**crossed eyes** strabismus in which eyes turn inward toward nose

**curvature of the spine** abnormal deviation in position of spine: scoliosis, lordosis, or kyphosis

**daltonism** color blindness, esp. difficulty in distinguishing red and green

**deaf muteness** inability to hear or speak

**deafness** partial or total inability to hear in one or both ears due to birth defect, disease, injury, or lesion

**debility** physical weakness or feebleness

**defect** abnormal functioning, physical flaw, or blemish

**deformity** abnormal or disfigured body part

**dementia** chronic mental disorder or incapacity due to organic brain disease

**deviated septum** abnormal position of wall or partition in anatomical part, esp. nose

**diplopia** double vision

**disability** condition that makes one unfit, incapacitated, or crippled

**double vision** vision disorder due to various diseases or drug reaction, causing doubling of perceived images

**Down's syndrome** chromosomal abnormality that causes oblique slant to eyes, round head, flat nose, small ears, short stature, and reduced mental capacity; mongolism

**dwarfism** abnormally short stature from pituitary deficiency, genetic defect, or cretinism

**dyslalia** speech disorder due to aphasia in which patient uses peculiar vocabulary or sounds

**dyslexia** developmental disorder that hinders the ability to learn to read and write

**elephant man's disease** neurofibromatosis

**Erb's palsy** partial paralysis of baby's arm due to injury during birth

**erectile dysfunction** inability to attain or maintain erection

**eunuchoidism** deficiency of testicular function that retards development of genitals and secondary sex characteristics

**farsightedness** hyperopia

**fetal alcohol syndrome** FAS; fetal abnormalities due to consumption of alcohol by mother during pregnancy, leading to retardation and severe behavioral disorders in later life

**galactosemia** genetic inability to convert galactose in milk into usable glucose, causing feeding difficulties and vomiting in newborn infants

**gigantism** abnormal growth to excessive height due to oversecretion of growth hormone by pituitary gland

**hammertoe** clawlike deformity of toe with permanent flexion of second and third joints

**handicap** physical malfunction that causes partial or total inability to perform an activity

**harelip** congenital cleft in upper lip due to failure of embryonic tissue of lip to fuse properly

**heart defects** congenital anomalies in circulatory system during embryonic development, causing murmurs and hypertension

**hemiplegia** paralysis of one side of body only

**hereditary defect** congenital defect inherited from one's parents through genes

**heterotropia** strabismus

**humpback** enlarged, rounded deformation of upper back; hunchback; kyphosis

**hunchback** humpback

**hyperopia** condition in which parallel light rays focus behind retina, causing blurred appearance of objects closer than 20 feet (6 m); farsightedness

**hypospadias** congenital abnormality in which opening of urethra is on underside of penis

**idiocy** severe mental subnormality with IQ under 20, due to physical brain damage

**knock-knee** abnormal incurving of legs that causes gap between feet when knees touch and leads to degenerative arthritis

**kyphosis** humpback

**lameness** condition of having a limb disabled enough to impair normal movement, esp. walking

**learning disabilities** various conditions, esp. nervous system disorders such as dyslexia, that interfere with the ability to learn to read and write

**lordosis** accentuation of inward curvature of lower back or neck, causing swaybacked appearance; swayback

**malformation** physical deformity or abnormality

**malocclusion** irregularity between teeth of upper and lower jaw that causes overbite or underbite

**mental retardation** deficiency from birth in some mental functions, often from congenital condition such as Down's syndrome

**microcephalic** (*adj*) having a smaller-than-normal head

**mongolism** Down's syndrome

**mutation** altered inherited characteristic due to genetic change

**muteness** inability to speak due to congenital condition, disease, or injury

**myopia** condition in which parallel light rays focus in front of retina, causing blurred appearance of objects farther than 20 feet (6 m); nearsightedness

**nearsightedness** myopia

**neural tube defect** any congenital abnormality caused by failure of closure of embryonic neural tube from which brain and spinal cord develop

**neurofibromatosis** inherited genetic disorder characterized by bumps and patches on skin and sometimes skeletal deformity; elephant man's disease

**nevus** birthmark

**night blindness** inability to see in dim light or at night, due to disorder of cells in retina, caused esp. by vitamin A deficiency

**nystagmus** congenital or acquired, persistent, rapid, involuntary movement of eyeball, usu. from side to side

**otosclerosis** deafness commencing in adulthood due to disorder of bones in middle ear

**palsy** rare term for paralysis

**paralysis** muscle weakness of varying severity due to injury or disease, total paralysis resulting in motor inability

**paraparesis** weakness of both legs due to central nervous system disease

**paraplegia** paralysis of both legs due to disease or spinal injury

**paresis** muscular weakness and mental deterioration, less severe than paralysis, due to neurological disease, esp. syphilitic infection

**phenylketonuria** PKU; birth defect in protein metabolism that causes damage to nervous system and severe mental retardation

**pigeon toes** toes with abnormal inward turning, associated with knock-knee

**PKU** phenylketonuria

**presbyopia** farsightedness in which lens of eye is unable to focus properly

**quadriplegia** paralysis of both legs and both arms due to disease or spinal injury

**scoliosis** S-shaped lateral curvature of spine due to congenital or acquired abnormalities of vertebrae or muscles

**senile dementia** progressive, irreversible impairment of cognitive function in old age

**Siamese twins** identical twins joined at birth

**speech disorders** language defects due to organic or sensory deficiency, poor speech mechanisms, or psychological disorders

**spina bifida** congenital cleft of vertebral column

**squint** strabismus

**strabismus** any abnormal alignment of eyes due to muscle imbalance; heterotropia; squint

**stuttering** speech disorder characterized by blocks or spasms that interrupt normal speech rhythm

**subnormality** state of arrested or incomplete mental development due to congenital defect, injury, or gross environmental deprivation

**swayback** lordosis

**talipes** clubfoot

**tardive dyskinesia** nervous system disorder characterized by facial tics and involuntary motor movements, often caused by antipsychotic drugs

**Tay-Sachs disease** inherited disorder of lipid metabolism that causes blindness, mental retardation, and death in infancy

**walleye** strabismus in which eye turns outward, showing more white than normal

## Injuries and Accidents

**abarticulation** dislocation of joint

**abrasion** wearing away of surface of skin or mucous membrane by rubbing or scraping; scrape

**accident** unexpected or unintended occurrence that causes physical harm or injury

**acute abdomen** emergency condition caused by damage to one or more abdominal organs that results in intense pain and shock

**aneurysm** balloonlike swelling of arterial wall

**avulsion** tearing or separation of part or tissue

**black eye** bruising of eyelid and area around eye's orbit

**blood blister** swelling just beneath skin filled with blood, caused by unaccustomed friction

**blow** sudden, hard stroke against body surface with hard object

**break** simple or compound fracture of bone

**bruise** skin discoloration caused by escape of blood under skin following injury; contusion

**bump** bruising blow to body without breaking of skin

**burn** first, second, or third degree injury and damage to skin and subcutaneous tissue caused by heat, fire, wind, radiation, or caustic substance

**cerebral hemorrhage** bleeding from cerebral artery into brain tissue

**charley horse** injury to arm or leg in which muscles, blood vessels, nerves, and other soft tissues are damaged and cramp up

**chilblain** red, round, itchy swelling of skin on fingers or toes due to exposure to cold

**chip** small, thin piece broken loose from bone

**collapsed lung** folding together and contracting of lung due to air in surrounding chest cavity; pneumothorax

**compound fracture** breakage of bone into multiple fragments, sometimes with bone end piercing overlying skin

**concussion** injury to brain from violent, jarring blow to head, often with limited period of unconsciousness and impaired brain function

**contrecoup** injury to body part due to blow on opposite side away from injury

**contusion** surface injury in which skin is not broken; bruise

**crack** minor fracture that causes fissure in bone but not separation of bone parts

**cut** pierced or broken skin

**detached retina** separation of retina from layer of eyeball, causing loss of vision

**dislocation** displacement of bone from proper position in joint

**embolism** obstruction of artery by lodged blood clot, fat, air, or foreign body carried by circulating blood

**first-degree burn** reddening of outer layer of skin

**fissure** crack in bone or thin cleft in tissue

**flash burn** destruction of body tissue by exposure to radiant heat, esp. from nuclear explosion

**fracture** simple or compound breakage of bone

**frostbite** tissue damage from exposure to intense cold, esp. freezing of tissue and cessation of blood circulation

**gash** deep, ragged cut through skin

**hernia** protrusion of tissue or organ outside cavity it normally occupies, esp. in lower abdomen, due to physical strain or coughing

**herniated disk** slipped disk

**injury** physical damage to body part by action of external force

**laceration** tear in flesh, esp. with irregular edges

**maiming** injury that causes loss or crippling of body part

**miscarriage** spontaneous abortion and expulsion of fetus, usu. between 12th and 28th weeks of pregnancy

**mutilation** removal of or severe damage to essential body part

**perforation** piercing of skin and underlying tissue, or of any hollow viscus, by sharp object; puncture

**pneumothorax** collapsed lung

**poisoning** condition produced by introduction of natural or synthetic toxic substance into body or sometimes by toxin produced by organism itself

**pull** strain of muscle or ligament

**puncture** wound made by sharp object, with small entry hole and little or no bleeding

**rupture** forcible tearing apart or bursting of organ; hernia

**scald** burn inflicted by hot liquid or steam

**scrape** abrasion

**scratch** superficial lengthwise abrasion

**second-degree burn** blistering of surface skin and damage to underlying dermis

**separation** disarticulation of bone from normal joint position

**simple fracture** clean breakage of bone at one site without piercing of skin

**slash** long, sweeping deep cut made with blade

**slice** thin cut through skin and underlying tissue

**slipped disk** abnormal protrusion of disk between abutting vertebrae, esp. in lumbar region, causing painful pressure against spinal cord; herniated disk

**soft tissue damage** generalized injury to tissue without damage to bones or organs

**spontaneous abortion** birth or expulsion of fetus before it has developed enough for independent survival

**sprain** excessive overstretching of ligament

**strain** excessive stretching of muscle

**stress fracture** hairline break, often in bone of lower leg, due to intense physical activity

**stub** bumping of foot or toe against immovable object

**suffocation** cutting off of supply of air, esp. by strangling of throat or smothering of mouth and nose

**sunburn** burn due to overexposure to sunlight, usu. first degree

**tear** ripping or pulling apart of muscle; ragged cut in skin

**third-degree burn** total destruction of skin and damage to tissue beneath

**trauma** physical wound or injury, esp. one causing shock

**whiplash** damage to ligaments, vertebrae, and spinal cord in neck caused by sudden jerking back of head, esp. in auto accident

**wound** external injury in which skin is broken, torn, or pierced

## SIGNS AND SYMPTOMS

**abscess** localized accumulation of pus surrounded by inflamed tissue

**adenoma** benign tumor of glandular origin or structure

**adhesion** union by fibrous connective tissue of two normally separate parts

**albuminuria** presence of protein albumin in urine

**anesthesia** loss of sensation in part or all of body

**angina** feeling of suffocation; chest pain

**angina pectoris** pain in center of chest that spreads to jaws and arms, due to insufficient blood supply to heart

**ankylosis** fusion of bones across joint

**anxiety** fear neurosis that dominates personality

**apnea** temporary cessation of breathing

**arrhythmia** irregularity or deviation from normal rhythm or force of heartbeat

**asphyxiation** suffocation; failure of oxygen to reach tissues due to respiratory obstruction

**asthma** difficulty in breathing due to recurrent bronchospasm

**ataxia** shaky movements and unsteady gait when brain fails to regulate posture or direction of limb movements

**atony** lack of normal elastic muscle tone

**atrophy** wasting away of normally developed organ or tissue due to degeneration of cells

**attrition** normal wearing away of surface of teeth

**bacteremia** presence of bacteria in blood, indicating infection

**bad breath** halitosis

**bedsore** skin ulceration due to continuous pressure and rubbing on body part

**belch** audible expulsion of intestinal gas through mouth

**bellyache** *Informal.* pain in stomach

**black-and-blue mark** ecchymosis

**blackhead** black clump of fatty sebum and keratin in outlet of sebaceous gland; comedo

**blackout** temporary loss of consciousness, vision, or memory

**blennorrhagia** heavy discharge of mucus, esp. from urethra

**blister** external swelling that contains watery fluid and blood or pus, caused by friction

**bradycardia** slowing of heart rate to under fifty beats per minute

**brain damage** congenital or acquired injury to tissues of brain, due esp. to inadequate oxygen supply, trauma, incomplete brain development, or disease, manifested by range of symptoms from impaired speech to retardation to vegetative state

**break wind** audibly expel intestinal gas through anus

**breathlessness** dyspnea

**bronchospasm** muscular contraction that narrows bronchi and causes difficulty esp. in exhalation

**bruit** any abnormal sound or murmur heard esp. with a stethoscope

**bubo** swollen and inflamed lymph node in armpit or groin

**burp** *Informal.* audible expulsion of intestinal gas through mouth

**cachexia** weight loss, weakness, and debility associated with chronic disease

**calculus** pebblelike mass, such as gallstone or kidney stone, formed within body; hard tartar layer formed on teeth by plaque

**callus** hard thickening of area of skin undergoing rubbing, esp. on hands or feet; mass of tissue forming around fractured bone ends

**cardiac arrest** abrupt cessation of heartbeat, causing loss of pulse, consciousness, and breathing

**caries** decay of bone tissue, esp. tooth; cavity

**catarrh** excessive secretion of thick phlegm or mucus by mucous membrane of nose

**cavity** hollow in tooth produced by carious decay

**cephalalgia** headache

**chancre** painless ulcer on lips, genitals, urethra, or eyelid

**Cheyne-Stokes respiration** cyclical slowing of breathing to cessation, then speeding up to peak

**chills** coldness and shivering, esp. during fever

**choking** obstruction of windpipe, causing partial or complete stoppage of breathing

**cicatrix** scar

**clubbing** thickening of tissue at base of fingernail or toenail, esp. enlargement of fingertip

**cold sore** small swelling or eruption of skin around lips that dries to leave crusty patch; fever blister

**colic** severe abdominal pain, usu. in waves, due to gas or intestinal obstruction; inexplicable crying in infancy

**collapse** sudden, severe failure of health; falling down from upright position

**collywobbles** *Informal.* bellyache

**coma** prolonged state of deep unconsciousness from which patient cannot be roused

**comedo** blackhead

**concretion** stony mass coated with calcium deposits in internal organ; calculus

**confusion** mental disorder, distraction, or inability to distinguish things clearly

**congestion** accumulation of blood within an organ; clogging of upper respiratory system with mucus

**constipation** infrequent, difficult, often painful bowel movements with hard feces; irregularity

**convulsion** involuntary muscle contraction that causes contorted movements of body and limbs

**cough** violent exhalation of irritant particles or congestive mucus from respiratory system; tussis

**cramp** prolonged painful contraction or spasm of muscle

**crepitation** soft crackling sound heard in lungs through stethoscope; rale

**crepitus** crackling sound made by grating of bone on bone or cartilage, esp. in arthritic joint

**crick** painful muscle spasm or cramp in neck or upper back

**cyanosis** bluish discoloration of skin and mucous membrane due to inadequate oxygenation of blood

**cyst** abnormal sac or cavity lined with epithelium and filled with liquid or semisolid substance

**decrepit** (*adj*) wasted away or weakened by, or as if by, old age

**dehiscence** splitting open of a wound

**detumescence** reduction or subsidence of swelling

**deviation** abnormal position, esp. of one or both eyes

**diaphoresis** excessive sweating, esp. when artificially induced

**diarrhea** frequent bowel evacuation, esp. of soft or liquid feces; Montezuma's revenge; runs

**dizziness** feeling off balance, unstable, confused, as though whirling in place

**dumping syndrome** faintness, sweating, and paleness due to rapid emptying of stomach, esp. in one who has had gastrectomy

**dyspepsia** digestive disorder with abdominal pain and gas after eating, sometimes with nausea and vomiting; indigestion

**dyspnea** labored or difficult breathing; breathlessness

**earache** pain in inner ear; otalgia

**ecchymosis** bluish black mark on skin from release of blood into tissues, usu. due to injury; black-and-blue mark

**eclampsia** convulsions, esp. due to toxemia during pregnancy

**efflorescence** skin eruption, rash, or other lesion

**emaciation** severe weight loss and wasting of body from malnutrition, cancer, tuberculosis, or parasites

**emesis** vomiting; vomited matter

**empyema** accumulation of pus in body cavity, esp. pleural cavity

**enervation** weakness, lack of energy

**epistaxis** attack of bleeding from the nose

**eruption** skin irritation, esp. rash

**excitation** state of uncontrollable mental activity

**exhaustion** extreme fatigue

**exophthalmic goiter** enlargement of thyroid gland accompanied by protrusion of eyeball from orbit

**fainting** temporary loss of consciousness due to insufficient flow of blood to brain; syncope

**fart** *Vulgar.* audible expulsion of intestinal gas through anus

**fatigue** intense, prolonged tiredness

**febrile** (*adj*) affected with fever

**fever** rise in body temperature above normal 98.6 degrees F, often accompanied by delirium when over 104 degrees F; pyrexia

**fever blister** swelling or eruption of skin around lips with high or prolonged fever; cold sore

**fibrillation** rapid, uncontrolled irregular twitching of heart muscle

**fissure** crack in membrane lining

**flatulence** expulsion of intestinal gas through mouth by belching or through anus by passing flatus

**flatus** intestinal gas

**flush** reddening of face and/or neck

**flux** abnormally copious flow from organ or body cavity

**gas** mixture of swallowed air and fermented contents of stomach; flatus; intestinal gas

**glycosuria** excretion of excess sugar in urine, as in diabetes

**goose bumps** goose flesh

**goose flesh** tiny puckers of skin with hair standing on end due to contraction of blood vessels and small muscle attached to base of each hair follicle; goose bumps; horripilation

**granuloma** nodule of connective tissue and capillaries associated with tuberculosis, syphilis, or nonorganic foreign bodies

**growth** abnormal formation on or in body; tumor

**halitosis** offensive breath, esp. from diseases of gums, teeth, throat, or lungs; bad breath

**hallucination** false perception of something not there, esp. visual image

**headache** pain within skull, commonly due to stress or fatigue; cephalalgia

**heartburn** pain rising from abdomen to throat, often accompanied by bitter fluid in mouth; pyrosis

**heart murmur** blowing or swishing noise produced by blood passing through defective heart valve

**hematoma** clotted accumulation of blood in tissue forming solid swelling

**hemolysis** abnormally high level of red blood cell destruction, usu. due to toxins or hereditary defects

**hemorrhage** outflow of blood from ruptured blood vessel, esp. internal bleeding

**hiccup** characteristic sound made by abrupt involuntary lowering of diaphragm and closing of upper end of trachea

**high blood pressure** elevation of pressure of blood in main arteries above normal range for age group; hypertension

**horripilation** goose flesh

**hydrocele** accumulation of watery fluid, esp. about testis

**hyperglycemia** excess of sugar in bloodstream, esp. due to diabetes mellitus

**hyperplasia** increase in number of fat cells, causing obesity

**hypersensitivity** uncommonly strong reaction to stimulus such as sunlight or a chemical, including most allergies

**hypertension** high blood pressure

**hyperthermia** exceptionally high body temperature of 105 degrees F or above; fever induced as treatment

**hypertrophy** increase in size of tissue or organ due to enlargement of cells

**hyperventilation** abnormally rapid breathing that lowers carbon dioxide concentration in blood

**hypopraxia** listlessness, enfeeblement, or lack of interest in activity

**hypotension** low blood pressure

**hypothermia** dropping of body temperature below normal range

**hysteria** extreme emotional excitation, sensory and motor disturbances, and outbursts of uncontrolled feeling

**illusion** false perception due to misinterpreted stimuli; belief in existence of that which does not exist

**incapacity** inability to perform some action

**incoherence** inability to produce intelligible, logical speech or thought

**incontinence** inability to control passage of urine

**indigestion** dyspepsia

**infirmity** feebleness, frailty

**inflammation** immediate defense reaction of tissue to injury or attack, involving pain, heat, redness, and swelling

**insomnia** inability to fall asleep or remain asleep

**intestinal gas** gas; flatus

**irregularity** constipation

**ischemia** insufficient blood flow to body part due to constriction or blockage of blood vessels

**itching** minor local skin irritation relieved by scratching; pruritus

**jaundice** yellowing of skin and whites of eyes from excess bilirubin in blood, often due to obstructed ducts or liver disease

**labored breathing** difficulty in inhaling air

**lesion** any localized, abnormal structural change in tissue or body part resulting in impaired function, including abscess, ulcer, or tumor

**leukocytosis** abnormal level in number of white blood cells, usu. due to infection

**leukopenia** reduction in number of white blood cells to below normal level

**lightheadedness** dizziness, mental confusion

**lividity** bluish coloration of skin

**low blood pressure** dropping of pressure of blood in main arteries below normal range for age

**low-grade fever** slight rise in body temperature above normal 98.6 degrees F

**lumbago** lower backache due to injury or sciatica

**macule** discoloration or thickening of skin in contrast to surrounding area

**malaise** general sense of being unwell, often accompanied by physical discomfort and weakness

**mania** excessive activity and euphoria

**Montezuma's revenge** *Slang.* diarrhea, usu. caused by eating contaminated food in foreign country

**mottling** blotches, streaks, or spots on skin

**mucus** viscous fluid secreted by mucous membrane, esp. in upper respiratory tract

**nasal discharge** drainage of mucus through nose

**nausea** feeling that one is about to vomit

**necrosis** death of cells in organ or tissue

**neoplasm** new tumor caused by uncontrolled reproduction of abnormal cells

**nephralgia** pain in kidney and loin area

**neuralgia** severe burning or stabbing pain along course of nerve

**neurasthenia** outdated or nontechnical term for fatigue, irritability, headache, dizziness, anxiety, and intolerance to noise due to head injury or mental illness

**night sweats** copious perspiration while sleeping

**nit** louse egg that attaches to body

**obesity** distinct, intense accumulation of excess fat in body

**otalgia** earache

**pain** sensation of strong discomfort in bodily part

**palpitation** abnormally rapid or violent heartbeat, esp. due to fear, exertion, neurosis, or arrhythmia

**papule** small, superficial bump or spot on skin, often part of rash

**paroxysm** sudden, violent spasm or convulsion; abrupt worsening of symptom

**perspiration** sweating

**phlegm** sputum

**pimple** small, pustulant, inflamed swelling on skin, often from bacterial infection

**plaque** sticky, colorless mixture of saliva, bacteria, and carbohydrates on surface of teeth that causes tartar and caries

**pock** small pus-filled eruption of skin

**poliosis** premature graying of hair

**polyp** benign growth on mucous membrane, esp. in nose, ear, or stomach

**postnasal drip** draining of mucus from nose onto pharynx

**proptosis** forward displacement of an organ, esp. eyeball

**prostration** total exhaustion

**pruritus** itching

**purpura** skin rash due to bleeding into skin from defective capillaries or blood platelet deficiency

**pus** thick yellow or green liquid containing blood cells and dead cells, formed at site of infection or inflammation

**pustule** small, pus-containing skin blister

**putrescence** foul smell caused by decomposition of tissue

**pyrexia** fever

**pyrosis** heartburn

**rale** crepitation

**rash** temporary skin eruption characterized by reddening and itching, esp. in form of pimples, hives, or wheals

**regurgitation** vomiting

**renal colic** severe pain in kidney

**respiratory arrest** cessation of breathing

**rheum** watery discharge from mucous membrane of mouth, eyes, or nose

**runny nose** discharge of mucus from nose

**runs** *Informal.* diarrhea

**scab** hard crust of blood, serum, or pus over healing wound

**scar** mark left on skin by healing wound where connective tissues replace damaged tissues; cicatrix

**seizure** sudden attack of disease or condition

**senescence** bodily degeneration after maturity

**senility** loss of intellectual faculties in old age

**shin splint** pain in front of shin, usu. caused by running on hard surface

**shivers** uncontrollable trembling

**shock** acute, progressive circulatory collapse, with blood pressure too low to maintain adequate blood supply to tissues, causing cold sweat, paleness, weak but rapid pulse, dilated pupils, irregular breathing, dry mouth, and reduced urine flow

**side effect**  incidental or secondary manifestation, esp. of medication

**sign**  physical, psychological, or behavioral manifestation of a disease, injury, condition, or disability

**skin eruption**  swelling, discoloration, or roughening of skin

**sneeze**  involuntary violent reflex expulsion of air caused by irritation of mucous membrane lining nasal cavity

**sore**  ulcer or open wound on skin or mucous membrane from injury or infection

**spasm**  sustained involuntary muscular contraction

**spasticity**  resistance to passive movement of limb; lack of motor coordination

**sputum**  mucus coughed up from respiratory tract; phlegm

**stitch**  sudden, sharp pain, usu. in muscle between ribs

**stomachache**  generalized intestinal pain, often accompanied by diarrhea, nausea, and vomiting

**strangury**  painful urination in which the urine is emitted in droplets due to muscle spasms

**stridor**  loud, harsh breathing noise due to partial obstruction of trachea or larynx

**suppuration**  formation and discharge of pus

**sweating**  secretion of salty, watery fluid by glands lying in dermis of skin; perspiration

**swelling**  growth of body part, curving outward from surface, esp. due to pressure from within; tumescence

**sycosis**  inflammation and itching of hair follicles

**symptom**  indication of disease or disorder, esp. one recognizable by patient

**syncope**  fainting

**syndrome**  combination of signs and symptoms

**tachycardia**  rapid heart rate

**tachypnea**  rapid breathing

**tartar**  calcareous deposit and encrustation on teeth

**tetany**  spasm and twitching of muscles of face, hands, and feet

**throw up** (*vb*)  vomit

**tic**  uncontrolled muscle twitch, esp. in face

**tic douloureux**  neuralgia of facial nerves

**tinnitus**  ringing in the ears

**toothache**  pain associated with teeth, gums, and surrounding tissue, usu. due to tooth decay or caries

**torpor**  sluggishness, unresponsiveness to stimuli

**toxemia**  accumulation of toxins in blood

**toxicosis**  reaction to toxin in body; poisoning

**toxic shock**  shock syndrome caused by toxin in body, often associated with tampon use

**tremor**  uncontrollable, rhythmical alternating movement of body part, esp. hands

**tubercle**  nodular lesion of lung due to tuberculosis

**tumescence**  swelling, esp. due to accumulation of blood or other fluid in tissue

**tumor**  abnormal growth of tissue in or on body part

**tussis**  cough

**unconsciousness**  lack of awareness of one's surroundings and unresponsiveness to stimuli; state of being asleep

**underweight**  state of insufficient or subnormal accumulation of body fat

**uremia**  toxic condition due to presence in blood of excess urea and other nitrogenous wastes excreted by kidney

**vesicle**  very small skin blister containing clear serum

**vital signs**  pulse rate, blood pressure, respiration, and body temperature, forming index of essential body functions

**vomiting**  reflex ejection of contents of stomach through mouth; emesis; regurgitation

**watery eyes**  eyes that discharge rheum or tears

**welt**  raised ridge on skin caused by slash or blow

**wheal**  temporary, itching, red or pale raised area of skin due to abrasion or allergy

**wheezing**  high-pitched breathing sounds due to bronchospasm

**withdrawal symptoms**  sweating, anxiety, nausea, vomiting, cramps, and tremors at cessation of addictive substance abuse

**withering**  drying out or shriveling of patch of skin

**xerostomia**  diminished secretion of saliva that causes abnormally dry mouth, esp. as drug reaction

**zit**  *Slang.* pimple

## DIAGNOSTIC TERMINOLOGY

**abnormality**  malformed part or dysfunctional process

**abruptio**  separation

**acquired** (*adj*)  designating condition or disorder contracted after birth, not hereditary

**active immunity**  production of antibodies by body's cells following attack of disease or immunization

**acute** (*adj*)  designating disease with rapid onset, severe symptoms, and brief duration, opposite of chronic

**affliction**  condition that causes pain and suffering

**agonal** (*adj*)  describing phenomena associated with death, such as cessation of breathing or heartbeat

**allergen**  antigen that causes allergy in sensitive person

**ambulatory** (*adj*)  designating patient who is able to leave bed and walk

**ameba**  single-celled, microscopic organism that may cause disease

**anodynia**  absence of pain

**antibiotic**  substance derived from a microorganism or fungus that destroys or inhibits growth of other microorganisms

**antibody**  special blood protein synthesized in lymphoid tissue in response to antigen, which it attacks and neutralizes

**antigen**  foreign substance, usu. protein, against which body produces an antibody

**arbovirus**  RNA-containing virus that can cause disease when transmitted from animals to humans by insects

**asepsis**  complete absence of disease-causing bacteria, viruses, fungi, or microorganisms

**asymptomatic** (*adj*)  showing no evidence of a disease

**atresia**  congenital absence or abnormal narrowing of body opening

**autoimmune** (*adj*)  designating disorder of body's defense mechanism in which antibodies are produced against body's own tissues, treating them as foreign substances

**autologous** (*adj*)  derived from same individual or organism

**autonomic** (*adj*)  occurring involuntarily, controlled by autonomic nervous system

**bacillus**  rod-shaped bacterium

**bacteria**  *pl., sing.* **bacterium;** primitive microorganisms, usu. unicellular with unique cell wall composition, that reproduce by simple division and often cause disease

**bacterial** (*adj*) designating disease, condition, or infection caused by bacteria

**bedridden** (*adj*) descriptive of patient unable to leave bed

**benign** (*adj*) consisting of localized mass of nonmalignant specialized cells within connective tissue that do not invade and destroy tissue or spread throughout body

**blood alcohol content** measure of alcohol concentration in blood; blood alcohol level

**blood pressure** pressure of blood in main arteries

**breech presentation** abnormal position of baby in womb, causing it to be delivered buttocks first

**carcinogen** substance that may produce cancer in living tissue

**carrier** individual that harbors pathogen without displaying symptoms

**cast** mass of dead, cellular, fatty material within body cavity that takes the shape of the cavity and can be released to appear elsewhere

**cerebral** (*adj*) of the brain

**chronic** (*adj*) designating disease of long duration with very slow changes and often gradual onset of recurrent symptoms, opposite of acute

**clot** soft, thickened lump formed in liquid, esp. blood

**coccus** spherical bacterium

**communicable** (*adj*) designating disease that can be transmitted from one person to another by physical contact, a carrier, or droplets exhaled into air

**condition** something causing state of poor health; official status of hospitalized patient, such as grave, critical, serious, poor, guarded, stable, fair, satisfactory, or good

**congenital** (*adj*) designating condition present at birth, often inherited

**contagious** (*adj*) designating any communicable disease, esp. one transmitted by physical contact

**contract** (*vb*) acquire a disease

**coronary** (*adj*) of or pertaining to arteries of heart

**cortical** (*adj*) involving external layers of brain

**cryptogenic** (*adj*) of unknown origin

**cytomegalovirus** DNA virus in herpes family that causes enlargement of epithelial cells and mononucleosislike disease

**defect** abnormal functioning, physical flaw or blemish

**deformity** abnormal or disfigured body part

**degenerative** (*adj*) designating disease or condition growing progressively worse due to deterioration in cell structure or function

**deterioration** worsening of condition

**diagnosis** process of determining by examination the nature of a disease or condition

**disability** condition that makes one unfit, incapacitated, or crippled

**discharge** liquid or semisolid substance emitted from body

**disease** particular disorder of organism with specific cause and recognizable symptoms

**disorder** any bodily abnormality or failure to function

**DOA** *dead on arrival:* describing patient's condition on reaching hospital

**dose-response phenomenon** condition in which there is increased risk with greater exposure to toxic substance

**dysfunction** abnormality, impairment, or cessation of bodily function

**dystrophy** faulty nutrition; disorder characterized by abnormal development of muscle

**embolus** blood clot, fat, air, amniotic fluid, or foreign body circulated by blood and lodged at some point in cardiovascular system

**endemic** disease that is constantly present in particular region but generally under control

**epidemic** contagious disease that spreads rapidly through population of a specific region

**etiology** cause of specific disease

**failure** total cessation of bodily function

**fastigium** point at which symptoms of disease are most pronounced

**fatal** (*adj*) causing death

**fistula** abnormal passage that leads from abscess or cavity to skin or to another abscess or cavity, caused by disease or injury

**genetic** (*adj*) designating condition inherited through chromosomes from one's parents

**germ** any disease-causing microorganism

**gusher** *Informal.* cut artery

**hereditary** (*adj*) designating condition transmitted from parents to offspring

**hypochondria** obsession with real and imagined physical ailments

**iatrogenic** (*adj*) resulting from treatment, esp. of a condition or disease

**idiopathic** (*adj*) describing condition of unknown cause or one that develops spontaneously

**immunity** ability of body to recognize and neutralize foreign matter, either natural or acquired

**impairment** damage to or weakening of body part or function

**inborn immunity** congenital resistance to specific disease

**incubation period** time between entry of disease organisms into body and onset of disease symptoms

**infarction** death of tissue due to oxygen deprivation

**infection** invasion of body by harmful pathogen

**infectious** (*adj*) designating a communicable disease, esp. one caused by invasion of harmful organisms such as bacterium, fungus, protozoan, or virus into body

**infestation** attack on body by parasitic microorganism

**injury** physical damage to body part by action of external force

**intervention** treatment or procedure designed to prevent disease from running its course

**intramuscular** (*adj*) situated in or administered by entering a muscle, used esp. of injections

**irreversible** (*adj*) impossible to halt or reverse by treatment

**languishing** (*adj*) failing in health, weakening, losing vigor

**life-threatening** (*adj*) designating a potentially fatal condition or procedure

**malabsorption** failure to digest certain nutrients or disruption of process by which digestive by-products are passed through intestinal wall into bloodstream

**malignant** (*adj*) consisting of a tumor that invades and destroys tissue in which it originates and can spread to other sites in body through vascular system

**metastasis** spread of malignant tumor far from site of origin, usu. through vascular system

**microbe** microorganism

**microorganism** any organism not visible to naked eye, such as bacterium, protozoan, fungus, and virus; microbe

**mold** multicellular filamentous fungus

**morbidity** state of being diseased

**morbific** (*adj*) causing disease

**moribund** (*adj*) dying

**mortify** (*vb*) cause body tissue to decay

**motor** (*adj*) designating muscular activity stimulated by impulses from central nervous system

**mutagen** external agent that increases mutation rate in cells

**mycosis** infection due to yeast or mold

**natural immunity** inborn lack of susceptibility to specific disease

**necrosis** death of discrete region of tissue

**nosocomial** (*adj*) hospital-induced, used esp. of a disease

**occlusion** closing or obstruction of hollow organ or body part

**opportunistic** (*adj*) designating disease or infection occurring only under certain conditions, as when immune system is impaired

**pandemic** (*adj*) designating epidemic disease that spreads to different countries over large region

**parasite** organism that lives in or on another living organism while contributing nothing to host's welfare, often causing irritation or interfering with function

**passive immunity** short-term resistance to disease from injection of another's antibodies

**pathogen** microorganism that produces a communicable disease

**pathogenic** (*adj*) disease-causing

**pathology** study of disease processes; course of a disease

**perfusion** passage of fluid through tissue, esp. blood through lungs

**plasma** liquid in which blood cells are suspended

**prognosis** assessment of future course and outcome of patient's disease

**progressive** (*adj*) growing steadily worse, often fatal

**psychomotor** (*adj*) relating to disorders of muscular activity affected by cerebral disturbances

**psychosomatic** (*adj*) designating a disease caused by interaction of physical and mental factors

**purulent** (*adj*) pustulant

**pustulant** (*adj*) containing and/or discharging pus; purulent

**referred pain** pain felt in unexpected part of body separate from its source

**reflex** automatic, involuntary activity caused by simple nervous circuits

**rejection** immune reaction to transplanted organ or foreign substance

**relapse** recurrence of disease symptoms after apparent recovery

**remission** lessening of severity of symptoms, esp. temporary disappearance during course of chronic or terminal illness

**resistance** measure of body's immunity to disease; degree to which disease is unaffected by antibiotics or drugs

**rickettsiae** group of parasitic organisms similar to bacteria that infest body through ticks or mites

**saprophyte** free-living organism that lives on dead or putrefying tissues

**scabbing** formation of hard crust of blood, serum, and pus over healing wound

**scourge** wasting disease that affects large region

**septic** (*adj*) affected with putrefactive destruction by disease-carrying bacteria or their toxins

**serum** fluid that separates from clotted blood or standing blood plasma

**spirillum** spiral bacterium

**spirochete** corkscrew-shaped bacterium

**spore** small reproductive body produced by microorganisms

**staphylococcus** any of several spherical, pathogenic bacteria in irregular clusters, both saprophytes and parasites

**stenosis** abnormal narrowing of blood vessel or heart valve

**streptobacillus** any of various rodlike bacteria that tend to form filaments

**streptococcus** any of several spherical, chain-forming pathogenic bacteria, mostly saprophytes

**stress** effect on human body of physical and mental demands and pressures

**subclinical** (*adj*) designating suspected disease or injury that is not developed enough to produce definite signs and symptoms

**symptom** characteristic indication of disease or disorder

**syndrome** set of signs and symptoms indicative of particular disease or condition

**systemic** (*adj*) affecting entire body, not just one part

**teratogen** substance or process that causes developmental abnormalities in fetus

**terminal** (*adj*) fatal; in or of final stage of fatal disease

**touch** *Informal*. mild onset of illness

**toxic** (*adj*) poisonous

**toxin** poisonous substance

**vector** any agent, such as insect or tick, that transmits parasitic microorganisms and infectious diseases from host to host

**viral** (*adj*) produced by a virus

**viral infection** infection caused by virus

**virulent** (*adj*) disease-producing

**virus** ultramicroscopic, metabolically inert agent composed of DNA or RNA core and protein coating, capable of replication only within living host cells; *Informal*. disease caused by a virus

**wasting** (*adj*) severely destructive to health

**yeast** unicellular fungus that usu. reproduces asexually by budding

**zoonosis** any infectious disease of animals, such as rabies, that can be transmitted to humans

# HEALTH, FITNESS, AND ENHANCEMENT

Activities and Treatments
Equipment and Resources
Nutrition for Fitness

**SEE ALSO**: Chap. 1: Hair and Grooming; Chap. 2: Biology; Chap. 4: Medicine; Chap. 9: Cooking and Cuisine; Chap. 17: Games, Activities, and Toys; Chap. 25: Truth, Wisdom, and Spiritual Attainment

## ACTIVITIES AND TREATMENTS

**acupressure** massage therapy technique that uses acupuncture points to release tension and promote relaxation and healing; shiatsu

**acupuncture** Chinese practice of puncturing body with

needles at specific points along meridians to relieve pain and cure disease

**aerobic dance** vigorous cardiovascular exercise that incorporates dance movements

**aerobics** vigorous exercise that induces accelerated heartbeat to improve cardiovascular health

**aikido** Japanese martial art form

**Alexander technique** *Trademark.* body alignment and co-ordination through efficient movement and stress release

**Ayurveda** ancient Indian medical system of classifying and treating somatic types for optimal health and functioning

**biofeedback** technique that involves instrument stress readings and training of bodily systems to increase awareness and control of pain and tension

**bodybuilding** development of muscle layer through program of weightlifting and nutritional supplements

**body contouring** cosmetic surgery to reshape body outline

**body mechanics** science and study of bodily motion, esp. for optimal benefits of exercise

**body work** physical therapy, healing, or relaxation treatments based on a particular system, such as polarity, yoga, Alexander, Reiki, acupressure, Rolfing, shiatsu, or massage therapy

**body wrap** herbal, steam, or heat weight-loss treatment

**breast augmentation** surgical silicone implantation in breast for cosmetic enhancement

**breast reduction** surgical removal of excess breast tissue

**breathing exercises** practice of deep, regular breathing to increase lung capacity, improve overall health, and relieve tension

**buddy system** pairing of two individuals for mutual safety in dangerous activity

**bulking** increasing size of muscles by weight work

**calisthenics** individual gymnastic exercises

**cap** artificial coating of teeth to enhance size, shape, and whiteness

**cardiopulmonary resuscitation** CPR; procedure to restore normal breathing and heart activity after cardiac arrest, by heart massage and often electrical and mechanical equipment

**cardiorespiratory endurance** stamina of heart and lungs during exercise

**cellulite reduction** treatment to diminish irregular fatty tissue deposits, esp. on thighs and buttocks

**chemical peel** cosmetic chemical burning of facial skin to promote new, smooth skin growth

**chiropractic adjustment** manipulation of spine to relieve tension, pressure, and imbalances in bones, muscles, and nerves

**circuit training** system that uses series of weight machines to work all muscle areas

**collagen injection** implantation of collagen into wrinkles and folds to improve appearance of skin

**colonic irrigation** treatment involving cleansing of colon with water to flush toxic impurities

**cooldown** period of gentle, reduced activity after vigorous exercise

**cosmetic surgery** surgical alteration of face or body for aesthetic enhancement; plastic surgery

**CPR** *cardiopulmonary resuscitation*

**crunch** sit-up in which one reaches out with arms toward bent knees

**dancercise** system of vigorous dance movements done to music for fitness

**dermabrasion** process of stripping top layer of facial skin to promote new, smooth skin growth

**detoxification** program of exercise, nutrition, and cleansing of system to remove pollutants from body, esp. narcotics or alcohol

**diet** specific program of food preparation and eating to enhance health and appearance

**endurance** stamina, capacity for prolonged exercise

**ergonomics** study or practice of adapting working environment to needs of body

**exercise** physical activity performed to enhance health and appearance

**eye tuck** cosmetic surgery to remove excess skin folds around eyes

**face-lift** cosmetic surgery to remove excess facial skin folds and wrinkles

**fast** period of abstention from food; (*vb*) abstain from eating for prolonged period

**Feldenkrais method** *Trademark.* system of exploration and adjustment of movement patterns for flexibility, coordination, and dynamic posture

**first aid** simple medical procedures for health and safety

**fitness** maintenance and improvement of health through exercise and proper diet; condition of being in good health

**flexibility** degree of movement, rotation possible in body and joints

**hamstring stretch** bending exercise for back of thigh

**Heimlich maneuver** procedure that involves clearing windpipe of choking victim by sudden upward pressure on abdomen

**herbalism** use of herbs for healing

**holistic health** approach that stresses complete system rather than treatment of specific parts and symptoms, based on theory that entity is more than sum of its parts

**isometric exercise** system that uses muscle groups acting in opposition or against a fixed object

**isotonic exercise** system that uses normal contraction of muscles

**jogging** gentle, medium-slow running gait, esp. as regular program of exercise

**jujitsu** Japanese martial art based on use of opponent's weight against him or her through leverage and understanding of anatomy

**jumping jack** calisthenic exercise that involves jumping and reaching up simultaneously

**karate** Japanese martial art form usu. used for defense by striking sensitive areas of attacker's body with hands, elbows, legs, or feet

**kinesiology** principles of anatomy and mechanics in human movement

**kung fu** Chinese martial art form usu. used for defense by striking vulnerable parts of attacker's body with hands and legs

**lifesaving** training in activities connected with saving of human life, esp. from drowning

**liposuction** surgical removal of excess body fat by suctioning it away through a tube

**low-impact aerobics** gentle form of aerobic exercise, with reduced stress to feet and joints

**marathon running** long-distance running, traditionally over twenty-six mile course

**martial arts** Asian forms of exercise and self-defense that emphasize balance and harmony of passive and active motions

**massage** system of relaxation using hands to knead, rub, stroke, and press body parts

**mouth-to-mouth resuscitation** method of blowing air directly into victim's mouth for artificial respiration

**nose job** *Informal.* rhinoplasty

**overstretching** excessively intense or abrupt stretching that results in torn or bruised muscle tissue

**passive exercise machine** electronic device that electrically stimulates muscles

**physiotherapy** massage, heat treatments, and other physical manipulations

**plastic surgery** cosmetic surgery

**polarity therapy** body work to balance magnetic polarization by manipulation, exercise, and diet

**power lifting** lifting substantial amounts of weight to increase muscle bulk

**pulse rate** heartbeats per minute; measure of exercise intensity and cardiovascular benefits

**push-up** exercise done by pushing upper body away from floor with arms to build upper body strength

**race walking** competitive speedwalking

**reflexology** massage of specific areas of foot, or sometimes hand, to treat ailments or relieve stress elsewhere in body

**regime** program or system of exercise and nutrition for better health; regimen

**regimen** regime

**Reiki** method of activating and balancing life force energy, used esp. by chiropractors and in massage

**rhinoplasty** cosmetic surgery on the nose; nose job

**Rolfing** *Trademark.* physical therapy system that emphasizes realignment of body's internal dynamics through intense deep massage and stretching of connective tissue

**rope jumping** cardiovascular exercise done by jumping over rope held by jumper and rotated around body

**rubdown** vigorous massage

**running** physical fitness regime of running either long distances or short intense distances for maximum speed

**shiatsu** Japanese massage system that involves bodily points and meridians responsive to pressure; acupressure

**silicone implant** cosmetic surgery that involves buildup of bodily proportions by addition of silicone, esp. in breasts

**sit-up** abdominal exercise in which one bends upper body from supine position with legs flat

**slimnastics** gymnastic exercises specifically for weight reduction

**speedwalking** vigorous, quick walking exercise with arms swinging

**stamina** power to sustain effort or activity

**steroid** any of various hormonal compounds that accelerate increase in muscle bulk from exercise, often with harmful side effects

**strength** ability to apply muscular force

**stress management** system of coping with stress and tension using biofeedback, relaxation techniques, and exercise

**sunbathing** exposing most or all of one's body to sun's rays, usu. for suntan

**suntan** darkened pigmentation of skin from exposure to sun

**Swedish massage** systematic massage that uses manipulation and gradual soothing of muscles and nervous system

**swimnastics** calisthenic exercises done while immersed in water

**tae kwon do** Korean martial art form that resembles karate

**ta'i chi chu'an** Chinese Taoist martial art form that emphasizes balance, graceful meditative movements, and coordinated breathing

**taking the waters** visiting a spa for beneficial effects of mineral spring water

**tanning** developing deeper skin tone from intentional exposure to sun's rays or sunlamp

**toning** firming muscles by moderate weight work without building bulk

**tooth bonding** cosmetic dental procedure of coating front surface of tooth for improved appearance

**tooth capping** cosmetic dental procedure of covering entire tooth with white enamel-like cap, for improved appearance

**training** regular pursuit of athletic activities to build strength and endurance or improve performance

**triathletics** exercise system that involves swimming, running, and bicycling over significant distances

**walking** least strenuous, most natural aerobic exercise

**warmup** brief period of stretching and loosening activity prior to vigorous exercise

**weightlifting** practice of lifting substantial amounts of weight to tone and strengthen muscles; weight work

**weight work** weightlifting

**work out** (*vb*) engage in period of strenuous exercise

**workout** strenuous exercise, esp. aerobic

**wushu** Chinese philosophical teachings that form the basis of certain martial arts

**yoga** system of physical postures and meditative breathing to tone muscles and organs, improve balance, flexibility, and strength, and create integration of mind and body

## EQUIPMENT AND RESOURCES

**ankle weights** weighted straps worn on ankles while one exercises

**barbell** rod with weighted disks at both ends

**dojo** karate or martial arts gymnasium

**dumbbell** hand-held weight; barbell

**earplug** piece of soft material inserted in outer ear to keep out noise or water

**exercise machine** mechanical device that aids weightlifting and muscle-toning exercises

**exercycle** stationary bicycle

**fat farm** *Informal.* weight-loss clinic at sanitarium or resort

**free weights** dumbbells or barbells; weights lifted without weight machines

**gravity boots** sturdy boots that hold wearer upside down

**gymnasium** enclosed area for physical activity, training, and contests

**health club** gymnasium, usu. for members only, with exercise and spa facilities

**heating pad** electric or water-heated pad for soothing sore muscles or injuries

**hot tub** whirlpool

**hot water bag** rubber container filled with hot water, used to soothe injured muscles

**ice pack** cold compress for sore or injured muscles or ligaments and pain reduction

**isolation tank** enclosed, sensory-deprivation container in which one floats, without stimuli, for deep relaxation

**Jacuzzi** *Trademark.* whirlpool spa with turbulent hot water

**jump rope** length of rope with handles, swung over head and under uplifted feet in jumping exercise

**leg warmers** knitted socklike garments that cover and warm lower legs during exercise

**leotard** tight, lightweight, knitted exercise garment for torso

**Lifecycle** *Trademark.* stationary exercise bicycle that measures rider's pulse and calories burned

**life jacket** buoyant, sleeveless jacket to prevent drowning; life vest

**life net** strong net used to catch people jumping from burning building

**life preserver** buoyant vest, jacket, or ring used to remain afloat in water

**life vest** life jacket

**Mae West** inflatable life jacket, esp. for aviator downed at sea

**masseur** male practitioner of massage

**masseuse** female practitioner of massage

**medicine ball** large, heavy ball for exercise and recreation

**mineral bath** immersion in mineral-rich waters, esp. at spa

**mud bath** immersion in mud formed by interaction of clay and hot spring water

**Nautilus machines** *Trademark.* system of weight training machines

**oxygen mask** covering for mouth and nose connected to oxygen tank

**parcourse** outdoor running and exercise course, esp. in urban areas

**prosthetic device** artificial replacement for body part

**punching bag** inflated leather bag suspended at eye level for punching

**rowing machine** device that simulates exercise of rowing a boat with oars

**running shoes** rubber-soled shoes with good support for running or jogging

**sauna** Scandinavian steam bath that uses dry heat

**spa** mineral spring resort; area of health club with sauna, steam room, and whirlpool

**Stairmaster** *Trademark.* stationary, adjustable electronic stairs for aerobic climbing exercise

**stall bar** series of horizontal wooden rungs between uprights, used for climbing or stretching exercises

**stationary bicycle** exercise bicycle for cardiovascular and muscular toning

**steam room** tiled room heated with abundant steam, for bathing, refreshment, sweating, and relaxation

**sudatorium** dry heat room, sauna

**sunlamp** electric light that produces ultraviolet tanning rays

**sweatband** headband worn to keep perspiration from dripping onto face during exercise

**tanning salon** establishment that uses sunlamps to cultivate artificial suntan

**track** path for runners, usu. oval

**treadmill** rotary track for running in place

**Turkish bath** steam bath

**Universal machines** *Trademark.* system of weight training machines

**weight belt** weighted strap worn around waist while exercising; wide leather belt worn as back support when lifting weights

**weight loss clinic** salon, spa, or gymnasium for weight reduction through diet and exercise

**weight machine** apparatus with weights suspended over pulleys and connected to handgrips, often with seat or bench

**whirlpool** tub in which jets or agitator propel current of hot water in soothing, swirling motion; hot tub

## NUTRITION FOR FITNESS

**additive** often chemical substance added to processed food to retard spoilage and improve appearance or taste of food

**alimentotherapy** treatment of disease through diet and nutrition

**banting** diet without sweets or carbohydrates

**basal metabolism** basic rate at which body expends energy to maintain itself in resting state

**calorie** measurement of energy provided by food

**carbohydrate** essential nutrient substance in sugars and starches

**carboloading** *Informal.* ingestion of large amounts of complex carbohydrates to produce extra energy reserves, esp. prior to exercise

**cholesterol** fatty substance found in foodstuffs, or formed by body itself, that coats and constricts arteries

**complementary proteins** proteins found in vegetables that, when combined, form nutritionally complete proteins otherwise normally found only in meats and milk

**complex carbohydrate** carbohydrate such as sucrose or starch in foods

**diet·** pattern of eating; range of foodstuffs ingested; programmed course of eating to gain or lose weight or improve health

**empty calories** highly caloric foods without significant nutritional value

**fad diet** eating regimen designed to appeal more to short-term weight loss goals than to sound nutritional principles

**fats** saturated, monounsaturated, polyunsaturated, and unsaturated essential nutrient material rich in calories

**fiber** dietary substance, usu. cellulose, found in plants, that promotes gastrointestinal fitness

**food combining** system of combining certain food groups in meals for health or weight control

**food group** basic category of nutritional foodstuffs, including milk, meat, vegetable and fruit, and bread and cereal groups

**health food** any food considered healthful, esp. natural, unprocessed, or organic food

**junk food** processed food rich in fats and sugars but low in nutrition

**macrobiotics** restricted diet program, primarily of whole grains, beans, and vegetables, based on balance of yin and yang natural cycles

**macronutrients** proteins, carbohydrates, and fats

**malnutrition** chronic lack of essential and beneficial nutritional foodstuffs

**megavitamin therapy** use of massive amounts of vitamins to treat illness and promote vitality

**micronutrients** vitamins and minerals

**minerals** chemical elements and compounds necessary in small amounts for health

**nutrient** dietary substance that provides chemical compounds necessary for growth and replenishment of body

**nutrition** process by which animals consume and process food; study of dietary requirements

**obesity** condition of having excess body fat

**omega-3 fatty acid** fatty acid, found esp. in fish oil, that reduces cholesterol levels in blood

**organic food** foodstuffs grown and prepared without chemical additives, pesticides, or fertilizers

**polyunsaturated fat** dietary fat, usu. vegetable fat

**protein** essential nutrient material composed of amino acids

**protein supplement** concentrated nutritional powder or liquid

**RDA** recommended *d*ietary *a*llowance of nutritional elements

**reducing pills** prescription drugs that cause appetite loss and promote weight reduction

**roughage** foodstuffs rich in fiber

**saturated fat** dietary fat, usu. animal fat, that increases cholesterol level in blood

**sitology** science of diet and nutrition

**starch** foodstuff rich in complex carbohydrates

**supplement** vitamin, mineral, or protein preparation that boosts intake of nutrients

**trace minerals** chemical elements necessary in minute amounts for health

**vegetarianism** practice of eating vegetables, fruits, and grains, and of eliminating animal products from diet

**vitamin** one of various organic nutrient elements and compounds necessary in very small quantities for health

**vitamin pills** nutritional supplements containing vitamins in condensed tablet or capsule form

**weight loss** reduction in body fat and weight, esp. by consumption of fewer calories relative to calories burned

# Hair and Grooming

Hair Styles
Beards and Mustaches
Grooming Aids and Processes

**See also**: Chap. 1: Health, Fitness, and Enhancement; Chap. 4: Medicine; Chap. 10: Hats, Headgear, and Hairpieces

## Hair Styles

**Afro** tight, bushy, natural curls, worn esp. by African Americans

**artichoke** full, teased hair cut tight at nape of neck

**auburn** (*adj*) having reddish brown hair, natural or dyed

**back combed** having hair teased or ratted

**bald** (*adj*) having no hair, minimal or thinning hair, or a shaved head

**bangs** fringe of hair above forehead cut straight across

**beckoning curl** single curl of hair hanging on forehead

**beehive** dome of teased hair piled high atop head

**blaze** streak of contrasting color through hair

**bleached blond** person with artificially lightened hair

**blond** person with gold or yellow-toned hair, natural or bleached

**bob** hair cut all one length, to shoulders or shorter

**bouffant** hair puffed to large volume, piled high

**braid** hair plaited singly or in pairs

**brunette** person with brown or black hair, natural or dyed

**brush cut** short, bristly haircut

**bun** long hair pulled into knot or roll at back of head

**burr cut** *Slang*. extremely short, bristly haircut; crew cut

**butch** extremely short haircut for men

**buzz cut** usu. short haircut done with electric clippers

**chignon** knot or roll of long hair at back of head

**clean-cut** (*adj*) having short, neat hair style

**close-cropped** (*adj*) having hair cut close to scalp

**coiffure** hair style

**coil** long hair pulled into roll at back of head

**coloring** adding streaks or highlights or totally changing one's hair color

**conk** naturally curly hair chemically processed to be straight, esp. among African Americans

**coquette bob** short, pixie bob haircut

**cornrows** small, tightly braided rows of hair along scalp, esp. for African Americans, sometimes with beads braided into rows

**cowlick** natural whorl or lock of hair standing straight up

**crest** plumelike tuft of hair

**crew cut** close-cropped hair, usu. on men; burr cut

**crimp** tight wave in hair made with crimping iron

**curls** tight coils or loose waves of hair

**DA** *duck's ass*; hair oiled and combed back over ears, dovetailing at rear; ducktail

**do** *Slang*. hair style, hairdo

**dreadlocks** long, unbrushed, woolly braids, worn esp. by Rastafarians

**ducktail** DA

**fade** *Slang*. modified raised or slanted flattop, sometimes with thin, close-shaven trails through it, worn usu. by African American men; variations include gumby, slope, high-top, high-low, and tribal

**feathercut** hair cut to resemble layered feathers

**finger wave** curl set by pressing fingers into damp hair

**fishtail braid** strand braid of hair

**flattop** short crew cut with flat, brushlike surface at crown

**fluff** hair puffed up and teased out from head

**forelock** lock of hair hanging down forehead

**French braid** braid with three strands pulled back from hairline

**French knot** long hair rolled into spiral at back of head; French twist; twist

**French twist** French knot

**fringe** bangs of hair on forehead

**frisette** frizz hair style (19th c.)

**frizz** very tightly curled hair that forms a wiry mass

**frosting** bleached hair ends prelightened to white

**fuzz cut** very short crew cut

**haircut** style of cutting and shaping hair

**hairdo** style in which hair is worn

**hair style** fashion in which hair is worn, cut, arranged, or combed

**henna** plant extract used to dye hair red

**jarhead** *Slang*. person with totally shaved head

**knot** hair rolled or twisted into tight mass

**layered cut**  hair cut in many different layers

**locks**  strands of hair

**lovelock**  long curl of hair hanging alone over shoulder (17th–18th c.)

**mane**  abundant or long, thick hair

**marcel**  deeply waved hair style consisting of tight waves set close to head

**mohawk**  narrow band of bristled, erect hair from forehead to nape of neck, surrounded by shaved scalp

**moptop**  shaggy hair style that partially covers brow or face

**natural**  very curly hair grown long and bushy, esp. by African Americans

**pageboy**  straight, chin-length hair turned gently under at ends

**part**  separation of hair falling along head, usu. at side of crown

**perm**  *Informal.* permanent wave in hair

**permanent wave**  chemical treatment that curls hair; perm

**peroxide blond**  person with very pale, bleached blond hair

**peyes**  long, uncut side curls worn by Hasidic Jewish men

**pigtails**  hair worn in several braids

**pixie**  short, layered haircut

**plait**  braid of hair

**platinum** (*adj*) having very pale, esp. bleached blond, hair

**pleach** (*vb*) braid hair

**pompadour**  hair fluffed and elevated at forehead

**ponytail**  long hair drawn into single tassel at back of head

**pouf**  hair piled high in rolled puffs

**Prince Valiant**  thick, straight bangs and chin-length, cropped hair around back of head

**process**  chemically straightened curly hair; conk

**psyche knot**  hair brushed and twisted into conical coil ending above nape of neck

**queue**  very long braid of hair down back

**quiff**  elaborate pompadour of hair

**ratted** (*adj*) having hair teased or back combed

**razor cut**  hair cut for layering with razor instead of scissors

**receding hairline**  balding at top of brow, causing hairline to move back on crown

**redhead**  person with reddish orange-toned hair, natural or dyed

**ringlets**  long, spiraling curls of hair

**roach**  roll of hair brushed straight back from forehead, sometimes to one side

**roll**  hair bunched and held together

**set**  hair styled by curling or waving on rollers

**shag**  usu. long, bushy, layered hair

**shingle**  hair bobbed and cut close in point at nape of neck, gradually longer up back of head, just covering ears

**shingling**  cutting hair with scissors over comb to create tapering effect

**shock**  bushy or tangled mass of hair

**shorn** (*adj*) having hair cut short, close to skull

**skinhead**  *Slang.* person with shaved head

**spikes**  hair formed into pointed projections with setting lotion or fixative

**spit curl**  precise curl of hair pressed against face, formed by saliva, water, or fixative

**split ends**  condition in which ends of hair split or fray from abuse or over time

**strawberry blond**  person with light reddish gold blond hair, natural or dyed

**streaking**  contrasting colors in strips through hair

**styling**  cutting, coloring, shaping, and manipulating hair into a specific, distinguishing form

**swirl**  long hair coiled into a circular shape

**tail**  few locks of nape hairs left long with the rest cut short

**teased** (*adj*) having hair ratted or back combed

**thatch**  thick growth of hair

**thinning**  early stage of baldness with loss of some hair

**tint**  chemical coloration of hair

**tint back** (*vb*) return tinted hair to natural color

**tone** (*vb*) subtly alter degree of light and dark shades in hair color

**tonsure**  ring of fringed hair around bald crown

**topknot**  tuft, roll, or fluff of hair at crown

**tortoiseshell**  warm, golden brown shade created by toning medium dark hair

**tousled** (*adj*) windblown, uncombed, or natural in hair style

**towhead**  person with extremely pale, whitish blond hair, esp. a young child

**tresses**  hair, esp. long and luxuriant; plait or braid of hair

**tuft**  projecting lock of hair

**twist**  French knot

**updo**  upsweep

**upsweep**  hairdo in which hair is combed or brushed upward to top of head; updo; upswept hairdo

**upswept hairdo**  upsweep

**wave**  hair formed into loose curls

**widow's peak**  point formed by hair on forehead

**wig**  artificial hairpiece

**windblown bob**  affectedly tousled hair style

## BEARDS AND MUSTACHES

**Abe Lincoln**  thin beard along jaw with mustache shaved

**beard**  man's facial hair, esp. when trimmed into shape, sometimes excluding mustache

**burnsides**  sideburns

**bushy** (*adj*) describing full, untrimmed beard

**chin whiskers**  short, thin beard at bottom of face only

**down**  soft, boyish growth of beard

**dundrearies**  long, flowing side whiskers

**facial hair**  beard and mustache

**five o'clock shadow**  growth of heavy beard several hours after shaving, giving unshaven appearance

**full beard**  untrimmed, abundant beard

**Fu Manchu**  thin, delicately trimmed beard and drooping mustache

**goatee**  close-trimmed, pointed beard on chin

**grizzled** (*adj*) having unkempt, unshaven appearance, esp. from several days' growth of facial hair

**handlebar mustache**  long, full mustache turning up at ends

**hirsute** (*adj*) having facial hair, esp. rough or coarse

**imperial beard**  single tuft of hair on chin and tufted mustache

**mustache**  facial hair between upper lip and nose; usu. worn by men

**mustaches**  former term for thick, long, or elaborately shaped mustache

**mustachioed** (*adj*) wearing a mustache

**muttonchops**  sideburns extending nearly to jaw line

**peach fuzz**  *Slang.* very soft down of facial hair

**sideboards**  *Chiefly Brit.* sideburns

**sideburns**  beard growth along sides of face below ears; burnsides

**sidelocks**  long sideburns, often extending off face

**side whiskers**  sideburns, esp. untrimmed

**stubble**  growth of beard or mustache shortly after shaving

**three day's growth**  dense stubble of facial hair that gives ungroomed, scruffy appearance

**tuft**  tassel-like beard

**unshaven**  *(adj)* having some growth of beard on one's face, giving unkempt appearance

**Van Dyke**  close-trimmed, pointed beard

**walrus mustache**  extremely long, bushy, drooping mustache covering upper lip

**weepers**  *Slang.* long, flowing side whiskers

**whiskers**  facial hair, esp. a beard

## GROOMING AIDS AND PROCESSES

**aftershave**  scented liquid tonic applied to face after shaving beard

**antiperspirant**  chemical solution used to suppress perspiration, esp. under arms

**astringent**  tonic lotion that tightens pores

**atomizer**  small bottle for spraying cologne or water

**baliage**  method of combing highlighting into hair

**balm**  ointment, lotion, or cream for soothing skin

**balsam**  soothing oil; balm

**bath**  immersion of body in hot water for cleanliness and relaxation

**bath oil**  scented skin oil placed in bath water

**bath salts**  scented chemicals dissolved in bath water

**bay rum**  popular, traditional aftershave lotion

**beautician**  manager or employee of beauty parlor; hairdresser

**beauty parlor**  business providing cosmetic treatments and hairstyling

**bikini waxing**  removal of stray pubic hairs by coating with hot paraffin and stripping off wax when cooled

**blow-dry**  *(vb)* dry and style hair with electric drying appliance that shoots hot air across hair

**blusher**  rouge

**bobby pin**  small, curved, metal or plastic hair fastener

**bracer**  stimulating liquid tonic applied to face after shaving

**brush**  bristles or hairs gathered into handle, used to apply cosmetics or groom hair

**bubble bath**  sudsing, oily powder placed in bath water

**cachou**  pastille for sweetening breath

**castile soap**  fine, hard, bland soap containing olive oil

**clipper**  small cutting implement for hair and nails

**coconut oil**  oil from coconut used to smooth and lubricate skin

**cold cream**  mineral oil compound used to remove cosmetics and soothe skin

**cologne**  fragrant liquid for scenting body

**coloring**  dyes or tints for altering hair color

**colorist**  hairdresser who alters color of all or some of one's hair with dyes or tints

**comb**  stiff-toothed implement for grooming hair

**compact**  small case holding face powder, puff, and mirror, sometimes also with rouge

**conditioner**  creamy softening lotion applied to hair after shampoo; creme rinse

**cosmetician**  professional trained in application of cosmetics

**cosmetics**  paints, powders, ointments, and lotions used to beautify face and body; makeup; maquillage; war paint

**cosmetology**  art, techniques, or profession of applying cosmetics

**cotton swab**  cotton-tipped stick used to apply or remove cosmetics

**creme rinse**  conditioner

**croquignole**  method of waving hair by winding it on rollers from ends of hair toward scalp

**curler**  small, usu. tubular framework used to set curl in wet hair

**curling iron**  heated metal rod used to curl hair

**curl relaxing**  chemical process that straightens naturally curly hair

**dental floss**  waxed string used to clean between teeth

**dentifrice**  tooth cleaning paste or powder

**deodorant**  chemical solution that neutralizes perspiration odors

**depilatory**  cream that removes facial or body hair

**diffuser**  attachment to blow drier used to dry hair

**eau de Cologne**  dilute solution of cologne

**eau de parfum**  dilute solution of perfume

**electric razor**  electrically powered shaving device, often with many small blades on movable head

**emery board**  abrasive surface used to smooth and shape fingernails

**eyebrow pencil**  colorant stick used to darken and define eyebrows

**eyelash curler**  small, clamping tool for curling eyelashes

**eyeliner**  paint in liquid or pencil form used to outline eyes

**eyeliner tattoo**  permanent dying of eyelash line around eyes

**eye shadow**  colored powder or cream applied to eyelid

**eyewash**  soothing chemical solution used to refresh eyes

**face powder**  cosmetic powder, often talc or cornstarch, applied to face to reduce shine and give matte finish

**facial**  deep cleaning of pores of face

**false eyelashes**  long lashes attached to eyelid

**false nails**  long fingernails attached at natural cuticle

**falsies**  artificial cosmetic aid, esp. breast pads

**fragrance**  perfume or cologne for scenting body

**friseur**  *French.* hairdresser

**grooming**  methods, practices, and techniques of creating and maintaining a neat, presentable appearance

**hairdresser**  person trained in cutting, setting, and styling hair; hair stylist

**hairdressing**  grooming of hair; shampoo or conditioner

**hair drier**  appliance that blows hot air to dry hair

**hair net**  fine mesh that holds hair in place

**hair spray**  sticky aerosol used to hold hair in place

**hair stylist**  hairdresser, esp. in cinema and advertising

**highlighter**  cosmetic used to emphasize some feature or portion of face

**highlights**  streaks of hair of different color or shade than rest of head of hair

**ice bag**  small bag that holds ice, for applying to face or eyes

**jojoba oil**  soothing oil made from wax of North American tree

**Kleenex**  *Trademark.* paper tissue

**kohl**  black eyelining pencil

**lanolin**  rich oil used to lubricate skin

**lip gloss**  creamy cosmetic used to give shine to lips, often tinted

**lipstick**  colorant cream for lips

**makeover**  extensive series of beauty and cosmetic treatments

**makeup**  cosmetics

**manicure**  grooming of fingernails

**maquillage**  cosmetics

**mascara**  darkening cream for eyelashes

**moisturizer**  cosmetic cream or lotion used to restore softness and moisture to skin

**mousse**  foam or gel that keeps groomed hair in place

**mouthwash**  chemical solution used to rinse and refresh mouth

**mudpack**  facial treatment that uses drying mud

**nail polish**  colored enamel for fingernails and toenails

**orange stick**  small, pointed wooden stick used to groom fingernails

**pancake**  thick cover-up cream for skin, esp. face

**pastille**  breath-sweetening drop

**pedicure**  grooming of toenails

**perfume**  volatile scented oil extracted from flowers or prepared synthetically, applied as fragrance

**polish remover**  solvent for removing old nail polish

**pomade**  fragrant, sometimes medicated ointment for hair and scalp

**pomander**  small ball or box of perfume

**powder**  fine grains of soothing colorant applied to skin, often made from talc

**powder puff**  soft applicator for powder

**razor**  small, sharp blade used to remove body or facial hair

**rinse**  temporary hair coloring

**rollers**  plastic or metal tubes for curling hair

**rosewater**  rose-scented water used to refresh skin

**rouge**  reddening colorant for cheeks; blusher

**roundbrush**  tubular brush with bristles extending in all directions, used to style hair

**safety razor**  handle with protective sheath for razor blade

**sandalwood oil**  perfume oil

**set**  (*vb*) style hair while wet so as to retain shape when dry; (*n*) hair thus shaped

**shampoo**  soap for hair, often scented and with various additives for health of hair

**shaver**  razor unit

**snood**  net for holding hair at back of head

**sunscreen**  chemical lotion for preventing or retarding sunburn

**swab**  small, flexible stick tipped in cotton for cleaning ears and applying makeup

**talc**  talcum powder

**talcum powder**  absorbent white powder used to refresh skin; talc

**tattoo**  art and practice of marking the skin with indelible designs and legends by puncturing the skin and inserting pigments; any design or legend so produced

**tinting**  altering natural hair color with dye or tint

**tissue**  thin, soft paper sheet used to clean skin and apply or remove cosmetics

**toilet**  general term for grooming aids and their use

**toilet paper**  tissue paper, usu. in roll, used esp. to wipe anus after defecating

**toilet powder**  absorbent, scented white powder for skin

**toiletries**  grooming aids

**toilet water**  scented liquid

**toothbrush**  small brush with handle, used to clean teeth

**toothpaste**  dentifrice in soft, moist form

**toothpick**  small, pointed stick used to clean between teeth

**tooth powder**  dentifrice in dry, granular, gently abrasive form

**tweezers**  small pincer tool used to grasp or remove hairs and other small particles

**unguent**  soothing ointment

**Vaseline**  *Trademark.* petroleum jelly ointment for soothing skin

**vent brush**  brush with air vents used in styling hair

**war paint**  colored ointments applied to face and body before going to war (Native Americans); *Informal.* cosmetics

**wash**  lotion

**waxing**  stripping away of body hair with hot wax

**witch hazel**  astringent lotion

**zinc oxide ointment**  creamy white paste for sun protection or soothing burns and rashes

# PHYSICAL APPEARANCE

Aspects and Components of Appearance
Physical Attributes
Small/Large
   Small, Short, or Thin
   Large, Tall, or Fat
Healthy/Sickly
   Healthy, Fit, Bright, or Strong
   Sickly, Out of Shape, Dull, or Weak
Beautiful/Ugly
   Beautiful, Attractive, or Well-Formed
   Ugly, Unattractive, or Malformed

**SEE ALSO**: Chap. 1: Anatomy; Hair and Grooming; Chap. 20: Insults, Slurs, and Epithets; Chap. 22: Personality and Behavior

Adjectives describing human physical appearance or physiological states have been grouped into three pairs of opposites, such as Healthy/Sickly. Each pair is broken down into two undefined lists of virtual synonyms and words with casually related meanings. The parameters for these lists are defined by the three or four adjectives forming the section title. While the meanings of the terms in each list vary, this category is intended to serve as a reminder of similar but slightly different and familiar words. The subcategory Physical Attributes includes adjectives describing a wide variety of physical states.

## ASPECTS AND COMPONENTS OF APPEARANCE

**air**  manifestation of some personal quality or emotion in one's appearance and bearing

**appearance**  outward, physical look

**aspect**  particular appearance or mien

**attitude**  arrangement or position of body parts

**aura**  impression given off of one's spiritual or emotional nature

**bearing**  manner in which one stands, moves, and acts

**body**  physical substance of a person; trunk as distinguished from limbs

**body language**  gestures and mannerisms, both intended and subconscious, that communicate one's feelings

**brow**  expression or mien, esp. on forehead

**build**  muscular development and posture; form of one's body

**bulk**  primary mass of one's body

**bust**  torso between neck and waist, esp. woman's breasts

**carriage**  posture and manner of carrying one's body

**cleavage**  area between a woman's breasts

**coloring**  complexion, natural skin tone

**complexion**  color and texture of skin, esp. on face

**comportment**  bearing, demeanor

**condition**  state of physical health and fitness

**conduct**  manner in which one behaves and carries oneself

**constitution**  one's physical makeup, both inherited traits and acquired characteristics

**corpus**  body, esp. when dead

**countenance**  demeanor and expression, esp. on face as indication of feelings

**demeanor**  outward manner, behavior toward others

**deportment**  manner of carrying and conducting oneself; bearing

**disposition**  prevailing mood and emotional makeup as revealed through expressions and actions

**expression**  arrangement of facial features, body posture, and use of vocal intonation to manifest a particular feeling

**extremities**  limbs, hands, and feet

**facade**  expression or image presented to others

**face**  front of head including chin, mouth, nose, cheeks, eyes, ears, and forehead

**features**  elements of face, esp. mouth, nose, and eyes

**fettle**  condition of body and mind

**figure**  shape, musculature, and posture of body

**form**  external appearance of body as distinct from face; figure

**frame**  physique or figure, esp. underlying skeletal structure

**gait**  manner of walking

**gestures**  movements of hands and limbs and expressions revealed through these movements

**girth**  size or measure around middle of torso

**grin**  open, wide smile

**grooming**  manner of caring for hygiene, hair, and body hair

**hairline**  point on forehead above which hair growth occurs

**hand**  terminal part of forelimb with five fingers used for manual operations and expressive gestures

**height**  distance from bottom of feet to top of head when standing erect

**image**  impression given off by facial expressions, bearing, posture, deportment, gestures, and voice

**impression**  outward physical appearance

**limbs**  arms and legs, ending in hands and feet; extremities

**looks**  physical appearance and countenance, esp. attractiveness

**manner**  distinct or characteristic air and bearing

**mannerism**  characteristic gesture or peculiarity of conduct

**mien**  expression of mood revealed through demeanor and bearing

**nature**  essential character as shown through physical traits

**pate**  crown or top of head, normally covered with hair

**person**  general image or impression given off by physical appearance and manner

**physique**  form and musculature of body; figure

**port**  *Archaic.* manner in which one bears oneself

**posture**  position and bearing of body, esp. when standing erect

**presence**  aura, impression, or sense of personality given off by physical appearance and manner

**profile**  side view of face

**proportions**  relation of parts of body to one another

**puss**  *Slang.* face, esp. mouth

**shape**  form and proportions of bodily parts; figure; physical condition

**skin**  smooth outer covering of body, forming complexion on face

**smile**  facial expression, usu. upward curl of corners of mouth and brightening of eyes

**stance**  posture, way of standing, esp. as expression of feeling

**stature**  natural height in upright position

**tic**  habitual spasmodic movement of facial muscles

**tone**  tautness of musculature

**torso**  trunk

**traits**  form and expression of body parts and facial features

**trunk**  central part of body to which limbs and head are attached; torso

**visage**  face and its expressions

**walk**  posture and manner of moderate forward movement in upright position

**weight**  relative measurement of one's mass

## PHYSICAL ATTRIBUTES

almond-eyed, androgynous, aquiline

bald, barefoot, blank, blind, blond, bowlegged, brachycephalic, bristling, brunette, buxom

chip-toothed, clubfooted, cross-legged, curled lip, curvaceous

dark, deadpan, deaf, dewy-eyed, doe-eyed, dolichocephalic, domed, downy

eagle-eyed, erect, exophthalmic

feline, flatfooted, flattened, flossy, fluffy, flushed, freckled, freckle-faced, full-mouthed, goggle-eyed

grimacing, grinning, gummy

hairy, hewn, hirsute, horny, horrent

irregular

jowly

knock-kneed

lambent, lanky, large, leathery, left-handed, life-size, limping, long-faced, loose-jointed, loose-limbed

microcephalic, mongoloid, mute

naked

oblong, open-eyed

pigeon-toed, pinched, poker-faced, popeyed, pouty, puckered, pug-nosed, pursed, pursy

rawboned, red-headed, retroussé, right-handed, roundheaded, round-shouldered, rubicund

saurian, scowling, setaceous, sharp-nosed, shorn, shovel-nosed, sinewy, sinuous, skinhead, slanted, slant-eyed, sloe-eyed, slow-footed, smirking, sneering, snub-nosed, speckled,

spindle-legged, splayfooted, squinty, straight-faced, stubbly, sulky, swarthy, swivel-hipped
taliped, throaty, toothy
vacuous, varicose veined
wavy, wide-eyed, widemouthed

## SMALL/LARGE

### SMALL, SHORT, OR THIN

bantam, bareboned, bony
compact
dainty, diminutive, dinky, dwarfish
elfin
flat-chested
gangling, gawky
half pint
infinitesimal, insubstantial, itsy-bitsy, itty-bitty
lanky, lean, Lilliputian, little
meager, measly, micro, microscopic, midget, miniature, minimal, minute
narrow, negligible, nipped
peewee, petite, puny, pygmy
reedlike, reedy, runty
sawed-off, scant, scanty, scarce, scraggy, scrawny, scrubby, short, shrimpy, shriveled, shrunken, sinewy, skinny, slender, slight, slim, slinky, small, spindly, spiny, squat, stringbean, stringy, stubby, stumpy, stunted
teensy-weensy, teeny, teeny-weeny, thin, tiny
undersized, underweight
wasp-waisted, wee, weedy, weeny, willowy, wiry, wispy

### LARGE, TALL, OR FAT

adipose, amazon, ample, Antaean
barrel-chested, beefy, behemoth, big, big-bellied, boundless, bovine, brawny, broad, broad of beam, Brobdingnagian, brutish, bulky, bull-necked, burly, buxom
capacious, chubby, chunky, clumpish, colossal, considerable, corpulent, cumbersome, Cyclopean
distended, dumpy
elephantine, elongated, embonpoint, endomorphic, enormous
fat, fleshy, fubsy, full, full-grown
gargantuan, generous, giant, gigantic, goliath, gross
heavy, hefty, herculean, huge, hulking, hunky, husky
immeasurable, immense, imposing
jumbo, Junoesque
large, leggy, leviathan, limitless, long, long-legged, long-limbed, lumbering, lumpish
mammoth, massive, mastodonic, meaty, mesomorphic, mighty, monumental, musclebound
obese, overblown, overdeveloped, overgrown, oversized, overstuffed, overweight
paunchy, plump, podgy, ponderous, porcine, portly, potbellied, prodigious, pudgy, pursy
rangy, roly-poly, rotund
sizable, squat, squdgy, stacked, stocky, stout, strapping, substantial, swollen
tall, thick, thickset, titanic, top-heavy, towering, tremendous, tubby
unwieldy
voluminous, voluptuous
wide
zaftig

## HEALTHY/SICKLY

### HEALTHY, FIT, BRIGHT, OR STRONG

able-bodied, agile
beaming, blooming, blushing, bouncing, bright, bright-eyed, bursting, bushy-tailed
chipper, clean, clear-eyed
dexterous
elastic, exercised
fit, fit as a fiddle, florid, flush
glossy, glowing
hale, hardy, healthful, healthy, hearty
in fine fettle, in shape, in the pink
light-footed, limber, lissome, lithe, lively, lusty
mighty, muscular
peppy, perky, pink-cheeked, pliable
radiant, red, ripe, robust, rosy, rosy-cheeked, rubicund, ruddy, rugged
scrubbed, shapely, shining, shiny, shipshape, sinuous, sleek, sound, spare, sparkling, spry, square-shouldered, stalwart, staunch, steady, stout, strapping, streamlined, strong, sturdy, sunny, supple, svelte
toned, trim, twenty-twenty, twinkling
vigorous, vital
well-fed, wholesome
youthful

### SICKLY, OUT OF SHAPE, DULL, OR WEAK

aged, ailing, amputee, anemic, attenuated
bedridden, bent, blanched, bleary-eyed, blind, bloated, bloodshot
cadaverous, chalky, corpselike, crippled
debilitated, decrepit, delicate, disabled, doddering, droopy, dull
emaciated, enfeebled, etiolated
faint, farsighted, feeble, feverish, flabby, flaccid, flimsy, flushed, fossilized, fragile, frail
gaunt, glabrous, glassy-eyed
haggard, hollow-eyed, humpbacked
ill, incontinent, infirm
lame, limp, lumpish, lurid
mute, myopic
nearsighted
obese, off-color, out of shape, out of whack, overweight
pale, pallid, palsied, paltry, peaked, peglegged, phthisic, pigeon-toed, pinched, pursy
ravaged, rheumy, rickety, rugose, run-down
scorbutic, shaky, shriveled, shrunken, sick, sickly, skeletal, skinny, slack, soft, sparse, spindle-legged, starved, stone-blind, stone-deaf, strabismic, sunken, swollen
tabetic, tottering, tubercular
underfed, undernourished, underweight
walleyed, wan, washed-out, wasted, waxen, waxy, weak, web-footed, wispy, withered, wizened, wraithlike, wrinkled

## BEAUTIFUL/UGLY

### BEAUTIFUL, ATTRACTIVE, OR WELL-FORMED

adorable, agreeable, alluring, angelic, appealing, appetizing, attractive

beaming, beauteous, beautiful, becoming,
    beguiling, bewitching, bonny, breathtaking, bright,
    built
callipygian, captivating, catching, charismatic, charming,
    classic, clear, clear-eyed, come-hither, comely, coquettish,
    curvaceous, cute
dainty, dashing, delectable, delicate, delicious,
    delightful, desirable, devastating, dimpled, divine,
    doll-like
enchanting, engaging, enticing, entrancing, enviable, exotic,
    exquisite, eye-catching
fair, fancy, fascinating, fetching, fine, flawless
glamorous, glorious, glossy, good-looking, gorgeous, graceful,
    great-looking
handsome, hot, hunky, hypnotic
immaculate, intoxicating, intriguing, inviting,
    irresistible
killer
light, lovable, lovely, luscious, lustrous
magnetic, magnificent, mignon, moon-eyed,
    mouth-watering
nifty
ornamental
perfect, photogenic, picturesque, pleasing, precious,
    prepossessing, pretty, provocative
redolent, regular, resplendent
scrumptious, sculptured, seductive, sensuous, sexy, shapely,
    showy, sightly, silky, slick, smiling, spellbinding, spotless,
    stacked, statuesque, streamlined, striking, stunning, sublime,
    sumptuous, symmetrical
taking, tantalizing, tasty, tempting, titillating, toylike
voluptuous
well-built, well-conditioned, well-favored, well-formed,
    well-groomed, well-made, well-proportioned, well-set,
    winning, winsome

## UGLY, UNATTRACTIVE, OR MALFORMED

angular, askew, awful, awkward
bandy-legged, beetle-browed, bent, blemished, blimpish,
    bloated, blowzy, blubbery, bovine, bucktoothed, bug-eyed
cadaverous, chalky, clammy, cleft, clumsy, crippled, crooked,
    cross-eyed, cumbersome
defaced, deformed, disfigured, disgusting, disheveled, droopy,
    dumpy
elephantine, emaciated
farinaceous, fat, foul, frightful, frowzy, fubsy
gap-toothed, gawky, geeky, ghastly, gnarled, goggle-eyed,
    graceless, grim-faced, grimy, grisly, grizzled, grotesque,
    grubby, gruesome, grungy
halt, harelipped, hatchet-faced, heavy-footed, hideous, homely,
    horrent, horrible, hulking, hunched
ill-formed, ill-made, irregular
jagged
leprous, loathsome, lopsided, lumpish
macabre, malformed, malodorous, mangy, marred, mealy,
    misshapen, moldering, monstrous, musty
offensive, oleaginous
pasty, pendulous, pitted, plain, pocked, ponderous, porcine,
    putrescent, putrid
ragged, repellent, repugnant, repulsive, revolting, rickety,
    rumpled, rumply, runty
sallow, scabby, scabrous, scaly, sclerotic, scorbutic, scraggy,
    scrawny, scrofulous, scruffy, shabby, shaggy, shapeless,
    sickening, simian, skew-eyed, sneering, splotchy, spoiled,
    spongy, squat, squinched, stooped, straggly, stumpy,
    stunted, sunken, swaybacked, swollen
tabescent, terrible, tubercular
ugly, unappealing, unattractive, ungainly, unprepossessing,
    unsavory, unsightly, unwieldy
walleyed, washed-out, wasted, waxen, withered

# CHAPTER 2

# Living Things

# Biology

Branches and Disciplines
Genetics, Heredity, and Evolution
Cell Structure and Function
Physiology
Environment, Ecology, and Animal Behavior
Reproduction and Development
Tools and Techniques
Taxonomy
  Five Kingdoms
  Major Taxonomic Subgroups

**see also**: Chap. 1: Anatomy; Medical Problems; Chap. 2: Animals; Plants; Simpler Life Forms; Chap. 3: Geology; Geography; Chap. 4: Chemistry; Chap. 8: Parents and Children; Chap. 12: Agriculture; Chap. 17: Gardening; Chap. 22: Sex, Love, and Romance

## Branches and Disciplines

**algology**  study of algae
**anatomy**  study of structures of organisms
**bacteriology**  study of bacteria
**behaviorism**  study of interaction between organism and organism or organism and environment
**biochemistry**  study of chemical processes necessary to sustain life
**biology**  science that deals with the morphology, physiology, origin, and distribution of living organisms
**biometry**  use of statistical techniques in biology
**bionics**  design of systems that duplicate living organisms
**bionomics**  ecology
**biophysics**  use of principles and techniques of physics to study biological phenomena
**biotechnology**  recombinant DNA, genetic engineering, cloning, and related applications of genetic research
**botany**  science of organisms of Kingdom Plantae, dealing with life, structure, growth, and classification of plants
**bryology**  branch of botany dealing with mosses and other bryophytes
**cell biology**  study of cell organelles, their functions and interactions
**cell physiology**  study of structure and functioning of cells
**comparative anatomy**  study of similar structures among organisms
**comparative biochemistry**  study of chemical similarities among organisms
**comparative embryology**  study of similar development among organisms
**conchology**  study of shells
**cytology**  study of structure and functions of cells
**dendrology**  study of trees and woody plants, esp. their taxonomy
**developmental biology**  embryology
**ecology**  study of relationships and balance between organisms and their environment; bionomics
**embryology**  study of development of organism from meiosis to birth; developmental biology

**endocrinology**  study of endocrine glands and hormonal control
**entomology**  study of insects
**environmental physiology**  study of adaptations of living things to environmental conditions
**enzymology**  study of structure and catalytic properties of enzymes
**epidemiology**  study of prevalence and spread of disease in a population
**ethology**  study of animal behavior
**evolution**  study of origin of species as process of development from earlier forms
**exobiology**  study of life beyond Earth's atmosphere
**genetics**  study of heredity
**helminthology**  study of parasitic worms
**hematology**  study of blood
**herpetology**  study of reptiles and amphibians
**histology**  study of tissues
**ichthyology**  study of fish
**immunology**  study of how body protects itself from invading organisms and chemicals
**life science**  any of a group of sciences dealing with living creatures and their life processes, esp. biology, zoology, and botany
**limnology**  study of freshwater lakes, ponds, and streams as discrete ecosystems
**malacology**  study of mollusks
**mammalogy**  study of mammals
**microbiology**  study of microscopic organisms and agents, such as bacteria, protists, and viruses
**molecular biology**  study of complex chemistry of biological macromolecules, esp. those involved in genetics
**morphology**  study of physical forms of living things
**mycology**  study of fungi
**natural history**  biology, physiology, origin, and distribution of living things as seen through perspective of time
**neurobiology**  study of nervous systems of animals
**nutrition**  study of foods and how they are used by body
**ornithology**  study of birds
**paleontology**  study of fossil record of living things
**parasitology**  study of animal parasites
**phycology**  study of algae
**physiology**  study of functions and vital processes of living organisms and their parts
**phytology**  former term for botany
**phytosociology**  ecology concerned with origin, composition, classification, and distribution of plant communities
**protozoology**  study of microscopic, usu. single-celled, protozoans
**systematics**  study of kinds, diversity, and relationships of living things
**taxonomy**  classification of living things
**zoology**  science of organisms of Kingdom Animalia, dealing with life, structure, growth, and classification of animals

## Genetics, Heredity, and Evolution

**abiogenesis**  discredited theory that living organisms can develop by spontaneous generation from inanimate material
**adaptation**  any feature that increases fitness of organism to

its environment; process of developing or altering these features by natural selection

**adenine** one of four nitrogenous bases used to carry genetic information in nucleotides of DNA and RNA

**albino** organism lacking normal coloration, usu. due to genetic factors

**allele** form that gene may take at one locus

**allopatry** populations, esp. species, with geographic ranges that show no overlap, often affecting speciation

**ameba** unicellular, microscopic protist that reproduces by fission

**analogy** resemblance in structure or function due to evolutionary adaptation rather than common ancestry

**anaphase** stage in meiosis or mitosis in which chromatids separate and move to opposite poles

**anticodon** set of three bases at end of tRNA that fits only with specific codon of mRNA

**autosome** any chromosome not carrying sex information

**bacterial transformation** form of genetic recombination in which one bacterium breaks open and part of its DNA enters another bacterium

**bacteriophage** virus that attacks bacteria only, used extensively in genetic research

**biogenesis** principle that living organisms originate from other living organisms similar to themselves

**book of man** projected mapping and sequencing of entire human genome

**capsid** protein coat surrounding nucleic acid core of virus

**cenogenesis** development of adaptive structures in embryonic or larval stage that are not part of evolutionary history of taxonomic group

**centromere** round body made of chromatin that holds two strands of chromosome together

**character displacement** state in which two related species become increasingly different in areas where both occur

**chromatid** individual strand of double-stranded chromosome in mitosis

**chromatin** stainable mass of material in nucleus that realigns into chromosomes during cell division

**chromosome** distinct body in nucleus that appears during cell division, composed of DNA and protein and containing genes

**chromosome map** diagram showing linear order of genes on chromosome

**cline** pattern of gradual change in character across species' geographic range

**clone** strain of genetically identical cells

**codon** sequence of three nitrogenous bases representing specific amino acid

**conjugation** transfer of nuclear material between two bacteria

**continuous variation** existence of varying degrees of a characteristic, controlled by more than one pair of genes

**convergence** two related species becoming increasingly similar over time

**cosmid** vector of DNA segment flanked by bacteriophage lambda, used in recombinant DNA technology

**crossing over** exchange of segments of chromosomal material between two strands of a tetrad during prophase of meiosis

**cytosine** one of four nitrogenous bases used to carry genetic information in nucleotides of DNA and RNA

**Darwinism** Charles Darwin's theory of evolution by variation and natural selection

**deoxyribonucleic acid** DNA

**diploid number** chromosome number equal to twice that found in gametes; found in somatic cells

**divergence** two related species becoming increasingly different over time

**DNA** deoxyribonucleic acid; nucleic acid that carries encoded message of gene, comprised of double helix ladder of paired nitrogenous bases bonded to phosphate group and deoxyribose sugar

**dominant trait** allele whose phenotypic trait dominates or prevents expression of recessive traits

**double helix** intertwining chains of nucleic acid linked by hydrogen bonds that constitutes basic structure of DNA

**ecotype** locally adapted variant of a species, genetically different from other ecotypes of that species

**endemic** species found only in limited geographic area

**evolution** development of species or organism from primitive state to present or specialized state

**exon** section of DNA that contains information that codes for protein product of gene

**extinction** dying out of species or population

**first filial generation** first offspring produced from parental cross

**fitness** measure of evolutionary success in terms of contribution to next generation

**fossil** remains of an organism long dead or direct evidence of it, such as its tracks, usu. preserved in rock

**fossil record** succession of fossilized living forms, usu. growing more complex, serving as evidence of macroevolution

**gene** segment of DNA responsible for transmitting hereditary traits

**gene pool** all genetic variability within a population

**genetic code** nucleotide triplet sequences in DNA and RNA that encode for protein synthesis

**genetic counseling** advising people of the probability of their having children with hereditary abnormalities

**genetic drift** changes in gene distribution due to random effects only

**genetic engineering** incorporation of new genes into an organism to alter it

**genetic isolation** absence of genetic exchange between populations due to geographical separation or mechanisms of behavior, anatomy, or physiology that prevent reproduction

**genetic map** diagram of gene locations on chromosome

**genetic recombination** change in gene combinations of offspring from that of parents

**genetics** study of heredity and similarities or differences between related organisms

**genome** one complete haploid set of chromosomes and their genes for an organism, containing all its inheritable traits

**genomic DNA** fragment or fragments of DNA produced by restriction enzymes acting on the DNA of a cell or organism

**genotype** genetic makeup of organism or cell

**geographic range** area inhabited by population

**guanine** one of four nitrogenous bases used to carry genetic information in nucleotides of DNA and RNA

**haploid** (*adj*) possessing only one set of chromosomes, in gametes

**Hardy-Weinberg principle** theory that frequencies of alleles and genotypes in population will remain constant in absence of evolutionary forces

**heredity**  transmission of genetic information from generation to generation

**heterosis**  hybrid vigor

**heterozygote**  organism carrying different alleles for the same trait

**histones**  positively charged proteins in chromatin

**homologs**  members of chromosome pair carrying corresponding genes

**homology**  similarity based on common descent that may or may not reflect functional similarity

**homozygote**  organism carrying identical alleles for the same trait

**hybrid**  offspring from parents of two different species

**hybrid vigor**  condition in which heterozygotes are more fit than either homozygote

**inbreeding**  mating of kin

**incomplete dominance**  state in which one allele only partially inhibits the expression of its alternate

**independent assortment**  tendency of unlinked genes to segregate independently

**intron**  nucleotide sequence that does not code for a protein

**isolation**  prevention of interbreeding between populations due to factors such as geography or behavior

**karyotype**  form, size, and number of chromosomes of an organism: in humans, forty-six chromosomes, including twenty-two pairs of autosomes and two sex chromosomes

**Klinefelter syndrome**  abnormal development toward female traits in males with XXY genotype

**Lamarckism**  inheritance of acquired characteristics, esp. theory that environmental change causes structural changes in organisms that are inherited by offspring

**law of dominance**  Gregor Mendel's rule that in certain traits, one allele in a heterozygote can be phenotypically expressed in preference to its alternate

**law of independent assortment**  principle that unlinked genes segregate independently

**law of segregation**  principle that alleles for a trait segregate independently during meiosis

**lethal gene**  mutation that causes early death when expressed

**life**  distinguishing characteristics of organisms, esp. growth capacity, metabolism, reproduction, and adaptation to environment

**linkage**  tendency of genes located near each other on chromosomes to be inherited together

**living things**  organisms distinguished from dead inorganic objects by basic characteristics of life: growth, metabolism, reproduction, and adaptability to environment

**locus**  position of allele on chromosome

**macroevolution**  long-term evolutionary phenomena occurring above level of species

**meiosis**  cell division in which the diploid chromosome number is reduced to the haploid as part of process of gamete formation

**Mendel's laws**  first law: alleles segregate in meiosis; second law: unlinked genes assort independently

**messenger RNA**  mRNA; single strand of RNA that carries genetic information from DNA to ribosome

**microevolution**  small-scale, rapidly occurring evolutionary phenomena in a single species

**modern synthesis**  merging of Darwinism and Mendelian genetics

**mRNA**  messenger RNA

**multiple alleles**  set of genes potentially occurring at one locus

**mutagen**  substance or condition that increases mutation rate

**mutation**  sudden inheritable change to new allelic form of gene

**natural selection**  process that results in survival of those organisms best suited to their environment, based on inherited favorable variations that increase from generation to generation; selection

**neo-Darwinism**  modern synthesis of Darwinism and Mendelian genetics

**nucleic acids**  main component of DNA and RNA, whose arrangement carries genetic code

**nucleoprotein**  protein associated with nucleic acids in nucleus of living cells

**nucleotide**  structural segment of nucleic acid chain, composed of phosphate group, five-carbon sugar, and purine or pyrimidine base

**operator gene**  segment of DNA to which repressor protein bonds, serving to regulate transcription activity

**operon**  set of structural genes related to single process and subject to the same repressor

**organism**  any discrete life form belonging to one of the five kingdoms

**palingenesis**  phase in development of individual that seems to repeat evolutionary history of its taxonomic group; recapitulation

**parental cross**  first cross in experiment to study genotypic and phenotypic characteristics of trait or traits

**phage**  bacteriophage

**phenotype**  observable characteristics of an organism

**phyletic group**  species related to each other through common descent

**phylogeny**  evolutionary history of taxonomic group

**plasmid**  small DNA molecule outside chromosome in prokaryotic organism that reproduces independently

**pleiotropy**  capacity of gene to assume several different phenotypic characteristics

**polymorphism**  occurrence in population of two or more distinct forms with no intermediate forms

**population**  interbreeding group of organisms

**population genetics**  study of gene movement and variation among interbreeding organisms

**prophase**  early stage in nuclear division during which chromosomes move toward equator of spindle

**protein synthesis**  transfer of encoded genetic information in DNA from nucleotides to amino acid sequence through initiation, elongation, and termination

**Punnett square**  graphic method for observing phenotypic and genotypic ratios

**purine**  either adenine or guanine

**pyrimidine**  cytosine, thymine, or uracil

**recapitulation**  palingenesis

**recessive trait**  allele whose phenotype is not expressed in heterozygous organism

**recombinant DNA**  DNA in which half of DNA double helix has been spliced from each of two different organisms to form new genetic code

**recombination**  change of gene groupings from generation to generation due to independent assortment and crossing over

**regulator gene** controller of transcription rate of other genes

**replication** method by which nucleic acids duplicate themselves

**repressor** functional protein of regulator genes

**restriction enzyme** enzyme that splits DNA double helix at specific nucleotide sequences

**ribonucleic acid** RNA; usu. single-stranded nucleic acid, characterized by nitrogenous bases bonded to phosphate group and ribose sugar, that acts as genetic material in viruses and as transcriber of genetic information in other cells

**RNA** *ribonucleic acid*

**second filial generation** offspring of first filial cross

**segregation** assortment of paired alleles into separate gametes

**selection** natural selection

**selection pressure** any environmental feature that results in natural selection

**sex chromosomes** pair of chromosomes that determines sex and sex-linked characteristics of organism

**sex-linked characteristic** any trait whose alleles are found on sex chromosomes

**sexual dimorphism** distinct differences between male and female in addition to primary sex characteristics

**sexual selection** differential abilities of individuals to acquire mates

**speciation** process of genetic diversification through which new species arise by natural selection

**spindle fibers** structural components of centromere

**splicing** separating two halves of DNA double helix and recombining each with strip from another organism

**structural gene** gene that produces a protein distinct from those of the operator and regulator genes of the same operon

**survival of the fittest** process of Darwinian natural selection

**sympatry** populations, esp. species, with geographic ranges that overlap at least in part

**telophase** final stage of mitosis and meiosis, in which chromosomes form two new nuclei

**tetrad** four chromatids of pair of replicated homologous chromosomes in prophase of meiosis

**thymine** one of four nitrogenous bases used to carry genetic information in nucleotides of DNA and RNA

**transcription** formation of RNA chain complementary to a DNA chain

**transduction** process in which genetic information in cellular DNA is transferred from one host cell to another by viruses or other filterable agents

**transfer RNA** tRNA; RNA that carries specific amino acids to messenger RNA

**transformation** genetic change induced by incorporation of DNA from one bacterial cell into another

**translation** construction of polypeptide through mRNA activity

**transposition** movement of gene or set of genes from one DNA site to another

**transposon** DNA segment that can insert copies of itself into other DNA sites within the same cell

**tRNA** transfer RNA

**Turner's syndrome** abnormality due to lack of one X chromosome in female, creating an XO genotype and retarding growth of gonads

**uracil** one of four nitrogenous bases used to carry genetic information in nucleotides of DNA and RNA

**variation** chance differences among individual organisms, some of them inheritable, that interact with environment to determine which individuals will survive and reproduce

**Watson-Crick model** double helix structure of DNA, first posited in 1953

**X chromosome** sex chromosome carrying female traits in mammals

**Y chromosome** sex chromosome carrying male traits in mammals

## CELL STRUCTURE AND FUNCTION

**A cells** glucagon-secreting cells in islets of Langerhans of pancreas; alpha cells

**active transport** energy-requiring, carrier-mediated transport system in which molecules can be moved across cell membrane against electrochemical gradient

**adenosine diphosphate** ADP; compound formed by hydrolysis of ATP

**adenosine triphosphate** ATP; major molecule that accepts energy from nutrients and donates this energy to cell functions

**adipocyte** fat cell specialized for synthesis and storage of triacylglycerol

**ADP** *adenosine diphosphate*

**aerobic** (*adj*) living, growing, or occurring in the presence of oxygen

**agonist** agent that produces a response that enhances the response of another agent

**agranular endoplasmic reticulum** smooth endoplasmic reticulum without ribosomes that modifies proteins and metabolizes barbiturates

**alpha cells** A cells

**anabolism** synthesizing of small molecules to form larger molecules

**anaerobic** (*adj*) living, growing, or occurring in the absence of oxygen

**angry macrophage** macrophage whose activity has been facilitated by chemicals released from T cells

**antagonist** molecule that competes for binding site with chemical messenger but does not trigger cell's response

**ATP** *adenosine triphosphate*

**axon transport** movement of materials along axons by means of intracellular filamentous structures

**basement membrane** thin layer of extracellular material associated with plasma membrane of epithelial cells

**basophil** granulocytic leukocyte whose granules stain with basic dyes

**B cell** lymphocyte in immune system that proliferates and differentiates into antibody-secreting plasma cells; insulin-secreting cell in pancreas

**beta cells** endocrine system B cells

**B lymphocyte** B cell

**calmodulin** intracellular protein that binds calcium and mediates many of calcium's second messenger functions

**cAMP** cyclic AMP

**carrier** integral membrane protein that combines with specific molecules, enabling them to pass through membrane

**catabolism** fragmentation of molecule into smaller parts

**cell** basic structural and functional unit of living organisms;

smallest unit into which living thing can be divided and retain characteristics associated with life

**cell division** process by which cellular material is divided between two new cells, either by meiosis or mitosis

**centrioles** two small bodies composed of nine fused sets of microtubules, located in cell cytoplasm, which participate in nuclear and cell division

**cGMP** cyclic GMP

**channel** passage formed by integral membrane proteins through which certain small-diameter molecules and ions diffuse across membrane

**chemosynthesis** synthesis of organic material within an organism in which chemical reactions serve as energy source

**chief cells** gastric gland cells that secrete pepsinogen

**chloroplast** chlorophyll-containing plastid surrounded by two membranes and having complex internal membrane system in which photosynthesis takes place

**cilia** hairlike projections from surface of specialized epithelial cells that sweep back and forth to propel material along cell surface

**citric acid cycle** Krebs cycle

**connective tissue cells** cells specialized for the formation and secretion of extracellular elements that connect, anchor, and support body structures

**cotransport** form of secondary active transport in which energy-producing substance and transported substance move in same direction

**countertransport** form of secondary active transport in which energy-producing substance and transported substance move in opposite directions

**creatine phosphate** molecule used to store energy in muscle cells, quickly converted to ATP for energy

**creatinine** waste product derived from muscle creatine

**cyclic AMP** cAMP; cylic form of adenosine monophosphate that serves as second messenger for many nonsteroid hormones and neurotransmitters

**cyclic GMP** cGMP; cyclic form of guanosine monophosphate that acts as second messenger in some cells, possibly in opposition to cyclic AMP

**cytochrome** carrier molecule in mitochondria that participates in transfer of electrons in oxidation reactions

**cytokinesis** stage of cell division following mitosis, in which cytoplasm divides to form two new cells

**cytoplasm** entire contents of cell excluding nucleus

**cytoskeleton** rodlike filaments of various sizes in cytoplasm of most cells, associated with cell shape and movement

**cytotoxic T cells** class of T cells that upon activation by specific antigen, directly attack cells bearing that type of antigen

**depolarization** change in value of membrane potential toward zero to make inside of cell less negative

**desmosome** cell junction consisting of fibers extending between plasma membranes of slightly separated cells, binding them together with flexible strength

**diffusion** movement of molecules by random motion from region of higher to one of lower concentration

**diffusion equilibrium** equality of diffusion fluxes in opposite directions

**ECF** extracellular fluid

**endocytosis** process in which plasma membrane invaginates, engulfing extracellular material and pinching off to form a vesicle around it

**endoplasmic reticulum** ER; organelle in cytoplasm made up of interconnected network of branched tubules and flattened sacs that assembles or modifies proteins: agranular or granular endoplasmic reticulum

**eosinophil** leukocyte involved with allergic responses and destruction of parasitic worms

**epithelial cells** cells forming tissue that covers body surfaces, lines body cavities, and comprises most glands

**ER** endoplasmic reticulum

**erythrocyte** enucleated cell that contains hemoglobin for transport of gases by blood; red blood cell

**eukaryote** any cell with membrane-bound nucleus containing genetic material in chromosomes and dividing by mitosis or meiosis, including all life forms except bacteria, blue-green algae, and some primitive organisms

**exocytosis** process in which membrane of intracellular vesicle fuses with plasma membrane, vesicle opens, and its contents are released into extracellular fluid

**extracellular fluid** ECF; fluid outside cells that forms environment in which cells live; interstitial fluid and plasma

**facilitated diffusion** transport system that moves molecules from high to low concentration across membrane until concentrations on both sides of membrane are equal

**flagella** threadlike organelles used for locomotion and feeding by some eukaryotic organisms

**gap junction** cell junction that allows ions and small molecules to move between cytoplasms of adjacent cells via small channels or tubes

**glial cell** cell that supports and nourishes neurons

**glycolysis** metabolic pathway of cellular reactions that break down glucose to form pyruvic acid, in presence of oxygen, or lactic acid, in absence of oxygen, plus ATP

**Golgi apparatus** cell organelle of membranes and vesicles near nucleus that processes and packages newly synthesized proteins for other organelles or secretion

**granular endoplasmic reticulum** endoplasmic reticulum with ribosome-studded membrane that assembles proteins

**granulocyte** white blood cell containing granules in cytoplasm

**ground substance** thin gel in intercellular substance of connective tissue

**helper T cell** one of class of T cells that enhances antibody production and cytotoxic T cell function

**histocompatibility antigens** antigenic protein molecules on surface of nucleated cells

**hypertonic solution** fluid whose osmolarity exceeds that of plasma

**hypotonic solution** fluid whose osmolarity is less than that of plasma

**intercellular fluid** liquid between cells

**interphase** stage between two meiotic or mitotic cycles

**interstitial fluid** cells between germinal cells in reproductive organs

**isotonic solution** fluid with same osmolarity as plasma

**Krebs cycle** stage of cellular respiration and energy metabolism that occurs in mitochondria; citric acid cycle; tricarboxylic acid cycle

**leukocyte** cell involved with immune response; white blood cell

**lymphocyte** agranular white blood cell

**lysosome** membrane-enclosed organelle in which digestive enzymes are confined

**macrophage** large white blood cell that engulfs invaders such as bacteria

**mast cell** connective tissue cell containing heparin and histamine

**matrix** connective tissue ground substance

**mediated transport** movement of substances with assistance of cell membrane components

**megakaryocyte** large bone marrow cell that produces platelets

**meiosis** cell division in which diploid chromosome number is reduced to haploid and received by gametes

**membrane** plasma membrane

**memory cell** agent of lasting immunity; long-lived lymphocyte that rapidly initiates immune response to previously encountered antigen

**microfilament** fibrous structure in eukaryotic cytoplasm that may be involved in cytoplasmic motion

**microphage** neutrophil, esp. one containing granulocytes

**microtubule** hollow tube in cytoplasm that provides structural support for cell

**mitochondria** organelles involved in cellular respiration and breakdown of energy into small units convenient for most cellular processes

**mitosis** cell division that forms two identical cells with original number of chromosomes

**monocyte** agranulocytic white blood cell that matures into macrophage

**mucopolysaccharide** gummy carbohydrate macromolecule

**myofibrils** contractile elements of muscle fiber

**NAD** nicotinamide adenine dinucleotide

**neutrophil** most common white blood cell, which protects body against infection

**nicotinamide adenine dinucleotide** NAD; coenzyme that accepts hydrogen and transfers it to cytochrome B

**nuclear envelope** double membrane surrounding nucleus of eukaryotic cell

**nucleolus** dense body in eukaryotic nucleus that is site of ribosomal RNA production

**nucleus** control center for all cellular activities

**organelles** membrane-bound compartments, nonmembranous particles, and filamentous structures that perform specialized functions and constitute internal structure of cells

**osmolarity** capacity for osmosis

**osmosis** diffusion of water across semipermeable membrane

**osmotic pressure** difference of solute concentrations on either side of semipermeable membrane

**osteoblast** bone-forming cell

**oxidative phosphorylation** use of electron energy released during cell respiration that yields energy-rich ATP

**oxyntic cells** parietal cells

**parietal cells** acid-secreting cells of stomach lining; oxyntic cells

**pathway** sequence of enzyme-catalyzed reactions by which energy-yielding substance is catabolized by protoplasm

**peroxisome** vesicle in which purines are broken down by cell

**phagocytosis** intake of solid particle by cell

**photosynthesis** process by which chlorophyll in green plant produces organic compounds from radiant light energy

**pili** rigid, cylindrical rods, comparable to flagella, that attach some prokaryotic bacteria to food sources

**plasma cell** antibody-producing cell cloned from B cell

**plasma membrane** outer layer of cell that separates it from environment; membrane

**plastid** any of various membrane-bound organelles in plants and algae that store starch, contain pigment, or are chlorophyll-containing site of photosynthesis

**platelet** protoplasmic blood cell fragment involved in clotting

**polymorphonuclear granulocytes** white blood cells with variable nuclei

**prokaryote** any cell that lacks distinct membrane-bound nucleus and organelles in its cytoplasm, including bacteria and blue-green algae

**red blood cell** erythrocyte

**RER** rough endoplasmic reticulum

**respiration** process that releases energy by breakdown of complex organic compound

**Rhesus factor** Rh factor

**Rh factor** group of antigens that may (Rh+) or may not (Rh-) be present on plasma membranes of erythrocytes; Rhesus factor

**ribosome** small cytoplasmic organelle and site of protein synthesis

**rough endoplasmic reticulum** RER; granular endoplasmic reticulum

**sarcoplasmic reticulum** network in muscle cell that transmits excitation to contractile proteins

**Schwann cells** cells forming neurilemma sheath around peripheral nerves

**secretory vesicles** membranous sac formed by Golgi apparatus, involved in exocytosis

**semipermeable membrane** membrane that allows only certain substances to pass through

**SER** smooth endoplasmic reticulum

**smooth endoplasmic reticulum** SER; agranular endoplasmic reticulum

**spindle** assembly of microtubules responsible for separating sister chromatids during mitosis

**suppressor T cell** T cell capable of inhibiting activity of B cells and other T cells

**T cell** lymphocyte originating in thymus gland, involved in cellular immunity; T lymphocyte

**tight junction** relatively impermeable discrete intercellular union

**T lymphocyte** T cell

**transport molecule** protein molecule involved in active transport and facilitated diffusion

**tricarboxylic acid cycle** Krebs cycle

**vacuole** membranous cavity within protoplasm, usu. containing watery fluid

**vesicle** intracellular membrane-bound sac that is much smaller than a vacuole

**white blood cell** leukocyte

**zymogen granule** particle that stores active enzymes

## PHYSIOLOGY

**abscess** microbes, leukocytes, and liquefied tissue debris walled off by fibroblasts and collagen

**absorption** passage of water or dissolved substance, esp. nutrient materials, into cell, blood, tissue, or organism

**absorptive state** period during which nutrients are entering bloodstream from gastrointestinal tract

**accommodation** adjustment of eye for viewing at various distances by changing shape of lens

**acetylcholine** ACh; a neurotransmitter

**acidosis** abnormal state of reduced alkalinity of blood and tissues

**ACTH** adrenocorticotropic hormone

**actin** protein located in thin filaments of muscle that, in conjunction with myosin, contracts muscle

**action potential** electrical signal propagated over long distance by nerve and muscle cells

**active hyperemia** increased blood flow through tissue as a result of increase in metabolic activity

**active site** area on enzyme to which substrate binds

**adaptation** decrease in frequency of action potentials fired by neuron despite stimulus of constant magnitude

**ADH** antidiuretic hormone

**adipose** fat in connective tissue

**adrenaline** epinephrine

**adrenergic** compound that acts like epinephrine or norepinephrine

**adrenocorticotropic hormone** ACTH; polypeptide secreted by anterior pituitary that stimulates adrenal cortex to secrete cortisol

**afferent neuron** neuron that transmits impulses to central nervous system and brain

**afferent pathway** component of reflex arc that transmits information from receptor to integrating center

**albumin** most abundant protein found in blood plasma

**aldosterone** steroid hormone secreted by adrenal cortex that regulates electrolyte balance in blood

**alkalosis** abnormal state of increased alkalinity of blood and tissues

**all-or-none response** event that occurs either maximally or not at all, usu. contraction of muscle fiber or firing of neuron

**allosteric enzyme** enzyme whose activity can be altered by modulator molecules binding to areas other than binding site

**alpha rhythm** prominent 8-13 Hz oscillation in EEG of awake, relaxed adult with closed eyes

**alveolar pressure** air pressure within alveoli of lungs

**alveolar ventilation** volume of air entering alveoli per minute

**amino acid** any of twenty-five organic acids containing an amino group that link together into polypeptide chains to form the proteins required for life, ten of which cannot be synthesized by the body and must be consumed

**amylase** enzyme that breaks down starch into disaccharides

**anabolism** constructive metabolism in which food is changed into living tissue

**androgen** male sex hormone

**antibody** protein secreted by plasma cells capable of combining with specific antigen that stimulated its production

**antidiuretic hormone** ADH; peptide hormone synthesized in hypothalamus and released from posterior pituitary; causing retention of more water in body

**antihistamine** chemical that blocks action of histamine

**antivenin** antidote to venom produced by venomous animal

**aortic-body chemoreceptor** sensor of oxygen and carbon dioxide pressure and acidity of blood, located in aorta

**apocrine secretion** release of substance by breaking away of entire top of gland cell

**arterial baroreceptors** nerve endings in arterial walls that sense changes in blood pressure

**arteriolar resistance** resistance to blood flow of arterioles

**atrophy** wasting away of muscle or organ, esp. from disuse

**automaticity** capacity for self-excitation

**autoregulation** independent ability of individual organs to self-regulate blood flow to the organ

**bacteria** pl., sing. **bacterium**; ubiquitous, unicellular organisms appearing singly or in chains in spherical, spiral, or rod-shaped form

**baroreceptor** neural receptor sensitive to pressure and rate of change in pressure; stretch receptor

**basal** (adj) at resting level

**basal metabolic rate** BMR; metabolic rate when subject is awake but at mental and physical rest, at a comfortable temperature, and without food for at least twelve hours

**beta rhythm** low, fast oscillations in EEG pattern of alert, awake adult who is actively paying attention or thinking

**bile** greenish liver secretion that is stored in gallbladder until released to emulsify fats in small intestine

**bile salts** steroid molecules in bile that promote solubilization and digestion of fats

**bilirubin** yellow substance that results from breakdown of red blood cells, excreted as component of bile

**binding site** area on protein with chemical groups that react with a specific substrate, binding it to surface of protein

**biological clock** internal factors that control innate body rhythms without external stimulation

**bioluminescence** emission of light produced by living organism

**biosynthesis** formation of organic compounds from elements or simple compounds by living organisms

**blocking antibody** antibody whose production is induced by cancer cells or tissue transplants and that blocks the killing of those cells by cytotoxic T cells

**blood** liquid that serves as an exchange medium between external environment and cells of organism

**blood-brain barrier** group of anatomical barriers and transport systems that tightly controls types of substances entering extracellular space of brain

**blood clot** network of fibers and other blood parts that covers wound and prevents additional blood loss

**blood pressure** pressure exerted by blood on walls of vessels

**blood sugar** glucose

**blood types** classification of blood by presence of A, B, O, or AB antigens on plasma membranes of erythrocytes, or presence of anti-A or anti-B antibodies in plasma

**BMR** basal metabolic rate

**bradykinin** peptide vasodilator that increases capillary permeability and probably stimulates pain receptors

**breathing** movement of air in and out of lungs

**bulk flow** movement of fluids or gases from region of higher pressure to one of lower pressure

**calcitonin** peptide hormone secreted by thyroid that reduces excess of calcium in blood by depositing it in bone

**carbohydrate** any of various organic saccharide sugars, starches, and celluloses that supply energy to body when consumed

**carbonic anhydrase** enzyme that catalyzes reaction combining water and carbon dioxide into carbonic acid, essential to effective respiration and production of stomach acid

**cardiac output** volume of blood pumped by either ventricle per minute

**carotid-body chemoreceptor** sensor of oxygen and carbon dioxide pressure and acidity in blood, located near origin of carotid artery

**catabolism** destructive metabolism in which living tissue is changed into energy and waste products

**catecholamines** chemically similar neurotransmitters dopamine, epinephrine, and norepinephrine

**CCK** cholecystokinin

**cell-mediated immunity** specific immune response mediated by cytotoxic T lymphocytes

**central thermoreceptors** temperature sensors located in hypothalamus, spinal cord, and internal organs

**chemical specificity** property of protein binding site such that only one or a few substrates can bind with it

**chemoreceptors** afferent nerve endings or associated sensory cells that respond to concentrations of certain chemicals

**chemotaxis** orientation and movement of cells in specific direction in response to chemical stimulus

**chitin** tough, horny substance that forms most of outer covering of insects and crustaceans

**cholecystokinin** CCK; peptide hormone secreted by small intestine that regulates motility and secretions of stomach, gallbladder contraction, and pancreatic enzyme secretion; pancreozymin

**cholesterol** steroid molecule that is precursor of steroid hormones and bile salts, component of plasma membranes, and present in fat and blood

**cholinergic** (*adj*) pertaining to or acting like acetylcholine

**chyme** solution of partially digested food in lumen of stomach and intestines

**clearance** volume per minute of plasma from which a specific substance has been completely removed

**climacteric** physical and emotional changes as sexual maturity gives way to cessation of reproductive function in female and testosterone decrease in male

**closed circulatory system** system in which blood is enclosed in vessels and does not directly bathe organs

**coenzyme** nonprotein organic molecule that temporarily joins with enzyme during reaction, serves as a carrier molecule, is not consumed in reaction, and can be reused until degraded; cofactor

**cofactor** coenzyme

**collagen** extremely strong fibrous protein that functions as structural element in connective tissue, tendons, and ligaments

**colloid** large molecule, such as plasma protein, to which capillaries are relatively impermeable

**command neuron** neuron whose activity initiates a series of neural events that result in a voluntary action

**compensatory growth** type of regeneration present in many organs after tissue damage

**complement** set of enzymes in bloodstream that work with antibodies to attack foreign cells and bacteria

**complex carbohydrate** polysaccharide

**compliance** distensibility of chest and lungs

**conducting portion** air passages whose walls are too thick to allow gas exchange between air and blood

**conducting system** network of cardiac muscle fibers specialized to conduct electrical activity to different areas of heart

**cone** one of two major photoreceptor types in retina that give rise to color vision

**contractility** force of contraction that is independent of fiber length

**contraction** tension-generating process of a muscle

**contraction time** interval between muscle action potential and development of peak twitch tension or shortening by muscle

**control system** interconnected components that function to keep physical or chemical value within predetermined range

**convergence** synapses from many presynaptic neurons acting on a single postsynaptic neuron

**core temperature** temperature inside of body

**corneal reflex** closure of eyelid in response to irritation of cornea

**corticotropin releasing hormone** CRH; hormone produced in hypothalamus that stimulates ACTH secretion by anterior pituitary

**cortisol** steroid hormone secreted by adrenal cortex that regulates organic metabolism by converting fats and proteins to glucose

**cortisone** steroid hormone secreted by adrenal cortex that counteracts pain and swelling

**countercurrent multiplier system** mechanism that creates high osmolarity in medulla of kidney, allowing higher urine concentration

**CRH** corticotropin releasing hormone

**cross bridge** projection of myosin molecule from thick filament of muscle that is capable of exerting force on thin filament, causing it to slide past thick filament

**crossed-extensor reflex** increased activation of extensor muscle on side of body opposite a limb flexion

**current** movement of electrical charge caused by movement of ions

**dark adaptation** improvement in sensitivity of vision after one is in darkness for some time

**dead space** area of respiratory system in which very little or no respiration occurs

**defecation** expulsion of feces from rectum

**deoxyhemoglobin** hemoglobin not combined with oxygen; reduced hemoglobin

**diastole** period of cardiac cycle in which ventricles are not contracting

**diastolic pressure** minimum blood pressure during cardiac cycle

**digestion** process of breaking down large particles and high-molecular weight substances into small molecules

**disaccharide** carbohydrate molecule consisting of two covalently bonded monosaccharides

**disinhibition** removal of inhibition from a neuron, allowing its activity to increase

**diuretic** substance that inhibits fluid reabsorption in kidney, causing increase in excreted urine

**divergence** single presynaptic neuron synapsing with and influencing activity of multiple postsynaptic neurons

**dominant hemisphere** cerebral hemisphere that controls hand used most frequently for intricate tasks

**dopamine** catecholamine neurotransmitter, precursor of epinephrine and norepinephrine

**dual innervation** innervation of organ or gland by both sympathetic and parasympathetic nerves

**ectopic focus**  region of heart other than sinoatrial node that assumes role of cardiac pacemaker

**edema**  accumulation of fluid in interstitial space

**EDV**  *end-diastolic volume*

**EEG arousal**  transformation of electroencephalogram pattern from alpha rhythm to beta rhythm, associated with increased level of attention

**effector**  cell or tissue whose change in activity constitutes response to stimulus

**efferent neuron**  neuron that carries information away from central nervous system to postganglionic neurons, muscles, or gland cells

**electrolyte**  substance that ionizes in solution and conducts electric current

**embolus**  mass of matter that obstructs blood flow

**emulsification**  maintenance of lipid droplets in solution

**end-diastolic volume**  EDV; amount of blood in heart just prior to systole

**endocrine gland**  ductless organ that synthesizes hormones and releases them directly into bloodstream

**endocrine system**  all ductless glands in body

**endorphin**  neurotransmitter that exhibits painkilling activity

**endoskeleton**  internal bony or cartilaginous supporting structure of vertebrates

**end-plate potential**  EPP; excitatory change in voltage across motor end plate of muscle cell membrane

**end-systolic volume**  ESV; amount of blood remaining in ventricle after ejection

**enzyme**  organic catalyst for physiological activity not used up in reaction

**enzyme induction**  process in which cell is induced to form enzyme in response to substance entering cell

**epinephrine**  hormone released by adrenal medulla that elevates blood sugar and initiates fight-or-flight response; adrenaline

**EPP**  *end-plate potential*

**equilibrium potential**  millivolts required to oppose movement caused by concentration gradient of specific ion

**erythropoiesis**  formation of erythrocytes

**erythropoietin**  hormone secreted mainly by kidney that stimulates erythrocyte production

**essential amino acids**  ten amino acids that cannot be synthesized in body and must be derived from diet

**essential nutrients**  substances necessary for normal body function that cannot be synthesized by body

**ESV**  *end-systolic volume*

**excitability**  ability to produce action potentials

**excitatory synapse**  synapse that, when activated, either increases likelihood of postsynaptic neuron reaching threshold and firing or increases firing frequency of existing action potentials

**excretion**  loss of substance through urine, feces, or other material expelled from body

**exocrine gland**  gland that secretes products through duct

**exoskeleton**  hard external supporting structure of invertebrates, such as shell of crustacean

**expiration**  movement of air out of lungs

**expiratory reserve volume**  supplemental air that can be forced out of lungs

**extension**  straightening of flexed limb

**extrinsic clotting pathway**  series of reactions by which clotting is initiated

**facilitation**  rendering excitation of nerve cells easier

**fat**  any of various mixtures of solid or semisolid triglycerides in adipose tissue, insoluble in water

**fatty acid**  organic compound whose carbon chain ends in a carboxyl group

**feces**  digestive waste products

**feedback**  change in quantity of substance that initiates either release or suppression of release of that substance

**fermentation**  conversion of complex carbohydrates or other organic substances into other chemicals by enzyme action

**ferritin**  protein in liver, spleen, and bone marrow that stores iron for metabolic use

**fever**  abnormal increase of body temperature

**fibrillation**  lack of coordination in contraction of muscle fibers

**fibrin**  insoluble protein formed during clotting

**fibrinogen**  soluble protein that transforms to fibrin

**fight-or-flight response**  adrenal-activated mobilization of body for extraordinary exertion

**filtration**  passing of fluid through membrane under pressure

**flexion**  bending of limb at joint

**flexion reflex**  contraction of flexor muscle; withdrawal reflex

**flexor muscle**  muscle that causes bending at joint by contraction

**flux**  excessive fluid discharge from bowels

**folic acid**  vitamin in B complex

**GABA**  *gamma-aminobutyric acid*

**gamma-aminobutyric acid**  GABA; inhibitory neurotransmitter of central nervous system

**gamma globulin**  IgG; globular protein antibody in plasma; most abundant class of plasma antibodies

**gastrin**  digestive system hormone that stimulates hydrochloric acid release by stomach and secretion of digestive enzyme by pancreas

**GFR**  *glomerular filtration rate*

**globulin**  protein insoluble in water; plasma protein complex comprised mainly of globulins

**glomerular filtration rate**  GFR; milliliters of plasma per minute filtered through kidney

**glucagon**  pancreatic hormone that increases blood glucose levels

**glucocorticoid**  adrenal cortex hormone that effects salt and water metabolism and stimulates conversion of noncarbohydrates to carbohydrates

**gluconeogenesis**  glucose formation from noncarbohydrates

**glucose**  monosaccharide six-carbon sugar in blood; blood sugar

**glutamic acid**  amino acid that may be brain neurotransmitter

**glycerol**  three-carbon alcohol derived from fats

**glycine**  simplest amino acid, present in most proteins

**glycogen**  white polysaccharide sugar, derived from glucose, that is principal form in which carbohydrate is stored in tissue

**glycogenolysis**  conversion of glycogen to glucose

**glycolipid**  sugar lipid containing short, water-soluble carbohydrate chain

**glycolytic fast fibers**  skeletal muscle fibers energized aerobically

**glycoprotein**  carbohydrate-protein complex

**Golgi tendon organs** sensory nerve fibers that monitor tension between tendons and muscle cells

**granuloma** mass of chronically inflamed tissue

**Hb** hemoglobin

**HDL** *high-*density *lipoprotein*

**hematocrit** percentage of total blood volume made up of blood cells

**heme** iron-containing pigment

**hemoglobin** Hb; iron-containing protein that carries oxygen in red blood cells and gives them red color

**hemostasis** stoppage of bleeding

**heparin** anticoagulant secreted by liver

**high-density lipoprotein** HDL; lipid–protein aggregate with low proportion of lipid or cholesterol that removes cholesterol from arteries

**histamine** amine derived from amino acid histidine that is released in allergic reaction, causing dilation of blood vessels and lowering of blood pressure

**histone** protein that is integral to chromosome structure

**holocrine secretion** process by which exocrine glands shed whole cells and their contents

**homeostasis** maintenance of constant internal environment

**hormone** chemical agent usu. released by ductless gland that has regulatory effect on functions in other parts of body

**humoral immunity** defense against disease by antibodies in body fluids

**hydrochloric acid** acid secreted by stomach during digestion

**hydrolysis** splitting of molecules by addition of water

**hydrostatic pressure** pressure exerted by a fluid

**hyperemia** increased blood flow

**hyperpolarization** presence of larger than normal number of oppositely charged ions on opposite sides of membrane

**hypersensitivity** allergic reaction

**hypertrophy** increase in size of cells, tissues, or organ

**hypoxia** oxygen deficiency at tissue level

**hypoxic hypoxia** hypoxia due to decreased oxygen pressure in arterial blood

**Ig** immunoglobulin

**IgG** gamma globulin

**immune responses** body's defense reaction through dual modes of antibody and cellular response

**immunity** resistance to specific disease

**immunoglobulin** Ig; any of five classes of antibodies: IgG, IgM, IgA, IgD, and IgE

**inspiration** taking of air into lungs

**inspiratory reserve volume** amount of air that can be drawn into lungs in excess of tidal volume

**insulin** pancreatic hormone that regulates blood sugar level

**interferon** molecule that inhibits viral replication in cells

**internal environment** conditions within an organism

**interneuron** internuncial neuron

**internuncial neuron** nerve cell connecting sensory and motor neurons in brain and spinal cord; interneuron

**intrinsic clotting pathway** series of reactions that initiate clotting of blood

**intrinsic factor** glycoprotein secreted by stomach and required for absorption of vitamin $B_{12}$

**ischemia** reduced blood supply to organ or tissue

**isometric contraction** increase of force in muscle whose length does not change

**isotonic contraction** development of force that remains the same during shortening of muscle

**ketone** product of lipid metabolism characterized by CO group

**kinesthesia** sensation of position and movement of limbs

**kinin** vasodilatory polypeptide

**lactase** enzyme that cleaves lactose into glucose and galactose

**lactic acid** three-carbon breakdown product of glucose

**latent period** elapsed time between stimulus and response

**lateral inhibition** inhibitory interaction between adjacent neurons

**LDL** *low-*density *lipoprotein*

**lecithin** phospholipid in nerve tissue and blood

**ligand** any molecule or ion that binds to protein surface by noncovalent bonds

**lipase** fat-splitting enzyme

**lipid** fat or fatlike substance insoluble in water, typically serving as energy-storage molecule

**lipoprotein** molecule combining protein and lipid

**low-density lipoprotein** LDL; protein–lipid aggregate that is major cholesterol carrier in plasma

**lumen** cavity within tubular structure

**lymph** colorless fluid derived from blood and carried in special ducts of lymphatic vessels

**lymphoid tissue** connective tissue containing lymphocytes

**lymphokine** regulatory soluble protein secreted by T cells

**mechanoreceptor** sensory cell or organ that receives mechanical stimuli

**metabolic acidosis** abnormal decrease in blood pH not caused by respiratory phenomena

**metabolic alkalosis** abnormal increase in blood pH not caused by respiratory phenomena

**metabolic rate** level of energy expenditure

**metabolism** sum of all chemical reactions in living cell or organism

**microorganism** any living organism too small to be viewed by unaided eye, including bacteria, viruses, protists, and some algae and fungi

**micturition** excretion of urine

**mineral** naturally occurring inorganic substance required for growth or functioning of organism

**mineralocorticoid** steroid salt-retaining hormone of adrenal cortex

**mononuclear phagocyte system** monocytes and macrophages

**monosaccharide** carbohydrate, such as glucose or fructose, consisting of a single sugar molecule, generally made up of five or six carbon atoms

**monosynaptic reflex** pathway involving single junction between two neurons

**motor** (*adj*) having to do with muscles and movement

**motor neuron** efferent neuron that innervates skeletal muscle fibers

**mucin** protein that forms mucus when mixed with water

**mucous membrane** mucus-secreting membrane lining body cavities and canals connecting with external air

**mucus** viscid, watery lubricating solution secreted by mucous membranes

**muscle fatigue** depressed metabolic activity of muscle cells due to increased concentration of lactic acid

**muscle spindle** modified skeletal muscle cell with stretch receptors that regulate muscle tone

**muscle tone** condition in which muscles are always slightly contracted

**myogenic** (*adj*) originating within muscle

**myoglobin** protein in muscles that binds oxygen

**myosin** contractile protein that forms thick filaments of muscle

**negative feedback** condition in which increase in substance over certain level produces responses which inhibit synthesis of that substance

**nerve growth factor** protein secreted by cells that attracts neurons to grow toward them

**neuron** functional unit of a nerve, including cell body, axon, and dendrites

**neurotransmitter** substance that transmits or inhibits nerve impulses from nerve cell to another cell at synapse

**neutrophil exudation** release of white blood cells

**night vision** higher than normal concentration of rods in retina, causing increased ability to see in darkness

**nociceptor** pain receptor

**norepinephrine** hormone of adrenal medulla that elevates blood pressure and blood sugar levels

**optimal length** length at which muscle fiber develops maximal tension

**organ** collection of tissues joined in structural unit to serve a common function

**organ system** group of organs with integrated functions

**osmoreceptor** hypothalamic neuron that responds to osmotic pressure changes in blood and influences sense of thirst

**oxidative** (*adj*) using oxygen

**oxidative fast fibers** skeletal muscle fibers energized aerobically

**oxidative slow fibers** slow-fatiguing skeletal muscle fibers energized aerobically

**oxyhemoglobin** globular protein with a molecule of oxygen bonded to iron

**pacemaker** area of vertebrate heart that initiates heartbeat; sinoatrial node

**pacinian corpuscle** deep-pressure sensory receptor

**palpitation** abnormally rapid heartbeat

**pancreozymin** cholecystokinin

**paradoxical sleep** sleep with rapid eye movement and intermittent muscular twitching, associated with dream state; REM sleep

**parahormone** chemical control agent that can be synthesized by more than one cell type

**parathyroid hormone** PTH; hormone that promotes vitamin D synthesis and elevates blood calcium

**pepsin** stomach enzyme that degrades proteins

**peptide** compound of two or more amino acids

**peripheral resistance** opposition to flow of blood in vessels

**peristaltic waves** successive contractions of tubular wall that move its contents forward

**permissiveness** potentiation

**phasic** (*adj*) intermittent, as opposed to tonic

**phospholipid** lipid compound containing water-soluble phosphate group

**phosphorylation** addition of phosphate to molecule

**photopigment** colored substance that absorbs light over narrow band of wavelengths

**photoreceptor** cell or organ capable of detecting light

**physiology** study of functions and vital processes of organisms and their parts or organs

**plasma** fluid portion of blood and lymph

**plasmin** enzyme involved in blood clotting

**pneumothorax** condition of having air in thoracic cavity outside of lungs

**polypeptide** protein, polymer of amino acid subunits

**polysaccharide** complex carbohydrate compound of chains of simple sugars, such as cellulose or starch

**positive feedback** stimulation by message to cell or organ of increased activity by original message sender

**postsynaptic neuron** neuron that conducts information away from synapse

**potential** voltage difference between two points

**potentiation** one event making possible the occurrence of another; permissiveness

**presynaptic neuron** neuron that conducts action potential toward synapse

**prion** infectious, viruslike particle composed solely of protein without a genetic component, found in animals

**prohormone** inactive substance converted to active hormone after release into bloodstream

**proprioception** awareness of position, balance, and movement

**prostaglandin** fatty, acid-derived parahormone

**protease** protein-splitting enzyme

**protein** any of a large class of organic nitrogenous substances containing amino acids that occur in all animal and vegetable matter and are essential to diet

**prothrombin** inactive precursor of clotting enzyme thrombin

**PTH** parathyroid hormone

**pulmonary ventilation** volume of air exchanged by lungs per minute

**pulse pressure** difference between systolic and diastolic arterial blood pressures

**P wave** deflection in electrocardiogram caused by depolarization of atria

**QRS complex** electrocardiogram pattern that occurs during ventricular depolarization

**rapid eye movement sleep** REM sleep

**RDA** recommended dietary allowance

**reactive hyperemia** increased blood flow that causes body temperature above normal range; fever

**receptor** sensory cell or organ

**receptor potential** potential transmitted from receptor to second neuron along way to central nervous system

**recommended dietary allowance** RDA; government estimate of minimal nutrient requirements of vitamins and minerals

**recruitment** involvement of excitable cells in process due to increase in stimulus strength

**red muscle fibers** tissues that bind and store myoglobin

**reduced hemoglobin** deoxyhemoglobin

**reflex** involuntary response to stimulus

**reflex arc** functional pathway of neuron system consisting of at least one afferent and one efferent neuron and usu. one interneuron

**refractory period** recovery time during which excitable neuron membrane is unresponsive to stimulus

**relative refractory period** recovery time during which excitable neuron membrane will respond only to stimulus that is stronger than initial stimulus

**relaxation time** period required for tension in muscle fiber to decrease from peak to zero

**REM sleep** rapid *eye* *movement* sleep; paradoxical sleep

**renin** enzyme secreted by kidneys

**residual volume** air left in lungs after forcible expiration

**respiration** exchange of gases between body tissues and surrounding environment, specifically intake of oxygen by tissues, which give off carbon dioxide and water

**respiratory acidosis** abnormal decrease in blood pH due to respiratory dysfunction

**respiratory alkalosis** abnormal increase in blood pH due to respiratory dysfunction

**respiratory quotient** RQ; ratio of carbon dioxide produced to oxygen consumed as food is metabolized

**respiratory rate** depth and frequency of exhalation and inhalation, related to carbon dioxide levels

**respiratory system** all organs involved in respiration

**resting membrane potential** all voltage measurable across membrane when it is not transmitting

**rod** visual cell of retina of eye sensitive to low levels of light

**RQ** respiratory *quotient*

**saliva** watery, slightly acidic secretion of salivary glands that moistens food and initiates its breakdown

**sarcomere** structural and functional unit of contraction in striated muscle

**saturated fat** fat in which carbon chains are bonded by single bonds while simultaneously bound to as much hydrogen as possible

**SDA** specific *dynamic* *action*

**secretin** duodenal hormone that promotes secretion of pancreatic juice

**secretion** synthesis and release of substance by cell or organ; such a released substance

**segmentation** division of body into more or less similar parts

**sensor** cell that receives signals

**serotonin** brain neurotransmitter that seems to have calming effect

**serum** liquid portion of coagulated blood

**sinoatrial node** pacemaker

**sliding-filament mechanism** contraction of muscle due to sliding past each other of thick and thin filaments

**slow-wave sleep** sleep pattern characterized by slow delta waves for four-fifths of total sleep time

**somatic receptor** neuron in voluntary nervous system connected directly to central nervous system

**spatial summation** increased response of nerve due to increased excitation

**specific dynamic action** SDA; increase of body temperature and basal metabolic rate after consumption of meal

**specificity** influence directed toward one response or body part

**split brain** division of brain into left and right hemispheres, which control different functions

**starch** complex molecule composed of many monosaccharides; main food storage substance in plants

**steady state** continuous exchange of substances in and out of cells with no apparent change in concentrations

**steroid** nonfat lipid characterized by four interconnected carbon rings

**stimulus** any change or phenomenon that causes response in organism or its component

**stress** stimulus that causes imbalance in homeostasis

**stretch receptor** baroreceptor

**striated muscle** voluntary muscle with cylindrical fibers that controls skeleton

**stroke volume** milliliters per heartbeat of blood pumped by either ventricle

**substrate** substance that is recipient of enzymic action

**summation** temporal or spatial addition of electrical effects of multiple stimuli

**surfactant** substance that reduces surface tension

**synapse** junction between two excitable cells, esp. point at which neurotransmitters send impulses in response to action potential in one neuron

**synaptic cleft** intercellular space between two excitable cells

**synergistic muscle** muscle with additive effects

**synthetic reactions** anabolic reactions in which food is synthesized into living tissue

**systemic circulation** movement of blood from heart to all tissues except lungs and back of heart

**systole** contraction of heart muscle

**systolic pressure** blood pressure produced when ventricles contract

**temporal summation** increase of nerve or muscle cell response due to increased frequency of excitation

**tetanus** continuous contraction of muscle due to fusion of twitches

**TH** thyroid hormone

**thermogenesis** production of heat within body

**thermoreceptor** sensory receptor that responds to temperature changes

**thick filaments** myosin molecules in muscle cells

**thin filaments** threads consisting of actin, troponin, and tropomyosin molecules in muscle cells

**threshold** minimal level at which stimulus excites a response

**thrombin** enzymatic molecule involved in blood coagulation

**thyroid hormone** TH; thyroxine

**thyrotropin** thyroid-stimulating hormone

**thyroxine** active thyroid hormone

**tidal volume** quantity of air moved during normal, quiet breathing

**tissue** group of similar cells that performs particular function

**tolerance** diminished response due to repeated exposure

**trace element** mineral present in body in extremely small amounts

**transferrin** protein that aids blood in transporting iron

**triacylglycerol** neutral fat lipid molecule composed of glycerol and three fatty acids; triglyceride

**triglyceride** triacylglycerol

**triiodothyronine** form of thyroxine

**tropomyosin** cablelike muscle protein in thin filaments

**troponin** structural muscle protein involved with contraction

**trypsin** pancreatic protein-cleaving enzyme

**T wave** electrocardiographic representation of electrical activity just prior to ventricular relaxation in diastole

**twitch** single contraction of muscle fiber

**ultrafiltrate** material separated from blood during filtering through renal capillaries

**unsaturated fat** fat in which some carbons are linked by double bonds

**urea** nitrogenous waste product of kidneys

**uric acid** nitrogenous waste product secreted in urine

**vasoconstriction** narrowing of blood vessel

**vasodilation** widening of blood vessel

**vasopressin** antidiuretic hormone

**ventilation** movement of air in and out of lungs

**vestibular system** sensory labyrinth of air in body cavities that responds to balance and movement

**vestigial organ** body part, such as tonsils or appendix, that no longer functions usefully

**viroid** infectious agent found in plants, consisting of single strand of RNA with no protein coat

**virus** ultramicroscopic, metabolically inert agent that can reproduce only within a host cell, containing RNA or DNA within protein coat

**vital capacity** maximal amount of air that can be moved by lungs

**vitamin** any of various organic compounds necessary for normal metabolic functions

**withdrawal reflex** flexion reflex

# ENVIRONMENT, ECOLOGY, AND ANIMAL BEHAVIOR

**abiotic factors** nonliving components that interact with and affect organisms in an ecosystem

**abyssal zone** deepest part of ocean where light is absent

**acclimatization** adaptive change in physiological system induced by prolonged exposure to environmental stress or a new environment

**acid rain** rain with abnormally high acid level, esp. due to combustion of fossil fuels

**agonistic** (*adj*) displaying any type of fighting behavior

**algal bloom** rapid growth of algae

**altitudinal succession** continuous succession of community types from low to high altitudes

**altricial** (*adj*) displaying condition in which young are born helpless and remain so for some time

**altruism** self-destructive behavior performed to benefit or protect others, esp. kin

**amphibious** (*adj*) capable of living both on land and in water

**anaerobe** bacterium that lives and grows without oxygen

**animal** multicellular, heterotrophic, usu. mobile organism

**aquatic** (*adj*) water-dwelling

**arboreal** (*adj*) tree-dwelling

**autotroph** organism that can produce its own food by using inorganic materials as its source of nutrients and usu. photosynthesis as its source of energy

**avifauna** bird life of particular area

**behavior** organism's observable responses to environment and stimuli

**biodegradable** (*adj*) capable of being broken down and absorbed in a natural environment, esp. susceptible to being broken down by microorganisms into simple compounds such as water and carbon dioxide

**biohazard** life-endangering substance, phenomenon, or activity

**biological magnification** increased concentration of chemicals along food chain

**biomass** total mass of organisms per unit area

**biome** discrete community and region, such as desert or tropical rain forest, characterized by same major life forms and climactic conditions

**bioremediation** use of biological means to restore biosphere or solve ecological problems, such as oil-eating microbes on an oil spill

**biosphere** sphere of life on Earth from crust into lower troposphere

**biota** flora and fauna of an area

**biotic factors** relationships among living organisms in an ecosystem

**biotic potential** reproductive potential of a species

**birthrate** number of organisms born per unit of time

**boreal forest** biome of wooded regions with cold, dry climate, sandy soil, and coniferous trees

**camouflage** any means of blending appearance with environment

**canopy** top layer of forest, where most food is produced

**carbon cycle** circulation of carbon in biosphere by plant photosynthesis, animal metabolism, and decomposition

**carnivore** meat-eating organism; consumer that feeds on other consumers

**carrying capacity** number of individuals of any species that a particular environment can support

**circadian rhythm** pattern in which a behavior occurs regularly in twenty-four hour cycle

**clear-cutting** logging of all trees in an area

**climax community** final stage in evolution of community

**cold-blooded** (*adj*) having body temperature that varies with approximate surrounding environment, as in fish and reptiles; poikilothermal

**colonial** (*adj*) designating species that occupies its habitat in groups

**commensalism** relationship in which one organism benefits from a host organism without affecting it

**communication** behavior that influences behavior of another organism in adaptive manner

**community** naturally occurring group of organisms living in a certain area

**competition** struggle between organisms of same or different species for access to limited resources

**competitive exclusion principle** rule that two populations cannot occupy the same ecological niche

**conservation** protection and preservation of natural environment and resources

**conspecific** member of same species

**consumer** organism that consumes other organisms as food

**courtship** behavior patterns used to attract potential mate

**cryptic coloration** type of camouflage in which color of organism blends with environment

**death rate** number of organisms that die per unit of time

**deciduous forest** biome with trees that lose their leaves in winter, forming belt through temperate latitudes, including monsoon rain forests of Asia and Africa

**decomposer** organism, such as bacterium, that causes decay

**desert** biome of arid regions with sparse, widely spaced vegetation and rainfall under 10 inches (25 cm) per year

**detritus** substrate litter composed of decaying organic matter

**dispersion** way in which species uses its habitat, such as colonial or solitary

**displacement behavior** activity, often due to ambivalence, not directly related to immediate stimulus

**display** behavior or series of behaviors modified by evolution for communication

**dominance** ability of one member of community to exercise control over other members and their environment

**dominant species** characteristic species of a community

**echolocation** determination of size, shape, and location of an object by bouncing high-frequency sound waves off it, used by organisms such as bats and porpoises

**ecological niche** specific role organism plays in community, esp. behavior and position in food cycle

**ecological succession** replacement of one community by another

**ecology** relationship and balance between organisms and their environment

**ecosystem** all interactions of a community of organisms with its physical environment

**ecotage** extreme measures, such as destruction of tree-cutting machinery, used in opposition to humanly caused ecological damage

**ecotone** transition zone between communities

**edge effect** increase in variety and density of organisms in ecotone

**effluent** outflow, usu. offensive, of human works and waste

**emigration** aggregate of movement of animals out of an area

**endangered species** species of organism in imminent danger of extinction, due usu. to destruction of its habitat, loss of food supply, evolutionary deselection, or destruction by humans

**endogenous** (*adj*) originating or developing from within the organism

**environment** all external factors acting on an organism

**environmental resistance** environmental factors that check biotic potential of a population

**estuary** semienclosed body of water along coast, often brackish

**ethogram** detailed description of behavior of an organism

**eusociality** presence of nonreproductive castes, such as worker bees, within a species

**eutrophication** aging and death of lake, esp. due to upset in ecological balance

**exogenous** (*adj*) originating or derived from outside the organism

**fauna** animal life of an area

**feeding level** level of energy transfer in ecosystem

**first-order consumer** consumer that feeds directly on producer; herbivore

**flora** plant life of an area

**food chain** route of passage of energy and materials through community of organisms, with successively larger ones feeding on smaller ones

**food web** all possible feeding relationships in an ecosystem

**forest floor** bottommost stratum of a forest

**geographic isolation** populations separated by geographical features

**global warming** increase in Earth's average atmospheric temperature and corresponding changes in climate, esp. due to greenhouse effect

**grassland** biome of plains regions, characterized by grasses

**greenhouse effect** increase of carbon dioxide in Earth's atmosphere that prevents radiated heat from dissipating, thereby raising its temperature

**grooming** manipulative cleaning of body surface

**growth** basic capacity of all organisms to develop or increase, usu. by assimilation of nutriments

**habitat** natural environment of an organism

**habituation** depletion of response to often repeated stimulus

**herbivore** plant-eating organism, consumer of producers

**heterotroph** organism that cannot produce food and that requires living or dead organic materials as its principal source of nutrition

**hibernation** period of dormancy during time of low temperatures when metabolic processes slow to minimum

**home range** area to which organism habitually restricts its movement

**homing** ability of displaced organism to return to its home range or place of birth

**homoiotherm** warm-blooded organism that maintains relatively constant body temperature

**host** organism that harbors and provides benefits to another organism

**imprinting** bonding of newborn, esp. bird, to first organism that mothers it

**insectivore** animal that feeds on insects

**insessorial** (*adj*) adapted for perching, as bird's foot

**instinct** innate behavior genetically keyed for and not learned

**interspecific competition** competition between populations of different species

**intraspecific competition** competition between members of same species

**jungle** dense forest community that results from secondary succession of rain forest

**K selection** process that favors competitive ability within a population and few offspring with great investment in each

**laterite** hard, impermeable crust formed by water leaching exposed soils in areas cleared of tropical rain forest

**latitudinal succession** continuous succession of community types from equator to poles

**learning** process by which responses and behavior of an organism are modified due to experience, as through conditioning and associative learning, imprinting in early life, and imitation

**lek** area repeatedly used for communal courtship displays

**limiting factor** component of environment that prevents population increase at given time

**littoral zone** area of ocean close to shore and subject to action of tides

**marine** (*adj*) sea-dwelling

**Mediterranean scrub** biome with mild winters and long, dry summers, characterized by small trees and spiny, evergreen shrubs, primarily in California and around Mediterranean Sea

**microenvironment** small area in ecosystem that differs from rest of area

**migration** seasonal movement of populations of animals

**mimicry** evolution of one species to resemble another for some selective advantage

**mobbing** group assault to drive off predator

**molting** regular shedding of all or part of outer layer of skin, esp. in snakes and crabs; shedding of feathers in birds

**mutualism** relationship in which two animals live in mutually beneficial, often necessary, association

**neritic zone** area of ocean along continental shelf beyond littoral zone

**niche** ecological niche

**nitrogen cycle** circulation of nitrogen through plants and animals in biosphere

**nitrogenous waste** nitrogen-containing animal waste product

**ocean** aquatic community covering almost three fourths of Earth's surface

**omnivore** plant- and animal-eating organism, feeding on both producers and consumers

**oxygen cycle** circulation of oxygen through biosphere by its release from plants during photosynthesis and utilization by animals during respiration

**pair-bonding** long-lasting association between male and female for cooperative rearing of young

**parasite** organism that lives in or on host from which it obtains nourishment

**parasitism** relationship in which parasite organism is completely dependent on host organism for nourishment and host is usu. harmed

**pecking order** social hierarchy, dominance

**pelagic** (*adj*) dwelling in the open sea

**pheromones** chemicals produced by one organism that influence behavior of another

**pioneering stage** first stage in ecological succession, usu. consisting of hardy autotrophs

**plankton** aggregate of microscopic, passively floating or slightly motile organisms in body of water, being primarily algae and protozoans that serve as food for marine animals

**poikilotherm** cold-blooded organism having body temperature that varies with that of environment

**pollutant** any substance that makes air, water, or soil unclean

**pollution** introduction of impurities and contaminants into environment, esp. air and water pollution

**population** group of organisms that naturally interbreeds, living in same locality

**population density** number of individuals per unit area

**population dynamics** combination of various factors affecting the size of populations

**population growth** changes in size of population with time

**precocial** condition in which young are able to move about and forage for food shortly after birth

**predation** feeding of one organism on another

**predator** animal that feeds on other organisms

**primary production** energy accumulated and stored in plants through photosynthesis

**primary succession** ecological succession that begins with lifeless terrain, first succession in an ecosystem

**producer** organism that can make its own food; autotroph

**pyramid of biomass** relationship revealing decrease of biomass with each successive feeding level

**pyramid of energy** relationship revealing loss of energy as it is transferred along food chain

**pyramid of numbers** relationship revealing decrease in number of organisms at each higher feeding level

**rain forest** tropical rain forest

**reciprocal altruism** seemingly altruistic social behavior performed in expectation that favor will be returned

**recycling** reprocessing of used materials, esp. nonbiodegradable ones

**red tide** overabundance of dinoflagellate protozoans in usu. subtropical marine waters, turning them reddish-brown and producing a fish-killing toxin

**renewable resource** resource that can be replaced naturally

**reproductive isolation** any barrier to interbreeding

**resource** anything humans take from environment; anything an organism needs to live

**resource partitioning** division of resources among similar species coexisting in same ecological niche

**ritualization** evolutionary modification of behavior patterns to serve as communication

**R selection** process that favors rapid population increase, with many offspring and little investment in each

**saprophyte** organism that feeds on dead and decaying matter

**savanna** biome consisting of tropical grasslands with scattered clumps of trees, found esp. in Africa

**scavenger** animal that feeds on dead animals

**secondary succession** series of ecological changes that occur when species of a climax community are removed

**second-order consumer** animal that eats a first-order consumer

**sedentary** (*adj*) not migratory; living in one place

**smog** fog and mist made heavier, darker, and more toxic by absorption of chemical fumes and smoke, usu. in urban areas

**social behavior** interactions among animals of one species living in structured, mutually dependent groups

**social hierarchy** series of dominance-subordination relationships in group; pecking order

**sociality** conditions and processes of social existence and interaction among organisms of species and among species

**solar collector** device for collecting and converting radiant energy of sunlight into electric power

**solar energy** radiant energy of sunlight, an abundant and nonpolluting alternative to fossil fuels

**solitary** species whose members live separately

**species diversity** number of species in community

**S-shaped curve** normal population growth curve

**stimulus** substance or phenomenon that causes or changes activity of an organism

**strip mining** laying bare of mineral deposits in earth to extract them, causing erosion

**substrate** surface on which an organism lives or moves

**succession** ecological succession

**symbiosis** relationship in which two organisms live in close, mutually beneficial association

**taiga** subarctic biome characterized by coniferous forests

**temperate deciduous forest** biome characterized by even distribution of rain averaging 39 inches (100 cm) per year; region in which trees periodically shed leaves

**temperate grassland** biome with flat to rolling terrain, covered by sod-forming grasses and legumes, forming transitional area to deserts, including plains, steppes, veld, and pampas

**terrestrial** (*adj*) ground-dwelling

**territory** area defended from intruders, usu. of same species, by organism or organisms

**tetrapod** four-legged vertebrate such as mammal or reptile

**third-order consumer** animal that eats a second-order consumer

**trophic levels** series of steps on food chain

**tropical rain forest** equatorial biome characterized by constant warm temperature, heavy rainfall, dense, varied, evergreen plant growth, and enormous diversity of life forms

**tropism** involuntary response of organism to stimulus

**tundra** arctic biome characterized by low average temperature and rainfall, permafrost, and few large plants

**vertical stratification** layers of a forest from top to bottom

**warm-blooded** (*adj*) having relatively constant body temperature regardless of surrounding environment; homoiothermal

**warning coloration** display of bright colors to announce rather than conceal animal's presence

**water cycle** worldwide circulation of water molecules throughout atmosphere, powered by sun through evaporation and precipitation

**weathering** mechanical process of freezing, thawing, and erosion

**zero population growth** birthrate equal to death rate

## REPRODUCTION AND DEVELOPMENT

**allantois** membrane for respiratory exchange in embryonic birds and reptiles; part of placenta in mammals

**amnion** membrane enclosing fluid-filled cavity containing embryo

**androgen** male sex hormone

**anisogamy** condition in most animals in which gametes are of different sizes

**baculum** slim bone supporting rigidity of penis in many mammals

**bilateral symmetry** mirroring of right and left halves of body

**blastula** hollow ball of cells formed from developing egg in early stage of noneutherian embryo

**budding** direct growth of new individual from body of old one

**CG** *chorionic gonadotropin*

**chorionic gonadotropin** CG; protein hormone secreted by blastocyst and placenta during first trimester of pregnancy

**cleavage** progressive subdivision of zygote by mitotic cell division

**clitoris** female erectile organ homologous to penis

**cloaca** combined urogenital and rectal chamber in most nonmammalian vertebrates

**coitus** sexual intercourse

**colostrum** thin, milky fluid secreted by mammary glands for several days after birth prior to onset of milk production

**copulation** sexual intercourse, esp. mammalian

**cytokinesis** stage of cell division in which cytoplasm divides to form two new cells

**deuterostome** animal, such as any chordate, in which anus and mouth form separately in the developing embryo

**development** stages of growth from conception through birth to maturity and death

**diapause** period in some species between fertilization of egg and beginning of development

**differentiation** development of specialized tissue from nonspecialized tissue

**ectoderm** outermost germ layer in early embryo that forms nervous system and integument

**egg** female gamete; protective reproductive structure enclosing ovum and nutrient supply, esp. of birds, fish, reptiles, and insects

**embryo** organism in early stages of development before birth

**endoderm** innermost germ layer in early embryo that forms gut and glands

**estradiol** estrogen hormone secreted by ovaries

**estriol** estrogen hormone secreted by placenta

**estrogen** group of steroid hormones secreted by female reproductive system

**estrous cycle** repeated series of changes in reproductive physiology culminating in estrus

**estrus** period of maximum sexual receptivity in female mammals, usu. related to release of eggs; heat

**eutherian** (*adj*) designating placental mammals or condition in which mammalian embryo is nourished by placenta

**fallopian tube** one of a pair of tubes that carries eggs away from ovaries in humans

**fertilization** union of two gametes that activates development of egg

**fetus** human embryo after third month

**follicle stimulating hormone** FSH; anterior pituitary hormone that stimulates maturation of ova and sperm

**FSH** *follicle stimulating hormone*

**fusion** joining of two gametes to form zygote

**gamete** mature sex cell: egg or sperm

**genitalia** reproductive organs, esp. external organs

**germ** formative structure

**germ cell** gamete

**gestation** developmental period of young in uterus of mammal

**GH** *growth hormone*

**gonad** organ that produces gametes: female ovary or male testis

**gonadotropic hormone** anterior pituitary hormone that stimulates sexual functions

**gonopodium** appendage used in fertilization

**Graafian follicle** ovarian follicle

**growth hormone** GH; anterior pituitary hormone that stimulates growth; somatotropin

**hatching** emergence of embryo as newborn from egg

**heat** estrus

**hermaphrodite** organism with both male and female reproductive organs

**implantation** settling of early mammalian embryo into uterine wall

**inbreeding** mating of closely related individuals within the same species

**incubation** development of egg by means of body warmth

**interstitial cells** cells between germ cells in reproductive organs

**in utero** unborn and developing in uterus

**in vitro** conceived and developing in isolation from living organism, as in test tube

**lactation** production of milk by mother's mammary glands

**larva** immature organism, such as caterpillar, that undergoes metamorphosis to become adult

**LH** *luteinizing hormone*

**lordosis** mating posture of many female mammals with back arched, rump raised, and vulva exposed

**luteinizing hormone** LH; anterior pituitary hormone that stimulates testosterone secretion in male and maturation of ovarian follicles in female

**maggot** larval form of certain insects, esp. flies

**maturity** stage in development at which organism's secondary sex characteristics and reproductive capacity are functioning

**menarche** onset of female menstrual cycle at puberty

**menopause** termination of female menstrual cycle and reproductive capability

**menses** menstruation

**menstrual cycle** hormone-regulated changes in uterine lining of human and certain other primate females

**menstruation** cyclical shedding of lining of uterus with loss of blood and fluid; menses

**mesoderm** middle germ layer in early embryo that forms muscles and supporting tissue

**metamorphosis** structural change from larval into adult form

**milk letdown** hormonal response to suckling of baby that ejects milk from mammarian nipples

**monogamy** practice of mating with only one partner

**morphogenesis** origin of form

**myoblast** embryonic cell that develops into skeletal muscle

**neonate** newborn

**neoteny** attainment of sexual maturity while still in larval form

**nest** structure in which organisms, esp. birds, lay eggs

**nidus** nest in which insects or spiders deposit eggs

**notocord** supporting axis in vertebrate embryo and in lower chordates

**nullipara** female that has never produced young

**ontogeny** development and life cycle of single organism or individual

**oocyte** cell giving rise by meiosis to an ovum, as in humans

**oogamy** sexual reproduction involving one large nonmotile, female gamete and one small, motile, male gamete

**oogenesis** origin and development of the ovum

**ovarian follicle** vesicle in ovary that contains developing egg; Graafian follicle

**ovary** female gonad

**oviduct** tube carrying egg from ovary to uterus or outside of body; fallopian tube in humans

**oviparous** (*adj*) egg-laying

**ovoviviparous** (*adj*) having membrane-enclosed eggs that remain in female until hatching

**ovum** egg; female gamete

**oxytocin** posterior pituitary hormone that stimulates milk letdown

**parthenogenesis** production of organism from unfertilized egg

**parturition** birth process

**penis** male erectile organ for copulation, esp. in mammals

**placenta** organ for nourishing embryo and removing waste products in most mammals

**planula** swimming larva of certain invertebrates

**polyandry** practice of female having more than one mate

**polygamy** practice of mating with more than one partner

**polygyny** practice of male having more than one mate

**postpartum** (*adj*) designating period immediately following birth

**progesterone** ovarian hormone that promotes continuation of pregnancy

**prolactin** anterior pituitary hormone that stimulates milk secretion

**pseudopregnancy** false pregnancy

**puberty** stage of life at which organism reaches sexual maturity and is capable of reproduction

**pupa** immobile, nonfeeding stage in metamorphosis of insect from larva to adult

**regeneration** regrowth of lost parts of organ or organism, as in worms

**reproduction** sexual or asexual process by which organisms produce new individuals of their species

**secondary sex characteristics** characteristics that distinguish between male and female of species, such as facial hair and enlarged breasts, but do not produce or convey gametes

**semen** male reproductive fluid that carries sperm

**Sertoli cell** cell that assists development of immature sperm

**sex hormone** any hormone that effects secondary sex characteristics or reproduction

**sexual reproduction** reproduction by fertilization and meiosis

**somatoplasm** reproductive cells of organism; germ plasm

**somatotropin** growth hormone

**sperm** spermatozoon

**spermatogenesis** origin and development of spermatozoon

**spermatophore** capsule of sperm passed to female during mating of some species

**spermatozoon** male gamete; sperm

**STH** *somatotropin hormone*

**syngamy** point in fertilization at which nuclei of sex cells meet and fuse

**testis** male gonad

**testosterone** primary male sex hormone

**umbilical cord** connection between embryo and placenta

**uterus** enlarged area of female mammalian oviduct where implantation occurs

**vagina** canal leading from uterus to outside of body that receives erect penis during copulation and acts as birth passage

**viviparous** (*adj*) giving birth to live young rather than laying eggs

**vulva** external genitalia in female mammals

**womb** uterus

**yolk** complex nutrient storage material in egg

**zygospore** cell formed by fusion of two similar gametes, as in certain algae and fungi

**zygote** cell formed by union of two gametes

## TOOLS AND TECHNIQUES

**agar** culture medium for growing bacteria

**aquarium** glass-sided container for holding aquatic organisms

**binomial** standard scientific name for organism, including genus and species in Latin, such as *Canis familiaris* for dog

**calipers** jawed instrument for measuring thickness or distance

**cast** plaster reproduction

**centrifuge** machine that removes moisture or separates different densities of substance by force directed outward from center of rotation

**chromatography** separation of chemical compounds on adsorbent material

**cladistics** classification of organisms based on lines of descent from common ancestor

**control** unmanipulated sample used for comparison with experimental group

**culture** laboratory growth of bacteria, microorganisms, or plant or animal cells in special nourishing fluid or solid

**dermestid** beetle used to remove dried flesh from skeletons for study collections

**dissection** cutting apart of specimen for study

**electron microscope** powerful optical instrument that uses electron beam to enlarge image of minute object

**electrophoresis** use of electrical field to separate chemical compounds into components

**ether** volatile, flammable liquid used as solvent and, formerly, as anesthetic

**field glass** binoculars; device for observing distant objects

**forceps** tweezerlike instrument for grasping small objects

**formalin** aqueous solution used for wet preservation of study specimens

**hydrophone** device for detecting underwater sounds

**hydroscope** instrument for viewing objects that are deep underwater

**life table** statistical device for studying population growth

**live trap** device for capturing an animal without harming it

**manometer** device for measuring pressure of gas

**medium** material, such as agar, on which a culture is grown

**metabolism chamber** controlled environment for studying metabolic processes

**microscope** optical device for enlarging images

**microtome** instrument for cutting very thin slices of tissue for microscopic examination

**model** simulation of natural event, used for prediction

**oscilloscope** device that shows electrical pulses as light flashes on screen, used for study of physiological processes

**paper chromatography** use of solvent to separate amino acids on filter paper

**perfusion** forcing of fluid into system of vessels

**petri dish** shallow glass vessel with loose cover, used for growing culture of microorganisms

**photomicrograph** photograph of enlarged image observed through microscope

**preservation** any method for permanently storing a scientific specimen

**press** device for drying and flattening botanical specimens

**radiocarbon dating** method of determining age of fossils by using disintegration rate of carbon-14 isotope

**radio telemetry** use of radio transmitter placed on organism to monitor its movement or physiological processes

**remote sensing** obtaining information on biosphere by noncontact method, esp. with satellites

**respirometer** instrument for measuring gas pressure

**scalpel** fine-bladed knife used for dissecting specimen

**scanning scope** electron microscope used to magnify image of surface structures

**Secchi disc** device for measuring light penetration into body of water

**slide** flat piece of glass used to hold object for observation through microscope

**sonogram** sound spectrograph

**sound spectrograph** visual representation of auditory communication; sonogram

**specimen** sample of organism for study and experimentation

**staining** use of various dyes to improve visibility of microscopic structures

**study skins** uniformly preserved dry specimens for systematic research

**synonymy** scientific names in different nomenclature systems used to designate same species or genus

**syringe** device for withdrawing or injecting fluids through needle

**taxidermy** preparing, stuffing, and mounting of animal skins

**terrarium** usu. glass-sided container enclosing garden of small plants

**type specimen** single specimen designated as one on which original taxonomic description and name are based

**vivisection** experiments conducted on living organisms

**zoo** parklike facility in which live animals are kept for public exhibition

**zymoscope** device that monitors fermentation by recording amount of carbon dioxide produced

## TAXONOMY

**taxonomy** system of classifying organisms into natural related groups based on shared features or traits, with categories in descending order from kingdom to species, as follows:

**kingdom** one of the five broadest, principal divisions of living things: Animalia (animals), Plantae (plants), Fungi, Protista (algae and protozoans), and Monera (bacteria)

**subkingdom** category of related phyla within a kingdom (as: Eumetazoa subkingdom of kingdom Animalia)

**superphylum** subkingdom (as: Schizomycetes superphylum of kingdom Monera)

**phylum** principal category within a kingdom, used in classification of animals, protists, and monerans (as: Chordata)

**division** principal category within a kingdom, used in classification of plants, algae, and fungi (as: Anthophyta, or vascular flowering plants)

**subphylum** intermediate category between phylum and class or superclass (as: Vertebrata)

**superclass** intermediate category between subphylum and class (as: Tetrapoda)

**class** category of organisms ranking below phylum and above order (as: Mammalia)

**subclass** intermediate category between class and order (as: Eutheria)

**order** category of organisms ranking below class and above family (as: Primates)

**superfamily** intermediate category between order and genus (as: Hominoidea)

**family** category of organisms ranking below order and above genus (as: Hominidae)

**genus** category of closely related species ranking below family and above species (as: Homo)

**species** basic unit of biological classification ranking below genus, including structurally similar organisms capable of interbreeding (as: Homo sapiens)

## FIVE KINGDOMS

**Animalia** kingdom of multicellular, eukaryotic organisms, usu. motile with ingestion as principal mode of nutrition and primarily sexual reproduction, including all animals: divided into thirty-two phyla

**Plantae** kingdom of multicellular, photosynthetic, eukaryotic organisms primarily adapted to life on land, including all plants: divided into ten divisions

**Fungi** kingdom of unicellular or filamentous, multinucleate, eukaryotic organisms, including molds, mildews, and mushrooms, that live by decomposing and feed on dead or living organic matter in which they grow and decompose: divided into four divisions

**Protista** kingdom of eukaryotic algae, amebas, and protozoans, consisting of photosynthetic autotrophs and heterotrophs: divided into ten divisions and five phyla

**Monera** kingdom of prokaryotic organisms, or cells without a membrane-bound nucleus and membrane-bound organelles, that reproduce by asexual budding or fission, including bacteria

## MAJOR TAXONOMIC SUBGROUPS

NOTE: *Orders of mammals and lists of species appear under Animals, Plants, and Simpler Life Forms. Latin names are used for entries, with English equivalents given in the definition.*

**Agnatha** class of cold-blooded, aquatic, jawless, boneless fish: about 60 species

**Amphibia** class of cold-blooded, scaleless amphibians born in water with gills but developing lungs and living on land, including the ancestors of reptiles: about 2500 species, including frogs, toads, and salamanders

**Annelida** animal phylum of segmented annelid worms with well-defined nervous systems: about 9000 species, including earthworms, leeches, and marine worms

**Anthophyta** division of flowering plants or angiosperms with ovules enclosed in carpels and mature seeds borne within fruits: about 235,000 species divided into two classes, Monocotyledones and Dicotyledones

**Arachnida** class of mostly terrestrial arachnid arthropods with four pairs of jointed legs: about 57,000 species, including spiders, mites, ticks, and scorpions

**Arthropoda** phylum of invertebrate arthropods with paired, jointed limbs, a segmented body, and a hard exoskeleton: over one million species, including insects, arachnids, and crustaceans

**Aves** class of warm-blooded, egg-laying, two-legged birds covered by feathers, with forelimbs used as wings and an embryo enclosed in an eggshell: about 9000 species

**Bryophyta** division of multicellular plants with photosynthetic pigments and food reserves similar to those of green algae: about 16,000 species, including mosses, liverworts, and hornworts

**Chondrichthyes** class of cold-blooded, aquatic, cartilaginous fish such as sharks and rays: about 625 species

**Chordata** phylum of animal chordates having a notochord at some stage of development, a hollow nerve cord, and a tail, including vertebrates: about 43,000 species

**Coniferophyta** division of seed plants with needlelike leaves: about 550 species of conifers, including gymnosperms

**Crustacea** class of mostly aquatic crustacean arthropods with two pairs of antennae, appendages on the thoracic segment, and a hard exoskeleton: about 25,000 species, including lobsters, crabs, crayfish, and shrimps

**Echinodermata** animal phylum of radially symmetrical, marine echinoderms, having an endoskeleton of ossicles and spines: about 6000 species, including starfish and sea urchins

**Eumetazoa** animal subkingdom of multicellular organisms with a true digestive cavity, including almost all animals; Metazoa

**Eutheria** subclass of all mammals other than marsupials and monotremes, broken down into seventeen orders with nearly 4500 species

**Insecta** class of mostly terrestrial insect arthropods that breathe by means of tracheae and have a tripartite body, one pair of antennae, three pairs of legs, and usu. two pairs of wings: about one million species, including bees, ants, fleas, flies, beetles, butterflies, and lice

**invertebrate** nontaxonomic grouping of all animals without a backbone or spinal column, comprising all thirty-one phyla of animals other than chordates

**Mammalia** class of warm-blooded, four-limbed, usu. hairy mammals that nourish their young with milk secreted by female mammary glands: about 4500 species divided into three subclasses

**Mesozoa** animal subkingdom of fifty species of extremely simple, wormlike organisms that are parasites of marine invertebrates

**Metatheria** subclass of marsupial mammals whose young are born undeveloped and are carried in the female's pouch: about 260 species, including kangaroos and opossums

**Metazoa** former term equivalent to Eumetazoa

**Mollusca** animal phylum of mostly aquatic, unsegmented mollusks with a muscular foot, soft body, and usu. one or more hard shells: about 47,000 species, with major classes being Bivalvia (clams, oysters, mussels, and scallops), Gastropoda (snails and slugs), and Cephalopoda (octopuses and squids)

**Nematoda** animal phylum of minute, free-living roundworms and plant and animal parasites: over 12,000 species

**Osteichthyes** class of cold-blooded, aquatic, usu. scaly, bony fish: about 19,000 species

**Parazoa** animal subkingdom of multicellular organisms without a true digestive cavity, primarily sponges of phylum Porifera

**Prototheria** subclass of mammals composed of egg-laying monotremes: only five living species

**Protozoa** nontaxonomic grouping, similar to superphylum, of animallike, eukaryotic organisms belonging to kingdom Protista that are primarily unicellular, colonial, and non-photosynthetic, formerly categorized as animals

**Pterophyta** division of primarily homosporous plants: about 12,000 species of ferns

**Reptilia** class of cold-blooded reptiles with lungs, completely bony skeletons, and bodies covered with scales or horny plates: about 6000 living species, including snakes, turtles, lizards, and crocodiles, and also extinct species such as dinosaurs

**Sarcodina** phylum of kingdom Protista, including unicellular heterotrophs with pseudopods: about 11,500 species, including amebas

**Vertebrata** subphylum of chordates whose notochord is replaced by a backbone or spinal column after its embryonic stage, and having a cranium enclosing a well-developed brain: about 41,700 species of mammals, birds, fish, amphibians, and reptiles

# ANIMALS

**SEE ALSO**: Chap. 2: Biology; Simpler Life Forms

Animals are categorized by shared characteristics provided in the definition for each descending level of the standard bio-logical taxonomy. Thus, users can infer that a "kangaroo" has the characteristics of a marsupial, a mammal, a vertebrate, and an animal. This largely eliminates the necessity for thousands of definitions, which would be primarily descriptive or provide only a Latin species name and the locale for each species. Where more than one term is frequently used to designate a single species, all such names appear, as for "platypus" and "duckbill platypus." The list of breeds (of chickens, dogs, cats, cattle, etc.) refer only to domestic breeds, not species.

## ANIMAL TYPES AND PARTS

**alley cat** mixed-breed domestic cat, esp. living unowned in city

**alter** (*vb*) neuter a male animal

**animal** member of kingdom of living organisms distinguished from plants by their ability to move about independently and to respond quickly to stimuli

**antler** branched, bony growth on head of deer and some other mammals, usu. shed annually

**ass** domesticated donkey or similar wild species

**avian** (*adj*) of or like a bird

**axilla** area under wing of bird

**baleen** horny substance attached along upper jaw of certain whales; whalebone

**bantam** miniature breed of chicken

**bay** brown horse with black mane and tail

**beak** bird's bill, esp. sharp, horny bill of bird of prey

**beast** large quadruped, esp. domesticated

**biddy** female chicken

**bilateral symmetry** body form in which right and left halves of organism are mirror images

**bill** hard jaws of a bird, usu. projecting to point

**billy goat** male goat

**biped** animal that moves on two feet

**bitch** female dog

**boar** male pig

**bovine** (*adj*) of or like an ox

**bronco** wild horse that resists being ridden

**brood** offspring from one hatching of bird's eggs

**broody** hen sitting on eggs

**broomtail** wild horse

**brumby** wild horse (Australia)

**buck** male deer, goat, rabbit, or kangaroo

**bull** male of various large mammals, esp. cattle

**bullock** castrated bull or steer

**bunny** *Informal.* rabbit

**calf** young of various large mammals, esp. cattle

**calico** domestic cat marked with black, orange, red, and white, usu. female; horse with similar markings

**canine** member of family of carnivores including dogs, wolves, and foxes; (*adj*) of or like a dog

**cannibal** animal that feeds on its own species

**capon** neutered rooster

**carnivore** animal that feeds on other animals

**caterpillar** wormlike larva of certain insects, esp. butterflies or moths

**cayuse** range horse

**chanticleer** rooster

**charger** horse ridden in battle or on parade; destrier

**chick** young bird, esp. chicken

**chordate** member of phylum comprising all true vertebrates and animals having a notochord

**claw** sharp, usu. hooked, horny structure or nail on foot of birds and some reptiles and mammals

**cloven-foot** mammal with hoof comprising two major toes for support

**clutch** group of eggs laid at one time by bird

**coat** natural outer covering of wool or fur

**cob** male swan

**cock** male chicken over one year old

**cockerel** male chicken under one year old

**colt** male horse before maturity

**comb** fleshy protuberance on head of chicken

**cony** small rabbit; Biblical term for hyrax

**corvine** (*adj*) of or like a crow

**covert** one of small feathers that cover bases of large feathers on wings and tail of bird

**cow** female of various large mammals, esp. cattle

**creature** animal

**crest** comb or feathered tuft on head of animal, usu. bird

**critter** *Informal.* animal

**cub** young of various large carnivores, esp. bears

**cud** food regurgitated from ruminant's stomach to be re-chewed

**cur** mixed-breed dog of little value

**cursorial** (*adj*) having limbs and feet adapted for running

**cygnet** young swan

**destrier** war-horse; charger

**dock** (*vb*) shorten tail or ears of animal

**doe** female deer, rabbit, goat, or kangaroo

**dogie** orphaned calf

**domestic animal** animal bred and raised in captivity as a pet, to perform work, or for food

**draft animal** animal used to pull wagon or plow

**drake** male duck

**drone** male bee or ant that serves only for reproduction and does no work

**duck** esp. female duck

**duckling** young duck

**eclipse plumage** dull plumage of birds, esp. adult males, that exhibit brilliant nuptial plumage when mating

**equine** (*adj*) of or like a horse

**ewe** female sheep

**fang** long, pointed canine tooth of carnivores, esp. used to tear flesh

**fauna** animals of a specific region or time

**fawn** young deer

**feather** one of horny shafts with soft branching barbs covering body of bird and comprising wing surface

**feline** member of the cat family of carnivores; (*adj*) of or like a cat

**feral** wild animal, esp. domestic animal gone wild

**filly** female horse under four years old

**fin** winglike membrane on body of fish, used for swimming

**fledgling** young bird just beginning to fly

**flipper** limb of pinniped or cetacean, broadened and flattened for swimming

**foal** young or newborn horse

**fowl** poultry

**gander** male goose

**gelding** neutered male horse

**gill** respiratory organ of fish and water animals

**gilt** young female pig

**gobbler** male turkey

**goose** esp. female goose

**gosling** young goose

**grimalkin** old female cat

**hand** unit of linear measure equal to four inches (10.2 cm), used to determine the height of horses

**hart** adult male red deer

**heat** estrus condition

**heifer** young cow

**hen** female chicken

**hind** adult female red deer

**hinny** offspring of a stallion and a jenny

**hoof** hard, horny foot of ungulate mammals

**horn** hard, hollow, bony, often pointed growth on head of certain hoofed animals; hard substance forming horns and other growths

**hound** any dog

**incisor** cutting tooth near front of mouth

**invertebrate** any animal without a backbone or spinal column

**jack** male donkey; jackass

**jenny** female donkey

**joey** baby kangaroo

**jumbuck** sheep (Australia)

**keet** guinea fowl chick

**kid** young goat

**kine** domestic cattle

**kitten** young cat

**kitty** kitten; pet name for cat

**lamb** young sheep

**leonine** (*adj*) of or like a lion

**liger** offspring of male lion and female tiger

**litter** several offspring from one birth, esp. in mammals

**livestock** domestic animals raised on a farm, esp. for profit

**lupine** (*adj*) of or like a wolf

**mandibles** upper and lower parts of bird's bill

**mane** long hair growing on animal's neck, esp. a horse or lion

**manx** tailless domestic cat

**mare** female horse

**marmalade** yellow cat

**maverick** unbranded range cow

**maw** stomach of ruminant, from which cud is regurgitated

**melanism** excess of dark pigmentation in skin, hair, or feathers

**minnow** any very small fish, usu. freshwater

**mongrel** mixed-breed dog; mutt

**mule** sterile hybrid between a horse and donkey, esp. between a mare and jack; any sterile hybrid

**mustang** wild horse

**mutt** *Slang.* mongrel

**muzzle** projecting portion of head of certain mammals, esp. dogs or horses, comprising mouth, nose, and jaws

**nag** broken-down old horse, esp. female; *Slang.* any horse

**nanny goat** female goat

**nest** structure made or place chosen for breeding or laying eggs, esp. by birds

**nuptial plumage** brilliant plumage exhibited by certain birds, usu. males, during mating season

**omnivore** animal that feeds on other animals and plants

**palfrey** saddle horse

**passerine** (*adj*) designating any small or medium-sized perching songbird with grasping feet

**paw** the foot of any quadruped with claws

**peahen** female peafowl

**pelt** skin of fur-bearing animal, esp. when stripped from carcass

**pen** female swan

**piebald** pinto

**piglet** young pig

**pileum** top of bird's head from base of bill back to nape

**pinto** horse with black and white patches; piebald

**piscine** (*adj*) of or like a fish

**plumage** feathers or cluster of feathers on head or body of bird

**polled** (*adj*) hornless

**pony** small breed of horse under 14.2 hands high

**pooch** *Informal.* dog, esp. one of mixed breed

**porcine** (*adj*) of or like a pig

**pouch** fold of skin on abdomen of female marsupial in which newborn young are carried

**poulard** spayed hen

**poult** young turkey

**poultry** domestic birds kept for meat or eggs; fowl

**predator** animal that lives by hunting and feeding on other animals

**prehensile tail** tail, as of certain monkeys, used for grasping or seizing

**prey** animal that is hunted and eaten by a predator

**proboscis** tubular organ, such as elephant's trunk, used for sucking, food-gathering, or sensing

**pullet** female chicken less than one year old

**pup** young dog; young seal

**puppy** young dog

**puss** any cat

**pussycat** any cat, esp. one of mixed breed

**quadruped** four-legged animal, usu. a mammal

**queen** female cat used for breeding; dominant mother bee in hive

**quill** stiff wing or tail feathers of bird; spine of porcupine or hedgehog

**radial symmetry** body form in which parts are arranged around central axis as mirror images to left and right of plane through that axis, as in coral and jellyfish

**ram** male sheep

**roan** horse of reddish-brown or black color with thick sprinkling of white

**rooster** male chicken; chanticleer

**ruminant** cud-chewing mammal with four-chambered stomach

**runt** smallest member of litter

**saurian** (*adj*) of or like a lizard

**scales** thin, overlapping, rigid plates forming protective covering of most fishes and reptiles and a few mammals

**scavenger** animal that feeds on refuse and decaying organic matter

**seal point** cat with pale body and dark brown face, ears, tail, and paws

**serpentine** (*adj*) of or like a snake

**shoat** pig under one year old

**sire** male parent of any quadruped, esp. a horse

**snood** fleshy appendage trailing from above the beak of a male turkey

**snout** projecting nose and jaws of various mammals

**songbird** any common passerine bird that makes musical vocal sounds

**sow** female pig

**spay** (*vb*) neuter female animal

**spine** sharp, stiff projection from body of a porcupine or from a fish's fin

**squab** fledgling pigeon

**stag** male deer

**stallion** male horse

**steer** neutered bull

**stray** lost or abandoned domestic animal

**stud** male horse used for breeding

**sunfisher** bucking horse, esp. one that falls on its rider

**tabby** cat with swirls of dark color on light background, esp. tigerlike stripes

**tadpole** larval, gilled stage of amphibious frog

**tail** flexible appendage at rear of animal's body; feathers extending from rump of bird

**tetrapod** any four-legged vertebrate, esp. mammals, birds, and reptiles

**thoroughbred** racing horse bred by crossing Arabian or Turkish stallion with English mare

**tiger** domestic cat with striped tabby markings

**tom** male cat or turkey

**tortoise shell** hard, mottled, yellow-and-brown shell of some turtles and tortoises; similar coloration of some female cats

**trunk** long, flexible snout or proboscis, as on elephant

**tusk** one of a pair of very long, large, pointed teeth projecting outside of the mouth of some mammals

**ungulate** hoofed mammal

**ursine** (*adj*) of or like a bear

**vermin** destructive, disease-carrying insects or small animals

**vertebrate** animal with backbone or spinal column, such as mammals, birds, fish, amphibians, and reptiles

**vixen** female fox

**vulpine** (*adj*) of or like a fox

**wattle** fleshy protuberance hanging below the head of chicken or turkey.

**wether** neutered ram

**whalebone** baleen

**whelp** young of a dog

**wing** either of the feathered forelimbs of a bird, used for flying; forelimb of a flying mammal, formed by membrane stretched between digits

**worker** sterile ant or bee that performs work for colony

## ANIMAL GROUPS

**bale** group of turtles

**bed** group of snakes

**bevy** group of quail

**bouquet** group of pheasants in flight

**cete** group of badgers

**charm** group of finches

**clowder** group of cats

**colony** group of ants, badgers, or frogs

**confusion** group of guinea fowls

**covert** group of coots

**covey** group of partridges, pheasants, or quail on the ground

**drove** group of animals moving together; group of oxen, sheep, or swine

**exaltation** group of larks

**flight** group of birds or insects

**flock**  group of birds; group of sheep

**gaggle**  group of geese on water or ground

**gam**  group of whales

**gang**  group of elk

**herd**  group of animals grazing together, esp. cattle or sheep; group of elephants

**hive**  group of bees

**host**  group of sparrows

**husk**  group of hares

**kennel**  group of dogs

**knot**  group of toads

**labor**  group of moles

**leap**  group of leopards

**murmuration**  flock of starlings

**muster**  group of peacocks

**nest**  group of rabbits; group of wasps; group of vipers

**pace**  group of asses

**pack**  group of wild animals moving together, esp. dogs or wolves; group of grouse

**parliament**  group of owls

**plague**  group of locusts

**pod**  group of seals or whales

**pride**  group of lions; group of peacocks

**sault**  group of lions

**school**  group of fish

**shoal**  group of fish, esp. bass

**shrewdness**  group of apes

**skein**  group of geese in flight

**skulk**  group of foxes

**sloth**  group of bears

**swarm**  group of insects, esp. bees

**team**  group of ducks in flight; group of oxen or horses

**trace**  group of hares or rabbits

**troop**  group of monkeys

**watch**  group of nightingales

# Vertebrates

**vertebrate**  member of the subphylum of chordates whose notochord is replaced by a backbone or spinal column after its embryonic stage, having a cranium enclosing a well-developed brain, including mammals, birds, reptiles, amphibians, and fish

## Mammals

**mammal**  member of a class of warm-blooded, usu. hairy vertebrates that nourish their young with milk secreted by female mammary glands

### Monotremes

**monotreme**  member of the most primitive, egg-laying order of mammals, comprising the subclass Prototheria
  duckbill, duckbill platypus
  echidna
  platypus
  spiny anteater

### Marsupials

**marsupial**  member of mammalian order whose young are born undeveloped and carried in the female's pouch, comprising the subclass Metatheria

  banded anteater, bandicoot, bettong
  cuscus
  dasyure, dunnart
  euro
  flying phalanger
  glider
  kangaroo, koala
  marsupial mole, marsupial mouse
  native cat, numbat
  opossum
  pademelon, phalanger, possum, potoroo
  quokka, quoll
  rabbit-eared bandicoot, rat opossum, ringtail
  Tasmanian devil, Tasmanian wolf, thylacine, tree kangaroo
  wallaby, wombat
  yapok

### Edentates

**edentate**  member of mammalian order without teeth or with single-rooted molars only
  ant bear, anteater, armadillo
  giant ground sloth (extinct)
  peba, peludo
  sloth
  tamandua, tatou, tatouay, tatoupeba

### Insectivores

**insectivore**  member of small, primitive, nocturnal order of mammals with weak eyesight that feed on invertebrates, esp. insects
  desman
  elephant shrew
  golden mole, gymnure
  hedgehog
  mole, moon rat
  otter shrew
  shrew, solenodon, star-nosed mole
  tenrec
  water shrew

### Dermopterans

**dermopteran**  member of mammalian order of nocturnal, herbivorous gliders that do not actually fly
  colugo
  flying lemur

### Chiropterans

**chiropteran**  member of mammalian order with forelimbs ending in membranes stretched between elongated digits, used for flying
  barbastelle, bat, brown bat
  chauvesouris
  false vampire, fishing bat, flittermouse, flying fox, free-tailed bat, fruit bat
  horseshoe bat
  leaf-nosed bat, little brown bat
  myotis
  noctule
  pipistrelle
  serotine
  vampire bat

### Primates

**primate**  member of mammalian order with flexible, grasping hands and feet with five digits, usu. omnivorous and arboreal

angwantibo, anthropoid ape, ape, aye-aye
baboon, bandar, Barbary ape, bonnet monkey, bush baby
capuchin, chacma, chimpanzee, colobus, cynomolgus
drill, dwarf lemur
entellus
galago, gelada, gibbon, gorilla, grivet, guenon, guereza
hamadryas baboon, hanuman, hominid, homo sapiens,
    howler, human being
indri
langur, lar gibbon, leaf monkey, lemur, lion-tailed monkey,
    loris
macaque, man, mandrill, mangabey, marmoset, monkey,
    mountain gorilla
night monkey
orangutan
patas monkey, potto, prosimian, proboscis monkey
quenon
rhesus monkey
saki, siamang, simian, snow monkey, spider monkey, squirrel
    monkey
tamarin, tarsier, titi, tree shrew
uakari
vervet
wanderoo, white-handed gibbon, woolly monkey

## CARNIVORES

**carnivore**  member of mammalian order of flesh-eating predators with prominent canine fangs and shearing molars, having retractable or unretractable claws on toed feet
aardwolf, American lion, Arctic fox
badger, bassarisk, bat-eared fox, bear, binturong, black bear,
    bobcat, brown bear, brush wolf, buffalo wolf, bush dog
cacomistle, canine, Cape fox, cape hunting dog, caracal, cat
    (Abyssinian, Angora, Archangel, Balinese, Birman, Burmese,
    color point, Cornish Rex, domestic shorthair, Egyptian, Havana
    brown, Himalayan, Korat, Maine coon, Maltese, manx, Persian,
    Rex, Russian blue, Siamese, Somali, Turkish swimming, Turkish
    van), catamount, cheetah, cinnamon bear, civet cat,
    clouded leopard, coati, coon, cougar, coyote, cuisimanse
dhole, dingo, dog (affenpinscher, Afghan hound, Airedale
    terrier, Akita, Alaskan malamute, Alsatian, American foxhound,
    American pit bull terrier, American water spaniel, Australian
    cattle dog, Australian heeler, Australian kelpie, Australian
    shepherd, Australian terrier, badger dog, Basenji, basset
    hound, beagle, bearded collie, Bedlington terrier, Belgian
    Malinois, Belgian sheepdog, Belgian Tervuren, Bernese
    mountain dog, Bichon Frise, black and tan coonhound,
    bloodhound, bluetick coonhound, boarhound, Border collie,
    Border terrier, borzoi, Boston bull terrier, Bouvier des Flandres,
    boxer, Boykin spaniel, Briard, Brittany spaniel, Brussels griffon,
    bulldog, bullmastiff, bull terrier, cairn terrier, cavalier King
    Charles spaniel, Chesapeake Bay retriever, Chihuahua, Chinese
    Shar-Pei, chow chow, clumber spaniel, Clydesdale terrier,
    cocker spaniel, collie, coonhound, corgi, Coton de Tulear,
    curly-coated retriever, dachshund, Dalmation, Dandie Dinmont
    terrier, deerhound, Doberman pinscher, elkhound, English
    bulldog, English cocker spaniel, English foxhound, English
    setter, English shepherd, English springer spaniel, English toy
    spaniel, Eskimo dog, field spaniel, flat-coated retriever,
    foxhound, fox terrier, French bulldog, gazelle hound, German
    shepherd, German shorthaired pointer, German wirehaired
    pointer, giant schnauzer, golden retriever, Gordon setter, Great
    Dane, Great Pyrenees, greyhound, griffon, Groenendael,
    harrier, hound, husky, Ibizan hound, Irish setter, Irish terrier,
    Irish water spaniel, Irish wolfhound, Italian greyhound, Jack
    Russell terrier, Japanese Chin, Japanese spaniel, keeshond,
    kelpie, Kerry blue terrier, King Charles spaniel, Komondor,

kuvasz, Labrador retriever, Lakeland terrier, Lhasa apso, lurcher,
    malamute, Malinois, Maltese dog, Manchester terrier, mastiff,
    Mexican hairless, miniature dachshund, miniature poodle,
    miniature pinscher, miniature schnauzer, Neapolitan mastiff,
    Newfoundland, Norfolk terrier, Norwegian elkhound, Norwich
    terrier, Old English sheepdog, otterhound, papillon, pariah
    dog, Pekingese, pharaoh hound, Plott hound, pointer,
    Pomeranian, poodle, Portuguese water dog, pug, puli, rat
    terrier, redbone coonhound, red setter, retriever, Rhodesian
    ridgeback, Rottweiler, Russian owtchar, Russian wolfhound,
    Saluki, Samoyed, schipperke, schnauzer, Scotch collie, Scottish
    deerhound, Scottish terrier, Sealyham terrier, setter, shepherd
    dog, Shetland sheepdog, Shiba-Inu, Shih Tzu, Siberian Husky,
    silky terrier, Skye terrier, soft-coated wheaten terrier, spaniel,
    spitz, springer spaniel, Staffordshire bull terrier, staghound,
    standard schnauzer, St. Bernard, Sussex spaniel, terrier, Tibetan
    mastiff, Tibetan spaniel, Tibetan terrier, toy fox terrier, toy
    poodle, toy spaniel, toy terrier, Treeing Walker coonhound,
    turnspit, vizsla, water spaniel, Weimaraner, Welsh collie, Welsh
    corgi, Welsh springer spaniel, Welsh terrier, West Highland
    white terrier, whippet, wirehair, wirehaired pointing griffon,
    wirehaired terrier, wolfhound, Yorkshire terrier)
ermine, eyra
feline, fennec, ferret, fisher, fitch, fossa, fox
genet, giant panda, glutton, gray fox, gray wolf, grison,
    grizzly bear
hyena
ice bear
jackal, jaguar, jaguarundi
kinkajou, kit fox, Kodiak bear
laughing hyena, leopard, leopard cat, linsang, lion, lynx
maned wolf, manul, margay, marten, meerkat, mink,
    mongoose, mountain lion
ocelot, olingo, otter, ounce
painter, Pallas's cat, panda, panther, polar bear, polar fox,
    polecat, prairie wolf, puma
raccoon, raccoon dog, ratel, red dog, red fox, Reynard,
    ring-tailed cat
saber-toothed tiger (extinct), sable, sand cat, sea otter,
    serval, silver fox, simba, skunk, sloth bear, snow leopard,
    spectacled bear, stoat, sun bear, suricate, swift fox, Syrian
    bear
tayra, tiger, timber wolf
weasel, white fox, white wolf, wildcat, wolf, wolverine
zoril

## PINNIPEDS

**pinniped**  member of mammalian order of aquatic carnivores that breed on land, with forelimbs adapted as flippers for swimming
eared seal, elephant seal
fur seal
hair seal, harbor seal
ross seal
sea cat, sea dog, sea elephant, seal, sea lion
walrus

## CETACEANS

**cetacean**  member of aquatic, nearly hairless order of mammals lacking hind limbs, with forelimbs adapted as flippers for swimming, a flat tail, and nasal blowholes on top of head, having either teeth or baleen
baleen whale, beaked whale, beluga, blackfish, blue whale,
    bottle-nosed dolphin, bouto, bowhead
cachalot, cowfish
dolphin
finback, fin whale

grampus, gray whale
humpback whale
killer whale
narwhal
orca
pilot whale, porpoise
right whale, rorqual
sea hog, sei whale, sperm whale, susu
toothed whale
whale, white whale

## SIRENIANS

**sirenian** member of herbivorous aquatic order of mammals
lacking hind limbs, with forelimbs modified as flippers for
swimming and a flat tail
dugong
manatee
sea cow

## PROBOSCIDS

**proboscid** member of mammalian order of large herbivores
with long, flexible trunk, incisors modified as tusks, and
huge, grinding molars
elephant
imperial mammoth (extinct)
jumbo
mammoth (extinct), mastodon (extinct)
pachyderm
tusker
woolly mammoth (extinct)

## PERISSODACTYLS

**perissodactyl** member of mammalian order of large herbivores with an odd number of toes on each hoof
ass
burro
donkey
horse (American quarter horse, American saddle horse, American
trotter, Andalusian, Appaloosa, Arabian, Barbary, Belgian,
Cleveland bay, Connemara, Clydesdale, French coach horse,
German coach horse, hackney, Haflinger, hunter, jennet,
Lippizaner, Morgan, palomino, Paso, Percheron, pinto,
Plantation walking horse, polo pony, pony of the Americas,
quarter horse, saddle horse, Shetland pony, Shire,
Standardbred, Suffolk, Tennessee walking horse, thoroughbred,
Trakehner, Turk, Waler, Welsh pony)
jackass
kiang, kulan
mule, mustang
onager
pony, Przewalski's horse
quagga (extinct)
rhinoceros
tapir, tarpan (extinct)
wild ass
zebra

## HYRAXES

**hyrax** member of herbivorous, rodentlike, hoofed order of
mammals related to proboscids
cony
dassie
hyrax
klippdach
rock hyrax

## TUBULIDENTATES

**tubulidentate** member of mammalian order of large, powerful diggers that eat ants and termites with a long, sticky
tongue and have teeth only in cheeks
aardvark, ant bear
earth pig

## ARTIODACTYLS

**artiodactyl** member of mammalian order of large herbivores, often ruminants, with even number of toes on
each hoof, often with antlers or horns
addax, alpaca, anoa, antelope, aoudad, argali, aurochs
(extinct), axis deer
babirusa, Bactrian camel, banteng, barasingha, Barbary
sheep, beisa, bezoar goat, bharal, bighorn sheep, bison,
blackbuck, blesbok, blue sheep, boar, bongo, buffalo, bull,
bushbuck
camel, camelopard, Cape buffalo, caribou, cattle (Aberdeen,
Angus, Ayrshire, beefalo, Brahman, Brown Swiss, cattalo,
Charbray, Charolais, Galloway, Guernsey, Hereford, Holstein,
Jersey, Longhorn, Santa Gertrudis, Scotch Highland, Shorthorn,
Texas Longhorn, West Highland, zebu), **chamois, chevrotain,
chital, cow**
dama gazelle, deer, dik-dik, dromedary, duiker
eland, elk
fallow deer
gaur, gazelle, gemsbok, gerenuk, giraffe, gnu, goat (Angora,
French Alpine, Kashmir, Nubian, Saanen, Toggenburg), **goat
antelope, goral, guanaco**
harnessed antelope, hartebeest, hippopotamus, hog
ibex, impala, Indian buffalo
javalina
kaama, kob, kudu
llama
Marco Polo's sheep, markhor, mazama, moose, mouflon,
mountain goat, mountain sheep, mouse deer, mule deer,
muntjac, musk deer, musk hog, musk ox
nilgai, nyala
okapi, oribi, oryx, ox
peccary, Père David's deer, pig, pronghorn, pronghorn
antelope, pudu
razorback, red deer, reindeer, river horse, Rocky Mountain
goat, roe deer
sable antelope, saiga, sambar, serow, sheep (Cheviot,
Corriedale, Dorset Horn, Hampshire, Karakul, Merino, Romney,
Scotch Blackface, Suffolk), **sika, springbok, stag, steenbok,
swine**
tahr, takin, topi
urial
vicuna, Virginia deer
wapiti, warthog, waterbuck, water buffalo, whitetail,
white-tailed deer, wild boar, wildebeest, wild goat, wild
ox, wild pig, wild sheep
yak
zebu

## PANGOLINS

**pangolin** member of mammalian order Pholidota of toothless, digging insectivores, with whiplike tongue and hairs
flattened into scales, that curls into a ball for defense
anteater
pangolin
scaly anteater

## RODENTS

**rodent** member of mammalian order of small, gnawing herbivores with one pair of evergrowing, chisellike incisors

agouti, antelope chipmunk, antelope squirrel

bandicoot, beaver, black rat, blesmol, brown rat

capybara, carpincho, cavy, chickaree, chinchilla, chipmunk, cloud rat, coendou, cotton mouse, cotton rat, coypu

deer mouse, degu, dormouse

edible dormouse

field mouse, flickertail, flying squirrel, fox squirrel

gerbil, gopher, grasshopper mouse, groundhog, ground squirrel, guinea pig

hamster, harvest mouse, house mouse, house rat, hutia

jerboa, jird, jumping mouse

kangaroo mouse, kangaroo rat

lemming

mara, marmot, meadow mouse, mole rat, mouse, muskrat

Norway rat, nutria

paca, pacarana, pack rat, Patagonian hare, pine mouse, pocket gopher, pocket mouse, pocket rat, porcupine, pouched rat, prairie dog

quill pig

rat, red squirrel, rice rat, rock squirrel, roof rat

sewellel, spiny rat, springhaas, squirrel, suslik

tree squirrel, tuco-tuco

viscacha, vole

wharf rat, whistle pig, whistler, woodchuck, wood mouse, wood rat

## LAGOMORPHS

**lagomorph** member of mammalian order of terrestrial herbivores with two pairs of evergrowing incisors and long hind limbs that are used for jumping

Arctic hare

Belgian hare

cony, cottontail

hare

jack rabbit

lapin, leveret

pika

rabbit

snowshoe hare, swamp rabbit

## BIRDS

**bird** member of a class of warm-blooded, egg-laying, two-legged vertebrates covered by feathers, with forelimbs used as wings and an embryo enclosed in an eggshell, that live on land, shore, or sea

## PASSERINE SONGBIRDS

**passerine** member of the order Passeriformes of land birds having feet adapted for perching, including all songbirds of Oscine and Suboscine suborders

**songbird** any passerine bird of Oscine suborder

### OSCINES

**oscine** member of suborder of passerine songbirds having highly developed vocal organs

Audubon's warbler

Baltimore oriole, bank swallow, barn swallow, blackbird, Blackburnian warbler, blackcap, bluebill, bluebird, blue jay, bobolink, bowerbird, brown thrasher, brown thrush, bulbul, bullfinch, bunting, bush tit, butcherbird

canary, cardinal, catbird, cedar bird, cedar waxwing, chaffinch, chat, chewink, chickadee, chiffchaff, chipping sparrow, cliff swallow, corbie, cotinga, cowbird, creeper, crossbill, crow

dipper, drongo

English sparrow

finch

gnatcatcher, goldfinch, grackle, grosbeak

hermit thrush, honeycreeper, house finch, house martin

indigo bunting

jackdaw, jay, junco

kingbird, kinglet

lark, linnet

magpie, martin, mavis, meadowlark, merle, mistle thrush, mockingbird, myna

nutcracker, nuthatch

oriole, ortolan, ouzel, oxpecker

pipit, purple finch, purple martin

quelea

raven, redbird, redpoll, redstart, redwing, red-winged blackbird, reedbird, reed bunting, ring ouzel, robin, rook

scarlet tanager, scissortail, shama, shrike, siskin, snowbird, solitaire, song sparrow, song thrush, sparrow, starling, sunbird, swallow

tanager, thrasher, thrush, tit, titlark, titmouse, towhee, tree swallow, troupial

veery, vesper sparrow, vireo

wagtail, warbler, water ouzel, water thrush, waxbill, waxwing, weaver, wheatear, white-eye, whydah, wood warbler, wren, wren-tit

yellowbird, yellow finch, yellowhammer, yellow-rumped warbler, yellowthroat

zebra finch

### SUBOSCINES

**suboscine** member of suborder of passerine songbirds having less well-developed vocal organs

antbird

bellbird, broadbill, bush wren

cock-of-the-rock

flycatcher

lyrebird

manakin

ovenbird

pewee, phoebe, pitta

tyrant flycatcher

woodcreeper

## OTHER LAND BIRDS

American eagle, ani

bald eagle, barbet, barn owl, bee-eater, bird of paradise, black grouse, bobwhite quail, brush turkey, budgerigar, bustard, button quail, buzzard

California condor, capercaillie, caracara, cassowary, cattle egret, chicken (Andalusian, Araucana, Australorp, Barneveler, Barred Rock, Brahma, Campine, Cochin, Cornish, Dominiker, Dorking, Frizzle, Game, Golden Sebright bantam, Hamburg, Japanese bantam, Jersey Giant, Lakenvelder, Leghorn, Mille Fleur bantam, Minorca, New Hampshire, Old English Game, Orpington, Phoenix, Plymouth Rock, Polish, Rhode Island Red, Rhode Island White, Rock Cornish, Rosecomb bantam, Silkie, Sultan, Sumatra, Sussex, Turken, White Leghorn, Wyandotte), chicken hawk, chimney swift, cockatiel, cockatoo, condor, crane, cuckoo, culver, curassow

dodo (extinct), dove

eagle, egret, emu, erne

falcon, flicker, francolin, frogmouth

goatsucker, golden eagle, goshawk, grouse, guacharo, guan, guinea fowl, gyrfalcon
harpy eagle, harrier, hawk, hawk owl, hemipode, hoatzin, hobby, honey guide, hoopoe, hoot owl, hornbill, horned owl, horned screamer, hummingbird
ivory-billed woodpecker
jacamar, jungle fowl
kea, kestrel, killdeer, kite, kiwi, kookaburra
lammergeier, lanner, lapwing, laughing jackass, lorikeet, lory, lovebird
macaw, mallee fowl, marabou, megapode, merlin, moa (extinct), motmot, moundbird, mound builder, mourning dove
nighthawk, nightingale, nightjar, notornis
oilbird, ostrich, owl
parakeet, parrot, partridge, passenger pigeon (extinct), peacock, peafowl, peregrine falcon, pheasant, pigeon (carrier, fantail, homer, homing pigeon, Jacobin, king, Modena, nun, pouter, roller, runt, trumpeter, tumbler), **pigeon hawk,** plover, poorwill, potoo, prairie chicken, ptarmigan
quail, quetzal
raptor, red grouse, red-headed woodpecker, rhea, ringdove, ring-necked pheasant, roadrunner, rock dove, roller, rosella, ruffed grouse
sage grouse, sage hen, sapsucker, screamer, screech owl, scrub fowl, secretary bird, seriema, snipe, snow bunting, sparrow hawk, stork, sun bittern, swift, swiftlet
tercel, tinamou, tody, toucan, touraco, tragopan, trogon, trumpeter, turkey, turkey buzzard, turkey vulture, turtledove
vulture
whippoorwill, whistler, woodcock, wood owl, woodpecker, wood pigeon, wryneck

### SEABIRDS AND WATERFOWL

**seabird** any bird living on the sea or along the coast and usu. able to swim, esp. gulls and terns

**waterfowl** swimming water birds, including ducks, geese, and swans

albatross, anhinga, auk, auklet
barnacle goose, belted kingfisher, bluebill, booby, brant, bufflehead
Canada goose, canvasback duck, coot, cormorant
dabbling duck, dabchick, darter, diver, dovekie, duck (Aylesbury, Blue Swedish, call, Cayuga, crested, Khaki Campbell, Muscovy, Pekin, Rouen, runner)
eider, erne
fish hawk, frigate bird, fulmar
gallinule, gannet, garganey, goldeneye, gooney bird, goose (African, Buff, Chinese, Embden, Pilgrim, Sebastopol, Toulouse), graylag goose, grebe, guillemot, gull
honker
jaeger
kingfisher, kittiwake
loon
mallard, mandarin duck, man-o-war bird, merganser, mew, moorhen, murre, mute swan
nene, notornis
osprey
pelican, penguin, petrel, pintail, pochard, puffin
razorbill, razor-billed, redhead, ring-necked duck, ruddy duck
scaup, scoter, sea duck, sea eagle, sea gull, sea raven, shearwater, sheldrake, shoveler, skua, snow goose, stormy petrel, swan, swan goose
takahe, teal, tern, tropic bird
waterfowl, water hen, whooper swan, widgeon, wood duck

### WADERS AND SHOREBIRDS

**wader** any of various long-legged, long-necked, long-billed birds adapted for wading in shallow waters, including bitterns, cranes, flamingos, herons, rails, and storks

**shorebird** any bird that frequents seashores and estuaries, esp. members of order Charadriiformes, including sandpipers and plovers

avocet
bittern
corn crake, crake, crane, curlew
dunlin
egret
flamingo
godwit, greenshank, gull
hammerhead, heron
ibis
jacana
killdeer, knot
lily-trotter, limpkin
marabou
night heron
oystercatcher
pewit, phalarope, plover
rail, redshank, ring ouzel
sacred ibis, sanderling, sandpiper, shoebill, skimmer, snipe, spoonbill, stilt, stint, stone curlew, stork, surfbird
turnstone
whimbrel, willet
yellowlegs

### BIRDS OF PREY

**bird of prey** any of various flesh-eating predator birds having a sharp, downwardly curved beak and talons, that live on land or sea

American eagle
bald eagle, barn owl, buzzard
California condor, caracara, chicken hawk, condor
eagle, erne
falcon, fish hawk
golden eagle, goshawk, gyrfalcon
harpy eagle, harrier, hawk, hawk owl, hobby, hoot owl, horned owl
jaeger
kestrel, kite
lammergeier, lanner
merlin
osprey, owl
peregrine falcon, pigeon hawk
raptor
screech owl, sea eagle, sparrow hawk
tercel, turkey buzzard, turkey vulture
vulture
wood owl

## REPTILES

**reptile** member of a class of cold-blooded vertebrates with lungs, completely bony skeletons, and bodies covered with scales or horny plates, including snakes and dinosaurs

**dinosaur** extinct herbivorous or carnivorous member of the reptilian orders Saurischia and Ornithischia of the Mesozoic era, including the largest known land animals

**snake** member of limbless, scaly, elongate reptilian suborder Serpentes, many of which are venomous agama, alligator, alligator lizard, alligator snapper, anole

basilisk, beaded lizard, blindworm, bog turtle, box turtle, butterfly agama

caiman, chameleon, chicken turtle, chuckwalla, cooter, crocodile

diamondback terrapin, dinosaurs (allosaur, ankylosaur, antrodemus, apatosaur, archaeopteryx, atlantosaur, brachiosaur, brontosaur, camarasaur, camptosaur, ceratopsian, coelophysis, diplodocus, elasmosaurus, hadrosaur, ichthyosaur, iguanodon, mixosaurus, oligokyphus, ornithiscian, ornithopod, peloneustes, plesiosaur, prosauropod, pterodactyl, quetzalcoatlus, saurischian, sauropod, scleromochlus, scolosaurus, stegosaur, steneosaurus, styracosaurus, tarbosaurus, theropod, titanophoneus, titanosaur, tylosaurus, tyrannosaur)

dragon

false map turtle, fence lizard, flying dragon

galliwasp, gavial, gecko, Gila monster, girdle-tailed lizard, glass snake, gopher tortoise, green turtle

hawksbill turtle, horned toad

iguana

Komodo dragon

leatherback turtle, lizard, loggerhead turtle

marine iguana, matamata, moloch, monitor, mugger

red-ear

sand lizard, sea turtle, side-necked turtle, skink, slider, slowworm, snake-necked turtle, snakes (adder, anaconda, asp, blacksnake, blind snake, boa, boa constrictor, boomslang, bullsnake, bushmaster, cobra, cobra de capello, constrictor, copperhead, coral snake, corn snake, cottonmouth, daboia, diamondback rattlesnake, egg-eating snake, fer-de-lance, garter snake, gopher snake, hamadryad, harlequin, hognose snake, horned rattlesnake, horned viper, indigo snake, king cobra, king snake, krait, mamba, massasauga, milk snake, moccasin, pine snake, puff adder, python, racer, rat snake, rattlesnake, rear-fanged snake, Russell's viper, scarlet snake, sea snake, sidewinder, spectacled cobra, spitting cobra, taipan, tic-polonga, tiger snake, timber rattlesnake, urutu, viper, water moccasin, water snake, worm snake)

snapping turtle, soft-shelled turtle, stinkpot, stump-tailed lizard, swift

tegu, terrapin, tokay gecko, tortoise, tuatara, turtle

wood turtle

## AMPHIBIANS

**amphibian** member of a class of cold-blooded, scaleless vertebrates born in water with gills but developing lungs and living on land, including the ancestors of reptiles

anuran, axolotl

blindworm, bullfrog

caecilian, clawed frog, congo eel, congo snake, cricket frog

edible frog, eft

fire salamander, frog

grass frog, green frog

hellbender, hop toad, horned frog

leopard frog

marine toad, midwife toad, mudpuppy

narrow-mouthed toad, natterjack, newt

paradoxical frog, pickerel frog, poison arrow frog

red-eyed tree frog

salamander, siren, spadefoot toad, spring frog, spring peeper, Surinam toad

toad, tree frog

urodele

waterdog, wood frog

## FISH

**fish** any of various cold-blooded, aquatic vertebrates with gills for breathing, fins, and usu. with scales, being a member of any of three classes: Agnatha (jawless, boneless fish), Chondrichthyes (cartilaginous fish such as sharks and rays), and Osteichthyes (bony fish)

albacore, alewife, alligator gar, amberjack, anchovy, angelfish, arapaima, arauana, archerfish, argusfish

balloonfish, barb, barbel, barn-door skate, barracuda, basking shark, bass, batfish, beluga, betta, black bass, blackfish, bleak, blenny, blindfish, blowfish, blueback salmon, blue catfish, bluefish, bluegill, blue shark, bonefish, bonito, bowfin, bream, brisling, brook trout, brown trout, buffalofish, bullhead, burbot, butterfish, butterflyfish

candlefish, capelin, carp, catfish, channel bass, channel catfish, char, characin, chimaera, Chinook salmon, chub, cichlid, cisco, clingfish, clown anemone, clown fish, cobia, cod, codfish, coelacanth, coney, conger eel, corydoras, cowfish, crappie, croaker, cutlassfish, cutthroat trout

dace, darter, devilfish, devil ray, discus, doctorfish, dogfish, dolphin, dorado, Dover sole, dragonfish, drumfish

eel, eelpout, electric eel, electric ray

filefish, flame tetra, flatfish, flounder, fluke, flying fish, flying gurnard, frogfish

gambusia, gar, garpike, giant bass, globefish, goatfish, goby, golden trout, goldfish, gourami, grayling, greenling, grouper, grunion, grunt, gudgeon, guitarfish, gunnel, guppy, gurnard

haddock, hagfish, hake, halfbeak, halibut, hammerhead shark, hatchetfish, headstander, herring, hogfish, horse mackerel, humuhumunukunukuapuaa

jack, jewfish

kelp bass, kelpfish, killifish, kingfish, koi

lake trout, lamprey, lanternfish, lingcod, loach, lumpfish, lungfish, lyretail

mackerel, mako shark, manta, marlin, menhaden, miller's-thumb, minnow, molly, Moorish idol, moray eel, mosquitofish, mudfish, mudskipper, mullet, muskellunge

needlefish, neon tetra, northern pike

oarfish, oscar

paddlefish, panchax, papagallo, paradise fish, parrotfish, pencilfish, perch, permit, pickerel, pike, pikeperch, pilchard, pilotfish, pipefish, piranha, plaice, platyfish, pollack, pollyfish, pompano, porbeagle shark, porgy, puffer, pupfish

rabbitfish, rainbow trout, rasbora, ray, redfin, redfish, red salmon, red snapper, remora, ribbonfish, roach, roosterfish, rudd

sailfish, salmon, salmon trout, sandfish, sardine, sawfish, scad, scat, scorpionfish, sculpin, scup, sea bass, sea bream, sea horse, seaperch, sea trout, sergeantfish, shark, shiner, shovelhead shark, shovelnose catfish, shovelnose sturgeon, Siamese fighting fish, silver salmon, skate, smelt, snapper, snook, sockeye salmon, sole, spadefish, Spanish mackerel, spearfish, speckled trout, sprat, squawfish, squirrelfish, steelhead, stickleback, stingray, stonefish, striped bass, sturgeon, sucker, Sunapee trout, sunfish, surffish, surfperch, surf smelt, surgeonfish, swordfish

tarpon, tautog, tench, tetra, thornback ray, thresher shark, tiger barb, tigerfish, tiger shark, tilapia, tilefish, toadfish, tope, torpedo fish, trevally, triggerfish, trout, tuna, tunny (*esp. Brit.*), turbot

veiltail goldfish

wahoo, walking catfish, walleyed pike, weakfish, whale

shark, whitebait, white bass, whitefish, white shark,
whiting, wolffish, wrasse
yellowtail, yellowtail flounder
zebrafish

## INVERTEBRATES

**invertebrate** any animal without a backbone or spinal column, including all thirty-one phyla of animals other than
chordates

## ARTHROPODS

**arthropod** invertebrate with paired, jointed limbs, a segmented body, and a hard exoskeleton that is molted from
time to time, including arachnids, insects, and crustaceans

### INSECTS AND ARACHNIDS

**arachnid** any of a class of mostly terrestrial invertebrate
arthropods, usu. with four pairs of jointed legs, no wings
or antennae, and simple eyes, that have a liquid diet, including spiders, mites, ticks, and scorpions

**insect** any of a class of mostly terrestrial invertebrate arthropods with a segmented body consisting of a head, thorax,
and abdomen, three pairs of jointed legs, usu. two pairs of
wings, and one pair of antennae, including bees, ants, fleas,
flies, beetles, butterflies, and lice

acarine, admiral butterfly, ant, ant lion, aphid, apple
maggot, assassin bug
bark beetle, bedbug, bee, bee fly, beetle, billbeetle, billbug,
blackbeetle, black fly, black widow, bloodworm, blow fly,
bluebottle, boll weevil, bombardier beetle, bookworm,
borer, botfly, bristletail, buffalo bug, buffalo carpet beetle,
bumblebee, buprestid beetle, butterfly
cabbage butterfly, caddisfly, cadelle, carpet beetle,
caterpillar, cattle grub, cattle tick, Cecropia moth,
centipede, chafer, chigger, chigoe, chinch bug, cicada,
cicala, click beetle, cockchafer, cockroach, codling moth,
Colorado potato beetle, conenose, copper butterfly, crane
fly, cricket, crotonbug, cucumber beetle, curculio
daddy-longlegs, damselfly, darkling beetle, deer fly,
dermestid, dipteran, dobsonfly, dor, dragonfly, drosophila,
dung beetle
earwig, elaterid, elm bark beetle, elm leaf beetle, emperor
butterfly, ephemerid
firefly, flea, flea beetle, flesh fly, flour beetle, flour moth,
flower fly, fly, frit fly, fritillary, fruit fly, fruit-tree bark
beetle
gadfly, gallfly, gall midge, gall mite, girdler, glowworm,
gnat, grain beetle, grasshopper, greenbottle fly,
greenbug, greenfly, ground beetle, grub, gypsy
moth
hairstreak butterfly, harlequin beetle, harlequin cabbage
bug, hawk moth, Hessian fly, honeybee, hornet, horn fly,
horntail, horse fly, housefly
ichneumon fly
Japanese beetle, jigger flea, June bug
katydid, khapra beetle, kissing bug
lacewing, ladybeetle, ladybug, lanternfly, leaf beetle,
leaf-cutting bee, leaf-footed bug, leafhopper, Lepisma,
locust, longhorn, long-horned beetle, long-horned
grasshopper, louse
mayfly, mealworm, mealybug, medfly, Mediterranean fruit
fly, Mexican bean beetle, Mexican fruit fly, midge, miller,

mite, mole cricket, monarch butterfly, mosquito, mosquito
hawk, moth, mourning cloak
oil beetle
painted lady, pill bug, podura, potatobug, praying mantis,
punkie
railroad worm, red admiral butterfly, rhinoceros beetle,
roach, robber fly, rose beetle, rose chafer, rove beetle
sawfly, sawyer, scarab, scorpion, scorpionfly, screwworm,
shadfly, silkworm, silverfish, skipjack, skipper, snapping
beetle, snout beetle, sow bug, spider, spider mite, spider
wasp, springtail, squash bug, stag beetle, stink bug, St.
Mark's fly, stonefly, swallowtail butterfly, syrphid fly
tabanid, tarantula, tenebrionid, tent caterpillar, tent fly,
termite, tettigoniid, thrips, tick, tiger beetle, tiger moth,
tiger swallowtail, tortoise beetle, tsetse fly, tumblebug,
twig girdler
viceroy, vinegar fly
walking stick, warble fly, wasp, water beetle, water bug,
water strider, weevil, whip scorpion, whirligig beetle,
white ant, wood nymph, wood tick, wood wasp
yellow jacket

### CRUSTACEANS

**crustacean** member of a subphylum of mostly aquatic,
invertebrate arthropods with gills, a hard outer shell, a
jointed body, appendages on the thoracic segment, and
two pairs of antennae

barnacle, beach flea
copepod, crab, crawdad, crayfish
Dungeness crab
fiddler crab
hermit crab, horseshoe crab
isopod
king crab, krill
lobster
prawn
sand hopper, shrimp, soft-shell crab, spider crab
water flea, wood louse

## MOLLUSKS AND AQUATIC INVERTEBRATES

**mollusk** member of a phylum of mostly aquatic invertebrates with an unsegmented body enclosed in one or more
hard shells, with a muscular foot for moving and usu. gills,
including clams, mussels, octopuses, oysters, scallops,
slugs, snails, and squid

**aquatic invertebrates** members of any of several phyla of
cnidarians, echinoderms, and sponges

**cnidarian** formerly coelenterate; member of a phylum of
invertebrates having a single, internal digestive cavity with
tentacles on the oral end, a primitive nervous system, and
special protective stinger cells, including jellyfish, sea
anemones, and coral

**echinoderm** member of marine invertebrate phylum having a body wall stiffened by calcareous protruding spines,
no head, and tubed feet, that lives on the seafloor, including starfish, sea urchins, sand dollars, and sea cucumbers

**sponge** member of the chiefly marine invertebrate phylum
Porifera having a porous structure and usu. a horny skeleton formed from hard substances that become stuck in its
body walls, that lives in large colonies attached to rocks

abalone, acorn worm, amphioxus, anemone, angel's wing
barnacle, bivalve, bloodworm, brain coral, brittle star
cannonball jellyfish, clam, cockle, comb jelly, conch, coquina,
coral, cowrie, crown-of-thorns starfish, cuttlefish
dead man's fingers, devilfish

elkhorn coral
gastropod, giant squid
hydra, hydrozoan coral
jellyfish
limpet, lion's mane
mussel
nautilus, nudibranch
octocorallian, octopod, octopus, oyster
periwinkle, polyp, pompano, Portuguese man-of-war
quahog
razor clam
sand dollar, sand flea, sandworm, scallop, scleractinian coral,
    sea anenome, sea cucumber, sea fan, sea feather, sea
    hare, sea nettle, sea slug, seasnail, sea star, sea urchin, sea
    wasp, sea whip, shellfish, shipworm, slug, snail, sponge,
    squid, staghorn coral, star coral, starfish
tubeworm
whelk
zoanthid

## WORMS

**worm** any slender, soft-bodied, legless, symmetrical invertebrate, often segmented, that lives underground, in water,
or as a parasite, esp. an insect larva
acanthocephalan, angleworm, annelid, armyworm,
    arrowworm
bloodworm, bollworm, bookworm
cankerworm, clamworm, cottonworm, cutworm, cysticercus
earthworm, earworm, eelworm
filaria, fireworm, flatworm, fluke
hairworm, hellgrammite, helminth, hookworm, hornworm,
    horsehair worm
inchworm
larva, leech, looper, lugworm
measuringworm
nemathelminth, nematode, nemertean
pinworm, planarian, platyhelminth, polychaete
red worm, ribbon worm, rotifer, roundworm
sandworm, sea mouse, sea worm, silkworm
tapeworm, teredo, threadworm, tobacco hornworm, tomato
    hornworm, trematode, tubeworm, tubifex, tussah
vinegar eel, vinegar worm
webworm, wireworm, woodworm

# PLANTS

Botany and Plant Parts
Trees
Shrubs
Flowering Plants
Grasses, Sedges, and Grasslike Plants
Herbaceous Plants
Ferns
Vines
Weeds

**SEE ALSO**: Chap. 2: Biology; Simpler Life Forms; Chap. 9:
Foods; Chap. 12: Agriculture; Chap. 17: Gardening

Plants are grouped under taxonomically distinctive subheadings with generic definitions, similar to the treatment accorded Animals.

## BOTANY AND PLANT PARTS

**algae** unicellular organism distinguished from plants by
having no true root, stem, or leaf; see under Algae in
Simpler Life Forms
**alternation of generations** life cycle in many plants, in
which diploid and haploid generations alternate
**angiosperm** flowering plant, esp. one having its seeds enclosed in an ovary
**annual** plant with life cycle of one year or season
**annulus** veil remnant on stalk of mushroom
**anther** part of stamen that produces and releases pollen
**articulation** joint in stem or between branch and leaf
**auxin** plant growth hormone
**axil** upper angle formed by leaf or twig and the stem from
which it grows
**axillary bud** bud formed at axil
**bark** outside covering of stems and roots of trees and woody
plants
**berry** small, fleshy fruit or dry seed or kernel of various
plants
**biennial** plant with two-year life cycle in which the vegetative first-year growth is followed by fruiting and dying
during second year
**blade** broad, expanded part of leaf
**botany** branch of biology dealing with life, structure,
growth, and classification of plants
**bract** leaflike structure growing below or encircling flower
cluster or flower
**bromeliad** member of the pineapple family of plants, usu.
epiphytic with stiff, leathery leaves and spikes of bright
flowers
**bryophyte** any member of the division of nonvascular
plants, including mosses and liverworts, that lack water-
gathering roots and tissues to conduct water
**bud** small swelling on plant from which shoot, leaf cluster,
or flower develops
**bulb** dormant underground bud stage of some plants
**bush** shrub
**Calvin cycle** sequence of reactions in second stage of photosynthesis by which carbon dioxide is reduced to carbohydrate
**calyx** outer whorl of protective leaves on a flower
**cambium** layer of formative cells beneath bark of tree
**cap** pileus of mushroom
**carpel** ovule-bearing leaf or leaflike structure that is primary
segment of pistil
**chlorophyll** pigment in chloroplast, needed for photosynthesis
**chloroplast** membrane-bound organelle that is site of photosynthesis
**club moss** any of various small, nonseed-bearing vascular
plants with conelike, spore-bearing structures on top of
stems; lycopod
**cohesion-tension theory** theory that upward movement of
water in plants results from negative pressure in leaf cells,
inducing water from vascular tissue to pull cohering chain
of water molecules up from root
**coleoptile** protective sheathing around young shoot in germinating grass seed
**composite** one of a large family of herbaceous plants with
flower heads of dense clusters of small florets surrounded
by ring of small leaves or bracts

**cone** reproductive structure of certain nonflowering plants with overlapping scales or bracts containing pollen, ovules, or spores

**conifer** cone-bearing gymnosperm, usu. with narrow, needlelike or small, scalelike leaves

**corm** underground stem base that acts as reproductive structure

**cormel** small corm

**corolla** flower petals

**corymb** flat-topped or convex cluster of flowers in which outer flowers open first

**cotyledon** first or second leaf of seedling

**crustose** (adj) having a thin thallus that clings to substratum of rock, bark, or soil

**cuticle** waxy layer on outer surface of plants

**cycad** any of the order of gymnosperms intermediate between ferns and palms, often with thick, columnar trunk crowned by large, tough, pinnate leaves

**cyme** inflorescence in which primary axis bears single central or terminal flower that blooms first

**cyst** sporelike cell with resistant, protective wall

**cytokinin** plant hormone that promotes cell division

**deciduous** (adj) designating any plant that sheds all its leaves once each year

**dehiscence** splitting open of pod or anther, esp. at maturity to discharge seeds

**dicot** dicotyledon

**dicotyledon** angiosperm having two seed leaves or cotyledons; dicot

**dioecious** (adj) having male and female flowers on different individuals

**division** major primary subdivision of plant kingdom, comparable to animal phylum

**dormancy** period of time in which growth ceases

**double fertilization** process in flowering plants in which one pollen sperm cell fertilizes egg cell and a second fuses with two polar nuclei

**endophyte** plant living within another plant, usu. as a parasite

**epiphyte** nonparasitic plant growing upon another plant for support

**evergreen** plant that maintains functional green foliage throughout year

**fern** nonflowering, vascular plant having roots, stems, and fronds and reproducing by spores instead of seeds

**fertilization** fusion of male and female sex cells, preceded by pollination in seed plants

**filament** stalklike portion of stamen, bearing the anther

**flora** plants of specific region or time

**floret** small flower; one of individual flowers comprising the head of a composite plant

**flower** seed-producing plant, usu. nonwoody, with shortened stem bearing leaflike sepals, colorful petals, and pollen-bearing stamens clustered around pistils; blossom; plant cultivated for its blossoms; reproductive organ of some plants; (vb) produce blossoms

**flowering plant** any angiosperm that produces flowers, fruit, and seeds in an enclosed ovary

**foliage** leaves of plant or tree

**foliose** (adj) covered with leaves

**frond** fern or palm foliage

**fructose** yellowish to white, crystalline, water-soluble sugar found in many fruits

**fruit** mature ovary of flowering plant, sometimes edible; see under Foods

**fungus** unicellular or filamentous organism that lives by decomposing, formerly classified with plants; see under kingdom Fungi in Simpler Life Forms

**funicle** stalk of ovule or seed

**gametophyte** gamete-bearing, haploid, multicelled stage of many plants, beginning with haploid spores and ending at fertilization

**germinate** (vb) sprout and start to grow from spore, seed, or bud

**gill** lamella

**grass** member of the family of flowering plants with long, narrow leaves, jointed stems, flowers in spikelets, and seedlike fruit

**gravitropism** growth or movement of plant in which force of gravity is determining factor

**gymnosperm** member of the division of seed plants having ovules on open scales, esp. cones

**gynoecium** pistil

**herb** nonwoody, seed-producing plant whose stem withers away to ground after one season's growth, often having medicinal or culinary uses

**herbaceous** (adj) designating nonwoody plant

**holdfast** portion of rootless plant that attaches to a surface

**horsetail** nonseed-bearing vascular plant with jointed stem, siliceous ribs, and a spore-bearing cone atop its stem; sphenopsid

**hypha** threadlike part forming mycelium of fungus

**indehiscent** (adj) not opening at maturity to discharge seeds

**inflorescence** production of blossoms; flower cluster on a common axis

**kernel** grain or seed, esp. inside fruit

**lamella** one of the radiating vertical plates on underside of cap of mushroom; gill

**lateral bud** bud growing on side of stem

**leaf** flat, thin structure growing from stem or twig of plant, used in photosynthesis and transpiration

**legume** any of the family of herbaceous plants, shrubs, and vines having compound leaves, clusters of flowers, and fruit in form of pod

**lenticel** spongy area of bark on woody plant that permits exchange of gases between stem and atmosphere

**lichen** fungus in symbiotic union with an alga, formerly classified with plants; see under kingdom Fungi in Simpler Life Forms

**ligneous** (adj) forming or having the nature of wood; woody

**lignin** organic substance that serves as binder for cellulose fibers in wood and certain plants

**liverwort** any of various small, flat bryophytes, usu. encrusting logs, rocks, or soil in moist areas

**lycopod** club moss

**meristem** undifferentiated tissue from which new tissue arises

**midrib** central vein of leaf

**monocot** monocotyledon

**monocotyledon** angiosperm having only one seed leaf or cotyledon; monocot

**monoecious** (adj) having male and female flowers on same individual

**moss** any of various small bryophytes without true stems, reproducing by spores, and growing in velvety clusters in moist areas on rocks, trees, and the ground

**mycelium** mass of threadlike tubes forming the vegetative part of a fungus

**mycorrhiza** close symbiosis between mycelia of certain fungi and root cells of some vascular plants

**nectar** sugary fluid in many flowers, which attracts animal pollinators

**nectary** organ of plant that secretes nectar

**nonvascular plant** bryophyte

**nut** dry, single-seeded fruit of various trees and shrubs, consisting of kernel enclosed in hard or tough shell

**nutation** spontaneous movement of plant parts during growth

**olfactory** (*adj*) affecting, emitting, or having to do with smell

**ovary** enlarged base of pistil in flowering plants that encloses ovules

**ovule** female germ cell or rudimentary seed prior to fertilization

**palisade cell** chloroplast-containing cell just below surface of a leaf

**palynology** study of pollen grains and spores

**panicle** loose, diversely branching flower clusters; compound raceme

**parenchyma** soft tissue forming chief substance of leaves and roots, fruit pulp, and center of stems

**pectin** white, colloidal carbohydrate, found in certain ripe fruits, that has thickening properties

**pedicel** stalk of single flower, fruit, or leaf

**peduncle** stalk supporting flower or flower cluster of an angiosperm or bearing the fruiting body of a fungus

**perennial** plant that lives more than two years, esp. herbaceous plant that produces flowers from the same root structure several years in a row

**petal** one of the circle of flower parts inside the sepals

**petiole** stem connecting a branch to a leaf blade

**phloem** nutrient-conducting tissue of vascular plants

**photoperiodism** capacity of plants to measure relative periods of daylight and darkness, thus anticipating and accommodating themselves to seasonal changes

**photosynthesis** production of organic substances from carbon dioxide and water in green plant cells which chemically transform radiant energy of sunlight

**phototropism** plant growth and movement toward light source

**phytochrome** light-detecting pigment involved in photoperiodism

**phytoplankton** aggregate of plants and other organisms in plankton

**pileus** horizontal part at top of mushroom stalk, bearing gills on its underside; cap

**pinna** one of the leaflets in featherlike arrangement along axis of a pinnate leaf

**pistil** central, seed-bearing part of flower, comprised of one or more carpels, each with style and stigma; gynoecium

**plankton** aggregate of passively floating or slightly motile organisms in a body of water, primarily algae and protozoa

**plant** member of the kingdom Plantae of multicelled organisms capable of carrying on photosynthesis in their cells, primarily adapted for terrestrial life

**pod** vessel enclosing one or more seeds, usu. splitting along two sutures at maturity

**pollen** fine, dustlike grains containing male sexual cells, produced in anthers or similar structures of seed plants

**pollination** transfer of pollen from stamen to upper tip of pistil

**raceme** diversely branching flowers lying along common axis

**ray** any of the flower stalks of an umbel

**receptacle** modified portion of stem or axis of flowering plant that bears the organs of a flower or flower head; torus

**reticulate** (*adj*) having veins arranged in netlike threads on leaves

**rhizome** creeping horizontal stem lying at or just beneath soil surface, which bears leaves at its tip and roots from its underside

**root** underground part of plant that functions in absorption, aeration, food storage, and as support system

**runner** long, slender stem growing from base of some perennials; stolon

**saprophyte** plant or fungus that feeds on dead and decaying organic matter

**scale** small leaf or bract covering and protecting the bud of a seed plant

**sedge** any of the family of rushlike or grasslike herbaceous plants growing in wet areas and having solid stems, slender leaves, and spikes of small flowers

**seed** fertilized plant ovule containing embryo, capable of germinating to produce new plant

**self-pollination** transfer of pollen from anther to stigma of same flower, another flower on same plant, or plant of same clone

**sepal** leaflike, usu. green outer circle of calyx

**sessile** (*adj*) attached at the base or without separate support structure

**shrub** woody perennial plant with several stems branching off near its base rather than a single trunk like a tree; bush

**sieve tube** longitudinal tube in phloem of flowering plants that conducts organic food materials through plant

**sorus** cluster of spore containers, esp. under a fern frond

**sphenopsid** horsetail

**spike** inflorescence in which flowers bloom along entire length of single stalk

**sporangium** organ or single cell producing spores

**spore** haploid reproductive cell that on germination develops into the gametophyte

**sporophyte** spore-bearing, diploid, multicelled stage of many plants that begins with fertilized egg and ends with production of haploid spores

**stalk** stem or main axis of plant; any slender, supporting or connecting part of plant

**stamen** pollen-producing part of central flower, comprised of filament and anther

**stem** main upward-growing axis of plant

**stigma** free upper tip of a flower style on which pollen falls and develops

**stipe** stalk or slender support, such as petiole of a fern or stem of a mushroom

**stolon** stem that takes root at intervals along ground, forming new plants; runner

**stoma** microscopic opening in plant epidermis, esp. one through which gases are exchanged with the environment

**style** slender, stalklike part of carpel between stigma and ovary

**succulent** plant with thick, fleshy tissues that store water

**taproot** deep main root from which lateral roots develop

**tendril** threadlike, often spiral part of climbing plant which clings to or coils around objects

**terminal bud** bud growing at end of stem

**thallus** nonvascular plant body without clear differentiation into stems, leaves, or roots

**torus** receptacle of a flower

**touch responses** twining, coiling, and other rapid movements in plants sensitive to touch

**translocation** transport of products of photosynthesis from leaf to other parts of plant

**transpiration** loss of water vapor from plant body

**tree** tall, woody perennial with single stem or trunk and branches that usu. begin at some height above the ground

**tropophilous** (*adj*) adapted to climate having marked environmental changes

**trunk** main stem of tree

**tuber** fat underground stem from which some plants grow, similar to but shorter and thicker than a rhizome

**umbel** cluster of flowers with stalks of nearly equal length that spring from the same point

**vascular bundle** arrangement of xylem and phloem that forms conducting system of a vascular plant

**vascular plant** any plant, such as the angiosperms, gymnosperms, or ferns, in which the xylem and phloem conduct water and organic nutrients

**vegetable** any plant, or part of a plant, that is used as food; see list under Foods

**vegetative** (*adj*) of plants, esp. pertaining to plant growth and nutrition; capable of growing as a plant

**veil** membrane that covers immature mushroom and breaks open, leaving veillike remnants usu. on stalk; annulus; velum

**velum** veil

**vessel** water-conducting tube in xylem

**vine** plant that grows along the ground or clings to a vertical support by means of twining stems, tendrils, or rootlets

**volva** membranous enclosure on base of certain mushrooms, formed when veil breaks

**weed** vigorous plant of rank growth that tends to overcrowd more desirable neighboring plants; any plant that is unwanted

**whorl** circular growth of leaves or petals

**woody** (*adj*) designating a plant consisting of or forming wood; ligneous

**xerophyte** plant adapted for growth in arid conditions

**xylem** water- and mineral-conducting woody tissue of vascular plants, found in stems, roots, and leaves, that supports softer tissues of plant

**zygophyte** plant that reproduces by means of zygospores

**zygospore** cell formed by fusion of two similar gametes, as in certain algae and fungi

## Trees

**tree** tall, woody perennial with single stem or trunk and branches that usu. begin at some height above the ground

acacia, ailanthus, alder, algarroba, allspice, almond, American elm, annatto, apple, apricot, araucaria, arborvitae, arbutus, ash, aspen, avocado

bald cypress, balsa, balsam fir, balsam poplar, banana, banksia, banyan, baobab, basswood, bay, bayberry, bean

tree, beech, betel palm, bigleaf maple, birch, black acacia, black alder, black ash, black cherry, black locust, black maple, black oak, blackthorn, black walnut, bombax, bottlebrush, box elder, boxwood, Brazil nut, brazilwood, breadfruit, bristlecone pine, buckeye, buckthorn, bumelia, butternut, buttonwood

cacao, California laurel, camphor tree, candleberry, carnauba, carob, cashew, cassia, catalpa, cedar, cercis, cherimoya, cherry, cherry plum, chestnut, chestnut oak, chinaberry, China tree, Chinese date, chinquapin, cinnamon, citron, citrus, clove, coconut, coffee tree, cork oak, cornel, cottonwood, cycad, cypress

dahoon, date palm, dogwood, Douglas fir, dungon

eastern hemlock, ebony, elder, elm, encina, eucalyptus

fig, fir, frankincense, fringe tree

gardenia, giant sequoia, ginkgo, gleditsia, grapefruit, guava, gum, gumbo-limbo

hackberry, hawthorn, hazel, hemlock, henna, hickory, holly, honey locust, hoptree, hornbeam, horse chestnut

Indian mulberry, ironwood

jacaranda, jarrah, Joshua tree, Judas tree, juniper

kauri, Kentucky coffee tree, kumquat

laburnum, lancewood, larch, laurel, lehua, lemon, lime, linden, litchi, locust, logwood, longleaf pine

madrone, magnolia, mahogany, manchineel, mango, mangosteen, mangrove, maple, mastic, medlar, mescal bean, mesquite, mimosa, ming tree, monkeypod, mountain ash, mulberry

Norway maple, nutmeg, nux vomica

oak, ohia lehua, Ohio buckeye, olive, orange, Osage orange

palm, palmetto, papaw, papaya, paper mulberry, paulownia, pawpaw, peach, pear, pecan, persimmon, pine, pistachio, plane, plum, pomegranate, pomelo, pond-apple, poplar

quince

raffia palm, rain tree, rambutan, redbud, red cedar, redwood, rosewood, rowan, royal poinciana, rubber

sago palm, sandalwood, sandarac, sapodilla, sappanwood, sassafras, satinwood, senna, sequoia, serviceberry, silk oak, silver maple, slash pine, snowbell, soapberry, sorb, sorrel tree, sour gum, soursop, speedwell, spruce, star apple, St. John's-bread, sumac, sweet cherry, sweet gum, sweetsop, sycamore

tacamahac, tamarack, tamarind, tangerine, tan oak, teak, thorn apple, thorn tree, thuja, tolu, tonka bean, toon, torreya, Torrey pine, tree of heaven, tulip oak, tulip tree, tupelo

upas

walnut, Washingtonia, Washington thorn, water elm, wattle, weeping willow, white fir, white poplar, white spruce, willow, willow oak, witch hazel

yellow pine, yellow poplar, yew

## Shrubs

**shrub** woody perennial plant with several stems branching off near its base rather than a single trunk like a tree

alder, allspice, aloe, althea, arbutus, azalea

barbasco, barberry, bayberry, bignonia, bilberry, blackberry, black currant, blackthorn, bladdernut, blueberry, box, bramble, broom, buddleia, buffalo berry, buttonbush

caper, cascarilla, cassia, cayenne, chokeberry, cinchona, clematis, cleome, coca, coffee, coffeeberry, coralberry, cranberry, crowberry, cubeb, currant

daphne, deerberry, divi-divi

elder, elderberry, erica, euonymus

farkleberry, firethorn, flowering maple, forsythia, frangipani, fuchsia, furze

gardenia, genista, germander, gooseberry, gorse, grape, greasewood, greenbrier, guava, guayule, guelder rose

haw, heath, heather, hemlock, hemp tree, henna, hibiscus, holly, honeysuckle, huckleberry, hydrangea

Indian currant, Indian hawthorn, indigo, Italian jasmine

jojoba, Juneberry, jute

kalmia, kat, kumquat

laurel, lavender, leadwort, leatherleaf, lespedeza, lilac, ling

magnolia, manzanita, milkwort, mistletoe, mock orange, mountain cranberry, mountain currant, mountain fetterbush, mountain holly, mountain maple, myrtle

nandina, night jasmine, ninebark

oleander, Oregon grape

partridgeberry, pepper, Persian berry, philodendron, photinia, poison haw, poison ivy, poison oak, poison sumac, prickly ash, privet, pussy willow

quassia

raspberry, rhododendron, rose, rosebay, rosemary, rose of Sharon

sad tree, sage, sagebrush, sand myrtle, scarlet sage, serviceberry, sheepberry, shrimp plant, silverberry, sisal, sloe, smilax, snowberry, spicebush, spirea, staggerbush, strawberry guava, strawberry tree, sumac, syringa

tamarisk, tea tree, titi, toyon

veronica, viburnum

whin, wild hydrangea, winterberry, winter cherry, wintercreeper, wintergreen barberry, wisteria, witch hazel

yaupon, yellowroot

zenobia

## FLOWERING PLANTS

**flower** seed-producing plant, usu. nonwoody, with a shortened stem bearing leaflike sepals, colorful petals, and pollen-bearing stamens clustered around pistils

**flowering plant** any angiosperm that produces flowers, fruit, and seeds in an enclosed ovary

acacia, adder's-tongue, African violet, agave, ageratum, ailanthus, amaranth, amaryllis, American Beauty rose, anemone, arbutus, arethusa, arnica, arrowhead, artichoke, asphodel, aspidistra, aster, atamasco lily, azalea

baby-blue-eyes, baby's-breath, bachelor's-button, begonia, berseem, betony, bird-of-paradise, bitterroot, black-eyed Susan, blazing star, bleeding heart, bloodroot, bluebell, bluebonnet, bluebottle, blue flag, bluet, boltonia, bridal wreath, broccoli, bromegrass, broom, brown-eyed Susan, buttercup, buttonbush

cactus, calendula, calla lily, calypso, camass, camellia, campanula, Canada thistle, candytuft, carnation, catalpa, cat's-paw, cattail, century plant, chamomile, Cherokee rose, Chinese lantern plant, Christmas rose, chrysanthemum, cineraria, clematis, clethra, cockscomb, colicroot, columbine, comfrey, compass plant, cornel, cornflower, corydalis, cosmos, cowslip, crocus, cyclamen

daffodil, dahlia, daisy, damask rose, dandelion, delphinium, dogwood, dragon's mouth, duckweed, Dutchman's-breeches, Dutchman's-pipe

edelweiss, eglantine, erigeron

fairy-slipper, figwort, fireweed, flax, fleur-de-lis, forget-me-not, forsythia, foxglove, foxtail, frangipani, fuchsia

gardenia, gentian, geranium, gladiolus, goatsbeard, golden aster, goldenrod, ground ivy, groundsel

harebell, hawkweed, hawthorn, heather, hepatica, hibiscus, hogweed, hollyhock, honeysuckle, horehound, horsemint, hyacinth, hydrangea

impatiens, Indian cress, Indian fig, Indian hemp, Indian paintbrush, Indian pipe, Indian strawberry, Indian warrior, indigo, iris, Italian aster

jack-in-the-pulpit, japonica, jasmine, jessamine, jonquil

knotweed

ladies'-tobacco, lady's-slipper, larkspur, lavender, lehua, lilac, lily, lily of the valley, lobelia, lotus, love-lies-bleeding, lupine

magnolia, mallow, marguerite, marigold, marsh mallow, marsh marigold, mayflower, maypop, mayweed, mignonette, mimosa, moccasin flower, mock orange, monkshood, morning glory, moss rose, motherwort, mountain laurel, mullein, myrtle

narcissus, nasturtium

ohia lehua, oleander, opium poppy, orchid, Oregon grape, Oswego tea, oxalis

pansy, pasqueflower, passionflower, pennyroyal, peony, periwinkle, petunia, phlox, pilewort, pink, pinxter flower, poinsettia, poppy, portulaca, prickly pear, primrose, pussy-toes, pyrethrum

Queen Anne's lace

rafflesia, ragwort, ranunculus, red fescue, resurrection plant, Rhode Island bent, rose, rose of Jericho, rudbeckia

safflower, saffron, saguaro, sansevieria, santonica, scarlet sage, shooting star, smilax, snapdragon, snowball, snowberry, snowdrop, snow plant, spirea, stock, strawflower, sunflower, swamp pink, sweet alyssum, sweet pea, sweet william

tamarisk, teasel, thistle, tidytips, trefoil, trillium, trumpet flower, trumpet vine, tulip

umbrella plant

vanilla, Venus's flytrap, verbena, vetch, viburnum, viola, violet

wallflower, water lily, wild rose, wisteria, wolfbane, woundwort

yarrow, yucca

zinnia

## GRASSES, SEDGES, AND GRASSLIKE PLANTS

**grass** member of the family of flowering plants with long, narrow leaves, jointed stems, flowers in spikelets, and seedlike fruit

**sedge** any of the family of rushlike or grasslike herbaceous plants growing in wet areas and having solid stems, slender leaves, and spikes of small flowers

alfalfa, alfilaria, Australian rye grass

Bahia grass, bamboo, barley, barn grass, barnyard grass, beach grass, beard grass, bengal grass, bent, bent grass, Bermuda grass, blue grama, bluegrass, bluejoint, bog grass, bristly foxtail grass, bromegrass, broomcorn, buckwheat, buffalo grass, bulrush, bunch grass

canary grass, cane, China grass, chufa, cock's-foot, corn, cotton grass, couch grass, crab grass

darnel, durra, durum wheat

eelgrass, English rye grass

feather grass, fescue, finger grass, flyaway grass, foxtail, frog's-bit

gama grass, grama, guinea grass

hair grass, hassock, hay, herd's grass, horsetail

Indian corn, Italian rye grass

Japanese lawn grass, Job's-tears

Kentucky bluegrass, khus-khus, Korean lawn grass

lawn grass, lemon grass, little quaking grass, lovegrass, lyme grass

maize, meadow fescue, meadow foxtail, meadow grass, mesquite grass, millet, myrtle grass

oat, oat grass, orchard grass

paddy, pampas grass, papyrus, peppergrass, pin grass, plume grass, pony grass

quitch

red fescue, redtop, reed grass, Rhode Island bent, ribbon grass, rice, rush, rye, ryegrass

scouring rush, scutch grass, sedge, sheep fescue, silk grass, slender foxtail, sorghum, spear grass, squirrel-tail grass, squitch, star grass, striped grass, sugarcane, switch grass, sword grass

tear grass, timothy, tule, twitch grass

umbrella plant

vetiver, viper's grass

wheat, wild oat, wild rye, windlestraw, wire grass, witch grass, wood meadow grass, woolly beard grass, worm grass

yellow-eyed grass

zebra grass, zoysia

## HERBACEOUS PLANTS

**herb** nonwoody, seed-producing plant whose stem withers away to the ground after season's growth, often having medicinal or culinary uses

ajuga, aluminum plant, amaranth, angelica, anise

balm, basil, belladonna, bellwort, bergamot, betony, birthwort, bitterroot, bladderwort, blue-curls, boneset, borage, bugle, bugleweed, burning bush, butterwort, button snakeroot

calamint, calendula, caraway, cardamom, carrot, castor-oil plant, catmint, catnip, cauliflower, celery, chamomile, charlock, chervil, chicory, cilantro, clover, coleus, coriander, corydalis, cowbane, cow parsnip, Cretan dittany, crowfoot, cumin

datura, deadly nightshade, death camass, dill, dittany, dropwort

eryngo

fennel, fenugreek, feverroot, figwort, finochio, Florence fennel, fool's-parsley, fraxinella

gas plant, germander, ginger, glasswort, ground ivy, ground pine

heliotrope, hemlock, hemp, hemp nettle, henbane, henbit, honewort, horehound, horsemint, hound's-tongue, hyssop

leadwort, lespedeza, licorice, lovage, lupine

mandrake, marijuana, marjoram, May apple, mint, monarda, monkshood, mullein, mustard

nutmeg

oregano, Oswego tea

parsley, parsnip, patchouli, pennyroyal, peppermint, perilla, philodendron

rattlesnake weed, rosemary, rudbeckia, rue

safflower, sage, salvia, samphire, sanicle, savory, scarlet sage, sea holly, sesame, sorrel, spearmint, spiderwort, sweet cicely, sweet woodruff

tansy, tarragon, teasel, thyme, tobacco, trefoil, turmeric

water hemlock, wild bergamot, wild marjoram, wintergreen, woodruff, wormwood, wort, woundwort

yarrow

## FERNS

**fern** nonflowering, vascular plant having roots, stems, and fronds and reproducing by spores instead of seeds

adder's-tongue

basket fern, bead fern, beech fern, bladder fern, Boston fern, boulder fern, bracken, bristle fern, brittle fern, buckler fern

chain fern, Christmas fern, cinnamon fern, cliff brake, climbing fern, crested fern, curly grass fern

fern, fragile fern

grape fern

hart's-tongue, hay-scented fern, holly fern

interrupted fern

lady fern, limestone fern, lip fern

maidenhair, male fern, marsh fern, moonwort, mosquito fern

New York fern

oak fern, osmund, ostrich fern

parsley fern, polypody, pteridosperm

rattlesnake fern, resurrection fern, rock brake, royal fern

seed fern, sensitive fern, shield fern, snuffbox fern, spleenwort

walking fern, walking leaf, wall fern, water fern, wood fern, woodsia

## VINES

**vine** plant that grows along the ground or clings to a vertical support by means of twining stems, tendrils, or rootlets

actinidia, Algerian ivy, ampelopsis, Amur grape, asparagus fern

balsam apple, balsam pear, bean, bittersweet, Boston ivy, bottle gourd, bougainvillea, boxthorn, bramble, bryony

cantaloupe, cape plumbago, casaba, catclaw vine, chayote, Chinese wisteria, clematis, convolvulus, coral greenbrier, creeping fig, cross-vine, cucumber, curly clematis

dewberry, dichondra

elephant's-foot, English ivy, everblooming honeysuckle

fleevine, fox grape

gloryvine, golden clematis, gourd, grape, grapevine, greenbrier

Hall's honeysuckle, honeysuckle, hop, horsebrier, Hottentot's bread

ipomoea, ivy

jackman clematis, Japanese creeper, Japanese wisteria, jasmine, jovin clematis

kudzu vine

liana, loofah

matrimony vine, melon, milkweed, monk's hood vine, moonseed, morning glory, muscat

pea, peppervine, poison ivy, poison oak, pokeweed, porcelain ampelopsis, primrose jasmine, pumpkin

rag gourd, rambler rose, Regel's tripterygium, runner bean

scarlet clematis, scarlet kadsura, sevenleaf creeper, silvervine, similax, squash, star jasmine, stephanotis, string bean, summer squash, sweet honeysuckle

teasel gourd, traveler's-joy, trumpet creeper, trumpet honeysuckle, trumpet vine

vanilla, vegetable sponge, vetch, Virginia creeper, virgin's bower

wandering Jew, watermelon, wintercreeper, winter jasmine, winter squash, wire vine, wisteria, woodbine

yam

# WEEDS

**weed** vigorous plant of rank growth that usu. reproduces profusely, is difficult to eliminate, and tends to overcrowd more desirable neighboring plants; any plant that is unwanted and interferes with growth of other plants, including many grasses, herbs, and mosses

barren strawberry, bedstraw, beggar-ticks, Bermuda grass, bindweed, bird's-eye pearlwort, bitter nightshade, black bindweed, bluegrass, blueweed, bracken, brake, broad-leaved dock, buckthorn, buckthorn plantain, bugleweed, bull thistle, bur, burdock

Canada thistle, Carolina horse nettle, carpetweed, cat's-ear, cattail, charlock, chickweed, chicory, cinquefoil, clover, cocklebur, corn spurry, cottonweed, couch grass, crab grass, crane's-bill, crazyweed, creeping buttercup, creeping cinquefoil, creeping speedwell, creeping veronica, curled dock

dandelion, devil's paintbrush, dewberry, dock, duckweed

English lawn daisy, Eurasian water milfoil

field bindweed, field chickweed, field horsetail, figwort, fireweed, foxtail

galinsoga, goose grass, goutweed, ground ivy, groundsel

hawkweed, heal-all, hedge bindweed, hemlock, hemp nettle, henbit, hogweed, horehound, horseradish, horsetail, horseweed, hydrilla

ice plant

Japanese fleeceflower, Japanese knotweed, jimson weed, Johnson grass

knawel, knotweed

lace grass, lady's-thumb, lamb's-quarters, liverwort, locoweed

mallow, mayweed, milfoil, milkweed, motherwort, mouse-ear chickweed, mouse-ear hawkweed, mustard

nettle, nut sedge

Oldfield cinquefoil, oxalis, oxeye daisy

pearlwort, peppergrass, pepperweed, pigweed, pilewort, pineapple weed, plantain, poison ivy, poke, pokeberry, pokeweed, prickly lettuce, prostrate knotweed, purslane

quack grass, quitch

ragweed, redroot pigweed, red sorrel, Russian thistle

sandbur, scarlet pimpernel, Scotch broom, self-heal, sheep sorrel, shepherd's-purse, skunk cabbage, smartweed, sorrel, sow thistle, spatterdock, speedwell, spotted lady's-thumb, spotted spurge, spurge, spurry, statice, stinging nettle, stinkweed, St.-John's-wort, strawflower, sulfur cinquefoil, swallowwort

tall buttercup, tansy, tarweed, tassel flower, thistle, thorn apple, tumbleweed

velvetleaf, Virginia pepperwood

water chestnut, water hyacinth, western sage, wheatgrass, white clover, wild carrot, wild garlic, wild lettuce, wild mustard, wild oat, wild onion, wild parsnip, wild radish, wild vetch, witch grass, witchweed

yarrow, yellow foxtail, yellow nut sedge, yellow wood sorrel

# SIMPLER LIFE FORMS

Fungi
  Zygomycota
  Ascomycota
  Basidiomycota
  Deuteromycota
Algae
  Photosynthetic Autotrophs
  Heterotrophs
Bacteria
  Bacterial Form Groups
  Eubacteria
  Archaebacteria
Viruses
  Bacteriophages
  Plant Viruses
  Animal Viruses

**SEE ALSO**: Chap. 1: Medical Problems; Chap. 2: Biology; Animals; Plants

Fungi, protists, monerans, and viruses are grouped under taxonomically distinctive subheadings with generic definitions, similar to the treatment accorded Animals and Plants.

## FUNGI

**fungus** member of the kingdom Fungi, consisting of unicellular or filamentous, multinucleate, eukaryotic organisms that live by decomposing and feed on dead or living organic matter in which they grow and decompose, formerly classified with plants, consisting of four divisions: Zygomycota, Ascomycota, Basidiomycota, and Deuteromycota

**lichen** fungus in symbiotic union with an alga

### ZYGOMYCOTA

**zygomycota** free-living terrestrial fungi, as well as plant and animal parasites, that reproduce sexually by formation of zygospores

black bread mold

dung fungus

zygomycetes

### ASCOMYCOTA

**ascomycota** sac fungi, having sexual spores in a sac

ascomycetes

black mold, blue-green mold, bread mold

cup fungus

dead-man's fingers, downy mildew

earth tongue

false mildew, false morel

lorchel

mildew, mold, morel, mushroom pimple

powdery mildew

red bread mold

sac fungus

truffle

yeast

### BASIDIOMYCOTA

**basidiomycota** club fungi, bearing spores at tips of slender projections on a basidium, including most forms commonly called mushrooms

basidiomycetes, bird's-nest fungus, boletus, bracket fungus, brittlegill
chanterelle, coral fungus, crumblecap
deathcap
earthstar
field mushroom
gill fungus, groundwart
inky cap
jelly fungus
meadow mushroom, milkcap, mottlegill, mushroom
oyster cap
parasol mushroom, pink gill, pore fungus, puffball
ringstalk, roof mushroom, rust
scalecap, sheath mushroom, shelf fungus, shiitake, slime mushroom, smoothcap, smut, stinkhorn
toadstool, tooth fungus, tricholoma
waxy cap, webcap, woodcrust

## DEUTEROMYCOTA

**deuteromycota** imperfect fungi, mostly parasitic with no sexual stage
aspergillus
blue mold
deuteromycetes
Fungi Imperfecti
green mold
moniliales
penicillium
ringworm fungus
thrush fungus
verticillium

## ALGAE

**alga** any unicellular, colonial, or filamentous eukaryotic organism belonging to kingdom Protista, with no root, stem, or leaf and having no nonreproductive cells in its reproductive structures, containing chlorophyll masked by red or brown pigment, and growing in water or damp places
**Protista** kingdom of algae, amebas, and protozoans, consisting of photosynthetic autotrophs and heterotrophs

## PHOTOSYNTHETIC AUTOTROPHS

**photosynthetic autotroph** organism capable of self-nourishment by using inorganic materials as its source of nutrients and photosynthesis as its source of energy
brown algae
carrageen, chlorophytes, chrysophytes, conferva, cryptomonads
diatoms, dinoflagellates, dulse
euglenas, euglenophytes
fucus
golden-brown algae, green algae, gulfweed
Irish moss
kelp
olive-brown seaweed
phaeophytes, pond scum, pyrrophytes
red algae, rhodophytes, rockweed
sargasso, sargassum, sea lettuce, sea moss, seaweed, sea wrack, stonewort
wrack
yellow-green algae

## HETEROTROPHS

**heterotroph** organism requiring living or dead organic materials as its principal source of nutrients
**protozoans** animallike, eukaryotic organisms of kingdom Protista, primarily unicellular, colonial, and nonphotosynthetic, categorized by means of motility as ciliates, flagellates, or pseudopods
acrasiomycetes, amebas
cellular slime molds, chytrids, ciliates
flagellates
myxomycetes
oomycetes, opalinids
plasmodial slime molds, protozoans, pseudopods
slime molds, sporozoans
water molds

## BACTERIA

**bacteria** *pl., sing.* **bacterium;** ubiquitous, unicellular organisms appearing singly or in chains in spherical, spiral, or rod-shaped form, forming major phylum of kingdom Monera
**Monera** kingdom of prokaryotic organisms, or cells without a membrane-bound nucleus and membrane-bound organelles, that reproduce by asexual budding or fission

## BACTERIAL FORM GROUPS

**bacilli** *pl., sing.* **bacillus;** rod-shaped bacteria
**cocci** *pl., sing.* **coccus;** spherical bacteria
**spirilla** *pl., sing.* **spirillum;** long, spiral, rod-shaped bacteria
**vibrios** *pl., sing.* **vibrio;** short, curved, or S-shaped bacteria

## EUBACTERIA

**eubacteria** true bacteria, including most free-living and parasitic bacteria with simple, undifferentiated cells having rigid walls
actinomycetes
blue-green algae
cyanobacteria
endospore-forming bacteria
green nonsulfur bacteria, green sulfur bacteria
lactic acid bacteria
mycoplasmas
purple nonsulfur bacteria, purple sulfur bacteria
spirochetes

## ARCHAEBACTERIA

**archaebacteria** surviving members of branch of prokaryotes adapted to earliest stages of biological evolution
halobacteria, halophiles
methanobacteria, methanogens
thermoacidophiles

## VIRUSES

**virus** ultramicroscopic, metabolically inert agent that can reproduce only within a host cell but is partially independent, consisting of nucleic acid enclosed in a protein coat, not fitting into any of the five kingdoms and classified by whether it infects bacteria, plants, or animals

## BACTERIOPHAGES

**bacteriophage**  any virus that infects specific bacteria; phage
  corticovirus, cystovirus
  inovirus
  levivirus
  microvirus, myovirus
  pedovirus, plasmavirus
  stylovirus
  tectivirus

## PLANT VIRUSES

alfalfa mosaic virus
bromovirus
carlavirus, caulimovirus, closterovirus, comovirus, cucumovirus

hordeivirus
ilarvirus
luteovirus
nepovirus
potexvirus, potyvirus
tobacco mosaic virus, tobacco necrosis virus, tobamovirus, tobravirus, tomato spotted wilt virus, tombusvirus, tymovirus

## ANIMAL VIRUSES

adenovirus, arbovirus, arenavirus
baculovirus, bunyavirus
coronavirus
enterovirus, Epstein-Barr virus
herpesvirus
influenza virus, iridovirus
orbivirus, orthomyxovirus
papovavirus, paramyxovirus, parvovirus, picornavirus, poliovirus, poxvirus
reovirus, retrovirus, rhabdovirus, rhinovirus, Rous sarcoma virus
togavirus

# The Earth

# GEOLOGY

Branches and Disciplines
Materials, Formations, and Substances
Processes, Phenomena, Events, and Techniques
Geological Time Scale
Mining

**SEE ALSO**: Chap. 2: Biology; Chap. 3: Geography; Minerals, Metals, and Rocks; Landscapes and Seascapes; Weather and Natural Phenomena; Chap. 4: Chemistry; Chap. 12: Agriculture

## BRANCHES AND DISCIPLINES

**astrogeology** geology of celestial bodies in our solar system

**chronostratigraphy** system of dividing geologic time into eras, periods, epochs, and ages

**crystallography** study of form, structure, and properties of crystals

**earth sciences** various sciences dealing with Earth and its nonliving components

**ecology** study of the relationship between organisms and their environments

**environmental geology** study of the interaction between human beings and the Earth

**geobotany** study of the distribution of plant species; phytogeography

**geochemistry** study of chemical composition and activity in Earth's crust

**geochronology** study of the age of Earth and dating of evolutionary stages of development

**geochronometry** measurement of geologic time by radioactive decay

**geodesy** branch of mathematics concerned with determining size and shape of Earth and position of points on its surface

**geodynamics** study of activity and forces inside Earth

**geognosy** study of composition of Earth and distribution of strata and mineral deposits

**geography** descriptive science that deals with Earth's surface

**geology** science of Earth's origin, evolution, and structure as recorded in rocks, crust, interior, and fossils

**geomorphology** study of nature, origin, and development of Earth's landforms

**geophysics** physics of phenomena occurring on Earth

**geopolitics** interrelationship of politics and geography

**historical geology** study of the history of Earth

**hydrology** study of Earth's water, its distribution and cycles

**lithology** study of rocks based on megascopic examination of samples

**magnetostratigraphy** use of magnetized rocks to determine record of changes in Earth's magnetic field

**marine geology** study of ocean's origin and structure, esp. its floor

**metallurgy** science and technology of metals and their separation from ores

**mineralogy** scientific study of minerals

**mining engineering** applied mineralogy and metallurgy

**oceanography** science of ocean movement and life

**orography** physical geography of mountains

**paleogeography** study of geography of the past

**paleontology** study of fossils

**pedology** soil science

**petrology** study of rocks

**physical geology** study of material composing Earth

**phytogeography** geobotany

**planetology** study of the planetary system

**seismology** study of seismic waves generated by earthquakes or other Earth vibrations

**soil science** applied study of soil and earth

**stratigraphy** study of deposition of sediments

**structural geology** study of structural features of rocks and geographical distributions of these features

**tectonics** study of movements that shape Earth's crust

## MATERIALS, FORMATIONS, AND SUBSTANCES

**abyssal plain** flat plain on ocean floor

**abyssal zone** lightless depths of open sea, usu. deeper than 12,000 feet (3700m)

**agglomerate** mass of heat-fused fragments of volcanic rock

**aggregate** rock composed of mixture of mineral fragments, crystals, and other materials

**alloy** two or more metals, or a metal and nonmetal, fused together when molten

**alluvial fan** cone-shaped deposit of earth made by flowing water

**alluvium** clay, silt, sand, or gravel sediment deposited by running water

**alpine glacier** valley glacier

**amalgam** alloy of mercury with another metal or metals

**anthracite** hard coal that burns almost without flame

**anticline** configuration of folded, stratified rocks in which rocks dip in two directions away from a crest

**aquifer** permeable rock that holds groundwater

**artesian well** well under pressure from weight of water in aquifer column

**ash** finely powdered volcanic lava

**asthenosphere** layer of Earth's crust near melting point, almost fluid

**atoll** coral island remaining after reef sinks below sea level

**axial plane** plane that divides rock fold symmetrically

**barrier beach** narrow strip of sand and rock separated from coast by channel

**batholith** large mass of intrusive, igneous rock extending very deep into Earth's crust

**bathyal zone** ocean area extending beyond continental shelf to depth of about 12,000 feet (3700m)

**beach** strip of loose, grainy material where land and large body of water meet

**bed** thin layer of sedimentary rock separating different materials lying above and below it

**bed load** heavy matter rolling along river bottom but not carried by upper layer of water

**bedrock** solid rock underneath soil layer

**berm** low ridge built up by storm waves

**bitumen** naturally occurring asphalt; hard or semisolid tar-like residue of petroleum or coal tar distillation

**bituminous coal** soft coal

**bole** easily pulverized, reddish clay

**boulder** detached, rounded, and worn large mass of rock

**breccia** rock composed of angular fragments of older rocks

**Bryozoa** phylum of attached and incrusting marine invertebrates

**caldera** crater formed by explosion and collapse of volcano

**calf** mass of ice broken off from glacier or iceberg

**caliche** crusted calcium carbonate formed on certain soils by evaporation of rising solutions in dry regions

**cannel coal** oily, compact coal that burns easily and brightly

**cast** mineral or mud deposited and hardened where body of an organism decayed to form a fossil

**catchment basin** drainage basin (Britain)

**cave** hollow area in earth with opening at surface

**cavern** large, roofed-over cave or passageway in rock, often formed by groundwater passing through cracks in limestone

**chatter mark** small, curved abrasion on surface of glaciated rock caused by passage of glacier over it

**cinder** rough piece of solid volcanic lava; slag from reduction of metal ores; intermediate state of burned matter not yet reduced to ash

**cinder cone** accumulated debris around volcanic vent forming steep-sided hill

**cirque** hollow mountain basin that collects snow, caused by glaciation

**clastic** rock containing rock particles, minerals, and crushed shells

**clay** soil composed of fine particles of hydrous aluminum silicates, plastic when wet, and hard when exposed to high temperature and/or pressure

**clod** lump of earth, clay, or loam

**coal** black, combustible mineral solid that results from partial decomposition of organic matter under heat and pressure over millions of years

**composite** rock made up of several distinct parts

**composite volcano** strato-volcano

**conchoidae fracture** fracture that produces curved surfaces similar to those of interior of a shell

**cone** peak of volcano

**conglomerate** rock, such as hardened clay, composed of rounded fragments of varying sizes in cement; pudding stone

**continent** large landmass on surface of Earth

**continental glacier** large glacier covering major part of a landmass

**continental shelf** edge of continental landmass covered by ocean

**continental slope** edge of continental shelf that slopes steeply down to ocean floor

**coral reef** structure on continental shelf made of shells of colonial marine organisms

**core** innermost part of Earth

**crag** steep, rugged rock projecting above rock mass

**crater** round pit, esp. at summit of volcano

**crevasse** deep crack in glacial ice

**crust** thin outer layer of Earth's surface, composed of sial and sima layers

**crystal** body created by solidification of chemical element or compound into regular atomic arrangement with plane faces; quartz that is close to transparent

**culm** carboniferous formation of beds of impure anthracite containing shale or sandstone; waste from anthracite coal mines

**delta** sediment deposited at river mouth

**deposit** sediment laid down in new location; pocket of mineral or ore in earth

**detritus** rock fragments resulting from disintegration by weathering and erosion

**diamond** mineral of nearly pure crystalline carbon, hardest natural substance known

**dike** igneous rock formation that cuts across another rock formation

**dip** acute angle that rock surface makes with horizontal plane

**dissected mountains** range formed by erosion of plateaus or plains

**divide** ridge separating two drainage basins

**dome volcano** small, steep volcano of rhyolite lava

**drainage basin** area drained by river and its tributaries; catchment basin

**drumlin** oval mound of till formed by glacier

**dune** mound or ridge of sand accumulated by wind

**earth** soft, granular, crumbly part of land; soil; land surface of the world

**eluvium** rock debris produced by weathering or disintegration

**erratic** large stone or boulder carried by glacier to place where it rests on bedrock of different composition

**esker** deposit formed by water running under glacier

**eugeosyncline** part of geosyncline in which the products of volcanism are associated with clastic sedimentation

**evaporite** rock formed by water evaporating from a mineral mass

**extrusive rock** igneous rock formed on Earth's surface or seabed, not underground

**facies** sedimentological record of depositional environment

**facies fossil** fossil species adapted to limited environment

**firn** granular ice formed by recrystallization of snow

**flint** hard quartz that produces spark when struck by steel

**fluvial** (adj) produced by rivers

**footwall** block of rock underlying a fault plane

**fossil** living thing preserved from previous geologic era in petrified rock form

**fossil fuel** fuel source, such as coal or petroleum, deposited in earth from organic remains during earlier geologic age

**freestone** stone, such as limestone or sandstone, that may be cut freely without splitting

**gemstone** hard mineral, crystal, or petrified material used as jewelry when cut and faceted, designated precious or semiprecious

**geode** hollow stone nodule lined by mineral crystals growing inward

**geosyncline** very large, troughlike depression in Earth's surface containing masses of sedimentary and volcanic rock

**geyser** thermal spring that intermittently ejects water with considerable force

**glacier** massive, moving ice layer formed in previous geologic era by accumulation and recrystallization of snow

**Gondwanaland** hypothetical continent that broke apart in Mesozoic era

**granite**  very hard crystalline igneous rock found in mountain cores

**gravel**  loose, rounded fragments of rock; stratum of gravel

**ground moraine**  debris remaining from melting of glacier and forming gently rolling surface

**groundwater**  water trapped in underground pores or fissures in earth

**guyot**  submerged, flat-topped seamount

**hadal zone**  the deepest trenches of the ocean bottom, usu. deeper than 20,000 feet (6000m)

**hanging wall**  block of rock overhanging a fault plane

**hard pan**  bedrock or cemented, compacted clayey layer unable to be penetrated by roots; hard, unbroken ground

**horn**  high, steep mountain peak formed by glaciers

**humus**  portion of soil made up of decomposed organic matter

**hydrocarbon**  compound of hydrogen and carbon, including fossil fuels

**hydrosphere**  Earth's water environment, including glaciers, oceans, atmospheric vapor, lakes, streams, groundwater, snow, and ice

**iceberg**  mass of ice detached from glacier and floating at sea

**icecap**  localized ice sheet

**ice pack**  expanse of floating ice formed over time due to compaction of ice by wind and currents

**ice sheet**  broad, moundlike mass of glacial ice of considerable extent

**igneous rock**  rock formed by cooling and hardening of magma

**index fossil**  fossil from specific time range, used to date rock layer surrounding it

**inner core**  innermost solid layer of Earth

**inorganic material**  matter that is not animal or vegetable, esp. compounds not containing carbon and derived from mineral sources

**inselberg**  monadnock

**intrusive rock**  igneous rock formed by magma cooling and hardening underground, esp. in cracks or cavities in existing rock

**joint**  break in rock mass with no movement of rock on opposite sides of break

**kame**  detrital mound left by retreating ice sheet, usu. stratified sand and gravel

**kettle lake**  body of water formed by melting glaciers moving over a basin

**laccolith**  large body of intrusive igneous rock, domed horizontally over surrounding rock mass, forcing overlying strata to bulge upward

**lava**  magma reaching surface of Earth, usu. through volcano

**lignite**  low-grade brown coal

**limestone**  calcium carbonate rock formed by accumulation of organic remains of sea animals

**lithosphere**  Earth's crust and upper part of mantle

**load**  soil particles and rock carried by running water, wind, or glaciers

**loam**  rich soil of clay, sand, and organic matter

**lodestone**  rock that possesses magnetic polarity

**loess**  fine, windblown dust particles that are unconsolidated and unstratified

**lopolith**  tabular igneous intrusion shaped like bowl with roof and floor sagging downward

**macle**  spot or discoloration in mineral; rough prism that shows cross or checkered pattern in cross section

**mafic magma**  readily flowing magma produced in mantle

**magma**  hot, molten rock within Earth

**mantle**  solid layer beneath Earth's crust to depth of 1800 miles (2900 km)

**mantle rock**  loose material, residual or transported, resting on solid rock of Earth's crust

**marl**  loose, crumbling earthy deposit of clay and limestone

**massif**  block of Earth's crust bounded by faults and displaced as unchanged unit to form principal mountain mass

**mélange**  heterogeneous mixture of rock materials

**meltwater**  water melted from glacial ice

**mesa**  hill with flattened top of hard sandstone or limestone

**metal**  opaque, fusible, ductile, conductive, lustrous substance, often a chemical element or compound yielding oxides or hydroxides

**metamorphic rock**  igneous or sedimentary rock that has been transformed by heat, pressure, or chemically active fluids

**meteorite**  small particle of matter from space that reaches surface of Earth without being vaporized

**mid-ocean ridge**  underwater volcanic mountain chain running parallel to edges of continents bounding ocean

**mineral**  inorganic chemical solid naturally occurring in Earth's crust and having definite chemical composition and tendency to form crystals

**miogeosyncline**  that portion of geosyncline in which volcanism is absent

**monadnock**  resistant rock hill standing well above surrounding peneplain; inselberg

**monolith**  single large block of stone

**moraine**  rock ridge left after disappearance of glacier, composed of till

**mountain**  natural landform or ridge in Earth's crust, elevated at least to 2000 feet (600 m)

**mountain core**  granite rock at center of mountain, surrounded by metamorphic rock

**native metal**  pure metal, usu. found in vein

**natural gas**  combustible mixture of gaseous hydrocarbons, largely methane, that accumulates in porous sedimentary rocks, used as a fossil fuel

**noble mineral**  precious, pure mineral, esp. corrosion-resistant metal such as gold

**nodule**  mineral lump composed primarily of chert or flint

**nonclastic rock**  sedimentary rock composed of interlocking rock that forms grains

**nonfoliated rock**  nonbanded metamorphic rock

**oolite**  spherical grain of sand size, usu. composed of calcium carbonate, originated by inorganic precipitation

**organic material**  substance derived from living organism

**outcropping**  emergence of rock formation from Earth to surface exposure

**outer core**  liquid part of Earth's core

**outwash**  material carried by glacier and laid down in stratified deposits

**Pangaea**  hypothetical continent that broke apart to form continents as they now exist

**peat**  partly carbonized decaying vegetable matter; first stage in formation of coal

**pebble**  small stone worn smooth and round

**peneplain**  flat area just slightly above sea level worn down by streams and mass wasting

**permafrost**  permanently frozen subsoil in arctic regions

**petroleum**  oily, flammable hydrocarbon found in rock strata, refined to produce gasoline

**piedmont**  flat expanse of land lying at foot of mountain

**piedmont glacier**  glacier formed at foot of mountain

**placer**  alluvial deposit containing heavy minerals

**plain**  flat, broad land area slightly above sea level

**plate**  one of huge, movable segments into which Earth's crust is divided and which float over mantle

**plateau**  flat, broad land area at least 2000 feet (600 m) above sea level

**playa**  flat-floored center of undrained desert basin

**playa lake**  temporary lake formed in playa

**plutonic rock**  igneous rock formed by slow crystallization, usu. at great depth

**porphyry**  rock with two or more grain sizes

**precious metal**  rare and therefore valuable metal, such as gold or silver, used in jewelry

**precious stone**  designation for most valuable gemstones, such as diamonds or emeralds

**precipitate**  rock formed from discharge or evaporation of water

**pudding stone**  *Chiefly Brit.* conglomerate

**quartz**  common, colorless, usu. transparent mineral of hexagonal crystals or crystalline masses; silicon dioxide

**range**  system of connected mountains

**reef**  wave-resistant structure composed of sedentary, carbonate-secreting organisms

**regolith**  mantle rock of loose material resting on solid bedrock

**residual**  soil with composition similar to that of bedrock below it

**rhyolite**  fine-grained volcanic rock produced by lava flow

**rill**  miniature stream channel carrying sheet wash

**rimrock**  top stratum of plateau that outcrops to form vertical face

**rock**  large mass of stone, concreted mass of stony material, or broken piece of such a mass

**rubble**  rough, irregular, loose fragments broken from larger mass of rock

**sand**  loose granular material formed by disintegration of rocks into particles smaller than gravel but coarser than silt

**sandstone**  sedimentary rock usu. of quartz sand cemented by silica or calcium carbonate

**schist**  metamorphic rock that can be easily split due to effects of heat

**scoria**  loose, cinderlike lava; slag left after smelting

**scree**  loose rock debris; talus

**seamount**  volcanic mountain at bottom of ocean

**sediment**  material deposited by water, wind, or glaciers

**sedimentary rock**  rock formed on Earth's surface from accumulation of material deposited by water, wind, or glaciers

**semiprecious stone**  designation for gems less valuable than precious stones, such as garnets or turquoise

**shale**  consolidation of clay, mud, or silt into finely stratified rock structure of unaltered minerals

**sheet wash**  thin sheet of water accumulating on slope

**shield**  large area of exposed Precambrian rock

**shield volcano**  volcano built on shield material

**shingle**  coarse, round detritus or alluvial material on seashore

**sialic magma**  thick, stiff magma forming just below crust, composed primarily of silicon and aluminum

**sial layer**  granitelike upper layer of Earth's crust

**silica**  silicon dioxide that occurs as crystalline quartz, opal, or sand

**silicon dioxide**  quartz

**sill**  thin layer of igneous rock extruded between layers of sedimentary rocks or volcanic ejecta

**silt**  loose sedimentary material with particles finer than sand and coarser than clay

**sima layer**  shell of dark, heavy rock composed primarily of silicon and magnesium, found throughout world; layer under sial layer

**slag**  refuse material separated from metal in smelting; lava resembling such refuse

**sludge**  muddy, slushy mass or sediment, esp. on riverbed

**slurry**  water mixture of insoluble mud or lime

**soil**  fragments of weathered rock combined with organic matter

**soil horizon**  layer of soil parallel to land surface

**spatter cone**  low, steep-sided volcanic cone built up from erupted droplets or blobs of lava

**stalactite**  columnar deposit of minerals hanging from cave ceiling

**stalagmite**  columnar deposit of minerals on cavern floor, caused by accretion of dripping mineral-rich water from ceiling

**stone**  concretion of earthy or mineral matter of indeterminate size and shape; one piece of such concretion

**stratified rock**  rock made up of many different layers

**strato-volcano**  steeply shaped volcano that emits fragmented material and viscous lava; composite volcano

**stratum**  sheetlike mass of sedimentary or igneous rock, usu. lying between other strata beds

**syncline**  fold in rock where strata dip inward from both sides

**talus**  sloping mass formed by pile of loose rock fragments and weathered matter collected at foot of cliff or on slope below rock face

**tarn**  lake formed at bottom of cirque after glacial ice has disappeared

**tarpit**  flat area in which natural bitumens, such as tar or asphalt, collect and are exposed to air so that animals fall in and have their bones preserved

**terminal moraine**  debris piled up at point of farthest glacial advance

**terrace**  flat platform at base of eroded sea cliff

**till**  mix of material dropped from melting glacier

**topsoil**  fertile soil made up mainly of humus

**trace fossil**  imprint left by animal track or burrow

**transported soil**  soil moved from its place of origin

**trench**  long, very deep trough in ocean floor bordering some continents

**tufa**  limestone deposited by springs

**tundra**  polar area soil, composed mainly of peat, whose top layer thaws each spring while base remains frozen year-round

**underground rock**  rock deposits not exposed at Earth's surface

**valley glacier**  glacier formed at high elevation, covering river valley; alpine glacier

**vent**  opening at Earth's surface from which volcanic material is emitted

**vesicle**  small cavity in rock formed by gas bubble, occurring in rock in its molten state

**volcanic rock**  igneous rock that solidified rapidly from molten lava at Earth's surface

**volcano**  cone-shaped mountain that vents hot, molten lava, gases, and rock fragments from Earth's interior

## PROCESSES, PHENOMENA, EVENTS, AND TECHNIQUES

**abrasion** wearing away of rock by solid particles carried by wind, water, ice, or gravity

**aftershock** minor earthquake following greater one and originating at same place

**age** interval of geologic time shorter than an epoch

**antipodes** two places at opposite sides of Earth

**avalanche** expanding mass of loosened material sliding suddenly and swiftly down mountain

**belt** elongated area, smaller than a zone, characterized by particular features or occurrences

**body wave** earthquake that moves underground

**Brinell hardness** measure of hardness of metal or alloy

**carat** unit of weight for diamonds or gemstones, equal to 200 mg (.007 ounce)

**carbon-14 dating** radiocarbon dating

**carboniferous** (*adj*) designating coal-making period of Paleozoic era

**cataclysm** great upheaval that causes sudden, violent changes in Earth

**cementation** binding of rock particles together

**chemical weathering** chemical transformation of original rock material into new chemical composition

**cleavage** pattern of breakage of rock or minerals along flat planes

**cleavage plane** smooth surface along which mineral breaks

**coal gasification** process by which coal is changed to gas

**coalification** process by which vegetable matter is transformed into coal

**columnar jointing** columns of rock formed by slowly cooling lava

**comminution** particle size reduction by physical processes

**compaction** reduction in pore space between individual grains due to pressure

**compression** stress force squeezing crustal rock together

**concretion** sedimentary rock with succeeding layers of minerals forming around a grain of sand or other nucleus

**contact metamorphism** metamorphism at contact between metamorphic and igneous rock

**continental drift** very slow motion of major landmasses around Earth's surface

**convergent boundary** area where two landmasses or plates move toward one another

**Coriolis effect** tendency of any moving body starting from surface of Earth to continue in direction propelled by Earth's rotation

**creep** gradual movement of soil particles downhill

**crystallization** process in which crystals separate from fluid, viscous, or dispersed structure

**decomposition** chemical formation of new compounds from elements within rock; chemical weathering

**deep ocean current** water motion caused by differences in temperature and density

**deflation** removal of loose particles from ground by action of wind

**dendrite** branching pattern made by one mineral crystallizing in another

**diagenesis** formation of sedimentary rock by compaction of sediment and chemical reactions

**disintegration** breakage of large rocks into smaller fragments; mechanical weathering

**divergent boundary** boundary between two landmasses pulling apart

**earthquake** sudden, violent shaking of Earth's crust

**elasticity** ability of material to recover from a deforming force

**elevation** height above sea level

**emergent coast** land exposed by lowering of sea level

**eolian** (*adj*) carried, deposited, or eroded by the wind

**epicenter** point on Earth's surface directly above focus of earthquake

**epoch** smallest major unit of geologic time; subdivision of period

**era** largest major unit of geologic time, divided into periods and epochs

**erosion** wearing down of natural landforms by wind, water, ice, or gravity

**eruption** sudden, often violent, outflow of lava from volcano

**eustasy** uniformly global change in sea level, due to change in quantity of water or shape of ocean basins

**fault** crack in Earth's crust from rock slippage up, down, or sideways

**fault block** large mass separated from surrounding material by faults on at least two sides

**fault zone** region of Earth's surface with high number of faults

**flood plain** river valley area flooded at high water

**focus** underground center of earthquake

**fold** bend or turn in crustal rock

**folded mountains** mountains formed by forces of flexing rock

**foliation** metamorphic rock banding

**foreshock** minor earthquake that precedes larger earthquake and originates at its focus

**fracture** characteristic manner of breakage of mineral

**geodetic survey** precise description of large land area corrected for Earth's curvature

**geologic column** layering of rock strata in order from oldest at bottom to youngest at top

**geologic time scale** convention of viewing geologic history in eras, epochs, and periods, based on fossil data

**geomagnetic** (*adj*) relating to magnetic properties of Earth

**geomorphic** (*adj*) pertaining to shape of Earth and its topography

**geotectonic** (*adj*) relating to structure, distribution, and shape of rock bodies in Earth's crust; pertaining to the conditions within Earth that resulted in movement of crust

**geothermal gradient** rate of increase of temperature downward into Earth

**geothermal power** energy from heat of Earth's interior

**geothermic** (*adj*) relating to heat of Earth's interior

**glacial varve chronology** determination of geologic age by reference to layers of silt and clay deposited by melting of retreating glaciers

**hade** angle between fault plane and vertical plane

**hardness** resistance of substance to scratching

**horizon** specific position in stratigraphic column that identifies stratum with a particular period; soil layer

**hydrologic cycle** movement of Earth's water from oceans to atmosphere to land and back to oceans

**hysteresis** retardation of recovery from elastic deformation after stress is removed

**ice age** any time of widespread glaciation, esp. Pleistocene glacial epoch

**induration** concretion of porous rocks and soils due to weather and chemical action

**interglacial age** historic period between ice ages

**isostasy** balancing of floating crustal rock on denser mantle

**joint** fracture plane in rocks, usu. arranged in parallel intersecting systems

**karst topography** irregular topography developed by action of surface and underground water in soluble rock such as limestone

**landslide** collapse of sloped or vertical face of earth or rock

**law of superimposition** rule that in layered beds of rock, oldest is deepest, youngest is closest to surface

**leaching** washing away of soluble minerals, esp. alkalines, from upper layers of soil by water

**lithification** hardening into rock

**luster** capacity of minerals to reflect light off their surfaces

**meander** curve formed in riverbed

**microseism** irregular wave caused by constant movement of Earth's surface

**Moho** Mohorovicic discontinuity

**Mohorovicic discontinuity** boundary between Earth's solid crust and soft mantle; Moho

**mold** fossil cavity left in rock after body of organism has decayed

**nonconformity** unconformity

**normal fault** fault formed when one side moves up, the other down

**oasis** fertile area in desert formed by erosion of surface down to water table

**orogeny** formation of mountains by folding of Earth's crust

**outwash plain** area with mineral and other deposits left by passing glacier

**period** second major unit of geologic time, subdivision of era, divided into epochs

**permeability** measure of the ease with which fluid can be passed through pore space of rock

**petrified** (*adj*) designating organic matter replaced by minerals over time

**phase** description of minerals present in a rock or soil sample

**plate tectonics** theory of formation and motion of Earth's crust and its moving plates

**plucking** erosion caused by glacier pulling rocks out of earth as it moves along surface

**porosity** percent of total volume of rock not occupied by solid mineral matter

**primary waves** seismic waves that move fastest through all forms of matter

**profile of equilibrium** shape of riverbank equally affected by erosion and deposition of material

**radioactive decay** breaking apart over time of atomic nucleus, with emission of radiant energy

**radiocarbon dating** dating of fossil remains by measuring ratio of remaining radioactive carbon 14 to total carbon; carbon-14 dating

**recrystallization** melting and recooling of rock, resulting in larger grain

**regional metamorphism** changes in rock over large area caused by increases in temperature and pressure deep in Earth

**relief** elevation differences among landforms

**Richter scale** logarithmic scale, ranging from 1 to 10, that indicates magnitude of an earthquake in terms of energy released

**rift valley** long, narrow valley formed between two faults

**rift zone** system of fractures in Earth's crust

**ring of fire** area of earthquake and volcanic activity around rim of Pacific Ocean

**rock cycle** change in form of Earth materials subjected to geological processes, esp. from magma to igneous, metamorphic, and sedimentary rock, and back to magma

**seafloor spreading** widening of ocean floor by addition of basaltic material at mid-ocean ridge

**secondary waves** seismic waves that pass through solids but not liquids or gases and that move slower than primary waves

**seismic wave** earthquake wave

**seismograph** instrument that records magnitude of earthquake as moving graph line

**shearing** force that changes shape of rocks but does not affect their volume

**sheeting** formation of joints parallel to ground surface by expansion of rock after removal of overlying material

**slump** downward movement of material caused by slippage of weak rock layer

**soil layer** horizon

**soil profile** cross section of soil horizons that shows different levels

**solfatara** volcanic fissure that emits vapors, steam, and sometimes hot mud, but not lava

**spit** curved sand deposit formed by current turning and slowing into a bay

**stable platform** area surrounding shield covered by relatively undisturbed sedimentary rock

**stack** vertical block of resistant rock cut off from mainland by wave action

**strain** change in dimensions of material due to stress

**stratification** formation into layers or beds

**stress** force applied to material that tends to change its dimensions

**structural mountain** mountain formed from uplift of crust

**subduction** act of one lithospheric block descending under another

**surface wave** earthquake moving on surface of Earth

**survey** detailed description of tract of land

**suspended load** sediment picked up from bed and carried off by water or air

**tension** stretching stress that tends to increase volume of a material

**texture** size, shape, and arrangement of particles that make up a rock

**thrust fault** fault in which hanging wall has moved upward relative to footwall

**topography** physical features of geographical area

**traction** process of carrying material along bottom of a stream

**transform fault** boundary where two plates slide past one another

**tsunami** huge ocean wave caused by underwater earthquake or volcanic eruption

**unconformity** break in continuity of geologic record; nonconformity

**uniformitarianism** concept that present is key to the past

**upheaval** powerful upward movement in Earth's crust

**upthrust** elevation of part of Earth's surface

**valley train** elongated formation of sand and gravel deposited in glacial channel

**vein** narrow water channel in rock or earth

**vent**  volcano opening from which lava erupts

**volcanism**  volcanic activity and phenomena

**water table**  level of water saturation into soil and rock; upper surface of zone of saturation below ground

**weathering**  changes in rock produced by heat, cold, wind, precipitation, and living matter

**zone**  large region of Earth's surface with distinctive characteristics

**zone of aeration**  area above water table where rock openings fill with air between rainstorms

**zone of saturation**  area above impermeable rock layer where all openings are filled with water

## GEOLOGICAL TIME SCALE

*NOTE: Entries for geological eras, periods, and epochs have been listed in chronological order, from the earliest to the most recent.*

**Precambrian era**  3800 million to 600 million years ago; Archeozoic and Proterozoic eras

**Azoic era**  earliest Precambrian era, preceding appearance of life; former term for Archeozoic era

**Archeozoic era**  early Precambrian era, beginning 3800 million years ago; Earth's crust solidifies; blue-green algae and earliest life forms appear

**Proterozoic era**  later Precambrian era, ending 600 million years ago; bacteria, algae, and primitive multicellular life

**Paleozoic era**  600 to 225 million years ago; Cambrian, Ordovician, Silurian, Devonian, Carboniferous, and Permian periods

**Cambrian period**  600 to 500 million years ago; age of marine invertebrates, shellfish, and echinoderms

**Ordovician period**  500 to 425 million years ago; primitive fishes, seaweeds, and fungi

**Silurian period**  425 to 400 million years ago; abundant shellfish; first land plants and modern fungi

**Devonian period**  400 to 345 million years ago; age of fishes; first amphibians, insects, and land animals appear

**Carboniferous period**  345 to 280 million years ago; Mississippian and Pennsylvanian periods

**Mississippian period**  345 to 320 million years ago; age of amphibians; shallow seas, low lands, and fern forests

**Pennsylvanian period**  320 to 280 million years ago; first reptiles; warm climate with swamps and cool forests

**Permian period**  280 to 225 million years ago; conifer forests; extinction of many marine invertebrates

**Mesozoic era**  225 to 65 million years ago; Triassic, Jurassic, and Cretaceous periods

**Triassic period**  225 to 190 million years ago; age of reptiles; active volcanoes

**Jurassic period**  190 to 135 million years ago; age of dinosaurs and flying reptiles; first birds and mammals

**Cretaceous period**  135 to 65 million years ago; last dinosaurs; modern insects; flowering plants

**Cenozoic era**  65 million years ago to present; Tertiary and Quaternary periods

**Tertiary period**  65 to 1.7 million years ago; Paleocene, Eocene, Oligocene, Miocene, and Pliocene epochs

**Paleocene epoch**  65 to 54 million years ago; age of mammals begins; mild to cool climate; first primates

**Eocene epoch**  54 to 38 million years ago; modern birds and mammals; warm climate; giant birds

**Oligocene epoch**  38 to 26 million years ago; browsing mammals and saber-toothed tigers

**Miocene epoch**  26 to 12 million years ago; widespread grasslands; grazing mammals; apes; whales

**Pliocene epoch**  12 to 1.7 million years ago; cool climate; mountain uplift; mammals increase in size and numbers

**Quaternary period**  1.7 million years ago to present; Pleistocene and Holocene epochs

**Pleistocene epoch**  1.7 million to 10,000 years ago; ice ages

**Holocene epoch**  10,000 years ago to present; modern humans

## MINING

**adit**  almost horizontal passageway into mine

**afterdamp**  mixture of gases left in mine after explosion of fire

**airway**  ventilating passage in mine

**assay**  analysis of ore or alloy to determine proportion and purity of components; (*vb*) make such an analysis

**bed**  layer, stratum, or substance in which minerals or ores are lodged

**bench**  working elevation platform in mine

**blackdamp**  chokedamp

**black lung**  disease caused by inhalation of coal dust

**bonanza**  rich vein of ore

**bore**  (*vb*) make mine tunnel by drilling

**borehole**  hole drilled in earth to extract core or release gas, oil, or water

**borrow pit**  excavated area from which material has been removed to fill another spot

**brattice**  air passage in mine formed of planks or cloth lining the tunnel

**breast**  face or heading where work is occurring

**cave-in**  collapse of mine shaft or tunnel

**chokedamp**  mine atmosphere that is low in oxygen, causing choking; blackdamp

**claim**  piece of land staked out by one person who has exclusive rights to mine it

**clinker**  hard mass of stony matter fused in furnace from coal impurities

**coal car**  open railroad car for transporting coal from mine

**coal gas**  gas produced by destructive distillation of bituminous coal

**collar**  topmost rim of vertical shaft in mine

**collier**  coal miner; ship for transporting coal

**colliery**  coal mine and its equipment

**continuous cutter**  machine that takes coal from mine face and loads it onto cars or conveyors

**core**  cylindrical sample of mineral or rock extracted from ground by hollow drill that leaves strata intact

**corf**  small cart for transporting coal or ore

**cradle**  box on rockers for washing sand or gravel to separate gold; rocker

**crosscut**  cut made across vein

**culm**  coal dust

**cupel**  small, shallow, porous cup used in assaying gold and silver

**deposit**  minerals or ores laid down by nature; location where minerals are found

**dig**  excavation

**distillation** purification by heating to separate more volatile parts of mixture, then cooling and condensing vapor to produce more refined substance

**drift** horizontal passageway in mine; gallery

**drill** (*vb*) bore deep hole into earth, esp. seeking oil

**excavation** hole or cavity dug into earth to find minerals

**extraction** removal or separation of mineral from ore

**face** front or end of excavation and location of mined substance

**firedamp** combustible gases in coal mine, esp. methane

**footwall** top of rock stratum beneath vein or bed of ore

**gallery** small tunnel for inspection or drainage; drift

**gangue** worthless mineral matter associated with valuable metallic mineral deposits; matrix

**gangway** primary, level passageway in mine

**gold rush** large, sudden influx of miners to area where large vein of gold has been discovered

**gondola** open railroad car with low sides used for carrying coal

**gusher** high-capacity, flowing oil well

**heading** road or level leading into coal deposit where mining occurs

**horse** mass of rock within lode or vein

**jack-up rig** floating offshore drill rig with retractable legs that lift hull above water level

**jig** device for separating ore by shaking in water

**kerf** deep cut a few inches high, used to undermine coal or mineral seam

**ledge** underground rock layer

**lode** ore deposit; vein; reef

**longwall** continuous face being mined, with roof supported by temporary supports

**matrix** gangue

**mine** large excavation in Earth from which to extract metallic ores, coal, precious stones, or salt

**mine car** small, open, low-sided vehicle for moving within mine, often on rails

**miner** person whose work is digging in a mine; mineworker

**mineworker** miner

**mining** process of removing ores, coal, and precious metals from Earth

**mining engineer** designer and builder of mines

**mother lode** main vein of ore in particular region

**muck** useless materials to be removed in order to get at desired mineral

**offshore drilling** sinking of oil wells into ocean bottom from floating platforms

**oil well** shaft into earth with pump for extracting crude petroleum

**open cut** designating mine in which excavation is performed from the surface

**ore** mineral embedded in the earth

**orebody** well-defined mass of ore-bearing rock

**panning** washing gravel in porous pan when searching for gold

**pay dirt** spot that can be mined successfully

**pillar** isolated mass of rock or ore that serves as roof support in early stages of mining operations

**pinch** (*vb*) diminish a vein to nothing

**pit** man-made cavity in ground for mining

**pithead** mine entrance and adjacent area

**placer** glacial deposit of gravel or sand that contains heavy ore minerals eroded from bedrock and that is concentrated as small particles that can be washed out

**pocket** usu. isolated body of ore in ground

**portal** entrance to mine tunnel

**power shovel** usu. diesel-powered excavating shovel

**prospect** place where mineral deposits are sought; (*vb*) search for ore

**prospector** person searching for valuable ores

**pulp** pulverized ore

**quarry** place where stone is excavated by cutting and blasting

**reef** lode or vein

**refinery** facility for purifying crude oil or raw metal

**riddle** coarse sieve for grading gravel

**riffle** grooved lining at bottom of sluice, used to collect particles of ore

**road** tunnel used for hauling excavated material

**rocker** cradle

**safety lamp** lamp designed so as to avoid ignition of mine gases

**salt** (*vb*) scatter minerals or ores in mine to deceive prospective buyers

**scuttle** deep bucket for carrying coal

**seam** relatively thin stratum or bed

**shaft** long, narrow, vertical or slanting passage sunk into earth

**shoot** small tunnel branching off from larger tunnel

**shortwall** mine with face one-third the length of a longwall, mined by continuous cutter

**slack** fine coal screenings

**sluice** sloping trough or flume through which water is run in washing gold ore

**smelt** (*vb*) melt or fuse ore to separate impurities and extract pure metal

**spoil** waste material from excavation

**stannary** *Chiefly Brit.* tin-mining region

**stope** steplike excavation formed by removal of ore from around shaft

**strike** discovery of rich deposit of ore, coal, or minerals

**strip mining** mining, esp. for coal, by laying bare deposits near surface rather than sinking shaft

**stull** timber prop between walls of stope

**tailings** residue of mining

**tailrace** channel for carrying off tailings

**tipple** apparatus for emptying coal from mine car

**tram** car on rails for conveying loads in mine

**trepan** heavy boring tool for opening shafts or quarrying

**trommel** revolving cylindrical sieve for screening ore

**tunnel** usu. horizontal passageway in mine

**vein** lengthy, regularly shaped bed of useful mineral matter that fills narrow water channel in rock and earth; lode; reef

**vug** cavity in rock or lode, often lined with crystals

**wash** (*vb*) separate ore or stones by passing water through gravel or earth

**well** shaft sunk into earth to tap underground supply of oil, gas, or water

**wellhead** machinery standing above opening of oil or gas well

**wellhole** shaft of oil or gas well

**well log** record of geological formations encountered while drilling a well

**wildcat** oil well drilled in area without known oil deposits

**winze**  inclined shaft that connects levels in mine
**workings**  active portion of mine or quarry

# GEOGRAPHY

Branches and Disciplines
Maps and Cartography
Earth's Atmosphere and Topographic Features
Populations and Resources
Nations of the World
States of the United States
Major World Cities

**SEE ALSO**: Chap. 2: Biology; Chap. 3: Geology; Minerals, Metals, and Rocks; Landscapes and Seascapes; Weather and Natural Phenomena; Chap. 4: Astronomy and Space Science; Chap. 8: Kinship and Family Relations; Chap. 12: Business and Economics; Agriculture; Chap. 13: Sociology

## BRANCHES AND DISCIPLINES

**cartography**  art and practice of making maps and charts
**chorography**  art of mapping and describing a region or district
**cultural geography**  human geography
**demography**  statistical study of distribution, density, and attributes of human populations
**economic geography**  study of how people use Earth's resources and their distribution
**geodesy**  mathematical determining of Earth's shape and location of points on surface
**geographer**  one trained in or practicing geography
**geography**  study of Earth's surface, physical features, climates, resources, products, and people
**geophysics**  study of materials of which Earth is composed
**geoscopy**  observational knowledge of earth and soil
**human geography**  study of people and their ways of life in different parts of Earth; cultural geography
**hydrography**  science of mapping and describing surface waters of Earth, esp. for navigation
**hypsography**  branch of geography involved with measurement and mapping of Earth's topography above sea level
**hypsometry**  measurement of elevations or altitudes
**meteorology**  study of Earth's atmosphere, climate, and weather
**orography**  branch of physical geography dealing with mountains
**physical geography**  study of nature and history of Earth's surface and atmosphere; physiography
**physiography**  physical geography
**soil science**  applied study of soils
**topography**  science of drawing maps and representing natural surface and man-made features of region

## MAPS AND CARTOGRAPHY

**aclinic line**  magnetic equator
**acre**  unit of area measure equal to 43,560 square feet (4047 square meters)
**Africa**  second largest continent, divided between Northern and Southern hemispheres, between Asia and South America, south of Europe, extending from Atlantic to Indian Ocean
**altitude**  height above sea level; elevation
**angle of declination**  angle between direction indicated by magnetic needle and true meridian
**angle of depression**  angle that descending line makes with horizon
**angle of elevation**  angle that ascending line makes with horizon
**Antarctica**  land area surrounding South Pole, forming fifth largest continent
**Antarctic Circle**  parallel of latitude 66 1/2 degrees south of equator, which is in perpetual daylight in midsummer
**Arctic**  land area surrounding North Pole
**Arctic Circle**  parallel of latitude 66 1/2 degrees north of equator, which is in perpetual daylight in midsummer
**arrow symbols**  map signs indicating motion and direction
**Asia**  world's largest continent, extending from Arctic to Singapore and from Bering Strait to Ural Mountains
**atlas**  bound maps showing different parts of world
**Australia**  island continent, smallest of seven continents, in Southern Hemisphere, between Africa and South America, extending from Indian to Pacific Ocean
**axis**  imaginary line through Earth's center from North to South Pole around which Earth rotates
**azimuth**  angular measurement clockwise around horizon from north or south to location of object or intersection of object's vertical circle with horizon
**azimuthal equidistant projection**  map projection in which great circles projected through a central point provide shortest distance from center to any point; zenithal equidistant projection
**bipolar** (*adj*) involving both North and South poles
**border**  dividing line between countries or other geographical units
**cardinal points**  four principal points of compass: north, south, east, and west
**cartogram**  type of map in which size of nations is based on something other than area
**celestial equator**  great circle of celestial sphere projected from plane of equator
**celestial globe**  sphere on which is depicted map of the heavens
**celestial horizon**  great circle on celestial sphere midway between zenith and nadir
**chart**  outline map, such as weather or resource map, with special information plotted geographically
**chorograph**  map or description of particular region
**circumpolar** (*adj*) surrounding or near either pole
**coastline**  point at which land meets ocean or sea
**compass**  directional device with magnetic needle pivoting freely and pointing north
**conformal** (*adj*) designating map or projection in which scale and angles are preserved

**conic projection** map in which Earth's surface is projected on conical surface which is unrolled to make plane surface

**continent** one of seven major landmasses of Earth

**Continental Divide** Rocky Mountain ridge forming North American watershed that separates rivers flowing east and west; Great Divide

**contour interval** vertical distance between contour lines on topographic map

**contour line** line on map that connects all points at same elevation or same ocean depth

**coordinates** location finders on map, marked by letters or numbers arranged horizontally and vertically along edges

**country** bounded territory of sovereign nation or state

**cylindrical projection** map projection of celestial sphere on cylinder that is then unrolled as plane

**degree** unit of measurement for latitude and longitude

**distortion** inaccuracies in size and shape of landmasses and oceans on flat map projections

**Earth** terrestrial globe on which all people live

**Eastern Hemisphere** half of Earth's surface, lying east of prime meridian

**elevation** altitude

**equal-area projection** map in which regions of Earth's surface that are of equal size are shown as equal in size

**equator** line of latitude halfway between North and South poles at zero degrees

**Eurasia** landmass made up of continents of Europe and Asia

**Europe** sixth and smallest continent except Australia, extending from Atlantic Ocean to Ural Mountains

**gazetteer** geographical dictionary that lists places in alphabetical order

**geopolitical map** map showing nonphysical as well as physical features

**globe** spherical model of Earth showing physical features

**graticule** network of parallels and meridians used as grid on map

**great circle** imaginary circle on Earth's surface formed by plane passing through its center, dividing Earth into two hemispheres; pair of opposing meridians

**Great Divide** watershed ridge forming continental divide, esp. Rocky Mountains of North America; Continental Divide

**Greenwich** English city through which prime meridian runs at zero degrees longitude

**grid** intersections of parallels of latitude and meridians of longitude around globe

**hachure** one of a series of short parallel lines used on map to represent sloping or elevated surface

**hemisphere** half of Earth, divided into northern and southern by equator, eastern and western by Atlantic and Pacific oceans

**high latitudes** areas more than sixty degrees north or south of equator

**homolosine projection** equal-area map projection in which ocean areas are distorted to reduce distortion of continents

**International Date Line** line based on 180-degree meridian that separates one calendar day from another, with west of line twenty-four hours later than east of it

**interrupted projection** map projection that breaks up oceans for accurate presentation and reduced distortion of continents

**isobar** map line that joins places having equal atmospheric pressure over or at a given time

**isobath** map line that joins places on seabed having equal depth below surface

**isoclinic line** map line that joins points at which magnetic needle has same inclination to plumb line

**isogloss** boundary on map between places with differing linguistic features or dialects

**isogonic line** map line that joins points at which magnetic declination is equal

**isogram** map line along which there is some constant value, such as that for temperature, pressure, or rainfall

**isohel** map line that joins points with equal duration of sunshine

**isohyet** map line that joins places having equal rainfall over a given period

**isometric line** map line that indicates true constant value for its extent

**isopach** isogram line that connects points of equal thickness of geological stratum formation

**isopleth** map line that connects points at which a given variable has specified constant value

**isotherm** map line that joins places having same temperature

**key** list of map's symbols and their meanings; legend

**latitude** north/south position of place, measured in degrees from zero to ninety in reference to equator by an imaginary arc passing through both poles

**legend** key

**longitude** east/west position of place, measured in degrees from zero to 180 along equator in reference to prime meridian

**low latitudes** areas less than thirty degrees north or south of equator

**loxodromic** (adj) noting or pertaining to a map projection in which rhumb lines appear straight

**magnetic equator** imaginary line around Earth near equator where lines of force of Earth's magnetic field are parallel with Earth's surface; aclinic line

**map** representation, usu. on flat surface, of physical characteristics of whole or part of some area

**Melanesia** portion of Oceania including Pacific Ocean islands south of equator

**Mercator projection** conformal map projection that shows meridians of longitude as parallel lines, thus distorting shapes of areas near poles

**meridian** line of longitude; imaginary line approximating semicircle around Earth through both poles at right angles to equator

**Micronesia** portion of Oceania including Pacific Ocean islands north of equator

**midlatitudes** areas between thirty and sixty degrees north and south of equator

**minute** one-sixtieth of one degree of latitude or longitude

**Mollweide projection** equal-area projection of Earth's surface as ellipse, with all parallels as straight lines more widely spaced at equator than at poles and all meridians equally spaced with central meridian half the length of equator

**nadir** point on celestial sphere opposite zenith and directly below observer

**North America** third largest continent, extending from Atlantic to Pacific oceans and from Arctic to Panama

**Northern Hemisphere**  half of Earth's surface, lying north of equator

**North Pole**  ninety degrees north latitude; point at northern end of Earth's axis

**Oceania**  Pacific Ocean islands

**parallel**  line of latitude; imaginary line on map or globe parallel to equator, connecting places on same latitude

**physical feature**  land or water form on Earth's surface, esp. as depicted on map

**polar projection**  map centered on one of poles

**poles**  two points at northern and southern ends of Earth's axis; North Pole and South Pole

**political feature**  national boundary or other feature showing how humans have divided Earth's surface

**polyconic projection**  map projection in which the parallels are arcs of circles equally spaced along a central straight meridian and the other meridians are curves equally spaced along the parallels

**Polynesia**  eastern portion of Oceania including Hawaiian Islands

**prime meridian**  line of longitude at zero degrees from which other longitudes are measured, running through Greenwich, England

**projection**  one of various ways in which Earth's curved surface is represented two-dimensionally: azimuthal equidistant, conformal, conic, cylindrical, equal-area, homolosine, interrupted, loxodromic, Mercator, Mollweide, polar, polyconic, sinusoidal, and zenithal equidistant

**relief**  elevation differences in land

**relief map**  map showing contour variations of land surface

**rhumb line**  curve on Earth's surface that cuts all meridians at same angle, such as constant compass direction course

**scale**  proportion between actual size of place and its representation on map

**sea level**  mean level of sea surface between high and low tides, used as standard for measuring elevations and ocean depths

**second**  one-sixtieth of one minute of one degree of latitude or longitude

**sinusoidal projection**  equal-area map projection with evenly spaced, straight-line parallels, a straight-line central meridian one-half the length of equator, and other meridians shown as curves symmetrical to central meridian

**South America**  fourth largest continent, largely in Southern Hemisphere, lying between Atlantic and Pacific oceans south of Panama

**Southern Hemisphere**  half of Earth's surface, lying south of equator

**South Pole**  ninety degrees south latitude; point at southern end of Earth's axis

**special-purpose map**  map showing neither physical nor political features but features such as population, vegetation, or climate

**state**  geographical and political division of nation

**strip map**  narrow map showing immediate area to be covered

**subantarctic** (*adj*)  bordering on the Antarctic

**subarctic** (*adj*)  bordering on the Arctic

**subcontinent**  major division of continent, often set off geographically

**subtropical** (*adj*)  bordering on the tropics

**surveying**  determining location, form, and boundaries of tract of land through application of geometry and trigonometry

**time zone**  one of twenty-four longitudinal divisions of one hour each that divide Earth

**topographic map**  detailed, large-scale map that shows physical and cultural features of one area

**transcontinental** (*adj*)  reaching from one edge of a continent to the other

**transoceanic** (*adj*)  reaching from one coast of an ocean to the other

**triangulation**  process of determining distance between points on Earth's surface by use of series of connected triangles and angles made by lines to points

**tropic of Cancer**  parallel at 23 1/2 degrees north

**tropic of Capricorn**  parallel at 23 1/2 degrees south

**tropics**  area of Earth closest the equator, between tropic of Cancer and tropic of Capricorn

**Western Hemisphere**  half of Earth's surface, lying west of prime meridian

**zenith**  point directly overhead on celestial sphere

**zenithal equidistant projection**  azimuthal equidistant projection

## EARTH'S ATMOSPHERE AND TOPOGRAPHIC FEATURES

**ab-polar current**  air current moving from either pole toward equator

**abyssal** (*adj*)  pertaining to dark, cold, lifeless ocean depths

**acclivity**  upward slope of ground

**aggrade** (*vb*)  raise level of valley or riverbed by deposit of sediment and detritus

**alluvial fan**  fan-shaped deposit of detrital material at place where swiftly flowing water enters plain or open valley

**alluvial plain**  plain formed by deposits of detrital material

**anthropomorphic soil**  soil altered from surrounding environment by human activity

**area**  amount of surface covered by a physical feature or region

**atmosphere**  air forming gaseous envelope that surrounds Earth, consisting of troposphere, stratosphere, mesosphere, thermosphere, ionosphere, and exosphere, which merges into outer space at altitude of several hundred miles

**badlands**  arid area cut by large number of deep gullies and nearly bare of vegetation

**catchment area**  area draining into river or reservoir

**chernozem**  fertile soil, rich in humus, found in temperate zones

**climate**  all weather conditions typical of a specific region

**climatic graph**  combined bar and line graph showing precipitation and average temperature for each month at specific place

**coast**  area where landmass meets body of water

**coniferous forests**  forests comprised of evergreen cone-bearing trees, growing across northern North America and Eurasia

**continental margin**  continent's edge

**continental shelf**  relatively flat seabed lying beneath shallow waters bordering continents

**continental slope** sharp descent between continental shelf and ocean basin

**cordillera** mountain system consisting of several parallel ranges

**Coriolis effect** change in path of object or fluid moving above Earth's surface due to Earth's rotation

**deciduous forests** forests with trees that lose their leaves at some point during year, found primarily in midlatitudes

**declivity** downward slope of ground

**deep zone** cold ocean water below thermocline

**deserts** extremely dry regions with little or no vegetation

**diastrophism** process that causes movement and reshaping of Earth's surface

**doldrums** low-pressure region near equator

**echo sounding** determination of water depth by measuring time required for sound wave to be reflected from bottom

**equinox** date in spring and fall on which day and night are of equal length

**estuary** river basin affected by ocean tides, having mixture of fresh and salt water

**exosphere** outermost portion of Earth's atmosphere, with air density so low that an air molecule is more likely to escape atmosphere than hit other molecules, beginning at altitude of 300 miles (483 km), forming outer portion of ionosphere

**fall line** line indicating edge of plateau, marked by waterfalls and rapids

**flood plain** low-lying area subject to flooding by river

**horizon** point in distance where sky seems to meet curve of Earth; soil layer

**horse latitudes** areas of high pressure over oceans between trade winds and westerlies

**hypolimnion** cold layer of water below thermocline in some lakes

**interfluve** land area separating adjacent stream valleys

**ionosphere** region of Earth's atmosphere beyond mesosphere, containing ionized layers of thermosphere and exosphere, extending outward from 50 miles (80 km) altitude

**island** landmass smaller than a continent, surrounded by water

**land** solid part of Earth's surface, not covered by water

**landmass** very large area of land, esp. a continent

**landscape** tract or characteristic aspect of Earth's surface, esp. as viewed extensively from one point

**littoral** (*adj*) designating intertidal zone along shore, below high-water mark and above low-water mark

**mainland** principal landmass of continent or country as distinguished from island or peninsula

**maritime** (*adj*) proximate to and influenced by sea or ocean

**massif** mountain mass of uniform height broken into individual peaks

**mesopause** boundary of transition between mesosphere and ionosphere, around 50 miles (80 km) altitude

**mesosphere** coldest layer of Earth's atmosphere, from 30 to 50 miles (48 to 80 km) altitude

**neritic zone** ocean life zone from low tide line to end of continental shelf

**oasis** fertile place with water in middle of desert

**ocean** great body of water covering almost three-fourths of Earth's surface; one of its four geographic divisions: Atlantic, Pacific, Indian, Arctic

**ocean basin** vast, deep hollow in Earth's surface filled by ocean waters

**ooze** liquid mud, largely of plankton remains, covering deep-sea plains

**ozone hole** any part of ozone layer that has become depleted by atmospheric pollution, permitting excess ultraviolet radiation to pass through and warm the atmosphere

**ozone layer** type of oxygen concentrated in stratosphere that blocks much of sun's ultraviolet radiation

**peneplain** land surface worn nearly flat

**peninsula** narrow land area almost completely surrounded by water except at point where it connects to mainland

**permafrost** permanently frozen ground underlying surface soil

**planetary winds** polars, westerlies, and trade winds; major winds on Earth's surface

**polar winds** very cold winds blowing from high pressure areas around poles

**pollutant** harmful substance in atmosphere

**pollution** contamination of environment with waste

**radial stream pattern** flowing of streams from central source

**rain forest** tropical rain forest

**range** system of connected mountains

**revolution** circling of Earth around sun

**ridge** long, narrow crest of elevated portion of Earth's crust

**rift valley** depression formed by land subsiding between parallel faults

**rotation** spinning of Earth on its axis

**runoff** water flowing over Earth's surface after rainfall or spring thaw

**salinity** amount of dissolved salts in body of water

**sea** large body of salt water, mainly enclosed by land and usu. connected to ocean

**snow line** line along mountain slope that represents lower limit of permanent snow

**soil layer** distinctive layer in a vertical cross section of soil

**solstice** one of two days each year when period of daylight reaches limit; longest or shortest day of year, June 21 or December 21

**stratopause** boundary of transition between stratosphere and mesosphere, around 30 miles (48 km) altitude

**stratosphere** layer of atmosphere from tropopause to inner edge of mesosphere, characterized by little change in temperature with increased altitude, extending from 10 to 30 miles (16 to 48 km) above Earth's surface

**subcontinent** landmass almost as big as a continent; India or Greenland

**taiga** extensive, subarctic coniferous forest beginning south of the tundra

**temperate** (*adj*) without temperature extremes

**temperate zone** midlatitudes between equator and poles

**thermocline** zone in body of water exhibiting rapid temperature decrease with increasing depth

**thermosphere** layer of upper atmosphere above mesosphere with very thin air and temperature that increases continuously with altitude, extending from 50 to 300 miles (80 to 483 km) above Earth's surface; inner portion of ionosphere

**tideland** land at seashore alternately exposed and covered by normal ebb and flow of tide

**timberline**  boundary marking highest altitude for natural growth of trees

**topsoil**  fertile soil, largely humus, in top horizon layer

**trade winds**  winds blowing from high pressure subtropics toward low pressure at equator

**tributary**  branch stream feeding main river

**tropical grassland**  area between tropical rain forest and desert

**tropical rain forest**  dense evergreen forest of equatorial regions; rain forest

**tropopause**  boundary of transition between troposphere and stratosphere, around 10 miles (16 km) altitude

**troposphere**  layer of atmosphere nearest Earth's surface, extending to altitude of 6 miles (10 km) over poles and 10 miles (16 km) over equator

**tundra**  vast, cold, nearly treeless region north of coniferous forests with permanently frozen subsoil

**Van Allen radiation belt**  doughnut-shaped region of high-energy particles trapped in Earth's magnetic field, extending from 2000 to 12,000 miles (3218 to 19,312 km) altitude

**wadi**  watercourse in arid region that contains water only after heavy rainfall

**watershed**  ridge separating runoff to two different river basins

**westerlies**  winds blowing from subtropical high pressure toward low-pressure midlatitudes

**wind erosion**  removal of powdery topsoil by wind, esp. in areas of prolonged heavy cultivation

**woodland**  forested region of Earth

## POPULATIONS AND RESOURCES

**aborigine**  original inhabitant of area or region

**avulsion**  separation of one's land by flooding or change in course of stream that cuts off part of property

**bioclimatic** (*adj*) relating to effect of climate on living things

**birthrate**  number of births per year per thousand of population for given region or population

**caste**  one of social groups into which population is divided, esp. among Hindus

**census**  official population count, often accompanied by collection of demographic information

**civilization**  organized society with developing art and technology

**clan**  group of families, often with common ancestor, who live and work together

**conservation**  actions taken to protect, preserve, or replenish natural resources

**conurbation**  group of towns or cities extended to form continuous urban area

**cultivation**  plowing of earth and planting of crops

**cultural region**  geographic area in which most people have common language and customs distinct from other peoples

**diversify** (*vb*) create and maintain variety of economic forms in one culture

**drainage system**  designation for region from which and means by which water flows off

**dynasty**  series of rulers over generations from single family line

**endangered species**  species of animal or plant in danger of becoming extinct

**environment**  surroundings as they affect living things

**ethnic group**  large group of people with shared heritage and more in common with each other than with other peoples

**extended family**  household or family unit including more than two generations and more than nuclear family

**extinct** (*adj*) no longer living

**extinction**  fact of being a species no longer living on Earth or no longer capable of regenerating

**fallow** (*adj*) designating cultivated land left unsown for one season or more

**fossil fuel**  fuel derived from organic material lying underground for millions of years

**greenbelt**  area surrounding city reserved for parks or farms

**heartland**  central or most important area of nation, esp. agricultural region

**homeland**  region or nation of one's birth

**homogeneous population**  people of one ethnic or cultural group

**hydroelectric power**  power of falling water used to generate electricity

**illiteracy**  inability to read and write

**immigration**  movement of peoples from one area to another

**independent nation**  self-governing, economically self-sufficient state

**indigenous** (*adj*) native to some place

**infant mortality**  percentage of children who die shortly after birth

**irrigation**  process of bringing water for cultivation to area with insufficient rain

**landlocked** (*adj*) having no border on or outlet to the sea

**land reclamation**  process of making land suitable for cultivation or other use, esp. through irrigation

**life expectancy**  statistical estimate of the number of years an individual is expected to live, based on such criteria as sex, race, health, and occupation

**malnutrition**  chronic, pervasive lack of proper food

**mestizo**  person of mixed Latin American Indian and Spanish descent

**metropolitan area**  urban center and its suburbs

**migration**  movement of peoples from their homeland

**minority people**  people belonging to a different ethnic group than most of nation's population

**mulatto**  person of mixed European and African descent

**nation**  group of people sharing a political system, culture, and territory

**natural harbor**  coastal area where land protects ships from open sea

**natural resource**  material found on or in Earth and used by people

**natural vegetation**  indigenous plant life

**nomads**  people who move from place to place as a way of life, with no permanent home

**nonrenewable resource**  useful and irreplaceable material coming from Earth's crust

**people**  collection of persons belonging to certain region or ethnic group

**plantation**  large farm specializing in one crop with many workers, often slaves

**polder** area reclaimed from sea or lake and protected from flooding by dikes

**polygamy** simultaneous marriage to more than one spouse

**population** total number of people in country or region; specific part of people in given region

**population profile** bar graph showing proportion of different age groups in total population

**raw materials** substances occurring in nature and used to manufacture goods

**reforestation** planting of new forests, esp. in areas where trees have been cut down or burned

**renewable resource** material that can be replaced by nature

**resource** any useful element of environment

**self-sufficiency** ability to produce all resources required to meet one's own needs

**solar energy** energy from sun used as fuel

**subsistence farming** raising just enough crops to feed one's own family

**sudd** floating mass of vegetable matter on White Nile River

**territory** large tract of land under jurisdiction of nation or government

**Third World** developing nations not allied with superpowers, primarily in Southern Hemisphere

**threatened species** a species likely to become an endangered species in the near future, within all or much of its range

**tree chart** chart showing people or things branching out from common source

**vegetation** plant life on Earth

**zero population growth** condition in which birthrate equals death rate and population remains constant

## NATIONS OF THE WORLD

NOTE: *The listings for Nations of the World provide the following information: country name — former name where appropriate; official name; location; capital; area in square miles; population; major language or languages; primary religion or religions; currency. The listings for States of the United States provide the following information: state name — postal code; order of admission, date admitted; location; capital; rank among states in area, population; nickname.*

**Afghanistan** Republic of; in central W Asia; capital Kabul; area 250,000 sq. mi., pop. 15,592,000; Pashtu; Sunni Muslim; afghani

**Albania** Republic of; in SE Europe; capital Tirana; area 11,100 sq. mi., pop. 3,268,000; Albanian; Muslim; lek

**Algeria** Democratic and Popular Republic of; in N Africa; capital Algiers; area 919,590 sq. mi., pop. 25,714,000; Arabic; Sunni Muslim; dinar

**Andorra** Republic of; in SW Europe; capital Andorra la Vella; area 191 sq. mi., pop. 51,000; Catalan; Catholic; franc and peseta

**Angola** People's Republic of; in W Africa; capital Luanda; area 481,352 sq. mi., pop. 8,802,000; Portuguese and Bantu; Catholic; kwanza

**Antigua and Barbuda** group of islands in Caribbean Sea; capital St. John's; area 170 sq. mi., pop. 64,000; English; Anglican; dollar

**Argentina** Republic of; in S South America; capital Buenos Aires; area 1,068,000 sq. mi., pop. 32,291,000; Spanish; Catholic; peso

**Australia** Commonwealth of; in S Pacific; capital Canberra; area 2,967,909 sq. mi., pop. 16,646,000; English; Christian; dollar

**Austria** Republic of; in central Europe; capital Vienna; area 32,375 sq. mi., pop. 7,595,000; German; Catholic; schilling

**Bahamas** Commonwealth of the; group of islands in W Atlantic; capital Nassau; area 5,380 sq. mi., pop. 251,000; English; Christian; dollar

**Bahrain** State of; in Persian Gulf; capital Manama; area 250 sq. mi., pop. 512,000; Arabic; Shi'a Muslim; dinar

**Bangladesh** People's Republic of; in S Asia; capital Dhaka; area 55,126 sq. mi., pop. 117,976,000; Bengali; Muslim; taka

**Barbados** island in West Indies; capital Bridgetown; area 166 sq. mi., pop. 260,000; English; Anglican; dollar

**Basutoland** Lesotho

**Bechuanaland** Botswana

**Belgium** Kingdom of; in W Europe; capital Brussels; area 11,781 sq. mi., pop. 9,895,000; Flemish and French; Catholic; franc

**Belize** formerly British Honduras; in Central America; capital Belmopan; area 8,866 sq. mi., pop. 180,400; English and Spanish; Catholic; dollar

**Benin** formerly Dahomey; Republic of; in W Africa; capital Porto-Novo; area 43,483 sq. mi., pop. 4,840,000; French and Fon; indigenous religions; franc

**Bermuda** Dependency of; British colony, island in W Atlantic; capital Hamilton; area 20 sq. mi., pop. 58,800; English; Christian; dollar

**Bhutan** Kingdom of; in E Asia; capital Thimbu; area 18,147 sq. mi., pop. 1,566,000; Dzongkha and Nepalese; Lamaistic Buddhist; ngultrum

**Bolivia** Republic of; in W central South America; capital Sucre and LaPaz; area 424,163 sq. mi., pop. 6,730,000; Spanish; Catholic; boliviano

**Bosnia and Herzegovina** formerly part of Yugoslavia; in SE Europe; capital Sarajevo; area 19,741 sq. mi., pop. 4,440,000; Serbian; Eastern Orthodox, Catholic and Muslim; dinar

**Botswana** formerly Bechuanaland; Republic of; in S Africa; capital Gaborone; area 231,804 sq. mi., pop. 1,218,000; English and Setswana; Christian and indigenous religions; pula

**Brazil** Federative Republic of; in E South America; capital Brasília; area 3,286,478 sq. mi., pop. 153,771,000; Portuguese; Catholic; cruzeiro

**British Honduras** Belize

**Brunei** Brunei Darussalam; in SE Asia; capital Bandar Seri Begawan; area 2,226 sq. mi., pop. 372,000; Malay; Muslim; dollar

**Bulgaria** Republic of; in SE Europe; capital Sofia; area 44,365 sq. mi., pop. 8,978,000; Bulgarian; Bulgarian Orthodox; lev

**Burkina Faso** formerly Upper Volta; in W Africa; capital Ouagadougou; area 105,870 sq. mi., pop. 8,941,000; French; indigenous religions; franc

**Burma** Myanmar

**Burundi** Republic of; in E central Africa; capital Bujumbura; area 10,747 sq. mi., pop. 5,647,000; Kirundi and French; Catholic; franc

**Cambodia** formerly Kampuchea; State of; in SE Asia; capital Phnom Penh; area 69,898 sq. mi., pop. 6,993,000; Khmer and French; Buddhist; riel

**Cameroon** Republic of; in W Africa; capital Yaoundé; area 185,569 sq. mi., pop. 11,109,000; French and English; indigenous religions and Christian; franc

**Canada** confederation in N North America; capital Ottawa; area 3,558,096 sq. mi., pop. 26,527,000; English and French; Catholic and Protestant; dollar; provinces: Alberta, British Columbia, Manitoba, New Brunswick, Newfoundland, Nova Scotia, Ontario, Prince Edward Island, Quebec, Saskatchewan; territories: Northwest Territories, Yukon

**Cape Verde** Republic of; group of islands in E Atlantic; capital Praia; area 1,557 sq. mi., pop. 375,000; Portuguese; Catholic; escudo

**Central African Republic** in central Africa; capital Bangui; area 240,535 sq. mi., pop. 2,879,000; French; indigenous religions and Christian; franc

**Ceylon** Sri Lanka

**Chad** Republic of; in N central Africa; capital N'djamena; area 495,754 sq. mi., pop. 5,064,000; French and Arabic; Muslim and indigenous religions; franc

**Chile** Republic of; in SW South America; capital Santiago; area 292,250 sq. mi., pop. 13,000,000; Spanish; Catholic; peso

**China** People's Republic of; in E Asia; capital Beijing; area 3,705,000 sq. mi., pop. 1,130,065,000; Mandarin; Taoist and Confucian traditions but officially atheist; yuan

**Colombia** Republic of; in NW South America; capital Bogotá; area 439,700 sq. mi., pop. 32,598,000; Spanish; Catholic; peso

**Commonwealth of Independent States** formerly part of the Union of Soviet Socialist Republics; in E Europe and N Asia; capital Minsk; area 8,555,000 sq. mi., pop. 273,-307,000; Russian, Ukrainian, and other indigenous languages; Russian Orthodox, Muslim, and others; ruble; republics: Armenia, Azerbaijan, Belarus, Kazakhstan, Kyrgyzstan, Moldova, Russia, Tajikistan, Turkmenistan, Ukraine, Uzbekistan

**Comoros** Republic of; group of islands in S Indian Ocean; capital Moroni; area 838 sq. mi., pop. 459,000; Comoran, French and Arabic; Sunni Muslim; franc

**Congo** People's Republic of; in W central Africa; capital Brazzaville; area 132,046 sq. mi., pop. 2,305,000; French; Christian and animist; franc

**Costa Rica** Republic of; in S Central America; capital San José; area 19,575 sq. mi., pop. 3,032,000; Spanish; Catholic; colon

**Côte d'Ivoire** Ivory Coast

**Croatia** formerly part of Yugoslavia; in SE Europe; capital Zagreb; area 21,829 sq. mi., pop. 4,680,000; Croatian; Catholic; dinar

**Cuba** Republic of; island in Caribbean Sea; capital Havana; area 44,218 sq. mi., pop. 10,582,000; Spanish; Catholic; peso

**Cyprus** Republic of; island in E Mediterranean Sea; capital Nicosia; area 3,572 sq. mi., pop. 708,000; Greek and Turkish; Greek Orthodox and Muslim; pound

**Czechoslovakia** Czech and Slovak Federative Republic; in central Europe; capital Prague; area 49,365 sq. mi., pop. 15,695,000; Czech and Slovak; Catholic; koruna

**Dahomey** Benin

**Denmark** Kingdom of; in N Europe; capital Copenhagen; area 16,629 sq. mi., pop. 5,134,000; Danish; Lutheran; krone

**Djibouti** Republic of; in E Africa; capital Djibouti; area 8,490 sq. mi., pop. 337,000; French and Arabic; Muslim; franc

**Dominica** Commonwealth of; island in West Indies; capital Roseau; area 290 sq. mi., pop. 85,000; English; Catholic; dollar

**Dominican Republic** part of an island in West Indies; capital Santo Domingo; area 18,703 sq. mi., pop. 7,253,000; Spanish; Catholic; peso

**East Germany** former German Democratic Republic, since 1990 part of united Germany

**Ecuador** Republic of; in NW South America; capital Quito; area 109,483 sq. mi., pop. 10,506,000; Spanish; Catholic; sucre

**Egypt** Arab Republic of; in NE Africa; capital Cairo; area 386,660 sq. mi., pop. 54,139,000; Arabic; Sunni Muslim; pound

**El Salvador** Republic of; in Central America; capital San Salvador; area 8,260 sq. mi., pop. 5,221,000; Spanish; Catholic; colon

**England** largest division of United Kingdom, part of Great Britain with Scotland and Wales

**Equatorial Guinea** Republic of; in W Africa; capital Malabo; area 10,831 sq. mi., pop. 360,000; Spanish; Christian and indigenous religions; franc

**Estonia** formerly part of the Union of Soviet Socialist Republics; Republic of; in N Europe; capital Tallinn; area 17,413 sq. mi., pop. 1,573,000; Estonian and Russian; Lutheran; ruble

**Ethiopia** People's Democratic Republic of; in E Africa; capital Addis Ababa; area 471,777 sq. mi., pop. 51,375,-000; Amharic; Muslim and Ethiopian Orthodox; birr

**Faeroe Islands** Danish island province in the N Atlantic; capital Torshavn; area 541 sq. mi., pop. 46,000; Faeroese and Danish; Lutheran; krona

**Fiji** Republic of; group of islands in SW Pacific Ocean; capital Suva; area 7,053 sq. mi., pop. 772,000; English and Fijian; Christian and Hindu; dollar

**Finland** Republic of; in N Europe; capital Helsinki; area 130,120 sq. mi., pop. 4,977,000; Finnish; Lutheran; markka

**France** French Republic; in W Europe; capital Paris; area 220,668 sq. mi., pop. 56,184,000; French; Catholic; franc

**French Polynesia** Territory of; French island territory in S Pacific; capital Papeete; area 1,544 sq. mi., pop. 185,000; Polynesian and French; Christian; franc

**Gabon** Gabonese Republic; in W Africa; capital Libreville; area 103,346 sq. mi., pop. 1,069,000; French and Fang; Christian; franc

**Gambia** Republic of the; in W Africa; capital Banjul; area 4,361 sq. mi., pop. 820,000; English and Mandinka; Muslim; dalasi

**Georgia** formerly part of the Union of Soviet Socialist Republics; Georgian Republic; in SE Europe and SW Asia; capital Tbilisi; area 26,872 sq. mi., pop. 5,449,000; Georgian; Georgian Orthodox; ruble

**Germany** formerly East Germany and West Germany; Federal Republic of; in central Europe; capital Berlin; area 137,616 sq. mi., pop. 77,555,000; German; Protestant and Catholic; mark

**Ghana** Republic of; in W Africa; capital Accra; area 92,099 sq. mi., pop. 15,310,000; English and Akan; Christian, Muslim and indigenous religions; cedi

**Gilbert Island** Kiribati

**Great Britain** England, Scotland, and Wales, three divisions within United Kingdom

**Greece** Hellenic Republic; in SE Europe; capital Athens; area 51,146 sq. mi., pop. 10,066,000; Greek; Greek Orthodox; drachma

**Greenland** Kalaallit Nunaat; semiautonomous colony of Denmark in NW Atlantic; capital Nuuk; area 840,000 sq. mi., pop. 55,415; Greenlandic and Danish; Lutheran; krone

**Grenada** group of islands in SE Caribbean Sea; capital St. George's; area 131 sq. mi., pop. 84,000; English; Catholic; dollar

**Guatemala** Republic of; in Central America; capital Guatemala City; area 42,042 sq. mi., pop. 9,340,000; Spanish; Catholic; quetzal

**Guinea** Republic of; in W Africa; capital Conakry; area 94,964 sq. mi., pop. 7,269,000; French; Muslim; franc

**Guinea-Bissau** Republic of; in W Africa; capital Bissau; area 13,948 sq. mi., pop. 998,000; Portuguese; Muslim and indigenous religions; peso

**Guyana** Co-operative Republic of; in NE South America; capital Georgetown; area 83,000 sq. mi., pop. 765,000; English; Christian and Hindu; dollar

**Haiti** Republic of; part of an island in Caribbean Sea; capital Port-au-Prince; area 10,714 sq. mi., pop. 6,409,000; French; Catholic; gourde

**Honduras** Republic of; in Central America; capital Tegucigalpa; area 43,277 sq. mi., pop. 5,261,000; Spanish; Catholic; lempira

**Hong Kong** Dependency of; British crown colony in E Asia on South China Sea; capital Victoria; area 402 sq. mi., pop. 5,700,000; Cantonese; Taoist, Confucian, and Christian; dollar

**Hungary** Republic of; in central Europe; capital Budapest; area 35,919 sq. mi., pop. 10,546,000; Hungarian; Catholic; forint

**Iceland** Republic of; group of islands in N Atlantic; capital Reykjavik; area 39,768 sq. mi., pop. 251,000; Icelandic; Lutheran; krona

**India** Republic of; in S Asia; capital New Delhi; area 1,266,598 sq. mi., pop. 850,067,000; Hindi and English; Hindu and Muslim; rupee

**Indonesia** Republic of; in SE Asia; capital Jakarta; area 735,269 sq. mi., pop. 191,266,000; Indonesian; Muslim; rupiah

**Iran** Islamic Republic of; on Persian Gulf in Middle East; capital Teheran; area 636,294 sq. mi., pop. 55,647,000; Farsi; Shi'a Muslim; rial

**Iraq** Republic of; in Middle East; capital Baghdad; area 167,923 sq. mi., pop. 18,782,000; Arabic; Muslim; dinar

**Ireland** Republic of; part of an island in NW Europe; capital Dublin; area 27,136 sq. mi., pop. 3,557,000; English and Irish; Catholic; pound

**Israel** State of; in Middle East; capital Jerusalem; area 8,019 sq. mi., pop. 4,371,000; Hebrew; Jewish; shekel

**Italy** Italian Republic; in S Europe; capital Rome; area 116,303 sq. mi., pop. 57,657,000; Italian; Catholic; lira

**Ivory Coast** Republic of; Côte d'Ivoire; in W Africa; capital Abidjan; area 124,503 sq. mi., pop. 12,070,000; French; Christian, Muslim and indigenous religions; franc

**Jamaica** island in Caribbean Sea; capital Kingston; area 4,243 sq. mi., pop. 2,513,000; English; Protestant; dollar

**Japan** Nippon; in E Asia; capital Tokyo; area 145,882 sq. mi., pop. 123,778,000; Japanese; Shinto and Buddhist; yen

**Jordan** Hashemite Kingdom of; in Middle East; capital Amman; area 37,738 sq. mi., pop. 3,065,000; Arabic; Sunni Muslim; dinar

**Kalaallit Nunaat** Greenland

**Kampuchea** Cambodia

**Kenya** Republic of; in E Africa; capital Nairobi; area 224,-960 sq. mi., pop. 25,393,000; English and Swahili; Christian; shilling

**Kiribati** formerly Gilbert Islands; Republic of; group of islands in S Pacific; capital Tarawa; area 277 sq. mi., pop. 65,000; English and Gilbertese; Christian; dollar

**Korea, North** Democratic People's Republic of Korea; in NE Asia; capital Pyong Yang; area 46,541, pop. 23,059,-000; Korean; Buddhist and Confucian traditions but officially atheist; won

**Korea, South** Republic of Korea; in NE Asia; capital Seoul; area 38,023 sq. mi., pop. 43,919,000; Korean; Buddhist, Confucian, and Christian; won

**Kuwait** State of; in NE Arabian peninsula; capital Kuwait; area 6,880 sq. mi., pop. 2,080,000; Arabic; Sunni Muslim; dinar

**Laos** People's Democratic Republic of; in SE Asia; capital Vientiane; area 91,428 sq. mi., pop. 4,024,000; Lao and French; Buddhist; kip

**Latvia** formerly part of the Union of Soviet Socialist Republics; Republic of; in N Europe; capital Riga; area 25,395 sq. mi., pop. 2,681,000; Latvian and Russian; Lutheran; ruble

**Lebanon** Republic of; in Middle East; capital Beirut; area 4,015 sq. mi., pop. 3,340,000; Arabic; Muslim; pound

**Lesotho** formerly Basutoland; Kingdom of; within Republic of South Africa; capital Maseru; area 11,720 sq. mi., pop. 1,757,000; Sesotho and English; Christian; loti

**Liberia** Republic of; in W Africa; capital Monrovia; area 38,250 sq. mi., pop. 2,644,000; English; Christian and indigenous religions; dollar

**Libya** Socialist People's Libyan Arab Jamahiriya; in N Africa; capital Tripoli; area 679,216 sq. mi., pop. 4,280,-000; Arabic; Sunni Muslim; dinar

**Liechtenstein** Principality of; in W central Europe; capital Vaduz; area 62 sq. mi., pop. 30,000; German; Catholic; franc

**Lithuania** formerly part of the Union of Soviet Socialist Republics; Republic of; in N Europe; capital Vilnius; area 25,174 sq. mi., pop. 3,690,000; Lithuanian; Roman Catholic; ruble

**Luxembourg** Grand Duchy of; in W Europe; capital Luxembourg; area 999 sq. mi., pop. 369,000; Luxembourgian, French and German; Catholic; franc

**Macao** Territory of; Portuguese dependency on South China Sea in E Asia; capital Macao; area 6 sq. mi., pop. 484,000; Cantonese and Portuguese; Buddhist; pataca

**Macedonia** formerly part of Yugoslavia; in SE Europe; capital Skopje; area 9928 sq. mi., pop. 2,090,000; Macedonian; Eastern Orthodox and Muslim; dinar

**Madagascar** Democratic Republic of; island in Indian Ocean east of Africa; capital Antananarivo; area 226,657 sq. mi., pop. 11,802,000; French and Malagasy; Christian and indigenous religions; franc

**Malawi** Republic of; in E central Africa; capital Lilongwe;

area 45,747 sq. mi., pop. 9,080,000; English and Chichewa; Protestant; kwacha

**Malaysia** Federation of; in SE Asia; capital Kuala Lumpur; area 127,316 sq. mi., pop. 17,053,000; Malay; Muslim; ringgit

**Maldives** Republic of; group of islands in N Indian Ocean; capital Male; area 115 sq. mi., pop. 219,000; Divehi and English; Sunni Muslim; rufiyaa

**Mali** Republic of; in W Africa; capital Bamako; area 478,764 sq. mi., pop. 9,182,000; French and Bambara; Muslim; franc

**Malta** Republic of; island in Mediterranean Sea; capital Valletta; area 122 sq. mi., pop. 373,000; Maltese; Catholic; lira

**Mariana Islands** Commonwealth of the Northern Mariana Islands; group of islands in Pacific Ocean; capital Saipan; area 184 sq. mi., pop. 22,591; Chamorro and English; Christian and indigenous religions; dollar

**Marshall Islands** Republic of; group of islands in Pacific Ocean; capital Majuro; area 70 sq. mi., pop. 40,609; English and indigenous languages; Christian and indigenous religions; dollar

**Martinique** Territory of; French dependency, island in Caribbean Sea; capital Fort-de-France; area 425 sq. mi., pop. 336,000; French; Catholic; franc

**Mauritania** Islamic Republic of; in W Africa; capital Nouakchott; area 397,954 sq. mi., pop. 2,038,000; Arabic and French; Muslim; ouguiya

**Mauritius** island in Indian Ocean; capital Port Louis; area 790 sq. mi., pop. 1,141,900; English; Hindu; rupee

**Mexico** United States of; in S North America; capital Mexico City; area 761,604 sq. mi., pop. 88,335,000; Spanish; Catholic; peso

**Micronesia** Federated States of; group of islands in Pacific Ocean; capital Kolonia; area 271 sq. mi., pop. 86,094; English and indigenous languages; Christian and indigenous religions; dollar

**Monaco** Principality of; on Mediterranean Sea, surrounded on other sides by France; capital Monaco-Ville; area 0.6 sq. mi., pop. 29,000; French; Catholic; franc

**Mongolia** Mongolian People's Republic; in central Asia; capital Ulan Bator; area 604,247 sq. mi., pop. 2,185,000; Khalkha Mongol; Buddhist; tugrik

**Morocco** Kingdom of; in N Africa; capital Rabat; area 172,413 sq. mi., pop. 26,249,000; Arabic and French; Sunni Muslim; dirham

**Mozambique** People's Republic of; in E Africa; capital Maputo; area 303,769 sq. mi., pop. 14,718,000; Portuguese; indigenous religions; metical

**Myanmar** formerly Burma; Union of; in SE Asia; capital Yangon, formerly Rangoon; area 261,789 sq. mi., pop. 41,279,000; Burmese; Buddhist; kyat

**Namibia** formerly South-West Africa; Republic of; in SW Africa; capital Windhoek; area 317,818 sq. mi., pop. 1,372,000; English and Afrikaans; Christian; rand

**Nauru** Republic of; island in S Pacific; capital Yaren; area 8 sq. mi., pop. 8,100; Nauruan; Christian; dollar

**Nepal** Kingdom of; in central Asia; capital Katmandu; area 56,136 sq. mi., pop. 19,158,000; Nepali; Hindu; rupee

**Netherlands** Kingdom of the; in NW Europe; capital Amsterdam and the Hague; area 15,770 sq. mi., pop. 14,864,000; Dutch; Protestant and Catholic; guilder

**Netherlands Antilles** Territory of; Dutch island dependency in Caribbean Sea; capital Willemstad; area 385 sq. mi., pop. 187,000; Dutch; Catholic; guilder

**New Zealand** group of islands in S Pacific; capital Wellington; area 103,736 sq. mi., pop. 3,397,000; English and Maori; Christian; dollar

**Nicaragua** Republic of; in Central America; capital Managua; area 50,193 sq. mi., pop. 3,606,000; Spanish; Catholic; cordoba

**Niger** Republic of; in W Africa; capital Niamey; area 489,189 sq. mi., pop. 7,691,000; French and Hausa; Muslim; franc

**Nigeria** Federal Republic of; in W Africa; capital Abuja; area 356,669 sq. mi., pop. 118,865,000; English and Hausa; Muslim; naira

**Northern Ireland** a division of the United Kingdom

**North Korea** Korea, North

**North Yemen** former Yemen Arab Republic, since 1990 part of Yemen

**Norway** Kingdom of; in N Europe; capital Oslo; area 125,181 sq. mi., pop. 4,214,000; Norwegian; Lutheran; krone

**Oman** Sultanate of; on SE Arabian peninsula; capital Muscat; area 82,030 sq. mi., pop. 1,305,000; Arabic; Muslim; rial

**Pakistan** Islamic Republic of; in S Asia; capital Islamabad; area 310,402 sq. mi., pop. 113,163,000; Urdu; Sunni Muslim; rupee

**Palau** Republic of; group of islands in Pacific Ocean; capital Koror; area 192 sq. mi., pop. 14,106; English and Palauan; Christian and indigenous religions; dollar

**Panama** Republic of; in Central America; capital Panama City; area 29,208 sq. mi., pop. 2,423,000; Spanish; Catholic; balboa

**Papua New Guinea** group of islands in SW Pacific; capital Port Moresby; area 178,221 sq. mi., pop. 3,613,000; Pidgin English; Christian; kina

**Paraguay** Republic of; in central South America; capital Asunción; area 157,047 sq. mi., pop. 4,660,000; Spanish; Catholic; guarani

**Peru** Republic of; in W South America; capital Lima; area 496,223 sq. mi., pop. 21,904,000; Spanish; Catholic; inti

**Philippines** Republic of the; in SE Asia; capital Quezon City (official), Manila (de facto); area 115,830 sq. mi., pop. 66,647,000; Tagalog; Catholic; peso

**Poland** Republic of; in N central Europe; capital Warsaw; area 120,724 sq. mi., pop. 38,363,000; Polish; Catholic; zloty

**Portugal** Republic of; in SW Europe; capital Lisbon; area 36,390 sq. mi., pop. 10,528,000; Portuguese; Catholic; escudo

**Qatar** State of; on Persian Gulf; capital Doha; area 4,247 sq. mi., pop. 498,000; Arabic; Muslim; riyal

**Rhodesia** Zimbabwe

**Romania** in SE Europe; capital Bucharest; area 91,700 sq. mi., pop. 23,269,000; Romanian; Romanian Orthodox; leu

**Russia** largest republic within Commonwealth of Independent States

**Rwanda** Republic of; in E central Africa; capital Kigali; area 10,169 sq. mi., pop. 7,603,000; Kinyarwanda and French; Catholic; franc

**San Marino** Most Serene Republic of; in Apennines, surrounded by Italy; capital San Marino; area 24 sq. mi., pop. 23,000; Italian; Catholic; lira

**São Tomé and Príncipe** Republic of; two islands in E Atlantic off W coast of Africa; capital São Tomé; area 372 sq. mi., pop. 125,000; Portuguese; Catholic; dobra

**Saudi Arabia** Kingdom of; on Arabian peninsula; capital Riyadh; area 839,996 sq. mi., pop. 16,758,000; Arabic; Muslim; riyal

**Scotland** a division of United Kingdom; part of Great Britain with England and Wales

**Senegal** Republic of; in W Africa; capital Dakar; area 75,-750 sq. mi., pop. 7,740,000; French and Wolof; Muslim; franc

**Seychelles** Republic of; group of islands in Indian Ocean; capital Victoria; area 176 sq. mi., pop. 71,000; English; Catholic; rupee

**Sierra Leone** Republic of; in W Africa; capital Freetown; area 27,925 sq. mi., pop. 4,168,000; English; Muslim and indigenous religions; leone

**Singapore** Republic of; in SE Asia; capital Singapore; area 225 sq. mi., pop. 2,703,000; Malay and Mandarin; Buddhist; dollar

**Slovenia** formerly part of Yugoslavia; in SE Europe; capital Ljubljana; area 7819 sq. mi., pop. 1,940,000; Slovene; Catholic; dinar

**Solomon Islands** group of islands in W Pacific; capital Honiara; area 10,640 sq. mi., pop. 314,000; English and Melanesian; Christian; dollar

**Somalia** Somali Democratic Republic; in NE Africa; capital Mogadishu; area 246,300 sq. mi., pop. 8,415,000; Somali; Sunni Muslim; shilling

**South Africa** Republic of; in S Africa; capital Pretoria (administrative), Capetown (legislative), Bloemfontein (judicial); area 472,359 sq. mi., pop. 39,550,000; Afrikaans, English, and Zulu; Christian; rand

**South Korea** Korea, South

**South-West Africa** Namibia

**South Yemen** former People's Democratic Republic of Yemen, since 1990 part of Yemen

**Soviet Union** Union of Soviet Socialist Republics

**Spain** Kingdom of; in SW Europe; capital Madrid; area 194,897 sq. mi., pop. 39,623,000; Spanish; Catholic; peseta

**Sri Lanka** formerly Ceylon; Democratic Socialist Republic of; island in S Asia in Indian Ocean; capital Colombo; area 25,332 sq. mi., pop. 17,135,000; Sinhala; Buddhist; rupee

**St. Kitts and Nevis** Federation of; twin-island state in Caribbean Sea; capital Basseterre; area 101 sq. mi., pop. 40,000; English; Anglican; dollar

**St. Lucia** island in W Atlantic; capital Castries; area 239 sq. mi., pop. 153,000; English; Catholic; dollar

**St. Vincent and the Grenadines** group of islands in W Atlantic; capital Kingstown; area 150 sq. mi., pop. 106,-000; English; Anglican; dollar

**Sudan** Democratic Republic of; in N Africa; capital Khartoum; area 966,757 sq. mi., pop. 25,164,000; Arabic; Sunni Muslim; pound

**Suriname** Republic of; in NE South America; capital Paramaribo; area 63,037 sq. mi., pop. 408,000; Dutch; Hindu and Christian; guilder

**Swaziland** Kingdom of; in S Africa; capital Mbabane; area 6,704 sq. mi., pop. 779,000; English and Siswati; Christian and indigenous religions; lilangeni

**Sweden** Kingdom of; in N Europe; capital Stockholm; area 173,731 sq. mi., pop. 8,407,000; Swedish; Lutheran; krona

**Switzerland** Swiss Confederation; in W Europe; capital Bern; area 15,941 sq. mi., pop. 6,628,000; French, German, and Italian; Catholic and Protestant; franc

**Syria** Syrian Arab Republic; in Middle East; capital Damascus; area 71,498 sq. mi., pop. 12,471,000; Arabic; Sunni Muslim; pound

**Taiwan** Republic of China; island in SE Asia in South China Sea; capital Taipei; area 13,885 sq. mi., pop. 20,-454,000; Mandarin; Buddhist and Taoist; dollar

**Tanzania** United Republic of; in E Africa; capital Dar es Salaam; area 364,882 sq. mi., pop. 26,070,000; Swahili; Muslim and Christian; shilling

**Thailand** Kingdom of; in SE Asia; capital Bangkok; area 198,456 sq. mi., pop. 54,890,000; Thai; Buddhist; baht

**Togo** Togolese Republic; in W Africa; capital Lomé; area 21,617 sq. mi., pop. 3,566,000; French and Ewe; indigenous religions; franc

**Tonga** Kingdom of; group of islands in SW Pacific; capital Nuku'alofa; area 270 sq. mi., pop. 108,000; Tongan; Catholic and Hindu; pa'anga

**Trinidad and Tobago** Republic of; two islands in West Indies; capital Port of Spain; area 1,980 sq. mi., pop. 1,270,000; English; Catholic and Hindu; dollar

**Tunisia** Republic of; in N Africa; capital Tunis; area 63,170 sq. mi., pop. 8,094,000; Arabic; Muslim; dinar

**Turkey** Republic of; in SW Asia and SE Europe; capital Ankara; area 301,381 sq. mi., pop. 56,549,000; Turkish; Muslim; lira

**Tuvalu** group of islands in S Pacific; capital Funafuti; area 10 sq. mi., pop. 9,000; Tuvaluan; Christian; dollar

**Uganda** Republic of; in E central Africa; capital Kampala; area 93,354 sq. mi., pop. 17,593,000; English and Swahili; Christian and Muslim; shilling

**Union of Soviet Socialist Republics** former country, now divided into Commonwealth of Independent States, Estonia, Georgia, Latvia, Lithuania

**United Arab Emirates** on Persian Gulf on N Arabian Peninsula; capital Abu Dhabi; area 32,278 sq. mi., pop. 2,250,000; Arabic; Muslim; dirham

**United Kingdom** United Kingdom of Great Britain and Northern Ireland; two islands in NW Europe; capital London; area 94,226, pop. 57,121,000; English; Anglican; pound; comprised of: England, Scotland, Wales, and Northern Ireland

**United States** United States of America; in central North America; capital Washington, D.C.; area 3,618,774 sq. mi., pop. 250,372,000; English; Christian; dollar

**Upper Volta** Burkina Faso

**Uruguay** Republic of; in SE South America; capital Montevideo; area 68,037 sq. mi., pop. 3,002,000; Spanish; Catholic; peso

**Vanuatu** Republic of; group of islands in W Pacific; capital Vila; area 5,700 sq. mi., pop. 150,000; Bislama and French; Christian; vatu

**Vatican City** Catholic state within Rome, Italy; area 109 acres, pop. 750; Italian and Latin; Catholic; lira

**Venezuela** Republic of; in N South America; capital Caracas; area 352,143 sq. mi., pop. 19,753,000; Spanish; Catholic; bolivar

**Vietnam** Democratic Republic of; in SE Asia; capital Hanoi; area 127,243 sq. mi., pop. 68,488,000; Vietnamese and French; Buddhist; dong

**Wales** division of United Kingdom, part of Great Britain with England and Scotland

**Western Samoa** Independent State of; part of an island in SW Pacific; capital Apia; area 1,133 sq. mi., pop. 169,000; Samoan; Christian; tala

**West Germany** former Federal Republic of Germany, since 1990 part of united Germany

**Yemen** formerly North Yemen and South Yemen; Republic of; on S Arabian peninsula; capital Sanaa; area 207,000 sq. mi., pop. 11,000,000; Arabic; Muslim; dinar

**Yugoslavia** Federal Republic of; in SE Europe; capital Belgrade; area 39,449 sq. mi., pop. 10,400,000; Serbian; Eastern Orthodox, Catholic and Muslim; dinar; comprised of: Serbia and Montenegro

**Zaire** Republic of; in W central Africa; capital Kinshasa; area 905,563 sq. mi., pop. 35,330,000; French; Catholic; zaire

**Zambia** Republic of; in S central Africa; capital Lusaka; area 290,585 sq. mi., pop. 8,119,000; English; Christian and indigenous religions; kwacha

**Zimbabwe** formerly Rhodesia; in S central Africa; capital Harare; area 150,803 sq. mi., pop. 10,205,000; English and Shona; indigenous religions; dollar

## STATES OF THE UNITED STATES

**Alabama** AL; 22nd state, admitted 1819; SE United States; capital Montgomery; ranks 29th in area, pop. 4,063,000; Camellia State

**Alaska** AK; 49th state, admitted 1959; NW of continental United States; capital Juneau; ranks 1st in area, pop. 552,-000; The Last Frontier

**Arizona** AZ; 48th state, admitted 1912; SW United States; capital Phoenix; ranks 6th in area, pop. 3,678,000; Grand Canyon State

**Arkansas** AR; 25th state, admitted 1836; S central United States; capital Little Rock; ranks 27th in area, pop. 2,362,-000; Land of Opportunity

**California** CA; 31st state, admitted 1850; W United States; capital Sacramento; ranks 3rd in area, pop. 29,840,000; Golden State

**Colorado** CO; 38th state, admitted 1876; W central United States; capital Denver; ranks 8th in area, pop. 3,308,000; Centennial State

**Connecticut** CT; 5th state, admitted 1788; NE United States; capital Hartford; ranks 48th in area, pop. 3,296,000; Constitution State

**Delaware** DE; 1st state, admitted 1787; E United States; capital Dover; ranks 49th in area, pop. 669,000; First State

**Florida** FL; 27th state, admitted 1845; SE United States; capital Tallahassee; ranks 22nd in area, pop. 13,003,000; Sunshine State

**Georgia** GA; 4th state, admitted 1788; SE United States; capital Atlanta; ranks 21st in area, pop. 6,508,000; Peach State

**Hawaii** HI; 50th state, admitted 1959; WSW of continental United States; capital Honolulu; ranks 47th in area, pop. 1,115,000; Aloha State

**Idaho** ID; 43rd state, admitted 1890; NW United States; capital Boise; ranks 13th in area, pop. 1,012,000; Gem State

**Illinois** IL; 21st state, admitted 1818; N central United States; capital Springfield; ranks 24th in area, pop. 11,467,-000; Prairie State

**Indiana** IN; 19th state, admitted 1816; N central United States; capital Indianapolis; ranks 38th in area, pop. 5,564,-000; Hoosier State

**Iowa** IA; 29th state, admitted 1846; N central United States; capital Des Moines; ranks 25th in area, pop. 2,787,-000; Hawkeye State

**Kansas** KS; 34th state, admitted 1861; NW central United States; capital Topeka; ranks 14th in area, pop. 2,486,000; Sunflower State

**Kentucky** KY; 15th state, admitted 1792; SE central United States; capital Frankfort; ranks 37th in area, pop. 3,699,-000; Bluegrass State

**Louisiana** LA; 18th state, admitted 1812; S central United States; capital Baton Rouge; ranks 31st in area, pop. 4,238,000; Pelican State

**Maine** ME; 23rd state, admitted 1820; NE United States; capital Augusta; ranks 39th in area, pop. 1,233,000; Pine Tree State

**Maryland** MD; 7th state, admitted 1788; E United States; capital Annapolis; ranks 42nd in area, pop. 4,799,000; Old Line State

**Massachusetts** MA; 6th state, admitted 1788; NE United States; capital Boston; ranks 45th in area, pop. 6,029,000; Bay State

**Michigan** MI; 26th state, admitted 1837; N central United States; capital Lansing; ranks 23rd in area, pop. 9,329,000; Wolverine State

**Minnesota** MN; 32nd state, admitted 1858; N central United States; capital St. Paul; ranks 12th in area, pop. 4,387,000; North Star State

**Mississippi** MS; 20th state, admitted 1817; S central United States; capital Jackson; ranks 32nd in area, pop. 2,586,000; Magnolia State

**Missouri** MO; 24th state, admitted 1821; NW central United States; capital Jefferson City; ranks 19th in area, pop. 5,138,000; Show-Me State

**Montana** MT; 41st state, admitted 1889; NW United States; capital Helena; ranks 4th in area, pop. 804,000; Treasure State

**Nebraska** NE; 37th state, admitted 1867; NW central United States; capital Lincoln; ranks 15th in area, pop. 1,585,000; Cornhusker State

**Nevada** NV; 36th state, admitted 1864; W United States; capital Carson City; ranks 7th in area, pop. 1,206,000; Sagebrush State

**New Hampshire** NH; 9th state, admitted 1788; NE United States; capital Concord; ranks 44th in area, pop. 1,114,-000; Granite State

**New Jersey** NJ; 3rd state, admitted 1787; E United States; capital Trenton; ranks 46th in area, pop. 7,749,000; Garden State

**New Mexico** NM; 47th state, admitted 1912; SW United States; capital Santa Fe; ranks 5th in area, pop. 1,522,000; Land of Enchantment

**New York** NY; 11th state, admitted 1788; NE United

States; capital Albany; ranks 30th in area, pop. 18,044,000; Empire State

**North Carolina** NC; 12th state, admitted 1789; SE United States; capital Raleigh; ranks 28th in area, pop. 6,658,000; Tar Heel State

**North Dakota** ND; 39th state, admitted 1889; NW central United States; capital Bismarck; ranks 17th in area, pop. 641,000; Peace Garden State

**Ohio** OH; 17th state, admitted 1803; NE central United States; capital Columbus; ranks 35th in area, pop. 10,888,-000; Buckeye State

**Oklahoma** OK; 46th state, admitted 1907; SW central United States; capital Oklahoma City; ranks 18th in area, pop. 3,158,000; Sooner State

**Oregon** OR; 33rd state, admitted 1859; NW United States; capital Salem; ranks 10th in area, pop. 2,854,000; Beaver State

**Pennsylvania** PA; 2nd state, admitted 1787; E United States; capital Harrisburg; ranks 33rd in area, pop. 12,000,-000; Keystone State

**Rhode Island** RI; 13th state, admitted 1790; NE United States; capital Providence; ranks 50th in area, pop. 1,006,-000; Ocean State

**South Carolina** SC; 8th state, admitted 1788; SE United States; capital Columbia; ranks 40th in area, pop. 3,506,-000; Palmetto State

**South Dakota** SD; 40th state, admitted 1889; NW central United States; capital Pierre; ranks 16th in area, pop. 700,-000; Coyote State

**Tennessee** TN; 16th state, admitted 1796; SE central United States; capital Nashville; ranks 34th in area, pop. 4,896,000; Volunteer State

**Texas** TX; 28th state, admitted 1845; SW central United States; capital Austin; ranks 2nd in area, pop. 17,060,000; Lone Star State

**Utah** UT; 45th state, admitted 1896; W central United States; capital Salt Lake City; ranks 11th in area, pop. 1,680,000; Beehive State

**Vermont** VT; 14th state, admitted 1791; NE United States; capital Montpelier; ranks 43rd in area, pop. 565,000; Green Mountain State

**Virginia** VA; 10th state, admitted 1788; SE United States; capital Richmond; ranks 36th in area, pop. 6,217,000; Old Dominion

**Washington** WA; 42nd state, admitted 1889; NW United States; capital Olympia; ranks 20th in area, pop. 4,888,-000; Evergreen State

**West Virginia** WV; 35th state, admitted 1863; E central United States; capital Charleston; ranks 41st in area, pop. 1,802,000; Mountain State

**Wisconsin** WI; 30th state, admitted 1848; N central United States; capital Madison; ranks 26th in area, pop. 4,906,000; Badger State

**Wyoming** WY; 44th state, admitted 1890; W central United States; capital Cheyenne; ranks 9th in area, pop. 456,000; Equality State

## MAJOR WORLD CITIES

**Accra** seaport capital of Ghana, on Gulf of Guinea in W Africa, pop. 949,000

**Addis Ababa** capital of Ethiopia in E Africa, pop. 1,412,000

**Ahmedabad** city in W India in central Asia, pop. 2,300,000

**Alexandria** ancient seaport in Egypt, in Nile delta on N coast of Africa, pop. 2,893,000

**Algiers** seaport capital of Algeria, on Mediterranean Sea in N Africa, pop. 1,483,000

**Amman** capital of Jordan, in Near East, pop. 900,000

**Amsterdam** capital of the Netherlands, in W Europe, pop. 691,000

**Ankara** capital of Turkey and ancient capital of Galatia, in Near East, pop. 1,700,000

**Athens** ancient city and capital of Greece, in SE Europe, pop. 3,027,000

**Atlanta** capital of Georgia in SE United States, pop. 425,-000

**Auckland** original capital of New Zealand, in SW Pacific Ocean, pop. 324,400

**Baghdad** capital of Iraq and ancient center of Islamic culture, on Tigris River in Near East, pop. 3,400,000

**Bandung** city on Java in Indonesia in SE Asia, pop. 1,400,-000

**Bangalore** city in India in central Asia, pop. 3,900,000

**Bangkok** seaport capital of Thailand, in SE Asia, pop. 4,700,000

**Barcelona** ancient seaport in NE Spain, on Mediterranean Sea in SW Europe, pop. 2,000,000

**Beijing** formerly Peking or Peiping; capital of People's Republic of China, in NE Asia, pop. 9,330,000

**Beirut** seaport capital of Lebanon and ancient Phoenician city, on Mediterranean Sea in Near East, pop. 500,000

**Belgrade** capital of Yugoslavia, on Danube River in SE Europe, pop. 1,250,000

**Belo Horizonte** city in Brazil in E South America, pop. 1,122,000

**Berlin** capital of united Germany in E Europe, pop. 3,050,-000

**Birmingham** industrial city in central England in W Europe, pop. 1,008,000

**Bogota** capital of Colombia, in N South America, pop. 3,968,000

**Bombay** seaport in W India, on Arabian Sea in central Asia, pop. 8,700,000

**Brazzaville** river port capital of People's Republic of Congo, on Congo River in central Africa, pop. 595,000

**Brussels** capital of Belgium, in W Europe, pop. 970,000

**Bucharest** capital of Romania, in SE Europe, pop. 1,900,-000

**Budapest** capital of Hungary, on Danube River in E Europe, pop. 2,115,000

**Buenos Aires** seaport capital of Argentina, in SE South America on Atlantic Ocean, pop. 3,000,000

**Cairo** capital of Egypt, on Nile River in N Africa, pop. 6,305,000

**Calcutta** seaport and former capital of British India, in central Asia, pop. 9,900,000

**Canberra** seaport capital of Australia, on E coast on Pacific Ocean, pop. 297,300

**Canton** Guangzhou

**Capetown** seaport and legislative capital of South Africa, in SW Africa on Atlantic Ocean, pop. 1,900,000

**Caracas** capital of Venezuela, in N South America, pop. 1,275,000

**Casablanca** seaport in Morocco, in NW Africa on Atlantic Ocean, pop. 2,600,000

**Chengdu** provincial capital in central China in E Asia, pop. 2,600,000

**Chicago** city in Illinois in central United States, on Lake Michigan, pop. 2,800,000

**Chongqing** formerly Chungking; city in S central China, in E Asia, pop. 3,890,000

**Chungking** Chongqing

**Copenhagen** seaport capital of Denmark, in N Europe on Baltic Sea, pop. 1,358,000

**Dakar** seaport capital of Senegal, in W Africa on Atlantic Ocean, pop. 1,300,000

**Dallas** city in Texas in SW United States, pop. 1,007,000

**Damascus** ancient capital of Syria in Near East, oldest continuously existing city in world, pop. 1,361,000

**Dar es Salaam** seaport capital of Tanzania in E Africa, on Indian Ocean, pop. 1,400,000

**Delhi** former capital of Mogul Empire adjacent to present capital of India (New Delhi), in central Asia, pop. 5,800,-000

**Detroit** river port in Michigan in N central United States, on Detroit River and Lake Erie, pop. 1,028,000

**Dhaka** capital of Bangladesh, in central Asia, pop. 3,400,-000

**Dublin** seaport capital of Ireland, in W Europe on Irish Sea, pop. 502,000

**Essen** industrial city in W Germany, in N Europe, pop. 622,000

**Glasgow** river port in Scotland in W Europe, on River Clyde, pop. 733,000

**Guadalajara** city in W Mexico in S North America, pop. 3,000,000

**Guangzhou** formerly Canton; seaport in SE China in E Asia, on Zhu Jiang River, pop. 3,300,000

**Hamburg** seaport in W Germany in N Europe, on Elbe River, pop. 1,600,000

**Han Cities** Wuhan

**Hanoi** capital of Vietnam, in SE Asia, pop. 3,100,000

**Harbin** provincial capital in NE China in E Asia, pop. 3,730,000

**Havana** seaport capital of Cuba, in Caribbean Sea, pop. 2,059,000

**Helsinki** seaport capital of Finland, in N Europe on Baltic Sea, pop. 487,000

**Ho Chi Minh City** formerly Saigon; seaport in Vietnam in SE Asia, pop. 3,900,000

**Hong Kong** seaport bordering SE China, in E Asia on South China Sea, pop. 5,700,000

**Houston** canal port in Texas in SW United States, on Gulf of Mexico, pop. 1,630,000

**Hyderabad** city in central India in central Asia, pop. 2,800,000

**Istanbul** port in Turkey in W Near East on Black Sea, at site of ancient Byzantium, pop. 5,800,000

**Jakarta** seaport capital of Indonesia on Java, in SE Asia on Java Sea, pop. 8,800,000

**Jerusalem** ancient holy city and capital of Israel, in Near East, pop. 457,000

**Johannesburg** city in South Africa in S Africa, pop. 1,600,000

**Kabul** capital of Afghanistan, in central Asia, pop. 1,200,000

**Kanpur** city in N India in central Asia, on Ganges River, pop. 1,688,000

**Karachi** seaport in Pakistan in central Asia, on Indus River delta and Arabian Sea, pop. 5,103,000

**Khartoum** capital of Sudan in N Africa, on Nile River, pop. 476,000

**Kiev** capital of Ukraine, in E Europe, pop. 2,400,000

**Kinshasa** formerly Leopoldville; river port capital of Zaire in central Africa, on Congo River, pop. 3,000,000

**Kobe** ancient seaport in Japan in E Asia, on Pacific Ocean, pop. 1,400,000

**Kuala Lumpur** seaport capital of Malaysia in SE Asia, on Strait of Malacca, pop. 1,000,000

**Lagos** seaport and former capital of Nigeria in W Africa, on Atlantic Ocean, pop. 1,243,000

**Lahore** Punjab capital in Pakistan, in central Asia, pop. 2,922,000

**La Paz** administrative capital of Bolivia in NW South America, pop. 955,000

**Leningrad** St. Petersburg

**Leopoldville** Kinshasa

**Lima** seaport capital of Peru in NW South America, on Pacific Ocean, pop. 5,493,000

**Lisbon** ancient Phoenician trading center and seaport capital of Portugal in SW Europe, on Atlantic Ocean, pop. 2,000,000

**London** ancient city and port capital of United Kingdom, in W Europe, on Thames River, pop. 6,700,000

**Los Angeles** seaport in California in SW United States, pop. 3,500,000

**Madras** seaport in India in central Asia, on Bay of Bengal, pop. 4,900,000

**Madrid** capital of Spain, in SW Europe, pop. 3,500,000

**Managua** capital of Nicaragua, in Central America, pop. 1,000,000

**Manchester** canal port in England in W Europe, on Irish Sea, pop. 451,000

**Manila** seaport capital of Philippines in E Asia, on South China Sea, pop. 1,700,000

**Melbourne** seaport in SE Australia, on S Pacific Ocean, pop. 3,000,000

**Mexico City** officially Mexico Distrito Federal; capital of Mexico in S North America, most populous city in world, pop. 18,000,000

**Miami** port city in Florida in SE United States, on Atlantic Ocean, pop. 347,000

**Milan** industrial city in N Italy, in S Europe, pop. 1,400,000

**Monterrey** industrial city in E Mexico in S North America, pop. 2,700,000

**Montevideo** seaport capital of Uruguay in S South America, on Atlantic Ocean, pop. 1,246,000

**Montreal** river port in E Canada, on St. Lawrence River, pop. 2,921,000

**Moscow** capital of Russia and former Soviet Union in E Europe, pop. 8,500,000

**Mukden** Shenyang

**Munich** Bavarian capital in SW Germany in central Europe, pop. 1,300,000

**Nagoya** industrial city in Japan in E Asia, pop. 2,100,000

**Nairobi** capital of Kenya, in E Africa, pop. 959,000

**Nanjing** formerly Nanking; river port and former capital of China, in E Asia, pop. 4,560,000

**Nanking** Nanjing

**Naples** ancient seaport in Italy in S Europe, pop. 1,200,000

**New York City** seaport in New York State in NE United States, on Atlantic Ocean, pop. 7,322,000

**Osaka** former capital of Japan, in E Asia, pop. 2,600,000

**Oslo** seaport capital of Norway in N Europe, on North Sea, pop. 449,000

**Ottawa** capital of Canada in N North America, pop. 819,-000

**Panama City** canal port on Panama Canal and capital of Panama in Central America, pop. 1,200,000

**Paris** capital of France in W Europe, on Seine River, pop. 2,200,000

**Peking** Beijing

**Philadelphia** city in Pennsylvania in E United States, on Delaware River, pop. 1,600,000

**Phnom Penh** capital of Cambodia, in SE Asia, pop. 300,-000

**Pôrto Alegre** seaport in Brazil in SE South America, on Atlantic Ocean, pop. 2,600,000

**Prague** capital of Czechoslovakia in E Europe, pop. 1,200,-000

**Pretoria** administrative capital of South Africa in S Africa, pop. 822,000

**Pusan** seaport in South Korea in E Asia, on Korean Strait, pop. 3,700,000

**Quezon City** former capital of Philippines in E Asia, pop. 1,300,000

**Quito** capital of Ecuador in N South America, pop. 1,200,-000

**Rangoon** Yangon

**Recife** seaport in N Brazil in E South America, on Atlantic Ocean, pop. 1,300,000

**Rio de Janeiro** seaport and former capital of Brazil, in E South America, on Atlantic Ocean, pop. 5,600,000

**Riyadh** capital of Saudi Arabia in Near East, pop. 1,380,-000

**Rome** ancient city and capital of Italy in S Europe, on Tiber River, pop. 2,800,000

**Saigon** Ho Chi Minh City

**San Diego** seaport in California in SW United States, on Pacific Ocean, pop. 1,110,000

**San Francisco** seaport in California in W United States, on Pacific Ocean, pop. 724,000

**Santiago** capital of Chile in S South America, pop. 4,858,-000

**Santo Domingo** seaport capital of Dominican Republic, in Caribbean Sea, pop. 1,700,000

**São Paulo** city in Brazil in SE South America, pop. 10,100,-000

**Seattle** seaport in Washington in NW United States, on Puget Sound, off Pacific Ocean, pop. 516,000

**Seoul** capital of South Korea in NE Asia, pop. 10,200,000

**Shanghai** ancient seaport and municipality in China in E Asia, pop. 7,000,000

**Shenyang** formerly Mukden; one-time Manchurian capital in N China in E Asia, pop. 4,200,000

**Singapore** capital of Singapore, at tip of Malay peninsula, in SE Asia, on South China Sea, pop. 2,600,000

**Sofia** capital of Bulgaria in E Europe, pop. 1,119,000

**St. Louis** river port in Missouri in central United States, on Mississippi River, pop. 453,000

**Stockholm** seaport capital of Sweden, in N Europe, on Baltic Sea, pop. 663,000

**St. Petersburg** formerly Leningrad; seaport in NW Russia in Europe, on Baltic Sea, pop. 4,800,000

**Surabaya** seaport in Indonesia on Java, in SE Asia, on Java Sea, pop. 2,500,000

**Sydney** seaport in E Australia, on S Pacific Ocean, pop. 3,500,000

**Taipei** capital of Taiwan in E Asia, on South China Sea, pop. 2,637,000

**Tashkent** capital of Uzbekistan and ancient Caucasian city in Near East, pop. 2,100,000

**Tbilisi** formerly Tiflis; capital of Georgian Republic in SE Europe, on Kura River, pop. 1,174,000

**Teheran** capital of Iran in Near East, pop. 6,022,000

**Tianjin** formerly Tientsin; ancient trading center and seaport in N China in E Asia, on Yellow Sea, pop. 6,000,000

**Tientsin** Tianjin

**Tiflis** Tbilisi

**Tokyo** ancient seaport and capital of Japan in E Asia, on Tokyo Bay, off N Pacific Ocean, pop. 8,300,000

**Toronto** lake port in Canada in N North America, on Lake Ontario, pop. 3,427,000

**Tripoli** seaport capital of Libya, in N Africa, on Mediterranean Sea, pop. 591,000

**Tunis** ancient Carthaginian seaport and capital of Tunisia, in N Africa, on Mediterranean Sea, pop. 1,000,000

**Vancouver** seaport in SW Canada in North America, on Pacific Ocean, pop. 1,380,000

**Venice** ancient seaport built on numerous small islands in N Italy, in S Europe, on Adriatic Sea, pop. 327,000

**Vienna** river port and capital of Austria, in central Europe, on Danube River, pop. 1,500,000

**Vientiane** capital of Laos, in SE Asia, on Mekong River, pop. 120,000

**Warsaw** capital of Poland, in E Europe, on Vistula River, pop. 1,600,000

**Washington** District of Columbia; capital of United States in North America, on Potomac River, pop. 607,000

**Wellington** seaport capital of New Zealand, on S Pacific Ocean, pop. 137,000

**Wuhan** conglomerate city and provincial capital in China in E Asia, pop. 3,400,00; also Han Cities

**Yangon** formerly Rangoon; ancient seaport capital of Myanmar in SE Asia, on Bay of Bengal, pop. 2,500,000

**Yokohama** ancient seaport in Japan in E Asia, on Tokyo Bay, pop. 3,100,000

# MINERALS, METALS, AND ROCKS

Minerals
  Mineral Compounds
  Gemstones
Metals
  Pure Metals
  Alloys
Rocks
  Igneous Rocks

Metamorphic Rocks
Sedimentary Rocks

**SEE ALSO**: Chap. 3: Geology; Chap. 4: Chemistry; Chap. 10: Ornaments and Accessories

# MINERALS

**mineral** inorganic chemical solid naturally occurring in Earth's crust and having definite chemical composition and tendency to form crystals

## MINERAL COMPOUNDS

acanthite, acmite, actinolite, adamite, alabaster, allanite, alunite, amblygonite, amphibole, analcime, andalusite, anglesite, anhydrite, anthophyllite, apatite, apophyllite, aragonite, argentite, arsenopyrite, asbestos, asphaltum, augite, aurichalcite, austinite, autunite, aventurine, axinite, azurite

babingtonite, barite, bauxite, benitoite, beryl, biotite, bismuth, bismuthite, bixbyite, borax, bornite, boulangerite, bournonite, brochantite, brookite, brucite

calaverite, calcite, cancrinite, carnallite, carnotite, cassiterite, celestite, cerargyrite, cerussite, chabazite, chalcanthite, chalcedony, chalcocite, chalcopyrite, chloragyrite, chlorite, chromite, chrondrodite, chrysoberyl, chrysocolla, cinnabar, clinozoisite, cobaltite, colemanite, columbite, conichalcite, copalite, cordierite, corundum, covellite, crocoite, cryolite, cuprite, cyanotrichite

danburite, datolite, dendrite, descloizite, diaspore, diopside, dioptase, dolomite, dumortierite

emery, enargite, enstatite, epidote, epsomite, erythrite

feldspar, fluorite, franklinite

gadolinite, galena, garnet, garnierite, gilsonite, glauberite, glauconite, glaucophane, goethite, graphite, gummite, gypsum

halite, hedenbergite, hematite, hemimorphite, heubnerite, heulandite, hornblende, howlite, hypersthene

idocrase, ilmenite, inesite

jadeite, jamesonite, jarosite

kaolinite, kernite, kyanite

laumontite, lawsonite, lazulite, lazurite, legrandite, lepidolite, leucite, limonite, linarite

magnesite, magnetite, malachite, manganite, marcasite, melanterite, mesolite, mica, millerite, mimetite, mineral coal, molybdenite, monazite, muscovite

natrolite, nepheline, neptunite, niccolite, nickeline

olivenite, olivine, orpiment, ozocerite

pargasite, pectolite, pentlandite, phenakite, phlogopite, plagioclase, polybasite, prehnite, proustite, psilomelane, pumpellyite, pyrargyrite, pyrite, pyrolusite, pyromorphite, pyrophyllite, pyroxene, pyrrhotite

quartz

realgar, rhodochrosite, rhodonite, riebeckite, rutile

scapolite, scheelite, scolecite, serpentine, shattuckite, siderite, sillimanite, skutterudite, smaltite, smithsonite, sodalite, soda niter, sperrylite, sphalerite, sphene, spinel, spodumene, stannite, staurolite, stephanite, stibnite, stilbite, strontianite, sulfur, sylvanite, sylvite

talc, tantalite, tephroite, tetrahedrite, thenardite, thomsonite, thorite, torbernite, tourmaline, tremolite, triphylite, trona

ulexite, uraninite, uranophane

vanadinite, variscite, vivianite

wavellite, willemite, witherite, wolframite, wollastonite, wulfenite

zincite, zoisite

## GEMSTONES

**gemstone** hard mineral, crystal, or petrified material used as jewelry when cut and faceted, designated precious or semiprecious

agate, alexandrite, almandine, amber, amethyst, amorzonite, andradite, aquamarine, aventurine

beryl, bloodstone

cairngorm, carbuncle, carnelian, cat's eye, chalcedony, chrysoberyl, chrysolite, chrysoprase, citrine

demantoid, diamond

emerald

fire opal

garnet, girasol

harlequin opal, heliotrope, hyacinth

jacinth, jade, jasper, jet

kunzite

lapis lazuli, lazurite

malachite, melanite, milky quartz, moonstone, morganite

nephrite

olivine, onyx, opal

peridot, pyrope

red jasper, rose quartz, rubasse, ruby, rutile

sapphire, sard, sardonyx, smoky quartz, smoky topaz, sodalite, spinel, star sapphire, sunstone

tiger's-eye, topaz, tourmaline, turquoise

white sapphire

zircon

# METALS

**metal** opaque, fusible, ductile, conductive, lustrous substance, often a chemical element or compound yielding oxides or hydroxides

## PURE METALS

aluminum, americium, antimony, arsenic

barium, beryllium, bismuth

cadmium, calcium, cerium, cesium, chromium, cobalt, columbium, copper

dysprosium

erbium, europium

gadolinium, gallium, germanium, gold

hafnium, holmium

indium, iridium, iron

lanthanum, lead, lithium, lutetium

magnesium, manganese, mercury, molybdenum

neodymium, nickel, niobium

osmium

palladium, phosphorus, platinum, polonium, potassium, praseodymium, promethium, protactinium

radium, rhenium, rubidium, ruthenium

samarium, scandium, silver, sodium, strontium

tantalum, technetium, terbium, thallium, thorium, thulium, tin, titanium, tungsten

uranium

vanadium

ytterbium, yttrium

zinc, zirconium

## ALLOYS

**alloy** two or more metals, or a metal and nonmetal, fused together when molten
> alnico, amalgam
> Babbitt, brass, bronze
> Carboloy, carbon steel, cast iron, chrome, coin nickel, constantan
> Damascus steel, damask
> electrum, elinvar
> graphite steel
> invar
> permalloy, perminvar, pewter, pinchbeck, pink gold
> solder, spiegeleisen, stainless steel, steel, sterling silver
> tombac
> white gold, wrought iron

## ROCKS

**rock** concretion of earthly or mineral matter of variable size, shape, and chemical composition

## IGNEOUS ROCKS

**igneous rock** rock formed by cooling and hardening of hot, molten rock within Earth
> andesite, anorthosite, aplite
> basalt
> carbonatite, clinkstone
> dacite, diabase, diorite, dolerite, dunite
> felsite
> gabbro, granite, granite pegmatite, granodiorite
> kimberlite
> lava
> monzonite
> nepheline syenite
> obsidian
> pegmatite, peridotite, phonolite, pitchstone, porphyry, pumice, pyroxenite
> rhyolite
> scoria, syenite
> trachyte, trap, traprock, tuff
> volcanic ash

## METAMORPHIC ROCKS

**metamorphic rock** igneous or sedimentary rock that has been transformed by heat, pressure, or chemically active fluids
> amphibolite
> calc-silicate
> gneiss, granulite, greenstone
> halite, hornblende schist, hornfels
> ironstone
> marble, metaquartzite
> phyllite
> quartzite
> schist, serpentine, skarn, slate, soapstone, steatite

## SEDIMENTARY ROCKS

**sedimentary rock** rock formed on Earth's surface from accumulation of material deposited by water, wind, or glaciers

> anhydrite
> breccia, brownstone, buhr, buhrstone
> chalk, chert, coal, conglomerate
> dolomite, dripstone
> flint
> grit, gypsum
> hematite
> limestone
> marl, mudstone
> oolite
> rock salt, rottenstone
> sandstone, shale, stalactite, stalagmite, stinkstone
> touchstone, travertine, tufa

# LANDSCAPES AND SEASCAPES

Hills, Hollows, and Valleys
Plains and Marshes
Woods and Brush
Inland Waterways and Lakes
Coastal Land, Islands, and the Sea

**SEE ALSO**: Chap. 3: Geography; Weather and Natural Phenomena

## HILLS, HOLLOWS, AND VALLEYS

**acclivity** upward slope of hill
**alp** high mountain
**arete** ridge in craggy mountains with sharp crest
**arroyo** steep-sided gully in arid region, carved by heavy rains
**badlands** highly eroded area of hills in fantastic shapes
**barranca** deep, steep-sided gully or arroyo
**barrow** pile of earth or rocks at location of ancient grave
**basin** depression in earth's surface, often with lake or pond at bottom; drainage outlet for river
**berm** narrow shelf at bottom, top, or along side of slope
**bluff** high, steep, broad-faced bank or cliff
**bowl** large, round hollow
**box canyon** narrow valley with vertical walls terminating in wall at upstream end
**brae** *Scot.* hillside above river
**bunker** mound of earth
**butte** sheer-faced, isolated, flat-topped hill with smaller summit than mesa
**caldera** large basin formed by explosion and collapse of center of volcano
**cañon** canyon
**canyon** deep, narrow valley with steep sides carved by river; cañon
**cave** underground hollow that opens into a hill
**cavern** underground chamber, usu. large
**cavity** hollowed space in rocks, cliffs, or hills
**cenote** deep limestone sinkhole
**chasm** deep cleft in earth; gorge
**chine** ridge or crest of ravine or gorge
**chink** small cleft, fissure

**chip**  deformity in earth's surface where piece has been displaced

**cirque**  deep, natural bowl in mountains; corrie; cwm

**cleft**  small fissure in earth

**cliff**  tall, steep, vertical face of rock overlooking lower area

**col**  depression in crest of ridge; mountain pass

**combe**  *Chiefly Brit.* valley or depression on side of hill

**cordillera**  series of parallel mountain ranges

**corrie**  cirque

**coulee**  dry streambed; shallow depression

**couloir**  mountainous gorge, esp. in Alps

**crag**  steep rocks or cliff with sharp outcroppings

**crater**  bowl-shaped depression, esp. at mouth of volcano

**crest**  highest ridge of mountain or hill

**crevasse**  deep cleft in glacier or earth

**crevice**  crack in earth

**cuesta**  ridge or hill with steep face on one side and long gentle slope on other

**cut**  slash in earth's surface; small, steep canyon

**cwm**  cirque

**dale**  valley, vale

**declivity**  downward slope of hill

**defile**  long, narrow passage between hills or cliffs

**dell**  small, secluded, wooded valley

**depression**  any hollow place or low point in earth's surface

**dingle**  small, wooded valley or dell

**divide**  mountain ridge from which streams drain in opposite directions

**donga**  narrow, steep-sided ravine, dry except in rainy season

**draw**  gully less deep than a ravine

**drift**  glacial deposit of gravel or boulders

**drumlin**  long, oval hill of glacial drift

**dune**  hill of sand formed by wind

**elevation**  height

**escarpment**  steep cliff separating two level surfaces

**esker**  elongated ridge of sand and boulders deposited by stream running beneath stagnant glacier

**fissure**  crack or split in earth

**foothills**  low-lying hills at base of mountain range

**gap**  mountain pass; ravine

**glacier**  large mass of moving ice

**glacis**  gentle slope; mound of earth, esp. before fortification

**glen**  secluded, narrow, grassy valley, usu. level at bottom

**gorge**  narrow, steep ravine with rocky walls

**grotto**  cave or cavern, usu. not deep

**gulch**  deep, steep-walled ravine formed by swift stream

**gully**  channel or small valley worn in earth by running water

**headland**  promontory

**height**  elevated tract of land, esp. mountain peak; elevation

**highland**  rolling hills in elevated tract of land

**hill**  usu. rounded elevation of land, smaller than a mountain

**hillock**  small hill

**hillside**  one slope of hill

**hilltop**  peak, crest, or ridge of hill

**hogback**  ridge with sharp crest and sides of steeply inclined strata

**hollow**  depression, low sunken place

**hummock**  low, rounded hillock

**intervale**  low-lying tract of land along river

**kloof**  deep gorge or ravine (South Africa)

**knap**  summit, hill top

**knoll**  small, rounded hill

**kopje**  small hill on veld (southern Africa)

**krantz**  steep cliff or precipice (southern Africa)

**massif**  central, compact portion of mountain range

**monticule**  secondary cone of volcano

**mound**  pile of earth or stones; knoll

**mountain**  landmass elevated far above surroundings, higher than a hill

**nunatak**  hill or mountain totally encircled by glacial ice

**overlook**  elevated land that affords view of surrounding flatlands

**palisade**  line of steep cliffs, esp. above river

**pass**  low point suitable for crossing mountain range

**peak**  top of mountain with distinct, pointed summit

**pike**  *Chiefly Brit.* mountain with pointed summit

**pinnacle**  tall mountain peak

**pit**  narrow, deep, steep-sided depression in earth

**piton**  sharp peak of mountain

**precipice**  vertical or near vertical face of hill or mountain; cliff

**promontory**  point of high land projecting out over water; headland

**puna**  treeless, wind-swept mesa or basin in high Andes (Peru)

**range**  series of connected mountains

**ravine**  narrow, steep-sided depression in earth's surface formed by running water, larger than a gully, smaller than a canyon

**recess**  cleft in earth, often concealed from view

**ridge**  range of hills or mountains; long, narrow elevation in earth's surface or ocean floor

**rift**  crack, fissure

**rincon**  small, secluded valley; sharp recess in cliff

**rise**  slope, hillside

**rut**  cut, furrow, or track in ground

**saddle**  mountain ridge connecting two peaks; col

**scarp**  line of cliffs formed by erosion or fracturing of earth

**serac**  tall peak or mass of ice projecting upward from glacier

**sierra**  mountain range, esp. with irregular contour of jagged peaks

**sink**  depression in earth's surface without drainage, often saline lake

**sinkhole**  limestone hollow connected to underground passage

**slough**  depression in swamp full of soft, deep mud

**spur**  ridge projecting from mountain or range; projection of elevated land

**steptoe**  isolated hill or mountain surrounded by lava

**strath**  *Scot.* steep-sided, wide, flat-bottomed valley

**submontane**  land at foot of or lying under mountain

**summit**  highest point of mountain or hill

**tableland**  flat-topped, elevated tract of land

**talus**  slope formed by pile of rock debris at foot of cliff

**tor**  high, rugged hill

**trench**  long, narrow furrow in ground or deep ocean floor

**trough**  long, narrow, shallow depression between ridges or slopes

**vale**  valley, esp. one hidden between hills

**valley**  long depression in earth's surface lying between hills or mountains, usu. formed by river flowing through it

**vista**  height affording view over large expanse of land

**wadi**  rocky desert riverbed, dry except for rainy season

**water gap**  gap across mountain ridge, cut by and giving passage to stream

**watershed**  area on one side of divide drained by rivers all flowing in same direction; ridge dividing two drainage areas

## PLAINS AND MARSHES

**alluvial plain**  flat plain where river leaves gorge or joins larger waterway

**barrens**  expanse of flat, treeless land

**bog**  small marsh or swamp; wet, spongy ground

**bottoms**  low-lying area at edge of waterway

**campo**  grassy plain (South America)

**champaign**  extensive area of level, open land

**chott**  shallow, brackish, saline marsh, usu. dry in summer (North Africa)

**clearing**  tract of land with trees and brush removed

**coastal plain**  flat expanse of land from coast to first range of mountains

**delta**  nearly flat alluvial plain at mouth of river, usu. triangular

**desert**  arid, barren region that may support sparse vegetation

**down**  rolling, open, upland region of grassy land

**erg**  vast area covered with shifting sands, esp. in Sahara Desert

**everglade**  swampy grassland, esp. in south Florida

**fen**  low boggy land partly covered by water

**field**  open land, usu. without many trees

**fjeld**  rocky, barren plateau (Scandinavia)

**flat**  expanse of level land

**flatland**  tract of level land

**glade**  open space in forest; marshy or grassy clearing

**grassland**  plain covered with grasses

**heath**  tract of open land with uncultivated vegetation such as heather and shrubs

**kipuka**  tract of land surrounded by recent lava flow (Hawaii)

**llano**  open grassy plain (southwestern United States or Latin America)

**mainland**  primary part of continent, as distinguished from islands

**marsh**  wet, boggy land; swamp

**meadow**  expanse of grassland, often in mountains or along river

**mesa**  small, high plateau; flat-topped, steep-sided, rocky land formation

**mire**  muddy bog, swamp

**moor**  tract of open wasteland often overgrown with low shrubs; heath

**morass**  marsh, swamp

**mud flat**  level area of muddy land, usu. at edge of body of water

**paludal**  (*adj*) marshy, swampy

**pampas**  broad, grass-covered plains in South America, esp. Argentina

**peat bog**  marsh of partially carbonized decomposing vegetable matter

**piedmont**  area lying at base of mountain range

**plain**  expanse of flat or rolling, usu. treeless, land

**plateau**  extensive tract of level land raised above adjoining land

**playa**  sandy, salty, or mud-caked flat floor of desert basin, usu. occupied by shallow lake following heavy rain (western United States)

**pocosin**  upland swamp of coastal plain

**polder**  tract of lowland reclaimed from sea or lake and protected by dikes or dams

**prairie**  large tract of rolling grassland

**quag**  quagmire

**quagmire**  marsh, bog; wet ground with difficult footing; quag

**quicksand**  deep bed of loose sand saturated with water that yields underfoot

**salina**  saline marsh or spring

**salt flat**  level tract of dried salt land left by evaporation of lake or sea

**salt marsh**  marshy tract in stage between saline lake and salt flat

**salt pan**  undrained natural depression in which evaporation of water leaves deposit of salt

**savanna**  grassy plain with scattered trees; treeless plain in tropics

**scabland**  tract of high, rocky land with no topsoil and dry streambeds

**solfatara**  level area surrounding volcano emitting vapors

**steppe**  vast plain of eastern Europe having few trees

**swale**  low, marshy depression or hollow

**swamp**  wet, boggy land

**sward**  grassy surface of land; turf, sod and soil with roots

**tarpit**  flat area filled with natural tar or asphalt which is exposed to air

**tickle**  land covered with grasses, esp. witch grass

**tract**  any expanse of land

**tundra**  level, treeless plain in arctic region with dark wet soil on base of permanently frozen subsoil

**vega**  flat, barren plain (Spain)

**veld**  field or plain (southern Africa)

**wallow**  soft, muddy area

**wash**  bog, marsh

**wasteland**  barren land, desert

**wetlands**  land with nonflowing surface water, such as marsh, swamp, or bog

## WOODS AND BRUSH

**backwoods**  remote, densely forested region

**bosc**  boscage

**boscage**  thicket or grove of shrubbery; bosc

**bracken**  thicket of large coarse ferns

**brake**  often marshy land overgrown with one plant, esp. ferns

**broom**  shrubbery, esp. with yellow flowers

**brush**  land covered with scrub vegetation

**brushwood**  thicket of shrubs or small trees

**bush**  dense growth of low shrubs; expanse of uncleared area

**canebrake**  thicket of cane

**chaparral**  dense thicket of stunted evergreen oaks

**clump**  cluster of trees or shrubs

**coppice**  thicket or wood of small trees; copse

**copse**  coppice

**covert**  thicket giving cover to game

**deadfall** tangled mass of fallen trees and branches

**forest** large tract of thickly wooded land

**furze** gorse

**gorse** growth of spiny, yellow-flowering shrub; furze

**grove** small wood or group of trees growing close together

**heath** shrubby evergreen plants covering tract of open land

**hedge** row of closely planted shrubs that forms a boundary

**jungle** wild land overgrown with dense mass of tropical vegetation

**motte** grove of trees on open prairie (southwestern United States)

**oasis** fertile area of vegetation in desert

**orchard** field of fruit or nut trees

**park** wooded tract of land, often cultivated

**rain forest** tropical woods covered by tall, dense canopy of branches in area of heavy rainfall

**rush** hollow-stemmed marsh grass

**scrub** growth of low trees and shrubs

**scrubland** dry tract of land covered with scrub

**sedge** tufted marsh plant

**shinnery** dense growth of small trees, esp. scrub oak

**shrubbery** growth of shrubs

**shrubs** short, multistemmed, woody plants

**spinney** *Chiefly Brit.* small wood with undergrowth

**stand** group of trees or shrubs growing together or in a line

**sylvan** (*adj*) covered with woods or groves of trees

**thicket** dense growth of shrubs and underbrush

**timberland** forested tract

**tussock** clump or tuft of sedge or marsh grass

**underbrush** shrubs, bushes, and small trees growing beneath taller trees; undergrowth

**undergrowth** underbrush

**underwood** small trees, shrubs

**vineyard** field of grapevines

**weald** forest, wilderness; rolling, upland region of woods; wold

**wild** wilderness

**wilderness** uncultivated, uninhabited region in natural state; wild

**windbreak** line or stand of trees affording protection from wind

**wold** weald

**wood** dense growth of trees, larger than a grove and smaller than a forest

**woodland** timberland, forest

**woods** region covered with trees and shrubs

## INLAND WATERWAYS AND LAKES

**bank** ground sloping upward from edge of lake, river, or sea

**bayou** creek or stream that is tributary of larger watercourse; marshy, stagnant body of water

**bed** bottom of body of water

**bend** curve in flowing waterway

**bight** bend in river; curved coast or bay

**billabong** dry streambed that fills in rainy season; stagnant pool in wilds (Australia)

**boca** *Spanish*. river mouth; harbor opening

**branch** small stream flowing into larger stream; one fork of divided waterway

**brink** riverbank

**brook** small stream of fresh water

**canal** artificial navigable waterway that connects bodies of water or is used for irrigation

**cascade** small waterfall, esp. one of a series

**channel** bed where natural stream runs; deeper part of river

**creek** small, usu. slow-moving stream

**current** swiftest part of stream

**cutoff** new channel in river, formed by water cutting across bend in its course

**debouchement** river mouth

**distributary** branch leading from main waterway and not rejoining it

**eddy** circular movement of water in pool in stream

**euripus** strait, esp. one with violent flow of water

**falls** waterfall; series of waterfalls

**feeder** tributary leading to larger watercourse

**floating island** mass of earth and decomposing vegetation held together by intertwined roots and floating on a lake

**ford** shallow part of stream that allows crossing by wading

**fork** point where river branches into two or more parts

**fountainhead** source of a stream, usu. a spring; wellspring

**freshet** stream springing from overflow of melting snow

**geyser** spring issuing intermittent jets of steam

**headwaters** small streams and freshets that converge to form source of river, often at high altitude

**kill** channel, creek

**lagoon** shallow body of water connected to larger body of water but cut off by atoll or sandbar

**laguna** small lake or pond

**lake** inland body of standing fresh water, usu. of considerable size

**loch** *Scot.* lake

**lough** *Irish*. lake, arm of the sea

**meander** curve or bend in river on level ground

**mere** small lake, pool

**millpond** pond created by damming of river

**mouth** point where stream enters lake or sea

**narrows** portion of stream decidedly less wide than other portions

**nyanza** lake in central or eastern Africa

**outlet** mouth of river

**oxbow** U-shaped bend in river

**oxbow lake** bow-shaped lake formed when river cuts across U-shaped neck of land

**pond** inland body of standing fresh water, smaller than a lake

**pool** deep, quiet place in stream; small body of water

**puddle** very small, shallow body of water

**race** strong current flowing through narrow channel

**rapids** shallow part of stream with strong current broken by obstacles such as rocks; white water

**reach** straight portion of river or stream

**reservoir** artificial, man-made lake, esp. for storing water supply

**riffle** shoal or reef in stream that causes choppy water or rapids

**rill** runnel

**ripple** shallow stretch of rough water in stream; rapids

**river** natural stream of significant length and volume that follows definite course

**riverbank** rising ground at edge of river; brink

**riverhead** source of river

**riverside** bank of river

**rivulet** small stream, brook

**run** creek

**runnel** very small brook; rill

**runoff** rainwater or melted snow flowing down mountain into streams

**salt lake** body of water in dry region, with no outlet, that has become saline through evaporation

**sandbar** ridge of sand accumulated by currents in stream

**sault** waterfall or rapids

**shallows** portion of stream with slight depth

**shoal** shallow place in river; sandbar

**sike** *Scot.* small stream, usu. dry in summer

**sink** saline lake with no outlet

**spout** waterspout

**spring** source of water issuing from ground

**strait** narrow waterway that passes between larger bodies of water

**stream** flowing body of water smaller than a river

**swash** narrow channel between sandbar and shore or within sandbar

**torrent** stream with strong, rapid current

**tributary** stream leading into larger stream, river, or lake

**vortex** whirlpool

**watercourse** any natural stream of flowing water; waterway

**waterfall** very steep or perpendicular stream of water, often over precipice; falls

**water hole** small hollow filled with standing water

**waterspout** geyser; spout

**water system** river with all its branches and tributaries

**waterway** watercourse

**well** pool filled by spring; flow of water from earth

**wellspring** source of a stream; fountainhead

**whirlpool** water spinning rapidly in a circle that produces downward sucking force at its center into which floating objects are pulled; vortex

**white water** rapids

## COASTAL LAND, ISLANDS, AND THE SEA

**archipelago** group of sea islands, esp. in curved row

**arm** narrow inland extension of sea

**atoll** ring-shaped coral reef enclosing lagoon

**barrier reef** coral reef separated from shore by lagoon

**bay** body of water forming indentation on shoreline of sea or large lake; wide inlet of sea smaller than a gulf

**beach** rocky or sandy area along edge of sea or ocean

**cape** point of land extending into water; peninsula

**cay** key

**channel** strait of sea between two landmasses

**coast** land along shore of ocean or sea

**coastline** boundary between land and sea

**côte** *French.* coast

**cove** small, sheltered recess in shoreline

**current** tidal movement of ocean waters

**estuary** point where river mouth meets sea's tide; arm of sea at river mouth

**firth** *Scot.* narrow arm of sea; mouth of river into sea

**fjord** long, narrow arm of sea with steep cliffs

**floe** large, flat mass of ice floating on sea

**gulf** section of ocean or sea that extends into land, larger than a bay

**harbor** coastal waters protected from open sea and deep enough for anchoring ships

**headland** high point of land projecting into sea; promontory

**high seas** open ocean several miles or more from shore

**holm** small inland or inshore island

**hook** curved spit of land

**horizon** distant point where sky seems to meet sea

**iceberg** large mass of ice broken off from glacier, floating in sea

**inlet** indent in shoreline, esp. narrow passage between points of land or islands, often forming entrance to lagoon

**island** land area completely surrounded by water, smaller than a continent

**isle** island

**islet** small island

**isthmus** narrow strip of land with water on both sides connecting two larger bodies of land

**key** low island or reef, esp. coral islet off south Florida; cay

**lagoon** shallow body of water connected to the sea

**littoral** (*adj*) of, on, or along the shore

**marine** (*adj*) of or at the sea or ocean

**neck** narrow strip of land, usu. between bodies of water

**ocean** any of vast, connected bodies of salt water that cover almost three-fourths of Earth's surface

**oceanfront** land directly along seashore

**offshore** (*adj*) designating area of sea lying a short way from beach

**pelagic** (*adj*) of or on the open sea

**peninsula** large land area almost completely surrounded by water, usu. connected to mainland by isthmus

**plage** *French.* beach

**playa** *Spanish.* beach

**point** land projecting into sea and narrowing at end

**polynya** area of open water enclosed by sea ice

**promontory** headland

**reach** narrow arm of sea that extends inland

**reef** ridge of rock or coral just under water surface

**ria** long, narrow inlet where sea has overflowed river valley

**riviera** coastal region of sea used as a resort area

**sandbank** large deposit of sand that forms a shoal

**sand bar** underwater ridge of sand formed in coastal waters

**sand dune** tall mound of sand on beach

**sea** large body of salt water, generally landlocked and smaller than the ocean; also used as synonym for ocean

**seaboard** seashore

**sea cliff** steep slope overlooking ocean

**seacoast** land situated along ocean

**seascape** view or scene of sea or ocean

**seashore** land at edge of sea, esp. beach; seaboard

**sea strand** long section of seashore

**seaway** deep inland waterway connecting with sea

**shingle** coarse alluvial material along seashore

**shoal** sandbar beneath shallow water, sometimes exposed at low tide

**shore** land bordering a sea or ocean; coast

**shoreline** edge of land where a large body of water meets land

**skerry** reef; rocky island

**sound** passage between bodies of water; long inlet or arm of sea; water separating island from mainland

**spit** narrow point of land extending into water; long, narrow reef

**strait** narrow waterway connecting larger bodies of water

**strand** land along body of water; beach; tidal land alternately covered and exposed by tides

**surf** waves breaking against rocks and beach at shore

**tidal basin** artificial body of water open to river and subject to tides

**tidal land** flatland at seashore exposed at low tide, covered at high tide; tideland

**tide** rise and fall of surface of ocean and connected bodies of water due to gravitational pull of moon and sun

**tideland** tidal land

**tide pool** tiny lagoon left in rocks along shore by withdrawing tide

**tidewater** ocean water that overflows land at high tide

**tideway** channel through which tide rises and falls

**tombolo** sandbar extending from an island to the mainland or another island

**waterfront** strip of land at edge of ocean or other waterway

# Weather and Natural Phenomena

Storms
Winds
Clouds
Disasters and Phenomena
Weather Conditions
Forecasting and Meteorology
Cyclical Events

**see also**: Chap. 3: Geology; Geography; Landscapes and Seascapes

## Storms

**anticyclone** wind system that rotates around high-pressure center in opposite direction from cyclone

**blizzard** severe snowstorm with large accumulations of snow

**cloudburst** sudden, intense rainstorm

**cyclone** advancing wind system with heavy rain that rotates around low-pressure pressure center clockwise in Southern Hemisphere, counterclockwise in Northern Hemisphere

**deluge** heavy rainstorm that causes flooding

**downpour** intense rainstorm

**dust storm** whirlwind of dust in dry region with hot, electrically charged air

**electrical storm** storm with atmospheric electrical discharge, thunder, and lightning

**gale** moderate windstorm, 32 to 63 mph, esp. at sea

**graupel** soft hail or granular snow pellets

**haboob** violent storm of dust or sand in North Africa, the Middle East, or India

**hail** shower of small lumps of snow or compacted ice pellets, graded by size: pea, marble, golf ball, hen's egg, tennis ball, grapefruit, football

**hurricane** tropical cyclone at sea with heavy rain and winds

over 72 mph, sometimes moving into temperate latitudes; tropical cyclone

**ice storm** storm with rain that freezes on contact with air

**line squall** thunderstorm along cold front

**maelstrom** powerful, turbulent whirlpool or whirlwind

**monsoon** seasonal windstorm that brings heavy rains off Indian Ocean

**neutercane** subtropical cyclone less than 100 miles in diameter

**rain** water droplets formed by condensation of atmospheric vapor falling to earth

**rainsquall** rain with gusty winds

**rainstorm** steady, prolonged rainfall

**shower** mild, brief rainfall

**sleet** frozen or partly frozen rain

**slush** partly melted, watery snow

**snow** precipitation formed into white ice crystals from water vapor at temperatures below freezing

**snow flurries** occasional windblown bursts of snowfall

**snowstorm** precipitation of small, dry crystals of water vapor

**squall** sudden, violent windstorm, often with rain or snow

**storm** atmospheric disturbance marked by wind and/or precipitation

**tempest** extensive, violent windstorm with rain or snow

**thundershower** mild thunderstorm

**thunderstorm** rainstorm with thunder and lightning

**tornado** violent whirlwind, advancing over land with funnel-shaped cloud; twister

**torrential rain** very heavy rainstorm

**tropical cyclone** hurricane

**tropical storm** tropical cyclone with winds under 73 mph

**twister** *Informal.* tornado

**typhoon** tropical cyclone in China Sea

**weather front** advancing storm

**willy-willy** severe tropical cyclone (Australia)

## Winds

**anemometer** wind-measuring instrument

**arctic** icy wind from north

**austral wind** southerly wind

**Beaufort scale** measure of wind force in miles per hour on scale from one (calm) to twelve (hurricane)

**berg** warm, dry wind blowing toward coast (South Africa)

**bise** cold, dry, northerly wind in Alps

**bora** cold, violent, northerly wind off Adriatic

**boreal** northerly wind

**breath** wind under 3 mph

**breeze** relatively gentle wind of 4–31 mph; any light wind

**cat's paw** light air that ruffles calm water surface

**chinook** warm, dry wind off eastern Rocky Mountains

**downwind** (*adv*) in direction toward which wind is blowing

**dust devil** small whirlwind of sand and dust

**favonian wind** west wind

**foehn** warm, dry wind blowing down mountainside

**fresh breeze** 19–24 mph wind

**fresh gale** 39–46 mph wind

**gale** 32–63 mph wind

**gentle breeze** 8–12 mph wind

**ghibli** hot desert wind of northern Africa

**gust** sudden, sharp burst of wind

**harmattan** dusty wind on Atlantic coast of Africa

**headwind** wind blowing against course of ship or aircraft

**howling wind** wild, loud gust of wind

**hurricane** storm with winds over 72 mph

**katabatic wind** wind blowing down mountain valley at night

**khamsin** hot southerly wind (Egypt)

**knot** measure of wind velocity equal to 1 nautical mile per hour

**levanter** strong easterly wind on Mediterranean

**light breeze** 4-7 mph wind

**mistral** cold, dry, strong northerly wind in southern France

**moderate breeze** 13-18 mph wind

**moderate gale** 32-38 mph wind

**nor'easter** wind from northeast

**norther** strong wind from north

**northerly** wind from north

**nor'wester** wind from northwest

**offshore** (*adj*) blowing from shore to sea

**onshore** (*adj*) blowing from sea to shore

**pampero** strong, cold westerly or southwesterly wind on pampas (Argentina)

**prevailing wind** general direction of swirling wind

**puna** cold mountain wind (Peru)

**samiel** hot, dry, violent, dusty desert wind (Africa)

**Santa Ana** hot, dry wind off desert in southern California

**sea breeze** moist wind off ocean

**simoom** hot, dry desert wind (Middle East and North Africa)

**sirocco** hot, oppressive wind from arid region, esp. on Mediterranean from Libyan desert

**solano** hot, easterly, Mediterranean wind that brings rain

**southeaster** wind from southeast

**southerly** wind from south

**southwester** wind from southwest

**squall** sudden, violent windstorm

**strong breeze** 25-31 mph wind

**strong gale** 47-54 mph wind

**tailwind** wind blowing in same direction as course of ship or aircraft

**tourbillion** whirlwind, esp. vortex of whirlwind

**trade wind** wind blowing almost continually toward equator

**tramontane** violent, polar wind from northwest (southern France)

**updraft** air pulling upward into atmosphere

**upwind** (*adv*) in direction from which wind is blowing

**violent storm** 64-72 mph wind

**vortex** whirlwind

**waft** light breath of moving air

**westerlies** winds from subtropical areas in west toward middle latitudes

**whirlwind** air current rotating violently upward around vertical axis and moving forward; vortex

**whole gale** 55 to 63 mph wind; windstorm

**williwaw** sudden, violent squall of cold wind, common on mountainous coasts at near-polar latitudes

**wind** natural movement of air at any velocity, esp. horizontal relative to Earth's surface

**windstorm** strong winds with no rain

**zephyr** gentle breeze from west

**zonda** warm, humid northerly wind (South America)

# CLOUDS

**altocumulus** white, globular cloudlets that appear in broken patches at altitudes around 10,000 feet (3048 m), usu. producing rain showers

**altostratus** dark, drab, thin cloud streaks at middle altitudes

**billowing** (*adj*) describing bulging masses of high clouds

**cirrocumulus** irregular, small, white sheets of cloud segments at altitudes around 20,000 feet (6096 m)

**cirrostratus** even layer of translucent, fibrous cloud streaks at altitudes of 20,000 feet (6096 m) or more, indicating that rain is coming

**cirrus** wispy, white cloud tufts and filaments at high altitudes up to 40,000 feet (12,192 m)

**cloud** visible mass of water or ice particles suspended at considerable height

**cumulocirrus** small, delicate cumulus at high altitude

**cumulonimbus** thunderstorm cumulus that spreads from dark portions at 5000 feet (1524 m) to towers rising upward to 50,000 feet (15,240 m)

**cumulostratus** cumulus with flat stratus base

**cumulus** cloud with flat, dark base around 2000 feet (610 m) and rounded, white mountainous outlines to altitudes of 10,000 feet (3048 m), that appears in a broken mass

**nimbostratus** low, dark gray rain cloud a few hundred feet above ground with ragged tops upward to 3000 feet (914 m), producing continuous precipitation

**nimbus** rain cloud of uniform gray that covers entire sky

**noctilucent cloud** luminous, thin, colored cloud seen at night

**nubilous** (*adj*) relating to clouds

**rack** wind-driven mass of high, broken clouds

**stratocumulus** large, rounded mass of dark cloud covering the entire sky, esp. in winter, at altitudes from 1500 to 6500 feet (457 to 1981 m), not producing rain

**stratus** flattened streaks of cloud at altitudes of a few hundred feet, similar to ground fog and producing drizzle

**thundercloud** electrically charged cloud that produces thunder and lightning; esp. cumulonimbus

**woolpack** cumulus cloud of fleecy appearance with flat base

# DISASTERS AND PHENOMENA

**acid rain** precipitation with excess acidity due to industrial pollutants

**aftershock** smaller tremor following main shock of earthquake

**air pollution** condition in which toxic substances are in atmosphere, esp. as a result of industrial and automobile emissions

**alpenglow** reddish glow at sunset and sunrise on mountain summit

**aurora australis** antarctic version of aurora borealis

**aurora borealis** streamers and bands of electrically caused radiant emissions that light up arctic night sky

**avalanche** large mass of snow, ice, and mud moving rapidly down mountain

**ball lightning** rare, luminous floating ball of lightning

**black ice** thin sheet of ice, often caused by freezing mist on roadway; transparent coating of ice on the sea

**bolt of lightning** common, streaking flash of lightning, usu. with thunder

**bore** tidal flood caused by rapid rise in water in channel

**corn snow** pellets or grains of snow formed by alternate melting and freezing

**corona discharge** storm phenomenon caused by discharge of electricity shaped like flames at surface of conductor; corposant; Saint Elmo's fire

**corposant** corona discharge

**dew** moisture condensed at night on surfaces of cool objects

**dewfall** nightly accumulation of dew

**dew point** temperature at which vapor condenses

**drizzle** very light, misty rain

**drought** prolonged period without rain

**earthquake** volcanic or tectonic crustal movement of Earth resulting in trembling, shaking, and fracturing; quake; temblor

**eclipse** total or partial obscuring of one celestial body by another

**ecocatastrophe** destructive upset in balance of nature, esp. from people's activities or negligence

**eddy** air or water current running against main current; whirlpool

**El Niño** unusually warm Pacific Ocean current that occurs periodically and often causes catastrophic weather conditions

**epicenter** Earth's surface directly above true center of earthquake

**erosion** wearing away of topsoil by wind and water

**eruption** violent release of steam and lava from volcano

**eye** calm region at center of cyclone or hurricane

**fault line** fracture in Earth's crust with displacement indicating and causing earthquakes

**flash flood** sudden, localized, massive rush of water due to heavy rainfall

**flood** overflow of body of water onto normally dry land; inundation

**flux** continuous flow of water, resulting in flood

**fog** thick mist or vapor suspended in lower atmosphere near ground

**freeze** drop in temperature below 32° F, or 0° C

**frost** minute ice crystals that form on surfaces; hoar

**frost heave** uplift of ground caused by freezing of moist soil

**frost hollow** low-lying area in which dense, cold air accumulates

**greenhouse effect** warming of Earth's surface and lower atmosphere when solar radiation is converted to heat and trapped in atmosphere by cloud layers and gases

**ground fog** low, often dense fog, esp. one through which sky and clouds above can be seen; radiation fog

**Gulf Stream** warm Atlantic current flowing from Florida to New England and Newfoundland

**haar** *Chiefly Brit.* cold sea mist or fog

**hailstone** pellet of compressed ice and snow

**hoar** frost

**hyperborean** (*adj*) of or relating to the extreme north; frozen

**hypocenter** focus of earthquake; epicenter

**ice floe** flat, floating mass of ice at sea

**ice fog** frozen fog vapor

**ignis fatuus** eerie light at night over marshland due to combustion of gas from decomposing organic matter

**Indian summer** unseasonably hot weather in autumn

**inundation** flood

**Jack Frost** personification of frosty weather

**jet stream** long, narrow, westerly 250 mph air current at high altitude in tropopause

**killing frost** last frost of spring or first frost of fall, limiting growing season for all but hardiest plants

**landslide** mass of rock and earth moving rapidly down slope

**lava** molten rock that issues from volcano

**lightning** flash of light from discharge of atmospheric electricity between clouds or between clouds and Earth

**lunar eclipse** condition produced by Earth lying directly between sun and moon so that moon passes through Earth's shadow

**meteor shower** cluster of falling rocks, incandescent from passage through Earth's atmosphere, generally burned up before reaching ground

**midnight sun** midsummer phenomenon at arctic and antarctic latitudes, where sun does not sink below horizon during night

**mist** fine light rain or thick fog

**mizzle** rain in very fine droplets; drizzle

**mudflow** mass of soil moved by rain and melting snow

**mud slide** mass of mud, swelled by rain or flood, moving down slope

**natural phenomenon** distinct, observable event, fact, or circumstance not caused directly by humans

**ozone depletion** chemical breakup in stratosphere of ozone layer, which absorbs sun's ultraviolet radiation

**pea soup** *Informal.* extremely thick fog

**pogonip** dense ice fog found in mountain valleys of western United States

**pollution** man-made contamination of Earth and atmosphere

**quake** earthquake

**radiation fog** fog produced by nocturnal cooling of surface boundary layer so that its content of water vapor condenses; ground fog

**rainbow** arc of prismatic colors in sky, formed by reflection and refraction of sun's rays through water vapor drops

**red snow** snow colored red by airborne dust and algae

**rime** frost, esp. coating of tiny granular ice tufts, due to supercooling and exposure to wind

**rip current** undertow

**riptide** strong, narrow surface current that opposes another tide and disturbs sea

**runoff** water from rain or melted snow flowing over land surface and reaching streams

**Saint Elmo's fire** corona discharge

**sea puss** swirling shore undertow

**seismic** (*adj*) of or relating to earthquakes

**sheet lightning** lightning obscured and diffused by clouds so that it appears over a broad area

**smaze** mixture of smoke and haze

**smog** fog augmented by smoke, chemical fumes, and automobile exhausts

**snowbank** mound of snow

**snowcap** snow covering mountain peak

**snowdrift** tall bank of windblown snow

**snowfield** broad expanse of snow

**snowflake** small, tabular, columnar, or otherwise geometrically regular, white ice crystal

**snowpack** accumulation of winter snow at high altitudes

**snowslide** landslide of snow and ice; avalanche

**solar eclipse** condition in which moon passes directly between sun and Earth

**spindrift** spray swept by wind from waves during storm at sea; spoondrift

**spoondrift** spindrift

**storm surge** sudden high tide, 10 to 20 feet (3 to 6 m) above normal, accompanying hurricane

**sunburst** flash of sunlight through break in clouds

**temblor** earthquake

**tephra** dust and solid matter ejected in volcanic eruption

**thunder** sudden, loud, booming noise following lightning, due to expansion of air heated by electrical discharge

**thunderbolt** single flash of lightning with accompanying thunder

**thunderclap** booming crash of thunder

**thunderhead** rounded upper mass of cumulonimbus clouds, signaling thunderstorm

**tidal wave** unusually high sea wave, often following earthquake; unusually high tide due to high winds and storm; tsunami

**total eclipse** complete obscuring of one celestial body by another

**tremor** mild earthquake

**tsunami** tidal wave

**undertow** current beneath ocean surface moving forcefully out to sea; rip current

**vapor** diffuse fog or smoke floating in air

**virga** streaks of precipitation that fall from cloud but evaporate before reaching ground

**volcano** vent in Earth's crust from which steam and molten rock are expelled

**waterspout** funnel-shaped column of mist and spray reaching from surface of sea or lake to underside of cloud

**whirlpool** eddy

**whiteout** severe blizzard condition with low visibility, no shadows, and only dark objects distinguishable

**zero-zero** condition of zero visibility in vertical and horizontal directions

**zodiacal light** luminous tract in sky in west after twilight and in east before dawn

## Weather Conditions

### Clear Weather

azure
blue skies
clear, cloudless
fair
high visibility
shiny, sunny, sunshine

### Cold Weather

arctic
biting, bitter, boreal, brisk
chilly, cold, cold snap, cold wave, cool
freezing, frigid, frosty
gelid, glacial
icy

nippy
subzero

### Hot Weather

close
dog days
hot, humid
muggy
sultry, sweltering
torrid, tropical

### Mild Weather

balmy
calm
dry
fair
mild
seasonable
temperate
warm

### Overcast Weather

cloudy
dark
foggy, foul
half-light, hazy
lowering, low visibility
misty, murky
overcast
partly cloudy
shady, smoggy, soupy, sunless

### Wet Weather

deluge, downpour, drizzle
freezing rain
inclement
rainy
showers, sleet, slush, snowing, soaking, sprinkles
torrential rains

### Windy Weather

blast, blow, blustery, breath, breeze
draft
flurry
gale, gusty
swirling
turbulent
windy

## Forecasting and Meteorology

**air mass** body of air hundreds of miles across and extending upward to the stratosphere, with uniform temperature and humidity

**air pressure** weight of air pushing down on Earth's surface

**anemometer** instrument for determining wind speed

**aneroid barometer** barometer in which atmospheric pressure moves pointer

**Antarctic** region surrounding South Pole, 66 1/2 degrees south of equator

**Arctic** region surrounding North Pole, 66 1/2 degrees north of equator

**arctic air mass** cold front moving from frigid to temperate zone in Northern Hemisphere

**atmosphere** entire mass of air enveloping Earth

**atmospheric pressure** pressure of air at any given point, equal to 14.7 pounds per square inch at sea level

**backing** counterclockwise change in wind direction at specific place

**barometer** instrument for measuring atmospheric pressure as indicator of weather change

**barometric pressure** pressure of atmosphere measured by height of column of mercury in which standard atmospheric pressure equals 29.92 inches (760 mm)

**ceiling** altitude of base of cloud layer obscuring at least half the sky

**ceilometer** photoelectric device for measuring and recording height of cloud ceiling above Earth

**Celsius** thermometric scale with zero degrees as freezing point of water and one hundred degrees as boiling point, designated C; Centigrade

**Centigrade** Celsius

**chill factor** windchill factor

**climate** prevailing temperature, wind velocity, humidity, cloudiness, and precipitation at given location over period of years

**col** area of intermediate pressure between two anticyclones or two depressions

**cold front** advancing edge of cold air mass

**depression** area in which atmospheric pressure is lower than surrounding areas, causing unsettled weather; low pressure

**equator** great circle of Earth, equidistant from two poles, dividing surface into northern and southern hemispheres

**Fahrenheit** thermometric scale of 180 degrees with freezing point of water at 32 degrees and boiling point at 212 degrees, designated F

**fogbound** (adj) surrounded by fog; unable to navigate because of fog

**forecast** prediction of weather based on meteorological data

**front** advancing edge of air mass

**gale warning** weather bureau prediction of gale force sea winds

**Groundhog Day** February 2, day on which legend has it that sunny skies mean six more weeks of winter, cloudy skies, an early spring

**heavy rain** significant rainfall

**heavy snow** significant snowfall

**high** high-pressure air mass

**high-pressure** (adj) designating air mass with barometric pressure exceeding atmospheric pressure

**horse latitudes** region thirty degrees north to thirty degrees south of equator, characterized by high pressure and relative calm

**humidity** measure of percentage of moisture in atmosphere

**inversion** increase of air temperature at higher altitude

**isobar** map line that connects locations of equal barometric pressure

**isohyet** map line that connects locations of equal rainfall

**isotherm** map line that connects locations of equal temperature

**low** low-pressure air mass

**low-pressure** (adj.) designating air mass with barometric pressure less than atmospheric pressure

**meteorology** scientific study of atmospheric phenomena, used to forecast weather

**occluded front** air mass forced aloft when cold front overtakes warm front

**occlusion** cutting off of contact between air mass and Earth's surface

**pluviometer** gauge for measuring rainfall

**polar front** boundary between cold arctic air and warm air of lower latitudes

**precipitation** falling to earth of hail, rain, or snow

**radiosonde** instrument that transmits meteorological data from balloon at high altitude

**rainfall** measure of total precipitation over specified period in given location

**rain gauge** instrument used to measure rainfall over given period of time; pluviometer

**relative humidity** ratio of moisture present in air to maximum moisture possible at given temperature

**ridge** elongated high-pressure area between two depressions

**saturated air** air containing maximum water vapor possible at given temperature

**seasonable** (adj) normal for time of year

**seeding** producing rain by sprinkling dry ice or silver iodide crystals in stratus cloud layers

**semitropical** (adj) subtropical

**sferics** electronic storm detection and tracking

**small craft warning** advisory of gale force winds at sea

**snowfall** total inches of accumulated snow

**stationary front** air mass holding fixed position

**storm warning** weather bureau notice of impending high winds and heavy precipitation

**subarctic** (adj) adjacent to Arctic Circle

**subtropical** (adj) typical of regions bordering the tropics; semitropical

**system** interacting fronts and air masses that cause weather conditions

**temperate zone** latitudes between tropic of Cancer and Arctic Circle, or between tropic of Capricorn and Antarctic Circle

**temperature** degree of hotness or coldness as measured on standardized scale

**temperature inversion** layer of warm air that surmounts cooler air and traps pollutants near ground

**thermal** rising current of warm air

**thermometer** device used to measure temperature, esp. by height of column of mercury

**torrid zone** area surrounding equator, extending north to tropic of Cancer and south to tropic of Capricorn; tropics

**tropic** either of two parallels of celestial latitude bounding torrid zone and marking sun's southernmost and northernmost declinations

**tropic of Cancer** latitude 23 1/2 degrees north of equator

**tropic of Capricorn** latitude 23 1/2 degrees south of equator

**tropics** latitudes between tropics of Cancer and Capricorn, extending 23 1/2 degrees north and south of equator; torrid zone

**troposphere** layer of atmosphere nearest Earth, where weather conditions occur

**trough** elongated low-pressure area between two areas of higher pressure

**unseasonable** (*adj*) abnormal for time of year

**veering** clockwise change in wind direction at specific place

**visibility** degree of atmospheric clearness; measure of greatest distance at which object can be seen by naked eye

**warm front** advancing edge of warm air mass

**wave** period of intense, unseasonable heat or cold

**weather** state of Earth's atmosphere at specific time with regard to heat, humidity, visibility, pressure, wind speed, and disturbance

**weather bureau** office for collecting weather information, making predictions, and compiling statistics

**weathercock** mounted, rotating vane in form of cock that indicates wind direction

**weather forecast** scientific prediction of weather

**weather front** mass of air with specific pressure and temperature

**weatherman** male weatherperson, formerly used for either sex

**weather map** chart with meteorological elements shown at specific times and places

**weatherperson** individual who reports and predicts weather

**weather station** installation for recording meteorological measurements and observations

**weather system** interacting fronts and air masses generating specific weather conditions

**weather vane** mounted, rotating object that indicates wind direction

**wedge** high-pressure area between two depressions, narrower than a ridge

**windchill factor** temperature felt on exposed skin equal to combination of actual temperature and wind speed; chill factor

**wind sleeve** mounted cone open at both ends, used to indicate wind direction; windsock

**windsock** wind sleeve

**zone** one of five major latitudinal divisions of Earth's surface with respect to temperature: frigid (north and south), temperate (north and south), torrid (equatorial)

## CYCLICAL EVENTS

**autumn** September 22 to December 20; fall

**autumnal** (*adj*) occurring in autumn

**autumnal equinox** first day of autumn, usu. September 22 in Northern Hemisphere

**blue moon** occurrence of two full moons in one month, taking place approximately every thirty-two months

**canicular** (*adj*) of or relating to dog days

**crepuscule** twilight

**crescent moon** phase of moon between new and first quarter or between last quarter and new

**dawn** hour during and after sunrise with first light

**daylight** hours between sunrise and sunset

**dog days** period of hot, sultry weather from July to late August in Northern Hemisphere

**dusk** hour during and after sunset with last light

**ebb tide** diminishing tide

**equinox** time of year when sun crosses equator, making day and night of equal length everywhere, usu. March 21 and September 22

**fall** September 22 to December 20; autumn

**full moon** phase in which entire visible disk of moon is illuminated by sun

**gibbous moon** phase between full and quarter moon, either waxing or waning

**gloaming** hour of darkness during and after sunset

**harvest moon** full moon nearest autumnal equinox

**hibernal** (*adj*) occurring in winter

**high tide** highest point reached by tide, usu. twice daily

**low tide** lowest point reached by tide, usu. twice daily

**moonrise** hour of moon's appearance in sky

**moonset** hour of moon's disappearance from sky

**neap tide** tide of minimum range at first and third lunar quarters

**new moon** phase in which dark side of moon faces Earth, with thin crescent moon seen a few days thereafter

**quarter moon** phase midway between full and new moon

**seasonal** (*adj*) occurring regularly during a specific season

**slack tide** period at turn of tide with little or no horizontal motion of tidal water

**solstice** time of year when sun is furthest north or south of celestial equator, June 21 or December 21

**spring** March 21 to June 20

**summer** June 21 to September 21

**summer solstice** June 21, being first day of summer and longest daylight period in Northern Hemisphere

**sundown** hour of sunset

**sunrise** hour of sun's appearance in east

**sunset** hour of sun's disappearance in west

**thaw** period in spring when snow and ice melt

**tide** twice daily alternate rising and falling of ocean waters due to unequal gravitational attraction of sun and moon

**twilight** hour after sunset; crepuscule

**vernal** (*adj*) occurring in spring

**vernal equinox** first day of spring, usu. March 21 in Northern Hemisphere

**wane tide** decreasing tide

**wax tide** increasing tide

**winter** December 21 to March 20

**winter solstice** December 21, being first day of winter and shortest daylight period in Northern Hemisphere

# PART TWO

# SCIENCE AND TECHNOLOGY

# The Sciences

# PHYSICS

Branches and Disciplines
Principles Of Mechanics, Waves, and Measurement
Electricity and Magnetism
Nuclear and Particle Physics
Cosmology
Heat
Optics
Acoustics

**SEE ALSO**: Chap. 3: Geology; Weather and Natural Phenomena; Chap. 4: Astronomy and Space Science; Chemistry; Chap. 5: Machinery and Fabrication; Electricity and Electronics

## BRANCHES AND DISCIPLINES

**acoustics**  study of production, control, transmission, reception, effects, and nature of sound waves

**actinology**  study of the chemical effects produced by electromagnetic radiation

**astrophysics**  study of physical and chemical constitution of the universe, esp. celestial matter

**atomic physics**  study of the nature of the atom and subatomic particles

**biophysics**  application of principles and methods of physics to biological problems

**chaos**  study of hidden, ordered structures or regularities in seemingly chaotic phenomena

**Copernican physics**  theories formulated by Nicolaus Copernicus that Earth revolves with other planets in orbits around sun

**cosmology**  study of structure, origin, evolution, and probable fate of the universe

**cryogenics**  study of production and application of effects of very low temperatures

**crystallography**  study of form, structure, properties, and classification of crystals

**dynamics**  branch of mechanics dealing with motion of material bodies under action of given forces

**electricity**  study of phenomena and laws governing attraction and repulsion of electrons and other charged particles

**electronics**  study of electron behavior

**fluid mechanics**  hydraulics

**geophysics**  branch of geology dealing with Earth physics: meteorology, oceanography, seismology, magnetism, radioactivity, geodesy

**gravitation**  study of the force of acceleration toward each other of two material particles or bodies

**heat**  study of production, properties, and effects of thermal energy

**heliology**  study of sunlight

**hydraulics**  study of mechanical properties of water and other liquids in motion and the engineering applications of these properties; fluid mechanics

**hydrodynamics**  study of fluids in motion and their interaction with their boundaries

**hydrostatics**  study of fluids at rest

**kinetics**  branch of mechanics dealing with all aspects of motion

**magnetism**  study of phenomena associated with magnets and electric currents

**mechanics**  study of energy and forces and their effect on matter

**Newtonian physics**  system based on laws of gravitation and motion developed by Sir Isaac Newton

**nuclear physics**  study of structure, behavior, and radioactive properties of atomic nuclei

**nucleonics**  study of nucleons and practical applications of nuclear phenomena

**optics**  study of propagation, control, transmission, reception, effects, and phenomena of light waves

**particle physics**  study of nature and interaction of subatomic particles

**physics**  study of properties and interaction of matter and energy

**pneumatics**  study of mechanical properties of air and other gases in closed systems

**quantum mechanics**  modern theory of matter which supersedes classical physics and concentrates on atomic and subatomic phenomena in terms of observable quantities

**relativity**  system of thought based on theories of Albert Einstein regarding universal character of propagation speed of light and consequent dependence of space, time, and other mechanical measurements on motion of observer performing measurements

**statics**  branch of mechanics dealing with action of forces on bodies at rest

**thermionics**  study of electron or ion emissions from heated surfaces

**thermodynamics**  study of quantitative relationship and conversion between heat and other energy forms, esp. mechanical energy or work

**wave mechanics**  form of quantum mechanics in which particle motion is described by wave motion

## PRINCIPLES OF MECHANICS, WAVES, AND MEASUREMENT

**acceleration**  rate of change in velocity with respect to time

**acceleration of gravity**  change in velocity due to gravitational attraction

**accuracy**  proximity of measurement to true or absolute value

**angular displacement**  amount of rotation of point, line, or body in specified direction about an axis

**angular impulse**  product of a torque and the time interval during which it acts

**angular momentum**  product of rotational inertia of a body and its angular velocity

**angular velocity**  time rate of change of angular displacement

**antinodal line**  line connecting points at which two waves interfere constructively at their maximum amplitudes

**Archimedes' principle**  object immersed in a fluid is buoyed up by a force equal to the weight of the fluid it displaces

**beat**  oscillation in amplitude of complex wave and interference resulting from it

**Bernoulli effect** pressure exerted by a fluid decreases as its velocity increases

**bond** electrostatic attraction between atoms or groups of atoms

**calculus** system of calculation using symbolic notations, essential to modern physics

**capillary attraction** tendency of liquid to rise in narrow tube or move through absorbent material, due to greater adhesion of liquid to solid than internal adhesion of the liquid itself

**center of gravity** fixed point in body through which force of gravitational attraction acts

**centrifugal force** force that tends to move particles rotating about an axis outward from center of rotation

**centripetal acceleration** acceleration always at right angles to velocity of particle

**centripetal force** force directed toward the center of a circle that keeps particles in uniform circular motion, assumed to be equal and opposite to centrifugal force

**cogeneration** simultaneous generation of electrical energy and low grade heat from same fuel

**components of a vector** two or more perpendicular vectors that when added together produce the original vector

**compression** reduction in volume of substance due to pressure

**concurrent forces** forces acting on same point

**coordinates** numbers that specify position in space and time

**correspondence principle** laws of quantum mechanics and any other new theory reduce to laws of Newtonian mechanics when Planck's constant is negligible, wavelengths are relatively small, and dimensions are relatively large

**crest** region of upward displacement in transverse wave

**damping** reduction in wave amplitude due to energy dissipation

**de Broglie principle** material particles have wavelike characteristics which can give rise to interference effects and diffraction

**deceleration** negative acceleration; rate at which motion slows

**density** mass per unit of volume; distribution per unit of space

**derived unit** unit of measurement defined in terms of other units

**dimensional quantities** physical measurements expressed in defined mathematical units

**direct variation** increase or decrease in one variable causing proportional increase or decrease in another variable

**displacement** vector quantity representing change in position of an object

**dissipative forces** frictional forces for which law of conservation of mechanical energy does not hold true

**distance** spatial separation of two points measured by length of hypothetical straight line joining them

**Doppler effect** amount of decrease or increase in frequency of radiation as source and observer of waves move toward or away from each other

**efficiency** ratio of machine's useful power output to power input

**elastic collision** collision in which total kinetic energy of two colliding objects is the same before and after collision

**elasticity** ability of object to return to its original form after removal of deforming forces

**endothermic** (*adj*) referring to process that absorbs energy

**energy** capacity to do work

**energy-matter relationship** energy is equal to mass times the velocity of light squared, expressed as $e = mc^2$

**entropy** measure of disorder of a system; internal energy of a system that cannot be converted to mechanical work

**equilibrant** force equal in magnitude to resultant, but opposite in direction, producing an equilibrium

**equilibrium** condition in which net force on object is zero and there is no change in its motion

**equivalence principle** gravitational and inertial masses are equal

**exothermic** (*adj*) referring to process that releases energy

**explosion** violent, outward expansion of forces

**extrapolation** extending of graph beyond measured points to infer values outside known range

**field** region of space containing lines of force with direction and strength; force that acts through space and time, as opposed to particle existing at one fixed point in space and time

**fluid** material that flows, such as liquid or gas

**force** action that results in acceleration or deformation of an object; measure of momentum gained per second by accelerating object

**frame of reference** coordinate system used to assign positions and times to events in describing motion

**friction** force resisting motion between two objects that are in contact

**fundamental forces** four basic forces acting in nature: strong force, electromagnetic force, weak force, gravitational force

**fundamental units** units of measurement defined in terms of a physical standard, not other units; seven basic units of measurement; International System of Units

**gas** phase of matter in which substance expands readily to fill any containing vessel, characterized by relatively low density

**general theory of relativity** Einstein's theory of gravitation, expressed in terms of curved space-time, which stipulates that the laws of science are identical for all observers regardless of their motion

**graph** plot on rectangular coordinates showing relationship of two variables

**gravitational field** region in space in which particles experience gravitational force

**gravitational force** mutual attraction between particles due to their masses

**gravitational potential energy** potential energy acquired by object when moved against gravity

**heat** energy resulting from disordered motion of molecules

**Hooke's law** stress applied to a solid body is directly proportional to strain produced

**ideal gas** theoretical gas composed of infinitely small molecules that exert no force on each other

**ideal mechanical advantage** ratio of distance through which effort is exerted to distance over which resistance is encountered in a machine

**imaginary time** measurement of time in complex numbers based on square root of –1

**implosion** opposite of explosion, in which forces are directed inward

**impulse** product of a force and the time during which it acts

**inclined plane** flat surface at angle to some force or reference line

**inelastic collision** collision in which total kinetic energy of colliding particles is not the same after collision as before it

**inertia** tendency of a body to remain at rest or in motion unless acted upon by an outside force

**instantaneous quantity** value at any given instant of a quantity that is changing

**International System of Units** SI; system of measurement based on these fundamental units: mass (kilogram), length (meter), time (second), temperature (kelvin), amount of substance (mole), electric current (ampere), luminous intensity (candela)

**inverse variation** increase in one variable that causes proportional decrease in another variable

**isolated system** system not being acted upon by outside forces

**joule** SI unit of work or energy equal to one newton acting through one meter

**kinetic energy** energy of an object due to its motion

**kinetic theory of matter** concept that all matter is made of small particles in constant motion whose collisions are perfectly elastic

**law** verbal or mathematical statement of relationship between phenomena that is always the same under the same conditions

**law of conservation of energy** energy can be neither created nor destroyed and is constant in a closed system

**law of conservation of mass-energy** sum of matter and energy in the universe is constant

**law of conservation of mechanical energy** sum of potential and kinetic energies of ideal energy system is constant

**law of conservation of momentum** total vector momentum of an object is always constant in a system free of external forces

**law of entropy** all natural processes tend to increase the measure of disorder in the universe

**law of universal gravitation** gravitational force between two objects is constant G times the product of the masses of the two objects and the distance between them

**length** distance between two points

**line of flux** line whose tangent indicates direction of magnetic field

**liquefaction** condensation of a gas or solid to a liquid

**liquid** state of matter in which particles are in proximity greater than that of a gas but less than that of a solid, restricting their random motions to vibrations around moving points

**longitudinal wave** wave in which vibrations are parallel to the direction of its propagation

**mass** quantity of matter in an object, measured by its resistance to a change in its motion

**mass density** mass per unit volume of a substance

**matter** any substance with mass and inertia

**mechanical advantage** ratio of resistance force to effort force in a machine

**mechanical impedance** ratio of applied wave-producing force to resulting displacement velocity in any wave-transmitting medium

**mechanical wave** displacement of portion of elastic medium that causes oscillation about an equilibrium position

**mechanics** effect of energy and other forces on matter

**meniscus** crescent-shaped surface of column of liquid

**metric system** internationally recognized system of weights and measures, based on decimal system

**moment** tendency to produce motion, esp. about an axis; product of physical quantity such as area or mass and its directed distance from axis

**momentum** product of the mass of a moving object and its velocity

**newton** SI unit of force required to accelerate a one kilogram mass at a rate of one meter per second per second

**Newton's first law of motion** object remains at rest or in motion with a constant velocity unless acted upon by an outside force

**Newton's law of universal gravitation** force of attraction between any two particles of matter is directly proportional to the product of their masses and inversely proportional to the square of the distance between their centers of mass

**Newton's second law of motion** the change in motion of an object acted upon by an outside force is directly proportional to the force and inversely proportional to the object's mass

**Newton's third law of motion** every action force has a reaction force equal in magnitude and opposite in direction

**nodal line** line that connects nodes

**node** point in medium or field that remains undisturbed when acted upon simultaneously by more than one disturbance

**normal force** force perpendicular to a surface

**orbital angular momentum** component of angular momentum of electron in atom or nucleon in nucleus, arising from its orbital motion rather than its spin

**parabolic relationship** one quantity varying as the square of another quantity

**parallax** shift in relative position of objects due to change in angle of perspective

**parity** symmetry property that expresses difference between wave function and its negative mirror image, expressed as +1 or –1

**pascal** SI unit of pressure, equal to one newton per square meter

**Pascal's law** external pressure applied to fluid in a closed vessel is transmitted uniformly throughout the fluid

**period** time duration of phenomenon or event, esp. one complete cycle, vibration, revolution, or oscillation

**periodic motion** identical motions that recur at equal time intervals

**phase** number describing wave position within each oscillation or cycle at specific time

**Planck's constant** fundamental determinant of values in quantum mechanics, expressing ratio of energy of one quantum of radiation to its frequency, equal to $6.624 \times 10^{-27}$ erg-seconds

**plasma** high temperature state of matter in which atoms, separated into electrons and positive ions or nuclei, produce conductive gas

**potential energy** energy based on position of object

**power** work done per unit of time

**precession** motion due to torque that displaces axis of rotation in spinning object

**precision** degree of exactitude and reproducibility in measured data; agreement between two or more measurements of same quantity made in same way

**pressure** force per unit area

**principle of parity** for every process in nature there exists an indistinguishable, mirror-image process

**projectile motion** motion of object moving in two dimensions under influence of gravity

**propagation** transmission of a wave through material or space

**property** any measurable aspect of matter

**pulse** single, nonrepeated disturbance in medium or field

**quantum** discrete, indivisible, and elemental unit of energy that emits or absorbs waves

**quantum jump** abrupt transition of system in quantum mechanics from one distinct energy level to another; quantum leap

**quantum leap** quantum jump

**quantum number** notation used to characterize discrete value and magnitude that a quantized physical variable may assume

**ray** line drawn to represent path traveled by a wave front; single line of light from luminous point

**relative deviation** average deviation of set of measurements, expressed as percentages

**resolution** location of vector force components acting in given direction

**rest mass** mass of an object not in motion

**resultant** single force that has same effect as two or more concurrent vectors applied at same point

**rotary motion** motion of a body about an internal axis

**rotational equilibrium** state of body in which sum of clockwise torques in given plane equals sum of counterclockwise torques about pivot point

**rotational inertia** resistance to change in angular velocity of rotating object

**scalar** quantity, such as time or mass, that has magnitude only

**scientific notation** method in which numbers are expressed in the form of $M \times 10^n$, where M is a number between one and ten and n is an integral power of ten

**second** fundamental SI unit of time measurement, equivalent to 9,192,631,770 emission cycles of cesium-133

**shear strain** ratio of amount of deformation of the side of a body to length of the side

**SI** Système Internationale; internationally recognized metric system of measurement

**simple harmonic motion** motion in which particle repeats the same path periodically

**simple machine** lever, pulley, wheel and axle, inclined plane, wedge, or screw

**solid** state of matter in which particles are close together and in fixed positions relative to each other

**special theory of relativity** theory formulated by Albert Einstein that physical laws remain constant in inertial reference systems for all freely moving observers, regardless of their speed

**standing wave** wave in which nodes are stationary; resultant of two identical waves traveling in opposite directions through same medium

**state** physical condition of matter

**stationary state** condition not changing with time and therefore appearing identical at any instant

**strain** amount of distortion produced in body under stress

**stress** distorting force per unit area

**sublimation** change from solid to gaseous state without intermediate liquid phase

**surface tension** strong attraction of surface particles for each other due to unbalanced forces; tendency of liquid surface to contract

**surface wave** surface disturbance with characteristics of both transverse and longitudinal waves

**symmetry** property that is unchanged by altered operations or reference frames; invariance

**Système Internationale** *French.* SI; International System of Units

**tensile strength** maximum stress any material subjected to a stretching load can withstand without tearing

**terminal velocity** velocity of falling object when flow of air resistance is equal to weight

**torque** force producing torsion or rotation in an object

**torque arm** perpendicular distance between force producing torque and axis of rotation

**trajectory** curve described by an object moving through space as it is affected by gravitational attraction of other objects

**translational equilibrium** state in which no unbalanced forces are acting on body

**transverse wave** wave in which disturbance is at right angles to direction of wave

**trough** region of downward displacement in transverse wave

**uncertainty principle** theory in quantum mechanics, formulated by Werner Heisenberg, that the more accurately the position of a particle is specified, the less accurately its momentum can be known, and that one can never be exactly sure of both

**unified field theory** principle that gravitational and electromagnetic forces can be expressed within single unified framework

**uniform circular motion** circular path described by particles that move at a constant angular velocity

**uniform quantity** quantity of constant value, such as acceleration or speed

**universal gas constant** constant of proportionality in ideal gas equation

**universal gravitational constant** constant of proportionality in Newton's law of universal gravitation

**vacuum** enclosed space out of which almost all matter has been removed

**vapor** gaseous phase of substance normally a solid or liquid

**vaporization** change of liquid or solid to gas or vapor by application of heat; volatilization

**vector** quantity that has both magnitude and direction

**velocity** rate of change of position in particular direction

**viscosity** resistance that a gas or liquid system offers to flow when it is subjected to shear stress

**viscous fluid** slow-flowing fluid

**volatile fluid** fluid that is easily evaporated

**volatilization** vaporization

**wave** traveling disturbance in a medium that does not create any permanent displacement in that medium

**wave equation** any of the fundamental equations of quantum mechanics whose solutions are possible wave functions of a particle

**wave front** real or imaginary surface at which phase of oscillation is identical for all adjacent points

**wavelength** distance between corresponding phase points, such as two adjacent troughs or crests, on two successive waves

**weight** measure of gravitational force of Earth or celestial body on an object, proportional but not equal to mass

**work** product of displacement and force in direction of displacement

**work function** energy needed to remove one electron from surface of material into field-free space

**Young's modulus** ratio of stress to strain in a solid

## ELECTRICITY AND MAGNETISM

**AC** alternating current

**acceptor** substance with three valence electrons added to semiconductor crystal to provide electron holes in lattice

**adhesion** attraction between unlike particles

**alternating current** AC; current that periodically changes direction at certain levels, measured in volts

**ampere** unit that measures rate of flow of charged particles, equal to one coulomb of charge per second

**angstrom** unit of linear measure used to express wavelengths of optical spectra, equal to $10^{-10}$ meter

**anode** positive terminal of electrolytic cell

**armature** coil of wire that produces current in generator and rotation in electric motor

**back electromotive force** potential difference created by motion of armature in operating motor; counter electromotive force

**battery cell** two dissimilar conductors that combine with an electrolyte to produce a potential difference

**cathode** negative electrode in electrolytic cell

**conductor** material that can transmit charged particles

**coulomb** SI unit of electric charge, equal to the charge found on $6.25 \times 10^{18}$ electrons; amount of charge that crosses surface in one second when current of one ampere flows across it

**Coulomb's law** product of the charges on two objects divided by square of the distance between the charges times constant K equals the force between the charges

**counter electromotive force** back electromotive force

**DC** direct current

**diamagnetism** property by which an object is repelled by a powerful magnet

**dielectric** nonconducting medium; insulator

**diode** solid-state device or tube with anode and cathode which rectifies alternating current and allows current to pass freely in one direction only

**direct current** DC; current that flows in one direction only and has virtually invariable magnitude

**domain** region of solid in which magnetic fields in atoms are aligned in common direction

**donor** substance with five valence electrons that provides free electrons in lattice structure of semiconductor crystal

**dynamo** generator

**effective resistance** resistance of a single resistor that could replace a combination of resistors

**electric charge** property of particle that attracts or repels other particles of opposite or like charge

**electric circuit** continuous path that can be followed by charged particles

**electric current** flow of charged particles

**electric field** space around charged object in which force acts on other charged objects

**electric field intensity** ratio of force exerted by electric field on charged particle per unit of positive charge

**electric field lines** lines representing direction of electric field

**electric force** force created between two objects due to their charges

**electricity** fundamental physical property caused by movement of electrons and other charged particles, manifested as attraction and repulsion

**electrode** grid

**electrolyte** conducting medium in which flow of current leads to movement of charged ions

**electromagnet** device in which magnetic field is generated by electric current

**electromagnetic force** fundamental force that exists between electrically charged particles

**electromagnetic induction** generation of electric current when magnetic flux lines cut through wire

**electromagnetic interaction** force that keeps electrons in orbit and forms bonds between atoms and molecules

**electromagnetic wave** wave composed of electric and magnetic fields that are perpendicular to each other and that move at speed of light in space

**electromagnetism** interrelationship of magnetic fields and electric currents

**electromotive force** EMF; potential difference generated by electromagnetic induction

**electron** subatomic particle of small mass and negative charge that orbits atomic nucleus

**electron collision excitation** collision between electron and atom that results in excited atom

**electron gas** free electrons moving through metallic conductor

**electronics** branch of physics dealing with behavior of electrons

**electroscope** device used to detect presence of electrostatic charges

**electrostatic charge** charge at rest, as on an object

**EMF** electromotive force

**excited atom** atom with one or more electrons at higher than normal energy level

**farad** unit of capacitance equal to one coulomb per volt

**faraday** quantity of electricity required to deposit one chemical equivalent of an element during electrolysis, equal to 96,500 coulombs

**Faraday's law** mass of an element deposited during electrolysis is proportional both to amount of charge passing through the electrolytic cell and to chemical equivalent of that element

**frequency** number of vibrations, oscillations, or cycles per unit of time

**fresnel** unit of frequency equal to $10^{12}$ cycles per second

**galvanic cell** battery cell

**galvanometer** instrument used to measure very small electric current

**generator** device that uses mechanical energy to produce electric energy; dynamo

**grid** element of electronic tube; electrode

**grounding** connection of charged object to Earth or other neutral site to remove object's charge

**henry** unit of inductance in closed circuit where electromotive force of one volt is produced by current variation of one ampere per second

**hertz** unit of frequency equal to one cycle per second

**impedance** total opposition to alternating current by circuit, expressed in ohms

**inductance** property of electric circuit by which varying current induces electromotive force in that circuit

**inductive reactance** opposition to alternating current due to self-induction

**insulator** material that greatly restricts the transmission of charged particles; dielectric

**interference** combination of two waves or disturbances that arrive at same point at same time

**inverse photoelectric effect** emission of photons from material bombarded by high speed electrons

**ion** charged atom or group of atoms resulting from loss or gain of one or more electrons

**ionization energy** energy required to remove an electron from an atom to an infinite distance

**Joule's law** amount of heat generated in watts when electricity flows through a substance, equal to the resistance of the substance in ohms times the square of the current in amperes

**law of conservation of charge** electric charge can be neither created nor destroyed

**Lenz's law** magnetic field generated by an induced current always opposes the field generating the current

**line of force** imaginary line in field of force positioned so that its tangent indicates direction of electric field

**magnetic field** region around a magnet in which magnetic forces can be detected

**magnetic flux** total of all magnetic flux lines through a region of a magnetic field

**magnetic flux density** number of magnet flux lines per unit area; magnetic induction

**magnetic flux line** line of force representing magnetic induction

**magnetic force** force between two objects due to magnetic flux of one or both objects

**magnetic induction** strength of a magnetic field; magnetic flux density

**magnetic moment** vector quantity that when multiplied by magnetic induction equals torque of given magnet or current acting on given object

**magnetism** fundamental phenomena in which magnets and electric currents exhibit force fields

**microwave** radio wave of a few centimeters' wavelength

**ohm** unit of electric resistance equal to one volt per ampere

**Ohm's law** current that flows in a circuit varies directly with the potential difference, or voltage, and inversely with the resistance

**oscilloscope** instrument with cathode-ray tube in which external voltages deflect electron beam simultaneously along vertical and horizontal axes to form image of wave

**paramagnetism** property exhibited by substances which, when placed in magnetic field, are magnetized in direct proportion to the field strength

**phase** angular relationship between current and AC voltage

**photovoltaic cell** device for converting light into electric energy

**piezoelectricity** production of electric current in certain crystals through deformation by mechanical stress

**plate** anode of electronic tube

**potential difference** difference in potential energy per unit charge between two points in electric field

**potentiometer** variable resistor

**primary** transformer winding that carries or induces current in one or more secondary windings

**radio waves** electromagnetic radiations produced by rapid current shifts in conductor

**reactance** opposition of inductance and capacitance to alternating current, expressed in ohms

**receiver** device used to detect electromagnetic waves and render them perceptible to the senses

**rectifier** device that changes AC to DC

**resistance** opposition to flow of electric current; ratio of potential difference across conductor to magnitude of current in it

**schematic diagram** map of electric circuit using symbols

**secondary** transformer output winding in which current is produced

**self-induction** production of voltage in a circuit, induced when the current is varied rapidly in that same circuit

**series circuit** circuit in which charged particles follow a single path through components

**siemens** SI unit of electrical conductance equal to reciprocal of the ohm

**storage cell** electrochemical cell that can be regenerated by external reverse currents

**superconductivity** state of some materials which exhibit zero resistance at very low temperatures; similar state exhibited by ceramic materials at higher temperatures

**temporary magnet** magnet produced by induction

**tesla** unit of magnetic induction equal to one weber per square meter

**thermionic emission** electron emission from surface of heated body

**thermocouple** electric circuit composed of two dissimilar metals joined at different temperatures

**thermoelectric effect** production of current in closed circuit composed of two dissimilar metals, in which the junctions are maintained at different temperatures

**transformer** device used to transfer energy from one circuit to another circuit by mutual inductance across two coils

**transistor** semiconductor device used as substitute for vacuum tube to control current flow in electronics

**triode** vacuum tube consisting of grid between anode and cathode

**vacuum tube** electron tube that contains grids and from which air has been evacuated to highest possible degree

**Van de Graaff generator** particle accelerator that transfers charge from electron source to insulated sphere on moving insulator belt

**volt** SI unit of potential difference between two points of conductor with constant one ampere current when one watt of power is dissipated between them

**voltaic cell** device that changes chemical into electric energy by immersion of two dissimilar metals in electrolyte

**voltmeter** device used to measure potential difference between two points in circuit

**watt** unit of power equal to one joule per second

**weber** SI unit of magnetic flux, equal to one volt x one second

# NUCLEAR AND PARTICLE PHYSICS

**accelerator** device that uses electromagnets to increase velocity and add energy to moving charged particles; atom smasher

**albedo** degree to which surface reflects subatomic particles that strike it

**alpha particle** helium nucleus that consists of two protons and two neutrons after it is emitted from radioactive atom's nucleus

**amu** atomic mass unit

**antimatter** substance composed of antiparticles

**antiparticle** particle that has the same mass and spin as its subatomic counterpart but opposite charge and magnetic moment

**antiquark** antiparticle of quark

**atom** basic unit of matter, composed of protons, neutrons, and electrons

**atomic mass unit** amu; unit of mass for atomic and subatomic particles, equal to 1/12 the mass of most common isotope of carbon, used to express atomic weight; dalton

**atomic number** number of protons in nucleus of an atom

**atomic theory** explanation of various phenomena by theory of properties and interactions of atoms and subatomic particles

**atomic weight** mass of atom expressed in atomic mass units

**atom smasher** accelerator

**atom-splitting** fission

**backscatter** reflection and reversal of direction of radiation by traversed medium

**baryon** subatomic particle with large rest mass undergoing strong interactions

**beta particle** high-speed electron or positron emitted from radioactive nucleus

**binding energy** energy required to separate nucleus into individual nucleons; separation energy

**Bohr theory** electrons revolve around nucleus in definite orbits and radiation is absorbed or emitted only when an electron moves from one orbit to another

**boson** subatomic particle, such as a photon or pi meson, that does not obey exclusion principle

**breeder reactor** nuclear reactor that produces more fissionable material than is consumed

**bubble chamber** container of superheated liquid in which paths of ionizing particles appear as strings of vapor bubbles

**calutron** early device for separating isotopes by atomic mass

**carbon 14** radioactive isotope of carbon used in radiocarbon dating

**cascade particle** least massive of xi particles

**chain reaction** self-sustaining series of nuclear reactions, in which products of reaction sustain process

**charm** quantum number assigned the value +1 for one kind of quark, -1 for its antiquark, and zero for all other quarks

**cloud chamber** closed vessel in which paths of charged subatomic particles appear as trails of liquid droplets

**cohesive force** attraction between like particles

**cold fusion** hypothetical fusion of atomic nuclei at much lower temperature and pressure than now required

**collider** particle accelerator in which positively and negatively charged particles circulate in opposite directions and collide head-on

**color** hypothetical force or charge on each type of quark that controls how they combine to form hadrons

**Compton effect** increase in X-ray wavelength due to interaction of X-rays and electrons as X-rays traverse matter

**control rods** devices in nuclear reactor used to regulate rate of nuclear reaction

**core** central part of reactor containing fissile fuel and rods

**critical mass** amount of particular fissionable material required to make fission reaction self-sustaining

**curie** unit of radioactivity equal to $3.7 \times 10^{10}$ disintegrations per second of any radioactive nuclide

**cyclotron** device that accelerates positively charged atomic particles by means of D-shaped electrodes, used to initiate nuclear transformations

**dalton** atomic mass unit

**decay** spontaneous radioactive disintegration in which nucleus undergoes transformation into one or more different nuclei and emits radiation, loses electrons, or undergoes fission

**dee** electrode of cyclotron

**deuterium** isotope which replaces hydrogen in heavy water

**deuteron** charged particle equivalent to nucleus of hydrogen isotope deuterium, consisting of one proton and one neutron

**dose** quantity of radiation absorbed by matter

**drift tube** tubular electrode placed in vacuum chamber of circular accelerator to accelerate charged subatomic particles

**dynamics** study of the motion of particles acted upon by forces

**dyne** unit of force that produces acceleration of one centimeter per second per second on mass of one gram

**electron cloud** region of high probability of finding an electron

**elementary particle** indivisible particle within atomic nucleus

**enrichment** process in which number of fissionable nuclei of an element such as uranium is increased

**erg** unit equal to work done by force of one dyne acting across one centimeter

**excited particle** atom or subatomic particle raised to higher energy state

**exclusion principle** no two identical particles in a system can carry the same quantum number

**fast neutron** neutron with kinetic energy greater than thermal energy

**fermion** subatomic particle, such as a lepton or baryon, that obeys exclusion principle

**fission** splitting of heavy nucleus into nuclei of intermediate mass; atom-splitting

**fusion** reaction in which nuclei of light atoms combine to form nuclei with larger mass numbers

**gamma ray** electromagnetic wave of extremely high frequency emitted by nucleus of radioactive atom; high-energy photon

**gas centrifuge** device used to separate enriched, fissionable isotopes of an element from nonfissionable isotopes by centrifugal action

**Geiger counter**  Geiger-Müller tube

**Geiger-Müller tube**  device that detects radiation of subatomic particles by use of ionizing property of radiation; Geiger counter

**gluon**  massless quantum of energy believed to carry force that binds quarks together within subatomic particles

**graviton**  theoretical subatomic particle, without charge or mass, believed to carry gravitational force between bodies

**hadron**  any heavy elementary particle that takes part in the strong interaction

**half-life**  length of time during which one half of a sample of radioactive nuclides decays

**heavy hydrogen**  hydrogen isotope with mass number greater than one; deuterium or tritium

**heavy water**  water in which hydrogen atoms are replaced by heavier deuterium isotopes

**hodoscope**  instrument that traces the paths of high-energy particles

**hypercharge**  property of some baryons and leptons conserved in strong electromagnetic interactions

**hyperon**  any baryon which has nonzero strangeness quantum number and relatively long lifetime

**inertial confinement**  method of producing fusion by laser implosion of deuterium or tritium pellets

**interaction**  change in quantum numbers of particles in close proximity

**isobar**  one of two atoms that have equal mass numbers but different atomic numbers

**isomer**  any of two or more nuclei with same number of neutrons and protons but different energy states

**isotone**  atom with same number of neutrons as another atom but different atomic number

**isotope**  any of two or more forms of an atom of some element with nearly identical chemical properties, but containing different number of neutrons and same number of protons, therefore having different mass

**isotopic spin**  quantum number related to number of different values of electric charge that given baryon or meson may have

**kaon**  any of four mesons that are positive, negative, or neutral, with mass 970 times that of electron; k meson

**k meson**  kaon

**lambda particle**  neutral baryon with strangeness number -1 and isotopic spin zero

**lepton**  subatomic particle with small rest mass

**linear accelerator**  device that accelerates charged particles in a straight line through many stages of small potential difference

**mass defect**  difference in mass between actual atomic nucleus and sum of particles from which nucleus is made

**mass number**  sum of protons and neutrons in nucleus of atom, being integer nearest to its atomic weight

**mass spectroscope**  device used to measure the mass of small, electrically charged particles

**meltdown**  melting of nuclear reactor core due to inadequate cooling of fuel, possibly leading to escape of radiation

**meson**  any hadron or subatomic particle with rest mass intermediate between lepton and baryon, consisting of a quark and antiquark

**moderator**  material used to decrease speed of fast neutrons in nuclear reactor

**Mössbauer effect**  phenomenon in which gamma rays do not lose energy from the recoil of certain radioactive isotope nuclei which are bound in a crystal lattice, resulting in sharply defined wavelength

**mu meson**  muon

**muon**  high-speed lepton, either positive or negative, with mass 207 times that of electron, that decays into electron and two neutrinos with very brief life; mu meson

**neutrino**  chargeless, nearly massless elementary particle affected only by weak force; type of lepton emitted along with beta particles

**neutron**  uncharged subatomic particle of approximate mass comparable to proton, making up half of the particles in all atomic nuclei except those of hydrogen

**nuclear binding energy**  energy required to separate an atom into its constituent nucleons

**nuclear equation**  equation representing a nuclear reaction; strong force equation

**nuclear force**  very short-range force that holds protons and neutrons together in atomic nucleus; strong force

**nuclear moderator**  substance used to slow neutrons in reactor

**nuclear reactor**  device used to obtain energy from controlled fission reaction; reactor

**nucleon**  proton or neutron in atomic nucleus

**nucleus**  positively charged, dense core of an atom, containing protons and neutrons

**nuclide**  any atom of a particular element

**omega particle**  particle that decays into cascade particle after colliding with pi meson

**pair production**  creation of electron-positron pair from energy

**particle**  piece of matter of negligible size that has both charge and mass

**photon**  massless quantum of electromagnetic radiation or light energy

**pile**  early term for nuclear reactor

**pi meson**  meson with mass 270 times that of electron and spin of zero

**Planck's law**  light or other waves can be emitted or absorbed only in discrete quanta whose energy is proportional to their frequency

**planetary model**  model of an atom in which the electrons orbit the nucleus as the planets orbit the sun

**positron**  positively charged antiparticle of electron

**protium**  most common hydrogen isotope, with mass number one

**proton**  positively charged subatomic particle of mass one atomic mass unit that is fundamental constituent of all atomic nuclei

**quark**  any of basic, hypothetical particles that, along with antiquarks, constitute all elementary particles: designated up, down, strange, charm, beauty or bottom, and truth or top

**rad**  measured dosage of absorbed ionizing radiation, equal to 100 ergs per gram

**radiation**  energy emitted as electromagnetic waves, gamma or X-rays, or as energetic nuclear particles

**radioactive materials**  substances that exhibit phenomenon of radioactivity

**radioactivity**  spontaneous decay of unstable atomic nucleus with emission of particles and rays

**radiocarbon dating**  determination of age of artifact based on known rate of decay of carbon-14 isotope

**radioelement** radioactive element occurring naturally or produced artificially

**radioisotope** radioactive isotope, usu. artificially produced

**reactor** nuclear reactor

**rem** measured dose of ionizing radiation whose biological effect is equal to that produced by one roentgen of X-rays

**rod** control rod in nuclear reactor

**roentgen** standard unit that measures ionizing radiation from X-rays or gamma rays

**Rutherford atom** atom in which negatively charged electrons revolve around a small, positively charged nucleus that constitutes nearly its entire atomic mass

**scintillation** flash of light or charged subatomic particle emitted when substance is struck by radiation

**secondary emission** emission of electrons due to bombardment of electrode by high-velocity electrons

**separation energy** binding energy

**sigma particle** unstable hyperon having strangeness number –1

**slow neutron** neutron with less kinetic energy than thermal energy

**solid state detector** device used to detect passage of charged subatomic particles by their ionizing or distorting effects on a non- or semi-conducting solid

**spark chamber** device used to detect passage of charged subatomic particles by light flashes they trigger

**spin** intrinsic angular momentum of each kind of elementary particle that exists even when particle is at rest, as distinguished from orbital angular momentum

**strangeness number** quantum number characteristic of a quark or a strongly interacting particle that is conserved in strong interactions with other fundamental particles, assigned a value of $+1$, $-1$, or zero

**strange quark** quark having strangeness –1 and a charge one-third that of an elementary charge, being more massive than up and down quarks

**string** hypothetical basic unit of matter, neither wave nor particle but thin, curved string with length dimension only

**string theory** theory of fundamental physics in which basic entity in four dimensions of space-time is one-dimensional object rather than zero-dimensional point of conventional elementary particle physics

**strong force** force that holds quarks together with protons and neutrons within atomic nucleus, independent of charge; strongest of four fundamental forces, but with shortest range

**strong force equation** nuclear equation

**strong interaction** interaction between gluons and between gluons and quarks that is responsible for strong force

**strontium 90** deadly radioactive isotope of strontium present in fallout from nuclear explosions and other fission-produced waste

**subatomic particle** one of several constituent parts of atoms: protons, neutrons, electrons, their component particles, and quarks

**supercollider** massive, extremely high-speed particle accelerator

**superstring theory** fundamental theory of subatomic particles in which all matter and energy are derived from vibration modes of one-dimensional strings that control all forces and matter; combination of string theory and supersymmetry

**supersymmetry** hypothetical symmetry among groups of particles containing fermions and bosons, esp. in theory of gravity as single unified force encompassing strong force, weak force, and electromagnetism

**synchrotron** particle accelerator with variable oscillating frequency

**thermonuclear reaction** nuclear fusion reaction

**tracer** radioactive isotope used to follow chemical process or determine physical properties

**transmutation** nuclear change of one element into another

**transuranic element** any element that has an atomic number greater than 92

**tritium** radioactive isotope of hydrogen with atomic weight three, used in thermonuclear devices and as tracer

**truth** elusive sixth quark, also designated top, believed to have a mass 90 to 250 times that of proton

**virtual particle** particle that cannot be directly detected but whose existence has measurable effects

**wave-particle duality** quantum mechanics theory that waves and particles are indistinguishable and sometimes behave alike

**weak force** force involved in decay of atomic nuclei and nuclear particles; second weakest of four fundamental forces, with very short range and no effect on force-carrying particles

**weak interaction** interaction between elementary particles and the bosons that carry the weak force from particle to particle

**weakly interactive massive particle** WIMP; small gravitational mass particle, believed to form cold, dark matter comprising ninety percent of universe

**WIMP** *weakly interactive massive particle*

**xi particle** baryon having strangeness number –2 and isotopic spin 1/2

**Z-zero particle** short-lived, very heavy particle, identical to photon except for mass, that conveys part of weak force between neighboring hadrons and leptons

## Cosmology

**anthropic principle** the universe appears as it does because if it were different we would not be here to observe it

**antigravity** hypothetical force by which one body would repel another; opposite of gravity, never detected experimentally

**big bang model** theory that universe originated in explosion of hot, dense core that rapidly expanded to cooler, more diffuse states

**big crunch** singularity at end of universe that reverses big bang effect

**black dwarf** cold remnant of white dwarf star after thermal energy is exhausted

**black hole** highly concentrated mass that has collapsed to such a degree that the escape velocity from its surface is greater than the speed of light, so that light and all other energy and matter is trapped in an intense gravitational field

**blue shift** shift of spectral lines toward shorter wavelengths, observed in celestial objects that are approaching observer

**Chandrasekhar limit** maximum possible mass of stable cold star, beyond which it will collapse to become a black hole

**chaos** phenomenon of unpredictability and randomness on all scales of physical structures, opp. of cosmos

**chaotic dynamics** time-dependent, nonperiodic regime in which individual histories corresponding to initially close states tend to diverge exponentially over time

**cold dark matter** fundamental particles with no force other than gravity that comprise ninety percent of universe

**cosmic background radiation** uniform radioactive hiss that fills space, measured at 3 degrees Kelvin

**cosmogony** study of possible origin and evolution of universe

**cosmological principle** assumption that universe would appear the same viewed from any point in it

**cosmology** study of structure of universe as a whole

**cosmos** orderly and harmonious universe that follows ascertainable laws, opp. of chaos

**critical density** mass density above which expansion of universe should slow down and reverse

**curved space** warping of space-time due to presence of massive bodies

**determinism** doctrine that every occurrence in universe is the result of a sequence of causes and effects

**differential microwave radiometer** device used to measure variations in brightness of cosmic background radiation

**event** specific point in space-time

**event horizon** boundary of black hole or other singularity

**expanding universe** model of universe based on big bang

**grand unification energy** energy above which electromagnetic, strong, and weak nuclear forces become indistinguishable

**grand unification theory** theory which unifies electromagnetic, strong, and weak forces

**Hubble constant** constant that represents rate of expansion of universe

**light cone** surface in space-time delineating possible directions for light rays that pass through given event

**matter era** period beginning 100,000 years after big bang, when universe had cooled so that electrons and protons could begin forming hydrogen atoms

**microwave background radiation** redshifted radiation from glow of early universe that does not appear as light but as microwaves of extremely high frequency

**naked singularity** space-time singularity not surrounded by an event horizon, thus kept from our view

**neutron star** cold or collapsed star in which gravitational force has caused combination of electrons and protons to form neutrons

**no boundary condition** theory that universe is finite but has no boundary

**primordial black hole** black hole created very early in life of universe

**pulsar** rotating neutron star whose radio emissions reach Earth in pulses, usu. at regular intervals

**pulsating universe theory** variation on expanding universe theory, in which cycle of expansion and contraction to and from primeval nucleus is endlessly repeated

**quasar** *quasi-stellar* radio source; powerful source of light and radio energy at limits of known universe, probably a highly luminous galaxy that has violently exploded

**radiation era** early stage of universe prior to matter era, when simple nuclei could be formed

**redshift** shift, due to Doppler effect, in spectral lines of object toward red end of spectrum as it recedes from observer, with degree of shift proportional to object's speed

**Schwarzschild radius** radius at which gravitationally collapsing celestial body becomes a black hole

**singularity** point in space-time at which space-time curvature becomes infinite and at which measurable quantities become exactly zero or infinitely large

**singularity theory** theory that universe started with a singularity

**space-time continuum** four-dimensional continuum with coordinates being three spatial dimensions and time; way of representing universe suggested by theory of relativity

**space-time curvature** conceptual form in which four-dimensional space-time is represented as a curve

**spatial dimension** any of three dimensions of space-time, other than time

**steady state model** theory of expanding universe stipulating continuous creation of matter, and stating that universe maintains uniform large-scale structure and constant average density at all times

**supermassive black hole** hypothetical singularity at center of some active galaxies or quasars

**supernova** explosion of massive star near end of its life, possibly due to gravitational collapse, causing greatly increased luminosity and loss of most of star's mass, sometimes leaving behind dense core; white dwarf star in close binary system producing explosions from mass taken from its companion star

**unified field theory** principle that all forces in universe are part of single concept

**universe** sum total of potentially knowable objects, matter, and energy, believed to be infinite in space and time

**white dwarf** very small, faint, cold star that has undergone gravitational collapse

**white hole** hypothetical time-reversed black hole

# HEAT

**absolute zero** temperature at which gas has zero volume and molecular kinetic energy is at minimum, equal to -459.7 degrees F, -273.2 degrees C, or zero degrees Kelvin

**adiabatic process** thermal process in which no heat is added to or removed from system

**advection** horizontal flow of atmospheric properties

**aneroid barometer** device that uses partially evacuated box to measure atmospheric pressure

**bimetallic strip** two dissimilar metals welded together so that thermal expansion causes strip to bend

**Boyle's law** volume of a fixed mass of gas kept at constant temperature varies inversely with pressure

**British thermal unit** BTU; quantity of heat equal to 252 calories

**Brownian motion** (or **movement**) random motion of colloidal particles due to bombardment of the particles by molecules of the surrounding medium.

**BTU** British *thermal unit*

**calorie** quantity of heat equal to 4.187 joules

**Celsius** temperature scale with zero degrees equal to freezing point of water and 100 degrees equal to boiling point of water at standard atmospheric pressure; Centigrade

**Centigrade** Celsius

**Charles' law** volume of a fixed mass of gas at constant pressure varies directly with its absolute temperature

**coefficient of expansion** change in area, volume, or length per unit area, volume, or length of a solid per degree change in its temperature

**condensation** change of state from gas to liquid

**convection** transfer of heat in a fluid, either by absorption or by rejection once the fluid has moved

**convection current** current caused by motion of a fluid, caused by differences in density due to thermal expansion

**critical constant** density, pressure, or temperature associated with critical point of pure element or compound

**critical point** point at which pure element or compound in one phase, as liquid, has same density, pressure, and temperature as in another phase, as gaseous

**cryogenics** production and effects of very low temperatures

**dew point** temperature to which air must be cooled at given pressure to reach saturation

**Edison effect** emission of electrons from metal when heated in a vacuum

**evaporation** change of state from liquid to gas or vapor

**Fahrenheit** temperature scale with 32 degrees equal to freezing point of water and 212 degrees equal to boiling point of water at standard atmospheric pressure

**first law of thermodynamics** when heat is converted to another form of energy, or vice versa, there is no loss of energy

**heat** quantity of thermal energy being added to an object, or moved from one object to another, because of a temperature difference

**heat capacity** quantity of heat required to increase temperature of a body by one degree

**heat engine** device that converts heat energy into mechanical work

**heat of fusion** energy required per unit mass to change substance from solid to liquid at its melting point

**heat of vaporization** energy required per unit mass to change substance from liquid to gas at its boiling point

**heat sink** entity that absorbs heat without significant temperature increase

**kelvin** SI unit of heat measurement, equal to 1/273 of Kelvin temperature scale

**Kelvin** temperature scale with zero degrees equaling absolute zero, and 273.16 degrees equaling freezing point of water

**kinetic theory of heat** theory that particles in a gas move freely and rapidly in straight lines and often collide, causing changes in their velocity and direction

**law of heat exchange** in any heat transfer system, hot materials lose amount of heat equal to that gained by cold materials

**mechanical equivalent of heat** conversion factor relating heat units to work units, equal to 4.19 joules per calorie

**melting point** temperature at which solid changes to liquid

**regelation** phenomenon in which a substance kept at constant temperature melts under pressure and refreezes when pressure is eliminated

**relative humidity** ratio of water vapor pressure in atmosphere to equilibrium vapor pressure at given temperature

**second law of thermodynamics** heat flows from area of high temperature to area of lower temperature unless work is done to reverse this process

**specific heat** energy required to change temperature of one kilogram of a substance one degree Kelvin

**standard pressure** pressure exerted by 760 mm of mercury at zero degrees Celsius

**supercooling** cooling of substance below normal phase-change point without inducing change of phase

**temperature** physical quantity measured by the average kinetic energy of particles in matter

**thermal energy** sum of potential energy and kinetic energy in random motion of particles of a material

**thermal excitation** act of stimulating and altering an atom by heating it

**thermal expansion** moving apart of particles as their temperature rises

**thermal unit** any of various standard measures of heat

**thermometer** device used to measure temperature

**third law of thermodynamics** temperature of a system cannot be reduced to absolute zero in a finite number of operations

**transition temperature** temperature at which resistance of some materials to electric current suddenly drops to zero

# OPTICS

**absorption spectrum** continuous spectrum of energy absorbed by gaseous atoms of element as white light passes through it

**achromatic lens** lens which forms images whose outline is free from prismatic colors

**actinic rays** light rays, esp. at ultraviolet end of spectrum, that produce chemical changes

**actinology** study of the chemical effects of light rays

**albedo** reflecting power of a body, expressed as ratio of reflected light to total light falling on surface

**angle of incidence** angle between light ray and line perpendicular to surface the ray is meeting

**angle of reflection** angle between reflected light ray and line perpendicular to the point of incidence

**angle of refraction** angle between refracted ray and line perpendicular to surface the ray is leaving

**band spectrum** emission spectrum consisting of fluted bands of color, characteristic of molecular gases and chemical compounds

**beam** parallel rays of light considered together

**black light** ultraviolet or infrared radiation used for fluorescent effects in the dark

**candela** SI unit of luminous intensity, equal to intensity of a source that emits monochromatic radiation of frequency $540 \times 10^{12}$ hertz

**candle** former standard unit of luminous intensity, equal to five square millimeters of platinum at 1773.5 degrees C

**candlepower** measure of luminous intensity

**center of curvature** center of sphere from which a spherical mirror is cut

**chromatic aberration** failure of a lens to bring all wavelengths of light in focus at the same point

**chromatics** study of hue and saturation of colors

**coherent light** light in which all waves leaving the source are in phase and have identical wavelengths

**color** property of an object with respect to light reflected by it in particular wavelengths forming a spectrum from red to violet

**complementary colors** primary and secondary colors that combine to produce white light

**concave lens** lens that diverges parallel light rays

**concave mirror** mirror that converges parallel light rays on its surface

**continuous spectrum** spectrum without dark lines or bands or with uninterrupted changes between colors

**converging lens** lens, thick in the middle and thin at the edge, that bends parallel rays toward common point

**converging mirror** concave mirror that causes parallel rays to converge

**convex lens** lens that converges parallel rays

**convex mirror** mirror that diverges parallel light rays on its surface

**critical angle** minimum angle of incidence that produces total internal reflection

**diffraction** bending of light waves around an object in their path into region behind obstacle

**diffraction angle** angle that diffracted wave front forms with grating plane

**diffraction grating** optical surface ruled with thousands of parallel, equally spaced grooves, used to diffract light

**diffuse reflection** irregularly reflected light scattered in many directions

**dispersion** refraction of polychromatic light into spectrum of its component wavelengths

**diverging lens** lens, thin in the middle and thick at the edge, that causes incident parallel rays to diverge as though from a common point

**diverging mirror** convex mirror that causes parallel light rays to diverge

**elementary colors** seven color regions in spectrum observed by dispersion of sunlight: red, orange, yellow, green, blue, indigo, and violet

**emission spectrum** spectrum produced by dispersion of light from excited atoms of an element

**fiber optics** branch of optics dealing with transmission of data or communications in form of light pulses through transparent fibers

**first law of photoelectric emission** rate of photoelectron emission is proportional to intensity of incident light

**fluorescence** emission of light by atoms excited during absorption of radiation from outside source

**focal length** distance from focal point to vertex or optical center of mirror or lens

**focal point** point of convergence, real or apparent, of rays reflected by mirror or refracted by lens

**focus** point at which light rays meet, or from which light rays appear to diverge or converge

**Fraunhofer spectrum** absorption lines that appear in the solar spectrum, due to gases in solar atmosphere

**hertz** SI unit of frequency, equal to one cycle per second

**illuminated body** object on which light is falling

**illumination** rate at which light energy falls on a given area of a surface

**image** optical counterpart of object formed by lenses or mirrors

**incandescence** emission of light due to thermal excitation

**incident light** light rays that fall upon or strike something

**index of refraction** number expressing speed of light in given medium, as ratio of either speed of light in a vacuum or speed in some specified medium to that in the given medium

**infrared light** electromagnetic waves longer than visible light and shorter than microwaves

**irregular reflection** scattering of light in many different directions from an irregular surface

**laser** light amplification by stimulated emission of radiation; device used to produce coherent light of great intensity

**law of reflection** angle of incidence is equal to angle of reflection when a light ray is reflected from a smooth surface

**light** electromagnetic radiation, ranging in wavelength from $4 \times 10^{-7}$ to $7 \times 10^{-7}$ meter, that causes sensation of vision

**line spectrum** electromagnetic spectrum made up of discrete lines, usu. characteristic of excited atoms or molecules

**lumen** unit of luminous flux on surface, all points of which are at unit distance from a point source of one candle

**luminescence** emission of light caused by absorption of radiant or corpuscular energy, not by incandescence

**luminous body** object visible due to emission of light from oscillating particles

**luminous flux** flow of light from a source

**luminous intensity** measure of light emitted by a source

**magnification** ratio of image distance or size to object distance or size

**monochromatic light** light of only one wavelength and color

**Nicol prism** one of a pair of prisms cemented together, used to produce and analyze light vibrating in a single plane as it passes through them

**objective lens** light-gathering and image-forming lens of microscope or telescope

**opaque material** material that does not transmit light

**optical density** property that determines the speed of light, and thus index of refraction, through a transparent medium

**optical fiber** very thin, flexible, transparent glass or plastic fiber that makes use of total internal reflection to transmit information in form of light pulses

**optics** study of propagation, control, transmission, reception, effects, and phenomena of light waves

**penumbra** partially illuminated portion of a shadow

**phosphorescence** emission of light from atoms excited by outside source that persists for a time after outside source is removed

**photic** (adj) of or relating to light

**photoelastic** (adj) of or pertaining to certain materials that are capable of double refraction when under stress

**photoelectric effect** ejection of electrons from surface, usu. of metal, exposed to light or electromagnetic radiation

**photoelectron** electron ejected by photoelectric effect

**photometry** quantitative measurement of visible radiation emitted from light sources

**photon** quantum of electromagnetic waves or light energy

**photon collision excitation** collision between photon and atom resulting in an excited atom

**photovoltaic cell** device used to convert light into electric energy

**plane polarization** polarization of light in which vibrations are confined to a single plane

**polarized light** light in which vibrations of all waves are in the same or parallel planes in optical region

**polychromatic light** light composed of several wavelengths and colors

**primary color**  red, yellow, or blue light, from which all other colors may be described or evolved by mixture

**primary pigment**  yellow, cyan, or magenta pigment; complement of primary colors

**principal axis**  radius connecting center of curvature of curved mirror with its geometric vertex, or center of curvature of lens with its optical center

**principal focus**  point at which rays parallel to principal axis either converge or diverge after reflection or refraction

**pumping**  excitation of very large number of atoms by laser

**quantum theory of light**  light is emitted and absorbed in small discrete packets called quanta; the energy in each quantum can be expressed as $E = hf$, where E is energy, h is Planck's constant, and f is frequency

**ray**  single line of light that radiates from a luminous point

**real image**  image formed by rays of light that actually recombine

**reflection**  return of light wave from boundary of a medium

**refraction**  bending of wave front as it passes obliquely from one medium to another

**resolving power**  ability of optical device to produce separate images of two closely spaced objects

**saturation**  degree of purity of a color, measured by absence of dilution by white

**secondary color**  color, such as orange, green, or violet, produced by mixing two primary colors

**secondary pigment**  red, green, or blue pigment; complement of secondary color

**second law of photoelectric emission**  kinetic energy of photoelectrons is independent of intensity of incident light

**Snell's law**  equation relating angle of incidence and index of refraction for ray incident on interface of two media

**solar ray**  ray of sunlight

**solar spectrum**  band of colors produced by dispersal of sunlight through a prism

**spectroscope**  optical instrument used to study spectra

**spectrum**  array of various wavelengths that compose light

**speed of light**  $3.00 \times 10^8$ meters per second in a vacuum, or approximately 186,000 miles per second

**spherical aberration**  failure of spherical mirror to focus all rays that are parallel to principal axis at the same point

**spherical concave mirror**  converging mirror formed of spherical segment of one base

**stopping potential**  potential difference needed to prevent photoelectric effect for specific metal and light of specific frequency

**threshold frequency**  lowest frequency of light that will cause photoelectric effect for specific substance

**total internal reflection**  reflection of a light ray at such a large angle that ray remains in its original medium

**translucent material**  material that transmits light but distorts it during passage

**transparent material**  material that transmits light undistorted

**ultraviolet light**  electromagnetic radiations of shorter wavelength than visible light but longer than X-rays

**umbra**  portion of a shadow from which all light rays are excluded

**vertex**  center of curved mirror

**virtual image**  image formed by light rays that appear to emanate from a point without actually doing so

**white light**  light, such as sunlight, that is mixture of wavelengths from red to violet

**X-ray**  invisible electromagnetic radiation that has a very short wavelength and great penetrating power

## ACOUSTICS

**acoustics**  science of the production, effects, and transmission of sound

**anechoic** (*adj*) completely absorbing sound waves, therefore free from echoes

**audio frequency**  band of audible sound frequencies between 15 hertz and 20,000 hertz

**audiogram**  graph of hearing loss in ear as measured by audiometer

**audiometer**  device used to measure sharpness and range of hearing

**aural** (*adj*) received through or relating to the sense of hearing

**consonance**  complex sound wave perceived as harmonious chord

**decibel**  unit of sound intensity level, one decibel being the smallest change of sound intensity perceptible to human ear

**dissonance**  sound waves perceived as inharmonious noise

**echo**  rebound of sound wave from impenetrable surface that results in repetition of sound

**fundamental**  lowest frequency of sound produced by an instrument or other tone source

**harmonics**  fundamental tone and tones whose frequencies are whole number multiples of the fundamental

**octave**  interval between given tone and one with double or half its frequency

**overtones**  sound waves of higher frequency than the fundamental, expressed in integral multiples only

**pitch**  perceived tonal characteristic that is equivalent to frequency

**resonance**  production of abnormally large vibration in response to external stimulus, occurring when stimulus frequency is at natural vibration frequency of system

**sonic** (*adj*) having to do with sound waves; equal to or being speed of sound in air

**sonic boom**  shock wave associated with object moving through fluid or gas at speed greater than that of sound

**sound wave**  longitudinal disturbance in matter that is audible to human ear; similar disturbance that exists above and below audible range

**sound intensity**  rate at which sound energy flows through given unit area

**speed of sound**  approximately 741 miles per hour in air at sea level

**subsonic** (*adj*) less than speed of sound

**supersonic** (*adj*) greater than speed of sound

**threshold frequency**  lowest sound intensity audible to average human ear

**timbre**  quality of sound

**ultrasound**  sound with frequency over 20,000 hertz, beyond upper limit of human hearing

**white noise**  blend of all audible frequencies distributed equally over range of frequency band

# ASTRONOMY AND SPACE SCIENCE

Celestial Bodies
Celestial Phenomena and Points
Branches, Laws, Theories, and Techniques
Signs of the Zodiac
Space Exploration and Rocketry

**SEE ALSO**: Chap. 3: Geology; Landscapes and Seascapes; Weather and Natural Phenomena; Chap. 4: Physics; Chap. 5: Weapons and Armaments; Chap. 6: Aircraft

## CELESTIAL BODIES

**Alpha Centauri** trinary star containing Proxima Centauri

**Andromeda Galaxy** large, spiral galaxy relatively close to Milky Way, with similar size and shape

**Ariel** satellite of Uranus

**asteroid** one of thousands of minor planets that revolve around sun, usu. between orbital paths of Mars and Jupiter; minor planet; planetoid

**asteroid belt** any group of asteroids that revolve around sun in orbital path between Mars and Jupiter

**barred spiral** spiral galaxy with barlike structure across its center

**binary star** two stars in orbit around one another; double star

**black dwarf** cold remains of white dwarf after thermal energy is exhausted

**brown dwarf** lump of celestial matter larger than a planet but not massive enough to be a star or produce thermonuclear reactions at its core

**Callisto** one of four Galilean satellites of Jupiter

**Canopus** second brightest star in heavens, 650 light years distant

**celestial body** celestial object

**celestial object** any solid or gaseous entity moving through space; celestial body; heavenly body

**Ceres** first and largest minor planet to be discovered

**Charon** only known moon of Pluto

**cluster star** one of a group of stars that share a common origin and common motion through space

**Coma cluster** large collection of galaxies located visually in constellation Coma Berenices

**comet** diffuse cluster of gas, dust, and ice moving about sun in eccentric orbit, with dust tail trailing in its path and ion tail pointing away from sun

**Crab Nebula** supernova remnant in constellation Taurus

**cynosure** Polaris; northern constellation Ursa Minor

**dark nebula** nebula that obscures background starlight and does not reflect starlight toward Earth

**Deimos** smaller of two moons of Mars

**diffuse nebula** luminous formation or irregular cloud of interstellar matter within Milky Way

**Dog Star** Sirius

**double star** binary star

**Dumbbell Nebula** planetary nebula consisting of faint star surrounded by cloud of gas shaped like dumbbell

**dwarf** star with small size or mass and low luminosity

**Earth** fifth largest planet of solar system and third from sun: orbits sun in 365 days and rotates on its axis in twenty-four hours

**eclipsing binary** binary star system in which one star appears to pass in front of the other

**elliptical galaxy** galaxy having round or lenticular shape, without spiral arms as internal structure

**equant** celestial body having equal diameters in all directions

**Europa** one of four Galilean satellites of Jupiter

**fireball** brilliant meteor that often trails bright sparks

**galaxy** vast system of about 100 billion stars, such as Milky Way, held together by gravity in spiral, elliptical, or irregular region about 100,000 light years across

**Galilean satellites** four largest moons of Jupiter, first seen by Galileo Galilei: Callisto, Europa, Ganymede, and Io

**Ganymede** largest of four Galilean satellites of Jupiter

**gas giant** large planet of low density, esp. one of major planets of our solar system; Jupiter, Saturn, Uranus, or Neptune

**globular cluster** large collection of closely grouped old and dead stars containing little or no gas between them

**Great Wall** huge chain of galaxies and superclusters stretching 500 million light years across universe

**Halley's Comet** famous comet visible from Earth every 76 years

**heavenly body** celestial object

**Horsehead Nebula** dark nebula in constellation Orion, silhouetted against bright nebula in shape of horse's head

**Io** one of four Galilean satellites of Jupiter, having active volcanoes

**irregular galaxy** galaxy having neither spiral nor elliptical shape

**Jovian satellites** system of at least seventeen moons that orbit Jupiter

**Jupiter** largest planet of solar system and fifth from sun, famous for its Great Red Spot: orbits sun in 11.9 years and rotates on its axis in 9 hours and 50 minutes

**Large Magellanic Cloud** larger of two irregular galaxies interacting with Milky Way as a satellite

**lenticular galaxy** elliptical galaxy in elongated form with nearly pointed ends

**Local Group** Milky Way, Magellanic clouds, Andromeda Galaxy, and other nearby galaxies forming a local cluster in the universe two million light years across

**local supercluster** supercluster of galaxies relatively near Milky Way

**Magellanic clouds** two irregular galaxies near Milky Way, visible only from Earth's Southern Hemisphere

**magnetic star** star that emits strong magnetic field, detected by its effect on spectrum

**major planets** four largest planets of solar system: Jupiter, Saturn, Uranus, and Neptune; gas giants

**Mars** seventh largest planet of solar system and fourth from sun: orbits sun in 687 days and rotates on its axis in 24 hours and 24 minutes

**Mercury** eighth largest planet of solar system and nearest to sun: orbits sun in 88 days and rotates on its axis in 59 days

**metagalaxy** entire system of galaxies including the Milky Way

**meteor**  very small particle of rock or metal orbiting sun, usu. in a swarm, that enters Earth's atmosphere and burns up; shooting star

**meteorite**  portion of meteor that enters Earth's atmosphere and reaches ground without disintegrating

**meteoroid**  small, solid chunk of iron, stone, or waxy material that flares to produce bright meteor

**Milky Way**  twelve-billion-year-old spiral galaxy of which our sun is one of 150 billion stars

**minor planet**  large asteroid in orbit around sun that is not large enough to be considered a planet

**Miranda**  satellite of Uranus

**Mira variable**  star whose overall brightness changes over period of about one year

**moon**  natural satellite of a planet, esp. the celestial body that revolves around Earth from west to east every 29 1/2 days

**nebula**  diffuse cloud of interstellar matter

**Neptune**  fourth largest planet in solar system, usu. eighth from sun, sometimes further from sun than Pluto: orbits sun in 165 years and rotates on its axis in 15 hours and 48 minutes

**Nereid**  large satellite of Neptune

**neutron star**  collapsed star of extremely high density, such as a pulsar, that is composed primarily of neutrons

**North Star**  Polaris

**nova**  star that increases in brilliance by several magnitudes in a few hours due to explosive ejection of surface material

**Oberon**  satellite of Uranus

**open cluster**  large collection of young, massive stars, loosely grouped with abundant gas between them

**Orion Nebula**  bright, diffuse nebula formed around stars comprising sword region of Orion constellation

**Phobos**  larger of two moons of Mars

**planet**  one of nine massive bodies in our solar system that revolve around sun and reflect its light; similar bodies that revolve around other stars

**planetary nebula**  star in last stage of life, surrounded by expelled outer layers of gas, originally thought to be planets

**planetoid**  asteroid; minor planet

**Pluto**  smallest planet of solar system, usu. furthest from sun, with highly eccentric orbit that sometimes brings it closer to sun than Neptune: orbits sun in 248 years and rotates on its axis in 6 days and 7 hours

**Polaris**  nearly stationary, bright, supergiant binary star located near north celestial pole; North Star; polestar

**polestar**  conspicuous star that lies nearest to north celestial pole; Polaris

**primary**  star or planet around which another celestial body revolves

**protoplanet**  whirling, gaseous eddy within gas and dust cloud rotating around a sun that gives rise to a planet

**protostar**  hypothetical, flat, circular, gaseous dust cloud in space that develops into a star

**Proxima Centauri**  closest star to sun

**pulsar**  rotating, collapsed neutron star of high density, composed primarily of neutrons, whose radio emissions or light reach Earth in pulses, usu. at regular intervals

**quasar**  quasi-stellar radio source; highly luminous galaxy at limits of known universe, probably undergoing violent explosion, being a powerful source of light and energy

**radio galaxy**  galaxy that emits stronger-than-normal radio waves

**radio source**  cosmic object or phenomenon that emits radio waves; radio star

**radio star**  radio source

**red dwarf**  small star of low spectrum-luminosity and surface temperature

**red giant**  large star of low surface temperature in late stage of stellar evolution, with absolute magnitude near zero

**red supergiant**  exceptionally luminous red giant having diameter 100 times that of sun

**reflection nebula**  nebula that reflects the light of nearby stars

**Ring Nebula**  planetary nebula consisting of faint star surrounded by ring of gas

**satellite**  one of many known moons of planets in solar system; artificial satellite set in orbit around planet

**Saturn**  second largest planet of solar system and sixth from sun, famous for its rings: orbits sun in 29.5 years and rotates on its axis in 10 hours and 39 minutes

**Seyfert galaxy**  one of several spiral galaxies with intensely bright nuclei and strong, broad spectral lines

**shepherd satellite**  satellite that keeps particles of a ring in their proper orbit around planet

**shooting star**  meteor

**Sirius**  brightest star in heavens, only nine light years distant in constellation Canis Major; Dog Star

**Small Magellanic Cloud**  smaller of two irregular galaxies interacting with Milky Way as a satellite

**solar system**  group of planets that orbit around common star or stars, esp. portion of Milky Way subject to gravity of our sun, including nine planets

**spectroscopic binary**  binary star in which shifting of lines in system's spectrum indicates orbital revolution

**spiral galaxy**  galaxy with central nucleus and concentrations of matter that extend in curved arms to create its spiral or pinwheel appearance

**star**  massive, very hot, luminous ball of highly ionized gases that derives its energy from continuous nuclear reactions

**starburst galaxy**  galaxy undergoing rapid wave of stellar birth

**sun**  any star that is center of a planetary system, esp. central star of Earth's solar system

**supercluster**  clusters of galaxies and local groups up to fifty million light years across

**supergiant star**  exceptionally luminous star of first magnitude, having diameter more than 100 times that of sun

**supernova**  explosion of massive star near the end of its life, possibly due to gravitational collapse, causing greatly increased luminosity and loss of most of star's mass, sometimes leaving behind dense core; white dwarf star in close binary system that produces explosions from mass taken from its companion star

**supernova remnant**  portion of supernova blown outward to form nebula

**terra**  Earth

**terrestrial planets**  four inner planets of solar system: Mercury, Venus, Earth, and Mars

**Titan**  largest satellite of Saturn and largest satellite in solar system

**Titania**  satellite of Uranus

**trinary star**  three stars bound to each other by gravitation

**Triton**  largest satellite of Neptune and only body in solar system with active ice volcanism

**Umbriel**  satellite of Uranus

**Uranus** third largest planet of solar system and seventh from sun: orbits sun in 84 years and rotates on its axis in 23 hours

**variable star** star that varies in intrinsic brightness

**Venus** sixth largest and brightest planet of solar system and second from sun: orbits sun in 225 days and rotates on its axis in 244 days

**Vesta** one of first two minor planets discovered in solar system

**Virgo cluster** large collection of galaxies located visually in constellation Virgo

**visual binary** double star in which separate components may be distinguished through powerful telescope

**whirlpool galaxy** interacting spiral galaxy connected to its companion galaxy by bridge of stars

**white dwarf** small, faint, cold star that has undergone gravitational collapse

## CELESTIAL PHENOMENA AND POINTS

**aberration** apparent displacement of star due to Earth's orbit and bending of star's light rays

**absorption lines** dark gaps in spectrum of sun or star due to layers of cooler gases in its atmosphere

**accretion disk** rapidly spinning disk of gas, usu. found around neutron star or black hole

**altitude** angular distance of celestial object located vertically above plane of celestial equator

**annular eclipse** solar eclipse in which the moon's angular diameter is smaller than the sun's

**antapex** point on celestial sphere from which sun appears to recede

**anthelion** bright white spot on parhelic circle opposite sun

**apex** point on celestial sphere toward which sun appears to move, relative to nearby stars

**aphelion** point in elliptical orbit of planet or comet that is farthest from sun

**apocenter** point on elliptical orbit that is farthest from body that is focus of orbit

**apogee** point in elliptical orbit of moon or artificial satellite that is farthest from Earth

**arc** apparent path of celestial body above and below horizon

**arroyo** channel formed by fluid erosion on Earth and sun

**asterism** pattern formed by stars on celestial sphere, esp. a constellation

**atmosphere** gaseous envelope surrounding star, planet, or other celestial body

**atmospheric layers** divisions of atmosphere that extend outward from surface of body: troposphere, stratosphere, mesosphere, thermosphere, and exosphere

**aureole** luminous area that surrounds sun as seen through thin cloud; corona

**aurora** display of changing colored light high in atmosphere at arctic and antarctic latitudes, caused by charged particles in Earth's magnetic field interacting with upper atmospheric gases

**axis** imaginary line through center of body about which it rotates

**azimuth** angle between celestial object and southern point of horizon, measured clockwise from horizon

**basin** huge, multiringed lunar crater, produced by asteroidal impact, later filled with lava to form mare

**Becklin-Neugebauer object** strong infrared source near Orion nebula

**Big Dipper** asterism within constellation Ursa Major formed by seven stars in shape of dipper

**biosphere** ecosphere

**black hole** highly concentrated mass that has collapsed to such a degree that the escape velocity from its surface is greater than the speed of light, trapping light and all other energy and matter in an intense gravitational field

**blue moon** occurrence of two full moons within one month

**blue shift** shift of spectral lines toward shorter wavelengths at blue end of spectrum, observed in celestial objects approaching Earth

**brightline spectrum** emission spectrum that appears as bright lines against dark background

**canals** linear grooves on surface of Mars once believed to be artificial waterways

**carbonaceous chondrites** uncommon meteorite class believed to be most primitive form of matter in solar system

**celestial equator** projection of Earth's equator on celestial sphere

**celestial sphere** apparent sphere of sky on which celestial bodies appear to lie, centered on observer on Earth

**chondrite** member of most abundant class of stony meteorites

**chromosphere** layer in sun's atmosphere between corona and photosphere

**collision** sudden, violent impact of two or more celestial bodies and ensuing reactions

**comet tail** tail of dust that trails away from path of comet nucleus and points away from sun, appearing when comet is near sun

**conjunction** occasion when two or more celestial bodies line up at same longitude on celestial sphere

**constellation** pattern formed by stars on celestial sphere, used to describe positions of celestial objects; area of celestial sphere enclosing such stars

**corona** layer of ionized gases that surround and extend a great distance from sun, visible as halo in solar eclipse; aureole

**cosmic noise** radio frequency radiations that emanate from Milky Way; galactic noise

**cosmic rays** highly charged ions that move at enormous speed and strike Earth continuously from all sides

**crater** circular rocky formation located on surface of moon and some other celestial bodies, caused by meteoritic impact

**crescent moon** phase of moon halfway between quarter and new moon

**declination** angular distance of celestial object north or south of celestial equator

**deferent** orbit of celestial body in Ptolemaic system

**dust** cloud of powdery matter floating in space

**eclipse** celestial event in which light from one celestial object is obscured by another object interposed between it and observer, esp. sun's light by moon on Earth or by Earth on moon

**ecliptic** great circle that represents apparent path of sun on celestial sphere

**ecosphere** zone of Earth or other celestial body in which living organisms could be supported

**electromagnetic spectrum** range of radiation wavelengths:

gamma rays, X-rays, ultraviolet rays, visible light, infrared rays, microwaves, and radio waves

**emission lines** bright lines in spectrum of light emitted by glowing gas

**equinox** one of two points in which great circle of ecliptic intersects great circle of celestial equator on celestial sphere: vernal on March 21, autumnal on September 22

**exosphere** outermost portion of planet's atmosphere

**extragalactic** (*adj*) outside the Milky Way system

**first point of Aries** position of celestial bodies on first day of zodiacal calendar

**flash spectrum** brightline spectrum that can be observed briefly before and after a total solar eclipse, produced by sun's reversing layer

**flocculus** one of the bright or dark patches on sun's surface, visible by spectroheliograph

**force field** space through which electric, gravitational, or magnetic force acts

**Fraunhofer lines** dark lines in solar spectrum

**full moon** phase of moon when it is on side of Earth away from sun, so that its entire face reflects sunlight to Earth

**galactic equator** great circle of celestial sphere halfway between galactic poles, parallel to and one degree north of centerline of Milky Way

**galactic noise** cosmic noise

**galactic pole** either of two opposite points of celestial sphere at greatest average distance from Milky Way

**geomagnetic axis** single diameter of Earth that is axis of Earth's magnetic field in conventionalized symmetrical approximation

**gibbous moon** phase of moon halfway between quarter and full moon

**gravitation** force by which celestial objects attract and are attracted by other celestial objects

**gravitational collapse** contraction of dying star that occurs when thermonuclear reactions cannot sustain force of self-gravitation

**halo** circle of definite size around sun or moon caused by ice particles in atmosphere

**horizon** great circle on celestial sphere perpendicular to hypothetical line that connects observer's zenith to nadir; distant line where sky seems to meet Earth

**interacting galaxies** two or more galaxies in such close proximity that their shapes are distorted by gravitational forces

**intercrater plain** flat surface of celestial body between craters

**intergalactic** (*adj*) existing or occurring between or among galaxies

**intergalactic medium** gas found between galaxies

**interplanetary** (*adj*) being or occurring within solar system but outside atmosphere of any planet or sun

**interplanetary medium** gas dust found between planets

**interstellar cloud** dense region of gas and dust from which stars are formed that lies between stars in galaxy

**ionosphere** very high layer in atmosphere of planets in which gases are largely ionized

**lines of force** field lines in force field: magnetic, electric, or gravitational

**Little Dipper** constellation Ursa Minor that contains Polaris and resembles a dipper

**luminosity** intrinsic brightness of any star when compared with sun

**lunar** (*adj*) of or relating to the moon

**lunar eclipse** passage of Earth between sun and moon that causes moon to be in Earth's shadow

**lunar occultation** disappearance of celestial body behind moon

**magnetic field** field arising from electric charge in motion that produces a force on another electric charge

**magnetosphere** region surrounding planet in which planet's magnetic field is stronger than interplanetary field

**mare** large, flat plain on moon, formerly called sea

**Mare Imbrium** round basin on near side of moon that is largest lunar sea

**meridian** great circle on celestial sphere that passes through zenith, nadir, north, and south points on horizon

**Messier object** one of 109 objects numbered from M1 as cataloged by French astronomer Charles Messier to distinguish clusters, nebulae, and galaxies from comets

**meteor shower** apparent divergence from single point by luminous paths of members as meteor swarm encounters Earth's atmosphere

**microwave background radiation** redshifted radiation from glow of early universe that appears not as light but as microwaves

**nadir** point on celestial sphere opposite zenith and directly below observer

**new moon** first phase of moon when it is between Earth and sun with side toward Earth in shadow

**nodes** two points at which orbit of celestial body intersects a reference plane, usu. ecliptic or celestial equator

**Northern Lights** aurora display in Northern Hemisphere

**nutation** slight, periodic oscillation in precession of Earth's axis in space

**occultation** passage of one celestial object in front of another, as in an eclipse

**Olympus Mons** largest volcano on Mars, probably largest in solar system

**optical double** pair of stars that form apparent binary double when viewed from Earth but are actually widely separated in space

**orbit** elliptical path of one celestial sphere or satellite around another larger body, in accordance with Newton's laws of gravitation and motion

**Orientale basin** youngest lunar basin

**outer space** space outside Earth's solar system

**outgassing** extrusion of gases from body of planet after its formation

**parhelic circle** luminous circle or halo parallel to horizon at altitude of sun

**penumbra** partly lighted area that surrounds complete shadow of celestial body during eclipse

**perigee** point closest to Earth in orbit of moon or other object around Earth

**perihelion** point closest to sun in orbit of member of solar system

**perturbation** disturbance in regular motion of one celestial body around another, esp. due to gravitational presence of third body

**phase** particular appearance of celestial body due to recurrent cycle in its illumination; recurrent stage in illumination and apparent shape of moon: new, quarter, full, and gibbous

**photosphere** visible surface of sun

**plasma** low-density, ionized gas with complex magnetic field that moves through space

**polar cap** large region of ice covering north or south polar region of planet, esp. Earth and Mars

**precession** slow shifting of celestial equator due to motion of Earth's axis from gravitational pull of sun and moon on Earth's equatorial bulge

**primordial black hole** black hole created very early in life of universe

**proper motion** apparent angular motion of star across observer's line of sight

**quarter moon** phase of moon halfway between new and full

**radiant** point on celestial sphere from which a meteor stream appears to come

**radio wave** electromagnetic wave that exists at radio frequency

**ray** beam of light from bright source; stream of particles emitted by radioactive substance

**redshift** shift, due to Doppler effect, in spectral lines of object toward longer wavelengths at red end of spectrum as it recedes from Earth, with amount of shift proportional to object's speed

**regolith** blanket of rubble on moon's surface from lunar impacts

**retrograde motion** motion in direction opposite usual orbit of similar celestial bodies

**rift valley** elongated depression of planet's crust between two faults

**ring plain** lunar crater of exceptional diameter with relatively smooth interior

**ring system** flat, thin, reflective band of dust and ice crystals that orbit and encircle a planet, esp. Jupiter, Saturn, Uranus, and Neptune

**Saturn's rings** wide system of visible rings around planet Saturn

**seeing** blurring of telescopic images of celestial bodies due to turbulence in Earth's atmosphere

**semimajor axis** one half the major axis of elliptical orbit described by a celestial body

**solar** (*adj*) of or relating to the sun

**solar corona** outer atmosphere of sun

**solar eclipse** interposition of moon between Earth and sun

**solar flare** sudden, brief increase in intensity of sun's light, usu. near sunspots, accompanied by increase in radiations

**solar nebula** large cloud of hot gas and dust from which sun and planets formed

**solar wind** stream of radiation and ionized gas that spirals outward from sun at high speed

**solstice** date on which sun reaches position farthest north or south of celestial equator; northern on June 21, southern on December 21

**space** three-dimensional continuous expanse in all directions that contains all matter; distance between and area not filled by celestial bodies

**space velocity** velocity of star's motion relative to sun

**spectrum** light emitted by star or other source, dispersed according to wavelength

**spicule** gas jet located in sun's chromosphere

**spiral arm** curved concentration of matter that extends from nucleus of spiral galaxy

**star cloud** large luminous patch of Milky Way that can be resolved with optical aid into dense concentration of stars

**sunspot** temporarily cooler region that appears as dark spot on sun's surface, accompanied by geomagnetic disturbances

**surface temperature** measure of heat at outer face of celestial object

**synodic month** interval between two successive conjunctions of same celestial bodies

**syzygy** straight alignment of three celestial bodies, esp. point in orbit at which moon is in conjunction or opposition with sun

**Tharsis ridge** principal area of Martian volcanic activity

**tidal friction** frictional effect of tides that very slowly retards rotational velocity of Earth

**tides** rising and falling of surface of bodies of water on Earth due to attraction of moon and sun as Earth rotates

**transit** passage of smaller body in front of larger one as seen from Earth

**umbra** dark central cone of shadow that projects from celestial body on side opposite sun; shadow of body in eclipse

**Van Allen radiation belts** doughnut-shaped regions around Earth in which high-speed, charged particles oscillate in Earth's magnetic field

**vertical circle** great circle of celestial sphere with plane perpendicular to horizon

**visible spectrum** portion of electromagnetic spectrum detectable by human eye

**waning moon** moon proceeding from full to new

**waxing moon** moon proceeding from new to full

**zenith** point on celestial sphere lying vertically above observer

**zodiacal light** faint glow above horizon, esp. at tropical latitudes, on clear moonless night after sunset in west and before sunrise in east

**zone** portion of spherical surface lying between two parallel circles

**zone of avoidance** region of sky where no galaxies can be seen due to light-absorbing clouds of dust

# BRANCHES, LAWS, THEORIES, AND TECHNIQUES

**absolute magnitude** astronomical measure of brightness of a star as it would appear at distance of 10 parsecs

**absolute zero** zero kelvins; temperature at which all molecular motion ceases

**albedo** ratio of amount of light reflected and scattered by a surface to amount of light falling on that surface

**apparent magnitude** brightness of star as seen from Earth

**armillary sphere** ancient instrument consisting of a set of rings, used to show relative positions of celestial equator and other circles on the celestial sphere

**astrobiology** study of living organisms beyond the atmosphere of Earth

**astrolabe** medieval instrument consisting of a graduated, vertical circle with movable arm, formerly used to find altitude of star

**astrology** study attempting to interpret the influence of celestial bodies on human events and individual personality, esp. at moment of birth

**astrometeorology** study of the theoretical effects of astronomical bodies and forces on Earth's atmosphere

**astrometric binary** binary system in which the existence of an invisible companion is inferred by its effects on orbital motion of a visible star

**astrometry** branch of astronomy that deals with measurement of the positions of celestial objects

**astronomer** person trained in and expert at the practice of astronomy

**astronomical unit** AU; measurement based on mean distance of Earth from sun, approximately 93 million miles (149.6 million km)

**astronomy** observation and theoretical study of celestial bodies, space, and the universe

**astrophotography** photography of celestial objects

**astrophysics** branch of astronomy dealing with physical properties of celestial objects, space, and the universe

**AU** *astronomical unit*

**big bang model** theory that universe originated in explosion of hot, dense core that rapidly expanded to cooler, less dense states; expanding universe

**big crunch** singularity at end of universe in which universe contracts, opposite to big bang

**binary accretion model** theory of formation of Earth-moon system due to accretion from one cloud of gas and dust

**Bode's law** mathematical relationship which agrees with distances of planets from sun in astronomical units

**Cassegrain reflector** compact, portable reflecting telescope, orig. 17th c.

**celestial mechanics** branch of astronomy concerned with motions and gravitational interactions of celestial objects

**Chandrasekhar limit** maximum possible mass of stable cold star, beyond which it will become a supernova or collapse to become a black hole

**chaos** disorderly and unpredictable universe

**coelostat** clock-driven mirror system in telescope that follows path of observed celestial object across sky

**Copernican system** first heliocentric theory of solar system, published by Nicolaus Copernicus in 1543

**coronagraph** disk in telescope used to create artificial solar eclipse that permits photography of sun's corona

**cosmogony** study of possible origin and evolution of universe

**cosmological principle** assumption that universe would appear the same viewed from any galaxy in it

**cosmology** study of structure of universe as a whole

**cosmos** orderly and harmonious universe

**coudé telescope** telescope in which focus remains fixed while observed object moves, used esp. with spectrograph

**dispersion** separation between different wavelengths in spectrum

**Doppler shift** change in wave frequency due to approach or recession of source relative to observer

**eccentricity** scale that expresses degree of flattening of elliptical orbit, with zero being circular and one being perfectly elliptical

**ephemeris** table giving computed position of celestial body for each day in given period

**epicycle** planetary motion described in Ptolemaic system as circle whose center moves along circumference of another larger circle

**epoch** time at which positions of celestial bodies are observed

**ether** quintessence

**expanding universe** big bang model

**Galilean telescope** first refracting telescope with positive objective lens and negative eye lens, developed by Galileo Galilei in 17th c.

**Geiger counter** Geiger-Müller tube

**Geiger-Müller tube** radiation detector that counts cosmic rays and gamma rays; Geiger counter

**geocentric** (*adj*) viewing universe as though Earth were its center

**gnomon** vertical plate of sundial, set parallel to Earth's axis; shaft perpendicular to horizon, used to find sun's meridian altitude

**gravitational lensing** bending of light of celestial body around another body closer to observer along same line of sight, so that the more distant body appears as ring or arc around closer body

**gravity anomaly** theory that force of gravity would be constant at surface of uniform spherical mass

**harmonic law** Kepler's third law, which states that the squares of periods of any two planets are in same proportion as cubes of their average distances from sun

**heliocentric** (*adj*) viewing universe as though sun were its center

**Hertzsprung-Russell diagram** graph that shows luminosities of stars plotted against their temperatures

**horizon system** system of celestial coordinates, such as altitude and azimuth, that are based on observer's horizon

**horoscope** positions of planets and stars relative to one another at time of person's birth, regarded in astrology as factor that determines one's character and destiny

**Hubble classification scheme** sequence of different types of galaxies: elliptical, spiral, and irregular

**image-intensifier tube** instrument used to increase brightness of image from telescope

**interferometer** instrument that produces interference patterns of light that enable precise measurement of minute wavelengths

**Kepler's laws** Johann Kepler's three laws of planetary motion: *first law* orbit of each planet is ellipse with sun at one of its foci; *second law* each planet revolves so that imaginary line between it and sun sweeps over equal areas of space in equal intervals of time; *third law* harmonic law

**light speed** distance light travels in one second, equal to approximately 186,000 miles (299,792 km)

**light year** astronomical unit of measurement equal to distance light travels in one year, approximately 6 trillion miles (9.5 trillion km), used as measure of astronomical distances

**magnitude** brightness of star in sky measured on logarithmic scale from zero (brightest) to five (faintest), with fifth-magnitude stars being 100 times fainter than zero-magnitude stars

**main sequence** band on Hertzsprung-Russell diagram that contains stage of stellar life in which star consumes hydrogen in its core through nuclear reactions, descriptive of majority of stars

**major axis** maximum diameter across an ellipse

**mascon** *mass concentration*; local concentration of very dense material beneath moon's surface

**mass-luminosity law** the greater the absolute magnitude of a star the greater its luminosity

**mass spectrometry** separation and measurement of molecules that have different masses by deflection of beam of ionized molecules

**monochromator** device with prism and slits, used to obtain desired narrow band of wavelengths from light source

**New General Catalogue** NGC; listing of galaxies, clusters, and nebulae that includes all Messier objects, numbered from NGC1

**Newtonian reflector** telescope with spherical or parabolic primary mirror and flat reflector set at 45 degree angle to optical axis to focus light at side of telescope tube

**Newton's first law of motion** an object remains at rest or in motion with a constant velocity unless acted upon by an outside force

**Newton's law of universal gravitation** force of attraction between any two particles of matter is directly proportional to the product of their masses and inversely proportional to the square of the distance between their centers of mass

**Newton's second law of motion** the change in motion of an object acted upon by an outside force is directly proportional to the force and inversely proportional to the object's mass

**Newton's third law of motion** every action force has a reaction force equal in magnitude and opposite in direction

**NGC** New General Catalogue

**no boundary condition** theory that universe is finite but has no boundary

**objective** lens in telescope nearest to object observed that focuses light to form image of object

**observable universe** portion of universe that can be viewed directly with telescopes or other optical aids

**observatory** building equipped with large telescope and other devices used for astronomical studies

**orrery** mechanical model that shows positions, motion, and phases of bodies in solar system, as in a planetarium

**parallax** apparent shift in position or direction of celestial body when viewed from Earth at changing points of its orbit around sun

**parsec** unit of astronomical measurement equal to 3.26 light years, distance required to produce parallax angle of one arc second

**period** time taken to complete cycle of events, esp. revolution of planet around sun

**period-luminosity relation** established relation between periods of certain stars and their intrinsic brightness

**photometry** process in which intensity of light or radiation emitted by celestial source is measured by electrical voltage or pulse counter

**photomultiplier tube** photometry device that amplifies electron current from photoelectric surface to permit accurate measurement of light from celestial source

**planetarium** complex revolving projector used to simulate motion and position of celestial objects inside a dome; building that houses projector and dome used for this purpose

**planetesimal** any of numerous small bodies that moved in orbits through space and may have formed planets

**plate tectonics** theory that planets and some other celestial bodies consist of crustal slabs that are in constant motion against each other

**Ptolemaic system** geocentric model of universe, postulated by Claudius Ptolemaeus in second century A.D., in which planets, moon, and sun revolve around Earth

**pulsating universe theory** variation on expanding universe theory, in which cycle of expansion and contracting to and from primeval nucleus is endlessly repeated

**quintessence** substance other than fire, air, water, or earth believed to compose celestial bodies in ancient and medieval philosophy; ether

**radial velocity** rate of linear motion of source toward or away from observer in line of sight, as in Doppler shift

**radio astronomy** study of radio energy sources in space by means of large, reflecting radio telescopes

**radio beam** steady stream of radio or radar signals sent from source location

**radio telescope** one or more radio antennas that receive and measure radio waves from celestial sources

**reflector** telescope with mirror as objective

**refractor** telescope with system of lenses as objective

**right ascension** angle in sky east of vernal equinox

**Roche limit** distance from planet's center below which a satellite cannot approach without suffering disruption

**Schmidt telescope** reflector telescope with spherical mirror as objective, used for wide-angle photography

**Schwarzschild radius** critical size that gravitationally collapsing mass must reach to be dense enough to trap light and become black hole

**seismometer** instrument that measures seismic waves on Earth or moon

**SETI** search for extraterrestrial intelligence

**sextant** instrument used, esp. by navigators, to measure angular distance of celestial object from horizon

**sidereal** (adj) expressed or measured in reference to stars

**sidereal period** time in which planet or satellite completes one revolution around its primary relative to a star seen from the primary

**sidereal time** time measured by rotation of Earth with respect to stars, not sun

**signal-to-noise ratio** error inherent in measurement of brightness of faint star based on background light or noise

**singularity** point in space-time at which space-time curvature becomes infinite, such as black hole

**space-time** four-dimensional order of universe specified by three spatial coordinates and one temporal coordinate

**space velocity** velocity of star's motion relative to sun

**spectral type** classification of star based on analysis of certain spectral lines and stated as letter (O, B, A, F, G, K, or M) in order of decreasing temperature and number within letter group, such as the sun, a G2 star

**spectrograph** combination of spectroscope and photographic equipment used in studying spectra of celestial objects

**spectroheliograph** spectrograph modified to study sun's spectrum

**spectroscopic parallax** distance of star indicated by absolute magnitude deduced from relative intensities of selected spectrum lines

**spectroscopy** study of radiative output of celestial source

**spectrum-luminosity diagram** graph that plots spectral type of each star against absolute magnitude

**stargazing** astronomy or astrology

**steady state model** theory of expanding universe stipulating continuous creation of matter, and stating that universe maintains uniform large-scale structure and constant average density at all times

**supermassive black hole** black hole that may exist at center of some active galaxies or quasars

**telescope** instrument used to collect light from celestial objects and resolve images of these objects: reflector, refractor, and Schmidt

**universe** sum total of potentially knowable objects, matter, and energy, believed to be infinite in space and time

**uranography** branch of astronomy that describes and maps the position of the heavens, esp. fixed stars

**uranology** former term for astronomy

**uranometry** measurement of positions, magnitudes, and distances of celestial objects

**Very Large Array** VLA; large set of radio telescopes arranged in Y-shape in New Mexico

**VLA** *Very Large Array*

**white hole** hypothetical time-reversed black hole

**Widmanstatten figures** designs appearing on etched meteoric iron and exhibiting its crystalline structure

**X-ray burster** source of intense X-ray flashes in Milky Way

**zodiac** band of twelve constellations on celestial sphere with ecliptic as its middle line that includes paths of every planet except Pluto, divided into twelve zones and used in astrology

## SIGNS OF THE ZODIAC

**Aquarius** the Water Bearer, a constellation between Capricorn and Pisces and eleventh sign of the zodiac; the fixed air sign and birth sign of persons born between January 20th and February 18th

**Aries** the Ram, a constellation between Pisces and Taurus and first sign of the zodiac; the cardinal fire sign and birth sign of persons born between March 21st and April 19th

**Cancer** the Crab, a constellation between Gemini and Leo and fourth sign of the zodiac; the cardinal water sign and birth sign of persons born between June 21st and July 22nd

**Capricorn** the Goat, a constellation between Sagittarius and Aquarius and tenth sign of the zodiac; the cardinal earth sign and birth sign of persons born between December 22nd and January 19th

**Gemini** the Twins, a constellation between Taurus and Cancer and third sign of the zodiac; the mutable air sign and birth sign of persons born between May 21st and June 20th

**Leo** the Lion, a constellation between Cancer and Virgo and fifth sign of the zodiac; the fixed fire sign and birth sign of persons born between July 23rd and August 22nd

**Libra** the Balance, a constellation between Virgo and Scorpius and seventh sign of the zodiac; the cardinal air sign and birth sign of persons born between September 23rd and October 22nd

**Pisces** the Fishes, a constellation between Aquarius and Aries and twelfth sign of the zodiac; the mutable water sign and birth sign of persons born between February 19th and March 20th

**Sagittarius** the Archer, a constellation between Scorpius and Capricorn and ninth sign of the zodiac; the mutable fire sign and birth sign of persons born between November 22nd and December 21st

**Scorpio** the Scorpion, the constellation Scorpius between Libra and Sagittarius and eighth sign of the zodiac; the fixed water sign and birth sign of persons born between October 23rd and November 21st

**Taurus** the Bull, a constellation between Aries and Gemini and second sign of the zodiac; the fixed earth sign and birth sign of persons born between April 20th and May 20th

**Virgo** the Virgin, a constellation between Leo and Libra and sixth sign of the zodiac; the mutable earth sign and birth sign of persons born between August 23rd and September 22nd

## SPACE EXPLORATION AND ROCKETRY

**abort** (*vb*) cancel or terminate mission or procedure prematurely, esp. due to equipment failure

**aerodynamic heating** surface heating of spacecraft produced by friction during reentry

**aerospace science** study and exploration of Earth's atmosphere and space beyond; rocket science; space science

**airlock** vacuum-tight door in cabin's pressure hull that can be opened to place equipment outside

**anti-G suit** totally enclosed uniform that equalizes G-force on astronaut

**A-OK** (*adj*) *Informal.* all systems go; okay to proceed as planned

**Apollo** series of manned NASA missions to moon

**artificial satellite** man-made object set in orbit around Earth

**astronaut** person sent on space mission

**astronautics** science of spacecrafts and outer space travel; cosmonautics

**Atlantis** space shuttle orbiter vehicle

**Atlas** family of launch vehicles; first-stage booster rocket

**atmospheric drag** frictional force that retards spacecraft or meteoroid moving through upper atmosphere

**backout** reversal of launch countdown due to poor weather or mechanical failure

**ballistic missile** unmanned military rocket with warhead; rocket bomb

**bearing** horizontal direction of object or point measured clockwise from reference line

**bird** *Informal.* rocket, spacecraft

**bits** radio transmission to and from spacecraft in binary code comprehensible to digital computers

**blastoff** launch; liftoff

**blowoff** separation of portion or stage of rocket by explosive force

**booster rocket** first stage of multistage rocket that provides thrust for liftoff

**Brennschluss** *German.* rocket's peak velocity

**burn** firing of rocket engine

**burnout** moment of final oxidation or combustion of fuel in a rocket engine

**burn rate** rate at which solid propellant is consumed

**capsule** small, pressurized compartment for astronauts

**cargo bay** unpressurized part of fuselage in which cargo is carried

**ceiling** altitude at which cloud cover limits vertical visibility

**centrifuge** apparatus with long arm in which individual is revolved to simulate effects of prolonged acceleration in space

**Challenger** NASA space shuttle which exploded in 1986

**CM** *command module*

**Columbia**  first space shuttle orbiter, launched in 1981

**command module**  CM; component of Apollo spacecraft attached to service module until reentry into Earth's atmosphere

**communications satellite**  satellite designed to reflect or relay electromagnetic signals used in communications; comsat

**Comsat**  *Trademark. communications satellite*

**cosmic particle**  cosmic ray

**cosmic ray**  highly energized particle moving at near speed of light that strikes spacecraft; cosmic particle

**cosmonaut**  Soviet astronaut

**cosmonautics**  astronautics, esp. Soviet space program

**Cosmos**  series of unmanned Soviet satellites

**countdown**  backward counting off of seconds before launch; operations during such a count

**counter**  radiation detection instrument or survey meter

**crawlerway**  heavily reinforced roadway for transport of rockets

**cutoff**  termination of propellant flow in rocket; stoppage of combustion

**decompression sickness**  disorder associated with reduced atmospheric pressure that causes gas bubbles in body and pain in chest and extremities

**deep space**  region beyond Earth's solar system

**descent**  drop from Earth orbit, reentry into atmosphere, and touchdown

**Discovery**  space shuttle orbiter vehicle

**docking**  maneuver in which two or more spacecraft or orbiting objects are joined together

**docking maneuver**  change in spacecraft path or trajectory to facilitate docking

**downlink**  radio or television transmission from spacecraft to Earth station

**drift**  lateral divergence from prescribed flight path

**drogue recovery**  system of spacecraft recovery after reentry that uses small and large parachutes to slow descent, stabilize vehicle, and decrease landing impact

**ESA**  *European Space Agency*

**escape velocity**  speed required to place spacecraft in orbit or break free of Earth's gravitational field

**European Space Agency**  ESA; cooperative organization of ten European nations for space exploration

**EVMU**  *extravehicular mobility unit*

**exobiology**  study of extraterrestrial environments for living organisms

**Explorer**  first series of NASA space probes

**external tank**  liquid oxygen or hydrogen propellant tank on space shuttle

**extraterrestrial**  (*adj*) not from Earth

**extravehicular activity**  space walks and other experiments conducted outside confines of spacecraft

**extravehicular mobility unit**  EVMU; space suit, including life support system and manned maneuvering unit; pressure suit; spacesuit

**failsafe**  design that ensures ability to sustain malfunction yet successfully terminate or abort mission

**flight**  movement of craft through space

**flight deck**  area of orbiter module occupied by crew

**flight path**  launch, orbit, and trajectory followed by spacecraft on mission

**flyby**  mission in which spacecraft passes close to target planet but does not orbit or impact it

**flying saucer**  unidentified flying object

**footprint**  area taken up by spacecraft on ground

**G**  acceleration due to gravity, equal to one G at sea level on Earth's surface

**Gemini**  series of NASA Earth orbital missions manned by two astronauts

**G-force**  force in excess of one G experienced by everything inside spacecraft during launch or reentry

**go/no-go**  (*adj*) being the point at which decision to launch or not launch must be made

**ground test**  procedure by which spacecraft, systems, or rockets are tested without launch

**guidance system**  control system that selects flight path of spacecraft and directs its movements in space

**gyro**  spinning wheel resistant to change of direction of its axis of rotation, used to steady orientation of spacecraft

**hangfire**  faulty condition in rocket engine ignition system that causes delay in firing

**hatch**  door in pressurized hull of spacecraft

**heat shield**  structural overlay that protects reentry body of spacecraft from aerodynamic heating

**heat sink**  material that absorbs heat, used for heat shield

**Hubble Space Telescope**  powerful telescope operating outside Earth's atmosphere that has capability to see much deeper into universe than telescopes on Earth's surface

**hydrogen**  gas used as fuel for space shuttle main engine when cryogenically cooled to liquid form

**ice frost**  layer of ice on outside of surfaces supercooled by cryogenic propellants such as oxygen and hydrogen

**impact**  rocket or spacecraft striking surface of planet or any other object

**impact area**  projected location of impact

**inclination**  angle between orbital plane of satellite and plane of ecliptic

**interplanetary travel**  hypothetical manned flights to other planets in solar system

**jacket**  shell around combustion chamber through which liquid propellant is circulated in regenerative cooling

**Jet Propulsion Laboratory**  JPL; center for basic and applied research in space science, located in Pasadena, California

**JPL**  *Jet Propulsion Laboratory*

**Jupiter**  three-stage booster rocket used to place first U.S. satellite Explorer I in orbit in January, 1958

**Kennedy Space Center**  KSC; primary launching base for U.S. spacecraft, located at Cape Canaveral, Florida

**KREEP**  set of elements found in lunar rocks and soil: K, symbol for potassium; REE, rare Earth elements; P, phosphorus

**KSC**  *Kennedy Space Center*

**launch**  initiation of space flight with takeoff of rocket from Earth's surface; blastoff; liftoff

**launch complex**  site and facilities at launching base

**launch crew**  technicians and engineers who prepare spacecraft for launch and run launch operation

**launcher**  structure with tubes and set of tracks from which rockets are launched

**launching base**  NASA station used to launch spacecraft

**launch pad**  area from which spacecraft and booster rockets are sent forth, either tower, tube, or platform

**launch window**  interval of time during which spacecraft can be launched to accomplish specific task or mission

**LEM**  *lunar excursion module*

**life-support system**  environmental control system that provides comfortable, shirtsleeve conditions for crew by control of temperature, pressure, humidity, and oxygen and nitrogen supply

**liftoff** moment in which rocket leaves launch pad on Earth; blastoff; launch

**liquid propellant** cryogenically cooled oxygen or hydrogen used in external fuel tanks of space shuttle

**LM** *lunar module*

**LOX** *liquid oxygen*, used as liquid propellant

**lunar excursion module** LEM; lunar module

**lunar module** LM; detachable vehicle on Apollo spacecraft used in manned moon landings; lunar excursion module

**lunar orbiter** command service module that remained in lunar orbit while lunar module landed on surface of moon

**lunar rock** rocks and soil returned to Earth by Apollo astronauts; moon rock

**Mach** number expressing ratio of speed of a body with respect to surrounding air or fluid; Mach 1 is speed of sound, supersonic being above Mach 1, subsonic below

**Magellan** unmanned spacecraft launched from shuttle to orbit and examine Venus during 1991

**manned flight** space mission with one or more humans on board

**Manned Space Center** MSC; NASA headquarters located in Houston, Texas, that serves as mission control for U.S. space flights

**manned station** orbiting space lab with crew on board

**Mariner** series of NASA spacecraft used for planet flyby missions

**Mercury** first series of NASA orbital and suborbital manned space missions

**microinstrumentation** telemetry equipment

**Mir** small Soviet space station used primarily for scientific experiments

**missile** unmanned military rocket aimed at target, usu. with warhead

**mission** space flight with prescribed goals and operations

**mission control** ground center that provides manned space missions with total support and control over all phases of flight

**module** self-contained unit attached to launch vehicle or spacecraft; pressurized manned laboratory

**moon rock** lunar rock

**MSC** *Manned Space Center*

**multistage rocket** space vehicle that uses two or more firing stages to boost payload into orbit, each stage being jettisoned when fuel is exhausted

**NASA** *National Aeronautics and Space Administration*; U.S. government agency administering space program

**NORAD** *North American Air Defense*; U.S. defense radar network covering North America

**nozzle throat** opening through which fuel from tanks is fed into engine

**orbit** path followed by satellite or spacecraft around Earth or other celestial body

**O-ring** plastic sealing ring on propellant tanks

**parking orbit** orbit around Earth maintained for long duration

**pass** single orbit of Earth by spacecraft or satellite

**payload** passengers, cargo, instruments, equipment, supplies, and support hardware carried by rocket over and above what is necessary to operate vehicle in flight

**photomosaic** space photograph composed of many individual images of segments of photographed objects

**Pioneer** series of unmanned NASA probes that explore solar system as far as Jupiter and Saturn

**plasma engine** hypothetical rocket engine powered by expelling jet of highly ionized plasma gas

**pod** detachable compartment of spacecraft

**pressure hull** main body of spacecraft comparable to aircraft fuselage

**pressure suit** extravehicular mobility unit

**probe** unmanned space mission on trajectory from Earth orbit to study another celestial object

**propellant** solid or liquid fuel used to provide thrust and launch rocket, place it in orbit, break it out of orbit, or slow its descent

**propulsion system** vehicle system of engines, fuel tanks, and lines providing thrust

**proving ground** testing ground

**radar tracking station** tracking station that maintains only radar contact with spacecraft

**Ranger** early series of NASA space probes

**reentry** return of space capsule into Earth's atmosphere

**retroengine** small engine used to produce retarding thrust and reduce velocity, esp. on reentry

**retrofire** ignition of retroengine

**retrograde** orbit of satellite in westerly direction, opposite easterly motion of earthbound observer

**retropack** group of retroengines

**retrorocket** rocket fired to reduce spacecraft motion, so that it descends from orbit or slows down in free fall

**rocket** portion of spacecraft in which combustible materials provide thrust for launch and orbit

**rocket bomb** ballistic missile

**rocketman** *Informal.* astronaut

**rocketry** study and practice of aerospace science

**rocket science** aerospace science

**Rover** vehicle used on lunar surface by astronauts

**satellite** artificial object sent into Earth orbit

**Saturn** first-stage booster rocket on Apollo missions

**scrub** (*vb*) cancel flight or mission

**sealing rings** mechanical devices designed to prevent loss of cabin atmosphere

**Sea of Tranquillity** large lunar basin and landing point of Apollo 11, first manned lunar expedition

**separation** stage in which launch vehicle booster rockets are jettisoned once fuel is exhausted

**service module** section of spacecraft containing propulsion and electrical systems and supplies

**shot** space flight to specific celestial body, such as moonshot

**shuttle** reusable spacecraft that replaced expendable launch vehicles and can return payloads and land on Earth

**silo** large, underground facility for storage and launching of long-range ballistic missiles

**Skylab** large NASA space workshop operated in the 1970's

**solid propellant** chemical mixture or compound containing fuel and oxidizer that burn to produce very hot gases at high pressure

**solid rocket boosters** two solid fuel rockets that augment thrust of shuttle from launch through first two minutes of ascent and are then separated and retrieved for reuse

**Soyuz** series of Soviet manned spacecraft

**Space Age** era of space exploration that began with launch of first Sputnik on October 4, 1957

**space colony** hypothetical large, semipermanent community living on space station or on another planet

**spacecraft** manned or unmanned platform or object placed in Earth orbit or in trajectory to another celestial body

**Spacelab** laboratory payload on shuttle, product of joint effort between ESA and NASA

**spaceman** astronaut; extraterrestrial being

**spaceport** space station

**space probe** probe

**space science** aerospace science; astronomy

**spaceship** spacecraft or satellite

**space station** permanently orbiting, large spacecraft designed to accommodate long-term human habitation; spaceport

**spacesuit** extravehicular mobility unit

**spacewalk** extravehicular activity in which astronaut, often connected by support umbilical, leaves confines of spacecraft

**spaghetti suit** *Slang.* long underwear worn by astronauts, having tubes that carry cooling water

**splashdown** spacecraft landing in ocean

**Sputnik** first Soviet artificial satellite series that began with October 4, 1957 launch

**staging** separation of spent stages of launch vehicle from capsule

**starship** interstellar spacecraft

**step rocket** multistage rocket with boosters

**suborbital flight** one of early manned Mercury flights that did not enter Earth orbit

**Surveyor** class of unmanned NASA space probes undertaken in preparation for manned Apollo lunar flights

**sustainer** small rocket engine that maintains spacecraft's speed after booster is jettisoned

**synodic period** time between two consecutive orbital passes over one reference longitude on Earth

**takeoff** launch; liftoff

**telemetry** coding and measuring of data obtained on spacecraft in form comprehensible to digital computers and transmission to Earth stations for interpretation

**terrestrial** (*adj*) of the Earth

**test flight** flight for controlled observation of operations, rocket, and spacecraft

**testing ground** area and facilities designated for test flights; proving ground

**test rocket** rocket designed for test flight only

**throttling** varying thrust of rocket engine during flight by fuel line constriction or changes in nozzle expansion and thrust chamber pressure

**thrust** propulsive force developed by rocket engines during firing, used to launch spacecraft and place it in orbit or on trajectory out of Earth's atmosphere

**thrust coefficient** ratio of engine thrust to product of nozzle throat area times nozzle inlet pressure

**Titan** first-stage booster launch vehicle

**touchdown** landing of spacecraft on Earth or another celestial body

**tracking station** facility that observes, plots, and monitors path of spacecraft

**trajectory** nonorbital flight path from one point to another

**t-time** specific time, plus or minus, that refers to launch time or zero at end of countdown

**UFO** *u*nidentified *f*lying *o*bject; hypothetical spacecraft from another solar system; flying saucer

**umbilical** electrical or fluid servicing line between tower on launch pad and upright rocket prior to launch, or between spacecraft and astronaut on spacewalk

**unidentified flying object** UFO

**unmanned flight** space mission without humans on board

**uplink** transmission path for sending signals from earth station to communications satellite or airborne platform

**upweight** spacecraft weight at launch, including payloads, support items, and unburned fuel

**Viking** series of NASA spacecraft designed to land on Mars

**visual tracking station** facility from which visual sightings of spacecraft are possible

**Vostok** series of manned Soviet spacecraft, used to make world's first manned space flights in 1961

**Voyager** series of NASA probes that explored outer planets on flybys of Jupiter in 1979, Saturn in 1980, Uranus in 1986, and Neptune in 1989

**V-2** German rocket bomb used in World War II

**weather satellite** unmanned spacecraft that returns meteorological data to Earth

**weightlessness** zero-G state

**window** gap in continuum; interval of time favorable to launch for specific mission

**yaw** angular motion of vehicle about vertical axis through center of gravity

**zero-G** condition of weightlessness and free fall experienced when no gravitational forces are acting on objects in spacecraft

# MATHEMATICS

Branches and Computational Systems
Quantities, Relationships, and Operations
Geometric Shapes and Mathematically Defined Forms
Mathematical Tools

**SEE ALSO**: Chap. 23: Spatial Positions and Relations; Shapes

## BRANCHES AND COMPUTATIONAL SYSTEMS

**algebra** theory and practice of arithmetic operations that uses symbols, esp. letters, to represent unknown variables in equations

**algorithm** set of rules for solving problems through finite repetitions of basic given procedure

**analysis** approach to functions and limits, esp. by use of differential and integral calculus

**analytic geometry** use of coordinate graphing system to demonstrate numerical relationships of algebraic equations; Cartesian geometry

**applied mathematics** study of physical phenomena using mathematical methods, as in mechanics, statistics, and physics

**arithmetic** study of usu. positive real numbers in addition, subtraction, multiplication, and division operations that yield sums, remainders, products, and quotients

**Boolean algebra** form of propositional calculus; algebra of elementary propositions in symbolic logic

**calculus** methods of calculation for continuously changing quantities, based on differentiation and integration of functions and related concepts

**Cartesian geometry** analytic geometry

**descriptive geometry** theory of geometry treated by means of projections on two planes at right angles to each other

**differential calculus** branch of mathematics dealing with rate of change of functions with respect to variables on which they depend

**elementary arithmetic** simple arithmetic computations that involve one- and two-digit positive integers

**Euclidean geometry** study of geometry within limits of Euclidean space, i.e. ordinary one-, two-, and three-dimensional space

**Fourier analysis** expression of periodic function as sum of infinite series of trigonometric functions

**game theory** field of study concerned with decision-making problems in competitive situations governed by rules

**geodesy** measurement and theory of curvature, shape, and dimensions of Earth's surface

**geometry** branch of mathematics that deals with deduction of properties, measurement, and relationships of points, lines, angles, surfaces, and solid figures in space

**group theory** study of the properties and relationships of mathematical groups, with associated operations that obey specific set of rules

**higher arithmetic** general theory of integers

**integral calculus** branch of mathematics used to find indefinite integrals of functions, evaluate definite integrals, determine dimensions, and solve simple differential equations

**linear algebra** algebra of vectors and matrices as opposed to real numbers

**math** mathematics

**mathematical biology** application of mathematics to problems in theoretical biology, esp. by construction of mathematical models

**mathematical physics** application of mathematics to problems in physics, esp. by construction of mathematical models

**mathematics** science dealing through symbolic representation with the relationship of numbers, magnitudes, and forms, including quantitative operations and the solution of quantitative problems

**matrix algebra** generalized algebra that deals with operations and relationships among ordered sets of elements arranged in rows and columns

**non-Euclidean geometry** geometry not in accordance with all of the postulates of Euclidean space, esp. the single parallel postulate

**number theory** advanced arithmetic devoted to study of properties of integers

**plane geometry** elementary form of geometry that deals with two-dimensional figures

**plane trigonometry** form of trigonometry that deals with triangles in the Euclidean plane

**political arithmetic** science of economic and demographic statistics that describe political units

**propositional calculus** branch of symbolic logic dealing with analysis of relationships between statements that have been reduced into conjunctions, disjunctions, and negations of more elementary statements

**quadratics** form of algebra that treats quadratic polynomial equations

**set theory** branch of mathematics and symbolic logic dealing with nature and relations of aggregates or sets

**solid geometry** geometry that deals with solid, three-dimensional figures

**statistics** collection, analysis, interpretation, and presentation of masses of empirical, numerical data

**symbolic logic** science of developing and representing logical principles by means of symbols to provide rules of deduction for computations

**systems analysis** study of an activity by mathematical means to determine how most efficiently to attain desired ends

**topology** investigation of those properties of a geometric configuration that remain unaltered when subjected to one-to-one transformations that are continuous in both directions

**trigonometry** branch of mathematics that measures relations between sides and angles of triangles

**vector analysis** study of the properties of vectors

## QUANTITIES, RELATIONSHIPS, AND OPERATIONS

**abscissa** horizontal coordinate of two-dimensional coordinate system in the Cartesian plane; x-axis

**addend** one of a group of numbers to be added together

**addition** arithmetic operation that combines numbers to generate sum

**aggregate** whole sum, total amount; set of mathematical elements with a common property

**algebraic function** sum, difference, product, quotient, or root of polynomial function

**antilogarithm** number of which a given number is the logarithm

**Arabic numeral** one of standard number symbols: 0,1,2,3,-4,5,6,7,8,9; digit

**area** number of unit squares required to cover surface; measurement of surface

**arithmetic mean** average

**arithmetic progression** sequence in which each succeeding term is derived by adding common difference to preceding term

**associative law** result of multiple operations does not depend on how they are grouped

**asymptote** straight line in relation to curve such that as point moves along infinite branch of curve the distance from point to line approaches zero

**average** result that occurs when sum of two or more quantities is divided by the number of quantities; arithmetic mean

**axiom** proposition assumed to be true without proof in order to study its applied consequences; self-evident truth

**axis** straight line for reference in graph, such as Cartesian coordinate; straight line through center of plane or solid around which it is symmetrically arranged

**base** number multiplied by itself in scientific notation; number that is raised to a power

**billion** one thousand million

**binary** (*adj*) designating system of numbers having two as its base

**binomial** expression that is a sum or difference of two unlike terms

**binomial distribution** probability function that indicates how often two outcomes with constant probability will occur in a succession of repetitive experiments

**bisection** division of angle or form into two equal parts

**cancel** (*vb*) remove either common divisor from numerator and denominator of fraction or equivalents from opposite sides of equation

**cardinal number** number used in simple counting to indicate an amount, such as how many of something are in a set

**Cartesian coordinate** either of two coordinates that locate point on Cartesian plane and measure its distance from x-axis or y-axis

**chain rule** rule for taking derivative of composite function in which second function is taken as independent variable in differentiating first function

**chi-square distribution** widely used probability density function that shows distribution of sum of squares of several independent random variables

**circular function** trigonometric function

**circumference** distance measured around outside of circle

**coefficient** number that multiplies another quantity; factor of a product

**common denominator** common multiple of denominators of two or more fractions

**commutative law** rule of combination in which an operation on two terms is independent of the order of the terms

**complement** angle or arc that when added to another angle or arc equals a right angle

**complex number** real or imaginary number expressed as a + bi where a and b are real numbers and i is the square root of –1

**composite function** function obtained from two given functions by applying one function to an independent variable and applying the second function to the result

**composite number** integer divisible by a whole number other than itself or 1

**compound number** number expressed in more than one denomination or unit, such as 6 feet, 2 inches

**computation** act or method of determining an amount, esp. by arithmetic

**concentric** (*adj*) designating two or more figures having a common center

**congruence** property of having exactly the same size and shape

**conjugate** (*adj*) having the same or similar properties, such as two lines; (*n*) one of two adjacent angles that total 360°

**constant** quantity with fixed value, opposite of variable

**continuous function** function whose value at each point is nearly the same as its values at nearby points

**conversion** change in form but not value of quantity or unit

**coordinates** numbers associated with points on number line or graph

**corollary** theorem proved by application of a previously proved theorem

**correlation coefficient** any measure of concomitant variation in two or more variables

**corresponding angles** pair of nonadjacent angles on same side of line that crosses two other lines, one interior and one exterior

**cosecant** trigonometric ratio expressed as secant of the complement of an arc or angle

**cosine** trigonometric ratio expressed as sine of the complement of an arc or angle

**cotangent** trigonometric ratio expressed as tangent of the complement of an arc or angle

**count** (*vb*) recite numbers in standard order; add units in group one at a time

**cross multiply** determine two products by multiplying numerator of each of two fractions by denominator of other

**cryptarithm** arithmetic problem with letters substituted for numbers, solved by finding all possible pairings of digits and letters that produce numerically correct answer

**cube** third power of a number; number multiplied by itself two times

**cube root** number whose cube is given number

**cubic equation** polynomial equation with no variable exponent higher than three

**data** numerical information

**decimal** (*adj*) designating system of numbers having ten as its base

**decimal point** mark indicating division between integers and fractions in mixed number

**degree** unit of angular measure; measure around fixed point, with total of 360 degrees in circle

**denominator** lower number of fraction, indicating number of parts into which the whole has been divided

**dependent variable** element in second set of a function associated with independent variable selected from first

**derivative** rate of change of mathematical function with respect to change in independent variable

**deviation** amount by which any single value differs from the mean

**diameter** straight line extending from edge to edge through center point of sphere or circle

**difference** amount of inequality between two quantities; result obtained when one quantity is subtracted from another

**differential** product of the derivative of a function of one variable times the small increment of an independent variable

**differential equation** equation containing derivatives

**digit** one of Arabic numeral symbols: 0,1,2,3,4,5,6,7,8,9

**distribution** arrangement of statistical population when one or more specific criteria are applied

**distributive law** rule of combination in which specified operation applied to combination of terms equals combination of that operation applied individually to each term

**dividend** number that is divided by divisor

**division** arithmetic operation that finds how many times one number is contained in another, producing a quotient

**divisor** number that divides dividend

**domain** set of elements by which a function is limited or defined

**eccentricity** number used to define form of a conic section as an ellipse, circle, parabola, or hyperbola

**equation** mathematical statement containing the equals (=) sign between two different but equal algebraic formulations

**even number** number that is divisible by two, where result is an integer

**expansion** replacement of an expression by the sum of its individual terms or by an infinite series

**exponent** superscript symbol used to indicate how many times a number is to be used as factor or multiplied by itself

**exponential function** function with independent variable as an exponent

**expression** symbol or combination of symbols representing a value or relationship

**extrapolation** estimating value of a function beyond range of its known values

**factor** two or more numbers multiplied together, each number being a factor of the product

**factor analysis** statistical method that reduces large number of measures or tests to smaller number of factors that account for all results

**factorial** product of all positive integers from given positive integer down to 1

**Fibonacci sequence** unending sequence of numbers, each of which is the sum of its two predecessors

**formula** equation illustrating rule for mathematical relationship of quantities

**fraction** quantity expressed as the ratio of two integers that is not itself an integer

**frequency distribution** grouping of observations or outcomes into classes and tabulation of number of occurrences of each class in given period

**function** exact association of one element from one set with element from another set

**geodesic** (*adj*) describing shortest line between two points on plane, esp. curved surface

**geometric mean** square root of product of two numbers

**geometric progression** sequence in which ratio of each succeeding term to preceding term is constant throughout

**Gödel's incompleteness theorem** theorem that within a given logical system there exists at least one mathematical formula that can be neither proved nor disproved

**googol** number that is equal to 1 followed by 100 zeros

**googolplex** number that is equal to 1 followed by a googol of zeros

**hypotenuse** side of right triangle opposite right angle

**hypothesis** provisionally true statement; supposition to be proved

**imaginary number** square root of negative number, esp. imaginary unit represented by square root of –1

**independent variable** element in function whose value is specified first and determines value of one or more other elements in expression of function

**infinity** boundlessly great number, amount, or geometric magnitude

**integer** any natural number, or positive or negative whole number, including zero; whole number

**interpolation** determination of the intermediate unknown values of a function between two known values

**inverse function** function that replaces another function when variables of first function are interchanged for set of values of independent variable

**inverse proportion** ratio of x to y when one unknown is multiplied by a number and its proportional unknown is divided by that number

**irrational number** any real number that cannot be expressed as the ratio of two integers

**least common denominator** smallest number that divides evenly into numerator of fraction; multiple of denomina-

tors of two or more specified fractions; lowest common denominator

**limit** value approached by function as its independent variable approaches some specific value

**linear equation** algebraic equation in which variables are in first power and whose graph is a straight line

**linear function** function with variables in first degree, multiplied only by constants, and combined by addition or subtraction

**locus** set of all points satisfying given conditions

**logarithm** exponent of that power of a fixed base number that equals another given number

**logarithmic function** inverse of exponential function

**lowest common denominator** least common denominator

**magic square** matrix in which each column, row, and both main diagonals produce same constant sum

**mantissa** decimal part of common logarithm

**mapping** examination of entities with no meaning beyond themselves as they relate to a different set of entities, in order to generate conclusions

**mathematical model** set of formulae or equations that describe behavior of physical system in mathematical terms

**matrix** ordered set of elements arranged in rows and columns, esp. one that can be combined with similar arrays having comparable number of rows and columns

**mean** average

**median** middle item in array of data ranked from smallest to largest, used as statistical measure of primary tendency

**million** one thousand thousand

**minuend** number from which another number is subtracted

**mixed number** number consisting of whole number and fraction

**mode** statistical measure of primary tendency made by determining item that occurs most frequently in a data set

**monomial** expression in form of single term that is either a constant, variable, or product of numbers and variables

**multiplicand** number to be multiplied by another

**multiplication** arithmetic operation in which additions of a number are repeated a specified number of times to produce a product

**multiplier** number by which multiplicand is multiplied

**natural number** positive integer

**number** abstract unit in numeral series that represents an arbitrarily determined quantity; arithmetic total, sum of units involved

**numeral** word, letter, symbol, or figure expressing or representing a number

**numerator** upper number of fraction, indicating number of parts taken of denominator

**odd number** number that is not evenly divisible by two

**one-to-one function** function in which change in value in domain always gives different value for function

**ordinal number** number indicating position in a series, as *first* or *third*

**ordinate** vertical coordinate of two-dimensional coordinate system in Cartesian plane; y-axis

**origin** point of intersection in coordinate system, esp. x-axis and y-axis system

**parameter** arbitrary constant whose values describe some member of a system of curves, expressions, or functions; independent variable used to express coordinates of variable point and their functions

**-opia** eye, sight
**-opsy** medical examination
**opto-** eye
**orchido-** testes
**ortho-** erect, straight, normal
**-osis** diseased or abnormal condition or state
**ossi-** bone
**osteo-** bone
**oto-** ear
**ovi-** egg
**patho-** disease, sickness, suffering
**-pathy** suffering, disease, or treatment
**pedi-** foot
**pedo-** child
**pharmaco-** drug or medication
**pharyngo-** pharynx
**-phasia** speech disorder
**phlebo-** vein
**-phrenia** lack, deficiency, disorder
**-plasia** growth
**-plast** cell, living substance
**-plasty** surgical repair or molding formation
**pleuro-** rib, side of body
**pneumo-** lung, air
**podo-** foot
**polio-** gray matter
**procto-** anus, rectum
**psycho-** mind
**pulmo-** lung
**pyelo-** pelvis
**reni-** kidney
**-rrhagia** rupture, profuse flow or discharge
**-rrhaphy** suture
**-rrhea** flow, discharge
**-rrhexis** rupture
**sangui-** blood
**sarco-** flesh
**schizo-** split
**-scope** instrument for viewing
**-sect** cut
**sero-** serum, blood
**somato-** body
**somni-** sleep
**stomato-** mouth
**-stomy** surgical operation involving creation of artificial
 opening
**tachy-** rapid
**thanato-** death
**thrombo-** blood clot, coagulation
**-tome** cutting instrument
**tomo-** cut, section
**-tomy** surgical incision or excision
**-tonia** muscle or nerve tension
**toxico-** poison
**toxo-** poison
**tracheo-** windpipe, trachea
**tricho-** hair
**-trophic** having nutritional requirements
**tropho-** nourishment
**urino-** urine
**uro-** urine
**utero-** womb, uterus
**vaso-** vessel

**veno-** vein
**ventro-** abdomen
**vermi-** worm
**zymo-** fermentation

# MEASURES AND WEIGHTS

Systems and Units
Measuring Devices
Measures and Standards of Time
U.S. System
Metric System
Special Measures
Foreign and Historical Measures
Combining Forms

**SEE ALSO**: Chap. 4: Physics; Mathematics; Chemistry; Chap. 5: Electricity and Electronics; Chap. 23: Time Perception; Spatial Positions and Relations

Definitions for historical, foreign, and special measures generally provide both U.S. and metric system equivalents. Within the U.S. system, metric conversion is provided. Conversion from metric to U.S. system is given only for basic units, such as meter to foot or gram to ounce, since other conversion factors can be derived by moving the decimal point to the left or right.

## SYSTEMS AND UNITS

**angular measure** units used to measure angles and sections of circles
**apothecaries' measure** units of weight used chiefly for dispensing liquid drugs
**apothecaries' weight** system of weights used chiefly in compounding and dispensing drugs
**avoirdupois weight** U.S. and British units of weight used for articles other than drugs, gemstones, and precious metals
**circular measure** units used to measure circles: quadrants, degrees, minutes, and seconds
**cubage** cubic measure
**cubic measure** units used to measure volume filled in three dimensions; cubage
**dry measure** units of capacity used to measure dry commodities
**land measure** units of linear and square measure, used to measure land
**linear measure** units used to measure length
**liquid measure** units of capacity used to measure liquids
**mariners' measure** units of linear measure used in navigation
**measures** units of standard systems, used to express dimension, extent, mass, and volume
**metrication** establishment of metric system as standard system of measurement
**metric system** decimal system of weights and measures, used in science and in most nations other than the United States, with basic units of meter, gram, and liter

**metrology**  science of weights and measures

**square measure**  units used to measure area covered in two dimensions

**surveyors' measure**  units of linear measure used in surveying

**time measure**  units used to measure the passage of time

**troy weight**  system of weights used for precious metals and gemstones

**U.S. units**  system of weights and measures, used primarily in the United States, with basic units of foot, ounce, and quart

**weights**  units used to measure mass or heaviness

**wood measure**  units of cubic measure used for wood

## MEASURING DEVICES

**analytical balance**  precision balance having sensitivity of 0.1 milligram

**balance**  weighing instrument that opposes a known weight to the object being weighed across a lever supported exactly in its middle

**bathroom scale**  small platform scale on which one stands to measure body weight

**beam**  balance, esp. its crossbar

**caliper**  tool with adjustable, usu. curved jaws on pivot, used to measure thickness or diameter

**compass**  instrument for drawing or measuring circles, consisting of two movable, rigid legs hinged at one end

**conversion table**  tabular arrangement of equivalent values of units of measure of different systems

**counterweight**  weight used to counterbalance an opposing object that is to be weighed

**cyclometer**  instrument that records the revolutions of a wheel to measure distance or speed

**extensometer**  instrument for measuring minute degrees of expansion, contraction, and deformation

**folding rule**  rule made of hinged sections, usu. of light wood, that fold out to increase length; zigzag rule

**measure**  instrument with graduated markings for measuring

**measuring cup**  cup with graduated markings, used to measure dry and liquid volume

**measuring spoons**  set of spoons in graduated sizes, used esp. in cooking

**micrometer**  device for measuring minute distances and angles, esp. in connection with a telescope or microscope

**platform scale**  scale with platform for holding object being weighed

**rule**  rigid strip of material having straight edge marked off with units of measure; ruler

**ruler**  rule

**scale**  balance, platform scale, or other device for measuring weight

**sonic depth finder**  device that uses sonar echolocation to measure underwater depths

**steelyard**  portable balance with two unequal arms, the shorter one having a hook or device for holding an object to be weighed and the longer one having a movable counterweight

**tape measure**  length of flexible material with graduated markings that unreels to measure linear dimension

**theodolite**  surveying instrument having telescopic sight for precise measurement of vertical and horizontal angles

**ultramicrometer**  micrometer calibrated to and capable of measuring extremely small magnitudes

**vernier**  small, movable, graduated scale running parallel to the fixed, graduated scale of a sextant or other measuring device

**weighbridge**  large platform scale standing flush with roadway, used to weigh trucks or livestock

**yardstick**  rule 36 inches in length

**zigzag rule**  folding rule

## MEASURES AND STANDARDS OF TIME

**ab urbe condita**  *Latin*. lit. from the founding of the city; used in dating system based on founding of Rome in 753 B.C.; AUC

**A.D.**  anno Domini; *Latin*. lit. in the year of the Lord; used to designate years of Christian era

**age**  measure of one's time alive

**alarm clock**  small clock that sounds alarm at set time to awaken sleeper

**a.m.**  ante meridiem; *Latin*. lit. before noon; morning

**analemma**  scale shaped like figure 8 showing declination of sun and equation of time for each day

**analog clock**  timepiece with hands revolving on face to indicate time

**ante meridiem**  *Latin*. lit. before noon; a.m.

**atomic clock**  extremely accurate timepiece whose operation is based on vibrations of certain atoms

**AUC**  ab urbe condita

**Aurora**  goddess of dawn (ancient Rome)

**B.C.**  before Christ; used to designate years before Christian era

**BCE**  before Christian (or Common) era; equivalent of B.C.

**beat**  musical measure of time

**bell**  device sounded on ship every half hour during each four-hour watch or segment of day

**calendar**  system or device for marking time by days, weeks, months, and years

**C.E.**  Christian (or Common) era; equivalent of A.D.

**Central time**  time zone in U.S. Middle West, one hour earlier than Eastern time

**century**  measure of time equal to 100 years

**chrono-**  Greek prefix meaning time

**chronograph**  instrument that measures and records time

**chronology**  science of computing and measuring time and sequentially ordering events

**chronometer**  instrument for measuring time; timepiece

**chronoscope**  instrument for measuring time

**clock**  mechanical timepiece marking passage of minutes, hours, and sometimes seconds

**date**  designation by number of each day of each month

**day**  basic unit of time equal to 24 hours

**daylight-saving time**  time attained by moving timepieces one hour ahead of standard time from spring to fall

**decade**  measure of time equal to 10 years

**dial**  face of clock, watch or sundial showing time of day

**digital clock**  timepiece indicating time by regularly changing display of numerical digits

**Eastern time**  time zone in U.S. Atlantic coast region, three hours later than Pacific time

**embolism** insertion of time period to regulate calendar, esp. day added for leap year

**gnomon** raised part of sundial that casts shadow to indicate time

**Greenwich mean time** worldwide standard time relative to time at meridian running through Greenwich, England

**Gregorian calendar** corrected Julian calendar incorporating leap year every fourth year

**horography** art of making timepieces

**horologe** timepiece, esp. sundial

**horologist** maker of clocks and timepieces

**horology** art or science of measuring time and making timepieces

**horometry** practice or science of measuring time

**hour** unit of time equal to 60 minutes

**hourglass** necked glass vessel containing sand or mercury, used to measure time, esp. period of one hour

**intercalary** (*adj*) inserted into calendar, as with leap year's added day

**International Date Line** imaginary line at 180 degrees longitude, exactly opposite Greenwich meridian, at which one day is added when passing westward across it

**Julian calendar** standard twelve-month, 365-day calendar introduced in ancient Rome

**minute** basic unit of time equal to 60 seconds, or 1/60 of an hour

**month** unit of time equal to 1/12 of a year, usu. 30 or 31 days, except February, which has 28 or 29 days

**Mountain time** time zone in U.S. Rocky Mountain area, one hour later than Pacific time

**o'clock** (*adv*) of the clock, used in telling time, as in one o'clock

**Pacific time** time zone along U.S. western seaboard, three hours earlier than Eastern time

**pendulum** suspended, swinging mechanism used in clockworks or as timepiece

**p.m.** *post* meridiem; *Latin*. lit. after noon; afternoon and evening

**post meridiem** *Latin*. lit. after noon; p.m.

**quartz clock** timepiece whose mechanical operation is based on electrical frequencies and resulting regular vibrations of quartz crystal

**real time** actual elapsed time, esp. when editing film

**second** unit of time equal to 1/60 of a minute

**sidereal time** time measured by rotation of Earth relative to a star on celestial sphere other than the sun

**solar time** time determined by calculating time required for sun to cross same point in sky a second time

**space-time** four-dimensional continuum incorporating time with three physical dimensions as means of locating events

**standard time** worldwide time system based on Greenwich meridian; time attained when daylight-saving time is reversed and clocks are turned back one hour in fall; time officially adopted by a country or region

**stopwatch** watch with hand that can be stopped or started at any instant for precise timing

**strike** (*vb*) make known the time by sounding, esp. a bell

**sundial** instrument indicating time of day by casting shadow of sunlight on dial

**tempo** rate of movement, speed; time in which musical passage is written and/or played

**time** dimension of reality characterized by sequential flow of events and phenomena through irreversible procession of moments from past to present to future; systematized demarcation of the passage of such moments into units of seconds, minutes, hours, days, and years; period or point in time; fourth dimension in space-time continuum

**time capsule** container holding records or objects of current culture, deposited for discovery at future date

**timecard** paper on which hours worked by employee are recorded

**time chart** chart showing standard times in various parts of world

**time clock** clock with mechanism to record time on timecard that employee begins and ends workday

**timekeeper** one appointed to record and announce time at event, esp. athletic contest

**time machine** hypothetical device permitting travel forward or backward through time

**timepiece** clock, watch, or other device for measuring and indicating time

**timer** device used to keep time or measure brief periods

**time sheet** paper for recording arrival and departure times of workers

**time signature** fractional sign used in musical notation to show number of beats per measure and kind of note lasting one beat

**timetable** schedule of times for some event, esp. arrivals and departures of railroads, buses, or airplanes

**time zone** longitudinal region within which same standard time is used

**watch** small timepiece worn on wrist or carried in pocket

**week** measure of time equal to 7 days

**year** measure of time required for Earth to complete one revolution around the sun, equal to either 365 or 366 days, or 12 months

## U.S. SYSTEM

**acre** unit of square measure, usu. for land, equal to 43,560 square feet (4047 sq. m)

**barrel** unit of cubic measure equal to 5.8 cubic feet; unit of liquid measure equal to 31.5 U.S. gallons (119 l) or 42 U.S. gallons (159 l) for petroleum

**board foot** cubic measure used for lumber, equal to 144 cubic inches or 12 inches by 12 inches by 1 inch

**bushel** cubic measure equal to 2150 cubic inches

**cental** hundredweight

**circle** circular measure equal to 360 degrees

**cloth yard** unit of linear measure for cloth, formerly equal to 37 inches (0.93 m), now equal to 36 inches (0.91 m) or 1 standard yard

**congius** unit of liquid measure used in prescriptions, equal to 1 gallon (3.7853 l)

**cord** cubic measure of wood, equal to 128 cubic feet (3.6 cu. m)

**cubic foot** 1728 cubic inches; 1/27 cubic yard

**cubic inch** 1 inch by 1 inch by 1 inch

**cubic yard** 27 cubic feet

**cup** unit of liquid measure equal to 8 fluid ounces (237 ml) or 16 tablespoons

**degree** unit of angular or circular measure equal to 60 minutes or 1/360 of a circle

**dram** unit of apothecaries' weight equal to 60 minims or 1/8 fluid ounce (3.89 g); unit of avoirdupois weight equal to 1/16 ounce (1.77 g)

**fathom** unit of linear measure equal to 6 feet (1.8 m), used in nautical and mining measurements

**fluid ounce** unit of liquid measure equal to 2 tablespoons or 1/8 cup (29.573 ml)

**foot** basic unit of linear measure equal to 12 inches; equivalent to 30.48 centimeters

**furlong** unit of linear measure equal to 220 yards (201 m) or 1/8 mile (0.2 km)

**gallon** unit of liquid measure equal to 4 quarts (3.7853 l)

**gill** measure of liquid volume equal to 1/2 cup or 4 fluid ounces (118 ml); noggin

**grain** smallest measure of weight, being 437.5 grains per avoirdupois ounce

**half-inch** unit of linear measure equal to 1/24 foot (1.27 cm)

**hogshead** unit of liquid measure usu. equal to 63 gallons (238 l)

**hundredweight** unit of avoirdupois weight equal to 100 pounds (45.359 kg); cental; short hundredweight

**inch** unit of linear measure equal to 1/12 foot; equivalent to 2.54 centimeters

**lb.** abbreviation for pound

**microinch** unit of linear measure equal to one-millionth of an inch

**mil** unit of length equal to one-thousandth of an inch (0.0254 mm), used esp. to measure diameter of wire or thickness of plastic

**mile** unit of linear measure equal to 5280 feet (1.609 km); statute mile

**minim** smallest unit of liquid measure, equal to 1/60 of a fluid dram, or approximately one drop

**minute** sixty seconds in angular measure; 1/60 of a degree

**nautical mile** unit of linear measure equal to 6080.20 feet (1853.25 m), used in navigation

**noggin** gill

**octant** the eighth part of a circle, equal to 45 degrees

**ounce** unit of avoirdupois weight equal to 16 drams or 1/16 pound; equivalent to 28.35 grams

**oz.** abbreviation for ounce

**peck** unit of dry volume equal to 8 quarts or 1/4 bushel (8.81 l)

**pennyweight** unit of troy weight equal to 24 grains or 1/20 of an ounce (1.555 g)

**pint** unit of liquid measure equal to two cups (0.6 l); unit of dry measure equal to 35 cubic inches

**pole** unit of square measure equal to 1 square rod or 30 1/4 square yards (25.3 sq. m)

**pound** unit of avoirdupois weight equal to 16 ounces; equivalent to 0.45359 kilogram

**quadrant** unit of circular measure equal to 90 degrees, or one quarter of a circle

**quart** unit of liquid measure equal to 1/4 gallon, or 57.749 cubic inches (0.946 l); two pints; unit of dry measure equal to 1/8 peck, or 67.201 cubic inches (1.101 l)

**road** unit of square measure equal to 1/4 acre

**rod** unit of linear measure equal to 5.5 yards or 16.5 feet (5.029 m)

**scruple** unit of apothecaries' weight equal to 20 grains or 1/3 dram (1.295 g)

**second** unit of angular measure equal to 1/60 of a minute or 1/3600 of a degree

**short hundredweight** hundredweight

**short ton** measure of avoirdupois weight equal to 2000 pounds (0.907 metric ton)

**square mile** unit of square measure equal to 640 acres (2.59 sq. km)

**statute mile** mile

**ton** short ton; 2000 pounds

**yard** unit of linear measure equal to 3 feet or 36 inches (0.9144 m)

## METRIC SYSTEM

**are** a; unit of land measure equal to 1/100 hectare or 100 square meters

**centiare** ca; one square meter

**centigram** cg; ten milligrams, 1/100 gram

**centiliter** cl; ten milliliters, 1/100 liter

**centimeter** cm; ten millimeters, 1/100 meter

**centner** fifty kilograms, or sometimes 100 kilograms

**decigram** dg; one hundred milligrams, 1/10 gram

**deciliter** dl; one hundred milliliters, 1/10 liter

**decimeter** dm; one hundred millimeters, 1/10 meter

**dekagram** dag; ten grams, 1/10 kilogram

**dekaliter** dal; ten liters, 1/10 kiloliter

**dekameter** dam; ten meters, 1/10 kilometer

**gram** g; basic metric measure of mass equivalent to 0.035 ounce or 15.432 grains

**hectare** ha; unit of surface or land measure equal to 100 ares, or 2.471 acres (10,000 sq. meters)

**hectogram** hg; one hundred grams, 1/10 kilogram

**hectoliter** hl; one hundred liters, 1/10 kiloliter

**hectometer** hm; one hundred meters, 1/10 kilometer

**kilogram** kg; one thousand grams; equivalent to 2.205 pounds

**kiloliter** kl; one thousand liters

**kilometer** km; one thousand meters; equivalent to 0.621 miles

**liter** l; basic metric unit of liquid volume equivalent to 1.057 quarts

**long ton** ton

**meter** m; basic metric unit of linear measure equivalent to 3.281 feet

**metric hundredweight** fifty kilograms

**microgram** ug; one-millionth part of gram, used primarily in chemistry

**micrometer** micron

**micron** u; one-millionth part of meter; micrometer

**milligram** mg; one-tenth centigram, one-thousandth gram

**milliliter** ml; one-tenth centiliter, one-thousandth liter

**millimeter** mm; one-tenth centimeter, one-thousandth meter

**nanogram** ng; one-billionth part of gram

**nanometer** nm; one-billionth part of meter

**picogram** pg; one-trillionth part of gram

**quintal** measure of weight equal to 100 kilograms or 1/10 ton

**ton** measure of weight equal to 1000 kilograms or 10 quintals; long ton

## SPECIAL MEASURES

**arpent** unit of area equal to one acre, orig. French, still used in Quebec and Louisiana

**assay ton** measure of weight used in assaying ore, equal to 29.167 grams

**baker's dozen** group of thirteen units or things; long dozen

**bale** large bundle of dry goods, approximately 500 pounds (U.S.)

**base box** unit of square measure, representing 112 sheets of tin each 14 by 20 inches (35 by 50 cm), equal to 31,360 square inches (196,000 sq. cm)

**bolt** linear measure for cloth equal to 40 yards (36.576 m)

**cable** nautical unit of length equal to 720 feet (219 m) in U.S. Navy and 608 feet (185 m) in British navy

**caliber** diameter of a gun's bore measured in hundredths of an inch

**capful** amount that a cap will contain

**carat** measure of weight for gemstones, equal to 206 milligrams (3 grains); measure of amount of gold per twenty-four parts of gold alloy

**case** carton containing usu. four, twelve, or twenty-four units or things

**centistere** one-hundredth part of stere

**chain** unit of linear measure used in surveying, equal to 66 feet (20 m) and divided into 100 links

**chiliad** group of one thousand

**cicero** printer's measure approximately equivalent to one pica or 0.1776 inch (4.5 mm)

**crate** quantity, esp. of fruit, packed in crate, approximately 2 cu. ft. (0.05 cu. m)

**dash** a few drops or grains, used as cooking measure, esp. for liquids

**double magnum** jeroboam

**dozen** group of twelve units or things

**em** printer's measure designating square width of given type size

**fifth** unit of liquid measure equal to approximately one-fifth gallon (750 ml), esp. for spirits

**frail** quantity of raisins contained in frail basket, approximately 75 pounds (34 kg)

**freight ton** unit of volume for shipping equal to 40 cubic feet

**gauge** diameter of a gun's bore measured in millimeters

**great gross** group of twelve gross, or 1728, units or things

**great pace** unit of linear measure representing distance between places at which same foot touches ground in walking, approximately 5 feet (1.5 m)

**gross** group of twelve dozen, or 144, units or things

**hand** linear measure equal to 4 inches (10 cm), used esp. for horses

**handbreadth** unit of linear measure equal to 2.5 to 4 inches (6.4 to 10 cm)

**hectostere** one hundred stere, equal to 130.8 cubic yards, used to measure cordwood

**jeroboam** unit of liquid volume equal to two magnums or approximately 4/5 gallon (3 l), esp. for wine; double magnum

**jerry can** can used as measure of liquid volume equal to five gallons (19 l) in U.S. or 4.5 imperial gallons (20.4 l) in Britain

**keel** measure of coal equal to 21 long tons and 4 hundredweight (21.5 metric tons)

**kip** dead weight load equal to 1000 pounds (453.6 kg)

**knot** rate of speed equal to one nautical mile per hour

**league** any of various units of linear measure equal to 2.4 to 4.6 statute miles

**light year** unit of linear measure used in astronomy, equal to distance light travels in one year in a vacuum, or approximately 5.878 trillion miles (9.46 trillion km)

**link** unit of linear measure used in surveying, equal to one hundredth of a chain

**long dozen** baker's dozen

**magnum** unit of liquid volume equal to approximately two-fifths gallon (1.5 l), esp. for wine

**megaton** one million tons, esp. an explosive force equal to one million tons of TNT

**military pace** unit of linear measure equal to 2 1/2 feet

**nail** unit of cloth measure equal to 2 1/2 inches

**nebuchadnezzar** unit of liquid measure equal to 20 quarts (18.9 liter), used esp. for wine

**pace** unit of linear measure representing span covered by feet in taking one step, approximately 30 to 40 inches (75 cm to 1 m)

**palm** unit of linear measure equal to 3 inches (7.5 cm)

**pica** unit of measure in typography equal to one-sixth inch or 12 points

**pinch** a few grains, used as dry measure in cooking

**pipe** cask used as measure of liquid volume, equal to 4 barrels, 2 hogsheads, or half a tun, containing 126 gallons (477 l), esp. of wine

**point** unit of measure in typography equal to one seventy-second inch or one-twelfth pica

**puncheon** cask used as measure of liquid volume, equal to 80 gallons (304 l)

**quire** twenty-five sheets of paper

**ream** five hundred sheets of paper or 20 quires

**rood** unit of linear measure varying from 5 1/2 to 8 yards (5 to 7 m); unit of land measure equal to 40 square rods (0.101 ha); unit of 1 square rod (25.29 sq. m)

**score** group of 20 units or things

**sextant** unit of circular measure equal to 60 degrees or one sixth of a circle

**span** unit of linear measure representing distance between fully extended tips of thumb and little finger, usu. equal to 9 inches (23 cm)

**stere** one cubic meter, used to measure cordwood; equivalent to 1.3080 cubic yards

**tablespoon** unit of measure equal to 3 teaspoons (14.8 ml)

**teaspoon** unit of measure equivalent to 4.9 milliliters

**township** unit of territory used in surveying, approximately six miles square (93.2 sq. km)

**troy ounce** unit of weight for precious metals and gemstones, equal to 31.103 g, with 12 troy ounces equal to 1 pound

## FOREIGN AND HISTORICAL MEASURES

**amphora** vase holding 10.3 gallons (38.99 l) (ancient Greece)

**ardeb** unit of dry measure equal to 5.62 U.S. bushels (Egypt)

**arroba** unit of avoirdupois weight varying between 25.37

**183**

pounds (9.5 kg) and 32.38 pounds (12 kg) in Spain, Portugal, and Latin America; unit of liquid measure equal to 4.26 gallons (16.1 liters) (Spain)

**arshin** unit of linear measure equal to 28 inches (71 cm) (Russia)

**aune** historical unit of measure for fabric equal to 47 inches (119 cm) (France)

**barleycorn** historical unit of length, equal to 1/3 inch (8.5 mm)

**bath** unit of liquid measure varying between 10 and 11 gallons (38 and 42 l) (Hebrew); 6.8 gallons (25.7 l) (ancient Rome)

**bovate** historical unit of land area varying between 7.5 and 20 acres, equal to one-eighth carucate (Britain)

**braccio** historical unit of length, usu. equal to 26 or 27 inches (66 or 68 cm) (Italy)

**braza** unit of length representing reach of outstretched arms, equal to 5.48 feet (1.67 m) (Spain, Latin America)

**cab** ancient liquid measure equal to 2 quarts (Hebrew)

**carucate** unit of land area varying between 60 and 160 acres (Britain)

**catty** measure of weight equal to about 1 1/2 pounds (680 g) (China, Southeast Asia)

**chopin** historical unit of liquid measure equal to one quart (Scotland)

**congius** unit of liquid measure equal to 0.8 gallons (3.2 liters) (ancient Rome)

**crore** total of ten million units, esp. rupees; 100 lacs (India)

**cubit** linear measure based on length of forearm, usu. equal to 17 or 18 inches (43 to 46 cm) (ancient Greece, ancient Rome)

**denarius** measure of weight equal to 4.6 grams (0.162 oz) (ancient Rome)

**dessiatine** unit of land measure equal to 2.7 acres (1.1 ha) (Russia)

**drachma** measure of weight equal to 4.36 grams (0.153 oz) (ancient Greece)

**ell** unit of linear measure for cloth equal to one thirty-second bolt or approximately 1 1/4 yards (114 cm) (Britain)

**ephah** unit of dry volume equal to 40 liters or approximately one bushel (Hebrew)

**fanega** unit of dry measure equal to 1.58 bushels (55.7 l) (Spain, Latin America)

**fanegada** unit of land measure equal to from 1.25 to 1.75 acres (0.5 to 0.7 ha) (Spain, Latin America)

**feddan** unit of area equal to 1.038 acres (0.42 ha) (Egypt)

**firkin** unit of liquid volume equal to 9 imperial gallons (41 l); one-half kilderkin (Britain)

**haikwan tael** customs unit equal to 1.20666 troy ounces of fine silver (China)

**hekat** unit of dry volume equal to 4.77 liters (4.33 qt) (Hebrew)

**hide** historical unit of land measure varying from 60 to 120 acres (24 to 49 ha) (Britain)

**homer** unit of volume equal to 10 baths liquid measure or 10 ephahs dry measure; kor (Hebrew)

**imperial gallon** 1.20095 U.S. gallons (Britain)

**imperial quart** 1.20095 U.S. quarts (Britain)

**kantar** measure of weight corresponding to hundredweight (Middle East)

**kilderkin** unit of liquid volume equal to 18 imperial gallons (82 liters), or 2 firkins (Britain)

**koku** unit of dry measure equal to 5.12 bushels (1.8 hl) (Japan)

**kor** homer

**kos** linear unit of land measure varying from 1 to 3 miles (1.6 to 4.8 km) (India)

**lac** total of 100,000 units, esp. rupees (India)

**liang** measure of weight equal to 1 1/3 ounce (37 g); tael (China)

**livre** measure of weight equal to 0.5 kilogram, equivalent to 1.1 pounds (France)

**long hundredweight** hundredweight equal to 112 pounds (50.8 kg) (Britain)

**mark** former measure of weight for precious metals equal to 8 ounces (249 g) (Europe)

**maund** measure of weight varying from 25 to 82.286 pounds (11 to 37.4 kg) (India)

**mina** ancient measure of weight and value equal to one-sixtieth part of talent

**mite** measure of weight equal to 1/20 grain (3.24 mg) (Britain)

**momme** measure of weight equal to 3.75 grams (0.13 oz) (Japan)

**morgen** old Dutch unit of land measure equal to 2 acres (0.8 ha) (South Africa)

**mutchkin** unit of liquid measure equal to slightly less than one pint (Scotland)

**obolus** measure of weight equal to 1/10 gram (Greece)

**oka** measure of weight equal to 2 3/4 pounds (1.25 kg) (Turkey)

**perch** measure of volume for stone equal to 24 cubic feet (0.7 cu. m) (Britain)

**pfund** measure of weight equal to 0.5 kilogram or 1.1 pounds (Germany)

**picul** measure of weight equal to 100 catties, or about 133 to 143 pounds (60 to 64 kg) (China, Southeast Asia)

**pocket** measure of weight, esp. for hops, equal to 168 pounds (76.4 kg) (Britain)

**pood** measure of weight equal to about 36 pounds (16 kg) (Russia)

**pottle** former liquid measure equal to two quarts

**quart** unit of liquid measure comparable to U.S. quart, equal to 69.355 cubic inches (1.136 l) (Britain)

**quartern** one-fourth part of certain weights and measures (Britain)

**reed** ancient unit of linear measure equal to 6 cubits

**Roman mile** unit of linear measure equal to 1620 yards (1480 m) (ancient Rome)

**rotl** measure of weight and dry measure varying widely, but approximately one pound (Islamic countries)

**rundlet** former measure of volume equal to 15 imperial gallons (68 liters) (Britain)

**ser** measure of weight usu. equal to one fortieth of a maund, varying in value but officially 33 ounces (950 gm) (India)

**shekel** measure of weight equal to 1/2 ounce (Hebrew)

**stack** unit of cubic measure, esp. for coal and wood, equal to 108 cubic feet (3 cu. m) (Britain)

**stadion** unit of linear measure equal to 622 feet (189.6 m) (ancient Greece)

**stadium** unit of linear measure equal to about 607 feet (185 m) (ancient Rome)

**stone** measure of weight equal to 14 pounds (6.4 kg) (Britain)

**tael** liang

**talent** ancient measure of weight equal to 3000 shekels or 6000 drachmas

**tierce** former unit of liquid volume equal to one-third pipe or 42 gallons (159 l), esp. for wine

**tod** measure of weight, esp. for wool, equal to 28 pounds (12.7 kg) (Britain)

**toise** former unit of linear measure equal to 6.395 feet (1.949 m) (France)

**tola** measure of weight equal to 180 grains (11.7 g) (India)

**tower pound** measure of weight equal variously to 12 ounces (350 grams), 15 ounces (437 grams), or 16 ounces (467 grams) (Britain)

**tun** unit of liquid volume equal to 252 gallons (953.9 l), esp. used for wine cask (Britain)

**vara** unit of linear measure varying from 32 to 43 inches (81 to 109 cm) (Spain, Portugal, Latin America)

**verst** unit of linear measure equal to 3500 feet (1.067 km) (Russia)

**virgate** former measure of land area equal to about 30 acres (12 ha) (Britain)

## COMBINING FORMS

**atto-** one-quintillionth part of given base unit

**centi-** one-hundredth part of given base unit

**deci-** one-tenth part of given base unit

**deka-** ten of given base unit

**exa-** one quintillion of given base unit

**femto-** one-quadrillionth part of given base unit

**giga-** one billion of given base unit

**hecto-** one hundred of given base unit

**kilo-** one thousand of given base unit

**mega-** one million of given base unit

**micro-** one-millionth part of given base unit

**milli-** one-thousandth part of given base unit

**myria-** ten thousand of given base unit

**nano-** one-billionth part of given base unit

**peta-** one quadrillion of given base unit

**pico-** one-trillionth part of given base unit

**tera-** one trillion of given base unit

# CHAPTER 5

# Technology

# MACHINERY AND FABRICATION

Machinery and Mechanical Devices
Fabrication and Manufacturing Processes
Types of Construction
Builders and Construction Workers

SEE ALSO: Chap. 4: Physics; Chap. 5: Structural Components;
Tools and Hardware; Electricity and Electronics; Chap. 6:
Aircraft; Automobiles

## MACHINERY AND MECHANICAL DEVICES

**absorbing dynamometer** device that absorbs and dissipates the power it measures

**aeolipile** early steam engine consisting of round vessel rotated by exhaust jets; simple turbine

**agitator** apparatus in machine that shakes and stirs objects

**air pump** machine that removes, compresses, or forces air into something

**alternator** alternating current generator or dynamo

**apparatus** complex device or machine that has a specific use

**appliance** device for specific purpose; machine for household task, usu. electric

**arc lamp** unit that produces light by maintaining arc between two electrodes, esp. carbon rods

**assembly** group of machine parts put together to form independent unit

**automatic machine** machine that regulates its own operation

**automaton** mechanical contrivance that appears to act by its own motive power; robot

**auxiliary device** unit that assists or supplements primary device, but is subordinate to it

**backhoe** hydraulic excavating tractor with hinged boom operating jawed bucket

**backup device** unit that takes over in event primary device fails and performs same task

**balance** instrument that opposes objects of known weight and object being weighed on lever supported exactly in middle, in order to measure weight

**balance crane** two-armed apparatus in which one arm counters the load on the other

**baler** device that compresses and wraps loose material into standardized bundles

**ball bearing** low-friction bearing in which moving parts revolve or slide on freely rolling metal balls

**ball cock** valve connected to hollow floating ball which rises and falls in tank to open and shut valve, controlling water supply to tank

**battery** device that generates electricity by chemical reaction

**bearing** machine part in or on which another part revolves or slides

**bellows** device that produces stream of air through narrow opening when sides are pressed together

**belt** endless, flexible band passing about two or more pulleys, used to transmit motion between pulleys or to convey materials

**bevel gear** gear having teeth cut into conical surface, usu. meshing with similar gear set at right angle

**blinker** warning light that flashes steadily on and off

**block and tackle** combination of fixed and movable pulley blocks with rope or cable, used to hoist large weights

**block gauge** hardened steel with ground faces, used to check accuracy of other gauges

**blower** device for supplying air at moderate pressure

**blowtorch** small torch that produces hot flame from liquid fuel with pressurized air to melt metals

**boiler** closed tank in which water is heated and converted to steam in order to power engine or supply heat

**brake** device that connects moving part to frame, used to hold parts in position, control direction of motion, or absorb energy; any device that slows or halts motion, esp. by friction

**buffer** padding device or cushion used to lessen or absorb shock

**burner** part that produces flame or direct heat

**business machine** machine for doing office work, such as computer, photocopier, or calculator

**butterfly valve** disk-shaped valve on axis at its diameter, used esp. as damper in pipe or choke in carburetor

**bypass engine** turbine or jet engine in which compressed air is diverted to join exhaust gases to increase thrust

**cableway** cables connecting two towers, used to move skip for transporting materials

**cam** rotating wheel or projection on wheel that gives or receives uneven rotation or reciprocating motion to or from another wheel

**camber** slight arching, upward curvature or convexity of member, for specific purpose

**capstan** rotating drum with cable used to hoist heavy weights

**carburetor** device in which air and gasoline spray combine to form explosive mixture in internal combustion engine

**carousel** flat machine that revolves

**caster** swivel wheel that supports movable weight, esp. heavy furniture

**centrifuge** machine that rotates to generate centrifugal force, used to separate particles of varying density or shed moisture

**clamp** device with two parts that can be brought together to grip, fasten, or brace something

**cogwheel** wheel with toothed rim that meshes with another wheel to transmit or receive motion

**combine** machine used to harvest crops

**compactor** device that crushes and compresses loose material into compact bundles

**compressed air machine** device operated by expansion of air under pressure in enclosed container

**compressor** pump that places air or gas under pressure

**computer** electronic device that stores information and performs complex calculations very rapidly

**contraption** mechanical device

**conveyor belt** endless mechanical belt used to transport objects along its path

**coupling** linkage between machine shafts

**crampon**  hooked device used to lift heavy weights

**crane**  long-armed machine used to lift or lower objects at great height

**crank**  arm bent at right angle and connected to shaft of machine, used to transmit or transfer circular motion to and from shaft

**crankshaft**  shaft with cranks that transmits motion

**cyclometer**  instrument that records revolutions of wheel to measure distance or speed

**cylinder**  chamber in which piston moves in reciprocating engine

**damper**  device that reduces shock, vibration, or air flow

**deadbolt**  lock bolt that closes and opens by turning of knob or key

**derrick**  hoisting beam with tackle rigged over it

**device**  mechanical contrivance used for specific purpose

**diaphragm**  dividing wall or partition between parts, usu. opening and closing to regulate entry or passage

**die punch**  sheet metal cutter used to make exact duplicates of die shape in heavy machinery; permanent mold

**diesel engine**  internal combustion engine that uses extremely high temperatures to burn fuel without spark

**differential gear**  series of gears that permit two or more shafts to rotate at different speeds

**differential motion**  movement in which speed of driven object equals difference in speeds of its connected parts

**dog**  mechanical gripping or holding device

**dredge**  apparatus used to scoop up mud and rocks from bottom of body of water

**drill**  pointed instrument that makes holes in hard substances

**drive belt**  endless loop that transmits power in engine

**driver**  mechanism that imparts motion to another machine or part

**dwell**  period in cycle of operation in which given machine part remains motionless

**dynamo**  device that generates electric current by using coiled wire in magnetic field

**electric motor**  motor that utilizes electric power to run machinery

**electromechanical**  (adj) designating a device activated electrically, as by a solenoid, and also working mechanically

**elevator**  platform or cage suspended on motor-operated cables to hoist or lower objects

**engine**  machine or device that uses fuel or energy to develop mechanical power, often to transmit motion to another machine

**epicyclic train**  series of gears or pulleys in which one or more axes revolve around central axis of sun gear

**extractor**  rotating device that draws off water by centrifugal force

**floodgate**  gate designed to control and regulate flow of water

**fluid coupling**  mechanism in which fluid, usu. oil, transmits torque from one shaft to another

**flywheel**  heavy, notched wheel used to regulate machine's speed and uniformity of motion

**four-stroke engine**  internal combustion engine with power stroke occurring once every four piston strokes

**fulcrum**  support point on which lever turns

**funicular**  device, esp. carriage, worked by overhead cable from which it hangs

**gantry**  frame on wheels that spans a distance, esp. used to carry cranes

**gauge**  device used to measure dimensions or test degrees

**gear**  device that transmits motion and power by contact between toothed wheels

**generator**  machine that creates electrical power

**Geneva wheel**  indexing device that provides period of motionlessness during operating cycle of machine

**gimmick**  ingenious mechanical device

**gin**  machine used to hoist heavy objects

**gizmo**  Informal. device or gadget

**go-devil**  flexible, jointed implement used to free pipes of obstruction

**governor**  device for maintaining uniform speed of engine, as by regulating fuel supply

**gyroscope**  wheel mounted in set of rings so that axis of rotation is free to turn in any direction

**harrow**  toothed device used to pulverize materials

**helical gear**  gear with teeth set at oblique angle to rotation of wheel

**hoist**  device that lifts objects

**hopper**  storage tank with discharge chute

**hydraulic engine**  engine powered by liquid, esp. by pressure created when liquid is forced through an aperture

**hydrostat**  instrument used to detect presence or monitor level of water

**hypoid gear**  bevel gear designed to mesh with similar gear, with axes at right angle

**idle gear**  gear placed between driving and driven gear to transmit motion between them

**idle wheel**  wheel gear for transmitting motion between driving part and driven part

**impeller**  rotating part of centrifugal pump

**implement**  tool or other device required to perform given task

**inclined plane**  simple machine: flat surface at angle to level ground

**induction motor**  electric motor in which rotation is induced by interaction of magnetic fields

**internal combustion engine**  fuel-burning reciprocating or rotary engine in which fuel/air mixture is converted into power in enclosed cylinder

**jack**  support, brace; ratchet device used to lift heavy weight

**jet engine**  engine that generates reaction force when compressed outside air and hot exhaust gases are forced through nozzle

**laser beam**  cutting or welding tool that uses highly concentrated beam of light made up of particles in excited energy state

**lathe**  machine that supports rotating object worked on by stationary cutting, boring, or drilling tool

**lever**  simple machine: rigid bar that transmits or modifies lifting force applied at one point and is supported by fulcrum at a fixed point

**linkage**  arrangement and coupling of simple machine elements into compound machines

**loom**  frame for weaving horizontal and vertical elements

**machine**  any device or instrument composed of interrelated functioning parts that aids in performing work by transmitting or modifying force or motion

**machinery**  working parts of a machine; assemblage of mechanical devices or machines

**machine tool**  heavy-duty power tool used to shape metal machine parts or wood, as on a lathe

**mainspring**  principal spring in mechanism

**mechanical advantage** ratio of resistance or load to applied force of machine

**mechanical device** anything produced or operated by machinery or a mechanism, esp. used to produce, transmit, receive, or alter motion

**mechanism** any device for performing work or transmitting motion; piece of machinery; assembly of moving parts performing one function within larger machine

**mill** device or machine used to cut, grind, mix, shape, or process

**mole** powerful boring machine used in construction of tunnels through earth and rock

**motor** small engine; electric-driven machine that powers a mechanical device

**muffler** device that reduces noise

**needle valve** valve in which opening is controlled by fine point that fits into conical seat

**nuclear reactor** device that releases energy from nuclear reaction in controlled form, used for large-scale energy production

**pallet** platform used to move and store goods

**parbuckle** doubled rope with middle secured at specific height and ends passed around cylindrical object that is to be raised or lowered

**pawl** device with hinged tongue whose tip engages notches of cogwheel or ratchet to allow one-directional rotation

**pendulum** weight suspended from fixed point so as to swing freely back and forth due to gravity and momentum

**permanent mold** die punch

**pile driver** machine with heavy drop hammer used to sink large timbers into ground

**pilot** device that guides action of machine or part

**pilot valve** valve that controls action of another valve

**plasma arc torch** machine that uses very hot gas to cut metal

**plow** device used to cut up, turn, and lift soil

**plug** electrical connection that fits into jack; device that closes off flow of liquid or gas

**pneumatic engine** engine powered by compressed air

**poppet** rising and falling valve consisting of disk on stem

**power tool** usu. electric device used to perform specific mechanical task

**power train** sequence of gears and shafting that transmits power from engine to driven mechanism

**press** device that uses pressure to form or manufacture

**pulley** simple machine: small wheel with rope or chain in grooved rim around its circumference, used to increase applied force, lift, or change direction of object at end of rope or chain

**pump** device that draws or moves liquids

**rack and pinion** large-toothed bar, or rack, that meshes with small gear, or pinion, to receive or transmit motion

**ratchet** device that converts continuous motion into intermittent motion, esp. toothed wheel on handle that imparts one-directional motion to tool

**reciprocating engine** engine in which back-and-forth movement of pistons causes rotary motion of crankshaft, either two-stroke or four-stroke

**reduction gear** combination of gears that reduces input speed to lower output speed

**retort** container with long tube used to distill substances

**robot** automaton

**rolamite** flexible, S-shaped metal loop in which two rollers are suspended with loop fastened to two parallel guide rails

**roller** rotating cylinder used to press or shape some object

**rotary engine** engine in which rotary motion is produced directly by triangular rotor, not as reciprocating motion from pistons

**rotor** any mechanism that rotates, esp. in motor or dynamo

**sander** machine or device that smoothes and polishes with sandpaper or abrasive material

**scale** balance or other device used to determine weight

**scope** instrument used to observe

**scraper** device that smoothes or cleans surfaces

**screw** simple machine: inclined plane turned around a cylinder

**screw conveyor** device for moving loose material, consisting of shaft with broad, helically wound blade rotating in tube or trough; worm

**self-regulating machine** automated machine in which feedback input determines changes in future output

**semaphore** apparatus that conveys information by means of visual signals

**servomechanism** automatic control system that compares input and output to regulate differential

**shunt** electrical switch or diverter

**simple machine** basic mechanical device, such as inclined plane, lever, pulley, screw, wedge, or wheel and axle

**siphon** tube bent into legs of unequal length with shorter leg placed in upper of two containers to draw liquid through and down into lower container by atmospheric pressure

**skidway** usu. inclined platform or path for sliding heavy objects, esp. logs or planks

**skip** basket or bucket, usu. suspended from crane or cables, used to transport materials

**solar cell** photovoltaic cell used to convert radiant energy of sunlight into electric power

**sonar** device that transmits sound waves through water and registers reflected vibrations

**spigot** stopper plug, often with valve to regulate flow

**spring** elastic contrivance, esp. coiled length of wire, that regains its shape after being compressed, bent, or stretched, used to impart force

**spring-loaded** (*adj*) designating machine part held in specific position by spring

**sprinkler** device that disperses drops of liquid over wide area

**spur gear** gear having teeth cut on rim parallel to its axis of rotation

**stator** part of machine that remains fixed with respect to its rotating parts

**steam engine** engine that derives its power from steam under pressure in a cylinder

**steam shovel** excavating machine with bucket on arm, operated by boiler-driven engine

**stopcock** plug, spigot, or valve that controls fluid flow

**subassembly** structural or functional group of machine parts that forms part of larger assembly

**sun gear** central gear around whose axis other gears in epicyclic train revolve

**switch** device used to open, close, or divert, esp. electric current

**synchronous motor** electric motor whose speed is proportional to frequency of current driving it

**tachometer** instrument that measures rate of rotation

**theodolite** surveying instrument used to measure vertical and horizontal angles

**thermometer** device that registers temperature

**thermosiphon** series of siphon tubes that circulate water in heating unit by convection

**thermostat** instrument that regulates temperature

**tool** instrument, esp. handheld, that works, shapes, cuts, or joins

**transformer** device that converts one form of electricity into another

**treadle** lever or pedal that turns wheel

**triple-expansion** (*adj*) designating power source using same fluid to do work at three successive stages of expansion

**truckle** small wheel or pulley

**turbine** engine with curved blades or vanes on spindle that rotates to convert energy from fluid entering enclosed casing into rotary motion

**two-stroke engine** internal combustion engine having compression and power stages only, with power stroke occurring once every two piston strokes

**universal joint** flexible connection used to transmit rotary motion from one shaft to another shaft not in line with it

**vacuum** enclosed space out of which nearly all air or gas has been pumped

**vacuum pump** pump used to draw air or gas out of enclosure to form vacuum

**valve** device that regulates flow through pipe or tube, esp. one that permits flow in one direction only

**vehicle** means of conveyance or transport, sometimes motorized, that moves on wheels, runners, or tracks

**ventilator** device that regulates air flow, used to maintain fresh air

**venturi** tube with concave sides that controls flow of liquid by producing suction

**vernier** small device with secondary, graduated scale, used to make fine adjustments on precision instruments

**waterwheel** wheel on shaft moved by weight of water hitting floats or paddles, used to transmit motion

**weapon** instrument or device for use in attack or defense in combat

**wedge** simple machine: two inclined planes joined to form device with pointed end and thicker base

**welding torch** device used to fuse metal parts by heat

**wheel** solid disk or circular frame connected by spokes to central axis, used to transmit power or motion in machinery

**wheel and axle** simple machine: grooved wheel or pulley fixed to shaft or drum, used to increase mechanical advantage or speed

**whorl** flywheel on spindle, used to regulate its speed

**widget** small mechanical device or gadget, esp. one whose name cannot be recalled

**winch** device with crank on handle, used to transmit motion, esp. for hoisting

**windlass** rotating drum with cable wound around it, used for hoisting

**windmill** mill operated by large oblique vanes that radiate from shaft and rotate by force of wind

**wind tunnel** tunnellike chamber through which air is forced to test airplanes and motors

**working part** machine, mechanical device, or element thereof that performs some function for a specific purpose, esp. related to motion

**worm** screw conveyor

**worm gear** mechanism consisting of rotating shaft cut with helical threads that engages with and drives toothed gear whose axis is at right angle to shaft

# FABRICATION AND MANUFACTURING PROCESSES

**automate** (*vb*) use only machine power in construction, assembly, production, or operation

**balance** (*vb*) even out weight distribution

**bale** (*vb*) compress and bind into standard-size bundle

**bevel** (*vb*) cut intersection of two faces to form third face at oblique angles to both

**blanch** (*vb*) bleach, clean in acid; coat with tin

**blast** (*vb*) blow up or move with explosives; polish or cut with stream of small particles projected by steam or air

**blend** (*vb*) mix or combine

**bond** (*vb*) connect or fasten together two or more parts

**bore** (*vb*) drill out a hole or cavity to increase its size

**braze** (*vb*) solder with soft flux

**broach** (*vb*) remove metal from surface with toothed cutting edge

**buff** (*vb*) polish, shine, smooth

**build** (*vb*) construct from different elements to form unified whole

**burn** (*vb*) transform with fire or intense heat

**burnish** (*vb*) polish, rub until shiny

**cannibalize** (*vb*) build or repair machine with parts salvaged from similar machines

**cant** (*vb*) tilt, pitch at an angle

**cantilever** (*vb*) construct as or support with projecting beam

**cast** (*vb*) form in a mold

**caulk** (*vb*) fill seam or joint with waterproof material

**check** (*vb*) hold back, restrain

**chill** (*vb*) harden by sudden cooling

**chop** (*vb*) cut into small pieces

**churn** (*vb*) agitate vigorously

**clarify** (*vb*) separate suspended particles from liquid

**cold-work** (*vb*) work metal at temperature below level at which recrystallization occurs

**collimate** (*vb*) make parallel or level; adjust line of sight

**compact** (*vb*) compress, reduce under pressure

**compress** (*vb*) flatten, change shape by pressure

**constrict** (*vb*) make smaller, esp. at one place; squeeze or limit

**construct** (*vb*) build from different elements into unified whole

**countersink** (*vb*) set below surface into fitted hole

**couple** (*vb*) join together, link, connect

**crate** (*vb*) box into large containers for shipping

**crush** (*vb*) pulverize, reduce to small bits

**crystallize** (*vb*) form crystals by evaporation

**cut** (*vb*) pierce with sharp object

**cybernate** (*vb*) use computers to control and carry out manufacturing or other operations

**dam** (*vb*) form barrier to flow of liquid

**distill** (*vb*) purify by vaporization into separate components

**dredge** (*vb*) enlarge or clear bottom of body of water

**drill** (*vb*) form hole in object with pointed instrument

**drop-forge** (*vb*) hammer hot metal into shapes between two dies

**elevate** (*vb*) raise to higher position

**extrude** (*vb*) force fluid material through press to shape objects

**fabricate** (*vb*) construct, esp. from standardized parts

**finish** (*vb*) apply final touches and embellishments

**fire** (*vb*) bake in oven to harden or glaze object, esp. pottery

**fit** (*vb*) join elements that conform in shape; insert; adjust elements to conform in shape

**forge** (*vb*) shape molten or heated metal

**form** (*vb*) give shape to

**found** (*vb*) lay the base for, begin to build

**frame** (*vb*) construct framework, support, or skeletal structure

**glaze** (*vb*) coat with smooth, impermeable finish

**grade** (*vb*) level, make smooth; sort by size or quality

**grind** (*vb*) cut and smooth surface with abrasive material; pulverize

**hoist** (*vb*) lift heavy weight mechanically

**hone** (*vb*) grind to smoothly finished surface

**install** (*vb*) fit fixture into housing; place machinery in position to function

**join** (*vb*) fit; bond

**knead** (*vb*) work into pliable mass by folding over, squeezing, and pressing

**knurl** (*vb*) form beaded or ridged metal surface

**lap** (*vb*) machine to an extremely fine, smooth finish

**lay** (*vb*) establish and prepare groundwork for

**machine** (*vb*) make or shape by action of machines

**manufacture** (*vb*) produce items in quantity with standardized, technologically advanced equipment

**mechanize** (*vb*) make mechanical; operate or perform by machinery

**mill** (*vb*) grind, cut, or shape; process

**mold** (*vb*) form in frame, cavity, or matrix

**plane** (*vb*) cut away large, flat surface area

**plaster** (*vb*) coat with layer of plaster

**press** (*vb*) exert force upon, esp. form by stamping on die or template

**produce** (*vb*) make, manufacture

**pump** (*vb*) move up and down, esp. move liquids by suction or pressure

**quarry** (*vb*) excavate stone by cutting or blasting at surface

**ream** (*vb*) widen a hole or opening

**refine** (*vb*) remove impurities

**regulate** (*vb*) systematically control operations

**retrofit** (*vb*) equip with parts not available at time of original construction

**salvage** (*vb*) repair and save from destruction

**sand** (*vb*) rub smooth with abrasive

**scrape** (*vb*) rub surface with rough tool or abrasive

**shape** (*vb*) cut and mold material into definite structure or form according to specific plan

**shear** (*vb*) stamp or cut into forms

**solder** (*vb*) join or cement with hot, liquefied metal

**splice** (*vb*) join by interweaving

**stamp** (*vb*) press and cut with a die

**strip** (*vb*) remove paint or finish, esp. from wood

**thread** (*vb*) apply ridges to smooth surface, usu. metal

**toenail** (*vb*) join with nail driven at oblique angle

**tool** (*vb*) work or shape with instruments or tools

**turn** (*vb*) form on rotating device, tool, or machine

**water-cool** (*vb*) cool engine or other machine part by water circulating around it in pipes

**weld** (*vb*) fuse metal components by application of heat

## Types of Construction

**bricklaying** art of building structures with fired clay blocks cemented together into walls

**bridge construction** process of building structures that span waterways or other geographical features

**cabinetmaking** construction of finished woodwork and furniture

**component building** construction from standardized, prefabricated parts

**construction** systematic devising, forming, and building of something with parts that fit together

**dam building** construction of barrier to water flow

**earthmoving** excavation of ground, esp. for highway or building

**excavation** formation of large hole or cavity in earth

**fabrication** making or constructing of something with parts that must be assembled

**finishing** applying outer layer and decorations to structure

**foundation** construction of base or support for structure

**frame construction** building a structural framework with wood, rather than masonry, steel, or concrete

**framing** process of using a wood frame for construction

**general building** construction of residential and commercial buildings without specialized features

**grading** moving earth to form smooth, even inclination, esp. for roadway

**heavy construction** building of large-scale structures with complex and powerful tools and machinery

**highway construction** building of paved roadways

**home building** construction of residential buildings

**HVAC** *h*eating, *v*entilation, and *a*ir *c*onditioning installation

**insulating** installation of insulating materials

**landscaping** development of land and foliage into decorative, useful arrangements

**masonry** building with stone, brick, or cemented elements: now also refers to plaster and concrete

**modular construction** design and building with units of standardized length and size

**painting** application of paint to finished surfaces

**platform framing** building process in which each story is framed and constructed independently

**plumbing** installation of water supply, drainage, and sewage system in buildings

**post-and-beam construction** wall construction of upright posts and crossbeams with planks laid crossways on beams

**prefab building** construction from standardized, prefabricated components

**remodeling** modification of existing structure to new needs or designs

**roofing** construction of protective top layer of building

**steel-frame construction** building a structure on a reinforced steel rod framework

**tilt-up construction** building method in which concrete walls are cast on site in horizontal frames, or wooden walls are preassembled, then lifted into final, vertical position

**timber framing** frame construction with heavy timbers as posts and beams, rarely done in 20th c.

**tooling** work done with one or more tools; arrangement of tools for particular manufacturing process

**tunnel building** excavation and surfacing of underground passageways

**wattle and daub** construction with upright rods or stakes interwoven with twigs or branches and plastered with clay and straw mixture

**wiring** installation of electrical facilities

**wood-frame construction** frame construction

## BUILDERS AND CONSTRUCTION WORKERS

**architect** one who designs and supervises the construction of buildings

**asbestos worker** person who covers surfaces, esp. pipes, with insulation materials

**boilermaker** worker who makes, assembles, or fixes boilers

**bricklayer** worker who builds with bricks

**builder** worker who constructs buildings, esp. supervisor of large construction projects

**building trades** trades such as carpentry, masonry, and plastering that are primarily concerned with construction and finishing of buildings

**cabinetmaker** worker who builds fine wooden furniture

**carpenter** worker who builds and repairs wooden things, esp. buildings

**cement mason** worker who applies finish to concrete floors, slabs, and other low concrete structures; worker who makes low forms in concrete

**construction worker** general laborer on construction of buildings or large structures

**contractor** one who agrees to purchase materials for and construct buildings at arranged price and time period

**designer** one who conceives and draws plans for construction or decoration

**drywaller** worker who cuts and installs plasterboard

**electrician** worker who installs and repairs electric wiring in buildings

**elevator constructor** worker who installs elevators, dumbwaiters, and escalators

**engineer** one who applies scientific and mathematical principles to design and build machines or structures

**equipment operator** worker who runs and manages operation of mechanical devices used in construction

**floor covering installer** worker who puts carpeting, linoleum, and rubber or vinyl tile on floors

**gardener** one who cultivates and maintains gardens

**glazier** one who cuts and fits glass panes in windows

**house painter** worker who applies paint to exterior or interior of buildings

**insulation worker** worker who installs insulation in buildings

**interior decorator** one who plans and decorates the inside of buildings, esp. furniture arrangement, fittings, and color schemes

**ironworker** one who makes iron decorations, esp. gratings, usu. by bending and joining iron rods

**laborer** general worker

**lathe operator** worker who cuts and shapes objects, usu. of wood or metal, on a lathe

**machine operator** worker who runs usu. heavy equipment used in construction

**marble setter** worker who cuts and sets marble

**mason** worker who builds with stones or bricks bonded by cement or mortar

**mechanical engineer** one who applies mathematical and scientific principles, esp. kinetics, to design and build machines, usu. with parts that move

**metalworker** one who makes objects of metal

**operating engineer** one who runs and maintains heavy construction machinery, such as bulldozers or cranes

**operator** worker who runs heavy machinery, such as bulldozers or cranes

**painter** worker who paints walls and ceilings

**paperhanger** worker who cuts and affixes decorative wallpaper

**pipe fitter** worker who installs or repairs pipes

**plasterer** worker who applies stucco and other plaster finishes to walls and ceilings

**plumber** worker who installs and repairs pipes and fixtures for sewage and water systems

**rigger** one who supervises the transport and installation of large machinery, such as conveyors, pumps, and heaters

**roofer** worker who covers roofs with shingles, slate, tile, or other materials

**sheet metal worker** person who makes and installs sheet metal products, such as ducts and gutters

**stonemason** mason who builds with natural stone

**subcontractor** worker who contracts to general contractor for specialized work, such as an electrician or plumber

**terrazzo worker** person who sets terrazzo or small marble tiles

**tilesetter** worker who lays tiles on floor or walls

**welder** worker who joins pieces of metal by application of heat and sometimes pressure until separate pieces fuse together

**woodworker** person who builds custom wooden structures, such as cabinets, fixtures, trim, and molding

# STRUCTURAL COMPONENTS

Building and Machine Parts
Carpentry

**SEE ALSO**: Chap. 5: Machinery and Fabrication; Building and Construction Materials; Tools and Hardware; Containers; Chap. 7: Exterior Structure; Interior Structure; Chap. 16: Architecture

## BUILDING AND MACHINE PARTS

**abutment** plane or point designed to give support or withstand thrust, esp. on projecting part of structure

**adapter** connector that enables different parts or devices to fit or function together

**anchor bolt** threaded rod embedded in foundation for support and stabilization of wood sill

**angle iron** metal brace used to reinforce corners or angles

**angle rafter** rafter in sloping roof

**aperture** usu. narrow opening, slit, or crack

**apron** plate or covering for mechanical device that protects its operator; interior trim beneath window stool

**arbor** short spindle that supports rotating machine part

**arm** small extension attached horizontally at angle to large base

**axle** shaft or spindle that supports rotating wheel

**backstay** supporting or checking piece in mechanism, esp. anchored tension member that supports compression member

**baffle** obstructing member, esp. used to hold back or turn aside flow of gas or liquid

**bail** supporting half hoop; hinged bar that holds paper to platen in typewriter

**ball-and-socket joint** joint between rods or links in which ball-like termination fits into concave, spherical socket

**baluster** small vertical member connecting stair tread and handrail

**band** ring or encircling strip, used esp. to bind something

**bar** straight supporting rod

**barb** sharp, hooked projection

**barb and shaft** point and length of weapon, missile, or tool

**base** bottommost component on which structure rests

**baseboard** finished interior trim where wall meets floor

**baseplate** steel plate at bottom of steel column

**baseshoe** molding placed against baseboard at floor

**batten** narrow wood strip that covers seam between boards

**batter boards** horizontal crosspieces nailed to posts in ground at corners of excavation to locate corners and establish level

**beam** horizontal structural member of wood or steel, used to support load

**beam pocket** notch that holds supporting beam

**bearing** sliding or turning machine part; point of support

**bearing pile** column sunk into ground or foundation to support vertical load

**bearing wall** wall that supports a floor or roof and walls above it

**becket** looped rope with large hook and eye, used to secure loose ropes and spars

**bed** horizontal layer of masonry mortar that holds bricks

**berm** narrow dirt ledge that supports beams

**bilge** point of largest circumference of cask or barrel

**bit** cutting or drilling part of tool

**block** enclosure for pulley; mold; building unit

**boom** projecting beam, spar, or supporting arm

**boss** raised knob on flat surface

**box beam** hollow structural member that supports loads

**brace** connecting or reinforcing element, usu. of wood

**bracket** projecting support fixture

**brake** machine element used to stop motion

**breather** vent, as in machine covering or storage tank, used to equalize pressure or permit entry or escape of vapor

**bridging** rows of small diagonal braces nailed between ceiling joists to support floor weight

**bristle** stiff hair, filament

**building block** component or part of structure

**building material** substance from which something is made or constructed

**built-ins** furniture and other nonstructural elements permanently incorporated in building

**built-up beam** support made of several smaller beams joined together

**bulkhead** partition; retaining wall

**bulwark** fortified wall or rampart

**bumper** shock-absorbing element

**bung** stopper in opening or spout of cask

**butt** thick end of something

**button** small, pressable control knob

**buttress** projecting support structure

**bypass** auxiliary pipe or channel connected to main passage, used to conduct gas or liquid around pipe or fixture

**cable** heavy-duty rope of wire strands, usu. wound together

**cage** openwork structure or frame, esp. of bars or wires

**caisson** underwater housing for structure or foundation

**cantilever** extension of structural member beyond point of support

**cap** tightfitting cover or top

**capstone** topmost stone in structure

**carriage** movable machine part designed to carry or convey something

**casing** trim or molding on doors or windows

**caster** small, swiveling wheel used to support or move furniture and heavy objects

**casting** part cast in mold

**ceiling joist** horizontal support piece for ceiling

**chain** rope or wire of connected metal links

**chamfer** beveled edge or channel on piece of wood

**channel** passageway, esp. for gas or liquid; three-sided, U-shaped element, usu. metal

**chase** vertical groove in masonry wall for pipes, ducts, or conduits; frame that holds paper in printing press

**chassis** framework or support for working parts

**chimney** vertical flue that draws off gases and heat from furnace or fireplace

**chock** wedge of hard material that prevents movement or fills gap

**chord** outside horizontal member of truss

**chute** inclined or vertical downward passageway

**clack valve** valve having hinged flap that permits flow in one direction only

**clasp** fastener, esp. clip

**cleat** wood brace

**clevis** U-shaped device with pin across opening

**clew** metal loop fastened to corner of hung canvas

**cog** tooth or radial support on wheel or gear

**coil** wire turned in loops

**coil spring** wire spring coiled helically into conical or cylindrical shape

**collar** ring or flange, esp. on pipe, to connect parts or prevent sideward motion

**collar beam** horizontal member placed between pair of opposing roof rafters to stiffen roof

**column** vertical structural support

**common rafter** rafter that extends from ridgepole to top plate

**component** part or element of structure

**conduit** tube, pipe, or channel, esp. for fluids or electric wiring

**connecting rod** reciprocating rod that connects two or more machine parts

**corner** point at which two or more surfaces meet, often a right angle

**corner board** exterior finish board at corner that abuts siding

**corner brace** diagonal structural support

**cornice** exterior trim at juncture of roof and wall, consisting of fascia, soffit, and molding

**cotter** split pin with spreadable ends

**counterflashing** metal surfacing, esp. for chimneys at roof line

**coupling** machine part that connects two rotating shafts at their ends to transmit torque between them

**cove molding** concave-faced molding, esp. between wall and ceiling

**cover** something placed over a part or structure, esp. to conceal or protect it

**cowling** removable metal housing or cover for engine

**cradle** supportive framework on which something rests

**creel** basketlike cage or rack

**crest** projecting ridge, top, or summit

**crib** framework of strips or planks, open at top

**cripple** short wall stud above or below door or window

**crossbar** connective bar placed in horizontal position

**crossbeam** transverse beam in structure, such as joist

**cross bridging** bridging of crisscross wood pieces; herringbone bridging

**crosshead** sliding member of reciprocating engine for maintaining straight motion between piston rod and connecting rod

**crosspiece** any element lying across another or connecting two or more parts

**cross section** side or end section of object

**crosstie** beam or rod placed crosswise for support

**crown** top point, part resting at top

**crutch** usu. forked support element on which another part rests

**culvert** drain or waterway under road or embankment

**curb** enclosing framework or border; element that restrains or checks

**curtain wall** exterior wall that protects interior wall from weather but bears no structural load

**dam** barrier to water flow

**deck** horizontal structure extending from exterior wall

**door frame** casing around door from which it is hinged or hung

**doorjamb** door frame cut into wall

**dovetail joint** projecting, wedge-shaped tenon that fits into mortise

**dowel** cylindrical length of wood used to fasten or hang

**downspout** vertical pipe that carries water from roof to ground

**drain** pipe or filter for removal of fluid

**drip cap** molding at exterior top side of doors and windows that sheds rain

**duct** pipe or channel for passage of gas or liquid

**ductwork** system of ducts used for heating, ventilation, or cooling

**edge** border; part farthest from middle

**elbow** L-shaped fastener or connective piece, esp. for pipes

**expansion joint** joint in masonry or concrete that accommodates expansion and contraction of materials without damaging structure

**exterior structure** elements and components of a structure that are visible from outside it

**exterior wall** flat, vertical surface that faces away from studs

**facade** exterior face on front of building

**facet** small cut face, as on precious stone

**facing** lining; finishing surface

**fairing** element that reduces wind drag

**fascia** flat, vertical member of cornice attached to outer edge of eave at end of rafter

**fastener** hardware device that holds separate parts together: bolt, nail, plug, screw, pin, toggle, clasp, or clamp

**felloe** rim or rim segment of spoked wheel that holds outer ends of spokes

**fender** guard, impact absorber

**ferrule** metal ring or cap at end of handle or tool

**filler** substance used to fill holes or smooth surface irregularities

**filter** device that separates particles from air or liquid

**firestop** fire-retardant element inside walls and floors, esp. horizontal wood member between studs to stop updrafts inside wall

**fire wall** partition made of fireproof material, used to prevent spread of fire within building

**fitting** small part or device, usu. of standardized size and shape

**fixture** plumbing or electrical unit

**flange** projecting rim or collar of wheel, pipe, rail, or beam, used to hold it in place or guide action

**flashing** sheet metal strip or wall for waterproofing or insulation, usu. by sealing joint

**flitch** bundle of veneer sheets; component of beam or girder

**floorboard** any of the strips of wood composing a floor

**floor joist** horizontal support piece for floor

**flue** enclosed passageway used to direct current of gas; chimney, channel for smoke or air

**fluke** pointed blade on anchor, barb

**flume** channel or inclined chute that carries water

**foliated joint** joint between overlapping, rabbeted edges of two boards, forming continuous surface

**footing** concrete pad that supports and distributes foundation weight

**forelock** cotter pin, split pin, or linchpin

**forms** panels joined as molds for concrete

**foundation** supporting part of structure beneath first floor joists, usu. concrete or masonry

**frame** open, supporting structure

**frieze** horizontal piece that connects siding to soffit, usu. decorative

**furnishings** usu. movable articles for use or decoration in structure

**furring** wood strips fastened to nonwood walls or ceiling to form straight surface for application of finished wall material

**gable end** end wall bearing a gable

**gain** notch, mortise, or groove, esp. to receive hardware

**gasket** flat sheet of material used to form gas-tight joint between engine parts

**gibbet** jib or projecting arm of crane

**girder** horizontal structural member that supports wall; floor joist between piers or columns; beam

**girder pocket** notch in foundation for base of girder

**grate** metal grid or frame of parallel bars, used for support, ventilation, and filtration

**grid** grate; metal openwork surface

**groove** long, narrow, hollow cut into surface

**gusset** plywood or metal plate that joins wooden members or reinforces joints

**gutter** trough to siphon fluid, esp. rainwater from roof

**guy** reinforcing wire, chain

**haft** handle, esp. of knife or ax

**handle** rod, knob, part to be grasped by hand

**handlebar** rod or bar with handle at each end

**hanger** iron strap used to suspend pipes and joists

**hank** coil, loop, or ring, esp. of rope

**hardware** metal fittings and utensils for building construction

**harness** assemblage of interconnected straps that restrain or fasten

**H-beam** long iron or steel I-beam with wide flanges

**head** top of door or window frame

**header** horizontal support that spans an opening in frame of wall or floor

**headpost** post at top of part

**herringbone bridging** cross bridging

**hilt** handle, esp. of knife or sword

**hinge** swiveling metal joint that fastens swinging element to stable support: butt, spring, strap, T-hinge

**hip rafter** diagonal rafter extending from ridgepole to corner intersection of top plates of two walls

**hoop** circular binding strip

**housing** frame or covering for part; recess in piece of wood for insertion of another piece

**hub** center part, esp. of wheel where it is fastened to axle

**I-beam** long iron or steel beam with cross section in form of I, used in heavy construction

**insulation** layer of material resistant to heat or sound conduction

**interior structure** elements and components of a structure that are visible from inside or functioning within it

**interior wall** flat, vertical surface facing inward from studs

**jack** brace, support

**jack rafter** shorter-than-common rafter

**jamb** side frame of door or window in wall

**jib** projecting crane arm

**joggle** joint formed between notch cut in one surface and projection made in another, usu. in wood or stone

**joint** point of contact between elements, usu. held by glue, nail, or screw

**joist** horizontal support beam for floor or ceiling

**journal** portion of shaft or axle contained by bearing

**keystone** central, uppermost stone of arch

**keystone joist** joist made of reinforced concrete with sloping sides and tip wider than bottom

**keyway** groove or slot cut in shaft or hub to hold key

**king post** vertical member between apex and base of triangular roof framework

**knob** round handle

**knuckle joint** joint permitting movement between parts in one plane only

**L** angled support beam, brace, or bracket

**Lally column** steel pipe with concrete-filled post used to support girders

**landing** floor area at top or bottom of stairs

**lap joint** joint between two members in which end or edge of one is partly cut away to be overlapped by end or edge of the other, resulting in a flush surface

**latch** fastener, esp. for door

**lath** narrow wood strips for lattice, trellis, and plastering base for wall; metal or gypsum panels nailed to studs on which plaster is applied

**lattice** wood strip framework

**leader** downspout connected to gutter

**leaf** sliding or hinged side or division, esp. of door or window

**leaf spring** long, multiple spring used in suspension systems of vehicles

**ledger** wood strip nailed to underside of wood beam or stud for support

**lever** bar used to lift heavy object or pry open something

**ligature** thread, wire, or small hoop that serves for binding or tying up

**linchpin** fastener that prevents slippage; linkage device

**lining** inner coating or layer

**lintel** horizontal, weight-bearing crosspiece above door or window

**load-bearing wall** wall that carries vertical load from above

**lookout** extending horizontal framing member that supports roof overhang, fascia, and soffit

**lug and slot** projection and hole into which it fits

**lumber** milled hardwood or softwood boards, used to build construction and cabinetry

**moldboard** flat or curved blade that pushes material aside as machine advances

**molding** wood strip with curved or decoratively cut surface

**mortise** notch or hole in wood that holds fitted tenon to form joint

**mullion** narrow bar that divides small windowpane glass or screen; vertical framing member that separates adjacent doors or windows

**muntin** wood member that separates glass panes in door or window

**newel** large post at foot of stairs

**nog** wooden peg, pin, or block, esp. one inserted into brickwork or between principal timbers of wall

**nonbearing wall** wall that supports no weight other than its own

**nosing** rounded edge of stair tread extending beyond riser

**notch** concave or V-shaped cut or indentation in edge or across surface

**nozzle** tube or vent used to expel fluid with force

**panel** flat piece of wood fitted into larger surface area

**part** component, one element of which something is made

**partition** interior wall

**peg** short, usu. tapered rod used to hold parts together or fill opening

**pier** vertical masonry column, usu. concrete, that supports beam or load from above

**pilaster** rectangular support or pier projecting from wall

**pile** concrete, steel, or wood column that supports building foundation

**piloti** column of iron, steel, or reinforced concrete that supports structure above open ground level

**pin** peg, post, or rod used to fasten objects

**pinion** small cogwheel, with teeth, that fits into large gearwheel or rack

**pintle** usu. upright pivot pin on which another part turns

**pipe** metal or plastic tubing used in plumbing and heating works

**plancier** underside of eave or cornice; soffit

**plank**  long, flat, wood member 2-4 inches (5.1-10.2 cm) thick and 6 inches (15.2 cm) or more wide

**plate**  horizontal structural member, usu. wood

**platen**  flat plate in printing press, or roller in typewriter, on which paper rides

**platform**  horizontal floor area, esp. midway up stairs

**plenum**  box on furnace from which ducts run to outlets

**pole**  shaft, narrow column

**post**  vertical structural member, esp. timber set on end to support beam

**projection**  part that juts out from surface

**purlin**  horizontal roof support between rafters

**pylon**  slender, towering structure flanking entrance or supporting wires

**queen post**  either of a pair of vertical posts extending from tie beam in roof framework, one on each side of center

**quoin**  block at corner of building; arch keystone

**raceway**  narrow channel for water; tube used to protect electric wires

**rack**  frame; toothed bar into which pinion fits

**rafter**  horizontal wooden support member for roof

**rail**  horizontal cross member of panel door or window sash

**railing**  several connected rails or posts

**rake**  flat, inclined edge on gable roof

**ramp**  sloping, sometimes curved, surface that joins different levels

**rampart**  barrier, bulwark

**rebar**  steel reinforcing rod for concrete

**register**  heating duct unit that directs airflow

**reinforcing rod**  round, steel bar used to strengthen concrete

**removable wood form**  framework used to form concrete slabs, removed once concrete hardens

**reservoir**  receptacle, usu. at bottom of structure, used to collect fluid

**revetment**  facing of stone or concrete to sustain embankment

**rib**  crosswise reinforcing element

**ribbon**  wood member joined to studs to support floor joists in balloon framing

**ridge beam**  ridgepole

**ridgepole**  highest horizontal timber in peaked roof to which rafters are nailed; ridge beam

**riffle**  bars or slats across bottom of sluice that catch nuggets, as of gold

**rigging**  system of ropes or chains used to support, suspend, or position equipment

**rim**  edge or border, esp. of something circular, often raised

**ring**  circular element used to bind, reinforce, or seal objects

**riser**  vertical part of stair

**rod**  straight, rigid piece of wood or metal

**roof**  top surface of structure

**roofing**  materials that form roof surface

**roof plate**  top plate

**rough opening**  gap in wall, floor, or ceiling formed by structural framing members

**rounce**  handle that moves printing press bed under platen

**rowel**  revolving disk with sharp points at end of spur

**rung**  supporting piece or crossbar, esp. on ladder

**rynd**  iron bar across upper millstone that supports it on spindle

**sally**  rafter projection notched to fit over and extend beyond plate or horizontal beam

**sandwich panel**  wall or other structural panel consisting of core of one material between two sheets of a different material

**sash**  movable frame that contains glass windowpanes

**scab**  wood piece nailed to two butting pieces of wood as splice

**scantling**  beam or timber of small cross section, such as 2x4

**scarf joint**  joint in which two timbers are fitted together with end laps and held together by bolts or straps

**sconce**  cover, protective shell

**scrap**  used metal parts reclaimed for other uses

**screen**  frame covered with mesh, usu. of wire

**scupper**  opening in building wall, used for drainage from flat roof

**shackle**  U-shaped fastener with pin

**shaft**  rotating cylinder; column that supports rotating machine elements

**shank**  straight or central element of fitting or tool; loop or eye on back of solid button

**sheathing**  material used to cover roof rafters or exterior wall studs

**shell**  outer covering or framework

**shim**  thin piece of material used to smooth, level, or finish area between two irregular surfaces

**shiplap**  siding boards with overlapping joints along edges, applied over sheathing

**shoring**  wood or metal braces used for temporary support during building construction

**shunt**  switch used to deflect motion

**shutter**  device that controls passage of light

**shuttle**  device that controls back-and-forth movement

**siding**  surface covering for exterior building walls

**sill**  horizontal member at base of window or door

**sill plate**  horizontal structure bolted to foundation beneath flooring

**skid**  plank or low platform on which load is supported

**slab**  strip of concrete, poured as single piece, esp. reinforced concrete floor

**slat**  flat, narrow strip

**sleeper**  wood member attached to concrete floor as base for wood floor

**sleeve**  tube that surrounds another part

**sluice**  gated or valved water channel

**soffit**  undersurface of cornice from fascia to wall; plancier

**soil pipe**  drainage system component that receives waste discharged from toilet and sometimes from other plumbing waste pipes

**soil stack**  vertical soil pipe

**soleplate**  horizontal member in subfloor below line of wall studs

**sound insulation**  section of insulating material that damps sound waves

**spar**  lengthwise support structure

**spider**  machine part consisting of several radiating spokes or arms, usu. not connected at outer ends

**spile**  peg or plug made of wood, often used as spigot

**spindle**  pin or shaft that holds rotating bit or wheel

**spit**  pointed, narrow rod

**splice**  joint made by weaving together rope ends

**spline**  thin wood strip fitted into grooves

**splint**  flexible strip used for weaving and bracing

**spoke**  radial reinforcement for wheel

**spool** cylindrical container used to wind and store rope and chain

**spout** chute used to move loose substances or liquids; projecting lip through which liquid is poured

**spring** flexible wire coil that provides resilience and absorbs shocks

**sprocket** one of series of teeth or points on wheel rim arranged to fit links of chain or another set of sprockets

**spur** projecting element

**stack** vertical shelves, pipes, or flues

**staff** shaft, rung

**stanchion** upright support bar or beam

**standard** upright support or support structure

**stave** strip of wood curved and bound with others to form vessel

**steel framing** structural frame made from steel members

**stem** shaft, support

**stile** vertical member, esp. of panel door

**stilt** pole that supports and elevates structure or load

**stock** main upright part of supporting structure

**stool** interior, horizontal molding on window sill between jambs

**stop** wood strip used to hold window in place or against which door closes

**story pole** pole cut to height between floor and ceiling and marked with minor dimensions for use in construction

**strake** single line of planking that extends the entire length of a structure, esp. ship

**strap** narrow, flexible band of leather or fabric that binds or secures objects

**strike plate** metal plate set in door frame to receive lock plunger

**stringer** side of stair cut to receive threads; long, horizontal timber connecting upright posts

**strip** long, thin section of material

**structural component** portion, element, or raw material used in something built or constructed

**strut** bar or piece that resists longitudinal pressure or stress along its length

**stud** vertical framing member for wall, usu. wood

**subfloor** boards nailed directly to floor joists, used as base for finished floorboards or carpets

**sump** pit, trap, or reservoir that collects liquid

**support** element that bears weight of another part or parts

**suspended ceiling** ceiling hung from floor or roof above it

**switch** device used to open or close flow, esp. electric current

**tackle** rigging; ropes and pulleys used to hoist objects

**tail** end of rafter that extends beyond exterior wall

**tappet** sliding rod struck by cam to move another part

**T-bar** iron or steel beam with flanges along one edge forming T-shaped cross section

**tee** T-shaped structural member

**template** horizontal member of wall that receives and distributes pressure of beam or girder

**tenon** projecting part cut in wood to insert in corresponding mortise as joint

**thill** vehicle shaft

**threshold** beveled strip, usu. wood or stone, fastened to doorsill directly below door

**tie** structural member that joins stress pieces in frame

**tie beam** horizontal beam that connects two structural members and keeps them in place

**tierod** steel rod that serves as structural brace

**timber** wood member, esp. one 5 inches (12.7 cm) or more in smallest dimension

**tine** slender, pointed projection of implement or weapon

**toe** part placed vertically in bearing, such as lower end of shaft

**toggle** pin or crosspiece placed across end of rope or chain to prevent slippage

**tongue** projecting piece of wood fitted into corresponding groove

**tongue-and-groove joint** joint between two boards, one of which is cut with a raised area on its edge that fits into corresponding groove in edge of other board to form flush surface

**tooth** regular projection on gear rim

**top plate** horizontal member at top of wall studs; roof plate

**trace** bar hinged to two parts of machine, for transferring motion between them

**track** belt or tread that guides line of motion

**transom** crosspiece in structure, esp. above window or door

**trave** crossbeam; section between crossbeams

**traverse rod** horizontal rod on which curtains open and close

**tread** horizontal part of stair on which one steps

**trellis** lath lattice support

**trestle** reinforced supporting framework

**trim** wood molding, strips for finish and decoration

**trimmer** beam or joist that forms rough opening in wall, floor, or roof into which header is framed

**tripod** three-legged support, usu. adjustable

**trippet** projection or cam that strikes another machine part at regular intervals

**truckle** small wheel or pulley

**trundle** small wheel or caster

**truss** rigid reinforcing framework; preassembled support unit used in roof construction, including rafters, joists, and bracing

**truss beam** beam that is part of truss

**tube** hollow cylinder, pipe

**tumbler** single cog or cam on rotating shaft that transmits motion to the part it engages

**underlayment** materials on top of subfloor that form smoother surface for finished flooring

**unit** single, distinct part with specific purpose; combination of elements into single part

**valley** V-shaped depression at intersection of two sloping roofs

**valley jacks** rafters that extend from ridgepole to valley rafter

**valley rafter** diagonal rafter that extends from ridgepole to top plate to form intersection of two sloping roofs

**valve** device that regulates flow of liquid or gas

**vane** flattened, curved piece on revolving wheel

**vapor barrier** section of material that resists passage of water vapor

**vent** opening, esp. in wall, serving as outlet for air, smoke, or fumes

**vent stack** top section of soil stack that extends out through roof

**volute spring** conical coil spring extending in direction of axis of coil

**wale bracket** horizontal timber or steel beam that braces vertical members

**waler** horizontal wood support used to cast concrete

**wall** vertical structure that forms interior or exterior side of room, attached to studs

**wall section** part of wall taken as structural or support unit

**waste pipe** horizontal pipe used to carry waste from bath and kitchen fixtures to soil pipe

**wattle** rod or stake interwoven with twigs or branches to form wall, fence, or roof

**W-beam** iron or steel beam with W-shaped cross section

**weather stripping** metal or fabric strips placed around edges of doors and windows to reduce heat loss

**web** internal, diagonal brace between chords in truss

**weep hole** water drainage opening in masonry wall

**weir** notch in dam or levee that regulates and directs flow of water

**winder** triangular tread on winding staircase

**winding** wire or thread coiled or wrapped around something, esp. single turn of such wire or thread

**wing** part extending laterally from main part

**withe** partition between flues of chimney

**wood roof truss** rigid framework of structural members to carry roof load

**worm** rotating shaft or cylinder cut with helical threads

**yoke** forklike end of rod or shaft within which another part is secured; viselike piece holding two parts firmly together

**Z-bar** steel bar with Z-shaped cross section

## CARPENTRY

**balloon framing** building with continuous studs from sill to roof plate

**benchmark** reference mark on construction site for land measurements and elevations

**bias** angle between construction lines

**blank** piece of material to be cut or worked into finished item

**blind nailing** placing of nails where they will be hidden when unit is complete

**blueprint** architect's detailed drawings of construction plan in standardized form; working drawings

**board foot** measure equal to 144 cubic inches of wood

**brick veneer** construction in which wood-framed building has layer of bricks as exterior siding

**building codes** local regulations for design and construction of buildings

**building permit** document issued by local government that grants the right to build

**built-up roof** roof of alternate layers of building paper and asphalt with final gravel layer

**carpenter** worker who builds large structures, esp. of wood

**carpentry** work and trade of building structures with wood

**catwalk** narrow elevated bridge, esp. temporary walkway around building site

**contractor** person who agrees to supply materials and do construction work for set price and hires subcontractors and laborers

**core** central layer of plywood sheet

**course** continuous row of bricks or shingles

**crossbands** layers of veneer glued at right angles to form plywood

**crosscutting** cutting wood across the grain

**cross section** side view through construction, esp. on drawings

**d** symbol for penny, indicating nail size

**dado** groove cut perpendicular to wood grain

**dead load** permanent load, such as roof, on structure

**dimension lumber** surfaced softwood milled to standard sizes, used to frame buildings

**dressed size** size of lumber after drying and planing ·

**elevation** drawing that shows design of exterior walls; height of building part above established point

**face nail** nail driven through board so that it is visible

**finish grade** elevation of ground relative to building after landscaping

**floor plan** detailed drawing that shows layout and dimensions of building interior as viewed from above

**foundation plan** detailed drawing of foundation that includes its dimensions and location of footings, piers, and walls

**framing** joining of wooden structural members as skeletal structure for building

**frostline** depth frost penetrates into earth

**grade line** level at which ground intersects foundation of building

**growth ring** layer of wood developed during annual period of growth

**half-timbered construction** exterior walls in which exposed heavy wood members are separated by masonry

**haunch** tapered end of tenon

**heartwood** hard, older wood at core of tree

**horse** support frame or stand with legs

**identification index** stamp on plywood that indicates its quality

**impact insulation class** material's ability to resist transmission of impact noise

**kerf** slot in wood formed by saw blade

**knocked-down** (*adj*) something delivered to job with parts cut to size but not assembled

**live load** load on building structure, such as furniture, that may be moved or removed

**lumbermill** place in which logs are milled and dressed as lumber

**lumberyard** place with open areas and structures in which lumber is stored for sale

**matched lumber** lumber with edges shaped as tongue-and-groove

**mil** measure of thickness equal to one thousandth of an inch (.0254 mm)

**millwork** cutting, sizing, shaping, and planing of lumber and wood parts

**miter** (*vb*) cut piece of wood on 45-degree angle

**mockup** model of structure, often full-size

**on center** measurement taken from center of one member to center of another

**out-of-plumb** (*adj*) not in proper vertical alignment

**penny** designation of nail length, shown as d

**pitch** ratio of rise to span of roof

**platform framing** framing in which studs extend for one floor only and rest upon subfloor of each story

**plot plan** drawing that shows size, slope, and location of structure on lot

**plumb** (*adj*) in true vertical position

**quarter-sawed** (*adj*) designating lumber cut at 90-degree angle to tree's growth rings

**rabbet** open groove cut into edge of board to form joint

**ripping** cutting wood in direction of grain

**rise** vertical height of stair

**roughing-in** installation of plumbing and electrical systems that will later be concealed by interior finishing

**run** total horizontal length, esp. of stairs

**R-value** measure of resistance of insulating material to heat flow

**sapwood** light-colored wood located between heartwood and bark in tree

**sawhorse** rack with two slanting legs at each end, used to support wood being sawed

**scaffold** movable platform supported by frame or suspended by ropes to support workers and materials above ground

**scale** proportion of drawings or blueprints to actual structure, represented by ratio

**scribing** marking material to be cut to fit irregular surface

**shear** force producing opposite but parallel sliding motion in each of the contacting planes in a structural member

**slope** rise of roof in inches per foot of run

**sound-transmission class** measure of material's resistance to passage of airborne sound

**span** distance between two supporting members, esp. between exterior walls

**specifications** architect's detailed instructions not shown on blueprints or working drawings

**subcontractor** person or company hired by contractor to do specialized tasks, such as plumbing or wiring

**superstructure** part of building above basement

**toenail** (*vb*) drive nails at slant

**true** (*adj*) precisely or accurately formed, fitted, placed, or calibrated, esp. to conform to pattern or form

**warp** variation in wood board from flat plane

**weatherize** (*vb*) secure structure against cold or wind by adding insulation, siding, strips, or storm windows

**working drawings** complete set of drawings that shows all details of structure to be built; blueprints

# Building and Construction Materials

Cuts, Sizes, Treatments, and Forms of Wood
Softwoods
Hardwoods
Paneling and Composite Boards
Stones, Bricks, Tiles, Glass, and Metals
Plastics, Paper, and Textiles
Adhesives and Binders
Surfaces and Finishing Materials

**see also:** Chap. 2: Plants; Chap. 3: Minerals, Metals, and Rocks; Chap. 5: Structural Components; Tools and Hardware; Chap. 7: Exterior Structure; Interior Structure; Ornamental and Functional Articles; Chap. 10: Fashion and Garment Parts

# Cuts, Sizes, Treatments, and Forms of Wood

**a/d** air-dried

**air-dried** (*adj*) a/d; designating lumber stacked out of doors so that air circulates between boards to remove moisture

**batten** sawed strip of wood, esp. used as seam or fastener

**beam** long, thick piece of lumber, used esp. as support for roof

**bevel siding** siding cut with sloping surface at edge

**board** milled, sawed piece of wood up to 2 inches (5.1 cm) thick and 2 or more inches wide

**board foot** standard measure of lumber, equal to 1x12x12 inches or 144 cubic inches

**caning** slender, flexible wood stems split into narrow strands and woven together, esp. for chairs

**ceiling board** cut board used in ceilings

**clapboard** narrow board thicker at one edge, used for outside walls; weatherboard

**close-grained** (*adj*) designating wood having fine, compact grain

**construction wood** dimension lumber

**cork** light, thick, soft, elastic bark of cork oak tree

**cut** amount of wood; style in which wood is sawed

**decking** construction boards for exterior use

**dimension lumber** usu. softwood lumber used for framing or as sheathing

**dowel** solid, cylindrical rod of wood

**dressed size** dimensions of lumber after drying and planing

**drop siding** siding with tongue-and-groove, rabbeted, or shiplap joint; matched siding

**edge-glued** (*adj*) designating flat-edged lumber bonded by gluing

**edge-matched** (*adj*) designating lumber with tongue-and-groove edges

**end-matched** (*adj*) designating lumber with tongue-and-groove ends

**excelsior** fine, curled wood shavings that form resilient mass, used for packing

**exterior plywood** usu. rough-grade plywood sheets with exterior glue, used under finishing materials

**fencing** long, thin posts or rails used to make fences

**finish lumber** high-quality softwood lumber to be left natural or stained for appearance

**flat-grained** (*adj*) designating wood having smooth, consistent grain

**flooring** long strips of tongue-and-groove finishing lumber, used for flooring

**framing** softwood construction lumber used for skeletal frame of structure

**furring strips** narrow, unfinished wood strips attached to masonry or concrete as base for finishing material

**grading** standardized system of rating and marking wood to indicate quality

**grape stakes** thick, unfinished posts used to support vines

**green lumber** undried lumber

**hardwood** lumber made from the wood of deciduous trees, used primarily for trim, finishing, and built-ins

**heartwood** mature wood at center of tree

**interior finish** material used to cover interior walls and ceiling surfaces

**jambs** strips used as side frame of door or window

**k/d** kiln-dried

**kiln-dried** (*adj*) k/d; designating lumber dried in kiln using regulated steam and hot air

**knotty** (*adj*) designating lumber with cross-grained, rounded areas, or knots, formed by lump where branch grew out of tree trunk

**lath** thin, narrow strips nailed to two-by-fours and rafters as foundation for plaster, tiles, and finishing boards

**lauan** Philippine mahogany, in trade usage

**log** long section of tree trunk or thick branch of felled tree to be cut and milled into lumber

**louver door** door with overlapping, horizontal slats

**lumber** timber sawed and milled into standard size beams, planks, and boards

**lumber sizing** standard sizes of lumber, in inches: 1x2, 1x3, 1x4, 1x5, 1x6, 1x8, 1x10, 1x12, 2x2, 2x3, 2x4, 2x6, 2x8, 2x10, 2x12, 3x3, 4x4, 4x8, 4x12

**matched siding** drop siding

**milling** cutting, shaping, and shaving of lumber and wood products on large scale in manufacturing plant

**mixed-grain** (*adj*) designating wood with both closed and open grains

**molding** shaped strip of wood used to finish or decorate walls: astragal, base, batten, bead, casing saddle, chair rail, corner guard, cove, crown, full round, half round, handrail, lattice, mantel, nose and cove, ogee, oval, picture frame, pilaster, quarter round, round edge, scalloped, sprung cove, stop, threshold, and window stool

**open-grained** (*adj*) designating wood having irregularly patterned grain, usu. wide

**paneling** broad, flat sections of wood from which panels are cut

**parquet** flooring squares in which grains of adjacent squares run at right angles

**partition** large sheet of wood or other material used to divide interior areas

**pinoleum** fine wooden sticks, stitched together as blinds

**plank** long, broad, thick board

**plywood** thin sheet of wood made by gluing and pressing together layers, often with grains at right angles; grades: AB, ACX, AD

**plywood circle** round plywood sheet

**plywood sizing** standard sizes of plywood: 4x8 feet or 4x10 feet by 1/4, 3/8, 1/2, 5/8, 3/4, or 1 inch thick

**pole** long, slender piece of wood, usu. cylindrical

**post** thick square or cylindrical beam section used in upright position

**pressure-treated** (*adj*) designating wood with resin compressed under great heat to increase hardness and resistance to moisture and decay

**puncheon** short post, used upright in framing

**rabbeted** (*adj*) designating board or plank with groove cut in edge to accept another piece of wood to form joint

**rattan** slender, tough stem of palm tree, used in furniture

**reed fencing** thick grass stalks plaited into fence

**roofing** rafter beams or plywood sheets used in roof frame; exterior material, such as shingles or shake, used on roof

**rush** round, pliant stem of certain marsh grasses, used in thatch roofs, furniture, and baskets

**sapwood** light-colored, living wood layer between heartwood and bark

**seasoning** aging and drying process that matures lumber to improve its workability

**sen** Oriental ash, in trade usage

**shake** long shingle split directly from log

**sheathing** layer of boards that covers roof rafters or outside wall studs

**sheeting** broad pieces of wood used to cover a surface

**shelving** thin, flat section of board to be fixed at right angles to wall

**shingle** thin, wedge-shaped piece of wood to be laid in overlapping rows over roof or wall sheathing

**shiplap** boards or siding rabbeted along edge to overlap and form joint

**shutter** louvered window covering

**siding** materials applied over wall sheathing as finished surface: hardboard, lap, metal, plastic, plywood

**siding shingle** shingle used over wall sheathing

**slat** thin, narrow wood strip

**softwood** lumber made from the wood of evergreen trees, used primarily for framing, construction, and some finishing

**split** flexible strip of wood or wood stem used in baskets or furniture

**stake** thin length of wood pointed at one end

**stock** tree trunk

**stud** boards, esp. 2x4s, used in upright position as framing to which sheathing, panels, or siding are nailed

**thatch** rushes or palm leaves used as roofing

**timber** heavy, dressed beam, usu. 5 inches (12.7 cm) or more in least dimension

**tongue-and-groove** (*adj*) designating lumber, esp. paneling and flooring, in which boards interlock along edges

**treatment** aging, drying, or seasoning done to improve quality of wood

**trim** finished interior and exterior moldings

**two-by-four** most common board used in framing, being 2 inches by 4 inches

**veneer** thin sheets of wood assembled in layers into plywood

**vertical-grained** (*adj*) designating lumber with grain running lengthwise

**walling** sheathing for walls

**weatherboard** clapboard

**weatherizing** treatment of exterior finish wood to conserve heat and resist water

**wicker** pliant twigs or rods plaited together into chairs or baskets

**windows** boards framed into windows

**wood** hard, fibrous substance beneath tree bark, cut and prepared as timber or lumber

**woodwork** interior moldings, doors, windows, and stairs

## SOFTWOODS

**softwood** lumber made from the wood of evergreen trees, used primarily for framing, construction, and some finishing

**appearance pine**

**balsam fir**

cedar, clear pine, cypress
Douglas fir
Englemann spruce
fir
hemlock
incense cedar
jack pine, juniper
knotty pine
larch, loblolly pine, lodgepole pine
mountain hemlock
Pacific yew, pine, ponderosa pine
red cedar, redwood
shortleaf pine, sound cedar, spruce, sugar pine
tamarack
white cedar, white fir, white pine
yellow pine, yew

# Hardwoods

**hardwood** lumber made from the wood of deciduous trees, used primarily for trim, finishing, and built-ins

acacia, alder, American ash, American beech, American elm, apple, ash, aspen
balsa, bamboo, banyan, basswood, beech, birch, black cherry, black walnut, black willow, brasswood, briarwood, burl birch, buttonwood
calamander, cherry, chestnut, Circassian walnut, concept oak, cork, cottonwood, crystal elm, cypress
dogwood
ebony, elite walnut, elm, eucalyptus
frontier birch
Garry oak, golden oak, gum, gumwood
harewood, hazel, heirloom cherry, hickory
ironwood
lauan, lemonwood, linden, locust, logwood
magnolia, mahogany, maple
Niagara ash
oak, olive, orangewood, Oriental ash
peach, pecan, Philippine mahogany, plane, poplar
red oak, rock elm, rosewood
sandalwood, satinwood, Savannah hickory, sen, shagbark hickory, spartan oak, sugar maple, sumac, sweet gum, sycamore
teak, tulipwood, tupelo
walnut, white ash, white oak, wicker, willow
yellow birch, yellow poplar
zebrawood

# Paneling and Composite Boards

**beaverboard** compressed wood fiberboard for walls and partitions
**buttonboard** hard, stiff paperboard
**ceiling tile** usu. 2x4 foot acoustic tile sheet of composite board
**Celotex** *Trademark.* insulation board made from sugarcane residue
**chipboard** compressed wood pulp, sawdust, and wood chips with resin binder
**Compoboard** *Trademark.* composite board
**composite board** class of high-strength, lightweight sheet materials made by combining various elements with a binder
**compreg** wood impregnated with resin, then compressed under great heat to increase hardness and resistance to moisture and decay; impreg
**corkboard** sheet of porous, elastic cork
**diffuser** panel mounted at angle to wall to absorb or disperse sound or light
**drywall** gypsum or hardboard panels joined as interior wall finish; plasterboard
**fiberboard** compressed wood or vegetable fibers in sheets
**gyp board** gypsum board
**gypsum board** laminate with gypsum core and layers of fibrous paper; gyp board; plasterboard
**hardboard** wood fibers placed under heat and pressure and pressed into sheets
**homosote** soft construction wallboard with crumbly edges, used esp. for displays
**impreg** wood impregnated with resin, then compressed under great heat to increase hardness and resistance to moisture and decay; compreg
**insulation board** sheets of material that resist transfer of heat or sound
**laminate** very strong or stiff multilayered material, esp. of plastic
**laminated board** sheets of multilayered material
**Masonite** *Trademark.* hardboard of pressed wood fibers for construction and insulation
**panelboard** composite board or laminate used as paneling
**paperboard** composite board of varying thickness and rigidity composed of layers of paper with binding
**particle board** panel of wood fibers, flakes, and shavings bonded together with synthetic resin
**pasteboard** layers of paper pressed together or pressed and dried paper pulp formed into sheets
**pegboard** composite or particle board pierced with holes into which pegs are placed for hanging objects
**perfboard** hardboard with holes into which hooks or pegs can be inserted for hanging objects
**pinboard** cork or soft board that can be pierced with pins to hold papers
**plasterboard** plaster of Paris core covered with heavy sheets of paper, used for walls or partitions; drywall; gypsum board
**plastic laminated wood** plastic coating bonded to plywood or particle board, used as countertop
**plastic plywood** layers of plastic pressed together as plywood
**plyboard** layers of composite board or plasterboard pressed together
**Pregboard** *Trademark.* compreg or impreg
**pressboard** variety of pasteboard
**pressed hardboard** wood fiber hardboard
**scagliola** imitation marble of ground gypsum with glue, used on floors and interior finishing
**Sheetrock** *Trademark.* popular brand of plasterboard
**Upson board** *Trademark.* easy-cutting, lightweight wallboard with clean edges of varying thickness, used esp. for displays
**wallboard** fibrous material made with gypsum in sheets for covering walls or ceilings or for displays
**weatherboard** laminate clapboard for exterior use

# STONES, BRICKS, TILES, GLASS, AND METALS

**acoustical tile**  sound-absorbent ceiling tiles made with slotted insulation board, polystyrene, or fiberglass

**adobe**  mixture of reddish clay, straw, and water, used for building walls

**aggregate**  cement formulation made from sand, gravel, and rock fragments, used esp. for tiles and shingles

**alloy**  metal that is a mixture of two or more metals or a metal and nonmetal

**aluminum**  lightweight, noncorrosive metal used in various forms

**aluminum screen**  fine mesh formed of aluminum wires

**aluminum shavings**  tiny, curled shreds of aluminum

**aluminum siding**  aluminum panels for exterior walls

**asbestos tile**  insulating tiles made from fireproof fibrous mineral

**ashlar**  thin, square-cut, dressed stone used for facing masonry walls

**asphalt**  brown or black bituminous coal tar residue used for paving and to make roofing tiles

**asphalt shingle**  asphalt sheet cut into flat shingles

**asphalt tile**  asphalt squares used in roofing

**barbed wire**  strands of twisted wire with sharp barbs projecting at regular intervals, used for fencing

**bead**  small, round piece of glass, metal, or wood, usu. strung with others like it

**bitumen**  natural asphalt; hard or semisolid, tarlike residue from distilled coal, wood tar, or petroleum

**blacktop**  bituminous asphalt mixture, used for road surfaces

**brass**  yellowish alloy of copper and zinc

**brick**  molded clay baked into hard oblong blocks, esp. of reddish-brown color, used as building blocks

**brickface**  flat material with appearance of red bricks, used for decoration, not structural support

**brownstone**  reddish-brown sandstone used in large blocks for building

**cable**  strands of heavy wire wound to form metal rope

**capstone**  stone in top layer of masonry wall

**castiron**  hard, molded iron alloy

**cast stone**  block of concrete made to resemble natural stone

**ceiling tile**  tile made from acoustical material or fiberboard, used in ceiling

**cement**  powder of lime and clay mixed with water and sand into mortar that hardens when dry; concrete

**ceramic**  clay pottery, earthenware

**ceramic tile**  fired clay tiles with hard glaze

**chain**  series of connected metal links

**chain link**  galvanized steel links interwoven into fencing

**chicken wire**  thin, flexible wire fencing with large, hexagonal mesh

**chrome**  chromium alloy used in plating

**chromium**  hard grayish-white metal, highly resistant to corrosion, used esp. in alloys

**cinder aggregate**  mixture of concrete and small rock fragments

**cinderblock**  concrete and cinder aggregate building block in any of various shapes, typically having a lateral hole through its center

**clay brick**  brick molded from clay

**cobble**  cobblestone

**cobblestone**  rounded stone used in paving; cobble

**common brick**  standard size, oblong, reddish-brown brick; red brick

**concrete**  mixture of cement, sand, gravel, and water that dries to form hard surface

**copestone**  stone used in top layer of masonry

**copper**  reddish-brown, conductive, corrosion-resistant metal

**cork tile**  square-cut piece of cork

**corrugated steel**  thin sheet of galvanized steel shaped into parallel grooves and ridges for added strength

**cullet**  glass scraps that can be remelted

**curbing**  stones or bricks used to form raised edge

**curbstone**  stone that makes up a section of curb

**cut glass**  ornamental flint glass with patterns cut into its surface by abrasive wheel

**cut stone**  flat stone cut to particular shape

**damask**  steel with wavy damascene markings

**face brick**  brick with specific color or surface treatment, used for building facades

**ferroconcrete**  high-strength, reinforced concrete, usu. layered in thin sheets

**firebrick**  highly heat-resistant brick, used esp. for fireplaces

**flag**  flat slab of stone; flagstone

**flagstone**  flat piece split from hard stone, used for paving

**freestone**  stone, such as limestone or sandstone, that may be cut freely without splitting

**glass**  hard, brittle, usu. transparent substance composed of fused and rapidly cooled silicates mixed with potash or soda and lime

**glass block**  square or oblong, hollow glass structure, used as decorative building block; glass brick

**glass brick**  glass block

**glass tile**  flat, hard, shatterproof glass square

**glass wool**  fine glass fibers woven into dense mass, used for insulation

**glazing**  panes or sheets of glass to be set in frames such as windows or mirrors

**gravel**  mixture of pebbles and rock fragments graded by size from coarse to fine, used for outdoor surfaces

**hanging wire**  thin, strong wire used to suspend or hoist objects

**iron**  common, strong, malleable metallic element that is basis of alloy steel

**limestone**  white calcium oxide used to make cement and mortar

**linoleum**  hard, smooth floor covering made of solidified linseed oil mixed with gum, cork dust, or wood flour set on a backing of burlap or canvas, often cut into kitchen tiles

**macadam**  rock fragments mixed with tar or asphalt to form roadway

**marble**  hard, crystalline limestone with white, streaked, or mottled surface that takes high polish

**marl**  brick composed of loose, crumbling earth

**masonry**  brick, cinderblock, stone, or tile bonded with mortar or concrete

**masonry veneer**  surface layer with appearance of stonework

**mirror**  glass coated on one side with reflective substance

**nickel**  silver-white, malleable metallic element used for plating and in alloys

**pane glass** transparent glass sheets cut to size for windows

**pantile** roofing tile that is curved in its width so as to overlap flanking tiles laid alternately convex and concave side up

**paving** gravel, stone, concrete, or asphalt, used to surface outdoor area or roadway

**pipe** hollow metallic cylinder

**piping** section or system of pipes

**pisé** rammed earth

**plate glass** clear ground glass in large sheets, used for windows; sheet glass

**prestressed concrete** concrete reinforced with embedded cables or wires under tension to increase strength

**quarry tiles** durable fired tiles of unrefined clay, used as flooring

**rammed earth** mixture of sand, loam, and clay rammed into forms; pisé

**rebar** reinforcing steel bars

**red brick** common brick

**reinforced concrete** concrete masonry embedded with steel bars or mesh for greater tensile strength

**reinforcing rod** steel bar used to reinforce concrete

**retarder** mixture of concrete or plaster with another ingredient that retards its set

**riprap** broken stone chunks used for foundations

**roofing** any of various ceramics, tiles, asphalts, or stones used to make roofs

**roof tile** ceramic or asphalt square of roofing material

**rough-cut stone** rubble; irregular, rough-dressed rock fragments

**rubble** masonry made of rough, irregular rock fragments; rubblework

**rubblework** rubble

**safety glass** shatterproof glass made by placing layer of resin or transparent plastic between two panes of glass

**scrap** discarded fragment, esp. of metal, that can be reused, often in altered form

**scrap iron** fragments of iron which can be recast

**screening** fine, close mesh composed of metal wires, used esp. to allow ventilation through doors or windows while excluding insects

**shake** rock fragments scattered about and set in mortar as roofing

**sheet glass** plate glass

**sheeting** any material, esp. metal or glass, cut into large, thin, flat pieces

**sheet metal** metal cut into large, thin, flat pieces

**slate** hard, bluish-gray, fine-grained rock used for roof tiles

**smoked glass** glass colored or darkened by smoke

**spun glass** fine threads of liquid glass

**stained glass** glass colored by fusing of metallic oxides, enameling, or burning pigments into its surface, used for decorative windows

**steel** hard, tough, rust-resistant iron alloy, used extensively for many purposes

**steel mesh** fine, interwoven strands of steel

**steel plate** hard, smooth sheets of steel

**stone** hard, solid, nonmetallic mineral substance of which rocks consist

**Syndecrete** *Trademark.* synthetic concrete

**terra cotta** hard, reddish-brown clay earthenware, used for ornamental facing

**tile** thin, usu. square or rectangular piece of stone, concrete, or fired clay, used for roofing or flooring

**tinfoil** paper-thin sheet of tin, or alloy of tin and lead, used for insulation

**wire** long, very thin metal thread

**wrought iron** tough, malleable, soft commercial iron with 1 or 2 percent slag content, used for furniture and fixtures

## PLASTICS, PAPER, AND TEXTILES

**asbestos** fibrous material of fireproof mineral, used for insulation and tiling

**Bakelite** *Trademark.* black plastic made of synthetic resin

**batting** cotton, wool, or synthetic fiber wadded and quilted into sheets

**batt insulation** insulation made of batting

**buckram** stiffened linen cloth

**bunting** thin, translucent cloth used for decorations

**burlap** coarse sacking; hessian

**canvas** coarse, dense hemp or cotton cloth

**cardboard** thick, stiff material made from paper pulp; paperboard

**carpeting** thick, heavy wool, cotton, or synthetic fiber woven with pile, used for floor covering

**cellophane** thin, transparent, moisture-proof material made from cellulose

**cellulose** chief substance in fibers of all plant tissue, used in making paper and textiles

**chamois** soft leather made from skin of goatlike, European antelope or sheep, used as polishing cloth

**cheesecloth** very loosely woven thin cotton cloth

**crepe paper** thin, stiff, crinkled paper

**fiber** slender, threadlike structure found in vegetable tissue or made synthetically

**Fiberglas** *Trademark.* brand of fiberglass

**fiberglass** finespun glass filaments woven into sheets, used with backing as thermal or acoustical insulation or pressed and molded with resin as plastic

**fibrous pad** thick, soft sheet composed of fibers

**flax** fibers of flax plant spun into thread

**foam rubber** rubber treated to form firm, spongy mass

**Formica** *Trademark.* laminated, heat-resistant plastic, used esp. for countertops

**grass cloth** soft fabric made from plant bark fibers

**grass paper** fine grass fibers plaited into paper

**hessian** coarsely woven cloth; burlap

**insulation** any of various, usu. fibrous, materials that do not conduct heat or sound

**jute** strong fiber used for rope, burlap, and mats

**kraft paper** strong, brown paper made from wood pulp prepared with sodium sulfate solution, used for wrapping

**leather** animal skin prepared by removing hair and tanning

**Lucite** *Trademark.* clear, synthetic resin that hardens when cooled, used for storefront windows instead of glass

**millboard** strong, heavy cardboard used for book covers or furniture panels

**muslin** cotton with plain weave, often heavyweight with coarse finish

**Mylar** *Trademark.* very thin sheets of reflective polyester with great tensile strength, used for insulation and fabrics

**Naugahyde** *Trademark.* imitation leather

**paper** very thin, flexible sheets made from wood pulp or other fibrous material

**paperboard** stiff, heavy material made from wood pulp, thicker than paper; cardboard

**papier-mâché** shredded paper mixed with glue to form highly plastic molding material

**pasteboard** stiff material made from pasted layers of paper or pressed and dried paper pulp

**Perspex** *Trademark.* hard, transparent, acrylic resin similar to Plexiglas

**plastic laminate** plastic glued to plywood or particle board, used for countertops

**plastics** various nonmetallic organic compounds produced synthetically by polymerization, which can be molded, hardened, or formed into pliable sheets, fibers, or foams

**Plexiglas** *Trademark.* lightweight, transparent, thermoplastic synthetic resin, used in place of glass

**polyester** polymeric synthetic resin used in making plastics and synthetic fibers

**polymer** natural or synthetic substance formed by chaining together many simple molecules to form giant molecules with different physical properties

**polypropylene** polymerized propylene, a very light, highly resistant thermoplastic resin, used for packaging and coating

**polystyrene** tough, clear, colorless plastic polymer of styrene, used esp. for containers and apparatus

**polyurethane** various synthetic polymers, used in elastic fibers, foam, insulation, molded products, and coatings

**quilt** fibrous material matted together between layers of heavy paper, used for heat insulation

**raffia** fiber obtained from Mediterranean palm, used for baskets or ropes

**rice paper** thin, translucent paper made from straw of rice grass

**rubber** hard, elastic substance obtained by coagulating and drying sap or latex of various tropical plants, or made synthetically

**rubber floor tile** hardened, flat rubber squares

**strawboard** coarse straw cardboard, used esp. for boxes

**styrene** easily polymerized aromatic liquid, used to make synthetic rubber and plastics

**Styrofoam** *Trademark.* rigid, lightweight polystyrene, used for insulation and commercial products

**tagboard** strong cardboard

**tarpaper** heavy paper impregnated with tar, used as base for roofing

**Teflon** *Trademark.* tough, insoluble polymer, used for non-stick coatings on cookware, in gaskets, and as insulation

**textiles** woven fabrics made of natural or synthetic fibers

**vinyl** compound derived from ethylene and polymerized into various resins and plastics

**vinyl floor tile** stiff, flat, vinyl plastic squares

**Vinylite** *Trademark.* any of various vinyl resins

**wallpaper** decorative strips of paper used to cover walls, usu. applied with glue

## ADHESIVES AND BINDERS

**acrylic resin** transparent, thermoplastic, polymeric resin, used in making molded plastics, paints, and textile fibers

**adhesive** any substance that binds or adheres

**adhesive tape** long, narrow, wound strip of tape with sticky substance on one side

**astringent** substance that causes binding by contraction

**binder** substance that holds things together

**birdlime** extremely sticky substance made from holly bark

**caulking** whitish tar or oakum putty used to stop crack or fill joint

**cement** soft substance that binds objects together when it hardens between them

**compo** composite mortar or plaster

**court plaster** adhesive plaster composed of silk coated with isinglass and glycerin

**creosote** brownish, oily liquid distilled from coal tar, used as wood preservative

**daubing** soft, sticky plaster or grease smeared on surface

**double-stick tape** tape with adhesive substance on both sides

**duct tape** wide, silver-gray, strong adhesive tape, used for Sheetrock work, household repairs, etc.

**electrical tape** strong, highly elastic, black adhesive tape

**epoxy** thermosetting, quick-drying chemical resin blended with other chemicals to form strong, hard, adhesive bond

**gaffer's tape** duct tape used esp. by TV and movie electricians

**gesso** white plaster of Paris or chalk mixed with glue, used as base for paint or gilding

**glue** sticky, viscous liquid made by boiling animal skins, bones, and hoofs to a jelly

**glycerin** syrupy alcohol used as a solvent or plasticizer

**grout** thin mortar or plaster, used to fill joints in masonry, tiles, or brick

**gum** adhesive substance made from sticky colloidal carbohydrate found in certain trees and plants

**gutta-percha** rubberlike gum latex, used for insulation and binding

**gypsum** naturally occurring hydrated sulfate of calcium, used in making plaster of Paris for binding plasterboard

**isinglass** semitransparent whitish gelatin derived from air bladders of fish, used as clarifier or glue

**joint compound** spackling compound

**lime** white calcium oxide obtained by heating limestone or shells, used in mortar and cement

**linseed oil** yellowish oil of flaxseed with unique drying qualities, used in paints, adhesives, and linoleum

**lute** clayey cement used as sealing agent

**masking tape** thin, weak, usu. beige adhesive tape

**mastic** yellowish tree resin used in adhesives and varnish

**mortar** mixture of lime or cement with sand and water, used to bind bricks or stones in building or as plaster

**mucilage** thick, sticky plant substance; watery gum or glue solution

**mud** *Slang.* joint or spackling compound

**oakum** loose, stringy hemp fiber treated with tar, used for caulking

**parget** plaster or mortar, used to coat masonry

**paste** mixture of flour or starch with water and alum or resin, used as adhesive on light materials

**pitch** dark, sticky substance distilled from coal, wood tar, or petroleum, used for waterproofing, roofing, or paving

**plaster of Paris** calcined gypsum in heavy, white powder form, mixed with water to form quick-setting paste

**pointing** mortar used for finishing brickwork

**Portland cement** cement that hardens underwater, made

by burning mixture of lime and clay, used to bind aggregate

**putty** mixture of powdered chalk and linseed oil, used to secure glass panes and fill cracks; cement composed of quicklime, water, and plaster of Paris or sand, used as plastering coat

**resin** any of various viscous, usu. clear or translucent, substances exuded from trees or plants, used in varnish, lacquer, and in making synthetic plastics

**sealant** wax, plastic, or silicone substance used for making a joint airtight or watertight

**sizing** thin, pasty substance used as glaze or filler on porous paper, plaster, or cloth prior to finishing

**solder** metal alloy melted and used to join or patch metal parts when it hardens

**Spackle** *Trademark.* spackling compound

**spackling compound** gypsum plaster mixed with glue, silica flour, and water, used as putty or filler; joint compound

**stucco** plaster applied as finish to interior walls and exterior surfaces

**tape** any of various adhesive tapes

**tar** thick, sticky, dark brown to black, viscous, liquid hydrocarbon obtained from distillation of wood, coal, or peat, used esp. in roofing and paving

**tarmac** bituminous binder used for surfacing roadways

**travertine** plaster made with light-colored Italian limestone

**viscin** clear, viscous substance obtained from mistletoe or holly sap

**viscum** birdlime made from mistletoe berries

**wax** plastic, dull-yellow substance, insoluble in water, used as sealant or to protect surfaces

**weather stripping** thin length of metal, fabric, wood, or composite, used to cover joint and keep out wind or water

## SURFACES AND FINISHING MATERIALS

**acrylic paint** pigments in solution of acrylic resin, quick-drying and brilliant

**alabaster** translucent, whitish, fine-grained gypsum

**blacking** black polish or stain

**bleaching** chemical substance used to remove color

**bluing** blue liquid or powder that prevents yellowing of white fabrics

**brecciation** process of giving surface the appearance of sharp rock fragments cemented together

**carnauba wax** hard brittle wax obtained from palm leaves, used in polishes

**cladding** process of covering one material, esp. metal, with another by bonding

**clinquant** imitation gold leaf

**cottage cheese** lumping plaster, used esp. for finishing ceilings

**damascene** wavy patterns like watered silk on metal; inlays of precious metals on iron or steel

**deck paint** strong, dense, hard-wearing exterior paint

**dye** natural or synthetic substance, esp. in solution, used to produce color

**enamel** opaque, usu. glossy, vitreous coating for metal, glass, and earthenware; paint drying to such a glossy finish

**faux bois** artificial wood grain finish made by swirling paint or stain; graining

**finish** manner in which surface is painted, varnished,

coated, smoothed, or polished; material applied to complete or perfect surface

**gild** (*vb*) overlay with very thin layer of gold

**gold leaf** very thin layer of gold overlaid on surface

**grain** pattern of fibers in wood

**graining** faux bois

**high-gloss** (*adj*) designating very bright, lustrous surface finish, esp. of enamel paint

**lacquer** durable, nonoily varnish, esp. of sumac, applied in layers to wood and polished to mirrorlike finish; comparable synthetic organic solution

**lamina** thin flake or scale of metal or animal tissue

**latex** waterbase paint made by suspending particles of synthetic rubber or plastic in water; milky, resinous liquid present in rubber trees

**leaf** very thin sheet of metal; lamina

**marbling** painting technique that gives veined, mottled, marblelike appearance to objects

**matte** flat finish without shine or luster, esp. in paints

**moire** watery, wavy design, as on silk

**oil** any of various greasy substances obtained from animal, vegetable, or mineral sources, used to treat absorbent surfaces

**oil-base paint** paint made by grinding pigment in drying oil, esp. linseed oil, not soluble in water

**paint** mixture of pigment with water, oil, or latex in liquid or paste form, applied to surfaces for protection and coloring

**parging** application of mortar to masonry surface to smooth and waterproof it

**patina** surface coating due to aging, esp. green coloration on copper

**pewter** alloy of tin with antimony, copper, or lead

**planish** (*vb*) toughen, smooth, or polish metal by hammering or rolling

**plaster** pasty mixture, made from lime or gypsum, sand, and water, that hardens on drying, used to coat walls and ceilings

**plate** thin, overlaid coating of metal, esp. gold, silver, or tin

**polish** wax, oil, or liquid plastic rubbed onto surface to provide bright, glossy finish

**primer** paint or sizing applied to raw surface prior to finishing coat

**rag-rolling** wiping wet painted surface with rag to create patterns in paint

**roughcast** coarse stucco used on exterior walls

**rubber cement** quick-evaporating, unvulcanized rubber in solvent, used to bind light materials

**semigloss** (*adj*) designating paint that dries to a finish more lustrous than matte and less lustrous than high-gloss

**shellac** thin, clear solution of refined lac resin in alcohol, used as wood filler and finish

**stain** liquid coating to darken or color wood and bring out grain

**stencil** design cut out of waxed paper or acetate and reproduced on surface below paper with paint or ink

**swirling** allowing undercoat of paint to show through top coat

**thinner** turpentine or other substance added to dilute paint or varnish

**tortoise shell** synthetic imitation of the hard, mottled, yellow-and-brown shell of certain turtles

**turpentine** colorless, volatile hydrocarbon used in paint and varnish

**Varathane** *Trademark*. oily wood varnish that dries to hard, clear, water-resistant surface

**varnish** resin dissolved in oil or thinner that dries to hard, lustrous, usu. transparent finish on wood

**veneer** thin overlay of finishing material, esp. wood, on base of another material

**verdigris** greenish-blue coating that forms naturally on brass, bronze, or copper

**waterbase paint** pigment mixed with water or latex, soluble in water

**wax** soft, resinous, water-resistant substance rubbed on surfaces, esp. wood and leather, to protect and shine

**whiting** powdered chalk used in paints and dyes; bleaching agent

# TOOLS AND HARDWARE

Common Tools and Tool Types
Edged, Pointed, Carving, and Turning Tools
Saws
Shaving, Shaping, Sharpening, and Smoothing Tools
Shovels and Digging and Lifting Tools
Drills and Bits
Hammers
Wrenches
Gripping, Tightening, and Fastening Tools
Measuring and Marking Tools
Miscellaneous Tools, Objects, and Supplies
Hardware and Supplies

**SEE ALSO**: Chap. 5: Machinery and Fabrication; Structural Components; Building and Construction Materials; Containers; Electricity and Electronics; Chap. 6: Automobiles; Chap. 10: Fashion and Garment Parts; Chap. 16: Graphic Design and Printing; Chap. 17: Gardening

Each subcategory lists and defines the major representatives of that tool type. These are followed by an undefined list of other tools of that type that are either less common or whose name is self-explanatory, such as "jeweler's saw."

## COMMON TOOLS AND TOOL TYPES

**bit** detachable, usu. interchangeable cutting, drilling, or boring part of a drill or other tool, available in various sizes suited to hole desired or specific need

**blade** broad, thin, flat, sharpened edge of cutting tool

**chisel** any of various wedgelike tools with cutting edge at end of blade, used for shaping solid materials, esp. wood or stone

**clamp** device that holds two or more objects tightly together between parts that draw together

**digging tool** any shovel, hoe, spade, or rake used for moving earth or rocks

**drill** shafted device, usu. affixed to handle, with point and two or more cutting edges for piercing hard surfaces, usu. by rapid rotations

**edged tool** tool with cutting edge or blade

**fastening tool** any screwdriver, clamp, vise, or cord used to hold parts together

**file** steel hand tool with abrasive surface for shaping and smoothing objects

**fixture** usu. decorative piece of hardware

**gauge** any device for measuring, testing, or registering measurements

**gripping tool** tool with jaws or pincers, such as pliers

**hammer** any of various handheld or power tools with hard, metal head at end of handle, used for pounding and nailing

**hardware** metalware usu. forming functional or decorative component part

**hook** curved, pointed, often barbed device for clasping or moving objects

**implement** any article used to facilitate some activity, such as a tool or utensil

**knife** blade, either attached to a handle or part of a machine, used for cutting, slicing, or shaping

**marking tool** device for scratching surface or applying mark at specific spot

**measuring tool** any device such as scale, rule, level, or square, used to determine magnitude, dimension, precision, or trueness

**plane** tool with horizontally mounted, adjustable blade in handle, used for smoothing or paring wood surfaces and for forming moldings, chamfers, and grooves

**pliers** small pincer tool with long, grasping jaws and two handles

**pointed tool** tool tapering to sharp point at one end

**power tool** any tool driven by more than human energy, esp. electrical power

**rule** length of straight hard material marked in units for measuring

**sander** power tool for smoothing surfaces with abrasive material, usu. on belt or disk

**saw** toothed blade attached to handle or in machine, used for cutting wood and other hard materials

**scraping tool** file or rasp for roughly removing surface material, esp. from wood

**screwdriver** handle with long, narrow, metal extension that tapers and flattens so as to fit into screwheads to turn and drive them

**shaping tool** any plane, sander, router, or lathe that precisely trims surface material to predetermined design

**sharpener** device for honing blade of edged tool

**shaving tool** device for removing excess material from surface

**shovel** broad, slightly hollowed, blade-edged scoop on handle for digging, scooping, or lifting heavy, often loose material

**smoothing tool** sandpaper, hone, or plane for finishing surface of shaped object

**square** instrument with straight edges and at least one ninety degree angle, used to plot right angles

**tightening tool** screwdriver, clamp, or vise for forcing parts together

**tool** any implement, instrument, or device held in hand or driven by machine power and used to facilitate some physical or mechanical task

**trowel** small hand tool with flat blade attached to handle, used to spread or smooth loose material

**wrench** any of various hand or power tools for holding or turning a bolt or nut in a set or adjustable mouth at end of handle

# EDGED, POINTED, CARVING, AND TURNING TOOLS

**adz** thin, curved blade mounted at right angles to handle, used for trimming and shaping wood

**awl** small, pointed instrument for marking and piercing holes, esp. in leather

**ax** heavy blade head attached to handle, used esp. for chopping and splitting wood

**ax head** heavy blade attached to ax handle

**bale breaker** bladed device for cutting and opening bales

**barb** sharp point projecting in opposite direction from main point of tool

**bill** curved blade set on handle, used for pruning or cutting; billhook

**billhook** bill

**blade** broad, thin, flat, sharpened edge of cutting tool

**bodkin** slender, pointed instrument for piercing cloth or leather

**bowl gouge** deeply fluted gouge

**bradawl** awl for making small holes in wood for brads

**burin** engraving tool with steel blade and sharp point

**caulking iron** chisellike edged tool for applying caulk to seams

**chisel** any of various wedgelike tools with cutting edge at end of blade, used to shape solid materials, esp. wood or stone

**church key** small, flat implement with pointed triangular head for penetrating beverage can tops

**cleaver** heavy cutting tool with broad blade, usu. used by butcher

**clipper** tool for cutting or shearing, often with multiple blades

**colter** sharp blade or wheel attached at front of plow, used for cutting earth

**cotter key puller** steel hook on short handle, used to remove cotter pins

**crampon** spiked plate attached to boot for use in climbing; device for lifting or grasping loads, usu. consisting of two hooks suspended from a cable or chain

**crotchet** small hook or hooked tool

**dagger** pointed blade on handle

**dibble** small, handheld, pointed device for poking holes in earth for plants or seeds

**drawknife** blade mounted between and at right angles to two handles and drawn over surface to be cut; drawshave

**edger** revolving blades set on long handle, used to trim edge of lawn

**frow** cleaving tool with wedge-shaped blade at right angle to handle

**gouge** grooving chisel with concave blade, used esp. in turning

**grapnel** small anchor with several flukes or claws

**grappling iron** hook for anchoring boat to dock or to another boat

**graver** any of various bladed tools, such as burin or scauper, used for engraving

**hardy** blacksmith's chisel with square shank for insertion into anvil

**hatchet** short-handled ax, often with a hammerhead

**hook** curved, pointed, often barbed device for clasping or moving objects

**inshave** curved blade set between and at right angles to two handles, used for removing surface of round objects

**knife** blade, either attached to a handle or part of a machine, used for cutting, slicing, and shaping

**machete** large heavy knife, often with blade widening at end away from handle

**nibbler** edged device for cutting sheet metal

**peavey** lever with spike and pivoting hook at one end, used by lumberjacks in handling logs

**pick** tool with heavy metal head, pointed at one or both ends, attached to wooden handle

**pickaroon** pike or hook at end of pole, used by lumberjacks, esp. on rivers

**pickax** head having ax blade and pick point attached to long handle

**pike** pointed head on long shaft

**pinking shears** shears with serrated edges for cutting fabric

**pipe cutter** hand tool with three wheels, one for cutting and two for guiding, that are pressed inward to cut through pipe as tool is rotated

**piton** spike pounded into rock fissure or ice for support in climbing

**punch** small, metal spike, used for perforating and stamping materials, marking layout lines, and driving nails

**puncheon** pointed stamping tool for goldsmith work

**razor** very fine-edged cutting blade, usu. of steel

**ripping bar** steel bar with clawed hook at one end and ripping wedge at the other

**round-nose scraper** scraper with blunt end, used for turning

**scissors** two hinged blades that cut when edges move past each other as handles are squeezed together

**scraper** edged tool used in turning on lathe

**scythe** long, curving blade on handle, esp. for cutting grass

**shears** large, powerful scissors for gardening or metalwork

**sickle** curved, hooklike blade on short handle, used for cutting grain

**skew** chisel with blade having angular front edge

**slick** large chisel for jointing large timbers; foundry tool for smoothing core or surface of sand mold

**spring shears** scissorslike cutting tool with nonpivoting jaws that spring open when released

**spur** pointed, sometimes barbed hook or metal device

**square-end chisel** chisel with blade ending square to its length

**stylus** hard-pointed needle for cutting or marking

**tang** projecting point or prong on chisel, file, or knife

**trier** hollow tube narrowing to point, used to withdraw samples of bulk material from sacks or other containers

**utility knife** razor blade held in small handle

**wedge** metal rod tapering to blade end, used for raising weights or splitting hard objects

**wire cutter** plierslike tool with edged jaws, used to cut through wire

### OTHER EDGED AND POINTED TOOLS

alpenstock

belt punch, bistoury, bob punch, bolster chisel, bread knife, bricklayer's chisel, brick set, broadax, bushwhacker, butcher knife, butt chisel

cant hook, carpet knife, carving chisel, carving knife, carving set, case knife, celt, chaser, chopping knife, clasp knife, claw hatchet, cold chisel, cold cutter, croze, cutting pliers

dogleg chisel, drawshave, drove chisel

eaves hook, electric razor

firmer chisel, fluted gouge, framing chisel, frowglass cutter

garnish awl, glazier's chisel, goosewing ax, groover, grub ax, grub hoe

hack, half hatchet, hedge trimmer, hook blade, hot cutter, hunting knife

iron

jackknife, jeweler's chisel

kranging hook

lance, lancet, letter-opener, linoleum knife

masonry chisel, mason's chisel, mat knife, mill knife, mortise chisel

nippers, nooker knife

palette knife, panga, paper cutter, paper knife, paring chisel, paring knife, penknife, plowshare, pocketknife, pole tree pruner, prick punch, pruner, pruning hook, pruning shears, putty knife

reed knife, rigger's knife, ripping chisel, roofing knife, roughing-out gouge

safety razor, saw knife, sax, scalpel, scauper, scoop, scorper, scraper, scuffle hoe, share, shearing hook, sheath knife, sheet metal punch, shingling hatchet, sidecutters, slotter, snips, spear, spindle gouge, surgical knife, swan neck chisel

table knife, taping knife, tin snips, turning chisel

wood chisel

Xacto knife

## SAWS

**backsaw** short saw with reinforced back

**band saw** saw consisting of endless, toothed steel band passing around two wheels

**bayonet** handsaw with long, deep-toothed, bayonetlike blade on small handle

**bench saw** circular saw mounted on workbench

**bucksaw** saw with blade mounted across upright frame, held in both hands for cutting wood on sawhorse

**buzz saw** stationary, power-operated, circular saw with teeth on large disk attached to shaft

**chain saw** usu. portable power saw with teeth set on endless, revolving chain

**circular saw** handheld electric saw with disk-shaped blade

**compass saw** small handsaw with narrow, tapering blade for cutting curves; keyhole saw

**coping saw** saw with thin, light blade in U-shaped frame with handle, used to cut small curves or do ornamental work in thin wood; fret saw

**crosscut saw** saw for cutting wood perpendicular to grain

**crown saw** rotary saw consisting of hollow cylinder with teeth at one end or edge; cylinder saw; hole saw

**dial saw** small blades mounted on circular plate whose diameter can be adjusted, used to cut holes

**dozuki** Japanese craftsman's saw with blade that widens away from handle and teeth that cut on the pull, not push, stroke

**flush cut saw** single-edged saw with extremely flexible, thin, unbacked blade that will bend to cut off pegs without marking adjacent surface

**frame saw** saw, often with multiple detachable blades that are attached to handle at both ends, used esp. for precision work

**friction saw** high-speed, usu. toothless, circular saw that cuts metals by melting them with frictional heat

**hacksaw** narrow, fine-toothed blade fixed in frame, used to cut metal

**handsaw** common saw with handle at one end for manual operation

**jigsaw** usu. stationary electric saw with narrow blade mounted vertically in frame, used to cut curves and other irregular lines

**keyhole saw** compass saw

**log saw** sturdy blade with large, deep teeth for cutting logs or timber

**miter saw** portable, electric, circular saw with adjustable guide for cutting miters

**panel saw** stationary power tool, either horizontal or vertical, used to cut large sheets of material accurately

**power saw** any of various electrical, gas-powered, pneumatic, or battery-driven saws

**radial arm saw** stationary, electrically powered saw with blade on overhead arm that moves across width of wood

**ripsaw** saw used for cutting wood with the grain

**ryoba** Japanese craftsman's saw with teeth on both sides of a blade that widens away from the handle and cuts on the pull, not push, stroke

**saber saw** portable, handheld electric jigsaw

**saw** toothed blade attached to handle or in machine, used for cutting wood and other hard materials

**scroll saw** narrow saw mounted vertically in frame and moved up and down in cutting curved ornamentation, usu. benchtop power saw

**stationary circular saw** power saw with disk-shaped blade, affixed to bench or in standing unit

**table saw** small, stationary power saw with benchlike table on which wood is placed for cutting

**veneer saw** small saw with a handle that is flat on one side and has a blade along its length, this blade having teeth facing in both directions, used for cutting veneer sheets

**whipsaw** saw operated between two persons, used to divide timbers lengthwise

### OTHER SAWS

azibiki

belt saw, board saw, bow saw, builder's saw, butcher's saw

contractor's saw, cordwood saw, cutoff saw, cylinder saw

diamond saw, double-cut saw, dovetail saw, dry-wall saw

electric saw

flooring saw, fret saw

helicoidal saw, hikimawashi, hole saw

jeweler's saw

kerf saw, kitchen saw

lightning saw, logging saw, lumberman's saw

marquetry saw, meat saw, mill saw, mortise saw

pad saw, panther-head saw, pitsaw, plumber's saw, plywood saw, pocket saw, portable saw, portable sawmill, pruning saw reciprocating saw

saw knife, saw machine, Sawzall, scribe saw, skewback saw, Skilsaw, splitsaw, surgeon's saw, sweepback saw

tenon saw, trim saw, trock saw, two-handed saw

utility saw

vertical saw

wallboard saw, wire saw, wood saw

## SHAVING, SHAPING, SHARPENING, AND SMOOTHING TOOLS

**abrader** handheld scraping tool

**anvil** heavy iron block on which metals are placed for shaping by pounding

**belt sander** electric sander with abrasive surface on continuous belt

**block plane** small plane for cutting across grain

**buffer** any of various polishing devices, usu. with smoothing surface attached to handle or other mechanism

**bullnose plane** small, blunt-ended planing tool

**butteris** L-shaped shank with flat blade, used for paring horse hooves

**chamfering plane** plane with blade that shaves and smooths wood at 45 degree angle to adjacent face

**circular file** file with cylindrical abrasive surface, often tapering toward end away from handle; round file

**darby** two-handled, wooden plasterer's float

**die** any of various tools for forming material into a specific shape, esp. by pressure of cutting

**disk sander** electric sander with abrasive surface attached to rotating disk head

**drum sander** usu. stationary power tool with rotating cylinder, used to smooth curved surfaces

**electric sander** electrically powered, orbital or straight-line hand tool for smoothing surfaces

**emery wheel** grinding wheel

**file** steel hand tool with abrasive surface for shaping and smoothing objects

**flatiron** device with flat metal bottom that is heated and used to smooth materials, esp. cloth

**flatter** blacksmith's flat-faced tool, laid on forging and struck with hammer to smooth surface of forging

**float** trowellike tool with thick rubber face attached at each end to handle, used for smoothing grout or similar material

**grinding wheel** circular head of abrasive material for sanding and grinding; emery wheel

**grindstone** revolving wheel of abrasive material, usu. Carborundum, for grinding and shaping

**half-round file** file that is flat on one side and rounded on the other

**hone** abrasive whetstone for sharpening bladed cutting tools

**honing guide** handles that attach to a chisel or plane blade to guide it across sharpening stone

**jack plane** any plane for rough surfacing

**jointer** large plane for smoothing wood surfaces; stationary power tool used to achieve smooth, flat surface on wood

**lapping kit** grains of silicon carbide in several sizes, used for lapping stones and finishing plane blades and chisels

**lathe** stationary power tool with fixed tool mechanism and machine that rotates work around axis, used for shaping cylindrical objects

**machine tool** power-driven device used to shape or trim objects

**multiplane** versatile plane, with up to forty interchangeable cutting blades, for large variety of uses

**oilstone** block of fine-grained stone, usu. oiled, for sharpening certain cutting tools by abrasion

**plane** tool with horizontally mounted, adjustable blade in handle, used for smoothing or paring wood surfaces and for forming moldings, chamfers, and grooves

**planer** power tool for surfacing rough wood

**power sander** high-speed electrical sander, either rotary, orbital, or straight belt, with attachments from fine to coarse grain

**punch press** power tool used to cut and shape metal sheets with dies under pressure

**putty knife** broad, flexible blade on short handle for spreading putty

**rabbet plane** plane for cutting deep notch or rabbet at edge of board to make joint with another board

**rasp** metal file with coarse raised nubs

**riffler** small file with curved abrading surface

**round file** circular file

**router** machine with rotating, milling, or cutting bits mounted on vertical spindle, used for gouging wood surfaces

**router plane** plane for cutting interior angles, as at bottom of groove

**sander** power tool for smoothing surfaces with abrasive material, usu. on belt or disk

**sandpaper** paper with sand or other abrasive glued to one side, used for smoothing surfaces, esp. wood

**scraper** any of various hand tools with blades that are usu. pulled, rather than pushed, to shape wood surface

**shaper** any of various tools or machines for shaping and pressing sheet metal; stationary power tool with cutters, used to contour edge of wood

**shavehook** small tool with blade set at right angle at end of shank, pulled for scraping effect, rather than pushed like plane

**slipstone** sharpening stone with rounded and tapering edges, used on gouges and other carving tools

**spokeshave** blade set between two winglike handles, used for forming and dressing curved edges of wood

**steel wool** matted mass of steel shavings used by hand for shaving and smoothing surfaces

**stone** grindstone or whetstone

**stroke sander** stationary power tool with continuous overhead belt, used to sand large panels or surfaces

**strop** strip of leather for sharpening razors

**swage** heavy tool for shaping metalwork, which is hammered against swage surface

**swage block** iron block used for shaping objects not easily worked on anvil

**tamper** wide blade set perpendicular to handle, used for flattening and evening out soft or loose materials

**thickness planer** plane with strong blade and wide cut, used for shaving deeply into wood surfaces

**trimming plane** plane with L-shaped body that hooks over board, used for trimming edges

**trowel** small hand tool with flat blade attached to handle, used for spreading or smoothing loose material

**trying plane** very long, wide-bladed plane for making tight-edged glue joints and leveling large boards

**waterstone** sharpening block, made of stone, that is used while wet

**whetstone** stone block for sharpening blades

**wood mill** stationary or portable device with multiple blades for making moldings

**OTHER SHAVING, SHAPING, SHARPENING, AND SMOOTHING TOOLS**

auger bit file

bastard file, beading plane, bench plane, bench stone, bending fork, brick trowel, buffing-and-polishing bonnet

cabinet scraper, cabinet rasp, capping plane, chuck, circle trowel, circular plane, combination plane, compass plane, contour sander, core box plane, corner trowel, cove trowel, curbing trowel

dado plane, dovetail plane

edge plane, electric plane

faceplate lathe, fillister plane, finger plane, finishing sander, flat file, fore plane

grinder, grooving plane, guttering trowel

hand plane, hand sander, hand scraper

jeweler's lathe

lute

match plane, mill file, molding plane, multiplane

needle rasp

orbital sander

pad sander, palm plane, perimeter sander, plasterer's float, plastering trowel, plough plane, plunge router, pointing trowel, portable handheld shaper, portable router, power plane

radius trowel, reed plane, rotary rasp, roughing plane, round bastard file

sanding belt, sash plane, scraper plane, scrub plane, seaming router, shoe rasp, shoulder plane, slick, smoothing plane, surform plane

tamping bar, tamping pick, tamping stick, tape file, thumb plane, tonguing plane, toothing plane, trenching plane, trimmer, trimming block

violin plane

warding file, wood plane, wood rasp

# SHOVELS AND DIGGING AND LIFTING TOOLS

**bail** scoop for removing accumulated water, esp. from boat

**bar** long, straight, rigid piece of metal for lifting or prying

**bull tongue** wide plow blade for cultivating or marking soil

**crowbar** metal bar with flattened wedge at one end, used as a lever

**cultivator** implement with flat blade, drawn between rows of plants to loosen earth and remove weeds

**fork** pronged tool for lifting, throwing, or piercing

**hoe** flat blade at end of long handle, used for working earth around plants

**lever** rigid bar on axis or fulcrum, used to lift weight or exert pressure to dislodge something

**loy** long narrow spade, esp. one with broad chisel point for digging post holes

**mattock** pickaxlike tool with one broad end, used for loosening soil by digging

**pinch bar** crowbar with projection at one end that acts as fulcrum, used for removing spikes or wedged under heavy wheel to be rolled; wrecking bar

**pitchfork** large, two- or three-tined fork on long handle, used for lifting and tossing

**plow** implement with blade for cutting or lifting soil or clearing away debris

**pry bar** tool similar to crowbar, used for lifting or moving heavy objects

**rake** head with multiple, sometimes splayed prongs on long handle, used for gathering loose material or leveling ground

**scoop** deeply concave shovel or hollowed spoon for digging and carrying earth

**scooper** shovel, scoop, or ladle

**shovel** broad, slightly hollowed, blade-edged scoop on handle, used for digging, scooping, or lifting heavy, often loose material

**spade** small, flat blade at end of long handle, pushed into ground with foot for digging

**spatula** spreading or scooping tool with flat, thin blade on handle

**spud** spadelike tool with narrow blade, used esp. for digging up weeds

**tire iron** crowbar used to remove hubcaps and lug nuts

**trowel** small, scooplike hand shovel

**wrecking bar** pinch bar

**OTHER SHOVELS AND DIGGING AND LIFTING TOOLS**

air shovel, air spade

bar spade

coal shovel

ditch spade, drain spade, draw hoe

entrenching tool

fire shovel

garden spade, garden trowel, gasoline shovel, grub hoe, gumming spade

irrigating shovel

peat spade, posthole digger, power shovel

salt shovel, scuffle hoe, split shovel, stump spud

trenching spade

wedge bar, Wonder bar

# DRILLS AND BITS

**auger** boring tool consisting of bit rotated by transverse handle

**auger bit** long bit with square tang at upper end, rotated by brace to bore through wood

**bench drill** large, stationary power drill

**bit** detachable, usu. interchangeable cutting, drilling, or boring part of drill or other tool, available in various sizes suited to hole desired or specific need

**bore** tool with bit, such as an auger, used for boring out holes

**bow drill** antique drill operated by cord wrapped around shank with ends attached to bowlike device

**brace** device for holding and turning a bit for boring or drilling

**breast drill** portable drill with plate at end of handle that is pressed against the chest to force drill against work

**center bit** bit with sharp, projecting point, easily centered in hole to be drilled

**chamfer bit** bit used to bevel edge of hole

**chaser** tool with multiple teeth for cutting screw threads

**chuck** threaded portion of drill that holds bit

**cordless drill** battery-operated power drill not requiring AC cord

**corkscrew** pointed, metal spiral on handle, inserted in corks to pull them from bottles

**countersink** drill bit or funnel-shaped metal piece used to enlarge upper part of hole, allowing a cone-shaped screwhead to lie flush with surface

**drill** shafted device, usu. affixed to handle, with point and two or more cutting edges for piercing hard surfaces, usu. by rapid rotations

**drill press** powerful, stationary drill with single vertical spindle and hand lever used to apply pressure in drilling accurate holes

**eggbeater drill** antique drill operated by rotary motion of handle similar to an eggbeater

**electric drill** any electrically powered hand tool for drilling holes

**gimlet** small boring tool with spiral point and cross handle

**hand drill** any small, hand-cranked drill

**jackhammer** powerful, portable drill operated by compressed air, used to break up rock or concrete

**keyhole router bit** bit that cuts keyhole-shaped hole in object to be hung over nail

**mandrel** metal rod or bar around which wood, metal, or glass is cast, molded, or shaped

**nail set** short steel rod used to drive nail below or flush with surface

**plug cutter** special bit that routs a circular groove

**push drill** hand drill operated by pressure of handle along line of shank

**reamer** rotary tool with helical or straight flutes, used for finishing or enlarging holes drilled in metal

**screw starter** threads on tapering point of short shank with bulb handle, used to make threaded holes for screws

**snake** device with head at end of flexible metal band, fed into curved pipes to remove obstruction

**tap** pluglike device with sharp ridges, inserted in opening and twisted to cut screw threads in it

**wimble** any of various boring devices, used esp. in mining to extract material from bored hole

**woodborer** boring tool for wood, operated by compressed air

### Other Drills and Bits

accretion borer, air drill, angle drill, automatic drill

beading bit, bench grinder, bevel trim bit, bitstock, bore bit, brad point bit, breast auger, broach, burr

carbide bit, circle cutter, compressed-air bit, core box bit, cross bit

diamond drill, disk drill, dovetail bit, dowling jig, drill set, drill stand

expansive bit, extensive bit

flat drill, Forstner bit

gimlet bit, glass bit

hinge bit

keyway drill

lockset bit

masonry bit, mortising bit, multispur bit

ogee fillet bit

panel pilot bit

parallel hand reamer, portable drill, post drill, posthole auger, Powerbore bit, power drill, pump drill, punch drill

raised panel bit, ratchet drill, roman ogee bit, rose reamer, rotary drill, round over bit, router bit

shell drill, shell reamer, spade bit, spade-handle drill, spike bit, star drill, strap drill

taper drill, tapping drill, tile bit, trepan, trephine, twist bit, twist drill

vix bit

## Hammers

**ball-peen hammer** machinist's hammer with one cylindrical and one hemispherical head

**battering ram** heavy beam or bar used to knock down walls and doors

**beetle** heavy, usu. wooden instrument for hammering, ramming, or driving wedges

**brad pusher** tool with long, narrow head on small bulb handle, used to drive brads while avoiding hammer marks on surface

**brick hammer** hammer having one broad flat head and one long, axlike head

**claw hammer** hammer with one head curved and forked into claw for pulling nails; rip hammer

**club** heavy, wooden rod, often narrowing at one end

**double-claw hammer** hammer with claws on both heads and no pounding surface

**drop forge** heavy object allowed to fall on piece of work placed on anvil; drop hammer

**fuller** hammer for grooving or spreading iron

**hammer** any of various handheld or power tools with hard, metal head at end of handle, used for pounding and nailing

**hammerhead** heavy, hard, usu. metal portion of hammer at end of handle, designed for striking

**hatchet** short-handled ax, usu. with one hammerhead

**mallet** hammer of wood, plastic, rubber, or metal, usu. with a barrel-shaped head, used esp. for driving a chisel

**maul** sledgehammer for driving piles, sometimes with wooden head, sometimes with one ax edge for splitting wood

**peen hammer** hammer with hemispherical or wedge-shaped head, used esp. for shaping material

**pestle** club-shaped device made of hard substance, used for grinding and pulverizing material in mortar

**ram** battering ram or other device for driving something by impact

**rammer** instrument for driving something by impact

**rip hammer** claw hammer

**scutch** hammer with elongated heads for shaping bricks

**sledge** sledgehammer

**sledgehammer** large, heavy hammerhead on long handle, swung with both hands

**small anvil** nonstanding, handheld anvil used to pound materials

**tack hammer** light hammer, often with magnetized head that holds tack

**tamp** tool for driving down an object or firmly patting down a filling

**tilt hammer** forging hammer with heavy head at one end of pivoted lever

**triphammer** heavy hammer raised and released by means of tripping device to fall on object being hammered

**Warrington hammer** light, balanced cabinetmaker's hammer with flat peen head and narrow tapering head

### OTHER HAMMERS

adz-eye hammer, air hammer
blacksmith's hammer, boilermaker's hammer, bushhammer
chipping hammer, cooper's hammer, cross peen hammer
demolition hammer, die hammer, drilling hammer, drop hammer, drywall hammer
electric hammer, engineer's hammer
framing hammer, goathead hammer
hand drilling hammer, hardie, high nailer
joiner's mallet
long-handled hammer
machinist's hammer
nail claw hammer
pile hammer
pneumatic hammer
raising hammer, ripping claw hammer, riveting hammer, rubber mallet
set hammer, shingler's hammer, shoemaker's hammer, soft-faced hammer, spalling hammer, steam hammer, stone hammer, stonemason's ax, stonemason's hammer, stud driver
tiler's hammer
upholsterer's hammer
veneer hammer
wooden mallet

## WRENCHES

**adjustable wrench** any wrench with adjustable jaws
**Allen wrench** hexagonal bar bent at right angle, used to turn Allen screw having axial hexagonal hole in its head
**alligator wrench** wrench with V-shaped, serrated jaws set at right angles to shank, used for turning cylindrical or irregularly shaped parts
**box-end wrench** wrench having closed ends that completely surround nut or bolthead
**box/open-end wrench** wrench having one closed box end and one open end
**Crescent Wrench** *Trademark.* hand wrench with parallel, adjustable jaws that have smooth surfaces
**crowfoot wrench** box or open-end wrench with opening set at right angle to shank
**lug wrench** wrench with hollow end, used to loosen or tighten lug nuts
**monkey wrench** wrench with adjustable jaws, used to grasp nuts or boltheads of different sizes
**obstruction wrench** wrench with bent shank for use in confined areas
**open-end wrench** wrench having partially open end that slips over nut or bolthead
**pipe-gripping wrench** any of various wrenches with differing jaw shapes, used to grip pipes
**pipe wrench** tool with two toothed jaws, one fixed and one free to grip pipes when wrench is turned in one direction only
**ratcheting box-end wrench** box-end wrench with teeth mounted in round openings and ratchet lever
**socket set** series of different-sized socket attachments for ratchet-style socket wrench
**socket wrench** wrench with hollow end, or socket, that fits nut or bolt, often ratchet-operated and equipped with socket set
**spanner** wrench having curved head with hook or pin at one end for engaging notches or holes in collars and certain nuts
**spark plug wrench** ratchet-style wrench with socket that fits over automobile spark plugs
**speeder wrench** socket wrench with long offset handle
**Stillson wrench** *Trademark.* monkey wrench with adjustable jaw that tightens as pressure is applied to its handle
**torque wrench** wrench having register that shows amount of torque, or rotational force, being applied
**wrench** any of various hand or power tools for holding or turning a bolt or nut in a set or adjustable mouth at end of handle

### OTHER WRENCHES

adjustable spanner
bicycle wrench
carriage wrench, chain wrench
end wrench
flare-nut wrench
gooseneck wrench
hexagonal wrench
lever wrench
Mack truck wrench
pin wrench,
ratcheting box
screw key, S-wrench
tappet wrench, tap wrench, tuning wrench
valve wrench

## GRIPPING, TIGHTENING, AND FASTENING TOOLS

**anchor** device that firmly binds one part of a structure to another, usu. by being implanted in one part
**bar clamp** clamp with two jaws attached to bar, one jaw fixed and one adjustable by means of a screw mechanism
**bench dog** device that fits in hole on workbench top and in moving face of bench vise, used to hold work in place
**bench vise** vise that clamps to bench or table
**brace** device that clasps or connects two pieces
**C-clamp** C-shaped clamp with a screw threaded through one end in the direction of other end
**chuck** device for centering and clamping work in a lathe
**clamp** device that holds two or more objects tightly together between parts that draw together
**claw** device with forked end for removing nails
**clip** gripping device using pinching action of two hinged arms
**cordless screwdriver** battery-operated power screwdriver not requiring AC wire
**diagonal-cutting pliers** pliers with clipping blades set at an angle in jaws
**electric riveter** power tool for fastening rivets
**forceps** hinged device for gripping small objects
**grip** pinching or grasping tool
**hand screw** clamp with two wooden jaws, tightened by two long screws passing through both jaws
**impact driver** screwdriver that turns when downward pressure is exerted on handle

**lineman's pliers**  pliers with reinforced jaws and insulated handles, used with electrical cable and wire

**locking pliers**  pliers whose jaws connect at sliding pivot that may be temporarily locked to aid in grasping and turning

**nail puller**  plierslike device with strong, wide, curved jaws for removing nails from wood

**needlenose pliers**  pliers with jaws tapering to point, used for grasping small objects

**Phillips screwdriver**  screwdriver with cross-shaped, pointed tip

**pincers**  two-handled gripping device with pivoting jaws

**pinchcock**  clamp for compressing flexible pipe or tube to regulate flow of liquid

**plate joiner**  electric doweling machine that fastens wooden members together using oval biscuits

**pliers**  small pincer tool with long, grasping jaws and two handles

**pneumatic stapler**  compressed-air powered staple gun

**power nailer**  automatic nailer driven by compressed-air chamber

**pucellas**  pointed gripping jaws on spring pivot, used for handling molten glass

**puller**  device for gripping and removing spikes or nails

**riveter**  device for pressing rivets together in order to fasten pieces of material together

**screw clamp**  any clamp tightened by a screw mechanism

**screwdriver**  handle with long, narrow, metal extension that tapers and flattens so as to fit into screwheads to turn and drive them

**screw gun**  power screwdriver

**slip-joint pliers**  pliers having sliding joint that permits adjustment of jaw span

**snap ring pliers**  tool with short jaws for removing and replacing snap rings on power tools

**spring clamp**  any clamp tightened by an elastic spring mechanism, rather than by a screw mechanism

**staple gun**  pneumatic or electrically powered stapler

**stapler**  small hand implement for affixing objects with thin wire staples

**stubby screwdriver**  screwdriver with very short shank and thick handle

**tongs**  two hinged arms used for grasping objects

**tweezers**  small device with two jointed arms held between thumb and forefinger, used to grasp small objects

**veneer press**  press frame for small veneering and assembly jobs

**vise**  tool with two clamping jaws that are brought together or separated by means of a screw or lever, used to hold objects and work tight and steady

**vise grip**  handheld vise that screws tight to hold work

**Yankee screwdriver**  *Trademark*. handheld tool with spiral ratcheting action

### OTHER GRIPPING, TIGHTENING, AND FASTENING TOOLS

adjustable bar clamp, auger screwdriver

band clamp, bent-nose pliers

cabinet-pattern screwdriver, channel-lock pliers, clamp-on vise, clutch-head tip screwdriver, corner clamp, cutting pliers

edging clamp, electric screwdriver, electric staple gun

flat-head screwdriver

glue gun

hammer staple, handspike, hand vise, holddown clamp

joint fastener

long-nose pliers

machinist's vise, magnetic screwdriver, miter clamp

nippers

offset screwdriver

patternmaker's vise, piling clamp, pin vise, pipe clamp, plastic tape, punch pliers

ratcheting screwdriver, ring pliers

saw vise, slab-handle screwdriver, spiral ratchet screwdriver

tacker, toggle clamp, tongue-and-groove pliers

utility tweezers

web clamp, welding clamp, wood bar clamp, wood hand screw

Z-bar, Z-clip

## MEASURING AND MARKING TOOLS

**bevel**  rule with adjustable arm that opens to form measured angles, used for drawing or shaping sloped edges

**butt gauge**  gauge with three cutters for marking mortise outlines, as for door butts

**caliper**  adjustable, often curved jaws on pivot, used for measuring thickness or diameter

**center punch**  small device with conical point for marking shallow impressions, used to center drill bits for making holes

**combination square**  adjustable device used as level, miter square, and try square

**compass**  instrument consisting of two movable legs hinged at one end, used to draw arcs and circles

**dividers**  pair of compasses used to measure lines or divide a large space into sections

**feeler gauge**  device for measuring gaps by inserting one of several arms of different thicknesses

**folding rule**  measuring device with multiple, pivoting lengths for compact storage

**level**  any of various devices for determining true horizontal lines, esp. one that has a bubble suspended in liquid in a glass tube set in a long straight board

**marking gauge**  any device for marking measurements with a sharp point, usu. having graduated scale on sliding arm

**micrometer**  precision instrument with spindle moved by finely threaded screw, used for measuring thicknesses and, by machinists, for turning shafts and boring holes

**miter box**  fixed or adjustable guide for saw angle, used in making a miter joint or crosscut

**miter square**  two straightedges joined at a 45 degree angle

**plumb bob**  weight hung on line, used to determine true vertical line; plummet

**plumb rule**  narrow board with plumb line and bob suspended from upper edge, used to determine verticality

**plummet**  plumb bob

**protractor**  device for measuring and marking off angles, esp. on drawings and plans

**rafter square**  roofer's square with premarked rafter tables for cutting hips and joists

**rule**  length of straight, hard material marked in units for measuring; straightedge

**ruler**  rule

**scale**  any of various devices for determining weight of objects

**scratch awl**  long blade tapering to sharp point for making fine marks

**screed** wooden strip that serves as guide for making a true level surface, esp. by dragging it across freshly poured concrete

**scriber** pointed tool for marking wood as guide for cutting or assembly

**slide caliper** pocket caliper with ruler along which one arm slides

**square** any instrument with straight edges and at least one ninety degree angle, used to plot right angles

**straightedge** length of straight, rigid material for measuring or marking; rule

**tape measure** narrow strip of flexible material, often in coil, marked off in measuring units

**try square** pair of straightedges fixed at right angles to one another, used to lay out right angles or test squareness

**T square** rule with perpendicular crosspiece at one end, used for marking parallel lines

**turning caliper** caliper into which a cutting or parting tool fits, used to make repetitive sizing cuts in turning

**vernier caliper** caliper in which two pieces slide across one another, one piece having a movable, graduated scale running parallel to the scale on the other piece

**wing divider** device consisting of adjustable arms and a graduated gauge for dividing lines and scribing circles

### OTHER MEASURING AND MARKING TOOLS

adjustable bevel, adjustable square, automatic center punch
bevel square
carpenter's level, carpenter's square, chalk, chalk line, charcoal
depth gauge, dial caliper, diameter gauge, dovetail square
flex, flex tape, framing square
grease pencil, guide
height gauge
machinist's rule, machinist's square, mortise gauge
pencil, power miter box
right angle
sizing caliper, sliding bevel, spirit level, steel rule, studfinder
T-bevel, trammel
zigzag rule

## MISCELLANEOUS TOOLS, OBJECTS, AND SUPPLIES

**bench** long table providing workspace and tool storage

**blowtorch** small, portable device blasting out intense gasoline flame, used in metalworking

**broom** stiff, bundled fibers attached to long handle, used for sweeping

**brush** close-set bristles on short handle, used for painting, sweeping, or cleaning

**cant hook** blunt-ended lumberjack's lever with hooked arm

**carpenter's apron** heavy, often canvas, protective covering for trunk and upper legs, having pouches, pockets, and loops to hold tools and supplies

**carpenter's belt** heavy leather belt with loops and other attachments for carrying tools

**dolly** wheeled platform, sometimes with handles, for moving heavy objects

**dust mask** small filter in frame that fits over mouth and nose, providing protection from dust and nontoxic fumes

**earplug** plug placed in ear to block out job noise

**extension ladder** adjustable ladder with two or more levels which may be extended and locked in place for greater height

**face guard** face shield

**face shield** protective visor covering entire face with transparent section for eyes; face guard

**flail** short, thick, wooden stick loosely attached to handle, for threshing

**flashlight** small, portable electric lamp, usu. battery-powered, that gives off a directed beam of light

**funnel** hollow cone narrowing to long tube for focusing downward flow of liquids

**gaff** barbed hook on handle, used esp. for lifting; spur attached to shoe for climbing

**glue gun** device that holds and fires stream of melted glue

**gluepot** double boiler in which glue is melted and stored

**glue press** large, stationary, multibeamed press for producing glue

**grease gun** handheld device for directing pressurized flow of thick lubricant

**hammer holster** leather loop attached to carpenter's belt, used to hold hammer

**hard hat** sturdy, framed, protective helmet made of metal or fiberglass

**hawk** small, square board on handle, used to hold mortar or plaster

**hearing protectors** earplugs or coverings for ears designed to reduce damage from exposure to noise of power tools

**hose** flexible tube through which fluids flow to a point

**jack** any of various portable devices for lifting or supporting weight

**jackscrew** jack operated by a screw that is steadied by a threaded support, having a plate to bear load

**jack stand** base with plate for supporting heavy object that has been lifted by a jack

**ladder** two long, rigid strips connected at intervals by crosspieces on which one steps to climb

**mop** absorbent cloth or fibers attached to handle, used for cleaning, esp. floors

**mortar** hard receptacle in which material is ground or pounded with pestle

**nail pouch** bag for carrying nails, as on carpenter's belt

**oilcan** metal container for oil, usu. with narrow spout

**padlock** detachable lock with pivoted or sliding shackle that can be passed through loop or ring

**paintbrush** closely bunched bristles on handle, used to apply paint

**paint pot** jar or other deep container for holding paint

**paint roller** cylinder of absorbent material set perpendicular at end of handle, used to apply wide swaths of paint

**paint tray** flat, wide receptacle for holding paint, esp. for use with roller

**platform truck** wheeled device with handles, used to move heavy objects

**plumber's helper** plunger

**plunger** rubber suction cup on handle, used to unblock obstructed pipes and traps by suction; plumber's helper

**respirator** protective mask used when spraying toxic finishes

**safety goggles** protective eyeglasses, sometimes tinted and ventilated at sides, encased in frames that rest on cheeks and brow

**sawbuck** sawhorse

**sawhorse** movable frame or trestle for supporting wood being sawed; sawbuck

**scaffold** elevated platform for supporting workers during building construction or repair

**soldering iron** often electrically powered device for melting and applying metal alloys used to fuse metal objects together

**sponge** chunk of porous skeletal matter from various marine animals, used to absorb liquid

**sprinkler** device for scattering liquid in fine drops

**squeegee** rubber blade on handle for spreading or wiping liquids over a surface

**stepladder** small, freestanding, portable ladder with hinged support stand

**straight ladder** usu. tall, single length of ladder that is leaned against a stationary surface for support

**toolbox** receptacle or case, often of metal, in which tools are stored

**tool cabinet** shelf with multiple compartments and hooks for storage and display of tools

**tool kit** small, portable tool container

**welder** gas-powered or electrical machine tool, used for cutting and joining metal parts by heating them to molten state

**wood-burning kit** electrical hand tool with multiple attachments, used to burn ornamental details and designs into woodwork

**workbench** sturdy table with broad surface at which work is performed

## Hardware and Supplies

**adapter** any of various pieces of hardware that permit non-matching parts to mesh, connect, or function together

**Allen screw** screw turned by insertion of Allen wrench into hexagonal hole cut into axis of screwhead

**alligator clip** clip with long, narrow, toothed jaws, used esp. for electrical connections

**anchor bolt** bolt inserted and fixed in masonry to hold timbers or shelves

**arbor** any spindle or bar that holds rotating cutting tools

**ball bearing** bearing composed of several hard balls running in grooves of two concentric rings, one of which is mounted on a rotating or oscillating shaft

**beam anchor** wall anchor

**bearing** supporting and guiding part of machine, in which another part moves smoothly

**bibcock** faucet with nozzle bent downward

**bit** detachable, usu. interchangeable cutting, drilling, or boring part of tool, available in various sizes suited to hole desired or specific need; drill bit

**blade** broad, thin, flat, sharpened edge of cutting tool

**boat nail** nail having convex head and chisel point

**bolt** metal fastening rod, threaded at one end, held in place by nut

**box nail** long nail with flat head

**box nut** nut with blind hole closed off at one end; cap nut

**brace** device that clasps or connects two pieces

**bracket** projecting support element, esp. for attaching a horizontally set piece to a vertical surface

**brad** thin wire nail with barrel head; thin nail, tapering in width, with lip at top of one side of head

**buckle** clasp consisting of rim with one or more movable tongues, fixed to one end of a strap and fastened to the other end

**bushing** removable lining or sleeve inserted in an opening to resist wear or serve as guide

**butt hinge** hinge secured to the butting surfaces of a door or the like

**cable** strong, heavy rope made of metal strands

**cap** fitted covering for end of something, esp. tube or pipe

**cap nut** box nut

**caster** small, swiveling wheel used to support and move heavy objects, esp. furniture

**catch** latch or other device for checking motion

**chain** length of connected metal links used for support or transmission of power

**chevron** L-shaped metal connector hammered into two pieces of wood to form strong miter joint, hidden beneath surface of wood and covered with putty; pair of pinch dogs connected at right angle

**chuck** clamplike device by which work to be turned is held; threaded portion of drill bit

**clamp** device holding two or more objects firmly together

**clevis** U-shaped yoke at end of chain or rod, through which hook or lever can be pinned or bolted

**clip** gripping device using pinching action of two hinged arms

**collar** protective or controlling ring or band at one end of a rod or shaft

**common nail** any of various size nails, distinguished from finishing nail by having wider head

**corner brace** L-shaped connecting piece

**cotter** pin, wedge, or key fitted or driven into opening to hold parts together

**cotter pin** split metal strip, whose arms are separated after insertion in hole to hold position

**crank** bent end of shaft by which circular motion is transmitted to or from shaft

**cross-garnet** T-shaped strap-hinge with stationary cross-piece

**cut nail** tapering, rectangular-shaped nail with blunt point

**doornail** large-headed nail formerly used for strengthening doors

**driftbolt** spike having round shank, used to fasten heavy timbers together; driftpin

**drill bit** bit

**elbow** pipe fitting or connection with right-angled bend

**expansion bolt** bolt inserted into hole in machinery and mechanically expanded to serve as anchor for something

**eye** loop through which hook slips to fasten something

**eyebolt** bolt with ring-shaped head

**eyelet** grommet

**female adapter** recessed element of connection that receives male adapter

**finishing nail** thin nail with very small, globular head, driven to point just beneath wood surface and concealed by filler or sawdust

**flange** strip along length or around end of object, such as pipe, for directing or strengthening

**gasket** ring, esp. of rubber or tallowed rope, placed or packed around piston or joint to make it fluid-tight

**gooseneck** iron pipe joint bent like neck of goose

**grommet** metal ring for lining small opening in soft material to protect or strengthen it; eyelet

**guide** device that regulates or controls motion or direction of another piece

**hanger bolt** bolt with tapered lag-screw thread on one end and machine-bolt thread on the other, used in timber construction

**hardware** metalware usu. forming functional or decorative component part

**hasp** fastening device consisting of hinged, metal strap held in place over staple by pin

**hinge** jointed device on which a movable part turns or swings freely

**hook** bent piece of inflexible material for restricting movement of attached object

**hook and eye** latching device consisting of hook and loop or screw eye through which the hook slips

**hoop** circular band of stiff material, used esp. to hold something together

**jam nut** thin, supplementary nut screwed down on regular nut to prevent it from loosening

**joint** connection, often reinforced, between two pieces of similar material, esp. between two sections of pipe

**knob** usu. rounded projection, esp. used as handle

**knuckle** cylindrical projecting part of hinge, through which a pin passes

**L** elbow or L-shaped support piece, usu. metal

**lag screw** wood screw with flat, boltlike head, used esp. with expandable metal anchor in concrete or stone

**latch** bar sliding into a catch, groove, or hole, used to hold movable part in place

**lock nut** nut with extra friction between itself and screw to prevent it from loosening

**lug nut** capped nut used esp. to attach automobile tires

**machine bolt** large bolt with square or hexagonal head and threads on lower portion for use with nut; machine screw

**machine screw** machine bolt

**male adapter** extending element of connection that enters female adapter

**nail** thin, tapering, pointed fastening device, usu. of metal, with head that is pounded to drive point into object that is to be held in place, made in various lengths designated by penny number, usu. up to sixty penny or 6 inches (15 cm) long

**nipple** piece of pipe threaded on each end, used for joining valves

**nut** any open ring-shaped, hexagonal, or square piece of metal with internal threads for tightening over end of bolt

**O-ring** ring made of rubber or other flexible material, used as gasket

**pad** soft, cushioning, protective insert

**Phillips head screw** screw with cross-shaped notches in its head

**pin** slender piece of hard material inserted into hole to secure something

**pinch dog** metal connector with points at either end that are driven below surface of two pieces of wood and covered with putty

**pipe** length of hollow, cylindrical tubing for conducting gas or liquid

**pipe fitting** coupling, such as elbow or tee, for connecting pipe sections

**plate** flat sheet of metal of uniform thickness, used as base or covering

**plug** small stopper that fits securely into opening to prevent passage of gas or liquid; wooden filler produced by plug cutter

**pull** handle, knob, or other piece of hardware that is pulled

**ring** fitted round band used for hanging, securing, or sealing

**ringbolt** bolt with ring fitted in an eye at its head

**rivet** metal pin or bolt passed through two or more pieces and pressed down at both ends to fasten them

**rod** length of straight, thin metal or other hard material for securing or connecting objects

**roofing nail** short nail with broad head, used for nailing down asphalt roofing shingles

**rubber washer** washer made of rubber that compresses to form tight seal

**screw** thin fastening device with spiral groove threaded around its length, secured by rotating it into object that is to be held: lag, machine, set, or wood

**screw eye** screw having ring-shaped head

**screw nail** fastener with helical thread and point that can be driven into wood with hammer and removed with screwdriver; drive screw

**setscrew** machine screw that passes through threaded hole in one part and into another to prevent movement

**shackle** U-shaped fastening or coupling piece, esp. bar of a padlock

**slide** moving part on track, channel, or guide rails

**snap ring** ring that must be forced open for use and snaps shut to make snug fit

**spike** long, heavy, naillike fastener for heavy timbers or railroad ties

**spring** spiral elastic device for exerting pressure by compression or contraction, recovering original shape when released

**square nut** nut with square sides

**staple** U-shaped loop of metal attached to something and through which a hasp, bolt, wire, or rope is secured fast

**stirrup** U-shaped or W-shaped rod for supporting longitudinal reinforcing rods

**strap-hinge** hinge having one long flap attached to face of movable object such as door

**stud** projecting rivet or infixed rod used for fastening or as a support

**switch** electrical device for altering, closing off, or releasing flow of current

**swivel** connecting device that allows both connected objects to pivot freely

**tack** short, sharp nail with broad head

**thumbscrew** screw with head shaped so that it can be turned with thumb and forefinger

**thumbtack** tack with wide flat head that can be pushed into material with thumb

**toggle bolt** bolt consisting of screw and two hinged arms which open when inserted, used to hold heavy objects in soft material

**trap** U- or S-shaped section of pipe under sink that seals off sewer gases treenail  wooden pin that swells when moist, used to fasten timbers together

turnbuckle  sleeve with swivel at one end and internal screw thread at other, or thread at each end, used for coupling or tightening two parts

U bolt  U-shaped bolt with screw thread and nut on each arm

upholstery tack  small tack used to attach material in upholstering furniture

valve  device for controlling flow of gas or liquid, as through pipe, by opening and closing

volute spring  conical coil spring extending in direction of axis of the coil

wall anchor  heavy-duty device used to tie walls together; beam anchor

washer  flat, thin ring used, esp. with bolt and nut, to increase tightness, prevent leakage, or distribute pressure

waste nut  internally threaded floor flange for pipe

wing bolt  bolt having flared head like wing nut

wing nut  nut with two flat, flared sides for turning between thumb and forefinger

wire nail  thin nail made of wire, designed for specific use such as finishing

wood screw  screw tapering to sharp point for use in wood

wye  Y-shaped connecting device, esp. for three-phase electrical circuit

### OTHER HARDWARE AND SUPPLIES

angle brace, angle bracket, astragal

backflap hinge, ball catch, bar bracket, barrel bolt, bell, bend, B nut, brad nail, brass screw, bullet catch, bullet latch, bumper, butterfly hook, buttonhook

cabinet knob, cabinet pull, cad cut washer, castellated nut, chain bolt, channel, climbing iron, coated nail, coil spring, concealed hinge, Condulet, continuous pull, corrugated nail, coupler, coupling, cover plate, crook, cross, cutoff riser

deadlock, deep thread screw, door slide, dowel screw, drawer slide, driftpin, drive screw, drop-leaf hinge, drop ring pull, drywall screw

edge pull, ell, extension bolt

fence bracket, finger pull, finish washer, flat head screw, flat washer, flex connector, flipper slide, flush mount, flush pull

galvanized nail, gate, glide

hexagonal nut

jet rail bracket, joist hanger

kep nut, kick plate, knife bracket

lazy Susan, lead shield, leg bracket, leveler, lock washer

magnetic catch, masonry nail, mending plate, metal screw, Molly fastener

nut-driver, nut-runner

outlet, oval head screw

panhead screw, piano hinge, pipe strap, pivot hinge, plastic shield, plate strap, plug clip, P-trap, pushpin

Rawl plug, riser extension, rod coupling, rope clip, round head screw

safety plate, sash lock, screw shield, sheave, shelf rest, socket head screw, Soss hinge, speed nut, spiral spring, spud washer, square U bolt, stanchion, standard, stay, strip, studfinder

tapping screw, tee, T hinge, threaded insert, threaded rod, Tite-joint, T nut, Toggler, touch bar, touch latch, track

union

wall box, wet post anchor, wire nut

# KNOTS

**SEE ALSO**: Chap. 6: Ships and Boats; Chap. 17: Hunting and Fishing

anchor knot  fisherman's bend

barrel knot  fisherman's knot used esp. to fasten together two strands of leader; blood knot

becket bend  sheet bend

bend  any loop or knot for joining end of one rope to another rope or to some other object, esp. nautical

bight  middle portion of rope, esp. when looped or bent, as distinct from ends

bitter end  inboard end of nautical line

Blackwall hitch  hitch for temporarily securing line to hook

blood knot  barrel knot

bow  knot comprised of two or more loops and two ends, used esp. to tie together ends of ribbon or string; bowknot

bowknot  bow

bowline  knot used to make nonslipping loop at end of rope

builder's knot  clove hitch

carrick bend  knot or bend for joining ends of two ropes

cat's-paw  nautical hitch in middle of rope forming two eyes to hold hook

clinch  knot in which eye is made by looping the rope and seizing one end to a standing part

clove hitch  knot for fastening rope to spar or larger rope, consisting of two half hitches made in opposite directions; builder's knot

crown  knot made by interweaving the strands at the end of a rope, usu. as first stage in tying knot

cuckold's neck  nautical hitch for holding spar, consisting of single loop with overlapping parts of rope held together; ring seizing; throat seizing

diamond hitch  knot for tying pack to an animal, in which interlacing ropes form a diamond atop the load

diamond knot  diamond-shaped knot tied in strands of rope

double knot  any knot formed by repeating the tying process

eye  loop formed at end of rope

figure of eight  knot resembling the numeral 8, formed by looping rope around itself twice, the second loop above the first

fisherman's bend  knot for attaching rope to an object, made by passing end of rope around object and the standing part and then under the round turn; anchor knot

flat knot  reef knot

flat seizing  seizing in which lines are parallel and a single binding layer is used

granny knot  faulty square knot in which bights cross each other in the wrong direction; lubber's knot

half hitch  knot made by forming loop and passing end of rope around the standing part and through the loop

half-knot  common knot joining the ends of two ropes, used to make square and other knots

harness hitch  hitch forming loop around rope, esp. at end of bowline

hawser bend  nautical knot joining the ends of two lines

**heaving-line bend**  nautical knot for attaching the end of a weighted heaving line to a hawser

**hitch**  any of various knots used to attach rope to something so as to be easily loosened

**inside clinch**  clinch knot with the seized end of line inside the noose

**knot**  interlacing, looping, bending, hitching, or folding together of pliant, slender length of cord or rope so as to fasten, bind, or connect two such lengths together or one length to something else

**lanyard knot**  stopper knot

**lash**  binding or fastening with rope or cord

**loop**  section of rope folded or doubled upon itself, leaving an opening between parts

**loop knot**  knot made by doubling over line at its end and tying both parts into square knot so as to leave a loop; open hand knot

**lubber's knot**  granny knot

**Magnus hitch**  knot for fastening rope to spar or larger rope, consisting of clove hitch with one more turn around object to which rope is bent

**manrope knot**  double wall knot with double crown, used to attach a manrope railing to its gangway or ladder

**marlinespike hitch**  hitch into which pointed metal implement is inserted in order to draw the seizing taut

**marling hitch**  one of a series of knots used to lash long rolls or bundles

**Matthew Walker**  knot formed at end of rope by retying loosened strands

**mesh knot**  sheet bend

**midshipman's hitch**  nautical hitch made by tying a rolling hitch with end of line to the standing part

**nail knot**  nooselike fisherman's knot that tightens when pulled and does not slip

**netting knot**  sheet bend

**noose**  loop with running knot that tightens as rope is pulled

**open hand knot**  loop knot

**outside clinch**  clinch knot with seized end of line outside noose

**overhand knot**  simple, small knot that slips easily, used as part of another knot or to prevent ends from fraying; single knot; thumb knot

**prolonge knot**  knot made up of three overlapping loops formed by passing a single rope over and under itself at crossings; sailor's breastplate

**reef knot**  nautical square knot used in tying down sails; flat knot

**reeving-line bend**  nautical bend for joining two lines so that they will pass easily through a hole or ring

**ring seizing**  cuckold's neck

**rolling hitch**  nautical hitch on a spar, composed of two round turns and a half hitch, that tightens under stress applied parallel to the spar

**rope-yarn knot**  knot made by splitting rope yarns apart and joining their ends in half-knots

**round seizing**  seizing in which lines are parallel and a double binding layer is used

**round turn**  complete turn of rope around object

**running bowline**  slipnoose made by tying end of bowline around its own standing part

**running knot**  knot made around and sliding along the standing part of the same rope, thus forming a noose

**running part**  part of rope or tackle that is hauled upon, separate from the standing part

**sailor's breastplate**  prolonge knot

**seizing**  method of binding or fastening together two ropes or parts of same rope by a number of longitudinal and transverse turns

**sheepshank**  knot, bend, or turn used to shorten rope, often temporarily

**sheet bend**  bend or hitch used to fasten rope temporarily to the bight of another rope or to an eye; becket bend; mesh knot; netting knot; weaver's knot

**single knot**  overhand knot

**slide knot**  knot formed by two half hitches on the standing part, the second hitch being next to the loop, which can be tightened

**slipknot**  any knot that rides easily along rope or cord around which it is made, esp. an overhand knot on the standing part

**slipnoose**  noose whose knot slides along the rope, tightening as the rope is pulled

**splice**  joining together of two ropes or rope strands by interweaving of strands

**square knot**  common knot formed of two half-knots, used to join two rope ends that emerge alongside standing part

**standing part**  length of rope that is in use and terminates in a knot or around which a knot is formed

**stevedore's knot**  stopper knot

**stopper knot**  knot forming a lump to prevent rope from passing through a hole or opening; lanyard knot; stevedore's knot

**stunner hitch**  double Blackwall hitch

**surgeon's knot**  knot similar to reef knot, used by surgeons to tie ligatures

**tack bend**  bend or loop used for temporary fastening

**throat seizing**  cuckold's neck

**thumb knot**  overhand knot

**timber hitch**  nautical knot or hitch formed by taking a turn on the spar, wrapping the end around the standing part, then several times around itself

**truelove knot**  elaborate, ornamental double knot formed by two interlacing bows

**Turk's-head**  turbanlike knot of small cords, formed around rope or spar

**turle knot**  fisherman's knot used to attach artificial fly or eyed hook to leader

**turn**  passing or twisting of rope or cord around itself, another rope or cord, or some object

**wall knot**  overhand or double knot made by interweaving strands at end of rope, terminating in crown or double crown

**weaver's knot**  sheet bend

**Windsor knot**  wide, triangular knot used for tying four-in-hand necktie

# CONTAINERS

Cases, Boxes, and Bags
Baskets

**SEE ALSO**: Chap. 7: Furnishings; Ornamental and Functional Articles; Chap. 9: The Kitchen; Chap. 10: Ornaments and Accessories

## RECEPTACLES AND CASKS

**ashcan** metal can for trash

**ashtray** small receptacle for tobacco ashes, cigarette and cigar butts

**barrel** bulging cylindrical vessel made of staves held together with hoops and having flat parallel ends the same size

**billycan** metal or enamel container with one open end, used for outdoor cooking or to carry food

**breaker** small water container in lifeboat

**bucket** pail

**butt** large cask for wine, beer, or water

**caddy** small box, can, or chest, used to store frequently used items

**cage** enclosure with wire or bars, used to confine people or animals

**can** cylindrical receptacle, usu. of metal, open at one end or closed off to seal in contents

**canister** cylindrical metal receptacle with removable, close-fitting top

**cannikin** wooden bucket; small can

**cask** barrel-shaped container for liquids

**catchall** container for miscellaneous articles

**cistern** large, underground reservoir for storing rainwater or other liquid

**coal scuttle** deep metal bucket with handle and lip, used to hold coal; hod

**coaster** small dish or mat placed under glass to protect furniture

**container** anything that holds other objects within itself

**crock** thick earthenware pot or jar

**crucible** vessel made of metal or refractory material, used to melt substances at high heat

**dinner pail** enclosed pail, carried by worker, that contains food

**drum** large, cylindrical receptacle, usu. for liquids

**Dumpster** *Trademark.* very large, metal trash container, usu. emptied directly into dump truck

**dustbin** *Chiefly Brit.* garbage can

**firkin** small, lidded, wood or metal cask

**gallipot** small ceramic vessel with small mouth, used by pharmacists for medicine

**garbage can** usu. metal container in variety of sizes, used to hold trash

**harness cask** tub on ship, used to soak and store salt meat prior to use

**hod** trough with pole handle, carried on shoulders for mortar or bricks; coal scuttle

**hogshead** large barrel or cask holding 63 to 140 gallons (238 to 530 l)

**hopper** funnel-shaped receptacle with opening at bottom, used for temporary storage and delivery of material; tank for liquids with mechanism that allows release of contents through pipe

**jemcan** container for liquids holding 5 gallons (18.9 l)

**keg** small cask or barrel holding 30 gallons (113.6 l) or less; rundlet

**kibble** iron bucket used in mines to hoist ore

**kilderkin** cask equal in size to half a barrel

**magazine** room or storage place for supplies, esp. ammunition

**mess kit** portable container used to cook and hold food, usu. by soldiers

**milk pail** receptacle into which cow's milk falls during milking

**mortar** small, bowllike porcelain vessel used to pound substances with pestle

**mortarboard** three-foot square board that holds mortar

**oilcan** can with long, slim spout, used to oil machinery

**pail** cylindrical vessel, usu. with handle, used to carry liquids or solids; bucket

**palette** thin oval or oblong board on which artist saves and mixes pigments

**piggin** wooden, pail-shaped vessel with one stave reaching above rim as handle

**pipe** cask, esp. for wine, holding two hogsheads, or 126 gallons (476 l)

**pipkin** small earthenware pot with horizontal handle

**pitcher** container that holds and dispenses liquids, made of glass, earthenware, or plastic, with wide mouth having lip on one side and handle on other

**plate** shallow, usu. round vessel of earthenware, glass, plastic, or metal that holds food

**powder horn** container for gunpowder made from horn of ox or cow

**puncheon** large cask in variety of sizes, usu. 80 gallons (304 l)

**receptacle** any open storage container

**rundlet** keg

**salver** tray used to serve food or drinks

**saucer** small plate, esp. with indentation at center for holding cup

**slop pail** bucket used for toilet or household wastes

**tank** large enclosed container, often cylindrical, used for storing or carrying gas or liquid

**tin can** can made of tin

**trash can** large metal container, esp. for dry refuse

**tray** flat receptacle with low rim, used to carry, hold, or exhibit objects

**trencher** wood tray used to serve food

**tub** wide, low receptacle with flat bottom

**tun** large cask that holds wine or beer

**vat** large tub or barrel, usu. for liquids

**waiter** tray on which tea service is carried

**wastepaper basket** small trash can, used for discarded papers

**watering can** metal can with long spout and narrow mouth, used to water plants by hand

## BASINS, LADLES, CUPS, AND POTS

**ashpan** pan under grate, used to collect ashes

**bail** container used to remove water from boat

**basin** shallow, round vessel with sloping sides, used to hold water, esp. for washing

**beaker** large, widemouthed drinking cup without handles

**biggin** percolator or pot with stand and lamp, used to warm coffee (19th c.)

**blackjack** large beer mug made of leather coated with tar

**bowl** deep, round dish with wide opening at top

**calabash** hard rind of inedible calabash fruit, used as dipper, bottle, or kettle; gourd

**caldron** large kettle

**cannikin** small can or cup

**cistern** large, silver vessel used to cool wine at dinner table

**cup** small, bowl-shaped drinking vessel with handle and base

**cuspidor** spittoon

**cyathus** long-handled ladle used to fill wine cups (ancient Greece)

**dipper** cup or ladle with handle, used to scoop up liquids

**flowerpot** usu. round container with small hole in bottom, used for growing plants

**gourd** hard rind from any of various fruits, used as dipper or kettle

**horn** hollowed animal horn used for drinking or for holding ink or gun powder

**jardiniere** large, round, decorative flowerpot

**jorum** large drinking vessel

**kettle** container for boiling liquids, cooking foods, etc.

**ladle** long-handled, cuplike spoon used for dipping or conveying liquids

**macock** horn in shape of animal's head, used for drinking (ancient Greece)

**mug** cylindrical drinking cup, usu. with handle

**pan** broad, shallow, open household container, usu. round

**patella** small pan or vase (ancient Rome)

**patera** metal or earthenware drinking saucer, once used for sacrificial libations (ancient Rome)

**pipkin** small metal or earthenware pot with horizontal handle

**porringer** small, shallow, one-handled bowl used to feed children; pottinger

**pot** deep, metal or earthenware container with handle, usu. round, used esp. for cooking

**pottinger** porringer

**rhyton** earthenware horn with base in shape of head of animal or mythological creature, used for drinking (ancient Greece)

**scoop** any of various open, hemispherical utensils used to remove liquid or loose materials

**shovel** large hand tool with broad scoop and handle, used for lifting or scooping

**spade** heavy digging tool with flat blade and long handle

**spittoon** low, round receptacle used for disposal of tobacco juice; cuspidor

**trough** long, shallow receptacle that holds animal's water or feed

**trowel** scoop-shaped hand tool used to dig in or plant gardens

**urn** vase on pedestal

**vase** tall, hollow vessel of porcelain, glass, metal, or earthenware, used to hold flowers or decoration

**vessel** hollow or deep container that holds objects, esp. liquid

**washbasin** bowl used for washing hands or face

**washtub** usu. round metal tub used to wash clothes

**water butt** receptacle for water, as in fountain or lavatory

## BOTTLES

**amphora** tall jar with narrow neck and base and two handles (ancient Greece)

**beaker** deep, thin, glass laboratory vessel with lip, used for pouring

**bottle** usu. glass or plastic rigid container for liquids with narrow neck and no handle, sometimes with cap

**canteen** hip flask used by soldiers or campers to carry water

**carafe** ornamental glass vessel with narrow neck and wider mouth, used for holding water or wine

**carboy** large bottle encased in protective wooden crate, used to hold corrosive liquids

**caster** small glass container used to serve condiments; cruet

**cruet** caster

**cruse** small earthenware container for oil, honey, or water

**decanter** ornamental glass bottle used to serve wine

**demijohn** glass bottle with capacity of 1 to 10 gallons (3.79 to 37.9 l), encased in wicker, with one or two handles

**ewer** wide-mouthed jug or pitcher made of brass or ceramics

**fifth** bottle that holds 1/5 gallon (0.76 l) of liquid

**flacon** small flask with tight cap, used to hold perfume

**flagon** large vessel with handle, spout, and lid, used to hold wine or liquor

**flask** flat container with neck and stopper, used for holding liquid, usu. carried in jacket or pants pocket

**flasket** small flask

**ginger jar** ceramic jar with wide mouth, globular body, and domed cover (China)

**jar** usu. cylindrical glass or earthenware container with no spout and large opening on top, capable of being sealed at top

**jeroboam** oversize wine bottle that holds 3 liters (3.17 quarts)

**jug** large, deep glass or earthenware container for liquids, with handle and small opening at top

**hip flask** flask worn attached to belt

**hot-water bottle** soft rubber container with stopper, used to hold hot water

**krater** jar with broad body, wide neck, and two handles (ancient Greece)

**lota** brass or copper water vessel (India)

**magnum** wine bottle that holds 2/5 gallon (1.52 l)

**olla** large earthenware jug with wide mouth and looped handles, used as water container or stewpot (Spain)

**phial** small, sealed glass container, used esp. to hold medicine; vial

**pocket flask** small flask carried in pocket

**potiche** vase or jar made of porcelain with rounded body that narrows at top

**rehoboam** oversize champagne bottle holding 5 quarts (4.73 l)

**stoup** flagon or tankard

**tankard** tall, one-handled vessel, esp. of pewter, often with hinged cover, used for drinking

**thermos** vacuum bottle

**vacuum bottle** tall, cylindrical container, usu. of metal or plastic, with glass or stainless steel vacuum liner and tight-fitting lid, used for maintaining liquids at original temperature for several hours; thermos

**vial** phial

# CASES, BOXES, AND BAGS

**ammunition box** container used to store firearm ammunition

**ark** orig. covered basket or small chest

**backpack** lightweight canvas or nylon sack, often on frame, used to carry objects on back while walking

**bag** flexible, pouchlike container that may be closed, used to hold, store, or carry objects

**bin** box, frame, or enclosure used for storage

**bindle** bundle that contains clothes and cooking utensils

**boot** leather case used to carry rifle; *Chiefly Brit.* trunk of automobile

**box** rigid, usu. rectangular container used to store or carry nonliquid articles

**bridget** leather pouch or pack carried on back

**bundle** package, usu. bound

**bunker** large bin, esp. one used to store ship's coal or oil

**caddie bag** bag used to carry golf clubs

**caisson** ammunition box; watertight enclosure used for underwater construction

**capsule** small gelatin shell, used esp. to enclose medicine

**card case** small rectangular receptacle used to carry business cards

**carton** cardboard box

**case** usu. flat box or receptacle that closes, used to store, ship, or carry objects

**casket** small ornamental chest; coffin

**cedar chest** large box made of cedar, used for protective storage of woolen items

**chest** storage box with lid, often with lock

**coffer** strongbox

**coffin** long, heavy box used for burial of corpse; casket

**cone** hollow, conical-shaped, baked cookie that holds scoop of ice cream

**crate** large, wood-framed container used for shipping wares

**crib** framework enclosure, esp. for animal or baby

**diplomatic pouch** sealed mail pouch, used to carry communications between diplomatic offices

**dispatch box** oblong box or case with lock, used to carry written dispatches

**envelope** flat paper container with gummed sealing flap

**file** metal or wooden cabinet used to organize stored papers for easy reference

**file folder** light, cardboard, folded cover or large envelope, used to hold loose papers stored in a file

**folio** case or folder that holds loose papers, often tied with ribbon

**footlocker** small, flat trunk with lock, esp. one that stands at foot of bunk in army barracks

**golf bag** bag used to carry golf clubs and balls

**gunny sack** loose burlap bag

**holdall** soft traveling bag

**holster** leather pistol case, open at the top, worn on belt or under one arm

**hope chest** box used to store young woman's collection of clothing and linen in anticipation of marriage

**housewife** pocketsize bag or roll of cloth that holds thread, needles, and scissors

**hussy** *Slang.* housewife

**kit** round, wood or metal shipping container with tapered sides

**kit bag** rectangular leather traveling bag with straps and sides that open

**letter file** file or file folder used for correspondence

**locker** usu. metal storage case, often built into wall

**mail pouch** large, reinforced envelope in which objects are sent through mails

**matchbox** small wood or cardboard box that holds matches

**moneybag** cloth sack used by banks to store and transport money

**money box** metal box with lock, used to store money

**monstrance** receptacle holding consecrated host for veneration by Catholics; ostensorium

**nesting box** one of a series of boxes in graduated sizes that may be stored within one another

**net** mesh of interwoven threads or ropes, used esp. to catch birds, fish, or insects

**nose bag** canvas bag that covers horse's muzzle and ties at top of head, used for feeding

**ostensorium** monstrance

**pack** bundle arranged for ease in carrying, esp. on back

**package** small or moderately sized bundle, usu. wrapped

**packet** small bundle, parcel, or thin package

**packing case** wooden shipping crate used for bulk goods

**packsack** leather or canvas backpack

**parcel** wrapped or tied bundle; package

**pillbox** small case that holds pills, usu. carried on person

**pod** protective pouch or removable housing

**portfolio** large, flat case with handle, used to carry papers or drawings without folding them

**pouch** sack or satchel of moderate size, used to store or transport goods

**powder box** heavy case, usu. metal, used to store gunpowder

**quiver** long, thin, cylindrical case, open at one end, used to carry arrows

**rack** framework on which bulky loads are arranged for carrying

**reliquary** casket or container used to exhibit relics

**sack** soft, large, usu. oblong bag

**sarcophagus** stone coffin with sculpture, placed in a church, tomb, or vault

**satchel** small bag, often with shoulder strap

**scabbard** leather or metal sheath that encloses blade of sword or dagger when not in use

**scrip** small bag or wallet carried by pilgrim or shepherd

**sheath** tightfitting, rigid case for sword or dagger

**skippet** small box that covers and preserves seal for documents

**sleeping bag** large, warmly padded bag in which to sleep outdoors

**socket** opening or hollow that forms receptacle for something

**strongbox** solid chest or case used to store money or valuables; coffer

**tea chest** square, wooden case lined with lead or tin, used for shipping tea

**till** money drawer behind counter in store or bank

**tinderbox** metal box that holds tinder, flint, and steel used in striking spark

**trunk** luggage with rigid frame, usu. too large to carry by hand, used for transporting clothes and personal items; enclosed storage compartment of car

**vanity bag** small case or handbag used to hold or transport toilet articles

**vanity case** rigid vanity bag

**vasculum** metal, cylindrical or flat box with lengthwise cover, used for collecting plants

**wallet** flat, folding leather case, used esp. for holding paper money

**wineskin** bag of animal skin, used to hold wine

## BASKETS

**basket** container made of interwoven cane, rushes, or strips of wood, open at top

**bassinet** small basketlike crib for infant, hooded at one end

**breadbasket** low basket, usu. of straw, used to hold and serve bread on table

**bushelbasket** round receptacle with capacity of 32 dry quarts (35.24 l)

**clothesbasket** oval basket used to hold and carry household laundry

**clothes hamper** wooden or plastic receptacle with lid, used to hold soiled laundry

**corbeil** sculptured basket of fruit or flowers, used as architectural ornament

**creel** wickerwork basket used to carry fish and fishing tackle

**dosser** pannier

**flower basket** wickerwork basket that holds or displays cut flowers

**frail** basket made of rushes, used for shipping figs or raisins

**fruit basket** basket that holds and displays fruit

**hamper** basket with lid, used for storage or to send food or other items; clothes hamper

**mocock** birch bark food basket (Algonquian Indian)

**pannier** wicker basket used to carry loads on back, often used in pairs when carried by pack animal or over rear wheel of bicycle; dosser

**punnet** *Chiefly Brit.* small fruit basket, often made of cardboard

**reed basket** basket woven of reeds

**rush basket** basket woven of rushes

**scuttle** shallow wood or wicker basket, used to carry or move loose substances

**sewing basket** small hamper used to store threads, needles, and thimbles

**skep** rough farm basket of twisted straw

**splint basket** rectangular basket of woven splints, with handle

**stave basket** basket formed of wood strips

**trug** coarse basket of wood strips, used to carry vegetables or flowers

**wash basket** often oval basket used to hold and carry household laundry

**wastebasket** small, open basket for discarded papers

**wastepaper basket** wastebasket

**wicker basket** basket of small flexible twigs

**wooden basket** basket of wood strips

# WEAPONS AND ARMAMENTS

Blades, Clubs, and Projectiles
Guns and Firearms
Firearm Parts, Accessories, and Processes
Bombs, Mines, and Explosives

**SEE ALSO:** Chap. 5: Tools and Hardware; Chap. 11: War and Military; Chap. 17: Hunting and Fishing; Chap. 24: Crime; Chap. 24: Violence

## BLADES, CLUBS, AND PROJECTILES

**anlace** tapering medieval dagger

**arbalest** crossbow

**archery** weaponry of bows and arrows

**armguard** band of leather or other material worn about wrist or forearm for protection and support, esp. while using bow

**arrow** pointed shaft, shot from bow

**arrowhead** wedge-shaped, stone or metal striking end of arrow

**assegai** slender, iron-tipped wood spear (southern Africa)

**atlatl** spear or throwing stick (ancient Mexico)

**ax** short, heavy blade affixed to long handle

**axe** ax

**backsword** single-edged sword

**ballista** crossbow; device used to hurl large missiles (ancient Rome)

**banderilla** decorated, barbed dart, used in bullfights

**barb** sharp, backward-extending projection on arrow

**barlow** sturdy, inexpensive jackknife

**barong** broad-bladed knife or sword (Philippines)

**bastinado** cudgel

**bat** stout stick or club

**baton** cudgel, truncheon

**battering ram** heavy beam used to beat down fortifications

**battle-ax** ax with heavy curved blade

**bayonet** short dagger; blade fitted on end of rifle

**bilbo** sword

**billy club** bludgeon

**blackjack** leather-covered club with flexible handle; cosh

**blade** flat, pointed, usu. sharp-edged piercing or slashing part of sword or knife

**blowgun** tube or pipe through which air is blown to propel dart or other missile; blowpipe; blowtube

**blowpipe** any of various blowguns used throughout Southeast Asia, on Malay Peninsula, and Indonesia: balasan, kahuk, kina, pocot, pucuna, sumpitan, tulup, zarabatana

**blowtube** blowgun

**bludgeon** club with thick, heavy striking end

**bola** two or more stones or iron balls at ends of cord, hurled at target (Latin America)

**bolo knife** long, heavy, single-edged knife, used for hacking

**bolt** missile or shaft shot from catapult; crossbow arrow, shorter than longbow arrow

**bombard** late-medieval cannon that hurled large stones

**boomerang** club bent at angle, thrown in arc; throwing stick (Australia)

**bow** curved, flexible frame used to propel arrow

**bow and arrow** curved, flexible frame fitted with arrow that is launched by spring tension

**bowie knife** foot-long, straight blade with slightly curved point

**brass knuckles** metal piece fitted over fingers at knuckles

**brickbat** hurled piece of brick

**broad arrow** arrow with flat, barbed head

**broadsword** broad-bladed sword

**butt shaft** target arrow without barbs

**catapult** ancient tension-powered device that hurled stones or other missiles

**clasp knife** pocketknife with one large, folding blade held open by catch

**claymore** large, two-edged, two-hand sword (Scotland)

**cleaver** butcher's heavy chopping knife, often with wood handle

**club** heavy stick or staff

**cosh** *Brit. slang.* blackjack

**crossbow** bow set horizontally on rigid stock or brace, used to fire arrows or bolts

**cudgel** heavy, short stick or club

**curtalax** cutlass

**cutlass** short, curved sword; curtalax

**dagger** weapon with short, straight, pointed blade attached to handle

**dart** short, slender, pointed missile, often ejected from blowpipe

**dirk** dagger

**dudgeon** dagger with handle of dudgeon wood

**elastic gun** cross between rifle and crossbow, having rifle-like body and crossbow firing mechanism

**elephant ax** heavy, sturdy ax hurled at big game, such as elephants

**epee** sharp-pointed sword with three-sided blade; fencing sword

**falchion** broad-bladed, slightly curved medieval sword

**flail** swinging bar attached to long handle, used in close combat

**flick-knife** *Chiefly Brit.* switchblade

**foil** blunt or button-pointed fencing sword with four-sided blade

**gladius** short, double-edged sword (ancient Rome)

**grip** handle or clasp portion of sword or knife

**halberd** long-handled, broad-bladed sword; pikestaff with axlike blade and spike

**handguard** lateral, protective piece dividing grip from blade of sword or knife

**hanger** light saber, often used by sailors (17th–18th c.)

**harpoon** large spear with barbed head

**harpoon gun** small cannon used to fire harpoons

**hatchet** ax with heavy, hammer-shaped head

**hilt** handle of sword or knife

**hunting knife** large knife with stout blade, used for skinning and cutting up game

**hunting sword** short, light saber with slightly curved blade (18th c.)

**Irish confetti** *Derogatory slang.* rocks used for stoning

**jackknife** small knife with folding blade

**javelin** light spear thrown long distances

**kard** knife with straight blade and no handguard (Southeast Asia)

**katana** samurai sword (Japan)

**kirpan** small dagger worn by orthodox Sikhs

**knife** any small, sharp-edged blade attached to handle

**knobkerrie** short wooden club with heavy round knob at one end, used hand-to-hand or hurled (southern Africa)

**kris** dagger with two scalloped edges and serpentine blade (Indonesia)

**kukri** short, curved sword of Gurkhas with broad blade that is sharp on its concave side (India, Nepal)

**kuttar** short dagger with handle consisting of two parallel bars joined by crosspiece (India)

**lance** long, spearlike, sharp-headed weapon

**Lochaber ax** pole with long ax head and hook attached (Scotland)

**longbow** large wooden bow, drawn by hand

**mace** spiked, heavy club, usu. metal

**machete** large, broad-bladed knife

**mangonel** medieval device for hurling stones, darts, or other missiles

**maul** heavy club with metal-studded head

**misericord** thin-bladed dagger

**nulla-nulla** Aboriginal hunting club or cudgel (Australia)

**nunchaku** two hardwood sticks joined at ends by short length of cord or chain (Japan)

**onager** heavy catapult

**panga** large, broad-bladed knife used as a weapon or like a machete to cut jungle growth (Africa)

**parang** short sword, cleaver, or machete (Malaysia)

**parazonium** dagger (ancient Greece)

**partisan** shafted weapon having spear blade as head with pair of curved lobes at its base (16th–17th c.)

**pikestaff** long shaft with pointed metal head

**pilum** long, heavy spear (ancient Rome)

**pocketknife** small knife with folding blade

**pogamoggan** flat, curved club with knobbed head or stone fastened at one end (American Indian)

**point** sharpened forepart of arrow, sword, knife, or spear

**poleax** battle-ax, esp. one with hook opposite blade

**pommel** knob on hilt of sword

**poniard** dagger with slender blade of triangular or square cross-section

**projectile** object fired or thrown through air, often long and pointed

**punji stake** sharp bamboo stake hidden in high grass to gash feet and legs of enemy, often coated with excrement so as to cause infection

**puntilla** small, sturdy dagger used to sever bull's spinal cord in bullfight

**quarterstaff** long, stout staff wielded with two hands

**quiver** sheath or long container for arrows

**rapier** straight, double-edged sword

**saber** long, curved sword

**sap** small club cut from sapling tree

**scabbard** sheath for sword, knife, or bayonet

**scimitar** saber with sharply curved, single-edged blade

**scythe** long, curved blade fastened at angle to long handle

**shaft** long pole forming body of weapon, as spear

**sheath** protective case for blade

**shillelagh** cudgel

**shiv** *Slang.* knife or blade

**skean dhu** small knife tucked into top of stocking in full Scottish Highland dress

**sling** device for hurling stones, consisting of short strap with long cords at each end, operated by placing stone in strap, which is then whirled until one cord is released to project the stone

**slingshot** forked, handheld bow used to launch stones or other projectiles

**slung shot** stone or chunk of metal fastened to strap or chain

**smallsword** light, tapering sword for thrusting, formerly used in dueling and fencing

**snickersnee** large knife used in cut-and-thrust fighting

**spatha** blunt-pointed sword (ancient Rome)

**spear** sharply bladed head mounted on long shaft

**spike** sharp-pointed piece of metal set with its point outward or upward

**spontoon** spear with crossbar at base of pointed blade on shaft (17th-18th c.)

**staff** club, lance, or spear

**stave** club, cudgel, or staff

**stick** crude wooden club

**stiletto** short dagger with thick blade

**Swiss army knife** *Trademark.* pocketknife with multiple, folding attachments

**switchblade** knife with folding blade that springs open; flick-knife

**sword** any long, bladed, pointed weapon

**throwing stick** short, straight or curved stick with hand grip, used for hunting in preliterate societies; *Australian.* boomerang

**Toledo** sword of fine-tempered steel (Spain)

**tomahawk** lightweight ax; combination pipe and ax (American Indian)

**trebuchet** medieval sling for hurling missiles

**trench knife** short knife for stabbing in close combat, sometimes equipped with brass knuckles as handguard

**trident** three-pronged spear, used for fishing

**truncheon** club, cudgel; spontoon

**twibill** double-edged battle-ax

**two-handed sword** heavy, broad-bladed sword swung with both hands on hilt

**waddy** heavy, tapered wooden war club (Australian Aborigine)

**war club** crude, club-shaped implement (American Indian)

**woomera** wooden rod with notched end, used to propel spear or projectile (Australian Aborigine)

**yataghan** long saber with doubly curved blade (Turkey)

## GUNS AND FIREARMS

**ack-ack** *Brit. slang.* antiaircraft gun

**air gun** air rifle

**air rifle** firearm powered by compressed air; air gun; toy rifle

**AK-47** automatic rifle

**antiaircraft gun** firearm used against attack by airplanes

**arms** weapons, esp. firearms

**assault rifle** usu. automatic rifle firing high-powered ammunition, often having pistol grip and long, detachable magazine

**autoloader** semiautomatic weapon, either gas-operated or recoil-operated

**automatic rifle** firearm that loads, fires, and ejects cartridges automatically while user depresses trigger

**basilisk** large, early cannon capable of firing a stone shot weighing 200 pounds (90.7 kg)

**bazooka** shoulder-fired rocket launcher

**BB gun** firearm that shoots small-sized shot, designated BB

**Big Bertha** *Informal.* large-bore cannon used by Germans (World War I)

**blunderbuss** short, old-fashioned, highly inaccurate firearm

**Bofors gun** usu. double-barreled, 40 mm automatic antiaircraft gun

**bolt-action rifle** firearm with hand-operated bolt as breechblock that unlocks to eject empty case and seals new cartridge in bolt assembly

**bombard** medieval cannon that threw stone balls

**break-action** basic single-shot shotgun

**breechloader** firearm loaded with cartridges at its rear or breech

**Bren gun** .303 caliber, gas-operated, clip-fed submachine gun

**Browning automatic rifle** .30 caliber, gas-operated, magazine-fed automatic rifle (World War II)

**Browning machine gun** .30 or .50 caliber, recoil-operated machine gun, fed by cartridge belt (World War II)

**burp gun** *Slang.* small submachine gun

**cannon** gun; large firearm mounted in place, firing explosive charges

**cap gun** toy pistol with paper holding very small explosive

**carbine** lightweight rifle of short overall length

**carronade** short, light iron cannon (Scotland, 18th c.)

**chassepot** bolt-action rifle that fires paper cartridges

**chokebore** shotgun with bore that narrows toward muzzle

**Colt** *Trademark.* brand of revolver

**culverin** early musket or long cannon (16th-17th c.)

**derringer** large caliber, very short-barreled pocket pistol

**double-barreled shotgun** double-action shotgun with two barrels, either side-by-side or over-and-under, often with two triggers

**elephant gun** very large caliber gun, .410 caliber or greater, used for hunting heavy, often dangerous game such as elephant, rhinoceros, lion, or Cape buffalo

**Enfield rifle** muzzle-loading .577 caliber rifle used by British in Crimean War; .30 caliber rifle used by U.S. troops (World War I)

**falcon** light cannon (15th-17th c.)

**field gun** gun mounted on wheels, used on field of war

**firearm** weapon that uses explosive charge to fire projectile at high speed

**firelock** gun having lock in which priming is ignited by sparks struck from flint and steel

**flamethrower** mounted or portable device that sprays ignited incendiary fuel at some distance

**flintlock** gun with old-fashioned firearm lock, esp. musket

**forty-five** .45 caliber pistol

**forty-four** .44 caliber pistol

**fusil** light flintlock musket

**Gatling gun** early, mounted machine gun with revolving cluster of barrels

**gun** any weapon consisting of metal tube (barrel) from

which projectile (bullet or shell) is discharged by force of explosive

**handgun** small, handheld firearm; pistol; revolver

**harpoon gun** mechanism used to fire harpoon

**harquebus** primitive, heavy matchlock or wheel-lock firearm (15th c.)

**heater** *Slang*. pistol

**Henry** .44 caliber, lever-action repeating rifle holding 16 rounds (U.S., 1860's)

**howitzer** lightweight, short cannon that fires charges with curved trajectory

**jingal** large musket fired from support, often mounted on carriage, formerly used in India and China

**lever-action rifle** early repeating firearm in which ejection of shell case and recocking are accomplished by hand-operated lever arm near trigger

**Long Tom** large, long-range gun mounted on ship's deck; towed 155 mm cannon (World War II)

**Luger** *Trademark*. brand of automatic 9 mm caliber pistol

**M-1** .30 caliber, gas-operated, clip-fed semiautomatic rifle (World War II)

**M-14** 7.62 mm gas-operated, magazine-fed automatic rifle

**M-16** 5.56 mm gas-operated, magazine-fed automatic rifle (1960's)

**machine gun** firearm that automatically loads and discharges cartridges for sustained periods

**machine pistol** fully automatic pistol; submachine gun

**magazine gun** repeater

**magnum** firearm using cartridges equipped with extra-large charge

**matchlock** firearm with old-fashioned slow-match mechanism as gunlock, esp. musket or handgun

**mitrailleuse** breechloading machine gun with several barrels

**mortar** short cannon

**musket** old-fashioned firearm with long barrel and smooth bore

**muzzleloader** firearm loaded through front end or muzzle by pouring powder in and stuffing rag patch down barrel

**over-and-under** double-action shotgun with barrels placed one above the other

**pepperbox** pistol with five or six revolving barrels (18th c.)

**percussion gun** firearm with percussion lock fired by detonation of cap that is struck by hammer

**petronel** large-caliber firearm that fired with butt resting against chest (15th-17th c.)

**piece** gun

**pistol** small, handheld firearm; handgun

**pompom** automatic antiaircraft cannon of 20 mm to 40 mm, esp. mounted on ships in pairs

**popgun** toy gun

**pump-action** *(adj)* designating manually operated repeating shotgun or rifle; slide-action

**pump gun** firearm operated by pumping action that advances new cartridges

**recoilless rifle** firearm without rebound motion from firing

**recoil-operated rifle** firearm that utilizes kickback movement of parts to operate action

**repeater** rapid-firing, small firearm; magazine gun

**revolver** small firearm with revolving chamber for cartridges; handgun; pistol

**rifle** firearm having long bore cut with spiral interior

grooves that spin and thus stabilize bullet's flight, usu. fired from shoulder

**rocket launcher** tube used to fire rocket shells; bazooka

**rod** *Slang*. pistol, revolver

**roscoe** *Slang*. gun

**Saturday night special** *Informal*. cheap, easily obtained handgun

**sawed-off shotgun** smoothbore firearm with barrel cut off to scatter shot more widely

**scattergun** shotgun

**self-loading firearm** semiautomatic weapon

**semiautomatic weapon** firearm that automatically ejects cartridges and reloads after each firing, activated by successive squeezing of trigger; autoloader

**serpentine** cannon of various calibers (15th-17th c.)

**Sharps** single-shot, lever-action breechloader, used by U.S. military and buffalo hunters (mid-19th c.)

**shotgun** smoothbore firearm, often double-barreled

**side arm** handgun; pistol; revolver; weapon worn at side in holster or in belt

**side-by-side** double-action shotgun with barrels placed side by side

**siege gun** field gun

**single-action** *(adj)* designating firearm that requires cocking of hammer before firing each shot

**six-gun** six-shooter

**six-shooter** six-chambered revolver; six-gun

**slide-action** *(adj)* designating rifle or shotgun with mechanism that ejects shell case and cocks and reloads firearm when slid back and forth quickly; pump-action

**small arm** handheld firearm

**Springfield rifle** .30 caliber, bolt-action repeating rifle (World War I)

**Sten gun** light submachine gun (Britain)

**stern chaser** cannon mounted at stern of sailing ship, facing aft

**Stinger** shoulder-fired antiaircraft missile that uses infrared guidance

**stun gun** battery-powered, handheld firearm that discharges nonlethal cartridges, darts, or electric charges to immobilize its target

**submachine gun** portable automatic firearm, fired from shoulder or hip; machine pistol

**submarine gun** firearm designed to function underwater

**swivel gun** gun mounted on pedestal or on wall so that it can be turned vertically or horizontally

**10-gauge** shotgun using shells of 2 cm diameter

**thirty-eight** .38 caliber handgun

**thirty-thirty** .30 caliber rifle that fires cartridge with thirty-grain powder charge

**thirty-two** .32 caliber handgun

**Thompson submachine gun** .45 caliber submachine gun with magazine, pistol grip, and detachable buttstock; Tommy gun

**Tommy gun** Thompson submachine gun

**trench gun** portable cannon or mortar fired from trenches in warfare

**twenty-two** .22 caliber firearm

**Uzi** short, 9 mm submachine gun

**Winchester rifle** *Trademark*. any rifle made by Winchester Arms Company, esp. magazine rifle of 19th c.

**zip gun** crude, homemade gun that fires real bullets

## FIREARM PARTS, ACCESSORIES, AND PROCESSES

**accuracy** measure of variation in group of shots or how close shot is to target

**action** mechanism by which firearm is operated

**ammo** *Informal.* ammunition

**ammunition** bullets, grenades, or bombs; explosive projectile fired from weapon; munitions

**armaments** weapons, military equipment

**armory** repository of arms

**arsenal** place of manufacture and storage of arms

**artillery** mounted missile-launching or projectile-firing weapons, esp. larger cannon, guns, and catapults

**ball** any of various spherical or conical projectiles or missiles

**ballistics** science and study of projectile motion; study and development of missile weapons

**barrel** tube of gun, through which bullet fires

**bead** careful aim

**bird shot** shot with diameter of less than 1/10 inch

**black powder** explosive powder containing saltpeter, sulfur, and charcoal, esp. for sporting guns

**blank** cartridge without projectile

**blast** explosive charge; explosion

**bolt** breech closure of gun that controls opening of bore

**bore** cylindrical, hollow part of gun barrel, usu. longer than it is wide; caliber measure

**breech** part of firearm at rear of bore

**buckshot** large-sized lead shot of .24 to .33 inches diameter, used in shotgun shells carrying nine to fifteen of such pellets

**bullet** small projectile discharged from firearm at great speed

**bullet drop** description of descending trajectory of bullet in flight, requiring that sightline be set above target depending on range

**butt** buttstock

**buttstock** shoulder end of firearm at rear of breech mechanism

**caliber** diameter of firearm bore; diameter of bullet

**canister** case of small projectiles to be fired at once from cannon; case shot

**cannonball** round, solid missile fired from cannon

**cap** explosive paper or metallic cap, used to ignite larger charge

**cartridge** cylindrical casing, usu. of brass, that holds primer, powder charge, and bullet

**cartridge belt** strap with loops that hold cartridges, worn around waist or over shoulder

**cartridge case** cylindrical, powder-holding element of cartridge

**case shot** canister

**chamber** firearm compartment that holds cartridge

**chape** metal mounting of scabbard or sheath of knife

**charge** (*vb*) load a weapon; (*n*) amount of powder or shot used to load weapon; load

**choke** narrowing of bore near muzzle of shotgun to concentrate shot pellets leaving muzzle; device that regulates muzzle constriction on shotgun

**cleaning rod** long rod, often with wire brush at one end, used to clean barrel of rifle

**clip** clasp that holds bullets to be fed into firearm chamber

**cock** hammer; (*vb*) pull back and set hammer prior to firing

**conventional weapons** nonnuclear weapons

**cradle** part of gun carriage on which recoiling gun slides

**detonator** device, esp. small amount of explosive, used to set off larger explosive

**double-O buck** common shotgun buckshot, used esp. for hunting deer

**drop at heel** term for measurement of shotgun length

**elevation** angle at which a weapon, esp. an artillery piece, points away from horizontal plane

**engines of war** military weapons

**firing pin** plunger in firing mechanism that strikes cartridge primer, thus igniting charge

**flint** gunflint

**flintlock** old-fashioned firearm lock that ignites powder charge when hammer holding a flint strikes spark from metal

**front sight** sight nearest muzzle of firearm

**fuse** flammable wick or tube made of combustible substance, used to ignite explosive

**gas** substance dispersed through atmosphere as poison, irritant, or asphyxiant

**gas-operated** (*adj*) using some of exhaust gases to operate action

**gauge** unit of measure of internal diameter, or bore, of shotgun barrel, 12 gauge being equal to approximately 3/4 inch (19 mm)

**grapeshot** cast-iron balls formerly used as cannon charge

**grenade launcher** device attached to muzzle of rifle that permits firing of rifle grenades

**group** series of shots on target, esp. pattern thus formed and span between centers of widest shots in group

**gunflint** small flint that produces spark, formerly used in firearm ignition

**gunlock** firearm mechanism that ignites charge: flintlock, matchlock, percussion lock, or wheel lock

**gunpowder** explosive chemical mixture used to propel firearm projectile

**gunstock** usu. wooden frame brace supporting firing mechanism and barrel of rifle or machine gun; stock

**hair trigger** sensitive firearm trigger

**hammer** firearm part that strikes firing mechanism of gunlock; cock

**hasty sling** method of inserting arm in sling to facilitate rapid firing of rifle

**holster** leather case for pistol, opening at top, usu. worn on belt

**home** (*vb*) proceed toward specified target, esp. under control of automatic guidance mechanism

**jacket** metal outer casing of bullet

**load** charge; single cartridge with bullet and powder; (*vb*) fill weapon with cartridges

**loaded** (*adj*) containing ammunition or explosive charge

**lock** gunlock

**magazine** sometimes removable or reloadable storage receptacle that holds extra cartridges in repeating rifles and shotguns; military storehouse for arms and ammunition

**magnum** (*adj*) designating a cartridge equipped with larger charge than other cartridges of comparable size; (*n*) firearm thus equipped

**matchlock** old form of gunlock in which priming is ignited by slow match

**Minié ball** bullet with cylindrical body, conical head, and hollow base (19th c.)

**munitions** ammunition; military equipment

**mustard gas** oily liquid used as chemical weapon

**muzzle** fore end of firearm barrel, point of departure for bullet

**muzzle energy** impact energy of bullet at muzzle velocity, expressed in foot-pounds

**muzzle velocity** speed of projectile as it leaves muzzle of gun, usu. expressed in feet or meters per second

**open sight** rear sight of firearm, consisting of notch in which gunner aligns front sight on target

**ordnance** large firearms; military supplies, esp. weapons, ammunition, and artillery

**pan** depressed part of lock that holds priming in older firearms

**patch** greased or moistened cloth formerly used as wadding for rifle ball; cloth used to clean bore of firearm

**payload** size of weapon's explosive charge

**peep sight** plate with small hole through which gunner makes sighting

**pellet** piece of shot

**percussion lock** lock of gun fired by percussive impact

**pin** metal peg that, when removed, activates fuse that detonates grenade

**pistol grip** handle, esp. of rifle, shaped like butt of pistol

**plug** single shot

**powder** gunpowder

**primer** cap or cylinder holding compound that may be exploded by percussion or other means, used for firing charge of powder

**propellant** explosive substance used to force projectile out of firearm barrel

**range finder** instrument used to determine distance to target

**rear sight** sight nearest breech of firearm

**recoil** distance through which a weapon moves backward after discharging

**recoil pad** cushion placed against shoulder to absorb jolt of recoil on high-powered rifles

**reloading** making one's own cartridge from shell casing, powder, primer, and bullet

**rifling** system of spiral grooves cut into gun barrel; process of cutting such grooves

**round** unit of ammunition equal to one shot

**saddle scabbard** sheath attached to horse saddle for storage of rifle

**safety** device on gun that prevents inadvertent firing

**scope** telescopic sight

**set trigger** trigger that can be adjusted to set pressure required to pull it; on some rifles with pair of triggers, the one set to very light touch

**shell** cylindrical casing that holds firearm charge; bullet, cartridge, or torpedo shell

**shot** lead pellets discharged from firearm: bird shot, buckshot, grapeshot

**shrapnel** cartridge filled with bursting charge; fragments from exploding charge

**side lock** method of discharging rifle in which hammer and percussion mechanism are on side of firearm rather than in line with barrel

**sight** mechanical or optical device used to guide aim of firearm; (*vb*) visually direct or aim firearm

**sight in** (*vb*) adjust sights to strike target at selected range

**silencer** attachment to muzzle of firearm that muffles noise

**sling** leather strap attached to fore and butt end of rifle, used to carry rifle on shoulder and esp. to steady aimed rifle when arm is placed through sling loop

**slug** bullet

**smokeless powder** any of various substitutes for ordinary gunpowder that emit little or no smoke, esp. one made of guncotton

**smoothbore** (*adj*) having a grooveless, unrifled bore

**soft point** bullet with point made of lead, not steel, which deforms as it enters object

**spitzer** pointed bullet

**star shell** shell that bursts in air and produces a bright light to illuminate enemy positions

**stock** gunstock

**tampion** protective plug placed in muzzle of firearm when not in use

**target practice** shooting at targets to test or improve accuracy in one's use of firearms

**telescopic sight** firearm aiming device equipped with magnifying lens; scope

**tracer** bullet that emits trail of smoke or luminous gas

**trigger** mechanism pulled by finger to fire gun

**trunnion** projection on either side of cannon, used to support it on its carriage

**wad** soft plug used to retain powder charge in muzzleloading gun

**wheel lock** obsolete gunlock in which revolving wheel strikes flint to make spark

**windage** degree to which gunsight must be adjusted to correct for deflection of projectile by wind

## BOMBS, MINES, AND EXPLOSIVES

**ABM** *antiballistic missile*

**A-bomb** atomic bomb

**aerial bomb** large explosive device dropped from airplane, esp. with parachute to slow descent

**antiballistic missile** ABM; missile designed to intercept and destroy ballistic missiles

**antimissile missile** ballistic missile designed to detect and destroy missiles in flight

**antipersonnel bomb** bomb that produces shrapnel designed to damage persons more than property

**ashcan** *Slang*. depth charge

**atomic bomb** immensely powerful bomb that utilizes nuclear fission reaction; A-bomb

**ballistic missile** unmanned military rocket with warhead

**blockbuster** aerial bomb that contains high explosives

**bomb** highly explosive charge thrown at or dropped on target

**buzz bomb** V-1 rocket

**castrator mine** explosive that detonates at crotch level

**cherry bomb** powerful, globular firecracker

**claymore mine** antipersonnel mine that produces fan-shaped fragment pattern

**cluster** numerous bombs dropped simultaneously over target and its immediate surroundings

**cluster bomb** canister that can be dropped from aircraft and opens to release large number of fragmentation explosives over wide area

**demolition bomb** bomb with powerfully destructive explosive charge

**depth charge** explosive charge detonated underwater against submarines

**dynamite** safe-handling, solid explosive that contains nitroglycerin, used esp. in mining, quarrying, and engineering

**dynamite bomb** explosive charge of dynamite or nitroglycerin embedded in stabilizing material

**explosive** substance that can blow up or detonate; weapon containing such a substance

**fireball** grenade, bomb

**firebomb** explosive device with incendiary effects

**firecracker** paper cylinder holding weak, noisy explosive and fuse, used in displays and celebrations, not as weapon

**fission bomb** bomb detonated by atomic fission reaction; atomic bomb

**floating mine** explosive charge used on water surface against ships

**fragmentation bomb** charge that detonates into many shrapnel fragments

**fougasse** mine attached to missile, stone, or launched object

**fuel-air explosive** explosive that achieves powerful, concussive blast effect by releasing and detonating highly volatile fuels in the air, used on troops in bunkers or tunnels and to clear mine fields

**fusion bomb** bomb detonated by atomic fusion reaction; hydrogen bomb

**gas bomb** bomb that contains poison or chemical gas

**grenade** missile or container with charge of explosive or chemical gas, launched or hand-thrown

**ground mine** land mine

**hand grenade** explosive device hurled by hand

**H-bomb** hydrogen bomb

**hydrogen bomb** immensely powerful bomb that utilizes atomic fusion reaction; H-bomb

**ICBM** intercontinental ballistic missile; supersonic missile with range of at least 3500 nautical miles (6500 km), usu. with thermonuclear warhead

**incendiary bomb** bomb that sets target on fire

**intercontinental ballistic missile** ICBM

**land mine** explosive charge shallowly buried underground, detonated by pressure from person or vehicle; ground mine

**mine** explosive charge in container buried underground or placed in sea, detonated by contact

**MIRV** multiple independently targetable reentry vehicle; missile with two or more warheads aimed at separate targets

**missile** projectile with explosive charge, launched through air toward target

**Molotov cocktail** homemade bomb consisting of gasoline-filled bottle ignited by rag in bottle neck

**napalm** incendiary bomb consisting of aluminum soaps in jelling gas

**neutron bomb** nuclear bomb that kills by radiation, with detonation that is destructive to persons but not property

**nitroglycerin** oily, highly explosive liquid

**nuclear bomb** violently explosive bomb with power derived from splitting nuclei of heavy chemical elements such as uranium or plutonium

**nuke** *Informal.* nuclear or thermonuclear bomb

**Patriot** U.S. antiaircraft missile with range of 37 miles (60 km), launched from a tracked vehicle with computer guidance, also effective against low-flying missiles

**petard** encased explosive charge attached to wall or gate

**pineapple** *Slang.* hand grenade

**pipe bomb** homemade or primitive bomb made with explosive charge inserted into lead pipe

**plastic explosive** puttylike substance holding and concealing explosive charge, detonated by fuse or remote control

**plutonium bomb** atomic fission bomb in which plutonium is bombarded by neutrons to produce explosive chain reaction

**pressure mine** explosive charge detonated by pressure

**report** loud noise of explosion

**robot bomb** rocket-propelled, gyroscopically steered bomb equipped with wings and control surfaces

**rocket** explosive charge inside missile

**rocket bomb** small bomb on missile fired by rocket launcher

**SAM** surface-to-air missile

**Scud** medium-range Soviet tactical missile with 200 pound (90 kg) warhead for surface-to-surface attacks

**Sidewinder** short-range, air-to-air missile that homes in on heat of target aircraft's engine exhaust

**smart bomb** *Slang.* steerable air-to-surface bomb guided to its target by television or laser beam

**smoke bomb** explosive charge yielding large amount of smoke

**sonic mine** explosive charge used in water against ships, activated by sound waves

**stink bomb** chemical charge that detonates to produce foul odor

**submarine mine** underwater mine that floats at predetermined depth

**surface-to-air missile** SAM; rocket launched from ground or water surface, aimed at aerial target

**tear gas bomb** grenade filled with chemical that causes extreme eye irritation

**thermonuclear bomb** bomb that utilizes nuclear fusion reaction; hydrogen bomb

**time bomb** explosive charge set to detonate at prearranged moment

**TNT** trinitrotoluene; highly explosive chemical used as charge in bombs

**torpedo** explosive underwater projectile

**TOW** tube-launched optically-guided wire-tracked missile; short-range antitank missile that trails thin wire

**V-1 rocket** pilotless, jet-powered plane with explosive warhead, used by Germans in World War II; buzz bomb

**V-2 rocket** early rocket with explosive charge, used by Germans in World War II

**warhead** front section of torpedo, missile, shell, or bomb, containing explosive charge

# ELECTRICITY AND ELECTRONICS

**SEE ALSO**: Chap. 4: Physics; Chap. 5: Machinery and Fabrication; Telecommunications; Computers; Chap. 7: Furnishings; Chap. 15: Popular Music; Television and Radio

**AC** alternating current

**accumulator** storage cell or battery of storage cells

**alternating current** AC; current that periodically changes direction at certain levels, measured in volts; current from wall socket

**alternator** electrical generator that produces alternating current

**ammeter** instrument that measures electric current in amps

**ammonium chloride** white crystalline salt used in dry cells

**amp** ampere; *Informal*. amplifier

**ampere** unit of electric current produced by one volt acting through one ohm, equal to one coulomb per second; amp

**Ampere's law** electric current and changing electric field create a magnetic field

**amplidyne** direct-current generator that magnifies small power input to create large power output

**amplifier** device or circuit that increases voltage or current of an input signal

**amplitude** maximum deviation of AC current from its average value during its cycle; peak value of waveform

**analog** (*adj*) designating electronic process in which data is represented by physical quantities that correspond to the variables involved

**anion** negative ion drawn to anode in electrolyzed solution

**anode** positive terminal of electrolytic cell; negative terminal of storage battery

**arc** luminous bridge formed between electrodes or across gap in circuit

**arc lamp** light in which current passes between electrodes through pressurized gas

**argon** colorless, odorless, inactive gas used to fill electric bulbs and lamps

**armature** wound rotor in generator that transforms electric current in coil into mechanical motion

**attenuator** device that reduces amplitude of signal with minimal distortion

**ballast** device used to maintain current in circuit by varying resistance in response to changes in voltage

**band** specific range of wavelengths or frequencies

**band-pass filter** filter that amplifies frequencies in specific range and reduces all others

**battery** number of primary or secondary cells that work together to produce flow of electric charge

**blackout** period of darkness due to electric power failure

**bombardment** stream of particles against surface, such as electrons against TV screen

**boost** (*vb*) raise voltage through circuit

**bridge** network configuration in which no two elements are in series or parallel; two-branch instrument that measures unknown impedance by balancing ratio of voltages in each branch to a known ratio

**brownout** enforced reduction of electric power usage

**bulb** rounded glass housing for filament of incandescent lamp

**bus** common path for multiple connections

**cable** strands of electrical conductor insulated from each other and laid together, often twisted around central core

**capacitance** measure of capacitor's ability to store a charge

**capacitor** device that accumulates and holds a charge of electricity; condenser

**carbon** carbon rod used in arc lamp

**cathode** negative electrode that emits stream of electrons and attracts positive ions in electrolytic cell; positive terminal of storage battery

**cathode-ray tube** CRT; heated filament that emits electron beam that can be controlled by externally applied potentials to produce luminous effect when electrons hit screen, as in a television or computer

**cation** positively charged ion drawn to cathode in electrolysis

**cell** housing for electrodes and electrolyte, used to generate electricity or in electrolysis

**cesium** alkali metal used in photoelectric cells; most electropositive element known

**charge** basis of electric energy, manifested in current, voltage, and electric field as positive or negative element that attracts unlike and repels like charged bodies

**chip** tiny electronic integrated circuit; microchip

**circuit** continuous path along which current flows: generator, resistors, conductors, other elements

**circuit breaker** switch that automatically interrupts electric circuit under abnormal conditions to prevent harmful, excessive current

**clip** waveform distortion due to excess level in circuit; something that attaches a wire to another element

**coaxial cable** insulated cable with two conductors, central signal line, and outer shield, used to transmit telephone, telegraph, and television signals

**coil** copper wire wound around solid object, used to produce electromagnetic effect and conduct current; inductor

**commutator** device for changing frequency or direction of a current

**condenser** capacitor that accumulates and holds a charge

**conductance** reciprocal of resistance, measured in mho units

**conductivity** capacity of a substance to conduct electric current

**conductor** material, esp. metal, through which electrons can flow as electric current

**contact** connection of touching but not soldered electric conductors, usu. metal

**controlled source** voltage or current source controlled by another circuit property

**converter** mechanical device that changes the form of electric energy or converts the frequency of radio signals

**copper wire** good conductor used in coils and wiring

**core** middle part of coil or solenoid, often a metal rod

**coulomb** quantity of charge transferred by one ampere in one second between two points in circuit

**coupling** connection of two electric circuits by part common to both; interaction of circuit elements

**CRT** cathode-ray tube

**cryotron** device based on fact that changing magnetic field causes superconductive element to oscillate between low and high resistance

**current** rate of flow of electric charge through solid or liquid, measured in amperes

**DC** direct current

**depolarizer** substance added to electrolyte to prevent polarization and remove gas deposits at electrodes

**diamagnetic** (*adj*) designating materials in which induced current field opposes applied magnetic field

**dielectric** (*adj*) designating insulating material for opposing electrical fields, esp. between plates in capacitors

**digital** (*adj*) designating an electronic process that defines frequencies and other data as discrete, binary bits of information

**diode** solid-state device or tube with anode and cathode that rectifies AC and allows current to pass freely in one direction only

**dipole** two equal but opposite charges held a small distance apart

**direct current** DC; current that flows in one direction only and has virtually invariable magnitude; current produced by a battery

**discharge** conversion of stored energy into electric energy

**discharge tube** glass vessel in which current passes from anode to cathode through a high vacuum

**doping** process in which impurities are added to semiconductors to control conductivity

**dry cell battery** one or more cells that work together in an ammonium chloride paste instead of a solution

**dynamo** *Chiefly Brit.* small direct-current generator

**electric** (*adj*) describing any device that uses or produces a charge of electricity

**electrician** specialist in the installation, maintenance, and repair of electrical equipment

**electricity** physical agency caused by movement of electrons and other charged particles, manifested as attraction, repulsion, light, and heat

**electrode** wire, rod, or plate that conducts electric current into or out of any device

**electrolysis** passage of current through electrolyte with migration of charged ions to like-charged electrodes

**electrolyte** conducting medium in which flow of current leads to movement of charged ions

**electrolytic cell** housing in which electrolysis occurs

**electromagnet** coil with soft iron core that acts as magnet when current flows through it

**electromagnetism** interaction of electricity and magnetism, esp. magnetic effects produced by currents

**electromotion** mechanical motion produced by electricity

**electromotive force** EMF; potential difference, expressed in volts, between terminals of a source of electric energy

**electron** negatively charged particle in all atoms that is basis of electricity

**electronics** branch of physics dealing with the emission and flow of electrons and the application of the energy produced to various devices

**electron tube** vacuum tube that controls passage of current through it by variations in grid potential; thermionic valve

**electrostatic** (*adj*) describing effects caused by charges at rest, such as electric charge on object

**EMF** *electromotive force*

**extension cord** long electric cord fitted with plug at one end and receptacle at other

**farad** unit of capacitance equal to one coulomb per volt

**faraday** quantity of electricity transferred in electrolysis and electric flux

**ferromagnetic** (*adj*) designating materials that retain magnetism

**field** region of space containing lines of force with direction and strength

**filament** thin, conductive heating element, usu. wire in vacuum tube, that produces light in light bulb

**filter** device that selectively damps or suppresses certain oscillations and frequencies while not affecting others

**flex** wire that bends to any shape to make connections, covered with insulating material such as rubber

**flux** field lines of direction and strength

**flux density** number of field lines per unit area

**frequency** number of complete oscillations per unit time of an electromagnetic wave or alternating current

**fuse** safety device that breaks circuit if current is too great, usu. a piece of wire that melts

**gain** ratio of increase in output over input in amplifier

**galvanometer** instrument used for comparative measurement of small currents in units other than amperes

**gamma ray** shortest wavelength of electromagnetic radiation

**gauss** basic unit of flux density; magnetic induction equal to magnetic flux density necessary to move electromotive force along wire at specific speed

**generator** machine used to transform mechanical energy into electric energy through electromagnetism

**gilbert** unit of magnetomotive force equal to 0.7958 ampere-turns

**grid** element that controls electron flow between anode and cathode in tube

**ground** large conductor connected to electric circuit as general return point; connection to such a body; circuit reference point at which potential is zero

**heating element** low resistance wire that heats when current flows through it

**henry** unit of inductance in which a variation of one ampere per second produces an induced electromotive force of one volt

**IC** *integrated circuit*

**impedance** total resistance to AC flow in circuit, combining resistance, inductance, and capacitance

**induced current** current that flows in coil moved in magnetic field

**inductance** flux in magnetic field caused by changing current in electric circuit or device, inducing voltage in that circuit or a nearby circuit

**induction** process by which electrification, magnetization, or electromotive force is produced in bodies and circuits through proximity to charge or field

**inductor** loop or loops of conducting material that produces oriented magnetic field when current is passed through it; coil

**infrared rays** electromagnetic waves with wavelengths longer than those of red light in visible spectrum

**input impedance** total opposition to AC by circuit, measured in ohms

**insulation** material that prevents current from escaping or entering where it is not wanted, used esp. to separate conductors

**insulator** material that prevents flow of current, including most nonmetals and gases

**integrated circuit** IC; electronic circuit conducted on single semiconductor wafer or microchip

**intensity** rate at which a wave transports energy across a unit area

**inverter** device that converts direct current into alternating current

**ion** electrically charged atom or group of atoms that results from loss or gain of one or more electrons by neutral atom

**ionization** conversion of atoms into positively or negatively charged particles

**jack** connecting device in circuit into which plug is inserted

**laser** *light amplification by stimulated emission of radiation*; device that excites atoms to higher energy levels in order to generate intense, coherent beam of light from electromagnetic radiation

**lead** common electrical conductor, usu. insulated, used esp. to connect wires to test instrument

**load** object of power delivery in circuit

**local action** effect caused by impurities in zinc plate of primary cell, making it less efficient

**loop** continuous current path

**magnetic field** condition of space in vicinity of magnetic substance or current-carrying body, in which forces can be found

**magnetomotive force** force that gives rise to magnetic flux

**maser** *microwave amplification by stimulated emission of radiation*; laser that functions only in microwave region of spectrum

**maxwell** unit of magnetic flux per square centimeter in which magnetic induction is one gauss

**microchip** chip

**microphone** device that transforms sound waves into current by use of vibrating diaphragm

**microwave** electromagnetic radiation with wavelength between infrared and radio waves

**modulation** alteration in waveform frequency or amplitude due to superimposition of another wave or signal

**motor** device that transforms electric energy into mechanical energy, esp. one that produces motion by means of coil of wire around armature turning between poles of a magnet

**moving coil** instrument that uses motion of coil in magnetic field

**mutual inductance** interactive inductance between inductive circuit elements

**node** network or circuit junction

**ohm** unit of resistance in circuit when potential difference of one volt produces current of one amp between two points

**Ohm's law** the ratio of voltage to current in a circuit is equal to the resistance

**open circuit** discontinuous circuit in which current cannot flow

**oscillator** wave generator

**oscilloscope** instrument that uses cathode-ray tube to display waveform images of periodic changes in voltage or current

**outlet** electric receptacle that leads to power source, into which electric devices are plugged

**parallel circuit** circuit in which positive and negative terminals connect to two distinct points, with voltage applied equally throughout

**paramagnetic** (*adj*) designating materials that have slight magnetic susceptibility

**Paschen's law** breakdown of voltage between electrodes in a gas is product of distance and pressure

**patchbay** patchboard

**patchboard** central jackfield that connects all elements in circuit configuration; patchbay

**patchcord** insulated connector in patchboard

**period** time required for one waveform cycle to be completed; inverse of frequency

**phase shift** time difference between waveforms

**phasor** diagram that illustrates phase and amplitude relations in AC circuits

**photoelectric cell** cell whose electrical properties are modified by illumination by light waves

**piezoelectricity** production of electric current in certain crystals through deformation by mechanical stress

**pile** several disks of two dissimilar metals stacked in alternating series and separated by pads of cloth or paper moistened with an electrolyte, used to produce current

**plate** positive anode toward which electrons are attracted in tube

**plug** fitting inserted into receptacle to establish contact connection in circuit

**polarization** effect produced when simple primary cell produces current; deposits of gas on plate that increase cell resistance during electrolysis

**potential** work needed to bring unit of positive charge from distance to given point

**potential difference** difference in electric force between any two points in circuit, with current flowing from high to low level

**potentiometer** variable resistor directly controlled by dial, knob, or lever

**power** time rate of electric energy in device or circuit, measured in watts

**power cord** insulated electric cord with specific current and material ratings, used as power supply line

**power supply** source of current and voltage

**primary cell** nonrechargeable device that produces flow of electric charge by means of chemical reaction of two different metals in acid

**probe** sensing device with lead tip, used for testing equipment

**raceway** tube used to protect electric wiring

**radio** use of electromagnetic waves to send message from microphone to receiver

**radio wave** longest wavelength of electromagnetic radiation

**reactance** impedance of AC circuit due to capacitance or inductance, expressed in ohms

**receiver** device that transforms electromagnetic radiation signals into electric current and voltage

**rectifier** device used to change AC to DC

**regulator** automatic device used to maintain current or voltage in circuit

**relay** device that uses small current to control greater current in another circuit by electromagnetic switching

**resistance** force that opposes flow of current through a conductor, measured in ohms; reciprocal of conductance

**resistor** passive circuit component that exhibits relatively constant resistance to current flow at all frequencies at same temperature

**resonance** peak frequency response characteristic of AC-driven circuit

**resonator** hollow enclosure of conductor resonated by certain frequencies of electromagnetic radiation

**rheostat** device that regulates current by means of adjustable resistors

**rotor** part of generator that turns

**sawtooth wave** serrated waveform with one slope steeper than the other

**schematic** standardized diagram of circuit

**secondary cell** device that produces current by chemical reaction, rechargeable by passing current in opposite direction from discharge; storage cell

**semiconductor** any of class of materials with conductivity near that of conductor at high temperatures and nearly absent at low

**series circuit** circuit with all parts connected in sequence so that same current flows through each part

**short circuit** abnormal condition caused by direct connection between points of low resistance on circuit, usu. resulting in bypass or break due to excess flow of current

**signal flow** impulse transmitted through circuit or network

**sine wave** waveform that represents periodic oscillations with same representation as sine curve

**socket** receptacle for plug or screw-in devices

**solenoid** coil with length very much greater than its diameter that acts as magnet when current passes through it; simple polar magnet equally magnetized along its full length

**solid-state** (*adj*) designating electronic device that utilizes properties of semiconductor materials, not electron tubes

**spark** instantaneous appearance of light and sound in electrostatic discharge of very short duration

**speaker** transducer that changes electric energy into sound waves

**spectrometer** instrument used to measure spectral wavelengths

**square wave** waveform that changes direction at right angle

**static** disturbance of radio or television reception by natural, atmospheric, or electrical phenomena

**stator** stationary part of generator

**steady state** long-term continuous circuit condition

**step-up/step-down** process in transformers that increases or decreases voltage depending upon turn ratio

**storage cell** secondary cell

**superconductivity** ability of certain metals to conduct current without resistance at very low temperatures

**surge control** multiple outlet plug that provides transient protection from sudden increases in current in electronic devices

**switch** device used to join or break parts of circuit, thus permitting or preventing flow of current

**target** surface at which stream of particles is directed

**terminal** point of current entry or departure from circuit; metal nut on screw or other mechanical device that connects wire to another apparatus

**tetrode** vacuum tube with four electrodes, a plate, two grids, and a cathode

**thermionic valve** *Chiefly Brit.* electron tube

**thermistor** semiconductor device that exhibits negative coefficient of resistance with temperature

**thermocouple** electric circuit composed of two dissimilar metals joined at different temperatures

**thermoelectric** (*adj*) describing production of electric current directly from heat

**thermopile** instrument with thermocouples connected in series behind cone, used to detect heat radiation and produce thermoelectric current

**tracer** device that follows current through circuit to locate trouble

**transducer** device that receives power from one system and supplies power in a different form to another system, usu. by converting physical quantity into electrical quantity

**transformer** two coils of wire on same core that induce AC transfer from one circuit to another at same frequency

**transient** (*adj*) designating an instantaneous peak

**transistor** small block of semiconductor with three terminals that acts like a vacuum tube in solid-state electronic devices

**transmission** emission of electromagnetic waves and their passage from one location to another

**transmitter** device that sends electromagnetic waves

**triode** three-electrode tube with negative grid between anode and cathode, used to increase voltage

**tube** device that controls passage of current through it by variation in grid potential, named for number of its electrodes: diode, triode, or tetrode

**tuner** device for receiving AM, FM, and shortwave radio signals

**turn ratio** ratio of number of turns of wire in primary and secondary windings of transformer

**turns** number of loops of wire in coil

**tweeter** small speaker that operates most efficiently at high frequencies

**ultraviolet rays** electromagnetic waves with wavelengths shorter than those of violet in visible spectrum

**vacuum tube** sealed glass bulb used to amplify, detect, or rectify AC to generate electrical oscillations, composed of plate, grid, and triode; electron tube; valve

**valve** *Chiefly Brit.* vacuum tube

**variable resistor** resistor whose resistance can be changed when contact slides around a length of wire

**volt** unit of potential difference between two points of conductor with constant one ampere current when one watt of power is dissipated between them

**voltage** measure of volts in a circuit, or energy per unit charge

**voltaic cell** two electrodes made from different metals in solution, used to produce electromotive force by chemical action

**voltmeter** instrument used to measure electromotive force or potential difference in volts

**watt** unit of power equal to one joule per second or one ampere flowing across potential difference of one volt

**wave** progressive disturbance or variation that propagates energy from point to point in a medium; undulating or jagged representation of this action

**waveform** repeating pattern of wave shape

**wavelength** distance along wave between points of same phase

**weber** practical unit of magnetic flux, equal to one volt second or $10^8$ maxwells

**Wheatstone bridge** test instrument that joins two branches of circuit to measure resistance by comparing it with a known resistance

**winding** wire wound around armature to act as coil

**woofer** large speaker that operates most efficiently at low frequencies

**X-ray** electromagnetic radiation of extremely short wavelength that penetrates solid bodies, acts like light on photographic film and plates, and ionizes gases

# TELECOMMUNICATIONS

Data Transmission
Voice Transmission and Telephony

**SEE ALSO**: Chap. 5: Electricity and Electronics; Computers; Chap. 15: Cinema; Television and Radio

## DATA TRANSMISSION

**bandwidth** smallest range of frequencies within which certain signal can be transmitted

**baud** unit of measure of speed at which information is transmitted in number of signal impulses or bits per second

**bulletin board** service accessed by modem, permitting users to leave, store, and retrieve messages

**cable** telegram; (*vb*) send a telegram

**cablegram** message transmitted by underwater cable

**channel** hardware device or path that transfers data between two elements of system

**coaxial cable** high-frequency telecommunications transmission line made up of insulated central conductor surrounded by conductive material that protects central conductor from interference

**communications network** interlocking system of lines, circuits, and organizations for telecommunications

**communications satellite** artificial satellite used in radio, telephone, and television transmission by means of reflection or amplification and retransmission of signals between Earth stations

**continental code** international Morse code

**converter** device for changing electric energy or data from one form to another

**cybernation** automatic, computer control of a process or operation

**cybernetics** science of communication and information theory, esp. automatic control and regulation of communication between humans and machines; information theory

**dash** telegraph signal of longer duration than dot, used in combination to represent letters in Morse code

**data transfer rate** speed at which information moves between two devices, measured in bits per second or bauds

**data transmission** sending of information, usu. in digital form, by coded electrical impulses

**day letter** low-priority telegram to be delivered on following day

**demodulation** conversion of alternating carrier wave or current into direct, pulsating current equivalent to transmitted data signal, esp. by modem; detection

**detection** demodulation

**dish** satellite dish

**dot** telegraph signal of shorter duration than dash, used in combination to represent letters in Morse code

**duplex** (*adj*) designating a telecommunications system capable of simultaneous transmission of messages in opposite directions on one channel

**Earth station** terminal equipped to receive from, and sometimes to transmit to, communications satellite

**electronic communications** telecommunications

**electronic mail** message system using telecommunications network lines between computers; E-mail

**E-mail** electronic mail

**facsimile** method or device for reproducing graphic material in permanent form and transmitting it over telephone line; fax; phototelegraphy

**fax** facsimile

**fiber optics** branch of optics that deals with thin, transparent, flexible glass or plastic fibers used for high-speed, clear transmission of signals carrying masses of data along their length

**full duplex** communication mode in which data can be transmitted and received simultaneously

**half duplex** communication mode in which data can be sent in only one direction at a time

**hardware** electronic systems and devices used in telecommunications

**information theory** mathematical theory concerned with statistical analysis of information and communications between humans and machines; cybernetics

**Intelsat** *In*ternational *Tel*ecommunications *Sat*ellite organization; global communications satellite network

**interface** meeting place of systems and means by which communication occurs there

**interference** imperfect or distorted signal reception, esp. due to stray or unwanted signals

**international Morse code** form of Morse code used in international telegraphy; continental code

**ISDN** *i*ntegrated *s*ervices *d*igital *n*etwork; digital transmission of voice and data simultaneously over several channels on one line

**jack** electrical device into which plug fits to make connection

**kilobaud** one thousand bits per second

**link** one element of telecommunications system or network

**log on** (*vb*) enter code or password to access telecommunications network

**modem** *mo*dulator/*dem*odulator; device for converting and transmitting or receiving digital computer signals over telephone lines linking computer to network or to another computer

**modulate** (*vb*) vary amplitude, frequency, phase, or intensity of carrier wave in accordance with signal wave of much lower frequency

**Morse code** code system of long and short sounds or dots and dashes used in transmitting telegraph signals

**multiplex** telecommunications system capable of simultaneous transmission of multiple signals over single channel

**network** service for electronic distribution of data to subscribers

**night letter** reduced-rate telegram sent in evening and delivered on following day

**packet switching** efficient data transmission system in which initial message is broken into relatively small units that are sent independently and subsequently reassembled

**phototelegraphy** facsimile

**plug** electrical device that fits into jack to make connection

**radiophotograph** graphic image transmitted by radio waves

**radiotelegram** message transmitted by radiotelegraphy

**radiotelegraph** telegraph in which messages or signals are sent by radio waves rather than through wires or cables

**remote** device that controls communications system without direct wire connection

**satellite dish** transmitter or receiving antenna in wide, concave, often round shape

**signal** sound or data conveyed over telephone or telegraph line, radio link, or optical fiber

**stock ticker** device for electronic transmission of stock prices from stock exchange receivers in brokerages and banks

**switch** device for establishing, breaking, or altering electrical connections in circuit

**switching** connecting, disconnecting, and redirecting of signals over network

**technetronic** (*adj*) pertaining to, shaped, or influenced by technological changes in society such as telecommunications and computers

**telecommunications** all forms of electromagnetic transmission and reception of data, sounds, and images; electronic communications

**telecommuting** working at home at computer terminal linked to another site, as by modem

**telefacsimile** facsimile

**telefoto** *Informal*. Telephoto

**telegram** message sent by telegraph

**telegraph** device that transmits messages by sending signals by electronic impulses through wire or by conversion to radio waves

**telegraph cable** insulated wires over which telegraph transmissions are sent

**telegraph codes** characters represented as groups of electrical pulses during telegraph transmission

**telegraph line** suspended wires carrying telegraph transmissions

**telegraph operator** person who types out coded messages in Morse code for telegraph transmission

**telegraphy** construction and operation of telegraph systems

**Telephoto** *Trademark*. apparatus for electronic transmittal of photographs

**teleprinter** device that types out material received as electrical impulses over communications system

**teleshopping** electronic shopping via videotex

**Teletype** *Trademark*. automatic printer connected to communications line

**teletypewriter** TTY; form of telegraph in which typewriter keys produce electrical impulses conveyed to receiving unit

**telex** *tele*printer *ex*change; service using teletypewriter to send and receive information

**terminal** originating or receiving point for signals in telecommunications system

**ticker** telegraphic receiver that prints messages on paper tape

**TTY** *teletypewriter*

**Unifax** *Trademark*. UPI wire service

**uplink** transmission path from Earth station to communications satellite

**videotex** system for transmission of data over telephone lines for display on video terminals

**Western Union** *Trademark*. national telegraph service company

**wire** telegram; (vb) send a telegram

**wireless** telegraphy without use of wires

**Wirephoto** *Trademark*. photograph transmitted by Telephoto equipment, esp. for use in newspapers

**wire service** press association news wire that transmits news dispatches via Teletype to radio, TV, and newspapers, esp. Associated Press, United Press International, and Reuters

## VOICE TRANSMISSION AND TELEPHONY

**access** ability to connect to line, circuit, or exchange, usu. denoting long-distance company's connection to local telephone company

**American Telephone & Telegraph** *Trademark*. AT&T; largest U.S. phone service company

**answering machine** electronic device that answers unattended phone and tapes incoming message

**answering service** service in which calls are picked up and messages taken by attendant when called party is unable to answer phone

**area code** prefix to phone number, specifying region in U.S. or Canada to which call is being made

**AT&T** *American Telephone & Telegraph*

**auto-dial** service feature whereby call is made automatically in response to pressing of single, preprogrammed button

**available line** telephone number not in use and obtainable by new customer

**Baby Bells** *Slang*. regional telephone companies formed out of breakup of Ma Bell, or AT&T

**bad connection** telephone transmission with distortion or interference

**beeper** device carried to alert bearer that phone call has been received at home or office; pager

**buried cable** underground telephone lines, esp. in large city

**business office** central administrative office handling customer billing, complaints, and service calls

**business phone** multiextension telephone for use in offices

**busy signal** standard, repeating tone indicating that telephone line is engaged

**busy verification** operator check to determine that busy line is actually being used and not out of order

**buzz** (*vb*) *Informal*. place phone call to someone

**cable** insulated assembly of copper wire or fiberglass strands for transmission of telephone signals or data

**call** (*vb*) attempt to contact another by telephone; (*n*) message delivered or contact made by telephone

**call box** *Chiefly Brit*. outdoor phone for calling police or fire department; public telephone booth

**caller ID** telephone service that allows subscriber to identify caller, whose telephone number is displayed on a small screen, before answering call

**call forwarding** automatic transfer of incoming calls to

another telephone line on which called party can be reached

**calling card** credit card with individualized customer number for billing calls to home or business phone when call is placed from another location

**calling party** person placing telephone call

**call waiting** system in which a tone alerts user that another incoming call is on line and allows user to switch from one call to another on a single line

**car phone** cellular or other radiotelephone installed in automobile

**cellular phone** mobile radiotelephone connected to computer-controlled communications system divided into small cells, each with its own transmitter

**central** local telephone operator who had to be contacted to place call prior to introduction of direct dialing

**channel** frequency bandwidth suitable for two-way telephone communication

**circuit** two-way communications path

**coin call** call placed from public or pay phone by insertion of coin

**coin-operated** (*adj*) describing public telephone requiring insertion of coin to place call

**collect call** operator-assisted call in which charges are paid by receiving party

**conference call** multiparty call requiring simultaneous connection of three or more telephone lines; teleconference

**cordless phone** mobile phone connected without wiring to base station that is connected by wire to standard telephone outlet

**cradle** part of telephone instrument in which handset rests when not in use

**crossed lines** electronic failure in which calls overlap, connect improperly, or otherwise interfere with each other

**cross talk** interference due to unintentional linkage to another communications channel

**custom calling** phone company designation for special services, such as call waiting or call forwarding, available at extra cost

**custom local-area signaling service** highly sophisticated custom calling service, esp. for businesses

**dead** (*adj*) having no dial tone on the line; nonfunctioning

**desk telephone** standard telephone instrument designed to rest on flat surface

**dial** usu. disk-shaped device on face of telephone instrument used to indicate number being called, now usu. replaced by keypad on touch-tone phone; (*vb*) place a call by using such a device

**dial-a-** designation used as prefix by businesses offering service or product over the phone (as: dial-a-prayer)

**Dial One service** selection of long distance company to provide service automatically accessed by dialing 1 prior to number

**dial tone** buzz heard when functioning phone receiver is lifted

**Dictograph** *Trademark.* device with highly sensitive transmitter, used for secretly listening to or recording conversations

**direct dialing** placing call without operator assistance, esp. long distance call

**direct line** number with direct access to called party at one of several extensions on same line without first going through general line answered by receptionist

**directory** book listing all residential and business telephone numbers in region or district

**directory assistance** assistance obtained by contacting special operator, usu. by dialing 411, to provide number that cannot be found in directory

**directory listing** individual or business entry listing name, address, and telephone number

**disconnect** breaking off of call due to electronic problem or intentional action to halt telephone service, usu. for nonpayment of bill

**disconnect notice** official telephone company warning that service will be discontinued on specific date, usu. due to nonpayment of bill

**800 number** special national system permitting calls to businesses without charge to calling party

**emergency number** special, often three-digit, number for use in emergency or to summon help

**exchange** central telephone office where local lines are connected and area served by it

**extension** one of several extra telephones connected to a single incoming line, often with its own number

**field telephone** early cellular telephone for military and business use

**flat-rate service** untimed service

**foreign exchange** central receiving station for all international calls to specific foreign country or region; any exchange outside local calling area

**411** standard three-digit code for local directory assistance

**handset** telephone mouthpiece transmitter and earpiece receiver mounted on handle

**hang up** (*vb*) replace telephone receiver in cradle, terminating call; do this abruptly while caller is speaking

**headset** earphone receiver and microphone transmitter for telephone mounted on attachment fitting onto head, used instead of handset

**hold** status on multiline phone in which call is removed from auditory circuit and caller waits without being disconnected

**hold the line** instruction to wait and not hang up

**home wiring** circuitry providing access from single residential phone to company line

**hookup** assembly and connection of parts linking single phone line to circuit or network

**horn** *Informal.* telephone

**hot line** direct line between two phones always kept open for instant access without dialing

**information** former term for directory assistance

**installation** process of activating single phone or phone system and connecting it to network

**instrument** single telephone with internal circuitry, bell, transmitter, mouthpiece, receiver, earpiece, and housing

**intercom** simple, two-way, short-range communication system with microphone and loudspeaker at each end

**international call** telephone call to location outside nation of origin

**international country code** routing code that directs call to correct nation without operator assistance

**international dialing prefix** three-digit code, usu. 011, giving caller access to international connection

**interrupt service** service that allows operator to cut in on call in emergency

**key** individual dialing button on touch-tone phone; switch that opens or closes communications circuit, moving from one line to another

**keypad** grid of numbered, lettered buttons used to indicate number being called on touch-tone phone

**LATA** *local access and transport area*; one of 161 local telephone calling areas established after breakup of AT&T: calls from one LATA to another are long distance

**life line** reduced rate telephone service for low-income customers in many states

**line** telephone wiring that connects individual, local, and national systems; single telephone connection

**line charge** cost of operating line to residence or business, usu. assessed monthly

**lineman** telephone repairman responsible for maintenance of aboveground lines strung between telephone poles

**listing** single entry of name, address, and telephone number in directory

**local access and transport area** LATA

**local call** call placed to phone within immediate area, usu. at no additional cost

**local loop** local line from business or residential phone to closest telephone company switch

**local network** telephone system handling calls in one city or region, usu. connected to larger network

**long distance** telephone service beyond local area, billed for timed toll

**Ma Bell** *Slang.* interlocking, national telephone company and system, formerly operated by AT&T

**memory phone** telephone instrument equipped with programmable memory that holds frequently dialed numbers accessed by punching a single key

**message rate** charge determined by time of day, distance, and duration of call

**mobile call** call placed from radiotelephone such as cellular phone

**modular equipment** standardized, interchangeable instruments, wiring, and jacks for easy removal and connection

**mouthpiece** end of handset containing microphone

**network** large, interconnected system of communications lines, central exchanges, and processing computers

**network interface** point at which network connects with individual line or system

**900 number** part of special system of toll call numbers used in marketing, public opinion surveys, and sales

**911** emergency number for police, fire, or ambulance

**nonpublished listing** telephone number not printed in directory at customer's request, also not revealed by directory assistance; unlisted number

**not in service** designating telephone line that has been disconnected or is not functioning properly

**off-premises extension** connection of telephone line and number to second location

**operator** person who controls routing, connection, and disconnection of calls through telephone switchboard

**operator-assisted call** call placed through operator rather than by direct dialing

**pager** beeper

**party line** shared telephone circuit that connects two or more customers to exchange

**pay phone** telephone in public place requiring coin deposit or credit card number for use

**PBX** *private branch exchange*; telephone system that functions within one business or building

**PCS** *personal communications service*

**personal communications service** PCS; any of a wide variety of proposed low-power, low-cost, mobile radio-telephones, representing an inexpensive alternative to cellular phones having fewer features

**person-to-person** (*adj*) designating operator-assisted call connected only to person designated by calling party

**phone** telephone instrument; (*vb*) place a telephone call

**phone book** directory of names, addresses, and phone numbers for specified area; telephone directory

**phone booth** small cubicle, generally with sliding door and often located outdoors, from which public may place coin-operated or credit card calls; telephone booth

**Picturephone** *Trademark.* device that combines telephone with television screen, enabling users to see each other, used briefly in 1960's

**PIN** *personal identification number*; computerized code used in placing credit card calls

**prefix** first three digits of seven-digit telephone number, often indicating location of line and exchange

**private line** telephone line intended for exclusive use of one person, family, or organization

**public telephone** telephone located in public place, operated by coin or credit card

**push-button phone** phone on which push-button keys bear numbers and letters used in placing a call

**radiotelephone** telephone in which communication is carried on through radio waves only

**random noise** unpredictable noise and interference in circuit

**receiver** portion of telephone equipment that converts incoming electrical signals into auditory sound waves

**reverse charges** charge toll for call to receiving party

**right of privacy** government-guaranteed right to freedom from interference with or eavesdropping on personal phone calls

**ring** bell-like tone generated by telephone to indicate incoming call; (*vb*) *Chiefly Brit.* place a phone call

**ring off** (*vb*) *Chiefly Brit.* hang up

**ring up** (*vb*) *Chiefly Brit.* place call

**rotary phone** traditional phone on which numbers and letters are arranged in circle beneath dial, which is rotated to indicate number being called

**scramble** (*vb*) alter signal to make it unintelligible without special unscrambling device

**service** installation, repair, maintenance, billing, and call-placing operations of telephone company

**service call** call to repairman to come to home or business to investigate and remedy problem with service

**service charge** basic monthly telephone company fee for use of system

**service order** request for service from phone company

**service rep** *Informal.* phone company employee who handles service orders, complaints, and installation and disconnect requests

**signal** sound conveyed over telephone or telegraph line

**speakerphone** telephone equipped with loudspeaker and microphone so that it can be operated without using handset or headset

**speed calling** service permitting memory storage of frequently called numbers and quick dialing with one or two digits

**station-to-station** (*adj*) designating operator-assisted call to anyone answering number dialed or any direct dial call

**subscriber** customer paying for use of telephone service

**surcharge** additional charge added to telephone fee

**switchboard** device for connecting, controlling, and disconnecting multiple phone lines, as in office

**tap** (*vb*) make secret connection into telephone circuit to eavesdrop on private conversations; wiretap

**tariff** schedule of rates charged by telephone company

**telco** *Informal.* local telephone company

**teleconference** conference call

**telephone** instrument for converting sound into electrical impulses to be transmitted over distances by wire; (*vb*) communicate by telephone

**telephone booth** phone booth

**telephone box** *Chiefly Brit.* phone booth

**telephone directory** phone book

**telephone man** one who repairs, installs, and maintains telephone service

**telephone number** basic seven-digit code by which calls are directed to each phone line

**telephone pole** tall wooden or metal pole from which telephone lines are suspended

**telephonics** science of conveying sound over distances, as by telephone

**telephony** construction and operation of telephone systems; telecommunications system based on telephone equipment that transmits speech or other sounds between two points, with or without wires

**three-way calling** service that allows customer to call two other parties and speak to them simultaneously

**tie-in** linkage between different lines, exchanges, or systems

**tie line** direct line connecting extensions in two or more PBX systems

**time and charges** service in which duration and fee information are provided by operator at termination of call

**toll** fee for telephone call

**toll call** call requiring payment of fee beyond basic service charge

**toll-free** (*adj*) requiring no additional fee beyond basic service charge

**touch-tone** tone-dialing system equipped with push-button keys for indicating number called by transmission of electronic beeps

**traffic** aggregate of calls handled by telephone company in given time

**transmitter** device, esp. mouthpiece, for converting sound waves into electrical impulses to be sent by telephone wire

**trunk line** circuit between two central telephone exchanges for making multiple connections; line from central office to PBX

**tympanum** diaphragm of telephone

**unlisted number** nonpublished listing

**unscramble** (*vb*) make telephonic message comprehensible by tuning receiver to frequencies used in transmission

**untimed service** telephone service that permits unlimited duration of certain local calls without additional per minute charge; flat-rate service

**videoconference** teleconference conducted via television equipment

**videophone** telephone with both audio and video capabilities

**voice mail** electronic system for recording and storage of voice messages, often in digitized form, for later retrieval by intended recipient

**wall phone** telephone instrument mounted on wall

**WATS** *W*ide *A*rea *T*elecommunications *S*ervice; special fixed-rate, long-distance service for companies making many toll calls, with cost unrelated to number of calls made

**white pages** alphabetical directory listing names and addresses with residential and business phone numbers in specific area

**wiretap** act or instance of tapping a telephone so as to eavesdrop on calls made or received; (*vb*) tap

**wrong number** undesired telephone connection due to dialing of incorrect digits

**yellow pages** directory listing business names, addresses, and telephone numbers in specific area, organized by category of business

# COMPUTERS

General Technology
Hardware and Peripherals
Software, Languages, and Programming
Memory

**SEE ALSO**: Chap. 5: Electricity and Electronics; Telecommunications; Chap. 11: Publishing and The Press; Chap. 16: Graphic Design and Printing

## GENERAL TECHNOLOGY

**abort** termination of program that returns control to operating system

**access code** password that allows entry into computer

**access time** interval required to retrieve information from memory or a disk

**A/D** conversion from analog signal to digital data

**ADP** *a*utomated *d*ata *p*rocessing

**AI** *a*rtificial *i*ntelligence

**algorithm** predetermined instructions for step-by-step solution to specific problem

**alphanumeric** (*adj*) consisting of both alphabetic and numeric characters

**Alt** key used alone or in conjunction with control and/or shift key to change meaning of another key with which it is used

**analog** signal with continuous range of values, opp. of digital

**applications** areas or operations of business, art, and technology in which computers are useful

**artificial intelligence** AI; capacity of machines to exhibit intelligent behavior and perform operations similar to learning and decision making

**automated data processing** ADP; processing data using computer program or system that reduces human intervention to a minimum

**automation** science and technology concerned with making self-regulating machines in which electronic devices replace or enhance human control

**backup** duplicate copy of program or file made as insurance against loss or damage

**bar code** light and dark lines readable by scanner, typically written on retail product packaging to represent price and other data

**batch** group of records or transactions that can be processed together

**batch processing** noninteractive computing mode in which input is gathered into groups or batches and additional input cannot be made once program is being executed

**baud** unit of measure of speed at which information is transmitted in number of signal impulses or bits per second

**BCD** binary coded decimal

**bells and whistles** *Informal.* unessential, but often attractive, features

**binary** system in which numbers are represented as sequences of zeros and ones, which is basis of digital computing

**binary coded decimal** BCD; method of encoding four bits of binary code to represent ten decimal digits

**bit vector** method of coding information as string of binary choices forming a vector

**Boolean** (*adj*) describing systems in which variable values are restricted to true and false

**boot** (*vb*) start up computer by loading operating system

**bootstrap** set of instructions that begin operation of operating system

**branch** program statement to control transfer to nonsequential instruction

**bug** error, esp. in program

**bulletin board** service, accessed by modem, that permits users to leave, store, and retrieve messages, shareware, and public-domain software

**bundling** selling hardware and software or several software programs together at set price

**burn** act of leaving new computer system turned on for several days or more to test for failure of electronic components

**bus** series of communications channels in which signals are passed, usu. sockets into which components are plugged

**CAD** computer-aided design; system that uses graphics display to design products

**CAI** computer-aided instruction; interactive teaching software system

**calculator** primitive numerical computer

**capture** (*vb*) record and enter data into computer for processing or storage

**card** printed circuit board or module; punch card used in keypunch encoding of data

**CAT** computer-assisted tomography; use of computer technology in assembling special X-ray

**CCD** charge coupled device; semiconductor sequential information storage technology

**chad** material punched out when holes are made along margins of perforated computer material; any wasted material

**channel** hardware device or path that transfers data between two elements

**character** letter, digit, or graphic symbol used to represent data

**chip** very small piece of silicon processed or burned to form integrated circuit; microchip

**chunk** conceptual unit of data or information

**CISC** complex instruction set computer; CPU able to recognize 100 or more instructions, slower and more common than RISC

**clear** (*vb*) erase stored or displayed data

**clock** electronic device that controls, measures, and monitors system functions

**coaxial cable** transmission wire composed of multiple layers of conductor and insulation

**cold boot** loading sequence in which entire operating system is loaded into computer at start-up or after reset

**command** coded instruction to computer

**compatible** (*adj*) able to use same programs or hardware, esp. matched to major brand but manufactured by smaller company

**computer-aided design** CAD

**computer-aided instruction** CAI

**computer-assisted tomography** CAT

**computerese** argot of computers, their users, and their designers

**computer game** usu. video game based on computer operations, often with joystick

**computer graphics** conversion of digital information into visual format for display on terminal or output on printer

**computerize** (*vb*) equip with or automate by computers

**computer literacy** nontechnical study and understanding of computers and basic familiarity with their uses in society

**computer science** study of design and use of computers and software

**concatenate** (*vb*) sequentially connect independent items

**configuration** computer and all devices connected to it; collection of set-up choices for software program

**control** Ctrl; command key that changes meaning of another key with which it is used

**control character** any keyboard character used as a command

**conversational** (*adj*) designating computer systems that engage user in two-way dialogue

**crash** system failure and shutdown due to software or hardware malfunction

**cross talk** interference between two signals

**crunch** (*vb*) perform many numerical calculations and manipulations of data

**crystal** piece of quartz whose piezoelectric vibrations are used to generate timing signals

**cursor** special character used to denote position on video display, usu. an underline, solid block, or highlight arrow

**cybernation** automatic control of a process or operation by computers

**cyberspace** virtual reality

**cycle time** time required by system to complete specific function

**D/A** conversion from digital data into analog signal such as voltage or sound

**data bus** set of communications channels that carry data between elements of computer

**data entry** inputting of information for processing by computer

**data management system** series of commands used to search and retrieve data and update or reference portions of database

**data processing** basic computer operations in general

**data transfer rate** speed at which information moves between two devices, measured in bits per second

**debug** (*vb*) locate and correct malfunction or error in program code

**dedicated** (*adj*) designed for specific application or function

**delimiter** blank space, comma, character, or symbol that indicates beginning or end of character string, word, or data item

**desktop publishing** DTP; use of personal computer with graphics and typographic layout programs, sometimes an image scanner, and usu. a laser printer to design and create publications

**digital** signal with two discrete values, zero and one, represented by presence or absence of electric pulse

**digital imaging** scanning and recording of visual images in digital form

**digitizer** device that converts images into numeric form comprehensible to computer

**DIP** *dual inline package*; standard method of switching integrated circuits, with pins carrying signals to and from circuit

**directory** table of contents that lists files

**documentation** written and graphic material describing and explaining use, operation, maintenance, or design of piece of hardware or software

**download** (*vb*) transfer programs or files from one computer to another device or computer

**downtime** interval when computer is inoperable due to malfunction

**drag** (*vb*) move cursor across screen by sliding mouse

**DTP** *desktop publishing*

**dump** (*vb*) print or display contents of internal storage on output medium, esp. during program failure

**dynamic range** levels of voltage or analog input signal needed to generate digital output

**EDP** *electronic data processing*; outmoded term for computer operations

**electronic mail** message system that uses telecommunications network links between computers; e-mail

**E-mail** electronic mail

**enable button** function on Macintosh screen that is lit up to indicate that it will work when double-clicked on by mouse, with gray indicating it is not enabled

**end user** person who uses specific hardware or software product

**enter** key command to perform operation

**escape** ESC; ASCII control key used in combination with others to provide added functionality, esp. to interrupt command or return to previous level of program

**even parity** scheme in which eighth bit in ASCII code is used to make sum of eight bits even so that it can be checked for errors

**execute** (*vb*) perform command or series of commands

**execution time** interval required to perform operation

**exit** (*vb*) leave specific context, often to return to system

**expert system** basis of artificial intelligence that captures information in particular domain through hierarchy of if/then questions

**fetch** (*vb*) read contents of specific memory location

**field** unit of data forming part of a record in structured database

**FIFO** *first in, first out*; processing of information in order received

**fifth generation** dawning new era of computer systems that use artificial intelligence and parallel processing by multiple CPUs capable of handling billions of calculations per second

**floating point** representation of numbers using scientific notation of decimal fraction times power of ten

**flow chart** symbolic, logical representation of program control

**footprint** area of desk or floor space occupied by piece of hardware

**format** (*vb*) prepare disk to receive information; (*n*) organization of data on disk into tracks and sectors

**fractal** geometrical structure that has regular or uneven shape repeated over all scales of measurement and a dimension that is greater than the spatial dimension of the structure

**function key** key designated to send specific command code

**fuzzy** (*adj*) approximate, not precise: used to describe search or operation that generates a set whose members lie across a spectrum of values approximating a central value

**generation** hardware developed at one period based on previous level of technology

**GIGO** *garbage in, garbage out*; output quality is dependent on input quality

**glitch** *Slang.* sudden, inexplicable malfunction

**graphics** use of computer to generate and display images on screen

**graphics tablet** wire grid in solid base that, when drawn on by stylus, inputs line drawings and graphics to computer

**hacker** *Slang.* person extremely knowledgeable about computers, frequently an amateur programmer

**handshaking** synchronization technique used to expedite transfer of data between two devices

**help level** portion of menu displayed on screen for user

**hexadecimal** sixteen-base number system commonly used in computers, employing numerals 0 through 9 and letters A through F

**hierarchical** (*adj*) describing any vertical, pyramidal organization of information in related levels and sublevels

**high resolution** video display system or printer that depicts images in great detail with high degree of accuracy

**housekeeping** administrative functions required for efficient system operation but not contributing to specific task execution

**hypermedia** combination of computer and hypertext system with CD audio, VCR, or laser disc capabilities

**IC** *integrated circuit*

**icon** graphic representation, esp. of option on computer menu accessed by mouse

**IDP** *integrated data processing*

**image scanner** graphics device that brushes over image to enter it entirely on disk without key commands

**index hole** hole in floppy disk that indicates beginning of first sector of track, used to trigger drive

**informatics** computer science and the study of information processing

**inheritance network** hierarchical organization of data for artificial intelligence in which elements in each descending level have characteristics of those in levels above them

**input** data received by computer from external source

**instruction** command; single operation to be executed

**integrated circuit**  IC; electronic circuit on single chip of material, usu. silicon; microchip

**integrated data processing**  IDP; processing data by using language common to all machines in system and requiring minimal human intervention

**integrated imaging**  combination of image scanning, graphic, and digital recording techniques

**interactive** (*adj*) designating any program or system that has a dialogue with human user and responds to input

**interactive page layout**  bidirectional desktop publishing process that establishes page layout

**interface**  hardware and/or software required to connect peripheral to computer system, one computer system to another, or for user's access to system; point at which any two parts of system connect

**interrupt**  signal from I/O device or peripheral to CPU to stop current processing and start new operation

**job**  program and data submitted to computer for execution

**joystick**  mechanical lever used to control cursor movement on video display

**jump**  programming instruction that stops sequential processing and transfers control to another point in program

**jumper**  nonmechanical switch that provides options on circuit board

**kerning**  capacity of certain programs, esp. when printing, to vary spacing between pair of letters, esp. reducing space to create balanced appearance

**keypunch**  outmoded system with keyboard-controlled device that encodes data by punching holes in card

**keypunch operator**  individual who enters data by encoding it on cards punched with holes

**keystroke**  single depression of one key on keyboard

**kilobaud**  one thousand bits per second

**kludge**  *Slang*. inelegant or sloppy but workable solution to problem in software or hardware

**label**  several characters that identify file or storage area

**LAN**  local area network; system for linking terminals, PCs, or work stations with each other or with mainframe to share data, peripherals, and programs, usu. in one building

**large scale integration**  LSI; placement of large number of integrated circuits on one silicon chip

**leading**  spacing between lines of type in computer-generated typeset output

**LED**  light emitting diode; feedback device permitting current to flow in one direction only

**LIFO**  last in, first out; most recently received information is processed first

**light pen**  photoelectric stylus that sends signals to computer by movement against CRT screen

**line drawing**  two- or three-dimensional graphic representation of objects on video display screen, esp. done with outlines

**line feed**  control key used as return or to advance to next line

**line surge**  sharp fluctuation in AC voltage that can damage computer circuits and magnetic media

**load** (*vb*) move data or program instructions from storage medium into computer memory for execution

**local area network**  LAN

**log on** (*vb*) enter personal identification data, such as name and/or password, into multiuser system so as to access it

**loop**  set of instructions designed to be repeated

**LSI**  large scale integration

**management information system**  MIS

**manual**  book containing operating instructions and sometimes design specifications for particular piece of hardware or software

**massively parallel processing**  use of thousands of processors acting together to create supercomputer

**microchip**  integrated circuit; chip

**MIPS**  millions of instructions per second; measure of processing speed

**MIS**  management information system; software or department in corporation that supports management in keeping track of and running organizations or departments under it

**mnemonic**  programming code or other shortened form that is easy to remember

**MOS**  metallic oxide semiconductor; material used to create high-density integrated circuits

**mouse**  small handheld device that is rolled across a surface to point at objects and control cursor movement on video display

**multimedia**  combination of text, graphics, video, animation, voice, and music in computer system using optical disc, videocassette, and compact disc audio

**multitasking**  ability of user to have multiple activities or programs in progress simultaneously

**multiuser** (*adj*) describing operating system that permits several users to share access to computer

**nesting**  programming technique that employs hierarchical levels of instruction

**network**  set of communications channels that connect computers

**neural network**  basis for advanced artificial intelligence by which computer forms and recognizes patterns, enabling it to reach conclusions not laid out for it by binary architecture

**noise**  random signals, interference, or nonmanaged data

**null cycle**  time required to scroll through entire program without introducing new data

**number crunching**  repetitive, arithmetic-intensive processing

**OCR**  optical character recognition

**octal** (*adj*) of or pertaining to an eight-base number system, sometimes used to encode data, employing numerals 0 through 7

**odd parity**  scheme in which eighth bit in ASCII code is used to make sum of eight bits odd so that it can be checked for errors

**off-line** (*adj*) designating equipment not directly linked to central computer or CPU

**on-line** (*adj*) designating equipment directly linked to central computer or CPU

**on-screen** (*adj*) designating data displayed on video terminal

**opening menu**  initial set of options that appear when program is loaded

**operand**  data unit or equipment item operated upon

**operator**  user of computer system

**optical character recognition**  OCR; process that optically scans printed text and converts it into machine-readable code

**optical reader wand**  mechanical device that reads bar codes

**output**  result of computer operation, usu. in form of hard copy or video display

**override** instruction that stops execution of previous command

**palette** complete range of colors available for display through computer graphics card

**parallel processing** data processing by multiple CPUs acting simultaneously

**parameter** definable characteristic or limit of system or program

**parity** error-detecting technique using eighth bit; odd parity or even parity

**parity bit** eighth bit in ASCII code that becomes zero or one to make sum of all eight bits even or odd as a data check

**password** code or sequence of characters used to protect system or specific file from unauthorized use

**patch** piece of program code inserted to debug or modify existing program

**pico** one thousandth of a billionth; one trillionth

**pixel** single dot and smallest element in visual display; square picture unit that is basis of computer graphics

**plotter** device used to make drawing on video display

**poke** program operation that loads specified value into specific memory location

**power down** orderly shutdown of computer and peripherals

**power supply** device that converts AC line voltage into DC voltage, used by computer

**power surge** sudden, dangerous fluctuation in AC voltage

**power-up** orderly start-up of computer and peripherals

**procedure** logical set of program commands called by single name

**program counter** CPU register storing address of next instruction to be fetched from memory for execution

**prompt** character displayed on terminal that indicates that computer is awaiting further instructions from user, often also identifying logged drive

**protocol** set of rules governing information exchange

**pseudobus** computer designed with all connective devices on single board and sockets for adding modules

**quad density** storage density of some disk media

**queue** FIFO-organized sequence of items awaiting processing or action by peripheral

**QWERTY** designation for traditional typewriter keyboard layout, named after six letters at upper left

**read** (*vb*) receive data into memory

**readout** manner in which computer presents processed information, such as visual display or line printer

**real time** actual time required for computer operations involving rapid analysis of data, esp. as it affects a physical process

**record** group of related fields forming unit of information in structured database

**recursion** repeated application of algorithm to define function or make calculation

**relational** (*adj*) describing development of database as large matrix

**response time** interval between input of data and computer output or response

**RISC** reduced instruction set computer; computer designed with chip that eliminates all but minimum number of instructions needed to perform most common tasks, providing increased processing speed

**robotics** control by computer of machine programmed to perform industrial or other tasks

**rollover** keyboard ability that allows rapid typing yet codes characters in order struck

**run** single, continuous execution of program by computer

**seek time** time required to move disk read/write head to specific track

**semiconductor** material that can be manipulated to improve its conductivity for the passage of electrons, esp. silicon used for integrated circuits

**sentinel** tag

**serial access** obtaining data sequentially by searching through all preceding data on that file or program

**serial processing** computer operations in which programs are run sequentially, not simultaneously

**Silicon Valley** area in northern California, south of San Francisco in the Santa Clara valley region, with concentration of semiconductor and computer companies

**silicon wafer** thin silicon disk used to make chips

**smoke test** checkout of new equipment

**solenoid** device that converts electric current into linear motion by magnetizing hollow coil

**spikes** sharp, temporary fluctuations in signal or voltage

**SPOOL** *simultaneous peripheral operations on-line*; technique that allows I/O operation of peripheral device such as printer while simultaneously executing another program

**stepper motor** rotating motor used to move read/write heads on floppy disk drives

**string** ordered sequence of data elements, usu. characters, treated as a unit

**stylus** light pen; scanning device used for input on graphics tablet

**support** personnel, documentation, or programs that complement hardware or software technology

**surge control** device that protects system from AC power surges

**sysop** *Informal.* *systems operator*; operator of bulletin board

**systems analysis** examination of operations in order to improve them or determine how to accomplish specific goals

**tag** indicator of beginning or end of unit of information; sentinel

**technical support** assistance offered by vendor of hardware or software to end user, usu. by telephone or through bulletin board

**telecommuting** working at home at computer terminal linked to another site, as by modem

**terminate** (*vb*) exit from program and usu. return to opening menu

**throughput** measure of system's execution efficiency in instructions per second

**timesharing** sharing of CPU by several users at once for different purposes through buffers and switching

**toggle** on/off switch with two positions that initiates or halts function

**tree structure** hierarchical organization of data for efficient search and retrieval

**turnaround time** interval needed to provide answer to question or execute task

**tweak** (*vb*) *Slang.* make fine adjustments to

**unbundling** pricing of system's hardware and software separately

**universal product code**  UPC; machine-readable bar code used for labeling merchandise

**UPC**  *universal product code*

**user**  individual who accesses a computer system

**user-friendly**  (*adj*) easy for user to understand and execute without extensive training

**user group**  people who share information on systems and software through meetings and publications

**variable**  named program entity capable of representing different values during program execution

**very large scale integration**  VLSI; placement of from one hundred thousand to one million circuits on single chip

**virtual reality**  creation of imaginary, animated, three-dimensional landscape that one may explore and change by means of sensors attached to one's body and connected to computer that generates scenes; cyberspace

**VLSI**  *very large scale integration*

**voice recognition**  ability of system to accept spoken words as input

**voice synthesis**  system capable of generating audio output responses in simulated voice using specific vocabulary of electronic phonemes

**wafer**  thin silicon disk used to make chips

**warm boot**  function that reads directories and reloads portions of operating system into RAM

**window**  individually controlled portion of screen on which information can be shown, esp. without exiting document file or program

**work station**  powerful, single-user computer, esp. one used for CAD, often networked

**WYSIWYG**  *what you see is what you get*; term designating video display that shows text as it will appear in printout

**zap**  *Informal.* unintentional overwrite of file; intentional use of command found in many programs to clear screen

## HARDWARE AND PERIPHERALS

**accumulator**  special purpose register of CPU that stores numeric data for arithmetic or logical operations

**acoustic coupler**  early type of modem, consisting of rubber cups that attached to earpiece and mouthpiece of telephone handset

**ALU**  *arithmetic/logic unit*; portion of CPU that performs arithmetic calculations and other logical operations

**arithmetic/logic unit**  ALU

**backplane**  motherboard

**bidirectional printing**  operation of printer from left to right and right to left for added speed; boustrophedon

**boustrophedon**  bidirectional printing

**buffer**  intermediate, temporary storage device for holding data until computer or peripheral such as printer is ready to process it

**card**  printed circuit board or module

**carriage**  moving portion of printer that carries paper

**cathode-ray tube**  CRT; common computer display screen

**CD drive**  disk drive that accepts compact disk storage medium

**central processing unit**  CPU; main part of computer system

**clone**  IBM-compatible computer

**coder-decoder**  chip used in analog-digital translation

**computer**  general purpose, digital, information processing device composed of a central processing unit, memory, input and output facilities, power supply, and housing

**computer system**  information processing package that includes computer and peripherals

**configure**  (*vb*) adjust printer, modem, or other peripheral to follow central processor; set up software with user-designated parameters

**console**  part of computer, such as keyboard and monitor, that enables operator to communicate with system

**continuous form**  unseparated sheets of paper with sprocket holes along margins, fed automatically into printer

**converter**  device that accepts data in one form and changes it into another, as from analog to digital

**CPS**  *characters per second*; designation of dot-matrix or daisy wheel printer speed

**CPU**  *central processing unit*; central intelligence of computer that processes and executes program instructions

**Cray**  *Trademark.* massive, parallel processing computer

**CRT**  *cathode-ray tube* used as monitor to display characters or designs

**daisy wheel**  rimless wheel with characters stored on ends of spokes, attached to moving carriage for use in letter-quality printing

**daisy wheel printer**  impact printer using daisy wheel for letter-quality printing

**digitizer**  device that converts information into numeric form comprehensible to digital computer

**disk drive**  electromechanical device that spins magnetic disk and allows data to be written to or read from disk through read/write head

**display**  video monitor, such as CRT or LCD, that temporarily shows information

**dot-matrix printer**  printer that forms characters with dots organized in matrix, usu. by impact process

**drive**  disk drive

**dual-processor**  (*adj*) designating computer system with two CPUs performing different operations simultaneously

**Dynabook**  *Trademark.* prototype of palmtop computer with handwriting recognition

**emulator**  hardware or software that allows one computer to simulate the behavior of another type of computer

**ENIAC**  *Trademark.* electronic numerical integrator and calculator; early mainframe computer that filled a large room

**execute**  (*vb*) run (a program)

**expansion slot**  connection to which new board can be added

**external slot**  point at which additional peripherals and modules can be connected to motherboard

**fanfold paper**  continuous form paper, folded on perforations and stacked in zigzag fashion

**file server**  computer acting as file storage for other networked computers, allowing multiple users access to individual file

**first generation**  earliest model of hardware in specific upgrade path

**form feed**  printer default parameter that controls automatic paper supply to printer through tractor feed

**486**  computer using full 32-bit microprocessor chip, currently fastest and most powerful personal computer

**front end processor**  small computer interfacing large host computer and peripherals that reduces I/O interruptions to host

**full-page display** vertically elongated video monitor able to display entire page of text

**graphics tablet** wire grid embedded in screen, activated by stylus to record points traced by stylus

**hard copy** computer output printed on paper; printout

**hard drive** device, either external or internal, that spins and reads high-capacity storage hard disk

**hardware** physical components of system: computer, external memory system, terminal, printer, modem

**hard-wired** (*adj*) built into hardware, as through electronic circuits, rather than functioning through software

**IBM-compatible** (*adj*) designating computer system that can interface with IBM hardware or software designed for IBM machines

**impact printer** printer that generates characters by character striking ribbon against paper

**ink-jet printer** printer that generates characters by squirting ink droplets against paper, controlled by deflection magnets

**input/output** I/O; devices or communications channels that move information into and out of computer

**I/O** *input/output*

**I/O port** data channel that connects peripherals to computer

**keyboard** device for inputting data by depressing keys that generate all standard characters (letters, digits, punctuation marks) and other keys that have special functions, such as cursor arrow keys or programmable function keys

**keypad** special purpose numeric keyboard to which other commands or characters may be assigned; numeric pad

**landscape** printing in which image or text is turned sideways, using top and bottom of page as sides

**laptop computer** very small personal computer, designed to fit on lap

**laser perf paper** continuous, fanfold paper with very fine perforations on edges

**laser printer** high-quality printer that forms images by focusing laser beam on photosensitive drum

**LCD** *liquid crystal display*

**letter-quality printer** impact printer that produces hard copy of high quality, comparable to that of electric typewriter

**line printer** impact printer capable of producing full line of 80 to 132 characters at one time

**liquid crystal display** LCD; flat-panel video screen that uses solution of liquid crystal subjected to voltage to block rear light transmission and generate display

**local network** computers in close proximity sharing peripherals

**logic board** motherboard for Apple and Macintosh computers

**Macintosh** *Trademark*. line of Apple computers, mouse-operated, with extensive graphics capabilities, hypertext, and graphical user interface

**mainframe** giant institutional computer that requires conditioned environment and allows for multiple users at work stations

**micro** microcomputer

**microcomputer** small home or office desktop computer that uses a CPU on a single chip, with power supply and I/O interfaces; micro

**microprocessor** complete CPU in integrated circuit on single chip

**mini** minicomputer

**minicomputer** intermediate size, usu. multiuser computer frequently used as work station or connected to work stations

**modem** *modulator/demodulator*; device linking two computers by telephone lines

**module** computer circuit board with specific function, used as building block in system

**monitor** high-resolution display screen; low-level CPU control that operates program

**motherboard** circuit board with series of parallel bus sockets into which computer modules and circuitry are plugged; backplane

**near-letter-quality printer** correspondence quality printer, such as dot-matrix, thermal, or ink-jet printer

**notebook computer** small laptop or portable computer, usu. under seven pounds in weight

**numeric pad** keypad

**open architecture** system design that permits easy replacement and upgrading of circuit boards, even the use of those made by third parties

**optical scanner** device that scans light from surface of printed matter and converts analog signals into machine-readable input for storage in computer

**overstrike** multiple striking of each character by impact printer to give darker impression

**page printer** printer that determines character pattern for entire page at once, rather than printing line by line

**palmtop** very small portable computer that can be held in one hand

**parallel configuration** interface between computer and peripheral that transfers entire byte or word of data at once, with separate line for each bit

**parallel port** actual connection in parallel configuration

**parallel printer** printer designed for parallel interface with computer

**PC** *personal computer*

**peripheral** device such as printer, modem, or hard drive, connected to and dependent on computer

**personal computer** PC; small, relatively low-cost microcomputer designed for home or business use

**port** channel connecting I/O device to computer

**portrait** normal printing in which image or text runs from top to bottom of page

**printout** hard copy; printed version of document file

**proportional spacing** printing technique in which character width determines space allowed

**PS/2** *Trademark*. IBM Personal System/2 computer that uses MS-DOS operating system

**rack-mountable** (*adj*) designating equipment designed for installation in standard nineteen-inch metal rack

**radiation shield** protective shield placed over video display to reduce eye strain and block radiation emissions

**read/write head** electromagnetic device used to read from or write to magnetic storage medium such as disk

**reconfiguring** resetting instructions that connect computer to peripheral such as printer

**retrofit** (*vb*) upgrade hardware, esp. with components that were not available at time of original manufacture

**reverse video** video display with dark characters on light background

**screen** video display terminal; contents of what appears on monitor

**SCSI** *small computer system interface*; pronounced

"scuzzy"; cable or other method of connecting peripheral to computer

**serial configuration** interface between computer and peripheral that passes information one bit or character at a time

**serial port** actual connection in serial configuration

**serial printer** printer designed for serial interface with computer

**sheet feeder** tray or other device that feeds paper into printer one sheet at a time

**single-board computer** computer with design placing CPU, main memory, and I/O controllers on single circuit board

**smart terminal** terminal with buffer to store certain amount of information and with microprocessor that allows for some processing capabilities

**split screen** screen divided into two or more windows that display independent or connected data

**stepper motor** rotating motor used to move read/write heads on floppy disk drives

**supercomputer** very fast, powerful mainframe, esp. for military and scientific research

**supermini** fastest and most powerful minicomputer, with capabilities nearly equal to those of a mainframe

**system** computer and all its related components

**terminal** peripheral device through which user communicates with computer, including keyboard for input and video display for output

**thermal printer** low-speed, moderate quality, small format, nonimpact printer that forms characters by applying heat to specially sensitized paper

**thimble printer** variation on daisy wheel printer with spokes bent up at 75 degree angle and two characters on each thimble-shaped spoke

**386** computer with 32-bit microprocessor chip

**tractor feed** device that moves continuous form, fanfold paper through printer

**286** computer with 16-bit microprocessor chip

**UNIVAC** *Trademark. universal automatic computer;* first generation, vacuum tube, mainframe computer introduced in 1951

**VDT** *video display terminal;* CRT monitor or other screen used to display computer output and communicate with computer; VDU

**VDU** *video display unit;* VDT

**video card** control device that runs color monitor

**word processor** dedicated computer used to write and process text documents

**XT** *Trademark.* second-generation IBM personal computer

## SOFTWARE, LANGUAGES, AND PROGRAMMING

**ALGOL** *algorithmic language;* early, high-level mainframe language, esp. used for teaching; forerunner of Pascal

**AppleDOS** disk operating system used in Apple computers

**application software** programs designed to handle particular types of information to achieve specific results, such as word processing or spreadsheet

**ASCII** *American Standard Code for Information Interchange;* code most commonly used to represent characters, using seven bits to represent each of 128 characters, including control codes

**assembler** program that converts assembly language into binary machine language

**assembly language** machine-specific, low-level, mnemonic language used to write efficient programs

**authoring system** group of programming tools used to develop usu. multimedia product

**background program** multitask program executed when CPU is not busy with priority task

**backslash** oblique stroke slanted to left, used as delimiter in some computer operating systems

**BASIC** *Beginner's All-purpose Symbolic Instruction Code;* simplified language for programmers on microcomputers

**benchmark program** standardized program used to compare speed of different computers

**beta** introductory version of new software program still being tested by outside users

**beta test** test of new or upgraded software conducted at select user sites just prior to release of product

**BIOS** communications medium between DOS and machine language

**block operation** task involving manipulation of information block

**bridgeware** software that serves as bridge between one kind of system or platform and another

**bundled software** several software programs sold together or sold with piece of hardware

**C** high-level programming language

**chaining** breaking up of program that exceeds memory capacity into smaller units that are executed sequentially

**COBOL** *common business oriented language;* high-level business language used on mainframes

**code** programming language that tells machine what to do

**compatibility** ability of software to run on specific computers

**compiler** program that translates high-level language into machine code that computer can execute

**compression** programming technique that compacts large amounts of data for storage on disks or inclusion in program

**conversion** translation of data from one operating system or program to another

**courseware** educational software designed esp. for classroom use

**CP/M** *Trademark. Control Program for Microcomputers;* early operating system for eight-bit microprocessors

**DA** *desk accessory*

**data bank** database or number of databases

**database** systematically structured collection of information organized for easy input, access, retrieval, storage, and update

**DBMS** *database management system;* program that creates, maintains, and accesses database

**DDT** *dynamic debugging tool;* program used to analyze and correct software problems

**default** option or value built into program or system in lieu of user input, but able to be overriden; default setting or parameter

**delete** word processing command to remove one or more characters

**desk accessory** DA; program built into Macintosh system

so that it is always available regardless of current process in operation

**diagnostic** program used to find source of errors or malfunctions

**disk operating system** DOS; program managing operation of entire disk drive–based system

**DOS** *disk operating system*

**dot command** printing and page formatting instruction in WordStar and some other word-processing programs, distinguished by period placed before command letters

**EBCDIC** *extended binary-coded decimal interchange code;* eight-bit character code for 256 characters, used by IBM mainframes instead of ASCII

**edit** (*vb*) make changes in document file

**emulation** real-time simulation program that allows one computer to mimic operations of another

**executable code** machine-readable version of code that machine can actually run, all in bits

**file management system** program or programs that facilitate creation and management of files

**Finder** *Trademark.* portion of operating system for Macintosh computers that locates elements to be processed

**firmware** program stored in ROM and built into computer, usu. to implement function previously provided in software

**FORTRAN** *formula translator;* early general-purpose, high-level compiled language, used primarily for mainframes and minis

**global search** program or command that searches for and acts upon every occurrence of a character, word, or phrase within file

**graphical user interface** GUI; video-display environment based on icons, WYSIWYG screen, and mouse operations, used orig. on Macintosh computers

**groupware** business or office software designed for use by network of users at connected work stations

**GUI** *graphical user interface*

**high-level language** programming language, such as C, COBOL, or Pascal, with form similar to English or mathematics

**hypertext** discrete units of information linked together for retrieval in nonsequential, associative form

**init** *initialization procedure;* usu. shareware utility that loads itself into RAM on start-up of Macintosh computer

**installed base** entire number of users of particular program

**intermediate compiler** program that translates high-level computer language into object code and saves it, prior to conversion into executable machine language

**interoperability** capacity of software to run on more than one platform, such as MS-DOS or Macintosh

**interpreter** program that translates high-level language into machine language to allow immediate execution of program

**JCL** *job control language*

**job control language** JCL; language that provides system with information needed to execute specific batch programs

**justify** (*vb*) align text against right and/or left margins

**language** arbitrarily designed and coded syntax and vocabulary that allows user to communicate with computer

**LISP** *list processing language;* high-level interpretive or compiled language used in artificial intelligence

**LOGO** powerful programming language for use by children

**Lotus 1,2,3** *Trademark.* powerful and popular spreadsheet program

**low-level language** coding specification that is close to language understood by computer and therefore more difficult for people

**machine language** binary code language that can be directly executed by CPU; basic language understood by computer

**machine-readable** (*adj*) encoded in or translated into form suitable for processing, such as ASCII

**macro** single command that expands into series of instructions temporarily or permanently saved as that command

**memory resident** designating program that remains in internal memory while other programs are being executed

**menu** list of program options displayed for user

**menu-driven** (*adj*) run by choosing from presented options rather than by entering commands

**merge** (*vb*) combine two files of ordered information into single file

**MS-DOS** *Trademark.* MicroSoft-Disk Operating System; dominant 16-bit disk operating system for IBM-compatible personal computers

**multiprogramming** process in which two or more programs are run simultaneously in same computer

**object code** intermediate stage between source code and executable code

**opening menu** initial set of options available when program is loaded

**operating system** OS; software that organizes and manages resources of system, communicates with peripherals, interacts with users, handles files, and accesses software

**operation code** assembly language that tells machine what to do

**OS** *operating system*

**output** information computer produces by executing program; means of displaying or extracting information from computer

**Pascal** popular, high-level structured programming language

**PC-DOS** standard operating system for IBM PC, marketed for compatibles as MS-DOS

**platform** major piece of software, such as an operating system, operating environment, or database, under which various smaller applications are designed to run

**pop-up window** window that can appear from background, remains hidden until needed, and goes away after use

**presentation software** graphics program designed for use in live presentation to audience

**print** command to send file to printer to produce hard copy of file

**productivity software** business applications that directly aid work of an organization, such as word-processing, spreadsheet, database, or desktop-publishing programs

**program** sequence of instructions to computer to perform specific work

**programmer** individual trained to design, write, and implement programs in any of various computer languages

**programming** study and practice of designing and building computer software programs; translation of problem from physical environment to a language computer can understand

**relational database** collection of data arranged logically into tables rather than hierarchically

**reprogram** (*vb*) rewrite or revise computer program

**retrofit** correction of one facet of program while program is in effect

**return** key that instructs computer to perform command just entered; key that produces hard-carriage return in word processing

**RPG** *report program generator*; business-oriented programming language used with databases

**scrolling** using screen as window on a file while moving vertically or horizontally through the file

**search and replace** capacity of editing program to find any appearance of specified character, word, or phrase in file and replace it with another specified character, word, or phrase

**shareware** often simple programs available at no charge, but for which a token donation is requested

**shell** large macro of saved keystrokes used as special commands

**SNOBOL** *string-oriented symbolic* language; high-level programming language used to manipulate character strings

**soft hyphen** hyphen automatically inserted in word at line break that will not appear if reformatted paragraph alters word placement

**software** instructions and programs that tell hardware what to do

**software package** computer program and documentation designed and marketed to fill a specific need, such as word processing

**source code** program in commonly understood, high-level language that must pass through compiler or interpreter to execute

**spell check** program designed to find and/or correct spelling errors in document, usu. used with word-processing program

**spreadsheet** program that simulates business or scientific worksheet and performs calculations when data is changed

**stand-alone** (*adj*) designating self-contained software program or computer system that operates independently

**structured language** high-level computer language such as Pascal or ALGOL that stresses logical flow of control and extensive self-documentation

**subscript** usu. small character printed below normal line of type

**superscript** usu. small character printed above normal line of type

**System** *Trademark*. operating system for Macintosh computers, working in conjunction with Finder

**systems software** collection of essential utilities programs for use with particular computer system

**text editor** program for revising stored documents and moving text

**TRS-DOS** *Trademark*. family of disk operating systems designed for Radio Shack computers

**UNIX** *Trademark*. multiuser operating system orig. developed at Bell Telephone Labs

**upgrade** new, improved version of previously released software program

**user assistance** help instructions built into program

**user interface** part of program that provides interaction between person and rest of software through video display and input devices

**utility** operating system-specific software used to perform routine tasks such as sorting, debugging, formatting, and copying

**vaporware** software that is promoted or marketed while still in development and may never be produced

**virus** self-replicating program intentionally designed to disrupt operations of one computer or computer network

**Windows** *Trademark*. operating environment featuring graphical user interface and mouse operation for MS-DOS computers

**Word** *Trademark*. popular word-processing program

**word processing** computer creation and manipulation of text by editing, formatting, storing, and printing

**WordPerfect** *Trademark*. popular word-processing program

**WordStar** *Trademark*. popular word-processing program

**word wrap** word-processing program's capacity to automatically place word on next line if it extends beyond margin

## MEMORY

**address** label designating numerical position of storage location in memory

**address bus** set of communications channels that determine amount of main memory computer can control

**bank** logical unit of memory

**batch** group of records or programs considered as single unit for processing

**bit** one binary digit, whose value is either zero or one; basic unit of computer memory

**block** logical unit of stored data

**bubble memory** high-capacity semiconductor memory technology that stores information in tiny magnetic bubbles

**byte** eight bits of information, usu. represents one character of data in memory

**cache memory** very high-speed, not addressable, semiconductor storage device for executing instructions

**cartridge** removable module holding secondary storage medium, esp. magnetic tape; similar module holding program stored in ROM, such as computer game

**cassette** cartridgelike tape storage device using 1/8 inch (3.2 mm) tape

**CD-ROM** *compact disc read-only memory*; compact disc used for permanent storage of massive amounts of data

**close** operation in which file is stored on external memory device and rendered unreadable until reopened

**copying** duplicating files or programs from one magnetic storage medium to another

**data** information that may be organized and processed by programs

**data file** information stored in external memory and recalled under unique file name

**direct access** random access

**directory** table of contents for files on disk

**diskette** floppy disk

**document file** collection of data stored on disk

**double density**  storage density of some disk media, greater than single density and less than high density

**double-sided disk**  disk able to store data on both sides

**DRAM**  dynamic random-access memory; fast-access, re-writeable, volatile memory chip

**drum**  cylinder coated with magnetic material, used as high-speed external memory device in mainframe computers

**dump** (vb)  copy or transfer contents of memory, esp. from one level to another

**dupe** (vb)  duplicate information, esp. from one disk to another

**EPROM**  erasable programmable read-only memory; read-only memory that can be erased under high intensity ultraviolet light and reprogrammed

**external memory**  disk drive, cassette, or other storage device not directly addressed by CPU and not part of main memory

**fetch** (vb)  read contents of specific memory location

**field**  sector of memory designated for specific kind of information

**file**  organized collection of data stored under single name

**file directory**  organized collection of information stored under single name; list of file names and sizes on disk

**flippy**  double-sided floppy disk turned over and used in single-sided drive

**floppy disk**  mylar disk storage medium in cardboard jacket

**GB**  gigabyte

**gigabyte**  GB; 1,024 x 1,024 x 1,024 bytes or approximately one billion bytes

**gulp**  Slang. group of bytes or bits

**hard disk**  high-speed, large capacity disk made of rigid substratum covered with magnetic oxide

**head**  device that reads or writes information on magnetic media

**high density**  storage density of some disk media, greater than double density

**index hole**  hole in floppy disk indicating beginning of first sector of track, used to trigger drive

**K**  kilobyte

**KB**  kilobyte

**kilobyte**  K or KB; 1,024 bytes

**laser disc**  optical disc

**load** (vb)  move data or program instructions from storage medium into computer memory for execution; move disk drive read/write head into operation

**logged disk drive**  engaged drive in dual drive system

**magnetic bubble**  tiny, mobile magnetized area that is basis of storage medium

**magnetic card**  flexible, plastic 3x7 inch card with magnetic surface used for data storage

**magnetic disk**  flat, round, magnetic-mechanical data storage medium coated with oxide that is selectively magnetized to record data and rotates on drive past read/write head which records data on concentric circles called tracks

**magnetic media**  material used to store information on cards, tapes, floppy disks, hard disks, or drums by magnetizing particles

**mailbox**  file for storing electronic mail

**main memory**  internal memory of computer, generally RAM

**mass storage**  external memory device such as a disk or cassette

**MB**  megabyte

**mechanical memory**  external memory device such as disk or drum

**megabyte**  MB; 1,024 x 1,024 bytes or approximately one million bytes

**memory**  internal or external storage area and capacity to store and retrieve binary data and programs; storage

**memory management**  use of hardware and software to control and allocate memory resources

**microfiche**  4x6 inch film used to store miniaturized photographic images of data

**microfloppy**  newer floppy disk, actually rigid, with 3 1/2-inch (8.9-cm) diameter

**minifloppy**  original 5 1/4-inch (13.3-cm) diameter floppy disk

**nibble**  four bits or half a byte

**nonvolatile memory**  memory that retains contents on storage medium when power is shut off

**optical disc**  grooveless disk on which digital data are stored as tiny pits in the surface and read by laser beam scanning the surface

**primary memory**  main storage area for data and programs

**punch card**  standardized, stiff paper card that stores information via punched holes denoting numerical values

**RAM**  random-access memory; volatile read/write memory that allows direct access to data and loses its data contents when power is turned off

**random access**  technique for storing or retrieving data in location where access does not require sequential search; direct access

**random-access memory**  RAM

**read-only memory**  ROM

**refresh** (vb)  maintain information stored in volatile memory

**register**  high-speed storage location in CPU that operates on small amounts of data

**reset key**  button or key that clears computer's volatile memory back to cold boot

**retrieval**  accessing of data in storage

**ROM**  read-only memory; memory storage device that can be written to once and not changed, used for nonvolatile, machine-specific instructions

**ROM chip**  integrated circuit with read-only memory implanted on it

**save**  place data on nonvolatile magnetic media for storage

**scratchpad**  small, fast, volatile storage in certain computers

**sector**  one of contiguous portions of disk track, so divided for rapid and efficient data storage

**sequential access**  storage method, such as on magnetic tape, that allows access to elements only in fixed order

**single density**  storage density of some disk media, less than double density

**single-sided disk**  disk that stores data on one side only

**SRAM**  static random-access memory; volatile memory technology using RAM chip that holds its contents without being constantly refreshed from CPU, faster and more expensive than DRAM

**storage**  memory

**storage capacity**  amount of data that can be stored in computer memory

**streaming mode**  magnetic tape system for copying data from hard disk as backup

**swapping**  technique for transfer of program and data code from one storage medium to main memory and back, or between levels of main memory

**tape memory** data-storage medium that consists of electro-magnetic tape

**TB** *terabyte*

**terabyte** TB; 1,024 x 1,024 x 1,024 x 1,024 bytes or approximately one trillion bytes

**TPI** *tracks per inch*; measure of disk storage density

**track** concentric circle on disk or drum surface for storage of data at designated address

**virtual storage** extension of addressable memory through secondary storage controlled by systems software that treats it as addressable main storage

**volatile memory** memory that does not retain data when power is turned off

**Winchester disk drive** original and sometimes alternate name for high-speed hard disk

**write** (*vb*) record data in memory

**write-protect** (*adj*) designating notch on 5 1/4-inch disk that, when covered, prevents inadvertent writing-over of stored information; designating similarly functioning mechanical switch on 3 1/2-inch disk

# CHAPTER 6

# Transportation

# AIRCRAFT

Types of Aircraft
Aviation and Aerodynamics
Airframe and Engines
Avionics and Instrumentation
Commercial Airlines, Airports, and Air Force

**SEE ALSO**: Chap. 4: Astronomy and Space Science; Chap. 11: War and Military

## TYPES OF AIRCRAFT

**ACV** *air cushion vehicle*

**aerodyne** early term for any heavier-than-air craft that derived lift from aerodynamic forces

**aerostat** balloon or other lighter-than-air craft lifted by container of gas

**Airbus** *Trademark*. large, short-range aircraft for mass transportation of passengers

**aircraft** structure designed to travel through the air; aerodyne or aerostat

**air cushion vehicle** ACV; Hovercraft

**airliner** large passenger aircraft operated by airline

**airplane** fixed-wing, heavier-than-air craft kept aloft by aerodynamic forces and powered by screw propeller or jet propulsion; also, *esp. Brit.* aeroplane

**airship** steered lighter-than-air craft with engine, esp. dirigible or blimp

**air taxi** small commercial airliner carrying passengers and mail to places not regularly served

**amphibian** aircraft capable of takeoff and landing on water and land

**autogiro** aircraft with freely rotating rotor in place of fixed wing and propeller for propulsion, cannot take off vertically or hover

**balloon** lighter-than-air, engineless aircraft propelled by airflow and lifted by enclosed bag of gas

**biplane** airplane with two sets of wings mounted one above the other

**blimp** nonrigid or semirigid airship

**Boeing 727** *Trademark*. most common midsize commercial jetliner, with three engines and capacity to hold 150 passengers

**bomber** air force plane designed to drop bombs

**chopper** *Informal*. helicopter

**crop duster** small aircraft that flies low over crops to spray pesticide

**Cub** *Trademark*. light, low-horsepower, high-wing Piper airplane

**DC-3** *Trademark*. most common propeller-driven commercial airliner, still in use

**dirigible** airship with lifting cells, as zeppelin

**dive bomber** aircraft that releases bombs while diving at target

**fighter** small, fast, highly maneuverable craft used in aerial combat

**gasbag** *Slang*. hot-air balloon

**gas balloon** hot-air balloon

**glider** heavier-than-air craft supported in flight by action of air against lifting surfaces, not dependent on engine and usu. not having one; sailplane

**grasshopper** *Slang*. small, light, military scouting and liaison plane

**gyrodyne** rotorcraft with engine-driven rotors and independent conventional propellers for propulsion

**gyroplane** rotorcraft with rotors started by engine but rotated by action of air, with independent propellers for propulsion

**heavier-than-air craft** aircraft that is heavier than air it displaces and is lifted by application of propulsion to aerodynamic forces

**heavy aircraft** class of aircraft capable of takeoff weights over 325,000 pounds

**helibus** helicopter used for short-range mass transportation of passengers

**helicopter** rotary-winged aircraft having one or more power-driven rotors on vertical axes, dependent for horizontal motion on rotors

**high-altitude reconnaissance plane** military surveillance craft capable of flying at altitudes over 50,000 feet (15,240 m)

**hot-air balloon** aerostat lifted by enclosure filled with heated air; gas balloon

**Hovercraft** vehicle that travels across land or water on cushion of air formed by downward thrust of jet engines; air cushion vehicle

**hydroplane** seaplane

**interceptor** fast-climbing fighter jet used defensively against attack

**jet** aircraft powered by jet propulsion

**jetliner** jet-powered commercial airliner

**jumbo jet** very large commercial jet airliner, such as the Boeing 747, DC-10, or Tristar L-1011, that holds over 300 passengers

**Lear jet** *Trademark*. small, powerful, noncommercial jet aircraft

**lighter-than-air craft** aircraft that rises and remains suspended by use of contained gas weighing less than the air it displaces, esp. balloon

**monoplane** aircraft or glider with one pair of wings

**ornithopter** experimental aircraft propelled by flapping wings

**pursuit plane** pre-World War II air force fighter plane

**rotorcraft** heavier-than-air craft principally dependent for flight on lift generated by one or more rotors

**sailplane** glider

**seaplane** aircraft designed to land on and take off from water; hydroplane

**747** jumbo jet manufactured by Boeing

**short takeoff and landing** STOL; aircraft capable of operating from short runway

**spy plane** high-altitude military reconnaissance plane

**SST** *supersonic transport*

**STOL** *short takeoff and landing* aircraft

**supersonic transport** SST; commercial airliner that flies faster than speed of sound

**tandem airplane** craft with two or more sets of wings with similar dimensions, placed one in front of the other on same level

**tanker** aircraft carrying fuel for in-air refueling of other aircraft

**tilt-rotor** amphibious military aircraft with rotors that stand vertically during takeoff and tilt to horizontal position to act as propellers in flight

**transport** large military aircraft used to convey troops or cargo

**triphibian** aircraft capable of takeoff or landing on land, water, or snow and ice

**ultralight** class of extremely low-weight, single-seat aircraft not requiring pilot's license for operation

**vertical takeoff and landing** VTOL; term applied to aircraft capable of taking off and landing vertically and flying horizontally, such as helicopter

**VTOL** vertical takeoff and landing aircraft

**warplane** military fighter or bomber

**widebody** jumbo jet with two aisles in passenger cabin, usu. able to carry over 300 passengers

**zeppelin** any rigid airship

## AVIATION AND AERODYNAMICS

**abort** (vb) terminate preplanned maneuver, esp. takeoff

**absolute altitude** vertical distance between aircraft and Earth's surface

**absolute ceiling** altitude beyond which aircraft cannot climb in standard atmospheric conditions

**aerial reconnaissance camera** camera with extremely long-range focus for high-altitude surveillance

**aero-** prefix meaning aircraft or flying

**aerobatics** intentional, abrupt maneuvers that alter normal flight pattern, esp. done in performance

**aerodonetics** science of flying gliders

**aerodynamics** science of the motion of air and other gases and the forces they produce on bodies in relative motion

**aeronaut** pilot of balloon or airship

**aeronautics** science, art, and business of designing, building, and flying aircraft

**aerophotography** long-range photography from aircraft

**afterburning** process of fuel injection and combustion for increasing thrust in turbojet exhaust, used only in military aircraft and SST

**airborne** (adj) carried through air by aerodynamic forces

**airflow** stream of air in motion relative to a body

**airframe icing** formation of ice on parts, esp. airfoil, due to certain moisture and temperature conditions, causing instability and control problems

**air lane** route regularly used by aircraft: jet route, victor airway

**airman** aviator

**airsickness** nausea, dizziness, headache, and cold sweat due to motion and altitude of air flight

**air space** space extending vertically above area of Earth's surface

**airspeed** speed of aircraft relative to air through which it is moving rather than Earth's surface

**airstream** airflow around aircraft in flight

**airway** specific route for air travel

**airworthy** (adj) safe and fit for flying

**altitude** height above Earth's surface or sea level

**angle of attack** angle between airfoil and relative flow of wind

**angle of incidence** angle between chord line of airfoil and thrust of aircraft

**approach** final period of descent prior to landing

**asymmetric landing** emergency landing in which engine on one side has failed

**attitude** position of aircraft expressed as inclination of its three axes (pitch, roll, and yaw) to frame of reference

**augmentation** increase of thrust by various methods

**autorotation** condition of flight achieved when lift is derived solely by effect of aerodynamic forces on unpowered rotor of autogyro or helicopter, or when power is lost

**aviation** art and science of flying aircraft; development of heavier-than-air aircraft

**aviator** flier; airplane pilot; airman

**aviatrix** female aviator

**bank** (vb) roll to attitude in which one wing tip is higher than the other; (n) condition of flight in which aircraft slopes laterally during turn

**barnstorm** (vb) tour country to give short demonstration airplane rides and stunt flying exhibitions

**barrel roll** complete roll by aircraft around longitudinal axis while simultaneously completing one spiral revolution in air

**bearing** horizontal direction to or from any point, measured in degrees clockwise from true north

**belly landing** emergency landing directly onto bottom of fuselage with landing gear retracted

**blind landing** instrument landing in zero visibility

**brake horsepower** actual horsepower of engine measured by brake attached to drive shaft

**buffeting** vibration of aircraft part caused by a burble

**burble** irregular flow of air around aircraft

**buzz** (vb) fly aircraft very low, esp. over structure

**calibrated airspeed** indicated airspeed corrected for installation error of cockpit gauge

**calibration** correction of airspeed

**CAT** clear air turbulence

**ceiling** height above Earth's surface of lowest significant cloud layer; altitude at which rate of climb of given aircraft falls to 100 feet (30 m) per minute

**center of gravity** point in body toward which every external particle of matter is attracted by gravity

**chandelle** abrupt, steep climb caused by aircraft's momentum

**chord line** imaginary line from leading to trailing edge of airfoil

**circling** flight pattern adopted by pilot while awaiting landing clearance or to position aircraft for landing

**clear air turbulence** CAT; unpredictable high-altitude turbulence with no clouds present, esp. wind shear due to jetstream

**climb** ascent, esp. to cruising altitude

**climbout** portion of flight between takeoff and initial cruising altitude

**close formation** flying in which several aircraft maintain relative positions near one another, often as exhibition

**contrail** white trail of condensed water vapor behind aircraft in flight; vapor trail

**corridor** flight route designated by international agreement

**crabbing** sideways motion of aircraft with respect to ground due to crosswind

**crash landing** forced landing in which aircraft is brought down without landing gear away from airport runway surface

**critical altitude** maximum altitude at which it is possible to maintain specified power and manifold pressure in standard atmosphere

**crosswind** wind not parallel to path of aircraft or runway

**cruise** (*vb*) maintain constant speed and altitude for period of time

**cruising altitude** constant altitude maintained for portion of flight

**decision height** point in ILS at which pilot sees runway and begins visual landing

**decompression** formation of nitrogen bubbles in blood or body tissues due to rapid ascent, causing pain in joints and convulsions

**density altitude** altitude corresponding to given air density in standard atmosphere; pressure altitude corrected for temperature

**depressurization** loss of cabin pressurization

**direct stability** propensity of aircraft to remain in stable flight attitude

**ditch** (*vb*) make crash landing in water and abandon aircraft

**dive** steep, sudden descent

**drag** sum of air resistance encountered in flight plus induced drag created by airfoil

**drag ratio** ratio of lift to drag as characteristic of wing; lift ratio

**drift** deviation from course, esp. due to crosswinds

**egress route** airway used for departure

**engine failure** loss of power in one or more engines, often necessitating emergency landing

**envelope** operating regime suited to particular aircraft

**equivalent airspeed** calibrated airspeed corrected for compressibility of air

**external load** cargo attached and carried outside fuselage

**feather** (*vb*) change pitch of propeller blades to reduce drag as engine is stopped

**final approach** period of final instrument approach from fixed point to landing, usu. last five to seven miles

**flame-out** failure of jet engine combustion in flight

**flight** distance covered by aircraft between takeoff and landing

**flutter** abnormal vibration in control surface due to aerodynamic force

**flying blind** flying by instruments only in low visibility

**forced landing** emergency landing on surface other than airport runway prior to completion of flight

**formation flying** flying in which several aircraft maintain positions relative to each other in simultaneous flight

**goaround** abandoning of approach just prior to landing in order to circle around airport

**ground speed** aircraft speed relative to ground it is passing over; airspeed corrected for headwind or tailwind

**guidance** direction of course of craft

**gust** sudden, brief change of wind speed or direction

**heading** compass reading expressing horizontal direction in which aircraft is facing

**headwind** wind blowing in direction opposite to course flown by aircraft

**hedgehop** (*vb*) fly very close to ground, esp. for crop-dusting

**hypersonic** (*adj*) designating supersonic speeds of Mach 5 and above

**icing** accumulation of ice on exterior of aircraft during flight; airframe icing

**IFR** instrument flight rules

**ILS** instrument landing system

**Immelmann** maneuver in which aircraft makes a half loop followed by a half roll to regain level flight position

**indicated airspeed** speed as shown on cockpit gauge

**induced drag** portion of wing drag resulting from generation of lift

**in-flight** (*adj*) done or occurring while aircraft is airborne

**instrument flight rules** IFR; type of flight plan and rules governing procedures for instrument flight

**instrument landing** avionic approach and landing in which ILS, PAR, or VOR is used

**instrument landing system** ILS; precision instrument approach based on beams transmitted from glide slope on ground that give vertical and lateral guidance by localizer up to decision height for visual landing

**JATO** jet-assisted takeoff

**jet-assisted takeoff** JATO; use of jet propulsion in takeoff only

**jet blast** jet engine exhaust

**jet propulsion** momentum derived from ejection of exhaust stream or rapid flow of gas from within propelled body by mechanical, thermal, or chemical process: turbojet, fanjet, ramjet, pulsejet, rocket

**jet route** high-altitude air lane

**jet stream** migrating stream of high-speed winds at high altitudes

**jettison** (*vb*) lighten load by dropping objects from aircraft in flight, esp. fuel in emergency

**jet wash** slipstream

**jump** specific instance of parachuting from aircraft

**lateral axis** axis from side to side of aircraft, perpendicular to direction of flight; pitch axis

**lateral stability** minimal pitch rotation; tendency of aircraft to return to equilibrium following forces applied to pitch

**lazy eight** maneuver in which aircraft gradually climbs, banks, and turns, tracing an imaginary figure eight on its side

**lift** upward aerodynamic force exerted on wing

**liftoff** vertical takeoff, esp. of helicopter or rocket

**lift ratio** drag ratio

**limit load factor** maximum pull of gravity to which airframe may be subjected in flight without structural damage

**load** in-flight weight carried by aircraft, including cargo, fuel, passengers, crew, and weight of aircraft when empty

**load factor** pull of gravity in absence of acceleration (load factor of 4 equals 4G); amount of load an aircraft can carry

**longitudinal axis** axis from nose to tail of aircraft, parallel to direction of flight; roll axis

**loop** circular figure performed as flight maneuver, beginning with aerobatic pull-up through vertical plane and ending with return to horizontal flight in same direction

**mach number** ratio of airspeed of an object to the speed of sound at given altitude and atmosphere, being 762 mph at sea level

**manifold pressure** factor used to determine grade of fuel required by aircraft engine

**mass ratio** ratio between mass of aircraft with fuel and after fuel has been used up

**Mayday** international radiotelephone distress signal, repeated three times to indicate imminent, grave danger

**missed approach** approach aborted by pilot at decision height when instrument approach cannot be completed safely

**moment** measure of aircraft's tendency to produce motion about an axis

**nose dive** swift, steep downward plunge of aircraft with nose toward ground

**octant** 45-degree angle, being one-eighth of a circle, used to state heading

**over-the-top** (*adj*) indicating position of aircraft above cloud layer or other obscuring phenomena forming ceiling

**Pan** international radiotelephone distress signal

**parachute** umbrellalike cloth contrivance used to retard falling speed of person or object dropped from aircraft

**payload** commercial revenue-producing load; expendable or deliverable load, such as bombs, used in military operations

**pilot** person who operates aircraft controls

**pitch** distance advanced by propeller in one revolution; movement of aircraft about lateral axis

**polar** (*adj*) having directional setting at north magnetic pole

**power loading** ratio of gross weight of airplane to its power

**precision approach** standard instrument approach in which electronic glide slope is provided by precision approach radar or instrument landing system

**pressure altitude** altitude relative to given pressure in standard atmosphere, uncorrected for temperature

**pressurization** regulation of cabin pressure for comfort of crew and passengers at high altitudes with low atmospheric pressure

**probe and drogue** method of in-air refueling in which tanker plane extends hose and funnel, or drogue, to which trailing plane extends intake pipe, or probe

**propulsion** driving force in engine that moves aircraft

**prop wash** slipstream

**pull out** (*vb*) exit from dive

**pull-up** maneuver in which nose of plane is lifted from level flight through vertical plane

**quadrant** quarter of circle centered on navigational aid, oriented clockwise from magnetic north

**ram** force of air being compressed into engine inlet by high velocity of aircraft

**ram effect** pressure resulting from ram

**range** distance aircraft is capable of flying without refueling or landing

**reaction propulsion** forward thrust due to engine expelling jet of fluid or particle stream

**roll** rotation of aircraft about longitudinal axis

**service ceiling** altitude at which rate of climb of given aircraft falls to 100 feet (30 m) per minute

**skyway** air lane, flight route

**skywriting** tracing words or figures in sky by trail of smoke released from small aircraft

**slipstream** current of air thrust backward by spinning propeller or jet; jet wash; prop wash

**solo flight** operation of aircraft by one person, esp. as part of pilot training

**sonic** (*adj*) designating speed of sound at given altitude

**sonic barrier** critical speed at which shock waves cause increased drag by exceeding speed of sound; sound barrier

**sonic boom** loud shock wave formed when speed of body exceeds speed of sound in same medium

**sound barrier** sonic barrier

**spin** nose-first descent along spiral path of large pitch and small radius; tailspin

**spiral** circling around longitudinal axis

**stall** loss of lift, sudden drop, and possible loss of control due to exceeding critical angle of attack and disruption of airflow around airfoil

**straight-in landing** landing on runway aligned within 30 degrees of final approach course

**stunt pilot** expert flier who performs exhibitions of formation flying and stunt maneuvers

**supersonic** (*adj*) greater than speed of sound at given altitude

**tailspin** nose-first spiraling descent with tail up

**tailwind** wind blowing in same direction as course flown by aircraft

**takeoff** act or moment of lifting off from ground to begin flight

**thrust** force in direction of motion of aircraft produced by jet exhaust

**torque** force that tends to produce rotation

**touchdown** point at which aircraft makes contact with landing surface

**transonic** (*adj*) just below or just above speed of sound

**true airspeed** indicated airspeed on cockpit gauge corrected for installation error, compressibility of air, pressure, and temperature; equivalent airspeed corrected for pressure and temperature

**turbulence** irregular motion of air that disrupts smooth flight

**vapor trail** contrail

**vector** compass heading; course followed by aircraft, provided by air-traffic control

**velocity** rate of motion in particular direction

**VFR** *visual flight rules*

**victor airway** low-altitude air lane

**visibility** distance at which unlighted objects can be seen under existing atmospheric conditions on ground or in flight

**visual flight rules** VFR; flight plan or maneuvering and rules governing conduct of flight based on pilot's visual observations in acceptable weather conditions

**volplane** downward glide with engine turned off

**wake turbulence** turbulence caused by passage of aircraft through atmosphere

**washin** increase in angle of incidence from root to tip of wing

**washout** decrease in angle of incidence from root to tip of wing

**wind shear** change of wind speed or direction over short distance, esp. due to thunderstorm

**wing flex** design of wings to flex and not remain rigid, providing smoother flight by allowing apparent flapping

**wing loading** gross weight of aircraft expressed as weight per unit area of wing surface

**wingover** flight maneuver beginning with climbing turn to point of stall, after which nose falls as turn continues so that aircraft emerges flying in opposite direction

**yaw** rotation of aircraft about vertical axis; deviation from line of flight, controlled by rudder

**zero-lift angle of attack** angle of attack at which no lift is created

**zero visibility** weather condition in which pilot can see nothing and must rely on instrument flight and air-traffic control

**zoom** (*vb*) climb suddenly and sharply at greater than normal angle

# Airframe and Engines

**accessory drive** drive shaft and gears for transmitting part of engine's power to generators, hydraulic pumps, and other accessories

**actuator** motor that moves elevators

**aft** (*adj*) toward the tail

**afterburner** device attached at exit of jet engine exhaust pipe to burn unburned fuel and exhaust gases, thus producing added thrust

**aileron** hinged or movable control surface, usu. on trailing edge of wing near tip, that regulates banking by causing movement about longitudinal axis

**air brake** airfoil that can be extended to produce additional drag for slowing aircraft

**airfoil** any surface, esp. wing, designed to produce a useful reaction when properly positioned in airstream

**airframe** any part of aircraft other than engine: fuselage, booms, nacelle, cowlings, fairings, airfoils, landing gear

**airscrew** propeller

**antitorque rotor** tail rotor on helicopter

**articulated blade** helicopter rotor blade hinged at hub

**athodyd** *aerothermodynamic duct*; continuous fuel-burning ramjet

**baffle** device for deflecting airflow

**balance tab** device that moves in opposite direction from control surface to which it is affixed

**ballonet** auxiliary air container on balloon or airship that can be inflated or deflated during flight to control altitude

**bay** compartment in fuselage

**belly** bottom of fuselage, esp. with landing gear retracted

**block** metal casting that houses engine cylinders

**boom** retractable metal tube for in-flight refueling

**booster** rocket engine that assists takeoff by supplementing main power supply

**bubble** transparent, hemispherical, seamless, unbraced cockpit canopy

**bulkhead** upright partition separating compartments and providing structural strength

**bypass duct** auxiliary channel through which compressed air is diverted around combustion chamber to join exhaust gases for added thrust

**cabane** struts used to support wing above fuselage

**cabin** enclosed portion of aircraft for passengers and crew

**cabin air intake** mechanism for drawing air into cabin

**camber** curvature of airfoil surface from leading to trailing edge

**canard** airframe with stabilizing and control surface ahead of main supporting surfaces and wings

**canopy** transparent, hinged cockpit cover

**cantilever** beam or member supported at one end only

**cermet** *ceramic-metal* alloy used to resist friction heat at supersonic speeds

**cockpit** compartment with controls for pilot and crew

**contraprop** pair of propellers mounted on coaxial shafts and geared to turn in opposite directions to reduce torque

**controls** devices that enable pilot to operate air control surfaces and various accessories in aircraft

**control stick** vertical lever used to operate elevator and ailerons in fighters and high performance aircraft; joy stick; stick

**control surface** movable surface used to control attitude or motion and guide aircraft: airfoil, aileron, elevator, or flap

**control tab** device that provides aerodynamic actuation of control surface

**control yoke** steering wheel with two arms used to operate elevator and ailerons in transports, bombers, and airliners

**cowling** metal cover, usu. faired, enclosing aircraft engine and portions of fuselage

**deceleron** aileron used to slow aircraft in flight

**delta wing** triangular wing with large sweepback and small thickness ratio

**diffuser** duct that converts high-speed gas flow to lower speed at increased pressure

**dihedral** up-and-down angle formed by aircraft wings relative to fuselage

**dorsal fin** long, narrow fin running aft on top of fuselage to leading edge of primary fin

**drag wire** wire in some wing structures running from forward inboard to aft outboard point to resist drag

**drogue** funnel-shaped device towed behind aircraft for in-air refueling

**effective span** measure of span of airfoil less corrections for tip

**ejection seat** emergency escape device by which both pilot and seat are catapulted from plane

**elevator** movable airfoil in tail assembly, usu. hinged to stabilizer, that controls vertical movements and rotation of aircraft about lateral axis

**elevon** one of a pair of control surfaces that act together as an elevator or separately as ailerons

**empennage** tail assembly, usu. comprised of vertical fin, rudder, elevators, and horizontal stabilizers; tail section

**engine pod** unit containing engine isolated from rest of aircraft, detachable in emergency

**envelope** folded outer covering of material for aircraft wing or for rigid airship

**fairing** secondary structure added to streamline aircraft part and reduce drag, usu. by covering nonstreamlined part

**fanjet engine** turbofan

**fin** fixed, vertical stabilizing surface on tail assembly; tail fin

**firewall** fire-resistant bulkhead separating engine from rest of aircraft

**flame damper** fitting on piston engine that hides exhaust flames, used to prevent detection of aircraft at night

**flap** hinged or pivoted airfoil on trailing edge of wing that increases lift by reshaping or fattening wing on takeoff and landing

**flaperon** airfoil surface hinged to wing and raised or lowered for lateral control

**flapperette** hinged rear half of flaperon, normally locked in line, but independently operative if flaperon fails

**flapping hinge** hinge that allows helicopter rotor blade to swing up and down within limits

**flex wing** nonrigid wing used on most aircraft

**flight deck** front compartment of aircraft housing crew; runway portion of aircraft carrier

**fore** (*adj*) toward the nose

**fuselage** elongated main body of airplane housing engines, crew, cargo, passengers, and equipment

**gas turbine** propulsion engine using hot, compressed gas as working fluid, consisting of compressor, combustion chamber, and turbine through which expanded gases are discharged to drive compressor and propel aircraft

**gondola** cabin suspended under airship or balloon for passengers and engine

**gull wing** wing that slants upward from fuselage for short distance, then levels out

**hatch** doorway in side or bottom of fuselage

**heat barrier** highest temperature at which skin can retain its strength

**hold** cargo storage area in belly of fuselage

**honeycomb** sandwich panel used for airplane skins: thin outer layers of metal, wood, or plastic with honeycomb core of metal, plastic, or paper for lightness and strength

**horizontal stabilizer** stabilizer mounted horizontally in tail assembly, to which elevators are attached for lateral stability

**horn** short lever fastened to control surface, to which operating cable or rod is attached

**hull** main body of airship

**hydroplane** attachment to bottom of fuselage of seaplane that allows it to glide across water

**inboard** (*adj*) close or closest to fuselage or body of aircraft

**inboard flap** flap closest to fuselage

**inboard spoiler** spoiler closest to fuselage

**inlet** throat

**interplane strut** strut between two wings or other surfaces

**jet** jet engine

**jet engine** any aircraft engine based on jet propulsion, always incorporating a gas turbine: turbojet, fanjet, ramjet, pulsejet, rocket

**joy stick** *Informal.* control stick, esp. one located between pilot's legs

**JP fuels** *jet propulsion fuels*, usu. petroleum derivatives

**jury strut** auxiliary strut bracing main strut

**landing gear** understructure, such as wheels and shock absorbers, capable of supporting weight of aircraft on ground; undercarriage

**lap joint** point at which sections of skin are connected

**leading edge** foremost edge of airfoil or propeller blade

**longeron** main longitudinal member of fuselage framing

**mixture control** control over fuel/air mixture in piston engine of light or older aircraft

**monocoque** fuselage relying on skin to carry most or all of load

**nacelle** wing housing for engine; enclosure other than fuselage for people, cargo, and engine; basket under balloon

**navigation lights** lights on ends of wings, red on left and green on right

**negative dihedral** airfoil displaced downward from level fuselage

**nose** foremost section of fuselage enclosing cockpit

**nose assembly** structural and mechanical parts comprising nose and cockpit enclosure

**nose cone** foremost portion of nose, usu. tapering to point and made of heat-resistant material

**nose landing gear** single, retractable wheel assembly beneath nose

**nose turret** observation or gun turret positioned at nose of military aircraft

**nozzle** portion of jet engine in which fuel is sprayed into burner can or tailpipe

**onboard** (*adj*) inside aircraft cabin, cockpit, or cargo hold

**outboard** (*adj*) far or farthest from fuselage or body of aircraft

**outboard flap** flap farthest from fuselage

**outboard spoiler** spoiler farthest from fuselage

**plating** heavy metal skin, esp. covering wings of large aircraft

**propeller** assembly with airfoil blades on hub of engine-driven shaft, used to propel aircraft; airscrew

**propjet** turboprop

**pulsejet** jet engine that burns fuel intermittently with air from outside that is compressed by ram effect due to forward motion

**pusher propeller** propeller mounted toward rear that pushes aircraft forward

**pylon** structure used to attach engine and fuel tank to aircraft, usu. under wing

**radar dome** radome

**radial engine** engine of older propeller-driven aircraft with cylinders arranged like spokes around crankshaft

**radome** housing for radar system on nose; radar dome

**ramjet** jet engine having no compressor and depending for operation on ram compression of air due to high forward velocity of aircraft

**RATO** rocket-*assisted* takeoff

**retroengine** engine capable of retrofiring to produce thrust in opposite direction of flight

**retrofire** (*vb*) reverse direction of thrust on engine or rocket

**reversible propeller** propeller with blades that may be reversed, usu. electrically, to aid braking

**rib** structural crosspiece attached to spar to strengthen wing

**rocket** jet engine carrying its own oxidizer along with fuel; missile propelled by rocket engine

**rocket-assisted takeoff** RATO; takeoff aided by auxiliary rocket device that provides extra thrust

**rod** thin strip of filler metal used to seal welded joint

**root** inboard end of wing where it joins fuselage

**rotor** one of rotating set of bladelike wings that provides lift for helicopter

**rudder** vertically hinged airfoil for yawing aircraft about vertical axis in flight

**ruddevator** control surface at wide dihedral angle that operates as both rudder and elevator; V-shaped tail

**sandwich** structural material with two skins stiffened by thick core; honeycomb

**shock absorber** device built into landing gear to absorb impact of landing

**skin** panels of metal riveted in place to cover fuselage

**slat** narrow auxiliary airfoil mounted ahead of wing or flap for better direction of airstream

**sound suppressor** equipment for reducing engine noise

**span** maximum distance from tip to tip of any airfoil

**spar** main lengthwise support member of wing or airfoil

**spinner** conical or parabolic fairing over propeller hub that spins with propeller

**spoiler** surface designed to be extended from wing under certain conditions to spoil airflow over it, decrease lift, or increase drag

**stabilator** horizontal structure serving as both stabilizer and elevator

**stabilizer** fixed or adjustable airfoil designed to give stability; vertical or horizontal stabilizer

**standby** auxiliary piece of equipment or system

**stick** control stick

**stick control** movement of elevator and ailerons by control stick

**stinger** sharp, pointed fairing at end of tail cone

**stressed skin** covering that contributes to strength of structure

**strut** supporting brace bearing compression and/or tension loads

**supercharger** engine-driven compressor that increases flow of air and fuel into cylinders to improve power in nonjet engines and maintains pressure in cabin and engine

**sweep** fore-and-aft angle of airfoil relative to fuselage

**sweepback** wing with leading edge at sharp angle to fuselage; swept-back wing

**swept-back wing** sweepback

**tab** small hinged surface on trailing edge of control surface, used to assist movement or to trim control surface

**tail** rear part of aircraft, providing stability

**tail assembly** empennage

**tail fin** fin; vertical stabilizer

**tail rotor** small rotor mounted on shaft at tail of helicopter to counteract torque of main rotor and provide directional control; antitorque rotor

**tail section** empennage

**tail wheel** small wheel that supports tail of aircraft with conventional landing gear on ground

**throat** most constricted part of jet exhaust nozzle; inlet

**throttle** hand-operated lever connected to valve that controls amount of fuel delivered to engine cylinders; fuel control for gas turbines in jet engines

**thrust chamber** chamber of jet engine, in which combustion of fuel and air, or oxidizer, takes place

**thrust spoiler** jet device used to reduce forward thrust without decreasing mass flow from engine

**tip** outboard end of wing farthest from fuselage

**tractor propeller** propeller mounted toward front that pulls aircraft

**trailing edge** rearmost edge of airfoil or propeller blade

**trim** tab attached to trailing edge of airfoil

**truss** assembly of structural members forming rigid framework for fuselage

**turbine** rotary engine with drive shaft powered by action of liquid or gas against curved vanes of wheel or escaping through nozzles located around wheel

**turbofan** turbojet engine that creates additional thrust by diverting secondary airflow around combustion chamber; fanjet engine

**turbojet** jet engine supplied with air from compressor driven by turbine that is activated by energy of jet exhaust gases

**turboprop** variation of turbojet in which gas turbine also drives conventional propeller to produce major portion of thrust; propjet

**turret** transparent dome for gunner on bomber or fighter

**undercarriage** landing gear

**vane** one of flat curved pieces rotating around axle in supercharger, used to compress air

**variable-sweep wing** sweepback whose angle can be changed during flight

**vertical axis** axis from top to bottom of aircraft, perpendicular to direction of level flight; yaw axis

**vertical stabilizer** section of airfoil on tail forward of rudder, providing longitudinal stability; fin

**wing** part of airplane that provides lift, esp. main lateral airfoil, usu. in pairs

**wing flap** flap

**wing rib** chordwise member that gives wing its shape and transmits load from skin to spars

**wingspan** lateral distance between tips of wings

**wing spar** principal spanwise structural member of wing

**wing tip** extreme outboard point of wing

**yaw control** equipment designed to reduce and control yaw: ailerons, elevators, rudder

**yoke** pilot's steering wheel with two upward-pointing arms

## Avionics and Instrumentation

**absolute altimeter** radar altimeter

**accelerometer** instrument that measures acceleration or deceleration

**ADF** automatic direction finder

**ADI** attitude direction indicator

**aerometer** instrument for measuring weight and density of gases

**aeroscope** device for gathering bacteria and dust from air for examination

**air log** instrument that records distance traveled by aircraft relative to air through which it moves, used to calculate true airspeed

**airspeed indicator** dial or gauge showing airspeed

**altigraph** altimeter that automatically records altitude on chart

**altimeter** device for measuring altitude, usu. above sea level

**anemograph** instrument for recording wind direction and speed

**anemometer** gauge for determining wind speed

**anemoscope** instrument for displaying direction of wind

**atmometer** instrument for measuring evaporating capacity of air; evaporimeter

**attitude direction indicator** ADI; instrument showing attitude of aircraft in space

**automatic direction finder** ADF; aircraft navigation radio

**automatic pilot** self-regulating control mechanism for keeping aircraft in level flight and on set course, or for executing maneuvers; autopilot

**autopilot** automatic pilot

**autosyn** type of gauge construction

**avionics** development and use of electronic equipment and control systems for aircraft

**avionics box** black box that plugs into avionics rack

**backup system** auxiliary instrument or device used to control aircraft if primary system fails

**bank indicator** instrument that tells pilot rate at which airplane is turning

**black box** flight data recorder and cockpit voice recorder encased in fire- and shock-resistant container, used in accident investigations; any replaceable unit that plugs into avionics rack

**bombsight** instrument on bomber that determines when to drop bomb in order to strike target

**Bourdon-tube gauge** crescent-shaped tube with one

closed end, used to measure pressure in high-pressure fluid systems

**ceilometer** automatic device for determining height of cloud ceiling by reflected light beam

**chronometer** device for precise measurement of time

**climatometer** instrument for measuring sensile temperature of atmosphere

**cockpit voice recorder** device in black box that records radio and direct conversations of crew

**compass** magnetic compass

**compass card** circular card on pivot to which magnetic compass is attached, marked in increments of 5 degrees

**console** cockpit instrument panel with controls, gauges, and meters; control panel

**control panel** console

**deviation** deflection of magnetic compass due to installation error

**directional gyro** gyro rotor mounted on pair of gimbals with horizontal spin axis, set to magnetic compass and used for directional reference

**direction finder** radio receiver with direction-sensing antenna, used in navigation and to take bearings

**distance measuring equipment** DME; instrument that measures nautical miles between aircraft and VOR station

**drift meter** instrument that shows drift of aircraft from left to right over ground

**Earth inductor** inclinometer

**emergency locator transmitter** ELT; automatic radio transmitter attached to aircraft structure and operating at set frequency on its own power source, used for locating downed aircraft

**evaporimeter** atmometer

**flight data recorder** device in black box that monitors flight data, used esp. in accident investigations; flight recorder

**flight recorder** flight data recorder

**fuel flowmeter** fuel pressure gauge marked in gallons per hour of usage or pounds per hour for gas turbines in jets

**fuel quantity indicator** gauge that indicates amount of fuel remaining

**galvanometer** device for detecting and measuring very small electric current

**gimbals** pair of rings pivoted on axes at right angles so that one swings freely within the other, used to support magnetic compass or gyro device

**glide slope** device that emits electronic signals to provide vertical guidance during approach or takeoff during ILS

**gyrocompass** motor-operated gyroscope whose rotating axis is kept parallel to axis of Earth's rotation and points to geographic, not magnetic, North Pole

**Gyropilot** *Trademark.* automatic pilot

**gyroscope** wheel mounted on spinning axis that is free to rotate around one or both of two axes perpendicular to each other and to the spinning axis, used as directional reference for keeping aircraft level in flight

**hub dynamometer** instrument for measuring power of engine in shop

**hygrograph** meter for continuously recording atmospheric humidity

**hygrometer** device for measuring absolute or relative humidity in air

**inclinometer** instrument that shows inclination of longitudinal axis of aircraft to horizontal plane of flight; Earth inductor

**inertial guidance** self-contained, automatic guidance system composed of gyroscopes, accelerometers, and computers used to maintain course in automatic pilot; inertial navigation system; INS

**inertial navigation system** INS; inertial guidance

**INS** inertial navigation system; inertial guidance

**instrument panel** cockpit console

**interference error** avionic error caused by unwanted or distorted radio signals

**intervalometer** device that controls frequency of exposures in aerial photography

**localizer** landing instrument that provides course guidance to runway, esp. in ILS

**LORAN** *long range navigation;* electronic navigational system that measures difference in time of reception of synchronized pulse signals from two transmitters

**machmeter** instrument that gives ratio of aircraft speed to speed of sound under existing atmospheric conditions

**magnetic compass** instrument with needle that indicates direction of North Pole due to action of Earth's magnetic field; compass

**manometer** gauge for measuring pressure of gases or vapors

**meteorograph** instrument that automatically records various weather conditions simultaneously

**NAVAID** *navigational aid;* visual or electronic device, airborne or on Earth's surface, that provides guidance or position data

**nephoscope** instrument for determining direction and speed of cloud movement

**ozonometer** device capable of measuring ozone level in cabin, not in general use

**PAR** *precision approach radar*

**pelorus** device for taking bearings that fits over compass card or gyrocompass

**photometer** device for measuring relative intensity of light

**Pitot-static system** method of providing or measuring pressure to operate altimeter, airspeed indicator, or other instrumentation

**pluviometer** instrument for measuring rainfall

**position indicator** navigational instrument that displays horizontal situation of aircraft

**power unit** onboard device that converts battery voltage to voltages required by various instruments

**precision approach radar** PAR; radar equipment used in final approach course to airport to provide precision instrument approach

**pressure altimeter** aneroid instrument that measures differences in atmospheric pressure to determine altitude

**pressure head** Pitot-static tube used to actuate air-speed indicator

**pyrometer** instrument for measuring temperatures above range of normal thermometer

**radar** *radio detecting and ranging;* system for determining direction, distance, height, and speed of aircraft by reflection of radio waves, also used as weather sensor on aircraft

**radar altimeter** instrument that uses reflection time of radio waves to and from ground to determine altitude of aircraft; absolute altimeter

**radio direction finder** little-used direction finder employing radio waves

**radiogoniometer** radio direction finder

**rate gyroscope** device sensitive to rate of angular motion

**rate-of-climb indicator** instrument that indicates rate at which aircraft is ascending or descending in feet per minute

**recording meter** any instrument that records readings on chart or traces them on screen: recording altimeter, anemometer, hygrometer

**sextant** simple navigational instrument for measuring angular distance of celestial body from horizon, rarely used on aircraft

**slip indicator** instrument for measuring longitudinal deviation about vertical axis; yawmeter

**sound ranging altimeter** instrument that determines altitude by timing sounds received from specific points

**squelch control** device that helps eliminate undesired noise in radio

**static tube** Pitot-static tube carrying static pressure of outside air

**synchroscope** instrument for determining difference in phase between two engines

**TACAN** *tactical air navigation*; ultra-high frequency electronic navigation aid used primarily on military aircraft

**tachometer** instrument that measures rate of rotation of revolving engine shaft

**telemetry** electronic tracking system, esp. for missile or experimental aircraft

**terrain clearance indicator** instrument for maintaining altitude above terrain of highest obstruction

**thermograph** instrument for automatically recording variations in temperature

**thermostat** device for automatically regulating temperature

**torquemeter** meter for measuring torque in shaft of nonjet engine

**transit instrument** sight level used to determine level line on fuselage as reference for repair

**transponder** electronic device that receives radio signals and generates distinctive reply pattern on radar

**turn-and-bank indicator** instrument for showing rate of turn of aircraft

**turnmeter** instrument for measuring angular velocity of aircraft about predetermined axis

**variometer** instrument that measures and records small variations in pressure

**venturi tube** suction gauge in slipstream that indicates reduction in pressure

**vertical-speed indicator** instrument that registers rate of climb

**very high frequency** VHF; band for radio communication and navigation

**very high frequency omni range** VOR; basic radio navigation system that relies on communications between aircraft and transmitting stations on ground, used esp. by military aircraft

**viscometer** instrument for measuring viscosity, esp. of fuel

**VOR** *very high frequency omni range*

**weather radar** system using radio signals to analyze weather conditions

**yawmeter** instrument that measures yaw of aircraft

# COMMERCIAL AIRLINES, AIRPORTS, AND AIR FORCE

**aerodrome** *Brit.* small airport

**air base** military facility for operation and maintenance of aircraft

**air cargo** air freight

**air carrier** person or company that undertakes transportation of cargo by air

**aircraft carrier** large warship that serves as floating air base

**airfield** landing area of airport, esp. military air base

**air force** aviation branch of armed forces

**Air Force One** jet aircraft used by U.S. president

**air freight** shipping of goods and cargo by air

**airline** company that moves freight and passengers on aircraft

**airliner** large passenger aircraft, usu. jet, operated by airline

**airmail** mail transported by air

**airman** enlisted person in Air Force or Naval Air Corps

**air piracy** skyjacking

**airport** area of land with control tower and runways for landing and takeoff of aircraft, facilities for storage and maintenance, and terminal for passengers

**airstrip** hard-surfaced area used as runway

**air-to-air** (*adj*) designating weapon launched from aircraft and directed at airborne object

**air traffic** aircraft in air near airport or on airport runways and approaches

**air-traffic control** ATC; radar facility with tower from which approaches and departures of air traffic in and around airports and along air routes are monitored and directed

**air-traffic controller** person trained and authorized by FAA to provide ATC services; controller

**approach lights** lights that indicate direction and termination of runway to approaching aircraft

**apron** area of land at airport used for loading and unloading of passengers and cargo, refueling, parking, and maintenance; ramp

**ATC** *air-traffic control*

**blast fence** barrier used to divert jet fuel blast

**blue room** *Slang.* lavatory on aircraft

**boarding** movement of passengers onto aircraft preparatory to flight

**boarding pass** ticket distributed at gate that permits passengers to enter aircraft

**bombardier** member of bomber crew who operates bombsight and releases bombs

**bug smashers** *Slang.* small private planes flying in congested traffic areas

**bumped** (*adj*) refused seating on flight for which one has reservation

**CAB** *Civil Aeronautics Board*

**captain** commanding officer of aircraft, esp. commercial airliner; air force commanding officer

**carousel** circular baggage conveyor from which passengers retrieve luggage at airport

**carrier** airliner; commercial airline

**carry-on luggage** small items of luggage taken on board by passenger and placed in overhead rack or under seat

**centerline** line marked down center of runway, imagined to extend beyond it onto clearway or stopway

**charter flight** flight on aircraft hired by group or organization for special trip not regularly scheduled

**chock** block or wedge set against wheel to keep it from turning

**Civil Aeronautics Board** CAB; federal agency that regulated airline industry activities until deregulation in 1978

**clearance** permission from air traffic control, esp. for approach, landing, takeoff, or routing

**clearway** area at least 500 feet wide around extended centerline of runway free of obstructions and under airport authority

**combat pilot** air force fighter pilot

**commercial pilot** pilot of commercial airliner who holds FAA commercial license

**commuter flight** frequently scheduled short flight between two nearby metropolitan areas; shuttle

**computer reservation system** CRS; computer linkup between all commercial airlines and travel agents for booking flight reservations

**controlled airspace** airspace within which aircraft may be subject to air-traffic control

**controller** air-traffic controller

**copilot** assistant pilot who relieves pilot; first officer

**deregulation** federal removal of certain restrictions on commercial airline practices, esp. ticket pricing and routes, in 1978

**direct flight** journey without change of aircraft but with one or more intermediate landings

**egress route** pathway out of aircraft in emergency evacuation

**ETA** estimated time of arrival; scheduled or anticipated time for completion of flight

**evacuation slide** inflatable chute used as emergency escape device from commercial airliner

**FAA** Federal Aviation Administration

**Federal Aviation Administration** FAA; federal government agency responsible for administering air-traffic control and investigating accidents

**first officer** copilot and second in command of commercial airliner

**flight** scheduled trip on airplane to fly specific route at certain time; such a scheduled route

**flight attendant** person on commercial airliner responsible for passengers' comfort and safety; stewardess or steward

**flight crew** pilot, copilot, flight engineer, and others who operate an aircraft during flight

**flight plan** information filed with air-traffic control that describes intended flight

**flight simulator** pilot training device that simulates flight conditions on ground

**forward cabin** first-class passenger compartment nearest cockpit

**frequent-flyer program** marketing incentive that rewards passengers with free flights for accumulated mileage

**gate** location where passengers board or disembark from airliner

**gate hold** air-traffic control instruction that requires loaded aircraft to remain at gate due to departure delay of over five minutes

**gosport** flexible tube formerly used for spoken communications between different compartments of aircraft, esp. in training

**ground crew** maintenance and repair workers

**hangar** large enclosure for storage, repair, and maintenance of aircraft

**helipad** landing and takeoff area used by helicopters

**heliport** small land or water area or structure used by helicopters for landing and takeoff

**hijacking** skyjacking

**holding procedure** maneuver by which aircraft remains in specified airspace while awaiting further ATC clearance

**hop** very short flight

**hostess** stewardess

**hub and spoke system** system of air transportation in which local flights are made to central hub airport from which connections are made to final local or long-distance destinations

**hub carrier** airline primarily serving specific hub airport

**jetway** tube-shaped bridge from terminal to aircraft for boarding passengers

**landing slot** airport runway space controlled by airline leasing slot from government

**landing strip** airstrip, often temporary runway surface

**layover** break partway through journey, esp. overnight away from home base

**local traffic** aircraft operating within sight of tower or under its control in IFR conditions

**Mae West** inflatable life jacket vest designed for use in water

**major carrier** large national or international commercial airline

**marker beacon** aural and visual signal transmitter that provides aircraft with its position on landing

**milk run** routine military mission, unlikely to be dangerous

**mission** flight by military aircraft, esp. bomber

**naval pilot** naval aircraft flier, esp. one based on aircraft carrier

**navigator** flight officer responsible for plotting course

**nonstop service** flight directly to final destination with no intermediate stops

**no-show** passenger with confirmed reservation who fails to arrive for flight

**off-line** (adj) designating travel on carrier other than one that sold ticket

**offset parallel runways** staggered runways with parallel centerlines

**outer marker** marker beacon located four to seven miles from runway threshold on extended centerline of runway

**overbooking** airline practice of selling more seats than are available based on statistical likelihood that some passengers will not show up

**overhead rack** compartment above seat for stowing carry-on luggage on airliner

**overshoot** (vb) fail to come to complete stop on runway; fly through final approach course

**oxygen mask** face mask connected to oxygen tank located above seat on commercial airliners, used in decompression emergency

**paratrooper** military parachutist

**radar contact** appearance of aircraft on radar display at air-traffic control

**radar service** services provided by air-traffic control to aircraft in radar contact

**ramp** apron

**red-eye** Informal. all-night, transcontinental flight arriving near dawn

**run** regularly scheduled flight between two points

**runway** defined rectangular area marked off on airport or aerodrome surface and prepared for landing and takeoff, usu. with centerline and marker lights on sides

**seat belt** protective restraining strap that buckles across passenger's lap

**second officer** member of flight crew with least seniority who monitors instruments and observes flight

**security search** physical search and X-ray examination of luggage and passengers prior to boarding flight, esp. to detect explosives or firearms

**shuttle** frequently scheduled flight between two nearby metropolitan centers; commuter flight

**skycap** airport employee who helps passengers with luggage or assists disabled passengers

**skyjacking** taking control of aircraft by force and making it alter destination by holding crew and passengers hostage; air piracy; hijacking

**standby** status of passenger waiting for open place on flight for which he or she does not have confirmed reservation

**stew** *Informal.* stewardess

**steward** male flight attendant

**stewardess** female flight attendant; hostess; stew

**stopover** brief landing at intermediate airport en route to termination point of flight

**stopway** area beyond takeoff runway and centered on its extended centerline, used in aborted takeoff

**stow** (*vb*) pack away in safe, orderly manner, esp. luggage

**taxi** (*vb*) move slowly on ground, esp. on airport ramps and aprons to and from runways (said of aircraft)

**terminal** airport structure used by arriving and departing passengers and for cargo handling; connection point on flight

**test flight** monitored flight on which new aircraft or equipment is tested

**test pilot** specially trained operator of experimental or new aircraft and equipment

**tower** tall airport structure from which air-traffic control services are provided

**traffic** routes and positions of aircraft in specific area

**tray table** small, flat surface that folds down from back of seat in front of passenger on commercial airliners

**turnaround** flight on which crew returns to home base on day of departure from it

**undershoot** (*vb*) miscalculate approach so that touchdown occurs before reaching runway

**upgrade** (*vb*) move to business or first-class seat from tourist or business class

**Valsalva maneuver** technique for relieving pressure in head due to imbalance of air pressure in ascending or descending aircraft by blowing hard with nose and mouth closed

**white knuckler** *Slang.* anxious passenger

**widebody** jumbo jet, usu. able to carry over 300 passengers

**wind tunnel** tunnellike structure used for testing aircraft parts or models by forcing wind past them at known velocity

# AUTOMOBILES

Types of Automobiles
Trucks and Buses
Internal Combustion Engine
Working Parts
Body Parts and Accessories
Driving and Repair

**SEE ALSO**: Chap. 5: Machinery and Fabrication; Electricity and Electronics; Chap. 6: Other Vehicles; Chap. 11: The City; Chap. 12: Insurance

## TYPES OF AUTOMOBILES

**ambulance** emergency conveyance to hospital

**automobile** four-wheel passenger vehicle, usu. having internal combustion engine; car

**beach buggy** dune buggy

**cab** taxicab

**car** automobile

**cement mixer** *Slang.* noisy old car

**cherry** (*adj*) *Slang.* describing older car in excellent condition

**coach** two-door enclosed sedan

**compact** small car

**convertible** automobile with retractable canvas roof

**coupe** small, enclosed, two-door, two-passenger automobile

**deuce** *Slang.* 1932 Ford coupe

**dragster** customized car modified for rapid acceleration racing

**dune buggy** roofless, recreational car with oversize tires for sand traction; beach buggy

**fastback** car with slanting aerodynamic roof that sometimes opens at rear

**flivver** *Slang.* small, cheap, old automobile

**go-kart** miniature, self-propelled chassis without body, esp. for racing

**golf cart** low power, open vehicle with canvas roof

**grand touring car** sporty two-passenger coupe; orig. large, vintage, open sedan with side rails

**gran turismo** *Italian.* sporty grand touring car for two passengers; GT

**GT** gran *turismo*

**gypsy cab** cab licensed to pick up passengers on call, but that often illegally cruises in search of passengers

**hack** *Informal.* taxicab

**hardtop** car with permanent, rigid top covering frame

**hatchback** usu. two-door car with roof lifting open at rear in lieu of trunk

**hearse** long station wagon for carrying corpse at funeral

**horseless carriage** early term for automobile

**hot rod** modified or souped-up, customized car

**jalopy** dilapidated automobile

**Jeep** *Trademark.* sturdy, four-wheel drive vehicle designed for rough terrain

**junker** *Slang.* old, dilapidated car

**landaulet** vintage convertible car with open driver's seat and folding top over rear seat

**Land Rover** *Trademark.* jeeplike vehicle designed for rough terrain

**lemon** *Informal.* bad car, esp. one that is new but has mechanical problems

**limo** limousine

**limousine** long, luxurious, chauffeur-driven sedan; limo

**lowrider** customized car fitted with specialized suspension that allows the chassis to ride just a few inches above pavement

**microbus** box-shaped station wagon similar to bus

**midget racer** tiny, open racing car

**motorcar** motorized automobile

**off-road vehicle** vehicle, such as a four-wheel drive Jeep, beach buggy, or snowmobile, designed for travel off public roads

**patrol car** squad car

**pimpmobile** *Slang.* large, ostentatious car, esp. limousine

**prowl car** squad car

**race car** specially designed, high-speed car for racing; racing car

**racing car** race car

**ragtop** *Slang.* convertible

**roadster** open, two-seater automobile with folding top and rear luggage compartment or rumble seat

**sedan** enclosed car seating four to seven persons, often four-door

**shandrydan** *Slang.* old, broken-down car or vehicle

**snowmobile** small, motorized vehicle equipped with ski-like runners and revolving tread

**sports car** low, small, high-powered, agile two-seater automobile

**squad car** police vehicle; patrol car; prowl car

**station wagon** passenger car with roof extended to rear to increase cargo and passenger space, seating up to ten persons; wagon

**stock car** factory-built passenger car modified for racing

**stretch** extra-long limousine with bar, TV, and other amenities

**subcompact** smallest automobile used in U.S.

**taxicab** sedan that carries passengers for fare determined by mileage; cab; hack

**touring car** vintage auto with two seats, four doors, and folding top

**town car** four-door car with rear passenger compartment separated from driver by sliding glass partition

**wagon** *Informal.* station wagon

**wheels** *Slang.* automobile, esp. one's own

**woodie** *Slang.* wood-paneled station wagon

## TRUCKS AND BUSES

**amphibian** flat-bottomed vehicle that moves over land or water on tracks with fins

**armored car** vehicle with bullet-resistant panels and doors, used by military or police

**autobus** bus

**big rig** *Slang.* multiunit or eighteen-wheeler truck

**bulldozer** tractor with broad, blunt blade for moving earth and debris, used in road building and construction

**bus** motorized, box-shaped vehicle used to transport numerous paying passengers, usu. on a fixed schedule; autobus

**camper** van with bed and kitchen

**caravan** large vehicle with living quarters

**carryall** passenger vehicle used as small bus

**Caterpillar** *Trademark.* tractor or construction vehicle propelled by two endless belts

**club cab** pickup truck with expanded cab that includes rear seat and/or storage area

**coach** *Chiefly Brit.* bus

**crawler** heavy construction vehicle that travels on Caterpillar treads

**delivery truck** enclosed freight-carrying truck

**diesel** large truck with diesel fuel engine

**dray** small truck for hauling goods

**duck** amphibious military truck with code designation DUKW (World War II)

**dump truck** heavy, open truck used to transport loose freight

**eighteen-wheeler** large tractor and semitrailer truck with eighteen wheels

**fire engine** heavy truck or tractor and trailer with fire-fighting equipment

**flatbed** truck with open platform or shallow box body

**float** trailer with platform for parade exhibit

**forklift** small work vehicle that hoists heavy loads on steel prongs

**garbage truck** municipal truck used for trash collection and removal

**grader** truck equipped with earth-leveling device

**haulaway** truck with two-level trailer, used to transport new automobiles

**hook and ladder** fire engine with ladders and other apparatus

**jitney** small passenger bus or van with flexible schedule over regular route

**juggernaut** *Chiefly Brit.* heavy truck

**limousine** van for transportation of passengers, esp. to airport

**lorry** *Chiefly Brit.* truck

**microbus** station wagon shaped like van

**mobile home** large van or trailer with living quarters; motor home

**motor home** mobile home

**moving van** large, enclosed truck used to haul household goods

**omnibus** public carrier for at least twelve passengers, usu. with door in rear

**paddy wagon** panel truck used to transport prisoners

**panel truck** enclosed, windowless van

**pantechnicon** *Chiefly Brit.* moving van

**pickup** small truck with cab, shallow box body, and tailgate

**recreational vehicle** RV; large van with living facilities

**RV** recreational vehicle

**semi** *Informal.* semitrailer truck

**semitrailer** freight trailer designed so that most of its weight rests on another vehicle, attached to tractor by fifth wheel or pivot

**six-by-six** six-wheeled truck with six driving wheels

**skidder** four-wheel tractor equipped with grapple, used to haul logs or timber over rough terrain

**steamroller** steam-powered tractor with heavy roller for roadwork

**tank**  military armored tractor propelled by two endless metal belts

**tow truck**  pickup equipped with winch for hauling other vehicles; wrecker

**tractor**  powerful vehicle with large rear wheels or endless belt treads, used to haul equipment or do work; cab and engine section that hauls semitrailer

**trailer**  engineless container drawn by tractor or other vehicle; auto-drawn highway vehicle with living facilities

**transfer**  passenger or baggage carrier used between locations by transfer company

**truck**  self-propelled motor vehicle designed for transportation of goods or special-purpose equipment, often with swivel for hauling trailer

**van**  multipurpose, enclosed, box-shaped vehicle having side panels, with or without windows in panels

**water wagon**  truck equipped with tank for hauling and sprinkling water

**weasel**  tractorlike vehicle used in snow

**wrecker**  tow truck

## INTERNAL COMBUSTION ENGINE

**afterburner**  auxiliary device that burns exhaust fumes from combustion

**air-cooled engine**  engine in which heat of combustion is dissipated by air flow, usu. by movement of fan

**automatic choke**  temperature- or time-controlled device that enriches air/fuel mixture for cold starts

**block**  aluminum or iron casting housing cylinders and crankshaft

**bore**  cylinder diameter

**cam**  one of rotating pieces along camshaft

**camshaft**  shaft that changes rotary motion into linear motion to operate valves

**carburetor**  device that controls and monitors air/fuel mixture fed to cylinders

**choke**  plate near top of carburetor that can be partially closed to restrict air entering carburetor and enrich fuel mixture

**combustion chamber**  area within cylinder above piston where fuel/air mixture ignites

**compression**  reduction in combustion chamber volume prior to power stroke on ignition

**compression-ignition engine**  diesel engine

**compression ratio**  ratio of maximum to minimum combustion chamber volume as piston strokes

**connecting rod**  linkage between piston and crankshaft; rod

**crankcase**  lower part of engine that contains lubricating oil

**crankshaft**  main engine shaft that converts linear motion of pistons into rotary motion

**cylinder**  hollow tube in engine block, containing piston

**cylinder head**  combustion chamber area of cylinders atop engine block; head

**dead center**  either of points at each end of stroke in reciprocating engine where crankshaft and connecting rod are in same line

**diesel engine**  compression-ignition engine in which air is heated by compression and diesel fuel is injected directly into the combustion chamber, where it then self-ignites

**displacement**  total volume swept by pistons in single stroke

**dual carburetor**  engine equipped with two carburetors operating together

**exhaust manifold**  metal casting that routes exhaust from each combustion chamber to common exhaust pipe

**exhaust valve**  device that opens to allow burned gases to be expelled from combustion chamber

**four-stroke cycle engine**  internal combustion engine working in four stages: intake, compression, power, and exhaust

**fuel injection**  fuel delivery system in which a high-pressure pump meters and atomizes fuel directly into diesel engine cylinder or into intake manifold of spark ignition engine

**glow plug**  element for each cylinder of diesel engine that heats incoming fuel and air to promote combustion when engine is cold

**head**  cylinder head

**head gasket**  packing element that seals cylinder head from engine block

**intake manifold**  tube or casting with combination of passages that routes fuel/air mixture from carburetor to combustion chamber in spark ignition engine

**intake port**  opening in cylinder wall of two-stroke cycle engine through which air or fuel/air mixture is forced into combustion chamber

**intake valve**  device in four-stroke cycle engine that opens to allow air or fuel/air mixture to be drawn into combustion chamber

**internal combustion engine**  reciprocating or rotary engine in which combustion of fuel is in direct contact with pistons or rotor

**lifter**  element connecting camshaft to pushrod or valve

**piston**  component moving up and down in cylinder, linked by connecting rod to crankshaft, and converting pressure of combustion into work

**piston ring**  circular device fitted into groove in piston to keep oil out and seal gases in; ring

**power stroke**  burning of fuel/air mixture in combustion chamber to force piston downward

**pushrod**  mechanical device through which camshaft activates rocker arm to open valve

**reciprocating engine**  two-stroke or four-stroke cycle engine

**ring**  piston ring

**rocker arm**  pivoting lever that pushes valve open

**rod**  connecting rod

**rotary engine**  internal combustion engine without pistons, in which triangular rotor moves orbitally and rotationally; Wankel engine

**slant six**  six-cylinder engine with row of cylinders mounted at an angle

**spark ignition engine**  engine in which spark or glow plug ignites an explosive air/fuel mixture

**stroke**  one phase in piston cycle

**supercharger**  engine-driven compressor that increases density of fuel/air mixture

**throttle**  device that controls volume of mixture delivered to spark ignition engine or quantity of fuel injected into diesel engine

**torque**  measure of twisting force generated by crankshaft

**turbocharger**  compressor driven by exhaust heat to increase density of fuel/air mixture

**two-stroke cycle engine**  internal combustion engine that works in two stages, compression and power, with blower or other means of delivering fresh air and fuel with piston at bottom dead center prior to compression stroke

**V-6**  six-cylinder engine with three cylinders in each of two banks set at ninety degree angle forming a V

**V-8**  eight-cylinder engine with four cylinders in each of two banks set at ninety degree angle forming a V

**valve**  device used to close off and meter flow of intake and exhaust into and out of combustion chamber

**valve clearance**  size of opening of valve necessary for proper engine operation

**valve guide**  hole through which stem of valve passes

**valve lifter**  cam extension that opens valves

**Wankel engine**  rotary engine

**water-cooled engine**  engine in which circulated coolant, or water and glycol mixture, extracts combustion heat

**wrist pin**  steel pin that links piston to connecting rod

## WORKING PARTS

**accelerator**  pedal operated by driver's right foot that varies amount of fuel fed to engine, thus controlling speed

**air cleaner**  device containing air filter and protecting against backfire

**air conditioner**  refrigeration and ventilation system for lowering temperature of passenger compartment

**air filter**  device that keeps solid particles out of fuel/air mixture

**alternator**  alternating current (AC) generator that supplies power to run car's electrical system

**automatic transmission**  gearbox that changes gear ratios independently of driver based on speed and load

**axle**  full shaft on which wheels revolve

**battery**  electrochemical storage unit of 6 or 12 volts

**bearing**  part, such as wheel bearing, on which another part revolves

**blower**  fan

**brake**  friction device used to slow or stop car

**brake drum**  metal arc mounted on hub against which shoes rub to stop car

**brake lining**  replaceable friction material attached to brake shoes and pressed by shoes against brake drums to stop car

**brake shoes**  arc-shaped pieces that fit inside and press against drums

**breaker points**  electrical switch in distributor used to control high voltage needed by spark plugs; points

**capacitor**  device for storage of electrical energy

**catalytic converter**  emission control device for converting pollutants to benign substances

**clutch**  coupling mechanism by which rotating shafts of engine and transmission may be engaged and disengaged; pedal operated by driver's left foot in manual transmission cars

**clutch plate**  flat coupling disc in clutch mechanism

**coil**  pulse transformer that increases voltage to fire spark plug

**condenser**  electrical device that prevents arcing

**cruise control**  automatic setting for continuous, high-speed driving

**CV joints**  *constant velocity* universal joints that keep input and output speed equal, contained in rubber boots into which grease is packed at each end of axle

**damper**  *Chiefly Brit.* shock absorber

**differential**  gear system that allows outer wheel to travel greater distance than inner wheel during turn

**disc brakes**  brakes whose friction is generated by pads rubbing rotor mounted on wheel assembly

**distributor**  device for directing high voltage from coil to appropriate spark plugs in turn

**distributor cap**  top of distributor with wires to each spark plug

**distributor rotor**  component that directs voltage to appropriate spark plug wire

**driveline**  drive train

**drive shaft**  shaft connecting transmission to rear axle in rear-wheel drive car

**drive train**  universal joint and drive shaft connecting transmission to axles; driveline

**drum brakes**  brakes with lined shoes that rub against inner circumference of metal, hub-mounted drums for friction

**electronic ignition**  spark ignition system without breaker points

**emergency brake**  manually operated brake that sets rear brakes in locked position, usu. while car is parked

**expansion strut**  steel or alloy segment cast into piston to control its expansion under heat and maintain constant piston-to-cylinder wall clearance

**fan belt**  engine-driven belt that operates fan

**fifth wheel**  pivot with which trailer attaches to tractor

**filter**  device that removes foreign substances from air, oil, gasoline, or water

**fluid drive**  power coupling between engine and transmission, consisting of two vaned rotors in sealed, lubricated casing, permitting smooth start in any gear

**flywheel**  heavy disk at rear of crankshaft that smooths separate power pulses from each cylinder

**four-wheel drive**  system in which differential conveys power to all four wheels

**front-wheel drive**  system in which differential conveys power only to front wheels, which steer and propel car

**fuel pump**  device that supplies fuel from gas tank to carburetor or fuel injection system

**fuse**  safety device that controls current flow to elements in electrical system

**gear**  one of toothed wheels in transmission that determine direction and relative speed of travel and mechanical advantage of engine

**gearbox**  transmission

**gear ratio**  ratio of speeds between input and output shafts of transmission in each gear

**generator**  direct current (DC) generating device

**half-shaft**  one of pair of half-axles that serves left or right wheel

**hand brake**  manually operated emergency brake

**header**  exhaust manifold designed for free flow of exhaust gases

**hydraulic brakes**  brake system operated by pressure of fluid in cylinders

**hydraulic clutch**  clutch operated by hydraulic pressure from engine cooling system

**ignition switch**  key switch in dashboard that sets ignition system in operation

**ignition system**  electrical system designed to produce spark in cylinders and ignite fuel, consisting of battery, coil, condenser, breaker points, distributor, spark plugs, and wires

**linkage** series of metal rods or levers that transmit motion from one unit to another

**manifold** exhaust manifold and/or intake manifold

**manual transmission** gearbox in which selection of gear is controlled by driver through clutch and gearshift

**master cylinder** brake fluid sump and piston that powers slave cylinders in hydraulic brake system

**muffler** baffle exhaust device used to lessen noise of combustion

**oil cooler** auxiliary radiator used to lower oil temperature

**oil filter** engine-mounted device that removes contaminants from engine oil

**oil pump** device that forces lubricating oil through engine

**overdrive** device used to lower overall gear ratio and hence reduce rpms necessary to achieve given road speed, thus decreasing fuel consumption

**PCV valve** *positive crankcase ventilation valve*; device that prevents crankcase vapors from discharging directly into atmosphere

**plug** spark plug

**points** breaker points

**power brakes** hydraulically actuated brakes with vacuum assist mechanism that reduces brake pedal pressure needed

**power steering** hydraulically assisted steering linkage that reduces turning effort

**rack-and-pinion steering** system in which rotation of steering wheel is translated into linear motion by pinion gear mounted in toothed rack

**radiator** unit of pipes that dissipates heat in engine coolant

**rear axle** axle connecting wheels at back of car

**rear-wheel drive** conventional system in which differential conveys drive power to rear wheels only

**reduction gear** combination of gears that reduce input speed so as to lower output speed

**regulator** device that controls voltage sent by alternator to battery

**seals** permanently installed rubber or leather components that keep lubrication from leaking

**shift** driver-operated lever that controls transmission

**shock absorber** device fitted to each corner of suspension to damp spring oscillations and smoothen ride

**slave cylinders** hydraulic brake cylinders on each wheel that convert hydraulic pressure from master cylinder into mechanical force applied to brakes

**solenoid** magnetic device that exerts force when current flows through coil

**spark ignition system** ignition system in which high-voltage current from coil is sent through distributor to appropriate spark plug at proper timing to ignite fuel/air mixture in combustion chamber

**spark plug** electrical component threaded into cylinder head whose spark initiates combustion; plug

**spark plug gap** opening across which spark jumps to ignite air/fuel mixture

**springs** main suspension units that absorb force of road shocks by twisting or flexing

**starter** high-torque electric motor used to start engine

**steering** system that transmits directional force from steering wheel to axle and wheels

**steering column** central pivoting unit of steering system

**steering wheel** wheel connected to steering column by which driver steers car

**stick shift** device by which driver controls gears in manual transmission

**suspension** springs, shock absorbers, and other components that connect wheels to car body

**sway bar** torsion coupling between right and left front-wheel suspensions to reduce roll and sway

**thermostat** device that regulates engine temperature by controlling flow of coolant through system

**timing** setting that initiates spark at appropriate point in piston's compression stroke

**torsion bar** flexible steel bar that twists to provide spring in suspension

**tranny** *Informal.* transmission

**transaxle** integrated transmission, differential, and drive unit on drive axle, front or rear

**transmission** assembly of gears and selector linkage that connects engine output shaft to rest of drive train by matching engine speed with desired road speed; gearbox; tranny

**universal joint** multidirectional joint in drive shaft that permits changes in angle while shaft is rotating

**water pump** device that circulates water coolant through engine

## BODY PARTS AND ACCESSORIES

**aerial** metal rod mounted on body for receiving radio signals

**air bag** bag that inflates during collision to prevent driver or passenger from being thrown forward

**antifreeze** glycol and water mixture used in water-cooled engine to lower freezing point of coolant

**antiknock** (*adj*) relating to any fuel additive that helps resist engine knocking

**ashtray** retractable metal receptacle in dash for extinguished cigarettes

**backseat** seat behind driver's seat in passenger compartment

**backup light** exterior light illuminated when car is in reverse gear

**belt tread** continuous band around sets of wheels on tanks and tractors

**bias-ply tire** tire with supporting cords embedded at angle to rotational direction

**body** external housing and structure of vehicle

**bonnet** *Chiefly Brit.* hood

**boot** *Chiefly Brit.* trunk

**brake fluid** viscous liquid used in hydraulic brake cylinders

**brake lights** rear lamps illuminated when brakes are in use

**brake pedal** foot control by which driver operates brakes

**bucket seat** low, individual, front seat for one passenger

**bulb** electric lamp

**bumper** protective member fitted over front and rear wheels; fender

**cab** enclosed passenger portion of truck

**camber** angle of wheel when viewed head-on

**caster** positioning that provides directional stability to front wheels

**chains** chain-link units attached to tires to increase traction on snow, ice, or mud

**chassis** substructure on which components of car are mounted

**chrome** shiny chromium alloy used to coat parts of body trim

**compartment** enclosed passenger seating area

**convertible top** retractable vinyl or fabric roof

**coolant** alcohol or glycol mixed with water to increase efficiency of cooling system

**cove** scooped-out area on side door or panel

**dash** dashboard

**dashboard** instrument panel facing driver in compartment; dash

**defroster** heating/ventilation system that directs air onto windshield to clear ice or condensation

**diesel fuel** fuel oil burned in diesel engine

**directional signal** turn signal

**emergency light** hazard light

**exhaust pipe** metal tube that routes exhaust fumes out of manifold

**fairing** custom part added to smooth contour of body and reduce drag

**fender** bumper

**fuel** gasoline or oil burned to supply power for engine

**gas** gasoline

**gasket** packing that seals joint, as between cylinder head and engine block

**gasohol** combination of gasoline and up to ten per cent alcohol, used as fuel

**gasoline** complex hydrocarbon blend used as fuel by internal combustion engines; gas

**gas tank** storage container for gasoline attached to chassis

**gearshift** mechanism by which gears are engaged and disengaged

**glove box** *Chiefly Brit.* glove compartment

**glove compartment** small storage area with door in dashboard; glove box

**grill** gridlike chrome covering placed over front of engine compartment to permit air to flow freely through engine

**hatchback** vehicle with rear hatch opening into passenger compartment

**hazard light** blinking front or rear light used when vehicle is stopped for mechanical trouble or in dangerous place; emergency light

**headlights** high-powered lamps that illuminate area in front of car for night driving

**headrest** unit attached to seat top as head support

**heater** unit using engine heat to warm passenger compartment

**high beam** second headlight for added illumination at distance

**hood** hinged cover over engine compartment

**horn** audible electric warning device controlled by driver

**hose** usu. rubber tube for carrying air or water from one unit to another

**housing** protective metal covering for engine part

**hub** wheel mounting on end of axle

**hub cap** often decorative chrome covering for lug nuts that attach wheel to axle

**inner tube** replaceable rubber lining that held air in old-fashioned tires

**instrument panel** dashboard with gauges and meters

**jack** device for lifting side of car to change tires

**Jaws of Life** *Trademark.* heavy-duty tool used to cut through and pry apart crumpled metal to free trapped accident victims

**jumper cable** insulated electrical cable for recharging battery or starting car with dead battery

**jump seat** removable or folding seat for extra passenger, esp. in limousine or taxicab

**lamp** electric filament bulb for illumination or signaling

**license plate** metal plate issued by state bearing car's identifying number

**loaded** (*adj*) having many optional features

**lubricant** engine oil or grease that reduces friction and heat on operating parts

**lug nuts** bolts that hold wheel on axle

**mag wheel** shiny magnesium wheel rim

**mud flap** splash guard

**mud guard** splash guard

**odometer** accumulated mileage gauge mounted on dashboard

**oil gauge** meter that indicates engine oil pressure

**oil pan** sump in which oil collects when not circulating through engine in operation

**panel** section of auto body

**parking light** small front or rear light

**pedal** foot control by which driver operates accelerator, brake, or clutch

**petrol** *Chiefly Brit.* gasoline

**premium** high-octane gasoline used in high-compression engines

**radial tire** tire with supporting cords embedded in line with direction of rotation

**raked** (*adj*) describing car, esp. hot rod, with lowered front end

**rearview mirror** small mirror affixed above windshield that allows driver to see what lies behind car

**recap** retread tire

**retread** used tire with new tread applied; recap

**rim** outer metal band on wheel to which tire is attached

**roll bar** protective bar over open driving compartment, esp. in racing cars

**roof** top of passenger compartment

**rumble seat** uncovered folding seat in back of car

**running board** footboard at base of door on side of car

**seat belt** safety device strapped across passenger to secure position in case of accident

**seat cover** vinyl, leather, or fabric placed over seat springs

**shift knob** end of gear shift handled by driver

**side mirror** rearview mirror mounted on side of car

**side pipes** chromed exhaust pipes mounted on side of exterior body of customized car

**side window** window on left or right side of car

**snow tire** special tire with deep tread or rubber cleats to provide traction on snow or ice

**spare tire** extra tire, usu. stored in trunk

**speedometer** road speed gauge mounted on dashboard

**splash guard** flap suspended behind rear wheel to prevent tire splash from muddying windows of following vehicles; mud flap; mud guard

**stick shift** upright gearshift protruding from floor, used to operate manual transmission

**stud** metal cleat inserted in snow tire to increase traction

**sump** part of oil pan containing oil

**sunroof** retractable section of roof

**sun visor** flap that may be lowered to shield passenger's eyes from sun

**tachometer** gauge mounted on dashboard that measures engine speed in revolutions per minute (rpms)

**tailgate** small gate at rear of vehicle that can be lowered to form horizontal surface

**taillight** rear light

**tailpipe** pipe that routes exhaust fumes from muffler to rear of car

**tire** pneumatic casing mounted on wheel forming interface between car and road: tubeless, tube, bias-ply, or radial

**tow bar** unit attached to rear bumper, used to haul another vehicle or trailer

**transmission fluid** viscous liquid used in hydraulic transmission

**tread** grooved portion of tire that touches road

**trim** decorations, chrome, and insignia attached to auto body

**trunk** enclosed storage compartment, usu. at rear

**tubeless tire** tire without inner tube

**turn signal** external, front and rear, driver-controlled lights used to indicate direction of turn; directional signal

**unleaded fuel** gasoline with low lead content, less polluting and forming fewer deposits than leaded fuel

**vanity plate** license plate customized with owner's initials, nickname, or other chosen letters or word

**wheel** circular frame at hub of axle to which tire attaches

**whitewall** tire with circular white strip on black

**windscreen** *Chiefly Brit.* windshield

**windshield** front window of passenger compartment; windscreen

**windshield wiper** motor-driven device with rubber blade for clearing water from windshield

**wiper blade** rubber attachment to windshield wiper

## DRIVING AND REPAIR

**automotive** (*adj*) self-propelled on land, sea, or air, usu. referring to land vehicles

**backfire** improperly timed explosion of fuel mixture, esp. occurring outside cylinder in exhaust system

**balance** (*vb*) adjust new tires for even rotation

**bleed** (*vb*) drain brake fluid to clear hydraulic brake lines of air

**blindside** (*vb*) strike another car without warning from rear or side

**blow-by** leakage of combustion gases between piston and cylinder wall into crankcase

**blown engine** *Slang.* general, extensive engine breakdown

**blowout** sudden, severe flat tire while driving

**Blue Book** *Trademark.* reference manual listing the standard, accepted values of used cars

**body shop** garage for repairs to body and repainting

**bodywork** nonmechanical repairs

**bottleneck** narrowing roadway that causes traffic congestion

**Botts dots** raised, reflective markers on roadway that alert driver when car drifts out of its lane

**broadside** (*vb*) strike another car full on side

**bumper-to-bumper** (*adj.*) describing long line of slow-moving traffic

**burn rubber** *Slang.* accelerate abruptly with tires squealing and leaving black marks on pavement

**center divider** barrier down center of two-way road

**chicken** game in which two drivers drive toward each other or toward obstacle, with first driver to turn away losing contest

**cornering** ability of driver or car to negotiate curves and turns

**crank** (*vb*) start engine

**crosswalk** lane marked off for pedestrian use while crossing street

**cruising** driving slowly back and forth along particular roadway in city

**curb** low bump at edge of roadway that separates it from sidewalk; also, *esp. Brit.*, kerb

**customizing** additions or alterations made by owner to standard body and engine

**dead battery** battery without stored voltage until recharged from external source

**Denver boot** device locked in place on wheel of illegally parked car to prevent it from moving

**detonation** knocking or pinging sound when gasoline is inadequate for acceleration or ascending grade

**dieseling** abnormal self-ignition in which engine continues running after ignition is turned off

**double clutch** pump clutch pedal twice in shifting gear

**double parking** illegal parking on street side of another parked car

**downshift** (*vb*) change to lower gear when decelerating

**driver's license** permit to operate car issued by state; license

**driveway** narrow private roadway leading to garage or residence from public roadway

**driving school** training institution for drivers

**drop the engine** remove entire engine for repairs; pull the engine

**drunk driving** driving recklessly while intoxicated; DUI

**DUI** *d*riving *u*nder the *i*nfluence; drunk driving

**emission control** smog control

**engine overhaul** complete replacement of working parts in engine

**EPA** *E*nvironmental *P*rotection *A*gency; government agency that sets smog standards and tests cars for gasoline mileage

**feeler gauge** tool with several blades, used to measure gap in spark plugs or valve clearance

**fender bender** *Informal.* minor car accident

**flat tire** punctured tire from which air has escaped

**freeway** divided highway with several lanes in each direction for fast driving

**garage** repair shop; place for storing car at one's home

**gas guzzler** *Informal.* car getting low mileage per gallon of gas

**grade** steep hill

**green light** signal to continue moving

**gun the engine** increase rpms

**hang** (*vb*) *Slang.* make a turn or U-turn

**head-on** (*adj.*) describing direct collision with car moving in opposite direction

**hit-and-run** (*adj.*) describing accident in which driver flees the scene

**hitchhike** (*vb*) stand by roadside with thumb extended seeking a ride

**horsepower** unit measuring power of engine, equal to 550 foot-pounds per second

**hot-wire** (*vb*) *Slang.* contact wiring around ignition switch to start car without key

**hydroplane** (*vb*) skid over very shallow water

**idle** running speed of engine with no load and closed throttle

**jackknife** accident in which tractor-trailer truck folds in half like knife blade closing

**jump-start** (*vb*) start car by using jumper cables to connect dead battery to good battery in another vehicle

**knock** noise from poorly controlled combustion in cylinder

**leadfoot** *Informal.* person who drives at high speed with foot pressed on accelerator

**learner's permit** state-issued permit to operate car only in presence of licensed driver

**license** driver's license

**lube** addition of lubricant and transaxle grease

**lug the engine** drive at rpm too low for engaged gear

**mechanic** person trained in auto repair

**mileage** miles traveled for each gallon of gasoline consumed

**moving violation** violation of driving laws cited by police; traffic violation

**no-fault insurance** insurance system in which liability is not dependent upon who is at fault in accident

**no parking** designation for roadway where parking is prohibited

**octane** measure of gasoline's ability to resist knock and detonation

**oil change** replacement of dirty crankcase oil

**one-way street** roadway with passage allowed in one direction only

**overhaul** engine overhaul

**parallel parking** parking in space parallel to direction of street

**parking lot** area reserved for parking of numerous cars

**parking ticket** citation issued by police for illegal parking

**passing lane** lane nearest center of roadway on two-way street, designed for cars traveling fastest

**pedestrian** person walking along or across roadway

**peel out** (*vb*) *Slang.* accelerate abruptly from a standstill

**ping** mild knock in detonation

**pit stop** *Informal.* stop for fuel and servicing, esp. on long drive or in race

**pop the clutch** *Informal.* disengage clutch abruptly, not smoothly

**pull the engine** drop the engine

**rear-end** (*vb*) strike another vehicle from behind

**rebuild** (*vb*) do complete engine overhaul

**reckless driving** dangerous, high-speed, drunk, or erratic driving

**red light** signal to stop and wait for green light

**registration** annual record of auto ownership filed with state

**rental car** automobile leased when no personal vehicle is available

**rev** (*vb*) increase engine rpms suddenly

**ride shotgun** *Informal.* ride in passenger seat located to driver's right

**roadway** usu. paved strip of land designated for use by automobiles

**roll start** roll standard-transmission car and pop clutch to achieve ignition when electrical system fails

**rpm** revolutions per minute; measure of engine speed

**rubberneck** (*vb*) strain to see accident scene from passing vehicle, causing slowing of traffic and danger

**rush hour** period of heavy traffic at beginning and end of workday

**school zone** area near school with special low speed limit

**scope** meter for measuring and monitoring operations of car's electrical system

**servicing** tune-up, oil change, lube, and other basic maintenance

**shunpiking** driving on back roads to avoid highways

**sideswipe** (*vb*) graze another car's side in minor accident

**skid** loss of control due to ice, water, or sudden stop

**slipstreaming** driving closely behind another vehicle to take advantage of reduced air resistance

**smog check** required monitoring of emission control system to ensure it meets certain standards

**smog control** system regulating automobile exhaust emissions; emission control

**smog device** emission control component

**souped-up** (*adj*) *Slang.* customized for increased power and speed; stroked

**specifications** precise measurements of proper settings for engine operations

**speeding** driving in excess of speed limit

**speed limit** maximum driving speed allowed by law on given roadway

**spin-out** rotating skid made by automobile, causing it to leave roadway

**stall** come to a halt though failure of enough fuel to pass through carburetor to engine, causing engine to cease operating

**sticker price** undiscounted price for car, usu. affixed to window as itemized list on sheet of paper

**stock** (*adj*) designating standard design, parts, and color of factory-manufactured automobile

**stop sign** usu. red, octagonal street sign reading "Stop"

**stroked** (*adj*) *Slang.* souped-up, esp. by lengthening piston stroke for greater power

**test drive** trial run to evaluate new car

**toe-in** slight forward convergence given to front wheels to improve steering alignment

**tool** (*vb*) drive, esp. down highway

**total** (*vb*) damage one's car beyond repair in accident

**towaway zone** no-parking area from which cars are removed to city or police garage, esp. at rush hour

**towing** pulling another vehicle or trailer with one's vehicle

**traffic** vehicles on roadway, esp. many vehicles

**traffic court** local court with jurisdiction over violators of traffic laws

**traffic signal** traffic control device usu. having red, yellow, and green lights

**traffic violation** violation of driving laws; moving violation

**tune-up** periodic adjustment of ignition, valve clearance, and fuel delivery system and replacement of electrical parts

**upshift** (*vb*) change to higher gear when accelerating

**U-turn** reversal of driving direction on same roadway

**vapor lock** boiling or vaporizing of fuel in lines due to excess heat, often causing stoppage of fuel flow

**vehicle ID** identification number stamped on engine block or dashboard

**wheel alignment** proper adjustment of wheel's caster, camber, and toe-in

**whiplash** neck strain due to sudden, violent accident involving rear-end impact

**winterize** (*vb*) prepare auto for cold weather by adding anti-freeze, thinner oil, and insulation

**wrecker** one who hauls away and disposes of cars after accidents

**yellow light** signal to slow down before proceeding or as warning of imminent red light requiring stop

# Railroads

Types of Trains, Cars, and Lines
Railroad Personnel
Parts, Practices, and Argot

**see also**: Chap. 6: Other Vehicles

## Types of Trains, Cars, and Lines

**air car** freight car with air brakes

**baggage car** freight car that carries baggage

**baggage train** train that carries freight and passenger baggage

**bar car** passenger train car in which refreshments are served

**booster** extra engine used to assist on steep grade

**boxcar** roofed freight car with sliding doors on its sides; crate

**branch** side road leading off main line

**buda car** *Slang*. automobilelike inspection car with small engine

**bullet train** very fast express train

**bunk car** sleeping car for loggers or track workers

**cable car** car powered by loop of underground cable

**caboose** last car on freight train, occupied by conductor, rear brakeman, and crew, in which their meals are taken; *Slang*: ambulance, anchor, ape wagon, bazoo wagon, bed house, brain cage, buggy, cabin car, cage, chariot, cook shack, cracker box, crib, den, doghouse, doodlebug, glory wagon, go-cart, hack, hearse, kipps, monkey cage, parlor, pavilion, penthouse, perambulator, saloon, shack, shanty, strawberry patch, sun parlor, van, zoo

**calliope** *Slang*. steam locomotive

**can** *Slang*. tank car

**cannonball express** *Slang*. fast express train

**car** individual railway vehicle, carrying passengers or freight, coupled to other cars to form train

**carriage** *Chiefly Brit*. railway car

**caterpillar** *Slang*. streamlined passenger train

**center dump ballast car** gondola car with chute beneath center of gondola, used to spread ballast on tracks

**chair car** passenger car with pairs of adjustable seats down each side of aisle

**choo-choo** *Baby talk*. train

**coach** car with seats for passengers

**coalburner** coal-burning locomotive

**coal car** freight car for coal, usu. gondola

**cog railway** rail line on steep mountain with locomotive that uses a cogwheel to engage cogs on tracks to gain traction

**crate** *Slang*. boxcar

**cut of cars** cars coupled together and/or attached to engine but without caboose

**day coach** ordinary passenger car

**diesel locomotive** engine powered by internal combustion engine that uses diesel fuel fired by compressed air in cylinders

**diner** dining car

**dinghy** *Slang*. sleeping car for train workers

**dining car** car in which meals are served to passengers; diner

**Donegan** *Slang*. old railroad car without wheels, used as office or residence

**doodlebug** *Slang*. caboose

**double-decked stock** stock car with two floors, esp. for sheep

**doubleheader** train hauled by two locomotives

**drawing room car** sleeping car with lounge areas

**drill** switch engine

**drop-bottom dump car** gondola with bottom that opens to disperse its load

**dummy** switching locomotive with housed boiler and running gear

**dump car** gondola that tips sideways to empty its load

**el** elevated

**electric car** single-car electric railway, such as trolley

**electric railway** railroad car or cars powered by electricity from cables or generator

**electric train** electrically powered urban railway

**elephant car** *Slang*. head brakeman's car behind locomotive

**elevated** railway raised above ground on trestle

**engine** locomotive

**express car** railway express cargo car on passenger train

**express train** fast train that makes few or no stops

**fantail** *Slang*. switch engine with sloping tender

**feeder line** secondary rail line connecting to main line

**flatcar** platform freight car without roof or sides; platform car

**flier** very fast train, esp. passenger express

**freight car** any of various cars designed to haul freight, usu. enclosed with sliding doors on sides

**freight train** nonpassenger train

**funicular** cable railroad that travels up and down a slope, often suspended from cable

**giraffe** *Slang*. mining car with one end elevated for inclines

**goat** *Slang*. engine that pushes cars around yard

**go-devil** handcar

**gondola** freight car with sides but no roof

**gravity car** unpowered car that runs downhill only

**handcar** small, flat, four-wheeled railway car propelled by two-handled pump, used to carry section gangs to work

**hand truck** hand car built like flat truck

**Hart convertible car** flat gondola car with drop bottom

**helper** auxiliary engine in doubleheader to aid on grade

**highline** main track

**high-sided gondola** freight car with tall sides and no roof

**hog** *Slang*. large steam locomotive for hauling freight

**hopper car** steel-sided freight car with chutes that discharge freight such as gravel or coal

**horse railway** street railway car drawn by horses

**house track** section of track at station, used for loading or unloading

**idler** unloaded flatcar placed ahead of or behind oversize load projecting from next car

**jimmy** *Slang.* four-wheel coal car

**jitney** four-wheel electric baggage car in terminal

**kettle** *Slang.* small steam locomotive, esp. decrepit one

**lay-by** *Chiefly Brit.* sidetrack

**limited** top-service train with few cars making selected stops

**line** track and roadbed following specific route

**liner** luxurious passenger train

**local** passenger train that stops at every depot along line

**local express** passenger train that stops at most depots

**locomotive** steam-, electric-, or diesel-powered railroad engine that pulls or pushes other cars; engine

**log car** flatcar for carrying piles of long logs

**lounge car** passenger car with seats at windows, bar, and refreshment facilities

**luggage van** *Chiefly Brit.* baggage car

**mail car** car for carrying postal freight

**main line** primary track

**metro** metropolitan underground railway (France)

**milk car** tank car for hauling milk

**milk train** *Informal.* train that makes frequent stops

**mill** *Slang.* steam locomotive

**mixed train** train with both passenger and freight cars

**model railroad** miniature-scale railroad built and run as hobby

**monorail** train running along single track

**Mother Hubbard** *Slang.* engine with cab over middle of boiler

**night owl** *Slang.* late-night passenger train

**observation car** passenger car with large sightseeing windows or elevated split-level section

**officers' car** private passenger coach for railroad company officials

**outfit car** boxcar with bunks for section men

**paddle wheel** *Slang.* narrow gauge locomotive with driving boxes outside wheels

**palace car** luxurious sleeping car

**parliamentary** train required by Parliament to run daily each way over entire length of system, stopping at every station and providing low-cost service (Britain, 19th c.)

**parlor car** first-class lounge or day car with plush seats

**passenger car** coach

**passenger train** train that carries only passengers and their baggage

**pike** *Slang.* railroad line, esp. short one

**platform car** flatcar

**plug run** *Slang.* local train, esp. one serving small towns

**postal car** enclosed freight car for hauling mail bags

**Prairie** locomotive with 2-6-2 wheel arrangement

**private car** passenger or parlor car owned or hired by group or individual for exclusive use

**produce car** ventilated or refrigerated boxcar specially equipped to carry fresh fruit and produce

**puller** switch engine that hauls cars around yard

**Pullman car** comfortable, well-appointed passenger car that converts into sleeping car or is divided into roomettes

**rack-and-pinion railway** railway with rack between rails that meshes with gear wheel or pinion on locomotive to assist on steep grades

**rack car** freight car with racks that hold lumber or pulpwood

**rail detector car** car equipped with instruments used to locate defects in rails

**railhead** farthest point from terminus to which rails have been laid

**rail line** route followed by particular railroad

**railroad** roadway of parallel steel rails that serve as track for passenger or freight cars drawn by locomotive; system of such tracks; company operating trains on railroad

**rails** railroads, their lines and equipment

**railway** railroad, esp. lightweight line operating locally

**rammer** *Slang.* extra engine on train

**reefer** *Slang.* refrigerator car

**refrigerator car** freight car with refrigerated compartment for perishables; reefer

**rocket sled** sled propelled along tracks by rocket engine, used to test effects of rapid acceleration and deceleration

**rolling stock** railroad cars of all types, esp. those owned by one company

**scoot** *Slang.* shuttle

**short line** train operating over short distance

**shuttle** train that makes short, frequent, round-trip runs over same track; scoot

**skeleton car** car for hauling logs in which truck carriages are held together by center beam without deck

**sleeper** sleeping car

**sleeping car** car outfitted with sleeping berths, esp. Pullman car; sleeper

**smoker** smoking car

**smoking car** passenger car in which tobacco smoking is allowed; smoker

**special** train running on irregular schedule or carrying unique cargo or passengers

**steam locomotive** engine powered by steam from boiler

**steam shovel** large mechanical shovel connected to motor in small enclosure on flatcar (snow plow and pile driver can also be thus connected)

**stemwinder** brakeless trolley; locomotive with special gear system

**stock car** ventilated or slatted car for livestock, esp. cattle, often with feeding mangers on sides

**streamliner** fast train

**streetcar** passenger car on municipal railway

**streetcar line** system of rails that provides public transportation on city streets

**street railway** rail system on city streets

**string** line of coupled cars

**stub** *Slang.* train that takes over part of another's schedule

**subway** underground municipal railway, usu. electric; underground

**supply train** train that gathers scraps and delivers supplies to all points along division

**switch engine** engine used solely to switch cars in yard; drill

**tangent track** portion of track adjacent to curve

**tank car** freight car for hauling fluids or gases in large, enclosed tank; tanker

**tanker** tank car

**tap line** short feeder line, owned by industrial concern, leading from regular tracks to factory or warehouse

**tender car** fuel and water supply car coupled directly behind engine

**trailer** flatcar pushed ahead of engine to couple to other cars on section unfit for locomotive

**train** several railroad cars coupled together

**tram** *Chiefly Brit.* streetcar; open railway car used in mines

**tramline** *Chiefly Brit.* streetcar line

**tramway** *Chiefly Brit.* streetcar line; system in which cars are supported by overhead cables

**trimmer** engine used to shove errant cars clear in hump yard switching

**trolley** street railway car

**truck** carriage with one or more pairs of wheels that guide one end of car or locomotive on sharp curves

**trunk line** main line of railroad system

**tube** *Chiefly Brit.* underground railway

**underground** subway

**varnish** *Slang.* highly lacquered wooden passenger car

**wagon** *Chiefly Brit.* railroad car

**wagon-lit** sleeping car (Europe)

**way car** local-line freight car

**work train** boxcars converted into living quarters with bunks, kitchen, and office for repair and maintenance crews, sometimes with flatcars that carry tools and supplies

**wrecking crane** flatcar with enclosure at one end holding steam boiler, engine, and hoisting mechanism

**wreck train** train equipped to clear tracks of debris or damaged equipment following storm or accident

**yard engine** engine used to switch and move trains in yard

**yard goat** *Slang.* yard engine

## RAILROAD PERSONNEL

**air jammer** worker who connects air hoses and air signals between coupled cars

**ash eater** *Slang.* fireman

**baggageman** person who handles passenger luggage

**baggage master** person who supervises baggage room at terminal

**bakehead** *Slang.* fireman

**boilermaker** person who assembles and maintains boilers

**boomer** *Slang.* itinerant railroad worker

**brakeman** person who operates train brakes; roughneck

**brotherhood** railroad workers' union, esp. one of Big Four: engineers, firemen, conductors, trainmen

**butch** *Slang.* person who peddles snacks and newspapers to passengers

**car inspector** person who checks for defects in cars

**chief clerk** person who handles correspondence, accounts, and paperwork

**conductor** person who supervises train crew and collects passenger fares; person in charge of street railway

**crew** track workers and trainmen

**dispatcher** person who manages train movements, schedules, and track assignments

**electric owl** *Slang.* night operator

**end man** rear brakeman

**engine driver** *Chiefly Brit.* engineer

**engineer** person trained to operate locomotive and drive train

**field man** yard brakeman

**fireman** person who shovels coal into firebox and puts water in boiler to maintain steam level; apprentice to engineer who works with him in cab

**flagman** person who gives signals at designated sites

**floater** *Slang.* migratory railroad worker

**gripman** porter

**guard** *Chiefly Brit.* conductor; elevated or subway brakeman

**head brakeman** brakeman at front of train who opens and closes switches, takes on water, and acts as flagman

**hoghead** *Slang.* engineer

**hop** *Slang.* porter

**hostler** roundhouse or terminal engine maintenance worker

**lineman** track inspector who reports damage to section gang

**news butch** *Slang.* peddler on passenger trains who moves down aisle with candy, fruit, drinks, snacks, and newspapers

**parlor brakeman** rear brakeman in caboose on freight train

**paymaster** railroad employee who travels about paying salaries

**pin lifter** *Slang.* yard brakeman or switchman

**pin puller** *Slang.* yard switchman

**porter** passenger baggage carrier at terminal; sleeping car attendant; gripman; hop; redcap

**railroader** one who works on railroad

**redcap** porter

**roughneck** *Slang.* brakeman

**roundhouse mechanic** engine service and maintenance worker in yard roundhouse

**section boss** foreman of section gang; warden

**section gang** group of section men who weed right of way, replace ties, reballast, and repair tracks

**section man** worker who maintains certain section of track

**signal maintainer** person who operates and services signals located at distance from depot

**signal man** operator of railroad signals

**smoke agent** *Slang.* fireman

**spiker** worker who drives spikes when laying rails

**stationmaster** operations supervisor at depot or terminal

**steel gang** *Slang.* crew that lays rails

**steward** passenger train crewman who manages provisioning of food and serves passengers

**stoker** fireman

**switchman** operator of switches that run cars from one track to another, either manually or electrically

**telegraph operator** person who sends messages over telegraph lines from yard or depot to train

**ticket agent** person in station or railroad office who sells passenger tickets

**train captain** former term for conductor

**trainman** member of train crew supervised by conductor

**trainmaster** person who maintains schedules and operates switch yards

**warden** section boss

**watchman** safety inspector, esp. in shack at junction of two tracks

**wrecking crew** relief crew

**yard clerk** assistant at yard office

**yardman** yardmaster

**yardmaster** supervisor of operations in railroad yard; yardman

## PARTS, PRACTICES, AND ARGOT

**adverse** uphill road grade

**air brake** system of continuous brakes worked by compressed air and pistons

**air pump** machine that compresses air in cylinders to drive air brake

**alley** *Slang.* clear track in yard

**alleyway** passage beside compartments in sleeping and parlor cars

**apron** flat, metal platform separating locomotive and tender

**atmospheric brake** original compressed air brake in 1869

**automatic air brake** standard air brake since 1871

**baggage room** terminal area in which incoming and outgoing luggage is held for pickup or shipment

**bail** (*vb*) *Slang.* fire up a locomotive

**ballast** gravel or slag bed for railroad ties

**ball the jack** *Slang.* increase speed

**barn** locomotive roundhouse

**berth** bed or bunk built into sleeping car

**blasting** burst of steam exhaust

**Blenkinsop rack** toothed third rail engaged by gear on some locomotives for traction on grade

**blizzard lights** two emergency lights flanking locomotive headlight

**block signal** signal at block entrance that controls trains entering and leaving

**block system** organization of railroad line into three- or four-mile sections governed by signals which assure that one train leaves block before another enters

**blue flag** warning that workers are repairing crippled car

**board** conductor's cry of "all aboard" as passenger train prepares to leave station

**boiler** metal tank in which water is heated and converted to steam to drive locomotive

**brake club** hard, three-foot club used to tighten hand brake

**broad gauge** road with rails wider than 4 feet 8 1/2 inches (1.43 m) apart

**bug** *Slang.* telegraph instrument; *Slang.* switchman's light

**bumper** retaining post at end of spur track that absorbs shock in collision

**bunk** elevated bed built into wall of sleeper compartment

**cab** enclosed area of locomotive in which engineer and fireman operate controls

**Casey Jones** *Slang.* engineer on fast-moving locomotive, named after legendary engineer who died in wreck

**cattle guard** device with projecting triangular spikes or widely spaced bars placed at road crossings to prevent cattle from passing

**catwalk** rungs or plank running board on boxcar or locomotive platform, used by brakeman to clamber between cars

**cinder** partly burned piece of fuel coal

**cinder pit** area in which cinder pans are dumped before train enters roundhouse

**clinker** fused mass of hot coals

**clinker hook** device that moves and breaks fused masses of hot coals

**commutation ticket** reduced fare, multitrip, time-limited ticket good on one line only

**consist** conductor's report by which yardmaster at next stop plans switchings

**couchette** fold-out, shelflike bed in low-fare compartment of European passenger train

**coupler** device used to fasten together individual cars; drawbar; pin

**cowcatcher** outthrusting metal bumper on front of locomotive that pushes aside obstructions, esp. cattle; pilot

**crossing** intersection of railroad tracks and public roadway

**crosstie** tie

**crown** (*vb*) couple caboose to line of freight cars

**cupola** observation area atop caboose

**dead freight** bulky, nonperishable freight

**deck** front part of cab; catwalk atop boxcar

**depot** train station or terminal for loading passengers and freight

**derailing** accident in which one or more cars slip off tracks; intentional forcing of car off tracks

**dirt track** roadbed without ballast under ties

**ditch** area beside and below roadbed

**division** section of line between terminals, approx. one hundred miles

**drawbar** coupler

**drop bottom** door and chute at base of hopper car or gondola for emptying cargo such as coal or gravel

**em** one thousand pounds of tonnage

**embankment** pile of earth holding up roadway

**engine cab** enclosed cab on locomotive

**extra** train not listed on timetable

**ferrophiliac** amateur lover of railroading

**flag** colored cloth signal used in daylight

**flange** inside projecting rim on wheel that guides it down track

**frog** implement used to derail car wheels or permit them to cross intersecting tracks

**full stroke** at top speed

**full throttle** at top speed

**gangway** space between rear of steam locomotive cab and tender

**gantlet** section of track through narrow passage in which two track lines overlap, one rail of each line lying between rails of the other

**gantry** bridgelike framework over tracks that supports signals or is used for loading

**gare** *French.* station

**gate** switch that may be opened or closed to control movement of trains on tracks

**gauge** recognized standard measure of distance between two rails: narrow 3' 6" (1.07 m), standard 4' 8 1/2" (1.43 m), broad 5' 6" (1.68 m)

**glory road** *Slang.* railroad

**go light** *Slang.* run engine without cars

**grab iron** steel bar on car or engine, used as handhold

**grade** tracks running up steep hill

**gravy train** *Slang.* short, easy haul

**green flag** signal indicating permission to proceed, displayed at front of train

**green light** nighttime permission-to-proceed signal

**highball** signal in which hand or lantern sweeps in high, wide semicircle to indicate full speed ahead

**hitch** (*vb*) couple cars together

**hobo** tramp who hitches free ride on freight train

**hump** rise built at end of freight yard from which cars roll to separate tracks for coupling

**hump yard** yard built on incline to allow switching by natural, gravitational momentum

**indicator** illuminated designation of train's number on locomotive and caboose

**ingersoll** trainman's open-faced watch

**iron** *Informal.* railroad track

**iron horse** former term for railroad, esp. steam locomotive

**jerkwater** *(adj) Informal.* designating small town at which train draws water from track pan without stopping

**jill pole** *Slang.* thick pole used to shove cars out of siding when engine is on main line and cannot pick up cars

**Johnson bar** reverse lever on locomotive

**joint** length of rail, usu. 33 to 39 feet (10 to 12 m)

**journal** part of axle that turns in shaft

**junction** intersection of two tracks or lines

**key** telegraph transmitting instrument; *(vb)* send a message by telegraph

**ladder** central track in yard, from which other tracks lead off

**lantern** flagman's night signal lamp

**layover** time lost in delay connecting with another train

**library** *Slang.* cupola of caboose

**marker** signal on rear of train, flag by day, lantern by night; signal on main line

**merry-go-round** *Slang.* roundhouse turntable

**Morse code** standard telegraphic code by which most railroad messages were sent prior to electronic telecommunications

**mudhole** *Slang.* small town or station

**mule** cable-operated device used to lift coal cars up incline for dumping

**narrow gauge** road with rails less than 4 feet 8 1/2 inches (1.43 m) apart

**off-peak** *(adj)* designating noncommuting hours with reduced passenger fare

**on the advertised** *Slang.* on schedule

**on the card** *Slang.* on schedule

**order** instructions telegraphed from dispatcher to conductor

**paddle** *Slang.* semaphore signal

**pass** free entry to car for passenger

**pick up** *(vb)* add cars at station

**pile** tall support member sunk into earth as foundation for trestle

**pilot** cowcatcher

**pin** coupler

**pod** intentional derailing to prevent cars on siding from entering main line

**point** intersection of gauge lines in switch or frog

**quill** *Slang.* railway whistle

**rack rail** third rail used for traction when engaged by gear on locomotive

**rail** long metal bar laid upon ground parallel to another such bar and connected to it by crossties, serving as track for railroad cars; railroad as means of transport

**rail anchor** device sprung into rail base to hold it in place

**railroading** construction and operation of railroads; travel by railroad

**railway bridge** trestle or covered bridge supporting tracks across land depression or water

**ride the bumpers** travel perched between freight cars

**right of way** land occupied by and immediately surrounding railroad main line

**roadbed** base upon which rails, ties, and ballast of railroad track rests

**roadway** railroad right of way with tracks, stations, and signals

**rods** underbracing of car

**roomette** individual compartment in Pullman car

**roundhouse** circular structure in yard housing idle locomotives for storage and repair

**round trip** journey to specific destination and back to starting point over same route

**run** regular route of train line

**runaway** train that is out of control and unstoppable by normal means, usu. due to mechanical failure

**runaway unit** individual car on runaway train

**saddle** first step of freight car under lowest grab iron

**sand dome** bin atop engine boiler filled with sand to be spread on tracks for traction

**scoop** fireman's shovel

**semaphore** apparatus giving signals to trains by position of movable arms

**service application** gradual reduction in speed

**sidedoor** sliding door on side of boxcar

**sidetrack** siding

**siding** short track connected by switch to main line and used for bypassing or unloading; sidetrack; turnout

**signal** marker, either flag or lantern

**smokestack** steel chimney for discharge of engine smoke and gases; stack

**snowfence** barrier placed along tracks to protect against snowslides

**snowshed** wooden shelter built over section of track, esp. in mountains, to protect against snowslides

**span** bridge or trestle

**spar** pole for clearing cars when switching; stake

**spot** *(vb)* place car in designated location, esp. for loading or unloading

**spur** short sidetrack connecting to main line, often dead end

**stack** smokestack

**stake** pole used to move cars in manual switching operation; spar

**standard gauge** railroad track and carwheel width of 4 feet 8 1/2 inches (1.43 m)

**stateroom** lavish, first-class suite of connected passenger compartments with separate sitting and sleeping areas

**station** regular stopping place for train line, with loading platform and usu. shelter for passengers

**steam brake** emergency braking procedure in which valve gear is reversed to slow engine

**steam stop** halting train by steam braking cars but not engine

**stroke** single movement of piston rod; measure of engine speed or drive

**stub** *Slang.* dead-end spur

**switch** device consisting of two movable rails that connect to tracks, used to direct cars from one siding to another or onto main line

**switchback** zigzag line over hill too steep for direct ascent

**switching** moving of cars or trains from one track to another

**switch shanty** small building in yard in which switchman rests and keeps lanterns

**switch tower** elevated lookout point in switch yard

**switch yard** yard in which cars are moved from one track to another to make up trains

**tack** coupling pin

**take water** draw water at overhead tank into storage container or boiler

**tank town** small town, often one in which only stop is to take water

**telegraph** traditional railroad communications system

**telltale** dangling ropes at approach to low bridge or tunnel entrance that warn of low overhead clearance

**temporary track** tracks laid for use while regular tracks are being repaired

**terminal** city or town at endpoint of line with station or depot; station at junction of lines; yard at end of division

**terminus** endpoint of line

**third rail** extra rail added on curves to prevent derailing

**throat** fan-shaped convergence of tracks at tunnel entrance

**throttle** equipment that determines amount of steam entering cylinders and thus controls speed of engine

**ticket punch** handheld device used by conductor to cancel tickets by perforation

**tie** wood plank supporting and connecting rails; crosstie

**timetable** folded sheet with schedule of arrivals and departures in both directions over one line

**tonnage** weight carried by entire train or individual car; amount of weight locomotive can pull

**trackage** lines of railroad tracks

**track layer** machine and vehicle used in laying tracks

**track pan** water dispenser hanging over tracks and attached to large tank

**tracks** pair of parallel metal rails, usu. with crossties, that guide car or engine wheels

**transfer table** flat, movable or rotating surface with single track that is turned to align with other tracks to transfer locomotive to new track

**trap** storage box that receives sand from sand dome and releases it onto rails below

**trestle** framework support on piles for tracks across river or depression; rudimentary railroad bridge

**turnout** siding

**turntable** platform with track used to rotate locomotives in yard at end of track and outside roundhouse

**undercarriage** frame and running gear of locomotive

**valve gear** device that directs steam in or out of cylinders to run locomotive forward or backward

**Wabash** *Slang.* big fire in locomotive firebox; (*vb*) *Slang.* hit car entering adjacent switch; slow for stop without completely stopping

**waiting room** area in station where passengers await trains

**walkway** area for walking along side of locomotive

**washout** emergency stop signal, in which arms or lamp are swung in wide, downward arc across track

**way bill** document prepared by carrier with details of shipment, routing, and charges

**way station** small, often remote station at which train stops only on signal

**Westinghouse** *Trademark.* original air brake, invented by George Westinghouse in 1869

**wheel base** distance from first pair of locomotive wheels to last pair of tender wheels

**whistle** railroad sound used to signal departure, arrival, approach to station, or crossing, also used to send message or warning by coded series of blasts

**whistle stop** small town at which passenger train does not normally stop

**Whyte classification** system that classifies locomotives by wheel arrangement, such as 4-8-2, 4-4-2, 2-8-8-4, etc.

**wigwag** grade crossing signal

**wye** tracks off main line arranged in Y-formation, used to reverse cars and engines without turntable

**X** designation for empty car

**yard** open area at terminus of line with network of tracks for storage of cars and assembly of trains

**zulu car** *Slang.* freight car ridden by immigrant farmers

# SHIPS AND BOATS

Types of Ships and Boats
Parts of Ships, Sails, and Equipment
Nautical Occupations
Seamanship and Port

**SEE ALSO:** Chap. 3: Landscapes and Seascapes; Weather and Natural Phenomena; Chap. 5: Structural Components; Chap. 11: War and Military; Chap. 17: Sports

## TYPES OF SHIPS AND BOATS

**airboat** light, flat-bottomed, aluminum vessel driven by propeller revolving in air

**aircraft carrier** very large, flat-decked seagoing airbase; carrier

**argosy** large, richly laden merchant ship; fleet of ships

**ark** large, flat-bottomed riverboat

**barge** flat-bottomed cargo vessel without power

**bark** three- or four-masted square-rigger

**bateau** *French.* boat

**bathyscaphe** submarine-shaped float filled with fluid lighter than water, used for deep-sea diving

**bathysphere** enclosed globe for deep-sea observations

**battleship** large, armored naval ship heavily outfitted for war

**bireme** galley with two banks of oars

**boat** small vessel used at sea or on inland waterway

**brigantine** two-masted ship with square-rigged topsail on mainmast

**bumboat** small boat used in port or at anchor to sell goods to ships' crews

**buss** rugged, square-sailed boat formerly used by herring fishery

**cabin cruiser** motorboat with enclosed cabin and living facilities

**caique** light rowboat or sailboat (Bosporus, eastern Mediterranean)

**canal boat** flat boat that operates on inland canals

**canoe** light, narrow boat with sharp or pointed ends, powered by one or more paddles

**caravel** small, fast sailing ship with narrow, high poop and lateen sails (Portugal and Spain, 15th–16th c.)

**cargo ship** power vessel that carries supplies, not passengers

**carrack** galleon or merchant vessel used in Mediterranean (15th–16th c.)

**carrier** aircraft carrier

**catamaran** twin-hulled sailing vessel

**clipper** speedy, fully rigged sailing vessel with sharp bow (19th c.)

**cockboat** small, oar-propelled boat used as ship's tender

**collier** ship outfitted for or employed in transporting coal

**container ship** freighter outfitted to carry large cargo containers

**coracle** small, round or very broad boat made of interwoven laths or wicker covered with skin or tarred or oiled cloth (Ireland, Wales)

**corsair** pirate ship

**corvette** small, fast warship, esp. for convoy; formerly a sailing warship larger than a sloop, smaller than a frigate

**craft** boat or vessel, esp. small one

**cruiser** speedy, armored warship with six to eight guns; cabin cruiser

**cutter** single-masted vessel with fore-and-aft rigged sails; sloop

**dahabeah** large passenger boat, orig. with lateen sails, used on Nile River

**destroyer** speedy warship armed with guns, torpedoes, and depth charges

**dhow** coastal ship with lateen sail and raised deck at stern (Indian Ocean)

**dinghy** small rowboat; small boat carried on ship or used as tender

**dink** small boat, esp. for duck hunting

**dogger** two-masted fishing vessel with blunt bow (Holland)

**dory** small, flat-bottomed boat with sharp bow and tapering stern

**dreadnought** large, armored battleship armed with heavy-caliber guns in turrets

**dredge** low workboat that scrapes bottom of waterway to make it navigable

**drogher** freight barge rigged as cutter or schooner (West Indies)

**dromond** large, fast, medieval galley or cutter

**dugout** boat or canoe hollowed out of large log

**escort** vessel accompanying and protecting another

**felucca** small, narrow ship propelled by oars or lateen sails (Mediterranean)

**ferry** vessel used to convey passengers and cargo back and forth across bay or stream

**fishing boat** any boat from which fish are caught

**fishing smack** fore-and-aft rigged vessel equipped with well for holding live catch

**flatboat** boat with flat bottom, esp. for use in shallow waterway

**fore-and-after** sailing vessel with fore-and-aft rigging

**freighter** large cargo vessel

**frigate** light boat orig. propelled by oars, later by sails; intermediate, square-rigged war vessel (18th-19th c.); heavy, missile-firing warship (20th c.)

**full-rigged** (*adj*) designating sailing vessel with three or more square-rigged masts

**galiot** small, swift ship propelled by sails and oars, formerly used in Mediterranean

**galleass** lateen-rigged fighting galley used in Mediterranean (15th-18th c.)

**galleon** heavy square-rigger with several decks and elaborate poopdeck; Spanish treasure ship (15th-18th c.); carrack

**galley** large, low, ancient or medieval ship propelled by sails and oars

**gig** captain's boat; long lifeboat rowed with four to eight oars

**gondola** small, flat canal boat sculled with single oar or hand-propelled by pole

**gufa** round rowboat of wickerwork (ancient Mesopotamia)

**hatch boat** small fishing boat equipped with covered wells for holding fish

**houseboat** boat outfitted with living quarters, usu. moored permanently in one place

**hoy** heavy harbor barge; sloop-rigged fishing vessel (17th-18th c.)

**hydrofoil** small, high-speed racing boat equipped with hydrofoils

**hydroplane** light, high-speed motorboat that skims along water on hydrofoils or flat bottom rising toward stern

**iceboat** triangular frame with sail mounted on runners, used on frozen waterways

**icebreaker** sturdy, powerful vessel for cutting channels through heavy ice

**ironclad** wooden warship armored with steel plate (19th c.)

**jangada** fisherman's log raft with sail, seat, and steering oar (Brazil)

**johnboat** flat-bottomed, square-ended fishing boat, used on inland waterways

**jolly boat** small boat carried at stern of sailing vessel

**junk** flat-bottomed boat with high stern and lateen sails (China, Japan)

**kayak** canoe made of skins that entirely cover frame except for paddler's seat in middle (Eskimo); small boat resembling this

**ketch** small, two-masted vessel rigged fore-and-aft

**knockabout** small, single-masted sailboat with no bowsprit

**launch** largest off-boat on warship; open motorboat

**lifeboat** small boat carried on ship or kept ready ashore for emergency use

**life raft** small, inflatable or balsa raft carried on ship for emergency use

**liner** large, elaborately outfitted passenger ship

**longboat** largest boat carried on merchant sailing ship

**longliner** commercial fishing vessel that uses long line with multiple hooks

**lorcha** three-masted sailing ship with lugsails (southeast Asia, Philippines)

**lugger** small ship rigged with lugsails on two or three masts

**man-of-war** warship

**market boat** vessel that transfers fish from fishing boats to market on shore

**merchant ship** commercial oceangoing vessel

**minesweeper** military vessel equipped to detect underwater explosive mines

**moleta** short-masted fishing boat with lateen sail and two outriggers (Portugal)

**motorboat** usu. small, open boat powered by internal combustion or electric engine; powerboat

**New Orleans lugger** broad-hulled fishing boat with single mast and large, dipping lugsail

**nickey** lug-sailed fishing boat (Isle of Man)

**nobby** small fishing boat (Isle of Man)

**nuggar** cargo boat with single square sail (Nile River)

**ocean liner** large, elaborately outfitted passenger ship for ocean crossings

**off-boat** small boat carried on ship, esp. for emergency use as lifeboat

**oiler** tanker

**paddle steamer** river-going steamboat propelled by wheels with paddles set at right angles about their circumference; paddle wheeler

**paddle wheeler** paddle steamer

**pinnace** small sailing ship, esp. tender to larger ship

**pirogue** dugout canoe or canoe-shaped boat having two masts

**polacre** two- or three-masted sailing ship (Mediterranean)

**pontoon** wooden, flat-bottomed boat or float used in building bridges; type of barge

**powerboat** motorboat

**pram** small, flat-bottomed sailboat with square bow

**proa** swift sailing boat with flat lee side and balancing outrigger (Indonesia)

**PT boat** patrol torpedo boat; small, speedy torpedo boat

**pulwar** light, keelless vessel (India)

**punt** small, flat-bottomed riverboat with square ends

**raft** flat structure of logs or boards fastened together; small, flat-bottomed, inflatable rubber boat

**riverboat** steam-powered passenger boat used on inland waterways, esp. paddle wheeler

**rowboat** small, oar-powered boat

**runabout** light, open motorboat

**sailboat** boat with at least one mast, propelled by wind in sails secured to mast

**sampan** small boat with sail, steered with stern oar, often with small cabin of mats (China, Japan)

**schooner** fore-and-aft rigged vessel with two or more masts, mainmast at aft, and square sails

**scow** large, flat-bottomed boat with square ends, used to carry coal or sand, often towed by tug

**scull** light, narrow racing boat for four or fewer rowers

**shallop** small, open boat fitted with oars and/or sails

**sharpie** long, narrow, flat-bottomed fishing boat with one or two masts rigged with triangular sails (New England)

**shell** long, narrow, thin-hulled racing boat rowed by team of up to eight

**ship** large vessel navigating sea or other deep waterway, powered by sails or engine

**ship of the line** largest class of warship, usu. with guns along two or more decks; battleship

**side-wheeler** vessel with paddle wheels on sides

**skeeter** small iceboat

**skiff** small boat, usu. rowed

**skipjack** small sailboat with flat, V-shaped hull and vertical sides

**slaver** Informal. slave ship

**slave ship** freighter used to transport slaves from their native home to market; slaver

**sloop** fore-and-aft rigged, one-mast vessel; cutter

**smack** small sailboat, usu. rigged as sloop; fishing boat, esp. trawler, with well for keeping fish alive

**speedboat** very fast motorboat

**sportfisherman** inboard motorboat, usu. 36 to 42 feet (12 m) long, used for offshore fishing

**square-rigger** sailing ship rigged with square sails

**steamer** steam-powered vessel

**steamship** ship driven by steam-powered engine

**sternwheeler** vessel with paddle wheel at rear

**sub** Informal. submarine

**submarine** warship carrying torpedoes and missiles that can function underwater; sub

**supertanker** extremely large tanker, usu. for oil

**tanker** cargo ship with large tanks in hull for carrying oil or other liquid; oiler

**tender** auxiliary vessel used in the supply and repair of other ships

**tern** three-masted schooner

**three-master** sailing vessel with three masts

**tin can** Slang. naval destroyer; old, rundown vessel

**torpedo boat** small, fast, maneuverable warship that fires torpedoes

**towboat** tugboat; boat for pushing barges on inland waterway

**tramp** vessel that will go anywhere for profitable cargo

**transport** ship used to carry soldiers or freight over long distance

**trawler** fishing boat that uses net to drag bottom of sea or lake

**trimaran** catamaran with three parallel hulls

**trireme** galley outfitted with three rows of oars

**tug** small, powerful vessel that aids in docking or towing larger ships

**twelve-meter** internationally recognized racing yacht

**U-boat** German submarine

**umiak** large, open rowboat of skins stretched on wooden frame (Eskimo)

**vaporetto** large motorboat for public transport on Venetian canals

**vedette** small naval launch used for scouting

**vessel** ship or boat

**warship** ship armed for combat, esp. battleship; man-of-war

**whaleboat** small, oar-powered boat used in whaling industry; whaler

**whaler** craft used in whaling

**wherry** light rowboat for rivers; one-person racing scull

**windjammer** large sailing ship

**xebec** three-masted sailing ship with long, overhanging bow and stern (Mediterranean)

**yacht** pleasure boat, esp. narrow-hulled sailboat

**yawl** ship's small boat; two-masted vessel with small aftermast behind wheel

# PARTS OF SHIPS, SAILS, AND EQUIPMENT

**abeam** (adj) directly outward from or at right angle to fore-and-aft line of ship

**aft** rear of ship; stern; (adj) toward the stern, behind

**aftermast** mast closest to stern

**alleyway** narrow passageway below decks

**anchor** large hook that grips bottom and holds ship in place

**anchor chock** casting through which anchor lines pass

**athwartships** (adv) running across ship from side to side

**backstay** line or cable running aft from masthead to side or stern

**ballast** heavy object used to maintain ship at proper draft

**batten** strip used to fasten canvas over hatchways or to stiffen sails

**beam** ship's breadth at widest point; side of ship; direction outward from fore-and-aft line

**becket** looped rope or grommet for securing lines, oars, and spars

**belowdecks** (*adv*) in area within hull beneath deck surface

**berth** bed or bunk mounted in wall of cabin belowdecks; dock space at wharf

**bibb** wooden support bracket fastened to ship's mast

**bight** any part within ends of line, esp. a bend

**bilge** low point of ship's hull

**binnacle** case, box, or stand for ship's compass and lamp

**bitt** one of twin deck posts to which cables or lines are secured

**block** heavy pulley used for rigging

**bobstay** rope, chain, or rod from outer end of bowsprit to cutwater

**boiler room** location of power-generating boilers belowdecks on steamship

**booby hatch** covering over small hatchway

**boom** long pole or spar that extends and holds bottom of sail

**bow** most forward part of ship

**bower** heavy anchor carried toward bow

**bowsprit** large spar projecting forward, used to carry headsail

**brace** any of various support pieces, esp. rope to sway yards on sailing vessels

**bridge** uppermost front cabin; platform for captain

**brig** place of confinement, ship's prison

**broadside** side of ship above waterline; volley fired simultaneously by all guns on one side of warship

**bulkhead** upright wall or partition separating compartments

**bulwark** rail around ship's deck

**buntline** rope used to haul square sail up to yard for furling

**burgee** swallow-tailed flag used for signals and identification

**burton** tackle made of single or double blocks, used to tighten rigging or hoisting

**buttock** convex, aftmost part of ship above waterline

**cabin** room used for passengers or officers

**camel** float between ship and pier that prevents chafing

**capstan** cylindrical spool revolving on shaft, used to wind cable

**carlings** fore-and-aft deck supports or frame for deck opening

**chock** metal casting on deck through which lines and hawsers pass

**cleat** small, metal or wood fitting with projecting ends, used to secure lines on deck

**clew** reinforced metal loop fastened to corner of sail

**coaming** raised steel frame around hatch or other opening on deck

**companionway** narrow stairway

**compass** navigational instrument with magnetized needle indicating north, used to determine heading

**conning tower** heavily armored pilothouse on warship

**container** very large receptacle of standard size for shipping

**course** sail on lower yard of square-rigger; direction to be steered

**crossjack** lowermost square sail set on mizzenmast of ship with four or more masts

**crosstrees** two short bars across masthead, used to spread rigging that supports mast

**crow's nest** lookout station atop mast on sailing vessel

**cuddy** small deck cabin; galley or pantry; platform on which fishing net is stored

**cutwater** forward edge of stem at and below waterline

**davit** crane projecting over side for hoisting lifeboats, anchors, or cargo on board

**deadlight** heavy plate glass window in portholes

**deck** flat, open surface of ship; floor

**deck chair** lightweight folding chair with arms, used on deck

**depth charge** underwater explosive directed against subs

**depth sounder** device for determining depth of water by measuring time required for sound wave to reach and return from bottom

**derrick** pivoting mast with tackle used to raise and lower boom

**engine room** room belowdecks housing engine works

**fantail** aft overhang of ship shaped like duck's bill

**fidley** framework or railing around hatch

**fluke** flat, triangular end of anchor that bites bottom

**flying jib** sail on extension outside jib

**fore** (*adj*) ahead, toward the bow

**fore-and-aft** sails rigged lengthwise from bow to stern; (*adj*) having no square sails; running lengthwise

**foredeck** deck area toward bow

**foremast** mast nearest bow

**foresail** sail rigged on mast toward bow

**futtock** curved timbers forming lower part of ship's ribs in wooden hull

**gaff** iron hook; spar rising aft from mast for sails

**galley** ship's kitchen

**gangplank** movable bridge used to board and leave ship; gangway

**gangway** gangplank

**garboard** lowest strake next to keel

**gennaker** oversized headsail behind mast on yacht, esp. for tacking in which wind crosses side of boat

**genoa** large jib overlapping mainsail on yacht; jenny

**gimbal** suspended setting for ship's compass that allows it to remain stable in rough seas

**gooseneck** curved member at foot of boom that pivots so that boom can be pointed in wide angle vertically or horizontally

**grapnel** light anchor with many hooks or prongs

**grappling iron** hooked iron used to pull another vessel alongside or for anchoring

**ground tackle** anchoring components

**gunwale** side rail where topsides and deck meet

**halyard** line or tackle for raising sails and flags

**hatch** door in deck or floor; covering over such a door

**hatch cover** closure that fits over hatch

**hatchway** covered opening in deck with stairs that lead belowdecks

**hawser** heavy line, esp. for towing or mooring ship to dock

**head** ship's toilet

**headsail** small sail rigged forward of mast

**heaving line** light line with weight on free end and other end attached to hawser, used to draw heavier line into position

**helm** lever or wheel for controlling rudder to steer ship; wheel

**hold** cargo area within hull belowdecks

**hull** frame or main body of ship that sits in water

**hydrofoil** winglike structure attached to hull that lifts boat to skim along water at high speed

**Jacob's ladder** portable ladder with wooden rungs and flexible rope or wire sides

**jenny** *Slang.* genoa

**jib** triangular sail forward of foremast, fastened to foredeck

**jigger** small hoisting tackle; small, aftmost sail of yawl

**kedge** light anchor used for getting off shoal

**keel** longitudinal structural member along center of ship's bottom, running from stem to stern

**keelson** beam or plates fastened longitudinally inside hull along keel to add structural strength

**kite** small sail set high on mast in light wind

**lanyard** line for fastening shrouds and stays or raising flags; cord around sailor's neck with knife hung on it

**lateen** triangular, fore-and-aft rigged sail on long yard suspended obliquely from short mast

**launch ramp** inclined chute for releasing launches into water

**lee** side of ship facing away from wind

**life preserver** buoyant, halterlike garment that keeps person afloat when overboard

**line** rope

**lugsail** four-sided sail with upper edge attached to yard, fastened obliquely to mast

**mainmast** principal mast of sailing vessel

**mainsail** primary sail rigged on mast

**mainstay** line extending forward from and stabilizing mainmast

**marlinespike** iron tool that tapers to point, used to separate strands of rope

**mast** long pole or spar rising from deck to support yards, booms, and rigging

**masthead** top part of mast

**midship** (*adj*) in or at middle of vessel

**mine** explosive charge in container placed in sea

**mizzen** fore-and-aft rigged sail on mizzenmast

**mizzenmast** mast nearest stern, esp. third mast from bow in ship with three or more masts

**moonraker** light, square sail rigged high on clipper ship mast in light winds

**oakum** strands of old tarred line used as caulking

**oar** long pole with flat blades for rowing boat; paddle

**orlop deck** lowest deck of ship with four or more decks

**outboard** (*adv*) in lateral direction from hull

**outboard motor** engine hung off stern of small, open boat

**outrigger** support, brace, or float extending from side of boat

**paddle** oar

**paddle wheel** wheel with paddles set at right angles about its circumference, used to propel steamboat

**paravane** pair of torpedo-shaped devices towed by cables from ship's bow, used to cut moorings of submerged mines

**pelorus** compasslike navigational instrument with two sighting vanes instead of magnetic needle

**pennant** small, triangular signal flag

**periscope** upright tube fitted with prisms and mirrors, extended upward from submarine for observation above sea level

**pink stern** sharp stern with narrow, overhanging transom

**pole** long slender piece of wood used to hand-propel raft, small boat, or gondola

**poop** raised deck at stern, usu. roofed

**port** left side of vessel when facing bow

**porthole** round window in ship's hull

**propeller** slanted blades turning on shaft extending from hull, used to propel ship

**prow** bow above the waterline

**quarterdeck** ceremonial open space on after deck

**ratline** small pieces of tarred rope or wood that join shrouds and serve as ladder rungs for climbing rigging

**reefed sail** sail reduced in size by rolling or tying

**ribs** framework of hull to which skin is attached

**rigging** cables, chains, lines, blocks, and tackle

**royal sail** small sail above topgallant sail

**rudder** pivoting vertical blade at vessel's stern, used for steering

**sail** large canvas or synthetic fiber sheet hung from mast to catch wind and propel ship forward: flying jib, foresail, gaff, gennaker, headsail, jib, lateen, mainsail, mizzen, moonraker, reefed sail, royal sail, skysail, spinnaker, square sail, staysail, studding sail, topsail

**scull** long oar mounted at stern and worked from side to side; one of a pair of light oars used on each side of boat

**scupper** drainage opening at deck level through ship's side

**sea anchor** large, canvas-covered frame let out as drag or float to reduce ship's speed

**seabag** sailor's large cylindrical bag for personal items

**sextant** optical instrument used to measure angular distances at sea to determine latitude

**shank** straight part of anchor above hooks or barbs

**sheave** grooved wheel inside pulley block

**sheer** upward curve of deck toward bow and stern

**sheet** line or chain at lower corner of sail that controls set

**shrouds** heavy lines bracing mast athwartships; stays

**sick bay** ship's infirmary

**skeg** after part of keel to which rudder is secured

**skin** outer surface of hull

**skysail** sail rigged above royal sail

**spanker** fore-and-aft sail on aftermost lower mast of ship with three or more masts

**spar** mast, gaff, or boom that supports sails

**spinnaker** baggy, triangular headsail on yacht, used to run before wind

**spring line** rope leading from bow or aft to dock to prevent movement ahead or astern while moored

**sprit** pole or spar reaching diagonally from mast to topmost corner of fore-and-aft sail to extend it

**square-rigged** (*adj*) having square sails as principal sails

**square sail** four-sided sail rigged on yard set athwart keel and horizontal to mast

**staff** post that supports flag or banner at stern or bow

**stanchion** upright bar or post that supports life line

**starboard** right side of vessel when facing bow

**stateroom** private cabin

**stay** heavy line or cable bracing mast

**staysail** fore-and-aft sail rigged on stay

**stem** front or bow of vessel, esp. upright piece at prow to which side timbers are attached

**stern** back or rear of vessel

**stopwater** canvas backed with lead or other material, fitted between metal parts for watertightness

**strake** plank extending length of ship from stem to stern

**strakework** lines of strakes

**stringer** longitudinal plank or plate for strengthening deck

**strut** outboard support piece between stern and propeller

**studding sail** light sail rigged outboard of major square sail

**swivel** freely rotating fastening device for lines and tackle

**tackle** blocks and rope lines used in rigging

**taffrail** upper, flat part of ship's stern with panels; rail around ship's stern

**thole** pin set vertically in gunwale as fulcrum for oar

**tiller** handle for turning rudder

**timber** wooden rib set lengthwise in hull

**toerail** extension of side planking above deck for safety

**topgallant mast** mast fixed to head of topmast on square-rigged vessel

**topgallant sail** sail set on yard of topgallant mast

**topmast** mast usu. formed as a separate spar above lower mast and used to support yards or rigging of topsails

**topsail** sail next above lowermost sail on mast of square-rigger

**topsides** deck and outer surface of hull above water

**torpedo** underwater projectile containing explosives

**transom** transverse part of squared stern

**truss** iron band around mast with gooseneck for securing yard

**turret** armored revolving platform for heavy guns on naval vessel

**vane** long streamer that indicates wind direction

**vang** steadying rope from peak of a gaff to ship's rail or mast

**ventilator** bell-mouthed tube on deck that provides fresh air belowdecks

**wales** strakes or heavy planks fastened to outside of hull

**warp** mooring line

**water line** one of several lines painted on side of hull that indicates submergence due to load

**wheel** helm

**winch** deck engine with drum for hoisting heavy objects

**windlass** crank-driven spindle for hoisting lines or hauling

**yard** long, slender rod fastened horizontally across mast to support sail

**yardarm** either half of yard supporting square sail

## NAUTICAL OCCUPATIONS

**able-bodied seaman** able seaman

**able seaman** experienced seaman qualified to perform routine duties, rating below boatswain's mate; able-bodied seaman

**admiral** top-ranking naval officer

**Argonaut** crew member sailing with Jason in search for Golden Fleece (Greek mythology)

**bilge rat** *Slang.* boiler worker or belowdecks sailor

**boatswain** foreman; warrant officer in charge of deck crew's work; bo's'n; pipes

**bo's'n** boatswain

**bowman** deck hand on yacht who sets spinnaker and works at bow

**buccaneer** pirate

**cabin boy** boy who serves officers and passengers on ship

**captain** officer who is master or commander of ship; skipper

**CB** *c*onstruction *b*attalion crewman in navy; Seabee

**chief petty officer** CPO; highest ranking naval enlisted man

**commander** captain of vessel

**commodore** naval captain commanding two or more vessels

**coxswain** naval petty officer in charge of steering small boat; person who steers racing shell and calls rhythm to rowers

**CPO** chief *petty* officer

**crew** personnel working on ship, usu. excluding officers

**crewman** individual member of ship's crew

**crew member** crewman

**deck hand** ship's lowest-ranking worker

**dockhand** longshoreman

**ensign** lowest-ranking naval commissioned officer

**ferryman** operator of ferryboat

**first mate** ranking crew member below captain

**fisherman** person who fishes from a boat for livelihood or recreation

**Flying Dutchman** legendary mariner condemned to sail seas until Judgment Day

**gondolier** operator of gondola

**grinder** crew member on yacht who turns handle on winch that hauls in lines and raises halyards

**gunner** naval warrant officer specializing in guns and torpedoes

**helmsman** person who holds helm and steers ship; pilot; steersman

**jack** *Slang.* seaman

**longshoreman** laborer who loads cargo from docks; dockhand; stevedore

**marine** member of military unit associated with navy, esp. Marine Corps

**mariner** person involved in navigation of ship; seaman or sailor

**mate** deck officer on merchant ship ranking below captain

**merchant seaman** crewman of merchant ship

**middy** *Informal.* midshipman

**midshipman** naval recruit, esp. student at Naval Academy

**navigator** person responsible for guiding ship's course

**oarsman** crew member who works oars to propel vessel

**pilot** harbor officer who boards and steers ship's entry into harbor; person who steers a ship into port; helmsman

**pipes** *Slang.* boatswain

**pirate** person who commits robbery on high seas; buccaneer; sea rover; rapparee

**privateer** crewman, esp, commander, of armed private ship or pirate ship cruising against commercial ships or warships of enemy

**purser** agent handling passengers' money and valuables

**quartermaster** steersman or signal and weather expert

**radio operator** communications officer or crewman

**rapparee** freebooter or pirate, esp. armed Irish plunderer of 17th c.

**sailmaker** person who designs, makes, and repairs sails, esp. for racing boats

**sailor** seaman; member of ship's crew; member of navy

**salt** *Informal.* crusty old mariner

**Seabee** CB; young sailor

**sea dog** seasoned sailor, mariner

**seafarer** mariner

**seaman** person who sails the seas; mariner

**sea rover** pirate

**shipbuilder** person who designs and constructs ships
**ship chandler** person dealing in ship's supplies
**shipfitter** welder who fits together structural parts of ships
**shipmaster** commander of vessel other than warship
**shipmate** fellow member of ship's crew
**shipowner** owner of ship or ships
**shipwright** carpenter skilled at shipbuilding and repair
**skipper** *Informal.* captain
**steersman** helmsman
**stevedore** longshoreman
**steward** waiter, porter, or kitchen help in crew
**swabby** *Slang.* deck hand
**tar** *Informal.* sailor
**Viking** Scandinavian sea rover or pirate (8th–11th c.)
**warrant officer** noncommissioned naval officer, usu. specialist such as electrician, pay clerk, machinist, or gunner
**watch** person responsible for observation duty on ship
**whaler** crewman on whaling ship
**windjammer** *Slang.* crewman on large sailing windjammer
**yachtsman** yacht owner; recreational sailor on yacht
**yeoman** naval petty officer with duties of clerk

## SEAMANSHIP AND PORT

**aboard** (*adv*) on board a vessel
**adrift** (*adj*) floating freely without being steered; not at anchor
**afloat** (*adj*) floating on surface of water; flooded
**aground** (*adv*) snagged on shore or bottom of waterway
**ahoy** (*interj*) call of attention; hello
**all hands** entire ship's personnel
**amphibious** (*adj*) used on both land and sea
**armada** fleet of warships
**ashore** (*adv*) to or on land
**avast** (*vb*) command to stop, cease, or give attention
**aweigh** (*adj*) designating anchor coming up
**backwater** reverse rowing stroke employed to halt vessel or propel it in reverse
**bail** (*vb*) empty accumulated water with paddle or bucket
**barnacles** hard-shelled sea growth on pier or ship bottom
**bear down** (*vb*) approach from windward
**bearing** navigational term indicating direction of one point with reference to another
**bear off** (*vb*) prevent vessel from touching or rubbing against dock or another vessel
**bear to** (*vb*) head in given direction
**belay** (*vb*) fasten or secure with lines; stop
**bells** indication of time on ship
**bend** any loop or knot for joining end of one rope to another rope or to some other object
**berth** mooring place or slip in docks
**bilge water** water accumulating in bilge
**bitter end** inboard end of ship's line
**Blackwall hitch** hitch knot for temporarily securing line to hook
**boat trailer** frame that supports boat, usu. on two wheels, and is hauled by vehicle
**bollard** post on pier, used to secure hawsers
**breakwater** offshore barrier that protects shore or docks from waves
**buoy** floating marker anchored to bottom, used to indicate channel or underwater object

**cabin class** accommodations better than tourist class, inferior to first class
**canal** artificial waterway for navigation
**cant** (*vb*) pitch to one side
**capsize** (*vb*) overturn at sea
**cast** (*vb*) throw
**cast off** (*vb*) let go of line; set sail
**cat's-paw** hitch in middle of rope, forming two eyes to hold hook
**celestial navigation** charting course by position of stars and planets
**change course** alter direction
**chart** navigational map
**circumnavigate** (*vb*) sail around, esp. the Earth
**clear the decks** send all idle crew belowdecks
**clove hitch** knot for fastening rope to spar or large rope
**colors** flag or flags
**come to** (*vb*) bring ship's prow nearer the wind; stop moving, drop anchor
**conn** (*vb*) direct ship's steering
**convoy** merchant vessels under protection of warships
**course** direction taken, stated in degrees from north
**crank** (*adj*) unstable, liable to capsize
**crest** top of wave that curls over
**cruise** pleasure voyage; (*vb*) sail from port to port
**current** horizontal flow of water
**dead ahead** located directly before bow
**dead reckoning** calculation of position from course and distance sailed
**debark** (*vb*) disembark
**disembark** (*vb*) go ashore from ship
**displacement** weight of water displaced by ship
**dock** long, often wood structure, extending into water, to which ships are moored; pier
**dockyard** storage and repair facility for ships
**downwind** (*adv*) in same direction as wind
**draft** depth to which ship is submerged, measured from keel
**draw** (*vb*) require specific depth of water to float
**dry dock** artificial, drainable basin in which ships are repaired
**embark** (*vb*) go on board ship
**even keel** condition of floating properly upright in water
**fag end** frayed or untwisted end of line
**fast** (*adj*) secured, tied, fastened, or arranged, esp. of lines
**fathom** unit of nautical measurement equal to six feet (1.8 m)
**fleet** large group of ships of various sorts
**flotsam** floating wreckage
**following sea** waves running in same direction as course
**founder** (*vb*) take on water to point of capsizing and sinking; struggle in storm, going nowhere
**free port** port where goods may be unloaded, stored, and reshipped without paying customs or duty
**furl** (*vb*) roll up or take in sails
**gale** strong wind of 30–55 knots (32–63 mph)
**go to sea** begin life as mariner
**harbor** protected body of water deep enough for anchoring, usu. with docks constructed along shore; port
**hawser bend** knot joining ends of two lines
**heading** compass direction of vessel
**heave** (*vb*) throw; (*n*) vertical oscillation of vessel

**heaving-line bend**  knot for attaching end of weighted heaving line to hawser

**heel**  (*vb*) list to one side

**high seas**  open ocean outside national territorial waters; international waters; open sea

**hitch**  knot used to secure line to spar

**hoist**  (*vb*) pull on line or halyard to raise something

**horse latitudes**  area on each side of equator where westerlies change to trade winds and reverse direction

**international waters**  high seas

**jetsam**  cargo and equipment, cast overboard to lighten load in storm, that sinks or is washed ashore

**jettison**  (*vb*) abandon or discard cargo overboard

**knot**  unit of speed equal to 6076 feet (1851 m) per hour or one nautical mph

**landfall**  sighting of land

**landlubber**  land-bound person not familiar with sea

**latitude**  distance measured in degrees north or south of equator

**leeward**  (*adj*) at side of vessel away from wind

**lie to**  (*vb*) remain stationary with bow to wind

**lighthouse**  tall structure topped by powerful, revolving signal light that marks land's end or danger area

**list**  (*vb*) tip to one side in water

**lock**  section of canal filled with water to carry vessels through

**log**  record of all events during voyage

**longitude**  distance measured in degrees east or west of Greenwich, England

**lubber's knot**  faulty square knot

**luff**  (*vb*) turn bow toward wind; sail close or closer to wind, causing sails to flap

**Magnus hitch**  knot for fastening rope to spar or larger rope

**make sail**  (*vb*) raise or set sails or additional sail; set out on voyage

**manifest**  itemized list of ship's cargo, esp. for customs

**marlinespike hitch**  hitch into which pointed metal implement is inserted in order to draw seizing taut

**Mayday**  international radiotelephone distress signal

**merchant marine**  personnel and ships of one nation used in commerce

**mole**  breakwater or stone barrier in harbor

**moor**  (*vb*) attach lines or cables, usu. to dock, to hold vessel in place

**mooring**  place where vessel is secured by lines or cables, esp. dock or slip; such securing lines or cables

**mothball**  (*adj*) designating vessel not in current use or held in reserve, often older vessel

**nautical**  (*adj*) of or pertaining to ships, sailors, or navigation

**nautical mile**  international unit of measurement for sea navigation equal to 6076 feet (1851 m) or 1.15 statute miles (1.85 km)

**navigable**  (*adj*) passable to vessels

**navigation**  plan and direct course of ship at sea

**open sea**  high seas

**overboard**  (*adv*) over ship's side and into the water

**passage**  travel on board ship, esp. from port to port

**pay out**  (*vb*) let out line

**pier**  dock

**pile**  upright post driven into bottom that shows above water

**pilot**  (*vb*) direct ship's course, esp. in and out of port or through difficult waters

**pitch**  rocking, fore-and-aft motion at sea

**plot**  (*vb*) plan course on map or chart

**port**  harbor

**prolonge knot**  knot made up of three overlapping loops formed by passing single rope over and under itself at crossings; sailor's breastplate

**put about**  (*vb*) reverse direction

**put out to sea**  begin voyage; join ship's crew

**quay**  stone dock, often parallel to roadway along edge of water

**range**  line determined by two or more objects on shore, used to plot safe course

**reach**  tack in which wind crosses side of boat

**reefed sail**  sail partly lowered and secured

**reef knot**  square knot used in tying in sails

**reeving-line bend**  knot for joining two lines so that they will pass easily through hole or ring

**registry**  certificate showing nationality of merchant ship

**ride at anchor**  float in position with anchor dropped

**roll**  tipping, side-to-side motion at sea

**rolling hitch**  hitch on spar that tightens under stress parallel to spar

**row**  (*vb*) power vessel by hand with oars

**run**  tack in which wind crosses stern of boat

**run aground**  (*vb*) encounter waters too shallow for depth of keel

**run before the wind**  sail swiftly in direction of wind

**sail**  (*vb*) travel by water, esp. on vessel propelled by wind in sails; manage or steer a sailing vessel

**sailing**  art and practice of navigation

**sailor's breastplate**  prolonge knot

**scrimshaw**  carved or engraved piece of ivory

**scud**  (*vb*) run before a gale

**sea biscuit**  hardtack biscuit eaten on long sea voyages

**seagoing**  (*adj*) made for use in open sea

**sea legs**  ability to walk on board ship, esp. in rough seas

**seamanship**  skill in sailing, navigation, and handling ships

**seasickness**  nausea and dizziness caused by roll and pitch

**seaworthy**  (*adj*) fit to travel on the open sea

**seizing**  means of binding together two objects or lengths of rope by number of longitudinal and transverse turns of thin line or wire

**set**  manner and position in which sails are rigged

**set sail**  begin voyage, depart from mooring

**shakedown**  initial test cruise for ship

**shipboard**  (*adj*) aboard ship

**ship out**  (*vb*) go to sea, esp. join ship's crew

**shipping**  commerce conducted by watergoing vessels

**shipshape**  (*adj*) having everything in good order

**ship's papers**  legally required papers carried on board, showing ship's registration and nature of cargo; registry

**shipwreck**  destruction or loss of ship in accident

**shipyard**  facility in which ships are built and repaired

**slip**  mooring place or berth in dockyard

**SOS**  save our ship; Morse code distress signal

**soundings**  depth measurements

**squall**  sudden, intense, localized storm at sea

**steamer rug**  heavy woolen blanket used to cover lap and legs of passenger in deck chair

**steerage**  space below forward deck, allotted to passengers paying lower fare

**stem-to-stern**  (*adv*) from front to back of vessel

**stowaway**  person concealed on board to secure free passage

**strike**  (*vb*) shorten or take down sails

**swab**  (*vb*) mop the deck

**sway** horizontal oscillation of ship's hull; (*vb*) heave object aloft

**swell** long, heavy undulation in sea's surface caused by distant disturbance

**tack** (*vb*) make course back and forth through wind by reversing after corner of sail; (*n*) direction of movement in relation to position of sails

**take bearings** determine one's position at sea relative to other objects

**take in sail** lower or remove sail from mast or yard

**tender** (*adj*) riding too high in water, therefore unstable; tending to heel excessively under sail

**territorial waters** area within three-mile (4.8-km) limit over which nation has jurisdiction

**three-mile limit** extent of territorial jurisdiction of any nation outward from its coastline

**tides** rise and fall of ocean level due to gravitational force of sun and moon

**timber hitch** knot formed on spar or other object by wrapping rope around object and itself

**trade winds** easterly winds prevailing at low latitudes and blowing toward equator

**trim** way in which boat floats in water; (*vb*) rig and put sails in order for sailing

**tumble home** inclination inward above waterline from greatest breadth

**turn turtle** capsize

**under sail** rigged and in motion

**upwind** (*adj*) sailing toward direction of wind; (*adv*) to windward

**voyage** journey by ship, esp. both outward and homeward

**wake** water disturbance pluming up behind moving vessel

**watch** observation of surrounding sea for storms, danger, or enemies, esp. four-hour period of such duty

**water line** line to which surface of water comes on hull

**weigh** (*vb*) hoist anchor

**westerlies** prevalent westerly winds of Temperate Zone

**wigwag** act of signaling by movement of two flags waved according to code

**windward** (*adj*) at side of vessel facing wind

**yachting** sport or recreation of sailing yachts

**yaw** (*vb*) deviate back and forth from course

# OTHER VEHICLES

Trolleys
Carriages
Wagons, Carts, and Sleds
Cycles
Litters

**SEE ALSO**: Chap. 5: Machinery and Fabrication; Containers; Chap. 6: Automobiles; Railroads

## TROLLEYS

**autobus** omnibus

**cable car** trolley operated by underground or overhead cable loop

**el** elevated trolley or railway

**elevated railway** urban passenger trolley suspended from overhead rail

**funicular** overhead cable railway up hill or mountain

**gondola** long, narrow boat serving as bus carrying passengers, esp. on canals of Venice

**herdic** small, horse-drawn omnibus with side seats and rear entrance (U.S., 19th c.)

**jitney** small passenger bus or van with flexible schedule over regular route

**monorail** trolley suspended from or balanced on single rail

**omnibus** public carrier for at least twelve passengers, usu. with door in rear

**streetcar** vehicle usu. on rails, esp. for city passengers

**subway** underground trolley or municipal railway, usu. electric

**tram** streetcar on overhead rail or cable

**trolley** wheeled carriage, usu. with overhead cable, often electric

**trolley bus** trackless, electric bus with overhead cable

**trolley car** trackless, electric streetcar with overhead cable

**wagonette** covered, four-wheel carriage bus with facing passenger seats for six or more

## CARRIAGES

**araba** cab or coach (Turkey)

**barouche** four-wheel carriage with facing double seats and folding top

**berlin** four-wheel carriage with suspended body (Germany, 18th c.)

**brougham** low, closed, four-wheel carriage for two passengers with driver's seat outside

**buckboard** four-wheel carriage with seat mounted on springlike board

**buggy** light, four-wheel, one-horse, two-passenger carriage

**cab** orig. cabriolet; light closed carriage for hire

**cabriolet** light, two-wheel, one-horse carriage with folding hood

**calash** caleche

**caleche** carriage with two small wheels in front and folding top; calash

**cariole** light, one-horse carriage

**caroche** luxurious, horse-drawn carriage

**carriage** any horse-drawn vehicle, esp. for private use

**carromata** light, two-wheel carriage with single pony (Philippines)

**carryall** light, covered carriage that seats four or more

**cart** heavy, horse-drawn, two-wheel carriage used for hauling freight

**chaise** small, usu. two-wheel carriage suspended on leather straps

**charabanc** large sightseeing coach

**chariot** ancient, two-wheel, seatless, horse-drawn battle car

**chuckwagon** large, closed supply wagon (U.S. West, 19th c.)

**clarence** closed, four-wheel, four-seat carriage with driver outside; growler

**coach** large, four-wheel, enclosed carriage with driver's seat outside

**Concord buggy** large, covered, four-wheel carriage with driver's seat outside and covered baggage compartment

**Conestoga** broad-wheeled covered wagon drawn by six horses

**coupe** enclosed, four-wheel carriage with driver's seat outside

**covered wagon** large, canvas-topped, four-wheel vehicle for moving families west (U.S., 19th c.)

**curricle** light, two-wheel carriage drawn by two horses abreast (18th-19th c.)

**diligence** four-wheel, four-horse public stagecoach (France, 18th c.)

**dogcart** light, usu. one-horse, two-wheel cart with two transverse seats back-to-back

**dos-a-dos** four-wheel dogcart with seats set back-to-back

**Dougherty wagon** passenger wagon on steel springs (U.S. West, 19th c.)

**drag** large, private, four-horse sporting coach with roof, rumble seats, and enclosed compartment

**dray** low, sturdy cargo cart with detachable sides

**droshky** low, open, four-wheel carriage with narrow bench (Russia)

**fiacre** small, four-wheel hackney coach

**fly** horse-drawn public coach or delivery wagon

**four-in-hand** carriage drawn by four horses

**Germantown** two- or three-seat carriage, esp. in Pennsylvania

**gharry** horse-drawn cab (India, Egypt)

**gig** light, two-wheel, one-horse carriage

**growler** *Brit. slang.* clarence

**hack** hackney

**hackney** four-wheel, two-horse, six-seat carriage kept for hire; hack

**hansom** two-wheel, two-horse, two-passenger, covered carriage with driver's seat elevated at rear; hansom cab

**hansom cab** hansom

**herdic** horse-drawn omnibus with side seats and rear entrance (U.S., 19th c.)

**jaunting car** light, two-wheel, open vehicle with lengthwise back-to-back seats

**landau** large, four-wheel carriage with top that folds into two parts (Germany)

**mudwagon** flat-sided, simple stagecoach, smaller than Concord

**phaeton** light, four-wheel carriage with seats front and rear, folding cover, and no coachman's seat

**post chaise** four-wheel coach, used to carry mail and passengers (18th-19th c.)

**prairie schooner** broad-wheeled covered wagon used in cross-country travel (U.S. West)

**quadriga** two-wheel chariot drawn by four horses (ancient Rome)

**rig** general term for carriage and horse

**rockaway** carriage with enclosed top (U.S., 19th c.)

**runabout** topless buggy

**shandrydan** hooded chaise; rickety carriage

**spider phaeton** very high, light carriage with covered seat and rear footman's seat

**spring wagon** light, versatile wagon with removable seats and canopy top

**stagecoach** public passenger and mail coach that ran on regular schedule (U.S. West, 19th c.)

**stanhope** light, open, one-seat, two-wheel carriage

**sulky** light, one-passenger, two-wheel carriage used in trotting races

**surrey** modest, four-wheel, two-seat carriage used for pleasure or to carry family, with or without top

**tandem** two-seat carriage drawn by team of horses harnessed one before the other

**tilbury** light, two-wheel gig

**tonga** two-wheel carriage (India)

**trap** light, one-horse carriage with springs

**troika** sleigh or carriage drawn by three horses abreast (Russia)

**victoria** large, luxurious, four-wheel, two-horse carriage

**volante** two-wheel carriage with axle behind body and driver riding horse (Cuba)

## Wagons, Carts, and Sleds

**baby carriage** covered crib on four springy wheels

**barrow** two-wheel cart with shallow body and shaft handles

**Bath chair** hooded, glassed wheelchair pushed by attendant

**bobsled** large, metal racing sled on runners

**caisson** two-wheel wagon used to carry artillery ammunition

**camion** strongly built cart or wagon for transporting heavy loads; dray

**cariole** light covered cart; dog-drawn toboggan

**carrier** device used to contain and transport articles; baby's reclining plastic seat, carried by a person

**cart** heavy, horse-drawn, two-wheel vehicle used to carry freight

**coaster** small sliding sled or wagon

**dogsled** small sled hauled by dogs

**dolly** platform on rollers for moving heavy loads

**dray** strong, low, sideless cart for hauling goods; camion

**fourgon** baggage wagon (19th c.)

**go-cart** lightweight handcart; small framework on wheels for children

**gurney** flat, wheeled cot for transporting disabled or injured person

**handcart** hand truck

**hand truck** small, hand-propelled, two-wheel carrier; handcart

**hay wagon** large, open wagon for hay

**jinrikisha** small, two-wheel passenger cab drawn by one or two persons (Japan, China)

**jumper** sled for hauling goods over bare ground

**kibitka** covered vehicle on wheels or runners (Russia)

**komatik** sled on wooden runners, with crossbars lashed with rawhide (Eskimo)

**laundry cart** upright, mesh vehicle on wheels, used to carry laundry

**luge** small racing sled driven in supine position down chute

**milk wagon** large wagon used to deliver milk

**oxcart** ox-driven freight cart

**perambulator** *Chiefly Brit.* baby carriage

**pram** *Brit. informal.* baby carriage

**pulka** one-man sledge on runners (Lapland)

**pung** sleigh with box-shaped body, drawn by one horse (Algonquian Indian)

**push cart** cart or barrow on wheels, pushed by hand

**ricksha** jinrikisha

**shopping cart** mesh, four-wheel grocery cart

**skid** low platform on wheels for moving heavy objects

**sled**  vehicle made of flat body on runners for use over snow and ice

**sledge**  any of various carts on runners for carrying goods over ice, often drawn by draft animals

**sleigh**  large passenger sled on runners, usu. open and horse-drawn, for use over snow and ice

**spring wagon**  light farm or ranch wagon on springs

**stroller**  seat on wheels for baby

**tipcart**  cart whose body tips to empty contents

**toboggan**  long, flat-bottomed sled with one end curved up and handrails

**trundle**  low hauling cart on wheels

**tumbrel**  farm tipcart, used to carry prisoners to execution (France, 18th c.)

**wagon**  any of various four-wheel vehicles, motorized, animal-drawn, or human-propelled, ranging in use from child's toy to transportation of bulky goods

**wain**  farm wagon or cart

**wheelbarrow**  single-wheel cart with shallow body, held and pushed by handles, used to transport small loads

**wheelchair**  chair on wheels for invalid or disabled person

## CYCLES

**ATV**  *all terrain vehicle*; sturdy three-wheel motorcycle for cross-country driving

**bicycle**  two-wheel cycle operated by foot pedals; bike

**bicycle-built-for-two**  two-wheel, two-seat, pedal-driven cycle; tandem

**bike**  *Informal.* bicycle

**chopper**  *Slang.* motorcycle

**cycle**  open, pedaled or engine-powered, single-passenger vehicle, usu. having two wheels in tandem

**dandy**  two-wheel velocipede

**dirt bike**  small, motor-driven cycle with extra-heavy tires

**hog**  *Slang.* large, heavy motorcycle

**minibike**  small motorcycle with raised handlebars

**monocycle**  unicycle

**moped**  pedal-started motor scooter with small engine

**motorbike**  low-power, lightweight motorcycle

**motorcycle**  two-wheel, motor-driven cycle; chopper

**motor scooter**  small, lightweight motorcycle; bicycle propelled by attached motor

**mountain bike**  rugged, fat-wheeled bicycle with deep tread for traction and stability on dirt trails

**ordinary**  early bicycle with a very large front wheel and a very small rear wheel

**pedicab**  tricycle with separate two-seat passenger compartment; trishaw

**penny-farthing**  *Chiefly Brit.* bicycle with large front wheel and small rear wheel

**quadricycle**  four-wheel cycle

**scooter**  small motorbike; child's two-wheel, self-propelled vehicle with long, narrow footboard

**sidewalk bike**  child's training bicycle with detachable set of extra rear wheels

**skateboard**  short board with pair of wheels at each end, powered by free foot while standing on board

**tandem**  bicycle-built-for-two

**ten-speed**  powerful, lightweight bicycle with ten gears

**trail bike**  small motorcycle designed for use on unpaved roads

**tricycle**  small, three-wheel, pedal-driven bicycle, esp. for young children; trike

**trike**  *Informal.* tricycle

**trishaw**  pedicab

**unicycle**  one-wheel bicycle with very tall seat, often used in circus; monocycle

**velocipede**  early, lightweight wheeled vehicle, self-propelled by rider

## LITTERS

**brancard**  stretcher

**camel litter**  seat fitted on camel's hump

**dooly**  enclosed palanquin litter (India)

**handbarrow**  light, flat, rectangular frame with handles at both ends

**horse litter**  seat carried by horse

**howdah**  covered seat carried by elephant or camel (India)

**jampan**  sedan chair borne on two poles (India)

**jinrikisha**  two-wheel passenger cab with fold-down top, pulled by one or two persons (Japan, China); ricksha

**kajawah**  litter (India)

**litter**  covered, often curtained couch on long shafts or poles, borne by animals or people

**norimon**  litter (Japan)

**palanquin**  enclosed litter (Asia)

**ricksha**  jinrikisha

**sedan chair**  portable, covered, single chair borne on poles

**stokes litter**  wire basket for transporting ill or injured person

**stretcher**  flat, open litter for carrying ill or injured person; brancard

**tonjon**  open litter (India)

**travois**  platform or net on two trailing poles drawn by animal (American Indian)

# PART THREE

# DOMESTIC LIFE

# The Home

# BUILDINGS

Living Places
Types of Buildings

**SEE ALSO**: Chap. 7: Exterior Structure; Chap. 11: The City

## LIVING PLACES

**abode**  place where one lives

**accommodations**  lodgings, sometimes including food

**apartment**  single unit within multiunit residential building, rented by person who usu. occupies the space

**building**  any enclosed structure with walls and roof

**camp**  group of tents or cabins used as temporary shelter

**caravan**  wagon or vehicle equipped with living quarters

**casa**  Spanish. house

**cave**  underground chamber opening at earth's surface, used as dwelling by prehistoric man

**cliff dwelling**  cavelike dwelling built into rock face of cliff

**condominium**  single unit within multiple-unit structure, owned by its individual deed holder, usu. its occupant

**co-op**  unit within multiunit structure jointly owned by residents of all units

**countryseat**  Chiefly Brit. usu. substantial rural house of urban dweller

**den**  shabby dwelling or cave, esp. used as hiding place

**digs**  Brit. slang. living quarters

**dive**  Informal. disreputable establishment, esp. commercial

**domicile**  customary, fixed, permanent dwelling; legal residence

**dump**  Informal. run-down, sloppy dwelling

**dwelling**  abode, living place

**edifice**  usu. large, elaborate building

**estate**  privately owned land with substantial residence on it

**farmhouse**  residential structure on farmland

**guesthouse**  small building separate from but near a main residence

**habitat**  one's regular place of residence

**habitation**  dwelling, residence

**hacienda**  primary dwelling on large ranch or estate (Spain, Latin America)

**haunt**  place regularly visited or inhabited

**home**  place where one lives

**homestead**  land and buildings in which a family dwells

**house**  building used as dwelling place

**household**  home and its occupants

**housing**  shelter or living accommodations

**lair**  hidden lodging place

**lodging**  place for dwelling, often temporary

**maison**  French. house

**nest**  safe, often secluded living place

**pad**  Slang. dwelling place

**place**  home, dwelling

**quarters**  lodging, dwelling place

**ranch**  rural house and surrounding land used for raising stock animals

**rancho**  ranch, hut for ranch workers (Spain, Latin America)

**residence**  place in which one regularly lives

**retreat**  hidden or secluded dwelling

**roof over one's head**  basic housing, shelter

**rooms**  portion of house used as living quarters

**roost**  place for resting or lodging, often temporarily

**shelter**  any protective structure used as temporary or permanent living place

**squat**  public or unoccupied dwelling used without permission

**structure**  building constructed for human use or occupation

**unit**  portion of structure partitioned for occupation by single person or group of persons

## TYPES OF BUILDINGS

**acropolis**  fortified, columned structure (ancient Greece)

**A-frame**  building constructed of a three-piece frame shaped like capital A

**alcázar**  fortress, palace (Spain)

**amphitheater**  roofless oval or circle with rising tiers of seats

**apartment**  building with several separate dwelling units

**arena**  large, open or enclosed building for contests, entertainments

**auditorium**  large room or hall for public gathering

**aviary**  place for confining birds, usu. screened

**balok**  small, fabric-covered, mobile cabin (Eskimo)

**barn**  large, open building for storing farm equipment, housing animals

**barracks**  set of buildings, often resembling sheds or barns, housing soldiers in garrison

**basilica**  oblong building with broad nave flanked by colonnaded aisles, ending in semicircular apse

**bathhouse**  structure containing baths, often also pools, steam rooms, and whirlpools; structure housing changing rooms for bathers, as at beach

**bi-level**  house having at least two levels of living space

**blockhouse**  heavy timber military structure with projecting upper story

**boardinghouse**  home converted to rooms for rent, with food sometimes included for tenants

**booth**  small enclosure isolating occupant

**bower**  rustic cottage

**bungalow**  one-story residence with low, sweeping lines, often with veranda

**cabana**  tentlike structure with projecting canopy

**cabin**  small, simple, one-story, low-roofed dwelling

**campanile**  tall, freestanding bell tower

**Cape Cod cottage**  compact, rectangular, one-and-a-half-story dwelling with steep gable roof and central chimney

**caravan**  Chiefly Brit. mobile home

**caravansary**  hotel or inn, orig. where caravans rested

**carriage house**  building for storage of carriages

**castle**  large, fortified building or group of buildings, usu. stone, housing ruler or nobleman

**chalet**  dwelling with unconcealed structural members emphasized by decorative carvings

**château**  large country house, esp. in French wine regions

**church**  Christian house of worship with spire, finial cross

**condominium**  multiple-unit residence jointly owned by deed holders, who are usu. its occupants

**conservatory**  glass-roofed house for plants

**coop** roofed cage or small enclosure for poultry

**cottage** small, detached dwelling, often rural

**crib** small, narrow dwelling; framework stall

**dacha** country cottage, summer house (Russia)

**dormitory** large residence hall with many bedrooms

**duplex** single residence divided into two units

**earth lodge** circular, dome-shaped dwelling made of posts and beams covered by branches, grass, and earth (American Indian)

**flat** apartment built on one floor of building

**garage** small, enclosed building for storing cars and equipment

**gazebo** freestanding, roofed summerhouse open on sides

**greenhouse** glassed enclosure for growing plants

**hall** large structure for public use; residence on country estate

**hangar** high-roofed, enclosed shed for repairing and storing aircraft

**high-rise** multistory apartment house or office building

**hippodrome** oval arena for equestrian events

**hogan** rough log and mud dwelling (Navajo)

**hostel** housing maintained by institution for specific group

**hotel** building of many rooms licensed to provide lodging

**house** building intended for human habitation

**houseboat** moored barge or low boat fitted for use as dwelling

**hovel** small, miserable shed or open-roofed structure

**hut** small, rudimentary structure for temporary habitation

**hutch** animal pen or coop; shack, shanty

**igloo** dome-shaped dwelling of ice blocks (Eskimo)

**inn** public house for lodging, usu. in countryside

**izba** traditional, rural log hut (Russia)

**jacal** thatched roof hut with walls of mud-plastered upright stakes (Mexico)

**kennel** shelter for dogs, with fenced yard

**kiosk** small structure with one or more open sides; open summerhouse or pavilion

**laura** monastery of Eastern orthodox church

**lean-to** rough shed, its roof having one slope

**lighthouse** tower with powerful light as signal of coastline to ships

**lodge** inn or resort hotel; house set aside from main house for hunting or other special use

**loft** upper floor of warehouse building converted to living area

**log cabin** rustic dwelling built of logs laid horizontally

**long house** long wooden communal dwelling (Iroquois)

**maisonette** *French.* small house or apartment

**mall** very large building housing stores, with adjacent parking lots

**manor** large hall on estate property

**manse** large, elegant residence

**mansion** grand, elaborate dwelling

**market** public building for wholesale trade

**mobile home** movable trailer with living facilities

**mosque** Islamic place of worship with rounded spires and minaret

**motel** hotel for automobile travelers, usu. long and low

**Nissen hut** prefabricated shelter, semicircular, with arching corrugated steel roof and concrete floor

**obelisk** upright, four-sided pillar tapering to pyramid top

**outbuilding** small structure, such as stable or woodshed, separate from main residence

**outhouse** small enclosed toilet set apart from main house, usu. without plumbing

**pagoda** structure resembling tower of several stories with projecting, concavely curved roofs (Asia)

**palace** large, stately house, usu. ruler's official residence

**palazzo** palace or large residence (Italy)

**pavilion** large, often sumptuous tent or canopy

**pen** small, open enclosure for animals

**pension** modest hotel or boardinghouse in Europe

**penthouse** dwelling unit built on roof of building

**pied-à-terre** temporary or second lodging; townhouse

**pile** large and lofty building or group of buildings

**plant** land, buildings, and equipment of factory

**port-a-potty** small, movable, enclosed booth used as toilet, esp. on construction sites

**posada** country inn (Spain, Latin America)

**possum-trot plan** house in two parts connected by breezeway

**prefab** structure built of interchangeable, prefabricated parts

**pueblo** communal dwelling, esp. contiguous flat-roofed adobe houses several stories high or arranged in terraces (Southwest American Indian)

**pyramid** massive stone structure, having square base with four triangular walls that meet in point at top (ancient Egypt)

**Quonset hut** prefabricated structure with semicircular arched corrugated steel roof on bolted steel truss foundation

**ranch house** low, sprawling, one-story suburban residence

**resort** complex of structures for recreational use

**rialto** exchange, marketplace, or theater building

**roadhouse** inn or hotel, usu. beyond city limits

**rotunda** round, domed building

**saltbox** frame dwelling, two stories in front, one in rear, with double-sloping roof extending farther in back

**semidetached** (*adj*) designating pair of residences joined by common wall

**shack** small, roughly built, crudely furnished house; shebang

**shanty** small, crudely built, shabby dwelling, usu. of wood

**shebang** primitive dwelling; shack

**shed** small structure, usu. for storage

**shop** small retail establishment

**skyscraper** very tall urban office or apartment building

**split-level** residence with rooms built on floor levels differing by about half a story

**stable** shelter for horses or stock animals

**stadium** very large, unroofed structure with tiered seats, used for sporting events

**stall** small booth or stand for retail sales, open at one side

**stand** small, open-air structure for retail business

**stupa** dome-shaped mound, tower, or Buddhist shrine

**supermarket** large, one-story store, with adjacent parking lots, that sells food and other household goods

**synagogue** Jewish house of worship

**tabernacle** usu. large meeting house or assembly hall, used esp. as place of worship

**tavern** building used as bar or saloon

**temple** edifice for non-Christian religious observance

**tenement** multiunit apartment building, usu. a cheap dwelling for urban poor

**tent** small shelter of canvas supported or suspended on poles

**tepee** conical tent of skin drawn on poles, used as dwelling (American Plains Indian)

**terminal** central transport station serving multiple lines

**theater** edifice that is site of various kinds of performances on stage

**tholos** circular building (ancient Greece)

**town house** often luxurious house in the city, esp. distinguished from house in country owned by same person; one of group of two- or three-story houses of uniform design joined by common sidewalls

**tract home** one of many identical, prefab residences in suburban cluster

**triplex** single residence divided into three units

**trailer** movable structure with living facilities

**tupik** sealskin tent used as summer dwelling (Eskimo)

**villa** large country estate; *Chiefly Brit.* small suburban house

**warehouse** large storage or manufacturing structure, often windowless

**washhouse** building equipped for washing clothes

**wickiup** elliptical hut used as residence by nomads (American Indian)

**wigwam** domed structure of poles overlaid with bark, used as residence (Great Lakes American Indian)

**woodshed** crude shed for storing wood

**yurt** circular, domed tent of skin on collapsible lattice frame, used by Mongol nomads (Mongolia, Siberia)

**ziggurat** temple pyramid built in successive stepped-back stages with shrine at top (ancient Mesopotamia)

# EXTERIOR STRUCTURE

## WINDOWS, WALLS, AND FACADES

**anta** support pier formed by thickening end of wall

**bailey** outer wall or space between two outer walls of castle

**bay window** large window set in bay or recess in room and projecting from outside wall, often three-sided

**bondstone** stone used to bond facing masonry to masonry backing

**bow window** rounded bay window; compass window

**bulkhead** retaining wall

**bull's-eye window** oeil-de-boeuf

**casement** hinged window frame with two windows opening outward from middle

**Catherine wheel window** small, round window with spokes extending outward from its center

**clapboard** narrow board, thicker at one side, used in covering outside of house, usu. painted white

**clerestory** outside wall carried above adjoining roof, pierced with windows

**compass window** bow window

**coping** finishing or protective cap to exterior masonry wall

**cornerstone** first stone laid where walls meet

**curtain wall** nonbearing exterior wall in framed building

**dead wall** wall without openings

**Diocletian window** Palladian window

**dormer** vertical window set in projection beneath sloping roof; entire projecting structure with such a window

**double-hung window** window with top and bottom sashes that move vertically

**embrasure** opening in wall for door or window, sloped or beveled to enlarge interior outline; reveal

**facade** outer surface of building, esp. front wall; face

**face** facade

**fanlight** semicircular window with radiating bars like ribs of fan, often above door or rectangular window

**French window** pair of casement windows reaching to floor and opening in middle

**front** building facade facing street

**frontispiece** highly ornamental, principle feature of a facade

**grille** grating forming barrier or screen over opening

**horizontal sliding window** window that opens sideways on tracks

**Judas hole** small window with sliding panel set in door, used as peephole

**lancet window** high, narrow, sharply pointed window set in lancet arch

**louver** opening in wall with overlapping slats that allow ventilation, prevent entry of rain, and provide privacy

**mullioned window** window with multiple panes divided by slender vertical strips

**oeil-de-boeuf** small circular or oval window; bull's-eye window

**oriel** large projecting bay window supported by corbel or bracket

**Palladian window** central arched window with two small flanking compartments, usu. mullioned; Diocletian window

**perpend wall** wall built of bricks or large stones passing through entire thickness of wall and acting as binders

**picture window** large, undivided window usu. opening onto scenic view

**porthole** small, round window, esp. on ship

**quarrel** small, quadrangular or diamond-shaped glass set diagonally in latticed window

**retaining wall** wall that resists lateral pressure, esp. from earth

**reveal** side of opening between frame and wall; embrasure; jamb

**revetment** stone or concrete facing used to protect embankment

**ribbon window** long, divided window forming continuous horizontal band across face of building

**rose window** circular window decorated with tracery that is symmetrical about the center

**roundel** small, round window

**scarp** vertical side of ditch below parapet of fortification

**sconcheon** reveal of window from frame to inner face of wall

**screen** frame holding fine wire mesh over door or window to exclude insects but permit ventilation

**shutter** movable cover or screen for window or door, often of wood slats

**siding** weatherproof boards or facings that form outer wall or facade

**skylight** opening in roof and ceiling covered with transparent material, usu. overhead window of glass

**storm window** protective window set in jamb outside permanent window in winter to conserve heat

**transom** window above door or other window, usu. hinged to horizontal crosspiece; such a crosspiece separating windows or door and window

**Trombe wall** glass-fronted, exterior masonry wall that absorbs solar heat for radiation into building

**wall** continuous upright surface connecting floor and ceiling or foundation and roof, subdividing interior space, or supporting other parts of structure

**window** opening in wall for admission of air and light, set with frame holding transparent substance, usu. glass

**windowpane** individual section filling a window sash, usu. of glass

## ROOFS AND TOWERS

**awning** rooflike covering extending outward from structure

**barbican** fortified tower at gate or bridge

**barrack roof** movable roof sliding on four posts, used to cover hay or straw brick

**bartizan** small, overhanging turret on wall or tower, esp. of castle

**bastion** projecting part of fortification

**battlement** parapet atop wall with alternating open spaces and merlons, used for defense or decoration

**belfry** tower, cupola, or turret in which bell is housed

**bell tower** tower in which bell is housed

**butterfly roof** roof with shallow valley and gently sloping sides

**buttress** projecting support structure providing stability for wall or building

**campanile** tall, straight, freestanding bell tower

**castellated** (adj) designating upward projection with battlements, like a castle

**chimney** vertical structure usu. of brick or stone, with flue for carrying off smoke from fireplace

**chimney pot** earthenware or metal pipe at top of chimney to increase draft and disperse smoke

**corbie gable** gable with corbie steps

**corbiestep** one of a series of steps terminating in upper part of gable wall

**cowl** hoodlike covering over chimney to improve draft

**crenel** opening in battlement between projecting merlons

**crenelation** series of open spaces and notches atop battlement

**crest** horizontal ridge of roof

**cullis** gutter in roof

**cupola** small dome on roof; rounded roof or ceiling

**curb roof** roof peaked at center with double slope on each side

**dome** hemispherical roof, usu. large

**donjon** massive central tower or stronghold in castle

**dormer** gabled extension off attic room, with sloping roof and vertical window

**eave** edge of roof projecting beyond side of building

**fastness** fortified, secure place, often elevated

**flat roof** roof without ridge, slope, or dome

**flèche** tall, thin church spire

**gable** extending, ridged roof section of triangular wall enclosed by sloping sides, usu. with window

**gambrel roof** roof having two slopes on each side, with lower slope steeper than upper

**geodesic dome** domed roof made of light, straight, structural elements forming polygons in tension

**gutter** metal drainage trough under roof eaves

**helm roof** four-faced, steeply pitched roof, rising to point from base of four gables

**hip-and-valley** roof shaped with hips and valleys

**hipped roof** roof with sloping ends and sloping sides

**jerkinhead** roof having hipped end over truncated gable

**lantern** decorative open structure admitting light at top of roof or dome; similar structure used for ventilation

**lean-to** roof having one slope, often projecting from wall

**lean-to hipped roof** single slope with hipped ends, usu. projecting from wall

**lou** wood-framed tower, forerunner of pagoda (China)

**louver** roof turret with slatted aperture for vent; slanted fins opening off attic to exclude rain and sun and admit light and air

**mansard** roof having two slopes on each of four sides, with lower slope steeper than upper

**Martello tower** circular stone fort with guns on top

**merlon** solid interval between battlement crenels

**minaret** tall, slender mosque tower with projecting balconies from which Moslems are called to prayer

**monopitch roof** single-slope lean-to atop freestanding structure

**obelisk** tapering, four-sided monolithic tower with pyramid at top

**observation tower** tall structure overlooking surroundings

**pagoda** tower with projecting, encircling roofs at each of several levels (Asia)

**pantile roof** roof of semicylindrical tiles laid with alternate concave and convex surfaces uppermost

**pitched roof** roof with sloping sides

**platform** raised, horizontal, flat surface

**pyramid roof** four triangular slopes rising to point from square base

**rainbow roof** gable roof with gentle convex slopes giving rounded appearance

**rainspout** pipe or duct that drains roof gutter

**roof** top covering of building

**sawtooth roof** two or more parallel roofs like teeth of a saw, with one slope steeper than the other

**scupper** water drainage opening in wall at floor or roof

**shed roof** roof forming single slope from peak to wall

**shingle roof** roof composed of overlapping strips of wood or other material

**skirt roof** small section of roofing between stories of building, usu. nonbearing and decorative

**slate roof** roof shingled with laminated rock material

**spire** tower or steeple tapering to point

**steeple** pointed tower, esp. atop church

**stupa**  domed-shaped tower, esp. on Buddhist shrine

**thatched roof**  roof made of thick layer of interwoven straw or reeds

**tile roof**  roof composed of semicylindrical strips of fired clay or stone

**tower**  tall, standing structure attached to larger structure or freestanding

**turret**  short, projecting tower, usu. at corner of building

**valley**  low point between two roof slopes

**watchtower**  tall lookout tower

**widow's walk**  railed lookout platform or walkway on roof

**ziggurat**  pyramidal temple tower in successive stories with winding outside staircase and shrine at top (ancient Mesopotamia)

## ENTRYWAYS AND LATERAL EXTENSIONS

**addition**  room or extension built onto already existing structure

**ambulatory**  sheltered place for walking in cloister

**archway**  entry or passageway beneath series of arches

**areaway**  sunken space leading to cellar or basement entrance or window

**atrium**  open court leading into building, often with a glassed side and roof

**backdoor**  entryway at rear of building

**balcony**  railed platform attached to upper story of building

**bay**  three-sided projection from side of building

**belvedere**  open, roofed, upstairs gallery, esp. overlooking pleasant scene

**breezeway**  roofed passage between two buildings or sections of one building

**bulkhead**  inclined door over stairway leading to cellar or shaft

**cloister**  covered walkway along wall of monastery, usu. opening through columns onto inner court

**deck**  broad, open balcony extending from house

**door**  solid, swinging or sliding barrier for opening or closing entryway to room or building

**doorway**  entryway to building in which door is set

**drawbridge**  bridge which may be raised or lowered to prevent or allow passage

**entrance**  point of entry

**entryway**  passage for or point of entry

**extension**  added portion of building attached to main structure

**fire escape**  structure of metal platforms and ladders or stairways down outer wall of structure, used for escape in case of fire

**French doors**  adjoining doors that open in middle, with rectangular glass panes

**front door**  main entryway at front of building; primary doorway

**frontispiece**  highly ornamented portico or principle entryway

**gallery**  outdoor balcony; roofed promenade or colonnade

**gate**  swinging, grated doorway in fence or exterior wall, usu. opening onto drive or grounds

**gateway**  entrance that may be closed by gate

**hatch**  small door or opening, esp. in airplane or ship; opening in ship's deck or in floor or roof of building

**lanai**  porch, veranda (Hawaii)

**lich gate**  roofed churchyard gate under which coffin rests while awaiting clergy during burial

**moon gate**  circular opening through wall (China)

**opening**  entryway or doorway

**pai-loo**  elaborate, monumental archway in three compartments (China)

**parvis**  enclosed court in front of building, esp. church court with row of columns

**passageway**  opening or hallway allowing entry to room

**perron**  outdoor platform with entrance door to building at top of stairway

**porch**  covered approach or appendage to building

**portal**  doorway or opening, esp. elaborate or imposing one

**portcullis**  grating of iron bars or timbers suspended over gateway, lowered to prevent passage

**porte-cochere**  arched entryway for carriages, leading from street to inner courtyard

**portico**  roof supported by columns and attached to building as porch

**revolving door**  two or more doors turning on common axis within cylindrical vestibule

**scaffolding**  elevated platform, esp. movable one for workers

**screen door**  doorway of fine mesh allowing ventilation but preventing entrance of pests

**skybridge**  skywalk

**skywalk**  enclosed elevated walkway connecting two buildings; skybridge

**sliding door**  door mounted on runners that slides aside to open

**storm door**  additional protective door placed outside regular door

**sun deck**  unroofed top surface of building

**torii**  post and lintel gateway of Shinto temple (Japan)

**trapdoor**  lifting or sliding door flush with surface of roof, ceiling, or floor

**turnstile**  four revolving arms pivoted atop post to permit single-file passage of people, usu. in one direction only

**veranda**  large balcony or open porch along side of building, often roofed and railed

**walkway**  open or covered passageway from area to area within or between structures

**wicket**  small gate or door

**wing**  section or room projecting from main structure

**zaguán**  *Spanish*. passageway from entrance into central patio

## ORNAMENTAL AND STRUCTURAL PARTS

**arch**  curved masonry support structure spanning an opening: basket-handle, flat, horseshoe, lancet, ogee, parabolic, round, shouldered, trefoil, Tudor

**bargeboard**  elaborately carved, ornamental wood that conceals projecting end of gable or sloped roof

**bracket**  projecting support element

**bridge**  elevated crossing between buildings

**capital**  upper end of column atop shaft, bearing weight of entablature

**caryatid**  sculptured, robed female figure used as column (ancient Greece)

**cheval-de-frises**  row of projecting spikes atop wall for defense

**colonnade**  series of columns at regular intervals

**column**  tall, round support member on pedestal in one of three basic types: Corinthian, Doric, or Ionic; other styles include Byzantine, Gothic, Moorish, Romanesque, and Tuscan

**corbel**  bracketlike member that supports weight, esp. one projecting upward and outward from wall surface

**Corinthian column**  column of late classical period characterized by high base, slender fluted shaft with fillets, and ornate capital with acanthus leaves

**cornerstone**  quoin

**cornice**  prominent, projecting horizontal member surmounting a wall or dividing it horizontally

**courtyard**  interior walled area surrounded by building

**crawlspace**  shallow, unfinished area beneath first floor or under roof, usu. for plumbing and wiring; crawlway

**crawlway**  crawlspace

**dentils**  series of small, rectangular, toothlike blocks beneath corona of classical cornice

**Doric column**  undecorated column of early classical period characterized by short fluted shaft and convex circular molding as capital, with no distinct base

**engaged column**  column attached to wall, not free-standing

**finial**  ornament atop spire or gable

**footscraper**  edged plate or bar fixed on doorstep for removing mud from boots

**gargoyle**  waterspout in form of elaborately carved creature projecting from gutter of building

**gingerbread**  showy, elaborate trim on house

**Ionic column**  column of middle classical period characterized by slender fluted shaft with molded base and volute or spiral capital

**jamb**  upright structural member at side of door or window

**lintel**  horizontal member carrying weight above opening or doorway

**miter**  covering on top of chimney to keep rain out

**mudsill**  lowest lip of structure, often embedded in mud

**parapet**  low wall or railing on balcony, bridge, or roof to prevent falls and provide cover from below

**pediment**  low, triangular gable with horizontal cornice set above colonnade or section of facade

**peristyle**  row of columns around outside of temple (ancient Greece)

**pier**  vertical, structural support

**pilaster**  upright, rectangular pier projecting less than half its width from wall

**pillar**  firm, upright support column or shaft

**platform**  raised, horizontal, usu. unroofed surface

**pylon**  massive structure flanking entry or towers by gate; tower or support post for bridge

**quoin**  one of several large stones forming corner of masonry wall; cornerstone

**sash**  frame in door or window in which panes of glass are set

**shaft**  column, esp. main cylindrical central portion of column

**skewback**  inclined surface of masonry against which stones of arch rest

**stilt**  pile or post supporting raised structure

**story**  any entire level or floor of a building

**telamon**  sculptured male figure, similar to female caryatid, used as column or pilaster

**trestle**  support brace with crossbar on two pairs of legs

**trough**  gutter under eaves of building for rain drainage

**vane**  movable device atop spire or tower that indicates wind direction; weather vane

**weathercock**  vane in shape of rooster

**weather vane**  vane

## OUTBUILDINGS, GARDENS, AND FENCES

**apiary**  collection of beehives; shed where bees are kept

**aqueduct**  elevated structure that supports water pipe or conduit

**arbor**  plot of grass, lawn, or garden; lattice trellis or vine bower for shade

**arboretum**  place where trees, shrubs, and herbs are grown for study or display

**artesian well**  deep-bored well in which water rises under pressure like a fountain

**backhouse**  outdoor toilet

**backyard**  outdoor area at rear of house, often fenced

**band pavilion**  open, roofed stage or gazebo on lawn

**band shell**  band pavilion, usu. semicircular

**barbed-wire fence**  fencing of twisted wires with sharp points

**barn**  large building for storage of farm equipment and feed and for housing of livestock

**barnyard**  usu. fenced area next to barn

**bed**  plot of soil where plants are cultivated

**belvedere**  small summerhouse

**botanical garden**  outdoor garden and greenhouses for growth, study, and display of unusual plants

**bower**  arbor or leafy shelter of twined boughs or vines

**cabana**  small cabin or tent opening onto beach or pool

**carport**  open-sided automobile shelter with roof, often extending from main building

**cesspool**  underground cistern or pit for household sewage

**chain-link fence**  fence of thin wire mesh

**chicken coop**  small enclosure or cage for poultry

**clothesline**  cord strung between two suspended points for hanging and drying laundry

**conservatory**  glass-enclosed greenhouse for growing or displaying plants

**corral**  pen or enclosure for livestock

**court**  open space surrounded wholly or partly by building

**curtilage**  enclosed area of land occupied by structure, gardens, and outbuildings

**cyclone cellar**  underground shelter used during windstorms

**Cyclone fence**  *Trademark.* type of chain-link fence

**doghouse**  small roofed enclosure for pet dog

**espalier**  trellis or lattice on which shrubs are trained to grow

**exedra**  covered area open on one side; semicircular outdoor alcove with bench seat (ancient Greece and Rome)

**flagstone**  large, flat slab of stone for paving garden or walk

**flower bed**  cultivated area for planting flowers

**fountain**  mechanical water spout, usu. in decorative, raised structure containing a pool

**front yard**  open area between house and roadway

**garage**  enclosed space for storage of automobiles and other equipment, usu. adjoining main building

**garden**  plot of cultivated, manicured lawns, plants, and flowers

**garden wall**  enclosure along one or more sides of garden

**garth**  enclosed yard or garden, esp. within cloister of religious institution

**gazebo**  open or screened pavilion or summerhouse set on lawn

**greenhouse**  glass-enclosed building for growing plants

**grotto**  cavelike summer structure or shrine

**grounds**  land surrounding house, esp. lawns and garden

**guesthouse**  small building separate from main structure, often with bathroom and kitchen, used to accommodate visitors

**hedge**  dense shrubbery forming boundary or enclosure; hedgerow

**hedgerow**  *Chiefly Brit.* hedge

**hothouse**  artificially heated greenhouse for tropical plants

**hutch**  animal pen

**incinerator**  container for burning refuse

**kennel**  series of cages or living quarters for dogs

**kiosk**  small pavilion, open on one or more sides, used as newsstand, bandstand, or covered entryway

**lathhouse**  structure with walls and roof of narrow lath strips

**latrine**  outdoor pit used as toilet, often enclosed; outhouse

**lattice**  openwork structure of crossed strips used as screen or support

**lawn**  flat expanse of mowed grass

**manger**  open food trough in stable, for horses or cattle

**mew**  *Chiefly Brit.* stables built along courtyard or alley

**moat**  wide trench around building or fortified place, usu. filled with water

**nursery**  building in which plants are grown, esp. for transplanting

**orchard**  field of cultivated fruit trees

**outhouse**  latrine

**paddock**  enclosed field for pasturing or exercising animals

**paling fence**  picket fence

**palisade**  stake or paling fence used for defense

**parterre**  ornamental flower beds set among paths

**path**  usu. unpaved walkway through grounds or garden

**patio**  usu. paved area adjoining house, used esp. for outdoor dining and recreation

**pavilion**  open tent, building, or shelter adjoining main body of building or separate from it

**pergola**  openwork arch or covering for walkway with plants trained on it; arbor or trellis

**picket fence**  fence of thin, white, vertical boards pointed at tops; paling fence

**pigpen**  fenced area for swine

**pool**  hole or large vessel lined with stones, concrete, or other material and filled with water, used for fish or swimming

**privy**  outhouse, latrine

**promenade**  public walk; gallery or balcony for walking

**quad**  *Informal.* courtyard surrounded by buildings on four sides

**rail fence**  barrier of crossed stakes connected by bars

**railing**  fence or barrier of horizontal rails and widely spaced supports

**rock garden**  ornamental garden laid out among rocks

**septic tank**  sunken container in which solid organic sewage is decomposed by bacteria

**snake fence**  zigzag fence of rails lying across one another at an angle; Virginia fence; worm fence

**snow fence**  barrier on windward side of structure, serving as protection from drifting snow

**stable**  building for housing livestock

**stake-and-rider**  fence with top bar supported by cross stakes

**stall**  compartment for domestic animal in barn; small booth or freestanding display stand

**stile**  series of steps for passing over fence or wall

**stoa**  usu. detached portico with colonnade, used for meetings or shelter (ancient Greece)

**stockyard**  large holding area for livestock being transported, often to slaughter

**stone wall**  barrier or boundary of piled rocks

**sunken garden**  cultivated area lying in ground depression

**sunk fence**  wall or fence set in ditch to create barrier without marring landscape

**swimming pool**  large water-filled tank for swimming, usu. made of concrete, set above or sunk into ground adjacent to house

**swing**  seat suspended freely at end of rope or chain

**tack room**  stable room for storage of riding gear and display of trophies

**tennis court**  measured area with net for playing tennis, adjacent to house and yard

**terrace**  unroofed, paved area adjacent to building

**toolshed**  small enclosure for storage of tools

**topiary**  hedge of trees or shrubs trimmed into ornamental, often fantastic shapes

**trellis**  open structure of thin crossed strips used to support vines or plants

**vegetable garden**  bed of earth for growing vegetables for personal use

**viaduct**  bridge of several short spans, supported on towers, that carries road or railroad across valley

**vineyard**  field of cultivated grapevines

**Virginia fence**  snake fence

**walkway**  open or covered passageway through garden

**weir**  stake fence or net enclosure in waterway for catching fish

**well**  hole sunk into earth to tap water supply

**woodshed**  small outbuilding for storing firewood

**worm fence**  snake fence

**yard**  open area adjacent to house, often walled and paved; lawns and unpaved grounds of building

**xyst**  long, covered portico for exercise in winter (ancient Greece); garden walk lined with trees (ancient Rome)

**zigzag fence**  fence running in series of sharp turns and bends

# INTERIOR STRUCTURE

Rooms
Parts of Rooms
Doors, Partitions, and Walls
Structural and Decorative Elements
Plumbing, Heating, and the Bathroom

**SEE ALSO**: Chap. 5: Structural Components; Chap. 7: Exterior Structure; Ornamental and Functional Articles; Chap. 16: Architecture

# ROOMS

**antechamber** outer room leading to another room, often used as waiting room

**anteroom** antechamber

**atelier** artist's studio or workshop

**atrium** central hall, often with open roof, off which other rooms open (ancient Rome)

**attic** room immediately below roof; cockloft; garret

**auditorium** large, open room used for public gatherings

**ballroom** large, open room for dancing

**banquet room** large room, esp. in hotel or restaurant, used to serve elaborate meals to numerous persons

**basement** room wholly or partly beneath ground level; cellar

**bathroom** room containing bathtub or shower, wash basin, and toilet

**bedchamber** bedroom

**bedroom** room containing bed, used for sleeping

**ben** inner room, esp. combined parlor and bedroom of two-room cottage (Scotland)

**boudoir** *French.* bedroom

**buttery** pantry; provision room off kitchen

**calefactory** warmed sitting room in monastery

**catacomb** burial vault beneath ground level

**cave** cellar; underground storage room, esp. for wine

**cavern** large underground chamber

**cell** small, single room for one person, esp. in prison or monastery

**cellar** storage room beneath ground level; basement; cave

**chamber** room

**chancellery** office of chancellor or secretary to high personage

**chapel** room for meditation, prayer, or religious services

**checkroom** place where baggage or clothing is left for safe-keeping; cloakroom; coatroom

**cloakroom** checkroom; anteroom to legislative chamber

**closet** small, private room

**coatroom** checkroom

**cockloft** small garret; attic

**conservatory** glass-enclosed room for growing and displaying plants or flowers; greenhouse

**corridor** hall

**cubiculum** small family burial chamber in catacombs (ancient Rome)

**cyclone cellar** storm cellar

**den** small room for solitary work; study

**dining room** room for eating, usu. between kitchen and living room

**drawing room** formal reception room; living room; sitting room

**dressing room** small room adjoining bedroom, with mirror, dressing table, wardrobe; backstage area in theater where actors put on costumes

**elevator** enclosure with sliding door, suspended on pulley system for transporting passengers or freight from one floor to another of structure; lift

**entertainment center** TV room

**exhibition hall** salon

**family room** informal living room for leisure activities, often with television; playroom

**foyer** vestibule

**garage** storage area outside main house, esp. for automobiles

**garret** room just below roof, esp. with sloping roof; attic; cockloft

**greenhouse** conservatory

**guest room** bedroom reserved for use by guests

**hall** passageway between rooms; entrance room of building; hallway

**hallway** hall

**hidden chamber** room with concealed entrance

**keep** strongest, most secure part of castle

**kitchen** room where food is prepared, usu. equipped with oven, range, refrigerator, sink, and counters

**landing** level area at end of flight of stairs

**larder** small room or closet for food storage

**laundry** small utility room with washing machine and dryer for laundering clothes

**library** room where books are stored on shelves; study

**lift** *Chiefly Brit.* elevator

**living room** room for common social usage, often largest room in house; drawing room; sitting room

**lobby** corridor or hall serving as passageway or waiting room adjoining larger rooms; hotel or theater foyer

**loft** attic; room above floor level within larger room

**master bedroom** large bedroom used by primary adult occupants of house

**multipurpose room** family room or utility room

**nursery** baby's room

**office** study; room designed or used for work

**pantry** small room for storage, esp. of kitchen supplies; serving room between kitchen and dining room

**parlor** room for entertaining guests

**pavilion** detached or semidetached division of building, often for display of objects

**playroom** family room; children's rumpus room

**porch** roofed or enclosed projection from main portion of structure, serving as entrance or sunroom

**powder room** women's rest room, esp. in restaurant or nightclub

**refectory** dining hall, esp. in monastery or convent

**repository** storage room

**rest room** bathroom, esp. in public building

**room** partitioned section of inside of building, usu. for some specific purpose

**rumpus room** room for parties, games, or recreation, often in basement

**sacristy** room in church for storing sacred vessels and vestments

**sala** large reception hall or sitting room

**salon** elegant apartment or living room; exhibition hall

**scullery** room adjoining kitchen, used for cleaning and storage of cookware and other rough kitchen work

**sitting room** drawing room; living room

**solarium** glass-enclosed sunroom

**stoop** small porch at entrance of house, often enclosed

**storeroom** room for storage of supplies

**storm cellar** basement room or excavation secured for protection against windstorms; cyclone cellar

**studio** artist's workroom; place in which audio or video recordings are made

**study** office, library, or room for studying

**sunroom** solarium

**throne room** formal audience room containing sovereign's throne

**tomb** subterranean chamber or vault, esp. for burial of the dead

**TV room** recreation or family room with television set; entertainment center

**utility room** laundry room

**veranda** roofed, screened porch or gallery

**vestibule** small entrance hall or room; enclosed passageway leading into building; foyer

**ward** section of prison; hospital room for several patients

**wine cellar** cool subterranean storage room for wine

**wing** portion of building that projects from main part

**workroom** workshop

**workshop** room for performing manual labor or making handicrafts; workroom

## PARTS OF ROOMS

**aisle** passage for walking between sections of seating or tall shelves

**alcove** recessed portion of room, open at one end; niche

**altar** raised structure for religious rituals

**ambry** recess in church wall for storage of sacramental vessels

**apse** recessed, usu. vaulted, semicircular portion of room, esp. at end of choir in church

**archway** passage beneath arch; arch over passage

**back stairs** stairs at rear of house

**balcony** railed platform extending from wall of second or higher story

**bandstand** platform in ballroom on which musicians perform

**bay** angular, recessed section of room projecting outward from exterior wall, often with windows on several walls

**bema** part of Eastern church containing altar

**built-in** immovable part of room that is integral to larger construction

**cabinet** case with doors and shelves, sometimes attached to wall

**ceiling** overhead inside lining of room adjoining tops of walls

**chancel** enclosed space around altar of church, designed for use by clergy and officials

**china closet** closet for storing dining supplies

**clavel** *Chiefly Brit.* mantel over fireplace

**closet** cabinet, recess, or small room for storage

**coffer** recessed panel in ceiling or vault

**corner** point where two converging walls meet

**counter** flat, built-in work surface

**cubbyhole** small space open on one side

**cubicle** small space partitioned off from main room

**cupboard** attached cabinet with shelves for storing kitchenwares and supplies; *Chiefly Brit.* any small closet

**dais** platform raised above floor level in hall or large room

**dumbwaiter** small elevator for conveying food, dishes, etc. from one floor to another

**entresol** mezzanine

**escalator** power-driven stairs on endless belt continuously ascending or descending

**fireplace** framed opening of stone or brick in chimney that holds open fire; hearth

**flight of stairs** staircase

**floor** underfoot inside base of room adjoining wall bottoms

**gallery** balcony or covered walk along wall at second story

**hearth** fireplace

**ingle** *Chiefly Brit.* large open fireplace

**ledge** narrow flat surface projecting from wall

**locker** storage cupboard or compartment secured with lock

**loft** raised section of room with floor, often reached by ladder

**loggia** roofed or open gallery, esp. facing inner court, often extending several stories

**mantel** facing of stone, marble, wood, or brick above and around fireplace; shelf above fireplace

**mezzanine** mid level of room between floor and ceiling, extending partway over ground floor; entresol

**mihrab** prayer niche facing Mecca in wall of mosque

**minbar** pulpit of Islamic mosque

**niche** alcove

**panel** flat, rectangular, distinct section of wall

**paneling** wall area composed of panels

**piano nobile** *Italian.* principal story of large building or villa

**platform** section of flooring raised above room level

**podium** speaker's platform

**pulpit** podium in church for minister

**riser** series of long, narrow platforms that are combined like steps for group of spectators or performers

**rostrum** raised platform, esp. for public speaker

**safe** secure receptacle for storage of valuables, often hidden in wall

**shelf** long, flat piece of material fastened horizontally to wall, used for storage

**shutter** movable, attached window shade of inflexible material

**split-level** section of room raised above floor level, reached by stairs

**stage** large platform, usu. at end of room, for performances

**staircase** structure containing stairs; flight of stairs

**stairs** series of steps leading from one level to another

**stairway** one or more flights of stairs with connective landings

**stairwell** vertical shaft in building containing stairway

**steps** stairs

**Tiepolo ceiling** decorative Italian Renaissance ceiling

**tokonoma** niche or shallow recess for display (Japan)

**trottoir** escalatorlike moving ramp on level floor

**walk-in closet** very large closet

**wardrobe** large closet for clothing

**window bench** window seat

**window seat** shelf attached to wall beneath window for sitting; window bench

## DOORS, PARTITIONS, AND WALLS

**back door** rear entrance to house

**baffle** screen or partition used to control passage of light or sound

**bulkhead** upright partition

**door** swinging or sliding barrier across entryway

**doorway** entrance into building, closed by door

**double leaves** two doors, hinged at sides, opening in middle

**Dutch door** door divided horizontally so that upper or lower half may be opened independently

**folding door** door with hinged sections that can be folded back, accordion style; one of pair of sliding doors between rooms

**French doors** two adjoining doors, hinged at sides, opening in middle, with glass panes throughout all or most of their length

**hopper casement** window frame with superimposed fanlights, used in hospitals

**jalousie** window shade or door made of adjustable slats to regulate flow of air or light

**partition** interior dividing wall, sometimes movable and not reaching to ceiling

**pier** wall between two openings; vertical structural support; section of wall between windows

**pocket door** usu. one of a pair of communicating doors that slides into and out of recess in wall

**reredos** back wall of fireplace or open hearth; ornamental wood or stone partition behind altar

**screen** movable partition used to conceal or protect area of room

**sliding door** unhinged door, frequently of glass, that slides open and shut, esp. between rooms

**standing wall** wall providing support to ceiling and floor above

**transom** small, hinged window directly over door

**trapdoor** lifting or sliding door covering opening in and flush with ceiling or floor

**wall** one side of room connecting floor and ceiling

## STRUCTURAL AND DECORATIVE ELEMENTS

**arch** curved structural support member spanning an opening: basket-handle, flat, horseshoe, lancet, ogee, parabolic, round, shouldered, trefoil, Tudor

**architrave** molded, decorated band of wood forming panel or opening for door or window; lowest part of entablature

**architvolt** ornamental molding around arch

**arris** sharp ridge formed at meeting of two surfaces

**backsplash** strip of water-resistant tile or formica above sink or beside bathtub

**baldachin** ornamental canopy over altar or important person

**baluster** upright, vase-shaped support for railing

**balustrade** row of balusters topped by railing

**band** narrow decorative or binding strip

**banister** handrail or balustrade

**barrel roof** ceiling having semicylindrical, vaulted form

**baseboard** molding covering juncture of wall and adjoining floor

**bas relief** raised ornamental molding, plasterwork, or sculpted stone on flat wall surface

**beam** principal horizontal support structure of building

**border** ornamental design along edge of wall or floor

**brace** structural element that transmits or supports weight

**bracket** projecting shelf support, often decorative

**bridgeboard** notched board acting as a string to support stair treads and risers

**canopy** rooflike covering of fabric on poles

**casement** hinged frame opening outward for French doors or double windows

**casing** enclosing frame around door or window

**chink** strip of wood used to cover gap between logs in log cabin

**colonnade** series of columns at regular intervals

**colonnette** small colonnade

**column** vertical supporting pillar; post

**compluvium** square opening in sloping roof over atrium through which rain falls into impluvium (ancient Rome)

**console** member projecting from wall to form bracket

**corona** crown-shaped projection above bed from which drapery is hung

**course** continuous horizontal layer of stone, bricks, or tiles in wall

**cover strip** decorative molding or length of material used to conceal structural parts

**coving** carved molding that connects ceiling and wall

**cresting** ornamental ridging on wall or ceiling

**curtain rod** horizontal suspension piece for curtain

**dado** lower part of wall separated from upper part by rail, molding, or border

**embrasure** side of window between frame and outer surface of wall; opening in wall sloped to large interior outline; reveal

**engaged column** column which is not freestanding but attached to wall

**fillet** flat molding separating other moldings

**fluted column** column with long, rounded, vertical grooves

**frieze** richly ornamented band; entablature between architrave and cornice

**girder** primary horizontal structural member supporting vertical load

**handrail** railing on staircase or gallery; banister

**hob** projection at back or side of fireplace on which pot is hung to be kept warm

**jamb** side post of doorway, window frame, or other opening

**lacunar** coffered vault, ceiling, or soffit

**machicolation** opening between corbels or in gallery floor for discharging missiles onto assailants below

**molding** ornamental strip of wood separating sections of wall or at juncture of wall and ceiling: bird's beak, cavetto, congé, cyma recta, cyma reversa, fillet and fascia, ovolo, plate rail, quarter round, reeding, scotia, torus

**mullion** slender, vertical dividing bar in window or screen

**newel** central upright pillar of winding staircase

**newel post** post supporting one end of handrail on flight of stairs

**nosing** usu. rounded edge of stair tread that projects over riser

**ogive** diagonal pointed arch or rib on Gothic vault

**parapet** protective low wall or railing

**pargeting** ornamental plasterwork on walls or ceiling

**parquetry** inlaid woodwork in geometric forms of different colors, esp. in floor

**pegboard** board perforated with holes for pegs on which objects are hung

**pelmet** valance

**pillar** firm, upright support or post; ornamental column or shaft

**plate rail** narrow shelf on upper wall for holding plates and ornaments

**post** upright piece, column

**rafters** angled crossbeams in roof, sometimes exposed

**railing** barrier, fence, or baluster of rails and supports; handgrip on baluster or gallery

**reglet** flat, narrow architectural molding

**reveal** embrasure

**ridgepole** highest horizontal member in roof

**riser** upright member between stair treads

**scalloping** continuous series of circle segments or angular projections forming border

**scrolling** spiral or convoluted ornamentation, esp. in wood

**scupper** opening in wall at roof or floor level for water drainage

**slat** thin, narrow, flat strip of wood or metal

**soffit** underside of structural member or part of building, such as overhang of staircase

**squinch** support at corner of room for superimposed mass such as arch, lintel, or corbel

**template** horizontal piece placed in wall under beam to distribute weight over door

**tracery** branching, interlacing ornamental work, esp. stonework in upper part of Gothic window or vault

**trave** division or bay in ceiling made by traverse beams

**traverse rod** horizontal metal rod on which curtains slide open and shut, controlled by lines and pulleys

**tread** upper horizontal part of stair

**valance** strip of fabric on frame that covers sides of bed or top of window frame; pelmet

**vault** arched, domed, usu. masonry structure forming ceiling

**viga** heavy rafter or log that supports roof in native Indian and Spanish architecture (Southwest U.S.)

**wainscoting** lower section of wall or story when distinct from top section, esp. when wood-paneled

**window frame** casement, jamb, and sill of window

**window sill** horizontal member at bottom of window frame

## PLUMBING, HEATING, AND THE BATHROOM

**basin** circular vessel with sloping sides and drain, used to hold water for washing

**bath** bathroom; bathtub

**bathroom** room containing bathtub and/or shower, plus wash basin and toilet; sometimes used to denote room with toilet and wash basin only

**bathtub** large, fixed tub for bathing

**bidet** chairlike fixture for bathing genitals and anus

**calidarium** hot-water room in public bath (ancient Rome)

**can** *Vulgar slang.* toilet bowl; bathroom

**cloaca** *Archaic.* sewer; toilet bowl

**comfort station** public bathroom

**commode** movable washstand with cupboard underneath; box holding chamber pot under open seat

**crapper** *Vulgar slang.* bathroom

**faucet** fixture through which water flows; tap

**Franklin stove** iron fireplace connected to chimney by funnel

**furnace** enclosed chamber, usu. in basement, where heat is produced to warm building

**half bath** bathroom with basin and toilet only

**hammam** communal bathhouse in Islamic countries, usu. with separate facilities for men and women

**head** toilet, esp. on ship

**impluvium** cistern, tank in floor of atrium that receives water from compluvium (ancient Rome)

**jakes** toilet

**john** *Slang.* toilet

**lavatory** toilet; bathroom

**loo** *Brit. informal.* bathroom

**ofuro** large Japanese-style bath, often of wood or stone, used by several people simultaneously

**radiator** nest of pipes for heating room by steam

**rest room** bathroom, esp. in public building

**sauna** hot, dry-air bath in enclosed wooden room, used to induce perspiration

**shower** enclosed stall with overhead water outlet for bathing

**sink** stationary basin connected to drain and water supply

**steam room** tiled room designed to expose user to steam in order to induce sweating

**tank** enclosed vessel holding water, esp. for toilet

**tap** *Chiefly Brit.* faucet

**toilet** bathroom fixture with seats over bowl through which water is flushed to dispose of human waste material; bathroom

**tub** bathtub

**wash basin** sink with running water used in bathing, esp. washing face and hands

**water closet** WC; toilet

**WC** *water closet*

**wet bar** counter for mixing drinks, with built-in sink and running water

**whirlpool** soothing bath in which jets agitate very hot water

**wood-burning stove** enclosed metal unit that burns wood for heat, with vent to dispense smoke out of house

# FURNISHINGS

Chairs and Sofas
Beds
Tables and Desks
Cases, Cupboards, and Chests
Stools and Stands
Curtains, Draperies, and Screens
Carpets and Rugs
Lamps and Mirrors
Accessories and Appliances

**SEE ALSO**: Chap. 7: Interior Structure; Ornamental and Functional Articles; Chap. 9: The Kitchen; Chap. 10: Ornaments and Accessories

## CHAIRS AND SOFAS

**Adirondack chair** wooden outdoor chair with sloping back and seat declining to rear

**armchair**  chair, often hardback, with sidepieces to support person's forearms or elbows

**banquette**  long, upholstered bench, often built into wall; sofa with one rollover arm

**barber chair**  heavy-duty, adjustable, swiveling chair with headrest and footrest

**Barcelona chair**  armless, leather-covered chair with cushioned seat on X-shaped stainless steel frame

**basket chair**  deep wicker chair with rounded back and adjoining arms

**Bath chair**  hooded, often glassed invalid's wheelchair

**bench**  long, backless seat for several persons

**Brewster chair**  heavy colonial chair with upright spindles in two tiers on the back and below the seat

**butterfly chair**  canvas or leather sling chair, with sling suspended from metal frame

**camp chair**  light, folding chair, often with canvas seat and back

**captain's chair**  chair with rounded back in which vertical spindles support rail that forms arms

**Carver chair**  heavy, turned colonial chair with three vertical and three horizontal spindles in back

**cathedra**  official chair or bishop's throne

**chair**  seat for one person, usu. four-legged, with backrest and sometimes armrests

**chaise**  couchlike lounging seat with leg and back supports

**chaise longue**  couchlike seat lengthened to form leg rest and with raised back support at one end

**channel back chair**  upholstered chair or sofa with deep vertical grooves in backrest

**chesterfield**  large, heavily stuffed sofa with upholstered upright arms

**Chippendale chair**  graceful, ornately ornamented chair in English style (18th c.)

**club chair**  deep, low, heavily upholstered easy chair with low back, solid sides and arms

**collapsible chair**  folding chair

**comb back chair**  Windsor chair with comblike vertical spindles topped by a curved top rail

**confidente**  sofa divided by armrests into large center section with triangular flanking seats (18th c.)

**contour chair**  chair designed to fit form of human body

**couch**  long, upholstered, stuffed seat for two or more persons, with back and armrests at one or both ends; sofa

**courting chair**  love seat

**curule chair**  folding, backless seat reserved for high dignitaries (ancient Rome)

**Dante chair**  Savonarola chair

**davenport**  large, upholstered sofa that converts to bed

**daybed**  armless couch with long seat and sloping back, for reclining or sleeping (18th c.)

**deck chair**  folding chair of metal or other durable material for outdoor use

**Derbyshire chair**  armless oak chair with broad carved top rail between square uprights; Yorkshire chair (Britain, 17th c.)

**desk chair**  upright chair designed for sitting at desk, often with armrests

**dining chair**  small upright chair for sitting at dining table, usu. armless

**director's chair**  folding armchair with canvas seat and back panel on wood frame

**divan**  large couch or sofa, usu. without back or arms

**dos-à-dos**  seat or sofa built so occupants sit back to back

**duchesse**  *French.* daybed with rounded, covered head, often in two or three pieces

**Eames chair**  armless chair with seat and back of molded plywood attached to tubular steel frame

**easy chair**  stuffed, upholstered, comfortable chair

**ergonomic chair**  work chair specially designed for comfort and support of back and neck

**fanback chair**  Windsor chair having spindle back spread like fan from seat to upper rail

**farthingale chair**  armless chair with high seat and low, straight back

**fauteuil**  *French.* stuffed arm chair

**folding chair**  usu. armless seat on legs that fold flat against it; collapsible chair

**Glastonbury chair**  small, light, folding chair, with two crossed straight legs at each side and arms connected to front seat rail

**highchair**  infant's chair on tall legs with attached shelf for food

**inglenook**  bench in nook by open fireplace

**lawn chair**  reclining chair, usu. of durable material, for outdoor use

**lounge chair**  long seat with headrest, used for reclining

**love seat**  small sofa with arms, suitable for two persons; courting chair

**méridienne**  *French.* short sofa with one arm higher than the other

**morris chair**  easy chair with adjustable back and removable cushions

**ottoman**  stuffed, long, low cushioned seat without back or arms, sometimes circular, able to accommodate several people

**overstuffed chair**  heavily padded, upholstered easy chair

**page chair**  porter chair

**parlor chair**  dining room chair with low back and no arms (18th c.)

**pew**  long wooden bench with back for seating in church

**platform rocker**  rocking chair with base set on curved rockers

**porch swing**  bench seat freely suspended from ceiling on porch

**porter chair**  straight-backed chair with enclosed side walls that form arch over seat; page chair (18th c.)

**potty-chair**  infant's low seat with removable bowl, used for toilet training

**pouf**  plumply cushioned, usu. circular, backless couch

**prayer chair**  low, stiff-backed, armless chair

**prie-dieu**  low bench fitted with shelf, used for kneeling during prayer

**recliner**  chair with adjustable reclining back

**rocker**  rocking chair

**rocking chair**  chair on two curved members that connect its front and back feet, allowing it to rock back and forth; rocker

**rout seat**  small, armless seat set along wall in ballroom

**Savonarola chair**  Renaissance chair with several pairs of interlaced curved slats extending from their intersection beneath the seat to form sides and legs; Dante chair; scissors chair (Italy)

**scissors chair**  Savonarola chair

**seat**  any chair, bench, or stool on which people sit

**sectional** sofa composed of modular sections that can be arranged in various combinations

**settee** medium or small seat or bench with back and usu. arms

**settle** wooden bench with arms and straight back

**sling chair** canvas or leather back and seat loosely fitted onto wood or metal frame

**slipper chair** low, armless bedroom chair with skirt covering short legs

**sociable** S-shaped sofa with two seats partially facing each other

**sofa** upholstered seat for three or more persons with fixed back and arms at each end; couch

**sofa bed** sofa with removable cushions and fold-out mattress

**spindle-back chair** chair with woven seat and carved rods from seat to top rail

**squab** couch with removable, thickly stuffed, soft cushions

**stall** fixed, enclosed seat in church for priest or choir

**stool** low seat without back or arms on three or four legs

**straight-backed chair** seat with upright, usu. high back

**studio couch** small, armless, backless, upholstered couch, convertible to double bed

**swing** seat suspended from frame or ceiling, usu. by chains at each end, for recreational use

**swivel chair** chair that revolves on its base

**tablet chair** seat with one arm widened for use as writing surface, esp. in schools

**tête-à-tête** S-shaped sofa that allows two people to face each other when seated

**throne** royal chair of state, usu. large and ornate

**triclinium** couch or set of couches surrounding three sides of table

**tub chair** *Chiefly Brit.* semicircular, upholstered easy chair with arms and back in one unit

**tuxedo sofa** overstuffed sofa with slightly curved arms at same height as back

**wagon seat** pair of attached, slat-back post chairs

**wicker chair** chair of plaited or woven twigs, often with high, fan-shaped back

**Windsor chair** wooden chair with curved spindle back, legs slanting outward, and saddle seat (18th c.)

**wing chair** large, upholstered armchair having high, solid back and winged sides

**Yorkshire chair** Derbyshire chair

# BEDS

**angel bed** bed with suspended canopy extending partway over it (French); bed without posts

**bassinet** infant's portable bed with hood over one end

**bed** usu. stuffed mattress with springs, in various sizes, for sleeping upon, often with frame of wood or metal

**bedroll** portable bedding that rolls up

**bedstead** frame and headboard for bed that supports springs and mattress

**berth** sleeping accommodation on ship or vehicle, often folding out from wall

**box spring** mattress base of spiral springs enclosed in cloth-covered frame

**bunk bed** two beds on frame set one above the other

**canopy** ornamental rooflike structure over bed, esp. cloth

**car bed** portable bed for infant, used in automobile

**charpoy** bedstead or cot frame strung with light rope (India)

**cot** flat, folding bed without padding, often of canvas

**cradle** infant's bed on legs with rockers

**crib** infant's bed, usu. having slatted sides

**davenport** large, upholstered sofa that converts to bed

**double bed** mattress and box spring for two persons, smaller than queen-size bed, 54 inches (137 cm) wide; full-size bed

**feather mattress** soft mattress stuffed with feathers

**foldaway bed** bed designed to double over and slide aside or out of view when not in use; folding bed

**folding bed** foldaway bed

**fourposter** traditional bed with upright post at each corner to support canopy or curtains

**French bed** postless bedstead with head and foot rolled outward in scroll form

**full-size bed** double bed

**futon** folding, Japanese-style sleeping pad stuffed with cotton batting

**gurney** rolling cot or stretcher for carrying sick or injured persons

**hammock** hanging bed of netting or canvas suspended from supports by cords attached at each end

**headboard** upright board forming head of bed

**hospital bed** adjustable bed with movable, criblike protective sides and variable positions, designed for hospital patients

**king-size bed** extra large mattress and box spring, at least 76 inches (193 cm) wide

**mattress** fabric case filled with resilient material, used as bed or on bedstead or box spring

**Murphy bed** bed on metal frame that folds into wall or closet when not in use

**paillase** straw mattress; pallet

**pallet** straw bed or hard mattress of poor quality; paillase

**poster bed** bed with upright posts at two or four corners

**queen-size bed** mattress and box spring larger than double bed, smaller than king-size bed, 60 inches (152 cm) wide

**rack** *Slang.* bed

**rollaway** bed on folding frame with wheels for easy storage

**single bed** narrow mattress and box spring for one person, 39 inches (102 cm) wide

**sofa bed** sofa with removable cushions and fold-out mattress

**tatami mat** thick, woven, straw floor mat, usu. grouped together in sections, on which futon rests (Japan)

**tester** bed with frame for canopy

**truckle bed** low bed on casters, rolled under higher bed when not in use; trundle bed

**trundle bed** truckle bed

**twin bed** one of pair of single beds, 39 inches (102 cm) wide

**waterbed** bed having large rubber or plastic sack filled with water and set in rigid frame, able to conform to sleeper's body position for comfort

# TABLES AND DESKS

**ambo** raised reading desk in nave of early Christian church

**banquet table** large dining table; long, flat serving table

**bar**  counter at which food and beverages are served

**basin stand**  small table with round hole in top surface to hold wash basin (18th c.)

**bed table**  nightstand

**bench**  long, flat worktable

**billiard table**  rectangular, felt-covered slate table of standardized dimensions for playing billiards

**buffet**  counter or table for serving food

**butterfly table**  small drop-leaf table with round or oval top, leaves supported by brackets shaped like butterfly wings

**capstan table**  drum table

**card table**  small, flat, square table with folding legs; folding table

**carrel**  table or desk with three sides raised above surface to serve as partitions for private study, esp. in library

**cocktail table**  coffee table

**coffee table**  long, low table usu. set before sofa

**computer table**  multilevel desk adapted to hold computer and printer

**console table**  small table supported by ornamental brackets fixed to wall

**counter**  level surface over which transactions are conducted or food served, usu. long and narrow

**credence**  small sideboard or table for valuables, esp. bread and wine used in Eucharist; credenza

**credenza**  credence

**davenport**  *Chiefly Brit.* small writing desk

**desk**  table with flat surface for writing, often with drawers or compartments

**dinette**  small table for informal dining, usu. in kitchen

**dining table**  large round, rectangular, or oblong table, often with leaves, at which meals are eaten

**door desk**  desk or tabletop formed by setting door across supporting drawers or legs

**drawing table**  flat surface adjustable to various heights and angles

**drop-leaf table**  table with hinged ends or leaves that may be lowered and insertible sections to increase length, esp. for dining

**drum table**  table having cylindrical top with drawers or shelves, rotating on a central post with three or four outwardly curving legs; capstan table

**end table**  small table, usu. with one drawer, that stands at end of couch or beside chair

**envelope table**  small table with triangular drop leaf or leaves

**escritoire**  writing desk

**extension table**  table with insertible leaf or leaves to increase length

**folding table**  usu. small, flat table with legs that flatten against the underside of the top surface when stored; card table

**gate-leg table**  table with movable paired legs on hinges that swing out to support drop leaves

**kitchen table**  informal dining table in kitchen; dinette

**kneehole desk**  flat-topped desk with space for knees between drawers

**lamp table**  small table that holds reading lamp beside chair

**leaf**  hinged or removable section of table that changes table's length

**lectern**  chest-high, stand-up reading desk for school or church

**nesting tables**  set of usu. three or four tables graduated in size so that they may be stacked together

**nightstand**  small, low table standing at bedside, often with single drawer; bed table; night table

**night table**  nightstand

**Parsons table**  square, contemporary table whose straight legs are flush with the edges of the top so as to appear jointless

**Pembroke table**  small table with two drop leaves and one drawer (18th c.)

**piecrust table**  round table with raised decorative edge like piecrust

**pier table**  table designed to stand against a wall between and below two windows

**pool table**  billiard table with pockets at corners and on sides, used for playing pool

**pouch table**  small worktable with fabric bag suspended under top to hold needlepoint, chess pieces, or other tools

**refectory table**  long, heavy, narrow table with trestlelike legs connected by a single strip

**rent table**  drum table with circular top and six drawers (18th c.)

**roll-top desk**  writing desk with sliding, flexible cover that rolls up beneath top

**salon table**  long, dining-height serving table

**secretary**  upright writing desk with bookshelves on top and foldout writing space

**sideboard**  dining room table with compartments and shelves for table service articles

**side table**  small table without drawers, usu. placed beside dining table or against wall

**step table**  small table topped by one or more progressively narrower shelves

**table**  smooth, flat surface supported usu. by four legs

**tambour**  rolling desk top of rounded wood strips glued to canvas

**teapoy stand**  small, ornamental, three-legged table that supports tea chest or caddy for tea service

**tray table**  small folding table with low rim around surface, often with crossed pairs of legs

**tripod**  stool, table, or altar with three legs

**trolley**  cart or stand on wheels used for conveying things

**TV table**  usu. metal, lightweight, folding tray table, used for eating in front of television

**typewriter table**  small, flat table, often on wheels, used to hold typewriter

**vargueno**  decorative, fall-front writing desk or chest on low table (Spain, 17th c.)

**workbench**  large, flat, sturdy table at which craftsman works

**writing desk**  flat-topped table with drawers or pigeonholes; escritoire

**writing table**  desk with retractable drawer used as writing surface and pigeonhole cupboard above, sometimes roll top

## CASES, CUPBOARDS, AND CHESTS

**armoire**  tall, movable cupboard or wardrobe

**Biedermeier cabinet**  cabinet, usu. of fruitwood with matched veneers, incorporating architectural motifs (Germany, 19th c.)

**bin** enclosed box, frame, or crib for storage

**bookcase** set of bookshelves in freestanding unit

**bookshelves** open, multilevel storage area for books

**breakfront** large cabinet with center section standing out from flanks

**buffet** drawers and cupboards for storage of dishes and linen; sideboard

**bunker** storage bin or compartment, esp. on ship

**bureau** chest of drawers for storage, often with mirror standing on top

**cabinet** standing storage unit with shelves and drawers

**caddy** container or rack for storing objects when not in use

**canterbury** small stand with tray top and upright partitions to hold music, magazines, or papers

**case** box or receptacle for enclosing objects

**cellarette** sideboard for bottles of wine or liquor

**chest** large, solid wood piece with lid and often interior drawers for storage; chest of drawers

**chest of drawers** upright set of enclosed storage receptacles on frame with short legs; dresser

**chiffonier** ornamental cabinet with shelves, drawers, and sometimes with mirror; tall, narrow chest of drawers

**chifforobe** combination wardrobe and chest of drawers

**china cabinet** standing storage shelves for china that requires protection or deserves display

**clothes chest** enclosed, heavy-topped container for clothing

**coffer** chest or strongbox for valuables

**commode** low, ornate chest of drawers; movable washstand with cupboard underneath

**console** large cabinet that rests on floor, esp. housing radio and/or television

**crate** wood slat storage or shipping box, usu. open on top

**credenza** large buffet or sideboard, often without legs; closed cabinet for papers and office supplies, often of desk height

**crib** rack or framework storage enclosure

**cupboard** small closet with storage shelves

**display case** enclosed, glass-faced unit for storage and exhibition of objects

**dresser** chest of drawers for clothing with flat top, often with mirror

**étagère** cabinet of tiered shelves open on all sides

**filing cabinet** vertical storage unit for papers, with two or more sliding drawers, usu. metal

**hamper** large, covered basket for storage or transport

**highboy** tall chest of drawers with legs; tallboy

**Hoosier cabinet** tall oak kitchen cabinet with drawers, shelves, breadboard, and enameled work surface

**hope chest** trunk in which young woman collects linens and clothing in anticipation of marriage

**hutch** bin or chest for storage

**kitchen cabinet** enclosed unit containing storage shelves, usu. mounted on kitchen wall

**locker** small drawer or compartment for secure storage when closed with lock

**lowboy** three-foot high dressing table with drawers on short legs

**mantel** shelf above fireplace

**playpen** small, often collapsible enclosure in which young child may play without close supervision

**poudreuse** small dressing table with mirror (18th c.)

**press** closet or cupboard, esp. large cupboard shelf with small cupboards behind it (16th c.)

**rack** framework of open shelves on which articles may be placed

**safe** sturdy, usu. cast-iron receptacle with strong lock, used for storing valuables

**sarcophagus** wooden, coffinlike wine cooler under sideboard

**shelf** thin, long strip of material, often wood, fastened horizontally on wall or in frame to support objects

**shelves** set of horizontal strips arranged vertically on wall

**sideboard** buffet or dining-room piece, used for storage of linen, silver, and china, or for serving food

**strongbox** sturdy receptacle with lock for storage of valuables

**tallboy** chest with seven or more drawers in two stacks and two small drawers on top; highboy

**tea caddy** small box, can, or chest for storing tea

**tea wagon** tea caddy on wheels for service

**trunk** large storage box of wood or metal

**vanity** lady's dressing table with small case for cosmetics; wide shelf around wash basin, often with shelves or drawers

**vitrine** glass showcase for memorabilia, valuables, and art objects

**wardrobe** freestanding closet fitted with hooks and bars for hanging clothes

**wet bar** small bar with sink and compartments, used for mixing and serving drinks

**whatnot** stand with open tier shelves on corner posts for books, papers, or ornaments

**Yorkshire dresser** dresser with clock

## Stools and Stands

**bar stool** tall stool, sometimes with low back, for sitting at bar

**bentwood hanger** Victorian-style hanger of wood bent to form hooks

**bier** stand for coffin

**campstool** small, portable folding stool with crossed legs and canvas seat

**cart** small stand with two wheels and two legs, moved by hand

**catafalque** elaborate stand for coffin

**clotheshorse** frame on which to hang laundry for drying

**clothes tree** upright pole with hooks at top for hanging clothes

**coatrack** tall wood or metal stand with hooks for hanging coats

**cricket** low wooden footstool

**cutty stool** low stool, esp. seat in church where offenders against chastity received public rebuke (Scotland)

**easel** upright support frame, often with three legs joined at top, esp. for artist's canvas

**foldstool** small stool that folds into compact unit for storage

**footrest** low stool set before chair for feet

**footstool** surface on short legs, used for resting feet while seated

**hall stand** small, flat table in hall

**hassock** firmly stuffed mat or cushion used as footstool

**hatrack** tall spindle with hooks for hanging hats

**lamp stand** small lamp table

**mora** low wicker stool or footstool (India)

**music stand** display case for sheet music with adjustable, inclined surface

**music stool** round stool with adjustable seat that swivels up or down

**pedestal** flat-topped base or stand for display of ornamental object

**prop** supporting stand

**sawhorse** rack for holding wood with crosspiece linking two sets of legs that form inverted V's

**smoking stand** ashtray mounted on tall wood or metal stand, usu. on single upright

**stand** support frame on or in which articles may be placed

**step stool** stool with one or two steps which fold away beneath seat

**stool** low seat without back or arms on three or four legs

**tabouret** cylindrical seat or stool without arms or back; small portable stand for holding work supplies

**tripod** three-legged stand

**truss** tripod of logs or timbers for farm use

**umbrella stand** low, open, often cylindrical receptacle for umbrellas

**work stand** small, metal stand with several movable leaves, covered with loops and hooks for holding supplies

## CURTAINS, DRAPERIES, AND SCREENS

**arras** hanging screen or tapestry on wall

**bamboo shade** hanging bamboo strips used as shade

**blind** roll-up or retractable window shutter or shade

**café curtains** pair of curtains that cover only lower half of window

**curtain** fabric hung on hooks or rod to cover window or adorn wall

**draperies** heavy, decorative material hung in long, loose folds on wall or opening and closing over window; drapes

**drapes** draperies

**fire screen** standing metal screen that keeps sparks from fireplace off rugs or floor

**jalousie** blind with adjustable horizontal slats that admit light and air while excluding rain and sun's rays

**panel** flat wall section used as partition to divide room

**partition** interior wall or barrier that divides room into sections

**priscilla curtains** pair of ruffled, tieback curtains

**purdah** screen or curtain used by Muslims and Hindus to seclude women from sight of men and strangers

**rollup shade** blind, often of cloth, that retracts onto spring roller

**roman shade** one-piece, pleated, fabric window shade

**screen** freestanding partition, often hinged, that shields or separates an area of a room

**shade** flexible screen or fabric mounted over window; window shade

**shoji screen** rice paper mounted on wood frame, used as sliding door or partition (Japan)

**shutter** solid, movable cover or screen for window or door

**tapestry** heavy woven cloth with designs, hung on wall or used as furniture covering

**tieback curtain** curtain held open by tie strip usu. of same material

**valance** drapery hung at top of window or along edge of bed, altar, table, or shelf to conceal another member

**veil** concealing curtain or cloth covering

**venetian blind** window shutter with overlapping, horizontal slats that may be opened, closed, raised, or lowered by pulling a cord

**window shade** flexible sheet covering for window; shade

## CARPETS AND RUGS

**area rug** small rug covering only part of floor; scatter rug

**Aubusson** ornate rug woven to resemble figured scenic Aubusson tapestry, often in pastel colors

**Axminster carpet** machine-woven carpet with pile tufts in variety of textures and many colors

**bearskin** fur of bear used as rug

**Belouch** type of Persian rug

**Bokhara** rich Persian rug

**broadloom** carpet woven on wide loom, esp. in solid color

**Brussels carpet** carpet of colored worsted yarns drawn up in uncut loops to form pattern

**carpet** heavy woven or felted fabric used as floor covering, usu. attached to entire floor and nonmovable

**Caucasian rug** rug woven in Caucasus mountains

**chenille** deep pile fabric used for rugs

**dhurrie** type of Indian rug

**drugget** coarse cotton or jute rug from India

**flokati** handwoven, woolen Greek rug with thick, shaggy pile

**flossa** handwoven Scandinavian carpet

**Heriz** type of Persian rug

**hooked** (adj) designating rug made by drawing loops through coarse fabric with a hook

**Indian rug** rug from India; American Indian rug (as: Navaho, Hopi, Zuni)

**Indo-Heriz** type of Persian rug

**Indo-Tabriz** type of Persian rug

**kilim** pileless woven rug from Turkey, the Caucasus, or Iran

**Kirman** Persian rug with ornate, flowing designs in soft colors

**Kurdistan** Persian-style rug from Kurdistan

**mat** coarse woven fabric or plaited reeds used as floor covering

**moquette** French carpet with velvety pile

**nap** hairy surface of rug

**Navaho rug** Southwest American Indian rug, often in geometric design

**nylon carpeting** machine-made carpet of synthetic nylon yarn

**Oriental rug** rug or carpet from Far East or Asia

**Persian carpet** distinctive rug or carpet in rich colors and intricate designs, made in area of Iran: Afshar, Ardabil, Aubusson, Bijar, Belouch, Farahan, Hamedan, Heriz, Indo-Heriz, Indo-Tabriz, Isfahan, Joshegan, Kashan, Kirman, Ladik, Mashad, Moud, Nain, Pak Persian, Sarough, Serapi, Taba, Yalameh

**pile** velvety surface of rug made by cutting off upright loops of yarn; rug with such a surface

**puma rug** rug of cougar fur

**rag** American folk art rug of cotton or garment scraps in cheerful colors, usu. with rounded ends

**rug** thick, heavy fabric, usu. with nap or pile, used as movable floor covering

**runner** long, rectangular hall rug

**rya** handwoven Scandinavian rug with deep, resilient, flat pile

**Savonnerie**  handmade, one-piece French pile carpet
**Saxony carpet**  rug of fine, closely twisted yarn
**scatter rug**  small rug that covers only part of floor; area rug
**shag**  rug with long, coarse, loose pile
**steamer rug**  warm covering for lap and feet, used esp. at sea
**Tabriz**  Persian rug with cotton warp and wool pile, in medallion design
**tapestry rug**  rug woven in intricate pattern, designed to hang on wall
**throw rug**  small rug
**Tientsin**  distinctive style of Chinese rug
**Turkish**  rug made in Turkey
**Turkoman**  rug made by peoples of eastern Turkey and Soviet Union
**wall-to-wall**  carpeting that covers entire floor of room
**Wilton**  carpet woven with loops and having velvet-cut pile

## LAMPS AND MIRRORS

**arc lamp**  arc light
**arc light**  electric light in which current passes in arc between two incandescent electrodes surrounded by gas; arc lamp
**arm lamp**  lamp with light source at far end of shaft attached to base
**bathing mirror**  small mirror, often attached to bathroom wall or above tub
**bedlamp**  small, focused reading light placed beside or above bed
**chandelier**  branched, ornate, multibulb lighting fixture suspended from ceiling
**cheval glass**  full-length mirror that can be tilted in hinged frame
**Chinese lantern**  light enclosed in translucent paper globe or shade
**desk lamp**  standing lamp beside desk or arm lamp on desk top
**floor lamp**  lamp that stands on floor; standing lamp
**fluorescent lamp**  tubular electric lamp coated on inner surface by fluorescent material and containing mercury vapor
**gaslight**  light fixture that burns illuminating gas
**girandole mirror**  mirror set in ornamental, branched, showy frame
**glass**  mirror
**gooseneck lamp**  desk lamp with long, thin shaft, usu. curved or flexible
**incandescent electric light**  lamp in which filament heated by electric current gives off light
**lamp**  device holding electric bulb, gas, or burning wick, used for illumination
**lampshade**  covering for lamp bulb, made of molded, translucent material; shade
**lantern**  light enclosed in portable, protective case with transparent openings
**light**  device for illumination by electricity
**looking glass**  small mirror, handheld or attached to wall
**mirror**  reflecting glass surface set in frame, usu. mounted on dresser, door, or wall; glass
**neon lamp**  discharge bulb containing neon gas that glows when voltage is applied across two electrodes

**night-light**  small light fixture that faces wall, providing dim light in dark room
**phoebe lamp**  shallow, early American, fat-burning lamp of metal or pottery, with spout for wick and cup to catch drippings
**pier glass**  tall mirror set in wall section between windows
**reading light**  small light placed above bed or beside chair
**searchlight**  light and reflector on rotating base, used to project beam to great distance
**shade**  device partially covering lamp to reduce glare; lampshade
**shaving mirror**  small mirror attached to bathroom wall
**speculum**  optical reflector; ancient mirror of polished bronze or silver
**spot**  spotlight
**spotlight**  lamp that produces powerful, focused beam of light; spot
**standing lamp**  floor lamp
**student lamp**  adjustable desk lamp with one or two arms, esp. oil-burning (19th c.)
**sunlamp**  electric lamp that emits ultraviolet radiations, used to tan skin indoors
**table lamp**  small lamp that stands on table
**task lighting**  lamp mounted to illuminate specific work area, such as kitchen counter or portion of desk
**Tiffany lamp**  lamp with shade of Tiffany stained glass
**toilet glass**  dressing table mirror, often with attached drawer
**torchiere**  tall floor lamp that emits indirect light from source within reflecting bowl that is open at top
**track lighting**  series of small, adjustable spotlights arranged along track, usu. mounted on ceiling
**trouble light**  device that provides emergency illumination or lights hard to reach places, esp. screened bulb on long power cord
**trumeau**  mirror with carved panel above or below glass set in same frame
**uplight**  lamp that projects illumination upward
**vanity lamp**  small, shaded lamp that stands on dressing table
**Venetian lamp**  delicate lamp with shade of Venetian glass
**wall mirror**  usu. tall reflecting glass mounted on wall
**wall washer**  lamp that evenly illuminates large area of wall

## ACCESSORIES AND APPLIANCES

**AC**  air conditioner
**air conditioner**  AC; electrical device that reduces interior temperature and humidity of building or room
**appliance**  any of various service units, usu. operated electrically, found in contemporary homes, esp. in the kitchen: refrigerator, freezer, stove, washing machine, dryer, dishwasher, vacuum cleaner, air conditioner, toaster, blender, food processor, can opener
**basin**  shallow, circular vessel with sloping sides for holding water
**bathtub**  large, usu. fixed vessel for bathing; tub
**bidet**  chairlike fixture for bathing genitals and anus
**ceiling fan**  large fan with circular blade motion, suspended from ceiling
**dishwasher**  enclosed electrical appliance for automatically washing and rinsing dishes
**dryer**  enclosed heater for drying washed clothing

**fan** electrical device for blowing air by movement of series of vanes or blades radiating from hub and revolving on its axis

**Franklin stove** iron, wood-burning stove with exhaust funnel running to chimney

**freezer** section of refrigerator or separate appliance with temperature low enough to freeze and preserve foods

**fridge** *Informal.* refrigerator

**Frigidaire** *Trademark.* type of refrigerator

**furnace** enclosed structure in which heat is produced by gas, oil, coal, or electricity to warm home

**icebox** insulated container with section for ice, used to cool foods

**meat locker** very large freezer, esp. for meat

**oven** fixed or freestanding chamber for baking, heating, roasting, or drying, using heat produced by gas or electricity

**potbelly stove** stove with rounded, bulging body, esp. wood-burning stove shaped thus

**punkah** ceiling fan (India)

**range** cooking stove with oven and flat top equipped with gas burners or electrical heating elements

**refrigerator** large, airtight cabinet or box for chilling foods by means of ice or electrical condensation

**stove** fixed or portable fuel-burning or electrical device for cooking food or heating room

**toilet** bathroom fixture with seat over bowl through which water is flushed to dispose of human waste material

**tub** bathtub

**washing machine** electrical apparatus with enclosed tub for cleaning clothing and linens

**water heater** apparatus with large storage tank where water is heated by gas or electricity for use in bathroom and kitchen

**wood stove** heavy metal heating and cooking apparatus, with heat supplied by wood burned in large chamber

# ORNAMENTAL AND FUNCTIONAL ARTICLES

Decorations, Ornaments, and Symbolic Objects
Functional Household Articles and Appliances
Linens and Fabrics
Glass and Ceramics

**SEE ALSO**: Chap. 5: Building and Construction Materials; Containers; Chap. 7: Interior Structure; Furnishings; Chap. 9: The Kitchen; Chap. 16: Architecture

## DECORATIONS, ORNAMENTS, AND SYMBOLIC OBJECTS

**accouterment** accessory item; trappings

**aigrette** heron's plume, sometimes placed in vase

**anthemion** flat, floral ornament in bas relief

**barber pole** cylinder with red and white spirals, used to indicate barbershop

**bas relief** sculptural relief in slight projection from surrounding surface

**beading** beaded molding; openwork trimming with beads

**bibelot** small household ornament or trinket; elegant miniature book

**bijou** small, dainty ornament of delicate workmanship, usu. jewelry

**birdbath** small, ornamental basin set outside for birds to bathe in

**bric-a-brac** small objects placed about room for ornamentation; curios; knickknacks

**cachepot** ornamental receptacle used to conceal flowerpot

**calabash** large, hard-shell gourd, used as utensil

**calami** cup for wine, used in Eucharist

**candelabrum** large, branched candlestick

**candleholder** candlestick

**candlestick** holder with socket for candle or candles; candleholder

**cartouche** ornate frame; oval or oblong figure enclosing sovereign's name (ancient Egypt)

**centerpiece** decorative display at center of table

**chalice** large cup or goblet, often of gold or silver, esp. for Eucharist wine

**chandelier** branched, ornate, multibulb lighting fixture suspended from ceiling

**chime** set of bells

**Chinese lantern** light with large paper shade, often globular

**ciborium** goblet-shaped vessel for storing Eucharist wafers

**cornucopia** curved goat's horn overflowing with fruit and grain, representing abundance

**crucifix** symbolic representation of Christ on cross, or cross itself

**cuckoo clock** clock equipped with mechanical birds that appear and emit sounds to announce hours

**curio** knickknack, bric-a-brac, or objet d'art

**cuspidation** decoration with horn or crescent moon

**decoration** any object used for its ornamental value

**diptych** two-leaved hinged tablet with pictures painted or carved on it

**epergne** ornate, tiered centerpiece with wrought metal frame bearing dishes, vases, and candleholders

**espagnolette** decorative metal knob on French door or window

**figurine** small carved, molded figure; statuette

**filigree** precious metal ornamentation of fine wire, applied to surfaces or in openwork setting

**font** receptacle for liquids, esp. holy water

**gaslight** gas burner affixed to wall with flame for illumination

**globe** spherical model of Earth on stand

**girandole** ornamental, branched candlestick or mirror frame

**grandfather clock** tall pendulum clock standing on floor

**jardiniere** ornamental stand for plants, often a large ceramic flowerpot

**knickknack** small, often trivial, ornamental object; curio; objet d'art

**lares and penates** treasured household belongings; household gods (ancient Rome)

**luster** glass pendant ornamenting candlestick or chandelier; object hung with such pendants

**menorah** candelabrum, esp. one holding nine candles for use during Jewish festival of Hanukkah

**modillion** ornamental block or bracket under corona of cornice

**monteith** large, silver punch bowl with scalloped rim

**napkin ring** metal ring for holding napkin in dining service

**niello** decorative object of metal with incised designs filled with black niello alloy

**objet d'art** decorative object of artistic value; curio; knick-knack

**objet trouvé** found object

**ornament** any object used to adorn or embellish

**paten** plate for wafers, used in Eucharist

**plume** decorative feather, cluster of feathers

**pontypool** decorative japanned metalware used esp. on trays

**quatrefoil** panellike ornament composed of four lobes radiating from common center

**salver** serving tray for food and drink; tray on which letters or calling cards are presented

**samovar** elaborate urn with spigot, used for heating water to brew tea

**sconce** bracket candlestick hung from wall; similar electric fixture

**speculum** ancient mirror of bronze or silver

**spray** ornamental cluster of flowers and greenery

**statuary** collection of statues

**statue** sculpted, modeled, or cast three-dimensional representation, usu. of person or animal

**statuette** small statue; figurine

**swag** suspended wreath or garland

**taper** squat, round candle used for religious observance

**tazza** ornamental cup or vase with large, flat bowl and pedestal or pillar, often with handles

**torchère** tall, ornamental candlestick on tripod base (18th c.)

**trappings** largely ornamental household articles

**trefoil** ornament in form of stylized trifoliate leaf

**trim** material used for decoration or embellishment along borders of larger piece

**trinket** small, inexpensive ornament

**triptych** picture or panel in three panels side by side

**urn** ornamental vase on pedestal, used for storage; closed vessel on stand with spigot for serving beverages

**vermiculation** decorative markings in irregular fine lines

**wind-bell** wind chimes

**wind chimes** cluster of small pieces of glass or metal that tinkle in wind; wind-bell

**wreath** ornamental circle of flowers and greenery

## FUNCTIONAL HOUSEHOLD ARTICLES AND APPLIANCES

**alarm clock** small bedside clock equipped with bell or buzzer set to sound at particular time

**ampule** sealed vial used to hold liquids

**andirons** metal supports with horizontal bar on legs, used to hold firewood on hearth

**appliance** any of various service units, usu. operated electrically, found in contemporary homes, esp. in the kitchen

**aquarium** enclosed, glass-sided container filled with water, serving as home to fish and other underwater life

**ashcan** metal refuse receptacle

**ashtray** small, flat, lipped receptacle for tobacco ashes

**basket** receptacle of interwoven material or light wood for trash, storage, transport, or display

**bed board** board placed under mattress for greater firmness

**bedpan** shallow vessel or receptacle used as toilet by bed-ridden person

**bed tray** stand with short, retractable legs, used for holding dishes and other objects while person is sitting up in bed

**bedwarmer** covered pan containing hot coals to warm bed

**bell** hollow metallic device that vibrates with ringing sound when struck; electronic signal device that simulates this sound

**bellows** blower that draws air through valve and expels it through tube, esp. to fan open fire

**bibcock** faucet having bent-down nozzle

**billet** chunky piece of firewood

**birdcage** grated enclosure that houses birds

**blotter** soft, spongy, unsized paper used to absorb ink

**bookends** heavy supports that hold books in place on shelf

**broom** bundle of firm, stiff fibers or twigs bound together on long handle, used for sweeping floor

**brush** bristles set into handle, used for scrubbing, sweeping, or smoothing

**bucket** round vessel for catching, holding, or carrying liquids

**bulletin board** soft board attached to wall for posting notices; pegboard

**caddy** small box, can, or chest for storage

**candle** molded or dipped mass of wax containing wick that may be burned for illumination

**candlelighter** long device for lighting ceremonial candles

**candlesnuffer** long device having hollow cone at end of handle, used for extinguishing ceremonial candles

**cantilever** bracket-shaped support for balcony or cornice; projecting beam supported at one end only

**carboy** protective rectangular container housing bottle with capacity of 5 to 15 gallons (18.9 to 56.8 l)

**carton** cardboard or wooden box

**censer** cup-shaped vessel with holes, suspended on chains and used for burning incense

**chamber pot** bedroom receptacle for human waste material

**circular file** *Slang.* waste basket

**clock** device for keeping and telling time, usu. circular, with hours around perimeter and two hands, one to show hours, one to show minutes

**coal scuttle** metal carrying pail with sloped lip and bail

**coaster** shallow container, small mat, or plate used to hold glasses and protect surfaces, esp. from moisture

**coat hanger** slender, arched device of metal, plastic, or wood, shaped like person's shoulders and used for hanging garments; hanger

**cresset** iron vessel or basket for holding illuminant, mounted as torch or suspended as lantern

**cuspidor** spittoon

**dry mop** long-handled mop with cloth, rope, or feather head, used for dusting floors

**dust mop** dry mop

**feather duster** soft feathers attached to handle, for dusting surfaces

**fixture** item of movable property incorporated into structure, both ornamental and functional

**flowerpot** container for growing plant, usu. of clay or plastic

**fly swatter** flat piece of rubber, plastic, or wire mesh attached to long handle, used for killing insects

**frog** small metal, glass, or plastic holder with spikes or perforations for holding flowers in place in vase

**garbage can** large metal or plastic container for trash; trash can

**grate** frame of parallel or crossed bars, esp. of iron, used to contain stove or furnace fire

**hanger** coat hanger

**hatrack** set of pegs or hooks that holds hats

**hose** long, flexible tube for conveying liquids

**iron** usu. electrical device with flat, long, metal base, heated to press clothes

**ironing board** flat, padded, cloth-covered surface on which clothes are pressed with an iron

**ladder** two long sidepieces joined by series of short crosspieces, used for climbing or reaching high places

**lampshade** any of various translucent, often fabric devices used to shield direct glare of lighted bulb in lamp

**lampstand** base on which shade and illuminating device rest

**lantern** portable, protective light case with transparent openings or covering, usu. with handle

**light fixture** device attached to wall or ceiling that holds lamp or light bulb

**mop** absorbent material fastened to long handle, used to clean floors

**nesting box** one of a series of boxes in graduated sizes that may be stored within one another

**oil lamp** usu. metal illuminating device that burns oil

**pail** bucket, usu. with handle, for carrying liquids

**pegboard** flat section of porous material attached to wall for posting notices; bulletin board

**planter** wood, ceramic, or glass receptacle used to hold live plant and earth

**plug** small object used to close opening; stopper

**plunger** rubber suction cup on handle for clearing plumbing traps

**pricket** candlestick with protruding point on which candle is impaled

**scuttle** shallow, open basket for carrying something, esp. metal pail for carrying coal

**shoe rack** hanging or floor device for storing shoes

**silent butler** receptacle with hinged lid for collecting table crumbs or emptying ashtrays

**sleeveboard** small ironing board for pressing garment sleeves

**spice rack** narrow storage shelves with front strips, usu. attached to wall

**spittoon** receptacle for expectorate; cuspidor

**steamer** enclosed container in which something is subjected to steam

**steam iron** clothes iron with compartment for holding water that is converted to steam and emitted onto fabric being pressed

**stopper** plug

**stoup** beverage container; basin

**stretcher** bedlike device on wheels for transporting sick or injured person

**terrarium** small glass enclosure for keeping, raising, and observing plants or animals

**tie rack** hanging device with slots or bars for storing ties

**torch** burning stick carried in hand for illumination

**towel rack** horizontal bar for hanging towels

**trash basket** small receptacle for dry trash

**trash can** garbage can

**tray** open, flat-bottomed receptacle with rim for carrying or holding objects

**vacuum cleaner** electrical device that sucks dirt and dust through hose into chamber

**valet** rack or tray for holding clothing and personal effects

**ventilation** system or means of providing fresh air to room

**wall bracket** usu. angle-shaped support attached to wall

**wastebasket** small garbage receptacle, esp. for paper

**whisk broom** small broom with short handle

**window box** box holding soil for growing plants on windowsill

**wine rack** wood frame with slots for storing bottles of wine on their sides

**wringer** device for pressing liquid out of washed clothes, usu. between two rollers, operated with crank handle

**zarf** ornamental holder for coffee cup without handle

## LINENS AND FABRICS

**antimacassar** delicate, often lace, protective covering on back or arms of chair

**arras** decorative wall hanging, screen, or tapestry

**backrest** pillow, bolster, or cushion placed behind back for support

**banderole** long, narrow, forked flag or streamer

**banner** strip of cloth on which sign is painted; flag, pennant

**bath mat** small, thick, fabric rug on bathroom floor

**bath towel** large towel for drying entire body

**beach towel** extra large towel for use at beach

**bedding** pillows, cases, sheets, blankets, and covers for bed

**bed pillow** stuffed fabric on which to support head while sleeping

**bedsheet** sheet

**bedspread** decorative fabric placed over blankets on bed

**blanket** large, usu. oblong woven fabric used as bed covering for warmth

**bolster** long, narrow cushion or pillow, sometimes with arm rests, used as prop on backless sofa or bed

**bunting** lightweight, loosely woven fabric for flags and patriotic decorations

**comforter** thick, often quilted, cloth blanket; duvet

**cover** blanket, quilt, bedspread, or sofa covering

**coverlet** bedspread, small cover

**crazy quilt** patchwork quilt without regular design

**cushion** small, often decorative, covered pillow on which people sit, lie, or recline

**dish towel** small cloth for drying dishes

**doily** small, protective and decorative napkin or linen, set on table or furniture

**doormat** flat piece of absorbent material on which people wipe their feet before entering house

**duvet** down- or fiber-filled quilt; comforter

**eiderdown** quilted blanket stuffed with duck feathers

**facecloth** very small towel, used wet to scrub face; washcloth

**fitted sheet** bedsheet that fits snugly over mattress

**flag** usu. rectangular piece of cloth with distinctive symbolic design; banner; pennant

**hand towel**  medium-size towel for drying hands and face

**hanging**  curtain, tapestry, or other suspended decoration

**lap robe**  heavy fur or blanket used to cover legs, usu. when outdoors

**linens**  general term for bedding, sheets, napkins, towels, and tablecloths

**mattress pad**  usu. quilted, protective cloth covering for mattress

**napkin**  usu. square piece of paper or cloth for wiping hands and lips, esp. after eating

**pennant**  flag or banner, esp. one tapering to a point at one end

**pillow**  fabric stuffed with feathers, foam, or fibers, used as soft resting place for head or back

**pillowcase**  protective or decorative cloth covering for pillow

**place mat**  decorative cloth, reed, or plastic sheet used by individual diner to protect table from plates and glasses

**quilt**  bedcover consisting of two cloth layers filled with cotton or down and stitched together in crisscrossed lines or patterns

**sampler**  decorative needlework with embroidered letters and verses

**sham**  covering, esp. for pillow, that provides altered outward appearance

**sheet**  oblong linen or cotton cloth placed between mattress and blanket on bed

**slipcover**  removable protective covering for article of furniture

**spread**  cover or cloth placed on top of bed or sofa; bedspread

**standard**  long, narrow, tapering flag bearing heraldic devices or symbols

**streamer**  banner or pennant; long, narrow, wavy cloth strip

**tablecloth**  decorative fabric used to cover and protect entire tabletop

**tapestry**  heavy, handwoven, highly decorative wall hanging

**throw pillow**  small, decorative pillow

**towel**  absorbent cloth of various sizes, used for wiping or drying the body

**upholstery**  material used to make soft covering, esp. for seat or sofa

**washcloth**  very small towel, used wet to scrub body; facecloth

**white goods**  bedding and linens

## GLASS AND CERAMICS

**amphora**  jar or vase with large oval body, narrow neck, and two handles rising near level of mouth (ancient Greece)

**ampulla**  glass or earthenware wine flask with two handles and globular body (ancient Rome)

**bell jar**  bell-shaped glass vessel for covering objects

**bottle**  usu. glass container for liquids with narrow neck and opening at top

**carafe**  liter or half-liter glass bottle, esp. for holding wine

**caster**  small glass bottle for serving condiments; cruet

**china**  plates, cups, and serving platters of delicate, translucent ceramic porcelain

**cistern**  large, usu. earthenware vessel for storing water

**crock**  thick earthenware pot or jar

**crockery**  earthenware plates, cups, and serving utensils

**cruet**  caster

**crystal**  objects, esp. bottles and drinking glasses, made of fine, cut glass

**cut glass**  glass with ornamental patterns cut into its surface

**decanter**  ornamental bottle for wine, port, or sherry, often made of cut glass

**etched glass**  decorative cut-glass objects

**ewer**  widemouthed jug or pitcher of brass or ceramics

**faience**  decorative, enameled French Renaissance earthenware

**jar**  widemouthed container, usu. of glass or earthenware

**jeroboam**  oversized wine bottle with capacity of 3 liters (3.3 quarts)

**jug**  large, deep, narrowmouthed container with handle, usu. of glass or earthenware

**Limoges**  enamelware or porcelain made at Limoges, France

**majolica**  glazed, richly colored, ornamental Italian earthenware

**pitcher**  container with lip and spout, used for holding and pouring liquids, usu. made of glass or earthenware

**porcelain**  hard, fine-grained, nonporous ceramicware, usu. translucent and white

**Satsuma vase**  large pottery vase over five feet tall, often placed by fireplace (Japan)

**Sèvres vase**  fine porcelain vase from Sèvres, France

**stoneware**  decorative white earthenware crocks, jugs, plates, and cups

**vase**  ornamental glass or earthenware vessel of greater depth than width, often used to hold flowers

**Wedgwood**  *Trademark*. type of bone china ceramicware

# CHAPTER 8

# The Family

# KINSHIP AND FAMILY RELATIONS

Kinship and Ancestry
Relationships by Blood and Marriage
Family Affairs

**SEE ALSO**: Chap. 3: Geography; Chap. 8: Marriage and Divorce; Parents and Children; Chap. 13: Anthropology; Sociology

## KINSHIP AND ANCESTRY

**affinity**  kinship relationship by marriage

**agnate**  paternal kinsman, esp. male relative on father's side

**ancestor**  person from whom one is descended, usu. more remote than grandparent; forefather

**ancestry**  line of descent or lineage

**antecedents**  ancestors

**blood**  relation by birth

**bloodline**  sequence of direct ancestors; family

**blood relation**  family member by birth

**branch**  division of family descended from common ancestor

**breed**  persons of the same stock

**breeding**  lineage

**clan**  extended family; tribe

**collateral**  kin descended by different line from same stock, such as uncle and nephew

**common descent**  blood relationship of two or more people with common ancestor; consanguinity

**congenital**  (adj) existing at birth

**consanguinity**  relationship by descent from common ancestor

**crossbreed**  (vb) interbreed

**descendant**  person born of same blood as ancestor in later generation; progeny

**descent**  extraction; lineage, derivation from an ancestor

**direct line**  descent by blood from parent to child

**distaff**  female side or branch of family; spindle side

**extended family**  ancestors and descendants by birth and marriage over several generations

**extraction**  ancestry; descent or lineage

**family**  persons of common ancestry or stock; persons related by birth or marriage; parents and their children by birth or adoption

**family tree**  generational chart of ancestry

**female line**  descent through mother

**filopietism**  excessive veneration of one's ancestors

**forefather**  ancestor

**fruit**  descendants

**full blood**  relationship between offspring of same parents

**full-blooded**  (adj) of pure, unmixed ancestry

**genealogy**  account of person or family's descent from first known ancestor

**generation**  persons constituting single step in line of descent

**gens**  clan, esp. one tracing patrilineal descent

**heir**  one receiving endowment from parent or predecessor

**heredity**  sum of qualities transmitted from ancestor to descendant

**heritage**  property or trait descending to heir, transmitted by immediate ancestor

**house**  family, including ancestors and descendants

**hybrid**  one born of mixed breeds, races, or diverse cultural traditions

**inbred**  (adj) born of closely related individuals; from the same stock

**incest**  sexual relations or interbreeding between two closely related persons, esp. between siblings or parent and child

**interbreed**  (vb) breed within closed population; crossbreed

**kin**  one's relatives; persons of common ancestry

**kindred**  group of one's relatives; kinship

**kinfolk**  one's relatives

**kinship**  state of being related

**kinship group**  individuals composing one's kin

**kinsman**  relative, esp. male

**kinswoman**  female relative

**kith**  close friends, neighbors, or relatives

**kith and kin**  close friends and relations

**line**  lineage; bloodline

**lineage**  descent in direct line from common progenitor; ancestry or extraction

**male line**  descent through father

**matriarch**  female, esp. mother, who rules or dominates family

**matriarchy**  family or group dominated by mother; state governed by woman

**matrilineal**  (adj) tracing descent through mother's line

**moiety**  one of two basic tribal or clan subdivisions based on unilineal descent

**next of kin**  one's closest relative

**nuclear family**  family unit composed of parents and children only

**offspring**  children

**origin**  ancestry; parentage

**parentage**  descent from parents or ancestors; lineage

**patriarch**  male, esp. father, who rules or dominates a family

**patriarchy**  family or group dominated by father; state governed by man

**patrilineal**  (adj) tracing descent through father's line

**patrimony**  anything derived from one's father, esp. an estate; heritage

**pedigree**  ancestral line, esp. of distinguished lineage

**people**  one's family and relations; racial, national, or tribal group

**philoprogenitive**  (adj) tending to produce offspring

**posterity**  all future generations descended from one progenitor; descendants

**progenitor**  forefather; ancestor in direct line

**progeny**  descendants; children

**pure blood**  one of unmixed ancestry, bred from members of recognized strain, group, or class

**race**  family, tribe, or people of same stock

**relation**  relative

**relative**  person connected to another by blood; relation

**seed**  ancestry or origin

**sire**  father; male ancestor or progenitor

**spear side**  male side or branch of family

**spindle side**  female side or branch of family; distaff

**stirp** line descending from common ancestor; stock

**stock** descendants of one individual; family, lineage

**strain** group with common ancestry producing physiological distinctions

**totem** emblem of family or clan, symbolic of its ancestry

**tree** chart of family lineage

**tribe** people of common stock; clan

**ultimogeniture** system of inheritance favoring youngest son

**unilineal** (*adj*) tracing descent through maternal or paternal line only

## RELATIONSHIPS BY BLOOD AND MARRIAGE

**aunt** sister of one's father or mother; uncle's wife

**auntie** *Informal.* aunt

**blood brother** brother by birth

**blood sister** sister by birth

**bro** *Informal.* brother

**brother** male sibling with one or both parents in common

**brother-in-law** brother of one's spouse; husband of one's sister; husband of one's spouse's sister

**cater-cousin** intimate friend; one not related

**child** son or daughter by birth or adoption

**cousin** child of one's uncle or aunt; relative descended from one's grandparents or ancestors in different line

**cousin-german** first cousin

**cousin once removed** cousin by marriage or by descent from grandparents, not through parents' line

**cousin twice removed** relative descended from grandparents' line through marriage or from more remote ancestors

**daughter** female child

**daughter-in-law** wife of one's son

**father** male parent

**father-in-law** father of one's spouse

**first cousin** child of one's uncle or aunt; cousin-german

**gaffer** *Informal.* grandfather

**gammer** *Informal.* grandmother

**grammy** *Informal.* grandmother

**grampa** *Informal.* grandfather

**gramps** *Informal.* grandfather

**grandaunt** great-aunt

**grandchild** child of one's child

**granddaughter** female child of one's child

**grandfather** father of one's parent

**grandma** *Informal.* grandmother

**grandmother** mother of one's parent

**grandnephew** male child of one's sibling's child; great-nephew

**grandniece** female child of one's sibling's child; great-niece

**grandparents** grandmother and grandfather; parents of one's parents

**grandson** male child of one's child

**granduncle** great-uncle

**granny** *Informal.* grandmother

**great-aunt** sister of one's grandparent; grandaunt

**great-nephew** grandnephew

**great-niece** grandniece

**great-uncle** brother of one's grandparent; granduncle

**half brother** brother related through one parent only

**half sister** sister related through one parent only

**husband** male spouse

**in-law** any relation by marriage

**kid brother** younger brother

**kid sister** younger sister

**maternal grandfather** mother's father

**maternal grandmother** mother's mother

**mother** female parent

**mother-in-law** mother of one's spouse

**nana** *Informal.* grandmother

**nephew** son of one's sibling or sibling-in-law

**niece** daughter of one's sibling or sibling-in-law

**novercal** (*adj*) relating to one's stepmother

**nuncle** *Chiefly Brit.* uncle

**parent** mother or father; progenitor

**paternal grandfather** father's father

**paternal grandmother** father's mother

**second cousin** cousin descended from grandparent, not through parent's line

**sibling** brother or sister

**sibling-in-law** brother or sister of one's spouse; spouse of one's sibling; spouse of spouse's sibling

**sis** *Informal.* sister

**sister** female sibling with one or both parents in common

**sister-in-law** sister of one's spouse; wife of one's brother; wife of one's spouse's brother

**son** male child

**son-in-law** husband of one's daughter

**spouse** husband or wife; person to whom one is married

**stepbrother** son of one's stepparent by former marriage

**stepchild** child of one's spouse by former marriage

**stepdaughter** daughter of one's spouse by former marriage

**stepfather** husband of one's mother by subsequent marriage

**stepmother** wife of one's father by subsequent marriage

**stepparent** spouse of one's parent by subsequent marriage

**stepsister** daughter of one's stepparent by former marriage

**stepson** son of one's spouse by former marriage

**unc** *Informal.* uncle

**uncle** brother of one's father or mother; aunt's husband

**wife** female spouse

## FAMILY AFFAIRS

**adult** one who has reached specified age of majority; grownup

**baptism** Christian sacrament of naming and admission to Christian community

**bar mitzvah** celebration of Jewish boy's coming of age

**bat mitzvah** celebration of Jewish girl's coming of age

**big daddy** representative of paternalistic authority

**birthday** date of one's birth; annual celebration of date of birth

**blood feud** multigenerational dispute between families

**bonding** formation of close personal relationship through constant association, esp. between mother and child

**breadwinner** one who earns money to support family

**change of life** climacteric; menopause

**charge** person, esp. child, committed to one's care

**chastity** abstention from sexual intercourse, esp. unlawful sexual intercourse

**climacteric** period in male of declining sexual activity; change of life

**close-knit** (*adj*) bound together by intimate social or familial ties

**cognomen** surname; last name

**come out** (*vb*) make one's debut

**connate** (*adj*) congenitally united; born together

**creature comforts** food, warmth, and shelter

**crèche** *Chiefly Brit.* foundling hospital; day nursery

**debut** formal entrance into society, usu. of teenage girl

**demoiselle** *French.* young lady

**domestic science** housekeeping

**dowager** widow holding property or title of deceased husband

**elder** respected, senior member of family or tribe

**ephebe** young man, esp. eighteen- to nineteen-year-old (ancient Greece)

**etiquette** social conduct prescribed by proper breeding

**family clinic** facility that provides counseling and medical care for family-related problems

**family counseling** therapy relating to family issues

**family likeness** physical appearance common to family members

**family planning** use of contraception to control number of children

**folk** people or tribes forming nation; group with common traditions and culture preserved over generations

**folks** *Informal.* persons of one's family; parents

**fraternal** (*adj*) brotherly

**given name** first name, chosen by parents

**grownup** adult

**guardian** adult who is legally responsible for another's child

**houseguest** overnight visitor in one's home

**household** those living together as a family in same dwelling

**housekeeping** management of home affairs; domestic science

**house sitter** person who occupies a home while tenant or owner is absent

**junior** child bearing same given name as parent

**kissing cousin** friend or relative known well enough to kiss upon meeting

**last name** surname

**majority** age at which child is legally an adult

**matchmaker** individual, esp. older woman, who arranges potential marriages

**matron** mature or distinguished married woman

**menfolk** males of a family or clan

**menopause** time of natural cessation of female menstruation and associated changes, usu. occurring between ages forty-five and fifty; change of life

**middle age** period of life from about ages forty to sixty

**midlife** period of emotional turmoil associated with aging; middle age

**minor** individual beneath age of legal majority, usu. eighteen to twenty-one years old

**name day** feast of saint for whom one is named

**naming** act of giving child a name

**noblesse oblige** obligation of honorable behavior associated with noble birth

**parricide** act of killing a member of one's family

**patronymic** name derived from father or paternal ancestor, usu. by addition of suffix or prefix

**propagate** (*vb*) breed or produce offspring

**purse strings** family finances or resources

**retirement** age at which one ceases working, usu. around sixty-five years old

**reunion** reconciliation or gathering of separated family members

**rite of passage** ceremony marking major transition in life, such as birth, puberty, marriage, or death

**senior citizen** elderly member of clan or society

**seniors** elders

**sterility** inability to conceive offspring

**surname** name borne in common by family members; cognomen; last name

**ties** associations or bonds between family members

**womenfolk** females of family or clan

# MARRIAGE AND DIVORCE

**SEE ALSO**: Chap. 8: Kinship and Family Relations; Parents and Children; Chap. 11: Law; Chap. 22: Sex, Love, and Romance

**adultery** sexual intercourse by married person with someone other than spouse

**affair** temporary, often secret romance outside marriage

**affiance** promise of marriage; betrothal

**alimony** legally required financial support paid to one marriage partner by the other as term of divorce

**anniversary** annual celebration on wedding date

**annulment** legal invalidation of marriage

**bachelor** unmarried man

**bachelor party** party given a bachelor by his male friends before his marriage, often a night of carousing prior to wedding day

**banns** public announcement of proposed marriage, esp. in church

**bedmate** spouse

**benedict** newly married man formerly a longtime bachelor

**best man** principal groomsman at wedding; paranymph

**betrothal** engagement to be married

**better half** one's spouse

**bigamy** illegal marriage to more than one person at a time

**bluebeard** man who marries and kills one wife after another

**bouquet** flowers carried by bride and tossed to single bridesmaids and guests after wedding

**bridale** usu. rustic wedding celebration

**bridal wreath** small, white, spring flowers used in bride's bouquet

**bride** woman just married or about to be married

**bridegroom** man just married or about to be married

**bride price** money or property given by prospective husband to bride's family

**bridesmaid** woman or girl attending bride at wedding; paranymph

**bride-to-be** woman engaged to be married; fiancée

**broken home** single-parent family in which child of divorced parents is raised

**celestial marriage** Mormon marriage held to be binding in present and future life

**celibacy** state of being unmarried

**cestus** bride's symbolic belt

**child support** payments made by one party following divorce for care and upbringing of children

**chuppah** *Hebrew.* canopy beneath which bride and groom stand during Jewish wedding ceremony

**church marriage** marriage performed by minister, priest, or rabbi

**civil marriage** marriage performed by magistrate

**cohabitation** living together, esp. while unmarried

**commitment** emotional and material trust that forms basis of marriage

**common-law marriage** marriage based on declaration, intent, or length of time living together without benefit of wedding

**community property** property acquired after marriage that is jointly owned by both partners and that by law must be divided equally upon divorce

**companionate marriage** form of marriage proposed in 1920's allowing birth control and uncontested divorce of childless couples, with no economic claims on partner

**compatibility** ability to live together in harmony

**concubinage** cohabitation of persons not legally married

**condonation** defense to prevent divorce; forgiveness for offense so it cannot be used as grounds for divorce action

**confirmed bachelor** never-married man; man living singly and not pursuing marriage

**conflict-habituated marriage** relationship dependent on conflict as part of its basic communication mechanism

**conjugal** (*adj*) pertaining to marriage or the relationship between husband and wife; connubial; marital; nuptial

**conjugal rights** rights of husband and wife to union and affection

**connivance** defense to prevent divorce

**connubial** (*adj*) conjugal; marital; nuptial

**consanguineous marriage** marriage between blood relatives

**consort** spouse of monarch

**consummate** (*vb*) complete or fulfill marriage bond by sexual intercourse

**contested divorce** legal proceeding for divorce that is challenged by party against whom proceedings are aimed

**contract** act of marriage; agreement to marry

**couple** married man and woman; (*vb*) join in wedlock

**courtship** social activities of potential mates culminating in engagement and marriage

**coverture** legal status of married woman

**cuckold** man with sexually unfaithful wife

**curtesy** right of husband, upon wife's death, to an interest in her property

**custody** immediate charge and care of children, usu. given to one partner in divorce

**Darby and Joan** very devoted elderly married couple

**desertion** abandonment of one's spouse and family

**deuterogamy** digamy

**digamy** second marriage after divorce or death of first spouse; deuterogamy

**dissolution** divorce

**divorce** legal termination of marriage; dissolution

**divorcé** divorced man

**divorcée** divorced woman

**dotal** (*adj*) pertaining to woman's marriage dowry

**double-ring ceremony** wedding in which both partners receive rings

**dowager** widow with title or property derived from dead husband

**dower** dowry; property woman brings to her marriage; right of widow to interest in husband's property

**dowry** money and real or personal property brought to marriage by woman

**dual-career marriage** marriage in which both spouses have full-time jobs or careers outside of household responsibilities

**dutch** *Slang.* wife

**eligible** (*adj*) single; available for marriage

**elope** (*vb*) run away to be married, esp. without parental consent

**endogamy** marriage traditionally within one's social, kinship, religious, or ethnic group

**engaged** (*adj*) describing one who has announced an intent to marry

**engagement** formal announcement of intention to marry; period or state of being pledged to marry

**Enoch Arden divorce** divorce based on disappearance of one partner for specified length of time

**epithalamion** song or poem in honor of wedding couple

**espousal** wedding; marriage ceremony

**estrangement** physical separation of married couple

**exogamy** marriage traditionally outside one's social, kinship, religious, or ethnic group

**extramarital** (*adj*) describing that which occurs outside the bonds of marriage

**family man** married man who is deeply involved in family life

**father-in-law** father of one's spouse

**fiancé** man to whom one is engaged to marry

**fiancée** woman to whom one is engaged to marry

**fling** extramarital affair

**flower girl** young girl who carries flowers before bride at wedding

**gay marriage** formalized, monogamous union between two persons of the same sex

**golden anniversary** fiftieth wedding anniversary

**Gretna Green** place where eloping couples are married

**groom** bridegroom

**groomsman** man attending groom at wedding

**group marriage** marriage between more than two persons, illegal in U.S.

**hand** bride's hand, given by her father, symbolizing his permission for her to marry; woman's agreement to marry

**happy couple** bride and groom at wedding

**hausfrau** housewife; married woman (Germany)

**helpmate** spouse

**henpeck** (*vb*) nag, esp. when done by wife

**hitched** (*adj*) *Slang.* married

**holy matrimony** state of being married

**homemaker** housewife

**homogamy** marriage among persons of similar age, social class, race, education, and religion

**honeymoon** vacation taken by newlyweds to begin their marriage

**honeymoon period** transitional time between single and married life; early, romantic period in marriage

**househusband** man who stays home to manage the household while his wife goes out to work

**housemate** spouse

**housewife** woman whose work is caring for home and children

**hubby** *Informal.* husband

**husband** married man; male spouse

**hypergamy** marriage into caste at least as high as one's own, esp. by Hindu woman

**hypogamy** marriage to person of lower socioeconomic status

**incompatibility** grounds for divorce based on mutual inability to live together with shared values, goals, and lifestyles

**inconstancy** fickleness in affections; infidelity

**infare** housewarming party for newly married couple

**infidelity** sexual unfaithfulness in marriage

**in-laws** relatives by marriage, esp. spouse's parents

**intended** one's future husband or wife

**interlocutory** preliminary divorce decree prior to final settlement

**intermarry** (*vb*) marry outside one's racial, religious, or ethnic group

**legal separation** legal arrangement to live apart made by estranged marriage partners

**levirate** ancient Hebrew marriage custom requiring brother of deceased man to marry his widow

**little woman** *Informal.* pejorative term for one's wife

**Lucy Stoner** married woman who keeps her maiden name

**maiden name** woman's surname prior to marriage

**maid of honor** principal unmarried woman attending bride at wedding ceremony

**man and wife** married couple

**marital** (*adj*) pertaining to marriage; conjugal; connubial; nuptial

**marriage** social and legal institution of formalized union between man and woman, typically foundation of family unit; matrimony; wedlock

**marriage counseling** therapy for partners in troubled marriage

**marriage license** document required for completion of legal establishment of marriage

**marriage of convenience** legal union based on circumstances other than love or affection, such as financial gain or naturalization

**marriage squeeze** demographic difference in number of eligible women and eligible men

**married** (*adj*) joined in marriage; conjugal

**marry** (*vb*) join in wedlock; unite man and woman in marriage; take another as one's spouse

**mate** spouse

**matrimony** marriage; rite, ceremony, or sacrament of marriage

**matron** long-married woman; wife; widow

**matron of honor** principal married woman attending bride at wedding ceremony

**mental cruelty** nonphysical abuse used as grounds for divorce

**miscegenation** marriage between persons of different races

**mistress** married man's regular female lover

**mixed marriage** marriage between persons of different races, religions, or ethnic groups

**monandry** practice and custom of having one husband at a time

**monogamy** practice of having only one spouse at a time

**morganatic marriage** union between person of high rank and person of lower rank in which children do not inherit higher-ranking parent's title or property

**mother-in-law** mother of one's spouse

**nest** (*vb*) settle into cozy, safe living place as couple or family; (n) family home

**newlyweds** recently married man and woman

**no-fault divorce** legal dissolution of marriage in which neither partner is blamed for its failure

**nonsupport** failure of one mate to provide financial support for spouse and family, as contracted in marriage agreement

**nubile** (*adj*) marriageable, esp. in reference to young girls

**nuptial** (*adj*) pertaining to marriage and the wedding ceremony

**nuptials** marriage ceremony; wedding

**old lady** *Informal.* wife

**old maid** *Derogatory slang.* elderly or confirmed spinster

**old man** *Informal.* husband

**on the rocks** *Slang.* failing, esp. in reference to a troubled marriage

**on the side** designating extramarital affair

**open marriage** arrangement whereby partners are free to have sexual relations outside marriage

**palimony** financial compensation paid to person previously lived with, but not married to, by more financially able partner

**paranymph** best man; bridesmaid

**partner** spouse

**philander** (*vb*) have sexual relations with no possibility of marriage

**play around** *Informal.* indulge in extramarital affairs

**plight one's troth** become engaged; take wedding vows

**polyandry** practice and custom of having more than one husband at a time

**polygamy** marriage to two or more spouses simultaneously

**proposal** offer of marriage

**prothalamion** song or poem that celebrates a marriage

**provider** spouse whose work generates income that pays family expenses

**proxy marriage** ceremony conducted with another person substituting for one of partners to be wed

**reception** party following wedding ceremony

**reconciliation** resolution of differences between estranged or separated couple

**rib** wife

**run around** play around; be unfaithful to one's spouse

**sannup** married man; husband (American Indian)

**scarlet letter** badge of an adulterer, esp. letter "A" worn as symbol of adultery

**separation** move to independent living quarters by couple with marriage problems, often prior to divorce action

**serial monogamy** series of monogamous relationships, none of which leads to marriage

**set up housekeeping** get married or cohabit

**seven-year itch** supposed temptation to have affair in seventh year of marriage

**shivaree**  noisy mock serenade to newly married couple

**shotgun wedding**  marriage compelled by bride's pregnancy

**shower**  celebration with gifts for bride-to-be, given by her female friends

**significant other**  mate or spouse

**soul mate**  empathic, loving spouse

**spinster**  unmarried woman past common age for marrying; old maid

**spousals**  nuptials; wedding

**spouse**  one's husband or wife

**squaw**  *Derogatory slang.* wife

**support payments**  money paid by one parent under terms of divorce settlement to care for children in custody of other parent

**suttee**  custom in which widow is cremated on funeral pyre of her husband (India)

**swap** (*vb*)  trade marriage partners with another couple for sexual activity; swing

**swing** (*vb*)  swap

**tie the knot**  *Informal.* get married

**traditional marriage**  union in which husband is breadwinner and head of household while wife is child rearer and housekeeper

**trial separation**  temporary break in cohabitation by married couple to determine whether they should separate permanently and initiate divorce proceedings

**troth**  pledge of fidelity at engagement or wedding

**trousseau**  bride's gown and accessories

**uncontested divorce**  dissolution of marriage without legal dispute between partners

**union**  joining in marriage; physical consummation of marriage

**unmarried** (*adj*)  single; not married

**uxorial** (*adj*)  wifely in behavior

**uxoricide**  murder of wife by husband

**uxorious** (*adj*)  inordinately submissive to one's wife

**viduity**  widowhood

**visiting privilege**  right of divorced person to visit children living in custody of other parent

**vital marriage**  relationship with high morale, mutual interest, affection, and emotional investment

**vows**  promise of fidelity; formal marriage pledge

**war bride**  woman marrying in wartime, esp. one whose husband leaves for military service immediately after wedding

**wear the pants**  display dominant behavior and control, esp. as exhibited by wife

**wed** (*vb*)  marry

**wedded** (*adj*)  married

**wedding**  marriage ceremony and festivities; nuptials

**wedding band**  wedding ring

**wedding day**  date on which marriage occurs

**wedding ring**  gold band presented at wedding and worn by one or both spouses to signify married status

**wedlock**  marriage; matrimony

**widow**  woman whose husband is dead

**widower**  man whose wife is dead

**widowhood**  state of being widowed

**wife**  married woman; female spouse

**wive** (*vb*)  take a wife; marry a woman

**woo** (*vb*)  court

**yoke** (*vb*)  join in marriage

# PARENTS AND CHILDREN

Pregnancy and Birth
Infancy
Upbringing and Development
Names and Relationships

**SEE ALSO**: Chap. 1: Anatomy; Chap. 2: Biology; Chap. 8: Kinship and Family Relations; Marriage and Divorce; Chap. 13: Psychology; Chap. 22: Sex, Love, and Romance

## PREGNANCY AND BIRTH

**abortion**  spontaneous or induced expulsion of fetus early in gestation period, usu. before twelfth week

**accouchement**  act of giving birth

**afterbirth**  placenta and fetal membranes expelled from uterus in parturition

**artificial insemination**  introduction of semen into uterus by other than sexual means

**barren** (*adj*)  unable to conceive or produce offspring

**bar sinister**  proof, condition, or stigma of illegitimacy

**bastard**  illegitimate child

**beget** (*vb*)  conceive and bear child

**biological clock**  woman's natural life cycle that controls ability to conceive and bear children

**biological parent**  parent who has conceived or sired child, though not always legal parent or guardian

**birth**  act or process of bringing forth child from mother's womb; parturition

**birth certificate**  official hospital record of birth

**birth control**  devices and methods used to prevent conception and reduce number of children born by woman

**birthday**  date of birth, celebrated annually

**birth defect**  physical defect present at birth that may be inherited or environmentally induced during pregnancy

**birthing**  art and practice of giving birth

**carry** (*vb*)  be pregnant

**Cesarean section**  delivery of child by surgical incision through walls of abdomen into uterus; C-section

**childbearing**  act of carrying and giving birth to children

**childbirth**  parturition; birth

**conception**  act of becoming pregnant, in which sperm fertilizes ovum and embryo begins growth in woman's uterus

**confinement**  period of lying-in immediately preceding birth of child

**congenital** (*adj*)  describing trait derived or inherited from parents through genes

**contraception**  devices and methods used to prevent pregnancy

**contraceptive**  device used to prevent pregnancy; (*adj*) tending to prevent conception

**couvade**  practice among some peoples in which husband enacts birth experience in his bed immediately preceding birth of his child

**C-section**  Cesarean section

317

**delivery**  act of giving birth to a child; assistance given to mother during childbirth

**embryo**  unborn child developing in mother's womb

**expecting** (adj) pregnant

**false pregnancy**  signs of pregnancy, esp. absence of menstruation, without presence of embryo, due to psychological or glandular disturbance or tumor

**family planning**  use of birth control to limit number of children in family

**family way**  pregnant

**fertile** (adj) able to conceive children

**fertility**  capability of reproducing; ability to conceive

**fertility drug**  medication used to enhance ability to conceive

**fetus**  embryo from three months after conception to birth

**fraternal twins**  twins of either sex, developed from separately fertilized ova, therefore not identical

**full term**  pregnancy lasting nine months

**gestation**  period of embryonic growth from conception to birth

**gravid** (adj) heavy with child; pregnant

**identical twins**  twins of same sex, developed from single fertilized ovum, very similar in appearance

**illegitimate** (adj) born out of wedlock; misbegotten

**inbreeding**  conception of children among closely related individuals

**in utero**  conception in uterus of woman; unborn

**in vitro**  fertilization and conception outside living body, in artificial environment

**knock up** (vb) Slang. make pregnant

**labor**  painful physical activities and sensations involved in giving birth

**Lamaze method**  system of special exercises and breathing used in childbirth

**legitimate** (adj) lawfully begotten and born in wedlock

**love child**  illegitimate child

**lying-in**  confinement; period immediately preceding childbirth

**maternity**  motherhood; hospital ward for childbirth and care of newborn infants

**midwife**  woman who assists mother during childbirth

**midwifery**  practice of being a midwife

**misbegotten** (adj) illegitimate

**miscarriage**  expulsion of underdeveloped fetus, usu. between twelfth and twenty-eighth weeks of pregnancy

**miscarry** (vb) have miscarriage

**morning sickness**  nausea associated with first months of pregnancy

**natal** (adj) relating to or associated with birth

**natal mother**  biological mother

**nativity**  birth

**natural childbirth**  birth in which mother does not use anaesthesia

**out of wedlock**  illegitimate

**ovum**  female germ cell that, when fertilized, develops into embryo

**parturition**  process of giving birth

**paternity**  fatherhood

**paternity test**  test to determine biological father of child by comparison of genetic traits

**placenta**  structure within uterus connected to umbilical cord through which fetus receives nourishment and eliminates feces

**Planned Parenthood**  Trademark. family planning organization that disseminates information and offers advice on birth control and sexually transmitted diseases

**preggers**  Brit. informal. pregnant

**pregnancy**  state of being with child

**pregnant** (adj) having unborn child in one's body; expecting; gravid; with child

**premature birth**  birth occurring after a gestation period of less than thirty-seven weeks

**prenatal** (adj) before birth

**primipara**  woman bearing a first child

**pro-choice** (adj) advocating legalized abortion

**procreation**  reproduction; act of begetting and bringing forth young

**pro-life** (adj) opposing legalized abortion

**quadruplets**  birth of four children from one pregnancy

**quintuplets**  birth of five children from one pregnancy

**sextuplets**  birth of six children from one pregnancy

**sire** (vb) beget as father

**spawn** (vb) reproduce, esp. in large numbers

**spermatozoon**  male germ cell in semen that fertilizes ovum to produce embryo

**sperm bank**  supply of spermatozoon used for artificial insemination

**sterile**  incapable of producing offspring; barren

**stillborn** (adj) describing infant dead at birth

**stork**  bird that in legend brings babies to parents

**term**  nine months of normal pregnancy

**test-tube baby**  embryo produced by laboratory fertilization and surgical implantation in uterus

**thalidomide baby**  child with birth defect caused by mother's use of drug thalidomide during pregnancy

**trimester**  one of three three-month periods during pregnancy

**triplets**  birth of three children from one pregnancy

**twins**  birth of two children from one pregnancy

**umbilical cord**  structure connecting navel of fetus with mother's placenta; emotional connection of mother and child

**unfertile** (adj) physiologically unable to conceive and reproduce

**unwed mother**  woman bearing child out of wedlock

**uterus**  womb

**war baby**  child conceived during war, often born when father is absent

**whelp** (vb) give birth to or bring forth young, usu. said of animals

**with child**  pregnant

**womb**  female uterus where embryo develops

## INFANCY

**babe**  infant

**baby**  infant

**baby food**  purée of easily digested food for toothless infant

**baptism**  Christian sacrament involving ritual use of water and naming of child, who is thus received into faith; christening

**bassinet**  infant's basketlike, hooded bed

**bottle feeding**  feeding of suckling child with sterilized, milklike formula from bottle

**breast feeding** suckling of child on milk from mother's breast

**bris** Jewish circumcision ceremony performed on eighth day following birth as rite of inclusion into religious community

**buggy** baby carriage

**burp** (*vb*) help infant expel gas from stomach by patting on back

**carriage** light-wheeled seat, often with hooded cover, for transporting infant

**change** (*vb*) replace child's soiled diaper with clean one

**chrisom child** infant that dies in first month of life

**christening** baptism, esp. naming of child in Christian faith

**circumcision** removal of prepuce from tip of male infant's penis

**cradle** infant's bed, often with spoke walls; infancy

**crib** baby's small bed with high sides

**crib death** inexplicable sudden infant death syndrome

**dandle** (*vb*) bounce baby playfully on one's knee

**diaper** folded cloth or absorbent material worn between legs and around waist by infant to collect urine and feces

**diaper rash** irritation that develops under wet diapers

**first step** initial indication of child's ability to walk, usu. around one year of age

**formula** milklike mixture used for bottle-feeding infants

**foundling** infant discovered when abandoned by unknown parents

**housebreak** (*vb*) toilet train, usu. said of animals

**infancy** period of early childhood

**infant** child in first year or two of life

**infanticide** murder of a baby

**lullaby** song sung to lull child to sleep

**mewling** (*adj*) crying weakly, whimpering; (*n*) an infant

**nap** brief period of sleep during daylight hours

**nappy** *Chiefly Brit.* diaper

**neonatal** (*adj*) relating to infant in first month of life

**newborn** child in first month of life

**nipper** *Chiefly Brit.* infant, baby

**nurse** (*vb*) suckle or breast-feed an infant

**nursery** infant's room in house

**pacifier** rubber nipple or teething ring for infant

**Pampers** *Trademark.* disposable diapers of soft, absorbent paper covered with thin layer of plastic

**perambulator** *Chiefly Brit.* baby carriage

**postnatal** (*adj*) referring to period after birth

**postpartum** (*adj*) referring to period following birth, esp. mother's depression during this time

**potty-chair** small seat with bowl used in toilet training

**potty training** training of child to use toilet

**preemie** *Informal.* prematurely born infant

**puling** (*adj*) whining, whimpering, mewling

**rocker** child's cradle on curved base

**stroller** seat on wheels for transporting infant

**suckle** (*vb*) breast-feed an infant

**suckling** infant still feeding on mother's milk; act of breast-feeding

**swaddling clothes** strips of cloth wrapped around infant to restrict movements

**teether** object for baby to bite while teething, esp. ring

**teething** painful first growth of teeth through infant's gums

**toddler** child who is beginning to walk, usu. aged one or two; tot

**toilet training** process of teaching child to control bladder and bowel functions and use toilet

**tot** toddler

**tyke** small child

**wean** (*vb*) accustom child to take nourishment other than by nursing

**wee tot** child (Scotland)

**wet nurse** woman who suckles infant not her own

## UPBRINGING AND DEVELOPMENT

**adolescence** period of growing up, from puberty to maturity

**adoption** legal taking of a child born to someone else as one's own

**adult** fully developed and mature person, esp. over age twenty-one

**age of consent** age at which child is legally allowed to give consent to sex or marriage, usu. eighteen years old

**allowance** weekly stipend given by parent to child as spending money, often earned by doing chores

**apron strings** state of being under dominance or control of one's parents at an advanced age

**au pair** foreign person, usu. young girl, living with family and serving as domestic and baby-sitter

**baby-sitter** person hired to care for children; sitter

**baby-sitting** act of caring for children during short absence by parents

**bedtime story** story told by parent to help child fall asleep

**bedwetting** inability of toilet-trained child to control urination in sleep

**biparental** (*adj*) relating to or derived from both parents

**bobbysoxer** preadolescent girl

**brat** spoiled, obnoxious, demanding child

**bring up** (*vb*) raise child to maturity

**changeling** child secretly substituted for another, usu. at birth

**chaperone** older person accompanying youngsters at social function to ensure proper behavior

**child abuse** physical mistreatment of children

**childcare** day care

**chip off the old block** child who closely takes after one parent

**chores** household tasks performed by child, often rewarded by payment

**Christian name** first name; name given by parents

**coming of age** reaching majority or age of consent

**corporal punishment** physical punishment, such as spanking

**curfew** time, set by parents, at which child must return home, esp. in evening

**custody** immediate charge and care of child; right to be child's guardian as determined in divorce or separation

**day care** supervision of preschool children, esp. while parents work; childcare

**day nursery** day-care facility

**development** stages of growth and maturation of child

**domestic** household help during day; maid

**duenna** chaperone or governess, esp. elderly woman serving in this capacity (Spain, Portugal)

**familial** (*adj*) of or relating to the family

**farm out** (*vb*) place children under care of paid guardian

**fatherhood** state of being a father

**favorite** child preferred by one or both parents

**filial** (*adj*) befitting relationship of child to its parent

**foster** (*vb*) provide parental care for a child not one's own

**foster home** place in which child lives with foster parents

**fosterling** foster child

**foster parents** individuals caring for a child not theirs legally or by birth

**gifted child** child with superior intelligence or talents

**godchild** child sponsored by godparents at baptism

**godparents** individuals who sponsor a child at baptism, thereby assuming certain responsibilities

**growing pains** emotional adjustments encountered during stages of development

**grownup** adult

**guardian** individual other than biological parents taking responsibility for child's upbringing

**infancy** first year or two of childhood

**JD** juvenile *delinquent*

**juvenile** teenager

**juvenile delinquent** JD; incorrigibly ill-behaved adolescent

**killcrop** former term for child who ate so much that parents feared he or she was descended from fairies

**latchkey child** young child of working parents who spends part of day at home unsupervised

**majority** age at which full civil rights are accorded, usu. twenty-one years

**maternal** (*adj*) characteristic of, related to, or inherited from mother

**matricide** act of killing one's mother

**maturity** final stage of development in which child is fully grown and able to care for itself

**minor** child under age of consent, which is usu. eighteen or twenty-one years of age

**minx** saucy young girl

**motherhood** state or quality of being a mother; maternity

**nanny** child's nursemaid

**nest** security of the family group; home

**nonage** period of youth before majority; immaturity

**nubile** (*adj*) of marriageable age, esp. young girl

**nursemaid** person employed regularly to care for children

**nymphet** sexually precocious adolescent girl

**only child** child with no siblings

**orphan** child whose parents are both dead or unknown

**paddle** (*vb*) spank

**parent** person who has begotten a child or is legally responsible for its upbringing; mother or father

**parentage** state of being a parent

**parenting** act and practice of raising children

**paternal** (*adj*) characteristic of, related to, or inherited from father

**patricide** act of killing one's father

**patrimony** estate inherited from father; anything derived from one's father

**phase** behavior and problems associated with particular period in child's development

**philoprogenitive** (*adj*) producing offspring; having deep affection for one's children

**playmate** play companion, esp. another child

**preadolescent** child just below age of puberty, approximately ages nine to twelve; preteen

**prepubescent** (*adj*) designating child just before age of puberty, about twelve years old

**preteen** preadolescent

**puberty** period marked by sexual development, when child is first capable of reproducing, usu. age fourteen in boys, age twelve in girls

**raise** (*vb*) bring up, educate, and nurture a child

**rear** (*vb*) raise a child

**restraint** device such as car seat or leash that restricts child's movement

**rite of passage** ritual associated with development stage, such as puberty

**runaway** unhappy adolescent fugitive from home

**sass** *Informal.* impudent backtalk from child to parent

**schoolboy** preadolescent male child

**schoolgirl** preadolescent female child

**scold** (*vb*) admonish misbehaving child

**sibling rivalry** natural hostility and competition between siblings

**single parent** individual raising child without spouse

**sitter** baby-sitter

**spanking** punishment consisting of slaps across buttocks, esp. with open hand

**spoiled** (*adj*) designating child overindulged by parents and lacking restraint or responsibility

**stripling** youth

**subadult** adolescent youth

**subdeb** adolescent girl

**subteen** preadolescent child

**talk back** (*vb*) make rude or impertinent answer to parent

**teenager** child between ages of twelve and twenty; juvenile

**teenybopper** *Slang.* teenager, esp. young girl

**terrible two's** difficult phase in child's life that occurs around age two, when child is first able to interact with environment and must learn limits

**tomboy** boyish preadolescent or adolescent girl

**transitional object** familiar object, esp. blanket or doll, carried by child in stage of early socialization

**unfathered** (*adj*) raised by mother only

**unfilial** (*adj*) not befitting child's relations with parents

**upbringing** manner in which parents supervise child's development

**waif** orphan; lost child

**ward** child under supervision of court or court-appointed guardian

**wetting** bedwetting

**working parent** parent who is unavailable to care for child while at job

**younger generation** those of same age as one's children

**youngster** member of younger generation

**younker** youngster (Holland)

**youth** young person, esp. child or adolescent but not infant

## Names and Relationships

**baby of the family** youngest child in family

**bairn** child (Scotland)

**bambino** *Italian.* infant

**big brother** older male sibling

**big sister** older female sibling

**boy** male child

**brat** child, esp. spoiled, troublesome one

**brood** family; children

**brother** male sibling

**bub** *Informal.* male child

**bubba** *Informal.* male child

**child** offspring; son or daughter between infancy and adolescence

**children** more than one child; sons and daughters born to or living with one set of parents; brood; kids; progeny

**chit** small child

**consanguinity** relationship by descent from common ancestor

**cub** child

**dad** *Informal.* child's name for father

**daddy** *Informal.* child's name for father

**daughter** female child

**daughter-in-law** wife of one's son

**dilling** *Chiefly Brit.* youngest child in family

**enfant** *French.* child

**father** man who has begotten a child; male parent

**father-in-law** spouse's father

**firstborn** eldest child in family

**flesh and blood** one's biological family, consisting of siblings and parents

**folks** *Informal.* parents

**forebear** parent or ancestor

**forefather** parent or ancestor

**girl** female child

**godchild** someone else's biological child whom one sponsors at baptism

**goddaughter** female godchild

**godfather** male godparent

**godmother** female godparent

**godparent** person who sponsors another person's child at baptism

**godson** male godchild

**half-blood** person related to another by having one common parent

**half-brother** male sibling with one common parent

**half-sister** female sibling with one common parent

**heirs** children; descendants

**issue** children

**junior** child, esp. male, having same first name as father

**kid** *Informal.* child

**kiddy** *Informal.* child

**kids** children

**lad** boy

**lass** girl

**little bugger** *Informal.* small child

**ma** *Informal.* child's name for mother

**mama** *Informal.* child's name for mother

**mammy** *Informal.* child's name for mother

**man-child** son

**man of the house** provider; father

**master** form of address for male youth too young to be called mister

**materfamilias** female head of household

**missy** *Informal.* pet name for girl child

**mom** *Informal.* child's name for mother

**momma** *Informal.* child's name for mother

**mommy** *Informal.* child's name for mother

**moppet** young child

**mother** woman who has given birth to a child; female parent

**mother-in-law** spouse's mother

**mum** *Chiefly Brit.* child's name for mother

**mummy** *Chiefly Brit.* child's name for mother

**mumsy** *Chiefly Brit.* child's name for mother

**namesake** child with same name as older family member

**nana** *Informal.* child's term for grandmother

**ne** *(adj)* born, used to indicate former name under which one was born

**nee** *(adj)* female form of ne

**nuclear family** parents and their children

**offspring** child or children

**old lady** *Informal.* mother

**old man** *Informal.* father

**pa** *Informal.* child's name for father

**papa** *Informal.* child's name for father

**papoose** young child (American Indian)

**pappy** *Informal.* child's name for father

**parent** mother or father of child; forebear

**paterfamilias** male head of household

**patronymic** name derived from father or paternal ancestor, esp. by addition of affix, such as Johnson, son of John

**peewee** *Informal.* child

**pop** *Informal.* child's name for father

**poppa** *Informal.* child's name for father

**poppy** *Informal.* child's name for father

**pops** *Informal.* child's name for father

**posterity** all future generations of offspring from one progenitor

**primogeniture** state of being firstborn

**progenitor** ancestor in direct blood line

**progeny** children; descendants

**punk** *Slang.* child

**scion** child; descendant

**sibling** brother or sister; one of two or more individuals with at least one common parent

**sire** male ancestor

**sister** female sibling

**small fry** young children

**son** male child

**son-in-law** husband of one's daughter

**sonny** male child

**stepbrother** male sibling by either parent's prior or subsequent marriage

**stepchild** child of one's spouse by prior or subsequent marriage

**stepdaughter** female stepchild

**stepfather** male stepparent

**stepmother** female stepparent

**stepparent** spouse of one's parent by prior or subsequent marriage

**stepsister** female sibling by either parent's prior or subsequent marriage

**stepson** male stepchild

**surname** name common to all members of family; last name

**venter** legal term designating maternal parentage

# CHAPTER 9

# Eating

# EATING VERBS

SEE ALSO: Chap. 9: Foods; Cooking and Cuisine; Chap. 17: Drinking and Alcoholic Beverages

**bolt**  swallow food or drink hurriedly
**break bread**  eat, esp. with another or others
**breakfast**  eat morning meal
**chew**  bite off and grind food between teeth; masticate
**chomp**  chew or bite down hard and noisily
**chow down**  *Informal.* eat, esp. main meal of day
**consume**  eat or drink, esp. in large amounts
**cram**  stuff with food
**devour**  eat voraciously, often to excess
**diet**  eat sparingly; restrict one's intake of food
**digest**  alter food by action of body chemicals into form that can be absorbed by body
**dig in**  *Informal.* begin eating
**dine**  eat dinner or any substantial meal
**dispatch**  eat up quickly
**drain**  drink everything in (container)
**drink**  consume a liquid
**eat**  place food in mouth, chew if necessary, and swallow
**eat out**  have meal in a restaurant
**eat up**  consume all of
**engorge**  eat greedily; gorge
**fall to**  begin eating
**feast**  eat rich, elaborate meal
**feast on**  enjoy eating (some specific, usu. lavish, food)
**feed**  eat, esp. out of hunger only, usu. said of animals
**finish off**  consume all of
**gobble**  eat hurriedly and sloppily
**gorge**  stuff oneself with food
**graze**  snack continuously or nibble small portions and samples of food
**gulp**  swallow hastily and greedily in large amounts
**guzzle**  drink greedily in large amounts
**imbibe**  drink, esp. alcoholic beverage
**ingest**  take food into body, usu. by swallowing
**ingurgitate**  consume greedily in large amounts
**inhale**  *Informal.* eat or drink very rapidly
**lap**  consume liquid food by licking it up with the tongue like an animal
**lap up**  eat or drink greedily with the tongue
**lunch**  eat midday meal
**masticate**  chew
**munch**  chew steadily and slowly; eat with pleasure
**nibble**  eat small amounts of something, esp. in quick bites
**nosh**  *Informal.* munch or eat a snack
**partake**  eat or drink one portion of a meal, esp. with others
**peck at**  eat in small amounts
**pick at**  eat sparingly and fussily
**pig out**  *Slang.* overeat
**polish off**  complete (a meal or dish)
**pork out**  *Slang.* overeat; pig out
**put away**  eat in large quantity
**quaff**  drink deeply and thirstily

**refect**  refresh with food or drink (archaic)
**refresh**  revive with food or drink
**relish**  eat with great pleasure
**sample**  eat small portions of (several different foods), esp. to taste quality
**savor**  enjoy the taste of one's food
**scarf**  *Slang.* eat greedily and very quickly
**set to**  begin eating
**sip**  drink slowly and carefully in small amounts
**slug down**  drink rapidly in large amounts
**slurp**  drink or eat noisily
**snack**  eat small portions of food, esp. between regular meals
**stuff oneself**  eat until one can eat no more
**sup**  dine; eat supper or evening meal
**swallow**  pass food or drink from mouth through throat to stomach
**swig**  drink in large mouthfuls or quantities
**swill**  drink greedily in large quantities
**take in**  consume; digest
**taste**  sense flavor of one's food; test flavor of by placing a little in one's mouth; eat or drink a small amount of
**toss down**  gulp or eat rapidly, almost without chewing
**tuck in**  *Chiefly Brit.* eat heartily
**wash down**  ease the swallowing of (food) by drinking liquid
**wine and dine**  entertain (guests) with food and drink
**wolf down**  eat ravenously and quickly

# FOODS

Food in General
Types of Food
Meats and Cuts of Meat
Sausage and Pâté
Poultry and Game
Fish and Shellfish
Dairy Foods
Cheese
Vegetables, Legumes, and Fungi
Fruits
Nuts and Seeds
Herbs and Spices
Grains and Flours
Pasta and Noodles
Cereals
Breads, Rolls, and Crackers
Cakes
Pastry
Cookies
Candy
Desserts
Dessert Sauces
Sweeteners
Cooking Fats and Oils
Additives and Thickening and Leavening Agents
Salad Dressings
Sauces
Condiments

Soups and Stews
Beverages

**SEE ALSO**: Chap. 2: Plants; Chap. 9: Cooking and Cuisine; Chap. 12: Agriculture; Chap. 17: Drinking and Alcoholic Beverages

## FOOD IN GENERAL

**aliment**  food as nourishment
**alimentation**  nourishment or sustenance
**board**  daily meals, esp. at table or provided for pay or with lodging
**bread**  food in general
**chow**  *Informal.* food
**chuck**  *Slang.* food, esp. in old West
**comestibles**  food; edibles
**cuisine**  prepared food; specific style of food
**daily bread**  basic sustenance
**delicacy**  very rare, costly, or fine food
**diet**  foods or cuisine one eats regularly, esp. when low in calories
**drink**  liquid food
**eats**  *Informal.* food
**edibles**  anything that may be eaten
**fare**  food, esp. specific kind of diet or cuisine
**feed**  one meal; animal food or fodder
**fodder**  food given to animals; feed
**food**  anything eaten as nourishment for sustenance; solid food as distinguished from liquid
**food and drink**  solid and liquid nourishment
**foodstuffs**  edible substances
**goodies**  *Informal.* foods one especially likes; treats
**grub**  *Slang.* food, usu. simple and basic
**leftovers**  food remaining after completion of meal, often saved
**meals**  food consumed at specific times of day
**mess**  food eaten by a group together, esp. soldiers
**morsel**  small portion of food
**nourishment**  food eaten for sustenance
**nutriment**  food taken as nourishment
**provisions**  supply of food
**rations**  supply of food, esp. for soldiers
**refection**  food eaten esp. after interval of hunger
**refreshment**  food and drink, esp. taken to restore energy
**scraps**  bits of food remaining after completion of meal, often discarded
**slop**  unappealing food, esp. leftovers
**sustenance**  any substance consumed to keep one alive
**swill**  unappealing food, often table scraps
**tidbit**  small morsel of food
**treat**  any food one particularly likes, esp. a sweet
**tucker**  food (Australia)
**viand**  food, esp. choice dish
**victuals**  food; provisions
**vittles**  victuals (colloq. spelling)

## TYPES OF FOOD

**additive**  often chemical substance added to improve some aspect of food, esp. as preservative or flavor enhancer

**aromatic**  any of certain herbs, spices, or vegetables, such as onions, garlic, or shallots, that give off a distinctive flavor and aroma
**beverage**  liquid food
**bread**  baked food, usu. made from flour or meal mixed with water and yeast
**cake**  baked, sweetened dough, often frosted
**candy**  flavored food sweetened with sugar or syrup, usu. in small chunks
**cereal**  grain produced from grass
**cheese**  solidified form of ripened curds of soured milk
**condiment**  substance eaten with another food to add flavor
**confection**  any sweet, esp. one prepared with fruit
**cookie**  small, sweet cake
**cracker**  thin, crisp, often unleavened bread
**cut**  part of an animal's flesh cut as one piece
**dairy**  food derived from milk, esp. cow's milk
**dessert**  usu. sweet substance eaten at end of meal
**dressing**  sauce or stuffing
**fat**  greasy substance forming most of adipose tissue of animals
**fish**  flesh of cold-blooded vertebrate animal living in water
**flour**  fine powder of ground grain
**fruit**  edible portion of mature, flowering plant
**fungus**  edible, growing, parasitic organism
**game**  flesh of wild birds or animals
**grain**  small, hard seed of certain cereal grasses
**herb**  seed plant used esp. as seasoning
**leavening**  substance that causes baked goods to rise
**legume**  pod or seed of certain herbs or shrubs
**meat**  flesh of animals, esp. mammals and fowl
**noodle**  flat strip of dough
**nut**  edible kernel of certain one-seeded fruits
**oil**  greasy liquid obtained from animal, mineral, or vegetable, used in cooking
**pasta**  flour or semolina dough dried in various shapes
**pastry**  fancy, sweetened baked goods
**pâté**  paste of meat, animal organs, and seasonings
**poultry**  flesh of fowl
**pulse**  edible seeds of certain legumes, such as peas, beans, or lentils
**roll**  small bread
**salad**  combination of usu. raw, chopped vegetables
**sauce**  liquid flavoring or dressing added to other foods
**sausage**  chopped, seasoned meat, usu. stuffed into thin casing
**seafood**  fish or shellfish and their parts
**seasoning**  herb or spice, used to enhance flavor of food
**seed**  edible, mature ovule of flowering plant
**shellfish**  flesh of invertebrate, aquatic animal covered by hard shell
**shortening**  butter, lard, or fat, used to make pastry or bread flaky and crumbly
**soup**  liquid food, usu. with bits of solid food, made by cooking meat, fish, vegetables, and seasonings in water
**spice**  portion of plant, esp. seed or leaf, used to season food
**stew**  mixture, esp. of meat and vegetables, cooked in liquid
**sweetener**  sugar or syrup used to make food sweet
**syrup**  thick, sweet liquid prepared from sugar, molasses, or glucose
**vegetable**  edible plant

# MEATS AND CUTS OF MEAT

**meat** flesh of mammals raised to be eaten, esp. cattle, pigs, and sheep

bacon, beef, beefburger, braciola, brains, breast, brisket, burger, butt, butterfly

Canadian bacon, center loin chop, charqui, Châteaubriand, chitterlings, chops, cold cuts, corned beef, cutlet

filet mignon, flanken, flitch

gizzards, goat

ham (Danish, picnic, prosciutto, Serrano, Smithfield, Virginia, Westphalian), hamburger, hock

jerky, joint

kid, kidney, knuckles

lamb, liver, loin chop

marrow, medallion, mountain oysters, mutton

noisette, numbles

oxtail

pastrami, pig's feet, pork, prairie oysters

rack, red meat, ribs, roast (blade, chuck, crown, eye of round, pot, rack, rib, rolled, round, rump, shoulder, sirloin tip, standing rib)

saddle, salt pork, short ribs, shoulder chop, slab bacon, spare ribs, steak (blade, club, cube, Delmonico, fillet, flank, hamburger, New York, porterhouse, rib, rib eye, round, rump, saddle, Salisbury, shank, shell, shoulder, sirloin, skirt, Spencer, strip, T-bone, tenderloin, top loin, top round), sweetbreads

tongue, tournedos, tripe

umbles

veal

# SAUSAGE AND PÂTÉ

**pâté** paste of meat, animal organs, and seasonings
**sausage** chopped, seasoned meat, usu. stuffed into thin casing

andouillettes

bangers, blood sausage, bologna, boudin blanc, boudin noir, Bratwurst, Braunschweiger

chicken liver pâté, chorizo

duck sausage

fish sausage, foie gras, forcemeat, frank, frankfurter

galantine, Genoa salami

head cheese, hot dog, hot link

Italian sausage

kielbasa, knockwurst, kosher salami

linguiça, liver pâté, liverwurst

merguez, mortadella, mulliatelle

pâté de foie gras, pâté de campagne, pâté en croute, pork sausage

salami, saucisse, saucisson, sausage, scrapple

terrine

Vienna sausage

weenie, wiener, wurst

zampone

# POULTRY AND GAME

**game** flesh of wild birds or animals
**poultry** flesh of fowl raised to be eaten

bear, boar

capon, chicken (broiler, free range, fryer, roaster, stewer), Cornish hen

deer, duck

fowl, frog legs

game, goose, grouse, guinea fowl

hare

partridge, pheasant, pigeon, pullet

quail

rabbit

squab

turkey

venison

wild turkey

# FISH AND SHELLFISH

**fish** flesh of cold-blooded vertebrate animals living in water
**shellfish** flesh of invertebrate, aquatic animals covered by hard shells

abalone, anchovy, angelfish

bacalao, bass, blackfish, bluefish, bonito, brisling, butterfish

calamari, catfish, caviar, clam, cod, codfish, conch, coral, crab, crawdad, crawfish, crayfish

eel, escargot

finnan haddie, flounder

gravlax, grunion

haddock, halibut, herring

John Dory

kipper

langoustine, lobster, lotte, lox

mackerel, mahimahi, milt, monk, mussel

octopus, orange roughy, oyster

perch, pompano, prawn

red snapper, roe

salmon, sand dab, sardine, scallop, scampi, scrod, scungilli, sea bass, sea urchin, shark, shrimp, skate, smelt, smoked salmon, snail, snapper, softshell crab, sole, sprat, squid, striped bass, sturgeon, surimi, swordfish

teal, terrapin, tile, tomalley, trout, tuna, turbot

weak, whitefish

yellowtail

# DAIRY FOODS

**dairy food** food derived from milk, esp. cow's milk

bonnyclabber, butter

cheese, clabber, cream, crème fraîche, curds

eggs

goat's milk

half-and-half, heavy cream

ice cream

kefir

leben, light cream

milk (buttermilk, condensed, dry, evaporated, homogenized, lowfat, nonfat, pasteurized, raw, skim, whole)

sour cream, sweet butter

ultrapasteurized heavy cream

whey, whipping cream

yogurt

# CHEESE

**cheese** solidified form of ripened curds of soured milk

American

Banon, Bel Paese, blue, Boursin, brick, Brie

Caciocavallo, Caerphilly, Camembert, cheddar, Cheshire, chèvre, Chevret, clabber, coeur à la crème, colby, comte, coon cheese, cottage cheese, cream cheese, crema Danica

Danish blue, Derby, Dunlop

Edam, Edelpilzkäse, Emmenthaler, Epoisses

farmer's cheese, feta, fontina, fromage blanc

Gammelost, Gjetost, Gloucester, goat cheese, Gorgonzola, Gouda, Gruyère

Havarti, hoop cheese

jack cheese, Jarlsberg

Kumminost

Lancashire, Leicester, Liederkranz, Limburger, Liptauer, Livarot, long horn

Maroilles, Mimolette, Monterey Jack, Montrachet, mozzarella, muenster

Neufchâtel

Parmesan, Pecorino, Pont L'Évêque, Port-Salut, pot cheese, processed cheese, provolone

Quargel

rat cheese, red Windsor, ricotta, Romano, Roquefort

sapsago, smoked cheese, Stilton, St. Marcellin, string cheese, Swiss

Teleme, Tillamook, Tilsit

Vacherin, Velveeta

Wensleydale, white cheddar

## VEGETABLES, LEGUMES, AND FUNGI

**fungus** edible, growing, parasitic organism
**legume** pod or seed of certain herbs or shrubs
**vegetable** edible plant, eaten raw or cooked

alfalfa sprout, artichoke, arugula, asparagus, aubergine

bamboo shoot, bean (aduki, black, broad, butter, chickpea, fava, garbanzo, green, haricot, kidney, lentil, lima, mung, navy, northern, pink, pinto, red, soya, string, wax, white), **bean sprout, beet, Bermuda onion, black-eyed pea, bok choy, broccoli, Brussels sprout**

cabbage, cactus, cardoon, carrot, cassava, cauliflower, celeriac, celery, chard, chayote, chicory, Chinese cabbage, chive, collard greens, corn, courgette, cowpea, cress, cucumber

daikon, dandelion greens

eggplant, endive, escarole

finocchio

green bean, green onion

Japanese eggplant, Jerusalem artichoke

kale, kohlrabi

leek, lettuce (Bibb, Boston, butter, corn salad, cos, curly, green leaf, iceberg, mache, red leaf, romaine), **lovage**

maize, manioc, mung sprout, mushroom (black, button, champignon, chanterelle, enoki, fungi, morel, oyster, porcini, shiitake, tree ear), **mustard greens**

nopal, nori

okra, onion, oyster plant

parsnip, pea (black-eyed, green, snow, split, sugar), **pearl onion, pepper** (bell, capsicum, chile, green, Italian, jalapeño, pimiento, red, serrano, wax, yellow), **potato, pumpkin**

radiccio, radish, rampion, ramson, red cabbage, red onion, rhubarb, rutabaga

salsify, scallion, seaweed, shallot, snap bean, sorrel, **soybean, spinach, sprout, squash** (acorn, butternut, crookneck, cymling, spaghetti, summer, winter, yellow, zucchini), **string bean, succory, sugar pea, sweet potato, Swiss chard**

taro root, tomatillo, tomato, truffle, turnip

water chestnut, watercress, wax bean

yam

zucchini

## FRUITS

**fruit** edible portion of mature flowering plant

ananas, apple (Baldwin, delicious, empire, golden, Granny Smith, gravenstein, Jonathan, Macintosh, macoun, pippin, Rome, winesap), **apricot, atemoya, avocado**

banana, berry (bilberry, bearberry, blackberry, black raspberry, blueberry, boysenberry, candleberry, checkerberry, cloudberry, cranberry, dewberry, elderberry, gooseberry, huckleberry, lingonberry, loganberry, mulberry, raspberry, strawberry, whortleberry), **black currant, blood orange, breadfruit, bullace**

calmyrna, canistel, carambola, cherimoya, cherry, citron, clementine, coconut, copra, crabapple, currant, custard apple

damson plum, date, durian

fig

granadilla, grape (Cabernet Sauvignon, cardinal Chardonnay, Chenin Blanc, Concord, Delaware, Italia, Merlot, Muscadet, muscat, Pinot Blanc, Pinot Noir, Riesling, seedless, Thompson seedless, Tokay, zinfandel), **grapefruit, greengage, guava**

jackfruit, jujube

kiwi, kumquat

lemon, lime, loquat

mandarin orange, mango, medlar, melon (cantaloupe, casaba, Crenshaw, honeydew, muskmelon, Persian, watermelon, winter melon)

naartje, navel orange, nectarine

olive, orange, ortanique

papaya, passion fruit, pawpaw, peach, pear (Anjou, Bosc, Bartlett, Comice, winter nellis), **pepino, persimmon, pineapple, pitahaya, plantain, plum, pomegranate, pomelo, prickly pear, prune, pummelo**

quince, quinoa

raisin, rambutan

sapodilla, sapote, satsuma, soursop, spanspek

tamarillo, tamarind, tangelo, tangerine

ugli fruit

Valencia orange

## NUTS AND SEEDS

**nut** edible kernel of certain one-seeded fruits
**seed** fertilized, matured ovule of certain flowering plants, usu. eaten dried

acorn, almond

beechnut, ben, betel, black walnut, Brazil, butternut

candlenut, cashew, chestnut, chinquapin, cobnut, corozo

dika

filbert

grugru

hazelnut, hickory, horse chestnut

kola

litchi

macadamia

palm, peanut, pecan, physic nut, pignola, pine, pistachio, pumpkinseed

quinoa

sassafras, sesame seed, souari nut, sunflower seed

walnut

327

**9. Eating**
Foods
Herbs and Spices / Grains and Flours / Pasta and Noodles / Cereals / Breads, Rolls, and Crackers / Cakes

**Part Three**

## Herbs and Spices

**herb**  seed plant used esp. as seasoning
**spice**  portion of plant, esp. seed or leaf, used to season food
   achiote, allspice, angelica, anise, asafetida
   basil, bay leaf, benne seed, berbere, black pepper, borage, bouquet garni
   cacao, calamint, capers, caraway seed, cardamom, carob, cayenne, celery seed, chervil, chicory, chili pepper, chili powder, Chinese parsley, chives, cilantro, cinnamon, cloves, coriander, cubeb, cumin, curly parsley, curry
   dill
   elephant garlic
   fennel, fenugreek, fines herbes, finochio, flaxseed
   garam masala, garlic, ginger, green peppercorn
   iodized salt, Italian parsley
   juniper berry
   kosher salt
   lemon basil, lemon grass, licorice, lovage
   mace, marjoram, mint, mustard
   nutmeg
   oregano
   paprika, parsley, pepper, pepper flakes, peppermint, pickling spice, poppy seed, pumpkin seed
   red pepper, rock salt, rosemary
   saffron, sage, salt, sea salt, sesame seed, shallots, sorrel, St. John's-bread, summer savory, sunflower seed, sweet basil
   table salt, tarragon, thyme, turmeric
   vanilla
   white pepper

## Grains and Flours

**flour**  fine powder of ground grain, used esp. in baking
**grain**  small, hard seed of certain cereal grasses
   barley, blue cornmeal, bran, buckwheat, bulghur
   corn, cornmeal, couscous
   farina, flour (bleached, enriched, gluten, pastry, rice, rye, semolina, unbleached, wheat, white)
   grits, groats
   hominy
   kasha
   masa, millet
   oat bran, oats
   polenta
   rice (basmati, brown, enriched, long-grain, minute, quick-cooking, short-grain, white), rye
   semolina
   wheat, wheat germ, wild rice

## Pasta and Noodles

**noodle**  flat strip of dough
**pasta**  flour or semolina dough dried in various shapes
   angel hair
   bucatini
   cannelloni, cappelletti, chow fun noodles, chow mein noodles, conchiglie
   dumpling
   egg noodles
   farfel, fettuccine, fettucelle, fusilli
   gelatin noodles, glass noodles, gnocchi

   knodel, kreplach
   lasagne, linguine, lo mein noodles
   macaroni, mafalde, manicotti, mostaccioli
   noodles
   penne
   quenelle
   ravioli, rice, rigatoni, rotelli, rotini
   soba, spaetzle, spaghetti, spaghettini
   tagliatelle, tortellini
   vermicelli
   won ton
   ziti

## Cereals

**cereal**  grain produced from grass, used esp. as breakfast food
   Cheerios, Chex, corn flakes, Cream of Wheat
   Frosted Flakes
   granola, Grape Nuts, grits, gruel
   mush
   oatmeal, porridge, puffed rice
   Raisin Bran, Rice Krispies, rolled oats
   Shredded Wheat
   Wheaties

## Breads, Rolls, and Crackers

**bread**  baked food, usu. made from flour or meal mixed with water and yeast
**cracker**  thin, crisp, often unleavened bread
**roll**  small bread
   anadama bread
   bagel, baguette, bialy, biscuit, black bread, bran muffin, breadcrumbs, breadstick, brioche, brown bread, bun
   challah, chapati, cheese bread, cornbread, corn dodger, cracknel, crisp, croissant, crouton
   egg bread, English muffin
   French bread
   garlic bread, graham cracker
   hardtack, hush puppy
   johnny cake
   matzo, melba toast, muffin
   nan, nut bread
   oatcake
   papadam, pita, poori, popover, pretzel, pumpernickel bread
   raisin bread, roll (cinnamon, dinner, hard, Kaiser, onion, Parker House, sourdough), rusk, rye bread
   saltine, seeded rye bread, semolina bread, ship biscuit, sippet, soda biscuit, soda bread, sourdough bread
   toast, tortilla
   unleavened bread
   wafer, water biscuit, whole-grain bread, whole-wheat bread
   yeast cake
   zwieback

## Cakes

**cake**  baked or pan-cooked, sweetened dough, often frosted
   angel food cake
   Banbury tart, Battenberg cake
   cheesecake, chocolate cake, coffeecake, cupcake

devil's food cake
fruitcake
gâteau, genoise, gingerbread
honey cake
jelly roll
kuchen
layer cake, loaf cake
marble cake
pancake (battercake, blini, blintz, buckwheat, crepe, flapjack, griddle cake, hotcake, johnnycake, latke, potato, waffle), pound cake
Sacher torte, sally lunn, savarin, shortcake, simnel cake, spice cake, sponge cake, stollen
tart, tartlet, teacake, torte
upside-down cake
waffle, wedding cake, white cake
yellow cake

## PASTRY

**pastry** fancy, sweetened baked good, often with filling
baba au rum, baklava, beignet, berry pie, Boston cream cake, cornet, cream pie, cream puff, crescent, cruller, crumpet
Danish, doughnut
Eccles cake, éclair
feuilletée, frangipane, fritter, fruit pie
jelly doughnut
madeleine, meringue pie, mille-feuilles
napoleon
pan au chocolat, pâté à choux, petit four, phyllo, pie, profiterole, puff
quiche
schnecken, scone, shoo-fly pie, sopaipilla, strudel, sweet roll
tart, timbale, turnover
Washington pie

## COOKIES

**cookie** small, sweet cake
animal cracker
bar, biscuit, brandy snap, brownie, butter
chocolate chip cookie
fig bar, florentine, fortune cookie
garibaldi, gingersnap
hermit
jumble
lady finger
macaroon
oatmeal cookie, Oreo
palm leaf, panettone, peanut butter cookie
ratafia
shortbread, sugar cookie
tollhouse
wafer

## CANDY

**candy** flavored food sweetened with sugar or syrup, usu. in small chunks
bark, bonbon, brittle, butterscotch
candy bar, candy cane, caramel, chocolate, chocolate bar, confection, cotton candy

fondant, frosting, fudge
halvah
icing
jawbreaker, jellybean, jimmies, jujube
kiss
lemon drop, licorice, Lifesaver, lollipop
marchpane, marshmallow, marzipan, mint, M'n'M
nonpareil, nougat
peanut brittle, penuche, peppermint, praline
rock candy
saltwater taffy, sweets
taffy, toffee, Turkish delight, tutti-frutti

## DESSERTS

**dessert** usu. sweet substance eaten at end of meal, often frozen or baked
apple pandowdy
baked Alaska, banana split, Bavarian cream, blacking pudding, blancmange, bombe, Boston cream pie, brown betty
cannoli, cassata, charlotte russe, clafoutis, cobbler, compote, coupe, crème brûlée, crème caramel, crêpe suzette, custard
deep dish pie, duff
Edinburgh fog, flan
floating island, flummery, frappé, frozen custard, frozen dessert, frozen yogurt, fruit cup, frumenty
gelato, glacé, granita
ice cream, ice cream bar, ice cream sandwich, Indian pudding, Italian ice
Jell-O
marrons glacés, meringue, moor-in-a-shirt, mousse, mud pie
parfait, pashka, peach Melba, pie, poached pear, pudding
rice pudding
Sacher torte, sherbet, snow cone, snow pudding, sorbet, soufflé, strawberry shortcake, streusel, sundae, syllabub
tiramisu, tortoni, trifle
vacherin
zabaglione, zuppa inglese

## DESSERT SAUCES

**dessert sauce** sweet liquid used as flavoring or dressing over dessert
butterscotch
charlotte russe, chocolate, crème Anglais, crème Chantilly, crème pâtissiere
frangipane
hard sauce, hot fudge
marshmallow
Nesselrode
pineapple
topping

## SWEETENERS

**sweetener** sugar or syrup used to make food sweet
corn syrup
fructose
honey
Karo syrup
maple sugar, maple syrup, molasses

sorghum, **sugar** (barley, brown, cane, caramel, castor,
confectioner's, cube, granulated, icing, light brown, powdered,
raw, spun, superfine), **syrup**
treacle

## COOKING FATS AND OILS

**fat** greasy substance forming most of adipose tissue of animals
**oil** greasy liquid obtained from animal, mineral, or vegetable source, used in cooking
almond oil, avocado oil
bacon fat, butter
chicken fat, cocoa butter, coconut oil, corn oil, cottonseed
oil, Crisco
drippings
extra virgin olive oil
fat
ghee, goose grease, grapeseed oil
hazelnut oil
lard
margarine
oleomargarine, olive oil
partially hydrogenated vegetable oil, peanut oil
rendered chicken fat
safflower oil, schmaltz, sesame oil, shortening, solid
vegetable shortening, soya oil, soybean oil, suet,
sunflower oil
vegetable oil, virgin olive oil
walnut oil, wheat germ oil

## ADDITIVES AND THICKENING AND LEAVENING AGENTS

**additive** often chemical substance added to improve some
aspect of food, esp. as preservative or to enhance flavor
**leavening** substance that causes baked goods to rise
agar, alum, arrowroot
baking powder, baking soda, brewer's yeast
cornstarch, cream of tartar
food coloring, flour
gelatin
hydrolyzed vegetable protein
isinglass
lecithin
monosodium glutamate, MSG
neat's-foot jelly
potato flour
rennet, roux
sago, sodium benzoate, starter
tapioca, tomato paste
yeast

## SALAD DRESSINGS

**salad dressing** usu. sharply flavored liquid mixture poured
over raw vegetable salad
aioli
blue cheese
creamy Italian
French
Italian

oil and vinegar
ranch, Russian
Thousand Island
vinaigrette

## SAUCES

**sauce** liquid flavoring or dressing of mixed ingredients
added to other foods
aioli, allemande, A-1 sauce, applesauce
barbecue, Béarnaise, béchamel, Bercy, Bordelaise, brown
chasseur, chili, cranberry, cream, curry
diable, duck
espagnole
giblet gravy, gravy
hoisin, hollandaise sauce, hot sauce
marinara, mayonnaise, mole, Mornay, mousseline, mushroom
nantua
oyster
pan gravy, pesto, pistou
ravigote, red-eye gravy, rémoulade
satay, soubise, soy sauce, suprême, sweet-and-sour sauce
Tabasco, tahini, tamari, tartar, tomato sauce
velouté
white, Worcestershire sauce

## CONDIMENTS

**condiment** substance eaten with another food to add flavor
anchovy, angostura bitters, aspic
bread and butter pickle, brine
caper, catsup, chutney, confiture, conserves, cornichon
dill pickle
gherkin
horseradish
jalapeño relish
ketchup
jam, jelly
lemon curd, lemon peel
marmalade, mustard
piccalilli, pickle, pimiento, preserves
relish, rosewater
salsa, sambal, sweet pickle
tahini
vinegar (balsamic, cider, malt, red wine, rice wine, white wine)
wasabi
zest

## SOUPS AND STEWS

**soup** liquid food, usu. with bits of solid food, made by
cooking meat, fish, vegetables, and seasonings in water or
milk
**stew** mixture, esp. of meat and vegetables, cooked in liquid
alphabet soup, avgolemono
beef broth, beef stew, bird's-nest soup, bisque, blanquette,
borscht, bouillabaisse, bouillon, broth, Brunswick stew,
burgoo
callaloo, caldo verde, chicken broth, chicken noodle soup,
chicken soup, cholent, chowder, cioppino, civet,
cock-a-leekie, consommé, cream soup, cullis
daube

egg drop soup
fumet
gazpacho, goulash, gumbo
hasenpfeffer, hot and sour soup
lobscouse
madrilène, matelote, matzo ball soup, menudo, minestrone, miso soup, mulligan, mulligatawny, mushroom, navarin
olla podrida, onion soup, oxtail soup
pepper pot, potage
ragout, ramen, rassolnik
Scotch broth, shark's fin soup, slumgullion, split pea soup, stock
tomato soup, turtle soup, tzimmes
vegetable soup, vichyssoise
won ton soup

## BEVERAGES

**beverage** liquid food
ambrosia, apple juice
barley water, beef tea, beer, birch beer, black tea, bouillon, buttermilk
café au lait, café filtre, café noir, caffè latte, cappuccino, chocolate milk, cider, club soda, cocoa, coconut milk, coffee, cola, cordial, cranberry juice, cream soda
egg cream, eggnog, espresso
float, frappe, fruit juice
ginger ale, ginger beer, ginseng tea, grapefruit juice, grape juice, green tea
herb tea, hot chocolate
ice cream soda
kava, kefir, kumiss
lemonade, limeade, lime rickey, liqueur
malted, maté, milk, milk shake, mineral water, mixer, mocha, mulled cider
nectar
orangeade, orange juice
phosphate, pineapple juice, punch
root beer
sarsaparilla, seltzer, shrub, soda water, soybean milk, spice tea, spirits, syllabub
tea, tisane, tomato juice, tonic water, Turkish coffee
vegetable juice
**water** (branch, distilled, mineral, seltzer, soda, sparkling, spring, tap, Vichy whiskey, wine)

# COOKING AND CUISINE

Preparations and Presentations
Cooking Techniques
Cuisines, Meals, and Restaurants
Cooks and Servers
Prepared Dishes

**SEE ALSO**: Chap. 9: Foods; The Kitchen

## PREPARATIONS AND PRESENTATIONS

**à la king** (*adj*) served with cream sauce
**à la mode** (*adj*) in the style of; served with ice cream

**al burro** (*adj*) served with butter
**al dente** (*adj*) firm to the bite
**amandine** (*adj*) served with almonds
**anglaise** (*adj*) boiled
**argenteuil** (*adj*) with asparagus
**aspic** jellied stock or juice
**au bleu** (*adj*) poached instantly upon being killed
**au fromage** (*adj*) with cheese
**au gratin** (*adj*) covered with sauce and crumbs; toasted
**au jus** (*adj*) served with natural juices
**au naturel** (*adj*) uncooked or cooked simply
**beurre blanc** butter, shallots, and wine
**beurre manie** flour kneaded with fat for sauce base
**beurre noir** browned butter with vinegar and capers
**bouquet garni** herb mixture in cheesecloth, removed after cooking
**broth** liquid in which meat, fish, grains, or vegetables have been cooked; stock
**brunoise** diced vegetables, used as sauce or stock base
**cacciatore** (*adj*) hunter's style; containing tomatoes, mushrooms, herbs, and other seasonings
**calzone** folded pizza
**canapé** small, savory sandwich appetizer on toast, cracker, or crustless bread
**chasseur** (*adj*) brown sauce usu. containing tomatoes, mushrooms, shallots, and white wine
**chiffonade** mixture of minced herbs and vegetables, used in soups
**clamart** (*adj*) with peas
**clean** (*vb*) remove unwanted portions of raw food prior to cooking or serving
**clotted cream** cream thickened by cooking; Devonshire cream
**consommé** clear soup made from stock
**cracklings** crisp residue left after rendering hog or chicken fat
**Crécy** (*adj*) with carrots
**creole** (*adj*) spicy sauce or dish, usu. with rice
**crepes** thin pancakes rolled with filling or jam
**croustade** baked or fried pastry shell, sometimes made of noodles, rice, or mashed potatoes, filled with ragout
**dauphine** (*adj*) with straw potatoes
**Devonshire cream** clotted cream
**dough** flour or meal combined with water or milk and shortening, to be shaped and baked
**drawn butter** melted, clarified butter, often seasoned
**dress** (*vb*) prepare for cooking or serving
**drippings** juices and fats from roast meat or poultry, used as base for gravy
**drizzle** (*vb*) sprinkle drops of liquid lightly over food
**dunk** (*vb*) dip a cake or bread into liquid before eating
**dust** (*vb*) sprinkle food with a dry ingredient
**duxelles** coarse hash of mushrooms and shallots sautéed
**en brochette** (*adj*) cut into chunks and broiled on a skewer
**en croûte** (*adj*) encased in pastry and baked
**entremets** vegetables or savories served with main course
**espagnole** (*adj*) with brown sauce
**estragon** (*adj*) with tarragon
**étouffée** (*adj*) smothered
**farci** (*adj*) stuffed
**flambé** (*adj*) served aflame after dousing with potable alcohol
**florentine** (*adj*) with spinach

**flute** (*vb*) form scalloped or undulating edge on pastry

**fondue** melted cheese with flavorings

**forcemeat** mixture of minced meat with egg white, used esp. as stuffing

**forestière** (*adj*) with mushrooms and bacon

**fumet** reduced stock, esp. fish

**galantine** boned, stuffed meat in aspic

**garnish** (*vb*) decorate with edible ornaments, such as parsley

**grecque** (*adj*) with olive oil and lemon

**grind** (*vb*) reduce solid food to small particles

**hash** fried, chopped meat and vegetables

**hold** (*vb*) serve dish without some usual ingredient or garnish, which is held back

**hull** (*vb*) remove leaves and stem of soft fruit

**Indienne** (*adj*) with curry

**jardiniere** (*adj*) with variety of fresh vegetables

**julienne** (*vb*) cut into matchstick-shaped pieces

**kabob** skewered, grilled cubes of meat and vegetables

**lardon** strip of fat drawn through meat with a needle

**lyonnaise** (*adj*) with onions

**macédoine** assortment of chopped fruits or vegetables

**maître d'hôtel** sauce of melted butter, minced parsley, and lemon juice or vinegar

**marinière** (*adj*) cooked in white wine, esp. fish

**mask** (*vb*) enhance appearance or taste of food by adding sauce or garnish

**meatballs** small spheres of ground meat cooked and served with sauce, soup, or pasta

**meunière** (*adj*) with browned butter, lemon, and parsley

**mirepoix** bed of cut vegetables on which to cook food

**nesselrode** (*adj*) with chestnuts

**Newburg** (*adj*) with cream, egg yolk, butter, and paprika sauce

**niçoise** (*adj*) with tomatoes, garlic, and olive oil

**normande** (*adj*) cooked with cider and cream

**omelette** sautéed eggs mixed with or folded around other ingredients

**over easy** (*adj*) describing fried egg that is flipped over and cooked briefly before serving

**pancake** egg and flour batter fried into circular cakes on griddle

**papillote** (*adj*) wrapped and cooked in greased paper or foil

**parmentier** (*adj*) with potatoes

**patty** thin, round, molded piece of ground or minced food; piece of food covered with batter and fried or baked

**peel** (*vb*) remove outer skin or layer of food, esp. of vegetable or fruit

**périgord** (*adj*) with truffles

**piccata** (*adj*) with lemon and parsley, also sometimes with capers

**pipe** (*vb*) squeeze soft mixture through pastry tube to form decorations or squeeze dough onto baking sheet

**pizza** circular, flat bread baked with cheese and tomato topping

**plump** (*vb*) soak dried fruits in liquid until they swell

**Provençale** (*adj*) with tomatoes, garlic, onions, and herbs

**quiche** savory egg custard tart with filling

**rare** (*adj*) cooked briefly, esp. meat

**ripieno** (*adj*) stuffed

**roast** meat, game, or poultry cooked over fire or in oven

**roulade** rolled, stuffed slice of meat or pastry

**roux** mixture of melted fat and flour, used as sauce base

**salad** fresh greens and other ingredients served cold and usu. raw: Caesar, chef's, coleslaw, composed, green, niçoise, pasta, potato, salmagundi, slaw, tabbouleh, tossed, Waldorf

**sandwich** assorted cold meats and fillings between bread slices: BLT, club, cold cuts, Cuban, Dagwood, double-decker, grinder, hero, hoagie, Italian sandwich, poor boy, Reuben, Sloppy Joe, submarine, torpedo, triple-decker, wedge

**sashimi** raw fish cut into very thin slices, arranged with ginger and wasabi horseradish

**savory** (*adj*) piquant and not sweet

**scallopine** thinly sliced, flour-dredged, sautéed meat

**short** (*adj*) crisp, flaky, and crumbling, esp. pastry

**stack** pile of pancakes

**sticks** food sliced or shaped into long pieces, often fried

**stock** meat, fish, or poultry broth, esp. when stored for use at later time

**stroganoff** (*adj*) with sour cream and mushrooms

**subgum** (*adj*) prepared with mixed vegetables in Chinese style

**sunnyside up** (*adj*) describing egg fried on one side only

**tandoori** (*adj*) baked in a clay tandoor oven

**temper** (*vb*) prepare egg for immersion in hot liquid

**unmold** (*vb*) remove from mold without losing shape

**vacuum-packed** (*adj*) sealed in a jar or can with nearly all air evacuated before sealing to preserve freshness

**Véronique** (*adj*) garnished with white grapes

**vol-au-vent** flaky pastry shell for filling with meat or vegetables and sauce

**well done** (*adj*) thoroughly cooked until all redness is gone, esp. meat

**whitebait** any small fish, esp. sprat, cooked whole without being cleaned

**zest** outer peel of citrus fruit, used for flavoring

## COOKING TECHNIQUES

**bake** (*vb*) cook with dry oven heat

**barbecue** (*vb*) cook over hot coals on grill or spit; grill

**bard** (*vb*) wrap meat with thin sheets of fat before roasting to prevent drying out

**baste** (*vb*) spoon liquid over food to moisten it while cooking

**batter** (*vb*) coat with flour, eggs, and breadcrumbs before frying

**beat** (*vb*) blend ingredients with rapid, rotary motion

**blacken** (*vb*) cook meat or fish over high, direct heat

**blanch** (*vb*) rinse or cook briefly in boiling water

**blend** (*vb*) stir ingredients together

**boil** (*vb*) heat to boiling point

**boil down** (*vb*) boil until reduced in volume

**braise** (*vb*) brown in fat, then cover and cook in liquid

**bread** (*vb*) coat with breadcrumbs

**broil** (*vb*) cook with hot coals or direct flame

**brown** (*vb*) sear surface of meat in pan, broiler, or oven to seal juices

**bruise** (*vb*) crush partially to release flavor

**butterfly** (*vb*) cut open and flatten

**can** (*vb*) preserve by sealing in airtight can or jar

**candy** (*vb*) cook in heavy syrup until glazed; coat with sugar

**caramelize** (*vb*) cook sugar until it forms brown syrup

**carbonado** (*vb*) score and broil, usu. meat

**casserole** (*vb*) bake mixed ingredients in casserole dish

**charbroil** (*vb*) broil or grill until blackened on outside

**chop** (*vb*) cut loosely and rapidly into small pieces

**churn** (*vb*) agitate milk in a container to make butter

**clarify** (*vb*) purify solid matter from fats or stock

**coddle** (*vb*) cook in water just below boiling point

**concentrate** (*vb*) make less dilute

**cream** (*vb*) blend until creamy and soft

**crisp** (*vb*) make brittle, usu. by frying

**crystallize** (*vb*) coat with sugar

**cube** (*vb*) cut into cube-shaped pieces

**curdle** (*vb*) coagulate, esp. milk; turn sour

**cure** (*vb*) prepare meat or fish for preservation by smoking, drying, or salting

**cut in** (*vb*) incorporate shortening into flour using two knives, so that mixture resembles uneven, coarse crumbs

**deep fry** (*vb*) cook by entirely submerging in hot fat

**deglaze** (*vb*) dissolve browned particles with liquid in sauté pan

**degrease** (*vb*) remove accumulated fat from surface of hot liquid

**dehydrate** (*vb*) remove moisture from, esp. to preserve

**desiccate** (*vb*) preserve by drying or dehydrating

**devein** (*vb*) remove dark dorsal vein from shrimp

**devil** (*vb*) season with mustard, cayenne, and other hot spices

**dice** (*vb*) cut into small cubes

**draw** (*vb*) remove entrails

**dredge** (*vb*) coat with flour, sugar, or crumbs

**dry** (*vb*) remove moisture from

**dry-roast** (*vb*) roast without oil, esp. nuts

**enrich** (*vb*) restore nutrients that have been lost in processing

**eviscerate** (*vb*) remove entrails from

**fillet** (*vb*) remove bones, esp. backbone from fish

**flake** (*vb*) break apart along natural separations

**flash-freeze** (*vb*) quick-freeze

**fold** (*vb*) blend ingredients lightly and gently so as to retain air

**force** (*vb*) stuff

**freeze-dry** (*vb*) dry a heat-sensitive food by freezing it and converting the ice to vapor in a high vacuum

**fricassee** (*vb*) cut up, brown, then cook in liquid

**frizzle** (*vb*) form into small, crisp curls, esp. by frying

**fry** (*vb*) cook in hot fat, either in deep fat or by pan-frying

**glaze** (*vb*) cover with glossy coating of juices, aspic, syrup, or egg

**grate** (*vb*) shred into particles or strips

**gratiné** (*vb*) bake or broil with sauce and crumbs in au gratin style

**grill** (*vb*) cook on open grid over hot coals; barbecue

**hard-boil** (*vb*) boil an egg until white and yolk solidify

**homogenize** (*vb*) prepare emulsion of milk by reducing size of fat globules to distribute them equally throughout

**knead** (*vb*) mix and work dough with one's hands

**lard** (*vb*) stuff meat with slices of fat

**macerate** (*vb*) steep in liquid, esp. liqueur

**marinate** (*vb*) soak in seasoned broth, juices, or wine

**mash** (*vb*) reduce food, usu. boiled, to soft, pulpy mass by pressure

**mince** (*vb*) chop finely

**mix** (*vb*) blend evenly

**mold** (*vb*) form into firm shape

**nap** (*vb*) cover with sauce that adheres to outline of food

**pan-boil** (*vb*) cook in uncovered frying pan over direct heat, using little or no fat

**pan-fry** (*vb*) fry in small amount of fat in skillet or shallow pan; sauté

**parboil** (*vb*) partially cook by boiling

**pare** (*vb*) remove skin or peel

**pickle** (*vb*) preserve in spiced brine

**poach** (*vb*) cook in liquid at or near boiling

**preserve** (*vb*) prepare fruit or vegetable by cooking with sugar, pickling, or canning, so as to resist spoilage

**purée** (*vb*) put solid food through sieve or blender or mash in mortar

**quick-freeze** (*vb*) freeze cooked or uncooked food very rapidly to facilitate lengthy storage; flash-freeze

**raise** (*vb*) make light by using yeast but not baking powder or soda

**reconstitute** (*vb*) return to liquid state by adding water

**reduce** (*vb*) cook liquid to decrease quantity and concentrate flavor

**refresh** (*vb*) plunge hot food into cold water to halt cooking

**render** (*vb*) remove animal fat

**rice** (*vb*) break soft food into small bits by forcing it through ricer

**ripen** (*vb*) advance or bring to maturity or best condition for use, esp. cheese

**roast** (*vb*) cook with dry oven heat, esp. meats

**salt** (*vb*) cure or preserve meat or fish by coating with salt

**sauté** (*vb*) brown quickly in small quantity of hot fat; pan-fry

**scald** (*vb*) heat food just to boiling point

**scallop** (*vb*) bake in layers topped with breadcrumbs

**score** (*vb*) cut surface of food

**scramble** (*vb*) stir vigorously and then cook in pan while stirring

**sear** (*vb*) brown surface quickly with high heat

**shirr** (*vb*) bake in shallow dish, esp. eggs

**shred** (*vb*) cut or grate into thin, irregular strips

**sift** (*vb*) remove lumps from dry ingredient by passing it through strainer or sieve

**simmer** (*vb*) cook in gently boiling water

**slice** (*vb*) cut lengthwise or crosswise into long or round pieces

**smother** (*vb*) steam slowly in heavy, closed vessel with minimal liquid

**soft-boil** (*vb*) boil an egg until white and yolk partially solidify, usu. for three to four minutes

**souse** (*vb*) pickle in vinegar or brine

**steam** (*vb*) cook over boiling water without allowing food to touch the water

**steep** (*vb*) pour boiling water over food and allow it to sit

**stew** (*vb*) simmer for a long time

**stir** (*vb*) mix with rotary motion

**stir-fry** (*vb*) cook quickly over high heat in wok or large fry pan

**stuff** (*vb*) fill cavity with seasonings, grains, or chopped vegetables; force

**sweat** (*vb*) cook vegetables or fruits slowly to release their juices

**thread** (*vb*) form a fine stream when poured boiling from a spoon

**toast** (*vb*) brown surface on grill, oven, or toaster, esp. bread

**toss** (*vb*) mix by flipping ingredients together

**truss** (*vb*) tie or sew legs and wings of poultry while roasting

**whip** (*vb*) beat lightly to incorporate air and increase volume

**whisk** (*vb*) beat vigorously until mixed or blended

## CUISINES, MEALS, AND RESTAURANTS

**à la carte** (*adj*) designating foods priced and chosen separately by dish

**alfresco** (*adj*) eaten outdoors

**antipasto** assorted Italian appetizers, esp. marinated vegetables and sliced meats

**appetizers** snacks; small items eaten before main course: antipasto, canapés, cold cuts, crudités, dim sum, dips, finger foods, hors d'oeuvres, kickshaw, rollmop, rumaki, spreads, starters, tapas, vorspeise

**Bake-Off** *Trademark*. contest in which baked goods are judged

**banquet** large, sumptuous spread of many dishes

**barbecue** outdoor meal consisting of meats cooked over charcoal; cookout

**bistro** small, unpretentious restaurant or tavern serving simple fare

**bite** small meal or snack

**blue plate special** restaurant main course at special low price

**box lunch** prepared lunch packaged in box

**brasserie** informal restaurant serving hearty food

**breakfast** morning meal

**brown bag** lunch carried in brown paper sack, esp. to office

**brunch** late morning meal, combining breakfast and lunch

**buffet** foods arranged for self-service

**cafeteria** self-service restaurant

**carryout** establishment that sells food to be eaten away from premises

**carte du jour** *French*. menu for the day

**carvery** roasted meats and poultry carved to diner's request in restaurant; restaurant providing such meats

**catering** food and service supplied at banquet

**charcuterie** delicatessen

**chophouse** restaurant that specializes in steaks and chops

**chuck wagon** provisions and cooking wagon used in American old west

**clambake** shellfish baked in sand on beach

**cocktail party** early evening gathering at which appetizers are served

**coffee break** snack taken on break from work, esp. mid-morning

**coffee shop** simple, low-priced restaurant serving plain fare

**convenience food** fast food

**cookery** cooking

**cooking** art and practice of preparing food; cookery

**cookoff** contest in which competitors prepare their specialties

**cookout** barbecue

**continental breakfast** breakfast of breads and coffee or tea

**course** one element of a meal, served at one time

**C ration** prepared, packaged soldier's meal

**crudités** sliced raw vegetables

**cuisine** manner of preparing food; style of cooking

**cuisine minceur** *French*. light foods prepared with minimal fat

**déjeuner** *French*. lunch

**deli** delicatessen

**delicatessen** shop serving prepared cooked meats, salads, and cheeses at counter; deli

**delivery** food delivered by restaurant to one's home

**dietetic** (*adj*) designating low-calorie food eaten to lose weight

**diner** small restaurant serving simple American fare

**dinner** main meal of day, eaten midday or evening

**dip** creamy mixture, esp. of savory ingredients, that is scooped up on chips or crudités

**dish** particular type, serving, or preparation of food

**doggie bag** bag supplied by restaurant in which leftovers are taken home

**drive-in** restaurant in which patrons are served or place orders while sitting in their cars

**early-bird special** reduced-price meal at restaurant for those seated early

**elevenses** *Brit. slang*. late-morning coffee or tea break

**entrée** dish served as main course of meal

**fast food** cheap, mass-produced dishes served quickly at walk-in or drive-in outlets; convenience food

**feast** banquet

**finger foods** appetizers that can be eaten with one's fingers, usu. in bite-size chunks

**first course** opening element of multicourse meal, usu. in smaller portion than entrée

**gourmet** food for connoisseur with sophisticated tastes

**greasy spoon** cheap diner or coffee shop

**haute cuisine** classic French cooking with rich sauces

**health food** natural or organic food with high nutritive value and low sodium or fat content, believed to promote good health

**high tea** *Chiefly Brit*. substantial late-afternoon snack with tea

**home cooking** simple, hearty fare

**hors d'oeuvres** appetizers

**junk food** low-quality, low-nutrition, starchy, sugary food

**kickshaw** tidbit or delicacy served as appetizers

**kosher** (*adj*) prepared according to Jewish dietary laws

**light meal** insubstantial meal, not a full-course meal

**lo-cal** (*adj*) *Informal*. designating cuisine or dish that is low in calories

**luau** outdoor Hawaiian feast with entertainment

**lunch** midday meal, usu. simpler than dinner or supper

**lunch counter** restaurant that serves meals, esp. lunch, to patrons seated at counter

**luncheon** formal midday meal, usu. with guests

**luncheonette** small diner serving lunch only

**macrobiotics** dietary philosophy based on yin and yang principles of balancing foods

**meal** customary time for eating, such as breakfast, lunch, or dinner; foods eaten at such a time

**meat and potatoes** plain, substantial fare

**mess** military self-service dining

**nouvelle cuisine** modern style of cooking emphasizing fresh, local ingredients and imaginative presentation

**on wheels** *Slang*. takeout food or food to go

**petit déjeuner** *French*. breakfast

**picnic** outdoor meal

**pit stop** *Informal*. roadside restaurant where one stops to eat on long car trip

**plat du jour** *French*. featured entrée of the day at restaurant

**pot luck** meal to which each guest contributes one dish

**power breakfast** breakfast meeting for usu. high-level business discussions

**prix fixe** *French.* meal served at restaurant at set price

**rabbit food** *Slang.* raw vegetables

**repast** meal; food consumed at one time

**restaurant** establishment serving and selling meals

**salad bar** self-service selection of ingredients for salad in restaurant or takeout establishment

**self-service** (*adj*) designating restaurant in which one takes food from serving area to table

**serving** amount of some particular food sufficient for one person

**servis compris** *French.* service charge included in price

**side dish** secondary dish served with entrée

**smorgasbord** Swedish cold buffet

**snack** small meal taken between regular meals

**soul food** southern U.S. African-American home cooking

**soup du jour** featured soup of the day at restaurant

**spread** extravagant, multicourse meal or feast

**square meal** substantial, full-course meal

**stay-on** cocktail party at which certain guests are invited to remain for full dinner

**supper** evening meal, lighter than dinner

**surf'n'turf** meat and seafood, esp. steak and lobster, served on same plate

**table d'hôte** *French.* complete meal served at stated time and set price

**takeout** food bought at restaurant to eat at home

**tapas** snack or appetizer served at bar in Spain

**tea** *Chiefly Brit.* late-afternoon snack with tea

**three-martini lunch** *Slang.* long business lunch on expense account, often with alcoholic beverages

**to go** (*adj*) describing food bought at restaurant to eat at home

**trattoria** small, inexpensive Italian restaurant

**TV dinner** frozen, prepackaged meal

**vegetarian** (*adj*) describing meals or cuisine without meat, chicken, or fish

**veggies** *Informal.* vegetables; meal of vegetables only

## COOKS AND SERVERS

**baker** person who makes and sells breads and cakes

**barkeeper** person who owns bar or serves alcoholic drinks; bartender

**barmaid** female who serves drinks at bar

**barman** bartender

**bartender** preparer and server of alcoholic drinks; barman

**busboy** person who clears dishes and resets tables in restaurant

**carhop** waiter or waitress at drive-in restaurant

**caterer** person who supplies, prepares, or serves food at large or private gatherings

**chef** chief cook, esp. one who plans menus and supervises others in preparation of food

**chef de cuisine** *French.* chef

**chief cook** chef

**confectioner** person who makes or sells candy and sweets

**cook** person who prepares food

**dishwasher** person who cleans dishes that have been used for cooking, eating, or serving food

**headwaiter** person who supervises waiters and busboys in restaurant

**host** person who receives and assists patrons at restaurant

**hostess** female host

**innkeeper** person who owns or operates an inn

**kitchen maid** female servant who assists cook and cleans up in kitchen

**maître d'** maître d'hôtel

**maître d'hôtel** headwaiter; maître d'

**pastry chef** person who prepares pastries; pastry cook

**pastry cook** pastry chef

**prep cook** kitchen assistant responsible for preparing ingredients to be used by chef

**publican** *Chiefly Brit.* proprietor or manager of tavern or bar

**restaurateur** owner or manager of restaurant

**scullery maid** female servant who prepares food for cooking

**server** waiter

**short-order cook** cook who prepares foods quickly, esp. at lunch counter

**soda jerk** *Informal.* person who prepares and serves ice cream dishes at soda fountain

**sommelier** wine steward

**sous-chef** person ranking next after chef in kitchen

**steward** person who supervises tables, wine, and waiters in restaurant or club

**waiter** person, esp. male, who serves food to others at tables

**waitress** female waiter

**wine steward** waiter responsible for serving wine in restaurant; sommelier

## PREPARED DISHES

**adobo** Philippine dish of marinated chicken or pork that is simmered and fried

**arroz con pollo** Latin American dish of chicken and rice cooked with saffron

**atole** cornmeal eaten as mush or gruel

**baba ghanouj** Middle Eastern mashed eggplant salad with olive oil, garlic, and tahini

**bacon and eggs** fried bacon strips, usu. with fried or scrambled eggs

**bangers and mash** British dish of sausage and mashed potatoes

**barbecued spareribs** pork ribs cooked over open fire and served with sauce usu. containing tomatoes, vinegar, and spices

**beef Bourguignonne** French beef dish with red wine, onions, and mushrooms

**beef en daube** French beef stew braised with vegetables, red wine, and herbs

**beef stroganoff** beef dish with sour cream, onions, and mushrooms

**beef Wellington** beef fillet with pâté de foie gras, covered with pastry

**bigos** mixed meat dish with sauerkraut

**blanquette de veau** veal stew served with egg sauce

**boiled dinner** meal of boiled meat, potatoes, and vegetables

**Boston baked beans** navy beans cooked with molasses and salt pork

**bouillabaisse** French stew of variety of fish and shellfish in seasoned vegetable broth

**bubble and squeak** British dish of fried cabbage and potato, sometimes with meat

**burrito** Mexican dish consisting of flour tortilla stuffed with meat, rice, beans, and cheese

**Caesar salad** salad of romaine lettuce, grated Parmesan cheese, and croutons in dressing of raw egg, lemon juice, and oil, sometimes with anchovies

**cannelloni** stuffed tubular pasta baked with sauce

**carbonara** pasta sauce of minced pancetta, egg yolks, and grated cheese

**cassoulet** French casserole of beans baked with meat

**cervelles au beurre noir** brains cooked with darkened butter sauce

**cheese soufflé** light, puffed, baked dish made with cheese, white sauce, and beaten egg whites

**chicken and dumplings** chicken served with small pieces of steamed or boiled dough

**chicken cacciatore** Italian chicken dish with herbs, tomatoes, and white wine

**chicken cordon bleu** breaded, sautéed chicken stuffed with ham and cheese

**chicken Marengo** chicken casserole with tomatoes, wine, onions, and mushrooms

**chicken paprika** chicken simmered in paprika and sour cream

**chicken Tetrazzini** baked dish of diced chicken, noodles, mushrooms, and cream sauce

**chili con carne** highly spiced Texas dish of beef, chilies, and usu. beans

**chili dog** hot dog covered with chili con carne

**chimichanga** crisp tortilla filled with meat and covered with salsa and sour cream

**chipped beef** dried, smoked beef sliced very thin

**cholent** Jewish stew of beef, beans, and potatoes, traditionally eaten on the Sabbath and cooked slowly for twenty-four hours

**chop suey** Chinese-American dish of bean sprouts, meat, mushrooms, and bamboo shoots, served with rice

**choucroute garnie** Alsatian dish of sauerkraut cooked with meats

**chowder** soup usu. with milk, salt pork, vegetables, and often seafood

**chow mein** Chinese-American stew of meat and vegetables, served with fried noodles

**churrasco** beef grilled under flames or broiled over open fire

**clams casino** broiled clams on the half shell, topped with bacon, breadcrumbs, and butter

**codfish balls** fried cakes of cod, potatoes, and egg

**colcannon** Irish dish of boiled cabbage, potatoes, and kale mashed together

**compote** dessert of fruit stewed in syrup

**confit** duck or goose cooked in its own fat and preserved

**coq au vin** French dish of chicken cooked in red wine with mushrooms and onions

**coquilles St. Jacques** scallops cooked in cream sauce with mushrooms, white wine, and Parmesan cheese

**corn dog** hot dog impaled on a stick and baked or deep fried in corn bread coating

**corned beef hash** mixture of diced corned or salted beef, potatoes, white sauce, and seasoning

**Cornish pasty** British dish of meat and vegetables wrapped in pastry and baked

**coulibiac** traditional Russian fish pie

**couscous** North African dish of steamed, cracked wheat, usu. served with lamb or chicken and sauce with vegetables

**creamed chipped beef** chipped beef simmered in milk and seasoned

**croquettes** small, rounded masses of cooked meat and vegetables coated with breadcrumbs and egg and deep-fried

**curry** Indian stew seasoned with combination of ground spices

**daube** stew of braised meat and vegetables

**deviled eggs** hard-boiled eggs with yolk mixed with mayonnaise or sour cream and paprika

**deviled ham** chopped, highly seasoned ham

**dhal** Indian sauce of puréed lentils and spices

**dirty rice** rice with Cajun spices, beans, and usu. sausage

**dolma** vine leaves stuffed with mixture of meat, rice, and spices

**egg foo yong** Chinese-American dish of beaten egg fried with meat and onions

**eggs Benedict** poached eggs and ham served on an English muffin and covered with hollandaise sauce

**enchilada** Mexican dish of rolled tortilla with meat or cheese filling, baked with chili-flavored tomato sauce

**fajitas** Mexican marinated beef or chicken cooked with variety of sauces and rolled in a tortilla

**falafel** Middle Eastern spicy, deep-fried patty of ground chickpeas or other vegetables

**fish and chips** British dish of fried, batter-coated fish with French-fried potatoes

**fondue** dish consisting of small pieces of meat, fruit, or bread dipped into a hot liquid such as melted cheese or chocolate

**French toast** bread dipped in egg-and-milk batter, then fried

**fried rice** Oriental dish of rice fried with meat and vegetables

**frittata** chopped vegetables or meat cooked in egg mixture

**fritter** battered, deep-fried food mixture

**gado-gado** Indonesian vegetable salad with peanut sauce

**gefilte fish** Jewish dish consisting of cakes of seasoned, chopped fish, eggs, and matzo meal cooked in fish broth

**gorp** trail mix

**goulash** Hungarian stew with meat, vegetables, and paprika

**guacamole** Mexican dip or salad of mashed avocado, lemon juice, salsa, garlic, and sometimes cilantro

**gumbo** Creole soup with okra, including seafood, vegetables, and meat

**haggis** Scottish dish of lungs, heart, and liver of a sheep or calf, with suet, oatmeal, and seasoning, boiled in the animal's stomach

**ham and eggs** traditional breakfast dish of cooked eggs served with slice of ham

**Hangtown Fry** omelet with bacon, fried oysters, and sometimes onions

**hasenpfeffer** marinated rabbit stew, usu. garnished with sour cream

**hot dogs and beans** baked beans cooked with sliced frankfurters

**hot pot** British dish of mutton or beef cooked in a pot with potatoes

**hummus** Middle Eastern dish of mashed chickpeas with olive oil, garlic, lemon juice, and tahini

**hush puppy** deep-fried cornmeal fritter

**jambalaya** Creole stew of rice, meat, vegetables, and spices

**kedgeree** Indian dish of rice, lentils, fish, seasonings, and sometimes egg

**kidney pie** British meat pie of kidney stew wrapped in dough

**kishke** animal intestine stuffed with flour, fat, onion, and seasoning; stuffed derma

**knish** dough stuffed with a filling, such as chopped meat and mashed potatoes, and baked

**kugel** baked pudding of potatoes or noodles

**lasagne** Italian baked dish consisting of layers of wide, flat pasta, tomato sauce, cheese, and usu. meat

**liver and onions** liver and onions sautéed together

**lobscouse** Scandinavian stew of meat, potatoes, onions, and ship biscuit

**lobster Newburg** dish of diced lobster cooked in cream sauce

**lobster thermidor** dish of lobster in cream sauce that is stuffed into lobster shell and browned

**macaroni and cheese** usu. tubular pasta baked with cheese sauce

**marinara** tomato sauce with garlic and spices served over pasta or seafood

**matelote** fish stew with seasoned wine sauce

**meatballs** small clumps of ground, seasoned meat, often served with gravy or sauce

**meat loaf** baked loaf of ground meat, egg, breadcrumbs, and seasoning

**moussaka** Greek dish with layers of ground meat and sliced eggplant, baked with seasoned sauce and cheese

**ossobuco** Italian dish of veal shanks stewed in white wine and tomatoes

**oysters Rockefeller** oysters topped with mixture of spinach, bacon, and seasonings and broiled on the half shell

**paella** Spanish dish of saffron-seasoned rice baked in stock with meat, seafood, and vegetables

**pakora** Indian fritter of chickpea flour

**pemmican** American Indian dish of powered dried meat mixed with hot fat and dried fruits and pressed into a loaf

**peperonata** Italian dish of peppers, tomatoes, onions, garlic, and olive oil

**pig-in-a-blanket** hot dog or sausage wrapped in dough and cooked; also, *esp. Brit.*, toad-in-the-hole

**pilaf** dish of seasoned rice or wheat

**piperade** Spanish omelet with strips of cooked ham

**piroshki** small pastry turnovers stuffed with meat, cheese, or vegetables

**pizza** thinly rolled dough covered with spiced mixture of tomatoes, cheese, and meat or vegetables and baked

**poi** Hawaiian dish of taro root that is baked, pounded, moistened, and fermented

**pork and beans** baked beans cooked with salt pork

**pork pie** pork stew covered with dough and baked

**potage** thick French soup, esp. made with cream

**potato chip** thin slice of potato fried crisp and usu. salted

**pot-au-feu** French dish of boiled meat and vegetables

**potpie** meat and vegetables covered with pastry and baked in a deep dish

**quennelle** poached dumpling of minced fish or meat

**raita** Indian dish of chopped cucumber or onion in yogurt

**ratatouille** seasoned vegetable stew of eggplant, tomatoes, zucchini, and peppers

**risotto** Italian dish of rice cooked in broth and seasonings

**rollmop** pickled herring, wrapped around an onion or pickle and skewed, served as an appetizer

**rumaki** chicken liver or water chestnut wrapped in bacon and broiled as appetizer

**saltim bocca** Italian dish of veal and ham wrapped together and sautéed in butter and sage

**sauerbraten** beef marinated in vinegar, onions, and spices before cooking

**sauerkraut** cut cabbage fermented in brine of its own juice with salt

**scallopine** thin slices of meat, esp. veal, sautéed in herbs and wine

**scampi** large shrimp broiled in garlic flavored sauce

**schnitzel** fried, breaded cutlet of veal or chicken

**Scotch egg** British dish of hard-boiled egg encased in sausage, breaded and deep-fried

**seviche** raw fish marinated in lime juice with tomatoes, peppers, and seasonings

**shepherd's pie** British meat pie baked with mashed potato crust

**souvlaki** Greek shish kabob consisting of small pieces of marinated meat and vegetables on a skewer

**spaghetti and clam sauce** Italian dish consisting of spaghetti pasta served with white or red sauce containing clams and garlic

**spaghetti and meatballs** Italian dish consisting of spaghetti pasta served with tomato sauce and meatballs

**Spanish rice** rice cooked with tomatoes, green peppers, and onions

**spoon bread** baked side dish of cornmeal, milk, eggs, and shortening

**steak and kidney pie** British meat pie of steak and kidney stew wrapped in dough

**stuffed cabbage** cabbage leaves wrapped around seasoned meat and rice mixture

**stuffed derma** Jewish dish consisting of animal intestine stuffed with matzo meal and onions, then roasted; kishke

**stuffed grape leaves** Greek dish of grape leaves wrapped around mixture of rice, herbs, and meat

**stuffed peppers** green peppers stuffed with rice, meat, or vegetables

**succotash** lima beans and corn kernels cooked together

**sukiyaki** Japanese dish of thinly sliced meat, vegetables, and bean curd, cooked with soy sauce, sugar, and sake

**sushi** Japanese dish consisting of cold cakes of rice flavored with vinegar and garnished with raw fish or vegetables

**Swiss steak** steak pounded with flour and browned with vegetables and seasonings

**tabbouleh** Middle Eastern salad of cracked wheat, parsley, and tomatoes in olive oil and lemon juice

**taco** Mexican dish of fried tortilla that is folded and filled with mixture of meat, cheese, and salad

**tahini** Middle Eastern sauce of sesame-seed paste

**tamale** Mexican dish of ground meat and peppers rolled in cornmeal, wrapped in cornhusks, and steamed

**tempeh** fermented soybean cake

**tempura** Japanese dish of seafood or vegetables dipped in egg batter and deep-fried

**teriyaki** Japanese dish of meat or fish marinated in spicy soy sauce and grilled or broiled

**terrine** chopped meat or vegetable mixture cooked in earthenware dish

**tofu** curdled, thickened soybean milk

**tostada** Mexican dish consisting of deep-fried, flat tortilla covered with meat, cheese, and salad

**trail mix** mixture of nuts, grains, seeds, and dried fruits, eaten as snack for energy; gorp

**tzatziki** Greek salad of yogurt and cucumber

**veal parmigiana** veal cutlets coated with breadcrumbs and fried, served with tomato sauce and Parmesan cheese

**veal scallopine**  veal cutlet dredged in flour and sautéed in butter and wine sauce

**Waldorf salad**  salad of chopped apple, celery, and walnut in mayonnaise

**Welsh rabbit**  melted, seasoned cheese, often mixed with beer, served on toast

**western**  omelette containing ham, green pepper, and onion

**Wiener schnitzel**  breaded veal cutlet that is fried and sometimes garnished with lemon slice and anchovy

**yakitori**  Japanese dish of small cubes of marinated chicken skewered and grilled

**Yorkshire pudding**  unsweetened batter of flour, salt, eggs, and milk, baked under roasting meat to catch drippings or baked alone with drippings from roast

# THE KITCHEN

Cookers
Pots and Pans
Utensils and Appliances
Dishes and Serving Containers
Glassware
Cutlery and Flatware
Linens and Accessories

**SEE ALSO**: Chap. 5: Containers; Chap. 7: Ornamental and Functional Articles; Chap. 9: Cooking and Cuisine; Chap. 17: Drinking and Alcoholic Beverages

## COOKERS

**autoclave**  pressure cooker

**barbecue**  grill or rack over hot coals, often on movable stand

**boiler**  vessel, esp. kettle, for boiling or heating

**brazier**  simple cooker containing live coals covered by a grill

**broiler**  oven compartment with overhead flame or heated coil

**burner**  gas or electric stove-top unit for heating food in pots and pans

**camp stove**  portable stove for outdoor cooking, usu. by gas

**convection oven**  oven unit with fan that circulates and intensifies heat, decreasing normal heating time

**cooker**  appliance or utensil for cooking food; *Chiefly Brit.* oven

**cooktop**  cooking surface consisting of a flat sheet of glass and ceramic material over a heating element, usu. electric

**corn popper**  enclosed vessel for popping corn kernels

**deep fat fryer**  often electric-powered basin with hot oil in which to immerse food

**espresso maker**  device that forces pressurized boiling water through finely ground coffee to make espresso, usu. with attachment for steaming milk

**griddle**  flat, wide, rimless cooking surface

**gridiron**  broiling grate in frame

**grill**  metal grid rack over coals

**hibachi**  small barbecue grid over hot coals (Japan)

**immersion heater**  electric heating coil dipped in liquids

**infrared broiler**  unit using infrared heat and having no flame

**microwave oven**  electronic cooker in which short microwave penetrations of food produce heat to cook food rapidly

**oven**  dry-heat cooker: electric, gas, pizza, tandoori

**pressure cooker**  airtight, steam-pressure cooking pot, usu. of reinforced steel or aluminum; autoclave

**rack**  grill

**range**  appliance with oven, broiler, and burners

**roaster**  oven or open fire for cooking with little liquid

**rotisserie**  small oven with attached spit, operated electrically

**salamander**  small browning or glazing broiler

**slow cooker**  electric cooking pot with tight-fitting lid, used for cooking meats at low temperatures over several hours

**smoker**  enclosure for flavoring or curing foods with smoke

**spit**  pointed skewer to hold meat over fire or coals

**steamer**  perforated rack fitted into pot containing boiling water

**steam table**  warming table on which food is held over boiling water

**stove**  cooking appliance with oven, broiler, and top burners; range

**tandoor**  cylindrical clay oven (India)

**toaster**  browning oven with electric heating coils, positioned vertically esp. for browning and crisping bread

**toaster oven**  electric appliance that toasts, broils, or bakes on heating coils positioned horizontally

**waffle iron**  two hinged metal griddles that close to cook batter

## POTS AND PANS

**baba**  small mold

**baking dish**  baking pan

**baking pan**  metal or glass ovenproof pan; baking pan

**baking sheet**  cookie sheet

**bean pot**  deep, round earthenware pot with narrow opening at top

**bread pan**  usu. rectangular pan for baking bread; loaf pan

**Bundt pan**  *Trademark.* tube-shaped cake pan with ridged surface

**cake pan**  round, square, or loaf-shaped ovenproof dish

**casserole**  deep, heavy pot with lid, used for baking

**cauldron**  very large pot or kettle

**chafing dish**  dish for cooking and keeping dishes warm on stand over low flame

**clay cooker**  large, round, tightly sealed earthenware casserole

**cocotte**  small ovenproof dish

**coffeepot**  electric or stovetop pot with internal mechanism for brewing coffee

**cookie sheet**  flat metal baking sheet

**cookware**  pots and pans

**coquille**  shell-shaped ovenproof dish

**cover**  flat, fitted top for pot or pan

**Crockpot**  *Trademark.* electric slow cooker

**dariole**  small, cylindrical mold

**double boiler**  pot fitted snugly atop another pot filled with boiling water

**Dutch oven**  cast-iron pot with lid

**electric frying pan**  frying pan with electrical heating unit

**feenjon**  small, metal pot with handle, used for boiling Turkish coffee

**frier**  frying pan

**frying pan**  shallow, long-handled pan for use above flame; frier; fry-pan; skillet

**fry-pan**  frying pan

**jelly-roll pan**  cookie sheet with one-inch-high lip around edge

**kettle**  metal pot for boiling water, often with narrow opening or spout at top

**loaf pan**  bread pan

**marmite**  large, steep-sided, metal or ceramic pot

**mold**  pan used to form food into shapes: butter, charlotte, chocolate, pâté, ring

**muffin pan**  baking pan with individual deep, round holders; muffin tin

**muffin tin**  muffin pan

**omelet pan**  slope-sided, long-handled frying pan for eggs

**paella pan**  very wide, shallow pan, often with two handles, used for baking

**pan**  broad, shallow, open, metal cooking container with handle

**percolator**  coffeepot in which boiling water bubbles up through tube and filters down through ground coffee held in perforated container near top

**pie pan**  shallow, round, ovenproof baking dish; pie tin

**pie tin**  pie pan

**pizza pan**  circular, flat, ovenproof metal plate

**poacher**  poaching pan

**poaching pan**  long, narrow pan with removable, porous tray; poacher

**pot**  usu. round, deep, covered cooking container with handle

**pudding mold**  round, heavy steaming dish with tight-fitting lid

**quiche pan**  shallow, circular baking pan with pinched edge

**ramekin**  small, shallow, ovenproof baking dish

**ring mold**  circular form used to set food into ring shape

**roasting pan**  cooking container for oven or open fire, usu. with rack or trivet inside

**samovar**  urn with spigot and heating element for boiling water to make tea

**saucepan**  medium-deep pot with handle

**sauté pan**  thick-bottomed, straight-sided skillet

**savarin**  ring mold

**skillet**  frying pan

**soufflé dish**  ovenproof, round, straight-sided baking dish

**spider**  cast-iron frying pan, orig. with legs to stand on hearth or over coals

**springform pan**  baking pan with detachable bottom

**steamer**  pot fitted with perforated insert that sits above water

**stew pan**  stewpot

**stewpot**  heavyweight pot for slow cooking, esp. of meat; stew pan

**stockpot**  large, tall, heavyweight pot

**tart tin**  vary small pie tin

**teakettle**  metal pot with small opening for boiling water

**Teflon pan**  *Trademark.* frying pan or pot coated with nonstick substance

**terrine**  earthenware baking dish, often rectangular

**timbale**  small, cylindrical mold

**tin**  metal baking pan

**tube pan**  deep, doughnut-shaped cake pan

**wok**  large, bowl-shaped frying pan (China)

## UTENSILS AND APPLIANCES

**apple corer**  pointed tube on handle for removing apple cores

**appliance**  usu. electrical device used in food preparation

**bain-marie**  warming dish using steam heat

**banquet cloth**  long, protective tablecloth for banquet table

**biscuit cutter**  deep, round device for cutting out dough

**blender**  electric appliance with rotary blades that chop, purée, or liquefy foods

**bottle opener**  metal lever for removing bottle caps

**breadboard**  solid wood slab for cutting bread and other foods; cutting board

**brochette**  spit or skewer

**brush**  small bristle brush for basting meat or buttering pastry

**bulb baster**  rubber tube and bulb for siphoning fats and liquids

**butcher block**  slab of wood up to three inches thick for cutting food, esp. meat; chopping block

**cake break**  wide-tined fork for slicing cake

**cake rack**  low grid for cooling baked items

**calabash**  large, hard-shell gourd used as scoop or ladle

**canister**  wide-mouthed container with tight-fitting lid, used for storing dry goods

**can opener**  manual or electrical device with rotary blade for cutting can lids

**cherry pitter**  small plunger for extracting pits

**china cap**  cone-shaped sieve; chinois

**chinois**  china cap

**chopping block**  butcher block

**chopping board**  wooden cutting surface

**chopsticks**  two small sticks for lifting food, operated in one hand

**church key**  device for opening cans by punching V-shaped hole in top

**churn**  container with paddle or agitating mechanism in which cream or milk is stirred to make butter

**cleaver**  heavy knife with broad blade, used esp. to cut meat through bones or joints or into large chunks

**coffee grinder**  closed container with rotary blades for grinding coffee, operated electrically or manually; coffee mill

**coffee mill**  coffee grinder

**colander**  perforated bowl for rinsing and draining

**cookie cutter**  form used to shape and cut cookie dough

**cookie press**  tube and plunger used to form cookie dough

**cooking fork**  long-tined fork on handle, used to move cooking foods

**cooler**  usu. insulated container for keeping foods cold

**corkscrew**  spiral, lever, or pincer used to extract cork from wine bottle

**Cuisinart**  *Trademark.* food processor

**cutting board**  breadboard

**dasher**  plunger with paddles at one end for mixing liquids in churn or ice cream freezer

**drum sieve**  round frame with screen in bottom through which food is forced with a pestle

**egg beater** rotary beater also used for whipping cream and smoothing batter

**egg slicer** parallel wires on hinged frame, used for cutting eggs

**food mill** perforated pot with crank for puréeing

**food processor** electric appliance with set of blades revolving inside container, used for cutting, blending, grating, and puréeing solid foods

**fork** tined spearing utensil

**frying basket** perforated enclosure on handle, used for dipping foods into deep fat

**funnel** cone open at top and leading into thin tube opening at bottom

**garlic press** small perforated masher with handle

**grapefruit spoon** teaspoon with serrated tip

**grater** punched metal surface for shredding foods, sometimes rotated by handle or freestanding with different size holes on each side

**grinder** manual or electrically powered tool used to pulverize, shred, or powder foods, esp. meats, coffee beans, and nuts

**hand beater** handheld rotary beater powered electrically

**ice cream maker** electric or hand-cranked device packed with ice around container that holds ice cream ingredients

**ice pick** pointed metal stick for breaking ice cubes

**jagging wheel** jagged-edged wheel on handle, used for cutting pastry into ornamental shapes

**jar opener** pliers with wide jaws that clamp around jar lids to loosen them

**juicer** electric appliance for extracting juice from fruit and vegetables

**kitchen shears** scissors for cutting foods

**knife** bladed instrument with handle, used for cutting, slicing, chopping: boning, bread, butcher, carving, chef's, chopping, coring, filleting, grapefruit, paring, serrated, slicing, utility

**ladle** deep, large spoon for serving soups

**mandolin** grater and slicer with wooden frame and adjustable blade

**masher** stiff wire instrument for puréeing, esp. potatoes

**measuring cup** marked or sized container for determining amounts

**measuring spoon** any of various sized spoons for determining amounts

**meat grinder** blades that rotate on handle to reduce meat to pulp

**meat pounder** wooden mallet with smooth and rough surfaces, used for thinning or tenderizing meat

**meat thermometer** gauge on pointed stem that is inserted in meat to register internal temperature and determine when it is properly cooked

**melon baller** bowl-shaped spoon for scooping melon

**mixer** manual or electric beating instrument for blending ingredients

**mixing bowl** round container for blending

**mortar and pestle** heavy bowl and grinding stick for pulverizing

**nutcracker** pliers for breaking nutshells

**nutpick** slender, pointed implement for removing meat from nut shells

**oven thermometer** temperature gauge that hangs on rack in oven

**oyster knife** short, rigid knife with hand guard at base of handle

**pastry bag** cloth bag with nozzled tube for shaping dough

**pastry blender** mixing utensil of wire tines bound at their ends on handle

**pastry brush** soft, small bristles bound to handle

**pastry jagger** notched wheel for decorating dough

**pastry scraper** flat blade on handle, used for manipulating pastry dough

**pastry tube** conical tube with patterned opening at one end, fitted on cloth bag for shaping icings and soft foods as they are squeezed through the bag

**pepper mill** peppercorn grinder

**peeler** rotating blade used to skin fruits and vegetables

**pitter** clamping device with small punch for removing fruit or olive pits

**pizza cutter** circular blade that rotates on handle, used for cutting pastry or pizza

**poultry shears** strong scissors for disjointing chickens and other poultry

**rack** wide grate used to support roast in pan

**reamer** ridged cone for juicing citrus fruits

**ricer** utensil with small holes through which soft food is forced to produce rice-size particles

**rolling pin** long, narrow cylinder for flattening dough

**rubber spatula** spatula with flexible rubber blade, used esp. for scraping bowls

**salad basket** mesh container used to wash and drain lettuce

**salad spinner** enclosed salad basket operated by handle

**scoop** small shovel, esp. used to take up dry materials

**scraper** serrated utensil for removing skins; rubber spatula for scraping sauces out of bowls

**sharpener** sharpening steel

**sharpening steel** solid block or long tube of steel on handle, used for sharpening knives; sharpener

**sieve** dome-shaped strainer with mesh bottom, esp. for separating coarse from fine parts of loose matter

**sifter** strainer for flour or sugar

**skewer** long, slender, pointed utensil of metal or wood, inserted through meat or other food while cooking

**skimmer** flat, very fine mesh strainer on handle, used for removing scum or particles from surface of liquid

**slotted spoon** large spoon with perforations, for removing solid pieces from liquid

**spatula** flat, usu. flexible-bladed device of metal, wood, or rubber, used for scraping or turning

**spoon** small, shallow bowl on handle: ice-cream scoop, measuring, slotted, table, tea, wooden

**spork** combination spoon and fork, esp. for removing spaghetti from water

**standing electric mixer** round bowl and mixing blades that attach to electric motor

**steamer basket** perforated basket on feet that holds food and stands above boiling water in steaming pot

**strainer** device for retaining solid bits and passing liquids

**tampon** absorbent cloth roll for wiping and tidying serving dishes

**tea ball** perforated enclosure on chain for brewing tea

**timer** device that can be set to make sound after set interval of time

**tongs** pincers for lifting and holding food

**trivet** metal support or rack, decorative or protective

**trussing needle** metal pin used to fasten meats while roasting

**utensil** implement, instrument, or vessel used in cooking

**vegetable parer**  pair of parallel blades on handle, joined at tip, used to peel fruits and vegetables

**whip**  whisk

**whisk**  beater consisting of several wire loops held together in handle; whip

**wood spoon**  long-handled spoon made of wood, used for stirring foods, esp. batter

**zester**  small knife with serrated lateral blade, used for cutting citrus rind

## DISHES AND SERVING CONTAINERS

**boat**  small, deep, usu. oblong serving dish

**bowl**  deep, rounded, hemispherical container that is open at the top: cereal, chopping, compote, cream, finger, fruit, porringer, punch, revere, salad, soup

**breadbasket**  often wickerwork container for serving bread, also made of wood or pottery

**charger**  large, shallow dish or platter

**coffee cup**  small cup, often with handle and matching saucer

**coffeepot**  pitcher or enclosed pot for serving coffee

**compote**  long-stemmed dish for serving fruit or sweets

**cookie jar**  lidded container for storing cookies

**creamer**  small pitcher with spout for serving cream or milk with coffee or tea

**cruet**  small glass bottle with stopper, used esp. for holding oil and vinegar

**cup**  small, open beverage container, often round and with handle: breakfast, coffee, custard, demitasse, egg, kylix, mug, noggin, tea

**decanter**  decorative, quart-size, glass bottle with stopper for serving wine

**demitasse**  small, delicate cup for serving strong black coffee

**dessert plate**  plate smaller than salad plate

**dinner plate**  large plate that holds individual portion of main course of meal

**dish**  shallow, slightly concave, usu. round container made of glass or ceramics, on which food is served

**eggcup**  small, deep-bowled cup for serving boiled egg

**finger bowl**  small, low bowl that holds water in which to rinse fingers at table

**gratin dish**  low, round baking and serving dish with two handles

**gravy boat**  medium serving pitcher with handle, often on saucer

**jar**  cylindrical container with large opening and no spout

**jug**  large container for liquids with small opening or spout and handle

**kylix**  shallow bowl with two handles, used as drinking cup (ancient Greece and Rome)

**lazy Susan**  revolving serving platter, usu. placed in center of table

**nappy**  small, shallow serving dish, often of glass, with flat bottom and sloping sides

**noggin**  small mug or cup

**pitcher**  large container with handle and lip or spout for pouring liquids

**plate**  shallow dish, usu. round, from which food is eaten: bread and butter, dessert, dinner, luncheon, salad, saucer, service

**platter**  large, flat serving dish, usu. with lip: charger, chop, fish, nappy, well-and-tree

**porringer**  low dish with handle, from which soup or porridge is eaten

**punch bowl**  large bowl from which punch is served, usu. with ladle

**revere bowl**  round, silver serving bowl with stand

**salad bowl**  large, deep bowl, often of wood, for tossing and serving salads

**salad plate**  medium-sized plate intermediate between dessert plate and dinner plate, holding one serving of salad

**salt cellar**  small container with perforated top for storing and shaking out salt

**salver**  tray on which food is served

**saucer**  small, round, shallow dish used under another container, esp. with indentation to hold cup

**scallop shell**  wide, flat shell of a scallop, used as a serving dish

**service plate**  large plate, often having lip, from which food is served to diners' plates

**serving container**  any vessel used for storing and serving food or drink

**soup bowl**  wide or deep bowl that holds one serving of soup

**sugar bowl**  small, decorative bowl for serving sugar

**teapot**  usu. round, ceramic or china container with top and spout for brewing and serving tea

**tea service**  complete set of china or silver pots, pitchers, bowls, cups, and saucers for serving tea

**thermos**  bottle with inner and outer walls enclosing vacuum to keep liquids at or near original temperature

**tray**  flat, wide surface, often with slightly raised edges, for carrying and serving food

**tureen**  large, deep serving dish with lid, esp. for soups

**well-and-tree platter**  platter with depression in shape of tree whose trunk ends in deep well for accumulation of liquids

**wine basket**  tall reed container for holding open wine bottle

## GLASSWARE

**balloon**  large, round, stemmed red-wine glass

**beer mug**  thick-walled glass cup, often with handle

**brandy snifter**  balloon-shaped, stemmed glass

**champagne coupe**  glass with shallow bowl, flared lip, and stem

**champagne flute**  narrow, conical, stemmed glass

**champagne saucer**  very wide, flat, stemmed glass

**champagne tulip**  gently curved, stemmed glass

**cocktail**  tall, narrow glass for mixed and iced drinks

**collins**  tall, narrow, iced drink glass

**cooler**  tall, narrow, iced drink glass

**copita**  stemmed sherry glass

**cordial**  small, stemmed glass

**flagon**  large metal or pottery vessel with handle

**footed pilsener**  tall, conical beer glass with wide base on stem

**glass**  any drinking vessel made of hard, brittle, transparent, crystallized material

**goblet**  large, round, stemmed wineglass

**heavy goblet**  thick-walled goblet

**highball** tall, straight-sided cocktail glass
**hock glass** thick or knobby-stemmed wineglass
**hourglass** glass that narrows in middle to stemmed bottom
**jigger** small glass used to measure 11/2 fluid ounces
**juice glass** plain, cylindrical glass for fruit juice
**mug** heavy drinking cup with handle, esp. earthenware
**mug stein** large, glass beer mug
**old-fashioned** short, squat tumbler
**parfait** small, narrow, stemmed glass
**Paris goblet** glass with large, round bowl and tall stem
**pilsner** tall, conical beer glass with short stem
**pony** small beer glass; small liqueur glass
**port glass** small, narrow, conical, stemmed glass
**punch cup** small, bowl-shaped cup with handle
**red-wine glass** large, stemmed wineglass
**rock glass** short glass for liquor over ice
**schooner** large beer mug
**seidel** large beer mug, often with hinged lid
**sham pilsner** short, conical beer glass
**sherbet** small, slant-sided glass
**sherry glass** flared-lipped, wide, conical glass with short stem
**shot** very small, heavy-bottomed, narrow glass
**snifter** balloon-shaped, stemmed glass
**sour glass** small, slant-sided glass, often with stem
**stein** large, usu. earthenware beer mug
**tankard** tall, one-handled, lidded mug, often pewter or silver
**Trier** stemmed, cut-glass, white-wine glass
**tulip goblet** round bowl glass with flared rim and stem
**tumbler** medium-tall, cylindrical glass
**whiskey sour glass** tall, narrow, stemmed cocktail glass
**white-wine glass** medium-size, stemmed wineglass
**wineglass** tall, rounded glass on stem, often of crystal
**zombie** very tall cocktail glass

## CUTLERY AND FLATWARE

**butter knife** small knife with dull blade, used for cutting and spreading butter
**carving fork** fork with two long tines and rim on which to rest thumb and forefinger at base of handle, used to hold meat being carved
**carving knife** large, sharp knife for slicing meat
**cheese knife** small knife, often with blunt end and wide blade
**chopsticks** two small sticks of wood or ivory held in one hand and used to lift food to mouth, esp. in Asia
**cocktail fork** small, three-tined fork
**cutlery** knives
**dessert fork** fork that is smaller than dinner fork
**dessertspoon** spoon intermediate in size between tablespoon and teaspoon
**dinner fork** large fork used for eating main course of meal
**flatware** eating tools, esp. forks, spoons, and knives
**fork** instrument with two or more prongs at end of handle, used to lift food to mouth: carving, cake break, cocktail, cold meat, dinner, fish, lemon, olive, oyster, pickle, salad
**grapefruit spoon** teaspoon with serrated tip, used to eat sections of grapefruit
**knife** small blade on handle, used for spreading and cutting: butter, carving, cheese, fish, jelly, oyster, pie, steak

**oyster fork** small, three-tined fork, used in eating shellfish
**runcible spoon** combination fork and spoon with concave body and pronglike tines
**serving spoon** large, often deep spoon with long handle, used for serving food
**silverware** cutlery and utensils of silver
**soupspoon** large spoon, usu. with rounded bowl, for eating soup
**spoon** device with small, shallow, concave bowl on handle, used for stirring or eating liquids: coffee, cream, dessertspoon, five o'clock, fruit, grapefruit, iced tea, nut, pierced, runcible, salt, serving, soupspoon, tablespoon, teaspoon, tomato
**steak knife** small knife with serrated cutting edge, used to slice meat
**tablespoon** spoon larger than teaspoon or dessertspoon, used in serving food and as standard measure
**teaspoon** small spoon, used esp. to stir coffee and tea or eat desserts

## LINENS AND ACCESSORIES

**aluminum foil** paper-thin sheet of aluminum on roll, used to wrap foods, line cookers, and serve as lid
**cheesecloth** fine mesh cloth for straining broth or binding herbs
**cookbook** book containing recipes and cooking instructions
**cozy** padded covering used to retain warmth of liquid in container, esp. in teapot
**dish drain** open rack used to stack drying dishes
**dish towel** small cloth for washing and drying dishes
**glove** insulated hot pad in form of glove that encloses entire hand
**hot pad** potholder
**linens** objects made of cloth, esp. napkins
**napkin** paper or cloth square for wiping hands and lips; serviette
**napkin ring** metal ring for holding napkin at place setting
**paper towels** thin sheets of absorbent paper, usu. on roll, for drying and cleaning surfaces
**parchment** thick parchment paper used to wrap certain baked items
**place mat** decorative cloth, reed, or plastic sheet for place setting, used to protect table
**place setting** cutlery, glassware, dishes, and napkin, often arranged on place mat
**plastic wrap** very thin sheet of clear plastic on roll, used to wrap foods and seal moisture or flavor
**potholder** heavy, insulated, usu. square piece of material for lifting very hot objects; hot pad
**serviette** *Chiefly Brit.* napkin
**silent butler** receptacle with hinged lid, used for collecting table crumbs and emptying ashtrays
**spice box** rack or box for holding spices
**tablecloth** large, decorative cloth covering entire table
**tidy** porous plastic container for collecting garbage in sink
**trivet** support or rack used to protect surfaces from hot serving dishes
**wax paper** thin sheet of waxed paper on roll, used to cover surfaces or placed on standing sauces to prevent formation of skin

# Clothing

# OUTER GARMENTS

Overcoats and Cloaks
Coats and Jackets
Suits and Uniforms
Sweaters and Vests
Shirts and Tops
Dresses and Skirts
Trousers, Shorts, and Leggings
Sporting and Exercise Wear
Liturgical Vestments
Armor

**SEE ALSO**: Chap. 10: Ornaments and Accessories; Footwear; Hats, Headgear, and Hairpieces

## OVERCOATS AND CLOAKS

**academic gown** long, flowing robe worn during college ceremonies, esp. graduation
**anorak** parka, often hooded (Eskimo)
**Aquascutum** *Trademark*. raincoat
**balmacaan** loose overcoat, single-breasted, with raglan sleeves
**benjamin** *Slang*. man's loose-fitting overcoat
**bertha** woman's loose, round-shouldered cape
**boubou** long, loose, often brightly colored outer garment worn by either sex (Africa)
**Burberry** *Trademark*. raincoat
**burnoose** man's hooded, cloaklike robe, worn by Arabs
**caftan** cotton, ankle-length, long-sleeved cloak (Middle East)
**cagoule** light, hooded raincoat
**cape** sleeveless garment with fitted neck that hangs loose over shoulders
**capelet** small shoulder cape
**capote** long, hooded overcoat
**capuchin** woman's hooded cloak
**car coat** hip-length overcoat or jacket
**cardinal** woman's short cloak with hood, orig. scarlet
**chesterfield** topcoat with fly front and velvet collar, often double-breasted
**chiton** rectangle of fabric, esp. gown or tunic, turned down at top and gathered at waist, knee- or full-length (ancient Greece)
**chlamys** man's thigh-length, oblong mantle (ancient Greece)
**cloak** long, sleeveless, capelike concealing robe
**covert coat** short topcoat
**cowl** monk's hooded cloak
**djellabah** loose-fitting, hooded gown or robe worn by men (North Africa)
**domino** loose, hooded cloak worn as costume with half-mask
**dreadnought** heavy woolen coat; fearnought
**duffle** hooded coat of heavy wool with toggle fasteners
**duster** lightweight protective driving coat
**fearnought** dreadnought

**frock** tunic, mantle, long coat, smock, or monk's robe
**fur coat** luxurious dress coat of animal fur
**fur-lined coat** overcoat lined with animal fur
**gaberdine** long, coarse coat or smock worn esp. by medieval Jews
**greatcoat** *Chiefly Brit*. heavy, full-length overcoat; long coat
**haik** long, loose, white cloth worn as outer garment (North Africa)
**hauberk** chain-mail tunic (12th–14th c.)
**himation** long, loose cloth draped over left shoulder (ancient Greece)
**Inverness** overcoat with detachable cape (Scotland)
**joseph** woman's long cloak (18th c.)
**jubbah** full-length outer garment with long sleeves (Middle East and North Africa)
**kaross** cloak of animal skins (southern Africa)
**kibr** hooded, sleeved robe (Middle East)
**kimono** long, wide-sleeved, sashed robe (Japan)
**kirtle** tunic; woman's long gown (medieval Europe)
**loden** coat of short-piled, waterproof, loden fabric
**London Fog** *Trademark*. brand of belted trench coat
**long coat** greatcoat
**macfarlane** heavy, caped overcoat with sides slit open for arms
**mackintosh** *Chiefly Brit*. lightweight raincoat
**manta** square blanket used as cloak (Latin America)
**manteau** loose coat, cloak, robe
**mantelet** very short cape or cloak
**mantle** loose, sleeveless cloak
**mantua** woman's loose-fitting cloak (17th–18th c.)
**monk's robe** long, usu. dark cloak worn in religious orders
**Newmarket** long, close-fitting coat worn as woman's overcoat or man's riding coat (19th c.)
**oilskin** raincoat of oiled, waterproof cloth; slicker
**opera cape** short, elegant evening cloak
**paletot** loose cloak with one or more capes (19th c.)
**pallium** man's draped rectangular cloth (ancient Greece and Rome)
**parka** fur, down, or nylon cold-weather jacket; hooded jacket
**peacoat** sailor's hip-length coat of dark blue wool; pea jacket
**pelerine** woman's narrow fur or fabric shoulder cape, with ends hanging down front (19th c.)
**pelisse** woman's long cloak with fur collar and trim
**peplos** woman's shawl (ancient Greece)
**petersham** man's bulky overcoat of petersham wool
**poncho** wool blanket with slit opening for head; similarly cut nylon or rubber raincoat
**raglan** topcoat with sleeves extending to collar, esp. for improved water resistance
**raincoat** waterproof overcoat
**rebozo** colorful wool shawl (Mexico)
**redingote** man's three-quarter-length, double-breasted coat with wide flat cuffs (18th c.)
**robe** long, loose outer garment, often ceremonial
**roquelaure** knee-length cloak that buttoned in front (18th–19th c.)
**ruana** wool covering with slit for head, like poncho (Colombia)
**serape** man's wool shoulder shawl (Mexico)

**shador** garment that covers all of body and head, worn by Muslim women

**shawl** heavy oblong, triangular, or square cloth worn over head and shoulders, esp. by women

**shearling** coat of sheepskin from recently shorn sheep

**shroud** burial garment

**slicker** oilskin

**smock** loose, protective, often yoked outer shirt garment

**sou'wester** sailor's long oilskin coat with buckles

**stole** long scarf or shoulder wrap with hanging ends in front

**surcoat** tunic worn over medieval armor; any outer coat

**surtout** man's long, fitted frock coat; woman's hooded mantle

**tabard** knight's short, loose, and sleeveless tunic; herald's cape emblazoned with lord's arms (medieval Europe)

**talma** long, circular cape or shoulder cape and hood (19th c.)

**tippet** fur or cloth shoulder cape

**toga** crescent-shaped fabric that is wrapped and draped around the body (ancient Rome)

**topcoat** lightweight overcoat

**topper** woman's short, loose-fitting topcoat

**topsider** heavy-duty, capelike, rubber raincoat

**trench coat** double-breasted raincoat with deep pockets, wide belt, and epaulets

**tunic** loose, draped gown, gathered at hips (ancient Greece and Rome)

**ulster** long, loose, belted, heavy coat, esp. with hood or cape (Ireland)

**watch coat** sailor's heavy overcoat

**wrap** outer garment worn wrapped and overlapping around body

## COATS AND JACKETS

**basque** woman's tight bodice jacket with attached skirt

**bi-swing** jacket with pleat or gusset at back of arms, allowing free movement

**blazer** single-breasted, informal coat with three patch pockets and metal buttons, in solid color or stripes

**blouse** loose, calf-length worker's garment

**bolero** very short, open jacket without lapels, often sleeveless

**bomber jacket** fitted leather jacket, orig. for bomber pilot; pilot jacket

**box coat** short, square-cut coat

**bush jacket** safari jacket

**car coat** protective coat for driving; coach coat

**cardigan** close-fitting, knitted jacket that opens down front

**claw hammer** *Informal.* swallow-tailed coat (18th c.)

**coach coat** car coat

**combat jacket** adaptation of close-fitting, waist-length woolen jacket with tight cuffs and waist, formerly worn by military personnel

**cutaway** single-breasted coat with knee-length skirts in back

**denim jacket** sturdy, fitted jacket of coarse blue twill fabric; jean jacket

**dinner jacket** short, dark coat with silk rolled collar and no tails; tuxedo jacket

**dolman** woman's coat with wide dolman sleeves tapering at the wrists

**double-breasted jacket** jacket having deep, overlapping front closure and two rows of buttons

**doublet** man's close-fitting jacket, sometimes sleeveless (16th c.)

**Eton jacket** short, black jacket with wide lapels and long sleeves

**flyaway jacket** loose, flowing jacket with fullness at back

**formal** man's evening jacket

**frock coat** close-fitting dress coat with no waist seam and long skirts front and back

**guernsey** man's heavy, close-fitting, knitted sporting jacket

**hacking jacket** riding jacket with tight waist and flared skirt having slit sides or back

**jean jacket** denim jacket

**jerkin** close-fitting, hip-length, sleeveless jacket

**justaucorps** fitted, knee-length coat with flaring and stiffened skirts (17th c.)

**kirtle** man's tunic (medieval Europe)

**lounge coat** single- or double-breasted informal coat with no waist seam; smoking jacket

**mackinaw** short, belted coat of heavy, nappy mackinaw wool, often in plaid

**Mao jacket** jacket with long, close-fitting cut and narrow, tight, stand-up mandarin collar, popular in China

**maxicoat** full-length coat

**mess jacket** fitted, waist-length uniform jacket; monkey jacket

**monkey jacket** mess jacket

**morning coat** coat with front cut away to tails at center-vented back

**Nehru jacket** lightweight, fitted jacket with band collar (India)

**Norfolk jacket** usu. tweed jacket with box pleats, patch pockets, and belt

**pilot jacket** bomber jacket

**pourpoint** padded, quilted doublet

**Prince Albert** long, double-breasted frock coat

**reefer** short, double-breasted jacket

**sack coat** man's straight-backed jacket of coarse black cloth

**safari jacket** long, belted cotton jacket with pairs of pleated pockets above and below belt; bush jacket

**sanbenito** Spanish sackcloth coat for penitents

**shell jacket** short, tight, front-buttoning military jacket

**shooting jacket** loose-fitting, durable hunting jacket

**shrug** woman's tight-fitting, one-button, waist-length jacket

**single-breasted jacket** jacket having single button row and no overlapping closure

**ski jacket** lightweight, waterproof jacket, insulated for protection from cold, usu. worn in snow

**smoking jacket** lounge coat

**spencer** waist-length jacket (19th c.)

**spiketail coat** tails

**sport coat** man's casual coat

**sport jacket** sport coat

**swagger coat** coat flaring from shoulder to hem

**swallow-tailed coat** tails

**tails** man's fitted dress jacket cut short in front, with two long, tapering skirts at back; spiketail coat; swallow-tailed coat

**tuxedo jacket** dinner jacket without tails

**Windbreaker** *Trademark.* thin jacket of wind-resistant material, esp. nylon

**woolly** wool jacket

**Zouave jacket** short, colorful military jacket, closed at neck only (French Algerian)

## Suits and Uniforms

**bib and tucker** *Brit. slang.* entire outfit of clothing, esp. formal

**black tie** man's semiformal evening wear, usu. tuxedo jacket worn with black bow tie

**blues** formal blue U.S. military uniform; dress blues

**bodysuit** close-fitting, one-piece torso garment, often with sleeves and snap crotch opening

**business suit** traditionally tailored, two- or three-piece suit

**butternuts** homespun overalls dyed brown with butternut extract

**cap and gown** ceremonial, full-length gown with sleeves and mortarboard cap, worn at commencement and other academic ceremonies

**casual suit** man's informal two-piece suit

**civvies** *Informal.* civilian clothes, as opposed to military uniform

**coverall** one-piece protective garment reaching from neck to ankles

**double-breasted suit** trousers and jacket with overlapping front closure and two rows of buttonholes

**dress blues** blues

**dress suit** man's formal or business suit

**dress whites** whites

**fatigues** heavy-duty military work uniform, often colored khaki or in camouflage design

**full dress** most formal military uniform

**gi** thick cotton jacket and loose trousers worn by martial arts practitioners (Japan)

**gray flannel suit** conservative gray wool business suit

**jumper** workman's jumpsuit

**jumpsuit** one-piece garment consisting of shirt with attached trousers; one-piece suit

**layette** newborn infant's complete outfit

**leisure suit** man's casual trousers and matching jacket styled like a shirt, often in pastel polyster (1970's)

**livery** identifying uniform of servants or workers

**lounge suit** suit with short-skirted jacket, slightly fitted; *Chiefly Brit.* man's suit for informal occasions

**mod suit** fitted suit in exaggerated fashion of 1960's, esp. with bell-bottom trousers and wide or no lapels

**olive drab** sturdy military field uniform

**one-piece suit** jumpsuit

**pantsuit** woman's suit with slacks instead of skirt matching jacket; slack suit

**pinstripe suit** dark suit with thin, white, vertical stripes

**regimentals** military uniform of particular regiment

**riding habit** fitted jacket and breeches worn while riding horseback

**sack suit** suit with short, loose-fitting sack coat

**sailor suit** traditional white or blue cotton naval uniform with wide collar and bell-bottomed trousers

**scrub suit** gown worn in surgery by doctors and assisting personnel

**seersucker suit** man's summer-weight suit in striped cotton

**slack suit** pantsuit

**snow suit** child's one- or two-piece cold-weather garment consisting of heavily lined pants and jacket

**sport suit** outfit of casual cut and cloth; town-and-country suit

**stripes** prison garb, traditionally wide-striped shirt and pants

**suit** jacket and trousers or skirt in matching material, sometimes including vest

**summer suit** suit of lightweight fabric

**tailor-made** jacket and skirt or trousers made to measure

**three-piece suit** jacket, trousers, and vest

**town-and-country suit** sport suit

**tropical suit** suit of very lightweight fabric and pale color, designed for comfort in tropics

**tuxedo** man's semiformal outfit consisting of single- or double-breasted jacket with satin lapels and trousers with stripe down their sides

**two-piece suit** suit consisting of jacket and trousers only, without vest

**undress** informal military uniform, as opposed to full dress

**whites** formal white U.S. military uniform; dress whites

**white tie** man's formal evening jacket with tails, usu. worn with white vest and white bow tie

**zoot suit** flashy suit with extremely baggy trousers, padded shoulders, and high waist

## Sweaters and Vests

**bodice** woman's laced vest worn over blouse or dress

**bulky** thickly knit, voluminous sweater

**bulletproof vest** protective vest of bulletproof mesh worn under shirt or jacket

**cardigan** close-fitting, casual sweater buttoning down front

**cashmere** sweater of soft cashmere wool

**crew neck** pullover with round, collarless neck

**fisherman sweater** heavy wool sweater knit in traditional patterns

**gilet** *Chiefly Brit.* woman's waistcoat

**hand-knit** sweater made by hand, not by machine

**Irish knit** hand-knit sweater of Irish wool, often white

**liberty bodice** sleeveless vest with buttons

**pullover** sweater with no fastenings, slipped on over head; slipover; *Chiefly Brit.* sweater

**shoulderette** woman's light, knit shawl, with ends formed into sleeves

**ski sweater** heavy wool sweater for cold weather

**slipover** pullover

**Sloppy Joe** girl's loose, baggy sweater

**sweater** knitted or crocheted jacket, usu. of wool, silk, acrylic, or cotton, in pullover or cardigan style

**turtleneck** close-fitting sweater with high, folded band collar

**vest** short, tight-fitting, sleeveless garment worn under jacket or coat, esp. by men

**V-neck** sweater with neck forming V open to sternum

**waistcoat** *Chiefly Brit.* vest

## Shirts and Tops

**aloha shirt** brightly colored sport shirt, usu. short sleeved (Hawaii)

**basque**  tight-fitting bodice
**bib**  protective cloth or plastic tied around neck under chin
**blouse**  woman's loose shirt extending from neck to waist-line, with or without collar and sleeves
**blouson**  voluminous shirt with close-fitted waistband
**body shirt**  woman's close-fitting top with attached panties that snap at the crotch
**bush shirt**  loose-fitting, cotton shirt with patch pockets
**bustier**  woman's tight-fitting, sleeveless, strapless, waist-length top
**button-down shirt**  shirt on which collar points button to shirt body
**camise**  lightweight, loose-fitting, long-sleeved shirt
**camp shirt**  short-sleeved shirt or blouse with notched collar, usu. having two breast pockets
**dashiki**  voluminous, collarless pullover shirt, often in bright colors (Africa)
**dickey**  detachable insert worn to fill neckline and simulate shirt front
**dress shirt**  man's shirt to be worn in evening or with necktie
**evening shirt**  formal white shirt
**evzone**  palace guard's pleated, white, gauze shirt (ancient Greece)
**flannel shirt**  durable work shirt of flannel cotton
**garibaldi**  woman's loose, high-necked, full-sleeved blouse, orig. red
**hair shirt**  rough shirt of animal hair, worn over skin as penance
**halter**  woman's top that covers breasts and leaves shoulders bare, often with straps around neck
**Hawaiian shirt**  loose-fitting, short-sleeved shirt of light-weight fabric printed in colorful, bold designs, usu. of nature scenes
**hickory shirt**  sturdy, cotton work shirt with vertical stripes
**jersey**  casual, close-fitting, stretchy-knit cotton or wool shirt
**jumper**  *Chiefly Brit.* loose blouse or pullover
**jupe**  man's shirt or woman's bodice (Scotland)
**jupon**  tight-fitting, padded garment worn under armor (medieval Europe)
**long-sleeved shirt**  shirt with sleeves ending at wrist
**middy blouse**  woman's or child's loose-fitting, hip-length, pullover blouse with sailor collar
**Pendleton**  *Trademark.* heavy, plaid wool shirt
**plaid shirt**  shirt in tartan pattern
**polo shirt**  close-fitting casual knit pullover with short sleeves and turned collar or banded neck
**romper**  child's one-piece garment with short, loose trousers gathered at knees
**rugby shirt**  knitted pullover sport shirt, usu. in broad, horizontal stripes with white collar
**Russian blouse**  hip-length shirt with full sleeves, tall collar, and embroidery (19th c.)
**sacque**  unfitted or semifitted bodice
**sark**  shirt (medieval Britain)
**shell**  woman's simple sleeveless blouse
**shirt**  cloth garment for upper part of body, usu. with collar, sleeves, and open front
**shirtwaist**  woman's blouse tailored like man's dress shirt
**short-sleeved shirt**  shirt with sleeves ending above elbow
**sport shirt**  casual, outdoor shirt
**tank top**  sleeveless, scoop-necked shirt of thin fabric

**top**  garment worn over chest and shoulders, sometimes with sleeves
**T-shirt**  collarless, short-sleeved, cotton-knit casual shirt
**tunic**  blouse extending to hips or knees and gathered at waist
**turtleneck**  long-sleeved jersey with high, turned down, tubelike collar

## DRESSES AND SKIRTS

**apron**  protective cloth panel tied around waist at back
**Beardsley gown**  formal gown (Britain, 19th c.)
**bouffant skirt**  extremely full, puffed-up skirt
**bridal gown**  elaborate white wedding dress
**bustle**  framework that supported full skirt (19th c.)
**cheongsam**  dress with slit skirt and high mandarin collar (Asia)
**coat dress**  dress with buttons in front, from neck to hem
**cocktail dress**  short-skirted party dress
**cotehardie**  man's or woman's long-sleeved, thigh-length, belted, buttoned, or laced garment (medieval Europe)
**crinoline**  petticoat of stiff netting and/or taffeta, worn under hoop skirt
**culottes**  full skirt divided into knee-length pants
**dirndl**  full skirt gathered at waist or dress with close-fitting bodice and full skirt
**dress**  woman's garment with top and skirt in one piece
**evening gown**  formal, full-length dress of high-quality fabric such as silk or satin
**fillebeg**  kilt
**float**  loose, flowing, sometimes fancy dress
**flounce**  wide ruffle attached to skirt
**formal**  full-length evening gown
**gown**  loose-flowing, usu. full-length, often formal dress
**granny dress**  old-fashioned, full-length, loose-fitting dress, esp. in black
**grass skirt**  skirt of grass reeds hung from waistband; hula skirt (Oceania)
**gymslip**  girl's knee-length school skirt
**harem skirt**  skirt divided into two parts and gathered at ankles
**hobble skirt**  narrow skirt tapering to ankles, with side slit
**hoop skirt**  full skirt stiffened with hoops
**housedress**  loose, casual cotton dress
**hula skirt**  grass skirt
**johnny**  hospital patient's gown that is open at back, collarless, and short-sleeved, usu. in white or green
**jumper**  sleeveless, one-piece dress
**jupe**  woman's skirt (Scotland)
**kilt**  man's plaid, wool, wraparound skirt, hanging to knees; fillebeg (Scotland)
**kirtle**  long gown or dress; man's tunic (medieval Europe)
**lavalava**  colorful cloth wrapped around body as skirt (Polynesia)
**maxiskirt**  ankle-length skirt
**microminiskirt**  skirt ending at top of thighs
**midiskirt**  midcalf-length skirt
**miniskirt**  midthigh-length skirt
**Mother Hubbard**  loose, shapeless dress
**muumuu**  loose, full-length dress, usu. of bright print fabric (Hawaii)
**pant dress**  dress with culotte-style skirt

**peplum** short, flared skirt with overskirt hanging in points

**petticoat** fancy underskirt, often with ruffled or lace hem

**pinafore** sleeveless dress with biblike bodice over blouse

**pleated skirt** girl's skirt with multiple pleats from waist to knees

**pollera** embroidered fiesta skirt with capelike top (Latin America)

**princesse dress** fitted one-piece dress without waist seam

**robe de style** long, formal gown with tight bodice and bouffant skirt

**sari** long, wrapped silk or cotton dress, worn with one end draped over head or shoulders (India)

**sarong** full-length, wrapped or draped skirt (Oceania and Malaysia)

**sheath** woman's close-fitting, unbelted dress

**shift** woman's loose-fitting dress that hangs straight and has no waistline

**shirtdress** dress tailored like shirt, with button-down front closure

**skirt** free-hanging outer garment that extends downward from waist

**slit dress** usu. close-fitting dress, cut open along one thigh at side

**sundress** sometimes strapless dress with bodice that exposes arms, shoulders, and back

**tea gown** semiformal, midcalf-length dress that has a yoke and full sleeves

**tent dress** loose-fitting dress without waistline that flares outward from shoulders to great fullness at hem

**trousseau** bridal gown and accessories

**tube dress** close-fitting, straight, full-length dress

**Turkish skirt** full skirt divided into loose trousers

**tutu** ballerina's very short, stiff, projecting skirt

**wraparound** skirt or dress that encircles body and overlaps at full-length opening

**wrapskirt** seamless piece of material worn wrapped around waist and legs as skirt

## TROUSERS, SHORTS, AND LEGGINGS

**antigropelos** waterproof leggings

**baggies** *Slang.* loose, knee-length swim trunks

**bell-bottoms** trousers widely flared at hem

**Bermuda shorts** knee-length shorts, often in bright plaids

**bloomers** woman's or child's full trousers, gathered at knee

**blue jeans** denims

**breeches** trousers, esp. knee-length

**britches** breeches; trousers

**buckskins** heavy leather trousers

**Capri pants** fitted casual pants to midcalf, with slit at bottom of sides

**chaps** cowboy's protective leather leggings, worn over pants and joined by belt or lacing

**chinos** casual trousers of polished chino cotton

**clam diggers** midcalf casual pants

**cords** corduroys

**corduroys** trousers of corduroy cotton with vertical wales; cords

**culottes** knee-length shorts, cut wide to resemble skirt

**cutoffs** full-length trousers cut off above knee to form shorts

**denims** pants of durable blue denim cotton; blue jeans; dungarees; jeans

**dhoti** man's long loin cloth (India)

**ducks** trousers of durable duck cotton

**dungarees** denims

**gabardines** dress trousers of gabardine wool

**gaiters** cloth or leather leggings buttoned over shoe tops and ankles

**galligaskins** loose, wide leggings (16th-17th c.)

**gamashes** horseback rider's leggings or gaiters (Scotland)

**gambados** horseman's leggings worn under jodhpurs

**high-waters** *Slang.* pants hemmed above ankles

**hiphuggers** woman's trousers that fit tight over hips and flare below knee

**hot pants** short shorts

**jeans** denims

**jodhpurs** riding breeches cut full at thigh, with stirrup foot strap; riding breeches

**kerseys** work pants of coarse, ribbed kersey wool

**knee breeches** pants fitted at knees like knickers

**knickerbockers** knickers

**knickers** short, loose pants, banded at knee, usu. for women and children; knickerbockers

**lederhosen** leather shorts with suspenders (Bavaria)

**leggings** protective covering for leg below knee, esp. of leather or canvas

**Levi's** *Trademark.* popular blue denim trousers

**loincloth** simple cloth wrapped around waist and groin

**long pants** pants hemmed at ankle

**matador pants** toreador pants

**moleskins** pants of durable cotton with thick nap on one side

**overalls** loose protective trousers with bib front and shoulder straps

**Oxford bags** extremely baggy trousers (1920's)

**pantaloons** short, loose-fitting trousers

**pants** outer garment covering each leg separately from waist to ankle; trousers

**pedal pushers** woman's tight-fitting, calf-length pants

**pegleg trousers** trousers cut full at hips and narrow at ankles

**plus fours** voluminous breeches hemmed four inches below knees

**puttees** cloth wrapped around lower leg; buckled leather leggings with straps; putts

**putts** puttees

**riding breeches** jodhpurs

**rompers** child's one-piece playsuit with bloomer pants

**shorts** casual trousers hemmed above knee

**short shorts** very brief shorts, barely covering buttocks; hot pants

**slacks** casual trousers

**spandex pants** skintight pants of spandex stretch fabric

**spats** cloth or leather gaiter over ankle and instep and attached to shoes

**spatterdashes** protective knee-high buckled leggings (18th c.)

**stretch pants** tight trousers of elasticized fabric

**tights** skintight, often sheer, knitted leggings extending from waist to toes or neck to toes

**toreador pants** fitted trousers banded at knee, patterned after bullfighter's trousers; matador pants

**trews** tight tartan shorts worn under kilt; full-length tartan trousers

**trousers** pants

**trunk hose** short, full breeches reaching to midthigh (16th-17th c.)

**tweeds** trousers of patterned tweed wool

**waders** waterproof trousers reaching from armpits to attached rubber boots, worn over regular trousers

## SPORTING AND EXERCISE WEAR

**bathing suit** man's or woman's swimming outfit: trunks, two-piece bikini, or one-piece leotard; swimsuit; swimwear

**bikini** woman's scanty two-piece bathing suit comprised of panties and brassiere

**body stocking** sometimes sheer, tight-fitting torso garment, often with sleeves and legs

**bodywear** leotard, tights, or body stocking

**gym pants** loose exercise pants

**gym suit** track suit or jogging suit

**jams** *Trademark.* long, baggy, brightly colored men's swim trunks

**jogging suit** usu. matching, loose-fitting top and pants, worn during athletic workout

**leotard** close-fitting torso garment, with or without sleeves, worn by dancers and acrobats

**muscle shirt** sleeveless T-shirt, usu. tight-fitting, worn typically by body builders

**one-piece bathing suit** sleeveless leotard for swimwear

**ski pants** pants of stretch fabric with foot stirrup

**ski suit** stretch pants and parka, worn for skiing and outdoor winter activities

**string bikini** skimpy two-piece bathing suit that barely covers crotch and nipples

**sweatpants** loose, fleece-lined, cotton athletic pants, gathered at waist with drawstring or elastic

**sweats** sweat suit

**sweatshirt** loose, long-sleeved, cotton-knit, fleece-lined shirt for athletic wear

**sweat suit** loose, cotton-knit exercise pants and pullover; sweats

**swimsuit** bathing suit

**swimwear** bathing suit

**track suit** loose-fitting sweat worn by athletes, esp. runners, before and after competition and during workouts

**trunks** shorts, esp. for swimming or boxing

**two-piece bathing suit** woman's bathing suit comprised of brassiere and panties; bikini

**unitard** close-fitting, clingy, full-body garment reaching from ankles to neck and wrists

**wetsuit** close-fitting rubber suit, sometimes worn in parts, that covers body from ankles to wrists and neck and retains body heat in cold water

## LITURGICAL VESTMENTS

**alb** priest's long, white, linen robe for Mass

**amice** priest's square cloth worn over shoulders

**cassock** priest's full-length garment with tight-fitting sleeves; soutane

**chasuble** priest's ornamented, knee-length outer garment without sleeves

**cincture** cord looped twice around waist to hold alb in place

**clerical collar** priest's narrow, stiff collar that buttons at back

**cope** bishop's long, open cloak

**cotta** altar boy or chorister's short, white, loose shirt

**dalmatic** deacon's tunic with wide sleeves and stripes descending from shoulders

**Geneva gown** loose, large-sleeved black gown worn by some Protestant clergy

**maniple** priest's long, silk band, worn looped over left arm

**miter** tall, pointed bishop's hat

**mozzetta** short shoulder cape with hood, worn by pope, cardinals, and bishops

**pallium** thin, ringlike band of wool across shoulders, with lappets in front and back, worn by pope and archbishops

**rochet** prelate's close-fitting, long-sleeved or winged, knee-length ceremonial garment

**soutane** priest's cassock or tunic

**stole** long, narrow scarf worn around neck and crossed over chest

**surplice** loose, white, knee-length outer garment with wide sleeves

**tunicle** long garment worn beneath dalmatic and over alb

**vestment** any garment worn by clergy or their assistants during religious service

## ARMOR

**ailette** protective shoulder plate of forged steel worn over coat of mail

**armor** protective body covering of metal, leather, or chain mail (medieval Europe)

**backplate** piece of armor covering back from shoulders to waist

**beaver** visor

**brassard** upper arm covering of armor

**breastplate** cuirass

**brigandine** medieval body armor of scales or plates

**chain mail** lightweight, flexible armor of interlinked metal rings

**coat of mail** upper body chain mail

**cubitiere** rounded elbow covering of armor; elbow piece

**cuirass** fitted leather or cloth bodice armor that protects breast and back; breastplate

**cuisse** plate armor for thigh front

**elbow piece** cubitiere

**epaulière** shoulder covering of armor; pauldron

**fauld** armor piece below breastplate, comprised of thin, overlapping plates

**footpiece** attached covering of armor for top of foot; solleret

**gauntlet** reinforced protective glove

**gorget** neck-encircling collar of armor on which helmet sits

**greave** lower leg protector of armor; jambeau

**hauberk** knee-length tunic of chain mail

**heaume** armor helmet outside mail hood that rests on shoulders

**helmet** rigid covering for head and neck with visor front

**jambeau** greave

**kneepiece** circular armor joint at knee; poleyn

**lame** one of several thin, overlapping plates that form a piece of armor

**pallette** round armor plate above heart, upper chest, and shoulder

**pauldron** epaulière

**placate** piece of armor that reinforces breastplate over lower torso

**plastron** plate armor for front of upper torso

**plate** individual section of suit of armor

**poleyn** kneepiece

**shoulder piece** connective armor joint between trunk and arm piece; epaulière

**skirt of tasses** armor plates hung around hips to which tasses and sword attach

**solleret** footpiece

**surcoat** garment worn over medieval armor, often embroidered with heraldic arms

**taces** tasses

**tasses** overlapping armor plates forming skirt at hips; taces

**tuille** hinged armor plate above thigh

**vambrace** piece of plate armor for forearm

**visor** protective helmet plate that lowers over face; beaver

# UNDERGARMENTS

Lingerie and Support Garments
Men's Underwear
Nightclothes and Dishabille
Hosiery

**SEE ALSO**: *Chap. 10: Ornaments and Accessories; Chap. 22: Sex, Love, and Romance*

## LINGERIE AND SUPPORT GARMENTS

**bandeau** strapless, band-shaped brassiere

**bikini** very brief, high-cut underpants

**bloomers** full, loose underpants, gathered at knee

**bodice** tight-fitting torso covering

**body stocking** close-fitting, one-piece torso garment with sleeves and legs

**bodywear** leotard, tights, or body stocking

**bra** brassiere

**brassiere** garment supporting breasts in two cups; bra

**bustle** framework used to support full skirt (19th c.)

**camisole** light, loose bodice worn over corset or brassiere; sheer blouse with shoulder straps and low neck

**chastity belt** belt of leather or forged metal that covered crotch to prevent sexual intercourse (medieval Europe)

**chemise** loose, short slip; shimmy

**chemisette** detachable, lace neckline filler

**combinations** one-piece undergarment with sleeves and legs

**corselet** combination brassiere and girdle

**corset** boned, laced, elasticized foundation garment, used to firm waist and hips, often including garter belt and brassiere

**crinoline** coarse, stiff petticoat worn under hoop skirt

**crotchless panties** bikini underpants with opening at crotch

**cutty sark** woman's short undergarment (Scotland)

**drawers** woman's knee-length undershorts

**dress shields** absorbent pads worn in armpits

**falsies** *Informal*. shaped pads worn inside a brassiere; padded bra

**farthingale** hoop or padded roll worn beneath skirt to extend hipline (16th c.)

**foundation garment** woman's support garment, such as corset

**garter belt** belt with straps attached, used to hold up stockings; suspender belt

**garters** elastic bands or straps that hold up hosiery

**girdle** light corset extending from waist to thighs

**G-string** backless panties covering crotch only, held up by cord at waist

**knickers** loose underpants, banded at knee; *Chiefly Brit*. panties

**leotard** close-fitting, skintight torso garment consisting of briefs and often sleeveless top

**lingerie** woman's underwear, often lacy or decorative

**merry widow** *Slang*. corset

**padded bra** brassiere with foam padding in each cup to make breasts appear larger

**pannier** hoop worn to extend skirts (19th c.)

**pantalets** long drawers with attached ruffle visible below knee (19th c.)

**panties** underpants

**panty girdle** girdle with sewn-in crotch, often with garters

**pasties** small, round coverings for woman's nipples, chiefly worn by striptease dancers

**peek-a-boo** brassiere with openings at each nipple

**petticoat** underskirt with ruffled or lace hem

**pettipants** thigh or knee-length underpants, banded in lace

**push-up bra** brassiere with added support under cups to lift breasts; uplift brassiere

**scanties** abbreviated bikini panties

**shimmy** chemise

**slip** dress-length undergarment with shoulder straps

**smock** yoked undershirt; chemise

**stays** *Chiefly Brit*. bone-stiffened corset

**step-ins** short panties

**support garment** usu. elastic device that binds or bears up part of body

**suspender belt** garter belt

**tap pants** loose-fitting underpants, similar to pants worn for tap dancing

**teddy** loose-fitting, one piece underslip with crotch; combination chemise and panties

**tournure** bustle worn for hip extension

**truss** extremely binding girdle, used esp. for treatment of hernias

**underall** garment that covers torso and hips

**underpants** woman's or child's underwear that covers groin, buttocks, and crotch; panties; undies

**underskirt** loose waist-to-knee undergarment

**undies** woman's or child's underwear, esp. underpants

**uplift brassiere** push-up bra

**wyliecoat** warm, woolen or flannel undershirt; petticoat (Scotland)

## MEN'S UNDERWEAR

**athletic supporter** tight-fitting support garment for genitals, esp. worn by dancer or athlete; cup; jockstrap

**baggies** *Informal.* loose, boxer-style underpants

**boxer shorts** loose-cut underpants reaching to midthigh

**breechcloth** loincloth

**briefs** abbreviated, jockey style underpants

**BVD's** *Trademark.* jockey shorts

**codpiece** bag or flap used to conceal opening of man's trousers; decorative external G-string (15th–16th c.)

**cup** athletic supporter

**drawers** underpants, esp. boxer style

**flannels** boxer shorts of flannel

**G-string** athletic supporter

**jockey shorts** brief, close-fitting underpants that end at top of thigh

**jockstrap** athletic supporter

**linens** linen underwear

**loincloth** cloth wrapped around waist and loins that covers genitals; breechcloth

**long johns** *Informal.* long underwear

**long underwear** full-length, usu. cotton-knit underwear that covers limbs, worn esp. in cold weather

**shorts** underpants

**singlet** *Chiefly Brit.* undershirt

**skivvies** *Informal.* man's underwear

**tank top** sleeveless, low-necked undershirt

**thermals** knitted cotton or wool long underwear, designed to retain body heat

**T-shirt** collarless, short-sleeved, cotton-knit undershirt

**underclothes** underwear

**underdrawers** undershorts

**underpants** undershorts

**undershirt** underwear for torso; undervest; union vest

**undershorts** underwear for groin, crotch, and buttocks; underdrawers; underpants

**undervest** *Chiefly Brit.* undershirt

**underwear** undergarments, shirt or shorts; underclothes

**union suit** *Chiefly Brit.* one-piece undergarment

**union vest** *Chiefly Brit.* undershirt

**unmentionables** undergarments

**vest** *Chiefly Brit.* undershirt

**woolens** heavy woolen long underwear

## NIGHTCLOTHES AND DISHABILLE

**at home** casual wear; lounging clothes

**baby doll** woman's sheer, two-piece nightgown

**bathrobe** loose, absorbent robe worn before or after bath or as dressing gown

**bed gown** sleeping gown

**bed jacket** upper body sleepwear

**boudoir dress** loose dressing gown

**brunch coat** casual housecoat worn at late breakfast

**camisole** woman's short negligee

**coverup** woman's loose, sheer robe or lounging coat

**creeper** infant's one-piece garment

**diaper** absorbent cloth folded between baby's legs and fastened around waist

**dishabille** casual, informal dress worn inside one's home

**dressing gown** robe, esp. of silk, worn while dressing or resting; morning dress

**dressing jacket** coat worn while dressing or resting

**gertrude** infant's pajama top that buttons across shoulders

**housecoat** woman's long-skirted, informal coat

**jammies** *Baby talk.* pajamas

**kimono** long, sashed, wide-sleeved traditional robe (Japan)

**lounging robe** loose, comfortable dressing gown

**morning dress** dressing gown

**negligee** woman's loose, diaphanous, often lacy nightdress

**nightclothes** sleeping garments

**nightdress** woman's sleeping garment

**nightgown** loose, dresslike garment worn in bed

**nightie** *Informal.* woman's or child's nightgown

**nightshirt** short nightgown

**pajamas** loose, lightweight sleeping shirt and trousers; also, *esp. Brit.,* pyjamas

**peignoir** negligee or dressing gown, esp. with fur cuffs, lace, or other decoration

**p.j.'s** *Informal.* pajamas

**robe** loose, informal garment for dressing, bathing, or resting

**robe de chambre** *French.* dressing gown

**sleeper** child's pajamas with attached foot coverings

**smoking jacket** man's loose-fitting lounging jacket

**wrapper** jacket or clothing wrapped around body

**yukata** dressing gown or robe of lightweight cotton (Japan)

## HOSIERY

**anklet** woman's short sock that reaches just above ankle

**argyles** socks knitted in varicolored diamond pattern

**athletic sock** thick cotton sock, usu. white

**bobbysocks** girl's socks that fold above ankle

**boothose** long socks worn under boots

**crew sock** short, bulky, ribbed sock

**dress sheer** woman's finely knit stocking

**fishnet stocking** full-length stocking woven in coarse mesh

**footlet** woman's thin, very low sock, worn as protective shoeliner instead of hosiery and not meant to be seen; Ped

**garter stocking** stocking extending to midthigh, held up by garter

**halfhose** elasticized stocking extending to just above knee

**hose** knitted coverings for foot and leg; hosiery

**hosiery** garments for foot and leg, esp. socks and stockings; hose

**knee high** sock or stocking that reaches to knee

**knee hose** stockings that reach to knee

**knee-sock** hose that reaches to knee

**leg warmer** footless knit legging for dancers or athletes

**lisle hose** hose of lisle cotton

**maillot** tights for dancers or acrobats

**mesh stocking** coarse-knit hose; fishnet stocking

**nylons** woman's stockings of synthetic material, esp. nylon

**pantyhose** woman's one-piece undergarment, combining panties and skintight, full-length hose

**Peds** *Trademark.* footlet

**rayon stocking** woman's stocking made from rayon

**seamless stocking** sheer stocking without seams

**sheers** *Informal.* sheer stockings

**sheer stockings** finely knit thin hose; sheers

**silk stockings** finely knit silk hose

**slouch sock**  sock with long top that is bunched around ankle

**sock**  knitted foot covering that extends above ankle

**stocking**  close-fitting knitted covering for foot and leg

**stretch sock**  hose of elastic material

**support hose**  elasticized stocking that provides support for leg

**sweat sock**  heavy wool or cotton sock

**tights**  skintight sheer garment that extends from waist to toes

**tube sock**  sock with unformed heel, knitted in cylindrical shape

**varsity sock**  athletic sock banded with school colors

**work sock**  sturdy wool or cotton sock

**woolens**  hose made from wool

# ORNAMENTS AND ACCESSORIES

Ornaments
Jewelry
Eyeglasses
Neckwear
Hand Wear and Gloves
Waistbands and Belts
Functional Attire and Accessories
Symbolic and Emblematic Attire
Luggage and Cases

**SEE ALSO**: Chap. 3: Minerals, Metals, and Rocks; Chap. 5: Containers; Chap. 7: Ornamental and Functional Articles; Chap. 10: Outer Garments; Clothing Materials; Hats, Headgear, and Hairpieces; Fashion and Garment Parts

## ORNAMENTS

**agrafe**  ornamental clasp on armor or costume

**armlet**  band around upper arm

**band**  narrow, decorative strip worn on arm, neck, or waist

**bodkin**  ornamental pin-shaped clasp for hair

**bouquet**  bunch of flowers fastened together

**boutonniere**  single flower worn in lapel buttonhole

**bow**  ribbon doubled into two or more loops, usu. worn in hair

**comb**  strip of hard material with teethlike projections, used to hold hair in place

**cordon**  decorative cord or ribbon

**corsage**  arrangement of flowers worn pinned to clothing, esp. by women

**crest**  plume on helmet; heraldic emblem

**epaulette**  often fringed shoulder ornament on military jacket

**feather**  bird's feather worn in hair or on hat

**festoon**  wreath or garland hanging in loop

**garland**  ornamental wreath or festoon of flowers

**netsuke**  small, finely carved toggle on kimono sash (Japan)

**nosegay**  small bunch of flowers; bouquet; posy

**panache**  tuft of feathers or tassel on helmet

**plume**  cluster of feathers

**pompom**  tuft or ball of fabric and fringe

**posy**  bouquet of flowers; nosegay

**shoulder knot**  ornamental knot or ribbon on shoulder of military uniform

**sporran**  fur pouch hung off belt in front of kilt (Scotland)

**tassel**  dangling fringed cords hanging from a roundish knob

**whim-wham**  fanciful object or ornament on clothing

**wreath**  braided, circular band of flowers worn in hair

## JEWELRY

**aigrette**  spray of gemstones depicting plume of feathers, worn in hair or on hat

**anklet**  band around ankle

**armlet**  jeweled armband above elbow

**band**  narrow ring encircling finger, usu. of precious metal

**bangle**  rigid, ring-shaped, slip-on or clasped anklet or bracelet

**bauble**  decorative trinket

**beads**  rounded, pierced pieces of glass, metal, wood, or stone strung together in strands

**bezel**  groove and flange holding gem in setting; slanting facets of exposed portion of cut gem in setting

**bibelot**  small trinket of curiosity, beauty, or rarity

**bijou**  small piece of delicate jewelry; trinket

**bracelet**  ornamental chain or band encircling wrist

**brooch**  large pin with clasp, worn at breast

**cameo**  gem carved in relief, esp. portrait

**carat**  unit of weight for gemstones equal to 200 milligrams

**carcanet**  jeweled ornamental collar or necklace

**chain**  series of small, connected, metal links, usu. worn around neck

**chaplet**  garland for head; string of beads

**charm**  representational item worn as protection from evil, token of luck, or to invoke magic powers

**chatelaine**  woman's ornamental clasp at waist for keys or purse; decorative chain suspended between two points

**coronet**  small crown

**costume jewelry**  inexpensive jewelry made from nonprecious substances

**crown**  jeweled royal headdress of precious metal

**crown jewels**  crown, scepter, and other royal regalia

**cuff links**  ornamental buttons joined by chain or shank for fastening French cuff

**diadem**  royal headdress; crown

**diamante**  synthetic diamond

**earring**  ornamental object hung from earlobe either by clasp or through hole pierced in lobe

**fob**  chain for pocket watch

**gem**  precious stone or pearl cut and mounted as ornament

**gemstone**  precious or semiprecious stone used as a gem

**gewgaw**  showy bauble or trinket

**gimcrack**  showy trinket of little value

**girandole**  earring or brooch with large gemstone surrounded by smaller ones

**glass**  *Informal*. precious stone; plain glass substituted for precious stone

**intaglio**  ornament with engraving beneath surface of material

**knickknack** trivial ornament

**labret** gemstone or other small ornament worn in hole pierced in lip

**locket** small, lidded case of precious metal on chain necklace, inside of which a memento or photograph can be placed

**money clip** two-armed metal fastener for holding paper money

**necklace** ornamental string or chain worn around neck

**nose ring** ring worn through hole pierced in one nostril of nose

**parure** set of jewelry worn together, such as earrings, bracelet, and necklace

**pearl** smooth, hard, rounded, white nacreous growth found within shell of some oysters, mounted or strung and used as jewelry

**pendant** decorative object hanging on chain or from earring

**pin** ornamental fastener attached to clothing with pointed wire or shaft

**pinkie ring** ring worn on little finger, esp. by men

**post** straight bar that pierces ear, often with attached setting that holds single pearl or stone as earring

**precious stone** class of gemstones of great value, esp. diamond, emerald, ruby, sapphire

**rhinestone** colorless synthetic gem, often of glass

**ring** band of precious metal worn on finger, often set with gem

**rivière** necklace of precious stones, usu. in several strands

**rondelle** small round bead used as spacer in necklace

**scrimshaw** carved, engraved object of whalebone

**semiprecious stone** any of a class of gemstones of moderate value, such as amethyst, garnet, opal, or topaz

**setting** decorated metal base in which stone or stones are placed, esp. on ring

**signet ring** ring bearing seal or initials

**solitaire** single gem set alone, esp. on ring

**stickpin** ornamental pin, esp. worn on necktie

**stone** gemstone

**stud** solid button mounted on metal post and inserted in garment as ornamental fastener

**tiara** small, crownlike, jeweled headdress, often in semicircular shape

**tie clip** tiepin

**tiepin** tie clasp or stud with ornamental head, used to attach tie to shirt; tie clip

**torque** metal collar or neck chain used in ancient Germany and Gaul

**trinket** small, cheap, ornamental object

**wampum** polished shells strung as beads (American Indian)

**wedding band** plain gold ring worn to indicate married status

**wristband** bracelet or ornament encircling wrist

**wristlet** close-fitting, knitted wristband often attached to glove or sleeve

## EYEGLASSES

**aviator glasses** contoured, metal-framed goggles worn by fliers

**bifocals** eyeglasses with lenses that have separate sections, one for seeing close up and one for distance

**blinkers** opaque sidepieces that reduce peripheral vision

**cheaters** *Slang.* eyeglasses

**contact lens** thin lens that fits directly on cornea

**dark glasses** sunglasses

**eyeglasses** glass lenses that correct impaired vision, set in a frame with earpieces; spectacles

**glasses** eyeglasses

**goggles** protective glasses in flexible frame fitting snugly against face

**granny glasses** round lenses in thin metal frames

**horn rims** glasses with frames of variegated animal horn or similarly colored plastic

**lens** glass portion of eyeglasses that is ground to correct vision

**lorgnette** eyeglasses with attached handle; opera glasses

**lorgnon** monocle, pince-nez

**monocle** eyeglass for one eye, attached to cord; lorgnon

**opera glasses** lorgnette

**peepers** *Slang.* eyeglasses

**pince-nez** eyeglasses attached by spring or clamp to bridge of nose; lorgnon

**Polaroids** *Trademark.* popular sunglasses of glare-reduction polarized glass

**quizzing glass** small, single eyeglass on handle

**reading glasses** glasses used exclusively to aid in reading or close work

**shades** *Slang.* sunglasses

**specs** *Informal.* spectacles; eyeglasses

**spectacles** eyeglasses

**sunglasses** glasses with dark lenses that protect eyes from sunshine; dark glasses

## NECKWEAR

**ascot** necktie or scarf knotted under chin, with broad ends hanging loose

**bandanna** large, colorful, patterned handkerchief tied around neck

**bertha collar** woman's wide, round shoulder cape and collar

**boa** long stole or scarf of fur or feathers

**bolo tie** thin cord with ornamental clasp; long string tie

**bow tie** small tie formed into bow at neck

**chemisette** lace filler for woman's shirt front

**choker** necklace that fits snugly around neck, often of velvet

**clerical collar** priest's narrow, stiff collar, buttoned at back; priest's collar; Roman collar

**clip-on tie** necktie that clips onto shirt collar instead of tying around neck

**collar** band, strip, or chain around neck

**comforter** heavy scarf, often of wool

**cravat** necktie or scarf worn around neck

**dickey** detachable collar and shirt front

**dog collar** chain with military identification tag

**fichu** woman's light, triangular scarf worn over shoulders and fastened in front, esp. to fill low neckline

**foulard** necktie or scarf of light foulard silk in small print design

**four-in-hand** long necktie or scarf tied in slipknot or Windsor knot with ends hanging

**fur** scarf, stole, or neckpiece of animal fur

**Geneva bands** two narrow strips of white cloth hanging from front collar of some Protestant clergy

**golilla** starched white linen collar standing out from neckline (Spain, 17th c.)

**guimpe** wide cloth covering nun's neck and shoulders

**jabot** lace cravat or frill on bodice front, often attached to neckband

**kerchief** square of cloth worn around neck or shoulders; neckerchief

**lei** necklace of flowers (Hawaii)

**muffler** wool or fur scarf

**neckband** cloth around neck

**neckerchief** kerchief

**necktie** narrow band of fabric looped around neck and fastened or tied in front

**old school tie** necktie with public school colors (Britain)

**polo neck** closed, round neckband of jumper or polo shirt

**priest's collar** clerical collar

**rabato** wide, stiff, lace-edged collar, standing at back on wire frame (17th c.)

**Roman collar** clerical collar

**ruff** stiff, wide neckpiece gathered in deep folds and radiating from neck

**scapular** band of cloth slitted for head opening and draped over shoulders by monks

**scarf** broad cloth or woven band worn over head or shoulders or around neck

**school tie** necktie with school colors or emblem

**shawl** rectangular or triangular piece of fabric worn over head and shoulders

**stock** clergyman's wide-banded scarf; long neckerchief worn with formal riding dress

**stole** woman's long, wide cloth worn around shoulders; priest's narrow scarf with ends crossed over chest

**string tie** narrow cord or cloth tie with ornamental clasp

**tallith** fringed prayer shawl worn by Jewish men

**tie** necktie

**tippet** long black prayer scarf of Anglican clergy; scarf or stole worn with ends hanging down front

**tucker** lace or cloth worn in neckline of dress

**vestee** ornamental front worn beneath woman's blouse or jacket and visible at neckline

**Windsor tie** broad necktie knotted in loose bow or wide triangular knot

## HAND WEAR AND GLOVES

**baseball glove** large leather glove for catching a baseball

**batting gloves** tight-fitting gloves worn when swinging a baseball bat

**boxing glove** heavily padded leather glove for boxing

**brass knuckles** set of connected metal rings worn as weapon on fist

**cesta** long, curved wicker basket worn on hand for jai alai

**cestus** boxer's leather hand covering reinforced with metal (ancient Rome)

**driving gloves** fitted leather gloves that end at knuckles, leaving fingertips uncovered

**gauntlet** high-cuffed glove; armored glove

**glove** hand covering with separate sheath for each finger and thumb

**hockey gloves** protective gloves for ice hockey

**kid gloves** soft kid leather gloves

**long gloves** woman's gloves that reach to elbow or upper arm

**mitt** fingerless glove; athletic glove, esp. baseball glove

**mittens** gloves with thumb sheath and single wide section for all fingers

**mousquetaire** woman's long glove with lengthwise buttoned opening at wrist

**muff** fur or wool cylinder open at both ends to insert hands for warmth

**suede gloves** gloves of napped leather

**weight gloves** tight-fitting leather gloves that terminate at knuckles, used for weightlifting

## WAISTBANDS AND BELTS

**baldric** ornamented belt worn over one shoulder, used to hold sword or bugle

**bandolier** ammunition belt worn over shoulder and across chest

**bellyband** band worn across stomach or around waist

**belt** waistband used esp. for holding up trousers or for decoration

**breechcloth** loincloth

**cartridge belt** belt holding ammunition, usu. worn around waist

**ceinture** belt or sash

**cestus** woman's symbolic belt, esp. for bride

**cincture** cord that holds priest's alb in place

**cummerbund** man's broad, tight-fitting waist sash, worn with formal attire

**fascia** broad, distinctly colored band worn at waist

**garter belt** undergarment belt with clips to hold up stockings

**girdle** close-fitting, elasticized support garment worn around waist and hips, usu. by women

**hamaki** wide, often elasticized belt worn for warmth (Japan)

**loincloth** cloth wrapped around loins and hips, often as only garment worn; breechcloth; waistcloth

**obi** broad sash for kimono (Japan)

**rope belt** belt of hemp or rope

**sash** ornamental band, ribbon, or scarf draped over shoulder and around waist

**surcingle** beltlike fastening for cassock or other garment

**suspender belt** garter belt with elastic straps for stockings

**waistband** strip of fabric attached to waistline of trousers or skirt, sometimes elasticized

**waist belt** strip of material worn around waist

**waistcloth** loincloth

## FUNCTIONAL ATTIRE AND ACCESSORIES

**accessory** article or set of articles added to basic clothing for decoration, convenience, or completeness

**apron** protective, skirtlike piece of material tied around waist

**atomizer** sprayer for medicine or perfume

**barrette** clip or comb with toothlike projections for holding hair

**bib** protective covering for shirt front

**blindfold** covering for eyes, tied at back of head

**brace** frame providing support for injured neck or limb

**braces** *Chiefly Brit.* suspenders

**bretelle** suspenderlike shoulder straps that attach to waistband of garment

**cane** stick, usu. wood, for support in walking

**crutches** tall supports fitting under armpits to aid walking in case of debility

**eyepatch** protective patch covering one eye, held in place by cord around head

**fan** folded, collapsible silk or paper semicircle on rods splayed from pivot, moved back and forth to create cooling air current

**handkerchief** soft square of linen, cotton, or silk for grooming face or wiping nose; hanky

**hanger** any of various devices for hanging garment when not in use, esp. shoulder-shaped frame with hook at top

**hanky** *Informal.* handkerchief

**hatpin** long stickpin with ornamental top, used to fasten hat

**holster** leather case for pistol, open at top, worn on belt or under one arm

**inro** small lacquer box containing cosmetics and medicines, worn on waist sash of traditional costume (Japan)

**money belt** waistband with pouch to conceal money

**parasol** woman's lightweight umbrella, used to shield sun's rays

**pomander** aromatic mixture in bag used to scent stored clothes

**sachet** small bag or pad holding potpourri or perfumed powder, usu. placed in drawer or closet to scent clothes

**scabbard** leather or metal sheath for tool or sword

**shield** broad piece of protective material, esp. armor, carried on arm as defense against blows and projectiles

**shoehorn** metal, horn, or plastic implement with troughlike blade, placed at heel of shoe to aid in insertion of foot

**shoe tree** form inserted in shoe to stretch it or maintain its shape when not in use

**sling** cloth looped around neck to hold injured arm

**spur** U-shaped attachment for heel of shoe with blunt, pointed, or roweled projection, used by rider to urge on horse

**suspenders** straps attached to trousers in front and back and slung over shoulders; braces

**swagger stick** short, metal-tipped stick covered with leather and carried in hand

**sweatband** strip of absorbent material worn around head and across forehead, esp. when exercising

**umbrella** protective, water-resistant, collapsible cloth dome on frame

**walking stick** cane or stick used for support in walking

**watch** small timepiece on wrist strap or carried in pocket

**watch fob** vest pocket for watch; watch chain

**wrist watch** small timepiece strapped to wrist

## SYMBOLIC AND EMBLEMATIC ATTIRE

**amulet** good-luck charm, often a necklace

**ankh** cross with looped upper arm, viewed as symbol of life (ancient Egypt)

**badge** emblem, often metal, denoting membership or rank of wearer

**blazon** coat of arms

**brassard** cloth armband with insignia

**caduceus** herald's staff

**chrisom** white baptismal robe denoting innocence

**cockade** hat ornament worn as badge

**cointise** article of apparel worn as emblem, esp. lady's scarf on knight's helmet as token of favor

**crepe** black band of crinkled silk fabric, worn as token of mourning

**fourragère** braided, decorative, military cord worn on shoulder

**mace** ornamental staff carried as emblem of authority

**menat** amulet believed to bring divine protection (ancient Egypt)

**orb** sphere surmounted by cross, carried as symbol of royal power

**orphrey** ornamental band or border on ecclesiastical vestment

**prayer shawl** cloth worn around neck during prayer

**phylactery** either of two square leather boxes containing scripture, worn on left arm and head by Jewish men during prayer

**rosary** string of beads used for counting Catholic prayers

**rosette** fabric gathered to resemble rose, worn as badge of office

**scarab** stone or faience beetle, used as symbol of resurrection (ancient Egypt)

**scepter** ornamental rod or staff denoting authority

**shoulder patch** cloth with insignia worn on uniform sleeve

**tallith** fringed prayer shawl worn by Jewish men

**zizith** fringe of tassels on Jewish man's ceremonial garments

## LUGGAGE AND CASES

**alforja** saddlebag

**aparejo** packsaddle of canvas or leather, used to hold load on pack animal

**attaché case** briefcase

**backpack** lightweight canvas or nylon sack, often on lightweight frame, carried on back while hiking

**bag** flexible sacklike container of paper, cloth, leather, or plastic, usu. capable of being closed at mouth

**baggage** luggage

**bandbox** cylindrical cardboard or wood box for lightweight items

**barracks bag** sturdy military cotton bag for personal items

**belt bag** small bag worn attached to belt

**Bermuda bag** round, cloth handbag with wooden handle

**billfold** leather case that folds flat, used to hold paper money

**Boston bag** traveling bag with two handles at top

**botta bag** leather wine sack carried over shoulder

**bridget** leather pouch or pack carried on back

**briefcase** flat, rectangular, usu. leather container for business papers and documents

**caddie bag** golf bag

**cargo bag** large, durable bag for freight

**carpetbag** small traveling bag made of carpeting

**carryall** large bag or case

**carry-on bag** small luggage taken on airplane

**case** small box or receptacle for storing items

**cedar chest** chest made of or lined with cedar, used for storage of clothing for protection against moths

**cigarette case** small, flat, often metal box for cigarettes

**club bag**  rectangular leather traveling bag that narrows to zippered top closure

**clutch**  woman's small, strapless handbag

**compact**  small cosmetic case, esp. for pressed face powder

**cosmetic bag**  small bag for holding cosmetics

**disco bag**  small handbag on long strap or chain

**ditty bag**  sailor's bag for small articles

**Dorothy bag**  open-topped handbag with drawstring

**duffel bag**  large, oblong, frameless, often canvas bag

**etui**  small ornamental case

**evening bag**  woman's elegant handbag of leather or fine fabric

**fanny pack**  small zippered pouch suspended from belt around waist

**flight bag**  small, lightweight travel bag, usu. with zippered outside pockets

**footlocker**  small trunk, usu. placed at foot of bed

**gamebag**  hunter's backpack with straps

**garment bag**  long, soft, folding bag with hangers for clothing

**Gladstone bag**  leather bag on rigid hinged frame that opens flat into two compartments

**glasses case**  small protective case for eyeglasses

**golf bag**  upright bag on frame, used for carrying golf clubs; caddie bag

**grip**  hand luggage

**gripsack**  traveling bag with handles

**gym bag**  small, usu. nylon bag for athletic wear and equipment

**handbag**  woman's small, leather bag for holding personal effects

**hatbox**  cylindrical, rigid box for storing a hat

**haversack**  knapsack with single strap worn over one shoulder

**holdall**  all-purpose luggage container

**housewife**  *Chiefly Brit.* pocket-size bag, esp. for carrying sewing implements

**impedimenta**  baggage and other encumbrances

**kit**  collection of matching bags used for travel

**kit bag**  rectangular leather traveling bag with straps and sides that open

**knapsack**  canvas or nylon bag strapped on back; rucksack

**locker**  storage chest with lock

**luggage**  suitcases or traveling bags; baggage

**lunchpail**  child's or workman's metal food container with lid

**musette bag**  small knapsack with one shoulder strap

**overnight case**  small traveling bag for brief journeys

**packsack**  *Chiefly Brit.* leather or canvas backpack

**pocketbook**  woman's handbag; wallet or billfold

**poke**  pouch, purse, or sack, esp. for gold dust and nuggets

**portfolio**  large, flat leather case for holding photographs or drawings

**portmanteau**  large leather trunk or suitcase that opens into two compartments

**pouch**  small drawstring bag; lockable case for diplomatic papers

**pullman case**  large suitcase

**purse**  woman's handbag; small bag or case for coins

**reticule**  woman's small handbag of beaded silk, brocade, or netting

**rucksack**  knapsack

**sack**  usu. rectangular pliable bag

**saddlebag**  two bags on straps slung over horse

**Saratoga trunk**  large traveling trunk with arched lid (19th c.)

**satchel**  small bag, often with shoulder strap

**schoolbag**  bag for schoolbooks and supplies

**seabag**  sailor's soft, cylindrical duffel bag

**shoulder bag**  bag with shoulder strap

**snuffbox**  small, ornamental, lidded case for snuff

**string bag**  mesh bag of heavy string or netting with two handles at top

**suitcase**  rectangular or oblong traveling bag with rigid frame

**tobacco pouch**  small folding bag for pipe and tobacco

**toilet kit**  usu. zippered bag for toiletries

**tote bag**  large handbag, esp. canvas

**traveling bag**  hand-carried bag for traveler's clothes and personal items

**traveling case**  small traveling bag

**trunk**  large, sturdy, boxlike luggage or storage container

**tucker bag**  food bag for outdoor use (Australia)

**valise**  traveling bag or suitcase that can be carried by hand

**vanity bag**  small case or handbag for toilet articles

**wallet**  small, flat, folding pocketbook with compartments for personal papers, currency, and credit cards

**wardrobe**  standing box or chest for clothes on hangers

**wardrobe trunk**  upright trunk with clothes hangers and storage compartments

**watchcase**  small, rigid box for storing watch

# CLOTHING MATERIALS

Fabrics and Cloth
Synthetic Fibers and Textiles
Laces
Furs, Leathers, and Pelts

**SEE ALSO**: Chap. 10: Ornaments and Accessories; Chap. 10: Fashion and Garment Parts

## FABRICS AND CLOTH

**alpaca**  long, soft, silky fleece of Peruvian llama wool

**Angora**  soft hair of Angora goat or rabbit, esp. for sweaters

**astrakhan**  lustrous, closely curled wool of young Russian lamb

**baize**  thick, soft, woolen cloth, usu. green, esp. for billiard table covers

**balbriggan**  plain-knit cotton, esp. for underwear and hosiery

**baldachin**  richly embroidered silk brocade, with gold and silver threads

**barathea**  silk, worsted, or synthetic fabric with pebbly surface

**barege**  sheer worsted cloth of silk or cotton, esp. for veils

**batik**  fabric that is hand-dyed, using wax to repel dye in a marblelike pattern

**batiste**  fine, sheer linen or muslin in plain or figured weave

**bayadere**  fabric with horizontal colored stripes

**beaver** heavy cloth of felted wool similar to beaver fur, esp. for overcoats

**bengaline** lightweight fabric with crosswise cord woven from coarse yarn

**bombazine** twilled silk or rayon dyed black, having worsted filling

**bouclé** tufted, nubby cloth with loose yarn loops

**brilliantine** lightweight, lustrous cotton and mohair warp

**broadcloth** densely woven fabric with soft finish in plain or twill weave

**brocade** heavyweight silk cloth with elaborate raised design, often in gold or silver

**brocatelle** heavyweight silk or linen fabric with figures in high relief, esp. for upholstery

**buckram** stiff, sized cotton or linen, esp. for linings or bookbinding

**bunting** coarse, open-weave worsted or cotton fabric, esp. for flags

**burlap** coarse cloth of jute, flax, or hemp, esp. for sacking or wallpaper; hessian

**byssus** fine linen cloth used for wrapping mummies (ancient Egypt)

**calico** plain-woven cotton cloth with figured pattern

**cambric** fine white linen, esp. for linings or handkerchiefs

**camel's hair** soft, silky, felted camel wool or fabric resembling it, esp. for coats

**camlet** durable, waterproof cloth for outerwear

**candlewick** usu. cotton fabric of loosely twisted yarn bunched and tufted to form design

**Canton crepe** soft, heavyweight crepe with finely wrinkled surface

**canvas** stiff, closely woven, heavy fabric of hemp or cotton, esp. for shoes, sails, and tents

**cashmere** very soft, downy wool from hair roots of Kashmir goat

**cassimere** smooth, twilled worsted for suits, often in stripes

**castor** heavy wool, esp. for overcoats

**cavalry twill** sturdy double twill fabric of cotton, wool, or worsted; tricotine

**cerecloth** wax-treated cloth for wrapping corpses

**challis** soft, lightweight cotton or wool in plain weave, esp. for neckties

**chambray** lightweight cotton, silk, or linen with colored warp and white weft

**charmeuse** lightweight, drapable silk with semilustrous satin face and dull back

**cheesecloth** lightweight cotton gauze in open mesh

**chenille** tufted, velvety cord of silk or worsted, esp. for trim, embroidery, spreads, and nightgowns

**cheviot** heavy, coarse wool of Cheviot sheep, for suits and coats

**chiffon** sheer, fluffy silk or synthetic fabric, esp. for blouses and dresses

**chiné** fabric with variegated Chinese designs dyed or printed on warp threads before weaving

**chino** durable, twilled khaki cotton

**chintz** often glazed, printed cotton, esp. for draperies and upholstery

**cloque** pique fabric with embossed or quilted design

**cloth** woven, knitted, felted, or pressed fabric of fibrous material, such as cotton, wool, silk, hair, or synthetic fibers

**combing wool** strong-fibered wool for manufacture of worsteds

**cord** corduroy

**corduroy** sturdy cotton with piled surface in lengthwise ridges; cord

**cotton** soft, white, absorbent fabric woven from fibrous hairs of cotton plant

**covert** durable cotton or woolen twill of mixed color yarns, sometimes waterproofed

**crape** crepe

**crash** rough, irregular fabric, esp. for draperies and toweling

**crepe** lightweight, crinkled fabric of silk, cotton, or rayon; crape

**crepe de Chine** soft, silky fabric with minute irregularities of surface

**crepon** heavy crepe fabric

**cretonne** heavyweight, unglazed cotton or linen in colorful prints, esp. for curtains or upholstery

**crinoline** coarse, stiffened horsehair or cotton, esp. for linings

**damask** fine, twilled, reversible silk, linen, or cotton in figured weave

**denim** heavyweight, durable twill cotton, esp. for blue jeans

**dimity** sheer, plain weave, usu. checked or striped cotton, esp. for curtains and bedspreads

**Donegal tweed** heavyweight, plain wool with colorful weft (Ireland)

**drill** durable twilled cotton; drilling

**drilling** drill

**drugget** coarse, durable wool (India)

**duchesse** highly lustrous satin

**duck** heavy, closely woven cotton, esp. for bags and outer garments

**duffel** rough, woolen, thickly napped cloth, esp. for coats and luggage

**dungaree** denim

**duvetyn** smooth, lustrous, napped fabric

**ecru** satin, unbleached linen, or raw silk of very pale brown color

**etamine** light, loosely woven cotton or worsted fabric

**fabric** material made from fibers or threads by means of weaving, knitting, or felting

**faconne** fabric with small, elaborate pattern, esp. velvet

**faille** semilustrous ribbed fabric of silk, cotton, rayon, or lightweight taffeta

**felt** nonwoven fabric of wool, cotton, or hair pressed together with heat

**fiber** slender, filamentous substance formed into threads for making fabric

**flannel** soft, loosely woven, napped wool or wool blend

**flannelette** lightweight cotton flannel, napped on one side

**fleece** soft knit or woven fabric with silky pile

**foulard** lightweight silk or rayon with printed design, esp. for ties and scarves

**frieze** heavyweight wool with rough, uncut nap

**fustian** stout cotton or linen in twill weave with short pile

**gabardine** firm woolen cloth in twill weave

**galatea** durable cotton, usu. striped, esp. for children's clothing

**gauze** thin, transparent cotton or silk

**Georgette** sheer silk or rayon crepe with pebbly surface

**gingham** striped or checked cotton in plain weave, esp. for housedresses

**gossamer** very thin, delicate cloth, esp. gauze for veils

**grenadine** thin silk or synthetic in leno weave

**grogram** coarse, loosely woven fabric of silk, silk and mohair, or wool

**grosgrain** heavy, closely woven, corded silk or rayon, esp. for ribbons

**gunny** coarse, heavy jute or hemp, esp. for sacks

**haircloth** stiff, wiry horsehair woven with cotton, used for stiffening and lining

**harrateen** English linen or wool, esp. for curtains or bed canopies

**Harris tweed** *Trademark.* tweed of fine, heavy Scottish wool from the Outer Hebrides

**herringbone** twilled fabric in pattern resembling fish skeleton, with series of V's in vertical row

**hessian** burlap

**homespun** plain-weave wool or linen made from homespun yarn

**hopsack** coarse, loosely woven cotton or wool

**horsehair** sturdy, glossy fabric woven from horse's mane

**huck** huckaback

**huckaback** absorbent, durable cotton or linen, esp. for towels; huck

**ikat** woven fabric in which warp and/or weft yarn has been tie-dyed (India)

**jaconet** thin cotton, esp. for bandages

**jacquard** intricate, variegated woven fabric

**jardiniere** multicolored material in floral or fruit print

**jean** denim

**jersey** soft, often elastic knit cotton, esp. for shirts

**Kendal green** coarse, woolen cloth, green in color

**kersey** heavy, coarse, ribbed wool, esp. for work clothes

**khaddar** handloomed cotton cloth (India)

**khaki** durable, twilled, dull yellow-brown cotton, esp. for military uniforms

**knit** any fabric made with interlocking loops of yarn

**lace** delicate, netlike, figured fabric of thread or yarn, esp. for trim

**lamé** fabric in which silver or gold threads are interwoven with silk, cotton, or rayon

**lawn** sheer linen or cotton in plain weave

**leno** firm, open-mesh weave in which warp yarns are paired and intertwined

**linen** cloth woven from flax yarns

**linsey-woolsey** coarse fabric of wool and linen

**lisle** twisted, hard cotton thread, esp. for hosiery and gloves

**lisse** lightly crinkled, gauzy silk, esp. for ruffles or trim

**loden** heavy, waterproof wool, esp. for coats

**luster** *Chiefly Brit.* cotton warp with wool or mohair filling

**mackinaw** heavy, napped wool in plaid design, esp. for coats

**mackintosh** lightweight, waterproof, rubberized cotton, esp. for raincoats

**madras** fine, hard cotton or durable silk, in colorful plaid or stripes

**malines** fine, stiff mesh of silk or rayon, esp. for veils

**marocain** heavy crepe of silk, wool, or rayon with strong rib effect, esp. for women's suits

**marquisette** sheer leno weave, esp. for curtains or netting

**marseilles** thick cotton that is figured or striped, esp. for coverings

**mat** tough, coarse, woven or plaited fabric

**material** any cloth or textile fabric

**matte jersey** jersey with a dull finish

**melton** heavy twilled wool with smooth face in solid colors

**merino** fine, soft wool of Spanish merino sheep, esp. for stockings

**mesh** woven, knit, or knotted material of open texture with evenly spaced strands

**messaline** soft, lightweight silk in satin weave

**mohair** long, silky wool made from fleece of Angora goat

**moiré** silky fabric with watered or wavy pattern; watered fabric

**monk's cloth** coarse, heavy cotton in a basket weave, orig. for monk's habit, now used esp. for draperies

**moquette** thick, velvety fabric, esp. for carpets and upholstery

**moreen** heavy wool or wool and cotton with moiré finish, for curtains or petticoats

**motley** varicolored cotton fabric, esp. for jester's costume

**mousseline** *French.* muslin; sheer rayon resembling muslin

**mousseline de laine** *French.* lightweight worsted wool or muslin with print

**mousseline de soie** *French.* gauzelike, stiff silk or rayon, esp. for blouses

**mull** soft, thin muslin

**muslin** plain-weave cotton with sheer to coarse finish, often printed or embroidered; mousseline

**nainsook** fine, lightweight cotton, often striped

**nankeen** durable, brownish-yellow Chinese cotton, esp. for trousers

**net** open-mesh fabric twisted or knotted at uniform intervals

**ninon** sturdy, sheer silk or rayon in plain or novelty weave

**oilcloth** cotton cloth waterproofed with oil and pigment, esp. for table or shelf covering

**organdy** very sheer, stiff, lightweight cotton with crisp finish, esp. for blouses

**organza** sheer silk, nylon, or rayon with crisp finish, stiffer than organdy, used for gowns and trim

**organzine** silk that has been additionally twisted in opposite directions, used warpwise in weaving silk fabrics

**oxford** cotton in plain, twill, or basket weave, esp. for shirts

**paisley** soft woolen fabric or silk printed with colorful, swirled designs

**panne** velvet or satin with lustrous, flattened pile

**paramatta** lightweight twilled dress fabric of wool, with cotton or silk warp

**pedaline** strawlike material of hemp core covered with cellulose, esp. for braids and ribbons

**percale** fine, closely woven cotton, esp. for bed sheets

**petersham** heavy wool for bulky outergarments

**Pima** fine broadcloth cotton, esp. for shirts

**pique** durable, ribbed cotton, rayon, or silk

**plaid** fabric in checkerboard, crossbarred pattern, esp. twilled wool

**plush** fabric with pile higher than 1/8 inch (3 mm), less dense than velvet

**pointelle** lacy, openwork fabric

**pongee** thin, soft, tan raw silk (China); similar cotton or rayon fabric in uneven weave

**poplin** sturdy, plain-weave cotton with fine ribs

**poult-de-soie** rich, shiny, ribbed silk and alpaca for dresses

**prunella** twilled, lightweight, worsted fabric

**qiviut** very soft, dense wool from undercoat of musk ox

**ragg** sturdy wool fiber blended with nylon to make flecked, grayish yarn

**ratine** loosely woven cotton or wool with nubby surface; ratteen

**ratteen** ratine

**raw silk** woven fabric of spun silk without sericin, a natural binder, removed

**rep** plain-weave fabric with prominent, rounded, crosswise cording

**russet** coarse, homespun, reddish-brown cloth

**sackcloth** coarse, rough cloth, orig. of goat's hair, now of hemp or jute, esp. for mourning clothes

**sailcloth** lightweight canvas, esp. for curtains and outer garments

**samite** rich medieval silk, interwoven with gold and silver

**sarcenet** soft, fine silk, esp. for veils and trim

**sateen** smooth, durable, lustrous cotton in satin weave

**satin** rich silk with glossy face and dull back; similar acetate, nylon, or rayon

**saxony** fine, closely knitted, soft wool for coats

**scrim** durable, open-weave cotton or linen, esp. for curtains

**seersucker** lightweight, crinkled linen or cotton, usu. striped

**serge** twilled worsted or wool, esp. for suits

**shahtoosh** very fine, brownish-gray wool from throat area of Indian goat

**shalloon** light, twilled wool or worsted, esp. for linings

**Shantung** medium coarse Oriental silk

**sharkskin** smooth wool or worsted with small woven design; similar fabric of acetate or rayon with dull appearance

**Shetland wool** soft, fine wool from undercoat of Shetland sheep

**shirting** cotton or other fabric, such as broadcloth or oxford, esp. for shirts

**shoddy** inferior fabric of reclaimed wool or shredded waste

**sicilienne** blend of silk and fine wool

**silk** soft, fine fabric of thread woven from fibers of silkworm cocoons

**slipper satin** sturdy satin for lightweight slippers

**stammel** coarse wool dyed red for penitents' undershirts

**stockinette** soft elastic cotton, esp. for bandages or infant wear

**stuff** *Chiefly Brit.* finished wool or worsted

**surah** soft, twilled, lustrous Indian silk or rayon, esp. for ties and dresses

**swansdown** heavy cotton flannel with thickly napped face; fine, soft, thick wool

**tabby** plain silk taffeta with watered moiré finish

**taffeta** finely woven, stiff silk, cotton, or rayon, with high sheen and fine crosswise ribs

**tapa** coarse cloth of pounded mulberry bark with geometric patterns (Pacific islands)

**tarlatan** thin, meshlike, stiffened cotton, sometimes glazed

**tartan** emblematic plaid-patterned, multicolored, twilled wool (Scotland)

**tattersall** fabric with colored crossbars on solid background

**terry** absorbent cotton fabric with uncut pile loops on both sides

**textile** fabric woven or knitted from natural or synthetic fiber

**ticking** durable linen or cotton, esp. for upholstery and covers

**tiffany** thin silk or cotton gauze

**tissue** fine, gauzy, sheer fabric

**toile** sheer, transparent linen or cotton

**toweling** narrow fabric of cotton or linen, in plain, twill, or huck weave, for towels

**tricot** plain, warp-knit fabric of wool, silk, or nylon, with fine ribs

**tricotine** cavalry twill

**tulle** thin, fine netting of silk, acetate, nylon, or rayon, esp. for veils and gowns

**tussah** tan, medium-coarse Oriental silk

**tweed** coarse woolen fabric in plain or herringbone weave

**twill** any fabric woven in parallel diagonal lines or ribs

**veiling** light, sheer netting for veils

**velour** cloth with velvetlike nap, esp. for upholstery and draperies

**velvet** richly woven fabric of silk, acetate, nylon, or rayon, with soft, thick pile

**velveteen** twilled, plain-weave cotton with short, velvety pile

**Venetian cloth** wool or worsted fabric in satin or twill weave, sometimes napped

**vicuna** very soft, light brown wool made from undercoat of South American llama

**vigogne** wool in twill weave and neutral color

**voile** sheer cotton, wool, silk, or rayon in plain weave, esp. for dresses or curtains

**wadmal** coarse, bulky, woolen fabric with heavy nap, esp. for protective clothing (Scandinavia)

**watered fabric** moiré

**whipcord** cotton, woolen, or worsted fabric with steep, diagonally ribbed surface

**wool** fabric woven from the soft, curly undercoat or fleece of mammals such as sheep, goats, and camels

**worsted** woolen fabric with smooth, hard surface and no nap

**zibeline** soft, lustrous fabric of wool mixed with alpaca or camel hair to form long, silky nap, esp. for coats, suits, and dresses

## SYNTHETIC FIBERS AND TEXTILES

**acetate** acetic ester of cellulose with satiny appearance

**Acrilan** *Trademark.* acrylic, wrinkle-resistant textile

**acrylic** quick-drying synthetic fiber made by polymerization of acrylonitrile

**Banlon** *Trademark.* synthetic textile

**Celanese acetate** *Trademark.* specially produced acetate textile

**Dacron** *Trademark.* resilient polyester fiber

**double-knit** polyester material

**durable press** permanent press

**fiberfill** resilient, lightweight, fluffy synthetic fiber, used esp. as filling for quilts or sleeping bags

**Fortrel** *Trademark.* bonded polyester fabric with acetate tricot backing

**Gore-Tex** *Trademark.* highly waterproof fabric laminated with thin membrane of stretched polytetrafluoroethylene (PTFE), which allows body to breath

**Lastex** *Trademark.* elastic material with latex rubber core covered by fabric strands

**leatherette** synthetic leather of paper and vinyl

**Lurex** *Trademark.* silver or gold synthetic textile

**nylon** strong, elastic, thermoplastic polyamide textile

**Orlon** *Trademark*. soft, lightweight, wrinkle- and sun-resistant acrylic fiber

**permanent press** textile treated with resin and heat to resist wrinkling; durable press

**polyester** synthetic, woollike knit material made from fibers formed by polymerization

**polypropylene** lightweight fiber that is a polymer of propylene, used in bonded fabrics

**polyvinyl** textile of polymerized vinyl compounds

**rayon** synthetic textile fiber of woven or knit cellulose that resembles wool, silk, or cotton fabric

**ripstop nylon** durable, tear-resistant nylon, esp. for parkas and tents

**Sarelon** *Trademark*. synthetic textile

**spandex** highly elastic, long-chain polymer fiber

**synthetic fiber** slender, threadlike structure derived from mineral or chemical components and used to make synthetic textile

**Thinsulate** *Trademark*. thin, versatile, spun-bonded fabric that is a good insulator

**Ultrasuede** *Trademark*. synthetic leather with suedelike texture

**Vicara** *Trademark*. wooly fiber for textile blends

**vinyl** polymer textile derived from vinyl

**vinyon** strong, easily molded, long-chain polymer vinyl textile fiber

**wash-and-wear fabric** permanent press fabric that can be washed and dries quickly

# Laces

**Alençon** delicate, fine mesh needlepoint in solid floral pattern

**bobbin lace** handmade lace formed by intertwisting threads on bobbins over patterns marked by pins in pillow; pillow lace

**bobbinet** machine-made net in hexagonal mesh

**Breton** handmade lace from Brittany

**Brussels lace** needlepoint or bobbin lace with floral design, orig. made near Brussels

**Carrickmacross** guipure appliqué lace with floral designs, from Ireland

**Chantilly** delicate silk or linen bobbin lace in hexagonal mesh with scrolled or floral design, usu. black, handmade in France

**Dieppe** lace in design originated at Dieppe, France

**duchesse** fine Flemish bobbin lace in delicate floral designs

**gros point** Venetian point lace with large, raised designs

**guipure** heavy, large-patterned lace of linen or silk

**illusion** delicate, gauzy tulle, esp. for veils

**lace** delicate, netlike, figured fabric of thread or yarn

**Mechlin** delicate bobbin lace from Belgium

**mignonette** narrow bobbin lace with scattered small designs, of French and Flemish origin

**Milan point** needlepoint Italian lace in braided floral pattern

**needlepoint lace** handmade lace worked entirely with needle over paper pattern in buttonhole stitch; point lace

**pillow lace** bobbin lace

**point lace** needlepoint lace

**raised point** needlepoint lace with padded floral design in high relief, orig. from Venice, Italy

**reticella** old-fashioned needlepoint lace in geometric pattern

**rose point** needlepoint lace in rose designs, orig. from Venice, Italy

**tambour** lace made on a frame of two interlocking hoops with designs embroidered or darned onto machine-made net

**tatting** lace made by hand looping and knotting a single, heavy thread

**Tenerife** handmade lace with spiderweb designs, from the Canary Islands, used for edging

**torchon** durable bobbin lace of coarse linen or cotton in simple, open, geometric patterns with scalloped edges

**Valenciennes** flat bobbin lace in simple floral pattern of fine, diamond-shaped mesh, with same thread forming ground and motif

**Venetian point** needlepoint lace from Venice, Italy, esp. raised and rose point laces

# Furs, Leathers, and Pelts

**alligator** skin of alligator with distinctive block pattern

**badger** short fur of badger

**bearskin** thick fur of bear, esp. for rugs

**beaver** soft, brown fur of beaver, esp. for hats

**black marten** soft, thick, very dark marten fur

**broadtail** fur of very young karakul lamb

**buckskin** pliable, suede-finished skin of deer

**buff** supple, oil-tanned cowhide

**cabretta** light, soft leather from skin of hairy sheep

**calfskin** young, domestic cowhide

**capeskin** flexible sheepskin with natural grain, esp. for gloves

**chamois** soft, pliant antelope or sheepskin

**chevrette** leather made from skin of young goat

**chinchilla** soft, pearly gray fur of chinchilla

**cony** rabbit fur

**coonskin** raccoon fur, esp. for hats

**Cordovan** fine-grained, dense, nonporous skin of horse, pig, or goat

**cowhide** sturdy hide of domestic cow

**doeskin** skin of female deer or sheep

**deerskin** skin of wild deer

**ermine** soft, white weasel fur, esp. for coats and trim

**fox** fox fur

**frosted mink** fur of mink with chemically lightened strands, giving it a streaked appearance

**fur** soft, thick mammal hair; skin bearing such hair, stripped and processed

**goatskin** skin of domestic or wild goat

**golden sable** golden fur of sable

**horsehide** dressed or raw skin of horse, esp. for baseballs

**kid** leather made from skin of young goat, esp. for gloves

**krimmer** dressed lambskin with loose soft curls of pale wool, from Crimea

**lambskin** soft skin of young sheep

**leather** animal skin prepared for use by removing all hair and tanning

**leopard** spotted fur of leopard

**Levant** morocco leather patterned with irregular creases

**maribou** thick fur of northern deer, esp. for capes

**marmot** coarse, woolly fur of marmot

**marten** soft, thick marten fur

**miniver** white fur of miniver, esp. for robes of state

**mink** brown, black, or white fur of cultivated mink

**mocha** pliable, suede-finished African sheepskin, esp. for gloves

**moleskin** furry, taupe-colored skin of mole

**morocco** fine, firm, flexible goatskin tanned with sumac, having pebbly grain and reddish color

**muskrat** glossy, dark brown fur of muskrat

**nappa** soft leather from sheepskin or lambskin, used for gloves and shoes

**nutria** beaverlike fur of coypu, used for coats, hats, and trim

**otter** dark brown fur of otter

**patent leather** stiff, shiny, varnished or lacquered leather, esp. for shoes

**pelt** skin of fur-bearing animal stripped from carcass, with hair removed

**pigskin** tough leather of swine skin, esp. for footballs

**pig suede** suede made from pigskin, used for jackets, shoes, and gloves

**puma** cougar fur

**rabbit** soft, light rabbit fur

**raccoon** long, coarse raccoon fur, esp. for coats

**ranch mink** fur of commercially raised, semiaquatic mink

**rawhide** untanned hide

**red fox** reddish-brown fox fur

**Russia leather** fine, smooth leather, esp. dyed dark red

**sable** rich, dark brown sable fur

**sealskin** slick, black fur of seal

**shagreen** untanned horsehide or sharkskin with granular surface

**shearling** tanned skin from recently shorn sheep or lamb

**sheepskin** hide of sheep, used esp. for parchment

**silver fox** silvery-white fox fur

**skunk** bushy, black-and-white skunk fur

**suede** tanned leather with flesh side buffed to a slight nap

**swakara** fur of karakul sheep, from Namibia

**vair** bluish-gray or white squirrel fur

**white fox** very pale or white fox fur

**white leather** animal hide bleached of natural color

**wild mink** brown fur of noncultivated mink

# FOOTWEAR

Parts of Shoes and Accessories
Shoes and Footwear

**SEE ALSO**: Chap. 10: Undergarments

## PARTS OF SHOES AND ACCESSORIES

**aglet** tag that covers end of shoelace

**arch** midsection of shoe that supports arch of foot

**breasting** inside forepart of heel

**bootjack** yokelike instrument for removing boot by catching its heel

**bootstrap** strip of material, esp. leather, sewn at top rear or sides of boot and grasped to help pull boot on

**buckle** latch fastening for two loose straps

**captoe** forepart of shoe, set off by line of stitching from one side of foot to other

**collar** top of shoe that encircles foot, ankle, or leg

**counter** stiffener inserted between liner and outside leather to shape shoe around heel

**creeper** attachment with iron points that is strapped to shoe to prevent person from slipping on ice

**cuff** trimming or finishing strip sewed around outside top of shoe

**eyelet** small hole through which shoelace passes

**facing** ornamental or protective lining

**French heel** high, curved heel used on women's shoes, characterized by heel breast that curves into shank

**heel** rigid attachment to sole beneath rear of foot

**hook** curved piece of metal throug'. which shoelace passes

**insole** thin support strip inside shoe

**lace hook** one of a series of hooks for lacing ankle portion of high-top shoe

**lace stay** part of oxford into which eyelets and laces are inserted

**lift** special arch support built into or inserted in footwear; one of the layers of leather forming heel

**mudguard** insert between sole and body of shoe

**outsole** sole

**platform** insert that adds height to heel

**quarter** rear part of shoe above heel

**seam** stitching where sections of shoe are attached

**shank** portion of sole of shoe beneath instep that provides support for arch section; metal or fiber piece that gives this part shape

**shoehorn** stiff, troughlike blade on handle, held at back of shoe to aid in inserting heel

**shoelace** cloth or leather string for binding shoe closed

**shoetree** form of wood or metal inserted in shoe to preserve its shape when not in use

**sole** thick bottom of shoe that rests on ground; outsole

**strap** cord of leather or cloth used to hold shoe on foot

**tassel** ornamental knob of loose, knotted strands of leather hanging over upper

**thong** upright piece between toes on certain sandals

**tip** front of toe

**toe** forepart of shoe over toes of foot

**toe box** piece of stiffened material placed between lining and toecap of shoe

**toecap** piece of leather or other material covering toe of shoe, sometimes of different color than upper

**tongue** attached piece across top of foot, esp. under laces

**upper** main part of shoe above sole

**vamp** upper covering forepart of foot, extending back

**wedge heel** heel on woman's shoe formed by triangular wedge that extends from front or middle to back of sole

**welt** strip of leather between insole and outsole through which they are stitched or stapled together

**wingtip** toecap perforated in wing-shaped design

## SHOES AND FOOTWEAR

**aerobic shoe** lightweight athletic shoe designed for high impact aerobic movement

**anklet** low woman's shoe with one or more ankle straps

**arctic** warm, waterproof overshoe

**athletic shoe** canvas or leather shoe with rubber sole

**babouche** ornamental heelless slipper (Middle East)

**ballet slipper** light, soft, close-fitting dance shoe

**balmoral** ankle-high laced boot or shoe

**basketball shoe** high-topped athletic shoe designed for playing basketball

**blucher** shoe with one-piece tongue and front vamp, overlapped by quarters that lace together

**boot** fitted leather upper reaching above ankle; waterproof rubber or plastic covering for shoe and ankle

**bootee** ankle-length boot; infant's knitted or crocheted sock worn as indoor shoe

**bootie** soft, sometimes disposable sock or bootlike covering for foot or shoe, for protection or informal wear

**brogan** heavy leather, ankle-high work shoe; stogy

**brogue** heavy shoe with punched design on uppers, such as wingtips or oxfords

**buck** light brown buckskin shoe

**bulldog shoe** shoe with deep, boxed toe

**buskin** thick-soled, laced, shin-high shoe

**button shoe** shoe with button closure and no laces

**chopine** woman's thick-soled shoe (16th-17th c.)

**chukka** ankle-high, laced, leather boot with two eyelets

**cleat** athletic shoe with metal or hard rubber grips on sole

**clodhopper** large, heavy, rustic shoe

**clog** shoe with thick wooden sole; klomp; wooden shoe (Holland and Scandinavia)

**combat boot** sturdy, high-laced military boot

**corespondent shoe** two-tone shoe, either tan or brown and white; buck

**cothurni** thick-soled elevator boots for dramatic costume (ancient Greece)

**cowboy boot** midcalf boot with high heels, pointed toe, and fancy stitching, traditionally for horseback riding

**Cuban heel** shoe with broad, medium-high heel with curved back

**dancing shoe** flexible, light, low-cut shoe

**decker** flat, rubber-soled sandal; flip-flop; zori

**desert boot** soft leather boot for walking

**docksider** casual, rubber-soled leather moccasin

**d'orsay** woman's pump or slipper with circular vamp

**dress shoe** formal, shiny leather shoe

**duck** casual slip-on, water-resistant shoe with canvas upper and rubber sole

**espadrille** shoe with hemp or crepe sole, canvas upper, and flat or wedge heel; rope-sole shoe

**everett** low-backed man's lounging slipper

**Faust slipper** high-cut house shoe with V-shaped sides

**flats** woman's casual, low-heeled shoes

**flip-flop** flat, loose, backless, rubber sandal held on with thong between first two toes; decker; zori

**flippers** broad, flat, usu. rubber attachments to feet, with toe end expanded into paddle for swimming, diving, or body surfing

**footwear** shoes, sandals, and slippers intended as outer covering for feet

**gaiter** ankle-high shoe of cloth or leather with elastic inserts in sides

**galoshes** high rubber overshoes for protection from snow and rain; overshoes

**geta** wooden clog elevated by transverse supports on bottom of sole (Japan)

**gillie** low-cut shoe with decorative lacing through loops and around ankle

**gumshoe** rubber overshoe or boot

**gym shoe** comfortable, rubber-soled athletic shoe, often with canvas upper

**half-boot** boot ending just above ankle

**heels** woman's high-heeled dress shoes

**Hessian boot** tasseled military boot ending just below knee (19th c.)

**high-button shoe** shoe buttoning to ankle

**high heels** woman's dress shoes with elongated heels and low-cut upper

**high-topped shoe** shoe with ankle-high upper

**high-topped sneakers** athletic shoe extending over ankle for extra support

**hiking boot** sturdy, lightweight boot with nonslip sole

**hip boot** tall boot extending above knee to top of thigh

**hobnail boot** rustic boot with short nails on sole to prevent wear

**huarache** woven leather sandal with rubber sole (Mexico)

**jackboot** heavy, glossy, midthigh military boot (17th-18th c.)

**jazz shoe** close-fitting, low-heeled oxford of soft leather or fabric, having thin, flexible sole, worn for jazz dancing

**kiltie** shoe with long tongue in tassels or fringe folding over instep

**klomp** wooden shoe; clog

**lace shoe** shoe with lace and eyelet closure

**larrigan** oil-tanned moccasin that extends up legs, used by lumbermen

**loafer** low-cut, slip-on shoe

**lounger** casual shoe

**military heel** woman's shoe with heel lower and thicker than Cuban

**moccasin** soft leather, heelless shoe with sole stitched to upper

**monk shoe** low, plain shoe with buckle closure

**mukluk** heavy sealskin or reindeer boot (Eskimo)

**mule** woman's low-heeled house shoe or lounging slipper, with upper across open toes

**overshoes** galoshes

**oxford** shoe laced over instep, with facings sewn on front of vamp for laces

**pac** laced, heelless sheepskin or felt shoe worn inside boot in cold weather

**pantofle** bedroom slipper

**paratrooper boot** sturdy boot that laces to knee

**patent leather shoe** dress shoe of shiny patent leather

**patten** clog or sandal with thick wooden sole for walking in mud

**penny loafer** casual slip-on shoe with flap in vamp, sometimes used to hold coin

**platform shoe** shoe with very thick, elevated sole

**plimsoll** light, rubber-soled shoe with mudguard and canvas top

**pump** woman's low-cut, low-heeled, thin-soled, casual shoe

**puttee** leather legging secured by strap or catch

**riding boot** high, close-fitting boot for horseback riding

**Roman sandal** flat-soled shoe with long straps tied around foot, ankle, and calf

**romeo** man's shoe or slipper with U-shaped elastic inserts at sides

**rope-sole shoe** shoe with thatched rope sole; espadrille

**rubber** low rubber shoe worn over regular shoes for protection from rain

**running shoe** athletic shoe with sole and support designed for running

**sabot** wooden shoe with strap across instep

**saddle oxford** saddle shoe

**saddle shoe** oxford-style, two-tone shoe, esp. in brown and white; saddle oxford

**sandal** usu. leather sole attached to foot by straps

**scuff** flat-soled slipper with no quarter or heel strap

**seaboot** high, waterproof wading boot for fishing and sailing

**shoe** outer covering for foot, usu. with sturdy sole and attached rigid heel

**ski boot** heavy boot that clamps to ski

**slip-on shoe** shoe without lace, button, or buckle closure, such as loafer

**slipper** soft, low-cut, slip-on shoe, esp. for indoor wear

**sneaker** canvas or leather sport shoe with pliable rubber sole

**snowshoe** oval, light, wooden frame strung with thongs that attaches to shoe for walking over deep snow

**soft-sole shoe** infant's shoe with moccasin seam and soft leather bottom

**spectator pump** woman's medium-heeled shoe with contrasting colors at heel and toe of upper

**spike** athletic shoe with metal spikes in sole

**spike heel** woman's very tall, narrow-heeled shoe; stiletto heel

**squaretoed boot** boot with squared-off toe

**steel-toed boot** work boot with steel-reinforced toe

**step-in** pump with high vamp and concealed goring

**stiletto heel** spike heel

**stogy** brogan

**tennis shoe** canvas athletic shoe with rubber sole

**thigh boot** boot extending to midthigh, flexible at knee

**thong** sandal with strip of material fitted between toes, strapped across foot

**toe shoe** woman's ballet slipper with wood block inside toe for en pointe dancing

**top boot** high riding boot with leather bands around upper

**track shoe** light, heelless shoe with steel spikes for running outdoors or rubber sole for running on indoor track

**veldschoen** heavy rawhide shoe without insole, made without nails

**wafflestomper** ankle boot with ridged sole, esp. for hiking

**wader** knee-high or chest-high waterproof boot for fishing and hunting

**Wallabee** *Trademark.* comfortable, hard-soled moccasin with soft leather or suede upper, orig. from Ireland

**wedgie** shoe with wedge-shaped heel joined to half sole

**Wellington boot** leather boot loosely fitted above knee

**white buck** casual oxford of white buckskin

**wingtip** man's dress shoe with toecap perforated in wing-shaped design

**wooden shoe** clog or other wood-soled shoe

**work shoe** durable leather shoe or boot

**zori** lightweight, usu. rubber, thong sandal (Japan)

# HATS, HEADGEAR, AND HAIRPIECES

Hats
Helmets, Headdresses, and Hairpieces

**SEE ALSO**: Chap. 1: Hair and Grooming; Chap. 10: Outer Garments; Ornaments and Accessories

## HATS

**astrakhan** hat of curly astrakhan wool (Russia)

**Balmoral** *Scot.* round, flat cap with projecting top all around

**bangkok** hat woven of fine palm fiber (Philippines)

**baseball cap** hat with close-fitted crown, front brim, and insignia

**beanie** small, close-fitting skullcap, formerly worn by college freshmen

**bearskin** large, military dress hat of bear fur

**beret** soft, round, flat, visorless, wool cap, banded to fit head

**bicorne** hat with brim turned up in two places

**biggin** child's cap; nightcap (16th–17th c.)

**billed hat** hat with visor

**billycock** *Chiefly Brit.* derby

**biretta** square cap with three corner points and tassel on top, worn by Catholic clergy

**bluebonnet** *Scot.* wide, flat, round cap of blue wool

**boater** flat-topped, stiff straw hat with round, flat brim

**bonnet** woman's brimless hat with chin ribbon

**bowler** felt hat with low, round crown and narrow brim

**brass hat** high-ranking officer's cap with gold braid

**Breton** round sailor hat with turned-up brim, for women

**brimmed hat** hat with projecting edge

**busby** tall, military dress hat of fur, with bag hanging on one side

**calash** woman's bonnet that folds back on top (18th c.)

**calpac** high-crowned cap (Turkey and Iran)

**campaign hat** broad-brimmed felt hat with four dents in crown, worn by members of U.S. Army and Marine Corps

**cap** usu. close-fitting hat, esp. with visor and no brim

**capote** stiff-brimmed hat with soft crown; bonnet

**castor** hat made of beaver or rabbit fur

**caul** woman's close-fitting net cap

**chapeau** *French.* hat

**chapeau bras** ceremonial, plumed bicorne carried under arm (18th c.)

**chaperon** round, stuffed hat with dangling cloth folds (15th c.)

**chéchia** cylindrical, brimless, tasseled Arab cap

**cloche** woman's bell-shaped, close-fitting hat worn well down on head

**cocked hat** tricorne with brim turned up in three places

**coif** nun's close-fitting skullcap worn under veil

**commode** woman's tall, ornate cap (17th–18th c.)

**coolie hat**  conical, straw sunhat (Asia)

**coonskin**  cap of raccoon skin, often with tail at back

**cowboy hat**  wide-brimmed hat with large, soft crown

**coxcomb**  jester's cap adorned with strip of red

**crusher**  soft, felt, crushable hat; crush hat

**crush hat**  crusher

**deerstalker**  close-fitting woolen cap with visor in front and back and earflaps that are tied across top of crown when raised, orig. worn for hunting

**derby**  man's stiff, felt hat with narrow brim and domed crown; billycock; pot hat

**dink**  beanie with button on top

**Dolly Varden**  woman's broad-brimmed, flower-trimmed costume hat (19th c.)

**dress cap**  cap worn with military dress uniform

**dunce cap**  tall, conical, brimless hat, formerly worn as punishment by poor students

**Dutch cap**  woman's cap of triangular cloth rolled back at each side

**fedora**  low, soft, felt hat with crown creased lengthwise

**felt hat**  soft fedora or other hat made of felt

**fez**  brimless, cone-shaped felt hat with tassel (Turkey)

**flowerpot**  hat with turned-down brim like upturned flowerpot

**fool's cap**  three-crowned or conical cap or hood with bells, worn by jesters; jester's cap

**forage cap**  small, nondress military cap with visor and round, flat crown

**fore-and-after**  cocked hat having visors front and back and earflaps

**fur hat**  head covering made of animal fur

**garrison cap**  overseas cap

**gibus**  collapsible opera or top hat

**glengarry**  woolen cap with straight sides, crease along top, and sometimes ribbon streamers at back (Scotland)

**hard hat**  protective rigid hat of metal or fiberglass worn by construction workers

**hat**  shaped head covering, usu. with brim (projecting edge) and crown (rounded or peaked top)

**havelock**  cloth cap with flap hanging down back of neck as sun shield

**helmet hat**  close-fitting hat with sides that extend over ears

**homburg**  hard felt hat with indented crown and rolled-up brim with ribbon edge

**jester's cap**  fool's cap

**jipijapa**  Panama hat made from leaves of jipijapa plant

**jockey cap**  lightweight cap with long visor worn by jockeys

**juliet cap**  close-fitting beaded or jewel-embroidered cap

**kamelaukion**  tall, brimless, flat-topped hat worn by Eastern Orthodox clergy

**kelly**  man's stiff, flat-topped straw hat

**kepi**  military cap with close-fitting band, round, flat top sloping toward front, and visor

**kossuth hat**  large hat with flat-topped crown and rolled brim (Hungary)

**leghorn**  hat or bonnet of fine leghorn straw

**liberty cap**  limp, close-fitting, conical cap worn as symbol of freedom in French Revolution

**lid**  *Slang.* hat

**millinery**  women's hats in general

**mobcap**  woman's indoor cap with full, high crown, tied with strap under chin

**monkey cap**  small pillbox hat with chin strap

**montero**  round hunter's cap with earflaps

**mortarboard**  close-fitting academic cap with flat, square top and tassel

**mutch**  *Scot.* woman's or child's close-fitting linen cap

**nightcap**  soft, brimless cap worn in bed

**opera hat**  silk top hat, often collapsible

**overseas cap**  visorless wool or cotton cap without stiffening; garrison cap

**Panama hat**  high-crowned, brimmed hat of pale, plaited jipijapa leaf fibers

**peaked hat**  hat with tall, peaked crown

**petasus**  broad-brimmed, low-crowned hat (ancient Greece and Rome)

**Phrygian cap**  close-fitting, conical cap (ancient Greece)

**picture hat**  woman's dressy, broad-brimmed day hat

**pillbox**  woman's small, stiff, brimless, cylindrical cap

**pinner**  woman's cap with long lappets (17th–18th c.)

**pixie**  woman's skullcap with pointed crown

**plug hat**  man's stiff bowler or top hat

**poke bonnet**  woman's bonnet with projecting front bill

**porkpie**  low-crowned felt hat with creased top and brim turned up in back, down in front; stingy brim

**postilion**  woman's hat with high, narrow crown and narrow, rolled brim

**pot hat**  derby

**rain hat**  waterproof or water-repellent hat

**sailor**  stiff straw hat with low, flat crown and circular brim; soft cotton sailor's hat with brim folded up

**scraper**  *Slang.* cocked hat

**service cap**  flat-topped military hat with visor

**shako**  stiff, high-crowned, plumed military hat with metal plate in front

**shovel hat**  clergyman's hat with shallow crown and wide brim curved up at side

**silk hat**  top hat

**skimmer**  flat-crowned straw hat with wide, straight brim

**skullcap**  close-fitting, brimless cap that fits high on head

**slouch hat**  soft felt hat with wide flexible brim

**snap brim**  soft felt hat with brim pulled down in front

**sombrero**  large, high-crowned, felt or straw hat with very wide, turned-up brim (Mexico)

**sou'wester**  waterproof hat with brim that is wide and slanted at back

**Stetson**  *Trademark.* broad-brimmed, high-crowned cowboy hat

**stingy brim**  porkpie

**stocking cap**  knitted conical cap with tassel or pompon on top, for winter wear

**stovepipe hat**  *Slang.* man's tall, silk top hat

**straw hat**  hat of woven straw, usu. flat and stiff, with straight brim

**sugarloaf**  conical-shaped hat, usu. with flat brim (17th–18th c.)

**sunbonnet**  ruffled cloth poke bonnet with protective neck cover

**sundown**  woman's broad-brimmed hat

**sun hat**  broad-brimmed hat with high crown for sun protection

**tam**  *Informal.* tam-o'-shanter

**tam-o'-shanter**  soft, flat, knitted wool hat with pompon on top; tam

**tarboosh**  red, fezlike Muslim hat

**ten-gallon hat** large cowboy hat

**terai** double felt, subtropical sun hat with wide, turned brim

**three-cornered hat** tricorne

**top hat** tall, formal hat, often collapsible, esp. of silk; silk hat; topper

**topper** top hat

**toque** woman's small, close-fitting, brimless hat (16th c.)

**tricorne** hat with brim turned up in three places; three-cornered hat

**trilby** *Chiefly Brit.* soft felt hat with indented crown

**tuque** knitted stocking cap, often pointed at top (Canada)

**Tyrolean hat** wide-brimmed felt or straw hat with feather on side

**watch cap** knitted, close-fitting, navy blue, cold weather cap worn by sailors

**Watteau hat** straw hat with feather and ribbon trim

**wide-awake** soft felt hat with low crown and wide brim

**yarmulke** skullcap worn by Jewish men

**zucchetto** skullcap worn by Catholic ecclesiastics, with color indicating rank

## HELMETS, HEADDRESSES, AND HAIRPIECES

**aigrette** long white heron's plume headdress

**anadem** *Archaic.* garland or wreath

**babushka** kerchief or scarf worn as woman's headdress (Russia)

**bagwig** wig with back hair enclosed in small, silk bag (18th c.)

**balaclava** hoodlike, close-fitting, knitted pullover mask that reaches to shoulders

**bandanna** large, colored kerchief tied around head

**bandeau** band or ribbon worn around head to hold hair

**basinet** lightweight, pointed steel helmet

**bathing cap** tight-fitting elastic cap, usu. of rubber, worn to keep hair dry while swimming or bathing

**burgonet** peaked armor helmet (16th c.)

**capuche** Capuchin monk's hood

**casque** armor helmet with eye slits

**chaplet** garland or wreath

**cornet** woman's tall, cone-shaped headdress, usu. of delicate fabrics with lace lappets (14th–18th c.)

**coronet** small, crownlike, jeweled headdress

**cowl** monk's hood

**crash helmet** usu. round, rigid, protective helmet for drivers and fliers

**crest** feather plume worn on helmet

**crown** jeweled headdress for royalty

**diadem** bejeweled cloth headband for royalty; type of crown

**earmuffs** soft, warm ear coverings connected by band across skull

**eyeshade** visor attached to head to shield eyes from sun

**fall** long, false hairpiece

**fanchon** kerchief folded into triangle and worn as cap

**fascinator** crocheted or lace scarf, narrowing toward ends, worn as head covering by women

**feathers** bird's feathers worn as headdress, esp. by American Indians

**fillet** narrow strip of material worn as headband

**football helmet** rigid, round helmet with faceguard and chin strap

**gas mask** close-fitting face piece connected to air canister, worn for protection from poisonous air

**garland** wreath of flowers or foliage

**hair net** mesh cap of fine material that holds hair in place

**hairpiece** section of false hair

**headband** fabric, leather, or flower headpiece that encircles head across forehead

**headcloth** kerchief, bandanna, or other cloth worn on head

**headdress** any decorative covering for head

**headgear** head covering of any kind

**heaume** armor helmet that rested on shoulders (13th c.)

**helmet** protective head covering of hard material

**hennin** woman's tall, conical, veiled headdress (15th c.)

**hood** soft fabric covering for head and neck

**kaffiyeh** square cloth folded into triangle and held on head by agal cord (Middle East)

**kerchief** small square of cloth used as head covering

**lambrequin** protective woven covering worn over helmet

**lappet** headdress with many folds, streamers, or flaps; one of these hanging flaps

**mantilla** woman's veil covering head and shoulders

**miter** bishop's tall, peaked headdress

**morion** visorless, high-crested, Spanish soldier's helmet (17th c.)

**panache** feather plume, esp. on helmet

**pelage** hair or feather head covering

**penna** headdress of feathers

**periwig** long, formal wig, often white (17th c.)

**peruke** wig (17th–19th c.)

**pith helmet** round, broad-brimmed, protective jungle helmet

**plumage** plumes and feathers worn as headdress

**plume** long bird's feather used as headdress

**postiche** artificial hairpiece

**pschent** Pharaoh's headdress (ancient Egypt)

**puggaree** light scarf wrapped around sun helmet as hat-band

**ramillie** wig with long plait at back, tied top and bottom with bows (18th c.)

**ribbon** strip of often colorful material tied around hair for decoration or to hold hair in place

**riding hood** loose, enveloping hood

**rug** *Slang.* wig

**rumal** man's checked cotton or silk kerchief worn as headdress (India)

**sallet** light helmet, with or without visor, with projection over neck (15th c.)

**scarf** cloth worn over head

**ski mask** pullover woolen hood with openings for eyes and mouth

**snood** fine material or net, pinned at back to contain hair

**sun helmet** topee

**switch** long, thick strand of usu. real hair, fastened together at one end and added to one's own, esp. by women

**tiara** crownlike headdress of jewels or flowers

**tin hat** metal helmet of tin

**topee** jungle helmet with cloth covering and cork insulation for protection from sun; sun helmet

**toupee** false hairpiece worn to cover baldness, usu. by men

**turban** long cloth wrapped around head or over cap by Muslims (Asia and Middle East)

**veil** length of cloth worn as woman's head covering, often covering face as well

**war bonnet** Native American headdress consisting of headband and tail of ornamental feathers

**welder's helmet** arc welder's helmet with tilting visor that covers face and a protective eye lens

**wig** synthetic hairpiece for entire skull

**wiglet** small wig used to supplement existing hair

**wimple** nun's headcovering of cloth that extends in folds over cheeks, chin, and neck

**wreath** braided foliage encircling head; anadem; chaplet; garland

**yashmak** Muslim woman's veil wrapped around upper and lower parts of face so that only eyes show

# FASHION AND GARMENT PARTS

Clothing in General
Garment Parts
Fashion, Trim, and Sewing
Fasteners

**SEE ALSO**: Chap. 10: Ornaments and Accessories; Clothing Materials

## CLOTHING IN GENERAL

**accouterments** personal clothes and effects

**activewear** sportswear designed for exercise, hiking, bicycling, and other sports activities

**apparel** clothing; garments; robes

**array** finery, fancy dress

**attire** clothing, esp. finery

**beachwear** bathing suits and other garments designed for use at beach or swimming pool

**bib and tucker** Brit. slang. entire outfit of clothing, esp. formal

**caparison** richly ornamental outfit of clothing

**clothes** clothing

**clothing** usu. cloth articles worn on body for covering and decoration; garments

**costume** complete outfit in specific style, esp. worn in some type of performance; robes

**disguise** outfit designed to conceal identity

**drapery** garments of cloth

**dress** clothing, esp. when suited to specific occasion

**duds** Informal. clothes

**ensemble** complete outfit, esp. when well-coordinated

**evening dress** complete outfit of formal clothing

**fashion** specific, esp. current, style of clothing

**fig** dress or apparel

**finery** fancy, decorative apparel

**formals** clothing suitable for ceremonies and elegant parties

**frippery** affected finery of low quality, considered to be in poor taste

**full fig** formal dress

**garb** attire, esp. in characteristic style

**garments** clothing, esp. outerwear

**garmenture** clothing; general attire (archaic)

**gear** clothing

**getup** Informal. outfit, often costume

**glad rags** Informal. showy or fancy clothing

**guise** style of dress

**habiliment** clothing, esp. for specific work or event

**habit** characteristic garb

**hand-me-downs** used clothing received from another

**fashion** current or specific style of dress

**mufti** ordinary clothes worn by person normally in uniform

**outfit** complete set of clothing

**playclothes** casual or functional clothing worn for leisure and recreational activities

**rags** old, tattered clothes

**raiment** clothing, general attire

**regalia** fancy or ceremonial attire

**rig** outfit, esp. unusual costume

**robes** apparel; costume

**robing** clothing

**soup-and-fish** Slang. man's formal evening clothes

**sportswear** activewear designed for exercise, hiking, bicycling, and sports; casually styled pieces of clothing that can be worn singly or in combination

**style** specific manner of dress, esp. current fashion

**suit** complete outfit of clothing, esp. formal

**Sunday best** one's finest outfit of clothing

**tatters** old, worn, ragged clothes

**threads** Slang. clothing in general

**toggery** Informal. clothing, esp. fancy dress; togs

**togs** clothing in general, esp. specific outfit; toggery

**toilette** formal outfit or specific costume

**trappings** articles of clothing, esp. decorative adornments

**trim** dress, esp. gear

**uniform** outfit of clothing characteristic of position or occupation

**vestments** official, esp. ecclesiastical, garments

**vesture** Archaic. clothing; garments

**wardrobe** one's complete supply of clothing

**wear** clothing, esp. of specific style or function

## GARMENT PARTS

**accessory** article or set of articles of dress that adds completeness, convenience, or decoration to basic outfit

**arm** tube of material from shoulder to wrist

**armhole** opening at shoulder for arm attachment

**barrel cuff** cuff formed from single band of material, usu. fastened by button

**batwing collar** man's high, flaring collar

**batwing sleeve** loose, long sleeve that fits into shoulder, ending at fitted wristband or cuff

**bell-bottom leg** trouser leg that widens at bottom

**bertha** woman's collar worn about shoulders, esp. over low-necked dress

**bishop sleeve** full sleeve gathered to fitted wristband

**bodice** blouse or upper part of dress

**body** torso covering

**bosom** front section across chest

**breast pocket**  usu. outside pocket sewn on one or both sides of upper front of shirt or jacket

**bretelle**  ornamental shoulder strap extending from front of dress to back

**bustline**  portion of garment covering woman's breasts

**button-down collar**  collar with points that button to shirt front

**button stand**  strip of cloth on front edge of coat for buttons or buttonholes

**cap sleeve**  short sleeve extending from bodice and covering top of shoulder

**caul**  network at back of woman's cap

**coattail**  rear skirts of dress, cutaway, or frock coat

**collar**  piece of fabric surrounding neck opening of shirt or coat

**cowl neckline**  loose, draped neckline

**crew neck**  round neckline without collar

**crotch**  point at which two pant legs meet

**cuff**  wristband on shirtsleeve; turned-back hem of trouser leg

**décolletage**  neckline, esp. woman's low-cut neckline

**Directoire**  empire waist

**dolman sleeve**  sleeve as an extension of bodice, with deep armhole tapering to fitted wrist

**dropped waist**  waistline set below natural waist

**drop seat**  rear section, as on children's pajamas, that may be opened and lowered independently

**earflap**  either of a pair of flaps attached to cap or hat, for covering ears in cold weather

**empire waist**  high, fitted waistline (France, 19th c.); Directoire; lifted waist

**epaulette**  decorative tab across shoulder, often fringed, esp. on uniform

**Eton collar**  broad, stiff collar worn folded outside of Eton jacket

**fastener**  device for joining or attaching garments or garment parts, such as zipper, button, or hook

**fly front**  cloth overlap concealing buttons or zipper, esp. from waist to crotch at front of pants

**French cuff**  folded double shirt cuff fastened by cuff links

**gigot sleeve**  sleeve with full shoulder and fitted wrist

**godet**  fluted pleat for fullness on lower skirt or sleeve

**gore**  tapering wedge of material that adds fullness to skirt or shoe

**gusset**  triangular expansion insert in seam

**high collar**  collar extending up to cover all or most of neck

**kimono sleeves**  large, square sleeves with underarm seam open, cut in one piece with garment

**lap**  loose, overhanging panel or flap

**lapel**  turned-back fold on front of coat, jacket, or blouse, joined to collar

**leg**  tube of material from hip to ankle

**lifted waist**  waistline set above natural waist; empire waist

**magyar sleeve**  very full sleeve cut in one piece with bodice

**mandarin collar**  narrow collar that stands up from neckline, often open at front

**Medici collar**  collar that stands high across back and low at front

**neck**  opening at top of garment, across upper chest

**neckline**  style of opening at top of garment

**notched collar**  collar forming notch with lapels of garment at seam where collar and lapels meet

**overskirt**  skirt worn over skirt of dress and draped or held up to reveal it

**pagoda sleeve**  long, narrow arm widening at wrist to show undersleeve

**patch pocket**  pocket made by sewing piece of material to outside of garment

**peg leg**  trouser leg that tapers to tight hem at ankle

**peplum**  short, flared flounce attached at waist of dress, blouse, or coat and extending over hips

**Peter Pan collar**  flat, attached, close-fitting collar with rounded ends meeting at round neckline

**placket**  faced slit at top of garment, esp. skirt, that facilitates putting it on and taking it off

**plunging neckline**  neckline cut very low in front

**pocket**  small, open-topped pouch sewn in or on garment

**pocket flap**  covering over top of pocket

**pouf**  fluffy, puffed part of garment

**Prussian collar**  high collar with ends almost meeting in front

**raglan sleeve**  sleeve cut in one piece with shoulder; set-in sleeve

**revers**  usu. wide lapels on jacket, coat, or dress

**rolled collar**  shirt collar that stands up slightly from neckline of garment and folds over on itself to lie flat

**roll-neck collar**  collar that turns back on itself

**saddle shoulder**  shoulder of raglan sleeve in which seam at neckline runs parallel to shoulder before angling down to armpit

**sailor collar**  collar with neckline that is square at back, narrowing to point at front closure

**seat**  material across buttocks

**set-in sleeve**  sleeve joined to body of garment at shoulder by seam at that juncture; raglan sleeve

**shawl collar**  attached collar and lapels in one piece, rolled back continuously along neckline to closure

**shirt front**  front of shirt that is exposed beneath jacket or vest

**shirttail**  part of shirt below waist, usu. worn inside trousers; tail

**shoulder**  cloth across shoulders to which sleeves attach

**shoulder pad**  cushion in shoulder providing protection or shape

**shoulder strap**  narrow band over shoulders, for decoration or to hold up pants, dress, or skirt; similar strap used to carry handbag or carryall

**skirt**  free-hanging material from waist down, either in single strip or encircling body

**slash pocket**  pocket set into garment, esp. below waistline, opening with exterior vertical or diagonal slit

**sleeve**  part of garment covering all or portion of arm between shoulder and wrist

**spaghetti strap**  very narrow shoulder strap on dress or blouse, sometimes decorative

**spread collar**  shirt collar with front points set widely apart

**stay**  strip of stiffening material in corset or shirt collar

**stiff collar**  starched or stiffened upright shirt collar

**stomacher**  embroidered center front of bodice (15th–16th c.)

**strap**  flat strip of material for securing, binding, or supporting

**tab collar**  shirt collar with small flap on one point that fastens to opposite point to hold both points in place

**tail** shirttail

**tails** divided skirts of man's formal jacket

**train** length of material attached to and trailing behind gown

**turtleneck** tall, close-fitting collar that rolls over on itself

**Vandyke collar** wide lace or linen collar with scalloped edge or deep points

**vent** small opening or section of permeable material allowing passage of air through garment

**V neck** neckline cut in deep V shape

**waist** torso covering that extends from neck to waistline

**waistband** belt or band of trousers or dress fitted around waist

**waistline** part of garment encircling natural waist at narrowest point of lower trunk

**watch pocket** small pocket just below front waistband of man's trousers or at front of vest

**Watteau back** loose, flowing back of woman's gown or robe, formed by box pleats falling from shoulder to hem

**welt pocket** pocket with reinforcing cord sewn to open edges

**wing collar** standing collar with high, stiff, turned-back corners

**wristband** lower sleeve covering wrist, esp. strip of fabric sewn to edge of sleeve

**yoke** fitted top of bodice, shirt, coat, or skirt to which lower part is sewn

## FASHION, TRIM, AND SEWING

**accordion pleats** narrow pleats resembling accordion folds

**acid washed** (*adj*) describing denim processed with bleach to fade color

**A-line** shape of woman's skirt, dress, or coat that is narrow at top and flaring to bottom, like letter A

**allover** (*adj*) describing a fabric with single repeating design motif

**applied casing** strip of fabric or bias tape sewn as casing

**appliqué** flat, decorative material or trim sewn on garment

**argyle** fabric with diamond-shaped designs, esp. in socks

**backstitch** hand stitching, one backward on garment front, two forward on reverse, to form solid line of stitching

**banded** (*adj*) having narrow cloth strips for decoration and to prevent raveling

**bargello** straight stitch used to form variety of zigzag and oblique designs in high and low relief; Florentine stitch

**basket weave** checkered weave resembling plaited basket

**baste** (*vb*) make long, loose, temporary stitches for fitting

**batting** layers of cotton or synthetic fiber for stuffing or lining

**beadwork** decorative beads stitched to fabric

**beson pocket** interior pocket with edging or stitching around opening

**bias** line at forty-five-degree angle to border in cutting for fit

**bind off** (*vb*) cast off knitting stitch to form an edge

**bird's-eye** textile pattern of small diamonds with center dot

**blanket stitch** embroidery or sewing stitch of variable size and width, often used to finish fabric edges decoratively

**bobbin** spool of thread or yarn on sewing machine

**bolt** measured roll of fabric of standard length

**bonded** (*adj*) made of two layers of the same fabric, or of a fabric and lining material, attached to each other by a chemical process or adhesive

**box pleat** parallel edges folded to face in opposite directions

**braiding** strips of interwoven yarn, fabric, or leather for binding or decoration

**burl** small knot of wool, thread, or yarn for imparting nubby texture

**buttonhole stitch** closely worked loop stitch making firm, finished edge; close stitch

**cable-stitch** series of knitting stitches used to produce cable appearance

**caddis** worsted ribbon or binding for garters and girdles

**candlewicking** series of knot stitches made in fabric with cotton embroidery thread

**casing** tunnel of stitched fabric holding elastic or drawstring

**cast off** (*vb*) make last row of stitches in knitting to prevent unraveling

**chain stitch** looped, ornamental stitch resembling chain links

**check** fabric woven or printed in checkerboard pattern

**ciré** highly glazed finish made by applying wax to fabric

**cleavage** revealing hollow between woman's breasts, esp. when revealed by low-cut neckline

**clew** ball of thread or yarn

**clocks** decorative embroidery on side of socks or stockings

**close stitch** buttonhole stitch

**collection** clothes produced by one designer, usu. for seasonal line

**colorfast** (*adj*) describing fabric with permanent color dyed into its yarn, so that it will not fade or run

**color scheme** selection of colors in outfit or garment to form some type of pattern

**coordinate** (*vb*) combine complementary elements and colors into outfit

**cording** ribbed surface of cord cloth

**couching** stitching with two threads, one of which stitches the other to the fabric

**crease** ridge or fold in garment

**crewel embroidery** loosely twisted wool yarn decoration

**crimping** act of pressing fabric into narrow, regular folds like pleats

**crocheting** needlework done with single strand of yarn or thread interlocked in loops to form fabric or garment

**cross-stitch** series of needlework stitches forming Xs

**crystal pleats** narrow, tightly pressed pleats, all facing in same direction

**custom-tailored** (*adj*) designed, manufactured, or fitted to individual specifications

**cutwork** openwork embroidery on linen, with pattern outlined in buttonhole stitch and ground fabric cut away

**damassé** (*adj*) woven in reversible, figured pattern like damask

**darn** (*vb*) mend with crossed or interwoven stitches; embroider with rows of running stitches

**dart** tapering tuck of fabric stitched down to improve fit

**designer** (*adj*) created by or carrying label of specific fashion designer, but often mass-produced

**diaphanous** (*adj*) transparent or translucent and gauzy

**double-knit** fabric made with double set of knitting needles that produce double-thick, ribbed fabric joined by interlocking stitches

**double stitch** two loops of single thread fastened in center of fold

**dressmaker** person who makes or alters women's dresses; (adj) having soft lines or elaborate detail

**dry cleaning** cleaning of garments with chemical rather than water

**dye** colorfast coloring agent for textiles

**ease** (vb) make seams narrower to allow fullness in garment or to permit free body movement

**embroidery** various types of decorative stitching with a needle

**engageantes** sleeve ruffles

**facing** plain or decorative lining at garment edge

**fagoting** openwork fabric decoration in which thread is drawn in crisscross stitches across open seam

**fashion** prevailing style or usage; design and manufacture of garments in this style

**fashion plate** person who wears latest fashions; drawing of specific style

**featherstitch** embroidered ornament in which succession of branches extends alternately on each side of central stem

**fell** seam with one raw edge folded under other, sewn flat on underside

**felting** nonwoven fabric of wool or hair, matted together by heat, moisture, and pressure

**fiber** slender, threadlike structure from which either natural or synthetic yarn is made

**figured** (adj) ornamented, marked, or formed into repeating pattern

**filling** yarn that interlaces the warp in fabric; yarn carried by shuttle

**Florentine stitch** bargello

**flounce** wide strip of material attached by one edge as trim, usu. at the bottom of skirt

**flue** soft, fluffy feathers, lint, or dusty debris

**fluting** long, round, ornamental grooves

**frayed** (adj) worn or ragged from use or age, esp. collars and cuffs

**French seam** seam in which raw edges of cloth are completely covered by sewing them together on both sides

**fringe** border or trim of loose or bunched threads

**frog** ornamental braided loop fastener with button

**froufrou** frilly ornamentation usu. on women's clothing

**full** (adj) having ample folds and abundant material

**furbelow** flounce on woman's clothing

**galloon** ornamental trim, esp. braid with gold or silver threads and scalloped edges

**garter stitch** knitting stitch that produces evenly pebbled texture on both sides of work

**gathers** soft folds in cloth formed by drawing fabric along a thread

**gauging** fullness gathered in parallel, stitched rows

**goffering** series of ornamental plaits, frills, and borders

**gray goods** unfinished fabric as it comes from loom

**gros point** large embroidery stitch

**hand** tactile quality of fabric

**hangtag** tag attached to garment providing information about its size, manufacturer, fabric, care, and sometimes price

**hardanger** openwork embroidery having elaborate symmetrical designs

**harlequin** variegated, often diamond-shaped color pattern on textiles

**haute couture** high fashion (France)

**hem** bottom of dress or pants folded back and stitched down

**hemline** height of skirt relative to leg and knee, changing with fashion

**herringbone** twilled wool weave in pattern resembling fish skeleton, with series of Vs in vertical rows

**high fashion** most up-to-date international styles

**hound's tooth** small, broken checks in cloth

**inseam** inner seam of trouser leg from crotch to bottom of leg

**intarsia** decorative pattern, as in knitted garments, resembling inlay

**interfacing** layer of fabric between facing and outer fabric

**inverted pleat** reverse of box pleat, with folds meeting on face

**jetted pockets** pockets piped and bound with same material

**kick pleat** inverted pleat extending as much as 10 inches (25 cm) upward from hemline at back of narrow skirt, to allow freedom in walking

**knife pleat** one-directional pleat folded so only one crease shows

**knit** (vb) make cloth by looping yarn or thread together with special needles

**knit and purl** make cloth by alternating knitted and purled stitches

**leno** weave in which paired warp yarns are intertwined in series of figure eights with filling yarn passed through each interstice to give fine, open mesh

**line** type of clothing available from one designer or during one season

**lining** inner garment, constructed separately and joined to outer garment at major seams

**list** band or strip of material

**locker loop** loop at back of garment near neck, orig. for hanging up garment

**long-waisted** (adj) having greater than average length between shoulders and waistline

**low-necked** (adj) having neckline cut low to leave neck and shoulders bare

**machine-stitch** (vb) sew on sewing machine

**macramé** decorative knots tied in geometrical patterns

**mannequin** model of human body used to design and display clothes; person who models clothes

**menswear** clothing designed for men

**mercerizing** treatment of cotton fiber with caustic alkali under tension to increase strength and luster

**missy** (adj) designating young girls' clothing sizes

**modiste** former term for female maker or seller of women's fashionable attire

**motley** (adj) of variegated material, like Renaissance fool's outfit

**nap** soft, hairy surface of fabric

**needle** slender, pointed, usu. steel instrument with eye in one end, used to draw thread through fabric in sewing

**needlepoint** embroidery worked on a gridlike formation of canvas

**needlework** process or result of stitching with a needle, esp. embroidery, needlepoint, and appliqué

**neutral color** white, black, tan, or gray, with no pigment added

**nonwoven fabric** material with fibers interlocked by heat, moisture, or adhesives, as in synthetics or felting

**notch**  V-shaped juncture of collar and lapel

**notions**  sundries or small articles, esp. trim, ribbon, and buttons

**nubby** (*adj*) having rough, knotted weave

**off-the-rack** (*adj*) readymade; not made to individual specifications

**orphrey**  rich, usu. gold embroidery, esp. band or border

**overcasting**  sewing along edges of material with long, spaced stitches to prevent raveling

**outer garment**  piece of clothing worn as protection or decoration and usu. visible to others

**overlock seam**  special stitch connecting fabric and finishing edge in one operation

**paillette**  ornamental spangle for costume

**passementerie**  ornamental trim combining braid, cord, beading, or metallic thread

**pattern**  instructional plan of design for sewing garment

**peekaboo** (*adj*) made of sheer and revealing material

**permanent press**  process in which fabric is treated with resin and heat to hold shape and resist wrinkling

**petit point**  small embroidery stitch

**pile**  upright yarn loops that produce velvety surface when cut

**pincushion**  small, soft, stuffed article into which pins are stuck when not in use

**pinstripes**  very thin, vertical stripes

**piping**  narrow, bias-cut cloth strip folded as edging or seam

**plaid**  checkerboard or crossbarred pattern

**plain weave**  most common and tightest weave, in which filling threads pass over and under successive warp threads

**platting**  weaving or braiding

**pleat**  fold of material doubled over on itself and stitched or pressed in place

**plissé**  puckered finish on fabric produced by caustic soda solution treatment that causes shrinkage

**polka dots**  pattern of regularly distributed round, solid markings

**preshrunk** (*adj*) designating a cotton garment shrunk to fit before sale

**prewashed** (*adj*) designating garments washed before sale, usu. to produce faded or worn look or soft texture

**primary color**  red, blue, or yellow

**print**  fabric on which color or design is printed rather than woven or resist dyed

**pucker**  crimp, wrinkle, or furrow in fabric finish

**purl** (*vb*) embroider or edge with twisted gold or silver thread; invert stitches in knitting for ribbed effect; finish a garment with looped edge

**quilling**  band of material fluted into small ruffles resembling a row of feather quills

**quill work**  quills stitched decoratively onto clothing

**quilting**  two layers of fabric stitched together over soft filling material

**rag trade**  *Slang.* fashion business

**raveled** (*adj*) unwoven, untwisted, or unwound

**readymade**  any garment made in advance for sale, not custom tailored

**ready-to-wear** (*adj*) designating mass-produced apparel, esp. synthetics

**resist dye**  fabric dye unaffected by water

**reversible** (*adj*) being a garment that may be worn with lining side out

**ribbing**  vertical ridge on cloth, esp. on knit material

**rickrack**  flat, zigzag braid or ribbon used for trim

**ruching**  strips of lace, ribbon, muslin, or net frilled or pleated for trim

**ruffle**  trim with ornamental pleats or gathers along one edge

**run**  ravel in knit fabric esp. hosiery

**running stitch**  small, consistent stitching made by passing needle in and out of fabric

**runway**  long platform down which models walk in fashion show

**saddle stitch**  decorative running stitch near edge of fabric

**sartorial** (*adj*) relating to tailoring and tailored clothes

**satin weave**  weave in which filling threads are interlaced with warp at wide intervals, giving effect of smooth surface

**Savile Row cut**  elegant, expensive, upper-class British style of tailoring

**scalloped edge**  waved pattern at border

**seam**  stitched line where two pieces of fabric are joined

**season**  spring or fall of single year when specific fashion styles appear

**seconds**  manufactured garments with small imperfections, sold at discount

**selvage**  narrow, woven border of heavy material finished so as to prevent raveling

**sennit**  straw, grass braid, or cord for hats

**sericeous** (*adj*) downy or silky in finish or appearance

**sequin**  small, shiny disk or spangle

**sewing**  act of forming and fastening by thread stitches

**shirring**  decorative gathering of fabric in parallel rows of short stitches to control fullness

**short-waisted** (*adj*) having less than average length between shoulders and waistline

**shuttle**  device that holds thread in place or passes woof through warp

**silkscreen printing**  dyeing method in which pattern is made by letting dye seep through unsealed areas of silkscreen

**sizing**  glutinous solution used for covering or stiffening fabric

**slip stitch**  concealed stitch for sewing hems; unworked knitting stitch

**smocking**  honeycomb stitches dividing and holding together tiny pleats

**soutache**  narrow, herringbone braid trim

**spangles**  small, shiny, metal disks sewn on fabric

**sprang**  weaving technique in which threads are intertwined and twisted to form mesh

**standaway** (*adj*) designed to stand upright or outward from the body

**static cling**  tendency of clothing to adhere to surfaces due to accumulation of static electricity, esp. in synthetic fibers

**step collar**  lapel joined to garment with V notch

**stitching**  small loops of thread or yarn used to fasten garment parts

**stonewashed** (*adj*) washed prior to sale with pebbles or stones to give worn appearance

**strapless** (*adj*) designating dress or woman's top made without shoulder straps

**stripes**  pattern of long, parallel bands, vertical or horizontal, on fabric

**style**  current fashionable way of dressing; distinctive flair or elegance in one's attire

**sunray pleats**  pleats radiating from one central point

**swatch**  fabric sample

**sweetheart neckline**  dress neck cut low in front and curved to resemble conventionalized heart shape

**tack**  (*vb*) fasten together with temporary stitches

**tailor**  (*vb*) make, style, fit, trim, mend, or adapt garments; (*n*) person who does this work

**tambour**  round embroidery frame consisting of two hoops, one fitting within the other; embroidery done on such a frame

**tanning**  processing of rawhides into soft leather by soaking in bath of tan bark

**tassel**  tuft of ornamental thread hanging from knot

**tatting**  cotton lace made by looping and knotting single heavy thread on hand shuttle

**template**  pattern for making garment, usu. a thin plate of wood or metal

**tent stitch**  short, slanting embroidery stitch

**terry**  loop forming uncut pile

**textile**  fabric woven or knitted from natural or synthetic fiber

**thimble**  small, protective cap worn on fingertip, used for pushing needle through cloth

**thread**  single strand of fibers used in making cloth or in sewing pieces of cloth together

**threadbare**  (*adj*) designating fabric having nap worn so that threads show

**tie-dyeing**  process of hand-tying portions of fabric or yarn to prevent absorption of dye and to produce pattern

**tinsel**  glittery, sparkling thread or strip in fabric

**topstitch**  line of stitches sewn on face side of garment along seam

**torsade**  twisted cord, esp. for draperies

**trademark**  logo or name of designer or manufacturer

**tram**  double, twisted silk thread used as weft in silk and velvet

**tuck**  fold of material stitched down partway or completely

**tuft**  cluster of closely drawn threads fastened at base

**turn-up**  edge or cuff of trouser (Britain)

**twill**  fabric woven in parallel diagonal lines or ribs

**two-ply**  (*adj*) designating fabric woven with two sets of warp thread and two of filling

**undergarment**  usu. protective item of clothing hidden under outer garments

**underlining**  fabric layer stitched to back of each piece of outer fabric

**understitching**  row of stitches that prevents facing from rolling to outside of garment

**unisex apparel**  clothing designed for men or women

**unisize**  (*adj*) made to fit all sizes or types in normal range

**vogue**  that which is currently in fashion; (*vb*) strike pose like a model

**vulcanization**  hardening of substance, esp. rubber, by heat

**wale**  even, lengthwise ridge in woven fabrics, esp. in corduroy

**wardrobe**  collection of clothing, esp. for one season or in possession of one person; storage cabinet or space for clothing

**warp**  yarns woven lengthwise in fabric and crossed by weft

**warp knit**  knit made with several yarns

**waterproof**  (*adj*) designating fabric treated so water will not penetrate it

**water repellent**  (*adj*) designating fabric treated to resist water absorption

**water resistant**  (*adj*) designating fabric sometimes slightly more absorbent than that which is water repellent

**wearing ease**  amounts by which sewing pattern should exceed body measurements to ensure comfortable fit

**weave**  any pattern of interlinking threads to form cloth; (*vb*) make cloth by interlacing strands of yarn or thread

**weaving**  fabric formed by interlacing two sets of yarn or thread at right angles to each other

**webbing**  sturdy, narrow, closely woven tape for straps and upholstery

**weft**  yarns carried horizontally by weaving shuttle, crossing and interlaced with warp

**welted pocket**  slit pocket with reinforcing cord sewn on open edge

**welting**  reinforcing strip or double edge at garment seam

**whipstitch**  stitch that passes over an edge for joining, finishing, or gathering

**Winnies**  annual industry awards for excellence in fashion design

**women's wear**  clothing designed for women

**woof**  yarn carried by shuttle and crossing warp in weaving; texture of woven fabric

**worsted**  smooth, hard, twisted thread used to make wool with smooth, hard surface

## FASTENERS

**band**  thin, flat, encircling strip of material

**barrette**  ornamental hair clip

**belt**  encircling strip of flexible material, esp. at waist

**bobby pin**  flat, metal or plastic hairpin with pinching arms

**brace**  clasp, connector

**braid**  cord or ribbon with three or more intertwined strips

**buckle**  fastener for two loose ends, attached to one end and grasping the other by catch or prong

**button**  small knob or disk attached to garment, passed through loop or buttonhole to connect two parts

**catch**  fastener that holds something in place, usu. by clamping or hooking

**chain**  series of connected metal links

**cinch**  tightly gripping belt or girth

**clamp**  fastener that presses two or more pieces together

**clasp**  hook and loop that holds objects together; brace

**clip**  clasping device, usu. with two pinching arms

**clothespin**  two wood or plastic arms on spring, esp. for clamping clothes to line

**connector**  device that connects one object to another; brace

**cord**  long, slender, flexible strip of twisted strands used for binding

**drawstring**  cord or thin rope that tightens to close an opening when its ends are pulled

**D-ring**  D-shaped metal ring through which belt or strap passes to close or secure something

**elastic**  fabric made of yarns containing rubber that stretches and returns to shape

**frog**  ornamental braided button and loop through which it passes

**hairpin**  long, open, U-shaped pin for holding hair in place

**hook**  rigid, curved or bent device for catching and holding

**lace**  cord or string used to draw together two flaps by passing through holes in opposite edges

**loop**  ring, curved piece, or doubled-back length of line through which hook passes

**peg**  short, pointed piece of wood or metal that holds parts together

**pin**  small, solid piece of wood or metal that clamps or pierces object to hold it in place

**ribbon**  narrow strip of material, usu. used for tying hair

**ring**  circular band, usu. of rigid material, used to gather and hold fabric

**rope**  cord of interwoven fiber strands

**safety pin**  pin bent back on itself to form spring, with guard covering point when pin is fastened

**stitch**  portion of thread left in material after in-and-out motion of needle

**strap**  loop or strip of flexible material

**string**  thin cord or rope

**stud**  small, buttonlike device with smaller button or shank on back, inserted through shirt front to fasten two sides together

**suspenders**  thin bands worn over shoulders, with clasps at end to hold up trousers or skirt

**tack**  temporary stitch holding materials together while they are being sewn

**thole**  pin or peg

**tie**  line, ribbon, or cord used for binding items together

**toggle**  ornamental, rod-shaped button passed through loop or frog

**twine**  sturdy string or thin rope for typing

**Velcro**  *Trademark.* nylon material with one surface of clinging pile so that matching strips can be pressed together

**zipper**  two parallel rows of interlocking teeth, metal or plastic, on strips of material drawn together by sliding pull piece

# INSTITUTIONS

# CHAPTER 11

# Social Order

# The City

Cities, Towns, Villages, and Districts
Roadways and Driving
Urban Structures and Phenomena

**See also**: Chap. 6: Automobiles; Chap. 7: Buildings; Chap. 11: Government; Chap. 13: Sociology

## Cities, Towns, Villages, and Districts

**arrondissement**  administrative district of city (France)

**banlieue**  *French.* suburb

**bedroom community**  suburb

**boom town**  town experiencing rapid unplanned growth due to economic activity

**borough**  one of five political divisions of New York City; *Chiefly Brit.* incorporated, self-governing urban area, comparable to municipality

**bourg**  town; market town (France)

**Bowery**  district of cheap bars and homeless persons in New York City

**burbs**  *Informal.* suburbs

**burg**  city or town

**burgh**  incorporated town with partial local jurisdiction (Scotland)

**capital**  city serving as seat of government; city renowned for some activity

**central city**  inner city

**city**  densely inhabited place larger and more important than town or village, usu. incorporated as an administrative and judicial unit

**ciudad**  *Spanish.* city

**commercial district**  nonresidential business district

**community**  group of individuals living together as a unit within larger population; area occupied by such people

**conurbation**  connected series of urban communities

**county seat**  city where county administrative offices are located

**cow town**  small, unsophisticated town, esp. within cattle-raising area

**crossroad**  town located at juncture of two or more roads

**district**  quarter, ward, or section of city

**dorp**  village

**downtown**  main business or government district of city or town

**dynapolis**  planned city consisting of several communities along central roadway

**enceinte**  town encircled by fortifications

**exurb**  area outside city and beyond suburbs, often inhabited by wealthy families

**exurbia**  region of exurbs

**faubourg**  suburb; outlying quarter of city (France)

**ghetto**  district occupied primarily by one religious or ethnic group, usu. poor

**ghost town**  once active town that is now deserted, usu. due to depletion of a natural resource

**greater**  *(adj)* designating metropolitan area surrounding city

**hamlet**  small village

**hick town**  small, often isolated, unsophisticated town

**hometown**  city or town of one's birth or principal residence

**inner city**  older, densely populated, often rundown central district; central city

**kampong**  small native village (Southeast Asia)

**kraal**  native village (South Africa)

**market town**  city to which farmers and artisans from surrounding countryside bring goods to sell at market

**megalopolis**  very large city; heavily populated region encompassing several cities

**metropolis**  large or important city, often a capital or center of business or cultural activity

**metropolitan area**  large city and its immediate suburbs

**midtown**  central section of city or town, esp. main shopping district

**mir**  *Russian.* village community collectively owned but cultivated by individual families

**municipality**  incorporated, self-governing, urban political unit

**neighborhood**  district with particular character or appearance, often covering very small area

**one-horse town**  small, rural town

**outskirts**  districts far from center of city

**Podunk**  small, insignificant, or remote town

**polis**  city-state (ancient Greece)

**precinct**  electoral subdivision of town, city, or ward; section of city for police control

**purlieu**  outlying district

**quarter**  division or district of town or city

**red-light district**  area with houses of prostitution

**residential area**  nonbusiness district of private homes

**satellite**  suburban community

**settlement**  place newly settled; small village

**shtetl**  *Yiddish.* formerly a small Jewish village in Eastern Europe

**suburb**  residential community lying just outside or within commuting distance of city; bedroom community

**suburbia**  outlying part of city or town

**thorp**  village or hamlet

**town**  any group of structures considered a distinct place with a distinguishing placename; closely populated area larger than a village but smaller than a city, having fixed boundaries that distinguish it from surrounding rural territory

**township**  small incorporated city

**trailer park**  area set up to accommodate house trailers on permanent basis

**uptown**  fancier residential or commercial district of city or town

**vicinity**  surrounding area or district; neighborhood

**village**  often rural community larger than a hamlet and smaller than a town; small incorporated municipality

**ville**  *French.* city

**ward**  administrative or electoral district of city

**whistle stop**  small rural town, esp. on railroad line

**zone**  division of city designated for specific purpose, esp. numbered postal delivery

# ROADWAYS AND DRIVING

**alley** narrow street, often providing access to rear of buildings

**alleyway** narrow street or passageway

**artery** principal roadway in branching system of roads

**asphalt** black bituminous composition used for paving roads

**autobahn** high-speed multilane expressway (Germany and Austria)

**autoroute** high-speed multilane expressway (France and Canada)

**autostrada** divided expressway connecting major cities (Italy)

**avenida** *Spanish.* avenue

**avenue** moderate-sized roadway wider than a lane and narrower than a boulevard; *Chiefly Brit.* driveway to house off main road

**back street** small, remote, obscure, or inaccessible roadway

**beltway** highway encircling an urban area; ring road

**blacktop** bituminous material used for surfacing roads; surface paved with this material

**blind alley** narrow, dead-end roadway

**boreen** *Irish.* narrow country lane

**bottleneck** narrowing point of traffic congestion

**boulevard** broad landscaped thoroughfare

**bumper-to-bumper** *(adj)* marked by heavy traffic with long rows of slow-moving cars

**bypass** route around town

**by-street** side street

**byway** rarely traveled roadway

**calastand** taxi stand

**camino** *Spanish.* boulevard

**carpool** arrangement among automobile owners to take turns driving a group to some common activity

**carrefour** crossroads, square, plaza

**carriageway** *Chiefly Brit.* highway

**car wash** area with facilities for washing automobiles

**cater-corner** *(adj)* diagonally opposed at an intersection; kitty-corner

**causeway** highway

**center strip** divider down middle of large roadway

**checkpoint** designated inspection place for vehicles

**chuckhole** rough hole or rut in road

**circle** rotary

**circus** *Chiefly Brit.* circular area at intersection of several roadways

**close** *Scot.* narrow passage running from street to court surrounded by houses; *Scot.* dead-end road

**cloverleaf** intersection of two highways where traffic is routed from one highway onto branches leading in a circle to another highway

**cobblestone** road paved with rounded stones larger than pebbles and smaller than boulders

**concourse** open space where roads or paths meet; junction

**congestion** excess traffic clogged or concentrated in too small a space

**corner** place or intersection of two streets or roads

**corniche** road built at top of a cliff running along a coast

**court** broad alley with single opening onto main street

**crescent** short roadway curved in a half-circle

**crossing** area designated for passage of pedestrians or vehicles across roadway; place where railroad track transects a roadway; crosswalk

**crossroads** intersection of two or more roads

**crosswalk** lane designated for pedestrians to cross road in safety

**cul-de-sac** street closed at one end; dead end

**curb** edging built along roadway forming lip of gutter; also, *esp. Brit.*, kerb

**dead end** street without exit at one end

**deck** roadway across multilevel bridge

**detour** roundabout route temporarily replacing section of roadway that is damaged or being repaired

**dirt road** unpaved roadway

**double-park** *(vb)* park vehicle on street side of vehicle already parked along curb

**drive** avenue, roadway

**drive-in** place of business laid out so that patrons can be served while remaining in vehicles

**driveway** road leading from public roadway to private building

**expressway** high-speed, divided, multilane highway for through traffic with limited access at intersections with other roadways; thruway

**filling station** service station

**flyover** *Chiefly Brit.* overpass

**freeway** toll-free highway

**frontage road** local road alongside expressway that provides access to property along it; service road

**garage** shelter or repair facility for automobiles, trucks, or buses

**gassen** *German.* lane or alley

**gas station** service station

**grade** sloping road; degree of inclination of sloping road

**grade crossing** crossing of rail or roadway or pedestrian walkway on one level

**gravel road** unpaved road covered with loose rock fragments

**green light** traffic signal indicating permission to proceed

**gridlock** traffic jam, esp. at intersection, in which all vehicles are blocked from moving

**gutter** recessed area at side of street to carry off surface water

**hairpin turn** extremely sharp U-shaped bend in road

**high road** *Chiefly Brit.* main street in village

**high street** *Chiefly Brit.* main or principal street

**highway** main direct roadway, usu. high speed and multilane

**impasse** dead end or cul-de-sac

**interchange** multilevel junction of two or more highways that makes it possible for traffic to change roadway without obstructing cross traffic

**interstate** multilane divided highway connecting major cities in several states

**jaywalk** *(vb)* cross roadway heedlessly or illegally so as to be endangered by traffic

**jersey barrier** strip of concrete at center of highway that divides oncoming traffic

**junction** intersection of roads, often where one terminates

**kitty-corner** *(adj)* cater-corner

**lane** narrow roadway, esp. between barriers or trees; strip of roadway designated for single row of vehicles

**macadam** roadway constructed by compacting a layer of small broken stone using bituminous binder

**manhole** opening in street that provides access to underground utilities

**main drag** *Slang.* principal roadway in town or city

**main street** principal business street, esp. in small town

**median strip** paved or planted area that divides highway into sections for traffic moving in opposite directions

**mew** back street, alley

**motor pool** several vehicles centrally based and dispatched for specific use

**motorway** *Chiefly Brit.* expressway

**one-way** (*adj*) designating roadway for movement in one direction only

**overpass** crossing of highways, or of highway and pedestrian crossing, at different levels, allowing traffic to pass on lower level; upper level of such a crossing

**park** (*vb*) temporarily leave vehicle at side of roadway or in parking lot or garage

**parking lot** open area or structure for parking vehicles

**parking meter** coin-operated register from which parking time is purchased for vehicle

**parkway** broad, usu. landscaped, thoroughfare

**paseo** *Spanish.* public walk or boulevard

**pavement** surface of roadway covered with asphalt or other hard substance; *Chiefly Brit.* sidewalk

**pike** turnpike

**pileup** serious collision involving several vehicles

**place** small, usu. residential, roadway

**plaza** point in toll road at which tollbooths are located

**post road** road used for mail conveyance

**pothole** large hole in road surface

**red light** traffic signal indicating that drivers or pedestrians must stop

**ring road** road encircling city; beltway

**road** long, open way with paved surface for traveling, esp. by vehicle

**roadblock** obstruction, usu. set up by police, to halt or impede passage on roadway

**road hog** aggressive driver of vehicle who invades others' traffic lanes

**road test** check of vehicle under normal operating conditions; test of driving ability required for obtaining license

**roadway** land over which road is built and on which vehicles travel

**rotary** circular roadway at multiple intersection around which all traffic moves counterclockwise; circle; traffic circle

**roundabout** *Chiefly Brit.* rotary

**route** course for travel from one point to another; highway

**row** *Chiefly Brit.* street

**rue** *French.* street

**rumble strip** one of a series of rough or raised strips of highway pavement, used to make drivers slow down speed of their vehicles

**rush hour** period at beginning or end of business day when traffic is at its peak

**safety island** portion of roadway from which vehicles are excluded

**safety zone** area of roadway for pedestrians or streetcar passengers only

**secondary road** feeder or artery to main roadway

**service road** frontage road

**service station** retail outlet for care of vehicles, esp. sale of gasoline; filling station; gas station

**shoulder** edge of roadway alongside driving area

**side street** small roadway; roadway leading off main street; by-street

**sidewalk** paved strip for pedestrians at side of street

**signpost** post with information or directions for drivers

**skyway** elevated highway

**speed limit** maximum legal driving speed permitted on given roadway

**speed trap** roadway patrolled by concealed police officers to catch drivers exceeding speed limit, esp. by radar

**speedway** public roadway for high-speed driving; expressway

**square** open area where two or more streets converge, usu. surrounded on all sides by buildings

**stop-and-go** slow driving in heavy traffic involving frequent stops

**stoplight** electric traffic signal

**stop sign** octagonal sign, usu. red, that requires drivers to come to full stop

**strasse** *German.* street

**street** roadway that is wider than alley or lane and usu. includes sidewalks; thoroughfare with abutting property

**streetlight** one of a series of lights mounted on poles spaced at intervals along public roadway

**subway** *Chiefly Brit.* underpass beneath street

**superhighway** wide highway designed for high-speed travel between major points

**switchback** zigzag road, esp. in hilly region

**tailgate** (*vb*) drive too closely behind another vehicle

**tarmac** roadway of tarmacadam

**taxi stand** place where taxis park while awaiting customers

**thank-you-ma'am** bump or hollow in roadway, esp. for runoff of surface water

**thoroughfare** main roadway

**through street** street that provides for continuous passage of traffic, with outlets at both ends

**thruway** expressway

**ticket** summons issued for traffic violation

**tie-up** stoppage of traffic due to congestion, construction, or accident

**toll** tax or fee paid for use of roadway

**tollbooth** enclosed stall on roadway where tolls are paid

**toll bridge** bridge at which toll is paid for crossing

**tollgate** barrier at which driver of vehicle must pay toll to pass

**toll road** roadway to which access requires payment of toll; tollway

**tollway** toll road

**towaway zone** no-parking area from which vehicles are removed by authorities

**traffic** vehicles or pedestrians moving between points or along roadway

**traffic circle** rotary

**traffic cone** conical, usu. rubber, brightly colored marker, placed in roadway as warning of danger to be avoided

**traffic island** paved or planted area in roadway that controls flow of traffic in opposite directions

**traffic jam** congestion and slow movement of traffic due to excess of cars on roadway, construction, or accident

**traffic light** traffic signal

**traffic signal** electrically operated visual device for controlling traffic by use of colored signals; traffic light

**trench** long ditch, esp. at side of roadway

**turnout** place where one road branches off another; space along highway where vehicles may park or pull over to allow passing

**turnpike** toll road or road that previously charged toll; pike

**two-way street** roadway that allows passage in both directions

**underpass** lower level of overpass roadway interchange

**U-turn** 180-degree change in direction

**van pool** carpool using multipassenger van

**via** *Spanish.* way, street

**way** route; course for travel from point to point

**white line** stripe painted on road to guide traffic

**wynd** *Scot.* very narrow lane

**zebra crossing** pedestrian crosswalk marked by series of thick white stripes

## URBAN STRUCTURES AND PHENOMENA

**agora** city marketplace (ancient Greece)

**alameda** public walkway lined by trees

**aqueduct** channel for large volume of flowing water

**arcade** long, arched gallery or passageway between shops

**arch bridge** span supported by series of arches and towers

**asphalt jungle** large, crowded urban area, esp. dangerous part where people must struggle to survive

**Bailey bridge** bridge constructed from interchangeable latticed steel panels joined by steel pins

**barrio** Spanish-speaking quarter in U.S. city

**bascule bridge** movable bridge in which rising section is counterbalanced by a weight

**bidonville** impoverished settlement of shanties on outskirts of city (France and North America)

**block** rectangular unit in city grid, enclosed by intersecting streets and occupied by buildings; length of one side of such a unit; row of houses between two streets

**boardwalk** raised promenade along beach

**bridge** structure carrying roadway for vehicles and/or pedestrians over depression, obstacle, or body of water: arch, bascule, cantilever, draw, flyover, foot, lift, pontoon, suspension, swing, toll, truss

**canal** man-made waterway for transportation or for draining and irrigating land

**cantilever bridge** span consisting of rigid construction elements that extend horizontally well beyond its vertical support members

**Casbah** native Arab section of North African city; Kasbah

**city hall** primary administrative building in city

**city planning** rational organization of urban growth

**cluster** group of buildings constructed close together on sizable tract to preserve open spaces

**commute** (*vb*) travel back and forth regularly between home in suburbs and work in city

**commuter** person who commutes regularly, esp. to work

**complex** large group of buildings or apartments

**compound** fenced or walled-in area containing group of buildings

**court** open space enclosed wholly or partly by buildings or surrounded by single building

**courthouse** building that houses law courts

**covered bridge** bridge with roofed or enclosed roadway

**crosstown** (*adj*) located at opposite points of town; (*adv*) from one side of town to the other

**deck** story or tier of building

**depot** storage place for cargo or motor vehicles; building for passengers and freight on public conveyances

**dike** bank of earth constructed to control or hold back water; ditch

**drawbridge** bridge built in sections that may be raised or lowered to permit or obstruct passage

**elevated railroad** urban or interurban railroad that runs along tracks raised above ground level

**elevator** enclosed box on pulley system for transporting passengers or freight in multistory building

**embankment** raised area along waterway or roadway

**embarcadero** landing place on bay or river

**emporium** commercial center; large retail establishment

**escalator** mechanical set of stairs arranged as endless belt that continuously ascends or descends

**esplanade** flat expanse of paved or grassy land along shore, esp. for driving or walking

**factory** large building with manufacturing facilities

**fairground** area where outdoor fairs, circuses, and exhibitions are held

**footbridge** bridge for use by pedestrians only

**forum** marketplace and central public area of city (ancient Rome)

**greenbelt** area of parkways or farmland encircling city

**high rise** multistory building with elevators

**hôtel de ville** *French.* city hall

**housing development** cluster of individual residences or apartment buildings of similar design under one ownership

**housing estate** *Chiefly Brit.* housing development

**housing project** publicly financed and administered housing development for low-income families

**interurban** (*adj*) between or connecting cities or towns

**Kasbah** Casbah

**kiosk** small, open, circular building used as newsstand or telephone booth

**landfill** low area of land that is built up from trash and garbage wastes embedded between layers of earth

**lift bridge** bridge having section that can be raised vertically to permit passage beneath it

**mall** large complex of shops and restaurants with attached passageways and parking space; public promenade lined with trees and closed off to motor vehicles; paved or planted divider in roadway; pedestrian passageway providing access to rows of stores

**marina** basin providing dockage for motorboats and yachts, with supply and repair facilities

**market** traditional urban center where goods are sold

**metro** subway system

**metropolitan** (*adj*) relating to or characteristic of a city

**mew** *Chiefly Brit.* houses built around a court

**minimall** group of small shops clustered around parking area, usu. on business street

**municipal** (*adj*) restricted to one self-governing locality

**noise pollution** environmental pollution consisting of bothersome or harmful noise; sound pollution

**off-hour** period of time other than rush hour or outside regular business hours

**off-peak** off-hour period with reduced public transportation fares

**park** tract of ground in or around city maintained in natural state or cultivated for recreational use

**passageway** path or narrow roadway that permits movement in, out, or through

**pedestrian** one who moves by foot

**people mover** movable sidewalk

**piazza** open square (Italy)

**pissoir** *French.* public urinal along street

**place** *French.* public square, plaza

**playground** outdoor area equipped with children's recreational facilities

**plaza** public square

**pontoon bridge** bridge supported by series of floats

**pound** depot for holding personal property until it is claimed by owner

**projects** *Informal.* housing project

**promenade** public walkway

**public transportation** buses, trolleys, and subways for use by general public for set fare, running on schedules over specific routes

**quay** paved bank or landing beside navigable waterway

**rapid transit** fast, modern, public transportation system

**residential** (*adj*) restricted to or occupied by private homes and apartments

**rialto** exchange or marketplace; theater district

**right of way** strip of land over which a public road is built; land used by a public utility

**row** area dominated by specific kind of structure or activity

**sewer** artificial underground channel to carry off sewage and surface water overflow

**shopping center** group of retail stores and service establishments with parking facilities, serving community or neighborhood

**shopping mall** shopping area with stores facing enclosed area restricted to pedestrians

**skid row** downtown district of cheap bars and hotels for transients

**skyscraper** very tall building

**skywalk** enclosed, elevated walkway that connects two buildings

**slum** densely populated urban area marked by crowding, poor housing, poverty, and social disorder

**slurb** shabby, ill-planned suburban area

**sound pollution** noise pollution

**span** bridge or overpass

**storefront** side of store or building facing street

**straphanger** person who commutes on public transportation, esp. while standing up holding a strap for support

**street railway** system of streetcars or buses

**strip** long stretch of land, often used as highway divider; commercially developed roadway

**subway** underground electric railway

**superblock** very large commercial or residential block, closed to through traffic and crossed by pedestrian walks and access roads, often with grassy malls

**supermarket** large, self-service retail outlet for food and household merchandise

**suspension bridge** bridge with roadway suspended from two or more cables that pass over towers and are anchored at ends

**swing bridge** bridge that opens by pivoting on central pier to permit passage

**telephone booth** enclosure on street within which one may sit or stand while making a telephone call

**telephone box** *Chiefly Brit.* public telephone booth

**tenement house** residential building that meets minimum standards of sanitation, safety, and comfort, occupied by poor families

**terminal** centrally located freight or passenger station of public carrier that serves as junction for several lines

**terrace** row of houses or apartments on raised ground; strip of park in middle of street; small avenue or lane

**town hall** building that houses administrative offices of town

**tram** *Chiefly Brit.* streetcar, trolley, or vehicle running on rails

**tramcar** *Chiefly Brit.* streetcar

**tramline** *Chiefly Brit.* street railway

**tramway** *Chiefly Brit.* streetcar line; overhead cable or rails for trams

**transfer** ticket that entitles passenger on public conveyance to continue journey on another line

**transfer point** junction at which passenger changes public transportation lines

**transit** local transportation of passengers by public conveyance

**truss bridge** bridge supported by bracketlike framework

**tube** *Chiefly Brit.* subway

**tunnel** hollow conduit or recess for passage; covered passageway through obstruction or under ground

**underground** *Chiefly Brit.* subway system

**urban** (*adj*) of, relating to, characteristic of, or constituting a city

**urban blight** decay and poverty of old inner city

**urban planning** systematic development of new urban areas or renovation of existing areas to improve conditions there

**urban renewal** planned renovation of older city districts

**urban sprawl** spreading of urban phenomena onto undeveloped land near city

**utility** service such as water, gas, or electricity provided by public or private company

**vacant lot** undeveloped and unused plot of land

**viaduct** bridge made up of several short spans supported by reinforced concrete arches and towers, carrying road or railroad over obstruction or valley

**walk-up** multistory building without elevator

**walkway** pedestrian passage

**warren** densely populated tenement or district

**waterfront** land or district adjacent to body of water

**water supply** facilities for bringing water to a community through reservoirs, aqueducts, tunnels, and pipelines

**wharf** structure built along shore of navigable waters at which ships may lie to receive and discharge cargo or passengers

**zoning** partitioning by ordinance of city, borough, or township into sections reserved for specific purposes

# GOVERNMENT

Forms, Systems, and Philosophies
Governmental Bodies and Institutions
Government Officials and Citizens
Acts, Powers, Conditions, and Procedures
Postal Service

**SEE ALSO**: Chap. 11: Politics; Law; International Relations; Titles of Rank; Chap. 12: Business and Economics; Finance

## FORMS, SYSTEMS, AND PHILOSOPHIES

**absolute monarchy** kingdom in which monarch has complete power

**absolutism** theory and practice of government by single absolute ruler

**anarchy** absence of government; advocacy of this state

**aristocracy** government by wealthy, privileged minority or hereditary ruling class

**autarchy** absolute sovereignty; autocracy

**autarky** economic self-sufficiency of a state

**authoritarianism** principle of submission to authority; concentration of power in hands of autocratic leader or powerful elite not constitutionally bound or responsible to the people

**autocracy** government power placed in hands of one ruler; autarchy

**autonomy** self-government, esp. state and local

**benevolent dictatorship** nonrepressive absolute rule that works for good of citizens

**bicameral** (*adj*) having two legislative houses in government

**caliphate** government ruled by Islamic civil and religious leader

**caretaker government** temporary regime during lapse in normal government functions

**centralism** assignment of power to central leadership

**centralization** organization under single authority; shift of political authority from local to state government

**checks and balances** principle of interdependency of governmental branches through power of limitation

**city-state** self-governing state composed of independent city and adjacent territory controlled by it, esp. in ancient Greece and Medieval Europe; polis

**civil government** government established by laws made by citizens or their representatives; nonmilitary, nonreligious authority

**civil liberty** freedom from arbitrary governmental interference, esp. as prescribed in U.S. Bill of Rights

**coalition government** temporary alliance of members of two or more parties to form governing majority

**collective** group or institution organized and run by all members equally

**colonialism** control by one state over dependent state or people

**commission plan** system of municipal government in which all powers lie in hands of elected commission

**common law** unwritten law developed over time and based on accepted notion of right and wrong

**commonwealth** government in which ultimate authority lies with people

**concurrent powers** rights exercised by both national and state governments

**constitutionalism** government based on written constitutional principles

**constitutional monarchy** government headed by monarch and regulated by constitution

**council-manager plan** form of city government in which strong elected council hires city manager to administer laws

**crown** monarch; government in constitutional monarchy

**decentralization** distribution of power among several groups

**democracy** government by the people, with majority rule exercised in periodic free election of representatives

**democratism** democratic government

**despotism** system of government in which ruler exercises absolute power

**dictatorship** government in which absolute power rests with one person or a few

**direct democracy** pure form of democracy in which people's will is expressed in mass meetings and becomes public policy

**dirigisme** *French.* theory that government should take part in direction of economic affairs

**divine right of kings** authority of sovereign considered to be granted by God, not people (16th-17th c.)

**dominion** sovereignty, authority over; self-governing member of British Commonwealth giving allegiance to British monarch

**duarchy** government by two equally powerful rulers; duumvirate

**duumvirate** government in which two persons rule jointly; duarchy

**dyarchy** dual responsibility shared by colonial government and native ministers

**empire** several territories, nations, or peoples governed by single sovereign authority

**fascism** government based on establishing oppressive, one-party, centralized national regime

**federal government** system in which political units surrender individual sovereignty to central authority but retain designated powers; such central authority

**federalism** principle of shared power between national and state governments

**feudalism** political system in Europe from 9th to 15th century in which lord owned all property worked by vassals

**gerontocracy** rule by elders

**governance** a method or system of government; exercise of government authority

**government** organized political institutions, laws, and customs by which state fulfills its authorized functions

**gynecocracy** government by women

**hagiocracy** government by group of persons believed to be holy

**hierocracy** rule by priest or clergy

**home rule** provision allowing local self-government while under state control

**isocracy** government in which all individuals have equal political power

**kingdom** monarchy ruled by a king

**limited government** constitutional principle that government may do only what people have empowered it to do

**local government** authority over town, city, county, or other small locale by citizens rather than state or federal government

**martial law** temporary suspension of law and use of military to maintain order during emergency

**matriarchy** government or monarchy in which power rests with females or descends through female line

**mayor-council plan** system of municipal government with elected mayor as executive and elected council as legislature

**meritocracy** government in which criterion for leadership is skill or intellectual achievement

**militarism** belief that war and its preparation are most important functions of state

**mobocracy** rule by mob

**monarchism** government by monarchy

**monarchy** government with absolute hereditary ruler who serves for life

**municipal** (*adj*) pertaining to local self-government

**nationalism** loyalty to interests of one's own nation

**neocolonialism** economic domination of one nation by a more powerful nation without imposition of colonial government

**ochlocracy** rule by multitude or mob

**officialism** rigid adherence to regulations and absence of creativity in government activities

**oligarchy** government by small group of privileged individuals

**one-man rule** despotism, dictatorship

**one world** philosophy and dream of a single world government

**pantisocracy** utopia in which all members rule equally

**parliamentary government** system in which executive (prime minister) is chosen by elected legislature (parliament) from among its members

**participatory democracy** democratic system permitting direct involvement of individuals

**paternalism** benevolent, fatherly control by authority of individuals' interactions with each other as well as with government

**patriarchy** government or monarchy in which power rests with males or descends through male line

**pluralism** governmental system that embraces cultural diversity and advocates general participation in decision making

**plutocracy** government by the wealthy

**police state** repressive system dominated by all-powerful police, esp. secret police, instead of elected officials

**polis** city-state (ancient Greece)

**popular sovereignty** principle that government exists only with consent of the governed, i.e., power lies with the people

**presidential government** system based on separation of powers between elected executive and legislative departments

**principality** state ruled by prince, often part of larger state or empire

**provisional government** temporary authority during lapse in normal government functions

**regency** reign of nonmonarch during youth or indisposition of monarch

**regime** system of administration and its practitioners

**representative democracy** indirect democracy in which people's will is expressed through elected representatives

**republic** government in which power is vested in elected representatives of citizenry

**republicanism** principles and advocacy of government by republic

**self-government** political power lying in hands of inhabitants of state or territory rather than outside authority; self-rule

**self-rule** self-government

**separation of powers** doctrine that division of responsibility among legislative, executive, and judicial branches is conducive to equitable government

**social contract** understanding between citizens and government on which government is based

**sovereignty** political autonomy and freedom of state from outside authority

**state government** authority over single state

**statism** highly centralized government control of economy

**stratocracy** government by the military

**technocracy** government run by experts and technicians

**thearchy** government based on divine sovereignty

**theocracy** government by church officials, who believe they have divine authority

**timocracy** government based on love of honor and military glory or on requisite ownership of property

**totalitarianism** authoritarian political system in which citizen is totally subject to will of state

**town meeting** oldest and most direct form of democracy, in which local citizens assemble to vote on issues

**triarchy** government ruled jointly by three persons; triumvirate

**tricameral** (*adj*) having three legislative houses or chambers in government

**triumvirate** triarchy

**tyranny** government by single absolute authority, esp. one exercising oppressive power

**unicameral** (*adj*) having a single legislative chamber in government

**unitary government** system in which power is held by single central source and local governments are merely administrative agents, the opposite of federalism

**welfare state** system in which ultimate responsibility of government is well-being of all citizens

**world federalism** principle of federal union of all nations with limited authority

**world government** principle of single governing authority for all nations

## GOVERNMENTAL BODIES AND INSTITUTIONS

**administration** activity and actions of all branches of government; collective body managing government affairs

**agency** unit of executive branch that administers programs, sets rules, and settles disputes in specific policy area

**Althing** oldest European legislature, the Icelandic parliament

**assembly** lower legislative house

**board** group of elected or appointed functionaries

**board of aldermen** governing body of city

**board of supervisors** governing body of county

**brain trust** informal group of advisers

**branches of government** tripartite division of U.S. government: executive, legislative, judicial

**Bundesrat** upper house of German parliament

**Bundestag** lower house of German parliament

**bureau** independent government office

**bureaucracy** large body of appointive government officials; complex structure of executive branch

**cabal** secret group seeking to exercise authority over government

**cabinet** chief advisory body to chief executive, president, or prime minister

**camarilla** secret group of advisers, often engaged in intrigue; cabal

**canton** small territorial division (France and Switzerland)

**capital** seat of government

**capitol** building where congress or state legislature meets

**Capitol** building in Washington D.C., in which Congress meets

**Capitol Hill** small hill on which U.S. Capitol stands; U.S. Congress, the Hill

**chamber** legislative house

**chamber of deputies** legislative body, usu. lower house

**city** large, usu. self-governing, municipality

**city council** legislative body of city

**city hall** building housing offices of city government

**civil service** nonmilitary governmental employees selected through merit system

**commissariat** major government division in Soviet Union prior to 1946

**commission** government agency with authority in one area; individuals appointed to investigate specific issues

**committee** body delegated to consider specific legislative matters

**committee of the whole** committee of all members of a legislative body, meeting under relaxed rules to expedite business

**commonwealth** federation of nations; official designation of four U.S. states: Kentucky, Massachusetts, Pennsylvania, and Virginia

**commune** smallest administrative district of some European nations; rural community based on collectivism

**confederacy** alliance for some specific purpose; eleven Southern states that seceded from United States in 1860; confederation

**confederation** confederacy

**conference committee** committee composed of members of both legislative houses

**congress** national legislative branch of government, esp. in republic; national or international representative assembly

**Congress** national legislative body of United States, consisting of Senate and House of Representatives

**Congressional committee** group of legislators chosen to consider details of legislation in one area and advise on Congressional action

**council** small governmental body, esp. for city

**county** political subdivision of state

**county board** governing body of county

**county seat** town that is site of county government

**court** judicial body; reigning sovereign with his or her family, retinue, and officers

**courthouse** building housing courts and local government offices

**D.C.** District of Columbia

**department** large administrative division of executive branch headed by cabinet member; regional division within nation comparable to state

**Department of Agriculture** U.S. executive department appointed to administer programs regarding farming

**Department of Commerce** U.S. executive department appointed to administer programs regarding domestic and foreign business

**Department of Defense** U.S. executive department appointed to administer programs regarding the military

**Department of Education** U.S. executive department appointed to administer programs regarding schools

**Department of Energy** U.S. executive department appointed to administer programs regarding sources and uses of energy

**Department of Health and Human Services** U.S. executive department appointed to administer programs regarding medicine and social welfare

**Department of Housing and Urban Development** U.S. executive department appointed to administer programs regarding city affairs and construction of dwellings

**Department of Justice** U.S. executive department appointed to administer programs regarding criminal and civil law

**Department of Labor** U.S. executive department appointed to administer programs regarding employer-employee relations

**Department of State** U.S. executive department appointed to administer programs regarding international relations

**Department of the Interior** U.S. executive department appointed to administer programs regarding land and natural resources

**Department of the Treasury** U.S. executive department appointed to administer programs regarding finance and money

**Department of Transportation** U.S. executive department appointed to administer programs regarding travel and shipping

**Department of Veterans Affairs** U.S. executive department appointed to administer programs regarding veterans of military service

**diet** national or provincial legislative body; assembly of princes

**District of Columbia** D.C.; seat of U.S. federal government

**divan** council of state or council chamber in Middle East

**duma** council or official assembly in pre-Soviet Russia

**duumvirate** coalition of two people in official capacity

**emirate** state or territory ruled by an Islamic emir or prince

**exchequer** national treasury and revenue department, as in Great Britain

**executive branch** law-enforcing and administrative branch of government, in United States headed by President

**federation** alliance of autonomous states

**floor** working area occupied by members of U.S. House or Senate

**folkmoot** general assembly of people of a town or shire in medieval England

**government corporation** public corporation that is government-owned but partially independent financially, organized to carry out a particular program

**grand duchy** territory ruled by grand duke or grand duchess

**Hill** *Informal.* short for Capitol Hill, where U.S. Congress is located

**home office** department responsible for administration of England but not the rest of United Kingdom

**house** one division of bicameral legislature

**House** U.S. House of Representatives

**House of Commons** elective lower house of British Parliament

**House of Lords** upper house of British Parliament, in

which peers and church officials sit for lifetime appointments

**House of Representatives** lower house of U.S. Congress, with two-year elective term

**inner circle** group of advisers closest to leader

**interest group** private organization attempting to influence government policy; lobby on specific issue

**interim committee** committee of Congress active between sessions

**joint committee** legislative committee composed of members from both houses

**judicial branch** section of government that administers justice and tries cases involving governmental or constitutional issues, composed primarily of judges

**judiciary** combined system of federal and state courts

**kitchen cabinet** unofficial, sometimes secret, advisers to head of state

**land office** government office for transaction of business relating to public lands

**legislative branch** lawmaking branch of government, usu. composed of elected representatives

**legislature** body charged with enacting laws

**lobby** interest group

**lower house** one branch of a bicameral legislature, usu. containing more members than upper house; U.S. House of Representatives; British House of Commons

**majlis** legislative body in Southwest Asia and North Africa

**ministry** department of government

**municipality** city, town, or village incorporated for self-government

**nation** independent, politically organized territory and its citizens

**national assembly** legislative body of nation

**office** public position or job

**Office of Management and Budget** OMB; U.S. executive agency that prepares federal budget

**OMB** Office of Management and Budget

**parish** political subdivision of Louisiana

**parliament** usu. bicameral elected legislature, as in Britain

**possession** territory ruled by government of another state

**privy council** board of personal advisers to monarch

**province** administrative division of a nation

**public** anything pertaining to the state or its subdivisions

**puppet government** government whose policies are orchestrated by another state

**regulatory commission** small board within executive chosen to manage particular government function

**Rules Committee** House committee that sets procedures for debate on bills

**rump** fragment of political group acting on behalf of original body after departure or expulsion of large number of its members

**secretariat** administrative department of government organization

**Secret Service** unit responsible for protecting U.S. President and Vice President

**select committee** legislative committee established for specific task and limited time

**senate** lawmaking assembly; state council

**Senate** upper house of U.S. Congress, with two senators from each state elected to six-year terms

**shadow cabinet** leaders of minority or opposition party in parliamentary system

**sinecure** public office requiring little or no work

**sovereignty** self-governing territory or state

**soviet** Communist government council and basic unit of political leadership of Soviet Union

**special committee** legislative committee established for specific task

**standing committee** permanent committee intended to consider specific subject

**state** politically organized community independent of other states; sovereign nation; major subdivision of United States

**statehouse** building housing offices of state government

**steering committee** committee of legislative or deliberative body that prepares agenda for session

**subcommittee** division of committee with limited purpose or authority

**supreme court** highest court in political unit with ultimate authority in judicial and constitutional matters

**Supreme Court** highest federal court in United States, consisting of nine judges

**synod** governing council or assembly of church

**territory** region over which government has authority

**think tank** institution conducting interdisciplinary research on issues of public policy

**town** municipal settlement larger than a village, smaller than a city

**town hall** location of mayoral and council offices; city hall

**town meeting** assembly of local citizens acting as legislative body

**township** New England territorial and political unit governed by town meetings

**triumvirate** group or association of three

**troika** administrative body of three

**union** combination of two or more autonomous political units

**upper house** one branch of bicameral legislature; U.S. Senate; British House of Lords

**village** smallest municipal corporation

**watchdog agency** commission responsible for protecting public by regulating an industry

## GOVERNMENT OFFICIALS AND CITIZENS

**administrator** one who manages and executes government programs

**alderman** city council member in some U.S. cities

**appointee** nonelective official, usu. chosen by executive branch

**assemblyman** member of legislative assembly, esp. male

**assemblywoman** female member of legislative assembly

**attorney general** chief law officer of nation or state; chief of U.S. Department of Justice

**autocrat** ruler possessing absolute authority

**backbencher** any member of British Parliament other than leaders of the party

**bureaucrat** member of bureaucracy

**burgess** former representative of borough or town in British Parliament

**burgher** inhabitant of borough or town

**burgomaster** mayor or chief magistrate of certain European cities

**caudillo** dictator, in Spanish-speaking countries

**chairman** official in seat of authority, esp. male

**chairwoman** female official in seat of authority

**chancellor** chief minister of state in certain parliamentary governments; prime minister; premier

**chief executive** principal administrative officer of government

**chief justice** ranking justice of court, esp. supreme court

**chief of staff** person responsible for supervising top executive's assistants and advisers

**chief of state** formal head of state, often not part of government process

**citizen** native or naturalized person owing allegiance to specific government

**city father** councilman or alderman

**city manager** official appointed by elected councilors to manage city administration

**civilian** person not in military or government service

**civil servant** member of civil service; elected or appointed government official serving the people

**clerk** record keeper

**commander in chief** supreme commander of armed forces; U.S. President

**commissar** supervisor of government department in Soviet Union before 1946

**congressman** member of House of Representatives, esp. male

**congresswoman** female member of House of Representatives

**constituent** resident of legislator's district

**coroner** county official responsible for investigating circumstances of deaths

**councilman** member of city council, esp. male

**councilor** member of city council

**councilwoman** female member of city council

**crown** office or person of monarch

**czar** absolute hereditary monarch of Russia until 1917; one having authority over major program

**deputy** member of lower legislative house; chief assistant to department head

**designate** (*adj*) used following title it modifies to indicate that person has been selected for office but not yet installed, as in ambassador–designate

**despot** absolute ruler

**dictator** absolute ruler, esp. oppressive tyrant

**disenfranchised** citizens denied right to vote

**doorkeeper** person in U.S. Congress who announces arrival of president and controls gallery passes

**duce** Italian fascist leader, esp. Mussolini

**dynasty** sequence of rulers from same family or group

**emperor** monarch governing an empire

**enfranchised** citizens granted right to vote

**etharch** ruler of a people or tribe

**fed** *Informal.* employee of federal government, esp. law enforcement officer

**federal agent** employee or representative of federal agency

**freeholder** one who has inherited and holds for life an estate of land

**freshman** newly elected member serving first term in U.S. Congress

**Führer** *German.* leader, esp. Hitler

**government employee** individual elected or appointed to work for any branch of federal, state, or local government

**governor** chief executive of U.S. state or imperial possession

**head of state** sovereign or chief executive, sometimes in ceremonial capacity only

**jemadar** any of various government officials in India

**king** male monarch

**lawgiver** member of legislature who draws up and enacts laws

**lawmaker** legislator

**legislator** member of legislature, usu. elected

**lieutenant governor** official next in line to state governor

**macebearer** official who carries ceremonial staff of office

**magistrate** public official entrusted with administration of law, often with judicial function

**manager** one who directs or supervises others

**mayor** highest executive official of city or town

**minister** high official managing government department or serving as diplomatic representative in foreign state

**minister without portfolio** government official with responsibilities in various areas

**monarch** hereditary ruler of kingdom, empire, or constitutional monarchy

**MP** *Member of Parliament* (Britain)

**official** middle- or high-level government employee

**ombudsman** government official who serves as intermediary between public and government and investigates complaints of misconduct by public officials

**page** person who carries messages and runs errands for members of legislature

**Pharaoh** absolute hereditary sovereign in ancient Egypt

**philosopher king** one who rules based on wisdom, proposed in Plato's *Republic*

**policymaker** top-level government official involved in creating and directing policy

**premier** prime minister

**president** head of executive branch

**President** chief executive of United States

**president pro tempore** presiding officer of Senate when vice president is absent, usu. senior member of majority party

**prime minister** first minister; head of cabinet in parliamentary government; chancellor; premier

**public servant** government employee owing first allegiance to citizens of nation he or she serves

**queen** female monarch

**recorder** official who sets down or transcribes information

**regent** one who rules monarchy when sovereign is disabled or too young

**representative** one elected to legislative body to serve interests of specific constituency

**secretary** executive official supervising operations of one department

**secretary-general** primary administrative official of organization

**selectman** municipal official in New England

**senator** member of senate

**Senator** member of U.S. Senate

**sergeant at arms** officer of legislative or judicial body charged with preserving order

**sky marshal** armed federal marshal responsible for preventing airline hijackings

**solon** member of legislature, esp. wise lawgiver

**sovereign** one exercising absolute power; monarch

**Speaker of the House** presiding office in U.S. House of Representatives

**statesman** one exercising leadership and conducting governmental business at a high level

**strongman** absolute ruler who rules by force; dictator

**subject** citizen governed by sovereign authority

**supervisor** member of county executive board

**treasurer** officer responsible for public funds

**tyrant** single absolute ruler, often oppressive or cruel and violent

**under secretary** second in command in executive department

**usurper** one who assumes and holds office without right

**vice-** prefix indicating official first in line to take place of immediate superior, as in vice-chancellor

**vice president** official next in line to president

**viceroy** governor of territory who represents monarch

**warlord** supreme military leader, often holding civil power by force

## ACTS, POWERS, CONDITIONS, AND PROCEDURES

**abdicate** (*vb*) give up throne or office

**abstain** (*vb*) withhold one's vote or participation

**acclamation** vote of legislature by voice only

**act** law passed by legislative body

**ad hoc** with specific or particular purpose

**adjourn** (*vb*) end legislative session

**advice and consent** constitutional power of Senate to approve all presidential appointments and treaties

**affirmative action** plan to rectify discrimination against minorities and women

**agenda** list of items to be brought before meeting

**allegiance** basic obligation of loyalty to state

**amendment** formal alteration of bill, law, or constitution

**amnesty** pardon by government authority, usu. head of state, to violators of federal law

**annexation** addition of territory into existing domain

**appointment** selection to fill nonelected office or function, usu. by president or executive

**apportionment** distribution and assignment of legislative seats

**appropriations** funds set aside by law for specific purpose

**arbitration** hearing or judgment of controversy by statutorily appointed body

**archives** collection of public documents

**articles** divisions of U.S. Constitution containing procedures for organization and implementation of government

**assessment** listing and evaluation of property for tax purposes

**authority** power to rule vested in government by people, constitution, or revolution

**bill** proposed piece of legislation

**bill of attainder** legislative act finding a person guilty of treason or felony without court trial

**Bill of Rights** first ten amendments to U.S. Constitution

**bloc voting** united voting of legislators or delegates to advance or obstruct action

**bond** certificate indicating government has borrowed money from individual or organization and will pay interest until bond is sold

**boondoggle** frivolous expenditure of public funds

**bribe** illegal payment to public official for favor

**briefing** act of providing information or instructions

**budget** financial plan for funding operations of government

**bull** decree of pope

**calendar** legislative schedule

**carry** (*vb*) secure passage or adoption; win majority of votes

**casting vote** deciding vote cast by presiding officer when other votes are equally divided

**caucus** closed meeting of legislative party members to decide status of forthcoming issues or select leaders

**censure** condemnation by vote of legislature

**census** official population count and informational survey taken every ten years

**charter** fundamental law or constitution granted cities by state legislature

**citizenship** full rights, duties, and privileges as a member of a nation, by birth or naturalization

**civil disobedience** refusal to obey government demands and laws, usu. passive resistance as matter of conscience

**civil law** laws pertaining to disputes between private parties or between private parties and government

**classified** (*adj*) secret

**clause** separate article of law or other formal document

**clearance** official authorization to know of or participate in classified activities

**cloture** procedure by which legislative body, esp. U.S. Senate, limits debate

**coalition** alliance of states or political parties

**committee hearing** publicly conducted information-gathering process by which committee reaches decision on issue

**commonweal** general welfare

**concurrent powers** powers held by both states and federal government

**concurrent resolution** congressional opinion requiring approval of both houses, but not a law

**confirmation** legislative approval of executive appointment

**conflict of interest** incompatibility between private interests and public responsibilities

**Congressional Record** official transcript of proceedings of both houses of Congress

**consensus** agreement by majority within group

**consent** willingness of people to submit to authority of civil government

**constitution** fundamental written law of state or nation

**Constitution** fundamental written law of United States

**constitutionality** accordance with constitution of a nation

**convene** (*vb*) come together as legislative body to commence session

**cooperative federalism** programs that feature joint effort of federal, state, and local governments to solve common problems

**coronation** act or ceremony of crowning a monarch

**debriefing** questioning and instruction of one privy to classified information

**debt ceiling** upper limit set for national debt

**Declaration of Independence** proclamation of liberty by American colonies in 1776

**decree** executive proclamation having force of law

**dedication** gift of private lands for public use

**delegated powers** constitutional powers of federal government

**deregulation** removal of established controls over business or industry

**devolution** transfer of power from central government to local government

**discharge petition** petition by half of House of Representatives to withdraw proposed bill from committee consideration

**dissenting opinion** written view on case by minority of U.S. Supreme Court

**domestic** (*adj*) pertaining to internal affairs of state

**domestic tranquility** state of peace within nation

**draft** compulsory selection of persons for military duty

**edict** official order or proclamation with force of law

**eminent domain** constitutional power of government to take private property for public use

**enactment** passage of bill into law

**enumerated powers** powers of federal government stated in U.S. Constitution

**exclusive powers** powers exclusive to federal or state government

**executive agreement** pact between U.S. President and head of foreign state not requiring senatorial approval

**executive order** rule issued by President, governor, or administrative authority that has force of law

**executive privilege** right of President to withhold certain information, usu. to protect national security

**executive session** hearing held by legislative body or committee that is closed to public

**expenditures** government spending of revenue

**extradition** return of criminal from one state or nation to another for trial

**fiat** authoritative government order or decree

**filibuster** delaying tactic to prevent legislative action

**first reading** initial submission of bill before legislature, often by number or name only

**fiscal policy** governmental use and manipulation of public revenues

**foreign policy** principles and goals determining one nation's relations with other nations

**forum** assembly for discussion of issues of public interest

**franking privilege** right to mail official papers without charge, enjoyed by members of Congress, President, and cabinet

**gag rule** any rule restricting open discussion or debate on a given issue in a deliberative body

**gavel-to-gavel** (*adj*) designating entire period from opening of legislative session to adjournment

**grant-in-aid** federal money given to state or local government for use in health, education, or public works

**hopper** box into which representatives drop bills to introduce them into the House

**impeachment** formal accusation brought to remove civil official from office; charges articulated in U.S. House of Representatives and tried in the Senate

**implied powers** authority of federal government based on indirect expression in U.S. Constitution

**inauguration** installation of President or other official into office

**inherent powers** authority of all national governments based on sovereignty as nation-states

**initiative** petition to place legislation or constitutional amendment on ballot for voters' direct approval

**internal revenue** money collected by government from citizens in form of taxes

**interpellation** procedure by which legislature asks government official to explain an act or policy

**interposition** doctrine that states may block enforcement of federal laws

**interregnum** temporary lapse in government functions, esp. during transition between two regimes or administrations

**item veto** executive veto of part of bill without rejection of entire measure

**joint resolution** formal expression of congressional opinion with force of law, esp. on unusual or temporary matter

**judicial review** power of courts to decide constitutionality of act of government

**junket** trip taken at public expense by government employee

**jurisdiction** authority over people or territory

**kill** (*vb*) prevent enactment of bill into legislation or veto enacted bill

**law** binding legislative act

**legislative power** constitutional authority allowing Congress to make laws

**lobby** (*vb*) attempt to influence government policy on specific issue, esp. by swaying legislative votes

**measure** legislative bill or enactment

**merit system** selection of civil servants on basis of demonstrated abilities rather than patronage

**minutes** written notes and record of meeting

**motion** formal proposal

**move** (*vb*) introduce a motion

**municipal charter** document creating city government and setting forth its powers and duties

**national supremacy** constitutional doctrine that national laws supersede state or local laws

**omnibus bill** all-inclusive or broad-ranging legislation

**ordinance** law, statute, or government regulation

**override** legislative vote to annul executive veto of legislative act

**pardon** legal forgiveness for crime granted by executive without judicial action

**parliamentarianism** study and practice of rules of conduct for legislative body

**parliamentary procedure** any of the rules and precedents governing proceedings of legislatures or meetings of other legislative bodies

**pass** (*vb*) approve

**passage** legislative enactment of bill into law

**patronage** awarding of government positions in return for support or other favors

**petition** formal written request, often signed by many citizens and submitted to government, esp. as means of placing referendum on ballot

**pigeonhole** (*vb*) set aside bill in committee and not bring it before legislature

**pocket** (*vb*) retain legislative bill without action to prevent it from becoming law

**pocket veto** process by which President prevents bill from becoming law by leaving it unsigned past end of legislative session

**portfolio** office and duties of minister of state

**position paper**  detailed report on an issue, usu. advising specific action

**prerogative**  exclusive, special right or privilege inherent in position or office

**prime the pump**  increase government funding to stimulate the economy

**private bill**  bill dealing with individual concern

**proclamation**  official public executive announcement

**progressive tax**  tax rate that increases as taxable income increases

**proportional representation**  allocation of legislative seats by party based on percent of popular or electoral vote received

**proviso**  clause stating conditions of bill or document

**public assistance**  government funds used to satisfy basic needs of poor citizens

**public lands**  territory owned by federal government

**public policy**  government programs approved by legislature or initiated by executive departments and agencies

**public service**  actions that supply essential commodity or service for benefit or welfare of people

**public works**  roads, dams, and other structures for public use that are paid for by government funds

**quorum**  number of members of body required to transact official business, usu. a majority

**railroad** (*vb*) rush legislation through without considering opposition

**ratify** (*vb*) vote approval; sanction formally

**reapportionment**  reorganization of electoral districts by new formula

**recall**  procedure by which public official is removed from office by popular vote

**recess**  suspension of legislative session or procedure

**redistricting**  revision of legislative district boundaries

**red tape**  excessive bureaucratic procedure that causes delay

**regalia**  emblems of office

**regulation**  executive actions to bring activities into conformity with law

**repeal** (*vb*) cancel or revoke legislative enactment

**report** (*vb*) send bill to full legislature with committee recommendation

**rescind** (*vb*) cancel, annul

**reserved powers**  powers not delegated to federal government by U.S. Constitution and not denied to states

**resolution**  formal expression of opinion or intent by governmental body

**revenue**  government income, primarily from taxation

**revenue sharing**  system by which state and local governments receive fixed amounts of federal tax revenues

**revoke** (*vb*) annul statute or recall official

**rider**  provision that might not pass on its own but that is likely to pass when attached to important bill

**roll call**  alphabetical recital of names of legislators on floor for vote on issue

**secession**  formal separation from organized body or government

**second** (*vb*) endorse another's parliamentary motion

**second reading**  legislative proceeding in which a bill is reported back from committee for full debate before vote

**sedition**  verbal incitement of resistance to lawful authority

**senatorial courtesy**  unwritten rule that U.S. Senate will approve an appointee only if acceptable to senators in President's party from state involved

**seniority system**  assignment of most important posts and committee chairmanships to members of U.S. Congress with longest service

**serfdom**  condition of being bound to land and subservient to feudal lord; thralldom

**session**  period of time during which legislative body meets

**sittings**  sessions of U.S. Supreme Court

**slavery**  ownership of persons who are absolutely subject to slaveholder's will

**special session**  legislative assembly at abnormal time

**states' rights**  governmental authority exercised by states, not to be infringed upon by federal government

**statute**  law; act of legislature

**statutory law**  law enacted by legislative body such as congress, state legislature, or city council

**strict construction**  interpretation of U.S. Constitution to mean that federal government has no powers or rights not expressly granted by Constitution, esp. limiting use of presidential power

**subjugation**  conquest or domination of a people or territory

**subsidy**  government funds paid to individual or group to enhance economic position

**succession**  order in which officials move up to vacated higher position, esp. procedure for filling presidential vacancy

**table** (*vb*) remove bill from consideration, usu. indefinitely; *Chiefly Brit.* place bill or motion on agenda

**tax**  monies collected by government from citizens to support government

**taxation**  government imposition of taxes; revenue derived from taxes

**term**  two-year session of House between elections; six-year incumbency in Senate before facing reelection

**thralldom**  slavery, serfdom

**top secret**  highly classified information requiring special clearance for access

**town meeting**  assembly of local citizens to discuss and vote on issues

**treason**  betrayal of one's government by making war on it or giving aid and comfort to its enemies

**ukase**  edict issued by Russian czar

**unconstitutional** (*adj*) in violation of constitutional principles

**undemocratic** (*adj*) not in accord with democratic principles, esp. totalitarian

**unincorporated area**  territory beyond any local jurisdiction

**unseat** (*vb*) remove from office, usu. by defeating in election

**unwritten constitution**  informal constitution based on series of laws over time

**vassalage**  condition of subordination to feudal lord as tenant

**veto**  power of executive to reject legislation passed by Congress; (*vb*) exercise such power

**veto power**  executive authority to reject legislation

**voice vote**  vote by acclamation

**vote**  exercise of political franchise in election of officials or expression of views on issues

**vote of confidence**  formal expression of political support for governing ministry by legislative majority in parliamentary system

**war powers** extended presidential powers of commander in chief in time of war

**ways and means** manner of raising and allocating revenues for conduct of government business

**white paper** detailed government report on specific subject

**yield** (*vb*) allow another member of body to express views in debate

## POSTAL SERVICE

**aerogram** sheet of lightweight paper folded to form its own envelope and bearing postal stamp imprint, sent via airmail, usu. overseas

**air express** system for overnight delivery of letters and packages by air

**air freight** shipment of packages by air

**airmail** postal transportation by aircraft, formerly at higher rate than first-class mail, now at standard rate

**APO** *Army and Air Force Post Office*; designation for overseas mail intended for military personnel

**Army and Air Force Post Office** APO

**bulk mail** low-cost, slowest class of postal service, esp. for large quantities of printed matter

**carrier** person who delivers mail

**certified mail** first-class mail for which proof of delivery is obtained and often returned to sender

**envelope** folded paper with sealing flap into which letters are placed for protection when sent by postal service

**express mail** guaranteed overnight delivery

**first-class mail** regular priority mail service, sent by air over long distances; priority mail

**forwarding address** new address given to post office when moving to guarantee mail forwarding

**general delivery** department at post office where mail is held for pickup at window

**indicia** postal markings or labels affixed to mail

**key** device that operator uses to send telegram

**letter carrier** mailman

**mail** nation's postal system; letters and other matter sent by mail; bags of postal matter; (*vb*) send a letter or package by post

**mailbag** canvas container used by postal service for gathering mail; letter carrier's shoulder bag

**mailbox** public receptacle for deposit of outgoing mail

**mail drop** receptacle for deposit of outgoing mail

**mail forwarding** postal service by which mail sent to person's old address is forwarded to new address

**mailman** one who delivers mail, esp. door-to-door on foot or by vehicle; letter carrier; postman

**mail order** business of selling of goods by mail; order for goods sent through mail

**parcel post** postal service and fees for handling packages

**PO box** *post-office box*

**post** national postal delivery system; single delivery of mail; (*vb*) send a letter or package

**postage** fee required for postal service; stamps

**postage due** additional fee required for delivery of letter with insufficient postage

**postage meter** device that prints postage on mail, records amount, and subtracts it from amount prepaid to postal service

**postage stamp** government-issued, adhesive-backed design on paper indicative of prepayment of specified postage fee; stamp

**postal** (*adj*) relating to or conducted by postal service

**postal money order** receipt issued by post office that is good for payment of cash at any post office

**postal scale** small scale for weighing letters and packages to determine required postal fee

**postal service** nation's institutions, regulations, and personnel for delivery of mail

**post-bag** *Chiefly Brit*. mailbag

**postcard** small card on which message is written and to which stamp is affixed for mailing without envelope

**postcode** *Brit*. code of numbers and letters for routing mail

**poste restante** direction written on envelope, esp. in Europe, that mail should be held at post office for addressee

**postman** mailman

**postmark** official mark showing date and place of mailing, printed over stamp as cancellation symbol

**postmaster** supervisor of post office

**postmaster general** director of national postal system

**post office** government department handling mail service; local branch of this department through which mail is processed; building housing local branch

**post office box** PO box; numbered box at post office used as address for receipt of mail

**postpaid** (*adj*) having postage prepaid by sender

**post road** route over which mail is transported

**priority mail** first-class mail

**railway express** system for shipment of packages by railroad

**registered mail** mail recorded in originating post office and at successive points of transmission for guarantee of special handling and safe delivery

**return to sender** postal designation indicating recipient is no longer at address and no forwarding address is known

**RFD** *rural free delivery*

**RR** *rural route*

**rural free delivery** RFD; designation for postal service to rural location

**rural route** RR; postal delivery route in rural area

**special delivery** mail delivery for extra fee by messenger immediately upon arrival at destination post office

**stamp** postage stamp

**star route** route in rural area serviced by private carrier under contract with postal service

**stationery** writing paper and envelopes used for letters and other mail

**surcharge** overprint on stamp that alters denomination

**zip code** five-digit postal code that indicates local post office through which mail should be routed to recipient

# POLITICS

Philosophies, Principles, and Parties
Party Functions and Political Practices
Politicians and Activists
Elections and Campaigns
Revolution and Antigovernment Activity

**SEE ALSO**: Chap. 11: Government; Law; Chap. 13: Sociology

# PHILOSOPHIES, PRINCIPLES, AND PARTIES

**anarchism** belief that all government authority is harmful; advocacy of government by voluntary personal cooperation

**anarcho-syndicalism** syndicalism

**art of the possible** politics based on practical expediency rather than theoretical visions

**Bill of Rights** basic human rights and privileges guaranteed in first ten amendments to U.S. Constitution

**Bolshevism** doctrine of wing of Russian Communist party advocating violent revolution, which seized power in 1917

**capitalism** political and economic system in which capital goods are privately or corporately owned and managed

**center** principles midway between liberal and conservative views

**centrist** (*adj*) being party of moderate views; positioned at middle of one's own party

**chauvinism** extreme, dogmatic patriotism

**civics** study of government, politics, and the duties and rights of citizenship

**civil rights** fundamental protections and nonpolitical rights, esp. individual freedoms, enjoyed by all citizens under Constitution

**collective** group or institution organized and run by all members equally

**collectivism** socialist system in which centralized group controls production and distribution of goods and services

**commons** third estate

**commune** usu. rural community organized on collective basis

**communism** political system based on elimination of private property and state ownership and control of means of production and distribution of goods and services

**Communist party** political party advocating principles of communism, esp. Marxism-Leninism

**conservatism** political posture based on preservation of traditional, established values and systems

**Democratic party** more liberal of two major U.S. parties

**domestic** (*adj*) relating to political affairs carried on within one's own country

**domination** exercise of authority or supremacy over another political entity

**egalitarianism** advocacy of removal of inequalities among people based on belief in human equality

**emancipation** granting of freedom, esp. from slavery

**enfranchisement** right to vote

**establishment** ruling class and institutions by which it maintains existing order in society

**evolutionary socialism** belief that transition from capitalism to socialism can be made through voting, without revolution

**extremism** political views of far right or far left

**Fabianism** gradual, nonrevolutionary change to socialism advocated by English Fabian Society (late 19th c.)

**Fourierism** social system based on small cooperative communities (mid-19th c.)

**fourth estate** the press, esp. as it wields political power and influence

**franchise** suffrage, right to vote

**freedom** individual option to make choices without coercion

**freedom of speech** right of citizens to express their opinions publicly without government interference, subject to laws against libel and incitement to violence

**freedom of the press** right to publish information or opinions without government restriction, subject only to laws of libel, obscenity, and sedition

**free enterprise** freedom of business activity from government interference or control

**free thought** unorthodox, independently formed, sometimes revolutionary notions

**geopolitics** influence of and concern with geography and demographics in nation's politics and foreign policy

**GOP** Grand Old Party; U.S. Republican Party

**Green party** liberal political party focusing on environmental issues, esp. in Germany

**guild socialism** socialism in which government contracts workers through national guilds and controls means of production (Britain)

**hard line** uncompromising or unyielding position or policy

**ideological party** minor party based on particular political, economic, and social views

**ideology** systematic body of sociopolitical theories and programs based on particular vision

**independence** freedom from political control or domination by others

**iron hand** often cruel authoritarian rule, esp. by military

**John Birch Society** ultraconservative, white supremacist, anticommunist political group

**Know-Nothing party** excessively patriotic group hostile to subversive foreign influence (U.S., mid-19th c.)

**laissez faire** opposition to government interference with personal freedom, esp. in economic affairs

**left wing** those supporting progressive reform and greater welfare of common man

**Leninism** principles and practice of communism developed by V. I. Lenin

**liberalism** belief in personal liberty and autonomy, progress, and government aid to those in need

**liberation** freeing of group or state from domination

**libertarian** advocate of absolute free will and freedom of thought

**liberty** freedom to exercise various rights, esp. choice of one's government and individual freedoms

**loyal opposition** minority party in legislature that maintains allegiance to government

**Magna Carta** charter of fundamental liberties granted to English barons by King John in 1215

**mainstream** predominant political views or trends

**majority rule** principle empowering that part of group with over fifty percent of vote to make decisions binding on all

**major party** party with sufficient electoral strength to win control of government with regularity; one of two major U.S. parties: Democratic or Republican

**Maoism** theory and practice of communism developed in China by Mao Zedong (mid-20th c.)

**Marxism** system of socioeconomic and political thought developed by Karl Marx that is basis of communism, esp. doctrine that class struggle will be main agency of change from exploitative capitalist system to classless society under socialist order

**middle-of-the-road** (*adj*) moderate

**minority party** loyal opposition; that major party with fewer members in legislature

**minor party** party with limited platform and following, unable to control government; any third party in United States

**moderatism** support for views midway between liberal and conservative

**multiparty system** sharing of political power among more than two parties

**national socialism** Nazism

**Nazism** totalitarian system of Third German Reich, based on racial supremacy; national socialism

**neofascism** fascist movement or principles promoted after defeat of fascist states in World War II

**New Left** movement advocating radical political and social change, begun by U.S. students in 1960's

**New Right** movement advocating conservative social values and nationalistic foreign policy, orig. 1960's United States

**nihilism** belief in nothing; advocacy of destruction of government without creation of something new

**nonpartisan** (*adj*) holding views and policies without regard to party

**Old Left** pro-Soviet socialist movement of 1930's in United States

**oppression** unfair, harsh exercise of authority

**partisan** (*adj*) advocating or based on views of one party

**party** group of like-minded individuals organized to direct and control government policy by winning elections

**party line** official, often standardized, policies and principles of one political party

**patriotism** love for one's country and loyalty to its government

**pinko** *Derogatory slang.* person with left-wing, often communistic, political views

**planned economy** socialist system advocating centralized government control of all economic functions

**political** (*adj*) of or relating to elections and government functions

**political economy** science dealing with interrelationship of political and economic processes

**political science** study of politics

**politics** art or science of guiding and controlling government, esp. in conjunction with attaining political office; principles and doctrines on which such activity is based

**polity** specific form of any political organization or unit

**populism** egalitarian political philosophy or movement that promotes interests of common people

**power elite** ruling class, esp. small group wielding inordinate political power

**proportional representation** system in which each party is represented in legislature in proportion to its percentage of electorate

**radicalism** advocacy of doctrines and policies for extreme change in political system

**reaction** resistance to change and clinging to old or outmoded social and political forms

**reactionary** (*adj*) holding ultraconservative political views that firmly support status quo and advocate suppression of those favoring change

**realpolitik** politics based on practical considerations, not theoretical objectives

**red** communist

**reform party** group advocating correction of abuses in government

**reign of terror** maintenance of power through violence and terrorism

**repression** prevention of unpopular or antigovernment views

**Republican party** GOP; more conservative of two major U.S. parties

**right wing** those supporting conservative positions, established order, and traditional values

**royalist** advocate of monarchy

**ruling class** privileged, wealthy individuals who collectively hold political and economic power

**self-determination** freedom of citizens to determine form of government of their home region

**social democracy** socialist state marked by gradual, peaceful, nonrevolutionary transition from capitalism to socialism

**socialism** various political and economic theories based on government ownership of all or most of means of production and distribution of goods, with control over aspects of social welfare and planning

**soft line** moderate or flexible position or policy

**splinter party** minor party that has split from major party

**state socialism** partial socialism introduced by moderate political action

**stewardship** obligation of ruling class to manage state with regard for welfare of all

**suffrage** right to vote

**suppression** prohibition or restraint of views unfavorable to government authority

**syndicalism** communism based on direct seizure of government control by workers; anarcho-syndicalism

**Tammany Hall** organized group exercising political control of a city through corruption, orig. 19th-century New York

**third estate** third class in threefold political division of kingdom; commons

**third party** independent party, often organized around one issue, that temporarily challenges major U.S. parties

**thought control** manipulation and suppression of public opinion and political perceptions

**Tory** political conservative, esp. 17th-19th c. British supporters of royal authority

**Trotskyism** branch of communism advocating worldwide revolution

**two-party system** American political system in which two major parties compete for control of government

**ultraconservative** (*adj*) reactionary, right wing, extremely conservative

**ultraliberal** (*adj*) radical, left wing, extremely liberal

**undemocratic** (*adj*) lacking in adherence to democratic principles

**universal suffrage** right of all members of society to vote

**utopian socialism** belief in transition to socialism by voluntary transfer of property from owners to state

**war party** legislative supporters of military action

**Whig** parliamentarian, esp. advocate of limited royal authority (Britain, 17th-19th c.)

**wing** opposing faction within legislature or party

# PARTY FUNCTIONS AND POLITICAL PRACTICES

**abdicate** (*vb*) give up office or throne

**acclamation** voice vote

**adapt** (*vb*) vote to pass or accept

**affiliation** association of like-minded individuals, esp. with specific party

**apparat** political organization or existing power structure

**appointment** nonelective office

**ascendancy** assuming position of increased power and dominance

**back room** meeting place for small inner circle to plan and manipulate political moves, often in secret

**beadledom** pointless, stupid, rigid bureaucracy

**bipartisan** (*adj*) pertaining to both major parties

**boodle** bribe money

**bossism** control of political organization by local boss

**cloakroom** anteroom to legislative chamber for informal conversations among legislators

**clout** political influence

**coalition** alliance among members of different parties for specific vote or cause

**corruption** use of political influence for personal gain

**cronyism** practice of granting political favors to friends

**deal** coherent series of programs set forth by one party, as in New Deal or Fair Deal

**declaration** statement of policy

**doctrine** basic political policy of party

**filibuster** delaying tactic, esp. lengthy speech to prevent passage of legislation

**front** coalition of divergent elements for common goals

**frying the fat** securing substantial political contributions

**fusion** coalition of political parties or factions

**gerrymandering** arranging legislative voting districts to favor one party

**graft** use of political influence or position to acquire personal gain

**issue** subject of dispute or debate

**jawboning** use of influence and office to affect behavior

**jobbery** corruption in public office

**junket** personal trip financed by public funds

**Komsomol** communist youth organization (Soviet Union)

**logrolling** trading of legislator's vote for reciprocal support on future votes

**machine** disciplined influential political organization, esp. under control of boss or clique

**movement** group pursuing organized actions to attain specific end

**national committee** group of leaders that controls party business between conventions

**nepotism** granting of political favors to relatives

**party line** official, established policies of one party

**patronage system** executive appointments reflecting partisan bias

**policy** overall plan embracing government goals

**pork barrel** legislation manipulated for political advantage to one's constituency or district, usu. public works projects

**power base** source of political power, usu. support of organized bloc of voters or ethnic minority

**pressure group** individuals with specific common interest organized to influence public policy

**program** plan of action

**propaganda** techniques used to influence or control the opinions of groups or individuals, esp. to promote one's views or damage an opponent's by dissemination of rumors and allegations

**proposition** idea set forth for debate

**prorogue** (*vb*) suspend or terminate legislative session, esp. of British Parliament, by royal prerogative

**public interest group** individuals organized to influence government policy for benefit of general citizenry

**public opinion poll** questions asked of random sampling of potential voters to determine views and preferences

**pull** influence

**purge** elimination of unfit or unfaithful party members

**roorback** libel for political effect

**seniority** legislative system by which members with longest continuous service achieve positions of privilege and power

**smoke-filled room** private gathering place where inner circle of politicians plan and scheme

**smoking gun** evidence of indisputable guilt

**special interest group** political group organized to further its specific common concerns; lobby

**spoils system** practice of appointing party loyalists to public office

**statecraft** skill at conducting political affairs

**statesmanship** skill and vision in governing; political acumen

**turn** (*vb*) to defect from one's party or professed view

**union** political unit formed by combination of two or more previously independent entities

**vest** (*vb*) imbue with authority

**vested interest** special interest in existing economic or political system for personal advantage

**war chest** campaign funds held in reserve by incumbent to defeat future challengers

**watchdog function** role of political party out of power in monitoring conduct of party in power

# POLITICIANS AND ACTIVISTS

**activist** individual engaged in direct action for political change or to influence specific issue; party worker

**agent provocateur** one who infiltrates suspect organization and incites its members into incriminating actions

**alternate** one who acts as substitute, esp. for convention delegate

**apparatchik** member of political organization, esp. Communist

**baby kisser** politician who endears himself or herself to voters by displays of personal warmth, as by kissing babies

**bedfellow** close political ally

**boss** powerful politician who controls votes or party, often by corrupt practices

**cabal** secret union of conspirators or advisers

**cacique** local political boss (Spain and Latin American)

**cadre** inner group of dedicated leaders who advocate particular views

**camp follower** politician who supports party solely for personal gain

**candidate** one who aspires to public elected office

**chairman** leader of party organization, esp. male

**chairperson** male or female leader of party organization

**chairwoman** female leader of party organization

**committeeman** member of party committee, esp. male

**committeewoman** female member of party committee

**conservative** adherent to political conservatism

**constituent** voter in defined electoral district represented by specific official

**dark horse** relative unknown; underdog in election

**delegate** representative

**demagogue** one who appeals to and manipulates mass prejudice

**Democrat** member of more liberal of two major U.S. political parties

**district leader** party leader within single district

**Dixiecrat** conservative southern Democrat who opposes civil-rights programs and advocates states' rights

**dove** opponent of military action as political solution

**elector** one entitled to vote in election

**éminence grise** individual with unofficial, secret powers

**extremist** advocate of extreme political positions

**fat cat** *Slang.* wealthy individual from whom large financial contribution is expected

**favorite son** state's candidate for presidential nomination and leader of delegation to party convention

**floater** person voting in more than one polling place

**floor leader** party member in charge of strategy during legislative sessions

**hack** experienced but unprincipled politician

**handler** one who manages political campaign, esp. media exposure

**hanger-on** one who associates himself or herself with politician for personal gain

**hatchet man** one employed to engage secretly in unscrupulous activities that would tarnish elected official

**hawk** supporter of military action as political solution

**heeler** local party worker or henchman for boss

**henchman** political supporter seeking personal gain or performing unsavory tasks

**holdover** one continuing in same office

**ideologue** political theorist rather than practitioner; zealous advocate of an ideology

**incumbent** officeholder

**independent** one not affiliated with any party

**jack-in-office** small-minded, disrespectful individual in position of authority

**jackleg** unprincipled, dishonest, or amateurish politician

**Jacobin** radical extremist, orig. terrorist supporter of democracy in French Revolution

**keynoter** one delivering keynote address

**kingmaker** person wielding sufficient political power to influence choice of candidates for office

**lame duck** officeholder who has been defeated in bid for reelection, during interval before inauguration of successor

**leadership** those who set party policies and strategy

**liberal** advocate of progressive reform

**lobbyist** person who works for special interest group

**machine politician** one owing allegiance to political machine

**majority leader** ranking member of party holding majority in legislature

**minority leader** ranking member of party in minority in legislature

**moderate** one supporting views midway between right and left

**mouthpiece** spokesperson, esp. for political leader

**mugwump** political independent, orig. one who left Republican party in 1884

**national chairman** head of national committee of major party

**new broom** individual new to power and zealous in duties

**nominee** one selected by party to oppose other party's candidates in election

**noncandidate** potential candidate for office who has officially announced that he or she will not run

**old guard** veteran political figures, usu. resistant to new ideas

**old-line** (*adj*) conservative, established, having seniority

**party boss** powerful individual who controls party operations, often by corrupt means

**party chairman** one chosen by party members to lead party

**party faithful** veteran, dependable, active party loyalists

**party hack** one blindly loyal to party and prepared to carry out orders

**placeman** *Chiefly Brit.* person appointed to office as reward for political support

**polemicist** one skilled in debate

**politician** person engaged in party politics or government, esp. one seeking or holding elected office; politico

**politico** politician

**pollster** one who polls public to determine preferences and advises candidates based on findings

**poll watcher** person who ensures legal voting process at poll

**powerbroker** influential individual who controls bloc of votes

**precinct captain** one responsible for overseeing party activities in one precinct

**precinct leader** chief member of party in precinct

**president-elect** one who has been elected president but not yet inaugurated into office

**progressive** one supporting political change and social improvement by moderate government policies

**radical** advocate of extreme, sometimes violent, measures to improve society or alter established form of government

**reactionary** advocate of ultraconservative political views, esp. suppression of those favoring change

**reformer** one seeking to change and improve political institutions and government policies

**regular** party member who can be depended on for votes or support

**Republican** member of more conservative of two major U.S. political parties

**running mate** candidate for lower office linked with candidate for higher office, usu. of same party, esp. vice president

**sachem** *Slang.* political party leader or boss

**seatwarmer** legislator appointed to fill vacancy with understanding that he or she will not run in next election

**stalking-horse** candidate put forth to draw votes from rival or to conceal candidacy of another person

**standard-bearer** head of party's slate in election

**state chairman** leader of party for single U.S. state

**statesman** skilled practitioner in art of governing

**suffragette** female activist advocating voting rights for women

**superdelegate** party leader or official chosen as uncommitted delegate to national political convention

**troubleshooter** one skilled at mediating political disputes

**ward heeler** worker in local political machine

**war-horse** *Informal.* experienced, dependable political veteran

**whip** party leader in legislature appointed to enforce party discipline and voting solidarity

**Young Turk** insurgent within group

## ELECTIONS AND CAMPAIGNS

**absentee ballot** vote cast by mail when voter is not at designated polling place on election day

**absolute majority** more than half of eligible voters

**acceptance speech** candidate's address to nominating convention

**at large** designating legislator, esp. member of British Parliament, elected by all voters rather than by voters of single district

**backlash** negative reaction to events among voters that causes swing to opposite view

**ballot** printed list of candidates and measures; voting

**ballot box** receptacle where ballots are placed after voting

**bandwagon** party, cause, or movement that readily attracts followers or supporters because of its mass appeal or apparent strength

**barnstorm** (*vb*) conduct campaign by making brief stops in many small towns

**big fix** citywide graft system for controlling votes

**blanket primary** open primary in which voter chooses between two or more parties

**bloc** group of voters

**body politic** people who compose a politically organized unit under a single government authority

**borough** *Chiefly Brit.* urban parliamentary constituency

**bunkum** insincere oratory by politician, designed to please constituents

**by-election** special parliamentary election between general elections (Britain)

**campaign** process undertaken to secure public office; (*vb*) actively run for office

**campaign button** small badge imprinted with candidate's name or slogan

**campaign trail** series of public appearances made by office seeker prior to election day

**canvass** count or sample of public opinion; soliciting of votes

**carry** (*vb*) win majority of votes or gain passage

**caucus** party meeting to choose candidates and plan strategy

**charisma** candidate's personal magnetism and charm

**closed primary** election to select party candidates limited to registered party members

**coattail effect** tendency of strong candidate for higher office to increase votes for weaker candidates of same party

**congressional district** territorial division of state whose residents elect member of House of Representatives

**constituency** defined electoral district

**convention** assembly of delegates to nominate candidates for office and draft platform, usu. for one party

**cross-file** (*vb*) register as candidate for more than one party or in primaries of more than one party

**crossover vote** vote of person registered in one party cast for another party's candidate

**declaration** formal announcement of candidacy

**delegation** representatives at convention from one state

**direct primary** preliminary election in which voters of one party select candidates for final bipartisan election

**dirty politics** corruption, bribery, deception, and covert activity on behalf of candidate

**district** electoral unit composed of precincts

**elect** (*vb*) choose public official through voting

**election** selection of public officials or expression of views on issue by poll of voters

**election day** day on which votes are cast

**electioneer** (*vb*) work for candidate or party; (*n*) one who does so

**electoral college** pledged presidential electors from each U.S. state, determined by popular vote in that state, assembled to elect president and vice president

**electoral votes** votes of each state in electoral college, equal to total of its Senate and House members

**electorate** total number of people qualified to vote

**ethnic vote** bloc of voters of specific racial or ethnic background who frequently vote alike

**fund-raiser** event held to raise money for candidate or cause

**general election** regularly scheduled election for state, local, or national officials

**glad-hand** (*vb*) greet voters with excessive cordiality to gain votes for one's candidacy

**grass roots** local organization or opinion, esp. as symbolized by constituents at district level

**hat in the ring** indication of candidacy

**hustings** any place from which campaign speeches are made; campaign trail in general

**initiative** procedure whereby voters sign petition to place issue or proposed law on ballot before electorate

**keynote address** opening speech that sets tone and outlines primary issues for convention

**landslide** overwhelming majority of votes

**local election** election for candidates and on issues governing small political unit such as town or city

**mandate** desires of constituents as expressed through votes and interpreted by politicians

**media campaign** extensive use of newspapers, radio, and television to reach voters

**minority** less than half of votes cast

**mudslinging** malicious personal attacks and invective directed against political opponent

**multiple voting** casting of ballots by one voter in different places in same election

**national convention** assembly every four years of major party's representatives to select presidential candidate and articulate a party platform

**national election** voting for candidates to govern entire nation, often with simultaneous voting for officials from many states

**nomination** selection of candidate to run in election

**nonpartisan election** election in which candidates are not identified by party

**off year** year without major, esp. presidential, election

**open primary** election to select party candidates in which any qualified voter may participate, regardless of party

**PAC** political *a*ction *c*ommittee

**plank** party policy on specific issue stated in platform

**platform** principles and policies supported by party or candidate in election

**plebiscite** vote in which district or nation expresses yes or no opinion, esp. choice of government or ruler

**plurality** largest number of votes, esp. when no one candidate receives a majority

**political action committee** PAC; organization that collects contributions and distributes funds to candidates and causes

**politicking** engaging in political activity, campaigning

**poll** survey of a scientifically selected sample of voters prior to election to determine preferences; expression of opinion by voting; (*vb*) process or count votes

**polling place** location where voters cast votes

**polling station** *Chiefly Brit.* location where voters cast votes

**poll tax** tax levied on every voter for right to vote

**popular** (*adj*) representative of majority of people

**precinct** smallest voting subdivision of city or ward

**preferential voting** system of voting in which voter indicates order of preference for candidates listed on ballot

**primary** preliminary election to determine party candidates in general election

**projected winner** election night estimate of eventual winner based on early returns and projection of trends

**proposition** statement of issue or suggested plan placed on ballot for direct popular vote on whether it will become law

**proxy** authority, esp. of deputy, to act for another

**public opinion** views on issues and candidates held by enough of electorate to be politically significant

**rally** meeting to arouse group enthusiasm or support for candidate

**recall** removal of unpopular elected official by special election

**recount** counting of votes a second time in case of possible mistakes or illegalities

**referendum** popular vote on measure proposed by legislature or by popular initiative

**registration** enrollment of individuals on voter lists, esp. during designated time period

**registration drive** movement to enroll those previously denied or not exercising voting rights

**returns** election results, voting totals

**run** (*vb*) place oneself before voters as candidate for office

**runoff** election held when primary is not conclusive

**safe seat** incumbency that faces only token opposition in election

**sample ballot** ballot distributed to voters before election to familiarize them with candidates and issues

**secret ballot** process by which voters' privacy is ensured

**slate** list of candidates, usu. all from one party; ticket

**slush fund** party campaign fund, the size and purposes of which are not necessarily legal

**smear campaign** crude, unsubstantiated attacks against opposing candidate

**special election** preliminary election held when issue must be decided by voters before primary or general election is held

**split ticket** votes cast for candidates of more than one party on same ballot

**stand** (*vb*) *Chiefly Brit.* run for office

**stand down** (*vb*) *Chiefly Brit.* step aside or withdraw from election, nomination, or office

**stepwinder** *Slang.* stirring political address

**straight ticket** vote for all candidates of single party

**straw poll** unofficial, random sample vote taken as measure of public opinion

**stump** (*vb*) move from town to town making speeches on behalf of issues or candidates

**swing vote** determining vote in close election, often one that changes at last moment

**ticket** list of candidates; slate

**turnout** percentage or number of eligible voters who cast ballots

**undecided voter** voter indicating no definite choice in political poll and therefore sought by all candidates

**vote** formal expression of opinion at ballot box

**voting booth** place where voter marks ballot

**voting machine** machine that registers and tallies votes

**ward** political subdivision of city, esp. as basis for election of city council members

**whistle stop** political stop in small community

**winner-take-all system** electoral college system in which candidate receiving majority of popular vote in state receives all of its electoral votes

**write-in** handwritten vote for candidate not listed on ballot

**write-in candidate** individual not on ballot but campaigning for office

## REVOLUTION AND ANTIGOVERNMENT ACTIVITY

**activism** direct, often intense, engagement in actions for political change

**anarchist** one who opposes all forms of authority and advocates violence to overthrow existing order

**antiestablishment** (*adj*) working against existing power structure

**assassination** murder of political officeholder

**blacklist** list of people or organizations considered undesirable, used to exclude them from jobs or organizations

**card-carrying** (*adj*) firmly identified with one party or group, esp. Communist party

**cell** smallest group within party organization, esp. Communist party

**civil disobedience** nonviolent refusal to obey authorities as means of political pressure

**civil disorder** riot or disruption of normal activities as means to political change

**counterrevolution** movement to overthrow government created by earlier revolution

**coup** coup d'etat

**coup d'etat** sudden exercise of political force, esp. violent overthrow of government by small group; coup

**demonstration** mass public meeting and display of opinion

**destructionist** person who advocates destruction of existing political institution

**direct action** action such as strike or boycott that seeks an immediate response from established authority

**dissent** opposition to established political order

**dissident** person expressing opposition to established government

**fellow traveler** Communist party sympathizer

**fifth column** group undermining a cause from within

**foco** small, rural, often secret group engaged in local revolutionary actions

**foquismo** Che Guevara's theory that revolution can be engendered from activities of many focos

**freedom fighter** person who battles against established forces of tyranny and oppression

**guerrilla** one conducting irregular warfare, sabotage, and terrorism to foment revolution

**incendiary** one who inflames or excites public to revolutionary acts

**insurgency** minor, often disorganized revolt against government

**insurrection** organized revolt against established government authority

**internal exile** banishment of person, esp. political dissident, to remote place within same country

**Jacobin** radical extremist, orig. terrorist supporter of democracy in French Revolution

**junta** small group controlling government after seizing power

**march** organized mass walk as demonstration of opinion or protest

**movement** coalition of groups and individuals seeking political change

**outside agitator** one who infiltrates group or situation to create greater disturbance

**popular front** coalition of leftist and sometimes centrist political factions to oppose common opponent, usu. reactionary government

**peacenik** *Slang.* antiwar demonstrator or activist

**proletariat** workers who will control government after Communist revolution

**protest** declaration, usu. accompanied by some action, of disapproval for politician or policy

**putsch** sudden surprise revolt against government

**radical** advocate of extreme, sometimes violent, measures to improve society or alter established form of government

**rally** mass gathering to express protest or opinion

**rebellion** direct defiance of established government, often armed and violent

**resistance** underground organization opposing government, esp. occupying force, through sabotage

**revolt** movement of dissent, esp. armed uprising against government

**revolution** activities intended to overthrow and replace existing government with preferred system

**ringleader** leader of small group, often engaged in illegal or rebellious act

**sabotage** destruction or obstruction aimed at disrupting government authority

**safe house** refuge for political fugitive

**sit-in** obstruction of public place through refusal to leave as nonviolent protest of government policy

**terrorism** systematic use of terror as political tool

**underground** secret, usu. antigovernment, terrorist group

**unrest** unhappiness with existing government that results in minor disturbances against it

**uprising** often localized or spontaneous act of violence against government

# LAW

Courts, Legal Bodies, and the Law
Judges, Lawyers, and Others in the Court System
Laws, Procedures, and Court Proceedings
Decisions, Judgments, and Conditions
Customs, Formalities, and Practices
Crimes, Criminals, and Civil Offenders

**SEE ALSO**: Chap. 8: Marriage and Divorce; Chap. 11: Government; Chap. 12: Business and Economics; Finance; Real Estate; Chap. 24: Crime

## COURTS, LEGAL BODIES, AND THE LAW

**adjective law** branch of law dealing with rules of procedure

**administrative law** statutes governing procedures before government agencies

**admiralty law** maritime law

**appellate court** higher court that reviews decision of lower court

**appellate jurisdiction** authority of appellate court to reverse lower court decision

**assizes** former periodic sessions of English superior courts

**bar** entire body of lawyers and counselors-at-law

**bar association** local or state organization of lawyers voluntarily or mandatorily registered in that jurisdiction

**bench** entire body of judges; where judge sits in court

**canon law** codified law governing church

**case law** precedent-setting judicial opinions

**chambers** judge's private office in courthouse

**chancery** separate judicial system that administers natural right or golden rule in courts of equity without jury, used esp. for obtaining relief other than financial

**circuit court** court sitting at two or more places

**civil law** codes, statutes, and case law governing civil actions; Roman law set forth in Justinian Code

**code** systematic statement of body of law

**commercial law** body of laws governing all business transactions not covered by maritime law

**common law** precedents set by court decisions, distinguished from statute law; body of English law forming foundation of legal system

**constabulary** body organized by government to preserve public order

**constitutional law** body of decisions and precedents that results from interpreting a constitution

**court** official assembly for transaction of judicial business; session of such an assembly; chamber for such an assembly

**courthouse** building in which court of law convenes

**court of appeals** court hearing appeals of lower court decisions

**court of claims** court with jurisdiction over claims, esp. against government

**court of common pleas** former English civil superior court; intermediate court in some U.S. states with civil and criminal jurisdiction

**court of inquiry** military court that investigates military matters

**court of law** court hearing and deciding cases based on statutes and common law

**court of record** court whose acts and proceedings are kept on permanent record and that has power to impose penalties for contempt

**court of sessions** state criminal court of record

**courtroom** chamber in which court proceedings are held

**criminal court** court with jurisdiction to try and punish violators of criminal law

**criminal justice** administration and enforcement of criminal law

**criminal law** statutes and common law of crimes and their punishment

**customs court** federal court having jurisdiction over tariff law cases

**district court** trial court with jurisdiction in specific judicial district

**divorce court** court handling dissolution of marriages

**equity** natural right or justice; flexible body of law and nonjury court system, esp. for gaining relief other than financial

**federal court** court established under U.S. Constitution, esp. to deal with violations of federal statutes

**firm** partnership or association of two or more lawyers

**forum** tribunal, court of law

**grand jury** body of usu. twelve to twenty-three citizens who investigate facts to determine whether a crime has been committed and return indictment

**Hammurabi Code** ancient Babylonian code of criminal and civil law written in cuneiform characters (18th C. B.C.)

**Inns of Court** four legal societies that admit persons to the practice of law in Britain: Inner Temple, Middle Temple, Lincoln's Inn, Gray's Inn

**international law** body of rules recognized as binding between national states, based on treaties, agreements, and customs; jus gentium

**judiciary** court system; governmental branch charged with administration of justice

**jurisdiction** scope of authority of specific court to hear particular cases

**jurisprudence** system, body, or philosophy of law

**jury** body of citizens sworn to weigh evidence and decide facts of case; petit jury as opposed to grand jury

**jus gentium** *Latin*. lit. law of nations; international law based on customs of all nations in Roman law

**justice** establishment and administration of rights based on rules of law and equity

**Justinian Code** Byzantine revision and codification of Roman law with addition of Corpus of Civil Law (6th c.)

**juvenile court** court with jurisdiction over children under age of legal responsibility regarding matters of delinquency or dependency

**kangaroo court** unauthorized, irregular court operating with disregard for normal legal procedures

**law** body of recognized rules of conduct and order established and enforced by government

**law office** place of business of lawyer or law firm

**law school** institution of graduate studies for instruction in law

**legal aid** legal assistance to those who cannot afford lawyers' fees

**lex talionis** *Latin*. law of retaliation; principle of correspondence between punishment and crime, as an eye for an eye

**maritime law** branch of commercial law relating to commerce and navigation; admiralty law

**military law** system of rules governing military personnel, including establishment of tribunals

**moot court** pretend student trial

**municipal court** city or town court with jurisdiction over local criminal and civil cases

**Napoleonic Code** civil code of France and basis of civil law (early 19th c.)

**patent law** legal system for issuance and court jurisdiction over patents that protect rights of invention

**petit jury** trial jury made up usu. of twelve citizens, as distinct from grand jury

**probate court** surrogate court

**pro bono** lit. for the good (Latin); legal work undertaken on behalf of public for little or no fee

**procedural law** prescribed steps and methods of enforcing one's rights in court, opposite of substantive law

**Roman law** legal system of ancient Rome that is basis of modern civil law and English common law

**small-claims court** special court handling disputes over minor debts

**special court** court created for exceptional and temporary purpose

**substantive law** law that describes what one's legal rights are, opposite of procedural law

**superior court** court of general jurisdiction in many states

**Supreme Court** usu. highest judicial tribunal of a political entity

**surrogate court** court with jurisdiction to prove wills and administer estates and guardianships; probate court

**tax court** court that decides tax cases

**tort law** form of law settling rights of monetary damages for injuries in civil and private cases

**trial court** court in which trials are conducted

**tribunal** court of justice; seat of particular judge

**unwritten law** law based on custom rather than legislative statute

**United States District Court** USDC; court with jurisdiction in specific region

**USDC** *United States District Court*

**venue** court's geographic jurisdiction; place where significant elements of cause of action took place or where case is tried

## JUDGES, LAWYERS, AND OTHERS IN THE COURT SYSTEM

**accused** one charged with an offense; defendant in criminal case

**adversary** opposite party in litigation

**advocate** lawyer, esp. one pleading client's cause in court

**agent** person authorized to act for principal in case

**alleged** one accused of crime before proven guilty

**alternate juror** jury member chosen to fill in should regular juror be unable to continue

**amicus curiae** *Latin.* lit. friend of the court; counselor assisting and seeking to persuade court on case to which he or she is not a party

**arbitrator** private, disinterested person chosen to conduct arbitration

**associate** subordinate member of law firm

**attorney** one who acts for another, esp. in legal proceedings

**attorney-at-law** lawyer admitted to bar and qualified to litigate in court

**attorney general** chief law officer of state or nation

**attorney-in-fact** one given power of attorney to act for another but not necessarily an attorney-at-law

**bailiff** court attendant charged with keeping order and escorting prisoners in court

**barrister** counsel admitted to plead at bar and in public superior court trials (Britain)

**bencher** *Chiefly Brit.* senior member of an Inn of Court

**bondsman** one who assumes responsibility of paying bond if defendant fails to appear in court

**character witness** one who verifies another's reputation as honest and law-abiding

**chief justice** presiding judge of court, esp. Supreme Court

**circuit judge** judge presiding over circuit court

**claimant** one asserting claim, esp. in civil case

**clerk** one who keeps records, has power to issue specific writs, and files documents

**client** person hiring attorney as representative

**competent party** individual who is legally able to enter into binding contracts

**condemned** criminal sentenced to death

**conservator** person designated to protect interests of an incompetent

**convict** one found guilty of a crime

**counsel** lawyer managing court trial; lawyer advising and representing an individual, corporation, or public body on legal matters

**counselor** lawyer; counsel

**counselor-at-law** lawyer

**court** judge as embodiment of a particular court

**court attendant** low-level functionary at legal proceeding

**court officer** bailiff or other official of court

**court reporter** stenographer who records and transcribes court proceedings verbatim

**DA** *district attorney*

**defendant** party sued by plaintiff or accused by state

**defense attorney** lawyer representing a defendant

**district attorney** DA; public officer acting as lawyer for government in prosecuting criminal cases; prosecutor

**executor** one responsible for administration of decedent's estate and for carrying out terms of a will

**executrix** female executor

**eyewitness** person who actually saw crime committed

**fiduciary** one entrusted to care for another's property

**garnishee** one in possession of another's property pending settlement of debts

**guardian** one legally empowered to manage affairs of a minor or incompetent person

**heir** one who would be entitled to inherit property of deceased by intestate succession under terms of will

**hostile witness** witness unfriendly to side calling him, subject to cross-examination by that side

**judge** presiding court officer, elected or appointed

**judiciary** judges of court system

**junior partner** lawyer with lesser status and seniority among partners in firm

**jurist** judge or lawyer

**juror** member of jury

**justice** judge; member of Supreme Court

**justice of the peace** local magistrate empowered to administer oaths, perform marriages, and handle minor cases

**law clerk** law student working for lawyer or judge, usu. at low pay to learn from experience

**lawgiver** legislator; one who enacts laws

**lawmaker** legislator; one who enacts laws

**lawman** police officer; one empowered to enforce laws

**lawyer** one licensed to represent people in court and advise on legal matters; attorney or counselor-at-law

**legal secretary** specially trained secretary for lawyer

**litigant** party to a lawsuit

**litigator** lawyer who participates in court trials; trial lawyer

**magistrate** public officer, esp. judge of lower criminal court

**maker** party executing a promissory note

**marshal** officer of judicial district who executes court processes, performing duties similar to those of sheriff

**master** court representative appointed to do specific act

**material witness** witness whose testimony is essential to case

**mediator** person who settles disputes and serves as intermediary between parties

**mouthpiece** *Slang.* lawyer, esp. criminal lawyer

**notary** officer of state authorized to administer oaths and acknowledge signing of documents; notary public

**ombudsman** government official who investigates complaints against public officials

**paralegal** specially trained aid to lawyer

**partner** member of law firm who shares ownership of firm

**party** one who sues or is sued in court

**petitioner** one seeking court remedies or making formal complaint or statement of cause of action in civil suit

**pettifogger** unethical lawyer who engages in petty arguments and obstruction of justice

**plaintiff** one who complains of another by bringing court action to obtain remedy

**presiding** (*adj*) designating judge who directs court proceedings, including assigning cases to be heard by other judges

**principal** one on whose behalf an agent acts; party to contract

**process server** person who hands over process to person sought by court

**prosecutor** lawyer hired by government to conduct criminal proceeding; district attorney

**public defender** lawyer hired by government to defend accused who cannot afford lawyer's fees

**receiver** person appointed to hold property to be disposed of by court order; one who receives goods knowing they are stolen

**referee** court officer appointed to hear argument on matter whose decision is final or is reported back to court

**respondent** defendant in certain proceedings; one required to answer appeal from judgment; party replying to petition

**security** person bound to pay debt if another fails

**senior partner** ranking partner in law firm

**sheriff** elected chief law enforcement officer of county

**solicitor** personal lawyer; lower court trial lawyer who prepares cases for barristers in higher courts (Britain)

**special prosecutor** individual appointed to investigate and indict in single, exceptional case

**surety** person promising to make good another's obligation

**surrogate** judge in court that administers estates and guardianships

**talesman** bystander summoned as juror when too few are called

**tenant** one who temporarily possesses another's real property

**trial examiner** person appointed to hold hearings, investigate, and make recommendations to court

**trial lawyer** lawyer who participates in trials; litigator

**trustee** one who holds property in trust for another as a fiduciary

**ward** minor child or incompetent person in care of guardian or conservator

**witness** one who testifies under oath in judicial proceeding as to what he or she has seen or observed; one present at some event, such as the signing of a document

## LAWS, PROCEDURES, AND COURT PROCEEDINGS

**accusation** charge of wrongdoing

**acknowledgment** formal declaration that one has executed a particular legal document

**action** lawsuit or court proceeding

**adjourn** (*vb*) suspend court proceedings until later stated time

**admission** voluntary declaration of facts made by one party in suit, esp. acknowledgment of guilt

**affidavit** written statement sworn under oath before authorized officer or notary

**allegation** contention or accusation; statement by party to legal action as to what will be proved

**amended complaint** written pleading that contains additional information, allegations, or causes of action in case

**amendment** legislative modification or addition to statute or constitution

**appeal** procedure by which case is brought from lower to higher court for revised ruling or rehearing

**arbitration** investigation and resolution of dispute by persons named by involved parties, usu. agreed on in contract as way to settle dispute without formal court trial

**argument** attorney's statements in support of client's case

**arraignment** calling of accused before court to hear charges and enter plea

**arrest** restraint or detention of person by legal authority

**assignment** transfer of rights from one person to another

**assize** legislative enactment, statute; judicial inquest

**assumpsit** action to recover damages for breach of contract or verbal or implied promise

**bail** payment of bond that is forfeited if one fails to appear in court

**bench warrant** arrest order issued by judge, usu. for failure to appear in court

**bill of attainder** unconstitutional legislative act that finds person guilty of high crime and imposes sentence

**bill of particulars** statement filed in court that gives details of claim or counterclaim

**binding arbitration** arbitration stipulated in contract as obligatory to all parties

**bind over** (*vb*) put under bond to appear in court for trial; shift case to grand jury or superior court from lower court

**case** court action, cause, suit, or controversy

**cause** case, claim, or lawsuit seeking recovery from another

**certiorari** *Latin.* lit. to be made more certain; higher court's review procedure on actions of lower court or government agency

**cessation** temporary adjournment of case

**challenge** objection to prospective juror during pretrial jury selection

**charge** judge's instructions to jury at close of trial regarding what to consider in reaching verdict

**charter** state grant allowing corporation to exist

**citation** writ issued by court commanding person to appear in court and perform some duty or show cause why not

**cite** (*vb*) issue citation; call upon to appear; hold someone responsible for objectionable conduct, such as contempt

**citizen's arrest** arrest made by private citizen rather than law officer

**civil action** lawsuit between private parties, usu. to recover money, property, or remedies, or to enforce rights

**civil case** lawsuit between private parties, as distinguished from criminal case

**claim** demand for something rightfully due but possessed by another

**class action** suit brought on behalf of many persons with similar interest in alleged wrong

**closing** final exchange of title and monies in real estate transaction

**codicil** amendment or addition to will

**commital** *Chiefly Brit.* commitment

**commitment** court order to take person into custody in penal or mental institution

**community property** property recognized in some states as owned in common by spouses

**confession** voluntary admission of guilt or responsibility

**constitution** fundamental law by which state governs

**contest** (*vb*) dispute or challenge by litigation

**continuance** deferral of court proceedings to future date

**contract** voluntary, lawful, mutual agreement to do or not do something in return for consideration

**cop a plea** *Informal.* plead guilty to lesser offense to avoid standing trial for more serious one

**copyright law** law protecting exclusive ownership of and rights to artistic and intellectual properties

**counterclaim** case brought against plaintiff by defendant

**counterplea** plaintiff's reply to defendant's plea or counterclaim

**court hearing** preliminary examination of arguments by judge

**court-martial** judicial court proceeding in armed forces

**court trial** trial by judge without jury

**criminal case** charge by state against individual, brought to punish violation of criminal laws

**cross-claim** claim made by defendant against plaintiff

**cross-complaint** complaint arising from original complaint, made by defendant against codefendant or third party

**cross-examination** questioning of witness by lawyer for other party in case

**cross-question** (*vb*) *Chiefly Brit.* cross-examine

**deed** document transferring ownership of real property

**defense** reasons of law put forth as to why adversary or claim should be denied

**deliberations** jury's consideration of case to reach verdict

**depose** (*vb*) elicit testimony outside court under oath or by affidavit; take witness's deposition

**deposition** sworn testimony of witness taken outside court proceedings

**direct examination** questioning of witness by lawyer who called him or her to stand

**direct testimony** statements of witness in answer to questions posed by attorney who called him or her to stand

**discovery** pretrial fact-finding through interrogatories, depositions, and other investigative procedures

**double jeopardy** repeat prosecution for same criminal offense, prohibited by U.S. Constitution

**enter plea** place plea in court record in proper form

**ex delicto** *Latin.* lit. out of wrong; cause of action arising from crime or tort

**ex post facto** *Latin.* lit. after the fact; fixing or changing punishment for act after it was committed, now forbidden by U.S. Constitution

**fair hearing** special administrative procedure required by court when person might otherwise be denied rights without due process

**file** (*vb*) perform first act of lawsuit; place among official records, return to office of court clerk

**gag rule** court order banning all parties involved in case from publicly disclosing anything about it or reporting on it in the media

**go to trial** determine that dispute warrants trial and commence proceedings

**habeas corpus** *Latin.* lit. have the body; court order requiring that detained prisoner be produced in court to inquire into legality of detention

**hearing** preliminary court examination of contested issues in criminal or civil proceeding

**impanel** (*vb*) select jury from official list of names

**impeachment of witness** providing evidence or engaging in questioning that attacks credibility of witness

**in camera** *Latin.* lit. in chambers; judicial proceeding from which public is excluded

**indictment** criminal charge made by grand jury

**information** criminal accusation made by prosecutor rather than by grand jury indictment

**in personam** *Latin.* lit. against the person; action directed against individual or owner of property

**inquest** official inquiry or examination before jury; coroner's investigation of cause of death

**in rem** *Latin.* lit. against the thing; action directed against specific piece of property

**instructions** judge's explanation of applicable law to jury

**interrogatories** written questions answered under oath by witness before trial

**intervention** third-party protection of alleged interest in legal proceeding begun by others

**jurat** notarized certification that affidavit has been sworn to

**jury is out** sequestering of jury while it reaches verdict

**jury trial** consideration of case by jury as opposed to by judge or arbitrator

**law** rule of conduct or action formally recognized as binding and enforced by controlling authority

**lawsuit** case in court instituted by one party to achieve justice from another

**legal age** minimum age at which person has capacity to enforce legal rights and fulfill obligations

**legality** quality of being legal; obligation imposed by law

**litigation** legal case contested in court before judge

**majority** age at which person is legally responsible for his or her actions

**minutes** official records and notes of proceedings

**motion** formal oral or written request to court, seeking judge's ruling

**nolle prosequi** *Latin.* lit. not wishing to prosecute; choice by district attorney or plaintiff not to proceed with action

**nolo contendere** *Latin.* lit. I do not wish to contest; essential admission of guilt by defendant, appealing to mercy of court

**novation** substitution of new contract or obligation for an old one

**objection** lawyer's protest to judge over statement or question by opposition

**offer of proof** lawyer's explanation to judge, away from jury, of intentions on some point

**open court** proceedings that are accessible to public

**own recognizance** condition of release of accused person without payment of bail

**patent** government grant of exclusive intellectual property rights for an invention

**peremptory challenge** veto challenge by lawyer to prospective juror that precludes any debate

**personal injury** physical damage to body, usu. as a result of accident or negligence, forming grounds for suit

**plea** legal suit or action; defendant's answer to plaintiff's declaration; accused's answer to criminal charge

**plea bargaining** agreement whereby defendant pleads guilty to reduced charge

**plead** (*vb*) argue case in court of law; make allegation or answer previous pleading

**post bail** pay bond to guarantee appearance in court

**power of attorney** written authority allowing one person to act for another in specific situations

**preliminary hearing** hearing before magistrate to determine whether sufficient evidence exists to justify trial

**presentment** accusation by grand jury, based on its own investigations

**press charges** pursue accusations into court action

**pretrial hearing** meeting in which lawyers and judge plan procedures for upcoming trial

**preventive detention** holding of prisoner without bail or on very high bail

**prior restraint** court order prohibiting publication or broadcast of certain material, generally not used in society committed to free speech and freedom of the press

**probate** proof that will is valid and genuine

**proceeding** legal action, esp. in court

**process** summons, subpoena, or warrant used to compel witness or party to appear in court

**process service** service

**prosecution** government proceeding in court against person accused of crime

**rebuttal** reply; evidence counter to that of opponent

**recess** brief break in court proceedings

**reconvene** (*vb*) continue court proceedings after recess

**recording** public filing of documents to give notice to interested parties

**reference** proceeding in which matter is heard by referee

**replevin** action to recover actual item of personal property rather than its value in damages

**restraining order** court order barring one party in suit from contacting, harassing, or acting against another

**RICO** *Racketeer Influenced and Corrupt Organization;* statute detailing laws relating to organized crime

**search warrant** court order authorizing search of certain premises or persons for stolen or illegal property

**sequester** (*vb*) isolate jury in private place for purposes of discussion and reaching a verdict

**service** physical act of handing warrant or subpoena to person who is required to appear in court; process service

**stand trial** defend oneself in court of law, usu. against criminal charges

**statute** legislative act with power of law

**statute of limitations** legislative act limiting time in which plaintiff may bring civil suit or state may bring criminal action and also limiting period of liability

**statutory** (*adj*) designating crime or law enacted by legislature

**stipulation** arrangement agreed upon between parties

**subpoena** (*vb*) *Latin.* lit. under penalty; command to appear in court and testify

**substituted service** process service by mail, newspaper publication, or to third party when person named cannot be found

**sue** (*vb*) bring suit against another, usu. to collect damages

**suit** court action or proceeding to recover rights or make claim

**summons** court paper announcing suit and stating time for court appearance

**tender** (*vb*) offer money or property to fulfill an obligation

**testimony** oral evidence given by witness under oath

**tort** civil wrong or injury, other than breach of contract, that is grounds for suit

**transcript** written record of court proceedings; copy of document

**trial** court examination of facts to decide issue in dispute

**trial by jury** usu. criminal trial decided by jury of citizens

**true bill** grand jury endorsement of indictment as warranting trial

**venire facias** *Latin.* lit. make come; writ summoning jurors to court

**voir dire** *French.* lit. to speak truly; preliminary examination of qualifications of juror or witness

**waiver** intentional abandonment of right

**warrant** court order authorizing action by public officer, usu. arrest or search and seizure

**writ** written court order issued to serve administration of justice, usu. stipulating that something be done or not be done

**writ of certiorari** request by higher court for case records for review

## DECISIONS, JUDGMENTS, AND CONDITIONS

**abandonment** relinquishing of possession of property without intent to recover it

**abatement** termination, esp. of nuisance; reduction from full amount, esp. of tax

**abeyance** temporary suspension or inactivity

**abolition** act of annulling or completely destroying

**accountable** (*adj*) answerable, responsible for some action

**acquittal** not-guilty verdict absolving accused party from guilt

**adjudication** judicial determination, decision, or sentence

**advisory opinion** nonbinding court opinion on legal question submitted by government official but not on specific case

**alimony** court-ordered payment to be made by one spouse to former spouse in divorce case

**amerce** (*vb*) punish by fine in amount fixed by court

**annul** (*vb*) cancel or make void, esp. marriage deemed void from beginning

**arrogate** (*vb*) claim, seize, or assume without justification

**assessment** determination of amount of damages, fine, or tax

**attachment** taking another's property by legal process, esp. as payment of debt

**award** final judgment; decision of arbitrators on case; document containing arbitrators' decision

**bailment** condition in which one person has possession of another's personal property, with responsibility for its protection

**bankruptcy** procedure used when person's total assets are insufficient to cover debts

**beat the rap** evade penalties connected with charge; receive not-guilty verdict (slang)

**bequest** gift by will of personal property

**binder** preliminary real estate or insurance agreement

**capital punishment** execution as criminal sentence

**cease and desist** order prohibiting a specific activity; mandatory injunction

**clear of charges** acquit; find not guilty

**clemency** reduction of sentence, usu. by executive branch

**community service** punishment requiring convicted person to perform unpaid work for community instead of serving term of imprisonment

**commutation** reduction of sentence after conviction

**compensatory damages** damages measured by harm suffered or loss incurred

**compurgation** clearing of accused by oaths of persons swearing to his or her innocence

**condemnation** unfavorable judgment, conviction; judgment by which authority confiscates private property

**conditions** terms of agreement or settlement

**condonation** forgiveness, esp. in spousal adultery

**consent decree** consent judgment

**consent judgment** judicial decree sanctioning voluntary agreement between parties in dispute to cease activity and drop action; consent decree

**consignment** delivery of property for sale by another with proceeds, less commission, returned to consignor

**conveyance** transfer of ownership title in real property

**conviction** guilty verdict in criminal trial

**costs** expenses other than attorney's fees incurred in litigation, sometimes awarded to prevailing party to be paid by losing party

**countermand** (*vb*) revoke an order or decree

**court order** decree issued by court, usu. requiring party to do or not do something

**cure** (*vb*) make acceptable any defective evidence or charges by admission of certain other evidence

**custody** care and keeping of something, esp. parent's right to raise child in divorce case

**damages** compensation sought by or awarded to litigant for loss or injury

**decision** verdict or determination in case

**declaratory judgment** determination stating legal rights or duties or interpretation

**decree** final decision and judgment of court

**default judgment** judicial decision rendered without trial proceedings, usu. due to default by one party, esp. failure to appear in court

**devise** gift of real property by will

**dictum** portion of opinion contained in court decision that is not essential for deciding narrowest construction of the facts

**directed verdict** judge's decision in civil case so one-sided that reasonable minds could not conclude otherwise and jury need not hear it

**disbarment** expulsion of attorney from legal profession; revocation of right to practice law

**disclaimer** act of declining to accept gift by will or trust, thereby allowing it to pass to next beneficiary entitled to it

**disculpate** (*vb*) acquit of charges

**dismiss** (*vb*) throw case out of court, drop charges; relieve hung jury of duties

**dissent** minority opposition to majority judgment

**dissenting opinion** written minority opinion in opposition to majority

**distrain** (*vb*) seize and hold goods as compensation due or to obtain satisfaction of claim

**divorce** legal dissolution of valid marriage

**drop charges** dismiss case; cease prosecution

**enforcement** effective carrying out of laws

**entail** rule of descent for estate beyond one generation, so that individual heir may not dispose of it

**entry of judgment** official statement and recording of decision

**escheat** turning of decedent's property over to state when no heirs are found

**execution of judgment** collection of award or enactment of sentence

**extradition** transfer of accused fugitive from state where arrested to state where charged

**finding** basis in fact or law for judgement

**fine** money payment required by decision

**foreclosure** procedure forcing sale of property to meet unpaid obligation

**garnishment** collection of judgment debt by interception of money owed to debtor

**grant** transfer of real property or interest therein

**guilty** (*adj*) found justly responsible for offense and liable to punishment

**hung jury** trial jury unable to reach minimum consensus needed for verdict

**immunity** protection of potentially incriminated witness or informer from prosecution based on information given

**indemnify** (*vb*) secure against loss or damage

**indemnity** exemption from penalties or liabilities; reimbursement for loss sustained

**injunction** court order directing someone to do or not do something

**instrument** formal legal document, such as deed, bond, or contract

**interdict** prohibitory act or decree of court

**interlocutory decree** temporary court decision that becomes final after certain time period

**intestate** (*adj*) having died without a will

**joint custody** sharing of child's upbringing by divorced parents

**judgment** court's final decision on matter in favor of plaintiff or defendant

**lease** agreement by which tenant rents property from landlord

**legacy** gift of property or bequest by will

**levy** seizure of property to satisfy judgment

**liability** legal obligation, duty, or accountability

**license** permissive right to do something granted by authority or by owner

**lien** claim on property for debt

**living trust** trust that takes effect during life of its creator

**mandamus** *Latin.* lit. we command; superior court writ ordering specific act or duty

**mandatory injunction** cease and desist order

**martial law** suspension of judicial procedures and imposition of military rule by executive branch of government in emergency circumstance

**mistrial** trial without legal effect due to error or prejudicial misconduct in proceedings

**mitigation of damages** steps taken by victim of wrongdoer to reduce monetary harm in civil case

**moratorium** legally authorized period of delay for performance of some obligation

**naturalization** granting of citizenship to one born in another country

**nominal damages** token award to party when court or jury finds in his or her favor but feels no serious damage has been sustained

**not guilty** designating defendant's plea or jury's verdict that law was not violated

**notice** formal indication between parties of intention to exercise right or terminate agreement at specific time; notification to person whose interests may be affected by upcoming proceeding

**nullity** state of being legally invalid

**obligation** duty or payment owed to another

**on the merits** judgment based on facts of case, not legal technicality

**opinion** formal court decision with factual determinations and legal reasons supporting it

**order** judgment or formal direction of court to do or not do something; request for silence in courtroom

**out-of-court settlement** agreement reached between parties in civil suit before or outside court proceedings

**pardon** executive act releasing convict from court sentence of punishment

**parole** release of prisoner after serving sentence, with assurance that he or she will abide by law

**per curiam** *Latin.* lit. by the court; unanimous decision of all judges on court

**precedent** former decision based on same or similar facts used as guide for judicial reasoning in current action

**probation** relief from all or part of prison sentence on promise of proper conduct

**promissory note** written promise to pay money to another

**property execution** enforcement of judgment involving property

**proprietary** (*adj*) having exclusive legal right to use, make, or market

**public policy** court's right to refuse to honor contract that undermines public good

**punitive damages** damages in excess of actual loss awarded to wronged plaintiff to punish defendant

**quash** (*vb*) set aside for insufficient grounds

**quit claim** deed releasing all claims against real property

**ratification** agreement that confirms previous action

**recovery** gaining by legal process

**redress** (*vb*) remove or make right a cause of complaint

**release** discharging or giving up of claim or rights in settlement

**remand** (*vb*) return to custody pending further trial or detention; return case from appellate to lower court for further proceedings

**remedy** legal means to recover right or obtain redress for wrong; relief given by court for wrong

**remittitur** *Latin*. lit. it is sent back; reduction of damages awarded at trial that are deemed to be excessive

**reprieve** delay in execution of sentence

**rescission** cancellation, annulment, or vacating of law, judgment, or contract, as by restoration to opposite party of what one has received from that party

**restitution** restoration to rightful owner; making good or providing equivalent for some harm

**reversal** judicial decision to overturn lower court ruling

**reversion** return of title to real estate to former owner or owner's heirs at termination of temporary grant

**review** judicial reexamination, esp. of lower court proceedings

**revoke** (*vb*) annul or rescind a document, decision, or offer

**satisfaction** discharge of legal obligation, esp. compensation for loss or injury

**sentence** court judgment stating punishment in criminal case

**set aside** (*vb*) annul or override jury's verdict, done by judge

**settlement** resolution of civil case, usu. without trial

**specific performance** obligation to carry out contractually promised performance when breach cannot be compensated by award of money

**stay** delay or suspension of legal proceedings, esp. execution of sentence

**stay of execution** limited suspension of judgment, usu. to allow appeal

**sub judice** *Latin*. lit. under a judge; awaiting judicial determination, therefore not open to public discussion

**summary judgment** judicial decision in civil case, usu. pretrial, deciding particular issues or entire matter

**supplementary proceedings** court action to collect judgment

**surcharge** award of damages imposed on one owing fiduciary duties to trust or estate

**suspended sentence** deferment of punishment, usu. over period of probation

**temporary restraining order** court order barring one party from action that might harm another, esp. through physical contact, until hearing on specific date

**testament** will, usu. restricted to personal property

**testamentary trust** trust created by will that comes into existence when probate court orders deceased's estate assets distributed to trustee

**trust** arrangement in which person or institution holds legal title to property with obligation to care for it for the benefit of another

**unanimous verdict** agreement of all jurors, required for criminal conviction

**verdict** decision of jury

**void** (*adj*) having no effect; without legal force to bind

**will** declaration on disposition of property and guardianship of minor children, taking effect upon death

**without prejudice** (*adv*) final and binding in accordance with res judicata

## CUSTOMS, FORMALITIES, AND PRACTICES

**abstract of title** compiled history of land ownership

**actus reus** *Latin*. wrongful act, as distinct from intent behind it

**admissible** (*adj*) allowable in court, being pertinent to case, esp. with regard to evidence

**alibi** proof that accused was not physically present at scene of crime; excuse

**ambit** sphere or limit of action or complaint

**amicus brief** statement or report by friend of court

**ancillary** (*adj*) supplementary, subordinate, esp. such evidence

**attest** (*vb*) witness a document in writing

**bail bond** obligation to pay bail if defendant fails to appear in court

**bar exam** lengthy test prospective lawyer must pass before being authorized to practice law in specific jurisdiction

**base fee** estate held from lord on condition of performing some service in feudal Britain

**bond** written, sealed obligation to pay sum of money

**bounty** payment promised for capture of fugitive outlaw

**brief** lawyer's written presentation of statutory and case law to support client's case

**burden of proof** duty to produce evidence to prove disputed facts, which lies with prosecutor in criminal case and with plaintiff in civil case

**calendar** schedule of cases coming to trial

**capacity** ability to understand facts and implications of one's behavior

**caseload** number of cases handled by court or lawyer in particular period

**causes of action** facts or specific complaints giving one party right to bring civil case against another

**caveat** *Latin*. lit. let him beware; warning

**charge** judge's instructions to jury; criminal accusation

**chattel** item of personal property other than real property and land

**circumstantial evidence** indirect evidence not based on direct observation that tends to prove other facts

**civil liability** legal obligations under civil law

**civil rights** personal liberties guaranteed by U.S. Constitution, its amendments, and acts of Congress

**closing statement** lawyer's summation of case to judge or jury

**collateral** (*adj*) incidental or additional to matter being discussed

**comity** courtesy rule by which courts recognize decisions of other courts and other states

**competency** minimum requirements to qualify as witness or party to contract or to serve in some capacity

**complaint** plaintiff's written claim in court proceedings

**compliance** conformity in fulfilling legal obligations

**confidential communications** exchanges, esp. between client and lawyer, protected from disclosure to others by legal privilege

**consensual** (*adj*) existing or made by mutual consent but usu. unwritten

**consideration** thing or act of value that one party provides another when entering into contract

**constitutional** (*adj*) in accordance with or authorized by constitution

**corpus delicti** *Latin*. lit. body of the crime; proof that crime has been committed and that charges should be brought

**corroboration** evidence from two or more witnesses that is identical or supports the other's word

**courtesy** rules of appropriate conduct in legal proceedings; favors and allowances granted by one lawyer to another

**covenant** written promise, esp. owner's obligations in deed on property

**cui bono** *Latin*. lit. to whose advantage; principle that probable responsibility for an act lies with one having something to gain by it

**de facto** *Latin*. lit. actual, in reality; how matters are by custom, though not required by law to be thus

**de jure** *Latin*. lit. by right, by law; how the law requires that matters be

**demonstrative evidence** evidence that is conclusive in proving something

**direct evidence** proof given by those who saw acts or heard words in question

**disclosure** descriptive information and revelations, esp. in patent application

**docket** court's official record of proceedings and calendar of upcoming cases

**document** (*vb*) provide written evidence as proof of something

**domicile** person's sole permanent legal residence

**due process** orderly administration of justice by proper court according to established rules and laws, entitling one to proper notice and fair opportunity to be heard

**earnest money** deposit or token sum paid as binder or to indicate intention to consummate deal

**eminent domain** government right to take private property for public use with just compensation

**encumbrance** right in real property held by third party that diminishes its value

**estate** grouping of all property of person, esp. deceased, in legal category

**estoppel** doctrine precluding change of one's previous position to detriment of others

**evidence** everything considered by court or jury to settle question of what truly is fact

**exclusionary rule** prohibition from use at criminal trial of evidence obtained by unreasonable search and seizure

**exhibit** physical object or paper used as evidence

**ex parte** *Latin*. lit. from or on one side; partisan communications with one party to dispute absent, as between one lawyer and judge

**extraterritoriality** immunity and exemption from arrest enjoyed by diplomats

**fair use** conditions under which copyright material may be used by another

**fee** lawyer's charge for his or her services

**fee simple** unencumbered ownership of real property without limitation to particular class of heirs

**fiduciary** position of high trust and confidence required of one entrusted with care of another's property

**flagrante delicto** *Latin*. lit. while the crime is burning; caught in the act of committing a crime

**forensics** relation of principles and facts from another profession, such as medicine, to legal proceedings

**freedom of the seas** principle of international law that holds that no state has sovereignty beyond its territorial waters

**gavel** wooden mallet used by judge to call court to order

**grandfather clause** legal provision that exempts a business or class of persons from new regulations that would affect prior rights and privileges

**gravamen** most significant part of grievance or complaint

**hearsay evidence** inadmissible secondhand evidence, usu. told to witness by another

**holograph** will or document in handwriting of its maker

**hornbook** general treatise or primer on some aspect of law

**immaterial evidence** facts of no consequence or relevance in deciding issues before court

**inadmissible evidence** facts not legally allowable as part of a case

**insanity plea** not-guilty plea based on accused's inability to comprehend wrongful conduct

**intellectual property** individual's creative or artistic work, protectable under copyright or patent law

**intent** design or resolve with which one acts; external manifestation of an inward will

**intestate succession** passage of ownership interests in property from decedent without will to successors determined by state law

**irrelevant evidence** evidence unrelated to issue before court

**J.D.** *Latin*. Juris Doctor; Doctor of Laws degree; Doctor of Jurisprudence

**J.D.S.** Doctor of Juridical Science degree

**jeopardy** defendant's risk of conviction and punishment when brought to trial

**judicial notice** court's acceptance of well-known facts as true without evidence

**judicial review** doctrine that court system may annul legislative or executive acts deemed unconstitutional

**jury duty** obligation of citizen to serve on jury

**laches** unreasonable delay that bars party from pursuing legal claim

**law-abiding** (*adj*) obedient to the law

**lawful** (*adj*) in accordance with established law

**law journal** publication of and for legal profession

**lawless** (*adj*) not regulated or restrained by law

**law review** law school publication with authoritative articles on legal trends or developments, written and edited by top students

**lawyering** practice of law; functions of an attorney

**leading question** question by lawyer that suggests answer desired from person being questioned

**legal** (*adj*) conforming to rules of law; related to practice of law

**legalese** jargon and argot of lawyers and court system

**legalism** legal term or expression; strict conformity to law

**lis pendens** *Latin.* lawsuit pending and listed on court docket; document announcing pending litigation

**litigious** (*adj*) prone to engage in lawsuits

**LL.B.** *Latin. Legum Baccalaureus*; Bachelor of Laws degree

**LL.D.** *Latin. Legum Doctor*; Doctor of Laws degree

**LL.M.** *Latin. Legum Magister*; Master of Laws degree

**malice aforethought** premeditated evil or antisocial intent

**material evidence** facts with significant bearing on case

**mens rea** *Latin.* lit. guilty mind; criminal intent required for conviction of particular crime

**merits** intrinsic nature of case apart from procedural matters

**mitigating circumstances** conditions under which crime was committed that reduce punishment due

**motive** implied reason for action, as distinct from intent

**non compos mentis** *Latin.* lit. of unsound mind; used to indicate insanity, temporary or permanent, and lesser forms of mental incompetence that make person unfit to stand trial

**oath** affirmation or solemn pledge binding one to tell the truth according to the law, after which false statements are punishable as perjury

**opening statement** outline of position and proposed proof by lawyer near start of trial

**overrule** (*vb*) refuse to honor lawyer's objection, esp. judicial refusal to do so

**personal property** all tangibles and intangibles in which one may hold interests of ownership other than real property

**physical evidence** objects presented to court that have bearing on trial

**pleadings** court papers in which parties assert allegations or contentions in support of positions

**polling the jury** asking each juror in open court to confirm concurrence with verdict

**practice** scope, priority, and manner in which one conducts legal suits, esp. the business of being a lawyer

**premeditation** prior intent or design to commit crime

**preponderance of proof** evidence that outweighs that of opposition

**presumption of law** rule binding judges or juries to draw certain inferences from facts

**prima facie** *Latin.* lit. at first sight; sufficient evidence to prove case unless contradicted

**privileged communications** statements and confidences that cannot be inquired into by others or made basis for suit, esp. between lawyer and client, husband and wife, or doctor and patient

**probable cause** having good reason to believe a crime has occurred and sufficient basis for arrest and accusation but not conviction

**pro forma** *Latin.* lit. as a matter of form; carried out with proper formality

**proof** establishment of fact in court by presentation of evidence

**property** something owned, esp. a piece of land or real estate; ownership or right of possession

**proxy** authority to act for another; document granting such authority

**public domain** unprotected status of intellectual property whose copyright has expired or that never had copyright

**quantum meruit** *Latin.* lit. according to what he deserves; reasonable value of services rendered

**read rights** state legal rights to person at time of arrest, required of arresting officer

**real property** real estate; land or buildings on it

**reasonable doubt** principle of law establishing criteria jury must apply to prosecution's case in order to return guilty verdict

**relevant** (*adj*) logically connected to case, esp. evidence

**represent** (*vb*) act as lawyer for client

**res ipsa loquitur** *Latin.* lit. the thing speaks for itself; rule of negligence based on occurrence itself though defendant was absent

**res judicata** *Latin.* lit. the matter has been decided; rule that case decided in court may not be pressed again by same parties and that decision is therefore final

**respondeat superior** *Latin.* lit. let superior give answer; doctrine transferring liability for agent's negligence to principal

**retainer** advance fee paid on hiring lawyer's services

**rights** proprietary interest in intangible thing; something one may claim as justly due; protections guaranteed by law and constitution

**scilicet** (*adv*) *Latin.* lit. to wit; used in affidavits at place of swearing

**seal** imprint on document certifying authenticity

**security** pledge of money or property as means of assuring payment of debt or performance of some act

**self-defense** act of repelling physical assault by force, used as plea to justify otherwise criminal act

**self-incrimination** statement that implicates oneself in a crime

**show cause** provide good reason why something should or should not be done in case, usu. ordered of litigant

**sovereign immunity** rule that government may not be sued without its consent

**speculation** expression of opinion for which one has no direct evidence; mere conjecture, esp. by witness

**ss** scilicet

**stand** witness stand

**stare decisis** *Latin.* lit. to stand by decided matters; doctrine of following rules and principles from previous judicial decisions unless they contravene general principles of justice

**strike** (*vb*) eliminate from official record of court proceedings

**subrogation** assumption of obligations of another party

**substantive** (*adj*) having a bearing on fundamental rights and merits as opposed to procedural aspects of case

**summation** lawyer's final argument and closing statement to jury

**suppress** (*vb*) keep secret by failure to disclose, esp. evidence

**sustain** (*vb*) grant lawyer's objection, esp. judicial decision to do so

**tangible property** physical objects taken as property, as distinguished from real and intellectual properties

**title** evidence or right of property ownership

**trademark** distinguishing design, symbol, or words used by manufacturer or dealer to identify product or service from competitors, registered by its owner and designated ™

**trial date** day set for commencing trial

**ultra vires** (*adj*) *Latin.* lit. beyond strength; designating acts beyond scope of corporate charter

**under advisement** with careful deliberation or consultation, esp. by judge

**unjust enrichment** doctrine that prevents profit at another's expense

**usufruct** legal right to use or enjoy profits of another's property

**vital statistics** public records of births, deaths, and marriages

**warranty** promise related to contract

**witness box** witness stand

**witness stand** space in courtroom occupied by witness while testifying; stand; witness box

**wrongful death** condition giving survivors right to sue for damages in death caused by some person or persons

**your honor** proper form of address to judge

## CRIMES, CRIMINALS, AND CIVIL OFFENDERS

**abduction** kidnapping, esp. of underage female for sex or prostitution

**accessory** one who unlawfully aids a criminal

**accessory after the fact** one who helps criminal elude arrest

**accessory before the fact** one who induces or counsels another to commit a crime

**accessory during the fact** one who witnesses a crime but does nothing to prevent it

**accomplice** criminal's active partner in crime

**adultery** voluntary sexual intercourse between married person and nonspouse

**aggravated assault** common assault combined with intent to commit another crime or with use of deadly weapon

**arson** willful and malicious burning of another's property

**assault** threat or attempt to inflict physical harm on another

**battery** unlawful act of touching, beating, or inflicting physical violence on another person; assault

**bigamy** state of having two or more living spouses

**blackmail** extortion by threat

**breach** violation of law, failure to meet obligation

**breach of contract** violation by one party having contractual duty or obligation

**breaking and entering** entry into another's property, forcibly or with criminal intent

**bribery** payment offered for favors, esp. to public officer

**brutality** unlawful ruthlessness or harshness, esp. by legal authorities

**burglary** unlawful presence in a building to commit crime, esp. theft

**capital crime** offense punishable by death

**civil offense** violation of civil statutes

**coercion** force or compulsion used to make person act against his or her will

**collusion** cooperation between persons to commit crime

**compounding a crime** offense of agreeing not to prosecute in return for a consideration

**concealment** fraudulent hiding of material facts

**condemned** (adj) sentenced to death for crime

**connivance** aiding in another's illegal act, thereby consenting to it

**conspiracy** agreement between two or more persons to commit illegal act or use unlawful means to carry out legal act

**contempt of court** willful disobedience or disdain for court rules

**contravention** opposition to or violation of a law

**contributory negligence** plaintiff's conduct held partly responsible for injury in negligence case

**convict** one found guilty of a crime

**crime** violation of public law punishable by state

**criminal** one found guilty of violating the law

**criminal liability** responsibility, with punishments due, for violation of criminal laws

**defamation** harm to another's reputation by libel or slander

**default** failure to fulfill legal obligation, esp. failure to appear in court when case is called

**delict** wrongful act, usu. misdemeanor, for which injured party is entitled to compensation

**disorderly conduct** any of various activities that disturb public peace

**duress** force, compulsion, threat, or pressure that deprives another person of free will

**embezzlement** appropriation of property by one to whom it has been entrusted

**extortion** act of taking another's money or property by threat or duress, esp. under pretext of authority

**false pretense** taking another's property by trickery or fraud

**felon** one convicted of serious crime or felony

**felony** serious crime, punishable by imprisonment in penitentiary and loss of some rights

**forgery** act of making, altering, or counterfeiting a document or signature with intent to deceive

**frame** (vb) Informal. contrive false evidence to make innocent party appear guilty

**fraud** perversion of truth with intent to deceive

**graft** bribery, esp. of public official

**grand larceny** theft of personal property exceeding specified value

**homicide** unlawful taking of human life

**infraction** violation of law, usu. a misdemeanor

**infringement** unauthorized use of patented or copyrighted invention or intellectual property

**injury** violation of person's rights so as to cause damage

**involuntary manslaughter** taking of human life through criminal negligence

**jury tampering** contact with jury member by lawyer to exert illegal influence

**kidnapping** willful abduction or detention of another against his or her will

**larceny** wrongful possession or use of another's property

**lawbreaker** one who violates the law

**lawless** (adj) not regulated or restrained by law

**libel** written statement defaming another's reputation

**malfeasance** act wrongful in itself or which perpetrator had no right to do, esp. performed by public official

**malicious mischief** willful or reckless damage to another person's property

**malpractice** wrongful conduct by a professional, through neglect or lack of ethics

**manslaughter** taking of human life without malicious intent

**mayhem** willful damage or violence to another person

**misdemeanor** lesser offense than felony, punishable by fine or imprisonment in jail but not penitentiary

**misfeasance** wrongful performance of lawful act

**moral turpitude** depraved, immoral, antisocial behavior

**murder** taking of another's life, esp. by deliberate and premeditated design

**negligence** failure to act in a reasonably prudent manner to protect interests of others, often encompassing recklessness

**nonfeasance** failure to do something one is duty-bound to do

**nuisance** wrongful use of one's property, causing damage or inconvenience to another

**obscenity** purveying of something having indecent, offensive content without redeeming value

**obstruction of justice** hindrance to or prevention of completion of the legal process

**offense** breach of criminal or civil law

**peculation** embezzlement of public funds

**perjury** false statement made under oath

**petty larceny** theft of personal property of less than legally specified value

**principal** chief wrongdoer in crime

**racketeering** operation of business characterized by systematically dishonest practices

**rape** sexual intercourse forced on another person, usu. a woman

**receiver** one who accepts goods knowing they are stolen

**reckless endangerment** action that could result in injury to another though it may not have

**resisting arrest** attempting to evade or physically prevent one's arrest

**robbery** theft aggravated by force or threat of assault

**skip bail** fail to appear in court after posting bail bond, which is then forfeited

**slander** defamation of another's reputation by spoken falsehoods

**smuggling** import or export of goods that are outlawed or in avoidance of customs duty

**sodomy** unnatural sexual intercourse, esp. anal or oral

**statutory rape** sexual activity with person under the age of consent

**subornation** inducement to commit illegal act, esp. perjury

**trespass** illegal entry of another's property or injurious encroachment on another's rights

**undue influence** threat or improper persuasion that overcomes one's free will to govern actions

**usury** practice of charging higher interest rate than allowed by law

**vandalism** wanton and malicious damage to another's property

**voluntary manslaughter** taking of human life with mitigating circumstances

# PUBLISHING AND THE PRESS

Publishing
Publications
Journalism
Newspaper Names

**SEE ALSO**: Chap. 5: Telecommunications; Chap. 12: Advertising; Chap. 14: Literature; Chap. 15: Television and Radio; Chap. 16: Graphic Design and Printing; Photography; Chap. 18: Grammar, Phonetics, and Linguistics

# PUBLISHING

**aa** designation for author's alterations on galley proofs, for which compositor must be paid

**ABA** *American Booksellers Association*; its annual spring trade convention for the publishing industry

**abridge** (*vb*) shorten or condense a text

**academic press** publishing house usu. specializing in scholarly works, often owned by university; university press

**acknowledgments** author's credit and thanks to family, colleagues, assistants, contributors, editors, and researchers, usu. in front matter

**acquisitions editor** publishing house editor who reviews and secures new writers and projects

**ad card** list of author's books, usu. facing title page; card page

**addendum** supplementary information published after book's initial publication

**advance** publisher's payment to author that is earned back from a percentage of book's income from sales and subsidiary rights

**advance copy** copy of book available before publication date

**appendix** supplementary information or material at back of book

**author** writer, esp. of books

**author's tour** promotional trip by author to publicize book's publication

**backlist** list of publisher's previous publications still in print

**back matter** information following main body of book text, including appendix, index, bibliography, and/or glossary

**bestseller** book that sells extremely well, usu. for a short period of time

**bibliography** list of source materials and related readings

**binding** spine, cover, and end papers of bound volume

**blockbuster** enormous bestseller

**blueline** contact print from offset negative that is final proof before press run; blues

**blue-pencil** (*vb*) make editor's corrections, usu. in blue pencil

**blues** *Informal.* blueline

**blurb** comment, usu. from well-known person or authority, praising book, used in promotion and advertising; puff

**boards** rigid covers for book, attached at spine

**bodice ripper** *Informal.* cheap, sensationalist, often hackneyed romantic or thriller novel

**BOM proof** cut and bound proof of uncorrected galleys, orig. made for submission to Book-of-the-Month Club

**bookbinding** process of fitting printed pages into protective covers to form book

**book club** membership organization offering books for sale through mail

**book jacket** often decorative, removable paper cover that protects book binding and usu. gives information about book and author

**bookman** one who sells books for a publisher; sales rep

**bookplate** label identifying book's owner

**bookseller** person in retail business of selling books

**bookstall** stand where books are sold, esp. outdoors

**bookstore** retail business establishment that stocks and sells books

**bound galleys** uncorrected galleys cut and bound in book-like form for final corrections and revisions

**buckram binding** coarse cotton or linen stiffened with glue or sizing for binding books

**bulk** thickness of book, based on weight of paper and number of pages

**caption** description under illustration or photograph

**card page** ad card

**caret** proofreader's mark indicating place where material is to be inserted

**case** book cover ready to be fitted with pages

**cast off** (*vb*) estimate number of pages a manuscript will make in book form

**censorship** practice of removing or restricting material published

**chain** national network of bookstores owned by one company

**chapter opening** first page of new chapter

**chapter title** heading for book chapter

**children's books** juvenile books

**clothbound** (*adj*) designating hardbound book with cloth-covered boards

**colophon** publisher's logo or identifying mark

**contents** list of book parts, including chapters, bibliography, index, and illustrations

**copy** material to be printed and published

**copyediting** correction and revision of grammatical, stylistic, and factual elements of book

**copyeditor** person who corrects and revises grammatical, stylistic, and factual elements of book

**copyreader** person who checks proofs or copy for errors

**copyright** exclusive legal right to publish and sell a written work, designated ©

**crane** cut and bound uncorrected galley proof

**crime novel** fiction genre that focuses on criminal acts and characters

**dedication** inscription of book to person or cause

**desktop publishing** publication of materials using personal computers and printers with graphic capabilities and various type fonts

**detective novel** fiction genre emphasizing crime detection

**dime novel** melodramatic or sensational novel of late 19th and early 20th century, sold in paperback for ten cents

**dust cover** protective paper jacket around hardbound book; dust jacket; jacket

**dust jacket** dust cover

**edit** (*vb*) work on written material, esp. with writers, to prepare it for publication

**edition** particular imprint or publishing run of book

**editor** person who works with writers and prepares written material for publication

**editorial director** supervisor of editorial staff and policies of publishing house; editor in chief

**editor in chief** policymaking executive and principal editor, esp. of magazine or journal; editorial director

**educational publishing** publication of textbooks

**end papers** decorative binding papers inside book cover

**epilogue** additional commentary at end of book

**errata slip** list of errors in a publication with their corrections, inserted on a separate sheet of paper slipped into book

**excerpt** passage of book reproduced, esp. for review

**ex libris** *Latin*. lit. from the library; owner's bookplate

**faction** blend of actual events and people into fictional story

**f and g's** printed, *folded*, *gathered* sheets ready for binding into book form

**fascicle** one section of book published in separate parts

**fiction** imaginative work involving invented prose narrative

**first edition** book printed in first print run of publication

**flyleaf** blank leaf in front or back of book

**folio** book page size; one-half sheet of foolscap

**footnote** note at page bottom with additional information or commentary on text

**foreword** introductory statement

**format** physical dimensions of publication

**frontispiece** illustrated page preceding title page of book

**front matter** material preceding book's main text, esp. acknowledgments, dedication, foreword, and introduction

**galley proof** first printed correction proof, orig. pulled from type in galley tray

**gathering** section in book, usu. a sheet cut into various leaves

**genre** distinct literary category such as poetry, thriller, detective novel, or gothic novel

**ghost writer** person who writes for another person, under that person's name, without receiving credit as author

**glossary** list of defined vocabulary terms used in text

**gothic novel** fiction genre using melodramatic, dark, romantic, and often frightening elements

**government press** state-operated publishing house

**hack** writer aiming at commercial success who produces banal and mediocre work; writer able to produce assigned work competently and quickly

**half title** title set on first page of book and before beginning of text

**hard copy** printout of text stored on computer

**hardcover** book bound in stiff boards rather than paper

**holiday reading** diverting books intended for readers on vacation

**house** publishing house

**house style** editorial style of particular publishing company

**imprint** publisher's name printed on book's title page; division within publishing house

**index** list of names, terms, ideas, and facts in book arranged alphabetically with page numbers for location in text

**in-print** (*adj*) designating book currently available for sale

**International Standard Book Number** ISBN; unique number code imprinted on book

**introduction** formal statement of intention or scope of book

**ISBN** International Standard Book Number

**jacket** dust cover

**juvenile books** books of fiction or nonfiction for children, often illustrated

**Kirkus Reviews** *Trademark*. book review service

**launch** promotional sales campaign at time of publication

**leader** book expected to sell best during particular season and receiving greatest attention and promotion from publisher, esp. paperback

**leaf** single sheet or page

**lexicon** listing of words in one language

**line editing** working line by line through manuscript to improve and clarify tone, text, sequence, phrasing, and style

**list** publisher's catalog of new titles to be published in particular season, esp. spring or fall

**literary agent** author's representative, esp. in sale and contract negotiations with publisher

**literary publishing** publication of literature, as opposed to purely commercial fiction and nonfiction

**literary work** written work of literary merit, esp. of imaginative or critical nature

**long discount** forty or fifty percent discount given by publisher when selling books in multiple quantities, usu. to wholesalers and retailers

**mail-order publishing** book publication or distribution by mail, esp. through book clubs

**manuscript** book in author's original form, usu. typewritten or word-processed

**mass market** (adj) designating small, rack-size paperback book, esp. for distribution on newsstands

**ms** manuscript

**mystery** fiction genre emphasizing suspense

**nonfiction** writing based on fact, not invention

**np** no pagination; designation for published work without page numbers

**option** right to develop published literary work for other media; publisher's right of first refusal on author's next work

**oral history** oral recollections of people representative of certain historic period, usu. tape-recorded

**out-of-print** (adj) designating book no longer available from publisher

**overrun** copies of book printed beyond actual orders received

**overstock** excess copies of specific book that publisher cannot sell

**over-the-transom** manuscripts submitted to magazine, publisher, or agent without prior arrangement

**packager** independent contractor who conceives idea for book, finds authors, illustrators, and designers, and makes business arrangement with publisher for publication and, sometimes, production

**page proofs** printed sheets in page form

**paperback** book bound in flexible, paper cover

**paperbound** (adj) designating paperback book

**part title** page showing title of major portion or part of book

**permissions** right to exploit published matter in some form

**piracy** illegal publishing of copyrighted material

**plagiarism** appropriation and publication of another's writing without consent

**pocket book** rack-size paperback book

**potboiler** fast-paced, heavily plotted popular fiction produced for financial gain only

**preface** introductory matter at front of book

**prepack** marketing package for store display containing several copies of book

**presales** planning session of sales force and management on development of sales campaign for books

**presentation copy** book copy to be formally presented by author as gift, often with special binding

**printer's error** error introduced into typeset copy by compositor, who cannot charge to correct it

**printing** mass production of printed material into book or periodical form

**proof** trial impression of type, for correction and revision

**proofreader** person who checks printed copy for errors

**proofreading marks** standardized symbols used to indicate corrections and revisions in text sent to printer

**proof sheet** trial printing of single page for correction and revision

**pub date** Informal. publication date

**publication** printing and distribution of book or periodical; something that is published

**publication date** date on which published book is first available for sale; pub date

**public domain** material that is not copyrighted and can be published without permission or payment

**publicist** person responsible for informing media and public of book's publication

**publicity** exposure and promotion of new book in media

**publisher** person or company engaged in publication of books and periodicals; chief executive of publishing house

**Publishers Weekly** Trademark. PW; news magazine of publishing industry

**publishing** business and practice of reproducing and issuing for sale books or periodicals

**publishing house** company engaged in soliciting, editing, publishing, and selling of books; house

**puff** blurb

**puff piece** uncritical article written to publicize book

**pulp** cheap, hackneyed fiction

**PW** Publishers Weekly

**rack-size** (adj) describing typical format of paperback for mass market

**reader** person who reviews manuscripts for publisher

**recto** right-hand page of book

**redact** (vb) edit or revise, adapt for publication

**reissue** newly printed edition of previously published book; reprint

**rejection slip** notice of publisher's rejection of manuscript

**release** date or act of publication; sheet sent out to media to publicize book, author, or event

**remainder** (vb) sell book at lowered price, usu. from overstock; (n) book that has been remaindered

**replacement** newly released book that replaces old book on store shelves

**reprint** reissue

**reserves** royalty payments withheld from author until it is certain that bookstores will not return distributed copies of book

**returns** unsold books returned by bookseller for credit from publisher

**review** published critical assessment of new book

**review copy** advance complimentary copy of book for reviewer

**revision** change in manuscript or edition

**rights and permissions** right to reprint, excerpt, condense, or otherwise exploit published matter in some form, negotiated by department of publishing company; permissions

**romance** fiction genre that presents melodramatic love story

**royalty** author's percentage of profits from book sale

**running foot** material printed at bottom of each page, usu. title, author's name, chapter title, or subject of page or section

**running head** material printed at top of each page, usu. title, author's name, chapter title, or subject of page or section

**sales conference** marketing meeting where new books are presented to publisher's salespeople, who then solicit orders

**sales force** publishing house employees involved with selling books to bookstores, wholesalers, and others

**scholarly publishing** publication of books and periodicals on academic, research, or scholarly topics

**science fiction** fiction genre focusing on speculation about future, other worlds, or highly advanced alien technologies

**self-publishing** books financed and published by author

**serial rights** commercial rights to publication of parts of work in magazine or newspaper, either before or after book publication

**shelf life** duration for which books are stocked by bookstores before being returned to publisher

**short discount** discount given by publishers to libraries, colleges, and other institutions who will not resell the books

**signature** folded, printed sheets to be bound into book pages

**sinkage** distance from page top to first line of type or illustration

**slush pile** *Informal.* unsolicited manuscripts submitted to publishing company, rarely published

**small press** publishing house with limited output, sometimes in specialized field

**special sales** sales of book other than through normal wholesale and retail channels, as in special outlets or to particular market

**spine** binding that connects book's covers along one edge

**spiral binding** binding with coiled wire through holed paper

**submission** manuscript offered to publisher, usu. by agent

**subsidiary rights** allied rights related to a book, including paperback, serialization, television and motion picture, electronic, and foreign publication rights

**synopsis** abstract of written work, as by reader in publishing house

**technical publishing** publication of research, educational, review, or report material in scientific and technological fields

**text** written body of book

**textbook publishing** publication and distribution to schools and universities of teaching manuals and textbooks

**thriller** fiction genre incorporating fantastic, suspenseful, or exciting situations

**title** name of publication; published book

**title page** book page with title, author's name, and publisher's imprint

**trade book** book for general market, distributed largely through bookstores and libraries

**trade paperback** large-size paperbound book for general market, distributed largely through bookstores

**trade publishing** publication of hardcover and paperback books of interest to general public distributed largely through bookstores and libraries

**translation** text rendered in language other than original language in which it was written and published

**trim size** page size after final cutting; dimensions of cover

**typescript** typewritten manuscript copy

**unabridged** (*adj*) designating complete text of book, story, or article; uncut

**uncut** (*adj*) unabridged

**unedited** (*adj*) not modified by editorial changes

**university press** academic press

**unpaginated** (*adj*) denoting book, usu. brief or for children, with no page numbers; np

**unsolicited manuscript** book or article submitted to publisher without prior arrangement

**vanity press** company that charges authors a fee to publish their work

**verso** left-hand page of book

**vetting** legal and expert checking of book's contents, esp. facts

**western** fiction genre featuring cowboy, Indian, and outlaw stories from U.S. West of 19th century

**young adult books** category of books for teenagers

## PUBLICATIONS

**almanac** book published annually, with seasonal information; yearly reference book with general information about countries of the world

**annals** written account of year's events in chronological order

**annual** yearbook, esp. of school or organization

**anthology** selection of poems, stories, or essays published together; compilation; treasury

**article** report, story, or essay complete in itself and forming part of a publication

**atlas** book of maps and charts

**audio book** book on cassette

**autobiography** story of one's own life

**bimonthly** periodical published once every two months or twice a month

**biography** story of another person's life

**biweekly** periodical published once every two weeks

**book** large number of sheets of printed material bound together along one edge between protective covers and published; text and graphic material printed on such pages

**booklet** small book, esp. paperbound

**book on cassette** audio recording of reading of a book; audio book

**boxed set** multivolume book packaged and sold as one unit

**broadside** large sheet of paper printed on one or both sides with advertisement or political message, usu. folded

**brochure** pamphlet, usu. promotional or descriptive

**bulletin** regular publication for members of organization or community group

**catalog** comprehensive descriptive listing, esp. of articles for sale or college courses

**circular** letter or advertisement printed for mass distribution

**codex** manuscript volume, esp. of classic text or scripture

**comic book** paperbound booklet of extended cartoons in series, usu. humorous or adventurous

**communiqué** official bulletin or correspondence

**compendium** brief treatment or account, usu. of extensive subject

**compilation** anthology

**concordance** alphabetical listing of significant words used in text or by particular writer, citing where they occur, used esp. with Bible

**cookbook** book of recipes

**daily** newspaper published each day

**diary** daily record of one's thoughts and experiences

**dictionary** alphabetical listing of words with definitions and etymological information

**digest** condensation or abridgment of material

**directory** listing of names, addresses, and other information about a specific group of people

**encyclopedia** book or set of books with information on many branches of knowledge, usu. arranged alphabetically

**gazette** newspaper; official publication with announcements

**gazetteer** dictionary of geographical terms

**guidebook** listing of directions and information for particular place, esp. for tourists

**handbook** manual of information on particular subject

**hornbook** book or primer providing basic information on particular subject

**house organ** in-house publication

**how-to book** manual or instruction book on particular subject

**incunabula** extant copies of earliest printed books, pre-1500

**index** extensive alphabetical listing of items, esp. in collection, with information on each

**in-house publication** bulletin or other regular publication of an organization, intended for employees or members; house organ

**irregular serial** serial not published at set intervals

**journal** any periodical or newspaper, esp. daily newspaper; regular publication of specific profession

**lexicon** dictionary or other vocabulary book

**magazine** periodic publication, usu. bound in paper, containing articles by various writers, often with photographs and illustrations, frequently focusing on some unifying theme or subject

**manifesto** public statement of policies and reasoning, esp. by government or political group

**manual** book of facts and instruction on particular subject

**monograph** scholarly book or long article on specific subject

**monthly** periodical published once a month

**newsletter** regular informational bulletin for subscribers, employees, or organization members

**newspaper** regular publication, esp. daily, containing news, opinion, general interest features, photographs, illustrations, and advertisements

**notice** formal announcement, esp. printed warning, rules, or information

**pamphlet** thin, simply bound or stapled collection of sheets, usu. on topic of current interest

**periodical** any publication appearing at regular intervals

**position paper** formal, detailed statement of policy

**primer** elementary handbook on particular subject or used to teach reading

**quarterly** periodical published every three months

**reference book** authoritative book used for research and information gathering on one or many subjects

**regional** magazine with coverage directed at readership in specific geographic area

**report** formal or official presentation of facts or record of proceedings

**self-help book** guidebook for personal development or improvement

**semimonthly** periodical published twice a month

**semiweekly** periodical published twice a week

**serial** something published in series of continuous segments at regular intervals

**slick** magazine printed on glossy paper; such a magazine regarded as possessing sophistication

**textbook** book giving detailed instruction in principles of some subject for students

**thesaurus** extensive listing of words and their synonyms, arranged alphabetically or topically

**tome** large, scholarly book

**tract** treatise, esp. proselytizing on politics or religion

**treasury** anthology

**volume** one of two or more separate books constituting a complete set; any single book

**weekly** periodical published once a week

**white paper** detailed authoritative report, esp. official government report

**who's who** listing of well-known people, in one specific field or many, with biographical information

**yearbook** periodical published once a year, esp. with information on previous year; annual publication of graduating class of school or college

**yellow pages** telephone directory of businesses, arranged topically

## JOURNALISM

**add** new copy added to already written article

**advance copy** story prepared before event it describes has occurred and held until release date

**advertorial** copy that is paid for by advertisers but laid out and written in style of regular copy

**agony column** newspaper advice column

**alternative press** journalism devoted to counterculture or antiestablishment interests

**angle** point of view taken in news story or feature

**AP** *Associated Press*

**article** complete written piece in newspaper or magazine

**assignment** news story or feature that a reporter or photographer is asked to cover

**Associated Press** AP; major American news cooperative that supplies news, photos, and soft features to newspapers and broadcasters by wire service

**attribution** credit given to source of news story

**banner** large, front-page headline extending width of page

**beat** reporter's regular, assigned geographical or topical territory

**bio** *Informal.* background material, often prepared by publicist, used in profile or feature on an individual

**blackout** absence of news coverage due to power failure, labor dispute, or strike, or at news subject's insistence

**blind lead** beginning of news story that does not identify its subject directly or by name

**blowup** enlarged photograph

**boilerplate** syndicated, standardized periodical material

**book** complete magazine or periodical

**book review** description and critique of recently published book

**box** straight lines of type formed into box to enclose copy or illustration

**break** division of word onto two lines

**broadcast journalism** news programming on radio and television

**bulldog edition** earliest daily edition of a newspaper

**bulletin** brief announcement of latest news, usu. coming directly from news source

**bureau** news department covering geographical or topical area

**bureau chief** supervising editor of newspaper office in foreign city or on specific news desk

**byline** author's printed name appearing with story

**canned copy** copy supplied by news agency, public relations firm, or other outside source

**caption** description under illustration or photograph

**carry** (vb) include or run a story

**cartoon** illustration, esp. for political commentary, amusement, or as space filler, in newspaper or periodical

**cause célèbre** news incident, often a legal case, that excites widespread public interest

**censorship** deletion of material deemed objectionable from publication

**centerfold** foldout double page at center of magazine, usu. containing illustration, sometimes featuring nude photographs

**center spread** pair of pages facing each other in center of publication that make up single unit

**circulation** publication's readership and subscribers

**city editor** newspaper editor in charge of local news and distribution of assignments

**city room** office of city editor and staff, where assembly of local news takes place

**classified advertisement** newspaper advertisement listed according to type of goods or services offered or desired; want ad

**clipping** article cut from journal

**clips** collection of journalist's published writings, used as résumé or portfolio in soliciting future work

**clipsheet** newspaper sheet reissued by another organization

**cold type** type set by a method that does not use the casting of molten lead

**column** feature in newspaper by regular writer, often including personal views; printed block of type, usu. justified between vertical lines

**column inch** one vertical inch of copy in one column

**columnist** writer of regularly featured article in periodical

**comics** part of newspaper devoted to comic strips

**comic strip** humorous series of illustrations with text, regularly featured in newspaper or magazine

**COMSAT** *com*munications *sat*ellite that relays news stories around the world

**contributing editor** frequent contributor to magazine who is not on staff

**contributor** writer whose name is not listed on masthead but who has article appearing in periodical

**copy** written text of article

**copyboy** errand person at newspaper, esp. one who carries copy for processing

**copy desk** newspaper room in which copyreaders edit copy and write headlines

**copyediting** correction, revision, and refinement of copy before publication

**copyeditor** person who corrects and revises grammatical, factual, and stylistic aspects of written news story

**correspondent** reporter covering stories in location distant from newspaper offices

**cover** (vb) report news or take pictures of event; (n) front outside binding of magazine

**coverage** extent to which news event is included in periodical

**cover copy** text for cover of periodical

**cover girl** attractive young woman photographed for magazine cover illustration

**cover story** magazine article featured on cover illustration

**critic** person who reviews artistic and literary works for newspaper or magazine

**cub reporter** beginning reporter

**cut** deletion of copy

**daily** newspaper published at least once each day

**dateline** line at beginning of news story indicating place and time of origin of story

**deadline** time at which prepared story must be submitted for editing and publication

**deep throat** *Slang.* highly placed, reliable, unattributable source

**diophead** headline beneath banner

**dispatch** news item filed by correspondent

**distribution** system of marketing newspapers and periodicals to points of sale

**double truck** photographs spread over two pages, as in centerfold

**edition** updated version of daily newspaper published at certain hour, such as morning, early, late, or final edition

**editorial** column by editor expressing newspaper policy or view on current issue

**editor in chief** supervisor of editorial policy of publication

**essay** often first-person column expressing writer's point of view on one subject

**exposé** news story revealing scandal or hidden corruption

**extra** special edition of newspaper, published between regular editions to cover news of unusual importance

**fanzine** usu. nonprofessional magazine produced by and for enthusiasts of specific field or person, esp. in pop music

**feature** general interest story, often of human interest or providing background on news, as distinguished from hard news

**feeding frenzy** ruthless attack on or exploitation of someone, esp. by media

**feuilleton** newspaper section, esp. in Europe, covering general features and serialized fiction

**filler** general-interest material plugged into empty newspaper space

**final** last edition of daily newspaper

**First Amendment** amendment to U.S. Constitution that guarantees freedom of the press

**first-time rights** sale of publication rights based on assumption that article or photograph has not been previously published

**flack** sometimes disparaging term for press agent

**flag** masthead

**follow-up** continuing coverage of ongoing news story

**fourth estate** the press

**freelancer** worker, esp. writer, not on staff of periodical

**free press** uncensored publication of newspapers and periodicals

**front page** first page of newspaper, devoted to major news stories of national, international, and local importance

**gossip columnist** writer who reports on real and rumored activities of celebrities

**graph** *Informal.* paragraph of copy

**graveyard shift** lobster shift

**hard news** current-events stories of importance

**headline** large-type descriptive heading over printed news story

**investigative journalism** in-depth coverage of news story and related background material, often requiring extensive interviewing and research

**issue** single edition of a periodical

**item** piece of news; single article

**journal** any periodical or newspaper, esp. daily newspaper

**journalism** factual writing, esp. news coverage, and photographs in support of such writing

**journalist** person who researches, photographs, or writes news, current events, or feature stories

**jump** continuation of article on another page or column

**kicker** brief head in small type above headline to indicate subject or draw reader's interest

**kill** (*vb*) abandon intention to publish story or article

**kill fee** reduced payment to writer or photographer for work that has been assigned but will not be used

**Kyodo** international news agency and wire service based in Japan

**layout** page design

**lead** introduction of news story, esp. its first sentence; most important news story of day; information or clue that draws reporter to story

**lead-in** introductory or transitional sentence in article

**leading** spacing inserted between lines by printer

**lead story** most important news story of the day

**legend** list of map or chart symbols

**libel** publication of false or defamatory statements

**lobster shift** *Informal.* night shift in newspaper office; graveyard shift

**makeup** layout of pages

**managing editor** person below editor in chief who oversees output of senior editors and regular production of periodical

**mass media** newspaper, radio, television, and movie media capable of reaching general public

**masthead** statement of staff, address, and other vital statistics of publication; flag

**media** all means of communication providing information to public

**media event** public event staged to gain publicity and media attention

**muckraking** search for and exposure of scandal, corruption, hidden crime, or abuse

**nameplate** newspaper name on top of front page

**news** important current events; reporting of current events

**news agency** organization for gathering and distributing news, features, and photos to subscribers

**newsdealer** person who sells newspapers and magazines

**news flash** news bulletin issued immediately after occurrence of event

**newsmagazine** periodical, esp. weekly, covering major news stories and features

**newsroom** office and information center for gathering news and housing writers and reporters

**newsworthy** (*adj*) interesting or important enough to warrant media attention

**obit** *Informal.* obituary

**obituary** announcement of person's death with information on his or her life; obit

**Op-Ed page** special features and commentary page *opposite editorial* page in newspaper

**pan** (*vb*) give highly negative review of event; (*n*) such a review

**paparazzi** photographers who pursue celebrities without regard for their willingness to be photographed

**personals** classified advertisements for those seeking personal relationships

**photo editor** person responsible for assigning and selecting photographs for publication

**photo essay** group of photographs, often with supplementary text, that conveys a unified story

**photojournalism** news coverage emphasizing photographic images that depict current-events stories; pictorial journalism

**pictorial journalism** photojournalism

**pipeline** channel for passing information to journalist

**play** (*vb*) determine angle of news story or amount of coverage

**plug** *Informal.* favorable publicity in news media

**political cartoon** newspaper illustration, usu. humorous, with political message

**press** newspaper publishing; news media; newspaper

**press agent** person who writes and circulates news items about organization or important person; publicist

**press association** organization of journalists and newspaper publishers

**press box** area set aside for members of press, esp. at sports events

**press card** newspaper reporter's credentials, used to cross police or security lines

**press conference** prearranged interview with reporters to provide requested information or generate publicity

**press corps** group of journalists from various publications and media who regularly cover the same beat

**press release** information on event, organization, or person written by publicist and circulated for use by news media

**press secretary** person responsible for handling press and public relations for prominent figure or organization

**profile** in-depth article focusing on one individual

**propaganda** persuasive, esp. biased, dissemination of information

**publicist** press agent

**puff piece** *Informal.* coverage of subject that is exaggerated in praise and totally uncritical

**put to bed** complete all editorial work on newspaper and send it to printer

**query** inquiry from writer to editor regarding acceptability of story, usu. presented in letter outlining or describing piece

**rave** (*vb*) give extremely positive review to event; (*n*) such a review

**report** (*vb*) cover and write a news story

**reportage** stories based on research or detailed coverage of documented observation of news events, including photo essays

**reporter**  person who investigates news event and writes story for media

**retraction**  printed statement reversing previously held position or relinquishing previously made claim

**Reuters**  major international news agency and wire service based in Britain

**review**  critique of current event, esp. in arts

**rewrite**  editorial revision of copy; (*vb*) revise copy

**rewrite man**  person whose job is to condense and revise articles written by other writers

**run**  (*vb*) carry a news story

**running head**  headline repeated on continuous pages

**runover**  story material exceeding allotted publication space and carried over to an extra line, column, or page

**scandal sheet**  cheap newspaper featuring tawdry stories about celebrities

**scoop**  *Informal.* major news story published ahead of one's competitors

**screamer**  newspaper headline with extremely sensational slant

**second-time rights**  rights to previously published article or photograph

**section**  part of newspaper covering sports, news, features, advertisements, or finance

**senior editor**  magazine or newspaper editor responsible for specific region, beat, or field

**sensationalism**  extreme reportorial style intended to arouse readership interest based on emotional appeal, often with questionable accuracy

**sensationalize**  (*vb*) publish news story with undue attention to sensational elements

**service piece**  article offering consumer information for specific industry

**sidebar**  additional material presented alongside major story

**silly season**  late summer news slump that inspires far-fetched news stories

**slant**  angle or approach to coverage of news story

**slipsheet**  paper fitted between freshly printed pages to prevent offsetting

**slug**  one- or two-word label for news story

**soft news**  background or feature stories of general interest

**source**  person supplying information to journalist

**sportswriter**  person who covers sports events for newspaper or magazine

**spread**  article or illustration covering large amount of space, esp. two facing pages

**squib**  filler or short news item

**staffer**  full-time reporter on newspaper

**stet**  *Latin.* lit. let it stand; proofreader's mark indicating that material marked for deletion should remain

**story**  single article appearing in periodical

**stringer**  part-time reporter for newspaper, often paid by the column-inch

**subhead**  small heading within text of story

**Sunday supplement**  feature magazine insert in Sunday newspaper

**syndication service**  company selling newspaper columns and features to many newspapers

**tabloid**  newspaper characterized by sensationalism; newspaper or journal with small page size, usu. half of regular size

**tag**  attention-grabbing item at end of story

**Tass**  state-owned Soviet news agency and wire service

**tear sheet**  sheet of newsprint or magazine copy retained for reference

**teaser**  headline that arouses curiosity

**thirty**  mark "30," used to indicate end of story

**thumbnail**  *Informal.* capsule news story or summary

**trade journal**  magazine catering to specific business, industry, or field

**underground press**  journalism devoted to counterculture and/or radical interests

**United Press International**  UPI; major U.S. news organization that supplies news, photos, and soft features to newspapers and broadcasters by wire service

**update**  follow-up article that brings news story up to date

**UPI**  United Press International

**volume**  year's issues of periodical, esp. bound into single volume

**want ad**  classified advertisement

**weekly**  newspaper or magazine published once a week

**Wirephoto**  *Trademark.* news photograph transmitted by special device over long distances by wire

**wire service**  news agency supplying news stories to newspapers

**write-up**  description of news event; story

**yellow journalism**  newspaper coverage in sensationalized, often irresponsible, style

## Newspaper Names (*usu. capitalized*)

**banner bulletin**
**call, capital, chronicle, clarion, courier**
**daily, diario, diary, dispatch**
**enquirer, examiner, exponent**
**free press**
**gazette, globe**
**herald**
**independent, inquirer, intelligencer**
**journal**
**leader, ledger, light,**
**mail, mercury, messenger, mirror, monitor**
**news**
**patriot, post, press**
**review**
**sentinel, star, sun**
**telegraph, times, tribune**
**union**
**weekly, world**
**zeitung**

# War and Military

Types and Techniques of Warfare
Soldiers and Military Life
War Machinery and War Zones
Military Ranks
Army, Air Force, and Marines
Navy and Coast Guard

**see also**: Chap. 5: Weapons and Armaments; Chap. 11: International Relations; Titles of Rank; Chap. 24: Violence

# TYPES AND TECHNIQUES OF WARFARE

**abort** (*vb*) cancel mission before completion

**action** military encounter or battle

**act of war** provocation by one nation of sufficient seriousness to start war

**advance** attack; forward movement of troops

**aggression** use of armed force to accomplish goals

**air cover** use of aircraft to protect ground or naval operations

**air raid** air strike

**air strike** attack using airplanes, esp. bombers; air raid

**air support** bombing used esp. to support ground forces

**alert** warning of impending attack; readiness for attack

**ally** army of another nation fighting one's common enemy

**amphibious operation** military maneuver using troops and vehicles able to travel on land and water

**armistice** general truce; cessation of war

**array** battle order; deployment of troops for battle

**assault** attack

**attack** sudden, violent armed aggression; assault

**balance of terror** mutual deterrence from engaging in hostilities based on both sides having relatively equal and devastating destructive capabilities

**barrage** wave of continuous artillery fire, often protective

**barricade** obstacle across roadway to prevent enemy advance

**battle** armed conflict between armies or forces

**besiege** (*vb*) surround with forces and attack continuously

**biological warfare** use of toxic organisms to kill and incapacitate enemy; germ warfare

**blitzkrieg** *German*. lit. lightning war; intense infantry attack spearheaded by tanks and supported by aircraft

**bloc** group of nations acting together for military and political purposes

**blockade** action aimed at restricting movement of enemy troops and supplies

**bloodbath** massacre, slaughter

**bombardment** attacks by artillery, bombs, or missiles

**broken-back war** continuing conflict between nations after use of devastating nuclear force

**brush-fire war** local, quickly escalating war

**camouflage** colors and materials such as nets, foliage, and special clothing used to make equipment or personnel blend in with natural setting

**campaign** specific stage or area of war

**cannonade** bombardment, heavy artillery fire

**capability** ability to implement military strategies and tactics

**capitulation** surrender

**capture** (*vb*) gain control of an area by force

**carpet bombing** massive bombing of specific area

**cease-fire** truce; temporary stoppage of attacks

**charge** sudden, rapid advance on enemy

**chemical warfare** use of weapons composed of toxic chemicals, generally recognized as illegal

**civil defense** organized system for protection of lives of noncombatants during wartime

**civil war** war between factions within one nation

**cold war** state of international tension with conflict expressed not in armed hostilities but in economic, ideological, and political measures

**collateral damage** civilian casualties and damage to nonmilitiary targets, esp. due to bombing raids

**column** long, narrow formation deploying troops in lengthwise direction

**conflict** armed hostilities, including undeclared war

**containment** policy and actions to prevent expansion of hostile forces or ideology

**controlled war** warfare conducted according to continuous flow of information to commanders of troops

**conventional war** war using no nuclear, chemical, or biological weapons

**convoy** ships or vehicles traveling together for mutual protection

**counterattack** attack in response to aggressor's attack

**counterinsurgency** organized activity in opposition to rebels

**counterintelligence** information gathering and processing to thwart or distort enemy's intelligence efforts

**counteroffensive** attack in response to enemy aggression

**crusade** military expedition undertaken with zeal for specific cause

**cryptanalysis** translation of enemy's secret encoded communications by breaking codes and ciphers

**decisive action** final battle of war; turning point in campaign

**deep interdiction** attacks on enemy communication and supply lines far behind battle zone

**defeat** state of being overcome by superior enemy force

**deployment** positioning of troops into place in readiness for battle or maneuvers

**deterrence** steps taken to prevent armed actions

**disarmament** reduction, by mutual agreement, of armed forces and weapons

**dogfight** engagement between two or more airplanes

**economic warfare** offensive or defensive use of trade and financial transactions to gain advantage against hostile forces or nations

**electronic warfare** use of electronic technology to thwart enemy weapons and disrupt communications

**enemy** adversary or opponent in military action

**engagement** battle or encounter with enemy

**escalation** increase in violence, arsenal, or area of conflict

**fail-safe** safety plan aimed at deterrence of accidental nuclear attack whereby bomber pilot must receive confirmation of attack plan at preordained stations before proceeding with attack orders

**firefight** intense, usu. brief, encounter with heavy gunfire between small tactical units

**first strike** use of one's nuclear weapons before enemy, esp. surprise attack

**flying column** troops equipped and deployed to move independently of principal unit

**formation** position of troops for battle or maneuvers

**friendly fire** artillery or other fire that causes damage or casualties to one's own forces

**general warfare** large-scale armed conflict between major powers, with national survival at stake

**germ warfare** biological warfare

**give ground** retreat

**global thermonuclear war** general warfare using nuclear weapons resulting in mass destruction and annihilation

**ground war** attack or operation by infantry and artillery only

**guerrilla warfare** small-scale military operations conducted inside hostile territory by irregular units

**gunboat diplomacy** policy employing threat of armed aggression

**holding attack** aggressive tactic to restrict enemy movement

**hostilities** instances of armed conflict

**hot-line agreement** arrangement between United States and Soviet Union to maintain instant communication line to deal with crisis or accident that might lead to war

**house-to-house battle** extremely close, hard ground fighting for a city or town that is strongly defended

**infiltration** passage of troops through gaps in enemy lines

**insurgency** insurrection

**insurrection** revolt against existing political structure and power; insurgency

**intelligence** collection and evaluation of military information regarding enemy

**interdiction** preventive action that blocks enemy's access to routes, areas, or supplies

**international conflict** armed hostilities between nations

**intervention** interference in affairs of another state, esp. insertion of military presence

**invasion** large-scale assault to take over enemy territory

**katabasis** retreat or backward march

**land power** military capability of forces mobilized on land

**launch-on-warning** policy of firing ballistic missiles immediately on detection of enemy missile attack without waiting for missiles to reach targets before retaliating

**laws of war** universal ethical guidelines governing basic conduct of forces toward enemies in wartime

**limited conventional warfare** general warfare without use of nuclear or biological weapons and with observance of voluntary restrictions on both sides; limited strategic warfare

**limited strategic warfare** limited conventional warfare

**local warfare** geographically confined conflict

**logistics** science of planning and executing troop movements, procurement and supply, provision, and related support services

**low-intensity conflict** isolated acts of violence, esp. hostage taking, terrorism, and counterinsurgency

**MAD** *Mutually Assured Destruction*

**maneuver** movement to place military supplies or personnel in advantageous position

**massacre** slaughter of many people

**mass destruction** widespread devastation, loss of life, and sometimes irrecoverable damage caused by conflict

**military intervention** introduction of armed force into state of tension or disagreement

**military posture** strength, capability, and readiness of armed forces

**military science** study of causative factors and tactical principles or warfare

**mobilization** preparations for war

**mutually assured destruction** MAD; deterrence based on capacity for total reciprocal annihilation

**national security** protection of state from external aggression and subversion

**neutrality** attitude of impartiality during period of tension or armed conflict

**nonalignment** policy of neutrality in situations of international armed conflict, esp. with respect to United States and Soviet Union

**nuclear club** *Informal.* nations possessing nuclear armaments

**nuclear nonproliferation** policy aimed at control and restriction of acquisition of nuclear weapons by nations that do not have them

**nuclear proliferation** process of additional nations acquiring nuclear weapons

**nuclear stalemate** deterrence from use of nuclear weapons based on mutual possession of them

**nuclear winter** global darkness and extreme cold over prolonged period due to dust cloud blocking sunlight following nuclear holocaust

**occupation** seizure of and continued presence in another state's territory by military force

**offensive** aggressive action

**operation** military action; combat, attack, defense, or maneuver

**order of battle** orderly disposition of military force in response to identification and assessment of enemy strength

**orders** military commands

**outgoing mail** *Slang.* friendly artillery fire

**overkill** excessive destructive capability beyond what could be required for victory; use of such capability

**peaceful coexistence** avoidance of armed conflict by adversaries

**penetration** aggressive advance into enemy territory

**phalanx** body of troops in close ranks and files

**pincers movement** maneuver using two-sided attack formation to enclose enemy

**pitched battle** intense conflict

**privateering** use of armed vessel by private person against hostile nation

**preemptive strike** nuclear attack in anticipation of enemy's nuclear attack; preventive strike

**preventive strike** preemptive strike

**proxy war** limited war between allies of actual enemies

**psychological warfare** use of propaganda and pressure to weaken and confuse enemy

**Pyrrhic victory** military supremacy won at debilitating cost

**raid** sudden attack on enemy by air on small land force

**rear guard** unit protecting rear of larger force

**reconnaissance** movement to gather information about enemy

**red alert** final stage of readiness when enemy attack appears imminent

**regroup** (*vb*) change military formation, esp. reorganize after defeat or retreat

**retreat** forced withdrawal of troops in face of enemy attack

**revolutionary war** military action aimed at seizing political power, esp. from existing government

**rout** decisive, overwhelming victory

**saber-rattling** show or threat of military force, used to intimidate other nations

**sabotage** destruction or injury to national defense, security, or resources through covert operations

**sally** rushing forward of troops from defensive position to attack enemy

**salvo** volley

**scorched-earth policy** devastation of property and agriculture in a region before abandoning it to enemy

**screen** protective arrangement of military vehicles and equipment

**sea power** military capability of naval forces mobilized at sea

**second strike** retaliatory nuclear attack in wake of first strike

**shock tactics** use of forceful, sudden assault on enemy

**show of force** intentional display of military strength to deter enemy action

**siege** blockade of enemy city or fort to force depletion of resources and ultimate surrender

**skirmish** brief, inconclusive battle

**sortie** sudden attack from defensive position; combat air mission

**spasm warfare** brief, cataclysmic conflict that uses all forces and resources without regard to consequences

**strafe** (*vb*) attack from the air with gunfire

**stratagem** tactical maneuver to surprise or deceive enemy

**strategic** (*adj*) pertaining to overall military power and goals

**strategy** long-term deployment and use of military forces and national resources with intent to achieve position of advantage

**strike** attack, esp. preemptive, preventive, first, or second thermonuclear attack; aircraft attack on surface target

**subversion** action from within to undermine military strength and national security

**surge capability** ability to generate and maintain greatly amplified military strength

**surgical strike** precisely planned and executed military attack on specific target area

**surprise attack** aggressive action that takes enemy by surprise

**surrender** formal declaration and acceptance of defeat; capitulation

**surveillance** observation for intelligence purposes, esp. from air or concealed position

**sweep** rapid movement of forces through area to assume control and eliminate enemy

**symbolic attack** show of force

**tactical** (*adj*) pertaining to battlefield operations or any immediate military objective

**tactical maneuver** purposeful operation involving deployment of forces and weapons in combat

**tactics** detailed plans and methods used to accomplish specific military objectives

**talionic attack** equal give-and-take exchange

**terrorism** employment of unethical tactics and violence in civilian settings, esp. hostage taking and assassination, for political or military advantage

**threat** declaration of intention and capacity to inflict injury

**thrust** advance rapidly against opposition

**tooth-to-tail ratio** proportion of combat forces to administrative or logistical support

**total war** complete involvement in war effort of nation's military, civilian, economic, and political resources

**treason** betrayal of one's country, esp. in wartime

**trench warfare** fighting from makeshift battlefield defenses over prolonged period

**triage** process of dividing war wounded into groups requiring immediate treatment, delayed treatment, and those beyond treatment

**truce** temporary cessation of hostilities

**unconventional warfare** military operations in enemy-held territory; clandestine hostilities and espionage; undeclared warfare; chemical, biological, or nuclear warfare

**underground** organized resistance to occupying army

**vanguard** troops at forefront of advancing army, sent to prepare main attack or maneuver

**victory** military supremacy in wartime or in specific battle

**volley** simultaneous discharge of numerous weapons; salvo

**war** sustained, often widespread, armed conflict, esp. between nations

**war crimes** unethical, criminal behavior and actions contrary to laws of war

**warfare** armed conflict between nations

**war games** simulations of battle or military operations that depict possible actual situations, used to test strategy and tactics

**war of independence** insurrection against colonial or oppressive powers; revolution

**wedge** troops arrayed in formation that tapers to a point at the front

**white flag** symbol of surrender

**withdrawal** retreat; backward movement of troops

**wolf pack** group of submarines or fighter planes making coordinated attack

**world war** extensive combat involving many nations around the world

## SOLDIERS AND MILITARY LIFE

**active duty** full-time military service

**adjutant** administrative assistant to commanding officer

**admiral** highest ranking naval officer

**aide-de-camp** assistant to commanding officer

**airborne** (*adj*) designating ground forces carried in aircraft

**air force** military branch of airborne forces

**Air Force** air force of the United States

**airman** enlisted member of Air Force or aircrew member in another service branch

**all hands** alert call in navy

**armada** fleet of warships

**armed forces** military personnel and resources used in protection of national interests against enemies and aggressive action against foreign powers

**armored division** military unit with tanks and other armored vehicles

**army** major national defense force; military branch of land forces; largest military unit, commanded by general

**Army** army of the United States

**attention** erect soldier's posture with heels together, arms at sides, eyes to front

**AWOL** absent *without leave*; unauthorized desertion of post or duty

**barracks** building used to lodge soldiers

**basic training** initial period of military training for molding recruits into soldiers

**battalion** tactical unit larger than company and smaller than regiment, commanded by lieutenant colonel

**battle fatigue** combat fatigue

**bells** designation for time or hour of day in navy

**billet** lodging for soldiers; official order to provide such lodging

**blockhouse** fortified structure; corner of stockade

**bluebonnet** soldier wearing a blue cap (Scotland)

**body count** count of enemy dead in battle, often used as morale booster to troops

**bombardier** member of bomber crew who releases bombs; noncommissioned officer in British artillery

**boot camp** training facility for recruits

**brass** *Informal.* officers of rank

**break ranks** move out of formation

**brevet** commission providing officer with higher nominal rank than that for which he or she is paid

**brig** jail on warship or naval base

**brigade** tactical unit larger than regiment and smaller than division, commanded by colonel

**brownshirt** Nazi storm trooper before World War II

**buck private** lowest grade of private

**cadet** student at military academy

**call-up** conscription of eligible civilians into military service

**camp follower** individual who profits off military camp, esp. as prostitute

**cannon fodder** foot soldiers who are subjected to greatest risk from enemy fire

**carabiniere** cavalry soldier armed with carbine, esp. in British 6th Dragoon Guards

**casern** military barracks in garrison town

**casualty** military person wounded or killed in battle

**cavalry** troops mounted on horseback

**centurion** commander of company of one hundred soldiers (ancient Rome)

**chaplain** military minister

**chesseur** cavalry or infantry soldier equipped for rapid movement (France)

**chevron** one of one or more inverted V-shaped stripes, worn on arm by noncommissioned officers

**Chief of Naval Operations** highest office of U.S. Navy

**chief of staff** ranking officer serving as commander's chief adviser; highest ranking officer of U.S. Army or Air Force

**chief petty officer** top-ranking naval noncommissioned officer

**chief warrant officer** top-ranking noncommissioned officer, below second lieutenant or ensign

**close order** exact arrangement of troops for drills or march

**coast guard** military forces that guard coastal waters and maritime traffic

**colonel** highest field grade rank in army

**color guard** honor guard that carries flags

**column** vertical array of troops into line

**combat fatigue** posttraumatic stress disorder among soldiers engaged in combat; battle fatigue; shell shock

**command and control** centralized decision-making, intelligence-gathering, and communications system of a military force

**commandant** senior officer and head of U.S. Marine Corps

**commander** ranking officer; commissioned naval officer below captain

**commander in chief** top-ranking leader of armed forces

**commanding officer** officer in charge of tactical unit

**commando** soldier specially trained for close combat, raids, and dangerous missions

**command post** headquarters of commander of military unit

**commissary** military supermarket and provisions store

**commissioned officer** military officer holding by commission a rank of second lieutenant or higher

**commodore** naval rank equivalent to that of brigadier general

**company** basic army unit, larger than a platoon and smaller than a battalion, commanded by captain and first sergeant

**condottiere** leader of band of mercenary soldiers (Italy, 14th–15th c.)

**conscientious objector** person who refuses to serve in armed forces on religious or moral grounds

**conscription** compulsory registration of selected individuals for military service; draft

**corps** any unit of soldiers; esp. tactical unit larger than a division and smaller than an army, commanded by lieutenant general

**court-martial** trial for military crimes presided over by military personnel; (*vb*) try by court-martial

**court of inquiry** court that inquires into and reports on alleged misconduct but does not pass judgment or impose sentence

**C ration** combat ration, usu. canned or powdered food

**deferment** temporary exemption from induction into military service

**Delta force** U.S. Army elite force trained in antiterrorist tactics

**deserter** soldier who intentionally abandons his or her post, disappearing from military authority without intention of returning

**detail** specific assigned task

**digger** Australian or New Zealand soldier of World War II

**Distinguished Service Cross** bronze medal awarded by United States for distinguished service in combat

**division** tactical unit larger than a brigade and smaller than a corps, commanded by major general

**dog biscuit** *Informal.* hard, dry biscuit, used as emergency ration

**dogtag** identification piece worn on chain around neck

**doolie** *Slang.* Air Force Academy cadet

**doughboy** *Informal.* U.S. infantryman, esp. in World War I

**dove** person opposed to war

**draft** conscription

**draftee** person conscripted into military service

**dragoon** orig. an infantryman mounted on horse; European cavalryman

**drill** exercise repeated in training

**drill sergeant** noncom who trains recruits in basic soldiering

**echelon** level of military command; military formation in parallel lines

**enlist** (*vb*) join military of one's own free will

**enlisted man** nonofficer in U.S. military

**enlisted woman** female nonofficer in U.S. military

**ensign** lowest-ranking commissioned officer in U.S. Navy

**escadrille** squadron on divisional unit of aircraft

**evzone** member of elite infantry corps (Greece)

**executive officer** second in command of unit or organization

**fall in** (*vb*) form up and come to attention as unit

**fall out** (*vb*) break ranks

**fatigues** drab uniform worn on fatigue duty, while laboring in camp, or in training

**fedayee** member of Arab commando unit operating esp. against Israel

**field grade officer** any mid-level officer, such as a major or colonel

**field marshal** highest-ranking military officer (Britain); officer of second-highest rank (France)

**five-star general** highest-ranking general of the U.S. Army

**flak** bursting shells fired from antiaircraft guns

**flank** extreme left or right side of array of troops

**FLASH** precedence code for urgent messages about combat or enemy contact

**fleet** group of ships under single command

**flight** basic Air Force unit, consisting of two or more aircraft

**flight pay** supplementary pay for minimum flight time per month for member of Air Force

**flyboy** *Informal.* airman

**foot soldier** infantryman

**frag** (*vb*) do violence against one's superior officer, esp. with fragmentation grenade

**frogman** underwater operative equipped with air tanks and wet suit, esp. for salvage, demolition, and reconnaissance

**fusilier** member of unit formerly armed with flintlock muskets (Britain)

**garrison** permanent military post or installation

**general** top-ranking army or air force officer

**generalissimo** supreme commander of armed forces (Italy, Spain, and Latin America)

**ghazi** Muslim soldier, esp. one fighting against non-Muslims

**GI** *government issue;* common soldier

**gob** *Slang.* sailor in U.S. Navy

**Green Berets** Special Forces

**ground forces** infantry and artillery, excluding naval and air forces

**group** administrative and tactical unit consisting of two or more battalions or squadrons and their headquarters

**grunt** *Slang.* low-ranking military man, esp. marine

**guard duty** duty as sentry

**guerrilla** member of unofficial or independent fighting unit operating in hostile territory

**guidon** soldier carrying small flag or streamer for signaling

**gunner** occupational title in artillery; Marine warrant officer

**hawk** person supporting war as national policy

**high command** highest headquarters of military force

**hitch** *Slang.* period of military service

**honor guard** ceremonial escort for important person or casket

**hoplite** heavily armed foot soldier (ancient Greece)

**hussar** European cavalry soldier, orig. Hungarian light cavalryman (15th c.)

**induction** act of drafting someone into military service

**infantry** armed foot soldiers

**inspection** formal, official scrutiny of assembled troops

**insubordination** disrespect and disobedience toward any person of higher rank

**irregular** member of unofficial or independent military unit

**janissary** soldier in Turkish army

**jarhead** *Slang.* member of U.S. Marine Corps.

**Joint Chiefs of Staff** principal military advisory board of U.S. president, including Chiefs of Staff of Army and Air Force, Marine Corps Commandant, and Chief of Naval Operations

**kamikaze** Japanese pilot who suicidally crashed airplane into target during World War II

**kern** soldier in Ireland and Scottish Highlands

**kitchen police** KP; soldiers assigned to assist cooks

**KP** *kitchen police*

**K ration** emergency field ration

**lance corporal** U.S. Marine enlisted rank between private first class and corporal; *Chiefly Brit.* corporal

**leatherneck** *Slang.* member of U.S. Marine Corps

**legionnaire** member of national association of former servicemen; Roman soldier

**letter of marque** government license to private person to outfit armed ship for warfare

**lieutenant** lowest-ranking commissioned officer in U.S. Army or Air Force

**lifer** soldier remaining in military for entire adult life

**lines** combatant forces on front lines, as distinguished from officers

**Luftwaffe** *German.* air force, esp. during World War II

**marine** member of elite branch of military serving in association with navy

**Marine Corps** branch of U.S. armed forces specially trained for land, sea, and air combat in conjunction with troops of other branches

**master sergeant** next-to-highest noncommissioned officer in Army, Air Force, and Marine Corps

**Medal of Honor** highest decoration awarded by United States for bravery in combat at risk of life above and beyond the call of duty

**medic** *Informal.* medical officer or member of military medical unit

**mercenary** soldier for hire, not fighting for his or her own nation; soldier of fortune

**mess** place where meals are prepared and eaten by military personnel; mess hall

**mess hall** mess

**mess kit** soldier's personal plate and utensils

**MIA** *missing in action;* military person lost in action whose fate is unknown

**middie** *Informal.* midshipman

**midshipman** cadet at U.S. Naval Academy; middie

**military** entire armed forces, its personnel and resources

**military police** MP; Army unit that fulfills police functions

**militia** military troops liable for call only during emergency, usu. civilians on nonactive duty

**Minuteman** member of group of American militia before and during Revolutionary War

**mission** operational task ordered by command to be completed before reporting back to headquarters

**MP** *military police*

**muster** (*vb*) assemble troops, esp. for inspection or discharge

**national guard** peacetime military force commanded by governor of each U.S. state, used for police work

**navy** military branch consisting of sea forces

**Navy** navy of the United States

**Navy Cross** decoration for outstanding heroism in U.S. naval operations

**NCO** *noncommissioned officer*

**noncom** *Informal.* noncommissioned officer

**noncombatant** soldier serving outside combat zone

**noncommissioned officer** NCO; enlisted person above rank of private, esp. corporal or sergeant; noncom

**oak leaf cluster** decoration in form of bronze twig with leaves and acorns, signifying second award of same medal to one person

**obstacle course** rigorous training field in boot camp consisting of various obstacles that must be overcome

**officer** commissioned military person

**olive drab**  military uniform made of woolen cloth in deep olive color

**pandour**  brutal, marauding soldier, orig. from Croatia

**panzer**  armored unit with tanks (Germany)

**parade rest**  position with feet one foot apart, hands clasped behind back, and head forward

**paratrooper**  soldier trained to parachute from airplane

**patrol**  small group of soldiers on reconnaissance

**petty officer**  noncommissioned naval officer

**pilot**  airplane flier

**platoon**  tactical unit larger than a squad and smaller than a company, commanded by lieutenant and sergeants

**plebe**  freshman at military or naval academy

**point man**  soldier who leads a patrol

**post exchange**  PX; department store on base for sales to military personnel and families only

**POW**  prisoner of war

**present arms**  salute position in which rifle in held vertically before chest with muzzle upward

**presidio**  garrison; military post

**prisoner of war**  POW; military person captured and held by enemy forces during war

**private**  soldier of the lowest rank

**pull rank**  exercise the power of one's rank over others

**Purple Heart**  medal awarded by United States for wounds received in action

**PX**  post exchange

**quartermaster**  officer who provides clothes and provisions for troops; petty officer who attends to ship's helm and signals

**R and R**  rest and recreation

**ranger**  soldier specially trained for raids, reconnaissance, and irregular warfare

**rank**  position in military hierarchy

**rear echelon**  troops removed from combat zone who are responsible for administration and matériel

**recruit**  person who recently joined armed forces

**recruitment**  campaign to generate enlistment in armed forces

**reenlist** (vb) rejoin military at end of tour of duty

**regiment**  tactical unit larger than a battalion and smaller than a brigade, commanded by colonel

**regular**  member of standing army

**Reserve Officers Training Corps**  ROTC; body of students being trained at college or university to become officers in armed forces

**reserves**  soldiers not on active duty but subject to call in emergency

**reservist**  member of the reserves

**resistance**  organized opposition to occupying enemy forces

**re-up** (vb) reenlist for another tour of duty

**reveille**  wake-up call, esp. played on bugle or drum

**revolutionary**  person who fights for violent overthrow of existing government

**rotate** (vb) return to home country after period of service overseas

**ROTC**  Reserve Officers Training Corps

**sailor**  enlisted person in naval military service

**salute**  formal gesture of respect, esp. by raising right hand to side of headgear

**sapper**  soldier who builds trenches or tunnels to undermine enemy positions

**sarge**  Informal. sergeant

**sawbones**  Slang. military surgeon

**SEALS**  sea-air-land forces; special forces of U.S. Navy

**section eight**  dishonorable discharge for physical or emotional incapacity

**selective service**  compulsory military service

**sentry**  soldier standing guard and preventing passage of unauthorized persons

**sepoy**  native infantryman formerly in service of British (India)

**sergeant**  noncommissioned officer in U.S. Army, Air Force, or Marines

**serial number**  identification number given to all military personnel

**service**  period as member of armed forces; military forces, collectively

**serviceman**  member of armed forces

**service stripe**  stripe worn on left sleeve indicating period of time on active duty

**shavetail**  Slang. second lieutenant

**shell shock**  combat fatigue

**shock troops**  elite corps trained to lead attack

**shore leave**  permission to leave ship and go ashore in port

**shore patrol**  U.S. Navy personnel having police duties similar to those of military police

**situation room**  area at headquarters through which latest reports are channeled

**soldier**  military fighting person; member of armed forces, esp. army

**soldier of fortune**  mercenary

**spahi**  member of native cavalry in service of French (Algeria)

**special forces**  specially trained elite fighting troops

**Special Forces**  U.S. Army personnel trained to work with indigenous forces engaged in guerrilla warfare and counterinsurgency operations and to conduct unconventional warfare; Green Berets

**specialist**  enlisted person with technical or administrative duties but no command, ranked in four grades comparable to corporal through sergeant first class

**Spetznaz**  special forces (U.S.S.R.)

**squad**  smallest tactical unit, consisting of ten or more people, commanded by staff sergeant

**squadron**  naval or airborne unit, esp. subdivision of fleet; armored cavalry unit; Air Force unit smaller than group, composed of two or more flights

**staff officer**  officer attached to commander's staff

**standard**  any of various military or naval flags

**standard-bearer**  soldier who carries flag

**star rank**  brigadier general or higher, having one or more stars

**stockade**  fortification; military jail

**storm trooper**  member of private Nazi army known for brutality; soldier resembling such Nazis

**stripes**  chevron or strip of cloth on sleeve indicating rank

**sutler**  civilian selling provisions on army post (18th–19th c.)

**swabby**  Slang. sailor or deckhand in U.S. Navy or Coast Guard

**tactical units**  subdivision of military; for U.S. Army, from smallest to largest, with commanding officer: squad (staff sergeant), platoon (lieutenant), company or battery (captain), battalion (lieutenant colonel), regiment (colonel), brigade (colonel), division (major general), corps (lieutenant general), army (general)

**taps** bugle sounded at end of day or at funeral

**terrorist** military or paramilitary person who employs extreme, unethical, often fanatical methods, esp. hostage taking, assassination, and murder of civilians, to gain political and military advantage

**tiger stripes** *Slang*. camouflaged uniform worn esp. in tropics

**top-secret** (*adj*) pertaining to security classification for information vital to national defense

**tour of duty** period of time on active military duty; period enlisted for

**troops** soldiers

**uhlan** lancer in light-cavalry unit

**unit** any of various subdivisions of military; tactical unit

**Unknown Soldier** unidentified soldier killed in combat whose tomb is a memorial to all unidentified dead service personnel

**veteran** former member of armed forces

**vexillary** one of a class of veteran soldiers (ancient Rome)

**volunteer** person who joins the military of his or her own free will

**war college** military training institution for teaching tactics and strategy of war

**war-horse** *Informal*. veteran soldier

**warison** bugle call to attack

**warpath** state of preparing for war or hostilities

**warrant officer** officer ranking above noncommissioned and below commissioned officer, holding rank by certificate

**weekend warrior** reservist who fulfills military obligation by attending weekend meetings of unit

**WIA** *wounded in action*; military person injured in action

**wing** administrative and tactical unit of U.S. Air Force consisting of two or more groups, headquarters, and support services

**wounded** soldiers who have been injured in combat

**yardbird** *Slang*. untrained soldier assigned to menial task or restricted to limited area for disciplinary reasons

**yeoman** naval petty officer who performs clerical duties

**Zouave** member of cavalry formerly in French army, orig. composed of Algerians, known for their dash and Oriental uniforms

## WAR MACHINERY AND WAR ZONES

**AAM** *air-to-air missile*

**ABC weapons** *atomic, biological, and chemical weapons*

**ABM** *antiballistic missile*

**air base** installation that services air force planes

**airburst** bomb explosion above ground surface

**aircraft carrier** large, flat-topped ship used as mobile airstrip

**air power** collective military strength of a nation in airplanes, bombers, jet fighters, pilots, and airborne technology

**all-terrain vehicle** vehicle with treads and/or wheels designed to traverse uneven terrain

**ammo** *Informal*. ammunition

**ammunition** projectiles fired from guns, including fuse, charge, and cartridge; any military explosive; ammo

**antiaircraft** artillery fired from ground or ships against enemy planes

**antiballistic missile** ABM; missile for interception and destruction of incoming ballistic missiles

**antimissile missile** ballistic missile used to detect and destroy enemy missiles in flight

**antipersonnel** (*adj*) designating weapons intended to maim or kill human beings rather than to damage property and equipment

**antitank** (*adj*) designating missile or artillery designed for use against armored vehicles

**area of war** geographical region involved in armed conflict

**armada** fleet of warships

**armaments** military equipment, esp. weapons

**armored personnel carrier** tracked vehicle with armored hull and light armament, for transporting troops in combat

**armory** place for storage of arms and equipment, esp. for training of reserves

**arms race** competitive development and proliferation of weapons, both conventional and nuclear

**arsenal** storage facility for weapons, sometimes also government manufacturing site for weapons; weapons stored there

**artillery** projectile-firing weapons

**ashcan** *Slang*. depth charge

**ASM** *air-to-surface missile*

**assault boat** portable boat for landing troops on beaches

**AWACS** *Airborne Warning And Control System*; sophisticated aircraft with powerful radar and computer, used to track other aircraft

**ballistic missile** self-propelled missile guided in trajectory ascent and falling freely in descent

**barrage balloon** one of several balloons anchored around military area to protect it from low-flying aircraft

**base** permanent center of military operations

**battery** tactical unit of artillery composed of six guns; two or more artillery pieces; guns on battleship

**battlefield** area of active armed conflict; battleground

**battlefront** front

**battleground** battlefield

**battle line** line of contact between opposing forces

**battleship** heavily armed and armored ship designed to shell other ships and shore targets

**beachhead** shore area in occupied territory seized as landing point for invading troops

**beaten zone** ground area that is receiving direct fire

**bivouac** temporary encampment, often with little or no shelter

**bomber** airplane designed principally to drop bombs

**bunker** fortified underground chamber of reinforced concrete with slant-sided openings

**caisson** two-wheeled vehicle for artillery ammunition

**cannon** large-caliber mounted gun

**cheval-de-frise** timber or iron barrel topped with spikes and barbed wire, used for defense

**clean weapon** nuclear bomb producing relatively little fallout

**combat drone** pilotless aircraft equipped with surveillance cameras, used to monitor battle areas; drone aircraft

**combat zone** area in which battle is occurring

**conventional weapons** traditional weapons and warheads, excluding nuclear, biological, and chemical weapons

**cross fire** gunfire from two or more points located so that lines of fire transect

**cruise missile** winged, jet-powered guided missile designed to fly low and carry a warhead

**D-day** day of planned military operation; June 6, 1944, day of Allied invasion of western Europe in World War II

**decoy** device that misleads soldier or weapon as to its target

**defensive weapons** armaments used for protection from attack

**defoliating agent** chemical that causes foliage to die, thus exposing hidden enemy

**delivery system** device, such as a missile, for transporting warhead to target

**demilitarized zone** DMZ; area forbidden to military installations and operations, often between opposing lines

**depth charge** powerful explosive dropped from ship or airplane that explodes underwater

**destroyer** speedy warship with guns, torpedoes, and depth charges

**direct fire** line-of-sight gunfire, esp. from close range

**dirty bomb** nuclear weapon producing large amount of fallout

**DMZ** demilitarized zone

**drone aircraft** combat drone

**field** area of active operations or combat, usu. away from command headquarters

**field artillery** mobile artillery that accompanies troops in combat

**fighter plane** small, maneuverable military plane equipped with automatic guns to attack other planes

**fire-and-forget weapons** electronically programmed weapons that require no human intervention to find targets and detonate

**firepower** amount of gunfire or explosives deliverable by weapon or armed forces unit

**flank** left or right section of army; wing

**fleet** organized unit of ships, aircraft, and marine troops under one administrative command

**fort** fortified structure occupied by troops, often surrounded by ditch, moat, rampart, or parapet

**foxhole** hastily dug pit for protection from enemy gunfire

**fratricide** nuclear warhead explosion that causes disturbance large enough to prematurely detonate other incoming warheads

**front** point of contact between two enemy forces; battlefront; battle line

**ground zero** area directly beneath a nuclear explosion

**gunnery** design, construction, and firing of heavy guns

**half-track** armored vehicle with rear driving wheels on caterpillar treads

**hard base** launching base protected against nuclear attack

**H-hour** specific hour of D-day when operation begins

**hunter-killer operation** offensive antisubmarine action

**ICBM** intercontinental ballistic missile

**interceptor** fighter plane utilized to divert or shoot down attacking enemy planes; missile used to explode incoming enemy missiles

**intercontinental ballistic missile** ICBM; rocket-propelled missile carrying warhead at long ranges

**jump jet** jet aircraft capable of nearly vertical takeoff that requires little or no airstrip

**laager** German. military camp or defensive position protected by circle or armored vehicles

**land-based missile** missile fired from site on land rather than air or sea

**landing force** amphibious assault unit

**line** military formation with several elements abreast of one another, esp. in closest contact with enemy

**Maginot line** line of fortifications built along French eastern frontier prior to World War II; any elaborate line of defense

**matériel** arms, ammunition, and other equipment

**medevac** helicopter used to evacuate wounded from battlefield

**minefield** area filled with hidden explosive charges

**Minuteman** ICBM with nuclear warhead

**missile** pilot, jet- or rocket-powered vehicle for delivering nuclear or conventional warhead

**mobile missile launcher** large truck and trailer used to launch missiles, allowing launch site to change rapidly

**MRV** multiple reentry vehicle

**multiple reentry vehicle** MRV; ballistic missile with two or more warheads

**mustard gas** oily liquid used as chemical weapon that causes blisters, blindness, and often death

**MX** ICBM with multiple nuclear warheads, capable of attack against bases, often concealed in underground silo

**nerve gas** often odorless and colorless, poisonous, easily absorbed liquid that interferes with nervous system and inhibits respiration

**nonnuclear weapons** tactical weapons

**nuclear weapons** bombs using atomic fission or fusion to create massive radiation doses and often irrecoverable damage to environment and property

**occupied territory** area under control of hostile armed forces

**ordnance** explosives, bombs, and ammunition

**paramilitary forces** troops similar to but separate from regular armed forces

**paravane** toothed, torpedo-shaped, protective device used by ship to cut moorings of underwater mines

**payload** warhead

**poison gas** nerve gas or other chemical weapon

**position** arrangement and disposition of troops at given time

**redoubt** secure, defended position; small, temporary, defensive enclosure

**round** cartridge or shell for single shot

**SADARM** sense-and-destroy armor

**SAM** surface-to-air missile

**SDI** Strategic Defense Initiative

**sense-and-destroy armor** SADARM; sensor-fused smart weapon

**silo** underground installation of concrete and steel that houses ballistic missile and mechanism for launching it

**situation map** map showing military plans and operations

**SLBM** submarine-launched ballistic missile

**smart weapons** steerable bombs and missiles electronically programmed to find target, esp. by heat detection

**soft base** target or launching base not protected against nuclear attack

**spoils** goods or property of defeated party claimed by victor

**Star Wars** program to use earth- and space-based weapons and technology to detect, intercept, and destroy enemy missiles; Strategic Defense Initiative

**stealth technology**  use of special design and materials to enable aircraft to evade detection, esp. by radar

**sternutator**  respiratory irritant used as chemical weapon

**stinkpot**  jar of combustibles that generate noxious odors, formerly used as weapon

**Strategic Defense Initiative**  SDI; Star Wars

**strategic weapons**  weapons intended to attack enemy's military and industrial facilities

**strike configured weapons**  delivery system arranged to carry out strike mission

**stronghold**  fortified position secure from enemy attack

**tactical aircraft**  planes providing air attack in support of ground forces

**tactical weapons**  armaments designed for limited or specific purposes, usu. nonnuclear weapons

**tank**  heavily armed, turreted, armored vehicle that moves on two continuous steel belts

**target**  area, object, or installation destined to be destroyed by bomb or missile

**theater**  geographical area of warfare

**trench**  long cut in ground with excavated earth thrown up in front to protect troops

**triphibian**  (*adj*) designed or equipped to operate on land, water, or in air

**turret**  low, armored, revolving structure for guns on fortress, warship, airplane, or tank

**vesicant**  burning and blistering agent used in chemical warfare

**warhead**  part of missile or rocket that contains explosive charge of nuclear, toxic, or detonating substance; payload

**war machine**  military hierarchy, infrastructure, weapons, technology, equipment, and personnel working together to wage war

**war zone**  combat area

**weapons of mass destruction**  nuclear, chemical, biological, and radiological weapons of massive lethal strength

**weapons system**  general type of weapon, esp. related series of weapons

**wing**  left or right section of army or fleet; flank

**wooden bomb**  *Informal.* reliable, stable, easily stored bomb

**yield**  force of nuclear explosion, measured in equivalent tons of TNT

## MILITARY RANKS (*IN DESCENDING ORDER*)

### ARMY, AIR FORCE, AND MARINES

general of the army (5-star)
marshal (Europe)
general (4-star)
lieutenant general (3-star)
major general (2-star)
brigadier general (1-star)
colonel
lieutenant colonel
major
captain
first lieutenant
second lieutenant
chief warrant officer (W-4)

chief warrant officer (W-3)
chief warrant officer (W-2)
warrant officer (W-1)
chief master sergeant
master sergeant
sergeant first class
specialist 7
sergeant major
first sergeant
gunnery sergeant
technical sergeant
staff sergeant
specialist 6
sergeant
specialist 5
corporal
specialist 4
lance corporal
private first class (PFC)
airman first class
private
airman
recruit
cadet

### NAVY AND COAST GUARD

fleet admiral
admiral
vice admiral
rear admiral
commodore
captain
commander
lieutenant commander
lieutenant
lieutenant junior grade
ensign
chief warrant officer (W-4)
chief warrant officer (W-3)
chief warrant officer (W-2)
master chief petty officer
senior chief petty officer
chief petty officer
petty officer 1st class
petty officer 2nd class
petty officer 3rd class
seaman
seaman apprentice
seaman recruit
midshipman

# INTERNATIONAL RELATIONS

Diplomacy and Diplomats
World Relations and Conditions
Security and Defense
Espionage and Intelligence

**SEE ALSO**: Chap. 11: Government; Law; War and Military; Chap. 12: Business and Economics; Finance

# DIPLOMACY AND DIPLOMATS

**accord** formal agreement; treaty

**agent-general** respective of a British dominion to England; chief representative

**alliance** agreement of mutual support between independent states

**ally** state or ruler associated with another by treaty

**ambassador** highest-ranking diplomatic officer

**ambassador-at-large** high-ranking diplomat not assigned to one particular foreign state

**amnesty** pardon granted to individual or group by government

**annexation** acquisition of another state or territory by a sovereign state

**Anschluss** political or economic union between nations, esp. Austria and Germany in 1938

**asylum** protection, esp. from extradition, given political refugees by state or agency with diplomatic immunity

**attaché** official of nondiplomatic government department attached to diplomatic post

**bilateralism** agreement between two nations to pursue common interests of mutual benefit

**bloc** group of aligned nations

**cahier** report of proceedings of any body

**cartel** international group joined together for common political or economic purpose; agreement between belligerents

**chancellery** office and personnel of embassy or consulate

**chargé d'affaires** envoy sent to state to which higher level diplomat is not sent; diplomat of lowest class who takes charge of business during temporary absence of ambassador or minister

**communiqué** official statement issued by parties at meeting

**compact** agreement between two or more states

**compromise** accord reached by mutual concession

**concession** yielding on some point so as to reach agreement

**concord** harmonious agreement among nations

**concordat** official agreement or compact; agreement to which pope is one party

**confederation** alliance or league of nations

**consul** official sent by one state to another to protect and assist its nationals in commercial relations

**consular agent** consular officer of lowest rank

**consulate** office or position of consul; premises occupied by consul

**consul general** top-ranking consul in key station or having authority over several consulates

**convention** general agreement among states regarding matters of common concern, less binding than treaty

**courier** diplomat bearing confidential documents

**covenant** formal, binding agreement between two or more nations

**delegate** representative of nation at conference or meeting

**deputy** substitute or assistant who assumes authority in absence of diplomatic superior

**detainee** person held for questioning, esp. civilian in wartime or political deserter

**détente** lessening of world tension

**diplomacy** art and practice of conducting international relations

**diplomat** political representative of one national government to another, appointed to conduct official negotiations and maintain relations between the two governments

**diplomatic corps** diplomatic personnel in residence in another state

**diplomatic immunity** special exemption from foreign laws afforded to diplomatic corps

**diplomatic mission** term served at foreign mission by diplomat; diplomat and his or her staff

**diplomatic pouch** case or package in which messages and information are transported

**diplomatic privilege** diplomatic mission's exemption from local jurisdiction

**diplomatic recognition** official acknowledgment of nation's sovereignty and legitimacy of its government

**diplomatic service** body of professional diplomats

**dispatch** message sent by diplomat from foreign post to home government

**doctrine** proclamation of basic governmental policy in international affairs

**dollar diplomacy** diplomatic activities to increase economic power of nation in foreign states

**embassy** ambassador's mission, entourage, and official residence in foreign nation

**emissary** representative, sometimes secret agent

**entente** international agreement of friendship or alliance, usu. stipulating common course of action; parties to such an agreement

**envoy** diplomatic agent of any rank

**exequatur** written recognition and empowerment of consul by government of nation in which he or she is stationed

**extradition** return of criminal to officers of state in which crime was committed

**foreign office** government ministry managing foreign affairs

**foreign policy** system of methods and objectives for maintaining relations with other states

**foreign service** diplomatic and consular staffs of one nation serving abroad

**General Assembly** highest deliberative body of United Nations, with representatives from all member nations

**Geneva Convention** internationally recognized rules for treatment of dead, wounded, and prisoners of war

**head of state** president, prime minister, sovereign, or other titular ruler of nation

**high seas** oceans and connecting waters not within territorial jurisdiction of any state

**international affairs** conduct and course of relations between two or more sovereign states

**International Court of Justice** judicial agency of United Nations that arbitrates disputes between nations; World Court

**international law** set of rules governing interactions of nations

**international relations** branch of political science concerned with military, economic, and diplomatic affairs between states

**internuncio** papal legate ranking below nuncio

**interpreter** person who provides oral translation between speakers of different languages such as diplomats from different nations

**league** association of nations with common purpose

**League of Nations** post-World War I organization of nations dedicated to promoting peace

**legate** emissary from one nation to another

**legation** diplomatic mission sent to foreign state; offices of diplomatic staff

**minister** diplomatic agent of second rank

**minister plenipotentiary** diplomat ranking below ambassador but wielding full powers

**mission** party sent overseas to conduct specific negotiations; permanent legation in foreign state

**nuncio** top-ranking papal legate to civil government

**pact** international agreement or treaty

**passport** official certificate issued to citizen by a government affirming his or her nationality and allowing foreign travel

**power politics** nationalistic policy based on military and economic coercion

**protocol** preliminary diplomatic agreement or records of diplomatic conference that form basis for final treaty

**secretary-general** principal officer of United Nations; principal officer of a secretariat

**secretary of state** appointed official who supervises department conducting U.S. foreign affairs

**Security Council** permanent peacekeeping council of United Nations, composed of five permanent and ten rotating two-year members

**shuttle diplomacy** negotiations between two hostile states conducted by intermediary traveling back-and-forth between them

**sovereign immunity** autonomy and independence of each sovereign state under international law

**sovereign state** self-governing, autonomous nation

**sovereignty** independence from external control by another nation

**State Department** U.S. executive department responsible for conduct of foreign affairs

**statesman** national leader with international respect

**statesmanship** exercise of astute national leadership based on world vision

**summit** conference of highest level officials from two or more states

**three-mile limit** ocean waters within three miles of coast considered part of national territory

**trade mission** delegates to foreign state seeking economic cooperation

**treaty** international agreement

**trust territory** nonself-governing region under authority of United Nations prior to becoming independent

**United Nations** post-World War II organization of nearly all nations dedicated to peace, economic development, and social welfare

**vice-consul** diplomatic officer subordinate to consul

**vice-legate** diplomatic officer subordinate to legate

**visa** license issued by nation permitting entry by foreigner, usu. in form of endorsement stamped in passport

**World Court** International Court of Justice

## WORLD RELATIONS AND CONDITIONS

**alien** resident of a state who is not a citizen or national of that state

**amity** international friendship or accord

**appeasement** unilateral concessions as means of pacifying hostile nation

**balance of power** world equilibrium in which no single power predominates

**Balkanize** (*vb*) divide a territorial entity into smaller, often hostile, units

**bamboo curtain** symbol of Chinese Communist ideological and political barrier to West

**banana republic** small Latin American state, dependent on foreign investment, often governed by despot

**banishment** expulsion from or relegation to a country or region by authoritative decree; exile

**border** national territorial demarcation

**carnet** customs document allowing automobile to be driven across international border at no cost

**client state** nation that is dependent on richer, more powerful nation for its political, economic, or military welfare

**colonialism** control of one state over other dependent territories or states

**colonization** acquisition and maintenance of dependent colonies

**colony** territory and citizens of state dependent on another state

**Common Market** European Economic Community

**compatriot** fellow countryman

**country** nation; fatherland; state

**crown colony** British colony without constitution or representative government, controlled directly by crown

**customs duty** tax on goods imported into country

**decolonize** (*vb*) allow a colony to become self-governing

**dependency** subject territory that is not an integral part of ruling country

**deport** (*vb*) expel, esp. an alien, from one country

**destabilize** (*vb*) take actions that render a government unable to function

**developed nation** industrialized state with well-developed economy and high standard of living

**developing nation** poor state in process of industrializing, with low standard of living

**domain** territory governed by single ruler or government; realm

**dominion** territory over which single government rules; sovereign authority over such territory

**domino theory** belief that unsuccessful containment, esp. of communism, in one state will be repeated in neighboring states

**dual citizenship** status of person who is legal citizen of two or more countries

**EEC** European Economic Community

**embargo** governmental prohibition on export of goods to specific foreign state

**emigrant** one who emigrates from native state

**emigration** departure of citizen of one state so as to become citizen of another

**enclave** territory completely enclosed by another state

**European Economic Community** EEC; cooperative economic partnership among states of western Europe, esp. for trade and finance; Common Market

**exile** compulsory or voluntary departure from homeland due to differences with government; banishment

**expatriation** citizen's voluntary renunciation of national allegiance

**extraterritoriality** right of state to extend its jurisdiction over its nationals into territory of another state

**fatherland** one's native country or that of one's ancestors; motherland

**foreign affairs** relations of one nation with others

**foreign aid** assistance, esp. economic, given to poorer nation by richer one

**free trade** international commerce without restrictive tariffs

**frontier** national boundary

**geopolitics** study of connections between geography and relations among nations

**glasnost** *Russian*. Soviet policy of openness about internal affairs and receptivity to Western influence during 1980's

**global** (*adj*) pertaining to entire world

**global economy** interrelated trade and development factors that affect all nations

**global interdependence** impact of each nation's foreign policy on all other states

**globalism** involvement of a country in international affairs and alliances, opposite of isolationism

**Good Neighbor Policy** U.S. policy toward Latin American states that pledges friendship and unified hemispheric defense

**Great Power** a nation that is predominant in international affairs

**hegemony** influence or authority of one nation over others

**human rights** basic freedoms and welfare of all world citizens, with which governments have no rights to interfere

**IMF** International Monetary Fund

**immigrant** one who immigrates into foreign state

**immigration** movement into country by noncitizens with intent to settle

**imperialism** policy of extending rule over other states

**imperium** area of dominion or empire; sphere of control

**incident** seemingly minor occurrence between nations that can lead to serious consequences

**international** (*adj*) that which involves two or more sovereign states

**International Bank for Reconstruction and Development** World Bank

**internationalism** principle of cooperation among nations to promote the common good

**International Monetary Fund** IMF; agency that promotes trade and development through contributions from member nations

**iron curtain** symbol of Soviet ideological and political isolation from West after World War II

**irredenta** territory historically or culturally related to one state but presently subjected to another

**isolationism** policy that peace and economic growth are best achieved by abstaining from alliances with and commitments to other nations

**Manifest Destiny** doctrine that it is U.S. destiny to expand territory in North America (19th c.)

**ministate** small, independent nation

**Monroe Doctrine** early 19th-century U.S. policy that opposed outside interference in Americas

**most-favored-nation** (*adj*) pertaining to treaty signatory that is accorded most favorable commercial benefits by another nation

**motherland** one's native country or that of one's ancestors; fatherland

**nation** people who share specific territory, have common customs, history, language, and culture, and are organized under a single government; country; sovereign state

**national** noncitizen who owes allegiance to a nation and enjoys its protection

**nationalism** allegiance to one's sovereign state

**nationality** status of citizenship in particular nation by birth or naturalization; people sharing common culture, organized to constitute sovereign state

**national supremacy** absolute military and economic power of one nation

**nation-state** sovereign state inhabited by fairly homogeneous group of people who share feeling of common nationality

**naturalization** process, other than by birth, through which citizenship is attained

**nonaligned nation** country not siding with one of the Great Powers

**OAS** Organization of American States

**OPEC** Organization of Petroleum Exporting Countries

**open door** policy of equal and impartial trade opportunities for all foreign nations

**Organization of American States** OAS; group that promotes cooperation and trade among nations of Latin America

**Organization of Petroleum Exporting Countries** OPEC; policy and price-setting cartel of oil-producing nations

**patriotism** love for or devotion to one's country

**power politics** nationalistic policy based on military and economic coercion

**protectionism** policy of restrictions on imported foreign goods to support domestic business

**realm** sphere of dominance, esp. royal domain over which monarch rules

**reciprocity** trade policy based on mutual benefit to both nations through exchange of special privileges

**refugee** one who has fled or been driven from his or her country to avoid persecution or danger

**refusenik** Soviet citizen refused permission to emigrate

**sanction** coercive economic or military action taken by one or several nations against another

**sovereign state** nation having supreme and independent power or authority in government

**sphere of influence** influence exerted by a Great Power over nearby states

**state** independent, sovereign nation

**superpower** extremely powerful nation with worldwide influence

**suzerain** nation controlling another state's foreign affairs

**tariff** government duty on imported goods

**territorial waters** waters, traditionally within 3 miles (4.8 km) of its shore, that are regarded as under jurisdiction of a state

**territory** geographical area under authority of single national government; area under U.S. authority that is not actually a state

**thalassocracy** dominion over the seas, esp. in trade

**Third World** underdeveloped nations of Asia, Africa, and South America

**trade balance** equilibrium of imports and exports between nations

**World Bank** international bank that makes loans to developing nations; International Bank for Reconstruction and Development

**world power** nation whose actions affect entire world

## SECURITY AND DEFENSE

**Allies** nations united against central European powers in World War I, or against Axis powers in World War II

**angary** international law permitting state at war to seize or destroy property of neutrals

**antiterrorism** strategy and actions to offset terrorism

**Arab League** confederation of Arab states formed in 1945 to promote unity and cooperation

**armistice** suspension of military operations between belligerents

**arms control** international agreements and diplomacy designed to regulate or stabilize use of weapons and armed forces

**arms race** competition between nations in building and stockpiling weapons to attain military superiority

**atomic age** period in history initiated by first use of atomic bomb and characterized by various uses of atomic energy

**atomic power** status of any nation that possesses nuclear weapons

**Axis** Germany, Italy, and Japan, opponents of Allies in World War II

**belligerent** nation at war that has been granted status in international law subjecting it to obligations and laws of war

**big stick** intimidation of smaller nations by threat of military intervention

**brinkmanship** tactic of maneuvering a dangerous situation to the limits of safety

**buffer state** small, neutral state separating two belligerents

**capitulation** act or terms of surrender

**chauvinism** excessive patriotism or nationalism

**coexistence** avoidance of warfare among hostile states

**Cold War** post-World War II ideological conflict between the United States and Soviet Union, conducted without direct military action

**collective security** multinational system in which members of alliance pledge mutual support against aggressors

**containment** policy that seeks to restrict influence of nation by confining it geographically

**détente** lessening of world tension

**deterrence** maintenance of large military arsenal to discourage belligerents from attacking

**disarmament** abolition, reduction, or limitation of arms

**dove** advocate of compromise and negotiation; supporter of peace and disarmament

**enemy** opposing state in war

**escalation** dynamic increase in tension, hostility, and conflict

**first strike** preemptive nuclear attack

**hawk** supporter of warlike defense posture

**insurgency** status in international law given to revolutionaries who possess insufficient organization to be granted the status of belligerency

**irenic** (*adj*) conducive to peaceful relations

**jingoism** aggressive, militaristic national policy

**limited war** hostilities conducted without resorting to use of nuclear weapons

**massive retaliation** use of nation's nuclear arsenal in response to attack

**militarism** belligerent international posture of intervention and intimidation

**mutual-defense treaty** agreement among nations to provide military assistance to any member coming under attack

**national security** nation's system of protection from foreign infiltration or attack

**National Security Council** NSC; U.S. executive agency that deals with defense, intelligence, and foreign affairs

**NATO** North Atlantic Treaty Organization; post-World War II organization formed among Western nations for mutual defense against Soviet aggression

**neutrality** state of impartiality and abstention from hostility in time of war

**nonaggression pact** pledge to refrain from acts of war

**nonaligned state** country not allied with one of prime belligerents

**North Atlantic Treaty Organization** NATO

**NSC** National Security Council

**peaceful coexistence** willingness or intention of belligerent nations to avoid armed conflict

**peace offensive** intensive diplomatic effort to achieve peace

**piracy** act of violence or theft committed at sea

**police action** localized military action undertaken without formal declaration of war, esp. against violators of international law

**preparedness** state of adequate advance planning for potential war

**rapprochement** reestablishment of friendly relations between hostile nations

**reprisal** retaliatory force short of war

**revanche** policy of regaining areas that have been lost to other states as result of war

**sabotage** action intended to disrupt or destroy nation's military or economic capabilities

**SEATO** Southeast Asia Treaty Organization; post-World War II alliance between United States and small Asian nations to protect those nations from Communist influence or attack

**security** measures taken to ensure national freedom from espionage, sabotage, and military attack

**Southeast Asia Treaty Organization** SEATO

**state of war** condition or period marked by armed conflict between nations, which are subject to international laws of war

**strategic nuclear weapons** long-range nuclear weapons capable of destroying enemy's civilian and military targets

**tactical nuclear weapons** nuclear weapons intended for specific, limited purpose

**terrorism** covert violent acts used to influence national policies

**treason** acts intended to overthrow government of one's own nation

**truce** temporary suspension of hostilities

**war** armed conflict between sovereign states

**Warsaw Pact** post-World War II organization formed by Soviet Union and eastern European nations for mutual protection from the United States and NATO states

**West** non-Communist countries of Europe and the Americas

## ESPIONAGE AND INTELLIGENCE

**agent** one engaged in intelligence operations

**Central Intelligence Agency** CIA; covert intelligence gathering agency of U.S. government since World War II

**CIA** *Central Intelligence Agency*

**cipher** secret code used in diplomatic communications

**collaboration** cooperation with enemy of one's state, esp. an occupying force

**collaborator** traitor who works with enemy state

**Company** *Informal.* Central Intelligence Agency

**counterespionage** spying intended to offset enemy espionage

**counterintelligence** actions intended to deceive or misinform enemy intelligence service and halt sabotage

**counterspy** one engaged in counterespionage

**courier** spy bearing secret documents

**covert** (*adj*) secret, hidden

**disinformation** deliberately false information, esp. about one's military strength or plans, released to confuse enemy government

**double agent** spy working for two opposed states

**espionage** spying to obtain information about plans and activities of foreign government

**Football** *Slang.* briefcase containing codes and options for use by U.S. President in launching nuclear attack

**infiltration** subtle or covert subversive involvement in another nation's affairs

**intelligence** political, military, economic, or other information about another state

**intelligence agency** government department engaged in obtaining secret information about other states

**Interpol** *International* Criminal *Police* Organization; international criminal investigative organization

**joe** *Slang.* espionage operative, usu. recruited from outside service

**laundered money** illicit funds given the appearance of legitimacy by passing through hands of third party

**listening post** location used for obtaining secret information about an enemy

**mole** undercover agent, esp. one who infiltrates another nation's intelligence agency

**quisling** traitor, collaborator with enemy

**reconnaissance** covert intelligence gathering, esp. regarding enemy military capabilities

**safe house** secret location where individuals may hide or plot sabotage and terrorism

**secret agent** spy, undercover operative

**spy** one who acts in a clandestine manner to obtain secret information about other states

**spying** secret intelligence-gathering activities against another nation

**traitor** person disloyal to his or her own nation

# TITLES OF RANK

**SEE ALSO**: Chap. 11: Government; Politics; War and Military; International Relations; Chap. 12: Occupations; Chap. 13: Education; Chap. 20: Terms of Endearment and Respect; Chap. 25: Religion

**abbé** French secular clergyman

**abbot** superior of men's monastery

**admiral** highest-ranking commissioned naval officer; naval commander in chief

**aga** general or leader in Ottoman Empire

**alcalde** chief administrative and judicial officer of Spanish town

**alderman** member of municipal council; magistrate ranking below mayor in English or Irish city

**ambassador** highest diplomatic representative of government serving as resident agent to foreign government or sovereign; special, temporary diplomatic representative

**amir** emir

**archbishop** bishop at head of ecclesiastical province

**archduchess** wife or widow of archduke; woman holding rank of archduke in her own right

**archduke** sovereign prince of imperial family in Austria

**archimandrite** dignitary of Eastern Orthodox Church ranking below bishop; superior of monastery or group of monasteries

**archon** chief magistrate in ancient Greece; presiding officer

**armiger** squire entitled to bear heraldic arms

**ataman** elected chief of Cossack village in Russia; hetman

**atheling** Anglo-Saxon prince or nobleman; heir apparent

**ayatollah** religious leader among Shiite Muslims, esp. one who is not an imam

**banneret** knight leading vassals into battle under his own banner, ranking above knight bachelor

**baron** lowest grade of peerage in Great Britain; continental European nobleman; lowest order of nobility in Japan

**baroness** wife or widow of baron; woman holding rank of baron in her own right

**baronet** peerage rank below baron and above knight

**bashaw** pasha

**beefeater** yeoman of the guard of English monarch

**bey** provincial governor of Ottoman Empire; title of respect in Turkey and Egypt

**bishop** high-ranking Anglican, Eastern Orthodox, or Roman Catholic clergyman having authority over other clergy and usu. governing a diocese

**boyar** Russian aristocrat ranking below ruling prince

**brigadier general** commissioned military officer with one star, ranking above colonel

**brother** male member of religious organization having a priesthood

**burgomaster** chief magistrate of certain European towns

**burgrave** hereditary governor of castle or town (Germany)

**cacique** native Indian chief in areas dominated primarily by Spanish culture; local political boss in Spain and Latin America

**caliph** spiritual head of Islam

**capo** chief of branch of Mafia family

**captain** commissioned army officer ranking above lieutenant and below major; naval officer with command of ship, ranking above commander and below commodore or admiral

**cardinal** highest official of Roman Catholic Church below pope

**castellan** governor or warden of castle or fort

**catholicos** primate of Eastern Orthodox Church, esp. Armenian

**caudillo** head of state in Spanish-speaking country, esp. military dictator

**centurion**  commanding officer of century unit in ancient Rome

**chamberlain**  chief officer in household of king or nobleman

**chancellor**  secretary of nobleman, prince, or king; chief secretary of embassy

**chaplain**  clergyman in charge of chapel or attached to branch of military, institution such as a college, important family, or royal court

**chatelaine**  wife of castellan

**chevalier**  lowest rank of French nobility, comparable to knight

**chief justice**  presiding judge of court having several members, esp. Supreme Court

**colonel**  commissioned military officer ranking above lieutenant colonel and below brigadier general

**commander in chief**  supreme commander of nation's military forces

**commissar**  Communist party official assigned to military unit to teach and ensure party loyalty

**commodore**  former commissioned officer in navy ranking above captain and below rear admiral

**constable**  warden or governor of royal castle or fortified town; police officer

**consul**  either of two annually elected chief magistrates in ancient Rome

**consul general**  highest-ranking consular officer

**corporal**  noncommissioned military officer ranking above private first class and below sergeant

**count**  European nobleman corresponding to British earl; former name for British earl

**countess**  wife or widow of earl or count; woman holding title of earl or count in her own right

**crown prince**  heir apparent to crown or throne

**crown princess**  wife of crown prince; female heir apparent or presumptive to crown or throne

**czar**  emperor of Russia until 1917 revolution; tsar

**czarevitch**  son and heir of czar

**czarevna**  daughter of czar or wife of czar's son

**czarina**  empress of Russia, wife of czar

**daimyo**  Japanese feudal baron

**Dalai Lama**  former ruler and chief monk of Tibet, believed to be reincarnation of Buddhist saint

**dame**  wife or daughter of lord; female member of order of knighthood

**dauphin**  eldest son of king of France

**deacon**  Roman Catholic cleric ranking below priest; layman elected by church to fulfill pastoral or administrative duties

**dean**  Roman Catholic priest supervising one district or diocese

**dewan**  prime minister of East Indian state

**dey**  ruling official of Ottoman Empire in northern Africa

**doge**  chief magistrate in republics of Venice and Genoa

**Don**  Spanish title equivalent to Mr. or Sir, prefixed to man's given name; Spanish nobleman or gentleman

**Dona**  Portuguese title equivalent to Madam or Lady, prefixed to woman's given name

**Doña**  Spanish title equivalent to Madam or Lady, prefixed to woman's given name

**dowager**  widow holding property and title from deceased husband

**duce**  *Italian.* leader; title of Benito Mussolini

**duchess**  wife or widow of duke; woman holding ducal title in her own right

**duke**  European nobleman of highest hereditary rank; member of highest rank of British peerage, ranking above marquis

**earl**  British peer ranking below marquis and above viscount, formerly called count

**effendi**  member of aristocracy or government official in Turkey

**Elector**  one of German princes entitled to elect emperor of Holy Roman Empire

**emeritus**  (*adj*) honorary title held after retirement and corresponding to that held during active service

**eminence**  person of high rank or attainment, esp. Roman Catholic cardinal

**emir**  native ruler in parts of Asia and Africa; amir

**emperor**  sovereign or supreme monarch of an empire

**empress**  wife or widow of emperor; woman who holds imperial title in her own right

**ensign**  commissioned naval officer ranking below lieutenant

**equerry**  officer of prince or noble charged with care of horses; attendant to British monarch

**esquire**  member of English gentry ranking below knight

**eupatid**  hereditary aristocrat of ancient Greece

**exarch**  Byzantine viceroy; Eastern Orthodox bishop ranking below patriarch and above metropolitan

**excellency**  title for certain high dignitaries of state and church

**Führer**  *German.* leader; used chiefly in reference to Adolf Hitler

**general**  highest commissioned military officer, ranking above lieutenant general

**generalissimo**  chief commander of army

**gentry**  condition or rank of being a gentleman

**governor**  official elected or appointed to act as ruler, chief executive, or nominal head of political unit

**governor general**  one who governs large territory or has deputy governors under him

**Graf**  *German.* count; title of nobility equivalent to British earl

**grand duchess**  wife or widow of grand duke; woman who holds rank of grand duke in her own right

**grand duke**  sovereign duke of certain European states

**grandee**  man of eminence and social status, esp. Spanish or Portuguese nobleman

**gunnery sergeant**  Marine Corps noncommissioned officer equivalent to first sergeant

**hakim**  Muslim ruler, governor, or judge

**headmaster**  man heading staff of private school

**headmistress**  woman heading staff of private school

**heir apparent**  next in line to title whose right to inheritance is indefeasible in law if he survives legal ancestor

**heir presumptive**  next in line to title whose right to inheritance may be eliminated by birth of nearer relative

**herald**  official of tournament of arms; ambassador acting as messenger between leaders during war

**hetman**  Cossack leader; ataman

**hidalgo**  member of Spanish lower nobility

**high commissioner**  principal or high-ranking commissioner; ambassadorial representative of government of one nation stationed in another

**highness**  title of address for person of exalted rank

**high priest** chief priest of Jewish Levitical priesthood; priest of Melchizedek priesthood in Mormon Church

**high priestess** chief female priest, esp. of ancient orders

**imam** Islamic ruler claiming descent from Muhammad and exercising spiritual and temporal leadership over region

**incumbent** holder of office or ecclesiastical benefice

**infanta** daughter of Spanish or Portuguese monarch

**inspector general** officer of military or naval corps of inspectors that investigates organizational matters

**jarl** Scandinavian noble ranking just below king

**judge** magistrate charged with administration of justice in court of law

**junker** member of Prussian landed aristocracy

**justice** judge or magistrate

**kaiser** emperor; ruler of Germany from 1871 to 1918

**khan** local chieftain or man of rank in countries of central Asia

**khedive** title of ruler of Egypt from 1867 to 1914, governing as viceroy of Turkish sultan

**king** male monarch of major territorial unit, usu. holding hereditary title and ruling for life

**knight** man honored by sovereign for merit, ranking in Great Britain below baronet

**lady** woman having proprietary rights or authority as feudal superior

**ladyship** title of address for woman having rank of lady

**laird** landed proprietor

**lama** Tibetan Buddist priest or monk

**lance corporal** enlisted man in Marine Corps ranking above private first class

**landgrave** count having jurisdiction over large territory; title of certain German princes

**legate** deputy or emissary

**lieutenant** official empowered to act for higher official; lowest ranking commissioned military officer

**lieutenant colonel** military officer ranking below colonel

**lieutenant commander** naval officer ranking below commander

**lieutenant general** commissioned military officer with three stars, ranking above major general

**lieutenant governor** deputy or subordinate governor

**lord** ruler by hereditary right or preeminence to whom service and obedience are due; holder of feudal tenure

**madame** title for woman of rank or office; French prefix for married woman

**mademoiselle** French prefix for unmarried woman

**magistrate** official entrusted with administration of laws; principal official exercising governmental powers over major political unit

**magnifico** Venetian nobleman

**maharajah** Hindu prince ranking above raja; also maharaja

**maharani** wife of maharajah; Hindu princess ranking above rani; also maharanee

**maître d'** maître d'hotel; majordomo; headwaiter

**majesty** form of address for reigning sovereign power, authority, or dignitary

**major** commissioned officer in military ranking above captain and below lieutenant colonel

**majordomo** man having charge of a large household; head steward; maître d'

**major general** commissioned military officer holding two stars, ranking above brigadier general

**malik** *Arabic.* king, leader

**manciple** steward or purveyor for college or monastery

**mandarin** public official of Chinese Empire

**marchesa** Italian woman holding rank of marchese

**marchese** Italian nobleman next in rank above count

**marchioness** wife or widow ·of marquis or marchese; woman holding title of marchesa in her own right; marquise

**margrave** military governor of German border province; German nobleman corresponding to British marquis

**marquess** marquis

**marquis** British peer ranking below duke and above earl; hereditary European or Japanese nobleman; marquess

**marquise** marchioness

**marshal** general officer of highest military rank; municipal or federal law enforcement officer; administrative head of police or fire department

**master-at-arms** petty officer charged with maintaining discipline aboard ship

**master sergeant** highest noncommissioned army officer, ranking above staff sergeant or sergeant major

**mayor** official elected or appointed to act as chief executive or nominal head of city or borough

**metropolitan** primate of ecclesiastical province

**mikado** emperor of Japan

**milady** term of address for Englishwoman of noble or gentle birth

**milord** term of address for Englishman of noble or gentle birth

**minister** Christian Protestant clergyman; diplomatic representative below ambassador; cabinet-level officer administering specific ministry in government

**minister plenipotentiary** plenipotentiary

**miss** conventional title for young unmarried woman

**mister** Mr.; conventional title for man not entitled to rank, honorific, or professional title

**Mogul** sovereign of 16th-century empire founded in India by conquering groups of Mongol, Turkish, and Persian origin

**monarch** hereditary sovereign or constitutional ruler of kingdom or empire

**monseigneur** French dignitary

**monsieur** French term of address for man, equivalent to mister; Frenchman of high rank or station

**monsignor** Roman Catholic prelate having dignity or titular distinction conferred by pope

**Most Reverend** term of address for archbishop or Roman Catholic bishop

**Mr.** conventional title before name of man not holding title of rank, honorific, or professional title; mister

**Mrs.** conventional title before name of married woman not holding title of rank, honorific, or professional title

**Ms.** title used instead of Miss or Mrs. when marital status of woman is unknown or irrelevant

**mullah** Muslim religious teacher of quasi-clerical class

**nabob** provincial governor of Mogul empire in India; man of great wealth or prominence

**nawab** viceroy or deputy governor in India

**negus** king or sovereign of Ethiopia

**Nizam** title of ruler of Indian state of Hyderabad until 1950

**nobleman** man of noble rank or birth

**noblewoman** woman of noble rank or birth

**nuncio** papal legate of highest rank, permanently accredited to civil government

**overlord** lord over other lords; lord paramount; absolute or supreme ruler

**padishah** chief ruler, sovereign, or shah of Iran

**padre** Christian clergyman; military chaplain

**palatine** feudal lord having sovereign power within domain; high officer in palace of Holy Roman Emperor

**pandit** wise or learned man of India

**parson** Protestant pastor

**pasha** Turkish or North African man of high rank or office; bashaw

**pastor** clergyman of local church or parish

**patriarch** Roman Catholic bishop ranking immediately below pope; bishop of Eastern Orthodox sees of Alexandria, Antioch, Constantinople, or Jerusalem, or of Western see of Rome; jurisdictional head of various Eastern churches

**patrician** person of high birth; orig. member of one of citizen families of ancient Rome

**peer** member of one of five ranks of British peerage: duke, marquis, earl, viscount, baron

**petty officer** subordinate officer in navy or coast guard appointed from among enlisted men

**pharaoh** sovereign ruler of ancient Egypt

**plenipotentiary** person, esp. diplomatic agent, invested with full power or authority to transact business; minister plenipotentiary

**podesta** medieval magistrate in Italian town or republic; mayor of Italian city under Fascist regime

**pontifex** member of council of priests in ancient Rome

**pontiff** Roman Catholic pope; pontifex

**pope** prelate who, as bishop of Rome, is head of Roman Catholic Church

**potentate** individual wielding great power; sovereign

**praetor** ancient Roman magistrate ranking below consul, having chiefly judicial functions

**prefect** any of various officials or magistrates of ancient Rome; chief officer or chief magistrate; student monitor in private school

**prelate** high-ranking ecclesiastic, such as bishop

**premier** prime minister; one who is first in position or rank

**president** chief executive of an organization; presiding officer of government body; elected chief of state and chief executive in most republics; ceremonial chief of state in republic with parliamentary government

**prexy** *Slang.* president, esp. of college or university

**priest** Anglican, Eastern Orthodox, or Roman Catholic clergyman ranking below bishop and authorized to perform certain rites

**priestess** female priest

**prime minister** chief minister of ruler or state; head of cabinet or ministry; chief executive in parliamentary government

**prince** male member of royal family, esp. sovereign's son or grandson; monarch or ruler of principality or state

**prince consort** husband of reigning female sovereign

**princeling** young, subordinate, or minor prince

**princess** female member of royal family, esp. daughter or granddaughter of sovereign; consort of prince; woman holding sovereign power

**principal** chief administrator of educational institution

**prior** officer ranking below abbot in monastery

**private** enlisted man of lowest military rank

**private first class** enlisted man ranking above private and below corporal

**proconsul** governor or military commander of ancient Roman province

**proctor** person appointed to supervise students, esp. during examinations

**professor** faculty member of highest academic rank at college or university

**provost** chief dignitary of collegiate or cathedral chapter; chief magistrate of Scottish burgh; keeper of prison; high-ranking university administrative officer

**purser** official on ship or aircraft responsible for papers, accounts, and comfort and welfare of passengers

**queen** wife or widow of king or tribal chief; female monarch

**queen consort** wife of reigning monarch

**queen mother** queen dowager who is mother of reigning monarch

**rabbi** Jewish master or teacher; Jew trained and ordained for professional religious leadership; leader of Jewish congregation; reb

**rajah** Indian or Malay prince or chief; Hindu title of nobility; also raja

**rani** Hindu queen; rajah's wife; also ranee

**rear admiral** commissioned officer in U.S. Navy or Coast Guard with two stars, ranking above captain

**reb** rabbi

**recording secretary** officer of organization charged with keeping minutes of meetings and other records

**rector** Episcopal clergyman in charge of parish; Roman Catholic priest directing seminary or college

**reeve** chief town officer of Anglo-Saxon king; medieval English manor overseer; head of council in some Canadian provinces

**regent** one who governs kingdom in minority, absence, or disability of sovereign; member of governing board of state university

**registrar** officer of educational institution responsible for registering students and keeping academic records; admitting officer of hospital, university, or other institution

**representative** elected member of legislative body, esp. U.S. House of Representatives

**reverend** member of clergy; clergyman's title preceded by "the" and followed by name

**sachem** North American Indian chief, esp. Algonquian; Tammany Hall political boss

**sacristan** sexton; person in charge of sacristy and ceremonial equipment of church

**sagamore** subordinate chief of Algonquian Indians

**sahib** word meaning sir or master among Hindus and Muslims in colonial India, used when addressing European of social status

**samurai** military retainer of Japanese daimyo practicing chivalric code of Bushido; aristocratic warrior of Japan

**satrap** governor of province in ancient Persia

**sayyid** title given to Islamic teacher or royal personage said to be descended from Muhammad

**scoutmaster** adult leader of band of boy or girl scouts

**secretary** officer of business or organization who keeps records of meetings; cabinet-level officer of state directing government administrative department

**secretary-general** principal administrative officer

**seigneur** seignior

**seignior**  man of rank or authority; feudal lord of manor; seigneur

**senator**  member of legislative body, usu. upper house, esp. member of U.S. Senate

**señor**  Spanish equivalent of Mr.

**señora**  Spanish equivalent of Mrs.

**señorita**  Spanish equivalent of Miss

**signor**  Italian equivalent of Mr.

**signora**  Italian equivalent of Mrs.

**signorina**  Italian equivalent of Miss

**sergeant**  police officer ranking below captain or lieutenant in United States and below inspector in England; noncommissioned army officer ranking above corporal and below staff sergeant

**sergeant major**  noncommissioned military officer serving as chief administrative assistant in headquarters, ranking above first sergeant

**sexton**  church officer who cares for church property, rings bell, and digs graves

**shah**  sovereign of Iran

**shammes**  sexton of Jewish synagogue

**sharif**  descendant of prophet Muhammad through his daughter Fatima; one of noble ancestry or political preeminence in Islamic countries

**sheik**  Arab chief or ruler

**sheriff**  important official of shire or county charged primarily with judicial duties; police officer for county

**shogun**  military governor ruling Japan until revolution of 1867–1868

**sir**  man of rank or position, esp. title before given name of knight or baronet

**sire**  man of rank or authority; lord; sovereign

**sister**  female member of religious community that observes vows

**sovereign**  one exercising supreme power in specific sphere; monarch, ruler, or king

**squire**  shield- or armor-bearer of knight; male attendant; member of British gentry ranking below knight and above gentleman

**sri**  conventional title of respect for distinguished Hindu Indian

**stadtholder**  viceroy in a province of the Netherlands; chief executive officer of the Netherlands

**staff sergeant**  noncommissioned military officer ranking above sergeant and below first sergeant or gunnery sergeant

**steward**  one employed on estate to manage domestic affairs; employee on ship, aircraft, or train who buys and obtains provisions and is responsible for comfort of passengers

**stewardess**  woman performing duties of steward

**subahdar**  governor of province in India; chief native officer of native company in British Indian army

**subaltern**  person holding subordinate position

**subdeacon**  cleric ranking below deacon; person ranked lowest in major orders of Roman Catholic and Eastern Orthodox churches

**suffragan**  Anglican or Episcopal bishop assisting diocesan bishop but not having right of succession

**sultan**  king or sovereign of Muslim state

**sultana**  female member of sultan's family, esp. wife

**superintendent**  top executive for jurisdiction or organization

**superior**  one who is above another in rank, esp. head of religious house or order

**supervisor**  administrative officer in charge of business, government, or school

**suzerain**  superior feudal lord to whom fealty is due

**swami**  Hindu ascetic or religious teacher

**taipan**  foreigner living in China and wielding economic power there

**tetrarch**  ruler of fourth part of a province in ancient Roman Empire

**thane**  free retainer of Anglo-Saxon lord; feudal Scottish lord

**title of rank**  descriptive or distinctive appellation accorded to a person by right of office, position, status, birth, or achievement

**trustee**  one of a body of persons appointed to administer affairs of a company or institution

**tsar**  czar

**tuchun**  Chinese warlord; provincial military governor in early 20th-century China

**'ulama**  member of body of Islamic mullahs

**vavasor**  feudal tenant ranking below baron; also vavasour

**veep**  *Informal.* vice president

**verger**  church official who keeps order during services and serves as usher or sacristan

**vicar**  Episcopal clergyman or layman having charge of mission or chapel; clergyman exercising broad responsibility as representative of prelate

**vicar of Christ**  Roman Catholic pope

**vice-**  prefix in title of official, such as vice-consul, who takes place of or succeeds a superior

**vice-admiral**  commissioned U.S. naval officer with three stars, ranking above rear admiral

**vice president**  person ranking below president and succeeding president in his or her absence

**vicereine**  wife of viceroy

**viceroy**  governor of country or province ruling as representative of king or sovereign

**viscount**  member of British peerage ranking below earl and above baron

**viscountess**  wife or widow of viscount; woman holding rank of viscount in her own right

**vizier**  high executive officer of various Muslim countries, esp. Ottoman Empire

**warden**  chief operating officer of prison; British governor or officer in charge of administrative department; chief administrator of college or governing officer of certain guilds in Britain

**warlord**  supreme military leader; military commander exercising civil power by force in limited area

**worship**  respectful term of address to British person of importance

**zamindar**  collector of land revenue for government in Muslim India; landlord in British India paying fixed revenue

CHAPTER 12

# The Economy

# BUSINESS AND ECONOMICS

Economics and Economic Theory
Commerce and Trade
Corporations and Business Practices
Labor
Employers, Employees, and Business People

**SEE ALSO**: Chap. 11: Government; Chap.12: Finance;
Advertising; Occupations; Chap. 13: Sociology

## ECONOMICS AND ECONOMIC THEORY

**accumulation**  addition to capital investment or capital stock from profits

**affluence**  substantial wealth and economic power

**aggregate**  total of some measured element of economy

**aggregate demand**  total spending on goods and services by all sectors, including consumers, business, government, and foreign

**aggregate equilibrium**  macroeconomic situation in which national demand for goods and services equals national supply of goods and services

**agribusiness**  growing, processing, and marketing of crops by large corporations instead of individual farmers

**agriculture**  growing crops and raising livestock, esp. as basis of economic structure

**antitrust** (adj) pertaining to policies or laws designed to curb monopolies

**assumed debt**  others' liabilities taken on, as in a merger

**austerity**  tightened economy characterized by shortages

**autarky**  national policy of self-sufficiency, including elimination of imports

**automation**  replacement of human laborers with machines, esp. self-regulating machines and computers

**balanced budget**  spending equal to revenue, esp. in government

**balance of payments**  periodic summary of difference between a nation's total payments to foreign countries and its receipts from them

**balance of trade**  difference in value between nation's imports and its exports

**bankruptcy**  inability to pay one's debts; legal insolvency

**belt-tightening**  measures to reduce expenditures, cut costs, and eliminate deficits

**bonanza**  source of great wealth or profits

**boom**  high level of economic activity; period of business expansion

**boondoggle**  wasteful or pointless business venture or government program

**bottom out** (vb) level out at low point of business cycle

**bourgeoisie**  middle class or class of owners

**boycott**  refusal to trade with a business, person, or nation as punishment or means of persuasion

**bread line**  line of destitute people awaiting free food

**break even**  achieve minimum sales needed to cover expenses and costs of production

**broke** (adj) bankrupt; having little or no available cash

**budget**  plan of expenditures based on anticipated revenues, as for a nation or company

**budget deficit**  state in which government expenditures exceed revenues

**business cycle**  periodic rise and fall in economic activity

**bust**  Informal. financial or economic collapse; state of bankruptcy

**buyer's market**  market in which supply exceeds demand, giving buyers leverage

**buying power**  purchasing power

**cap**  upper limit to spending

**capital**  money, assets, or property used as means of production or for investment

**capital-intensive** (adj) designating production using more capital than labor

**capitalism**  economic system based on private ownership and profit incentive

**cartel**  group of producers acting cooperatively to control production and prices

**chattel**  movable item of personal property; slave

**cheap** (adj) low-priced; reluctant to spend money

**circular flow diagram**  schematic representation of relationship between major economic sectors

**class**  social rank or caste as determined by income or economic status

**class struggle**  Marxist view of conflict between labor and capital, personified by workers and owners

**clean up** (vb) Informal. reap large profits

**collectivism**  political/economic system based on public ownership of production

**command economy**  system, such as communism, in which government controls factors of production and policy

**commercialism**  practice and spirit of commerce or business, esp. high regard for profits

**common market**  association of countries seeking economic cooperation, esp. through tariff concessions

**Common Market**  European Economic Community

**communism**  economic system based on collective ownership of means of production and control of distribution of goods and services

**company town**  town whose inhabitants are largely dependent on a single company for jobs and services

**compensation**  payment for services or labor, esp. wages

**competition**  rivalry between similar businesses for customers or clients

**conspicuous consumption**  acquisition and use of goods and services beyond one's needs as a display of wealth

**consumer goods**  products purchased by individuals for personal use

**consumerism**  consumption of goods and services; protection of consumers from poor products or misleading claims

**consumer price index**  measure of fluctuation in prices of common consumer goods and services over fixed time period

**containerization**  packaging and shipping large amounts of merchandise in single container

**convergence theory**  theory that capitalist and socialist societies are becoming more alike

**cost-benefit analysis**  ratio of dollar cost of project to dollar benefit it will produce, used to compare worthiness of various proposed projects

**cost of living**  average cost for basic necessities of life

**creeping inflation** barely noticeable but persistent increase in prices

**cut corners** trim inessential budget items

**dear** (*adj*) expensive

**decline** period of reduced business activity

**deficit** budget imbalance in which expenditures exceed revenues

**deficit financing** financing of budget deficit by borrowing

**deficit spending** government spending in excess of revenues, esp. to stimulate national economy

**deflation** decrease in money supply, causing sharp fall in prices

**demand** capability and desire of consumer to purchase goods and services

**demand curve** graph showing amounts purchased at different prices

**demand elasticity** measure of change in quantity demanded caused by change in price

**demand-side economics** Keynesian economic theory emphasizing stimulation of aggregate demand

**democratic socialism** economic system based on socialist government regulated by democratic electoral process

**depression** severe, prolonged decline in business activity

**deregulation** planned, usu. gradual, removal of governmental control over business

**destitution** extreme poverty

**devaluation** official lessening of value of currency relative to other currencies

**developed nation** industrial and/or technological society with high standard of living

**developing nation** agricultural society with low standard of living and little technological development

**diminishing returns** any additional unit of one factor of production that yields a smaller increase in production while other factors remain constant; law of diminishing returns

**disadvantaged** (*adj*) deprived of decent standard of living by poverty or lack of opportunity

**discomfort index** statistic combining rate of inflation with unemployment rate

**discretionary income** money available for luxuries after basic needs have been met

**disposable income** income remaining after paying all taxes

**distribution** marketing of merchandise; process by which products reach ultimate consumers; portions or shares of total income received by different groups

**diversify** (*vb*) expand business or economy by increasing number of goods produced or operations undertaken

**down-and-out** (*adj*) poor, destitute

**downside** downward trend, esp. loss on investment such as securities

**dumping** selling goods below cost to other nations to eliminate surpluses or offset competition

**duopoly** market controlled by two sellers only

**earning power** potential for earning wages, income, or profits, esp. over a lifetime

**easy money policy** loose money policy intended to expand money supply and lower interest rates

**econometrics** statistically oriented economic theory and models used in forecasting changes

**economic model** simplified representation of a real-world phenomena based on likely reactions to economic changes

**economics** study of wealth and its creation, dissemination, and consumption

**economic system** manner in which a nation uses its resources and manages production and distribution

**economist** student and practitioner of economic theory; someone so trained serving as policy adviser, esp. in business or government

**economy** organization of social and political institutions and businesses for production, distribution, and use of goods and services; frugality or careful spending

**elasticity** amount of change in purchases or production caused by small change in price or another variable

**embargo** ban on import or export of specific item to or from particular nation

**entitlement** government transfer payment guaranteed to all members of a group

**expansion** period of recovery and growth in business cycle

**expensive** (*adj*) high in cost or price

**extravagance** excessive spending beyond one's means, esp. on unnecessary items

**factors of production** essentials in generating goods and services, esp. natural resources, labor, capital, and management

**false economy** seemingly effective but misguided efforts to save or cut back on costs

**farm economy** national economy based on agriculture

**feudalism** primarily medieval economic and political system based on relationship of lord to vassal living and working on lord's land

**fiefdom** in feudal system, heritable land held from lord in return for work and loyalty

**Five-Year Plan** economic plan specifying goals to be reached in five years, esp. in China and Soviet Union

**food stamps** coupons for food at reduced prices, issued monthly by government to qualifying poor persons

**forecast** analysis and prediction of market trends

**foreign aid** monetary and other assistance given by one nation to another

**Fourth World** nations without wealth or valuable resources and showing little economic growth

**free enterprise system** economic system based on private individual ownership of production with decision making based on profit motive in competitive market; capitalism

**freehold** land held for life with right to pass it on through inheritance

**free trade area** nations that have agreed to reduce or eliminate trade barriers and tariffs among themselves while external tariffs vary

**freeze** fixing of some economic factor, such as prices, employment, expenditures, or taxes, at a given level

**full employment** economic condition in which unemployment is deemed minimal and acceptable, usu. under six percent

**gainful employment** work for which one is paid wages

**galloping inflation** sudden, rapid, or extreme and uncontrollable increase in prices

**GNP** gross *n*ational *p*roduct

**goods** things produced and purchased

**goods and services** end results of production: things people buy and activities performed for others

**Gresham's law** statement of tendency of inferior currency to circulate more freely than superior currency, which is hoarded

**gross national product**  GNP; combined annual monetary value of all goods, services, and products sold on markets of national economy

**guaranteed annual income**  proposed program in which family income is supplemented by government to reach base level

**hand-to-mouth** (*adj*) relating to bare existence with nothing to spare

**hard up** (*adj*) *Informal.* lacking resources

**have-nots**  persons or nations with relatively little wealth

**haves**  persons or nations with relatively great wealth

**heir**  person who will inherit or does inherit another's property upon his or her death

**hunting and gathering society**  primitive, preagricultural civilization or people that subsists through hunting and collecting wild plants

**hyperinflation**  extremely rapid inflation and major shortages due to panic buying

**index**  number showing percentage variation over time of economic factors from an arbitrary standard, usu. 100

**index of leading indicators**  statistical measure capable of predicting economic conditions in near future, based on several factors

**indigence**  poverty

**industrialization**  replacement of hand tools by machine and power tools and development of large-scale production, beginning in late 18th c.

**inelasticity**  change in price that causes little change in purchases or production

**inflation**  sustained rise in price of goods and services

**inflationary spiral**  continuous increase in prices, costs, and wages

**inheritance**  property, wealth, or business acquired at death of another

**input-output model**  matrix in which rows and columns represent input or output of goods from various sectors of economy

**insolvency**  inability to pay bills and debts

**Keynesian economics**  theory emphasizing stimulation of aggregate demand over supply

**labor-intensive** (*adj*) designating production using more labor than capital

**Laffer curve**  economic model relating lower tax rates to higher tax collections

**laissez faire**  economic system with minimal government regulation of business, trade, and competition

**landed class**  members of society who own property

**latifundium**  great estate operated on feudal basis (Latin America)

**law of diminishing returns**  diminishing returns

**loose money policy**  stimulation of economy by making credit inexpensive and abundantly available

**Lorenz curve**  graph showing variance between equal and actual distribution of income

**lottery**  game of chance in which people buy numbered tickets and prizes are awarded by lot, used to raise funds by some states

**lower class**  people occupying bottom rung of socioeconomic ladder

**lumpenproletariat**  lowest level of society, comprised of unskilled workers, tramps, beggars, and criminals who lack solidarity with proletariat

**macroeconomics**  economic branch dealing with broad aspects of the economy, esp. aggregates on national level

**make ends meet**  keep one's expenditures equal to or less than one's income

**Malthusian** (*adj*) pertaining to the theories of T.R. Malthus regarding dichotomy between geometric population growth and arithmetic increase in means of subsistence, causing shortages unless war or famine intervenes to eliminate the imbalance

**mammon**  wealth and material gain as an object of worship and evil

**manufacturing**  production of commodities for sale

**market**  activity of buying and selling; trade; potential customers for a product

**market economy**  economic system ruled by opportunity of consumers to buy and producers to sell

**market equilibrium**  condition of equal supply and demand with stable prices

**market mechanism**  interaction of supply and demand that determines market price and output level

**market share**  percentage of total sales in specific market accounted for by one company

**market socialism**  public ownership of means of production and use of market mechanism for distribution

**Marxism**  socioeconomic theories of Karl Marx, esp. as basis of communism

**mass production**  manufacture of large quantities of goods using standardized parts and assembly lines

**material assets**  wealth, property, or businesses owned

**materialism**  belief that accumulation of wealth and material objects is of primary importance in life

**measure of value**  function of money as standard unit measure for value of commodities

**mechanization**  substitution of machinery for human labor in production process

**mercantilism**  preindustrial economic system emphasizing controlled balance of exports and imports (16th-18th c.)

**microeconomics**  branch of economics dealing with single units of production and consumption

**middle class**  heterogeneous socioeconomic group with common values, comprised of business and professional people, bureaucrats, farmers, and skilled laborers

**mixed economy**  system combining elements of market and command economies

**monetarism**  theory that level of economic activity depends primarily on quantity and growth rate of money supply

**money**  medium of exchange and measure of value in economy

**money supply**  amount of money in circulation at a given time

**monopoly**  domination of market by single company

**national debt**  total amount owed by federal government at given time to other nations, businesses, and individuals

**nationalization**  government assumption of control over privately owned industry

**natural resources**  industrial materials and capacities found in nature

**needy**  those living in poverty

**negative income tax**  guaranteed minimum income provided by government for all families existing below set income level

**nest egg**  reserve fund of money

**oligopoly** market condition in which there are few sellers, enabling them to influence price and other factors

**open market** competitive market free from price control and not restricted to any individual or group

**ophelimity** economic satisfaction

**out-of-pocket** (*adj*) owed or paid out in cash

**ownership** lawful title or possession; proprietorship

**panic** public fear that economic entity, market, or system is failing, and consequent rush to liquidate assets

**paper profit** unrealized profit due to appreciation in value of something owned but not yet sold

**pauperism** condition of extreme poverty

**pay** wages or salary given for services

**peak** highest point in business cycle; boom

**penury** extreme poverty

**per capita income** total national income or GNP divided by total population

**petite bourgeoisie** lower middle class, such as small shop-keepers and artisans

**Phillips curve** statistical measure of increasing rate of inflation as unemployment decreases

**physiocrats** political economists who held that an inherent natural order governs society and advocated a laissez-faire system (France, 18th c.)

**planned economy** socialist or other economic system with centralized government control of production and distribution

**plutocracy** system of government controlled by wealthy

**political economy** social science that deals with economics in connection with politics and society

**poor** that portion of society with little wealth, low standard of living, and few opportunities

**possession** ownership of property or wealth

**poverty** lack of socially acceptable amount of money and material possessions; indigence

**poverty level** poverty line

**poverty line** government standard for personal or family income used for measuring portion of population living in poverty; poverty level

**PPI** producer *price* index

**price controls** government ceiling set on prices of basic goods and services to fight inflation

**price index** measure of fluctuation in prices from arbitrary standard over period of time

**price supports** government payments, esp. to farmers, to maintain minimum prices by buying up surpluses

**prime cost** that part of cost of commodity derived from labor and materials directly used in its manufacture

**private enterprise** capitalist economic system with minimal government interference, allowing individual ownership of property and encouraging competition and profit incentive

**private property** property owned by individuals, corporations, or organizations privately, without government intervention; right to own property that is basis of capitalism

**private sector** part of economy that is composed of individuals and privately owned businesses

**privileged class** property-owning, landed, wealthy members of society

**producer price index** PPI; scale that compares cost of producing goods now with cost in past year

**production** process of creating or making goods and services

**productivity** measure of ability to produce more output from given input

**profit** net amount earned after deducting costs in business enterprise

**proletariat** working class

**propertied class** members of society who own land or businesses

**property** land or other items of value owned by business or individual

**property rights** government guarantees of individual freedom to own, buy, and sell private property

**proprietary rights** right to ownership of a tangible or intangible thing or idea

**proprietorship** ownership, esp. of one's own business

**prosperity** high point of business cycle; state of wealth

**public sector** part of economy composed of federal, state, and local governments

**public utility** industry providing essential public service, such as electrical, water, or telephone service, in which single firm is granted local monopoly

**purchasing power** value of currency in terms of what it can buy compared with buying power at time established as base period; ability to purchase goods and services; buying power

**purse strings** control over funds

**quotation** current price of commodity or security

**rationing** limited distribution of a product so that everyone receives a fixed amount

**raw goods** materials gathered in original state from nature for use in production

**Reaganomics** supply-side economics espoused by former U.S. President Ronald Reagan

**real dollars** value of money in terms of what it can purchase

**real property** land and buildings and structures on it

**real wages** amount that can be purchased at given time with one's income, computed by dividing money wages by consumer price index

**recession** period of no growth in national economy for at least six months; stage in business cycle with decreased demand for goods, increased unemployment, and decline in GNP

**recovery** increase in business activity following recession or depression; upturn in business cycle

**reflation** restoration of economic health and higher levels of activity, usu. by changes in monetary policy

**regulation** government control and supervision of certain economic activities

**remuneration** payment in cash for goods or services

**renewable resources** natural resources that are not exhausted by use

**reparation** compensation paid to make up for something, esp. payments by defeated nation in war for economic losses suffered by victor

**restitution** making good for a loss; giving back something to rightful owner

**restrictive practices** trade agreements deemed to be unfair to competitors or against public interest

**revaluation** government increase in exchange rate to increase value of currency relative to other currencies

**revenue** total income of business, government, or individual before expenses

**ruin** total economic collapse; bankruptcy

**sanctions**  coercive economic restrictions placed on one nation by another

**scarcity**  lack of resources or funds; absence of a certain commodity in demand

**seasonal fluctuations**  regular, predictable changes in business activity at certain times of year

**sector**  any of the elements that interact in process of supply and demand, namely consumers, businesses, governments, and foreign countries

**secular trend**  long-term economic direction

**service**  work performed for another for payment

**service economy**  economy emphasizing services over industrial production, esp. automated, cybernetic services

**shakeout**  drop in economic activity that eliminates marginal or unprofitable businesses and products

**shortage**  situation in which demand for goods exceeds supply, esp. at given price

**shortfall**  shortage or deficiency

**slavery**  former economic system based on ownership of workers by masters

**sliding scale**  variable scale, as for wages or prices charged, based on changes in other factors or ability to pay

**slump**  decline in business activity; slow portion of business cycle

**smokestack industry**  heavy manufacturing, such as steel or automobile manufacturing

**socialism**  state ownership of all or most of means of production and distribution, with control over aspects of social welfare and planning

**social security**  federal government payments to elderly, unemployed, and disabled persons, financed by contributions from employers and employees

**socioeconomic** (*adj*)  involving interrelation of social and economic factors

**splurge** (*vb*)  indulge in excessive spending

**squander** (*vb*)  spend resources extravagantly or foolishly

**stagflation**  inflation and stagnation or high unemployment occurring together

**standardization of parts**  use of interchangeable parts in mass production

**standard of living**  quality of life measured by general level of consumption of material goods

**stipend**  regular payment

**storming**  practice of accelerating production to fill quotas (Soviet Union)

**subsidy**  government payment to business or individual to improve economic condition

**subsistence level**  level of production and consumption barely adequate for survival

**subvention**  government or foundation grant for public benefit

**supply**  quantity of goods or services available

**supply and demand**  basic economic law stating that as price of a good increases, suppliers will be willing to produce more but consumers will demand less, so that price and quantity are both directly and inversely related

**supply curve**  graph showing amount producers will supply at different prices

**supply elasticity**  measure of change in supply caused by change in price

**supply-side economics**  macroeconomic theory emphasizing stimulation of production as basic factor in growth

**surplus**  situation in which supply of goods exceeds demand, esp. at given price

**surplus value**  in Marxist theory, difference between value of work done or commodities produced and value of labor and other inputs, generally equal to profit under capitalism

**technological monopoly**  exclusive rights held by developer company to patented product or process

**tenancy**  possession of land or property by right

**tight money policy**  slowing down of economy by making credit expensive and limiting money supply

**title**  right of ownership, esp. document stating such right

**trade barriers**  tariffs, quotas, and customs regulations used by one country to discourage importation of certain goods

**trade deficit**  imbalance in which nation's imports exceed its exports

**trade imbalance**  condition in which nation's exports and imports are not equal

**transfer payment**  disbursement, such as social security or unemployment payment, for which no goods or services are received

**trickle-down theory**  theory that government financial incentives to big business will eventually benefit smaller businesses and general public

**trough**  lowest portion of business cycle before recovery

**trust**  several companies acting together to control production, pricing, and distribution of a product

**underdeveloped nation**  nation having weak economy and low standard of living

**underprivileged**  persons at social disadvantage, esp. due to poverty

**unemployment rate**  percentage of measured civilian labor force without jobs but actively seeking work

**upper class**  social class at top of society, possessing wealth and owning means of production

**urban economy**  economy in which most wealth and economic activity is centered in cities

**value**  market price; worth of something in money at specific time; purchasing power of unit of currency; Marxist expression of labor embodied in commodity

**wage-price controls**  laws intended to stabilize economy by limiting increase in wages or prices

**waste**  reckless or excessive spending, esp. on unnecessary things

**ways and means**  methods of raising money and obtaining resources for use by company or nation

**wealth**  money, real property, or human resources; assets

**welfare**  government assistance to poor; state or degree of well-being

**welfare capitalism**  modified capitalism that incorporates government-funded social welfare programs

**welfare state**  social system based on political responsibility for improvement in condition of all citizens

**wholesale price index**  measure of changes in commodity prices at all stages of production; producer price index

**work ethic**  belief system emphasizing social and personal value of work

**working class**  those who work for a living with little control over working conditions, esp. unskilled manual and factory laborers; proletariat

**working poor**  employed persons earning below poverty level wages

**worth**  material value expressed in terms of money

**worthless** (*adj*)  lacking monetary value

## COMMERCE AND TRADE

**ad valorem tax**  tax levied on certain goods as percentage of their value

**army-navy store**  retail store that sells surplus military apparel and supplies at discount prices

**asking price**  amount initially sought for goods or services

**auction**  public sale at which items are sold one by one to highest bidder

**automat**  restaurant with food in small compartments opened by inserting coins

**bait and switch**  scam in which inexpensive merchandise is advertised but customer is then pressured to buy more expensive items

**bar code**  set of vertical bars printed on consumer product with coded information to be read by computerized scanner

**bargain**  something sold at price favorable to buyer; (*vb*) negotiate terms of sale to one's advantage

**bargain basement**  basement floor of department store, where goods are sold at reduced prices

**barter**  (*vb*) exchange commodities, goods, or services without use of money

**bazaar**  shop selling various goods; outdoor market or street of stalls, esp. in Middle East; sale of miscellaneous articles to benefit a charity

**bid price**  amount initially offered in payment for goods

**bill**  itemized statement of charges for goods or services; check; tab

**bill of lading**  document issued to shipper by carrier describing goods shipped and terms of carriage

**bill of sale**  written certification of transfer of ownership

**black market**  illegal trade to avoid government regulation or taxation

**blister pack**  display package in which clear plastic seals product against cardboard sheet

**blue law**  law forbidding business transactions on Sunday

**board of trade**  association of business people

**bodega**  *Spanish.* grocery store, usu. small neighborhood shop

**boiler room**  *Slang.* place where illicit brokers engage in high-pressure selling by telephone, esp. of securities

**booth**  enclosed stall for display and sale of goods, esp. at outdoor market or fair

**boycott**  organized effort to deter customers from patronizing a business or industry

**brand name**  identifiable product label, esp. of a widely advertised and distributed item

**buyer's market**  market in which supply is plentiful and prices are favorable to consumers

**buyer's remorse**  regret or anxiety experienced immediately after making a purchase

**cabotage**  trade in coastal waters or air space between two points within one country

**callback**  recall of defective product by manufacturer

**carriage trade**  wealthy patrons or elite clientele

**cartage**  act or cost of delivering goods, esp. by truck

**case goods**  products shipped and sold in multiple units in cardboard box

**case sale**  sale of cased goods in large quantities at reduced prices

**cash-and-carry**  (*adj*) sold for cash payment with no delivery included

**cash down**  portion of total cost paid to hold goods or as first installment on credit sale

**cash on delivery**  COD; payment due when shipped goods are received

**cash register**  business machine with money drawer and tapes that display and tabulate amount of each sale

**catalog**  published booklet containing list of items for sale and prices, often with pictures

**catalog sales**  distribution of merchandise by mail with orders placed from catalogs

**caveat emptor**  *Latin.* lit. let the buyer beware; principle that one buys at one's own risk

**chaffer**  (*vb*) bargain; haggle over price

**chain**  business with many retail locations

**chain store**  individual outlet of retail chain

**chamber of commerce**  organization of business people promoting economic development in particular area

**charge account**  credit account in which merchant allows customer to pay for purchases over time

**charm price**  price set just below even dollar amount, such as $9.99

**check**  itemized statement of charges for goods or services; bill; tab

**CIF**  *c*ost, *i*nsurance, and *f*reight; seller's designation that quoted price includes packing, shipping, and insurance charges

**classified ads**  compact advertisements in newspaper columns arranged by subject

**clearance**  sale to get rid of old goods and make room for new ones

**clientele**  all of one's customers

**closeout**  sale to dispose of all goods, esp. when ending business venture

**COD**  *c*ash *o*n *d*elivery

**cold call**  telephone sales call to stranger who is unfamiliar with product or service

**come-on**  *Slang.* incentive to buy

**come to terms**  settle on price

**commerce**  organized exchange of commodities on large scale, usu. involving transport from place to place; trade

**commissary**  food and supply store, esp. in army camp

**commission**  percentage of sales price paid to broker by owner of merchandise sold

**commodity**  good traded in marketplace, esp. one that is transportable

**common carrier**  company in business of transporting goods at uniform rates

**comp**  *Informal.* free service or good, esp. admission ticket to event; (*adj*) complimentary

**company store**  retail outlet operated by company for convenience of its employees, who often must shop there

**comparison shopping**  collecting information on prices and quality of similar products from different outlets

**competitive pricing**  practice, esp. by large companies, of setting prices slightly higher than competition while offering other advantages, usu. on brand name products

**concession**  right granted to engage in activity for profit on grantor's premises

**concessionaire**  person exercising a concession

**consignment**  shipment of items to be sold; sale of personal items through a merchant on commission

**consumer** individual or group purchasing goods or services in marketplace

**consumer goods** products made for and sold directly to individuals to be used as sold

**consumerism** movement to educate consumers to obtain better, safer products from manufacturers

**contraband** unlawful or prohibited goods; trade in such goods

**convenience store** store open very long hours, carrying limited selection of goods, usu. at inflated prices

**co-op** cooperative store owned by and operated for benefit of members

**corner the market** attain a monopoly or predominant share of sales of a particular commodity

**cost** amount paid for goods or services, esp. wholesale price paid by retailers

**counter** long table in store for display of goods

**coupon** certificate or ticket entitling holder to reduced purchase price or redemption for cash

**cover charge** cost of admission to bar or club

**cover the territory** solicit orders from all potential customers in one area

**cross sell** (*vb*) attract customer by offering one product or service while selling another

**curb service** service for customers who remain in their cars, esp. at drive-in restaurant

**customer** person who buys, esp. regularly at same place

**customs** government duty on imported goods

**cut-rate** (*adj*) at reduced price

**deal** bargain, favorable price; (*vb*) trade, do business; bargain so as to reach favorable price

**dealer** buyer and seller of goods; franchise holder

**department store** large retail store with departments selling many kinds of goods

**dicker** (*vb*) haggle over price

**discount** price below standard retail or list price

**discount house** store that sells merchandise at less than standard price

**door-to-door** (*adj*) selling by calling at each house or apartment in an area; shipped directly from point of pickup to point of delivery

**drive-in** service establishment in which customers remain in cars

**dry goods** cloth or clothing products

**dumping** below-cost sale of goods, esp. to kill competition

**durable goods** consumer items with long-term market life, esp. cars or furniture; hard goods

**ego goods** expensive luxury items

**emporium** marketplace, trading center; large store selling variety of products

**exchange** place of trade; barter, trade; (*vb*) return one purchased item and replace it with another

**excise tax** tax on manufacture, sale, or consumption of goods and services

**expense** any of various costs of operating a business

**export** product sold outside country of origin; (*vb*) sell goods outside one's own country

**factory outlet** warehouse serving as point of sale for discount goods

**fair** gathering for exchange and sale of goods among individuals

**fair market value** price something can be expected to bring on open market at given time

**fire sale** sale of commodities actually or supposedly damaged in fire at greatly reduced prices

**five-and-dime** low-priced general merchandise store

**flagship** central or largest store in chain

**flea market** usu. outdoor market with numerous stalls selling used or handmade new articles

**flood the market** greatly increase available supply of some good to force price down

**fly-by-night** unreliable business (slang)

**FOB** *free on board*; assumption of responsibility by shipper for all costs until goods are placed on carrier

**franchise** contract or license permitting regional distributor to use name and sell products of another company or manufacturer

**free** (*adj*) available at no cost

**freebie** *Informal.* something available at no cost

**frequency marketing** rewarding consumer loyalty by offering an incentive or discount for frequent use of product or service

**full-service** (*adj*) offering broad range of services in one basic line of business

**functional goods** utilitarian articles such as tools or clothing

**futures** purchases or sales of commodities at speculative prices for future delivery or receipt

**garage sale** sale of used household and personal articles held at seller's home, usu. in yard or garage

**general store** usu. small store selling different kinds of goods

**generic product** lower-priced version of brand name product with plain label indicating kind of product only

**give-and-take** exchange on an even basis

**giveaway** product offered for free, usu. to attract potential customers for other goods

**glut** large oversupply of goods

**good buy** product whose value equals or surpasses its price

**gouge** (*vb*) grossly overcharge

**gratis** (*adj*) at no cost, free

**gray market** discount market that operates somewhere between legitimacy and the black market

**guarantee** seller's assurance that product is as represented and will be repaired or replaced if defective

**haggle** (*vb*) argue over price

**half-price** (*adj*) reduced to half of original price

**handout** *Informal.* something given at no cost

**hard goods** durable goods

**hard sell** high-pressure salesmanship

**hawk** (*vb*) sell goods in public, esp. by shouting advertisements

**hedonic goods** pleasure-oriented consumer items such as art, musical recordings, or toys

**high-pressure** (*adj*) pertaining to sales effort involving insistent arguments, forceful persuasion, or refusal to take no for an answer

**import** product bought from another country; (*vb*) buy products made in other countries

**impulse buying** sudden purchase of goods without prior intent, usu. stimulated by display or advertising

**installment purchase** purchase made on credit and paid off in series of payments over time

**in stock** (*adj*) available for sale at the present time

**interstate commerce** trade among and between states, regulated by federal government

**inventory**  all items of merchandise in stock at given time

**invoice**  itemized list of goods or services to be paid for

**IOU**  informal written memorandum of indebtedness

**job lot**  random assortment of goods for sale as one unit

**juice**  *Slang*. exorbitant interest or commission

**keystone** (*vb*) price goods at twice their cost as standard practice

**kiosk**  small structure open on one side for street sales

**lading**  load of freight, shipment of goods

**license**  legal right to use or sell another's patented or copyrighted material

**line**  stock of goods of particular type carried by store

**liquidation**  disposal of all remaining merchandise at reduced prices

**list price**  official retail price; nondiscounted price

**loss leader**  popular item sold at a loss or negligible profit to attract customers to retail outlet

**low-pressure** (*adj*) pertaining to sales effort involving subtle persuasion and soft-spoken arguments

**low-price** (*adj*) available at little cost

**mail order**  technique of selling items and taking orders through the mail

**mall**  large, usu. completely enclosed shopping complex comprised of many different shops and restaurants

**manufacturing**  production of commodities

**markdown**  reduction in price to promote sales

**market**  place where people gather to sell and trade goods; store or shop for sale of provisions; (*vb*) offer for sale

**marketable** (*adj*) fit for sale

**marketing**  activities involved in moving goods and services from producer to consumer: market research, advertising, promotion, distribution, and sales

**marketplace**  world of trade and business; site where goods are offered for sale

**market research**  collection and analysis of information to determine goods and services preferred by certain groups

**markup**  amount added to cost by retailer to set price for customer

**mart**  market, trading center

**merchandise**  consumer goods for sale

**merchandising**  advertising, display, promotion, and direct selling methods

**mom-and-pop** (*adj*) designating small, family-owned business, usu. retail

**money's worth**  good value obtained for cost

**monopsony**  existence of only one buyer for goods or services

**nominal price**  stated price when bargaining or reduction is possible

**nondurable goods**  items that will be consumed in a relatively short time, such as clothing or food

**nonrefundable** (*adj*) final and not subject to return or refund

**notions**  small, useful items sold in store, esp. for sewing

**OEM**  outside *e*quipment *m*anufacturer; company that exploits or develops another company's product as part of its own

**oligopsony**  existence of only a few consumers for a product

**on the block**  for sale

**on the house**  offered gratis or free, with compliments of selling establishment

**on time** (*adj*) purchased on credit with payments to be made over fixed period of time

**outbid** (*vb*) offer better price than others seeking to purchase the same item

**outlet**  store selling goods for specific manufacturer or distributor

**outlet store**  retailer selling defective, damaged, or surplus goods at reduced price

**overcharge** (*vb*) set price higher than value of goods; charge more than stated price

**overprice** (*vb*) set price too high to sell

**package store**  retail store selling alcoholic beverages for consumption off premises

**packaging**  container or wrapping in which product is sold; design of such wrapping, often intended to attract customers

**packing slip**  form listing items included in shipment

**patent**  right granted by government that prevents others from using idea or invention or making same product as originator for seventeen years

**patron**  person who is customer or client, esp. regular one, of store or other establishment

**patronage**  clientele; business or trade

**patronize** (*vb*) be a regular customer

**peddle** (*vb*) sell, esp. travel about selling small items

**penetration pricing**  pricing of new product at low level to lure customers away from established product

**pennyworth**  bargain, value for price paid

**peril point**  lowest possible import duty short of damaging domestic industry

**pitch**  salesperson's discourse intended to persuade customers to buy

**planned obsolescence**  design of consumer goods for limited use, necessitating frequent replacement or repair

**plaza**  public marketplace in town

**point-of-purchase** (*adj*) relating to place where sales are made or purchases paid for

**popular prices**  pricing designed to attract general sales

**premium**  something offered free or at low price as inducement to buy something else

**price**  quantity of money demanded in exchange for goods or services

**price-cutting**  selling an article at a price reduced from prior or advertised level

**price discrimination**  selling of same product to two different buyers at different prices

**price fixing**  setting of prices by government or among competing businesses contrary to free market dictates

**price tag**  label attached to commodity indicating its price

**price war**  business competitors' repeated lowering of prices

**product differentiation**  any of various devices that enable consumers to distinguish one firm's product from others in the same industry

**product manager**  person who oversees all aspects of marketing of specific product

**profit**  amount of sales revenues left for business after paying cost, overhead, taxes, and operating expenses

**profit margin**  excess of income over expenses and costs

**promotion**  something devised to advance a product or service in order to persuade consumers to buy or use it

**prospect**  potential customer

**protectionism**  policy of strict trade regulations to support domestic industry

**purchase**  anything obtained by buying; act of buying; (*vb*) obtain by paying price

**purchase order**  itemization of items being bought

**purchase price**  amount paid for commodity

**quality control**  maintenance of standards in production by checking product at stages during manufacture

**quota**  fixed limit, esp. government limit on imports and exports

**racket**  easy, profitable source of income, often illegal

**rebate**  discount made by refunding percentage of purchase price

**recall**  removal of defective product from market for correction

**receipt**  written acknowledgment that payment has been received

**reduced** (adj) at less than original price

**refund**  return of money previously paid for commodity

**repo**  Informal. repossession

**repossession**  taking back of commodity from buyer who has failed to make payments when due

**retail**  sale of goods directly to consumers

**retailer**  business or individual that offers retail sales directly to consumers

**rock bottom**  at the lowest possible price

**rollback**  action that returns prices to earlier, lower level, as by government order

**rummage sale**  sale of contributed items, used or new, to raise money, esp. for charitable organization

**sale**  exchange of goods or services for agreed sum of money; special offering of goods at reduced prices

**sales force**  employees engaged in selling

**salesman**  person engaged in selling, esp. male; salesperson

**salesmanship**  ability, skill, or technique of selling

**salesperson**  person engaged in selling; salesman

**sales slip**  receipt or form listing details of sale

**sales tax**  tax levied by city or state on retail sales of merchandise

**self-service**  practice of serving oneself without assistance of salesperson

**seller's market**  market in which demand exceeds supply, with prices rising

**selling**  act, practice, or technique of making sales

**sell short** (vb) underestimate value in setting price

**service center**  authorized establishment for repair and purchase of replacement parts, esp. for cars and appliances

**service charge**  amount added to price of goods to pay for service

**service mark**  trademark applied to service offered, designated <sup>SM</sup>

**shop**  usu. small outlet for retail sales; (vb) purchase goods

**shop around** (vb) search for bargains or special items in several places

**shopping**  visiting one or more stores to look at, price, and buy items

**shopping center**  outdoor complex of stores, restaurants, and movie theaters usu. grouped around common parking lot

**shopping spree**  outing during which multiple purchases are made

**shortage**  condition in which demand for goods exceeds available supply

**showroom**  place where merchandise is displayed for sale

**show window**  large store window in which merchandise is displayed

**shrink wrap**  clear, flexible, plastic film that shrinks when exposed to heat, used to wrap and seal products

**slash** (vb) drastically reduce prices

**smuggling**  importing of prohibited or outlawed goods

**soft goods**  items lasting a relatively short time, esp. clothing

**soft sell**  low-pressure sales technique

**stall**  booth, table, or counter in market

**staple**  chief commodity of region; item regularly stocked due to constant demand

**steal**  Informal. product obtained at very low price, often less than its value

**steep** (adj) expensively priced

**stock**  finished goods on hand or in storage and available for sale

**stock in trade**  resources, abilities, or goods on hand required for carrying on specific business

**store**  retail outlet selling consumer goods, such as chain, convenience, department, discount, specialty, or surplus store

**storefront**  ground-level room with display windows, usu. used as retail store

**storewide** (adj) throughout all departments of store, used esp. of a sale

**sublicensing**  granting of licenses to other companies to exploit, develop, or market one's product

**supermarket**  large, self-service retail food store, often part of a chain

**surcharge**  additional amount added to price

**surplus store**  retail outlet selling extra or leftover goods at discount prices

**swap** (vb) barter, exchange

**swap meet**  flea market, esp. one based on barter system

**tab**  Informal. price, total cost; bill; check

**territory**  area in which traveling salesman solicits orders

**test marketing**  offering new product for limited time in small area to assess national sales potential

**thrift shop**  retail store selling used items at low prices, often to support charitable organization

**ticket**  slip of paper serving as evidence that holder has paid fare or admission and is entitled to some service

**tickler file**  special file used to remind salesperson of customers requiring attention at certain dates in future

**tie-in**  sale at which two or more items, only one of which is in demand, must be bought together as a unit

**till**  money drawer at shop counter

**trade**  commerce; exchange of goods for money

**trademark**  symbol, design, or name used to distinguish product from its competitors, designated <sup>TM</sup>

**trader**  person who engages in commerce or sells goods

**trade show**  convention at which related companies in single industry show and compare new products and ideas

**trading post**  store in remote region or settlement

**trading stamp**  stamp given as premium by retailer, having specific value when redeemed for articles

**traffic**  exchange of goods

**transaction**  business deal; sale or exchange of items

**transfer**  ticket entitling bearer to change from one public vehicle to another at no additional charge

**traveling salesman**  business representative soliciting orders in assigned territory

**truck** (vb) exchange or barter

**twofer**  Informal. card or ticket entitling bearer to two items for price of one

**underbid** (*vb*) offer less than competition for commodity

**undercharge** (*vb*) ask less than normal or accepted price

**undersell** (*vb*) set price for a product that is lower that one's competition

**unit pricing** standard measurement for pricing different brands of same product

**Universal Product Code** UPC; computer code of bars and numerals printed on merchandise to identify it and confirm price

**unload** (*vb*) sell off unwanted merchandise, usu. at reduced price or in large quantities

**UPC** *Universal Product Code*

**upset price** minimum permissible bid at auction

**used property** commodity resold after period of use

**variety store** retail outlet selling many different commodities, esp. small, nondurable goods

**vend** (*vb*) sell

**vending machine** coin-operated machine selling merchandise, esp. candy or cigarettes

**vendor** one who sells

**vendue** public auction

**voucher** written document showing expenditure or receipt of money

**warehouse** building where merchandise is stored before shipment to retailers

**wares** commodities

**warranty** guarantee on product for limited time after purchase

**waybill** list of goods sent by common carrier with shipping directions

**wholesale** sale of goods in large quantity to retail businesses at cost substantially below retail price

**wholesaler** business or person purchasing goods from producers for resale to other businesses

**will-call** department in a store where merchandise is held for payment and pickup by customer

**window shopping** looking at merchandise without purchasing

**yard sale** garage sale held outdoors, esp. in yard

## CORPORATIONS AND BUSINESS PRACTICES

**advance** partial payment of amount due on signing of contract

**affairs** matters of business

**alien corporation** company operating under foreign nation's charter

**amalgamation** combining of corporations into a new business entity

**annual report** corporate management's financial report to shareholders at end of fiscal year

**annual review** supervisor's regular assessment of job performance of subordinates

**ante** stake to be paid to begin participation in business

**application** business activity suitable for computerization

**articles of incorporation** formal document establishing corporation, describing its business, directors, finances, and stock issued

**assembly line** manufacturing process in which each worker performs specialized task in assembling product that passes by on moving belt or track

**assignment** transfer to another of one's claim or right, esp. to income

**bailout** instance of government coming to assistance of failing business

**bankroll** (*vb*) finance, supply with money

**bankruptcy** legal insolvency; inability to pay debts; procedure to dissolve company and be released from certain debts

**belly up** *Slang*. collapse or failure of a business

**big business** major corporations with political interests

**board of directors** group of top managers setting corporate policies and direction

**bonus** payment over and above salary given to employee, esp. executive, as incentive or reward

**bottom line** last line of financial statement, indicating net profit

**bubble company** fraudulent cover operation posing as legitimate business

**budget** schedule of expenses adjusted to estimated revenue for set period

**budgeting** curtailing expenses so as not to exceed income

**business** commercial, mercantile, or industrial enterprise conducted to make a profit

**buyout** outright purchase of business, esp. by management or employees with borrowed money

**capital-intensive** (*adj*) requiring large capital investment or expenditure relative to need for labor

**capitalization** total funds of corporation, including stocks, bonds, undivided profits, and surplus

**cash cow** *Informal*. business with dependable source of income

**cash flow** measure of liquidity equal to excess or deficiency of net income relative to cash expenses

**ceiling** upper limit set for spending

**channels** formalized hierarchical lines of communication of responsibility between managers and subordinates

**Chapter 11** bankruptcy code section that applies to a corporation going out of business which may require restructuring

**charter** legal form establishing corporation and defining its purpose

**close** (*vb*) officially conclude business transaction

**closed corporation** company whose stock is held by a small group, usu. persons also involved in management

**collapsible corporation** company set up to be dissolved before realizing profits, thus avoiding taxes

**collection division** department responsible for obtaining payments due to company

**collusion** agreement between competitive companies, esp. to fix prices or limit production output

**commission** fee paid to broker or agent for services in business transaction

**compagnie** *French*. company

**company** organization formed for doing business

**concern** company, business firm

**concession** entitlement to operate business granted by government or other business

**conglomerate** corporation composed of smaller corporations in diverse business fields

**consideration** something of value given or done in return for comparable action by another as part of contract

**consolidation** organization combining two or more companies, each of which retains partial autonomy

**consortium** business alliance of companies

**contract** legally binding agreement between parties

**controlling interest** ownership of enough stock in company to set policies and make decisions

**co-op** membership-owned business

**corner** monopoly ownership of commodity, stock, or security

**corporate veil** protection of corporate owners from personal liability

**corporation** business organization existing and treated as legal entity independent of its individual owners

**cost-effective** (adj) producing good results for amount invested; efficient in use of funds

**cost overrun** amount by which project exceeds estimated cost

**cottage industry** small or home-based business

**crapshoot** Informal. speculation on business enterprise

**cut a check** Slang. write a check on business funds

**cutback** reduction in production, personnel, or budget

**dba** doing business as; fictitious business name

**deal** business transaction or agreement

**dealings** business affairs or relations

**diminishing returns** additional investments resulting in smaller proportion of profits

**dissolution** dismantling of business, contract, or partnership

**diversification** broadening of large corporate holdings into wide variety of investments

**divestiture** sale or dissolution of subsidiary business or investment

**dividend** portion of corporation profits distributed regularly to stockholders

**economize** (vb) cut costs to increase profits; reduce spending

**endowment** money placed in tax-exempt foundation by corporation

**enterprise** quality of risk-taking or initiative in business; company, venture, or firm

**escalator clause** contract provision requiring increases in payments based on economic fluctuations

**establishment** business or company, esp. its physical plant

**fee** amount charged for professional services

**firm** business or company

**Fortune 500** list of 500 largest American corporations published annually by Fortune magazine

**foundation** tax-exempt institution, funded by corporate profits, that contributes to charities, arts, and education as means of avoiding corporate tax and generating goodwill

**franchise** government permission for company to carry on particular business in certain place, often involving partial monopoly

**funding** money available for use by company

**golden parachute** substantial compensation given to top executive as severance bonus when dismissed due to corporate merger or takeover

**goodwill** intangibles belonging to business, esp. its trade reputation

**go public** (vb) offer stock of privately owned company for sale to public

**ground floor** Informal. advantageous position or opportunity based on early involvement in new venture

**growth area** section of firm's business experiencing expansion and providing revenue base for operations

**growth company** company growing faster than economy in general and reinvesting most of profits into business

**grubstake** money provided by investors to individual starting a business

**hardball** Slang. highly competitive or ruthless business activities

**headhunting** search by professional recruiters for executives to fill high-level positions

**holding company** corporation whose business is buying and selling stock in other companies

**home office** headquarters of business with branches

**honorarium** payment in lieu of professional fee, usu. token amount

**horizontal merger** merger involving competitive companies that perform or produce the same or similar functions or products

**house** business establishment

**incentives** financial or other benefits offered for labor or services

**industry** large-scale business activity; particular branch of manufacturing

**institution** established corporation, esp. one serving public needs

**interlocking directorates** boards of directors of different corporations having common members

**investment** business expenditure made for eventual profit

**labor-intensive** (adj) requiring large supply of labor relative to need for capital investment

**license** government permission to operate business

**liquidation** sale of business in which all assets are converted to cash

**lose one's shirt** Slang. make a bad investment; fail at business

**management** organizational and administrative aspect and personnel of business

**market research** collection and analysis of data on consumer habits, trends, and preferences

**market share** percentage of sales controlled by one company in specific industry or segment of an industry

**memorandum** written communication within company relating to business operation, goal, or project

**memo to the file** written record on decisions for file of author only

**merger** assimilation of one business or corporation into another

**mommy track** career path in which woman forgoes rapid advancement in order to spend time with family

**moneymaker** business enterprise that generates profits

**multinational corporation** large company based in one country with interests, investments, and operations in others

**nonprofit corporation** business operating for reasons other than profit making, and paying no taxes

**number-cruncher** Informal. person or thing that performs numerous numerical calculations, such as an accountant or computer

**operating expenses** ongoing, recurring costs of conducting business, not including costs of production

**operations research** systematic analysis, usu. mathematical, of problems in business operations

**organization** administrative personnel and executive structure

**overbudget** (*adj*) describing venture in which costs exceed estimated costs

**overhead** total direct expenses in operating a business

**Pac-Man defense** attempt to prevent hostile takeover in which targeted company bids to take over hostile firm

**Parkinson's law** statement that work expands so as to fill the time available for its completion

**parlay** (*vb*) successfully exploit asset or position

**partnership** association of two or more individuals or business entities joined as part owners in business

**patent** right granted by government to exclusive rights to invention for certain number of years

**pension fund** fund created and maintained by corporation or government to provide benefits under pension plan, with assets usu. invested in securities

**perk** *Informal.* perquisite

**perquisite** nonmonetary benefit for employee, such as free trip or company car; perk

**personnel** employees; department responsible for hiring new employees

**Peter Principle** statement that every employee in a hierarchy tends to rise to the level of his or her incompetence

**petty cash** cash fund on hand for small daily expenses

**philanthropy** gifts and endowments of foundations or charitable organizations

**plant** machinery, buildings, and grounds of factory or business

**poison pill** *Slang.* mechanism, such as issuing a new class of stock, by which company averts hostile takeover

**positioning** placement of company within industry or product within company

**privately held corporation** corporation not offering stock for sale to public, usu. family owned

**profit motive** impetus to engage in business activity for financial gain

**prospectus** description of company, its property, and its operations, circulated to prospective investors

**proxy fight** contest between factions of stockholders for control of company, in which each group solicits signed proxy statements for votes needed to gain control

**public corporation** corporation whose stock is traded on stock exchange

**public relations** activities intended to create favorable public opinion about company or product

**public-service corporation** private corporation chartered to provide essential commodity or service to the public

**quality assurance** quality control guarantees

**quality control** maintenance of production standards by checking product at stages during manufacturing process

**realize** (*vb*) convert into money; bring in profit

**receivership** status of bankrupt business placed in hands of receiver appointed to settle its debts

**reinvest** (*vb*) use profits to build company rather than disburse them to shareholders

**retainer** fee paid to lawyer or other professional adviser as advance on services

**royalty** payment for rights to property based on percentage of revenue generated by it

**seed money** funds for starting business venture

**sole proprietorship** unincorporated business with one owner

**speculation** engagement in transaction or venture involving risk in hopes of large gains

**spin-off** new company created by distribution to stockholders of stock of another company

**staff** regular, full-time, permanent employees

**start-up company** newly established company

**start-up expenses** costs involved in establishing a business

**stock** equipment, materials, and supplies of a business; shares of a company sold to public with value based on company assets and income

**subcontract** (*vb*) hire secondary company or individual to do part of contracted job

**subsidiary** business owned by parent company

**sunrise industry** industry with high growth potential, such as electronics industry

**sunset industry** industry, such as heavy manufacturing, with declining market due to social or technological changes

**syndicate** association of corporations formed to carry out costly financial project

**syndication** sale or licensing of commodity to network of similar businesses

**take a bath** *Slang.* lose everything on a business venture

**takeover** merger forced on one business by another

**tender** offer of money made to satisfy obligation

**trade association** organization with representatives from companies in same industry or business

**trade convention** gathering of representatives from many companies in same business, esp. to introduce new products

**undercapitalized** (*adj*) lacking sufficient operating funds

**undertaking** venture, enterprise

**underwrite** (*vb*) guarantee financial support for business

**up-front** (*adj*) invested or paid before service is rendered or product is delivered

**upside** measure of financial gain on investment

**venture** business enterprise, esp. one with high degree of risk but potential for large profits

**venture capitalism** financing of new businesses for eventual share in profits

**vertical merger** purchase by one company of a supplier or distributor

**wheel and deal** *Informal.* arrange business deals in aggressive, flamboyant manner

**white knight** *Informal.* business that prevents hostile takeover of another company by offering better terms

**windfall profit** unexpected return on investment

**working capital** portion of company's capital readily convertible into cash for paying expenses and wages

**working vacation** businessman's vacation in which mail, phone calls, and office problems intrude

## LABOR

**affirmative action** government-regulated program ensuring that employers hire women and minorities

**AFL-CIO** *American Federation of Labor and Congress of Industrial Organizations*

**agency shop** work situation in which worker need not be union member but must pay union an amount equal to its dues

**American Federation of Labor and Congress of Industrial Organizations** AFL-CIO; umbrella organization for most American labor unions

**arbitration** negotiation between management and labor mediated and decided by neutral third party

**backsheesh** tip or gratuity, esp. bribe

**base pay** basic rate of pay before overtime, bonuses, or raises

**benefits** payments under annuity, pension plan, insurance, unemployment, or disability

**blacklist** roster of workers excluded or persecuted by management for pro-union views

**blue-collar** (adj) pertaining to factory or manual labor

**bonus** amount above regular salary given as reward or for motivation

**Boulwareism** "take it or leave it" collective bargaining technique of management

**ca'canny** Brit. slang. deliberate work slowdown to express discontent

**calling** profession or trade, esp. one's natural vocation

**casual labor** temporary or part-time work, often unskilled

**closed shop** business prohibited from employing nonunion members, outlawed by right-to-work laws

**codetermination** mutual setting of policy by labor and management

**collective bargaining** negotiations between employer and union representatives, esp. over wages or benefits

**common labor** manual or unskilled work

**common situs picketing** picketing of entire construction site by union in dispute with only one subcontractor

**company town** city or town whose economy is dominated by a single business enterprise or factory

**company union** workers in union in single company, not affiliated with group of unions, often under employer's control

**compulsory arbitration** negotiations requiring union and management to accept binding decision of outside mediator

**contract** labor-management agreement renegotiated regularly to determine wages, benefits, and working conditions

**cost-of-living allowance** guaranteed annual pay raise based on increase in cost of living

**craft** occupation requiring special training or skill

**craft union** union of skilled workers in specific trade or industry

**crew** small group of workers under direction of foreman

**day job** temporary or part-time position, esp. in field other than one's primary vocation

**day shift** regular hours of employment, usu. 8 or 9 a.m. to 5 or 6 p.m.

**disability insurance** guarantee of continued income for worker seriously or permanently disabled on the job

**double time** pay scale at twice the normal rate for work done on holidays, weekends, or after hours

**earning power** lifetime potential for earning wages, income, and profits

**earnings** total amount of wages during pay period

**employable** (adj) physically or mentally fit for work; meeting minimum job requirements

**employment** job or occupation at which one works; number or percent of persons holding jobs

**farm labor** unskilled agricultural work

**featherbedding** practice of forcing an employer to create unnecessary jobs

**fringe benefit** benefit in addition to wages, esp. health insurance, profit sharing, or paid vacation

**gang** work crew directed by foreman

**general strike** work stoppage by entire labor force of city or nation

**giveback** union agreement to relinquish benefits previously granted as part of new contract

**gratuity** amount given freely by customer above cost of service rendered, esp. to waiter or driver

**graveyard shift** hours of night employment, usu. midnight to 8 a.m.; lobster shift; night shift

**guild** union of people in same craft or trade

**independent union** union not affiliated with AFL-CIO or other association

**injunction** court or executive order, usu. requiring strikers to return to work

**job** position and duties of employment

**labor** work force; work performed by laborers

**laborer** worker, esp. semiskilled or unskilled

**labor force** total number of persons over age sixteen who hold or are looking for jobs

**labor union** organization of workers for protection, representation, and benefits in dealings with employers

**layoff** dismissal of workers, esp. temporarily

**line of work** vocation, trade, or profession

**lobster shift** graveyard shift

**lockout** shutdown of business by management to pressure workers and union into agreement

**malingering** pretending to be ill to avoid work

**manual labor** unskilled, physical work

**mechanization** use of machines in combination with semiskilled workers to replace unskilled workers

**mediation** arbitration of union-management dispute by neutral third party

**minimum wage** legally fixed lowest hourly rate payable to certain types of workers

**moonlighting** working at a second job, often at night

**National Labor Relations Board** NLRB; federal agency regulating and investigating unfair labor practices

**night shift** graveyard shift

**NLRB** National Labor Relations Board

**occupation** job, trade, or profession

**occupational hazard** danger inherent in particular job, esp. unsafe working conditions

**on spec** (adj) performed or made without guarantee of payment for work or service

**overtime** payments at higher than normal rate for extra hours worked during day or week

**paycheck** regular payment of wages or salary

**payday** day on which paycheck is received

**pay period** regular interval between paydays

**payroll** roster of employees and record of their wages

**pension** regular payments made to employee upon retirement

**pension plan** systematic plan by which corporation or government makes regular payments to retired or disabled employees, sometimes partially funded by employee contributions

**picket** (vb) stand or march with signs in front of workplace as display of dissatisfaction during strike; (n) striking worker who does this

**piecework** work done and paid for by unit produced instead of at hourly rate

**pink-collar** (*adj*) pertaining to low-paid work usu. done by women, esp. secretarial work

**pink slip** notice of dismissal from one's job

**post** specific position or duty on job

**preferential shop** shop in which management hires only union members as long as they are available

**premium** additional wages paid for overtime or dangerous work

**profit sharing** division of portion of company profits among employees

**proletariat** Marxist term for workers with no capital or means of production

**raise** increase in wages

**rank and file** all regular union members

**retirement** permanent termination of employment; pension benefits paid to former employee

**right-to-work law** state law allowing workers to work whether or not they join a union and outlawing a closed shop

**salary** money earned for regular work, paid periodically

**scab** strikebreaker who works for company being struck

**seasonal unemployment** annual, temporary loss of jobs due to seasonal conditions, esp. absence of farm work in winter

**semiskilled labor** usu. manual work requiring some training

**seniority** status obtained from length of time worker has been on job, usu. rewarded with higher pay and other benefits

**serf** person of feudal class bound to land and subject to will of lord

**severance pay** payment made to employee at time of termination of employment

**shape-up** method of selecting longshoremen from assembled group of available workers

**shift** regularly scheduled hours of work

**sit-down strike** strike in which workers remain idle in workplace until settlement is reached

**skilled labor** work, such as craft or trade, that requires training

**slowdown** intentional reduction in output by workers to force employer concessions without a strike

**social security number** nine-digit number issued when person registers for social security system, required to gain employment and used as identification number for taxation and banking

**specialization of labor** condition in which workers learn and perform very specific tasks

**specialty** skill or specific job performed by worker

**split shift** workday divided into two periods, with intervening break longer than meal or rest period

**starvation wages** wages barely sufficient to provide subsistence

**steel-collar worker** robot

**stoop labor** poorly paid farm labor, esp. immigrants harvesting crops

**straight time** standard work hours without overtime

**strike** organized and deliberate work stoppage used to attain benefits, esp. changes in working conditions or wages

**strikebreaker** worker hired to replace striking employee

**sweatshop** exploitative workplace characterized by long hours, low pay, and substandard conditions, esp. employing immigrants

**sweetheart agreement** agreement between employer and union on terms favorable to employer, often without approval of union members

**swing shift** work period between day and graveyard shifts, usu. 3 or 4 p.m. to midnight

**sympathy strike** work stoppage by laborers in support of striking workers elsewhere

**syndicalism** worker ownership and management of industries achieved by revolutionary movement and general strike

**Taft-Hartley Act** federal law protecting public welfare during labor disputes by allowing president power of injunction to halt certain strikes

**take-home pay** gross wages less deductions for taxes, insurance, union dues, retirement, or savings

**time and a half** pay scale at one and half times normal rate, for hours worked beyond normal workday; overtime

**timecard** card on which hours worked by each employee are recorded by time clock

**time clock** clock with mechanism for recording hours of arrival and departure of employees

**tip** gratuity received for service

**trade** occupation, esp. craft of skilled work

**trade union** organization of workers within craft, trade, or industry

**Trade Unions Congress** TUC; British umbrella organization for most trade unions

**TUC** *Trade Unions Congress*

**turnover** number of employees leaving jobs in given time period

**underemployed** overqualified or part-time workers

**unemployable** (*adj*) designating person unable to find work because of age, lack of skills, or disability

**unemployed** those who are out of work

**unemployment** lack of work; number or percent of persons not holding jobs

**unemployment compensation** regular payments, usu. from state funds into which employers have paid, to qualified unemployed persons

**unfair labor practices** union and employer activities banned by legislation to promote peaceful industrial relations

**union** workers' mutual benefit and protection organization

**union card** card identifying person as member of specific union

**unionism** principle of trade unions as protectors of workers' rights

**union scale** minimum wage for particular category of worker as fixed by union contract

**union shop** business employing union members and requiring nonmembers to join within stated time, often three months

**unskilled labor** manual or factory work requiring little or no training

**vocation** trade, profession, or occupation, esp. one for which one feels a calling

**wage** payment for labor on hourly or piecework basis

**walk of life** trade, profession, or occupation

**walkout** spontaneous strike

**white-collar** (*adj*) pertaining to office, sales, or professional work, usu. involving people, information, and ideas

**wildcat strike** work stoppage not authorized by labor union

**work** occupation, profession, trade, or business

**workday** regular hours during which work is performed

**worker** person employed to perform physical or mental activity in return for wages

**workers** labor force

**workers' compensation** protection provided by state governments for workers injured on job

**working class** proletariat, esp. unskilled manual and factory laborers

**workingman** industrial or manual laborer

**workplace** person's place of employment; any or all places where people are employed

**work stoppage** cessation of work by employees to protest working conditions; strike

**workweek** total number of hours worked at regular salary each week

**yellow-dog contract** illegal requirement that worker not join union

## Employers, Employees, and Business People

**administrator** business executive; manager

**agent** one authorized to represent another; traveling salesman

**apprentice** person in process of learning trade

**arbitrator** third party called in to settle dispute

**artisan** craftsman in skilled trade

**assistant** helper serving in subordinate position

**associate** fellow worker of equal or slightly subordinate position

**auctioneer** person who conducts public sales at auction

**backer** supporter, sponsor, or provider of funds

**bagman** *Chiefly Brit.* traveling salesman

**baron** person with great or absolute power in one particular field

**blue-collar worker** crafts, manufacturing, or common laborer

**boss** person in authority; foreman, manager, or owner

**breadwinner** worker whose earnings support family

**broker** businessperson connecting buyers and sellers for fee or commission

**bureaucrat** official in large organization, esp. one following inflexible routine

**businessman** owner, manager, or business executive, esp. male

**businessperson** person in business of either sex

**businesswoman** female owner, manager, or business executive

**CAO** chief administrative officer

**capitalist** owner of business, esp. supporter of free enterprise system

**captain of industry** major figure in one particular industry and business leader

**CEO** chief executive officer

**CFO** chief financial officer

**chairman of the board** top corporate officer, appointed by board of directors, charged with supervision of high-level affairs of company

**chief** boss, top person in business hierarchy

**chief administrative officer** CAO; corporate executive responsible for day-to-day operations of business

**chief executive officer** CEO; corporate executive responsible for overseeing administration and setting policy

**chief financial officer** CFO; corporate executive responsible for financial operations

**clerk** low-level office worker; person who sells in store

**common laborer** unskilled manual worker

**comprador** native Chinese agent of foreign business serving as liaison to native employees

**comptroller** controller

**controller** chief accountant of business; comptroller

**counsel** adviser to business management, esp. attorney

**craftsman** skilled worker or artisan

**dealer** person who sells or trades some product

**director** member of board of directors; top corporate executive

**distributor** agent for business responsible for getting goods from producer to consumers

**domestic** person employed in another's home

**employee** worker hired for wages

**employer** person who hires workers and pays their wages, often owner of business

**entrepreneur** financial backer, often manager, of business enterprise

**executive** upper-level business administrator or manager

**exporter** person who sells goods in foreign countries

**fat cat** *Slang.* wealthy, powerful business executive

**field rep** *Informal.* outside salesman, usu. with some management responsibility

**financier** person engaged in large-scale financial operations

**foreman** person in charge of small group of workers

**freelancer** self-employed person contracting his or her services

**fund-raiser** person who solicits money for new or established business

**hand** manual worker, laborer

**headhunter** personnel agent who recruits executives, esp. from other companies

**help** casual workers in subordinate positions

**high roller** *Informal.* person or institution spending money freely or extravagantly

**hired help** part-time or temporary laborers

**hireling** person available for any work; mercenary

**importer** person who sells goods made in foreign countries

**industrialist** owner or manager of industrial enterprise

**intrapreneur** corporate employee given free rein to develop new products and services within company without observing normal protocols

**Jaycee** member of Junior Chamber of Commerce, a civic group for young business leaders

**jobber** middleman between manufacturer and retailer; distributor

**journeyman** skilled, experienced worker

**laborer** person doing manual, unskilled, or semiskilled work

**lackey** person in subordinate position, esp. servant

**magnate** powerful, successful businessperson

**management** employees hired to administer company policy

**manager** director or administrator of business operations; person responsible for running single retail outlet

**mediator** outsider brought in to settle dispute

**mercenary** person who works merely for money or reward

**merchant** seller of merchandise; retailer; trader

**middleman** dealer buying from manufacturer and selling to retailer

**middle management** middle echelon of business administrators

**migrant worker** farm laborer who travels about harvesting seasonal crops

**mogul** powerful businessperson

**moneychanger** person in business of exchanging currencies of different nations

**monger** dealer or trader

**movers and shakers** people who initiate actions and get things done

**nabob** rich, powerful person

**officer** person in position of authority in business, usu. with title

**office worker** clerical or subordinate white-collar worker

**official** executive, manager, or corporate officer

**operator** worker trained to run specific machinery

**organization man** person who identifies strongly with ideas and ethics of his or her employer

**overseer** manager; foreman

**owner** person with legal and financial rights of proprietorship over company

**part-time worker** person employed temporarily or less than full-time

**patron** wealthy person who finances or supports business or institution

**paymaster** person authorized to pay wages or salaries

**peddler** person who carries articles from place to place to sell them

**player** *Informal.* active and influential participant in business dealings

**plutocrat** powerful, wealthy member of ruling class

**president** top executive officer of company

**professional** person trained and engaged in highly skilled occupation

**profiteer** person who sells a product or service at excessive prices

**prole** *Informal.* proletarian; laborer

**proletarian** worker or laborer

**proprietor** owner of business

**rainmaker** *Slang.* executive with extraordinary ability to attract clients and use connections to increase profits

**rep** *Informal.* representative

**representative** salesperson or authorized agent for business

**retailer** person who sells directly to consumers

**retainer** person serving another

**robber baron** ruthless, exploitative capitalist (late 19th c.)

**salesman** person employed as sales clerk or sales representative, esp. male salesperson

**salesperson** male or female who sells goods or services

**sales rep** *Informal.* sales representative

**sales representative** person employed as sales agent for company in particular area

**saleswoman** female salesperson

**secretary** clerical office worker, esp. one subordinate to a single superior

**self-employed** *(adj)* designating person owning a business or working freelance

**servant** person employed to perform personal and household services

**service worker** person who provides services directly to consumers or clients

**shopkeeper** owner or manager of small retail business

**silent partner** partner investing capital in business but not taking part in decision making or operations

**slave** worker who is owned by master

**small businessman** owner of modest or personally run company

**sponsor** person who helps finance business or business activity

**staff** full-time, permanent company employees

**subordinate** person under authority or direction of another

**superintendent** person in charge of department or institution

**superior** person with authority over another

**supervisor** superintendent, manager, or director of unit within business

**taskmaster** person responsible for assigning and supervising rigorous tasks performed by others

**team player** person who respects organizational hierarchy and works well with others

**temp** *Informal.* temporary worker hired for specific job and excluded from union or fringe benefits

**trader** merchant, salesman; broker, agent

**tradesman** *Chiefly Brit.* shopkeeper

**traveling salesman** business representative who solicits orders by traveling through assigned territory

**treasurer** chief financial officer of company

**tycoon** powerful, successful businessperson

**underling** person working in subordinate capacity

**unskilled laborer** manual or factory worker with no training

**vassal** feudal serf; subordinate or servant

**vendor** one who sells

**venture capitalist** financier investing in high-risk and start-up companies in hopes of reaping large profits

**wage earner** salaried employee

**wage slave** person utterly dependent on current, often inadequate, salary

**white-collar worker** office, sales, or professional worker

**wholesaler** person who sells products to other businesses

**wildcatter** person who promotes risky or unsound business venture

**workaholic** compulsively hard worker to the exclusion of other interests

**worker** person employed to perform labor for wages

**working girl** sometimes disparaging term for female office or clerical worker

**workingman** laborer, esp. industrial or manual worker

**working mother** woman serving as both parent and employee

**working stiff** *Slang.* hardworking common laborer or factory worker

**workingwoman** female who is regularly employed

# FINANCE

Accounting
Spending, Receiving, and Possessing Wealth
Money, Currency, and Denominations
World Currencies

**SEE ALSO:** Chap. 11: Government; Chap. 12: Business and
Economics; Insurance; Real Estate

# BANKING AND FINANCIAL SERVICES

**ABA number** *American Banking Association* number

**acceptance** short-term credit arrangement used in financing trade in which banks substitute their credit for the customer's

**account** record of all financial transactions for specific person or entity

**accrued interest** interest owed but not yet paid

**acquittance** document or receipt held as evidence of discharge of debt

**adjustable rate** interest rate, esp. on mortgage, that varies with predetermined factors

**agio** fee paid to exchange one currency for another

**American Banking Association number** ABA number; bank's identification number in upper right corner of check

**amortization** paying off of debt in installments over time, with each payment covering current interest and part of principal

**annuity** investment plan providing guaranteed retirement income

**appraisal** estimate of property's true value, esp. by expert

**arrears** overdue debts

**ATM** *automated-teller* machine

**automated-teller machine** ATM; computerized electronic device for depositing and withdrawing funds from account; cash machine

**bad debt** uncollectable bill or loan

**balance** amount standing as credit in checking or savings account

**balance due** amount standing as debit on charge account

**balloon payment** large final loan payment after many smaller payments

**bank** institution receiving money on deposit, lending money on interest, and simplifying fund exchanges by use of checks and notes

**bankbook** small booklet in which account transactions are recorded

**bank card** personalized, magnetically imprinted plastic card used in combination with secret code for ATM transactions

**bank check** check drawn by bank on itself and signed by authorized bank officer; cashier's check

**bank clerk** *Chiefly Brit.* teller

**bank draft** check drawn by bank against funds deposited to its account in another bank

**banker** owner or manager of bank

**banker's acceptance** draft or bill of exchange drawn on bank and accepted by it

**banking** business and practice of operating a bank

**banking house** company in business of banking

**bank note** paper note issued by bank for use as money; currency

**bank paper** bank notes collectively

**bank rate** standard discount interest rate set by central bank, esp. in Britain

**bank run** series of large withdrawals made by bank depositors fearful of bank failure

**bankrupt** (*adj*) designating person or entity whose total property and assets are insufficient to pay debts

**bank statement** list of transactions and charges on customer's account during regular period, usu. issued monthly

**bearer** holder of note or other financial instrument

**beneficiary** person for whom funds are placed in trust, in whose favor letter of credit is issued, or who receives income from estate, insurance policy, or annuity

**blind trust** trust in which public official, to avoid conflict of interest, places assets under control of independent trustee who manages them without owner's oversight

**borrow** (*vb*) take out a loan with understanding that it will be repaid in specified time, usu. with interest

**bounced check** check returned by bank due to insufficient funds

**branch bank** bank office operating at distance from main bank

**building and loan association** savings and loan association

**bursar** treasurer, esp. of college

**call loan** loan repayable on demand

**call money** funds loaned by bank to stockbrokers that may be demanded at any time

**capital** money, assets, and property used as means of production; owner's equity in business plus creditors' advances

**capital funds** total capital accounts of bank, including par value of capital stock, surpluses, undivided profits, and capital reserves

**cash** (*vb*) turn in check at bank and receive currency

**cashier** bank officer responsible for receipts and disbursements

**cashier's check** bank check

**cash machine** automated-teller machine

**CD** *certificate of deposit*

**central bank** banker's bank, such as Federal Reserve

**certificate of deposit** CD; receipt for funds deposited, usu. for specified amount of time at fixed interest rate

**certified check** check with bank guarantee that sufficient funds are on deposit to cover it, usu. indicated by special stamp

**charge** purchase made on credit to be paid in cash over specified time, often with interest

**charge account** account, usu. with retail store, that allows customer to buy merchandise on credit

**check** written order for bank to pay funds held for depositor; also, *esp. Brit.*, cheque

**checkbook** book containing detachable forms for writing checks on bank account

**checking account** account at bank against which checks may be drawn

**chit** voucher for small sum of money owed

**Christmas club** savings account from which funds are withdrawn at Christmas to pay for shopping

**clearinghouse** central bank in which representatives of local banks meet daily to exchange checks and settle balances

**collateral** assets pledged by borrower to guarantee repayment of loan

**collection** recovery of loans in default of regular payments; department or agency responsible for this

**collection items** drafts or notes subject to collection before proceeds are credited to depositor's account

**comaker** person signing another's note to strengthen credit

**commercial bank** bank primarily involved in taking demand deposits for checking accounts and offering short-term loans

**commercial paper** short-term negotiable debt instrument arising out of corporate commercial transactions

**commute** (*vb*) substitute single payment for series of smaller payments

**compound interest** interest calculated on total of principal plus accrued interest

**consumer credit** credit offered to individuals rather than institutional borrowers

**correspondent bank** bank that carries deposit balance for bank in another locality and exchanges services with that bank

**cosigner** person signing loan contract and promising to repay loan if borrower defaults

**counter check** check available at counter for use of depositors in making withdrawals

**counterfoil** *Chiefly Brit.* check or receipt stub

**countersign** (*vb*) sign another person's document in order to verify authenticity

**courtesy card** personalized card entitling bearer to special banking privileges

**creative financing** financing that combines different instruments, such as bonds and mortgages

**credit** arrangement for future payment, usu. with interest, on goods or money obtained immediately; funds available to borrower

**credit bureau** agency providing information to lenders on credit rating of individuals or companies

**credit card** plastic card certifying bearer's entitlement to charge purchases to credit account

**credit limit** largest amount that can be borrowed on credit card or account

**credit line** line of credit

**creditor** person or business to whom amount is owed

**credit rating** measure of past credit reliability, used to gauge degree of risk involved in loan or extension of credit to individual or business

**credit union** cooperative association for pooling savings of members or employees and making loans to them at low interest

**debt** amount owed to lender by borrower

**debt service** total interest on loan over full term of payments

**default** failure to make timely loan payments

**deferred payment** money withheld until certain date

**delinquency** failure to meet agreed-upon time for debt repayment

**demand deposit** bank deposit that may be withdrawn without notice

**deposit** money stored in bank or financial institution; partial payment for goods, services, or property

**depository** place where funds and valuables are placed for safekeeping

**deposit slip** written record of amount placed in bank on specific date

**depreciation** gradual devaluation or drop in price

**deregulation** elimination of government regulatory controls on deposits and loans, allowing freer banking activities

**discount** interest paid at beginning of loan period, deducted from principal in advance

**discount rate** interest charged by Federal Reserve Bank on loans to member banks

**dishonor** (*vb*) refuse check presented as payment; refuse to make due payment on debt

**down payment** initial payment required on credit purchase

**draft** written order for payment

**Dun & Bradstreet** agency furnishing information to subscribers on financial standing and credit rating of businesses

**dunning** harassment of debtor for payment

**duty** tax on imports or exports

**early withdrawal** withdrawal of funds from timed deposit before maturity, usu. involving interest forfeiture

**earnest money** funds given as partial payment and binding pledge in agreement

**EFT** electronic funds transfer

**electronic funds transfer** EFT; banking transaction via telecommunications network

**embezzlement** illegal appropriation of property or funds entrusted to one's care

**encashment** act of cashing a check

**endorsement** signature on back of item, usu. check, authorizing payment or transferring rights to someone else

**equity** money invested in property or business entity with mortgages, debts, and liens deducted

**escrow** written agreement deposited with third party, usu. bank, as custodian, to be delivered upon fulfillment of some condition

**exchanges** items presented for collection through clearinghouse or exchanged directly by local banks

**exchequer** treasury, esp. funds in British treasury

**extortion** obtaining money illegally, esp. by misuse of authority

**FDIC** Federal Deposit Insurance Corporation

**Fed** *Informal.* Federal Reserve System, esp. its Board of Governors

**Federal Deposit Insurance Corporation** FDIC; government agency guaranteeing funds placed in banks

**Federal Reserve System** federal banking system that regulates flow of money and acts as central clearinghouse for banks

**fiduciary** trustee administering estate, executing will, or serving as guardian of minor's assets

**finance** dealings concerning money in the business world, including circulation of currency, granting of credit, banking, and investment

**finance charge** monthly interest on revolving credit account

**finance company** institution specializing in consumer loans and lines of credit to businesses

**financial services** services provided by banking and investment banking institutions, savings and loan associations, mortgage companies, and brokerage houses

**financial statement** report summarizing impact of business transactions during fiscal period

**financier** person trained and engaged in large-scale financial operations

**float** uncollected amount of check cashed by one bank on another bank's account; brief interim before collection when bank on which check is drawn has use of depositor's money for free

**floating debt** short-term debt arising from current operations and having no specific time of repayment

**foreclose** (*vb*) deprive mortgagor of right to redeem property mortgaged for failure to fulfill conditions

**frozen assets** funds made unavailable to their owner

**guaranty** written promise to creditor by guarantor to be liable for debt should principal debtor fail in his or her obligations

**high finance** practices and institutions involved in banking and investment

**honor** (*vb*) accept and pay an obligation when called for

**IMF** *International Monetary Fund*

**insolvency** lack of resources to pay one's debts

**installment loan** note repaid in equal periodic payments, each including interest and part of principal

**instrument** formal legal document, such as deed, bond, note, or draft

**insufficient funds** deposits that are inadequate to cover check or withdrawal

**interest** fee charged for use of capital or extension of credit; sum paid as percentage of money on deposit

**interest forfeiture** loss of interest accrued on account, esp. due to early withdrawal of time deposits

**internal revenue** taxes collected on wages and business profits by government

**international banking** large-scale financial operations, esp. involving debt and credit to nations

**International Monetary Fund** IMF; international agency established to promote trade and economic cooperation and to stabilize balance of payments by making loans to member nations

**investment** outlay of money for income or profit

**investment banking** activities of financial institutions whose primary business is issuing and trading securities of other companies

**IOU** informal promissory note; written acknowledgment of indebtedness

**joint account** bank account held by more than one person

**juice** *Slang.* money loaned at exorbitant interest, esp. by bookmaker

**kiting** writing check against insufficient funds or moving funds from bank to bank to create temporarily expanded credit

**land bank** bank financing real estate transactions, esp. federal bank providing long-term loans to farmers

**laundering** concealing source of large sums of money, usu. by moving it through several accounts

**layaway plan** method of making installment purchase on revolving credit account

**lending institution** savings and loan association, mortgage company, or bank specializing in business and consumer loans

**letter of credit** document from one bank to correspondent bank requesting that letter bearer be given credit

**line of credit** credit limit set by lending institution; credit line

**liquidity** ease with which asset can be converted to cash

**loan** amount of money borrowed or lent on interest

**loan office** place where loans are made

**loan officer** bank employee responsible for interviewing loan applicants and approving and setting terms of loans

**loan shark** *Informal.* lender charging excessive interest

**Lombard** banker or moneylender

**long-term loan** loan with maturity date many years in the future

**M-1** money held by public for use in current spending, including coins, paper currency, demand deposits, and traveler's checks

**M-2** M-1 plus savings and time deposits, money market funds, overnight repurchases, and Eurodollars

**M-3** M-2 plus large time deposits, institutional money market funds, and term repurchases

**magnetic ink character recognition number** MICR number; electronically coded number printed at bottom of check

**maker** person who signs and executes note or promise to pay

**maturity** due date of mortgage, note, draft, acceptance, or bond

**MICR number** *magnetic ink character recognition number*

**MO** *money order*

**moneychanger** person who exchanges national currencies at established rates

**money market** high-interest, unregulated, nonbanking investment entity that originated in 1970's

**money market mutual fund** entity that pools assets of investors and puts funds into short-term, high-interest bank CDs, treasury bills, and commercial paper

**money order** MO; order for payment or draft sold by bank for fee

**mortgage** method of pledging property as guaranty of payment of debt with interest

**mortgage company** lending institution specializing in large, long-term loans on real estate

**mortgage holder** institution or person holding mortgage on property

**national bank** federally chartered bank

**near money** assets with high degree of liquidity, such as savings deposits

**negotiable instrument** note or other instrument legally transferable to another by proper endorsement

**negotiable order of withdrawal account** NOW account; checking account in which unused money earns interest

**never-never** *Brit. slang.* installment plan

**nonpar** (*adj*) describing items on which payer bank deducts exchange charge before paying them to collecting bank

**note** promissory note issued to creditor (note payable) or accepted from customer owing money (note receivable)

**noteholder** one to whom loan payments and interest are due

**NOW account** *negotiable order of withdrawal account*

**numbered account** bank account identified by number only, to conceal identity of depositor, esp. in Swiss bank

**obligation** debt security, such as mortgage or corporate bond

**on-demand** (*adj*) pertaining to note payable immediately upon receipt

**outstanding check** check that has been written but not yet paid by bank on which it was drawn

**overdraft** bank withdrawal in excess of funds available

**overdraw** (*vb*) draw on an account in excess of available funds

**par** (*adj*) describing items that payer bank remits without charge

**par value** amount agreed to be repaid, exclusive of interest, on bond, note, or other obligation

**passbook** bankbook recording deposits, withdrawals, interest, and service charges on account

**pawn** something deposited with another as security for a loan; (*vb*) make such a deposit

**pawnbroker** person licensed to lend money at specified rates on items of personal property deposited as collateral

**pawnshop** place of business of pawnbroker

**payback** return on investment; period of time required to recoup investment

**periodic payments** regular, usu. monthly, payments of interest and principal required by terms of loan

**PIN** *p*ersonal *i*dentification *n*umber; secret code used to access ATM

**plastic** credit card

**points** small percentage of loan, esp. mortgage, prepaid as origination fee and deemed interest

**postdated check** check dated in future and not payable until that date

**premium** amount paid for loan in addition to interest

**prepayment penalty** additional fee charged for paying off loan before it is due

**price** rate of interest charged on loan

**primary deposit** cash deposited in the bank

**prime rate** rate of interest charged by banks on loans to major borrowers, esp. businesses

**principal** face amount of loan, excluding interest

**promissory note** written contract to pay specified amount at set future date

**protest** notarized document giving notice that note or draft was presented for payment and refused

**quittance** discharge from debt

**rate** percentage of money returned as interest

**receivership** process by which assets of company in bankruptcy are held and administered by bank or other appointed trustee

**recoup** (*vb*) recover original investment

**recourse debt** negotiable instrument for which maker or endorser is liable

**rediscount** commercial paper discounted a second time

**redlining** discriminatory refusal or limitation of loans based on geography, esp. within inner-city neighborhoods

**regulation** control of U.S. banking operations by government

**reimburse** (*vb*) pay back, esp. for money already spent

**remit** (*vb*) make payment

**remittance** money paid, esp. sent as payment

**repossession** taking back of article by creditor when debtor fails to make payments

**repurchase agreement** contract between bank and investor in which bank agrees to buy back security it has sold to investor at fixed price on designated date

**reserve bank** bank holding money reserves of other banks

**reserve requirement** percentage of their deposits that member banks must keep as cash or on deposit with district Federal Reserve Bank

**reserves** funds set aside by bank to enable it to pay depositors in cash on demand

**return item** item returned unpaid by payer bank

**return on capital** profit or yield achieved on investments

**revolving credit** charge account in which portion of total is due each month and interest is added monthly

**rubricated account** special bank account, esp. one with special designation or title

**run** sudden large number of bank withdrawals

**safe-deposit box** rented space in bank vaults to which only renter has access, used for secure storage of valuable property

**S and L** savings and *l*oan association

**savings** assets set aside for future use

**savings account** interest-bearing bank account

**savings and loan association** S and L; institution owned by depositors and making long-term real estate and other loans; building and loan association

**savings bank** institution specializing in small, timed deposits

**secondary reserves** bank assets, such as government securities or commercial paper, that can quickly be converted into cash

**secured loan** cash loan based on collateral that ensures repayment of borrowed money

**security** item standing as means of assuring payment of debt; person bound to pay debt if another fails

**service charge** fee charged by bank on depositor's account statements for services rendered, usu. in connection with checking account

**share draft** interest-bearing checking account in a credit union

**shave** (*vb*) purchase a note at rate discounted to illegal level

**short-term loan** loan with maturity date usu. under one year

**Shylock** person charging exorbitant interest on loans

**signature card** card containing signatures of individuals authorized to write checks on bank account

**simple interest** interest computed by multiplying principal by rate and by number of years

**smart card** plastic credit card with memory chip for financial transactions

**smart money** investments made with advantage of inside information

**solvency** ability to pay one's debts and meet one's financial responsibilities

**speculation** high-risk investment in hopes of rapid high return

**spendthrift trust** trust account in which principal is made inaccessible to one who might spend it recklessly

**stale check** check invalidated by lapse of time between writing and cashing

**state bank** bank chartered by nation or state, regulated by its laws

**statement** regular, usu. monthly, description of all transactions, deposits, and running balance in account

**stop payment** request by depositor that his or her bank refuse payment of check written on account

**subordinated** (*adj*) designating debt obligation whose holder is placed in precedence below preexisting creditors

**surety** person liable for another's debts

**surety company** institution that insures against various types of losses and executes bonds

**survivorship account** account in name of two persons that belongs to either survivor on death of other

**Swiss account** numbered account, esp. in Swiss bank

**teller** bank clerk who pays out and receives money directly from public

**term** length of time over which promissory note must be paid

**terms** conditions of promissory note, obligation, or contract

**thrifts** thrift institutions, savings and loan banks, or credit unions

**till** place for keeping cash; ready cash

**time deposit** savings account deposit that may not be withdrawn without penalty until specified time

**time payments** payments on installment

**transit items** cash items payable outside city of bank receiving them and transmitted to payer bank

**transit number** number printed on check identifying bank, its location, and proper routing

**traveler's check** replaceable check sold by banks, to be countersigned and used as money by those traveling away from home bank

**treasurer** person in charge of funds or finances of business or institution

**treasury** place where funds are kept; funds of corporation or state; agency administering treasury

**treasury house** building housing treasury offices

**trust** obligation on person (trustee) to hold and use property according to terms of special grant, esp. for benefit of others

**trust account** money deposited by one person and held in trust for another

**trust company** bank that handles trusts and all banking operations except issuance of notes

**trustee** person legally empowered to administer on behalf of beneficiary

**trust fund** trust account, esp. held for use by children after depositor's death

**trust officer** bank employee responsible for operations of trust department

**unsecured** (*adj*) not guaranteed by collateral

**usury** charging of excessive interest on loans

**variable-rate mortgage** mortgage with adjustable rate, often linked to prime rate

**venture capital** funds used for investment in high-risk enterprises, usu. for start-up companies

**void** (*vb*) invalidate check, as by writing "void" across it

**voucher** written statement attesting to expenditure or receipt of money and accuracy of account

**welsh** (*vb*) *Informal*. fail to pay one's debts

**withdrawal** removal of funds from account

**World Bank** U.N. agency established to make loans to underdeveloped member nations

**yield** percentage of money returned on investment

## SECURITIES

**acquisition** purchase of one company by another, including gaining control of its stock

**actionnaire** *French*. stockholder

**agiotage** *French*. speculation, esp. dealing in foreign exchange and stockjobbing

**American Stock Exchange** AMEX; exchange for stocks not listed on New York Stock Exchange

**AMEX** *American Stock Exchange*

**arbitrage** selling of assets in one market after purchase in another to profit by price differential; purchase and sale of large block of securities in company in expectation of profit, esp. when engaged in discussions of merger or takeover

**arbitrageur** one who engages in arbitrage

**baby bond** bond with value of less than $1,000

**bearish** (*adj*) pessimistic about security prices; causing or describing a fall in stock prices

**bear market** market in which stocks are declining

**bid-and-asked price** highest price offered and lowest price accepted for security at specific time

**bid price** amount initially offered for block of stock

**Big Board** *Informal*. New York Stock Exchange

**block** very large number of shares in one company sold as unit to one buyer

**blue chip** high-quality, generally nonspeculative stock or security

**blue-sky law** law designed to prevent sale and promotion of fraudulent securities

**bond** security certificate of loan, with principal to be repaid by issuing body, usu. government or corporation, at specified maturity date, with interest usu. paid at intervals

**bond issue** offering of bonds for sale with set interest rates and maturity dates

**book value** theoretical value of security based on company balance sheet

**bourse** stock exchange in European city

**broker** one who buys and sells stocks as agent for others, receiving a commission for this service

**brokerage** business that buys and sells stocks as agent for others

**bullish** (*adj*) optimistic about security prices; causing or expecting a rise in stock prices

**bull market** upward trend indicating stock market vigor

**buy back** purchase by corporate management of stock in its own company to reduce number of outstanding shares

**buy-out** purchase and retirement of outstanding securities of a company, which is thus taken private

**call** option to buy given quantity of stock at stated price within a specified time, purchased in anticipation of increase in price

**capital gain** profit on sale of a security: sales price less commissions less cost or basis

**capital gain distribution** regular payments to stockholders by corporation, similar to dividends

**capital stock** total value of corporate capital divided into negotiable shares of stock

**Chicago Board of Trade** major exchange that deals in futures, esp. of grains and metals

**churn** excessively fast turnover of securities for purpose of generating broker's commission, often for little gain

**closely held** describing securities not available for trading

**commission** broker's fee on stock sale or purchase

**commodities broker** individual licensed to trade on commodities exchange

**commodities exchange** place where trading in contracts on staple products is conducted

**common stock** share of ownership in company, providing eligibility for dividends and vote on company decisions

**convertible security** security that can be exchanged for another kind of security

**correction** brief movement of market in opposite direction from general trend, esp. to offset sharp advance or decline

**coupon** detachable printed statement specifying interest due on bond at given time

**crash** abrupt, sharp decrease in asset prices, esp. stocks

**cross trade** simultaneous, offsetting buy and sell orders taken by single broker without recording trade, often depriving investor of chance to trade at more favorable rate

**curb** market dealing in securities not listed on exchange

**debenture** unsecured bond

**discount** difference between issuing price and selling price of security

**discretionary account** account that empowers broker to make transactions on own discretion, without consulting client

**diversify** (*vb*) place investments in several different companies and forms to guard against collapse of one

**dividend** regular return on investment paid to stockholders from business profits

**Dow Jones Average** *Trademark.* index of relative price of securities based on daily price of selected industrial, transportation, and utility stocks traded on New York Stock Exchange

**employee stock ownership plan** ESOP; system by which employees acquire stock in company for which they work and receive distribution at retirement

**ESOP** *employee stock ownership plan*

**exchange** place where trading of securities or commodities is conducted by brokers; commodities exchange; mercantile exchange; stock exchange

**ex dividend** recently declared dividend that is not paid to recent purchaser of security

**Fannie Mae** FNMA; any of various publicly traded securities backed by a pool of mortgages held by federal agency

**financial district** area where banks, investment houses, brokerages, and exchange are located, esp. Wall Street in New York City

**fixing** scheduled time for stock market status report

**float** (*vb*) place securities, esp. bond issue, on market; (*n*) amount of common stock not closely held and available for trading

**floor** area of stock exchange occupied by brokers and traders

**FNMA** *Federal National Mortgage Association;* Fannie Mae

**futures** contracts to buy specific commodity at set price, to be delivered at future date

**futures exchange** exchange that sells futures contracts on indexes for future value

**gilt-edged** (*adj*) designating highest quality securities and bonds

**Ginnie Mae** GNMA; bond or certificate issued by federal agency based on mortgages purchased from lenders

**glamour stock** popular, usu. blue-chip stock that rises quickly or steadily in price

**GNMA** *Government National Mortgage Association;* Ginnie Mae

**go private** (*vb*) take company private by buying back all public-issue securities

**go public** (*vb*) offer stock of privately owned company on market

**government bond** bond issued by municipal, state, or federal government as means of obtaining capital

**greenmail** practice of purchasing large block of company's stock at special rate, either to force rise in stock prices or as offer to buy back stock at premium, often to thwart possible takeover

**growth stock** common stock in company with significant sales and earnings, having some degree of instability but opportunity for substantial increase in price

**high yield** strong return on investment, usu. anything over ten percent

**high-yield security** security that pays interest at significantly higher rate than government or corporate bonds, often carrying lower credit rating

**holding company** corporation whose sole business is to acquire, hold, and sell stock ownership in other companies

**holdings** securities one owns

**hostile takeover** assumption of control of company against wishes of management by appealing directly to shareholders, often for purpose of reselling stock at significant gain

**income fund** mutual fund providing current income

**income stock** stock in relatively stable company that produces regular return on investment with small chance of rapid price increase

**indenture** document detailing terms of bond issue

**index arbitrage** form of program trading based on manipulation of fleeting differentials between share price and futures price contracts

**industrials** stocks of industrial corporations, esp. those listed on New York Stock Exchange

**insider information** information that is not publicly available, used to obtain large, often illegal, profits on stock transactions

**institutional trading** buying and selling of large blocks of securities by banks, pension and mutual funds, and other financial intermediaries

**investment** outlay of money for income or profit

**issue** circulation or offering of securities for sale

**junk bond** high-yield, speculative bond often issued by lower credit-rated company, sometimes to finance corporate takeover

**LBO** *leveraged buyout*

**leverage** use of credit in business activity, esp. to enhance speculative capacity; borrowed capital used in business

**leveraged buyout** LBO; change of company ownership through purchase of large block of stock financed by debt to be paid off out of future revenue

**listed** (*adj*) designating a security traded on one of the exchanges

**margin** cash or collateral required to be deposited with broker to protect broker and allow client to purchase securities on credit

**margin account** brokerage account in which trading on margin can occur

**market** institution of and place where trading of securities occurs; stock market

**market index** number showing percentage variation from arbitrary standard, used to measure rise and fall of market

**market order** instructions to buy or sell at current market price

**market price** prevailing price for security or commodity in given market

**mercantile exchange** place where trading in securities occurs, as distinguished from commodities exchange

**merger** combining of two or more companies by issuing

stock of controlling corporation to replace most of stock of other companies

**mergers and acquisitions**   department of investment banking firm or brokerage handling corporate mergers and acquisitions

**municipal bond**   bond sold by local or state government

**mutual fund**   investment company owned by shareholders and using funds to purchase stocks and bonds of other corporations

**NASDAQ**   National Association of Securities Dealers Automated Quotations; system for quoting and trading over-the-counter securities

**New York Stock Exchange**   primary security trading exchange, located on Wall Street in New York City

**obligation**   debt security with required fixed payment, such as mortgage or corporate bond

**odd lot**   quantity of stock purchased in units other than 10 or 100 shares

**offering**   security made available for purchase at specific price for set period of time

**option**   right to buy or sell security at fixed price within specified time

**OTC**   (adj) over-the-counter

**outstanding**   (adj) of securities, publicly issued and in circulation

**overpriced**   (adj) designating securities priced above true value with potential to decline in price

**over-the-counter**   (adj) OTC; designating stocks not listed on any exchange, sold directly to buyers

**paid-in-kind security**   PIK security

**panic**   sudden, widespread fear of financial collapse that results in attempts to sell off securities at any price

**par issue**   security offered at face value

**par value**   face value of share of stock or bond

**penny stock**   highly speculative common stock, usu. selling for less than one dollar per share

**PIK security**   paid-in-kind security; usu. high-yield security on which interest accrues as additional securities, not as interest, dividends, or cash

**pit**   area of commodities exchange where brokers and traders work

**point**   unit of variation in security market prices

**portfolio**   investor's sum total of stocks, bonds, and securities

**preferred stock**   share of ownership in business that provides first claim on assets after creditors, priority in receipt of dividends, but not necessarily a voice in company management

**premium**   amount over par value for which preferred stock is sold

**price-earnings ratio**   current price of a share of common stock divided by earnings per share over one-year period

**proceeds**   earnings from security sale less commissions

**profit taking**   selling of securities to take advantage of temporarily inflated price

**program trading**   large, computerized security transactions, usu. made by institutional investors, that occur automatically at predetermined prices

**public issue**   offer of securities for sale to public on exchange

**publicly traded**   designating stock available for sale on exchange or over-the-counter

**put**   option to sell given quantity of securities at specific price and within specified time, purchased in anticipation of decline in price

**quotation**   current price of stock or commodity; record of opening and closing prices and number of shares traded on particular day

**raider**   financier who uses greenmail, leveraged buyout, and arbitrage in attempt to purchase publicly owned entity against the wishes of its management

**rally**   period of rising stock market prices

**risk arbitrage**   investment in securities or commodities subject to takeover or other speculation

**Sallie Mae**   SLMA; student loans issued by federal agency based on mortgages purchased from lenders

**SEC**   Securities and Exchange Commission

**securities**   government-regulated class of investments, including bonds, notes, stock certificates, and mortgages

**Securities and Exchange Commission**   SEC; federal agency that regulates stock and commodity market transactions and conduct of market participants

**sell-off**   decline in prices of certain securities due to pressure to sell

**sell short**   (vb) sell securities that seller does not yet own but expects to cover later at lower price

**Series E bond**   widely held bond issue of U.S. Treasury

**Series H bond**   widely held bond issue of U.S. Treasury

**shakeout**   rapid decrease in value of certain securities, often forcing speculators to sell holdings

**share**   single unit of stock or other security

**shareholder**   owner of share or shares in company

**shares**   Chiefly Brit. stocks

**SLMA**   Student Loan Marketing Association; Sallie Mae

**slump**   general decrease in stock prices over period of time

**soft market**   weak, declining market

**speculation**   buying or selling of securities at high risk in anticipation of rise or fall in price

**speculator**   one who speculates in securities

**split**   dividing of securities by substituting multiple of original shares with equal par value but proportionately lower value per share

**spot market**   market in which cash is exchanged for actual delivery of commodities

**spots**   Informal. commodities

**stock**   unit of ownership of corporation; outstanding capital of a company

**stock bonus**   payment in company stock in addition to wages, esp. to corporate executive

**stockbroker**   agent buying and selling shares of ownership in corporations for clients who pay sales commission

**stock certificate**   written evidence of ownership of shares of stock

**stock exchange**   market for trading in stocks; association of brokers who meet daily to buy and sell securities; stock market

**stockholder**   owner of share or shares in capital of corporation

**stockjobbing**   sales and promotion of often worthless securities

**stock market**   market for stocks throughout a nation; stock exchange

**stock option**   put or call

**stock parking**   concealing one's ownership of securities

**stocks and bonds**   securities in general

**straddle** option in which a put and a call are combined at same market price for same set period

**street name** broker's as opposed to owner's name on security, usu. for convenience

**subscription** agreement to pay certain amount for fixed number of securities

**surety company** company that insures against various types of losses and executes bonds

**takeover** assumption of management or ownership of company through acquisition of its stock

**tax-exempt bond** government obligation on which interest is exempt from federal and/or state income tax

**T-bill** U.S. Treasury bill or note

**technical correction** brief movement of market counter to general trend due to mechanics of pricing

**tender offer** offer at stated price for stock purchase from shareholders in takeover, often with promise of better management

**ticker** computer recording and displaying current stock prices

**trader** person whose business is buying and selling of commodities or securities

**trading** exchange, purchase, and sale of stocks and bonds

**trading pit** area of intense activity where trading occurs at exchange

**Treasury bill** short-term, interest-bearing obligation of U.S. Treasury, maturing in one year or less; T-bill

**Treasury bond** any of various series of bonds issued by U.S. Treasury, maturing over long periods of time

**Treasury note** interest-bearing obligation of U.S. Treasury, maturing in one to ten years

**triple witching hour** last hour of trading on any of four Fridays each year when options and futures expire, regarded as highly volatile time

**underpriced** (*adj*) priced below true value with potential to increase in price

**underwrite** (*vb*) agree to buy or guarantee purchase of securities issue on given date at fixed price

**utilities** stocks issued by corporations that provide power, water, or telephone services, forming a separate market index

**voting stock** shares of stock that give owner right to vote on certain corporate decisions

**Wall Street** street at center of New York City financial district serving as location of New York Stock Exchange; U.S. financial interests and business in general

**war bond** government bond issued to obtain revenue to support war effort

**warrant** call option with much longer maturity period than option, usu. up to two years or more

**wash sale** sale of stock at a loss and repurchase within thirty days for tax purposes; simultaneous purchase and sale of same stock or commodity to give impression of activity

**water** (*vb*) increase par value of shares without having assets to support this increase

**watered stock** stock illegally issued at above face value without corresponding increase in corporate assets

**yield** ratio of annual dividends or earnings per share to market price

**zero-coupon bond** bond sold at discount from face value and paying no regular interest, which is paid in full at time of maturity

# TAXATION

## TYPES OF TAXES

**ad valorem tax** tax applied to value of what is being taxed, esp. imports

**alcohol tax** tax on sale of alcoholic beverages

**alternative minimum tax** special income tax on certain tax preference items

**amusement tax** tax on movies, plays, and other performances, included in admission price

**capital gains tax** tax on disposition of securities, business assets, or real property

**capitation tax** poll tax

**customs duty** tax on goods imported from another country

**death tax** inheritance or estate tax

**direct tax** tax levied directly on person by whom it is to be paid, as income or estate tax

**douane** *French.* customs duty; customs house

**duty** tax on imported, exported, or manufactured goods

**estate tax** tax on assets of deceased person

**estimated tax** income tax paid quarterly by persons not subject to withholding, esp. self-employed people

**excess-profits tax** special tax on profits over fixed amount

**excise tax** tax on the manufacture, use, or sale of certain goods, esp. alcohol, tobacco, or firearms

**federal tax** tax levied by national government

**franchise tax** tax levied on corporations for right to do business in state or locality

**gas tax** tax on sale of gasoline as fuel

**gift tax** tax on very large gifts, paid by giver

**graduated tax** income tax with rates increasing at higher levels of income

**hidden tax** tax paid by manufacturer, supplier, or seller and passed on to consumer in market price; indirect tax

**income tax** federal, state, and local government tax on individual and business earnings, providing most of government revenues

**indirect tax** hidden tax

**inheritance tax** state tax on assets of deceased person, usu. paid by beneficiary

**land tax** tax on real property

**levy** imposition and collection of tax; amount of tax

**local tax** tax levied by city or county government

**luxury tax** excise tax on certain luxury items, such as boats

**maximum tax** tax computation that limits rate of taxation on net capital gains

**minimum tax** special minimum income tax

**municipal tax** tax levied by city government

**personal property tax** tax paid on movable items such as automobiles, furniture, or machinery used in business

**poll tax** tax sometimes levied for right to vote; capitation tax

**progressive tax** variable income tax rate that increases as amount to be taxed increases

**property tax** tax paid by owner of real property based on assessed value; real estate tax

**proportional tax** income tax that takes same percentage of income at all income levels

**protective tariff** tax on imports, intended to give domestic producers advantage in competitive pricing

**real estate tax** property tax

**regressive tax** tax rates that tax lower incomes at higher rates than higher incomes; tax rates equal at all levels of income, effectively taxing lower incomes more heavily

**revenue stamp** government stamp indicating payment of tax on commodity such as alcohol or tobacco

**revenue tax** tax usu. imposed on alcohol or tobacco

**sales tax** tax levied by city, county, or state on retail sales of merchandise

**school tax** local tax, usu. on property, with revenues used for support of schools

**self-employment tax** Social Security tax paid as percent of net income by usu. self-employed persons not subject to FICA withholding by employers

**severance tax** tax on lump-sum distribution at termination of employment

**single tax** tax on land ownership that constitutes sole source of revenue (19th c.)

**sin tax** *Informal.* tax on alcohol, tobacco, gambling, or other activities considered to be neither luxuries nor necessities

**Social Security tax** tax withheld from wages by FICA or paid as self-employment tax by sole proprietors

**state tax** tax levied by state government

**surtax** extra tax or charge; tax levied on income exceeding specified amount

**tariff** schedule of taxes on imports

**tax** compulsory federal, state, or local charge levied on income, imports, or retail purchases and used to finance government expenditures

**taxation** act of taxing; revenues derived from tax

**toll** tax or fee paid for privilege such as crossing bridge or driving on highway

**unemployment tax** amount paid by employer, and sometimes by employee, to be used as unemployment compensation to workers who lose their jobs

**value-added tax** sales tax on producer based on value of contribution to final product

**windfall profits tax** federal excise tax on profits from domestically produced crude oil

**withholding tax** tax deducted by employer from wages as income and Social Security tax

## INCOME TAX

**ability to pay** basis of principle that highest tax burden should fall on those with greatest ability to pay

**abusive tax shelter** investment scheme involving transactions that generate artificial losses in excess of actual investment for purpose of creating tax credits

**accelerated cost recovery system** ACRS; method of calculating depreciation, giving larger deductions in earlier years and smaller ones in later years

**ACRS** accelerated cost recovery system

**active participation** income-producing entity in which individual is directly involved

**adjusted basis** cost of asset less certain expenses and salvage value and/or plus improvements

**adjusted gross income** AGI; total taxable income before deductions and exemptions but after certain adjustments

**adjustments** reductions to gross income in determining AGI

**AGI** adjusted gross income

**amended return** corrected version of return previously filed based on new or corrected information

**amortization** method of deducting intangible expenses by prorating them over fixed period, similar to depreciation

**assessment** amount of tax liability as determined by taxing authority

**at-risk loss** net loss on business for which taxpayer is ultimately liable

**audit** examination of books and records by taxing authority to determine validity of return

**backup withholding** federal tax withheld at source on nonwage income such as interest, dividends, or pensions

**bad debt** loan determined to be uncollectable, deductible as an expense

**basis** cost or value when placed in service of depreciable asset plus or minus certain adjustments

**boot** nonlike-kind property included in like-kind exchange to balance value

**Bureau of Customs and Excise** tax-collecting authority in Great Britain

**capital gain** profit on sale of business assets, securities, real property, personal property, or intangible property

**capitalization** transferring cost of certain assets to balance sheet rather than taking full expense in year of purchase

**capital loss** loss on sale of business assets, securities, real property, personal property, or intangible property

**carryback** application of tax benefit or credit to previous year's tax return

**carryforward** application of unused tax benefit, credit, or capital loss to following year's tax return; carryover

**carryover** carryforward

**casualty loss** loss not reimbursed by insurance due to act of God or criminal act, partially accepted as an itemized deduction

**charitable contribution** itemized deduction allowed for cash or goods donated to nonprofit organization

**collection** formal process of requiring payment of overdue tax to revenue service

**contract labor** business expense for payments to individuals subcontracting on job but not regular employees of taxpayer

**corporation** business entity that is organized under incorporation laws of one state and usu. pays taxes on net profits

**cost of goods sold** initial amount, either cost of merchandise and warehousing or direct labor and materials, by which gross income is reduced in determining gross profit before expenses

**credit** any of various amounts by which tax liability is reduced

**decedent** for tax purposes, a person who died in previous tax year

**declare** (*vb*) report received income on return

**declining balance depreciation** depreciation figured as percent of remaining undepreciated basis, which declines each year

**deductible** (*adj*) designating an amount or type of expense that may be used to reduce adjusted gross income before calculating tax

**deduction** standardized or itemized amount by which adjusted gross income is reduced in determining taxable income

**dependent** person half of whose support is paid by taxpayer, who claims an exemption for this person

**depletion** depreciation of certain intangible assets, esp. oil and natural gas

**depreciation** allowance made for decrease in value of capital assets over time; various means of prorating the cost of such assets as an expense over fixed number of years

**distribution** amount paid out by pension, IRA, profit-sharing plan, trust, estate, or corporation to shareholders

**dividend** annual taxable payment to shareholders on earnings of securities

**earned income credit** amount added to withholding and estimated payments in determining overpayment or tax due, for low-income persons with dependents

**EID** employer identification number

**employee business expense** unreimbursed expenses incurred in course of work by salaried employee, an itemized deduction; such expenses reimbursed in W-2 as an adjustment

**employer identification number** EID; government-issued number that identifies corporation, partnership, trust, or individual who employs others

**enrolled agent** person who has passed IRS examination and is officially recognized as a tax preparer

**estimated tax** quarterly payment of income tax in lieu of withholding, made esp. by self-employed persons

**exciseman** Brit. government excise tax collector

**exemption** set amount allowed as deduction from income or credit on taxes for taxpayer, spouse, dependents, and those over sixty-five or blind

**expense** any of various costs associated with income production or a business, deductible from income

**expensing** taking entire cost of depreciable asset as expense in year of purchase

**extension** application for or permission granted to file return after due date

**Federal Insurance Contributions Act** FICA; legislation under which taxes are levied for support of Social Security

**FICA** Federal Insurance Contributions Act

**fiduciary return** tax return filed by trustee of an estate or trust

**filing** act of filling out and submitting tax return to taxing authority

**filing date** date on which return must be mailed in

**foreign earned income exclusion** amount of foreign earned income not liable to U.S. tax but subject to foreign tax

**foreign tax credit** reduction of U.S. tax liability based on taxes paid to foreign country on income from that country

**gain** profit on sale or exchange of asset

**garnishment** deduction of person's unpaid taxes or other debts directly from paycheck or bank account by order of court

**gross income** total income received before deductions

**head of household** unmarried person who pays over half the cost of maintaining home for child or other dependent

**holding period** period of time between acquisition and disposition of capital asset, used to determine whether asset is short or long term

**income** various forms of taxable and nontaxable revenue received by taxpayer

**income property** commercial or residential real property on which rent is paid to taxpayer

**independent contractor** self-employed person responsible for payment of own taxes

**individual retirement account** IRA; tax-free savings account into which annual contributions are made that allows deferment of tax payments until retirement

**informational return** tax return showing income and expenses but no tax liability, such as partnership or fiduciary return

**in-kind contribution** value and cost of services rendered to charitable organization, an itemized deduction

**Inland Revenue** federal taxing authority in Great Britain

**interest income** income derived as percentage of return on bank or savings deposits, bonds, or mortgages

**internal revenue** money collected by government from sources within country

**internal revenue agent** employee of IRS who audits, examines tax returns, and determines assessments

**Internal Revenue Service** IRS; tax-collecting agency of U.S. government

**investment expense** deductible amount, such as margin interest, incurred in production of investment income

**involuntary exchange/conversion** casualty, theft, or condemnation resulting in loss or decreased value of capital asset

**IRA** individual retirement account

**IRS** Internal Revenue Service

**itemized deduction** personal expense, such as medical or charitable outlay or mortgage interest paid, allowed as deduction from adjusted gross income in determining taxable income

**joint return** tax return reporting income for both members of married couple

**Keogh plan** personal retirement plan for self-employed individual, with contribution based on net income

**K-1** form issued by partnership, trust, fiduciary, or subchapter S corporation showing individual's share of net profit or loss and certain other income, distributions, and deductions

**like-kind exchange** nontaxable exchange of the same type of property

**limitation** standardized amount or amount based on individual return that credit or deduction may not exceed

**limited partnership** partnership with at least one general partner who has unlimited liability and at least one limited partner who is liable only for his or her investment

**long-term capital gain** profit on sale of assets held over one year

**loophole** means of reducing taxes by careful use of laws; law written to benefit one class or group of taxpayers

**lump-sum distribution** single payment from pension or profit-sharing program to which employee contributed, usu. received at time of separation from job

**MACRS** modified accelerated cost recovery system

**modified accelerated cost recovery system** MACRS; method of calculating depreciation that allows smaller deductions in early years than ACRS

**moving expense** expense allowed as itemized deduction for cost of moving personal belongings and family when employee moves over 35 miles to take new job

**net operating loss** NOL; condition in which business expenses exceed total income for year, resulting in loss applicable to previous or later year's tax return

**net profit** gross income less all expenses

**NOL** net operating loss

**nonemployee compensation** amounts paid to self-employed person, subject to self-employment tax

**nonprofit organization**  tax-exempt corporation filing informational return

**nonresident**  taxpayer who is part-year resident or not a resident of taxing authority

**nontaxable** (*adj*) not liable to taxation

**office-in-home**  portion of residence used for business, with percentage of housing costs taken as expense

**ordinary income**  noncapital gains income that is taxable in full

**out-of-state return**  tax return filed for income received from state of which one is not a resident

**overpayment**  tax payment in excess of amount owed, generating refund or credit

**partner**  active or passive member of partnership reporting portion of partnership's income on individual return

**partnership return**  informational return filed by general or limited partnership, showing profit or loss, portions of which are transferred to each partner's individual return

**part-year resident**  person who moved into and/or out of state during tax year

**passive activity**  any source of income, esp. a limited partnership with real estate investment or a trust, in which taxpayer has no active involvement

**penalty**  additional assessment for failure to file on time, underpayment, or underestimation of tax liability

**personal interest**  interest and finance charges paid on credit cards, charge accounts, and other personal loans, no longer deductible

**points**  percent of face value of mortgage paid at closing and fully deductible as itemized deduction when paid on principal residence

**portfolio income**  income derived from investments and securities, considered unearned income

**preenactment** (*adj*) designating property acquired or activities begun prior to tax reform act of October 23, 1986

**premature distribution**  taxable distribution from retirement plan or IRA prior to designated age of collection

**preparer**  professional trained and usu. licensed to fill out tax returns for others

**preparer penalty**  IRS assessment against preparer for sloppiness, negligence, or fraud

**recapture**  adding back of investment tax credit or depreciation taken on asset that has been disposed of before end of useful life

**refund**  amount of overpayment returned to taxpayer after filing of return

**reimbursement**  payment received for out-of-pocket expense that reduces deduction

**rental income**  income derived from rental of business or residential real property

**retirement credit**  credit for low-income, elderly, retired and totally disabled persons

**return**  forms, schedules, and statements used to report income and expenses and determine tax liability

**rollover**  reinvestment of distribution, esp. from pension or IRA, to postpone payment of tax

**salvage value**  estimated remaining value of asset once it is fully depreciated

**schedule**  tax form listing itemized expenses or showing income from various sources

**self-employment tax**  Social Security tax paid as percentage of net income by those not subject to FICA withholding by employers

**SEP**  *s*implified *e*mployee *p*ension

**short form**  simplified tax form for those with wages and unearned income but no enumerated deductions or credits

**short tax year**  tax year of less than twelve months for tax entity existing less than full year or one changing from calendar-year to fiscal-year accounting

**short-term capital gain**  profit on sale of securities, business assets, or real property held less than one year

**simplified employee pension**  SEP; tax-deferred pension identical for all employees and distributable from outset of employment

**sole proprietorship**  unincorporated business operated by one person with net income after expenses taxed on individual return and subject to self-employment tax

**special agent**  experienced IRS agent responsible for investigating cases involving possible fraud or tax evasion

**standard deduction**  specified amount allowed to all taxpayers as deduction from AGI when not itemizing

**straight-line depreciation**  traditional depreciation in which basis is divided equally by number of years over life of asset

**subchapter S corporation**  corporation with less than thirty-five shareholders that elects not to be taxed at corporate level but to have each shareholder's portion of net income taxed individually, as in a partnership

**taxable income**  income subject to taxation after subtracting deductions, adjustments, and exemptions

**tax base**  taxpayer's regular residence

**tax bracket**  income range with set tax rate

**tax break**  legal means of reducing one's tax liability by taking advantage of specific regulation

**tax code**  complete listing of all laws and regulations relating to income taxes

**tax collector**  agency or individual responsible for calling for and receiving tax payments

**tax court**  body that reviews and decides on serious tax issues and audits

**tax dodge**  illegal or apparently illicit means of avoiding tax liability

**tax evasion**  any attempt to illegally avoid paying taxes

**tax-exempt** (*adj*) not liable to taxation

**tax-exempt status**  condition or requirement by which entity, usu. nonprofit organization, makes its income not liable to taxation

**tax farmer**  one who collects taxes for taxing authority and receives commission or fee

**tax-free exchange**  usu. like-kind exchange of business assets or real property in which transaction is nontaxable

**tax haven**  nation or state with very low or no income tax

**taxing authority**  federal, state, or municipal government empowered to collect taxes

**tax liability**  amount of tax due

**tax lien**  claim on or confiscation of wages, bank deposits, or other property by taxing authority for payment of overdue tax

**taxman**  *Informal.* tax assessor or collector

**taxpayer**  individual required to pay tax or file return

**tax rate**  specified percentage of commodity, income, or service that is taxed

**tax rate schedule**  list of variable taxes at different levels of income or assessed value

**tax return**  annual report on earnings and calculation of tax due federal and state governments

**tax shelter** investment designed to postpone or avoid payment of taxes rather than generate taxable income

**tax structure** laws, codes, and regulations determining basic method of taxation for specific taxing authority

**tax year** twelve-month period taken as annual taxing period, not necessarily beginning January 1

**TIN** *taxpayer identification number*; either social security number or employer identification number

**triple tax-exempt bond** government bond whose interest is exempt from federal, state, and local taxes

**trust** taxable entity controlling assets for benefit of individual beneficiaries, with trust distributions being deductions to trust and usu. taxable to beneficiaries

**unemployment compensation** payment received by individual from unemployment insurance, often taxable in full or part

**useful life** period over which capital asset may be depreciated

**wages** salary paid to employee by employer, subject to withholding tax

**wash sale** transaction in which cost basis and proceeds are equal

**W-4** form filed by employee indicating number of exemptions, used by employer to determine withholding

**windfall profit** profit on domestically produced crude oil, subject to special tax

**withholding** payroll deduction for taxes and other items made by employer for direct payment to government

**withholding tax** income tax deducted by employer from wages

**write-off** expense allowable as tax deduction

**write off** (*vb*) take expense as tax deduction

**W-2** form prepared at year's end by employer, and filed with government, showing employee's compensation and taxes withheld

## ACCOUNTING

**account** subdivision of basic accounting system used to record assets, liabilities, equity, sales, or expenses

**accountancy** keeping or inspecting of business accounts; work of an accountant

**accountant** person trained in accounting methods, general bookkeeping, and tax preparation

**accounting** system of recording and summarizing business and financial transactions

**accounting clerk** entry-level bookkeeping position in company

**accounts payable** amounts owed to creditors

**accounts receivable** amounts to be received from customers for credit purchases

**accrual** entering in books items of income or expense that have been earned or incurred but not yet received or paid; such an item of income or expense

**accrual method** accounting system that matches accruals to period in which they were earned or incurred rather than period in which they were received or paid

**adjusted trial balance** statement of debt and credit balances and all transactions on all ledger accounts, used to complete balance sheet at end of fiscal period

**adjustment** amount added to or subtracted from account to bring balance up to date

**allowance** amount set aside for specific purpose, actual or budgeted

**annualize** (*vb*) project income or expenses for full year based on results for part of year

**appreciation** increase in value of asset over time

**assessment** determination of income or value of property for purpose of fixing tax

**assets** articles or property of value; property, materials, and economic resources owned by business or individual

**at risk** (*adj*) denoting the amount an owner or investor stands to lose should business go bankrupt

**audit** examination of business financial accounts

**auditor** person trained to examine accounts

**balance** amount standing as debit or credit on account

**balance sheet** report of total assets, liabilities, and owner's equity accounts at specific time

**bank reconciliation** tracing of all discrepancies until account books match bank statements

**bar graph** graph of differences between items at one point in time or the change at different times

**basis** cost adjusted by certain expenses, salvage value, and excess depreciation, used in calculating gain or depreciation

**beginning inventory** value of merchandise on hand at opening of fiscal period

**black** (*adj*) showing a profit; in the black

**bookkeeper** person responsible for keeping financial records

**bookkeeping** systematic recording of financial business transactions and records

**books** general accounts or records of business transactions

**books and records** general accounts, posting of transactions and balances, and substantiating evidence

**book value** value of asset at specific point in time, equal to initial cost less accumulated depreciation

**bottom line** net profit or loss after expenses, shown at bottom of profit and loss statement

**business entity** organization existing independent of its owner's personal holdings

**calendar year** accounting year running from January 1 to December 31

**capital account** total amount of investment in business entity by each owner or all owners

**capital contribution** investment of capital or value of goods invested in business entity

**cash basis method** accounting system in which income and expenses are entered in books only when paid and no accruals are made

**cashbook** book in which record of all receipts and disbursements of money are kept

**cash disbursements journal** special journal with record of all transactions involving cash payments

**certified public accountant** CPA; accountant who has passed state licensing examination

**circle graph** graph showing percentages of revenue or expenses in different areas of activity

**clerk** bookkeeper or record keeper for business

**close an account** reduce account to zero balance when no further transactions are anticipated

**close the books** balance out all income and expense accounts at end of period

**closing entries** net income or loss transferred to capital account as necessary to close books

**compound entry** journal entry having two or more debits and/or two or more credits

**comptroller** controller

**constructive receipt** condition in which funds not yet collected, such as an uncashed check, are deemed to have been received because they are controlled by recipient

**continuous budget** rolling budget

**controller** chief accounting officer of business or government, esp. responsible for internal auditing of books; comptroller

**cook the books** *Slang.* manipulate financial records to conceal profits, avoid taxes, or give false impression in audit

**cost** amount of money paid for goods or services

**cost accounting** system of recording, analyzing, and allocating production and distribution costs for internal use by business; managerial accounting

**costing out** *Informal.* applying cost accounting methods

**CPA** certified public accountant

**credit** amount of liability, equity, or revenue recorded as entry into account books on right side of T account

**current assets** liquid and semiliquid assets, such as cash, accounts receivable, and inventory

**current liabilities** business debts coming due for payment within next accounting period

**current ratio** relationship between current assets and current liabilities

**daybook** chronological record of each day's transactions

**debit** amount of asset or expense recorded as entry into account books on left side of T account

**deficit** net loss

**disbursement** payment of funds

**double-entry accounting** financial recordkeeping in which there must be an equal credit for each debit

**draw** withdrawal of capital from unincorporated business entity by owner or partner

**ending inventory** value of merchandise on hand at close of fiscal period

**entry** recording of single item in account book or ledger

**equity** owner's financial claim to or investment in assets or property of business

**expense** cost of goods or services that reduces owner's equity or profits for accounting period

**face value** principal amount of promissory note

**factor** entity that buys accounts receivable at discount from firm unable to carry them

**financial accounting** system of accounting used for reporting to investors, banks, and taxing authorities

**financial statement** report summarizing changes due to transactions during accounting period

**fiscal year** annual accounting period for business, either calendar year or sometimes July 1 to June 30 or October 1 to September 30

**fixed costs** expenses that are not variable during an accounting period, many of which are paid regularly

**general ledger** journal in which all business transactions are recorded and accounts balanced

**gross** total revenue before deduction of costs and expenses

**gross profit** difference between total sales revenue and cost of merchandise sold before deduction of other expenses

**horizontal analysis** comparison of changes in accounting statements from one period to next

**income** money received in sales, wages, or profits

**independent contractor** one who does work for another without being a regular employee, usu. setting own hours and conditions and hiring own workers

**intangible asset** property, such as patent, that represents value but has no physical form

**in the black** (*adj*) operating at a profit; black

**in the red** (*adj*) operating at a loss; red

**inventory** value of items of merchandise in stock at given time

**invoice** itemized list and billing statement of goods shipped or services rendered

**journal** entry book for recording daily transactions and indicating to which accounts they apply

**journal entry** orderly, usu. chronological, record of business transactions

**journalize** (*vb*) record transactions as journal entries

**ledger** book containing each business account on separate page, to which all journal entries are transferred

**liabilities** amounts owed to creditors; accounts payable

**limited liability** risk of loss fixed at some maximum amount, such as total investment

**liquidation** closing of business by collecting assets and settling debts

**liquidity** ease with which assets can be converted to cash

**log** (*vb*) enter transaction in journal or daybook

**managerial accounting** cost accounting

**multicolumn journal** journal using standard system of keeping books for several accounts

**negative amortization** increase of principal of loan by amount by which periodic loan payments fall short of interest due, usu. because of interest rate increase

**negative cash flow** excess of expenses over income

**net** money free from all charges, costs, and expenses

**net income** total revenue less costs and expenses

**net loss** amount by which expenses exceed revenue; deficit

**net profit** amount by which revenues exceed expenses

**net sales** total sales for period less returns, allowances, and discounts

**net worth** total assets minus liabilities of individual or business

**notes payable** promissory notes on loans issued to creditors

**notes receivable** promissory notes received by business from those who owe it money

**number-cruncher** *Informal.* accountant or clerk involved in bookkeeping and computer or statistical operations, but not management or decision making

**outstanding account** balance of unpaid debt, amount owing on loan

**owner's equity** owner's capital account in business

**P and L** *profit* and *loss* statement showing gross income, expenses, and net profit

**payment schedule** agreement between debtor and creditor for repayment of loan in installments over specified time

**payroll** list of employees and payments made to each for specific pay period

**payroll deduction** amount subtracted from gross earnings before payment of salary

**payroll register** form summarizing employee's earnings for each pay period

**pencil footing** *Informal.* column total written in small penciled figures, to be carried forward

**positive cash flow** excess of income over expenses

**posting** transference of transactions from journal entry to ledger account

**post up** (*vb*) transfer journal transaction into general ledger

**proceeds** amount of cash received from transaction after commissions, costs of sale, and interest deductions

**profit** revenue earned less expenses incurred

**public accounting** accounting services provided to clients for fee by licensed practitioners

**quarterly tax return** regular payment of sales, unemployment, and other business taxes

**ratio analysis** numerical comparison of items on financial statement to evaluate their relationships

**realize** (*vb*) convert into money; gain as net result of transaction

**reconciling** process of determining and accounting for discrepancies between accounts, balances, or statements

**red** (*adj*) showing a loss; in the red

**retained earnings** corporate earnings not paid out as stockholders' dividends

**revenue** money earned from sales of goods, services, or other business transactions

**rolling budget** budget prepared month by month instead of annually; continuous budget

**ruling** horizontal line beneath column of figures to indicate that entries above line are complete

**sales allowance** price reduction on damaged goods

**sales return** merchandise returned to vendor for credit or refund

**selling expenses** costs incurred in selling or marketing goods

**sole proprietorship** noncorporate business with one owner

**spreadsheet** worksheet on which financial information is presented in two-dimensional matrix; computer program for maintaining such a record

**statement** regular, usu. monthly, record of all transactions, deposits, and balances of account

**stockholders' equity** value of stockholders' claims to corporate assets

**subsidiary ledger** separate ledger containing detailed accounts for each creditor, debtor, customer, or vendor

**suspense account** account into which items are temporarily placed until their disposition is determined

**T account** account record shaped like a T, used in analyzing transactions, with left side showing debits and right side showing credits

**tangible assets** items having material form and intrinsic value

**temporary capital accounts** records of contributions, draws, and other changes during fiscal period, to be transferred to permanent capital account at end of period

**trial balance** statement of debit and credit balance on all open accounts, used to check their equality and make adjustments in double-entry accounting

**uncollectable account** account receivable that cannot be collected and that may be written off as bad debt

**valuation** assessment of value

**value** worth in financial terms

**vertical analysis** restating of dollar amounts on financial statement as percentage of base amount

**weighted average cost method** method of calculating inventory by adding purchases to beginning inventory and dividing by total units to obtain average cost per unit

**withdrawal** return of cash or other business assets to owner

**worth** value of assets and securities

**worthless** (*adj*) lacking all value, bankrupt

**write-down** reduction of asset's value, as with damaged but not worthless inventory

**write-off** uncollectable debt; worthless asset

**zero base accounting** method in which each item is justified on basis of cost and need

## SPENDING, RECEIVING, AND POSSESSING WEALTH

**acquisition** accumulation and retention of wealth

**acquisitiveness** eagerness for and skill at attaining and holding wealth

**advance** payment made or received before due

**affluence** abundance of wealth or riches

**aid** financial help, esp. institutional assistance to poor

**alimony** regular payments made by one spouse to the other as required by divorce decree

**allotment** one's portion; amount due to one

**allowance** amount of money given regularly, esp. to child

**alms** money or supplies given to the poor

**angel** *Informal.* financial supporter for a particular enterprise

**annuity** payment of fixed sum at regular intervals, usu. yearly

**appanage** person's rightful gain, perquisite; amount added to endowment

**appropriation** money given over or set aside for specific use; amount taken for one's own use, often improperly

**assets** all that one owns, all wealth possessed

**assignee** person to whom rights have been transferred and payments are due

**assignment** transfer of claim on certain rights or funds to another

**avarice** excessive desire for wealth; greed

**award** amount given by court decision, as result of judgment in competition, or for merit

**backing** financial support for some enterprise

**banausic** (*adj*) mundanely concerned with making money

**barter** direct exchange of goods and services without use of currency

**benefactor** person giving financial help to another

**beneficiary** person named to receive income, inheritance, or proceeds of trust or insurance policy

**benefit** public event or performance held to raise funds for specific group, person, or cause

**bequest** legacy

**bestowal** gift made to another

**billionaire** person whose net worth exceeds one billion dollars

**blackmail** extortion of payment by threat, esp. to reveal embarrassing information

**bonanza** source of great wealth

**bounty** generous gift given freely; substantial riches

**brass ring** *Informal.* wealth and success as a goal or prize

**bribery** giving of money to another to induce illegal act

**capitalist** person who has extensive capital, esp. invested in business enterprises

**charity** money given voluntarily to help those in need

**cheap** (*adj*) stingy

**closefisted** (*adj*) stingy, miserly

**come into** (*vb*) receive one's inheritance; unexpectedly obtain wealth

**commission**  percentage of proceeds from sale or transaction paid in addition to or in lieu of wages

**compensation**  wage, salary, fee, commission, or other payment received for services or product

**consideration**  money given as part of business transaction, esp. for services rendered

**Croesus**  very rich man

**cumshaw**  gratuity or tip, sometimes obtained illegally

**cut off** (vb) disinherit

**deep pockets**  abundance of wealth

**disinherit** (vb) exclude from inheritance

**dole**  allotment of money or aid to those in need

**donation**  contribution or gift, esp. to charity

**donor**  one who gives money, esp. to an organization

**double-dipping**  practice of receiving more than one form of compensation from same employer or organization

**dowry**  wealth and property brought by bride to husband at time of marriage

**economy**  careful management of wealth; restraint in spending

**endowment**  gift or bequest used to provide income for institution or person

**estate**  one's fortune or property, esp. when deceased

**expenditure**  outlay of money for particular purpose

**fat cat**  Slang. wealthy person, usu. politically influential

**fee**  payment given, esp. for professional service or license

**fellowship**  sum paid for support of graduate student

**fixed income**  uniform rate or amount of income received over period of time

**flush** (adj) abundantly supplied with money

**fortune**  large quantity of wealth

**frugality**  thrift, economy, and care in spending

**generosity**  willingness to give to others; giving in abundance

**gift**  something freely handed over to another

**giving**  act of making a gift, often associated with charity

**Golconda**  rich mine or other source of great wealth

**graft**  illicit profits gained by taking advantage of privileged position

**grant**  formal gift, usu. by institution or government

**grant-in-aid**  funds given, usu. by government or foundation, to support work of scholar, scientist, artist, or institution

**gratuity**  money given for service provided in excess of regular price; tip

**gravy**  Slang. money obtained easily, sometimes illegally

**greed**  avarice

**heir**  person who receives property, esp. great wealth, of dead person by will or law

**heiress**  female heir

**hemorrhage**  rapid loss of assets in large amounts

**honorarium**  payment for acts or services for which custom or propriety forbids a price to be set

**inheritance**  wealth and property received upon another's death

**investment**  use of one's existing capital to generate income or profit and thus increase wealth

**kickback**  reimbursement of funds based on secret collusion, often illegal or unethical

**largess**  generous gifts

**lavish** (adj) generous, often extravagant, in giving or spending

**legacy**  money or property left to another by will; bequest

**liberality**  generosity in giving or spending

**loaded** (adj) Slang. very wealthy

**lot**  one's due portion or fortune

**lucrative** (adj) profitable; tending to or likely to make money

**man of means**  wealthy individual

**means**  available wealth, resources

**Midas**  one whose touch seems to turn everything to gold

**millionaire**  person whose net worth exceeds one million dollars

**millions**  great wealth

**miser**  stingy person who hoards money, even at expense of own comfort

**moneybags**  very wealthy person

**moneyed** (adj) wealthy, well-to-do

**munificence**  generosity in giving

**nabob**  very rich and influential person

**net worth**  total value of one's possessions, property, and wealth

**niggardly** (adj) stingy, miserly

**opulence**  great wealth, characterized by lavish spending

**parsimony**  great caution in spending, stinginess

**patron**  wealthy person who provides financial support for an activity, person, or institution

**pay**  money handed over for work done or services performed

**penny-pinching**  extreme frugality

**penny-wise** (adj) thrifty and careful over small sums or matters

**pension**  regular payment given to one who has fulfilled certain conditions, esp. worked at a particular job until a certain age

**penury**  extreme poverty

**per diem**  Latin. lit. by the day; daily expense allowance received while traveling or being employed at some distance away from one's home

**philanthropy**  charitable donations or gifts to needy individuals or nonprofit institutions

**plutocracy**  group of wealthy, politically influential persons; rule by the wealthy

**pop** (vb) Slang. pay for something, esp. another's share

**portion**  one's proper due or lot

**possession**  ownership; condition of holding wealth

**possessions**  wealth, property

**pourboire**  French. tip, gratuity

**premium**  additional amount paid for something

**pretty penny**  Informal. large amount of money

**prodigality**  free spending

**prosperity**  accumulation or possession of wealth

**public assistance**  government aid to the needy

**purse**  sum of money offered or collected as prize, reward, or gift

**purse-proud** (adj) proud of one's wealth, esp. in a showy manner

**quota**  one's proportional share of wealth or pay

**ransom**  money paid for release of confiscated property or kidnap victim

**rebate**  portion of payment returned at time of purchase

**recipient**  person who receives money

**relief**  public assistance or welfare payments

**remuneration**  payment or reward for work, service, or trouble

**resources**  available wealth, capital

**retirement benefits** money paid regularly at termination of one's employment by former employer or government

**riches** wealth, money in one's possession

**salary** payment received regularly for work performed

**save** (*vb*) avoid expense so as to put money aside for future use

**savings** funds set aside for future use

**scholarship** gift of money to assist needy student in paying for education

**scotch** (*adj*) *Informal*. (sometimes offensive) frugal; cheap

**scrimp** (*vb*) economize, try to save when little is available; skimp

**skimp** (*vb*) keep expenses low; scrimp

**skinflint** miser, niggardly person

**slush fund** money set aside for illicit or corrupt purposes

**sparing** (*adj*) frugal, cautious in spending

**spending** paying out of money

**spendthrift** person who spends money wastefully or carelessly

**sponsor** person responsible for providing financial support for an individual, activity, or institution

**spring** (*vb*) *Informal*. pay another's cost or expenses

**squander** (*vb*) spend money wastefully or extravagantly

**stingy** (*adj*) frugal, miserly, spending money grudgingly

**stipend** regular payment for service; allowance

**subsidy** grant of money, esp. from government for public benefit

**testament** will

**thrift** frugality, care in spending

**tight-fisted** (*adj*) stingy, reluctant to spend

**tightwad** *Informal*. miser, stingy person

**tip** gratuity

**treasury** accumulated and stored wealth

**treat** (*vb*) pay another's share

**tribute** regular, often forced, payment as show of subjugation

**underwrite** (*vb*) agree to pay costs and cover losses of undertaking or institution

**ungenerous** (*adj*) stingy, reluctant to spend money on others

**usance** income and other benefits derived from ownership of wealth

**wages** regular payments by employer for work performed

**wastrel** person who squanders money or spends extravagantly

**wealth** large amount of money and property

**welfare** government aid granted to those in need

**well-to-do** (*adj*) prosperous, wealthy

**will** legal statement of person's wishes for disposition of money and property following death; testament

**worth** value of one's assets, property, and money

## MONEY, CURRENCY, AND DENOMINATIONS

**agio** fee paid to exchange one currency for another

**almighty dollar** characterization of money as source of power

**arm and a leg** great sum of money

**bale of hay** *Slang*. large amount of money

**bank note** promissory note issued by bank, used as form of paper money

**bankroll** conspicuous wad of bills

**bean** *Slang*. one dollar

**bill** one piece of paper money

**bill of exchange** written order to pay specific sum of money to particular person

**bob** *Brit. informal*. shilling

**boodle** *Slang*. money, esp. taken in robbery or given as bribe

**bouncing paper** *Slang*. bad check

**bread** *Slang*. money

**buck** *Slang*. one U.S. dollar

**bucks** *Slang*. large amount of money

**bullion** gold or silver ingots or bars, held as standard for currency

**cambio** *Spanish*. foreign exchange bank

**cambist** dealer in foreign currencies

**capital** accumulated wealth, esp. used to increase wealth

**cash** paper currency and metal coins; actual money

**cash in hand** money available at given moment

**cent** basic fractional unit or coin in most countries, usu. one-hundredth of primary unit of currency; one-hundredth of a U.S. dollar

**centavo** cent in various Spanish-speaking countries

**centime** cent in various French-speaking countries

**centimo** cent in various Spanish-speaking countries

**change** coins

**chicken feed** *Slang*. insignificant amount of money

**circulation** paper currency and coins passed from person to person

**clam** *Slang*. dollar

**C-note** *Slang*. hundred-dollar bill

**coin** small, flat metal disk used as money

**coinage** metal currency; making of coins

**coin collection** accumulation of old, rare, or foreign coins as a hobby

**coin of the realm** legal tender

**cold cash** money paid in full at time of business transaction

**Confederate note** paper money produced by Confederate states during U.S. Civil War

**copper** a coin made of copper, bronze, or the like, esp. U.S. cent or British penny

**counterfeit** forged money not printed and issued by government

**crown** former coin of Great Britain, equal to twenty-five new pence

**currency** money circulated as medium of exchange in any country, esp. paper money

**demonetization** stoppage of use of gold or silver as currency standard

**denarius** silver coin and monetary unit of ancient Rome

**devaluation** reduction of currency's value relative to international monetary values

**dime** ten-cent U.S. coin

**dinero** *Slang*. money

**dollar** basic unit of U.S. currency; one hundred cents; smallest value of single bill

**dollars** money in one's possession

**do-re-mi** *Slang*. money

**double eagle** twenty-dollar U.S. gold piece

**doubloon** obsolete gold coin of Spain and Spanish America

**dough** *Slang*. money

**drachma** principle silver coin of ancient Greece; monetary unit of modern Greece

**ducats** *Slang.* money, esp. cash; gold or silver coins formerly used in Europe

**eagle** ten-dollar U.S. gold piece

**Eurodollar** U.S. dollar deposited in or credited to European bank

**exchange** conversion of one nation's currency into another's

**exchange rate** value of one nation's currency in relation to that of another; cost of exchanging one currency for another

**farthing** one-quarter penny, formerly used in Great Britain

**Federal Reserve note** paper currency issued by individual Federal Reserve Bank in denominations from one to ten thousand dollars; prevailing form of currency in circulation in United States

**fen** basic fractional unit or coin of China

**fiat money** currency without gold or silver backing, issued by government decree

**fido** coin with minting error

**fin** *Slang.* five-dollar bill

**fiver** *Slang.* five-dollar bill; five-pound note

**five-spot** *Slang.* five-dollar bill

**floating exchange rates** uncontrolled exchange rates in which currencies of various nations rise and fall based on supply and demand for each currency

**florin** coin equal to two shillings in Great Britain; former gold coin of Florence

**Fort Knox** site of U.S. gold bullion depository

**four bits** *Slang.* fifty U.S. cents

**funds** money resources available; capital

**gelt** *Slang.* money

**G-note** *Slang.* thousand-dollar bill

**gold** yellow precious metal formerly used for coins, often held by nation as standard for issued currency

**gold certificate** former U.S. paper currency redeemable for gold

**gold dust** tiny bits of gold as it is normally found in placer mining

**gold piece** single gold coin

**gold standard** monetary system in which value of nation's currency is based on and backed by gold

**grand** *Informal.* one thousand U.S. dollars

**green** *Slang.* money, esp. paper currency

**greenback** U.S. legal-tender note, printed in green on the back

**green stuff** *Slang.* paper currency

**groat** former coin of Great Britain, equal to four pennies

**guinea** former coin of Great Britain, equal to twenty-one shillings

**half C-note** *Slang.* fifty-dollar bill

**half crown** former coin of Great Britain, equal to two shillings and sixpence

**half dollar** fifty-cent coin (U.S.)

**ha'penny** *Brit. informal.* half penny

**hard cash** actual coins and paper currency, as opposed to credit or other notes

**hard currency** paper money in circulation

**K** one thousand U.S. dollars

**kale** *Slang.* money

**kitty** small, informal savings fund; money pooled for specific purpose

**kopeck** basic fractional unit or coin of Soviet Union

**legal tender** official form of money, recognized as national medium of exchange in payment for purchases or debts; coin of the realm

**lettuce** *Slang.* paper currency, greenbacks

**long green** *Slang.* paper currency

**lucre** monetary gain or riches, often used in derogatory sense

**mad money** *Informal.* extra spending money for emergencies or impulse buying

**mammon** personification of riches as deity or evil spirit

**mark** former money of account in medieval England, equal to thirteen shillings, fourpence; monetary unit of Germany

**medium of exchange** currency used as measure of value in exchange for goods and services

**megabucks** *Informal.* very large amount of money

**mill** one-tenth U.S. cent

**minor coin** coin of nonprecious metal, neither gold nor silver

**mint** manufacturing site, depository, and government agency responsible for authorized coinage from metal

**mintage** process of making coins from metal; money produced at mint

**monetary system** coinage and circulation of currency

**money** medium of commerce, exchange, and banking that serves as recognized measure of value; paper currency and coins

**money order** order for payment of specified sum issued by bank or post office, serving as cash in exchange

**moola** *Slang.* money

**mopus** *Slang.* cash, ready money

**napoleon** former French coin with picture of Napoleon, equal to twenty francs

**nest egg** savings

**new pence** monetary unit of Great Britain, equal to one-hundredth of a pound since 1971

**nickel** five-cent U.S. coin

**noble** former coin of Great Britain, equal to half a mark

**note** single piece of paper currency issued by bank or government

**numismatics** science and study of coins and coinage

**obol** silver coin of ancient Greece, equal to one-sixth of a drachma

**paper money** authorized currency printed on paper

**pecuniary** (*adj*) pertaining to money

**pelf** money, esp. ill-gotten

**pence** *Brit.* plural of penny

**penny** one-cent coin, equal to one-hundredth of a dollar in United States or of a pound in Great Britain

**petrodollars** accumulation of surplus dollars by petroleum-exporting nations

**petty cash** small fund of money kept on hand for incidental expenses

**pfennig** one-hundredth of a mark (Germany)

**piaster** former Spanish dollar; *Informal.* money

**piggy bank** coin bank in shape of pig; any small bank of coins

**pin money** extra money; small savings

**pocket money** small amount of spending money kept on person

**pot** *Slang.* large sum of money; amount of money wagered at one time

**pound** basic monetary unit of United Kingdom, equal to one hundred new pence; prior to 1971, equal to twenty shillings or 240 pence

**purse** financial resources, money

**quarter** twenty-five cent U.S. coin

**queer** *Slang.* counterfeit money

**quid** *Brit. informal.* pound

**ready money** cash available for spending

**real** former silver coin of Spain and Spanish America

**red cent** *Informal.* penny

**revaluation** increase in currency's value relative to international monetary values

**roll** *Informal.* large number of paper bills, esp. rolled into bundle

**rubber check** bad check

**sawbuck** *Slang.* ten-dollar bill

**scrip** temporary paper to be exchanged for money; paper money in amounts less than one dollar, formerly issued in United States

**shekel** half-ounce gold or silver coin of ancient Hebrews; basic monetary unit of Israel

**shekels** *Slang.* money

**shilling** former monetary unit of United Kingdom, equal to one-twentieth of a pound or twelve pence

**shoestring** very small amount of available cash

**silver** white precious metal used in manufacture of coins and as monetary standard

**silver certificate** former U.S. paper currency redeemable for silver

**simoleon** *Slang.* dollar

**sixpence** former British coin equal to six pennies or one-half shilling

**smacker** *Slang.* dollar

**small change** coins of low denomination

**solidus** gold coin of ancient Rome and the Byzantine Empire

**sou** former coin of France, equal to five or ten centimes; *Slang.* small amount of money

**sovereign** former British gold coin valued at twenty shillings or one pound

**specie** coined money, as opposed to paper notes

**spending money** cash available for immediate use

**sterling** standard of British coinage in silver; British money

**subsidiary coin** U.S. coin with value under one dollar

**tanner** *Brit. slang.* sixpenny piece

**tenner** *Informal.* ten-dollar bill; ten-pound note (Britain)

**ten-spot** *Slang.* ten-dollar bill

**token money** coins with lower actual value as metal than their face value

**treasury** place for deposit and disbursement of funds, esp. government agency holding public tax funds

**tuppence** *Brit. informal.* twopence

**two bits** *Slang.* twenty-five U.S. cents

**two-spot** *Informal.* two-dollar bill

**wad** *Informal.* large amount of cash on hand

**wampum** *Informal.* money; beads used as medium of exchange by American Indians

**wherewithal** money for specific purpose

**xenocurrency** currency circulated and traded outside its country of issue

# WORLD CURRENCIES

**afghani** currency of Afghanistan

**austral** currency of Argentina

**baht** currency of Thailand

**balboa** currency of Panama

**birr** currency of Ethiopia

**bolivar** currency of Venezuela

**cedi** currency of Ghana

**colon** currency of Costa Rica, El Salvador

**cordoba** currency of Nicaragua

**cruzado** currency of Brazil

**dalasi** currency of Gambia

**dinar** currency of Algeria, Bahrain, Iraq, Jordan, Kuwait, Libya, Tunisia, Yugoslavia

**dirham** currency of Morocco, United Arab Emirates

**dobra** currency of São Tomé and Principe

**dollar** currency of Antigua and Barbuda, Australia, Bahamas, Barbados, Belize, Bermuda, Brunei, Canada, Dominica, Fiji, Grenada, Guyana, Hong Kong, Jamaica, Kiribati, Liberia, Nauru, New Zealand, Singapore, Solomon Islands, St. Kitts-Nevis, St. Lucia, St. Vincent and the Grenadines, Taiwan, Trinidad and Tobago, Tuvalu, United States, Zimbabwe

**dong** currency of Vietnam

**drachma** currency of Greece

**escudo** currency of Cape Verde, Portugal

**forint** currency of Hungary

**franc** currency of Andorra, Belgium, Benin, Burkina Faso, Burundi, Cameroon, Central African Republic, Chad, Comoros, Congo, Djibouti, Equatorial Guinea, France, Gabon, Guinea, Ivory Coast, Lichtenstein, Luxembourg, Madagascar, Mali, Martinique, Monaco, Niger, Rwanda, Senegal, Switzerland, Togo

**gourde** currency of Haiti

**guarani** currency of Paraguay

**guilder** currency of the Netherlands, Netherlands Antilles, Suriname

**inti** currency of Peru

**kina** currency of Papua New Guinea

**kip** currency of Laos

**koruna** currency of Czechoslovakia

**krona** currency of Iceland, Sweden

**krone** currency of Denmark, Greenland, Norway

**kwacha** currency of Malawi, Zambia

**kwanza** currency of Angola

**kyat** currency of Myanmar

**lek** currency of Albania

**lempira** currency of Honduras

**leone** currency of Sierra Leone

**leu** currency of Romania

**lev** currency of Bulgaria

**lilangeni** currency of Swaziland

**lira** currency of Italy, Malta, San Marino, Turkey, Vatican City

**loti** currency of Lesotho

**mark** currency of Germany

**markka** currency of Finland

**metical** currency of Mozambique

**naira** currency of Nigeria

**ngultrum** currency of Bhutan

**ouguiya** currency of Mauritania

**pa'anga** currency of Tonga

**pataca** currency of Macao

**peseta** currency of Andorra, Spain

**peso** currency of Bolivia, Chile, Colombia, Cuba, Dominican Republic, Guinea-Bissau, Mexico, the Philippines, Uruguay

**pound** currency of Cyprus, Egypt, Ireland, Lebanon, Sudan, Syria, United Kingdom

**pula** currency of Botswana

**quetzal** currency of Guatemala

**rand** currency of South Africa

**rial** currency of Iran, Oman, Yemen

**riel** currency of Kampuchea

**ringgit** currency of Malaysia

**riyal** currency of Qatar, Saudi Arabia

**ruble** currency of Russian Republic and former Soviet Union

**rufiyaa** currency of the Maldives

**rupee** currency of India, Mauritius, Nepal, Pakistan, Seychelles, Sri Lanka

**rupiah** currency of Indonesia

**schilling** currency of Austria

**shekel** currency of Israel

**shilling** currency of Kenya, Somalia, Tanzania, Uganda

**sucre** currency of Ecuador

**taka** currency of Bangladesh

**tala** currency of Western Samoa

**tugrik** currency of Mongolia

**vatu** currency of Vanuatu

**won** currency of North Korea, South Korea

**yen** currency of Japan

**yuan** currency of China

**zaire** currency of Zaire

**zloty** currency of Poland

# AGRICULTURE

Farming and Crops
Ranching and Animal Husbandry
Soils and Soil Management
Tools, Machinery, and Structures
Business and Science of Agriculture

**SEE ALSO**: Chap. 2: Biology; Animals; Plants; Chap. 3: Geology; Geography; Landscapes and Seascapes; Chap. 9: Foods; Chap. 17: Gardening

## FARMING AND CROPS

**agrarian** (*adj*) pertaining to the land or farmers

**agrichemical** fertilizer, pesticide, or feeding supplement

**alfalfa** deep-rooted perennial of pea family used for fodder and as cover crop

**annual** plant that lives for only one year or one season

**barley** cultivated cereal grass, one of man's first grains

**berry crops** small, juicy, fleshy fruits

**bone meal** fertilizer made of fine bone, a natural source of phosphorus

**bracero** seasonally contracted Mexican migrant agricultural worker

**bushel** unit of dry measure for grain or fruit equal to 4 pecks or 32 quarts

**campesino** *Spanish*. farmer or farm laborer in Latin America

**cereal** any grain produced from grass and used as food

**chaff** useless husks of wheat or other grains, separated in threshing

**citrus** thorny trees and shrubs that grow in warm climates and produce pulpy edible fruit

**clear-cutting** removing all trees in a stand of timber

**cocoa** beans of small evergreen cacao tree, used primarily in making chocolate

**coffee** beans of coffee tree, grown in tropical highland regions, used to make beverage

**complete fertilizer** fertilizer containing three primary plant nutrients: nitrogen, phosphorus, and potassium

**corn** tall cereal plant whose kernels are used extensively for fodder and human food; maize

**cotton** most important textile fiber, produced from seed pods of shrubby tropical plant

**cover crop** grass or legume that improves soil by adding organic matter and discouraging erosion

**crop** plant or agricultural product grown and harvested for profit or subsistence; yield in a single season or place

**crop rotation** rotation of crops

**cultivate** (*vb*) prepare and till soil for planting of crops

**cultivation** growing of plants or crops from seeds, bulbs, or shoots

**cutover** land cleared of vegetation, esp. trees

**cutting** plant section from leaf, stem, or root capable of developing into new plant

**DDT** *dichlorodiphenyl trichloroethane*; hazardous pesticide in widespread use on crops

**Demeter** goddess of agriculture and fertility (ancient Greece)

**dirt farmer** owner of small farm who works his or her own land

**disseminate** (*vb*) sow or scatter seed

**dry farming** agriculture without irrigation, relying on drought-resistant crops and moisture-conserving soil cultivation techniques

**dust** (*vb*) sprinkle crops with insecticides, esp. from a low-flying airplane

**everbearing** (*adj*) continuously producing or bringing forth fruit

**extensive cultivation** farming system in which limited work is put into relatively large area of land

**fallow** (*adj*) designating cultivated land left unsown for one season or more

**farm** tract of land devoted to any agricultural purpose; (*vb*) engage in raising crops or animals

**farmer** person who cultivates land or raises crops or livestock, esp. one who owns farmland; grower

**farm hand** hired farm worker

**farmhouse** residence on farm for farmer and family

**farming** business of agriculture and farm operation

**farmland** land under cultivation

**farmstead** farmland and the buildings on it

**farmyard** enclosure within or connected to farm buildings

**fertile** (*adj*) rich in resources, fruitful; able to reproduce by seeds or spores

**fertility gods** supernatural beings to whom ancient primitive farmers turned for aid with crops

**fertilizer** organic or chemical soil additive that increases or accelerates growth

**field** cleared area of land used for pasture or growing

**field crops** crops grown on large tracts of land

**first fruits** earliest fruit of the season

**fish meal** dried, ground fish used as fertilizer or feed

**flax** annual plant grown for its fiber and seed

**force** (*vb*) cause plants to grow faster by artificial means

**fruit** edible plant structure of mature ovary of flowering plant or tree, usu. sweet and pulpy

**fruit grower** farmer who raises fruit trees or berries

**furrow** narrow groove in ground made by plow

**Future Farmers of America** community organization for young people in rural districts

**garden** plot of land where vegetables, fruits, flowers, or herbs are grown, esp. small plot for personal use

**gardener** person who tends plants in garden

**germination** sprouting of spore, seed, or bud as growth begins

**glean** (*vb*) collect grain after reaping

**grain** seed or fruit of some plants, including cereal grasses

**grain farming** cultivation of grain crops, usu. requiring large tracts of land

**granary** repository for grain storage

**grow** (*vb*) develop a plant from germination through maturity

**grower** farmer

**growing season** period in year during which crops can be raised in given region

**hacienda** large landed estate or plantation in Latin America

**harvest** crop gathering season; process of reaping and gathering crops; season's yield of crops

**harvest moon** full moon nearest to autumnal equinox

**headland** strip of unplowed land at ends of furrows

**herbage** nonwoody vegetation, esp. grasses upon which animals graze

**hull** outer covering of seed or fruit; (*vb*) remove this covering

**husk** dry outer covering of various crops, such as corn; (*vb*) remove this covering

**insecticide** pesticide that kills insects living on plants

**inseminate** (*vb*) sow seeds in earth

**intensive cultivation** farming system in which significant and continuous work is lavished on relatively small area to maximize yield

**intercrop** (*vb*) grow one crop between rows of another

**irrigation** any of various systems of bringing water to plants, including flood, border, furrow, sprinkler, drip, or surface irrigation systems

**legumes** plants with fruits or seeds in dry pods with two sutures, such as beans or peas, used for food or forage

**lumber** milled strips of wood cut from trees, used for building

**lumbering** work and business of tree farming or felling trees to make lumber

**maize** corn

**manure** fertilizer of livestock excrement

**migrant worker** seasonal farm laborer who moves from place to place to get work

**monoculture** growing only one type of crop on a piece of land

**mowing** cutting down of grass or grain

**muck** farmyard dung and decaying vegetable matter; manure

**nitrogen** one of three essential plant nutrients

**no-tillage** direct seeding without plowing of soil

**nut** dry fruit or seed with kernel inside separable rind, shell, or hull

**open-field cultivation** system in which farmer owns and cultivates strips of land, unfenced and scattered over several large fields

**orchard** area planted with trees that bear fruit or nuts

**organic farming** farming that relies on natural materials to control pests and for use as fertilizers

**paddy** plot of continuous wetland, esp. where rice is grown

**pastoral** (*adj*) characteristic of the rural life of farmers and shepherds, esp. in idealized state

**patch** small plot of ground for growing

**peck** unit of dry measure equal to 8 quarts or one-quarter bushel

**pest** insect, small animal, fungus, or weed that damages or kills crops

**pesticide** any of various pest killers, including fungicides (kill fungi), insecticides (kill insects), miticides (kill mites), molluskicides (kill snails and slugs), and ovicides (kill eggs), esp. chlorinated hydrocarbons (organochlorines), organic phosphates (organophosphates), and carbamate compounds

**phosphate** any substance containing salt and phosphoric acid, used as fertilizer

**plant** tree, shrub, or herb put into soil and grown to maturity, esp. an herb in context of farming; (*vb*) begin growing process by putting seed or seedling into ground

**plantation** large farm or estate on which cultivated crops are grown by resident workers, usu. in tropical or semitropical region

**planter** owner of plantation or large farm

**planting** one season's crop

**plot** small planted area of land

**plow** (*vb*) work the soil; till or furrow

**plowboy** boy leading team of animals pulling a plow

**produce** fresh agricultural products, esp. fruits and vegetables

**pruning** pinching, heading, thinning, or shearing plants to direct growth or improve health or appearance

**raise** (*vb*) cause to grow

**reap** (*vb*) gather a crop, esp. grain, by cutting

**rear** (*vb*) grow or breed

**rest** (*vb*) lie fellow

**rice** starchy seeds or grain of marsh grass, requiring much moisture and warm temperatures, used to feed more people than any other cereal

**rotation of crops** cultivation system in which crops are systematically changed on each plot to prevent nutrient loss in soil and to discourage weeds, pests, and diseases; crop rotation

**rye** main bread grain in parts of northern Europe, where wheat cannot be cultivated due to cold weather

**seed** (*vb*) sow; plant with seeds from which plants grow

**seedbed** plot of ground prepared for seeding

**seeding** scattering of seeds

**seedling** plant grown from seed, esp. young tree

**semination** propagation or dissemination by seed

**sharecrop** (*vb*) farm as a sharecropper

**sharecropper** farmer who exchanges works for share of crop's value less credited expenses

**sheaf** bound bundle of reaped grain, esp. wheat

**shifting cultivation** primitive system in which crops are grown in one area until it is exhausted and growers move on

**side dressing** plant nutrients used to fertilize at crop roots

**slash-and-burn** (*adj*) of a cultivation technique in which land is made usable by burning trees and undergrowth, thereby clearing as well as nourishing the land

**slit planting** tillage method in which seeds are dropped into narrow openings cut into soil

**smudge** smoky fire used to protect fruit trees from frost

**soil** surface of earth capable of supporting plant life

**sow** (*vb*) scatter or plant seed for growing

**spading** digging in earth with a spade

**spring wheat** wheat grain sown in spring to avoid harsh winter weather

**stand** group of trees growing together

**stone fruit** any fruit, such as a plum, having a hard, stone-like seed

**strip farming** planting of strips of closely growing plants, such as grasses or clover, between crops to hold up rainwater, thereby reducing erosion

**stubble** stumps of cut grain left in ground

**subsistence crops** crops grown for farmer's own food needs

**subsistence farming** cultivation of crops for one's own use only

**sugar** product of crystallization of juice of crops, esp. sugar beets and sugarcane

**swath** strip of space from which grain plants have been cut down

**swidden** tract of land cleared for planting by burning vegetation on it

**tea** white-flowered evergreen plant, grown throughout Asia, whose dried leaves are used to make a beverage

**team** two or more horses or oxen harnessed together to pull plow or other vehicle

**terrace cultivation** system of cultivating mountains and hills by carving out and reinforcing small fields with low embankments

**thin** (*vb*) remove weaker plants to maximize growth of remaining crop

**threshing** separating grains or cereals into usable and nonusable parts

**till** (*vb*) plow, cultivate, and fertilize land for the purpose of raising crops

**tilth** cultivation of land; land that is tilled

**timber** forest trees used for lumber

**top dressing** plant nutrients applied to surface of land

**tract** large area of land used for cultivation

**transplant** (*vb*) dig up growing plant or tree and place it in ground elsewhere

**tree farming** business and practice of growing trees, esp. for lumber

**vegetable** any herbaceous edible plant

**vernalize** (*vb*) shorten plant's growth period, usu. by chilling it or its seeds or bulbs

**vine** woody climbing plant, esp. grapevine

**vineyard** land used for cultivating grapevines, esp. for winemaking

**weed** undesirable plant that harms or inhibits growth of crop plants; (*vb*) remove such plants from soil

**wheat** cereal grass with dense, erect spikes that produces grain used as staple food throughout temperate regions

**windrow** row of hay or sheaves of grain raked together to dry

**winnow** (*vb*) blow off undesirable chaff from grain by current of air

**winter wheat** wheat grain sown in fall in regions where it can survive winter weather

**work** (*vb*) cultivate, plow, and till earth for planting

**yield** amount of crop produced in specific area by cultivation

# RANCHING AND ANIMAL HUSBANDRY

**animal husbandry** care and raising of domesticated animals, esp. cattle, horses, and sheep

**barn raising** gathering of local people to help their neighbor build a barn

**beast of burden** domesticated animal used to carry loads or pull tools or wagons

**beef** full-grown ox, cow, bull, or steer bred and fattened for meat; flesh of this animal as food

**beekeeper** one who raises bees and gathers honey

**branding iron** long-handled metal rod with distinctive design at one end, used for marking livestock

**break** (*vb*) tame and train a horse

**breed** (*vb*) supervise the sexual propagation of animals; (*n*) group of animals of one species differentiated by common characteristics and descent

**browsing** grazing

**cattle** domesticated ruminant bovines raised for their meat or milk

**cattle drive** herding of large number of cattle from one place to another

**coop** small cage or pen housing poultry

**cornfed** (*adj*) designating beef cattle raised on diet of corn, believed to improve health and flavor

**corral** enclosure for domesticated animals, esp. horses

**cote** pen or enclosure for livestock

**cowboy** ranch worker on horseback who herds and tends cattle; cowpoke; rancher

**cowhand** ranch worker

**cowpoke** cowboy or cowgirl

**cowpuncher** cowboy or cowgirl

**creamery** dairy

**cud** mouthful of swallowed food regurgitated by cattle for second chewing

**dairy** farm or ranch for raising dairy cattle, producing milk and milk products; creamery

**domestic animal** animal tamed or bred for human purposes

**dovecote** cage or pen housing pigeons

**eggs** shelled ovum laid by hens, collected and sold for food

**ensilage** green fodder preserved in a silo

**feed** food or fodder for livestock

**feedlot** place where animals are fattened for slaughter

**fodder** domestic animal food

**forage** food eaten by browsing or grazing animal; fodder

**free-range** (*adj*) designating livestock and poultry permitted to graze or forage freely outside a small confinement

**gaucho** cowboy of the South American pampas

**grass** herbaceous vegetation upon which animals graze

**grassland** tracts of land covered with grass for grazing

**grazing** feeding of animals on growing grass or herbage; browsing

**hatch** (*vb*) bring forth young from an egg

**hatchery** place for hatching eggs

**hay** grass, alfalfa, or clover cut and dried for fodder

**haycock** conical stack of hay drying in field

**hayrick** *Chiefly Brit.* haystack

**haystack** large heap of hay piled outdoors; hayrick

**herd** group of cattle, sheep, or other animals living together under human supervision; (*vb*) control movement of livestock, esp. from horseback

**herdsman** one who tends or supervises a herd

**hog** large domestic swine

**horse** large domesticated mammal used for transportation and work

**hutch** animal pen, esp. for rabbits

**incubation** sitting on or keeping eggs in warm environment favorable for hatching

**keep** (*vb*) raise, as livestock

**livestock** domestic animals kept for work, by-products, or sale, esp. cattle, sheep, hogs, and horses

**meadow** expanse of grassland used as pasture or hayfield

**milk** dairy product secreted by lactating mammals, esp. cows and goats

**oats** cereal grass, used esp. for fodder

**pack animal** animal bred for strength and used to carry loads, esp. mule, donkey, or horse; sumpter

**pasturage** practice of grazing livestock on a pasture

**pasture** land on which livestock graze

**pen** small yard or enclosure for domestic animals

**poultry** birds raised for their meat or eggs

**predator** animal that feeds on other animals

**raise** (*vb*) cause to breed

**ranch** large farm, esp. in U.S. West, for raising cattle, horses, or sheep; (*vb*) operate or work on a ranch, esp. raise livestock

**rancher** owner or manager of ranch; cowboy

**ranchero** rancher in Latin America or U.S. West

**ranch hand** employee on ranch

**rancho** farm or ranch

**range** large open area over which livestock can roam and graze

**rangeland** tract of land suitable for livestock grazing

**ruminant** (*adj*) cud-chewing, esp. cattle and sheep

**shearing** cutting or clipping of animal hair, esp. for use as wool

**sheep** ruminant animals domesticated for wool and meat

**sheepshearing** clipping wool from sheep

**sheepwalk** *Brit.* sheep pasture

**shepherd** herdsman, esp. for grazing sheep

**silage** succulent feed made from fermented fodder in silo

**silo** usu. cylindrical, airtight tower for making and storing silage

**sire** male parent of four-legged animal, esp. horse; (*vb*) father a horse

**slaughterhouse** structure in which livestock are butchered

**stall** compartment in stable for one animal

**stock** strain or related group of animals; livestock

**stock horse** horse used in herding cattle

**stockman** person who raises livestock

**stockyard** enclosure for livestock, esp. where cattle, sheep, hogs, or horses are held before slaughter or shipment

**straw** mass of grain stalks, dried and used as fodder

**stud** male animal, esp. horse, used for breeding

**sumpter** pack animal

**swine** domesticated pig or hog

**transhumance** seasonal movement of livestock from valley to mountain pastures and back again

**winterfeed** feed given to livestock in winter when pasturage is impossible

**wool** soft, curly hair shorn from sheep; cloth made of this hair

**workhorse** horse used for plowing and hauling, not for riding

## SOILS AND SOIL MANAGEMENT

**adobe soil** heavy clay soil

**aeration** supplying abundant oxygen to soil through cultivation

**alluvial soil** sand or clay deposited at shore of waterway

**amendment** soil-conditioning substance that promotes plant growth by addition of vitamins, fertilizer, or other additive

**arable** (*adj*) fit for cultivation

**available moisture** water in soil that may be absorbed by plant roots

**available nutrient** nutrient in soil that may be absorbed by plant roots

**backfill soil** soil, sometimes amended, used to refill planting hole

**bog** wet, spongy soil with decaying mosses and peat

**bole** easily pulverized, reddish clay

**chernozem** fertile soil, rich in humus, covering large areas of temperate regions

**clay** firm, fine-grained soil, plastic when wet

**clunch** hardened clay

**contour plowing** erosion-prevention technique in which land is plowed around rather than up and down a slope, creating rain-catching furrows

**cropland** land suitable for cultivation of crops

**decalcified soil** soil deprived of lime or calcium compounds

**deflocculated soil** soil lacking well-aggregated structure, caused by soft water

**desertification** spread of desertlike conditions on previously arable land

**diatomaceous earth** soil amendment formed by skeletal remains of microscopic organisms

**dispersed soil** soil in which clumped aggregates are separated into individual components

**drought** prolonged period without rain that causes soil failure and crop death

**dust bowl** region that endures long droughts and intense dust storms

**erosion** gradual eating or wearing away of soil by water, wind, snow, or ice

**fertile soil** earth capable of sustaining growth

**friable** (*adj*) describing easily crumbled soil

**ground water** water stored within porous rock in earth, esp. near surface

**horizon** layer of soil with distinct characteristics

**humus** organic matter in soil resulting from decomposition of plants and animals

**illuviation** accumulation in one layer of soil of materials leached from another layer

**land** Earth's surface and its resources

**laterite** red, residual soil in well-drained tropical rain forest

**leaching** washing away of soluble plant foods from topsoil by rain

**leaf mold** rich soil composed largely of decayed leaves

**loam** fertile soil consisting of humus, clay, and sand

**loess** particles of soft, porous rock, carried by wind, that mix with humus to form loam

**marl** soft, friable mixture of clay and limestone, used as fertilizer in lime-deficient soil

**mold** loose, soft, easily worked soil rich with decayed animal or vegetable matter

**mulch** leaves, straw, or peat moss spread on ground around plants to prevent evaporation of water from soil and to protect roots

**peat** brownish, fibrous substance resulting from vegetative decay

**pedology** soil science

**plow sole** compressed layer at bottom of furrow resulting from repeated plowing

**podsol** grayish, relatively infertile soil in coniferous forest

**reclamation** making dry or useless land capable of cultivation

**regosol** soil composed of unconsolidated material without stones and without distinct horizons

**rill erosion** formation of numerous small channels that occurs on recently cultivated soil

**sand** soil composed of loose, gritty particles of worn or disintegrated rock

**scarify** (*vb*) loosen soil with a cultivator

**sheet erosion** type of soil erosion, esp. on sloping farmland, in which rain washes away thin layer of topsoil

**silt** soil composed largely of sediment carried by moving water, with particles larger than clay but smaller than sand

**soil** source of food and moisture for plants, consisting of small particles of rock together with humus

**soil bank** government program subsidizing farmers to stop growing surplus crops and enrich idle land

**soil conservation** protection of fertile topsoil from erosion and replacement of its nutrients

**soil erosion** wearing away of soil, esp. by wind and water

**soil management** organized soil conservation and care programs

**spodosol** acidic forest soil of low fertility, found in cool, humid areas of Northern Hemisphere

**subsoil** layer of harder soil beneath topsoil

**terracing** forming of hillside into series of flat, raised mounds to reduce erosion in growing areas

**tillage** land that is tilled

**tilth** land that is tilled; cultivation of land

**topsoil** upper layer of soil, usu. darker and richer than subsoil

**wind erosion** type of soil erosion in which powdered topsoil, due to cultivation, is carried away by wind

## Tools, Machinery, and Structures

**aqueduct** large pipe or conduit for bringing water from distant source

**backhoe** excavating vehicle with hinged bucket on arm for digging

**baler** machine for compressing, binding, and wrapping grasses and hay in standardized bundles

**barn** storage building for feed, equipment, and other farm products; structure housing farm animals

**barnyard** usu. fenced area adjoining barn

**billhook** curved blade set on handle, used for pruning or cutting

**binder** attachment to harvester or reaper that binds cut grain

**canal** artificial waterway for drainage or irrigation

**cannery** factory for processing food and sealing it in metal containers

**chisel plow** plow that exposes minimal soil, aiding moisture retention and reducing soil runoff and wind erosion

**colter** sharp blade or wheel used to cut ground ahead of plowshare

**combine** multiprocess, in-field grain harvesting machine

**crop duster** device for spreading chemical dust over crops, often from low-flying airplane

**cultivator** tool drawn between rows of plants to loosen earth and uproot weeds

**dibble** pointed tool for making holes in soil for seeds, bulbs, or small plants

**flail** short, thick wooden stick loosely attached to handle, used for threshing

**glasshouse** greenhouse

**grader** machine that levels a slope, roadway, or plot of ground

**grain elevator** tall, cylindrical warehouse for grain

**grange** farmhouse and its outbuildings

**greenhouse** glass building with controlled temperature and humidity for cultivating plants out of season, sprouting seeds, or forcing plants; glasshouse

**grub hoe** heavy hoe used for digging up roots and stumps

**harness** assemblage of leather straps and metal pieces by which horse or mule is fastened to plow or other vehicle

**harrow** horse or tractor-drawn frame with spikes or sharp-edged disks for breaking up and leveling plowed ground

**harvester** machine for cutting and gathering crops or grain

**hayfork** mechanical device for moving hay; pitchfork

**hayloft** elevated area in barn for storage of hay

**hayrack** frame from which livestock eat hay

**hay rake** tool used to rake hay from swath into windrow

**hoe** thin, flat-bladed, long-handled cultivation tool

**hovel** open shed, esp. for cattle or tools

**incubator** enclosed, warm environment for keeping and hatching eggs

**lathhouse** structure of thin narrow wood strips for support or protection of plants

**manger** trough in stable holding feed for livestock

**mattock** pickaxlike tool with one broad end, used for loosening soil by digging

**mill** building and machinery for grinding grain into flour or meal

**moldboard** curved metal plate attached to plow for turning soil

**pick** heavy tool with pointed iron or steel head on long handle, used to loosen and break up soil

**pitchfork** long-handled tool with sharp prongs for lifting and tossing hay or straw; hayfork

**plow** implement used to cut, turn up, and break soil

**plowshare** furrow-cutting blade of moldboard plow

**reaper** machine for cutting standing grain, often with mechanism for bundling and tossing out bundles of cut grain

**rick** stack of hay or straw in field, usu. covered for protection from rain

**rotary plow** implement with spinning blades set on power-driven shaft, used to break up unplowed soil prior to planting

**rototiller** electrically powered device with spinning blades for cultivating soil

**scuffle hoe** spadelike hoe that is pushed instead of pulled

**scythe** long, single-edged blade set at right angle to long curved handle, for hand-cutting grass or grain

**self-feeder** hopper and trough that automatically dispenses feed for livestock

**shadoof** long, suspended rod with bucket at one end, used for raising water for irrigation (Egypt)

**shears** device with multiple sharp edges for cutting wool, esp. from sheep

**shelterbelt** protective barrier of trees or shrubs; windbreak

**sickle** crescent-shaped blade on short handle for cutting tall grass or weeds

**spade** flat blade on long handle for digging or turning soil by pressing blade into ground with foot

**spike-tooth harrow** harrow with straight teeth set horizontally, used to smooth soil for planting or sowing

**thresher** machine for beating out grain from husks

**tiller** machine used to plow and cultivate soil

**tractor** vehicle with powerful engine and large rear wheels or endless treads, for pulling farm machinery

**trough** low, narrow receptacle for food for animals

**windbreak** hedge, row of trees, or fence for protection from wind

**windmill** machine for grinding grain powered by wind's rotation of large oblique vanes radiating from shaft

## BUSINESS AND SCIENCE OF AGRICULTURE

**aeroculture** practice of growing plants without soil by suspending them above spraying outlets that constantly moisten their roots; aeroponics

**aeroponics** aeroculture

**aggie** *Informal.* agricultural school or college; student at such a school

**agribusiness** business associated with processing, manufacturing, producing, and distributing of agricultural products

**agricultural engineering** design of farm machinery, mechanization of farming, and soil management

**agricultural extension service** government organization providing information and consultation services, often at state's land-grant university

**agricultural sciences** disciplines related to agricultural production, including mineralogy, virology, plant physiology, animal nutrition, microclimatology, and watershed management

**agriculture** science and practice of cultivating soil, raising crops, and raising livestock; farming

**agrobiology** science of plant growth and nutrition as applied to improvement of crops and soil management

**agrology** study of agricultural production

**agronomy** science and economics of soil management and crop production

**agrostology** branch of botany dealing with grasses and grains

**angiosperm** part of seed-producing plant that produces seeds in enclosed ovary within flower; any flowering plant

**animal nutrition** science and practice of feeding livestock, esp. to accelerate growth and improve quality of meat

**aquaculture** cultivation and regulation of water plants and water animals for human consumption

**arboriculture** cultivation of trees and shrubs, esp. for ornamentation

**asexual propagation** reproduction without union with another member of species

**biomass** living material

**biomass conversion** use of organic matter to create energy

**botany** science of plant life, structure, growth, and classification

**breadbasket** region that supplies most of nation's grain

**canning** preserving food in airtight containers of metal or glass

**cash crops** crops grown for income rather than subsistence

**citriculture** cultivation of citrus fruits

**collective farm** cooperative

**commodity** agricultural product seen as economic unit

**Commodity Credit Corporation** Department of Agriculture-sponsored market price-support organization that makes loans to farmers

**cone** conical-shaped, pollen-bearing fruit of tree, characterized by scales or bracts; seed-bearing fruit

**conservation** management of natural resources for their protection and preservation

**conservation tillage** erosion-reducing techniques, including plowless farming, reduced-tillage, no-till, eco-till, and slit planting

**cooperative** farm with several owners or group of farms organized by and operated for benefit of owners or members; collective farm

**Corn Belt** region in midwestern United States between Iowa and Indiana that is ideal for raising corn

**croft** *Chiefly Brit.* tenant farm

**cross-pollination** exchange of pollen between two plants, naturally or artificially

**deforestation** clearing of trees from tract of land

**dehydration** process of removing water from soil or products

**demesne** land legally held in one's possession

**ecology** science concerned with the interrelationship of organisms and their environment

**enclosure** transitional step in land use that replaces unfenced strips of land held in common with individually owned property with defined boundaries

**environmental protection** programs and techniques of assuring continued balance and abundance of Earth's resources

**famine** acute, widespread lack of food, esp. due to crop failure or drought

**farm management** techniques by which large, modern farms are run

**fishery** place where fish are bred

**food** basic human nourishment, usu. satisfied by agricultural products

**food processing** post-harvest handling of agricultural products, including milling, fermenting, freezing, drying, canning, dehydrating, pasteurizing, and radiating

**forestry** science of planting and caring for trees, esp. systematic management of timber production with regard for conservation

**Four-H Club** Department of Agriculture youth program providing training in agriculture, conservation, and home economics

**Future Farmers of America** community organization for young people studying vocational agriculture

**gathering** primitive system of collecting nuts and crops that are growing wild

**genetic engineering** technique of producing new, improved hybrid species by cutting and splicing of genetic units of DNA from different organisms

**geoponic** (*adj*) having to do with agriculture

**grain reserve** grain storage to offset crop failure

**grange** farmers' association

**granger** member of grange

**green revolution** introduction of high-yield crops and use of improved agricultural techniques, esp. in underdeveloped nations, to increase food production

**gymnosperm** part of seed-producing plants that produces seeds on open scales, usu. in cones

**herbicide** plant-killing agent

**horticulture** cultivation of fruits, vegetables, shrubs, and herbaceous and ornamental trees and plants

**husbandry** cultivation of plants and animals

**hybrid** offspring of two plants with different genetic material

**hydrology** science dealing with properties, distribution, and circulation of water on Earth's surface

**hydroponics** growing of plants in nutrient-rich solutions without soil

**integrated pest management** ecological pest control based on preventive measures and minimal use of pesticides

**kibbutz** collective farm (Israel)

**land-grant school** college or university given federal government aid, esp. in form of land, to offer agricultural studies

**logging** cutting trees for lumber

**market garden** farm on which vegetables are grown for market in local industrial areas; truck farm (Britain)

**microclimatology** study of weather and its impact on a small region

**milling** grinding of grain into flour; cutting of timber into lumber

**mineralogy** science of minerals found in soil and rocks

**mixed farming** farming of both crops and livestock

**nitrogen fixation** transformation of nitrogen from air into nitrates by certain plants; self-fertilization

**nursery** place where young plants are raised

**nutrients** nourishing substances

**olericulture** production, storage, and marketing of vegetables for home market

**pasteurization** method of destroying bacteria in milk by heating

**peasant** small farmer, tenant farmer, or farm laborer

**pedology** soil science

**pisciculture** artificial breeding and transplantation of fish

**plant physiology** study and experimentation on functions and growth of plants

**pollution** harmful waste material discharged into air, water, or soil

**pomology** fruit-growing science

**precipitation** rain, hail, snow, or mist; amount of water thus deposited

**production limits** voluntarily accepted limits established as eligibility for commodity loans

**ranger** warden of forest or park

**reforestation** planting of forests on denuded land

**rubber** product obtained as liquid latex by tapping trees, which is then treated to produce solid rubber

**rural** (*adj*) designating farming and ranching regions with small towns, away from large urban centers

**serf** person bound to feudal master's land

**sharecropper** tenant farmer paying rent in form of crops

**silviculture** cultivation of forest trees

**stoop labor** physical labor associated with picking of fruit and vegetables from low-growing plants

**subsidy** government payment to farmers to support prices, esp. on surplus products

**tapping** making hole in tree to draw off liquid, esp. sap or syrup

**target prices** income supplements, set higher than loan rates, calculated to reflect national average cost of producing crop

**tariff** government tax on imported or exported product

**tenant farmer** person farming land owned by another and paying rent in cash or share of crops

**truck farming** growing of vegetables or fruit to be marketed locally

**vegetative propagation** asexual plant reproduction

**vermiculture** raising and production of earthworms and their by-products

**viniculture** cultivation of wine grapes

**virology** study of viral diseases, esp. as they affect livestock

**viticulture** science and cultivation of grapes

**water** ubiquitous natural liquid essential to plant growth

**watershed** ridge dividing areas drained by different river systems; area drained by river system

**weather** atmospheric conditions at given time and place

**zoology** science of animal life, structure, growth, and classification

# Advertising

**SEE ALSO**: Chap. 5: Telecommunications; Computers; Chap. 11: Publishing and the Press; Chap. 12: Business and Economics; Chap. 15: Television and Radio; Chap. 16: Graphic Design and Printing; Photography

**A-board** display in which two sloping boards are joined at top, used for outdoor signs

**accordion** hinged display structure that folds like an accordion and expands or contracts to fill space

**account** client or person employing agency to create ads

**account coordinator** person responsible for maintaining good relations between client and media

**account executive** advertising agency employee who oversees marketing and administrative efforts for one or more clients' campaigns and deals directly with client

**account supervisor** person who oversees account executives

**action cards** mail-order device in which set of postcards with order forms and return addresses for a variety of products and companies is sent to potential customers

**ad** advertisement

**AD** art director

**admass** *Chiefly Brit.* high-pressure marketing using mass media advertising to reach large numbers of people

**advertisement** paid public announcement describing something for sale

**advertising** calling public attention to a particular product by paid announcements so as to arouse desire to buy it; any public notice

**advertising manager** client representative responsible for overseeing marketing efforts related to product, including budgeting, creative activities, and liaison with agency

**advertising sales representative** media planner who contacts publications

**advertorial** advertisement that resembles newspaper editorial but promotes advertiser's product, service, or point of view

**agate line** measure of advertising space, 1/14 of an inch by one column wide

**age group** target audience based on age

**agency** company in business of creating advertisements, packaging, and product names for clients' products and services

**airplane banner** flag or banner bearing advertisement, trailing behind low-flying airplane

**appeal** approach used to promote sales

**art direction** general approach to and look of an advertisement

**art director** AD; person responsible for creative positioning and graphic design of advertisement

**audiovisual** (*adj*) A/V; pertaining to simultaneous use of tape recordings, slides, and video to support pitch, presentation, or display

**A/V** audiovisual

**billboard** very large outdoor printed sign

**billings** gross income to agency from one account or several accounts

**blister pack** display package in which clear plastic seals product against cardboard sheet

**book** talent agency listing, with pictures, of actors and models

**booking** scheduling of talent and staff offered work on shoot or photo session

**brainstorming** meeting to generate creative ideas

**broadside** sheet printed on one or both sides with advertising message

**brochure** folded leaflet with advertising message, usu. illustrated

**bumper sticker** advertising strip attached to automobile-bumper

**bus card** advertising poster attached to side or back of bus, esp. in city public bus system

**business-to-business** (*adj*) designating communications or dealings by agencies or between companies

**buzzword** word or phrase that takes on added significance or new meaning through repetition or special usage

**calling card** small card with person's name, business name, telephone number, and address; any identifying symbol, trademark, or object

**campaign** total planned sales effort on behalf of specific client, usu. multimedia and over period of time

**catalog** illustrated booklet listing available products

**classified ad** brief listing in periodical of items for sale and services offered, arranged by category; want ad

**client** company, or its representative, that employs agency to create advertisements

**Clio** annual award given for excellence in radio and television advertising

**color separation** photographic process using separate plates for each color

**commercial** advertising announcement on television or radio or in movie theater; (*adj*) designating product or service suitable for wide, popular market

**competitive bid** anticipated charges requested by agency from suppliers for preparing materials for advertising, compared with bids of other suppliers

**concept** general idea behind slogan, pitch, or campaign

**consumer** private individual at whom advertisements are aimed

**consumer market** defined group of consumers

**cooperative advertising** sharing of cost of advertisement between manufacturer and retailer

**copy** written part of advertisement

**copywriter** person responsible for writing advertising copy and creating concept with art director

**corporate identity** words and graphics that project image that corporate client wishes to convey to public

**cost per thousand** CPM; cost of advertising per thousand potential customers reached through publication, broadcast, or outdoor advertisement

**CPM** cost per thousand (roman numeral *M*)

**creative director** person responsible in agency for developing concepts, coordinating production of art and copy, and executing campaign

**creative team** art director, copywriter, and creative director involved in initial development of advertisement

**cycle** schedule of periodic, often quarterly, residual payments to actors, models, and singers

**dealer spot** spot advertisement placed by retail dealer of product rather than manufacturer

**decal** specially prepared paper from which graphics can be transferred to another surface

**direct mail** direct marketing exclusively by mail

**direct marketing** marketing via leaflets, brochures, letters, catalogs, or print ads mailed or distributed directly to potential consumers; any medium used to elicit responses directly from consumers

**display** any of various structures used to describe or show product being advertised

**display ad** illustrated advertisement in newspaper or magazine

**dog and pony show** *Informal.* elaborate pitch, presentation, or campaign

**drive time** *Slang.* ads directed at commuters in cars, esp. during morning and late afternoon

**dummy** rough layout of assembled work for print advertisement

**dump-bin** floor display holding an assortment of loose items

**electronic billboard** electronic sign that displays animated, full-color messages in a public place

**estimate** proposed or expected budget of campaign

**exclusivity** prohibition on performing in commercial for product that is competitive with one for which actor has commercial currently on hold or running; right to use specific talent, art, music, etc., in advertising

**exhibition** public show or display

**exposure** number of potential consumers reached through specific medium

**flack** press agent or publicist, sometimes considered disparaging

**flier** fly sheet

**flip chart** chart with series of illustrated pages bound at top so that pages can be lifted vertically and dropped behind other pages, used in presentation

**fly sheet** handbill, loose sheet with printed advertisement; flier

**focus group** group of potential consumers used in market research to determine likely effectiveness of advertising

**freelance** copywriter, graphic artist, or creative person employed by agency or client on intermittent basis

**giveaway** promotion involving free novelties or gifts

**graphic design** any form of visual artistic representation of product or layout of advertisement

**graphic designer** person responsible for implementing art direction of print advertisement

**grinder** *Slang.* actor impersonating doctor or other professional authority on television commercial

**halftone** printed image formed by close-set dots of varying sizes

**handbill** small, printed advertising sheet distributed by hand

**hard sell** aggressive advertising technique

**head shot** glossy 8 x 10–inch picture of actor's or model's face

**hidden persuaders** subtle or subliminal advertising messages and techniques

**hold** period during which commercial is held by agency prior to release

**hook** clever phrase or melody used to capture consumer's attention; peg; slant

**huckster** *Informal.* person who works in advertising industry

**hymn** *Slang.* hidden or subliminal message

**hype** *Informal.* extravagant promotion of person, idea, or product

**IBM** *Slang.* advertisement with corporate look

**impact** degree of success of campaign; reaching of consumers

**impulse buying** buying for momentary pleasure rather than out of genuine need, sometimes encouraged by advertising

**independent** agency functioning alone, without control by larger corporation

**ink** *Slang.* print publicity; press coverage

**insert** printed sheet or sheets inserted into publication or enclosed with mailing

**jiffy hanger** metal hook attached by grommet to piece of buckram coated with adhesive that is applied to wall or display surface

**jingle** catchy, repetitious musical refrain used in radio or TV advertising

**junk mail** unsolicited advertising material sent by post

**kickapoo** *Slang.* client's product

**knockdown** display or exhibit that can be disassembled easily for shipping

**launch** introduction of new product or service

**layout** design for graphic advertising production, roughly depicting look of advertisement

**linage** total lines of advertising placed in publication in one issue over period of time

**live tag** voice-over at end of prerecorded commercial that provides current or local information

**logo** recognizable trademarked design and lettering for trade, product, or organization; logotype

**logotype** logo

**Madison Avenue** advertising in general; New York City street that is location of many large agencies

**magalog** *Informal.* mail-order catalog that carries editorial matter and advertisements for other companies

**mailer** advertisement sent by mail

**mailing list** list of prospective customers organized by location, income, or other aspect of consumer profile

**mail order** retail sales conducted by mail

**mall-fixture advertisement** poster advertisement mounted in glassed frame in kiosk or other public place in mall or transportation depot

**market** prospective customers for given product

**marketing** strategy and specific techniques used in reaching consumers

**market profile** characteristics of group or area targeted for campaign

**market research** study of consumer groups and business competition used to define projected market

**market share** percentage of specific market reached or sold by given product, advertisement, or agency

**marquee** billboard advertising theater performance

**media** forms of mass communication that carry advertising, esp. newspapers, magazines, television, and radio

**media buying service** company that specializes in buying print and television or radio time for advertisements

**media planner** employee of advertiser or advertising agency who coordinates media aspects of campaign and selects which media to use

**media research** study of radio, television, and magazines for purpose of reaching optimal consumer audience

**mention** brief item in press or on broadcast referring to person, product, or service

**merger** combining of two or more agencies to pool accounts and staff; takeover of one agency by another

**Merry Andrew** *Slang.* actor impersonating victim of headache or indigestion in commercial

**message** underlying theme or idea in advertisement

**Middle America** conservative, middle-class segment of U.S. population that makes up largest consumer group

**mockup** scale-dimensional display model used in planning

**model** actor employed by agency to appear in advertisement

**mom-and-pop** (*adj*) having a traditional, rural look in advertisements; designating a small advertising agency

**MOS** supposedly from Germanism *mit-out* sprache; commercial filmed without recording sound and without speaking actors

**multimedia** (*adj*) involving use of several media simultaneously in single advertisement or campaign

**national** advertising spot running throughout the country

**novelties** free items, such as matches, calendars, or buttons, bearing advertiser's logo

**outdoor** *Informal.* billboard, bus card, mall-fixture, or other outdoor advertisement

**P and G** *Slang.* lit. Proctor & Gamble; advertisement with Middle American appeal, style, and art direction

**paste-up** formation of graphic design or layout by pasting objects to stiff board; mechanical

**payback** return on investment; success of advertisement

**payoff** results of advertising campaign

**peg** *Informal.* strong, appealing, notable element of press release or campaign; hook; slant

**penalty payment** required payment, usu. to actors, models, and singers, for violation of standard booking practices

**photo opportunity** sometimes staged event having visual appeal or interest to photographers, used to generate publicity and free advertising

**piggyback** (*vb*) run group of commercials back to back, usu. for same client, in time frame such as four fifteen-second spots for price of one sixty-second spot

**piggy spot** *Slang. pain is good* spot; radio or television commercial for painkiller featuring actor impersonating pain sufferer

**pitch** presentation of advertising message

**planned obsolescence** method of stimulating consumer demand by designing products to become outdated or broken after limited use

**plug** *Informal.* favorable mention or picture of product in nonadvertising portion of media presentation

**point-of-purchase advertising** signs, displays, and other techniques of attracting attention and promoting products at their point of sale, such as at the counter of a retail store

**point-of-purchase display** arrangement of goods in retail store with conspicuous advertising copy

**POP** *point-of-purchase*

**pop-up** display or mailer, part of which automatically moves or lifts from surface as it is opened

**portfolio** large, bound volume containing pictures from ads, used by agency or talent to generate new jobs

**poster** graphic advertisement attached to flat surface or standing up with clip backing

**PR** *public relations*

**premium** something offered free or at reduced price as inducement to buy something else

**presentation** pitch, description of advertising campaign

**press agent** publicist

**press kit** collection of editorial and promotional materials distributed to press

**principal** performer in commercial who can be recognized or identified, including but not limited to speaking parts

**print** advertising in newspapers, magazines, catalogs, or mailers, usu. photographs or other graphic material

**production manager** person responsible for overseeing details in making of video or print advertisement

**promotion** method of increasing sales of merchandise through advertising; any activity aimed at increasing sales

**propaganda** promotion of specific ideas or views, esp. political

**publicist** person hired to promote cause, individual, or product by generating free advertising; flack; press agent

**publicity** dissemination of promotional material to draw interest or generate sales

**public relations** PR; business of inducing goodwill and acceptance in public toward individual, cause, company, or product

**puffery** undue or exaggerated praise or claims used in advertising and publicity

**rates** cost per inch of print advertising; cost per minute of radio and TV advertising

**rating** measure of audience for television show, used to establish rates

**refusal** right of first actor or model selected for advertisement to refuse or accept assignment

**regional** advertisement appearing in one region only

**release** signed permission given by person to use his or her photo, voice, name, or testimonial statement commercially

**remnant space** unsold print advertising space sold at a discount

**residual** payment to model, actor, or singer each time advertisement is played, shown, or run

**rollout** *Informal.* geographic expansion of campaign from test market, as to regional or national market

**sale** offering of retail goods at reduced prices to induce increased consumption

**sandwich board** two hinged boards with advertising messages on them, worn hung over shoulders

**SAU** standard advertising unit

**scatter package** arrangement to air television commercials at various times or intervals

**sell** (*vb*) promote an idea, product, or concept

**session** recording session for radio or TV commercial; photograph-taking session

**session fee** amount paid to talent or artist for day's work on single session

**shill** person planted in audience to lure onlookers into buying product or participating in activity

**shoot** taping or filming of commercial in studio or on location

**show bill** advertising poster

**sizzle** *Slang.* image rather than substance

**skywriting** writing across sky with chemically produced smoke emitted from airplane, usu. for purposes of advertising

**slant** emphasis of a campaign or advertisement; hook; peg

**slice-of-life** (*adj*) denoting advertisement that depicts naturalistic, everyday activities

**slogan** short, memorable advertising phrase

**sniping** pasting up outdoor posters over billboards or on empty structures, walls, and traffic poles, often without permission

**soft sell** subtle advertising technique

**space** page or section of page bought for advertisement in newspaper, magazine, or catalog

**spokesperson** well-known person serving as regular advocate of specific product or cause

**spot** spot announcement

**spot advertising** advertising in selected locales rather than nationally

**spot announcement** radio or television commercial of fifteen, thirty, or sixty seconds; spot

**stabile** display that is suspended or that rises from pedestal at different levels and on different planes, none of which move

**staff** permanent, full-time agency employees

**standard advertising unit** SAU; system of standard dimensions for print advertising based on six columns, each 2 1/16 inches wide

**static ad** photographic or print advertisement

**storewide sale** sale in all departments of large store

**storyboard** series of panels roughly depicting scenes, copy, and shots in television commercial

**streamer** long, narrow sign with message in bold type hung across open area, window, or doorway

**stylist** hair and makeup artist on television shoot

**subliminal advertising** concealed appeal to consumers' unconscious to buy product

**subway card** advertising poster attached to interior or exterior side of subway car

**sweepstakes** lottery in which winners are randomly selected, often used to induce purchase of product as means of entering contest

**tabletop** type of shoot in which product is photographed on a table, either life-size or in miniature

**table topper** exhibit arranged on table rather than floor

**talent** actors, models, and singers employed in advertisements

**talent agency** organization that represents actors and models appearing in advertisements

**target audience** consumer group most likely to buy product, identified by region, age, demographics, or economic status; target market

**target market** target audience

**teaser** advertisement or publicity that arouses interest or curiosity about forthcoming product or event, sometimes without naming it

**telemarketing** selling, advertising, or market research done by telephone

**tent** display card folded and set up with two sloping sides, like inverted V, esp. for small displays on tables

**testimonial** statement, often by celebrity or prominent person, affirming truth, fact, character, or value of a product, event, or service

**test market** consumer group interviewed to determine target audience

**test market spot** spot used exclusively on test market and monitored for its effectiveness

**throwaway** handbill or other printed matter that is distributed free to residences and contains local advertising; novelty item used to entice consumers into buying more costly item

**tie-in** campaign to link products, media, or markets

**time slot** specific time bought for airing of commercial on radio or television

**trade name** name used by company to describe and distinguish its brand of a generic product, usu. trademarked

**trade-out** barter arrangement for exchange of commercial time, advertising space, products, or services

**trade show** convention at which advertising agencies or related companies show and compare products and ideas

**triptych** three-sided display with central element and two wings

**turntable** revolving mechanical display platform

**upscale** (adj) Informal. having a look aimed at the well-to-do urban market

**VO** voice-over

**voice-over** VO; recorded offscreen voice heard on television or radio commercial

**volume** dollar amount of billings or revenue

**want ad** classified ad

**wild spot** spot appearing in various slots and locales, neither regional nor national, or on nonnetwork station

**window display** merchandise and/or advertising attractively arranged in store window

# INSURANCE

SEE ALSO: Chap. 12: Finance

**accident** unplanned event causing injury, death, or damage

**accident insurance** coverage for loss due to accidental bodily injury

**act of God** usu. catastrophic event arising from natural causes

**actuarial tables** tables showing life expectancies

**actuary** statistical specialist who computes insurance rates

**adjustment** estimate of loss; settlement of claim

**adjustor** insurance company representative trained to make accurate estimates of loss or liability

**advertiser's liability** protection for risk inherent in advertising claims

**agent** representative selling policies for insurance company

**annuity** periodic payments of specific amount made by insurer, often for life

**assigned risk** high-risk client assigned to insurance company by lottery-style method

**assurance** Chiefly Brit. insurance, esp. life insurance

**automobile insurance** coverage for drivers of automobiles

**aviation insurance** insurance against loss of life on air flight

**beneficiary** person eligible to receive insurance payments

**benefits** payments to insured person or his or her beneficiary

**bond** guarantee against financial loss caused by default of third party or by circumstance over which guarantor has no control

**bordereau** computerized billing statement used in international insurance claims

**carrier** insurance company, insurer

**catastrophe** sudden, violent loss

**claim** insured's application to receive benefits

**cleanup fund** life insurance policy covering expenses after insured's death

**coinsurance** jointly held insurance policy; policy in which insured pays portion of costs or losses

**collision insurance** protection against damage to one's own property in case of accident

**comprehensive** auto or health insurance policy covering all risk contingencies

**coverage** inclusion within scope of policy; insurance

**damages** amount paid to cover loss

**deductible** that part of loss to be paid by insured party, deductible from insurer's payment

**dental insurance** health insurance coverage for dental work

**disability insurance** government payments to cover loss of employment due to injury or sickness

**disaster insurance** coverage for damage due to act of nature, such as flood, hailstorm, or earthquake

**double indemnity** clause in policy providing for payment of twice the basic benefit

**draft** order issued by insurer for payment of benefits

**dramshop law** liquor liability law making server of alcohol liable for possible loss caused by intoxicated person

**dramshop liability insurance** coverage for sellers of alcoholic beverages

**endorsement** provision added to insurance policy altering its scope or application

**endowment insurance** life insurance policy that matures on set date or at death of insured, whichever occurs first

**errors and omissions** coverage for mistakes made in documents, esp. instances of libel and copyright infringement

**estimate** appraisal of loss for claim

**excess carrier** company that insures insurance company for losses in excess of policy liability limit

**exclusion** contingency not covered by policy

**exposure** maximum amount company may have to pay on claim

**fair market value** estimated value of lost property at time of loss, used for determining cost of replacement

**fault** liability under coverage

**fine print** often overlooked small type on policy outlining exclusions or limitations

**fire insurance** coverage for loss due to fire

**gravamen** essential part of claim

**group insurance** coverage for all members of organization or employees of company

**hazard** situation that increases possibility of loss

**health insurance** coverage for medical expenses

**health maintenance organization** HMO; health coverage in specific region in which doctors hired by HMO provide services for prepaid subscribers

**HMO** *health maintenance organization*

**homeowner's policy** coverage for fire, theft, or other damage to one's home

**indemnification** protection from loss or damage and promise to pay for what has been lost or damaged, usu. seen as basic premise of insurance

**indemnity** payment, repair, or replacement of insured loss

**inland marine insurance** coverage for freight on inland waterways

**insurance** system or business of insuring property or persons against loss or harm due to specific contingencies; contract providing for indemnification against loss

**insurance policy** printed contract between insured and insurer stating terms and limits of agreement

**insured** person paying premiums and receiving guarantee of indemnities

**insurer** insurance company or entity providing indemnities

**jumping juvenile** life insurance for child in which cost increases sharply when child reaches majority

**lapsed policy** policy that has expired due to nonpayment of premiums

**liability** insurance coverage for loss arising from insured's actions; insured's responsibility for damage or loss

**lien** charge or claim on policy by third party

**life insurance** coverage guaranteeing payment of specified sum to beneficiary on death of insured

**limitations** areas excluded from or not covered by policy

**line** particular type of insurance offered by company

**loading** extra charge above premium to cover special risks

**major medical** coverage of all medical and hospital expenses resulting from illness or injury

**malpractice insurance** coverage for professionals, esp. doctors, for damage caused by neglect or poor treatment, usu. at very high premium

**marine insurance** coverage for shipping and freight by sea

**maturity** date at which policy becomes payable

**Medicaid** government-subsidized medical insurance

**Medicare** government-subsidized medical insurance for aged

**midnight clause** clause setting expiration of policy at midnight on certain date

**moral hazard** insurance company's risk as to insured's honesty or trustworthiness

**mortality table** graph of selected population's death to age ratio, used to calculate risk

**mortgage insurance** government coverage for institutions making loans for purchase of property

**multiple employer trust** collection of insurance programs managed by intermediary organization under contract to actual insurance companies

**natural death** death other than from accident, homicide, or suicide

**newspaper policy** limited health insurance policy sold by newspapers to boost circulation

**no-fault** insurance covering loss regardless of responsibility for accident

**nuisance value** amount paid by insurer to dispose of claim

**occurrence** event or events, sometimes ongoing, constituting single loss

**overage** excess coverage

**overinsured** (*adj*) having coverage beyond value of insured objects

**payable** indemnity due on claim

**peril** cause of possible loss, such as fire or flood

**personal injury** condition that is basis for claim against carrier for damages or suffering resulting from accident

**policy** contract stipulating terms of insurance coverage

**policyholder** insured person

**premium** periodic payment made by insured to maintain coverage

**primary insurer** company issuing policy to insured

**property damage insurance** protection against liability for damage to another's property

**redlining** discriminating in issuing property insurance based on location

**reinsurance** insurance taken by insurance company with another insurer to deflect excess costs in case of catastrophic loss

**renter's insurance** coverage for furnishings and other property kept in rented premises

**reparation** compensation paid on claim

**reserves** cash amounts held by insurance company to pay potential and pending claims

**rider** attachment or amendment to policy

**risk** uncertainty of outcome of situation; likelihood of loss

**schedule** list in claim of losses; items covered by policy with corresponding values

**self-insurance** insurance of one's property or interest by creating special fund instead of seeking coverage with underwriter

**settlement** payment by insurer on claim for loss

**shock loss**  immense loss that causes adverse effect on insurer's assets

**Social Security**  government program of economic benefits to qualifying retired, elderly, surviving, or disabled persons

**spendthrift clause**  clause preventing beneficiary's creditors from attaching life insurance benefits paid to beneficiary

**statement**  breakdown of premium costs provided by insurer

**subrogation**  assumption by third party of insured's right to seek reimbursement on policy

**surety**  guarantor, usu. insurance company

**surety bond**  bond guaranteeing performance of contract

**surrender**  voluntary termination of policy by insured for cash payment from company

**term**  time during which policy is in effect

**term insurance**  policy that provides coverage for limited period

**term life insurance**  policy with premiums paid until death of insured

**theft insurance**  coverage for loss of property stolen from house or automobile

**tontine**  life insurance in which chief beneficiaries are those whose policies are in force at end of specified term

**uncovered** (*adj*)  unprotected under insurance policy

**underinsured** (*adj*)  having insufficient insurance

**underwrite** (*vb*)  determine rates and assign coverage of policy

**underwriter**  expert in evaluating risks and assigning rates and coverage

**unemployment insurance**  periodic payments, usu. by state government from payroll contributions, to qualified unemployed person

**uninsured** (*adj*)  having no insurance

**uninsured motorist coverage**  automobile insurance protection against losses incurred in accident caused by driver without insurance

**vis major**  *Latin*. lit. greater force; act of God; accident without human cause

**workman's compensation**  government disability insurance for workers

# REAL ESTATE

Real Estate Practice
Deeds, Leases, and Real Property Law
Mortgages and Financing

**SEE ALSO**: Chap. 5: Structural Components; Building and Construction Materials; Chap. 7: Buildings; Chap. 11: The City; Law; Chap. 12: Finance; Insurance

## REAL ESTATE PRACTICE

**abatement**  decrease in property tax due; improvement

**absentee owner**  owner living away from site of property

**abutment**  bordering of two pieces of property

**abutting owner**  one whose land touches another's

**acreage**  land measured in units equal to 43,560 square feet

**acreage zoning**  zoning that permits development at low-density locations only

**addition**  expansion of building to include new rooms or outbuildings

**ad valorem**  *Latin*. lit. according to value; usual manner in which taxes are assessed on real property

**agent**  person legally empowered to represent owner, buyer, or landlord in sale or rental of real estate

**alligator**  *Slang*. investment property producing less income than expenses

**apartment building**  structure with three or more rental units

**apartments**  *Chiefly Brit*. set of rooms used as dwelling by one person or one family

**appraisal**  authorized valuation of property based on market value, cost of replacement, or multiplying income derived from it by chosen constant

**appreciation**  increase in property value over time

**as is** (*adj*)  designating property to be purchased in its present condition with no guarantee of its future state

**assessed value**  value placed on property by government for purpose of taxation

**assessment**  valuation of property; appraisal, esp. for taxation

**bachelor**  one-room rental unit in apartment building

**Baltimore method**  appraisal of corner lot to equal total of all surrounding lots

**beachfront property**  building with one side facing directly onto beach

**bedsit**  *Chiefly Brit*. one-room studio apartment without kitchen

**birdbath**  *Slang*. low, paved area that collects water

**bird dog**  *Informal*. person finding new listings for real estate broker

**blockbusting**  illegal scheme to induce property sale by owners fearing decreased value due to minority encroachment

**boardinghouse**  building in which rooms are rented and meals served

**board of realty**  local agency or council supervising real estate transactions

**bottom fisher**  *Slang*. person seeking bargain prices on real property, usu. from distressed sellers

**broker**  agent licensed to sell, rent, or manage property on commission

**building codes**  local ordinances regulating standards of building construction

**building inspector**  licensed official who checks construction sites to guarantee compliance with building codes

**capital gain**  taxed portion of profit on property sale

**caretaker**  one who cares for property of absentee owner

**chartulary**  register of estate titles and deeds

**commission**  fee paid to agent or broker on sale or rental

**condo**  condominium

**condominium**  individually owned property, usu. apartment that is part of larger, multiple-unit structure having other owners and often having common elements; condo

**conversion**  change of building's use and status, as from rental to condominium

**co-op**  cooperative

**cooperative**  multiple-unit property collectively owned by owners of individual units, who hold proprietary leases on their apartments; co-op

**Department of Housing and Urban Development** HUD; federal agency responsible for providing low-cost housing

**depreciation** decrease in value of property over time

**develop** (*vb*) purchase real property with intention of increasing its value, usu. by subdivision, improvement, and construction

**developer** owner who improves and subdivides land into building lots

**development** tract of land subdivided into building lots

**dockominium** boat marina operated like a condominium, with each member owning his or her own slip

**duplex** single building divided into two residences

**estate agent** *Chiefly Brit.* real estate agent

**exclusive listing** listing given to one broker only while reserving right to sell property oneself

**exclusive right to sell** listing in which broker receives commission no matter who sells property

**fair market value** highest attainable asking price for property at a given time

**finder's fee** reward paid to third party for locating buyer or seller of property

**first-and-last** payment of two month's rent on commencement of rental

**fixer-upper** *Informal.* run-down property in need of substantial remodeling and repair, purchased at bargain price; handyman's special

**fixing-up expenses** final costs of minor improvements by owner prior to sale, deductible from taxable profit

**fixture** any article permanently attached to building or property

**flat** *Chiefly Brit.* apartment on one floor of building

**flip** immediate resale of property, usu. at a profit, sometimes before closing

**frontage** property line abutting public street or waterway

**garden apartment** apartment on ground floor of multiple-unit dwelling with private landscaped area; low-level apartment building surrounded by landscaped areas

**greenbelt** land zoned to prohibit construction

**ground cover** landscaped foliage planted to prevent erosion

**habitable** (*adj*) capable of being inhabited, usu. according to law

**handyman's special** fixer-upper

**hectare** measurement of land equal to 2 1/2 acres

**high rise** multistory building with elevators

**home owner's insurance** guarantee against property loss made by company to which owner pays regular premiums

**homestead** tract of federally owned land awarded to claimant meeting statutory requirements

**housekeeping** care and management of property

**HUD** Department of *H*ousing and *U*rban *D*evelopment

**hundred percent location** business area with greatest land value and highest rents

**improved land** property offered with necessities such as lights, sewers, sidewalks, and water lines

**improvements** facilities or amenities added to property to increase its value

**income property** property held primarily or exclusively for production of revenue

**industrial park** industrial complex, usu. in suburban or rural area, dominated by manufacturing plants, warehouses, and offices

**inside lot** parcel between corner lots

**key lot** parcel with increasing worth due to location

**key money** lump sum paid on moving into rental unit

**land value** worth of land as distinct from structures on it

**leasehold improvements** permanent, depreciable improvements made to leased or rented property, usu. for business

**let** (*vb*) offer for rental or lease

**listing** property offered for sale by one or more real estate brokers

**loft** floor of warehouse transformed into residence, usu. above ground level

**low-cost housing** moderately priced housing made available to poor families, esp. in urban areas

**management company** company owning and renting more than one building

**manager** landlord's representative living on premises and overseeing rental units

**market value** amount a piece of property is likely to bring when offered for sale on open market

**model home** decorated, vacant residential structure shown to prospective buyers of similar units

**neighborhood** small district with homogeneous income level, land value, and ethnic profile

**occupancy** use to which property is put; possession of land taken to acquire ownership

**open house** house or apartment open during specified hours for inspection by prospective buyers or tenants

**open listing** listing given to brokers on nonexclusive basis

**option** right but not obligation to purchase or lease property

**outbuilding** independent structure considered part of real property along with primary building

**parcel** tract or plot of land with set boundaries

**penthouse** dwelling unit on top floor of building

**pied-à-terre** residence used only part-time

**project** group of houses or apartments built and arranged in defined area, often low-cost housing

**property tax** tax levied on real property

**rack-rent** (*vb*) exact the highest possible rent

**railroad flat** long, narrow apartment in which one room follows another

**raw land** vacant, unimproved, unused land

**real estate** property in form of land and buildings; practice and business of selling, renting, and developing real property

**Realtor** *Trademark.* person who works in real estate and is a member of the National Association of Real Estate Boards

**realty** real estate; practice and procedures involved in disposition of real estate

**record of title** title to piece of real estate shown in public record

**rent** monthly payment by tenant to landlord for occupation or use of property

**rental** amount paid on rented property; act of renting; property rented

**rental property** property occupied by tenant for regular payment of set amount to landlord

**rent control** government regulation of rental charges

**rent stabilization** rent increases regulated by law

**residence** building in which people live

**row house** one of a series of uniformly built homes connected by common sidewalls

**security** deposit or pledge made to guarantee contractual obligation

**security deposit** amount deposited on rental as guarantee against damage to property

**showplace** building or estate shown as example of available properties

**single** one-room studio apartment

**site** parcel of land

**slum** area of substandard, overcrowded, decaying housing

**slumlord** absentee landlord who profits by charging exorbitant rents for neglected properties

**snob zoning** exclusionary residential zoning requiring large lots or prohibitively costly design standards

**starter home** relatively inexpensive, low-end home that is buyer's first owned property, purchased with the intent to sell it for a profit and acquire a better property in future

**steering** illegal direction of potential buyers toward or away from minority neighborhoods

**studio** one-room apartment with kitchen and no separate bedroom

**subdivision** tract of land divided into several lots for construction of individual residences

**super** superintendent

**superintendent** person living in building, managing rentals, and making repairs for absentee owner; super

**tax break** tax benefit allowed for property ownership

**tax shelter** property that generates negative income, held for purpose of obtaining tax deduction

**tenement** apartment house barely meeting minimum standards of sanitation, safety, and comfort

**time-share unit** single property, esp. vacation home, with multiple owners, each allocated specific amount of time for occupancy

**title search** examination of public records for liens prior to granting title to new owner

**townhouse** single-family, multistory urban dwelling, usu. attached to adjacent dwelling by common wall

**tract house** dwelling on defined area of land, usu. in development, built on similar model to that of adjacent dwellings

**triplex** single residence divided into three living units

**vacation property** dwelling used only for vacation, often rented as income property

**valuation** assessment of value of land and buildings

**variance** exception permitting noncompliance with normal building codes

**walk-up** apartment above ground floor in building without elevator

**zero lot** property in which edge of structure is edge of property lot

**zoning** dividing city or town into areas by specifying uses, such as commercial or residential, to be made of property in each zone

## DEEDS, LEASES, AND REAL PROPERTY LAW

**abstract of title** official records giving history of title to piece of property

**accession** addition to property by growth or improvement

**access** right to enter and leave property

**accretion** increase in property by gradual natural addition, esp. due to water, as by river silt

**adverse possession** legal acquisition of someone else's real property through prolonged, open, exclusive, unauthorized occupation

**air rights** legal right to use air space above building

**alienation** transfer of title of ownership to property from one person to another

**assurance** act and instrument of conveying real property

**attorn** (*vb*) agree to remain as tenant under new owner at same property

**boilerplate** *Informal.* standard legal language for deeds, contracts, or leases

**cadastre** official register of size, ownership, and value of property, used in determining taxes

**certificate of occupancy** municipal issuance stating that property meets minimum requirements for intended use

**chain of title** documentary history of ownerships of real estate parcel

**clear title** ownership free of all limits or conditions

**cloud on title** outside encumbrance or condition that impairs title of ownership

**common element** area or element of condominium in which each owner has an undivided interest

**condemnation** legal process by which government purchases private property for public use

**conveyance** instrument by which property title is transferred

**cotenancy** ownership or rights to property shared by two or more persons

**curtilage** enclosed, fenced space immediately surrounding dwelling

**deed** legal document transferring or establishing ownership of property

**deed restriction** provision in deed permanently restricting use and development of property

**devise** (*vb*) assign or transfer real property by will

**easement** privilege allowing use of or access to another's property for specific purpose

**encroachment** unauthorized occupancy or trespass upon another's property, esp. by structure or improvement

**encumbrance** hindrance that delays clearing of title

**escalator clause** provision in lease that increases or decreases rent under stated conditions

**escheat** reversion of property to state when no heir or legal claimant can be found

**estate** all property, real and personal, owned by a person

**estate at will** leasehold that can be terminated at will by either party

**eviction** legal dispossession of tenant by landlord

**fee simple estate** real estate with absolute ownership and no binding restrictions

**foreclosure** legal procedure depriving mortgagor of right to sell mortgaged property other than to pay debt

**free and clear title** property ownership with no claims against it

**freehold** estate in land, inherited or held for life

**future estate** right to property contingent on some future event

**grant** transfer of property

**grantee** person receiving deed to property

**grantor** person conveying deed to property

**ground lease** lease on land only, whether or not there are or will be structures on it

**holdover tenant** tenant whose lease has expired and against whom eviction action may be brought

**index lease** lease with rate escalation provision

**joint tenancy** property or lease held by two or more parties with right of survivorship

**landlady** female landlord

**landlord** owner of rented or leased property

**lease** terminating agreement covering possession, use, or occupancy of property

**leasehold** property acquired under a lease; rights in such property

**lessee** tenant to whom lease is granted

**lessor** landlord, grantor of rights to property through lease

**lien** claim on property to satisfy outstanding debt or duty

**life tenancy** right to use property that terminates with death of user or holder of right

**lot** legally identified parcel of land

**marketable title** title to property that is free of encumbrances and can be readily sold or mortgaged

**mechanic's lien** lien secured on property by contractor who has repaired or built it in order to ensure payment for labor and materials

**metes and bounds** system for describing boundaries and orientation of a piece of land

**month-to-month tenancy** rental agreement without set term of lease, terminated at any time, usu. with one month's notice

**mortmain** ownership of land by perpetual corporation, esp. religious organization

**notice to quit** landlord's notification that tenant must vacate premises

**owner** legal holder of property

**property** single piece of real estate owned or possessed

**proprietary lease** lease granted to shareholders of a cooperative for use and occupancy of their individual space

**quiet enjoyment** covenant in lease stating that tenant will peaceably enjoy possession of property

**quitclaim** transfer of all one's interests in property without warranty of title

**real property** land and permanent structures on it

**recording** act of entering a document into abstract of title of property

**reliction** increase in land area due to withdrawal of water

**retaliatory eviction** illegal eviction action by landlord in response to tenant's complaint

**reversion** return of property to original owner or heirs at expiration of temporary grant

**right of survivorship** right of one joint tenant to inherit real estate interest of a deceased joint tenant

**riparian rights** rights of owners of land adjoining a body of water

**sandwich lease** three-party rental agreement between landlord, original tenant, and subtenant

**sky lease** agreement to use air space above property

**squatter** person occupying public or private land or residence without benefit of legal title

**squatter's right** legal right to occupy property based on long-term tenancy

**sublease** lease by tenant to third party on already leased premises

**subtenant** person occupying subleased property; undertenant

**survey** legal description of land based on observations of licensed professional surveyor

**tenancy** occupation of building or land by rental or lease

**tenancy in common** ownership of undivided shares of real property by two or more persons without right of survivorship

**tenant** person with temporary, conditional use of property owned by another

**tenants' rights** legal rights of tenants

**title** all elements and written documents constituting legal ownership of property

**title deed** document constituting evidence of legal ownership

**trust** property interest held by one party for benefit of another

**trust deed** document that conveys interest to a trust as security for loan

**undertenant** subtenant

**undivided share** part ownership applied to entire property, rather than ownership of part of property

## MORTGAGES AND FINANCING

**acceleration clause** provision of mortgage that advances date for payment of balance under certain circumstances

**adjustable-rate mortgage** variable-rate mortgage

**assumable mortgage** mortgage taken over from seller by buyer

**balloon payment** single, large, final payment on loan

**binder** preliminary, temporary agreement to make down payment and purchase property pending formal contract

**bonus** amount above interest charged for loan on transfer of property

**buy-down** arrangement in which mortgage carries below-market interest rate for first few years

**chattel mortgage** loan secured by personal property

**clear escrow** receive approval of application for mortgage loan, required to gain title to property

**closing** final approval of escrow in property purchase; gathering of all parties to consummate real estate transaction; settlement

**deposit** amount paid to hold property until escrow clears

**down payment** initial cash sum paid at time of real estate purchase; front money

**earnest money** good-faith sum of cash used as binder

**equity** value of property in excess of claims and loans against it

**equity of redemption** right of mortgagor to regain property lost through failure to make timely payments

**escrow** deed held by neutral party, such as bank, for delivery upon fulfillment of certain conditions, usu. making of payments

**financing** arranging purchase of property through down payment and mortgage loan

**first mortgage** mortgage having priority over other mortgages on property

**Freddie Mac** Federal Home Loan Mortgage Corporation, which buys mortgages from lenders

**front money** down payment

**Ginnie Mae** GNMA; Government National Mortgage Association; agency of federal government that buys pools of mortgages from lender institutions and sells interest in them to the public

**home loan** mortgage given for purchase of home

**indexing** method of adjusting interest rate on loan based on agreed-upon index or indicator

**installment purchase** loan paid off in multiple payments at set intervals over time

**interest** charge made at set rate on money borrowed to purchase property, added to principal amount borrowed

**kicker** loan surcharge

**law day** due date on mortgage after which debt is in default

**loan-to-value ratio** fraction of appraised value that lender will loan on property

**Maggie Mae** Mortgage Guarantee Insurance Corporation; federal agency that insures institutions making mortgage loans

**mortgage** transfer or conveyance of real property as security for debt; written instrument for such transfer

**mortgagee** person to whom property is mortgaged

**mortgage insurance** guarantee of mortgage payment to mortgagor by third party

**mortgage tax** local tax on face value of mortgage

**mortgagor** person who mortgages property

**origination fee** points charged on face value of mortgage at time of purchase

**points** percentage of loan principal added to cost of purchase, one point equaling one percent

**principal** amount of money borrowed from mortgagor, on which interest is computed; authorized party to sale, lease, or rental agreement

**refinance** (*vb*) borrow additional funds against equity in property

**satisfaction of mortgage** recordable document stating that loan has been repaid

**second mortgage** mortgage taken by third party on property already mortgaged

**settlement** closing

**variable-rate mortgage** loan on which interest rate changes with predetermined factors, such as prime rate; adjustable-rate mortgage

**workout** process by which a borrower, esp. one near bankruptcy, fulfills a debt commitment by modifying the terms of repayment

**wraparound mortgage** mortgage that contains obligation to repay a smaller, previously existing mortgage; second mortgage

---

# OCCUPATIONS

General Titles, Positions, and Status
Trades and Crafts
Occupations and Job Titles

**SEE ALSO**: Chap. 11: Titles of Rank; Chap. 12: Business and Economics

## GENERAL TITLES, POSITIONS, AND STATUS

**agent** one who represents the interests of another

**amateur** one who is not paid for work

**analyst** one skilled in the examination of specific problems

**apprentice** one learning trade under experienced worker

**artisan** craftsman or skilled tradesman

**assembler** one who fits parts together

**assistant** one who helps or aids another; one subordinate to another in rank or function

**associate** partner or fellow worker

**attendant** one who serves customers

**blue-collar worker** laborer, nonoffice worker

**boss** supervisor, owner, or person with authority over others

**broker** agent or intermediary in sale

**businessman** man engaged in commerce, esp. owner or executive

**businesswoman** woman regularly employed in business, esp. white-collar worker

**chairman** presiding officer or top executive of company

**chairwoman** female presiding officer

**cleaner** one whose work is cleaning

**clerk** low-ranking official responsible for recordkeeping; one engaged in retail selling

**coach** one who instructs others in how to perform duties, esp. in sports

**common laborer** unskilled, blue-collar worker

**counselor** one who advises others

**craftsman** one working in skilled trade or craft

**director** one entrusted with overall supervision

**employee** one who works for an individual or institution

**employer** one who has others working for him or her

**engineer** one who builds or manages machinery or complex systems

**executive** one with administrative or managerial responsibility

**fabricator** one who builds or puts things together

**fitter** one who installs or adjusts machinery

**foreman** chief worker leading crew or production workers

**forger** one who works with metal

**freelancer** one who is self-employed or works for various employers

**functionary** minor official who performs specific tasks

**hand** helper, esp. at unskilled jobs

**helper** general assistant

**installer** one who puts machinery into operation

**instructor** one who teaches another a skill

**jack** common worker, esp. one with more than one trade

**journeyman** one experienced in a trade

**laborer** unskilled worker

**layman** one outside some skilled profession

**machinist** one who makes or repairs machines; one who uses machine tools

**maker** one who manufacturers or creates something

**manager** one who directs others

**master** highly skilled worker; manager or director

**mover** one who transports things from place to place

**office worker** white-collar worker

**official** one with rank and specific responsibilities
**operator** one who handles functioning machinery
**overseer** supervisor
**partner** one of two or more owners of business
**performer** one who entertains others
**practitioner** one skilled in and engaged in trade or profession
**producer** one who makes something; one who finances the making of something
**professional** one who is paid for work; one engaged in work requiring advanced education
**proletarian** worker, esp. blue-collar worker
**public servant** government employee
**repairman** one who maintains and fixes equipment
**representative** one who acts as agent for another
**researcher** one who undertakes careful investigation
**salesperson** one who sells some product to public, usu. retail
**secretary** clerical assistant
**skilled laborer** one who works at job requiring special training
**slave** one who is forced to work for no pay
**smith** forger or fabricator, esp. in metals
**sole proprietor** self-employed owner of business having no partners
**steward** one who manages provisions or affairs
**superintendent** one in charge and having executive overview
**supervisor** administrative officer; one who oversees other's work; overseer
**technician** specialist in technical details of job
**tender** one who provides support
**tester** one who examines and evaluates a product
**tradesman** one skilled in a trade or craft
**trainer** one who instructs and prepares others for a job
**unskilled worker** laborer at job requiring no training
**vendor** one who sells; salesperson
**white-collar worker** office worker
**worker** one engaged in manual or industrial labor
**wright** skilled worker, esp. in wood and other materials
**yeoman** one attending or assisting another

## TRADES AND CRAFTS

**armorer** maker and repairer of armor and arms
**arrowsmith** maker of arrows
**artisan** skilled craftsman
**baker** maker of breads, biscuits, and cakes
**barber** beardcutter and hairdresser
**blacksmith** maker of forged iron objects
**boatwright** maker of seagoing vessels
**boilermaker** maker of boilers, esp. for engines
**bookbinder** maker of bindings for book pages
**bookwright** maker of books
**brazier** brass worker
**brewer** maker of malt liquors
**bricklayer** setter of bricks
**butler** house servant in charge of wines and table service
**cabinetmaker** maker of fine, finished woodwork, esp. furniture

**candlewright** maker of candles
**carpenter** cutter and framer of wooden structures
**cartwright** maker of carts and wagons
**carver** cutter of meat at table
**chandler** candle maker; dealer in provisions and small wares
**cobbler** shoemaker
**collier** coal miner
**cooper** maker of barrels and casks
**die maker** maker of dies or cutting and shaping tools
**doll maker** maker of dolls
**draper** maker and seller of cloth
**farrier** *Chiefly Brit.* blacksmith
**fletcher** maker of arrows
**founder** caster of metal objects
**fuller** maker of gathers in cloth garments
**gatewright** maker of gates
**glassblower** maker of glass vessels or sheet glass through blowing process
**glazier** maker and installer of glass
**goldsmith** gold worker
**haberdasher** retail dealer in men's furnishings
**joiner** one who does finishing woodwork, esp. construction by joining pieces of wood
**lather** worker on a lathe
**luthier** maker of stringed instruments
**mason** builder using stone or brick
**mercer** dealer in expensive fabrics
**miller** keeper or operator of mill or processing plant for grain, wood, coffee, or cotton
**millwright** builder of mills; one tending workshop fixtures
**monger** trader or dealer
**pitwright** carpenter working in or about a mine
**playwright** writer of dramatic pieces
**plowright** maker and repairer of plows
**potter** maker of fired earthenware vessels
**puttier** cementer; glazier
**rigger** scaffolder; person tending to rigging, esp. of ships or aircraft
**saddler** maker of horse saddles
**shipwright** builder of ships
**silversmith** forger or shaper of silver objects
**smith** worker who shapes or forges, esp. in metals, including: anvilsmith, blacksmith, bladesmith, boilersmith, clocksmith, coppersmith, goldsmith, gunsmith, hammersmith, ironsmith, jobsmith, knifesmith, locksmith, sawsmith, scissors smith, silversmith, stonesmith, swordsmith, tinsmith, toolsmith
**steeplejack** repairer of steeples and chimneys
**stonecutter** cutter, carver, and dresser of stone
**stonemason** cutter of stone or builder in stone
**tanner** maker of prepared animal hides
**tilewright** maker of tiles
**tinker** mender of metal objects
**turner** maker of articles turned on a lathe
**vintner** maker and seller of wines
**wainwright** maker of carts and wagons
**weaver** maker of textiles by loom or by mechanical or manual interlacing of threads
**welder** joiner of metals by use of heat
**wheelwright** maker and repairer of wheels
**woodcutter** chopper or engraver of wood
**wright** workman in construction; mechanic

## OCCUPATIONS AND JOB TITLES

accountant, account executive, acrobat, actor, actress, actuary, adjustor, adman, administrator, adviser, aeronautical engineer, aerospace engineer, agricultural engineer, agronomist, air traffic controller, ambassador, anthropologist, apartment manager, apparel salesperson, appraiser, archaeologist, architect, architectural engineer, archivist, arc welder, army engineer, artisan, artist, asbestos worker, astrologer, astronaut, astronomer, astrophysicist, athlete, attorney, auctioneer, auditor, au pair, author, automotive engineer, auto repairman, auto worker

babysitter, baggage handler, bailiff, baker, ballerina, banker, bank teller, barber, bartender, bath attendant, beautician, beekeeper, bellboy, bellhop, bench carpenter, billing clerk, biochemist, biologist, biophysicist, blacksmith, boarding housekeeper, body worker, boilermaker, boniface, bookbinder, bookie, bookkeeper, bootblack, botanist, bouncer, bounty hunter, brakeman, braze welder, brewer, bricklayer, brickmaker, bridge operator, broadcaster, broker, budget analyst, builder, bus driver, businessman, butcher, butler

cabdriver, cabinetmaker, calligrapher, candy maker, carny worker, carpenter, cartographer, carver, cashier, caster, caterer, cement mixer, ceramic engineer, ceramicist, chairman, chauffeur, checkout clerk, chef, chemical engineer, chemical worker, chemist, chief administrative officer, chief executive officer, chief operating officer, chimney sweep, chiropractor, choreographer, cinematographer, city manager, civil engineer, civil service employee, clergyman, clerk, clockmaker, clothier, clown, cobbler, commercial artist, commodities broker, common laborer, communications engineer, communications specialist, composer, comptroller, computer programmer, computer technician, concessionaire, conductor, confectioner, con man, construction engineer, construction worker, consul, contractor, cook, cooper, coppersmith, copyeditor, copywriter, coremaker, coroner, correctional officer, cosmetologist, costermonger, counselor, courier, couturier, cowboy, crier, critic, cryptographer, curator, custodian

dancer, data processor, dealer, decorator, defender, dental hygienist, dental supply salesman, dental technician, dentist, designer, detective, die maker, dietitian, diplomat, director, disc jockey, dishwasher, distiller, distributor, docent, doctor, doll maker, domestic, doorman, door-to-door salesman, drafter, drainage worker, dramatist, dramaturge, driver, dustman

ecologist, economist, editor, educator, electrical engineer, electrician, electronics engineer, electroplater, elevator operator, embalmer, embroiderer, employment agent, engine driver, engraver, ensign, entertainer, entrepreneur, etcher, evangelist, excavator, extra

farmer, farm hand, fashion designer, federal employee, field hand, fieldworker, file clerk, filmmaker, filtration worker, financier, firefighter, fireman, fire-protection engineer, firer, fisherman, fishery worker, fitter, flier, floor layer, food processor, forester, forest ranger, forger, forklift operator, founder, foundryman, freight operator, fuel engineer, furnace engineer, furniture maker

gamekeeper, game maker, garbageman, gardener, garment worker, gas fitter, gas welder, gate clerk, gem cutter, gem dealer, geneticist, geographer, geological engineer, geologist, glassblower, glazier, goldsmith, governess, government worker, grammarian, graphic artist,

gravedigger, groundskeeper, guard, guide, guru, gynecologist,

haircutter, hairdresser, hand sewer, handyman, hardware salesman, harvester, hatcheck person, hat maker, heat-treater, high school teacher, highway engineer, highwayman, historian, hod carrier, home economist, homemaker, horologist, hostess, hostler, houseboy, housecleaner, housekeeper, housewife, hunter, hydraulic engineer

illuminating engineer, illustrator, indexer, industrial engineer, industrialist, information clerk, inspector, installer, instrumentalist, insulation worker, insurance salesman, interior designer, intern, interpreter, interview clerk, investigator, investor, irrigation engineer

jailor, janitor, jester, jeweler, jewelry maker, journalist, judge, juggler, jurist, juror, justice

keypunch operator, kitchen worker, knitter

labor leader, lab technician, laundress, lawyer, layout artist, leatherworker, legal secretary, legislator, lexicographer, librarian, lighting technician, linguist, liquor salesman, lithographer, locker room attendant, locksmith, logger, logician, longshoreman, lumberjack

machine operator, machinist, magician, maid, mailroom worker, maintenance man, maître d'hôtel, manicurist, manufacturer, marine, marine biologist, marine engineer, marine mechanic, marshal, mason, masseur, master, mate, mathematician, meat cutter, mechanic, mechanical engineer, melter, mental health worker, mercer, mercerizer, merchandise displayer, messenger, metallurgical engineer, metallurgist, metal processor, metalworker, meteorologist, meter maid, midwife, migrant worker, military engineer, miller, miner, mining engineer, minister, model, model maker, molder, mold maker, mortician, municipal employee, municipal engineer, musician

nanny, naval engineer, navigator, net fisherman, newscaster, night watchman, novelist, nuclear engineer, nuclear physicist, nurse, nursemaid, nutritionist

obstetrician, occupational therapist, oceanographer, ombudsman, opera singer, ophthalmologist, optician, optometrist, orderly, ordnance engineer, ore refiner, orthopedist, osteopath

page, painter, paleontologist, paperhanger, park ranger, patternmaker, paver, payroll clerk, personnel officer, pest control worker, petroleum engineer, petroleum worker, pharmacist, philosopher, photoengraver, photographer, physical therapist, physician, physicist, physiologist, pickler, pilot, pimp, plasterer, plastics worker, playwright, plumber, poet, policeman, political scientist, politician, pornographer, porter, potter, power engineer, power plant operator, power supply engineer, practical nurse, president, press agent, press secretary, priest, printer, private investigator, producer, product engineer, production clerk, professor, projectionist, proofreader, proprietor, prosecutor, prostitute, psychiatrist, psychoanalyst, psychologist, public administrator, publicist, public relations man, public servant, publisher, puddler, purchasing agent

quality control officer

rabbi, rack jobber, radar engineer, radio commentator, radio engineer, radio operator, railroad conductor, railroad engineer, rancher, real estate broker, receptionist, refrigerator engineer, registered nurse, rehab counselor, repairman, research assistant, research engineer, researcher, retail clerk, rigger, riveter, road worker, rocket engineer, rocket scientist, roofer, rubber worker

sailor, sanitary engineer, screenwriter, scribe, sculptor,

seamstress, seaweed gatherer, secretary, securities analyst, security guard, semanticist, semiotician, serf, servant, service station attendant, sheet metal worker, shipper, ship's captain, ship's mate, shoemaker, shopkeeper, silversmith, slave, smuggler, social worker, sociologist, solderer, soldier, sole proprietor, solicitor, sound engineer, sound man, speech pathologist, spinner, sponge gatherer, sporting goods salesman, spotter, stainer, stand-in, state employee, statistician, steam engineer, steam fitter, steeplejack, stenographer, stevedore, stewardess, stockbroker, stock clerk, stonecutter, stonemason, stoneworker, street sweeper, structural engineer, stunt man, stylist, subcontractor, surgeon, surveyor, swami, systems analyst

tactician, tailor, talent agent, talent scout, tax collector, tax preparer, teacher, teamster, telegraph operator, telephone engineer, telephone operator, telephone repairman, teller, textile engineer, textile worker, therapist, thermal cutter, thief, ticket agent, ticket taker, tile setter, tinner, tinsmith, tobacconist, tobacco worker, toll taker, tool engineer, tour guide, tractor driver, trader, tradesman, trade unionist, traffic officer, translator, transportation engineer, transport worker, trapper, travel agent, traveling salesman, treasurer, tree farmer, truck driver, trucker, tutor, type-caster, type composer, typesetter, typist

undertaker, unskilled laborer, upholsterer, urban planner, usher, utility worker

valet, vending machine operator, vendor, ventilation engineer, venture capitalist, veterinarian, vice president, videotape engineer, vintner, vocalist, vocational therapist

waiter, waitress, wallpaperer, warden, warder, wardrobe attendant, warehouseman, waterproofer, water-supply engineer, waxer, weatherman, weaver, welder, welding engineer, wet nurse, wholesaler, winemaker, woodworker, wrecker, writer

yeoman

zookeeper, zoologist

# CHAPTER 13

# Social Sciences

# ANTHROPOLOGY

Branches and Disciplines
Ages, Species, and Races of Humankind
Kinship, Marriage, and Other Customs
Practice, Techniques, Artifacts, and Tools

**SEE ALSO**: Chap. 2: Biology; Chap. 3: Geology; Chap. 5:
Weapons and Armaments; Chap. 8: Kinship and Family
Relations; Marriage and Divorce; Chap. 13: Sociology;
Psychology; Chap. 25: Mythology and Folklore

## BRANCHES AND DISCIPLINES

**anthropogeography** study of geographical distribution of
humankind and relationship of peoples to their environment

**anthropological linguistics** study of relationship between
language and culture, esp. in preliterate societies

**anthropology** study of physical and sociocultural aspects of
humankind, including human origins, evolution, biological characteristics, customs, and belief systems

**applied anthropology** purposive study of specific, often
primitive society, esp. by authorities making practical decisions about it

**archaeology** scientific study of early historic and prehistoric cultures by excavation and analysis of their artifacts,
monuments, and other remains

**business anthropology** study of group behavior, workplace design, and other human problems derived from
corporate environments

**cultural anthropology** study of characteristics, similarities,
and differences among various human cultures, based esp.
on fieldwork and empirical data

**dendrochronology** method of dating past events by analysis of annual rings of trees

**epigraphy** study of ancient inscriptions

**ethnoarchaeology** study of contemporary primitive cultures, esp. as means of understanding prehistoric cultures

**ethnobiology** study of how different human cultures use
plants and animals

**ethnobotany** study of agricultural customs and plant lore of
a culture

**ethnography** systematic description of individual cultures

**ethnohistory** study of development of cultures, esp.
through analysis of archaeological findings

**ethnolinguistics** study of interplay between language and
culture

**ethnology** analysis of cultures, esp. with regard to their
historical development, similarities, and dissimilarities

**ethnomethodology** study of rules and rituals on which
most social interactions are based

**ethnomusicology** study of relationship between primitive
or folk music and culture to which it belongs

**ethnoscience** study of systems and concepts of knowledge
and classification of objects and concepts among primitive
peoples

**paleontology** study of life forms existing in earlier geologic
periods, based on their fossil remains

**philosophical anthropology** study of basic nature and essence of humankind

**physical anthropology** branch of anthropology concerned
with fossil origins of man, evolution, and human behavior

**praxeology** study of human conduct

**social anthropology** branch of anthropology concerned
with social relationships, esp. those institutionalized into
fixed behavior patterns such as ritual, religion, kinship,
marriage, and political and economic structures

**structural anthropology** branch of anthropology based on
principles of structural linguistics

## AGES, SPECIES, AND RACES OF HUMANKIND

**anthropoid** member of primate suborder Anthropoidea,
including monkeys, apes, and human beings

*Australopithecus* extinct genus of small-brained, large-toothed, bipedal hominid near-men whose fossil remains
date back to four million years in Africa and who had the
ability to stand fully erect

*Australopithecus afarensis* earliest species of *Australopithecus* that lived four million years ago in East Africa

*Australopithecus africanus* species of *Australopithecus*,
characterized by small stature and use of simple weapons,
that lived three million years ago

*Australopithecus boisei* species of rugged *Australopithecus*,
characterized by large teeth, that lived one to two million
years ago

*Australopithecus robustus* species of *Australopithecus*,
larger in stature but probably less intelligent than *Australopithecus africanus*, that lived two million years ago

**bipedalism** locomotion on two feet, characteristic of hominids

**Bronze Age** period beginning around 4000 B.C. characterized by use of bronze tools, the wheel, and ox-drawn
plows, and by growth of first civilizations in Egypt and
Sumeria

**Caucasian race** one of three traditional human racial
groupings, characterized by light skin pigmentation,
straight to curly hair, and light to dark eyes, inhabiting
Northern Hemisphere, esp. Europe

**cave man** cave dweller, esp. of Stone Age

**Copper Age** cultural period between Neolithic and Bronze
ages, characterized by ability to extract copper for use in
making tools

**Cro-Magnon man** tall, erect Upper Paleolithic prototype
of modern *Homo sapiens* in Europe between 40,000 and
30,000 years ago, that used stone tools and produced cave
paintings

**Eolithic Age** Dawn Stone Age, between 2.5 and two million years ago, in which hominoid near-men used primitive, fractured stone tools

**Folsom culture** early North American hunting-gathering
culture that flourished about 9000 B.C., characterized by
use of fluted stone spearheads

**Heidelberg man** species of primitive hominid contemporary with *Pithecanthropus* around 500,000 years ago, having
massive teeth but undeveloped chin

**hominid** any of modern or extinct bipedal primates of family Hominidae, including genera *Homo* and *Australopithecus*

**hominoid** member of superfamily Hominoidea, including modern great apes, humans, and their extinct ancestors

*Homo* genus of bipedal primates in family Hominidae, including modern *Homo sapiens* and several extinct species

*Homo erectus* extinct species of hominid, formerly known as *Pithecanthropus erectus*, known from Peking and Java man discoveries, having erect stature and postcranial skull but smallish brain, low forehead, and protruding face, characterized by use of crude stone tools and possibly simple speech, that lived from 500,000 to 250,000 years ago

*Homo habilis* extinct species of upright hominid in East Africa that existed two to 1.5 million years ago

*Homo sapiens* species of bipedal primate to which modern human beings belong, beginning 250,000 years ago during Stone Age with *Homo sapiens neanderthalensis*, characterized by use of tools and language

**humankind** all members of human race

**Iron Age** period following Bronze Age, in which humankind learned to smelt iron for tools and weapons, beginning around 2000 B.C. in Near East

**Java man** extinct race of early hominid, *Pithecanthropus erectus*, with apelike skull and human limb structure, whose skeletal remains were found in Java

**Lower Paleolithic period** earliest portion of Old Stone Age, between two million and 200,000 years ago

**Mesolithic period** Middle Stone Age following Paleolithic age, from 10,000 to 8000 B.C. in Europe, characterized by first food-producers, development of boats and sleds, and use of microliths

**Middle Paleolithic period** middle portion of Old Stone Age, between 200,000 and 40,000 years ago

**missing link** hypothetical species assumed to bridge evolutionary gap between anthropoid apes and human beings, sometimes identified as *Australopithecus*

**Mongoloid race** one of three traditional human racial groupings, characterized by yellowish complexion, straight black hair, and epicanthic folds about eyes, esp. inhabiting Asia

**Neanderthal man** extinct race of Middle Paleolithic man, powerful and physically robust with brain capacity comparable to modern man, that inhabited Europe and western Asia between 100,000 and 40,000 years ago

**Negroid race** one of three traditional human racial groupings, characterized by dark skin pigmentations, curly hair, and wide features, primarily inhabiting Southern Hemisphere, esp. Africa

**Neolithic period** New Stone Age preceding Bronze Age, between 8000 and 4000 B.C. in Near East, characterized by settlement into villages, domestication of animals, grain cultivation, pottery, textile weaving, cave painting, and flint-mining

**Olmec** (*adj*) of or pertaining to an early prehistoric New World civilization, from 1500 to 500 B.C. in Mexico, characterized by extensive agriculture, dating system, pyramids, trade, and fine artwork

**Paleolithic period** Old Stone Age period from two million years ago through 10,000 B.C., characterized by hunting-gathering society and use of increasingly sophisticated stone tools, divided into Lower, Middle, and Upper Paleolithic periods

**Peking man** extinct, early *Homo erectus* whose fossil remains were discovered in China, characterized by hunting and use of fire and stone tools

**Piltdown man** hypothetical early modern human being whose existence was based on skull fragments found in England, believed to be missing link between apes and man but later exposed as fake

*Pithecanthropus* former genus of extinct hominids now assigned to proposed species *Homo erectus*

**prehistoric man** certain hominid species of genus *Homo* that lived before recorded history

**prehistory** period of human development prior to recorded events, known through archaeological discoveries

**Proconsul** extinct hominoid subgenus that lived 17 to 20 million years ago and may have been ancestral to modern chimpanzees and apes

**protohistory** period of transition between prehistory and earliest recorded history

**pygmy** term denoting groups whose typical male averages less than 59 inches (150 cm) in height, generally hunter-gatherers with few crafts, found esp. in central Africa and Philippines

**race** one of the three major human groupings whose members tend to breed among themselves and share inherited physical characteristics: Caucasian, Mongoloid, Negroid

*Ramapithecus* extinct genus of late Miocene hominoid, formerly believed to have been ancestral to hominids, that lived about twelve million years ago

**recorded history** written record of history made by culture having formal language

**Stone Age** period beginning around two million years ago, characterized by use of increasingly sophisticated stone tools and weapons and, in latter ages, by development of food cultivation, villages, and crafts, usu. divided into Paleolithic, Mesolithic, and Neolithic periods and ending with dawn of civilization in Bronze Age around 4000 B.C.

**subrace** division within one of the three major human racial groupings, usu. inhabiting specific region

**Sumer** ancient region in Near East in which city-states and written language first developed in late Neolithic period, after 4000 B.C.

**troglodyte** prehistoric cave dweller

**Upper Paleolithic period** latter portion of Old Stone Age, between 40,000 and 10,000 B.C.

# KINSHIP, MARRIAGE, AND OTHER CUSTOMS

**affinity** kinship relationship based on marriage

**ancestor worship** veneration of spirits of dead ancestors believed to influence affairs of the living

**animism** belief in spiritual beings and esp. that natural objects and phenomena possess souls

**anthropophagy** cannibalism

**bigamy** accepted practice of marriage to more than one person at a time among certain cultures

**bride price** money or goods given by bridegroom or his family to bride's family

**cannibal** person who eats human flesh, esp. as part of tribal religious or magical ceremony

**cargo cult** any messianic native religious system found in southwestern Pacific islands, formed in response to white civilization, and characterized by belief that ancestors will return with cargoes of modern goods

**caste system**  any endogamous, hereditary social grouping based on status, economic position, and mores

**clan**  unilineal kinship descent group, either through male (patrilineal) or female (matrilineal) line

**collateral**  kin descended by different line from same stock

**conventionalized art**  art based on accepted manner of depicting subject matter; stylized art

**death rites**  ceremonies, burial, and mourning that accompany passage of person from world of the living to the dead

**decorative art**  ornamental designs applied to enhance beauty of objects having practical uses

**dietary laws**  secular or religious rules for what foods may be consumed under certain conditions, used to maintain group's unique social identity

**dominance relationships**  status systems within social groups based on power, possessions, and prestige

**dowry**  money or goods given by bride's family to bridegroom at marriage

**endogamy**  rules defining boundaries of marriage within specific tribe or social group; marriage within such tribe or group

**exogamy**  rules defining social unit within which marriage is forbidden; marriage outside specific tribe or social group

**extended family**  kinship group including nuclear family and relatives, esp. when living in one household

**family**  group of persons related by blood, esp. parents and children, forming basic biosocial unit

**head deformation**  changing of head shape in infancy by binding infant's soft head, practiced esp. in Pacific Northwest and Borneo

**headhunting**  taking and preserving the heads of one's enemies, practiced by certain primitive peoples

**henotheism**  worship of particular god by family or tribe without precluding belief in other deities

**hetaerism**  social system in which women are considered common property

**incest taboo**  prohibition and accompanying horror of sexual relations within defined exogamous kinship group

**kinship**  family relationships and system of social rules governing descent, inheritance, marriage, residence, and sexual relations within kinship groups

**marriage**  state in which two persons are bonded together under socially prescribed rules, esp. for procreation and child-rearing

**marriage rites**  religious, civil, and cultural traditions surrounding marriage ceremony

**matriarchy**  social organization in which mother is head of family and descent is traced through female line

**matrilineal** (*adj*) having descent traced through female line

**matrilocal** (*adj*) designating extended family in which husband joins household of wife's parents; uxorilocal

**moiety**  one of two divisions of tribe based on unilineal descent through either mother's or father's line

**monogamy**  social practice of marriage with only one person at a time

**naturalistic art**  realistic art

**neolocal** (*adj*) living away from both husband's and wife's relatives

**nuclear family**  basic family unit restricted to parents and their offspring

**patriarchy**  social organization in which father is head of family and descent is traced through male line

**patrilineal** (*adj*) having descent traced through male line

**patrilocal** (*adj*) designating extended family in which wife joins household of husband's parents; virilocal

**pecking order**  hierarchical social organization based on dominance relationships and submission of those lower in status

**polyandry**  practice of having more than one husband at a time

**polygamy**  socially approved practice of having more than one spouse at a time

**polygyny**  practice of having more than one wife at a time

**realistic art**  art that strives to represent objects with exact likenesses; naturalistic art

**representative art**  art that portrays nature and life in recognizable manner

**rite**  formal or ceremonial act or procedure prescribed in solemn and religious occasions

**rites of intensification**  ceremonies or rituals associated with periodic and seasonal events of crisis or special significance to a people

**rites of passage**  ceremonies or rituals that accompany individual's passage from one social status to another, such as puberty, initiation, marriage, and burial

**ritual**  established procedure or ceremony prescribed by custom for solemn occasions, such as rite of passage

**stylized art**  conventionalized art

**symbolic art**  art that employs symbols to signify objects and convey meaning

**taboo**  culture-specific prohibition of certain behavior, word, or object

**totem**  animal, plant, or object with which clan, tribe, or people identifies in its rituals, often believing it to be an ancestor

**tribe**  group of persons, usu. of common descent, occupying one community and sharing common language, customs, and traditions

**unilineal** (*adj*) having descent traced through either male or female line

**uxorilocal** (*adj*) matrilocal

**vendetta**  private, multigenerational family feud in which kin are obliged to avenge wrongs done their relatives

**virilocal** (*adj*) patrilocal

## PRACTICE, TECHNIQUES, ARTIFACTS, AND TOOLS

**aborigine**  one of original inhabitants of a region

**acculturation**  process of cultural change due to friendly or hostile interchange between two societies

**anthropometry**  measurement of size and proportions of human body using calibrated instrument

**artifact**  object made or used by human beings, esp. one found at archaeological excavation, providing evidence of an earlier culture's existence

**band**  group of wandering people, usu. from one tribe and comparable in size to village

**barrow**  tumulus

**bladelet**  small, blade-shaped, sometimes reworked piece of stone used as cutting edge of tool or weapon in late Stone Age

**cave dwellings** Stone Age dwellings, located in caves during Upper Paleolithic period

**cave paintings** art form characteristic of Upper Paleolithic period, practiced in European caves from around 30,000 B.C.

**cephalic index** measurement of head used in physical anthropology, consisting of ratio of maximum width to maximum length, with results classified as dolichocephalic (long-headed), mesocephalic, or brachycephalic (short-headed)

**cist** prehistoric tomb or casket with stone walls

**civilization** stage of cultural development marked by written records, development of cities, and advanced levels of science, government, and art; one culture or people of a specific place and time

**cliff dwellings** shelters in caves or on cliff ledges built by members of prehistoric people in southwestern United States

**convergent evolution** tendency of different lines of descent to develop similar characteristics in adapting to specific environmental conditions

**core tool** stone tool made by chipping flakes from stone core until it has assumed desired size and shape

**crannog** lake dwelling built on artificial island

**cromlech** megalithic chamber tomb

**cross dating** method of determining age for archaeological site of unknown age by comparing its distinguishing traits to those of another site of known age

**cultural relativism** concept that cultural traits and values derive from social context peculiar to specific culture

**culture** shared knowledge, beliefs, and ways of living built up by members of group and transmitted from one generation to next; specific group sharing such knowledge, beliefs, and ways of living over defined period of time

**culture area** geographical region in which neighboring groups share distinct patterns of culture

**culture complex** number of interrelated culture traits dominated by one essential trait

**culture diffusion** spread of culture traits or cultural patterns from central point and borrowing from one culture by another

**culture hero** mythical or idealized historical figure embodying goals and ideals of a people

**culture trait** any single characteristic of human activity acquired through social life and communicated across generations

**cuneiform** triangular or wedge-shaped pictographic writing system characteristic of cultures of ancient Near East from around 3500 B.C.

**Darwinism** theory of origin and evolution of species which postulates survival of the fittest individuals or species through natural selection, based on works of Charles Darwin

**dig** excavation

**dolmen** megalithic tomb consisting of stone slab laid across two or more large, upright stones

**enculturation** process of learning the culture of one's group or society, through observation, experience, and instruction

**ethnic group** people distinguished by common racial or cultural background

**ethnocentrism** belief in inherent superiority of one's own ethnic group or culture; tendency to view alien groups or cultures through prism of one's culture

**evolution** theory of development of species from simpler forms, based on work of Charles Darwin

**excavation** archaeological site at which layers of earth have been systematically exposed by digging to uncover human artifacts or remains of earlier cultures; dig

**flint** piece of hard stone used as primitive tool or to strike spark for making fire

**folklore** traditional beliefs, customs, and legends of a people, esp. those expressed orally through memory and practice

**folkways** patterns of behavior and belief common to particular group of people, learned from other members of group

**genealogy** study and record of family origins and history of descent

**geographical race** people or peoples isolated from other groups by major geographical barrier such as ocean or mountain range

**graffito** drawing or writing scratched on wall or other surface

**hand ax** large, bifacial stone tool of Lower Paleolithic period

**henge** Neolithic monument consisting of circular area enclosed by ditch and containing circles of upright stone or wood pillars, used for ritual purposes or astronomical observations

**hieroglyphics** pictographic script of ancient Egyptians, in which the symbols used are conventionalized, recognizable pictures of the things represented

**hunting-gathering society** any of the small-scale societies, primarily located in Southern Hemisphere, that subsist through hunting and collecting plants rather than by cultivation

**indigenous** native to or characteristic of a particular region

**kitchen midden** shell mound

**kiva** large, underground chamber used in Pueblo Indian religious ceremonies

**lake dwellings** remains of prehistoric settlements built on piles at shores of lakes in central Europe from Neolithic period into Iron Age

**Lascaux Cave paintings** fine Paleolithic wall paintings dating from 13,000 to 8500 B.C., found in cave in southwestern France

**megalithic monuments** large stone tombs and dolmens of undressed stone, such as Stonehenge, built in Europe during Neolithic period and early Bronze Age

**menhir** upright monumental stone standing alone or in arrangement with others

**microlith** tiny flint scraping tool for dressing skins, characteristic of Mesolithic cultures

**migration** movement of peoples from one geographical area to another

**monolith** monument such as obelisk constructed of a single, huge stone block, typical of Neolithic period

**nomadism** pastoral lifestyle in which group with no fixed residence moves from place to place on seasonal circuit

**nonliterate** (*adj*) preliterate

**pastoralism** often nomadic mode of subsistence, usu. among small groups, based on herding of domesticated livestock

**people** entire body of human beings forming one community, tribe, clan, nation, or other grouping

**petroglyph** prehistoric drawing or carving on stone

**potsherd** pottery fragment used in dating excavation sites or tracing cultural contacts, esp. in Neolithic period

**preliterate** (*adj*) designating culture or people who lack any writing system; nonliterate

**primitive** (*adj*) pertaining to preliterate or tribal people with strong cultural and physical similarities to their early ancestors

**primitive communism** way of life practiced among preliterate groups who shared possessions and cooperated closely to survive

**racial characteristics** physical traits such as skin pigmentation, hair quality, facial shape, or eye shape and coloring that distinguish one race

**Rosetta stone** stone slab, discovered in Egypt, bearing parallel inscriptions in Greek, Egyptian hieroglyphs, and demotic characters, facilitating decipherment of hieroglyphs

**seminomadism** pastoral lifestyle, esp. among Middle Eastern camel and goat herders, in which groups have settled abodes for part of year

**shell mound** prehistoric refuse heap containing remains of shellfish and human artifacts; kitchen midden

**site** exact location of single unit of territory studied by archaeologists

**society** autonomous community of persons sharing common customs, beliefs, goals, and attitudes, organized together under accepted rules

**sociocultural** (*adj*) of or pertaining to interaction of social and cultural elements

**stele** monumental, upright stone slab or pillar bearing an inscription or design

**Stonehenge** prehistoric, megalithic monument erected by a Bronze Age culture in England around 1500 B.C.

**tablets** flat rock slabs bearing hieroglyphs or cuneiform characters, used to reconstruct Bronze Age and Iron Age history

**Tepe Gawra** major excavation site in northern Iraq with twenty-six levels of cities dating to before 4000 B.C.

**trilithon** prehistoric structure consisting of two upright stones supporting a horizontal stone

**tumulus** artificial mound, esp. over grave; barrow

**village** small, settled community of several hundred people living together

**woodhenge** Neolithic henge monument constructed of upright timbers

# SOCIOLOGY

Attitudes and Behavior
Cultural Movements, Events, and Institutions
Social Types, Norms, and Symbols
Social Structure and Conditions
Schools and Doctrines
Tools and Techniques

**SEE ALSO**: Chap. 11: The City; Government; Politics; Chap. 12: Business and Economics; Chap. 13: Psychology; Education

## ATTITUDES AND BEHAVIOR

**ableism** discrimination against people having some physical or mental disability

**adaptation** ability to learn behavior that helps in adjusting to individuals, groups, and technology

**ageism** discrimination based on age

**agnosticism** belief that human beings cannot know whether there is a God or understand things beyond the material world

**American dream** popular belief that perseverance and hard work will bring forth America's bounty in the form of material well-being

**anthropocentric** (*adj*) regarding human beings as center of the universe

**anthropomorphism** attribution of human shape and character to animals, deities, or inanimate objects

**anti-Semitism** prejudice against and persecution of Jews

**antisocial** (*adj*) holding beliefs or taking actions harmful to well-being of society

**apartheid** policy of strict racial segregation and discrimination in South Africa

**apolitical** (*adj*) having no interest in politics

**atheism** conviction that there is no God

**bias** prejudice

**bigotry** intolerance of those different than oneself

**blackball** (*vb*) exclude socially

**brave new world** grand vision of benevolent, technological future in novel by Aldous Huxley, now considered ironic

**chauvinism** unreasoning devotion to one's race, sex, or country

**chic** (*adj*) pertaining to elegance and up-to-date style; (*n*) elegance and style

**civility** politeness, esp. as mere formality

**class consciousness** awareness of belonging to one class in the social order

**classism** discrimination based on class

**collective behavior** responses and reactions of groups, esp. crowds, to same stimuli

**color bar** barrier preventing nonwhites from living and working with whites

**conformity** living according to social expectations and norms

**convention** customary social practice or rule

**conventional** (*adj*) conforming to accepted social standards

**craze** latest passing popular fashion or idea

**crime against humanity** crime or crimes, such as genocide, directed against particular group that has committed no criminal act

**crusade** actions pursued zealously and vigorously to further some cause

**custom** traditional social convention enforced by general disapproval of its violation

**decorum** propriety and good taste; polite behavior

**dehumanize** (*vb*) make inhuman or machinelike

**deviance** marked divergence from society's accepted norms

**discrimination** different treatment for certain racial, ethnic, religious, or sexual groups

**double standard** moral code applying more stringent standards to one group than to another, esp. between sexes

**doxy** accepted belief, esp. religious

**ethnocentrism** belief that one's nation, culture, or ethnic group is superior

**ethos** characteristic and distinguishing attitudes and habits of group

**etiquette** established conventions of polite social intercourse

**fad** passing popular fashion

**fashion** current style, mode, or custom

**fellowship** companionship, generosity toward others

**flag-waving** display of zealous patriotism

**folklore** traditional beliefs, legends, and customs of one culture

**folkways** beliefs, preferences, and customs of social unit or group

**formality** propriety in observing prescribed customs

**general will** collective desire of a community

**groupthink** conformity to group values and ethics

**hard-line** (*adj*) uncompromising or unyielding in adherence to a dogma or plan, esp. in politics

**hero worship** idolizing of an individual, esp. a sports star or entertainer

**honor system** system that trusts people, esp. students or prisoners, to work honestly, without supervision

**horse-and-buggy** (*adj*) old-fashioned

**iconoclasm** opposition to accepted ideas and beliefs

**ideology** body of beliefs and ideas of one person, group, or culture

**individualism** view that society's primary goal is promotion of the individual over group welfare

**indoctrination** training others in one's beliefs

**internalization** incorporation of cultural values and attitudes within oneself, consciously or unconsciously

**ism** distinctive cause, doctrine, school, or principle

**isolationism** opposition to involvement in affairs external to one's community or nation

**Jim Crow** discrimination against blacks

**jingoism** excessive, often warlike, national chauvinism

**latest thing** fad or current fashion

**left** political liberalism; radical end of political spectrum

**lifestyle** consistent pattern of one's life, attitudes, customs, values, and economic standing

**manners** prevailing customs of polite, conventional behavior

**martyrdom** willingness to die rather than renounce one's beliefs or principles

**mass hysteria** irrational behavior on a wide scale caused by unfounded belief or fear

**master race** race that is supposedly biologically equipped to rule all others

**middle-of-the-road** (*adj*) favoring a point of view midway between extremes

**mode** current fashion or style

**mores** essential folkways and binding customs of a society

**nationalism** patriotism, belief in one's country

**networking** developing and maintaining a system of professional contacts aimed at furthering one's career

**nihilism** belief that there is no purpose to existence; rejection of established laws and institutions

**nonviolence** abstention from use of violence on moral grounds

**particularism** exclusive adherence to one doctrine, system, or interest

**passive resistance** opposition to established government by nonviolent acts of noncooperation

**Peter Principle** tendency in large organizations for people to rise to their level of incompetence

**politically correct** (*adj*) marked by or conforming to typically progressive, orthodox views such as environmentalism, pacifism, and social equality for those outside the white male power structure and Western, Judeo-Christian tradition

**preferential treatment** treatment of one person or group better than others based on social status

**prejudice** predisposition toward baseless intolerance and hatred for particular group; bias

**pro-choice** (*adj*) supporting the right to legal abortion

**pro-life** (*adj*) opposing the right to legal abortion

**propriety** socially acceptable conduct

**provincialism** narrow concern with one's own locale or people

**public service** work in the public interest, often for government

**purge** elimination of those regarded as undesirables, esp. from government without due process

**race riot** riot motivated by racial fear or hatred

**racism** segregation and persecution based on doctrine of superiority of one race over others

**rage** extremely popular fashion, usu. short-lived

**redbait** (*vb*) accuse an individual or group of being communist

**regionalism** devotion to culture of one's native area

**religious tolerance** acceptance of those practicing faith different from one's own

**reverse discrimination** bias against majority as a result of efforts to improve lot of minority

**right** political conservatism; reactionary end of political spectrum

**right-to-life** (*adj*) pertaining to opposition to right to legal abortion based on belief that fetus is a person

**right-to-work** (*adj*) pertaining to right of workers to employment regardless of labor union status

**ritualistic** (*adj*) performed according to a rigidly prescribed order

**role** pattern of expected behavior for individual in given situation in relation to social status

**role conflict** problems that occur when a person's roles conflict with each other or with his or her values

**scapegoating** blaming members of minority group for social or economic problems

**sectionalism** devotion to interests of one's native region

**segregation** social separation, esp. of races

**separatism** policy of racial, cultural, or national autonomy

**sexism** discrimination and denial of opportunity on basis of sex, esp. against women

**sexual harassment** unwanted advances and persistent pestering for sexual favors, esp. by person in position of authority such as employer

**social perception** manner in which people's perceptions of others are shaped by previous experience, attitudes, and expectations

**states' rights** rights belonging to each state rather than to federal government, esp. in connection with social policies

**style** current fashionable way of dressing, speaking, or acting

**suppression** forceful quelling of an idea or movement

**taboo** prohibition or superstition established through accepted social custom

**taste** attitude or style reflecting group preference at particular time

**territoriality** powerful attachment to physical area perceived as one's own property

**terrorism** use of wanton violence for political goals

**Titanism** open revolt against established social standards

**tokenism** practice of making a token gesture by hiring or admitting a small number of minority group members

**tolerance** liberal attitude toward differing lifestyles, cultures, and beliefs

**tradition** long-established custom or practice of a society

**trendy** (*adj*) following the latest fashion

**tribalism** intense loyalty to one's own group

**un-American** (*adj*) opposed to or inconsistent with the accepted notion of American ideals and institutions

**unfashionable** (*adj*) out of date

**universal** (*adj*) held by everyone

**up-to-date** (*adj*) conforming to latest styles and beliefs

**upward mobility** ascension of the socioeconomic ladder

**values** principles, standards, and goals given high intrinsic worth by society

**vogue** latest fashion

## CULTURAL MOVEMENTS, EVENTS, AND INSTITUTIONS

**affirmative action** program to increase presence of women and minorities in public and private sectors

**antinuke** (*adj*) *Informal.* opposed to development and use of nuclear weapons or energy

**asphalt jungle** the city, esp. crowded, urban neighborhoods regarded as dangerous

**baby boom** burst of population in generation born just after World War II

**backlash** reaction opposite to that intended by a particular social movement

**Bible Belt** area of United States, particularly in South and Midwest, noted for religious fundamentalism

**Big Brother** officials of authoritarian state that erodes privacy of the individual to exercise control

**blacklist** privately circulated list of those to be denied employment because of allegedly subversive views

**Black Muslims** militant Islamic sect of black Americans who advocate racial separation, asceticism, and formation of a black state

**black nationalism** advocacy of establishment of separate black nation in United States

**Black Panthers** radical black power organization of 1960's

**black power** political and economic power sought by black Americans

**boom** swift and vigorous economic growth with accompanying societal euphoria

**boycott** group refusal to patronize a business or another person or group for economic or political reasons

**brain drain** ebbing of nation's intellectual and professional resources through emigration

**busing** transferring schoolchildren out of their neighborhoods to achieve racial balance in schools

**Camelot** the White House under John F. Kennedy from 1961 to 1963

**cause** principle or movement vigorously upheld and supported

**childcare** care for preschool children of employed parents, esp. at day-care center

**civil disobedience** nonviolent refusal to comply with laws or official policy on moral grounds

**civil rights** rights guaranteeing equal opportunity to all citizens, regardless of race, religion, sex, or national origin

**consciousness-raising** increasing awareness, esp. among women, of their secondary status and particular group needs and goals through interaction with other women

**conspicuous consumption** extravagant spending to enhance social status

**cooptation** winning over of an adversary to one's own belief

**counterculture** culture and lifestyle of late 1960's, esp. among young, characterized by opposition to war and society's prevailing values

**credibility gap** difference between official pronouncements and what is believable

**crisis intervention** intervention by group offering immediate help to potential suicides, addicts, and other troubled persons

**Cultural Revolution** radical sociopolitical movement in China during 1960's in which Mao Zedong attempted to restructure society and reinvigorate his revolution

**culture of poverty** values, attitudes, and behavior believed to be common to the poor

**culture shock** trauma resulting from movement from one culture or society to another

**current affairs** events, movements, institutions, and trends in political and social life at present time

**deracination** uprooting from one's social or cultural environment

**designer** (*adj*) originally designed by and carrying label of fashion designer, now used to describe various products considered unique or superior

**environmentalism** active concern for state of Earth's natural resources

**equal opportunity employment** hiring of employees without regard to race, sex, or national origin

**establishment** society's ruling class, representing all vested interests

**ethnic group** minority group linked by language, origin, culture, or religion within larger society

**fallout** radioactive residue that falls to Earth after nuclear explosion; repercussions of any event

**feminism** doctrine and programs promoting rights and interests of women, esp. in male-dominated society

**food stamps** government-provided food coupons for low-income families

**freedom rides** bus trips made by activists traveling south to work for racial integration, esp. in 1960's

**free university** institution for study of nontraditional subjects, usu. in unstructured curriculum

**free world** non-Communist world

**future shock** disorientation and anxiety due to inability to cope with continual, rapid, technological change and breakdown of old values

**gay liberation** sociopolitical movement to combat legal and social discrimination against homosexuals

**gay power** organized political influence exerted by homosexuals as a group, esp. to achieve equal rights and social justice

**genetic engineering** biological creation of improved species through recombining of spliced DNA from different species

**genocide** organized attempt to destroy an entire people or race

**gentrification** restoration of run-down urban neighborhoods by upper- or middle-income families

**global village** the world as one single community, esp. owing to mass media, communications, and rapid transportation

**Götterdämmerung** collapse of society linked with catastrophic violence and disorder, orig. from German mythology

**green revolution** increased food production for underdeveloped nations through improved agricultural methods

**grievance committee** group chosen to represent employer and employees to resolve workers' problems

**groundswell** rapidly growing wave of popular sentiment or opinion, often lacking overt leadership

**halfway house** place for societal readjustment after institutional confinement

**haut monde** high society

**hip-hop** *Slang*. popular subculture of urban youth, esp. African Americans, based in part on rap music, break dancing, and graffiti art

**hippies** youth culture of 1960's, alienated from society and interested in mysticism, psychedelic drugs, nature, pacifism, and sexual freedom

**holocaust** large-scale destruction of human life

**Holocaust** systematic murder of European Jews by the Nazis during World War II

**hotline** direct telephone line to assistance, for use in personal crisis

**hunger strike** refusal to eat, usu. by prisoners or demonstrators, until certain demands are met

**information explosion** computer-generated rapid increase in data available in all fields

**inner city** blighted, poor section of metropolitan area

**iron curtain** former military and ideological barrier isolating Soviet-controlled Eastern Europe

**Kremlinology** study of government and policies of Soviet Union

**Ku Klux Klan** anti-black, anti-Semitic, anti-Catholic, white supremacist secret organization advocating violence

**land reform** redistribution of agricultural land to peasants and small farmers

**legal aid** free representation by attorney for those unable to pay fees

**lib** *Informal*. liberation, usu. used after group name, as in women's lib

**life-care** (*adj*) designed to provide for basic needs of elderly residents, usu. in return for a regular fee

**love-in** gathering of people for purpose of demonstrating mutual love or protesting inhumane policies

**lunatic fringe** extreme minority on periphery of any larger movement

**Main Street** provincial, conservative small-town life

**mammon** material wealth seen as evil

**McCarthyism** use of sensationalism and accusations to uncover supposed Communists in government in 1950's

**Me Decade** decade of 1970's, supposedly reflecting self-indulgence, narcissism, and lack of social concerns in youth, esp. as reaction to 1960's

**movement** organized actions taken by group working together to achieve specific goal

**nativism** policy of reviving or maintaining a native culture

**New Left** political movement of young people, esp. in 1960's and 1970's, seeking social change

**old-world** (*adj*) pertaining to traditional European customs and values

**peaceful coexistence** policy of cooperation and noninterference between United States and Soviet Union

**Planned Parenthood** *Trademark*. organization that disseminates information on birth control and sexually transmitted diseases

**pop culture** contemporary style, art, and media

**population explosion** rapid rise and continued increase of population

**pronuclear** (*adj*) supporting the development and use of nuclear energy

**radical chic** patronage of extremists and left-wing radicals by the rich and famous, sometimes without genuine conviction

**rally** mass demonstration in support of specific cause

**recycling** reprocessing of used paper, metals, and other waste materials to conserve national resources

**redevelopment** renovation of urban slum area

**rent strike** tenant refusal to pay rent until housing is improved

**resistance** organized underground movement opposing foreign occupation or government repression

**revolution** violent overthrow of government resulting in change in social order

**riot** violent, large-scale public disturbance, often for purposes of protest

**samizdat** clandestine circulation of banned manuscripts in former Soviet Union

**Satyagraha** Gandhian way to social reform through tolerance and nonviolent passive resistance (India)

**sect** faction of larger group or movement

**sexual revolution** era of promiscuity and open sexuality beginning in 1960's

**shelter** place where homeless people can sleep; underground refuge for use in event of nuclear attack

**sit-in** occupation of an institution to protest its policies

**soup kitchen** place set up in run-down neighborhood to feed poor and homeless

**special interest group** group seeking to advance specific cause by gaining government favors

**storefront group** self-help community action group housed in storefront

**Sunbelt** southern and southwestern United States, characterized by political conservatism since 1960's

**teach-in** lectures and debates at university or college to protest school's policy

**technetronic** (*adj*) influenced or characterized by advances in technology and electronics applied to social problems

**test ban** multinational agreement to stop nuclear testing

**think tank** government- or business-sponsored group organized for problem solving and intensive research

**Third World** underdeveloped countries of world

**ticky-tacky** (*adj*) *Informal*. relating to dull uniformity of style, esp. in housing development

**tobacco road** poor southern rural area, characterized by hopelessness and despair

**underground** secret resistance organization, esp. in totalitarian country

**urbanization** transformation of rural or suburban areas to urban ones

**urban renewal** redevelopment of run-down parts of city

**women's liberation** movement to combat sexual discrimination and achieve full rights and opportunities for women equal to men, orig. late 1960's

**women's movement** broad-ranging activities and beliefs involving legal, social, economic, vocational, educational, and personal rights of women in male-dominated society

## SOCIAL TYPES, NORMS, AND SYMBOLS

**African American** preferred term for black Americans of African descent and for their culture

**apologist** one who justifies a questionable cause or doctrine

**Asian American** preferred term for Americans of Asian descent and for their culture

**baby boomer** person born just after World War II

**bag lady** poor, homeless, usu. old woman living in streets and carrying belongings in shopping bag; shopping bag lady

**battered child** child physically abused by his or her parents

**battered wife** woman physically abused by her husband

**beatnik** member of Beat Generation of 1950's, who were nonconformist in dress, attitude, and artistic expression

**beautiful people** wealthy or famous trendsetters

**Bircher** member or follower of John Birch Society, an extremely conservative political group

**bitch goddess** stereotype of dominating, complaining, beautiful woman

**black** preferred term from 1960's to 1980's for Americans of African descent, formerly called Negroes

**blue blood** member of aristocratic or socially prominent family

**blue book** directory of socially prominent persons

**blue-collar** (adj) pertaining to class of workers who perform manual and unskilled labor or factory work

**boat people** refugees who fled Southeast Asia in boats, and to whom few countries granted asylum

**bohemian** person living unconventionally, esp. an artist

**brother** term denoting comradeship, esp. among blacks

**café society** fashionable high society

**canaille** riffraff

**colored** former term for American blacks, now considered pejorative

**conscientious objector** person who refuses to serve in armed forces on religious or moral grounds

**cracker** *Derogatory slang.* poor southern white person

**DINK** *dual income, no kids;* married couple without children, both of whom work

**dissenter** person who rejects established doctrines

**dissident** person who rejects establishment and often attempts to sway others into opposition

**dominant group** those in society setting norms, values, and standards

**dropout** person who leaves a program, esp. school, before completion; one who lives by norms alien to society

**empty nester** parent whose child or children have moved away from home

**everyman** typical or common man

**expatriate** person who has rejected allegiance to native land and lives elsewhere

**fellow traveler** Communist party sympathizer

**flapper** young woman of 1920's who behaved and dressed boldly and unconventionally

**flower child** hippie

**folk** common people

**football widow** woman whose husband ignores her on weekends or certain weekday nights to watch football on television

**fugitive** person who has run away from danger or justice

**gaybasher** heterosexual, often homophobic male, who physically assaults or defames gays

**glitterati** chic, wealthy, famous people

**golf widow** woman whose husband ignores her to play golf

**good old boy** *Informal.* stereotypical white male of U.S. South who drinks beer, hunts, jokes, and socializes with his friends

**gray eminence** one who exercises great power unofficially

**Grundy** personification of conventional social disapproval and narrow-mindedness

**hard-hat** *Informal.* working-class person, often holding politically conservative ideas

**high society** those who are fashionable, wealthy, and famous

**hillbilly** person from backwoods or remote rural area, esp. in U.S. South

**hippie** member of 1960's youth culture, alienated from society and interested in mysticism, pacifism, nature, psychedelic drugs, and sexual freedom; flower child

**hoi polloi** common people

**homeland** mother country

**homeless** those who have no permanent place to live and frequently sleep in streets

**honky** *Derogatory slang.* white person, esp. as referred to by nonwhites

**in-crowd** group with common interests and feelings of solidarity and exclusivity; in-group

**indigenous** (adj) native

**in-group** in-crowd

**intelligentsia** intellectual and academic leaders

**jet set** rich, fashionable group frequently traveling in pursuit of pleasure

**John Doe** anonymous average man

**John Q. Public** average person

**junta** military group that takes power after coup

**Latino** person of Latin-American or Spanish-speaking descent; preferred term for such Americans and for their culture

**leading edge** forefront of movement; new ideology or theory

**leftist** radical of political Left

**liberal** one who favors progressive, democratic political reform

**life of Riley** *Informal.* comfortable, carefree lifestyle

**literati** persons of letters

**lonely-hearts** (adj) pertaining to persons seeking companionship or love

**loose cannon** person whose reckless behavior endangers efforts or welfare of others

**lumpenproletariat** segment of underclass degraded by nonproductivity and shiftlessness, including tramps, beggars, and criminals

**lynch mob** mob that murders an accused person, esp. by hanging

**man about town** worldly man who is a member of fashionable society

**man in the street** average person

**mass society** impersonal modern society

**Middle American** middle-class Americans, esp. living in Midwest

**minority group** group within larger society with different language, culture, or religion, often subject to discrimination

**mob** disorderly or riotous crowd of people, often bent on or engaged in lawless violence

**moral majority** largely fundamentalist, conservative Christians of Middle America

**mother country** one's native land or that of one's ancestors

**needy** poor, destitute persons

**Negro** member of the peoples traditionally classified as the Negro race and usu. of sub-Saharan African descent, now called black or African American

**out-group** all those not part of the in-crowd or in-group

**pecking order** hierarchy of social dominance within group

**people** all citizens of one state or nation or of the world

**power elite** those in control of nation's government, economy, and resources

**pressure group** collection of like-minded people seeking to influence policies

**public** people of one community or nation as a whole

**rabble** disorderly crowd

**rank and file** ordinary people constituting major part of an organization, esp. a labor union

**reference group** social group that an individual views as the standard against which to judge his or her own actions

**refugee** person who flees his or her home or country to seek safety from war or persecution

**refusenik** *Informal.* Soviet citizen, esp. a Jew, who was denied permission to emigrate

**role model** person whom others copy when developing attitudes, values, and behavior patterns

**sacred cow** individual or institution deemed exempt from criticism or questioning

**scab** worker who refuses to honor strike or join a labor union

**semiskilled worker** manual laborer with some training

**senior citizen** person who is elderly or aged, esp. one living on a pension

**shopping bag lady** bag lady

**significant other** live-in lover, mate, or spouse

**silent majority** large, conservative group of Middle America whose views are supposedly unheard due to vocal protests on left and right

**silk-stocking** member of wealthy or aristocratic class

**single parent** one person, usu. divorced or never married, supporting and caring for a child or children

**slumlord** owner of substandard housing

**smart set** fashionable high society

**social outcast** person outside of or excluded from normal society

**squatter** unlawful settler on land or in abandoned housing

**stereotype** oversimplified, often unfavorable, commonly held picture of all members of certain group

**storm trooper** member of violent, brutal army corps, orig. a Nazi

**stowaway** one who hides on a vehicle to get free passage

**straw boss** member of work crew who supervises his or her colleagues

**street person** homeless person living on city streets

**strikebreaker** worker who returns to work during strike

**suffragette** militant female advocate of women's right to vote

**teenybopper** *Slang.* female teenager, esp. one following adolescent fashions and trends

**temp** *Informal.* temporary worker

**Tom, Dick, and Harry** common man; people generally

**transient** homeless person looking for work or place to live

**troglodyte** individual with reclusive habits or outmoded behavior; outcast from society

**turnover** number of employees replaced in given time period

**Ugly American** American visitor or diplomat abroad who behaves in an offensive manner and is insensitive to foreign customs

**Uncle Sam** personification of U.S. government as bearded man in red, white, and blue top hat

**Uncle Tom** black whose behavior is regarded as servile

**underage** (*adj*) below legal age, usu. for drinking or sex

**underdog** victim of social injustice; one attempting to overcome adversity

**underprivileged** (*adj*) socially and economically deprived

**unperson** someone treated as if he or she does not exist

**unskilled** (*adj*) having no job training or vocation

**untouchable** person outside and below the Hindu caste system

**upper crust** aristocratic, wealthy high society

**urban guerrilla** member of violent, terrorist, underground political group in urban area, esp. in 1970's

**vanguard** leaders or advance position of political or artistic movement

**wannabe** person who idealizes successful individuals and imagines being like them

**WASP** *w*hite *a*nglo-*s*axon *p*rotestant; member of dominant group setting standards and values of American society

**Woodstock nation** generation of baby boomers who came of age in 1960's, esp. those subscribing to counterculture epitomized by Woodstock music festival

**working mother** employed mother of young child

**working poor** employed persons living at subsistence level

**Yuppie** *y*oung *u*rban *p*rofessional characterized as ambitious, materialistic, and faddish

## SOCIAL STRUCTURE AND CONDITIONS

**acculturation** adaptation to the customs of a culture

**age groups** divisions of society based on custom and age of members

**anomie** condition in which social norms have weakened or disappeared

**assimilation** integration of customs and values from previously distinct cultures into dominant culture

**atomism** society composed of clearly distinct elements and factions

**biculturalism** presence of two distinct cultures in one society

**biracial** (*adj*) involving or including two races

**birthrate** number of births per thousand in given population

**bondage** servitude or subjugation

**bracket** division of society based on age, income, or other demographic factor

**bureaucracy** authority concentrated in complicated structure of administrative bodies

**caste** station in life defined by birth, more rigid than class and allowing no chance for change

**centralization** power and authority in hands of one central agency

**circle** group bound together by common interests and activities

**clan** group with interest in common, often related persons

**class** social rank according to status, economic interest, and way of life

**classless** (*adj*) free from social class distinctions

**clique** small, exclusive circle of people; coterie

**collective behavior** common, spontaneous reaction of a group of people to the same event

**colony** community of those with similar interests, often isolated or concentrated in particular place

**commonweal** general welfare

**communalism** system of collective groups devoted to their own interests rather than to those of society as a whole

**commune** small group living together, usu. sharing work, earnings, and specific value system

**community** any group with shared interests, feelings, values, or geographic location

**community center** meeting place offering recreational and educational activities for community

**coterie** clique

**counterculture** segment of society with values and lifestyle opposed to those of prevailing culture

**crosscurrents** conflicting tendency or movement that may impede functioning of an institution

**cross-fertilization** exchange of values, customs, and ideas between different societies or groups within a society

**culture** values, beliefs, customs, and art of a specific society; civilization

**disempowerment** loss of influence, significance, or rights by individual or group

**dominant group** group setting society's norms, values, and standards

**dynamic culture** society undergoing rapid change

**enculturation** socialization into cultural mainstream

**endogamy** mating within one's social group

**environment** social conditions and surroundings as they affect behavior and attitudes

**ethnic group** societal subgroup with common cultural, religious, national, or racial heritage

**etiquette** established conventions of polite social intercourse

**extended family** relatives of different generations living together or in close proximity

**favela** shantytown or slum in or near a Brazilian city

**ghetto** section of city to which minority group is confined or lives by choice

**ghost town** permanently abandoned town, esp. in U.S. Old West

**group dynamics** intersection of individuals within group

**guild** association for promotion of common aims

**heterogeneous** (*adj*) composed of varied elements

**homeostasis** tendency of society to maintain social stability

**homogeneous** (*adj*) composed of similar elements

**humanity** entire human race; humankind;

**humankind** all members of the human race; humanity; mankind

**indigenous** (*adj*) native to a specific society or region

**individuation** loss of class identity by individuals

**industrial** (*adj*) related to industry; nonagricultural

**inequality** lack of fairness or justice in society

**infrastructure** basic facilities and systems serving country, region, or city, including transportation, communications, power, and schools

**institution** established pattern of norms and values; organization that meets important group or social needs

**institutional family** family in which propagation of race and care of children take precedence over happiness and personal freedom of parents

**institutionalization** making permanent certain patterns of behavior and values

**institutionalized racism** racial discrimination not based on individual attitudes but inherent in social structures and institutions

**interaction** coming together of individuals with mutual influence

**kibbutz** collective farm in Israel

**kinship group** extended family

**kolkhoz** collective farm in Soviet Union

**labefaction** decline in public morality and social order

**lily-white** (*adj*) exclusive of all nonwhites

**living standard** level of comfort, economic security, and stability

**lower class** working class, characterized by low standard of living

**macrocosm** model that is a large-scale and complex representation, often of one of its components

**mankind** humanity; humankind

**matriarchy** society in which mother is family or tribal head and descent is traced through female line

**melting pot** society that incorporates diverse social and cultural groups

**microcosm** group believed to be representative of a much larger entity

**middle class** socioeconomic group with comfortable standard of living and conventional beliefs and lifestyle

**mythos** underlying and enduring attitudes and beliefs characteristic of a society, esp. in connection with supernatural forces

**neighborhood** community of people living near one another

**norms** customary standards of behavior in a society, reflecting its values

**nuclear family** usu. married couple and their children

**paternalism** firm, fatherly control of government or employees

**patriarchy** society in which father is family or tribal head and descent is traced through male line

**peer group** those of same age and social position

**petite bourgeoisie** lower middle class

**phenotype** appearance of an organism resulting from interaction of heredity and environment

**pluralism** existence of diverse cultural groups within one society

**polarization** concentration of group interests around opposite extremes rather than along a continuum

**police state** country in which police suppress activities that conflict with government policy

**poverty line** economic level beneath which people are considered to be living in poverty

**power structure** those established in ruling positions in government or other institutions

**primary group** those with close, intimate relationships, such as family groups

**Procrustean bed** pattern into which one is arbitrarily forced

**psychosocial** (adj) relating psychological development to social environment

**public** the people as a whole; the community at large

**public assistance** government-funded social welfare programs for the needy; relief

**race** group of people with traits transmitted by descent sufficient to distinguish distinct human type

**rat race** Informal. intense, exhausting, usu. competitive urban business life that leaves little time for leisure life

**relief** public assistance

**reservation** public land on which American Indians are resettled

**rite** traditional, customary, often ceremonial or formal observance or procedure

**ritual** established practice or procedure performed regularly as a rite

**royalty** hereditary social class that rules certain countries

**rural** (adj) lying outside developed cities, in the countryside

**scarcity** period or condition of inadequate supply of food or other raw material

**secondary group** people relating on an impersonal, formal level, such as business colleagues

**secret police** undercover police used by totalitarian governments to observe and apprehend dissenters

**sect** faction of larger group

**servitude** subjection to a master or mistress

**shantytown** section of city with substandard housing, esp. rickety little huts

**skid row** area of city frequented by alcoholics and vagrants

**slavery** involuntary servitude

**slum** densely populated urban area marked by crowding, poverty, poor housing, and social disorder

**social codes** accepted, often unwritten, rules of behavior and value systems

**social contract** theoretical agreement between people to establish government and abide by its laws

**social convention** norm of behavior or belief

**social intercourse** exchange of thoughts or feelings

**socialization** process by which a child acquires and internalizes society's beliefs, values, and habits, so as to become functioning member of group

**Social Register** Trademark. book that lists members of high society

**social structure** framework of society's institutions governing interpersonal and group relations

**social welfare** system of services for improving condition of the disadvantaged

**society** institutions and value systems of people with similar traditions and customs who inhabit same geographical area over several generations; autonomous structure based on such institutions and value systems that provides group identity and basis for community living

**squalor** poverty, filth, and moral degradation

**standard of living** level of subsistence, esp. with regard to basic economic necessities

**starvation wages** wages too low to provide subsistence

**status** relative position within group or society

**status quo** existing state of affairs

**stock** race or ethnic group

**strain** subdivision within general race or ethnic group

**strata** specific socioeconomic level of society

**subculture** group within society whose social status, ethnic background, religion, or shared values and interests distinguish it from others in that society or culture

**subsistence** basic means required to support life

**substandard** (adj) beneath legal or acceptable levels

**suburbia** social and cultural aspects of life in residential communities lying just outside a city

**system** unity formed of diverse parts arranged according to a common plan

**technology** application of science to practical affairs

**telesis** planned progress through use of natural and social forces

**trend** prevailing direction in which society is moving at a given time

**underclass** lowest level of society, consisting of impoverished persons with low social status, often self-perpetuating from generation to generation

**underdeveloped** (adj) designating poor countries of Third World

**upper class** highest level of society, made up of those with wealth, power, and prestige

**urban** (adj) relating to cities

**vacuum** isolation from society

**victimless crime** illegal act, such as prostitution, to which all parties have consented

**zero population growth** condition in which birthrate and death rate are equal and population remains constant, esp. due to family planning

## SCHOOLS AND DOCTRINES

**anomie** state or condition marked by breakdown or absence of social norms and values

**behavioral science** study of human activity in attempt to discover recurrent patterns and postulate rules

**behaviorism** theory that all human behavior is learned or based on conditioning and that observed behavior forms only valid data

**biosociology** study of interactions between human biological characteristics and social behavior

**conflict theory** view of society as groups in conflict

**criminology** scientific study of crime, criminal nature, and its impact on society

**cultural diffusion** spread of cultural characteristics from one society to another

**determinism** theory that choice of action is determined by causes other than human will

**ekistics** scientific study of human settlements and communities

**environmental determinism** theory that social environment rather than hereditary factors determines personality

**ergonomics** study of adjustment to environment, esp. in workplace

**eugenics** science dealing with improvement of hereditary factors through social control of reproduction

**euthenics** science dealing with improvement of hereditary factors for human welfare through environmental control

**evolutionary theory** belief in gradual, sequential development of society

**functionalism** social theory of Emile Durkheim emphasizing integration of institutions, their interaction with society, and consensus of values that is external to individual and influences his or her actions

**human ecology** study of how human beings relate to their political, economic, and social environment

**humanism** nontheistic, rationalist belief that people are capable of self-fulfillment and ethical conduct without recourse to the supernatural

**industrial sociology** study of social relationships and institutions as influenced by industry

**interactionist doctrine** belief that social processes and institutions derive from one person reacting to action of another

**labeling theory** view that society creates deviance by prematurely labeling a person as inadequate or undesirable

**linguistics** study of structure, development, social impact, and interrelationship of languages

**looking-glass theory** theory that people develop their sense of self in response to how they think others see them

**metalinguistics** study of relationship of language to other culturally determined behavior

**mutualism** social dependence for general welfare

**occupational sociology** study of working roles on a broader scale than in industrial sociology

**penology** branch of criminology that evaluates programs and institutions dealing with criminals

**Protestant ethic** theory of Max Weber that the hard work and frugal life conducive to capitalism developed from the Calvinist doctrine of predestination

**rising expectations** theory that revolutions are more likely to occur as social and economic conditions begin to improve, causing increased expectations and frustration

**Social Darwinism** view that individuals will advance in society based on their ability to adapt to living conditions

**social pathology** study of social factors, such as poverty or crime, that tend to increase social disorganization and inhibit personal adjustment

**social science** scientific study of different aspects of society, including disciplines of political science, anthropology, sociology, criminology, and economics

**sociocultural approach** propaganda theory based on defining cultural norms that guide people's social behavior

**sociology** application of specific doctrines and techniques to systematic study of social institutions, collective behavior, and human relationships

**sociology of knowledge** study of relationships between social and political structures and intellectual life

**sociology of leisure** study of social impact of increased leisure as by-product of technology and modernization

**structural functionalism** analysis of social phenomena within narrowly defined concepts of observable structures and functional consequences

**structuralism** theory based on study of social status systems and interdisciplinary analysis of social behavior, used to define the patterns of interaction between diverse modes of behavior that form society's underlying structure

**urban sociology** study of the relationship between urban environment and social structures within it

## TOOLS AND TECHNIQUES

**case study** study and research that analyzes a single group, person, or institution

**casework** social work that deals directly with individuals' specific needs and problems

**census** official population count and collection of demographic information on general population

**cohort** group having one demographic factor in common

**content analysis** study of document to learn about culture, esp. to determine number of times one term or value appears in given context

**control group** group of participants used as basis of comparison in controlled experiment

**controlled observation** research technique in which situation is set up and resulting phenomena observed

**cultural base** total number of cultural traits in given culture at one time

**cultural relativity** evaluation of culture's customs and their functions in context of entire culture

**culture trait** specific tool, act, or belief related to particular situation or need in one culture

**demography** study of relationship between human populations and vital and social statistics, esp. marital status, age, sex, and employment, usu. by statistical and quantitative methods

**historical analysis** study of historical records and writings to support or disprove a cultural hypothesis

**participant observation** research method in which researcher actively takes part in daily activities of group under study

**population** all people, things, ideas, or traits that possess those characteristics being measured or studied

**population base** total number of persons in society at a given time

**random sample** portion of population chosen at random to ensure impartiality in a study

**real-life laboratory** observation of people in arranged settings or natural environments without their awareness of being observed

**sampling** technique of drawing random and representative sample from a population

**scientific method** application of empirical, objective, and systematic data collection and analysis to study of culture and society

**secondary document** document written by someone not actually present at described event

**secondary research** research based on previously generated or collected data

**social engineering** application of findings of social science to solution of social problems

**social service** actions by professionals to improve social circumstances of people and communities

**sociogram** sociometric diagram representing pattern of relationships between group members

**sociography** use of statistical data to describe social phenomena

**sociometry** measurement of attitudes of social acceptance or rejection as expressed by group preferences

**statistical analysis** research technique using statistical data to formulate and test hypotheses

**stratified random sampling** method of selecting sample for survey that reflects proportions of different groups in population being studied

**survey research** method of obtaining information about population through interviews and questionnaires filled out by random sample

**universe** distinct field of thought or reality forming a closed system; all-inclusive group or population from which sample can be drawn for analysis

# PSYCHOLOGY

Schools and Doctrines
Syndromes, Disorders, and Conditions
Phobias
Manias
Tools, Techniques, Principles, and Practitioners
Mental States, Processes, and Behavior

**SEE ALSO**: Chap. 1: Medical Problems; Chap. 2: Biology; Chap. 4: Medicine; Chap. 8: Parents and Children; Chap. 13: Sociology; Education; Chap. 22: Sex, Love, and Romance; Chap. 24: Mental Disturbances; Chap. 25: Truth, Wisdom, and Spiritual Attainment

## SCHOOLS AND DOCTRINES

**abnormal psychology** branch of psychology concerned with basic theory, but not treatment, of psychotic and personality disorders

**Adlerian psychotherapy** theory of psychotherapy developed by Alfred Adler emphasizing overcompensation in denial of feelings of personal weakness or inferiority

**analytic psychology** school of psychoanalysis developed by Carl Jung

**applied psychology** use of psychological knowledge and skills to solve problems

**associationism** theory that holds that development proceeds from association of simple ideas gained from sensory data

**behaviorism** doctrine that emphasizes observable data, esp. from stimulus and response studies, as foundation for theories of behavior

**bioenergetics** school of therapy that employs breathing exercises, physical movement, and free expression to relieve stress and muscle tension

**blank-slate hypothesis** theory that human thought and behavior are based on experience, not innate components

**child development** child psychology focusing on weaning, feeding, and toilet training and acknowledging both environmental and hereditary factors

**client-centered psychotherapy** treatment in which client talks without direction or interpretation from therapist, whose attitude is characterized by unconditional empathy

**clinical psychology** branch of psychology that focuses on human development and interaction and supports therapeutic intervention to aid the problem solving of individuals, couples, families, and groups

**cognitive psychology** branch of psychology that bases research and treatment on analysis of mental processes in all aspects of human thought or cognition

**community psychology** subdivision of clinical psychology concerned with individuals' adaptation to their community

**comparative psychology** study of comparative behavior of different animal species to enhance understanding of human behavior

**constitutional psychology** psychological doctrine that attributes behavior patterns to body type

**consulting psychology** study and relief of individual problems in business, school, and government settings

**cultural relativism** belief that no absolutely correct standards of behavior exist against which varying cultural and personal behavior patterns can be measured

**demonology** superstitious belief in demons and evil spirits as cause of abnormal behavior

**depth psychology** study of unconscious mental processes

**developmental psychology** specialty that focuses on the course of social, emotional, moral, and intellectual growth over a lifetime

**eclectic psychology** branch of psychology drawing information, theories, and intervention techniques from different schools of thought

**engineering psychology** design of man-machine systems to fit human physiological and psychological needs

**ethology** scientific study of animal behavior

**existential psychotherapy** therapy emphasizing patient's subjective experience of existence, based on philosophical systems associated with Sartre, Heidegger, Jaspers, and Kierkegaard

**experimental psychology** research aimed at better knowledge of learning, memory, perception, and other basic mental processes

**Freudian psychoanalysis** psychoanalytic theories developed by Sigmund Freud, emphasizing importance of early stages of development, the dynamic unconscious, and the interplay of id, ego, and superego

**functionalism** psychological approach stressing mental functioning rather than mental structure

**gestalt** school of psychology that asserts that perceptual experience is a configuration or pattern in which the whole is more than the sum of its parts

**hedonism** theory that pleasure is the primary principle motivating human behavior

**holistic approach** approach emphasizing person as a whole, not isolated functions or disorders

**humanistic psychology** branch of psychology emphasizing individual and collective human behavior and its improvement

**individual psychology** branch of psychology emphasizing

uniqueness of human personality and psychological struggle

**industrial psychology** specialty that focuses on issues and problems specific to organizations and deals with questions of management and power distribution within such groups

**Jungian psychology** psychological doctrines of Carl Jung regarding mythological, cultural, and racial inheritance and the collective unconscious

**metapsychology** high-level speculation on the origin, structure, and function of the mind

**nativism** theory that personality and behavior are primarily inherited, not learned

**neoanalytic psychology** psychoanalytic theory based on Freud and incorporating modern science

**parapsychology** study of phenomena beyond range of normally observable psychological events

**personality theory** integrated set of principles that explains the development of those characteristics that make each person unique

**phenomenological approach** psychological approach that focuses on individual's way of perceiving and interpreting the world

**phrenology** method of studying personality by measurement of skull shape and its irregularities (19th c.)

**physiognomy** outmoded theory of personality based on belief that outward appearance indicates inner character

**psychoanalysis** study and long-term treatment of personality disorders using free association, interpretation of dreams, transference, and empathic neutrality; Freudian psychoanalysis

**psychobiology** study of anatomy and biochemical processes as they affect behavior

**psychodrama** psychotherapy using role-playing

**psychology** scientific study of the mind, mental states and processes, and human behavior

**psychopathology** science of causes and development of mental disorders

**psychophysics** study and measurement of relationship between intensity of stimuli and of sensations they produce

**psychophysiology** study of interaction between physiological and psychological processes

**psychotherapy** treatment of mental disorders and difficulties by psychological methods

**sleep and dreams** psychological discipline concerned with interrelated phenomena of sleep and dreams

**social psychology** study of effects of social interaction on group behavior, individuals, and mental processes

**somatopsychology** study of effects of physical problems and disfigurement on behavior and methods of treating related adjustment problems

**structuralism** psychological school that emphasizes definition and structure of consciousness in formation of human behavior

**Sullivanian theory** theoretical approach that focuses on interactions between patient and therapist

**theoretical psychology** branch of psychology that emphasizes formulation of a general integrated set of principles rather than treatment of patients

**transactional analysis** psychotherapy emphasizing interpersonal exchanges, psychological games, and roles played over a lifetime

## SYNDROMES, DISORDERS, AND CONDITIONS

**abnormal behavior** unhealthy, disturbed, or disintegrated behavior that interferes with normal, positive functioning

**abulia** loss of will or ability to act

**acting out** unconscious expression of previously repressed feelings through specific behavior

**addiction** physical dependence on chemical substance

**affective disorder** neurotic disorder involving disturbances in mood

**aggression** hostile, destructive behavior toward others

**agita** condition of general anxiety or agitation

**alienation** psychological isolation from interaction or identification with society and its values; withdrawal

**amentia** mental deficiency, esp. low intellectual capacity

**amnesia** partial or complete memory loss

**animality** expression of animal instincts in human behavior

**anomie** feeling of isolation or disconnectedness from social norms; cultural alienation

**anorexia nervosa** pathological fear of obesity, esp. in young women, leading to inability to retain food, loss of appetite, malnutrition, and sometimes death

**antisocial personality** disorder characterized by chronic violation of rules and customs of social group

**anxiety** state of general fear or dread, not necessarily connected to particular object or idea

**anxiety neurosis** neurositic disorder typified by feelings of pervasive anxiety

**asthenic reaction** fatigue as response to anxiety

**autism** condition marked by infantile onset of pervasive lack of responsiveness to others, with gross deficiency in language development

**battle fatigue** posttraumatic stress disorder affecting soldiers engaged in combat

**bedwetting** urination in bed at night by children who have been toilet trained, usu. due to repressed anxiety or resentment

**belle indifference** anxiety-free state of certain hysterical neurotics; calm, inappropriate attitude toward some physical symptom

**bestiality** act or fantasy of engaging in sexual relations with animals

**bipolar disorder** disorder involving alternation or intermixture of manic and depressive episodes

**block** psychological obstacle to doing what one has set out to do and is capable of doing; sudden interruption of speech or thought processes

**borderline personality** disorder characterized by impulsiveness, intense and unstable relations with others, identity disturbance, marked mood shifts, and chronic feelings of emptiness or boredom

**bruxism** unconscious grinding and gnashing of teeth, usu. during sleep

**bulimia** constant, abnormal craving for food followed by self-induced vomiting, accompanied by preoccupation with weight

**catatonia** syndrome, usu. in schizophrenia, marked by stupor with musculature rigidity or agitated overactivity

**character disorder** deeply ingrained, habitual, rigid reaction pattern that is maladaptive and limits optimal functioning in society

**combat fatigue** trauma following acutely stressful conditions of warfare

**compensation** defense mechanism in which sense of weakness or lack is offset by emphasizing positive traits

**complex** specific constellation of psychological symptoms arising from powerful emotions buried in unconscious mind and affecting behavior

**compulsion** repetitive behavior serving no rational purpose; need to act without understanding motives

**compulsive personality** disorder marked by rigid, inhibited, excessively orderly, and often unemotional character and inability to relax

**condition** state of one's mental health, esp. abnormal or unhealthy state

**conversion disorder** neurosis characterized by the conversion of psychological disturbances into physical symptoms

**cretinism** mental deficiency caused by thyroid disorder

**cultural alienation** anomie

**cyclothymic personality** disorder in which normally extroverted person suffers fluctuations in mood between sadness and elation

**defense mechanism** any of various mental processes, including compensation, denial, displacement, negation, procrastination, projection, rationalization, reaction formation, regression, repression, and substitution, used by the ego for protection against instinctual demands and to reduce anxiety

**delusion** false or distorted belief firmly maintained though contradicted by reality

**dementia praecox** schizophrenia

**denial** defense mechanism in which one refuses to acknowledge the existence of an unpleasant reality, esp. the significance of one's behavior

**depersonalization** disorder involving the experience of self as unreal or strange

**depression** depressive neurosis or psychosis

**depressive neurosis** disorder involving chronic feelings of sadness, lethargy, and hopelessness; depression

**depressive psychosis** major depressive episode involving feelings of self-hate and negativity, sometimes marked by hallucinations, delusions, or mutism; depression

**deviance** extreme or marked difference from the norm

**disorder** abnormality, unhealthy condition, or dysfunction of mental health

**disorientation** disturbance in understanding one's position in time or place or one's identity

**displaced aggression** transference of hostility from true object to another object

**displacement** defense mechanism in which repressed emotion or idea is transferred to more acceptable object

**dissociative disorder** separation or disunity among aspects of single personality

**dysfunction** abnormality or failure of mental process

**Electra complex** psychological consequences of girl's sexual attraction to her father and feelings of competition with mother

**escapism** behavior and fanciful thought processes induced to escape from reality

**euphoria** unstable feeling of well-being; in manic depression, elevated end of cycle

**exhibitionism** need to shock others, esp. those of opposite sex, by exposing one's genitals or engaging in overt sexual behavior when inappropriate

**existential neurosis** disorder involving sense of meaninglessness and isolation

**fetishism** sexual dysfunction in which object or body part is essential to sexual arousal

**fixation** extreme attachment to objects or ideas associated with earlier stage of psychic development; halting of stage of personality development

**flattened affect** general impoverishment of emotional reaction in which victim appears distant and removed

**flight of ideas** disorder involving inability to keep to point of narrative; constant digression and lack of continuity

**frigidity** inability of woman to achieve orgasm through coitus

**fugue** combination of temporary amnesia with apparent rational behavior

**functional disorder** mental disturbance without known organic brain disorder or disease

**guilt** recurrent feeling of self-reproach or self-blame for something wrong, often something beyond one's control

**hallucination** sense impression for which there is no real external stimuli, either visual, auditory, or olfactory

**hebephrenia** form of schizophrenia involving disintegration of personality, giggling and grinning, and childish behavior

**hyperactive child syndrome** syndrome involving inability of child to pay attention, sit still, or be calm or quiet

**hypochondria** neurotic preoccupation with one's own health; formation of imaginary symptoms and exaggeration of minor discomforts

**hypomanic personality** disturbance pattern in which person displays mixture of elevated mood and restless agitation

**hysteria** anxiety reaction involving dissociation and conversion, characterized by excitability, high anxiety, and sensory and motor disturbances

**infantilism** abnormal regression to childish behavior in adulthood

**inferiority complex** feelings of inadequacy, negative self-perception

**insanity** legal definition of personality disturbance that causes an inability to bear responsibility for one's actions

**insomnia** chronic or extreme sleeplessness

**involutional psychosis** severe disturbance, often of middle age, involving depression, guilt, and insomnia

**koro** syndrome found chiefly in China and Southeast Asia, characterized by anxiety over retraction of penis or breast and labia into body

**learning disability** any condition that interferes with the learning process or ability to learn specific skills

**malaise** persistent, vague feelings of unease and listlessness

**mania** extreme, chronic obsession with something; excessive excitability; manic or excited phase of manic depression

**manic depression** psychosis affecting moods, alternating between extremes of elation and dejection

**martyrdom** tendency to take blame or burdens upon oneself, esp. to elicit sympathy or guilt in others; self-victimization

**masochism** condition in which pleasure, esp. sexual, is derived from pain inflicted by another on oneself

**melancholia** deep sadness

**minimal brain dysfunction** nervous system impairment that may cause hyperactivity in children

**multiple personality** extreme dissociation resulting in belief that two or more distinct personalities reside within oneself, each taking conscious control at different times; split personality

**narcissism** immature self-love manifested by grandiose sense of importance, need for constant attention and admiration, hidden sense of shame, and difficulty in relating to or having true feelings for others

**narcolepsy** frequent, uncontrollable desire for sleep

**nervous breakdown** lay term for temporary, abrupt impairment of normal functioning due to psychotic or neurotic disorder

**neurosis** emotional disorder involving basic repression of primary instinctual urge and reliance on defense mechanisms that results in symptoms or personality disturbance; psychoneurosis

**neurotic depression** common disorder involving inability to recover speedily from depression

**noctambulism** somnambulism

**nymphomania** compulsive desire for sex in females

**obsession** persistent, pervasive, disturbing fixation on an emotion, idea, object, or person

**obsessive-compulsive neurosis** disorder involving fixation on disturbing ideas and impulsive repetition of certain acts

**Oedipus complex** psychological consequences of boy's sexual attraction to his mother and feelings of competition with father

**overcompensation** extreme, unbalanced effort to overcome feelings of inadequacy or guilt

**paranoia** persistent delusions of persecution or suspicion of others

**paranoid schizophrenia** disintegration of perception of reality combined with delusions of grandeur or persecution

**paraphilia** disorder characterized by preference for unusual sexual practices and perversions

**passive aggressive personality** personality marked by extreme passivity combined with hostility, stubbornness, lack of cooperation, and uncommunicativeness

**pathology** any abnormal condition or mental disease

**pedophilia** desire for sexual activity with children

**persecution complex** tendency to feel that one is being unfairly and constantly harassed

**personality disorder** fixed, rigid, and ingrained patterns of relating to others that limit effective functioning and impair relationships and are usu. at odds with basic values of one's culture or community

**phobia** unfounded, persistent fear of something based on externalization of anxiety

**postpartum depression** depressive symptoms in mothers associated with period immediately following childbirth; similar feelings experienced after completing some task

**posttraumatic stress syndrome** pattern of reactions and disorders that appears some time after a traumatic experience, esp. in soldiers after combat; battle fatigue

**procrastination** defense mechanism involving postponement or avoidance of stressful task or situation

**projection** defense mechanism involving attribution of one's own unacceptable or unwanted qualities and motives to others

**psychological dependency** dependency characterized by attachment to person or thing that results in severe distress if object is removed

**psychoneurosis** neurosis

**psychopathic personality** individual with personality disorder involving stunted or nonexistent moral values, antisocial or violent behavior, and inability to identify with others

**psychosexual disorder** sexual disorder in which psychological rather than organic factors are of major importance

**psychosis** severe mental illness, such as manic depression, paranoia, or schizophrenia, involving loss of contact with reality and breakdown of comprehensible behavior, speech, and thought

**psychosomatic disorder** physical illness or perception of illness arising from psychological disturbances

**rationalization** defense mechanism involving substitution of rational motive for genuine, but irrational, motive as excuse for one's behavior

**reaction formation** defense mechanism involving denial of unacceptable unconscious urges by behavior contrary to one's own feelings

**reactive disorder** abnormality or dysfunction appearing suddenly, as if in response to specific situation

**real anxiety** anxiety produced by situations of actual danger in the external world

**reality anxiety** disorder involving fear of punishment for behavior judged wrong only by oneself

**regression** defense mechanism involving return to behavior expressive of earlier developmental stage, usu. due to trauma, fixation, anxiety, or frustration

**repression** defense mechanism in which threatening or unacceptable ideas or urges are forgotten

**resentment** feeling of displeasure toward source of supposed injury or offense

**retardation** congenital subnormality of intelligence or lack of normal mental capacity or development

**reversion** return to former or regressed condition

**SAD** seasonal affective disorder

**sadism** condition in which pleasure, esp. sexual, is derived from inflicting pain on others

**sadomasochism** condition in which pleasure, esp. sexual, is derived from inflicting pain on others and from pain inflicted on oneself

**satyriasis** compulsive desire for sex in males

**schizokinesis** disorder involving lack of coordination between body's perception of stimulus and appropriate reaction

**schizophrenia** psychosis involving break with reality and disintegration of rational thought and communication; dementia praecox

**seasonal affective disorder** SAD; phenomenon in which mood changes are alleged to correspond to the seasons, esp. depression in winter

**self-victimization** tendency to view oneself as a victim of unfair treatment; martyrdom

**senile psychosis** disorder in elderly involving memory loss, irritation, and regressive behavior

**sleepwalking** somnambulism

**sociopath** psychopathic personality who exhibits extreme asocial and antisocial behavior

**somatic delusion** individual's false perception of his body

**somatoform disorder** neurosis involving physical symptoms without physical cause

**somnambulism** walking in one's sleep; noctambulism; sleepwalking

**speech dysfunction** speech abnormality or incapacity

**split personality** multiple personality

**sublimation** defense mechanism involving substitution of socialized behavior for unacceptable acting out of primary urge

**substance use disorder** chronic abuse of chemical stimulants or alcohol

**substitution** defense mechanism involving replacement of unacceptable behavior with acceptable behavior

**suicidal** (*adj*) having intense, uncontrollable, self-destructive impulses, often due to depression

**superiority complex** condition in which one considers oneself better than others, often due to lack of genuine self-esteem

**syndrome** group of symptoms characterizing ongoing disease or disorder

**tic** involuntary muscle twitch, esp. of face, usu. indicating unreleased tension

**transient situational disorder** temporary disruption of personality due to external stress or overwhelming circumstances

**traumatic anxiety** disturbance based on present situation instead of memories of trauma or unhappiness

**vertigo** dizziness and loss of balance

**victimization** tendency to view oneself as victim of unfair treatment; martyrdom

**voyeurism** practice of deriving sexual gratification from watching others naked or engaged in sexual acts

**waxy flexibility** symptom of catatonic schizophrenia in which person permits limbs to be positioned by others, then retains that posture for long periods of time

**withdrawal** detachment from meaningful relationships with others and retreat into inner world; cessation of consumption of addictive substance and attendant unpleasant symptoms

**word salad** disturbed and incomprehensible speech of schizophrenics

# PHOBIAS

**acrophobia** fear of heights
**aerophobia** fear of drafts of fresh air
**agoraphobia** fear of crowds or open places
**agyrophobia** fear of crossing the street
**ailurophobia** fear of cats
**algophobia** fear of pain
**amathophobia** fear of dust
**androphobia** fear of men
**Anglophobia** fear or dislike of England or anything English
**anthophobia** fear of flowers
**apiphobia** fear of bees
**arachnaphobia** fear of spiders
**astraphobia** fear of lightning and thunder
**autophobia** fear of loneliness
**bathophobia** fear of deep places
**brontophobia** fear of thunder
**chrometophobia** fear of money
**claustrophobia** fear of enclosed places
**clinophobia** fear of going to bed
**coitophobia** fear of coitus
**coprophobia** fear of feces
**cremnophobia** fear of precipices

**cryophobia** fear of cold
**cynophobia** fear of dogs
**dipsophobia** fear of drunkenness
**doraphobia** fear of fur
**dromophobia** fear of crossing streets
**eisoptrophobia** fear of mirrors
**eleutherophobia** fear of freedom
**emetophobia** fear of vomiting
**entomophobia** fear of insects
**eremiophobia** fear of being alone
**ergophobia** fear of work
**erythrophobia** fear of blushing and the color red
**galeophobia** fear of sharks
**gametophobia** fear of marriage
**gephyrophobia** fear of crossing bridges
**gerascophobia** fear of old age
**gymnophobia** fear of nudity
**gynephobia** fear of women
**hedonophobia** fear of pleasure
**helminthophobia** fear of worms
**hematophobia** fear of blood
**hippophobia** fear of horses
**hodophobia** fear of travel
**homophobia** fear or dislike of homosexuals
**hydrophobia** fear of water
**hypegiaphobia** fear of responsibility
**hypnophobia** fear of sleep
**ichthyophobia** fear of fish
**ideophobia** fear of ideas or reason
**lalophobia** fear of speaking, esp. in public
**logophobia** fear of words
**lyssophobia** fear of madness
**maieusiophobia** fear of pregnancy
**microphobia** fear of germs
**musophobia** fear of mice
**mysophobia** fear of dirt or contamination
**necrophobia** fear of death
**neophobia** fear of novelty
**nyctophobia** fear of night or darkness
**ochlophobia** fear of crowds
**onomatophobia** fear of a name or particular word
**ophiciophobia** fear of snakes
**ornithophobia** fear of birds
**pathophobia** fear of disease
**pedophobia** fear of children
**peniaphobia** fear of poverty
**phasmophobia** fear of ghosts
**phobophobia** fear of fear
**phonophobia** fear of noise
**photophobia** fear of light
**pneumatophobia** fear of spirits
**pnigophobia** fear of choking
**pyrophobia** fear of fire
**scotophobia** fear of dark
**siderodromophobia** fear of trains
**tachophobia** fear of speed
**tapephobia** fear of being buried alive
**teratophobia** fear of monsters
**thalassophobia** fear of the sea
**thanatophobia** fear of death
**thermophobia** fear of heat
**tocophobia** fear of childbirth
**tomophobia** fear of surgery

**topophobia**  fear of a particular place
**toxiphobia**  fear of being poisoned
**traumatophobia**  fear of injury
**triskaidekaphobia**  fear of the number thirteen
**xenophobia**  fear or dislike of foreigners
**xerophobia**  fear of dry places, esp. deserts
**zoophobia**  fear of animals

## MANIAS

**ablutomania**  chronic obsession with bathing
**ailuromania**  intense enthusiasm for cats
**anthomania**  inordinate interest in flowers
**arithmomania**  craze for counting and numbers
**automania**  compulsion toward solitude
**bibliomania**  inordinate interest in acquiring books
**cacodemonomania**  inordinate obsession with demonic possession
**cheromania**  compulsion toward gaiety
**choreomania**  craze for dancing
**chrematomania**  obsessive desire for money
**coprolalomania**  obsession with foul speech
**cynomania**  intense enthusiasm for dogs
**dipsomania**  irresistible craving for alcoholic beverages
**dromomania**  intense enthusiasm for traveling
**egomania**  inordinate obsession with oneself
**eleutheromania**  irresistible craving for freedom
**entheomania**  obsessive zeal for religion
**entomomania**  inordinate fascination with insects
**eremiomania**  irresistible craving for stillness
**ergomania**  obsessive zeal for work
**erotomania**  uncontrollable obsession with sexual desire
**florimania**  intense interest in plants
**gephyromania**  irresistible fascination with bridges
**glazomania**  inordinate fascination with listmaking
**gymnomania**  compulsion toward nakedness
**gynecomania**  obsessive and uncontrollable desire for sex in males; satyromania
**hedonomania**  irresistible craving for pleasure
**heliomania**  uncontrollable craving for the sun
**hippomania**  fascination with and enthusiasm for horses
**homicidomania**  irresistible impulse to commit murder
**hydromania**  uncontrollable fascination with water
**hypnomania**  uncontrollable desire for sleep
**ichthyomania**  excessive fascination with fish
**kathisomania**  uncontrollable compulsion to sit
**kleptomania**  irresistible impulse to steal
**letheomania**  obsessive fascination with narcotics
**logomania**  obsession with talking
**megalomania**  uncontrollable obsession with grandiose self-importance and extravagant acts
**melomania**  excessive fascination with music
**monomania**  obsessive zeal for one topic or interest in one idea
**mythomania**  irresistible impulse toward exaggeration and lying
**necromania**  excessive interest in the dead
**nesomania**  intense obsession with islands
**noctimania**  intense fascination with night
**nymphomania**  obsessive and uncontrollable desire for sex in females
**ochlomania**  intense obsession with crowds

**oikomania**  irresistible craving for home
**oinomania**  inordinate fascination with wine
**oniomania**  uncontrollable compulsion to buy
**ophidiomania**  excessive interest in reptiles
**ornithomania**  inordinate fascination with birds
**paramania**  irresistible impulse to derive joy from complaints
**parousiamania**  obsessive zeal for the second coming of Christ
**phagomania**  irresistible craving for food and interest in eating
**phaneromania**  uncontrollable impulse to pick at a spot or growth on one's body
**pharmacomania**  chronic fascination with medicines
**phonomania**  obsession with noise or sound
**photomania**  irresistible craving for light
**plutomania**  uncontrollable craving for great wealth
**pyromania**  compulsion to set things on fire
**satyromania**  obsessive and uncontrollable desire for sex in males
**scribomania**  obsessive zeal for writing
**siderodromomania**  intense fascination with railroad travel
**sitomania**  abnormal craving for food
**sophomania**  inordinate estimation of one's own wisdom
**thalassomania**  intense fascination with the sea
**thanatomania**  inordinate obsession with death
**timbromania**  inordinate enthusiasm for postage stamps
**tomomania**  inordinate interest in surgery
**trichomania**  intense fascination with hair
**xenomania**  obsessive interest in foreigners
**zoomania**  craze for animals

## TOOLS, TECHNIQUES, PRINCIPLES, AND PRACTITIONERS

**achievement test**  structured series of questions measuring progress or knowledge in specific field
**analysand**  person treated by psychoanalysis
**analysis**  method in which therapist treats subject through long-term series of regular psychoanalytic sessions
**analyst**  psychotherapist or psychiatrist whose training qualifies him or her through analysis, courses, and supervision to analyze others
**anima**  in Jungian theory, female aspect of a male's personality
**animus**  in Jungian theory, male aspect of a female's personality
**aptitude test**  structured measurement of capabilities, esp. through a series of questions
**archetype**  in Jungian theory, primal character and predisposition to behavior within collective unconscious of individuals
**aromatherapy**  use of scented oil to influence mood and treat stress
**atomism**  theory that reduces all psychological phenomena to simple elements
**autohypnosis**  practice of hypnotizing oneself
**autosuggestion**  idea arising within oneself and affecting one's thinking and behavior
**aversion therapy**  technique of linking deeply felt revulsion with a behavior to be reduced or eliminated

**bataca** stuffed pillow with handles used for pummeling to release aggression without causing damage

**battery** combination of various tests and measurements

**behavior checklist** list of personality traits used in psychological testing

**behavior modification** altering of behavior through conditioning and behavior therapy

**behavior therapy** treatment aimed at eliminating unacceptable symptoms or behavior rather than exposing underlying causes

**Bender-Gestalt test** test for neurological disorders in which subject must copy nine geometrical designs

**bibliotherapy** use of reading materials as aid in therapy

**biofeedback** behavior therapy technique involving control of health and personality problems by sensitization of individual to internal body mechanisms to reduce stress

**birth trauma** theory that explains neuroses in terms of shock experienced by infant during birth

**brainwashing** extreme psychological conditioning used to change ideological attitudes

**case study** detailed psychoanalytic history of an individual used for teaching or reporting purposes

**catharsis** therapy that allows pent-up, socially unacceptable emotions to be expressed

**choice point** area of maze requiring test subject to choose between alternative directions

**classical conditioning** process linking a conditioned stimulus with a conditioned response; Pavlovian conditioning

**client-centered therapy** therapy that emphasizes nonjudgmental support of client's point of view and encouragement of expression of feelings and growth needs

**clinical judgment** professional's trained personal judgment in evaluating case and recommending treatment

**clinical psychologist** professional in field of counseling individuals with psychological problems

**conditioned response** acquired response to stimulus not originally capable of causing it; Pavlovian conditioning

**conditioned stimulus** stimulus at first incapable of arousing response but later capable of eliciting one

**conditioning** form of learning that produces automatic response to stimulus

**confederate** assistant in experiment posing as subject

**control group** experimental group equal in all respects to other groups being tested but not subjected to experimental conditions

**couch** bedlike furnishing on which patient lies during psychoanalytic session

**counseling** therapeutic psychological treatment program involving professional testing, interviews, and guidance

**counselor** therapist specializing in providing advice on patient's specific problems

**countertransference** transference on part of analyst of repressed emotions aroused by patient during course of treatment

**couple counseling** treatment that focuses on problems in the relationship between two people, usu. romantically involved or married

**culture fair** test or measurement whose content has been scrutinized to eliminate cultural or ethnic bias

**desensitization therapy** therapy emphasizing reduction of unwanted behavior by gradual pairing of another response with original stimulus

**diagnosis** clinical identification of disorder affecting patient

**dream interpretation** psychoanalytical technique involving symbolic explanation of dream content

**ECT** electroconvulsive therapy

**educational therapy** treatment aimed at improving patient's learning skills

**electric shock therapy** therapy that uses passage of electric current through patient's brain; electroconvulsive therapy

**electroconvulsive therapy** ECT; electric shock therapy

**encounter group** small group that meets, usu. with professional leader, for collective therapy through open exchange of intimate thoughts and feelings

**extinction** elimination of learned response when reinforcement is no longer given

**family therapy** treatment of family members as a group

**feedback** information on results of behavior used to influence future behavior

**figure-ground** perceptual tendency for portion of field to stand out more clearly than less distinct background

**free association** technique requiring patient to speak freely about anything coming to mind so as to explore the unconscious

**goal box** box at end of experimental maze in which animal being tested finds food or reward

**group leader** therapist trained in and leading group therapy sessions

**group therapy** treatment of several patients at one time by therapist, with emphasis on group interaction

**halfway house** residence offering supportive environment and counseling in which patients live following release from mental institution to ease reentry into society

**headshrinker** *Slang.* psychotherapist; shrink

**Holtzman technique** projective technique for personality evaluation based on interpretation of ninety ambiguous inkblots

**horizontal study** study of individual's current status, not history

**hypnotherapist** psychotherapist specializing in hypnotherapy

**hypnotherapy** therapy employing hypnosis to treat symptoms and make suggestions for improvement of future behavior

**idiographic** (*adj*) involving study or explication of individual cases or events

**implosion therapy** technique of reliving frightening event in therapeutic setting until original trauma has lessened or disappeared

**inkblot test** Rorschach test; Holtzman technique

**intelligence quotient** IQ; ratio of mental age to chronological age, multiplied by 100

**intelligence test** measurement of intellectual abilities

**intermittent reinforcement** in operant conditioning, a sporadic pattern of administering reinforcement after a particular response occurs

**IQ** intelligence quotient

**learning theory** comprehensive theory of factors affecting learning, memory, and forgetting, drawing elements from Pavlov to the behaviorists and cognitive psychology

**longitudinal study** long-term study of individual development

**manual arts therapy** treatment involving use of industrial arts skills

**maze** device consisting of box with many pathways, one leading to goal or reward, used to study learning behavior

**medication** administration of any of various depressants, tranquilizers, stimulants, or other substances to alter behavior, ease symptoms, or enhance treatment

**memory drum** mechanical device used to display items to be memorized in psychological study

**mental age** average level of mental ability for specific age group

**mental hospital** facility for treatment of severely disturbed patients, many of whom are committed for duration of treatment

**mental hygiene** development and maintenance of a wholesome, integrated personality

**Minnesota Multiphasic Personality Inventory** MMPI; elaborate true/false test showing personal and social adjustment

**MMPI** *Minnesota Multiphasic Personality Inventory*

**naturalistic observation** behavioral observation in natural, not experimental, setting

**negative reinforcement** reinforcement obtained by stopping of punishment after a response, thus increasing appearance of that response

**noise box** small device emitting low-level white noise to drown out external sound during therapy session

**nomothetic** (*adj*) involving study or formulation of general or universal laws

**nonschedule-standardized interview** interviewing technique based on standard questions interpreted or phrased for each interviewee's maximum comprehension

**nonstandardized test** test not meeting all requirements of standardized test due to absence of dependable norms

**norm** average performance or score on psychological test

**occupational therapy** treatment using crafts, sports, and skills development to restore confidence and build social skills

**operant conditioning** form of learning based on immediate reward for response

**organic therapy** physical treatment of disorder

**organismic theory** belief that all behavior stems from a whole, integrated personality guided by the drive for self-actualization

**paired-associate learning** learning task in which one of a pair of items previously presented is shown to subject who must try to give its associated match

**paradoxical effect** effect opposite the normal effect, as with certain stimulant drugs given to calm hyperactive children

**patient** person undergoing treatment or therapy

**Pavlovian conditioning** conditioning that creates reflex in which response is occasioned by secondary stimulus that has been repeatedly associated with primary stimulus

**peer** person regarded as equal to another or to others in group

**performance test** measure of nonverbal abilities, such as hand-eye coordination

**personality inventory** standardized questionnaire providing information about attitudes and behavior, evaluated with reference to norms

**personality test** measure of development of personality in areas of insight, goal definition and attainment, and interpersonal relationships

**phallic symbol** any long or tall narrow object that may resemble or represent the penis, esp. as symbol of power

**phone therapy** therapy session conducted by telephone

**pigeonhole error** tendency to slot people into invalid behavioral categories

**placebo** treatment that has no effect except in patient's own mind

**play therapy** treatment based on self-expression using dolls and puppets, esp. for children

**pleasure principle** id-motivated drive or instinct seeking immediate satisfaction of all needs and desires

**positive reinforcement** rewarding stimulus that strengthens learned behavior

**posthypnotic suggestion** instruction given during hypnosis in regard to behavior or experience to take place after hypnosis has terminated

**prefrontal lobotomy** surgical severing of neural connections in brain to control extremely violent patients

**primal scream therapy** treatment in which patient reenacts disturbing past experiences, esp. of infancy, and expresses repressed anger through screams, hysteria, or violence

**profile** diagram showing results of individual's psychological testing and evaluation

**projective technique** unstructured testing method using ambiguous material to elicit projected responses

**proxemics** study of human spatial requirements and effects of population density

**psychiatrist** medical doctor specializing in treatment of mental disturbances, including by prescription of medications

**psychoanalyst** professional therapist practicing psychoanalysis as originated by Freud and later developed and modified by others

**psychological test** measurement and assessment of various aspects of personality

**psychologist** professional who has completed graduate training in any branch of psychology and fulfilled state requirements for licensing

**psychologize** (*vb*) reason or theorize psychologically, esp. in a naive way

**psychometric test** standardized, structured test measuring mental functioning in precise, uniform way

**psychosurgery** brain surgery used to treat chronic mental disorder

**psychotherapist** professional therapist who treats psychological disorders through verbal methods; therapist

**reality principle** mechanism by which child realizes postponement of immediate gratification is sometimes required in exchange for greater rewards

**reciprocal inhibition** behavior therapy technique using mutual exclusivity of certain responses to overcome behavioral problems

**recreation therapy** treatment emphasizing relaxation, games, outdoor activities, or lectures to promote free and expressive activity

**reductionism** explanation of complex phenomenon by analyzing its simplest basic mechanisms and components

**rehab counselor** therapist providing counseling on problems of rehabilitation

**rehabilitation** restoration of normal health and functioning following period of impairment due to mental or physical disorder

**reinforcement** reward that increases likelihood of appearance of a particular response

**reinforcing stimulus** in operant conditioning, reward for a particular behavior

**rhesus monkey** macaque monkey of India used extensively in medical and psychological research

**role-playing** assumption and acting out of role to resolve conflicts and practice appropriate behavior, usu. in group therapy

**Rorschach test** personality evaluation involving patient interpretation of inkblot images; inkblot test

**sample** selected members of population whom researchers wish to observe or study so as to formulate generalizations about that population

**scapegoat** substitute object for aggression

**schedule-standardized interview** printed, questionnaire-style interview with established reliability and validity that is presented to all subjects in invariable form

**security blanket** child's blanket used as transitional object

**self-examination** intense scrutiny of one's personality and behavior; self-review; self-criticism

**selfness** state of possessing a distinct, developed, individual personality

**sensitivity training** group therapy in which patients seek deeper understanding of themselves and others by exchange of intimate thoughts and feelings, sometimes through physical contact

**sensory deprivation** experimental technique in which subject is confined in soundproof chamber and deprived of variation in sensory stimuli

**sex surrogate** person provided by therapist for sexual activity with patient in unorthodox treatment of sexual disorders

**shaping** procedure in operant conditioning in which abnormal behavior is encouraged by rewards

**shock therapy** use of electric shock in cases of severe disorder, catatonia, or depression; electric shock therapy

**shrink** *Slang.* psychotherapist

**Skinner box** laboratory device for study of operant conditioning in which animal learns to press lever for reinforcement such as food

**speech therapist** person who specializes in treatment of speech dysfunctions

**standardized test** psychological measure whose administration, scoring, and interpretation are identical for all who take it, providing a reliable and valid norm for comparison

**stimulus** signal received by sense organ

**straitjacket** coatlike device that binds arms against body, used to restrain violent patients

**stress** psychological or physiological pressures that threaten health, stability, or functioning of personality

**structured test** measurement designed to evoke specific responses

**subject** person or animal in psychological test or experiment

**subliminal** (*adj*) involving stimuli intended to take effect below level of consciousness

**suggestion** induction of an idea that is accepted and readily acted on, esp. under hypnosis; idea so induced

**support group** group of people who meet regularly to discuss problems affecting them in common, such as alcoholism or bereavement

**systematic desensitization** technique for reduction or elimination of oversensitivity, esp. fear

**TAT** *t*hematic *a*pperception *t*est

**team** group of professionals working toward common goal

with patient, often including persons from different disciplines

**T-group** group engaged in sensitivity training

**thematic apperception test** TAT; measurement of personality and motivation based on subject's construction of a story based on a series of standardized pictures

**therapeutic community** treatment and rehabilitation center providing supportive environment for drug detoxification and recovery from mental disorders

**therapist** psychotherapist

**therapy** treatment intended to improve psychological condition and assist in understanding and resolving emotional problems

**time-binding** process of relating past and future to present behavior and increasing understanding of consequences

**touchy-feely** *Slang.* pertaining to sensitivity training

**transference** patient's identification of therapist with pivotal person in his or her life and subsequent transferral of feelings about that person to therapist

**transitional object** familiar object to which child clings during early socialization and that substitutes for mother's care

**trial** each attempt made to learn in learning study

**twelve-step program** method of recovery from addictive and obsessive-compulsive conditions through group reinforcement and spiritual awareness

**unconditioned response** response occurring naturally, without training or reinforcement

**unconditioned stimulus** stimulus eliciting innate response

**unstructured test** test designed with ambiguous stimuli that evoke individualized responses

**verbal learning** experimental psychology concerned with how humans learn and remember through language

**verbal test** measurement of ability to retain and use knowledge and express ideas verbally

**visualization** technique of encouraging subject to imagine or picture self in altered and improved condition, having achieved desired goal

**vocational interest test** measure of job or career aptitude and interest

**vocational rehab** therapy and counseling intended to assist person in resuming former work activities

**word association** technique involving subject's pairing of given word with whatever word comes to mind

## MENTAL STATES, PROCESSES, AND BEHAVIOR

**abandonment** feeling of having been forsaken or neglected, esp. by one's parents

**abreaction** release of repressed feeling by mentally reliving experience causing that feeling

**adaptation** capacity to alter one's behavior to conform to social norms

**addictive personality** person who has a tendency toward compulsive behavior associated with one specific activity or object

**affect** emotion attached to ideas, objects, or mental representations

**aggression** drive characterized by anger, hostility, or territoriality

**anal phase** second stage of psychophysical development during which child, usu. at age 2, becomes preoccupied with defecation, dealing with issues of control and autonomy

**angst** anxiety

**anticipatory grief** experience of grief or mourning in period leading up to expected tragic event, which is often experienced as a relief when it occurs

**apperception** conscious perception

**aptitude** ability and natural skills in certain areas

**archetype** Jungian characterization of fundamental personality trait held in collective unconscious

**attitude** learned tendency toward pattern of response in accordance with deep feelings

**automatic writing** symptom of disturbed functioning in which subject writes things without being aware of the act or of what is written

**avoidance** behavior characterized by evasion and/or withdrawal

**basic anxiety** feelings of loneliness or helplessness toward a potentially hostile environment

**behavior** actions and activities of humans and animals

**body language** body movements, positions, and gestures that communicate an attitude

**bonding** development of close and powerful relationships with family or friends based on initial attachment of infant and mother

**brutalization** physical and mental abuse, esp. when inflicted by family or mate

**castration complex** unconscious male fear of castration or emasculation, esp. as punishment for oedipal feelings

**cathexis** concentration or buildup of mental energy and emotional significance in connection with an idea, activity, or object

**civilian catastrophe reaction** extreme stress suffered by victims of natural disasters

**codependency** any of various problems or disorders based on one person's close association with another's habits or addictions, resulting in blurred individuation

**cognition** perception

**cognitive development** stages of growth in thinking and perception from childhood concern with objects to adult use of symbols and logic

**cognitive dissonance** psychological discomfort resulting from individual's conflicting beliefs or desires

**cognitive learning** learning by understanding rather than by conditioning

**collective unconscious** Jungian characterization of major part of unconscious mind, containing ancestral memories and images from humanity's history

**compensation** effort to replace feelings of inadequacy with feelings of adequacy

**concept learning** ability to form an abstraction from some aspect of a group of objects or common events, which increases from childhood to maturity

**conflict** state of tension arising from opposing desires or tendencies

**conscience** moral sense of right and wrong and accompanying desire to do right

**coping** ability to function in society despite any of various conditions or disorders

**creativity** ability to perceive new combinations of information for problem solving or invention

**death instinct** destructive, aggressive compulsion to achieve nonexistence; thanatos

**defense** ego mechanism used to channel energy to middle area between id's wishes and ego's reality

**disengagement** shift from active to passive mode

**disturbance** departure from normal emotional state, esp. state of anxiety

**dream** images and thoughts in mind of sleeping person

**drive** condition of urgent basic need that causes motivation to satisfy need

**dysfunctional family** family in which emotional and physical support needed for individuation and healthy development are missing and family members are sacrificed to the family group itself

**ego** reality-oriented, structured component of personality that enables individual to function autonomously in the world; one of three divisions of psyche in psychoanalytic theory

**eidetic imagery** photographic memory in which vivid mental images can be described in detail

**emasculation** deprivation or reduction of male's sense of power, esp. by mate

**emotion** strong psychophysical response of individual

**episode** specific instance of behavior or condition

**externalization** perception of one's own difficulties as being caused by external forces, not innate characteristics

**extrasensory perception** phenomenon of perception or communication occurring independent of powers of sense organs

**extroversion** tendency to direct one's interest toward things outside the self

**facade** surface behavior

**fantasize** (vb) create mental world through one's imagination, esp. to fulfill a psychological need

**Freudian slip** statement or action that inadvertently reveals unconscious motive or desire

**frustration** disturbed state occurring when individual cannot attain goal or relieve tension

**functional fixedness** inability to perceive and use objects in innovative ways or engage in alternative thinking processes

**genital phase** final stage of psychophysical development, occurring at puberty, in which affectionate relationship with sexual partner can be achieved; childhood stage between ages 2 1/2 and 7, marked by increased sexual and genital interest

**gestalt** unified whole, esp. the psyche, having properties that cannot be derived from the sum of its parts

**gratification** basic, often sensual, satisfaction

**group dynamics** ways in which group members interact, esp. to achieve group goals

**hang-up** Slang. fixation or psychological block

**homeostatic drive** motivation to maintain constant or stable internal environment

**hormone** any of various chemicals secreted by glands that affect behavior

**hyperactive** (adj) abnormally animated or active, esp. in relation to children

**id** unconscious, unsocialized component of personality, containing unexpressed desires and motivations and driven by pleasure principle; one of three divisions of psyche in psychoanalytic theory

**identification** unconscious process of adopting attributes of another

**identity crisis** period or episode of psychological distress during which questions of self-definition become paramount

**imagination** ability to apply creative thought to real situations, forming unique mental images

**imago** idealized mental picture of another, esp. one's parent

**imprinting** early learning that occurs quickly and thoroughly

**impulse** wave of psychic energy that is either discharged, inhibited, directed, or sublimated

**individuation** development of a distinct personality, separate from one's mother's, and a sense of boundary between self and others

**inhibition** process of stopping an impulse

**inner child** part of a person's self that remains as it was in childhood and influences the way that person sees and relates to the world as an adult

**instinct** inborn, universal, biological drive

**intelligence** range of attributes centering around reasoning skills, knowledge of one's culture, and problem-solving abilities

**internalization** adoption of values through identification

**introjection** replacement of relationship with external object with relationship with internal, imagined object

**introversion** tendency to withdraw from others and turn inward upon the self

**intuition** ability to understand quickly through feeling, not analysis

**kinesthesis** sensory ability to feel body positioning

**learning** adaptive change in behavior caused by training, experience, or observation

**leveling** forgetting; failing to perceive adequate detail

**libido** in Freudian terms, sexual energy; in Jungian terms, psychic energy

**looking-glass self** self-image based on perceived view of other's, esp. child's perception of parent

**merging** loss of one's individual identity through intense and overly close association with another

**midlife crisis** feelings of anxiety and uncertainty about one's identity, relationships, and values, usu. experienced between ages 35 and 55

**mind-set** fixed point of view, attitude, or mood

**mneme** retentive basis in the mind accounting for memory

**mood** ongoing or passing emotional state

**morale** condition of confidence, enthusiasm, and good cheer, esp. in face of hardship

**motivation** desires and needs that inspire behavior

**nesting** forming strong relationships and creating secure home environment, esp. for rearing family

**networking** developing personal contacts for exchange of information or furthering of one's career

**nightmare** vivid, unpleasant, terrifying dream, often recurring

**nocturnal emission** ejaculation, esp. among boys undergoing puberty, usu. after erotic dream; wet dream

**nurturing** care and warmth that promote healthy development

**nurturing environment** conditions that encourage sense of security

**nympholepsy** frenzy of emotion, esp. for something unattainable

**onychophagia** habitual nail-biting, usu. as sign of anxiety neurosis or other suppressed feeling

**oral phase** first stage of psychophysical development after birth, in which mouth is main source of pleasure and stimulation

**paramnesia** distortion of memory in which fact and fantasy are confused

**peak experience** point of great joy, wonder, or surrender

**penis envy** in Freudian theory, female feelings of inadequacy and jealousy because of repressed wish to have a penis

**perception** process of conscious sensory input; cognition

**persona** in Jungian view, individual's facade or mask of socialized behavior

**personality** totality of traits, feelings, values, and expressions that characterize an individual

**personal unconscious** in Jungian view, unconscious mental contents unique to individual and not part of collective unconscious

**phallic phase** stage of development, usu. ages three to five, in which focus of pleasure shifts to genitals

**preconscious** (*adj*) referring to mental activity that is not immediately conscious but can easily be recalled

**primal** (*adj*) having to do with basic, primitive urges and emotions

**process** course of action or form of behavior

**psychasthenia** neurosis characterized by phobias and obsessions

**psyche** mental or psychological structure of an individual, esp. in connection with motivation

**psychic energy** in Jungian theory, general life force

**psychodynamics** in Freudian view, interplay of unconscious mental processes that determine human thought, feelings, and behavior

**psychogenic** (*adj*) caused by mental conflict

**psychosexual stages of development** in Freudian theory, sexual development in oral, anal, and genital phases

**psychotropic** (*adj*) altering one's mental functions, used esp. of tranquilizers and hallucinogenic drugs

**reflex** inborn natural response

**REM sleep** rapid *eye movement* sleep; cyclical sleep state characterized by increased brain activity, dreams, and rapid eye movements

**response** activity resulting from stimulus

**schema** belief system or experience that produces specific mode of perception and behavior

**self-abuse** accusation and blame of oneself; masturbation

**self-actualization** fulfillment of individual's potential as independent, functioning, healthy, adjusted person

**self-conscious** (*adj*) awkward and embarrassed in presence of others due to excessive concern with others' opinions

**self-control** ability to curtail or sublimate one's natural desires and behavior

**self-denial** sacrifice of one's own desires or needs

**self-examination** deep study of one's personality, behavior, thoughts, and feelings

**self-fulfilling prophecy** unconscious tendency to make behavior and events conform to anticipated outcomes

**self-love** regard for oneself and one's feelings

**self-pity** excessive and self-indulgent sorrow for oneself

**self-worth** healthy sense of oneself as a valuable individual

**sensation** sense impression of sight, sound, smell, taste, or touch and resultant feelings

**sentiment** positive or negative feeling about idea, object, or person

**set** attitude or readiness to perceive in certain way

**sex identity** feelings of comfort with and adjustment to one's maleness or femaleness

**shadow** in Jungian theory, unsocialized, primitive, idlike aspect of self

**sibling rivalry** competition among brothers or sisters within family structure

**sleep deprivation** reduced sleep over prolonged period, causing personality disorganization, diminished cognitive abilities, and sometimes psychotic delusions and hallucinations

**slough of despond** hopeless dejection and depression

**soma** body or physical self

**somatotype** body type, classified as endomorphic (heavy), ectomorphic (frail), or mesomorphic (muscular), each associated with a type of temperament or personality

**soul-searching** deep, often painful, introspection and self-examination

**state** specific mental or emotional condition

**stream of consciousness** personal conscious experience regarded as an uninterrupted series of events

**stress** bodily reaction to danger, difficulty, or threat

**strung-out** (*adj*) *Slang*. debilitated from addiction to drug or alcohol; extremely anxious

**subconscious** mental activity and impulses occurring below threshold of active awareness; (*adj*) existing in mind beyond conscious level

**superego** aspect of personality involving conscience, guilt, imposition of moral standards, and introjected authoritative and ethical images; one of three divisions of psyche in psychoanalytic theory

**suppression** conscious attempt to forget unpleasant idea or object or inhibit an impulse

**symbiosis** intense mutual interdependence

**synesthesia** experiencing a sensation in one sense organ from stimulus to another organ, such as hearing colors or seeing music

**tantrum** violent, uncontrollable outburst of rage, esp. in children

**temperament** characteristic mental, physical, and emotional aspects of an individual

**thanatos** death instinct, esp. as expressed in violent aggression

**trance** state of altered and diminished consciousness, esp. under hypnosis, in which voluntary movement is lost

**unbalanced** (*adj*) having disturbed or uneven mental functions

**unconscious** aspect of mind and personality that holds thoughts, desires, images, and urges of which individual is not aware; (*adj*) not actively aware of oneself

**unstable** (*adj*) emotionally unsettled or unpredictable

**verbal intelligence** grasp of ideas, language, information, and numbers

**Weltschmerz** *German*. sentimental melancholy over state of world

**wet dream** nocturnal emission

**wish fulfillment** attainment in dreams or fantasies of often unconscious or unattainable desire or impulse

# PHILOSOPHY

Schools, Doctrines, and Movements
Notions, Ideas, and Methods
Logic

**SEE ALSO**: Chap. 11: Government; Chap. 13: Sociology; Psychology; Chap. 23: Reasoning and Intuition; Chap. 25: Religion; Mythology and Folklore; Eschatology; Truth, Wisdom, and Spiritual Attainment

## SCHOOLS, DOCTRINES, AND MOVEMENTS

**aesthetics** branch of philosophy concerned with beauty and values in the judging of beauty, esp. in art; esthetics

**Age of Reason** Enlightenment

**analytic philosophy** highly structured approach to philosophical problems through modern logic, developed by Ludwig Wittgenstein (20th c.)

**animism** belief in the conscious life, or soul, of inanimate objects as well as living beings

**anthroposophy** doctrine that cultivating spiritual development is humankind's most important task

**antinomianism** doctrine that rejects conventional moral law and maintains that salvation derives from faith and grace alone

**Aristotelianism** practical, empirical philosophy of Aristotle, highly influential throughout course of Western history (Greece, 4th c. B.C.)

**atomism** theory that reality consists of minute, independent material units or atoms (Greece, 5th c. B.C.)

**axiology** science of and inquiry into values, as in aesthetics and ethics

**bioethics** study of ethical issues arising from medical and biological research (late 20th c.)

**Cartesianism** doctrine of René Descartes that all knowledge can be firmly established based on certain truths (France, 17th c.)

**conceptualism** theory that universal ideas exist as mental objects available to all minds

**Confucianism** quasireligious ethical system of China, based on sayings of Confucius (6th c. B.C.)

**cosmology** study of origin and totality of universal realities as basis for metaphysical speculation

**critical philosophy** doctrine of Immanuel Kant that the world is understood only insofar as it conforms to the mind's structure

**Cynicism** school originating with Diogenes, professing moderation and virtue as sole good, later based on protest and opposition to prevailing philosophical ideas (Greece, 5th c. B.C.)

**Cyrenaics** hedonistic philosophy of bodily pleasure, precursor to Epicureanism (Greece, 4th c. B.C.)

**deontology** ethical doctrine of duty as basis of moral obligation

**determinism** theory that reality and events unfold according to a predetermined, inevitable course

**dialectical materialism** Marxist form of materialism based on Hegelian dialectic applied to philosophy of social history

**dualism** theory that two basic, irreducible opposites, such as light and dark, good and evil, or mind and matter, constitute reality

**Eleaticism** Presocratic doctrine of Parmenides that absolute reality is undifferentiated and immutable while change is merely apparent (Greece, 6th c. B.C.)

**empiricism** view that sense perception and experience are sole foundations of knowledge, esp. held by John Locke (Britain, 17th c.)

**Encyclopedism** rationalist, humanistic movement to compile an encyclopedic compendium of knowledge, edited by Denis Diderot (France, 18th c.)

**Enlightenment** Age of Reason; intellectual movement toward tolerance, positive social action, and humanism, based on belief in perfectibility of people through reason (18th c.)

**Epicureanism** ethical doctrine of Epicurus, holding pleasure to be highest good, with pleasure deriving from moral conduct (Greece, 3rd c. B.C.)

**epistemology** theory of knowledge; critical study of nature, limits, and validity of knowledge

**esthetics** aesthetics

**ethics** science and study of morality and human conduct

**eudaemonism** ethical system defining moral behavior in terms of happiness and well-being

**existentialism** philosophy emphasizing free will in coming to terms with subjective meaning and meaninglessness in one's existence, based on teachings of Sören Kierkegaard (20th c.)

**fatalism** doctrine that all events and occurrences are predetermined and inevitable

**formal logic** branch of logic that emphasizes form and principles of deductive reasoning rather than content of propositions

**hard determinism** theory that there is no free will or nonpredetermined action

**hedonism** ethical doctrine of pleasure as highest or only good

**historical materialism** historicism

**historicism** deterministic explanation of phenomena in terms of their origins and development, associated with Hegel and Marx (19th c.); historical materialism

**humanism** any philosophical doctrine emphasizing human concerns, motives, and aspirations rather than other natural or spiritual forces, holding human reason to be the source of its authority

**hylozoism** doctrine that life is inherent in all matter, whether animal, vegetable, or mineral

**idealism** theory that reality is a creation of mind, and that mental and spiritual values, rather than matter, constitute reality; immaterialism

**ideology** scope of ideas within a particular theory or belief system

**immaterialism** idealism

**individualism** political philosophical theory emphasizing personal freedom and autonomy

**instrumentalism** school of pragmatism that maintains that the value of ideas lies in their practical application to human problems

**logic** philosophical inquiry into principles and methods of validity and proof

**logical empiricism** logical positivism

**logical positivism** school rejecting metaphysics and emphasizing methods of criticism and analysis of science, with reliance on principle of verifiability in experience or language (20th c.); logical empiricism

**materialism** theory that reality consists solely of matter, without separate reality of mind or spirit

**metaphysics** branch of philosophy concerned with ultimate nature and categories of reality; study of being, existence, and essence; ontology and cosmology

**monism** doctrine that reality of mind and body are fundamentally one and undifferentiated and can be reduced to one fundamental force, advocated by Spinoza in 17th c.

**mysticism** doctrine of direct, inexplicable knowledge and experience of truth and reality without rational processes or reliance on creed, orthodoxy, or belief system

**naturalism** theory that reality consists solely of the natural, observable world, with no supernatural or spiritual realm

**Neoplatonism** school synthesizing Platonic, Aristotelian, Christian, Jewish, and mystical traditions (3rd-5th c. A.D.)

**nihilism** doctrine that social and economic order is inherently corrupt and morality cannot be justified (Russia, 19th c.)

**nominalism** theory emphasizing that ideas and objects exist only in particular, not in abstract or general forms, influenced by William of Occam (14th c.)

**objectivism** theory emphasizing external, objective, rather than internal, subjective, aspect of reality; ethical theory that good is of value independent of human feelings but based on universally valid moral truths

**optimism** doctrine holding that reality is fundamentally good and the world is governed by benign forces

**ordinary-language school** movement advocating use of everyday language to resolve philosophical problems (20th c.)

**perspectivism** doctrine that reality and truth are known only from perspective of individual or group viewing them at particular moment

**pessimism** doctrine holding that reality is fundamentally evil and the world is governed by malevolent forces

**phenomenalism** empirical theory that knowledge exists solely in the appearance of phenomena, or sense data, rather than in the ultimate reality of objects themselves

**phenomenology** science of describing and analyzing classes of phenomena and consciousness (20th c.)

**philosophes** leading thinkers of the Enlightenment (France, 18th c.)

**philosophy** study and pursuit of fundamental principles underlying knowledge, conduct, and universal reality, esp. disciplines of aesthetics, epistemology, ethics, logic, and metaphysics

**Platonism** idealistic philosophy of Plato, derived from teaching of Socrates; classic idealism and belief that the human mind can attain absolute truth (Greece, 4th c. B.C.)

**pluralism** theory that reality consists of several distinct, fundamental realities

**political philosophy** study of people as political animals and relationship between government and citizens

**positivism** theory that truth or knowledge is based solely on what is scientifically verifiable by direct experience, based on teachings of Auguste Comte (19th c.)

**pragmatics** branch of semiotics concerned with causal relationships between symbols and words and their users

**pragmatism** philosophical view emphasizing consequences and practical results of one's conduct rather than principles and categories of reality (19th c.)

**pre-Socratics** those Greek philosophers of nature who lived before Socrates, esp. the Pythagoreans

**Pythagoreanism** doctrines of Pythagoras, esp. that universe is manifestation of various combinations of mathematical ratios (Greece, 6th c. B.C.)

**Ramism** opposition to Aristotelianism and advocacy of new logic in doctrines of Ramus

**rationalism** theory emphasizing reasoned, not empirical, foundations of knowledge; truth apprehended by deductive reasoning independent of experience or observation (17th c.)

**realism** theory that universal concepts and reality exist independently of perception

**relativism** theory that truth and ethical values are relative, not absolute and independent, and are contingent on nature of mind

**scholasticism** medieval, Christian philosophical school based on empiricism of Aristotle and teachings of Thomas Aquinas (11th-13th c.)

**scientific method** empirical, experimental approach to proof and the analysis of phenomena

**semantics** branch of semiotics concerned with signs and things they signify

**semiotics** theory of signs and symbols used in communication

**skepticism** theory that man can never attain certain knowledge and that all knowledge should be questioned

**soft determinism** theory that although events are determined by cause and effect, free will is possible

**Sophists** wandering teachers who emphasized rhetoric over truth and taught whatever their students wanted to learn (Greece, 5th-4th c. B.C.)

**Stoicism** pantheistic philosophy founded by Zeno of Citium encompassing doctrine of submission to divine will and freedom from passions (Greece, 3rd c. B.C.)

**subjectivism** doctrine limiting knowledge of reality to that which is consciously apprehended, with moral values dependent on personal and subjective tastes; truth seen as relative to human nature and ability to comprehend

**syntactics** branch of semiotics concerned with formal properties of language or symbolic systems

**Thomism** theological philosophy of Thomas Aquinas; rational system teaching that at some point reason fails and faith provides revelation (13th c.)

**transcendentalism** philosophy emphasizing thought processes in discovery of reality; philosophy emphasizing intuitive and spiritual rather than empirical basis of knowledge, developed by Ralph Waldo Emerson and Henry David Thoreau (U.S., 19th c.)

**utilitarianism** theory of moral conduct based on attainment of maximum good for greatest number of people (19th c.)

**utopianism** often impractical belief in and advocacy of ideal state

**vitalism** theory that living beings are governed by a vital force and by laws separate from those governing inanimate objects

## NOTIONS, IDEAS, AND METHODS

**absolute** single, eternal explanation for all reality

**abstraction** that which is theoretical, dissociated from specific instances or phenomena

**academicism** purely speculative thoughts and opinions

**a fortiori** (*adj*) *Latin*. lit. from a stronger; even more certain, for an even stronger reason

**agnosticism** belief that we cannot know whether God exists

**altruism** principle or practice of unselfish concern for the good of others, esp. as a moral act

**analytic** (*adj*) being of a type of proposition or statement inherently true by virtue of its terms' meanings

**antithesis** second stage of dialectical process, being a proposition directly opposite and apparently contradictory to the thesis

**a posteriori** (*adj*) *Latin*. lit. from what comes later; derived from experience, based on empirical data; from a particular instance to a general law

**appearance** sensory aspect of existence to an observer

**a priori** (*adj*) *Latin*. lit. from what precedes; independent of and prior to experience; based on reason or inherent logic, independent of empirical data; from a general law to a particular instance

**archetype** original model from which all others follow, esp. perfect example of type

**association of ideas** basic principle explaining all mental activity in terms of combining and recombining of certain component elements

**atheism** rejection of all belief in God

**automatism** view of body as a machine and consciousness as noncontrolling element of body

**becoming** that which exists only temporarily or changes from one form to another

**being** that which has unchanging actuality or substance or is logically conceivable

**casuistry** skill in science and application of moral decisions and judgments; employment of specious reasoning in moral questions

**categorical imperative** unconditional moral rule of conduct, not dependent on personal preferences

**category** basic form or mode of existence

**cause** that which is responsible for an effect in deterministic thinking; in Aristotelian thinking, that which is based on something's substance, design, maker, and purpose or function

**chain of being** hierarchical notion of universe as ordered structure of diminishing complexity from God on down

**cogito ergo sum** *Latin*. lit. I think, therefore I am; fundamental argument for idealism, attributed to René Descartes

**concept** idea capable of being defined and recognized; general idea or class

**concretion** that which is founded in fact; hard evidence, specific instances, or phenomena

**connotation** implication of a term, as distinguished from its denotation

**consciousness** awareness, sentience

**contingence** condition of being not necessary or of essence

**corporeal** (*adj*) relating to the body or physical matter

**debate** formal argument, esp. between those taking opposite views on single proposition

**deduction** mode of reasoning leading from general observation to particular conclusion

**denotation** specific meaning of a term, as distinguished from its connotation

**dialectic** orig. Socratic philosophic discourse or style of inquiry based on critical examination, later developed by Hegel as dynamic process of thesis, antithesis, and synthesis; Hegelian dialectic

**dichotomy** division into two classes; distinction based on a basic dissimilarity

**ding an sich** *German*. lit. the thing itself; essential being, prior to secondary qualities

**discourse** orderly, systematic communication, esp. in philosophic discussion

**discursive** (*adj*) characterized by analysis

**dysteleology** assumed absence of purpose and design in nature and phenomena

**eclecticism** combining of elements from different philosophical systems without resolving their conflicts

**effect** that which results from a cause in deterministic thinking

**emotivism** idea that ethical behavior is an expression of feelings and emotions

**empirical** (*adj*) pertaining to the senses; dependent on experience and direct observation

**entelechy** motive force for realization, completion, and perfection

**epiphenomenalism** idea that body can alter mind, but mind cannot alter body

**essence** inherent nature of an object, inseparable from its identity and contingent on nothing

**ethical pluralism** notion that more than one basic moral system can exist

**evil** moral wrongdoing; malevolence or ethical perversion

**exegesis** critical explanation

**existence** being; all that has being and continues to be

**experience** totality of what is perceived and thought

**Forms** absolute, eternal, immutable, and perfected Platonic models of which all earthly things are imperfect copies

**four elements** basic constituents of physical world: earth, air, fire, and water

**free will** option and power of moral choice in determining one's behavior

**golden mean** Aristotelian ethical doctrine of moderation as way to virtuous action

**good** character or behavior that is a model of moral order of the universe; that which promotes or inspires actions and attitudes supporting happiness and well-being

**Gordian knot** intricate and difficult problem or circumstance best resolved by cutting through it boldly and imaginatively

**Hegelian dialectic** dialectic

**hermeneutics** science of interpretation and explanation

**heuristic** (*adj*) characterized by ability to persuade or reveal rather than to convince logically

**Hobson's choice** choice between unacceptable alternatives; absence of real alternatives

**holism** notion that fundamental entities have existence beyond sum of their parts

**hypothesis** assumption, theory, or proposition made to account for some phenomena

**hypothetical imperative** conditional rule of conduct: if certain results are desired, certain actions must be taken

**idea** something present in consciousness; in Platonic terms, an archetype or essential concept

**ideal world** world of permanent truth

**immanent** (*adj*) existing within the mind only

**indeterminism** notion that some events do not have any cause

**induction** mode of reasoning leading from particular observations to general conclusions

**inference** mode of reasoning in which conclusion is derived from premises accepted as true

**infinite regress** endless series of arguments connected by interdependent premises and conclusions

**innate ideas** inborn ideas not based on experience

**intellect** ability to think

**intuition** direct apprehension of knowledge, without application of reason

**knowledge** understanding based on experience, intuition, and reason

**li** ultimate embodiment of good in Confucianism

**Logos** universal rational principle that orders the universe

**maieutic** (*adj*) pertaining to the Socratic method for clarifying ideas

**methodology** study of the nature of inquiry

**mind-body duality** idea that mind and body are distinct

**model** ideal form of image, object, or argument

**monad** *Greek*. lit. unit; ultimate, indivisible force center that is unit of all existence

**moral skepticism** notion that ethical principles have no objective basis

**natural law** naturally occurring moral rules that form universal law higher than man-made law

**natural rights** innate rights of humanity, such as life, liberty, equality, and the pursuit of happiness, that cannot be denied by society

**noetics** science of the intellect or of pure thought

**noncontradiction** principle that statement cannot be both true and false and object cannot both have and not have some quality

**noumenon** *Greek*. lit. that which is conceived; reality that cannot be experienced, as opposed to appearance or phenomena

**nous** *Greek*. lit. mind; universal principle of reason, embodied in God

**Occam's razor** principle that simplest explanation or theory is correct and should not be needlessly multiplied

**ontological argument** attempt to prove existence of God by analysis of definition of God

**ontology** metaphysical study of the essence of being and reality

**organon** system of rules or principles for demonstration or examination

**pantheism** belief that God and universe are identical

**particular** individual, specific instance, object, or term for a universal or general class

**percept** sense perception rather than idea of an object

**perceptual error** false or distorted sense perception

**perceptual judgment** judgment based on sense perception

**Peripatetic** follower of Aristotle, so called from practice of walking while teaching

**petitio principii** *Latin*. lit. postulation of the beginning; assumption of a premise identical with the conclusion

**phenomena** objects and events known through sensory experience

**phenomenal world** world of appearances

**philosopher king** Platonic ideal of philosopher ruling and leading society

**physicalism** theory that all factual statements can be reduced to observations of phenomena

**poetic** (*adj*) apprehended by the emotions

**praxis** action and practice rather than theory

**primary quality** characteristic inherent in an object, such as its shape, size, or mass

**quintessence** essence of a substance; substance other than four elements believed to compose celestial bodies

**reality** that which exists independently of ideas about it and independently of all other things, but from which all else derives

**reason** intellectual faculty, ability to comprehend by rational powers; systematic thinking, judgment of truth of propositions

**secondary quality** characteristic in object capable of stimulating sense perception, such as color or sound

**sensationalism** empiricist view that sensations are both source and verification of all knowledge

**sentience** ability to sense or feel

**situation ethics** moral evaluation of any action in relation to specific circumstance

**social contract** concept that society is based on agreement among people to be governed

**Socratic method** dialectic technique of inquiry developed by Plato's teacher Socrates (Greece, 5th c. B.C.)

**solipsism** theory that one can be aware of nothing outside the self and one's personal perceptions and feelings

**sophistry** use of persuasive but misleading or unsound argument

**spiritualism** view that the spirit is ultimate reality in universe

**state of nature** concept in political philosophy describing condition of humankind without government

**substance** that which exists by itself or is the essential part of something

**sufficient reason** principle that there is a reason for every phenomenon being as it is and not otherwise

**summum bonum** *Latin*. lit. highest good; moral principle of action based on effecting the greatest good

**superman** ideal, superior being described in work of Friedrich Nietzsche

**synthesis** dialectical combining of thesis and antithesis into higher stage of truth

**synthetic** type of proposition or statement in which predicate adds, or synthesizes, knowledge

**tabula rasa** *Latin*. lit. blank tablet; empiricist description of human mind at birth, with no innate ideas, awaiting experience to develop ideas

**teleology** belief in purpose and design in nature and phenomena

**theorem** principle, rule

**theory** hypothesis or speculation rather than action

**thesis** proposition held for proof by argument

**transeunt** (*adj*) producing an effect outside the mind

**truth** accord between internal and external realities; established and accepted principles of observation, action, or behavior; reality itself

**unexamined life** existence apart from philosophical inquiry, deemed not worth living by Plato

**universal** general concept having unrestricted application; proposition true for all members of its class

**values** moral standards and social goals held worthy for their own sake

**verifiability** ability of statement to be confirmed as true or refuted as false

**vice** moral corruption or evil

**virtue** moral integrity or excellence

**will** ability to make choices

**will to power** Friedrich Nietzsche's view that power is the prime motivating force in human nature

**zetetic** (*adj*) seeking; (*n*) seeker

# LOGIC

**ambiguity** possibility of having more than one meaning

**amphiboly** argument in which statement's meaning can be interpreted in more than one way

**analogy** relation based on similarity; inference based on shared qualities

**antecedent** conditional element in proposition

**antinomy** contradiction or opposition of one law to another

**argument** set of reasoned statements leading from assumptions and premises to conclusion

**assumption** statement taken to be true without proof

**axiom** assumption accepted as basis for deductive reasoning

**biconditional** (*adj*) designating a proposition that asserts the mutual interdependence of two things or events

**circular** (*adj*) describing reasoning in which apparently proved conclusion has been assumed as premise

**compound proposition** combination of at least two simple propositions using conditional word such as "if," "or," or "then"

**conclusion** reasoned deduction drawn from argument's premises

**conditional** "if-then" proposition in which existence or occurrence of one phenomenon or event depends on existence or occurrence of another phenomenon or event

**constant** term with invariable meaning

**contradiction** logically false statement

**converse** statement with elements expressed in reverse order of original proposition; reverse

**counterexample** fact that refutes a generalization

**deduce** (*vb*) draw conclusion by reasoning process

**deductive logic** formal logic; study of relationship between premises and conclusions of arguments; reasoning in which premises necessarily lead to particular conclusions

**demonstration** proof of an argument

**dilemma** syllogism in which major premise contains two or more conditional propositions and minor premise is a disjunction

**disjunction** compound proposition, either inclusive or exclusive, produced by joining two simple propositions by the word "or"

**enthymeme** incomplete argument, missing premise or conclusion

**Euler diagram** overlapping circles representing classes of objects, used to illustrate syllogisms

**fallacy** incorrect reasoning; invalid argument; instance of false conclusion drawn from premises

**generalization** proposition applying to all members of certain class of things or indefinite portion of that class

**ignoratio elenchi** *Latin*. lit. ignorance of the refutation; fallacy of offering irrelevant proof

**implication** relation between two propositions whereby one may be logically deduced from the other

**indisputable** (*adj*) incontestable, self-evidently true

**induce** (*vb*) conclude by induction

**inductive logic** study of relationship between premises and conclusions of inconclusive arguments

**invalid** (*adj*) incorrectly argued; not logically based on premises

**inverse** statement reversed in order, directly opposite form of original

**irrefragable** (*adj*) irrefutable, undeniable

**irrefutable** (*adj*) not capable of being refuted or disproved

**lemma** subsidiary proposition that helps prove another proposition

**logic** study and use of formal reasoning process for analyzing relationship between premises and conclusions of arguments

**Lull diagram** concentric circles and overlapping triangles used to illustrate circle of interconnected syllogisms

**major premise** premise in syllogism containing predicate of conclusion

**metamathematics** study of general properties of logical systems

**minor premise** premise in syllogism containing subject of conclusion

**modal logic** logic that classifies propositions according to their necessity and probability

**obverse** proposition inferred from another by denying the opposite of that which given proposition affirms

**ordered pair** set of two objects in definite order of first and second

**paradox** self-contradictory statement

**postulate** statement or proposition assumed to be true without proof

**predicate** that which is affirmed or denied concerning subject of proposition

**premise** general statement used as basis for argument and to support conclusion

**proof** series of statements used to show validity of argument

**proposition** point to be discussed, proved, disproved, or maintained in argument

**QED** *quod erat demonstrandum; Latin.* lit. that which was to be demonstrated; designation for conclusion, equivalent to "therefore" or "thus"

**quantifier** term, such as "all" or "some," that establishes or restricts the quantity of a proposition

**rational** (*adj*) having reason; capable of reasoning

**rationale** explanation of principles or opinion

**reciprocal terms** terms with same signification

**reductio ad absurdum** *Latin.* lit. reduction to absurdity; refutation of proposition by arguing to false conclusion from its premise

**relationship** connection by means of conditionals and/or quantifiers between two or more propositions

**reverse** converse

**set** group of things

**sorites** series of related syllogisms forming closed circle of premises leading to conclusion that connects back to original premise

**sound** (*adj*) having premises that are true and a conclusion that is valid

**statement** true or false sentence existing as part of argument

**subject** term of proposition concerning which predicate is affirmed or denied

**syllogism** form of deductive argument based on two premises or assumptions and conclusion drawn from them

**symbolic logic** mathematical logic using symbols to express propositions, quantifiers, and relationships; propositional calculus and functional calculus

**tautology** proposition necessarily true by virtue of its components; redundant proposition adding no new knowledge

**truth-functional logic** form of logic using connective terms "and" and "or"

**truth table** diagram or list of truth-value of each component of compound statement

**truth-value** truth or falsity of a statement

**universe of discourse** all objects possibly referred to in establishing and proving argument

**valid** (*adj*) correctly argued as a conclusion based on premises

**variable** term with different meanings depending on context

**vice versa** (*adj*) expressed as contrary of original statement

**vicious circle** two propositions that establish each other or two terms that define each other

# EDUCATION

**SEE ALSO**: Chap. 8: Parents and Children; Chap. 13: Sociology; Psychology

## COLLEGES AND UNIVERSITIES

**A and M** *A*gricultural and *M*echanical college

**academe** academia

**academia** community life or environment of a university; academe

**academic** (*adj*) relating to an institution of higher education

**accredited** (*adj*) issuing degrees recognized as valid

**advanced degree** degree beyond baccalaureate

**advanced standing** credit given to students for classes completed elsewhere

**alma mater** college or school from which one received a degree

**art school** college providing instruction in fine arts

**B.A.** *B*achelor of *A*rts degree

**baccalaureate** bachelor's degree

**bachelor's degree** degree given at completion of studies at four-year college; baccalaureate; undergraduate degree

**B.S.** *Bachelor of Science* degree

**B school** *Informal.* business school

**bursar** financial officer at college

**business school** school for professional training in business theory and methods

**certificate** special degree, lower than bachelor's, awarded by junior college or training institution

**chancellor** university president; chief executive of state educational system

**cluster college** small college that specializes in one field of study and is affiliated with a university

**college** institution of higher education that provides general course of studies leading to bachelor's degree; part of university offering specific course of study

**college try** *Informal.* all-out effort

**collegiate** (*adj*) of or relating to college

**colloquium** conference or informal meeting at which specialists speak and answer questions on designated topic

**commencement** ceremonies surrounding awarding of degrees and graduation

**community college** junior college serving local residents

**convocation** ceremonial gathering of members of college

**cow college** *Informal.* agricultural college; small, rural college

**credential** degree awarded in professional field, such as teaching, after or separate from bachelor's degree

**cum laude** (*adv*) *Latin.* lit. with praise; designation on diploma indicating graduation with honors

**dean** official in charge of division, faculty, or school within a college

**degree** title conferred by college for completion of course of study or in honorary recognition

**department** division of college offering instruction in specific field

**diploma** official document bearing seal and recording receipt of degree

**divinity school** division within college providing training for ministerial candidates

**D. Litt.** *Latin. Doctor Litterarum;* Doctor of Letters degree

**doctoral program** studies leading to Ph.D. degree

**doctorate** highest university degree, esp. Ph.D.; doctor's degree

**doctor's degree** doctorate

**D.Th.** Doctor of *Theology* degree

**fellowship** stipend given to support advanced study

**free university** unaccredited institution established by students for discussion of nonacademic and often controversial subjects

**graduate** (*vb*) complete course of study; confer or receive degree; (*n*) student who has completed studies and received degree

**graduate school** university division in specific field attended after receipt of bachelor's degree

**graduation** ceremony of conferring degree at completion of studies

**groves of academe** academic environment

**higher education** college and university studies

**honorary degree** degree awarded in recognition of achievement, not for completion of studies

**institute** educational establishment usu. devoted to technical field

**interdisciplinary major** course of study involving two or more academic disciplines

**intersession** period between academic terms

**ivory tower** place remote from worldly things, esp. institution of higher education

**ivy halls** *Informal.* educational institution, esp. old university on East Coast

**junior college** two-year community college not issuing degrees, often a vocational or technical school

**land-grant college** government financed college providing low-cost higher educations, esp. in agriculture and mechanical arts

**law school** graduate school for training to be lawyer

**lecture hall** large room or auditorium for addressing groups of students

**liberal arts** college studies emphasizing general knowledge rather than professional or vocational training

**LL.D.** *Latin. Legum Doctor;* Doctor of Laws degree

**lower division** first two years of college

**M.A.** *Master of Arts* degree, achieved after B.A.

**magna cum laude** (*adv*) *Latin.* lit. with great praise; designation on diploma indicating graduation with great honors

**major** student's primary field of study; (*vb*) select one's primary field of study

**master's degree** university graduate degree received after bachelor's and before doctorate

**matriculation** enrollment as student in college or university as degree candidate

**M.D.** Doctor of Medicine; doctoral degree awarded at completion of medical school

**medical school** four-year graduate program of studies and work experience for training as a doctor

**minor** student's secondary field of study; (*vb*) select secondary field of study

**M.S.** *Master of Science* degree, received after B.S.

**multiversity** large university composed of many schools, colleges, or divisions

**normal school** formerly, a teachers college

**Oxbridge** *Brit.* Oxford and Cambridge, the two most prestigious British universities

**Ph.D.** Doctor of Philosophy; highest university postgraduate degree

**Phi Beta Kappa** national university honor society for scholars

**postdoctoral** (*adj*) designating work and study undertaken after receipt of doctorate

**postgraduate** student who takes advanced work after graduation; (*adj*) designating study leading to postgraduate degree

**postgraduate degree** master's degree or doctorate, received after bachelor's degree

**predoctoral** (*adj*) designating student or course of study leading toward doctoral degree

**premed** program of undergraduate studies preparatory to medical school admission; student enrolled in such a program

**professional school** postgraduate division of university for training in profession such as medicine, law, or business

**provost** high-ranking university administrator

**regent** member of governing board of some state universities

**registration** enrollment in specific classes at beginning of term

**research institute** postgraduate academic institution devoted primarily to research, not instruction

**sabbatical** leave of absence for professor, originally granted every seventh year

**Sc.D.** *Latin. Scientiae Doctor;* Doctor of Science degree

**scholarship** funding granted to student, esp. on basis of need or merit

**semester** either of two, usu. eighteen-week, divisions of academic year, September to January or February to June

**seminary** institution that trains candidates for ministry or priesthood; theological seminary

**Siwash** small college with provincial outlook

**S.J.D.** *Latin. Scientiae Juridicae Doctor;* Doctor of Juridical Science degree

**state college** government-funded college, esp. for students of one state

**summa cum laude** (*adv*) *Latin.* lit. with highest praise; designation on diploma indicating graduation with highest honor

**symposium** formal meeting at which specialists deliver papers on given topic

**teachers college** college for training elementary and secondary school teachers, usu. in two-year program

**tenure** permanent employment granted to college or university professor after trial period

**term** division of academic year during which courses begin and end

**theological seminary** seminary

**trimester** segment of academic year divided into three quarters or semesters, usu. September to December, January to March, and April to June

**tuition** fee required for registration at educational institution

**undergraduate degree** bachelor's degree

**university** public or private educational institution operating at highest level, with facilities for teaching and research, undergraduate colleges granting bachelor's degrees, and graduate programs and professional schools granting master's degrees and doctorates

**upper division** third and fourth years of college

**war college** institution that provides training in military theory and practice

## SCHOOLS AND CLASSES

**academic year** period of school sessions, usu. September through June

**academy** high school or college emphasizing specific subjects; private high school

**adult school** institution providing education for adults, usu. without college credit

**alternative school** nontraditional elementary or secondary school

**Bible school** parochial school, esp. one run by fundamentalist religious order

**boarding school** school at which students reside during school year

**board of education** local government agency that supervises activities of public schools

**church school** educational institution run by church

**class** specific course of study, group of students, or period of instruction

**classroom** place where instruction takes place; schoolroom

**common school** public school usu. including both primary and secondary grades

**conservatory** school or academy offering training in one of the fine arts, esp. music

**consolidated school** public school created by merging students and faculty from several discounted schools, usu. in rural area

**continuation school** school for students who have been excluded from regular school for academic or disciplinary reasons

**convent** girls' school run by community of nuns

**country day school** private, nonboarding elementary or secondary school outside city limits

**course** lectures, assignments, class meetings, and tests on particular subject over set period of time

**day care** daytime supervision of preschool children

**day nursery** day school

**day school** place where day care is provided; nursery school; nonboarding private school; day nursery

**école** *French.* school

**elementary school** grades one through six or eight, often including kindergarten; grade school; grammar school; primary school

**finishing school** exclusive girls' private school emphasizing social and cultural activities, not academics

**form** grade in secondary school (Britain)

**free school** loosely structured alternative school, often allowing students decision-making power

**grade** one year's stage in elementary or secondary education

**grade school** elementary school

**grammar school** elementary school, grades one to six

**gymnasium** secondary school for students planning to go to university (Germany)

**Hebrew school** school for instruction in Jewish traditions and Hebrew language, usu. holding weekly sessions for Jewish children

**high school** secondary school, usu. grades nine through twelve, sometimes grades ten through twelve

**homeroom** classroom where students begin and sometimes end day

**institution** established, generally public, organization and facilities providing education

**intermediate school** elementary school, grades four through six; junior high school

**junior high school** seventh and eighth grades

**kindergarten** first year of school, for five-year-olds, before first grade

**language institute** school providing intensive training in foreign language

**Latin school** secondary school emphasizing instruction in Latin and Greek

**lycée** public secondary school, esp. in France

**magnet school** public school with specialized curriculum that draws students from broad region

**middle school** school between elementary and high school, usu. grades six through eight

**military academy** institution providing training in war and soldiering as well as academic disciplines

**Montessori school** institution following system of training young children developed by Maria Montessori, stressing free-form physical activity, individual instruction, and early literacy

**night school** school offering evening classes in continuing education, generally for older students employed during day

**nursery school** prekindergarten facility providing day care and some training for children from about three to five years of age

**palestra** sports school (ancient Greece)

**parish school** school run by local church

**parochial school** private elementary or secondary school supported and administered by religious body, esp. Catholic Church

**playgroup** informal preschool with adult supervision but no instruction

**preparatory school** usu. private secondary school aimed at preparing students for college; prep school

**prep school** preparatory school

**preschool** day-care or nursery school instruction for children prior to entering kindergarten

**primary school** elementary school

**private school** school maintained by nongovernment funds, including students' tuition fees

**public school** government-supported, usu. tuition-free, school (U.S.); privately endowed secondary school offering classical curriculum (Britain)

**scholarship** money granted to student to help pay tuition

**school** institution providing instruction, esp. for children in grades one to twelve and kindergarten

**school board** local public school administrative body

**school district** administrative unit of public school system

**schoolhouse** building used to house school, esp. elementary school

**schoolroom** classroom

**secondary school** institution after elementary school and before college, particularly grades nine to twelve, public or private

**seminary** parochial, usu. Roman Catholic, secondary school, esp. for girls

**senior high school** four-year secondary school, grades nine through twelve

**session** hours in day or months in year when classes are given

**storefront school** urban school meeting in store fronting on street

**summer school** classes held between June and August, when school is normally not in session

**Sunday school** class held on Sunday for religious instruction, esp. Christian

**trade school** secondary school teaching vocational skills

**training school** school that prepares students for specific occupation

**ulpan school** school for intensive study of Hebrew, esp. by immigrants to Israel

**upper school** division of secondary school, usu. final two years

**vocational school** school providing instruction in industrial or commercial skills needed for particular trade or profession

**yeshiva** school for Talmudic study; Orthodox Jewish school for religious and secular studies

## TEACHERS AND STUDENTS

**adviser** teacher or school administrator who counsels students on academic or personal difficulties

**alumna** female graduate of institution; *pl.* **alumnae**

**alumni** collective term for all graduates of institution

**alumnus** male graduate of institution; *pl.* **alumni**

**apprentice** individual receiving training in specific profession through work experience

**assistant professor** lowest level of university professor

**associate professor** intermediate level of professor, below full professor

**autodidact** self-taught person

**bookworm** extremely serious student with few other interests

**cadet** undergraduate at military academy

**chairperson** head of university department, formerly and sometimes still chairman

**class** group of students graduating in same year

**classmate** member of one's own class

**clock watcher** student eager for class to end

**coach** tutor or trainer providing special instruction to individual student or help with specific problem

**coed** female college student

**collegian** student at college or university

**docent** college or university teacher or lecturer

**doctoral candidate** student participating in doctoral studies leading toward a degree

**don** college or university professor; tutor or fellow of Oxford or Cambridge (Britain)

**donnish** (*adj*) professorial in manner or disposition

**educable** (*adj*) capable of learning, though sometimes mildly retarded

**educator** teacher or school administrator

**emeritus** (*adj*) designating retired college professor holding honorary title

**exchange student** high-school or college student studying at foreign institution, usu. for one year, as part of reciprocal program between two schools or countries

**faculty** teaching staff of educational institution

**faculty meeting** closed-door gathering of teaching staff

**fellow** individual appointed to position and receiving allowance to pursue research or advanced study

**freshman** first-year student at high school or college; frosh

**frosh** *Informal.* freshman

**Fulbright** *Informal.* grant awarded to postgraduate scholar to study abroad; recipient of such a grant

**full professor** tenured professor of highest rank

**gifted child** child with exceptional intelligence and aptitude for learning

**graduate student** student in graduate program or school

**greasy grind** *Slang.* obsessively hardworking student with no interests other than academics

**grind** *Informal.* industrious, serious student

**hall monitor** student assigned to control student activities in elementary or secondary school hallways

**handicapped child** child who is limited by physical, intellectual, or emotional problems, causing difficulty in learning

**headmaster** man heading staff of private school

**headmistress** woman heading staff of private school

**instructor** teacher

**intern** advanced or graduate student in professional field, esp. medicine, receiving supervised work experience in addition to academic training

**junior** third-year student at high school or college

**lector** college lecturer

**lecturer** teacher who instructs class through long, formal discourses; university teacher below rank of assistant professor

**licentiate** person who has received license to practice an art or profession; holder of intermediate degree between baccalaureate and doctorate

**master** *Chiefly Brit.* male teacher, esp. in preparatory school

**mentor** teacher or older student who provides guidance and support for less experienced student

**monitor** student appointed to assist teacher

**novice** beginning student, esp. in specific field

**opsimath** person who begins to learn late in life

**overachiever** individual performing above expected capacity

**pedagogue** teacher

**philomath** lover of learning

**plebe** freshman at military academy

**practice teacher** student teacher

**praepostor** senior student at public school who has authority over other students (Britain)

**preceptor** headmaster or principal of school; teacher

**prefect** student monitor in private school

**preppy** student at preparatory school

**preschooler** child under five attending nursery school

**principal** chief executive officer of school

**privatdocent** university teacher who is receiving no salary, being compensated instead by fees

**proctor** individual chosen to monitor or supervise students, esp. at examination

**prodigy** extraordinarily talented child; wunderkind

**professor** highest-ranking university faculty member

**professoriate** body of professors at college; faculty

**protégé** student receiving special attention and encouragement from teacher or elder

**pundit** teacher; learned individual

**pupil** student

**reader** one who lectures to students (Britain)

**rector** chief administrator of school or university, esp. parochial school

**Rhodes scholar** holder of prestigious scholarship awarded to candidates from United States and British Commonwealth for postgraduate study at Oxford

**salutatorian** student ranking second in graduating class behind valedictorian

**scholar** student, esp. one doing advanced study in some subject; learned, erudite person

**school-age** (*adj*) old enough to begin school, generally six years old

**schoolboy** male schoolchild

**schoolchild** elementary and sometimes secondary school student

**schoolgirl** female schoolchild

**schoolmarm** female schoolteacher, esp. in small town school

**schoolmaster** man who teaches school

**schoolmistress** woman who teaches school

**schoolteacher** teacher, esp. at elementary level

**seminarian** student in seminary, esp. Roman Catholic

**senior** final-year student at high school or college

**sophomore** second-year student at high school or college

**staff** faculty and other school employees

**student** individual who attends school; one who studies so as to learn; pupil

**student body** all students at school or college

**student teacher** assistant teacher still studying to receive teaching credential or degree; practice teacher

**substitute teacher** elementary or secondary school teacher hired as interim replacement for absent teacher

**swot** *Brit. slang.* (*vb*) study hard; (*n*) very industrious student; grind

**TA** *teaching assistant*

**teacher** one trained to be and employed as an instructor of students; instructor; pedagogue

**teacher's aide** noncredentialed assistant to teacher

**teacher's pet** teacher's favorite student

**teaching** act, practice, and profession of instructing students

**teaching assistant** TA; graduate student aiding professor in instruction of undergraduate class

**teaching fellow** graduate student granted free tuition in return for assisting professors in class or laboratory

**tenured** (*adj*) designating college professor holding permanent employment

**trainee** student learning skills in specific field

**transfer** student who has changed from one school to another; (*vb*) change schools

**truant** student inexcusably or habitually late or absent from school

**truant officer** official charged with identifying and apprehending truant students

**tutor** private teacher for one individual; individual providing personalized instruction in British university

**tyro** novice or beginner in some field

**underachiever** individual performing at less than expected level

**underclassman** first- or second-year college student

**undergraduate** student in four-year college program

**upperclassman** third- or fourth-year college student

**valedictorian** student with highest grade ranking in class, selected to present valedictory address

**wunderkind** precociously bright child or prodigy

## CURRICULA, STUDIES, LEARNING, AND TESTS

**ABC's** the alphabet; basic primary education

**abecedarian** (*adj*) relating to the alphabet; (*n*) person learning the alphabet

**achievement test** test that measures learning in a specific area

**adult education** courses offered to adults who have completed or discontinued formal education; continuing education

**A level** second of two standardized secondary school examinations required for university admission (Britain)

**alphabet** ordered letters used to form words of language

**aptitude** innate ability, capacity for learning

**aptitude test** measure of various abilities, esp. verbal and mathematical

**assignment** work to be completed in designated time

**associative learning** process by which discrete ideas become linked to each other

**audiovisual aids** educational materials and teaching devices, such as films and recordings, that appeal to both sense of hearing and sense of sight

**audit** (*vb*) attend class as an observer, without receiving credit

**basal** (*adj*) fundamental, esp. of a reading book

**bilingual education** classes given in two languages

**blackboard** hard, dark surface in classroom for writing and drawing on with chalk; chalkboard

**black studies** college curriculum on history and culture of African Americans

**blue book** small notebook with blue cover, often used for taking college examinations

**bone up** (*vb*) *Informal*. study diligently for test, esp. at last minute

**brushup course** refresher course in subject previously studied

**busywork** effort expended on useless, irrelevant study

**CAI** computer-*assisted* instruction

**career education** vocational education

**CEEB** *College Entrance Examination Board*

**chalkboard** blackboard

**civics** study of government and politics, esp. in high school

**classical education** traditional academic course of study, sometimes including study of Greek and Latin; classicism

**classicism** classical education and study

**cloze** reading comprehension test in which test taker supplies words deleted from text

**College Boards** *Trademark*. aptitude and achievement tests used in determining college admission; SAT

**College Entrance Examination Board** CEEB; organization that administers SAT and achievement tests used to judge applicants for college admission

**colloquy** serious conversation or discourse

**communications skills** ability in language arts

**compensatory education** programs designed to make up for experiences missed by disadvantaged children

**computer-assisted instruction** CAI; instruction in which computer leads student through programmed lesson

**continuing education** adult education

**core study** basic curriculum of subjects related to central theme

**correspondence course** class conducted by mail

**course** series of lectures, assignments, class meetings, and tests on particular subject over set period of time

**course of study** curriculum

**cram** (*vb*) *Informal*. prepare for test at last minute

**crash program** intensive course for rapid learning of material

**credit** acknowledgment that student has completed a class requirement leading to a degree; unit of such acknowledgment, accumulated toward graduation requirement

**crib** (*vb*) *Informal*. plagiarize, copy, or cheat

**criterion-referenced scoring** scoring of test against predetermined specific set of scores by unique group

**Cuisenaire rod** *Trademark*. one of a set of colored rods used in teaching arithmetic

**curriculum** all courses offered by an institution; set of courses in area of specialization; course of study

**curve** grading system based on relative position of student within class, not raw score

**dean's list** honor roll of students with high grades

**dialectic** formal debate, esp. Hegelian or Platonic

**didactic** (*adj*) designed to instruct

**discipline** field of study or special knowledge

**dissertation** extended written treatment on subject, usu. involving research, esp. by degree candidate

**drill** repetitive practice in particular subject

**dyslexia** condition characterized by impairment of reading ability

**early childhood education** instruction at preschool and early elementary school level

**education** act and process of acquiring learning; knowledge and growth produced by schooling

**Education Testing Service** division of CEEB that administers SAT and achievement tests

**educational television** ETV; noncommercial television channels reserved by Federal Communications Commission for educational programs

**elective** course outside student's major field of study

**ESL** English as a second language; course of study in English for nonnative speakers

**essay** written examination or paper

**ETV** educational television

**exam** examination

**examination** scheduled classroom test of students' knowledge and progress; exam

**exceptional children's education** special programs for gifted, retarded, or other children with abnormal or unusual abilities

**exercise** something performed, studied, and repeated to develop skill

**extension** program that makes courses available to those without normal access to them, as by correspondence

**fail** (*vb*) receive grade indicating failure to pass a course

**fescue** long stick for pointing to letters to aid children learning to read

**field** area of study or specialty

**field trip** visit by students to site away from classroom to gain firsthand knowledge of subject

**fill in the blanks** designating an examination that requires student to add appropriate word or phrase omitted from sentence

**final exam** examination given at conclusion of course, covering all material studied

**finals** final examinations in all subjects at end of term

**flashcard** small card with words, numbers, or pictures on it, used in learning drills

**flunk** (*vb*) receive failing grade

**4.0** perfect, straight-A grade point average

**functional illiterate** person with reading ability less than that needed to function in modern society

**grade** measure of knowledge gained in class, given on tests and written work and at end of course

**grade-equivalent score** measurement of test score by decimal representation of year and month of student's grade level, such as 7.3 for third month of seventh grade

**grade point average** average of total earned grade points on scale from zero to four divided by total class credits

**gut** *Slang*. easily passed course

**home ec** home economics; theory and practice of cooking and homemaking

**homework** assignments to be completed outside class

**honor roll** list of students with high grades

**honors class** accelerated class for advanced students

**hornbook** children's primer, orig. 16th century

**humanities** branch of learning concerned with human activities and institutions

**illiteracy** inability to read and write

**independent study** course of study designed by student outside normal curricula or requirements of major

**indoctrination** instruction in fundamentals of partisan point of view

**industrial arts** training in use of tools and machinery

**Initial Teaching Alphabet** expanded phonemic alphabet of forty-three characters, used to teach reading

**innumeracy** difficulty or inability in using mathematics

**instruction** teaching, lectures

**intelligence quotient** IQ; person's mental age, based on standardized intelligence test, multiplied by 100 and divided by chronological age

**intelligence testing** tests designed to identify exceptional children, measure intelligence levels, and diagnose disturbed children

**IQ** intelligence *quotient*

**lab** laboratory

**laboratory** period set aside for scientific experiments and instruction in use of equipment; lab

**language arts** reading, writing, spelling, and speech skills

**language laboratory** facility in which taped, question-and-answer material is used to aid learning of foreign language

**learning** acquisition of knowledge and understanding, esp. by study

**learning disability** physiological or emotional impairment of capacity for learning

**lecture** instructive discourse given to class

**lesson** one day's class instruction

**lesson plan** teacher's outline of class session and assigned work

**lessons** studies and homework

**lexicon** book containing alphabetical arrangement of words and definitions

**literacy** ability to read and write

**makeup test** examination given at later date for those unable to take it initially

**master class** advanced seminar, esp. in music or performing arts

**memorization** learning by rote

**mick** *Slang.* from Mickey Mouse; an easy class

**midterm** exam given halfway through course; midyear

**midyear** midterm

**mnemonic device** trick or technique used to assist memory

**multiculturalism** attempt to avoid racism, sexism, ageism, and ethnocentrism and to encompass various cultures and value systems, esp. in college curriculum

**multiple-choice test** examination offering several possible answers to each question, one of which is correct

**multiplication tables** chart used in elementary school to teach multiplication of numbers one through twelve

**new math** theory of mathematics instruction based on set and number theory leading to principles of arithmetic

**norm-referenced scoring** scoring of test against set of scores compiled by typical group of students

**O level** first of two standardized secondary school examinations required to continue education (Britain)

**open classroom** spacious teaching area shared by groups of students in elementary school, permitting movement from activity to activity and individualized instruction

**orals** oral examination by panel of professors as final test in doctoral program

**paper** written homework assignment

**pass** (*vb*) receive satisfactory grade on examination or for class

**pass-fail grading** system of grading in which students either pass or fail a course and do not receive a letter or number grade

**pedagogy** art, science, and profession of teaching

**phonics** rote memorization of syllable and letter sounds to learn reading

**placement test** entrance examination used to assign students to appropriate class level

**polytechnic** (*adj*) relating to instruction in technical arts and applied sciences

**practice** drills or homework assignments used to achieve proficiency in subject

**practicum** curriculum that includes supervised practical experience and training, esp. for teachers

**précis** brief written summary

**Preliminary Scholastic Aptitude Test** PSAT; SAT-type test taken by high school students in years prior to year of college application

**primer** brief introductory book on some subject, esp. reading

**programmed learning** instruction in which student proceeds through a series of highly structured materials at his or her own pace, receiving immediate feedback and testing from materials

**progressive education** instruction that rejects rote learning and strict discipline in favor of individual stimulation, group discussion, and more diverse curriculum

**propaganda** ideas and information intended to promote or degrade some group or viewpoint

**proseminar** graduate seminar open to advanced undergraduates

**PSAT** *Preliminary Scholastic Aptitude Test*

**quadrivium** upper division studies in medieval university, comprising arithmetic, music, geometry, and astronomy

**question-and-answer** (*adj*) designating a test given in the form of interrogation of student by teacher

**quiz** brief, often unannounced, test on material recently studied

**raw score** actual score on test unadjusted for student's relative position in group tested; number of correct answers on test

**read** (*vb*) study a specific field, esp. in Britain

**reading disability** learning problem that impairs person's reading skill

**reading period** period prior to final examinations during which classes are suspended, usu. for intensive study

**realia** objects used by teacher to illustrate everyday life

**refresher** brief course in subject previously studied

**remedial** (*adj*) designating courses intended to correct poor study habits or improve skills in specific field

**report card** periodic record of student's grades issued by school to parents

**research** systematic study of some topic, often involving accumulation of information and reference materials

**responsions** examination required for enrollment as undergraduate at Oxford

**review** study of all material covered during course, usu. in preparation for examination

**rote** learning mechanically by memory without really understanding

**SAT** Scholastic Aptitude Test

**scholarship** learning, knowledge, study in general

**scholastic** (adj) relating to schools or students

**Scholastic Aptitude Test** Trademark. SAT; standardized test used by colleges in evaluating reading and mathematics skills of applicants for admission

**schoolbook** textbook for specific class

**schooling** education

**school without walls** nontraditional educational program that uses community facilities as learning resources

**schoolwork** lessons, homework, and tests; general studies

**score** measure of test results, determined by one of various methods

**self-paced** (adj) designed so that student can learn at his or her own rate

**self-taught** (adj) having acquired learning or skills without formal education

**semiliterate** (adj) barely able to read and write

**seminar** small group of students pursuing advanced studies with professor

**shop** high school class providing vocational training, esp. in automobile mechanics, metalwork, or carpentry

**skip** (vb) pass over next grade in school and advance to higher level

**slate** small, handheld blackboard

**social studies** study of government, history, and culture; civics

**special education** course of study aimed at group of students with particular needs, problems, or goals

**specialty** primary field of study or interest

**speed-reading** technique for rapid reading by skimming without appreciable comprehension loss

**speller** manual used to teach spelling

**spelling bee** elimination contest to determine best speller

**spoon-feed** (vb) present information so thoroughly that independent thought is curbed and initiative destroyed

**standardized test** achievement test that measures knowledge in specific skill or subject without taking into account other factors

**Stanford-Binet test** intelligence test and scale for evaluating children

**straight A's** perfect report card; 4.0 grade point average

**study** use of one's mind for the gaining of knowledge; such activity in a particular field

**study group** several students studying together regularly, exchanging notes and information

**study hall** schoolroom set aside for individual study, not class discussion

**subject** department or field of knowledge and skills

**Summerhill** famous English school specializing in progressive education

**syllabus** outline or summary of course of study

**tardy** (adj) late for beginning of class

**teach** (vb) give instruction, guide studies, and offer knowledge or information to others

**team teaching** program in which two teachers incorporate their subjects into one course which they teach together

**term paper** lengthy written assignment in high school or college that displays student's progress and knowledge at end of course

**test** examination, measurement, and evaluation of student's knowledge and progress in course

**text** textbook

**textbook** book containing principles of subject, used in its study; text

**theme** written assignment, essay

**thesis** lengthy essay based on original research written by candidate for degree, esp. doctorate

**Three R's** reading, writing, and arithmetic; basic primary education

**tracking** assignment of students to specific curriculum based on aptitude level

**tripos** final honors examination (Britain)

**trivium** lower division studies in medieval university, comprising grammar, rhetoric, and logic

**true-false test** examination in which student must indicate whether answer is correct or incorrect

**tutorial** class conducted for one student or small number of students

**valedictory** farewell address at commencement ceremonies

**visual aid** instructional device, such as a map, chart, or model, that depicts the visual aspect of subject being studied

**viva** oral examination at university in Britain or Europe

**vocational education** vocational training; career education

**vocational training** instruction in industrial or commercial skills needed for particular trade or profession; vocational education

**Wechsler Scales** intelligence tests for adults, children, and preschoolers, used to show subject's strengths and weaknesses

**whole language** basis for method of teaching reading, used as alternative to phonics, in which students read interesting books, write stories before they can spell, and learn correct usage through correction of their work

**workbook** notebook used for homework, notes, or lab work

## EXTRACURRICULAR ACTIVITIES AND CONCERNS

**academic freedom** education without government or other external interference

**beanie** skullcap formerly worn by freshmen at some colleges

**busing** transportation of students from one area to another to achieve racial balance in schools

**cafeteria** school lunchroom

**campus** grounds and facilities of school or university

**cap and gown** mortarboard and full-length gown worn at commencement

**coeducational** (adj) being an institution for male and female students

**common room** lounge for use by faculty or residents of dormitory

**commons** plot of land on campus for general use by students

**corporal punishment** physical punishment of students

**counseling** professional advice for students on career planning and personal problem solving

**custodian** janitor

**debate** contest involving discussion of topic by teams presenting opposing arguments

**detention** keeping students at school after school hours as punishment

**dorm** dormitory

**dormitory** residence building for students at college, university, or boarding school; dorm

**extracurricular** (*adj*) designating student activities not receiving academic credit or engaged in outside classroom

**extramural** (*adj*) relating to extension courses (Britain)

**ferule** lit. flat strip of wood used to punish children; school discipline

**fraternity** selective men's social organization, usu. with its own residence, at college

**Greek** person who belongs to Greek-letter fraternity or sorority

**gym** physical education classes; building for indoor sports

**hazing** cruel pranks and harassment, esp. as fraternity initiation rite

**homecoming** annual weekend during which alumni return to college, usu. highlighted by athletic contest

**hooky** nonattendance at school

**intercollegiate** (*adj*) designating contests or activities conducted among or between colleges

**interscholastic** (*adj*) designating contests or activities conducted among or between schools

**intramural** (*adj*) designating contests or activities conducted within a single university or school

**janitor** person who cleans and maintains school grounds; custodian

**jayvee** *j*unior *v*arsity athletic team

**locker** student's personal storage compartment at school

**mortarboard** cap with flat top and tassel, worn at commencement

**open enrollment** voluntary enrollment in public school other than one indicated by residence; college acceptance of students regardless of qualifications

**Parent-Teacher Association** PTA; national society that brings parents in contact with their children's teachers

**parietals** rules regulating visiting hours for members of opposite sex in college dormitories

**phys ed** *Informal.* physical education classes

**playing fields** open areas for athletic contests

**pledge** person who has promised to join a fraternity or sorority; (*vb*) make such a promise

**Pledge of Allegiance** oath of loyalty to U.S. flag, repeated by class at beginning of day in some elementary and secondary schools

**Project Head Start** government program to help disadvantaged children

**prom** formal dance, esp. at high school

**PTA** *Parent-Teacher Association*

**recess** brief suspension of studies for exercise and recreation

**reunion** gathering of alumni to commemorate graduation

**roommate** person sharing one's dormitory room

**rush** recruiting drive by fraternity or sorority

**schoolbag** case for carrying books and supplies

**school bus** vehicle that picks up and delivers children to and from school

**school prayer** brief prayer recited at beginning of day in some schools, but banned in others

**show and tell** period in elementary school during which students describe or display things of interest to class

**sorority** selective women's social organization at college, usu. with its own residence

**student government** organization of students elected as decision-making body on student affairs

**student newspaper** student-run journal of campus affairs

**student union** college building devoted to extracurricular student activities; center of student affairs; union

**teach-in** lengthy meeting on college campus for debate of controversial issues

**union** student union

**varsity** athletic team representing school or college in contests against other schools

**work-study program** program that offers high school or college students work experience and income in addition to schooling

**yearbook** annual publication that reviews year's activities and lists all students or all graduating students in high school or college

# ARTS AND LEISURE

# CHAPTER 14

# Fine Arts and Literature

# PAINTING

Schools and Styles of Fine Art
Painting Tools and Techniques
Kinds of Paintings
Display of Art

SEE ALSO: Chap. 12: Advertising; Chap. 14: Sculpture; Chap. 16: Architecture; Graphic Design and Printing; Photography; Crafts; Chap. 23: Colors

## SCHOOLS AND STYLES OF FINE ART

**abstract art** nonrepresentational and nonfigurative style emphasizing formal values over representation of subject matter

**abstract expressionism** nonrepresentational style emphasizing emotion, strong color, and giving primacy to the act of painting (mid-20th c.)

**academic art** officially sanctioned art; traditional art, emphasizing grand themes and a rational approach to form and content

**action painting** active, aggressive methods of applying paint; tachism (U.S., mid-20th c.)

**aestheticism** movement characterized by eclectic search for beauty and interest in Japanese and classical art (U.S. and Britain, late 19th c.)

**analytical cubism** fragmented, multifaceted, and simultaneous depiction of a subject in several planes (early 20th c.)

**antiart** self-conscious, nihilistic break with traditional art forms and content (late 20th c.)

**archaism** use of old styles in contemporary art

**art brut** direct, primitive style, as found in the art of children or the mentally disturbed (France, 20th c.)

**art deco** style characterized by repetitive, ornamental, and highly finished curvilinear and geometric designs, esp. in synthetic materials such as plastics (1920's-1930's)

**art nouveau** decorative style emphasizing fluid, biomorphic lines and swirling motifs (late 19th c.)

**ashcan school** antiacademic, realistic depiction of the grimmer aspects of everyday life (U.S., early 20th c.)

**avant-garde** innovative art in advance of popular ideas and images, characterized by unorthodox and experimental methods

**Barbizon School** style emphasizing idyllic landscapes and nature (France, 19th c.)

**baroque** emotional, dramatic style, anticlassical in form and spirit (late 16th-18th c.)

**Bauhaus** school emphasizing the functional and geometric by incorporating craft elements in design (early 20th c.)

**Blaue Reiter** *German.* expressionist group; Blue Rider School (early 20th c.)

**Brucke** expressionist group (Germany, early 20th c.)

**Byzantine** (*adj*) designating a style with Oriental and Occidental elements and strong religious content (2nd-13th c.)

**cave art** prehistoric paintings and engravings on Paleolithic-era cave walls

**classical** style with emphasis on symmetry, proportion, and harmony of line and form (ancient Greece and Rome)

**cloissonism** style with flat colors, black-outlined forms, and a lack of modeling; synthetism (France, 19th c.)

**colorfield** (*adj*) characteristic of abstract, minimal styles without representation, line, form, or modeling, in which color is the sole element (mid-20th c.)

**computer art** electronically produced images displayed on video screens (late 20th c.)

**conceptual art** avant-garde, idea-oriented style with emphasis on performance, theory and criticism, and attitude (late 20th c.)

**concrete art** realism, opposed to abstract art (early 20th c.)

**constructivism** style with geometric abstraction and emphasis on three-dimensionality (Russia, early 20th c.)

**cubism** departure from traditional, naturalistic view of reality, emphasizing multifaceted, simultaneous views of subject and distorted perspectives (early 20th c.)

**dada** style with antirational approach and nihilistic, absurdist, and incongruous themes (1915-1925)

**decadent art** style with artificial, neurotic, sometimes bizarre themes (late 19th c.)

**de Stijl** school of art characterized by minimalism, geometric abstraction, and use of primary colors; neoplasticism (Netherlands, early 20th c.)

**distressed art** style utilizing materials, often found materials, that are abused or battered by the artist (late 1980's)

**divisionism** neo-impressionism

**earthwork** artistic work consisting of large-scale alteration or modification of area of land or artist's installation of soil and rock in display space; aboriginal, nonpermanent paintings done in dirt

**expressionism** style emphasizing emotional expression, strong color and composition, and a distorted, theatrical treatment of image (early 20th c.)

**fantastic realism** highly imaginative, magical subject matter rendered with academic, realistic technique (Austria, mid-20th c.)

**Fauvism** style with brilliant, unrestrained color and offhand approach to composition (France, early 20th c.)

**fin de siècle** *French.* sophisticated stylization (late 19th c.)

**folk art** any untrained, nonacademic, or unschooled style

**Fontainebleau School** style emphasizing the elegant and decorative (France, 16th c.)

**funk art** combination of painting and sculpture, deliberately messy and rough, often humorously depicting provocative or kitsch subjects (U.S., mid-20th c.)

**futurism** style glorifying modern technology, speed, and the machine age (Italy, early 20th c.)

**Gothic** style emphasizing Christian imagery, brilliant color, and strong verticality in composition (12th-16th c.)

**grand manner** academic painting style with adherence to traditional, often noble themes and reliance on formal rules of depiction

**hard-edge** (*adj*) characteristic of a style with geometric abstraction, a flat picture plane, perfection of surface, and graphic precision (U.S., mid-20th c.)

**Hellenic** (*adj*) of the classical style of Greek antiquity (8th-4th c. B.C.)

**Hellenistic** (*adj*) of the post-classical Greek style before the Roman conquest (4th-2nd c. B.C.)

**Hudson River school** group of American painters whose

style was characterized by idyllic landscapes, esp. of the Hudson River area (19th c.)

**hyperrealism** extension of photorealism in which depiction of subject is indistinguishable from reality (late 20th c.)

**Impressionism** style emphasizing the depiction of light and its effects, with the act of seeing as its primary subject (France, 19th c.)

**international style** style with detailed depiction of Christian subjects and Gothic verticality in composition (14th c.)

**intisme** style with intimate interior scenes of domestic life (France, late 19th c.)

**Italianate** (*adj*) conforming to the style of the Italian Renaissance masters

**Jugendstil** art nouveau (Germany, early 20th c.)

**Kamakura** (*adj*) denoting high classical period (Japan, 13th-15th c.)

**kinetic art** art marked by incorporation of painted and sculpted mechanical parts into art piece that moves or creates the impression of movement (mid-20th c.)

**light art** art characterized by incorporation of steadily beaming or blinking electrical and neon lights (mid-20th c.)

**lyrical abstraction** nonfigurative, expressionistic, poetic style, lighter than abstract art in tone and theme (mid-20th c.)

**Mannerism** anticlassical style characterized by dramatic gestures and poses of figures, intense color, and complex perspective (16th c.)

**merz** collage style using junk or found objects (early 20th c.)

**metaphysical painting** pittura metafisica

**Ming** (*adj*) characteristic of a highly academic classicism, esp. in porcelains (China, 14th-17th c.)

**minimal art** abstract, simple, reductionist style with absence of all but basic formal elements and primary colors (U.S., mid-20th c.)

**modernism** style that breaks with traditional art forms and searches for new modes of expression (early 20th c.)

**Mogul school** Islamic art style (India, 16th-19th c.)

**Nabis** style with emphasis on painter's personal vision (France, late 19th c.)

**naturalism** style emphasizing the depiction of the actual appearance of nature and the visible world

**neoclassicism** style modeled after proportion and restraint of Greek and Roman classical antiquity (late 18th-early 19th c.)

**neo-expressionism** style using expressionistic emotionalism in post-expressionist era (mid-20th c.)

**neo-impressionism** style with emphasis on the scientific application of the optical effects of light and color (France, late 19th c.); divisionism

**neoplasticism** de Stijl

**neue wilde** new wave (Germany, late 20th c.)

**new objectivity** style with detailed, realistic depictions emphasized over expressionist values (Germany, early 20th c.)

**new secession** style modeled on the Post-Impressionist sensibility of form, content, and color (Germany, early 20th c.)

**new wave** combination of cartoon, graffiti, and performance art in a minimalist, unsophisticated style (late 20th c.)

**New York school** abstract expressionism practiced by artists in New York City that emphasized the emotional, dramatic, and heroic in scale and theme (mid-20th c.)

**nonobjective** (*adj*) characteristic of a style in which emotional, formal values are emphasized over representation of objects (20th c.)

**nouveau realisme** style characterized by a return to realistic forms in an abstract era (France, mid-20th c.)

**op art** style with graphic abstraction and pattern-oriented optical effects (mid-20th c.)

**Orphism** geometric, cubist-derived style using a broad color spectrum (early 20th c.); synchromism

**performance art** use of paintings, sculpture, and video in live theatrical performance by artist (late 20th c.)

**photorealism** style emphasizing the meticulously realistic depiction of banal contemporary subjects, esp. suburban, snapshotlike scenes (mid-20th c.)

**pittura metafisica** style with mysterious, symbolic, metaphysical subject matter; metaphysical painting (Italy, early 20th c.)

**plein-air** (*adj*) pertaining to a style of painting that represents luminous effects of natural light and open-air atmosphere as contrasted with artificial light and the atmosphere of work produced in a studio (France, 19th c.)

**pointillism** neo-impressionism employing tiny, closely spaced points of color that blend to produce a luminous quality (France late 19th c.)

**pop art** style-making use of images from popular culture and commerce, often reproduced exactly (mid-20th c.)

**Post-Impressionism** emotionally expressive, formally modern style with nontraditional approach to color and composition (late 19th-early 20th c.)

**postmodernism** style reflecting the exhaustion of modernist experimentation and a partial return to more traditional forms (late 20th c.)

**postpainterly abstraction** nongestural, nonrepresentational style with emphasis on clean, perfect surface (mid-20th c.)

**pre-Columbian** (*adj*) of or pertaining to native American art before the arrival of Columbus (pre-16th c.)

**prehistoric** (*adj*) pertaining to cave painting and other forms of Paleolithic art

**pre-Raphaelite** (*adj*) designating a style modeled on romanticized vision of medieval, pre-Renaissance styles (19th c.)

**primitivism** style with unsophisticated, pretechnological, simple approach to form and content

**proletarian art** social realism depicting working class life (early 20th c.)

**Quattrocento** art of Indian Renaissance (15th c.)

**realism** depiction of reality as it appears, without idealization or stylistic, imaginative distortion

**Renaissance** (*adj*) pertaining to humanistic art that is classical in form and content; (*n*) revival of aesthetics of classical antiquity (14th-17th c.)

**representational** (*adj*) designating art concerned with accurate, naturalistic depictions of reality

**rococo** style with ornamental, poetic, curvilinear forms and lyrical themes (18th c.)

**Romanticism** style characterized by an emotional, intuitive exaltation of nature over culture and imagination over realism (late 18th-early 19th c.)

**seicento** classical high Renaissance art (Italy, 17th c.)

**social realism** depiction of ordinary life as emblematic of social and political truths (20th c.)

**suprematism** style emphasizing geometric abstraction (Russia, early 20th c.)

**surrealism** style using subconscious mental activity as its subject matter, characterized by dreamlike, hallucinatory imagery (early 20th c.)

**Symbolism** movement that rejected realism and expressed subjective visions through evocative images (France, late 19th c.)

**synchromism** Orphism

**synthetic cubism** late cubism emphasizing surfaces, altered perspective, and often strong colors

**synthetism** cloissonism

**tachism** action painting

**T'ang** classical period (China, 7th-9th c.)

**Tantra art** mystical, diagrammatic, and symbolic art (Buddhist, Hindu)

**tenebrism** chiaroscuro style that depicted dramatic imagery in dark tones (17th c.)

**verism** fantastic, often disturbing subjects rendered with photographically accurate realism (Germany, early 20th c.)

**video art** use of filmed or videotaped material displayed alone or with other media (late 20th c.)

**vorticism** style characterized by abstract, geometric designs and energetic, machine-age themes (Britain, early 20th c.)

**Yamato-e** narrative painting style characterized by continuous illustrations executed on long scrolls (Japan, 12th-14th c.)

## PAINTING TOOLS AND TECHNIQUES

**abstract** (*adj*) designating reliance on pure form rather than representation of subject matter for effect

**acetate color** opaque, waterproof pigment

**acrylic paint** synthetic, fast-drying pigment

**advancing color** warm colors at red end of spectrum

**aerial perspective** type of perspective involving subject perceived from above by viewer

**airbrush** nozzled tube used to apply paint in spray form

**alla prima** completing oil painting in one sitting

**aniline dye** coal-tar dye used as paint pigment

**appliqué** application of foreign material to surface of painting for ornamentation

**aquarelle** transparent watercolor

**aquatint** etching of spaces rather than lines, producing tonal effect like wash or watercolor

**architectonic** (*adj*) controlled, linear, geometric in rendering

**atelier** artist's studio

**base** inert pigment used in manufacture of lakes

**batik** painting on wax-treated cloth

**binder** substance combining pigment particles into pliable, fluid medium

**black glass** small, convex black mirror for reducing landscape views, dulling color as compositional aid; Claude glass

**brilliance** radiance or intensity of color

**brush** bristles fixed on handle for applying paint or varnish: angular liner, bamboo, blender, bright, bulletin cutter, camel's hair, cutter, dabber, dagger striper, easel, fan blender, filbert, fitch, flat, highliner, lettering, limp, liner, mop, oval, poster, quill, red sable, round, script, shader, varnish, wash

**brushwork** artist's distinctive way of applying paint with brush

**canvas** woven fabric of linen, cotton, or hemp stretched on frame and used as painting surface; completed painting

**cartoon** full-size, preliminary painting or sketch for completed work

**cerography** painting using wax as pigment binder

**chalk** soft, white limestone, sometimes with color added, used in drawing

**charcoal** pencil made from chunk of soft, porous, black carbon

**chiaroscuro** technique of depicting light and dark tones to create an illusion of depth and modeling

**chih-hua** finger painting technique (China)

**chinoiserie** work patterned after Chinese art

**chroma** strength or purity of a color, measured by its departure from neutral color

**chromolithograph** colored picture printed from impressions made by a series of stone or metal plates, each in a different color

**Claude glass** black glass

**coat** single application of paint on surface

**collage** pasting together bits of found objects, newspaper, and cloth over other materials on a single surface

**color** paint, pigment, or dye that reflects light waves of a particular length

**coloration** color arrangement or manner in which colors are used in painting

**complementary colors** two colors at opposite points on color scale, such as red and green

**composition** aesthetically pleasing, harmonious, and effective arrangement of parts to form whole

**construction paper** heavy colored paper, esp. for cutouts

**contrast** use of striking differences, esp. in color or tone, between adjacent parts of painting

**cool colors** blue-green portion of spectrum

**craquelure** network of small cracks in painted or varnished surface of old painting

**crayon** small stick of chalk, colored wax, or charcoal used for drawing

**crepe paper** thin, crinkled paper

**crosshatching** shading technique that uses many parallel strokes

**dab** (*vb*) apply paint in light, quick strokes or dots

**decoupage** cutting out designs from paper or other material, mounting them on surface, and applying varnish or lacquer

**designer's colors** opaque watercolors

**distemper** water-base paint with glue binder; mix of powdered pigment and size

**drawing** picture, design, or sketch done with lines in pen or pencil; skill at using lines to depict something

**drying oil** oil painting medium that dries to form solid surface for pigment

**easel** vertical frame for supporting painting in progress

**eclectic** (*adj*) composed from disparate elements in many styles

**emulsion** liquid suspended in another liquid, esp. oil and varnish

**enamel** pigment mixed with varnish that dries to a hard, glossy finish

**encaustic** (*adj*) designating painting done with pigment mixed with beeswax and blended with heat

**ferrule** metal tube clamping brush hairs to handle

**figurative** (*adj*) designating identifiable representation of human figure or object

**finger paint** water-soluble, nontoxic, creamy paint applied with fingers, esp. for children and crafts

**finish fetish** emphasis on high-gloss, perfectly and smoothly rendered surface

**foreshortening** technique of creating the illusion of a painted object projecting through the picture plane; use of linear perspective to depict three-dimensionality

**forgery** copy of an artwork, intended to pass as an original

**framing** designing and fashioning borders for paintings, usu. of wood, often ornamental

**fresco** technique of painting directly on a wet, plaster surface

**fugitive color** pigment with tendency to fade

**gesso** plaster of Paris used as white primer for painting surface, esp. canvas

**gilding** application of gold leaf to picture surface

**glaze** thin, translucent layer of color

**golden section** aesthetic formula expressed as ratio between two portions of a line, or two dimensions of a plane figure, in which lesser is to greater as greater is to sum of both

**gold watercolor** water-soluble gold in tablet form, for watercolor, illumination, or lettering

**gouache** opaque watercolor bound with gum

**graphic art** art and technique by which copies of an original design are printed, as from a plate or block

**grisaille** monochrome in primarily gray tints, esp. on glass, having appearance of relief

**ground** prepared painting surface

**hachure** hatching

**hatching** shading technique that uses parallel lines; hachure

**highlight** bright, light area emphasizing modeling

**historiated** (*adj*) having human or animal figure ornament

**hue** distinct qualities of a color that position it in the spectrum

**iconography** representation by images; study of such images

**illumination** decorative, esp. miniature, painting in books

**impasto** thick application of paint that forms an opaque relief surface

**imprimatura** painting surface prepared with a thin glaze of color

**japan** varnish mixed with pigment

**lacquer** protective, transparent, resinous liquid that dries to a glossy surface

**lake** pigment prepared with metallic compounds

**limn** (*vb*) represent in painting or drawing

**line** contour or shape of drawing

**linear perspective** type of perspective involving view perceived from in front of subject by viewer in arbitrarily fixed position

**line drawing** drawing done in lines only, showing gradations of tone through variations in width and density of lines

**liver** oil paint that has thickened into an insoluble, rubbery mass inside tube

**long paint** thin, watery paint

**madder** redroot used as pigment

**mahlstick** support piece for steadying painter's hand and brush while at work

**malerisch** (*adj*) *German*. painterly; emphasizing form over outline

**mandorla** halo of light on holy figure (Buddhist, Christian)

**medium** liquid in which pigment is mixed to form paint; type of paint or coloring matter used in painting

**model** person who poses for a drawing, painting, or sculpture

**modeling** technique of depicting three-dimensional objects on two-dimensional surface

**monochromatic** (*adj*) having a one-hued color scheme

**monumental** (*adj*) indicating scale, grandeur, and nobility of form or content

**muller** tool for grinding pigments

**oeuvre** *French*. entire body of an artist's work

**oil paint** pigment mixed with drying oil, esp. linseed oil

**opalesce** (*vb*) exhibit a play of colors

**oxgall** wetting agent used to improve pliability of water paints

**paint** pigment ground to a powder, then mixed with a liquid binding medium

**painterly** (*adj*) having qualities distinctive of painting, esp. rendering images in terms of color or tone rather than contour or line

**painting** art and technique of applying colored pigments and other materials to a flat surface, esp. stretched canvas, to depict an image or represent a feeling with consideration for composition, form, and color

**palette** handheld board for mixing paints

**palette cup** small container that clips onto palette to hold oil or water

**palette knife** thin, flexible blade for mixing and applying paint

**pastel** crayon made of color ground with chalk and compounded with gum water into paste, often of pale color

**pastiche** jumble of different styles

**pentimento** emergence of traces of oil paint underlayer as overlay dries to transparency

**perspective** system of realistically depicting three-dimensional objects or views onto two-dimensional, flat surfaces through convergent lines and planes; portrayal of objects in space

**picture plane** surface behind which a painting's subject is situated in space

**pigment** coloring matter mixed with binder to form paint

**planes** successive stages of depth within a painted image, foreground to background

**polychromatic** (*adj*) painted in many colors

**poster paint** opaque, water-base paint with gum or glue-size binder, sold in large jars, typically in bright colors

**primary colors** red, yellow, and blue, from which all other colors in spectrum can be mixed

**proportion** aesthetic relation of parts to whole

**receding color** cool color at blue end of spectrum

**reducing glass** double concave lens that reduces image seen through it

**representational** (*adj*) depicting recognizable objects, figures, or scenes

**restoration** repair of damaged or worn painting

**rosin** hard resin used as varnish ingredient

**sand painting** painting composed of colored sands spread on the ground

**saturation** degree of purity of a color; intensity of hue

**scumbling** brush technique that softens a painted surface by overlaying it with a light, irregular, textured, semiopaque color

**secco** painting on dry plaster on wall or ceiling

**secondary colors** orange, green, and purple, being those colors produced by mixing two of the primary colors

**section d'or** ideal proportion between the side of a square and a diagonal drawn inside the same square, giving a sense of design and harmony, based on golden section ratio

**sfumato** technique used to depict hazy, smoky shadows or outlines

**sgraffito** technique in which surface layer of paint is scratched through to reveal color beneath

**shellac** thin, clear varnish made from lac resin and alcohol

**short paint** thick paint

**sinopis** reddish brown pigment, esp. for drawings

**size** glue and water preparation for canvas

**sizing** process of applying a surface with size

**sketch** quick, preliminary drawing used as basis for painting

**solvent** liquid component of paint that evaporates to leave dried pigment on surface painted

**spectrum** series of colored bands arranged in order of respective wavelength from infrared to ultraviolet

**stretcher** backing frame for canvas

**study** detailed drawing or painting of a section of the planned work

**taboret** artist's chest with shelves and tabletop palette

**tempera** pigment mixed with water and an albuminous or gelatinous material, esp. egg yolk

**tessera** small tile or stone for mosaic illustration

**texture** characteristic visual and tactile quality of surface of work of art, resulting from manner in which materials are used

**texture paint** paint of heavy consistency and coarse grain consisting of gypsum and sand with binder, used for creating rough surfaces

**thinner** solvent used to dilute paint

**tinctorial** (*adj*) relating to colors, dyes, and stains

**tint** gradation of a color relative to the amount of white mixed into it

**tone** general coloration or balance of dark and light in a painting, creating harmony

**tracing** copy made by following lines as seen through transparent paper superimposed on original

**traction** cracking or fissuring of dry paint surface

**trompe l'oeil** extremely deft illusion in which a painted object appears real through depiction in fine detail

**turpentine** colorless, volatile oil used in paints and for cleaning brushes

**underpainting** preliminary coat of paint

**value** degree of lightness or darkness in a color

**varnish** protective film composed of resin dissolved in drying oil

**wash** thin coat of water-base paint

**water-base paint** pigment soluble in water; watercolor

**watercolor** pigment in binder of gum arabic, water, and glycerin; translucent stain of color on paper

## KINDS OF PAINTINGS

**altarpiece** devotional image or shrine in church or temple

**anastasis** depiction of Christ harrowing hell

**cabinet picture** small easel painting

**calathus** bowl of fruits, in art symbolizing abundance; kalathos

**capriccio** depiction of fantastic architecture (18th c.)

**cherub** representation of a winged angel, or chubby child clothed in red, who supports the heavenly throne

**cityscape** depiction of an urban scene

**contrapposto** depiction of a strongly twisted human torso

**deiesis** depiction of Christ enthroned between Mary and St. John

**diablerie** depiction of hell and its inhabitants

**diptych** two-paneled altarpiece

**dreamscape** depiction of a fantasy world or figments of dreams

**easel painting** canvas painted at an easel, then framed and hung

**ecce homo** *Latin.* lit. behold the man; depiction of Christ in judgment before Pontius Pilate

**ex-voto** *Latin.* lit. out of a vow; image or painting giving thanks or left as offering to God

**figure** drawing of a human body and face

**fusuma** painting on a sliding screen (Japan)

**genre** realistic depiction of scenes from everyday domestic life

**grotesque** work combining animal, human, plant, and fantastical forms

**hieratic** (*adj*) designating a style characterized by prescribed religious content

**history painting** usu. academic depiction of scenes from mythology, history, or the Bible

**icon** image, esp. portrait

**illuminated manuscript** miniature painting used as decoration in a handwritten text; psalter

**kakemono** vertical scroll painting (Japan)

**kalathos** calathus

**kwacho** depiction of birds and flowers (Japan)

**landscape** depiction of natural landforms, sometimes allegorical

**life drawing** drawing of human figure, often nude

**maesta** depiction of Madonna and Child (Italy)

**makemono** horizontal scroll painting (Japan)

**mandala** schematized representation of the cosmos, usu. in form of concentric geometric shapes, in Oriental art

**memento mori** depiction of objects that are reminders of mortality

**miniature** very small painting

**mosaic** illustration composed of small, colored stones or tiles set into cement

**mural** large-scale painting, usu. on a wall or ceiling

**namban** portrait of foreigners, esp. Europeans (Japan)

**nature morte** *French.* lit. dead nature; still life

**nocturne** night scene

**nude** undraped human figure, sometimes allegorical

**panel painting** painting supported on freestanding framework, as distinct from a mural or fresco

**pantocrator** depiction of Christ as universal ruler (Byzantine)

**pastoral** (*adj*) designating painting that depicts rural life, often in idealized manner

**pictograph** picture symbolizing an idea or object, used as early form of writing

**Pietà** depiction of the Virgin Mary mourning over the dead Christ

**polyptych** altarpiece with more than three panels

**portrait** depiction of a person, esp. the face

**psalter** illuminated manuscript

**putto** stylized, decorative depiction of nude male child, often winged

**rotulus** illuminated manuscript in scroll form

**seascape** depiction of scene at sea

**self-portrait** depiction of artist's own face

**silhouette** side view of subject, esp. figure or head, filled in with black

**stick figure** depiction of human figure as single lines with circle for head

**still life** realistic depiction of inanimate objects, esp. flowers, fruit, or domestic items; nature morte

**tanka** scroll painting of a deity (Tibetan Buddhism)

**tondo** circular picture

**triptych** three-paneled altarpiece

**triskelion** figure composed of three curved or bent arms, legs, or branches radiating from the center

**uchiwa-ye** fan-shaped picture (Japan)

**ukiyo-e** depiction of scenes from everyday life (Japan)

**vanitas** still life representing mortality

**vignette** small, decorative painting used at intervals in a book

**wall painting** mural painted directly on wall

**wen-jen-hua** scholarly, literary painting (China)

## DISPLAY OF ART

**artist's rep** person responsible for selling artist's work on commission or arranging shows

**auction** showing of valuable artwork offered for sale to highest bidder

**collector** person who owns and displays artwork in his or her home

**cooperative gallery** noncommercial gallery run by artists

**curator** person in charge of a museum and the objects in it

**docent** tour guide at museum

**gallery** building devoted to exhibition and sale of artworks

**group show** showing of works by more than one artist

**hanging** aesthetic placement of paintings on wall, using considerations of light, shadow, and height

**juried show** show for which works are selected by panel of judges

**museum** large institution devoted to the acquisition, study, care, and permanent exhibition of works of art

**opening** first day of show

**patron** individual who supports the arts and artists

**portfolio** large, flat case for carrying drawings or paintings

**private collection** large number of valuable artworks owned by individual, sometimes lent out for public showing

**retrospective** show covering several phases in artist's career

**show** display of artworks in gallery or museum for specific length of time

**studio** artist's workroom, also used for casual display of works

**vernissage** varnishing day; the day before an opening, used for last-minute touch-up of paintings

# SCULPTURE

Types of Sculpture
Sculpture Tools and Techniques

**SEE ALSO**: Chap. 5: Tools and Hardware; Chap. 14: Painting; Chap. 16: Architecture; Crafts

## TYPES OF SCULPTURE

**akrolith** statue made of two materials, esp. with wooden body and stone head

**anaglyph** ornament sculptured or embossed in low relief

**assemblage** sculptural collage of unrelated parts, materials, or objects

**bas-relief** sculpture projecting less than half its depth from matrix; low relief

**bust** sculpture of upper part of body, esp. head and shoulders

**collage** composition of seemingly unrelated parts, materials, or objects

**colossal** extremely large-scale sculpture, larger than heroic

**discobolus** statue of athlete about to toss discus (ancient Greece)

**heroic** sculptural scale larger than life-size

**high relief** sculpture projecting more than halfway out from matrix

**ice sculpture** carving made from ice block in freezing environment

**installation** placing of sculptures and other objects in physical environment or room, which becomes part of piece

**low relief** bas-relief

**mezzo-relievo** sculpture projecting half its depth from matrix

**mobile** freely moving, three-dimensional sculpture made of several counterbalanced objects suspended at different levels and moving in the air

**relief** sculpture attached to a matrix or flat background, not freestanding

**sculpture in the round** freestanding piece with no supporting backing or matrix

**stabile** abstract sculpture constructed of stationary parts attached to fixed supports

**statuary** groups of statues; art of making statues

**statue** three-dimensional sculpture of human or animal form

**statuette** small statue

**totem** carved emblem, esp. animal or plant form

**video sculpture** three-dimensional piece incorporating prerecorded videotape

**wax sculpture** carving in wax

**wood sculpture** carving and assembling in wood

## SCULPTURE TOOLS AND TECHNIQUES

**acrylic resin**  thermoplastic polymer used in making molded plastic

**alabaster**  translucent, marblelike stone for carving

**alloy**  mixture of two or more metals or a metal and non-metal, such as bronze or brass

**annealing**  softening of hammer-hardened metal by heating and gradual cooling

**anodize** (*vb*)  coat metal with protective oxide film by electrolysis

**armature**  framework used to support sculpture in modeling process

**banker**  sculptor's workbench for dressing stones

**base**  lowest part of sculpture, often separate part on which it rests

**boss**  projecting volume to be carved or cut

**boucharde**  toothed, metal, stone-carving hammer

**brazing**  method of joining metals; coating with brass or giving brasslike appearance

**bronze**  alloy of copper and tin for casting statuary

**bronzing**  process of coloring a plaster cast to make it appear like bronze

**burnishing**  rubbing or polishing to a high gloss

**bush chisel**  toothed, stone-carving hand tool

**carving**  cutting away of wood or stone to create three-dimensional forms, as opposed to modeling

**casing**  plaster reinforcing shell used to hold flexible, negative mass

**casting**  reproduction technique using a mold

**casting plaster**  white plaster of Paris

**cavo-relievo**  relief carving within recessed surface, in which highest point is flush with background stone

**charge** (*vb*)  fill negative mold with positive material

**chase** (*vb*)  finish metal surface

**chisel**  sharp, metal carving tool: bush, claw, oval, pointed, or T-shape

**chryselephantine** (*adj*)  covered with ivory and gold, esp. antique Greek statuary

**cire perdue**  lost-wax process

**coil method**  technique of construction with clay coils

**core**  solid, internal portion of mold in metal casting

**damascene**  decorative inlay of one metal on another

**dead stone**  stone ruined by exposure to weather

**drill**  tool for boring holes in wood, metal, or stone

**electrum**  alloy of gold and silver for fine sculptural details

**emboss** (*vb*)  decorate with low relief design

**fabricate** (*vb*)  assemble parts into sculptural whole

**file**  abrasive metal tool for smoothing and shaping

**filler**  inert ingredients used to add bulk to mixture

**foundry**  process of melting, casting, or molding metals

**galvanize** (*vb*)  add zinc plating to metal

**ganosis**  application of colored wax to stone sculpture to dull glare during carving

**goggles**  transparent, protective eye coverings, esp. used when welding metal

**gouge**  curved chisel

**gradine**  toothed chisel

**grounding**  finely polished marble

**hammer**  malletlike tool for applying force to chisel

**lathe**  device for shaping a piece by holding it against an abrading or cutting tool

**lost-wax process**  technique for casting metal, in which modeled wax form is melted away and space between core and outer mold is filled with molten metal such as bronze

**mallet**  cylindrical wooden block on handle

**mantle**  clay mold around a wax model

**maquette**  small, preliminary model of finished work

**marble**  very hard limestone rock used as classic carving material

**marmoreal** (*adj*)  resembling marble or marble statue

**matrix**  base material to be carved

**modeling**  building up of three-dimensional form, as opposed to carving

**mold**  form for making cast of sculptural form

**moulage**  process of making a mold, esp. with plaster of Paris

**negative**  shell-like mold or impression into which casting material is poured or pressed

**niello**  deep-black alloy of sulfur and lead or copper for decorative inlays on metal

**origami**  art of folding paper to depict objects (Japan)

**papier-mâché**  shredded paper soaked in water and glue to form pulpy medium

**paraffin**  colorless, odorless, waxy hydrocarbon used for casting

**patina**  usu. green film on surface of old bronze, caused by exposure to atmosphere or chemicals

**pedestal**  base or stand for sculpture, esp. bust

**peen**  wedgelike or spherical striking surface of hammerhead, used to shape material

**pick**  pointed, metal hammer for removing large areas of stone

**piece mold**  negative made in several parts to preserve original and permit many positive castings

**plaster of Paris**  mixture of calcined gypsum with water to form quick-setting paste used for casts, moldings, and statuary

**plastic** (*adj*)  capable of being shaped, molded, cast, or pressed into different shapes; (*n*) synthetic material with malleable quality

**Plasticine**  *Trademark.* oil-base modeling paste used instead of clay or wax

**plasticity**  flexible or shapable quality of a material

**pointing**  system of copying from three-dimensional model by drilling holes to required depths

**pointing device**  apparatus that marks or drills into a sculpture to set proportionate volumes in order to make copies on any scale

**polychromy**  use of many colors, esp. on statuary

**positive**  cast formed by filling negative mold with casting material

**quarry**  excavation site for marble or stone

**quenching**  quick-cooling of heated metal by immersion in brine, oil, or water

**rasp**  sharply toothed carving and finishing tool

**repoussé**  process of hammering metal into decorative forms in relief

**sandblasting**  etching glass, or cleaning and grinding metal or stone surface, by application of sand carried at high speed by air or steam

**sander**  hand or power tool for smoothing surfaces

**sand molding**  coating the inside of a mold with sand to prevent material from sticking

**sculpture**  art and technique of carving, molding, or welding plastic or hard materials into three-dimensional works of art

**site-specific** (*adj*) designating a sculpture which is created, designed, or selected for a specific location

**slush casting** casting of hollow, metal shape by pouring metal into mold and immediately pouring it out, leaving thin layer that hardens on walls of mold

**soapstone** soft, easily carved stone

**spall** chip or splinter broken from stone in carving

**stainless steel** rust-resistant steel alloy with high luster

**stereotomy** technique of cutting solids to form geometric shapes

**stone** mass of rock broken off from its matrix rock bed

**stone carving** cutting away of stone from a block to form three-dimensional shape

**temper** (*vb*) achieve desired consistency or hardness by mixing or treating, esp. by suddenly cooling heated metal

**term** pedestal supporting a bust or merging into a biomorphic shape

**torch** welding and heating tool

**turn** (*vb*) work on a lathe

**vent** passage in mold through which gases escape during casting

**waste mold** negative mold that must be destroyed to free positive cast

**welding** process of uniting metals by fusing them when molten or pressing them together when soft

# LITERATURE

Schools, Styles, and Forms
Devices, Techniques, and Elements
Books and Pages
Literary Characters and Practitioners

**SEE ALSO:** Chap. 11: Publishing and the Press; Chap. 15: Theater; Chap. 18: Grammar, Phonetics, and Linguistics; Rhetoric and Figures of Speech

## SCHOOLS, STYLES, AND FORMS

**abstract poetry** poetry emphasizing use of sound rather than the meaning of words to convey emotional tone

**accentual verse** poetry based on number of accents rather than duration of sounds or syllabic recurrence

**aestheticism** literary movement emphasizing aesthetic values over social and moral values (19th c.)

**Amerind** written and oral literary tradition of native American Indians

**angry young man** one of a group of writers whose works were characterized by an iconoclastic style reflecting bitter dissatisfaction with traditional society (Britain, mid-20th c.)

**animal epic** medieval narrative form using animal characters

**antinovel** piece of prose fiction lacking some elements of novel structure, such as plot or character development

**Apollonian** (*adj*) emphasizing formal elements and rationality

**apologue** allegorical fable typically containing a moral

**Attic** (*adj*) emphasizing clear, lucid, elegant prose

**autobiography** account of author's own life; memoirs

**avant-garde** innovative style that challenges traditional and established forms

**ballad** poem that tells a story, often meant to be performed out loud

**ballad stanza** four line stanza of iambic tetrameter with second and fourth lines rhymed

**baroque** style emphasizing dramatic or distorted elements presented in classical ordered form (17th-18th c.)

**Beat Generation** rebellious style emphasizing colloquial language and nonconformist values (U.S., 1950's)

**belles-lettres** literature, esp. with creative and artistic style and content; letters

**Bildungsroman** novel narrating story of young person's coming of age and development

**biography** narrative of another person's life

**Bloomsbury group** group of writers and intellectuals, including Virginia Woolf and John Maynard Keynes, associated with Bloomsbury district in London (1920's)

**Byronic** (*adj*) characterized by romantic melancholy and melodrama, as in the works of Lord Byron

**Celtic Renaissance** revival of Gaelic language and literature (late 19th-early 20th c.)

**chanson** song; poem to be sung

**chanson de geste** song of great deeds; epic poem

**chronicle** medieval and Renaissance historical writing

**classical** (*adj*) pertaining to a style with great scope, depth, clarity, and elegance; pertaining to Greek and Roman classics

**classicism** adherence to classical principles, esp. in contrast with Romanticism (19th c.)

**comedy** literary and dramatic form emphasizing humor, treating events lightly or satirically, and having a happy ending

**comedy of intrigue** comic style emphasizing plot and situation more than characterization

**comedy of manners** comic style emphasizing use of manners and conventions of sophisticated society

**comedy of morals** comic style emphasizing ridicule of bad moral practices, aiming to instruct in moral improvement

**comic relief** humorous episode or scene intended as contrast in serious drama or literary work, often to emphasize primary action

**concrete poetry** unconventional, graphic arrangement of letters, words, and symbols to convey meaning

**confession** autobiography addressing very private topics

**courtly love** stylized code of conduct between lovers, esp. as described in medieval literature

**criticism** analysis and evaluation of literary works

**cyberpunk** science fiction characterized by violence, computer technology, and nihilism (1980's)

**cycle** collection of poems or narratives related by common subject matter, usu. a central character

**dada** literary and dramatic artistic movement emphasizing nihilism, irrationality, absurdism, and sometimes violent opposition to conventional values (Europe, 1915-25)

**decadent** member of literary and artistic movement emphasizing aesthetic values of art over nature and freedom from moral restraints (late 19th c.)

**deconstruction** literary analysis based on rejection of notion of hierarchy and belief that nature of language and usage prevents any text from having a fixed, coherent meaning that represents reality (mid-20th c.)

**detective story**  literary form with crime and the apprehension of criminals as its subject

**diary**  daily journal of personal activities and reflections

**dime novel**  cheap paperback fiction, esp. detective story or melodrama; penny dreadful

**drama**  composition in verse or prose, usu. for theatrical performance, that portrays character through story involving conflicts in which emotions are expressed through dialogue and action

**eclogue**  pastoral poem

**elegy**  song, poem, or speech lamenting one who is dead; poem in elegiac couplets

**Elizabethan** (*adj*) of or pertaining to drama and literature of the reign of Elizabeth I of England, including the works of Shakespeare (late 16th c.)

**epic**  literary work recounting deeds of legendary hero

**epic poem**  traditional form of long narrative poem recounting deeds of legendary hero

**epigram**  terse, witty, often paradoxical saying, often in form of concise poem with ingenious ending

**epistle**  letter, esp. formal or elegant one

**epistolary novel**  novel written in the form of letters

**epithalamium**  song or poem honoring bride and groom

**epos**  epic poetry; group of poems, transmitted orally, concerned with facets of a common epic theme

**erotica**  literary works devoted to sexual themes

**essay**  brief, analytic, interpretive prose composition dealing, often formally, with a single subject from a subjective viewpoint

**exemplum**  anecdote or short narrative with moral point, esp. used to sustain argument

**Expressionism**  depiction by nonnaturalistic means of subconscious thoughts, subjective realities of characters, and the struggle of abstract forces (20th c.)

**fable**  narration demonstrating a useful truth, esp. in which animals speak as humans; legendary, supernatural tale

**fabulism**  writing of fables

**faction**  *Informal*. novel or other writing that treats real events and people as if fictional; roman à clef

**fairy tale**  story about fairies or other magical creatures, usu. for children

**fantasy**  fiction with strange or otherworldly settings or grotesque characters

**farce**  light, dramatic composition with improbable plot, broad satirical comedy

**festschrift**  collection of learned essays by students and colleagues honoring a scholar on a special occasion

**fiction**  invented or imagined story

**fin de siecle**  *French*. style characteristic of the end of the 19th century, esp. fashionably sophisticated despair

**Gongorism**  style characterized by ornate language and artificial diction

**Gothic**  fiction with emphasis on horror and macabre, mysterious, or violent events, often in desolate, remote settings

**graveyard school**  melancholy, romantically gloomy style (18th c.)

**grotesque**  fanciful, fantastic, and bizarre representations of human life and events (19th-20th c.)

**Grub Street**  literary hacks collectively (18th c.)

**haiku**  unrhymed verse form with 17 syllables, usu. in three lines (Japan)

**heroic** (*adj*) dealing with or describing the deeds and attributes of heroes

**high comedy**  comedy that employs subtle characterizations and witty language, often to satirize upper class lifestyles

**historical novel**  fictional account of historical events or story of fictional characters and events in historical setting

**idyll**  short lyrical poem or prose composition describing pastoral scenes or any charming episode of everyday life •

**Jacobean** (*adj*) of or pertaining to the literary style characteristic of the age of James I of England (early 17th c.)

**jeremiad**  prolonged lamentation or complaint

**journal**  daily record of experiences and reflections, esp. for private use

**juvenilia**  works suitable or designed for the young

**kaleyard school**  school of writers who described homely life in Scotland (late 19th c.)

**lampoon**  harsh satire usu. directed against an individual

**letter**  personal, written message directed to a person or organization

**letters**  literature; belles-lettres

**limerick**  humorous verse rhymed aabba, usu. with a's of three anapestic feet and b's of two anapestic feet

**literature**  writings in which ideas of permanent or universal interest are expressed through artistic use of forms such as novels, poetry, plays, histories, biographies, or essays

**Lost Generation**  American writers living in post-World War I Europe

**low comedy**  often farcical comedy of action with simple characters, burlesque, and horseplay

**lyric poetry**  poems expressing intense personal emotion

**masque**  short, allegorical drama performed by masked actors (16th-17th c.)

**melic** (*adj*) pertaining to an elaborate form of lyric poetry (ancient Greece)

**melodrama**  work of extravagant theatricality, unlikely plot, and overwrought and simplistic characterizations

**memoir**  record of events written by person having intimate knowledge of them; biography or biographical sketch

**memoirs**  autobiography; recounting of one's life and experiences

**minimalism**  style characterized by spare, simple, often impersonal and repetitive tone (mid-20th c.)

**miracle play**  medieval drama based on the life of a saint or martyr

**missive**  letter, usu. formal or official

**mock-heroic** (*adj*) of or pertaining to a form of satire in which trivial subjects, characters, and events are treated in the heroic style

**modernism**  self-conscious break with past and search for new forms of expression (early 20th c.)

**monograph**  scholarly work on some specific subject

**mystery**  fiction dealing with the solution of a crime or the unraveling of secrets

**mystery play**  medieval drama based on Scriptural incidents

**myth**  legend or traditional narrative, often based in part on historical events, that reveals human behavior and natural phenomena by its symbolism

**naturalism**  literature based on scientific observation of life, without idealization

**New Criticism**  style of literary criticism emphasizing close textual analysis (mid-20th c.)

**New Humanism** works that reflects a belief in moderation, dignity, permanent values, and dualistic existence (20th c.)

**nonfiction** prose composition dealing with noninvented, nonimagined subject

**novel** extended fictional prose narrative, usu. involving a central character: novel of character, of incident, of manners, of sensibility, of the soil, or psychological novel

**novelette** brief novel or long short story

**novella** brief novel with compact plot

**nursery rhyme** short, simple, traditional rhymed poem or song for very young children

**occasional verse** poetry created for particular occasion

**ode** lyric poem marked by exalted feeling, varying line length, and complexity of form

**Parnassian** (*adj*) denoting school of poets who emphasized form over emotion (France, late 19th c.)

**parody** composition that imitates the style of another author or work for comic effect

**pasquinade** publicly posted lampoon or satire

**pastel** short, light prose sketch

**pastiche** literary work that borrows from or mimics the style of one or more sources

**penny dreadful** *Chiefly Brit.* dime novel

**Petrarchan sonnet** sonnet consisting of an octave with the rhymed scheme abbaabba and a sestet in one of several rhyme schemes, such as cdecde or cdcdcd

**picaresque novel** episodic adventures of usu. roguish protagonist

**poem** verse composition

**poetry** sometimes rhymed, usu. rhythmic writing with concentrated imagery in language selected to create an emotional response to its sound and sense; metrical writing; verse

**polemic** art of disputation; an argument

**polyphonic prose** rhythmic prose containing many poetic devices

**postmodernism** any of various reactions to modernist explorations and austere forms, often entailing some return to past forms, minimalism, fantasy, complexity, and pessimism

**poststructuralism** any of various theories of literary criticism, such as deconstruction, that hold that there is no single true reading of a text

**potboiler** usu. inferior work written for profit, esp. fiction

**prose** unrhymed, nonmetrical writing

**prosody** system or style of versification and metrical structure; science and art of versification

**prothalamion** song or poem written to celebrate a marriage

**psychobiography** biography that stresses childhood trauma or other bases for the unconscious motives of its subject

**psychological novel** novel delving deeply into characters' feelings and motivations

**quantitative verse** poetry based on temporal quantity or duration of sounds

**Rabelaisian** (*adj*) characterized by coarse, broad humor, suggestive of the work of François Rabelais

**realism** nonidealized fidelity to accurate literary representation of real or everyday life

**Renaissance** (*adj*) designating literature marked by the humanistic revival of classical influence in Europe (14th-17th c.)

**Restoration comedy** farcical comedies of manners written in the period following the Restoration of Charles II to the English throne (17th c.)

**rhyme** verse composition that rhymes

**roman** *French.* novel

**roman à clef** *French.* novel depicting real persons and actual events under fictional names

**roman-fleuve** *French.* saga

**Romanticism** period and style emphasizing emotional and imaginative intensity (19th c.)

**rondeau** verse based on two rhyme sounds, composed of ten or thirteen lines in three stanzas, in which the opening words of the first stanza are used as a refrain after the second and third stanzas

**rondel** short poem, usu. of fourteen lines on two rhymes, of which four are made up of the initial couplet repeated in the middle and at the end

**saga** heroic narrative about historic or legendary figures; lengthy, multigenerational, fictional narrative; roman-fleuve

**satire** work holding up human vices and follies to ridicule; ironic, witty work exposing or discrediting vice or folly

**science fiction** stories based on impact of actual, imagined, or potential science, usu. set in future or on other planets

**semiotics** study and analysis of the relationship of signs and symbols, esp. in language

**serial** work appearing in installments

**Shakespearean sonnet** sonnet having the rhyme scheme abab, cdcd, efef, gg, and consisting of three quatrains and one couplet

**short short story** highly condensed work of prose fiction

**short story** compact, fictional narrative with few characters, unified effect, and often more mood than plot

**sirvente** medieval poem or song, either heroic or satirical, composed by a troubadour

**sketch** short, usu. descriptive composition, intentionally slight, discursive in style, and familiar in tone

**soap opera** serialized melodrama for TV or radio

**socialist realism** state-approved literary style that glorifies worker's life in socialist country

**song** short musical composition with lyrics

**sonnet** fixed verse form of fourteen lines, usu. in iambic pentameter with set rhyming pattern, often ending in rhymed couplet

**speech** public address or discourse

**Sturm und Drang** German literature characterized by rousing action and high emotionalism, often featuring individual revolt against society (18th c.)

**surrealism** style emphasizing production of fantastic, incongruous imagery through unnatural juxtapositions (1920's)

**Symbolism** French reaction to realism, exalting symbolic representation over actuality (late 19th c.)

**tanka** five-line poem consisting of 31 syllables (Japan)

**technothriller** action-suspense novel featuring use of sophisticated technology, esp. weapons systems

**tetralogy** literary composition in four connected parts

**textual criticism** close analysis of a literary work, often aiming to determine author's original text

**thriller** gripping work with intrigue, adventure, and suspense

**tongue twister** amusing phrase, line, or verse that is difficult to pronounce due to a succession of similar consonantal sounds

**tragedy** serious narrative or drama having a sad or disastrous ending; in ancient drama, downfall of a great person due to a tragic flaw or fate

**tragicomedy** drama blending tragedy and comedy

**translation** rendering of literary work from one language into another

**trilogy** literary work in three connected parts

**true life** realistic narrative or drama, esp. of everyday life

**verse** poetry; metrical writing in general

**versification** act of composing verses; particular metrical structure or style; prosody

**Victorian** (*adj*) denoting writing often associated with strict moral standards and conduct in Britain during reign of Queen Victoria (late 19th c.)

**vita** brief, autobiographical sketch

**western** simple, action-packed narrative set in old American West, usu. involving cowboys

**whodunit** *Informal.* mystery story

# Devices, Techniques, and Elements

**agon** dispute or debate between chorus and characters in classic Greek tragedy

**Alexandrine** verse with six iambic feet; iambic hexameter

**allegory** extended metaphor using objects, characters, and events to represent larger meanings

**alliteration** repetition of initial sound in two or more consecutive words

**allusion** figure of speech employing reference to famous or identifiable person, place, event, or literary passage

**ambiguity** expression of an idea in words that may be interpreted in more than one way

**amphigory** nonsense verse or composition

**amplification** figure of speech using restatement for emphasis

**ana** anecdotes, sayings, or literary curiosities about a particular subject

**analects** literary fragments or passages

**analogy** comparison of apparently or largely dissimilar objects to reveal similarities

**anapest** metrical verse foot with two short or unstressed syllables followed by one long or stressed syllable

**anecdote** brief narrative describing a particular interesting event or person

**anticlimax** narrative moment involving a small or trivial resolution in place of the expected larger and more significant resolution

**antiphrasis** irony; use of word or description to convey the opposite of its normal or literal meaning

**antithesis** figure of speech using emphatically contrasting images or words

**arsis** lighter, shorter part of poetic foot in quantitative verse; accented, longer part of poetic foot in accentual verse

**assonance** juxtaposition of similar sounds without actually rhyming, esp. vowels

**atmosphere** dominant mood or tone of a work

**bathos** unsuccessful attempt at profundity, resulting in ridiculous or humorous effect

**bibliotics** analysis of handwriting to authenticate a document or determine its authorship

**blank verse** unrhymed verse; unrhymed iambic pentameter, often with each second line accented

**bombast** inflated, extravagant expression

**bowdlerize** (*vb*) censor or abridge by cutting offensive sections

**bucolic** (*adj*) pertaining to descriptions of an idyllic, rural life

**cacophony** harsh, discordant sounds in recited poetry

**cadence** measured, rhythmic emphasis of language

**caesura** break in poetic rhythm

**canto** one of the main divisions of a long poem

**caricature** description employing extreme and comic exaggeration

**carmen figuraturum** poem printed to form the physical shape of its subject matter

**character** convincing, imaginary personality developed and realized in fiction

**characterization** creation, presentation, and exposition of personalities in literature

**character sketch** brief essay or story that describes a person

**clerihew** light verse quatrain rhyming aabb, usu. dealing with person named in first line

**cliche** timeworn and commonplace expression; trite description

**climax** culmination of dramatic narrative, often turning point in story

**coda** concluding or summary part of literary work

**cognomen** distinguishing name or epithet

**collate** (*vb*) compare two texts or editions

**colloquialism** informal usage of word or phrase, usu. not acceptable in formal use

**common meter** four-line stanza with lines one and three in iambic tetrameter, lines two and four in iambic trimeter

**complaint** lyric poem on subject of unrequited love or sadness

**conceit** dramatic, witty, ingenious metaphor or analogy

**conflict** struggle or contrast of opposing forces in plot

**controlling image** image or idea forming basic nature or structure of work

**couplet** two rhyming lines of verse

**dactyl** metrical foot with one long or stressed syllable followed by two short or unstressed syllables

**dead metaphor** overused figure of speech drained of its original power to evoke analogy

**denouement** final unfolding of plot; resolution or outcome

**device** word pattern, figure of speech, or dramatic convention used to evoke desired effect in literary work

**diatribe** bitter argument, accusation, or harangue

**digression** insertion of material unrelated to main body of work

**dipody** prosodic measure or unit of two feet

**dithyramb** short poem or chant in wild, irregular strain

**ditty** short, simple, or whimsical lyric

**doggerel** trivial or bad poetry

**double rhyme** rhyme consisting of two syllables of which the second is unstressed

**effect** language designed to produce distinctive, desired impression

**elegiac** couplet of dactylic hexameters with second lacking arsis in third and sixth feet

**elision** omission of unstressed vowel or syllable to achieve metrical uniformity

**encomium** expression of enthusiastic praise

**epilogue** concluding section after main body of work

**epithet** characterizing word or phrase used with or in place of name, esp. a disparaging or abusive term

**euphony** pleasantness of sounds in recited poetry

**euphuism** elegant Elizabethan style characterized by the frequent use of antithesis, alliteration, and mythological simile

**exegesis** critical interpretation of text

**explication de texte** *French*. close analysis of a literary text with focus on language, style, content, and textual interrelationships

**exposition** dialogue or descriptive material intended to convey information or background or to explain something

**eye dialect** use of misspellings to convey character's poor education or humorous dialectal pronunciations

**falling rhythm** stress occurring on first syllable of each foot

**fantasy** fanciful design or imaginative creation

**feminine rhyme** rhyme of two or three syllables of which only the first syllable is stressed

**figurative language** metaphorical expression abounding in figures of speech

**flashback** narrative device by which an event that takes place outside the narrative framework is brought into the chronology of the story

**flash-forward** narrative device by which a future event or scene is inserted into the chronology of a story

**flyting** dispute or exchange of personal abuse in verse form

**foil** one character serving as contrast to another

**foot** basic unit of verse meter, consisting of any of various fixed combinations of stressed and unstressed, long and short syllables

**footnote** explanatory comment or reference to documentation at bottom of page

**free verse** unrhymed verse of irregular meter and nonmetrical rhythm

**fustian** pretentious or banal writing

**genre** category of composition with particular style, form, and content

**georgic** poem with agricultural theme

**gloss** brief marginal explanation of difficult or obscure passage; continuous commentary accompanying text; interlinear translation

**hamartia** tragic flaw that causes hero's misfortune in Greek tragedy

**hapax legomenon** word or phrase occurring one time only in a text or works of an author

**heading** title or caption of page or chapter

**heroic couplet** rhyming couplet in iambic pentameter

**hexameter** line of verse with six metrical feet

**hiatus** two vowel sounds that come together without pause or intervening consonantal sound

**Hudibrastic verse** mock-heroic verse in humorous octosyllabic couplets

**hyperbole** extravagant exaggeration for effect

**iamb** metrical foot of one short or unstressed syllable followed by one long or stressed syllable

**iambic pentameter** poetry consisting of five metrical feet per line, each foot having one short or unstressed syllable followed by one long or stressed syllable

**imagery** figurative language used to evoke mental picture or create atmosphere

**interactive fiction** adventure or mystery story in which reader is given choices as to how story line will develop

**interior monologue** extended representation in monologue form of a fictional character's thoughts and feelings; stream of consciousness

**internal rhyme** correspondence of sounds within units of composition

**introduction** opening section of work containing essential matter

**irony** literary form in which words express something other than, or opposite to, their literal meaning

**kenning** metaphorical compound word used in place of the usual name of a person or thing, esp. in Old English or Norse poetry

**lampoon** harsh satire directed against an individual

**leitmotif** dominant recurring theme

**locale** scene or setting of story or composition

**macaronic** (*adj*) composed of Latin words mixed with vernacular words or non-Latin words given Latin endings

**metaphor** word or phrase used in place of another to suggest likeness or analogy between them

**meter** rhythm in verse with continuously repeating basic pattern

**metonymy** figure of speech in which the name of one thing is used in place of something else with which it is associated

**metrics** study or theory of verse meter

**mimesis** imitation or mimicry of another's style or language

**monologue** long speech by one individual; dramatic soliloquy

**motif** recurring thematic element, esp. one dominant idea

**narrative** story or account of events, either fictional or true, usu. in chronological or linear order

**obscurantism** intentional obscurity and vagueness in writing

**octave** verse stanza of eight lines

**octet** first eight lines of Petrarchan sonnet

**onomatopoeia** formation of a word that names a thing or action by imitation of a sound associated with it; use of words whose sounds suggest or imitate their meaning

**pandect** treatise on an entire subject

**parable** short story illustrating moral attitude or principle

**paraenesis** written piece containing advice

**passim** (*adv*) *Latin*. lit. here and there; used to indicate repetition of phrase or idea throughout book or article

**passus** section or division of story or poem

**pathetic fallacy** ascription of human traits and feelings to inanimate objects or nature

**pathos** evocation of sympathetic pity

**pentameter** verse line with five metrical feet

**personification** representation of an object or abstraction in human form or as an imaginary being

**plagiarism** literary theft; stealing another's work without giving credit, passing it off as one's own

**plot** plan or main story of work; story line

**poeticism** poetic expression that is trite or artificial

**poetic license** deviation from fact, rule, or convention for effect

**point of view** perspective of character from whose standpoint narrative events are seen

**polymythy** inclusion of many diverse subplots in literary work

**preface** introduction to larger work

**proem** preface or introduction

**prolegomenon** formal essay or critique introducing extended work

**prologue** preface or introduction; speech addressed to audience at beginning of play

**purple prose** excessively affected or sentimental writing intended to manipulate reader's feelings

**pyrrhic** metrical foot of two short or unstressed syllables

**quatrain** four lines of verse

**recension** critical revision of a text, esp. based on a study of its sources

**refrain** regularly recurring phrase or verse, esp. at end of each stanza in poem

**rhyme** correspondence in sounds of units of composition, esp. terminal sounds

**rhythm** ordered, recurrent alternation of strong and weak elements in flow of language

**rising action** narrative building to a climax

**rising rhythm** stress occurring on last syllable of each foot

**roundelay** poem with regularly repeated refrain

**sarcasm** caustic, ironic language directed esp. against an individual as a taunt

**satire** wit and irony used to expose and discredit a vice or folly

**scansion** metrical analysis of verse

**scene** subdivision of play, representing continuous action in one locale; place in which action occurs

**sestina** lyrical form of six six-line, unrhymed stanzas, in which endwords of first stanza recur in each following stanza in successively rotating order

**simile** figure of speech comparing two unlike things

**soliloquy** dramatic monologue expressing unspoken thoughts

**spondee** metrical foot of two long or stressed syllables

**sprung rhythm** poetic rhythm approximating natural speech

**stanza** division of poem; series of lines arranged together in recurring pattern

**story** fictional narrative or dramatic plot

**story line** plot

**stream of consciousness** continuous, unedited flow of conscious experience and thoughts; interior monologue

**strophe** two or more lines of verse constituting rhythmic unit; stanza; movement of the classical Greek chorus, characterized by turning from side to side of orchestra

**style** distinctive manner of expression, tone, or use of language, esp. characteristic of one author or genre

**stylized** (*adj*) conforming to established, conventional pattern or style rather than natural style

**subplot** subordinate story line in fiction or drama

**subtext** implicit, unstated, metaphorical meaning behind literary text, esp. dialogue

**suspense** use of uncertainty and anxiety as to outcome to heighten excitement

**symbol** something that stands for or suggests something else by association or convention

**tetrameter** verse line of four dipodies or metrical feet

**text** original words of written composition; main body of written work

**theme** unifying subject or topic of composition

**tragic flaw** defect in tragic hero's character that causes downfall

**trimeter** verse line of three dipodies or metrical feet

**triple rhyme** rhyme consisting of three syllables of which the second and third are unstressed; feminine rhyme

**trochee** metrical foot of one long or stressed syllable followed by one short or unstressed syllable

**tropology** use of figurative language in speech or writing

**tushery** affected writing characterized by archaic language

**verisimilitude** depiction of characters and setting, giving them the appearance of truth; realism

**vignette** brief incident, scene, or story

**villanelle** short poem of fixed form, usu. five groups of three rhyming lines followed by a quatrain

**voice** author's distinguishing style, tone, point of view, and use of language

**wordplay** use of rhetorical figures of speech and verbal wit to enhance literary work

**writer's block** psychological inhibition that prevents writer from continuing or completing work

## BOOKS AND PAGES

**abridgment** shortened version of work

**adaptation** rewriting an original work to fit another form

**almagest** any of various medieval works of a like kind, as on astrology or alchemy

**almanac** book with calendar, tables, information, and forecasts on various fields

**anonymous** (*adj*) published with no author's name; written by unknown author

**anthology** collection of writings by different authors

**atlas** book of maps and geographical charts

**bestiary** medieval collection of moralized fables about real and mythical animals

**bibelot** miniature book of elegant design

**bible** publication accepted as the preeminent authority in any given field

**bibliography** list of resources used in compiling a text, or works relating to a subject

**binding** manner and material in which printed book is covered and held together

**canon** works ascribed to author and accepted as genuine

**chapbook** small book or pamphlet, esp. of popular poetry or ballads

**chrestomathy** collection of selected literary passages, often by one author, and esp. from a foreign language

**classic** work of universally recognized and enduring excellence, great authority, and importance

**codex** manuscript book, esp. Biblical writing or other classic text

**commonplace book** reference book with organized collection of quotations, statements, essays, or treatises

**compendium** concise but comprehensive treatise or abstract

**concordance** alphabetical index of principal words in book, esp. the Bible; alphabetical index of subjects or topics

**dictionary** alphabetical list of words in one language with their definitions; list of defined terms in a given field

**draft** unfinished, preliminary version of manuscript

**duodecimo** book page size, equal to one-twelfth sheet of foolscap

**edition** particular form or version in which text is published; redaction

**encyclopedia** book or set of books containing information on many branches of knowledge in alphabetically arranged articles

**fascicle** one section of a book being published in separate parts

**folio** book page size, equal to one-half sheet of foolscap

**foolscap** large sheet of paper folded to form book pages

**forgery** fraudulently made or altered document

**glossary** alphabetical list of difficult, technical, or occupational terms with definitions, esp. for one field

**Gutenberg Bible** generally accepted as first book printed with movable type (15th c.)

**hornbook** rudimentary treatise on some subject; child's primer

**incunabula** copies of work of early art or industry, esp. book printed before 1501

**inedita** unpublished literary works

**lexicon** any wordbook or dictionary, esp. of an ancient language; the vocabulary of a particular field, subject, social class, or person

**little magazine** usu. noncommercial literary magazine featuring works of little-known authors

**magnum opus** one author's classic masterpiece

**manuscript** written or typewritten work, as distinguished from printed copy

**marginalia** marginal notes in book

**masterpiece** supreme intellectual or artistic achievement

**minor classic** extraordinary work of less significance or notoriety than a classic

**octavo** book page size, equal to one-eighth sheet of foolscap

**octodecimo** book page size, equal to one-eighteenth sheet of foolscap

**omnibus** volume containing collection of previously published works by single author or on single theme

**onymous** (*adj*) bearing the author's name

**opus** literary work

**palimpsest** parchment or tablet used more than once, from which the earlier writing has been erased

**passage** paragraph, verse, or brief section of written work

**primer** small introductory book on one subject, esp. for children

**quartet** tetralogy

**quarto** book page size, equal to one-quarter sheet of foolscap; book printed on quarto pages

**redaction** something put in writing; edition; version

**reference** authorative work containing many useful facts of organized information

**reprint** reissue of book previously published

**signature** sheet of foolscap folded into leaves of book pages

**tetralogy** set of four works connected by theme, subject, character, or setting

**thesaurus** extensive listing of words and their synonyms

**tome** very large or scholarly work

**tour de force** work of great skill, ingenuity, and brilliance

**treatise** systematic exposition of arguments, principles involved, and conclusions reached

**trilogy** three connected works

**variorum** edition of a text containing notes or different versions of the text by various editors or scholars

**version** edited, annotated, abridged, expanded, or revised form of previously published work; redaction

## LITERARY CHARACTERS AND PRACTITIONERS

**amanuensis** one employed to take dictation or copy manuscripts

**anonymous** ascription on work of unknown authorship

**antagonist** character opposed to protagonist; rival

**antihero** modern protagonist without traditional heroic qualities

**archetype** character embodying basic, universal human qualities

**author** writer who has composed a literary work

**bard** composer, singer, or declaimer of epic verse

**belletrist** author of amusing, sophisticated works

**bibliognost** person with comprehensive knowledge of books

**bibliophile** lover of books and literature

**biographer** one who writes history of another's life

**bluestocking** woman with bookish or learned tendencies (18th c.)

**Boswell** devoted biographer and caretaker of another's literary legend

**bouquiniste** person who buys and sells used books

**character** literary depiction of a fictional person, esp. one having some recognizable human trait or symbolizing an archetype or universal personality

**chorus** character or group of characters commenting on the action of a drama

**confidant** character emotionally close to protagonist, but relatively uninvolved in story's action

**confidante** female confidant

**copywriter** writer of advertising or magazine copy

**critic** person who assesses the value or merit of literary works

**deuteragonist** character second in importance to protagonist in classic Greek drama

**dramatis personae** list of characters in a literary or dramatic work

**dramatist** playwright

**editor** person who revises and corrects manuscripts and advises authors on their work

**essayist** writer of essays

**fabulist** person who writes or relates fables

**farceur** writer of broad, satirical comedy

**fictioneer** prolific writer of generally mediocre works of fiction

**ghost writer** one who writes for another without receiving credit

**goliard** one of a class of wandering scholar-poets noted for composing satiric Latin verses (Europe, 12th-13th c.)

**hack** writer working for hire, usu. producing material of little merit

**hagiographer** biographer of the saints

**hero** usu. male protagonist, esp. of epic, tragedy, or adventure

**heroine** female protagonist, esp. of epic, tragedy, or adventure

**journalist** writer for magazines or newspapers

**literati** persons concerned with, and knowledgeable about, literature

**man of letters** author, often in more than one form or genre; literary scholar

**metaphrast** person who translates or changes a literary work from one form to another, as prose into verse

**nom de guerre** *French*. lit. war name; pseudonym

**nom de plume** *French*. lit. pen name; pseudonym

**novelist** author of book-length fictional narratives

**pen name** pseudonym

**persona** character in a play, novel, or poem

**playwright** writer of dramas for theatrical performance; dramatist

**poet** writer of poems and verse

**poetaster** inferior poet

**poet laureate** most eminent poet of one nation during a specific time, often having official standing

**protagonist** main character in narrative; hero or heroine

**pseudonym** fictitious name used for writing; nom de guerre; nom de plume; pen name

**screenwriter** author of scripts for movies or television

**scribe** official clerk and copier of manuscripts before invention of printing; author, esp. journalist; scrivener

**scrivener** professional or public copyist or writer; scribe

**secretary** general assistant to writer, esp. one who takes dictation and types manuscripts

**skald** bard, esp. ancient Scandinavian poet

**speechwriter** author of public speeches for another

**stock character** standard character in many literary works, easily recognized and classified by the reader or audience, who requires little or no development by the author

**storyteller** one gifted at reciting or writing tales and anecdotes

**troubadour** lyric poet and musician who told of courtly love in France and Italy (11th–13th c.)

**wordsmith** author, esp. one skilled at the use of language; writer

**writer** person engaged in composing books, articles, and other literary works as an occupation or profession; author; journalist

# CHAPTER 15

# Performing Arts

# CLASSICAL MUSIC

Types of Music and Composition
Harmony, Melody, and Structure
Time and Tempo
Opera and Vocal Music
Musicians and Performance

**SEE ALSO:** Chap. 15: Popular Music; Musical Instruments;
Dance

## TYPES OF MUSIC AND COMPOSITION

**accompaniment** vocal or instrumental part that complements melody

**adaptation** piece based on existing melody or composition

**air** simple tune, melody, or song

**allemande** composition in moderate duple or quadruple time, basis for German court dance (17th-18th c.)

**arabesque** short, highly ornamented composition, esp. for piano

**aubade** sunrise music, esp. love song

**bagatelle** short, simple piece, usu. for piano

**ballade** piano composition in romantic mood suggesting epic ballad

**ballet** music written to accompany balletic dance

**baroque** (adj) designating music of period 1600-1750

**berceuse** lullaby

**bourrée** composition in quick duple time, basis of French dance (17th c.)

**cantata** vocal work in several movements, based on religious or dramatic subject

**capriccio** instrumental composition in free, unusual form

**cavatina** simple song or melody, usu. without second part or repeat

**chaconne** musical form characterized by continuous variation in a progression of chords which form the harmonic basis for each variation, usu. in triple time

**chamber music** instrumental music for small group in which each performer has a different part

**classical** (adj) denoting music of the European tradition marked by sophistication of structural elements and embracing vocal, symphonic, chamber, and solo music, esp. as distinguished from popular and folk music and jazz; designating typically homophonic music of the period 1750-1830

**composition** any written piece of music, esp. one of scope and complexity

**concertino** short concerto

**concerto** composition for one or more solo instruments with orchestral accompaniment, usu. in three movements

**concerto grosso** baroque composition contrasting small group of solo instruments with full orchestra

**dirge** slow, mournful piece, esp. accompanying funeral

**divertimento** instrumental form similar to suite and symphony, containing dances and short movements

**divertissement** short ballet used as interlude between acts of opera

**duet** composition for two instruments or voices; duo

**duo** duet

**écossaise** Scottish country dance in 2/4 time

**étude** piece intended to aid student in learning instrument

**evensong** evening prayer, vespers music

**fantasia** composition in fanciful improvisational form

**fugue** contrapuntal composition with melodic themes announced or imitated by each voice entering in succession

**gavotte** French dance music used in suites (18th c.)

**gigue** early Italian dance in various triple times

**humoresque** whimsical or playful composition

**incidental music** music performed during play to project mood or accompany action

**interlude** brief musical passage played between parts of longer piece, drama, or religious service

**intermezzo** movement between main sections of longer work, such as an opera

**invention** short keyboard composition that develops single motif in counterpoint

**march** music for marching, usu. in 4/4 time

**minuet** early French dance in 3/4 time

**modern** (adj) designating music composed in classical forms during the 20th century

**music** art and science of combining tones or sounds in single line (melody), in combination (harmony), and in time relationships (rhythm) to express ideas and emotions in a structurally complete and unified work having an appealing sound when produced by one or more voices or instruments, or both

**musique concrète** French. recorded montage of electronically manipulated and transformed natural sounds presented as a composition

**nocturne** dreamy, romantic piece, esp. for piano (19th c.)

**nonet** composition for nine instruments or voices

**octet** composition for eight instruments or voices

**opus** composition, usu. numbered to indicate order in which composer's work was published

**overture** musical introduction to ballet, opera, or oratorio that foreshadows themes that appear later

**partita** suite or series of variations

**pastorale** piece of music, esp. opera or cantata, suggestive of simple, rural life

**pavane** music written to accompany a stately European court dance (16th c.)

**piece** composition

**polonaise** music for stately Polish dance in triple time

**prelude** orig. a musical introduction, later an independent piece

**quadrille** French dance alternating between 6/8 and 2/4 time (early 19th c.)

**quartet** composition for four instruments, usu. two violins, viola, and cello, or voices

**quintet** composition for five instruments or voices

**raga** music following traditional formula for melody, rhythm, and ornamentation (Indian)

**requiem** composition written for funeral Mass

**rhapsody** composition in free, irregular form

**romantic** (adj) designating music of the late 19th century marked by free expression of imagination and emotion, virtuosic display, and some experimentation with form

**rondo** piece that alternates main and contrasting themes, usu. gay, playful, and fast

**roundelay** song in which phrase or line is continually repeated

**sacred music** compositions for religious services

**saraband** stately dance music in triple time (17th-18th c.)

**scherzo** playful piece in rapid triple time

**semiclassical** (*adj*) designating composition combining classical and contemporary, popular elements

**septet** composition for seven instruments or voices

**serenade** romantic song; instrumental piece for small group of string and wind instruments

**serial composition** nonmodal music using any or all of twelve chromatic tones in an arbitrarily set pattern (20th c.)

**sextet** composition for six instruments or voices

**sinfonia concertante** concerto for two or more solo instruments

**sinfonietta** symphony for small orchestra, esp. strings only, or of less than normal length

**solo** piece for single instrument or voice

**sonata** composition for one or two instruments, esp. piano, usu. in three or four movements in contrasting forms and keys

**sonatina** short, simplified sonata

**string quartet** composition for two violins, viola, and cello

**suite** instrumental music in several movements, each in a different dance form, all in the same key

**symphonic poem** large narrative orchestral work in one movement; tone poem

**symphony** composition for orchestra, usu. in four movements in contrasting tempos, moods, and keys

**toccata** keyboard piece with bold, rapid passages in contrapuntal style

**tone poem** composition for symphony orchestra, usu. in one movement, based on literary or historical subject; symphonic poem

**transcription** arrangement of composition for voice or instrument other than that for which it was written

**trio** composition for three instruments or voices

**twelve-tone** (*adj*) pertaining to serial composition using all twelve chromatic tones (early 20th c.)

**villanella** instrumental piece in style of rustic Italian dance (16th c.)

**voluntary** musical piece, sometimes improvised, performed by organist as prelude to larger work or church service

**waltz** music for German dance in triple time (19th c.)

## HARMONY, MELODY, AND STRUCTURE

**accent** recurring stress or emphasis

**accidental** sharp or flat not found in key signature

**affettuoso** (*adv*) with tenderness and affection

**agitato** (*adj*) restless or hurried in manner

**alto clef** clef placing middle C on third line of staff

**amoroso** (*adv*) with love

**anacrusis** upbeat; note or notes preceding downbeat of musical phrase

**animato** (*adj*) with spirit, lively

**appassionato** (*adj*) with emotion or passion

**appoggiatura** grace note or brief, ornamental tone sounded before another

**arpeggio** playing notes of chord in succession rather than simultaneously

**arrangement** orchestration and structure of composition

**attack** approach or manner of approach in beginning to play a musical phrase

**atonal** (*adj*) without reference to key or mode, using all twelve tones of chromatic scale at random

**augmentation** modification of theme by increasing time value of all its notes

**augmented** triad with fifth tone raised one-half step

**bar** measure of set number of beats

**bass clef** clef placing F below middle C on fourth line of staff

**basso continuo** continuo

**beat** metrical or rhythmic accent

**cadence** chords at end of phrase or piece that suggest harmonic resolution

**cadenza** brilliant virtuoso passage at end of solo

**cantabile** (*adv*) in a songlike manner

**canto** melody in choral or instrumental music

**cantus firmus** fixed melody to which other voices are added

**chord** two or more notes sounded together

**chromatic** (*adj*) containing all twelve half steps in octave

**clef** sign at beginning of musical staff that indicates pitch of notes

**coda** passage added to final section of piece

**coloratura** florid ornamentation in vocal music, esp. runs, trills, and arpeggios

**composition** art and practice of writing pieces of music

**con amore** (*adv*) in a tender manner

**con anima** (*adv*) in a spirited manner

**con bravura** (*adv*) with boldness

**con brio** (*adv*) in a vigorous manner

**con dolore** (*adv*) sadly, sorrowfully

**con espressione** (*adv*) with feeling

**con moto** (*adv*) with animation and spirit

**consonance** interval or chord that provides a feeling of satisfaction and resolution: third, fourth, fifth, sixth, octave

**con sordino** (*adv*) in a muted manner

**con spirito** (*adv*) with spirit or animation

**continuo** figured bass part for keyboard or strings, esp. in baroque ensemble; basso continuo

**contrapuntal** (*adj*) based on counterpoint

**countermelody** secondary melody sounded simultaneously with primary melody

**counterpoint** several independent but related melodies played simultaneously

**crescendo** gradual, steady increase in volume; (*adj*) gradually increasing in volume

**da capo** (*adv*) repeated from the beginning

**decrescendo** gradual decrease in volume; (*adj*) growing softer

**degree** tone or step of the scale

**development** elaboration of theme through counterpoint, modulation, rhythm, and tempo changes

**diatonic** (*adj*) designating major and minor scales; designating eight-tone scale without chromatic deviation

**diminished** triad with fifth tone reduced one-half step

**diminuendo** (*adj*) decreasing in volume

**dissonance** interval or chord that is restless and discordant

**dolce** (*adj*) soft and sweet

**dominant** fifth step of diatonic scale

**double flat** lowering of note's pitch two chromatic half-steps from natural

**double sharp** raising of note's pitch two chromatic half-steps from natural

**downbeat** first beat of measure

**enharmonic** (*adj*) designating tones that have same pitch but different notation, such as C-sharp and D-flat

**exposition** statement of material on which movement or piece is based

**fanfare** trumpet flourish, esp. at dramatic entrance

**fifth** tone on the fifth degree from a given tone; interval from tonic to dominant

**figure** shortest musical idea or motif in composition

**final bar** heavy, vertical, double line indicating end of piece

**finale** closing part or movement of composition

**flat** lowering of note's pitch one chromatic half step from natural

**forte** (*adj*) loud, forceful

**fortissimo** (*adj*) very loud

**fourth** tone on the fourth degree from a given tone; interval from tonic to subdominant

**fundamental** root note of a chord

**glissando** gliding effect, esp. series of adjacent tones sounded in rapid succession on keyboard

**grace note** brief, ornamental tone sounded before another; appoggiatura

**grazioso** (*adj*) graceful, flowing

**Greek modes** ascending musical scale consisting of two disjunct tetrachords: Dorian, hypodorian, Phrygian, hypophrygian, Lydian, hypolydian, mixolydian

**harmonic** overtone

**harmony** chord or combination of tones sounded together; structure of music that deals with the arrangement, voicing, and modulation of chords

**homophony** music in which one melody and set of chords predominates

**ictus** recurring stress or beat

**interval** difference in pitch between two tones

**intonation** production of a tone with a voice or instrument

**inversion** chord with tones in other than standard order

**key** major or minor scale with set flats and sharps, used as basis for composition

**key signature** flats and sharps on staff that indicate key of composition

**leading tone** major seventh

**legato** (*adv*) in a smooth, even style, with no breaks between notes

**ligature** slur

**maestoso** (*adj*) majestic

**major scale** diatonic scale composed of five whole steps and two half steps

**major seventh** note in diatonic scale one-half step below tonic

**marcato** (*adj*) accented, stressed, marked

**martellato** (*adj*) detached, strongly accented, or hammered with stroke of bow on stringed instrument

**measure** notes and rests contained between two bar lines

**mediant** third step of diatonic scale

**melody** tune, air, or theme composed of tones arranged in a pleasing succession

**meno mosso** (*adv*) less rapidly, slower

**microtone** any interval less than a semitone, esp. a quarter tone

**middle C** C note nearest middle of standard piano keyboard

**minor scale** diatonic scale starting on sixth note of relative major scale and composed of the same notes

**minor seventh** note in diatonic scale one full step below tonic

**modal** (*adj*) of or relating to a diatonic eight-tone scale other than major or minor; pertaining to mode, as distinguished from key

**mode** any of various arrangements of the diatonic tones of an octave, differing from one another in the order of whole and half steps; one of the Greek modes; scale

**modulation** change from one key to another within a single composition

**molto** (*adv*) very

**monophony** music consisting of unaccompanied melody

**mordent** trill made by rapid alternation of a principal tone and another tone a half step below it

**motif** recurring subject, theme, or idea; motive

**motive** motif

**movement** section of sonata, symphony, suite, or concerto

**musicology** scholarly study of music history, theory, and acoustics

**natural** return of a sharp or flat tone to its original pitch; original or normal pitch of note

**non troppo** (*adv*) without excess

**notation** standardized system of characters and symbols used to represent musical composition

**note** written character indicating duration and pitch of tone with value that is relative and dependent on time signature of piece; a single tone

**obbligato** subordinate solo instrument or melody line above or behind main melody

**octave** interval of eight diatonic tones

**orchestration** arrangement of composition for instrumental ensemble, esp. full orchestra

**ornament** embellishing note not part of basic melody or harmony

**ostinato** musical figure regularly repeated at the same pitch

**overtone** acoustical frequency higher in frequency than the fundamental; harmonic

**parlando** (*adj*) sung or played as though speaking or reciting

**part** notes performed by one instrument or voice as solo or in combination with other parts

**partial** overtone or harmonic

**passage** section of composition

**pedal** prolonged or continuously repeated tone

**pentatonic** (*adj*) designating five-tone scale, esp. one arranged like a major scale with the fourth and seventh deleted

**phrase** complete musical figure

**pianissimo** (*adj*) very soft

**piano** (*adj*) soft, subdued

**pitch** frequency of tonal vibrations per second

**pizzicato** (*adj*) played with plucked strings

**poco** (*adv*) somewhat, rather

**polyphony** music consisting of two or more independent melodic lines sounding together

**polyrhythm** simultaneous use of contrasting rhythmic patterns

**portamento** continuous gliding from note to note, sounding all intervening tones, usu. by voice or stringed instrument

**progression** series of chords

**quarter tone** interval equivalent to half a semitone

**rallentando** (*adj*) gradually slowing

**range** limits of pitch encompassed by a melody; full extent of tones falling within capacity of a voice or instrument

**refrain** regularly recurring musical figure

**register** different parts in the range of a voice or instrument

**relative keys** major and minor keys composed of the same notes and having the same key signature

**repeat** vertical arrangement of two dots on staff, indicating that preceding passage is to be repeated

**reprise** repetition of musical phrase

**resolution** progression from dissonance to consonance, esp. to the tonic note

**rest** interval of silence between tones; sign indicating duration of such silence, with value relative and dependent on time signature of piece

**rhythm** temporal relationship of successive notes; regular tempo, grouping, and accenting of tones that impel music forward

**ritardando** (*adj*) with gradual slowing of tempo

**root** tone on which a chord is built; fundamental

**roulade** series of rapid notes inserted in composition as ornamentation, esp. vocal coloratura

**rubato** (*adj*) having variation in speed within musical phrase, esp. juxtaposed against steady rhythm

**scale** series of notes arranged in steps at fixed intervals; mode

**scherzando** (*adj*) lively, brisk, playful

**second** tone on the next degree from a given tone; interval between such tones

**segue** seamless transition between sounds, themes, or pieces

**semitone** interval equal to one half of major second; half of a whole tone

**semplice** (*adj*) simple, straightforward

**sempre** (*adv*) always

**seventh** tone on the seventh degree from a given tone; interval from tonic to subtonic

**sforzando** (*adv*) with force

**sharp** raising of note's pitch one chromatic half step from natural

**signature** arrangement of sharps and flats on staff to indicate key; numerical indication of beats per measure

**sixth** tone on the sixth degree from a given tone; interval from tonic to superdominant

**skip** melodic interval greater than a second

**slur** curved line indicating that notes be sounded without pause; ligature

**sostenuto** (*adj*) sustained in time value of tones

**spiccato** (*adj*) performed with short, rapid bow stroke that allows bow to rebound between notes, giving detached effect to tones

**staccato** (*adj*) with abrupt, distinct breaks between notes

**staff** five horizontal lines and four spaces on which music is written; stave

**stanza** division in a vocal composition, formed by a recurring pattern of words

**stave** staff

**step** one degree of a scale; interval between two adjacent scale degrees, as a second

**strain** passage of composition; melody

**stretto** overlapping of response and call parts in fugue

**subdominant** fourth step of diatonic scale

**subito** (*adv*) suddenly

**submediant** sixth step of diatonic scale; superdominant

**subtonic** seventh step of diatonic scale, one degree below tonic

**superdominant** submediant

**supertonic** second step of diatonic scale, one degree above tonic

**swell** gradual increase followed by gradual decrease in loudness

**syncopation** accenting of normally unaccented beats to create rhythmic displacement

**tablature** notation indicating string, fret, key, or finger to be used rather than note to be played

**tacet** be silent

**tenuto** (*adj*) designating note or chord held to full extent of its time value

**tessitura** register including most notes of melody or vocal part or range of instrument where most tones lie

**tetrachord** diatonic series of four tones with perfect interval between first and fourth

**theme** complete musical idea; basis of musical variations

**third** tone on the third degree from a given tone; interval from tonic to mediant

**tie** slur connecting two held notes of same pitch

**timbre** characteristic quality of sound produced by an instrument; degree of resonance

**tone cluster** group of notes played simultaneously on keyboard with forearm, elbow, or fist

**tone row** set but arbitrary sequence of notes in serial composition

**tonic** first note of a scale

**transition** modulation; passage that connects one part of a piece to the next

**transpose** (*vb*) write or perform a piece in a key other than the original

**treble** upper register of vocal or instrumental range; highest part in harmonic music

**treble clef** clef with G above middle C on second line of staff

**tremolo** rapid reiteration of tone or alternating tones to produce a tremulous effect

**triad** chord made up of three tones, usu. first, third, and fifth

**trill** ornament consisting of rapid alternation between note and another note one half step above

**triplet** three notes played in amount of time normally required for two notes of same duration

**tune** melody

**turn** melodic embellishment or grace note consisting of principal tone with auxiliary tones above and below it

**tutti** (*adj*) all; performed by all voices or instruments together

**unison** simultaneous performance of identical parts by several instruments or voices

**upbeat** unaccented beat, often last beat of measure, sometimes beginning phrase or composition

**variation** change in key, meter, rhythm, harmony, speed, or mood of basic theme

**vibrato** slight, rapid alternation in pitch that produces a pulsating effect less pronounced than tremolo

**vigoroso** (*adj*) vigorous or spirited in manner

**vivace** (*adv*) lively

**voicing** arrangement of notes in chord or parts in composition

**volante** (*adv*) moving with light rapidity

**whole tone** interval of a major second, equal to two semitones

**whole-tone scale** scale progressing entirely by whole tones

## TIME AND TEMPO

**accelerando** (*adj*) gradually faster

**adagio** (*adv*) slowly, in a leisurely manner, (*adj*) slow; slower than andante, faster than lento

**alla breve** 2/2 time with one breve per measure

**allegretto** (*adj*) light and moderately fast; faster than moderato, slower than allegro

**allegro** (*adj*) brisk or rapid; faster than allegretto, slower than presto

**andante** (*adj*) moderately slow and flowing; faster than adagio, slower than moderato

**andantino** (*adj*) slightly faster than andante

**assai** (*adv*) very, as applied to tempo directions

**breve** note equal to two whole notes

**common time** 4/4 time

**compound time** time in which each beat of bar is divisible into three

**courante** music in quick triple time; mixture of 3/2 and 6/4 time

**crotchet** *Chiefly Brit.* quarter note

**demiquaver** *Chiefly Brit.* sixteenth note; semiquaver

**demisemiquaver** *Chiefly Brit.* thirty-second note

**dotted note** note with dot after it, indicating it is to be prolonged by one-half its length

**duple time** two, or multiple of two, beats per measure, such as 2/4 or 4/4

**eighth note** note having duration equal to one eighth of whole note; quaver

**eighth rest** rest equal in duration to eighth note

**4/4 time** time signature indicating four beats per measure with quarter note lasting one beat; common time

**grave** (*adj*) serious; slower than lento, faster than largo

**half note** note having duration equal to one half of whole note; minim

**half rest** rest equal in duration to half note

**hemidemisemiquaver** *Chiefly Brit.* sixty-fourth note

**larghetto** (*adj*) slow; faster than largo, slower than grave

**largo** (*adj*) very slow; slower than grave

**lento** (*adj*) somewhat slow; faster than larghetto, slower than adagio

**meter** regular, recurrent grouping of beats and accents, indicated by time signatures such as 4/4 and 6/8

**minim** half note

**moderato** (*adj*) at moderate speed; faster than andante, slower than allegretto

**presto** (*adj*) very fast; faster than allegro

**quarter note** note having duration equal to one quarter of whole note; one quarter of entire measure in common time; crotchet

**quarter rest** rest equal in duration to quarter note

**quaver** *Chiefly Brit.* eighth note

**semibreve** *Chiefly Brit.* whole note; one half of breve

**semiquaver** *Chiefly Brit.* sixteenth note; demiquaver

**sixteenth note** note having duration equal to one sixteenth of whole note; demiquaver; semiquaver

**sixteenth rest** rest equal in duration to sixteenth note

**sixty-fourth note** note having duration equal to one sixty-fourth of whole note; hemidemisemiquaver

**sixty-fourth rest** rest equal in duration to sixty-fourth note

**tempo** pace or rate of speed of piece, from slowest to fastest: largo, larghetto, grave, lento, adagio, andante, andantino, moderato, allegretto, allegro, presto

**thirty-second note** note having duration equal to one thirty-second of whole note; demisemiquaver

**thirty-second rest** rest equal in duration to thirty-second note

**time** time signature or rhythm of piece

**time signature** numerical fraction, such as 3/4 or 9/8, that shows number of beats per measure and kind of note that lasts one beat

**triple time** three, or multiple of three, beats per measure, such as 3/4 or 6/8

**whole note** note equal in duration to four quarter notes, lasting entire measure in common time; semibreve

**whole rest** rest equal in duration to whole note, lasting entire measure in common time

## OPERA AND VOCAL MUSIC

**a cappella** (*adj*) without instrumental accompaniment

**alto** female voice or voice part lower than soprano; male countertenor voice or voice part

**anthem** sacred vocal composition with words from the Scriptures; song of praise

**antiphony** alternate or responsive singing or chanting of psalm or verse by two sections of choir

**aria** solo song in opera, cantata, or oratorio

**aria da capo** operatic aria in three sections with first and third matching and middle part contrasting

**art song** song usu. set to poem and performed in recital with interdependent vocal and piano parts

**ballad** vocal song telling story, usu. of love

**barcarole** song of Venetian gondoliers

**baritone** male voice or voice part lower than tenor and higher than bass

**bass** lowest normal male voice or voice part; basso

**basso** bass

**basso profundo** exceptionally deep bass voice

**bel canto** agile, operatic vocal technique that stresses even tone

**bravura** florid, virtuoso composition or performance

**buffo** male opera singer who specializes in comic parts

**canon** strict form of composition in which each voice has same melody starting at different times

**cantata** vocal composition with instrumental accompaniment in several movements, based on religious or dramatic subject

**canticle** liturgical song based on Biblical text

**canto** part of choral work that carries melody

**canzonet** light song, less elaborate than madrigal

**carol** traditional song of faith, esp. heard at Christmas

**cavatina** operatic solo less elaborate than aria

**chanson** song (France)

**chant** sacred song and oldest form of choral music

**chanteuse** singer, vocalist (France)

**choir** group of singers, esp. one employed in church service; chorale

**choirboy** boy who sings in choir, esp. church choir

**choral** vocal music performed by chorus or choir; (adj) relating to or composed for a chorus or choir

**chorale** hymn or psalm sung to traditional melody in religious service; choir

**chorister** member of choir, esp. its leader

**chorus** organized group of singers, esp. singing in unison; such a group singing in connection with soloists in opera or oratorio; piece of music to be sung in unison

**coloratura** florid ornamentation, esp. runs, trills, and arpeggios, in vocal music; one who sings such music

**comic opera** light, humorous, often sentimental opera

**contralto** lowest female voice or voice part

**countertenor** adult male able to sing in alto range

**descant** counterpoint sung above main melody

**falsetto** artificial method of singing used by males to obtain notes above their normal vocal range

**fioritura** melodic ornamentation, often extemporized in Italian opera

**glee** simple part song, usu. for male voices

**glee club** choral group, usu. large

**Gregorian chant** unharmonized liturgical chant with free rhythm, used in ritual of Roman Catholic Church

**hymn** religious or sacred song

**Kyrie** musical setting for brief liturgical prayer that opens Mass

**leitmotif** short, recurring phrase associated with single character or situation in opera

**libretto** words and text of opera or oratorio

**lieder** stylized German song

**light opera** operetta

**madrigal** unaccompanied choral music in counterpoint, based on nonsacred text

**Magnificat** musical setting for the canticle of the Virgin Mary in Luke 1:46-55

**Mass** music for solemn Roman Catholic service in sequence of established parts

**melisma** ornamental phrase of several notes sung to one syllable of lyric, esp. in plainsong

**mezzo-soprano** female voice between alto and soprano

**monody** elegy or dirge sung by one person

**motet** vocal composition in contrapuntal style without accompaniment, based on sacred text

**opera** drama in which the text is entirely sung and acted to orchestral accompaniment, usu. with elaborate scenery and costumes

**opera buffa** farcical comic opera (Italy, 18th c.)

**opera seria** dramatic, classical opera (Italy, 18th c.)

**operetta** light, romantic, comic opera with songs and spoken dialogue

**oratorio** fairly long, usu. religious work for solo voices, chorus, and orchestra, performed without action, costume, or scenery

**part song** contrapuntal composition for three or more unaccompanied voices

**pasticcio** medley or opera made up of portions taken from other operas

**plainsong** liturgical chant, esp. Gregorian

**precentor** choir leader

**presa** cue marking the entry point for each voice in a canon

**processional** hymn or organ solo performed in church during entry procession of choir and clergy

**recessional** hymn sung at conclusion of religious service

**recitative** speechlike vocal composition without fixed rhythm, used for dialogue in opera

**requiem** funeral Mass

**round** canon in which voices enter at regular intervals repeating the same melody

**Sanctus** ancient Christian hymn of adoration

**singer** vocalist

**sol-fa syllables** tones of scale sung as syllables: do, re, mi, fa, sol, la, ti

**solfège** solfeggio

**solfeggio** vocal exercise using the sol-fa syllables; solfège

**song** short, simple composition with words and music

**soprano** highest female vocal range or voice part

**tenor** male voice or voice part above baritone and below alto or countertenor

**threne** threnody

**threnody** dirge, song of lamentation at funeral; threne

**tremolo** prominent vocal vibrato

**vocal** portion of composition written for voice

**vocalist** person who has received formal voice training to perform lieder, opera, or choral music; singer

**zarzuela** comic Spanish operetta

## MUSICIANS AND PERFORMANCE

**absolute pitch** ability to sing or name a single isolated note out of context

**accompanist** single instrumentalist, usu. pianist, who plays for dancer or singer

**baton** conductor's light rod, used to keep time

**beat** tempo indicated by conductor to musicians and singers

**bowing** act or art of playing notes on stringed instrument with down or up motion of bow

**chamber orchestra** small ensemble for performing chamber music

**choirmaster** director of choral group

**collegium musicum** group of usu. amateur musicians who meet to perform old or obscure music, often at a university

**coloration** subtle variation in intensity or tone by performers

**composer** person who creates and writes down musical compositions

**concert** live performance of music before audience

**concertmaster** assistant to orchestra conductor; first violinist of orchestra

**conductor** leader of orchestra

**consort** ensemble of singers and instrumentalists

**ensemble** several musicians who perform together

**improvisation** composition of music while performing

**instrumentalist** performer on specific instrument

**maestro** respected conductor, orchestra leader, or composer

**musicality** sensitivity to and aptitude for music

**music director** creative director of a group of performers

**musician** composer, conductor, or instrumental performer

**orchestra** large group of musicians performing on many instruments of all sorts, usu. over 100 members

**philharmonic** symphony orchestra

**pit** sunken area in front of stage in which orchestra sits during opera or ballet performance

**pitch pipe** small reed pipe used to tune instruments or establish pitch for singer

**player** instrumental performer

**program** printed information about compositions and performers, handed out to audience; sequence of compositions to be performed

**quartet** ensemble of four instruments or singers, esp. string quartet

**recital** concert given by individual performer

**score** written copy of composition with all parts arranged on staves, used during performance

**sheet music** printed copy of composition

**sight-read** (*vb*) play or sing written music on sight without rehearsal

**sinfonietta** small orchestra, often composed solely of stringed instruments

**string quartet** ensemble of two violins, viola, and cello

**symphony** full orchestra

**touch** musician's innate feel for instrument

**tuning** adjusting pitch of instrument

**virtuoso** performer with great technical skill and artistry

# POPULAR MUSIC

Styles and Genres
Performance, Airplay, and the Record Industry
Sound Reproduction Technology
Rock Era Dances
  1950's
  1960's
  1970's
  1980's

**SEE ALSO**: Chap. 5: Electricity and Electronics; Chap. 15: Classical Music; Musical Instruments; Television and Radio

## STYLES AND GENRES

**a cappella** singing without instrumental backing

**acid house** intense, urban, black-influenced dance music of late 1980's, often with portions of different songs mixed together

**acid rock** free-form, psychedelic music of 1960's

**acoustic rock** rock-'n'-roll played on nonelectric instruments, esp. acoustic guitar

**ambient music** background music; music used as an environmental element

**anthem** highly emotional and dramatic song, often patriotic or devotional

**ballad** slow, sentimental, romantic song; song that tells a narrative story in short, repetitive verses

**barrelhouse** jazz piano style with lively beat, orig. 1920's

**bebop** jazz style emphasizing aggressive, energetic playing, esp. rapid and difficult chord changes, orig. 1940's; bop

**big band** style associated with large jazz orchestras, orig. popular in 1920's and 1930's

**bluebeat** 1950's precursor of reggae and ska

**bluegrass** traditional acoustic country style

**blues** spiritual and melancholy folk music song form originated by blacks in rural southern United States, derived in part from field hollers; major source of jazz, urban blues

**boogie** blues rock style popular in 1960's

**boogie-woogie** frenetic blues style, usu. on piano

**bop** bebop

**bossa nova** Brazilian jazz interpolations on samba dance music

**bubblegum** *Slang.* light, trendy, innocuous pop music

**cabaret** song style typical of nightclub entertainment

**Cajun** country music style of Cajun or French-Canadian residents of southern Louisiana

**calypso** popular Caribbean dance music, sometimes with improvised lyrics

**chantey** sailor's work song; shantey

**country** popular style derived from traditional English folk music, blues, and rock-'n'-roll, orig. a regional style

**country-and-western** recording industry designation for country music

**cradlesong** lullaby

**disco** dance-oriented pop music emphasizing heavy backbeat, simplistic lyrics, and polished production techniques, orig. late 1970's

**ditty** brief, simple, often humorous, song

**Dixieland** upbeat, brass-oriented jazz, orig. 1920's

**doo-wop** a capella, harmony-oriented rock-'n'-roll vocal style, orig. 1950's

**electronic music** music performed on electronic instruments such as synthesizers, orig. 1970's

**elevator music** Muzak

**folk music** traditional and ethnic songs usu. performed on acoustic instruments

**folk rock** modern or traditional folk songs played on electrified instruments

**funk** dance-oriented, predominantly black soul music, usu. with horns and irregularly accented beat

**fusion** combination of jazz and electric rock, orig. 1970's

**glitter rock** highly theatrical rock with showy costumes, spectacular staging, and decadent themes, orig. early 1970's (U.S. and Britain)

**gospel** popular Christian church music, esp. influenced by black spirituals from American rural south

**hard rock** rock with a simple, driving, repetitive dance beat and usu. accessible lyric themes

**heavy metal** highly dramatic, guitar-based rock featuring costumed musicians and lyrics about authority, teenage rebellion, machismo, violence, and sexual fantasy

**high life** urban West African mixture of jazz and indigenous musical forms

**hip-hop** rock and dance style emphasizing spoken lyrics, contemporary urban themes, and acrobatic steps; rap

**honky-tonk** white, country-inflected rhythm-and-blues

**house music** dance-oriented club music of late 1980's with derivative elements and intense, discolike backbeat

**jazz** major modern popular music form originating in New Orleans around 1900, derived from blues, ragtime, and gospel roots, characterized by free improvisation, virtuoso solo performances, syncopated rhythm, and a variety of original vocal and instrumental styles of varying complexity: bebop, big band, cool, Dixieland, fusion, hot, modern, New Orleans, progressive, ragtime, and swing

**jug band** blues and jazz style using primitive instruments such as washboards or jugs, orig. 1920's

**juju** guitar-driven West African dance music

**klezmer** Yiddish folk music of Ashkenazi Jews performed by small band featuring clarinet and accordion

**lullaby** song sung to lull a child to sleep; cradlesong

**mbaqanga** rhythmic pop music of South Africa, derived from Zulu music and jazz, played on electric instruments and drums; township music

**Motown** upbeat, pop-influenced rhythm-and-blues originally produced by group of black artists recording in Detroit, esp. in 1960's-70's

**Muzak** *Trademark.* string-based adaptation of classical, show, and pop tunes, recorded as unobtrusive, environmental background music; elevator music

**New Age** repetitive, ambient acoustic jazz and serene background music, orig. 1980's

**new wave** punk-derived, dance-oriented pop, emphasizing uninhibited performance and antiauthority lyrics, orig. late 1970's

**patriotic** marches and other dramatic songs with lyrics zealously supporting one's country

**polka** Bohemian dance and folk music in distinctive duple rhythm

**pop** pop music

**pop music** popular music; contemporary music aimed at a mass audience and receiving wide exposure while evolving rapidly; pop

**power pop** strong, rhythmic, infectiously melodic, usu. guitar-driven pop music

**protest music** folk-derived, political reform songs of 1960's

**psychedelic music** hallucinogenic, drug-influenced 1960's rock

**punk rock** fast, loud, anarchic rock popular in late 1970's and early 1980's

**ragtime** syncopated jazz piano style of 1890's to 1920's

**R&B** rhythm-and-blues

**rap** dance-oriented pop style with insistent beat and rhyming, spoken lyrics, often couplets, that treat modern urban themes, esp. social protest and commentary, orig. 1980's among young blacks in inner cities; hip-hop

**reggae** uniquely syncopated, Rastafarian-influenced popular music of Jamaica

**rhythm-and-blues** R&B: urban, dance-oriented form derived from blues and rock-'n'-roll, orig. late 1940's

**rock** rock-'n'-roll

**rockabilly** country-influenced, white rhythm-and-blues style of rock, orig. 1950's

**rock-and-roll** rock-'n'-roll

**rock and soul** rock-'n'-roll with strong rhythm-and-blues roots

**rock-'n'-roll** blues-influenced, popular, youth-oriented, usu. electric dance music emphasizing strong beat and repetitive phrasing, orig. 1950's; rock; rock-and-roll

**roots music** indigenous popular music of a specific region

**salsa** modern Latin-American dance music

**scat** jazz vocal style in which singer imitates the sound and style of a horn playing without using words

**scratch** urban, black dance music similar to rap but using rhythmic sound made by manually moving a record back-and-forth under a turntable needle, orig. 1980's

**shantey** chantey

**shockabilly** rock style influenced by punk and rockabilly

**show tunes** popular songs from Broadway musical shows

**ska** Jamaican dance pop of 1950's, precursor of reggae

**skiffle** unsophisticated, acoustic folk music using washboard, jug, and other homemade instruments

**soca** Trinidadian roots music with blues and Brazilian influences

**soft rock** melodic pop rock without driving beat, not emphasizing electric guitars, and often having soothing or romantic lyrics

**soukous** popular dance music of the Congo and Zaire, using electric instruments

**soul** pop music derived from rhythm-and-blues, orig. 1960's

**soundtrack** musical score for film

**sprituals** gospel music

**stadium rock** widely popular commercial rock, esp. performed in large sports arenas

**steel band** rhythmic Caribbean music played on tuned steel drums

**stride piano** jazz and blues piano style with energetic, syncopated beat

**surf music** rock-'n'-roll, esp. from California during 1960's, featuring close treble harmonies and exuberant lyrics about beach life

**swing** big band jazz of 1930's-1940's, esp. for dancing

**synthpop** glossy, elegant pop emphasizing electronic synthesizer sound, orig. early 1980's

**thrash** frenetic, loud, aggressive punk rock

**torch song** steamy love song or ballad

**township music** popular dance music originating in townships of South Africa, played on electric instruments and drums; mbaqanga

**urban contemporary** slick, blues-based, romantic pop of 1980's

**washboard** lively blues style using primitive instruments; jug band music

**work song** folk song sung by workers to the rhythm of their work

**world beat** indigenous, usu. third-world musical forms, such as reggae and African popular music, sometimes influenced by another culture's music, esp. Western rock and pop styles and electric instrumentation

**zouk** popular dance music from French Antilles, based on Caribbean rhythms and played on electric instruments

**zydeco** blues-influenced Cajun dance music popular with French-speaking black people in Louisiana and Texas

## PERFORMANCE, AIRPLAY, AND THE RECORD INDUSTRY

**A&R** artist and repertory; record company employee responsible for signing and developing acts, matching songs to artists

**air guitar** imaginary guitar played by singer or dancer, usu. with wild, highly expressive mannerisms

**airplay** exposure of record on radio program

**album** group of six to fifteen songs released together on record, cassette, and/or compact disc; esp. a 33-rpm, long-playing record in a cardboard jacket

**American Bandstand** *Trademark.* weekly television program since 1950's featuring teenagers dancing to records

**AM radio** amplitude modulation radio broadcasting, generally associated with popular music programming

**AOR** album oriented rock; easy listening, light pop or soft rock radio programming

**arranger** person responsible for orchestrating a song for performance or recording

**artist and repertory** A&R

**A-side** primary hit side of 45-rpm single record

**ax** *Slang.* musical instrument, esp. guitar

**backbeat** danceable beat characteristic of rock-'n'-roll

**backup singer** harmony or background singer who complements featured vocalist

**band** group of musicians performing together

**beat** accent in rhythm; backbeat

**belt** (*vb*) *Informal.* sing a song loudly and energetically

**Billboard** *Trademark.* weekly trade magazine of the recording industry, including news, features, and charts

**boogie** (*vb*) become animated by dance music; play with soulful feeling

**bootleg record** pirated record

**bottleneck** glass or metal cylinder, orig. the neck of a bottle, used to create sliding guitar notes; guitar-playing style using bottleneck

**bottom** *Slang.* bass part of pop song

**break dancing** very acrobatic, urban, black dance style, orig. late 1970's

**bridge** segment of pop song that connects verses and chorus

**B-side** secondary side of 45-rpm record, not the hit; flip side

**cartage** transport of musical equipment to performance or recording session

**casual** informal performance at party or wedding

**charts** written musical arrangements; record industry tabulations on sales of popular records

**chops** *Slang.* level of musical skill and virtuosity; solo passage

**chorus** recurring segment of song, usu. after each verse, often containing the song's title or hook

**clam** *Slang.* musician's mistake, bad note

**club** small bar in which musicians perform

**combo** group of musicians playing together

**concept album** long-playing record with songs united by theme, narrative, and style

**cook** (*vb*) *Slang.* play an instrument with fire and inspiration

**cover version** new rendition of an older, familiar song; white version of black song in the 1950's

**crooner** easy, smooth-styled, romantic singer

**crossover hit** song belonging to a particular genre that achieves commercial success in another genre

**cut** individual song on an album; (*vb*) record a song

**date** recording session, esp. for jazz

**deejay** disc jockey

**def jam** *Slang.* excellent sound or record, esp. hip-hop

**demo** demonstration record or tape submitted by musicians seeking recording contract; rough version of a song, to be polished for finished recording

**dinosaur** rock performer or band emphasizing thunderous, formulaic rock, esp. with out-of-date style

**disc** phonograph record

**disc jockey** DJ; radio announcer who hosts a record-playing program or dance; deejay

**discography** descriptive listing of recordings by category, artist, composer, label, or date

**discotheque** dance club with recorded music

**DJ** disc jockey

**dub** technique of mixing record or performance for very heavy bass line; mix without lead vocals

**ear candy** *Slang.* light, syrupy, easy-listening music

**ears** *Slang.* ability to recognize potential hit song based on keen appreciation of pop sensibility

**easy rock** light pop or soft rock

**EP** extended play

**extended play** EP; four-song, 45-rpm single

**fan club** organization devoted to following a particular group or performer

**fanzine** rock or pop music fan magazine

**festival** outdoor pop music event featuring many performers, often taking place over a period of several days

**festival seating** nonreserved seating, usu. on floor or ground

**flip side** B-side

**folkie** *Informal.* enthusiast or performer of folk music

**format** radio programming style and content

**45** seven-inch, 45-rpm record, usu. with one song on each side; single

**funky** (*adj*) dirty, down-home, bluesy, or unsophisticated

**fuzz** electronic sound distortion, popular in 1960's

**garage band** rough, amateur pop group

**ghetto blaster** *Slang.* very large, powerful cassette player, usu. carried on street

**gig** *Slang.* musicians' job, usu. a performance date

**go-go** (*adj*) describing style of pop music fashion, orig. 1960's

**golden oldie** *Informal.* hit pop song from earlier years, esp. rock-'n'-roll from the 1950's; oldie

**Grammys** annual awards given by music industry for excellence and achievement in various categories of popular and classical music

**groove** *Slang.* period of inspired, easy collaboration and performance among musicians; coherent rhythmic sense

**groupie** *Informal.* pop music fan, esp. female, who follows the fortunes of a particular band, hoping to become intimate with its members

**headbanger** *Slang.* fan or performer of heavy metal; metalhead

**hip** (*adj*) knowledgeable about current trends in pop culture, esp. music; (*n*) up-to-date, latest sounds

**hit** song achieving large commercial success

**hit parade** current crop of hit songs, esp. used in the 1950's

**honky-tonk** rural or western-style bar

**hook** immediately memorable and appealing musical catch phrase

**hootenanny** folk song festival or sing-along

**horn section** trumpets, trombones, and saxophones backing a combo on recordings or performances

**jam** jam session; (*vb*) improvise with other musicians

**jam session** impromptu musical performance; jam

**jingle** brief, catchy song advertising a product

**jukebox** mechanical record-playing machine, esp. in bars and dance halls

**juke joint** roadhouse, esp. in rural South, in which blues and rhythm-and-blues music is performed

**label** company producing records, identified by a distinctive label featuring its trade name on every disc it releases

**lead** short, instrumental passage over rhythm parts

**lick** *Slang.* musical phrase; riff

**liner notes** text on an album cover, esp. offering background on musical content of record

**lip-sync** (*vb*) mouth lyrics in sync with recording during performance

**live recording** recording made at live performance

**LP** long-playing record, usu. 33 1/3 rpm with a 12-inch diameter

**lyricist** person who writes words that are set to another person's music to form song

**metalhead** headbanger

**monster hit** pop recording with very great commercial and popular success

**MOR** middle-of-the-road; radio programming style, precursor of easy rock or AOR

**MTV** Trademark. Music Television; twenty-four-hour-a-day channel playing music videos

**music video** commercial or promotional videotape featuring a performance of a song, often incorporating dancing, a narrative line, action, or animation, orig. 1980's; video

**novelty record** humorous pop song, often capitalizing on a topical subject

**oldie** pop song from earlier years; golden oldie

**open tuning** tuning guitar strings so that chords may be played without fretting individual strings

**original** song composed by its performer

**part** arrangement for each instrument used in a song

**payola** Informal. bribe taken by disc jockey from record company to promote a recording on radio

**pickup** electric amplification device on an instrument, esp. a guitar

**pirate** (vb) illegally record, manufacture, or sell records and tapes

**platter** Slang. a phonograph record

**playlist** specified songs to be aired on radio show

**producer** individual responsible for overseeing recording sessions by handling budget, hiring musicians and singers, choosing and arranging songs, and shaping the final sound

**product** record or tape to be sold; music in general

**race record** recording by black musicians in 1920's–1930's, esp. in southern United States

**record** grooved disc on which music has been imprinted; (vb) register music on tape from which such a disc is made

**record club** mail order membership club for the purchase of records, cassettes, and compact discs

**release** distribution of a record; date such distribution begins

**reverb** echo effect popular on many rock-'n'-roll recordings

**riff** short melodic passage played on an instrument; lick

**rim shot** Informal. comic punctuation played by drummer after punch line of joke

**roadie** Slang. equipment handler for touring band

**scratch** (vb) make rhythmic sound by moving record back-and-forth under a turntable needle

**section** group of horn or string players backing up band

**session** musical recording period, esp. one day

**set** complete performance for audience, including selection of songs played

**set list** order of songs to be performed during set

**sideman** musician employed on recordings or performances, usu. not member of band

**single** 45-rpm record; song released off album to promote album sales or performance tour

**slam dance** punk music dance in which dancers bump into and strike one another

**sleeve** envelope covering record inside album jacket

**solo** single instrument lead played over rhythm section, usu. in absence of vocals

**songwriter** composer of music and sometimes lyrics for short musical pieces usu. made up of verses, chorus, and bridge

**soul** ability to convey depth of feeling in musical performance

**soundalike** recording that imitates successful artist, attempting to pass as the original upon casual listening

**standard** familiar, often-played popular song with widely known lyrics

**swing** (vb) perform freely, with feeling, and in tempo

**sync** (vb) Informal. synchronize

**talent** performers, singers, musicians

**Tin Pan Alley** popular music, esp. of the recent past, named after New York street housing many songwriters and music publishers

**top 40** AM radio format emphasizing the forty most-popular pop songs; list of these songs calculated and distributed weekly

**topical song** narrative song that comments on a current event

**tour** extensive series of performances in different cities

**track** one song on album; single recording; each element of instrumental music behind vocals

**verse** basic unit of a song, providing narrative and setting up chorus

**video** music video

**video jockey** VJ; host on music video program

**VJ** video jockey

**vocal** singer's part of popular song

**wah-wah pedal** pedal that distorts guitar sound, orig. 1960's

**Walkman** Trademark. very small, portable cassette player with earphones

**wall of sound** full, lush sound quality in pop record production, originated by Phil Spector in 1960's

**wax** (vb) Informal. record

## SOUND REPRODUCTION TECHNOLOGY

**amp** Informal. amplifier

**amplifier** device that increases voltage of sound waves

**analog recording** storage of sound waves directly on tape in form of electromagnetic energy; record or tape made this way

**cartridge** small, closed container for cassette tape; case on phonograph holding needle and apparatus for converting stylus motion into electrical voltage

**cassette** small, enclosed tape cartridge

**CD** compact disc

**channel** recording track on tape recorder

**compact disc** CD; means of sound reproduction that uses laser to read digitally encoded disc

**compressor** device that controls dynamic range of frequencies

**console** mixing console

**deck** tape recorder

**digital delay** conversion of analog signal into digital information, which is stored briefly on a memory chip then released in analog form

**digital recording** sound recording in which a frequency or waveform is sampled at regular intervals, then assigned numerical value, usu. a binary notation; record or tape made this way

**direct box** device that converts high impedance level instrument output into lower microphone level input

**Dolby** *Trademark.* noise reduction system that reduces tape hiss

**drum machine** digital synthesizer with stored samples of drum sounds that can be reproduced in any sequence

**dub** (*vb*) copy mix onto cassette; (*n*) such a copy

**echo chamber** empty chamber in recording studio for live creation of echo effects

**emulator** digital computer synthesizing sounds from voice or other source

**EQ** *equalizer*

**equalizer** EQ; tone control that divides the audio range into intervals and accentuates its parts

**filter** device for suppressing or minimizing certain frequencies

**flanging** slight slowing of tape machine produced by touching flange of reel with thumb; phase shifter

**half-track** tape recorder with two tracks, both in same direction, covering entire width of tape, used for final mix to stereo

**headphones** small speakers in frame that fits over ears

**hi-fi** *Informal.* high fidelity

**high fidelity** reproduction of sound with high degree of faithfulness to original; system doing this; hi-fi

**horn** *Slang.* loudspeaker

**isolation booth** chamber in studio for recording vocals or single instruments

**limiter** compressor with high ratio of gain reduction

**loop** endlessly repeating section of tape

**master** (*vb*) transfer taped recordings onto lacquer mold, disk, or tape from which other copies will be pressed or duplicated; (*n*) such a disk or tape; matrix

**matrix** master

**mic** *Informal.* microphone

**microphone** transducer that changes sound waves into electric current measured in voltage: condenser, crystal, dynamic, or ribbon; mic; mike

**MIDI** *musical instrument digital interface*; language used by keyboard instruments to talk to each other and to computers or sequencers

**mike** *Informal.* microphone

**mix** blending of tracks to produce completed recording; mixdown; (*vb*) execute such a blending

**mixdown** mix

**mixing console** master board that controls the mixing of all specialized functions on all recording tracks; console

**monophonic** (*adj*) designating sound recording having single transmission path

**multitrack recorder** tape machine used in recording: 2-track, 4-track, 8-track, 16-track, or 24-track

**noise gate** dynamic range control that permits shutting off of signal when too low

**oscillator** tone generator, either sine or square wave

**overdub** track added in sync with already existing tracks

**PA** public-address system

**pan** *Informal.* panoramic; variation of volume sent to two or more speakers, so that sound seems to move between speakers when played together

**patchbay** central field of jacks connecting all elements of recording system

**phase shifting** electronic flanging achieved by shifting waves slightly out of sync, creating whooshing effect

**playback** act of reproducing a newly made recording to check it

**playback head** part of tape recorder that is used to pick up magnetic pattern on tape in order to play back recorded material

**pot** *Informal.* potentiometer

**potentiometer** variable resistor directly controlled by dial, knob, or lever on recording console; pot

**power supply** source of alternating current voltage

**preamp** *Informal.* preamplifier

**preamplifier** device that increases signal strength for detection and further amplification; preamp

**public-address system** PA; combination of microphones and speakers that makes sound audible to many people

**quadraphonic** (*adj*) designating sound reproduction system using four speakers, usu. set in four corners of room

**receiver** radio tuner with built-in amp and preamp

**record head** part of tape recorder that is used to imprint a magnetic pattern based on sound waves onto tape

**reel-to-reel** (*adj*) of or pertaining to a system using large, open spools of tape: quarter-inch, half-inch, or three-quarter inch

**reverb** electronically produced echo effect

**sampler** device that allows digital encoding of any signal picked up with microphone or direct recording box

**sequencer** digital keyboard computer that records sequences of notes and tells other keyboards when to play them

**speaker** transducer that changes voltage into sound waves

**stereophonic** (*adj*) designating sound recording having two transmission paths

**tape** plastic magnetic tape impregnated with metal oxide, used to record sound waves in form of voltage

**tape recorder** means of storing sound in form of voltage on magnetic tape; deck

**track** one channel on multitrack recorder

**transducer** device, such as microphone or speaker, that is activated by power from one system to supply power in either the same or a different form to another system

**tuner** device that receives AM and FM radio signals

**turntable** revolving platform carrying phonograph record

**tweeter** speaker that is most efficient at high frequencies

**twenty-four track** state-of-the-art multitrack recording studio console, sometimes used in tandem with another machine to create forty-eight tracks

**vibrato** device that electronically produces slight, rapid variations in pitch to impart a tremulous effect to sound

**volume** degree of loudness or intensity of sound

**woofer** speaker that is most efficient at low frequencies

## ROCK ERA DANCES

**1950's** (birdland, continental walk, handjive, hucklebuck, hully gully, Madison, shake, slop, stroll)

**1960's** (alligator, bird, boogaloo, Boston monkey, camel walk, dear lady twist, dog, fly, frug, freddie, funky chicken, funky pigeon, hitchhike, jerk, loco-motion, mashed potatoes, monkey, Philly dog, pony, skate, slauson, swim, temptation walk, twine, twist, Watusi)

**1970's** (bump, disco, hustle, L.A. hustle, Latin hustle, line dance, New York hustle, night fever, popcorn, rocking chair, roller coaster, roller disco, shuffle, special K, sway)

**1980's** (acid house, bedrock, break dancing, dirty dancing, Egyptian, ET, file dance, guess, le freak, moonwalk, nasty, neutron dance, pogo, salsa, slam dance, snake, vogue, walk)

# MUSICAL INSTRUMENTS

Instrument Types and Groupings
Drums
Percussion
Mirlitons
Keyboards
Stringed Instruments
Wind Instruments
Accessories

**SEE ALSO**: Chap. 15: Classical Music; Popular Music

## INSTRUMENT TYPES AND GROUPINGS

**band** group of musicians playing together

**big band** brass, winds, piano, and drums

**brass** any wind instrument made of metal with a metal mouthpiece

**chamber orchestra** small orchestra of less than twenty-five players, largely strings and woodwinds

**combo** small jazz or dance band

**dance band** up to twenty musicians, primarily winds

**drum** membranes stretched on a frame, esp. a hollow cylinder, that are struck with hand or stick

**gagaku ensemble** shawms, flutes, gongs, drums, koto, and biwa, used to perform classical music (Japan)

**gamelan orchestra** tuned percussion, fiddle, and drums (Indonesia)

**instrument** any contrivance or apparatus that produces musical sounds

**jazz band** horns, drums, woodwinds, guitars, and keyboards

**jug band** band with strings, rudimentary percussion, and jug, playing folk music

**keyboard** any instrument composed of strings of varying lengths held taut and struck or plucked mechanically

**marching band** horns, drums, woodwinds, and percussion instruments played while marching before crowd or in parade

**mariachi** guitars, percussion, and brass (Mexico)

**mirliton** any instrument composed of membranes stretched and vibrated by air, not struck

**orchestra** large musical ensemble, with woodwind, brass, percussion, and string instruments, that performs symphonic music

**palm court orchestra** small string group and piano

**percussion** any instrument that is a solid or hollow object struck, shaken, or scraped

**piano trio** piano and violin with either viola or cello; piano, drums, and bass

**rock band** electric guitars, bass, drums, and keyboards

**string** any instrument composed of strings, usu. of uniform length, stretched on a frame and bowed or plucked by hand

**string quartet** two violins, viola, and cello

**wind** any instrument composed of a hollow tube made of wood or metal, with small holes and a mouthpiece that is blown into while fingers cover the holes

**wind quintet** flute, oboe, clarinet, bassoon, and horn

**woodwind** any wind instrument made of wood with a reed mouthpiece

## DRUMS

**banana drum** long, narrow, tubular drum (Congo)

**barrel drum** drum with convex sides

**bass drum** large, double-headed, cylindrical drum used in modern orchestra

**bata** one of a set of long, conical drums (Cuba)

**bendir** skin drum (Morocco)

**bhaya** left-hand drum of tabla set

**bodhran** drum with shallow frame, used in folk music (Ireland)

**bongo** one of a set of small, cylindrical, single-headed drums played with the hands (South America)

**changko** double-headed drum made of lacquered wood (Korea)

**conical drum** drum that tapers to a point or small head

**cylindrical drum** hollow frame drum with same diameter top to bottom

**da-daiko** very large frame drum used in gagaku ensemble (Japan)

**daibyoshi** Shinto temple drum (Japan)

**darabukke** small, goblet-shaped drum (Middle East)

**dauli** cylindrical, double-headed drum (Greece)

**dhola** barrel drum played horizontally (India)

**double drum** two drums bound together

**dugdugi** double-headed pottery drum (India)

**footed drum** drum that stands on legs, often with carved bases in form of human feet

**frame drum** any drum with membrane stretched on a rigid frame

**friction drum** drum in which cord or stick pierces drum membrane and vibrates to form sound

**gong drum** single-headed cylindrical drum used in modern orchestra

**human skull drum** two skulls mounted top to top (Tibet)

**ingungu** friction drum made from gourd (South Africa)

**isigubu** cylindrical drum made from a hollow log (South Africa)

**kakko** barrel drum, mounted on stand, used in gagaku ensemble (Japan)

**kalungu** wooden talking drum (West Africa)

**kelontong** small frame drum, equipped with long handle, that forms sounds when pellets on strings strike its surface (Indonesia)

**kettledrum** single membrane stretched over large pot or container

**kit** set of drums and percussion instruments used by pop or jazz bands: snare drum, tom-toms, side drum, bass drum, suspended cymbals, and hi-hat cymbals

**koboro** conical church drum (Ethiopia)

**mridanga** ancient, elongated barrel drum with tuned heads, used for performing formal, traditional music (India)

**murumbu** pot-shaped drum (South Africa)

**nakers** small kettledrum of Arabic origin (medieval Europe)

**naqara** small pair of kettledrums (Arabia)

**ngoma** wooden kettledrum usu. played by women (South Africa)

**ntenga** conical drum (Uganda)

**o-daiko** Shinto barrel drum (Japan)

**okedo** Kabuki theater drum (Japan)

**peyote drum** iron pot drum, filled with water (American Indian)

**rommelpot** friction drum made from household pot (Europe)

**side drum** small cylindrical drum equipped with snares, used in modern orchestra

**snare drum** small, double-headed drum with wires across bottom for amplified reverberation

**steel drum** metal barrel cut to form drum: ping-pong, guitar pan, bass pan, rhythm pan, cello pan

**tabla** pair of drums with variable pitch, played with hands (India)

**tabor** small cylindrical drum hung around neck (Europe)

**taiko** folk music drum (Japan)

**talamba** small, metal kettledrum (Yugoslavia)

**talking drum** any of various, usu. hollow, percussion instruments used to play rhythms and tones that have specific meanings (Africa)

**tambour** circular drum

**tambourine** shallow frame drum with metal disks attached for added percussion (Spain and Portugal)

**tenor drum** high-toned cylindrical drum used in modern orchestra

**terbang** shallow frame drum (Java)

**timbale** one of a set of single-headed cylindrical drums mounted on stand (South America)

**timpanum** tuned, orchestral kettledrum, mounted on footed base; *pl.* timpani

**tom-tom** hand-beaten drum (American Indian); medium-pitched drum in trap set

**trap set** pop or jazz drum and percussion kit: snare drum, tom-toms, side drum, bass drum, cymbals, high-hat

**tsuri daiko** barrel drum decorated and suspended on frame, used in gagaku ensemble (Japan)

**tsuzumi** small, hourglass-shaped, double-headed drum, used in Nō drama (Japan)

**uchiwa daiko** frame drum with handle (Japan)

# PERCUSSION

**bell** metal, cup-shaped resonator with clapper or pellet inside that strikes wall to produce tone: cowbell, camel bell, temple bell, handbell, wind-bell, church bell

**bell-lyra** portable glockenspiel mounted on lyre-shaped frame, used by marching bands

**bones** pair of small bones that make a clicking sound when struck together

**bonnang** set of gong chimes in box frame (Java)

**bull-roarer** wood disk or blade spun on cord

**buzz disk** disk spun on twisted cord

**carillon** set of tuned bells

**castanets** hand-held wood or bone clappers, clicked together

**chimes** set of bells on pole or frame

**clappers** pair of sticks or blocks, held and struck together

**clave** one of a pair of wood sticks or blocks, struck together

**cowbell** large, metal bell struck with stick

**cymbals** conical or dished metal disks, struck together or with stick

**electric xylophone** vibraharp

**gambang kayu** xylophone (Java)

**gamelan gong** xylophone (Bali and Java)

**gansa gambang** metallophone (Bali)

**glass harmonica** water-filled wineglasses in box or set, resonated by rubbing rims

**glockenspiel** metallophone on stand, carried in marching band

**gong** metal disk struck by stick

**high-hat** two cymbals on stand, crashed together by foot pedal

**humming top** hollow vessel with holes, spun to produce sound

**Jew's harp** small frame with flexible metal tongue, plucked by finger while instrument is held to mouth

**jingle** small bell or rattle, often worn as ornament

**kalimba** marimba, zanza (Africa)

**kenong** bowl-shaped gong over resonating box (Java)

**lithophone** set of graduated stones in box frame

**maraca** gourd filled with beans or seeds that rattle when shaken (South America)

**marimba** xylophone with wood resonators under bars (Latin America)

**mbira** gourd resonator with tuned metal or wood strips, plucked with fingers (Africa)

**metallophone** set of graduated metal bars over resonating box, struck with mallet

**rattle** hollow form with seeds or stones inside, shaken to produce raspy sound

**rhythm stick** small wood stick struck against any surface; child's rudimentary percussion instrument

**sansa** thumb piano; zanza (Africa)

**slit drum** log or pole hollowed through slit, beaten with sticks

**suspended cymbal** single cymbal loosely attached to stand

**tam-tam** large bronze gong

**thumb piano** hollow resonating box with tongues of various lengths to be plucked; sansa

**triangle** metal rod bent into triangle, struck with stick

**vibraharp** percussion instrument that resembles a marimba, played with mallets and having metal rather than wooden bars and electrically powered resonators that create vibrato effect; electric xylophone; vibraphone

**vibraphone** vibraharp

**washboard** washing board scraped with rod or stick

**woodblock** resonant, hollow block of wood, struck with wooden sticks

**xylophone** set of tuned bars in box frame, struck with sticks or mallet

**zanza** wood box with graduated wood or metal tongues, plucked with fingers and thumbs; kalimba; sansa (Africa)

## MIRLITONS

**comb and paper** hair comb with paper folded around it
**eunuch flute** tube with membrane-covered aperture; onion flute (Europe)
**kazoo** toy horn with membrane-covered blowhole
**onion flute** eunuch flute
**zobo** kazoo-like toy horn in shape of conventional horn

## KEYBOARDS

**accordion** keyboard that controls vibrating reeds set in motion by bellows-forced air; piano accordion
**baby grand** small grand piano
**barrel organ** mechanical organ with revolving cylinder turned by hand
**calliope** steam-powered organ
**celesta** set of graduated steel plates struck with hammers that are activated by a keyboard
**cembalo** harpsichord or keyed dulcimer
**chord organ** simplified organ on which each key sounds a full chord
**clavichord** early keyboard, smaller than piano, having strings struck by bass pins attached to key ends
**clavicytherium** early, upright spinet
**clavier** any of various keyboard instruments, including piano and harpsichord
**concert grand** largest, highest-quality grand piano with richest tone
**concertina** small accordion
**geigenwerk** mechanical harpsichord (Germany)
**grand piano** large piano with horizontal frame and strings, supported on three legs
**Hammond organ** *Trademark.* electronic organ with double keyboard that produces sound of a pipe organ
**harmonium** small reed organ powered by bellows
**harpsichord** early wire-stringed double keyboard with seven stops, having strings plucked by quills; cembalo (17th-18th c.)
**hurdy-gurdy** mechanical violin with strings activated by keyboard
**melodeon** small reed organ; accordion
**Moog** *Trademark.* one of the earliest electronic synthesizers
**ondes martenot** electronically vibrated strings controlled by keyboard
**organ** set of pipes resonated by air: barrel, electric, mouth, pipe, portative, reed
**orphica** small portable piano (Europe, 19th c.)
**piano** steel strings struck by felt hammers operated from keyboard: grand, baby grand, upright, spinet, player, table, electric; pianoforte
**piano accordion** accordion
**pianoforte** piano
**Pianola** *Trademark.* brand of player piano
**pipe organ** large organ in which tones are produced by passage of air through sets of variable-length pipes operated by keyboard
**player piano** upright piano operated by moving scroll perforated with notations

**reed organ** organ in which tones are produced by set of free metal reeds
**regal** small, portable organ (16th-17th c.)
**spinet** compactly built, upright piano; early harpsichord with one keyboard
**square piano** piano with rectangular, horizontal body
**squeezebox** *Informal.* accordion or concertina
**synthesizer** electronic console that produces sounds using keyboard-controlled oscillators, filters, mixers, and amplifiers, and sometimes by digital computer
**theremin** electronic tone generator controlled by distance between player's hands and two metal antennas
**Tippoo's tiger** mechanical organ in the shape of a tiger attacking an Englishman (Britain)
**upright** piano with vertical frame and strings
**virginal** small spinet with no legs, one wire per note (16th-17th c.)
**vocoder** electronic instrument that resolves human voice signals and transmits tones of same pitch by keyboard

## STRINGED INSTRUMENTS

**aeolian harp** rectangular zither on which strings are not plucked but rather sounded by air currents
**archlute** lute with two pegboxes, one for bass strings
**Autoharp** *Trademark.* zither with dampers on strings controlled by buttons
**bagana** box-shaped, ritual lyre (Ethiopia)
**balalaika** flat, triangularly shaped lute with two to four strings (Russia)
**bandore** ancient lute, cittern, or pandora
**bandoura** large lute with many strings that produces continuous, low tones (Russia)
**banjo** shallow, circular body with parchment belly, long neck, and one short and four long strings
**baryton** bass viol
**bass fiddle** double bass
**bass viol** viola da gamba; double bass
**biwa** four-stringed lute (Japan)
**bolon** three-stringed harp lute with spherical gourd resonator and belly of animal skin with hair (Sierra Leone)
**bouzouki** lute with strings in double courses (Greece)
**bow** string attached to flexible stick
**bull fiddle** double bass
**bumbass** long, single string that is bowed or plucked (Europe, 17th c.)
**cello** large, bass violin with floor stand; violoncello
**ch'in** long, classical zither (China)
**chitarra battente** early, deep-bodied guitar (Italy)
**chitarrone** long-necked lute with two pegboxes
**cittern** flat-bodied, long-necked, pear-shaped instrument, similar to guitar (Europe, 15th-18th c.)
**clarsach** ancient harp (Ireland and Scotland)
**cobza** lute with strings in two groups around sound holes (Romania)
**colascione** very long-necked lute with three strings (Italy)
**contrabass** double bass
**crowd** crwth
**crwth** ancient lyre with shallow body, either plucked or bowed; crowd (Ireland)
**cymbalom** dulcimer in table frame (Hungary)

**Dobro** *Trademark.* lap guitar with metal resonator plate on body

**double bass** largest, deepest-pitched member of violin family; bass fiddle; bass viol; bull fiddle; contrabass; string bass

**dulcimer** zither struck with mallets or sticks

**fiddle** any stringed instrument bowed rather than plucked, esp. violin

**fidla** bowed zither (Iceland)

**gittern** early four-stringed guitar made from single piece of wood; cittern (Britain)

**guitar** flat-backed, long-necked, stringed instrument, usu. with waisted shape to soundbox that produces sounds when plucked: acoustic, electric, double-neck, electric bass, pedal steel, Hawaiian

**guittaron** very large bass guitar (Mexico)

**gutbucket** crude bass made of gut string attached to bucket, used in folk and some jazz music

**hammer dulcimer** set of tuned strings in frame, struck with hammer

**harp** angled strings set in frame attached to soundbox: bow, angle, frame, double, orchestral

**harp lute** any of various instruments in which plane of strings is at right angles to belly of instrument (West Africa)

**Irish harp** bow-shaped medieval harp (Ireland)

**kantele** traditional, five-stringed lute (Finland)

**kerar** bowl-shaped folk lyre (Ethiopia)

**kit** very small, narrow violin

**kithara** large, box-shaped lyre (ancient Greece)

**ko-kiu** shallow, square-bodied, long-necked fiddle (Japan)

**kora** harp lute with sixteen to twenty-one strings and skin belly (West Africa)

**koto** long zither with thirteen silk strings (Japan)

**lira** three-stringed, pear-shaped folk fiddle (Greece)

**lirica** small, pear-shaped fiddle (Yugoslavia)

**lute** pear-shaped resonating box with long, often bent neck holding strings stretched over bridge, plucked to produce sound

**lyre** resonating box with attached strings on two curved arms joined by a yoke, struck with plectrum (ancient Greece and Egypt); solid wooden box with strings stretched over bridge (Europe)

**machete** fish-shaped guitar (Portugal)

**mandola** small lute with curved pegbox (Italy)

**mandolin** classical lute with usu. four pairs of strings (Italy)

**mandolone** bass mandolin

**monochord** ancient, single-stringed instrument with oblong sounding box, used esp. to determine intervals

**moon guitar** flat-backed, short-necked, silk-stringed lute (Asia)

**obukano** large, bowl-shaped lyre (East Africa)

**orpharion** ancient cittern with six to nine paired metal strings

**oud** short-necked lute (Middle East and North Africa)

**pandora** large, bass cittern; bandore

**pedal steel guitar** box-shaped guitar on legs, having ten strings altered in pitch by foot pedal and plucked while being pressed by movable steel bar

**pipa** shallow, silk-stringed, fretted lute (China)

**psaltery** medieval board zither that was plucked (Europe)

**ramkie** simple folk guitar (South Africa)

**rebab** medieval bowed fiddle with one to three strings (Middle East)

**rebec** pear-shaped fiddle with bowed strings (medieval Europe)

**ruan** long-necked, flat-backed lute (China)

**samisen** long-necked, shallow-bodied, three-stringed lute (Japan)

**santir** dulcimer with trapezoidal box and strings struck by curved beaters (Middle East)

**sarod** bowed lute (Northern India)

**sintir** dulcimer of santir family (Egypt)

**sitar** large lute made from a gourd, having arched metal frets on a long neck (India)

**string bass** double bass

**tambura** fretted, long-necked lute (Yugoslavia, India)

**tamburitza** plucked, guitar-shaped mandolinlike instrument (Yugoslavia)

**theorbo** bass lute with bass strings on second pegbox (Renaissance Europe)

**ukulele** very small, four-stringed guitar (Hawaii)

**uti** short-necked lute (Yugoslavia)

**valiha** tube zither (Malagasy)

**vina** stick-shaped zither with two gourd resonators (India)

**viol** predecessor to violin with flat back, broader bow, and fretted fingerboard (Europe, 17th c.)

**viola** four-stringed member of violin family, slightly larger than violin and with deeper pitch

**viola da gamba** cello; bass viol (17th c.)

**viola d'amore** fretless tenor viol with seven gut strings and seven wire sympathetic strings (Europe, 18th c.)

**violin** small, finely shaped, curved, resonating body with four strings that are bowed or occasionally plucked

**violoncello** cello

**yang chin** zither with movable bridges (China)

**zither** long resonator body with many strings attached over its entire length: raft, stick-shaped, trough, tube

## WIND INSTRUMENTS

**alpenhorn** long, powerful horn of wood with curved bell that produces single note

**arghool** oboe with two pipes, one a drone (Arabia)

**aulos** double pipe with double reed (ancient Greece)

**bagpipe** air-filled bag with reeded mouth pipe, drone pipe, and melody pipe

**basset horn** bent or curved, reeded horn (Bavaria)

**bassoon** double-tubed bass horn with double reed mouthpiece

**bombardon** E-flat bass tuba

**bosun's pipe** whistle with variable pitch

**bugle** simple metal horn with reedless mouthpiece

**chalumeau** progenitor of orchestral clarinet (Europe)

**clarinet** horn or tube with reed inserted in mouthpiece that vibrates when blown

**clarion** ancient, curved trumpet

**contrabass** largest orchestral clarinet

**contrabassoon** double bassoon that reaches very low octaves

**cor anglais** English horn; curved, belled alto oboe (Europe, 17th c.)

**cornet** trumpet-shaped, flared metal horn played with valves

**cornett** wood horn with finger holes

**cornu** long trumpet curved into circle (ancient Rome)

**crumhorn** narrow, curved, double-reed horn (Renaissance Europe)

**cuckoo whistle** simple whistle flute

**didgeridoo** large, aboriginal bamboo pipe (Australia)

**doodlesack** goatskin bagpipe (Germany)

**English horn** large, deep-pitched oboe having pear-shaped bell; cor anglais

**euphonium** large, valved tenor tuba

**fife** small, side-blown flute

**fipple flute** any instrument with tubular body, finger holes, and whistle mouthpiece

**flageolet** six-holed whistle flute with bone or ivory mouthpiece (Europe)

**flügelhorn** valved, flared brass horn, esp. for military bands

**flute** tube producing tones by air blown through or across mouthpiece hole, with or without keys

**French horn** valved brass horn with coiled tube ending in flared bell

**fujara** very long, wood whistle flute (Slovakia)

**glass flute** tube made of glass

**harmonica** set of reeded tubes in box-shaped, metal shell; mouth organ

**hautboy** early oboe

**helicon** coiled tuba carried over shoulder in marching bands

**horn** curved, conical animal horn with reedless mouthpiece; any flared metal tube with reedless mouthpiece

**hornpipe** folk clarinet, often of animal horn

**hunting horn** earliest form of modern horn, consisting of coiled conical tube with flaring bell

**jug** large, deep, glass container with small opening at top, across which player blows

**lituus** curved military trumpet (ancient Rome)

**lyricon** wind synthesizer fingered like clarinet that controls analog synthesizer

**megaphone** cone-shaped device for intensifying or directing voice

**mellophone** valved, flared metal horn

**mouth organ** harmonica

**musette** early bagpipe with air supplied by bellows (France, 17th–18th c.)

**nose flute** tube played with breath from nostril instead of mouth

**oboe** keyed wood pipe with double-reed mouthpiece and conical tube

**oboe d'amore** oboe pitched a minor third below the conventional oboe, much used in music of baroque period

**ocarina** simple, oval-shaped flute with finger holes and mouthpiece

**ophicleide** conical metal tube bent double

**panpipe** set of small flutes of graduated sizes joined together in one unit; syrinx

**piccolo** small flute that reaches high octaves

**pipe** small whistle flute held in one hand

**post horn** straight or coiled metal horn with no valves or slide

**recorder** wood whistle flute in one of various pitches (Europe)

**sackbut** trombone (medieval Europe)

**salpinx** narrow ivory trumpet (ancient Greece)

**sarrusophone** brass horn with double-reed mouthpiece

**saxhorn** any of a family of brass instruments similar to cornet and tuba

**saxophone** metal horn with reed mouthpiece: sopranino, soprano, alto, tenor, baritone, bass, contrabass, subcontrabass

**saxtuba** large, bass saxhorn

**serpent** intricately curved wood horn with finger holes (18th c.)

**shakuhachi** bamboo flute (Japan)

**shawm** folk pipe with double-reed mouthpiece (Eastern Europe and Asia)

**shiwaya** vessel flute made from hollow fruit shell (South Africa)

**shofar** curved ram's horn that produces tones one-fifth apart, used to signal Jewish High Holidays

**sousaphone** large bass tuba

**syrinx** panpipe

**talinka** medieval, one-hole flute (eastern Europe)

**ti-tzu** bamboo flute (China)

**tonette** small, end-blown flute

**trombone** brass tube with a reedless mouthpiece and a slide for varying tube length

**trumpet** flared brass tube with reedless mouthpiece, usu. with three valves

**tuba** large, valved, deep-pitched brass horn with flared bell

**urua** very long double folk clarinet (Brazil)

**whistle flute** flute in which air is blown into mouthpiece rather than across it

## ACCESSORIES

**bell** large end of tube of wind instrument, usu. with edge turned out and enlarged

**bocal** curved metal piece holding reed and connected to body of bassoon

**bottleneck** glass tube slid along guitar strings for glissando effect

**bow** horsehairs stretched on wood rod for playing stringed instrument

**box** soundbox

**bridge** thin, arched support over which strings are stretched at belly of stringed instrument

**brush** metal bristles on handle for playing drums

**capo** movable bar attached to fingerboard of fretted, stringed instrument to raise pitch

**chanter** melody pipe of bagpipe

**damper** device that deadens sound, esp. by halting vibration of string

**drumhead** stretched membrane struck by drumsticks

**drumstick** wood stick for striking drumheads

**f-hole** either of two f-shaped slits in body of stringed instrument, esp. of violin family

**fingerboard** fretboard of guitar or lute

**finger hole** opening in tube or body of wind instrument, covered by finger to regulate pitch

**fret** lateral ridge on fingerboard of stringed instrument, used to regulate pitch and finger placement

**fretboard** fingerboard of guitar with lateral ridges that regulate pitch

**key** elements depressed by fingers and connected to strings in keyboard

**ligature** metal binding that holds reed on wind instrument

**mallet** drumstick with padded, rounded head

**membrane**  thin, pliable sheet of animal or vegetable tissue stretched to form drumhead

**metronome**  device for exactly measuring tempo through regular, repeated clicking sounds

**mouthpiece**  detachable end of wind or brass instrument that goes into player's mouth

**mute**  device used to muffle tone, esp. inserted in bell of brass instrument

**neck**  narrow extension from body to peghead of string instrument

**nut**  ledge at upper end of fingerboard of stringed instrument over which strings pass

**peg**  device that controls tension of strings

**peghead**  base for arrangement of pegs that control tension on strings

**pick**  plectrum

**pipe**  tube forming essential part of wind instrument; tube from which tones of organ are produced

**pitch pipe**  small reed pipe used to tune instruments or establish pitch for singer by producing specific tone; tuning pipe

**plectrum**  thin piece of ivory, wood, metal, horn, quill, or plastic, used to pluck strings of stringed instrument; pick

**purfling**  ornamental, inlaid border on back of violin and other stringed instruments

**reed**  thin, elastic tongue of wood fastened over mouthpiece in wind instrument and set vibrating by air current

**soundbox**  hollow, bell-shaped, resonating body of stringed instrument; box

**spit valve**  valve that opens to release saliva, as from trumpet

**string**  thin cord of nylon, gut, or metal stretched and plucked or bowed

**tube**  long, hollow body of wind instrument, usu. with finger holes or valves

**tuning fork**  two-pronged metal device that produces specific tone when struck, usu. 440 frequency A

**tuning pipe**  pitch pipe

**valve**  hole in body of brass instrument closed off by depression of key

**yoke**  crosspiece that connects or binds other parts

# Dance

Dances of the World
Ballet
Events, Steps, and Dancers

**see also:** Chap. 15: Classical Music; Popular Music; Theater

## Dances of the World

**abstract dance**  modern dance form in which pure movements have no implied narrative or symbolic meaning beyond themselves

**alegrias**  oldest and purest form of flamenco (Spain)

**allemande**  court dance performed with interwound arms, developed from German folk dance (17th-18th c.)

**ballet**  classical dance form based on conventional steps and positions with precise, graceful movements; a theatrical

entertainment that conveys story or atmosphere through such dance and music

**ballo**  standard popular dance and its music (Italy, 15th-16th c.)

**barn dance**  rural American social dance, variation on schottische in triple time, sometimes held in barn

**basse danse**  court dance that preceded minuet (16th-17th c.)

**beguine**  vigorous, popular ballroom dance in bolero rhythm, similar to rumba (Caribbean)

**belly dance**  solo dance performed by woman that emphasizes undulations of stomach (Middle East)

**bergamasca**  fast, rustic dance in duple time, similar to tarantella (Italy)

**Bharat Natya**  ancient, classical Vedic cult dance for women (India)

**bocane**  sedate dance for couple in duple time

**bolero**  lively dance in triple time, performed with sharp turns, stamping feet, and sudden stops (Spain)

**bop**  shufflelike dance to modern bebop jazz

**bossa nova**  dance similar to samba, with jazz influence (Brazil)

**bourrée**  dance in quick duple time (France, 17th c.)

**breakdown**  lively folk or jazz dance

**bugaku**  classical dance for men, performed in the imperial palace to gagaku music (Japan)

**bunny hug**  ragtime dance that is variation on Charleston

**cachucha**  lively solo dance resembling the bolero, performed with castanets in triple time (Andalusia)

**cakewalk**  African-American stage dance with eccentric strutting followed by solemn processional walk (19th c.)

**canary**  lively European court dance (16th c.)

**cancan**  high-kicking stage dance performed by women while holding up skirt front (France, 19th c.)

**carioca**  variation on samba (Brazil)

**carmagnole**  meandering street dance performed to lively song of French Revolution

**cha-cha**  fast, rhythmic, ballroom dance, based on three quick steps and a shuffle (Latin America)

**Charleston**  vigorous 1920's ballroom dance in which knees are swung in and out and heels turned outward on each step

**clog**  dance in which performer beats out rhythm on floor with heavy wood shoes

**conga**  ballroom dance for group in single line doing three steps forward and a kick (Cuba)

**contredanse**  folk dance in which couples face each other in two lines

**cooch**  hootchy-kootchy

**cotillion**  lively social dance similar to quadrille with frequent changing of partners under leadership of one couple (France, 18th c.)

**country dance**  traditional dance in which dancers form facing lines (Britian)

**courante**  dance in quick triple time with running or gliding step (Italy, 17th c.)

**czardas**  dance in duple time with slow first movement and fast, whirling second movement (Hungary)

**djanger**  vigorous, dramatic children's dance in which dancers cry out (Bali)

**écossaise**  country dance in quick duple time (Scotland)

**erotic dance**  striptease

**fan dance** solo dance performed by nude or seminude woman using one or more large fans to cover her body

**fandango** dance in lively triple time performed by one couple with castanets to guitar accompaniment (Spain, Latin America)

**farandole** dance in lively sextuple time, in which couples join hands and follow leader in various figures (Provence)

**flamenco** vigorous, rhythmic gypsy dance performed with stamping of feet and clapping of hands (Spanish Andalusia)

**fling** Highland fling

**foxtrot** two-step ballroom dance in quadruple time

**galliard** spirited, five-step dance for two dancers, performed in triple time (Europe, 16th-17th c.)

**galop** lively round dance in duple time (France and Germany, 19th c.)

**gavotte** dance of peasant origin performed in quick quadruple time (France, 18th c.)

**ghost dance** ritual native dance that calls on ancestors to assist in revival of power of a people

**gigue** jig; suite dance in triple time (Italy)

**gopak** folk dance performed with stomping of heels (Ukraine)

**habanera** dance in slow duple time (Cuba)

**haka** traditional Maori dance (New Zealand)

**Highland fling** lively folk dance characterized by tossing of arms and legs; fling (Scotland)

**hoedown** square dance

**hootchy-kootchy** pseudo-Oriental carnival dance that involves suggestive torso movements performed by woman dancer; cooch

**hora** traditional round dance (Israel and Romania)

**hula** dance with sinuous hip movements and mimetic hand gestures that tell story to drumming and chanting accompaniment (Hawaii)

**interpretive dance** highly personal form of modern dance

**jazz dance** modern dance form performed to jazz music, esp. in quadruple time, based on standardized movements

**jig** lively, springy folk dance in triple time; gigue

**jitterbug** American jazz two-step, performed by couples in the 1940's, consisting of standardized patterns with acrobatic swings, twirls, splits, and somersaults

**joropo** ballroom dance in rapid triple time (Venezuela)

**jota** folk dance performed by a couple in triple time with complex rhythms made with castanets and heels (Spain)

**juba** American southern plantation slave dance, accompanied by rhythmic clapping and slapping of knees and thighs

**kathak** classical dance form of Mongol era (India)

**kathakali** dance for men wearing facial makeup and using intricate hand gestures and expressions (India)

**kazatsky** lively Slavic folk dance for single male dancer

**kebiyar** popular children's fan dance (Bali)

**khon** dramatic dance for men performed to orchestral music (Thailand)

**kolo** folk dance in which a circle of dancers moves around a soloist who performs elaborate steps (Serbia)

**lambada** ballroom dance that combines elements of merengue, samba, and salsa, in which partners' bodies interlock closely to strong, sensual rhythm (Brazil)

**Lambeth walk** spirited 1930's ballroom dance combining jaunty strut with square dance figures

**ländler** folk dance in moderate triple time, antecedent of waltz (Austria and Germany)

**legong** elegant, traditional dance-pantomime, performed by girls in elaborate colorful costumes and accompanied by gamelan orchestra (Bali)

**limbo** competitive, acrobatic dance in which dancer bends backward from knees and moves under horizontal pole at progressively lower heights (West Indies)

**lindy** energetic jitterbug (1930's)

**malaguena** lively dance similar to fandango (Spain)

**mambo** ballroom dance similar to rumba and cha-cha with more complex steps (Cuba)

**manipuri** traditional folk dance (northern India)

**maxixe** syncopated ballroom dance in duple time (Brazil)

**mazurka** lively folk dance in triple time (Poland)

**merengue** ballroom dance performed with one stiff leg dragged on every step (Haiti)

**Mexican hat dance** lively courtship dance for solo male performed around brim of sombrero placed on ground (Mexico)

**minuet** slow, stately dance in triple time, performed with bowing and toe pointing (18th c.)

**modern dance** expressionistic, theatrical dance, developed after 1915 as alternative to ballet, with no formal conventions and unorthodox movements, done to eclectic music and based on one of various specialized techniques for using the entire body

**morris dance** vigorous rural dance for men wearing Robin Hood costumes, performed esp. on May Day (Britain, 16th c.)

**nautch dance** sinuous dance for female performer (India)

**nihon buyo** blend of ancient dance forms performed in Kabuki theater (Japan)

**one-step** ballroom round dance in duple time, performed to ragtime with quick walking steps backward and forward

**ox dance** comic men's folk dance like mock duel (Sweden)

**pas de deux** ballet dance for couple

**passacaglia** moderately slow dance in triple time (Italy, Spain, 17th c.)

**pavane** stately court dance in slow duple time (Europe, 16th c.)

**peabody** lively ballroom dance

**polka** lively dance for couples, performed in duple time using hop-step-close-step pattern (Bohemia)

**polonaise** stately promenade or march in slow triple time (Poland, 19th c.)

**quadrille** square dance with five complete parts, performed by four couples in duple and sextuple time

**rain dance** ritual native dance invoking rain

**reel** lively, traditional Highland folk dance (Scotland)

**rigadoon** lively, popular dance for one couple, performed in quick duple time (17th-18th c.)

**round dance** folk or ballroom dance in which couples move in circular motion around room

**rumba** ballroom dance performed in duple or quadruple time with step-close-step pattern and complex shifting of weight (Cuba)

**salsa** popular dance performed to rhythmic, big band jazz (Latin America)

**saltarello** lively dance for soloist or couple, in which a hop step begins each measure (Italy, 17th c.)

**samba** dance of African origin, consisting of a step-close-step-close pattern with dips and leaps on the beat, performed to relaxed jazz music (Brazil) saraband  stately court dance, similar to minuet, in slow triple time (Spain, 17th–18th c.)

schottische  round dance resembling a slow polka (Scotland)

seguidilla  folk dance in triple time, performed to guitar and castanet accompaniment (Spain)

shag  dance performed with vigorous hopping on each foot in turn (1930's–1940's)

shimmy  ragtime dance characterized by shaking of shoulders and hips (1920's)

shuffle  dance characterized by scraping feet across floor

siciliano  folk dance in which partners are joined by a handkerchief (Sicily)

Sir Roger de Coverley  country dance for two rows of dancers facing each other (Britain)

skirt dance  folk dance performed in full, flowing skirts

slow dance  contemporary popular dance in which couples embrace and sway gently to slow ballads

snake dance  ritual dance performed with snakes, or in which their images are invoked or imitated by sinuous movements

soft-shoe  tap dance steps in soft-soled shoes without metal taps

square dance  set folk dance for four couples arranged in a square; hoedown

stomp  dance to jazz music with driving rhythm, usu. marked by stamping of feet

strathspey  slow folk dance in quadruple time, similar to reel (Scotland)

striptease  burlesque dance in which performer suggestively removes clothing piece by piece; erotic dance

swing  jazz dance performed in moderate, lilting syncopation to big band music

sword dance  native male ceremonial dance performed around swords or in circle with flourished swords

tambourin  dance in duple time accompanied by drone bass or steady drumbeat (Provence)

tango  ballroom dance performed by couple in quadruple time with long pauses, varied steps, and stylized poses (Latin America)

tap dance  rhythmic variations tapped out audibly by dancer usu. wearing shoes with metal taps or special hard soles

tarantella  rapid, whirling folk dance in sextuple time (Italy, 18th c.)

Texas two-step  variation on two-step done to country-and-western swing music

toe dance  women's ballet executed on tips of toes while wearing pointe shoes with reinforced toes

trepak  vigorous men's folk dance featuring leg flings and kicks (Ukraine)

turkey trot  ragtime round dance having springy steps with straightened knees, body swings, and up-and-down shoulder movements

two-step  ballroom dance performed in duple time with sliding step-close-step pattern

valse à deux temps  French. bright, gliding ballroom dance similar to galop (19th c.)

villanella  rustic, free-form dance performed to unaccompanied song (Italy, 16th–17th c.)

Virginia reel  dance in which two facing lines of couples execute a series of figures in turn (19th c.)

waltz  classical ballroom dance performed in moderate triple time with accent on first beat of step-step-close pattern and dancers revolving in circles (19th c.)

war dance  native ritual dance performed prior to battle or in celebration of victory

Washington Post  ballroom dance in sextuple time (19th c.)

zapateado  solo dance performed with rhythmic foot tapping (Spain and Latin America)

## BALLET

adagio  slow, sustained movement stressing grace, balance; ballerina's lyrical performance in second part of grand pas de deux

allegro  rapid movements accompanied by jumps, turns, and batteries

allongé  extension of arms in arabesque

arabesque  standing on one leg with raised leg extended in straight line to rear and foot pointed

assemblé  rising off floor, straightening both legs in air, and returning to fifth position

assoluta  (adj) extraordinary

attitude  standing on one leg with raised leg behind body and knee bent; same position with raised leg in front of body

balance  light, rocking waltz step in which weight is shifted from side to side

ballerina  female dancer, esp. company's principal ballerina

ballet d'action  ballet that tells a story, often tragic

ballet master  ballet company's principal instructor, often also choreographer

balletomane  enthusiastic and knowledgeable follower of ballet

ballon  dancer's spring and lightness in leaps

ballonné  broad leap with battement kick

barre  horizontal bar opposite mirrors and along wall in studio for class exercises

battement  high or low kick: grand battement or petit battement

batterie  beating together of feet or legs, esp. in midair

bourrée  traveling movement with feet moving in tiny steps from tight fifth position

brisé  jump in which one leg beats against the other in midair

cabriole  man's batterie with one leg kicked high and the other leg rising to beat against it one or more times

cambré  bending back or to one side

Cecchetti method  classic Italian style of ballet, as distinguished from French and Russian schools

chaîné  series of short, usu. rapid turns made while moving across the floor

changement de pied  jump begun in fifth position, ending in fifth position with opposite foot forward

character dance  comic, semiserious dance, often a folk dance step or part performed with classical technique

chassé  traveling movement in which one foot follows and displaces the other

choreographer  creator of steps and patterns for ballet set to specific piece of music

choreography  art of devising form, sequence, and purpose of ballet movements

ciseaux  scissorslike leap with legs wide apart in midair

**closed positions** first, third, and fifth positions, in which feet are in contact with each other

**coda** final section of classical grand pas de deux

**combination** several movements in succession

**contretemps** step taken in counter time

**corps de ballet** ensemble or chorus of company dancers who perform together, not solo, usu. the junior members of a company

**coryphée** performer dancing in small group instead of solo or in corps de ballet

**count** measure of beats on which movements take place

**coupé** linking movement between steps, in which one foot replaces the other on a spot

**couru** (*adj*) running

**croisé** movement with body at oblique angle to audience and working leg crossing behind or in front of body

**danseur** male ballet dancer

**danseur noble** principal male dancer, equal to prima ballerina

**dégagé** freeing of foot prior to taking step, with working leg brushed out so that toes rise a few inches off the floor

**demi-plié** movement in which knee or knees are half-bent with heels on floor

**demi-pointe** dancing with weight of body on toes and ball of foot

**developpé** slowly bending and then straightening knee as leg is raised in extension from floor

**divertissement** dance or series of short dances without plot

**écarté** separated body position; position with perfectly square head and body leaning away from raised leg turned out to extreme

**échappé** jump with feet moving from a closed fifth to an open second position

**effacé** position with torso and hips at oblique angle to audience, working leg extended to front or back, and opposite arm raised above head

**elevation** apparent ability to remain suspended in midair while performing movements

**emboîtés** little hopping steps from leg to leg with working leg lifted in low front attitude

**en arriere** (*adj*) to the back; backward

**en avant** (*adj*) to the front; forward

**enchaînement** linking together of two or more movements to fit phrase of music; combination

**en dedans** (*adj*) moving arms or legs inward, toward body

**en dehors** (*adj*) moving arms or legs outward, away from body

**en face** (*adj*) facing body directly forward

**en l'air** (*adj*) performed off the ground

**en seconde** (*adj*) performed in second position

**entr'acte** interlude between main parts of a ballet

**entrechat** directly upward jump with body straight and feet reversing position several times in midair, named by number of reversals, as in entrechat quatre or entrechat six

**épaulement** bringing one shoulder forward in presenting step to audience with head turned over forward shoulder

**extension** dancer's ability to lift leg above head in nearly straight line from hip

**failli** linking movement between steps in which dancer jumps into quarter-turn

**fifth position** closed position with feet fully turned out and crossed one in front of the other, so that the heel of each touches the big toe of the other

**figure** step, leap, small combination

**first position** closed position in which feet form straight line perpendicular to body with heels touching

**fish dive** forward dive in which ballerina is caught by partner with her head and shoulders just above the floor

**fondu** lowering of body by slowly bending the knee of supporting leg with working foot pointing frontward

**fouetté** spin on one leg in which body is propelled by whipping motion of raised leg, performed by ballerina, usu. in series

**fourth position** open position with feet turned out from hip and placed horizontally, one in front of the other, a foot apart

**frappé** movement beginning with small beat with foot extended out strongly from knee

**glissade** gliding step from fifth to second to fifth position, performed on floor in low leap or prior to leap

**grand battement** high kick in any direction

**grand jeté** high leap covering a long distance in air

**grand pas de deux** formal, five-part pas de deux: entrée, ballerina's partnered adagio, male solo, female solo, coda

**grand plié** knees bending as deeply as possible with heels rising off floor

**jeté** leap made by pushing off on one leg and landing on the other

**Labanotation** standard choreographic notation technique, devised by Rudolf von Laban

**open positions** second and fourth positions, in which feet are placed apart

**par terre** (*adj*) performed on the ground

**partnering** strength, grace, rhythm, and certainty with which danseur assists and supports ballerina

**pas** formalized step; designation for type of dance

**pas de basque** linking movement between steps

**pas de bourrée** traveling step in any direction on pointe or demi-pointe

**pas de chat** leap from plié in fifth position

**pas de cheval** movement from fourth position that resembles a horse pawing the ground

**pas de deux** dance for two dancers, esp. grand pas de deux

**pas de quatre** dance for four dancers

**pas de trois** dance for three dancers

**passé** movement with working leg raised to side and knee bent, in which foot is pointed downward and brushed against standing leg

**pas seul** solo dance

**penché** (*adj*) leaning forward

**petits battements** small, quick movements with foot beating from front to back of ankle

**petit tours** short, fast turns made while progressing in straight line or circle

**piqué** stepping out onto pointe; little hop preparatory to traveling movement

**pirouette** turn of body while standing on one leg with raised leg held in position, performed on pointe for female, demi-pointe for male

**placement** good posture, turnout, and proper leg alignment

**plié** bending of knees while back is held straight with hips, legs, and feet turned out

**pointe** dancing on tips of toes; ballerina's dancing while maintaining continuous straight line from tips of toes to hip

**pointe shoes** ballerina's slippers with hard block in toes, used for standing on pointe

**port de bras** carriage and movement of arms

**posé tours** series of turns executed diagonally, around, or straight across floor

**positions** five basic positions of feet and arms

**premier danseur** principal male dancer

**première danseuse** principal ballerina

**prima ballerina** ballet company's principal ballerina

**principals** prima ballerinas and premier danseurs of ballet company

**promenade** slow turn of body on planted foot in adagio

**régisseur** stage manager who supervises performances

**relevé** rising onto pointe or demi-pointe

**répétiteur** rehearsal coach

**révérence** deep bow or curtsy

**rond de jamb** rotary movement of leg on floor or in air

**rosin** translucent, brittle turpentine resin used on shoes to prevent slipping on floor

**royale** changement de pied in which calves are beaten together before feet change position

**saut de basque** jump straight up, made with one leg bent at knee

**saut de chat** jump similar to grande jeté but with front leg passing through attitude

**second position** open position in which feet form straight line perpendicular to body while a foot apart

**sissonne** jump with legs straight and one leg extended to side

**soloist** dancer who performs occasional solos, ranked above corps de ballet and below principals in company hierarchy

**soubresant** leap from both feet to landing on both feet in fifth position

**sous-sous** rising from fifth position on flat feet to fifth position on pointe

**soutenu** (*adj*) sustained, esp. of battement rising into fifth position demi-pointe with equal weight on both legs

**stulchak** move in which male dancer holds ballerina above his head on one straight arm

**sur le coup de pied** position of pointed foot lightly wrapped around front of ankle or touching back of calf near floor

**temps** step in which weight is not transferred from foot to foot

**temps de flèche** sharp, hitch-kick jump in which legs pass in the air

**temps levé** hop taken from one foot starting in any of various positions

**temps lié** connected movement that combines leg and arm movements on second, fourth, and fifth positions of feet

**tendu** (*adj*) stretched and extended straight, esp. a leg

**third position** closed position with feet placed horizontally, one in front of the other, each heel at midpoint of the other foot

**tour** turn

**tour à la seconde** turn in second position

**tour en l'air** complete turn or turns executed in the air, begun and ended in fifth position

**tour jeté** high jump combining fast turn in the air and whiplike change of leg positions, ending in arabesque demi-plié

**turnout** outward rotation of legs at as close to 180-degree angle from hips as possible

**tutu** ballerina's short, flaring, fluffy skirt

**variation** solo dance, esp. third and fourth solo parts of classical grand pas de deux

**vole** traveling movements

# EVENTS, STEPS, AND DANCERS

**agitando** heel work used in Spanish dances

**balance** balancing step in place, usu. in triple time

**ball** large, formal party featuring social dancing

**ballroom dance** any social or recreational dance, such as the foxtrot, tango, or waltz, performed by couples often in a ballroom

**bump** abrupt, suggestive forward hip thrust

**bunny hop** short leap forward to toe of one foot, followed by quick step onto other foot

**chassé** sliding dance step

**chorus line** group of background dancers who perform in unison in musical theater

**country dance** informal social dance in rural area

**cut in** (*vb*) tap another person's shoulder and take their dancing partner

**dance** succession of rhythmic steps and bodily movements in set patterns performed to music

**dancercise** aerobic exercises and calisthenics performed to intensely rhythmic music

**discotheque** nightclub featuring highly amplified, recorded popular dance music and lighting effects

**do-si-do** square dance figure in which woman passes around her partner and then the man on her right

**figure** dance step, position, or combination of steps

**folk dance** indigenous dance common to one region or people

**formal** ball; large social gathering with ballroom dancing

**go-go dancer** dancer who performs on platform raised above patrons of disco or nightclub

**heel-and-toe** (*adj*) pertaining to locked knee step in which heel of one foot touches ground before toe of other foot leaves it

**hoofer** *Slang.* dancer

**hop** informal dance, esp. 1950's teenage rock-'n'-roll dance held to live or recorded music

**masked ball** ball at which participants wear disguises, esp. face masks

**mixer** informal dance and social gathering

**paso doble** Latin march step associated with bullfighting

**percussive movement** modern dance movement whose original staccato force is not carried through

**poussette** figure in which couples dance in circle with hands joined

**prom** formal dance or ball for high school students

**record hop** hop held to recorded music

**sashay** square dance figure in which partners sidestep in circle around each other, man moving behind woman

**set** basic formation in country or square dance

**splits** move in which dancer sinks to floor with legs extending straight out at right angles to body

**spotting** fixing of dancer's eyes on single spot by moving head during series of rapid turns

**square dance** stylized form of country dance in which four couples respond to steps announced by caller

**stag dance** gathering to which men and women come separately, not as couples

**step** specific dance movement or figure

**swing** dance figure in which partners revolve with arms or hands joined

**taxi dancer** woman employed to dance with patrons, as of cabaret or club, who pay her a fee

**tea dance** dance held in late afternoon

**Terpsichore** Greek muse of dance

**terpsichore** choreography; the art of dancing

**terpsichorean** dancer; (*adj*) pertaining to dance

**variation** combination of dance steps or figures

# THEATER

Theatrical Forms and Venues
Stagecraft, Production, and Dramatic Structure
Actors, Characters, and Theater People

**SEE ALSO**: Chap. 14: Literature; Chap. 15: Classical Music; Dance; Cinema; Television and Radio; Chap. 17: Entertainments and Spectacles

## THEATRICAL FORMS AND VENUES

**Actors Equity Association** AEA; union for theatrical actors and stage managers

**agitprop** informal drama supporting radical leftist ideology

**amphitheater** large, esp. round, outdoor space with raised tiers of seats around a stage; originally a natural dip

**arena theater** central stage surrounded by seats without proscenium; performed in the round

**auditorium** room, hall, or building used for performances

**avant-garde** experimental or new drama

**ballet** theatrical form that uses dance and music to convey a story without words

**benefit** performance given to raise money for some charity, cause, organization, or person

**big time** *Informal.* Broadway and legitimate theater, esp. successful

**black comedy** comedy emphasizing morbid, gloomy, grotesque, or calamitous themes and events

**borscht belt** resorts in New York's Catskills region known for distinctive Jewish comedy and cabaret entertainment

**Broadway** professional, legitimate, mainstream theater; the street in New York City where such theater occurs

**bunraku** puppet theater (Japan)

**burlesque** satire; variety entertainment featuring comic skits, striptease, and magic

**cabaret** dancing, singing, and skits performed in a bar or café

**chronicle play** play based on loosely connected chronological episodes that depicts historical theme or events

**circus** traveling troupe of acrobats, clowns, and trained animals, usu. performing in oval arena

**classical theater** Greek tragedies, Shakespearean plays, or other long-established dramas or comedies

**closet drama** play intended to be read, not performed

**comedy** dramatic form using wit, humor, and satire; narrative with happy ending

**comedy of manners** dramatic form depicting and satirizing fashionable society

**commedia dell'arte** popular, folk-based comedic tradition of masked carnival mimes and acrobats, based on stock characters and situations (Italy, 16th-18th c.)

**community theater** little theater

**dinner theater** theater in which production is performed for audience that has been served dinner

**drama** theatrical form based on exposition of conflict through dialogue and actions of performers

**experimental theater** avant-garde; new and nontraditional dramatic form and narrative

**farce** low comedy, based on horseplay and absurd situations

**floor show** cabaret or nightclub theater; entertainment staged in conjunction with drinking and revelry in audience

**fringe theater** politically provocative or experimental theater in Britain, similar to U.S. off off Broadway

**Globe Theatre** traditional, round, open-air theater in London where Shakespearean drama was performed (early 17th c.)

**Grand Guignol** style of dramatic production that emphasizes grisly, frightening, violent, or morbid themes

**Great White Way** Broadway theater district in New York City

**guerrilla theater** performance, sometimes in streets, used esp. for social protest or propaganda; street theater

**happening** improvised, spontaneous theatrical performance, popular in 1960's

**high comedy** dramatic form characterized by witty, satiric depictions of upper class life

**improv** *Informal.* improvisation

**improvisation** unrehearsed, impromptu performance, usu. within larger dramatic structure or in rehearsal; type of entertainment featuring spontaneous, unrehearsed skits by a troupe of actors; improv

**Kabuki** highly choreographed, stylized, all-male theater (Japan)

**legitimate stage** professionally produced, traditional theater, as opposed to burlesque, vaudeville, and nonprofessional stagings

**little theater** amateur, neighborhood theater; community theater

**low comedy** dramatic form that employs burlesque, farce, and slapstick, usu. involving common folk, without clever or witty dialogue

**masque** elaborate costume play, orig. traditional folk theater and dance spectacles

**melodrama** dramatic form that exaggerates emotions and emphasizes plot over characterization

**minstrel show** theatrical entertainment featuring white performers in blackface who sing, dance, and tell stories, based on stereotypes of African-American culture (U.S., late 19th c.)

**miracle play** medieval drama based on the Bible or the life of a saint or martyr

**morality play** medieval, allegorical dramatic form that provided instruction in Christian orthodoxy

**musical** light dramatic entertainment featuring musical interludes, story told largely through song and dance

**musical comedy** comic musical play

**music hall** theater or room for variety shows; in Britain, form of popular entertainment consisting of variety acts

**mystery play** medieval drama based on Scriptural events, often illustrating points of religious doctrine and faith

**national theater** repertory company drawing on nation's best actors, technicians, and writers, often government-funded

**neighborhood playhouse** small, often semiprofessional local theater

**Nō** classical, all-male theater, elegant and serious in tone and form (Japan)

**odeum** small theater or concert hall

**off Broadway** low-budget, theatrical productions performed in modest venues, esp. in New York, sometimes as a pre-Broadway venture

**off off Broadway** highly experimental, sometimes nonprofessional theatrical productions performed in small venues far outside realms of legitimate theater

**olio** program consisting of musical numbers and skits; backdrop or curtain with advertisements; revue

**one-acter** *Informal.* play consisting of one, usu. uninterrupted, act

**open-air theater** performance in unenclosed auditorium or amphitheater, esp. Globe-type theater

**opera** musical drama composed of vocal pieces sung to orchestral accompaniment, esp. with tragic themes on grand scale

**operetta** romantic, light opera with songs and dance

**pageant** elaborately staged, open-air dramatic production, often with historical theme

**pantomime** performance without spoken words

**passion play** medieval religious drama dealing with Christ's passion

**performance art** often experimental, dramatic form combining theatrical performance, visual art, music, dance, cinema, or video in non-narrative, multimedia piece, originated in 1970's

**performance space** often bare, open area designed for performances, sometimes without seats for audience

**play** dramatic work performed by actors before an audience, usu. on stage and usu. from a written script

**playhouse** modest local theater used for live performances

**playlet** short play

**puppet theater** dramatic production using puppets instead of human actors

**repertory company** company that presents several works regularly or alternately using same performers

**revue** series of unrelated, often comic, skits, songs, dances, and monologues; olio

**road show** theatrical performance that travels from city to city

**send-up** mocking parody or spoof of another work

**shadow play** theater in which the shadows of puppets are cast on a screen between puppets and audience

**showboat** floating riverboat used as theater (U.S., 19th c.)

**showcase** small production used to expose actors to talent agents, producers, and directors; equity waiver

**sketch** brief, comic play or skit

**skit** short, informal, comic piece, esp. in imitation of longer, serious work; sketch

**slapstick** low comedy dependent on physical humor or horseplay

**stand-up** (*adj*) designating comedy in form of monologue delivered while standing alone before audience

**strawhat** (*adj*) pertaining to summer theater

**street theater** theatrical form using public areas or streets as a stage, often politically radical in theme; guerrilla theater

**summer stock** acting company that produces plays during summer

**theater** building in which plays are performed, usu. having stage and audience seating area

**theater-in-the-round** theatrical presentation in which the audience sits on all sides of an open stage; arena theater

**theater of cruelty** theatrical form using violence, sadism, and suffering to explore the cruelty of human existence and similar themes

**theater of fact** documentary theater

**theater of the absurd** theatrical form that dispenses with linear narrative and realistic dialogue and explores existential dimensions of life, esp. popular since 1950's

**tragedy** dramatic form dealing with a flaw, moral weakness, or maladjustment of the central character, resulting in downfall or catastrophe

**tragicomedy** dramatic form mixing elements of tragedy and comedy

**variety show** entertainment consisting of a series of different acts, orig. performed in music halls

**vaudeville** theatrical entertainment that featured a variety of performances by different singers, dancers, comedians, and other specialty acts (early 20th c.)

**Yiddish theater** traditional plays of eastern European Jews, performed in Yiddish

## STAGECRAFT, PRODUCTION, AND DRAMATIC STRUCTURE

**act** major division of play; (*vb*) perform in dramatic stage production

**action** what a character does in order to reach his or her objective

**ad lib** spontaneous line or lines not part of script

**anagnorisis** critical moment of recognition leading to denouement in Greek tragedy

**applause** expression of audience approval by clapping hands

**apron** section of stage floor closest to audience, usu. in front of proscenium; forestage

**aside** actor's lines spoken to audience, not other actors

**audience** spectators viewing a performance

**audition** brief trial performance held to appraise actor's talent and suitability for role

**backdrop** curtain painted as scenery, hung at rear of stage

**backlight** lighting of stage from upstage area behind actors used to create visual depth

**backstage** wings, dressing rooms, and other areas behind proscenium out of audience view

**balcony** elevated seating area in auditorium, usu. jutting out over orchestra floor

**barnstorm** (*vb*) travel about country performing plays

**beat** small segment of a scene in which character has one specific objective

**bill** performance or piece being shown in theater

**bit** short theatrical routine

**blackface**  black facial makeup, orig. burnt cork, worn by performers esp. in minstrel shows

**blackout**  abrupt switching off of all stage lights at end of scene

**blocking**  director's charting of actor's stage movements

**boards**  stage floor; the theater in general

**bomb**  play meeting with critical and/or commercial failure; (*vb*) fail badly

**book**  words of a musical or opera

**border**  narrow curtain or strip of canvas hung above stage to mask flies

**born in a trunk**  *Slang*. born into a theatrical family

**bow**  actor's acknowledgment of applause, usu. by bending head and body forward

**box**  private seating compartment in theater, esp. an elevated one

**box office**  small room near theater entrance in which tickets are sold; number and value of tickets sold for show

**bravo**  audience shout of approval

**break a leg**  actor's traditional expression of good luck

**business**  minor piece of stage action, such as gesture or movement, used to create effect or portray character

**callback**  actor's second audition for same part

**cast**  actors chosen to perform parts in a play; (*vb*) select actors to play parts

**cast party**  celebration of opening or closing night

**catharsis**  purging of emotions through viewing play

**cattle call**  *Slang*. publicly announced audition open to all comers

**character**  person portrayed in play

**circuit**  locations at which touring company gives dramatic performances

**close**  (*vb*) end play's performance run

**cold reading**  audition or rehearsal of previously unseen script

**comic relief**  brief, humorous interlude in serious drama

**costume**  actor's outfit, worn to create appearance of the character being played

**cothurnus**  grave and elevated style of tragic acting; one of a pair of thick-soled boots worn in ancient Greek tragedy

**coulisse**  side flat; space between two side flats

**counterweight system**  a vertically tracked weight arbor corresponding to pulleys and pipe (baton) for hoisting scenery

**cue**  word, phrase, or action signaling actor's line, entrance, or exit, or change in lighting or sound

**curtain**  drapery separating audience from stage; descent of stage curtain at end of play or act

**curtain call**  return of actors to stage to take bows in response to applause at play's end

**curtain raiser**  short play or other selection presented before main play in a program

**curtain warmer**  curtain raiser

**cut drop**  drop scene that has been cut to reveal part of upstage area

**cyclorama**  curved backdrop used to create the illusion of sky, space, or distance

**dark**  (*adj*) description of theater on night without performance

**debut**  actor's first performance, as in the professional theater or in a particular role

**decor**  scenery, sets, or backdrops

**denouement**  resolution of plot; outcome or dramatic unraveling of story complications and conflicts

**deus ex machina**  *Latin*. lit. god from a machine; character or device introduced from outside the story to resolve plot

**dialogue**  words spoken by characters in play

**dimmer**  device by which the intensity of a lighting unit may be varied

**dimmer board**  a panel of dimmers

**downstage**  area of stage nearest audience

**drama**  literary works written for the theater; theatrical presentation involving the creation, exploration, and resolution of conflict

**dramatic structure**  traditional, formal composition of dramatic piece, based on resolution of conflict

**dramaturgy**  art of dramatic composition

**dress circle**  first balcony seating area above boxes

**dress rehearsal**  rehearsal in full costume just prior to opening night

**drop curtain**  curtain that is lowered from flies into position as rear wall of stage area

**drop scene**  drop curtain used as background for scene played downstage while upstage set is being changed behind it

**engagement**  run of scheduled performances

**ensemble piece**  play or performance in which all actors share equal billing and size of part

**entr'acte**  short performance, as music or dance, between acts of a play; interval between acts of a play or other production

**epilogue**  brief section at conclusion of play

**epitasis**  portion of Greek tragedy in which main action moves toward climax

**finale**  final scene or musical number of performance

**flat**  theatrical unit covered in muslin or lawn used as walls

**flies**  area above stage with weights and ropes for manipulating scenery down and up

**flop**  unsuccessful play or performance

**footlights**  row of lights set along front edge of stage floor; acting profession in general

**forestage**  apron

**fourth wall**  imaginary wall at front of stage separating actors from audience

**French scene**  division of a scene according to character entrances and exits

**fright wig**  wig with spikey hair standing out in all directions, worn for comic effect

**front of house**  audience area of theater

**gallery**  top balcony, usu. containing the cheapest seats

**gel**  colored plastic sheeting used to tint stage lights

**gobo**  pattern inserted into lighting instrument and projected at stage

**grease paint**  theatrical makeup

**green room**  backstage room in which performers relax before, between, or after appearances on stage

**ground plan**  overhead scale view of set that includes all scenery and set pieces

**hall**  auditorium, stage, theater, music hall, or performance space

**hamartia**  tragic flaw that causes hero's misfortune in Greek tragedy

**histrionics**  acting in highly theatrical or exaggerated, dramatic style

**hit**  extremely popular play or performance

**hit one's mark**  stop movement in precisely designated spot marked on stage

**house**  auditorium in which audience sits during performances

**houselights**  theater lights in auditorium, not those on stage

**house seat**  theater seat reserved by management for special guest or professional

**instrument**  Method term for actor's body or theatrical light

**intermezzo**  short, light interlude between acts

**intermission**  interval between acts

**jack**  stage brace for scenery

**knee play**  *Slang*. intermission

**leg drop**  narrow scenery flat or drop, often used in pairs to form inverted U

**light bridge**  platform or elevated room from which lights are positioned

**lighting board**  control panel for lighting stage and auditorium

**limelight**  brilliant stage light that illuminates major characters; center of attention

**lines**  words spoken during performance of play, esp. by one character

**lobsterscope**  punched metal disk rotating in front of spotlight for lighting effects

**loge**  balcony seating area of theater

**makeup**  cosmetics and other materials applied to face, hands, and areas of body not covered by costume

**marks**  tape or chalk marks on stage indicating actor positioning

**marquee**  canopy on front of outside theater advertising play

**mask**  face-covering of molded material or cloth, often used to indicate character

**matinée**  afternoon performance

**Method**  naturalistic acting technique, developed by Konstantin Stanislavski, that emphasizes actor's personal exploration of and identification with character

**mezzanine**  lowest balcony in theater, esp. first few rows in this balcony

**mise en scène**  *French*. props and scenery used in a performance; setting of play

**monologue**  speech delivered at length by one actor

**motley**  multicolored garment traditionally worn by jester

**mug**  (*vb*) make exaggerated, often comic, facial expressions while acting

**Muse**  mythological spirit believed to inspire poetry and drama (ancient Greece)

**no-show**  person holding reservation who does not claim ticket

**number**  song performed in theatrical production

**objective**  what a character wants in scene or play

**obstacle**  whatever prevents a character from reaching an objective, thereby forwarding the action of the play

**off book**  (*adj*) designating rehearsal for which actors must have lines memorized

**one-night stand**  single performance in one locale by touring company

**one sheet**  paper work recorded and used by light and sound board operators to run show

**open**  (*vb*) begin series of performances

**opening night**  first performance of play, often a gala occasion

**orchestra**  audience seats on ground floor of theater

**overact**  (*vb*) perform in exaggerated, unconvincing manner

**paper the house**  increase audience size by distributing free tickets

**parados**  passageway between sets and wings

**paraskenae**  projecting wings of stage building (ancient Greece)

**parquet circle**  parterre

**part**  role in play for which actor is cast

**parterre**  seats on main floor of theater behind orchestra; parquet circle

**patch**  manual or computer assignment of dimmers to channels on control board

**peanut gallery**  *Informal*. rear balcony seating in theater; cheaper seats, from which rabble traditionally threw peanuts

**perform**  (*vb*) act, sing, or dance before an audience

**performance**  any entertainment presented before an audience; act of performing a theatrical piece; particular instance of presenting a theatrical piece

**periactoid**  three side scenic unit conveying different scenes, usually used in a series

**peripeteia**  sudden and unexpected turn of events or plot twist

**pit**  sunken area directly in front of stage in which orchestra musicians sit

**platform**  3/4" plywood covered frame used for flooring or levels on a set

**playbill**  theatrical program; handbill identifying cast and production members for audience

**plot**  arrangement of narrative events in play or plan of lighting design

**premiere**  first performance of play

**preparation**  technique an actor uses to create an emotional state of being before entering a scene

**preview**  performance of play given before official opening

**production**  all elements involved in one particular staging of a play

**program**  brochure or sheet describing play and listing performers and production staff, handed out before performance begins

**project**  (*vb*) speak so that voice carries to entire audience

**prologue**  introduction to play or performance

**prompt**  (*vb*) supply (an actor) with forgotten line or missed cue from offstage

**prompt script**  master script with all acting and technical cues, used by stage manager to supervise show during performance

**prop**  property

**property**  any article used to dress the stage for scenes, or any object carried by an actor; prop

**proscenium**  arched part of stage, located in front of curtain, that separates stage from auditorium

**protasis**  opening portion of ancient drama in which characters and plot are introduced

**rake**  slope of stage floor from apron to rear wall

**rave**  extremely favorable review

**rehearsal**  practice performance; preparation of production by cast, crew, and director

**rehearsal studio**  large room or hall for rehearsing

**repertoire**  stock of plays performed by actor or company

**repertory**  presentation of a stock of plays by a theater company over a regular season; company or troupe that presents plays this way

**review** critical description of performance, usu. by a member of the media

**revolving stage** stage set on circulating platform which turns 120 or 180 degrees, providing fast, smooth scene changes

**ring down the curtain** lower the curtain

**ring up the curtain** raise the curtain

**riser** stairlike theater seating or stage area

**role** actor's part; character in play

**routine** theatrical skit; dance combination; comedian's material

**run** total number of consecutive performances of a play at one theater or on tour

**run-through** rehearsal of entire piece

**scenario** outline of play's action, including notes on scenery and special effects; skeleton plot

**scene** uninterrupted action within play; division of an act

**scenery** backdrops or structures on stage that represent the play's locale

**scene shop** area in which scenery is constructed and painted

**scrim** open-weave cotton fabric, opaque when front lit and translucent when back lit

**script** working version of play's text

**sensory** technique used by actors in Method training in which specific sensory input is re-created by imagination

**set** scenery, flats, and properties composing play's environment

**show** play; production of play

**show business** entertainment industry, including the theater

**show-stopper** dramatic or musical moment during performance that draws prolonged applause, halting action

**shtick** *Slang.* comedian's or actor's unique style or material

**sides** pages of a script with lines and cues for one role only, commonly used at auditions

**sight gag** funny bit without dialogue

**sightline** line of vision from audience to extreme corners of stage

**slapstick** comedy stressing farce, horseplay, or sight gags

**smash** successful, long-running play

**soliloquy** monologue expressing character's inner thoughts, addressed to no one

**sotto voce** (*adv*) in a low, soft voice

**spike marks** taped marks for furniture, prop, or set placement

**spirit gum** solution of gum arabic in ether, used to attach false hair or beards

**spotlight** powerful light used to illuminate individual actor, manually operated on a rotating axis

**SRO** *standing room only*; designating a sold-out performance

**stage** area on which plays are performed before an audience

**stagecraft** skill in theatrical performance; art and practice of staging plays; art of set construction

**stage direction** instruction in script of play indicating production requirements or performer's action or appearance

**stage door** actors' and production crew's entrance, located away from audience's street entrance to theater

**stage fright** extreme fear and anxiety at prospect of performing before audience

**stage left** stage area on actor's left when facing audience

**stage right** stage area on actor's right when facing audience

**stagestruck** (*adj*) infatuated with performing and the theater

**stage whisper** loud, easily overheard, mock whisper

**stall** theater seat with back and sides; *Chiefly Brit.* orchestra seat

**standing room** area at rear of orchestra in which audience may stand during sold-out performance; SRO

**steal the show** perform so brilliantly as to draw most of the audience's attention to oneself

**stock scenery** scenery of a standard size that is stored for reuse

**strike** (*vb*) take apart and remove (scenery or set) from stage

**striplights** encased set of lights on 3 or 4 separate circuits, used for color washes of cyclorama

**subtext** meaning and motivations underlying spoken text

**supertitle** translation of text or brief plot summary projected on screen above stage during performance

**swan song** actor's final performance

**tableau** stage picture created by actors posing motionless

**tableau curtain** curtain that opens in center, with sections drawing up and to side, creating draped effect

**teaser** drapery or flat member across top of proscenium arch that frames stage opening and conceals flies

**tech rehearsal** internal rehearsal held to check sound and lighting

**theater** art and practice of writing, producing, staging, and performing plays; building in which plays are staged; also, *esp.Brit.*, theatre

**theatricality** sense of what will work on stage

**throwaway line** unimportant line of dialogue lost in action

**thrust stage** stage extending beyond the proscenium, usu. surrounded by audience on three sides

**Tony awards** theatrical awards given annually by American Theatre Wing for best Broadway shows, performances, etc.; Antoinette Perry awards

**top billing** first or most prominent spot in a list of actors on a program or marquee

**tormentor** fixed curtain or flat on each side of stage that prevents audience from seeing into wings

**touring company** group of performers moving from city to city to present a play or musical, esp. one already successful on Broadway

**trap** removable section of stage floor through which actors can enter or exit or scenery be brought in or removed

**tryout** actor's audition; test performance of play before official opening

**turkey** *Slang.* disastrous production or performance

**turn** brief performance

**twofers** *Informal.* two tickets for the price of one

**typecasting** assigning role to actor based on actor's appearance, personal style, or previous experience

**upstage** rear portion of stage; (*vb*) to move upstage from another actor, forcing him or her to turn away from audience; to draw audience's attention from another actor by distracting behavior

**vehicle** theatrical work with role designed or well-suited to display or exploit the talents of particular performer

**venue** type of performance space

**vomitory** large opening through banks of seats in auditorium that permits large members of people to enter or leave theater

**walk-through** early or casual rehearsal

**whiteface** white pancake makeup, used esp. by mimes

**wings** sides of stage beyond view of audience

**workshop** exchange of ideas and application of skill among director, writer, actors, and others involved in development of new play or work in progress

## ACTORS, CHARACTERS, AND THEATER PEOPLE

**acrobat** expert performer of physical tricks or feats

**actor** stage performer, esp. male, but may also apply to female; player; Thespian

**actress** female stage performer

**alazon** swaggering braggart, stock character in classic Greek comedy

**angel** *Informal.* financial backer, as of play production

**antagonist** adversary of leading character or hero

**backer** investor in production

**bard** epic poet, national minstrel

**Bard** William Shakespeare

**barker** person who stands at entrance to show, esp. carnival, attracting passersby

**barnstormer** traveling actor; actor in road production

**bit player** actor who performs a small role, usu. with few lines of dialogue

**booking agent** person who arranges venues for performances

**buffoon** fool

**busker** street performer

**cameo** small role played by a famous actor; brief appearance in play

**cast** actors who portray all the roles in play

**character** specific role in play, portrayed by actor

**character actor** player who specializes in roles depicting strong or memorable personalities, but not hero

**child actor** preadolescent who works as an actor

**choragus** leader of chorus; coryphaeus (ancient Greece)

**chorus** group of actors in ancient Greek drama speaking lines in unison, commenting on action of play but not interacting with characters; group of dancers and singers performing together in musical

**chorus line** chorus dancing in line across stage, esp. in musical comedy

**coach** acting teacher hired to help with specific part

**comedian** comic actor

**comedienne** female comic actor

**comic** comedian or comedienne

**company** group of actors, esp. stock company

**comprere** master of ceremonies

**contortionist** circus acrobat capable of assuming unnatural positions

**coryphaeus** leader of chorus; choragus (ancient Greece)

**costume designer** person responsible for costuming the actors

**crew** all nonperformers; stagehands and technicians involved in a production

**dancer** performer who specializes in graceful movements done to music, often without speaking or while singing

**director** person responsible for blocking stage movements, motivating actors, and providing unity to production

**diseuse** actress skilled at dramatic monologues

**diva** leading woman singer in grand opera

**dossenus** sharp-witted hunchback character in classical Roman comedy

**dramatis personae** cast of characters in a dramatic work

**dramaturge** composer of dramas; company's script analyst

**dresser** personal assistant responsible for helping actor into costume at time of performance

**emcee** master of ceremonies

**ensemble** group of actors performing together; full company

**entertainer** performer, esp. one skilled in singing and dancing

**extra** actor in minor, nonspeaking role

**flyman** member of set crew who works in the flies

**foil** role that provides contrast or opposition to hero

**fool** comic role in folk or morality play; buffoon; jester

**gypsy** *Slang.* singer/dancer who works in chorus line; experienced background player

**ham** actor with contrived, overworked, or insincere style

**harlequin** masked, comic character, usu. dressed in multicolored, diamond-patterned tights and carrying a sword or magic wand, in commedia dell'arte

**heavy** villain

**hero** principal male character in drama

**heroine** principal female character in drama

**impresario** manager, director, or fund-raiser for theater company

**ingénue** role of innocent, naive young woman in drama

**jester** fool

**juggler** performer skilled at tossing several objects in the air in rapid rotation and catching them

**juvenile** young actor or one who plays young parts

**lead** principal character in drama

**leading lady** actress playing heroine or principal female character in drama

**leading man** actor playing hero or principal male character in drama

**librettist** writer of song lyrics for a musical

**lighting designer** person responsible for technical and aesthetic arrangement of lights used in production

**magician** entertainer who performs feats of sleight of hand

**makeup artist** person who applies makeup to actors

**master electrician** person responsible for hanging, focus, and integrity of designer's plot

**master of ceremonies** MC; person who presides over revue or variety show, esp. introducing acts and filling breaks with patter; comprere; emcee

**matinée idol** handsome actor popular with female audiences

**MC** master of ceremonies

**merry-andrew** clown or fool

**mime** actor who uses gestures and bodily movements to silently portray a character or communicate moods and ideas

**minstrel** medieval entertainer who traveled from place to place singing and reciting stories

**monologist** actor who performs a monologue

**mummer** masked, traveling performer of northern European folk plays (18th-19th c.)

**pantomime** actor in dumb show or silent performance

**patron** person who provides the major portion of funding for a company

**Pierrot** stock male character in French pantomime who wears loose white costume and whiteface

**player** actor

**playwright** author of plays

**prima donna** orig. principal woman singer; vain performer who wants all of the audience's attention

**producer** person responsible for financial and administrative aspects of production, esp. fund-raising

**prompter** person hidden from audience who supplies next line of dialogue or other cue when actor forgets

**protagonist** main character in drama; hero or heroine

**puppet** doll or figure manipulated by hand on small stage

**repertory** company in which actors share leading roles in several different plays performed in rotation; stock company

**saltimbanque** street performer, esp. juggler or contortionist

**Scaramouch** cowardly braggart who is easily vanquished in farce and commedia dell'arte

**scene-stealer** performer who draws audience attention away from other actors on stage; prima donna

**set designer** person responsible for design and creation of stage sets and scenery

**singer** performer who specializes in rhythmic, melodic speech set to music

**song-and-dance man** entertainer who specializes in musicals

**soubrette** role of lady's maid, esp. flirtatious intriguer

**sound designer** person responsible for acoustic setup of speakers and special sound effects

**spear carrier** extra

**stagehand** person who sets up and changes scenery before and during performance

**stage manager** theater staff person responsible for functional details of production during rehearsal and performance

**stand-by** actor prepared to substitute for regular performer in part as needed but usually not a member of cast

**stand-up comic** entertainer who performs comic routine while standing alone onstage

**star** very popular, successful, and well-known actor who performs leading roles

**stock** stock company

**stock company** troupe of actors, each specializing in certain types of roles and sharing others, who perform a series of plays, usu. at one theater; repertory company

**stooge** *Slang.* comic foil, esp. one who feeds lines to other actors

**straight man** actor whose lines set up jokes for comedian

**stripper** burlesque performer who removes garments one at a time during elaborate dance set to music

**supernumerary** actor in walk-on part; extra

**supporting actor** person in role supporting, or secondary to, leading man or lady

**talent scout** person employed to find new performers

**technical director** person responsible for coordinating technical aspects of show including set, lights, and sound effects

**Thespian** actor

**tragedian** actor who specializes in tragic roles; writer of tragedies

**tragedienne** female actor who specializes in playing tragic roles

**troubadour** wandering medieval minstrel who wrote and performed poetry and songs

**troupe** company of actors

**trouper** dedicated, selfless, and versatile performer

**tummler** combined comedian, activities director, and master of ceremonies at borscht belt resorts

**understudy** actor versed in another's part, ready to step in if needed, usu. a member of the cast

**usher** theater attendant who guides audience members to their seats

**vaudevillian** performer of usu. comic vaudeville routines

**villain** character who opposes hero; bad guy; heavy

**walk-on** small, nonspeaking part; actor playing such a part

# CINEMA

Genres and Types of Pictures
Cinematography Tools and Techniques
Movie People and Show Business

**SEE ALSO**: Chap. 15: Theater; Television and Radio

## GENRES AND TYPES OF PICTURES

**action adventure** fast-paced, exciting narrative of some dangerous or bold undertaking

**animation** series of drawings that depict action by means of slightly progressive changes, each photographed separately to create movie; cartoon

**A picture** high-budget, high-quality feature film, usu. with stars

**art film** low-budget, nonstudio, often nonnarrative film utilizing experimental techniques

**biographical film** film based on life story of actual person

**blaxploitation** film exploiting blacks

**blue movie** pornographic film

**B-picture** low-budget studio film, often in genre and without major stars, formerly shown as added feature on bill with A picture

**buddy picture** narrative about adventures shared by two friends, usu. male

**cartoon** animated film

**chiller** *Informal.* horror film

**cinéma vérité** documentary filmed with handheld camera without added effects, authentic and candid in action and style

**costume film** period piece

**cowboy picture** western

**crash and burn film** *Slang.* violent action film featuring a series of spectacular vehicular explosions

**detective picture** story involving criminal investigation

**disaster picture** narrative about effects on characters of natural or man-made catastrophe

**documentary** nonfiction narrative about actual event or characters in journalistic vein

**epic** long, episodic, large-scale story with heroic characters

**experimental film** avant-garde, unconventional, or abstract film

**exploitation film** film with highly commercial appeal to specific audience, esp. particular sex, race, or age group

**fantasy** fanciful departure from known realities

**film noir** 1940's American black-and-white style of film, esp. with a private detective as hero, that emphasized dark, sinister moods and bleak viewpoints

**gangster film** melodramatic narrative film about a violent, criminal antihero, esp. popular in the Depression era

**genre** film using a specific technique, style, story, or setting, such as western, gangster, or science fiction film

**hard-core** (*adj*) pruriently explicit, as in pornography that vividly depicts sex acts

**horror** films with strange, frightening events that threaten characters, esp. those emphasizing bloodshed or supernatural forces

**horse opera** western

**independent film** usu. low-budget film not produced by major studio

**industrial** promotional film for product or company

**law-and-order film** action-adventure story in which criminals are brought to justice by law officials

**melodrama** sensational story emphasizing emotional content over characterization

**musical** story told in large part through musical productions, esp. song-and-dance numbers

**newsreel** short documentary account of current events

**new wave** movement characterized by abstraction, subjective symbolism, improvisation, and experimental techniques, orig. France, late 1950's, early 1960's; nouvelle vague

**nouvelle vague** *French*. new wave

**oater** *Slang*. western

**period piece** narrative occurring in another era, with appropriate historical sets and costumes; costume film

**porn** *Informal*. pornography

**pornographic film** low-budget picture designed for sexual titillation; blue film; porn; skin flick

**prequel** sequel that depicts events preceding those of the original work

**remake** new version of old film

**romantic comedy** light comedy involving love interest

**science fiction** film depicting effect of science on society, esp. future society or other planets; sci-fi; space opera

**sci-fi** *Informal*. science fiction

**screwball comedy** light, imaginative, fast-paced film with witty dialogue and improbable plot line

**sequel** continuation of story or characters depicted in an earlier film

**serial** episodic motion picture, usu. seen in installments

**sexploitation** *Informal*. film that exploits sex

**shocker** horror, thriller, or monster film

**shoot-'em up** *Informal*. film that emphasizes gunplay and violent action

**short subject** short motion picture, usu. of less than 3000 feet of 35 mm film (or half an hour), often a documentary

**silent film** motion picture without sound, either from pre-1930 era or for effect

**skin flick** *Slang*. pornographic film

**slapstick comedy** humorous film that features boisterous, physical jokes and mugging

**slasher movie** film depicting violent killer who runs amok maiming or dismembering other characters, esp. young females

**snuff film** *Slang*. pornographic film that shows actual murder of performers

**soft-core** (*adj*) sexually stimulating, as in pornography that features nudity but not explicit sex acts

**space opera** science fiction involving space travel

**spaghetti western** *Informal*. Italian-made, low-budget cowboy film

**stag movie** pornographic film intended for male audience

**student film** production directed by film-school students

**talkie** early film produced with sound (1920's-1930's)

**tearjerker** *Informal*. sentimental melodrama

**teen picture** film depicting teenage characters and lifestyles, aimed at teen audience

**thriller** suspense drama

**travelogue** documentary motion picture showing and describing travels

**western** narrative set in lawless, 19th century American frontier; cowboy picture; horse opera; oater

**whodunit** *Informal*. detective or thriller film

## CINEMATOGRAPHY TOOLS AND TECHNIQUES

**academy leader** countdown from 9 to 2 that appears on screen before film begins

**acetate base** plastic strip supporting emulsion in film

**action** director's command to actors to begin playing scene

**ADR** automatic dialogue replacement; looping and dubbing process

**anamorphic lens** type of lens that compresses wide camera angles into standard frame widths, used in CinemaScope

**angle on** shot of specific person, place, or thing

**animation** process of creating moving graphic images on film by small progressive changes between each drawing cel

**answer print** first acceptable, color-balanced print made from original negative

**aperture** camera shutter opening that admits light to expose film

**arc light** high-powered light for set illumination

**aspect ratio** ratio of width of a projected image to its height

**assembly** editing and splicing for rough cut

**automatic dialogue replacement** ADR

**backlighting** illumination from behind subject

**back projection** projection from rear of previously photographed material on translucent screen, used as background for shot

**BCU** big closeup

**beep tone** beep lasting 1/24 of a second that occurs at number 2 in academy leader countdown

**big closeup** BCU; shot of face filling screen

**blackout** abrupt fade to black at end of scene

**blimp** soundproof cover over motion-picture camera

**blow-up** enlargement

**boom mic** overhead microphone on extendible crane

**bridging shot** film shot connecting discontinuous images

**camera angle** angle of view: high, low, or wide

**camera car** vehicle equipped with camera mounts for filming while moving at traffic speed

**camera mount** any of various bases for a camera: crane, dolly, specialty mount, sticks

**camera track** camera's path of motion in following a scene

**cel** transparent celluloid sheet used for animation drawing, constituting one frame of an animated film

**celluloid** film; plastic formerly used for photographic film

**century stand** equipment used to support camera

**changeover marks** white circles that appear twice for a split second in upper right corner of frame just before reel ends

**CinemaScope** *Trademark*. wide-screen process using anamorphic lenses in photographing and projecting a film

**cinematography** art and science of motion-picture photography

**Cinerama** *Trademark*. wide-screen film photography and projection process using three synchronized cameras and three projectors

**Claymation** *Trademark* animated film made by taking series of photographs of clay figures set in different positions

**clip** film clip

**close medium shot** photo of person from head to knees

**close shot** closeup

**closeup** CU; full screen shot of subject, esp. a person's head

**composite print** married print

**continuity** editing technique yielding smooth, coherent narrative from scenes shot out of sequence

**crane** mobile, counterweighted camera mount allowing camera great height and vertical movement

**creeping titles** titles or credits scrolled over film image

**crosscutting** jumping back and forth between two scenes happening simultaneously

**cross-fade** merging of images from end of one scene into beginning of next

**cut** quick transition from one shot to another

**cut** director's command to actors to cease playing scene

**cutaway** quick movement of camera away from shot; shot focusing on something other than main action

**cut-in** still shot inserted in film and interrupting the action or continuity; insert

**cyclorama** studio or stage background creating illusion of open scenery

**dailies** hastily printed footage from previous day's shooting, assembled for daily viewing by director and producer before editing or sound synchronization; rushes

**day for night** simulation of night scenes actually shot during daylight with filters

**dialogue track** recorded dialogue to be run in sync with picture

**diffuser** light-softening screen of silk, gelatin, or frosted glass

**dissolve** one shot gradually fading into another

**dolly** movable camera mount, usu. a small wheeled platform

**dolly in** shot in which dolly approaches subject

**dolly shot** shot taken from a moving dolly

**dupes** inexpensive black-and-white copies made from work print for use by various postproduction specialists

**ECU** extreme closeup

**edge code** code imprinted after filming at one-foot intervals on picture and sound to facilitate editing in sync

**editing** arrangement, splicing, and assemblage of film footage into desired sequences and synchronization of film with soundtrack

**emulsion** sensitive chemical solution that forms coating on film

**establishing shot** shot setting time and place of scene; master shot

**exterior shot** scene shot outside in natural or artificial light

**extreme closeup** ECU; closeup showing only subject's face or part of face

**fade-in** gradual emergence of image from black ground

**fade-out** gradual disappearance of image into black ground

**fast motion** effect of speeded-up action achieved by undercranking camera, then replaying film at normal speed

**favoring shot** shot focusing on specific person or object

**file footage** stock film footage, such as scenes of crowds and natural backgrounds, kept on file for use

**film** strip of cellulose acetate coated with sensitive emulsion for recording images when exposed to light, usu. 35 mm wide

**film clip** brief section extracted from film; clip

**film gate** device that holds film flat and steady as it passes through camera

**final cut** edited version of film that is approved and nearly ready for distribution

**Foley** *Trademark*. technique for adding special effects to soundtrack

**footage** section of film

**frame** single picture on strip of film, usu. 16 frames per foot of film; (*vb*) compose a single shot

**freeze frame** optical effect in which single frame is held as persistent, still image in film; stop motion

**full frame** shot of entire subject filling frame

**FX** *Slang*. special effects

**gauge** width of film in millimeters

**glass shot** part of scene painted on glass and inserted into scene

**gobo** black wooden screen used to block unwanted light; sound-absorbent screen used to shield microphone from external sounds

**ground** background or foundation behind or under focus of shot

**head shot** closeup of person's face and head

**hold** sustained shot on specific person or object

**inky dink** *Slang*. small lamp used to light limited area

**insert** close shot of an object, such as a newspaper headline or clock; cut-in

**intercut** (*vb*) move back and forth between two shots

**interior shot** scene shot inside, usu. on a sound stage, with artificial light

**iris-in** gradual appearance of on-screen image through an expanding circle, esp. in silent films

**iris-out** gradual disappearance of on-screen image through a contracting circle, esp. in silent films

**jump cut** sudden transition out of scene to speed narrative

**key light** main light on photographed subject

**kinetoscope** old-fashioned film loop viewer

**klieg light** carbon arc lamp producing intense light

**library shot** stock shot taken from film library

**lighting** cinematographer's art and skill of illuminating scenes for filming

**locked cut** final edited version of film, ready for postproduction work

**long shot** scene filmed from considerable distance, usu. wide angle

**looping** editing process in which speech and sound effects are synchronized to film already shot

**magazine** lightproof film container

**M and E** *m*usic and *e*ffects on soundtrack

**married print**  image, sound, and dialogue tracks synchronized for projection or reproduction; composite print

**master shot**  establishing shot

**matte**  device that blocks part of film, to be exposed later

**medium close**  shot showing subject from head to chest or waist

**montage**  fast-moving sequence of superimposed images

**Movieola**  *Trademark.* film editing machine

**moving shot**  shot in which camera focus moves, as in dolly or pan shots

**offscreen**  (*adj*) OS; taking place away from the screen, as a character's voice

**optical effect**  special visual effect: dissolve, fade, wipe, freeze

**original negative**  film that was actually loaded into camera, after it is developed, from which all copies are generated other than dupes

**OS**  (*adj*) offscreen

**outtake**  footage deleted from final edit of film

**overcranking**  photographing more than 24 frames per second of film, for slow motion effect

**pan**  panoramic shot of wide, horizontal view; movement of camera eye across wide area as camera moves horizontally on mount

**parallax**  slight difference between image in camera viewfinder and actual image seen through lens

**pixilation**  technique using stop-action camera to move subjects between takes and shots, in order to achieve comic effect of jerky motion

**point of view**  POV; camera angle on subject that places the viewer in the desired relationship to the character

**POV**  *point of view*

**print**  reproduction of original film

**process cinematography**  special effects illusion in which foreground action or scene is superimposed on separately shot background

**projection**  display of film images on screen

**rack**  (*vb*) adjust film through projector gate

**rack focus**  pulling of focus plane from one area to another on same frame

**raw stock**  unused film

**reaction shot**  shot showing subject reacting to action of preceding shot

**rear projection**  special effect using prefilmed background against which scene is set and photographed; rear-screen projection

**rear-screen projection**  rear projection

**reel**  flanged spool for film; one section of feature film consisting of more than one reel

**release print**  clean film print released for projection to audience

**reshoot**  retake

**retake**  shot or scene that needs to be taken more than once; reshoot

**reverse shot**  change in point of view from previous shot

**rolling**  (*adj*) indication that cameras are shooting scene

**rollover**  written text scrolling over scene, often offering historical exposition

**rotoscope**  device used to transfer live-action shot to animation

**rough cut**  preliminary edit; first version of motion picture following initial cutting and editing

**rushes**  dailies, esp. East Coast usage

**safety film**  nonflammable film

**sequence**  series of scenes or shots tied together by single idea, concept, or event

**set design**  creation and construction of scenery

**70 mm**  film size twice as large as standard 35 mm

**shoot**  period of filming; (*vb*) film a scene

**shooting**  filming of scenes

**shooting script**  final version of screenplay with all camera angles, shots, and scene numbers included

**shot**  continuous shooting of scene without stopping camera

**skip frames**  technique in which every other or every third frame is omitted, giving film a faster, jagged look

**skypan**  big, bowl-shaped light used to illuminate wide area

**slo-mo**  *Informal.* slow motion

**slow motion**  effect of very slow action achieved by overcranking camera, then replaying film at normal speed; slo-mo

**smash cut**  jarring visual transition to next shot, often accompanied by loud sound

**special effects**  visual and sound effects added to film by various laboratory techniques; FX

**splice**  joining of two film sections; an edit

**split screen**  process shot showing two different scenes at same time

**squeezed print**  anamorphic process print

**stereoscope**  optical instrument used to create a three-dimensional projection effect

**sticks**  *Slang.* camera mounts

**stock**  film used to make a motion picture, usu. 35 mm

**stock shot**  prefilmed shot taken from newsreels or travelogues to insert into film as establishing shot

**stop-action photography**  special effect technique in which performers stop moving and camera is stopped while something or someone is added to or removed from set, creating illusion of sudden appearance or disappearance

**stop motion**  freeze frame

**sweetening**  enhancing soundtrack quality electronically after filming and recording are complete

**synchronize**  (*vb*) align picture and soundtrack

**take**  shot filmed without stopping camera or action

**Technicolor**  *Trademark.* color motion-picture process

**telecine projector**  device for transferring 35-mm motion-picture film to television videotape format

**3-D**  processing of film to give illusion of three-dimensional action when viewed through special lenses

**three-point lighting**  basic lighting setup that includes front, back, and side lights

**tilt**  vertical movement of camera on stationary mount

**time code**  series of marks along edge of film used to synchronize sound and other effects

**time-lapse photography**  technique in which slow, continuous process is photographed by exposing one frame at a time, creating speeded-up effect when projected at normal speed

**titles**  written text on screen often superimposed over filmed images, usu. stating time and place of action or credits

**tracking shot**  shot in which camera and action both move in parallel direction; dolly shot

**traveling matte**  special-effect photography combining two separate film sequences into single shot

**trucking shot**  image filmed with mounted camera on moving truck; movement of camera mount while filming

**two-shot**  image of two people in frame

**undercranking** photographing fewer than 24 frames per second of film, thus creating fast-motion effect

**wide-screen** (*adj*) denoting panoramic dimension in film projection

**wipe** technique in which one image pushes another off-screen

**workprint** first, unmarried print made from original negative that editor splices together

**zoom** effect created by camera action or use of lens with variable focal length, not by moving camera or camera mount

## MOVIE PEOPLE AND SHOW BUSINESS

**above-the-line** designating those on film budget not considered part of crew, such as the director, producer, and actors

**Academy Awards** Oscars

**AD** *a*ssistant *d*irector

**adaptation** screenplay with story taken from another medium

**agent** actor's, writer's, or director's representative for finding work, making deals, and creating packages

**art direction** direction that results in overall look of a film

**art director** person responsible for designing the look of a film

**art house** theater that shows primarily art films, foreign films, and classics

**assistant cameraman** person in charge of operating camera, usu. behind viewfinder

**assistant director** AD; person on set responsible for implementing the director's orders and overseeing the actors; first or second assistant director

**associate director** first AD for video production

**associate producer** person attached to project but not functioning as producer; line producer

**auteur** film director with strong personal style

**backdrop** flat scenery set up behind actors

**back-end deal** arrangement by which all or some of one's compensation for work on a film comes from final profits after all expenses have been met

**background** part of a scene or set situated behind the actors; extras

**background music** incidental music on soundtrack

**backlot** outdoor area, usu. adjoining studio, for shooting exterior scenes that depict locations

**bankable star** actor whose presence in film guarantees production and likely financial success

**below-the-line** designating crew, equipment, and production costs of film

**best boy** *Slang*. gaffer's assistant

**billing** order in which actors' names appear in credits, on marquee, and in advertising for film

**bit** small part for actor, sometimes with a few lines

**boffo** (*adj*) *Slang*. highly successful, esp. as designating a box office hit

**boom operator** technician who controls crane equipped with boom mike

**breakdowns** regular listing of upcoming parts to be cast, circulated to agents

**buzz** *Slang*. advance word on film in industry; heat

**call** arrival time at shoot

**cameo** small part played by actor who is usu. featured

**cameraman** chief operator of camera

**cast** actors, bit players, and extras

**casting director** person responsible for preauditioning and selecting right actor for each role

**chase scene** action sequence involving pursuit

**cheat to camera** turn one's face so that more of it can be seen on camera

**cineaste** devotee of films; person professionally involved in making films

**cinema** art, technique, and business of making motion pictures; movies

**cinematheque** small movie house showing avant-garde films

**cinematic** (*adj*) characteristic of films or the art of filmmaking

**cinematographer** person responsible for photographing film; director of photography

**clapboard** boards hinged at one end and banged together to mark filmed sequences with scene numbers for synching; clapperboard

**clapperboard** clapboard

**clapper loader** *Chiefly Brit*. third assistant cameraman

**closing credits** long list of all actors and technicians involved in production, shown at end of film

**colorization** addition of color to films originally shot in black and white

**coming attractions** trailers previewing upcoming films

**commissary** dining room or cafeteria on motion-picture studio lot

**continuity** *Chiefly Brit*. script supervisor

**coproduction** arrangement to cofinance picture between two or more producers or companies

**cover** (*vb*) read and synopsize script, story, or novel

**credits** lists of actors, artists, and technicians involved in making film, shown at beginning and/or end of movie

**crew** technicians, artists, and other workers involved in production

**development** stage after purchase of script or idea by studio leading toward production

**dialogue** words spoken by characters on soundtrack

**director** creative overseer of motion picture who guides actors, determines narrative style, and selects camera angles

**director of photography** head cameraman who determines ways to achieve director's desired effects; cinematographer

**director's chair** canvas on wood frame chair typically used on set

**distribution** placement of released film in theaters, usu. by studio acting as distributor

**dolly grip** crew member who helps move dolly

**double bill** double feature

**double feature** two films shown in theater for the price of one; double bill

**dresser** actor's wardrobe assistant on set

**drive-in** outdoor theater where audience remains inside cars

**dubbing** replacing part or all of an existing soundtrack, esp. with a translation into another language, or adding background music or special effects

**editor** creative organizer of film footage into assembled sequences of scenes

**executive producer** person responsible for raising money and initiating project, but not for daily administrative tasks

**extra** actor without speaking part, usu. hired by the day as part of a crowd scene; background

**featured** (*adj*) designating an actor with a significant part, often named in opening credits

**feature film** motion picture at least 3000 feet long in 35 mm film

**film** motion picture

**filmmaker** individual who creates movies, esp. director

**first run** film recently released for first time, esp. in wide distribution

**flashback** narrative device in which action taking place in the past is inserted into the chronological structure of the story

**flash forward** narrative device in which future scenes are inserted into a film's present time structure

**flick** *Slang*. motion picture

**flying rig** operator of special effects device used in stunts to create the illusion of falling

**focus puller** second assistant cameraman, who adjusts camera focus

**Foley artist** person who integrates special sound effects into soundtrack

**front-end deal** arrangement by which one's compensation for work on a film comes out of money that is available before or during production

**gaffer** electrician who operates and rigs lights

**genre** group of films defined by style or theme

**green light** go-ahead to commence production, given by studio head

**greensman** crew member who tends trees and plants

**grip** member of film crew who moves equipment, esp. lighting

**hammer** *Slang*. handyman on movie set

**head of production** top studio executive responsible for coordinating all projects in development and production

**heat** *Slang*. good word of mouth about a new movie; buzz

**heavy** male villain

**high concept** story idea for popular film that can be summarized in one catchy line or phrase

**in-between** assistant artist responsible for animation frames inserted between main frames drawn by chief animator

**indie** *Informal*. independent motion picture production company outside major studio system; film made by such a company

**Industry, the** the motion picture business in Hollywood

**ingénue** young, attractive female character; actress who plays such a part

**in production** (of a film) in the shooting stage, after development

**in the can** (of a film) completed but not yet ready for distribution

**key grip** head of grip crew

**lead** primary male or female part in film

**leading lady** actress playing only lead roles

**leading man** actor playing only lead roles

**legs** *Slang*. strength and longevity at the box office

**lighting director** person responsible for placement of lights to achieve director's desired effects

**line producer** studio executive responsible for day-to-day coordination of production and staying within budget

**location** place for filming scene outside studio or sound stage

**location scout** person who finds and arranges for use of shooting locations

**log line** one sentence description of story

**lot** motion-picture studio and its surrounding property

**love interest** provision for romance in narrative; star's romantic opposite

**low-budget film** usu. nonstudio production with minimal financing

**majors** large Hollywood studios

**marquee** rigid canopy of movie theater advertising film currently showing there

**matinée** screening of a film during daytime, usu. afternoon

**McGuffin** *Slang*. plot device for setting story into motion, esp. missing object or person

**merchandising** development and sale of products related to particular film and its characters

**method actor** student or practitioner of the naturalistic Stanislavski method of acting, which emphasizes a personal exploration of the character being played

**motion picture** series of photographic images projected in rapid succession on a screen to give the illusion of continuous action; film; flick; movie; moving picture; picture; picture show

**motion pictures** motion-picture industry; silver screen

**movie** motion picture

**movies** cinema

**movie theater** building in which films are displayed for public viewing; picture palace; picture show

**moving picture** motion picture

**multiplex** movie theater with several screens in different rooms showing different films

**nickelodeon** early movie theater, in which films were viewed individually through a small machine operated by a nickel

**on location** filming at a site away from studio or sound stage

**opening credits** names of primary actors, technicians, director, and producer shown at beginning of film

**option** purchase by individual, company, or studio of exclusive right to develop film project during designated time

**Oscars** annual awards for excellence in acting and filmmaking given by Academy of Motion Picture Arts and Sciences; Academy Awards

**PA** production assistant

**package** proposed combination of script, actors, and director, presented to studio, esp. by agent

**pass** free ticket to a screening; studio decision not to develop project or not to produce project already in development

**persistence of vision** short-term retention of image on retina, producing illusion that a series of rapidly changing images are in motion

**picture** motion picture

**picture palace** movie theater

**picture show** motion picture; movie theater

**pitch meeting** meeting at which screenwriter and/or producer proposes film idea to potential financier or studio

**player** actor

**postproduction** editing, dubbing, and addition of special effects after conclusion of filming

**post punch supervisor** person who supervises photocopying of cels and drawings used in animation

**premiere** opening night screening of new film

**preproduction** work done prior to filming and production, such as casting, selecting locations, designing production, and rewriting script

**preview** advance screening of new film before general release

**principal** leading actor in specific film

**producer** executive and financial overseer of film production; packager of film idea for sale and distribution

**product** film idea, script, novel, or completed film

**production** creation and shooting of film from script

**production assistant** PA; person responsible for carrying out day-to-day assignments given by line producer

**production company** company that develops projects for sale to studios or networks or for independent financing

**production manager** person who oversees daily activities during filming

**production values** quality of set, costumes, lighting, sound, and atmosphere of film

**projection booth** room in movie theater from which film reels are projected onto screen

**projectionist** technician who operates film projector in theater

**property** story idea, concept, novel, or script, the rights to which are owned by potential producer or studio

**ratings** system of motion picture grading based on age of admissible audience: G (general); PG (parental guidance suggested); PG–13 (no one under 13); R (restricted admission if under 17); NC–17 (no one under 17)

**release** distribution of completed film to theaters

**revival house** movie theater showing old films only

**rewrite** thorough revision of screenplay

**rigger** crew member who hangs suspended equipment, esp. lights

**scale** minimum pay approved by union for a specific job

**scene** division of film in which continuous action takes place in a single location

**scenery** painted screens, backdrops, hangings, and props

**score** musical background for film; (*vb*) compose background music for film

**screen** flat, reflective white surface on which films are projected; (*vb*) show a film to an audience

**screening** showing of a film before an audience

**screenplay** written form of film containing dialogue, description of scenes, characters, and action; script

**screen test** audition in which actor is filmed to check appearance on film and suitability for role

**screenwriter** person who conceives, writes, and rewrites screenplays

**script** screenplay

**script doctor** writer who makes usu. minor revisions of someone else's script

**script girl** director's assistant who holds shooting script

**script reader** person hired to read and synopsize new scripts submitted to producer, studio, or agent

**script supervisor** person who takes notes on arrangement of set for continuity and editing

**second-assistant cameraman** person who pulls focus while camera is operating

**second unit** crew filming minor scenes or extras, often without director present

**set** sound stage or location where filming takes place

**sex goddess** female star whose fame is based on sex appeal

**shooting script** final version of screenplay indicating all details of camera shots

**show** single projection of film from beginning to end, esp. at designated time

**show business** *Informal.* art, practice, and business of making films; entertainment industry in general

**sides** pages of scene given to actor at casting audition

**silent bit** small part without lines, distinct from extra

**silver screen** motion pictures

**sneak preview** unadvertised screening of new film before release

**sound editor** person who builds reels of sound effects and dialogue for mixing

**sound effects** sounds other than dialogue and music added to film soundtrack, usu. artificially produced

**sound mix** electronic blending of elements on soundtrack

**sound stage** cavernous, soundproof building or room on studio lot for shooting films

**soundtrack** band on edge of film carrying music, dialogue, and sound effects synchronized with picture

**spin-off** project developing as adjunct to existing film

**stage manager** second assistant director for video production

**stand-in** actor who substitutes for another during setup of scene for camera and lighting

**star** celebrated actor commanding major roles and high salary

**starlet** ingénue; young, up-and-coming actress being promoted as future star

**star system** practice of casting and promoting stars because of their ability to attract audiences

**star vehicle** film project developed specifically to exploit popularity of one star

**still photography** publicity photographs of actors taken on set

**storyboard** graphic representation of each scene in film sequence, serving as guide for production

**story editor** person responsible for development of story from initial concept to shooting script

**studio** buildings and grounds where films are made; company owning such, engaged in financing and distributing films

**stunt** dangerous or difficult feat required by scene; *Informal.* person who performs such feats

**stunt man** stand-in trained to perform stunts, esp. for male actors

**stunt woman** stand-in trained to perform stunts for female actors

**stylist** hairdresser and wardrobe assistant on set

**subtitles** text at bottom of screen providing continuous translation of foreign language film

**superstar** major star who enjoys wide recognition

**supporting actor** actor with featured nonleading role

**supporting actress** actress with featured nonleading role

**take a meeting** *Slang.* attend a meeting

**talent** actors and other performers

**talent scout** casting director or studio employee who looks for new talent

**teamsters** union truckdrivers employed on all studio productions

**theater** movie theater

**third-assistant cameraman** person who loads film in magazine, operates clapper, and cleans filter; clapper loader

**tie-in**  project related to existing film

**Tinseltown**  *Informal.* Hollywood, as center of the movie industry

**Titan crane**  large, movable crane with seat for director

**toon**  *Informal.* character in animated cartoon

**trades**  movie industry journals, esp. *Variety* and *Hollywood Reporter*

**trailer**  film clip used as in-theater advertisement; preview of upcoming release

**treatment**  detailed outline of script not in screenplay form

**turnaround**  status of projects which studio no longer wishes to produce but still owns

**typecasting**  selecting actor based on physical appearance or previous parts rather than acting skills

**unions**  representatives of actors and technicians in film industry that set wage scales and working conditions

**unit**  production crew on location or in sound stage

**unit publicist**  press and media liaison responsible for publicizing specific film during production and release

**usher**  person who escorts audience to seats in theater

**VO**  *voice-over*

**voice-over**  VO; narration heard over film sequence, not spoken as dialogue by actors on screen

**wardrobe**  actors' costumes; department responsible for them

**world premiere**  first public screening of film

**wrangler**  crew member responsible for horses and any other animals used on set

**wrap**  conclusion of filming day and esp. of entire production

**X-rated**  *(adj)* rating designating sexually explicit film not to be viewed by persons under seventeen, now replaced by NC-17; still used in reference to pornography

# TELEVISION AND RADIO

Television Programming and Institutions
Broadcast Journalism
Television Technology
Radio Programming
Radios and Radio Technology

**SEE ALSO**: Chap. 5: Electricity and Electronics; Telecommunications; Chap. 11: Publishing and the Press; Chap. 12: Advertising; Chap. 15: Popular Music; Theater; Cinema; Chap. 17: Sports

## TELEVISION PROGRAMMING AND INSTITUTIONS

**ABC**  *Trademark.* American Broadcasting Company; one of the three major national U.S. television networks

**across-the-board**  scheduled daily at same time

**action line**  phone-in service for television viewers with consumer problems

**affiliates**  local stations across nation associated with a major network and receiving its feed

**AFTRA**  *American Federation of Television and Radio Artists*; primary union for broadcasting performers

**air**  *(vb)* broadcast

**air date**  scheduled broadcast date

**airtime**  hour at which broadcast is scheduled to begin; duration of program; total broadcast time devoted to programming of one type or from one source

**announcement**  commercial or promotional spot

**announcer**  person who introduces programs, identifies station, or reads news reports

**anthology show**  nonepisodic series connected by genre or theme instead of characters

**audience participation**  program in which audience members take active role

**BBC**  British Broadcasting Corporation; major British network that produces programming seen on educational and public television in United States

**blackout**  mandated interruption or restriction on broadcast, esp. local sporting event

**bleep**  sound covering censored material on soundtrack or tape

**blooper**  *Informal.* embarrassing gaffe made on the air

**boob tube**  *Informal.* television set

**break**  program interruption, esp. for a commercial or station identification

**broadcast**  presentation of a program; *(vb)* transmit by radio or television waves

**broadcasting**  transmission of programs by television or radio over wide area

**broadcast journalism**  news reporting by television or radio

**bumper**  *Slang.* ID of show displayed briefly before commercial or next segment; brief news announcement so displayed

**cable television**  station or network broadcasting programs receivable only by paying subscription fee for hookup

**candid camera**  program showing unwitting or unrehearsed subjects reacting to situations, filmed with small, hidden camera

**canned laughter**  prerecorded laugh soundtrack for comedy program

**casting director**  individual responsible for auditioning and selecting performers for shows

**CBS**  Columbia Broadcasting System; one of the three major national U.S. television networks

**clip**  specific section of film or tape

**close**  end of program; wrap-up

**cold open**  unnarrated piece of film or video used to begin documentary or news segment

**commercial**  paid advertisement broadcast during breaks in programming

**commercial television**  station or network in business for profit by selling advertising time to sponsors

**Corporation for Public Broadcasting**  federally chartered organization that promotes development of public radio and television, esp. by serving as a conduit for Congressional appropriations and a buffer between the government and Public Broadcasting System

**couch potato**  *Slang.* chronic television viewer

**counterprogramming**  offering a different type of program from others in given time slot in order to attract specific audience

**credits**  graphics at beginning or ending of program that list names of performers, crew, and staff

**daytime drama** soap opera

**dead air** unintentional period of silence or a blank screen

**dedicated channel** cable channel for local government, educational, or public use

**docudrama** narrative, fictionalized treatment of actual event, person, or topic

**documentary** nonfiction program covering current events, issues, or personalities

**docutainment** documentaries that sacrifice information for sensationalism and entertainment values

**dramatic series** noncomic, recurring weekly program

**dramedy** dramatic comedy, as opposed to situation comedy

**educational access channel** small, local, noncommercial channel offering the public an opportunity to transmit educational programs

**emcee** MC

**Emmys** annual awards given by National Academy of Television Arts and Sciences for excellence in programming and performing

**episode** regular installment of ongoing program

**episodic role** actor's appearance in single episode of on-going show

**fairness doctrine** policy mandated by FCC, requiring that stations grant equal time to political views and candidates in opposition to these already aired

**FCC** Federal Communications Commission; government agency that licenses and regulates operations of radio and television stations

**font** on-screen graphic or super; typeface used for on-screen graphics

**footage** shots of an actual event or scene

**format** specific type of programming provided by station or shown at particular time of day or week

**Fox Network** *Trademark.* major commercial network competing with ABC, CBS, and NBC

**game show** program in which contestants compete for prizes by playing a game

**giveaway** type of game show with prizes given to contestants or audience members

**graphics** mixture of designs and words used esp. to introduce and close shows, also during shows and in commercials, often computer-generated

**guest star** well-known actor playing episodic role

**idiot box** *Slang.* television set

**infomercial** program-length commercial cast in standard format, as a documentary or talk show, to disguise that it is an advertisement

**infotainment** programming that is both informative or educational and entertaining

**instant replay** immediate video rerun of section of broadcast event, esp. live sport

**in-the-can** *(adj)* designating a completed program or material that has been shot

**kidvid** *Slang.* television programs intended for children

**laugh track** canned laughter, esp. for sitcom

**live** *(adj)* broadcast as event or performance occurs, as opposed to prerecorded

**local station** affiliate of network in specific region, or small, independent broadcasting entity

**magazine** documentary show covering several topics in single broadcast; newsmagazine

**makeover** thorough course of beauty, hair, and cosmetic treatments for performer

**mass communications** activities of mass media

**mass media** means of communication, such as television and radio, that reach and influence large numbers of people

**MC** *m*aster of *c*eremonies; host of variety, talk, or game show; emcee

**media** means of public communication, such as television and radio, providing public with news, entertainment, and advertisements

**medium** television or radio as media

**miniseries** specially programmed, serialized drama or documentary broadcast over two or more days

**MTV** *Trademark. M*usic *Tele*vision; first and most popular cable channel exclusively broadcasting music videos

**music video** short, colorful, often narrative videotaped accompaniment to pop song

**NAB** *N*ational *A*ssociation of *B*roadcasters

**NABET** *N*ational *A*ssociation of *B*roadcast *E*mployees and *T*echnicians

**narration** voice-over description of events on screen or gaps in visual story

**narrowcast** *(vb)* aim a program at specific, limited audience or market

**National Association of Broadcast Employees and Technicians** NABET; primary nonperformers' union

**National Association of Broadcasters** NAB; voluntary broadcasting group promoting self-regulatory codes

**National Association of Television and Radio Announcers** NATRA; organization of broadcast announcers

**NATRA** *N*ational *A*ssociation of *T*elevision and *R*adio *A*nnouncers

**NBC** *Trademark. N*ational *B*roadcasting *C*ompany; one of the three major national U.S. television networks

**network** association of stations affiliated with one of the major broadcasting companies; ABC, CBS, CNN, Fox, or NBC

**network executive** representative of network charged esp. with monitoring or directing creative work on programs

**newsmagazine** magazine show

**Nielsen rating** widely accepted estimate of relative audience share for particular program, based on monitoring of preselected sample of viewers by A.C. Nielsen Company

**noncommercial broadcasting** publicly funded programs

**OC** *(adj)* on-camera

**open** beginning of program

**outro** wrap-up of program comparable to tag but for longer programs

**paid political announcement** advertisement for political candidate or cause

**pay-per-view** ppv; special cable hookup requiring single payment for one broadcast

**pay television** commercial service that broadcasts programs to viewers who pay monthly charge or per-program fee; subscription television

**PBS** *P*ublic *B*roadcasting *S*ervice; network of publicly funded, noncommercial stations

**people meter** device for recording in-home response to programming

**personality** actor famous for particular role or work as host or MC

**phonathon** prolonged, on-air fund-raiser soliciting phone-in participation by viewers

**pilot** introductory test episode of proposed new program

**plug** *Informal.* advertisement, esp. mention of product within context of program, not in paid commercial spot

**ppv** *pay-per-view*

**preempt** (*vb*) replace with another program

**prerecorded** (*adj*) taped or filmed prior to broadcast

**prime time** midevening hours of broadcast time, when largest audience is watching; 8 p.m. to 11 p.m.

**producer** person responsible for preparing, supervising production of, and editing program or news spot

**production company** company that develops pilots for networks and creates and produces programs

**program** single scheduled television broadcast

**program analysis** dissection of program content, success, and viewership, aimed at increasing ratings

**programming** determination or nature of broadcast content and balance of news, talk shows, sitcoms, dramas, documentaries, variety shows, movies, or sports programs

**public access television** local cable television station providing free time for low-budget, often nonprofessional programs; system of such stations

**public service announcement** advertisement or announcement done for public good with time donated by station

**public television** nonprofit television station or broadcast network emphasizing educational and cultural programming

**quiz show** program in which contestants compete for prizes by answering questions

**rating** measure of relative audience size for competing programs at same hour, used esp. to set price for commercials

**reality show** entertaining coverage of real-life events, including those staged for show

**recurring** (*adj*) occurring regularly, esp. of characters on program

**renewal** FCC approval of extended broadcast license

**repeat** reshowing of program in same season

**rerun** repeat broadcast of program, usu. in later year

**season** annual run of new shows, usu. beginning in September or January

**segue** seamless transition from program to program or segment to segment

**serial** program appearing in regular installments

**share** percentage of viewers watching particular show

**shoot-'em-up** *Informal.* western

**sign off** (*vb*) make closing announcement and show station identification at end of broadcast day

**simulcast** program broadcast over cooperating radio and television stations at same time to provide improved audio, esp. for televised music program

**sitcom** *Informal.* situation comedy

**situation comedy** usu. half-hour, comedic show with recurring characters in simplistic situations

**skitcom** *Informal.* comedy format in which star or stars perform in series of unrelated skits

**slot** time slot for regularly scheduled program

**soap** soap opera

**soap opera** melodrama series, usu. showing five days a week during daytime hours; daytime drama; soap

**sound bite** brief segment of audio and video transmission, esp. on talking-head show

**space opera** futuristic, melodramatic fantasy involving space travel and extraterrestrials

**special** program that appears one time only or is not part of regular schedule

**specialty station** station with single-format programming

**spin-off** series or program derived from a previously popular show or its characters

**spokesperson** popular or compelling individual who speaks on behalf of product or cause

**sponsor** advertiser buying time on particular show to promote product

**sportscast** broadcast of sporting event

**sportscaster** person who delivers sports news or describes sports event

**spot** spot announcement

**spot announcement** brief advertisement or promotional blurb on upcoming program, newsbrief, or station break; spot

**standards and practices** network department responsible for insuring that program content meets specific moral standards

**stand by** instruction to hold for further information or continuation of broadcast

**station** facility for producing and broadcasting programs

**station break** interruption of network program for local station identification and information on upcoming programs

**station identification** brief spot giving call letters and channel number of station or name of network, usu. before and after program or on the hour and half-hour

**strip show** program scheduled five days a week in same time slot

**studio** offices, engineering rooms, and originating site of live programs and news broadcasts

**studio program** broadcast recorded or transmitted live from stage in studio

**STV** *subscription television*

**subscription television** STV; pay television

**subtitle** written translation of foreign language program appearing on-screen simultaneously with audio

**summer repeat** rerun aired during summer months

**super** on-screen image superimposed on original video image

**superstation** independent, local television station that is distributed and broadcast nationally via satellite to cable systems

**sweeps** thrice-yearly rating surveys that coincide with highly competitive programming weeks for networks

**syndication** reissue of series for broadcast after show has ceased production of new episodes; marketing of show on station-by-station basis and not to networks

**tag** identification of producer or syndicator at end of program

**talent** actors, performers

**talking head** *Slang.* closeup shot of someone talking or being interviewed; programming based on such shots

**talk show** program with host interviewing unusual guests and celebrities

**talk-show host** engaging person who serves as regular moderator of talk show

**taped show** program prerecorded for later broadcast

**target** (*vb*) aim program at particular audience

**telecast** single television broadcast or program

**teleplay** script for a television program

**telethon** lengthy, uninterrupted program raising money for charitable cause

**televangelist** religious minister preaching over television and frequently soliciting donations for a church

**television station** facility for producing and broadcasting programs

**television time-out** time-out taken in sports event to accommodate television commercials

**telly** *Brit. informal.* television or a television set

**tie-in** program with content that relates to another program

**time slot** hour of day and day of week when weekly program is scheduled

**TV** *television*

**under-five** *Informal.* actor's part with less than five speaking lines

**variety show** program with host presenting several different entertainers and acts, such as music, dance, comedy, and magic

**vast wasteland** *Slang.* pejorative term for television programming

**video game** computer-controlled game attached to and played on television set

**video jockey** VJ; announcer for music-video program

**viewer** person who watches television

**viewing public** those who watch television and are potential consumers for advertised products

**VJ** *video jockey*

**VO** *voice-over*

**voice-over** VO; voice of offscreen narrator heard while other visuals are on screen

**western** dramatic program set in 19th-century American West

**whodunit** *Informal.* mystery program

## BROADCAST JOURNALISM

**add** news story added to broadcast, esp. at last minute

**advance** news story circulated ahead of scheduled release date

**air personality** engaging announcer who attracts viewers to newscast

**all-news** station exclusively airing news programs

**anchor** principal journalist on news program

**anchorman** male anchor

**anchorwoman** female anchor

**A roll** interviews and stand-up portion of news broadcast

**ARTNA** *Association of Radio and Television News Analysts*

**Association of Radio and Television News Analysts** ARTNA; organization of broadcast journalists

**BAN** *Black Audio Network*

**Black Audio Network** BAN; news service for black radio stations

**blind interview** interview with unnamed source

**blurb** brief news release

**bridge** transition within story, esp. use of stand-up or walk and talk to relate portion of report

**broadcast journalism** reporting of news events on radio or television

**B roll** footage used to illustrate reports during news broadcast

**bulletin** report of news development important enough to warrant interruption of regular programming

**CNN** *Trademark.* Cable News Network; network of all-news cable channels

**coanchor** one of two anchorpersons on same news show

**color commentary** interpretation and background during sports play-by-play

**commentary** editorial analysis and interpretation of news

**commentator** news analyst

**copy** written text of news story

**correspondent** person supplying news and broadcasting from remote location

**cover** (*vb*) gather and report news

**coverage** pictures and accounts of an event broadcast live

**depth interview** interview characterized by intensive questioning of one individual on specific subject or subjects

**electronic news gathering** ENG; use of video equipment instead of film to expedite news gathering and eliminate delays in processing

**ENG** *electronic news gathering*

**equal access** broadcasters' desire for equality with newspapers in access to courtrooms and other news sources

**equal time** legal requirement that stations grant equal airtime to qualified political candidates and others with opposing viewpoints

**eyewitness news** news format stressing casual responses by news anchors

**flash** brief news report on something extraordinary that has just occurred; bulletin

**follow-up** news story providing additional or new information on previously broadcast item

**group interview** interview of individual by several journalists simultaneously

**hard news** serious events of immediate, general interest and value

**hold for release** agree not to air news story until specified date

**human-interest story** report designed to engage attention and sympathy of audience members who identify readily with people and situations described

**interpretive reporting** in-depth analysis of news events

**interview** questioning of individual by one or more reporters, esp. on personal views or activities

**kicker** cheery final story on newscast

**kill** (*vb*) decide not to air story

**lead** newscast's opening and most important or attention-grabbing story

**lead-in** introduction to news story

**local news** news broadcast based at local station, covering regional news and human-interest stories

**meat** essence of a news story

**media coverage** degree of attention given certain event by media

**media event** public appearance or event staged deliberately to gain attention from media

**national news** news of national and international significance broadcast by network from central studio

**news** reports of recent events of general interest or importance that are collected and broadcast on news programs

**newsbreak** station break typically consisting of two or three brief news items

**newsbrief** very short news item, often interrupting regular programming

**newscast** regularly scheduled news broadcast

**newscaster** person who reads news on broadcast

**news hour** time, usu. in early evening, when day's primary news broadcast occurs

**news program** regular newscast or special public-affairs broadcast

**newsreel** short film of recent news events, formerly shown as part of program in theaters

**newsroom** room in which news is written and edited prior to broadcast

**news team** anchorperson, weatherperson, sportscaster, and reporters who appear on news show

**nonevent** media-induced or -conceived news story

**open-ended question** broadly framed question allowing for freely formulated answer

**panel show** news show in which several journalists interview knowledgeable person on given issue

**parachute journalism** practice in which reporter arrives on location after producer has prepared story, tapes segment for on-screen appearance, and departs immediately

**personal interview** one-on-one, in-depth conversation between reporter and public personality

**play-by-play** live description of sporting event

**press conference** appearance of person, esp. government official, for questioning by group of reporters

**public affairs program** news or news analysis broadcast, esp. dealing with timely subjects related to general public welfare

**public forum** program providing opportunity for discussion of current events

**recap** news summary, esp. at end of broadcast

**release copy** advance copy or announcement of impending news story

**reporter** newsperson covering individual stories from field

**rip and read** tear news item from wire service teletypewriter and broadcast it immediately

**segment** relatively brief but complete treatment of specific news story, comprising portion of news broadcast

**segment producer** person responsible for single segment

**sidebar** brief item dealing with secondary aspect of news story

**slant** (*vb*) distort information to express a particular bias or viewpoint

**soft news** local human-interest stories of passing interest

**spin control** *Slang.* attempt to give bias to coverage of political candidate, esp. by casting potentially damaging information in a more favorable light

**stand-up** portion of news broadcast in which standing reporter faces camera and delivers report

**straight news** serious stories relating esp. to politics, business, and international affairs

**structured interview** interview in which reporter allows person being interviewed to set parameters for questions

**tag** newscaster's final on-screen words added to taped news story

**update** news story rewritten to include latest developments

**use** television appearance by legally qualified political candidate

**vérité** action portions of report, without narration or talking head

**walk and talk** stand-up in which reporter walks along while delivering report with camera following

**weatherperson** member of news team who describes and forecasts weather

**wrap-up** summary of day's news, esp. in final few minutes of broadcast

## TELEVISION TECHNOLOGY

**across the mike** speaking from side of microphone to muffle plosive and sibilant sounds

**aerial** antenna

**airwaves** pathways of broadcast frequencies

**antenna** metallic rod or wire for receiving radio or television waves, often placed on top of building; aerial

**audio** electronically reproduced sound

**audio frequency** wavelength of sound

**band** group of communication frequencies, such as VHF or UHF

**beam** stream of radio waves sent continuously in one direction

**Beta** *Trademark.* secondary videocassette recorder format, now largely abandoned

**big-screen television** television with screen over 23 inches across

**black-and-white** (*adj*) displaying monochrome reproduction of television images

**blip** interruption of sound reception; spot of light on the screen

**boom** device from which microphones are suspended above performers out of camera view

**booster** radio-frequency amplifier for television set

**brightness control** knob on television set used to regulate amount of light emitted from tube

**broadcast television** signal sent via airwaves, as distinguished from cable or closed circuit

**cable** alternate way of transmitting television signals by cable lines rather than through air, requiring hookup to cable for reception

**cable system** local company that supplies cable channels to its subscribers

**camcorder** small, portable videotape recorder and camera

**cameraman** operator of video camera

**cathode-ray tube** CRT; electronic tube used as television screen

**CC** (*adj*) closed-captioned

**channel** band of broadcasting frequencies used by station

**character generator** small computer producing letters and graphic images directly on screen, without use of camera

**chroma key** electronic special effects system that permits insertion of image onto another image already present on screen

**chrominance signal** color-coded video signal

**closed-captioned** (*adj*) CC; designating programs having subtitles for hearing-impaired viewers, with captions appearing only on specially equipped television sets

**closed circuit** broadcasting signal sent only to televisions connected by cable to transmitter

**coaxial cable** electronic cable used to transmit television signals to cable subscribers

**color** polychrome reproduction of television images

**color bars** series of strips representing colors in spectrum, used for adjusting color on set; horizontal bars

**colorcast** television program broadcast in color

**color control** knob on color television set regulating mixture of red, blue, and green

**contrast**  degree of difference between black and white or colors of picture

**control room**  room adjacent to studio from which production is directed and engineered

**crew**  technical staff working on broadcast

**CRT**  cathode-ray tube

**cue**  off-camera signal to performer; signal from control booth to cameraman

**cue card**  large card with dialogue held near camera to prompt performers

**dead mike**  microphone that is not working; period of silence

**definition**  clearness with which televised images are reproduced

**detail**  degree of sharpness of visual image

**distortion**  image deformity caused by lens imperfection

**dot pattern**  image formed by closely placed, tiny dots of shaded or colored light

**dub**  duplicate tape of broadcast

**engineer**  operator of technical broadcasting equipment

**fade**  gradual reduction in picture from brightness to black

**feed**  program transmitted by network to affiliates for broadcast, usu. sent out before airtime; recording of event or live report transmitted to studio

**fidelity**  accuracy and clarity of image and sound reproduction

**film**  (vb) record program on film rather than videotape

**flagging**  diagonal shift of top portion of picture, which seems to bend left or right

**flicker**  fluctuations in picture

**footage**  section of film or tape

**frame**  one picture in series; complete image being transmitted by television

**frequency**  number of oscillations of wave per second

**generation**  number of duplications separating tape or film from original

**ghost**  secondary image that repeats main picture image, caused by signal interference

**glitch**  Slang. broadcast interference or malfunction

**grain**  size of silver particles on film image

**HDTV**  high-definition television

**headphones**  device worn over head with tiny speakers positioned over ears to receive audio transmission

**headset**  device with headphones and attached microphone

**high-definition television**  HDTV; receiver with high number of scanning lines per frame, producing extremely sharp image and resolution

**hookup**  connection to assemblage of circuits used for radio or television transmission

**horizontal bars**  color bars

**horizontal hold**  control that regulates back-and-forth image

**image**  picture on television screen

**intensity**  strength of screen image

**interference**  static or unwanted signals that distort image or audio

**key light**  primary light focused on subject

**lapel mike**  tiny microphone attached to clothing on chest; lavaliere microphone

**lavaliere microphone**  small microphone clipped to person's clothing or placed around neck; lapel mike

**lighting**  illumination of set

**line recording**  recording both picture and sound at the same time

**luminance signal**  black-and-white video signal

**microphone**  electronic device for picking up, magnifying, and converting sound waves to electric signals

**minicam**  small, portable videotape camera

**mix**  electronic blending, esp. of audio signals

**mobile camera**  small, portable videotape camera

**mobile unit**  truck equipped with videotape recording and transmission equipment for on-the-spot coverage of events

**monitor**  television set with no audio output, used on stage to show performers and technicians what is being shot and/or broadcast

**off-camera**  (adj) designating activity unseen by viewers

**on the air**  designation that studio is in taping or broadcast mode

**outtake**  section of tape not used on broadcast

**pickup**  reception of network transmissions by individual station or affiliate

**picture**  visual element of television program

**picture tube**  electronic device that transforms broadcast signals into patterns of light on screen; cathode-ray tube

**playback**  reproduction and rebroadcast of videotaped pictures

**portapak**  lightweight, portable video camera system

**projection television**  television with very large screen

**pulse**  very short burst of electromagnetic waves

**rabbit ears**  dipole receiving antenna on television set

**rain**  vertical marks interfering with clarity of image

**range**  full extent of area covered by transmission

**rear-screen projection**  television in which image is projected onto screen from behind

**receiver**  television set with cathode-ray tube

**reception**  process by which radio or television waves are transformed into images on screen; clarity of these images

**relay links**  devices activated by signal and operating other devices that connect elements in transmission path

**remote control**  device for tuning television set from short distance away

**resolution**  measurement of picture sharpness

**satellite**  artificial station orbiting Earth and relaying television signals from one point on Earth to another

**satellite dish**  large, shallow hemisphere used to receive transmissions relayed by satellite

**scan lines**  electronic beam pattern of parallel lines translated by television set into screen image

**scramble**  (vb) encode audio or visual signal so that only certain subscribers can receive it

**screen**  television monitor displaying image

**separation**  distinction of shades or colors in image

**set**  television set

**sharpness control**  device that regulates clarity of image

**shoot**  (vb) to film or tape something

**signal generation**  origination and production of radio or television waves to be transmitted

**small screen**  television in general, as distinguished from cinema, which is big screen

**snow**  fluctuating white spots that partially obscure image on screen due to weak signal

**splice**  (vb) join together two pieces of film or tape

**static**  atmospheric electrical discharges that interfere with television waves

**steadycam** portable video or film camera attached to operator by harness and frame to eliminate wavering of tracked image

**subscriber terminal** set receiving cable broadcasts

**super** (*vb*) superimpose one image on another

**sweetening** improvement of sound and image quality after original recording

**swell** gradual increase in sound volume

**sync** *Informal.* synchronization

**synchronization** exact alignment of audio and picture; sync

**tape** videotape; (*vb*) to record program on videotape

**taped** (*adj*) prerecorded, not live

**technician** television engineer

**telecine** device that converts film or slides into television signal

**telecommunications** electromagnetic transmission and reception of data to produce sound and images

**TelePrompTer** *Trademark.* device displaying cue cards to aid performers in remembering lines

**teletext** broadcast information services, esp. for news, stock market, and consumer goods; videotext

**televise** (*vb*) broadcast pictures and sound via television

**television** TV; electronic system for transmitting images and sound over wires or through space by conversion of light and sound into electrical waves and reconversion at receiving set into visible light projected by CRT and audible sound; receiving set in such a system

**television channel** specific broadcast frequency

**television receiver** TV set

**test pattern** fixed picture, often color bars, broadcast by station to assist viewers in adjusting reception

**transmission** passage of radio or television waves through space between transmitter and receiver

**transmitter** tower sending wave transmissions from source to viewers

**tube** *Informal.* cathode-ray tube used for projecting television images; television set; television in general

**tuning control** device for determining which channel or frequency is received by set

**TV** television set or receiver

**TV set** receiver for television transmissions, with cathode-ray tube for generating images

**UHF** ultrahigh frequency; frequency range between 300 and 3000 megahertz

**VCP** videocassette player; device that plays but does not record cartridge tapes

**VCR** videocassette recorder; device that plays and records cartridge tapes

**vertical hold** control of up-and-down image

**VHF** very high frequency; frequency range between 30 and 300 kilohertz

**VHS** *Trademark.* Video Home System; primary videocassette format

**video** television production in general, outside major commercial and subscription systems; film process used in television production

**videocassette** plastic tape cartridge on which VCR records

**videodisk** flat disk storing and playing back recorded image and sound

**videotape** (*vb*) record visual images and sound as electronic impulses on magnetic tape for television broadcasting; (*n*) magnetic tape used for such recordings

**videotext** teletext

**VTR** videotape recorder; device used for recording noncassette tapes

**wavelength** measurement of sound or light wave; frequency

**wild** (*adj*) designating recording of sound separately from picture

## RADIO PROGRAMMING

**all-news** radio format airing news programs only

**all-talk** talk radio

**alternative radio** avant-garde, noncommercial programming

**announcer** person employed to speak on radio broadcasts

**AOR** radio format emphasizing album-oriented rock music

**black radio** programming aimed at black listeners

**call-in** show in which listeners telephone host to discuss issues live on the air

**call letters** initials identifying radio station

**countdown** playing of top pop hits in reverse order up to number one

**country-and-western** station broadcasting country-and-western and bluegrass music

**disc jockey** DJ; radio announcer for music program

**DJ** disc jockey

**drive time** periods in morning or evening when commuters typically are in their cars and listening to radio broadcasts

**easy listening** programming consisting of relaxing, bland music; middle-of-the-road

**Emergency Broadcast System** radio frequencies reserved for use by government and police agencies in an emergency

**format** emphasis and content of broadcasting, such as all-news, country music, talk show, Top 40 call-in, AOR, or classical

**handle** *Slang.* citizens band operator's nickname

**listener-sponsored radio** local noncommercial radio station funded by voluntary donations from listeners

**middle-of-the-road** MOR; easy listening

**MOR** middle-of-the-road

**Muzak** *Trademark.* environmental background music, usu. adaptations of classical, show, and pop songs, available to subscribers

**National Public Radio** NPR; noncommercial, publicly funded, educational and cultural radio network

**newscaster** announcer for news program

**NPR** National Public Radio

**pirate radio** unlicensed radio station

**program director** person responsible for establishing format and determining programming of station

**radio drama** dramatic show broadcast over radio

**Radio Free Europe** federally funded U.S. network that broadcasts news and entertainment to eastern Europe from European locations

**radio wire** news wire supplying up-to-date news to stations

**segue** seamless transition, esp. from one song to the next

**sigalert** traffic advisory warning broadcast

**signature** station identification, jingle, or slogan

**soap opera** old-fashioned radio melodrama, orig. sponsored by soap manufacturer

**studio** offices, engineering rooms, and originating site of broadcasts over radio station

**talk radio** broadcasting format featuring phone-in audience participation and guest interviews by radio personality; all-talk

**talk show** discussion-style program where host and guests converse

**10-4** *Slang.* Citizens Band designation for okay

**top 40** programming format featuring current popular-music hits and issuing weekly list of forty most popular songs

**topless radio** talk show specializing in sexual topics

**underground radio** unconventional, politically progressive, and musically avant-garde programming format

**USIA** United States Information Agency, operator of Voice of America overseas

**Voice of America** politically oriented U.S. station, broadcast overseas by USIA

## RADIOS AND RADIO TECHNOLOGY

**aerial** arrangement of wires or metal rods for receiving radio transmissions

**airwaves** radio waves transmitted at various frequencies

**AM** amplitude *modulation* broadcasting band

**amplifier** radio component that strengthens signal received

**band** group of broadcasting frequencies, such as AM or FM

**beacon** radio transmitter; signal transmitted by radio transmitter

**boom box** *Informal.* very large but portable radio/cassette player

**bug** *Informal.* hidden radio transmitter

**capsule radio** tiny radio transmitter, swallowed for medical diagnosis; radio pill

**car radio** radio receiver in automobile with external antenna

**CB** *Citizens Band*

**channel** radio wave frequency of sufficient width for one- or two-way communication, used by broadcasting station

**circuit** means of transmitting interactive communications signals, usu. comprising two channels

**Citizens Band** CB; short-range, two-way radio frequency

**clear channel** strong signal on frequency with no interference; frequency cleared for long-distance transmission

**clock radio** alarm clock that turns on radio at designated hour

**console** often decorative enclosure for radio receiver, tuner, and amplifier

**continuous wave** CW; electromagnetic wave of constant amplitude and frequency, used to carry information by being modulated

**crystal radio** nonelectric receiver sensitive to radio waves

**CW transmitter** *continuous-wave* transmitter

**descrambler** device that makes radio signals intelligible by systematically tuning receiver to transmitted frequencies

**detector** device that rectifies alternating current in radio receiver

**engineer** person responsible for off-air activities that permit announcer to keep program running smoothly

**equalization** electronic amplification or reduction of particular ranges of audio frequencies

**FM** *frequency modulation* broadcasting band

**frequency** number of oscillations of wave per second

**ghetto blaster** *Slang.* portable radio with large speakers

**ham** amateur two-way radio operator

**hertz** measurement of frequency in vibrations per second

**hi-fi** high fidelity

**high fidelity** radio with excellent sound reproduction; hi-fi

**kilohertz** one thousand hertz

**link** radio relay station serving as connection in communications system

**megahertz** one million hertz

**multiplex** (*vb*) transmit two signals of sound over one channel, esp. for stereophonic radio reception

**pocket radio** small, battery-operated or transistor radio

**power pack** source of direct current to operate radio

**power plug** device that connects wire from radio to source of AC current

**power transformer** device for transferring AC current from one winding to another at constant frequency

**quadcast** four-channel FM broadcast

**quadraphonic** (*adj*) designating transmission of FM signals using four channels

**radio** conversion of sound signals into electromagnetic waves and transmission of these waves through space to receiving set, which then converts them back into sound; such a receiving set

**radiophone** equipment, such as a walky-talky or CB, for carrying on two-way communication by radio waves

**radio signal** particular frequency of transmitted radio wave

**radiotelegraphy** transmission of messages by radio waves rather than through wires or cables

**radio wave** electromagnetic wave moving at radio frequency, between 10 kilohertz and one million megahertz

**receiver** device for transforming radio waves into sound

**recording engineer** technician who operates equipment in recording studio

**recording studio** soundproofed, acoustically controlled room for radio broadcasting or recording of audio

**shortwave radio** radio that transmits or receives radio waves shorter than used in AM broadcasting, corresponding to frequencies over 1600 kilohertz

**signal** power of sound transmitted by station

**speaker** device for changing electrical signals into sound waves

**station** specific frequency or band assigned to a broadcaster; individuals and offices responsible for originating broadcasts; studio or building from which broadcasts originate

**stereophonic** (*adj*) designating transmission of FM radio signals using two channels

**tower** very tall structure transmitting station's programs as radio waves

**transceiver** combination radio transmitter and receiver

**transistor** tiny electronic device that controls flow of electricity in radio equipment

**transmitter** radio wave broadcasting device

**tuner** device sensitive to different radio wave frequencies, which permits selection of specific radio station by receiver

**tuning** adjustment of radio dial to specific frequency of given station

**Walkman** *Trademark.* small, portable, speakerless radio–cassette player utilizing earphones for listening

**walky-talky** portable, two-way radio receiver and transmitter, often battery-operated

**wireless** *Chiefly Brit.* radio; transmission of sound waves through air without wires or cables

# Applied Arts

# ARCHITECTURE

Schools and Styles
Classical Elements and Design
Building Construction and Design

**SEE ALSO**: Chap. 5: Structural Components; Building and
Construction Materials; Chap. 7: Exterior Structure;
Interior Structure; Ornamental and Functional Articles;
Chap. 11: The City

## SCHOOLS AND STYLES

**architecture** art and science of designing and building habitable structures, esp. with aesthetically pleasing, coherent forms

**arcology** fusion of architecture with ecology

**art deco** architectural style using stylized, repetitive geometric designs, esp. zigzags and lozenges, with emphasis on facades in tile and relief (early 20th c.)

**art nouveau** architectural style using decorative, biomorphic forms with curved, irregular lines (late 19th c.)

**baroque** architectural style using strong, dramatic design with imaginative use of theatrical, chiaroscuro effects (Europe, 17th-18th c.)

**Bauhaus** architectural school characterized by clean geometry and functionalism (Germany, 1920's)

**brutalism** use of exaggeration and distortion in architecture to create effect of massiveness and power (mid-20th c.)

**Byzantine** synthesis of Oriental and Occidental architectural styles, marked by domes and minarets (eastern Europe, 4th-13th c.)

**churrigueresque** (*adj*) of a baroque architectural style with elaborate surface decoration (Spain, 18th c.)

**classical** (*adj*) of the architectural style of ancient Hellenic Greece and imperial Rome, emphasizing columniation

**Colonial** variation of Georgian architectural style prevalent in colonial America (18th c.)

**Directoire** (*adj*) noting or pertaining to a style of architecture and decoration in France similar to Regency style in Britain (late 18th c.)

**Egyptian** (*adj*) of an architectural style prevalent from the third millennium B.C. through the Roman era, characterized by the use of massive, pillared stonework with emphasis on religious monuments

**Egyptian Revival** architectural style using monolithic, columnar forms, flat roofs, and ancient Egyptian decorative motifs (19th-early 20th c.)

**flamboyant** (*adj*) of a highly decorative Gothic style (France, 15th-16th c.)

**Georgian** (*adj*) of a style incorporating classical, Renaissance, and baroque elements of architecture, emphasizing formal, symmetrical design (U.S. and Britain, 18th c.)

**Gothic** architectural style with emphasis on verticality and intricate, decorative, pointed arches (Europe, 12th-16th c.)

**Gothic Revival** architectural style marked by a resurgence of Gothic verticality and sharply pitched roof forms (U.S. and Britain, late 18th-19th c.)

**Greek Revival** architectural style marked by a resurgence of classical Greek and Roman forms, with columns supporting pedimented roofs (U.S. and Britain, early 19th c.)

**Hellenic** (*adj*) of a monumental style of religious architecture, characterized by columnar supports of pediment-roofed temples (Greece, 8th-4th c. B.C.)

**Hellenistic** (*adj*) of a classical style that influenced imperial Roman architecture (Greece, 4th-2nd c. B.C.)

**International Style** modern architectural style and construction, emphasizing horizontal bands of windows, undecorated glass, curtain-wall facades, and skyscrapers (20th c.)

**Moorish** (*adj*) of an architectural style emphasizing overall decoration, carving, arabesque design, and intricate stuccowork (Spain, 11th-14th c.)

**neoclassical** (*adj*) marked by a return to classical architecture in response to romantic themes (Europe, 18th-19th c.)

**Norman** (*adj*) of an architectural style using massive stonework and rounded arches (Britain, 11th c.)

**Palladian** (*adj*) of an architectural style patterned after northern Italian Renaissance (Britain, 18th c.)

**postmodern** (*adj*) of an architectural style with eclectic, sometimes whimsical use of a variety of styles, esp. classical elements, often large-scale for corporate or institutional use (late 20th c.)

**Prairie School** group of American architects who emphasized a style using low-pitched roof and long horizontal lines (early 20th c.)

**Queen Anne** (*adj*) of a style of architecture and furnishing characterized by simplicity and restraint, esp. using red brick (Britain, 18th c.)

**Regency** (*adj*) of a style of architecture, furnishing, and decoration characterized by simple lines and increasing use of Greco-Roman forms (Britain, early 19th c.)

**Renaissance** resurgence and reinterpretation of classic forms of architecture with focus on symmetry, balance, and elegance (Europe, 15th-16th c.)

**rococo** architectural style using fanciful, carved spatial forms and excessively elaborate ornamentation (Europe, 18th c.)

**Romanesque** architectural style using massive forms and geometrical patterns (Europe, 11th-12th c.)

**Tudor** (*adj*) characteristic of a transitional style between Gothic and Palladian, with emphasis on privacy and interior design (Britain, 16th c.)

**Victorian** (*adj*) characteristic of a highly decorative architectural style with Gothic elements (U.S. and Britain, late 19th c.)

## CLASSICAL ELEMENTS AND DESIGN

**abacus** flat slab forming uppermost member of capital of column

**acanthus** decorative scrolled leaf form

**amphistylar** (*adj*) having columns at both ends

**annulet** ring-shaped molding or ridge

**anthemion** decorative palmlike leaf form

**apse** vaulted, semidomed end of aisle or building

**arabesque** abstract, curled, or plantlike decorative forms

**arcade** series of arches bounded by columns

**arch** curved structural member spanning an opening and serving as support, esp. of stone blocks: barrel, basket-handle, bell, blunt, cinquefoil, cusped, elliptical, equal, flat, horseshoe, inflected, keel, lancet, ogee, parabolic, pointed, primitive, rampant, relieving, round, rowlock, scalloped, segmental, shouldered, trefoil, Tudor

**architrave** beam across tops of columns, forming base of the entablature

**archivolt** molding along curve or underside of arch

**arcuate** (*adj*) structurally dependent on arches

**arris** sharp edge or angle where two surfaces meet

**atrium** open courtyard bordered by walkways

**attic** part of the entablature above cornice that hides the roof

**baldacchino** canopy supported by columns

**ballflower** ornament consisting of ball placed in flower-shaped hollow of circular molding

**barrel vault** continuous, semicircular, arched vault

**base** bottom of column taken as architectural unit, consist-ing of torus, scotia, plinth, and fillets

**basilica** church with aisles and elevated nave

**bas-relief** sculptured relief on wall or pediment

**bay** area between columns; deeply recessed window

**bezant** flat discus used as ornament

**boss** ornamental projecting stud; raised block

**buttress** masonry supporting arch or vault

**campanile** freestanding bell tower

**canopy** decorative, rooflike covering over altar, tomb, or doorway

**cantilever** extension of beam, floor, or roof beyond its vertical support

**capital** decorative cap atop column, supporting entablature

**capstone** keystone of arch

**caryatid** column sculpted in form of standing female figure

**chapiter** capital of column

**chigi** finials on Shinto temple roof (Japan)

**cloister** courtyard bounded by walkways

**colonnade** series of columns at regular intervals

**column** round, vertical, supporting pillar with pedestal, shaft, and capital: Byzantine, Composite, Corinthian, Doric, Gothic, Ionic, Moorish, Romanesque, Tuscan

**Composite column** Roman order combining Corinthian acanthus with Ionic volutes

**console** member extending from wall to form bracket

**corbeil** ornamental, sculptured basket of fruit or flowers

**corbel** short, decorative cantilever projecting from wall

**Corinthian column** late-style column having high base, slender, fluted shaft with fillets, ornate capital, and acan-thus

**corona** projecting part of cornice

**cornice** projecting top level of building or entablature

**course** single, continuous row of bricks, stones, or masonry

**crenellation** repeated indentations in molding or ornament

**crossette** projection at corner of architrave of door or win-dow

**crown** uppermost part of column

**cupola** small, rounded structure atop roof

**cusp** pointed projection at intersection of two arcs or foils

**cyma** uppermost projecting molding with partly concave and partly convex profile

**cymatium** uppermost member of classical cornice, usu. a cyma recta molding

**dado** section of pedestal below shaft base and above ground base

**dentil** small, rectangular, toothlike blocks projecting under corona of cornice

**Doric column** earliest known style of column, undecorated, without base, and having short, fluted shaft

**dosseret** clearly defined block resting on capital of Byzan-tine or Romanesque column

**echinus** rounded molding forming bell of Doric capital

**egg and dart** closely set, alternating series of oval and pointed forms, used to enrich echinus

**engaged column** column attached to wall, not freestanding

**entablature** horizontal element above columns, including architrave, frieze, and cornice

**entasis** slightly convex curve in column, giving it the ap-pearance of perfect verticality

**extrados** exterior curve or surface of arch

**facade** exterior face of building

**fan vault** vault composed of concave conoidal surfaces in-tersecting or touching at top and usu. decorated with curved ribs

**filigree** ornamental work of delicate, intricate design

**fillet** flat molding that separates others; space between two flutings in column shaft

**finial** ornament atop spire or gable

**fluting** vertical grooves in column shaft

**flying buttress** arch or arch segment projecting from wall and transmitting the thrust of a roof or vault outward and downward to a solid buttress or pier

**foliation** decorative member resembling leaves or flowers

**folly** fake ruin; structure built as functionless whimsy

**frieze** horizontal band in entablature between architrave and cornice, usu. ornamented

**gable** triangular area of wall at end of pitched roof

**gargoyle** waterspout in form of elaborately carved creature projecting from gutter

**gopuram** massive gateway to Hindu temple (India)

**groin** curved line or edge formed by intersection of two vaults

**grotesque** decorative design of human or animal figures and fanciful motifs

**imbrication** ornament with overlapping edges, such as tiles

**impost** post from which arch springs from pier, column, or wall

**intrados** interior curve or surface of arch or vault

**Ionic column** middle period column with an elegant base, tall, slender, fluted shaft, and a volute or spiral capital

**keystone** center stone of arch

**lintel** horizontal beam over door or window

**loggia** gallery or balcony open on at least one side

**lunette** round window; rounded niche for sculpture

**masonry** construction with stones or bricks

**metope** Doric frieze panel between triglyphs

**minaret** tall tower attached to mosque

**molding** decorative recessed or contoured strip used for finishing, usu. at juncture of wall and ceiling: beak, cavetto, congé, cyma recta, cyma reversa, echinus, facia, fillet, ovolo, plate rail, quarter round, reeding, scotia, torus

**narthex** porch at church main entrance of church

**nave** main axis of church or cathedral

**niche** recessed area in wall

**oculus** circular wall opening

**order** one of the classical styles of base, column, and entablature: Corinthian, Doric, or Ionic

**pantheon** classic domed temple form in ancient Greece and Rome

**parquetry** geometrically patterned, inlaid wood, esp. for floors

**pedestal** support at foot of column

**pediment** triangular shape at end of pitched roof

**pendentive** curved support in form of spherical triangle between dome and its supporting masonry

**peristyle** colonnaded courtyard behind entrance

**pier** isolated masonry support

**pilaster** flat, columnar form against wall

**pillar** upright support column or shaft

**plinth** projecting block at base of building or column

**portico** covered entryway or porch with columns

**pylon** monumental temple gateway (ancient Egypt)

**quoin** corner of building; stone forming building corner

**relief** moldings and ornamentation that stand out from a surface

**reticulation** ornamental design resembling a net

**sarcophagus** ornamental stone coffin

**scotia** concave molding in column base

**shaft** cylindrical pillar between capital and base of column

**skewback** course of masonry with a sloping surface against which stones of arch abut

**soffit** undersurface of arch

**spandrel** wall area above curved sides of arch

**spire** tall, tapering Gothic tower

**springer** first stone of arch above impost

**squinch** arch placed diagonally between two walls

**steeple** tall, narrow, conical tower

**stellate** (adj) star-shaped

**stereobate** foundation or base upon which building, esp. classical temple, is erected

**stringcourse** decorative, horizontal band, as of stone, projecting beyond or flush with face of building, often molded

**stupa** domed, Buddhist shrine

**stylobate** course of masonry forming foundation for a colonnade, esp. outermost colonnade of building

**summer** stone laid upon top of pier, column, or wall, from which arch springs

**supercilium** fillet above cyma of a cornice

**tabernacle** highly decorated niche

**telamon** male figure, similar to caryatid, used as column or pilaster

**tholos** circular building (ancient Greece)

**tomb** structure over or housing a grave

**torii** monumental post-and-lintel gateway to Shinto shrine (Japan)

**torus** large convex molding used as lowest molding in column base

**trabeated** (adj) dependent on upright-and-horizontal or post-and-lintel construction, not on arches

**tracery** ornamental pattern in Gothic architecture

**transept** transverse arms of cross-shaped church, usu. perpendicular to nave

**trefoil** decorative, three-lobed design

**triglyph** grooved projecting panels in Doric frieze

**triumphal arch** monumental gateway

**tumulus** earth or stone mound over grave

**Tuscan column** Roman order of column, similar to Doric with fluted shaft

**tympanum** area above doorway or arch, esp. triangular face of pediment

**vault** arched, domed, usu. masonry ceiling or roof: barrel, dome, fan, groin, ribbed

**viga** wooden beam that supports roof of adobe structure

**vomitory** aislelike entrance through bank of stadium or theater seats

**voussoir** one of the wedge-shaped stone blocks used to form arch

**westwork** monumental, Romanesque church front formed of porches and towers and containing an entrance with vestibule below and a chapel above

**ziggurat** mound built with stepped sides

## BUILDING CONSTRUCTION AND DESIGN

**attic** space between ceiling joists and roof rafters

**backfill** replacing earth around foundation

**balloon frame** one-piece studs extending from foundation to roof of two-story structure

**baseboard** wooden finish strip where interior wall meets floor

**bearing wall** wall that supports a vertical load, esp. the floors and walls above; load-bearing wall

**blocking** placement of wooden framing members between other members to add strength and provide nailing surface

**blueprint** detailed architectural design diagram

**board measure** system for measuring lumber, in which each board foot is equal to one inch by twelve inches by twelve inches

**breast wall** retaining wall

**building codes** ordinances regulating construction standards

**casement window** window hinged on one side, swinging outward

**center to center** distance from center of one member to center of next as shown on drawings

**central heating** single heat source supplying several ducts

**compressive strength** ability of material to withstand forces tending to shorten it

**contractor** builder responsible for implementing architectural designs and drawings, purchasing materials, and hiring labor

**crawlspace** area between floor joists and earth beneath building

**curtain wall** exterior wall that protects an interior wall from weather, but bears no structural load

**dead load** weight of materials used to build structure

**deflection** vertical distance that beam moves under load stress

**double glazing** door or window made of two panes of glass sealed together with a dead air space between them to provide insulation

**double-hung window** window with two sashes that move vertically

**drafting** mechanical drawing

**dry wall** interior wall composed of gypsum board panels

**elevation** building face; front drawing of structure projected geometrically on vertical plane parallel to one of its sides

**ell** wing of building at right angle to main structure

**excavation** pit dug in earth for foundation

**fascia** vertical boards at end of rafter forming face of cornice and attached to overhanging outer edge of roof

**fixture** plumbing or electrical equipment

**floor plan** drawing that shows the top view of one floor of a house

**foundation** masonry or concrete substructure of building beneath first-floor joists

**grade** elevation above sea level of building site; slope of ground for building site

**half-timbered** (*adj*) relating to exterior walls with exposed, heavy, wooden members separated by masonry

**house drain** large horizontal sewer beneath house that receives wastes from soil pipes

**house sewer** sewer line that connects house drain to city sewer or septic tank

**interior trim** molding, casing, and bargeboard used to finish walls, doors, or windows

**kip** deadweight load equal to 1000 pounds (453.6 kg)

**knee wall** short wall used in constructing top floor of one-and-one-half-story structure

**landing** platform at top, bottom, or between flights of stairs

**live load** weight of variable, movable loads placed on a building

**load-bearing wall** bearing wall

**maquette** small, preliminary model of designed structure

**mechanical drawing** stylized, precise drawing of plans and blueprints done with aid of rulers, scales, and compasses; drafting

**mockup** scale model of structure with full detail

**modular construction** construction of buildings from standardized units

**modular unit** factory-built finished section of building, room-size or larger, for modular construction

**module** standardized unit of measurement for determining building proportions

**monolithic** (*adj*) constructed of concrete, with all members cast at the same time as a single unit

**nonbearing wall** wall that bears only its own weight

**orientation** positioning of building with regard to sun, wind, or view

**outlet** electrical unit providing source of AC

**overhang** horizontal distance between fascia and exterior wall

**perspective** drawing of building to give same appearance as in three-dimensional space

**plat** drawing showing layout of housing development or mall

**platform frame** building in which each story is built on the story below but framed independently

**plot** piece of land with specific dimensions for construction

**post-and-beam construction** wall construction in which beams rather than studs support heavy posts

**prefabricated** (*adj*) assembled into complete, standardized, structural units at factory

**radiant heating** heating by direct heat rays, without blowers

**retaining wall** wall built to resist lateral pressure, esp. to hold back soil; breast wall

**rise** vertical height of roof from ground

**sandwich wall** masonry wall with two panels separated by insulation

**scale** use of proportional measurements in drawings

**schedule** list of parts for construction

**section** vertical cross-section diagram of building

**service entrance** access point for electric lines leading from power company pole to building

**setback** zoning regulation that limits how near to a street a building can be

**shear** force that produces opposite but parallel sliding motion on contacting planes in a structural member

**slab** flat concrete block laid as foundation or reinforced concrete floor

**soil pipe** part of drainage system that receives waste flow from all fixtures, esp. toilet, leading to house drain

**solar heat** heat generated by collected rays of sun

**sound transmission class** means of specifying ability of material to resist sound transmission

**specifications** record of design and construction details not shown on drawings

**stress** force acting upon a structural member

**subfloor** floor material nailed directly to floor joists and covered by finished wood or carpet

**sump** pit in basement that collects water

**tensile strength** ability of structural member to withstand forces tending to lengthen it

**thermostat** self-regulating device controlling heat and air conditioning

**tilt-up** (*adj*) designating concrete walls cast in horizontal frames, then lifted into vertical position

**veneer** facing one material with another finishing surface

**waste pipe** horizontal pipe that carries waste from fixtures to soil pipe

**water table** level of underground water beneath structure

**weather stripping** metal or fabric strips placed at edges of doors and windows to reduce heat loss

**weep hole** small opening at bottom of wall that permits moisture to drain out

**working drawings** drawings with design details, from which construction is done

**zoning** (*adj*) of or pertaining to ordinances regulating type, size, and uses of buildings which may be constructed in specific area

# Graphic Design and Printing

Graphic Design
Graphic Arts
Printing and Typefaces

**See also**: Chap. 5: Computers; Chap. 11: Publishing and the Press; Chap. 12: Advertising; Chap. 14: Painting; Chap. 16: Photography; Chap. 23: Colors

## Graphic Design

**acetate** flexible, plastic film used to protect artwork

**air** white space

**airbrush** handheld tool for spraying paint and touching up artwork

**artwork** any graphic image prepared for reproduction

**asymmetry** dynamic compositional principle that states that design not be identical on both sides of central line

**binding** adhesive or other means of keeping pages and cover of published work together

**bleed** extension of image up to or beyond edge of page

**burnishing** transfer of color overlay or dry transfer letters by rubbing with hard, smooth edge

**calendered paper** paper glazed and pressed to glossy finish

**calligraphy** beautiful, stylized, highly decorative handwriting, often with many flourishes

**camera lucida** prismatic device used to project image for tracing; lucie

**camera-ready** (*adj*) designating project that is ready to be photographed for reproduction

**caricature** exaggerated drawing, esp. of human subject, portraying humorous or grotesque qualities

**cartoon** preliminary drawing; humorous sketch or drawing, as in comic strip

**center spread** copy and illustration that spread across facing pages at the center of a publication

**chart** any organizational or quantitative diagram containing information and revealing relationships in visual arrangement of elements

**china marker** colored wax pencil for marking glazed or coated surfaces

**Chinese ink** India ink

**close crop** (*vb*) silhouette

**collage** compositional technique using various materials not normally associated with one another

**Color Key** *Trademark*. color acetate proofs of line negatives

**color overlay** transparent sheet of color film transferred by burnishing

**color separation** composite negative used to reproduce separate plates or layers for primary colors and black

**column** vertical unit of grid for type and images, separated by gutters

**comp** comprehensive; detailed mock-up of a layout for presentation purposes

**compass** instrument for drawing arcs and circles

**comprehensive** comp

**copy** textual matter; artwork to be photographed for reproduction

**crop** (*vb*) trim edges of illustration or photograph

**crop marks** indicators used to establish parameters of area to be reproduced

**Day-Glo** *Trademark*. fluorescent paint or ink

**desktop publishing** creation and printing of graphic presentations and designs using a computer

**diagram** graphic visualization of abstract data designed to reveal relationships

**die** steel rule with edge for cutting out paper or cardboard shapes very precisely; metal stamp for impressing or embossing a design

**drafting** mechanical drawing

**drawing board** work surface that can be secured by user at angles from horizontal to vertical

**drop cap** bold or stylized initial letter of chapter or paragraph set into body of text

**dry-transfer letters** sheet imprinted with letters of alphabet in various styles for transfer to surface by rubbing

**dummy** prototype layout of assembled graphic work

**duotone** reproduction of image in two colors, one for darker shade with greater detail, one for lighter flat tint

**electrostatic printing** process such as xerography in which images are produced by attraction between electrostatic charge and particles of toner

**emboss** (*vb*) raise printed design in relief by pressure of plate on which image is engraved below surface

**eraser** mildly abrasive material or tool used to remove marks on paper

**felt-tip pen** pen with absorbent cloth nib, filled with ink that dries instantly

**figure-ground** principle of perception in which parts of a visual field tend to appear as solid and well-defined against a less-distinct background

**final art** camera-ready version of project

**fixative** aerosol varnish

**flop** (*vb*) reverse an image by turning original back to front

**flow chart** plan that forecasts appearance and process of design job

**folio** page number

**foundry** establishment in which typefaces originate through casting or technical encryption prior to distribution

**four-color process** reproduction of a wide range of colors by printing superimposed sequence of cyan, magenta, yellow, and black in varying intensities

**French curve** drafting instrument for tracing curved lines

**gestalt** entire configuration of visual elements, having properties not ascribable to its component parts

**glitter** shiny, decorative flakes of light-reflecting material

**graph** any diagram representing interrelations among two or more things

**graphic** (*adj*) represented visually, esp. by drawing or printing; (*n*) visual representation or design

**graphic design** art, discipline, and profession of visual communication that combines images, words, and ideas to purposefully convey information to an audience, esp. to produce specific effect or achieve desired goal

**graphite** soft, black, shiny form of carbon used for marking, esp. as pencil lead

**grid** horizontal and vertical divisions of page surface, used as organizational system for type and illustrations

**gutter** empty space between and around columns of type and images on page

**hairline** thinnest of printing rules

**halftone** simulation of solid or continuous tone image by breaking it into pattern of dots of varying sizes

**halftone screen** field of tiny dots used to produce halftone print

**hand composition** setting of a galley of lead type by hand

**ichnography** drawing with compass and rule

**illumination** detailed hand-decoration of manuscript books

**illustration** graphic image, esp. used for explanation or clarification of a text

**India ink** permanent dye composed of lampblack and glue or size; Chinese ink

**ink** viscous fluid or powdered substance used for writing, printing, and graphic reproductions

**justification** spacing of letters and words within text lines so that all full lines in type column have even margins on both right and left sides

**kerning** fine adjustment of spacing between letter forms to attain uniform appearance

**laid finish** paper with watermarks in close parallel stripes or which shows wire marks of mold used in its manufacture

**layout** design of text and images for reproduction

**lead** thin strip of graphite used as marking part of pencil

**lead holder** mechanical pencil

**letterspacing** insertion of additional space between letters of words for balance or emphasis

**light box** display unit for viewing color transparency, consisting of frosted glass with diffuse light from incandescent bulb beneath it

**line art** high-contrast rendering for reproduction without screening, consisting of lines or areas of solid black and solid white

**line copy** graphic design consisting of two tones without intermediate gradations

**logo** distinctive design, emblem, and trademark of product or organization; logotype

**logotype** logo, esp. one made of letter forms

**loupe** small, freestanding magnifying lens used to inspect transparent and reflective surfaces

**lucie** camera lucida

**markup** instructions for typesetting or color treatment

**mat** stiff cardboard frame for photo or artwork

**mat knife** blade on handle for cutting paper or art boards

**mechanical** artwork and type pasted into position on boards, ready for photo-transfer to printing plate or silkscreen; paste-up

**mechanical drawing** precise drawing done with aid of rulers, scales, and compasses; drafting

**mechanical pencil** tube holding thin pencil lead; lead holder

**moiré** interference pattern of dots arising from overlaying regular patterns while printing four-color process

**montage** image made of composite graphic elements that are overlaid and superimposed

**negative** film on which values of a recorded image are the reverse of the original, used for duplication

**negative space** air; white space

**pantograph** device for enlarging or reducing drawing size

**Pantone Matching System** *Trademark.* PMS; color organization and numbering specification system that dictates quantity and type of inks needed to make specific colors

**paper** thin, felted sheet of wood, vegetable, or synthetic fiber in varying weights and qualities

**parallel rule** hinged straightedges for drawing parallel lines at varying widths

**paste-up** mechanical

**pen** drawing implement composed of ink-bearing tube and point or nib: ballpoint, dip, felt-tip, fountain, metal nib, quill, reed, reservoir

**pencil** drawing tool with marking substance made of graphite, lead, or colored wax encased in paper or wooden tube

**Perspec** *Trademark.* colored, acrylic sheets

**photo collage** technique in which photographs and portions of photographs are pieced together and overlayed to form single piece

**Photostat** *Trademark.* process using special graphic camera to produce paper positives

**photostat** copy made using Photostat process and camera

**picture** visual representation or image of something

**pixel** picture element; single dot, or smallest element in visual display; square picture unit that is basis of computer graphics

**planography** art or technique of printing from flat surface directly or by offset

**PMS** *Pantone Matching System*

**portfolio** flat case use to carry samples of work for presentation, usu. made of leather

**positive** film or paper print made from photographic negative

**printing** reproduction of image using inked surface to make copies: intaglio, lithography, offset, planography, relief

**proof** printing impression made for examination, correction, or approval

**protractor** instrument for measuring and drawing exact angles

**pull** (*vb*) take impression or proof from block, plate, or type

**Rapidograph** *Trademark.* technical pen used for precise renderings of line art, esp. rules and stipples

**relief** printing or design in which image stands out from surface

**repro** image or type proof ready for paste-up

**reproduction** exact copy of visual image

**retouch** (*vb*) change details of negative or photographic print with pencil, brush, airbrush, or computer

**rivers** combination of spaces in consecutive lines of type that creates vertical streaks of white space

**rough** preliminary sketch of concept, layout, or job

**rubber cement** bonding agent that permits removal of mounted work and rubbing away of excess cement

**rubilith** usu. red acetate transparency that photographs black and occupies place in mechanicals that will ultimately be filled by art to be reproduced

**rules** metal strips of various widths, used to draw straight lines; the lines themselves

**saddle stitch** binding method in which pages are stitched through their middle folds

**scale** proportion that the representation of something bears to the object itself

**Scotchlite** *Trademark.* chemical coating that gives signs their highly reflective properties

**screen** creation of tonal value in artwork by regular pattern, usu. measured as dots per square inch

**seal** embossed design or symbol, often impressed on wax by stamp or medallion engraved with such design

**set square** flat, triangular tool used to ensure correct alignment of paste-up

**signage** environmental graphics created to assist identification and way-finding

**silhouette** (*vb*) outline an image so that it is separated from its background; close crop

**sketch** rough, preparatory drawing, usu. done quickly

**specifications** specs

**specs** *Informal.* complete description of job, esp. for printing; specifications

**stamp** die or block for impressing or imprinting

**stat** *Informal.* paper positive produced by Photostat process

**stationery** writing paper and materials in general; family of letterhead, envelopes, notepaper, and business cards

**stencil** waxed cardboard or thin metal or plastic with letters or designs cut out, so that ink may be applied to surface through cut-out area

**stipple** gradation of light and shade produced by separate touches of small points, larger dots, and longer strokes

**stock** specified quality or kind of paper for printing

**straightedge** blade guide for drawing or cutting very straight lines

**surprint** overprinting of one image on top of another

**swatch** sample of paper or ink color

**symmetry** classical principle that states that design be identical on both sides of center line

**template** drawing guide for shapes, symbols, or lettering

**tracing paper** thin, semitransparent paper laid over earlier artwork to compare or relate parts of design

**transparency** image recorded on color film, viewed by projection of light shining through it, as on light box

**T square** drawing guide for parallel and perpendicular lines

**vellum** translucent paper used for tracing; thin, treated calfskin used for writing or printing

**Velox** *Trademark*. brand of photographic print, prepared from line negative, that has been screened for reproduction

**washed-out** (*adj*) having poor color reproduction; faded

**wax** (*vb*) apply heated beeswax as adhesive to repro for paste-up

**weight** degree of boldness of typeface

**white space** empty space or white area that gives contrast to layout; air; negative space

**X-acto knife** *Trademark*. thin blade or razor in knife handle, used for cutting stencils and mats

**xerography** electrostatic printing technique in which areas on paper are sensitized with static electrical charge so that they attract oppositely charged dry-ink particles from toner, which are then fused onto the copy paper

**Xerox** *Trademark*. brand name for copying machine using xerography; commonly used synonym for all photocopying by xerography

# GRAPHIC ARTS

**abbozzo** sketch, first draft

**aquatint** engraved printing process in which tones resemble watercolor

**block print** design printed by means of one or more wood or metal blocks

**bow pen** drafting pencil

**brayer** small rubber roller for inking printing blocks or plates by hand, usu. for making proofs

**burin** pointed engraving tool

**cartouche** oval or rounded decorative border around frame

**cerography** process of engraving design or text by incision into wax surface

**chalcography** art of copper engraving

**chalk** calcium carbonate powder formed into drawing stick

**chamois** soft leather cloth used to blend charcoal lines

**crayon** powdered pigment in waxy binder molded into drawing stick

**decal** design or picture printed on special paper for transfer to another surface

**decalcomania** art or process of transferring images from paper to other surfaces

**Ditto machine** *Trademark*. machine that copies text and drawings by ink-transfer process

**drypoint** engraving technique using a sharply scratched, inked copperplate

**enchase** (*vb*) decorate with inlay, embossing, or engraving

**engrave** (*vb*) produce image or design on printing plate by scratching it with a sharp tool

**engraving** graphic reproduction technique in which lines are cut into a metal or wooden surface, which is then inked and printed; design so produced

**etch** (*vb*) form image or design on a metal plate or glass by corrosive action of acid

**etching** process of making graphic design on a metal plate or glass by corrosive action of acid instead of with a pointed tool as in engraving; design so produced; impression made from such an etched plate

**etching tools** points, scrapers, and burnishers

**fitch** lettering brush, made of bristle, with straight chiseled edges

**frottage** technique of obtaining textural effects or images by rubbing pigment on paper stretched over an irregular surface

**glyptography** art and process of engraving on gems

**gold point** drawing on slightly abrasive surface with gold point or wire

**graphic arts** arts and techniques by which copies of an original are printed, as from blocks or plates; printmaking

**gravure** intaglio process of photomechanical printing

**hachure** series of parallel lines for shading or modeling; hatching

**hatching** hachure

**hyalography** technique of etching or engraving on glass

**incision** cutting into, as linoleum or wood block

**inlay** design or decoration made by inserting or applying fine materials in surface of object

**intaglio** engraving process in which ink-retaining lines are cut into metal surface

**linocut** linoleum cut

**linoleum block** piece of thick, soft, cork linoleum mounted on block of wood, incised or carved in relief with design, and used to make prints

**linoleum cut** image carved into surface of linoleum, often mounted on wood block, then inked and printed; linecut

**lithography** printing and reproduction process using stone slab marked with greasy ink; similar process using another substance, such as aluminum or zinc

**mezzotint** engraving process using coarse, random-dot screen burred by chisel on a metal plate, which is then inked and printed

**monotype** single print made from engraving process

**overlay** decoration or layer of some material applied onto another surface

**pastel** chalk or crayon stick of ground pigment and nonoily binder

**photogravure** process by which intaglio engraving is formed on metal plate, from which ink reproductions are made

**pounce** cleaning powder for drafting paper; copying technique using fine powder and perforated paper

**print** picture or design printed from engraved or otherwise prepared block or plate

**printmaking** art and technique of making prints, esp. by engraving, etching, drypoint, woodcut, or serigraphy

**rag paper** high-quality paper made from cotton and linen mixed with wood pulp

**repoussé** relief design on paper

**reproduction** copy or duplication made from an original work

**resist** protective layer applied to parts of printing plate

**restrike** new print made from old engraving, woodcut, or lithographic stone

**sanguine** reddish chalk or pastel for drawing

**serigraph** silkscreen print

**serigraphy** printing technique using silkscreen process

**silkscreen** printing technique that uses inked silk cloth, mounted on frame, to which stencil film is affixed; serigraphy

**silverpoint** drawing made with sharp, pointed silver tool on coated paper

**spline** flexible guide for drawing long curves

**steel engraving** graphic reproduction made by incising design on steel plates, then imprinting on paper

**stump** rolled chamois for blending chalk or pencil on paper

**sumi** *Japanese*. black ink used by calligraphers

**tooth** abrasive quality of paper that helps it to hold pigment, charcoal, or chalk

**tortillon** small stump made of paper, used in drawing

**tusche** greasy liquid used as medium receptive to lithographic ink

**wash drawing** broad areas of color used in conjunction with line forms, as in watercolor painting

**woodblock** image carved into surface of wood, then inked and printed

**woodcut** technique of printmaking from woodblock; print or impression formed this way

**zincography** process of producing printing surface using zinc plate etched by acid

## PRINTING AND TYPEFACES

**ascender** part of lowercase letter that rises above x-height, as in b, d, f, or h

**beard** sloping part of type that connects face with shoulder of body

**bed** surface on which printing form holding type is locked on flat-bed press

**bleed** (*vb*) print so that material runs off edge of page after trimming

**blueline** (*vb*) check for and mark typos on first run of laid-out page with blue pencil; (*n*) proof of final negatives made on light-sensitive paper, used for checking specifications before making plates

**boldface** thick, heavy typeface, used for emphasis

**bond paper** superior quality paper, usu. with high cotton fiber content

**capitals** uppercase letters

**card out** (*vb*) add extra space between lines of text to fill out column or page exactly

**chase** rectangular metal frame in which composed type is secured for printing

**chromolithography** printing in color by lithography using a series of plates or stones

**cold type** type set by any method other than casting of molten lead, esp. handset composition

**composing stick** small, handheld, adjustable tray in which compositor places type before fitting it in galley

**composition** typesetting

**computer typesetting** high-speed phototypesetting, eliminating need for mechanical setting of type

**condensed** (*adj*) designating type that is narrow and elongate in proportion to its height

**copy** any issue of a given publication printed from the same plate or plates

**cursive** style of typeface simulating handwriting

**cylinder press** flat-bed press

**descender** part of lowercase letter that goes below main body of letter, as in g, j, p, or y

**dingbat** typographic symbol or ornament such as fist, arrow, or heart

**dummy** prototype layout that shows length and placement of items indicated for sizing

**elite** letter size measuring twelve characters per inch, widely used in typewriters

**em** unit of measure of column width in terms of type size

**en** unit of measure equal to one half the width of an em

**engraving** graphic reproduction technique in which lines are cut into a hard surface such as metal or stone, which is then inked and printed

**expanded** (*adj*) designating type that is wider in proportion to its height, having a flattened, oblong appearance

**f and g's** folded and gathered, unbound printed sheets in proper sequence for binding

**flat-bed press** printing device in which horizontal printing surface, or bed, moves against rotating cylinder that carries paper; cylinder press

**flexography** relief printing technique using soft plastic or rubber plates and fast-drying ink

**font** full assortment of letters and symbols in one size and family of type

**form** type assembled and secured in chase for printing; any made-up sequence of pages ready for printing

**four-color process** reproduction of range of colors by printing a superimposed sequence of cyan, magenta, black, and yellow in varying intensities

**frame** device that holds type, esp. galley

**furniture** pieces of wood or metal, less than type high, used to fill spaces on bed not occupied by type

**galley** sheets of final type proofs; with hot type, shallow tray holding typeset pages

**gatefold** spread that opens from center to reveal additional pages

**grain** direction of long fibers in sheet of paper

**graphics** photographs or illustrations to be printed

**gravure** process of intaglio printing, in which plate is inked only beneath its surface

**hot metal** type cast from molten lead; hot type

**hot type** hot metal

**imposition** arrangement of page plates in proper order on press to ensure correct sequence when folding and gathering at bindery

**impression** all copies of publication printed in one operation

**indent** (*vb*) set type in or back from margin

**italics** scriptlike style of letters or type

**justify** (*vb*) line up margins evenly in type column

**kern** portion of typeface projecting beyond body or shank; (*vb*) adjust space between specified letter pairs for printing

**laser printing** high-speed computer printing technique using laser to form dot-matrix patterns and electrostatic process to fuse metallic particles to paper

**leading** insertion of thin strips of type metal for spacing between lines of text; space so created

**letterpress**  method of printing from raised type

**ligature**  character or type combining two or more letters, such as

**line-casting**  casting of entire line of type in a slug

**Linotype**  *Trademark.* typesetting machine that sets each line of type in single slug

**lowercase**  small letters in font of type

**mackle**  blur in printing, as from double impression

**majuscule**  uppercase letter

**matrix**  mold for casting typefaces

**mimeo**  *Informal.* mimeograph

**mimeograph**  printing machine using waxed stencil wrapped around rotating, ink-fed drum, past which sheets of paper are fed; mimeo

**minuscule**  lowercase letter

**mold**  framed page of cast type from which plate is made

**Monotype**  *Trademark.* brand of machine for setting and casting type, based on paper tape containing holes in coded pattern

**Multigraph**  *Trademark.* rotary typesetting and printing machine, used esp. for duplicating written matter

**newsprint**  cheaply produced, disposable wood pulp paper, used chiefly for printing newspapers

**offset lithography**  printing process in which stone or metal or paper plate makes inked impression on a rubber blanket, that in turn transfers it to the paper being printed, instead of taking direct impression of plate on paper; photo-offset

**offset printing**  printing method in which image is photographically engraved on metal sheet and then offset onto paper

**orphan**  poor line break that dangles first line of new paragraph at end of column or bottom of page

**overrun**  copies in excess of specified pressrun; overs

**overs**  *Informal.* overrun

**pallet**  typeholder

**photocomposition**  method of composition in which type is set photographically

**photoengraving**  reproduction technique using light-sensitive, emulsion-coated metal plates

**photo-offset**  offset lithography

**phototypography**  any of various techniques for making printing surfaces by light or photography

**pi**  typefaces mixed together at random

**pica**  letter size measuring ten characters per inch; unit of measure equal to twelve points or 1/6 of an inch

**plate**  cast to be printed from, made from mold of set type or photo-offset negative

**point**  standard unit of type measurement, approximately equal to 1/72 of an inch

**press**  printing press

**pressroom**  room in publishing establishment in which printing presses are located

**pressrun**  operation of printing press for specific job; number of copies so printed

**print**  (*vb*) produce impressions of inked type or plates on paper; publish large numbers of book or periodical in printed form

**printer**  person who runs printing operations

**printer's devil**  young worker below level of apprentice in print shop

**printer's mark**  individual printer's identifying mark, usu. on copyright page

**printing**  technique, process, and business of reproducing written or graphic material, esp. by impression from movable types or plates

**printing press**  any of various machines for printing in mass form from inked type, plates, or rollers; press

**print shop**  facility in which type is set, plates or rollers are made, and printing is done

**proof sheet**  inked page made from galley or plate, used to check for errors before printing

**quoin**  wedge of wood or metal for securing type in chase

**reglet**  thin wood strip less than type-high, used to produce blank space around page of type

**reprography**  duplication of documents or designs by any process using light rays and photography, such as offset printing or xerography

**roller**  cylinder in rotary press to which plate is attached for printing

**roman**  (*adj*) designating common, upright style of typeface

**rotary press**  printing press with plates mounted on cylinders that pass over paper fed from continuous roll

**rotogravure**  intaglio printing process using rotary presses

**run**  quantity printed in pressrun

**sans serif**  style of letters or type without serifs, or typefaces without serifs, such as Helvetica and Franklin Gothic

**score**  (*vb*) make furrows in paper to facilitate folding

**serif**  fine cross-stroke that terminates main stroke at top and bottom of letters; style of typefaces having serifs, such as Bodoni, Garamond, and Times Roman

**shank**  body or stem of piece of type

**signature**  letter or symbol placed at foot of first page of every sheet to guide binder in folding and gathering; printed sheet folded to page size for binding

**slug**  line of type cast in single piece by Linotype machine

**small capitals**  capital letters that are smaller than standard size for that font, designed to align visually with ordinary type line

**swash**  extending ornamental flourish on letters of certain fonts of italic or cursive type

**thermography**  technique for imitating embossed appearance by dusting printed areas with powder that adheres to wet ink, then fusing ink and powder to paper by heat

**toner**  cartridge containing dry ink particles, used in xerography and laser printing

**type**  piece of metal with raised letter or symbol in reverse on one end and used collectively, inked, and pressed against paper to leave impressions

**typeface**  any of various distinctive styles of letters to be reproduced by printing or photography; alphabet designed with specific attributes that unify the character set

**typefaces**  common text and display faces include:

Baskerville, Bembo, Bodoni
Caledonia, Caslon, Century, Cheltenham, Clarendon
Electra, English
Fraktur, Franklin Gothic, Futura
Garamond, Goudy
Helvetica
Janson
Melior
Old English, Optima
Palatino, Plantin
Renaissance
Times Roman
Univers

**type family** grouping of printing types with common design but different weights and styles, such as roman, italic, bold, condensed, or expanded

**typeholder** small device that holds a few lines of type, used esp. to stamp titles on covers; pallet

**typesetting** arrangement of type for printing, usu. by computer or machine; composition

**typography** art and process of setting and arranging type for printing; creation of typefaces

**underlay** sheets of paper placed under type to bring it to required height for printing

**uppercase** letters in font of type that differ from corresponding lowercase letters in form and height; capitals

**watermark** paper mark indicating maker or trademark of stock

**web press** printing press using continuous roll of paper

**widow** poor line break in which a single word or short line ends a paragraph; last line of paragraph when it is carried over to next column or page

**x-height** height of letters having no ascender or descender, typified by lowercase *x* in given typeface

# PHOTOGRAPHY

Types of Photography
Cameras
Lenses
Tools and Techniques

**SEE ALSO**: Chap. 11: Publishing and the Press; Chap. 15: Cinema; Television and Radio; Chap. 16: Graphic Design and Printing

## TYPES OF PHOTOGRAPHY

**aerial photography** pictures taken from airplane or satellite

**animation** graphic images sequenced for motion effect

**architectural photography** pictures displaying building design

**black and white** pictures using monochrome black-and-white film, without color; b/w

**b/w** black and white

**calotype** paper-negative photography, now obsolete

**cinematography** motion-picture photography

**collodion** wet-plate photography, now obsolete

**color** prints, slides, and film utilizing the full color spectrum

**composite** several shots of model or actor in different poses, printed together with head shot on reverse side

**daguerreotype** silver-plate photography, now obsolete

**electron micrography** image seen and photographed through electron microscope

**fashion photography** pictures of clothing and accessories on models for advertising

**ferrotype** iron-plate photography, now obsolete; tintype

**fine-art photography** work emphasizing aesthetic composition and emotional substance rather than some specific purpose

**holography** three-dimensional photography, using split laser beam

**infrared photography** exposures using infrared light, often at night

**laser photography** holography and other photography using lightwave amplification by stimulated emission of radiation

**macrophotograph** extreme closeup

**microphotograph** extremely small-scale photograph requiring optical enlargement

**photocopy** photographic reproduction of graphic material or document

**photogram** silhouette produced by direct exposure of paper, without lens or negative

**photography** reproduction of images of objects on sensitized film by exposure to light and chemical processing

**photojournalism** form of journalism in which pictures associated with news events, specific editorial content, or documentary features dominate the written material

**portraiture** photographs of posed individuals, done in selected environment or studio

**print photography** fashion and commercial photography for publications

**product photography** stylized, precise photographs of an object for advertising

**radiography** x-ray photography

**reportage** photojournalism, esp. photo essays based on research or detailed coverage of documented observation

**scenic photography** pictures of landscapes or seascapes

**stereophotography** simulation of binocular vision that produces two images

**still life** pictures of inanimate objects for product, tabletop, or fine-art photography

**still photography** still shots taken on the set of a movie or television show, or a single frame of film used like a still shot; unit photography

**stroboscopic photography** photography of moving subjects, using pulsing light source to apparently freeze movements

**tabletop photography** still life, product, or food photographed on tabletop

**tintype** ferrotype

**travel photography** photographs displaying beautiful locales around world

**underwater photography** photographs of underwater environment and fish, taken with special enclosed camera

**unit photography** still photography

**xerography** photocopying directly onto paper

## CAMERAS

**aerial-reconnaissance camera** long-range camera designed for military and defense use

**animation camera** camera designed to expose one frame at a time, used for animated sequences

**autofocus camera** camera that automatically sets aperture and shutter speed for operator, sometimes also equipped with automatic flash

**box camera** simple, low-cost camera

**camera lucida** instrument using prism and mirrors to project image of object on plane surface for tracing

**camera obscura** primitive camera in which light aperture projects image on surface

**8x10** camera format using eight-inch by ten-inch sheet film to produce same-size negatives

**5x7** camera format using five-inch by seven-inch sheet film to produce same-size negatives

**flash** camera using high-powered burst of illumination

**folding camera** camera in which bellows collapses into fold when camera is not in use

**4x5** camera format using four-inch by five-inch sheet film to produce same-size negatives

**minicam** portable, handheld video camera

**panoramic camera** camera equipped with motor that swivels it to take panoramic view in one exposure on 35 mm negative

**pinhole camera** rudimentary camera having tiny aperture and no lens

**Polaroid** *Trademark.* camera that develops film immediately within itself

**portrait camera** camera fitted with portrait lens

**single-lens reflex camera** camera in which image appears on ground-glass viewer after being reflected by mirror or passing through prism or semitransparent glass

**6x9** camera format using 120 mm film to produce 6 mm by 9 mm negatives

**6x7** camera format using 120 mm film to produce 6 mm by 7 mm negatives

**6x6** camera format using 120 mm film to produce 6 mm by 6 mm negatives

**stop-action** camera that stops at intervals to allow for manipulation of photographed subject

**35 mm camera** any camera that uses standard 35 mm film

**twin-lens reflex camera** camera with two lenses in single focusing mount, using 2 1/4-inch format

**underwater camera** camera mounted in waterproof container or self-contained, using O-rings for waterproofing

**video camera** camera for electronically processed videotape that requires no developing

**viewfinder camera** viewing lens system that separates image from shutter lens system

## LENSES

**achromatic lens** finely made, expensive lens with no chromatic aberration

**anamorphic lens** lens for wide screen effects

**anastigmatic lens** lens with vertical, horizontal lines focused in same plane

**aplanatic lens** lens free from spherical aberration

**apochromatic lens** lens in which all colors are focused at a common point

**convertible lens** lens for different focal lengths

**fisheye lens** short focal-length, wide-angle lens of over 180 degrees, used to create distorted image

**fixed-focus lens** usu. wide-angle lens with nonvariable focus

**long-focus lens** lens with narrow angle of view for greater magnification

**normal lens** lens with angle of view approximately equal to human vision, or 50 to 55 degrees

**portrait lens** moderately soft-definition, medium-long focal- length lens

**process lens** lens with precise color-separation capacity for reproduction and engraving work

**standard lens** normal lens usu. provided with camera at time of purchase, such as 50 mm lens with 35 mm camera

**telephoto lens** lens that reduces depth of field for distant objects: with 35 mm camera, telephotos are 80 mm, 105 mm, 135 mm, 180 mm, 200 mm, and 300 mm

**wide-angle lens** lens with wide field of view

**zoom lens** lens with focal length continuously variable to close in on small or distant objects or open up for wide view

## TOOLS AND TECHNIQUES

**actinic light** part of light spectrum that exposes photographic film and paper

**albumen paper** printing paper coated with egg white, salt, and critic acid, and sensitized with silver nitrate

**ambrotype** positive picture made from photo negative on glass backed by dark surface

**angle of view** degree of camera lens' width of vision

**aperture** opening that controls amount of light admitted into camera through lens

**aperture-priority** (*adj*) designating semiautomatic exposure system in which aperture is preset and camera selects shutter speed

**ASA** *American Standards Association;* organization that rates light sensitivity for film exposure

**barn door** *Slang.* adjustable blinder attached around light to prevent spillage

**bellows** accordion-pleated cloth that insulates camera body and lens from light

**black back** film holder

**blimp** soundproof plastic covering over camera being used to take stills on movie set

**blow-up** photo enlargement

**book** photographer's portfolio containing clippings and samples of work

**boom** projecting arm used to support lights over a subject while remaining out of the camera's view

**bulb** camera setting that keeps shutter open while release is pressed

**burn in** (*vb*) allow more light on certain photo areas while printing

**buy out** selling of all photos and future rights of photo shoot to one buyer

**cable release** wire that activates the shutter from a distance

**camera** lightproof box that records the image of an object viewed through the aperture of a lens onto light-sensitive film

**candid** snapshot taken without staging, lighting, or special effects, often of unsuspecting subject

**century stand** light stand with wide base composed of legs that fold together

**cibachrome** positive-to-positive color printing method

**circle of confusion** area outside focal point that is not in focus

**click stop** turnable control on diaphragm that engages with distinct click at setting positions

**closeup** photograph taken at very close range

**collotype** process for making prints directly from hardened colloid film with ink-repellent and ink-receptive parts

**color separation** separate negative containing portion of picture to be printed in one color

**color transparency** color positive on transparent film or glass, viewed by projected light

**contact sheet** print consisting of all frames of a developed roll of film on one sheet of paper, with prints the same size as actual negatives; proof sheet

**contrast** variance of light and dark tones in photo

**coppertoning** (*adj*) designating chemical additives that give warm, brownish tinge to black-and-white photo

**cove** curved inset used to create illusion of infinite depth

**crop** (*vb*) remove outer portion of print

**C-type** color print made from negative by color-producing organic substance, or chromogen

**cyan** greenish blue color used in color printing

**darkroom** lightproof processing laboratory for film and prints

**definition** clarity of detail, image sharpness

**depth of field** zone between focal point and unfocused area in which image is reasonably sharp

**develop** (*vb*) chemically process latent image on exposed film or print paper

**developer** chemical solution producing images on exposed film or paper

**diaphragm** variable opening that allows light onto film in camera

**dip and dunk** method used in most color and some black-and-white film processing in which film is draped or dipped into chemical and rinsing baths

**dodge** (*vb*) shade area of photo from light to reduce density of dark areas during printing

**emulsion** light-sensitive chemical coating on film and paper

**enlargement** print made larger than original negative

**enlarger** magnifying device used in printing

**exposure** opening of shutter to allow light onto film, producing latent image; allowing light onto paper, producing print

**exposure meter** light meter

**film** light-sensitive chemical coating on flexible, plastic ribbon: black and white, color, microfilm, negative, nonchromatic, panchromatic, sheet, sound

**film holder** black receptacle for sheet film used in 4x5 or 8x10 camera; black back

**filter** glass or plastic gel or disc that screens certain light frequencies or colors from film exposure, also used in printing to alter contrast

**finder** camera indicator of focus or light

**fixative** chemical solution that makes negative or print exposure permanent by removing light-sensitive silver halides; fixer

**fixer** fixative

**flag** unit composed of metal frame with stretched black cloth, used to direct light

**flash** any device providing high-powered bursts of illumination

**flashbulb** single electric lamp that flashes when metal filament burns

**flashcube** four flashbulbs attached to camera

**flashgun** device that holds and repeatedly ignites flashbulb for taking continuous pictures without changing bulbs

**focal length** distance between lens and corresponding plane, where its subject is focused

**focus** point at which image is seen distinctly

**format** negative size, such as 35 mm

**f-stop** ratio of aperture opening to lens focal length

**glossy** shiny photographic print

**glycerin sandwich** badly scratched negative between glycerin-coated glass plates that obscure scratches for printing

**grain** size of silver particles in photographic film or paper, determines fineness of image

**grease pencil** marker for contact sheets, prints, and negatives

**grid spot** honeycomb grid placed over light to focus it in one direction

**ground glass** textured, flat pane of glass in camera, used to focus image

**halation** glow on photo resulting from overexposure

**head shot** close-up of face, esp. for actors or models; mug shot

**hypo** chemical solution used as fixative for film and prints

**hypo clearing agent** solution used to remove excess fixative from film or paper

**iris diaphragm shutter** shutter having group of overlapping blades that open and close at center when exposing film

**leader** black or transparent strip at end of film roll

**lens** curved-glass device that directs light rays from object onto camera plate to create image

**lens cap** protective cover for lens

**lens shade** hood to keep direct light off lens

**light box** container for color-corrected lights with one translucent side, used to view negatives or slides

**light meter** device that indicates light intensity; exposure meter

**light stand** usu. three-legged, adjustable support for strobe or tungsten light

**loupe** small magnifying lens worn directly on eye to inspect photos

**magazine** unit loaded with film that can be removed from camera and replaced by another unit in order to change film in use in middle of roll

**matte** photographic print lacking gloss and luster

**microfilm** film containing miniaturized copy of graphic material, esp. newspapers for archives

**monopod** light, compact, one-legged camera stand that must be held, designed for use when shooting in confined space

**mug shot** *Slang.* identification photo, esp. for police use

**negative** exposed film image with light and shade tones opposite original image

**Newton's rings** colored rings on photo caused by sun's glare

**nonchromatic** (*adj*) designating film that is not sensitive to colors

**orthochromatic** (*adj*) designating film that is sensitive to all colors except red

**overexposure** film or photographic paper exposed to too much light or radiation

**panchromatic** (*adj*) designating film that is sensitive to all colors

**panning shot** technique of moving camera at same speed as subject to blur background while subject remains in focus

**paparazzo** freelance photographer who pursues celebrities for candid photos

**paper** light-sensitive paper used for making photographic prints

**parallax** slight difference in fields of view between lens and viewfinder

**passport photo** small head shot in standard size for use on passport

**photograph** image produced on sensitized surface by action of radiant energy, esp. light; shot

**plate** glass or plastic sheet coated with light-sensitive emulsion to be exposed, developed, and printed as photograph

**platinum process** contact printing process that gives photograph a very beautiful, silver hue with long tonal ranges, used for long-lasting archival pictures for museums

**positive** film that records light and shade tones similar to original image

**power pack** portable DC power supply, esp. for flash

**print** exposed, developed image on photographic paper; (*vb*) project image onto light-sensitive paper or contact sheet

**projection** display of slides or transparencies on screen by shining light through them

**proof sheet** contact sheet

**range** distance from camera to subject

**range finder** focusing system that measures distance from camera to subject, sometimes coupled to camera lens so that both work together

**reel** revolvable cylinder around which film is wound for development

**reflector** any substance used as background to reflect light

**resolution** sharpness of photographic image; ability of camera to record distinct detail

**reversal** any positive-to-positive, rather than negative-to-positive, printing process

**safelight** darkroom light that has no effect on film and paper

**seamless** *Informal.* backdrop consisting of no-seam paper

**semigloss** (*adj*) designating most common surface of paper for color prints

**sepia** print or photograph made in a brownish hue that resembles sepia

**sheet film** film that comes in single sheets, each of which produces one negative, as for 4x5 or 8x10 camera format

**shoot** (*vb*) take a photograph; (*n*) photographic session

**shot** photograph

**shutter** mechanical system that controls the length of time that light acts on sensitive emulsion by opening and closing aperture

**shutterbug** *Slang.* photography enthusiast

**shutter-priority** (*adj*) designating semiautomatic exposure system in which shutter speed is selected and camera sets aperture, used esp. to convey motion

**slave unit** mechanism that simultaneously fires a flash source when a photoelectric cell is activated by illumination from the camera linked to the flash

**slide** developed, mounted color-film exposure

**snapshot** informal, nonstudio photograph

**snoot** cone-shaped shield on strobe or spotlight that directs light over smaller, controlled area

**soft box process** process in which flash or spot is thrown through box, instead of using umbrella as light diffuser

**soft focus** photograph with indistinct outlines of images

**solarization** full or partial reversal of image by extreme overexposure

**speed** length of time shutter remains open to record image; sensitivity of film, expressed numerically as ASA rating

**spotlight** intense light directed on specific area

**still** photographic print of motion picture scene

**stock house** photo agency that sells photographer's stock photos to periodicals but does not make assignments

**stop bath** chemical solution that halts development of film or print

**strobe** electronic flash, balanced like blue daylight at 5200° K

**studio** professional photographer's specially equipped room for shooting photographs

**tank** cylinder or box containing developing solution

**tear sheet** proof sheet of single or multiple images torn from printed matter

**time exposure** exposure of film for more than one-half second, usu. to take photograph without sufficient light

**toner** solution used to impart color or hue to silver photographic image, such as in cyanotype, gold tone, palladium, platinum, or selenium process

**transparency** film negative viewed by projection of light shining through it

**tripod** three-legged support used to hold camera steady

**tungsten light** orange, halogen-quartz light source at 3200° K, used esp. for motion pictures and portraits

**umbrella** color-corrected white, silver, or gold concave material used to bounce light onto subject

**underexposure** film exposed to insufficient light or radiation

**viewfinder** finder indicating focus

**vignette** photograph gradually lightened or darkened at its edges to leave no definite line at border

# CRAFTS

Ceramics and Glassmaking
Other Crafts

**SEE ALSO**: Chap. 10: Fashion and Garment Parts; Chap. 14: Painting; Chap. 16: Graphic Design and Printing; Chap. 17: Hobbies

## CERAMICS AND GLASSMAKING

**agateware** pottery variegated to resemble agate

**argil** potter's clay

**ash glaze** semitransparent glaze containing wood ashes

**aventurine** opaque, brown glass with fine, golden particles

**banding wheel** hand-operated turntable for coiling or decorating pots

**basaltware** unglazed Wedgwood stoneware, usu. black with dull gloss

**bat** removable disc atop potter's wheel

**batch** raw materials mixed in proper proportions for making glass

**bat wash** flint wash used on kiln shelf to prevent sticking during glost firing

**Belleek ware** fragile, Irish porcelain with bright luster

**biscuit** once-fired clay object, before glazing; bisque

**bisque** biscuit

**blister** glaze fault caused by impurities

**bloat** ceramic fault caused by impurities in clay

**blow** (*vb*) shape glass with steady current of air

**blow mold** hinged mold for shaping molten glass

**blowpipe** long metal tube used to gather and blow molten glass

**blunger** tank with mechanical arms for blending clay and water

**bone china** fine, naturally white china made with bone ash

**celadon** greenish, iron-containing glaze used in Oriental porcelain and stoneware

**ceramics** manufacture of works of art by firing of earthenware, porcelain, or brick at high temperature; works so produced

**china** delicate porcelain ceramic ware

**clay** potter's clay

**cone** pyrometric cone

**crackle** cracking of glaze after firing; craze

**crackleware** ceramic ware with finely cracked glaze

**crank** kiln shelf

**craze** crackle

**crockery** earthenware

**cullet** glass scraps that can be remelted

**dead clay** overly wet clay

**delft** glazed earthenware, usu. blue and white

**dod box** device for forming pottery handles

**Dresden china** porcelain ware produced near Dresden, Germany, characterized by dainty design

**dunt** (*vb*) crack because of sudden cooling, said of ceramic ware

**earthenware** coarse wares of kiln-baked clay; crockery

**elephant ear sponge** fine-grained surfacing tool for working clay

**enamelware** metalware or pottery covered with a glassy, opaque enamel surface

**engobe** coating of white slip

**faience** glazed earthenware for blocks or tiles

**fat clay** plastic, easily workable clay

**fettling knife** sharp, pointed blade for finishing surfaces

**fictile** (*adj*) made of earth or clay by a potter

**firing** baking ceramic objects in hot oven

**flux** material used to lower melting point of glaze

**frit** flux and silica compound for strengthening porcelain

**gaffer** master glassblower who shapes glassware

**glacure** thin glaze for fine pottery

**glass** hard, transparent substance formed by melting silica and soda ash

**glassblowing** art and practice of shaping a mass of molten glass by blowing air into it through a tube

**glassmaking** art and technique of making glass, usu. by fusing silicates containing soda and lime

**glaze** glossy, vitreous, waterproof coating fused by heat to pottery; glost; (*vb*) apply such a surface to a ceramic

**glost** clay ware with glaze applied but not yet fired

**graffito** technique of scratching design through glaze

**graniteware** pottery with speckled, granitelike appearance

**greenware** unfired ceramics

**grog** fired and crushed clay, added to fresh clay to reduce plasticity and shrinkage or give texture

**hard** (*adj*) fired at high temperature

**hollowware** deep ceramic dishes

**impasto** enamel or slip forming low-relief decoration on ceramic object

**ironstone** hard, white ceramic ware

**jasperware** fine, hard Wedgwood stoneware, stained in various colors by metallic oxides, with raised designs in white

**jigger** machine for forming ceramic objects in a plaster mold rotating beneath a template

**kaolin** pure, fine-grained white clay

**kiln** oven for firing pottery

**lead glass** glass containing lead oxide

**lean clay** unpliable clay; short clay

**limekiln** kiln in which limestone and shells are burned

**luster** metallic, iridescent sheen of glaze

**majolica** enameled, richly colored Italian pottery

**Ming** (*adj*) designating fine porcelains in brilliant colors made during Ming dynasty (China, 15th-17th c.)

**mishima** decoration of pottery by carving raw clay and filling the cuts with different-colored clay

**muffle** protective box around kiln flames

**nankeen** Chinese porcelain having blue ornament on white background

**overglaze** additional glaze or color applied to an existing glaze

**oxidation** firing with oxygen-rich flame

**paddling** beating clay with stick to shape or decorate it

**pallet** flat board or metal plate used to support ceramic objects during drying

**Parian** (*adj*) denoting fine, unglazed, marblelike porcelain

**porcelain** hard, white, nonporous ceramic ware composed of kaolin, feldspar, and quartz

**pot** usu. round earthenware vessel of any size

**potsherd** broken pottery fragment

**potter's clay** finely textured, pliable earth that is free of impurities and suitable for making ceramic objects: argil, ball, china, fire clay, kaolin, petuntse, porcelain, refractory, terra cotta

**potter's wheel** revolving disc for throwing pottery forms, usu. foot-operated; wheel

**pottery** clay objects, either glazed or unglazed, shaped and hardened by heat: Albin ware, basalt, biscuit, blackware, bone china, china, crackleware, delft, Dresden china, earthenware, eggshell porcelain, faience, Imari ware, ironstone, Leeds pottery, Limoges, lusterware, majolica, Meissen, porcelain, saltglaze, Satsuma ware, Sèvres ware, Spode, spongeware, stoneware, terra cotta, Wedgwood

**pressed glass** molded glass shaped while molten by thrusting plunger into mold

**primary clay** clay found at natural site

**prunt** small lump of glass fused to larger glass piece

**pug mill** machine used to mix clay

**punty** iron rod used in handling hot glass in glassmaking

**pyrometer** device used to measure kiln temperature

**pyrometric cone** ceramic cone calibrated to melt at exact temperature, giving visual indication of kiln temperature; cone; Seger cone

**raku** open-air, high-firing technique that produces rough, dark, lead-glazed earthenware (Japan)

**raw** (*adj*) unfired

**reduction** high-temperature firing

**refractory** (*adj*) having high heat resistance

**relief** decoration raised above surface of piece

**resist** decoration by treating selected areas so that they reject slip or glaze

**sagger** box of clay for packing ceramic ware in kiln

**salt glaze** process in which salt is vaporized in kiln to leave pebbly texture on piece

**Seger cone** pyrometric cone

**semiporcelain** vitreous ceramic ware similar to but less hard and translucent than true porcelain

**short clay** lean clay

**sieve** sifter for removing clay lumps

**slip** watery, liquid clay for decorating and cementing biscuit

**slip glaze** glaze containing plastic clay, applied to raw earthenware

**slob** lumpy waste clay

**slurry** watery clay

**smalt** blue coloring agent for vitreous materials

**soft** (*adj*) fired at low temperature

**Spode** *Trademark.* fine porcelain or china

**spun glass** blown glass in which fine threads form surface texture

**stoneware** high-fired clay pottery, often glazed with salt

**terra cotta** hard, brown-red, unglazed earthenware

**terre verte** glazing clay

**throw** (*vb*) form pottery on wheel

**underglaze** color or decoration applied to piece before glazing

**vitreous** (*adj*) resembling glass in transparency, brittleness, hardness, or glossiness

**vitrification** fusing of clay body to state of glasslike imperviousness

**ware** ceramic objects

**wash** thin coating of glaze

**wedge** (*vb*) pound clay to remove air bubbles and improve workability

**Wedgwood** *Trademark.* brand of ceramic ware orig. made in 18th century by Josiah Wedgwood, typically basaltware and jasperware in blue-gray color

**wheel** potter's wheel

**willowware** china using decorative design of willow tree, bridge, and two birds (Britain, 18th c.)

**zaffer** cobalt oxide mixture that produces blue color in glass and ceramic glazes

## OTHER CRAFTS

**amber craft** making jewelry from brownish-yellow fossil resin

**appliqué** decoration, as a cutout design, sewn on to a piece of material

**assemblage** arrangement of a collection of objects in aesthetic relationships or curious juxtapositions

**basketry** crafting of functional or decorative containers by interweaving strips of grass, reed, or other flexible material

**batik** technique of hand-dyeing patterns on fabric by using wax to resist dyes

**beadworking** decorative working or weaving of beads onto surface of clothing, accessories, or household objects; stringing of beads, as to produce a necklace

**block printing** printing with ink from engraved blocks of wood or other hard material

**boneworking** making of jewelry and other decorative objects from animal bones

**bookbinding** craft of encasing books, esp. in fine leather or buckram

**bookcraft** making of books with particular attention to paper, printing techniques, folding of pages, and binding

**burlap crafting** making of objects, such as lampshades or wall hangings, out of burlap, which is often painted or decorated with other materials

**cabinetmaking** process or craft of making fine furniture and other woodwork

**calligraphy** art of highly decorative handwriting, as with many flourishes

**candlemaking** forming of candles by dripping, pouring, rolling, or casting wax, paraffin, or tallow around a cotton wick

**caning** making of articles by interweaving slender, flexible stems of certain plants

**carving** making of articles by cutting, shaping, or chipping a hard substance, as a block of wood

**casting** process or craft of making forms in plaster or resin from a mold

**ceramics** craft of making fired earthenware, porcelain, or brick pottery; pottery

**chenille work** making of small figures from a wire core covered with soft chenille fabric

**cloissoné** enamelwork in which the enamel surface is set in hollows between wires soldered on metal

**copper enameling** process in which heat is used to fuse enamel powder colored with copper oxide to surface of articles; etui

**coralworking** making jewelry from the pinkish, hard skeletal deposit of certain marine polyps

**cork pictures** making decorative objects by burning holes in a cork surface with a hot wire or bradawl, then inserting other substances, such as moss or bark, into the holes

**corrugated cardboard crafting** cutting and shaping three-dimensional decorative objects out of corrugated cardboard

**craft** any art, trade, or occupation requiring the skilled working of materials to form decorative or useful objects, often practiced as a recreational activity; handicraft

**crewelwork** decorative embroidery done with crewel yarn on cotton or linen, employing simple stitches worked in floral patterns

**crocheting** knitting with a hooked needle that draws thread or yarn through intertwined loops

**cut-paper collage** decoupage

**damascening** craft of making gold inlays

**decalcomania** process of transferring designs from specially prepared paper to wood, metal, or glass

**déchirage** making of collages with torn paper, esp. Japanese paper

**decoupage** technique of decorating a surface with paper cutouts; cut-paper collage

**discharge printing** bleaching designs onto dyed fabric

**doll making** making of small figures shaped like humans, usu. as toys, esp. out of paper, fabric, rag, or wood

**dyeing** process of tinting fabric or other absorbent material with colorants derived from plant extracts or synthetic chemicals

**egg decorating** painting on the shells of eggs whose contents have been blown out through a tiny hole

**embossing** decorating surfaces with raised ornamentation

**embroidery** working of raised and ornamental designs with a needle on woven fabric using contrasting or brightly colored thread

**enameling** fusing of clear, glassy flux of silica and potash, colored with metal oxides, to surface of metal or pottery as ornamentation

**engraving** cutting or corroding of designs into hard surfaces, such as metal or wood, which are usually inked for making impressions

**etching** technique of making designs on a metal plate or glass by the corrosive action of acid

**etui** copper enameling

**fabric making** weaving

**fabric painting** process of painting designs on fabric

**featherwork** making of decorative objects out of feathers

**felt crafting** cutting of designs and decorative objects out of felt, which is sometimes painted on

**fiber arts** design and crafting of objects from natural fibers or fibrous materials

**flower making** art or technique of making artificial flowers out of cut, folded, and mounted crêpe, tissue paper, or other stiff fabric

**fraktur** stylized and highly decorative watercolor painting, often bearing elaborate calligraphy

**frottage** technique in which textural effects or images are obtained by rubbing lead, chalk, crayon, or charcoal over paper laid on a granular or relief surface; rubbing

**gem cutting** craft of cutting and engraving gemstones; lapidary

**glassblowing** shaping of molten glass by blowing air into it through a tube

**glass etching** etching of designs onto glass with acid

**glass painting** painting of images and designs on plate glass

**handicraft** craft

**ikat** method of printing woven fabrics by tie-dyeing warp yarns, weft yarns, or both before weaving, used esp. in Malaysia and Africa

**ikebana** Japanese art of arranging flowers in highly aesthetic designs, based on one of four traditional styles: Moribana, Nageire, Rikka, or Seika

**inlay** design or decoration made by inserting or applying layers of fine materials, such as gold or silver, in surface of object

**intaglio** process by which a design is incised or engraved into surface of plate or other object

**ivoryworking** carving of decorative objects out of elephant tusks

**jetworking** craft of making beads, jewelry, buttons, or other items from polished, dense, black coal

**jewelry making** design and production of ornamental objects, such as rings, earrings, or necklaces, worn for adornment, using materials such as precious and semiprecious stones and metals, glass, bones, feathers, shells, beads, and wood

**jewelsmithing** making of jewelry, esp. with cut stones

**kitemaking** design and construction of kites that are both aesthetically pleasing and aerodynamically sound

**knitting** interlacing loops of yarn to form decorative or functional garments and accessories

**lacemaking** crafting of fine, openwork fabrics in ornamental designs

**lacquerwork** process of coating wood with resinous varnish obtained as sap from Japanese tree

**lapidary** gem cutting

**leathercrafting** methods or techniques of making clothing and accessories, esp. for decorative or functional use, from animal hides that have been stripped of hair or wool

**lithography** printing process using stone slab, or zinc or aluminum plate, marked with greasy ink

**macramé** technique of making elaborately patterned knotwork with hand-knotted twine or rope, used esp. for wall decorations and hangings

**marbling** process of coloring or staining in imitation of marble by swirling ink or oil colors on water, then lowering paper onto its surface to pick up the design

**maskmaking** craft of forming coverings for the face from papier-mâché, wood, plaster of Paris, or other materials

**metalworking** process of shaping articles out of metal

**mizuhiki** Japanese craft in which bundles of wire are covered tightly in gold or silver paper and interwoven into delicate, symmetrical shapes

**mobile making** arranging of delicately balanced metal, paper, or plastic shapes that are suspended in midair from wire so as to move freely in air currents

**mosaic** making of designs by inlaying small pieces of colored stone, tile, or glass in mortar

**needlecrafts** handicrafts involving sewing with cloth or threads: crocheting, knitting, embroidery, crewel, needlepoint, quilting, rug hooking, trapunto

**needlepoint** embroidery using woolen yarn, esp. on canvas, usu. with uniform spacing of stitches

**needlework** art and process of working with a needle, esp. in embroidery, needlepoint, tapestry, quilting, and appliqué

**niello** ornamental work produced by inlaying metal with a black metallic substance consisting of silver, copper, lead, and sulfur

**origami** Japanese decorative art of folding paper to form recognizable shapes, esp. animals

**papercraft** making of decorative objects by cutting and folding paper; making of fine paper products

**paper flower making** craft or technique of forming artificial flowers from paper

**papermaking** handmaking of fine paper from pulp and size that is mixed with rag, linen, leaves, or other materials

**paper sculpture** making of decorative objects by cutting and folding paper into shapes

**papier-mâché** forming decorative objects from substance made of pulped paper or of rags or paper soaked in glue, formed into shapes when moist and becoming hard when dried

**patchwork** sewing together of pieces of cloth of various colors and shapes

**pebble-and-stone polishing** burnishing the surfaces of pebbles or small stones to produce smooth sheens and bring out their colors

**perfumery** art of blending natural and synthetic scents to make perfume

**pin and thread** process in which many pins are pushed into a soft base, such as cork or padded fabric, and thread is stretched back-and-forth around the pins to create intricate geometric patterns

**plaiting and braiding** interlacing of three or more lengths of yarn to create strong, decorative strips

**plastics** making of objects from molded plastic

**pokerwork** pyrography

**poonah work**  painting or stenciling on velvet; theorem painting

**potato printing**  cutting of relief designs in raw potato and using it to make prints

**pottery**  making or collecting of decorative and functional vessels of fired clay; ceramics

**printmaking**  art or technique of impressing designs on cloth or other material

**puppetry**  making of and performing with small, painted, clothed figures operated by finger, hand, rod, sticks, or strings

**pyrography**  process of burning designs on leather, wood, acrylics, or foam with heated tool such as electric pen; pokerwork

**quillwork**  craft in which stiff paper is cut in strips, rolled tightly, and glued on surface such as small box to form patterns

**quilting**  creation and collection of needlework or patchwork bedcovers, often antique

**raffia**  fiber obtained from raffia palm, used to make baskets, hats, and mats

**repoussage**  embossing by hammering designs on metal

**resist printing**  process of printing designs on cloth with paste of flour and water that acts like wax in batik to resist dyes

**rubbing**  frottage

**rug hooking**  creating patterned rugs with a hooked tool

**rugmaking**  weaving of rugs

**rushwork**  weaving of rush stems into chair bottoms or mats

**scrapcraft**  cutting and assembling of discarded and found objects, such as egg cartons, bottle caps, corks, ice cream sticks, paper clips, nut shells, pine cones, or leaves, into decorative objects

**scrimshaw**  carving or engraving of ivory, bone, or shell

**seed collage**  sorting and arranging colored seeds into mosaic pattern on some surface

**serigraphy**  silkscreening

**sewing**  process of creating or repairing garments by stitches

**shell carving**  forming of decorative objects from shells

**shellwork**  coloring, assembly, and arranging of shells to form decorative designs and shapes

**silhouetting**  making of cutout profiles of figures in black paper

**silkscreen**  printing process using inked silk cloth, mounted on frame, to which stencil film is affixed, esp. used for posters and clothing; serigraphy

**spinning**  making of yarn or threads from fibers or filaments

**stained glass work**  design and creation of objects, esp. windows and lampshades, from colored glass pieces, usu. joined by leaded strips

**stenciling**  printing process in which ink or paint is applied to sheets perforated with designs or letters

**stitchery**  decorative needlework, including embroidery or crewelwork

**straw working**  practice of weaving, cutting, and assembling dried straw to form baskets and other objects

**string pictures**  technique of gluing various types of string, thread, and yarn on surface to form design

**textiles**  making cloth by weaving or knitting

**theorem painting**  poonah work

**tie-dyeing**  creating of designs on textiles by tying parts of the cloth so they will not absorb dye or forming barrier to dye with a clip or rubber band

**tincrafting**  making of objects out of tin, sometimes using tin cans, often with patterns cut or punched into the metal

**toymaking**  handcrafting of children's playthings

**trapunto**  quilting done in high relief through two or more layers of cloth, produced by padding a stitched pattern with yarn or cotton

**tritik**  form of tie-dying in which strong thread is stitched along line through fabric and pulled tight to exclude dye

**watermark design**  making designs on paper by laying wire in the sieve on which paper pulp is poured, so that where wire touches pulp it dries to a more compact surface than surrounding paper, resulting in a design that shows up in light

**weaving**  design and creation of fabrics, rugs, or textiles on a loom by interlacing threads or yarns; fabric making

**whittling**  carving of decorative or functional objects by trimming and shaping a stick of wood

**wickerworking**  making objects consisting of interlaced willow, twigs, or rods

**wood engraving**  cutting of designs in end-grained block of wood

**woodworking**  carving and shaping of articles in wood

**yarn making**  spinning of natural fibers to make yarn

# CHAPTER 17

# Leisure and Recreation

# HOLIDAYS, CELEBRATIONS, AND VACATIONS

Annual National and Religious Holidays
Celebrations, Observances, Rites, and Gatherings
Parties and Partying
Vacations and Interludes
Travel and Tourism

**SEE ALSO:** Chap. 17: Entertainments and Spectacles;
Drinking and Alcoholic Beverages; Chap. 25: Religion

## ANNUAL NATIONAL AND RELIGIOUS HOLIDAYS

**Admission Day** U.S.: date on which state entered Union, which varies by state

**Advent** Christian: beginning fourth Sunday before Christmas, period of fasting and prayer through Christmas celebrating Jesus' birth and anticipating his second coming

**Allhallows** All Saints' Day

**All Saints' Day** Christian: November 1, feast day to honor martyrs and saints; Allhallows

**All Souls' Day** Christian: November 2, day to pray for and honor departed souls

**American Indian Day** U.S.: fourth Friday in September, honoring Native Americans

**Anzac Day** Australia and New Zealand: April 25, commemorating landing of troops on Gallipoli, Turkey, in World War I

**April Fools' Day** April 1, traditional day for playing jokes

**Arab League Day** March 22, observed by most Arab nations

**Arbor Day** U.S.: last Friday in April, set aside for preserving trees, often by planting, and encouraging environmental awareness

**Armed Forces Day** U.S.: third Saturday in May, honoring the members of armed forces

**Armistice Day** Veterans Day

**Ascension Day** Christian: tenth day before Pentecost, forty days after Easter, feast day commemorating Christ's departure from Earth to heaven

**Ash Wednesday** Christian: first day of Lent, forty days before Easter

**Assumption Day** Christian: August 15, feast day commemorating Virgin Mary's ascension to heaven

**Australia Day** Australia: January 29, national holiday commemorating arrival of British

**autumnal equinox** U.S.: September 22, first day of fall

**Bairam** Id al-Adha Islamic, festival following Ramadan

**Bastille Day** France: July 14, celebrating beginning of French Revolution

**Bon** Japan: July, feast of lanterns honoring ancestral spirits

**Boxing Day** Great Britain: December 26, day after Christmas, originally celebrated by giving Christmas boxes or gifts to service workers and domestics

**Canada Day** Canada: July 1, commemorating union of provinces into a nation; Dominion Day

**Candlemas** Christian: February 2, celebrating presentations of Christ child and purification of Virgin Mary

**Carnival** Mardi Gras

**Chinese New Year** first new moon after sun enters Aquarius, in late January or early February, festive celebration of new year in Chinese calendar

**Christmas** Christian: December 25, holiday honoring the birth of Christ; Noel

**Christmas** Christian: January 6 on Eastern Orthodox Julian calendar

**Christmas Eve** Christian: December 24, day or evening before Christmas

**Cinco de Mayo** Mexico: May 5, holiday commemorating the defeat of Napoleon III's forces in 1867

**Columbus Day** U.S.: second Monday in October, orig. October 12, commemorating of Columbus's landing in America in 1492

**Commonwealth Day** British Commonwealth: May 24, anniversary of Queen Victoria's birthday

**Confucius's birthday** China: around September 28, commemorating birth of Confucius

**Constitution Day** formerly in Soviet Union: December 5

**Corpus Christi** Christian: eleventh day after Pentecost, festival celebrated by Catholics honoring the Eucharist

**Decoration Day** Memorial Day

**Diwali** Hindu: late October, festival of lights celebrated in India

**Dominion Day** Canada Day

**Easter** Christian: first Sunday after full moon, occurring on or after March 21, celebrating resurrection of Christ

**Election Day** U.S.: first Tuesday after first Monday in November, reserved for electing public officials

**Emperor's birthday** Japan: April 29, day honoring birth of emperor

**Epiphany** Christian: January 6, twelfth day after Christmas, celebrating the Magi's visit to Jesus and Jesus' baptism

**Father's Day** U.S.: third Sunday in June, honoring fathers

**Flag Day** U.S.: June 14, anniversary of adoption of American flag in 1777

**Flower Festival** Japan: April 8, Hana Matsuri, the spring flower festival

**Fourth of July** U.S. Independence Day

**Gandhi's birthday** India: October 2, honoring India's independence leader Mahatma Gandhi

**Good Friday** Christian: Friday before Easter, commemorating Christ's crucifixion

**Groundhog Day** U.S.: February 2, traditional day for predicting spring's arrival by observing a groundhog's shadow, indicating six more weeks of winter, or lack of shadow, indicating spring is imminent

**Guy Fawkes Day** Great Britain: November 5, celebrating capture of Guy Fawkes, who blew up Parliament in 1605

**Halloween** U.S. and Canada: October 31, festive tradition including dressing in costume, trick-or-treating, and playing pranks

**Hanukkah** Jewish: eight days beginning twenty-fifth day of Kislev (December), festival of lights marking rededication of Temple of Jerusalem and miracle of oil lamp that burned for eight days on a one-day supply of oil

**High Holy Day** Jewish: Rosh Hashanah or Yom Kippur

**Holi** Hindu: spring festival celebrated in India by lighting of fires on Holi eve and throwing of water and colored powders during day

**Human Rights Day** December 10, observed by member states of United Nations

**Immaculate Conception** Roman Catholic: December 8, honoring Virgin Mary's freedom from original sin in conception

**'Id al-Adha** Islamic: major four-day festival beginning on tenth day of last month of calendar; Bairam

**Inauguration Day** U.S.: January 20 following presidential election, day of inauguration of newly elected president

**Independence Day** Israel: celebrated in April or May

**Independence Day** Mexico: September 16, celebrating revolution of 1810

**Independence Day** U.S.: July 4, honoring adoption of Declaration of Independence by American colonies in 1776; Fourth of July

**Islamic New Year's Day** vernal equinox, around March 21, celebrating first day of Islamic calendar

**Jefferson Davis's birthday** southern U.S.: June 3, celebrating birth of president of the Confederacy

**Kenyatta Day** Kenya: October 20, honoring Jomo Kenyatta

**Kwanza** African: December 26 to January 1, harvest festival

**Labor Day** U.S. and Canada: first Monday in September, honoring workers

**Lammas** Christian: August 1, in memory of St. Peter's imprisonment and deliverance; English harvest festival

**Lenin Memorial Day** formerly in Soviet Union: April 22, honoring Vladimir Ilyich Lenin, leader of socialist revolution of 1917 in Russia

**Lent** Christian: forty days from Ash Wednesday to Easter Sunday, period of penitence and fasting in preparation for Easter

**Lincoln's birthday** U.S.: February 12, celebrating birth in 1809 of U.S. President Abraham Lincoln, now celebrated on Presidents' Day

**Mardi Gras** Christian: Tuesday immediately before beginning of Lent, celebrated by feasting, carnivals, and parades; Carnival

**Martin Luther King Day** U.S.: January 15, celebrating birth of civil rights leader Dr. Martin Luther King, Jr.

**Martinmas** Christian: November 11, celebrating feast of St. Martin

**Maundy Thursday** Christian: Thursday before Easter, commemorating Christ's Last Supper

**May Day** May 1, traditional spring festival, also international holiday honoring workers

**Memorial Day** U.S.: May 30, honoring soldiers who died in battle; Decoration Day

**Michaelmas** Christian: September 29, feast of the archangel St. Michael

**Midsummer Day** Great Britain: June 24, feast of St. John the Baptist; traditional night when spirits are believed to wander

**Moharram** Islamic: first month of Islamic calendar, festival held during first ten days of new year

**Mother's Day** U.S.: second Sunday in May, honoring mothers

**Muhammad's birthday** Islamic: June 8, celebrating birth of prophet Muhammad

**National Day** People's Republic of China: October 1

**National Day** Spain: July 18

**National Unity Day** Italy: November 4

**New Year's Day** January 1, first day of new year on Gregorian calendar

**New Year's Eve** December 31, celebrating last day and night of year on Gregorian calendar

**Noel** Christmas

**October Revolution Day** formerly in Soviet Union: November 7, celebrating socialist revolution of 1917, when Bolsheviks seized power in Russia

**Omisoka** Japan: December 31, Grand Last Day celebration, equivalent to New Year's Eve

**Palm Sunday** Christian: Sunday before Easter, commemorating Christ's triumphal entry into Jerusalem

**Pan American Day** U.S. and Latin America: April 14, honoring understanding and cooperation among the Americas

**Passover** Jewish: eight days beginning fourteenth day of Nisan (March or April), commemorating Hebrews' deliverance by Moses from slavery in Egypt; Pesach

**Peach Festival** Japan: March 3, day when young girls decorate ceremonial dolls with peach blossoms to symbolize peacefulness

**Pentecost** Christian: seventh Sunday after Easter, commemorating arrival of Holy Spirit to the apostles; Whitsunday

**Pesach** Passover

**Posadas** Christian, esp. Mexico: December 16 to 24, commemorating Joseph and Mary's search for shelter

**Presidents' Day** U.S.: third Monday in February, interim date celebrating birthdays of Washington (February 22) and Lincoln (February 12)

**Purim** Jewish: fourteenth day of Adar (March), celebrating Persian Jews' deliverance by Esther from massacre by Haman

**Queen's birthday** Great Britain: April 21, but celebrated in June, honoring birthday of queen

**Ramadan** Islamic: ninth month of Islamic calendar, period of fasting commemorating revelation of the Koran to Mohammed

**Reformation Sunday** Protestant: Sunday nearest October 31, commemorating day Martin Luther began the Reformation

**Republic Day** India: January 26, commemorating founding of Republic of India

**Respect for the Aged Day** Japan: September 15, honoring the elderly

**Robert E. Lee's birthday** southern U.S.: January 19, celebrating birth of Confederate commander in chief

**Rosh Hashanah** Jewish: New Year, first day of Tishri (September or October)

**Sadie Hawkins Day** U.S.: first Saturday after November 11, when women invite men to dance or celebrate

**Saint Patrick's Day** March 17, honoring Saint Patrick, patron saint of Ireland

**Saint Stephen's Day** Roman Catholic: December 26, honoring patron saint of bricklayers in Europe

**Saint Valentine's Day** Valentine Day

**Shavuot** Jewish: sixth or seventh day of Sivan (June), commemorating revelation of Ten Commandments to Moses at Mount Sinai

**Shrovetide** Christian: three days before Ash Wednesday, time of feasting in preparation for Lent

**Shrove Tuesday** Christian: last day of Shrovetide

**Simon Bolivar's birthday**  Latin America, esp. Ecuador and Venezuela: July 24, honoring leader of South American revolt against Spain in early 19th century

**Spring Bank Holiday**  Great Britain: last Monday in May, official public holiday in spring originating from Christian holiday Whitsuntide

**Sukkoth**  Jewish: beginning fifteenth day of Tishri (October or November), Feast of Tabernacles, celebrating fall harvest and commemorating period when Hebrews wandered in wilderness after Exodus, marked by building of shelters

**summer solstice**  June 21 in Northern Hemisphere, first day of summer

**Tet**  Vietnam: New Year, ocurring first new moon after sun enters Aquarius, late January or early February

**Thanksgiving Day**  U.S.: fourth Thursday in November, day of giving thanks, commemorating Pilgrims' harvest festival

**Trinity Sunday**  Christian: seventh day after Pentecost, honoring the Holy Trinity

**Twelfth Night**  Christian: January 5 or 6, eve of Epiphany

**United Nation's Day**  October 24, celebrating ratification of U.N. Charter in 1945

**Valentine Day**  February 14, day for sending messages or gifts of love; Saint Valentine's Day

**V-E Day**  May 8, anniversary of Allied victory in Europe at end of World War II

**vernal equinox**  March 21 or 22, first day of spring

**Veterans Day**  U.S.: November 11, honoring veterans of armed forces and commemorating end of World War I; Armistice Day

**V-J Day**  August 14, anniversary of Allied victory in Japan at end of World War II

**Walpurgis Night**  eve of May Day, April 30, believed in medieval times to be night when witches celebrate their sabbath

**Washington's birthday**  U.S.: February 22, celebrating birth in 1732 of George Washington, first U.S. president, now celebrated on Presidents' Day

**Whitsunday**  Pentecost

**Whitsuntide**  Christian: week beginning with Whitsunday or Pentecost, esp. first three days of that week

**winter solstice**  December 21 in Northern Hemisphere, first day of winter

**Women's Day**  March 8, honoring work of women, esp. in socialist states

**World Health Day**  April 7, observed by member states of the United Nations

**Xmas**  Christmas

**Yom Kippur**  Jewish: tenth day of Tishri (September or October), day of atonement marked by fasting and prayer

## CELEBRATIONS, OBSERVANCES, RITES, AND GATHERINGS

**affair**  social gathering or event

**anniversary**  annual recurrence of special date, esp. wedding day

**assemblage**  gathering of persons for specific purpose

**at home**  reception at one's residence; open house

**ball**  large, lavish, usu. formal dance

**bank holiday**  legal holiday on which banks close (Britain)

**banquet**  lavish meal for many people, esp. ceremonial or honorific

**baptism**  sacrament of admission into Christian church, enacted by sprinkling of water on child

**bar mitzvah**  initiation ceremony marking coming of age of thirteen-year-old Jewish boy

**barn dance**  American social dance, orig. held in barn

**bas mitzvah**  bat mitzvah

**bat mitzvah**  initiation ceremony marking coming of age of thirteen-year-old Jewish girl; bas mitzvah

**beanfeast**  *Chiefly Brit. slang.* formerly, annual dinner given by employer for employees

**bee**  gathering for specific purpose, often for a competition; such as a spelling bee

**benefit**  public performance, dinner, or gathering, proceeds of which go to certain person, group, or cause

**birthday**  annual observance of day one was born

**black-tie** (*adj*) designating formal affair to which tuxedo is worn

**bonfire**  large, open-air fire, usu. at night, around which people gather

**box social**  fund-raiser auction with box lunches

**bris**  Jewish rite of circumcision

**call**  social visit paid to another's home

**callithump**  noisy parade

**carnival**  period, usu. several days, of feasting and merrymaking, esp. before Lent

**cavalcade**  formal procession of vehicles

**celebration**  instance or observation of holiday, religious ceremony, or festivity

**ceremony**  formal act in observance of ritual or holiday

**church feast**  festive observance of religious holiday, esp. saint's day

**clambake**  outdoor social gathering, esp. at beach with food baked on hot rocks

**cocktail party**  informal gathering, usu. in early evening, where refreshments are served but not a complete meal

**coffee klatsch**  informal gathering for conversation at which coffee is served; kaffee klatsch

**coming out**  debut in formal society

**commemoration**  celebration in memory of someone or something

**commencement**  ceremony at which school or college degrees are conferred

**communion**  Christian sacrament commemorating Christ's death by taking bread and wine

**confirmation**  generally nonsacramental Christian rite of admission to full church membership

**corroboree**  nocturnal festivity with song and ceremonial dance (Australian aborigine)

**cotillion**  formal dance, esp. honoring debut

**dance**  social gathering for purpose of dancing to music

**date**  appointment for social engagement, esp. with member of opposite sex; such an engagement

**debut**  party and dance honoring young woman's entrance into formal society; coming out

**dinner**  gathering to eat evening meal, esp. feast or banquet

**event**  noteworthy social occasion

**extravaganza**  extremely elaborate or lavish social event

**fair**  gathering, often over several days at one place, for feasting and amusements, usu. with exhibition of goods for sale

**feast** elaborate meal or banquet, often ceremonial

**feria** *Spanish*. market fair or festival, often on church holiday

**-fest** suffix added to indicate festival or celebration, as in sunfest or lovefest

**festival** period of celebration, feasting, and special observances

**festive occasion** joyous celebration that usu. includes feasting

**festivity** festival or festive gathering

**fête** *French*. festival; elaborate party or outdoor gathering, often commemorative

**fête champêtre** *French*. outdoor entertainment

**fiesta** processions, festivities, and dances on saint's day (Spain, Latin America)

**formal** dance to which men wear tuxedos and women wear gowns

**function** formal ceremony or large social gathering

**funeral** ceremony of burial or cremation of the dead; procession accompanying corpse to final resting place

**gala** celebration marking special occasion, esp. opening of public entertainment

**gathering** any assemblage of several persons for a specific, often social or ceremonial, purpose

**gaudy** joyous celebration, esp. reunion (Britain)

**get-together** informal social gathering

**harvest home** feast at end of harvest season

**high tea** substantial late afternoon snack at which tea is served, esp. in Britain

**holiday** day commemorating an event, usu. by suspension of work and other regular activities; *Chiefly Brit*. vacation

**holiday season** last two months of the year in United States, including Halloween, Thanksgiving, Christmas and Hanukkah, and New Year's Eve

**homecoming** occasion marking return of group of people to their home, esp. annual celebration of university alumni

**honeymoon** vacation taken by newlyweds immediately after wedding

**hootenanny** informal folk or country song performance, often with audience sing-along

**hop** informal dance, often to recorded music

**house party** gathering at one's residence, often over more than one night

**housewarming** party celebrating one's move to a new home

**jamboree** large, festive gathering, often with mixed entertainment

**jubilee** special anniversary, esp. twenty-fifth, fiftieth, or sixtieth

**kaffee klatsch** coffee klatsch

**kermis** outdoor festival or charitable fair (Netherlands)

**klatch** small, informal gathering, esp. for idle chitchat

**last rites** Roman Catholic sacrament administered to person near death

**legal holiday** nationally established holiday on which banks and government offices are closed

**luau** feast or banquet (Hawaii)

**luncheon** formal midday meal, esp. as part of meeting

**masked ball** large dance to which guests wear masks

**masquerade** social gathering, esp. dance, at which guests wear masks and costumes

**Mass** celebration of Catholic church service and the Eucharist

**matinée** performance or gathering in the afternoon

**meet** assembly of persons, groups, or teams for competition or organized activity

**memorial** gathering to commemorate something or someone, esp. after death

**mixer** friendly, informal get-together

**movable feast** religious feast that occurs on a different date in different years

**name day** church feast honoring saint after whom one is named

**national holiday** legally established government holiday

**observance** standardized ceremony or rite honoring something

**Oktoberfest** fall beer-drinking festival (Germany)

**open house** informal, daylong hospitality offered at one's home to invited and uninvited guests

**opening night** celebration of first performance of public entertainment

**pageant** extravagant display, esp. procession with floats

**parade** formal public procession, usu. with floats and other displays, esp. on holiday

**party** informal social gathering for amusement or celebration, often with refreshments and entertainment

**picnic** excursion on which meal is eaten outdoors

**potlatch** ceremonial feast of Pacific Northwest Indians in which gifts are given by host and guests attempt to exceed them

**powwow** Native American ceremony with feasting and dancing, usu. in expectation of some beneficial result

**procession** orderly, often ceremonial or decorative movement of group of people

**prom** formal dance at school or college

**promenade** procession of guests beginning formal ball; leisurely walk, esp. in public square

**receiving** announced time when one welcomes visitors at one's home

**reception** social gathering of welcome, esp. for guests after formal event such as wedding

**red-letter day** special day

**religious holiday** holiday commemorating event observed by church

**reunion** gathering of persons after period of separation

**revel** uproarious, wild festivity

**rite** standardized, ceremonial act or occasion

**rite of passage** ceremony performed to mark person's change of status, such as at puberty or time of marriage

**ritual** observation of ceremony or event prescribed by custom for solemn occasions and rites of passage

**roast** gathering to humorously honor or kiddingly defame someone

**Sabbath** day of rest and religious observance; Saturday for Jews, Sunday for Christians

**Sadie Hawkins** party or dance to which females invite males

**salute** ceremonial honor and praise for someone

**saturnalia** wild, orgiastic, excessive celebration

**séance** gathering to communicate with spirits

**seder** Jewish dinner service on first evening of Passover

**Shabbat** *Hebrew*. Jewish Sabbath, observed from sunset Friday to sunset Saturday

**shindig** *Informal*. lavish social gathering, usu. with dancing; shindy

**shindy** *Informal*. shindig

**show** performance, entertainment, or public spectacle

**shower** party at which gifts are given to guest of honor, esp. bride-to-be or mother-to-be

**sing-along** gathering at which group of people sing songs informally, often under direction of leader; songfest

**sit-down dinner** formal dinner at which one is served while seated at table

**soiree** social gathering in evening

**songfest** sing-along

**square dance** lively folk dance in which couples perform designated steps and figures

**stay-on** cocktail party at which certain guests are invited to remain for full dinner

**sun dance** summer solstice ceremony of Plains Indians

**tea** light, late afternoon meal at which tea is served, esp. in Britain

**tea ceremony** traditional, formal, highly stylized Japanese green tea service for guests

**tea party** late afternoon gathering at which tea is served

**testimonial** formal expression of admiration

**tribute** formal expression or show of support and respect

**vacation** period of rest from normal activities, often spent away from home

**wake** often festive vigil over corpse prior to burial; *Chiefly Brit.* annual holiday or vacation

**walkabout** brief respite from regular work and period of roaming the bush among Australian aborigines

**wayzgoose** printers' annual celebration

**wedding** ceremony and festivities marking marriage

**welcome** warm reception of newly arrived person or persons

**white-tie** (*adj*) designating extremely formal affair to which men wear swallow-tailed coats and white bow ties

**whoop-de-do** *Informal.* uproarious festivity or revel

**yuletide** feast of Christmas

## PARTIES AND PARTYING

**after-hours** (*adj*) occurring or operating in early morning hours after regular bars close, when only a few, sometimes private, social clubs are open

**bacchanalia** drunken feast, orig. honoring Roman god Bacchus

**bachelor party** gathering of men honoring friend about to be married

**bash** *Informal.* wild party

**birthday cake** cake given to person on his or her birthday, usu. with one burning candle for each year in age

**blast** *Slang.* exciting event or party

**blowout** *Slang.* uninhibited, often lengthy party

**bon vivant** highly sociable person with well-developed tastes, esp. in food and drink

**boogie** (*vb*) dance to rock music; *Informal.* have a raucous good time

**bridge party** gathering at which groups of four people play bridge

**BYOB** bring your own bottle/booze/beer; designation that host will not supply drinks at party

**card party** social gathering at which card games are played, usu. with refreshments

**carouse** (*vb*) take part in noisy, merry, drinking party

**carrying-on** *Informal.* foolish, excited behavior

**casual** informal, sometimes spontaneous, social gathering

**catering** act or business of supplying and serving food and drink at parties

**celebrate** (*vb*) mark happy occasion by festivity and pleasurable activity

**chaperon** one delegated to insure proper behavior, esp. in young people

**cheers** greeting or toast indicative of hospitality and good times

**chic** (*adj*) stylish, elegant; following the latest trends

**circulate** (*vb*) move from person to person at party

**clubhouse** building or enclosed area used as regular gathering place by group

**co-host** one of two persons hosting party

**company** group of people gathered for social event, esp. guests in one's home

**confetti** bits of colored paper scattered about as form of decoration at celebration

**costume party** party at which guests wear clothes different from their normal attire

**crash** (*vb*) *Informal.* attend a party uninvited

**cut in** (*vb*) take another's place, esp. as a dance partner

**cutup** *Informal.* person who clowns and plays practical jokes, esp. to gain attention in a group

**debauch** orgy

**dinner party** social gathering featuring evening meal

**Dionysian** (*adj*) frenzied and orgiastic

**dissipation** excessive indulgence in pleasure

**diversion** amusing activity that distracts one's attention

**do** *Chiefly Brit.* affair, party

**dress-up** (*adj*) designating a gathering to which one dresses formally or in costume

**engagement** arrangement to attend social function

**epicure** person who enjoys and has discriminating taste in food and drink

**fast lane** *Informal.* social life marked by attendance at many parties and social functions, esp. the trendiest and most boisterous affairs

**favor** small gift or trinket given to guests at party

**fling** brief period of unrestrained pleasure and dissipation

**frat party** *Informal.* party at college fraternity house

**fun and games** good times, party activities, and merrymaking

**gaiety** good cheer, merriment, and festivity

**garden party** outdoor gathering in garden or backyard

**gate-crasher** *Informal.* person attending party uninvited, often forcing way into gathering

**get down** (*vb*) *Informal.* have a good time, esp. boisterously

**get together** (*vb*) assemble for social event

**good cheer** merrymaking and revelry; feasting

**good times** pleasurable social activities and entertainments

**guest of honor** person in whose honor party is thrown

**hedonism** dedication to self-indulgent pursuit of pleasure

**hen party** *Informal.* gathering for women only

**high jinks** *Informal.* boisterous fun, esp. lively pranks

**high time** *Informal.* good time, esp. while intoxicated

**hobnob** (*vb*) associate on very friendly terms

**hoedown** rollicking dance party, esp. one featuring square dancing

**hoopla** *Informal.* gay and excited commotion or celebration; whoopla

**hospitality** friendship and kindness extended to guests

**host** man who entertains others, esp. at his home

**hostess** woman who entertains others, esp. at her home

**jollity** gaiety, good times; *Chiefly Brit.* party, jolly occasion

**key club** private club where each member has key to premises

**la dolce vita** *Italian.* the sweet life; hedonism, good times, and dissipation

**lark** playful merrymaking, sometimes involving pranks

**lawn party** outdoor gathering on grass field, often under tents

**life of the party** gregarious, charming, entertaining individual at social affairs

**lion** prominent person or celebrity in demand socially

**live it up** *Informal.* enjoy oneself, have a boisterous good time

**maffick** (*vb*) *Chiefly Brit.* celebrate with boisterous public display

**man about town** worldly man who frequents fashionable clubs and parties

**merriment** gaiety, fun, amusement

**merrymaking** convivial festivity, fun

**no-host bar** bar at which party guests must pay for drinks

**noisemaker** horn or cowbell sounded or rung at celebration

**orgy** unrestrained merrymaking and dissipation in group, esp. with free sexual activity; debauch

**pajama party** slumber party

**party** informal social gathering for amusement or celebration; (*vb*) *Informal.* engage in social activities in boisterous, unrestrained manner

**party down** (*vb*) *Informal.* participate uninhibitedly at a party

**party hearty** *Informal.* participate boisterously at a party

**partying** *Informal.* indulging in and enjoying parties

**party planner** person hired to organize, orchestrate, and stage parties

**pay a visit** make social call at another's home

**place card** small card with guest's name indicating where guest is to sit at dining table

**playboy** often rich man given to pleasure-seeking, sexual promiscuity, and dissipation

**pranks** mischievous party games and practical jokes

**regale** (*vb*) entertain others with splendid feast or amusing stories

**revel** wild party or celebration

**revelry** noisy party or merrymaking

**ripsnorter** *Informal.* wild, boisterous party

**roister** (*vb*) engage in noisy revelry and carousing

**rollick** (*vb*) behave in lively, carefree manner, esp. with others

**Roman holiday** time of debauchery and licentiousness

**RSVP** *French.* repondez s'il vous plait; request on invitation that one indicate whether he or she will attend

**salon** regular gathering of distinguished guests in private drawing room, esp. in celebrity's home

**slumber party** overnight house party, esp. for teenage girls; pajama party

**smoker** informal social gathering for men only

**sociable** (*adj*) friendly, enjoying the company of others; (*n*) informal social gathering

**social** informal gathering, esp. for group or organization

**social call** informal visit to another's home

**social club** group organized for recreation and entertainment

**social intercourse** conversation and interaction with others

**stag party** party for men only; bachelor party for bridegroom, often with pornographic movies

**step out** (*vb*) leave one's home seeking a good time

**supper club** expensive nightclub serving fine food and drink

**surprise party** party kept secret from guest of honor until last moment

**table-hopping** *Informal.* act of moving quickly from table to table at large party or club

**taxi dancer** girl employed by dance hall to dance with patrons for a fee

**tea party** social gathering in late afternoon at which tea is served

**tear** *Informal.* spree of carousing and dissipation

**tête-à-tête** *French.* intimate conversation between two people

**TGIF** thank God it's Friday; expression of relief at end of work week

**treat** meal or drinks paid for by another; (*vb*) to pay for another's meal or drinks

**trendy** (*adj*) fashionable in the latest social mode; faddish

**Tupperware party** gathering in home at which salesperson distributes samples and tries to sell Tupperware products to other women

**vanity fair** place or group characterized by pursuit of idle pleasures, decadence, and ostentation

**wallflower** shy or unpopular person who remains at periphery of social gathering

**whirl** series of parties in rapid succession

**whoopee** *Informal.* boisterous revelry and fun

**whoop it up** *Informal.* have a rollicking, boisterous good time

**whoopla** hoopla

**wing-ding** *Slang.* festive, lively party or event

**work the room** *Informal.* move from person to person at party, esp. seeking advantage or influence

# VACATIONS AND INTERLUDES

**absenteeism** deliberate or habitual absence from work or school

**AWOL** absent without leave; unauthorized absence from military service

**break** cessation of normal activities, esp. work

**breather** pause for rest, esp. from difficult task

**busman's holiday** vacation spent pursuing one's regular activities

**cocktail hour** early evening, at end of workday

**coffee break** brief pause in workday for rest and refreshment

**cut** (*vb*) stay away without excuse, esp. from school

**day off** single day's paid vacation from work

**day of rest** day off, esp. Sunday

**downtime** period of worker inactivity or equipment repair, esp. on machinery such as computer or communications system

**entr'acte** *French.* intermission

**escape** getaway from regular activities, esp. to exotic place for relaxation

**excursion** brief, often one-day pleasure trip, esp. at bargain rates

**expedition** journey with specific purpose

**field trip** excursion, esp. to place under study for observation

**free time** period without normal duties or responsibilities

**furlough** leave of absence from duty, esp. for soldier

**getaway** departure from home for vacation

**great escape** long-anticipated vacation, esp. to exotic locale

**halftime** midpoint intermission during sports event

**happy hour** early evening, at end of workday, when bars reduce price of drinks

**hiatus** interruption or break in normal activities

**holiday** *Chiefly Brit.* vacation away from home

**hooky** unexcused absence from school

**idyll** romantic or bucolic interlude

**interim** period of time between two events

**interlude** brief respite from normal activities

**intermission** brief, scheduled interval between two events, esp. between acts of a performance; entr'acte

**jaunt** usu. short pleasure trip

**journey** trip taken away from home

**junket** trip or journey, esp. one taken by politician at public expense

**knock off** (*vb*) *Informal.* leave work at end of day

**leave** authorized absence from work or military duty, esp. for extended period; leave of absence

**leave of absence** leave

**leisure time** period free from normal duties, when one may rest, play, or travel

**liberty** brief, authorized absence, esp. from naval duty

**Lord's day** for Christians, Sunday, traditionally a day off from work

**lull** short period of calm or lessened activity

**outing** brief pleasure trip, usu. to outdoor location

**paid vacation** scheduled, authorized absence from work without loss of salary

**pause** temporary break or cessation of activity

**playtime** free or leisure time for recreation

**R and R** rest and recreation

**recess** temporary break in work or school day

**respite** temporary interval of relief from duties

**rest** refreshing period of inactivity after work or travel

**rest and recreation** R and R; regular vacation period from military duty

**retreat** act of withdrawing into seclusion or retirement; place of refuge or seclusion

**sabbatical** leave from regular work, esp. for extended period with pay

**safari** journey or hunting expedition, esp. in eastern Africa

**shore leave** authorized permission for sailor to go ashore briefly

**sick leave** authorized absence from work, with full or partial pay, due to illness or injury

**sojourn** temporary stay away from home

**spare time** unoccupied time available for leisure activities and recreation

**take five** (*vb*) *Informal.* stop activity briefly for rest

**tea break** brief pause in workday for tea, esp. in Britain

**time off** authorized break from regular duties

**tour** journey through several places, often led by guide, ending at starting point

**travels** journeys, often to places far from home

**trip** journey away from home for pleasure or business

**truancy** unexcused absence, esp. from school

**vacation** period of rest from normal activities, often spent traveling away from home

**visit** journey and stay at place away from home

**voyage** journey or period of travel, esp. by sea

**weekend** days between end of one work week and beginning of next, Saturday and Sunday in United States and Europe

## Travel and Tourism

**accommodations** lodgings, sometimes including meals

**Baedeker** guidebook to foreign country, orig. published by Karl Baedeker in Germany during 19th century

**bed-and-breakfast** overnight accommodation, esp. in private home, that includes breakfast

**bellboy** man or boy employed to carry luggage and run errands at hotel; bellhop

**bellhop** bellboy

**bon voyage** *French.* lit. pleasant journey; expression of farewell to traveler

**booking** advance reservation for lodging or travel

**business class** travel at level between first class and coach class

**cabin class** accommodations on passenger ship superior to tourist class but inferior to first class

**caravan** company of persons traveling together, esp. in series of vehicles following one another

**charter** hire or lease of ship, bus, or airplane to transport large group at reduced fare

**check in** (*vb*) register at hotel; announce arrival for journey by public conveyance

**check luggage** turn over baggage for transport in cargo area

**check out** (*vb*) settle one's bill and leave hotel

**Club Med** *Trademark.* organization offering group vacation at relaxing tropical location

**coach class** standard travel facilities

**Cook's tour** guided, often cursory sightseeing tour

**cruise** ocean trip on comfortable passenger ship

**double occupancy** travel accommodation designed for two persons

**emigrate** (*vb*) leave one's country and settle in another

**excursion fare** low fare with special requirements

**expatriate** (*vb*) leave one's native country and take up permanent residence abroad

**expedition** journey or voyage for some definite purpose

**exploration** traveling in unknown region for educational purposes

**first class** finest accommodations in hotel or on public conveyance

**gadabout** person who wanders restlessly in search of pleasure

**globetrotter** person who travels widely and frequently

**grand tour** journey through continental Europe, usu. at completion of education

**guide** person hired to lead tourists or travelers through unknown area, usu. providing information about it

**hike** vigorous walk of some distance, often for observation, recreation, and health

**hostler** person who cares for horses at an inn

**hotel** commercial establishment providing lodging and often meals for travelers

**immigrate** (*vb*) arrive in new country and settle there

**inn** establishment providing lodging and often food and drink for travelers, usu. smaller than hotel

**itinerary** detailed plan or record of journey

**jet set** wealthy people who travel frequently to fashionable, exclusive places

**joyride** automobile ride merely for pleasure, usu. at high speed, often in stolen vehicle

**leg** one stage of journey

**lionize** (*vb*) *Chiefly Brit.* visit interesting sights

**lodging** facility for temporary, overnight stay

**motel** hotel for automobile travelers at which car can be parked close to one's room

**motoring** vacation or travel by automobile

**no-show** person who makes reservation but does not appear

**odyssey** extended, often wandering journey

**one-way ticket** ticket valid for travel from one place to another without return

**on the road** engaged in ceaseless travel

**open return** round-trip ticket with unspecified return date

**overbook** (*vb*) accept more reservations than places available in expectation of no-shows

**package tour** group travel in which all accommodations and activities are organized and paid for in advance

**passage** journey from place to place, esp. by water

**pension** modest European hotel or boardinghouse, esp. one serving meals

**peregrination** travel, esp. on foot

**peripatetic** (*adj*) moving from place to place, itinerant

**pilgrimage** long journey to religious shrine or place of historical interest

**pleasure trip** journey taken for amusement only

**porter** person employed to carry one's baggage, esp. at hotel or depot

**progress** forward movement, esp. on official journey

**remigrate** (*vb*) return to country of one's birth after prolonged absence

**reservation** arrangement by which hotel room or seat on public conveyance is set aside and held

**resort** place where people go for vacations, esp. to rest and relax

**return ticket** *Chiefly Brit.* round trip ticket

**round-the-world** (*adj*) designating ticket for passage or trip around the world

**round trip** travel from starting point to destination and back again; fare or ticket providing for such a journey

**route** course followed on travels

**rubbernecking** sightseeing by twisting one's head to gaze about

**safe passage** successful journey through dangerous region

**Sherpa** member of Tibetan people who serve as porters and guides on mountain-climbing expeditions

**sightseeing** visiting places of interest for pleasure and education

**slumming** visiting poor urban slums, esp. out of curiosity

**spa** resort with mineral spring or health facilities and sauna, esp. fashionable spot

**spin** usu. brief pleasure trip in motor vehicle

**steerage** portion of ship occupied by passengers paying lowest fare

**Sunday drive** pleasure trip by auto on Sunday, esp. to view the countryside

**tour** journey or trip of some duration, usu. for sightseeing, esp. in organized group

**tour bus** vehicle carrying group of tourists

**tour guide** person leading others to points of interest, usu. providing relevant information

**tourism** travel of foreign visitors to another nation and income derived therefrom; similar travel within one's own country

**tourist** person who visits another country or region for pleasure and sightseeing

**tourist class** lowest-priced accommodations on ship or train

**touristy** (*adj*) typical of or intended for tourists, therefore often tasteless or banal

**travel agency** company that arranges itineraries, lodging, and transportation for tourists and other travelers

**traveler** person who journeys about

**traveler's check** replaceable bank draft issued to traveler, signed at issuance and again at time of cashing

**travelogue** lecture, accompanied by slides or film, about travel to foreign or out-of-the-way place

**travels** journeys, often to faraway places

**trek** slow, laborious travel, often by foot over long distance

**turista** *Informal.* acute intestinal infection and diarrhea, usu. caused by bacteria in food or water of foreign country

**walk** period or course of walking for pleasure or exercise

**wayfarer** person who travels from place to place, esp. on foot

**world traveler** person who journeys to many lands

**year abroad** year spent living in foreign country, esp. by college student

# ENTERTAINMENTS AND SPECTACLES

**SEE ALSO**: Chap. 15: Dance; Theater; Chap. 17: Holidays, Celebrations, and Vacations; Sports; Hobbies; Games, Activities, and Toys

**acrobatics** art and performance of gymnastics and tumbling

**aerialism** performance of feats in the air, esp. on a trapeze

**aerobatics** spectacular flying stunts and maneuvers such as rolls and dives by an airplane

**amateur night** entertainment featuring nonprofessional performers, often in competition for prizes

**amusement** any pleasurable or entertaining diversion

**amusement park** outdoor facility providing rides, shows, exhibitions, and other amusements

**animal act** circus act involving tricks by wild and domestic animals

**aquacade** swimming and diving to musical accompaniment

**aquarium** building in which live aquatic organisms are exhibited

**aquatics** water sports and performances

**arm wrestling** contest in which opponents face each other gripping hands and attempt to force each other's arm down

**beauty contest** staged show, usu. made up of women, in which panel selects most beautiful contestant

**belly dancing** solo performance, usu. given by woman, involving gyrations of abdomen and hips

**big top** circus; main tent of circus

**botanical garden** outdoor garden and greenhouses for study and exhibition of plants

**buffoonery** clown show

**bullfight** public spectacle in which men excite, fight with, and ceremonially kill bulls

**bumper cars** amusement park ride in which padded electric cars purposely collide with each other

**burlesque** broadly comic theatrical entertainment of short skits and sometimes striptease acts

**callithump** noisy, boisterous parade

**card section** large group seated in bloc at outdoor public event, turning multicolored cards in unison to form patterns when viewed from afar

**carnival** traveling program of amusements, exhibitions, and sideshows

**carousel** merry-go-round

**casino** facility for gambling, sometimes featuring floor show

**cavalcade** parade; procession of riders or carriages

**chute the chute** amusement park ride similar to roller coaster, often ending in water

**circus** public performance, often in tent, of feats of skill, acrobatics, animal acts, and clown shows

**cirque** *French.* circus

**clown show** performance by buffoons, jesters, and comics

**concours** *French.* public competition or contest

**conjuring** practicing magic

**contest** activity in which teams or individuals compete for victory

**contortionism** acrobatics in which performer twists body into unusual postures

**convention** annual gathering of members of an industry or trade to exhibit new products

**county fair** annual exhibition at county fairgrounds featuring displays of livestock, stage shows, and rides

**crafts fair** gathering for display and sale of handmade crafts

**cyclorama** large pictorial representation encircling viewer, often with real objects as foreground; panorama

**demolition derby** exhibition in which old automobiles are intentionally rammed until just one is left running

**diorama** scenic representation blending sculpted figures and details, often in miniature, with painted background

**display** exhibition

**diversion** pastime or amusement that agreeably distracts attention from daily routine

**drum corps** marching band, esp. of drummers, under direction of drum major and majorettes, who often twirl batons

**entertainment** diverting, amusing, and engaging public performance

**equestrian show** exhibition of horsemanship, esp. jumping

**escape artist** person who breaks free of seemingly impossible confinement

**exhibit** public display of objects

**exhibition** public showing of performance skills or objects of interest; display

**expo** exposition

**exposition** public exhibition or show, esp. of commodities; expo

**extravaganza** lavish or spectacular show

**fair** exhibition designed to acquaint buyers or public with products; gathering for exchange and display of articles

**fantoccini** puppet show using string-operated or mechanical puppets

**fashion show** display of stylish clothing on models

**Ferris wheel** amusement park ride consisting of a tall, rotating, upright wheel with attached cars for riders

**figure skating** dance performance on ice skates

**fireworks** pyrotechnics; explosive devices with loud discharge and spectacular appearance

**float** low, flat, decorated vehicle that carries exhibits or tableaux in a parade

**floor show** variety performance on stage, esp. dancing

**freak show** public exhibition of oddities or freaks of nature

**funambulism** tightrope walking

**fun house** building in amusement park containing devices designed to startle, amuse, or frighten visitors

**gala** public entertainment marking special occasion

**girlie show** *Informal.* striptease acts

**gladiators** slaves who fought other slaves or wild animals in arena (ancient Rome)

**gymkhana** automotive meet with several events that test driving skills

**harlequinade** pantomime or farce featuring Harlequin character in multicolored, diamond-patterned tights

**high-diving** diving from very high platform into small pool

**high jinks** boisterous, unstructured carrying-on

**high-wire act** tightrope walking and acrobatics

**Icecapades** *Trademark.* figure skating show performed by company of ice skaters to musical accompaniment

**jamboree** noisy, festive gathering; assembly of Boy Scouts or Girl Scouts

**jongleur** itinerant, medieval acrobat, juggler, and minstrel (France)

**jousting** tilting

**jugglery** juggling

**juggling** keeping several objects in motion in the air by alternately catching and tossing them; jugglery

**legerdemain** magic, esp. sleight of hand

**light show** kaleidoscopic display of colored lights and film loops

**lists** medieval tournament enclosed by high stake fence

**loop-the-loop** airplane ride that makes vertical loop; ride simulating this

**magic** producing illusions by sleight of hand or conjuring

**marching band** band composed of brass, woodwind, and percussion that performs while marching before crowd in parade or at athletic event

**marine park** public display of marine animals and fish in outdoor tanks

**masquerade** performance or party with guests in disguise

**medicine show** former traveling variety show that used entertainers to attract crowd to whom remedies were then sold

**merry-go-round** amusement park ride with seats, often in form of animals, on revolving platform; carousel

**mime show** pantomime

**mummery** comic or ridiculous pantomime performance

**music hall** vaudeville or variety theater

**pageant** elaborate exhibition or spectacle with music, dramatic tableaux, and a procession of floats

**panorama** cyclorama

**pantomime** act conveying a story or idea without words

through facial gestures, hand movements, and dance; mime show

**parade** public procession of marching bands, performers, motorized displays, and floats

**peep show** often pornographic film or other object viewed through a small opening; raree show

**planetarium** facility housing a large model of the solar system, which is projected onto its ceiling or dome for view from seats below

**prestidigitation** sleight of hand

**prom** promenade

**promenade** strolling or walking through a public square; formal dance or ball; prom

**psychedelic show** light show imitating visual effect of psychedelic drugs, often to rock music

**public contest** competitive event or events staged before spectators

**public spectacle** unusual, notable, and entertaining acts performed in public or before audience

**Punch-and-Judy show** traditional puppet show depicting battling couple

**puppetry** puppet show

**puppet show** manipulation of small, handheld, string-operated or mechanical jointed figures in staged show; puppetry

**pyrotechnics** spectacular display, esp. of fireworks

**raree show** peep show; unusual carnival or street show

**regatta** series of rowing, sailing, or speedboat races

**revue** stage performance consisting of a series of skits, songs, and dances; variety show

**ride** any of various mechanical devices at amusement park or carnival that provide frightening or amusing rides for patrons

**rodeo** public performance by cowboys, featuring broncobusting, Brahma bull riding, calf roping, and steer wrestling

**roller coaster** elevated railway constructed in curves and inclines as frightening amusement park ride

**roller derby** staged contest between two roller-skating teams on oval track

**rope dancing** acrobatics performed on suspended rope

**roundabout** *Chiefly Brit.* merry-go-round

**saltimbanque show** European street performance by clowns, acrobats, and contortionists

**scavenger hunt** party contest with time limit for locating several difficult-to-obtain articles

**scenic railway** brief, elevated railway for viewing scenery

**shadow play** show in which shadows of puppets or performers are cast on screen

**show** any public performance

**sideshow** incidental diversion offered with main show

**sketch** brief, often comic, theatrical piece

**skit** brief burlesque or comic sketch included as part of revue, sometimes in imitation of a serious work

**sleight of hand** magic and conjuring tricks requiring deception through manual dexterity and skill; prestidigitation

**snake charming** entertainment involving professed power to charm and control venomous snakes

**son et lumière** *French.* sound-and-light show

**sound-and-light show** outdoor spectacle at historic sight using recorded narration with sound and light effects

**spectacle** public exhibit or performance of something

unusual, striking, notable, or entertaining, often on a large scale

**spectacular** spectacle or astonishing performance

**spectator sport** athletic contest performed before audience

**sports** organized, competitive athletic activities engaged in by trained athletes for the diversion of spectators

**squib** small firecracker

**stage show** performance, esp. song and dance, on stage, usu. inside a facility designed for such performances

**street show** performance staged in public street, esp. clown show or acrobatics

**striptease** act in which usu. female performer removes clothing piece-by-piece to musical accompaniment; girlie show

**stunt** act of daring, dexterity, and skill

**synchronized swimming** water ballet

**tableau** striking staged scene, usu. involving persons who remain in fixed positions

**talent show** amateur revue aimed at discovering talented new performers

**thaumaturgy** magic, performance of miracles

**theme park** amusement park in which structures and displays focus on central theme or motif

**three-ring circus** large circus with three acts performing simultaneously

**tightrope walking** balancing act performed on wire or rope suspended at some height; funambulism

**tilting** medieval contest in which two riders attempt to knock each other off horses with lances; jousting

**tournament** medieval contest between mounted knights armed with lances; series of contests leading to a championship in various sports and competitive fields

**trapeze act** acrobatic circus performance on horizontal bar suspended at some height from two parallel ropes

**tumbling** acrobatics involving somersaulting, rolling on floor, and handsprings

**variety show** revue

**vaudeville** traditional form of broad, comic revue

**ventriloquism** performance in which voice seems to come not from speaker but from dummy or other source

**water ballet** synchronized movement to music by performers in a pool of water; synchronized swimming

**water park** amusement park in which most or all of rides involve passing through water

**wax museum** exhibit of life-size wax effigies of famous people; waxworks

**waxworks** wax museum

**Wild West show** performance depicting scenes of U.S. Old West and displaying feats such as horsemanship, marksmanship, and rope twirling

**wrestling** staged athletic contest involving physical combat

**zoo** parklike facility for public display of living animals; zoological garden

**zoological garden** zoo

# SPORTS

Team Sports
Individual Sports and Competitive Events
General Sports Terminology

**17. LEISURE AND RECREATION**
SPORTS
TEAM SPORTS / INDIVIDUAL SPORTS AND COMPETITIVE EVENTS / GENERAL SPORTS TERMINOLOGY

**PART FIVE**

Auto Racing
Baseball
Basketball
Bowling
Boxing and Wrestling
Football
Golf
Gymnastics and Calisthenics
Hockey
Horse and Dog Racing
Skiing
Soccer
Surfing
Swimming and Diving
Tennis
Track and Field

**SEE ALSO**: Chap. 15: Television and Radio; Chap. 17: Entertainments and Spectacles; Games, Activities, and Toys

Basic definitions are provided for the names of twenty major competitive sports and games. The extensive lists of specialized technical and slang terms that follow these generic definitions are intended as a prompt or memory jog for users already familiar with the games they describe.

## TEAM SPORTS

Australian Rules football
bandy, baseball, basketball, bobsledding
Canadian football, crew, cricket, curling
doubles tennis
field hockey, flag football, football
handball, hardball, hockey, hooverball, hurling
ice hockey
kickball
lacrosse
polo, pushball
relay race, Roller Derby, rounders, rugby
shinny, slow pitch softball, soccer, softball, speedball, stickball, stoolball, stoop ball
tag football, team handball, touch football
volleyball
water polo, whiffleball
yachting

## INDIVIDUAL SPORTS AND COMPETITIVE EVENTS

acrobatics, Alpine skiing, archery, arm wrestling
balance beam, bareknuckle boxing, barrel racing, baton twirling, biathlon, biathlon relay, bicycling, bobsledding, boloball, bowling, boxing, Brahma bull riding, broad jump, broncobusting, bullfighting, bull riding
calf roping, candlepins, canoeing, court tennis, cross-country, cross-country skiing, cycling
decathlon, deck tennis, discus, distance running, diving, downhill skiing, draw, dressage, duckpins
enduro biking, equestrian
fencing, field events, figure skating, fives, foot racing, freestyle wrestling
giant stride, golf, Greco-Roman wrestling, gymnastics

hammer throw, handball, high jump, hurdling
ice dancing, ice skating, Indian wrestling
jai alai, javelin, judo
kayaking, korfball
lawn bowling, lawn tennis, long jump, luge
marathon, martial arts, medley relay, miniature golf, modern pentathlon, motocross
ninepins, Nordic skiing
paddle tennis, pancratium, parallel bars, pelota, pentathlon, ping-pong, platform diving, platform tennis, pole bending, pole vault, pugilism
racquetball, relay race, rings, road racing, rowing, running
sambo wrestling, shooting, shot put, side horse, skiing, ski jumping, slalom, sled-dog racing, speed skating, springboard diving, sprint, squash, stall bar, steeplechase, steer-wrestling, sumo wrestling, surfing, swimming
table tennis, tennis, tenpins, track, track and field, triathlon, triple jump
ultramarathon
vaulting
walking, water skiing, weightlifting, wrestling, wrist wrestling

## GENERAL SPORTS TERMINOLOGY

AAU, all-American, All-Pro, all-star, all-star team, amateur, Amateur Athletic Union, America's Cup, anchorman, arena, athlete, athletic scholarship, at large, attackman (lacrosse, rugby), average
backup, ball, ballpark, barnburner, batsman (cricket), bench, bench press (weightlifting), bench warmer, best-of-five series, best-of-seven series, big game, bird cage, black belt (karate), blackout, blank, bleachers, bluff, body English, bonus, boo, boobirds, book, booster, box seat, breeze, Bronx cheer, brown belt, bulk up, bull's-eye (archery), burn, bush, bye
call, cape work (bullfighting), captain, carom, cash in, cellar, champion, championship, chaw, cheap shot, cheat, cheerleader, chukker (polo), chula (jai alai), circuit, clean and jerk (weightlifting), cleats, clock, club, clubhouse, clutch, clutch play, coach, cocaptain, colors, comeback, competition, conference, consolation prize, coxswain (crew), crosse (lacrosse), cuadrilla (bullfighting), cup
dark horse, deadlock, defender, dog it
eligibility, épée (fencing)
fan, field, field house, finesse, first division, first string, fix, forfeit, formation, free agent, fronton (jai alai), front runner
game ball, gamer, goal, good hands, go the distance, grandstanding, groundskeeper, guile, gym, gymkhana, gymnasium
halftime, Hall of Fame, homecoming, home field, home stand, host, hot dog
innings (cricket), in play, instant replay, iron man
jackpot, jam (roller derby), jammer (roller derby), jayvee, jib (yachting), jock, juice, junior varsity
keel (yachting), kill shot, kill the clock
laugher, light tower, lock, locker room, longshot
mainsail (yachting), manager, matador (bullfighting), match, match play, miscue, misplay, muff
NAIA, National Association of Intercollegiate Athletics, National Collegiate Athletic Association, NCAA
odds, odds-on favorite, official, officiate, off-season, Olympics, on a roll, out-of-play, overmatched, overtime
Pan American Games, parry (fencing), pase (bullfighting), phenom, phys ed, physical education, picador (bullfighting), pickup game, play, play-by-play, play catch-up, playing field,

play-off, point, position, prelims, press box, pro, professional, promoter, prospect, psyched, psych-out, psych-up, push

quarter, quarterfinal, quickness

razzle-dazzle, recruiting, redshirt, ref, referee, regatta (yachting), rematch, repechage (crew, cycling), replay, reserve, ringer, roll, rookie, roster, round robin, rover (archery), rugger (rugby), runner-up, run out the clock

saber (fencing), score, scoreboard, scorecard, scrub, scrum (rugby), scull (crew), season, season ticket, second division, second effort, second string, second wind, seed, seesaw, semifinal, semipro, semiprofessional, series, set a record, shave points, shirts'n'skins, shoo-in, shuttlecock (badminton), side, sleeper, slump, snatch (weightlifting), spark plug, spectator, spoiler, spot points, spotter, spread, squad, stadium, standings, standoff, stiff, streak, stroke (crew), sub, substitution, sudden death, suit up, Summer Games, Summer Olympics, sweep

tailgate party, tally, taw (marbles), team, team play, teamwork, television time-out, test match (cricket), the wave, throw (rodeo), throw-in, thrust (rodeo), tie, timekeeper, time-out, to play, tossup, tote board, touché (fencing), tournament, tourney, trade, trading deadline, trainer, training, try (rugby), tryout, tune-up

underbird, underdog, upset

varsity, versus, vigorish

wager, waivers, walk-on, warmup, water boy, white belt, wicket (cricket), wild card, wind sprint, Winter Olympics, world champion, world championship, world class

yell leader

zip

# AUTO RACING

**auto racing** racing of stock or specialized automobiles by drivers competing over racing course or on closed public roadways

apron, autocross

black flag

checkered flag, cyclocross

demolition derby, draft, drag race, dragster

formula one, funny car

go-carting, Grand Prix, green flag, groove

Indianapolis 500, infield

kick

lap, lap money, LeMans

midget racer, motocross

NASCAR, nitro-fueled

off-road race

pace car, pace lap, pit, pit crew, pit stop, pole position

qualifying

rally

spin-out, stock car racing

winner's circle

yellow flag

# BASEBALL

**baseball** game of ball between two nine–player teams played for nine innings on field built around a diamond, with home plate and three other bases at its points, around which a runner must pass after successfully hitting a pitched ball with a wooden or metal bat in order to score one run, the object being to score more runs in nine innings than one's opponent

ace, AL, alley, all-star, All-Star Game, American League, apple, artificial turf, assist, Astroturf, at bat, average, away

Babe Ruth league, backstop, backup, balk, ball, ball boy, ball club, ball game, ball girl, ball hawk, ballpark, ballplayer, Baltimore chop, barehanded, base, baseball, baseball bat, baseball cap, baseball card, baseballer, baseball game, baseball glove, baseball player, base hit, baseline, base on balls, base path, baserunner, basket catch, bat, bat boy, batter, batter's box, batter up, battery, batting average, batting cage, bean, bean ball, beat out, big league, blank, bleachers, bloop, blooper, bobble, book, boot, bottom, bottom of the ninth, box, boxscore, box seat, broken bat, brush, brushback, bull pen, bunt, bush league, bushleaguer

cage, called strike, catch, catcher, catcher's mask, caught looking, center field, center fielder, chance, change-of-pace, change-up, chase, check swing, chin music, choke up, chopper, classic, cleanup, cleanup hitter, clear the bases, closed stance, closer, clothesline, clout, club, clutch hit, coach, comebacker, commissioner, complete game, concessions, connect, control, Cooperstown, count, cover a base, curve, curve ball, cut, cut fastball, cutoff, cutoff man, Cy Young Award

day game, dead ball, deck, deep, designated hitter, DH, diamond, dinger, dish, doctor the ball, double, doubleheader, double play, double play depth, double steal, double switch, drag bunt, drive, ducks on the pond, dugout, dying quail

earned run, earned run average, ERA, error, extra-base hit

fadeaway, fadeaway slide, fair ball, fall classic, fan, farm, farm club, farm system, farm team, fastball, field, fielder, fielder's choice, fielding average, fireman, first base, first base coach, first baseman, fly, fly ball, fly out, follow through, force, force out, force play, forkball, foul, foul ball, foul line, foul out, foul pole, foul territory, foul tip, fourbagger, frame, free agent, free pass, free trip, fungo

game-winning hit, gapper, glove, glove man, go-ahead run, gold glove, good eyes, gopher ball, grand slam, ground ball, grounder, groundout, ground rule double, ground rules, gun

Hall of Fame, handle, hang, hardball, head-first slide, heat, heater, heavy hitter, hickory, hidden-ball trick, high, high-and-inside, high-and-tight, high hard one, high heat, hill, hit, hit-and-run, hit batsman, hit by pitch, hit for the cycle, hitter, hit the corner, hold, hold the runner, home plate, homer, home run, home stand, hook, horsehide, hot corner, hot-stove league, hummer, hurler

infield, infield back, infielder, infield fly rule, infield hit, infield in, infield out, inning, inside, inside pitch, inside-the-park home run, insurance run, intentional walk, in the hole

junior circuit, junk, junkball pitcher

K, keystone, knock, knuckle ball, knuckleballer, knuckler

LCS, lead, lead off, leadoff hitter, league, league lead, League Championship Series, leather, leatherman, left field, left fielder, left-handed batter, left-hander, leg out a hit, line drive, line out, liner, line score, lineup, little league, load the bases, long relief, low, low-and-away, low-and-outside

major league, major leaguer, manager, middle relief, minor league, minor leaguer, mitt, most valuable player, mound, move, MVP

nail the runner, National League, night game, nine, NL, no hits, no runs, no errors, no-hitter

official at bat, on, on base, on base percentage, on deck, one-bagger, one-base hit, one-hitter, open stance, opposite

field, out, outfield, outfielder, outside, outside pitch, overthrow
pass, passed ball, payoff pitch, peg, pennant, pennant race, pepper, perfect game, pick-off, pick-off move, pill, pinch-hit, pinch hitter, pine tar, pitch, pitcher, pitcher's mound, pitchout, pivot, plate, play ball, pocket, Pony League, pop, pop fly, pop-up, power hitter, prospect, pull, pull hitter, pull the string, punch, put-out
rain check, rain delay, rainout, rally, rbi, reached on error, relay, relief pitcher, reliever, retire the batter, rhubarb, ribby, rifle, right field, right fielder, right-handed batter, righthander, rip, road trip, rocket, rookie, Rookie-of-the-Year, rosin bag, rotation, Rotisserie League, rounders, round-tripper, rubber, rube, run, run batted in, rundown, runless, runner, runners at the corners, running catch, run through the sign
sack, sacrifice, sacrifice bunt, sacrifice fly, safe, safety squeeze, sandlot, save, score, scorecard, scorekeeper, scoring position, scout, scratch hit, screwball, scuff, season, second base, second baseman, senior circuit, series, shag, shell the pitcher, shift, shinguard, shoestring catch, short relief, shortstop, show, shutout, side, sidearm, single, sinker, slam, slice, slide, slider, slow pitch softball, slug, slugfest, slugger, slugging percentage, slurve, smash, smoke, softball, southpaw, speed gun, spitball, spitter, split-fingered fastball, spring training, squeeze bunt, squeeze play, stadium, stand, starter, steal, stickball, stolen base, stoopball, stopper, straightaway, stretch, stretch drive, strike, strikeout, strike zone, stroke, stuff, suicide squeeze, swat, swing, swinging strike, swipe, switch hit, switch-hitter
tag, tag up, take, take an extra base, take the pitch, tee off, Texas leaguer, third base, third base coach, third baseman, three-bagger, three-base hit, three up, three down, throw, throw behind the runner, throw out, tip, top, top of the inning, toss, total bases, trap, trip, trip to the mound, trip to the plate, triple, triple-A, Triple Crown, triple-header, triple play, turn a double play, tweener, twin bill, twi-night, twirler, two-bagger, two-base hit
ump, umpire, uncork, underarm, underhand, unearned run, up, up-and-in, uppercut, upper deck, upswing, utilityman
waivers, walk, warmup, warning track, webbing, wheel, wheels, whiff, wide, wild pitch, win, windup, winning percentage, World Series
yield

double-team, downtown, draw iron, dribble, drive, dunk, dunk shot
ejection, elbow, endline
fadeaway, fadeaway jumper, fast break, field, field goal, field goal percentage, fill the lanes, Final Four, finger roll, five second violation, flagrant foul, follow shot, forty-five second clock, forward, foul, foul line, foul out, foul shot, free throw, free throw attempt, free throw lane, free throw line, front, front court, full-court press
give-and-go, glass, goaltending, guard, gun
hack, half-court game, hand check, hanging on the rim, hang time, high post, hit, holding, home court, home court advantage, hook shot, hoop
illegal defense, in and out, inbounds, inbounds pass, inside, in your face, iron
jam, jump ball, jump circle, jumper, jump shot
key
lane, lane violation, lay-up, line, loose ball foul, low post
man-to-man defense
National Basketball Association, National Invitation Tournament, NBA, net, NIT, no-look pass
offensive foul, offensive rebound, off guard, off the dribble, one-on-one, outlet pass, outside, over the limit, over the top
paint, palming, pass, penetration, perimeter, perimeter shooting, personal foul, pick, pick-and-roll, pivot, platoon, playmaker, point, point guard, post, post position, post up, power forward, press
quarter
reaching in, rebound, rejection, reverse dunk, rim, rotation, run-and-gun
screen, set a pick, set a screen, set shot, shoot, shooter, shot, shot clock, shot selection, sixth man, skyhook, slam dunk, small forward, spot up, steal, stuff, swingman, swish, switch
tap-in, team foul, team rebound, technical foul, ten-second rule, three-point line, three-point play, three-point shot, three-second violation, tip-in, tipoff, top of the key, touch, transition, transition game, trap, trap defense, traveling, triple double, turnaround jumper, turnover, twenty-four second clock, twenty second timeout
uptempo game
walking
yo-yo
zone defense

# BASKETBALL

**basketball**  game played between two teams of five players each on a rectangular court with a raised basket at each end, points being scored by shooting a round, inflated ball through the opponent's basket
air ball, alley-oop, assist, at the buzzer
backboard, backcourt, backcourt foul, backcourt violation, bank, bank shot, baseline, basket, basketball, bench, block, blocked shot, blocking, boards, bonus situation, bounce pass, boxing out, break, breakaway foul, brick, bucket
carom, carrying-over, center, charge, charging, charity stripe, cherry pick, chest pass, coast-to-coast, cold, continuation, conversion, cords, court, courtside, crosscourt pass
dead ball foul, defensive rebound, delay of game, deliberate foul, dish, disqualification, double dribble, double pump,

# BOWLING

**bowling**  game in which a heavy ball is rolled down an alley toward ten pins standing in a triangular pattern, the object being to knock down all the pins at once
alley
bedposts, boccie, break
candlepins
duckpins
foul line, frame
guide marks, gutter
hook
kingpin
lane, lawn bowling, league bowling
open
perfect game, pin, pinsetter, pocket, poodle
scratch, seven-ten split, skip, spare, split, strike
tenpin, triple, turkey

# BOXING AND WRESTLING

**boxing**  contest between two fighters who punch each other with gloved fists over the designated number of rounds or until one has been knocked out

**wrestling**  contest between two opponents who struggle hand to hand in order to pin each other's shoulders to a mat, held under varying styles and rules

airplane spin, apron, arm wrestling

back-pedal, bantamweight, bareknuckle, bicycle, body slam, bout, boxer, break, bum, butt

canvas, card, cauliflower ear, clinch, club fighter, combination, contender, corner, count, counterpunch, cross, crown, cut man

dance, decision, dive, draw, duck

fall, featherweight, fight, fighter, fisticuffs, flyweight, footwork, freestyle wrestling, full nelson

glass chin, glass jaw, glove, Golden Gloves, gouge, Greco-Roman wrestling, guard

half nelson, hammerlock, handler, hand lock, haymaker, headlock, heavyweight, hook

Indian wrestling

jab, judge, junior weight

kayo, kick boxing, kidney punch, knockdown, knockout, KO

lace finger, left, light heavyweight, lightweight, lock, low blow

Marquis of Queensberry rules, mat, match, middleweight

nelson, neutral corner

one-two, on the ropes

pin, point, prefight instructions, preliminary, press, prizefight, prizefighter, promoter, pug, pugilism, pugilist, puncher, punching bag, punchy

rabbit punch, rassling, referee, reversal, right, ring, ringside, roadwork, rope-a-dope, ropes, round, roundhouse

scissors, scissors hold, second, semifinal, shadowbox, sleeper hold, slugfest, spar, sparring partner, speed bag, speed work, split decision, stop, stranglehold, sumo wrestling

tag team, takedown, tandem, technical knockout, ten point must system, throw, thumb, title fight, titleholder, titlist, TKO, toehold, trainer, trunks

undercard, unranked, uppercut

weigh-in, welterweight, white hope, windmill, wrestler, wristlock

# FOOTBALL

**football**  game in which two opposing teams of eleven players each defend goals at opposite ends of a 100-yard rectangular field, points being scored by carrying an inflated oval ball across the opponent's goal line or by kicking this ball over the crossbar between the posts of the opponent's goal

AFC, American Football Conference, armchair quarterback, audible, automatic

back, backfield, backfield in motion, back judge, ball-carrier, batting the ball, blindside, blitz, block, blocker, blocking back, bomb, bootleg, bowl, bowl game, breakaway, bring a load, broken field, bump and run, buttonhook

Canadian Football League, carry, catch, center, CFL, chair pattern, cheap shot, chip shot, clip, clipping, clothesline tackle, coffin corner, completion, conversion, convert, cornerback, corner pattern, Cotton Bowl, counterplay,

coverage, crackback, crawling, crossbar, cut, cutback, cutoff block

deep, defense, defensive back, defensive coordinator, defensive end, defensive tackle, delay, dive play, double-team, down, down-and-out, downfield, down lineman, draft, draft pick, draw, draw play, drive, drive block, drop back, drop kick

eat the ball, encroachment, end, end around, end line, end run, end zone

face mask, fade, fair catch, fake, field goal, field judge, first-and-goal, first down, flanker, flanker back, flare pass, flare pattern, flat pass, flats, fleaflicker, flex, flex defense, flow, fly pattern, football, footballer, football player, formation, forward pass, fourth down, free kick, free safety, fullback, fumble

gain, game plan, gap, goal line, goal line stand, goalpost, goal-to-go, grass drills, Grey Cup, gridder, gridiron, guard

Hail Mary pass, halfback, halftime, hand-off, hash mark, head linesman, Heisman Trophy, helmet, hit, holding, hook pattern, huddle

I formation, illegal procedure, inbounds, ineligible receiver, in motion, in play, inside, inside linebacker, instant replay, intentional grounding, interception, interference

juke, jump pass

keeper, kick, kicker, kickoff, kickoff return, kick return specialist

lateral, left side, line, linebacker, line judge, lineman, line of scrimmage, linesman, look-in pass

man-to-man defense, middle linebacker, misdirection, Monday morning quarterback, motion, muff

National Football Conference, National Football League, neutral zone, NFC, NFL, nickel defense, no-huddle offense, nose guard, nose tackle

offensive coordinator, offensive lineman, official, offside, off tackle, onside kick, open field, option, Orange Bowl, outlet pass, out-of-bounds, out-of-play, outside linebacker

pass, PAT, pay dirt, penalty, personal foul, physical, pigskin, pileup, pitchout, pits, place kick, placekicker, placement, platoon, play-action pass, playbook, pluggers, pocket, point after touchdown, post pattern, power play, power sweep, prevent defense, Pro Bowl, pulling guard, punt, punter, punt formation, punt return

quarter, quarterback, quarterback sneak, quick kick, quick read, quick release

read, receiver, reception, red-dog, red zone, ref, referee, release, replay official, return, reverse, right side, ring his bell, roll, rollout, Rose Bowl, run, run-and-shoot, runback, runner, running back, running play, rush, rushing

sack, safety, safety blitz, sandwich, scatback, scramble, screen pass, scrimmage, seam, secondary, second down, set position, shift, short, short yardage, shotgun, shovel pass, side judge, sideline, single wing, slant, snap, sneak, soccer-style kicker, special teams, spike, spiral, split backs, split end, spread formation, sprint-out, squib kick, Statue of Liberty play, stick-um, stiff-arm, straight-arm, strong left, strong right, strong safety, strong side, stunt, stutter step, sudden death, Sugar Bowl, suicide squad, Super Bowl, sweep, swing pass, swivel hips

tackle, tailback, taxi squad, TD, T formation, third down, throw, tight end, touchback, touchdown, touch football, touch-tackle, trap, trap block, trenches, triple option, triple threat, try for point, turf, turnover, two-minute warning

umpire, unnecessary roughness, unsportsmanlike conduct, upfield, upright, up the middle

veer offense

weak safety, weak side, wedge, wide receiver, wig-wag, wind field, wingback, wishbone
yardage, yard line, yards gained, yards per carry
zebra, zone, zone defense

# Golf

**golf** game in which a small, white ball is struck with wooden or metal-headed clubs over a course of usu. eighteen holes placed at some distance from one another around natural or artificial obstacles, the object being to sink the ball into each successive hole in as few strokes as possible
address the ball, approach shot, apron
back nine, backspin, backswing, bag, best-ball foursome, best-ball match, birdie, bisque, bogey, brassie, bunker
caddie, carry, chip, chip shot, club, clubhouse, country club, course, cup, cut shot
divot, dogleg, dormie, double bogey, double eagle, downswing, drive, driver, driving range, drop, dub, duffer
eagle, eighteen holes
fade, fairway, fairway trap, fairway wood, flag, flagstick, follow-through, foozle, fore, foursome, fringe, front nine
gallery, gimme, golden ferret, golf ball, golf club, golf course, golf widow, Grand Slam, green, greens fee, grip
hacker, handicap, hazard, heel, hit up, hole, hole in one, hole out, hook
iron
leader board, lie, links, lip, loft
mashie, Masters, match play, medal play, mulligan
nassau, niblick, nineteenth hole
out-of-bounds, overplay, overshoot
par, pass-through, penalty stroke, pill, pin, pin high, pitch shot, play through, plus fours, press, pro-am, pull, putt, putter, putting green, putt out
rim, rough, round, run
sand trap, sclaff, shaft, shag, shank, shoot, skull shot, slice, slope, snap hook, spoon, stableford, stance, stroke, stroke play, stymie, swipe
tee, tee off, tee shot, three-ball match, threesome, toe, top, topspin, trap, triple bogey, twosome
unplayable lie
waggle, water hazard, wave up, wedge, wiff, wood
yips

# Gymnastics and Calisthenics

**calisthenics** conditioning exercises usu. performed with little or no special apparatus
**gymnastics** performance of physical exercises that require strength, balance, and agility, esp. on special apparatus, usu. in judged competition
ariel
backflip, balance beam
chin-up, crossbar, crunch
dismount
flip, floor exercise, freestyle
gymnast
handspring, handstand, high bar, horizontal bar, horse
Indian club, iron cross
jumping jack
parallel bars, pommel horse, pull-up, push-up
rings, roadwork

scissors, setting-up exercises, sit-up, somersault, springboard, straddle
tilt board, trapeze, tuck, twist
uneven bars
vault, vaulting horse
walkover

# Hockey

**hockey** game played on round-ended rectangle of ice between two teams of six skaters each, object being to shoot hard rubber puck past defenders and goalkeeper into opponent's net using bent wooden stick
assist
back-check, blades, blue line, board check, boards, body check, break, breakaway goal
Campbell Conference, center, change-on-the-fly, charging, check, chippy, crease, cross-check, cross-ice
defenseman, draw, dribble, drop pass
empty net goal, end
face, face mask, face-off, fore-check, forward
glove save, goal, goalie, goalkeeper, goaltender, goon
hat trick, high-sticking, hip-check, holding, hooking
icing, interference
left wing, line, line change, linesman
major penalty, minor penalty
National Hockey League, net, neutral zone, NHL
offside
pass, penalty, penalty box, penalty killer, penalty shot, period, playmaker, point, power play, puck
rebound shot, red light, red line, right wing, rink, roughing
save, shorthanded, shot on goal, skate, slap shot, slashing, spearing, Stanley Cup, stick, sticked, stickhandler, stickhandling, stick save
tripping, T-stop
Wales Conference, white line, wing
Zamboni machine, zone

# Horse and Dog Racing

**dog racing** contest of speed over track between dogs, usu. chasing a mechanical rabbit
**horse racing** contest of speed over oval track between horses either ridden by jockeys or pulling sulkies and their drivers
allowance race, also-ran
backstretch, Belmont Stakes, blind bet, blinders, blinkers, box bet, boxed-out, break, break away, break-from-the-gate, break stride, Breeder's Cup, buggy
chicane, claiming race, closer, colors, course
daily double, derby, distance, double play
exacta
fast track, favorite, feature race, filly, finish line, furlong, futurity
gelding, grandstand, grass, greyhound
handicapping, handle, head
jock, jockey, juvenile
Kentucky Derby
length, long shot
maiden race, mudder
neck, neck and neck, nose
odds-on favorite, off and running, offtrack betting, OTB

pacer, paddock, parimutuel, parlay, perfecta, photo finish,
place, post, post race, post time, Preakness, prohibitive
favorite
quarter horse, quinella
rabbit, race, racecourse, racehorse, racetrack, racing form,
railbird
saddle, saddling barn, scramble, short odds, show, silks,
simulcast, sire, speed horse, stable, stake horse, stake race,
starting gate, starting price, steeplechase, steward,
stretch, stretch run, stretch runner, string, stud, sulky
thoroughbred, tote, trainer, trial horse, trifecta, Triple
Crown, trotter, turf, turfman, turn, twin double
walking ring, walkover, water jump, weigh-in, wheel bet,
whip, win, winner's circle, wire, wire-to-wire
yearling

# SKIING

**skiing** racing over snow on a pair of long, narrow runners
of wood, plastic, or steel; maneuvering between obstacles
or jumping for distance on such runners over snow
Alpine skiing, au alement
bathtub, bunny
cement, chairlift, christie, cover, cross-country skiing
downhill
fall line
gate, giant slalom
hot dog
jumping
kick turn
langlauf
mogul
Nordic skiing
off-piste
piste, powder
rope tow
schuss, ski, ski bob, ski boots, skijoring, ski jump, ski lift, ski
mask, ski pants, ski pole, ski run, ski suit, ski tow, slalom,
snowplow, stem, stem turn, super giant slalom, swing
telemark, traverse, tuck
unweight
Vorlage
wedeln, wedge

# SOCCER

**soccer** game played between two teams of eleven players
each on a long rectangular field in which a round inflated
ball is advanced by kicking or bouncing it off any part of
the anatomy except the hands and arms, the object being
to put the ball in the opponent's net, which is defended by
a goalkeeper who may use his hands to stop shots
association football
center, corner kick, crossbar
defenseman, dribble
football, footballer, forward, free kick, fullback
goal, goalie, goalkeeper, goal kick, goal kicker, goalmouth,
goaltender
halfback, hat trick, header
kickoff
left wing, linesman
midfield, midfielder
NASL, North American Soccer League, nutmeg

offside
pass, penalty, penalty kick
right wing, roughing
tiebreaker, touchline
volley
winger, World Cup
yellow card
zone

# SURFING

**surfing** riding shoreline ocean waves while standing on a
long, shaped board of wood or foam and fiberglass coated
with resin, sometimes in judged competition
aggro
baggies, barney, beach break, bellyboard, board, body surf,
body whomping, boogie board
choppy, close out, come up, crank a turn, crash and burn,
curl
ding, drop, drop in
flat
glass-off, glassy, gnarly, goofy-foot, gremmie, gun
hang five, hang ten, ho-dad, hot curl, hot dog
jams
kick-out
leash, left, lineup, locked in, long board
noseride, noserider
offshore wind, onshore wind, outside, overhead
paddleboard, pearl
quasimodo
radical turn, rail, reef break, right, rip
set, shaper, shoot the curl, shoot the pier, shoot the tube,
shore break, short board, stoked, surfboard, surfer,
surfriding, swell
thruster, tube, tubed, turn
wahine, walk the nose, wall, wet suit, wipeout

# SWIMMING AND DIVING

**diving** judged competition in which contestants plunge
headfirst into water after leaping from an elevated platform
and performing specified maneuvers in the air
**swimming** racing contest in which swimmers propel themselves across surface of water over designated distance, usu.
in one of four strokes
back dive, backstroke, bathing cap, belly flop, breaststroke,
butterfly
cannonball, crawl
diver, diving board, dolphin kick
flip turn, flutterboard, flutter kick, freestyle, frog kick, full
gainer
gainer
half gainer, heat
individual medley
jackknife
kick lap, kick turn
medley relay
overarm
paddleboard, pike position, platform diving, pool, poolside
scissors kick, scull stroke, sidestroke, splits, springboard
diving, starting block, stroke, swan dive, swimming pool,
synchronized swimming
triathlon, tuck, twist
whip kick

## TENNIS

**tennis** game played on a rectangular court between two players or pairs of players who use strung rackets to bat a small, hollow ball back and forth across a low net that divides the court in half, the object being to place an unreturnable shot within the opponent's half of court

ace, advantage, approach

backcourt, backhand, backspin, backstroke, ball boy, baseline, bisque, break, break point, break service

charge the net, clay court, country club, courtside, crosscourt

deuce, dink, double fault, doubles, drop shot

fault, fifteen, follow-through, footwork, forecourt, forehand, forty

game point, good, Grand Slam, grass court, ground stroke

hack, hard court

lawn tennis, let, line judge, linesman, lob, long, love

match, match point, mishit, mixed doubles

net, netball, net judge, netman

on serve, overhand, overhead smash

paddle, passing shot, placement, placement shot

racket, racquet, rally, retrieve, return

seed, serve, server, service, service break, service court, set, set point, sideline, singles, skein, slice, stop volley, stroke

tennis ball, tennis elbow, tennis shoe, thirty, tiebreaker, topspin

undercut, unforced error

volley

webbing, Wimbledon

## TRACK AND FIELD

**track and field** indoor or outdoor contest made up of several competitive events, including running races, hurdling, vaulting, jumping, and tossing objects

anchor, anchor lap

baton, break, broad jump

cinder track, cross-country

dash, decathlon, discus, distance medley, distance runner, distance work

fast start, field event, finish line, flying start, Fosbury flop

get set, go, gun lap

hammer throw, heat, heptathlon, high hurdles, high jump, homestretch, hop, step, and jump, hurdles

individual medley, infield, intermediate hurdles

javelin

kick

lap, long jump, low hurdles

marathon, medley relay, metric mile, middle distance, miler

neck and neck

on your mark

pacesetter, pentathlon, pole vault, prelim, pull up, put

qualifying race

relay, run, running start

shakedowns, shot put, speed work, splits, sprint, start, starter, starting block, steeplechase, stopwatch, straddle, straightaway

thin clads, time trial, track meet, track shoe, track suit, triple jump

walk, water jump, weightman, wind sprint

# HUNTING AND FISHING

Hunting Practice and Techniques
Fox Hunting
Hunting Equipment
Fishing Practice and Techniques
Fishing Equipment and Tackle

**SEE ALSO:** Chap. 5: Knots; Weapons and Armaments; Chap. 6: Ships and Boats; Chap. 13: Anthropology

## HUNTING PRACTICE AND TECHNIQUES

**airplane hunting** hunting with shotgun and usu. .00 buck from airborne craft, illegal except for game control officers

**archery** hunting with bow and arrow

**bag** (*vb*) *Informal.* kill or capture game; (*n*) amount of game taken during one hunting trip

**battue** *Chiefly Brit.* beating ground to drive game from cover

**bay** position of stag or any cornered animal that has turned to face pursuers

**beagling** hunting with beagle hounds, esp. for cottontail or rabbit

**beater** person who flushes game birds or hoofed game to guns

**big game** any large game that is hunted, esp. deer, elk, bear, moose, bison, caribou, antelope, sheep, mountain goat, mountain lion, jaguar, peccary, or wild hog

**blooding** *Chiefly Brit.* smearing of initiate's face with blood of first fox or stag he or she has seen killed

**blood sport** any sport in which animals are killed, esp. hunting

**boat hunting** shooting game from a boat

**bow hunting** hunting with bow and arrow

**canoe hunting** hunting in areas reached by canoe on inland waterway but inaccessible overland

**chase** act of searching out and pursuing game and wild animals for purpose of killing them; *Chiefly Brit.* private game preserve, sometimes stocked with animals and birds to be hunted

**chasse gardée** *French.* private hunting preserve

**chevy** *Chiefly Brit.* hunting cry; a hunt

**closed** (*adj*) restricted as to permissible time, place, and game that may be hunted

**closed season** time of year when hunting for particular game is prohibited

**cold scent** scent left by quarry some length of time before hounds pick it up

**competition shooting** skeet, trap, or target shooting as competitive event

**coon hunting** hunting for racoons with hounds, usu. at night

**course** (*vb*) hunt game with dogs by sight rather than scent

**covert** hiding place of fox or upland game, esp. shrubs or thicket

**curing** preparing of animal flesh for preservation, usu. by drying or salting

**dead set** stiff posture of hunting dog indicating presence and location of game

**drag** scent left by fox or other animal

**dress** (*vb*) cut up, trim, and remove skin, feathers, and viscera from game prior to storage or transportation

**drive** portion of hunt in which beaters drive birds over hunters or in which deer are driven toward concealed standers

**earth** (*vb*) chase an animal into its burrow or den

**falconer** person who practices falconry

**falconry** hunting with falcons, hawks, or eagles; training hawks to hunt

**fault** loss of scent; break in line of scent

**ferreting** using ferrets to drive rabbits and other rodents from underground

**fetch** (*vb*) of hunting dogs, retrieve game

**field dressing** rough dressing of game, often hung from tree, immediately after killing

**flush** (*vb*) cause game, esp. birds, to break cover or take flight

**foil** (*vb*) *Chiefly Brit.* obscure scent with another scent

**fowl hunting** hunting of waterfowl

**fox hunting** traditional sport in which mounted hunters follow hounds in pursuit of fox

**game** wild animals and birds that are hunted and killed for sport and/or meat

**game birds** hunted land birds, esp. blackcock, capercaillie, dove, grouse, partridge, pheasant, pigeon, ptarmigan, quail, snipe, turkey, wild turkey, and woodcock

**gamekeeper** person employed to maintain game preserve, prevent poaching, and nurture animal life

**game preserve** area set aside for propagation of game

**gillie** *Scottish.* hunting or fishing guide

**give tongue** of hounds, bay while following a scent

**gunning** hunting of game with shotgun, not rifle

**hounds** pack of hounds used for hunting; huntsman's call to hounds

**hunt** (*vb*) pursue or search for game for purpose of catching or killing it; (*n*) act or practice of hunting game or other wild animals

**hunter** person who hunts game or other wild animals, esp. for sport

**hunter's moon** first full moon after harvest moon, in late September or early October

**hunting** practice and techniques associated with the pursuit and search for game for purpose of killing them

**hunting ground** region set aside for hunting game

**huntress** woman who hunts

**huntsman** hunter; manager of hounds during hunt

**hunt's-up** call formerly played on hunting horn to rouse participants in hunt

**incomer** duck or pheasant that flies directly toward shooter

**kill** end of run in which quarry, esp. fox, is caught and killed; any dead game

**limit** maximum number of game that may legally be taken in designated time or locale

**open season** time of year when hunting for certain game is permitted

**plinking** shooting at tine cans or other stationary targets with handgun

**poach** (*vb*) hunt or kill game illegally on another's property or preserve

**poacher** one who poaches game

**point** (*vb*) of hunting dog, stand rigid, facing in direction of located game to indicate its position; (*n*) *Chiefly Brit.* distance between two extreme ends of hunt in straight line

**predator** any animal that exists by hunting other animals for food, esp. bobcat, coyote, crow, fox, lynx, skunk, or wolf

**preserve** area designated for maintenance of game for hunting

**prey** hunted animal

**pursuit** act of following game so as to overtake and kill it

**quarry** game hunted, esp. by hounds or falconry

**quartering** cutting up of carcass of killed game into four pieces prior to transporting it

**quest** (*vb*) of hunting dogs, bay or give tongue in pursuit of game; search for game

**reloading** making of one's own bullets from shell casings, powder, and primer

**retrieve** (*vb*) of hunting dogs, fetch killed or wounded game

**riot** (*vb*) pursue animal other than intended quarry

**safari** hunting expedition for big game in Africa

**scent** distinctive odor left by animal that has passed, used by dogs in tracking prey

**season** legally designated time of year when specific game may be hunted in given region

**set** (*vb*) of hunting dogs, indicate position of game by standing stiffly and pointing muzzle

**shikari** person who hunts big game, esp. professional guide or hunter (India)

**shoot** trap or skeet shoot; *Chiefly Brit.* hunting expedition, esp. for game

**shooting** hunting with a gun for sport

**shorebirds** hunted birds that live by water, esp. curlew, plover, snipe, rail, gallinule, and yellowlegs

**skeet shooting** trapshooting in which clay targets are propelled singly or in pairs from several different positions at varying heights and speeds to simulate flight of game birds

**small game** any small, wild animal that is hunted, such as hare, rabbit, racoon, squirrel, woodchuck, groundhog, opossum, or prairie dog

**snap** (*vb*) fire shot without raising gun to eyes to aim; fire gun on an empty chamber

**sporting** (*adj*) engaging in or related to open-air sports such as hunting and fishing

**sportsman** person who engages in open-air sports such as hunting and fishing, esp. with sense of fairness and courtesy

**spring** (*vb*) *Chiefly Brit.* flush game bird from cover

**stalking** following prey or quarry closely with intent to kill or capture, esp. hunting game in open, broken country with little or no cover, as in stag hunting

**stander** hunter with gun over whom beater drives birds or toward whom deer hunter pushes deer

**still-hunt** (*vb*) hunt game alone, usu. in heavy, wooded cover and as silently as possible, esp. without a dog

**surround** hunting method in which prey is chased into location where it is encircled and cannot escape

**tanning** process of converting hides into leather

**track** (*vb*) follow scent left by animal

**tracking** pursuing prey by following readable track or physical markings, or by using hounds to follow scent

**trapper** one who engages in trapping

**trapping** capturing game and wildfowl by setting mechanical contrivance that springs shut when triggered

**trapshooting** shooting at clay pigeons hurled into air from mechanical trap

**upland game birds** hunted game birds such as grouse, pheasant, pigeon, quail, and wild turkey

**venatic** (*adj*) of or pertaining to hunting

**venery** *Archaic.* sport of hunting

**waders** hunted wildfowl, such as coots, curlews, and plovers, found in shallow waters

**warrantable** (*adj*) of legal age for being hunted, esp. deer

**waterfowl** hunted birds that live on water, such as brant, bufflehead, canvasback, coot, duck, eider, gadwall, goose, mallard, scoter, shoveler, teal

**white hunter** person who guides big game hunters in Africa

**wildfowl** hunted game birds such as wild ducks, geese, swans, or waders

**wild fowling** hunting wildfowl such as ducks, geese, or waders

**wildlife management** organized protection, preservation, and propagation of game and other wild animals

**winged predators** birds that live by feeding on other animals, such as crow, eagle, hawk, jaeger, or owl

**woodsman** person skilled at hunting and trapping

## FOX HUNTING

**all on** cry of whipper-in indicating that all hounds are accounted for

**bait** (*vb*) set dogs on prey

**bolt** (*vb*) force fox out of hiding place into open

**call** sound made on horn to encourage hounds

**capping fee** fee paid to hunter's association by nonmember for one day's hunting rights

**carry** (*vb*) hold or catch scent

**challenge** cry of hound on picking up scent

**chop** (*vb*) attack and kill fox that has not begun to run; mob

**course** (*vb*) run fox into full view

**crop** whip

**cry** (*vb*) of hounds, bay continuously while following scent

**entered hound** foxhound that has hunted in prior seasons

**find** discovery of prey, esp. fox

**foxhound** hound

**fox hunting** traditional sport in which mounted hunters follow hounds in pursuit of fox

**gone away** huntsman's cry indicating hounds are in pursuit and hunt is on

**groom** person who cares for horses used in fox hunting

**halloa** huntsman's cry used to incite hounds

**hound** breed of dog trained to pursue game by scent, used esp. in fox hunting; foxhound

**hounds** pack of hounds used for hunting; huntsman's call to hounds

**hunting with hounds** fox hunting

**line** trail of scent left by fox

**mob** (*vb*) chop

**mort** note played on hunting horn signifying that hunted animal has been killed

**mute** (*adj*) of a hound, following scent of fox without crying out

**pink coat** usu. scarlet coat worn by members of fox hunt

**ratcatcher** *Chiefly Brit.* informal costume, usu. tweed jacket and tan riding breeches, worn while fox hunting

**run** chase of fox from find to kill

**run at hounds** engage in fox hunting with hounds

**tally ho** cry of huntsman indicating that fox or other prey has been sighted

**tantivy** cry of huntsman when chase is at full tilt

**thruster** rider who remains at front of field in fox hunt

**view halloa** cry of huntsman on seeing fox break cover

**whip** whipper-in

**whipper-in** member of hunt responsible for hounds; whip

**worry** action of hounds in tearing fox carcass apart

**yoicks** huntsman's cry used to encourage hounds

## HUNTING EQUIPMENT

**action** mechanism by which firearm is operated

**blind** hiding place for hunting ducks or geese

**block** *Slang.* set of decoys

**bow and arrow** curved, flexible frame bent by string stretched between its ends to fire pointed shafts

**bow net** clam-shaped net that springs shut to trap hawks, usu. baited with pigeon

**buckshot** lead shot, larger than BB, used in shotgun shells for hunting deer, boar, and similar game

**butt** stand concealed by thicket or sunk in ground and used for shooting driven birds

**camouflage** clothing or other gear made of material with mottled design in brown and green that simulates forest environment

**coursing hound** hound used to run game into view, such as greyhound, whippet, or Afghan

**cover** underbrush or woods that conceal wild animal

**deadfall** trap in which disturbance of bait triggers fall of heavy weight onto prey

**decoy** lifelike dummy or model of hunted species, esp. game bird or wildfowl, set out to attract others of species; trained bird or animal used for same purpose, now illegal

**double-O buck** common buckshot, used esp. for hunting deer

**float** flat-bottomed, wide boat such as johnboat, used for hunting shorebirds and waterfowl

**floating blind** boatlike concealment used for hunting ducks or geese

**gamebag** bag with shoulder strap, usu. of canvas or leather, used to carry dead game birds

**goose block** set of decoys used to attract geese

**hakapik** iron or steel hook on long wooden pole, used in seal hunting

**hide** *Chiefly Brit.* small place of concealment for gun, built esp. of straw or camouflage netting

**hip boots** waterproof boots reaching to midthigh or hips, used for wading through water

**hood** cover for a hawk's head, used in falconry when bird is not pursuing game

**hound** breed of dog trained to pursue game by scent, used esp. in fox hunting

**hunting box** *Chiefly Brit.* house in hunting area used during hunting season

**hunting dogs** any dog used for hunting game, such as pointers, retrievers, setters, hounds, spaniels, beagles, bassets, and weimaraners

**hunting horn** small copper horn carried by huntsman during fox hunt

**hunting knife** large, sturdy knife with blade curved toward tip, used to skin and dress game

**hunting scope** telescopic sight on hunting rifle

**jacklight** portable lantern or electric light used to spot game at night and transfix it while hunter shoots, generally illegal

**license** formal permission authorizing bearer to hunt in specified place or time or for specific game

**lure** feathered decoy swung at end of line, sometimes baited with raw meat, used in falconry

**natural blind** natural growth or formation used as concealment while hunting ducks and geese

**packhorse** horse used for carrying equipment and supplies, esp. into remote hunting areas in mountains

**pointer** any of certain breeds of dog used for pointing birds

**pointing dog** any of various breeds of dog, including setters and Brittany spaniels, used for pointing game

**profile** decoy depicting bird in profile

**purse net** net with drawstring that fits over rabbit hole

**rail boat** low, flat-bottomed boat with protective rails, used in hunting waterfowl

**recurve bow** bow that is bent backward from its primary curvature at the tips

**retriever** dog used for retrieving game

**rifle** firearm with spiral grooves cut inside long bore, imparting more precise trajectory to bullet, usu. fired from shoulder

**setter** dog used to set game, including breeds such as long-haired pointing bird dogs

**shooting stick** devise resembling walking stick, with folding seat on one end and pointed tip, which is imbedded into ground

**shotgun** smoothbore firearm, often double-barreled, firing either single slug or multiple-pellet loads

**silhouette** two-dimensional representation of game animal or bird, used as target

**snare** nooselike trap used esp. for rabbits

**spring trap** trap that springs shut on prey when triggered

**stool** *Slang.* decoy, esp. set of decoys

**straight bow** bow that curves in one direction only

**trap** mechanical contrivance that springs shut or open when triggered by prey

**trophy** antlers, hide, or body part kept to memorialize successful hunt

**tumbler** dog similar to small greyhound, formerly used in rabbit hunting

**waders** waterproof boots reaching to mid-chest, used esp. by duck hunters for wading through water

## FISHING PRACTICE AND TECHNIQUES

**amadou** absorbent fungus used to dry waterlogged dry flies

**angle** (*vb*) fish with hook and line

**angler** fisherman who is skilled in the art and practice of angling

**angling** art and practice of fishing with hook and line

**backcast** in fly casting, action of lifting line off the water through an upward and backward flip of fly rod's tip prior to forward cast of line that presents fly to quarry

**backhand cast** fly-fisherman's cast made across own body

**backing** between 100 and 250 yards of lighter, usu. braided line tied in behind heavier fly line as margin of safety against long run by big fish

**backlash** overrun of reel spool resulting in snarled line

**bait casting** casting of artificial lure or plug, as well as bait, with revolving-spool reel on fiberglass rod 4 to 7 feet long

**beach** (*vb*) bring fish in without net or gaff

**beginner's luck** initial success supposed to come to inexperienced and unskilled fishermen

**bite** action of fish taking hook and bait

**boat** (*vb*) bring fish into boat with net, gaff, or tailer

**bottom-fishing** fishing with live or dead bait for fish that are bottom feeders, such as ocean fish like flounder and sole or freshwater fish like catfish and carp

**bowfishing** shooting fish in shallow water with bow and arrow, esp. freshwater carp or bottom fish such as stingrays, skates, and sharks

**casting** act of projecting and placing artificial lure, fly, or bait within intended area and distance

**catch** all fish landed by an angler in one day

**charter** lease of boat by party for fishing expedition; any boat so leased

**clamming** digging for clams in mud flats and shallows with rake

**closed season** time of year when fishing for particular species is prohibited

**coarse fishing** *Chiefly Brit.* fishing for any freshwater fish other than salmon, trout, or grayling

**cock** (*vb*) of a float, turn up at one side; (*n*) male salmon or trout

**crabbing** fishing for crabs by dropping baited metal cage to bottom of water

**dap** (*vb*) allow fly to bounce lightly over surface of water using long rod up to 17 feet (5 m) in length

**deep-sea fishing** fishing from boat in ocean waters at some distance from shore

**double haul** fly casting technique used to achieve distance

**drag** unnatural movement of fly across water due to pull of current on line, often exceeding speed of current

**drag adjustment** device in reel mechanism that slows the pull of running fish

**dress** (*vb*) prepare a fly or bait a hook for use

**drift-fishing** fishing in which the fly's action is due entirely to current; still fishing with bait from a moving boat

**electric fishing** catching fish by submerging positive and negative electrodes, causing fish to swim toward positive electrode and become unconscious, illegal for sportfishing but used to move fish to other waters

**false cast** cast in which line and fly are prevented from hitting water by switching line forcefully back and forth

**fillet** (*vb*) remove flesh of fish from backbone in two strips for cooking

**fingerling** small trout

**fish** plural usage of fish except in scientific and technical context or to refer to several species, not individuals, where "fishes" is preferred

**fish culture** artificial breeding and propagation of fish to provide stock for angling or commercial sale

**fisherman** person who fishes, either for profit or pleasure

**fishery** fish hatchery

**fish hatchery** place where fish culture is carried out; fishery

**fishing** technique, practice, and diversion of catching fish for sport, usu. with line, hook, and rod

**fishing banks** shallow area of sea with abundant fish

**fishing ground** body of water designated, set aside, or preferred for commercial fishing

**fish story** *Informal.* exaggerated tale of fishing exploits

**float-fishing** river fishing in which boat continuously drifts while angler casts

**fly-fishing** method of fishing with artificial flies, in which weight of line, not lure, is propelled through air by switching it back and forth from a long rod to achieve velocity, with reel mounted below rod grip and used primarily to store line

**freshwater fish** most popular fish for freshwater fishing: esp. trout (brook, brown, golden, rainbow) also bass, bluegill, bullhead, carp, catfish, char, crappie, gar, grayling, perch, pike, salmon, sauger, shad, walleye, whitefish

**game fish** any species of fish that may legally be taken for sport and tends to resist capture

**gentle craft** sport of fishing or angling

**greased-line method** fishing for salmon in stream with fly that sinks just beneath surface and plastic-coated line that floats with no drag; formerly, this line was greased to make it float

**gut** (*vb*) remove entrails from fish

**hand line** line that is pulled in by hand rather than reeled in, used esp. to extricate fish from weeds

**harl** (*vb*) *Chiefly Brit.* troll with flies, spoons, or prawn on a long line in boat or estuary or inland seaway, used. for salmon and sea trout

**haul** commercial catch, esp. all fish caught by seine in one day

**hit** strike

**hole** still, deep place in stream where fish feed; pool

**hook** (*vb*) catch fish when hook is planted in its mouth

**horizontal cast** method of casting line beneath overhanging branch or rock by swinging rod parallel to surface of water

**ice fishing** tecnique of fishing through a hole cut in ice, usu. in frozen lake in winter

**jag** (*vb*) *Informal.* touch fish with hook, but not hook it

**jigging** imparting up and down motion to lure or bait, esp. in ice fishing

**keeper** fish that is legally big enough to keep

**kite fishing** method of offshore fishing in which airborne kite trolls skipping bait or holds live bait at surface of water

**lake fishing** fishing in freshwater lake, from shore or by trolling from boat

**land** (*vb*) bring hooked fish in to shore or net

**laying on** *Chiefly Brit.* fishing in nearly still water by resting baited hook on bottom with half-cocked float

**ledgering** *Chiefly Brit.* type of fishing in which a ledger is used to hold bait on bottom

**margin fishing** technique of fishing under bank on side of lake toward which wind is blowing food by placing rod on rests and floating bait, which is blown back under bank

**neck** upstream end of pool

**nibble** response of fish preparing to take bait on line

**nymph fishing** most difficult form of wet-fly fishing, usu. for trout using nymphs cast upstream

**permit** official license granting an individual permission to fish

**piscary** place for fishing

**piscatory** (*adj*) relating to fishing or fishermen

**play** amount of slack in a line, allowing it to move freely in response to fish

**playing fish** maintaining proper tension on line to tire out and bring in fish without breaking line

**plug casting** bait casting using plug as lure

**pool** still, deep place in stream where fish feed; hole

**present** (*vb*) offer fly to fish by casting it

**reef-fishing** fishing on or from shallow ridge of rocks or sand in ocean

**retrieve** (*vb*) reel in or pull back fishing line by hand

**rise** act of fish coming to fly; circular ripples on water's surface indicating fish coming up to feed

**roll cast** fly-casting technique in which line does not go behind angler, used on streams with close overhangs

**run** (*vb*) of fish, take hook or bait and swim quickly away from fisherman

**saltwater fish** most popular fish, for saltwater fishing: esp. tuna, cod, salmon, and striped bass; also albacore, barracuda, blackfish, bluefish, croaker, dolphin, flounder, mackerel, marlin, pollock, pompano, red snapper, sailfish, shark, whiting

**seiner** commercial fisherman using seine

**shoot line** in fly casting, act of allowing forward cast of fly line to pull out extra loops of line held by noncasting hand, used to lengthen cast

**sidearm cast** cast performed by swinging rod parallel to ground at side of body, esp. to avoid overhang

**sink-and-draw** fishing with dead bait that is alternately allowed to sink, then drawn up to surface

**skipper** captain of boat

**snag** (*vb*) catch fly or lure in underwater obstruction or overhang when casting

**snatch** (*vb*) *Chiefly Brit.* use weighted triangle on hand line to poach fish

**spin casting** fishing with lure or bait and closed-face reel with fixed spool from which line peels off at end of long spinning rod, different from spinning

**spin fishing** spinning

**spinning** method of casting light lure with fixed-spool reel, mounted on underside of rod, in which line uncoils but spool remains stationary; spin fishing; thread-line fishing

**sportfishing** fishing for sport with rod and reel, usu. from motorboat for saltwater fish

**squidding** surf casting for squid

**still fishing** fishing with stationary bait from shore or boat

**stock** supply (stream or lake) with fish for fishing

**stream fishing** fishing in fresh waterway, either from shore or by standing in boots in water

**strike** moment when fish attacks and takes fly, lure, or bait and must be hooked; hit

**surf casting** technique and practice of using 8- to 12-foot spinning or bait-casting rod to cast heavy-duty line into sea while standing at shoreline

**switch** (*vb*) move fishing line with swift, lashing motion

**tail** downstream end of pool

**take** (*vb*) of fish, strike bait, lure, or fly and become hooked

**taking fish** fish rising to take bait, or one whose actions indicate it to be likely to strike

**test** designation for weight of line

**thread-line fishing** *Chiefly Brit.* spinning

**tie** (*vb*) design and make artificial fly

**trawl** (*vb*) fish by dragging net along bottom of sea, or with buoyed trawl line having numerous baited hooks spaced at intervals along it

**troll** (*vb*) tow baited hook or lure, either submerged or on surface, behind slow-moving boat, usu. in lake or sea

**trolling** fishing from slow-moving boat with lure or bait trailing behind at varying depths and speeds in lakes or saltwater

**trotting** angling in fast-moving water, using float and line that holds bait near bottom

**tying** art and practice of designing and making flies

**underhand lob** casting technique in which rod tip is raised vertically to propel bait or lure outward from fisherman

**warp** (*vb*) move boat about by pulling anchored rope

**whaling** hunting for and capturing whales with harpoons at sea

**X** designation for leader diameter in gut or monofilament, expressed in multiples of X

## FISHING EQUIPMENT AND TACKLE

**angleworm** earthworm commonly used as live bait

**antenna float** float with long tip on top that shows above water surface

**archer tackle** spinning tackle used with dead bait

**arlesey bomb** streamlined ledger weight with swivel that slips through weeds

**artificial bait** object made to resemble fly, worm, fish, or animal and placed on hook

**artificial fly** imitation of fly, insect, or larva made from feathers, fur, silk, thread, and/or tinsel, with hook attached; fly

**backlash** snarled line on reel due to improper casting; bird's nest

**bait** living creatures such as minnows, earthworms, grubs, or grasshoppers attached to hook and used to entice fish into striking

**bait-casting rod** fiberglass rod for bait casting, usu. 5 to 6 feet (1.5 to 1.8 m) long

**baitfish** small fish such as minnow or shiner used as bait for larger fish

**bait kettle** *Chiefly Brit.* can used for carrying live bait

**balanced tackle** tackle used esp. in fly-fishing, in which relationship between rod action and reel-and-line weight is essential to effective casting

**barb** point projecting off hook in opposite direction from point, used to prevent fish from spitting out hook

**barbless hook** hook without barb, easier to remove from fish than barbed hook

**barrel knot** knot used esp. for fastening together two strands of leader gut or monofilament; blood knot

**barrel swivel** swivel consisting of two connected eyes, used to absorb twisting of line

**bass bug** large fly-rod lure with cork or deer-hair body that imitates bass food such as frog, bee, dragonfly, or mouse

**bend** crook in fishhook, often ending at barb

**bird's nest** backlash

**black gnat** artificial fly used for trout or salmon

**blood knot** barrel knot

**boat rod** rod for casting or trolling with lure or bait from boat, usu. 5 to 6 1/2 feet (1.5 to 2 meters) long

**bob** bobber

**bobber** float usu. made of cork and quills, used in still fishing to suspend bait at set depth and indicate strike; bob

**boulter** long, heavyweight line with several hooks attached

**bubble float** transparent, spherical float partly weighted with water

**bucktail** artificial fly with long wing, often of hair from deer's tail, that imitates minnow or other small baitfish

**bucktail jig** lure with weighted head and bucktail wings

**bung** *Brit. slang.* cork float

**bunt** bagging portion of fishing net

**cast** *Chiefly Brit.* leader

**casting rod** fishing rod, usu. 4 to 8 feet (1.2 to 2.4 m) long, for casting bait or spinning lure, usu. fitted with revolving reel that allows angler to control line with thumb during cast

**check** adjustable ratchet system on reel that prevents line from running freely when fish takes it

**chugger** plug that rests on water's surface and makes popping sound when retrieved; popper; popping plug

**chum** ground bits of bait or food discarded into water to attract game fish

**clinch knot** knot in which eye is formed by looping rope and seizing end to standing part, used as hook eye line knot

**close-faced reel** reel enclosed in housing with hole at center or edge of cover through which line passes

**cloudbait** finely minced bait discarded into water to attract fish

**corkball float** float made of ball of cork

**cork bug** fly with solid cork body that floats and imitates action of frog, mouse, or grasshopper, used in bass fishing

**courge** *Chiefly Brit.* perforated box hung over side of boat to keep bait alive

**crawlers** rubber cleats that attach to boots to prevent slipping on rocks

**creel** basket, esp. of wicker, for holding fish, often carried by strap over shoulder

**cut bait** bait-sized chunks of fish that are too large to be used whole as bait

**cuttyhunk** twisted linen fishline, esp. one laid by hand

**Darter** *Trademark.* plug that floats horizontally when at rest and submerges up to three feet (1 m) when wobbling slowly

**dead bait** any dead fish or insect used as bait

**deep diver** plug for bass and walleye that sinks upon hitting water; sinking plug

**devon** spinner with vanes at head and triangle at tail

**diamond sinker** long, slender sinker, tapering at each end, used for trolling

**dipsey sinker** small, teardrop-shaped, lead sinker

**disgorger** rodlike device with forked end, used to remove hook from fish's throat

**diving plug** plug that darts at surface of water, then plunges

**dobber** float or bob

**doctor** type of artificial fly, often silver

**double-taper line** leader line that tapers at both ends so that it can be reversed when wear requires it

**drifter** fishing boat using drift net

**drift net** fishing net held upright in water by floats at upper edge and sinkers at bottom edge, so as to be carried by current or tide

**drop net**  circular net lowered by weighted cords at four points into water to catch fish and small crustaceans for bait

**dry fly**  fly that imitates appearance and action of floating insect, with hackles projecting at right angles from hook to keep fly on surface

**dusty miller**  artificial fly used esp. for trout and salmon

**eye**  loop at end of fishhook shank through which line or leader passes

**farm**  waters devoted to propagation of fish

**ferrule**  any of several fitted, usu. metal joints, composed of socket and plug, that are spaced along length of rod so that it can be dismantled and reassembled

**fiberglass rod**  basic material used for fishing rods, replacing bamboo after 1948

**fighting chair**  seat attached to deck at stern of fishing boat, used by angler in landing very large fish

**fish box**  covered box sunk into floor of boat to hold catch

**fish eggs**  roe

**fishfinder**  surf fishing device with pyramid sinker and barrel swivel that allows bait to cover broad area

**fishhook**  slender, recurved, usu. barbed piece of metal wire at end of lure or on which fly is tied or bait placed for catching fish; hook

**fishing line**  line of braided or twisted silk, cotton, or monofilament, used to connect hook to rod and reel; fishline

**fishing pole**  rudimentary gear consisting of long, thin rod with line and hook fastened to one end for catching fish

**fishing rod**  long, thin, flexible rod of bamboo, fiberglass, or graphite with reel attached, used with line and hooks for catching fish; rod

**fishing smack**  large, usu. commercial fishing vessel containing well to keep catch alive

**fishing vest**  armless jacket, usu. waterproof, with several pockets and places where fishing tackle may be stored or attached

**fishline**  fishing line

**fish stringer**  length of rope or line run through mouths and gills of catch and draped in water, esp. over side of boat or from shore

**fixed-reel seat**  frame by which fixed spinning reel is attached to rod

**fixed-spool reel**  spinning reel with open top

**float**  cork, hollow plastic, or bobber used to buoy up baited line in water

**floating-diving plug**  lure that dives beneath water's surface when retrieved

**fly**  artificial fly

**fly book**  folding case for storing flies, often containing several waterproof envelopes or lining of lamb's wool

**fly box**  container in which artificial flies are stored in compartments with clear lids or on snap catches or cloth

**fly leader**  monofilament between a hook or fly and a heavier line, used to reduce alarm in fish

**fly line**  heavy test line, used in fly-fishing, whose weight propels the cast

**fly reel**  reel used to store backing and fly line

**fly rod**  long, light, flexible rod of bamboo or fiberglass, used in fly-fishing

**gaff**  large, barbless steel hook on handle, used for landing or boating fish

**gang hook**  hook with several points

**gear**  tools, apparatus, and other equipment used in fishing; rig; tackle

**gill net**  mesh wall held vertically in water by corks on top and lead weights on bottom, capturing anything too large to slip through it

**golden shiner**  freshwater minnow used as live bait

**grasshopper**  artificial fly resembling grasshopper

**grip**  portion of end of rod below casting reel or above fly reel that angler holds while fishing, usu. having nonslip surface

**gut**  embryo silk in varying thickness used for leader or tippets, now largely replaced by monofilament nylon

**hackle**  legs and feet of artificial fly made by wrapping long neck or saddle feathers, usu. from a cock or hen, around hook shank

**hackle fly**  artificial fly made with hackles, usu. without wings

**hand line**  hook at end of line dropped into water by hand, without rod or reel

**harpoon**  barbed, spearlike missile attached to rope, fired or thrown at whales or large fish

**hatch boat**  *Chiefly Brit.* small fishing vessel with covered wells for holding fish

**hip boots**  waterproof boots reaching to hips

**hook**  fishhook

**ice auger**  device used to cut hole in ice for ice fishing

**ice skimmer**  slotted, ladlelike device used to clear ice chips from hole and surrounding area in ice fishing

**ice spud**  device with chisel-like blade on heavy handle, used to punch hole in ice for ice fishing

**ice sounder**  device consisting of lead weight with spring clip on line, used to determine depth of water beneath ice in ice fishing

**jig**  lure with weighted head, fixed hook, and tail made of feathers or nylon, often attached by wire leader; jigging lure

**jig and eel**  narrow-bodied metal squid lure up to 12 inches (30.5 cm) long with eel rigged onto it, used for striped bass and sea trout

**jigging lure**  jig

**jigging rod**  spinning rod used with jigs

**Jock Scot**  artificial fly with yellow and scarlet coloring in body and tail, and hackle of guinea fowl and grouse feathers, esp. for salmon

**keeper ring**  small wire ring positioned at rod butt just above grip, used to attach hook when not fishing

**keep net**  long, cylindrical net used to keep catch alive

**Kendal sneck bent**  fishing hook with wide, square bend

**landing net**  any baglike net on handle large enough to lift exhausted fish from water and land or boat it

**leader**  length of wire or monofilament that protects line from fish or forms invisible link between main line and lure, bait, or fly; *Chiefly Brit.* cast

**ledger**  *Chiefly Brit.* sinker designed to hold bait at bottom and allow line to run freely through it, usu. ball of lead with hole bored through it

**ledger line**  *Chiefly Brit.* line set so that bait and sinker rest on bottom

**line**  part of tackle that connects cast lure or baited hook to rod in fisherman's hand, usu. monofilament, also: braided nylon, copper, cotton, cuttyhunk, Dacron, linen, nylon, silk, or wire

**live bait** any natural organism placed on a hook and used to catch fish: angleworm, caterpillar, crayfish, cricket, darter, dragonfly, fish egg, frog, grasshopper, grub, hellgrammite, mayfly, minnow, night crawler, worm

**lobster pot** baited box trap dropped to seafloor for catching lobsters

**lock-snap swivel** swivel composed of wire, the end of which hooks onto itself

**loop knot** knot made by doubling over line at its end and forming square knot with loop from both thicknesses

**lure** any artificial bait used to attract fish, usu. distinguished from artificial flies

**mayfly** widely found insect used as bait and as prototype for artificial dry flies

**midge** mosquitolike insect whose larvae are used as bait for trout in streams and mountain lakes

**monofilament** single strand of extruded nylon used for fishing line

**multiplier** very free-running reel used for bait casting and spinning

**muskie rod** heavy bait-casting rod with offset handle

**nail knot** nooselike knot that tightens when pulled and does not slip, sometimes tied around nail for attaching sections of leader or attaching leader to fly line

**net** any of various mesh devices with handles, used to snare fish in water for landing or boating

**nymph** artificial fly modeled after any subaqueous insect and its larva, having no wings, soft hackle at head, tapered body, and sparse tail

**palmer** artificial fly with bushy body made entirely from wound hackle feathers

**pencil float** long, hollow, often plastic float

**phantom** spinning lure similar to devon

**pillars** cross bars from one plate to the other in reel frame

**pirn** Brit. dial. fishing reel

**plastic ball float** round, hollow float made of plastic

**plastic lure** lure made of plastic, as distinguished from metal or wooden lures

**plug** lure made of wood, plastic, or metal that darts through water imitating a small fish, fitted with one of more gang hooks

**plummet** Chiefly Brit. cork-bottomed lead weight used to plumb deep water such as in lakes

**plunker** casting lure that makes plunking sound as it hits water

**point** last section of tapered leader in fly fishing; tippet

**popper** chugger

**popping plug** plug that floats on surface and creates bubbles and popping sounds when it is jerked by moving rod tip; chugger

**popping rod** bait-casting rod with straight handle

**pork rind** strips of hog's skin preserved in liquid, used with lure or alone when shaped into lure that makes fishlike wiggle when retrieved

**pounds test** weight that a fishing line can lift without breaking

**priest** Brit. slang. cudgel for dispatching fish that have been landed or boated

**purse line** line used to close bottom of purse seine

**purse seine** large seine drawn by two boats around school of fish and closed at the bottom by means of a line passing through rings

**pyramid sinker** medium-sized lead sinker in form of pyramid

**quill** hollow stem of bird's feather, used for floats

**reel** device with rotating or fixed spool attached to butt of fishing rod, used to let out or bring in line

**reel crank** handle used to turn spool of line on reel

**revolving-spool reel** standard bait-casting reel in which spool drum revolves when casting or reeling in line

**rig** gear or tackle

**rod** fishing rod

**rod butt** end of rod behind grip and furthest from tip

**rod guide** one of several metal rings attached along length of rod so that line follows action of rod and can be controlled from reel to hook

**rod rest** Chiefly Brit. device used to support rod, often in tandem with other rod rests, esp. when ledgering

**rod ring** Chiefly Brit. ring at end of rod through which line runs; tip-top

**rod tip** attachment to end of rod farthest from butt with guide through which line runs

**roe** eggs of fish used as bait

**saltwater bait** live bait used for deep-sea fishing and surf casting: baitfish, crab, cut bait, herring, mullet, shrimp, squid

**seaboot** tall, waterproof wading boot

**seine** vertical fishing net suspended in water between floats at surface and submerged sinkers

**shank** straight body of fishhook, leading from eye to bend

**single-action fly reel** fly reel whose spool makes one turn with each turn of the reel handle

**sinker** metal weight, usu. made of lead, molded in various shapes and sizes, used to lower, troll, or anchor bait or lure at desired depth

**sinking plug** deep diver

**sliding-clamp reel seat** pair of clamps on butt of spinning rod that hold reel in place

**sliding float** float that is free to run along line between topmost weight and rubber stop, used in deepwater fishing

**snap swivel** swivel in shape of safety pin that snaps shut

**spear** long staff with sharply pointed metal head, used for stabbing fish

**spent wing fly** dry fly with extended wings

**spider fly** wet or dry fly with no tail or wings, an overlong hackle body, and long legs resembling spider

**spinner** lure with oval metal blade mounted on shaft that revolves when drawn through water

**spinning reel** fixed-spool reel with adjustable drag and antireverse lock, mounted on underside of rod

**spinning rod** lightweight bamboo, fiberglass, or graphite rod for spinning with small lure, lure-fly combination, or bait

**split shot** small lead shot partially split for easy placement on leader or line as weight

**split-shot sinker** sinker made of partially split lead shot

**spool** revolving apparatus in reel, around which line winds and unwinds

**spoon** brightly colored, spoon-shaped lure with one or more hooks that swivels and flashes to imitate small baitfish, used in casting or trolling

**sproat** fishhook having circular bend

**stink bait** sponge or dough impregnated with slime from decomposed matter, cheese, or small dead fish, used for catfish and carp

**streamer fly** artificial fly having long hackle wings extending beyond bend of fishhook, representing minnow or small baitfish

**surface disturber** type of floating plug shaped to splash on retrieval

**surface plug** nonspinning lure that darts along surface of water

**surf rod** long, sturdy rod used in surf casting

**swivel** two metal eyes joined by pin so that entire swivel unit revolves freely and absorbs torsion of lure or bait to minimize twist on line

**tackle** equipment and apparatus used in fishing; gear; rig

**tackle box** sturdy, waterproof, metal or plastic box in which fishing tackle is stored, usu. having several compartments

**tag** small piece of shiny material wound on hook shank at rear end of body of fly

**tailer** flexible noose on handle, slipped over fish's tail to land or boat it without net or gaff

**tapered leader** leader that is thinner at tippet end

**terrestrial** wet or dry fly representing a land insect such as an ant, beetle, or grasshopper in water

**tilt** ice-fishing device with crosspieces that span hole in ice, used to hold baited line leading from underwater revolving-spool reel and attached to cocked arm that releases when fish strikes; tip-up

**tip guide** metal ring at end of rod through which line runs and is controlled by movement of rod; tip-top

**tippet** finest end of tapered leader; tail or wing of artificial fly made from shaft of certain cock feather; point

**tip-top** tip guide

**tip-up** tilt

**trace** *Chiefly Brit.* section of spinning line between reel line and hook

**trammel net** three-layered net with a fine-meshed middle layer between two coarser outer layers, so that fish become entangled in one or more of the nets

**trawler** fishing boat used to haul trawl net

**trawl line** buoyed fishing line with baited hooks attached at intervals

**trawl net** net dragged along sea bottom to catch fish

**treblehook** hook terminating in three bends and three barbed points

**trident** fishing spear having three-pronged point

**trolling reel** sturdy, open-spool reel for trolling from boat

**trotline** sturdy fishing line suspended across or submerged in stream with individual hooks attached at intervals by separate lines

**tube fly** artificial fly with tubular body that resembles a lure, used for salmon or trout fishing

**turle knot** knot used to attach artificial fly to leader

**ultralight spinning tackle** specialized spinning tackle orig. from France, no heavier than a 3-ounce rod and 3-pound test line, used for small game fish

**waders** thigh-high rubber boots, often with studded soles to provide traction over rocks; chest-high, waterproof boot trousers with suspenders

**wading staff** rod used to test bottom firmness while wading through water

**waist boots** waterproof boots reaching to waist

**wet fly** sparsely dressed, usu. flat fly that imitates action and appearance of submerged insect

**worm fly** *Chiefly Brit.* artificial fly with two bodies and two hooks but only one eye, used esp. beneath overhanging foliage

# GARDENING

Gardens and Gardening Systems
Practice, Tools, and Techniques
Plants and Plant Parts

**SEE ALSO**: Chap. 2: Biology; Plants; Chap. 12: Agriculture

## GARDENS AND GARDENING SYSTEMS

**alpine garden** garden of plants native to high altitudes

**arboretum** garden in which trees and shrubs are grown and displayed

**bonsai** garden of dwarf trees artfully cultivated in pots (Japan)

**botanical garden** collection of plants and trees kept for exhibition and scientific study

**conservatory** elaborate greenhouse where plants are grown and displayed

**dry garden** garden of cactus and other plants requiring little water for cultivation

**flower bed** small area of ground planted with flowers, often part of larger garden

**flower garden** garden of decorative, blossoming plants

**formal garden** elaborate, manicured, and carefully pruned decorative garden

**garden** plot of ground where plants are cultivated

**Garden of Eden** Biblical paradise home of Adam and Eve

**glasshouse** *Chiefly Brit.* greenhouse

**greenhouse** translucent structure in which environment is controlled to allow delicate plants to develop and thrive

**hanging garden** garden with plants suspended in pots rather than growing from ground

**hedge** dense row of shrubs used to form boundary

**herbarium** collection of dried plants, esp. for botanical study

**hortorium** museum for collection, preservation, and study of plant specimens

**Japanese garden** manicured garden with bonsai, teahouse, and still water

**jardin** *French.* garden

**kitchen garden** small vegetable garden for personal use

**landscape** viewable portion of terrain and its features; (vb) manipulate a natural environment for aesthetic purposes

**lawn** ground covered with closely mowed grass

**orchard** cultivated fruit or nut trees

**ornamental garden** garden of flowers and decorative shrubs

**park** area of public land, esp. in or near city, with lawns, gardens, trees, paths, and recreational facilities

**patch** small garden; flower bed

**rock garden** artificial landscape containing natural-looking rock outcrops and soil surfaces

**roof garden**  potted plants growing on roof of building, esp. in urban area with no open land surrounding buildings

**rose garden**  ornamental garden of carefully pruned rose bushes

**sunken garden**  garden built below level of surrounding land

**tea garden**  Japanese garden with teahouse

**terrarium**  miniature garden enclosed in glass container

**truck garden**  garden in which vegetables are grown to be marketed

**vegetable garden**  garden of cultivated, edible plants

**victory garden**  home vegetable garden grown during wartime to supplement crop production

**vineyard**  plantation of cultivated grapevines

**xeriscape**  garden for drought-tolerant plants

**yard**  cultivated area beside residence

## PRACTICE, TOOLS, AND TECHNIQUES

**acidity**  state of having excessive acid, or a relatively low concentration of hydrogen atoms in soil, esp. in areas of heavy rainfall and abundant organic matter

**agronomy**  science and management of crop production

**air layering**  propagation method by which roots develop on stems while attached to mother plant

**alkalinity**  state of having high concentration of calcium and other minerals in soil, esp. in areas of light rainfall

**arbor**  latticework bower on which vines are trained

**arboriculture**  cultivation of trees and shrubs for ornament

**arborist**  tree specialist

**backfill**  soil returned after being dug up to cover positioned roots, often mixed with additives to improve its condition

**balanced crotch**  two tree branches growing equally, rendering each branch weak

**balled and burlapped**  designating soil-covered roots bundled and wrapped for protection until planting

**bare root**  condition of dormant plant whose root is devoid of soil

**bed**  area of ground prepared for plants

**blanch** (vb)  shield plant, esp. vegetable, from sunlight to promote paler color in stems or leaves

**blower**  power sweeper, esp. for leaves

**bolt** (vb)  produce flowers or seeds prematurely

**bone meal**  fertilizer of crushed bone

**botany**  science of plant life, including structure, growth, and classification; characteristics of a plant or plant group

**broadcast** (vb)  toss out seed by hand

**brush cutter**  pruner

**budding**  putting forth of buds; asexual propagation technique

**chlorosis**  iron deficiency in plant

**cloche**  transparent protective covering for delicate plants

**cold frame**  low, transparent, unheated greenhouse box

**compost**  nutrient-rich decomposed organic matter

**cordon**  tree pruned to have only one main stem

**crown**  soil level just below ground where stem and root join

**cultivate** (vb)  prepare soil for plants and care for them to foster growth

**cutting**  portion of plant removed and induced to propagate

**damping-off**  condition caused by fungal disease in which stems of small seedlings wilt and rot

**deadhead** (vb)  pinch off dead flower heads from stems to promote blooming

**defoliation**  unnatural and often unhealthy loss of leaves

**Demeter**  goddess of agriculture and fertility (ancient Greece)

**dibber**  dibble

**dibble**  pointed tool used to make holes in soil for insertion of plants or seeds; dibber

**dieback**  death of plant stems, starting at tips

**drainage**  movement of water through soil in plant's root area

**drill**  straight furrow for sowing seeds in rows

**drip line**  imaginary circle drawn around plant under its outermost branches, where rainwater is likely to fall

**edger**  revolving blade on long handle, used for trimming lawn or flower bed

**espalier**  lattice or trellis on which tree or shrub branches are trained to grow in flat pattern

**etiolation**  bleaching of plant due to light deprivation

**evapotranspiration**  process of transferring moisture from earth to atmosphere by evaporation of water and transpiration from plants

**fertilize** (vb)  apply nutrient-rich materials to soil

**fertilizer**  material containing one or more plant nutrients

**flat**  rooting box for cuttings or seeds

**floriculture**  cultivation of ornamental and flowering plants

**florist**  person who grows and sells flowers

**floristry**  growing and selling of flowers and ornamentals

**flower pot**  plant container, usu. plastic, wood, or ceramic

**force** (vb)  artificially induce rapid growth or blooming of plant

**forestry**  science of planting and cultivating trees

**friable soil**  easily crumbled soil

**fruition**  bearing of fruit

**furrow**  planting trench made by plow

**gardener**  person who enjoys or is skilled at tending gardens

**gardening**  process of making, caring for, and working in gardens

**germination**  sprouting of seeds for planting

**girdling**  act of cutting around plant through bark and cambium in order to kill it

**graft**  union of one plant to another so that two will grow as one

**greenhouse**  hothouse

**green thumb**  exceptional facility for gardening and growing plants successfully

**ground cover**  low, dense-growing plants used to cover ground where grass will not grow

**groundskeeping**  care of gardens, playing fields, and lawns

**grow light**  artificial indoor light for growing plants

**harden-off** (vb)  gradually expose greenhouse seedlings to outdoor weather

**harrow**  tool with spikes or sharp-edged disks for cultivating soil

**heading back**  pruning to shorten branches

**herbaceous** (adj)  designating nonwoody plant

**hoe**  hand tool with thin, flat blade on handle for loosening soil and weeding

**honeydew**  sticky, sweet substance produced by aphids and other insects

**horticulture** science and art of growing plants

**hose** flexible tube used to convey water to garden

**hotbed** plot of earth covered with glass and heated to accelerate plant growth

**hothouse** glass building artificially heated for growing plants; greenhouse

**humus** organic part of soil resulting from decomposition of plant or animal matter

**hydroponics** growing of plants without soil in nutrient-rich solutions of moist, inert material

**inarching** grafting while plants are still rooted

**intercropping** space-saving method of planting fast-growing crop between rows of slower-growing crop

**irrigation** bringing of water to plant beds, esp. by ditches or channels

**landscape gardening** practice of arranging lawns, flower beds, and bushes in attractive manner for human use, esp. as a profession

**lath house** overhead structure of narrow wood strips providing protection from sunlight or frost

**lawn mower** manual or power machine for cutting grass

**leaching** loss of soluble matter from soil due to filtering through of water

**leaf mold** rich soil composed largely of decayed leaves

**lime** calcium compound used as soil amendment to enhance crop growth

**loam** friable mixture of sand and clay

**loppers** long-handled pruning shears

**manure** fertilizer of animal excrement

**mulch** protective ground cover of leaves, straw, and peat moss

**nozzle** spout at end of hose for directing flow of water

**n-p-k** initials for ingredients in complete fertilizer: nitrogen (n), phosphorus (p), and potassium (chemical symbol k)

**nursery** place where young trees or plants are raised

**offset** small new plant at end of stem sent out from base of mature perennial

**organic** (*adj*) designating plants grown with animal or vegetable fertilizers only

**peat moss** mulch of slightly decomposed plant remains

**perlite** light, porous soil additive composed of volcanic material

**pest** destructive or troublesome insect, small animal, or weed

**photosynthesis** production of organic substances from carbon dioxide and water in green plant cells, which chemically transform radiant energy of sunlight

**pinching** removal of tips of twigs and branches to force bushy growth

**plant classification** standard botanical classification system: family, genus, species, variety (subspecies), strain, hybrid

**planter** decorative container for growing plants

**plant food** nitrogen-rich chemical mixture used to fortify plants and accelerate growth

**pleaching** training of plant growth so that plaited branches form hedge or arbor

**plug** small wedge or segment cut from plant for testing

**pollard** tree pruned to produce dense, leafy dome

**pollination** transfer of pollen from stamens to pistils

**potted plant** any plant grown in soil enclosed in a container, esp. indoors

**propagation** multiplication of an organism by natural reproduction

**prune** (*vb*) control growth of plant by trimming at top to increase quality and yield of flowers or fruit

**pruner** bladed device for cutting back plant growth; brush cutter

**rake** long-handled, toothed tool for gathering loose material or smoothing surface

**root-bound** (*adj*) designating potted plant whose roots have no room to grow

**rootstock** portion of grafted or budded plant containing root

**salinity** excess salt; measure of salt content

**scree** rocky debris, sometimes re-created as rock garden habitat

**shade** shelter or protection from light or sun

**shearing** pruning of outer foliage

**shovel** handled tool with broad scoop or hollowed-out blade for digging in earth

**shredder** compost maker

**silt** soil composed primarily of sediment that accumulates on bottoms of rivers and bays, with particles smaller than sand but larger than clay

**sod** carpet of grass; turf

**soil** upper layer of earth that may be cultivated, and that can support plant growth; this material collected and placed in gardens or pots, consisting of small particles of rock together with humus

**soil amendments** substances added to improve soil texture and fertility, such as compost, manure, peat moss, bark, perlite, lime, or chemicals

**spade** digging instrument with blade that is pushed into ground with foot

**spading fork** spade with forklike tines

**species** naturally existing population of organisms that interbreed; botanical classification between genus and variety

**sphagnum** long-fibered, highly absorbent peat moss

**sprinkler** device for distributing water evenly over large area of garden

**staking** providing support for plants with thin strips of wood stuck upright in ground

**standard** plant trained to form treelike shape with single trunk and crown of foliage

**terrace** raised, flat mound of earth with sloping sides, often in series of descending levels

**thinning** pruning by removing whole branches to create less density; removal of some seedlings to foster growth of others

**tillage** land that has been tilled

**tiller** machine designed for digging, cultivating, aerating, and mixing soil

**tilth** cultivation of land

**top-dress** (*vb*) apply mulch to protect seeds

**topiary** pruning of hedges into unique or formal shapes; hedge so pruned

**topsoil** rich, relatively fertile top layer of soil

**transpiration** loss of water from plant leaves into air

**transplant** (*vb*) transfer plant from one home to another

**trellis** structure of thin strips on which climbing plants are trained

**trowel** small tool with curved, scooplike blade on handle, used in turning earth and digging

**turf** sod

**weed** (*vb*) remove unwanted growth from garden

**weed trimmer**  tool for cutting back weeds
**wheelbarrow**  shallow, open container on single wheel with handles, used for moving soil and plants
**wilting**  limpness in plant due to lack of water, poor root function, or disease
**windbreak**  plants used as barrier to wind
**window pot**  planter placed on or outside window sill

## Plants and Plant Parts

**annual**  plant with life cycle of one year or season
**anther**  part of stamen that produces and releases pollen
**bark**  outside covering of stems and roots of trees and woody plants
**bedding plant**  plant adapted for open-air bed
**biennial**  plant with two-year life cycle, in which vegetative first-year growth is followed by fruiting and drying during second year
**bloom**  flower
**blossom**  flower, esp. of fruit-bearing plant
**bole**  tree trunk
**bolt**  (vb) prematurely produce flowers and seeds, esp. in hot weather
**bonsai**  potted tree or shrub that has been dwarfed, usu. by pruning roots and pinching
**bract**  leaflike structure growing below or encircling flower cluster or flower
**broad-leaved**  (adj) describing a plant having leaves that are not needles
**bromeliad**  plant with stiff, leathery leaves and spikes of bright flowers
**bud**  small swelling on plant from which shoot, leaf cluster, or flower develops
**bulb**  dormant underground bud stage of some plants
**bush**  shrub
**cactus**  fleshy-stemmed plant with reduced or spinelike leaves, living in dry places and requiring little water
**calyx**  outer whorl of protective leaves of flower
**cambium**  layer of formative cells beneath bark of tree
**carpel**  ovule-bearing leaf or leaflike structure that is primary segment of pistil
**climber**  vine or climbing plant with tendrils
**conifer**  cone-bearing evergreen, usu. with narrow, needle-like or small, scalelike leaves
**corm**  underground stem base that acts as reproductive structure
**cormel**  small corm
**corolla**  petals of a flower
**cosmopolite**  plant living throughout world
**cotyledon**  first leaf or two of seedling
**crab grass**  weedy annual grass that roots and spreads rapidly in lawns and gardens
**creeper**  plant whose stem puts out tendrils or rootlets and that moves along surface as it grows
**crown**  topmost portions of tree's leafy canopy
**cultivar**  plant variety originating in cultivation and persisting as species
**deciduous**  (adj) designating any plant that sheds all its leaves once each year
**dendroid**  (adj) treelike in form
**double flower**  flower with petals that are numerous and clustered to cover center

**epiphyte**  nonparasitic plant that lives on another plant
**everbearing**  (adj) producing fruit throughout growing season
**evergreen**  plant that maintains functional green foliage throughout year
**exotic**  plant that is not native to growing area
**eye**  bud of root or tuber
**fern**  nonflowering plant having fronds instead of leaves and reproducing by spores instead of seeds
**filament**  stalk of stamen bearing the anther
**flora**  plants of specific region or time
**flower**  (n) seed-producing plant with stem that bears leaf-like sepals, colorful petals, and pollen-bearing stamens; plant cultivated for its blossoms; reproductive organ of some plants; bloom; blossom; (vb) produce blossoms
**flower bud**  bud that produces a flower only, no fruit
**flowering plant**  plant that produces flowers, fruit, and seeds
**foliage**  groups of leaves, flowers, or branches; greenery
**foliage plant**  plant cultivated for decorative foliage
**frond**  fern or palm foliage
**fruit**  mature ovary of flowering plant, usu. edible
**fruit tree**  tree bearing fruit
**go to seed**  pass to stage of producing seeds at end of growth cycle, used esp. of seasonal crops
**grass**  member of family of flowering plants with long, narrow leaves, used for food and fodder or as lawns
**greenery**  green vegetation; foliage
**hardy**  (adj) designating a plant with high resistance or tolerance to cold or freezing temperatures
**herb**  seed-producing plant with little or no woody tissue, valued for its medicinal, aromatic, or savory qualities
**houseplants**  ornamental plants that can live indoors in small pots
**kernel**  grain or seed, esp. inside fruit
**latent bud**  dormant bud in stem or beneath bark
**lateral bud**  bud growing on side of stem
**leaf**  flat, thin structure growing from stem or twig of plant, used in photosynthesis and transpiration
**leaflet**  small or young leaf
**moss**  any of various small, green plants without true stems, reproducing by spores and growing in velvety clusters in moist areas on rocks, trees, or the ground
**native**  plant indigenous to region
**orchid**  perennial epiphyte cultivated for its brightly colored flowers
**ornamental**  plant or shrub grown for its decorative effect
**perennial**  plant that lives two years or more; herbaceous plant that lives beyond its flowering stage
**petal**  one of the circle of flower parts inside the sepals
**petiole**  stem connecting branch to leaf blade
**pistil**  central, seed-bearing part of flower, comprised of one or more carpels, each with style and stigma
**plant**  member of kingdom of living things capable of carrying on photosynthesis in cells, primarily adapted for terrestrial life
**pollen**  fine, dustlike grains containing male sexual cells, produced in anthers or similar structures of seed plants
**rhizome**  creeping horizontal stem lying at or just beneath soil surface, bearing leaves at its tip and roots from its underside
**root**  underground part of plant that functions in absorption, aeration, food storage, and as support system

**runner** long, slender stem growing from base of some perennials; runner

**seed** fertilized plant ovule containing embryo and capable of germinating to produce new plant

**seedling** plant grown from seed rather than cutting; young plant or tree

**sepal** usu. green, leaflike outer circle of calyx

**shoot** new growth, sprout, or twig on plant

**shrub** woody perennial plant with several low-branching stems; bush

**shrubbery** cluster of shrubs

**spike** stem with flowers directly attached to its upper portion

**spore** reproductive cell in mosses and ferns, capable of producing new adult individual

**sprout** young growth on plant; new growth from bud, rootstock, or germinating seed

**spur** projection from rear of flower, arising from sepal or petal

**stalk** stem or main axis of plant; any slender, supporting or connecting part of plant

**stamen** pollen-producing part of central flower, comprised of filament and anther

**stem** main upward-growing axis of plant

**stigma** free upper tip of flower style on which pollen falls and develops

**stolon** stem that takes root at intervals along ground, forming new plants; runner

**style** slender, stalklike part of carpel between stigma and ovary

**succulent** plant with thick, fleshy tissues that store water

**sucker** strong offshoot from roots or lower stem of plant

**taproot** deep, main root from which lateral roots develop

**tendril** threadlike, often spiral part of climbing plant that clings to or coils around objects

**terminal bud** bud growing at end of stem

**thorn** sharp-pointed, leafless branch of plant

**tree** tall, woody perennial with single stem or trunk and branches usu. beginning at some height above ground

**tropical plant** plant that occurs naturally in tropical climate

**trunk** thick, primary stem of tree

**truss** compact flower cluster at tip of stem

**tuber** fat, underground stem from which certain plants grow, similar to but shorter and thicker than rhizome

**tuberous root** thickened underground food storage structure

**twining stem** tendrillike stem of certain climbing plants

**variegated** (*adj*) designating plant with patterned or bicolored leaves and petals

**vegetable** any herbaceous plant all or part of which may be used as food

**vine** plant that grows along the ground or clings to vertical support by means of twining stems, tendrils, and rootlets

**water sprout** nonflowering shoot springing from bud of main plant branch

**weed** undesired, uncultivated plant for which no purpose has been found, often growing in profusion and interfering with growth of desired plants

**xerophyte** plant adapted to growth in arid conditions

# HOBBIES

**SEE ALSO:** Chap. 1: Health, Fitness, and Enhancement; Chap. 9: Cooking and Cuisine; Chap. 12: Occupations; Chap. 16: Crafts; Chap. 17: Holidays, Celebrations, and Vacations; Entertainments and Spectacles; Sports; Gardening; Games, Activities, and Toys; Chap. 25: Magic and the Occult

Many of these hobbies are also practiced as crafts.

**angling** fishing with hook and line

**antique collecting** accumulating old and valuable items, esp. furniture, pottery and porcelain, silver, glass, and art

**antique refinishing** restoring old, finely crafted furniture to its original condition

**aquarium building** design, creation, and maintenance of small, glass-enclosed aquatic environments for fish and plants

**audiophile** one who studies and collects state-of-the-art electronic audio equipment

**avocation** hobby

**backpacking** rural or wilderness hiking, with equipment and tents carried in rucksack on back

**ballooning** riding aloft in observation basket borne upward by large, spherical bag filled with gas or hot air

**bingo** board game of chance played socially

**bird-watching** observing wild birds in their natural habitat

**board games** competitive, amusing diversion involving manipulation of objects on a board

**bridge** card game played by two sets of partners

**camping** excursion, with provisions, into rural or wilderness area

**cards** games of chance and skill played with ordered deck of playing cards

**carpentry** cutting, joining, and framing of wood to form cabinetry or buildings

**ceramics** craft of making fired earthenware pottery

**climbing** mountaineering

**coin collecting** accumulating valuable or historical metal currency; numismatics

**collecting** act of accumulating of specimens of antiques, autographs, bottles, buttons, china, coins, dolls, glass, matchbooks, postcards, rocks and minerals, stamps, wine labels, or other articles

**cooking** preparation of food dishes for entertainment as well as nourishment

**crafts** skilled working of materials to form decorative or useful objects; handicrafts

**crewel embroidery** needlework employing twisted stitch

**crocheting** needlework done with hooked needle

**crossword puzzle** written word game in grid format, solution to which is based on definition clues

**customizing** process of modifying mass-produced item to specific requirements for performance or finish

**decoupage** technique of decorative surfacing with paper cutouts

**do-it-yourself** (*adj*) pertaining to practice of building or repairing items oneself, esp. household objects

**drying flowers** hanging and preserving dead flowers as decorative objects

**embroidery** decorative needlework using threads of high gloss, bright color, or hues contrasting with cloth

**fabric painting** applying designs to fabric in paint

**fiber arts** design and crafting of objects from natural fibers or fiber materials

**fishing** sport of catching fish with rod and line, hook, spear, or net

**fly fishing** sport of catching fish with line attached to floating hook dressed with feathers to resemble an insect

**folk dancing** traditional ethnic dances performed socially

**gambling** playing at any game of chance for money or other stakes; wagering on the predicted outcome of any event; gaming

**games** structured, often competitive activities for amusement: games of chance, games of skill, athletic, board, card, and indoor and outdoor games

**gaming** gambling

**gardening** creation, design, and maintenance of decorative and edible plants, esp. for domestic use and enjoyment

**glass painting** painting of images and designs on plate glass

**handicrafts** crafts

**hang gliding** riding aloft in harness attached to large kite, esp. leaping off elevated place and floating down to flat ground

**hobby** leisure activity, skill, or sport engaged in for enjoyment and enrichment; avocation

**home decorating** practice of designing and furnishing domestic interiors

**hunting** pursuit, capture, and killing of game animals for sport rather than subsistence

**ice-skating** sport of gliding over ice wearing metal-bladed shoes

**ikebana** Japanese art of flower arranging

**in-line skating** roller-blading

**jewelry making** design and production of ornamental objects, such as rings or necklaces, worn for adornment

**jogging** running for health purposes

**kite flying** hoisting aloft and sailing of frame covered by light material attached to long string

**knitting** interlacing of yarn to form decorative or functional garments and accessories

**landscaping** design and maintenance of outdoor areas adjacent to buildings, esp. for use and enjoyment

**macramé** elaborate, mesh knotwork done with twine or rope

**manège** training and skilled riding of horses

**mask making** craft of forming masks from papier-mâché,-wood, plaster of Paris, or other materials

**mobile making** making arrangements of wire and metal, paper, or plastic shapes that are suspended to move in air currents

**model airplanes** miniature replicas of aircraft that are handmade and collected as a hobby

**model cars** miniature replicas of automobiles, often historical, that are handmade and collected as a hobby

**model trains** working miniature replicas of railroad cars and trains that are collected and displayed as a hobby

**mountain climbing** mountaineering

**mountaineering** ascent of difficult mountain slopes with aid of equipment; mountain climbing

**needlecrafts** handicrafts involving sewing or weaving with cloth or threads: crocheting, knitting, embroidery, needlepoint, quilting, rug hooking, trapunto, weaving

**needlepoint** embroidery with yarn, esp. on canvas

**numismatics** coin collecting

**orchid growing** cultivation of tropical orchids in hothouse environment

**origami** Japanese art of decorative paper folding

**paper flower making** craft of forming artificial flowers from paper

**paperworking** making of decorative objects by cutting and folding paper; making of fine paper products

**papier-mâché** craft of forming decorative masks or objects from rags or paper soaked in glue, formed into shapes, and dried

**pastime** activity pursued for pleasure and enrichment during leisure hours

**pets** care and feeding of household and domestic animals kept for pleasure

**philately** stamp collecting

**phillumenism** collecting matchbooks and matchbook covers

**photography** process of creating or collecting photographic images, esp. of nature, travel, and family

**pottery** making or collecting of decorative and functional vessels of fired clay

**pressing flowers** placing fresh flowers or leaves between sheets of blotting paper or absorbent tissue and flattening them between pages of a heavy book

**puppetry** making, collecting, and performing with hand-operated dolls

**puzzles** collection and us of toys, objects, and games designed to amuse and test ingenuity

**quilting** creation and collection of needleworked or patchworked bedcovers, often antique

**recreation** leisure activity pursued for pleasure, relaxation, or enrichment

**riding** using of horses for recreational touring of the countryside

**rock climbing** ascending rock faces and cliffs, usu. with equipment such as rope, pick, and petons

**roller-blading** skating on Rollerblades, a brand of in-line skates with a single row of wheels, like an ice skate blade

**roller-skating** skating on wheeled shoes for recreational exercise

**scouting** organized group recreation and education, esp. for development of social and out-of-doors skills in young people

**scrimshaw** decorative engraving of ivory, bone, or shell

**scuba diving** ocean diving with oxygen tank and breathing apparatus for extended underwater exploration

**sewing** design and creation of garments by needlework

**shell carving** forming decorative objects from shells

**skateboarding** use of small, wooden board on wheels for recreation and locomotion

**skeet shooting** firing of guns at clay targets thrown to represent birds in flight

**skin diving** underwater diving without aid of special breathing apparatus or oxygen tanks

**17. LEISURE AND RECREATION**
GAMES, ACTIVITIES, AND TOYS
ATHLETIC EVENTS AND ACTIVITIES / PUBLIC CONTESTS AND PERFORMANCES / OUTDOOR GAMES

**PART FIVE**

**skydiving** jumping out of flying airplane to coast freely and perform maneuvers before opening parachute

**sledding** riding on vehicle with runners over snow and ice

**snorkeling** exploring coastal underwater areas using a breathing tube extending above surface of water

**spelunking** exploring caves

**stained glass** objects, esp. windows and lampshades, crafted of colored glass pieces, usu. joined by leaded strips

**stamp collecting** selection and accumulation of postage stamps, esp. historical, rare examples, or first printings; philately

**stenciling** printing by applying ink or paint to sheets perforated with designs or letters

**stitchery** decorative needlework, including embroidery or crewelwork

**surf fishing** fishing along shoreline of ocean

**surfing** sport of riding shoreline ocean waves on wooden or foam and fiberglass surfboard, or using body to ride such waves without board

**taxidermy** art of preserving stuffed, dead animals in lifelike form

**terrarium building** design, creation, and collection of small, glass-enclosed garden environment

**tie-dyeing** creating designs on textiles by tying parts of the cloth so they will not absorb dye

**toymaking** making of children's playthings

**trapshooting** sport of shooting at clay pigeons or pigeons released from cages

**trapunto** quilting done in high relief through two or more layers of cloth, produced by padding a stitched pattern with yarn or cotton

**weaving** design and creation of fabric, rugs, or textiles on loom

**whittling** carving of decorative or functional objects by trimming and shaping a stick of wood

**windsurfing** riding of wind-propelled, oceangoing apparatus resembling surfboard with attached sail

**woodworking** shaping of articles in wood

**yachting** recreational sailing of pleasure boat

# GAMES, ACTIVITIES, AND TOYS

**SEE ALSO**: Chap. 17: Holidays, Celebrations, and Vacations; Sports; Entertainments and Spectacles; Hobbies

## ATHLETIC EVENTS AND ACTIVITIES

acrobatics, aerobics, aikido, aquaplaning

backpacking, ballooning, bareback riding, bellyboard riding, body-surfing

caber, calisthenics, canoeing, cartwheels, climbing

fishing, fly-fishing

gliding, gym

handsprings, hang gliding

iceboating, Indian wrestling

judo, jujitsu

karate, kendo, kung fu

martial arts, mountaineering

ninjutsu

riding, rock climbing

sailing, sailplaning, sculling, shooting, skateboarding, skating, skeet shooting, skin diving, skydiving, snorkeling, somersaulting, surf casting

tae kwon do, tobogganing, trapshooting, tumbling

whitewater rafting, windsurfing

## PUBLIC CONTESTS AND PERFORMANCES

aerobatics, aquacade, aquatics

beauty contest, bullfighting

carousel, cavalletti, cockfighting, contortionism

demolition derby, dog racing

equestrian events

funny cars

Grand Prix racing

harness racing

jousting

lists

Maypole celebrations

quarterhorse racing, quintain

rodeo, rope walking

Soap Box Derby, stock-car racing, synchronized swimming

thoroughbred racing, tightrope walking, trampoline jumping, trapeze performing, trot racing

## OUTDOOR GAMES

badminton, bandy, boccie, broomball, bumper cars, bungee jumping

capture the flag, catch, croquet, curling

dodge ball, Dodgem

Frisbee

gliding

hare and hounds, hide-and-seek, hopscotch, horseshoes

jacks, jump rope

keepaway

leapfrog

marbles, merry-go-round, miniature golf, muss

obstacle race

paddleball, paddle tennis, pall-mall, pepper, punchball, pushball

quoits

racquets, ring-a-lievio, ring-around-the-rosey, ring taw, ringtoss, roller-skating

sack racing, shuffleboard

tag, teetertotter, tetherball, three-legged race, tipcat, trapshooting, tug of war

# INDOOR GAMES

acrostics, anagrams
bagatelle, billiards, bingo, blindman's buff, bluff, board games,
    bo-peep
cards, cat's cradle, charades, consequences, crambo, craps,
    crossword puzzle
darts, dice, dominoes
fan-tan
games of chance, games of skill, ghosts
hazard
jacks, jackstraws
keno
lotto
mumbletypeg, musical chairs
nine ball, Nintendo
pachinko, parlor games, peekaboo, pick-up-sticks, pinball
    machines, pin the tail on the donkey, pocket billiards, pool,
    post office, put-and-take, puzzles, pyramids
raffle, reversi, roulette
skittle, slot machine, snooker, spillikins, spin the bottle
tic-tack-toe
video games

## POOL AND BILLIARDS

**billiards**  game played with hard ivory balls that are driven
    with a cue stick on cloth-covered, rimmed table without
    pockets
**pool**  game played with fifteen numbered balls and white
    cue ball that is driven with a cue stick into other balls, the
    object being to sink balls into pockets at the perimeter of
    a cloth-covered, rimmed table
    balkline, bank shot, break, bumper
    carom, chalk, combination shot, crutch, cue, cue ball, cushion
    eight ball, English
    massé
    nine ball
    object ball
    pocket
    rack, rotation, run
    scratch, shot
    table scratch, topspin

# CARD GAMES

**cards**  any game played with a set of marked pieces of
    cardboard, usu. in a deck of fifty-two divided into four
    suits (clubs, diamonds, hearts, and spades), each suit num-
    bered one through ten plus a jack, queen, and king
    all fours
    baccarat, beggar-my-neighbor, bezique, blackjack, blind
        poker, Boston, brag, bridge
    canasta, casino, chemin de fer, clubs, concentration,
        conquian, contract bridge, cooncan, crazy eights,
        cribbage, cutthroat contract
    draw poker, duplicate bridge
    Earl of Coventry, euchre
    fan-tan, faro, fish, frog
    gin, gin rummy, go fish
    hearts, high-low
    loo, lowball
    Michigan, monte
    nap

old maid, ombre
pairs, patience, penny ante, pinochle, piquet, poker, Pope
    Joan, primero
quadrille
rouge et noir, rubber bridge, rummy, Russian bank
seven-up, skat, slapjack, snap, snipsnapsnorum, solitaire,
    speculation, straight poker, strip poker, stud poker
tarak, three-card monte, twenty-one
vingt-et-un
war, whist

## CARD TERMS

ace, ante
bank, banker, bid, bluff, bug, bullet
call, check, contract, cowboy, crossruff, croupier, cut
deal, dealer, dealing box, deuce, deuces wild, discard, double,
    draw, draw poker
face card, fill up, flop, flush, four of a kind, full house
hand, hole card, house, hoyle
inside straight, in the hole
joker
lead, limit
major suit, manille, mechanic, meld, misdeal, moriah
nob, no trump
odd trick, one-eyed, overtrick, overtrump
pair, pam, pan, pass, penny ante, picture card, playing card,
    pot, pot limit, preemptive bid
raise, royal flush, rubber, ruff
singleton, shoe, shoot the moon, shuffle, slough, spadille,
    straight, straight flush, strong suit, stud poker, suit
three of a kind, trey, trump, two pair
underbid, undertrick
wild card
Yarborough

# BOARD GAMES

**board game**  game played on flat sheet of wood or card-
    board with markings, usu. requiring moving of pieces
    about the board
    acey-deucy
    backgammon
    checkers, chess, Chinese checkers, Clue
    draughts
    fox-and-geese
    go
    mah-jongg, merels, Monopoly, morris
    Parcheesi
    Risk
    Scrabble, shogi
    tiddlywinks, tivoli, trick-track, Trivial Pursuit
    Yahtzee

## CHESS

**chess**  game played by two persons, each having sixteen
    pieces that are moved about a board having sixty-four
    squares
    advance
    bishop, black
    capture, castle, check, checkmate, chessman
    develop, draw
    end game, en passant, en prise

fianchetto, fork
gambit, grandmaster
horse
jeopardy
king, knight, kriegspiel
master, mate
opening
passed pawn, pawn, perpetual check, piece
queen
rook
stalemate
white

## TYPES OF TOYS

balls, board games
cards
dolls
mechanical toys, models
novelties
playthings, pull toys, puzzles
soldiers, stuffed animals
windup toys

## TOYS AND PLAYTHINGS

**toy** usu. small object, often representing something familiar, for children to play with
   air rifle, alphabet blocks, arrows
   Barbie doll, battledore, beachball, beanbag, bell ringers, bells, bicycle, blocks, bobblehead doll, boomerang, building blocks
   Cabbage Patch doll, cap gun, carriage, chemistry set, Chinese puzzle, clockwork toy, cockhorse, coloring book, comic book, counters, crayons
   darts, dice, doll carriage, doll clothes, doll furniture, dollhouse, dreidel
   expression blocks
   gyroscope
   hand puppet, historiscope, hobbyhorse, hoop, hula hoop
   Irish mail
   jack-in-the-box, jack-o'-lantern, jigsaw puzzle, jolly jumper, jungle gym
   kaleidoscope, kewpie doll, kite
   magic lantern, marionette, marbles, maze, mechanical bank, model airplane, model railroad, music box, myriopticon
   nested blocks, ninepins, Noah's ark
   pail and shovel, paints, paper doll, picture car, piggy bank, pinwheel, pogo stick, pop gun, puppet, puzzle
   rag doll, Raggedy Ann doll, rattle, rocking horse, roller skates, rubber ball
   scooter, seesaw, shoufly, shuttlecock, skateboard, skatemobile, sled, sleigh, slide, slingshot, Slinky, slot car, soapbox, space toys, squirt gun, stilts, swing
   tanagram, teddy bear, teetertotter, tiddlywinks, Tinkertoys, tin rattle, tin soldier, top, toy animal, toy book, toy car, toy drum, toy soldier, toy train, toy truck, trading cards, tree house, tricycle
   velocipede
   wading pool, wagon, water pistol, wheels, whirligig, whistle, windmill
   yo-yo
   zoetrope

# SMOKING AND TOBACCO

**SEE ALSO:** Chap. 24: Drug Abuse and Alcoholism

**ambeer** tobacco juice
**ash** powdery, burned tobacco, esp. burned portion of a cigar or cigarette
**ashtray** small receptacle for collecting ash and extinguishing smoking materials
**baccy** *Informal.* tobacco
**black tobacco** dark, strong-tasting cigarette tobacco
**bong** water pipe
**boogie** *Slang.* thin-bodied, air-cured tobacco from Kentucky
**book** pile or package of tobacco leaves
**briar** pipe carved from root burl of evergreen brier shrub
**Burley** light-colored tobacco with low nicotine content, grown esp. in Kentucky
**butt** portion remaining after cigarette or cigar has been smoked and stubbed out; *Slang.* cigarette
**calean** Persian water pipe
**calumet** ornamental, ceremonial pipe of American Indians; peace pipe
**canaster** coarse pipe tobacco
**cancer stick** *Slang.* cigarette
**carton** box containing ten standard packets of cigarettes
**cavendish** pressed cake of tobacco that has been sweetened, esp. with molasses
**chain-smoke** (*vb*) smoke cigarettes compulsively
**chaw** *Informal.* plug of chewing tobacco
**cheroot** cigar cut square at both ends
**chew** plug of chewing tobacco
**chewing tobacco** tobacco leaf treated and pressed into small cakes, portions of which are broken off and chewed
**chibouk** pipe with long stem and clay bowl (Turkey)
**chillum** part of water pipe containing tobacco
**cigar** cylindrical roll of cured tobacco encased in tobacco leaf wrapper
**cigar cutter** device with blade and point for clipping and piercing cigars before smoking
**cigarette** thin tube of finely chopped, cured tobacco encased in thin paper, often with filter at one end
**cigarette case** small, flat container for holding cigarettes
**cigarette girl** young woman who sells cigarettes from tray carried around restaurant dining room or cabaret
**cigarette holder** long, thin, hollow device, often with built-in filter, used to smoke cigarette that is inserted in one end
**cigarette machine** vending machine that dispenses packages of cigarettes
**cigarette paper** rolling paper
**cigarillo** small, thin cigar
**cigarro** *Spanish.* cigar
**cigar-store Indian** wooden likeness of Native American, usu. standing outside tobacco shop
**cinder** portion of burned tobacco not yet reduced to ashes
**claro** light-colored, mild cigar

**clay pipe**  pipe with bowl made of clay

**coffin nail**  *Slang.* cigarette

**colorado**  cigar of moderate strength and color

**corncob pipe**  pipe made from dried cob of corn

**corona**  cigar with long, straight sides and roundly blunted, unsealed end

**cubeb**  dried tropical berry crushed and smoked in cigarettes

**cud**  individual portion of chewing tobacco

**curing**  process of treating and aging raw tobacco to improve its burn and flavor as smoke

**cuspidor**  open receptacle for expectoration of tobacco juice; spittoon

**dip** (*vb*)  place snuff against one's gums

**dottle**  unburned or partially burned tobacco caked in bowl of pipe

**drag**  single draw on cigarette

**dudeen**  short, clay tobacco pipe

**fag**  *Slang.* cigarette

**filter**  porous substance used to remove impurities from smoke

**filter tip**  cigarette with one end of cellulose or charcoal for filtering smoke

**Flip-Top**  *Trademark.* cardboard cigarette box with hinged cover

**gasper**  *Brit. slang.* cigarette

**hand rolling**  making one's own cigarettes from loose tobacco and rolling papers

**hard pack**  cigarette box made of thin cardboard

**Havana**  high-quality Cuban cigar

**hookah**  water pipe, usu. with long, flexible tube for inhaling smoke (Middle East)

**humidor**  jar or receptacle for storing tobacco and cigars and maintaining their moistness

**inhale** (*vb*)  breathe tobacco smoke into one's lungs, esp. from cigarette

**kinnikinnick**  mixture of dried leaves, bark, and tobacco smoked by Native Americans

**Latakia**  highly aromatic Turkish tobacco

**lighter**  device, usu. with flint, wick, and flammable fuel, used to ignite smoking material

**light up** (*vb*)  ignite and begin smoking, esp. a cigarette

**low tar** (*adj*)  containing less tar than usual or standard, therefore less unhealthy

**maccaboy**  high-quality, usu. rose-scented snuff formerly, aromatic tobacco from Martinique

**maduro**  cigar with dark brown leaf wrapper

**meerschaum**  pipe with bowl made of the white, claylike mineral meerschaum

**menthol**  cigarette containing menthol, which has cooling effect on mucous membranes

**mundungus**  tobacco with unpleasant smell

**nargileh**  water pipe of Near Eastern origin

**navy plug**  compressed cake of strong, dark tobacco

**nicotiana**  tobacco grown for its ornamental flowers

**nicotine**  chief active ingredient of tobacco

**nicotine addiction**  physical and psychological dependence on nicotine due to regular smoke inhalation

**nicotinism**  addiction and other effects of regular, prolonged use of nicotine

**nonsmoking section**  area of public space, esp. restaurant, where smoking is prohibited

**no smoking**  admonition that smoking is prohibited

**pack**  rectangular, paper or soft cardboard container usu. containing twenty cigarettes

**packet**  cigarette pack

**panatela**  long, slender, flat-sided cigar

**passive smoking**  inhalation of cigarette, cigar, or pipe smoke of others, esp. by nonsmoker in enclosed area

**peace pipe**  calumet

**perfecto**  cigar tapering nearly to a point at each end

**pigtail**  twisted strand of tobacco

**pinch**  small amount of chewing tobacco or snuff

**pipe**  smoking device consisting of hollow stem with bowl-shaped receptacle for tobacco at one end and mouthpiece at other

**pipe bowl**  rounded portion of pipe, open at top and connected to one end of pipestem at bottom, into which smoking tobacco is placed

**pipe cleaner**  flexible wire coated with cotton and inserted through pipe stem to remove tar

**pipe rack**  usu. wood device for storage and display of pipes

**pipestem**  long, hollow portion of pipe with bowl at one end and mouthpiece at the other

**pipe tobacco**  tobacco leaves cut in shreds suitable for smoking in a pipe

**plug**  flat, compressed cake of tobacco

**puff**  single drag on cigar, cigarette, or pipe; (*vb*) smoke, esp. cigar or pipe

**quid**  plug of chewing tobacco

**rappee**  snuff made of dark, pungent tobacco

**rolling paper**  thin slip of paper, usu. gummed at one edge, for hand rolling cigarettes; cigarette paper

**roll-your-own**  cigarette that has been hand rolled

**secondhand smoke**  smoke from someone else's cigarette to which one is exposed secondhand through proximity, as in office or restaurant

**seegar**  *Informal spelling.* cigar

**shag**  strong, coarse pipe tobacco cut in fine shreds

**smoke** (*vb*)  inhale and exhale fumes of burning tobacco, esp. do so habitually; (*n*) cigarette or other smoking material

**smoke-free zone**  area in public place in which smoking is prohibited

**smokeless ashtray**  receptacle for extinguished smoking material with lid to contain smoke

**smokeout**  day during which smokers are encouraged to abstain from smoking as part of widespread campaign

**smoker**  railroad car designated for smoking; smoking car; person who smokes regularly

**smoke room**  room designated for smoking, usu. in public place or club

**smoker's cough**  cough typical of cigarette smokers, due to habitual inhalation of smoke

**smokes**  *Informal.* cigarettes

**smoke shop**  retail store selling tobacco, pipes, and smoking supplies

**smoking**  act of inhaling and exhaling fumes of burning tobacco

**smoking car**  smoker

**smoking jacket**  man's casual lounging jacket

**smoking lamp**  ship's lamp, illuminated when smoking is permitted

**smoking room**  room in public building or club designated for smoking

**smoking section** area of public place, esp. restaurant, designated for smoking
**smoking stand** ashtray set on top of wood or metal support
**smoking zone** area in public place designated for smoking
**snipe** *Slang.* cigar or cigarette butt
**snort** single inhalation of snuff
**snuff** tobacco preparation to be inhaled, chewed, or placed against gums
**snuffbox** small, lidded container for holding snuff
**soft pack** cigarette packet made of folded paper
**spittoon** cuspidor
**stogy** cigar, esp. roughly made, inexpensive one
**stub out** extinguish cigarette or cigar by crushing its burning portion against a surface
**Surgeon General's Report** published findings of U.S. government study regarding health dangers of cigarette smoking
**tabac** *French.* tobacco
**tar** dark, viscous, bituminous residue present in smoke and containing poisonous by-products
**tobacco** leaves of cultivated plant of the nightshade family, cured for smoking, chewing, or use as snuff
**tobacco barn** tobacco shed
**tobacco juice** discolored, brown saliva from chewing tobacco or snuff
**tobacconist** dealer in tobacco and smoking supplies
**tobacco pouch** soft, folding receptacle for pipe tobacco
**tobacco shed** long structure in which tobacco is hung for aging, drying, and curing; tobacco barn
**tobaccosis** nicotine addiction
**tobaccoey** (*adj*) like tobacco; filled with tobacco smoke
**toke** *Slang.* single drag of a marijuana cigarette
**Turkish tobacco** dark, aromatic cigarette tobacco, grown esp. in Turkey
**twist** hand-rolled cigarette
**Virginia tobacco** tobacco cultivated in eastern United States and cured by heat or dry air, stronger and darker than Burley
**water pipe** any of various devices in which smoke is cooled by passing through water before being inhaled
**weed** *Informal.* tobacco smoking material

# DRINKING AND ALCOHOLIC BEVERAGES

# DRINKING TERMS

**abstinence** total restraint from consumption of alcohol
**after-dinner drink** liqueur taken after a meal; digestif
**aging** process of maturing liquor by long-term storage
**alcohol** colorless, inflammable liquid intoxicant in wine, beer, and spirits
**ale** liquor infusion of malt by fermentation, flavored with hops, and stronger than beer
**apéritif** drink taken as appetizer before meal
**bacchanalia** drunken revel, esp. honoring Roman god Bacchus
**banger** *Slang.* shot of straight spirits, such as vodka, on ice
**bathtub gin** homemade spirit made from raw alcohol and essential oils
**beer** alcoholic beverage brewed by slow fermentation from malt and hops; brew; suds
**bitters** alcoholic liquor flavored with astringent, aromatic, strong-tasting herbs
**blue law** law restricting alcoholic use, sale, or consumption
**bock beer** strong, dark beer, aged very short time, drunk esp. in spring
**bond** designation for government-supervised distilled spirits, aged at least four years, and 100 proof
**bootlegger** one who smuggles or illegally sells liquor
**booze** *Informal.* liquor; (*vb*) drink alcohol
**bracer** drink taken as stimulant or refresher
**brew** *Informal.* beer
**brewer** one who makes beer
**brewsky** *Informal.* beer
**brut** (*adj*) designating very dry champagne
**bubbly** *Informal.* champagne
**BYOB** bring your own booze; designation on party invitation that drinks will not be supplied by host
**carding** *Informal.* requiring proof of age from customer before selling him or her alcoholic beverage
**cask** wooden container for aging and storage of alcoholic beverages
**cellar** stock of wines, usu. stored in cool basement
**chaser** drink taken immediately after another kind of drink, esp. beer after whiskey
**chug-a-lug** (*vb*) drink entire contents of container in one gulp
**cocktail** mixed alcoholic drink
**cocktail party** early evening gathering at which drinks and snacks are served
**compotation** rousing drinking party
**cordial** liquor sweetened with fruit
**cork** stopper for wine bottle made from tough outer tissue of cork oak
**corkage** charge by restaurant for opening bottle of wine purchased elsewhere
**corn whiskey** mash made from eighty percent corn
**corpse reviver** *Slang.* alcoholic drink
**digestif** after-dinner drink, esp. liqueur, that aids digestion
**distillation** purification of alcoholic liquor by heating, separation, and condensation
**distiller** one who makes alcoholic liquor by distillation, vaporizing and extracting its essence
**distillery** place where whiskey and other liquors are made
**doctor** (*vb*) alter or dilute composition of drink

**double** two shots of liquor in one drink

**draft** amount drunk in one swallow

**dram** small drink of liquor

**drink** alcohol in general; single serving or glassful of liquor; (vb) consume alcoholic beverage

**drinking** consumption of alcoholic beverages, usu. for pleasure; such consumption to excess

**dry** (adj) designating locale or time in which sale and consumption of alcohol is forbidden; describing wine that is opposite of sweet

**eighty-six** common measure of alcoholic content or proof in hard liquor

**eyeopener** drink taken on awakening or early in the day, esp. when suffering a hangover

**fifth** one-fifth gallon, standard U.S. bottle size for spirits

**finger** measure indicating drink filled to width of one finger

**firewater** Native American slang for alcoholic liquor

**forbearance** abstinence; temperance

**gill** measure equal to four fluid ounces

**gulp** single large swallow of drink

**hangover** unpleasant aftereffects of too much drink, esp. headache and nausea, experienced following day

**hard liquor** liquor with alcoholic content higher than that of wine and beer

**highball** liquor, esp. whiskey, mixed with soda in a tall glass

**hogshead** large cask, holding from 63 to 140 gallons (238 to 530 l)

**home brew** homemade alcoholic drink

**hooch** Slang. alcoholic liquor, esp. of inferior quality

**imbibe** (vb) drink, esp. to excess

**jeroboam** oversized wine bottle holding approximately 3 liters (3.3 quarts)

**John Barleycorn** personification of alcoholic liquor

**jug** large, narrow-mouthed, earthenware container, esp. for liquor; contents of jug or alcoholic liquor

**juice** Slang. alcoholic liquor

**keg** small barrel, esp. for beer on draught

**keg party** Informal. gathering at which beer is served from keg

**knock back** (vb) Slang. take a drink, esp. aggressively

**lace** (vb) fortify drink with alcohol

**libation** alcoholic drink, esp. wine, poured as offering to god

**likker** Informal spelling. liquor

**liqueur** usu. flavored, sweet, thick alcoholic liquor

**liquor** alcoholic drink, usu. distilled rather than fermented; booze

**little brown jug** Slang. alcoholic drink

**long neck** (adj) Informal. designating beer bottle with long neck

**magnum** large wine or champagne bottle holding 2/5 gallon (1.5 l)

**malt liquor** strong beer made by fermenting malt

**maraschino cherry** cherry preserved in sweet liqueur distilled from juice of bitter wild cherry, served in certain cocktails

**mash** crushed malt or meal mixed with hot water and fermented to form beer or whiskey

**Mickey** Slang. alcoholic drink doctored with knockout drug; Mickey Finn

**mixer** nonalcoholic beverage, often carbonated, combined with spirits in cocktail

**moonshine** Informal. low-quality, illegally distilled or smuggled whiskey, esp. corn liquor

**must** pulp and skins of crushed grapes before or during fermentation into wine

**near beer** malt liquor with very low alcohol content

**neat** (adj) straight up

**nectar** alcoholic drink

**nightcap** drink taken just before going to bed

**nip** small drink, sip of liquor

**nog** strong English ale

**noggin** small quantity of drink, esp. one-fourth pint

**nondrinker** one who practices temperance

**off the wagon** Slang. having drunk an alcoholic beverage after a period of abstinence

**one for the road** final drink before leaving bar or party

**on the rocks** poured over ice

**on the wagon** Slang. denying oneself alcoholic drink; designating a period of abstinence

**package store** outlet selling alcoholic beverages for consumption elsewhere

**pick-me-up** Informal. drink taken to restore one's energy, esp. at end of workday

**potable** something fit to drink

**potation** alcoholic drink or brew

**potion** mixture of liquors

**prohibition** legal forbidding of manufacture and sale of alcoholic drinks

**proof** arbitrary standard measure of alcoholic strength of beverage, often twice percent of alcohol content

**pull** swig or sip of drink

**punch** mixture of juice, soda, and liquor

**punt** hollow in exterior bottom of wine bottle

**quaff** (vb) drink copiously

**redeye** Slang. cheap, strong whiskey

**refraining** (adj) practicing temperance

**refresher** refill of empty drink

**rocks** Informal. ice cubes

**rotgut** Slang. inferior, cheap liquor

**sauce** Slang. alcoholic drink

**sec** (adj) designating wine, usu. white

**shandygaff** Chiefly Brit. beer diluted with nonalcoholic drink such as ginger beer

**shooter** shot of spirits to be drunk in one gulp

**sip** small taste of drink

**six-pack** standard unit in which beer is sold

**snort** Slang. drink taken in one shot

**sober** (adj) not drunk, esp. habitually temperate in use of alcohol

**sobriety** quality of being sober

**social drinking** moderate drinking at gatherings

**soft** (adj) designating wine and beer, as opposed to hard liquor

**soft drink** nonalcoholic beverage or mixer

**sparkling wine** champagne and other effervescent wines

**spike** (vb) Informal. add alcohol to drink or increase amount of alcohol contained therein

**spirits** alcoholic beverages; liquor

**splash** tiny amount of one spirit or water or soda added to a mixed drink

**split** small bottle, esp. of champagne, usu. 6 ounces (177 l)

**stiff** (adj) strong, in describing drink; high in alcoholic content

**stone cold sober** *Informal*. absolutely unintoxicated

**straight up** (*adj*) designating an alcoholic drink without mixer or chilled drink without ice, such as a martini; neat

**strong drink** alcoholic beverage

**suds** *Slang*. beer

**swear off** (*vb*) cease drinking for period of time

**sweet** (*adj*) describing fruity wines, opposite of dry

**swig** large swallow of drink

**swill** (*vb*) drink in great gulps or guzzle, esp. beer

**teetotaler** one who does not drink alcohol

**temperance** moderation or abstinence from alcoholic drink

**toast** drink taken in honor of person or event, accompanied by words of praise or good wishes, often a standardized phrase

**uncork** (*vb*) remove cork stopper from wine bottle

**unintoxicated** (*adj*) abstinent, free of alcohol

**vintage** year in which wine grapes were grown

**vintner** winemaker

**wassail** riotous drinking and revelry

**wet** (*adj*) designating locale or time in which consumption of alcoholic drinks is permitted

**whiskey** distilled liquor made from fermented mash of cereal grain, such as barley, rye, or corn

**white lightning** *Informal*. moonshine; illegal, low-quality liquor

**wine** fermented grape juice

## BARS, BAR TOOLS, AND HABITUÉS

**after-hours** (*adj*) designating establishment serving alcohol after normal bar hours

**alehouse** place where beer and ale are sold

**back** (*adj*) designating nonalcoholic drink served on the side with a shot of spirits

**backbar** shelves and counter space along wall behind bar, used for storing bottles and glasses

**bar** place where drinks are served across a long counter; such a counter

**bar back** busboy who brings supplies and cleans up for bartender

**barfly** *Slang*. person who frequents bars

**barhop** (*vb*) *Informal*. visit and drink at series of bars over course of evening

**barkeep** barkeeper

**barkeeper** person who owns or tends bar; barkeep

**barmaid** female serving drinks at bar

**bar rag** cloth for wiping surface of bar counter

**barrelhouse** cheap drinking and dancing establishment

**barspoon** long spoon for stirring drinks, often with spiral handle

**barstool** tall seat at bar counter, usu. without back or arms

**bartender** preparer and server of alcoholic drinks at bar counter

**beer garden** outdoor bar serving beer

**beer hall** large bar primarily or solely serving beer, esp. German

**bistro** small bar or tavern, esp. European

**bottle club** often private club serving drinks after normal legal closing hours

**bouncer** person employed to maintain order in bar, as by removing unruly customers

**buvette** *French*. small bar

**buy back** (*vb*) provide free drink to customer

**cabaret** club serving food and drink and providing entertainment

**café** small, informal barroom or cabaret

**call drink** brand-label spirits requested by customer

**cantina** small barroom or saloon, esp. in southwest U.S. or Mexico

**cash bar** bar at special, often private function that sells drinks to those in attendance

**champagne saucer** very wide stemmed glass for champagne

**cocktail lounge** public room where drinks are served, esp. in hotel or restaurant

**cocktail napkin** small, square napkin served with drink

**cocktail shaker** glass or metal container for shaking certain chilled, mixed drinks

**cocktail stirrer** tall spoon or straw used to mix drink

**cocktail strainer** device to retain ice in shaker from which chilled drink is poured

**cocktail waitress** female serving drinks in bar

**corkscrew** spiral device with handle for removing cork stopper from wine bottle

**cover charge** entry charge, usu. for entertainment, in club or bar

**crushed ice** granulated bits of ice used in certain drinks

**dive** *Informal*. cheap, tawdry bar

**dramshop** bar or saloon

**draught** drawing of beer from large container or keg; beer so drawn

**flight** *Slang*. samples of three different wines offered for a set price

**glass** container for single drink

**happy hour** early evening hours, usu. between four and seven p.m., when bar serves drinks at reduced price or with free snacks

**honky-tonk** cheap, often disreputable bar or club

**ice tongs** hinged device for lifting ice cubes

**jigger** small glass used to measure one and a half ounces of spirits

**last call** final chance to order drinks before bar closing

**meat rack** *Slang*. singles bar where primary objective is to find sexual partner

**no-host bar** bar, usu. at private party, requiring payment for drinks

**on tap** designating beer stored in keg or barrel and drawn off through tap

**on the house** designating drink purchased for customer at bar's expense

**pitcher** usu. glass container holding several servings of beer or other drink

**pony glass** short, narrow, stemmed glass for cordials and straight up cocktails

**pourer** spigot attachment for bottles allowing one serving to pour each time bottle is upended

**pouring whiskey** house brand kept on speed rack

**pub** public house; tavern or bar , esp. in Britain

**pub-crawler** one who drinks at one bar after another

**publican** *Chiefly Brit*. proprietor or manager of pub or tavern

**rathskeller** restaurant patterned after German beer hall, usu. in basement

**roadhouse** tavern or nightclub located on main thorough-fare outside city limits

**rock glass** short, stout glass for straight liquor on ice

**round** single serving of drinks for all present

**rumshop** *Informal.* cheap bar

**run a tab** accumulate bill for drinks, to be paid at end of evening or later time

**saloon** public room for sale and consumption of alcoholic drinks

**service bar** bar area where only waitresses pick up drinks

**shaker** container in which certain drinks are mixed

**shot** small measure of undiluted liquor, usu. one and a half ounces

**shot glass** small glass used to measure one shot

**singles bar** bar or tavern catering primarily to single men and women, esp. those seeking sexual partner or lover

**snifter** balloon-shaped, stemmed goblet that narrows at top, esp. for brandy

**soda gun** bar device with hose and selector for adding nonalcoholic beverages to drinks

**sour mix** lemon juice and sugar used in mixed drinks

**speakeasy** saloon or club selling alcohol illegally, esp. during Prohibition

**speed rack** bartender's device, on runners, with slots that hold bottles of house brands most frequently used

**stand drinks** (*vb*) *Informal.* buy a round of drinks for all present

**steward** supervisor of storage and service of wine in restaurant or large household

**strainer** flexible mesh device on handle for straining drink into glass

**swizzle stick** long rod, often in spiral shape, used to mix drinks

**tab** unpaid portion of bill accumulating at bar

**tap** (*vb*) draw off liquid, esp. beer, from keg or barrel; (n) device that does this

**taproom** bar serving beer on tap

**tapster** bartender, esp. in taproom

**tavern** place where liquor is sold and consumed; formerly an inn

**tip cup** container placed on bar for bartender's gratuities

**top shelf** name brands of spirits displayed above bar

**twist** slice of lemon peel curled over and served in certain drinks

**water back** glass of water served on side with shot of spirits

**watering hole** *Informal.* bar or tavern

**well drink** inexpensive, generic house brand of spirits

## Toasts

**toast** drink taken in honor of person or event, accompanied by words of praise or good wishes, often a standardized phrase
a votre sante
bottoms up
cheerio, cheers, chin chin
down the hatch
gesondheid, gun-bei
health, here's looking at you, here's mud in your eye, here's to you
kam pai
l'chaim

many happy returns
na zdorovye
prosit, prost
salud, sante, skal, skoal
to your health
wassail

## Beers

**beer** alcoholic beverage brewed by slow fermentation from malt and hops
ale
beer, bitter, bock beer
dark beer, dortmunder
kumis, kvass
lager, light beer
malt liquor, mead
near beer
Pilsner, porter, pulque
stout
weiss

## Wines

**wine** fermented grape juice
Alsace, amontillado, amoroso, apple wine, Asti Spumante
Barbera, Bardolino, Barolo, Beaujolais, Bergerac, blanc de blancs, blanc de noirs, blush, Bordeaux, Burgundy
Cabernet Sauvignon, Chablis, Champagne, Chardonnay, Chenin blanc, Chianti, claret, cold duck, Cotes du Rhone
dandelion wine, dessert wine, Do, Dolcetto, Dom Perignon (trade name), Dubonnet (trade name)
fortified wine, Frascati
Gewurztraminer, Graves
hard cider, hock
Johannisberg Riesling, jug wine
Lachryma Christi, Lambrusco, Liebfraumilch
Macon, Madeira, Malaga, Marsala, Mateus Ros, Medoc, Moselle, Muscadet, Muscat
Navarra
oloroso, oporto, Orvieto
Pinot Blanc, Pinot Noir, port, Pouilly-Fuisse, Pouilly-Fume
red wine, Riesling, retsina, Rhine, Rhone, Rioja, rose, ruby port
sack, sake, Sancerre, Sauterne, sherry, soave, sparkling wine, Sylvaner
table wine, tawny port, Tokay
Valdepeas, Valpolicella, vermouth, vinho verde, Vouvray
white cabernet, white wine, white zinfandel
zinfandel

## Spirits

**spirits** alcoholic beverages; liquor
absinthe, advocaat, applejack, aquavit, Armagnac
bathtub gin, blended whiskey, bourbon, brandy
campari, Canadian whiskey, Cognac
gin, grain alcohol, grappa, grog
Irish whiskey
kirsch
mao-tai, marc, mash, mescal, moonshine
negra

ouzo
peppermint schnapps, pulque
raki, rum, rye
schnapps, Scotch whisky, slivovitz
tequila
vodka
whiskey

## LIQUEURS AND CORDIALS

**cordial** liquor sweetened with fruit
**liqueur** usu. flavored, sweet, thick, alcoholic liquor
alcool blanc, amaretto, anisette, apricot brandy, Asiago
B and B, Benedictine, bitters
Calvados, cassis, Chartreuse, Cointreau, crème de bananas, crème de cacao, crème de cassis, crème de fraise, crème de framboise, crème de menthe, crème de violette, curaçao
Drambuie
Galliano, Grand Marnier
Irish Mist
Kahlua, Kir, kummel
mocha liqueur
pastis, pear William, Pernod
ratafia
sambuca, sloe gin, Strega
triple sec

## MIXED DRINKS

**alexander** gin, crème de cacao, and light cream
**angel's kiss** crème de cacao, sloe gin, brandy, and light cream
**Bacardi cocktail** Bacardi rum, juice of lime, and grenadine
**banshee** crème de banana, crème de cacao, light cream
**bay breeze** vodka, pineapple juice, and cranberry juice
**between the sheets** brandy, triple sec, rum, and a squeeze of lemon
**B-52** Kahlua, Irish Mist, Grand Marnier
**Black Russian** vodka and coffee liqueur
**black velvet** Guinness stout and champagne
**Bloody Mary** vodka, tomato juice, lemon juice, Worcestershire sauce, Tabasco, and salt and pepper
**blue whale** vodka, blue curacao, orange juice, and lemon juice
**bocce ball** amaretto, orange juice, and soda
**brandy alexander** crème de cacao, brandy, and heavy cream
**Bronx cocktail** gin, dry vermouth, sweet vermouth, and orange juice
**bullshot** vodka, beef bouillon, and salt and pepper
**buttered rum** hot buttered rum
**Cape Codder** vodka or rum, cranberry juice, and squeeze of lime
**champagne cocktail** champagne, sugar, and bitters
**chi-chi** vodka, pineapple juice, and cream of coconut
**cobbler** wine or liquor, fruit, and shaved ice
**cocktail** any mixed drink containing liquor
**collins** liquor, squeeze of lemon or lime, soda water, and powdered sugar

**cooler** wine or other spirits, fruit juice, and carbonated water
**Cuba libre** rum, cola, and a squeeze of lime
**daiquiri** rum, squeeze of lemon or lime, and sugar
**eggnog** liquor, milk, beaten egg or crème, and sugar
**firefly** light crème de cacao, cream, and rosemint
**fizz** liquor, carbonated beverage, citrus juice, and sugar
**flip** liquor or wine, egg, and sugar
**frappe** liqueur poured over shaved ice
**French connection** Cognac and amaretto
**fuzzy navel** peach schnapps and orange juice
**Gibson** gin, dry vermouth, and a pearl onions
**gimlet** gin or vodka, lemon or lime juice, and sugar
**gin and tonic** gin and quinine water
**gin fizz** gin, squeeze of lemon, sugar and soda
**godfather** scotch and amaretto
**godmother** vodka and amaretto
**golden Cadillac** crème de cacao, Galliano, and light cream
**grasshopper** crème de cacao, crème de menthe, and light cream
**greyhound** vodka and grapefruit juice
**grog** rum and water, served hot with lemon and sugar
**Harvey Wallbanger** vodka, Galliano, and orange juice
**highball** liquor and water or carbonated beverage
**hot buttered rum** rum, sugar, butter, and hot water; buttered rum
**hot toddy** toddy
**Irish coffee** whiskey, hot coffee, sugar, and whipped cream
**Jack Rose** apple brandy, lime juice, and grenadine
**kamikaze** vodka, triple sec, and lime juice
**King Alphonse** dark crème de cacao and cream
**Kir** white wine and crème de cassis
**Kir royale** champagne and crème de cassis
**Long Island iced tea** rum, gin, vodka, triple sec, lemon juice, and cola
**madras** vodka, orange juice, and cranberry juice
**mai tai** rum, curaaao, grenadine, lemon and pineapple juice, almond syrup, and sugar
**Manhattan** whiskey and sweet vermouth
**Margarita** tequila, triple sec, and lemon or lime juice
**martini** gin and dry vermouth
**melon ball** melon liqueur, vodka, and pineapple juice
**Mexican coffee** coffee liqueur, tequila, coffee, and whipped cream
**mimosa** champagne and orange juice
**mint julep** bourbon, crushed ice, sugar, sprigs of mint, and water
**Moscow mule** vodka, ginger ale, and a squeeze of lime
**negus** wine, hot water sugar, nutmeg, and lemon
**nutcracker** amaretto, hazelnut cream, and coconut
**old fashioned** whiskey, sugar, bitters, and water
**orange blossom** gin, orange juice, and sugar
**Pimm's cup** Pimm's No. 1 Cup and lemonade or ginger ale
**piña colada** rum, coconut milk, and crushed pineapple
**pink lady** gin, grenadine, and egg white
**pink squirrel** crème de noyeaux, crème de cacao, and light cream
**planter's punch** rum, squeeze of lime, sugar, and carbonated water
**posset** hot milk curdled with ale or wine, sweetened and spiced

**presbyterian** rye or bourbon, soda, and ginger ale

**punch** any combination of alcoholic beverages, fruit juices, and other beverages, usu. in a large bowl

**Ramos gin fizz** gin, egg white, cream, lemon juice, and sugar

**rickey** gin or vodka, soda, and a squeeze of lime

**Rob Roy** scotch and sweet vermouth

**rum and coke** rum and cola

**rusty nail** scotch and Drambuie

**salty dog** gin or vodka, grapefruit juice, and salt

**sangre** tequila, tomato juice, lemon juice, Worcestershire sause, tobasco, and salt and pepper

**sangria** red wine, fruit juice, fruit chunks

**Scotch and Soda** Scotch whiskey and Soda

**screwdriver** vodka and orange juice

**sea breeze** vodka, grapefruit juice and cranberry juice

**Seven and Seven** Seagram's Seven Canadian Whiskey and 7-UP

**shandy** *Chiefly Brit.* beer and lemonade

**sidecar** brandy, cointreau, and lemon juice

**Singapore sling** gin, cherry-flavored brandy, sugar, and carbonated water

**slam dunk** Southern Comfort, orange juice, and cranberry juice

**sling** liquor, sugar, lemon or lime juice, and water

**slippery nipple** sambuca and Bailey's Irish Mist

**sloe gin fizz** sloe gin, squeeze of lemon, and powdered sugar

**smash** liquor, sugar, sprigs of mint, water, and ice

**sombrero** coffee flavored brandy and milk or light cream

**sour** liquor, squeeze of lemon or lime, sugar, and sometimes soda water

**spritzer** white wine and carbonated water

**stinger** brandy and crème de menthe

**syllabub** sweetened milk or cream mixed with wine or cider

**tequila sunrise** tequila, grenadine, and orange juice

**toddy** rum or other liquor, boiling water, and sugar; hot toddy

**Tom and Jerry** rum, spices, milk, egg, and sugar

**Tom Collins** gin, squeeze of lemon or lime, sugar, and carbonated water

**velvet hammer** vodka, crème de cacao, and light cream

**vodka and tonic** vodka and tonic water

**vodka martini** vodka and dry vermouth

**Wassail** spiced ale or wine, sometimes with baked apple

**whiskey sour** whiskey, squeeze of lemon, and powdered sugar

**white lady** gin, creamm, egg white, and powered sugar

**White Russian** vodka, coffee liqueur, and milk or cream

**white spider** vodka and white crème de menthe

**wine cooler** wine and carbonated beverage

**wu-wu** vodka, peach schnapps, cranberry juice, and grapefruit juice

**zombie** rum, apricot-flavored brandy, pineapple juice, squeeze of lime, squeeze of orange, and powered sugar

# PART SIX

# LANGUAGE

# CHAPTER 18

# Structure and Usage

# GRAMMAR, PHONETICS, AND LINGUISTICS

Grammar and Usage
Parts of Speech
Punctuation and Diacritics
Phonetics
Linguistics and Writing Systems

**SEE ALSO**: Chap. 13: Anthropology; Education; Chap. 14: Literature; Chap. 16: Graphic Design and Printing; Chap. 18: Rhetoric and Figures of Speech

## GRAMMAR AND USAGE

**ablative** case indicating noun is starting point, means, instrument, or agent

**abstract noun** noun describing something general or not perceivable by sense

**accidence** study of grammatical inflection

**accusative** case indicating noun is direct object of verb

**active voice** verb form indicating that subject is performing action expressed by verb

**agreement** parallelism, as between subject and verb, in person, number, gender, or case

**antecedent** substantive that is replaced by pronoun, usu. later in same or subsequent sentence

**aorist** verb tense, as in Classical Greek, expressing past action without reference to its completion or duration

**apodosis** clause expressing result in conditional sentence

**apposition** placing of word or phrase after a substantive to explain or identify it

**article** modifier "a," "an," or "the" used to signal presence and definiteness or indefiniteness of following noun

**aspect** verb form indicating nature of action expressed by verb with regard to duration, repetition, beginning, or completion

**attributive** adjective or noun placed adjacent to noun it modifies

**auxiliary verb** verb used with main verb to indicate tense, mood, or voice

**case** role of noun, pronoun, or adjective in relation to rest of sentence, usu. shown by inflection

**causative** word noting causation

**clause** group of words containing subject and predicate

**collective noun** noun that is singular in form but denotes a group

**comma fault** use of comma between related main clauses in absence of conjunction, usu. considered incorrect in formal usage; comma splice

**comma splice** comma fault

**common gender** class of words that may refer to either a male or female

**common noun** noun that refers to any or all members of a class of beings or things rather than a particular individual

**comparative** second degree of comparison of adjectives or adverbs, indicated by ending "-er" or the word "more"

**comparison** inflection of adverbs and adjectives to show degrees: positive, comparative, superlative

**complement** word or phrase that completes a grammatical construction in the predicate and describes or is identified with the subject or object

**complex sentence** sentence containing one independent clause and one or more dependent clauses

**compound-complex sentence** sentence containing more than one independent clause and one or more dependent clauses

**compound sentence** sentence composed of two or more simple sentences joined by coordinating conjunctions

**compound word** word formed by combining two or more existing words

**concrete noun** noun describing something that can be perceived by sense

**conditional** (*adj*) designating clause, word, mood, or sentence that expresses a condition or hypothetical state

**conjugation** inflection of a verb

**connective** word that joins words, phrases, clauses, and sentences

**construction** arrangement of two or more words or morphemes in grammatical unit

**contraction** shortened form of word or phrase, with omitted letters replaced by apostrophe

**coordinating conjunction** conjunction that connects two words, phrases, or clauses of equal grammatical rank

**copula** verb that links subject and predicate; linking verb

**copulative** (*adj*) designating a verb functioning as a copula; designating a conjunction that connects words or clauses of equal rank or function

**correlative** word used regularly in association with another word, such as the conjunctions "either" and "or"

**count noun** noun that refers to countable thing and can be used in the singular or plural, such as "bus"

**dangling participle** participle that appears from its position to modify a word other than the one intended

**dative** noun case for indirect object in inflected languages

**declarative sentence** sentence that makes a statement

**declension** inflection of nouns, pronouns, and adjectives for gender, number, and case; class of nouns or adjectives having similar inflected forms

**definite article** article "the" that classes modified noun as identified or specific

**demonstrative** pronoun or adjective that points out the person or thing referred to

**dependent clause** clause unable to function as complete sentence on its own; subordinate clause

**determiner** word that modifies or restricts a noun and is placed before any other adjectives

**diagram** grammatical analysis of sentence in graphic form

**direct address** form of noun used to address person or object directly in a sentence

**direct object** word or phrase representing person or thing that receives action denoted by transitive verb

**dual** form in some languages that indicates reference to two persons or things

**dvandva** compound word composed of comparable, nonsubordinate elements, such as "bittersweet"

**emphatic** (*adj*) designating a form used to add emphasis, such as "do" in "I do like it"

**epicene** (*adj*) designating a noun or pronoun capable of referring to either sex

**exclamatory sentence** sentence expressing surprise or strong feeling

**exophora** use of word or phrase that refers to something

outside its linguistic environment, such as "that" in "Look at that"

**expletive** word used to introduce a subject, esp. "there" or "it" used as introductory word

**factitive** (*adj*) pertaining to verb expressing process of making or rendering in a certain way

**feminine** grammatical gender that includes most nouns referring to females, as well as other nouns

**first person** form of pronoun or verb indicating speaker or group including speaker, as "I" or "am"

**form class** group of words or forms in specific language that have one or more grammatical features in common

**function word** word that expresses grammatical relationships and has little semantic content

**future** verb tense indicating action or state in the future

**future perfect** verb tense indicating action to be completed by or to extend up to specified time in the future

**gender** grammatical distinction applied to nouns and pronouns, often correlated with sex, but sometimes based on arbitrary assignment

**genitive** noun case indicating possession or origin

**gerund** verb form ending in English in "-ing" and functioning as verbal noun

**govern** (*vb*) require the use of a particular form of another word

**grammar** study of the way sentences of a language are constructed; these features or constructions themselves; set of rules accounting for these constructions

**grammarian** expert in grammar

**grammatical** (*adj*) relating to grammar; conforming to standard usage

**head** chief member of grammatical construction, which determines grammatical role of entire construction or upon which other members depend

**helping verb** auxiliary verb

**heteroclite** (*adj*) irregular in inflection

**historical present** present tense used in narrating past event

**hypotaxis** dependent or subordinate relation or construction

**imperative** verb mood indicating command or request

**imperfect** verb tense indicating habitual or incomplete action continuing at some temporal point of reference in past

**impersonal** (*adj*) being a verb with only third person singular forms and having an unspecified subject

**inceptive** verb form or aspect expressing beginning of an action; inchoative

**inchoative** inceptive

**indefinite article** article "a" or "an" that classes modified noun as singular but unidentified

**indefinite pronoun** pronoun such as "some" or "any" that does not specify the identity of its referent

**independent clause** main clause

**indicative** verb mood indicating statement or question

**indirect object** word or phrase representing person or thing with reference to which the action of verb is performed

**infinitive** basic verb form that does not show person, number, or tense and is often preceded by "to"

**inflection** change in grammatical function of word, as in case, number, or person, esp. by adding affix

**intensifier** intensive

**intensive** linguistic element, esp. an adverb, indicating increased emphasis or force; intensifier

**interrogative** word or construction used in asking a question

**intransitive verb** verb having no direct object of its action, which is complete

**inversion** change in usual word order, as in placement of auxiliary verb before subject

**irregular** (*adj*) not conforming to the usual pattern of inflection in a language

**linking verb** copula

**locative** noun case indicating place or position

**loose sentence** sentence in which subordinate clause or modifiers follow completion of main clause

**main clause** clause that could stand alone as complete sentence

**marker** element indicating grammatical class or function of construction

**masculine** grammatical gender that includes most nouns referring to males, as well as other nouns

**mass noun** noun that refers to indefinitely divisible substance or abstract notion, such as "electricity" or "truth"

**middle voice** verb form, as in Greek, indicating that the subject is acting on or for itself

**misplaced modifier** word, phrase, or clause erroneously placed in sentence so that it modifies a different noun from that intended

**modal auxiliary** auxiliary verb used with another verb to express mood, such as "can" or "must"

**modifier** word or phrase qualifying or describing meaning of another word, esp. adjective and adverb or prepositional phrase

**mood** indication of condition or manner of verb's action: indicative, imperative, subjunctive, optative

**neuter** grammatical gender for nouns not classed as masculine or feminine

**nominative** case usu. indicating that noun is subject of verb

**nonrestrictive clause** relative clause that describes or supplements modified element but is not essential to its basic meaning

**noun phrase** grammatical construction that functions as a noun, consisting of a noun and any modifiers or a noun substitute, such as a pronoun

**number** indication whether noun, verb, etc., refers to one or more than one: singular, plural, dual

**object** noun or noun substitute that receives or is affected by action of verb; noun or pronoun representing goal of preposition

**objective** grammatical case used for object of transitive verb or preposition

**optative** verb mood expressing a wish or desire

**paradigm** set of all inflected forms of a word

**parataxis** joining together of clauses or phrases without conjunctions

**parse** (*vb*) analyze, describe, and grammatically label the parts of a sentence

**participle** verb form that can be used as adjective or with auxiliary verb to form certain tenses

**particle** small, usually uninflected word that has grammatical use rather than lexical meaning, esp. a word that does not fit into part of speech categories

**part of speech** basic class of words in given language to which any word can be assigned based on meaning, form, or function in a sentence

**passive voice** verb form indicating that subject is receiver of action expressed by verb

**past** verb tense referring to events or states in times gone by

**past participle** verb form usu. ending in "-ed" or "-en," used as adjective or in forming passive voice or perfect tenses

**past perfect** verb tense indicating action or state completed before specific time in past

**perfect** verb tense noting action or state terminated prior to some temporal point of reference

**perfect participle** past participle

**periodic sentence** sentence in which completion of main clause is suspended until end

**periphrastic** (*adj*) using two or more words instead of an inflected word to express a grammatical function

**person** indication of person speaking, spoken to, or spoken about: first (I, we); second (you); third (he, she, it, they)

**personal pronoun** any pronoun that distinguishes speaker or one spoken to or about: I, we, you, he, she, it, they

**phrasal verb** unit consisting of verb and one or more adverbs or prepositions, often having idiomatic meaning

**phrase** sequence of grammatically related words lacking subject and predicate

**pluperfect** past perfect

**plural** form designating more than one

**positive** first degree of comparison of adjectives or adverbs, being the basic form

**possessive** form or case indicating ownership or possession

**postposition** placing of word, particle, or affix after another word to modify it or relate it to other elements of sentence

**predicate** that which is said about subject of sentence

**predicate nominative** noun or pronoun that has same referent as subject and is used in predicate with copula

**prepositional phrase** phrase made up of preposition and its noun or pronoun object with any modifiers

**present** verb tense indicating action or state occurring or existing now

**present participle** verb form ending in "-ing" used as modifier or in forming the progressive

**present perfect** verb tense indicating action completed at present time or continuing from past into present

**preterit** verb tense indicating action or state, esp. completed action or state, in past

**principal parts** verb forms from which all other inflected forms can be derived, consisting of infinitive, past tense, and past participle

**privative** affix indicating negation or absence, such as "a-" in "apolitical"

**progressive** verb form indicating continuing action

**proper noun** name of specific person, place, or thing, usu. indicated by capitalization

**qualifier** adjective or adverb used to qualify or limit meaning of word modified

**quantifier** modifier that establishes amount or extent of word modified

**reduplication** doubling of syllable or other element, sometimes in modified form, to generate derivative or inflected form

**reflexive** verb taking subject and object with same referents; pronoun used as object to refer to subject of verb

**regular** (*adj*) conforming to usual pattern of inflection in a language

**relative clause** subordinate clause that modifies antecedent noun or pronoun

**relative pronoun** pronoun used to introduce relative clause

**restrictive clause** relative clause that identifies or limits

meaning of word modified and is essential to meaning of sentence

**run-on sentence** sequence of two or more main clauses not separated by semicolon, conjunction, or period

**second person** form of pronoun or verb used in referring to one or ones addressed, as "you"

**sentence** grammatically independent unit expressing a statement, question, command, or exclamation, usu. consisting of subject and predicate

**sentence fragment** phrase or clause written as sentence but lacking subject or verb

**serial comma** comma used after next to last item and before conjunction in series of three or more items

**simple sentence** sentence consisting of only one main clause and no dependent clauses

**singular** form designating just one

**split infinitive** placing of word or phrase, usu. adverb, between "to" and its verb in infinitive form

**strong verb** verb that forms past tense and past participle by internal vowel change

**subject** word or phrase about which something is stated in sentence

**subjunctive** verb mood indicating doubt, wish, or hypothetical state

**subordinate clause** dependent clause

**subordinating conjunction** conjunction joining independent clause and dependent clause

**substantive** word or group of words functioning as a noun

**superlative** highest degree of comparison, of adjectives or adverbs, indicated by ending "-est" or the word "most"

**suppletive** (*adj*) describing inflected form of word entirely different from stem, such as past tense of "go"

**tense** verb form indicating time of action or state denoted by verb

**third person** form of pronoun or verb indicating person or thing spoken of, as "he" or "goes"

**transitive verb** verb indicating action upon direct object and able to form passive voice

**verbal** word derived from verb and used as noun or adjective: gerund, infinitive, or participle

**verb phrase** verb and its modifiers, objects, or complements functioning together in a sentence; main verb and auxiliary verbs functioning together as a verb

**vocative** noun case indicating direct address

**voice** verb form indicating whether subject acts or is acted upon

**volitive** (*adj*) pertaining to verb expressing a wish or permission

**weak verb** verb that forms past tense and past participle by adding suffix

**word order** sequence in which words are arranged in sentence or construction

## PARTS OF SPEECH

**adjective** word modifying a noun usu. by describing, delimiting, or specifying quantity

**adverb** word modifying a verb, adjective, other adverb, or clause, usu. by indicating where, when, how, or to what degree

**conjunction** word connecting words or word groups

**interjection** word used by itself to express emphatic feeling, such as "hurrah" or "yikes"

**noun** word naming a person, animal, object, idea, quality, act, or place

**preposition** word expressing relation between its object and another word or phrase in sentence

**pronoun** word taking place of a noun or noun phrase

**verb** word expressing action, state of being, or a relation between things

## PUNCTUATION AND DIACRITICS

**accent mark** mark used to show emphasis on a particular syllable or how a letter is to be pronounced

**acute accent** ´ short line slanting up to right placed over vowel to show that it has a certain sound quality or has the main stress

**ampersand** & standing for the word "and"

**angle brackets** < > used to set off what is enclosed

**apostrophe** ' used in contractions and possessives

**asterisk** * placed in printed matter as reference or to indicate omission of material found elsewhere; star

**bang** *Slang.* exclamation point (Printing and Computers)

**braces** { } used to connect words or items to be considered together

**brackets** [ ] used to enclose and set off matter within text, to indicate aggregation, or as parentheses within parentheses

**breve** ˘ small, open, U-shaped symbol placed over letter to indicate short vowel or short or unstressed syllable

**bullet** • large, solid, vertically centered dot placed in printed matter to call attention to particular passage, or used for syllable divisions in dictionaries

**caret** ∧ used to indicate where something is to be inserted

**cedilla** ¸ hooklike mark placed under consonant, usu. "c," to indicate modification of usual phonetic value, as in French "façade"

**circumflex** ˆ placed over vowel to show that it is long, pronounced with rise or fall in pitch, or pronounced with particular sound quality

**colon** : used to direct attention to matter that follows, esp. list, quotation, or explanation, and indicating a nearly full stop

**comma** , used to set off word, phrase, or clause or to separate items in list, and indicating slight pause

**dagger** † vertical cross widening at top of upright used as reference mark or to indicate person has died

**dash** — used to indicate break or shift in thought or sentence, around a parenthetical element, or prior to attribution of quote

**diacritic** mark placed over, under, or through a letter to indicate pronunciation or stress, or to distinguish words with identical spellings

**diacritical mark** diacritic

**diagonal** virgule

**dieresis** ¨ placed over second of two vowels to show that it is pronounced separately, as in "naïve"

**diesis** double dagger

**ditto mark** " placed on next line under word or phrase to indicate repetition

**double dagger** ‡ vertical cross with two horizontals used as reference mark; diesis

**ellipsis** . . . used to indicate omission of letters or words

**exclamation mark** exclamation point

**exclamation point** ! used to replace period for emphasis at end of sentence; exclamation mark

**fistnote** index

**full stop** *Chiefly Brit.* period

**grave accent** ` short line slanting up to left placed over vowel to show that it has certain sound quality, has secondary stress, or is pronounced rather than silent

**haček** ˇ small V-shaped symbol over consonant, usu. indicating palatalized sound

**hamza** ' indicating glottal stop in Arabic

**hyphen** - used to divide or join compound words, to break word between two lines, and in writing out compound numbers

**index** ☞ stylized hand with one finger extended horizontally and other fingers curled, used to point out important note or paragraph in text

**interrobang** ‽ question mark overlaid on exclamation point used at end of exclamatory rhetorical question

**interrogation mark** question mark

**leaders** series of spaced dots or hyphens used to lead eye horizontally

**macron** ¯ horizontal line placed over vowel to indicate it is long or over syllable to indicate long or stressed syllable

**obelisk** dagger

**paragraph mark** ¶ used to indicate beginning of new paragraph

**parallels** ‖ used as reference mark in printing

**parentheses** ( ) used to enclose amplifying or explanatory word or phrase or alternative term

**period** . indicating end of sentence, also used after abbreviations and initials

**pilcrow** paragraph mark

**prime** ′ placed after letter or character to distinguish from another of the same kind, as A, A′, or to show primary stress

**punctuation** system of standardized graphic symbols inserted in written matter to clarify meaning and separate structural units

**question mark** ? used to replace period at end of interrogative sentence

**quotation marks** " " used to set off and surround spoken or quoted material, some titles, and special or borrowed words; ' ' used to set off and surround a quotation within a quotation

**quotes** quotation marks

**section mark** § pair of S's stacked vertically and interlocking, used to indicate beginning of text subdivision or as reference mark

**semicolon** ; used to separate major elements of sentence, such as independent clauses, and to separate elements of series which themselves contain commas

**slash** virgule

**solidus** virgule

**square brackets** brackets

**star** asterisk

**stress mark** mark placed before, over, or after syllable to indicate stress in pronunciation

**subscript** any symbol written below normal line of letters

**superscript** any symbol written above normal line of letters

**swung dash** ~ used in place of word or part of word previously spelled out

**tilde** ˜ placed over letter "n" in Spanish to indicate palatal sound (ny) or over vowel in Portuguese to indicate nasalization

**umlaut** ¨ two dots placed above vowel, esp. in German, to indicate modification of its sound, as in "Lübeck"

**virgule** / placed between words to separate alternatives, indicate "or," "and or," or "per"; diagonal, slash, or solidus

**vowel point** dot, line, or other mark placed above or below consonant symbol to indicate vowel sound, as in Hebrew

# PHONETICS

**accent** variation in pronunciation of words due to regional, class, or cultural factors; emphasis on particular syllable of word or word within phrase

**affricate** consonant sound involving complete closure in vocal tract gradually released with audible friction

**allophone** one of the alternate phonetic forms of a phoneme, depending on its environment

**alveolar** consonant sound made by tongue against bony ridge behind upper front teeth

**apheresis** loss of one or more sounds or letters at beginning of word

**apocope** omission of last letter, syllable, or part of word

**aspirate** sound characterized by audible breath accompanying sound's articulation

**assimilation** process by which speech sound becomes more like neighboring sound

**bilabial** consonant sound formed by coming together of both lips

**breath** expiration of air through open glottis, without vibration of vocal cords

**brogue** Irish accent in English pronunciation; any strong regional accent

**buccal** (adj) pertaining to sounds made in cavity of cheeks

**cardinal vowel** any of eight primary, sustained vowel sounds used as reference points for describing vowel sounds of a language

**click** sound formed by suction of air into mouth and sudden plosive or affricate release

**close** (adj) designating vowel produced with tongue close to roof of mouth

**closed** (adj) designating syllable ending with consonant

**cluster** succession of two or more consonants in a syllable

**complementary distribution** relationship between speech sounds that do not occur in the same environment

**consonant** one of two basic categories of speech sounds, based on closure or near-closure in vocal tract to produce blockage of air or audible friction

**continuant** consonant sound that may be prolonged without change in quality

**coronal** (adj) articulated with blade, or front, of tongue raised

**dental** consonant sound made by pressure of tongue against teeth

**devoice** (vb) pronounce a normally voiced sound as voiceless or with reduced vibration of vocal cords

**digraph** pair of letters representing single speech sound, such as "sh" in "show"

**diphthong** complex vowel sound characterized by gliding change in tone during articulation of single syllable

**dissimilation** process by which speech sound becomes different from neighboring sound or disappears because of identical sound nearby

**distinctive feature** phonetic property serving to characterize and distinguish between phonemes in a language

**disyllable** word consisting of two syllables

**dorsal** speech sound made by pressure of back of tongue on roof of mouth

**egressive** (adj) generated with exhalation of breath from lungs

**ejective** voiceless stop or fricative produced with air compressed above closed glottis

**elision** omission of sounds in connected speech

**enclitic** unstressed word or form closely connected in pronunciation with preceding word and not normally used on its own

**epenthesis** insertion of extra sound in middle of word

**excrescent** (adj) designating sound inserted in word due to articulation but without grammatical or etymological justification

**flap** consonant sound produced by rapid flip of tongue against roof of mouth or upper teeth

**fortis** (adj) designating consonant sound characterized by relatively strong, forceful breath or effort

**free variation** relationship between speech sounds such that one may occur in place of the other with no change in meaning

**fricative** consonant sound characterized by audible friction of moving air forced between vocal organs; spirant

**geminate** doubled consonant sound

**glottal** (adj) articulated in opening at upper part of larynx, between vocal cords

**glottal stop** consonant sound made in larynx by closing glottis or vocal cords

**guttural** (adj) articulated in back of mouth or with tongue against soft palate

**haplology** omission of one of two similar sounds or syllables in a word

**implosive** consonant sound formed by inward-moving air, closure of mouth, and vocal cord vibration

**inflection** quality or variation of tone or pitch of voice

**ingressive** (adj) produced with air taken into mouth

**interdental** consonant sound made with tip of tongue between upper and lower teeth

**International Phonetic Alphabet** IPA; symbols used as universal system for transcribing speech sounds of any language

**intonation** pattern or form of pitch in articulation of words

**intrusive** (adj) designating speech sound inserted in connected speech where it is not present in the spelling

**IPA** International Phonetic Alphabet

**labial** speech sound formed by active use of lip or lips

**labiodental** speech sound formed by lower lip in contact with upper teeth

**lallation** lambdacism

**lambdacism** substitution of "l" for "r" or mispronunciation of "l"; lallation

**laminal** speech sound formed using blade of tongue

**laryngeal** (adj) articulated in the larynx

**lax** (adj) designating vowel pronounced with muscles relatively relaxed

**lenis** (adj) designating consonant sound characterized by relatively weak muscular tension and breath pressure

**liaison** linking of words, esp. in French, in which otherwise silent final consonant is pronounced as initial sound of following word that begins with vowel

**liquid** speech sound, such as "l", pronounced without friction and capable of being prolonged like a vowel

**long vowel** vowel sound relatively long in duration

**metathesis** transposition of letters, syllables, or sounds in a word

**modulation** variation in pitch and loudness of the voice

**monophthong** vowel retaining same quality throughout its duration

**monosyllable** word consisting of only one syllable

**mouillé** (*adj*) pronounced as a palatal or palatized sound, as the sounds spelled "ll" and "ñ" in Spanish

**mutation** phonetic change in initial consonant of a word under certain conditions, as observed in the Celtic languages; umlaut

**nasal** speech sound formed by audible passage of air through nose

**obstruent** speech sound characterized by stoppage or obstruction of exhalation: stop, fricative, or affricate

**occlusion** brief complete closure in vocal tract, resulting in stoppage of exhalation and ensuing pressure

**open** (*adj*) designating vowel produced with relatively large opening above the tongue; designating syllable ending with vowel

**orthoepy** study of pronunciation; standard pronunciation of a language

**palatal** speech sound formed with tongue close to or touching hard palate

**paragoge** addition of letter or syllable to end of word without changing meaning

**pharyngeal** speech sound produced in the pharynx

**phone** single speech sound

**phoneme** smallest unit of sound in a language that can distinguish one word from another

**phonemics** study of phonemes and phonemic systems of languages

**phonetic alphabet** alphabet having separate symbol for each distinguishable speech sound

**phonetician** specialist in phonetics

**phonetics** study of speech sounds and their production, transmission, reception, and transcription

**phonology** study of distribution and patterns of speech sounds in a language or languages

**phonotactics** patterns in which sounds of a language may combine to form sequences

**pitch** acoustic character of speech based on high or low quality of sound frequency

**plosive** consonant sound characterized by sudden release of complete closure in vocal tract, with audible expulsion of compressed air

**polysyllable** word consisting of two or more syllables

**primary accent** primary stress

**primary stress** strongest, principle stress of a word; primary accent

**proclitic** unstressed word or form closely connected in pronunciation with a following word and not normally used on its own

**pronunciation** act or manner of producing speech sounds; accepted way in which a word, syllable, or letter is sounded in a given language; phonetic transcription of word

**prothesis** addition of sound or syllable at beginning of word

**quality** characteristic timbre of a vowel sound

**quantity** relative duration, or length, of a sound or syllable

**Received Pronunciation** RP; prestigious, regionally neutral pronunciation of British English derived from educated speech of S England, widely used in British broadcasting

**resonance** amplification of speech sound by vibrations of air in vocal tract

**retroflex** (*adj*) designating speech sound made with tip of tongue curled up and back toward hard palate

**rhotacism** excessive use or misarticulation of the sound "r"

**rounded** (*adj*) designating speech sound pronounced with rounded lips

**RP** *Received Pronunciation*

**sandhi** modification of phonological entity determined by phonetic environment

**schwa** neutral, unstressed vowel sound made in center of mouth; symbol (ə) for this sound

**secondary accent** secondary stress

**secondary stress** stress in word weaker than primary stress but not unstressed; secondary accent

**short vowel** vowel sound relatively short in duration

**sibilant** speech sound characterized by "s" or hissing sound

**sonant** speech sound that is voiced; speech sound that forms syllable by itself

**sonorant** voiced speech sound made with relatively free passage of air, such as vowel or nasal

**sound spectrogram** graphic representation made by sound spectrograph

**sound spectrograph** electronic device that produces graphic representation of component frequencies and other acoustic features of a sound

**spirant** fricative

**stop** consonant sound made with complete closure at some part of vocal tract; plosive

**stress** degree of force applied in pronouncing sound, syllable, or word, producing relative loudness

**suction stop** click or implosive

**surd** (*adj*) voiceless; unvoiced

**syllable** basic uninterrupted unit of pronunciation consisting of vowel sound, vowel sound with one or more consonant sounds, or consonant pronounced alone

**synaloepha** blending of vowel at end of one word with vowel at beginning of next

**syncope** dropping of sounds or letters from middle of word

**syneresis** contraction of two syllables or vowels into one, esp. to form diphthong

**synizesis** combination of two vowels that do not form diphthong

**tense** (*adj*) designating vowel pronounced with muscles relatively tense

**tonic** syllable in an utterance having principal stress, usu. accompanied by change in pitch

**transcription** writing of speech sounds using phonetic symbols

**trigraph** three letters representing single speech sound

**trill** speech sound formed by rapid rolling or tapping motion of tongue or uvula

**triphthong** monosyllabic speech sound composed of three different vowel qualities

**umlaut** change in vowel sound in a Germanic language

under influence of vowel originally occurring in following syllable

**unstressed** (*adj*) pronounced without stress or emphasis

**unvoiced** (*adj*) voiceless; surd

**uvular** speech sound made by placing back of tongue against fleshy process on soft palate

**velar** speech sound formed by placing back of tongue against soft palate

**vocalic** (*adj*) relating to or containing a vowel or vowels

**voiced** (*adj*) produced with vibration of vocal cords

**voiceless** (*adj*) produced without vibration of vocal cords; unvoiced; surd

**voiceprint** graphic representation of acoustic features of person's voice; sound spectrogram

**vowel** one of two basic categories of speech sounds, based on free passage of air through vocal tract

## LINGUISTICS AND WRITING SYSTEMS

**abbreviation** shortened or contracted form used to represent entire word or phrase

**ablaut** regular alternation of internal vowel, reflecting change in grammatical function; apophony

**acrolect** variety of creole that approximates most closely the standard language

**acronym** word formed from initial letters of set series of words

**affix** morpheme added before, after, or within base word to create new word; prefix, suffix, or infix

**Afroasiatic** family of languages including Semitic, Egyptian, Berber, Cushitic, and Chadic

**agglutination** word formation in which distinct morphemes are combined without fusion or change, esp. addition of affixes to base word

**allomorph** alternate phonological shape of morpheme, such as plural form "-en" in "oxen" and "-s" in "goats"

**alphabet** letters of a language, arranged in set order; system of symbols or characters representing individual speech sounds of language

**alphabetize** (*vb*) arrange words in order of letters of alphabet, either letter-by-letter or by word

**alternation** variation in form of linguistic unit as it occurs in different environments or under different conditions

**amelioration** melioration

**American Sign Language** language consisting of manual signs and gestures, used by deaf people in the U.S. and parts of Canada

**analogy** process by which words or phrases are created or altered on model of existing language patterns

**analytic** (*adj*) designating a language that uses function words and changes in word order, rather than inflected forms, to express grammatical relations

**Anglo-Saxon** Old English

**antepenult** third syllable from the end in a word

**anthropological linguistics** study of relationship between language and culture, esp. in preliterate societies

**antonym** word opposite in meaning to another

**apophony** ablaut

**applied linguistics** use of linguistic theory in teaching, psychology, lexicography, and data processing

**Aramaic** ancient Semitic language from whose script were derived Hebrew, Arabic, and many other scripts

**archaism** word, form, or usage no longer in common use

**argot** special, often secret vocabulary and idiom of one group

**artificial language** language invented for specialized use, esp. for international communication or computer programming

**Austronesian** family of languages spoken in Malay Peninsula, Indonesia, Philippines, Vietnam, Madagascar, and Oceania; Malayo-Polynesian

**baby talk** style of speech addressed to children, characterized by eccentric pronunciations and simplified sentence structure

**Baltic** branch of Indo-European languages including Latvian, Lithuanian, and Old Prussian

**Bantu** subbranch of Niger-Congo family of languages spoken in central and southern Africa, comprising over two hundred languages including Kikuyu and Swahili

**base** root or stem

**basilect** variety of creole that is most distinct from acrolect or standard language

**bilingual** (*adj*) fluent in two languages

**blend** word formed from parts of other words, such as "brunch" or "motel"

**bound form** linguistic form that occurs only in combination with other forms, such as most affixes

**boustrophedon** ancient form of writing in which lines alternate running right to left and left to right

**Braille** system of writing using combination of raised dots that are read by touch, for use by the blind

**Briticism** word or usage characteristic of British English, esp. when employed in American English

**calque** loan translation

**cant** special language used by underworld group or by members of a profession

**Celtic** branch of Indo-European languages including Irish, Scottish Gaelic, Welsh, and Breton

**citation** quotation or excerpt showing particular word or phrase in context

**code-switching** alternate use of two or more languages or varieties of a language within same conversation or passage

**cognate** language related to another by descent from same language; word related to another by descent from same root word

**coinage** newly invented word

**collocation** regular co-occurrence of lexical items together, such as "commit crime"

**colloquial** (*adj*) designating language characteristic of or suitable to familiar, casual conversation

**combining form** linguistic form that occurs only in combination with other forms

**comment** rheme

**comparative linguistics** study of patterns of similarities and differences between languages

**competence** unconscious internalized knowledge of the rules of a language enabling speaker to produce and understand the language

**computational linguistics** study of the applications of computers in processing and analyzing language, as in automatic machine translation

**connotation** associated or secondary meaning of word in addition to its explicit or primary meaning

**contamination** alteration in linguistic form due to influence of related form

**corpus** collection of spoken or written utterances taken as representative sample of a given language and used for linguistic analysis

**creole** pidgin that has developed in complexity over time and has become the native language of a group of speakers

**cuneiform** system of writing using wedge-shaped characters, used by the ancient Assyrians, Babylonians, and others

**cursive** (*adj*) designating handwriting or printing in which letters are joined together in flowing style

**Cyrillic** Greek-based alphabet used in Russian and other Slavic languages

**dead language** language no longer in use as sole means of oral communication in a community

**deep structure** (in transformational grammar) underlying semantic or syntactic representation of sentence from which surface structure may be derived

**definiendum** term to be defined at head of dictionary entry

**definiens** defining part of dictionary entry

**demotic** current, everyday form of a language, esp. the Modern Greek vernacular; simplified form of ancient Egyptian hieroglyphic writing

**denotation** explicit or direct meaning of word

**derivation** formation of new words by adding affixes or changing shape of base word

**descriptive grammar** approach to grammar concerned with actual usage of speakers rather than with norms of correctness

**descriptive linguistics** study of structure of one language without reference to its history or comparison with other languages

**Devanagari** alphabetic script with some syllabic features, used for writing Hindi and other languages of India

**diachronic** (*adj*) relating to study of a language as it changes over time

**dialect** regionally or socially distinct variety of a language

**dialect atlas** linguistic atlas

**dialectology** study of dialects

**dictionary** book containing alphabetical listing of words in a language with their meanings and other information

**diglossia** use in a society of widely differing formal and informal varieties of a language

**direct discourse** exact quotation of speaker's words

**discourse analysis** study of patterns and rules governing units of connected speech or writing longer than one sentence

**doublet** either of two different words ultimately deriving from the same source

**Dravidian** language family of South Asia, spoken mainly in S India

**eponym** person or mythological figure after whom something is named

**Esperanto** invented language intended for international use, based on words common to major European languages

**etymology** study of history and development of form and meaning of words; derivation of a word

**etymon** linguistic form from which another is historically derived

**expression** unit of speech composed of several elements

**eye dialect** use of spellings that are intended to convey speaker's dialectal or uneducated pronunciations but are actually respellings of standard pronunciations

**fingerspelling** communication in sign language by means of manual alphabet

**fluency** ease and proficiency of expression in specific language

**folk etymology** modification of word based on false assumption about its origin or irrelevant analogy with familiar word

**formal** (*adj*) referring to language use typical of impersonal and official situations, characterized by complex vocabulary and sentences, careful grammar, and avoidance of colloquial expressions

**franglais** French spoken with large admixture of English words

**free form** linguistic form that can be used by itself as an independent word

**generative grammar** formalized set of rules that can generate all acceptable grammatical sentences of a language to explain tacit understanding native speaker has of that language

**Germanic** branch of Indo-European languages including German, English, Dutch, and Scandinavian languages

**ghost word** word that has come into existence through error, as through a misprint

**glossary** alphabetical listing of specialized terms and their meanings, usu. for one particular field

**grapheme** smallest distinctive unit of a writing system, esp. one representing a single phoneme

**graphology** study of writing systems

**Grimm's law** pattern of consonant correspondence between Germanic and other Indo-European languages demonstrated by Jakob Grimm in 1822, establishing regular process of change in language as basis for future linguistic analysis

**Hangul** alphabet used in writing Korean

**hapax legomenon** word that appears only once in a text, the works of an author, or the written record of a language

**headword** word or phrase used as heading of chapter or as dictionary or encyclopedia entry

**Hellenic** branch of Indo-European languages including ancient and modern Greek

**heteronym** word spelled the same as another but having different sound and meaning, such as "lead" the metal and the verb

**hieratic** (*adj*) designating simplified form of hieroglyphics used by priests in ancient Egypt

**hieroglyphic** pictorial symbol used in ancient writing to represent word or sound

**hieroglyphics** system of writing, as that of ancient Egypt, that uses pictorial symbols

**historical linguistics** study of language as it changes over a period of time

**Hobson-Jobson** alteration of word borrowed from foreign language to fit patterns of borrowing language

**holophrase** single word functioning as phrase or sentence

**homograph** word with same spelling but different meaning from another word

**homonym** word with same pronunciation and spelling but different meaning from another word; homophone

**homophone** word with same pronunciation but different meaning from another word

**honorific** title or grammatical form showing respect

**hypercorrection** use of an inappropriate pronunciation,

form, or construction to avoid using a seemingly incorrect form

**ideogram** written symbol representing idea or thing directly; ideograph

**ideograph** ideogram

**idiolect** individual person's distinct manner of speaking

**idiom** expression having a meaning not predictable from usual meanings of its constituent words; language or style of speech peculiar to a people

**illiteracy** inability to read and write one's native language

**Indic** Indo-Aryan

**indirect discourse** inclusion of speaker's words in altered form in longer sentence

**Indo-Aryan** subgroup of Indo-Iranian branch of Indo-European languages including Sanskrit, Hindi, and Urdu

**Indo-European** widespread family of languages spoken primarily in Northern Hemisphere, including Italic, Germanic, Slavic, Baltic, Hellenic, Celtic, and Indo-Iranian branches

**Indo-Iranian** branch of Indo-European languages including Indic and Iranian subgroups

**infix** affix added within base word

**informal** (*adj*) referring to language use suitable to or typical of casual or familiar speech or writing

**informant** native speaker of language who supplies utterances or other data for someone analyzing or learning the language

**interlingual** (*adj*) using two or more languages, as some dictionaries

**Iranian** subgroup of Indo-Iranian branch of Indo-European languages including Persian, Pashto, Avestan, and Kurdish

**isogloss** line on map marking limits within which particular feature of speech occurs

**Italic** branch of Indo-European languages including Latin and modern Romance languages such as French, Spanish, and Italian

**Japlish** Japanese spoken or written with large admixture of English words

**jargon** technical or specialized terminology of group or profession; obscure or unintelligible language

**jive** special slang jargon, often flippant or misleading

**kana** Japanese writing system using syllabic characters, having two varieties

**kanji** Japanese writing system based on Chinese characters

**king's** (or **queen's**) **English** correct, standard speech and usage of educated persons in England

**Kufic** early form of Arabic alphabet used in writing Koran

**language** system using combinations of vocal sounds, written symbols, or gestures with accepted meanings to express thoughts and feelings common to one people of specific region or culture; communication using such a system

**language family** group of related languages descended from common parent language

**language universal** property or feature common to all languages

**Latin** Italic language of ancient Rome that is primary source of Romance languages

**Latin alphabet** twenty-three letter alphabet of ancient Rome that is basis for English and other European alphabets

**lemma** form of word or phrase that represents its entire inflectional range, such as the form glossed in a dictionary

**letter** written symbol representing speech sound in particular alphabet

**lexeme** smallest distinct lexical unit in language system; item of vocabulary

**lexical** (*adj*) pertaining to the words or vocabulary of a language

**lexicographer** writer or editor of dictionaries

**lexicography** art and practice of making dictionaries

**lexicology** study of formation and use of words

**lexicon** vocabulary; listing of words in a language; total stock of words in a language

**lingo** language, esp. jargon or slang, of a particular field, group, or individual

**lingua franca** language used for communication between persons who ordinarily speak different languages

**linguist** specialist in linguistics; polyglot

**linguistic atlas** set of maps showing distribution of linguistic features in the speech of an area; dialect atlas

**linguistics** study of sound, structure, meaning, vocabulary, and development of language, including fields of phonetics, phonology, morphology, syntax, semantics, pragmatics, comparative, and historical linguistics

**lipreading** understanding of spoken words from movement of speaker's lips without hearing sounds made

**literacy** ability to read and write

**literatim** (*adv*) letter for letter; literally

**loan translation** compound word or phrase formed by translation of each of the elements of a compound from another language

**loanword** word borrowed from another language

**logogram** character or symbol that represents entire word

**longhand** normal handwriting in which words are spelled out in full

**macaronic** (*adj*) made up of Latin words mixed with vernacular words often given Latin endings

**Malayo-Polynesian** Austronesian

**manual alphabet** set of finger signals representing letters of alphabet, used in sign language

**melioration** semantic change in a word over the course of time to a more approved or respectable meaning

**metalanguage** language used to describe or analyze language

**metalinguistics** study of relation of language to other culturally determined behavior

**Middle English** English language of period c1150–1475

**Modern English** English language since c1475

**morpheme** smallest distinctive grammatical unit of a language that is meaningful in itself and indivisible

**morphology** branch of linguistics involving forms and structure of words and patterns of word formation in particular language; these patterns of word formation themselves

**morphophoneme** abstract phonological entity representing corresponding allomorphs of one morpheme

**morphophonemics** study of relationship between morphemes and their phonological form

**mother tongue** language first learned by a person

**multilingual** (*adj*) able to speak several languages

**native speaker** person speaking particular language learned naturally during childhood

**natural language** language that is the native language of a group of speakers

**neologism** new word or existing word with new meaning introduced into language

**Niger-Congo** large family of African languages

**nonce word** word invented or formed for particular occasion

**nonstandard** (*adj*) designating grammar, word choice, etc., used and considered acceptable by most educated native speakers

**nonverbal communication** communication without words, as by gestures, postures, and facial expressions

**Old English** English language before c1150; Anglo-Saxon

**onomastics** study of origin and use of proper names

**orismology** science of defining technical terms of a field of study

**orthography** representation of language sounds by written symbols or letters; study of letters and spelling; correct or standard spelling

**paradigmatic** (*adj*) referring to a relationship among linguistic elements that can substitute for each other in a given context

**paragraph** subdivision of written composition set in block, usu. beginning on indented line, and having some coherence

**paralanguage** vocal qualities, gestures, and facial expressions that accompany speech and contribute to communication but are not part of actual language system

**parlance** specified style of speaking, esp. involving choice of words

**paronym** word derived from same root as another; cognate

**patois** provincial dialect differing from standard form of the language; jargon

**patronymic** name derived from name of one's father or ancestor, esp. by addition of affix

**pejoration** semantic change in a word over the course of time to a less favorable or less respectable meaning

**penult** next to the last syllable in a word

**performance** person's actual use of language in speaking or writing

**philology** study of written texts to determine meaning and authenticity; older term for linguistics, esp. historical and comparative linguistics

**phonogram** symbol representing word, sound, or syllable

**phraseogram** written symbol that represents phrase, as in shorthand

**pictograph** pictorial symbol representing idea or thing, as in picture writing

**picture writing** system using pictures or pictorial symbols to record events or express ideas

**pidgin** auxiliary language with simplified grammatical structure and vocabulary drawn mostly from one language, used by speakers of two different languages for communication

**pinyin** system for romanizing Chinese into Latin alphabet

**pochismo** English word borrowed into Spanish use

**polyglot** (*adj*) multilingual; composed of numerous linguistic groups; (*n*) person who knows several languages

**polysemous** (*adj*) having many meanings

**polysynthetic** (*adj*) designating language that uses long words with many affixes to express grammatical relations and meanings

**portmanteau word** blend

**pragmatics** branch of linguistics concerned with language in context, including speaker's intent and relation to listener; branch of semiotics concerned with relations between symbols and their users

**prefix** affix added before base word

**prescriptive grammar** approach to grammar concerned with establishing norms of correct and incorrect usage or rules based on these norms

**protolanguage** assumed parent form of language

**provincialism** word, phrase, or sound distinct to particular region or dialect; regionalism

**proxemics** study of varying patterns of physical proximity in interpersonal communication

**psycholinguistics** study of relationship between language and psychological processes of its users

**queen's English** king's English

**reconstruction** determination of hypothetical earlier form of a language by comparison of data from a later stage of the language

**reflex** element in a language that has developed from corresponding element in earlier form of the language

**reformed spelling** simplified spelling that eliminates unpronounced letters, such as "thru" for "through"

**regionalism** provincialism

**rheme** portion of sentence providing new information about topic; comment

**rhotacism** change of speech sound to "r" as language evolves

**romaji** system of writing Japanese using letters of Latin alphabet

**Roman alphabet** Latin alphabet

**Romance language** one of the group of Indo-European languages descended from Latin, including French, Spanish, Italian, Portuguese, and Romanian

**romanization** use of Latin alphabet to write a language usu. written in a different alphabet

**root** morpheme that is the basic element of a word, underlying inflected or derived forms

**rune** character of ancient Germanic alphabet

**Sapir-Whorf hypothesis** theory that language shapes behavior and thinking of those who speak it

**script** distinctive formation of letters by hand; handwriting; any system of writing

**semantics** branch of linguistics concerned with nature, structure, and development of meaning in language; branch of semiotics concerned with relationship between signs or symbols and what they denote

**semiotics** study or theory of signs and symbols in language and other communicative behavior

**Semitic** subfamily of Afroasiatic languages including Akkadian, Aramaic, Arabic, and Hebrew

**shorthand** rapid writing system using simple strokes and symbols to represent letters, words, and phrases

**sign** meaningful gestural unit belonging to a sign language; sign language

**signed English** form of communication using the signs of American Sign Language but using English grammar

**signing** communication by sign language

**sign language** system of hand motions and finger configurations representing letters, ideas, and things, used in communication among deaf

**Sino-Tibetan** family of Asian languages including Mandarin and other Chinese dialects, Burmese, and Tibetan

**slang** informal, often nonstandard language consisting of newly coined words and extended meanings; specialized vocabulary, jargon, or vernacular

**Slavic** branch of Indo-European languages including Russian, Polish, Czech, Bulgarian, Serbo-Croatian, and Slovene

**sociolect** dialect used by particular social group

**sociolinguistics** study of interactions of language and society

**sound symbolism** nonarbitrary connection between phonetic features of words and their meanings

**source language** original language of text to be translated

**speech community** all people using one language or dialect

**spelling** standardized arrangement of letters to form specific words

**Sprachgefühl** sense of established usage and what is linguistically effective or appropriate

**standard** (*adj*) designating relatively unified, institutionalized form of language accepted as norm to be spoken and taught

**stem** part of inflected word which remains unchanged, to which inflections are added

**structuralism** structural linguistics

**structural linguistics** study of nature and structure of language as network of coherent systems of formal units

**substandard** (*adj*) designating colloquial usage differing from standard dialect and deemed incorrect

**substratum** set of features of a language traceable to influence of earlier language that it has replaced

**suffix** affix added after base word

**Sumerian** language of ancient Mesopotamia, attested in pictographic and cuneiform writing

**superstratum** set of features of a language traceable to influence of a language formerly spoken in the society by a dominant group

**surface structure** representation of final syntactic form of sentence derived from deep structure in transformational grammar

**syllabary** system of written symbols each representing a syllable

**synaesthesia** direct relation or association between word's meaning and its form or sound

**synchronic** (*adj*) relating to study of a language as it exists at one point in time

**syncretism** merging of two or more different inflected forms into one

**synonym** word with same or essentially similar meaning as another word

**syntactics** branch of semiotics dealing with formal properties of symbol systems and relationship of signs to each other

**syntagmatic** (*adj*) referring to relationship among linguistic elements that occur sequentially

**syntax** rules for arranging words to form phrases, clauses, and sentences; study of this

**synthetic** (*adj*) designating language that uses affixes, rather than separate words, to express grammatical relationships

**tagmeme** grammatical unit based on relationship between a grammatical function and the class of items than can fill that function

**tagmemics** school of linguistics using tagmeme as basic unit of grammatical analysis

**target language** language into which text is to be translated; language that one is learning

**taxeme** feature of arrangement of elements in construction, such as selection, order, or phonetic modification

**theme** first major element in a sentence, about which the rest of the sentence communicates information; topic

**thesaurus** book listing words and their synonyms and antonyms

**tone language** language in which otherwise phonologically identical words are distinguished by different pitches, such as Chinese

**toneme** phoneme consisting of contrasting tone in tone language

**tongue** language or dialect

**topic** portion of sentence containing item about which information will be provided by rest of sentence

**transformational grammar** system of grammatical analysis, esp. a form of generative grammar, concerned with process by which surface structure is derived from deep structure

**translation** rendering of passage from one language into another

**transliteration** representation of letters or words from one language in characters or letters of another language

**ultima** last syllable of a word

**uncial** style of writing using large, rounded letters, esp. in Greek and Latin manuscripts of the 3rd to 9th centuries A.D.

**usage** actual or customary manner in which language is used in a community; way in which particular word or phrase is used, esp. when choice of words is involved

**variant** one of two or more different spellings, pronunciations, or forms of the same word

**verbatim** (*adv*) word for word

**vernacular** language or dialect indigenous to place; common spoken language, distinct from formal written language

**vocabulary** words of a language; body of words known or used by an individual or group; list of words, usu. arranged in alphabetical order and defined or translated

**vulgar** (*adj*) designating the popular or informal variety of a language, esp. Latin

**vulgarism** commonly used word or phrase regarded as substandard, coarse, or obscene

**Wade-Giles system** system for the romanization of Chinese, widely used esp. before the adoption of pinyin

**word** basic, discrete unit of meaning in language, composed of one or more speech sounds or their written representation

**word-hoard** individual's vocabulary

**zoosemiotics** study of communication systems used by animals

# RHETORIC AND FIGURES OF SPEECH

**SEE ALSO:** Chap. 13: Philosophy; Chap. 14: Literature; Chap. 18: Grammar, Phonetics, and Linguistics

**accismus** insincere refusal

**adage** proverb; traditional wise saying

**agnomination** echoing of word's sound or repetition of word in different sense for emphasis or as pun

**allegory** extended metaphor; representation of idea with concrete, structured image

**alliteration** succession of words or stressed syllables of word group beginning with same consonant sound or with same letter

**allocution** address; formal speech

**allusion** reference to famous, historical, or literary person or event

**ambages** roundabout form of speaking the truth in misleading manner

**ambiguity** expression of idea in words that may be interpreted more than one way

**amplification** figure of speech that emphasizes ideas through reiteration, embellishment, or elaboration

**ana** miscellaneous sayings or bits of information on some topic

**anacoluthon** deliberate failure to complete sentence, followed by shift to another thought or construction

**anadiplosis** repetition of last word in phrase or sentence, to constitute first word in following phrase or sentence

**anagram** rearrangement of letters in one word to form another

**analogy** comparison of things alike in certain respects to establish basis for exposition or argument

**anaphora** repetition of same word or phrase to begin consecutive sentences or clauses

**anastrophe** deliberate reversal of usual, logical order of sentence parts for emphasis

**anathema** formal denunciation

**anecdote** short narrative or description revealing point of interest about person or event

**anonym** pseudonym formed by backward spelling of real name

**antiphrasis** ironical description meant to convey impression opposite that normally conveyed by words used

**antithesis** use of strongly contrasting words and images

**antonomasia** substitution of epithet or appellative for proper name, or proper name for common noun or general class of words

**aphorism** succinct, memorable statement of a truth; maxim

**apophasis** statement of assertion while denying intention of mentioning that subject

**aposiopesis** abrupt interruption that leaves thought incomplete

**apostrophe** direct form of address aimed at someone or something not present

**apothegm** tersely worded maxim

**appellative** descriptive name, designation, or epithet

**ara** long, formally worded curse

**archaism** old, obsolete diction or vocabulary, esp. when used for effect

**argumentation** form of discourse emphasizing persuasion

**assonance** juxtaposition of similar word sounds, esp. vowels

**asyndeton** condensed expression characterized by omission of conjunctions

**atticism** concise and elegant expression

**aureate** (*adj*) distinguished by flowery rhetoric

**axiom** self-evident truth, succinctly stated

**banality** expression devoid of originality or wit; cliché

**bathos** unsuccessful attempt at lofty, dignified style, resulting in triteness, triviality, or unintentional humor

**bombast** inflated, grandiloquent language

**bon mot** clever remark or comment; witticism

**brachylogy** concise expression or diction

**brief** summary of ideas or points of argument

**brocard** short, proverbial rule

**bromide** commonplace saying or turn of phrase

**buzzword** slogan or catchword conjuring popular idea or image

**byword** proverb; word or phrase associated with a person or thing

**cacology** poor diction or pronunciation

**cadence** rhythm and measure of written or spoken language

**cant** insincere language intended to convey impression of genuine feeling

**catachresis** wrong use of one word for another that sounds similar to it or has similar meaning

**catchword** commonly repeated word or phrase; slogan

**chestnut** old and familiar anecdote or joke

**chiasmus** reversal of word order in two otherwise parallel constructions

**circumambages** instance of indirect or evasive speech or writing

**circumlocution** roundabout mode of expression; use of unnecessary verbiage

**cliché** stereotyped expression; trite description; banality; platitude; truism

**cognomen** distinguishing name or epithet

**conceit** ingenious idea expressed as elaborate, fanciful metaphor or analogy

**concinnity** harmony of tone and logic in discourse

**connotation** shades and variety of meanings attached to word or phrase in addition to specific denotation; implication

**conundrum** question or riddle whose answer involves a pun

**curse** invocation of evil upon someone; imprecation; malediction

**dead metaphor** figure of speech drained of its power of analogy; metaphor grown colorless with overuse

**debate** formal argumentation

**declamation** recitation as exercise in oratory or elocution

**denotation** specific, literal meaning

**description** form of discourse emphasizing portrayal

**diatribe** abusive, bitter style of speech

**diction** selection and use of words to convey meaning; quality, style, and sound of an individual's speech relative to prevailing standards

**digression** departure from subject at hand to another, unrelated one

**discourse** speech; lengthy, formal discussion of subject

**dithyramb** wildly enthusiastic speech or writing, usu. of irregular form, esp. impassioned poem or chant

**double entendre** intentionally ambiguous statement, esp. with one possibly indecent meaning

**double-talk** intentional ambiguity; mixture of sense and nonsense

**dysphemism** harsh or unpleasant language used as substitute for more direct or neutral expression, opposite of euphemism

**echoism** onomatopoeia

**effect** distinctive impact or impression that language produces

**elaboration** development of theme or image

**ellipsis** omission of words essential to meaning and structure, but easily filled in by reader or listener

**elliptical** (*adj*) tending to be ambiguous, unclear, or round-about

**elocution** practice of oral delivery or public speaking

**eloquence** artful, persuasive, elegant, or vivid language

**emphasis** rhetorical weight given to ideas by placement, repetition, elaboration, or contrast in words used

**enallage** intentional replacement of one grammatical form with another

**endearment** affectionate form of address

**epigram** concise, vivid saying

**epilogue** concluding remark or statement; last of seven parts of oration in classical rhetoric

**epistrophe** repetition of word or phrase at end of consecutive sentences or clauses

**epithet** descriptive, often disparaging phrase characteristically applied to a person or thing because of its accuracy and color

**equivocation** use of ambiguity in order to deceive or evade

**equivoque** amusing usage of word that suggests several other similar meanings; pun

**eulogy** formal, extended statement of praise, esp. to honor deceased person; panegyric

**euphemism** indirect, mild language used as substitute for direct, possibly offensive description; opposite of dysphemism

**euphuism** florid, affected, artificial style of speech

**exclamation** sharp, sudden utterance; vehement protest or complaint

**excursus** long, formal digression

**exordium** introduction to oration; first of seven parts of oration in classical rhetoric

**expatiation** speaking or writing at great length

**expletive** emphatic interjection

**exposition** form of discourse emphasizing explanation

**expression** particular word or phrase used to represent something verbally

**figurative language** metaphorical language used outside its usual forms of construction and meaning for purposes of description, persuasion, or originality of expression

**figure of speech** expressive language construction in which word meaning differs from literal sense of words

**flourish** fine language used merely for effect

**flowery** (*adj*) ornate, excessive, or showy in expression

**forensics** art, study, and use of argumentation and debate

**glossolalia** unintelligible, ecstatic speech; speaking in tongues

**grandiloquence** pompous, bombastic language

**harangue** bombastic ranting; extended attack or complaint; Philippic

**hendiadys** separation of an idea into two parts, which are then joined by a conjunction

**homily** morally instructive speech

**hypallage** reversal of expected syntactic relation between two words

**hyperbaton** transposition of normal sentence order

**hyperbole** extravagant exaggeration for comic or colorful effect or emphasis

**hypocorism** pet name; diminutive form imitating baby talk

**hypothesis** tentative assumption to be tested in argument

**hysteron proteron** reversal of logical order of two-part statement

**illeism** excessive use of pronoun "he" or "she" in reference to oneself

**implication** connotation

**imprecation** curse

**innuendo** insinuation; words with an unpleasant connotation

**invective** abusive language

**inversion** change in normal word order for effect

**invocation** address to God or higher power

**Irish bull** apparently sensible but actually incongruous expression

**irony** figure of speech conveying intent or reality different from, or opposite to, literal meaning of words used; speech employing elements of restraint, humor, sarcasm

**lingo** strange, obscure language or jargon peculiar to one group

**litany** prayer or supplication

**litotes** understatement, such as "not bad," in which affirmative is expressed by negating contrary statement

**locution** style of expression

**logodaedaly** arbitrary and capricious coinage of words

**malapropism** incorrect use of word similar to appropriate word

**malediction** curse

**maxim** aphorism, proverb

**meiosis** understatement, esp. for humorous effect

**metaphor** identification of one thing by another; trope, or turn of phrase, describing one idea in terms of another idea or image analogous to it

**metonymy** substitution of name of an object associated with a word for the word itself

**mot** brief, witty saying

**motto** word or phrase used regularly to characterize something or some group

**mouthful** very long word or phrase; statement rich in meaning, full of impact

**narration** form of discourse emphasizing recounting of event

**nonsense** expression lacking meaning, logic, or clarity of thought

**nutshell** brief statement reducing something to its essence

**oath** any profane expression, esp. one irreverent toward God

**obiter dictum** *Latin*. lit. saying by the way; incidental, uncalculated remarks

**onomatomania** obsession with words, their sounds, and meanings

**onomatopoeia** use of words whose sounds imitate or suggest their meaning; echoism

**oration** formal speech intended to persuade; in classical rhetoric, a speech divided into seven parts: exordium, narration, exposition, proposition, confirmation, confutation, and epilogue

**ornate** (*adj*) florid, overly embellished, or high-flown

**oxymoron** combination of two contradictory terms

**palindrome** word, phrase, or sentence reading the same backward or forward

**panegyric** eulogy

**pangram** sentence or verse containing all letters of the alphabet

**parable** short story that illustrates a moral attitude or principle

**paradox** apparently contradictory statement that is actually true

**paralipsis** concise treatment of subject suggesting that much is being omitted; preterition

**paraphrase** restatement of thought to retain meaning while changing form of expression

**parenthesis** remark made as explanation

**paronomasia** pun or play on words

**password** secret word or phrase used to gain admission to restricted area; shibboleth

**pathetic fallacy** assigning of human traits and feelings to natural or inanimate objects

**pedantry** style of expression emphasizing allusions, quotations, and ostentatious or inappropriate displays of erudition

**periphrasis** indirect, wordy style of expression

**peroration** summation of major points and persuasive concluding remarks occurring at end of speech

**persiflage** banter; light chatter

**personification** act of verbally endowing animals, objects, or abstractions with human attributes

**phatic** (*adj*) designating speech used to express goodwill or sociability rather than to impart information

**Philippic** harangue

**phraseology** style of expression

**platitude** trite or commonplace remark; cliché

**play on words** pun

**pleonasm** redundancy

**polemic** argument set forth, esp. on controversial subject

**polysyndeton** use of number of conjunctions in close succession

**preterition** paralipsis

**profanity** common or vulgar language, esp. characterized by irreverence toward God or sacred things

**prolepsis** anticipation and response to opponent's argument before it is actually stated

**prologue** introductory remark or statement

**prosopopoeia** personification of absent or dead person as present and speaking

**proverb** brief popular saying, usu. of unknown origin, expressing a commonplace truth; wise saying succinctly stated; adage; maxim; saw

**pun** wordplay based on similarity of sound but difference in meaning between words; paranomasia; play on words

**punch line** concluding phrase or line of joke, pun, or riddle

**quibble** pun or device used for evasion of argument

**quip** witty retort

**rebuttal** reply to argument

**redundancy** use of more words than needed to express idea; pleonasm

**repartee** conversation characterized by wit; clever reply

**repetition** reiteration of word, phrase, or idea for emphasis

**retort** sharp, incisive, often retaliatory reply; reply in kind

**rhetoric** theory and use of clear, persuasive, vivid language in presentation of argument or point of view; principles of oratory; undue use of exaggeration or bombast

**rhetorical figure** nonstandard usage that does not alter meaning of words

**rhetorical question** question asked solely for effect, and not to elicit a reply

**riposte** quick, sharp reply

**sarcasm** caustic, ironical language intended to wound or belittle another

**saw** sententious saying; maxim

**saying** formulation grown familiar through repetition; adage; saw

**scheme** rearrangement of words for effect of changed sound

**sesquipedalianism** use of very long words

**shibboleth** phrase characteristic of particular group; password

**shop talk** jargon or lingo of particular occupation

**simile** expression showing similarity between two unlike things, generally begun with comparison word "like" or "as"

**slogan** catchword

**slur** disparaging remark or characterization

**Socratic method** question and answer format of discourse; assumption of ignorance in debate for ironical effect

**solecism** ungrammatical combination of words; error in diction

**speaking in tongues** utterance of incomprehensible sounds while in ecstatic state, usu. believed to be words of deity

**speech** theory and practice of oral communication, esp. before an audience

**spoonerism** intentional or accidental transposition of initial sounds of two or more words; confusion resulting from such transposition

**syllepsis** construction placing one word in relationship to two other words, effecting two different senses

**symploce** simultaneous use of anaphora and epistrophe

**synecdoche** metaphoric form in which a part signifies the whole and less general stands for more general, or vice versa

**synthesis** dialectic combination of thesis and antithesis to deduce solution or truth

**thesis** position set forth for argument by speaker or writer

**threnody** dirge, lamentation

**trope** figure of speech; turn or twist on ordinary, literal sense of word or words

**truism** commonplace statement of truth; cliché

**understatement** form of irony in which something is represented as less than it really is

**verbigeration** continual repetition of words and phrases

**vitriol** extremely caustic speech or writing

**watchword** motto used as sign of recognition within group or as guiding principle for action

**wellerism** well-known quotation followed by facetious sequel

**wordplay** verbal wit; use of rhetorical figures of speech

**zeugma** syllepsis in which modifier is inappropriate in relation to one term or appropriate to each term in a different way

# QUALIFIERS AND CONNECTIVES

Comparisons
Approximations and Generalizations
Emphasizers
Maximizers and Superlatives
Absolutes and Guarantees

**SEE ALSO:** Chap. 18: Prefixes and Suffixes; Chap. 23: Time Perception; Spatial Positions and Relations

Qualifiers are those familiar words, phrases, and idioms that we use, often without thinking, to alter the intensity of another word or phrase, to modulate the language, and to provide subtle gradations and shadings of meaning. Connectives are words, such as conjunctions and prepositions, that express a relation or connection between two things, especially a relation involving place or time. This list includes all the conjunctions and prepositions and nearly a thousand other words and phrases, primarily adverbs and adjectives, that function to qualify and connect other words. Subcategory titles describe the impact on a sentence of the words in that particular list.

## CONJUNCTIONS

according as, afore, after, against, albeit, also, altho, although, an, and, and also, and/or, as, as far as, as how, as if, as long as, as though, as well as
because, before, being, both, but
considering
directly
either, ere, ergo, except, excepting
for, forasmuch as, fore
gin
how, howbeit, howe'er, however
if, immediately, inasmuch as, insofar as, insomuch as, instantly
lest, like
much as
neither, nor, notwithstanding, now
once, only, or, otherwise
plus, provided, providing
save, saving, seeing, since, sith, so, sobeit, so long as, still, supposing, syne
than, that, then, tho, though, till
unless, unlike, until
well, what, when, whence, whencesoever, whene'er, whenever, whensoever, where, whereabout, whereabouts, whereas, whereat, whereby, where'er, wherefore, wherefrom, wherein, whereinto, whereof, whereon, whereso, wheresoe'er, wheresoever, wherethrough, whereto, whereunder, whereunto, whereupon, wherever, wherewith, whether, while, whiles, whilst, whither, whithersoever, why, without
yet

## PREPOSITIONS

a, abaft, aboard, about, above, absent, according to, across, adown, afore, after, against, agin, à la, aloft, along, alongside, amid, amidst, among, amongst, an, anent, après, around, as, aside, aslant, as of, as to, astraddle, astride, at, athwart
bar, barring, bating, because, before, behind, below, ben, beneath, beside, besides, between, betwixt, beyond, but, by
chez, circa, concerning, considering, contra, cum
despite, down, during

ere, ex, except, excepting, excluding
failing, for, forby, fore, forth, frae, from
in, including, inside, instead of, into
less, like
maugre, mid, midst, minus, mongst
near, neath, next, next to, nigh, notwithstanding
o', o'er, of, off, on, onto, opposite, or, out, outside, over
pace, past, pending, per, plus
re, regarding, respecting, round
sans, save, saving, since, sith, syne
than, thorough, thro, throughout, thru, thwart, till, times, to, touching, toward
under, underneath, unless, unlike, until, unto, up, upon
versus, via, vice, vis-à-vis
wanting, while, with, withal, within, without, worth

## LIMITATIONS AND CONDITIONS

a bit, a breath, a couple, additionally, admitting, a few, albeit, a little, all but, all the same, all things considered, alone, although, a mite, as far as, as good as, aside from, as is, as it is, as long as, as soon as, as the case may be, as well, at all, at best, at least, at most, a trifle, at worst, au contraire
barely, barring, below, besides, be that as it may, bit by bit, briefly, but, by any chance, by any means, by chance, by degrees, by hook or by crook, by no means, by the same token
catch, circumstantially, conceivably, conditionally, considering, contingent on, cursory
decreasingly, demi-, depending, discounting
else, even, even so, even still, even though, even with, ever less, everything being equal, except, except for, excepting, except that, excluding, exclusive of, exempting, expressly
faintly, few, for all one knows, for all that, for aught one knows, formerly, for my part, for the most part
God willing, gradually, grain of salt, granting
half, halfway, handful, hardly, hardly ever, hedged, hemi-, hen's teeth, hereby, how, howbeit, however, howsoever
if, if and only if, if and when, if at all, if it so happens, if not, if only, if possible, if then, ill, in, in addition, in any case, in any way, in a way, in brief, in case, infrequently, in no way, in part, insofar as, in some measure, in spite of, in that case, iota, irregardless
just, just in case, just so, just the same
kicker, kind of
latter, least, leastways, leastwise, leaving aside, less, less and less, less than, let alone, like, little by little
maybe, mayhap, mere, merely, midway, might, mildly, mini-, minimus, minus, minutely, mite, moderately, modestly, modicum, momentary, mostly
namely, nary, nay rather, needless, negligible, neither, never, nevertheless, nohow, no less than, nominal, no more than, nonetheless, nor, not hardly, not in the least, not much, not often, notwithstanding, nowhere near, null
occasionally, off, on balance, once, on condition that, only, only if, on the whole, otherwise, overly, overmuch
part by part, partial, partially, partly, partway, passing, pending, pennyworth, perchance, perhaps, personally, picayune, piddling, piecemeal, pittance, possibly, pretty, pretty much, provided, providing, provisionally, purely
qualifying, quasi, quite the contrary
rarely, rather, regardless, relatively, remote, restricting, restrictive
sans, satisfactory, save, saving, scarcely, seldom, semi-, several, short of, slightly, sliver, smattering, smidgen, so as, sobeit, so far, so long as, so many, some, somehow, somehow or

LANGUAGE

18. STRUCTURE AND USAGE
QUALIFIERS AND CONNECTIVES
REFLECTIONS AND REFERENCES / COMPARISONS / APPROXIMATIONS AND GENERALIZATIONS / EMPHASIZERS

other, someway, somewhat, soon, sort of, soupçon, sparely, sparsely, speck, sporadically, spot, step by step, still, still and all, stipulated, strings, subject to, submarginal

tad, temporary, that being said, that being so, that is to say, though, thumbnail, tittle, to, to a certain point, to a degree, token, to some degree, to some extent, trace

under, under par, under the circumstances, unless, upon my word, up to

verge, videlicet, viz

waiving, waning, wee, well, were it not, when, whereof, whichever, whit, with a catch, withal, without, with reservations, with strings, with the proviso, with the stipulation, worse

yet

## REFLECTIONS AND REFERENCES

according, accordingly, according to, aforementioned, again, against, allowing for, all the same, all things considered, along, along with, amid, amidst, among, amongst, and so, and so forth, and so on, anent, apart, apparently, arguably, around, as, as a result, as being, as far as, as if, as they say, as though, as to, asunder, as well as, attended by, at the same time

because, because of, between, betwixt, by, by and by, by dint of, by the way, by virtue of, by way of

concerning, conjointly, consequently, considering, contrary to, counter to, coupled with

ditto, due to

either, else, elsewise, ergo, etcetera, evidently

finally, for each, for example, for instance, for that reason, for this reason

given

hence, henceforth, henceforward, hereat, hereby, herein, hereinafter, hereinbefore, hereinbelow, hereon, heretofore, hereunder, hereunto, hereupon, herewith, hither, hitherto, how come

ibid, imprimis, in addition to, inasmuch as, incidentally, incidental to, including, in conjunction, indeed, in keeping with, in lieu of, in line with, in other respects, in other words, in passing, in re, in relation to, in return, insofar as, insomuch as, instead, instead of, in the matter of, intro-, in turn, in twain, in two, in view of, irrespective

jointly

loc cit

midst, mongst, much as, much less, mutually

natch, naturally, naturellement

of, of course, on account of, only, on that account, on the other hand, op cit, or, or else, other than, otherwise, outwardly

penultimate, per, peripheral

qua

re, readily, regarding, respecting, respectively

secondary, seeing that, selectively, self-styled, separately, severally, side, since, snap, so, so as, soever, sofar as, so forth, so much, so on, specified, spotty, square, stated, subsidiary, such, supposed, supra, surfeit

tacit, that is to say, then again, thence, there, thereat, thereby, therefore, thereinafter, thereof, thereon, thereto, theretofore, thereunder, thereupon, thus, thus and so, thusly, together with

uncommon, undue, unduly, unusual, unusually, upon

variable, various, variously, veritable, vice, virtual

what for, what if, whence, where, whereat, wherefor, wherefrom, whereinto, whereon, wheresoever, whereupon, whichever, while, why, with, with regard to, with relation to, with respect to

yet

## COMPARISONS

about, above, à la, alike, all get-out, all that, almost, and then some, another, as, as much as, as well as

beside, better

close to, comparably, comparatively, compared to, complementary

different

either, either-or, enough, equally

farther, further

in comparison, increasingly, in kind, in like manner

just about

like, like so, like that, likewise

mainly, middling, mixed, moiety, more

nearly, near miss, next to, nigh, no less than, nor

opposite, or, over, over against, over and above

premium

rather, relatively

same, second best, second class, second fiddle, second rate, similar, so, somewhat, so-so, sufficient, super, surpassing

tantamount, than, third rate, to-and-fro, to wit

unlike, unparalleled, unprecedented

vice versa, vis-à-vis

well-nigh, what, whereas, whether, while, worse

## APPROXIMATIONS AND GENERALIZATIONS

about, a few, after all, again, a little, all in all, a lot, any, anyhow, anyway, apparently, approximately, around, as a rule, as a whole, as it were, as much as, at all events, at any rate, at large, aught

ballpark, before long, belike, be that as it may, borderline, broadly, by and large

circa, close, close to, collectively, commonly, comparatively

en masse, essentially, ever

fairly, for all that, for that matter, for the most part

generally

here and there

in all, in any case, in any event, in a way, in general, in short

just about, just the same

kind of

lately, latterly, like, long and short of it

mainly, mas o menos, mezzo-mezzo, more or less, much

near, neither here nor there, now and then

often, only just, on the whole, overall

possibly, primarily, probably, proportionately

relatively, reputedly, roughly, roundly

say, seeming, seemingly, simply, some, sometimes, somewhat, somewhere, somewhere near, soon, sooner or later, sort of, so-so, so to speak, such and such, sundry

then again, thereabouts, to a degree, to an extent, to the tune of, truth of the matter

virtually

whatever, what have you, whatnot, wherever

## EMPHASIZERS

above, after all, again, all, all-around, all of, all told, a lot, also, altogether, and how, as well, awfully

beside, besides, big deal, by far

decidedly

either, especially, even, evermore so, ever so, exceedingly, expressly

far and away, fine, further, furthermore

increasingly, indeed, in detail, in particular, in the main

just, just so
lastly
mainly, mighty, moreover, more than ever, mostly
namely, no matter, notably, not to mention
obviously, on top of, over, over and above
particular, particularly, plus, primarily, pronounced
quite
real, really, resounding, respective, right
simply, singularly, so, specially, specifically, still, strong, such
tall order, telling, terribly, to boot, too, to say nothing of, to say the least
up
very
well, whopper

## MAXIMIZERS AND SUPERLATIVES

all, all along, all-embracing, all get-out, all-inclusive, all over, a lot, always, aplenty, a sight, at length
best, bevy
chiefly, chock-full, commonly, considerable, copious
decidedly, doozie
ever, evermore, every, exceedingly, extremely
far, far and away, farthest, first water, foremost
galore
head and shoulders, head over heels, hook, line, and sinker, hyper
ideally
jillion
lickety-split, likely, lots
major, many, maxi-, mighty, more and more, most, much, multiplicity, myriad
nth, numerous
oft, often, oftentimes, oodles
part and parcel, plenteous, plentiful, premium
radically, rattling, real, rife, right, rip-roaring, roaring
scads, slew, smashing, socko, spanking, spate, staggering, stiff, strong, super, super-duper, supreme, surpassing, sweeping
thumping, thundering, tiptop, top
ultra-, unbounded, unbridled, unmitigated, unremitting, unrivaled, untold, up
vast, vaulting, very
walloping, waxing, way, whacking, whopping, wide-ranging, widespread, withering
zillion

## ABSOLUTES AND GUARANTEES

above all, absolutely, actually, after all, all, all along, all out, all over, all the while, altogether, always, as a matter of course, as a matter of fact, at any cost, at first, at last, at long last, at that
bar none, by all means
cap-a-pie, certainly, clean, clearly, complete, completely, conclusively
dead on, decidedly, definitely
entirely, even, eventually, exactly, expressly
fare-thee-well, finally, first, first and foremost, firstly, first of all, first things, forever, forever and ever, forevermore, for good, for keeps, forsooth, for sure, full-out, fully
granting
hands down, head to toe
identically, immeasurably, in all respects, in a word, in conclusion, indeed, indubitably, inevitably, in fact, infinitely,

in full, in no way, in particular, in point of fact, in reality, in the first place, in the long run, in toto, invariably, irrespective of
just, just so
lastly, literally, literatim, lock, stock, and barrel
minimus
nada, naught, necessarily, needless to say, never, nil, nix, nohow, no ifs, ands, or buts, no more, none, not a bit, not at all, not a whit, now and forever, no way, nowise, null, null and void
of course, once, once for all, one and all, only, out-and-out, outright
paramount, par excellence, perfectly, plain, plenary, plumb, precisely, premier, prime, primo, principal, proper, purely
quite
really, right
same, selfsame, sheer, simply, smack-dab, solely, solid, so much as, squarely, stark, stock-still, stone, supreme, sure, sure enough, surely
thoroughly, through and through, to a tee, top flight, topnotch, total, totally, to the limit, to the utmost, truly
ultimately, unadulterated, unconditional, unconditionally, undeniably, under no circumstances, unlimited, unmistakably, unqualified, unreservedly, uppermost, utmost, utter, utterly, uttermost
verbatim, verily, veritably, versal, void
well, whatever, whatsoever, wherever, whole, whole hog, wholly, wide, without exception, word-for-word, world, worst
zero, zilch

# PREFIXES AND SUFFIXES

Prefixes
Suffixes

**SEE ALSO:** Chap. 4: Medicine; Chap. 18: Abbreviations

NOTE: *When used before a vowel in combining form, most prefixes drop or change the final o, i, a, or y. Only the full combining form, with the final vowel, is listed here. Where a prefix or suffix has two or more distinct meanings, examples are given that reflect each usage.*

## PREFIXES

**a-**  not (*asocial*)
**ab-**  away from (*absent*)
**acantho-**  spine, thorn (*acanthus*)
**aceto-**  vinegar, acetic acid (*acetometer*)
**acro-**  top, tip (*acrophobia*)
**actino-**  ray, beam (*actinometer*)
**adeno-**  gland (*adenovirus*)
**aero-**  air, gas (*aerodynamic*)
**agri-**  farming (*agribusiness*)
**agro-**  field, soil, crop production (*agronomy*)
**algo-**  pain (*algolagnia*)
**allo-**  other (*allotrope*)
**alti-**  high (*altitude*)
**ambi-**  both (*ambidextrous*)
**amphi-**  both, around (*amphibious*)
**amylo-**  starch (*amyloplast*)
**an-**  not, lacking (*anarchy*)

**ana-** up, against, back (*anabasis*)
**andro-** male (*androgenous*)
**anemo-** wind (*anemometer*)
**angio-** container (*angiosperm*)
**aniso-** unequal (*anisotropic*)
**ante-** before (*antebellum*)
**antho-** flower (*anthophore*)
**anthropo-** human (*anthropology*)
**anti-** against (*antibody*)
**apo-** away, apart (*apogee*)
**aqui-** water (*aquifer*)
**arbori-** tree (*arboriculture*)
**archeo-** ancient, old (*archeology*)
**archi-** first, most basic (*architrave*)
**arterio-** artery (*arteriosclerosis*)
**arthro-** joint (*arthropod*)
**asco-** sac (*ascomycete*)
**astro-** star (*astronomy*)
**atmo-** vapor, gas (*atmosphere*)
**audio-** hearing, sound reproduction (*audiophile*)
**auri-** gold (*auriferous*); ear (*auriform*)
**auto-** self, same (*automatic*)
**avi-** bird (*aviculture*)
**bacterio-** bacteria (*bacteriophage*)
**baro-** weight, pressure (*barometer*)
**batho-** deep (*bathosphere*)
**bene-** good (*benevolent*)
**biblio-** book (*bibliography*)
**bio-** life (*biography*)
**blasto-** bud, embryo (*blastosphere*)
**brachio-** arm (*brachiopod*)
**brachy-** short (*brachylogy*)
**brady-** slow (*bradycardia*)
**branchio-** gills (*branchiopod*)
**broncho-** throat (*bronchoscope*)
**caco-** bad (*cacology*)
**calci-** calcium (*calcify*)
**calli-** beautiful (*calligraphy*)
**cardio-** heart (*cardiology*)
**carpo-** fruit (*carpophore*)
**cata-** down, against, back (*cataclysm*)
**ceno-** common (*cenobite*)
**centi-** hundred (*centigram*)
**centri-** center (*centrifuge*)
**cephalo-** head (*cephalothorax*)
**cerebro-** brain (*cerebrospinal*)
**cero-** wax (*ceroplastic*)
**chalco-** copper (*chalcocite*)
**cheli-** claws (*cheliped*)
**chilo-** lip (*chiloplasty*)
**chiro-** hand (*chiropractor*)
**chloro-** green (*chlorophyll*)
**choreo-** dance (*choreography*)
**chromo-** color (*chromolithography*)
**chrono-** time (*chronometer*)
**chryso-** gold (*chrysolite*)
**circum-** around (*circumference*)
**cis-** near to, on near side of (*cisalpine*)
**clado-** branch (*cladogenesis*)
**clino-** slope (*clinometer*)
**co-** variation of com–, used esp. to form new words (*co-worker*)
**coel-** cavity (*coelenteron*)

**com-** with, together with (*combine*)
**contra-** against (*contravene*)
**copro-** excrement (*coprophilia*)
**cortico-** cortex (*corticosteroid*)
**cosmo-** universe (*cosmology*)
**costo-** rib (*costotomy*)
**cranio-** skull (*craniotomy*)
**cruci-** cross (*cruciform*)
**cryo-** – cold (*cryogenics*)
**crypto-** hidden (*cryptography*)
**cteno-** rake, comb (*ctenophore*)
**cupri-** copper (*cupriferous*)
**cysto-** bladder (*cystoscope*)
**cyto-** cell (*cytoplasm*)
**dactylo-** finger, toe (*dactylomegaly*)
**de-** negation (*dehumidify*)
**deca-** ten (*decagon*)
**deci-** tenth (*decimeter*)
**demi-** half, lesser (*demitasse*)
**demono-** devil, demon (*demonolatry*)
**dendro-** tree (*dendrology*)
**denti-** tooth (*dentifrice*)
**dermato-** skin (*dermatology*)
**deutero-** second (*deuteropathy*)
**di-** two, double (*dicotyledon*)
**dia-** thorough, opposed, completely (*diagnosis*)
**dicho-** in two parts (*dichotomy*)
**dino-** terrifying (*dinosaur*)
**diplo-** double (*diplopod*)
**dis-** apart, asunder, away, or having a general negative or reversing force (*disability, discontent, dislike*)
**dodeca-** twelve (*dodecahedron*)
**dorsi-** back of body (*dorsiflexion*)
**duo-** two (*duologue*)
**dyna-** force, power (*dynamotor*)
**dys-** evil, bad, impaired (*dysfunction*)
**eco-** ecology (*ecosystem*)
**ecto-** outside, external (*ectoderm*)
**electro-** electric (*electromagnetic*)
**enantio-** opposite (*enantiomorph*)
**encephalo-** brain (*encephalogram*)
**endo-** within (*endogenous*)
**ennea-** nine (*enneahedron*)
**entero-** intestine (*enterology*)
**entomo-** insect (*entomophagous*)
**eo-** early, dawn (*eolith*)
**epi-** on, over, near (*epidermis*)
**equi-** equal (*equilateral*)
**ergo-** work (*ergonomic*)
**eroto-** sexual desire (*erotogenesis*)
**erythro-** red (*erythrocyte*)
**ethno-** race, nation (*ethnography*)
**eu-** good (*eugenics*)
**eury-** broad, wide (*euryphagous*)
**ex-** former (*ex-president*); out of, thoroughly (*extract, exhaust*)
**exo-** outside, external (*exogamous*)
**extra-** outside, external (*extraterrestrial*)
**febri-** fever (*febrifuge*)
**ferro-** iron (*ferromagnet*)
**fibro-** fiber (*fibroblast*)
**fissi-** split, cleft (*fissiped*)
**flori-** flower (*floriculture*)
**fluoro-** fluoride (*fluorocarbon*)

**fructi-** fruit (*fructiferous*)
**galacto-** milk (*galactophorous*)
**gameto-** mature reproductive cell (*gametogenesis*)
**gamo-** joined, united (*gamopetalous*)
**gastro-** stomach (*gastronomy*)
**geo-** land, earth (*geology*)
**geronto-** old age (*gerontocracy*)
**glosso-** tongue (*glossolalia*)
**glotto-** tongue (*glottochronolgy*)
**glyco-** sugar, sweet (*glycogen*)
**gono-** sexual, reproductive (*gonophore*)
**grapho-** writing (*graphomotor*)
**gymno-** naked, nude (*gymnogynous*)
**gyneco-** woman (*gynecology*)
**hagio-** holy (*hagiography*)
**halo-** salt (*halogen*)
**haplo-** single, simple (*haplology*)
**hecto-** hundred (*hectoliter*)
**helico-** spiral (*helicospore*)
**helio-** sun (*heliotherapy*)
**hema-** blood (*hemagglutination*)
**hemato-** blood (*hematocyst*)
**hemi-** half (*hemisphere*)
**hemo-** blood (*hemoglobin*)
**hendeca-** eleven (*hendecagon*)
**hepato-** liver (*hepatotoxin*)
**hepta-** seven (*heptagon*)
**hetero-** different (*heterogeneous*)
**hexa-** six (*hexagon*)
**hiero-** sacred (*hierogram*)
**histo-** tissue (*histology*)
**holo-** complete, whole (*hologram*)
**homeo-** similar, like (*homeostasis*)
**homo-** same (*homogeneous*)
**homoio-** similar, like (*homoiothermal*)
**hyalo-** glass (*hyaloplasm*)
**hydro-** water (*hydrodynamic*)
**hyeto-** rain (*hyetograph*)
**hygro-** wet (*hygrometer*)
**hylo-** matter (*hylotheism*)
**hyper-** above (*hyperactive*)
**hypno-** sleep, hypnosis (*hypnotherapy*)
**hypo-** under (*hypothermia*)
**hystero-** womb (*hysterectomy*)
**iatro-** medicine (*iatrogenic*)
**ichythyo-** fish (*ichthyology*)
**icono-** image, likeness (*iconology*)
**ideo-** idea (*ideology*)
**idio-** peculiar (*idiosyncrasy*)
**il-** not (*illogical*)
**ileo-** intestinal ileum (*ileocolitis*)
**ilio-** ilium portion of hipbone (*iliofemoral*)
**im-** not (*impartial*)
**immuno-** immune (*immunology*)
**in-** not, used to give negative or privative force, esp. to adjectives (*inexpensive*)
**inter-** between (*interscholastic*)
**intra-** inside, within, interior (*intracellular*)
**ir-** not, against (*irreducible*)
**irido-** rainbow, iris of eye (*iridotomy*)
**iso-** equal (*isometric*)
**jejuno-** jejunum portion of intestine (*jejunostomy*)
**juxta-** close, near, beside (*juxtaposition*)

**karyo-** cell nucleus (*karyolysis*)
**kerato-** horn (*keratogenous*)
**kineto-** movement (*kinetoscope*)
**labio-** lip (*labiovelar*)
**lacto-** milk (*lactogenic*)
**lamelli-** plate, scale (*lamelliform*)
**laparo-** abdominal wall (*laparoscope*)
**laryngo-** larynx (*laryngoscope*)
**lepido-** scale (*lepidopteron*)
**lepto-** thin, fine (*leptodactylous*)
**leuko-** white (*leukocyte*)
**levo-** left (*levorotatory*)
**ligni-** wood (*ligniform*)
**litho-** stone (*lithography*)
**logo-** word, spoken (*logomachy*)
**longi-** long, length (*longicorn*)
**luni-** moon (*lunitidal*)
**lympho-** lymph (*lymphocyte*)
**lyso-** decomposition, dissolving (*lysosome*)
**macro-** large (*macrocosm*)
**magni-** great, large (*magnify*)
**male-** evil, bad (*malevolent*)
**masto-** breast (*mastopathy*)
**matri-** female (*matriarchy*)
**mechano-** machine (*mechanoreceptor*)
**mega-** great (*megalopolis*)
**megalo-** great (*megalomania*)
**melano-** black (*melanocyte*)
**mero-** part (*merogony*)
**meso-** middle (*mesopause*)
**meta-** after, beyond, changed (*metaphysics*)
**metro-** measure (*metronome*)
**micro-** small (*microorganism*)
**milli-** one thousandth (*millimeter*)
**mis-** wrong, ill, incorrect (*misprint, mistrust*)
**miso-** hatred (*misogyny*)
**mono-** single, one (*monotone*)
**morpho-** shape (*morphology*)
**muco-** mucus (*mucopurulent*)
**multi-** many (*multifaceted*)
**musculo-** muscle (*musculoskeletal*)
**myco-** fungus, mold, mushroom (*mycotoxicosis*)
**myelo-** marrow, spinal cord (*myelocyte*)
**myo-** muscle (*myocardium*)
**myria-** ten thousand (*myriagram*)
**mytho-** myth (*mythology*)
**myxo-** mucus, slime (*myxovirus*)
**nano-** one billionth (*nanosecond*)
**narco-** stupor, drugged state (*narcoanalysis*)
**naso-** nose (*nasolacrimal*)
**necro-** dead body (*necrophilia*)
**nemato-** thread (*nematocyst*)
**neo-** new (*neologism*)
**nepho-** cloud (*nephometer*)
**nephro-** kidney (*nephrology*)
**neuro-** nerve (*neurology*)
**neutro-** neutral (*neutrosphere*)
**nocti-** night (*noctilucent*)
**nomo-** custom, law (*nomology*)
**non-** not, freely implying negation or absence of something (*nonprofessional, nonpayment*)
**noso-** disease (*nosogeography*)
**noto-** back of body (*notochord*)

**nucleo-** nucleus (*nucleotide*)
**nycto-** night (*nyctophobia*)
**ob-** against (*obverse*)
**octa-** eight (*octagon*)
**oculo-** eye (*oculomotor*)
**odonto-** tooth (*odontogeny*)
**oleo-** oil (*oleomargarine*)
**oligo-** few (*oligopoly*)
**omni-** all (*omnipotent*)
**oneiro-** dream (*oneiromancy*)
**onto-** being, existence (*ontology*)
**oo-** egg (*oocyte*)
**ophio-** snake (*ophiolatry*)
**ophthalmo-** eye (*ophthalmology*)
**opistho-** back, behind (*opisthograph*)
**opto-** eye (*optometry*)
**organo-** body organ (*organoleptic*)
**ornitho-** bird (*ornithology*)
**oro-** mountain (*orography*); mouth (*oropharynx*)
**ortho-** straight (*orthopedic*)
**ossi-** bone (*ossiferous*)
**osteo-** bone (*osteopath*)
**oto-** ear (*otolaryngology*)
**out-** beyond, to an end point, abnormal (*outdoors, outlast, outmoded*)
**over-** too much, to excess (*overweight*)
**ovi-** egg (*oviparous*)
**oxy-** sharp, acute (*oxymoron*)
**pachy-** thick (*pachyderm*)
**paleo-** ancient, old (*paleolithic*)
**pan-** all (*pantheism*)
**para-** beside, beyond; guard against (*parallel, parachute*)
**pari-** equal (*paripinnate*)
**partheno-** without fertilization (*parthenogenesis*)
**patho-** disease, suffering (*pathological*)
**patri-** male (*patriarchy*)
**pedi-** foot (*pedicab*)
**pedo-** child (*pedophilia*)
**penta-** five (*pentagon*)
**per-** through, very (*pervade*)
**peri-** around, very (*perimeter*)
**petro-** stone (*petrology*)
**phago-** eating (*phagocyte*)
**pharmaco-** drug (*pharmocology*)
**pharyngo-** pharynx (*pharyngoscope*)
**pheno-** shining, appearing (*phenotype*)
**philo-** loving (*philosophy*)
**phlebo-** vein (*phlebotomy*)
**phono-** sound (*phonograph*)
**photo-** light (*photography*)
**phreno-** brain (*phrenology*)
**phyco-** seaweed, algae (*phycology*)
**phyllo-** leaf (*phyllotaxy*)
**phylo-** race, tribe, species (*phylogeny*)
**physio-** nature (*physiology*)
**phyto-** plant (*phytogenesis*)
**piezo-** pressure (*piezoelectric*)
**pinni-** web, fin (*pinniped*)
**pisci-** fish (*pisciculture*)
**plagio-** oblique (*plagiotropic*)
**plano-** flat (*planogamete*)
**pleo-** more (*pleomorphism*)
**pleuro-** side, lateral (*pleurocarpous*)

**pluto-** riches, wealth (*plutocracy*)
**pluvio-** rain (*pluviometer*)
**pneumato-** air, breath (*pneumatophore*)
**pneumo-** air, breath (*pneumococcus*)
**pod-** foot (*podiatry*)
**polio-** gray matter (*poliomyelitis*)
**poly-** many (*polygon*)
**post-** after (*postmortem*)
**pre-** before (*preproduction*)
**preter-** beyond (*preternatural*)
**primi-** first (*primipara*)
**pro-** before, forward (*prologue*); for, favoring (*proslavery*)
**proprio-** one's own (*proprioceptive*)
**proto-** first (*prototype*)
**pseudo-** false (*pseudonym*)
**psycho-** mind, spirit, soul (*psychosomatic*)
**pterido-** fern (*pteridology*)
**ptero-** wing (*pterodactyl*)
**pyelo-** pelvis (*pyelonephritis*)
**pyo-** pus (*pyorrhea*)
**pyro-** fire (*pyromania*)
**quadri-** four (*quadrilateral*)
**quinque-** five (*quinquevalent*)
**re-** again (*revitalize*)
**recti-** straight (*rectilinear*)
**reni-** kidney (*reniform*)
**retro-** backward (*retroactive*)
**rhabdo-** rod, wand (*rhabdovirus*)
**rheo-** flow, current (*rheostat*)
**rhino-** nose (*rhinoplasty*)
**rhizo-** root (*rhizogenic*)
**rhodo-** rose (*rhodolite*)
**racchar-** sweet, sugar (*saccharide*)
**sangui-** blood (*sanguiferous*)
**sapro-** rotten, decomposed (*saprogenic*)
**sarco-** flesh (*sarcophagous*)
**scato-** excrement (*scatology*)
**schizo-** split (*schizophrenia*)
**sclero-** hard (*scleroderma*)
**seleno-** moon (*selenography*)
**self-** of or by oneself (*self-analysis*); to, with, or toward oneself (*self-abnegating*); independent or automatic (*self-governing, self-operating*)
**semi-** half, partially, somewhat (*semiweekly, semidetached*)
**septi-** seven (*septilateral*)
**sero-** serum (*serology*)
**sesqui-** one and a half (*sesquicentennial*)
**sex-** six (*sexpartite*)
**shm-** used to form jocular variations as replacement for initial consonant in standard form of word (*fancy shmancy*)
**sidero-** iron (*siderolite*)
**siphono-** tube (*siphonostele*)
**socio-** society (*sociology*)
**somato-** body (*somatotype*)
**somni-** sleep (*somnifacient*)
**spermato-** seed (*spermatozoon*)
**spermo-** seed, germ (*spermophyte*)
**spheno-** wedge (*sphenography*)
**sphygmo-** pulse (*sphygmometer*)
**spiro-** respiration (*spirograph*); coil, spiral (*spirochete*)
**sporo-** spore (*sporophyte*)
**steato-** fat, tallow (*steatopygia*)
**stego-** cover (*stegosaur*)

**stelli-** star (*stelliform*)
**steno-** close, narrow (*stenography*)
**stereo-** solid (*stereoscope*)
**stomato-** mouth (*stomatoplasty*)
**strati-** stratum (*stratification*)
**strepto-** twisted (*streptococcus*)
**stylo-** column, pillar (*stylolite*)
**sub-** below, under (*subarctic*); secondary (*subplot*)
**super-** above (*supernatural*)
**supra-** above, beyond (*supraorbital*)
**sus-** under, beneath, secondary (*suspend*)
**syl-** with (*syllepsis*)
**sym-** with (*symmetry*)
**syn-** with (*synoptic*)
**synchro-** occurring together (*synchrotron*)
**tacho-** speed (*tachometer*)
**tachy-** rapid (*tachycardia*)
**tauto-** same (*tautology*)
**techno-** technique, skill (*technology*)
**tele-** distant (*telekinesis*)
**teleo-** final (*teleology*)
**telo-** end (*telophase*)
**teno-** tendon (*tenotomy*)
**tera-** trillion (*terabyte*)
**terato-** monster (*teratology*)
**terri-** land, earth (*terricolous*)
**tetra-** four (*tetralogy*)
**thanato-** death (*thanatology*)
**thaumato-** miracle, wonder (*thaumatology*)
**theo-** god (*theology*)
**thermo-** heat (*thermoplastic*)
**thrombo-** blood clot, coagulation (*thrombocyte*)
**toco-** birth, child (*tocopherol*)
**tomo-** cut, section (*tomography*)
**tono-** stretching, tension (*tonometer*)
**topo-** place, local (*topology*)
**toti-** entire (*totipalmation*)
**toxico-** poison (*toxicology*)
**toxo-** poison (*toxoplasmosis*)
**tracheo-** trachea (*tracheotomy*)
**trachy-** rough (*trachycarpous*)
**trans-** across, through, on far side of (*transverse*)
**tri-** three (*trilateral*)
**tribo-** friction (*triboluminescence*)
**tricho-** hair (*trichocyst*)
**tropho-** nourishment (*trophosome*)
**tropo-** turn, response, change (*troposphere*)
**ultra-** beyond (*ultrasonics*)
**un-** not, freely used to give negative or opposite force to adjectives (*unhappy*); used to reverse action or state of verb (*unfasten*)
**under-** beneath, below, or lesser in place, grade, or extent (*undersized*)
**uni-** single, one (*unicycle*)
**urino-** urine (*urinoscopy*)
**uro-** urine (*urology*)
**vaso-** vessel (*vasoconstrictor*)
**veno-** vein (*venostasis*)
**ventro-** abdomen (*ventrodorsal*)
**vermi-** worm (*vermiform*)
**vini-** wine (*viniculture*)
**vitri-** glass (*vitriform*)
**vivi-** living, alive (*vivisection*)

**xantho-** yellow (*xanthophyll*)
**xeno-** foreign (*xenophobia*)
**xero-** dry (*xeroderma*)
**xylo-** wood (*xylophone*)
**zoo-** animal (*zoology*)
**zygo-** yoke, double (*zygomorphic*)

## SUFFIXES

**-ability** combination of -able and -ity for nouns corresponding to adjectives ending in -able (*capability*)
**-able** capable of, fit for, tending or given to (*laudable, singable*)
**-ably** combination of -able and -ly for adverbs corresponding to adjectives ending in -able (*tolerably*)
**-acea** used in formation of names of zoological classes and orders (*Crustacea*)
**-aceae** used in formation of names of botanical families (*Rosaceae*)
**-aceous** resembling, made of (*herbaceous*)
**-acious** used in formation of adjectives corresponding to nouns ending in -acy or -acity (*fallacious, audacious*)
**-acity** quality of, having characteristics of (*tenacity*)
**-acy** ending for nouns of quality, state, or office (*delicacy, papacy*)
**-adelphous** having stamens growing together in bundles (*monadelphous*)
**-agogue** leader, bringer of, practitioner (*demagogue*)
**-aholic** one who has addiction to or obsession with something (*workaholic*)
**-al** having form or character of, pertaining to (*autumnal, natural*); used to form nouns from verbs (*refusal*)
**-ales** used in formation of names of botanical orders (*Cycadales*)
**-algia** pain (*neuralgia*)
**-amine** variation of amino- in chemical compounds (*chloramine*)
**-an** used to form adjectives, esp. of place and membership (*American, Elizabethan*)
**-ana** collection of items (*Americana*)
**-ance** used to form nouns corresponding to verbs or to adjectives ending in -ant (*brilliance*)
**-ancy** combination of -ance and -y denoting state or quality (*brilliancy*)
**-androus** male (*polyandrous*)
**-andry** used in nouns corresponding to adjectives ending in -androus (*polyandry*)
**-ane** used in names of hydrocarbons of methane or paraffin series (*propane*)
**-anthous** having flowers of specified type or number (*monanthous*)
**-arama** variation of -orama (*foodarama*)
**-arch** chief, leader, ruler (*matriarch*)
**-archy** rule, government (*monarchy*)
**-arian** used to form personal nouns from adjectives or nouns ending in -ary (*librarian*)
**-aroo** variation of -eroo (*buckaroo*)
**-arooni** variation of -aroo, diminutive or additionally jocular (*sockarooni*)
**-asis** used in scientific and medical words from Greek (*psoriasis*)
**-ast** one connected with or given to (*enthusiast*)

**-ate** use to form nouns that denote office or function or a person who exercises function (*consulate, magistrate*); used in chemistry to indicate salt of acid ending in –ic (*nitrate*)

**-athon** used in compound words to indicate event drawn out to unusual length (*danceathon*)

**-ation** combination of –ate and –ion used to form nouns corresponding to verbs with stem –ate (*separation*)

**-ative** combination of –ate and –ive to form adjectives corresponding to verbs with stem –ate (*regulative*) or from other stem words (*normative*)

**-biosis** mode of life (*aerobiosis*)

**-blast** bud, sprout (*ectoblast*)

**-carp** part of fruit or fruiting body (*endocarp*)

**-carpic** used in formation of adjectives from stems ending in –carp (*endocarpic*)

**-carpous** having fruit (*apocarpous*)

**-cele** tumor (*variocele*)

**-cene** variation of –ceno (*Pleistocene*)

**-ceno** new, recent (*cenogenesis*)

**-cephalic** variation of –cephalous (*brachycephalic*)

**-cephalous** having a specific kind of head (*brachycephalous*)

**-chroic** variation of –chroous (*monochroic*)

**-chrome** color (*polychrome*)

**-chroous** having a specific kind of color (*isochroous*)

**-cide** killer, act of killing (*suicide*)

**-clase** used in formation of compound words for minerals with specified cleavage (*plagioclase*)

**-clasis** breaking (*thromboclasis*)

**-cle** used to form diminutive nouns (*particle*); used to form nouns that denote place appropriate to action of verb from which they are formed (*receptacle*)

**-coccus** spherical bacterium (*streptococcus*)

**-coele** cavity (*enterocoele*)

**-colous** inhabiting specified place or thing (*nidicolous*)

**-cracy** rule, government (*democracy*)

**-crat** ruler, supporter of particular form of government (*autocrat*)

**-cule** variation of –cle (*molecule, ridicule*)

**-cyst** cyst sac (*statocyst*)

**-cyte** cell (*leucocyte*)

**-dactyl** used to form nouns corresponding to adjectives ending in –dactylous (*pterodactyl*)

**-dactylous** having toes or fingers (*tridactylous*)

**-dendron** tree (*rhododendron*)

**-derm** skin (*pachyderm*)

**-drome** running; racecourse or other large structure (*hippodrome, airdrome*)

**-ectomy** excision or removal of particular part (*appendectomy*)

**-elle** used to form diminutive or derivative nouns (*bagatelle, organelle*)

**-emia** blood condition (*anemia*)

**-ence** used to form nouns from verbs or from adjectives ending in –ent (*abstinence, difference*)

**-ensis** pertaining to or originating in, usu. in scientific terms (*carolinensis*)

**-eous** composed of, resembling (*igneous*); used to form adjectives from nouns, esp. those ending in –ty (*beauteous*)

**-er** used to form comparative degree of adjectives or adverbs (*smaller, faster*); used in formation of nouns of person from object of occupation, place of origin, or specific characteristic (*hatter, villager, teetotaler*); used to form agent nouns

from verbs (*employer*); used to form occupation names (*butcher*)

**-ergic** activated by, sensitive to, releasing (*allergic*)

**-ern** used to form adjectives from directions (*northern*)

**-eroo** used to form familiar, usu. jocular nouns (*switcheroo*)

**-ers** *Chiefly Brit.* informal variation of noun or adjective (*preggers*)

**-ery** used to form nouns denoting occupation, condition, place, products, things collectively, actions, or qualities (*archery, bakery, cutlery, trickery*)

**-esce** used to express beginning of action of verb (*convalesce*)

**-escence** used to denote nouns of action or process, change, or condition corresponding to verbs ending in –esce or adjectives ending in –escent (*convalescence*)

**-escent** used in formation of adjectives expressing beginning of action (*convalescent*)

**-ese** used to form adjectival derivatives of place names, esp. for inhabitants or language of place (*Japanese, Viennese*); used to characterize jargon (*computerese*)

**-esis** used in nouns of action or process (*genesis*)

**-esque** indicating style, manner, or distinctive character of adjective or individual (*picturesque, Kafkaesque*)

**-ess** used to form feminine nouns (*countess*)

**-est** used to form superlative degree of adjectives or adverbs (*smallest, fastest*); formerly used to form second person singular indicative of verbs (*knowest*)

**-eur** used to form agent nouns or occasionally adjectives from verbs (*masseur, provocateur*)

**-euse** used to form feminine nouns corresponding to nouns ending in –eur (*masseuse*)

**-ey** variation of –y, esp. after words end in "y" (*clayey*); used informally or to denote little one (*Charley*)

**-fest** assembly of people for common purpose (*songfest*)

**-fex** maker (*spinifex*)

**-fic** making, producing, causing (*honorific*)

**-fication** used to form nouns of action or state corresponding to verbs ending in –fy (*specification*)

**-fid** split, divided (*bifid*)

**-florous** having flowers (*uniflorous*)

**-fuge** that which repels or drives away something specified (*vermifuge*)

**-fy** make, cause to be, render (*beautify*)

**-gamy** marriage (*monogamy*)

**-gen** that which produces (*hydrogen*)

**-genesis** origin, beginning (*parthenogenesis*)

**-genetic** used to form adjectives from nouns ending in –genesis (*parthenogenetic*)

**-genic** producing or causing, produced or caused by, used to form adjectives corresponding to nouns ending in –gen or –geny (*hallucinogenic, cosmogenic*)

**-genous** giving rise to the thing specified (*androgenous*)

**-geny** origin (*phylogeny*)

**-glot** having a tongue or speaking, writing, or written in a language (*polyglot*)

**-gnathous** having a jaw (*prognathous*)

**-gnomy** knowledge (*physiognomy*)

**-gnosis** knowledge (*prognosis*)

**-gnostic** used to form adjectives from nouns ending in –gnosis (*diagnostic*)

**-gon** angled (*polygon*)

**-gony** production, origination (*cosmogony*)

**-grade** walking or moving in specified manner (*retrograde*)

**-gram** something written or drawn (*epigram, diagram*); message, bulletin (*telegram*)

**-graph** drawn or written, esp. instrument used to produce writing (*telegraph*)

**-graphy** process, science, or art of drawing, writing, recording, or representing (*biography, photography, choreography*)

**-gynous** taking an attitude toward women (*misogynous*)

**-gyny** used to form nouns corresponding to adjectives ending in -gynous (*misogyny*)

**-hedral** used to form adjectives from nouns ending in -hedron (*polyhedral*)

**-hedron** figure with faces or sides of specified number (*octahedron*)

**-holic** variation of -aholic (*chocoholic*)

**-ia** used in names of diseases, places, Roman feasts, and Latin plurals (*malaria, Romania, Saturnalia, Reptilia*)

**-ial** variation of -al (*editorial*)

**-ian** variation of -an, esp. denoting type, engagement in, or practice of (*reptilian, Episcopalian, electrician*)

**-iasis** disease (*psoriasis*)

**-iatrics** medicine, treatment (*pediatrics*)

**-iatry** specific area of healing or medical practice (*psychiatry*)

**-ibility** variation of -ability when base adjective ends in -ible (*responsibility*)

**-ible** variation of -able (*horrible*)

**-ibly** combination of -ible and -ly for adverbs corresponding to adjectives ending in -ible (*visibly*)

**-ic** used to form adjectives from other parts of speech (*poetic*); having some attribute of, in the style of (*sophomoric, Byronic*); used in chemistry to show higher valence in opposition to -ous (*ferric chloride*)

**-ical** combination of -ic and -al to form adjectives corresponding to nouns or adjectives ending in -ic (*economical*)

**-ician** used to form personal nouns denoting occupation (*beautician*)

**-ics** field of study, body of knowledge or principles, usu. corresponding to adjectives ending in -ic or -ical (*ethics, physics*)

**-id** descendant of, esp. for names of dynasties (*Abbasid*); name of zoological family or class or adjective pertaining to taxonomic division (*arachnid*); used to form adjectives corresponding to nouns ending in -or (*pallid*)

**-idae** denoting names of zoological families (*Candiae*)

**-ide** indicator of chemical compounds (*chloride*)

**-idine** denoting names of chemical compounds derived from other chemical compounds (*guanidine*)

**-idion** variation of diminutive -idium (*enchiridion*)

**-idium** diminutive for scientific terms (*peridium*)

**-ie** variation of -y or -ey, esp. denoting little one (*birdie*)

**-iensis** variation of -ensis (*mississippiensis*)

**-ier** indicating person engaged in trade or occupation (*cashier*); used on loanwords from French, often with loss of final "r" sound (*dossier*)

**-iform** shaped like (*cruciform*)

**-iformes** taxonomic names of animals (*Passeriformes*)

**-ify** variation of -fy used to form verbs from adjectives (*intensify*)

**-il** variation of -ile (*civil*)

**-ile** used to form adjectives expressing capability, susceptibility, liability, or aptitude (*agile, docile, fragile, prehensile*)

**-ility** used to form abstract nouns corresponding to adjectives ending in -le, -ile, or -il (*ability, agility, civility*)

**-illion** indicating numerals of specified exponential degree (*trillion*)

**-ine** like, pertaining to, made of (*marine, crystalline*); names of chemical substances (*chlorine*)

**-ing** used to form nouns that express action, result, or product of verb (*building*) or participial adjective form of verb (*thinking man*); belonging to, descended from (*farthing*)

**-ious** used to form adjectives corresponding to nouns ending in -ity (*atrocious*)

**-isation** *Brit.* variation of -ization (*organisation*)

**-ise** *Brit.* variation of -ize (*specialise*)

**-ish** used to form adjectives from nouns denoting belonging to, having characteristics of, or inclined to (*British, childish, bookish*); used to form adjectives from adjectives meaning somewhat or rather (*sweetish*)

**-ism** used to form nouns denoting action, condition, doctrine, or usage (*criticism, barbarism, Darwinism, realism, witticism*)

**-ist** used to form personal nouns corresponding to verbs ending in -ize or nouns ending in -ism (*apologist, socialist*)

**-istic** used to form adjectives from nouns ending in -ist or -ism (*socialistic, altruistic*)

**-istical** combination of -istic and -al to create additional adjectival form (*linguistical*)

**-istics** combination of -ist and -ics to form collective noun (*linguistics*)

**-ite** denoting person associated with place, group, belief, or system (*Israelite, laborite*); mineral and fossil names (*anthracite, ammonite*); names of chemical compounds (*sulfite*); used to form adjectives and nouns from adjectives and some verbs (*opposite*)

**-itious** used to form adjectives from nouns ending in -ition (*ambitious*)

**-itis** inflammation (*arthritis*); abnormality or excess (*computeritis*)

**-itive** used in substantives of Latin origin (*transitive*)

**-ity** used to form abstract nouns expressing state or condition, esp. adjectives (*insincerity*)

**-ium** used on nouns borrowed from Latin (*tedium*), certain compound words (*equilibrium*), and associative derivatives of personal nouns (*collegium*)

**-ization** combination of -ize and -ation (*civilization*)

**-ize** added to adjectives and nouns to form transitive verbs meaning make, give form to, or subject to some process (*fossilize, dramatize, terrorize*), or to form intransitive verbs denoting change of state, kind of behavior, or activity (*crystallize, apologize, philosophize*)

**-kinesis** movement (*telekinesis*)

**-lalia** abnormal or disordered speech (*glossolalia*)

**-latry** worship of (*idolatry*)

**-lepsy** seizure, fit (*epilepsy*)

**-less** without (*childless*)

**-like** used to form adjectives denoting similarity, preceded by hyphen if base word ends in double "l" (*childlike, bell-like*)

**-ling** denoting one concerned with, often pejoratively or diminutively (*hireling, duckling*); used with adverbs to express direction, position, or state (*underling, darkling*)

**-lith** stone (*paleolith*)

**-lithic** used in names of archaeological ages (*Neolithic*)

**-logue** used in names of kinds of discourses or writing (*monologue, travelogue*)

**-logy** science of, body of knowledge (*biology, theology*)

**-ly** used to form adverbs from adjectives (*slowly*); added to nouns denoting every time (*hourly*); used to form adjectives meaning like (*cowardly*)

**-lysis** dissolving, breaking down, decomposing (*electrolysis, analysis, paralysis*)

**-lyte** something subjected to a process, often where process ends in -lysis (*electrolyte*)

**-lyze** used in verbs corresponding to nouns ending in -ysis (*analyze*)

**-machy** battle, fighting (*logomachy*)

**-mancy** divination (*oneiromancy*)

**-mania** obsession with, craving for (*pyromania*)

**-megalia** variation of -megaly (*hepatosplenomegalia*)

**-megaly** abnormal enlargement of specified part (*cardiomegaly*)

**-ment** used in nouns denoting action, product, or means (*refinement, fragment, ornament*)

**-mer** member of particular chemical group (*polymer*)

**-merous** having parts of specified kind or number (*pentamerous*)

**-metric** used to form adjectives based on nouns ending in -metry (*geometric*)

**-metry** process of measurement (*chronometry*)

**-morph** form or structure (*allomorph*)

**-morphic** variation of -morphous (*anthropomorphic*)

**-morphism** used to form nouns corresponding to adjectives ending in -morphous or -morphic (*isomorphism*)

**-morphous** having specified shape, form, or structure (*polymorphous*)

**-mycete** fungus, mushroom (*ascomycete*)

**-mycetes** taxonomic names of fungi, esp. classes (*Myxomycetes*)

**-ness** used to form abstract nouns denoting quality and state from adjectives and participles (*darkness, preparedness*)

**-nomy** distribution or arrangement (*economy, taxonomy*)

**-oate** denoting names of chemical compounds (*benzoate*)

**-ock** used to form descriptive and diminutive names (*bullock, hillock*)

**-odont** having or relating to teeth, esp. used as base in combination with -ia or -ics (*orthodontia*)

**-odus** variation of -odont, used for names of zoological genera (*ceratodus*)

**-odynia** pain (*pododynia*)

**-oid** similar to, like (*ovoid*)

**-oidea** used for names of zoological classes (*Echinoidea*)

**-ola** used in various commercial coinages and jocular variations of other words (*granola, crapola*)

**-oma** tumor (*melanoma*)

**-onym** word, name (*synonym, pseudonym*)

**-oon** used in formation of nouns from Romance languages (*bassoon*)

**-opia** eye, sight (*myopia*)

**-opic** used to form adjectives corresponding to nouns ending in -opia (*myopic*)

**-opsia** variation of -opia (*hemianopsia*)

**-opsis** likeness, esp. to named thing (*coreopsis*)

**-opsy** medical examination (*biopsy*)

**-opy** variation of -opia (*amblyopy*)

**-or** denoting condition or property, sometimes in noun form corresponding to adjective ending in -id (*squalor*); used to form animate or inanimate agent nouns, often as variation of -er (*traitor, projector*)

**-orama** used in compound words, esp. in advertising and journalism (*scoutorama*)

**-orial** used to form adjectives based on nouns ending in -tor or -tory (*editorial, valedictorial*)

**-ory** used to form adjectives that imitate words ending in -tory or -sory (*excretory, sensory*); used in nouns denoting place or receptacle (*crematory*)

**-ose** full of, given to (*verbose*); used in chemical names of sugars and carbohydrates (*fructose, lactose*)

**-osis** denoting action, condition, or state, esp. abnormal one (*hypnosis, tuberculosis*)

**-ota** used in plural form of taxonomic names, esp. phyla (*Eukaryota*)

**-ote** used to form singular nouns from taxonomic names ending in -ota (*eukaryote*)

**-otic** used to form adjectives denoting relationship to indicated action, process, state, or condition, often based on nouns ending in -osis (*hypnotic*)

**-our** *Brit.* variation of -or (*honour*)

**-ous** used to form Anglicized adjectives, generally meaning possessing or full of (*nervous, tremendous*); used in chemistry to show lower valence in opposition to -ic (*ferrous chloride*)

**-pagus** used in names of malformed conjoined twins (*thoracopagus*)

**-parous** bearing, producing (*oviparous*)

**-pathic** used to form adjectives from nouns ending in -pathy (*homeopathic*)

**-pathy** suffering, feeling, disease, or treatment (*antipathy, sympathy, psychopathy, homeopathy*)

**-ped** having specified feet (*biped*)

**-pede** variation of - ped (*centipede*)

**-penia** lack, deficiency (*leukopenia*)

**-phage** thing that devours (*bacteriophage*)

**-phagia** variation of -phage (*hemophagia*)

**-phagous** eating, feeding on, devouring (*creophagous*)

**-phagy** eating, devouring (*anthropophagy*)

**-phany** appearance, manifestation (*epiphany*)

**-phasia** denoting names of speech disorders (*aphasia*)

**-phil** variation of -phile (*esosinophil*)

**-phile** lover of (*bibliophile*)

**-philia** affinity for or tendency toward, also unnatural attraction (*hemophilia, necrophilia*)

**-philiac** used to form adjectives from nouns ending in -philia (*hemophiliac*)

**-philic** used to form adjectives from nouns ending in -phile (*bibliophilic*); affinity for, among class of substances (*acidophilic*)

**-philism** used to form abstract nouns based on nouns ending in -phile (*bibliophilism*)

**-philous** liking, having affinity for (*dendrophilous*)

**-phily** variation of -philia (*hydrophily*)

**-phobia** fear (*acrophobia*)

**-phone** speech sound or instrument of sound transmission (*homophone, microphone*)

**-phony** used to form abstract nouns corresponding to nouns ending in -phone (*telephony*)

**-phore** bearer of (*gonophore*)

**-phorous** used to form adjectives corresponding to nouns ending in -phore (*gonophorous*)

**-phrenia** indicating names of mental disorders (*schizophrenia*)

**-phyllous** having leaves (*monophyllous*)

**-phyte** plant (*lithophyte*)

**-plasia** growth (*hypoplasia*)

**-plasm** living tissue, cell substance (*ectoplasm*)

**-plast** cell, living substance (*chloroplast*)

**-plasty** molding formation or surgical repair (*rhinoplasty*)

**-plasy** variation of -plasia (*homoplasy*)

**-plegia** paralysis (*paraplegia*)

**-ploid** having chromosome sets (*hexaploid*)

**-pnea** breath (*dyspnea*)

**-pod** having specified kind or number of feet (*cephalopod*)

**-poda** having specified feet, used in names of zoological classes (*Cephalopoda*)

**-pode** variation of -podium (*pseudopode*)

**-podium** footlike part (*monopodium*)

**-podous** used to form adjectives from nouns ending in -pod (*cephalopodous*)

**-poiesis** making, formation (*hematopoiesis*)

**-poietic** used to form adjectives from nouns ending in -poiesis (*hematopoietic*)

**-pterous** having wings (*dipterous*)

**-rel** used in diminutive or pejorative noun (*scoundrel*)

**-rhiza** variation of -rrhiza (*coleorhiza*)

**-rrhagia** rupture, profuse flow or discharge (*bronchorrhagia*)

**-rrhaphy** suture (*herniorrhaphy*)

**-rrhea** flow, discharge (*diarrhea*)

**-rrhexis** rupture (*enterorrhexis*)

**-rrhiza** root (*mycorrhiza*)

**-rrhoea** variation of -rrhea (*melanorrhoea*)

**-saur** used in names of extinct reptiles (*dinosaur*)

**-saurus** variation of -saur (*tyrannosaurus*)

**-scope** instrument for viewing (*microscope*)

**-sepalous** having specified sepals (*polysepalous*)

**-ski** jocular or informal addition derived from Slavic names (*Russki*)

**-sky** variation of -ski (*buttinsky*)

**-some** used to form adjectives from verbs and nouns (*burdensome*); meaning body in compounds (*chromosome*); collective used with numerals (*threesome*)

**-sophy** science of, wisdom (*philosophy*)

**-sperm** one having specified seeds (*angiosperm*)

**-spermal** used to form adjectives from nouns ending in -sperm (*gymnospermal*)

**-sporous** having specified spores (*helicosporous*)

**-stichous** having specified rows (*distichous*)

**-stome** organism having a mouth (*cyclostome*)

**-stomous** having specified mouth (*monostomous*)

**-stomy** surgical operation involving creation of artificial opening (*colostomy*)

**-taxis** arrangement or order (*heterotaxis*)

**-taxy** variation of -taxis (*epitaxy*)

**-teen** used to form cardinal numerals from 13 to 19 (*fifteen*)

**-therm** heat (*isotherm*)

**-thermy** heat, heat generation (*diathermy*)

**-tion** used to form abstract nouns, esp. from verbs, expressing action, state, or associated meanings (*revolution, relation*)

**-tious** added to various stems to form adjectives (*facetious, bumptious*)

**-tome** cutting instrument (*osteotome*)

**-tomous** cut, divided (*dichotomous*)

**-tomy** cutting, incision, surgical excision (*appendectomy*)

**-ton** used to form nouns from adjectives (*simpleton*)

**-tonia** muscle or nerve tension or personality disorder (*hypertonia, catatonia*)

**-tonic** used to form adjectives from nouns ending in -tonia (*catatonic*)

**-trix** used to form feminine, esp. of nouns ending in -tor (*executrix*)

**-trope** one turned toward (*heliotrope*)

**-troph** nutrient matter or organism with specified nutritional requirements (*embryotroph, heterotroph*)

**-trophic** having nutritional requirements, maintaining an activity (*autotrophic, gonadotrophic*)

**-trophy** used to form nouns meaning feeding or growth (*mycotrophy, hypertrophy*)

**-tropic** turned toward, having an affinity for (*geotropic, psychotropic*)

**-tropism** variation of -tropy (*heliotropism*)

**-tropous** turned, curved (*anatropous*)

**-tropy** used to form abstract nouns corresponding to adjectives ending in -tropic or -tropous (*psychotropy*)

**-tude** used in abstract nouns and formation of new nouns (*platitude*)

**-ty** used in nouns denoting quality or state (*unity*); added to numerals to denote multiples of ten (*twenty*)

**-type** having a particular characteristic, regarded as a group or class (*prototype, phenotype*)

**-urgy** technique or art of dealing or working with something (*chemurgy*)

**-vore** one that eats (*carnivore*)

**-vorous** eating (*omnivorous*)

**-ward** used to denote spatial or temporal direction (*backward, afterward*)

**-wards** variation of -ward (*towards*)

**-xion** *Brit.* variation of -tion (*connexion*)

**-y** characterized by, inclined to (*juicy, dreamy*); added to usu. monosyllabic bases to create informal nouns (*granny, cabby*); used to denote little one (*Billy*)

**-yer** variation of -er in formation of occupational names (*lawyer*)

**-zoa** used in names of zoological classes (*Protozoa*)

**-zoon** animal or organism, esp. single member of zoological class name ending in -zoa (*protozoon*)

# ABBREVIATIONS

**SEE ALSO**: Chap. 3: Geography; Chap. 4: Physics; Chemistry; Medicine; Chap. 5: Weapons and Armaments; Computers; Chap. 11: Government; War and Military; Titles of Rank; Chap. 12: Finance; Chap. 13: Education; Chap. 15: Popular Music; Television and Radio; Chap. 17: Sports; Chap. 24: Crime; Chap. 25: Religion

This section does not include acronyms and initials for organizations, entities, and trademarked products such as AMA, FCC, MS-DOS, NATO, and SDI, which appear in their appropriate categories. Most of the abbreviations listed here have been normalized to one form, without periods, except where the period is required, as in certain titles, academic degrees, or A.D. and B.C., or to distinguish the abbreviation from a word, as a.m. or mach. In practice, there is great variety in the use of periods and capitalization for abbreviations.

**A.B.** *Latin.* artium baccalaureus; Bachelor of Arts

**abbrev** abbreviation

**abr** abridged

**AC** alternating current; air conditioning

**ack**  acknowledge, acknowledgment
**A.D.**  *Latin.* anno Domini; in the year of the Lord
**adj**  adjective
**admin**  administration
**adv**  adverb
**aeron**  aeronautics
**agcy**  agency
**agric**  agriculture, agricultural
**aka**  also known as
**alt**  alternate; alternation; altitude
**a.m.**  *Latin.* ante meridiem; morning
**AM**  amplitude modulation
**amb**  ambassador
**ammo**  ammunition
**amp**  ampere; amplifier
**anat**  anatomy
**anon**  anonymous
**approx**  approximate
**Apr**  April
**apt.**  apartment
**arch.**  architecture
**arith**  arithmetic
**art.**  article
**ASAP**  as soon as possible
**assoc**  associated, association
**asst**  assistant
**astron**  astronomy
**att**  attached; attorney
**aug**  augmented
**Aug**  August
**aux**  auxiliary
**ave**  avenue
**avg**  average
**AWOL**  absent without leave
**B.A.**  Bachelor of Arts
**bal**  balance
**b and w**  black and white
**bbl**  barrel
**B.C.**  before Christ
**B.C.E.**  before Christian (common) era
**bd**  board
**bet**  between
**bf**  boldface
**bibliog**  bibliography
**biog**  biography
**biol**  biology
**blvd**  boulevard
**bot**  bottom; botany
**bro**  brother
**B.S.**  Bachelor of Science
**bskt**  basket
**BTU**  British thermal unit
**bu**  bushel
**bull.**  bulletin
**bur**  bureau
**BYOB**  bring your own booze/beer/bottle
**C**  Celsius, centigrade
**c**  cent; century; copyright
**ca**  circa
**cal**  calorie
**calc**  calculate
**cap.**  capitalize
**capt**  captain
**cat.**  catalog

**CB**  Citizens Band
**cc**  cubic centimeter
**Cdr**  Commander
**C.E.**  common era, same as A.D.
**cent.**  century
**CEO**  chief executive officer
**cert**  certificate, certified
**cf**  *Latin.* confer; compare
**cg**  centigram
**chap.**  chapter
**chem**  chemistry
**chm**  chairman
**chron**  chronology
**cie**  *French.* compagnie; company
**circ**  circular
**cl**  centiliter
**class.**  classified, classification
**cm**  centimeter
**CNS**  central nervous system
**co**  company
**c/o**  care of
**COD**  cash on delivery
**Col.**  Colonel
**col**  colony; column
**collab**  collaboration
**colloq**  colloquial
**comb.**  combination, combining
**comm**  commander; commerce; committee
**conc**  concentrated
**cond**  condition
**conf**  conference
**confed**  confederate
**Cong**  Congress
**conj**  conjunction
**const**  construction; constitution
**contd**  continued
**contemp**  contemporary
**contr**  contraction
**contrib**  contributor, contribution
**coroll**  corollary
**corp**  corporation
**corr**  correct; correspondence
**CPA**  certified public accountant
**CPI**  consumer price index
**cpl**  corporal
**CPR**  cardiopulmonary resuscitation
**cr**  credit; crown
**crim**  criminal
**crit**  critical, criticism
**CRT**  cathode-ray tube
**ct**  court
**ctr**  center
**cu**  cubic
**cum**  cumulative
**CYA**  cover your ass
**d**  *Latin.* denarii; penny (Britain); diameter; dime; dollar
**DA**  district attorney
**dba**  doing business as
**dbl**  double; decibel
**DC**  direct current
**D.D.**  Doctor of Divinity
**D.D.S.**  Doctor of Dental Science
**Dec**  December

**dec**  deceased
**def**  definition
**deg**  degree
**Dem**  Democrat
**denom**  denomination
**dept**  department
**deriv**  derivative, derived
**dial.**  dialect
**diam**  diameter
**dict**  dictionary
**dim.**  diminished; dimension
**DINK**  dual income, no kids
**dip.**  diploma
**dir**  director
**dist**  district; distance
**div**  division; divorced
**do.**  ditto
**DOA**  dead on arrival
**doc.**  document
**dol**  dollar
**doz**  dozen
**Dr.**  Doctor
**DST**  daylight-saving time
**dt's**  delirium tremens
**dup**  duplicate
**E**  east, eastern
**ea**  each
**eccl**  ecclesiastical
**ecol**  ecology
**econ**  economics
**ed**  editor
**educ**  education
**EEG**  electroencephalogram
**e.g.**  *Latin.* exempli gratia; for example
**EKG**  electrocardiogram
**el**  elevation
**elec**  electric
**elem**  elementary
**elev**  elevation
**enc**  enclosure, enclosed
**encyc**  encyclopedia
**env**  envelope
**eq**  equal, equalization
**equiv**  equivalent
**ERA**  earned run average
**esp.**  especially
**ESP**  extrasensory perception
**Esq.**  Esquire
**est**  estimated
**et al**  *Latin.* et alia; and others
**etc.**  *Latin.* etcetera; and so forth
**et seq**  *Latin.* et sequens; and the following one
**etym**  etymology
**ex.**  example
**exam**  examination
**exc**  except
**exec**  executive
**ex lib**  *Latin.* ex libris; from the books of
**exp**  expense; express
**ext**  extension; exterior
**F**  Fahrenheit
**f**  feminine; father; feet
**fac**  facsimile

**fath**  fathom
**Feb**  February
**fec**  *Latin.* fecit; he made it
**fed**  federal; federation
**fem**  feminine
**ff**  and following
**fid**  fiduciary
**fig**  figurative
**fin.**  finance; finish
**fka**  formerly known as
**FM**  frequency modulation
**fn**  footnote
**f.o.b.**  freight on board
**fol**  folio; following
**foll**  and the following entry
**for.**  foreign
**freq**  frequent
**Fri**  Friday
**frt**  freight
**frwy**  freeway
**Ft.**  fort
**ft**  foot, feet
**fur.**  furlong
**furn**  furnished
**fut**  future
**fwd**  forward; foreword
**fx**  special effects
**FYI**  for your information
**g**  gram
**gal.**  gallon
**gaz**  gazette
**gds**  goods
**gen**  general
**geneal**  genealogy
**geog**  geography
**geol**  geology
**geom**  geometry
**GIGO**  garbage in, garbage out
**gloss.**  glossary
**gm**  gram
**GOP**  Grand Old Party
**Gov.**  governor
**Govt**  government
**gp**  group
**GQ**  General Quarters
**gr**  gram; gross; grade
**grad**  graduate
**gram.**  grammar
**gtd**  guaranteed
**guar**  guarantee
**ha.**  hectare
**hdqrs**  headquarters
**hf**  half
**HMS**  His (or Her) Majesty's Ship
**Hon.**  Honorable
**hor**  horizontal
**hosp**  hospital
**hq**  headquarters
**hr**  hour
**HRH**  His (or Her) Royal Highness
**ht**  height
**hwy**  highway
**ibid**  *Latin.* ibidem; in the same place

**id.** *Latin.* idem; the same
**i.e.** *Latin.* id est; that is
**illus** illustrated
**imper** imperative
**in.** inch
**inc** incorporated
**incl** including
**incorp** incorporated
**ind** independent; index
**indic** indicative
**inf** infinitive
**init** initially
**in loc cit** *Latin.* in loco citato; in the place cited
**insp** inspector
**inst** institute
**instr** instructor
**int** interior; interim
**interj** interjection
**interrog** interrogative, interrogation
**inv** invoice
**I/O** input/output
**IOU** I owe you
**IQ** intelligence quotient
**irreg** irregular
**ISBN** International Standard Book Number
**isl** island
**ital** italics
**Jan** January
**jct** junction
**J.D.** *Latin.* Jurum Doctor; doctor of law
**Jly** July
**Jn** June
**jour** journal
**JP** justice of the peace
**jr** junior
**juv** juvenile
**k** kilogram; thousand; karat; kilobyte
**kg** kilogram
**kHz** kilohertz
**kilo.** kilogram
**km** kilometer
**kn** knot
**KO** knockout
**Kt** knight
**kW** kilowatt
**L** *Latin.* libra; pound (Britain)
**l** liter
**lab** laboratory
**lang** language
**lat** latitude
**lb.** *Latin.* libra; pound
**l.c.** lower case
**lect** lecturer
**lex** lexicon
**lf** lightface; left field
**lg** large
**lic** license
**Lieut** lieutenant
**ling** linguistics
**liq** liquid
**lit.** literally
**Litt. D.** *Latin.* litterarum doctor; doctor of letters
**LL.B.** *Latin.* legum baccalaureus; bachelor of law

**LL.D.** *Latin.* legum doctor; doctor of laws
**ln** lane
**loc cit** *Latin.* loco citato; in the place cited
**long.** longitude
**LPN** licensed practical nurse
**Lt.** lieutenant
**lt** light
**Ltd** limited
**m** meter; masculine; million
**M.A.** Master of Arts
**mach.** machine
**mag** magazine
**Maj.** Major
**Mar** March
**masc** masculine
**math** mathematics
**max** maximum
**MC** master of ceremonies
**M.D.** Doctor of Medicine
**mdse** merchandise
**meas** measure
**mech** mechanical, mechanics
**med** medicine
**memo** memorandum
**met.** metropolitan
**M.F.A.** Master of Fine Arts
**mfd** manufactured
**mfr** manufacturer
**mg** milligram
**mgr** manager
**mi** mile
**mid** middle
**milit** military
**min** minimum; minister; minute
**misc** miscellaneous
**ml** milliliter
**mm** millimeter
**MO** *Latin.* modus operandi, method of operation; money order; mail order
**mo.** month
**mod.** moderate
**Mon** Monday
**MP** Military Police; Member of Parliament
**mph** miles per hour
**Mr.** mister
**Mrs.** title of respect for a married woman
**Ms.** title of respect for a woman regardless of marital status
**M.S.** Master of Science
**ms** manuscript
**MSG** monosodium glutamate
**Msgr** Monsignor
**M.S.W.** Master of Social Work
**Mt.** Mount; mountain
**mtge** mortgage
**mtn** mountain
**muni** municipal
**N** north, northern
**n** noun; neuter; noon
**N/A** not applicable
**nat** national; natural
**naut** nautical
**NB** *Latin.* nota bene; note well
**NE** northeast; northeastern

**neg** negative
**neut** neuter
**no.** *Latin.* numero; number
**nom** nominative
**Nov** November
**np** no pagination
**nr** near
**num** numeral
**NW** northwest; northwestern
**OBE** Order of the British Empire
**obit** obituary
**obj** object; objective
**obs** obsolete
**occas** occasional, occasionally
**Oct** October
**off.** officer; official
**op** opus
**op cit** *Latin.* opere citato; in the work cited
**opp.** opposite
**orch** orchestra
**org** organization
**orig.** originally, origin
**ot** overtime
**oz.** ounce
**p** page
**PA** public address (system)
**P and L** profit and loss
**par.** paragraph
**paren** parentheses
**Parl** Parliament
**part.** participle
**pat.** patent
**PC** personal computer; politically correct
**pc** parsec
**pd** paid
**PE** physical education
**per.** period; person
**perh** perhaps
**perm** permanent
**pers** personal
**pfd** preferred
**ph** phase; phone
**pharm** pharmacy
**Ph.D.** Doctor of Philosophy
**philos** philosophy
**photo** photograph
**phr** phrase
**phys ed** physical education
**pk** peck
**pkg** package
**pl** plural; place
**p.m.** *Latin.* post meridiem; afternoon
**PO** post office
**poss** possessive
**POV** point of view
**pp** pages
**ppd** postpaid; prepaid
**pref** preface; preferred
**prelim** preliminary
**prep.** preposition
**pres** president
**priv** private

**prod.** product
**pron** pronoun; pronunciation
**pronun** pronunciation
**pro tem** *Latin.* pro tempore; for the time being
**prov** province
**P.S.** postscript
**Ps** Psalms
**pseud** pseudonym
**psych** psychology
**Pt.** Point
**pt** part; pint
**p/t** part time
**pub.** publication
**pvt** private
**pwr** power
**PX** post exchange
**q** quart
**QED** *Latin.* quod erat demonstrandum; which was to be demonstrated
**qt** quart
**qty** quantity
**qv** *Latin.* quad vide; which see, in reference to
**R** *Latin.* Rex, Regina; king, queen
**R and R** rest and recreation/recuperation
**rbi** run batted in
**rd** road
**rec** recipe; receipt
**ref** reference
**refrig** refrigerator
**reg** registered; regulation
**rel** relative
**REM** rapid eye movement (sleep)
**Rep** Republican
**res** reserve; residence
**ret.** retired
**rev** reverse; review; revised
**Rev.** Reverend
**RFD** Rural Free Delivery (postal route)
**rh** relative humidity
**rhet** rhetoric
**RIP** rest in peace
**riv** river
**R.N.** registered nurse
**rnd** round
**rpm** revolutions per minute
**RR** railroad
**RSVP** *French.* répondez s'il vous plaît; please answer
**rt** right
**rte** route
**Rx** pharmaceutical prescription
**S** south, southern
**s** second
**SASE** self-addressed stamped envelope
**Sat** Saturday
**S.B.** *Latin.* scientiae baccalaureus; bachelor of science
**sci** science
**sd** sound
**SE** southeast; southeastern
**secy** secretary
**Sept** September
**seq** *Latin.* sequens; the following
**sgd** signed
**sing.** singular

**sm** small
**S.M.** *Latin*. scientiae magister; master of science
**soc** society; sociology
**sol.** solution
**SOP** standard operating procedure
**soph** sophomore
**SOS** save our ship, international distress signal
**spec** special; specification
**specif** specifically
**SPQR** *Latin*. senatus populusque romanus; the senate and Roman people
**sq** square
**SS** steamship
**St.** Saint; street
**st** state
**std** standard
**Ste.** Saint (female)
**stet** *Latin*. it stands; let the original stand
**sub.** subject; subtract
**subj** subject; subjunctive
**Sun** Sunday
**supp** supplement
**supr** supreme
**supt** superintendent
**sur** surface
**surv** survey
**SW** southwest; southwestern
**sym** symbol
**syn** synonym
**t** ton
**tba** to be announced
**tbs** tablespoon
**TCB** take care of business
**TD** touchdown
**tech** technical
**tel** telephone; telegraph; telegram
**temp** temporary
**terr** territory
**Test.** Testament
**TGIF** thank God it's Friday
**theol** theology
**therm** thermometer
**Thurs** Thursday
**tit.** title
**TKO** technical knockout
**tkt** ticket

**TNT** trinitrotoluene (explosive)
**tot.** total
**Tpke** turnpike
**tr** translation; transpose
**treas** treasury
**trib** tributary
**tsp** teaspoon
**Tues** Tuesday
**u.c.** upper case
**UFO** unidentified flying object
**ult** ultimately
**unan** unanimous
**uncert** uncertain
**univ** universal
**u.s.** *Latin*. ut supra; as above
**usu.** usually
**util** utility
**v** verb; versus
**val** value
**var** variable, variety
**vb** verb
**ver** verse
**vet** veteran
**vi** intransitive verb
**VIP** very important person
**viz** *Latin*. videlicet; that is to say, namely
**voc** vocative
**vocab** vocabulary
**vol** volume; volunteer
**VP** vice president
**vs** versus
**vt** transitive verb
**vv** verses; *Latin*. vice versa, conversely
**W** west, western
**w** week; wide; watt
**Wed** Wednesday
**whsle** wholesale
**wk** week
**wt** weight
**X** extra
**x** cross
**Xmas** Christmas
**yd** yard
**yr** year
**z** zero; zone
**zool** zoology

# CHAPTER 19

# Action and and Sense Words

# Verbs of Motion

Gaits
Mood and Intent
Directions

**see also**: Chap. 23: Spatial Positions and Relations

## Gaits

**amble** walk at an easy pace or in a leisurely manner
**barrel** move along rapidly and heavily; roll along
**bounce** move in a lively manner, as if by sudden leaps
**bound** move by leaping forward
**bustle** hurry with a great show of energy and purpose
**canter** move with a three-beat gait, easier than a gallop, used esp. of horses
**caper** skip along gaily
**clamber** climb using both hands and feet
**clomp** clump
**clump** walk clumsily and noisily
**crawl** move slowly or laboriously; move in a prone position without the use of hands or feet
**curvet** prance or canter, used esp. of horses
**dander** saunter; stroll at a leisurely pace
**dart** move suddenly and rapidly
**dash** move with a sudden burst of speed; flash
**dogtrot** move at a quick, easy gait, like a dog
**drift** float smoothly or effortlessly; move in an aimless or casual way
**flash** dash
**flit** move swiftly and lightly in irregular motion; skim along
**flitter** move lightly, like a bird; flutter
**flow** glide smoothly, as though in fluid
**flutter** move with quick, irregular, or flapping motions; flitter
**fly** move very quickly
**foot it** *Informal*. walk, run, or dance
**footslog** tramp or march heavily, esp. through mud
**frogmarch** force a person to walk forward with arms grasped behind the back
**gallop** bound quickly in a three-beat gait, like a horse
**gallumph** tromp heavily in clumsy gait
**glide** move smoothly and effortlessly
**goose-step** move in high-kicking soldier's march with stiff knees
**hobble** proceed unevenly or haltingly; walk lamely, with a limp
**hoof** *Slang*. walk; move on one's feet
**hop** move in short, bounding leaps, like a rabbit
**hotfoot it** *Informal*. hurry
**hurdle** bound over (obstacles)
**hurry** go quickly
**hurtle** rush forward recklessly
**inch** move slowly, bit by bit
**jog** run at a moderate pace
**jounce** move joltingly in an up-and-down manner; bounce
**jump** spring; leap; bound

**leap** spring forward through the air
**limp** walk lamely or jerkily, favoring one leg
**lope** move in a long, easy, bounding gait
**lumber** move slowly with heavy feet and drooping shoulders
**march** move with a regular, measured gait, in step with others; proceed with purpose
**maunder** move in a dreamy, aimless way
**mince** walk with short steps in a dainty, affected manner
**mosey** stroll, amble, or saunter; leave quickly
**pace** walk with a slow, measured tread, often back and forth
**pad** walk with dull, muffled footsteps
**patter** move as though on little feet, making a light noise
**plod** walk heavily, slowly, or tediously; trudge
**prance** move by springing forward; strut about in a spirited manner
**prowl** move about stealthily; pace nervously
**ramble** roll along in a leisurely, aimless manner
**reel** walk unsteadily
**run** spring forward quickly so that both feet are off the ground between each step
**sashay** glide or move in a nonchalant way
**saunter** strut or stroll in a leisurely manner
**scamper** run or dash quickly, lightly, or playfully; scurry; skelter
**scrabble** scratch and claw; grope and clamber for a foothold
**scramble** move or climb quickly, using hands and feet
**scuff** walk without lifting one's feet
**scuffle** shuffle; scrape one's feet
**scurry** scamper
**scuttle** run or move with hasty steps, esp. away from danger
**shamble** walk in a lazy, awkward manner, dragging one's feet
**shlep** *Slang*. drag or haul oneself along in an awkward, heavy manner
**shuffle** drag one's feet; move along rhythmically; scuffle
**skelter** scamper
**skip** spring or leap lightly in bounding gait
**skitter** move quickly and lightly over a surface; skip
**slide** move easily and smoothly over a surface
**slither** slip or glide over a surface; slide along smoothly
**slog** plod heavily; tramp over a difficult path
**slosh** flounder and splash about in mud, water, or slush
**spring** leap forward through the air
**sprint** run at top speed, esp. for a short distance
**stagger** reel, sway, or totter along unsteadily
**stamp** proceed by bringing one's feet down firmly with each step
**step** move by lifting each foot and setting it down in a new position
**step lively** move lightly, with springy step
**stomp** stamp; step down hard
**straddle** walk with legs spread apart
**stride** move vigorously with long, measured steps
**stroll** proceed idly, at a leisurely pace
**strut** walk with vain, pompous, or affected air
**stumble** walk unsteadily or clumsily; trip over one's own feet
**stump** walk heavily and clumsily
**swagger** walk with an arrogant strut
**tiptoe** walk quietly or cautiously, with weight on one's toes
**tittup** *Chiefly Brit*. prance or caper like a spirited horse
**toddle** walk with short, uncertain steps

**totter** proceed weakly, wobbling with faltering steps
**tramp** walk, tread, or step heavily; tromp
**trample** tread heavily and noisily, esp. while crushing things under one's feet
**tread** step or walk on, along, or over something
**trip** stumble and fall
**tromp** tramp
**trot** move in a quick, steady, bouncy gait between a walk and a run
**trudge** walk wearily or laboriously; plod
**waddle** move with slow, short steps, rocking from side to side like a duck
**wade** walk through water or mud
**walk** advance at a moderate pace in steady steps; move along by foot
**waltz** move in a breezy, conspicuous manner; dance along
**wamble** move in unsteady, shaky, or staggering gait
**whisk** move lightly and rapidly
**wobble** proceed with an unsteady rocking motion, esp. clumsily, from side to side
**zip** move with great speed and vigor
**zoom** move quickly, esp. with loud hum or buzz

## MOOD AND INTENT

**accelerate** move more rapidly; quicken one's step
**ambulate** walk easily from place to place
**balk** hold back or hesitate
**barge** move forward heedlessly or clumsily, often colliding with things
**bestride** stand, ride, or walk across
**blunder** move unsteadily, in confusion
**bob** move up and down with a short, jerky motion
**bop** shuffle along as if to music; go quickly
**brush** touch lightly in passing
**buck** charge against; spring into the air
**budge** move slightly; begin to move
**buzz off** *Slang.* move rapidly; depart unceremoniously
**caper** leap or skip about playfully
**careen** swerve from side to side while moving forward
**career** go at full speed
**catapult** move quickly or forcefully through the air
**cavort** frolic playfully; romp
**charge** rush to attack; bear down on
**chase** pursue hastily
**chug** move laboriously and noisily
**clip** move swiftly
**coast** move forward under acquired momentum
**convoy** escort for protection
**course** move swiftly through or along designated path
**cover ground** move quickly across distance
**cower** crouch and pull away in fear
**creak along** move slowly, unsteadily, and squeakily
**creep** go timidly or cautiously so as to escape notice
**cringe** shrink in fear or deference
**crouch** bend low to the ground
**crowd** press forward; advance by pushing
**cruise** move at controlled speed; wander about with little purpose
**crumple** collapse in a heap
**dally** tarry
**dance** move lightly in time to music

**dawdle** loiter; waste time; piddle
**decelerate** slow down
**dillydally** loiter
**dither** move in a trembling, agitated manner
**dive** plunge headfirst
**dodder** proceed feebly and unsteadily
**dodge** move to and fro on irregular course
**drag** dawdle; proceed laboriously
**drift** float smoothly or effortlessly; move in aimless or casual way
**duck** bend over to avoid some object
**ease** maneuver carefully; move against slight resistance
**elude** evade skillfully
**escape** get away from danger or restraint; evade
**escort** accompany as protection
**evade** avoid deftly; escape
**falter** stumble; walk unsteadily
**fiddle about** putter aimlessly; dally
**fidget** move nervously or restlessly
**flail** move or toss about freely, often to no effect
**flap** flutter; toss about ineffectually
**flee** run away in haste
**flick** go or pass abruptly and swiftly
**flip** leap up and turn over in air
**float** move gently and lightly, as though suspended in fluid
**flock** assemble and move together in a group
**flounce** move with jerky motions or angry impatience
**flounder** struggle with stumbling movements
**flump** fall suddenly and heavily
**flurry** move in an excited, confused manner
**frisk** jump, skip, or frolic in a playful manner
**frolic** romp about in a frisky, merry way
**gad** move about restlessly and to no purpose
**gallivant** roam frivolously
**gambol** frolic, jump, or skip playfully
**glissade** glide down slope in standing or squatting position
**grovel** crawl in a submissive, facedown position
**gush** issue forth suddenly, forcibly, or copiously
**halt** come to a stop
**hasten** move rapidly; hie
**herd** assemble and move together in a group
**hie** hasten
**hike** walk a great distance for exercise or pleasure
**hover** hang suspended in place above something
**hulk** move heavily and clumsily
**hunch** push forward in bent posture
**hustle** proceed in aggressive, hurried manner
**idle** saunter aimlessly; loiter
**intrude** enter a place uninvited, often by force
**jaunt** make short journey for fun
**jet** move very rapidly, in a rush
**jostle** push or shove one's way forward roughly, esp. through a crowd
**journey** travel to a set destination; voyage
**knife** move through something swiftly and easily, like a knife
**leapfrog** vault over the backs of others
**linger** remain in place longer than expected
**loaf** lounge lazily or idly
**loiter** remain in place for no apparent reason; move slowly and idly; dillydally; idle; loll
**loll** loiter; lounge; sprawl
**lollop** bound or leap forward

**lounge** move idly or lazily; loll

**lunge** thrust oneself forward suddenly

**lurk** move furtively to avoid notice; slink; sneak

**make way** allow another to pass or enter

**maneuver** change direction or position adroitly for specific purpose

**maunder** move in a dreamy, aimless way

**meander** wander aimlessly, without direction; ramble or drift along a winding course

**mooch** wander about without purpose in a slow, lazy manner

**moonwalk** *Slang.* slide backward, apparently without lifting one's feet

**motor** *Informal.* move in haste

**muddle through** work one's way clear of obstacles without planning or direction

**muscle** *Informal.* force one's way by strenuous effort

**nip up** spring to one's feet from supine position

**obtrude** force oneself in where one is not welcome

**paddle** move through water by flailing one's hands and feet

**parade** march as if in procession, esp. to show off

**patrol** move about to observe an area or maintain security

**piddle** dawdle

**plane** glide across a surface; fly along effortlessly

**play** move in a lively, cheerful manner

**plow** proceed steadily or laboriously; push through

**plug away** keep moving against one or more obstacles

**poke along** move slowly, without direction

**post** move rapidly

**potter** wander vaguely; putter

**promenade** take a leisurely public walk, esp. to show off

**prowl** roam stealthily; pace restlessly

**pursue** follow intently so as to overtake

**pussyfoot** tread cautiously or stealthily

**putter** move aimlessly or idly among objects; potter

**quicken one's step** accelerate

**quickstep** make energetic march

**ramp** rear up and advance menacingly, used esp. of four-legged animals

**rampage** rush about wildly

**range** pass across large area

**rip** rush headlong

**ripple** flow in small undulations

**roam** wander without purpose; rove

**rock** move oneself rhythmically to and fro

**romp** run in a lively, effortless, energetic manner; cavort

**rove** roam

**rumble** move heavily, esp. with a deep, muffled sound

**rush** move in great haste; dash forward in attack

**rush headlong** move rapidly and out of control

**sail** skim across a surface as through propelled by wind

**scoot** move hastily; dart lightly

**scrieve** *Scot.* move rapidly and smoothly

**seep** flow or pass slowly through something

**settle** become fixed in one position

**shadow** follow someone secretly, at a distance, for the purpose of observation

**shilly-shally** dawdle; go indecisively

**shimmy** shake, vibrate, or wobble with a dancelike motion

**shoot** move rapidly; pass rapidly over

**shoulder** push one's way roughly through a crowd

**shunt** force or turn someone aside or out of the way

**skate** glide along smoothly, as if crossing ice

**ski** glide over a surface as if wearing skis on snow

**skid** slide out of control sideways

**skim** glide lightly across a surface

**skulk** sneak or lurk about in a stealthy or cowardly manner; slink

**sled** slide across a surface as though on runners

**slink** move stealthily or furtively; lurk

**slouch** move idly, drooping with hunched back

**slump** fall or sink suddenly; assume drooping posture

**snake** make one's way quietly along a winding course

**sneak** slink; lurk

**souse** plunge into liquid

**speed** move rapidly

**splash** flail or move about noisily in water

**sprawl** lie back carelessly with limbs outspread

**spurt** gush forth; rush forward

**squirm** wriggle or twist about

**stalk** pursue a quarry or prey; walk stiffly and proudly

**stampede** flee headlong in panic as a group

**steal** come or go secretly, unexpectedly, and unobserved

**stir** begin to move from position of rest

**straggle** hang back; fall farther behind

**streak** rush past rapidly

**stream** issue forth or flow from someplace

**surge** rise and fall in waves

**swarm** move in great numbers, hovering like bees

**swim** propel oneself smoothly as through water

**swoop** rush down upon suddenly, esp. in attack

**swoosh** move swiftly with a rustling sound

**tail** *Informal.* follow

**tarry** remain in place; wait for something; dally

**tear** move with great haste

**toodle** *Slang.* move along in an easygoing manner

**tool** cruise or drive along

**toss** move restlessly; jerk about

**tour** range over an area for pleasure or inspection

**track** follow the footprints or path of

**trail** follow; come after

**traipse** tramp about; wander aimlessly without reaching one's destination; proceed haphazardly

**trek** make slow, difficult progress over long route

**trespass** enter upon another's property uninvited

**trickle** move slowly, bit by bit

**troop** gather together and move in a group

**truck** *Slang.* roll along in an easy, untroubled manner

**trundle** roll along

**twinkle** flutter lightly about

**twitch** move erratically or jerkily; fidget

**undulate** move with a sinuous, wavelike motion

**upspring** bound up from place

**usher** lead the way to help others find their place

**vamp** move in a bewitching manner

**visit** come or go to see someone or someplace

**voyage** journey

**waft** move or float lightly as though through air

**wag** move jerkily from side to side or up and down

**wallow** move slowly and with difficulty, as though through mud

**wash** flow along; run up against

**welter** toss or heave about

**wheel** roll along easily and swiftly

**whid** *Scot.* move deftly and quietly

**whiz** move swiftly and effortlessly

**whoosh** rush past with a sudden hissing noise
**wiggle** move from side to side with quick, jerky motions
**wince** shrink back from a blow, recoil
**wing** fly as if on wings; move swiftly
**worm** creep along in a devious, stealthy manner
**wrench** move aside with a violent twist
**wrestle** move by force
**wriggle** writhe; squirm from side to side
**writhe** move in twists and bends
**zap** *Informal*. move with great speed or force

## DIRECTIONS

**about-face** turn in the opposite direction
**absquatulate** *Slang*. depart or flee
**advance** move forward
**angle** move indirectly toward or away from a person or object; turn sharply in a new direction
**approach** draw near
**arise** move upward from lower position
**arrive** reach one's destination
**ascend** move or climb upward
**attain** arrive at
**back off** step away from
**back-pedal** step back rapidly
**backtrack** return over course already covered
**back up** move backward
**bear down on** catch up with; approach rapidly
**beat it** *Informal*. leave hastily
**begone** depart
**betake oneself** cause oneself to go
**blast off** *Slang*. depart abruptly
**blow in** *Slang*. arrive from somewhere, esp. unexpectedly
**bolt** make sudden, hasty departure or escape
**bounce** strike a surface and rebound
**bowl along** move along smoothly and quickly
**burst forth** issue forth suddenly from spot
**bypass** circumvent (an obstacle)
**carom** strike and rebound
**cast** veer
**catch** overtake
**check out** *Informal*. depart quickly or abruptly
**circle** revolve around
**circumambulate** circle on foot, esp. ceremonially
**clear out** depart permanently or abruptly
**climb** ascend; make steady upward progress
**close in on** begin to overtake
**come** move toward something; approach; arrive at
**come about** reverse direction; tack
**come along** *Informal*. arrive
**come back** return
**come down** move from higher to lower position
**come forth** emerge
**come in** enter
**come out** emerge
**come up** move from lower to higher position
**commute** travel back and forth regularly between two points
**continue** keep on same course as before
**converge** tend or incline toward a single point
**crab** move sideways, diagonally, or obliquely, esp. with short bursts of speed

**crisscross** move in many intersecting lines across a given space
**cross** move or traverse from one side or place to another
**cruise** be on one's way; travel
**cut** move abruptly at a sharp angle
**debouch** march out into open ground from confined place, used esp. of troops
**decamp** depart from resting place, often quickly or secretly
**decline** slope downward from straight course
**deflect** turn from true course or straight line
**depart** begin a journey; go away; leave; set out
**descend** move downward
**desert** depart from someplace, often permanently
**deviate** turn aside from normal course
**diddle** move rapidly back and forth or up and down
**divagate** stray from course
**double back** return over same course
**draw away** increase distance from given place
**draw near** reduce distance from given place; approach
**ebb** recede, like the tide
**eddy** move against current; move in a circle
**edge** advance gradually; move sideways
**egress** depart
**embark** set out from a place, esp. on a voyage
**emerge** rise; appear; come forth from concealment; come out
**emigrate** leave one's native country and settle elsewhere
**enter** arrive at; come in
**evacuate** depart rapidly from an endangered place
**exit** leave; go out
**fade** drift away from focus of activity
**fall** descend freely under force of gravity
**fall back** lag
**fall down** collapse to ground
**fishtail** swerve or slide from side to side out of control while moving forward
**flinch** pull back in abrupt movement
**follow** come behind or after, moving in same direction
**ford** wade across body of water
**gain** arrive at; follow more closely
**gain ground** lessen distance between oneself and another so as to follow more closely
**get along** depart
**get going** move faster; depart
**go** move along; proceed; move on a set course, esp. depart from someplace
**go away** depart
**gravitate** move toward; tend toward
**gyrate** revolve around fixed point or on axis
**hang back** remain at some distance behind
**head** move forward toward set point; go in certain direction
**head out** *Informal*. depart
**hightail it** *Informal*. depart hastily
**hit the road** *Informal*. begin a journey; depart
**hunker down** squat or stoop on one's haunches
**immigrate** enter and settle in a foreign country
**issue forth** pass or come out from enclosed place
**jag** change direction repeatedly in irregular pattern
**jerk** move with abrupt, erratic motion
**jibe** shift suddenly from one side to the other, used esp. of ships
**jiggle** move with short jerks up and down or back and forth

**jink** move unexpectedly with abrupt turns and shifts

**juke** move evasively through obstacles; fake another out of position, esp. in football

**lag** fail to keep up; fall back

**land** attain one's destination, esp. from above

**lap** overtake another in race, increasing lead by one full circuit of course

**lead** go before others

**leave** depart

**light** arrive at and come to rest

**light out** *Slang*. depart hurriedly

**list** veer to one side

**loop** move in curves or arcs

**lose ground** follow less closely; fall farther behind

**lunge** rush forward with sudden thrust

**make tracks** *Informal*. run away; go in a hurry

**migrate** move from one country to another

**mizzle** *Brit*. depart suddenly

**mount** ascend; climb on top of

**move** go or pass from one place to another; progress

**move along** proceed in one direction

**move it** *Slang*. depart hastily and under pressure

**navigate** set one's course at sea

**negotiate** maneuver through, around, or over

**nip away** *Chiefly Brit. slang*. sneak away; leave stealthily

**outpace** exceed in speed and pass

**outstrip** get ahead of; leave behind

**overhaul** overtake

**overtake** catch up with and pass; overhaul

**pass** move; proceed; depart; move past another going in the same direction; come up to, then move beyond

**peel off** veer sharply aside from group moving in one direction

**peel out** *Informal*. depart quickly

**perambulate** travel or walk over or through

**peregrinate** wander; traverse; travel over on foot

**piss off** *Slang*. depart hastily and unceremoniously

**pitch** plunge forward, often rising up abruptly afterward

**pivot** turn in place as if on a shaft

**plummet** descend rapidly

**plunge** rush or fall violently, with headlong haste

**pounce** swoop down upon suddenly

**press on** move forward despite obstacles

**proceed** continue forward in same direction

**progress** move forward, upward, or onward

**pull back** move away from

**put about** turn in new direction

**quit** leave someplace

**radiate** proceed from or toward a center

**rappel** descend steep incline by sliding down rope passed around one's body

**rear** rise up on one's hind legs like a horse

**rebound** reverse direction; bounce back

**recede** pull back; withdraw

**recoil** draw back, esp. in alarm or disgust

**reel** fall back from a blow; recoil

**reenter** come in again

**regress** move backward

**repair** go; betake oneself

**retire** withdraw; fall back

**retract** draw back

**retreat** draw back from a dangerous situation; flee; turn tail

**return** come back to a place formerly visited

**reverse** change direction of one's movement, usu. to opposite direction

**revolve** turn in a complete circle on an axis in place

**ricochet** bounce back or off

**rise** get up or move upward

**roll** move by turning over and over

**rotate** turn in circles on central axis in place

**run away** retreat; move off rapidly

**sally forth** set out; depart

**scale** climb over

**scat** *Informal*. go away quickly, often under compulsion

**scatter** disperse in all directions

**schuss** make straight, high-speed downhill run on skis

**scram** *Informal*. depart unceremoniously and in haste

**scrooch** crouch down on one's haunches, leaning forward

**scrunch** crouch; hunker down

**scud** move or run swiftly, like a ship driven by a gale

**seesaw** move up and down or back and forth

**separate** move away from

**set foot in** enter (new region or place)

**set forth** begin a journey; leave someplace

**set off** start moving

**set out** depart; begin journey

**sheer** deviate from one's course

**shift** change place or position

**shin** draw oneself up by holding fast with hands and legs

**show up** arrive

**shunt** travel back and forth

**shuttle** move or transport to and fro

**sidestep** step around so as to avoid

**sidle** move sideways

**sink** descend slowly toward the bottom

**skedaddle** *Informal*. depart hastily and unceremoniously

**skiddoo** *Informal*. depart hastily; skedaddle

**skirt** pass around; move along the border of

**slalom** zigzag between and around obstacles

**slant** move at an angle

**slip away** retreat; depart quietly

**soar** rise up to great height

**somersault** tumble head over heels

**spin** revolve rapidly in place

**spiral** move in circles around axis

**split** *Slang*. leave; depart abruptly

**squat** crouch near ground without sitting

**stand forth** move forward

**start out** begin progress; set out

**steer** direct one's course

**steer clear of** stay away from; avoid

**step out** depart at energetic pace

**stray** wander from set course; roam about

**stretch** extend over distance in particular direction

**strike out** set out; depart

**sway** swing slowly and rhythmically to and fro

**sweep** move steadily in wide circuit or curve

**swerve** alter one's course abruptly; turn aside

**swing** move freely in wide curve; move back and forth

**swivel** turn as if on pivot

**tack** change direction, used esp. of ships

**tag along** come after someone; follow another closely

**take a powder** *Slang*. depart hurriedly, esp. without taking leave

**take off** begin to move; depart; rise up into the air

**teeter** move back and forth, esp. near an edge

**topple** fall down

**travel** move or go from one place to another; depart from current location

**traverse** move along or across, from one side to the other

**tumble** turn end over end, esp. in flight

**turn** reverse or alter direction; veer from course; rotate on axis

**turn about** veer from course

**turn back** reverse direction; retrace one's steps

**turn tail** *Informal.* retreat

**twine** wind about in twisting course

**twirl** revolve rapidly in place

**twist** follow winding course; change direction sharply

**up** *Informal.* start out abruptly

**vamoose** *Slang.* depart in haste

**vault** leap over, esp. with aid of hands or pole

**veer** change direction; turn to one side; cast

**verge** move or incline in some direction

**waggle** move from side to side shakily

**walk** *Informal.* depart, split

**wander** move without direction or purpose; roam about in irregular course

**wave** waver

**waver** sway in place; move to and fro; wave

**weave** follow zigzag or side-to-side course

**wend** proceed over long, winding course

**whirl** spin in a circle; turn rapidly in place; move or be carried along quickly

**wind** proceed by twists and turns, changing direction constantly

**windmill** move like a windmill, esp. by rotating one's arms in wide arcs

**withdraw** pull back; retreat

**wobble** proceed with unsteady, rocking motion; go clumsily in side-to-side motion

**wreathe** turn in circles or spirals

**yaw** deviate from a straight course, used esp. of ships

**yo-yo** *Informal.* move back and forth or up and down between two points

**zag** execute sharp turn

**zig** alter direction sharply

**zigzag** proceed in zigs and zags, making sharp turns first to one side, then to the other

# VERBS OF SIGHT

**SEE ALSO**: Chap. 23: Verbs of Thought; Judgment and Criticism

**admire** regard with respect or wonder

**assay** examine and evaluate

**avert one's eyes** look away to avoid another's glance or some unpleasant sight

**bat an eye** blink with surprise or emotion

**behold** gaze upon; see

**bird-dog** *Informal.* watch carefully

**blear** make one's eyes dim or watery

**blink** look glancingly; close and open one's eyes quickly

**browse** look over in a casual, leisurely manner

**canvass** examine carefully; survey entire area

**cast about** seek by looking around

**cast a glance** direct one's gaze at something

**catch sight of** become aware of; distinguish; manage to see

**check** examine carefully

**check out** examine and evaluate

**command a view of** overlook, esp. from strategic position

**compare** examine two or more items to determine differences or similarities

**contemplate** view thoughtfully and with steady attention

**descry** catch sight of; discover

**detect** note; discover the true nature of; spot

**discern** come to recognize; perceive by sight

**distinguish** single out; perceive clearly; recognize differences; spot

**draw a bead on** focus one's aim at

**drop one's eyes** lower one's eyes before another person's gaze

**envisage** visualize in a specific way

**envision** picture in one's mind

**espy** catch sight of

**examine** look over closely; inspect

**eye** view; gaze at

**eyeball** *Informal.* observe closely

**face** look at directly

**fix one's eyes on** gaze at intently

**focus** adjust one's eyes to produce a clear image at a particular range

**follow** watch the movements of

**gape** gaze dumbly, esp. with mouth open

**gawk** stare stupidly

**gaze** look at intently, eagerly, or steadily

**get a load of** *Slang.* take notice of

**give the evil eye** stare at with malicious intent

**give the once-over** scrutinize rapidly in detail, from top to bottom

**glance** look quickly

**glare** stare angrily or relentlessly

**glaze** get a blurred, glassy look in one's eyes

**glimpse** take or get a brief look at; identify quickly

**glint** glance briefly; have bright emotion in one's eyes

**gloat** observe with unpleasant, superior satisfaction

**glower** stare with brooding, sullen anger

**goggle** stare with wide, protuberant eyes

**identify** observe to establish the identity or nature of a person or thing

**inspect** examine carefully and thoroughly

**keep tabs on** watch closely or maintain surveillance on

**leer** cast a lascivious, wanton look; ogle suggestively; make eyes

**look** use one's power of vision so as to see something

**look askance at** take a sidelong glance at

**look away** avert one's eyes; turn one's eyes from object

**look daggers** glare or glower sullenly and with hostility

**look for** search

**look on** observe passively

**look out** be watchful

**look over** examine or inspect, usu. briefly

**look sideways at** glance sidelong at, usu. implying disapproval

**look up** lift one's eyes toward the sky

**look upon** view; regard; scrutinize

**make eyes at** ogle or leer at

**make out**  see and identify, esp. with difficulty
**mark**  take note of
**marvel**  gaze with amazement or curiosity
**mind**  notice; heed attentively
**monitor**  observe over time; check for specific reason
**moon**  gaze at dreamily or longingly
**note**  observe with attention
**notice**  mark with attention; take note of
**observe**  regard with attention, esp. to form judgment
**ogle**  eye amorously or lewdly; make eyes at
**overlook**  gaze down on from above; look past; fail to see
**oversee**  survey, inspect, or supervise (some activity)
**overview**  survey generally
**peek**  look quickly or furtively from a concealed place
**peep**  look cautiously or stealthily, esp. through a small opening
**peer**  gaze searchingly, with difficulty or curiosity
**perceive**  observe so as to understand; become aware of the presence of
**pick out**  distinguish one among many
**pick up**  catch sight of
**pore over**  gaze at or study intently
**preview**  view in advance
**pry**  look at carefully or inquiringly, esp. against another's will
**read**  observe so as to discern the true nature of; scan; study
**recognize**  see to be that which is already known
**reconnoiter**  appraise and examine so as to gain information
**regard**  heed with attention; look attentively
**register**  perceive; take note of
**remark**  observe with attention
**review**  view or examine again, esp. to form judgment
**rivet**  fix the eyes in a steady, intent gaze
**roll one's eyes**  shift gaze continuously; turn eyes up in sockets as sign of disapproval
**rubberneck**  *Informal.* stare with exaggerated curiosity by craning one's neck
**scan**  examine or search hastily from point to point
**scope**  *Slang.* check out; observe closely
**scour**  pass eyes over in search of something
**scout**  observe to acquire information
**scowl**  contract one's brow and glower in disapproval
**screen**  examine in detail to differentiate
**scrutinize**  inspect closely; look upon
**search**  look over carefully for purpose of discovery; look for
**see**  perceive with one's eyes; examine; recognize; watch
**seek**  search out
**set eyes on**  catch sight of, esp. for first time; look at
**sift**  pass one's eyes over so as to differentiate
**sight**  look carefully in one direction; catch sight of; aim at
**size up**  examine closely to evaluate
**skim**  pass one's eyes over swiftly; give a cursory glance to
**skirr**  search about; glance over rapidly; skim
**snoop**  look into or pry in a sly or intrusive manner
**spectate**  observe passively
**spot**  distinguish; take note of; detect
**spy**  catch sight of; observe in secret, esp. with hostile intent
**squint**  look with one's eyes partly shut
**stare**  gaze fixedly or intently, often with wide eyes
**stare down**  gaze at with fixed stare to force another back down
**study**  consider and examine carefully or in detail
**supervise**  oversee

**survey**  examine overall; inspect and evaluate
**take a gander**  *Slang.* take a look
**take note of**  observe with particular attention; spot; take notice of
**take notice of**  take note of
**take stock of**  examine and appraise
**tend**  pay close attention to; observe closely
**trace**  follow or examine carefully, in step-by-step detail
**view**  watch attentively; regard in a special light; survey or inspect
**visualize**  see and form a mental image of
**watch**  observe closely; look at; see
**watch out**  be vigilant and watchful
**wink**  close and open one eye quickly, esp. as a signal or hint
**witness**  see by personal presence or perception

# Verbs of Speech

Modes and Manners of Expression
Intonation and Inflection
Speech Sounds and Noises
Expressions of Feeling
Reasoning and Informing
Judgments Pro and Con
Questions and Answers

**SEE ALSO**: Chap. 19: Sounds and Noises; Chap. 20: Nonsense, Confusion, and Trouble; Chap. 23: Reasoning and Intuition; Judgment and Criticism

## Modes and Manners of Expression

**add**  speak further; go on to say
**affect**  feign; make a pretense to
**air**  express publicly or aloud; ventilate
**announce**  proclaim, esp. publicly; foretell; give notice of; annunciate
**annunciate**  announce
**assert**  declare forcefully as true; postulate
**babble**  talk foolishly, excessively, and unintelligibly
**banter**  address in a playful, joking, or teasing manner
**beckon**  call to; attract attention of
**bicker**  argue incessantly over petty issues
**bid**  command another's action; greet; make an offer
**blab**  reveal indiscreetly; chatter thoughtlessly
**blabber**  blab; speak foolishly
**blather**  talk foolishly
**blatter**  talk noisily and rapidly
**blither**  talk foolishly
**blurt**  utter suddenly and inadvertently
**break**  begin uttering a sound or series of sounds
**broach**  mention for first time
**bubble**  gurgle; speak excitedly
**bullshit**  *Vulgar slang.* talk nonsense, esp. intended to deceive; talk foolishly, boastfully, idly, or vulgarly; shovel shit; sling shit; wank
**burble**  babble excitedly; prattle
**call**  command or order; summon or invite
**chat**  talk informally, lightly, and familiarly

**chatter**  talk incessantly and rapidly

**chew the fat**  *Informal.* make friendly, familiar conversation; chew the rag

**chew the rag**  *Informal.* chew the fat

**chime in**  insert remark into others' conversation

**chitchat**  chat idly; gossip

**chorus**  speak in unison with others

**clam up**  cease speaking and remain silent

**command**  give an order; direct with authority

**comment**  utter brief opinion or explanation

**confab**  confabulate

**confabulate**  speak at an informal, impromptu conference; confab

**confide**  tell a secret; entrust information

**continue**  add to; resume after interruption

**converse**  hold a dialogue; speak with others

**couch**  phrase in specific language

**coze**  converse informally or familiarly

**declaim**  speak impressively or dramatically

**declare**  state firmly; announce formally and openly

**deliver**  bring forth in words; utter; enunciate

**demand**  request as if by right; insist on

**deny**  say something is untrue or does not exist; refuse to acknowledge; disown

**dictate**  order with force of authority; speak aloud for another to write down

**echo**  repeat another's words exactly

**embellish**  add entertaining details

**evoke**  call up or inspire a particular response

**exaggerate**  overstate; make unfounded claims; speak of something as greater than it is

**excuse**  pardon; justify a fault or error; release from obligation

**express**  put into words; make known; state

**falter**  stammer; speak hesitantly

**fib**  speak dishonestly; lie on unimportant issue

**footle**  *Informal.* gab foolishly

**gab**  *Informal.* chatter

**go**  *Informal.* say

**greet**  receive another in specified way, usu. upon meeting

**harangue**  make lengthy, often pompous and bombastic, speech

**harp**  speak repeatedly and tiresomely about something

**hem and haw**  speak hesitantly and evasively

**herald**  proclaim the approach of

**hesitate**  speak slowly and uncertainly, esp. with pauses

**indite**  put into words; compose

**ingeminate**  repeat

**insist**  declare or demand emphatically

**interject**  interrupt; throw in a remark

**interrupt**  stop a person in the midst of something, esp. by inserting a remark; speak while another is speaking

**introduce**  announce (a speaker); present to another to make acquainted; acquaint with a subject

**invoke**  call upon God in prayer; summon up a spirit by incantation

**issue**  send out; put forth, usu. officially; state

**iterate**  repeat

**jabber**  talk rapidly and unintelligibly

**jaw**  *Slang.* talk; scold

**jive**  *Slang.* attempt to deceive through fast talk; talk foolishly and unintelligibly; use hip jargon, esp. of jazz

**kibitz**  *Informal.* offer unsought advice; make unsolicited comments

**lie**  tell an untruth; deceive another

**maintain**  assert as true; affirm in agreement

**maunder**  ramble; mumble incoherently

**mention**  speak of briefly; refer to by name

**mimic**  imitate another's speech; repeat words exactly

**muster**  summon; call

**narrate**  give an account of; recount events; tell a story

**natter**  chatter

**note**  remark upon; speak of attentively

**observe**  remark; take note of

**orate**  speak pompously; make a formal speech

**order**  command; ask for

**outspeak**  speak frankly or boldly; excel in speaking

**overstate**  exaggerate

**page**  summon by calling name

**palaver**  chatter idly; talk aimlessly and profusely

**parody**  mimic humorously

**parrot**  mimic or imitate; repeat words mechanically

**pass**  change the subject of conversation

**patter**  speak rapidly and mechanically; employ the glib, rapid speech of salesman or comedian

**perorate**  deliver lengthy, rhetorical speech

**persist**  continue to repeat or press an opinion

**phrase**  express in words or in appropriate terms

**piffle**  *Informal.* talk nonsense

**pipe up**  begin talking

**pontificate**  speak pompously, pretentiously, and dogmatically

**portray**  describe in words; represent verbally

**prattle**  chatter childishly

**predict**  forecast or prophesy

**present**  introduce one to another; bring before the public; bring formal charge in court

**prevaricate**  speak evasively; lie

**proclaim**  declare loudly; announce officially

**profess**  claim; pretend

**promise**  declare that one will or will not do something

**prompt**  incite to action; assist with words

**prophesy**  predict with assurance based on mystical knowledge; speak as if divinely inspired; vaticinate

**put it**  state something in particular way

**quip**  utter witty or sarcastic remark

**quote**  repeat exact words of

**ramble**  talk disconnectedly at length; wander from the subject

**rap**  *Slang.* talk, esp. freely and openly

**rattle**  ramble quickly and obliviously; chatter incessantly

**recount**  narrate story; tell in detail

**rede**  *Chiefly Brit.* give counsel, advise; interpret, explain

**reel off**  list rapidly

**refer**  allude to; call attention to

**regale**  entertain with stories

**rehash**  express old material in new form with little change

**reiterate**  say again or repeatedly

**relate**  narrate; tell in detail

**remark**  say; comment on

**repeat**  say again; say something said by another; say over; ingeminate; iterate

**require**  order or oblige to do something; claim by right or authority

**say**  express in words; state opinion or belief; utter or pronounce

**schmooze**  *Slang.* gossip and chat familiarly, esp. to endear oneself

**sermonize** give long, moralizing talk

**shoot off one's mouth** talk too freely or indiscreetly

**shoot the breeze** chat casually

**shovel shit** *Vulgar slang.* talk nonsense, esp. to deceive; bullshit

**simper** say with a weak, silly smile

**sling shit** *Vulgar slang.* bullshit

**slobber** fawn over; speak with spittle running from one's mouth

**smatter** speak words of a language with little or no knowledge of the language

**sneer** speak with upper lip curled, usu. contemptuously

**soft-pedal** *Informal.* de-emphasize or avoid stressing

**soliloquize** utter one's thoughts without addressing anyone, esp. in stage performance

**sound** utter or pronounce

**speak** utter words to express something; make a public speech; converse politely; use one particular language to communicate

**speak out** speak loudly, freely, and frankly

**spell out** name letters of word aloud in order; explain methodically

**spiel** *Informal.* talk glibly and at length, esp. to persuade

**spit it out** say what is on one's mind without delay

**squib** utter in an offhand manner; speak in brief, satiric bits

**state** express in words; declare; report particulars of

**stretch** exaggerate or extend beyond the truth

**stumble** make blunders in speech; speak haltingly and awkwardly

**summon** send for; call together; call upon

**swear** promise on an oath; state emphatically; curse

**talk** convey or exchange ideas or information with spoken words; express, utter, or discuss in words; have the power of speech; use one particular language to communicate

**talk down** silence another by speaking loudly and persistently

**tell** inform; reveal

**title** provide a name for

**touch on** mention briefly

**trifle** talk frivolously; toy with; treat casually

**turn a phrase** speak gracefully and precisely

**twaddle** talk nonsense

**twitter** talk rapidly, in an anxious manner

**utter** make a sound with the mouth, esp. a word

**vaticinate** prophesy

**ventilate** air

**venture** dare to utter; suggest

**verbalize** put into words

**vocalize** express aloud in words; use one's voice in speech or song

**voice** express in words; utter aloud; pronounce

**vouchsafe** grant in gracious or condescending manner

**vow** promise solemnly

**waffle** talk vaguely, indecisively, and evasively

**wank** *Vulgar slang.* speak foolishly and boastfully; bullshit

**warn** inform of danger; advise of action to avert danger

**warrant** guarantee or assure

**wrangle** argue, quarrel noisily or angrily

**yabber** *Australian.* talk foolishly; jabber

**yak** *Slang.* chatter persistently and foolishly

**yammer** *Informal.* persist in talking loudly; wail; grumble

**yarn** tell tales, esp. invented and grandiose ones

## Intonation and Inflection

**accent** stress (a particular sound or syllable)

**articulate** utter distinctly; give clear expression to

**bawl** cry loudly

**bellow** roar; speak in a loud, deep voice

**belt** *Informal.* sing out loudly

**blare** utter raucously and noisily

**blubber** weep noisily

**bray** cry harshly, like a donkey

**breathe** whisper; speak softly

**buzz** hum, like a bee; murmur or whisper; speak dully and continuously

**cachinnate** laugh loudly or excessively

**cackle** laugh shrilly, with sound like a hen's

**call** speak loudly and distinctly, so as to be heard at a distance

**cant** talk or beg in whining singsong

**catcall** express disapproval loudly

**caterwaul** cry out harshly; quarrel noisily

**chant** recite in monotonous, repetitive tones

**cheer** encourage or applaud with shouts

**chuff** make noisy explanations or grunts

**chunter** *Brit. informal.* talk in a low, inarticulate way; mutter

**clatter** talk noisily

**croon** sing sweetly and softly

**cry** shout shrilly; call out like an animal

**devoice** pronounce a formerly voiced sound without vibration of vocal cords

**drawl** speak slowly, usu. prolonging vowels

**drone** make sustained murmur or humming sound; utter at length in monotonous tone

**enounce** pronounce distinctly; articulate

**enunciate** pronounce words clearly and distinctly

**gabble** talk quickly and indistinctly

**groan** make long, deep sound of pain, grief, or disapproval

**growl** make low, threatening, animal-like sound

**grumble** make low, unintelligible sounds in throat

**hammer** make point emphatically and repeatedly

**holler** shout

**hoot** cry out in scorn or disapproval with long "o" sound, like an owl

**howl** utter long, wailing cry, like a dog's, in amusement, pain, or scorn; weep loudly; yowl

**incant** utter magical words or sounds

**inflect** alter tone or pitch of speaking voice

**intone** recite as a chant, esp. in monotone

**jabber** chatter, like a monkey

**keen** utter high, wailing tones

**lilt** speak in light, pleasant rhythm

**mince** speak affectedly, esp. to appear refined

**mispronounce** utter word sounds incorrectly

**moan** emit or speak with low, mournful, inarticulate sound of pain or suffering

**modulate** vary pitch or tone of voice, esp. to softer level

**mouth** form words with lips only; declaim with exaggerated distinction

**mumble** speak indistinctly

**murmur** speak in low voice with continuous sound

**mutter** utter subdued grumbles, often in low, unclear tones

**nasalize** speak with a twang, as though pushing voice through one's nose

**proclaim** declare loudly

**pronounce** utter distinctly, correctly, or in a particular way

**pule** whimper softly and plaintively

**raise one's voice** speak loudly; shout

**rasp** speak in rough, grating voice

**rhyme** speak in words with identical sounds, esp. at end of lines of speech

**roar** utter long, deep, loud sound, like a lion's; laugh loudly

**roll off one's tongue** be uttered eloquently, smoothly, and glibly

**rumble** utter with heavy, deep, rolling sound

**scream** utter a sudden, sharp, loud cry

**screech** utter a high, shrill, piercing cry, esp. in terror or pain

**shout** speak loudly, esp. to attract attention or to express strong emotion; holler; yell

**shriek** utter a shrill cry or scream

**shrill** utter in high, thin, piercing tone

**sigh** utter a long, audible exhalation expressing grief, exhaustion, or relief

**sing** speak in musical sounds and rhythm, esp. to set melody

**slur** pronounce indistinctly, running sounds together

**snarl** growl angrily, esp. with bared teeth, like a beast

**sob** utter through uneven breaths caused by heavy weeping

**speak up** speak more loudly

**splutter** speak rapidly and indistinctly, esp. with rapid series of spitting sounds; sputter

**sputter** speak in series of quick, explosive sounds; splutter

**squeak** speak in a high-pitched cry

**squeal** speak with a long, shrill crying sound, like a pig

**stammer** speak with a series of involuntary pauses or rapid repetitions of one syllable

**stress** place accent on particular syllable

**stutter** suffer involuntary disruption of speech, esp. repeating first consonant sound of words

**sustain** prolong sound of word

**susurrate** whisper

**tongue** produce speech effects with one's tongue; sound certain words

**trill** speak with vibrating sound in one's voice, like a bird's song

**troll** sing in carefree, jovial way

**trumpet** proclaim in bright, rising tone

**twang** speak with nasal intonation

**ululate** howl or wail; hoot

**wail** utter a long, sad cry

**warble** sing with a gentle trilling sound, like bird's song

**whimper** make feeble frightened or complaining sounds; whine softly

**whine** make a long, high, complaining cry

**whisper** speak softly, using breath but not vocal cords

**whoop** utter a loud, excited cry; holler

**yammer** persist in talking loudly; wail; grumble

**yell** shout

**yowl** howl

## SPEECH SOUNDS AND NOISES

**bark** cry out sharply and gruffly, like a dog

**bay** howl; make a prolonged barking noise

**bell** speak in ringing tones, resembling a bell's

**blat** make sharp, loud noise

**bleat** cry pathetically, like a sheep

**boo** utter a long exclamation of disapproval by sounding the syllable "boo'

**boom** make prolonged, deep, resonant sound

**caw** utter harsh, raucous call, like a crow's

**cheep** utter faint, shrill sound, like a bird's

**chirp** emit short, sharp sound, like a bird's

**chitter** twitter

**clack** chatter; prattle; make abrupt, sharp sound

**cluck** utter throaty cry or laugh, like a hen's

**coo** make soft, murmuring sound

**cough** emit sharp, rasping sound from the chest

**crack** emit sharp, sudden, explosive sound

**croak** make deep, hoarse sound, like a frog's

**crow** make loud, shrill cry, like a crow

**gargle** make sound like liquid bubbling in throat

**gasp** speak with sudden, short intakes of breath, esp. out of fear or shock

**gibber** make meaningless, unintelligible sounds, esp. in fear

**giggle** laugh in silly, nervous way, often shrilly

**gobble** speak with guttural sound, like a turkey

**grunt** make gruff, snorting sound, like a pig

**gulp** suppress words by swallowing hard; choke or gasp for air; swallow hard in shock or fear

**gurgle** make low, bubbling sound in throat

**hawk** clear throat noisily

**hem** make sound of clearing throat, esp. while searching for words

**hiss** speak, esp. expressing disapproval, with prolonged "s" sound, like a snake

**huff** blow or bluster, esp. in annoyance; breathe heavily

**hum** utter prolonged "m" sound; drone like an insect

**lisp** speak defectively, with "s" and "z" sounds pronounced as "th'

**mew** speak weakly, with a cry like a cat's

**mewl** cry weakly; whimper

**moo** emit low, deep sound, like a cow

**neigh** make long, high-pitched cry, like a horse

**oink** make grunting sound, like a pig

**peep** make high, weak, chirping sound, like a bird

**puff** emit short, light exhalations; breathe hard

**purr** make low, soothing, vibrating sound, like a cat

**quack** utter harsh cry, like a duck

**roll** emit deep, prolonged sound, like a drum's

**scat** improvise nonsense syllables, esp. to jazz

**snap** make sharp cracking sound

**sniffle** speak while repeatedly drawing air up into nose

**snuffle** speak with noisy sniffs through partly blocked nose

**squall** utter harsh cry or scream, esp. like a baby

**squawk** utter loud, harsh cry, like a bird

**titter** giggle with high-pitched sound

**twitter** make a rapid series of light, chirping sounds, like a bird's; chitter

**wheeze** speak with audible hoarse whistling sound from the chest

**whinny** speak with low, gentle neighing sound, like a horse would make

**yap** bark shrilly, like a dog

**yelp** utter sharp, shrill cry or bark, like a dog's; yip

**yip** yelp

**yodel** utter prolonged musical call, with voice alternating between falsetto and normal pitch

**zing** utter high-pitched, shrill sound

# EXPRESSIONS OF FEELING

**avow** declare openly or assuredly

**bait** tease; torment maliciously

**bellyache** *Informal.* complain or find fault peevishly

**bemoan** complain; express regret

**bewail** express sorrow over; cry about

**bitch** *Slang.* complain noisily and incessantly; rag

**blarney** flatter, wheedle, or con

**bluster** boast; talk loudly or boisterously

**boast** exaggerate oneself; speak with unwarranted pride; vaunt

**brabble** squabble; argue noisily

**burst out** express suddenly with feeling

**chaff** tease good-naturedly; banter

**cheer** encourage or applaud with shouts

**chortle** laugh loudly and gleefully

**chuckle** laugh quietly, half suppressing the laughter

**clamor** protest or demand loudly

**complain** express dissatisfaction or pain; find fault; protest wrongs; gripe; grouse; squawk

**confess** admit to sins, errors, or weaknesses; state one's attitude reluctantly

**crack** make a joke; wisecrack

**crow** express gleeful triumph

**cry** call out in pain or grief; emit a loud, wordless expression of grief

**curse** exclaim violently in anger; call evil upon another; utter oath or obscenity; cuss

**cuss** *Informal.* curse

**dish** *Slang.* gossip nastily

**enthuse** express with enthusiasm

**exclaim** cry out suddenly from pain, pleasure, or surprise

**exhort** urge on energetically

**exult** rejoice greatly

**fume** seethe and splutter angrily

**gam** engage in friendly conversation

**gibe** jeer or ridicule

**giggle** laugh in silly, nervous way

**greet** speak in a friendly or respectful manner, esp. upon meeting

**gripe** complain

**groan** make long, deep sound of pain, grief, or disapproval

**grouse** complain

**grumble** complain with ill temper; grump

**grump** grumble

**gush** talk with extravagant enthusiasm or flattery, esp. in an affected manner

**harass** attack or annoy repeatedly

**heckle** interrupt and harass a public speaker

**howl** utter long, wailing cry in amusement, pain, or scorn; weep loudly

**hurl** utter vehemently, esp. abuse or curses

**hype** exaggerate merits of; mislead by sensationalizing

**imprecate** utter curses; invoke evil

**insult** speak ill so as to hurt another's feelings or arouse anger; treat with insolence or contempt

**jape** joke

**jeer** shout at rudely or scornfully

**jest** joke, esp. lightly

**joke** make humorous remarks; poke fun at; make light of; jape; jest

**jolly** keep another in good humor to win cooperation

**josh** joke, tease, or kid

**kid** tease; deceive in fun

**lament** express great sorrow or regret

**lash out** attack violently; hurl insults

**laugh** utter sound of mirth with a smile and expulsion of air

**moan** emit or speak with low, mournful, inarticulate sound in pain or suffering

**needle** annoy; provoke intentionally

**obsess** speak of continuously and at undue length

**paint** describe in vivid detail

**pledge** promise solemnly

**pop off** *Informal.* speak loudly or indiscreetly; express anger

**pour out** express freely

**preach** deliver a public religious address; urge people to adopt certain moral ways, esp. in an obtrusive manner

**profess** declare openly or affirm, esp. one's belief

**promise** vow or pledge to do or not do something; declare emphatically

**protest** express disagreement or disapproval; declare firmly

**psych** *Informal.* arouse to action, urge on, or inspire, esp. oneself

**quip** utter clever or witty remark

**rag** *Informal.* complain incessantly; bitch

**rage** talk angrily or wildly; rave

**rail** speak loudly or insistently; scold harshly; complain bitterly

**rally** rouse; urge on

**rant** speak loudly, violently, and theatrically

**rave** talk wildly, furiously, and nonsensically; speak about with great admiration; rage

**razz** tease or ridicule good-naturedly

**reassure** restore confidence; remove fears of

**refuse** express unwillingness to do something

**regret** express sorrow over loss; state disappointment, repentance, or annoyance

**renounce** reject; refuse to abide by; formally give up claim

**repent** express regret over one's actions

**repine** fret; express discontent or longing

**repudiate** deny; disown utterly; reject

**rhapsodize** speak of ecstatically

**rib** tease

**ridicule** make fun of; laugh at another's weaknesses or faults, esp. in malicious, scornful way

**rip** tear apart verbally; utter violently; spit out

**rouse** urge on, awaken, or excite

**sass** speak rudely or impertinently

**scoff** express scorn, derision, or contempt

**scorn** reject as unworthy or contemptible; express contempt

**scream** utter a sudden, sharp, loud cry; express intense hysteria

**share** describe something so that others may experience it

**sigh** utter a long, audible exhalation expressing grief, exhaustion, or relief

**simper** utter weakly or sadly

**slash** speak of cuttingly or harshly

**slight** insult by discourtesy or lack of respect

**snap** speak with sudden irritation

**snarl** speak in a bad-tempered manner

**sneer** express scorn or contempt, esp. with curled upper lip

**snicker** giggle slyly; laugh at covertly, in a suppressed manner; snigger

**snigger**  snicker

**snivel**  cry miserably; complain with a whine

**snub**  speak unkindly or scornfully to reject or humiliate another

**sob**  utter through uneven breaths caused by heavy weeping

**spit**  utter violently, often while saliva is ejected from mouth

**spout**  gush forth; speak at length

**spur**  urge on, arouse, or incite

**squawk**  complain

**squeal**  protest sharply, esp. in long, loud, high cry

**swear**  promise on an oath; state emphatically; curse; use profanity

**sweet-talk**  Informal. flatter

**talk back**  reply defiantly

**talk down**  speak condescendingly

**taunt**  try to provoke with scorn or criticism; jeer at

**tease**  try to provoke playfully by jokes, questions, or sarcasm

**threaten**  express intention to punish or harm another

**unburden oneself**  confess to relieve one's conscience

**unleash**  make (unrestrained verbal assault); let loose (a torrent of words)

**unload**  release one's emotions through words

**urge**  encourage; try hard to persuade; recommend strongly

**vaunt**  boast

**vent**  give verbal outlet to, esp. one's feelings

**wail**  utter long, sad cry; lament or complain persistently

**weep**  express sadness or sorrow by shedding tears; cry at length

**welcome**  greet with pleasure or ceremony

**whimper**  make feeble, frightened, complaining sounds; whine softly

**whine**  complain in petty, feeble way

**wisecrack**  make witty, clever remarks

**wish**  express one's desire, aim, or hope

**yawn**  express boredom by inhaling deeply with mouth wide open

**yawp**  squawk noisily; clamor; complain

**yowl**  utter loud, wailing cry; howl

## REASONING AND INFORMING

**accent**  stress or emphasize

**advise**  counsel; warn; recommend

**allege**  assert without proof; give as reason or excuse

**allude**  refer to indirectly

**apprise**  inform; give notice

**attest**  affirm to be true; bear witness or testify

**attribute**  assign cause, characteristic, or origin to

**bandy**  exchange comments, esp. argumentatively

**beat around the bush**  speak evasively; wander from subject to subject

**belabor**  make a point to absurd lengths

**break the news**  make something known

**cajole**  persuade by flattery

**cant**  speak hypocritically

**chaffer**  bargain for; haggle over

**chew over**  discuss at length

**clarify**  explain or make understandable

**clear the air**  speak openly to remove hostility, tension, or confusion

**coax**  persuade gently

**collogue**  confer privately

**communicate**  succeed in conveying information or feelings; transmit; make known

**con**  Informal. persuade after gaining confidence

**confer**  discuss with others

**confide**  tell a secret; entrust information

**constate**  assert positively

**contend**  assert or argue a point

**contrast**  compare or appraise differences

**convey**  impart information; communicate

**convince**  persuade by argument; overcome doubts

**counsel**  advise, esp. professionally

**decree**  order based on lawful authority

**define**  state or explain precisely, esp. meaning of word or thing

**delineate**  describe clearly in accurate detail

**depict**  describe

**describe**  set forth the nature of something; depict

**disclose**  reveal or make known

**discourse**  speak extensively on same subject; lecture

**discuss**  talk about with others; examine by means of argument

**divulge**  reveal something unknown

**elucidate**  clarify; explain

**emphasize**  stress the importance of

**enounce**  state as a proposition

**equivocate**  speak ambiguously to conceal truth or avoid commitment

**explain**  show meaning of, make clear; state reasons for

**expound**  explain in detail

**fill in**  inform more fully; provide additional information

**get across**  make one's point clear

**get over**  get across; convince another

**gloss over**  cover up, esp. a mistake

**gossip**  reveal personal or sensational facts; spread rumors

**hash over**  discuss further, esp. when already settled

**hint**  suggest; refer to indirectly

**hold forth**  speak at length; lecture about

**illustrate**  explain by giving examples

**imply**  suggest indirectly, hint at

**import**  imply; indicate

**impute**  attribute or ascribe

**induce**  persuade

**inform**  provide information

**insinuate**  imply or hint, esp. artfully or unpleasantly

**instruct**  inform; teach another; direct or command

**interpret**  explain meaning of; analyze; translate speech to another language

**itemize**  state in list form

**lay down**  assert, allege; set down, impose

**lecture**  discuss formally and at length, often before a group

**limn**  describe, portray

**list**  state as a series of names or items

**name**  mention specifically; provide the word that designates something

**narrate**  give an account of; tell a story

**notify**  inform; report on; make known

**offer**  propose or suggest; declare oneself ready

**open**  broach subject; declare ceremoniously

**outtalk**  surpass verbally; get the better of in talking

**parley**  discuss or confer, esp. with enemies or to settle dispute

**persuade**  convince by reasoning; induce

**philosophize** speak thoughtfully on moral issues

**pitch** attempt to sell by persuasion

**plead** make an appeal or entreaty; address court as an advocate

**postulate** state as true as the basis for reasoning

**powwow** *Informal.* discuss in group or at conference

**preface** introduce; lead up to

**prelect** discourse formally and publicly; lecture

**prescribe** lay down a course to follow

**proffer** propose; offer

**propagate** transmit or spread widely; publicize

**propose** offer for consideration; declare as one's plan

**proselytize** try intensely to convert others to one's point of view

**psychologize** analyze motives and feelings of oneself or others

**read** utter written words aloud; interpret

**reason** discuss calmly and thoughtfully

**rebut** refute; disprove

**recant** formally withdraw one's former statement

**recap** recapitulate

**recapitulate** state again, esp. main points of discussion; recap

**recite** state in order, esp. facts; repeat aloud from memory

**recount** tell in detail; narrate

**refute** prove a statement wrong

**relate** narrate; tell in detail

**relay** pass on a message or information

**repeat** tell another what one has heard or learned

**report** give an account of; describe as news

**represent** describe as; declare to be

**resolve** settle an issue

**restate** say again, often in altered form

**retell** inform of again; narrate again

**retract** withdraw statement or opinion; unsay

**reveal** make known; uncover

**snitch** *Informal.* give incriminating information against; inform on

**specify** mention or state in detail

**spell out** explain explicitly; detail unmistakably

**spill** *Informal.* divulge or reveal

**spill one's guts** *Informal.* reveal one's inner emotions or deepest secrets

**spill the beans** *Informal.* disclose a secret, either accidentally or imprudently, esp. so as to ruin a surprise or plan

**squeal** *Slang.* inform on

**stipulate** insist on as part of agreement

**stress** emphasize a point

**submit** offer or propose for consideration; contend

**suggest** propose for consideration

**summarize** list key points of; sum up; synopsize

**sum up** summarize; state essentials of

**sustain** confirm; uphold validity of

**sway** influence

**synopsize** summarize

**take back** withdraw or deny earlier statement

**talk into** persuade to do or think something

**talk out of** discourage from doing or thinking something

**talk over** discuss; review

**talk sense** speak reasonably

**talk turkey** *Informal.* speak frankly

**tattle** reveal another's secrets, esp. misbehavior; gossip

**tell** inform; reveal

**tell all** reveal everything, including secret information

**testify** express personal conviction; attest to; bear witness, esp. in court

**transmit** convey to another, esp. information

**treat** deal with some subject; discuss

**typify** represent in essentials common to a group

**understate** describe in restrained terms; represent something as less than it is

**unsay** retract

**unswear** retract; recant on an oath

**unveil** disclose or make known publicly

**validate** confirm truth of

**verify** check or confirm truth of

**voice** express a given position or point of view

**vouch** guarantee certainty or accuracy of

**wheedle** persuade or obtain by coaxing and flattery

**withdraw** take back an earlier statement

**witness** testify or attest to, esp. in court

**word** phrase carefully; select words that best express something

**work in** find place for something in conversation

## Judgments Pro and Con

**acknowledge** recognize as valid

**affirm** validate or confirm; state positively

**agree** accept; concede as true; assent

**animadvert** make critical remarks

**argue** dispute or contend; give reasons pro or con; discuss; give evidence for or against

**assent** agree

**attack** criticize with great vigor; denounce

**aver** assert in pleading; verify

**avouch** declare as a matter of fact; confirm; acknowledge; confess

**backbite** say mean or spiteful things

**bad-mouth** *Slang.* criticize severely

**barrage** subject to repeated verbal attacks

**belittle** speak slightingly of; disparage; decry

**berate** scold vigorously and repeatedly

**carp** complain about; find fault with

**castigate** criticize severely, esp. as punishment

**comminate** denounce

**complain** express dissatisfaction or disapproval

**concur** approve; express agreement

**confront** face boldly; take opposing position

**contradict** disagree or state opposition, esp. in an arbitrary, impatient manner

**criticize** comment unfavorably; express judgment on; discuss critically

**decry** belittle

**demur** object mildly

**denigrate** sneer at; blacken the reputation of

**denounce** speak against; accuse; proclaim publicly to be guilty or evil; comminate

**deplore** regret deeply; express shock or distaste over

**discredit** damage reputation of; cause to be disbelieved

**disparage** belittle

**dispute** argue, debate; quarrel; question truth of

**dissuade** persuade against; alter another's opinion

**espouse** support position or cause

**execrate** declare to be evil

**flatter** compliment excessively, esp. to gain favor

**fulminate** utter with denunciation; issue censure or invective

**fuss** complain vigorously or pettily

**hector** intimidate with bullying attacks; bluster

**judge** state one's considered opinion on, esp. critical opinion

**laud** praise

**lecture** address another reprovingly, esp. to correct faults

**make fun of** ridicule, esp. jokingly

**malign** say unpleasant and untrue things about; castigate

**mock** scoff or jeer contemptuously; ridicule by mimicry of speech

**moralize** speak of right and wrong conduct

**nag** complain or find fault incessantly

**niggle** find fault in petty way; fuss over details

**object** express disfavor; protest or disagree

**opine** express judgment

**poke fun at** ridicule or tease

**praise** speak highly of and express approval; laud

**profane** speak of irreverently and disrespectfully

**promote** publicize; speak well of

**put down** *Informal.* criticize harshly; ridicule

**question** express doubt about

**quibble** raise petty objections

**rate** scold angrily

**rebuke** scold sharply; reprove

**recommend** advise an action; endorse; praise one to another

**remonstrate** protest; complain

**reprehend** rebuke; blame

**reprimand** rebuke, esp. formally

**reproach** express disapproval of another's fault

**reprove** condemn for a fault or offense

**revile** criticize angrily and abusively

**ridicule** make fun of another's faults, esp. in scorn

**salute** express respect or admiration for

**scandalize** slander, defame, or speak maliciously of

**scold** rebuke or censure severely; find fault with noisily

**score** berate; denounce

**slander** utter false statements damaging to another's reputation

**slash** criticize cuttingly and harshly

**slur** speak ill of

**smirch** discredit another's reputation

**sound off** *Informal.* express opinions loudly and freely

**speak one's mind** express opinions frankly; speak one's piece

**speak one's piece** speak one's mind

**speculate** express an opinion without knowledge

**support** state one's approval of; corroborate

**talk up** discuss favorably; promote

**tout** praise highly

**trash** *Informal.* subject to invective or harsh criticism; attack

**upbraid** reproach; criticize

**vilify** speak evil about

**vindicate** clear of blame or suspicion; prove to be valid

**vote** give formal expression of one's opinion or choice

**wig** *Brit. informal.* rebuke

**zing** *Slang.* criticize harshly

## QUESTIONS AND ANSWERS

**acknowledge** admit agreement with

**admit** concede as true; acknowledge; allow

**allow** *Informal.* suppose to be; admit

**answer** respond to question or accusation; reply

**appeal** request earnestly; ask for corroboration or vindication

**ask** call for an answer; put a question to; request; invite

**ask about** pose question on

**badger** question persistently

**beg** ask for earnestly and humbly; evade; sidestep

**beseech** beg for earnestly; implore

**come back** respond; answer quickly

**concede** admit truth of something; admit defeat

**confess** admit to sins, errors, or weaknesses

**consult** seek advice or opinion of

**cross-examine** pose a series of questions, esp. to court witness

**cross-question** *Chiefly Brit.* cross-examine

**demand** request as if by right; insist on

**deny** refuse to acknowledge

**divulge** reveal something unknown

**entreat** beg, implore

**examine** inquire into; ask questions of

**explain** elaborate on a brief answer

**grant** admit that something is true

**grill** question intensely at length

**impetrate** ask for; entreat

**implore** request earnestly, beg for

**importune** request persistently

**inquire** ask, question; investigate; also, *esp. Brit.*, enquire

**interrogate** question, esp. formally and at length

**investigate** inquire systematically in close examination

**invite** ask another for comments or to do something

**offer** propose or suggest an answer

**pester** annoy with frequent requests or questions

**petition** request earnestly and formally

**plead** make an appeal or entreaty

**pose** state a question

**pray** entreat someone, esp. God

**press** demand insistently; urge or pressure; beseech

**proffer** offer, esp. in answer

**pry** inquire into, often furtively or impertinently

**pump** question persistently for information

**put a question to** ask; inquire

**query** ask a question; express doubt

**question** ask for information; seek or demand an answer

**quiz** question or examine briefly or rapidly

**react** respond to a question

**rebut** prove false or oppose by evidence or argument

**refuse** deny request or demand; answer "no'

**rejoin** reply sharply or critically

**reply** answer

**request** ask for something

**respond** answer, esp. a specific question

**retort** answer, esp. with quick, witty, or angry reply; riposte

**retract** change or withdraw statement or opinion; unsay

**riddle** pose question that is both amusing and puzzling

**riposte** retort

**supplicate** ask for humbly; beseech

**talk back** answer or respond defiantly

**temporize** evade direct answer, esp. to gain time
**testify** bear witness, esp. in court
**unsay** retract, esp. a previous statement

# Sounds and Noises

Sound, Hearing, and Deafness
Actual Sounds
Descriptions of Sounds
Speech Sounds
Comic Sound Effects

**SEE ALSO**: Chap. 1: Anatomy; Medical Problems; Chap. 4: Physics; Chap. 15: Classical Music; Chap. 18: Grammar, Phonetics, and Linguistics; Chap. 19: Verbs of Speech; Chap. 20: Exclamations; Nonsense, Confusion, and Trouble

## Sound, Hearing, and Deafness

**acoustic** (adj) pertaining to the sense or organs of hearing or to sound
**acoustics** branch of physics that deals with sound and sound waves
**attend** (vb) listen to
**audio** (adj) pertaining to transmission, reception, or reproduction of sound
**audiology** study of hearing disorders and rehabilitation of those with hearing impairments
**audiometer** instrument for recording acuity of hearing
**audition** act, sense, or power of hearing
**auditory** (adj) pertaining to hearing, sense of hearing, or organs of hearing; perceived through the sense of hearing
**aural** (adj) pertaining to the ear or sense of hearing; auricular
**auricular** (adj) perceived by the ear; aural
**babel** confused mixture of sounds or noises
**be all ears** listen with all one's attention
**bend an ear** listen attentively; give ear
**bug** hidden, electronic listening device
**cacophony** harsh discordance of sound; dissonance
**clamor** loud and continuous noise
**closed-captioned** (adj) designating television program broadcast with captions visible with use of a decoder, intended for the hearing-impaired
**consonance** harmony of sounds
**deaf** (adj) partially or wholly deprived of sense of hearing
**deaf-mute** person who is unable to hear or speak
**decibel** unit of measure used to express differences in power in acoustics, designating degree of loudness
**din** loud, confused, continuous noise
**discord** inharmonious or confused combination of sounds; harsh noise; dissonance
**dissonance** inharmonious or harsh sound; cacophony; discord
**dumb** (adj) mute
**ear** organ of hearing in human beings and other vertebrates; sense of hearing
**earshot** distance within which a sound or voice can be heard

**eavesdrop** (vb) listen secretly to a private conversation
**euphony** agreeableness of sound, esp. harmonious or pleasant sounding combinations of tones
**faint** (adj) lacking loudness
**frequency** number of cycles per unit time of a sound wave, determining its pitch
**give ear** listen carefully; bend an ear
**hard-of-hearing** (adj) hearing-impaired
**hark** (vb) listen attentively
**harmony** pleasing combination of tones
**hear** (vb) perceive sounds by the ear; listen to; have the faculty of perceiving sound vibrations
**hearing** sense by which sounds are perceived; act of perceiving sound
**hearing aid** compact electronic amplifier, usu. placed behind one's ear to improve hearing
**hearing-impaired** (adj) having reduced or deficient hearing ability; hard-of-hearing
**hertz** unit of frequency equal to one cycle per second
**hush** silence or quiet, esp. after noise; (vb) make silent
**inaudible** (adj) incapable of being heard
**lend an ear** listen carefully
**listen** (vb) give attention with the ear for purpose of hearing; wait attentively in expectation of perceiving a sound
**listen in** (vb) overhear; eavesdrop
**loud** (adj) designating a sound or tone having exceptional volume; noisy or clamorous
**loudness** measure of a sound's intensity, independent of its pitch and timbre
**lull** temporary quiet or stillness; soothing sound
**muffle** (vb) deaden sound, esp. by wrapping that which is producing it
**mum** (adj) silent
**mute** (adj) silent, esp. refraining from speech; not emitting sound; incapable of speech, dumb
**noise** sound, esp. loud, harsh, or confused one; clamor
**noisy** (adj) making much noise; loud
**otology** study and treatment of diseases of the ear
**overhear** (vb) hear, esp. speech, without speaker's intention or knowledge; eavesdrop; listen in
**pitch** degree of height or depth of a tone or sound, depending on the relative rapidity of its frequency
**prick up one's ears** listen attentively
**quiet** (adj) making little or no sound or noise; silent
**racket** loud, disturbing noise or uproar; clamor; din
**register** tonal range of a voice, instrument, or sound-producing device
**resonance** prolongation of sound by reflection or reverberation; characteristic quality of a particular voiced sound
**resonant** (adj) deep and full of resonance; sonorous
**resonate** (vb) resound
**resound** (vb) echo or ring with sound; sound loudly; resonate
**reverberate** (vb) reecho, resound; be reflected repeatedly, as sound waves from walls of a confined space
**ring** (vb) give forth a clear, resonant sound; resound or reverberate
**sibilation** hissing sound
**silence** absence of sound; stillness
**soft** (adj) designating sound or tone having very little volume; low or subdued in noise level
**sonant** (adj) sounding; having sound
**sonic** (adj) pertaining to sound

LANGUAGE

**19. ACTION AND SENSE WORDS**
SOUNDS AND NOISES
ACTUAL SOUNDS / DESCRIPTIONS OF SOUNDS / SPEECH SOUNDS / COMIC SOUND EFFECTS

**sonority**  condition of being resonant or sonorous

**sonorous**  resonating with sound; loud and deep-toned; rich and full in sound

**sound**  sensation produced by stimulation of organs of hearing by vibrations transmitted through air or other medium; mechanical vibrations transmitted through an elastic medium that produce stimulation of organs of hearing; particular auditory effect thus produced; any noise, vocal utterance, or musical tone; (*vb*) make or emit a sound

**soundproof**  (*adj*) impervious to sound

**still**  (*adj*) free from sound or noise; silent; subdued or hushed in sound

**stone-deaf**  (*adj*) totally deaf

**stridor**  harsh, grating, or creaking sound

**timbre**  characteristic quality of a sound, independent of its pitch and loudness

**tone**  any sound considered with reference to its pitch, strength, timbre, and source; quality of a sound

**tone-deaf**  (*adj*) unable to distinguish differences in pitch in musical tones

**turn a deaf ear to**  refuse to listen to

**ultrasound**  sound with frequency greater than 20,000 hertz, approximately the upper limit of human hearing

**voice**  sounds uttered through mouth of living creature, esp. human being; such sounds as distinctive to an individual

**volume**  degree of sound intensity or loudness

## ACTUAL SOUNDS

ahh, arf, arp

baa, beep, birr, blap, blat, boing, boo, bowwow, burp, buzz

caw, cheep, chink, chirp, chirr, chirrup, churr, clang, clank, clap, click, cling, clink, clinkety-clank, clip, clip-clop, clomp, clonk, clop, clop-clop, clunk, coo, cuckoo

ding, ding-a-ling, ding-dong, dong, drivit

eek

fizz

gong, goo

haw, hem, hiccup, hiss, honk, hoo, hum, hurrah

ick

meow, mew, mewl, moo

oink

pat, ping, pit-a-pat, pitter-patter, plink, plonk, plunk, pop, pow, purr

quack

rat-a-tat, ring, ring-a-ling, riprap

splat, splish, squish, swish, swoosh

tantara, tap, tat, tick, ticktock, ting, ting-a-ling, toot, tweet

varoom

whap, whirr, whish, whizz, whomp, whoop, whoopee, whoosh, woof, wow

yahoo, yikes, yip, yo, yoo-hoo, yow

zap, zing

## DESCRIPTIONS OF SOUNDS

baffle, bang, bawl, bay, belch, bell, blare, blast, bleat, bleep, bong, boom, boop, bray, bruit, buffet, bugle, bump, burble

cacophony, catcall, caterwaul, cheer, chime, chip, chuff, chug, chunk, clack, clamor, clangor, clash, clatter, cluck, clump, conk, crack, crackle, crash, creak, crinkle, croak, cronk, crool, croon, crow, crump, crunch

drill, drone, drum

fart, flick, flump, flutter

gag, gaggle, gargle, glop, gnash, gobble, grate, grind, gulp, gurgle, guzzle

hammer, hawk, hoot, howl, huff, hush

jangle, jingle

keck, keen, knell, knock

lap, lisp, low

mash, mizzle

neigh, nip

pad, paradiddle, patter, peal, pestle, pip, pipe, pitter, plash, plop, pound, pule, pummel

racket, rap, rasp, rattle, report, roar, rollick, rumble, rustle

scrape, scratch, screak, scream, screech, shake, shatter, shriek, shrill, shush, sizzle, skirl, slam, slap, slur, slurp, smack, snap, snarl, sneeze, sniff, sniffle, snivel, snore, snort, snuffle, sob, splash, splatter, squall, squawk, squeak, squeal, squib, stertor, stomp, strum, swat

tamp, thill, throstle, thrum, thud, thump, thunder, thunk, thwack, ticktack, tinkle, tintinnabulate, tirl, toll, tootle, tramp, tread, trill, tromp, trumpet, twang

ululate

warble, whack, wham, whang, wheeze, whinny, whistle, whiz, whop, whump, winnow, wolf

yak, yakety-yak, yawp, yelp, yodel

zip, zoom

## SPEECH SOUNDS

babble, bark, bellow, blab, blabber, blather, blatter, bleat, blither, blubber, blurt, bluster, brattle, bray, bubble, bumble, burble

cackle, caw, chat, chatter, chitter, chuff, cry

gab, gabble, gibber, giggle, groan, growl, grumble, grunt, guffaw

holler, hoot

jabber

murmur, mutter

natter, nicker, noodle

patter, prattle, pribble

quibble

shout, simper, sing, snicker, splutter, sputter, squeal, stammer, stutter, susurrate

tattle, titter, trill, twaddle, twitter

wail, warble, whimper, whine, whisper

yabber, yammer, yap, yell, yelp, yowl

## COMIC SOUND EFFECTS

aaaa, aaargh, aaarrgh, ack, ahchoo, ak

babrom, bada, ba-da-bam, badow, baff, balump, bam, bammm, bang, bash, ba-wroo, bawww, bdlm, bdlmp, bdmp, beep, bep, bida-bom, biff, bing, blaff, blam, blamma, blang, bl-eech, bleed, bleeed, bllam, bllom, blm, blodom, blog, blom, bloo, blop, blouw, blrashh, blug, bof, boing, bom, bong, bonk, boom, boom-ba-doom, bop, bounce, boyng, bradada, brat, brrrrram, brrt, burble

chomp, chonk, chop, chsh, chugalug, clang, clank, clash, clik, clikety, clrrash, coff, crack, crackle, crak, crash, creak, crunch, cut

dang-a-lang, danglang, dig, ding, dingdong, dinggg, dong, doof, drinnggg, dzzzz, dzzzzz

ech, eeeeeeeee, eeeeek, eep, ert

feh, flink, floom, floosh, foomf, fooosh, foosh, froosh, fsst, fwadoom, fweet

gag, gah, gasp, ge-boom, gha, ghaaa, gleh, glig, glk, glook, glub, glug, go, gong, gonng, goo, gop, gring, grinngg, grrr
hack, ha-ho, hf, hmf, hnf, honk, hrf, huf, huh, humph
inng
jab
kaf, kchow, kchunk, klak, klaket, klakkety, klek, klik, klink, klomp, klop, kneek, kortch, kpow, krak, kree, kreet, krk, krr-oomf, kr-rumf, krumf, kruuungg, ktak, kweeg
mf, mff, mhf, nf, nfs, nggg, ngs, nok, nyaaoooo
oof, oop, ooze, oww
paf, piu, plip, ploosh, pok, poof, poom, poot, pop, pow, ptung, ptweeeeng, punt
rap, rat, rat-tat, rattle, ring, room, rowf, rrinngg, r-rip, rrip, rrowr, rrrooaar, runch
schplivartz, scree, screeech, screeee, shmek, skeee, skloorgle, skntch, skramm, skreech, skrotch, skwee, skweee, slam, slap, slap-ap-ap, slash, slep, slosh, smak, smash, smashh, smeeeeeeer, smek, smesh, smooch, snap, snf, snick, snif, snuf, sob, spa-bam, spla-poom, splash, splat, splinter, sploog, sploosh, splow, splush, spong, sponggg, spung, sput, squeee, sreiikk, stomp, swish, swok, swop
tap, tat, thud, thunk, tick, tilt, tinkle, toot, treee, tromp, trompitty, tsk, tsss, tsssboom, twang, twee, tweep, twerp
ugh, ung
vaaaagglum, vash, va-va-voom, voof, voom, vroooom, vrrumm
waa, waaah, waf, wak, wee, weoooeeeoooee, wham, whap, whirr, whom, whomp, whoom, whoosh, whuf, wok, woop, wrraaammmm, wurf
yap, yappa, yatata, yayter, yeaaaaa, yeeeaaaakk, yhaaa, yitti, yoop, yotter, youch, yyp
z, zaaaaa, zap, zetz, zing, zip, zok, zop, zot, zzap, zzip, zzz, zzzzz

---

# Smells and Tastes

Smells
Tastes

**SEE ALSO**: Chap. 1: Anatomy; Chap. 9: Foods; Chap. 17: Smoking and Tobacco

## Smells

**air** (*vb*) ventilate by exposure to open air
**ambrosia** something appealing to smell or taste, orig. food of the gods
**anosmic** (*adj*) having complete or partial loss of sense of smell
**aroma** usu. agreeable odor, often arising from spices or plants; bouquet of wine
**aromatic** (*adj*) having a pleasing scent or odor
**attar** perfume or essential oil obtained from flowers
**bad breath** halitosis
**balm** aromatic fragrance or sweet odor, esp. in resinous, oily substance exuding from certain plants
**balsam** fragrant or aromatic substance exuding from certain trees
**BO** *body* odor
**body odor** BO; natural smell of human body, esp. unpleasant odor of perspiration

**bouquet** distinctive aroma of wines and liqueurs
**breath** hint or mere suggestion of scent, esp. carried on a light current of air
**cologne** mildly perfumed toilet water
**corky** (*adj*) having a spoiled scent, esp. from tainted cork
**deodorant** any agent used for eliminating odors
**deodorize** (*vb*) eliminate unpleasant odor
**eau de toilette** perfumed toilet water; cologne
**effluvium** slight trace or invisible exhalation of vapor, usu. noxious or disagreeable
**emanation** breath or issuing forth of vapor
**essence** perfume or scent; basic or intrinsic smell of something
**ester** fragrant volatile liquid found in essential oils and synthesized for use as scent
**exhalation** vapor or emanation
**fetid** (*adj*) having a strong, unpleasant smell; olid
**fetor** strong, offensive smell; stench
**foul** (*adj*) unpleasant smelling
**fragrance** sweet or pleasing odor
**fragrant** (*adj*) having a sweet or pleasing odor
**fresh** (*adj*) well-ventilated and airy
**fulsome** (*adj*) sickening or disgusting to the senses
**fume** usu. vaporous smokelike exhalation, esp. of odorous or harmful nature
**fumigation** exposure to smoke or vapors, usu. in disinfectingprocess
**funk** strong, offensive smell
**fust** strong, musty, or moldy smell
**gamy** (*adj*) having the tangy, slightly tainted odor of uncooked game
**graveolent** (*adj*) having a rank smell
**halitosis** condition of having foul-smelling breath
**heady** (*adj*) intoxicating and exhilarating to the sense of smell
**incense** aromatic substance that produces sweet odor when burned; any fragrant scent or perfume
**malodorous** (*adj*) foul-smelling
**mephitic** (*adj*) noxious and stinking
**mephitis** any poisonous stench, esp. noxious exhalation from the earth
**miasma** noxious exhalation, esp. from decomposing organic matter
**musk** strong odor of substance secreted in gland of male musk deer, or synthesized, used in making perfume; must
**must** musk, esp. powdered form
**nares** nostrils or nasal passages
**nasal** (*adj*) pertaining to the nose or nostrils
**nidor** strong smell, esp. of burning meat or fat
**nidorous** (*adj*) rank-smelling, esp. like burning or decaying animal matter
**nose** organ of smell
**nostril** one of two external openings of nose; one of nares
**odor** sensation perceived by sense of smell, either agreeable or disagreeable
**odoriferous** (*adj*) yielding or diffusing an odor
**olfaction** sense of smell; act of smelling
**olfactory** (*adj*) pertaining to sense of smell
**olid** (*adj*) fetid
**perfume** agreeable scent, odor, or volatile particles emitted by a substance; (*vb*) impart a pleasant fragrance

**pomander** ball-shaped mixture of aromatic substance
**pong** *Brit. informal.* disagreeable smell, stink
**potpourri** fragrant mixture of dried flower petals and spices
**putrefy** (*vb*) cause to rot or decay with offensive odor
**putrescent** (*adj*) becoming putrid, undergoing putrefaction
**putrid** (*adj*) in state of foul decay and decomposition with accompanying odor of rot
**rancid** (*adj*) having an unpleasant, stale smell
**rank** (*adj*) having an offensive, foul smell or taste
**redolent** (*adj*) fragrant, having a pleasant odor; smelling of
**reek** strong, unpleasant smell, esp. vaporous stink; (*vb*) give off strong, unpleasant odor
**rose** (*adj*) sweetly scented like a rose
**rot** state of putrefaction and decay and its attendant unpleasant odor
**rotten eggs** distinctive smell of decaying, uncooked eggs, used to indicate particular foul smell
**sachet** small bag or case of perfumed powder, used for scenting clothes or linens
**savor** quality of a substance that affects sense of smell; particular smell
**savory** (*adj*) agreeable in smell, esp. fragrant
**scent** distinctive, usu. agreeable odor; perfume; sense of smell; (*vb*) imbue with odor or perfume
**skunk** animal that emits noxious scent when endangered, used to represent any powerfully unpleasant stink
**smell** odor or scent that may be perceived through the nose by the olfactory nerves; (*vb*) perceive by sense of smell or inhale odor of
**smelly** (*adj*) having or emitting a strong, unpleasant odor
**sniff** scent or odor perceived; (*vb*) smell something by short inhalations through the nose
**snuff** (*vb*) perceive by smelling; sniff
**snuffle** (*vb*) draw air into nose so as to smell something
**spoor** scent left by a wild animal, used in tracking
**stench** foul or offensive smell
**stink** (*vb*) emit a strong, offensive smell; (*n*) a strong, offensive smell
**stinking** (*adj*) foul-smelling
**stink to high heaven** smell extremely unpleasant or foul
**stinky** (*adj*) foul-smelling
**stuffy** (*adj*) poorly ventilated, stale, lacking fresh air
**sweet** (*adj*) fragrant, perfumed, or fresh to the smell
**trace** hint or suggestion of a particular scent; whiff
**unscented** (*adj*) having no smell; without scent or odor added
**vapor** visible exhalation of gaseous particles into the air
**ventilate** (*vb*) provide fresh air to enclosed place
**waft** faintly perceived odor; trace of scent in the air
**whiff** slight trace of odor or smell of something

## TASTES

**acerbic** (*adj*) sour or astringent in taste
**acidic** (*adj*) sharp and biting in flavor
**acrid** (*adj*) sharp, biting, or bitterly pungent
**aftertaste** sensation of taste remaining after substance causing it is no longer in mouth
**appetizing** (*adj*) appealing to the taste
**astringent** (*adj*) harshly biting, esp. constrictive to taste buds
**biting** (*adj*) sharp, somewhat acidic, producing harsh taste

**bitter** (*adj*) having a harsh, disagreeably acrid taste; being one of the four basic taste sensations
**brackish** (*adj*) having a slightly salty or briny flavor
**briny** (*adj*) salty in flavor
**caustic** (*adj*) sharp and acidic
**delectable** (*adj*) delicious or appetizing
**delicious** (*adj*) very pleasing to taste
**dry** (*adj*) of wines, not sweet or fruity
**dulcet** (*adj*) *Archaic.* sweet to the taste
**dulcify** (*vb*) sweeten
**flavor** distinctive taste; additive imparting specific taste
**flavorful** (*adj*) possessing strong flavor; tasty
**flavoring** something that imparts a particular taste
**four basic tastes** elemental taste sensations that are mediated by sense organs and form basis of most other tastes: bitter, salt, sour, sweet
**fruity** (*adj*) tasting of fruit; of wines, sweet
**full-bodied** (*adj*) at full strength or flavor, esp. of wines
**gamy** (*adj*) having the tangy, tainted flavor of uncooked game
**goût** *French.* taste, relish
**gustation** act of or faculty for tasting
**gustatory** (*adj*) pertaining to taste or tasting
**honey** (*adj*) sweet
**hot** (*adj*) sharply pungent or peppery
**juicy** (*adj*) succulent, mouth-watering
**mouth-watering** (*adj*) appetizing
**nip** biting or tangy taste
**palatable** (*adj*) good-tasting
**palate** sense of taste
**peppery** (*adj*) hot and pungent, tasting of pepper
**pickled** (*adj*) preserved in and tasting of brine
**piquant** (*adj*) pleasingly sharp, biting, or tart
**pungent** (*adj*) biting or acrid; having a sharp affect on taste organ
**rancid** (*adj*) having an unpleasant, stale taste
**rank** (*adj*) having an offensive, foul taste
**relish** pleasing or appetizing flavor; enjoyment of the taste of something
**saccharine** (*adj*) very sweet; artificially sweet
**saline** (*adj*) salty
**salt** (*adj*) producing that one of the four basic taste sensations that is not sweet, sour, or bitter ·
**salty** (*adj*) tasting of salt
**sapor** flavor; quality of substance affecting sense of taste; savor
**saporific** (*adj*) imparting or producing flavor
**savor** quality of substance affecting sense of taste; sapor
**savory** (*adj*) agreeable to the taste, sometimes piquant
**scrumptious** (*adj*) delicious
**seasoning** salt, herbs, or spices that enhance flavor of food
**sec** (*adj*) of wines, dry, not sweet
**sharp** (*adj*) strongly pungent or biting
**smack** taste or flavor, esp. hint of flavor
**sour** (*adj*) tart, acidic, lemony; being one of the four basic taste sensations
**spicy** (*adj*) piquant or pungent; seasoned with spices
**strong** (*adj*) having a powerful, dominant, specific flavor
**succulent** (*adj*) juicy and full of good flavor
**sugary** (*adj*) sweet like sugar
**sweet** (*adj*) tasting of sugar or honey; being one of the four basic taste sensations

**sweet-and-sour** (*adj*) combining the tastes of sugar or honey and vinegar or lemon juice

**syrupy** (*adj*) very sweet, esp. of viscous liquids

**tang** strong, distinctive taste or flavor

**tart** (*adj*) sour or acidic, sharp to the taste

**taste** sense by which flavor or savor of things is perceived and appreciated; (*vb*) perceive or try the flavor of something

**taste buds** small bodies, primarily on tongue, that are perception organs for sense of taste

**tasteless** (*adj*) having no distinct flavor

**tasting** act of perceiving or testing the flavor of something

**tasty** (*adj*) good-tasting, delicious, savory

**tongue** movable organ on floor of mouth used in eating and containing taste buds that perceive flavors

**toothsome** (*adj*) agreeable to the taste, palatable

**treacly** (*adj*) extremely, sometimes sickly, sweet

**whet one's appetite** stimulate one's appetite through pleasing taste or smell

**yummy** *Informal.* very tasty

**zest** agreeable or piquant flavor imparted to something

**zesty** (*adj*) agreeably piquant

# CHAPTER 20

# Common Expressions

**20. COMMON EXPRESSIONS**
EXCLAMATIONS / GREETINGS AND FAREWELLS
GRUNTS, CALLS, AND SOUNDS / INTERJECTIONS / CURSES AND OATHS / GREETINGS

**PART SIX**

# EXCLAMATIONS

Grunts, Calls, and Sounds
Interjections
Curses and Oaths

**SEE ALSO**: Chap. 19: Sounds and Noises; Chap. 20: Nonsense, Confusion, and Trouble

## GRUNTS, CALLS, AND SOUNDS

aah, achoo, ack, ah, aha, ahem, ah-ha, aw
baa, bah, blah, boo, bowwow, brrr
cheep
eek, eh
guffaw
hah, ha-ha, harrumph, haw, heehaw, heigh-ho, hem, hi-ho, hmmm, ho, ho-hum, hoo, hoy, huh, humph, hunh, hup, hut
ick
la-di-da, lo
nah
o, oh, oink, oof, ooh, ooh-la-la, oompah, oomph, ooo, ow
peugh, pip-pip, poof, pshaw
rah
shh
ta-da, tut, tut-tut
ugh, uh-huh, uh-oh, umph, unh-unh
varoom
wahoo, wha, whee, wo, wow, wowee
yah, yahoo, yay, yech, yikes, yo, yoikes, yoo-hoo, yow, yuck, yum, yummy, yum-yum
zap

## INTERJECTIONS

alack, alas, alleluia, amen, and how, avast, aw-shucks, aye
banzai, boy, bravo, by jingo
cheerio, cheers, chop-chop
dear, dear me, ditto
egads, eh, what, eureka
fiddlesticks, fore, forsooth
gadzooks, gee, gee whillikers, gee whiz, gesundheit, giddyap, golly, golly gee, golly whillikers, good golly, good gracious, goody, gracious, gracious me
hallelujah, hark, heads up, hear ye, hear ye, heave-ho, heavens, heavens to Betsy, here here, hey, hip-hip, holy cow, holy mackerel, holy moly, holy toledo, hooray, hosanna, hurrah, huzzah
jeepers
lackaday, lo and behold
mama, marry, my gracious, my my, my stars, my word
nah, nay, nerts, nope, nuts
oh boy, oh dear, oh my, okay, okey-doke, okey-dokey, ole, oops, oopsy-daisy, ouch, oy, oyez
peekaboo, phew, pooh, prithee, prosit
rah, rah-rah, roger, rot
salud, scram, shaddup, shucks, shush, skoal

tallyho, ten-four, there, there, timber, touché, tsk tsk, tush, tut-tut
viva, voila
whatever, well, whew, whoa, whoop-de-do, whoopee, whoops, why, woe is me, wowie, wowie-zowie
yea, yeah, yep, yippee, yo mama, yup
zooks, zounds, zut

## CURSES AND OATHS

arse, ass, asshole
bastard, bejesus, blame, blast, bleep, blimey, bosh, brother, bull, bullroar, bullshit, by cracky, by Jove
Christ, cockadoodie, cocksucker, cottonpickin', crap, crapola, crikey, criminy, cunt
dad-blamed, dadburn it, dad-gummed, dammit, damn, damnation, damn it, dang, darn, dash, dod, doggone, doodie, drat, durn
faugh, feh, fie, for Christ's sake, frig, frigging, fuck, fuckin', fuckin'-A, fucking, fuckin'-hell, fuck it
God, goddamn, goddamnit, gol blame, gol darn, good God, good Lord, gramercy
heck, heckuva, hell, hellacious, hell's bells, helluva, holy gosh
jeez, jeez Louise, Jesus, Jesus Christ, Jesus H. Christ
merde, motherfucker, mother of God, my ass
noogie
Od
phooey, pish, piss, piss off, poop, pox
sacre bleu, Sam Hill, sheesh, shit, shoo, shoot, son of a bitch, son of a gun, sumbitch
tarnation
what the dickens, what the hell, what the Sam Hill

# GREETINGS AND FAREWELLS

Greetings
Farewells
Interchangeables

**SEE ALSO**: Chap. 20: Exclamations

## GREETINGS

ahoy, all hail
bonjour
glad to see you, good to see you, greetings
hail, halloa, have a good one, hello, hello there, hey, hey-ho, hi, hi, there, hi ya, hola, how are you?, how do?, how do you do?, howdy, howdy-do, howdy-doody, how d'ye do?, how goes it?, how's by you?, how's everything?, how's it going?, how's the world treating you?, how's things?, how you be?, how you been?, how you doing?, hullo
many happy returns
que pasa?
salud, salutations, shake
welcome, what it is?, what's happening?, wie gehts?
yo

## FAREWELLS

à bientôt, à demain, adieu, adios, arrivederci, à toute à l'heure, Auf Wiedersehen, au revoir

be good, be seeing you, bless you, bonne nuit, bon voyage, buenas noches, buona notte, bye, bye-bye

catch you later, come again

das vedanya

enjoy

fare thee well, farewell

God be with you, God bless, Godspeed, good-bye, good luck, good night, gute Nacht

happy trails, hasta la vista, hasta luego, hasta mañana, have a good one, have a nice day

later, later on

mañana

over, over and out

peace

regards, roger

sayonara, see ya, see you later, see you later alligator

take care, take it easy, ten-four, toodleoo

## INTERCHANGEABLES

all hail, aloha, ave

bonjour, bon matin, bon soir, buenas tardes, buenos dias, buona sera, buon giorno

check, cheerio, cheers, ciao

good afternoon, good day, good evening, good morning, good to see you, guten Abend, guten Morgen, guten Tag

hail

konbanwa, konichiwa

pip-pip

regards

salaam, shalom

# INSULTS, SLURS, AND EPITHETS

Appearance or Style
Intelligence or Aptitude
Behavior or Personality
Morality or Character
Sexuality or Gender
Ethnic Origin, Race, or Religion

**SEE ALSO**: Chap. 1: Physical Appearance; Chap. 20: Terms of Endearment and Respect; Chap. 22: Personality and Behavior; Sex, Love, and Romance; Strategy, Intrigue, and Deception; Chap. 23: Judgment and Criticism; Mental Disturbances; Crime; Violence

Insults, Slurs, and Epithets are grouped into six lists of virtual synonyms, each representing insults to a specific characteristic. Thus, all the definitions under Appearance or Style essentially mean "unattractive," while all the insults under Intelligence or Aptitude essentially mean "ignorant" or "stupid." Definitions would tend to be repetitive. Vulgar and derogatory labels apply to virtually all the insults under Sexuality or Gender and Ethnic Origin, Race, or Religion, and thus have been omitted.

## APPEARANCE OR STYLE

Amazon, ape, armpit

baboon, bag, bag lady, bear, beggar, behemoth, beldam, biddy, blastie, blimp, blob, bohunk, booger, bruiser, brute, bug, bumpkin, bunny, burrhead, butterball, buzzard

chit, city slicker, clotheshorse, codger, Colonel Blimp, conehead, coot, cootie, cornpone, cow, cripple

dandy, dinosaur, dirt bag, dog, dotard, dwarf

eyesore

fancyass, fatso, fatty, feeb, ferret face, fleabag, fogy, fop, fossil, four-eyes, Frankenstein, freak, frump

geek, geezer, ghost, ghoul, gimp, golem, golliwogg, goon, gorgon, gorilla, grease monkey, greaser, guttersnipe

hag, have-not, hayseed, heifer, hick, hillbilly, hobbledehoy, hobo, ho-dad, hog, homunculus, hoyden

invalid

jarhead

lard, lardass, Little Lord Fauntleroy, longhair, lummox, lump, lunger

malkin, mannequin, measle, meatball, Medusa, monkey, monstrosity, moose, mossback, mug, mutant, mutt

Neanderthal

old bag, ox

peacock, peewee, picklepuss, pig, pilgarlic, pimple, pimpleface, pinhead, pipsqueak, pizzaface, plain Jane, plugugly, porker, preppy, prune, pus bucket, pustule, pygmy

ragabond, ragamuffin, ragtag, relic, reptile, ronyon, rooster, rube, runt

sad sack, scarecrow, scrag, shlump, shorty, shrimp, shriv, skinhead, slattern, slicker, slob, slouch, sloven, small fry, sow, spas, spastic, specter, spud, squirt, stick, string bean, stumblebum, sweat hog, swell

tank, tawpie, Teddy boy, toad, toff, tomboy, troglodyte, troll, tub

ugly duckling

waif, wallflower, wart, weenie, whale, whiffet, white bread, wombat, wraith

yokel

zit

## INTELLIGENCE OR APTITUDE

addlebrain, addlehead, addlepate, airhead, ament, April fool, automaton

bananahead, basket case, beefhead, beetlehead, bimbo, birdbrain, blatherskite, blockhead, blubberhead, blunderhead, bonehead, boob, bozo, brain, bubblehead, bufflehead, buffoon, butthead

cabbagehead, chawbacon, chickenbrain, chowderhead, chucklehead, chump, clod, clodhead, clodpate, clodpoll, clot, cluck, conehead, crackbrain, cretin, criticaster, cuckoo

deadhead, dimwit, ding-a-ling, dingbat, dingdong, ditz, dodo, dodo brain, dolt, dolthead, donkey, doofus, dope, dork, dullard, dullhead, dumbbell, dumb bunny, dumb cluck, dumbhead, dumbo, dumdum, dummkopf, dummy, dunce, dunderhead, dunderpate, dupe

easy mark, egghead

fathead, fatwit, featherbrain, featherhead, feeb, flathead, flibbertigibbet, fool
gaby, gawk, gudgeon
half-wit, hammerhead, harebrain, highbrow
idiot, ignoramus, imbecile
jackass, jiggin, jobbernowl, jolterhead, jughead
klutz, know-nothing, knucklehead
lackwit, lamebrain, lightweight, loggerhead, loon, lowbrow, lumpkin, lunkhead
meatball, meathead, mental midget, mongoloid, moron, muddlehead, mumpsimus, musclehead, mushhead, muttonhead
nincompoop, ninny, ninnyhammer, nitwit, no-brainer, noddy, noodlehead, nudnik, numskull
patzer, peabrain, peahead, pinbrain, pinhead, pointyhead, potatohead, puddinghead, puttyhead
rattlebrain, rattlehead, retard, rockhead
sap, saphead, scatterbrain, sciolist, shit for brains, silly fool, simp, simpleton, slobbering idiot, slowpoke, softhead, stupe, submoronic twit, sucker
techie, thickhead, thickwit
vegetable, void
witling, woodenhead
yoyo
ziphead

# BEHAVIOR OR PERSONALITY

acidhead, agent provocateur, agitator, airy-fairy, alky, alien, also-ran, amateur, android, animal, annoyance, appendage, apple polisher, archenemy, artiste, artsy-fartsy, ass, asshole, ass-kisser
backbreaker, badass, baggage, bag lady, banana, banshee, barbarian, barfly, bastard, bear, beast, beggar, bellyacher, bête noir, bighead, bigmouth, big shot, bindle stiff, bitch, blabbermouth, black sheep, blatherskite, blellum, blow-hard, Boeotian, boaster, bookworm, boor, bore, botcher, brat, brawler, bruiser, brute, bugbear, bugger, bullshit artist, bullshitter, bully, bullyboy, bungler, buster, busybody, butt, butterfingers, buttinsky, buzzard
carper, chatterbox, chauvinist, cheapo, cheapskate, chicken, chimp, chiseler, chowhound, chuff, chump, churl, cipher, clam, clochard, clod, clodhopper, clown, clunk, clunker, cold fish, Comstocker, copycat, cornball, couch potato, cousin, crab, crackpot, crank, crazy, cream puff, creature, crumb, crybaby, cube, cur, curmudgeon, cuss, cutup
dabbler, deadwood, dick, dickhead, dilettante, dinosaur, dip, dipshit, ditz, dog breath, dog meat, do-gooder, dogsbody, donkey, do-nothing, doofus, doormat, dork, dotard, doubting Thomas, drag, draggle-tail, dreamer, drifter, drip, drone, dropout, drudge, druggie, drunk, dud, duffer, dweeb
earbender, eightball, enfant terrible, extremist
fart, fat cat, fathead, fawner, featherweight, finagler, firebrand, fish, flake, flamer, flâneur, flash in the pan, flibbertigibbet, floater, flop, flubber, flunky, fogy, fox, fraidy-cat, freak, freebooter, freeloader, fucker, fuckface, fuckhead, fuckup, fuddy-duddy, fumbler, fungus, fussbudget, fusspot
gadfly, galoot, gasbag, gawk, geep, geezer, glutton, goat, goldbrick, golem, goody-goody, goody two shoes, goof, goofball, goof-off, goon, goose, gossipmonger, gourmand, gowk, grease monkey, greenhorn, griper, grobian, grouch, groupie, grump, gull
hack, ham, hambone, hamburger, hangdog, hanger-on, hard case, hardhead, hard-nose, harridan, has-been, head, heathen, hedonist, hellion, hellhound, hell-raiser,

high-muck-a-muck, hippie, homebody, horse's ass, hot dog, hothead, hotshot, hoyden, hypochondriac, hypocrite
iceberg, icicle, idler, incendiary, incubus, inebriate
jackal, jackanapes, jackass, jack-off, jailbird, jay, jerk, jerk-off, jester, Johnny-come-lately, joker, juicehead, juicer, junkie
kibitzer, killjoy, klutz, knave, knight-errant, know-it-all, know-nothing, kook
lackey, laggard, lamb, lame, lame duck, landlubber, larrikin, layabout, lazybones, lemming, lemon, leper, lightweight, litterbug, loafer, loggerhead, lollygagger, looby, loon, loser, lotus-eater, loudmouth, lounge lizard, lout, lowbrow, lubber, lug, lunatic, lurdan, lush
madman, madwoman, maenad, malcontent, mama's boy, maniac, marshmallow, Martian, martinet, masher, meanie, meatball, meddler, megalomaniac, mercenary, merry-andrew, meshugene, milksop, milquetoast, mimic, misanthrope, mischief-maker, miscreant, miser, misfit, misogynist, mobster, mole, mollycoddle, Momus, moneybags, monger, mongrel, mooch, mooncalf, mother, motherfucker, motor-mouth, mouse, muck-a-muck, muckraker, mugwump, mule, mutt
nag, namby-pamby, name-dropper, narc, nebbish, nemesis, nerd, nervous Nellie, nibs, niggard, ninny, nit, nitpicker, nobody, nomad, nonentity, nonperson, noodle, no one, Nosy Parker, nothing, nouveau riche, novice, nut, nutter
oaf, oddball, odd man out, old fart, old fogy, outcast, outsider, oyster
pack rat, pain, pain in the ass, pain in the neck, palooka, panhandler, pantywaist, pariah, patch, patsy, pauper, pawn, peasant, peckerwood, pedant, penny pincher, peon, pepper pot, pest, petticoat, pettifogger, pharisee, philistine, pigeon, piker, pill, pinchbeck, pip, pipsqueak, pisher, pisser, playboy, playgirl, plebe, plunderer, poetaster, polecat, Pollyanna, pollywog, poltroon, poop, poseur, prankster, pretender, prima donna, princess, procrastinator, profiteer, provocateur, pseudo, psycho, pub-crawler, puckfist, pug, punching bag, punk, pussy, putty, putz
quicksilver, quidnunc
rabble-rouser, rake, rapscallion, reb, rebel, recluse, redneck, reject, renegade, revisionist, reynard, riffraff, roach, roadhog, robot, roughneck, roundheel, roustabout, rover, rowdy, rube, ruffian, rummy, rumormonger, runabout, runagate
sad sack, sap, sawney, scapegoat, scaramouch, scaredy-cat, scavenger, scofflaw, scrapper, screwball, scrooge, scrounger, scut, seadog, second banana, second fiddle, sheep, shit, shithead, shlemiel, shlep, shlimazel, shlub, shlump, shmegege, shmo, shmuck, shmutz, shnook, showboat, show-off, shrink, shrinking violet, silly ass, sissy, sitting duck, skinflint, skunk, slacker, slasher, slave, slave driver, slowpoke, slug, slugabed, sluggard, slut, sly boots, smart aleck, smarty-pants, smellfungus, snail, snip, snitch, sniveler, snob, snoop, so-and-so, SOB, sob sister, social climber, sod, sodbuster, soft touch, softy, son of a bitch, sop, sorehead, sot, sourball, sourpuss, souse, speedfreak, spendthrift, spider, spoilsport, sprat, spud, spy, square, squealer, squirt, stick, stick-in-the-mud, stickler, stiff, stinkard, stinker, stockjobber, stooge, straight arrow, stranger, stray, street arab, street person, strutter, stuffed shirt, succubus, sucker, swab, swagman, swellhead, swine, sycophant
tagalong, taskmaster, tattletale, tease, tenderfoot, termagant, terror, tightwad, tinhorn, tinker, toad, toady, tomboy, tomfool, tool, toper, tosspot, touch, toughie, tourist, tout, townie, tramp, tramper, transient, trickster, tripe, troublemaker, truant, tumbleweed, turd, turkey, twerp, twit, Typhoid Mary, tyro

LANGUAGE

**20. COMMON EXPRESSIONS**
INSULTS, SLURS, AND EPITHETS
MORALITY OR CHARACTER / SEXUALITY OR GENDER / ETHNIC ORIGIN, RACE, OR RELIGION

ulcer, underling, unperson, upstart

vagabond, vagrant, vandal, varlet, vassal, Venusian, vulture

wacko, waffler, wag, wage slave, Walter Mitty, wangler, wanker, war-horse, washout, weakling, weenie, weirdo, wench, wet blanket, wethead, wheedler, wheeler-dealer, whiffler, whippersnapper, whipping boy, white trash, wildcatter, wild man, wimp, windbag, wino, wiseacre, wise guy, wise-ass, wisenheimer, witch, wolf, workaholic, worm, worrywart, wowser, wreck, wretch, wuss

Xanthippe

yahoo, yardbird, yenta, yes-man, yobbo

zany, zealot, zero, zombie, zonker

## MORALITY OR CHARACTER

adulterer, Ananias, Antichrist, archfiend, arriviste

Babbitt, backbiter, backstabber, bamboozler, bandit, betrayer, bigamist, bigot, bilker, blackguard, blank, bloodsucker, Bluebeard, bogeyman, bounder, brigand, brown-noser, buccaneer, bum, burglar, butcher

cad, caitiff, cancer, cannibal, cardsharp, carline, cateran, charlatan, cheat, chintz, chiseler, churl, commie, comsymp, con artist, con man, counterfeiter, coward, creep, crook, crud, culprit

dastard, deadbeat, debauchee, deceiver, delator, demagogue, demon, desperado, despot, devil, dictator, dissembler, dodger, dog, double-crosser, double-dealer, dregs, dreck, dross

failure, faitour, faker, fascist, felon, fibber, fiend, finagler, fink, flimflam man, fly-by-night, forger, fraud, freeloader

ganef, goldbrick, gold digger, good-for-nothing, gouger, grafter

heel, heretic, highwayman, hilding, hoaxer, hoodlum, hooligan, huckster, humbug, hypocrite

idolator, impostor, Indian giver, indulger, infidel, informer, ingrate, insurgent, interloper, intruder

jackal, jailbird, jellyfish, JD, judas, juvenile delinquent

kaffir, killer, kleptomaniac, knave

leech, liar, libertine, lily-liver, louse, lout, lowlife

mafioso, malingerer, mammon, miscreant, miser, monster, monstrosity, mountebank

ne'er-do-well, no-account, no-goodnik

ogre, operator, opportunist, outlaw

pagan, pariah, parasite, Peeping Tom, perjurer, pervert, philanderer, philistine, phony, picaro, pickpocket, pimp, pinko, piranha, pirate, pissant, plagiarist, plague, poacher, poltroon, ponce, prevaricator, profligate, psychopath, puke, pusher

quack, quisling, quitter

racketeer, rake, rapist, rat, ratfink, recreant, recusant, red, reprobate, ringleader, robber, robber baron, rodent, rogue, rotter, roué, rustler

saboteur, sadist, saltimbanco, savage, scab, scalawag, scandalmonger, scoundrel, scourge, scum, scumbag, scumsucker, scuzz, scuzzball, serpent, sham, shark, sharp, shill, shirker, Shylock, shyster, sickie, sicko, Simon Legree, sinner, slanderer, slave driver, sleaze, sleazebag, sleazeball, slime, slimebag, slimeball, slime bucket, slumlord, slyboots, snake, snake in the grass, sneak, snipe, snitch, snollygoster, sociopath, sponge, stoolie, stool pigeon, swindler, swine

thief, thug, traitor, transgressor, trash, trickster, troublemaker, turncoat, two-timer, tyrant

usurer, usurper

vampire, vermin, vicemonger, villain, viper, vulture

warmonger, waster, wastrel, weasel, whoreson, witch, worm, wrongdoer

yellowbelly

## SEXUALITY OR GENDER

Amazon

bawd, bearded clam, bitch, brazen hussy, bugger, bull dyke, butch

castrato, cat, chicken, chicken hawk, chippy, closet queen, cock, cocksucker, concubine, coquette, courtesan, cow, cream puff, cuckold, cunt, cyprian

deviate, dick, diesel dyke, dildo, dingleberry, dink, dong, douche bag, drag queen, dyke

fag, faggot, fag hag, fairy, fetishist, flit, floozy, fox, fruit, fruitcake, fucker

gigolo, gunsel

hag, harlot, harpy, harridan, heifer, hen, homo, hooker, hussy

jade, john

lech, lecher, les, lesbo, libertine, lily, Little Lord Fauntleroy

mama's boy, masher, meat, minx, mo, motherfucker

nance, nancy, nympho

old maid

pansy, pantywaist, pecker, pederast, pedophile, Peeping Tom, pervert, philanderer, piece, pimp, playboy, playgirl, ponce, poof, poofter, prick, prig, procurer, prong, prostitute, prude, punk, pussy, puta

queen, queer, quim

rosy piglet, rut hostess

satyr, shmuck, shrew, sissy, slattern, slit, slut, snatch, sodomist, spinster, stag, streetwalker, stripper, strumpet, stud, swinger, swish, switch hitter

tail, tart, tomboy, tramp, transvestite, trick, trollop, twat

vamp, virago, vixen, voyeur

wanker, wanton, weenie, wench, whore, wiener, wienie, wolf, woman of the street

## ETHNIC ORIGIN, RACE, OR RELIGION

abo, alien, arkie, Aunt Jemima, Auslander

babu, blackie, bohunk, Brit, buck, burrhead

Charlie Chan, Chinaman, Chink, cockney, coolie, coon, cracker

dago, darky, dink

foreigner, Frenchy, frog

ginzo, gook, goomba, goy, gringo, Guinea

half-breed, Hebe, heinie, high yeller, honky, howley, hun, hymie

immigrant, Injun

Jap, JAP, Jew boy, jig, jigaboo, jungle bunny

kike, kraut

limey

Mick, moke, Mr. Charlie

nigger, niggra, Nip

ofay, okie

pachuco, paddy, paleface, picaroon, Polack

redskin

Russki

sheeny, shegatz, shikse, slant, slant-eye, slope, spade, spic, squaw

Ubangi, Uncle Tom

WASP, wetback, whitey, wog, wop

yid

Zulu

**20. COMMON EXPRESSIONS**
TERMS OF ENDEARMENT AND RESPECT
PET NAMES / FRIENDLY OR FAMILIAR ADDRESS / TITLES AND HONORIFICS / AFFECTIONATE REFERENCE

**PART SIX**

# TERMS OF ENDEARMENT AND RESPECT

Pet Names
Friendly or Familiar Address
Titles and Honorifics
Affectionate Reference
Respectful or Admiring Reference

**SEE ALSO**: Chap. 8: Kinship and Family Relations; Chap. 11: Titles of Rank; Chap. 20: Insults, Slurs, and Epithets; Chap. 22: Sex, Love, and Romance

## PET NAMES

acushla, angel, angel baby
babe, baby, baby doll, baby face, beau, boo-boo, bubaloo, bubbles, bubehleh, buttercup
calf, candy, cara mia, cherry, chickabiddy, chickadee, cookie, corazon, cupcake, cutie, cutie pie
daddy, daisy, darling, dear, dearest, dear heart, dearie, dimples, doll, dollface, dove, dreamboat, duck, duckie, duckling, ducks, dumpling
goose
hon, honey, honeybunch, honey child
kitten
lamb, lambchop, lambkin, liebschen, loosker, love, lover, luv
mi amore, monkey, monkey face, muffin, my dear, my love, my pet, my sweet
noodles
pet, pigeon, pooch, pooh, poppet, precious, puddin' head, pumpkin, punkin, puss, pussy willow
snooks, snookums, sugar, sugarpie, sugarpie honeybunch, sweetheart, sweetie, sweetie pie, sweetkins, sweetness, sweet patootie, sweet pea, sweet potato, sweets, sweet thing, sweetums
tomato, toots, tootsie, turtledove
valentine

## FRIENDLY OR FAMILIAR ADDRESS

ace, amigo, auntie
big fella
big guy, binky, boyo, brat, bro, brother, bub, bubba, bud, buddy
cap, captain, champ, chap, chief, chuck, chum, cock, cousin, cove, coz, curly
dad, daddy, deadeye, doc, dude
fella, friend
gaffer, gal, gill, girl, girlie, girlie-girl, goofus, gov, governor, gramma, grammy, grampa, gramps, granny, guy
hombre, home, homeboy, homes, hotshot
jack
kid, kiddo
lad, laddie, lady, lass, lassie, little one
ma, ma'am, mac, maestro, mama, master, mate, mio, missy, mom, momileh, mommy, monkey, moose, muchacho, munchkin, my main man, my man

neighbor, nuncle
old bean, old boy, old chap, old fellow, old man, old scout, old thing, old timer, old top padre
pa, pal, pal o' mine, papa, pard, pardner, peewee, pooh-bah, pop, poppa, pops
rascal
sarge, shrimp, sis, sister, scout, skip, skipper, skippy, sleepyhead, slick, slim, slugger, son, sonny, sonny boy, soul brother, speedy, sport, sprout, squirt, stretch
tot
unc, uncle
whippersnapper, whiz, whizzer
youngster

## TITLES AND HONORIFICS

babu, Brother, bwana
Dame, dean, diva, Dom, don, dona
Eminence, Esquire, Excellency
Father, Frau
grace
Herr, Highness, Holiness, Holy Father, Holy Mother, Honor, Honorable
Imperial Highness, Imperial Majesty
lady, ladyship, liege, lieutenant, lord, lordship
ma'am, madam, madame, mademoiselle, maharishi, majesty, massa, master, memsahib, milady, miss, mister, mistress, monsieur, monsignor, most honorable, most reverend, Mother, Mr., Mrs., Ms., my lady, my liege, my lord
officer
padre
rabbi, reverence, reverend, right honorable, right reverend, rinpoche, Royal Highness, Royal Majesty
sahib, sergeant, señor, señora, señorita, Serene Highness, Serene Majesty, signora, signore, signorina, sir, sire, sirrah, Sister, sister, sri, swami
taipan
worship
yogi, Your Eminence, Your Excellency, Your Grace, Your Highness, Your Holiness, Your Honor, Your Majesty, Your Reverence, Your Worship

## AFFECTIONATE REFERENCE

alter ego, apple of my eye
beauty, belle, beloved, best friend, best girl, blood brother, boy, boyfriend, brat, brother
calf, candy, card, Casanova, chap, character, charmer, cherub, chick, chit, choice, chum, cohort, colleen, colt, companion, comrade, confidant, confrere, cowpoke, crackerjack, crème de la crème, critter, crony, cub, Cub Scout
damsel, darb, diamond in the rough, dilly, dish, Don Juan, doozer, dream, dreamboat, dulcinea, dynamo
eager beaver, eagle, elf, enchantress, enchilada
familiar, fatso, favorite, fellow, filly, fireball, firecracker, flash, fox
gal, gamine, geezer, gem, girl, girlfriend, go-getter, goose, green thumb, guy
handyman, heartthrob, hepcat, highroller, hombre, honcho, hotshot, humdinger, hunk
idol, imp, inamorata, ingenue
jewel, jim-dandy, junior
kingpin

lad, lady love, lamb, lass, lefty, light, live wire, looker, love, lovebird, lucky devil, lucky stiff, lulu
main squeeze, mensch, minikin, minx, monkey, moose, moppet
neighbor, number one, numero uno, nymph
old duffer, old geezer, old lady, old man
partner, peach, pearl, pigeon, pip, pippin, pixie, playmate, plum, pollyanna, pooch, pooh-bah, posy, powerhouse, prince, protégé, puck, pud, pup, puppy
raconteur, rascal, Romeo, rose
scamp, sensation, sharpy, showman, sidekick, slim Jim, smoothie, sophisticate, soul brother, spring chicken, sprite, spud, steady, sugar daddy, swan, sylph
teammate, top banana, top dog, tops, tot, treasure, trouper, trump
urchin, vamp, Venus
water nymph, whippersnapper, whiz, whizbang, whiz kid, whizzer, wiz, wonder, wrangler
Yankee Doodle dandy, youngster, yours truly

## RESPECTFUL OR ADMIRING REFERENCE

ace, adept, aficionado, agha, all-American, all-around girl, all-around guy, all-star, altar boy, Atlas, avatar
bahadur, ball of fire, bellwether, big name, big timer, blockbuster, blood brother, blue blood, blue ribbon, boy wonder, Brahman, brownie, buck
captain, celeb, chief, classic, colleague, colonel, connoisseur, crackerjack
deadeye, diva, doyen, dynamo
eagle scout, elder, elder statesman, expert
fashion plate
genius, gentleman, gentlewoman, gourmet, governor, grand dame, gray beard, guru
handyman, Hercules, hero, heroine, homecoming queen, honcho, humanitarian
impresario, individual, insider, intellectual, iron man
jack-of-all-trades, jack rabbit, journeyman, judge
keeper, king, knockout
lady, laureate, leader, leading lady, leading man, leatherneck, liege, lifesaver, lion, luminary
Madonna, maestro, maiden, man about town, man of God, man of letters, martyr, marvel, master, mastermind, matinée idol, matron, maven, maverick, mentor, millionaire, muse
natural, nonesuch
old hand
padrone, paladin, paragon, past master, patriot, patron, phenom, phrasemaker, pick, pilot, pioneer, poet laureate, pres, president, pro, prodigy, pundit
queen
rara avis, reformer, Robin Goodfellow, Robin Hood, role model
sage, saint, samaritan, Samson, savant, savior, seer, select, self-starter, senator, sensei, sharpshooter, sleuth, smart cookie, socialite, soldier, solon, somebody, sovereign, spark plug, specimen, spitfire, sponsor, standard bearer, star, statesman, strongman, stud, superman, superstar, superwoman, supremo, swami, swashbuckler
teacher, thoroughbred, titan, torchbearer, trailblazer, trendsetter, troubleshooter, tutor, tycoon
up-and-comer
veteran, VIP, virgin, virtuoso, visionary, volunteer
warrior, watchdog, winner, wise man, wit, wizard, wonder, wonder-worker, workhorse, worldbeater, worthy, wunderkind
yeoman, yogi
zaddik

# NONSENSE, CONFUSION, AND TROUBLE

Foolishness, Bunkum, and Trifles
Drivel and Silly Talk
Fusses and Troubles
Confusion
Nonsense Words and Cutesies

**SEE ALSO:** Chap. 19: Verbs of Speech; Chap. 19: Sounds and Noises; Chap. 20: Exclamations; Chap. 20: Insults, Slurs, and Epithets; Chap. 21: Yiddish Borrowings; Chap. 24: Violence

## FOOLISHNESS, BUNKUM, AND TRIFLES

airy-fairy
bagatelle, balderdash, ballyhoo, baloney, bauble, bilge, blah, blahs, blatherskite, bluff, blunder, bluster, bogus, bollocks, bosh, braggadocio, bravado, brummagem, buffoonery, bull, bullshit, bunkum, bunk, burlesque
caacaa, cheek, claptrap, cock, cockalorum, cockamamie, codswallop, corn, cow pat, crambo, crap, crock, crud, curliewurly
diddlyshit, diddly-squat, doodad, doodle, doo-doo, doohickey, dreck, dregs, drool, dung
fancy, fanfaronade, farce, fiddlededee, fiddle-faddle, fiddlesticks, fig, flapdoodle, flimflam, flotsam, flubdub, fluff, flumadiddle, flummery, flummox, folderol, foofaraw, foolishness, footle, foozle, fribble, frills, frippery, froth, fudge
gadget, gammon, gas, gewgaw, gibberish, gimcrack, glob, goop, guff, gunk
hambone, hanky-panky, hem and haw, hogwash, hokum, hooey, hoot, horseshit, hot air, humbug, humdinger, humdrum
idiocy, inanity
jabberwocky, jazz, jetsam, jiggery-pokery, jingle, jive, joke, jot, junk
kitsch, kludge, knavery
lampoonery, lip
malarkey, meshuge, mickey mouse, mishegaas, mockery, monkeyshine, muck, mush
nonsense, non sequitur
oddment
pap, piddle, poop, poppycock, puffery, pulp, put-on
quackery
raffle, raillery, rattletrap, razzmatazz, refuse, ribbing, rigmarole, rodomontade, roguery, rot, rubbish, Rube Goldberg
sap, sass, scat, scum, scuttlebutt, send-up, sham, shit, shlock, shtick, skullduggery, slag heap, slapdash, slobber, slop, slurry, slush, sob story, spoof, sport, stuff, swagger, swill
taradiddle, tittle, tomfoolery, tommyrot, tongue-in-cheek, tosh, trangam, trash, trickery, trifle, trinket, tripe, trivia, trumpery
vapors
waggery, wank, waste, whatnot, whigmaleerie, whim, whimsy, white elephant, whoopla, whopper, widget, wind, wisecrack
yuck

**20. COMMON EXPRESSIONS**
NONSENSE, CONFUSION, AND TROUBLE
DRIVEL AND SILLY TALK / FUSSES AND TROUBLES / CONFUSION / NONSENSE WORDS AND CUTESIES

**PART SIX**

## DRIVEL AND SILLY TALK

babble, badinage, bibble-babble, blabber, blather, blatter, blither

chatter, chitchat, chitter, chitter-chatter, claptrap, cliché

ditty, doggerel, drivel

footle, fribble, fustian

gab, gabble, gibber, gibber-gabber, gibberish, gibble-gabble, gobbledegook, gossip

jabber, japery

logorrhea

natter, nitpicking

palaver, persiflage, piffle, pleasantries, prattle, prittle-prattle

scribblings, silliness, small talk, squiggles, stultiloquence

tittle-tattle, twaddle, twiddle-twaddle, twitter

verbiage

yabber, yak, yakety-yak, yikety-yak

## FUSSES AND TROUBLES

ado

bear, bickering, billingsgate, blooey, bobbery, boo-boo, boondoggle, bother, brannigan, brawl, broil, brouhaha, bug, bugaboo, bugbear, bummer

callithump, cattawumpus, collywobbles, commotion, conniption, crash

delirium, derring-do, disturbance, dither, donnybrook, doozie

feud, fit, fix, flap, flurry, fluster, foible, foul-up, fracas, fray, free-for-all, frenzy, furor, fuss

glitch

haggle, hash, hassle, hell, helter-skelter, high jinks, hoopla, hubble-bubble, hubbub, hullabaloo, hysteria

imbroglio

jam, jumble

katzenjammer, kibitzing, kink

lather, loggerheads, logjam

madhouse, maelstrom, megillah, melee, mess, mishmash, mix-up, moil, muss

no-no

peeve, pickle, pother, pratfall

quarrel

racket, rage, raise Cain, raise hell, rat's nest, rattrap, rhubarb, roughhouse, row, rowdydow, ruckus, ruffle, rumble, rumpus

scramble, scrap, scrape, screwup, seizure, set-to, shambles, shenanigan, shindig, shindy, short circuit, slam-bang, snafu, snarl, snit, spasm, spat, squabble, stew, stink

tamasha, tiff, tizzy, to-do, trouble, tsimmes, tsores, tumult, tussle, twitter

unrest, uproar

vendetta

whoop-de-do, whoopee, whoopla, wingding, wormwood, wrangle, wreckage

## CONFUSION

absurdity, addlement, agitation, anarchy, ataxia

bafflement, bewilderment, blooper, bollix, boner, boo-boo, botch, bungle

cacophony, catawumpus, chaos, churn, clinker, cloud, cloudland, clutter, confusion

daze, disorder

embranglement, entropy

farblondjet, farmisht, farrago, fartumlt, flutter, fog, folly, fret

gaffe, gallimaufry, goof

haze, higgledy-piggledy, hocus-pocus, hodgepodge, hokey-pokey, hotchpotch

jumble, jungle

ludicrousness

maze, medley, mishmash, mist, mix-up, motley, muddle, mumbo jumbo

olio, olla podrida

pandemonium, pastiche, patchwork

ridiculousness, rummage

scattershot, shambles, slaphappy, swirl, switcheroo

tintamarre, tohubohu, topsy-turvy, Tweedledum and Tweedledee

unset

voodoo, vortex

waffling, whirligig, whirlpool, whirlwind

## NONSENSE WORDS AND CUTESIES

artsy-craftsy

bleep

caboodle, chichi, comfy, coo, cuckoo, cutesy

dingus, doodad, doodle, doohickey

gaga, gizmo, gussy up

harum-scarum, heebie-jeebies, ho-hum, hoity-toity, hugger-mugger, hunky-dory, hurly-burly, hurry-scurry

itsy-bitsy, itty-bitty

kit'n'caboodle, knickknack

lardy-dardy

mollycoddle

namby-pamby, newfangled, niminy-piminy

okey-dokey, oodles

palsy-walsy, peekaboo, pell-mell, p's and q's

raggle-taggle, razzle-dazzle, rinky-dink

screaming-meemies, shilly-shally, skimble-scamble

teensy, teensy-weensy, thingamabob, thingamajig, thingummy, tidbit, tutti-frutti

whatchamacallit, whatsis, whim-wham, whoosis, willies, willy-nilly, wishy-washy

# Foreign Expressions

# LATIN WORDS AND PHRASES

**SEE ALSO**: Chap. 4: Medicine; Chap. 8: Kinship and Family Relations; Chap. 11: Law; Chap. 13: Philosophy; Chap. 14: Literature; Chap. 15: Theater; Chap. 18: Qualifiers and Connectives; Chap. 23: Time Perception; Chap. 25: Mythology and Folklore

**ab initio**  from the beginning
**ab intra**  from within, from inside
**ab origine**  from the origin or source
**ab urbe condita**  lit. from the foundation of the city; Roman dating system; AUC
**ad astra per aspera**  to the stars through difficulties
**ad extremum**  to the extreme; at last
**ad hoc**  lit. for this; for this purpose
**ad hominem**  lit. to the man; argument directed at man's character, not his position
**ad infinitum**  to infinity; endlessly
**ad interim**  temporarily
**ad libitum**  at one's pleasure, without restriction; ad lib.
**ad nauseam**  to the point of nausea; repeatedly; endlessly
**ad patres**  lit. to his fathers; deceased
**adsum**  I am here, used in response to a roll call
**ad valorem**  according to value, esp. tax thus imposed
**ad verbum**  lit. to the word; worded exactly as the original
**Agnus Dei**  lamb of God, i.e., Christ
**alma mater**  lit. nourishing mother; one's academic institution
**alter ego**  other self; best friend
**alumna**  female graduate of academic institution
**alumnus**  male graduate of academic institution
**amor vincit omnia**  love conquers all
**anno Domini**  in the year of the Lord
**annuit coeptis**  God favored our undertaking
**annus mirabilis**  notable, remarkable year or event
**ante bellum**  before the war
**ante meridiem**  a.m.; before midday
**a posteriori**  from what comes after; cause deduced from effect
**a priori**  from what comes before; deduced from what is known
**ars gratia artis**  art for art's sake
**ars longa, vita brevis**  art is long, life is short
**ave**  be well; farewell
**bona fide**  in good faith
**carpe diem**  seize the day
**caveat emptor**  let the buyer beware
**caveat lector**  let the reader beware
**cave canem**  beware of the dog
**ceteris paribus**  other things being equal
**circa**  ca; around or about, esp. of time
**cogito ergo sum**  I think therefore I am
**compos mentis**  of sound mind
**con**  against, opposite of pro
**cornucopia**  horn of plenty

**corpus delicti**  body of the crime; evidence of crime
**cui bono**  to whose advantage?; legal principle that responsibility for act lies with one gaining by it
**cum**  with
**cum grano salis**  with a grain of salt
**cum laude**  with praise or honors
**curriculum vitae**  lit. course of life; resumé
**de facto**  from fact; in reality
**Dei gratia**  by the grace of God
**de jure**  by right
**delirium tremens**  dt's; advanced, trembling alcoholic delirium
**Deo volente**  God willing
**de profundis**  from depths of despair
**desideratum**  something much wanted or needed
**deus ex machina**  lit. god from a machine; divine intervention
**Dominus vobiscum**  the Lord be with you
**dramatis personae**  cast of a drama
**ecce homo**  lit. behold the man; Christ crowned with thorns
**ecce signum**  lit. behold the sign; behold the proof
**editio princeps**  first edition
**emeritus**  one who has served with honor
**eo nomine**  by or under that name
**e pluribus unum**  one out of many, inscribed on U.S. coins
**ergo**  therefore
**errare humanum est**  to err is human
**erratum**  error
**et alia**  and others
**et cetera**  etc.; and the rest; and so on
**et sequens**  and the following
**et tu, Brute**  lit. and you, Brutus; even you are guilty of betrayal
**ex cathedra**  lit. from the chair; with authority
**excelsior**  higher; ever upward
**exeunt**  they go out, esp. leave stage
**exit**  he or she goes out, esp. leaves stage
**ex libris**  from the books or library of
**ex nihilo nihil fit**  from nothing comes nothing
**ex officio**  by virtue of office
**ex parte**  lit. from one side, used esp. of partisan legal communications
**ex post facto**  derived from what was done after
**ex tempore**  lit. out of time; spontaneously, without preparation
**factotum**  person, esp. servant, who does various chores
**fiat lux**  let there be light
**gaudeamus igitur**  therefore let us rejoice
**habeas corpus**  lit. you may have the body; esp. a writ used by defense lawyer to require formal pressing of charges against accused
**hic jacet**  here lies, used on tombstones
**homo sapiens**  lit. rational man; species of modern human beings
**homunculus**  miniature man, thought to reside within humans or in spermatozoon by 16th-century scientists
**horribile dictu**  horrible to relate
**humanum est errare**  to err is human
**ibidem**  ibid.; in the same place, used in bibliographies and footnotes
**idem**  the same; something previously mentioned
**id est**  i.e.; that is

**ignoramus**  lit. we ignore; extremely ignorant person, know-nothing

**illuminati**  persons possessing enlightenment

**imprimatur**  lit. let it be printed; license to print; sanction or approval in general

**in absentia**  in one's absence

**incunabula**  lit. swaddling clothes; origin or earliest stages, esp. of printed books

**in excelsis**  in the highest degree

**in extremis**  at the moment of death

**in flagrante delicto**  while the crime or act is occurring

**infra dignitatem**  beneath one's dignity

**in loco citato**  in loc. cit.; in the place cited, used in bibliographies and footnotes

**in loco parentis**  in place of the parent

**in medias res**  in the middle of things

**in memoriam**  in memory of

**in omnia paratus**  prepared for all things

**in re**  in the matter of; regarding

**in situ**  in place; in its natural or original position

**in statu quo**  in the former state

**inter alia**  among other things

**inter nos**  between ourselves

**inter se**  among themselves

**in toto**  in all; entirely

**in utero**  in the womb

**in vino veritas**  in wine lies the truth

**in vitro**  in glass, esp. a test tube

**in vivo**  in that which is living

**ipse dixit**  lit. he himself said it; statement made but not proved

**ipso facto**  by or based on the fact itself

**jacta alea est**  the die is cast

**lapsus linguae**  slip of the tongue

**lex talionis**  law of corresponding retaliation, as an eye for an eye

**literati**  highly educated, literate persons

**locus**  place

**lusus naturae**  freak of nature

**magna cum laude**  with great praise or honors

**magnum opus**  one's great work

**mala fide**  in bad faith

**mandamus**  lit. we demand; writ commanding specific act or duty

**margaritas ante porcos**  pearls before swine

**materfamilias**  female head of household

**mea culpa**  my fault

**memento mori**  lit. remember you must die; reminder of death

**mens rea**  lit. guilty mind; criminal intent

**meum et tuum**  mine and thine

**mirabile dictu**  wonderful to relate

**mirabile visu**  wonderful to behold

**mittimus**  lit. we send; warrant of commitment to prison

**modus operandi**  method of operating

**modus vivendi**  way of living

**mons veneris**  lit. mound of Venus; round protuberance beneath female pubic hair

**mutatis mutandis**  after changing what had to be changed

**ne plus ultra**  lit. not more beyond; highest level of perfection

**nolens volens**  whether unwilling or willing

**noli me tangere**  touch me not

**nolo contendere**  lit. I do not wish to contend; legal plea of no contest to charges

**non compos mentis**  not of sound mind

**non possumus**  lit. we cannot; statement of inability to do something

**non sequitur**  it does not follow

**nota bene**  note well; pay attention

**obiter dictum**  passing remark without legal weight

**omnia vincit amor**  love conquers all

**opere citato**  op. cit.; in the work cited, used in bibliographies and footnotes

**opus**  work, esp. musical composition

**passim**  lit. here and there; repeated in many places

**paterfamilias**  male head of household

**paternoster**  our father

**pax**  peace

**pax vobiscum**  peace be with you

**per annum**  per year; annually

**per capita**  lit. per head; per person

**per diem**  daily

**per se**  in itself; inherently

**persona non grata**  unwelcome person

**post meridiem**  p.m.; after midday

**post mortem**  after death, esp. an examination

**postscriptum**  lit. written after; used to tag addition to a letter

**prima facie**  at first view

**primus inter pares**  first among equals

**pro**  in favor of

**pro bono publico**  for the public benefit

**pro et contra**  for and against

**pro forma**  lit. for form; done perfunctorily, as a formality

**pro patria**  for one's country

**pro rata**  proportionately according to an exact formula

**pro tempore**  for the time being; temporarily

**qua**  lit. who; in the capacity of; as

**quid nunc**  what now?

**quid pro quo**  something given for something; an exchange

**quod erat demonstrandum**  Q.E.D.; which was to be demonstrated

**quod erat faciendum**  which was to be done

**quodlibet**  lit. whom it pleases; philosophical point for disputation

**quod vide**  q.v.; which see, referring to something

**quorum**  lit. of whom; minimum attendance at assembly or meeting

**quo vadis**  where are you going?

**rara avis**  lit. rare bird; anything unusual or rare

**re**  regarding, short for in re

**reductio ad absurdum**  leading logically to an absurd conclusion

**redux**  brought back

**regina**  queen

**requiescat in pace**  rest in peace

**res**  thing; matter; fact

**res ipsa loquitur**  the thing speaks for itself

**res publica**  popular affairs; commonwealth

**rex**  king

**rigor mortis**  stiffness of death

**sanctum sanctorum**  lit. holy of holies; sacred place

**saturnalia**  revelry or uproarious festivities

**semper fidelis**  always faithful

**sequitur**  it follows

**sic**  thus, esp. to note a textual mistake

**sic passim**  thus throughout, used of word or idea found throughout text

**sic semper tyrannis**  thus always to tyrants

**sic transit gloria mundi**  so passes the glory of the world

**sine die**  indefinitely, with no set date in the future

**sine qua non**  lit. not without which; indispensable thing or condition

**status quo**  conditions as they are now

**stet**  lit. it stands; let the original stand, used in proofreading

**stupor mundi**  wonder of the world

**subito**  immediately; suddenly, esp. as a musical direction

**sub rosa**  lit. under the rose; in secret, covertly

**sui generis**  of its own kind; one of a kind

**summa cum laude**  with the highest praise or honors

**summum bonum**  the highest or chief good

**tabula rasa**  clean slate

**tempus fugit**  time flies

**terra firma**  solid ground; dry land

**terra incognita**  unknown ground, uncharted territory

**ultra vires**  exceeding legal authority

**ut infra**  as below

**ut supra**  as above

**uxor**  wife

**vade mecum**  lit. go with me; pocketbook carried for ready reference

**veni, vidi, vici**  I came, I saw, I conquered

**verbatim**  word for word

**verbum sap**  enough said, inferring something left unsaid

**versus**  lit. toward opposite; against or in competition with

**via media**  middle way

**vice versa**  conversely; the opposite way

**vide**  see, used to direct or refer a reader elsewhere

**videlicet**  lit. it is permitted to see; namely

**viva voce**  lit. with the living voice; by word of mouth

**vox populi**  lit. the voice of the people; popular opinion

**vox populi, vox Dei**  the voice of the people is the voice of God

# FOREIGN WORDS AND PHRASES

French
Other Romance Languages
German, Greek, and Other Languages

**SEE ALSO**: Chap. 9: Foods; Cooking and Cuisine; Chap. 11: Titles of Rank; Chap. 15: Classical Music; Musical Instruments; Chap. 20: Greetings and Farewells; Chap. 21: Latin Words and Phrases; Yiddish Borrowings

Many foreign words have been naturalized in the English language to such a degree that they no longer have the feel or sound of a foreign expression. Such words as "debutante" and "séance" are not included in this section. Words like "voilà" and "déclassé," which sound French when used in English speech, and foreign phrases used as English idioms (such as "bon voyage"), form the bulk of this list.

# FRENCH

**à bas**  down with

**à bientôt**  see you soon

**adieu**  good-bye, farewell

**affaire d'amour**  love affair

**agent provocateur**  outside agitator who incites others to criminal acts or riot

**aide de camp**  senior military officer or confidential adviser

**à la carte**  lit. on the card; priced separately on the menu

**à la mode**  in the fashion

**amour**  love

**ancien régime**  the old or former regime

**à propos**  relative or pertaining to; fitting; to the purpose

**au contraire**  on the contrary

**au courant**  up to date

**au fait**  well-versed, expert

**au naturel**  in its natural state, esp. nude

**au revoir**  good-bye, until we meet again

**avant-garde**  the vanguard, esp. in the arts

**à votre santé**  to your health

**beau geste**  fine gesture, often for effect

**beau idéal**  model or conception of excellence

**beau monde**  fashionable society

**beaux arts**  fine arts

**belles lettres**  serious literature

**bête noire**  pet peeve

**billet-doux**  love note

**bon appétit**  good appetite; enjoy your meal

**bonhomie**  good nature

**bonjour**  hello, good day

**bon marché**  inexpensive

**bon mot**  witty turn of phrase

**bonne chance**  good luck

**bon vivant**  person who lives well and enjoys socializing

**bon voyage**  have a good journey

**bric-à-brac**  trinkets, baubles

**cachet**  sign or expression of approval; superior status

**canaille**  common people, rabble

**canard**  insult or hoax

**ça ne fait rien**  no matter, it is not important

**carte blanche**  unrestricted authority or access

**cause célèbre**  notorious incident

**c'est la guerre**  that's the way of war, used to express resignation

**c'est la vie**  that's life

**chacun à son goût**  each to his own taste

**chef-d'oeuvre**  masterpiece

**chez la famille**  at home with one's family

**chez moi**  at my home

**comme ci, comme ça**  so-so, neither one way nor the other

**comme il faut**  proper, appropriate

**contretemps**  unfortunate mishap or inconvenience

**coup d'état**  usu. violent overthrow of government

**coup de grâce**  final blow

**crème de la crème**  very best or top level, usu. used of people

**cul de sac**  dead end

**danse macabre**  dance of death

**déclassé**  reduced to or having low status

**décolletage**  low-cut neckline on dress

**déjà vu**  lit. already seen; illusory sense of having previously experienced something

**demimonde**  group whose activities are ethically or legally questionable, esp. prostitutes

**dénouement**  resolution or outcome, esp. of story

**de rigueur**  strictly according to the rules

**dernier cri**  the last word

**déshabillé**  state of being poorly or carelessly dressed

**désolé**  heartbroken, disconsolate

**double entendre**  word or expression having two meanings in context

**éclat**  flair, dash

**élan vital**  creative force

**embarras de richesses**  embarrassment of riches

**éminence grise**  person wielding power in the background

**en famille**  just among the family

**enfant terrible**  irresponsible person, esp. incorrigible child

**en garde**  on guard

**en masse**  as a group

**en passant**  in passing

**entr'acte**  intermission

**entrée**  main course of meal

**entre nous**  just between us

**esprit de corps**  spirit of and loyalty to one's group

**fait accompli**  accomplished fact

**faute de mieux**  for lack of something better

**faux pas**  social error

**femme fatale**  dangerous, enticing woman

**fin de siècle**  end of the century, usu. decadent

**gaucherie**  vulgarity, awkwardness

**grande dame**  aristocratic elderly lady

**habitué**  one who frequents some establishment

**haute couture**  high fashion

**haute cuisine**  elegant, often rich food

**hauteur**  snobbish, aloof manner

**haut monde**  high society

**hors d'oeuvre**  appetizer

**idée fixe**  obsession

**je ne sais quoi**  lit. I do not know what; that indescribable something

**joie de vivre**  exuberant high spirits

**laissez faire**  policy of government in which affairs are allowed to run their own course

**lèse majesté**  attack on ruler or established authority

**l'état c'est moi**  I am the state

**longeur**  tedious, dreary passages of language

**ma chère**  my dear, said of females

**madame**  married woman

**mademoiselle**  unmarried woman

**maison**  house

**maître d'hôtel**  chief waiter

**manqué**  having failed

**Mardi Gras**  lit. fat Tuesday; pre-Lenten festival on Shrove Tuesday

**mélange**  mixture

**ménage à trois**  three-way relationship, usu. sexual

**merci**  thank you

**merci beaucoup**  thank you very much

**métier**  vocation or calling

**mon chère**  my dear, said of males

**monsieur**  mister, sir

**mot juste**  word that conveys precise meaning

**n'est-ce pas?**  isn't it so? don't you agree?

**noblesse oblige**  obligations of noble birth

**nom de guerre**  lit. war name; pseudonym, stage name

**nom de plume**  pen name

**nouveau riche**  person who is newly rich

**objet d'art**  work of art

**objet trouvé**  found object, usu. of artistic value

**papier-mâché**  paper and glue mixture used to form sculptures

**par example**  for example

**par excellence**  superior, preeminent

**parti pris**  point of view determined in advance; prejudice

**parvenu**  newcomer, upstart

**passé**  out of date, no longer in fashion

**petit bourgeois**  person who belongs to lower middle class, usu. made up of shopkeepers and clerks

**pièce de résistance**  principal or showpiece object or event

**pied-à-terre**  temporary or part-time residence

**plat du jour**  featured dish of the day

**plus ça change, plus c'est la même chose**  the more things change, the more they remain the same

**potpourri**  medley, usu. of scented herbs and spices

**prix fixe**  set price

**protégé**  person under's one care or tutelage

**provocateur**  one who challenges or agitates others

**raconteur**  storyteller

**raison d'être**  reason for being

**recherché**  esoteric, rare; mannered, affected

**répondez s'il vous plaît**  please respond

**risqué**  indelicate or suggestive

**roman à cléf**  novel depicting historical figures under fictional names

**sacré bleu**  exclamation meaning good God

**sang-froid**  composure, self-possession

**sans souci**  without concern or worry

**savoir-faire**  knowledge of what to do or say, esp. in social situation

**s'il vous plaît**  please

**soi-disant**  so-called

**son et lumière**  sound and light show

**succès d'estime**  critical success, esp. for work of art

**table d'hôte**  set meal served at fixed time and place

**tant mieux**  so much the better

**tant pis**  so much the worse

**tête-à-tête**  intimate, private conversation

**touché**  lit. touched; signifying strike in fencing or comment that is on the mark

**tour de force**  display of power, skill, or virtuosity

**tout de suite**  immediately

**tout le monde**  everyone

**trompe l'oeil**  fooling the eye, esp. illusion of perspective in painting

**vis-à-vis**  regarding, relating to

**voilà**  there it is, look at that, it is so

**volte-face**  reversal, turnabout

## OTHER ROMANCE LANGUAGES

**a cappella**  *Italian*. sung without instrumental accompaniment

**adios**  *Spanish*. good-bye

**aficionado**  *Spanish*. fan, enthusiast

**al dente** *Italian*. lit. to the tooth; firm to the bite, said esp. of food

**alfresco** *Italian*. in the open air

**amigo** *Spanish*. friend

**arrivederci** *Italian*. good-bye, until we meet again

**auto-da-fé** *Portuguese*. lit. act of faith; execution of condemned heretics after public declaration of judgment

**bambino** *Italian*. baby, child

**basta** *Italian*. enough! stop it!

**bodega** *Spanish*. wineshop; small market

**buenas dias** *Spanish*. hello, good day

**caballero** *Spanish*. horseman, gentleman, cavalier

**campesino** *Spanish*. farmer, peasant

**cantina** *Spanish*. bar, café

**caramba** *Spanish*. exclamation of amazement, anger, or dismay

**che sarà sarà** *Italian*. what will be, will be

**ciao** *Italian*. good-bye, see you later

**cognoscenti** *Italian*. those in the know, esp. intellectuals

**compañero** *Spanish*. male companion or partner

**con mucho gusto** *Spanish*. with great pleasure

**conquistador** *Spanish*. conqueror

**desperado** *Spanish*. bold, reckless bandit or outlaw

**diva** *Italian*. exalted female singer

**dolce far niente** *Italian*. sweet inactivity

**dolce vita** *Italian*. the good life

**gaucho** *Spanish*. cowboy, mounted herdsman

**gracias** *Spanish*. thank you

**hacienda** *Spanish*. ranch

**hombre** *Spanish*. man, fellow

**inamorata** *Italian*. female sweetheart or lover

**incognito** *Italian*. anonymously or in disguise

**incommunicado** *Spanish*. isolated from any contact with others

**junta** *Spanish*. usu. military council serving as government

**machismo** *Spanish*. strong sense of masculinity and virility

**maestro** *Italian*. master, esp. of music

**magnifico** *Italian*. great man

**mañana** *Spanish*. tomorrow

**mas o menos** *Spanish*. more or less

**mucho** *Spanish*. much

**olé** *Spanish*. shout of approval or encouragement

**padre** *Spanish*. father, esp. clergyman

**peccadillo** *Spanish*. minor offense, venial sin

**pentimento** *Italian*. appearance of earlier stages or images, esp. in painting

**per favore** *Italian*. please

**por favor** *Spanish*. please

**posada** *Spanish*. inn

**prego** *Italian*. please

**presto** *Italian*. quickly, right away

**prima donna** *Italian*. principal female, leading lady

**pronto** *Spanish*. quickly, right away

**que pasa?** *Spanish*. what's happening?

**que sera sera** *Spanish*. whatever will be will be

**quién sabe?** *Spanish*. who knows?

**salud** *Spanish*. to your health

**señor** *Spanish*. sir, mister

**señora** *Spanish*. married woman

**señorita** *Spanish*. unmarried woman

**siesta** *Spanish*. afternoon nap or rest

**sotto voce** *Italian*. softly, under one's voice

**toro** *Spanish*. bull

**vamos** *Spanish*. let's go

**vaya con Dios** *Spanish*. God be with you

**vertù** *Italian*. love of arts and fine things

**virtuoso** *Italian*. person skilled in one field, esp. a performer

**viva** *Spanish*. exclamation of approval

## GERMAN, GREEK, AND OTHER LANGUAGES

**acedia** *Greek*. listlessness, sloth

**Achtung** *German*. attention

**agape** *Greek*. God's love for man

**ahimsa** *Hindi*. doctrine of nonviolence

**aloha** *Hawaiian*. hello or good-bye

**angst** *German*. anxiety

**anomie** *Greek*. lawlessness and loss of purpose leading to despair

**apocrypha** *Greek*. secret, hidden things, esp. in texts

**ataxia** *Greek*. lack of control or order

**auf Wiedersehen** *German*. good-bye, until we meet again

**babushka** *Russian*. grandmother, old woman; head scarf

**banzai** *Japanese*. lit. 10,000 years; cry of victory or salute

**Blitzkrieg** *German*. sudden, violent attack

**bwana** *Swahili*. sir, master, father

**catharsis** *Greek*. cleansing or purification, esp. from guilt through drama or art

**charisma** *Greek*. capacity to inspire and lead others

**cosmos** *Greek*. orderly universe

**danke schön** *German*. thank you very much

**ding hao** *Chinese*. very good, excellent

**Doppelgänger** *German*. phantom double

**do svidaniya** *Russian*. good-bye, until we meet again

**Dummkopf** *German*. dummy, blockhead

**ersatz** *German*. fake, imitation

**eureka** *Greek*. I've found it; it is real or true

**Frau** *German*. married woman

**Fräulein** *German*. unmarried woman

**geisha** *Japanese*. young woman trained as companion for men

**Gemütlichkeit** *German*. good-natured, friendly cordiality

**Gestalt** *German*. unified whole that cannot be inferred from its component parts

**Gesundheit** *German*. good health to you, used esp. after someone sneezes

**glasnost** *Russian*. openness, esp. social and political

**gnothi seauton** *Greek*. know thyself

**gulag** *Russian*. forced-labor camp

**guru** *Hindi*. venerable teacher

**halcyon** *Greek*. lit. kingfisher; calm, peaceful

**hara-kiri** *Japanese*. ritual suicide by disembowelment

**hausfrau** *German*. housewife

**hoi polloi** *Greek*. common people

**hubris** *Greek*. excessive pride and arrogance

**iota** *Greek*. atom; small amount

**jawohl** *German*. yes, definitely

**kamikaze** *Japanese*. person on a suicide mission, orig. a pilot; any reckless person

**kaputt** *German*. finished, ruined, broken

**kismet** *Turkish*. fate

**Kitsch** *German*. vulgar, trashy, valueless work

**kowtow** *Chinese*. fawn, bow low

**kudos** *Greek.* fame, glory, adulation

**l'chaim** *Hebrew.* to your health

**Lebensraum** *German.* additional room needed for expansion

**logos** *Greek.* rational principle that governs the universe

**Lumpenproletariat** *German.* vagrants, criminals, and rabble without class consciousness

**mazel tov** *Hebrew.* congratulations

**nabob** *Hindi.* man of wealth and power

**nirvana** *Sanskrit.* extinction of desire and achievement of perfect holiness

**pariah** *Hindi.* outcast

**perestroika** *Russian.* policy of Soviet economic and political reform

**pogrom** *Russian.* massacre or persecution

**pundit** *Hindi.* authoritative, scholarly commentator

**Putsch** *German.* insurrection

**Rathskeller** *German.* basement tavern

**sahib** *Arabic.* master

**salaam** *Arabic.* peace

**samurai** *Japanese.* member of feudal warrior caste

**sayonara** *Japanese.* good-bye, farewell

**Schadenfreude** *German.* pleasure derived from another's misfortune

**shalom** *Hebrew.* peace

**skoal** *Swedish.* to your health

**stasis** *Greek.* cessation of movement or circulation

**Sturm und Drang** *German.* storm and stress

**swami** *Sanskrit.* master, esp. religious teacher

**taboo** *Polynesian.* prohibited act

**tovarishch** *Russian.* comrade

**Übermensch** *German.* superman

**uhuru** *Swahili.* freedom

**ukase** *Russian.* command or edict

**verboten** *German.* forbidden

**Wanderjahr** *German.* year of travel

**Wanderlust** *German.* desire to travel

**Weltanschauung** *German.* comprehensive world view or outlook

**Weltgeist** *German.* spirit of the times

**Weltschmerz** *German.* world-weary sorrow

**Wunderkind** *German.* prodigy

**yogi** *Sanskrit.* practitioner of yoga

**Zeitgeist** *German.* spirit of the time

# YIDDISH BORROWINGS

**SEE ALSO**: Chap. 8: Kinship and Family Relations; Chap. 20: Insults, Slurs, and Epithets; Terms of Endearment and Respect; Nonsense, Confusion, and Trouble; Chap. 22: Sex, Love, and Romance

**baleboste** efficient, competent housewife or hostess

**beheyme** cow, or big dummy, used esp. of women

**bube** grandmother

**bubele** little bube; dear, sweetie

**bubkes** lit. beans; nothing

**chazerei** lit. pig food; junk, unpalatable stuff

**chutzpah** gall, nerve, or brashness

**drek** *Vulgar.* shit, literally or figuratively

**farblondzhet** (*adj*) wandering aimlessly; confused or out of it

**farmisht** (*adj*) confused, mixed up

**farshtunkener** stinking, nasty one

**fartumlt** (*adj*) disoriented, confused

**feigel** lit. bird; *Slang.* homosexual male

**futz** (*vb*) *Vulgar.* screw around; mess with

**gelt** money

**gevalt** lit. violence, force; outcry of alarm, as in "oy gevalt"

**golem** robot, lifelike creature; clay icon

**goy** gentile, non-Jew

**goyim** gentiles, non-Jews

**goyish** (*adj*) non-Jewlike

**haimish** (*adj*) homey, cozy

**kibitz** (*vb*) meddle, offer gratuitous advice

**kishke** intestine, gut; stuffed derma

**kish meyn tokhes** *Vulgar.* kiss my ass

**klutz** dullard; clumsy person

**knish** lit. stuffed dumpling; *Vulgar slang.* vagina

**kosher** (*adj*) fit to eat under Jewish dietary laws; proper, legitimate

**kreplach** lit. triangular dumplings; *Slang.* nothing

**kvell** be delighted

**kvetch** (*vb*) complain, whine, nag; (*n*) crotchety person

**luftmensch** person whose head is in the clouds, dreamer

**macher** wheeler-dealer, big shot

**mamzer** lit. illegitimate child; despicable individual; *Slang.* con man

**maven** expert, connoisseur

**megillah** long story, rigmarole

**mensch** admirable human being, person of dignity and integrity

**meshugas** insanity, nonsense

**meshuge** (*adj*) crazy, mad, or nuts

**meshugene** crazy person

**mishpoche** family, clan

**nakhes** good feeling, pride and joy; pleasure

**nebbish** nobody, loser, drip, or hapless one

**nogoodnik** bum to be avoided at all cost

**noodge** (*vb*) nag, pick at; (*n*) nagger, badgerer

**nosh** (*vb*) snack, nibble, or eat a bit; (*n*) tidbit or snack

**nosher** one who nibbles constantly

**nu** (*interj*) well? so? so what?

**nudnik** talkative bore; dummy

**ongeblozn** (*adj*) puffed up, conceited, or arrogant

**oy** (*interj*) oh!

**parnose** livelihood

**patsh** slap

**patshke** (*vb*) fiddle about lazily

**pisher** little squirt; someone of no consequence

**plotz** (*vb*) burst, explode

**punim** face

**pupik** bellybutton

**putz** *Vulgar.* lit. penis; jerk

**schmooze** (*vb*) have a heart-to-heart talk; chitchat or gab with one's associates

**shadchen** marriage broker, matchmaker

**shegetz** non-Jewish boy or young man; Jewish boy who fails to observe religious practices

**shiksa** non-Jewish woman, esp. girl or young woman

**shlemazel** born loser, someone always unlucky

**shlemiel** fool, social misfit, or failure; awkward person

**shlep** (*vb*) drag, haul around; trudge; (*n*) slob, bum

**shlock** shoddy, poorly crafted items

**shlong** *Vulgar.* penis

**shlump** slob, drip

**shmaltz** lit. rendered chicken fat; mawkish oversentimentality, maudlin mush

**shmate** rag, cheap dress; shoddy garment or object

**shmeer** (*vb*) bribe, grease the palm of; (*n*) complete array of things

**shmegege** buffoon, idiot

**shmendrik** weak, ineffectual person

**shmo** boob, dummy

**shmuck** *Vulgar.* lit. penis; bad person, idiot, fool, or bastard

**shmutz** garbage, dirt

**shnook** pathetic but lovable fool, easy mark, or sucker

**shnorrer** beggar, panhandler; miser, wheedler, or cheapskate

**shnoz** nose, esp. large one

**shpritz** (*vb*) lit. spray; inject life into, poke fun at

**shtick** verbal bit, esp. comic routine; one's special interest or talent

**shtunk** something that smells unpleasant; louse

**shtup** (*vb*) stuff; push; *Vulgar.* have sex with

**shvitzer** someone who sweats a lot; braggart

**tchatchkes** knickknacks, trinkets

**tokhes** rear end, buttocks; tush

**tsimes** fuss, big to-do, or brouhaha

**tsores** worries, woes, or afflictions

**tush** toches

**vey** pain, as in "oy vey"

**vitz** joke, wisecrack

**yenta** gossipy person, busybody

**yid** derogatory term for a Jew

**zaftig** (*adj*) juicy, plump; voluptuous, sexy

**zhlub** someone insensitive and boorish

# PART SEVEN

# THE HUMAN CONDITION

# CHAPTER 22

# Character and Behavior

# PERSONALITY AND BEHAVIOR

Appealing/Unappealing
   Appealing, Elegant, Neat, Rich, or Fancy
   Unappealing, Shabby, Messy, Poor, or Clumsy
Warm/Cold
   Warm, Friendly, Sensitive, or Loving
   Cold, Unfriendly, Irritable, or Cruel
Extroverted/Introverted
   Extroverted, Outgoing, Outspoken, or Dramatic
   Introverted, Reserved, Isolated, or Mysterious
Dominant/Submissive
   Dominant, Stubborn, Proud, or Confident
   Submissive, Uncertain, or Tentative
Strong/Weak
   Strong, Bold, or Tough
   Weak, Fearful, or Anxious
Active/Inert
   Active, Lively, Awake, or Limber
   Inert, Lazy, Tired, or Insensate
Happy/Sad
   Happy, Playful, Optimistic, or Elated
   Sad, Serious, Pessimistic, or Discontented
Calm/Angry
   Calm, Gentle, or Easygoing
   Angry, Emotional, Aggressive, or Passionate
Moderate/Excessive
   Moderate, Sane, Conservative, or Old-Fashioned
   Excessive, Mad, Insane, or Radical
Proper/Vulgar
   Proper, Courteous, Refined, or Puritanical
   Vulgar, Rude, Degenerate, or Wild
Intelligent/Stupid
   Intelligent, Informed, Clever, or Articulate
   Stupid, Ignorant, or Confused
Special/Ordinary
   Special, Bright, Skillful, or Unusual
   Ordinary, Dull, Plain, or Banal
Wise/Foolish
   Wise, Mature, or Experienced
   Foolish, Immature, Bigoted, or Trivial
Good/Bad
   Good, Sincere, Honest, or Just
   Bad, False, Evil, Insincere, or Dishonest
Giving/Demanding
   Giving, Trusting, Innocent, or Generous
   Demanding, Critical, Calculating, or Selfish
Helpful/Troublesome
   Helpful, Positive, Responsible, or Nice
   Troublesome, Negative, Irresponsible, or Unpleasant

**SEE ALSO**: Chap. 1: Physical Appearance

Nearly 4000 adjectives describing human personality and behavior have been grouped into sixteen pairs of opposites, such as Happy/Sad. Each pair is broken down into two undefined lists of virtual synonyms and words with casually related meanings. The parameters for these lists are defined by the four or five adjectives forming the section title. While the meanings of the terms in each list vary, the category is intended to serve as a reminder of similar but slightly different and familiar words and to help provide variety in the adjectives one might use in describing a person. While this system of categorizing adjectives is by no means scientific, and is not based on accepted psychological standards, it is hoped that the associations and divisions of these words will prove stimulating and useful to readers and writers, especially those engaged in creative writing.

## APPEALING/UNAPPEALING

### APPEALING, ELEGANT, NEAT, RICH, OR FANCY

adorable, affluent, alluring, appealing, aristocratic, arresting, attractive
beautiful, becoming, beguiling, bewitching, breathtaking
caparisoned, captivating, charismatic, charming, chic, Circean, classy, clean, clubby, couth, crisp, cuddly
dandy, dapper, dashing, dazzling, dear, debonair, decorous, desirable, devastating, dignified
elegant, enchanting, engaging, enthralling, enticing, entrancing, exquisite
fancy, fashionable, fetching, finished, flowery, flush
galluptious, glamorous, glorious, graceful, gracious
handsome, healthy, highborn, hygienic
immaculate, impeccable, imperial, ingratiating, intoxicating, inviting, irresistible
kempt, kingly
lardy-dardy, lavish, lush, luxuriant, luxurious
magnetic, mellifluous, mod, modish
natty, neat, nifty, nobby, nubile
opulent, ornate
patrician, photogenic, picturesque, plush, plushy, polished, posh, prepossessing, pretty, princely, privileged, prosperous
redolent, refined, regal, resplendent, rich, ritzy, royal
sanitary, sartorial, scrumptious, seductive, select, sexy, silk-stocking, sleek, slick, smart, smooth, snazzy, soigné, sophisticated, spanking, spellbinding, spiffy, splashy, splendid, spotless, spruce, stainless, stately, sterling, striking, stunning, stylish, suave, sumptuous, surefooted, sure-handed, svelte, swank, swanky, swell, swish
tantalizing, tasty, tidy, trendy, trig, trim
ultrachic, ultramodern, ultrarich
voguish
wealthy, well, well-groomed, well-heeled, well-off, winning, winsome
yummy

### UNAPPEALING, SHABBY, MESSY, POOR, OR CLUMSY

abysmal, accident-prone, all thumbs, angular, askew, awkward, awry
blowsy
cadaverous, chunderous, clumsy, contaminated, crumpled
déclassé, decrepit, derelict, destitute, dingy, disfigured, disgusting, dowdy, down-and-out, drippy, dumpy

fiddle-footed, filthy, frightful, frowzy, funky
gaudy, gawky, geeky, ghastly, gnarly, graceless, grisly, grotesque, gruesome
hard-up, heavy-footed, hideous, homely, horrid, horrific
icky, imperfect, impoverished, impure, incondite, incongruous, indecorous, indigent, inelegant, infelicitous, insolvent
lowborn, lowly
macabre, malodorous, meretricious, messy, monstrous
odious, oily, oleaginous, overdressed
penniless, penurious, plain, poor, putrescent, putrid
ragged, ragtag, rancid, ratty, repellent, repugnant, repulsive, revolting, rough, rugged
scabrous, scandalous, scraggly, scummy, scuzzy, seedy, shabby, shaggy, shocking, shoddy, sickening, simian, slatternly, slavering, sleazy, slimy, slobbery, sloppy, slovenly, slummy, sordid, squalid, stinky, subhuman
tacky, tatty, tawdry, tenth-rate, tousled
ugly, ulcerous, unappealing, unbecoming, unclean, uncoordinated, uncouth, underprivileged, undesirable, undignified, unfashionable, unfit, unhandy, unhealthy, unkempt, unpolished, unsanitary, unsavory, unsightly, untidy, unvarnished, unwashed
weather-beaten, woolly
yucky

## WARM/COLD

### WARM, FRIENDLY, SENSITIVE, OR LOVING

adoring, affable, affectionate, agreeable, amatory, amenable, amiable, amicable, amorous, appreciative, approachable, ardent, avuncular
chummy, companionable, compassionate, congenial, convivial, cordial
devoted, disarming
earthy, empathic
familiar, favorable, fond, forgiving, friendly
genial, good-humored, good-natured, gracious, gregarious
heartwarming, hearty, hospitable
ingratiating, intimate
kind, kindhearted, kindly, kindred
largehearted, likable, lovable, loving
merciful
neighborly
open, open-hearted
pally, palsy-walsy, personable
reverent, romantic
sensitive, sensual, sentimental, sociable, soft, soft-hearted, summery, sympathetic
tender, tender-hearted, touching
warm, warm-hearted, well-disposed, worshipful

### COLD, UNFRIENDLY, IRRITABLE, OR CRUEL

abrupt, alien, aloof, arctic, arid, asexual, ashen, astringent, atrabilious, austere
bad-tempered, bilious, bitter, bleak, bloody, blunt, brusque, brutal
callous, cantankerous, catty, cheap, chilly, chintzy, chippy, churlish, closed, cold, cold-blooded, cold-hearted, contemptuous, crabby, cranky, cross, crotchety, cruel, crusty, cryptic, curmudgeonly, cursed, curt, cussed, cutthroat, cynical
dispassionate, distant, domineering, dour, Draconian, dry, dyspeptic

egocentric, empty, envious
forbidding, formidable, freezing, frigid, frosty
gelid, glacial, glowering, gray, greedy, grouchy, grudging, gruff, grumpy
hardened, hardhearted, hateful, haughty, heartless, hollow, huffish, humiliating
icy, ignoble, ill-humored, ill-natured, ill-tempered, impersonal, inconsiderate, indifferent, inhospitable, insensitive, insulting, insusceptible, intolerant, inured, irreconcilable, irritable
jealous
liverish
matter-of-fact, mean, mechanical, merciless, misanthropic, miserly
nasty, niggardly, nippy
ornery
parched, parsimonious, peckish, peevish, penurious, persnickety, petty, piercing, pinchbeck, pitiless, Procrustean, psychopathic
raw, reactionary, remorseless, remote, ruthless
sadistic, salty, self-serving, sere, sexless, sharp-tongued, shrewish, snappish, snarly, snippety, snippy, snitty, snotty, sour, spiteful, spleenful, splenetic, stark, steely, stern, stiff, stingy, stoical, stony, strict, surly, suspicious
testy, tetchy, thick-skinned, tight, tight-fisted, touchy, troglodytic, truculent, tyrannical
uncharitable, uncommunicative, uncongenial, unfeeling, unforgiving, unfriendly, ungrateful, unkind, unkindly, unmerciful, unmoved, unsympathetic
vengeful, venomous, vexatious, vicious, vitriolic
waspish, wintry, withholding, wizened, wooden, wrongheaded

## EXTROVERTED/INTROVERTED

### EXTROVERTED, OUTGOING, OUTSPOKEN, OR DRAMATIC

ambitious, assertive, atwitter
blatant, bloviating, blustering, boisterous, bold, bombastic, brash, brazen, breathy
chatty, choleric
defiant, dramatic
emphatic, evangelical, excited, exhibitionistic, expansive, expressive, extemporaneous, extroverted, exuberant
flagrant, flamboyant, flashy, flirtatious, forward, freewheeling
garrulous, grandiloquent, gregarious, gushy
high-profile, histrionic
immodest, indiscreet, intrusive
jabbering
lippy, logorrheic, loquacious, loud, loudmouthed
madcap, malapert, meteoric, militant, multiloquious
noisy
obstreperous, obtrusive, orotund, outgoing, outspoken, overbearing, overt, overweening
pert, petulant, presumptuous, prolix, protrusive, protuberant, public, pugnacious, pushy
rah-rah, raucous, red-hot, rousing
shrill, sonorous, spectacular, splashy, stagestruck, stagy, stentorian, strident, stridulous, swinging, switched-on
talkative, theatrical, throaty, turgid
uninhibited, unreserved, unselfconscious, uproarious
verbose, visible, vitriolic, vocal, vociferous, voluble
wordy

## INTRODUCED, RESERVED, ISOLATED, OR MYSTERIOUS

abashed, alien, alienated, alone, aloof, anonymous, antisocial, ascetic, asocial, austere, autonomous, awkward
bashful
chary, clannish, claustral, cloistered, cloistral, concealed, confidential, covert, coy, crafty
delitescent, detached, discreet, distant
elliptical, elusive, enigmatic, eremitic, estranged, evasive
ghostly, guarded
hermitic,
incommunicado, indirect, inhibited, inner-directed, inscrutable, insular, introspective, introverted, invisible, inward, isolated
laconic, latent, lone, lonely, low-profile
misty, misunderstood, modest, monastic, monkish, mum, mute, mysterious
nebulous, nonverbal
oblique, obscure, occult
paradoxical, passive, phantom, private
quiescent, quiet
reclusive, reluctant, remote, repressed, reserved, restrained, reticent, retiring
secluded, secretive, self-absorbed, self-conscious, self-effacing, sensitive, sequestered, shadowy, shamefaced, sheepish, short-spoken, shy, silent, smoky, sneaky, soft-spoken, solitary, solo, spectral, sphinxlike, spooky, standoffish, stay-at-home, stealthy, still, stolid, strange, sub rosa, subterranean, surreptitious, suspicious
taciturn, tactful, tight-lipped, tiptoe
ultracool, unapproachable, unassertive, unassuming, unclear, uncommunicative, undemonstrative, understated, unexpressive, unfathomable, unobtrusive, unsociable
vanishing, veiled, voiceless
wary, watchful, wistful, withdrawn, wordless, wraithlike
xenophobic

## DOMINANT/SUBMISSIVE

### DOMINANT, STUBBORN, PROUD, OR CONFIDENT

abusive, adamant, ascendant, assuming, assured, authoritative, autocratic
bossy, bullheaded, bumptious
certain, cock-a-hoop, cocksure, cocky, commanding, compelling, conclusive, confident, controlling, contumacious
decisive, determined, direct, directed, dogged, dogmatic, dominant, domineering, do-or-die
egoistic, egotistic, emphatic, enduring, entitled, entrenched
firm, fixed, focused, forceful, formidable
grandiose
hard-ass, hard-bitten, hard-boiled, hard-edged, hardened, hardheaded, headstrong, hellbent, high and mighty, high-flown, high-handed, high-powered
immovable, impenetrable, imperative, imperious, impervious, implacable, impregnable, independent, indestructible, indomitable, inexorable, inflated, inflexible, insistent, insuperable, intent, intimidating, intractable, intransigent, invincible, invulnerable, ironbound, ironclad, irresistible
lordly
macho, magisterial, magistral, messianic, mighty, militaristic, mulish

obdurate, obstinate, omnipotent, one-sided, opinionated, orgulous, orotund, ossified, overweening, overwhelming
persistent, persuasive, pertinacious, pervicacious, pigheaded, poised, portentous, possessive, predominant, preponderant, presumptuous, prideful, prodigious, proprietary, proud, purposeful, pushy
ramrod, recalcitrant, redoubtable, refractory, relentless, renitent, resolute, rigid
secure, self-assured, self-confident, self-important, self-involved, self-possessed, self-righteous, self-satisfied, self-seeking, single-minded, smug, stiff, strident, strong-minded, strong-willed, stubborn, sure, swaggering, swashbuckling, swellheaded
take-charge, tenacious, territorial, thick-skinned, turgid
unassailable, unbending, undaunted, unfaltering, unflagging, unflinching, unreceptive, unregenerate, unrelenting, unstinting, unstoppable, unswerving, unwary, unwieldy, unwilling, unyielding
vain, vainglorious, vehement, volitive
whole hog, willful

## SUBMISSIVE, UNCERTAIN, OR TENTATIVE

accommodating, acquiescent, adaptable, ambivalent, apologetic, apprehensive, assailable, awkward
balky
caducous, chameleonic, changeable, chary, chivvied, compliant, concessive, conciliatory, culpable, cursory
dainty, deferential, dependent, diffident, doubtful, downtrodden, dubious, ductile
effeminate, equivocal, exposed
fatalistic, fawning, flexible, flimsy
halfhearted, halting, haphazard, harmless, hesitant, humiliated
ill at ease, impalpable, inconclusive, inconstant, incredulous, indecisive, indirect, inoffensive, insecure, irresolute
labile, lambent, loath, lost
malleable, masochistic, mealy-mouthed, meek, mousy, mutable
noncommittal, nude
obedient, obeisant, obsequious
penitent, phlegmatic, plastic, pliable, pliant, prostrate, protean
qualmish, queasy, questioning, quizzical
receptive, reconciled, reluctant, repentant, reserved, resigned, respectful
self-abnegating, self-denying, sequacious, serviceable, servile, shackled, slavish, solicitous, squishy, subdued, submissive, subservient, suggestible, supple, suppliant, susceptible, sycophantic
tentative, tenuous, thin-skinned, timid, tongue-tied, tractable, tremulous
unresisting
vacillating, vague, vulnerable
wavering, wishy-washy
yielding

## STRONG/WEAK

### STRONG, BOLD, OR TOUGH

able-bodied, adventuresome, adventurous, all-powerful, audacious
ballsy, belligerent, bluff, blunt, bold, brash, brave, brawny, burly
clutch, courageous
daring, dauntless, decisive, doughty, durable

effective
fearless, firm, flinty, forbidding, formidable, full-blooded
gritty, gutsy, gutty
hale, hard-ass, hardball, hard-nosed, hardy, heavy,
    hell-for-leather, hoydenish
indestructible, inexhaustible, intrepid
lionhearted, lusty
manly, massive, mettlesome, mighty, militant, motivated,
    muscular
nervy
oppressive
physical, plucky, potent, powerful
ready, red-blooded, reliant, resilient, robust, rocky, rough,
    rugged, ruthless
scrappy, self-made, self-reliant, self-sufficient, self-supporting,
    self-sustaining, skookum, solid, spartan, spirited, spunky,
    stalwart, staunch, steadfast, steely, stout, stout-hearted,
    strapping, street-smart, streetwise, strong, sturdy, substantial
thriving, tough, truculent
unblinking
valiant, valorous, venturesome
warlike
yeomanly

## WEAK, FEARFUL, OR ANXIOUS

abashed, afraid, ailing, alarmed, anemic, anxious,
    apprehensive, ashamed, asthmatic
bedridden, bloodless, brittle
candy-ass, clinging, consumptive, cowardly, craven, creaky,
    cringing
debilitated, decrepit, delicate, desperate, dilute, disconcerted,
    doddering
effete
faint, fainthearted, faltering, fearful, feckless, feeble, fidgety,
    fitful, flimsy, fragile, frail, frangible, frightened, futile
gimpy, gutless
hagridden, helpless, horrified, horror-struck, humbled,
    humiliated, hung-up
ill, impotent, impoverished, impuissant, incapacitated,
    ineffective, inept, infirm, insecure, insufficient
jittery
lame, lily-livered, limp, limp-wristed
mawkish, meager, milk-livered, mortified
namby-pamby, needy, nervous, neurotic
oversensitive, overwhelmed
pale, pallid, paltry, panicked, panic-stricken, paranoid, pathetic,
    pavid, petrified, phthisic, pitiful, plaintive, poor-spirited,
    punchless, puny, pusillanimous
recreant
scared, shaky, sheepish, short-winded, shrinking, sickly,
    simpering, skimpy, skittish, slight, sniveling, snuffling,
    spasmodic, spineless, spooked, squeamish, stressed,
    stressed-out, sulky
terrified, timid, timorous, toothless, tottering, trapped,
    trembling, tremulous
uncomfortable, undernourished, uneasy, unnerved, unwell,
    uptight
vertiginous
wan, wary, washed-out, washy, watery, weak, weakhearted,
    weak-kneed, wet, whining, whiny, white, white-livered,
    wimpy, wispy, wormy
yellow

# ACTIVE/INERT

## ACTIVE, LIVELY, AWAKE, OR LIMBER

acrobatic, active, adroit, agile, alert, alive, ambulatory, athletic,
    attentive, avid, awake
bouncy, breezy, bright-eyed, brisk, bubbly, bustling, busy,
    buxom
catalytic, chipper, crisp, curious
deft, diligent, dynamic
eager, effervescent, elusive, energetic, energized, enterprising,
    errant, exhilarated, exuberant
fecund, feisty, fervent, fleet, fleet-footed, fluent, fluid,
    footloose, free, fresh, frisky, frolicsome
galvanic, go-go, gymnastic
hale, high-spirited, high-strung, hurried
industrious, interested, intrigued, irrepressible, itinerant
jaunty, jingly
kinetic
lambent, liberated, light, limber, lissome, lithe, lively, lyric
mercurial, mobile, motile
nimble, nomadic
operose, outdoorsy
peppy, peripatetic, perky, productive, prolific, prompt
quick, quicksilver
rambunctious, rapid, raring to go, ready, reborn, renascent
saltatory, sassy, saucy, sentient, sinuous, skittish, snappy,
    speedy, spirited, sprightly, springy, spruce, spry, strenuous,
    supple, swift, switched-on, sylphlike
tireless
unencumbered, up-and-coming
vibrant, vigilant, vigorous, vital, vivacious, volant, volatile
wakeful, whippy, wide-awake, wide-eyed, willowy
zappy, zestful, zesty, zingy, zippy

## INERT, LAZY, TIRED, OR INSENSATE

abstracted, aged, apathetic, asleep, atrophied
barren, beat, benumbed, blank, blasé, bored, bovine, bushed
cadaverous, comatose, complacent
dazed, dead, delitescent, dilatory, disinterested, docile, doltish,
    dopey, dormant, draggy, dreamy, drooping, droopy, drowsy,
    drugged, dull, dulled
emotionless, empty, enervated, exhausted
fallow, fatigued, flat, floppy
glassy, glassy-eyed, groggy
haggard, hazy, hoary, hypnotic, hypnotized
idle, immobile, impassive, impervious, inactive, inanimate,
    inattentive, incapacitated, indifferent, indolent, inert,
    insensate, insipid
jaded
kaput
lackadaisical, languid, languorous, late, latent, lazy, leaden,
    lethargic, lifeless, listless, logy, lymphatic
malingering, moribund, mute
numb
otiose, overripe
paralyzed, passive, phlegmatic, placid, pococurante, poky,
    porcine, punch-drunk, punchy
rusty
sagging, sapped, satiated, sedentary, semicomatose,
    semiconscious, senseless, shiftless, shot, slack, sleepy,
    slothful, slow, sluggish, sodden, somnolent, spaced-out,
    spent, spiritless, stagnant, static, stiff, stuporous, supine
tardy, tepid, tired, torpid, truant

uninterested, unmindful, unmotivated, unresponsive
vacant, vacuous
weary, wizened, world-weary, worn-out
yawning
zomboid, zonked

## HAPPY/SAD

### HAPPY, PLAYFUL, OPTIMISTIC, OR ELATED

agrin, airy, amazed, amused, amusing, astonished
beatific, bemused, blissful, blithe, bonhomous, buoyant
carefree, cavalier, cheerful, cheery, chipper, content,
    contented, convivial
delighted, devil-may-care, droll
ebullient, ecstatic, elated, enchanted, enraptured, enthusiastic,
    espiègle, euphoric, expectant, exuberant, exultant
fanciful, fancy-free, festive, flying, frolicsome, fulfilled,
    fun-loving, funny
gamesome, gay, gemütlich, giddy, giggly, glad, gleeful, glowing
happy, happy-go-lucky, harmonious, hilarious, hopeful,
    humorous
impish, infectious
jaunty, jocose, jocular, jocund, jolly, jovial, joyful, joyous,
    jubilant
laughing, lighthearted, lilting, ludic
merry, mirthful, mischievous
optimistic, overjoyed
perky, playful, pleased, psyched, puckish
radiant, rapturous, ravished, relieved, rhapsodic, riant, risible,
    roguish, roseate, rosy
sanguine, sated, satisfied, silly, sky-high, spirited, sportive,
    starry-eyed, stoked, sunny
thankful, triumphant
up
waggish, whimsical, wishful

### SAD, SERIOUS, PESSIMISTIC, OR DISCONTENTED

abject, absorbed, abysmal, achy, afflicted, aggrieved,
    agonizing, anguished
beleaguered, bereaved, bereft, bleak, blue, brokenhearted,
    brooding, bummed, bummed out
chagrined, cheerless, contrite, crestfallen, crushed
dark, dejected, demure, depressed, deprived, desolate,
    despondent, disconsolate, discontented, discouraged,
    disenchanted, disgusted, disillusioned, dismal, dissatisfied,
    distraught, distressed, disturbed, doleful, dolorous, doomed,
    dour, down, down-at-heel, downbeat, downcast
elegiac, embittered
fatalistic, forlorn, fretful, funereal
gloomy, glum, grave, grief-stricken, grieving, grim, grouchy,
    grum, grumpy, guilt-ridden, guilty
hapless, harried, heartbroken, heavy-hearted, homesick,
    hopeless, humorless, hurt
inconsolable, indisposed, injured
joyless
lachrymose, languishing, lonely, lonesome, lovesick, lugubrious
maudlin, melancholy, miserable, misty-eyed, moody, mopey,
    morbid, morose, mournful
nostalgic
oppressed, out-of-sorts, owlish

pained, pathetic, pensive, perturbed, pessimistic, pining,
    pitiable, pitiful, plaintive, plangent, poignant, pouty, pungent
regretful, remorseful, repentant, rueful, ruthful
sad, saturnine, serious, severe, sighing, sober, solemn, somber,
    soppy, sorrowful, sorry, stern, stricken, Stygian, subdued,
    suffering, suicidal, sulky, sullen, surly
teary, teary-eyed, tortured, tragic, tristful, troubled
unfortunate, unfulfilled, unhappy, unlucky
wailful, weepy, wistful, woebegone, woeful, wounded,
    wrecked, wretched, wronged

## CALM/ANGRY

### CALM, GENTLE, OR EASYGOING

apollonian
calm, casual, composed, constrained, cool, cool-headed
dégagé, demure, dewy, dispassionate, dry-eyed
easygoing, emollient, even-tempered
gentle
imperturbable
laconic, laid-back, lenient, levelheaded, low-key, low-pressure
matutinal, meditative, mellow, mild, muted
neutral, nonchalant, nonviolent
objective
pacific, pacifistic, passive, patient, peaceful, poised
quiet
relaxed, restrained, reticent
sedate, self-disciplined, self-possessed, serene, soft, steady,
    stoical, subdued
taciturn, tame, temperate, tempered, tranquil
unbothered, unemotional, unflappable, unforced, unhassled,
    unhurried, unruffled, unstirred, untroubled

### ANGRY, EMOTIONAL, AGGRESSIVE, OR PASSIONATE

aggravated, aggressive, aghast, agitated, amorous, angered,
    angry, animated, annoyed, antsy, appetent, argumentative,
    avid
bellicose, belligerent, blooming, brash, breathless
choleric, combative, competitive, contentious
dedicated, defiant, dramatic
edgy, effusive, emotional, engagé, enthusiastic, excitable,
    excited, explosive
ferocious, feverish, fierce, fiery, fire-eating, flighty, flustered,
    frazzled, free-swinging, frenzied, fuming, furious
harried, hassled, henpecked, hepped-up, het up, high-keyed,
    high-pressure, high-strung, hostile, hot, hot-blooded,
    hotheaded, huffy, hungry, hyper, hysterical
impassioned, impetuous, impulsive, incensed, indignant,
    inflammatory, intemperate, intensive, intent, irascible, irate,
    irrepressible
jealous
livid, lusty
mad, manic, miffed, militant, militaristic
overwrought, overzealous
passionate, peeved, peppery, perfervid, piqued, pissed, pissed
    off, pugnacious, pushy
quarrelsome
rabid, raddled, raging, rambunctious, rash, resentful, restive,
    restless, ruffled, rumbustious
scrappy, seething, self-indulgent, sensuous, short,
    short-tempered, sick and tired, snappish, sore, soulful,

spontaneous, steaming, stewing, sthenic, stir-crazy, stirred up, stormy, strained, subjective, sulfurous, sultry
temperamental, tempestuous, tense, testy, ticked, ticked-off, ticklish, torrid, touchy, trigger-happy, troubled, truculent, tumultuous, turbulent, turned-on
unglued, unreasonable, unreconciled, unremitting, unrestrained, unsettled, unstable, upset
vehement, Vesuvian, vexed, violent, visceral, volcanic
warm-blooded, white-hot, worked-up, wound-up, wrathful, wrought-up, wroth
zealous

quirky
rabid, radical, raging, rakish, rapacious, rash, ravening, raving, reckless
screwy, spasmodic, strange, streaky, surreal, sybaritic
temerarious
ultra, ultraist, unbalanced, unbridled, unconventional, uncurbed, unfettered, unhinged, unrestrained
voracious
wacky, warped, wasteful, way-out, weird, wiggy, wild-eyed, wired
zany, zooey

# MODERATE/EXCESSIVE

## MODERATE, SANE, CONSERVATIVE, OR OLD-FASHIONED

abstemious, abstinent, adjusted, assiduous
balanced, businesslike, buttoned-down
careful, cautious, celibate, chary, circumspect, clocklike, closemouthed, collected, composed, concise, concrete, conscientious, conservative, consistent, constant, controlled, conventional, cool-headed
diplomatic, down-to-earth
equitable
factual, frugal
gingerly, gradual
inveterate
laconic, levelheaded
matter-of-fact, middle-of-the-road, mild, moderate, modest
no-nonsense
objective, obsolete, old-fashioned, orderly, orthodox, ossified, outdated, outmoded
passé, penny-wise, pious, practical, pragmatic, prudent
rational, reasonable, regimented, regular
safe, sane, sensible, sober, sound, sparing, square, stable, standardized, standpat, steady, stick-in-the-mud, sticky, stodgy, strait-laced, stringent, studied, superannuated
tactful, temperate, thrifty, tough-minded
ultraconservative, utilitarian
workmanlike

## EXCESSIVE, MAD, INSANE, OR RADICAL

aberrant, abnormal, addictive, alcoholic, amok, anarchic, anarchistic, apoplectic, avaricious
berserk, brash
chaotic, crazed, crazy
daffy, daft, delirious, demoniacal, deranged, deviant, dizzy, dotty, dysfunctional
eldritch, epicurean, erratic, esurient, excessive, extravagant, extreme
fanatic, fanatical, febrile, fey, flagrant, flaky, florid, frantic, freakish, frenetic, frenzied
gonzo, greedy
headlong, hedonistic, heedless, hog-wild, homicidal, hyper, hysterical
immodest, incendiary, inordinate, insane, insatiable, irrational
kamikaze, kooky
loco, lunatic
mad, madcap, maniacal, monomaniacal
nihilistic
obsessive, odd, off, off-the-wall, overwrought
perfervid, phrenetic, pinko, pixilated, potty, prodigal, profuse, psycho, psychotic, punk

# PROPER/VULGAR

## PROPER, COURTEOUS, REFINED, OR PURITANICAL

aesthetic, appropriate, auspicious
ceremonious, chaste, citified, civil, civilized, classical, clubby, conforming, conventional, correct, courteous, courtly, couth, cultivated, cultured
decent, decorous, delicate, demure, dignified, diplomatic, discreet
effete, elitist, established, esthetic, ethical
fastidious, felicitous, finicky, formal, fussy
gallant, genteel, gentlemanly, gracious
hoity-toity, holier-than-thou, honorable
ingratiating, irreproachable, Ivy League
kosher
law-abiding, legitimate
maidenly, mannered, matronly, modern, modest, moral, moralistic
obedient, official, orthodox
pietistic, polite, pompous, precious, presentable, priggish, prim, prissy, pristine, professional, proper, prudent, prudish, pudibund, punctilious, punctual, puritanical
refined, religious, reputable, respectable, respectful, rhetorical, righteous, right-thinking, rigid
safe, sanctimonious, seemly, self-righteous, smooth, smug, snobbish, snooty, soapy, sporting, sportsmanlike, squeamish, stable, staid, starchy, stiff, stilted, straight, straight-arrow, strict, stuffy, suave, suitable
tactful, tasteful, taut, tight-assed, too-too, traditional, tweedy
U, unflappable, upright, uptight, urbane
Victorian
well-behaved, well-bred, well-mannered, white, white-bread

## VULGAR, RUDE, DEGENERATE, OR WILD

abandoned, aberrant, abnormal, abominable, aboriginal, abusive, animalistic, anomalous, atavistic
barbaric, base, bawdy, beastly, bibulous, bizarre, blasphemous, blooey, blunt, boorish, brash, brazen, brutish
caddish, cannibalistic, carnal, cheap, cheeky, coarse, common, concupiscent, coquettish, crass, crude
debauched, decadent, degenerate, depraved, deviant, dirty, dirty-minded, discourteous, disobedient, disorderly, disreputable, dissipated, dissolute
egregious, erotic
farouche, feral, flatulent, flip, flippant, flooey, foul, fresh
garish, gauche, gross
heathenish, heteroclite, heterodox, hoggish, hokey
ill-bred, illicit, ill-mannered, immoderate, immoral, impertinent,

impolite, impolitic, improper, impudent, inappropriate, incestuous, incongruous, indecent, indecorous, indelicate, inexcusable, informal, insolent, intoxicated, irregular, irreverent

kinky, knockabout

lascivious, lawless, lecherous, lewd, libertine, libidinous, licentious, loose, loud, low, lowbrow, lubricious, lustful

mannerless, meretricious

native, naughty, non-U

obscene, obstreperous, offbeat, offhand, opprobrious, outlandish, outrageous, outré, overdressed

perverted, plebeian, pornographic, primitive, profane, profligate, promiscuous, prurient, prying, purple

queer

Rabelaisian, racy, raffish, rakish, rambunctious, randy, rank, raucous, raunchy, raw, rebellious, recherché, refractory, revolutionary, ribald, riotous, ripped, rip-roaring, risqué, roily, rough, rough-and-tumble, rough-hewn, rowdy, rowdydowdy, rude, rumbustious, rustic, ruttish

salacious, sassy, savage, scabrous, scandalous, scurrilous, self-abandoned, shameless, showy, slutty, smutty, steamy, swinish

tactless, tasteless, tawdry, tipsy, trashy

unbecoming, unblushing, uncivil, uncivilized, uncontrollable, unconventional, uncool, uncouth, uncultured, undiplomatic, ungracious, unmanageable, unmannered, unmannerly, unnatural, unrefined, unruly, unseemly, unsportsmanlike, untamed, untoward

vulgar

wanton, weird, whorish, wild

## INTELLIGENT/STUPID

### INTELLIGENT, INFORMED, CLEVER, OR ARTICULATE

abreast, accurate, acute, analytical, apt, argute, articulate, astute, au fait, authoritative

bookish, bright, brilliant, broad ranging

canny, cerebral, clear, clearheaded, clear-sighted, clever, cogent, cognizant, coherent, comprehensive, concise, conscious, conversant, cunning

discerning, donnish, droll

educated, erudite, expert

facile, fluent

glib, heads-up, heady, highbrow, high-minded, hip

imaginative, incisive, informed, ingenious, innovative, inquiring, inquisitive, insightful, intellectual, intelligent, interpretive, inventive

keen, knowing, knowledgeable

learned, limpid, literate, logical, lucid, luminous

mental

observant, omnilegent, omniscient, organized

pawky, pedagogic, penetrating, perceptive, percipient, perspicacious, piercing, pithy, precocious, prescient, proficient, profound

quick-witted

rational, recondite, reflective, retentive, right, ruminant

savvy, serious-minded, sharp, sharp-witted, shrewd, silver-tongued, smart, smooth-tongued, subtle, succinct

terse, trenchant, tuned-in

ultrasmart, uncanny, understanding, unerring, urbane

versed

well-advised, well-informed, well-read, well-rounded, well-spoken, with-it, witty, worldly, worldly-wise

### STUPID, IGNORANT, OR CONFUSED

absent-minded, abstracted, addlebrained, addled, agog, amnesiac

backward, baffled, befogged, befuddled, benighted, besotted, bewildered, blithering, bovine

confounded, confused, cretinous

dense, dim, dimwitted, disorganized, disoriented, doltish, dull, dumb, dumbfounded, duncical

empty-headed, erroneous

fallible, fatuous, fat-witted, feeble-minded, foggy, fuzzy

hazy

idiotic, ignorant, illiterate, imbecilic, inarticulate, incognizant, incoherent, incompetent, inconscient

lumpish

maundering, mindless, mixed-up, moronic, muddled, muddleheaded, myopic, mystified

nescient, numb

oblivious, obtuse, opaque

perplexed, preoccupied, purblind, puzzled

rambling, rattled, retarded

scatterbrained, senile, simple, simpleminded, slaphappy, slow, slow-witted, sophomoric, spaced, spaced-out, spacey, speechless, stunned, stunted, stupefied, stupid, stuporous, subliterate, subnormal

thick, thickheaded, thick-witted, turbid

unclear, unconscious, undiscerning, unfocused, uninformed, unknowing, unlearned, unlettered, unorganized, unread, unschooled, unskilled, untutored, unversed

vacant, vacuous

witless, woodenheaded, woozy, wrong

zoned out, zonked out

## SPECIAL/ORDINARY

### SPECIAL, BRIGHT, SKILLFUL, OR UNUSUAL

ablaze, able, acclaimed, accomplished, adept, adequate, admirable, admired, ageless, aglow, all-around, amazing, ambidextrous, anointed, artful, artistic, arty, atypical, auspicious, avant-garde

bedazzling, blessed, bodacious, breathtaking, bright, brilliant

capable, celebrated, charismatic, colorful, competent, conspicuous, consummate, controversial, coordinated, corking, creative, creditable

dazzling, different, distinct, distinctive, distinguished, divine

eccentric, efficient, effulgent, eminent, esteemed, estimable, excellent, exceptional, exclusive, exemplary, exotic, extraordinary

famous, fascinating, favored, fine, first-class, first-rate, flashing, foremost, fortunate

glimmering, glittering, glorious, glossy, glowing, grand, great

handy, heavenly, hip, honored

iconoclastic, idiosyncratic, illuminated, illustrious, imaginative, imperial, important, imposing, impressive, incandescent, incomparable, incredible, individual, indubitable, inimitable, inspiring, invaluable, inviolate, iridescent

jazzy

light, lucky, luminous, lustrous

magical, magnificent, majestic, major, marquee, marvelous, masterful, matchless

nonpareil, notable, noted, noteworthy, novel

original, otherworldly, outstanding

peculiar, peerless, perfect, phenomenal, praiseworthy,

preeminent, prepared, prestigious, priceless, primary, Promethean, prominent, protean, proverbial

quaint, qualified, quality

radiant, rare, refulgent, remarkable, renowned, resourceful, respected, resplendent, reverential, ripe

sacred, saintly, scintillating, select, sensational, serendipitous, sexy, shining, signal, significant, singular, skillful, sole, sovereign, sparkling, special, spicy, splendid, startling, stellar, storied, stupendous, sublime, successful, super, superb, superhuman, superior, superlative, supernatural, supreme, surefooted, sure-handed

talented, terrific, tiptop, titled, together, top, topflight, topnotch, top-of-the-line, tops, towering, transfigured

uncommon, unconventional, unequaled, unexcelled, unique, unmatched, unorthodox, unprecedented, unusual, unwonted, utopian

valuable, valued, varied, vast, versatile, victorious, vintage, vivid

well-known, well-spoken, well-thought-of, whiz-bang, wonderful, wondrous, worthwhile, worthy

## ORDINARY, DULL, PLAIN, OR BANAL

automatic, average

banal, bland, blank, boring, bourgeois

characterless, colorless, common, commonplace, conventional, cursory, customary

dated, derivative, dim, dingy, dismal, down-to-earth, drab, dreary, dull

empty, everyday, expressionless

faded, fair, fallible, familiar, faulty, flat

garden-variety, glib, gratuitous

habitual, hackneyed, homespun, humble, humdrum

imitative, inartistic, inconclusive, inconspicuous, indifferent, inefficient, inept, inferior, inglorious, innocuous, insignificant, insipid

jejune

lackluster, lifeless, low-class, lowly, low-quality, lukewarm, lusterless

matter-of-fact, mediocre, menial, middling, mild, minor, modest, mortal, mundane, musty

negligible, nondescript, normal

obvious, okay, one-dimensional, ordinary

passable, pedestrian, perfunctory, petit bourgeois, plain, plain-spoken, plastic, plebeian, proletarian, prosaic, prototypical

regular, repetitive, rinky-dink, run-of-the-mill

secondary, second-class, second-rate, shoddy, simple, small-time, soggy, soporific, spare, stagnant, stale, standard, stereotypical, sterile, stock, stripped-down, subordinate, superficial, superfluous

tarnished, tasteless, tedious, tepid, terrestrial, timeworn, tiresome, tolerable, trite, typical

unadorned, unassuming, undistinctive, undistinguished, unexceptional, unexciting, unhip, unimaginative, uninspiring, uninteresting, unprepared, unpretentious, unqualified, unsung, untalented, untitled, useless, usual

vapid

workaday, working-class, would-be

## WISE/FOOLISH

### WISE, MATURE, OR EXPERIENCED

actualized, adult, all-knowing, all-seeing, august, aware, awesome

balanced, broad, broad-minded

centered, clear, clear-sighted, cogent, coherent, complex, contemplative

deep, discriminating, disinterested, dispassionate

eloquent, enlightened, ethereal, exalted, experienced

farseeing, farsighted, focused

grand, grown-up

immortal, impartial, infallible, infinite, influential, integrated

judicious, just

large-minded, levelheaded, lofty, lucid

magisterial, majestic, mantic, masterful, masterly, mature, metaphysical, mystical

noble

old, Olympian, omnipresent, omniscient, open-minded, orbicular, oriented

patriarchal, perfect, philosophical, practiced, prescient, profound, prophetic, psychic

realized, resonant

sacred, sacrosanct, sagacious, sage, sapient, serene, sophisticated, spiritual, sublime, supernal, supreme, sybilline

telepathic

unassailable, unbiased, understanding, universal

vatic, venerable, veteran, visionary

weathered, weighty, wise, wizardly

### FOOLISH, IMMATURE, BIGOTED, OR TRIVIAL

abstract, absurd, adolescent, affected, amateurish, anthropocentric, anti-intellectual, artless, artsy, asinine, awe-struck

balmy, barmy, bathetic, bedazzled, biased, bigoted, blind, bumbling

callow, capricious, careless, childish, chumpish, clownish, comical, corny, cretinous, cute, cutesy

daffy, daft, distracted, dopey

ethnocentric

farcical, flabbergasted, flatulent, flighty, foolhardy, foolish, foppish, frivolous, frothy

garrulous, gibbering, giddy, goofy

half-assed, half-baked, half-cocked, harebrained, harum-scarum, hasty, highfalutin, homophobic

idiotic, ill-advised, imbecilic, immature, impetuous, impractical, imprudent, inane, indiscreet, inexperienced, infantile, injudicious, in the clouds, irrational

juvenile

kooky

la-di-da, laughable, lightheaded, long-winded, loquacious, ludicrous

melodramatic, mincing, minor, misanthropic, misogynous, moronic, mushyheaded, muzzy

naif, naive, narrow, narrow-minded, nattering, nerdy, nonplussed, nutty

parochial, pedantic, petty, picayune, piddling, pinchbeck, prejudiced, preposterous, pretentious, prolix, provincial, pubescent, puerile

quixotic, quizzical

rash, rattlebrained, redundant, repetitious, ridiculous

sappy, sectarian, sententious, shallow, shortsighted, sightless, silly, singsong, skin-deep, small-minded, small-time, soft-headed, sophistic, speechless, spoony, superficial, superstitious

trifling, trivial

unfledged, ungrounded, unrealistic, unwise, unworldly

verdant

waggish, wide-eyed, windy, woolly-headed

yeasty, youthful

zany

# GOOD/BAD

### GOOD, SINCERE, HONEST, OR JUST

aboveboard, angelic, authentic
benevolent, bona fide
candid, capital, choice, conscientious, constant
dear, decent, deserving, devout, direct
earnest, ethical
fair, fair-minded, fine, first-rate, forthcoming, forthright,
    foursquare, frank, free
genuine, God-fearing, good, guileless
harmonious, high-minded, holy, honest, honorable, humane
idealistic, impartial, incorruptible, irreproachable
judicious, just
loving, loyal
magnanimous, moral
natural, noble
organic
prelapsarian, principled, pure
real, reliable, reverent, righteous, right-minded
scrupulous, selfless, seraphic, simon-pure, sincere,
    straightforward, sublime
true, true-blue, truthful
unimpeachable, up-and-up, up-front, upright, upstanding
veracious, veridical, vestal, virtuous
wholehearted, wholesome, worthy

### BAD, FALSE, EVIL, INSINCERE, OR
### DISHONEST

accursed, adulterous, affected, amoral, apocryphal, apostate,
    arch, artificial, awful
backhanded, bad, baleful, baneful, barefaced, base, bent,
    bloodthirsty, bogus
calumnious, canting, casuistic, contemptible, corrupt,
    counterfeit, crafty, crooked, cunning, cursed
damned, debased, deceitful, deceptive, delusive, demoniacal,
    despicable, detestable, devilish, devious, diabolical,
    disgraced, dishonest, disingenuous, disloyal, dissembling,
    duplicitous
egregious, ersatz, evasive, evil, execrable
fake, fallen, false, fatuous, feigned, fell, fiendish, flagitious,
    flagrant, foul, foxy, fraudulent, fulsome, furtive
guileful
hangdog, heinous, heretical, hexed, high-sounding, hollow,
    horrid, hypocritical
ignoble, ignominious, infamous, infernal, insidious, insincere,
    irredeemable
Janus-faced, jive
loathsome, lowdown
malefic, malevolent, malignant, mealy-mouthed, mendacious,
    miscreant, misleading, mock, monstrous, moralistic,
    murderous
nefarious
odious, ostentatious
perfidious, pernicious, perverse, pharisaic, phony, piacular,
    predatory, pretentious, pseudo, purulent
recreant, reprobate, rotten
sanctimonious, scurvy, selfish, serpentine, shady, sham,
    shameful, shifty, sinful, sinister, slanderous, slippery, sly,
    smarmy, sneaky, sophistic, sorcerous, specious, spurious,
    stealthy, synthetic
tainted, terrible, traitorous, treacherous, two-faced
unashamed, unconscionable, unctuous, underhanded, unfair,

ungodly, unholy, unjust, unpardonable, unprincipled,
    unscrupulous, untruthful, unworthy
vain, venal, venomous, vile, villainous, viperous, virtueless,
    vulpine
wicked, wily, worthless

# GIVING/DEMANDING

### GIVING, TRUSTING, INNOCENT, OR
### GENEROUS

accessible, accommodating, adaptable, approving, artless
beatific, believing
candid, careless, childlike, complaisant, compliant, credulous
democratic, dewy-eyed, doting, dulcet
easy
faithful, frank, free
game, generous, giving, good-natured, gracious, grateful,
    guileless, gullible
hopeful, humble
impressionable, inconsistent, indiscriminate, indulgent,
    ingenuous, innocent, insouciant, instinctive, intuitive
lax, liberal
naive, natural
obliging, open
permissive
rapt, reciprocating
saccharine, selfless, simple, sugary, sweet, syrupy
tender, tolerant, transparent, trustful, trusting
ultraliberal, unabashed, uncritical, understanding,
    undesigning, unguarded, unquestioning, unsophisticated,
    unsparing, unsullied, unsuspecting, unwitting
virginal
young

### DEMANDING, CRITICAL, CALCULATING, OR
### SELFISH

abrasive, accusatory, acerbic, acidic, acquisitive, admonishing,
    agnostic, anal, aporetic, arbitrary, arrogant, assiduous,
    assumptive, atheistic, attentive
biting, blameful, bumptious
cagey, calculating, captious, carping, categorical, caustic,
    caviling, censorious, challenging, cheap, chiding, choosy,
    clinical, compulsive, conceited, condescending, constipated,
    contemptuous, contradictory, contrary, costive, covetous,
    crafty, critical, cryptic, cutting
definite, deliberate, demanding, deprecatory, derogatory,
    dictatorial, didactic, disabused, disapproving, disbelieving,
    disciplined, discriminating, disdainful, disparaging,
    distrustful, doctrinaire, dogmatic
edacious, egocentric, exacting, exigent
facetious, fastidious, fault-finding, fussy
gluttonous, grabby, greedy, guarded
hard, harsh, high-and-mighty, hubristic, huffy, hypercritical
impatient, incisive, insistent, ironic
judgmental
logical
materialistic, measured, methodical, meticulous, mocking,
    mordacious, mordant
narcissistic, niggling
obsessive, omnivorous, opinionated, opportunistic
painstaking, particular, patronizing, pejorative, peremptory,

perseverant, persistent, pertinacious, picky, pointed, political, precise, procacious

querulous

ravenous, rebuking, reproving, Rhadamanthine, rigorous

sanctimonious, sarcastic, sardonic, satiric, satirical, scolding, scornful, scrimping, scrupulous, sedulous, selective, self-centered, selfish, self-serving, self-willed, set, sharp, sharp-edged, skeptical, slashing, specific, supercilious, superior, systematic

tactical, tendentious, thorough, tireless, trenchant

ultracritical, unbelieving, ungenerous, unrelenting, unstinting, uppish, uppity, usurious

vain, vituperative, voracious

withholding, wolfish, wry

## HELPFUL/TROUBLESOME

### HELPFUL, POSITIVE, RESPONSIBLE, OR NICE

accessory, accommodating, aggrandizing, altruistic, amenable, amicable, attached, avuncular

beneficent, benevolent, benign, big-hearted, brotherly

caring, charitable, chivalrous, civic-minded, clement, compassionate, concerned, conciliatory, conscientious, considerate, constructive, cooperative

dutiful

eager, equable, equitable

faithful, fatherly, felicitous, fortunate, fraternal

good-hearted

helpful, heroic, humane, humanitarian, hunky-dory

indulgent, instructive, intimate

large, lenient, loving, loyal

magnanimous, maternal, merciful, motherly, munificent

neighborly, nice

obliging

paternal, patriotic, philanthropic, pleasant, positive, progressive, propitiatory, propitious, protective, provident

reliable, responsible, responsive

selfless, self-sacrificing, sensitive, sharing, sisterly, social, social-minded, solicitous, soothing, sunny, supportive, sympathetic

tender, thoughtful, tonic, tried-and-true, trustworthy, trusty

unfailing, unselfish, upbeat, useful

valuable, voluntary

well-intentioned, well-meaning, wholesome, worthwhile

### TROUBLESOME, NEGATIVE, IRRESPONSIBLE, OR UNPLEASANT

abrasive, abusive, acrid, acrimonious, annoying, antagonistic, arch, argumentative, avaricious, averse

balky, baneful, bilious, bitter, bothersome, bullying

cagey, capricious, carking, cloying, comminatory, complaining, covetous, crafty, crappy, creepy, crotchety, crummy, cutthroat

dangerous, designing, destructive, difficult, discontented, disquieting, disturbing, divisive, dour, downbeat

envious

fearsome, feral, fickle, fierce, foxy, fractious

harsh, horrendous, horrible, horrid, horrific

importunate, incompatible, infamous, inhumane, invidious, irksome, irreconcilable, irresponsible

jackleg, jangly, jaundiced

libelous, lousy, lupine

maddening, maladjusted, manipulative, mean, meddlesome, menacing, minatory

nagging, nauseating, negative, negligent, nerve-racking, nettlesome, nihilistic, nosy, notorious, noxious

objectionable, obnoxious, odious, offensive, officious, ominous, onerous, oppressive

parlous, pernicious, pesky, pestilent, pesty, petulant, polypragmatic, pompous, prankish, preachy, prickly, provocative, pugnacious

querulous

rancid, rancorous, rapacious, rascally, remorseless, renitent, reprehensible, restrictive, rivalrous, roguish

sacrilegious, savage, scary, scathing, scurrilous, seditious, self-destructive, severe, sharp, sick, slanderous, slashing, slinking, sly, small, smirking, snide, sniffish, sniffy, snobbish, snoopy, snotty, sordid, sour, spiteful, spleenful, sticky, stroppy, stuck-up, subversive

terrifying, thorny, thoughtless, toxic, treacly, tricky, troublesome, truculent, trying

unconcerned, undependable, unfaithful, ungrateful, unpleasant, unsympathetic, useless

venomous, vicious, vindictive, virulent, vitriolic, vituperative, vulpine

wayward, wearisome, wily, worrisome, wrongheaded

---

# SEX, LOVE, AND ROMANCE

Love and Romance
Flirtation, Dating, and Courting
Sexuality and Libido
Homosexuality
Anatomy and Physiology of Sex
Contraception and Fertility
Sex Acts
Perversions, Fetishes, and Titillations
Pornography and Prostitution

**SEE ALSO:** Chap. 1: Anatomy; Medical Problems; Chap. 2: Biology; Chap. 4: Medicine; Chap. 8: Marriage and Divorce; Parents and Children; Chap. 13: Psychology; Chap. 20: Insults, Slurs, and Epithets; Terms of Endearment and Respect

## LOVE AND ROMANCE

**adoration**  great love and devotion; worship

**affection**  warmth, liking

**amative** (adj) inclined to love and lust

**amatory** (adj) pertaining to love and lovemaking

**amorist**  lover, devotee of love

**amorous** (adj) full of love; feeling sexually aroused

**amour**  love affair, esp. illicit one

**Aphrodite**  ancient Greek goddess of love and beauty

**ardor**  enthusiasm in love

**Astarte**  ancient Semitic goddess of fertility and sexual love

**beloved**  greatly loved person

**break a heart**  reject or wound one's lover

**brokenhearted** (adj) rejected in love

**caring**  concern and esteem for loved one

**carry a torch**  endure unrequited love

**Casanova** man engaging in many love affairs

**celibacy** state of being unmarried; abstention from sexual love

**cheat** (*vb*) deceive one's lover with another, secret lover

**chemistry** animal attraction; sympathetic understanding; rapport

**cherish** (*vb*) love devotedly

**chivalry** courageous, honorable, supportive attitude toward women

**cohabit** (*vb*) live together

**commitment** bond of love and responsibility

**compatibility** harmonious coexistence

**concubine** mistress, kept woman; secondary wife of polygamous male, usu. of inferior rank

**conjugal love** affection and relations between married couple

**constancy** faithfulness in love

**corazón** *Spanish.* heart; love and affection; lover

**cotton to** (*vb*) *Informal.* take a liking to

**couple** two people who are in love with each other or relating erotically

**courtly love** polite, formal, old-fashioned love

**crush** *Informal.* infatuation

**cuckold** husband of woman who is having sex with another man

**Cupid** ancient Roman god of love

**Dear John** *Informal.* letter from woman telling her lover she is ending the relationship

**devotion** faithful, enduring love

**Don Juan** seducer of women

**dote on** (*vb*) care for excessively or foolishly

**ecstasy** sexual bliss

**enamor** (*vb*) charm, fill with love or desire

**enchant** (*vb*) delight with love

**enthrall** (*vb*) enslave with love

**Eros** ancient Greek god of love

**fair sex** women collectively, sometimes considered offensive

**fall for** (*vb*) *Slang.* fall in love with; take a shine to

**fancy** (*vb*) be attracted to or fond of

**fascination** state of being spellbound by love

**favor** token of love

**fondness** tender affection

**forbidden love** any prohibited form of love

**game of love** typical give-and-take in developing romantic relationship

**go for** (*vb*) be attracted to

**goo-goo eyes** *Slang.* foolishly amorous glances

**have eyes for** *Slang.* be attracted to

**head over heels in love** extravagantly in love

**heartache** pain caused by being in love

**heartbreaker** person causing pain to lover

**heartsick** (*adj*) extremely unhappy in love

**heartthrob** person attracting much romantic attention

**honor and keep** love vow taken by married couple

**illicit love** prohibited acts or forms of love

**inamorata** woman who loves or is loved

**inamorato** man who loves or is loved

**infatuation** temporary, intense feeling of love

**intimacy** special, deep closeness growing from mutual love

**item** *Slang.* couple known to be together

**jealousy** resentment caused by real or imagined rival

**keep company** be involved in love relationship with another

**knight** courtly male lover

**lady** courtly female lover

**Lolita** extremely seductive young girl

**longing** desire for love or beloved person

**lose one's heart** fall in love

**Lothario** seducer and deceiver of women

**love** strong emotional attachment to another person; sexual passion or desire based on such feelings; intense affection or caring for another

**love at first sight** instantaneous attraction on meeting

**lovebirds** loving couple

**lovelorn** (*adj*) heartsick, rejected, or unhappy in love

**lover** person who is in love with another, esp. one having a sexual or romantic relationship with another; person with whom one is having an extramarital affair

**lovers' quarrel** stormy and emotional fight between lovers

**lovesick** (*adj*) anxious or emotionally unbalanced from love

**main squeeze** *Slang.* primary lover or mate

**make up** (*vb*) patch up a lovers' quarrel; reconcile

**mate** spouse; lover

**mistress** lover of man married to another

**moonstruck** (*adj*) dreamily romantic; in love

**mush** overly sentimental affection

**obsession** overriding preoccupation with beloved

**other woman** love interest of married or attached man

**paramour** married person's lover

**passion** strong emotional response to lover

**philander** (*vb*) engage in love affair without willingness to marry

**pine** (*vb*) long for one's lover

**platonic love** nonsexual love

**puppy love** youthful, immature love

**rapture** ecstasy of love

**reconciliation** settlement of differences with one's lover and resumption of romantic relationship, as after a separation

**rejection** lack of acceptance by or of lover; failure to elicit love from an object of one's love

**relationship** involvement of two persons in love

**romance** close emotional and physical relationship; love affair

**romantic** (*adj*) pertaining to sexual love; inspiring emotions of romance; (*n*) romantic person

**Romeo** male lover, esp. man preoccupied with or noted for amatory success

**run after** (*vb*) pursue lover or would-be lover

**seduction** enticement of another into having sex

**seductress** woman who entices men into having sex

**shack up** (*vb*) *Slang.* live together as a couple without marriage

**smitten** (*adj*) infatuated, in love

**soul mate** cherished lover, true love

**stardust** naively romantic quality

**sugar daddy** *Informal.* man using his wealth to attract young woman as his lover

**swept off one's feet** fallen madly in love

**swoon** (*vb*) faint with love

**take a shine to** fall under the spell of another's attraction; fall for

**take up with** (*vb*) *Informal.* begin romantic relationship with

**toy with** (*vb*) play at love with no commitment

**triangle** situation involving two people who are both in love with a third person

**true** (*adj*) faithful

**true love** deep, abiding love

**turtledoves** sweethearts, lovers

**two-timer** *Informal*. person who is unfaithful to lover or spouse

**under one's thumb** (*adj*) dominated by one's lover

**unfaithful** (*adj*) betraying a lover or spouse by taking another

**unrequited love** love for someone who does not love in return

**Venus** ancient Roman goddess of love

**womanizer** man pursuing women for sexual purposes

**worship** intense love and adoration

**yearn** (*vb*) long for love or lover

**yen** craving for someone or for love

## FLIRTATION, DATING, AND COURTING

**admirer** person making obvious show of affection

**advances** overtures made in hopes of starting a relationship or sexual encounter

**affair** temporary romantic relationship

**assignation** lovers' arrangement to meet

**attraction** sexual and romantic interest

**babe** *Derogatory*. girl or woman

**beau** male suitor; boyfriend

**belle** beautiful, charming lady

**bewitch** (*vb*) charm or delight with feelings of love

**billet-doux** love letter

**bird** *Brit. slang*. attractive young woman

**bird-dog** (*vb*) *Slang*. steal or attempt to steal another person's date

**bitch** *Slang*. aggressive, difficult, critical, or unavailable woman

**blade** dashing, jaunty young man

**blind date** arranged meeting between previously unacquainted people

**boyfriend** frequent or favorite male companion; beau

**boy toy** *Derogatory slang*. young man who serves as sexual plaything, esp. to a famous or wealthy person

**bunny** *Derogatory slang*. pretty, alluring young woman

**buss** (*vb*) kiss

**caress** (*vb*) fondle gently

**chaperon** older escort of dating couple

**charm** (*vb*) attract and please another

**chase** pursuit of loved one

**chick** *Slang*. girl, young woman

**cockteaser** *Vulgar slang*. female who purposely arouses males sexually but refuses to have intercourse; male homosexual who acts similarly

**come-hither** (*adj*) beckoning in a flirtatious manner

**come-on** *Slang*. flirtatious advance

**computer dating** service that matches couples based on personal information put into computer

**coo** (*vb*) speak gently, lovingly

**coquetry** flirtation

**coquette** coy, teasing, flirtatious girl

**cosset** (*vb*) fondle as one would a pet

**court** (*vb*) woo, be suitor to

**courtship** act and process of seeking to become another's lover; wooing of one person by another

**cruise** (*vb*) *Informal*. travel about in search of sexual companionship

**cuddle** (*vb*) lie close together affectionately

**dalliance** flirtation; fondling, amorous foreplay

**darling** sweetheart, lover

**date** arrangement to meet for pleasant or romantic activity; romantic partner; (*vb*) see a romantic partner on regular basis

**dear** sweetheart, lover

**double date** *Informal*. social engagement involving two couples

**Dutch treat** date on which each person pays his or her own costs

**embrace** (*vb*) hold another in one's arms

**endearment** word or term of affection; pet name

**femme fatale** irresistibly attractive woman

**filly** *Informal*. girl or young woman

**fling** inconsequential love affair

**flirt** (*vb*) court playfully; (*n*) person who tempts others through playful courting

**flirtation** frivolous or playful love affair

**fondle** (*vb*) caress, stroke gently

**forbidden fruit** attractive but unavailable love interest

**French kiss** deep kiss with tongue inserted in partner's mouth

**gallivant** (*vb*) run around in search of sexual companionship

**girlfriend** frequent or favorite female companion; sweetheart

**going steady** (*adj*) regularly dating one person

**hanky-panky** *Informal*. questionable sexual conduct

**hit it off** *Informal*. find each other attractive or compatible as lovers

**hit on** (*vb*) *Slang*. make persistent sexual advances to

**holding hands** gently gripping each other's hands as a gesture of affection

**honey** *Informal*. sweetheart, lover

**hug** enthusiastic, affectionate embrace

**indiscretion** coy or ill-advised reference to sexual encounter

**jilt** (*vb*) abandon one's sweetheart

**kiss** (*vb*) press mouths together as sign of love, affection, or desire; (*n*) such an act

**ladies' man** extremely flirtatious, sexually interested male

**lady-killer** *Informal*. devastatingly attractive man who fascinates women

**liaison** sexual encounter or affair

**liberties** impertinent or unwarranted sexual actions

**love letter** affectionate, passionate correspondence to one's beloved

**make out** (*vb*) *Slang*. kiss and fondle passionately for extended time

**meat rack** *Derogatory slang*. singles bar

**minx** pert young girl

**Mr. Right** man who is viewed as ideal romantic partner or potential spouse (sometimes used with Miss, Mrs., or Ms. when referring to a female)

**necking** prolonged kissing and fondling

**nuzzling** lying close and snuggling affectionately, esp. with heads

**oeillade** *French*. amorous glance

**ogling** closely eyeing the object of one's affection

**one-night stand** *Informal.* casual, unrepeated sexual encounter

**on the make** searching for a sexual partner; on the prowl

**on the prowl** on the make

**osculation** kiss

**parietal** (*adj*) having to do with rules governing contact between sexes and dating hours, esp. at institution

**pass** *Informal.* approach to another with intimated offer of sex

**paw** (*vb*) *Informal.* handle roughly with sexual intent

**peck** small kiss

**personals** classified advertisements for sexual partners

**pet** sweetheart, lover

**pet name** affectionate term of address

**petting** fondling, foreplay

**pickup** *Informal.* casual sexual partner, esp. one met in public place

**pick up** (*vb*) *Informal.* become acquainted with informally, usu. in expectation of sexual encounter

**pin** (*vb*) formalize steady dating arrangement with girl by giving her one's fraternity pin

**play the field** *Informal.* have numerous sexual partners or romantic attachments

**pucker up** (*vb*) *Slang.* prepare to kiss

**put the make on** aggressively court with intention of having sex

**reconcile** (*vb*) resolve differences and renew affection

**rendezvous** meeting between lovers, sometimes in secret

**roving eye** interest in having many sexual encounters

**run around** (*vb*) pursue sexual partners, esp. in addition to primary partner

**seduce** (*vb*) entice or persuade doubtful or unwilling person into sexual intimacy

**serenade** courting song

**singles** unmarried persons interested in dating

**singles bar** drinking establishment designed for meeting of singles

**skirt** *Disparaging slang.* woman or girl

**smack** loud kiss

**smooch** (*vb*) *Informal.* kiss; pet

**smoothie** *Informal.* person who is seductive in manner and speech

**snow job** *Slang.* extreme, often manipulative, persuasion to have sex

**snuggle** (*vb*) cuddle affectionately

**soul kiss** passionate, open-mouthed kiss with tongue of one partner in mouth of the other; French kiss

**spark** (*vb*) *Informal.* court or woo

**spoon** (*vb*) *Informal.* court by caressing and kissing, esp. in a sentimental manner

**squire** (*vb*) escort woman to social gathering, esp. in a proper manner

**stand up** (*vb*) *Slang.* fail to appear for a date with

**steady** regular date or lover

**step out** (*vb*) go on date

**string along** (*vb*) *Informal.* encourage suitor with no intention of responding

**suitor** man courting a woman; swain

**swain** suitor

**sweetheart** darling, lover

**sweet nothings** *Slang.* sweet talk, esp. whispered in lover's ear

**sweet talk** *Informal.* endearments spoken to one's lover

**swinger** *Slang.* extremely sexually active person

**tease** (*vb*) engage in coy, playful flirtation; (*n*) flirt, coquette

**temptress** female who entices or allures

**tête-à-tête** intimate talk

**tomato** *Slang.* attractive young woman

**tongue wrestling** *Slang.* French kissing

**tryst** romantic meeting, rendezvous

**valentine** sweetheart; greeting card or note sent to one's lover or object of one's affection on February 14

**vamp** seductive woman

**walking out** *Brit. slang.* going steady

**wolf** *Informal.* sexually aggressive male

**wolf whistle** man's whistle of appreciation for woman's appearance

**woo** (*vb*) attempt to win affection or favor; court

## SEXUALITY AND LIBIDO

**age of consent** age when one may legally engage in sex

**animal** person with abundant sexual energy

**animal magnetism** erotic attraction

**aphrodisiac** substance that increases sexual desire and performance

**asexual** (*adj*) having no sexual orientation

**birds and bees** euphemism for basic information about sexuality and reproduction

**bisexual** (*adj*) attracted to both males and females

**carnal** (*adj*) relating to physical desire

**chastity** virginity, sexual innocence

**Circean** (*adj*) dangerously or fatally attractive

**cold** (*adj*) sexually unresponsive

**concupiscence** strong sexual desire

**conjugal rights** sexual rights of husband and wife

**continence** total abstinence from sexual activity

**craving** desire for sex

**dark meat** *Vulgar slang.* African-American considered as sexual partner

**desire** intense sexual urge

**dirty old man** mature or elderly man with lewd or obscene preoccupations

**easy** (*adj*) available for indiscriminate sex

**emasculate** (*vb*) deprive male of his power and sexuality, literally by castration or figuratively

**epicene** (*adj*) with characteristics of both sexes; sexless, neither male nor female

**erotic** (*adj*) pertaining to sexual love; strongly sexual

**erotica** art and literature with erotic content

**eroticism** sexual quality or character

**estrus** period of sexual heat or rutting

**facts of life** basic information about sexuality and reproduction

**fast** (*adj*) easily available for sex

**female** woman; (*adj*) characteristic of women

**feminine** (*adj*) characteristic of women; female

**fox** *Slang.* extremely sexually attractive young female or male

**free love** uninhibited sexual behavior, generally without expectation of conventional social contracts such as marriage

**frigid** (*adj*) sexually unresponsive, said esp. of women

**gender** sexual identity, both biological and learned

**heat**  period of sexual arousal and interest in mating; estrus

**he-man**  *Informal.* virile, macho male

**heterosexual**  one attracted to opposite sex

**homosexual**  one attracted to same sex

**horny** (*adj*) *Vulgar slang.* craving sex; sexually aroused

**hot** (*adj*) *Slang.* sexy; aroused, stimulated

**hot number**  *Slang.* sexy, attractive woman

**hots**  *Slang.* usu. **the hots**; intense sexual desire or attraction

**hunk**  *Slang.* attractive man with well-developed physique

**impotent** (*adj*)  unable to achieve erection for sexual intercourse

**itch**  *Slang.* sexual urge

**ithyphallic** (*adj*)  lewd, obscene; displaying an erect penis

**jade**  wanton woman

**keep one's honor**  resist sexual temptation, remain chaste

**Kinsey scale**  sevenfold numerical scale of sexual orientation, devised by Alfred Kinsey, in which zero is exclusive heterosexuality and six is exclusive homosexuality

**lascivious** (*adj*)  lustful, lewd

**lechery**  lewdness, lustfulness

**letch**  *Slang.* lecherous individual

**lewd** (*adj*)  lustful, lecherous, obscene in desires

**liberated** (*adj*)  without sexual inhibition

**libertine**  one who indulges freely in sex

**libido**  sexual desire and energy

**Lord Fauntleroy**  effeminate man

**love potion**  magic substance that creates desire; aphrodisiac

**lubricity**  wanton lechery

**lust**  strong sexual desire, esp. without deep affection

**lusty** (*adj*)  filled with sexual desire

**machismo**  exaggerated, showy claims of virility

**macho** (*adj*)  overly assertive, virile, and domineering

**magnetism**  fundamental sexual attractiveness

**maiden**  virgin

**male**  man; (*adj*) characteristic of men

**manly** (*adj*)  virile, macho

**masculine** (*adj*)  characteristic of men; male

**masher**  *Slang.* man who makes passes at women

**misogyny**  hatred of women

**musth**  sexual excitement or frenzy, esp. in rutting season among certain animals

**neuter** (*adj*)  having no sex

**nubile** (*adj*)  ready for marriage, said esp. of young women

**nymphet**  sexually precocious girl in early teens

**oversexed** (*adj*)  having excessive sexual interest and energy

**pantywaist**  *Informal.* weak, effeminate man

**passion**  intense emotion and sexual desire

**philter**  magic substance that arouses passion; love potion

**piece**  *Vulgar slang.* person regarded as sex object, esp. a female; piece of ass

**piece of ass**  *Vulgar slang.* piece

**piece of meat**  *Derogatory slang.* man or woman regarded as sex object

**potency**  virility, sexual ability

**prig**  person tending to see pornographic content where it does not exist

**promiscuity**  indiscriminate, casual, frequent sexual activity

**prudery**  extreme modesty, sexual restraint

**prurience**  lewd, lascivious desire or thought

**pudibund** (*adj*)  prudish

**pure** (*adj*)  chaste

**racy** (*adj*)  spirited, sexually zestful

**randy**  craving sex; sexually aroused; horny

**raunchy** (*adj*)  coarse, earthy

**rutting**  mating urge; estrus; heat

**ruttish** (*adj*)  salacious; lustful

**salacious** (*adj*)  lewd, lascivious

**satyr**  lecherous man

**scabrous** (*adj*)  risqué; obscene

**sensual** (*adj*)  carnal; devoted to sensory pleasure

**sensuality**  fondness for and indulgence in sensory pleasure; lasciviousness

**sex appeal**  sexual attractiveness

**sex fiend**  person excessively intent on having sex

**sex goddess**  woman revered as ultimate sex object

**sex kitten**  *Informal.* sensuous, seductive young woman

**sex object**  person, esp. woman, valued only for sex

**sexpot**  *Informal.* person with sex appeal

**sex surrogate**  professional who has sex with clients for therapeutic purposes

**sex symbol**  celebrity known for sex appeal

**sexuality**  state of being or feeling sexual

**sexually active**  regularly engaging in sex

**sexual orientation**  gender preference in sexual partners

**sissy**  weak or effeminate man

**slut**  loose, promiscuous woman

**Spanish fly**  preparation used as aphrodisiac

**stag** (*adj*)  designating all-male event, esp. with lewd entertainment

**steamy** (*adj*)  sexually arousing

**straight** (*adj*)  *Informal.* heterosexual

**stud**  *Slang.* exceptionally sexually competent male

**sultry** (*adj*)  characterized by or arousing passion

**supermacho** (*adj*)  given to extreme displays of virility

**superstud**  *Slang.* extremely sexually active male

**sybarite**  sensualist, voluptuary

**tail**  *Vulgar slang.* woman viewed as a sex object; piece

**thigh**  *Derogatory slang.* female as sex object

**throbbing** (*adj*)  pulsing with sexual arousal

**tramp**  loose, promiscuous woman

**transsexual** (*adj*)  sexually oriented as if one's body were of the opposite sex

**trollop**  promiscuous woman

**undersexed** (*adj*)  having inadequate sexual interest and energy

**unisexual** (*adj*)  of one sex

**unsexual** (*adj*)  not sexual

**urge**  sexual desire

**urge to merge**  *Informal.* sexual desire

**vamp**  wily, seductive woman

**vanilla sex**  *Slang.* ordinary, nonkinky sexual activities

**vestal virgin**  chaste woman

**virgin**  person who has not experienced sexual intercourse, used esp. of women

**virginity**  state of being chaste and without sexual experience

**virile** (*adj*)  manly, masculine

**virility**  manly strength and sexual potency

**virtue**  traditional chastity, esp. in female

**voluptuary**  person given over to sensual gratification

**voluptuous** (*adj*)  devoted to sensual gratification

**wanton** (*adj*)  loose, lewd, promiscuous, immoral

**wench**  lewd woman

**wimp**  *Informal.* weak, effeminate man

# Homosexuality

**AC/DC** (adj) Slang. bisexual

**age-differentiated** (adj) designating homosexuality involving usu. bisexual adult male and sexually passive young boy prized for his androgynous qualities, predominant in Islamic world, ancient Greece, and pre-industrial Europe

**androphilia** homosexuality involving two adults, both of whom self-identify as males, predominant in 20th-century United States and Europe

**auntie** Slang. older male homosexual

**baby butch** Slang. young, boyish lesbian

**bear** Slang. hirsute, often husky gay male

**beefcake** Informal. photographs of nude or nearly nude young men in magazines, posed to display their muscles or genitals

**bent** (adj) Chiefly Brit. slang. homosexual

**bisexual** (adj) attracted to and sexually active with both males and females; (n) such a person

**bugger** (vb) Vulgar slang. have anal intercourse with

**bull dyke** Derogatory slang. masculine-appearing lesbian

**butch** (adj) Slang. designating a masculine-appearing or -behaving female; designating a masculine-behaving male homosexual; (n) lesbian

**camp** something involving self-conscious and extravagant humor, irony, or amusement, often with playful inversion of values; (vb) behave in an extravagantly theatrical and stereotypically effeminate manner

**catamite** boy or youth in homosexual relationship with man; gunsel

**chicken** Slang. young male homosexual, esp. one sought by older men

**chicken hawk** Slang. older homosexual male who prefers young men

**clone** homosexual male who adopts stereotypical appearance featuring short hair, clipped mustache, flannel shirt, and denim trousers, often with leather accessories

**closet queen** Disparaging slang. man who keeps his homosexuality a secret

**cock ring** Vulgar slang. ring worn at base of penis, used to prolong erection

**cocksucker** Vulgar slang. person who performs fellatio, esp. male homosexual

**come out** (vb) declare one's homosexuality to family and friends or publicly; enter gay subculture

**daisy chain** Slang. line of males joined penis-in-anus or sometimes penis-in-mouth

**diesel dyke** Derogatory slang. masculine-appearing lesbian

**drag** clothing worn by one sex that is characteristic of the other sex

**drag queen** male transvestite

**dyke** Derogatory slang. lesbian

**effeminate** (adj) not masculine in appearance or behavior, said esp. of homosexuals

**ephebophobia** male homosexuality involving age-differentiated attraction

**fag** Derogatory slang. faggot

**faggot** Derogatory slang. male homosexual; fag

**faggotry** Derogatory slang. state, condition, and acts of homosexual males

**faggy** (adj) Derogatory slang. of or resembling male homosexuals; effeminate

**fag hag** Derogatory slang. heterosexual woman who cultivates friendships with gay males

**fairy** Derogatory slang. male homosexual

**feigele** Yiddish derogatory slang. male homosexual

**fem** Slang. very feminine lesbian, in contrast to butch

**fish** Derogatory slang. usu. heterosexual woman

**fist fuck** Vulgar slang. insert one's closed fist into another's anus

**flaming** (adj) Slang. blatantly or outlandishly gay

**flit** Derogatory slang. male homosexual

**fruit** Derogatory slang. male homosexual

**gay** (adj) homosexual, either male or female, sometimes restricted to males only

**gay liberation** sociopolitical movement to combat legal and social discrimination against homosexuals, begun in late 1960's

**gay power** organized political influence exerted by homosexuals as a group, esp. to achieve equal rights and social justice

**gay pride** communally nurtured sense of self-esteem and self-assertion among homosexuals

**gay subculture** social environment of self-identified homosexuals, comprising neighborhoods, events, organizations, and other formal and informal institutions that promote a sense of community and identity

**gender-differentiated** (adj) designating homosexuality involving fixed sexual roles in which one partner is passive and the other active-penetrative or one butch and the other fem

**glory hole** Vulgar slang. hole in men's room wall used to perform fellatio

**go both ways** Slang. engage in bisexual acts

**granola dyke** Slang. New Age lesbian who rejects cosmetics and feminine beauty accessories

**gunsel** Slang. catamite

**heterosexism** prejudicial discrimination against non-heterosexual practices based on tacit belief in universality of heterosexual norms

**homo** Derogatory slang. homosexual, usu. male

**homoeroticism** sexual arousal caused by member of same sex

**homophile** one who is homosexual; (adj) supportive of gay rights and interests

**homophobia** irrational fear of or aversion to homosexuals

**homosexual** person sexually attracted to and usu. sexually active with members of the same sex

**homosociality** male bonding without implication of sexual contact

**in the closet** secretly homosexual

**lace** Vulgar slang. foreskin on penis

**latent** (adj) in popular usage, designating one who appears heterosexual while repressing unconscious homosexual tendencies

**leather scene** sub-subculture involving suggestion of sadomasochistic activities and wearing of leather accessories

**lesbian** female homosexual

**lesbian separatism** extreme lesbian movement advocating complete separation from males

**lesbo** Derogatory slang. lesbian

**lez** Derogatory slang. lesbian

**licorice stick** Vulgar slang. black man's penis

**limp wrist** Derogatory slang. male homosexual

**lip service** *Vulgar slang.* fellatio

**mary** *Derogatory slang.* homosexual male

**mo** *Derogatory slang.* homosexual, usu. male

**nance** *Derogatory slang.* effeminate male; homosexual male

**nellie** *(adj) Slang.* designating an effeminate male; *Derogatory slang.* designating a homosexual male

**outing** public exposure of another's homosexuality against his or her will

**out of the closet** having revealed one's homosexuality

**pansy** *Derogatory slang.* male homosexual; effeminate male

**pederasty** sexual relations between a man and an boy, usu. under sixteen

**poof** *Brit. slang.* male homosexual; effeminate male

**Princeton style** *Vulgar slang.* ejaculation achieved by friction between another male's thighs

**punk** *Slang.* young male coerced into passive sexual role by older, often heterosexual, male prison inmate; any young, passive male partner of older homosexual

**queen** *Derogatory slang.* effeminate male homosexual, esp. one who dresses in woman's clothing

**queer** *Derogatory slang.* homosexual, esp. male

**queer bashing** physical and verbal assault on gays, usu. by young homophobic males who self-identify as heterosexual

**rim** *(vb) Vulgar slang.* lick or suck anus

**salt-and-pepper** *(adj)* designating interracial couple

**sapphist** lesbian

**seafood** *Slang.* sailors with reputed fondness for oral sex

**service** *(vb) Slang.* perform fellatio on nonreciprocal basis

**situational** *(adj)* designating homosexuality that occurs in sex-segregated situations, such as prisons, ships, or boarding schools, where heterosexuals are deprived of contact with the opposite sex, usu. temporary and without homosexual self-identity

**stud** *Slang.* very sexually active male homosexual or butch lesbian

**sucked dry** *(adj) Vulgar slang.* fellated with great passion

**swish** *Derogatory slang.* effeminate male homosexual; *(vb)* employ effeminate body language

**switch-hitter** *Slang.* one who is bisexual

**tearoom** *Slang.* men's bathroom in public place

**trade** *Slang.* usu. self-identified heterosexual or bisexual male who restricts himself to penetrative role in sex with passive homosexual

**transvestite** person who dresses in clothing of opposite sex, esp. drag queen

**tribade** lesbian

**tribadism** sexual practices of lesbians

**tubs** gay bathhouse

**twinky** *Slang.* handsome, young, gay male

**vegetable** *Derogatory slang.* rare term for lesbian, as distinguished from male "fruit"

**well-hung** *(adj) Vulgar slang.* having a large penis

## ANATOMY AND PHYSIOLOGY OF SEX

**AIDS** acquired immune deficiency syndrome; usu. fatal disease characterized by inability of body to fight various infections due to HIV virus, which attacks immune system, transmitted by direct contact of body fluids

**androgen** male hormone

**androgynous** *(adj)* having both male and female characteristics

**ARC** AIDS-related complex; various diseases and infections to which AIDS sufferers are susceptible

**areola** pigmented area around nipple

**arousal** condition in which there are physiological signs of sexual stimulation, such as erection

**ballocks** *Vulgar slang.* testicles

**balls** *Vulgar slang.* testicles

**basket** *Vulgar slang.* man's genital area

**bazongas** *Vulgar slang.* woman's breasts

**bearded clam** *Vulgar slang.* female genitals

**beaver** *Vulgar slang.* woman's pubic area

**beget** *(vb)* generate (offspring)

**bone** *Vulgar slang.* penis, esp. in erection

**boner** *Vulgar slang.* erection

**boob** *Vulgar slang.* woman's breast, esp. large

**booby** *Vulgar slang.* woman's breast

**bosom** woman's breast

**box** *Vulgar slang.* woman's pubic area, esp. vagina

**breast** woman's mammary gland

**brick house** *Slang.* well-built woman

**brown eye** *Vulgar slang.* anus

**bum** *Chiefly Brit. slang.* buttocks

**bunghole** *Vulgar slang.* anus

**buns** *Slang.* buttocks

**bush** *Vulgar slang.* woman's pubic hair

**bust** woman's breasts

**buxom** *(adj)* describing woman having large breasts and full body

**callipygian** *(adj)* having shapely buttocks

**castration** removal of man's testicles

**cervix** neck of uterus

**cheeks** *Slang.* buttocks

**cheese** *Vulgar slang.* smegma

**cherry** *Vulgar slang.* hymen; *(adj)* virginal

**chlamydia** gonorrhealike venereal disease caused by parasite

**clap** *Vulgar slang.* gonorrhea

**cleavage** area between woman's breasts

**climax** orgasm

**clit** *Vulgar slang.* clitoris

**clitoral orgasm** woman's climax, centered in clitoral tissue

**clitoris** small, sensitive, erectile protuberance at upper end of female vulva

**cock** *Vulgar slang.* penis

**cojones** *Spanish vulgar slang.* testicles

**come** *Vulgar slang.* ejaculation; *(vb) Informal.* have orgasm

**conception** fertilization of egg by sperm

**cooze** *Vulgar slang.* vagina

**crabs** pubic lice

**crack** *Vulgar slang.* vagina

**cramps** pain caused by menstrual period

**crotch** genital area

**cryptorchidism** undescended testicles

**cum** *Vulgar slang.* semen

**cumstain** mark left by semen, esp. on bedding

**cunt** *Vulgar slang.* vulva

**dental dam** device placed in mouth to prevent entrance of body fluids during oral sex, used as an AIDS preventative

**dick** *Vulgar slang.* penis

**dink** *Vulgar slang.* penis, esp. small one

**dong** *Vulgar slang.* penis

**dork** *Vulgar slang.* penis

**ejaculation** male orgasm with emission of sperm

**erection** stiffening of blood-filled penis due to sexual arousal

**erogenous** (*adj*) designating areas of body that are sensitive to sexual stimulation; erotogenic

**erotogenic** (*adj*) erogenous

**estrogen** female hormone

**estrous cycle** period of increased sexual interest and activity

**eunuch** castrated male

**fallopian tube** female internal tube that carries eggs from ovaries to uterus

**family jewels** *Slang.* man's genitals

**fern** *Vulgar slang.* female genitals

**foreskin** fleshy covering of head of penis

**fur** *Vulgar slang.* woman's pubic hair

**gash** *Vulgar slang.* vagina

**genitalia** genitals

**genitals** external sexual organs, male or female; genitalia

**get** (*vb*) beget

**gonad** organ producing eggs or sperm

**gonorrhea** infectious venereal disease characterized by inflammation of and discharge from mucous membrane

**goose bumps** raised body hairs due to intense sexual excitement

**G spot** extremely sensitive and erogenous spot in front wall of vagina, instrumental in orgasm

**gynandrous** (*adj*) having physical characteristics of both sexes

**hard-on** *Vulgar slang.* erection

**heinie** *Slang.* buttocks

**hermaphrodite** person with physical characteristics of both male and female

**herpes simplex** recurrent, incurable venereal disease affecting mouth or genitals with sores

**hickey** *Slang.* love bite; purplish bruise made by vigorous sucking of skin

**honeypot** *Vulgar slang.* vagina

**hung** (*adj*) *Vulgar slang.* having a large penis

**hymen** membrane that partly closes vagina of virgin; maidenhead

**jelly roll** *Vulgar slang.* vagina

**jewels** *Vulgar slang.* man's genitals

**jissom** *Vulgar slang.* semen

**Johnnie** *Vulgar slang.* penis

**joint** *Vulgar slang.* penis

**jugs** *Vulgar slang.* woman's breasts, esp. large ones

**knockers** *Vulgar slang.* woman's breasts

**labia majora** outer folds at vaginal opening

**labia minora** inner folds at vaginal opening

**lingam** *Sanskrit.* lit. male gender; penis, phallus

**load** *Vulgar slang.* sperm in one ejaculation; wad

**love drop** *Slang.* small quantity of semen emitted prior to full ejaculation; preorgasmic ejaculation

**love juice** *Slang.* semen

**maidenhead** hymen

**mammary** (*adj*) pertaining to woman's breasts

**meat** *Vulgar slang.* penis

**member** penis

**merkin** false hair for female pudenda

**mons veneris** female pubic mound

**muff** *Vulgar slang.* female pubic area

**multiply** (*vb*) have sexual intercourse, conceive, and bear children

**nipple** dark, sensitive, protuberant opening of breast through which milk flows

**nooky** *Vulgar slang.* vulva

**nuts** *Vulgar slang.* testicles

**organ** penis

**orgasm** convulsive climax of intercourse

**ovary** egg-producing organ of female

**ovulation** monthly dropping of egg from ovary to uterus

**ovum** egg produced by female

**pecker** *Vulgar slang.* penis

**pelt** *Vulgar slang.* woman's pubic hair

**penis** male erectile organ of copulation and bonding, used esp. by heterosexuals for insertion of sperm into uterus

**period** monthly menstruation

**peter** *Vulgar slang.* penis

**phallic** (*adj*) pertaining to the penis

**phallus** penis; object that represents or symbolizes penis

**pizzle** animal penis

**PMS** premenstrual syndrome

**pole** *Vulgar slang.* penis

**premenstrual syndrome** PMS; physical and emotional changes associated with hormonal fluctuations prior to menstruation

**preorgasmic ejaculation** small quantity of semen emitted prior to full ejaculation

**prepuce** foreskin

**priapic** (*adj*) pertaining to the penis

**priapism** abnormal, persistent erection without accompanying sexual desire

**Priapus** god of male sexuality (ancient Greece and Rome)

**prick** *Vulgar slang.* penis

**primary sex characteristic** feature differentiating male from female in relation to reproduction

**private parts** external sexual organs; genitals

**procreate** (*vb*) have sexual intercourse resulting in childbirth

**prong** *Vulgar slang.* penis

**prostate gland** gland at base of urethra in males

**prunes** *Vulgar slang.* testicles

**puberty** onset of sexual maturity

**pubes** pubic hair

**pubescence** arrival at puberty

**pubic** (*adj*) pertaining to or situated in area of pubis

**pubic hair** hair appearing at puberty around lower abdomen and genitals

**pubic lice** small parasitic insects living in pubic hair and transmitted by sexual contact

**pubis** lower abdomen, covered with hair and forming bony protuberance above genitals

**pudenda** external female genitals

**pussy** *Vulgar slang.* female genitals

**putz** *Vulgar slang.* penis

**quim** *Vulgar slang.* female genitals

**racks** *Vulgar slang.* female breasts

**reproduction** sexual process of conception, pregnancy, and birth of young

**rim** *Vulgar slang.* anus

**rocks** *Vulgar slang.* male genitals

**rod** *Vulgar slang.* penis

**root** *Vulgar slang.* penis

**safe sex** use of condom during intercourse as protection against disease; practice of oral sex or mutual masturbation for same purpose

**scrotum** sack holding testicles

**secondary sex characteristic** feature, such as body hair or breasts, that differentiates males and females but is not directly connected to production of egg or sperm

**semen** male ejaculate containing sperm

**sex** basic division of a species into male and female, for purpose of reproduction; sexual activity; instinct or attraction drawing one sex toward another; sexual intercourse; genitals

**sex change operation** surgical reconstruction of one's sexual organs as those of the opposite sex

**sexually transmitted disease** any of various infections acquired through contact of sexual organs, including AIDS, ARC, chlamydia, crabs, gonorrhea, herpes simplex, pubic lice, syphilis, trichomoniasis, venereal disease, and yeast infection; venereal disease

**short hairs** *Slang.* pubic hair

**slit** *Vulgar slang.* vagina

**smegma** sebaceous matter secreted around penis or clitoris; cheese

**snatch** *Vulgar slang.* female genitals

**social disease** venereal disease

**spado** castrated man

**sperm** spermatozoon, male seed in semen

**spotting** menstrual discharge occurring between periods

**stacked** (*adj*) *Slang.* having voluptuous, sexually appealing body, esp. large breasts

**sterile** (*adj*) barren, incapable of procreating

**syphilis** infectious degenerative venereal disease acquired through sexual contact or congenitally

**T and A** *tits and ass*

**testicle** sperm-producing gland at base of penis; testis

**testis** testicle; *pl.* **testes**

**testosterone** male hormone

**tit** *Vulgar slang.* breast

**tool** *Vulgar slang.* penis

**trichomoniasis** parasitic infestation of vagina causing heavy discharge

**tumescence** stiffening and engorging of penis

**tush** *Slang.* buttocks

**twat** *Vulgar slang.* female genitals

**uterus** organ of conception and nurturance of fetus; womb

**vagina** canal from vulva to uterus

**vaginal orgasm** orgasm occurring in vagina

**vas deferens** tube carrying sperm from testicle to penis

**venereal disease** disease transmitted by sexual contact with infected person; sexually transmitted disease; social disease

**Venus mound** *Slang.* female genitalia; mons veneris

**vulva** external female genitals

**wad** *Vulgar slang.* unejaculated sperm; sperm in single ejaculation

**wet dream** ejaculation during sleep

**wet spot** semen-soaked mark on sheets after sex, or on man's underpants

**whang** *Vulgar slang.* penis

**wiener** *Vulgar slang.* penis

**wieny** *Vulgar slang.* penis

**willy** *Vulgar slang.* penis

**wing-wang** *Vulgar slang.* penis

**womb** uterus

**wong** *Vulgar slang.* penis

**yeast infection** fungus living in vagina

**yoni** *Sanskrit.* vulva

## CONTRACEPTION AND FERTILITY

**abortion** induced expulsion of fetus from mother's womb

**artificial insemination** insemination of woman for purposes of conception through medical procedure rather than intercourse

**barren** (*adj*) infertile; unable to conceive

**bilateral tubal ligation** BTL; surgical sterilization of female

**birth control** prevention of conception by chemical or mechanical means; contraception

**birth-control pill** contraceptive hormone, usu. estrogen and progesterone, taken daily in tablet form by women, that causes temporary infertility

**BTL** bilateral *tubal ligation*

**catcher's mitt** *Slang.* diaphragm

**cervical cap** diaphragmlike device used with spermicidal jelly to prevent sperm from entering uterus

**climacteric** period of major physiological change, such as menopause

**coil** intrauterine contraceptive device

**coitus interruptus** contraception through withdrawal of penis before ejaculation

**condom** usu. rubber sheath worn on penis to capture semen during intercourse and thus prevent conception

**contraception** prevention of pregnancy

**contraceptive sponge** absorbent material containing spermicide placed on cervix for contraception

**curse** *Slang.* monthly menstrual period

**diaphragm** rubber disk worn on cervix during intercourse for contraception by preventing sperm from entering uterus

**douche** water or cleansing agent used for washing semen from vagina after intercourse, considered ineffective contraceptive method

**emmenagogue** substance or practice that promotes menstruation

**false pregnancy** symptoms of pregnancy without having actual embryo in womb

**fertility** ability to conceive or impregnate

**fertility drug** hormonal substance used to induce ovulation and produce pregnancy

**flying Baker** *Slang.* menstrual period

**foam** spermicidal substance placed in vagina for contraceptive purposes

**French tickler** *Slang.* condom

**geld** (*vb*) castrate, usu. in reference to animals

**glove** *Slang.* condom

**gravid** (*adj*) pregnant

**hysterectomy** surgical removal of uterus

**impregnate** (*vb*) make (a female) pregnant; cause (an egg) to be fertilized

**infertility** inability to conceive or impregnate; barrenness; sterility

**intrauterine device** IUD; contraceptive device worn continuously for up to several years inside uterus to prevent fertilization or implantation

**in trouble** *Slang.* pregnant and unmarried

**in utero** (*adj*) in the womb or uterus

**in vitro** (*adj*) *Latin.* lit. in glass; artificially inseminated and maintained, as in a test tube

**IUD** intrauterine device

**knock up** (*vb*) *Slang.* impregnate

**loop** type of IUD
**menarche** first menstruation, at beginning of fertility
**menopause** end of menstruation and fertility
**menses** monthly menstruation
**menstruation** monthly discharge of blood from uterus when conception has not occurred
**morning-after pill** contraceptive chemical taken after intercourse to prevent implantation of embryo
**Norplant** *Trademark.* contraceptive device implanted under woman's skin, where it slowly releases hormone progestin for five years
**pessary** contraceptive device worn in vagina
**pill** birth-control pill
**pregnant** (*adj*) carrying fetus inside womb; with child
**prophylactic device** something that prevents conception and venereal disease, esp. a condom
**rag** *Vulgar slang.* menstrual period
**rhythm method** contraceptive method that gauges likelihood of fertility during woman's menstrual cycle
**rubber** *Slang.* condom
**salpingectomy** surgical severing of fallopian tubes to sterilize a woman
**skin** *Slang.* condom
**spermicidal jelly** sperm-killing, jellylike substance placed in vagina during intercourse
**spermicide** substance that kills sperm
**sterility** inability to produce living offspring
**sterilization** surgical procedure that prevents conception
**Trojan** *Trademark.* condom
**tubal ligation** sterilization of female by sealing off of fallopian tubes to prevent ovum from reaching uterus
**tying one's tubes** *Slang.* tubal ligation
**vasectomy** surgical procedure for sterilizing men by cutting vas deferens
**with child** pregnant

## SEX ACTS

**action** *Slang.* sexual activity
**act of love** intercourse
**adultery** sex act by married person with someone other than spouse
**anal intercourse** penetration of anus by penis
**anilingus** oral anal sex
**ass** *Slang.* sexual intercourse
**astride** (*adj*) taking a dominant position during penetration
**autoeroticism** self-stimulation, masturbation
**ball** (*vb*) *Vulgar slang.* have sexual intercourse
**bang** (*vb*) *Vulgar slang.* have sexual intercourse
**beat off** (*vb*) *Vulgar slang.* masturbate
**bed** (*vb*) take to bed for sexual activity
**blow** (*vb*) *Vulgar slang.* perform fellatio on
**blow job** oral penile sex, fellatio
**boff** (*vb*) *Vulgar slang.* have sexual intercourse
**bundling** cuddling in bed without undressing
**circle jerk** *Vulgar slang.* mutual masturbation among three or more persons
**coition** coitus
**coitus** sexual intercourse; coition
**come** (*vb*) *Informal.* reach orgasm
**congress** sexual intercourse
**consummation** sexual intercourse, esp. on wedding night

**cop a feel** touch another's body sexually, often in quick and surreptitious way
**copulation** sexual intercourse
**cornhole** (*vb*) *Slang.* perform anal intercourse
**couple** (*vb*) have sexual intercourse
**cream** (*vb*) *Vulgar slang.* come, reach orgasm
**cream one's jeans** *Vulgar slang.* reach orgasm
**cunnilingus** oral vaginal sex
**deflower** (*vb*) have sexual intercourse with a virgin
**diddle** (*vb*) *Slang.* have sexual intercourse
**do it** (*vb*) *Slang.* have sexual intercourse
**eat** (*vb*) *Vulgar slang.* perform fellatio or cunnilingus on
**ejaculate** (*vb*) emit sperm at orgasm
**feel** act of touching another sexually
**feel up** (*vb*) *Vulgar slang.* fondle someone in a sexual manner, esp. touch a woman's breasts
**fellatio** oral penile sex
**fingerfuck** (*vb*) *Vulgar slang.* manually stimulate female's genitals
**foreplay** fondling and caressing before actual intercourse
**fornication** sexual intercourse, esp. between unmarried persons
**frig** (*vb*) *Vulgar slang.* have sexual intercourse
**fuck** (*vb*) *Vulgar slang.* have sexual intercourse
**fucking** *Vulgar slang.* sexual intercourse
**get down** (*vb*) *Slang.* have sexual relations
**get it on** *Vulgar slang.* have sexual relations
**get it up** *Vulgar slang.* achieve erection of penis
**get off** (*vb*) *Vulgar slang.* reach orgasm
**give head** *Vulgar slang.* perform oral sex
**go all the way** *Slang.* have sexual intercourse
**go down on** *Vulgar slang.* have oral-genital sex with
**hand job** *Vulgar slang.* stimulation by hand of another's genitals; masturbation
**have sex** (*vb*) engage in sexual intercourse
**hide the salami** *Vulgar slang.* have sexual intercourse
**hump** (*vb*) *Vulgar slang.* have sexual intercourse
**inseminate** (*vb*) ejaculate into (vagina); impregnate (a female)
**intercourse** copulation between male and female
**in the saddle** having mounted one's usu. female partner
**irrumation** oral penile sex, esp. involving active thrusting of penis; fellatio
**jack off** (*vb*) *Vulgar slang.* masturbate
**jerk off** (*vb*) *Vulgar slang.* masturbate
**jump** (*vb*) *Vulgar slang.* engage in sexual intercourse with
**know** (*vb*) have sexual intercourse with (biblical)
**lay** (*vb*) *Vulgar slang.* have sexual intercourse with
**lie with** (*vb*) have sexual intercourse with
**lovemaking** sexual relations
**make** (*vb*) *Slang.* have sexual relations with
**make it** *Slang.* have sexual intercourse
**make love** have sexual intercourse
**masturbation** self-stimulation of one's sexual organs
**mate** (*vb*) have sexual relations
**ménage à trois** sex act among three people
**missionary position** sexual intercourse with man on top and woman underneath lying face to face
**mount** (*vb*) position oneself atop female
**muff diver** *Vulgar slang.* cunnilingus enthusiast
**mustache ride** *Vulgar slang.* oral sex
**nooky** *Vulgar slang.* sexual intercourse
**onanism** masturbation; uncompleted intercourse

**peel** (*vb*) *Slang.* undress prior to having sex
**penetration** entry of male into female
**play with oneself** masturbate
**pork** (*vb*) *Vulgar slang.* have sexual intercourse
**pound off** (*vb*) *Vulgar slang.* masturbate
**premarital sex** sexual relations before marriage
**pull a train** *Vulgar slang.* have uninterrupted sex with a series of male partners, esp. bikers
**pump** (*vb*) thrust with pelvis during intercourse
**quickie** *Informal.* brief, often secretive sex act
**ravish** (*vb*) force someone to have sexual relations
**ream** (*vb*) *Vulgar slang.* have sexual intercourse with a woman
**relations** sexual intercourse
**rim job** *Vulgar slang.* anilingus
**rocks off** *Vulgar slang.* ejaculation
**romp** (*vb*) have playful sexual relations
**rut** (*vb*) *Vulgar slang.* have sexual intercourse
**safe sex** sexual relations using condoms or other devices as precautionary measure against disease, esp. AIDS
**score** (*vb*) *Slang.* entice another into having sexual intercourse
**screw** (*vb*) *Vulgar slang.* have sexual intercourse
**seduce** (*vb*) entice unwilling or doubtful person into sex
**service** (*vb*) *Vulgar slang.* have sexual intercourse to satisfy another's needs
**sexual intercourse** copulation between male and female
**sexual relations** intercourse and related sexual activities
**shoot one's wad** *Vulgar slang.* ejaculate
**shtup** (*vb*) *Vulgar slang.* have sexual intercourse
**sixty-nine** *Vulgar slang.* simultaneous, mutual oral genital sex
**slam** (*vb*) *Vulgar slang.* have sexual intercourse with
**slam bang** *Vulgar slang.* quickie
**sleep around** (*vb*) *Informal.* have casual sex with numerous partners
**sleep with** (*vb*) have sexual intercourse with, make love to
**statutory rape** sex with person under legal age of consent
**suck** (*vb*) pull gently with mouth, esp. on partner's genitals
**swive** (*vb*) *Archaic.* have sexual intercourse
**take** (*vb*) have sexual intercourse with
**take a lover** find or accept sex partner
**twiddle** (*vb*) *Vulgar slang.* have sexual relations
**union** sexual intercourse
**venery** gratification of sexual desire
**wank off** (*vb*) *Vulgar slang.* masturbate
**whack off** (*vb*) *Vulgar slang.* masturbate

## PERVERSIONS, FETISHES, AND TITILLATIONS

**algolagnia** pleasure and gratification derived from inflicting or suffering pain; sadism
**bestiality** sexual activity with animals
**bondage** sex involving forcible restraint or tying up of partner
**breather** person excited by telephoning someone, often unknown, and breathing heavily over phone
**bugger** (*vb*) *Vulgar slang.* sodomize
**buggery** *Vulgar slang.* anal intercourse
**child abuse** sexual molestation of child by adult

**clitoridectomy** excision of clitoris to curb female sexual desire
**coprophilia** sexual stimulation from feces
**crime against nature** sexual perversion
**date rape** rape inflicted by person with whom victim is socializing voluntarily
**defile** (*vb*) humiliate or brutalize sexually
**delicate self-cutting** usu. female perversion in which normal cosmetic tweezings and pluckings are extended to self-infliction of small cuts
**deviance** behavior that is socially disapproved of and considered unnatural or abnormal
**deviant** (*adj*) departing from the norm, considered perverse or unnatural; (*n*) one who acts thus
**dildo** *Slang.* artificial penis, used as sexual aid
**dominance** sex in which one partner humiliates, degrades, or intimidates the other for sexual stimulation
**exhibitionism** exposing oneself to others for sexual stimulation
**exploitation** degradation, victimization, or profit making from sexual activity
**fetish** sexual obsession with a specific object or usu. nonerogenous body part
**fig leaf** coy covering of genitals on nude body or statue
**flagellation** sexual stimulation by whipping or beating
**flashing** sudden public exposure of one's nudity for sexual stimulation
**frottage** practice of deriving stimulation by rubbing up against another person, as in a crowded place
**gangbang** *Vulgar slang.* sexual intercourse, usu. forcible, engaged in by several persons successively with one partner
**golden shower** urination that causes sexual stimulation
**group grope** *Slang.* orgy
**homeovestism** dressing oneself as a sexual object, esp. among women, to derive sexual excitement
**incest** sexual relations among family members
**incubus** evil male spirit who has sex with women in their sleep
**indecent exposure** public nudity
**infibulation** sewing shut of vagina
**jailbait** *Slang.* person under legal age of consent taken as sexual partner
**kinky** (*adj*) perverse, decadent, or unusual in one's sexual habits
**masochism** derivation of sexual pleasure from undergoing pain, abuse, or cruelty
**molestation** sexual assault, esp. of defenseless person or child
**mooning** *Slang.* exposing one's bare buttocks in public
**necrophilia** sexual stimulation from corpses
**nymphomania** insatiable sexual craving in women
**off-color** (*adj*) somewhat offensive, indecent
**orgy** group sexual relations
**panty raid** college prank involving males' theft of females' underwear
**paraphilia** mental disorder characterized by preference for unusual sexual practices and perversions
**pedophilia** sexual desire in an adult for children
**Peeping Tom** voyeur
**perversion** deviance or sexual maladjustment; such an act; paraphilia

**pervert** person who is sexually maladjusted, with abnormal tastes and habits

**rape** forcible sexual relations

**renifleur** person sexually aroused by odors

**sadism** derivation of sexual pleasure from inflicting pain on others

**sadomasochism** derivation of sexual pleasure from inflicting and undergoing pain or cruelty; S and M

**S and M** sadomasochism

**satyriasis** insatiable sexual craving in men

**scopophilia** sexual pleasure derived by looking at nude bodies or erotic photographs

**sex crime** immoral, illegal sex act; sexual outrage against another

**sexual assault** rape or molestation

**short eyes** *Slang.* pedophile

**sodomy** anal intercourse; intercourse with animals

**stimulator** electric dildo; vibrator

**streaking** running naked through public place as form of exhibitionism

**submission** allowing oneself to be dominated to derive sexual stimulation

**succubus** female demon who has sex with men in their sleep

**swinging** *Slang.* exchanging partners with another couple

**taboo** (*adj*) forbidden due to indecency or bad taste

**telephone sex** stimulation through verbal sexual fantasies heard over telephone

**titillate** (*vb*) excite sexually

**titillation** erotic stimulation

**transsexuality** predisposition to identify with opposite sex, often accompanied by sex change operation

**transvestism** practice of dressing in attire of opposite sex, esp. among men

**unnatural act** sexual practice considered abnormal

**urolagnia** deriving sexual stimulation from urination, esp. drinking of urine

**vibrator** electric dildo

**vice** immoral or illegal sexual practice

**voyeurism** watching others disrobe or engage in sex for purposes of sexual stimulation

**vulgarity** coarse sexual behavior and language

**water sports** *Slang.* erotic urination; urolagnia

**zoophilia** sexual excitement derived from animals

## PORNOGRAPHY AND PROSTITUTION

**bagnio** brothel

**bawd** female procurer, madam

**beefcake** *Informal.* photographs of nude or nearly nude young men in magazines, posed to display their muscles or genitals

**bordello** brothel, whorehouse

**brothel** whorehouse; bagnio

**call girl** *Slang.* often high-class prostitute who arranges appointments for sex by phone

**camp follower** prostitute on military base

**cat** *Slang.* prostitute

**cathouse** *Slang.* whorehouse

**centerfold** photo of nude woman or man featured in magazine

**cheesecake** *Informal.* photographs of nude or scantily clad women posed suggestively

**chicken** *Slang.* young prostitute, esp. homosexual

**chicken hawk** *Slang.* older male customer for young male prostitute

**chippy** *Slang.* prostitute

**concubine** woman serving as mistress or member of harem

**courtesan** prostitute for upper classes of society

**demimondaine** female prostitute

**demimonde** society of female prostitutes

**easy woman** prostitute

**escort service** service providing call girls under guise of being public dates

**fallen woman** prostitute

**floozy** *Slang.* disreputable woman, usu. prostitute

**geisha** professional hostess for men's parties, often mistakenly thought to be prostitute (Japan)

**gigolo** man supported by women in return for sex

**groupie** *Informal.* female who pursues celebrities, esp. rock musicians, for sex

**hard-core** (*adj*) graphic and explicit in pornographic content

**harem** group of wives or concubines belonging to polygamous male

**harlot** prostitute

**hetaera** highly-cultured courtesan or concubine (ancient Greece)

**hooker** *Slang.* prostitute

**hustler** *Slang.* prostitute

**john** *Slang.* person paying prostitute for sex

**knocking shop** *Chiefly Brit.* house of prostitution

**lady of the night** *Slang.* prostitute

**madam** woman managing whorehouse

**massage parlor** business usu. providing sexual services for sale in addition to nonsexual massage

**obscenity** indecent, offensive sexual behavior or content

**odalisque** female slave, harem concubine

**pander** (*vb*) solicit customers for prostitutes

**peep show** lewd entertainment featuring nude women

**pimp** procurer

**pinup girl** usu. naked or scantily clad woman posing seductively for photographs

**ponce** *Brit. slang.* pimp

**pornography** writing or pictures portraying sexual activity and intending to arouse

**procurer** man who solicits customers for prostitute; pimp

**prostitute** person who sells sexual acts to strangers

**prostitution** sexual intercourse or acts for payment

**red-light district** area of city with whorehouses and prostitutes

**seraglio** Muslim harem; whorehouse

**skin flick** *Slang.* film that features nudity and explicit sexual activity

**smut** pornography

**snuff film** *Slang.* pornographic film involving real, not staged, killing of performers

**soft-core** (*adj*) having borderline pornographic content

**solicit** (*vb*) offer sexual services for hire

**streetwalker** prostitute doing business on public streets, usu. cheaper than call girl

**stripper** person doing striptease dance

**striptease** lewd entertainment featuring woman or man removing clothes in time to music

**strumpet** prostitute

**tart** prostitute
**tramp** prostitute
**trick** *Slang.* prostitute's customer
**trollop** prostitute
**turn a trick** perform sex act with customer
**wench** former term for prostitute
**white slavery** prostitution ring using young, often rural girls kidnapped into bondage
**whore** prostitute
**whorehouse** building where prostitutes are available for hire
**X-rated** (*adj*) pornographic, used esp. of a book or film
**zenana** harem, seraglio

# STRATEGY, INTRIGUE, AND DECEPTION

Strategy and Tactics
Intrigues, Plots, and Corruption
Secrecy and Concealment
Pranks and Tricks
Falsehood, Pretense, and Exaggeration
Fraud, Treachery, and Deception

**SEE ALSO**: Chap. 11: War and Military; Chap. 20: Insults, Slurs, and Epithets; Chap. 23: Judgment and Criticism; Chap. 24: Crime

## STRATEGY AND TACTICS

**about-face** sudden reversal of position
**aggrandizement** actions intended to increase power or wealth
**angle** secret motive; (*vb*) attempt to gain advantage, often by improper or illicit means
**approach** preliminary steps taken in setting about task or problem
**arm-twisting** application of direct, personal pressure to achieve desired result
**arrangement** informal, often secret agreement or plan
**artfulness** skill and cunning in adapting means to ends
**artifice** clever, artful stratagem
**baffle** (*vb*) confuse, perplex
**bait** (*vb*) tease or torment with persistent, malicious attacks to generate desired response
**bedevil** (*vb*) utterly confuse and harass so as to take advantage of
**befuddle** (*vb*) confuse, perplex
**bewilder** (*vb*) utterly confuse or puzzle by number or complexity of considerations
**bind** situation in which one is obstructed or held in check; predicament
**blow hot and cold** change from favorable to opposing view and back again
**blueprint** detailed plan
**brain-picking** *Informal.* act of gaining information from another by careful questioning
**brinkmanship** pushing a risky situation to the limit of safety

**buttonhole** (*vb*) detain in conversation as if by physical restraint
**buy off** (*vb*) persuade to action or restraint by payment or other inducement
**cage** trap or ensnaring device
**cagey** (*adj*) shrewd, esp. cautious not be entrapped
**calculated** (*adj*) carefully thought out to accomplish an end
**call one's bluff** confront and expose another's empty threat or pretense
**canny** (*adj*) clever, calculating, or shrewd
**capitulation** act or condition of surrender and submission
**captious** (*adj*) designed to confuse or ensnare, esp. in argument
**capture** (*vb*) take or attain domination of by stratagem or guile
**carrot** something used as a lure or incentive
**cash in on** (*vb*) obtain advantage or profit from
**cat and mouse** act of teasing and playing with something before destroying it
**catch** concealed drawback, complication, or means of entrapment
**Catch-22** paradoxical problem whose solution is made impossible by circumstances inherent in it; senseless and self-contradictory policy or bureaucratic regulation
**change of heart** reversal of opinion or point of view
**chart** (*vb*) carefully plan out (a course of action)
**chink** *Informal.* small opening permitting evasion or escape
**circuitous** (*adj*) indirect or evasive in deeds or language
**clout** predominant influence within particular circle
**coax** (*vb*) persuade or influence by flattery; manipulate to desired end by prolonged effort and adroit handling
**coercion** use of force or intimidation to obtain compliance
**competition** rivalry between two or more parties to secure the favor of a third party
**complicate** (*vb*) make more difficult or complex than necessary
**compromise** (*vb*) make mutual concessions to achieve overall end or reach agreement
**concession** act of yielding on or acknowledgement of disputed point
**concoction** scheme or plan that has been devised; fabrication
**conduit** person who serves as means of transmitting or distributing information or goods
**confound** (*vb*) perplex, baffle, or throw into confusion
**confrontation** face-to-face encounter with adversary
**confuse** (*vb*) make unclear or blurred; perplex or bewilder
**contrivance** artificial arrangement or scheme
**convoluted** (*adj*) tortuously involved, complex, or confusing
**cook up** (*vb*) *Informal.* concoct, devise, or improvise
**corner** (*vb*) drive into a position without escape; entrap
**countermine** (*vb*) devise stratagem or counterplot, esp. for halting enemy attack
**coup** swift, cunning, and successful action
**craft** skill or cunning in achieving ends or deceiving others
**create** (*vb*) devise, fabricate, or make up
**cross** (*vb*) oppose, contradict, or thwart
**cunning** ingenuity, craftiness, and subtle skill, often used for deception
**curve** deceptive or misleading maneuver
**dare** (*vb*) meet boldly or defiantly; challenge another to prove himself or herself

**deploy** (*vb*) spread out, place, use, or arrange strategically

**design** specific purpose; plans and schemes formed to achieve some purpose

**device** stratagem or trick, esp. method of deception

**devise** (*vb*) contrive or plan to bring about

**diagram** detailed plan or outline in graphic form

**disown** (*vb*) refuse to acknowledge as pertaining to oneself; deny responsibility for

**distraction** something intended to divert attention away from something else

**diversion** pretense or feint that draws attention away from one's true purpose or primary action

**dodge** clever expedient or contrivance, used to evade or gain advantage

**double** duplicate; counterpart of another

**edge** advantage over an adversary

**embarrass** (*vb*) involve in public shame or difficulty; place in doubt; impede by obstacles or difficulties

**encroach** (*vb*) advance gradually or stealthily beyond proper limits; trespass into another's territory

**engineer** (*vb*) manage by skillful contrivance

**enticement** temptation that leads on or excites false hopes

**entrap** (*vb*) place in position from which there is no escape; corner

**evasion** elusion or escape by trickery or clever stratagem; avoidance of one's obligations

**expediency** adherence to what is advantageous in achieving a specific end, often without regard for what is ethical or just

**expedient** means to an end

**fabrication** concoction

**feather one's nest** take advantage of opportunities for gain, esp. at another's expense

**feint** attack aimed at one point as a distraction from the real point of attack

**fence** (*vb*) parry arguments by avoiding direct answers

**finesse** (*vb*) handle situation with skill and adroitness

**flip-flop** *Informal.* abrupt, often repeated, change of position

**foil** (*vb*) keep from succeeding; thwart

**foment** (*vb*) promote or incite, esp. to create discontent or rebellion

**forestall** (*vb*) obstruct or thwart by prior action

**fox** (*vb*) trick or outwit by cunning

**frame** (*vb*) contrive or devise, as a plan

**freeload** (*vb*) *Informal.* take advantage of another's generosity

**gag** (*vb*) restrain from speaking freely

**gambit** maneuver calculated to gain an advantage, esp. at the outset

**gamble** venture of uncertain outcome or involving risk

**game** stratagem, often tricky or illegal

**game plan** carefully thought out, long-range strategy or course of action toward a specific end

**gamesmanship** use of ethically dubious or improper but not strictly illegal means and expedients to achieve an objective

**gimmick** ingenious scheme or device; hidden feature

**guideline** general indicator for future course of action

**haggle** (*vb*) bargain or wrangle, esp. in petty or quarrelsome way

**hatch** (*vb*) invent, fabricate, or initiate

**hedge** intentionally evasive, vague statement; line of retreat left open in order to avoid commitment

**hogtie** (*vb*) make helpless so as to hamper or thwart

**hook** something that entices or attracts others

**horse trading** crafty negotiating or self-serving compromise

**house of cards** scheme or plan that is delicately balanced and vulnerable to imminent collapse

**hucksterism** use of aggressive or flashy methods to influence others, esp. to make a sale

**hunch** strong premonition; guess

**impede** (*vb*) hinder or retard in progress by means of obstacles

**incite** (*vb*) urge on to action

**infringe** (*vb*) encroach upon and violate, esp. the rights of others

**instigate** (*vb*) incite or provoke to action

**interlope** (*vb*) intrude upon another's rights or territory

**inveigle** (*vb*) obtain, persuade, or entice by flattery and artful talk

**invention** original idea, concept, or plan

**jockey** (*vb*) maneuver cleverly for position of advantage

**juggling act** process of skillfully managing several elements at once

**jury-rig** (*vb*) construct or arrange temporarily in haphazard manner

**knack** clever method or stratagem

**labyrinth** complex, sometimes devious arrangement or maze

**lead on** (*vb*) induce to follow unwise course; draw into trap

**live by one's wits** achieve one's goals through cunning, guile, and mental quickness

**loophole** means of escape, esp. through an ambiguity or omission in a document permitting an evasion or misconstruction of its intent

**low blow** unscrupulous or unfair attack

**lull** (*vb*) cause to feel a false sense of security, esp. prior to attack

**lure** (*vb*) attract or entice into danger by false promise or decoy

**Machiavellian** (*adj*) devious, cunning, or unscrupulous

**machination** scheme or crafty design with evil purpose

**maneuver** (*vb*) employ clever stratagems or schemes to achieve an end; skillfully manipulate a person or situation to one's advantage

**manipulate** (*vb*) manage skillfully, esp. control by cunning or insidious means to one's advantage

**map out** (*vb*) envision and plan beforehand

**mastermind** (*vb*) provide skillful direction and supervision for (an important activity)

**meddle** (*vb*) interfere with or involve oneself in another's activity without right or invitation

**method** system, technique, or specific plan of action

**nepotism** favoritism shown toward one's relations

**nickel-and-dime** (*vb*) defeat by small, gradual incursions

**obstruction** something that impedes another's course

**obviate** (*vb*) eliminate (a difficulty) before it arises

**on the make** seeking to improve one's position by any means necessary

**operate** (*vb*) exert a force or influence, often by following an irregular course of action

**opportunism** unscrupulous or unprincipled exploitation of opportunities

**orchestrate** (*vb*) arrange so as to achieve best result

**outflank** (*vb*) bypass (one's adversary)

**outfox** (*vb*) outwit

**outguess** (*vb*) outwit by anticipating others' actions

**outline** general or preliminary plan indicating only its essential features

**outmaneuver** (*vb*) outdo or defeat by skillful planning

**outreach** (*vb*) take advantage of through deception

**outsmart** (*vb*) outwit

**outwit** (*vb*) use superior cunning or ingenuity to get the better of; outfox; outsmart

**parlay** (*vb*) use (one's assets) to achieve greater success or wealth

**parry** (*vb*) evade or adroitly ward off

**pass the buck** shift one's responsibility to another

**pawn** person used or manipulated to further another's purposes

**perpetrate** (*vb*) execute or commit (an act, esp. a crime)

**perplex** (*vb*) hamper with complications or confusion

**pitch** *Informal.* persuasive line of reasoning

**pitfall** trap or hidden danger

**placebo** inert substance substituted for active one in experiment as trick or test control

**plain dealing** direct and honest conduct in one's transactions with others

**plan** procedure, design, or method of action with specific objective

**play both ends against the middle** maneuver opposing groups against each other to one's own advantage

**play possum** gain advantage of someone by feigning sleep or death

**ploy** maneuver or stratagem, esp. used to frustrate adversary

**ply** (*vb*) supply or offer something so as to gain advantage

**political** (*adj*) adept at influencing and manipulating allies and adversaries

**posture** viewpoint or attitude regarding specific condition

**program** detailed, long-range plan for achieving an end

**projection** visualization of a plan to its anticipated end; scenario

**prospectus** initial description and projection of a venture

**provoke** (*vb*) stir up intentionally

**pull strings** exercise covert influence or control

**put up to** (*vb*) incite or instigate

**raid** surprise attack; daring escapade, esp. against adversary; sudden incursion by legal authorities

**ransack** (*vb*) search thoroughly, esp. during a robbery

**rejigger** (*vb*) *Informal.* change or rearrange in a new or different way, esp. by using techniques not always considered ethical

**retaliate** (*vb*) exact revenge upon an adversary

**retraction** disavowal of previous view or statement

**retreat** tactical withdrawal from difficulty or danger

**retrench** (*vb*) reduce, diminish, or curtail to economize or shift emphasis of plans

**revenge** (*vb*) inflict injury in return for

**sandbag** (*vb*) *Informal.* coerce by threat or force; treat harshly; thwart

**scenario** description of possible outcome based on projected actions

**scheme** cunning, usu. secret plan of action

**scuttle** (*vb*) abandon, withdraw from, or eliminate (prior plans or resources)

**shrewd** (*adj*) astute, keen, clever

**skull session** meeting held to plan strategy

**sly fox** crafty, cunning, often devious individual

**smooth operator** one who maneuvers and manipulates with deft cunning

**snaffle** (*vb*) *Brit. informal.* acquire by devious or odd means

**song and dance** long, misleading or irrelevant statement, often used as distraction

**stratagem** clever trick or device for outwitting or gaining advantage over adversary or attaining objective

**strategy** careful, cleverly devised plan or series of maneuvers for attaining a specific goal or result

**string along** (*vb*) *Informal.* draw into a circumstance and keep in an unresolved state

**subtlety** astute perception in handling others

**system** highly organized method or procedure for attaining an end or maintaining a position

**tactic** plan, procedure, or expedient for promoting a desired end or result

**tactics** system or method for achieving success or advantage by use of one's means and resources

**tantalize** (*vb*) torment by tempting with something unattainable

**tap** (*vb*) draw on (one's resources)

**tease** (*vb*) tempt, tantalize, or taunt, esp. with persistently petty annoyances

**temptation** something that entices another to do wrong

**throw off** (*vb*) mislead or distract

**thwart** (*vb*) successfully frustrate (another's purpose)

**tinker** (*vb*) adjust or arrange in an unskilled manner

**toy with** (*vb*) amuse oneself at another's expense

**trimmer** one who alters his or her view to achieve ends

**trip up** (*vb*) detect in a fault or mistake; expose

**trump card** *Informal.* final, conclusive factor that gives advantage to one group or person

**turn** (*vb*) change or cause to change allegiance

**twist** clever and unexpected device or development

**undermine** (*vb*) subvert and weaken in degrees by insidious, often secret actions

**use** (*vb*) manipulate; take advantage of

**vacillate** (*vb*) alter one's opinion or position frequently; hesitate in one's decisions

**vantage** position of advantage or superiority

**venture** speculative undertaking

**vex** (*vb*) puzzle or confound

**volte-face** *French.* about-face; reversal of position

**vulpine** (*adj*) foxy, cunning or sly

**waiting game** delaying of an action in hopes of a better opportunity to come

**weave** (*vb*) contrive by an elaborate combination of elements

**wheel and deal** *Informal.* pursue one's goals without restraint by using personal power

**wheeler-dealer** *Informal.* shrewd, unrestrained operator

**wild card** unpredictable person or element with determining impact

**window of opportunity** most advantageous moment for doing something or implementing a plan

**work** (*vb*) exploit; make use of

**wrangle** (*vb*) obtain by petty, persistent argument

**wrinkle** innovative device, trick, strategy, or aspect

## INTRIGUES, PLOTS, AND CORRUPTION

**agent provocateur**  one who associates with and incites suspected persons to incriminating acts

**agitator**  one who stirs up public feeling, esp. inciting unlawful acts

**baksheesh**  tip or bribe

**bane**  curse; source of harm

**barratry**  purchase or sale of preferment or office in church or state

**Black Hand**  any of various secret criminal societies, orig. Italian

**blood feud**  persistent conflict between families or clans

**boiler room**  *Slang*. central location for telephone salesmen using high-pressure techniques to sell things of dubious value

**boodle**  *Slang*. bribe money

**bookmaking**  determining odds and accepting illegal bets

**brew**  (*vb*) contrive, plot, or scheme

**bribe**  something given secretly to influence opinion, esp. money; payoff

**Byzantine**  (*adj*) characterized by devious, surreptitious, intentionally convoluted operation

**cabal**  plot, esp. persons secretly united against their government

**camarilla**  *Spanish*. group of secret, scheming advisors

**camorra**  secret society with dishonorable ends, orig. 19th-century Italy

**catch up**  (*vb*) cause to be apprehended for illicit activities

**cell**  small group acting as a unit within larger organization, often in secret

**Chinese puzzle**  something complicated, obscure, and perplexing

**choplogic**  convoluted, often sophistic reasoning

**cloak-and-dagger**  (*adj*) pertaining to melodrama, intrigue, and espionage

**close call**  narrow escape

**close shave**  *Informal*. near miss; narrow escape

**coalition**  temporary alliance of distinct parties for specific purpose

**cobweb**  network of confusion, deception, or complexity

**co-conspirator**  one who joins another in a conspiracy

**cohort**  companion or colleague, esp. in some scheme

**collaborator**  one who cooperates and assists in a scheme

**collogue**  (*vb*) conspire; confer privately

**collusion**  secret agreement to cooperate for deceitful purpose

**complicity**  taking part in or having knowledge of another's illicit activity

**conclave**  private meeting or secret assembly of a group

**confederacy**  conspiracy or agreement among persons, often for unlawful purpose

**connivance**  knowledge of, consent to, or cooperation in illegal or deceitful act

**consort**  (*vb*) associate with someone, esp. in criminal or illicit activities

**conspiracy**  secret agreement or scheme among several parties to perform wrongful act

**conspirator**  one taking part in a conspiracy

**conspire**  (*vb*) form a conspiracy with one or more people

**contract**  secret arrangement for hired assassin to commit murder

**conventicle**  unauthorized assembly, esp. for unsanctioned worship

**corruption**  inducement to or engagement in improper or wrongful acts

**counterplot**  scheme devised to thwart opponent's plot

**coup d'état**  secret plot by small group to overthrow existing government in sudden, decisive action

**covin**  conspiracy to defraud or harm others

**cult**  secret organization intensely devoted to promotion of specific goals, individuals, or beliefs

**deal**  private arrangement with another for mutual advantage

**defection**  desertion, esp. betrayal of one's national allegiance

**depose**  (*vb*) remove from office

**dethrone**  (*vb*) remove from power, esp. from royal throne

**dive**  faking of knockout in boxing match that has been prearranged for benefit of wagerers

**double agent**  one pretending to serve one government while secretly serving its enemy

**éminence grise**  *French*. lit. gray eminence; confidential agent wielding unofficial power

**escape**  (*vb*) avoid evil, danger, or threat; find a way out of confinement before release date

**espionage**  intelligence gathering by agents of one government or company about plans and actions of another

**feud**  bitter, prolonged opposition

**fix**  (*vb*) illegally predetermine or prearrange outcome of something, usu. for profit

**fixer**  *Informal*. one who arranges the outcome of an event through bribery or influence

**gang**  group secretly organized to perform illegal acts; ring

**gerrymandering**  inequitable division of political territory

**grease someone's palm**  give a bribe to someone

**grudge**  prolonged and deep-seated feeling of ill will

**guerrilla**  one engaged in sabotage, terrorism, and irregular warfare

**heeler**  ward heeler

**henchman**  unscrupulous, often violent, subordinate

**in cahoots**  *Informal*. in league; having a partnership, esp. to deceive

**infiltrate**  (*vb*) enter unobtrusively and establish oneself for purpose of subversion

**inside information**  details or plans known only to select individuals and held in confidence

**insurgency**  often disorganized and sporadic revolt against a government

**insurrection**  organized, open rebellion against a government

**intrigant**  one who engages in intrigues and schemes

**intrigue**  secret scheme or plot; underhanded or deceitful stratagem, often very intricate

**jimmy**  (*vb*) force open with a crowbar, esp. for purpose of robbery

**jobbery**  unscrupulous conduct by public officials for private gain

**kickback**  reimbursement of funds based on secret collusion, usu. to defraud another

**load**  (*vb*) alter balance of (dice) to make them predictable

**maze**  intricate, confusing, often misleading sequence of actions or purposes

**mole**  double agent whose cover is established before spying begins

**morass** something that entraps or obstructs

**mutiny** organized opposition to authority, esp. on ship

**net** entrapping device or circumstance

**network** interconnected group of individuals with common goal

**on the take** *Slang.* accepting bribes or payments for favors granted

**outbreak** initiation of uprising or insurrection

**pack** (*vb*) influence makeup of (an institution or body) to secure one's purpose

**patronage** awarding of official jobs to gain political advantage

**payoff** *Informal.* bribe

**payola** *Informal.* secret payments for promotion or service, esp. to radio disc jockeys by record companies

**perquisite** bonus or fringe benefit in excess of regular salary

**plant** something or someone secretly put in place for later discovery to create a desired effect

**plot** secret plan, usu. for evil or unlawful end; intrigue

**powerbroker** person whose influence is based on control of votes or individuals

**power play** maneuver or strategy in which concentrated power is used to control a situation or rival

**propaganda** information and ideas spread deliberately to further one's goals or hinder those of one's adversary

**provocateur** one who incites or arouses others to illegal acts

**push** (*vb*) urge support for (specific position or cause); engage in sale of (illicit substance, esp. drugs)

**putsch** secret plot to overthrow a government, usu. relying on a sudden and swift uprising

**rebellion** defiance of or resistance to established authority

**revolt** organized uprising against a government

**rig** (*vb*) manipulate in advance to one's advantage

**ring** group organized, often in secret, for unethical or illicit purposes; gang

**ringleader** chief member or leader of a gang or ring

**sabotage** destruction of property or interference with the operation of a business or government so as to undermine it

**saboteur** one who engages in sabotage

**salt** (*vb*) enrich appearance of (a mine) by secretly introducing minerals to be found there

**scandal** disgraceful or discreditable action or circumstance; public slander

**sedition** incitement of public disorder or insurrection against legal authority

**simony** sale of church office or preferment

**sinecure** office providing income for little or no work

**slush fund** money used for buying influence and corrupt political favors

**smoke-filled room** back room in which small group of politicians make secret deals

**snitch** (*vb*) *Informal.* inform; (*n*) informer

**spy** (*vb*) observe others or act in secret to obtain information about one's adversaries

**stack** (*vb*) prearrange secretly for purpose of cheating, esp. a deck of cards

**subversion** systematic efforts to undermine an organization by working secretly within it

**terrorism** coercion by use of systematic, random violence and intimidation

**thick** (*adj*) in an intimate, often secret association with someone

**tokenism** practice of making only insignificant, symbolic actions to satisfy demands

**tong** secret Chinese fraternal organization engaged in gang warfare and racketeering

**treason** violation of allegiance to one's government, esp. an attempt to overthrow it or kill its leader

**Trojan Horse** something with a deceptive appearance, intended to undermine an adversary from within

**underground** secret organization plotting disruptions of civil order and concealing fugitives

**unwholesome** (*adj*) corrupt

**uprising** popular, often regional acts of opposition to authority

**usurpation** taking of another's office without right

**venal** (*adj*) open to corruption and bribery

**vendetta** prolonged, bitter feud involving revenge killings

**vice** corruption, esp. habitual moral failing

**villainy** state of depravity, corruption, and vice

**ward heeler** henchman working for local politician or party machine; heeler

**web** intricate network; snare

**whitewash** (*vb*) gloss over or excuse the wrongdoings of

**wirepulling** using one's influence with superiors to gain objective or manipulate others

## SECRECY AND CONCEALMENT

**abscond** (*vb*) depart secretly

**alias** assumed name

**alphanumeric** (*adj*) utilizing both numbers and letters, esp. designating such a code or cipher

**ambuscade** ambush

**ambush** trap in which persons lie concealed and attack by surprise

**arcanum** secret mystery unknowable without initiation

**backdoor** (*adj*) indirect, concealed, or devious

**background** less obvious or somewhat obscured information

**backstage** (*adj*) secretly or in private

**backstairs** (*adj*) secret or furtive; scandalous

**beard** decoy or disguise in social situation

**befog** (*vb*) confuse or render obscure that which is clear or true

**behind-the-scenes** (*adj*) working in secret

**between you and me** in confidence

**black market** illicit trade in regulated goods

**blind** activity or organization used to conceal another, often illicit, purpose

**blow one's cover** reveal one's true identity, esp. inadvertently

**blow the whistle on** inform on, reveal secrets of

**blur** (*vb*) obscure (the truth); make dim or unclear

**booby trap** bomb or mine concealed from the unwary in an apparently harmless object; any hidden trap set for an unsuspecting person

**bug** concealed device for eavesdropping

**burke** (*vb*) suppress quietly or indirectly; keep quiet

**bury** (*vb*) conceal by covering from view

**bushwhack** ambush, esp. by those hiding out in the woods

**buzz** (*vb*) speak softly, as if concealing secrets; gossip

**cache** hiding place, esp. for concealed provisions; something hidden or stashed away

**camisado** ambush, esp. a night attack

**camouflage** deception or concealment by disguise and artifice

**carapace** disguising, often ornamental shell

**cipher** message in code; method of altering a text to conceal its meaning

**clandestine** (*adj*) done in secret; surreptitious

**classified** (*adj*) designating information not to be revealed publicly, esp. for reasons of national security

**cloak** (*vb*) disguise; conceal completely

**cloud** (*vb*) hide or conceal; confuse, make unclear or dim

**code** system of arbitrary symbols with assigned meanings, used to communicate in secret

**code name** name assigned to conceal person's true identity, or to conceal true purpose of a plan

**code word** secret password, esp. allowing entry into code

**conceal** (*vb*) hide; prevent disclosure of the truth

**concealment** means, place, state, or act of concealing or being concealed

**confidence** secret communication

**contraband** smuggling or illegal trafficking in prohibited goods

**cover** disguise; something that conceals or obscures the truth

**cover one's tracks** hide traces of oneself to evade detection or pursuit

**covert** (*adj*) secret or veiled; undercover

**coverup** stratagem for concealing, esp. conspiracy to prevent public disclosure of illegal or unethical act

**cryptic** (*adj*) intentionally obscure; used to conceal

**cryptography** writing and analyzing of messages written in secret code or cipher

**decipher** (*vb*) decode; determine the meaning of (anything obscure or difficult to understand)

**decode** (*vb*) translate (encoded message) into intelligible form

**decoy** something used to entice unsuspecting victim into trap

**disguise** clothing and makeup used to conceal one's identity; misrepresentation of how something really is; masquerade

**dissemble** (*vb*) conceal facts or true motives by some pretense; give or put on a false appearance; dissimulate

**dissimulate** (*vb*) dissemble

**divulge** (*vb*) reveal; leak (secrets)

**doggo** (*adj*) *Informal.* lying in hiding, esp. concealed at a distance

**eavesdrop** (*vb*) listen in secret to what others are saying in private; listen in

**exposé** public revelation of damaging information

**expose** (*vb*) reveal or display to public view; deprive of protection

**fine print** something deliberately obscure, esp. limitations of agreement

**foxhole** hiding place

**fugitive** one who runs away, hides, or assumes a disguise to evade capture

**furtive** (*adj*) sly or shifty; obtained by stealth

**get away with** (*vb*) evade apprehension or punishment for (wrongdoing)

**get out** (*vb*) become publicly known, esp. leaked secrets

**grapevine** secret source of news; informal channel of gossip

**hide** (*vb*) screen from view, keep secret; conceal; obscure

**hideaway** hideout

**hideout** place where one is safe or concealed, esp. from the law; hideaway

**hole up** (*vb*) take refuge, as from pursuers; hide

**hugger-mugger** (*adj*) secret; muddled or confused

**hush-hush** (*adj*) highly secret

**hush-up** intentional suppression of information to avoid consequences

**imposture** practice of deception under an assumed name or character

**incognito** (*adj*) having one's identity concealed

**indiscretion** failure to maintain secrecy or propriety

**informant** informer

**informer** one who provides incriminating information against others or reveals group secrets; informant

**innuendo** vague hint or insinuation; indirect intimation about another's reputation

**inside information** true or essential facts about something, often not widely known

**insinuation** indirect, subtle derogation; stealthy introduction of oneself into a situation

**intelligence** information gathered covertly about enemy activities

**in the dark** in secrecy; lacking knowledge of something

**in the know** possessing inside information

**leak** (*vb*) surreptitiously reveal (secret information); (*n*) something or someone that allows secret information to become public

**lie low** (*vb*) remain in hiding or out of sight for a period of time

**listen in** (*vb*) eavesdrop

**low-profile** (*adj*) in a deliberately inconspicuous or anonymous manner; without attracting attention

**lurk** (*vb*) sneak about; conceal oneself and wait for chance to do evil or harm another

**mask** part of a disguise; something that conceals the truth

**masquerade** false or misleading appearance; disguise

**mum** (*adj*) silent; kept secret

**nose out** (*vb*) discover by investigation, esp. through prying into others' secrets

**obfuscate** (*vb*) confuse or cause to become obscure

**oblique** (*adj*) indirect, devious, or underhanded; obscure

**obscurantism** deliberate withholding of knowledge to gain advantage

**obscure** (*vb*) conceal or hide by making dim and unclear; (*adj*) dim, concealed from view, or unclear; oblique

**on the lam** escaping or hiding from authorities, esp. as a fugitive

**palimpsest** writing material erased and written over

**password** secret word or phrase, usu. used to gain entry to something

**pig in a poke** something offered with its true value concealed

**private** (*adj*) not to be generally disseminated; out of public view or knowledge

**pry** (*vb*) inquire into others' business

**pussyfoot** (*vb*) move stealthily and with great care

**recess** partly concealed area

**reconnaissance** covert information-gathering, esp. preliminary observation of enemy territory

**reveal** (*vb*) make known (that which was secret)

**rifle** (*vb*) search through with intent to steal or take something away

**rumor** statement or opinion in general circulation but of unknown source and dubious authenticity

**rumormonger** one who spreads rumors

**safe house** haven where one may hide or safely engage in secret activities

**score** (*vb*) *Slang.* acquire, esp. illicit drugs

**screen** something that shelters, protects, or conceals

**second-story man** burglar skilled at entering through upstairs window

**secrecy** state or condition of being secret or concealed; ability to keep secrets; habit of being secretive

**secret** (*adj*) hidden, obscure, or covert

**secretive** (*adj*) given to keeping things concealed

**shadow** (*vb*) observe another over time from a distance without being noticed; (*n*) one who does this

**shirk** (*vb*) evade (one's obligations)

**sing** (*vb*) *Slang.* provide information or evidence against others; act as an informant

**skulk** (*vb*) move in stealthy, furtive manner

**slyboots** one who engages in stealthy trickery and mischief

**smell a rat** detect tricky or dishonest behavior

**smoke screen** something intended to obscure or mislead

**sneak** (*vb*) move or act in a stealthy, furtive manner; (*n*) one who moves or acts in this fashion

**sneak thief** one who steals what is available without violence and by entering open buildings

**snoop** (*vb*) meddle or pry into another's affairs; (*n*) one who does this

**spill** (*vb*) divulge a secret

**spill the beans** *Informal.* indiscreetly disclose all known information

**spy** (*vb*) observe secretly with hostile intent; (*n*) one who does this

**squeal** (*vb*) turn informer

**Star Chamber** secret, arbitrary, unfair tribunal

**stash** (*vb*) keep concealed for future use; (*n*) something so concealed

**steal** (*vb*) take (another's property); come and go in secret

**stealth** furtive or secret movements or procedures

**stonewall** (*vb*) *Informal.* act in an evasive, obstructive manner; refuse to cooperate, esp. with official inquiry

**stool pigeon** *Slang.* person acting as a decoy or informer

**stowaway** someone concealed on a vehicle so as to obtain transport

**sub rosa** (*adv*) covertly or secretly

**subterfuge** deceptive artifice or stratagem, esp. to conceal or evade

**subterranean** (*adj*) operating secretly outside normal society

**suppress** (*vb*) keep hidden or withhold from the public

**surreptitious** (*adj*) stealthy and underhanded; clandestine

**surveillance** concealed observation, esp. of an adversary

**tail** (*vb*) secretly observe or follow; (*n*) one who does this

**tap** (*vb*) cut in on (electric circuit or telephone line), usu. to eavesdrop

**tattle** (*vb*) disclose someone's secrets

**tittle-tattle** gossip

**top-secret** (*adj*) designating secret information, the revelation of which would pose grave danger to authority or security

**track** (*vb*) follow traces of and observe secretly; trail

**trail** (*vb*) track

**ulterior** (*adj*) beyond what is shown or avowed; intentionally kept concealed

**undercover** (*adj*) acting in secret; engaged in spying; covert

**underhanded** (*adj*) secretive or deceptive; sly; dishonest

**under-the-counter** (*adj*) clandestine, usu. involving illicit transaction or merchandise

**under-the-table** (*adj*) secret, underhanded; as a bribe

**under wraps** *Informal.* hidden away; kept concealed

**unearth** (*vb*) discover and bring to public attention

**unmask** (*vb*) recognize and disclose the true character of (a person or action)

**up one's sleeve** kept hidden, esp. for last-minute use, as a trick

**veil** something that serves to conceal or obscure

**vizard** disguise or mask

**watch** surveillance or close observation, esp. at night

**waylay** (*vb*) ambush; attack by surprise

**weasel** *Slang.* informer or stool pigeon

**whistle-blower** one who informs on another or publicly reveals wrongdoing and corruption

**wind** (*vb*) entangle, insinuate, or introduce by stealth

**wiretap** device attached to telephone line in order to eavesdrop

**wise** (*adj*) *Slang.* possessing inside information

**wriggle out** (*vb*) escape from difficult situation by shifts or expedients

## PRANKS AND TRICKS

**antic** attention-grabbing, playful prank

**caper** frivolous prank; illegal or questionable act

**caprice** impulsive, unpredictable change or action

**chicanery** deception by cunning artifice or trickery

**culprit** one guilty of wrongdoing or mischief

**deviltry** mischief or wicked behavior

**dido** mischievous antic; prank

**elf** mischievous, often magical troublemaker

**escapade** unconventional and reckless adventure

**fourberie** trickery, esp. underhanded maneuvers

**frolic** (*vb*) act in a playful manner; (*n*) playful, carefree behavior

**hocus-pocus** nonsense, sleight of hand, or trickery used to conceal deception

**imp** small, mischievous person

**joke** (*vb*) toy playfully with someone

**knavery** mischief or rascality

**lark** carefree adventure, escapade, or frolic

**legerdemain** sleight of hand; trickery

**mischief** conduct causing minor harm or trouble; knavery; naughtiness; rascality; waggery

**monkeyshine** prank

**naughtiness** mischief or minor rascality

**playfulness** sense of fun, mischief, and caprice

**practical joke** prank intended to cause minor harm or embarrassment

**prank** mildly mischievous act or playful trick; dido; monkeyshine

**prankster** one given to pranks, practical jokes, and playful mischief

**prestidigitation** sleight of hand

**Puck** mischievous scamp in English folklore

**pull a fast one** perpetrate a trick or fraud

**rapscallion** mischievous trickster; rogue

**rascality** mischievous character or conduct; knavery

**rogue** playful mischief-maker or scamp

**roguery** playful mischief

**ruse** trick or subterfuge

**scamp** impish prankster; rogue

**shenanigan** *Informal.* mischievous trick or nonsense

**skulduggery** unscrupulous activity; devious tricks

**sleight of hand** cleverly executed, deceptive tricks or conjuring, usu. requiring manual dexterity; legerdemain; prestidigitation

**slippery** (*adj*) untrustworthy, devious, or tricky

**spoof** good-natured hoax, often a parody

**sportive** (*adj*) playful or mischievous

**sprite** elf, imp, or prankster

**trick** clever and deceptive maneuver; mischievous prank; delusive appearance

**trickery** deception by crafty ingenuity and artifice; legerdemain

**trickster** one who deceives others by using tricks

**trouble** difficulty or annoying circumstance that causes disturbance or worry

**waggery** mischief; inclination to play practical jokes

**wild-goose chase** futile pursuit, esp. one intentionally induced by someone

**wile** trickery, guile, or ensnaring stratagem

**witchcraft** use of sorcery or magical influence

## FALSEHOOD, PRETENSE, AND EXAGGERATION

**adulterate** (*vb*) alter so as to make less pure or less valuable

**affected** (*adj*) not genuine in manner

**apocrypha** writings or statements of doubtful authenticity

**apostasy** total departure from one's beliefs

**audacity** bold, arrogant disregard for conventional thought or restrictions

**backhanded** (*adj*) indirect and devious

**baloney** *Slang.* trivial lies and exaggeration

**belie** (*vb*) give false impression of

**bend** (*vb*) distort to one's own ends

**big lie** major distortion of truth, esp. for propaganda use

**bill of goods** *Informal.* something intentionally misrepresented

**bogus** (*adj*) not genuine; counterfeit

**brown-nose** (*vb*) *Slang.* ingratiate oneself; seek favor

**bull** *Slang.* vain, empty talk intended to mislead

**bum rap** *Slang.* false accusation; frame-up

**bum steer** *Informal.* intentionally bad advice or misdirection

**butter up** (*vb*) *Informal.* gain favor of through lavish flattery

**by hook or by crook** by any available means

**cajole** (*vb*) persuade by flattery or false promises

**calumny** misrepresentations that injure another's reputation

**canard** false, fabricated, or exaggerated story or report

**cant** insincere statements; private language of some group, esp. the underworld

**careerism** devotion to advancement in one's profession at the expense of integrity and one's personal life

**castle in the air** idealized condition or unrealizable dream

**charade** deceptive act; pretense

**chimerical** (*adj*) wildly improbable and imaginative

**cock-and-bull story** outrageous fabrication related as truth

**contrive** (*vb*) fabricate or invent, esp. in crafty manner

**cook the books** manipulate financial records to give a false impression

**cop out** (*vb*) *Informal.* back down on agreement or back out of unwanted responsibility

**coquetry** flirtatiousness; coy, insincere attempts to gain favor, usu. by female

**counterfeit** (*vb*) make imitation of with intent to deceive; feign; (*adj*) bogus; fake; imitation; phony

**cozen** (*vb*) win over or influence by shrewd trickery and artful persuasion

**cozy up** (*vb*) ingratiate oneself or try to become familiar for personal advantage

**crocodile tears** hypocritical sorrow; false tears

**crooked** (*adj*) insincere, indirect, or dishonest

**cry wolf** (*vb*) give false or needless alarm

**defamation** injury to another's reputation by libel or slander

**delude** (*vb*) deceive or trick, esp. mislead the mind or judgment of

**dirt** *Informal.* malicious gossip

**dirty pool** *Informal.* underhanded behavior; misconduct

**dishonesty** inclination or willingness to defraud or deceive; falsehood; mendacity; untruth

**disloyalty** absence of devotion or faithfulness; failure to fulfill one's obligations to another

**distortion** lacking, or altered from, a true sense or proportion

**doctor** (*vb*) tamper with or falsify, as a document

**double-talk** deliberately ambiguous or contradictory language with the appearance of sense, intended to deceive or confound

**duplicity** dishonesty about one's true motives or meaning

**elusion** skillful evasion of an adversary or difficulty

**embellish** (*vb*) add to or adorn for effect; exaggerate

**equivocation** use of ambiguous statements in order to mislead others or evade the truth

**evasion** means or instance of escape

**exaggeration** enlarging on truth or reality; overemphasis; baloney; fish story; hokum; tall talk

**exorbitant** (*adj*) exceeding the bounds of what is proper or customary

**extravagance** excessive, unrestrained behavior or notion

**fabricate** (*vb*) invent, esp. concoct so as to deceive

**facade** false appearance; false front

**facsimile** exact copy or forgery

**fairy tale** exaggerated, implausible story

**fake** impostor, charlatan; worthless imitation of something; (*adj*) counterfeit

**fallacy** deceptive or delusive appearance; mistaken idea

**false** (*adj*) intentionally untrue; treacherous or disloyal; counterfeit

**false front** facade

**falsehood** dishonesty, lies; extreme exaggeration; untruth

**falsify** (*vb*) misrepresent; make false by alteration; fudge

**fast and loose** (*adv*) in a cunning and deceptive manner

**fast-talk** (*vb*) influence or deceive by glib, deceitful speech

**Fata Morgana** mirage or illusion

**feign** (*vb*) give false appearance of; pretend

**fib** trivial lie; (*vb*) tell a trivial lie

**fictitious** (*adj*) false, assumed, or imaginary

**fish story** *Informal.* tall tale; exaggeration of true facts

**fishy** (adj) questionable or suspicious

**flannelmouthed** (adj) speaking in a shifty, ingratiating way

**fob off** (vb) pass off (inferior substitute) as genuine

**foist** (vb) assert surreptitiously, by stealth or deceit; pass off as genuine

**fool's paradise** condition of imaginary satisfaction

**forgery** fabricating or altering of a document for purpose of fraud; document so produced

**frame** (vb) incriminate (an innocent person) by prearranged trick

**fudge** (vb) fail to meet responsibilities or commitments; welsh; exaggerate or falsify

**funny money** Slang. counterfeit or artificially inflated currency

**gammon** Brit. informal. deceptive talk; humbug

**gilding** making things appear better than they are

**gin** trap

**glad hand** Informal. insincere, ingratiating greeting

**gloss** deceptively appealing appearance

**goldbrick** one who malingers or shirks duties

**gossip** false or misleading statements made covertly to defame another's reputation

**guise** false appearance; pretext

**half-truth** statement that mixes truth with falsehoods in order to deceive

**hokum** silly, nonsensical exaggeration and lies

**hook** something intended to attract and entrap

**huckster** one who employs showy methods or extravagant claims to promote and peddle merchandise or ideas

**humbug** something intended to deceive or mislead; someone pretending to be what he or she is not; gammon

**hype** (vb) promote by extravagant, often misleading propaganda; (n) such propaganda and exaggerated claims

**hyperbole** extreme exaggeration for effect

**hypocrisy** false appearance or pretense of virtues and beliefs one does not hold

**illusion** state of being intellectually deceived; misleading image

**illusory** (adj) deceptive; producing illusion

**imitation** (adj) counterfeit

**impersonation** disguising oneself or pretending to be another

**impostor** someone assuming false character or name for purpose of deception; fake

**indirect** (adj) tending to evade or misrepresent what really is; backhanded

**inflation** increase out of proportion to normal

**jive** false, misleading, or insincere and deceptive talk

**lay it on** (vb) exaggerate in order to impress or persuade

**levant** (vb) Brit. slang. evade one's debts

**libel** written or published defamation of another's reputation

**lie** (vb) make dishonest, misleading statement, esp. with intent to deceive; (n) dishonest statement

**line** Informal. dishonest, evasive, or misleading statement

**lip service** insincere statement of devotion or support

**lowball** (vb) state deceptively low price or estimate

**magnify** (vb) make seem greater; overstate

**make believe** (vb) pretend or feign

**malinger** (vb) pretend illness in order to avoid duties

**mealy-mouthed** (adj) inclined to use indirect or devious language

**mendacity** deception; dishonesty

**mirage** something that appears other than it is or seems to exist when it does not

**mislead** (vb) deceive; give false impression or advice to

**misrepresent** (vb) provide false information about or mistaken impression of

**overdo** (vb) exaggerate in the extreme

**overreach** (vb) take advantage of by cunning or unscrupulous methods

**overstate** (vb) exaggerate

**pass off** (vb) offer or sell with intent to deceive; misrepresent

**perjury** dishonest statement under oath in court of law

**phantom** (adj) fictitious or illusory

**phony** (adj) false; counterfeit; (n) insincere or deceitful person

**pipe dream** unrealizable aspiration

**piracy** unauthorized appropriation or use of another's property, esp. in copyright infringement

**plagiarize** (vb) represent (another's work) as one's own

**playact** (vb) pretend to be other than one is

**pose** attitude or appearance assumed for effect

**pretend** (vb) give false appearance; feign; make believe

**pretender** one who claims position of authority that is not his or her right

**pretense** false, professed, or make-believe act or intent; charade

**pretext** assumed appearance or purpose used to conceal true intent

**prevaricate** (vb) equivocate; veer from truth

**prodigal** (adj) reckless, extravagant, or excessive

**pseudo** (adj) false or spurious

**pull someone's leg** trick or deceive another playfully

**put on** (vb) mislead deliberately; feign

**put something over on** deceive

**quasi** (adj) resembling or seeming

**questionable** (adj) doubtful or suspicious; likely to be false

**razzmatazz** Informal. misleading or ambiguous speech or actions; double-talk

**recant** (vb) go back on one's beliefs or renounce former position

**recreant** one who deserts friends or betrays beliefs

**red herring** distraction or false clue

**ringer** impostor, esp. one entering competition under false pretense

**roorback** defamatory, published political lies

**scalp** (vb) Informal. buy and resell at greatly increased price

**seduction** something that attracts irresistibly; temptation or enticement into unwise act

**shadowy** (adj) unreliable, doubtful, or illicit

**shady deal** arrangement of dubious merit and authenticity

**shifty** (adj) given to deception, evasion, and fraud

**shuck and jive** Slang. insincere, deceptive talk that gives false impression

**shuffle** (vb) act in shifty, evasive manner

**simulation** act or object that is counterfeit or feigned

**slander** false oral statements that defame another's reputation

**snare** something deceptively appealing; trap

**so-called** (adj) misrepresented as such

**soi-disant** (adj) French. so-called

**sophistry** false though apparently valid argument used to deceive

**spoof** good-natured hoax, esp. parody

**spurious** (adj) superficially similar but innately false

**story** fabricated excuse, explanation, or evasion

**stretch** (*vb*) amplify or exaggerate beyond the norm for one's own advantage

**suborn** (*vb*) induce another to lie or commit perjury

**subreption** intentional misrepresentation or concealment of truth and the resulting inferences

**sweet talk** *Informal.* insincere flattery

**synthetic** (*adj*) contrived as a substitute for the real thing

**tale** intentionally untrue or exaggerated report

**tall tale** extremely fanciful or highly exaggerated story; yarn

**tall talk** exaggeration

**tampering** altering of something so as to falsify it; engaging in secret improprieties

**tergiversation** equivocation or evasion

**tortuous** (*adj*) characterized by indirect tactics; tricky, crooked, or devious

**traduce** (*vb*) betray with falsehoods and thus defame

**trap** (*vb*) entrap, snare; (*n*) something devised to trick or capture unsuspecting persons

**trifle** (*vb*) deal lightly or in a mocking manner

**trump up** (*vb*) concoct or invent for purpose of deception

**two-time** (*vb*) *Informal.* jilt or betray, esp. one's lover

**untruth** lie or falsehood

**veneer** superficial, deceptively pleasing appearance

**warp** (*vb*) falsify or distort

**wheedle** (*vb*) influence or persuade by smooth or artful flattery

**whiffle** (*vb*) vacillate or change position easily

**whole cloth** total and utter fabrication

**whopper** extravagant lie or deception

**window dressing** misrepresentation intended to give favorable impression of something

**yarn** highly embellished story; tall tale

# FRAUD, TREACHERY, AND DECEPTION

**abuse** corrupt or improper practice or custom

**alibi** excuse used to avert blame

**arrogate** (*vb*) claim or appropriate for oneself without right

**backslide** (*vb*) fail to live up to one's beliefs or moral values

**bamboozle** (*vb*) dupe or deceive by trickery or flattery; hoodwink

**banditry** activities and practices of bandits, such as plunder and robbery

**barefaced** (*adj*) unscrupulous; not concealing one's vices

**baseness** lack of noble qualities of mind or spirit; villainy

**beat** (*vb*) *Slang.* swindle; cheat

**befool** (*vb*) delude or deceive

**beguile** (*vb*) influence by deception; cheat out of by cunning

**betrayal** disloyalty in time of need, esp. treacherous exposure to an enemy

**bewitch** (*vb*) influence or charm as if by witchcraft

**bilk** (*vb*) cheat by evading payment due

**blackmail** extortion through intimidation or by threat of public revelation or exposure

**blind** subterfuge intended to mislead; agent acting as decoy or distraction for another person

**bluff** (*vb*) deceive or frighten by pretense of strength

**bounce** (*vb*) draw (check) on insufficient funds

**bucket shop** *Slang.* gambling house or brokerage that does not execute orders, profiting at customer's expense by fluctuations in price

**bunko** *Informal.* swindle or scheme that takes advantage of another's ignorance

**burn** (*vb*) *Slang.* deceive or cheat in transaction, esp. by overpricing or failing to deliver goods

**capper** *Slang.* shill

**cardsharp** one who habitually and successfully cheats at cards

**catchy** (*adj*) clever and beguiling, often tricky

**cat's-paw** person used to serve the purposes of another; dupe; tool

**caught napping** duped by trickery, usu. due to lack of vigilance

**charlatan** person making extravagant pretense of knowledge or skill; fraud; mountebank; quack

**cheat** (*vb*) practice fraud and trickery; influence or deprive of something expected by using deceit

**chiaus** *Slang.* swindler

**chisel** (*vb*) get by cunning or trickery; cheat, esp. out of funds

**chump** *Informal.* dupe; easy mark

**clip** (*vb*) *Slang.* profit unfairly from, esp. by overcharging

**clip joint** *Slang.* place of business that overcharges customers

**con** *Informal.* confidence game; swindle

**con artist** *Informal.* one who cheats others in confidence games; con man; swindler

**confidence game** appropriation of funds by making false promises of quick profits, usu. from unethical investment; con; sting; swindle

**confiscation** appropriation of another's property

**con man** *Slang.* con artist

**cop** (*vb*) *Informal.* purchase or obtain (illicit goods); steal or swipe

**crib** (*vb*) *Informal.* plagiarize, steal, or cheat on examination by use of concealed notes

**cully** *Archaic.* (*vb*) cheat or deceive; (*n*) one so deceived; dupe

**deceit** act of deception; trick; state of falseness

**deceive** (*vb*) mislead by false appearance or statement that is passed off as true, usu. to gain advantage or as a trick; befool

**deception** act of deceiving; that which deceives

**decoy** someone or something used to lure an unsuspecting victim into danger or distract attention from some other action

**defraud** (*vb*) cheat out of something by deception

**desertion** abandonment of proper post or responsibilities

**devious** (*adj*) scheming, cunning, or deceptive

**diddle** (*vb*) *Informal.* cheat, swindle, or fool; toy with

**dirty trick** *Informal.* fraudulent or unscrupulous secret act

**discredit** (*vb*) injure the reputation of; cast aspersions on the authenticity of

**do a job on** cheat, swindle, or take advantage of

**do a number on** confound thoroughly so as to swindle

**dodge** clever expedient or contrivance used to evade, trick, or deceive

**double-cross** (*vb*) *Informal.* betray by treachery; cheat by acting contrary to expectations

**double-dealing** (*adj*) marked by duplicity; deceitful

**dupe** one easily deceived or fooled; object of a swindle;

cat's-paw; chump; easy mark; fool; gull; mark; patsy; pigeon; pushover; sap; sucker; tool

**easy mark** one highly susceptible to fraud or swindle; dupe

**embezzle** (vb) steal or appropriate to one's own use, as funds entrusted to one's care; peculate

**extort** (vb) obtain from another by intimidation, misused power, or ingenuity

**fair-weather** (adj) loyal only during good times

**faithless** (adj) disloyal; deceitful

**fall guy** Slang. one who takes the blame for another's misconduct

**filch** (vb) steal casually or furtively

**finagle** (vb) get by using trickery or deception; swindle, cheat, or trick

**fink** (vb) Slang. betray or inform on someone; (n) one who does this; ratfink

**fink out** (vb) Slang. cop out or renege

**fleece** (vb) defraud or extort money from; gaff; overcharge

**flimflam** Informal. deception or fraud, esp. one involving misleading talk

**fool** (vb) deceive or trick; (n) dupe

**foul play** any treacherous, deceitful, our unfair dealing

**fraud** deception and trickery, esp. a breach of confidence to gain an advantage, or an inducement to part with something of value; impostor; one who practices trickery and deception

**fraudulence** deceit by falseness and trickery

**front** one who serves as a cover for illegal activity, or induces victims to engage in scheme perpetrated by another

**fuck over** (vb) Vulgar slang. misuse; take advantage of deceitfully

**gaff** (vb) Slang. cheat or fleece

**go back on** (vb) betray; renege on

**gouge** (vb) extort from or overcharge

**graft** use of dishonest or illegal means for gain or profit

**greenhorn** naive person who may easily be swindled or tricked

**grift** methods used to obtain illicit profits, esp. from confidence game

**guile** craft, duplicity, or cunning

**gull** dupe; (vb) take advantage of or deceive

**gyp** cheat or swindle by some sharp practice

**highway robbery** Informal. exorbitant profit or gain derived from business transaction

**hoax** act intended to deceive or trick, esp. into accepting as real that which is not; mischievous deception

**hocus** (vb) perpetrate a hoax on someone

**hoodwink** (vb) deceive by false appearance

**hornswoggle** (vb) Slang. swindle, cheat, or perpetrate a hoax on

**ill-gotten** (adj) acquired by improper or evil means

**illicit** (adj) prohibited by law or custom; not permitted or authorized

**Indian giver** Informal (offensive). person who gives something away and then takes it back

**infidelity** lack of faith; betrayal, esp. of one's spouse

**insidious** (adj) designed to draw another into a trap or fraud

**jerk around** (vb) Slang. mislead; take advantage of

**jilt** (vb) abruptly abandon, esp. one's lover

**Judas** one who betrays another while acting as a friend

**juggle** (vb) manipulate to achieve desired end or give false appearance

**kangaroo court** court that disregards legal principles and justice, esp. so as to make fair trial impossible

**lame** Slang. one not in the know; unsophisticated person

**launder** (vb) Informal. disguise source of (illicit funds) so that they appear legitimate

**lift** (vb) Informal. steal; plagiarize

**loan shark** Informal. person charging excessive interest on loans

**mark** Slang. target or victim of swindle; dupe; easy mark

**milk** (vb) exploit illicitly or excessively for advantage; drain someone or something of resources

**monte** gambling card game, usu. a swindle

**mooch** (vb) Slang. scrounge, steal, or sponge

**mountebank** unscrupulous trickster; charlatan

**nemesis** formidable, persistent, and vengeful adversary who cannot be defeated

**nick** Brit. slang. steal or cheat

**nobble** Brit. slang. swindle, cheat, or steal

**operator** Informal. person who accomplishes his or her purposes by devious means, esp. by evading difficulties or regulations

**palm off** (vb) dispose of (something valueless) by deception

**palter** (vb) haggle, equivocate, or act deceitfully

**parlous** (adj) dangerously shrewd and cunning

**patsy** Slang. dupe

**pawky** (adj) Chiefly Brit. cunning or crafty

**peculate** (vb) embezzle

**perfidy** treachery, esp. disloyalty or betrayal

**pervert** (vb) turn or lead astray; put to improper use; corrupt

**pettifogger** shyster, esp. disreputable lawyer

**pigeon** Slang. dupe

**pilfer** (vb) steal

**pinch** (vb) Slang. steal

**plunder** (vb) loot; take by theft or fraud

**Ponzi** investment swindle in which early investors receive return from money of later ones, who never see return

**predatory** (adj) preying upon or living off others

**prey** (vb) attack for booty; exert harmful influence upon; (n) victim unable to resist attacks

**profiteering** making exorbitant profit, esp. on scarce or rationed articles

**pull a fast one** enact a trick or fraud

**pull the wool over someone's eyes** prevent another from seeing true circumstances; hoodwink

**purloin** (vb) take dishonestly, by breach of trust

**pushover** Informal. dupe; easy mark

**pyramid** (vb) speculate in securities by using paper profits as margin for additional trading

**quack** fraudulent or ignorant pretender to medical skills; charlatan

**quisling** traitor who betrays his or her country to an invading enemy

**racket** organized illegal scheme or activity; swindle

**racketeer** one engaged in organized illegal activities, esp. extortion through intimidation

**rat** (vb) Slang. inform on or betray one's associates

**ratfink** Slang. informer; fink

**renege** (vb) deny or renounce; fail to fulfill one's obligations

**rip off** (vb) Slang. steal, cheat, or defraud

**robber baron** businessman profiting by exploitation of unscrupulous but legal activity

**rook** (vb) cheat or defraud by swindle

**runner** smuggler or distributor of illicit goods

**sap** *Slang*. dupe

**scam** fraudulent operation or swindle

**scoundrel** deceitful, unscrupulous person

**sell** (*vb*) gain acceptance for; betray; cheat

**sell out** (*vb*) betray

**setup** arrangement that draws unsuspecting party into swindle

**shaft** (*vb*) *Informal*. treat poorly by taking advantage of or betraying

**shake down** (*vb*) extort money from

**sham** deceptive trick or hoax; spurious imitation or counterfeit object; impostor

**shark** shrewd individual preying upon others through extortion and trickery

**shell game** fraud involving sleight-of-hand substitution of valueless item for one of value; thimblerig, using walnut shells instead of balls

**shill** *Slang*. decoy for pitchman, gambler, or con game; capper

**shlemiel** *Yiddish slang*. awkward, unlucky person, often taken advantage of by swindler or con artist

**shortchange** (*vb*) cheat by returning less than correct change

**short con** *Slang*. simple confidence game perpetrated by single operator, involving small amount of money

**shyster** *Informal*. one unscrupulous in professional duties, esp. a lawyer

**sitting duck** helpless or easy target or victim of swindle

**skim** (*vb*) *Slang*. fraudulently conceal or underestimate (profits, as from gambling), esp. to avoid paying taxes

**skin game** swindle or con game

**slicker** *Informal*. cunning swindler

**snooker** (*vb*) *Slang*. deceive, cheat, or dupe

**sponge** (*vb*) acquire without paying for or by taking advantage of another's generosity

**squeeze** (*vb*) pressure so as to obtain or extort something

**steal** (*vb*) vengefully take (something that belongs to another), esp. in secret or by force; pilfer; pinch; swipe; walk off with

**sting** *Slang*. apparent swindle used by authorities in investigation of fraud or racket; confidence game

**string along** (*vb*) *Informal*. perpetrate hoax upon; fool by misleading

**sucker** dupe

**Svengali** one using physical force and mind control to dominate another

**swindle** (*vb*) obtain (another's assets or money) by fraud or deceit; (*n*) action or scheme intended to defraud or deceive; con; confidence game; racket; skin game

**swipe** (*vb*) *Informal*. steal

**take** (*vb*) *Informal*. cheat, swindle, or victimize

**take advantage of** exploit; get the better of; impose swindle on

**thimblerig** sleight-of-hand swindle involving small ball that must be found under one of three cups, similar to three-card monte

**three-card monte** sleight-of-hand swindle in which mark must identify one of three cards that have been moved around facedown by dealer

**tool** one used by another; cat's-paw; dupe

**traitor** one who betrays his or her country or another person or reneges on responsibilities

**treachery** failure of faith or trust; act of perfidy or treason

**turncoat** one who betrays a cause or supports an enemy

**two-faced** (*adj*) double-dealing; inconstant in allegiance; hypocritical

**unconscionable** (*adj*) unscrupulous; done without conscience

**unscrupulous** (*adj*) lacking principles; willing to do anything to achieve one's goal

**victimize** (*vb*) defraud, cheat, or take advantage of

**walk off with** (*vb*) steal

**wangle** (*vb*) obtain by underhanded methods; manipulate for fraudulent ends

**water** (*vb*) artificially increase value of without necessary assets as basis

**weasel** (*vb*) evade one's obligations; manipulate situation to one's advantage; (*n*) *Slang*. informer

**welsh** (*vb*) *Informal*. renege on one's obligation or debt, esp. a bet

**wildcat** (*adj*) financially reckless and conducted in violation of normal business practices

**wrong** (*vb*) do harm to; defraud or discredit

# CHAPTER 23

# Cognition

# TIME PERCEPTION

Fixed Times
Periods of Time
Relative Time

**SEE ALSO**: Chap. 3: Weather and Natural Phenomena; Chap. 4: Physics; Chap. 18: Qualifiers and Connectives

## FIXED TIMES

**anniversary** commemoration of each full year's passage since original event

**annual** (*adj*) yearly, once a year

**appointment** meeting at designated time

**autumnal equinox** September 22 in Northern Hemisphere

**bedtime** hour of going to sleep for night

**biannual** (*adj*) occurring twice a year; occuring every two years; semiannual

**bicentennial** (*adj*) occurring every 200 years; (n) 200th anniversary

**biennial** (*adj*) occurring every two years; (n) two-year anniversary; event that occurs once in two years

**bimensal** (*adj*) bimonthly

**bimonthly** (*adj*) occurring every two months; twice a month; bimensal; semimonthly

**birthday** annual commemoration of day of one's birth

**bissextile day** February 29, occurring every fourth year

**biweekly** (*adj*) occurring every two weeks; twice a week; semiweekly

**calends** first day of a month (ancient Rome)

**canonical hour** any of certain times of the day set apart for prayer and devotion

**centenary** observation of hundred-year anniversary

**centennial** hundredth anniversary; (adj) occurring every hundred years

**Christmastide** holiday season from Christmas until after New Year's Day; period from Christmas Eve to Epiphany, esp. in Britain

**Christmastime** holiday season in December commemorating Christ's birth

**cockcrow** dawn

**cockshut** *Chiefly Brit.* dusk

**curfew** time designated by authority to retire or stay indoors for the night

**daily** (*adj*) occurring each day

**dawn** sunrise

**deadline** final moment at which something must be done

**decennial** (*adj*) occurring every ten years

**dinnertime** time for main meal of day, in afternoon or evening

**diurnal** (*adj*) daily

**dog days** hottest part of summer

**duodecennial** (*adj*) occurring every twelve years

**dusk** twilight, darkening hour during and after sunset

**eleventh hour** last possible moment for some action

**equinoctial** (*adj*) pertaining to equinoxes

**equinox** moment in year when center of sun is in line with equator and day and night are of equal length: about March 21 and September 22

**estival** (*adj*) pertaining to summer

**eve** evening

**evening** period of time from sunset to end of twilight; eve; eventide

**eventide** evening

**first light** sunrise

**gloaming** twilight, dusk

**halcyon days** peaceful, happy, or prosperous times

**harvest moon** full moon nearest autumnal equinox

**hebdomadal** (*adj*) weekly, every seven days

**heyday** time of greatest flourishing

**high noon** exactly twelve o'clock noon

**high tea** *Chiefly Brit.* time of late afternoon snack or light supper, usu. five o'clock

**horary** (*adj*) pertaining to hours; hourly

**hourly** (*adj*) occurring every hour

**ides** fifteenth or thirteenth day of each month in ancient Roman calendar

**inception** beginning

**in the nick of time** just at the last minute

**last-ditch** (*adj*) done in final moment out of desperation

**last-minute** (*adj*) done when time is running out

**latter Lammas** day that will never come

**lunchtime** hour for eating light midday meal

**mañana** *Spanish.* tomorrow

**matinal** (*adj*) pertaining to morning

**matutinal** (*adj*) early, pertaining to morning

**midday** noon, middle of day, when a.m. turns to p.m.

**midnight** middle of night; twelve o'clock at night, when p.m. turns to a.m.

**midweek** middle day or time of week, esp. Wednesday

**millennial** thousandth anniversary; (adj) occurring every thousand years

**monthly** (*adj*) occurring every month

**morn** morning, dawn

**morrow** tomorrow

**nocturnal** (*adj*) pertaining to night; nightly

**nonce** present occasion

**noon** twelve o'clock midday, when a.m. turns to p.m.; noontime

**noontime** noon

**now** (*adv*) at the present moment

**once** (*adv*) one time only; at one time in past

**on time** (*adj*) punctual, at the specified time

**perennial** occurring year after year

**post time** time of day's first horse race at track

**premiere** first occurrence of event

**present-day** (*adj*) contemporary, modern

**punctual** (*adj*) prompt, on time

**quadrennial** (*adj*) occurring every four years; lasting four years

**quadricentennial** 400th anniversary; (adj) occurring every 400 years

**quarterly** (*adj*) occurring four times per year

**quincentennial** 500th anniversary; (adj) occurring every 500 years

**quinquennial** (*adj*) occurring every five years

**quotidian** (*adj*) daily, everyday

**salad days** time of youth, exuberance, or innocence

**semiannual** (*adj*) occurring every half year or twice a year; semiyearly

**semicentennial** (*adj*) occurring every fifty years

**semidiurnal** (*adj*) occurring every half day or twice a day

**semimonthly** (*adj*) occurring every half month or twice a month

**semiweekly** (*adj*) occurring every half week or twice a week

**semiyearly** (*adj*) semiannual

**septennial** (*adj*) occurring every seven years

**small hours** extremely late at night; hours after midnight and before dawn

**solstice** time in year when sun is farthest north or south of celestial equator, in Northern Hemisphere about June 21 or December 21, respectively; longest or shortest period of sunshine during year

**stitch in time** timely or punctual act or repair

**summer solstice** June 21 in Northern Hemisphere

**sundown** sunset

**sunrise** time in morning when sun appears over eastern horizon; dawn; first light; sun up

**sunset** hour in early evening when sun disappears over western horizon; sundown

**sun up** *Informal.* sunrise

**suppertime** time designated for evening meal

**teatime** time for light late afternoon repast of tea and cakes, generally four o'clock

**time** dimension of reality characterized by flow of events and phenomena through irreversible procession of moments; systematized demarcation of the passage of such moments into units of seconds, minutes, hours, days, and years; period or point in time; fourth dimension in space-time continuum

**today** this present day

**tomorrow** day after today; morrow

**tonight** present or coming night

**tricennial** (*adj*) occurring every thirty years

**tricentennial** 300th anniversary; (*adj*) occurring every 300 years

**triennial** (*adj*) occurring every three years; continuing or persisting for three years

**trimonthly** (*adj*) occurring every three months

**triweekly** (*adj*) occurring every three weeks; occurring three times a week

**twilight** period of dimming light just after sunset

**under the wire** at last possible moment

**vernal equinox** March 21 in Northern Hemisphere

**vespers** prayer said at evening; sixth canonical hour

**vicennial** twentieth anniversary; (*adj*) occurring every twenty years

**vintage** one season's harvest of wine grapes

**vintage year** year in which something outstanding is made or done, esp. wine harvest

**weekly** (*adj*) occurring once a week

**winter solstice** December 21 in Northern Hemisphere

**yearly** (*adj*) occurring once a year

**yesterday** day before today

**zero hour** moment for commencement of plan; beginning of ordeal or crisis

# PERIODS OF TIME

**aeon** eon

**afternoon** period from noon to evening

**age** period of time corresponding to life of object or individual; period in Earth's history

**all-day** (*adj*) lasting from morning to evening

**all-night** (*adj*) lasting from evening to morning

**always** (*adv*) forever; all the time

**annus mirabilis** *Latin.* notable or remarkable year

**April** fourth month of year, containing 30 days, following March, preceding May

**around-the-clock** (*adj*) at all times of day and night

**August** eighth month of year, containing 31 days, following July, preceding September

**autumn** season of shortening days ending in winter solstice, extending from September 22 to December 20; fall

**awhile** (*adv*) for a short time

**bicentenary** *Chiefly Brit.* bicentennial

**bicentennial** (*adj*) lasting 200 years

**bimillenary** (*adj*) lasting 2000 years

**bimillennium** 2000 years

**blue moon** long period of time

**calendar year** 365 days, beginning January 1 and ending December 31; 366 days in leap years

**centenary** 100 years; one century

**century** 100 years

**chiliad** 1000 years

**circadian** (*adj*) occurring in twenty-four-hour cycles

**coffee break** period of short rest in morning or afternoon, usu. at place of work

**coon's age** *Informal.* long time

**cycle** regular, recurring interval of time; set period of days or years

**day** period of twenty-four hours; sunrise to sunset

**daytime** time in which there is sunlight

**decade** period of ten years

**December** twelfth and last month of year, containing 31 days, following November, preceding January, including first day of winter

**donkey's years** *Informal.* long period of time

**duration** extent of time during which something takes place

**elapse** (*vb*) pass away, said of period of time

**elapsed time** time measured from beginning to end of event

**eon** extremely long period of time; aeon

**epoch** significant time period marked by historical events; geologic time division smaller than period

**era** significant period of time marked by historical events; major geologic time division including periods

**eternal** (*adj*) lasting forever

**eternity** forever, time without end; immeasurable time

**everlasting** (*adj*) endless, unceasing, eternal

**fall** autumn

**February** second month of year, containing 28 days or 29 days every fourth year, following January, preceding March

**fiscal year** twelve-month-period, used in business and accounting, usu. beginning July 1 or October 1

**forever** (*adv*) always, eternally, in perpetuity

**for good** permanently

**for keeps** forever

**fortnight** period of two weeks

**Friday** sixth day of week, following Thursday, preceding Saturday; last day of regular workweek in United States

**future** time yet to come

**hiatus** break or gap in continuity

**historical year** year beginning with January 1

**hitch** *Slang.* period of time served in military

**hour** one twenty-fourth of one day; sixty minutes

**immemorial** (*adj*) extending beyond memory

**indiction** repeating cycle of fifteen years, used in Roman Empire

**infinity** boundless, limitless time

**instant** moment, time period of extremely short duration

**interim** interval of time

**interlude** short time intervening between events or dramatic acts

**intermittent** (*adj*) periodic, interrupted in time, recurrent

**interregnum** period of vacancy of throne or royal office; period of time when there is lapse in normal government functions

**interval** pause, break, recess

**January** first month of year, containing 31 days, following December, preceding February

**jiffy** *Informal.* brief amount of time

**July** seventh month of year, containing 31 days, following June, preceding August

**June** sixth month of year, containing 30 days, following May, preceding July, including first day of summer

**lasting** (*adj*) enduring, unending

**lead time** time period allotted between start-up time of task and emergence of results

**leap year** 366-day year, occurring every fourth year, in which February has 29 days

**lifelong** (*adj*) for the duration of one's life

**life span** period of life from birth to death

**lifetime** period of time that life of someone or something lasts

**long-drawn-out** (*adj*) lasting or seeming to last a very long time

**longevity** length of a life span

**long haul** extended period of time

**long-run** (*adj*) extended over a long period of time

**longstanding** (*adj*) of great duration or age

**long-term** (*adj*) of extensive duration

**lustrum** period of five years

**March** third month of year, containing 31 days, following February, preceding April, including first day of spring

**May** fifth month of year, containing 31 days, following April, preceding June

**Metonic cycle** period of nearly 19 years, after which phases of moon return to some calendar date, used in Gregorian calendar

**microsecond** one millionth of a second

**millenary** (*adj*) lasting 1000 years

**millennium** 1000 years

**millisecond** one thousandth of a second

**minute** sixty seconds; one sixtieth of an hour

**moment** brief span of time; second, instant

**Monday** second day of week, following Sunday, preceding Tuesday; first day of regular workweek in United States

**month** period of approximately thirty days, based on time required for one complete revolution of the moon; one of twelve divisions of year

**moratorium** period of delay

**morning** period of day from dawn to midday

**nanosecond** one billionth of a second

**Neolithic** (*adj*) designating period of cultural development from about 10,000 to 3000 B.C.

**night and day** (*adj*) all the time, at all hours

**nine-to-five** (*adj*) *Informal.* pertaining to standard working day in forty-hour week

**November** eleventh month of year, containing 30 days, following October, preceding December

**October** tenth month of year, containing 31 days, following September, preceding November

**olympiad** period of four years

**overnight** period of time from night until next morning

**past** period of time already gone by

**period** duration or division of time; geologic division within era including epochs

**perpetual** (*adj*) eternal, everlasting

**perpetual day** period at North and South poles when sun does not set

**perpetual night** period at North and South poles when sun does not rise

**perpetuity** endless time; state of lasting forever

**picosecond** one trillionth of a second

**playtime** leisure time, free time

**posterity** the future; subsequent generations

**prehistoric** (*adj*) pertaining to period before written history

**present** period of time occurring now

**protracted** (*adj*) extended over time, drawn out

**quarter-hour** one quarter of an hour; fifteen minutes

**round-the-clock** (*adj*) at all hours of the day or night

**Saturday** seventh and last day of week, following Friday, preceding Sunday; first day of weekend; Jewish Sabbath

**season** period of time characterized by particular weather, events, and holidays; one of four major divisions of year

**second** one sixtieth of a minute; fundamental unit of time equal to 9,192,631,770 emission cycles of cesium-133

**sempiternal** (*adj*) eternal, perpetual

**September** ninth month of year, containing 30 days, following August, preceding October, including first day of autumn

**short-run** (*adj*) occurring over a short span of time

**sidereal day** time taken for one complete rotation of Earth

**since** (*adv*) from a time in the past until the present

**sojourn** temporary period spent in one place

**split second** very short time; fraction of a second

**spring** season of lengthening days ending in summer solstice, extending from March 21 to June 20

**stint** limited period of time, esp. for accomplishment of some task

**stretch** duration of time; *Slang.* term of incarceration

**summer** season of shortening days ending in autumnal equinox, extending from June 21 to September 21

**Sunday** first day of week, following Saturday, preceding Monday; last day of weekend; Christian Sabbath

**take five** *Informal.* stop working for a few minutes' rest

**term** fixed period of time in which an activity, office, tenure, or agreement is valid and ongoing

**Thursday** fifth day of week, following Wednesday, preceding Friday

**time frame** period of time designated for completion of something; timespan

**time immemorial** time before recorded history or beyond memory; time out of mind

**time-lag** interval between two related events or phenomena

**time-lapse** (*adj*) designating photography in which very slow process is made to appear rapid by taking multiple exposures over time

**time limit**  maximum duration allowed for something

**time-out**  cessation of activity for specified duration, esp. in athletic contest

**time out of mind**  time immemorial

**timespan**  period of time; time frame

**trice**  very brief time; moment

**Tuesday**  third day of week, following Monday, preceding Wednesday

**twelvemonth**  *Chiefly Brit.* one year

**twinkling**  very short time

**Wednesday**  fourth day of week, following Tuesday, preceding Thursday; midweek

**week**  period of seven days

**weekday**  working day; any day of week except Saturday or Sunday

**weekend**  end of week; Saturday and Sunday; nonwork days

**while**  period or interval of time; (conj) during or throughout the time that

**window**  period of time considered highly favorable for beginning or accomplishing something

**wink**  brief period of time

**winter**  season of lengthening days ending in vernal equinox, extending from December 21 to March 20

**workday**  weekday; Monday through Friday and sometimes Saturday

**year**  period of 365 days, during which Earth makes one full revolution around sun; twelve months

## RELATIVE TIME

**after** (*prep*) later in time than; (*adv*) later in time

**aftertime**  future time

**afterward** (*adv*) subsequently

**again** (*adv*) once more

**ago** (*adj*) time past

**ahead of time** (*adj*) early

**already** (*adv*) before a specific time

**anachronism**  misplacement or incongruity in time

**ancient** (*adj*) of very great age

**anew** (*adv*) again, repeated

**anon** (*adv*) at once; soon

**ante-**  prefix meaning before or prior to

**antiquated** (*adj*) of great age, obsolete

**antique** (*adj*) very old, belonging to bygone age

**anymore** (*adv*) any longer; nowadays

**anytime** (*adv*) without restriction or regard to time

**aperiodic** (*adj*) not periodic, with no regular recurrence

**après** (*prep*) *French.* after

**archaic** (*adj*) old-fashioned, of an earlier time

**asynchronous** (*adj*) not concurrent

**atemporal** (*adj*) outside of time

**at once** (*adv*) immediately; at the same time

**at the drop of a hat**  promptly, as soon as the slightest opportunity is given

**at times** (*adv*) occasionally

**auld lang syne**  *Scottish.* good old days

**before** (*prep*) prior to, at a previous time

**belated** (*adj*) delayed, too late

**betimes** (*adv*) in a short or good time; occasionally; early

**betweentimes** (*adv*) during intervals

**borrowed time**  time that is overextended or overdue

**brief** (*adj*) of very short duration

**by-and-by**  future

**by turns** (*adj*) alternately

**chronic** (*adj*) constant, continuing over time

**chronological** (*adj*) arranged in order of time

**circa** (*prep*) about

**coeval** (*adj*) of the same age

**conclusion**  ending

**concurrent** (*adj*) at the same time

**constant** (*adj*) perpetual, occurring continually

**contemporaneous** (*adj*) existing at the same time

**contemporary** (*adj*) at the same time; belonging to the same or current time period

**continual** (*adj*) chronic, constant, unceasing, uninterrupted

**continuous** (*adj*) without break or interruption

**current** (*adj*) at present, now

**dated** (*adj*) antiquated, old enough to be out of fashion

**delay** (*vb*) postpone, cause to wait, slow down; (*n*) instance of such postponement or slowing

**directly** (*adv*) at once, immediately

**during** (*prep*) at the same time as, in the time of

**early** (*adv*) at or near the beginning; before or ahead of time; (*adj*) occurring in the first part of a period of time

**ephemeral** (*adj*) lasting for one day; short-lived

**ere** (*prep*) before

**erelong** (*adv*) soon, before long

**erenow** (*adv*) before now

**erewhile** (*adv*) some time ago

**erst** (*adv*) previously, earlier

**erstwhile** (*adj*) former, of times past

**eve**  evening or day before

**eventually** (*adv*) finally, in the end

**ever** (*adv*) always, at any time

**first** (*adv*) earliest, preceding others; (*adj*) before all others

**fore** (*adj*) coming first, prior to

**forenoon**  morning, before noon

**former** (*adj*) prior, earlier, preceding in time

**formerly** (*adv*) in a previous time

**for the time being**  temporarily

**frequent** (*adj*) often

**from time to time**  occasionally, not often

**fugitive** (*adj*) not durable, transient

**henceforth** (*adv*) from the present time forward

**hereafter** (*adv*) in the future, after the present

**heretofore** (*adv*) previously, up to the present time

**immediate** (*adj*) without delay or interval, next

**imminent** (*adj*) about to happen immediately

**impermanent** (*adj*) temporary, lasting for a limited time

**impromptu** (*adv*) extemporaneously; (*adj*) done without previous preparation

**in a flash**  instantaneously, extremely quickly

**in a moment**  very soon, right away

**in a trice**  at once, in a moment

**in a twinkling**  at once, immediately, quickly

**in a wink**  at once, in an instant

**infrequent** (*adj*) seldom, not often

**in good time**  on time; early, in advance

**in no time**  almost at once

**instantaneous** (*adj*) happening and concluding in an instant; without duration

**interim** (*adj*) temporary; (*n*) intervening time

**intermediate** (*adj*) in an intervening time

**in the meantime** temporarily

**in the offing** occurring in the near future; soon

**in time** sooner or later; early enough

**in turn** eventually; in due order of succession

**isochronal** (*adj*) occurring at regular intervals

**last** (*adj*) final; time immediately prior to the present

**late** (*adj*) after the appointed or usual time, tardy

**lickety-split** (*adv*) very quickly, right away

**long ago** far in the past

**long since** long ago

**meantime** (*adv*) meanwhile

**meanwhile** (*adv*) in the intervening time; at the same time; meantime

**meta-** prefix meaning after or beyond

**ne'er** (*adv*) never, at no time

**never** (*adv*) not ever, at no time

**never again** (*adv*) not to occur anymore

**nevermore** (*adv*) never again, no more

**new** (*adj*) not existing prior to this moment; of recent origin

**nonce** present or immediate occasion or purpose

**nowadays** (*adv*) in the present, currently

**now and then** occasionally

**occasional** (*adj*) occurring infrequently or irregularly

**occasionally** (*adv*) now and then; sometimes

**off and on** intermittently

**off-peak** (*adj*) pertaining to time period of less than maximum use, frequency, or duration

**off-season** less busy season

**often** (*adv*) frequently, many times

**ofttimes** (*adv*) frequently, often

**old** (*adj*) having lived or existed for a long period of time

**on again, off again** intermittently

**ongoing** (*adj*) enduring or continuing

**parachronism** chronological error, usu. placing event later than correct time

**part-time** (*adj*) lasting fewer hours than full-time, usu. said of employment

**permanent** (*adj*) continuing without change, not temporary

**post-** prefix meaning after or behind

**postdate** (*vb*) date after time of transaction or occurrence, esp. a check

**posthaste** (*adv*) speedily, with haste

**pre-** prefix meaning before or prior

**precedence** act or state of going before; right to priority

**preceding** (*adj*) going before

**precursor** person or thing that goes before

**predate** (*vb*) date or affix before actual time of transaction or occurrence

**preliminary** (*adj*) preceding, before

**preprandial** (*adj*) relating to time just before dinner

**presently** (*adv*) soon

**presto** (*adv*) in rapid tempo; immediately

**previous** (*adj*) before, preceding, former

**primeval** (*adj*) from original time, ancient, primal

**prior** (*adj*) before, preceding, previous to

**procrastination** habit of delaying or postponing

**prolong** (*vb*) lengthen, extend, continue

**promptly** (*adv*) without delay, quickly

**pronto** (*adv*) *Informal.* quickly, right away

**proximo** (*adv*) in the next month after this month

**rare** (*adj*) not frequent

**rarely** (*adv*) not often, infrequently

**recent** (*adj*) pertaining to the near past, lately; new

**recurrent** (*adj*) returning periodically

**remote** (*adj*) distant

**repeatedly** (*adv*) at intervals, again and again

**respite** postponement, delay, pause

**retrospective** (*adj*) directed toward looking backward

**right away** immediately, without delay

**seldom** (*adv*) not often, rarely

**semipermanent** (*adj*) lasting, but not permanent; durable

**simultaneous** (*adj*) occurring at same moment

**someday** (*adv*) at some future time

**sometime** (*adv*) at an unknown or unspecified point of time; (*adj*) having been formerly

**sometimes** (*adv*) now and then, on occasion

**soon** (*adv*) promptly, immediately; earlier than usual

**sooner or later** eventually

**sporadic** (*adj*) happening in scattered instances

**spur-of-the-moment** (*adj*) impromptu; occuring without planning or rehearsal

**straightaway** (*adv*) immediately, without delay; straight off

**straight off** straightaway

**subsequent** (*adj*) following, later

**successive** (*adj*) following in order

**sudden** (*adj*) abrupt, happening unexpectedly; quick

**summary** (*adj*) quickly done, without delay

**tardy** (*adj*) late; slow

**temp** *Informal.* temporary employee

**temporal** (*adj*) pertaining to, defined, or limited by time; transitory

**temporary** (*adj*) of certain limited duration, not permanent

**tempus fugit** *Latin.* time flies

**terminal** (*adj*) final, occurring at the end

**then** (*adv*) at that time; following, next

**thence** (*adv*) from that time; thereafter

**thenceforth** (*adv*) from that time forward

**thereafter** (*adv*) subsequently; after that

**theretofore** (*adv*) before or until then

**thereupon** (*adv*) immediately following that

**therewith** (*adv*) thereupon

**time after time** repeatedly

**time and again** repeatedly

**time-consuming** (*adj*) requiring or taking up a great deal of time

**time-honored** (*adj*) esteemed due to age or longstanding use

**timeless** (*adj*) outside limits of time; unrestricted by time period or era; undated; eternal, with no beginning or end

**timely** (*adj*) early, seasonal, opportune, or executed on time

**time of life** one's age

**timesaver** something intended to expedite an action

**time-tested** (*adj*) having effectiveness proved over a long period of time

**time warp** hypothetical peculiarity in progression of time that would allow movement back and forth in time

**transience** state of being limited by time; impermanence

**transitory** (*adj*) temporary, fleeting

**unceasing** (*adj*) continuous, without interruption

**until** (*conj*) up to the time of; at any time before

**untimely** (*adj*) premature, unseasonable; occurring at improper time

**upcoming** (*adj*) about to occur; coming to pass

**upon** (*prep*) without interval or delay

**up-to-the-minute** (*adj*) extending to the present moment; new, modern

**urgent** (*adj*) requiring immediate attention

**vestigial** (*adj*) relating to or indicating something formerly present

**vintage** (*adj*) old, antique

**well-timed** (*adj*) propitious

**when** (*adv*) at a particular time; at which time

**whenever** (*adv*) at any time; as soon as

**whensoever** (*adv*) at whatsoever time

**while** (*conj*) during the time that

**yesteryear** year past; recent past

**yestreen** *Scottish.* last evening or night

**yet** (*adv*) present time; any time until the present; at some future time; in the time remaining

**yore** time past; (*adv*) long ago

# SPATIAL POSITIONS AND RELATIONS

Fixed Positions and Points
Dimensions and Directions
Relative Positions

**SEE ALSO**: Chap. 4: Mathematics; Chap. 18: Qualifiers and Connectives; Chap. 23: Shapes

## FIXED POSITIONS AND POINTS

**acme** highest point

**aloft** (*adv*) high in the air

**angle** point at which two lines converge

**antinode** area of maximum amplitude between adjacent nodes

**apex** highest point

**apical** (*adj*) at the highest point

**apogee** highest or most distant point

**attitude** position in space determined by relationship of object's axis and a reference point

**balanced** (*adj*) in equilibrium due to even distribution of weight on all sides

**base** bottom point or position

**beginning** origin; point at which something starts

**benchmark** point of reference for making measurements

**blind spot** area that cannot be seen

**capsheaf** highest point, acme

**center** middle, esp. point around which circle is drawn

**chink** narrow opening or division

**circumcenter** center of circumscribed circle

**cleft** split; depression between ridges

**corner** point where converging lines, edges, or sides meet

**crest** highest point

**crisscross** (*adj*) intersecting; having a number of crossing lines or paths

**crossed** (*adj*) intersecting at a specific point

**crown** highest point

**depth** farthest or innermost part or point

**dorsal** (*adj*) near or on the back

**dorsolateral** (*adj*) on both the back and sides

**edge** line at which area begins or ends; border

**end** point marking most extreme extent; part lying at limit

**endpoint** either of two points at ends of line segment

**epicenter** exact center, esp. Earth's surface beneath focus of earthquake

**erect** (*adj*) in upright or vertical position

**extremity** farthest point

**farthest** (*adj*) at the greatest possible distance

**first** (*adj*) situated at the beginning or in front

**fissure** narrow break in surface produced by separation of parts

**fix** charted position or bearings

**focal point** focus

**focus** point at which lines or rays come together, cross, or diverge; focal point; hub

**fork** point of branching

**gap** break in space; empty space in continuity

**grade** position on scale or hierarchy

**hanging** (*adj*) suspended from a point

**here** (*adv*) in or at this place

**hereat** (*adv*) at this place

**hindmost** (*adj*) nearest the rear position

**hub** focus

**innermost** (*adj*) farthest inward

**in the way** located so as to be an obstacle in one's course

**inverted** (*adj*) with top and bottom parts reversed

**last** (*adj*) situated farthest to the rear, after all others

**low** (*adj*) lying close to or at the bottom point

**metacenter** intersection of lines through centers of buoyancy of a floating body at rest and when tipped to one side

**midpoint** point at or near the center or middle

**nadir** lowest point, esp. opposite zenith in celestial sphere

**navel** central point, middle

**node** point at which parts begin or focus; point at which curve crosses itself at different tangents

**omphalos** center or navel

**outmost** (*adj*) farthest from the center

**outrance** *French.* ultimate extremity

**pendent** (*adj*) suspended, hanging

**perigee** point in orbit of heavenly body at which it is nearest to Earth

**perihelion** point in orbit of celestial body at which it is nearest to sun

**plumb** (*adj*) perpendicular; exactly vertical

**point** definite, unique position on scale; geometric element positioned by ordered set of coordinates

**polycentric** (*adj*) having more than one center

**position** space occupied by an object at a given moment

**prone** (*adj*) having front surface facing downward

**prostrate** (*adj*) lying facedown on the ground

**quadrant** one of four parts into which an area is divided by two perpendicular lines

**quincunx** arrangement of five items around a square or rectangle with one at each corner and one in the center

**reclining** (*adj*) leaning backward from vertical position

**recumbent** (*adj*) lying down, reclining; leaning

**ridge** line where two slopes meet at their highest points

**ringside** (*adj*) located around a ring

**rolled** (*adj*) turned around itself

**section** distinct part of something, esp. solid cut by plane

**sector** portion of circle bounded by two radii

**segment** portion of larger figure, esp. circle, cut off by one or more lines or planes

**site** specific location

**situated** (*adj*) having or designating a specific location

**slit** long, narrow opening

**somewhere** (*adv*) to or at an unspecified place

**square** (*adj*) exactly aligned; straight, level

**stationary** (*adj*) fixed in position

**stone's throw** *Informal.* short distance

**summit** highest point

**supine** (*adj*) on back with front surface facing upward

**suspended** (*adj*) hanging freely from a point

**terminus** end of a line

**there** (*adv*) in, to, or at that place

**thereat** (*adv*) at that place

**tip** top, summit, or apex

**top** highest point

**transverse** (*adj*) reaching across, esp. at right angles to front-back axis of object

**ultimate** (*adj*) farthest, esp. most remote; last in series

**ultima Thule** *Latin.* lit. ultimate Thule; farthest point or limit of a journey, esp. point farthest north

**underside** surface on bottom, usu. hidden from view

**up** (*adv*) in or toward a higher position; facing upward; in vertical position

**uppermost** (*adj*) located at the highest position

**ventral** (*adj*) situated on the front side of a body

**verge** something that limits, borders, or bounds something else; edge

**vertex** highest point; point opposite and farthest from base; termination of line; intersection of two or more lines

**whereabouts** general place where something is

**whereat** (*conj*) at or toward which point

**zenith** highest point, esp. point in celestial sphere opposite nadir

**zonal** (*adj*) pertaining to or having the shape of a zone

**zone** specifically defined and bounded area of a surface


## DIMENSIONS AND DIRECTIONS

**aligned** (*adj*) arranged in a straight line; set in order

**allover** (*adj*) extending over an entire surface

**altitude** distance upward from surface

**anyplace** (*adv*) anywhere

**anywhere** (*adv*) at or to any place or point

**approach** (*vb*) come near or closer to

**area** extent of space or surface bounded by fixed lines

**ascending** (*adj*) moving upward from lower to higher level

**askew** (*adv*) to one side

**aslant** (*adv*) obliquely, at a slant

**aslope** (*adv*) in a slanting position

**asymmetrical** (*adj*) lacking symmetry, irregular; unsymmetrical

**atilt** (*adv*) in an inclined position

**axis** straight line about which a body rotates or around which parts of body are symmetrical

**azimuth** arc of horizon measured clockwise from fixed point at north or south

**back-and-forth** (*adj*) backward and forward, from side to side; to-and-fro

**backward** (*adv*) in reverse of normal direction; with back foremost; toward the rear

**bearing** horizontal direction of one point measured in degrees from another point

**beeline** direct course, straight line

**bidirectional** (*adj*) capable of moving in two, usu. opposite, directions

**bilateral** (*adj*) having or concerning two sides

**bilevel** (*adj*) divided horizontally into two usu. equal parts

**bisect** (*vb*) divide into two usu. equal parts

**border** outer edge or boundary of a space

**boundary** indicator that sets limit or extent; edge

**breadth** dimension from side to side; width

**brink** edge, esp. of steep place

**broad** (*adj*) extending to a great range or width

**bulk** three-dimensional magnitude

**cavity** hollowed space

**centrifugal** (*adj*) moving away from center or axis

**centripetal** (*adj*) moving toward center or axis

**chasm** wide, deep gap

**chockablock** (*adj*) crowded together; extremely full

**circuit** circular line bounding an area

**circuitous** (*adj*) following an indirect path

**circumambient** (*adj*) lying on all sides

**circumference** outer boundary, esp. perimeter of circle

**clockwise** (*adj*) in direction in which clock hands rotate

**coast-to-coast** (*adj*) extending across an entire nation or continent

**compass** enclosing limits of any space; space within such limits

**contour** general outline of a shape

**counterclockwise** (*adj*) in direction opposite that in which clock hands rotate; backward

**country mile** *Informal.* long distance

**cross-country** (*adj*) extending across an entire country

**dangling** (*adj*) hanging loosely

**decline** gradual downward movement

**depth** dimension downward from top, horizontally inward, or from back to front

**descending** (*adj*) moving downward from higher to lower position

**dextral** (*adj*) on or leaning to the right

**diagonal** (*adj*) running in an oblique direction from a reference line

**diameter** straight line from one side of circle to the other through center point

**dimension** magnitude measured in one direction, esp. width, length, or thickness that determines a position in space

**direct** (*adj*) from point to point by shortest course; straight

**direction** line along which something is pointing, facing, or moving

**directional** (*adj*) designating direction in space

**distance** extent of space between two points, lines, surfaces, or objects, usu. along shortest path

**drop** distance from one level to some lower level

**east** direction of sunrise; direction to one's right when facing north

**edgewise** (*adj*) sideways

**elevation** distance upward from fixed surface

**elongation** condition of being stretched or lengthened

**encircling** (*adj*) running completely around in a circle

**equiangular** (*adj*) having all angles equal

**equilateral** (*adj*) having all sides equal

**everywhere** (*adv*) in all places or parts

**extension** stretching or enlargement in scope

**extensive** (*adj*) covering a great area or scope

**extent** maximum space across or through which something stretches out or reaches

**facedown** (*adv*) with the front side down

**faceup** (*adv*) with the front side up

**falling** (*adj*) descending freely, usu. straight downward

**far and wide** (*adv*) covering great distances in all directions

**far cry** great distance

**field** region covered by a feature or through which a force acts

**forward** (*adv*) moving toward a point in front

**fourth dimension** time dimension used as coordinate with length, depth, and breadth in space–time continuum

**frontal** (*adj*) located at or moving against the front

**frontward** (*adv*) moving forward

**geocentric** (*adj*) having Earth as center

**geodesic** (*adj*) pertaining to the geometry of curved surfaces

**grade** degree of inclination of slope

**heading** specific direction, esp. compass point toward which something is moving

**height** distance from bottom to top; extent upward above surface; highest part or point

**high** (*adj*) reaching upward, esp. to great extent; elevated from a surface

**high and low** (*adv*) everywhere possible

**horizontal** (*adj*) parallel to the horizon or level ground; level; at right angles to vertical

**inch** (*vb*) move by small degrees

**incline** grade, slant, or deviation from vertical or horizontal position

**inclined** (*adj*) at an angle with another surface

**indirect** (*adj*) deviating from straight line or path

**infinite** (*adj*) boundless in all directions; immeasurable

**infinity** immeasurable extent of space

**involute** (*adj*) curled or curved inward

**inward** (*adv*) toward or at the inside or center

**isometric** (*adj*) having equality of measure

**isosceles** (*adj*) having two sides equal and nonparallel

**latitudinal** (*adj*) having side-to-side extent, esp. as measure of distance from Earth's equator

**left** (*adj*) located toward the west when facing north

**length** longest linear extent or dimension of object

**lengthways** (*adv*) lengthwise

**lengthwise** (*adv*) longitudinally, in direction of length; lengthways

**level** (*adj*) flat; horizontal; having all parts at equal height

**light-year** distance light travels in one year, used in astronomical measurements

**limit** greatest extent

**linear** (*adj*) consisting of or moving in a straight line; having a single dimension

**long** (*adj*) of a considerable extent; extending to greater length than breadth; far, distant

**long-distance** (*adj*) situated at or extending a great distance

**longitudinal** (*adj*) placed or moving lengthwise; having top-to-bottom extent

**mile** unit of linear distance equal to 5280 feet or 1760 yards (1.609 km)

**multilateral** (*adj*) having many sides

**nationwide** (*adj*) extending across an entire country

**north** cardinal point of a compass in direction of north terrestrial pole, to the left of a person facing the rising sun and directly opposite south

**nowhere** (*adv*) not at any place; (*n*) unknown or distant place

**oblique** (*adj*) neither perpendicular nor parallel to another surface; slanting or sloping

**obtuse** (*adj*) designating an angle greater than 90 but less than 180 degrees

**off** (*adv*) away from a course or path

**on** (*prep*) used to indicate location or immediate proximity; (*adv*) toward a place; forward or along a given course

**out** (*adv*) in a direction away from the center or normal position

**outline** general shape or boundaries of something

**out-of-bounds** (*adj*) outside designated limits or boundaries

**outreach** length or extent of reach

**outward** (*adj*) directed away from the center; situated on the outside

**outwardly** (*adv*) toward or on the outside

**parallax** apparent displacement of moving object as viewed from two different points

**parsec** 3.26 light-years

**patulous** (*adj*) spreading widely from the center

**perimeter** boundary of closed plane figure

**pervasive** (*adj*) spread throughout every part

**plane** flat or level surface; two-dimensional body

**prolate** (*adj*) extended in line joining the poles

**protracted** (*adj*) extended in space, esp. forward or outward

**radial** (*adj*) extending from a center; moving along a radius

**radiating** (*adj*) extending in a direct line away from or toward a center

**radius** line extending from center of circle to its boundary

**range** maximum extent outward

**ray** line extending from point or center

**rearward** (*adv*) toward the back

**rectilinear** (*adj*) moving in or forming a straight line

**retroflex** (*adj*) turned sharply backward

**retrograde** (*adj*) directed or moving backward, against the general direction

**reverse** (*adj*) moving opposite to the regular direction; having backside forward

**revolution** movement around center or axis and return to original position

**right** (*adj*) located toward the east when facing north

**ringed** (*adj*) encircled; formed of rings

**rising** (*adj*) moving to a higher position

**rotary** (*adj*) turning on an axis

**rotation** turning of body on an axis; single complete turn around axis

**seesaw** (*vb*) move back and forth or up and down

**shouting distance** relatively short distance

**sideways** (*adv*) facing to the side; toward or from one side; edgewise

**sinistral** (*adj*) on or leaning to the left

**skew lines** nonintersecting straight lines in different planes

**slant** slope or incline away from level

**slope** slant, oblique course; measure of upward or downward inclination

**south** cardinal point of a compass in direction of south terrestrial pole and directly opposite north

**space** particular extent in one, two, or three dimensions; distance between two or more objects

**space-time** four-dimensional continuum having three spatial coordinates with which to locate an event or object

**span** distance between two points, esp. endpoints

**statewide** (adj) extending throughout an entire state

**straight** (adj) moving or extending continuously in one direction without turning

**straightforward** (adj) moving in a direct line

**stratified** (adj) forming layers in a graded series

**stretch** considerable extent, length, or area

**sweep** continuous, entire range; curving course of line

**symmetrical** (adj) corresponding in size, form, and relative position on opposite sides of line, plane, point, or axis

**tabular** (adj) arranged in vertical and horizontal rows

**tangential** (adj) digressing suddenly from one course and turning to another

**three-dimensional** (adj) having height, width, and depth

**throughout** (prep) in or to every part

**tilt** surface slanting from level position

**to-and-fro** (adj) back-and-forth

**trajectory** curve followed by body projected through space

**triangulation** technique for determining location through bearings from two fixed points at a given distance

**two-dimensional** (adj) having height and width only

**ubiquitous** (adj) existing everywhere

**uniaxial** (adj) having one axis

**unidirectional** (adj) moving in one direction only

**unilateral** (adj) arranged on one side

**universal** (adj) existing everywhere; distributed throughout space without limit or exception

**unsymmetrical** (adj) asymmetrical

**up-and-down** (adj) moving alternately upward, then downward

**upright** (adj) having main axis perpendicular or vertical

**vector** line segment with both magnitude and direction in space

**vertical** (adj) perpendicular to horizon or level surface; upright; designating an extent to the highest point; at right angles to horizontal

**void** empty space

**-ward** suffix meaning moving or located in a direction, as in homeward or upward

**way** path from one place to another; length of such a course

**-ways** suffix meaning in or toward a direction or position, as in sideways

**west** direction of sunset; direction to one's left when facing north

**wherever** (conj) toward or in any place at all

**wide** (adj) of specific extent from side to side; covering a large area

**width** extent from side to side, at right angles to length

**worldwide** (adj) extending throughout the world

## Relative Positions

**abeam** (adv) at right angles to, esp. a ship's keel

**about** (adv) near to; on every side

**above** (adv) in a higher place, over

**abutting** (adj) touching at border, esp. ending at contact point

**across** (prep) from side to side; on the other side

**adaxial** (adj) on the same side as or facing the axis

**adjacent** (adj) nearby; just before or facing; adjoining

**adjoining** (adj) connected at point or along line

**advance** (adj) located before others

**afar** (adv) at a great distance

**afield** (adv) away from a base

**after** (prep) following behind

**against** (prep) directly opposite; close beside or in front of; in contact with; in an opposite direction to

**ahead** (adv) in front of

**alongside** (adv) at or by the side of

**ambit** boundary or limit of a place

**amid** (prep) in the middle of, among; amidst

**amidst** (prep) amid

**among** (prep) surrounded by, in the midst of; amid

**anent** (prep) *Chiefly Brit.* alongside; in line with

**anterior** (adj) located toward the front; before

**antipodal** (adj) at the opposite side of the globe

**apart** (adv) separately, at some distance

**apposed** (adj) placed side by side or in proximity

**around** (adv) on all sides; nearby; here and there

**aside** (adv) toward or on one side

**astraddle** (adv) with one extension or leg on each side; astride

**astride** (prep) on both sides of from above; with a leg on each side of

**at** (prep) situated in, on, or near

**at hand** (adj) in close proximity

**athwart** (adv) across; from side to side

**atop** (adv) above, on, or at the top

**away** (adv) at a distance, far off; aside

**axial** (adj) forming, situated on, or in the direction of an axis

**back** (adv) toward or at the rear

**back-to-back** (adj) facing in opposite directions from a common point

**before** (adv) in front, ahead

**behind** (adv) in or toward the back or rear; in the place already passed

**below** (adv) in or toward a lower place; underneath

**beneath** (adv) in a lower position; directly below

**beside** (prep) by the side of, usu. nearby

**between** (prep) occupying the intermediate space or interval that separates; 'tween

**betwixt** (prep) between, in a middle position; 'twixt

**beyond** (prep) on or to the farther side; more distant than; outside the reach of

**bordering** (adj) located or in contact at the edge

**bottom** under or lower side; lowest point or place

**by** (prep) near, close to; in the direction of; aside, away

**cater-corner** (adj) located diagonally opposite; kitty-corner

**caudal** (adj) at or toward the tail or posterior end

**central** (adj) at or near the center, in the middle

**centric** (adj) in or at the center; central; focused on a center

**close** (adj) being near; having little space between elements

**coaxial** (adj) having a common axis

**coextensive** (adj) having identical spatial extent or boundaries

**coincident** (adj) filling the same space

**colinear** (adj) having corresponding parts arranged along the same straight line

**collateral** (adj) parallel or conforming in position or order; running side by side

**collinear** (adj) lying in or sharing the same straight line

**concentric** (adj) having a common center

**configuration** arrangement of parts relative to one another

**confocal** (adj) having a common focus

**consecutive** (adj) following one another in unbroken order

**conterminous** (*adj*) having a common boundary; lying within one common boundary

**contiguous** (*adj*) touching along one side or at some point; adjacent

**convenient** (*adj*) close at hand, accessible

**converse** (*adj*) reversed

**coplanar** (*adj*) occupying the same plane

**coterminous** (*adj*) having the same boundary

**covering** (*adj*) entirely enclosing or overlaying

**decussate** (*adj*) crossed or intersected

**deep** (*adj*) extending far from surface or edge, esp. downward

**detached** (*adj*) not connected, separate

**discontinuous** (*adj*) not continued, discrete; out of or without sequence

**discrete** (*adj*) consisting of separate, unattached elements; constituting a distinct individual or entity

**distal** (*adj*) farthest from the point of attachment or origin; terminal

**distant** (*adj*) far away, separated by a wide space

**distinct** (*adj*) separate, clearly differentiated from others

**down** (*adv*) in or to a lower position; toward or at the bottom

**elsewhere** (*adv*) some place other than here

**encircling** (*adj*) forming a circle around

**enclosed** (*adj*) surrounded on all sides

**enclosing** (*adj*) surrounding on all sides, encircling

**encompassing** (*adj*) enclosing, forming a border around

**enveloping** (*adj*) completely enclosing

**equidistant** (*adj*) equally spaced from a fixed point

**even** (*adj*) at the same level or point

**exterior** (*adj*) situated on or outside a surface, beyond the bounds of

**external** (*adj*) outside, beyond the surface of

**face-to-face** (*adj*) in direct contact, with front sides directed toward each other

**facing** (*adj*) with front surface directed toward

**far** (*adj*) at a great distance

**far and away** by a significant margin

**farther** (*adj*) more distant, more remote

**flanking** (*adj*) lying beside, often on both sides

**flush** (*adj*) even with the edge of, directly in contact

**foot** bottom

**fore** (*adj*) toward the front, forward

**fore and aft** in or at both front and rear

**forth** (*adv*) forward, from one place

**forward** (*adj*) situated at or toward the front

**fringe** (*adj*) at the edge

**from** (*prep*) indicating a starting point, esp. beginning at; indicating separation from a starting point

**front** part or surface facing forward

**fronting** (*adj*) lying before; facing

**further** (*adv*) to a greater extent; farther

**halfway** (*adj*) at the midpoint

**hard by** near, in close proximity to

**hence** (*adv*) from this place, away

**hereabout** (*adv*) nearby, in close proximity

**here and there** (*adv*) in a number of places

**hither** (*adv*) to or toward this place; (*adj*) being on the closer or adjacent side

**hithermost** (*adj*) nearest on a specific side

**immediate** (*adj*) present, near at hand; without intervening space

**indoors** (*adj*) situated or occurring within a roofed structure

**inferior** (*adj*) lower

**infra-** prefix meaning below

**inner** (*adj*) situated farther within; being closer to the center

**inside** (*adv*) in the inner part; within

**interior** (*adj*) located within fixed boundaries

**intermediate** (*adj*) in the middle; between two points

**interposed** (*adj*) placed between, intervening

**intersecting** (*adj*) crossing at a point

**interspersed** (*adj*) scattered at intervals among

**interstice** space situated between things, esp. a narrow interval

**intervening** (*adj*) lying or placed between

**kitty-corner** (*adj*) cater-corner

**lateral** (*adj*) situated at or directed to the side

**leeward** (*adj*) facing away from the source of wind

**levitated** (*adj*) elevated into the air in apparent defiance of gravity

**long-distance** (*adj*) located at a great distance

**lower** (*adj*) situated below; in a lesser position than another

**maximum** upper limit, greatest value attained

**mean** position midway between extremes

**medial** (*adj*) in the middle

**median** (*adj*) being in the middle or in an intermediate position

**mid** (*adj*) situated in a middle position; amid, amidst

**midair** any point in the air that is more than just above the ground

**middle** (*adj*) halfway between extremes; intermediate

**midline** median line or median plane

**midst** central or interior position

**midway** (*adj*) halfway, in the middle of a distance

**near** (*adv*) within or at a short distance

**nearby** (*adj*) close at hand

**next** (*adj*) immediately before or following; nearest

**next to** directly beside, sometimes bordering at the edge

**nigh** (*adv*) near

**nip and tuck** so close that advantage alters rapidly between competitors

**not far** relatively near or close

**obverse** (*adj*) facing the observer, often in opposition

**off** (*adv*) at a distance, away from

**on** (*adv*) in contact with or in close proximity to a surface

**onward** (*adv*) forward, moving ahead

**opposite** (*adj*) situated across from or at the other side of an intervening space

**out** (*adv*) away from, at a distance

**outdoors** (*adj*) situated or occurring outside any enclosure or beneath open air

**outer** (*adj*) situated relatively farther out or distant from center

**outside** (*adj*) located beyond a boundary or outer surface; external; outdoors

**over** (*prep*) higher than or above another; (*adj*) beyond the upper surface or edge

**overlying** (*adj*) situated directly above and entirely covering

**parallel** (*adj*) extending in the same direction, at all points equidistant, and not converging

**peripheral** (*adj*) situated at the external boundary or surface

**perpendicular** (*adj*) exactly at right angles to a flat surface or plane

**point-blank** (*adj*) direct, at very close range

**port** (*adj*) located on the left side, esp. of a vessel

**position** location relative to other places at any given moment

**posterior** (*adj*) located toward the rear; behind

**propinquity** nearness, proximity

**proximal** (*adj*) near, esp. close to the center

**proximate** (*adj*) next to; very near

**proximity** nearness

**rear** (*adj*) toward or at the back

**remote** (*adj*) far or distant

**retral** (*adj*) located at or toward the back; posterior

**retro-** prefix meaning backward or behind

**separate** (*adj*) disconnected in space, distinct from others

**side by side** next to each other, esp. facing in same direction

**spatial relation** connection or relative position in space of one point or object with reference to one or more other points or objects

**starboard** (*adj*) located on the right side, esp. of a vessel

**sub-** prefix meaning below, beneath, or under

**successive** (*adj*) following one after another

**super-** prefix meaning over, above, or on top

**superior** (*adj*) located higher up or above

**superjacent** (*adj*) overlying

**supra-** prefix meaning above or over

**surrounding** (*adj*) enclosing or overlaying on all sides

**thence** (*adv*) from that place

**thenceforth** (*adv*) onward from a given place

**thereabout** (*adv*) somewhere close or near to a given place

**therefrom** (*adv*) away from that place

**therein** (*adv*) in or into that place

**thither** (*adv*) to or toward that place; there; (*adj*) on the farther side

**through** (*prep*) in one side and out the other; from one edge to another

**toward** (*prep*) in the direction of; in the vicinity of; turned to, facing

**trans-** prefix meaning across, beyond, or through

**traverse** (*adj*) extending across

**'tween** (*prep*) between

**'twixt** (*prep*) betwixt

**ulterior** (*adj*) lying on the far side; more remote

**under** (*prep*) below or beneath something, esp. so as to be covered, enveloped, or hidden

**underneath** (*prep*) directly below the surface or level of, esp. so as to be hidden

**up** (*adv*) in or toward a higher position; relatively higher than

**upside down** having upper and lower parts reversed from normal position

**upward** (*adv*) in or toward a higher position

**via** (*prep*) by way of

**vicinity** area in proximity; state of nearness

**whence** (*adv*) from what place? (*conj*) from what place

**where** (*adv*) at, in, or to what place? (*conj*) in or at what place

**whereto** (*conj*) to which place

**whither** (*adv*) to what place? where? (*conj*) to which place

**windward** (*adj*) facing toward the source of wind

**within** (*adv*) in the interior, inside; enclosed

**within an inch** very close but not quite touching

**without** (*adv*) on the exterior, outside; external to

**yon** (*adv*) yonder

**yonder** (*adv*) over there, at some distance; yon

# Shapes

**SEE ALSO**: Chap. 4: Mathematics; Chap. 23: Spatial Positions and Relations

In addition to adjectives that describe the shapes of physical and natural objects, and mathematically defined forms, this section includes certain concrete nouns, such as "anchor," "bell," and "doughnut," that have distinctive and distinguishing shapes.

**acicular** (*adj*) needle-shaped

**acuminate** (*adj*) tapering to a slender point

**acute** (*adj*) of an angle of less than ninety degrees

**amygdaloid** (*adj*) almond-shaped

**anchor** object that has a broad, hooklike arm

**angular** (*adj*) sharp-cornered; having points from which two lines diverge

**annular** (*adj*) ring-shaped

**apical** (*adj*) narrowing to a pointed tip

**arc** unbroken segment of a curved line

**arcuate** (*adj*) curved like a bow

**asymmetrical** (*adj*) lacking balance; not the same on both sides of central axis

**attenuated** (*adj*) tapering to long, slender point

**awry** (*adj*) turned or twisted from a central axis

**bacillary** (*adj*) rod-shaped

**ball** round or spherical shape

**bell** hollow, curved shape with open, circular base and surface curving to a central apex

**biconcave** (*adj*) concave on both sides

**biconvex** (*adj*) convex on both sides

**bifurcate** (*adj*) divided into two branches

**bilateral** (*adj*) two-sided; symmetrical on both sides of an axis

**biradial** (*adj*) having both bilateral and radial symmetry

**block** cube

**bolus** lumpy, rounded mass

**botryoidal** (*adj*) formed like a bunch of grapes

**bowl** concave hemisphere opening upward

**box** rectangle with upright sides; cube

**branching** (*adj*) forming subdivisions like a tree

**brick** rectangular solid longer than it is wide

**bulbous** (*adj*) round like a bulb

**bump** swelling or lump in flat surface

**bursiform** (*adj*) pouch-shaped

**campanulate** (*adj*) bell-shaped

**capitate** (*adj*) enlarged at the head and spherical; forming a head

**catenary** curve formed by flexible, nonelastic cord hanging freely between two points

**catenulate** (*adj*) chainlike in shape

**chevron** V or inverted V

**circinate** (*adj*) rolled up on the axis at the apex; ring-shaped

**circle** curved line every point of which is equidistant from a fixed center

**circular** (*adj*) circle-shaped

**clavate** (*adj*) club-shaped and thicker at one end; claviform

**claviform** (*adj*) club-shaped; clavate

**clothoid** (*adj*) tear-shaped loop

**cloverleaf** figure formed by four leaves on one stem

**club** stylized cloverleaf figure on playing cards

**coil** series of loops, spiral

**columnar** (*adj*) arranged in vertical rows

**compass** (*adj*) curved; forming a curve or an arc

**concave** (*adj*) hollowed, rounded, or curved inward

**concavo-convex** (*adj*) concave on one side and convex on the other, esp. with greater curvature on concave side; convexo-concave

**cone** solid with circular base and vertical surface of line segments that join every point of base circumference to common vertex

**conical** (*adj*) cone-shaped

**conoid** (*adj*) conelike or nearly conelike

**contour** outline of curving, irregular figure

**convex** (*adj*) curved or rounded outward, as with exterior of sphere or circle

**convexo-concave** (*adj*) concavo-convex, esp. with greater curvature on convex side

**convoluted** (*adj*) twisted; coiled

**cordate** (*adj*) heart-shaped; cordiform

**cordiform** (*adj*) heart-shaped; cordate

**crenate** (*adj*) having margin or surface cut into scallops or notches

**crenulate** (*adj*) having irregularly wavy or serrate outline

**crescent** shape bounded by convex and concave edges of less than half a hemisphere

**crook** bent or hooked form

**cross** two lines intersecting, esp. at right angles; X-shaped figure

**cruciform** (*adj*) cross-shaped; (*n*) cross

**cube** regular solid of six equal square sides

**cubical** (*adj*) cube-shaped

**cucullate** (*adj*) hooded; hood-shaped

**cuneal** (*adj*) wedge-shaped

**cuneate** (*adj*) triangular at base and tapering toward a point; cuneal

**curlicue** figure with multiple, nonduplicating curves and spirals

**curvature** amount or state of being curved

**curve** path of a point not moving in a straight line

**cusp** point or apex; tip of crescent

**cuspidate** (*adj*) terminating in a point

**cycle** circular or spiral arrangement

**cycloid** curve generated by point on circumference of circle as it rolls along a straight line

**cylinder** straight tube joining two equal, parallel, circular bases

**cylindrical** (*adj*) cylinder-shaped

**decagon** ten-sided polygon

**decahedron** ten-faced polyhedron

**decurved** (*adj*) curved or bent downward

**decussate** (*adj*) X-shaped

**deltoid** (*adj*) triangular

**dendriform** (*adj*) resembling a tree; dendroid

**dendroid** (*adj*) tree-shaped; dendriform

**dentiform** (*adj*) tooth-shaped

**diamond** four-sided figure with long diagonal vertical; lozenge

**discoid** (*adj*) disk-shaped

**disk** flattened, circular object, sometimes thicker at center than at edge

**dodecagon** twelve-sided polygon

**dodecahedron** twelve-faced polyhedron

**dogleg** course that takes a sharp bend or abrupt turn

**dome** convex hemisphere, usu. opening downward and attached at base

**donut** doughnut

**double helix** pair of intertwined helixes

**doughnut** ring-shaped solid; donut

**egg** oval

**elbow** otherwise straight shape that is bent, esp. at ninety-degree angle near its center

**ellipse** elongated closed circle, oval

**elliptic** (*adj*) ellipse-shaped; elliptical

**elliptical** (*adj*) elliptic

**elongate** (*adj*) stretched out

**ensiform** (*adj*) sword-shaped

**falcate** (*adj*) hooked or curved like a sickle; falciform

**falciform** (*adj*) sickle-shaped; falcate

**fastigiate** (*adj*) narrowing toward the top; having upright clustered branches

**foliate** (*adj*) branching, esp. into leaves

**frustum** part of solid cone or pyramid left by cutting off top portion by plane parallel to base

**fungiform** (*adj*) mushroom-shaped

**fungoid** (*adj*) funguslike in form

**funnel** hollow cone with tube extending from base

**globe** sphere, esp. the Earth

**globose** (*adj*) globular

**globular** (*adj*) globe-shaped, spherical; globose

**gurge** spiral, whirlpool

**hastate** (*adj*) triangular or arrow-shaped with two spreading lobes at base

**heart** standardized representation of heart as matching curves joined at vertical axis and tilted upward to form V-notch at top

**helical** (*adj*) spiral, helix-shaped

**helicoid** (*adj*) forming or arranged in a flat coil or flattened spiral

**helix** spiral; curve traced on cylinder or cone by point moving at constant oblique angle across right sections

**hemihedral** (*adj*) having half the number of planes required by symmetry

**hemisphere** half a sphere

**heptagon** seven-sided polygon

**heptagonal** (*adj*) having seven angles and seven sides

**hexagon** six-sided polygon

**hexagonal** (*adj*) having six angles and six sides

**hexagram** figure formed by completing externally an equilateral triangle on each side of a regular hexagon

**horn** curved ends of a crescent

**hump** rounded, protruding, often irregular lump

**hyperbola** plane curve generated by a point moving so that the difference of its distances from two fixed points is constant

**icosahedron** twenty-faced polyhedron

**infundibuliform** (*adj*) funnel- or cone-shaped

**involute** (*adj*) curled or spiraling inward

**knot** interlacing or tying of strands

**lanceolate** (*adj*) narrow and tapering at one end, like the head of a lance

**ligulate** (*adj*) strap-shaped

**linear** (*adj*) narrow and elongated

**lobate** (*adj*) having roundish projections or divisions

**loop** curving or doubling of line to form closed or partly open curve within itself

**lozenge** diamond

**lump** often irregular bump, hump, or knob

**lunette** crescent or half-moon shape

**meniscus** crescent; concave or convex upper surface of column of liquid

**moline** (*adj*) having the end of each arm forked and recurved

**moniliform** (*adj*) resembling a string of beads

**napiform** (*adj*) globular at top and tapering off gradually; parsnip- or carrot-shaped

**nodular** (*adj*) in shape of rounded or irregular mass

**nodule** small, rounded lump or irregular mass

**nonagon** nine-sided polygon

**notched** (*adj*) having V-shaped or rounded indentation, esp. at edge

**obcordate** (*adj*) heart-shaped with notch at apex

**oblate** (*adj*) flattened or depressed at poles

**oblique** (*adj*) inclined; neither parallel nor perpendicular; having no right angle

**oblong** square, circle, or sphere elongated in one dimension

**obovate** (*adj*) ovate with narrower end at base

**obovoid** (*adj*) ovoid with broad end toward apex

**obtuse** (*adj*) being an angle of more than 90 but less than 180 degrees

**obverse** (*adj*) having base narrower than top

**octagon** eight-sided polygon

**octagonal** (*adj*) having eight angles and eight sides

**octahedron** eight-faced polyhedron

**ogee** pointed arch with reversed curve near each side of apex

**ogival** (*adj*) ogee or ogive-shaped

**ogive** pointed arch

**ophidiform** (*adj*) resembling snakes

**orb** circle; spherical body

**orbicular** (*adj*) spherical, circular

**oval** (*adj*) broadly elliptical; egg-shaped

**ovate** (*adj*) shaped like longitudinal section of an egg with basal end broader

**ovoid** (*adj*) egg-shaped; ovate

**palmate** (*adj*) resembling a hand with fingers spread

**parabola** plane curve that is the path of a moving point whose distance from a fixed point remains equal to its distance from a fixed line

**parabolic** (*adj*) parabola-shaped; bowl-shaped

**parallelepiped** prism with six faces that are parallelograms

**parallelogram** quadrilateral with opposite sides parallel and equal

**parted** (*adj*) divided into distinct portions by deep, lengthwise cuts

**peaked** (*adj*) coming to a point at top

**peltate** (*adj*) shield-shaped

**pentacle** pentagram

**pentagon** five-sided polygon

**pentagonal** (*adj*) having five angles and five sides

**pentagram** five-pointed star with alternate points connected by a continuous line; pentacle

**pentahedron** five-faced polyhedron

**pentangle** pentagram

**pinnate** (*adj*) resembling a feather, with similar parts arranged on opposite sides of an axis

**plane** flat, two-dimensional surface; (*adj*) two-dimensional

**plano-concave** (*adj*) flat on one side, concave on the other

**plano-convex** (*adj*) flat on one side, convex on the other

**polygon** closed plane figure bounded by three or more straight lines

**polygonal** (*adj*) shaped like a plane bounded by three or more straight lines

**polyhedral** (*adj*) having the shape of a polyhedron

**polyhedron** solid figure having many faces

**pretzel** shape that resembles a loosely tied knot

**prism** polyhedron with two polygonal faces lying in parallel planes and other faces being parallelograms

**prismatoid** (*adj*) polyhedral with all vertices in two parallel planes

**prismoid** (*adj*) prismatoid with parallel bases having the same number of sides

**prolate** (*adj*) elongated in direction of a line joining poles

**pyramid** polyhedron with polygonal base and triangular sides with common vertex

**pyriform** (*adj*) pear-shaped

**quadrangle** quadrilateral

**quadrangular** (*adj*) quadrilateral-shaped

**quadrilateral** four-sided polygon; quadrangle

**rectangle** parallelogram all of whose angles are right angles, usu. with adjacent sides of unequal length

**rectangular** (*adj*) rectangle-shaped

**rectilinear** (*adj*) forming a straight line

**reniform** (*adj*) kidney-shaped

**retroflex** (*adj*) turned or bent abruptly inward

**retuse** (*adj*) having apex that is rounded or obtuse with a slight notch

**rhomboid** (*adj*) rhombus-shaped

**rhombus** equilateral parallelogram having oblique angles

**right angle** angle bounded by two lines perpendicular to each other

**right triangle** three-sided polygon with two sides meeting at right angle

**ring** circular shape

**rondure** circle or sphere; graceful curving roundness

**round** (*adj*) circular; ring- or ball-shaped

**sagittate** (*adj*) shaped like an arrowhead

**scalloped** (*adj*) having a border formed by a continuous series of circle segments or angular projections

**scroll** spiral, rolled, or convoluted form

**scutate** (*adj*) shield-shaped

**semicircle** half a circle

**serrate** (*adj*) notched or toothed along edge

**shape** specific external surface or outline of an object having a distinct form

**shell** upright concave shape, usu. hemispherical, often open horizontally

**sickle** curve in a half circle

**sigmoid** (*adj*) curved like the letter C; curved in two directions like the letter S

**solid** three-dimensional shape; (*adj*) three-dimensional

**spade** stylized spearhead shape used on playing cards

**spatulate** (*adj*) thin and flat like a spatula

**sphere** solid bounded by a surface on which all points are equidistant from a fixed central point; ball

**spherical** (*adj*) sphere-shaped

**spicate** (*adj*) arranged in the form of a spike

**spiral** three-dimensional curve generated by a point moving in one or more turns about an axis; (*adj*) winding around a fixed line in a series of planes; coiling around a center while receding from or approaching it; helical

**square** parallelogram with four equal sides and four right angles; (*adj*) having four equal sides and four right angles in plane figure

**star** figure with five or more points formed by overlapping triangles with common center

**stellate** (*adj*) star-shaped

**straight line** series of points arranged without angles; direct line between two points

**styliform** (*adj*) bristle-shaped

**switchback** zigzag arrangement

**tapering** (*adj*) becoming narrower at one end than the other

**terete** (*adj*) cylindrical or slightly tapering

**ternate** (*adj*) arranged in threes

**tetartohedral** (*adj*) having one-fourth the number of planes needed for symmetry

**tetrahedron** four-faced polyhedron

**toothed** (*adj*) having series of notches resembling teeth

**toroid** surface generated by a closed plane curve rotated about a line lying in the same plane as the curve but not crossing it

**toroidal** (*adj*) torus-shaped

**torus** doughnut-shaped surface

**trapezium** four-sided plane having no two sides parallel

**trapezoid** four-sided plane having two parallel sides

**trapezoidal** (*adj*) having the form of a trapezoid

**triangle** three-sided plane figure with three angles

**triangular** (*adj*) three-sided and plane

**trifoliate** (*adj*) having three lobes

**trifurcate** (*adj*) branching into three

**trihedral** (*adj*) having three faces

**trilateral** (*adj*) having three sides

**trochoid** curve generated by a point on the radius of a circle as the circle rolls on a fixed straight line

**truncated** (*adj*) having the end square or even

**tube** hollow, elongated cylinder, often flexible

**tubular** (*adj*) tube-shaped

**turtleback** raised, convexly arched surface

**unciform** (*adj*) hook-shaped

**uncinate** (*adj*) bent at the tip like a hook

**V** two equal line segments diverging upward at an acute angle from a point

**vermiculate** (*adj*) having irregular, thin, wavy lines like the trail of a worm

**villiform** (*adj*) closely set and resembling bristles or velvet pile

**virgate** (*adj*) shaped like a rod or wand

**volute** (*adj*) spiral- or scroll-shaped

**wheel** round, circular form

**whorl** something that whirls, coils, or spirals

**winding** (*adj*) describing a line that is curved, sinuous, or irregular

**worm** irregular spiral or tube; vermiculate; zigzag

**X** two crossed line segments, usu. of equal length

**zigzag** series of sharp, angular turns; switchback

# COLORS

White
Gray
Black
Brown
Reddish Brown
Red
Pink
Orange
Yellow
Green
Blue
Purple

**SEE ALSO**: Chap. 4: Physics; Chap. 14: Painting; Chap. 16: Graphic Design and Printing

The names of colors are often evocative or refer to an object in nature distinguished by a particular color or shade. While elaborate numbering systems based on hue and chroma exist to differentiate colors, actual definitions tend to be circular and self-referential (such as a greenish blue darker than teal and greener than aquamarine).

## WHITE

alabaster, argent
blond, bone
chalk, Chinese white, columbine
dove
eggshell
flake white
gauze
ivory
milk-white
nacre
off-white, oyster
pearl, platinum, pure white, putty
silver, snow
white
zinc white

## GRAY

ash
battleship
charcoal, cinder, cinereous, cloud
dark gray, dove
flint
granite, gray, greige
iron
lead, light gray
merle, moleskin, mouse, mushroom
neutral
obsidian
pale gray, pelican, plumbago

salt-and-pepper, silver gray, slate, smoke, steel
taupe

## BLACK

black, blue-black, Brunswick black
carbon
ebony
ink
jet
lampblack
pitch, pure black
raven
sable, soot

## BROWN

acorn, amber, anthracene, autumn leaf
beige, biscuit, bistre, brindle, bronze, brown, brunet, brunette,
  buff, burnt almond, burnt umber, butternut
café au lait, camel, Cologne brown
dark brown, doeskin, Dresden, dun
earth, ecru
fallow, fawn, fox
hazel
khaki
leather, light brown
manila, maple sugar, Mars brown, mink, mocha
negro, nougat, nutria
otter
peppercorn, pongee, putty
raffia, raw sienna, raw umber
sandalwood, seal
tan, tanaura, tawny, toast, topaz
umber
Vandyke brown
walnut

## REDDISH BROWN

auburn
baize, bay, brick, burgundy, burnt ocher, burnt sienna
caramel, Castilian brown, chestnut, chocolate, cinnamon,
  cocoa, cordovan
fulvous
ginger
henna
light red-brown, liver
mahogany
nutmeg
ocher, oxblood
piccolopasso
reddish brown, roan, russet
sand, sedge, sepia, sienna, sorrel
terra cotta, titian
Venetian red

## RED

alizarin crimson, alpenglow, annatto
blood-red, bois de rose, bougainvillea, Bourdeaux, brick red,
  brownish red

cadmium red, cardinal, carioca, carmine, carnelian, Castilian
  red, cerise, cherry, Chinese red, cinnabar, claret, cochineal,
  cranberry, crimson, crimson lake
damask, dark red
faded rose, fire-engine red
garnet, geranium, grenadine, gules
Indian red, iron red
jockey
light red, lobster
madder lake, maroon, Mars red, murrey
orange-red
paprika, peach, Persian red, pinkish red, ponceau, poppy,
  Prussian red, puce
red, rhodamine, rose madder, ruby, rust
scarlet, stammel, strawberry
tile red
Venetian red, vermilion
wild cherry, wine

## PINK

begonia, blush
cameo, carnation, casino pink, coral
deep pink
fiesta, flamingo
hot pink
incarnadine
livid pink
mallow pink, melon, moonlight
nymph
ombre, orchid rose
pale pink, peach, petal pink, pink
reddish pink, rose, royal pink
salmon, shell pink, shocking pink
tea rose

## ORANGE

apricot, aurora
burnt Roman ocher
cadmium orange, carotene, carrot, chrome orange, copper
dark orange
helianthin, hyacinth
mandarin, marigold, mikado
ocher, orange
pale orange, pumpkin
realgar, red-orange, Rubens' madder
Spanish ocher
tangerine, terra cotta
yellow-orange

## YELLOW

amber, auramine, aureolin, azo yellow
barium yellow, blond, brass, brazen, brazilin, buff, butter
cadmium yellow, calendula, canary, Cassel yellow, chalcedony,
  chamois, champagne, chrome yellow, citron, corn, cream,
  crocus
dandelion
flax
gamboge, gold, goldenrod, green-yellow
honey

Indian yellow
jonquil
lemon, linen
maize, mustard
Naples yellow
orange-yellow, orpiment
pale yellow, palomino, pear, primrose, purree
quince
reed
saffron, safranine, sallow, sand, snapdragon, straw, sulphur,
   sunflower
wheaten
yellow, yellow ocher, yolk

## GREEN

absinthe, aqua, avocado
bay, beryl, bice, blue-green, brewster, Brunswick green
cadmium green, celadon, chartreuse, chrome green, clair de
   lune, corbeau, cucumber, cypress
dark green, drake
emerald
fir green, flagstone, forest green
grass, gray-green, green, gunpowder
holly
jade
kelly green, Kendal green
leaf, light green, lime, Lincoln green, lizard, loden, lotus
malachite, marine, mint, moss, myrtle
Niagara green, Nile green
olive
pale green, parrot, patina, pea green, pistachio green
reseda
sea green, serpentine, shamrock, spruce
teal, terre verte, tourmaline, turquoise
verdigris, viridian
willow green
yellow-green, yew

## BLUE

aquamarine, azure
baby blue, blue, blueberry, bluebonnet
calamine blue, cerulean, cobalt blue, copenhagen blue,
   cornflower, cyan
delft blue, Dresden blue
flag blue
gentian, greenish blue
havana lake, helvetia blue, huckleberry, hydrangea
ice blue, Indanthrene, indigo
jouvence
lapis lazuli, light blue, lucerne, lupine
marine, midnight blue, milori
napoleon blue, navy blue
pale blue, peacock blue, powder blue, Prussian blue,
   purple-blue
reddish blue, royal blue
saxe blue, sea blue, sky blue, smalt, steel blue
teal blue
ultramarine
Venetian blue
water blue, Wedgwood blue, wisteria, woad
zaffer

## PURPLE

amaranth, amethyst, Argyle, aubergine
blue-violet, bluish purple, bokhara
campanula, clematis
dahlia, damson, deep purple
fuchsia
grape, gridelin
heliotrope, hyacinth
imperial purple
lavender, light purple, lilac
magenta, mauve, monsignor, mulberry
orchid
pale purple, pansy, periwinkle, phlox, plum, prune, purple
raisin, raspberry, reddish purple, royal purple, rubine
solferino
tulip, Tyrian purple
violet, violetta

---

# VERBS OF THOUGHT

Thinking, Judgment, and Consideration
Reasoning and Examination
Learning and Memory
Knowledge and Understanding
Belief and Conception

**SEE ALSO:** Chap. 23: Reasoning and Intuition; Judgment and
   Criticism

## THINKING, JUDGMENT, AND CONSIDERATION

**appraise**  estimate the nature or merit of
**assess**  appraise, judge
**assume**  suppose to be true
**attend**  consider, give heed to
**attitudinize**  form opinion
**brainstorm**  (n) sudden idea; exchange ideas with others to
   stimulate creative thinking
**brood**  meditate quietly; ponder moodily, think persistently
   about
**browse**  consider casually
**chew over**  mull, think over at length
**cogitate**  meditate, ponder hard
**concentrate**  focus one's thoughts
**conceptualize**  think about, interpret
**conjecture**  conclude or suppose from scant evidence; surmise, guess
**consider**  think about carefully
**contemplate**  meditate on, consider thoroughly with deep
   attention
**count**  consider
**decide**  arrive at conclusion or solution
**dope out**  Slang. figure out
**dwell on**  linger over in thought
**engross**  occupy the mind or attention completely
**entertain**  take into consideration

773

**esteem**  consider or believe to be of a certain value; regard highly

**estimate**  guess extent of, conjecture about

**figure**  regard, consider

**fret**  worry, brood

**gather**  conclude from observation or hints

**gauge**  estimate, judge

**grope**  search for answer or comprehension

**guess**  arrive at a conclusion by intuition and without sufficient evidence; surmise; conjecture about accurately

**hazard**  guess, estimate

**heed**  pay attention to, mind

**interpret**  construe in a certain way, conceive; explain the meaning of

**judge**  form an opinion of, esp. by weighing evidence

**look into**  consider, explore

**meditate**  think contemplatively; center one's thoughts; muse, reflect

**mind**  heed closely

**mull**  ponder at length

**muse**  reflect on something from all sides, often inconclusively

**note**  give careful attention to

**occupy one's thoughts**  totally engage one's mind

**occur**  come to mind

**opine**  form an opinion about

**outfox**  outsmart

**outguess**  anticipate another's plans or motives

**outsmart**  get the better of by thinking; outfox; outthink; outwit

**outthink**  excel in thinking; get the better of by thinking

**outwit**  get the better of by superior ingenuity and clever thinking; outsmart

**percolate**  penetrate; brood over

**perpend**  reflect on carefully

**ponder**  meditate on; consider quietly, deeply, and thoroughly

**predetermine**  decide on beforehand

**prejudge**  form an opinion prematurely

**premeditate**  consider or plan out before acting

**preoccupy**  engross to the exclusion of all else

**psych**  *Informal.* intimidate psychologically

**rack one's brain**  strain for solution

**read**  make out the significance of

**reappraise**  evaluate again

**reckon**  estimate; figure, assume

**reconsider**  consider again with a view toward change of decision or action

**reevaluate**  reconsider; appraise again

**reflect**  consider quietly

**regard**  take into account or consideration

**rethink**  consider again

**revise**  reconsider, change one's opinion

**revolve in one's mind**  mull over, consider at length

**ruminate**  ponder, muse; go over in one's mind repeatedly and slowly

**second-guess**  use hindsight to criticize or correct; predict

**select**  choose one over another

**simmer**  be in initial stages of consideration

**sink**  become deeply absorbed, as in thought

**size up**  appraise, evaluate, judge

**sleep on**  consider overnight

**speculate**  reflect or meditate on some subject; indulge in idle conjecture; guess, surmise

**stew**  *Informal.* brood over

**surmise**  guess; infer without strong evidence

**tackle**  think seriously about some problem

**take into account**  consider

**theorize**  speculate

**think**  employ one's powers of judgment or reason; consider; remember; ponder; occupy one's mind in reflection on

**think about**  consider

**turn over**  consider; revolve in one's mind

**view**  examine, survey, consider

**weigh**  consider carefully, evaluate

**wonder**  think or speculate curiously or doubtfully; ponder over

**worry**  fret; experience concern over

**wrestle with**  occupy oneself in serious thought about; consider all sides of; debate internally

## REASONING AND EXAMINATION

**abstract**  determine and summarize essentials; consider as general instance apart from specific examples

**adduce**  offer as evidence

**analyze**  subject to careful scrutiny

**arrive at**  conclude by reasoning

**attribute**  regard as based on or having specific meaning

**belabor**  apply unreasonable scrunity

**calculate**  consider logically and dispassionately

**canvass**  examine carefully in detail

**cast about**  contrive, plan

**cerebrate**  use reason, think about

**check**  test validity by examining closely

**check out**  examine and approve; consider carefully

**clarify**  make intelligible; free from confusion

**clear up**  explain so as to eliminate confusion; clarify

**compare**  examine for differences or similarities

**conclude**  determine or decide by reasoning

**construe**  analyze and explain

**contrast**  compare with something else

**convince**  prove by argument

**correlate**  determine and establish an orderly connection between two or more things

**crack**  puzzle out and resolve

**debate**  consider from all sides

**deduce**  infer or conclude by reasoning from something known or assumed

**deliberate**  consider carefully and thoroughly

**derive**  infer, deduce

**diagnose**  analyze to determine the cause of

**dig into**  *Informal.* study, examine thoroughly

**dissect**  examine minutely in all component parts; analyze

**educe**  deduce from something undeveloped

**establish**  determine, prove

**evaluate**  study and determine value or amount of

**examine**  inspect or investigate carefully

**explore**  analyze, study, investigate

**figure**  calculate; conclude

**figure out**  solve, determine

**find out**  discover truth of by study or observation

**follow**  keep one's mind on, attend to

**hypothesize** make an assumption as premise in an argument

**infer** derive a logical conclusion from premise or evidence; guess, surmise

**inspect** examine critically

**integrate** bring together and unite information and thoughts into a coherent whole

**intellectualize** consider the rational content or form of

**interpolate** estimate unknown from known

**interpret** explain the meaning of; construe or conceive in a specific way

**investigate** examine closely and systematically

**metagrobolize** tackle a difficult or puzzling problem

**observe** examine carefully; consider from all sides

**penetrate** discover the true nature of by careful examination

**place** estimate the nature of; determine proper order or position of

**plumb** examine deeply, closely, and critically

**pore over** study attentively; meditate on intently

**probe** investigate thoroughly

**prove** establish the truth or accuracy of

**puzzle** exercise one's mind to understand something mysterious; attempt a solution by guesswork

**question** analyze, examine; doubt, dispute

**rationalize** consider logically; invent plausible reasons for

**reason** think logically so as to reach a conclusion

**redefine** clarify meaning; reexamine

**reduce** comprehend something complex by analyzing its component parts

**research** investigate thoroughly

**review** evaluate critically; examine or study again

**scrutinize** examine very closely

**search** look into carefully in an effort to find something hidden; examine

**sift through** separate and examine various possibilities

**solve** determine the answer to a problem

**sort out** examine and place in order

**strategize** plan carefully toward a specific end

**study** investigate carefully and in detail; think deeply, reflect on

**surmise** imagine; infer from scant information

**survey** inspect or consider comprehensively

**syllogize** reason by means of premises that support a logical conclusion; deduce

**synthesize** combine elements to reach a conclusion

**think over** evaluate from all sides for possible action

**think through** consider thoroughly and reach a conclusion

**trace** follow logically from beginning to end

**work out** devise or arrange by careful calculation

**work over** consider at length; examine thoroughly

## LEARNING AND MEMORY

**absorb** take in, learn

**acquaint oneself with** become familiar with, furnish oneself with knowledge about

**ascertain** discover, learn with assurance

**assimilate** absorb and comprehend

**bear in mind** remember, consider

**bethink oneself** think, consider; remind oneself; remember

**bone up** *Informal*. refresh one's memory; study intensely to assimilate quickly

**call to mind** remember

**catch on** grasp mentally, understand

**commit to memory** memorize

**digest** assimilate information; arrange methodically in the mind

**discover** gain knowledge of for the first time; realize

**evoke** call up or produce memories

**fix in one's mind** remember; settle on

**get wise** *Slang*. become informed

**glean** gather information slowly and patiently

**inquire into** investigate, seek information about

**learn** acquire information, knowledge, or understanding

**master** become adept through understanding and study

**memorize** learn exactly by rote; commit to memory

**pick up** learn; acquire understanding of through light study

**recall** remember

**recollect** remember

**remember** call back to the level of consciousness; think of again; retain in one's memory; recall; recollect

**reminisce** think about past experiences, often wistfully

**retain** hold in one's mind or memory

**sink in** have something penetrate one's mind

**soak up** absorb and fill one's mind with

**study** apply one's mental faculties so as to acquire knowledge

**summon up** recall, evoke

**take in** grasp the meaning of, comprehend; absorb

**wise up** *Slang*. learn or become aware of or knowledgeable about, esp. something unknown or known to others

## KNOWLEDGE AND UNDERSTANDING

**appreciate** be fully aware of nature or value of

**apprehend** understand, perceive

**collect one's thoughts** organize one's thinking

**comprehend** understand

**crystallize** give one's thoughts a definite form

**dawn on** begin to be perceived

**determine** resolve conclusively

**dig** *Slang*. understand; recognize

**discern** recognize or understand, esp. as distinct or different

**distill** determine the essence of

**distinguish** separate mentally; recognize as different

**familiarize** make known to oneself

**fathom** penetrate and understand thoroughly

**get at** penetrate, determine the truth of

**get it** *Informal*. understand

**grasp** comprehend

**grok** *Slang*. understand, comprehend

**identify** determine the particular nature or identity of; recognize

**ken** *Scottish*. recognize, know

**know** perceive clearly with certainty; recognize, be acquainted with; understand the nature of; be convinced of

**make out** decipher meaning of, comprehend

**perceive** become aware of; gain understanding of

**pierce** see into and understand against resistance

**prehend** apprehend

**realize** understand clearly or fully, apprehend

**recognize** perceive clearly, realize to be real or true; identify from past experience

**resolve** reach conclusion or solution

**savvy** *Informal.* understand, catch on to

**see** perceive, comprehend

**see through** recognize the true nature of

**sense** become aware of; comprehend, grasp

**suss out** *Chiefly Brit. slang.* reach an understanding of; figure out

**understand** grasp the idea or meaning of; comprehend

## BELIEF AND CONCEPTION

**believe** have confidence in the truth of without proof; hold an opinion

**buy** *Informal.* believe or accept

**conceive** originate, imagine

**concoct** originate, fabricate, conceive

**conjure up** imagine or contrive as if by magic

**contrive** fabricate, invent

**create** conceive, originate; imagine

**daresay** believe or assume to be probable

**deem** believe; hold as an opinion

**divine** discover or perceive intuitively, not by reason

**dream** fantasize or imagine; consider as a remote possibility

**dream up** conceive or devise an idea or plan

**envisage** have a mental picture of

**envision** imagine, picture to oneself

**evoke** re-create from memory or imagination; conjure up

**expect** imagine; suppose

**fabricate** conceive, create, concoct

**fancy** form a conception of; believe without assurance

**fantasize** imagine; dream

**feel** believe, think

**find** feel; discover

**foresee** know beforehand, esp. by intuition

**harbor** maintain a thought or feeling about

**hatch** conceive or concoct an idea or plan

**have a hunch** guess, intuit

**hold** believe, have an opinion

**ideate** form an idea or thought; conceive

**imagine** form mental image or notion of; guess or conjecture; create

**incline** lean toward one view or plan of action

**incubate** hatch; give form to an idea

**intuit** understand or know without rational thought; feel

**invent** imagine, contrive

**make up** conceive, imagine, devise

**moon** indulge in dreams over

**opine** hold an opinion on; suppose

**originate** conceive, create

**picture** envision in one's mind, imagine

**preconceive** form an opinion in advance without real knowledge

**prefigure** picture or imagine beforehand

**presume** assume or suppose to be true as a matter of fact

**realize** become fully aware of; conceive of

**reify** ascribe concrete qualities to an abstraction

**rely on** believe, trust

**suppose** assume, often for the sake of argument

**suspect** believe to be true or likely

**take it** assume, imagine

**tend** pay heed to; exhibit disposition toward

**think up** imagine, contrive, devise

**trust** believe

**visualize** envision or form a mental image of

**weave** form by elaborate combining of elements into a connected whole

# REASONING AND INTUITION

Reason and Rationale
Order, Hierarchy, and Systems
Intuition and Imagination

**SEE ALSO:** Chap. 13: Philosophy; Chap. 13: Education; Chap. 22: Strategy, Intrigue, and Deception; Chap. 23: Verbs of Thought; Chap. 23: Judgment and Criticism; Chap. 25: Truth, Wisdom, and Spiritual Attainment

## REASON AND RATIONALE

**adduce** (*vb*) bring forward, cite, allege

**analogy** inference derived from likeness between two or more things

**analysis** systematic separation and examination of parts

**antithesis** contrast or opposition, esp. of ideas or argument in dialectic process

**apologia** reasoned defense or justification

**apprehension** understanding

**argument** chain or sequence of reasons leading to conclusion

**assumption** statement accepted as true before being proved

**axiom** generally accepted truth or principle

**biconditional** (*adj*) pertaining to the relation between two statements that is valid only when both are true or false

**brainstorm** (*vb*) engage in a session of energetic thinking, often in a group; (*n*) sudden valuable idea

**circumscribe** (*vb*) define clearly

**clarification** something that reduces confusion or makes an issue understandable

**clincher** final, irrefutable statement that wins an argument

**cogent** (*adj*) compelling, persuasive; relevant

**cogitation** deep thinking

**cognition** process of knowing or gaining knowledge, esp. intellectual process

**cognitive** (*adj*) involving the acquisition of knowledge

**coherent** (*adj*) logically clear and consistent

**comprehension** intellectual understanding, mental grasp

**conception** ability and process of forming ideas

**confutation** refutation of an argument

**conjecture** inference, guess

**construe** (*vb*) explain, interpret; understand

**contend** (*vb*) argue, contest

**contest** (*vb*) challenge, attempt to refute

**contradiction** assertion of contrary statement; opposition

**contradistinction** distinction by contrast or opposition

**contraposition** antithesis, opposition

**controvert** (*vb*) dispute, deny, contradict, contest

**convention** general agreement in principle

**convince** (*vb*) prevail in argument, persuade

**correct** (*vb*) remove errors, rectify; (*adj*) factual, true

**counterexample** example that refutes another statement

**counterproposal** alternative proposal made after rejecting initial proposal

**criterion** measure or standard of judgment

**crux** central or decisive point in argument

**cumulative** (*adj*) increasing by successive additions; tending to lead to the same conclusion

**cut-and-dried** (*adj*) done according to routine, formula, or set plan

**data** facts or information; material providing grounds for discussion

**datum** given fact on which argument or premise is based or from which conclusion may be drawn

**debate** (*vb*) dispute, deliberate; examine question or issue verbally; (*n*) formal argument or discussion of opposing views

**deduction** reasoning process that proceeds from general to particular

**define** (*vb*) determine or describe in specific terms

**definition** formal statement or explanation of meaning

**definitive** (*adj*) conclusive; most reliable or complete

**delimit** (*vb*) set boundaries or limits

**demystify** (*vb*) explain clearly so as to remove confusion

**determine** (*vb*) define, settle, fix, ascertain, limit

**dialectic** art or practice of logical discussion, esp. in investigating truth of a theory or opinion

**didactic** (*adj*) instructive, pertaining to teaching

**differentiate** (*vb*) distinguish; mark or perceive differences

**discursive reasoning** reasoning that draws inferences from logical thought patterns

**disjunction** separation into elements

**disprove** (*vb*) refute

**dispute** (*vb*) contend, argue

**disquisition** formal inquiry or discourse

**dissect** (*vb*) analyze

**dissertation** disquisition, discussion; essay

**egghead** *Informal.* intellectual person, often with pretentious manner

**epistemic** (*adj*) concerning knowledge

**esemplastic** (*adj*) capable of shaping diverse elements into a unified whole

**examination** thorough, detailed investigation or study

**excogitate** (*vb*) think out, contrive

**explicate** (*vb*) interpret, explain

**expostulate** (*vb*) reason earnestly, usu. against something

**extrapolate** (*vb*) infer an unknown from something that is known

**fact** something known to be true or real

**facultative** (*adj*) relating to mental activity or capacity

**fallacy** false idea, error in reasoning

**forensic** (*adj*) pertaining to argumentation

**forethought** premeditation

**generalization** general inference derived from particular

**gist** essential point of argument or story

**grasp** comprehension

**hypothesis** unproved assumption for debate or discussion; proposition

**idea** concept, mental impression, or notion

**ideation** process of forming ideas or images

**ignoratio elenchi** *Latin.* lit. ignorance of proof; type of fallacy using irrelevant proof

**implausible** (*adj*) not particularly believable

**implication** something implied or suggested as naturally inferred or understood

**induction** reasoning process that proceeds from particular to general

**inference** logical conclusion drawn from premise

**information** knowledge, data

**intellect** mental faculty for knowing, judging, perceiving, and reasoning

**intellection** intellectual activity

**intellectualize** (*vb*) seek or consider rational content or form of; apply reason and ignore emotional or psychological significance of

**interpretation** explanation of meaning

**irrelevant** (*adj*) not pertinent, immaterial

**ken** (*vb*) *Scottish.* know, discern

**last word** conclusive point in discussion

**logic** method of sound reasoning that relates sequence of facts, events, or notions

**lucid** (*adj*) clearly expressed

**middle ground** reasonable position between extremes

**moot** (*adj*) open to discussion or debate; irrelevant to an issue in debate

**notion** idea, proposition, theory

**nub** point, gist

**perception** capacity for comprehension; keen mental faculty or observation

**perspicacious** (*adj*) endowed with keen mental perception

**perspicuous** (*adj*) presented in clear and precise manner

**pertinence** relevance to the matter at hand

**polemic** controversial argument; person who argues in opposition to another

**position** point of view; statement of proposition or thesis

**postulate** hypothesis assumed as basis for line of reasoning

**prehension** mental understanding

**premise** something assumed as basis for argument or position

**proposition** anything stated for consideration or discussion or to be proved

**proviso** conditional stipulation

**ratiocination** process of careful, precise reasoning

**ratio cognoscendi** *Latin.* lit. grounds of knowledge; grounds by which something is known

**rational** (*adj*) conforming to reason

**rationale** fundamental reason, basis, or explanation

**reason** power to form logical conclusions and sound judgments

**reasoning** orderly use of mental faculties to reach conclusions and draw inferences

**reductionism** simplification of a complex concept, phenomenon, or issue, esp. oversimplification or distortion

**reflection** careful consideration of something

**refutation** use of evidence to prove something false

**relation** connection between things that belong or function together

**riddle** cleverly puzzling or confounding question

**rumination** extended meditation; going over of something in one's mind

**sophistry** deceptive or fallacious reasoning

**sound reasoning** valid thinking

**specious** (*adj*) unsound though appearing to be true

**speculation** assumption of truth based on insufficient evidence

**standard** criterion for judgment; established rule or measure

**statement** proposition, presentation of point

**sticky wicket** *Chiefly Brit.* difficult problem requiring sound reasoning for solution

**stipulation** specific, essential condition or accepted point

**syncretism** reconciliation of conflicting beliefs or forms

**synthesis** combining of disparate elements into a whole

**tangent** sudden change or digression in reasoning process

**tenable** (*adj*) defensible; reasonable

**theorem** proposition that can be drawn from premises or is part of general theory

**theory** coherent series of plausible propositions that serve as explanation for something

**thesis** position or proposition set forth for proof or argument

**thought** act or process of thinking; cogitation; reasoning power

**thought-out** (*adj*) derived by careful mental consideration

**thrust** essential element or principal goal of argument

**treatise** systematic exposition of essentials of argument and its conclusion

**unilateral** (*adj*) one-sided, imbalanced

**viable** (*adj*) having likely chance of working

**watertight** (*adj*) flawless; having no possibility of evasion or misunderstanding

**well-founded** (*adj*) based on sound or valid reasoning

**well-grounded** (*adj*) having a sound basis or foundation

**well-taken** (*adj*) justified, based in truth or fact

**wit** mental soundness or ability, esp. facility for making unusual connections and brief, clever expressions

## ORDER, HIERARCHY, AND SYSTEMS

**agenda** outline or list of things to be considered

**antecedent** conditional element in proposition

**antinomy** contradiction or opposition between two apparently true statements

**aperçu** *French.* brief outline or summary

**aspect** particular phase or light in which something is viewed

**basis** principal component of something; essential condition

**breakdown** classification into categories

**canon** system of rules or laws; body of criteria and standards

**case** set of circumstances or conditions

**case history** recorded details and past, used for analysis

**catalog** list, register of items arranged systematically

**category** specific division within classification system

**catena** chain or sequence of linked things, events

**chain** sequence of connected things, events

**check** criterion used for testing or evaluation

**circular reasoning** reasoning involving unproved conclusion of argument as proof

**class** large, inclusive set sharing common characteristics

**classification** systematic arrangement into classes, groups, or categories with specific characteristics

**clause** particular section

**codify** (*vb*) organize systematically

**coherence** logical or natural consistency

**cohesion** unity, coherence

**collate** (*vb*) place in order; compare critically

**collateral** (*adj*) corresponding, esp. in parallel sequence; secondary

**colligation** bringing together of separate facts under unifying principle, idea, or theme

**columniation** organization of material into rows and columns

**comparison** examination of two or more items to determine similarities and differences

**compartmentalize** (*vb*) separate into distinct categories

**compendium** collection of information; brief summary of larger work

**component** element or facet

**comprise** (*vb*) constitute; include within scope; be made up of

**concatenation** connected series or chain

**concinnity** harmony or elegance of structure

**condition** something that defines, limits, or changes a more general case or set

**connection** causal or logical relation between objects or ideas

**consecutive** (*adj*) in order

**consequence** inference or logical conclusion; result

**construct** something organized or structured by mental activity

**content analysis** classification and evaluation of material to determine its meaning or likely effect

**continuity** unbroken connection or succession

**continuum** consistent series or whole, esp. sequence progressing by small gradations

**convention** standard rule or practice

**corollary** one proposition that is proved incidentally by another

**correlative** (*adj*) related as reciprocal proofs

**correspondence** relation by similarity or congruence

**course** usual procedure; progression in steps

**delineate** (*vb*) outline; set forth in precise detail

**design** arrangement of elements or details

**dichotomy** division into two mutually exclusive or contradictory parts

**division** distinct group forming portion of larger group

**doctrine** basic principle in branch of knowledge or belief system

**domino effect** cumulative effect that results when one action initiates a series of events

**element** basic constituent part

**example** single instance that shows character of larger set

**explicit** (*adj*) fully demonstrated, expressed, or explained

**extrinsic** (*adj*) external; inessential, not part of

**facet** element, aspect, component

**feedback** automatic furnishing of data from the output of a system or process and evaluation of such information by a control device to shape future output

**flow chart** diagram using symbols to display step-by-step procedure or system

**form** distinguishing shape or component; established method of proceeding; formula

**formula** standard statement; general fact or rule

**framework** basic underlying structure or plan

**full circle** series of developments that return to source, original position, or opposite position

**fundamental** minimum determining aspect or part of something

**go/no-go** (*adj*) requiring a decision to continue or halt

**gradation** arrangement in levels or stages; single level within such a series

**grade** level within hierarchy

**gradient** measure of rate of change

**grid** network of evenly spaced horizontals and perpendiculars; any system so organized

**hierarchy** organization into a branching or ranked structure

**hyponym** term used to denote subcategory of a more general class

**increment** something added, esp. very small amount or series of regular successive additions

**index** list of specific data or items, usu. arranged alphabetically

**infrastructure** basic, underlying framework or feature of an organizational system

**instance** example, case; one stage viewed as part of process

**interconnectedness** cohesive relation between elements

**interface** point at which independent systems meet and interact

**interlocking** (*adj*) connected, interrelated

**interpenetration** mutual penetration between two things

**intrinsic** (*adj*) essential to nature of system or object

**jigsaw** complex, intricate puzzle

**juxtapose** (*vb*) place side by side

**key** guide providing explanation to system and its symbols

**knot** cluster of things together

**labyrinth** something extremely complex in structure; maze

**lattice** network of elements or design organized in crossed pattern like a matrix

**level** grade or rank within structure

**limit** point or number that may not be exceeded

**linear** (*adj*) proceeding logically or sequentially in a straight line

**list** meaningful sequence of items

**logistics** detailed planning, implementation, and coordination of an operation, esp. military

**matrix** arrangement of elements into rows and columns

**maze** confusing, intricate network; labyrinth

**method** systematic procedure or mode of inquiry in a field or discipline

**model** structural design for system or object

**moiré** irregular, wavy pattern

**morphology** science of structure, form, and patterns

**network** interlocking or interconnected system

**nexus** connection; connected group or series

**nomenclature** system of terms and symbols for describing something

**non sequitur** *Latin*. lit. it does not follow; inference or conclusion that does not follow logically from premises or evidence

**norm** average, standard

**offshoot** collateral branch; secondary element

**order** arrangement or sequence of things or events; category, class, rank, or level

**ordonnance** arrangement or disposition of parts, esp. of artistic creation

**organization** act or process of arranging systematically into logical or consistent form

**outline** hierarchical organization of material; summary; plan

**paradigm** model, example

**paradox** statement, belief, or idea apparently contrary to truth, reality or itself, but actually possible or true

**parameter** limit or boundary; characteristic defining element

**partition** division into constituent elements

**patchwork** organization into an interconnected network

**pattern** coherent design or arrangement of parts

**pertinent** (*adj*) essential, basic, or relevant

**plan** design; detailed program; orderly arrangement of parts

**point** most important element of argument, story, or line of reasoning

**position** order or place within structure or hierarchy

**position paper** detailed report advising plan of action on given issue

**precedent** established standard or rule

**précis** concise summary of essential points or facts

**premise** proposition previously proved or assumed; basis for argument

**prerequisite** something required before proceeding to the next level

**principium** *Latin*. lit. that which is first; fundamental principle

**principle** comprehensive, fundamental law or assumption

**probability** chance or likelihood that given event or result will occur

**qualitative** (*adj*) pertaining to the essence or inherent nature or character

**quantitative** (*adj*) measuring an exact or specified amount or quantity

**random** (*adj*) without order or sequence

**rank** (*vb*) organize into hierarchy of relative positions; (*n*) position in such a hierarchy

**reciprocal** (*adj*) shared by or affecting both sides equally

**reference** definitive source of information relating to something

**relative** (*adj*) associated, relevant; referring or connected to another thing

**relevant** (*adj*) having importance to the matter at hand; providing conclusive evidence

**reticulate** (*vb*) divide, arrange, or mark into network

**rudiment** basic principle or element

**salient** (*adj*) prominent, conspicuous

**section** separate part or portion

**sector** distinctive portion of larger system, esp. one bounded by specific lines

**sequence** continuous, connected series

**sequitur** *Latin*. lit. it follows; conclusion, consequence

**set** number of things with common characteristics classed together

**side effect** secondary response, often adverse

**sift** (*vb*) separate out or sort

**skeleton** structural framework

**solution** explanation or answer; process of finding answer or resolving problem

**spectrum** continuous sequence or range

**spider web** complex network of interconnected elements

**step** one stage in process; grade or rank in scale

**step-by-step** (*adj*) taken in proper sequence, one at a time

**stratagem** cleverly contrived scheme or plan, esp. to surprise, deceive, or gain advantage over an adversary

**strategy** detailed plan or method for obtaining specific goal

**structure** defined organizational pattern or arrangement

**structuring** act of forming something according to a structure

**subcategory** division of category within structure

**subdivision** smaller set within larger set forming division of whole

**subset** set each of whose components is part of a larger, inclusive set

**subsidiary** secondary part ranked lower in hierarchy

**succession** sequence; process of following in order

**sui generis** *Latin.* lit. of his, her, or its own kind; constituting a class unto itself

**summary** concise, general description of larger argument or system

**superstructure** overlying framework or extension built on top of or added to basic structure

**switchery** network

**syndetic** (*adj*) connective; interconnected

**synoptic** (*adj*) characterized by general overview; pertaining to a brief or condensed statement

**syntax** connected, organized system; harmonious placement of parts, esp. linguistic

**system** interacting or interdependent combination of things forming unified whole

**systemic** (*adj*) relating to or common to a particular system

**tactics** strategy, esp. careful or devious planning and maneuvering to gain advantage

**template** model or pattern for duplicating existing object or system

**test** critical evaluation to prove or disprove; criterion for such evaluation

**thread of an argument** course or outline of ideas expressed

**track** course or sequence of argument or discussion

**train of thought** course of argument, discussion, or reasoning

**tree** branching hierarchical structure

**trusswork** latticelike network of interconnected elements

**unity** state of being complete in itself or combining with others to form a whole

**vicious circle** chain of events in which each response generates a new problem

**warp and woof** foundation composed of interlocking elements

**web** complex network; spider web

**well-ordered** (*adj*) organized into logical and coherent form

**workable** (*adj*) capable of functioning properly

**wrinkle** change in traditional or routine procedure or method

## INTUITION AND IMAGINATION

**air castle** castle in the air

**aperçu** *French.* sudden intuitive insight

**caprice** sudden, unpredictable, apparently unmotivated idea

**castle in the air** daydream; impractical idea; air castle

**chimerical** (*adj*) imaginary; visionary; wildly fanciful

**clairvoyance** ability to perceive matters beyond one's senses; precognition; second sight

**collective unconscious** genetically determined part of unconscious common to all members of one race or people

**common sense** sound practical judgment not based on reasoning or special knowledge

**conation** impulse or tendency to act with resolution

**conceit** fanciful idea or thought

**conception** inception and understanding of ideas and abstractions

**concoction** fabrication, fanciful creation

**conjecture** guess; speculation

**conjuring** imagining or contriving ideas

**creation** act of making, imagining, or inventing something new

**creativity** ability to imagine and make new or original forms, ideas, or things, esp. by transcending traditional thinking

**daydream** wishful product of one's imagination

**delirium** hallucinatory, visionary mental disturbance

**dream** visionary product of one's unconscious imagination

**eidolon** ideal; phantom of imagination

**enchantment** state of imaginative rapture

**ESP** extrasensory perception

**extrasensory perception** ESP; ability to perceive another's thoughts or things beyond one's normal senses

**fabrication** creation, invention, or construction

**fabulous** (*adj*) being the product of imagination

**fancy** whim, notion

**fantastical** (*adj*) conceived by unrestrained imagination

**fantasy** creation of unrealistic images and dreams; caprice

**feeling** intuitive sense separate from rational process

**fiction** creation or invention of the imagination

**figment** something invented or contrived

**flash** sudden intuitive perception

**flight of fancy** extravagant indulgence in whim and imagination

**guess** opinion not based on specific evidence

**hallucination** fantastic, unrealistic vision or impression

**haptic** (*adj*) denoting one who draws primarily on cutaneous sense data and tactile experience

**humor** sudden, inexplicable whim or notion

**hunch** strong intuitive feeling about future

**idea** newly formulated or original thought or notion

**idealization** overestimation of something in its ultimate, perfected form

**illusion** misapprehension, hallucination, or misleading image

**image** mental representation of something not present

**imagination** creative faculty to produce mental images of things not present, previously unknown, or suggestive of something stored in memory

**implicit** (*adj*) unexpressed but essential to nature of something

**impression** distinct image of something; reaction

**impulse** sudden, spontaneous inclination or idea

**ingenuity** skill and cleverness in conception or design

**innovation** new way of doing or viewing something

**insight** clear, deep perception

**inspiration** power of arousing intellect or emotions, esp. to receive or conceive new insights or ideas; such a new insight or idea

**instinct** perceptions or impulses coming from below the conscious mental level; natural aptitude or faculty

**intimation** indirect or subtle communication of idea

**intuition** direct knowledge or insight independent of any reasoning process

**invention** creation, fabrication, contrivance

**juice** essence, strength, or vitality

**make-believe** fancy, daydream, illusion

**mind's eye** inner eye that provides the ability to conceive of or remember imaginary scenes

**myth** fanciful, usu. traditional, imaginary tale serving as basis for commonly held belief

**mythopoeia** creation of myths

**notion** one's opinion or view of something, often fanciful or vague; personal theory, whim, or inclination

**novelty** innovation, fresh idea

**passing fancy** notion or whim held briefly

**perception** awareness of one's environment, esp. recognition by intuition or senses

**phantasm** fantasy, illusion, figment of imagination

**phantasmagoria** constantly shifting, hallucinatory succession of images

**precognition** clairvoyance

**premonition** intuitive anticipation of an event without reason; presentiment

**presentiment** premonition

**pretend** (*adj*) make-believe or imagined

**psychic sense** sensitivity to immaterial or supernatural powers and influences

**quixotism** capricious, impractical devotion to ideals and dreams

**rapture** powerful experience involving heightened perception and sensations, as of another sphere of existence

**reverie** daydream; state of being lost in thought

**second sight** clairvoyance

**sixth sense** extraordinary intuitive power of perception beyond the five senses; intuition

**spark** something that ignites one's imagination or thoughts

**speculation** conjectural consideration of a matter; guess; surmise

**surmise** conjecture; speculation

**telepathy** extrasensory communication from one mind to another, as by ESP

**theory** imaginative but unverifiable speculation serving as explanation for something

**vagary** erratic or unpredictable action or idea

**visile** (*adj*) denoting one who draws primarily on visual data and input

**vision** perception with one's imagination; extraordinary or vivid discernment or insight; supernatural appearance that provides insight

**visualization** ability to imagine or conceive

**whim** sudden, unusual, or capricious notion or thought

**whimsy** imaginative, playful, and fantastic creation; whim or caprice

**wishful thinking** unrealistic dream; ascribing reality to one's hopes and wishes

# JUDGMENT AND CRITICISM

Judgments and Critiques
Approval, Respect, and Recognition
Support, Encouragement, and Agreement
Praise, Exaltation, Flattery, and Applause
Disapproval, Disrespect, and Denial
Opposition, Disagreement, and Attack
Blame, Censure, Ridicule, and Contempt

**SEE ALSO:** Chap. 11: Law; Chap. 19: Verbs of Speech; Chap. 20: Insults, Slurs, and Epithets; Terms of Endearment and Respect; Chap. 23: Verbs of Thought

## JUDGMENTS AND CRITIQUES

**adjudge** (*vb*) deem; decide, rule upon, sentence

**analysis** critical evaluation of whole or parts

**appraise** (*vb*) estimate value, worth, or significance

**arbitration** act of hearing and determining the outcome of a controversy by a mediator

**argue** (*vb*) give reasons pro and con

**assess** (*vb*) form opinion of, appraise

**attitude** mental position, feeling toward something

**auto-da-fé** pronouncement of judgment

**candor** forthrightness; lack of prejudice

**censor** supervisor of morals and conduct; official who passes judgment on material

**chord** individual feeling or reaction

**commentary** explanation and evaluation, usu. written

**conclusion** reasoned determination or inference

**consensus** general or unanimous agreement; majority of opinion

**contention** point put forth in argument or debate

**criticism** act of passing judgment as to the merits of anything; faultfinding; analysis and evaluation of a literary or artistic work or performance; critique

**criticize** (*vb*) consider and assess merits of; find fault with

**critique** critical evaluation; usu. written; review

**decide** (*vb*) reach choice or pass judgment

**decision** resolution reached after consideration; conclusion, judgment

**deem** (*vb*) judge; hold an opinion of

**designate** (*vb*) indicate or choose for specific purpose

**discretion** personal choice or judgment; ability to form free and responsible decisions

**discriminate** (*vb*) distinguish between, exercise selective judgment

**disposed** (*adj*) inclined, tending toward or against

**distinguish** (*vb*) discern a difference; separate from others

**editorial** expression of opinion on some subject, esp. in newspaper

**estimation** opinion, judgment

**evaluate** (*vb*) assess, form opinion on

**forejudge** (*vb*) prejudge

**frame of reference** point of view, basis for judgment

**free will** exercise of free or voluntary choice or decision

**gauge** (*vb*) estimate, judge

**guess** (*vb*) estimate; reach opinion with little evidence

**hairsplitting** making overly fine distinctions; quibbling

**inclination** disposition, esp. favorable; slant

**intercede** (*vb*) intervene to reconcile conflict

**judge** (*vb*) form an opinion through careful deliberation

**judgment** pronouncement of one's opinion; process or capacity for forming opinions

**judicious** (*adj*) having or exercising sound judgment

**misjudge** (*vb*) form an unjust or mistaken opinion

**misread** (*vb*) misinterpret, judge incorrectly

**notice** critical review

**opine** (*vb*) form, hold, or express opinion

**opinion** point of view, appraisal of particular matter

**option**  power or freedom to choose or make independent judgment

**outlook**  point of view, opinion

**overlook** (*vb*) inspect and examine so as to reach judgment on

**partiality**  bias, predisposition

**parti pris**  *French.* preconceived prejudice or bias

**partisan**  adherent to cause, supporter of point of view

**pass** (*vb*) render favorable judgment or verdict

**pass judgment**  express firm, irrevocable opinion

**peremptory** (*adj*) allowing no contradiction, precluding all debate

**point of view**  opinion; position from or manner in which something is considered or appraised; viewpoint

**position**  firm point of view or opinion on something

**preconception**  opinion formed without knowledge or experience

**predisposed** (*adj*) inclined in advance, pro or con

**prejudge** (*vb*) form opinion in advance; forejudge

**prepossession**  prejudice or opinion formed beforehand, esp. favorable one

**rank** (*vb*) determine relative value or position of

**rate** (*vb*) set value of; assign rank to

**reconsider** (*vb*) assess previous judgment and form new opinion

**referee** (*vb*) arbitrate as judge; (n) one who so arbitrates

**regard** (*vb*) consider and appraise from one point of view

**reservation**  exception; act of withholding

**reserve judgment**  defer opinion until later time

**review** (*vb*) provide critical analysis, esp. written or broadcast

**second thoughts**  reservations about previous position or judgment

**sentence**  formal judgment arrived at by deliberation, esp. in court of law and specifying punishment

**sentiment**  judgment based on feeling; opinion

**settle** (*vb*) decide, resolve conclusively

**slant**  personal opinion, point of view

**snap** (*adj*) designating judgment reached hastily and without deliberation

**sound judgment**  reasonable opinions free of error

**speculate** (*vb*) form or express opinion without knowledge of subject

**suppose** (*vb*) hold as one's opinion; think likely to be true

**surmise** (*vb*) infer on scant grounds; conjecture

**tendency**  leaning in one direction

**think better of**  reconsider

**turn the tables**  reverse relative positions of opposing parties

**two cents worth**  opinion offered on topic being discussed

**umpire** (*vb*) wield authority to resolve disputes; (n) one who has such authority

**unbiased** (*adj*) fair, free from prejudice

**undercurrent**  concealed viewpoint or feeling, esp. opposite of that expressed

**vacillate** (*vb*) hesitate or waver in opinions

**value judgment**  opinion as to worth of something

**vantage point**  point of view, position

**verdict**  opinion based on evidence

**vet** (*vb*) appraise, verify, or check

**view**  opinion or judgment on something

**viewpoint**  position from which or basis on which judgment is made; point of view

**vote** (*vb*) state one's opinion, esp. express formal opinion in political process

**will**  disposition, inclination

**winnow** (*vb*) separate useful from useless elements

## APPROVAL, RESPECT, AND RECOGNITION

**accept** (*vb*) approve of, admit to; recognize as true

**acknowledge** (*vb*) recognize as rightful or genuine; state agreement with

**admire** (*vb*) regard with approval and respect

**appreciate** (*vb*) recognize value of; hold in high esteem

**approbation**  approval, esp. formal approval

**approval**  ratification; favorable opinion

**approve** (*vb*) express favorable opinion; give formal consent

**begrudge** (*vb*) view with reluctant approval

**bow** (*vb*) incline head or body in respect

**carte blanche**  full discretionary power; unconditional authority

**choose** (*vb*) select freely; have preference for

**cite** (*vb*) give credit to

**coddle** (*vb*) treat with extreme care

**command respect**  deserve and receive respect as one's due

**commemorate** (*vb*) honor memory by ceremony or observance

**compassion**  sympathetic awareness and concern for others' distress

**condone** (*vb*) pardon, excuse

**consideration**  esteem, regard; opinion based on matters taken into account

**coopt** (*vb*) assimilate as one's own

**cotton to** (*vb*) *Informal.* take a liking to

**countenance** (*vb*) extend approval, sanction

**credence**  mental acceptance as true

**credibility**  capacity for belief; ability to instill or evoke belief

**credit** (*vb*) consider favorably as source of action or possessor of trait

**cup of tea**  something one likes or is well-suited to

**curtsy**  slight dip of body and bending of knees as show of respect by women

**deference**  respect for another's wishes

**deserving** (*adj*) deemed worthy

**dignify** (*vb*) give distinction to, show respect for

**elect** (*vb*) choose or select, esp. by formal vote

**esteem**  high regard

**estimation**  esteem, honor

**exemplary** (*adj*) commendable, deserving imitation

**fancy** (*vb*) take a liking to, often capriciously

**favor** (*vb*) support, view positively, prefer; (n) partiality, warm regard

**favorable** (*adj*) expressing approval or partiality

**favoritism**  partiality, showing of special favor

**genuflect** (*vb*) touch knee to floor as show of respect or reverence

**grant** (*vb*) accord another his or her due

**gratuity**  something given freely as show of recognition for service or favor

**high opinion**  esteem, respect or regard for

**honor** (*vb*) hold in high regard, show recognition of

**idealize** (*vb*) hold in excessively high regard, esp. as model for imitation

**imprimatur** formal approval, sanction
**inclination** liking, disposition toward
**indulge** (*vb*) take pleasure in; treat with excessive consideration
**kowtow** (*vb*) show servile deference; touch forehead to ground as sign of deep respect
**laurels** honors
**like** (*vb*) approve, feel inclined toward, prefer
**love** (*vb*) feel strong or active affection, admiration, and respect for; enjoy greatly
**obeisance** gesture of respect
**oblige** (*vb*) perform a favor; put another in one's debt by doing favors
**opt** (*vb*) decide in favor of
**pardon** (*vb*) forgive; excuse; tolerate another's fault
**partiality** favorable bias or predisposition
**pass muster** obtain approval or acceptance
**pay respects** express esteem and regard for
**pet** one favored with great kindness or consideration
**pick** (*vb*) select one out of many
**pick over** (*vb*) select the best and discard the unwanted
**play up** (*vb*) exaggerate merits of
**popular** (*adj*) widely approved of or preferred
**pourboire** *French*. gratuity
**predilection** favorable opinion or bias
**prefer** (*vb*) like better, promote over others
**preference** special choice; favorable view
**presume** (*vb*) assume to be true without proof
**prize** (*vb*) value highly, hold in esteem
**proclivity** inclination, predisposition toward
**propensity** strong inclination or tendency
**prostrate** (*vb*) lie facedown on ground as show of submission and respect
**ratify** (*vb*) formally approve, usu. by vote
**recognition** acknowledgment; special attention
**red carpet** show of exceptional courtesy
**regard** esteem, respect
**relish** (*vb*) appreciate, be pleased by
**reputation** one's place in public esteem, overall character as judged by others
**repute** condition of being known, esp. in positive light
**respect** (*vb*) consider worthy of high regard and esteem
**reward** something given in return for service or merit
**rubber-stamp** (*vb*) approve routinely or automatically
**salaam** ceremonial salutation and show of respect made by bowing with right palm on forehead
**salute** (*vb*) express respect and admiration; make any of various gestures of respect; (*n*) gesture of respect, esp. with right palm at forehead
**sanction** authoritative approval or permission
**satisfaction** state of contentment or gratification; confident acceptance of something as good or true
**save face** maintain dignity, prestige, or reputation
**say-so** authoritative approval
**seal of approval** official indication or mark of approval
**select** (*vb*) choose, express preference, discriminate
**self-pride** sense of satisfaction at one's own character and achievements
**self-regard** consideration for oneself
**self-respect** proper regard for oneself and one's dignity and value as a person
**smile on** (*vb*) look favorably on

**submit** (*vb*) yield, abide by another's judgment or authority
**superiority** quality or state of having higher status or worth
**take kindly to** develop a partiality toward
**take to** respond favorably to
**testimonial** expression of appreciation; recommendation
**think better of** improve one's opinion of
**thumbs-up** *Informal*. act or gesture of approval or assent
**tribute** show of respect, gratitude, or affection
**untouchable** (*adj*) above criticism
**valuation** assessment of worth
**value** (*vb*) place high relative worth on
**vote of confidence** expression of support or approval
**vouchsafe** (*vb*) grant as privilege or special favor, esp. in condescending manner
**warm** (*vb*) grow to like, view favorably
**well-disposed** (*adj*) favorably inclined
**wow** (*vb*) elicit enthusiastic approval or delight from

## SUPPORT, ENCOURAGEMENT, AND AGREEMENT

**adopt** (*vb*) accept formally
**advocate** (*vb*) plead a cause; (n) one who pleads a cause
**aegis** support, esp. formal guidance and protection
**affirm** (*vb*) declare as valid or confirmed
**agree** (*vb*) settle by mutual consent; concur
**appoint** (*vb*) select officially
**assent** (*vb*) agree
**assist** (*vb*) help, support
**aver** (*vb*) assert; verify
**avouch** (*vb*) guarantee as factual or provable; affirm
**beau geste** *French*. fine but often empty gesture
**beneficent** (*adj*) resulting in good; kindly or charitable
**beneficial** (*adj*) conducive to well-being; producing an advantage
**benefit** (*vb*) produce well-being or an advantage
**bonhomie** geniality
**boon** timely benefit, blessing
**boost** (*vb*) assist, promote
**booster** enthusiastic supporter
**buck up** (*vb*) raise morale of; become more cheerful
**buoy** (*vb*) support or sustain; raise spirits of
**champion** (*vb*) actively support or defend
**choice** act of selecting; best part; one selected
**cold comfort** limited sympathy or encouragement
**comfort** consolation in time of affliction; feeling of encouragement
**commiserate** (*vb*) express sympathy or condolences
**concur** (*vb*) agree
**condolence** expression of sympathy
**confirm** (*vb*) ratify, sanction; establish the validity of
**congratulate** (*vb*) salute another's success or good fortune
**console** (*vb*) comfort another in distress or sorrow
**corroborate** (*vb*) support with evidence; confirm
**embrace** (*vb*) accept readily, gladly
**encourage** (*vb*) inspire with courage or confidence; give assistance to
**encouragement** support, inspiration, aid
**endorse** (*vb*) express definite, public approval
**espouse** (*vb*) embrace or adopt a cause
**exculpate** (*vb*) clear of alleged fault

**exhort** (vb) urge strongly

**exonerate** (vb) relieve of obligation or duty; free from blame

**find for** (vb) decide in favor of

**hold up** (vb) bring to notice for support

**hold with** (vb) agree, concur with

**hortatory** (adj) giving encouragement, urging on

**humor** (vb) accommodate another by indulgence

**indulgence** act of great consideration

**ingratiate** (vb) gain favor or acceptance by a deliberate act

**mollify** (vb) appease, soften in temper or feeling

**name** (vb) decide on, choose

**nod** indication of one's support or assent

**nominate** (vb) designate, propose for honor or office

**nurture** (vb) further the development of through kind support

**OK** informal expression of support or approval; (adj) all right; (vb) express or give one's support or approval to

**okay** OK

**okey-doke** (adj) OK

**on behalf of** on the side of, in support of

**palliate** (vb) excuse; mitigate gravity of

**partisan** adherent to a cause; supporter of point of view

**pass** (vb) approve formally, as by a legislative body

**pep talk** brief, emotional talk calculated to arouse support or foster determination

**persuade** (vb) prevail on by argument or entreaty

**placate** (vb) appease, calm by concessions

**please** (vb) give pleasure or satisfaction to

**prelation** promotion to higher status, grade, or rank

**preselect** (vb) choose in advance

**pro** (adv) favoring or supporting; (n) argument in affirmation; proponent of an issue

**promo** Informal. something devised to advertise or promote

**promote** (vb) encourage or advance a person or thing through one's support

**prop up** (vb) support or sustain

**proponent** supporter, advocate

**proselytize** (vb) attempt to convert others to one's opinion

**protestation** solemn declaration or affirmation

**pump up** (vb) fill with enthusiasm and excitement

**recommend** (vb) support or represent as worthy

**reinforce** (vb) strengthen by support or assistance

**relent** (vb) become less severe, give in

**second** (vb) give support or encouragement; endorse a motion

**see eye to eye** agree in all ways

**side with** agree with, support

**single out** (vb) select, distinguish from group

**soothe** (vb) appease by attention or concern

**suit** (vb) be agreeable, satisfactory, or appropriate to

**support** (vb) uphold, advocate; aid, help; corroborate

**swallow** (vb) accept without opposition

**unanimous** (adj) having the agreement and consent of all

**uphold** (vb) support

**validate** (vb) give official approval or confirmation of; support, corroborate

**vindicate** (vb) relieve of blame; justify; defend, support

**vouch for** (vb) attest, guarantee; supply supporting evidence for

**whitewash** (vb) cover up the faults of, protect from blame

**win over** (vb) convince of one's opinion

**witness** (vb) affirm, support

**yea** (interj) expression of affirmative response or vote

**yea-say** (vb) agree, affirm something

**yes-man** one who always agrees with a superior

## Praise, Exaltation, Flattery, and Applause

**acclaim** shouted approval or praise

**acclamation** approval loudly expressed, esp. by applause; cheers, or shouts

**accolade** expression of praise; award or honor

**adore** (vb) esteem, worship, or honor

**adulate** (vb) flatter or admire excessively or servilely

**aggrandize** (vb) make great or greater in power, wealth, or honor

**apotheosize** (vb) elevate to divine status, deify

**applause** display of public approval, esp. hand clapping

**awe** fearful reverence, admiration, or submission

**belaud** (vb) praise excessively

**bepraise** (vb) praise

**blandish** (vb) cajole with gentle flattery

**blarney** clever, often coaxing flattery; cajolery

**bless** (vb) speak kindly of; wish well; extol

**boast** (vb) brag, praise oneself

**bow and scrape** submit oneself before a superior

**brag** (vb) boast, indulge in self-glorifying talk

**bravo** (interj) shout of praise

**butter up** (vb) Informal. charm with flattery or praise to gain favor

**cajole** (vb) persuade with clever flattery

**canonize** (vb) sanction by authority, esp. ecclesiastical

**celebrate** (vb) honor; present for widespread public notice and praise

**cheer** (vb) comfort, restore hope to; encourage or salute with shouts; (n) shout of encouragement or praise

**commend** (vb) praise; present as worthy of confidence

**compliment** (vb) express respect, affection, or admiration for; flatter; praise

**court** (vb) seek to attract or win over by flattery and attention

**crown** (vb) bestow favor on as a mark of honor

**curry favor** seek advancement through flattery and fawning attention

**dote** (vb) bestow lavish, excessive fondness

**elevate** (vb) exalt in rank or status

**encomium** glowing, enthusiastic praise

**encore** demand, as by audience, for reappearance or additional performance as expression of approval for performer

**eulogize** (vb) speak or write high praise for

**eulogy** formal commendation or high praise, esp. for deceased person

**exalt** (vb) glorify or elevate by praise

**extol** (vb) praise highly, glorify

**fawn** (vb) show excessive affection, esp. by servile flattery

**flatter** (vb) praise excessively or insincerely

**flattery** insincere or excessive praise

**glorify** (vb) extol, elevate

**grace** (vb) confer favor or honor on

**hail** (vb) acclaim, greet with approval

**hallow** (vb) respect highly, venerate

**hand** outburst or round of applause

**here-here** (*interj*) *Chiefly Brit.* expression of support or encouragement

**hip-hip hooray** (*interj*) signal for applause or intensifier of cheers

**homage** reverential regard, respect, or tribute

**hooray** (*interj*) expression of appreciation or encouragement; hurrah

**hosanna** (*interj*) shout of praise or acclamation

**hurrah** (*interj*) hooray

**huzzah** (*interj*) hurrah

**hype** extravagant promotion; excessive praise

**idolatry** excessive or blind devotion or reverence

**idolize** (*vb*) admire to excess; worship

**immortalize** (*vb*) confer undying fame on

**inflate** (*vb*) expand or puff up, esp. unjustifiably

**kudos** honor, praise

**laud** (*vb*) praise, acclaim

**lionize** (*vb*) treat as person of importance

**make much of** treat with great affection or special consideration

**merit** (*vb*) possess praiseworthy qualities and virtues

**olé** (*interj*) shout of approval; bravo

**ovation** prolonged, enthusiastic applause

**paean** song of praise or tribute

**panegyric** formal, elaborate written or oral praise

**pay a compliment** express favorable opinion, praise

**plaudits** enthusiastic expression of approval; round of applause

**plug** (*vb*) *Informal.* promote insistently; praise highly

**praise** (*vb*) express approval; commend

**praiseworthy** (*adj*) deserving of praise

**put on a pedestal** elevate, exalt

**rave** extravagantly enthusiastic appraisal or review

**resound** (*vb*) be celebrated

**revere** (*vb*) regard with high esteem or awe

**root for** (*vb*) wish success; applaud noisily

**salvo** round of cheers or applause

**self-congratulation** uncritical satisfaction with one's own accomplishments

**self-flattery** exaggeration of one's strengths along with denial of one's weaknesses

**self-glorification** boastful exaggeration of one's strengths

**set up** (*vb*) extol as model

**stroke** (*vb*) *Informal.* flatter, promote feelings of self-approval in

**sweet-talk** (*vb*) *Informal.* coax or persuade by flattery and cajolery

**talk up** (*vb*) praise, extol

**tout** (*vb*) flatter loudly or extravagantly

**venerate** (*vb*) regard with reverence and deference

**viva** (*interj*) *Spanish, Italian.* exclamation of approval

**worship** (*vb*) regard with high honor and reverence

## DISAPPROVAL, DISRESPECT, AND DENIAL

**adverse** (*adj*) unfavorable; opposed to one's interest

**animosity** feeling of strong dislike or enmity, esp. when displayed in action

**animus** strong dislike, often prejudiced and hostile; animosity

**antipathy** aversion, dislike

**askance** (*adv*) with disapproval, suspicion, or mistrust

**aversion** repugnance coupled with a strong desire to avoid; dislike

**avoid** (*vb*) shun or keep away from as indication of distaste

**bias** prejudice

**brush-off** *Informal.* curt, rude dismissal

**censorious** (*adj*) given to censure

**chasten** (*vb*) discipline by inflicting suffering on so as to improve or purify

**cold shoulder** intentionally unsympathetic and disrespectful treatment

**confound** (*vb*) refute or contradict

**contradict** (*vb*) assert the contrary, imply the opposite; deny directly

**correct** (*vb*) point out another's errors; punish with a view to improving

**correction** rectification of errors

**critical** (*adj*) inclined to find fault

**criticism** unfavorable observations or comments

**cross out** (*vb*) eliminate from consideration; x out

**debase** (*vb*) lower another in status or esteem

**decry** (*vb*) express strong disapproval of

**deflate** (*vb*) reduce in size or importance

**denial** refusal to recognize or acknowledge something; disavowal or disowning of

**deny** (*vb*) refuse to recognize or acknowledge; disavow, disown

**deprecate** (*vb*) express earnest disapproval of; belittle

**detest** (*vb*) dislike intensely, loathe

**detract from** (*vb*) take away a part from

**dim view** skeptical or unfavorable attitude

**disapproval** unfavorable judgment or condemnation

**disapprove** (*vb*) express unfavorable judgment on

**disavow** (*vb*) deny knowledge of

**discard** (*vb*) reject as useless

**disclaim** (*vb*) deny interest in or connection with; disavow

**discommend** (*vb*) cause to be viewed unfavorably; disapprove of

**discontent** dissatisfaction with

**discount** (*vb*) view with doubt; underestimate importance of

**discountenance** (*vb*) treat or view with disfavor

**discredit** (*vb*) deprive of good repute; destroy confidence in accuracy of

**discriminate** (*vb*) treat unfavorably without justification

**disenchantment** state of freedom from illusion, esp. from overoptimism

**disesteem** disfavor, low regard

**disfavor** disapproval, dislike

**disgruntled** (*adj*) discontented; having ill humor

**dishonor** (*vb*) bring shame on, deprive of honor or prestige; treat in degrading manner

**disillusionment** condition of being free of illusions

**dislike** (*vb*) regard with displeasure

**dismiss** (*vb*) put aside from serious consideration, make light of

**disown** (*vb*) repudiate, refuse to acknowledge

**displease** (*vb*) incur disapproval or dislike

**disqualify** (*vb*) deprive of right or privilege; render unfit

**disregard** (*vb*) treat as worthless by ignoring

**disrepute** state of being held in low regard

**disrespect** lack of consideration; low regard

**dissatisfaction** condition of displeasure or discontent

**distaste** dislike, aversion

**downgrade** (*vb*) minimize or depreciate in quality or importance

**embarrass** (*vb*) place in state of confusion or self-conscious discomfort

**enmity** feeling of ill will or extreme dislike and animosity

**eschew** (*vb*) abstain from or avoid on moral or practical grounds

**fair game** deserving of or susceptible to criticism

**frown on** (*vb*) express disapproval of or displeasure toward

**harp on** (*vb*) dwell on persistently, esp. by voicing criticisms

**hate** (*vb*) dislike intensely

**hiss** sibilant sound made as expression of disapproval

**hoot** cry or shout of derision or objection

**hypercritical** (*adj*) excessively critical, censorious

**ignore** (*vb*) refuse to notice; deem unworthy of consideration

**inconsequential** (*adj*) unimportant, insignificant

**inexcusable** (*adj*) incapable of being justified

**inferiority** sense or state of having low status or worth

**in the dog house** *Slang.* in a state of disfavor

**judgmental** (*adj*) tending to pass moral judgment and view others as inferior to oneself; quick to judge

**knock** (*vb*) *Informal.* find fault with, esp. with trivial criticisms

**libel** unjustly damaging or unfavorable opinion expressed in written or printed form; anything defamatory

**lose face** be deprived of one's dignity, prestige, or reputation

**low opinion** lack of regard or respect for

**make light of** (*vb*) treat as object of little importance

**muckrake** (*vb*) search for and expose misconduct, esp. of officials

**nay** (*interj*) expression of negative reply or vote; denial or dissent

**naysay** (*vb*) deny; reject; express negative opinion

**neglect** (*vb*) disregard, ignore

**one-upmanship** art or practice of maintaining an advantageous position over others

**ostracize** (*vb*) exclude from group by common consent

**pass up** (*vb*) neglect to take advantage of; decline, reject

**pejorative** (*adj*) tending to disparage or devalue

**pet peeve** frequent subject of complaint

**pharisaism** hypocritical and judgmental self-righteousness

**pick apart** (*vb*) find fault with all aspects of

**pick at** (*vb*) criticize repeatedly, esp. for minor faults

**pick on** (*vb*) single out for undeserved criticism and harassment

**play down** (*vb*) understate merits or significance of

**pooh-pooh** (*vb*) express disdain for; dismiss lightly

**potshot** random or aimless critical remark

**prejudice** preconceived judgment or opinion, esp. unfavorable

**question** (*vb*) express doubt about

**reduce** (*vb*) downgrade, demote

**reject** (*vb*) refuse to accept or consider; rebuff; turn down

**reprehend** (*vb*) voice disapproval or censure

**reproach** (*vb*) express disappointment or displeasure

**reproof** expression of censure or criticism

**reprove** (*vb*) scold or correct gently; express disapproval of

**repudiate** (*vb*) disown, refuse to accept, reject with denial or condemnation

**riot act** firm reprimand or warning

**segregate** (*vb*) distinguish and separate from others

**serve one right** treat as one deserves, esp. criticize or punish justly

**shun** (*vb*) deliberately avoid or look down on

**skepticism** attitude of doubt

**slight** (*vb*) treat with disdain or indifference

**slough over** (*vb*) treat as slight or unimportant

**snobbishness** air of superiority coupled with rebuffing of those deemed inferior to oneself

**snooty** (*adj*) showing disdain and snobbishness

**snub** (*vb*) slight, disregard, or insult

**spank** (*vb*) strike on buttocks with open hand as expression of disapproval

**stereotype** oversimplified characterization; unjustified generalization

**stigma** mark of shame or discredit; stain or reproach

**stigmatize** (*vb*) bring disgrace or infamy on

**stricture** adverse criticism

**stuck-up** (*adj*) *Informal.* self-important, snobbish

**stultify** (*vb*) cause to appear stupid, foolish, or irresponsible

**supercilious** (*adj*) patronizing and haughtily disdainful of others

**take to task** criticize for shortcomings

**talk down** (*vb*) deprecate, criticize

**target** (*vb*) set as object, esp. for criticism

**tease** (*vb*) disturb or provoke by persistent irritating remarks and distractions

**thumbs-down** gesture of disapproval

**toy** (*vb*) act with indifference; trifle

**turn down** (*vb*) reject, show disfavor toward

**uncomplimentary** (*adj*) unfavorable, derogatory

**underrated** (*adj*) valued at less than true worth

**undervalue** (*vb*) depreciate, treat as though of little worth

**undeserving** (*adj*) not worthy of consideration, respect, or assistance

**unfavorable** (*adj*) adverse, contrary; not propitious

**unflattering** (*adj*) unfavorable, derogatory

**unpopular** (*adj*) disapproved of or disliked in general or by a particular group

**unpromising** (*adj*) appearing unlikely to succeed

**unsatisfactory** (*adj*) inadequate; worthy of disapproval or rebuke

**unsung** (*adj*) insufficiently praised

**unworthy** (*adj*) lacking in value, undeserving

**veto** (*vb*) refuse to approve; reject or prohibit emphatically

**vitiate** (*vb*) debase or corrupt; make ineffective or weak

**write off** (*vb*) depreciate; regard as lost or worthless

**wrong** (*vb*) treat unfairly or disrespectfully

**x out** (*vb*) cross out

## OPPOSITION, DISAGREEMENT, AND ATTACK

**abjure** (*vb*) repudiate or renounce firmly and solemnly

**admonish** (*vb*) express warning or disapproval, esp. gently

**adversary** person or group that opposes or attacks; opponent

**afflict** (*vb*) assault or attack repeatedly

**argue** (*vb*) dispute, contend

**assail** (*vb*) attack violently with ridicule or abuse

**assault** (*vb*) attack violently

**at odds** (*adj*) of opposing viewpoints

**attack** (*vb*) direct unfriendly words or unfavorable criticism against; set upon in hostile manner

**ban** censure, condemnation

**banish** (*vb*) remove by authority or force; exile

**blackball** (*vb*) vote against; ostracize or exclude socially

**blast** (*vb*) attack vigorously with vehement words

**boo** (*interj*) sound exclaimed as disapproving shout

**brand** (*vb*) stigmatize, mark with disapproval

**bring to terms** compel to agree or submit

**buck** (*vb*) *Informal.* oppose, resist

**carp** (*vb*) find fault, complain unreasonably

**cavil** (*vb*) raise trivial objections

**challenge** (*vb*) dispute, call in question

**chuck** (*vb*) discard or set aside as unwanted

**combat** (*vb*) oppose

**complain** (*vb*) express displeasure

**con** (*adv*) in opposition, against

**confront** (*vb*) oppose or challenge directly

**contest** (*vb*) dispute, challenge

**contumacious** (*adj*) obstinately disobedient or rebellious

**counter** (*vb*) act in opposition

**cow** (*vb*) intimidate with threats

**cross** (*vb*) oppose, run counter to, contradict

**damage** (*vb*) do harm or injury to

**daunt** (*vb*) lessen the courage of

**debunk** (*vb*) expose and strip of falseness

**decline** (*vb*) withhold consent

**demur** (*vb*) object or hesitate based on one's scruples

**differ** (*vb*) disagree in opinion or belief; be at variance

**disagree** (*vb*) differ in opinion; fail to agree; dissent

**discourage** (*vb*) hinder by disfavoring

**dispute** (*vb*) argue, debate, quarrel with

**dissent** (*vb*) speak out against; differ in opinion, esp. with the majority (*n*) expression of disagreement

**dissidence** disagreement

**dissuade** (*vb*) deter through advice or persuasion

**division** separation by disagreement or difference of opinion

**exclude** (*vb*) bar from consideration or inclusion

**excommunicate** (*vb*) exclude from membership, esp. from church group

**exile** expulsion from one's native land

**fight** (*vb*) oppose

**find against** (*vb*) decide for opposite view or side

**flak** annoying criticism or opposition

**forbid** (*vb*) prohibit, rule against

**gainsay** (*vb*) deny, dispute; contradict, oppose

**harass** (*vb*) annoy, attack, or impede repeatedly

**heckle** (*vb*) harass with questions or gibes

**hostile** (*adj*) critical, antagonistic toward, opposed

**hostility** enmity or antagonism; opposition or resistance to an idea or project

**hound** (*vb*) harass or attack without respite

**impeach** (*vb*) accuse of misconduct in office; challenge the credibility of

**impugn** (*vb*) oppose or assail as false or without integrity

**lash out** (*vb*) make severe verbal attack, esp. reproach

**niggle** (*vb*) find fault constantly in petty way

**nitpick** (*vb*) engage in petty, unjustified criticism

**object** (*vb*) oppose firmly; express distaste for

**obstruct** (*vb*) hinder, impede by blocking

**offend** (*vb*) cause dislike, anger, or resentment

**offense** assault, attack; something that insults, displeases, or outrages

**onslaught** furious attack or assault

**opponent** person who is on the opposing side; adversary

**oppose** (*vb*) take contrary view; resist, combat

**opposed** (*adj*) contrary; set in contrast to

**oppugn** (*vb*) assail by criticism; dispute

**plaint** lamentation, protest, complaint

**polemic** controversial refutation of another's opinion; person who makes such a refutation

**press** (*vb*) assail, harass, afflict

**protest** complaint, objection, expression of dissent

**quibble** (*vb*) equivocate, hedge; cavil, carp

**rebut** (*vb*) contradict or oppose by argument

**recriminate** (*vb*) retort bitterly, make retaliatory accusation

**redbait** (*vb*) attack as communistic

**renounce** (*vb*) withdraw or abandon one's previous support; repudiate

**reprobation** condemnation or rejection as unworthy or evil

**repudiate** (*vb*) reject as untrue

**resist** (*vb*) exert force against

**resistance** opposition by one to another

**run counter to** oppose, be contrary to

**squelch** (*vb*) put down with crushing force

**stymie** (*vb*) hinder or block

**taboo** (*adj*) forbidden; banned as evil; (*n*) prohibition

**take issue with** oppose, form contrary opinion

**take on** (*vb*) contend against

**take sides** state opinion in opposition to another

**tear into** (*vb*) attack without restraint

**tee off** (*vb*) *Slang.* make angry denunciation

**torment** (*vb*) afflict, cause severe distress

**variance** disagreement, dispute, or quarrel

**verboten** (*adj*) forbidden; prohibited by law

**withstand** (*vb*) resist or oppose with determination, esp. successfully

**write down** (*vb*) depreciate or disparage in writing

**wrong** (*adj*) incorrect, judged to be false

## BLAME, CENSURE, RIDICULE, AND CONTEMPT

**abuse** (*vb*) attack verbally, revile; maltreat

**accursed** (*adj*) under a curse, damned

**accuse** (*vb*) find fault with, blame

**affront** (*vb*) insult

**allegation** assertion, esp. of culpability, made with little or no proof

**anathema** something detested; ban or curse, esp. by ecclesiastical authority

**animadversion** unfavorable or censorious comment or criticism

**arrogance** feeling of superiority over others, esp. offensive display of superiority

**aspersion** derogatory remark or malicious charge

**backbite** (*vb*) slander, speak ill of

**backstab** (*vb*) attempt to discredit by underhanded means

**bad-mouth** (*vb*) *Slang.* criticize severely; speak disloyally of

**barb** pointed or biting and openly unpleasant remark

**baste** (*vb*) scold soundly; denounce vigorously

**bawl out** (*vb*) *Informal*. reprimand severely

**belittle** (*vb*) portray as little or less than might seem; mock; disparage

**beneath contempt** at the lowest possible level of respect; utterly degraded

**berate** (*vb*) condemn vehemently at length

**besmirch** (*vb*) tarnish or detract from another's honor

**blacken** (*vb*) defame, sully, ruin the reputation of

**blame** (*vb*) find fault with; hold responsible

**blasphemy** insult to, contempt for, or irreverence toward something sacred

**blot** mark of reproach, stain of infamy

**booby prize** prize given in good-natured acknowledgment of poor performance or achievement

**brickbat** uncomplimentary or unkind comment

**bring to account** reprimand

**Bronx cheer** raspberry

**burlesque** (*vb*) imitate derisively or mock, esp. by caricature

**butt** victim of abuse or ridicule

**calumniate** (*vb*) malign with false statements or misrepresentations

**calumny** false and malicious statements damaging to another's reputation

**caricature** distortion or exaggeration to make someone or something appear ludicrous

**castigate** (*vb*) punish or criticize severely; chastise

**censure** (*vb*) find fault with in a harsh or vehement manner; (*n*) vehement expression of condemnation

**chaff** (*vb*) ridicule in a good-natured, teasing manner

**charge** (*vb*) accuse of wrongdoing; blame

**chastise** (*vb*) criticize severely

**chew out** (*vb*) *Slang*. reprimand, scold harshly

**chide** (*vb*) voice disapproval; reproach, rebuke

**comeuppance** *Informal*. deserved rebuke or penalty

**commination** denunciation

**condemn** (*vb*) express strong disapproval or adverse judgment; pronounce guilty; declare to be wrong

**contemn** (*vb*) scorn, treat with contempt

**contempt** disdain, lack of respect; disgrace

**contumely** insulting or humiliating behavior based on contempt

**correction** punishment, rebuke

**criticize** (*vb*) find fault with; censure

**crucify** (*vb*) persecute or treat cruelly with gross injustice

**culpable** (*adj*) deserving condemnation or blame

**curse** (*vb*) invoke evil or harm upon; revile profanely

**cuss** (*vb*) *Informal*. curse

**damn** (*vb*) condemn harshly as a failure

**debase** (*vb*) reduce in status or value

**defamation** calumny, disgrace, or harm done to another's reputation

**defame** (*vb*) use malicious statements to disgrace or harm another's reputation

**degrade** (*vb*) bring into contempt or low esteem

**demean** (*vb*) degrade; lower in status or dignity

**denigrate** (*vb*) defame, cast aspersions on

**denounce** (*vb*) condemn publicly as evil or blameworthy

**depreciate** (*vb*) disparage, represent as of little value

**derision** bitter, contemptuous ridicule

**derogate** (*vb*) express low opinion of

**desecrate** (*vb*) treat irreverently or contemptuously; profane that which is sacred

**despise** (*vb*) look down upon with contempt; regard as worthless

**detest** (*vb*) dislike intensely

**diatribe** bitter, abusive, sarcastic criticism

**disdain** (*vb*) view scornfully, treat with contempt

**disgrace** (*vb*) humiliate; cause to lose favor; bring shame upon

**disgust** marked aversion, total repugnance

**disparage** (*vb*) degrade, speak slightingly of

**dress down** (*vb*) censure severely

**dump on** (*vb*) *Informal*. belittle; bad-mouth

**effigy** crude figure representing and ridiculing a hated person

**epithet** descriptive word or phrase, esp. one that is disparaging or abusive

**excoriate** (*vb*) censure severely; scathe

**execrate** (*vb*) detest utterly; denounce as evil

**fault** (*vb*) criticize, blame

**find fault** criticize

**flay** (*vb*) criticize harshly

**fleer** (*vb*) sneer or laugh at derisively; mock

**flout** (*vb*) scorn, treat with contemptuous disregard

**fulminate** (*vb*) utter denunciations and invective

**fustigate** (*vb*) criticize harshly

**gibe** (*vb*) deride, taunt; (*n*) mocking, sarcastic remark

**gloat** (*vb*) view with triumphant and often malicious satisfaction, esp. another's misfortune

**goat** one who takes blame for something, often undeservedly; victim

**going-over** severe scolding

**grill** (*vb*) question intensely; torment

**harangue** passionate, critical, or scalding speech; tirade or vehement attack

**hatchet job** forceful, malicious critique

**high horse** contemptuous, superior attitude or manner

**humble** (*vb*) destroy another's prestige, spirit, dignity, or power

**humble pie** embarrassing humiliation and submission under pressure

**humiliate** (*vb*) cause another a painful loss of dignity or self-respect

**implicate** (*vb*) show incriminating connection; blame

**imprecate** (*vb*) curse, invoke evil upon

**impute** (*vb*) lay blame on; discredit

**incriminate** (*vb*) charge with or show evidence of involvement in wrongdoing

**indict** (*vb*) formally charge with wrongdoing; criticize, accuse

**infamy** bad public reputation or reproach received for evil ways

**insolence** insulting and contemptuous behavior or attitude

**insult** (*vb*) treat or speak of with contempt or indignity; affront

**irreverence** lack of proper or accustomed respect

**irrision** derision

**jape** (*vb*) make mocking fun of

**jeer** (*vb*) taunt, mock, or speak of with derision

**lambaste** (*vb*) *Informal*. berate harshly; censure

**lampoon** (*vb*) ridicule harshly with satire

**laugh at** (*vb*) express scorn or derision for by laughter; make fun of

**laughingstock** object of ridicule

**loathe** (*vb*) feel intense contempt and aversion for; abhor

**make fun of** ridicule, mock; make sport of

**make sport of** make fun of

**malediction** curse

**malign** (*vb*) speak evil of; utter injurious, often false, statement; defame, slander

**mock** (*vb*) treat with contempt or ridicule

**Momus** god of censure and mockery (ancient Greece); carping critic

**moralize** (*vb*) express opinion on right and wrong conduct; chastise others for misconduct

**mortify** (*vb*) subject to severe embarrassment and shame

**mud** *Informal.* abusive, malicious remarks

**mudslinging** using offensive epithets and false attacks to discredit one's opponent

**name-calling** using offensive terms to humiliate and induce condemnation of another

**needle** (*vb*) *Informal.* tease, torment, or goad repeatedly

**objurgate** (*vb*) denounce or berate harshly; castigate

**obloquy** abusive, condemnatory language, esp. by numerous persons

**odium** intense loathing and contempt

**onus** disagreeable burden or blame

**opprobrium** disgrace or reproach due to shameful conduct; cause or object of infamy

**pan** (*vb*) *Informal.* criticize severely, esp. in review of a performance

**Philippic** speech full of bitter condemnation

**piece of one's mind** *Informal.* severe scolding or rebuke

**pillory** (*vb*) expose to public ridicule

**pink** (*vb*) wound by piercing criticism or ridicule

**poison-pen** (*adj*) written with malice, usu. anonymously

**poke fun at** ridicule

**pollute** (*vb*) debase, defile, make impure

**pox** curse, evil; expression of distaste or aversion

**profane** (*vb*) desecrate or defile with abuse or irreverence

**put down** (*vb*) *Informal.* disparage, belittle; criticize, esp. contemptuously

**put to shame** expose faults of, censure, or humiliate

**rag** (*vb*) *Informal.* scold; subject to prolonged torment; tease

**rail** (*vb*) revile; denounce vehemently and bitterly

**rap** (*vb*) *Slang.* rebuke, criticize sharply

**raspberry** *Informal.* expression of disapproval, esp. contemptuous sound made through compressed lips; Bronx cheer

**razz** (*vb*) *Slang.* heckle, deride, tease

**rebuff** (*vb*) snub or reject peremptorily

**rebuke** (*vb*) reprimand; express strong disapproval to

**reprimand** (*vb*) reprove or censure sharply, esp. from position of authority

**revile** (*vb*) subject to verbal abuse

**revulsion** strong sense of distaste and repugnance

**ridicule** (*vb*) make fun of, mock, deride

**roast** (*vb*) *Informal.* criticize mercilessly, often in public

**roorback** defamatory falsehood published for political effect

**rub it in** *Informal.* emphasize something unpleasant to tease or annoy

**sacrilege** gross irreverence toward sacred person or thing

**sarcasm** sharply ironical utterance or cutting remark

**satirize** (*vb*) censure or ridicule by ironic description of human vices and follies

**scald** (*vb*) subject to heated criticism or censure

**scapegoat** one who bears blame for others

**scathe** (*vb*) assail with severe denunciation

**scoff** (*vb*) mock; express scorn or derision

**scold** (*vb*) censure severely or find fault with, esp. from position of authority

**scorch** (*vb*) censure, attack harshly

**score** (*vb*) berate, censure, denounce

**scorn** (*vb*) reject or dismiss disdainfully as unworthy; deride

**self-criticism** harsh assessment of oneself

**self-flagellation** extreme criticism of oneself

**self-incrimination** act of incriminating oneself, esp. by giving evidence

**shame** (*vb*) cause to feel guilt or humiliation

**shoot down** (*vb*) *Informal.* deflate, ridicule, discredit

**show up** (*vb*) embarrass, discredit, expose faults of

**silent treatment** aloof expression of disapproval made by completely ignoring another

**slam** (*vb*) *Informal.* criticize harshly

**slander** (*vb*) damage another's reputation by uttering falsehoods

**slap down** (*vb*) assault verbally, insult

**slash** (*vb*) criticize viciously

**slur** (*vb*) insult, disparage

**smear** (*vb*) maliciously attack another's reputation; vilify

**smirch** (*vb*) discredit, disgrace

**sneer at** (*vb*) laugh at scornfully; jeer and mock

**soil** (*vb*) damage or disgrace another's reputation

**spurn** (*vb*) scorn, reject disdainfully

**stain** (*vb*) bring dishonor or blame on; blemish

**sully** (*vb*) defile, tarnish

**supercilious** (*adj*) patronizing; haughtily disdainful

**swipe** *Informal.* sharp, critical remark

**taint** (*vb*) contaminate morally, corrupt; tarnish

**talking-to** reprimand, scolding

**tarnish** (*vb*) bring disgrace on; sully

**taunt** (*vb*) reproach or challenge in a mocking or insulting manner

**tear down** (*vb*) vilify, denigrate

**tell off** (*vb*) *Informal.* reprimand, scold

**thumb one's nose** *Informal.* express contempt, esp. through rejection

**thunderbolt** sudden, severe attack

**tick off** (*vb*) *Chiefly Brit.* scold severely; rebuke

**tirade** prolonged outburst of verbal abuse

**tongue-lashing** harsh verbal criticism or scolding

**traduce** (*vb*) speak maliciously or falsely of, slander

**trash** (*vb*) *Informal.* censure, revile; utterly destroy by criticism; dismiss as worthless

**travesty** grotesque or debased imitation

**twit** (*vb*) subject to light ridicule or reproach

**umbrage** vague feeling of resentment over perceived insult

**upbraid** (*vb*) find fault with; criticize harshly, scold vehemently

**vilify** (*vb*) defame or slander with abusive statements

**vilipend** (*vb*) regard with low opinion; disparage, depreciate

**vituperate** (*vb*) censure severely, revile harshly

**walk all over** treat contemptuously and without regard

**whispering campaign** systematic dissemination of derogatory rumors

**wig** (*vb*) *Brit. informal.* scold severely, rebuke

**wipe one's boots on** treat contemptuously with no regard

# The Dark Side

# Drug Abuse and Alcoholism

Drug Names and Forms
Drunkenness, Drunkards, and Alcoholism
Paraphernalia and Behavior
Users and Abusers

**See also**: Chap. 4: Medicine; Chap. 13: Psychology; Chap. 17: Drinking and Alcoholic Beverages; Chap. 24: Mental Disturbances; Crime

## Drug Names and Forms

**Abbott** *Slang*. hypnotic Nembutal manufactured by Abbott Laboratories

**A-bomb** *Slang*. heroin and marijuana cigarette

**Acapulco gold** *Slang*. powerful Mexican marijuana; gold

**ace** *Slang*. barbiturate or amphetamine capsule or pill

**acid** *Slang*. LSD

**addictive drug** substance inducing physical or psychological dependence

**Amanita muscaria** hallucinogenic mushroom; death's-head; fly agaric

**amphetamine** central nervous system stimulant; amphetamine sulphate

**amphetamine sulphate** amphetamine

**amyl nitrite** pharmaceutical drug that dilates blood vessels, producing brief exhilaration

**Amytal** *Trademark*. barbiturate depressant amobarbital sodium

**anabolic steroid** muscle-building hormonal substance with dangerous side effects

**analgesic** painkilling drug

**angel dust** *Slang*. PCP

**antidepressant** pharmaceutical treatment for depression or apathy

**aphrodisiac** drug that increases sexual arousal

**ataraxic drug** tranquilizer

**atropine** antispasmodic drug

**Aunt Emma** *Slang*. morphine

**bag** *Slang*. small measure of a drug, esp. heroin

**bale** *Slang*. pound of marijuana

**balloon** small measure of heroin stored in toy balloon

**bam** *Slang*. barbiturate and amphetamine combination

**bang** *Slang*. drug injection or sniff of cocaine

**banji** *Slang*. marijuana

**bar** *Slang*. block of pressed marijuana

**barbital** addictive hypnotic sedative taken as white powder

**barbiturate** pharmaceutical central nervous system depressant and muscle relaxer

**B-bomb** *Slang*. benzedrine inhaler

**belladonna** psychoactive depressant derived from deadly nightshade

**benny** *Slang*. benzedrine

**Benzedrine** *Trademark*. pharmaceutical amphetamine

**Bernice** *Slang*. cocaine

**bhang** *Slang*. mild preparation of marijuana leaves, drunk with milk or water

**bindle** paper in which drugs are wrapped

**Biphetamine** *Trademark*. pharmaceutical stimulant combining two amphetamines

**bird's eye** *Slang*. tiny package of narcotics

**black** *Slang*. opium

**black beauty** *Slang*. Biphetamine in black capsule

**blackstuff** *Slang*. opium

**blank** *Slang*. nonnarcotic substance sold in place of real drug

**blow** *Slang*. cocaine

**blowzeen** *Slang*. cocaine

**body drug** physically addictive substance

**bomber** *Slang*. thick marijuana cigarette

**boo** *Slang*. marijuana

**bouncing powder** *Slang*. cocaine

**boy** *Slang*. heroin

**brick** *Slang*. block of pressed marijuana, usu. one kilo

**brown** *Slang*. Mexican heroin

**bud** marijuana, esp. the resinous flower of the female plant

**bullet** *Slang*. line or snort of cocaine

**bundle** *Slang*. package of small, preweighed bags of heroin

**bush** *Slang*. marijuana

**button** *Slang*. peyote or mescal top

**caffeine** mild stimulant in coffee and tea

**California sunshine** *Slang*. form of LSD

**Cam red** *Slang*. Cambodian marijuana

**can** *Slang*. ounce of marijuana

**candy** *Slang*. cocaine

**Cannabis indica** powerful hybrid of cannabis sativa; indica

**Cannabis sativa** hemp plant from which marijuana is derived

**cantharides** supposed aphrodisiac Spanish fly

**cap** *Informal*. capsule of any drug

**cargo** load of drugs

**cartwheel** *Slang*. amphetamine tablet

**Cecil** *Slang*. cocaine

**cephalotropic drug** drug that changes physiological functions of the brain

**Chinese molasses** *Slang*. opium

**chloral hydrate** crystalline compound used as sedative

**Christmas tree** *Slang*. hypnotic sedative Tuinal

**clear light** *Slang*. very pure, powerful LSD

**coca** plant with stimulant alkaloids from which cocaine is derived

**cocaine** addictive central nervous system stimulant derived from coca leaf; *Slang*: Bernice, blow, blowzeen, bouncing powder, candy, Cecil, coke, crack, flake, girl, lady snow, nose candy, Peruvian perfume, snow, toot, white girl

**codeine** painkilling depressant

**coke** *Slang*. cocaine

**cola** caffeine-containing seeds or nuts of African tree

**Colombian gold** *Slang*. potent marijuana grown in South America

**controlled substance** any behavior-altering or addictive drug whose possession and use are restricted by law

**crack** extremely powerful and addictive form of smokable cocaine

**crank** *Slang*. methamphetamine

**crystal meth** *Slang*. methamphetamine in crystalline form

**cube** *Slang*. LSD-dosed sugar cube

**dagga** *Slang*. marijuana from Africa

**datura** plant with strong hallucinogenic and intoxicant effects; jimson weed; locoweed

**death's-head** *Slang.* hallucinogenic mushroom *Amanita muscaria*

**deck** *Slang.* small, folded packet of heroin

**Demerol** *Trademark.* highly addictive pharmaceutical painkiller, or synthetic opiate

**desoxyn** pharmaceutical amphetamine

**DET** *d*iethyl*t*ryptamine

**Dexamyl** *Trademark.* pharmaceutical amphetamine with added barbiturate sedative; purple heart

**Dexedrine** *Trademark.* pharmaceutical amphetamine; dexie

**dexie** *Slang.* Dexedrine

**diet pill** drug taken to reduce appetite, esp. amphetamine

**diethyltryptamine** DET; synthetic derivative of tryptamine hallucinogenic effects

**Dilaudid** *Trademark.* morphine-derived painkiller

**dime bag** *Slang.* small container of heroin or other drug sold for $10

**dimethyltryptamine** DMT; intensely hallucinogenic synthetic drug

**DMT** *d*imethyl*t*ryptamine

**doll** *Slang.* amphetamine or barbiturate

**doobie** *Slang.* marijuana cigarette

**dope** *Slang.* any drug or narcotic, esp. heroin or marijuana

**dose** amount of drug to be taken by one person at one time

**dot** *Slang.* microdot

**downer** *Informal.* any depressant or sedative-hypnotic drug

**drug** any habit-forming, behavior-altering, or damaging illicit substance, esp. narcotic

**dust** *Slang.* PCP

**ecstasy** *Slang.* mild hallucinogen

**eighth** *Slang.* one-eighth ounce of heroin

**fireplug** *Slang.* large pellet of opium

**flake** *Slang.* cocaine

**flea powder** *Slang.* extensively cut heroin

**fly agaric** *Amanita muscaria*

**freebase** *Slang.* ether-purified cocaine

**gage** *Slang.* marijuana

**gangster** *Slang.* marijuana

**ganja** *Slang.* marijuana

**girl** *Slang.* cocaine

**gold** *Slang.* Acapulco gold

**goofball** *Slang.* barbiturate

**gow** *Slang.* opium or heroin

**grass** *Slang.* marijuana

**H** *Slang.* heroin

**hallucinogen** any drug producing intense visual and sensory distortion

**hard drugs** physically addictive substances, esp. heroin, morphine, and cocaine

**hash** *Informal.* hashish

**hashish** concentrated form of marijuana resin; hash; resin

**hash oil** oil derived from hashish

**hay** *Slang.* marijuana

**head drug** *Informal.* psychologically addictive substance, esp. hallucinogen

**heart** *Slang.* amphetamine

**hemp** *Cannabis sativa* plant, source of marijuana

**herb** *Slang.* marijuana

**heroin** addictive narcotic opium derivative produced by treating morphine with acetic acid; *Slang:* boy, dope, gow, H, horse, junk, noise, poison, scag, skag, smack, tecata

**homegrown** (*adj*) locally grown or nonimported, as of marijuana

**hooch** *Slang.* marijuana

**hop** *Slang.* opium

**horse** *Slang.* heroin

**hotshot** *Slang.* lethal mixture of heroin and poison, or overdose of pure heroin injected to kill user

**hypnotic** sleep-inducing drug

**ibogaine** plant-derived stimulant

**ice** *Slang.* smokable methamphetamine with prolonged effect

**indica** *Cannabis indica*

**jay** *Slang.* marijuana cigarette

**jelly bean** *Slang.* stimulant pill

**jimson weed** datura

**joint** *Slang.* hand-rolled marijuana cigarette

**jolt** *Slang.* heroin injection

**junk** *Slang.* heroin

**K** *Slang.* kilo, esp. of marijuana

**kef** marijuana

**key** *Slang.* kilo of marijuana

**killer weed** *Slang.* marijuana

**kilo** *Slang.* pressed bundle of marijuana weighing one kilogram; one kilogram of any drug

**lady snow** *Slang.* cocaine

**laudanum** opium in solution

**laughing gas** nitrous oxide

**leaper** *Slang.* amphetamine pill

**Librium** *Trademark.* pharmaceutical tranquilizer

**lid** *Slang.* ounce of marijuana

**line** *Slang.* small amount of chopped cocaine, arranged in a strip for inhalation

**locoweed** datura

**L-pill** lethal potassium cyanide pill

**LSD** *l*ysergic acid *d*iethylamide; powerful, psychedelic, synthetic hallucinogen

**'lude** *Informal.* Quaalude

**Luminal** *Trademark.* barbiturate pill

**lysergic acid** LSD

**M** *Slang.* marijuana; morphine

**magic mushroom** *Slang.* mushroom containing the hallucinogen psilocybin

**majoon** *Slang.* hallucinogenic drug in candy form

**mandrake** narcotic herb

**mannite** milk sugar for cutting heroin

**marahoochie** *Informal.* marijuana

**marijuana** dried *Cannabis sativa* or *Cannabis indica* leaves and flowers, smoked or eaten as mild hallucinogen; *Slang:* banji, bhang, boo, bush, dagga, gage, gangster, ganja, grass, hay, herb, hooch, kif, killer weed, M, marahoochie, Mary Jane, mezz, mota, muggle, pot, reefer, shit, smoke, tea, 13-m, viper's weed, weed, yerba

**Mary Jane** *Slang.* marijuana

**matchbox** *Informal.* small container of marijuana, esp. empty kitchen matchbox

**Maui wowie** *Slang.* extremely potent marijuana from Hawaii

**MDA** *m*ethyl*di*amphetamine, a stimulant

**meperidine** crystalline narcotic used as sedative and painkiller

**meprobamate** nonbarbiturate sedative; Miltown

**mescal** small succulent with hallucinogenic, buttonlike tops

**mescaline** hallucinogen derived from succulent mescal plant or peyote cactus

**meth** *Informal.* methamphetamine

**methadone** synthetic opiate used to replace heroin in treatment of addicts

**methamphetamine** amphetamine, esp. street drug in powder form; crank

**methaqualone** nonbarbiturate sedative-hypnotic substance used to induce sleep; Quaalude

**Methedrine** *Trademark.* pharmaceutical amphetamine

**mezz** *Slang.* marijuana

**michoacán** *Slang.* potent green marijuana from Mexican state of Michoacán

**microdot** *Slang.* tiny LSD tablet; dot

**mike** *Informal.* one microgram, esp. of LSD

**milk sugar** white lactose crystals for cutting cocaine or heroin

**Miltown** *Trademark.* pharmaceutical minor tranquilizer meprobamate

**MMDA** amphetamine with hallucinogenic properties

**morning glory seeds** mildly hallucinogenic plant seeds

**morphine** painkilling opium alkaloid narcotic; *Slang:* Aunt Emma, M, unkie, white nurse

**mota** *Slang.* marijuana

**mother's helper** *Slang.* Valium

**muggle** marijuana

**narcotic** painkilling or sleep-inducing substance, esp. opiate or pharmaceutical hypnotic, usu. addictive

**Nembutal** *Trademark.* pharmaceutical barbiturate

**neuroleptic drug** antipsychotic drug that reduces anxiety and tension; tranquilizer

**nickel bag** *Slang.* small container of heroin or other drug sold for $5

**nicotine** poisonous alkaloid present in tobacco leaves

**nitrous oxide** inhaled anesthetic with hallucinogenic properties; laughing gas

**Nixon** *Slang.* poor quality drug passed off as high quality

**noise** *Slang.* heroin

**nonbarbiturate sedative** pharmaceutical depressant that affects the central nervous system

**nose candy** *Slang.* cocaine

**number** *Slang.* marijuana cigarette

**nutmeg** mildly hallucinogenic plant seed

**opiate** narcotic derived from or containing opium

**opium** narcotic derived from poppy plant; *Slang:* black, blackstuff, Chinese molasses, gow, hop, poppy

**orange wedge** *Slang.* LSD in tall orange tablet

**Owsley** *Slang.* high-quality LSD of 1960's, named for its chemist

**o-z** *Informal.* ounce of drugs, esp. marijuana

**Panama red** *Slang.* reddish marijuana from Panama

**paper** *Informal.* folded paper containing dose of drugs

**paregoric** soothing opium extract

**PCP** phencyclidine; addictive drug orig. used as animal tranquilizer, acting as depressant, anesthetic, stimulant, convulsant, and hallucinogen; angel dust

**peace pill** *Slang.* LSD or sometimes PCP

**pep pill** stimulant

**Percodan** *Trademark.* morphine-derived narcotic painkiller

**Peruvian perfume** *Slang.* cocaine

**peyote** hallucinogenic cactus, chewed or used as source of mescaline; top

**pharmaceutical** drug manufactured legally by company but acquired without prescription

**phencyclidine** PCP

**pill** *Slang.* pellet of opium

**pinks** *Slang.* barbiturates

**pink wedge** *Slang.* powerful LSD in tall pink tablet

**pinner** *Slang.* very thin marijuana cigarette

**poison** *Slang.* heroin

**popper** vial of amyl nitrite

**poppy** opium

**pot** *Slang.* marijuana

**psilocin** substance produced after ingesting psilocybin

**psilocybin** hallucinogen derived from *Psilocybe mexicana* mushroom

**psychedelic** intensely mind-altering substance that produces heightened awareness and hallucinations, esp. LSD, psilocybin, and mescaline

**psychoactive drug** depressant, stimulant, or hallucinogen that affects central nervous system

**psychotropic drug** substance affecting mood or behavior, without central nervous system stimulation or depression, esp. tranquilizers, antidepressants, marijuana, and hashish

**pure** *Slang.* unadulterated heroin

**purple haze** *Slang.* LSD in purple tablet

**purple heart** *Slang.* Dexamyl

**Quaalude** *Trademark.* pharmaceutical sedative methaqualone; 'lude; soaper

**quack** *Slang.* Quaalude

**quinine** substance used in cutting heroin

**rainbow** *Slang.* red and blue Tuinal capsule

**rainy-day woman** *Slang.* marijuana cigarette

**red** *Slang.* Seconal capsule

**red chicken** *Slang.* Chinese heroin

**reefer** *Slang.* marijuana cigarette; marijuana

**resin** *Slang.* hashish

**roach** *Slang.* small butt end of marijuana cigarette

**rock** *Slang.* crack cocaine

**roller coaster** *Slang.* combination of stimulant and tranquilizer in one pill

**rope** *Slang.* marijuana cigarette

**San Francisco bomb** *Slang.* cocaine, heroin, and LSD mixture

**scag** *Slang.* heroin

**Seconal** *Trademark.* pharmaceutical depressant-hypnotic secobarbital sodium

**sedative-hypnotic** drug that depresses central nervous system

**shake** *Slang.* loose, mildly intoxicating leaves of dried marijuana that have fallen from flowering stems

**shit** *Slang.* drugs; marijuana

**shot** hypodermic injection of a drug

**sins** *Slang.* sinsimilla

**sinsimilla** seedless, unpollinated, female marijuana with high THC content; sins

**skag** *Slang.* heroin

**sleeping pill** pill or capsule containing a barbiturate for inducing sleep

**smack** *Slang.* heroin

**smoke** *Informal.* marijuana

**snop** *Slang.* marijuana cigarette

**snow** *Slang.* cocaine

**soaper** *Slang.* Quaalude

**soft drug** nonaddictive or psychologically addictive substance

**soma** legendary hallucinogen made from intoxicating plant

**soporific** hypnotic or sleep-inducing drug

**Spanish fly** preparation of powdered blister beetles, used as an aphrodisiac; cantharides

**speed** *Slang.* any central nervous system stimulant, esp. amphetamine

**speedball** *Slang.* injected mixture of cocaine or amphetamine and heroin

**spliff** *Slang.* large marijuana cigarette, esp. of Jamaican ganja

**spoon** *Slang.* tiny heroin dose, usu. one-sixteenth ounce

**stick** *Slang.* marijuana cigarette

**stimulant** any drug that increases central nervous system activity; upper

**STP** *Slang.* legendary, powerful hallucinogen used esp. in 1960's that causes three-day trips, often with permanent bad side effects, orig. 2.5 dimethoxy-4-methylamphetamine

**stuff** *Slang.* drugs, esp. illicit ones

**sugar cube** *Slang.* form of liquid LSD dropped on cube of sugar

**synthetics** narcotics produced in laboratory

**tab** single drug dose in form of compressed powder

**taste** minute quantity of a drug, often offered to entice buyer

**tea** *Slang.* marijuana

**tecata** *Slang.* heroin

**ten-cent pistol** *Slang.* bag of poisoned heroin

**tetrahydrocannabinol** THC; active substance in marijuana and hashish

**Thai stick** *Slang.* powerful marijuana in stick form from Thailand

**THC** *tetrahydrocannabinol*

**13-m** *Slang.* marijuana

**toot** *Slang.* cocaine

**topi** *Slang.* peyote

**toye** *Slang.* small container of opium

**trank** *Informal.* tranquilizer

**tranquilizer** pharmaceutical drug that alleviates anxiety; trank

**Tuinal** *Trademark.* hypnotic barbiturate combining amobarbital and secobarbital

**twist** *Slang.* marijuana cigarette

**unkie** *Slang.* morphine

**upper** *Informal.* stimulant

**Valium** *Trademark.* pharmaceutical minor tranquilizer diazepam

**viper's weed** *Slang.* marijuana

**weed** *Slang.* marijuana

**white girl** *Slang.* cocaine

**white lightning** *Slang.* LSD in small, white tablet form

**white nurse** *Slang.* morphine

**whites** *Slang.* amphetamine pills

**windowpane** *Slang.* form of LSD

**yellow** *Slang.* yellow jacket

**yellow jacket** *Slang.* yellow capsule of Nembutal

**yenshee** *Slang.* opium residue

**yerba** *Slang.* marijuana

**z** *Slang.* ounce of any drug

**Zacatecas purple** *Slang.* purple marijuana from Zacatecas, Mexico

## DRUNKENNESS, DRUNKARDS, AND ALCOHOLISM

**AA** Alcoholics Anonymous

**addled** (*adj*) drunk; confused by drink

**alcoholic** one suffering from alcoholism; beverage containing alcohol; boozer; chronic drunk; drunkard

**Alcoholics Anonymous** AA; organization that helps alcoholics to stop drinking by following twelve-step program

**alcoholism** condition of uncontrollable continual or sporadic heavy drinking of alcohol

**Antabuse** *Trademark.* pharmaceutical treatment for alcoholism

**bender** prolonged period of drunkenness

**besotted** (*adj*) stupefied by drink

**bibber** one addicted to drink

**bibulous** (*adj*) inclined or addicted to drink

**binge** drinking spree

**blasted** (*adj*) *Slang.* very drunk

**blind drunk** (*adj*) extremely inebriated

**blotto** (*adj*) *Slang.* very drunk

**bombed** (*adj*) *Slang.* drunk

**boozer** *Informal.* one who drinks to excess; alcoholic

**brannigan** drinking spree

**canned** (*adj*) *Slang.* drunk

**cheap drunk** one who becomes intoxicated on one or two drinks

**chronic drunk** alcoholic

**cockeyed** (*adj*) *Slang.* drunk

**crapulence** drunkenness to point of sickness

**crapulous** (*adj*) sick from overindulgence in liquor

**crash** (*vb*) *Slang.* experience aftereffects of intoxication

**crispy** (*adj*) *Slang.* hung over

**crocked** (*adj*) *Slang.* drunk

**debauchery** indulgence in excessive drinking or other immoral pleasures

**delirium tremens** dt's; violent hallucinations and seizures induced by prolonged alcohol abuse

**Dionysian** (*adj*) drunken and orgiastic, after Greek god Dionysus

**dipsomania** uncontrollable craving for alcohol

**dissipation** excessive consumption of alcohol

**drunk** (*adj*) intoxicated by alcoholic drink; temporarily impaired, excited, or stupefied by alcoholic drink; *Slang:* blasted, blotto, bombed, canned, cockeyed, crocked, fried, high, in one's cups, lit up, loaded, oiled, pickled, pie-eyed, pissed, plastered, polluted, potted, ripped, shitfaced, shnockered, skunk drunk, sloshed, smashed, sotted, sozzled, squiffed, stewed, stinko, stoned, swacked, tanked, tiddly, tight, tipsy, wasted, wiped out, woozy, wrecked, zonked

**drunkard** person often or habitually drunk

**dt's** delirium *tremens*

**ebriosity** habitual intoxication

**enabler** one who permits and encourages an alcoholic to drink

**fantods** jitters; delirium tremens

**fried** (*adj*) *Slang.* very drunk

**fuddle** (*vb*) stupefy with alcoholic drink

**giddy** (*adj*) somewhat inebriated

**grog blossom** alcoholism

**hair of the dog** *Informal.* drink of liquor supposed to relieve a hangover

**hangover** severe headache, nausea, or other unpleasant aftereffects of too much drink

**high** (*adj*) *Informal.* intoxicated

**hit the bottle** *Slang.* drink heavily

**hit the sauce** *Slang.* drink heavily

**hooch hound** *Slang.* drunkard

**hung over** (*adj*) feeling unpleasant aftereffects of too much drink

**immoderation** excessive drinking

**indulgence** act of drinking, esp. to excess

**inebriated** (*adj*) drunk

**in one's cups** *Slang.* drunk

**intemperance** excessive drinking of alcohol

**intoxication** loss of control, excitement, or stupefaction due to consumption of alcohol

**jake leg** *Slang.* paralysis from drinking strong liquor

**jimjams** *Slang.* delirium tremens

**juicer** *Slang.* drunkard

**katzenjammer** severe headache due to hangover

**liquor up** (*vb*) *Informal.* make drunk; drink to excess

**lit up** (*adj*) *Slang.* drunk

**loaded** (*adj*) *Slang.* drunk

**lush** one who drinks to excess; alcoholic

**morning after** period upon awakening when aftereffects of night of drinking are felt

**muzzy** (*adj*) *Informal.* muddled or confused, esp. by drink

**oenophile** lover of oenomel, a drink of wine and honey (ancient Greece)

**off the wagon** *Slang.* having returned to drinking after period of temperance

**oiled** (*adj*) *Slang.* drunk

**one too many** extra drink that pushes one over edge into drunkenness

**pass out** (*vb*) become unconscious from drunkenness

**pickled** (*adj*) *Slang.* drunk

**pie-eyed** (*adj*) *Slang.* very drunk

**pissed** (*adj*) *Vulgar slang.* very drunk

**plastered** (*adj*) *Slang.* very drunk

**polluted** (*adj*) *Slang.* drunk, intoxicated

**potted** (*adj*) *Slang.* drunk

**problem drinker** alcoholic, one who cannot control drinking

**ripped** (*adj*) *Slang.* very intoxicated, drunk

**rummy** *Slang.* alcoholic, esp. one intoxicated on cheap liquor

**shiker** *Yiddish.* drunkard

**shitfaced** (*adj*) *Vulgar slang.* very drunk

**shnockered** (*adj*) *Slang.* drunk

**skunk drunk** (*adj*) *Slang.* extremely inebriated

**sleep it off** overcome aftereffects of drink by sleep

**sloshed** (*adj*) *Slang.* very drunk

**smashed** (*adj*) *Slang.* very drunk

**soak** (*vb*) *Informal.* become drunk

**sober up** (*vb*) take action or pass time to end a state of drunkenness

**sot** chronic drunkard

**sotted** (*adj*) drunk

**soused** (*adj*) *Slang.* drunk

**sozzled** (*adj*) *Slang.* very drunk

**spree** prolonged period of drunkenness

**squiffed** (*adj*) *Slang.* very intoxicated, drunk

**stewed** (*adj*) *Slang.* drunk

**stinking** (*adj*) *Slang.* very inebriated

**stinko** (*adj*) *Slang.* drunk

**stoned** (*adj*) *Slang.* intoxicated

**swacked** (*adj*) *Slang.* very dunk

**swizzle** (*vb*) drink to excess

**tanked** (*adj*) *Slang.* drunk

**tank up** (*vb*) take drink; become inebriated

**tiddly** (*adj*) *Brit. slang.* slightly drunk

**tie one on** *Slang.* drink until inebriated

**tight** (*adj*) *Slang.* drunk

**tipple** (*vb*) drink liquor habitually or excessively

**tippler** one habitually drunk

**tipsy** (*adj*) slightly intoxicated

**toot** *Slang.* drinking spree

**tope** (*vb*) drink to excess

**toper** one who drinks to excess

**tosspot** drunkard, sot

**twelve steps** step-by-step program for recovery from addiction, originated by Alcoholics Anonymous

**under the influence** inebriated, esp. while driving a car

**under the table** so intoxicated as to be lying on floor; outdrunk by another

**wasted** (*adj*) *Slang.* intoxicated

**wino** *Informal.* one chronically addicted to drink, esp. cheap wine

**wiped-out** (*adj*) *Slang.* drunk to the point of unconsciousness

**woozy** (*adj*) intoxicated; slightly dizzy

**wrecked** (*adj*) *Slang.* drunk

**zonked** (*adj*) *Slang.* extremely intoxicated, drunk

## PARAPHERNALIA AND BEHAVIOR

**abuse** (*vb*) use any drug to excess; (*n*) excessive use of drug

**acid trip** *Slang.* experience of taking LSD

**addiction** physical or psychological dependence on drug

**army disease** *Slang.* morphine addiction, esp. among military personnel who first received drug to alleviate pain

**bad trip** *Slang.* negative response, including panic, fear, and psychosis, due to hallucinogenic drug; bummer

**bang** (*vb*) *Slang.* inject drugs

**bang a gong** *Slang.* sniff cocaine

**black market** covert, illegal sale of drugs

**blow** (*vb*) *Slang.* inhale drugs; smoke marijuana

**bogue** *Slang.* withdrawal symptoms

**bong** *Slang.* water pipe for smoking marijuana

**boot** technique of injecting heroin gradually to prolong euphoric sensation

**bummer** *Slang.* bad trip

**burn** (*vb*) *Slang.* cheat someone on drug deal; (*n*) drug swindle

**bust** *Slang.* arrest for possession or sale of drugs

**buzz** *Slang.* initial mild effect of drug

**cap** gelatin capsule for holding drug dose; (*vb*) insert drug into capsules

**carry** (*vb*) have drugs on one's person

**charge** *Slang.* sudden, exhilarating effect of drugs

**chillum** short clay marijuana pipe

**chipping** *Slang.* occasional or recreational use of hard drugs

**clean** (*adj*) *Slang.* not in possession of drugs; (*vb*) remove stems and seeds from marijuana

**cold turkey** *Informal.* sudden withdrawal from addictive drug use

**come down** (*vb*) feel drug high depart, return to normal state

**connect** (*vb*) *Slang.* buy or find source for drugs

**contact high** mildly altered state caused by proximity to marijuana smoke or smokers

**cook** (*vb*) dissolve heroin powder in water over heat prior to injection

**cop** (*vb*) *Slang.* buy drugs; score

**cotton** cotton filter for straining cooked heroin prior to injection

**cotton mouth** *Slang.* dryness in mouth due to inhibited salivation caused by marijuana smoking

**crack house** building used as crack distribution center, usu. in poor urban area

**crack pipe** small glass pipe used for smoking crack cocaine

**crash** (*vb*) *Slang.* fall asleep or come down from effect of drug

**cross-tolerance** tolerance to effects of one drug because of tolerance to a similar substance

**crutch** device for holding butt of marijuana cigarette

**cut** (*vb*) dilute a drug, esp. heroin or cocaine, with adulterating inactive substance

**deal** (*vb*) *Slang.* sell drugs

**dependency** physical or psychological addiction to drugs

**detox** *Informal.* detoxification

**detoxification** period of treatment and counseling during which addict overcomes drug dependency

**do dope** (*vb*) use or take drugs

**drop** (*vb*) *Slang.* swallow a pill or drugs; take LSD

**dropper** medicine dropper used as homemade drug injection equipment

**drug abuse** excessive use of any drug or narcotic

**drug testing** examination and analysis, usu. of blood or urine, to determine presence of drugs, usu. conducted by government or employer

**dusted** (*adj*) under the influence of PCP, or angel dust

**dusting** *Slang.* addition of heroin to marijuana cigarette

**fix** (*vb*) *Slang.* inject oneself with narcotic; (*n*) single injection of a drug

**flash** *Slang.* rush

**flip out** (*vb*) *Slang.* experience psychotic state, or extreme mental or physical reaction, as a result of taking a drug

**fly** (*vb*) *Slang.* experience intoxication due to drugs

**freak** (*vb*) *Slang.* freak out

**freak out** (*vb*) *Slang.* hallucinate uncontrollably; experience dramatic, frightening, drug-induced distortion of perception and feeling; freak

**freebase** (*vb*) *Slang.* process cocaine with ether and heat to intensify its effects; smoke freebased cocaine

**geeze** (*vb*) *Slang.* inject drugs, esp. heroin

**get high** (*vb*) *Slang.* achieve euphoria or other drug-induced state

**get off** (*vb*) experience effects of drugs, esp. by injection

**glue sniffing** breathing glue fumes for hallucinogenic or euphoric drug effect

**goof** (*vb*) *Slang.* be under the influence of narcotics or barbiturates; nod out

**habit** physical dependence on addictive drug; amount required each day to satisfy dependency

**hassle** (*vb*) *Informal.* buy drugs, bargain for drugs

**high** (*adj*) euphorically under the influence of drugs; (*n*) *Slang.* such a state

**hit** *Slang.* (*vb*) inject drugs; (*n*) single drug injection; one drag on a marijuana cigarette

**holding** (*adj*) *Slang.* carrying drugs on one's person

**hookah** water-cooled pipe for smoking marijuana or hashish

**hooked** (*adj*) *Informal.* physically dependent on drug

**hustle** (*vb*) *Slang.* get money for drugs, esp. by prostitution or other illegal means

**hypo** *Informal.* hypodermic syringe

**hypodermic syringe** small glass syringe used to inject drugs; hypo

**ice-cream habit** *Slang.* moderate social use of hard drugs

**jag** state of intense, protracted drug stimulation

**jones** *Slang.* drug addiction, esp. to heroin

**joypop** (*vb*) *Slang.* inject heroin occasionally, esp. subcutaneously instead of into vein

**kick** (*vb*) *Slang.* give up or break drug habit or dependency

**kick the gong around** *Slang.* sniff cocaine

**kick the habit** *Slang.* give up drug use; kick

**kit** *Slang.* hypodermic needle and equipment for injecting drugs

**kitchen** *Slang.* drug laboratory

**life** *Slang.* **the life;** syndrome of drug addiction and attendant patterns of behavior and activity

**loaded** (*adj*) *Slang.* high on drugs

**mainline** (*vb*) *Slang.* inject drug into vein

**methadone maintenance** program of legally administered methadone provided to prevent recidivism of former heroin addicts

**miss** drug injection that misses vein

**monkey on one's back** *Slang.* drug addiction or dependency

**munchies** *Slang.* intense craving for food, esp. sugar, experienced after smoking marijuana

**nail** *Slang.* hypodermic needle for drug injections

**narcoterrorism** terrorist tactics employed by drug dealers against government agents

**narghile** type of water pipe

**needle** hypodermic needle used for drug injections

**needle park** *Slang.* meeting place in which heroin addicts inject drugs

**nod out** (*vb*) *Slang.* be under the influence of narcotics; doze off into drug stupor

**OD** overdose

**outfit** equipment for injecting drugs

**overdose** OD; intake of quantity of drugs above one's tolerance, producing debilitation or death

**panic** bad reaction to drug; heroin shortage

**paraphernalia** implements and objects used in preparing and ingesting drugs

**physical dependence** physiological addiction to drug

**pinned** (*adj*) *Slang.* having constricted eye pupils due to narcotics use

**pipe** device for smoking marijuana, hashish, or crack cocaine; *Slang.* easy-to-inject vein

**plant** (*vb*) place drugs on premises or on person set up to be arrested for drug possession

**pop** (*vb*) *Slang.* inject heroin under skin, not into vein

**possession** having drugs on one's person or property

**potentiate** (*vb*) cause drug to act more powerfully by action or use of another drug

**psychological dependence** drug craving based on desire for pleasure, not physical addiction

**reverse tolerance** increased sensitivity to smaller doses of drug the more it is taken, as with marijuana

**rig** equipment for injecting drugs

**roach clip** *Slang*. gripping device for holding end of burning marijuana cigarette; roach holder

**roach holder** *Slang*. roach clip

**run** *Slang*. period of intense drug use

**rush** *Slang*. sudden sensation of drug's effects, esp. from injection; flash

**score** *Slang*. (*vb*) buy or obtain illicit drugs; (*n*) any drugs so purchased; any illicit drug transaction

**scrip** *Informal*. prescription for drugs, esp. narcotics

**setting** environment and mental state of person preparing for hallucinogenic drug experience

**shoot** (*vb*) *Slang*. shoot up

**shooting gallery** *Slang*. location where addicts inject drugs

**shooting gravy** *Slang*. reinjection of blood backed up into needle during drug injection

**shoot up** (*vb*) *Slang*. inject drugs into vein

**sick** (*adj*) suffering from drug withdrawal

**skin-pop** (*vb*) *Slang*. inject drugs subcutaneously, not into vein

**snort** (*vb*) *Slang*. inhale powdered drug through nose

**spaced-out** (*adj*) *Slang*. feeling floating sensation or numbing effects of drug use

**spike** *Slang*. hypodermic needle

**spoon** *Slang*. small measure of heroin

**stash** hiding place for drugs; hidden supply of drugs

**stem** *Slang*. glass pipe for smoking crack or ice

**stoned** (*adj*) *Slang*. intoxicated by drugs

**straight** (*adj*) *Informal*. not using illicit drugs

**straw** thin tube used for sniffing drugs in powdered form, esp. cut-off straw

**street** *Slang*. usu. **the street;** world of drug use, abuse, and hustling required to acquire money for drugs

**strung-out** (*adj*) *Slang*. severely addicted to drugs

**substance abuse** long-term addiction to or excessive use of narcotics or controlled substances

**tea pad** *Slang*. room or other location for smoking marijuana

**tie off** (*vb*) wrap cord or strap around upper arm to force veins into prominence for injection

**toke** *Slang*. single puff on marijuana cigarette

**tolerance** resistance to the effects of a drug, resulting in the need to use increasingly large doses of that drug for the same effect

**toot** *Slang*. a snort of a drug, esp. cocaine

**tracks** *Slang*. needle marks from repeated drug injections

**trip** *Slang*. (n) hallucinogenic drug experience; (*vb*) take a hallucinogen, esp. LSD

**turn on** (*vb*) *Slang*. take drugs; become intoxicated from drug use

**using** (*adj*) *Slang*. taking drugs; addicted to drugs

**wasted** (*adj*) *Slang*. intoxicated; very high

**water pipe** device in which marijuana smoke is cooled by passing through water before entering hose leading to smoker's mouth

**white light** *Slang*. sensation of intense light produced by hallucinogenic drugs

**wig out** (*vb*) *Slang*. experience dramatic mental effects from drug use

**wings** *Slang*. first drug injection

**wired** (*adj*) *Slang*. very high on drugs, esp. stimulants

**withdrawal** cessation of use of addictive drug with painful or unpleasant symptoms

**works** *Slang*. equipment for drug injection

**yen-shee** *Slang*. painful opium-induced constipation

**Zig-Zag** *Trademark*. brand of cigarette rolling papers

**zoned out** (*adj*) *Slang*. very intoxicated, nearly senseless from drug use

**zonked out** (*adj*) *Slang*. very intoxicated, nearly senseless from drug use

## USERS AND ABUSERS

**acid freak** *Slang*. LSD user

**acid-head** *Slang*. habitual user of LSD

**addict** person who is physically or psychologically dependent on some drug; junkie

**A-head** *Slang*. habitual user of amphetamines

**bagman** *Slang*. drug seller

**burnout** person who is apathetic and disoriented from prolonged drug use, esp. from marijuana smoking

**candy man** *Slang*. drug seller

**chef** *Slang*. chemist, esp. in illicit amphetamine laboratory

**connection** *Slang*. drug seller; supplier of drugs

**cook** *Slang*. chemist in illicit drug laboratory; chef

**copilot** *Slang*. guide

**croaker** *Slang*. doctor supplying narcotics to addicts

**dealer** *Slang*. drug seller

**dope fiend** *Slang*. drug addict

**dopehead** *Slang*. drug addict

**dope peddler** *Slang*. drug seller

**dope pusher** *Slang*. drug seller

**doper** *Slang*. regular drug user, esp. marijuana smoker

**drug seller** person who buys and sells drugs illegally; *Slang*: bagman, candy man, connection, dealer, man, pusher, source

**explorers' club** *Slang*. group of LSD users

**flower children** youthful psychedelic drug users in the 1960's, esp. in San Francisco's Haight-Ashbury district

**freak** *Slang*. person using particular kind of drug on frequent basis, such as a speed freak

**gee head** *Slang*. paregoric user

**ground control** *Slang*. guide

**guide** person experienced in LSD use who guides another's LSD trip; copilot; ground control

**head** *Slang*. drug user or addict, esp. one using a particular drug, such as a pothead

**hustler** *Slang*. drug addict forced into stealing or prostitution to support habit

**junkie** *Informal*. heroin addict; drug addict

**man** *Slang*. **the man;** one's drug supplier; the police

**mother** *Slang*. one's regular drug supplier

**narc** *Slang*. police officer on narcotics detail

**pillhead** *Slang*. habitual amphetamine or barbiturate user

**poison people** *Slang*. heroin addicts

**pothead** *Slang*. regular marijuana user

**pusher** *Slang*. drug seller

**shmecker** *Slang*. heroin user

**source** one's drug supplier; dealer

**speed freak** *Slang.* regular user of amphetamines

**square** *Slang.* user's term for person not using drugs

**straight** *Slang.* person not using drugs

**take-off artist** *Slang.* heroin addict who supports habit by robbing other addicts

**tea head** *Slang.* marijuana user

**trafficker** large-scale drug seller or importer

**travel agent** *Slang.* LSD seller

**vice squad** narcotics division of police

**viper** *Slang.* marijuana smoker

# MENTAL DISTURBANCES

Insanity
Mental Institutions
Agitation, Abnormality, and Instability

**SEE ALSO:** Chap. 1: Medical Problems; Chap. 13: Psychology; Chap. 20: Insults, Slurs, and Epithets

## INSANITY

**amok** (*adj*) in a murderous frenzy; raging violently

**ape** (*adj*) *Slang.* crazed, nuts, or wildly overactive; apeshit

**apeshit** (*adj*) *Vulgar slang.* ape

**around the bend** *Slang.* crazy

**balmy** (*adj*) *Informal.* crazy

**bananas** (*adj*) *Slang.* crazy, deranged

**barmy** (*adj*) *Brit. slang.* balmy

**batty** (*adj*) crazy; demented

**bent** (*adj*) abnormal, esp. somewhat crazed or perverse

**berserk** (*adj*) frenzied; crazed

**bonkers** (*adj*) *Slang.* crazy; mentally unbalanced

**cracked** (*adj*) *Slang.* insane

**crackpot** *Informal.* one given to eccentric or lunatic notions

**crazed** (*adj*) distracted, overexcited, slightly nuts

**crazy** (*adj*) mentally deranged or demented; insane; (*n*) *Slang.* one who acts or is insane

**criminally insane** prone to criminal acts or threats; dangerous

**cuckoo** (*adj*) *Slang.* crazy

**daffy** (*adj*) *Slang.* nutty, screwy

**demented** (*adj*) perversely insane; mad

**dementia** insanity, esp. severe mental impairment due to brain damage

**demoniac** (*adj*) behaving as though possessed by the devil

**deranged** (*adj*) insane

**feeble-minded** (*adj*) mentally deficient; moronic

**flip** (*vb*) *Slang.* lose one's mind

**flip out** (*vb*) *Slang.* go crazy or become frenzied

**flipped** (*adj*) *Slang.* deranged; crazy

**frenzied** (*adj*) marked by violent agitation; berserk

**frenzy** temporary madness; intense agitation and compulsive activity

**fruitcake** *Slang.* crazy or eccentric person; nut

**go ape** *Slang.* become violently emotional

**go mad** become insane; suffer a breakdown

**gone** (*adj*) *Informal.* lost in madness, outside reality

**goofy** (*adj*) *Slang.* nutty, silly

**go to pieces** break down, suffer an emotional collapse

**have a screw loose** be crazy

**haywire** (*adj*) *Slang.* out of control; disordered

**homicidal** (*adj*) having murderous intent or making threats

**idiot** one who is severely mentally deficient

**insane** (*adj*) mentally disordered or deranged; suffering from insanity; *Slang:* around the bend, balmy, bananas, barmy, batty, bonkers, cracked, crazy, deranged, loco, loony, nuts, off one's rocker, out of one's tree, psycho, wacko

**insanity** various deranged states of mind, mental disorders, conditions, and incapacity; dementia; lunacy; madness

**kook** *Slang.* one who is odd, eccentric, or unbalanced

**kooky** (*adj*) *Slang.* eccentric or peculiar

**lather** *Informal.* agitated or overwrought state

**loco** (*adj*) *Slang.* insane

**loony** *Informal.* (*n*) lunatic; (*adj*) crazy; insane

**lose one's mind** go insane

**lunacy** insanity

**lunatic** insane person

**mad** (*adj*) mentally disturbed or deranged; insane; completely senseless or disordered

**madman** insane person; lunatic

**madness** insanity

**maniac** one who is totally, often dangerously, insane

**mental** (*adj*) affected with a disorder of the mind

**moonstruck** (*adj*) mentally deranged

**moron** one of very low mental capacity

**moronic** (*adj*) feeble-minded

**nut** mildly crazy or eccentric person, usu. harmless; fruitcake

**nuts** (*adj*) *Slang.* crazy; insane

**nutter** *Brit. slang.* mildly crazy person

**nutty** (*adj*) *Slang.* eccentric, mildly crazy; daffy

**oddball** *Informal.* eccentric or abnormal individual

**off** (*adj*) *Slang.* slightly crazy; abnormal

**off one's head** crazy

**off one's rocker** *Slang.* crazy

**out of one's head** crazy

**out of one's mind** crazy

**out of one's tree** *Slang.* crazy

**overdrawn** (*adj*) *Slang.* oddball, nuts

**over the edge** gone crazy

**possessed** (*adj*) behaving as though controlled by supernatural power or powerful subconscious impulse

**potty** (*adj*) *Brit. slang.* slightly insane or eccentric

**psycho** (*adj*) psychopathic; insane; (*n*) psychopathic person

**psychopath** *Slang.* one who is mentally ill, esp. exhibiting amoral and antisocial behavior

**psychopathic** (*adj*) exhibiting amoral and antisocial behavior, including the inability to tell right from wrong

**psychosis** major, severe form of mental disorder

**psychotic** one afflicted with severe mental disorder; insane person

**rabid** (*adj*) frenzied, raging uncontrollably

**raving** (*adj*) speakingwildly, deliriously

**schizoid** (*adj*) suffering from schizophrenia or multiple personality; schizy

**schizy** (*adj*) *Informal.* schizoid

**screaming-meemies** *Informal.* extreme terror or nervous hysteria

**screwy** (*adj*) *Slang.* slightly insane; daffy

**sick** (*adj*) mentally ill

**sicko** *Slang.* perverse, deranged person

**sociopath** psychopathic personality with extremely asocial or antisocial behavior

**stark raving mad** *Slang.* completely insane

**touched** *(adj)* unbalanced or slightly crazy

**twisted** *(adj) Slang.* perverse, diabolical

**unbalanced** *(adj)* mentally disordered, deranged

**unglued** *(adj) Slang.* mentally unstable or upset

**unhinged** highly distraught or unsettled

**wacko** *Slang. (adj)* insane, crazy *(n)* one who is insane

**wacky** *(adj) Slang.* slightly crazy or eccentric

**weirdo** *Informal.* extraordinarily strange individual

**whacked-out** *(adj) Slang.* strung out, agitated, or slightly insane

**wigged out** *(adj) Slang.* agitated, anxious, or slightly insane

**zany** *(adj)* eccentric or mildly abnormal in behavior

## MENTAL INSTITUTIONS

**asylum** institution for the relief and care of the mentally ill

**bedlam** *Archaic.* lunatic asylum

**booby hatch** *Slang.* insane asylum

**bughouse** *Slang.* insane asylum

**commit** *(vb)* place someone in mental hospital

**committed** *(adj)* required to enter and remain in mental hospital

**funny farm** *Slang.* mental hospital

**halfway house** residence for formerly institutionalized patients that helps to facilitate their readjustment to normal life

**home** mental hospital

**insane asylum** institution for the care and treatment of the mentally ill; booby hatch; bughouse

**institution** mental hospital

**loony bin** *Slang.* mental hospital

**lunatic asylum** mental hospital

**madhouse** mental hospital

**mental home** low-security mental hospital

**mental hospital** institution for the care and treatment of the mentally ill; funny farm; home; institution; loony bin; lunatic asylum; madhouse; nut house; snake pit

**mental ward** section of hospital reserved for mentally ill

**nut house** *Slang.* mental hospital

**padded cell** heavily padded, individual holding room for confinement of psychotic patient

**psychiatric ward** section of regular hospital reserved for the mentally ill; psycho ward

**psycho ward** *Slang.* psychiatric ward

**sanatorium** sanitarium

**sanitarium** hospital for the treatment of the mentally ill; sanatorium

**snake pit** *Informal.* mental hospital

## AGITATION, ABNORMALITY, AND INSTABILITY

**abandon** freedom from normal restraints in behavior

**aberrant** *(adj)* departing substantially from standard behavior

**abnormality** deviation from normal, accepted behavior

**agita** *Informal.* anxiety; agitation

**agitated** *(adj)* overly excited or anxious

**agitation** mental excitement or disquiet; perturbation

**agony** intense mental pain or tortured state of mind

**amentia** mental deficiency, esp. low intellectual capacity

**analgesia** insensibility to pain while conscious

**angst** feeling of anxiety, apprehension, and insecurity

**anguish** extreme mental distress

**anomaly** any abnormality or deviation from the norm

**anxiety** distress, uneasiness, apprehension, and psychic tension caused by fear of impending or imagined danger or misfortune

**at loose ends** distracted, unsettled, uncertain

**at sea** confused, dazed, or disoriented

**attack** fit of disorder; active episode of recurrent illness

**at wit's end** perplexed, esp. having exhausted one's mental resources

**baffled** *(adj)* confused; confounded

**bewildered** *(adj)* extremely confused and disoriented

**bizarre** *(adj)* odd, extravagant, or eccentric in behavior

**black out** *(vb)* undergo temporary loss of consciousness, vision, or memory

**blow one's mind** *Slang.* become overwhelmed with wonder or bafflement, esp. when drug-induced

**brainsick** *(adj)* mentally disordered

**breakdown** physical, mental, or nervous collapse; nervous breakdown

**breaking point** point at which one succumbs to stress

**broken** *(adj)* completely crushed in mind and spirit

**brooding** *(adj)* depressed, moody

**bugaboo** imaginary object of fear, causing disproportionate anxiety

**bundle of nerves** extremely anxious individual

**butterflies** *Informal.* queasy feeling due to nervousness or agitation

**cabin fever** restless irritability from isolation or prolonged confinement

**catatonic** *(adj)* marked by stupor, rigidity, muteness, and bizarre or purposeless activity; *(n)* one suffering from catatonia

**cold sweat** concurrent chills and perspiration from fear or shock

**collapse** nervous breakdown or extreme depression

**comatose** *(adj)* in a state of prolonged unconsciousness

**come to** *(vb)* awaken from unconsciousness

**compulsive** *(adj)* unable to control an irrational impulse to do something

**confounded** *(adj)* baffled or confused

**confused** *(adj)* unable to differentiate reality; disturbed in mind or purpose; muddled

**conniption** fit of hysteria, rage, or alarm

**consternation** amazement or dismay causing confusion

**crack up** *(vb) Informal.* suffer a breakdown; go insane

**crisis** turning point in mental disorder

**crumble** *(vb)* suffer emotional collapse; go to pieces

**death wish** conscious or unconscious desire to die

**delirious** *(adj)* suffering from delirium

**delirium** state of confusion, disordered speech, hallucination, and frenzy

**delusion** persistent false belief regarding self or others

**depression** condition of general despondency, dejection, and withdrawel

**despair** utter loss of hope and confidence

**deviant** *(adj)* straying from normal behavior; *(n)* one who so strays

**diabolical** *(adj)* perverse, as though possessed by devil

**disorientation** displacement from a normal sense of time, place, and identity

**distracted** (*adj*) confused, unfocused, at loose ends

**distraught** (*adj*) extremely agitated

**distress** mental pain or suffering

**disturbed** (*adj*) showing symptoms of emotional illness and distress

**dither** nervous, disoriented, or indecisive state

**dizzy** (*adj*) mentally confused

**doldrums** spell of inactivity or depression

**dotty** *Informal*. mentally unbalanced; amiably eccentric

**eccentric** one who behaves abnormally; oddball

**eccentricity** bizarre or abnormal, but harmless, activity

**erratic** (*adj*) peculiar, inconsistent, or unpredictable in behavior

**euphoria** feeling of extreme elation

**fanatic** (*adj*) marked by excessive behavior

**fantasy** delusive view or idea

**fantods** emotional outburst or fit

**fazed** (*adj*) disturbed or disconcerted

**fit** sudden, violent emotional reaction or outburst

**flustered** (*adj*) confused, anxious, or agitated

**frantic** (*adj*) mentally deranged, out of control, or very nervous

**frazzled** (*adj*) in state of extreme nervous fatigue

**freak** *Slang*. abnormal individual

**freak out** (*vb*) *Slang*. behave irrationally, withdraw from reality, or experience nightmarish hallucinations, esp. when drug-induced

**hallucination** perception of objects not really there

**heebie-jeebies** *Slang*. condition of extreme anxiety and nervousness; jitters; willies

**hysteria** uncontrollable, irrational outburst of emotion or intense anxiety

**hysterics** fit of hysteria

**imbalanced** (*adj*) mentally disturbed or abnormal

**instability** tendency to behave in an unpredictable or erratic manner

**insufficiency** lack of mental fitness

**jangled** (*adj*) tense, irritated, nervous

**Jekyll and Hyde** person marked by dual personality, one good and one evil

**jimjams** *Slang*. jitters

**jitters** extreme sense of panic and nervousness; heebie-jeebies; screaming-meemies; willies

**kamikaze** (*adj*) recklessly self-destructive

**lobotomized** (*adj*) sluggish, dull-witted, or calmed due to lobotomy

**maladjusted** (*adj*) poorly adapted to normal society; eccentric

**malcontent** one rebelliously opposed to societal norms

**manic** (*adj*) hyperactive; excessively excited or agitated

**mental** (*adj*) *Informal*. affected with a disorder of the mind

**mental illness** disorder of the mind

**mixed-up** (*adj*) completely confused or emotionally unstable

**muddled** (*adj*) confused

**nervous breakdown** breakdown

**neurotic** (*adj*) excessively anxious or indecisive

**non compos mentis** *Latin*. lit. not of sound mind; mentally incompetent or unsound

**obsessive** (*adj*) unable to escape some persistent idea or need

**off-the-wall** (*adj*) *Informal*. extreme terror or nervous hysteria; jitters

**on pins and needles** experiencing nervous anxiety or anticipation

**on tenterhooks** in a state of uneasy suspense or anxiety

**overwrought** (*adj*) extremely anxious or agitated

**paroxysm** sudden emotional outburst

**peculiar** (*adj*) odd or eccentric in behavior

**perturbation** agitation

**perverse** (*adj*) obstinately unreasonable, willful, or evil

**phobic** (*adj*) suffering from exaggerated, illogical fears

**pixilated** (*adj*) slightly unbalanced

**prostration** state of overwhelming exhaustion or helplessness

**queer** (*adj*) peculiar or eccentric in behavior

**rage** uncontrollable anger directed at any available target

**rattled** (*adj*) confused, disconcerted, and anxious

**retarded** (*adj*) severely mentally deficient

**rocky** (*adj*) *Informal*. unstable, upset, or unsteady

**screaming-meemies** *Informal*. extreme terror or nervous hysteria; jitters

**shaken-up** (*adj*) disoriented or confused

**shattered** (*adj*) in a state of mental, emotional, or nervous collapse or disintegration

**shock** sudden, violent emotional disturbance, usu. caused by traumatic event or injury

**slough of despond** state of extreme depression

**spell** period of mental distress

**spooked** (*adj*) *Slang*. fearful over imagined threats

**state** abnormal condition of mind

**stressed-out** (*adj*) *Informal*. exhausted or extremely anxious

**strung-out** (*adj*) *Slang*. addicted to a drug; in an extreme state of nervous exhaustion

**stupor** state of extreme apathy or torpor from stress or shock

**swivet** state of extreme agitation

**tangled** (*adj*) disoriented or bewildered

**tantrum** uncontrollable fit of rage or hysteria

**tizzy** *Slang*. state of disorientation, anxiety, or upset

**trance** sleeplike state of suspended animation

**trauma** disordered psychic state due to emotional stress or physical injury

**turmoil** state of extreme agitation and confusion

**turn** *Informal*. nervous shock, as from fright

**twitter** state of anxiety, agitation, or extreme upset

**unsound** (*adj*) abnormal or disordered, as in the mind

**unstable** (*adj*) unable to control one's emotions or behave within accepted norms

**up the wall** extremely anxious or agitated

**willies** *Slang*. extreme state of anxiety and jitters; heebie-jeebies

**worked-up** (*adj*) agitated, unable to contain emotions

**zoned** (*adj*) *Slang*. dazed, disoriented, or confused

# CRIME

**SEE ALSO**: Chap. 11: Law; Chap. 22: Strategy, Intrigue, and Deception; Chap. 24: Drug Abuse and Alcoholism; Violence; Death

## CRIMES

**abduction** carrying off of person by force, esp. for sex or prostitution or as hostage

**adultery** engaging in extramarital sex

**aggravated assault** severe physical attack

**air piracy** skyjacking

**arson** intentionally setting fire to property

**assassination** murder of public figure

**assault** personal physical attack or threat of violence

**assault and battery** assault with actual physical contact or violence upon other person

**battery** physical violence upon another person, esp. beating

**bigamy** marrying while already legally married

**blackmail** demand for payment based on threat of embarrassment, exposure, or harm; extortion

**bootlegging** illegal production, distribution, or sale of something already owned or copyrighted, or something unregistered or outlawed; piracy

**break-in** illegal entry of another's property

**breaking and entering** entry into another's property, forcibly or with criminal intent

**bribery** offering payment for favors or corrupt behavior, esp. involving a public official

**bunko** confidence game or swindle that takes advantage of victim's ignorance

**burglary** breaking into and entering private property for purpose of crime, usu. theft

**capital crime** crime punishable by death

**chop shop** *Informal.* garage where stolen cars are dismantled so that their parts can be sold separately

**collusion** action by two or more persons to commit crime, esp. fraud

**confidence game** fraud or swindle involving misleading trickery; bunko

**conspiracy** secret plan among two or more persons to commit unlawful act

**contempt of court** willful disrespect for rules and orders of a court

**counterfeiting** manufacture of fake money

**crime** illegal act against person or property for which offender is liable to punishment

**crime against humanity** sinful act of monstrous proportions, such as genocide, directed against a group because of race, religion, or national origin

**crime of commission** illegal act involving specific violation of law

**crime of omission** illegal act involving failure to perform specific requirement of law

**crime of passion** illegal act committed in heat of anger or jealousy

**defalcation** failure to meet promise; act of embezzlement

**defamation** injury to person's character; spoken slander or written libel

**disorderly conduct** any of various activities that disturb public peace

**drive-by shooting** usu. gang-related shooting by unseen assailant in passing car

**embezzlement** theft of money or appropriation of property entrusted to one's care

**extortion** demand for payment based on threat of embarrassment, exposure, or harm; blackmail

**felony** serious crime, punishable by imprisonment

**forgery** fraudulent imitation of documents or signatures

**frame** (*vb*) falsely accuse or incriminate an innocent party

**fraud** deception or trickery for illegal gain

**graft** bribery, esp. of public officials

**grand larceny** theft of personal property exceeding specified value

**gunrunning** smuggling of firearms

**hijacking** takeover of public vehicle by violent means

**hit-and-run** (*adj*) guilty of leaving the scene of an auto accident to avoid responsibility for injuries and damage caused

**holdup** armed robbery

**homicide** taking of human life, usu. intentionally

**hot** (*adj*) *Slang.* stolen

**infraction** violation of a law

**involuntary manslaughter** taking of human life through criminal negligence

**job** *Slang.* crime

**justifiable homicide** killing person for defensible reason

**kidnapping** holding person, esp. child, captive in exchange for ransom

**killing** taking of human life

**larceny** theft of personal property

**libel** publication of statement damaging to another's reputation

**lift** (*vb*) *Informal.* steal

**looting** stealing from locations left unprotected after violent event or natural catastrophe

**malfeasance** wrongdoing or misconduct, esp. an act in violation of public trust committed by a public official

**malicious mischief** intentional or reckless harm or damage to property of another

**manslaughter** taking of human life by accident or negligence

**mayhem** willfully inflicting bodily injury on another person; deliberate violence or damage; state of rowdy disorder

**misconduct** intentionally improper behavior by a public official, esp. malfeasance

**misdemeanor** illegal act less serious than a felony, usu. punishable by fine or probation

**mugging** robbery, esp. in public place

**murder** taking of human life for no defensible reason

**mutiny** rebellion against authority, esp. military

**nuisance** use of one's property to damage or inconvenience another

**numbers racket** illegal lottery run by organized crime syndicate

**obstruction of justice** act that hinders or prevents completion of legal process

**offense** breach of criminal laws

**organized crime** network of criminals acting systematically in illegal activities; syndicate

**payola** *Informal.* bribery to promote commercial product, esp. music

**peculation** embezzlement of public funds

**perjury** lying while under oath, esp. giving false testimony in court

**petty larceny** theft of personal property of less than a specified value

**pickpocketing** theft from unsuspecting victim's person, esp. from a pocket

**pilferage** theft of small amounts of goods done over time to avoid detection

**piracy** bootlegging

**plunder** robbery by force, esp. in wartime; taking of property by force or fraud

**poaching** taking of fish or game from private property or protected reserve

**premeditated crime** crime planned and committed with malice aforethought

**prostitution** sexual intercourse for payment

**purse snatching** forceful theft of woman's handbag from her arm

**pyramid scheme** confidence game in which first investors are paid off with investment of later ones, who never see a return

**racketeering** operation of a business characterized by systematically dishonest practices

**rackets** *Informal.* often **the rackets**; businesses controlled by racketeering

**rape** forcible sexual intercourse without consent, esp. committed by a man against a woman

**reckless endangerment** action that could result in injury to another though it may not have

**resisting arrest** attempt to evade or physically prevent arrest

**robbery** theft aggravated by force or threat of assault

**roll** (*vb*) *Slang.* rob a helpless person, esp. an insensible drunk

**rumrunning** smuggling of liquor

**rustling** *Informal.* stealing, usu. cattle or horses (U.S. Old West)

**safecracking** forcible entry into locked safe to steal its contents

**sedition** incitement to rebellion against government

**shanghaiing** kidnapping a person into service aboard ship, esp. by drugging

**shoplifting** theft from store by person posing as customer

**skyjacking** forcible, violent seizure of aircraft; air piracy

**slander** making of false and malicious verbal statements damaging to another's reputation

**smuggling** import or export of goods that are outlawed or in avoidance of customs duty

**sodomy** performance of unnatural sex acts, usu. anal sex or sex with an animal

**soliciting** seeking clients for prostitute

**stealing** wrongfully taking another's property; theft

**subornation** inducing another to commit an illegal act, esp. perjury

**swindling** performing fraudulent business transactions

**syndicate** organized crime

**terrorism** use of intimidation and random violence, esp. as a political weapon

**theft** stealing

**tong war** violence between Chinese secret societies seeking to control organized crime

**treason** betrayal of one's country or government

**trespass** illegal use or occupation of another's property, esp. entry upon another's land

**vagrancy** wandering idly in a public place without home or money

**vandalism** defacing or damaging of another's property, often random and purposeless

**voluntary manslaughter** taking of human life with mitigating circumstances

**white-collar crime** illegal acts by professionals or office workers against institutions, government, or businesses

**white-slave trade** organized recruitment or abduction of victims, usu. women, into prostitution

**wilding** *Slang.* wanton, random assault and vandalism

## CRIMINALS

**accessory** person who, though absent, assists another to commit a crime or evade capture

**accomplice** criminal's active partner in crime

**arsonist** person who intentionally sets a fire

**bandit** robber, esp. one who attacks victims in public places

**bluebeard** any man who allegedly murders a series of women he has married

**bookie** person accepting illegal bets

**bootlegger** seller of illegal items; smuggler

**brigand** bandit, esp. member of gang operating in forest or mountains

**burglar** thief

**call girl** high-class prostitute reached by telephone

**cannon** *Slang.* pickpocket

**career criminal** one who habitually engages in crime

**cat burglar** one skilled at breaking into buildings, even those secured against theft, by climbing through upstairs windows or across roofs

**cateran** member of gang of roving brigands

**con artist** confidence man

**confidence man** swindler or instigator of fraudulent business schemes; con artist; con man

**con man** confidence man

**Cosa Nostra** *Italian.* lit. our affair; Mafia

**criminal** person engaging in illegal acts; crook

**crook** criminal

**dacoit** robber and murderer in organized gang (India)

**delinquent** person who violates the law

**Fagin** fence; trainer of pickpockets

**family** *Slang.* Mafia

**felon** person guilty of a felony

**fence** receiver of stolen property

**first offender** person guilty of crime for first time

**fugitive** person fleeing arrest or imprisonment

**gang** organization of street criminals, usu. young

**gangster** person working in criminal organization; highbinder

**gun moll** *Slang.* gangster's girlfriend; female criminal

**gunslinger** *Informal.* violent criminal who wore gun on hip (U.S. Old West)

**hardened criminal** habitual criminal committed to life of crime

**highbinder** gangster

**highwayman** person who stops travelers to rob them

**hit man** *Slang.* hired assassin

**hoodlum** violent young ruffian; member of organized crime syndicate

**hook** *Slang.* pickpocket; (*v*) work as a prostitute

**hooker** *Slang.* prostitute

**hooligan** violent young ruffian; street gang member

**horse thief** stealer of horses

**juvenile delinquent**  criminal under age of legal majority; youthful offender

**killer**  murderer

**kleptomaniac**  person unable to stop stealing

**loan shark**  *Informal.* lender charging illegally high interest rates

**Mafia**  organized crime syndicate, orig. Sicilian; Costa Nostra

**mafioso**  member of Mafia

**mass murderer**  killer of many people

**mob**  gang of criminals; organized crime syndicate

**mugger**  person attacking and robbing others on street

**murderer**  person who willfully takes another's life; killer

**Peeping Tom**  person who spies on sexual or private activities of others

**peterman**  *Slang.* safecracker

**pickpocket**  person who steals money or valuables from victim's pocket, esp. in crowded place; cannon; hook

**pimp**  person soliciting for prostitutes

**poacher**  person who steals fish or game from another's land or protected reserve

**point**  *Informal.* person who occupies lookout position during illegal activity or crime

**prostitute**  person engaging in sex for pay

**prowler**  person entering another's home for purpose of robbery or violence

**public enemy**  dangerous criminal widely sought by law enforcement agencies

**racketeer**  person involved in rackets, organized crime, or illegal business operations

**safecracker**  robber specializing in forcing open safes; peterman

**scofflaw**  person who violates the law with contempt, esp. one who fails to pay fines owed

**second-story man**  burglar specializing in entering buildings through upstairs windows

**serial killer**  mentally unbalanced person who kills one victim after another

**smuggler**  transporter of illegal goods, esp. across borders; bootlegger

**squatter**  person illegally occupying another's vacant property

**streetwalker**  prostitute who solicits on the streets

**thief**  one who steals; burglar

**thug**  brutal, petty criminal; professional strangler

**tong**  member of secret Chinese gang

**underworld**  segment of society engaged in crime as profession

**vandal**  person engaged in wanton violence to property, usu. not motivated by theft

**youthful offender**  defendant who may be sentenced with special consideration due to age; juvenile delinquent

## POLICE PROCEDURES AND DETECTION

**AKA**  *also known as*; prefix before alias

**alias**  false name used by criminal

**all-points bulletin**  APB; description of wanted criminal issued to all police in area

**APB**  *all-points bulletin*

**apprehend**  (*vb*) catch suspect or criminal

**arrest**  (*vb*) lawfully detain suspect; (*n*) act of apprehending and detaining suspect; bust

**arrestee**  person arrested on suspicion of crime

**at large**  describing a criminal who is free, having evaded arrest

**badge**  *Informal.* policeman

**ballistics**  study of firearms and bullets, used in detection and identification of weapons used in crimes

**beat**  police officer's assigned area of duty

**Bertillon system**  fingerprinting and identification system

**billy club**  policeman's heavy wooden stick or baton; night stick

**blotter**  book in station house in which arrests are recorded as they occur

**bobby**  *Brit. informal.* policeman

**book**  (*vb*) register arrestee at jail or place of detention

**bounty**  payment offered for capture of criminal at large

**break**  piece of luck that helps to solve a crime

**bust**  *Slang.* arrest

**canary**  *Slang.* person confessing a crime or offering information to police

**case**  unsolved crime or one being tried

**citizen's arrest**  arrest made not by police but by person whose authority rests on fact of citizenship

**clamp down**  (*vb*) increase police activity, usu. on specific problem

**clue**  piece of information leading toward arrest of criminal

**collar**  (*vb*) *Informal.* arrest

**comb**  (*vb*) thoroughly inspect scene of crime; search intensely for clues

**confession**  admission of guilt

**cop**  *Informal.* policeman

**copper**  *Informal.* policeman

**coroner**  public officer investigating deaths likely to be due to criminal acts

**crack**  (*vb*) solve a case

**crackdown**  intensification of police efforts to control crime

**crime lab**  laboratory in which evidence is examined scientifically to aid in apprehension of suspects

**criminology**  study of crime, its causes, detection, correction, and prevention

**custody**  arrest and detention of suspect or criminal

**dactyloscopy**  method of studying fingerprints to establish identification

**delator**  professional informer

**detection**  art and practice of finding solutions to crimes

**detective**  police officer or private individual skilled at acquiring information about crimes and tracking down suspected criminals; dick; hawkshaw; shamus

**detention**  holding of suspect or criminal in custody to await charges, trial, or sentencing

**deterrence**  prevention of crime

**dick**  *Slang.* detective

**DNA fingerprinting**  identification of criminal suspect by matching genes in known segment of labeled DNA with those in forensic sample, as blood or hair, obtained from suspect

**dragnet**  systematic police search for criminal

**evidence**  facts or objects leading to apprehension of suspect or solution of crime

**facial identification system**  FIS; computerized method of identifying suspects

**false arrest** improper arrest without legal cause or due process

**FBI** Federal Bureau of Investigation

**Federal Bureau of Investigation** FBI; U.S. national police and investigative agency

**finger** (*vb*) *Slang.* identify someone as a suspect; inform on someone

**fingerprints** inked impression of lines on tips of fingers, used in identification of suspect

**fink** *Slang.* informer

**first degree** designation for police procedure involving initial arrest of suspect

**FIS** *facial identification system*

**forensics** investigative procedures used in deciding legal matters; scientific examination of evidence for use in criminal case

**frisk** police search of person believed to be carrying concealed weapon or stolen or illegal goods, usu. by patting suspect's clothing

**fuzz** *Slang.* police

**gendarme** police officer, esp. in France

**get small** *Slang.* evade arrest and flee

**G-man** government man; law enforcement officer

**handcuffs** metal bands that lock around wrists, used to restrain hands of prisoner or suspect

**hawkshaw** detective

**heat** *Slang.* police

**informer** person giving information on crime to police; fink; stool pigeon

**K-9 corps** dogs used in law enforcement

**lead** clue aiding in apprehension of suspect

**lie detector** polygraph

**lineup** technique in which victim or witness is asked to identify suspect from several people standing in line

**Mace** *Trademark.* nonlethal chemical spray used to temporarily incapacitate or subdue a person

**manhunt** intense police search for suspect or fugitive

**marshal** federal judicial officer who performs duties of sheriff; police officer

**Miranda rule** law requiring that police inform persons being detained or interrogated of their constitutional rights

**MO** *modus operandi*

**modus operandi** *Latin.* mode of operating; characteristic procedure followed by habitual criminal, useful in detection; MO

**most wanted list** FBI's roster of criminals with highest priority for arrest

**moulage** taking of plaster impression as evidence in criminal investigation

**MP** *military police*

**mug shot** *Slang.* photo taken of suspect in custody and filed for future reference

**nab** *Informal.* catch and arrest suspect

**narc** *Slang.* narcotics law enforcement officer

**night stick** policeman's billy club

**paddy wagon** *Informal.* police van for transporting arrestees

**pinch** (*vb*) *Slang.* arrest

**police** governmental organization concerned with maintaining public order and safety, enforcing laws, and apprehending criminal suspects

**policeman** member of a police force, esp. male; *Slang* or *Informal:* badge, bobby, cop, fuzz, heat, the man

**police officer** member of a police force

**polygraph** machine registering biological stress signals when subject is questioned about suspected activities; lie detector

**posse** group empowered by law to pursue and apprehend criminal suspect

**precinct** police headquarters for section of city

**private detective** investigator for hire, with no legal authority to make arrests; private eye

**private eye** *Slang.* private detective

**rap** *Slang.* criminal charge; (*vb*) arrest, detain

**rap sheet** *Slang.* record kept by law-enforcement officials of a person's arrests and convictions

**roll over on** (*vb*) inform on one's accomplice to help police make arrest

**run in** (*vb*) *Slang.* arrest suspect and bring to jail

**Scotland Yard** metropolitan London police

**search and seizure** search of person or premises by police with probable cause warrant

**search warrant** legal document empowering police to search premises for evidence of illegal activity

**second degree** designation for police procedure involving transport of suspect to jail or detention

**shamus** *Slang.* detective

**sheriff** law-enforcement officer of county or other civil subdivision of state

**snitch** *Informal.* informer

**stakeout** waiting in hiding for suspect to appear or illegal act to occur

**stool pigeon** *Slang.* informer; person acting as decoy to trap suspect

**suspect** person suspected of committing crime but not yet convicted by legal due process

**sweep** movement of large number of police across area where suspected crimes are occurring or criminals hiding

**third degree** designation for police procedure involving interrogation of suspect; brutal or unethical methods of police questioning

**vice squad** police unit enforcing laws against immoral acts, esp. prostitution and drugs

**vigilante** individual or group attempting to enforce law and punish offenders without legal authority

**voiceprint** method of coding human voice into electronic pattern, used for identification of suspects

**warrant** legal document authorizing police action

**wired** (*adj*) carrying a concealed microphone or recording device in order to collect evidence

## LEGAL PROCEDURES AND TRIALS

**acquittal** act of relieving accused from charge of alleged crime; not-guilty verdict

**alibi** excuse intended to avert blame, esp. one in which accused person claims to have been elsewhere at time crime was committed

**arraignment** appearance in court for indictment on charges

**attorney** practitioner in court of law, trained and qualified to prosecute or defend accused persons

**bail** money or security deposit paid to court for release of person awaiting trial, guaranteeing defendant will appear for trial or forfeit bail money

**bail bondsman** person in the business of posting for suspects bail in return for a fee, usu. ten percent of posted amount

**bailiff** court officer serving as messenger or usher

**bar-and-grill** *Slang*. criminal legal system, esp. the handing down of harsh sentences

**chambers** judge's private office adjoining courtroom

**charges** crimes of which suspect is accused

**circumstantial evidence** evidence that implies one fact by proving other events or circumstances suggesting it

**complicity** association or participation in crime

**confession** suspect's admission of guilt

**conviction** legal establishment of guilt in committing crime, usu. after trial

**cop a plea** *Informal*. plead guilty to lesser crime than the one that is charged

**courtroom** chamber in which trial takes place

**custody** charge and control over suspect, exercised by court and esp. by police

**defendant** suspect on trial in court of law

**detainer** writ or order for further detention of a person already in custody, sometimes from another jurisdiction

**entrapment** illegal method of enticing suspect into committing or revealing crime

**evidence** legally admissible facts or objects that help to establish guilt or innocence of defendant

**exonerate** (*vb*) clear of all charges or guilt

**extradition** transfer of criminal suspect from place of apprehension to location of legal jurisdiction

**eyewitness** person who actually saw a crime committed

**finger** (*vb*) *Slang*. identify to authorities as having committed a crime

**frame** (*vb*) set up innocent person to appear guilty of crime

**grand jury** jury with power to indict only

**guilty** (*adj*) justly charged with and convicted of the commission of a crime

**hearsay evidence** testimony given as secondhand information rather than by eyewitness

**incrimination** showing evidence or proof of involvement in crime

**indictment** formal charging with commission of crime

**insanity plea** seeking exoneration on basis of temporary insanity or lack of responsibility for actions

**judge** official overseeing courtroom proceedings and sentencing individuals convicted by jury

**jump bail** fail to appear in court after bail bond has been posted

**jury** panel of citizens sworn to pass judgment on accused

**misconduct** improper behavior by attorney or judge

**penal code** body of law dealing with punishment of crime

**plaintiff** filer of legal complaint against defendant

**plea** formal declaration of guilt or innocence by defendant

**plea bargaining** reduction of criminal charges in exchange for guilty plea to lesser offense

**preventive detention** holding a prisoner without bail or on very high bail

**probable cause** reasonable grounds for assuming validity of criminal charge

**probation** suspension of sentence, allowing convicted offender freedom based on accountability to authorities

**prosecutor** government official responsible for presenting case against accused

**protective custody** detention of person solely for his or her safety

**public defender** government official appointed by court to defend accused person unable to afford attorney

**remand** (*vb*) return accused to custody pending further action

**self-defense** defense of criminal act by claiming danger to accused existed at time of commission

**sentence** punishment handed down by judge on convicted offender

**sequester** (*vb*) isolate jury in private place for discussion or to pass judgment

**state's evidence** testimony of accomplice in crime, who becomes voluntary witness for the prosecution in return for reduced sentence

**subpoena** writ commanding a person to appear in court or face penalty

**substantiate** (*vb*) verify another's testimony; give proof

**summation** attorney's concluding remarks to jury

**summons** written notice requiring appearance in court

**suspended sentence** court's permission for convicted offender not to serve prison sentence

**testify** (*vb*) provide sworn statement in court

**testimony** statements by witness under oath during trial

**trial** legal procedure for hearing testimony, weighing evidence, deciding guilt or innocence of criminal suspect, and setting sentence

**verdict** decision of jury as to suspect's guilt or innocence

**warrant** writ issued by court, esp. to make arrest

**witness** person giving evidence at trial

**Witness Protection Program** program of U.S. government designed to insure safety or anonymity of witnesses, esp. informers

**writ** formal legal document or instrument

## PRISON AND PUNISHMENT

**administrative segregation** placement in solitary confinement of prisoner not accused of any disciplinary infraction

**amnesty** pardon handed down to group or class of offenders

**bastinado** punishment by beating soles of feet with stick

**behind bars** *Informal*. imprisoned or in jail

**big house** *Slang*. penitentiary or prison

**bilboes** shackles attached to long iron bar for prisoner's feet

**black hole** any wretched place of imprisonment or confinement

**break** escape from jail or prison

**brig** naval prison, esp. on ship

**cage** prison cell

**calaboose** *Slang*. jail

**can** *Slang*. jail or prison

**cangue** large wooden yoke formerly fastened about neck as punishment (China)

**capital punishment** sentence of death; death penalty

**captive** prisoner

**cat-o'-nine-tails** whip of nine knotted cords attached to handle, used for flogging

**cell** small room in which prisoner is held or lives

**cellblock** prison unit consisting of a number of cells

**chain gang** group of convicts chained together, esp. when doing manual labor outside

**chair** *Informal*. electric chair

**city hotel** *Slang.* jail

**clemency** mercy shown to prisoner by authorities

**clink** *Slang.* jail or prison

**commitment** sentencing of criminal to prison term

**commute** (*vb*) reduce sentence

**con** *Informal.* convict

**concentration camp** enforced labor and execution center, esp. one run by Nazis in World War II

**condemned** (*adj*) sentenced, esp. to death

**confinement** imprisonment

**conjugal visit** private visitation privilege extended to prisoner for exercise of conjugal rights with his or her spouse

**convict** person found guilty of crime serving time in prison; con

**cooler** *Slang.* jail

**coop** *Slang.* prison

**correctional institution** prison or penal colony for long-term incarceration

**count** census of prisoner, during which all other prison activity halts

**county jail** local center for short-term incarceration of persons awaiting trial or sentencing or convicted of minor offenses

**death penalty** capital punishment

**death row** area in prison housing convicts sentenced to death

**debtor's prison** prison in which debtors were formerly held until able to pay debts

**detention facility** jail, camp, or hall for inmates awaiting trial or sentencing and for aliens awaiting deportation

**dime** *Slang.* ten-year prison sentence

**do time** *Slang.* serve a sentence

**drunk tank** *Informal.* city jail cell in which persons arrested for public drunkenness, and other arrestees, are held overnight

**dungeon** prison, esp. dark and forbidding one

**electric chair** seat in which condemned prisoner is strapped for electrocution

**electrocution** execution by electric charge

**ex-con** *Informal.* former convict, now released from prison

**execution** putting to death of person convicted of crime, usu. by electrocution, gas chamber, firing squad, hanging, injection, or guillotine

**executioner** prison officer charged with carrying out execution

**false imprisonment** illegal confinement of someone against his or her will and without cause

**firing squad** group of soldiers who execute prisoners by simultaneously shooting them

**fish** *Slang.* new prisoner

**flogging** whipping as punishment

**gas chamber** airtight prison room in which execution by poison gas takes place

**gibbet** upright post with projecting arm at top for hanging bodies of executed criminals as warning

**guillotine** instrument for execution by beheading, in which a heavy blade is dropped between two grooved uprights

**hack** *Slang.* prison guard

**hanging** execution by strangulation or breaking of neck, usu. by suspending prisoner from rope tied around his or her neck

**hangman** public executioner who administers hangings

**hitch** prison term

**holding cell** prisoners' temporary place of confinement

**hole** solitary confinement

**house arrest** confinement under guard in one's normal living quarters instead of prison

**house of correction** place of confinement and reform for criminals convicted of minor offenses

**house of detention** place of confinement for alleged criminals awaiting trial, and sometimes for witnesses

**incarceration** imprisonment

**injection** execution by injection of toxic substance

**inmate** prisoner

**inside** (*adv*) *Slang.* in prison

**jacket** *Slang.* prisoner's file or arrest record; prisoner's reputation

**Jack Ketch** *Brit. slang.* official hangman

**jail** building for short-term confinement of prisoners and those accused of crimes; county jail; *Slang:* calaboose, can, city hotel, clink, cooler, jug, poky; also, *esp. Brit.*, gaol

**jailbird** inmate, esp. longtime or repeat inmate

**jailer** official overseeing jail operations and guarding prisoners; turnkey; warder

**jailhouse lawyer** prisoner who does legal research and writing for others while serving time

**joint** *Slang.* usu. **the joint**; prison

**jug** *Slang.* jail

**keeper** jailer, prison guard

**kite** *Slang.* note passed from one cell to another

**knout** (*vb*) flog

**lam** *Slang.* escape from prison or flight to evade authorities

**lifer** *Slang.* prisoner sentenced to life term

**life sentence** prison term lasting for entire life span

**lockdown** confinement of all prisoners to their cells

**lynching** illegal execution of suspect, usu. hanging by mob

**man** *Slang.* usu **the Man**; police officer or prison guard

**maximum-security prison** heavily guarded prison housing prisoners with long sentences and dangerous or hardened criminals

**medium-security prison** prison with moderate security, less than maximum and more than minimum

**minimum-security prison** moderately guarded or unguarded prison, such as a work farm, housing white-collar and less serious offenders and those serving short sentences or nearing release

**mittimus** warrant of commitment to prison

**mule** *Slang.* person who smuggles contraband, esp. into jail or prison

**nickel** *Slang.* five-year prison sentence

**on ice** *Slang.* imprisoned, esp. in solitary confinement

**oubliette** concealed dungeon with trapdoor in its ceiling

**pardon** official cancellation of sentence or punishment for crime

**parole** release from prison before full sentence has been served

**parolee** prisoner who has been set free but must maintain contact with authorities

**pen** *Informal.* penitentiary

**penal** (*adj*) pertaining to or constituting legal punishment

**penal colony** prison, esp. one in isolated area

**penal institution** jail, reformatory, or prison

**penitentiary** maximum-security prison, esp. one maintained by a state or the U.S. government for serious offenders

**pillory** wood frame used to restrain head and hands as punishment

**poky** *Slang.* jail

**political prisoner** person deemed politically dangerous by state and falsely imprisoned for supposed crimes

**population** prisoners who are not in segregation and are allowed to mix with others

**POW** *prisoner of war*

**prison** state or federal institution for long-term confinement of convicts, usu. felons; *Slang:* big house, can, clink, coop, joint, slammer, stir

**prisoner** person accused or convicted of crime and held in jail or prison; captive; inmate

**prisoner of war** POW; person held captive by enemy during wartime

**prison riot** violent outburst by prisoners against prison conditions

**probation** suspension of prison sentence on guarantee of good behavior and regular reporting to authorities

**protective custody** administrative segregation of prisoner deemed in danger if allowed to mix with other prisoners

**punishment** penalty imposed by legal system on convicted offender

**punk** *Slang.* male prisoner coerced into sexually passive or submissive homosexual role

**quarter** *Slang.* twenty-five-year prison sentence

**rack** torture device in which victim's body is bound to frame and stretched

**rat** *Slang.* (n) informer; (vb) inform on

**recidivism** repetition of, or chronic engagement in, criminal acts; return to confinement for any reason, including technical parole violations

**reformatory** penal institution for reform and rehabilitation of young offenders, esp. minors; reform school

**reform school** reformatory

**rehabilitation** preparation of prisoners for reentry into society by eliminating criminal impulses

**reprieve** delay in execution of sentence

**segregation** locked-down housing apart from other prisoners, usu. in solitary, either disciplinary or administrative

**sentence** punishment determined by law

**serve time** pass time of sentence in prison

**shakedown** search of prisoner or prison cell, undertaken by guards, esp. for contraband or weapons

**short time** *Informal.* period of sentence just prior to prisoner's release; brief sentence

**slammer** *Slang.* prison

**solitary confinement** holding of prisoner alone in isolated cell for extended period

**stir** *Slang.* prison

**stockade** military prison

**stocks** heavy wooden frame with holes for confining ankles and wrists, formerly used for punishment

**street** *Slang.* usu. **the street**; world outside confinement

**tank** *Slang.* prison or jail cell for more than one prisoner, usu. temporary holding cell

**tar and feather** cover offender's body with hot tar and feathers as punishment, usu. by mob action

**time** prison sentence

**torture** cruel and unusual punishment, esp. infliction of extreme pain

**trusty** well-behaved and trustworthy prisoner given special privileges and responsibilities, often having power over other prisoners

**turnkey** jailer

**up the river** *Slang.* serving time in prison

**violate** (*vb*) *Slang.* return to incarceration as a parole violator

**warden** prison administrator

**warder** jailer

**ward of the state** minor or incompetent person under protection or custody of court

**water torture** punishment in which water is dripped slowly onto victim's forehead

**whipping** punishment by flogging with whip

**work camp** work farm

**work farm** minimum-security prison in which inmates are allowed out of their cells to work, esp. outdoors; work camp

**yard** enclosed outdoor area for exercise of inmates, where prisoners can mingle

**yardbird** *Slang.* convict or prisoner

**yard hack** *Slang.* guard in prison yard

# VIOLENCE

Violent Events
Fights
Attacks
Violent Actions
Violent Persons

**SEE ALSO**: Chap. 5: Weapons and Armaments; Chap. 11: War and Military; Chap. 22: Strategy, Intrigue, and Deception; Chap. 24: Mental Disturbances; Crime; Chap. 25: Magic and the Occult

## VIOLENT EVENTS

**annihilation** total destruction; extinction

**atrocity** cruel, inhumane act

**barbarity** brutal or inhuman conduct; cruelty

**bastinado** beating with stick or cudgel

**bedlam** place or occasion of uproar and commotion

**bloodbath** violently gory conflict

**bloodshed** slaughter; taking of life, as in war or murder

**brouhaha** uproar

**brutality** savagery; cruel or harsh treatment

**butchery** brutal, heartless killing

**carnage** large-scale destruction of life

**collision** violent meeting of opposites; striking or crashing together

**commotion** agitated or disturbed activity; fray; tumult

**conflagration** extensive, extremely destructive fire

**contest** conflict, fight, or struggle for victory over opponent; altercation

**coup de grâce** *French.* lit. blow of mercy; deathblow; final, decisive stroke

**deathblow** coup de grâce

**decimation** large-scale destruction

**demolition** act of destruction

**despoilment** forceful, violent deprivation or destruction of goods or property

**destruction** tearing down or totally eliminating something

**devastation** total destruction; laying waste

**disturbance** outbreak of public disorder; disruption of the peace

**explosion** sudden, violent expansion or outburst, esp. involving combustion and loud noise, as with explosive material

**extinction** annihilation

**fight** physical conflict between opponents

**furor** rage or frenzy of activity or feeling

**fury** anger, rage, or wrath

**fuss** tumult, or small disturbance; a quarrel over something trivial

**havoc** ruinous destruction or devastation; chaos

**holocaust** destruction or sacrifice, esp. of human life on grand scale

**inferno** hellishly violent conflagration

**internecine** (*adj*) mutually destructive, esp. due to conflict within a group

**massacre** indiscriminate mass killing; widespread butchery

**mass murder** large-scale killing; slaughter

**mayhem** maiming or disfiguring of another person; random or deliberate violence

**monstrosity** very large-scale, severe, shocking event

**outbreak** sudden instance of violence

**outburst** sudden expression of violent emotion or action

**outrage** instance of violent brutality

**paroxysm** convulsive and uncontrollable seizure; fit of violent action or emotion

**rage** intense, uncontrollable anger

**reign of terror** period of violence and fear; situation of ruthless oppression

**revolt** violent attempt to overthrow established authority

**rhubarb** *Slang.* argument or conflict

**riot** violent disruption of public order or peace; uproar

**ruin** destruction by defeat or decay

**savagery** barbarity or cruelty

**shambles** place of slaughter or wreckage

**slaughter** ruthless killing, esp. in large numbers

**spoliation** robbery and plunder, esp. during war

**Sunday punch** knockout punch; one's most powerful blow

**tumult** violent and noisy disturbance; commotion

**upheaval** widespread social unrest or agitation

**uproar** disturbance or tumult; outbreak of chaos; brouhaha

**violence** exertion of rough physical force to injure or abuse

**war** organized, armed conflict between nations

**wrack and ruin** state of destruction or wreckage

**wreckage** remains of something after a violent event resulting in extensive damage to it

# FIGHTS

**altercation** dispute; contest

**argument** dispute between proponents of opposing views

**battle** conflict between soldiers or armies

**battle royal** battle distinguished by great valor and bloodshed

**brawl** noisy fight or quarrel

**broil** quarrel, dispute, noisy argument or fight

**clash** hostile meeting of opponents; conflict

**combat** fight, esp. armed military encounter; fray

**conflict** fight or struggle between enemies

**contention** struggling or striving together in a contest; rivalry

**contest** conflict, fight; struggle for victory over an opponent; altercation

**contretemps** inopportune occurrence; dispute

**dispute** combat or controversy over a difference of opinion; altercation; contretemps; quarrel

**dogfight** rough physical fight

**donnybrook** riotous event with uncontrolled fighting

**duel** fight between two persons, esp. with witnesses and rules of conduct

**duke it out** fight, esp. with fists; do battle

**feud** protracted hostility between two parties, with alternate strikes against each other

**fight** physical conflict between opponents

**fisticuffs** striking with the fists

**flap** noisy argument

**fracas** noisy fight or brawl

**fray** combat, fight; commotion; contest

**free-for-all** wild and uncontrolled fight with many participants

**go to the mat** engage in physical struggle, as in wrestling

**gunfight** fight between opponents armed with pistols or rifles; shootout

**hammer and tongs** vigorously, with great violence or force

**horseplay** playful fighting

**infighting** battle at close quarters

**joust** contest between knights mounted on horseback and armed with lances

**knock-down-drag-out** (*adj*) describing esp. violent and prolonged fight

**melee** confusing crush of battling opponents

**mix-up** fight or brawl

**quarrel** angry disagreement; dispute

**roughhouse** (*vb*) engage in playful, boisterous fighting

**row** noisy quarrel; abusive, quarrelsome dispute

**ruckus** noisy commotion; fracas; rumpus

**rumble** *Slang.* battle between two groups or gangs

**rumpus** noisy disturbance; ruckus

**run-in** unexpected, violent encounter

**scrap** *Informal.* fight, usu. casual or brief

**scrape** fight or quarrel

**scuffle** confused, disordered fight; tussle

**set-to** brief, sharp fight or argument

**shootout** gunfight

**shoving match** fight conducted by rough pushing

**skirmish** light, brief conflict

**spat** petty quarrel

**squabble** noisy dispute or brawl

**strife** contest; fight

**struggle** difficult, exhausting fight, often prolonged

**tiff** small, angry outburst; petty quarrel; spat

**tussle** physical contest between opponents

**vendetta** prolonged feud involving killing for revenge

**war** sustained, widespread conflict, esp. between nations or peoples, with heavily armed and equipped soldiers

# ATTACKS

**accost** (*vb*) approach in challenging manner

**aggravated assault** severe attack

**ambush** surprise attack by concealed force

**assail** (*vb*) attack vigorously or violently; assault

**assault** sudden attack or invasion; physical attack on a person; (*vb*) assail; attack

**attack** (*vb*) set upon in a forceful, aggressive, violent manner; begin hostilities against; (*n*) hostile and aggressive action; assault

**battery** physical beating of a person

**blitz** lightning quick, all-out attack

**blow** sudden, hard stroke with hand or weapon

**bombard** (*vb*) attack with projectiles or bombs

**breathe down someone's neck** chase menacingly and begin to overtake

**charge** (*vb*) rush at or advance aggressively

**cheap shot** attack from blind side or at weakest point

**close in on** (*vb*) surround; gain ground on

**crowd** (*vb*) close in on or press against

**foray** raid, esp. for booty in war

**go at** (*vb*) advance aggressively on an opponent

**harass** (*vb*) badger or persecute repeatedly

**harry** (*vb*) raid, invade, harass, or torment

**have at** (*vb*) make hostile advance upon

**intrusion** entry without permission or invitation; invasion

**inundate** (*vb*) overcome by superior force

**invasion** forceful or hostile intrusion, infringement, or entry, esp. by an army

**lash out** (*vb*) strike or kick suddenly and aggressively

**light into** (*vb*) *Informal.* attack suddenly and vigorously

**lunge** (*vb*) thrust or plunge forward

**noogie** *Slang.* light, often playful blow, esp. to the head, struck with extended knuckle of curled-up second or third finger

**onrush** strong forward rush or movement

**onslaught** vigorous, powerful attack

**pay back** (*vb*) retaliate against or punish

**pillage** robbery or plunder, usu. in war; rapine

**raid** sudden invasion, esp. by surprise

**rapine** pillage

**sneak attack** surprise attack, esp. by hidden forces

**start something** *Informal.* pick a fight

**storm** (*vb*) attack with overwhelming force

**strafe** (*vb*) attack with machine-gun fire from the air

**strike** (*vb*) hit with force; (*n*) sudden attack

**swing at** (*vb*) aim blow at an opponent

**thrust at** (*vb*) move aggressively toward an opponent

**tilt** (*vb*) charge at an opponent

# VIOLENT ACTIONS

**abuse** do wrongful harm to someone; maltreat

**accost** approach forcibly

**act up** behave uncontrollably and unpleasantly

**afflict** inflict injury or distress

**annihilate** destroy completely, make extinct

**annoy** harass repeatedly in quick attacks

**antagonize** provoke; act in hostile manner

**avenge** exact satisfaction for a wrong

**batter** beat repeatedly

**beat up** strike forcefully with hands or weapon

**belt** hit, often with a belt or strap

**blast** ruin, destroy; afflict with blight

**blight** ruin; cause to wither or decay

**blow off steam** *Informal.* forcefully vent strong feelings

**blow one's top** *Informal.* explode with anger

**blow up** *Informal.* lose one's temper

**bludgeon** hit with a clublike weapon

**boil over** lose one's temper

**bomb** drop bombs on; bombard; shell

**bombard** bomb

**bop** *Slang.* hit over the head

**bother** purposefully annoy or irritate

**brain** *Slang.* hit over the head, dash out opponent's brains

**brandish** wave a weapon menacingly

**brawl** argue noisily

**break** smash or split violently into pieces

**broadside** hit from side

**browbeat** intimidate

**brutalize** treat cruelly

**buffet** hit with hand or fist; cuff repeatedly

**bug** *Slang.* bother, annoy

**bulldoze** overpower with intimidating force

**bully** intimidate

**burn** set fire to; incinerate

**burst** break apart with sudden violence

**bust** *Informal.* hit or break

**butcher** chop up or kill brutally

**butt** strike with head

**cane** strike with thin stick

**chafe** rub against so as to wear away

**choke** strangle by applying pressure around neck

**chop** cut up with knife

**churn** shake violently, stir up

**clap** hit across back

**claw** strike or tear with something sharp or pointed, esp. fingernails

**clobber** strike hard blow

**clout** strike

**club** hit with heavy weapon

**coerce** compel by force

**collar** seize by neck

**come to blows** engage in physical fight

**commandeer** seize arbitrarily, often for military or public use

**confront** face an enemy; provoke hostile encounter

**conquer** take by force, defeat opponent

**consume** destroy completely, esp. by fire

**countervail** exert equal force against

**crack** strike so as to break open

**crash** collide violently, shatter or break in pieces

**cream** *Slang.* defeat decisively in a fight

**crucify** execute by crucifixion; defeat utterly

**crunch** grind or press with crunching sound; step on

**crush** squeeze or press until damaged or destroyed; oppress

**cudgel** beat with heavy stick

**cuff** strike with one's hand; slap

**cut** penetrate, divide, or detach with a sharp-edged instrument

**cut up** damage or injure, esp. by lacerations; slice into pieces

**damage** cause injury to; impair

**dash**  hurl or throw forcefully

**decimate**  destroy a significant portion of, orig. every tenth person

**deck**  *Informal.* strike forcefully to the ground

**defeat**  overcome, esp. in battle

**defile**  pollute

**demolish**  destroy, ruin, or take apart

**dent**  make a depression or hollow in something

**depopulate**  destroy or reduce the number of inhabitants of

**deracinate**  uproot from home or native culture

**desecrate**  treat without respect

**despoil**  plunder or ravage

**destroy**  ruin, demolish, or exterminate; reduce to fragments or useless form

**devastate**  lay waste; destroy utterly

**devour**  destroy by consuming

**disembowel**  eviscerate

**dismantle**  take apart

**dismember**  cut limb from limb

**do mischief**  commit intentional harm

**drill**  bore a hole in; hit dead on

**drub**  cudgel; defeat soundly in battle

**drum**  hit repeatedly

**embroil**  engage in battle

**eradicate**  wipe out

**erupt**  burst out, break into rage or anger

**eviscerate**  remove innards of; disembowel; gut

**explode**  burst violently

**expunge**  obliterate

**exterminate**  destroy completely, annihilate

**extirpate**  root out, eradicate, or expel

**fell**  cause to fall, knock down; kill

**fire**  cause to burn; shoot a gun

**flail**  beat, esp. with free-swinging stick attached to handle

**flay**  skin, strip off surface

**flog**  whip

**fly at**  rush, attack

**force**  coerce, impose, or take violently

**fracture**  break, crack

**fragment**  break into parts

**gash**  cut deeply

**gnash**  grind

**gouge**  force or scoop out, esp. an eye

**grapple**  fight closely; seize and hold opponent in physical contest

**graze**  strike glancing blow upon

**grind**  wear down to powder or fragments; gnash

**gut**  eviscerate

**hack**  chop up, mangle

**hammer**  strike or beat heavily

**have it out**  engage in a fight

**hew**  cut or strike forcibly with ax

**hit**  strike, knock, or deliver blow to

**horsewhip**  flog with whip

**hurt**  wound, cause pain or injury

**impair**  damage, harm, or injure

**impale**  pierce with sharp stick or rod

**impinge**  collide with or strike

**implode**  burst inward

**incinerate**  burn

**infect**  contaminate or pollute with disease

**injure**  harm or damage

**intimidate**  frighten with threats of harm; browbeat; bully

**invade**  make an assault on; enter forcefully and with hostility

**irritate**  provoke, annoy; attack sore spot

**irrupt**  violently burst or break in

**jab**  poke, punch

**jar**  conflict or clash; shake

**jolt**  shake roughly, knock

**jump on**  leap upon in attack

**kayo**  *Slang.* knock out

**kick**  strike with foot

**kick ass**  *Vulgar slang.* defeat opponent soundly and forcefully to gain desired result

**kick butt**  *Vulgar slang.* kick ass

**kill**  take another's life by violence

**knee**  jab with knee

**knife**  strike or attack with blade

**knock**  hit; make a striking blow

**knock out**  KO; strike hard to render unconscious; kayo

**knuckle**  press or strike with knuckles or fists

**KO**  knock out

**lacerate**  tear or cut

**lash**  strike suddenly, esp. with a whip

**lather**  *Informal.* beat or whip severely

**lay low**  knock down, beat

**level**  demolish completely, raze to the ground

**lick**  hit repeatedly, defeat in fight

**liquidate**  eliminate opponents, esp. by killing

**loot**  rob, plunder

**lop off**  cut off

**maim**  disfigure, mutilate

**maltreat**  abuse

**mangle**  mutilate, injure

**manhandle**  treat roughly

**mar**  injure, damage

**maraud**  plunder, raid

**mash**  smash, reduce to pulp

**maul**  beat up, injure

**mess up**  dishevel, disarrange

**mistreat**  abuse

**mob**  attack in group

**molest**  bother, intrude on, or interfere with; attack sexually

**mug**  attack and rob in public place

**mutilate**  damage, esp. by cutting off a body part

**nab**  *Informal.* seize

**nail**  *Slang.* hit; *Informal.* seize

**nettle**  irritate, sting, or provoke

**nip**  sever, bite off, or snap at

**nuke**  *Informal.* obliterate with or as if by nuclear weapon

**obliterate**  destroy completely, erase; expunge

**off**  *Slang.* kill

**oppress**  master by superior force; control through intimidation or by force

**oust**  forcibly eject, drive out

**overpower**  overcome by superior force

**overrun**  trample, run over, or overwhelm

**overwhelm**  oppress or overpower

**paste**  *Slang.* hit or smack hard, esp. on the face

**paw**  *Informal.* handle roughly

**pelt**  strike repeatedly

**pepper**  assault or hit repeatedly with small blows

**persecute**  harass, oppress

**pestle**  grind or pulverize

**pick a fight**  incite another into conflict
**pierce**  penetrate sharply, as if by stabbing
**pillage**  plunder or rob
**pinch**  squeeze or compress tightly and painfully
**pistol-whip**  strike repeatedly with gun
**plague**  torment; infest
**plaster**  *Informal.* strike hard; defeat decisively
**plow under**  force out of existence; overpower
**plunk**  *Informal.* strike; hit with a ball or other object
**poison**  harm or kill with poisonous substance
**poke**  thrust, intrude
**pollute**  poison, taint, or make foul
**pound**  batter or hammer
**powder**  beat into small pieces; pulverize
**prod**  jab or poke, with or as if with pointed object
**pulverize**  reduce to fragments
**pummel**  beat or pound
**pump**  strike rapidly and repeatedly
**punch**  strike with fist; sock
**punch out**  *Slang.* beat up or knock out with one's fists
**puncture**  pierce with pointed object
**punish**  injure in retaliation; do severe harm to
**push**  thrust or press forcefully
**push around**  shove from place; bully
**quash**  suppress, subdue
**rabbit punch**  (*n*) quick, sharp blow to neck or base of skull
**rack**  torture or torment; stretch body of another on rack
**rage**  show or proceed with violent anger
**raid**  invade or attack suddenly
**ram**  batter; strike with great force
**rampage**  act wildly and recklessly
**ransack**  plunder, search for booty
**rap**  hit with sharp blow
**rape**  seize or plunder; assault sexually
**ravage**  devastate, plunder
**raven**  seize violently; devour
**raze**  tear down or demolish
**ream**  *Informal.* batter, esp. by stretching apart
**rend**  tear apart, split; rive
**retaliate**  injure someone in return for injury inflicted
**riddle**  attack repeatedly, esp. with bullets
**riot**  disturb the peace or public order
**rip**  tear, cut
**rive**  rend
**rock**  knock backwards with a blow
**rough up**  abuse; handle harshly
**rout**  set to flight, drive from place
**rub**  abrade
**ruin**  destroy, wreck
**run amok**  behave wildly, with uncontrollable violence
**rupture**  tear apart, break open
**rush**  assault
**sack**  plunder or loot
**sail into**  *Informal.* assault vigorously
**savage**  attack in a ferocious, barbarous way
**scald**  burn, esp. with boiling liquid
**scalp**  cut or pull skin from skull of
**scar**  cut and disfigure; wound permanently
**scathe**  damage or harm as if by scorching
**scorch**  parch or shrivel with heat
**screw**  twist into strained position; abuse
**sear**  burn or char surface of
**seize**  grasp forcefully, confiscate; nab; nail

**set upon**  attack suddenly
**shatter**  break into fragments; destroy violently
**shed blood**  engage in savage, bloody fighting
**shell**  bomb
**shellac**  *Slang.* beat soundly
**shoot**  hit with a bullet or arrow
**shove**  push roughly
**shred**  tear into strips
**sic**  attack (used esp. to incite dog upon victim)
**sideswipe**  strike along side with glancing blow
**sink**  destroy by submerging
**skewer**  pierce with sharp object
**slam**  strike or shove forcefully
**slap**  strike with open hand; cuff
**slash**  cut or gash, esp. with sharp blade
**slay**  destroy, esp. kill by violence
**slice**  cut
**slit**  cut to strips; make long, narrow slice in
**slug**  *Informal.* hit hard with fist
**smack**  strike with loud sound
**smash**  crush, shatter, or break up
**smite**  strike hard with hand or weapon; strike down or slay
**smother**  stifle; suffocate
**snip**  cut to bits, clip
**snipe**  shoot at from a distance
**sock**  *Slang.* punch
**spank**  beat on buttocks
**spike**  pierce with pointed object
**spill blood**  fight so as to cause bleeding
**splinter**  break or split into long, narrow pieces
**split**  tear apart, divide forcefully
**squash**  mash or crush; suppress
**squeeze**  apply pressure to
**squelch**  crush down; suppress or stamp out
**squish**  squash or squeeze
**stab**  puncture with knife or sharp object
**stamp**  beat upon with foot; crush or pound
**stave**  break a hole in; splinter or smash
**steamroller**  flatten in a fight; roll over an opponent with superior force
**stick**  pierce with pointed object
**sting**  pierce or wound with poison
**stomp**  stamp or step on heavily
**stone**  hit repeatedly with rocks, esp. to kill
**storm**  attack suddenly with superior force
**strafe**  attack with machine-gun fire from the air
**strangle**  suffocate or choke by squeezing around neck
**strike**  hit with one's fist or an object; clout
**strong-arm**  use violence or intimidation to persuade
**stun**  daze or deaden with blow
**subdue**  beat into submission
**subject**  bring under domination, force to submit
**suffocate**  (*n*) choke; smother
**sunder**  rend, split, or break apart
**swamp**  overwhelm by submerging; sink
**swat**  strike or hit
**take on**  oppose (another); entice (someone) to fight
**tap**  hit lightly
**tear**  rip, split, or pull apart
**thrash**  beat or flog
**thresh**  thrash, beat, or cut up
**throttle**  choke or strangle
**thump**  beat or pound; *Informal.* thrash severely

**thwack**  strike or hit with something flat
**tilt**  cause to fall over; upset the balance of
**torment**  torture
**torture**  cause extreme pain to, inflict suffering on; torment
**trample**  crush under one's feet
**trash**  *Informal.* lay waste, ruin, or vandalize
**trim**  administer beating to
**trounce**  beat soundly
**tussle**  scuffle; struggle at close range
**tweak**  pinch and pull with a twist or jerk
**twist**  wrench and turn with rotary motion
**tyrannize**  oppress, intimidate
**vandalize**  destroy or desecrate property with malicious intent
**vanquish**  conquer or defeat in battle
**violate**  ravish, rape; mistreat
**wallop**  beat soundly; *Informal.* hit hard
**waste**  devastate or totally demolish; *Slang.* murder
**whack**  strike with solid blow
**whale**  strike soundly; beat on repeatedly
**wham**  hit hard
**whip**  strike with a lash, flog; defeat decisively
**whomp**  *Informal.* inflict loud, heavy blow or slap
**whop**  *Informal.* strike forcibly
**whump**  thump
**whup**  regional variation of *whip*; beat or defeat decisively
**work evil**  cause damage or injury, esp. by immoral or wicked means
**work over**  *Informal.* beat up; hit repeatedly
**wrack**  wreck, destroy
**wreak**  inflict or exact punishment, injury, or vengeance
**wreak havoc**  cause destruction or chaos
**wreck**  ruin, destroy
**wrench**  twist or pull sharply
**wrest**  wrench or seize violently
**wring**  twist (another's neck) with the hands
**yank**  pull sharply
**zap**  *Informal.* strike or stun with sharp blow
**zonk**  *Slang.* knock out; strike soundly

## VIOLENT PERSONS

**aggressor**  initiator of unprovoked attack
**agitator**  one who incites others to violence; firebrand
**anarchist**  one who resists all authority, esp. by terrorism
**animal**  brutish person
**annihilator**  one who utterly destroys
**arsonist**  one who sets things on fire; incendiary
**assailant**  attacker
**assassin**  murderer, esp. the fanatical or hired killer of a politically prominent person
**attacker**  one who uses force to harm others or start a fight; assailant
**barbarian**  cruel, uncivilized brute; Goth
**beast**  brutal, animallike person
**berserker**  frenzied and ferocious warrior of Norse legend
**bomber**  one who sets off explosions
**brute**  savage, cruel, unfeeling person
**bully**  blustering, overbearing person who terrorizes weaker people
**butcher**  brutal or indiscriminate killer
**cannibal**  person who eats human flesh

**cutthroat**  merciless murderer, esp. one who cuts throats
**destroyer**  one who crushes, kills, and totally wipes out opponents; exterminator
**devil**  cruel, evil, remorseless person
**dynamitard**  political terrorist who uses dynamite
**exterminator**  destroyer
**fiend**  cunningly evil person; hellhound
**firebrand**  agitator
**fire-eater**  angry person always ready to attack others
**fury**  raging, vengeful person
**goon**  *Informal.* hoodlum or thug, esp. one hired to attack others
**gorilla**  *Slang.* large, brutish, animallike person
**Goth**  barbarian
**hard-nose**  *Slang.* tough, obstinate person
**hellcat**  evil, vengeful woman
**hellhound**  fiend
**hellion**  *Informal.* mischievous troublemaker
**hell-raiser**  *Informal.* one who stirs up trouble
**henchman**  person hired to perform violent acts for another
**hijacker**  terrorist who commandeers planes and other vehicles
**holy terror**  *Informal.* uncontrollable troublemaker
**hood**  *Slang.* hoodlum
**hoodlum**  tough, young street ruffian, esp. member of lawless gang; hooligan
**hooligan**  hoodlum
**hothead**  person easily aroused to anger or attack; hotspur
**hotspur**  hothead
**Hun**  savage barbarian
**incendiary**  arsonist
**invader**  one who attacks another's territory
**killer**  murderer
**knave**  unprincipled, untrustworthy, or dishonest person; rascal
**mad dog**  *Slang.* vicious, uncontrollable person
**maniac**  wildly insane person
**monster**  cruel, vicious person
**mugger**  one who assaults others with intent to rob
**murderer**  one who takes another's life; killer
**predator**  one who lives by plunder and robbery
**raider**  one who suddenly attacks or invades
**rapist**  one who forces another to have sexual intercourse
**rascal**  mischievous troublemaker; knave; rogue
**rogue**  rascal; scoundrel
**rough**  *Chiefly Brit.* ruffian
**roughneck**  crude, rowdy person
**rowdy**  rough, disorderly, quarrelsome person
**ruffian**  brutal, lawless person, esp. hoodlum; rough; tough
**savage**  ferocious, brutal, beastly person; rogue
**scoundrel**  wicked, disreputable person; rogue
**she-wolf**  evil, vicious, predatory woman
**slasher**  one who attacks with knife or blade
**spitfire**  easily angered person, esp. woman
**terminator**  cold-blooded killer, esp. one for hire
**terror**  *Informal.* wildly uncontrollable person
**terrorist**  one who uses force, often random, to intimidate or gain political ends
**thug**  brutal hoodlum, thief, or murderer, esp. gang member
**tiger**  fiercely belligerent person
**tigress**  ferocious woman
**tinderbox**  highly excitable or inflammable person who is potential source of widespread violence

**tough** ruffian
**troublemaker** one who agitates or incites others to quarrel
**vandal** malicious, destructive person
**villain** wicked person, criminal
**virago** quarrelsome, foul-tempered woman
**vixen** ill-tempered, evil woman
**warrior** person with fighting spirit
**witch** evil, devilish person, esp. a woman, who professes to have supernatural powers
**wolf** fierce, cruel person

# DEATH

Dead or Dying
Unnatural Deaths
Murder and Suicide
Dead Bodies
Burial and Funerals
Beyond the Grave
Language of Death

**SEE ALSO**: Chap. 1: Medical Problems; Chap. 24: Crime; Chap. 25: Magic and the Occult; Eschatology

## DEAD OR DYING

**asleep** (*adj*) dead; into the state of death
**at peace** (*adj*) dead
**bite the dust** die
**buy the farm** *Slang*. die or be killed
**cash in one's chips** *Slang*. die
**casualty** person killed in war or accident
**croak** (*vb*) *Slang*. die
**dead** (*adj*) no longer living; (*n*) **the dead**; dead persons collectively
**death** act of dying; total and permanent cessation of life
**deceased** (*adj*) dead
**demise** death
**departed** (*adj*) dead
**die** (*vb*) experience death; cease living
**DOA** dead on arrival; term used to indicate person was dead on arrival at hospital
**done for** *Informal*. dead or close to death
**done in** *Informal*. dead, esp. from unnatural causes
**drop dead** *Informal*. die suddenly
**dying** (*adj*) about to die; approaching death
**eclipsed** (*adj*) having died
**eighty-sixed** (*adj*) *Slang*. dead, esp. killed
**elapsed** (*adj*) having died
**end** death
**expire** (*vb*) die, esp. after prolonged disease
**extinct** (*adj*) no longer living, esp. of a species
**fatality** person who has died, esp. in accident, war, or crime
**final rest** death
**final sleep** death
**goner** *Informal*. one who is dead or about to die
**gone to Davy Jones's locker** *Slang*. dead, esp. at sea
**have one foot in the grave** be dying
**iced** (*adj*) *Slang*. dead, esp. from unnatural causes

**in extremis** (*adj*) at the point of death
**kick in** (*vb*) *Slang*. die
**kick off** (*vb*) *Slang*. die
**kick the bucket** *Slang*. die
**late** (*adj*) recently deceased, used as reference with person's name
**lost** (*adj*) dead
**meet one's Maker** die
**moribund** (*adj*) dying, about to die
**mortal** living being who must eventually die; (*adj*) causing or liable to cause death
**on ice** *Slang*. dead
**pass away** (*vb*) die
**pass on** (*vb*) die
**perish** (*vb*) die, esp. in violent or untimely manner
**pop off** (*vb*) *Informal*. die, esp. suddenly
**rest** state of death
**six feet under** *Slang*. dead and buried
**sleep** state of death
**succumb** (*vb*) die, esp. from disease
**terminal** (*adj*) dying, esp. from fatal illness
**waste away** (*vb*) die slowly from disease
**wither and die** degenerate from disease until death

## UNNATURAL DEATHS

**asphyxiation** death by lack of oxygen or from breathing obstruction; smothering; suffocation
**beheading** executive by decapitation
**Black Death** bubonic plague
**brain death** cessation of brain activity, indicated by flat EEG reading
**buried alive** asphyxiated beneath the ground
**burn** (*vb*) *Slang*. die in the electric chair
**choking** windpipe obstruction by physical pressure or due to breathing of poisoned air
**crucifixion** nailing of hands and feet to cross
**decapitation** removal of head from neck
**disease** fatal wasting or impairment of body function
**electrocution** death by electric shock
**evisceration** death by disembowelment
**execution** putting to death as legal punishment for crime
**fatal illness** disease that results in death
**firing squad** execution by several rifles fired at once
**gallows** structure for hanging by the neck
**guillotine** structure with large blade for decapitation
**hanging** execution by strangulation or breaking of neck in suspended noose wrapped around neck
**immolation** death by fire
**murder** unlawful taking of another's life with malicious intent
**natural causes** old age, infirmity, or general debility
**noose** loop of rope for hanging
**OD** overdose
**old age** general infirmity resulting from aging
**overdose** OD; ingestion of toxic amount of drug
**pestilence** devastating epidemic of contagious disease
**poisoning** ingestion of a toxic substance
**sacrifice** being offered to deity as victim
**smothering** being deprived of air or overcome by smoke or fumes; asphyxiation
**stake** wood post to which person is tied and burned

**starvation**  total deprivation of food

**stoning**  being beaten by thrown stones

**strangulation**  stoppage of breath by compression of throat

**suffocation**  being deprived of oxygen or prevented from breathing; asphyxiation

**suicide**  taking of one's own life

**vaporization**  dissipation into small particles due to pressure or molecular disturbance

**widdy**  *Scottish.* hangman's noose

## MURDER AND SUICIDE

**assassination**  murder of a public figure

**bloodshed**  taking of life; slaughter

**blow away**  (*vb*) *Slang.* murder

**bump off**  (*vb*) *Slang.* murder

**butcher**  (*vb*) slaughter or kill in a barbarous or indiscriminate manner

**carnage**  bloody slaughter of large numbers of people; massacre

**chill**  (*vb*) *Slang.* murder

**-cide**  suffix meaning killer or killing of

**contract**  *Slang.* agreement to commit murder for payment

**disembowelment**  evisceration; removal of the bowels or entrails

**dispatch**  (*vb*) murder deftly; eliminate quickly

**dispose of**  (*vb*) murder or eliminate

**do away with**  (*vb*) murder

**do in**  (*vb*) *Informal.* murder

**dust**  (*vb*) *Slang.* murder

**euthanasia**  merciful, painless killing of hopelessly sick person; mercy killing

**extermination**  complete and immediate elimination by killing

**felo-de-se**  one who kills himself or herself or dies as a result of committing an unlawful malicious act

**fratricide**  killing one's brother

**garrote**  method of strangulation in which iron collar is tightened around neck

**genocide**  killing of entire race or nation

**grease**  (*vb*) *Slang.* murder

**hara-kiri**  ritual suicide by disembowelment; seppuku (Japan)

**hecatomb**  sacrifice or slaughter of numerous victims

**hit**  *Slang.* murder by hire, esp. by organized crime

**hit list**  *Slang.* list of those contracted to be murdered

**hit man**  *Slang.* hired murderer, esp. by organized crime

**holocaust**  genocide, esp. of Jews by Nazis in World War II

**homicide**  taking another's life with malicious intent; murder

**ice**  (*vb*) *Slang.* murder

**infanticide**  killing a baby

**kill**  (*vb*) take another person's life by violence

**knock off**  *Slang.* murder

**liquidate**  (*vb*) eliminate by killing

**lynching**  execution, usu. hanging, by mob without legal sanction

**manslaughter**  accidental murder without malicious intent

**martyrdom**  self-sacrifice for the sake of some principle or cause

**massacre**  indiscriminate, ruthless killing of numerous, often helpless persons

**mass murder**  murder of numerous individuals, usu. by one person

**matricide**  killing one's mother

**mercy killing**  euthanasia

**murder**  unlawful taking of another's life with malicious intent; (*vb*) commit an act of murder; *Slang:* blow away, bump off, chill, dispatch, dispose of, do away with, do in, dust, grease, knock off, off, rub out, snuff out, stretch out, whack, waste, wax, zap

**off**  (*vb*) *Slang.* murder

**parricide**  killing one's parent or close relative

**patricide**  killing one's father

**pogrom**  organized massacre of a minority people, esp. Jews

**poisoning**  secret administering of toxic substance to cause another's death

**purge**  elimination of undesirable elements in group or society

**regicide**  killing one's king or queen

**ritual murder**  killing by group in ceremonial rite

**ritual suicide**  killing oneself in a prescribed manner

**rub out**  (*vb*) *Slang.* murder, often by organized crime

**sacrifice**  taking victim's life as religious offering

**self-immolation**  burning oneself to death

**self-slaughter**  suicide

**seppuku**  hara-kiri

**serial killing**  murder of one victim after another over time by same killer

**shooting**  killing by gunshot

**slaughter**  brutal or violent killing of single person or large numbers of people

**slay**  (*vb*) murder

**snuff out**  (*vb*) *Informal.* murder

**strangulation**  killing by choking or cutting off air supply

**stretch out**  (*vb*) *Slang.* murder

**suffocation**  killing by smothering or strangulation

**suicide**  taking one's own life; self-slaughter

**suicide pact**  agreement between two people to commit suicide simultaneously

**waste**  (*vb*) *Slang.* murder

**wax**  (*vb*) *Slang.* murder

**whack**  (*vb*) *Slang.* murder

**wrist-slitting**  killing oneself by cutting arteries in wrists

**zap**  (*vb*) *Slang.* murder

## DEAD BODIES

**bones**  dead body, esp. one decomposed

**cadaver**  dead body, esp. one prepared for dissection

**carcass**  *Slang.* human body, esp. when dead

**carrion**  dead body left out for animals and birds to eat

**clay**  *Slang.* dead and buried body

**corpse**  dead body

**crowbait**  *Slang.* dead body left unburied

**dead body**  remains of a person who has died

**dead man**  corpse

**deceased**  polite or formal term for one who is dead

**decomposition**  natural decay of dead body

**dust**  one who is dead and decomposed into dust

**dust and ashes**  one who is dead and decomposed into dust

**loved one**  overly polite euphemism for dead person

**mortal remains**  corpse

**remains**  corpse

**rigor mortis** temporary stiffening of body shortly after death
**skeleton** bones of body after decomposition of flesh
**stiff** *Slang.* corpse

## BURIAL AND FUNERALS

**autopsy** examination and dissection of corpse to determine cause of death; necropsy; postmortem
**barrow** mound of earth and stones over grave
**bereaved** family and friends of deceased
**bier** stand or pedestal for a coffin or the coffin itself
**body snatcher** graverobber
**boneyard** *Slang.* cemetery
**burial** interment of dead body in grave
**burial ground** cemetery, esp. tract of land set aside for primitive cemetery
**burial mound** mound built over burial ground or grave
**cairn** heap of stones set up as memorial to the deceased
**canopic jar** vessel containing deceased's entrails for burial with mummy (ancient Egypt)
**casket** elaborate coffin
**catacomb** underground cemetery consisting of tunnels with recesses for tombs
**catafalque** ornamental bier on which body lies in state
**cemetery** area set aside for burying the dead in graves or tombs; boneyard; burial ground; graveyard; necropolis
**cenotaph** honorary tomb for person buried elsewhere
**cerecloth** waxed cloth for wrapping corpse
**cerement** waxed shroud or graveclothes
**charnel house** repository for bodies and bones of the dead
**cinerarium** vessel, esp. urn, used to receive ashes of the cremated dead
**cist** neolithic burial chamber with stone walls
**coffin** box or case for burying corpse; pall
**columbarium** vaulted structure with recesses for cinerary urns
**coronach** funeral dirge played on bagpipes (Scotland)
**coroner** public official who investigates deaths not due to natural causes
**cortege** funeral procession
**cremains** ashes of cremated body
**cremation** reduction of body to ashes for interment
**crematorium** crematory
**crematory** place, such as funeral establishment, at which cremation is done; furnace for cremation; crematorium
**cromlech** circle of stone monoliths on burial mound
**crypt** underground vault or burial chamber
**death march** funeral procession
**death watch** vigil kept over dead or dying person
**deep six** burial at sea
**dirge** song of lamentation at funeral
**dolmen** prehistoric tomb, usu. consisting of two upright stone slabs supporting one horizontal slab (Britain and France)
**elegy** funeral song or poem of lamentation for the dead
**embalming** treatment of corpse to prevent decay
**entomb** (*vb*) place corpse in burial tomb
**epitaph** memorial inscription on tomb or grave
**eulogy** praise for the deceased at funeral service
**exequies** funeral rites or ceremonies
**exequy** funeral procession
**exhumation** digging up of corpse from grave

**extreme unction** anointment of dying person with oil and prayer for recovery, administered by priest; final Catholic sacrament before death; last rites
**funeral** observance held for dead person before interment
**funeral director** manager of funeral home
**funeral home** establishment for embalming and preparation of dead for burial or cremation
**funerary** (*adj*) associated with burial
**grave** excavation in ground for burial of body
**gravedigger** person who digs graves
**graverobber** person who steals corpses after burial, as for medical dissection or profit; body snatcher
**gravestone** monument marking burial site
**graveyard** cemetery
**hearse** large automobile used to convey corpse to burial place
**in dust and ashes** mourning
**inhume** (*vb*) bury, inter
**in memoriam** in memory of, written in epitaph
**inter** (*vb*) perform interment; bury
**interment** disposition of dead body in earth or tomb, or by cremation
**inurn** (*vb*) place ashes in a burial urn
**Kaddish** Jewish prayer of mourning
**keen** loud, wailing lamentation for the dead
**knell** bell tolled to signal death or funeral
**kurgan** burial mound (Eastern Europe and Siberia)
**lamentation** mourning aloud for the dead
**last rites** extreme unction
**lay out** (*vb*) prepare corpse for viewing prior to interment
**lay to rest** bury corpse
**lich gate** roofed gateway at entrance to churchyard under which coffin rests at beginning of burial service
**lie in state** be laid out on public display in official recognition of one's stature in life
**mausoleum** large building for aboveground entombment
**memorial** service in honor of the deceased after burial or interment
**monument** tombstone or other grave marker
**morgue** storage place for dead bodies pending identification and burial
**mortician** undertaker
**mortuary** building for storing dead bodies and preparing them for burial
**mourning** customary show of grief for deceased person
**mummy** body embalmed and wrapped in cloth for burial (ancient Egypt)
**necropolis** cemetery
**necropsy** autopsy
**obsequy** funeral rite or ceremony
**pall** coffin; cloth draped over coffin, bier, or tomb
**pallbearer** one of several persons carrying coffin to grave
**plot** individual burial site in cemetery
**postmortem** autopsy
**pyre** combustible heap for burning dead body as part of funeral rite
**Requiem Mass** Catholic Mass and liturgy celebrated for the repose of the dead
**requiescat** prayer for the repose of the dead
**rest in peace** RIP; standard acknowledgment of death; wish or prayer for the deceased
**RIP** rest in peace
**sarcophagus** coffin, esp. one of stone

**sepulcher** tomb or other place of burial

**shrine** tomb or other receptacle for the dead

**shroud** cloth or sheet in which corpse is wrapped for burial; cerecloth; cerement; winding sheet

**taps** bugle call at military funerals

**threnody** elegy or song of lamentation, esp. for the dead

**tomb** place of interment; excavation for a grave; burial vault or chamber

**tombstone** stone marker placed on or over burial site

**tumulus** ancient grave; artificial mound over burial site

**undertaker** one who prepares the dead for burial and manages funerals; mortician

**urn** ornamental vessel containing ashes of cremated dead person

**vault** underground burial chamber or tomb

**vigil** long, prayerful watch over dead or dying person

**wake** often festive vigil held over body of dead person prior to burial

**winding sheet** shroud

## BEYOND THE GRAVE

**abyss** bottomless pit, gulf of nonexistence after death

**afterlife** existence of the soul in heaven; great beyond

**below** (*adv*) in hell

**damnation** condemnation of soul to hell

**dark** void beyond life, esp. hell

**devil, the** ruling spirit of hell; Satan

**Erebus** mythological place of darkness on the way to Hades (ancient Greece)

**Final Judgment** determination of soul's fate by God

**ghost** soul of deceased returning in bodily likeness; specter; wraith

**ghoul** evil being that robs graves and feeds on corpses

**great beyond** afterlife

**Grim Reaper** personification of death as cloaked skeleton holding scythe

**Hades** mythological underworld (ancient Greece)

**heaven** dwelling place of God and joyful abode of the souls of the dead

**hell** dwelling place of the devil and abode of the condemned souls of the dead

**hellfire** fire in hell

**hereafter** life after death or beyond mortal existence

**infernal** (*adj*) relating to or inhabiting the eternal inferno of hell

**manes** venerated, appeased spirit of dead person (ancient Rome)

**nether world** hell

**purgatory** intermediate state after death in which the souls of sinners become fit for heaven

**resurrection** act of rising from the dead, esp. for Final Judgment

**revenant** one who returns from death

**rise from the dead** achieve resurrection; return as a ghost

**saint** one of the dead entered into heaven, esp. the canonized or holy dead

**Satan** the devil

**soul** nonbodily spirit of deceased that exists after death

**specter** visible yet incorporeal spirit or ghost; wraith

**spirit** soul of deceased, esp. malevolent being or ghost

**Styx** principal underworld river in myth (ancient Greece)

**transmigration** passage of soul at death from body of one being to another

**underworld** hell

**upstairs** *Informal*. heaven

**vampire** reanimated corpse that returns at night to drink blood of living people

**void** unknown darkness beyond life

**wraith** apparition of living person in exact likeness, seen just before death; ghost, specter

## LANGUAGE OF DEATH

**amort** (*adj*) *Archaic*. at the point of death

**antemortem** (*adj*) preceding death

**black humor** morbid comedy, esp. relating to death

**body bag** large receptacle made of heavy material, used to transport corpse from battlefield or death scene

**capital punishment** legal execution for certain crimes

**condemned** (*adj*) sentenced to death for crimes committed

**coup de grâce** *French*. lit. blow of mercy; deathblow

**cryonics** freezing of recently deceased people in hopes of resuscitation when cure exists for their fatal disease

**dead duck** person or thing about to fail or die

**deathbed** bed on which someone dies

**deathblow** destructive stroke or event; coup de grâce

**death camp** concentration camp to which prisoners are sent for execution

**death instinct** self-destructive impulse based on desire to achieve state of harmonious nonexistence in death; Thanatos

**death mask** cast taken from face of dead person

**death rate** number of deaths per thousand in specific group or at given place and time

**death rattle** gurgle of air passing through mucus in throat of dying person

**death's-head** human skull as symbol of mortality

**death toll** number of casualties from particular incident

**dying breath** last breath at moment of death

**dying day** end of life; last day of life

**Enoch Arden** missing person who is presumed dead but is later found alive

**fey** (*adj*) *Scottish*. fated to die

**intestate** (*adj*) without a valid will at time of death

**kiss of death** action or relationship ultimately causing one's ruin

**lethal** (*adj*) deadly

**memento mori** object, esp. skull, serving as reminder of mortality

**morbidity** dwelling on gloomy thoughts of death

**mortality** being subject to death; death in large numbers; proportion of deaths in population due to specific cause

**necrology** list of those who have died within a given period; obituary

**necrophilia** achieving erotic stimulation from corpses

**obit** *Informal*. obituary

**obituary** biographical notice of person's death published in newspaper; necrology

**on one's deathbed** in the last few hours before death

**posthumous** (*adj*) occurring after one's death

**post-obit** (*adj*) effective after particular person's death

**predecease** (*vb*) die first; die before another person or event

**quietus** removal from activity, as in death

**skull and crossbones** emblem of death depicting skull and two crossed skeleton bones, esp. on pirate flag or as warning sign for poisons

**stillbirth** birth of dead child

**stillborn** (*adj*) dead at birth

**swan song** farewell appearance or last act, sometimes before death

**testament** will or act relating disposition of one's property after death

**testate** (*adj*) having made and left a valid will

**thanatology** study of death and its circumstances

**Thanatos** primal, instinctual desire for death; personification of death (ancient Greece)

**vanishing point** point at which one ceases to exist

**vital signs** index of essential body functions, including pulse, breathing, and body temperature, that indicate life

**widow** surviving wife of dead husband

**widower** surviving husband of dead wife

**will** legal directions for disposition of one's property after death

# CHAPTER 25

# Faith

# RELIGION

World Religions
Christian Denominations and Sects
Christianity
Judaism
Islam
Eastern Religions
God and Divinity
Practice and Doctrine
Individuals and Titles
Structures and Institutions
Sacred Texts and Objects
Religious States and Experiences

**SEE ALSO:** Chap. 10: Outer Garments; Ornaments and
Accessories; Chap. 11: Titles of Rank; Chap. 13:
Philosophy; Chap. 25: Mythology and Folklore; Magic
and the Occult; Eschatology; Truth, Wisdom, and Spiritual
Attainment

## WORLD RELIGIONS

**Baha'i** modern religion developed in Iran in 1863 by
Baha'Allah, emphasizing universal brotherhood, social
equality, and the unification of all religions

**Brahmanism** pantheistic religious system of highest Hindu
caste, based on the Brahmanas and Upanishads text commentaries on the Vedas, source of pre-Hindu religion
introduced in 2nd millennium B.C.

**Buddhism** religion and philosophic system founded in
India in 6th c. B.C. by Siddhartha Gautama, the Buddha,
teaching that meditation and the Eightfold Path enable
one to escape suffering and achieve Nirvana

**Byzantine Church** Orthodox Eastern Church

**Catholicism** Roman Catholicism

**Christianity** doctrine, faith, and monotheistic religious
practice based on belief in Jesus Christ as Messiah and Son
of God and on Old and New Testaments of Bible

**Christian Science** Christian religious movement and system of healing through prayer founded in 19th c. America
by Mary Baker Eddy

**Church of Jesus Christ of the Latter-day Saints** Mormon
Church

**Church of Rome** Roman Catholicism

**Confucianism** ethical and social teachings based on sayings
of Confucius in China in 6th c. B.C., later incorporated
into Taoist and Buddhist religions

**Druze** independent religious sect founded in 11th c. and
containing elements of Islam, Christianity, and Judaism,
believing in transmigration of souls, now practiced chiefly
in Syria, Lebanon, and Israel

**Eastern Orthodox Church** Orthodox Eastern Church

**Gnosticism** esoteric salvational system from 2nd c., based
on secret knowledge combining elements of mythology,
ancient religions, and Christianity

**Hinduism** religion and social system of Hindus of Indian
subcontinent, recognizing authority of Vedas and other

sacred texts, emphasizing karma and reincarnation and
worship of various deities, based on four goals and four
stages in human life and socially rooted in four castes

**Islam** doctrine, faith, and practice of monotheistic Muslim
religion in which Allah is supreme deity and Koran is
sacred revelation, devoted to worship of Allah through
Five Pillars, founded by prophet Muhammad in 7th c.
Arabia; Muhammadanism

**Jainism** ancient monastic religion of India, influential on
Hinduism, founded by Mahavira in 6th c. B.C., emphasizing asceticism, reverence for all living things, and cycles of
rebirth

**Judaism** doctrine, faith, and practice of ancient monotheistic Israelite religion based on written Torah (first five
books of Hebrew Bible or Old Testament) and teachings
of the Talmud, which view religion as part of everyday
family life, founded around 2000 B.C.

**Lamaism** form of Mahayana Buddhism and Tibetan Bo-
nism, with elaborate ritual and strong hierarchy under
Dalai Lama, practiced in Tibet, Nepal, and Mongolia

**Latter-day Saints** Mormon Church

**Mazdaism** Zoroastrianism

**Mormon Church** Christian religion founded in United
States in 1830 by Joseph Smith and now centered in Utah,
based on Book of Mormon accounts of ancient American
peoples who were to found Zion, emphasizing revelation
and proselytizing; Church of Jesus Christ of the Latter-day
Saints

**Muhammadanism** Islam

**Orthodox Eastern Church** Christian church comprising
local and national churches in southwest Asia and eastern
Europe that split from Western church in 5th c. because
of its rejection of the Roman pope and communion with
patriarch of Constantinople, marked by elaborate ritual
and iconography: includes Albanian, Bulgarian, Greek,
Rumanian, Russian, Serbian, Syrian, and Ukrainian Orthodox churches; Byzantine Church; Eastern Orthodox
Church

**Protestantism** any of various Christian denominations established during or following the Reformation against
papal authority and Roman Catholicism in 16th c.

**Roman Catholicism** highly ritualistic, dogmatic Christian
doctrine and faith based on Scripture and tradition, with
hierarchy of celibate clergy under an infallible pope claiming direct historical line from apostle Peter, formal sacraments and Mass, and veneration of saints and Virgin Mary;
Catholicism; Church of Rome

**Shinto** polytheistic, highly ceremonial, native religion of
Japan, influenced by Confucianism and Buddhism, emphasizing worship of nature and ancestors and formerly
divinity of emperor

**Sikhism** institutional mixture of Hinduism and Islam,
founded by Nanak in northern India in 16th c., that rejects
caste system

**Taoism** Chinese religion and philosophy based on 6th c.
B.C. teachings of Lao-tzu, advocating simplicity and self-
lessness in following the Tao or path to enlightenment
through balance of yin and yang

**Theosophical Society** eclectic belief system founded by
Madame Blavatsky in 1875, based largely on Brahmanic
and Buddhist teachings

**Vedanta Society** nondualistic Hindu philosophical system
in fulfillment of the sacred Vedas and Upanishads

**Zen** variety of Mahayana Buddhism seeking intuitive illumination of satori through simplicity, meditation, and instruction from masters, practiced esp. in Japan and Korea

**Zoroastrianism** religious system of Persia prior to founding of Islam, established by Zoroaster in 6th c. B.C. and based on Avesta as holy scripture, emphasizing continuous apocalyptic struggle between good and evil; Mazdaism

## CHRISTIAN DENOMINATIONS AND SECTS

**Amish** strict Mennonite community distinguished by self-sufficient living style that rejects technology, inspired by 18th c. Swiss bishop Jacob Amman

**Anabaptist** Protestant sect important in 16th c. advocating adult baptism and separation of church and state, precursor to Mennonites and Baptists

**Anglican Church** Protestant denomination developed after Henry VIII of England separated from Roman Catholic Church in 1534 and consolidated in reign of Elizabeth I, retaining many theological and hierarchical elements of Catholicism; Church of England

**Armenian Apostolic Church** Monophysite Christian church organized in United States in 1899

**Assemblies of God** largest of Pentecostal churches founded in early 20th c., practicing faith healing, speaking in tongues in enthusiastic services, and believing in second coming of Christ

**Baptist Church** Christian Protestant denomination whose evangelical beliefs include religious liberty with no creeds or hierarchy, priesthood of all believers, and adult baptism by total immersion, founded by John Smyth in 1609

**Calvinism** religious doctrine, based on beliefs of 16th c. Reformation leader John Calvin, advocating austere morality, predestination and election, and piety

**Christian Science** Christian religious sect and system of healing founded in 19th c. by Mary Baker Eddy; Church of Christ, Scientist

**Church of Christ** offshoot of Presbyterian Church founded in 1804, emphasizing literal interpretation of New Testament

**Church of Christ, Scientist** Christian Science

**Church of England** Anglican Church

**Church of God** any of various Christian denominations that emphasize personal conversion, imminent return of Christ, and sometimes speaking in tongues

**Church of the Brethren** Dunkers

**Church of the New Jerusalem** Swedenborgians

**Congregational Church** Christian church organization, developed from 16th c. separatist revolt in England, in which each local congregation is independent in governance and recognizes only Christ as its head

**Coptic Church** Christian Egyptian and Ethiopian Monophysite Church recognizing St. Mark the Evangelist as its founder and using Arabic in its services, known as Coptic Orthodox since 19th c.

**Dunkers** Christian denomination founded in 1708 in Germany that practices trine immersion and opposes taking of oaths and military service; Church of the Brethren

**Episcopalian Church** Christian denomination that evolved from Church of England within Anglican communion that developed in United States in 1784, with worship based on Book of Common Prayer

**Friends** Quakers

**Greek Orthodox Church** autonomous branch of Eastern Orthodox Church that consists of Church of Greece, patriarchate of Constantinople, and churches using Greek in the liturgy and Byzantine rite

**Huguenots** French Protestant denomination of 16th and 17th c. comprised of followers of John Calvin

**Jehovah's Witnesses** evangelical Christian sect, founded in United States in 19th c. by Charles Russell, that refuses to participate with the government, actively proselytizes, and believes in imminent second coming of Christ

**Lutheran Church** conservative Protestant denomination based on teachings of Martin Luther, 16th c. German leader of Reformation, emphasizing authority of Scripture with justification and salvation by faith alone

**Mennonites** evangelical Protestant denomination, descended from Anabaptists, named after 16th c. Dutch religious reformer Menno Simons, that emphasizes simplicity and separation from worldly things, including military service, and adult baptism

**Methodist Church** Christian Protestant denomination, founded as 18th c. evangelical movement by Anglican John Wesley, emphasizing God's grace, individual responsibility, and study of the Bible as interpreted by reason and tradition

**Metropolitan Community Church** Christian congregation of gay men and lesbians

**Millenial Church** Shakers

**Moravians** Christian denomination descended from Bohemian Brethren, holding Scriptures to be only rule of faith and practice

**Presbyterian Church** Christian Protestant denomination founded by John Knox in Scotland in 1557 as British form of Calvinism, governed by its ministry and congregationally elected elders

**Puritans** Protestant group in England and American colonies in 16th and 17th c. that wanted to reduce Roman Catholic elements of Church of England, characterized by strict religious and moral discipline, influenced by John Calvin

**Quakers** Christian religion founded in 17th c. England by George Fox, emphasizing individual's spiritual inner light and rejecting sacraments and ordained ministry, associated with pacifism and social activism; Friends; Religious Society of Friends

**Reformed Church** Christian Protestant denomination governed by its ministry and congregationally elected elders and serving as continental European form of Calvinism

**Rosicrucians** occult group founded in 1868 by R.W. Little, claiming descent from ancient brotherhood said to be founded by 15th c. Christian Rosenkruez

**Russian Orthodox Church** autocephalous branch of Eastern Orthodox Church whose liturgy is in Old Church Slavonic, headed by patriarch of Moscow in communion with patriarch of Constantinople

**Seventh Day Adventists** Christian denomination whose evangelical doctrine anticipates the imminent return of Christ to Earth and observes Saturday as Sabbath, founded in United States in 1863

**Shakers** religion founded in England in 1747, led by Ann Lee, advocating celibacy, communal property, and simple way of life; Millenial Church; United Society of Believers in Christ's Second Appearing

**Swedenborgians** religious sect founded in 18th c., influenced by Emanuel Swedenborg, a Swedish mystic who claimed to receive divine revelations; Church of the New Jerusalem

**Uniates** Eastern Orthodox church that is in union with Roman Catholic Church, acknowledges the Roman pope, but maintains its own liturgy, discipline, and rites

**Unitarianism** Christian denomination that arose during the Reformation that rejects doctrine of the Trinity, posits universal salvation, emphasizes religious tolerance and congregational autonomy, and incorporates humanism and nontheistic thought

**Unitarian-Universalism** American liberal religious denomination in Christian tradition, formed by merger of Unitarians and Universalists in 1961

**United Church of Christ** American Protestant denomination formed by merger of Evangelical and Reformed churches and Congregational Christian Church in 1957, with simple services and governing synod

**United Society of Believers in Christ's Second Appearing** Shakers

**Universalism** liberal Christian denomination founded in 1779, emphasizing universal fatherhood of God and final salvation of all souls

**Zwinglianism** religious system following doctrines of Ulrich Zwingli, 16th c. Swiss Protestant reformer, maintaining that Eucharist is merely symbolic and not literally the body of Christ and that church should model itself on ancient Christianity

## CHRISTIANITY

**Abel** second son of Adam and Eve, killed by his brother Cain

**Adam** first human, father by Eve of Cain and Abel

**Advent** period of prayer and fasting beginning four Sundays before Christmas

**agape** divine love of God or Christ for humankind

**Agnus Dei** liturgical prayer to Christ the Savior

**Agony** Christ's suffering in garden of Gethsemane

**agrapha** sayings of Jesus other than those in Gospels

**Annunciation** announcement of Christ's coming birth, made by archangel Gabriel to Mary

**Antichrist** principal opponent of Christ; Satan

**apostolic succession** unbroken chain of succession from apostles, perpetuated through pope and other bishops by laying on of hands in ordination of clergy in Catholic, Orthodox, and Anglican churches

**Ascension** Christ's bodily ascent into heaven following Resurrection

**Assumption** the bodily taking up of the Virgin Mary to heaven

**aureole** halo

**Ave Maria** Roman Catholic prayer to the Virgin Mary; Hail Mary

**beatification** official papal recognition of dead person as blessed, often prior to canonization

**beatitudes** blessings spoken by Jesus in Sermon on the Mount

**Beelzebub** chief devil, Satan

**bull** edict from pope in form of sealed letter

**Cain** eldest son of Adam and Eve, murderer of his brother Abel

**Calvary** place where Christ was crucified

**canonical hours** periods of day designated for prayer and devotion: matins and lauds, prime, tierce, sext, nones, vespers, and compline

**canonization** official recognition by Roman Catholic Church of dead person as a saint

**canticle** liturgical song based on Biblical text

**catechism** formal Catholic religious instruction in form of questions and answers

**christen** (*vb*) bring into the church by baptism

**Christendom** Christian church and its congregation throughout world

**Christmas** celebration of birth of Christ on December 25 among Western Christians and on January 6 in Eastern Orthodox Church

**Christology** study of nature of and deeds of Jesus Christ

**church** lit. members of the body of Christ, used to designate Christian house of worship

**communion** Holy Communion

**compline** final canonical hour, following vespers

**confession** Catholic sacrament received on admitting one's sins to priest and receiving absolution and doing penance

**confirmation** Catholic sacrament received at and Protestant rite performed at ceremony of acceptance of membership into church at time of adolescence

**consubstantiation** actual presence of Christ, embodied in bread and wine of the sacrament of the Eucharist

**Counter Reformation** movement in Catholic Church in response to Protestant Reformation

**credo** statement of beliefs recited in unison at Mass

**cross** symbol of Christianity, Christ's Crucifixion and death, and the redemption of humankind

**crown of thorns** wreath placed on Christ's head before Crucifixion

**crucifix** representation of Christ crucified on cross

**Crucifixion** Christ's death on the cross

**Crusades** Christian wars of Middle Ages to reclaim Jerusalem from Islam

**denomination** religious body with particular name and practices, esp. one of various Protestant sects

**Doxology** words of praise for God beginning "Praise God from whom all blessings flow"

**Easter** celebration of Resurrection of Christ

**ecumenism** Christian movement toward unity that transcends denominational distinctions

**Eden** paradise in which Adam and Eve resided before the Fall

**encyclical** letter from pope to all bishops on religious or civil matters

**Epiphany** commemoration of manifestation of Christ to the Magi

**eschatology** doctrine of last things; second coming of Christ and Judgment Day

**Eucharist** sacrament of Holy Communion; sacrifice of the Mass; Lord's Supper

**evangelical counsels** vows taken by members of religious order, including poverty, chastity, and obedience

**Eve** first woman, wife of Adam, mother of Cain and Abel

**ex cathedra** *Latin.* lit. from the chair; from seat of authority, applied to infallible pronouncements of pope

**excommunication** expulsion from Catholic Church

**Fall, the** lapse of humans into state of sinfulness through sins of Adam and Eve

**Father** one of three-part aspect of God

**fundamentalism** beliefs and practices based on literal interpretation of Bible, esp. among Protestants

**genuflection** bending of knee and crossing of oneself in reverence

**Gloria in Excelsis Deo** liturgical hymn based on Psalms

**golden rule** Christ's maxim that we should do unto others as we would have them do unto us

**gospel** good news message of salvation and kingdom of God, esp. as announced to world by Christ; story of Christ's life and teachings

**Great Schism** rift in Roman Catholic Church from 1378 to 1417, characterized by two and sometimes three claimants to papacy

**Hail Mary** Catholic prayer repeated as atonement for sins; Ave Maria;

**halo** radiant light surrounding head of Jesus, Mary, or any saint

**heaven** dwelling place of God and resting place of souls of the faithful dead

**hell** dwelling place of Satan and place of eternal torture for souls of the damned

**High Mass** Catholic Mass in which celebrant and choir sing specified parts

**Holy Communion** sacrament in which one eats body and drinks blood of Jesus Christ; communion; Eucharist

**Holy Grail** cup or platter used by Christ at Last Supper

**Holy Mother** Virgin Mary

**holy rood** cross or crucifix symbolizing cross on which Christ died; rood

**Holy Spirit** one of three-part aspect of God

**holy water** water blessed by Catholic priest

**Homoiousian** believer in 4th c. creed that essence of Son is similar to, but not same as, that of Father

**Homoousian** believer in 4th c. creed that Son and Father are made of same substance

**host** wafer representing flesh of Christ in communion

**Immaculate Conception** Catholic dogma that Mary was conceived without sin and that Christ was born to Virgin Mary through miraculous agency of God

**indulgence** removal of punishment for sin based on penance or on certain prayer practices; writ of forgiveness sold at one time by Catholic Church, protested by Martin Luther in 95 Theses

**indult** privilege given by Catholic ecclesiastical authority

**infallibility** principle of papal immunity from liability to error and pontiff's unfailingly correct judgment in matters of faith

**Inquisition** medieval tribunal of Catholic Church intent on persecution of nonbelievers and those seen as heretics

**Jansenism** movement in Holland and France during 17th c. that advocated reform of Catholic Church rather than abandonment of it

**Jesuits** largest Roman Catholic order of men, founded by Ignatius Loyola in 1540, which played a role in Counter Reformation and later in missionary work; Society of Jesus

**Jesus** 1st century Jewish prophet from Nazareth and founder of Christianity

**John the Baptist** Nazarite prophet who baptized Jesus, later executed by Herod Antipas

**Judas Iscariot** one of Christ's twelve apostles, who betrayed him to Romans

**Judeo-Christian tradition** Western religion, culture, and heritage based on both Judaism and Christianity

**Kyrie eleison** short Greek liturgical prayer used in Mass

**Last Supper** Passover meal eaten by Jesus and his disciples on the eve of his Crucifixion

**Latin** language of Roman Catholic liturgy and Mass

**lauds** canonical hour in early morning, accompanied by psalms of praise, usu. recited with matins

**Lent** forty-day period of penitence prior to Easter

**logos** word of God; actively expressed, revelatory, creative wisdom and will of God through Christ

**Lord's Prayer** prayer beginning "Our Father" that Jesus taught his disciples; Paternoster

**Lord's Supper** Eucharist; Holy Communion

**Lucifer** angelic form of Satan

**Madonna** Virgin Mary

**Manicheanism** Gnostic Christian movement of 3rd c. based on teachings of Persian sage Mani that universe is characterized by struggle between good and evil, influenced by Zoroastrianism

**Mary** Virgin Mary

**Mary Magdalene** follower of Christ who witnessed his Crucifixion and was first to see him resurrected

**Mass** central religious rite of Roman Catholic Church, which reenacts Christ's Last Supper in celebration of Eucharist

**matins** first canonical hour of day, designated for morning prayer and psalms of praise

**Melchite** Christian in Egypt and Syria who accepts definition of faith adopted by Council of Chalcedon in 451 A.D.

**miracle** event deviating from laws of nature and being sign of God's power or presence

**Mithraism** Persian mystery cult centered on benevolent god Mithra, supplanted by Christianity in 4th c.

**Mother of God** Virgin Mary

**Nativity** birth of Christ, esp. as depicted in art

**Nicene Creed** statement of Christian faith in 325 A.D. stipulating that Jesus is only begotten Son of God and of one substance with the Father

**Ninety-Five Theses** document written by Martin Luther in 1517, protesting sale of indulgences, which began Protestant Reformation

**nones** fifth canonical hour, orig. midafternoon

**novena** Roman Catholic devotion consisting of nine separate days of prayer or services

**obsecration** prayer of supplication

**Our Lady** Virgin Mary

**passion** sufferings of Christ between night of the Last Supper and his death

**Paternoster** Lord's Prayer

**patristics** study of writings of church fathers

**Pentecost** festival celebrating descent of Holy Spirit on apostles

**Peter** chief among Christ's twelve apostles, founder of church in Rome and first pope

**Pietism** Lutheran movement of 17th c. Germany that emphasized personal devotion

**prelapsarian** (*adj*) before the Fall

**Prince of Darkness** Satan

**proof text** Biblical text used as evidence for assertion

**Protestant** any of various Christian churches outside Roman Catholic Church

**Protestant Reformation** Christian schism within Catholic Church in 16th c. that resulted in Protestantism; Reformation

**Providence** divine guidance and care of God over earthly creatures

**purgatory** place where penitent souls are purified for ascent to heaven

**Rastafarianism** religious sect, orig. Jamaican, holding Haile Selassie to be the Messiah and Ethiopia to be Eden, and anticipating eventual return of blacks to Africa

**Reformation** Protestant Reformation

**Requiem Mass** Catholic funeral Mass

**requiescat** prayer for repose of the dead

**Resurrection** rising of Jesus from the dead after his Crucifixion and burial, an essential event in Christian belief

**Roman Catholicism** Christian church headed by pope as bishop of Rome

**rood** holy rood

**rule** document on which religious order bases its practice

**Sabbath** holy day consecrated to worship of God, Sunday for Christians

**Salvation Army** evangelical and social service organization founded in England in 1865 by William Booth

**Satan** supreme evil spirit residing in hell

**Second Coming** Christ's promised return after Ascension

**Society of Jesus** Jesuits

**Son** Jesus Christ, Son of God

**stations of the cross** images representing fourteen stages of Christ's passion

**stigmata** bodily marks resembling wounds of crucified Christ that appear supernaturally on bodies of certain inspired persons

**strict interpretation** literal interpretation of events described in Bible

**synod** ecclesiastical council

**Te Deum** hymn of praise to God in form of psalm beginning "Te Deum laudamus"

**transcendentalism** liberal Protestant movement of 19th c. that sought direct contact with deity outside institutional church

**transubstantiation** change during consecration of bread and wine of Eucharist into Christ's body and blood

**Trinity** three aspects of God, as Father, Son, and Holy Spirit

**Vatican** see of bishop of Rome; city-state serving as headquarters of Roman Catholic Church

**vespers** evening religious service

**virgin birth** conception of Jesus by Virgin Mary through miraculous agency of God

**Virgin Mary** Mary, mother of Jesus by virgin birth; Holy Mother; Madonna; Our Lady

**wafer** thin piece of unleavened bread used in Eucharist; host

## Judaism

**Abraham** patriarch and founder of ancient Hebrew nation

**Aggadah** nonlegal, narrative material in Talmud and Midrash containing parables and illustrative anecdotes

**ark** sacred gilded wood chest containing stone tablets bearing the Covenant; enclosure for Torah in synagogue

**Ashkenazim** German and Eastern European Jewry

**bar mitzvah** ceremony marking boy's reaching age of religious responsibility and maturity

**bas mitzvah** bat mitzvah

**bat mitzvah** ceremony marking girl's reaching age of religious responsibility and maturity; bas mitzvah

**bris** brith milah

**brith milah** rite of circumcision for male infant performed on eighth day after birth; bris

**cabala** mystical interpretation of Scriptures, with emphasis on secret meanings in text, by medieval Jews; kabala

**Canaan** ancient land promised by God to Abraham, occupying region that is now Israel; Holy Land

**Chanukah** Hanukkah

**Chasidim** Hasidim

**Chosen People** the Israelites, according to the Old Testament

**Conservative** form of the practice of Judaism, adapting ritual and traditional forms to modern life, less strict than Orthodox practice in adherence to rituals

**covenant** God's agreement to protect the faithful of Israel, as revealed in the Torah

**daven** (*vb*) recite Jewish prayers, esp. with nodding motion of upper body

**David** second king of Israel, who unified Jewish tribes and established capital at Jerusalem circa 1000 B.C.

**Decalogue** Ten Commandments

**Diaspora** historical exile of Jews from Israel to Babylonia in 6th c. B.C., when Judaism became distinguishable in modern form

**Essenes** Palestinian sect of Roman period characterized by ascetic practices and apocalyptic theology

**Exodus** flight of Israelites from Egypt led by Moses, forming second book of Pentateuch

**First Temple** Solomon's Temple at Jerusalem, destroyed by the Babylonians in 6th c. B.C.

**Flood** great deluge that covered Earth, described in Genesis

**Gabriel** archangel of Hebrew tradition, serving as divine messenger

**Haggadah** book containing liturgy and songs for Seder service at Passover

**Halakhah** body of Jewish law contained in the Bible, Talmud, and oral tradition

**Hanukkah** festival of lights celebrating victory of the Maccabees over the Syrians, observed for eight days to commemorate miracle of oil lamp in temple at Jerusalem; Chanukah

**Hasidim** followers of form of Jewish mysticism that emphasizes strict rituals and religious zeal, originating in Eastern Europe in 18th c.; Chasidim

**Hebrew** classical language of Judaism; in modern form, an official language of Israel

**Hebrews** Semitic people of Palestine traditionally descended from Jacob and considered ancestors of modern Jewry; Israelites

**Herod** king of Judea from 37 to 4 B.C., builder of Second Temple at Jerusalem

**High Holy Day** Rosh Hashanah (New Year) and Yom Kippur (Day of Atonement)

**Holy Land** Canaan; Palestine

**holy of holies** innermost part of tabernacle

**Israel** northern kingdom of the Hebrews traditionally descended from Jacob, including ten of the Twelve Tribes;

modern Jewish state founded in 1948; chosen people of God; name given to Jacob

**Israelites** Hebrews descended from Jacob and inhabiting ancient kingdom of Israel

**Jacob** second son of Isaac and father of patriarchs of twelve tribes, forefather of Hebrew people

**Jewish calendar** lunisolar calendar reckoned from 3761 B.C., containing twelve months and 353 to 355 days, adjusted every nineteen years to match solar cycle, used to determine religious holidays

**Jewry** Jewish people

**Judah** southern kingdoms of the Hebrews, including the tribes of Judah and Benjamin; fourth son of Jacob or the tribe descended from him

**Judeo-Christian tradition** Western religion, culture, and heritage based on both Judaism and Christianity

**kabalah** cabala

**Kaddish** Hebrew prayer for the dead

**Kol Nidre** opening prayer of Yom Kippur

**kosher** (*adj*) following dietary and ceremonial laws governing what is fit to eat by Jews

**Maccabees** Jewish family led by Judas Maccabaeus, who regained Jerusalem from the Syrians in 164 B.C., as commemorated by Hanukkah, and lost it to Rome in 63 B.C.

**Magen David** Star of David

**manna** miraculous food supplied to Israelites during their journey through the wilderness

**Masada** mountaintop fortress overlooking Dead Sea that was site of Zealots' last stand against Romans circa 70 A.D.

**Midrash** rabbinic explanation and exegesis of Jewish Scripture focusing on nonliteral meaning of text

**mikvah** *Hebrew*. ritual bath of purification

**minyan** *Hebrew*. quorum of ten men needed for Jewish worship

**Mishnah** formal code of Jewish law, finalized in 3rd c.

**mitzvah** act that fulfills a commandment or injunction; in modern usage, any kindness

**Moses** prophet who led Israelites out of slavery and received God's law on Sinai

**Noah** tenth descendant of Adam, chosen by God to survive the Flood with sons and animals in ark

**Orthodox** form of Judaism strictly conforming to rituals and traditions of Torah and Talmud

**Passover** commemoration of deliverance of Israelites from slavery; Pesach

**Pesach** *Hebrew*. Passover

**Pharisee** member of ancient Jewish sect who strictly adhered to oral laws and traditions, distinguished from the Sadducees

**Purim** festival in which costumes and masks are worn in celebration of Jews' deliverance by Esther from massacre in Persia

**Rabbinical Judaism** form of Jewish practice founded after destruction of Second Temple in 70 A.D.

**Reform** modern practice of Judaism that does not require observance of rituals and emphasizes ethical aspects and rational thought

**Rosh Hashanah** Jewish New Year

**Sabbath** holy day consecrated to worship of God, Saturday for Jews

**Sadducee** member of ancient Jewish sect, composed chiefly of priests and aristocrats, who opposed the Pharisees

**Sarah** wife of Abraham

**Saul** first king of Israel

**Second Temple** Herod's temple at Jerusalem, destroyed by Romans in 70 A.D. except for Western Wall

**Seder** Passover service that recounts story of Exodus from Egypt through Haggadah

**Sephardim** medieval Spanish and Portuguese Jews who emigrated to North Africa, Turkey, and Palestine to escape the Inquisition; their descendants

**shalom** *Hebrew*. peace, used as a greeting or farewell

**Shavuoth** holiday commemorating revelation of Ten Commandments to Moses on Mount Sinai

**Shema** liturgical prayer recited daily expressing love of God

**shtetl** *Yiddish*. Jewish village or community in Eastern Europe

**shul** *Yiddish*. synagogue

**Star of David** six-pointed star that is symbol of Judaism, formed from two equilateral triangles; Magen David

**Sukkoth** Jewish holiday celebrating the fall harvest and commemorating shelters of Hebrews during Exodus

**synagogue** Jewish house of worship; shul

**Ten Commandments** fundamental rules for life, given by God to Moses; Decalogue

**Twelve Tribes** original groups of Hebrews descended from Jacob, who settled kingdoms of Israel and Judah

**Wailing Wall** Western Wall

**Western Wall** holy stone wall remaining from Second Temple, destroyed in 70 A.D., used as site of Jewish prayer in Jerusalem; Wailing Wall

**yeshiva** all-day school of religious and secular learning

**Yiddish** Germanic language with mixture of Hebrew words, written in Hebrew letters, used primarily by Ashkenazim of Eastern Europe

**Yom Kippur** day of atonement and repentance following Rosh Hashanah, observed by fasting and prayer

**Zealots** Jewish sect of Roman period, characterized by revolutionary political ideology, that violently resisted Roman rule

**Zion** Palestine as Jewish homeland and symbol of Judaism, orig. hill in Jerusalem on which temples were built

**Zionism** worldwide Jewish movement, begun in late 19th century, that resulted in establishment of state of Israel

## ISLAM

**adhan** call to prayer five times daily

**Allah** God; Supreme Being

**Allah akbar** God is great; rallying cry and call to faith of Islam

**Ash-Shaytān** Satan; the devil

**ayatollah** teacher, judge, and leader of Shi'ite sect

**azan** call to prayer made five times a day by the muezzin

**baqa** in Sufism, the pure spiritual state remaining after extinction of the self

**Black Muslims** Nation of Islam

**caliph** spiritual leader claiming succession from Muhammad

**dervish** mystic, esp. Sufi, engaging in ecstatic whirling and dancing

**fana** in Sufism, annihilation of the self and union with the Divine

**Fatiha** first chapter of the Koran, recited at beginning of each of the five daily prayers

**fatwa** authoritative opinion or judgment in Islamic law

**Five Pillars of Faith** five requirements of faith in Islam: profession, worship, alms-giving, pilgrimage to Mecca, and fasting during Ramadan

**giaour** person outside Islamic faith, esp. an infidel

**hadith** tradition, esp. relating to sayings and deeds of Muhammad and his followers

**hafiz** title of respect for a Muslim who knows the Koran by heart

**hajj** pilgrimage to Mecca

**hajji** Muslim who has made pilgrimage to Mecca

**Hegira** Muhammad's exodus from Mecca to Medina in 622 A.D.

**'Id al-Adha** major four-day festival in last month of calendar

**ihram** white robes worn by male Muslims on their pilgrimage to Mecca

**imam** Muslim religious leader

**iman** act of faith in God

**jihad** holy war or crusade undertaken as Islamic duty

**Ka'ba** shrine in Great Mosque at Mecca that is objective of Muslim pilgrimage, regarded as House of God

**kafir** infidel or unbeliever

**kamal** perfection of Allah

**kashf** revelation

**Koran** Allah's revelation to Muhammad, arranged in written form as sacred Islamic text; Qur'an

**Mahdi** Muslim messiah who will establish reign of righteousness throughout world

**Mahomet** Muhammad

**marabout** hermit or holy man, esp. in North Africa

**maulvi** term of respect for expert in Islamic law in India

**Mawlid** celebration of birthday of Muhammad

**Mecca** holy city of Islam and birthplace of Muhammad, in what is now Saudi Arabia, toward which Muslims bow in prayer

**Mohammed** Muhammad

**Moharram** Islamic new year festival, in first month of lunar calendar

**mosque** Islamic house of worship

**muezzin** caller of faithful to prayer

**mufti** jurist who explains Islamic law

**Muhajirun** people who accompanied Muhammad on the Hegira

**Muhammad** 6th-7th c. A.D. Arab prophet and founder of Islam; Mahomet; Mohammed

**mujtahid** Shi'ite teacher with authority to interpret Islamic law and religion

**mullah** teacher of religious law; 'ulama

**Muslim** follow of Islam

**nabi** prophet

**namaz** ritual prayer

**Nation of Islam** organization of African-Americans advocating teaching of Islam and racial separatism

**qadi** Islamic scholar and judge in primarily religious court with civil authority

**Qiyama** last judgment

**Qur'an** Koran

**Ramadan** sacred month of fasting from sunrise to sunset during ninth month of lunar calendar

**sayyid** title of teacher descended from prophet Muhammad

**shari'ah** religious law and practical ordinances based on the Koran

**sherif** governor of Mecca, claiming descent from Muhammad

**Shi'ah** Shi'ite

**Shi'ite** member of the smaller of two major Islamic sects, given to fundamentalism, led by succession of imams; Shi'ah

**Sufi** follower of Sufism

**Sufism** mystical Islamic sect and system that seeks union with God through ecstatic trance, associated esp. with Iran

**Sunni** member of the larger of two major Islamic sects, based on orthodox law and theology of Koran and other works

**sura** any one of the 114 chapters of the Koran

**tariqah** spiritual path of Sufism

**'ulama** teacher and doctor of Muslim law and religion; mullah; Muslim religious teachers collectively

**ummah** people of the Muslim world

**Wahhabi** member of conservative Muslim group, found mainly in Saudi Arabia, practicing strict interpretation of Koran

**wali** saint

**zahid** ascetic

**zuhd** asceticism

## Eastern Religions

**ahimsa** principle of nonviolence to living things (Hinduism, Jainism)

**amrita** beverage of immortality (Hinduism)

**ananda** perfect bliss (Hinduism)

**anatta** doctrine of nonexistence of personal soul (Buddhism)

**anekantavada** seeing issues from more than one side (Jainism)

**anicca** doctrine of impermanence through cycle of birth, growth, decay, and death (Buddhism)

**atman** individual self; principle of life (Hinduism)

**Atman** World Soul, from which individual souls derive

**bardo** plane of intermediate existence between death and rebirth, basis of Tibetan *Book of the Dead* (Vajrayana Buddhism)

**bhakti** devotional acts (Hinduism)

**Bhakti** religious movement centered around worship of gods (Hinduism)

**bhikshu** monk, esp. disciple of Buddha (Buddhism)

**bodhi** supreme knowledge and Enlightenment (Buddhism)

**Bodhisattva** enlightened person who postpones Nirvana in order to help others attain enlightenment (Buddhism)

**bo tree** sacred fig tree, under which the Buddha is believed to have attained enlightenment

**Brahman** ultimate reality, characterized as pure being, consciousness, and bliss (Hinduism)

**Buddha** 6th c. B.C. Indian, Siddhartha Gautama, whose teachings are basis of Buddhism; first of three Tisarana, or sources of refuge

**bushido** spiritual path of samurai class (Japan)

**caste** one of many subdivisions of the four religious and social classes of Hinduism: Brahman or priest, warrior, merchant/farmer, artist; varna

**chakra** one of seven sources of spiritual energy within

body, tapped by yoga, lying at the intersection of cosmic order and human order (Hinduism)

**cit** pure consciousness (Hinduism)

**Confucius** Chinese philosopher of 6th-5th c. B.C. whose *Analects* and sayings form basis of Confucianism

**dagoba** shrine housing sacred relics

**Dhamma** teachings of the Buddha; truth; second of three Tisarana, or sources of refuge (Buddhism)

**dharma** cosmic law; everyday duty; spiritual doctrine (Hinduism)

**dhyana** meditation (Hinduism, Buddhism)

**Diwali** festival of lights in October (Hinduism)

**dukkha** first noble truth of Buddhism, that life is suffering caused by craving and attachment (Hinduism)

**Eightfold Path** eight pursuits leading to Enlightenment: understanding, motives, speech, action, livelihood, effort, intellectual activity, and contemplation (Buddhism)

**Enlightenment** spiritual awakening; awareness that releases one from cycle of dependent origination (Buddhism)

**Ganges** sacred river in northern India in which Hindus bathe

**Golden Temple** principal site of Sikh worship in India

**guna** three aspects of nature: passion, inertia, and purity (Hinduism)

**Hare Krishna** Vedic sect whose members engage in group chanting of Krishna's name, founded in United States in 1966

**hatha yoga** physical discipline using postures and breathing to effect changes in awareness (Hinduism)

**Hinayana** Theravada

**jiva** individual soul or ego self taken as manifestation of Atman (Hinduism)

**jnana** wisdom acquired through meditation and study (Hinduism)

**karma** action and results of action; moral cause and effect (Hinduism, Buddhism, Jainism, Sikhism)

**karma yoga** yoga of action (Hinduism)

**koan** baffling aphorism that inspires awakened mental state or disrupts discursive thought (Zen Buddhism)

**lama** monk or priest (Mahayana Buddhism)

**Lao-tzu** Chinese teacher of 6th c. whose *Tao Te Ching* forms basis of Taoism

**Lingayat** sect of southern India that does not recognize caste distinctions (Hinduism)

**lotus** symbolic water lily (Buddhism)

**Mahavira** last of Tirthankara and consolidator of Jainism in 5th c. B.C.

**Mahayana** later of Buddhism's two main branches, predominant in China, Japan, Korea, Tibet, and Vietnam, encompassing Vajrayana

**mandala** complex design of circle surrounding square, with symbolic and ritual power, used in temple design and as art form (Hinduism, Buddhism)

**mantra** holy word or sound used in meditation (Hinduism)

**maya** illusion; phenomenal world seen without awareness (Buddhism, Hinduism)

**Middle Path** middle way of life, between asceticism and luxury (Buddhism)

**moksha** liberation, release from cycle of ordinary experience and reincarnation of samsara (Buddhism, Hinduism, Jainism)

**mudra** sacred hand gesture (Hinduism, Buddhism)

**Nanak** founder of Sikhism in 16th c. India, who combined elements of Islam and Hinduism

**naos** ancient temple or shrine

**neti neti** *Sanskrit.* lit. neither this nor that; ineffable and undifferentiated nature of Brahman (Hinduism)

**Nirvana** release from endless cycle of rebirth into state of cosmic bliss (Buddhism)

**Om** mantric sound that is complete expression of Brahman (Hinduism); also used in Vajrayana Buddhism

**panth** community of Sikhs

**parinirvana** Nirvana achieved at death of physical body

**prajna** knowledge, wisdom, spiritual insight, and enlightenment (Hinduism, Buddhism)

**prana** breath, sacred life force (Hinduism)

**rahit** ritual and ethical code enumerating five signs of faith: uncut hair, dagger, breeches, comb, and bracelet (Sikhism)

**raja yoga** yoga of kingly discipline and spirituality (Hinduism)

**samadhi** union of meditator with object of meditation; transcendence (Hinduism, Buddhism)

**samsara** cycle of rebirth and transmigration of souls (Hinduism); rebecoming and reexistence (Buddhism)

**Sangha** greater community of Buddhist practitioners; monastic order founded by the Buddha; third of three Tisarana, or sources of refuge

**Sankhya yoga** one of six leading systems of Hindu philosophy, stressing duality and reality of spirit and matter

**sat** realm of existence or being (Hinduism)

**Satcitananda** reality, combining sat (being), cit (consciousness), and ananda (bliss), seen through qualities of Brahman (Hinduism)

**satori** enlightenment, awakening (Zen Buddhism)

**stupa** memorial mound that may contain relics of saint (Buddhism)

**Sunyata** that which exists absolutely and without predication (Buddhism)

**t'ai chi ch'uan** neo-Confucian concept of single, ultimate principle and source of all things; stylized meditation exercise based on this concept (China)

**Tantra** tradition incorporating secret ritual with mystical practices rooted in harmony of masculine and feminine aspects of cosmos, often expressed in sexual ritual (Hinduism, Buddhism)

**tantrayana** Vajrayana (Hinduism)

**Tao** the way or path to self-realization and enlightenment (Taoism)

**tapas** yoga techniques of breath control and bodily conditioning for greatest creative power (Hinduism)

**Theravada** earlier of Buddhism's two main branches, predominant in Sri Lanka, Burma, and Southeast Asia; Hinayana

**Tirthankara** twenty-four chronologically sequential Jain sages, last of whom is Mahavira, consolidator of Jainism

**Tisarana** three levels or sources of refuge: Buddha, Dhamma, and Sangha (Buddhism)

**tope** shrine or stupa (Buddhism)

**Trimurti** divinity in three aspects of Brahma, Vishnu, and Shiva (Hinduism)

**upaya** instructional device such as koan (Buddhism)

**Vaishnava** Bhakti sect devoted to worship of Vishnu (Hinduism)

**Vajrayana** tantric Buddhism, with mystical aspects, emphasizing male and female symbolism and deities, predominant in northern India, Tibet, and Nepal; tantrayana

**varna** caste (Hinduism)

**Vedanta** classical philosophy in fulfillment of Vedas, dealing with nature of Brahman in dualistic (Dvaita) and non-dualistic (Advaita) doctrines (Hinduism)

**vinaya** monastic code of discipline (Buddhism)

**Way, the** Tao (Taoism)

**yang** cosmic force of masculine, active, light, warm, contracting, creative energy of heaven (Taoism)

**yantra** diagram for meditation (Hinduism)

**yin** cosmic force of feminine, passive, dark, cold, expansive, material energy of earth (Taoism)

**yin and yang** two modes of cosmic energy that form dynamic Tao, or way of the universe, and combine in various proportions in all things

**yoga** spiritual discipline and practice involving meditation, physical postures, breathing exercises, and devotional acts: hatha (physical), jnana (wisdom and intellect), karma (action), raja (kingly spirituality), and sankhya (philosophic) (Hinduism)

**zazen** cross-legged meditation practice (Zen Buddhism)

**zendo** retreat for meditation; monastery (Zen Buddhism)

## GOD AND DIVINITY

**Adonai** *Hebrew.* the Lord, God

**Agnus Dei** figure of a lamb as representation of Jesus Christ

**Ahura Mazda** Supreme Being, representing forces of good and evil (Zoroastrianism)

**Allah** God, Supreme Being (Islam)

**All-Knowing** God the omniscient (Christianity)

**Almighty** God the omnipotent (Christianity)

**anima mundi** *Latin.* world soul

**Atman** soul, self (Hinduism)

**Brahma** god of creation, mediating between Vishnu and Shiva (Hinduism)

**Buddha** enlightened being (Buddhism)

**Christ** anointed Jesus Christ, Savior and Son of God, second element of Trinity (Christianity)

**Creator** Supreme Being, God

**dea** *Latin.* goddess

**deity** supreme being, god, divine being

**demigod** half divine being, born of union of god and mortal

**deus** *Latin.* god

**deva** a god or divinity (Buddhism, Hinduism); one of an order of evil spirits (Zoroastrianism)

**Divine Mind** Supreme Being (Christian Science)

**divinity** deity, god, divine being

**Dominus** *Latin.* God, the Lord

**earth mother** great mother, goddess

**Elohim** *Hebrew.* God

**Father** God, first element of the Trinity (Christianity)

**First Cause** Supreme Being as creator of universe

**god** immortal being or personification of natural or psychic force

**God** Supreme Being (Christianity)

**God Almighty** God

**goddess** female god or deity

**godhead** divine being

**Godhead** essence of God, Supreme Being; Holy Trinity

**godhood** state of being a god

**God the Father** Christian God in aspect of creator of universe and humankind

**God the Son** Jesus Christ

**Good Lord** usu. **the Good Lord**; God (Christianity)

**Good Shepherd** Jesus Christ

**Great Mother** ancient nature goddess (pre-Hellenic Europe, Near East)

**Holy Ghost** Holy Spirit

**Holy Spirit** spirit of God, third element of the Trinity; Holy Ghost; Spirit

**Holy Trinity** tripartite nature of God: Father, Son, and Holy Spirit; Godhead (Christianity)

**idol** image or representation of deity, or object made into god

**Immanuel** *Hebrew.* lit. God is with us; name attributed to Christ by Christians

**immortal** being with eternal life

**incorporeal** (*adj*) pertaining to nonbodily attribute of God

**Indra** sky, storm god (Hinduism)

**Jahweh** Yahweh

**Jehovah** Yahweh, God (Judaism)

**Jesu** Jesus

**Jesus Christ** Son of God and Savior of humankind, both fully human and fully divine

**kami** gods, spirits of the divine (Shinto)

**King of Heaven** God (Christianity)

**King of kings** Jesus Christ

**Krishna** avatar of Vishnu (Hinduism)

**Lamb of God** Jesus Christ

**living Christ** Christ as present through the Eucharist

**Lord** Supreme Being, God; Christ

**Lord of hosts** Jehovah, God

**Lord of lords** Jesus Christ

**Mahdi** expected restorer of Islam

**Maker** God

**Messiah** Jesus Christ; expected deliverer of Jewish people

**Nazarene** Jesus Christ

**numen** divine spirit

**Omnipotent** (*adj*) all-powerful: attribute of God (Christianity)

**Omnipresent** (*adj*) all-present: attribute of God (Christianity)

**Omniscient** (*adj*) all-knowing: attribute of God (Christianity)

**pantheon** group of gods

**Paraclete** Holy Spirit

**Prince of Peace** Jesus Christ

**Rama** incarnation of Vishnu (Hinduism)

**Redeemer** Jesus Christ

**Sat Guru** God (Sikhism)

**Savior** Jesus Christ

**Shaddai** *Hebrew.* God

**Shiva** god of destruction (Hinduism); Siva

**Siva** Shiva

**Son of God** Jesus Christ

**Son of Man** Jesus Christ

**Spirit** Holy Spirit

**Supreme Being** God; deity responsible for creation

**Tathagata** Buddha's name for himself

**theos** *Greek.* god

**Trimurti** triad of gods Brahma, Vishnu, and Siva (Hinduism)

**Trinity** god in three aspects: Father, Son, and Holy Spirit (Christianity); creator/mediator, preserver, and destroyer (Hinduism); Holy Trinity

**unmoved mover** God; supreme being as creator

**Vishnu** god the preserver (Hinduism)

**Yahweh** *Hebrew.* God in Old Testament; Jahweh

**Yama** god of the dead (Hinduism)

## PRACTICE AND DOCTRINE

**ablution** ritual bathing of body or washing of object or person

**absolution** forgiveness for sins

**agnosticism** belief that God's existence is unknowable; nescience

**amen** solemn ratification of faith used at end of prayer by Christians and Jews

**anathema** curse, ban, or excommunication pronounced by religious authority; offering consecrated to deity

**animism** belief that natural objects and phenomena have souls

**anthropomorphism** investing God or divinity with human attributes

**antinomianism** belief in Christian faith alone as necessary for salvation, without necessity of moral law

**apotheosis** deification, esp. by elevating mortal to god

**asceticism** religious practice of strict discipline and self-denial

**atheism** nonbelief in God

**atonement** reconciliation with God through forgiveness of sins; suffering and death of Jesus for human sins Christ

**autocephalous** (*adj*) having its own chief bishop but in communion with other Orthodox churches

**baptism** Christian sacrament of admission into church shortly after birth; immersion in water to symbolize such admission

**belief** itemized codification of religious assertions or affirmations of faith

**benediction** blessing

**benison** benediction or blessing

**blasphemy** sacrilege; intentional offense to God

**blessing** act of consecrating or wishing God's favor upon; benediction; benison

**camp meeting** religious gathering, often evangelical, held in tent or outdoors; tent meeting

**canon** religious code or doctrine; canon law, authoritative texts

**catechism** elementary guidebook for Christian religious instruction

**celibacy** abstention from marriage and sexual relations, as by priest

**charismatics** followers of Christian movement who believe in ecstatic religious experience, sometimes manifested by speaking in tongues and instantaneous healing

**chastity** abstention from sexual activity

**collegial** (*adj*) marked by sharing of authority among Roman Catholic bishops

**commandment** one of Biblical Ten Commandments

**communion** Holy Communion

**conclave** meeting of Roman Catholic cardinals to select pope

**concordat** ecclesiastical agreement between pope and sovereign

**confession** disclosure of sins to achieve absolution

**consecration** dedication of person or object to sacred use

**conventicle** assembly for worship, esp. secret or unsanctioned one

**conversion** formal change from one religion to another

**Creation** formation of Earth and beginnings of humanity as told of in sacred texts, esp. fundamentalist view that God created world in seven days as in Genesis

**creationism** doctrine that matter and all its forms were created by an omnipotent God, esp. literal belief in story of Creation in Genesis

**creed** formal statement or system of religious beliefs, esp. for specific denomination

**cult** particular system of religious practice or religious group, usu. unorthodox or deviating from major faith and practicing in an absolute, oppressive, or obsessive way, often under the direction of a charismatic leader

**deadly sins** seven sins held to be fatal to spiritual progress: pride, covetousness, lust, anger, gluttony, envy, and sloth

**deism** belief in transcendent God as creator without further intervention in human affairs

**devotions** religious practices, esp. prayers

**dispensation** God's ordering of affairs of the world; exemption from practices authorized by religious authority

**ditheism** belief in two equally powerful gods; belief in existence of antagonistic forces for good and evil, as in Zoroastrianism

**doctrine** religious teaching

**dogma** religious teaching formally stated as creed or article of faith

**dualism** doctrine of two independent eternal principles; distinction between conventional and ultimate reality in Hinduism

**ecclesiastical** (*adj*) relating to church as formal and established institution

**ecumenical** (*adj*) pertaining to whole Christian church, esp. promoting its unity

**ethics** fundamental moral principles that guide one's behavior toward others and world at large

**Eucharist** sacrament of Holy Communion; sacrifice of the Mass; Lord's Supper

**evangelize** (*vb*) spread the gospel

**Evensong** evening prayer

**exegesis** analysis and interpretation of Scripture

**expiation** atonement for one's sins

**extreme unction** Christian sacrament of anointing one who is near death; sacrament of the sick

**faith** emotional belief in divine order as ultimate reality, usu. involving existence of God and practice of specific religious doctrine, not requiring proof

**faith healing** miraculous healing by power of God

**fast** abstention from food, usu. as religious discipline

**fideism** exclusive reliance on faith and exclusion of science and philosophy in religious matters

**grace** undeserved love and mercy of God toward humankind; sanctifying energy mediated by God's word in Protestantism and through sacraments in Catholicism

**hagiography** writings and critical studies of saints

**hagiology** literature or biography dealing with lives of saints

**hajj** pilgrimage to Mecca (Islam)

**hallelujah** expression of praise for God

**healing** curing of physical affliction through faith and prayer

**henotheism** allegiance to one god while allowing worship of any of several other gods by family or tribe

**heresy** unorthodox or dissenting religious belief

**hermeneutics** science of theological interpretation

**heterodoxy** unorthodox theological views

**Holy Communion** sacrament in which one eats body and drinks blood of Jesus Christ; Eucharist; communion

**holy orders** Christian sacrament of ordination as priest or deacon

**hosanna** cry of love for God

**hymn** sacred song in praise of God

**idolatry** worship of physical image of deity

**indigenous religion** religion limited to a particular region

**insufflation** rite of breathing on person to symbolize spiritual inspiration

**interdenominational** (*adj*) common to or involving different religious denominations

**invocation** act of calling upon deity, usu. in prayer

**isagogics** branch of theology introductory to Bible study and exegesis

**kenosis** doctrine that Christ gave up His divine attributes to experience human suffering

**laying on of hands** rite in which cleric places hands on head of person being confirmed or ordained, also used in faith healing

**libation** pouring out of wine to honor deity

**libertinism** indulgence of flesh as religious expression

**litany** prayer in form of call and response, usu. between minister and congregation

**literalism** literal interpretation of Bible

**liturgy** rites of religious worship

**love feast** meal of fellowship and charity taken as rite

**lustration** ritually purifying bath

**mantra** holy word or sound used in meditation (Hinduism)

**matrimony** Christian sacrament of marriage before God

**meditation** spiritual and mental discipline or exercise involving contemplation and awakened state of awareness

**monasticism** system and way of life of monks

**monotheism** belief in a single God

**morals** specific attitudes and behaviors derived from broad ethical principles and beliefs

**mortal sin** serious, willful transgression against law of God that deprives soul of divine grace until absolution and possibly results in eternal damnation

**native religion** any of various religions indigenous to a particular region, particularly one inhabited by preliterate people; primitive religion

**nescience** agnosticism

**nondualism** lack of distinction between conventional and ultimate realities (Hinduism)

**oblation** offering to God of bread and wine in Eucharist

**observance** recognition and celebration of religious rite

**offertory** offering of bread and wine before consecration at Eucharist service; period for collection during worship service

**ordination** Christian sacrament received upon joining priesthood

**original sin** sin or evil innate in humankind, stemming from Adam's sin

**orthodoxy** correct religious belief according to specific doctrine

**orthopraxy** correct religious behavior and rituals according to specific doctrine

**paganism** belief in god other than Christian, Jewish, or Muslim God

**pantheism** belief that God is manifested by and throughout the universe; worship of eclectic body of deities

**path** spiritual process of discipline and manner of conduct

**penance** specific act of repentance for sins; Catholic sacrament

**Pentecostalism** belief in and practice of revivalism, baptism, speaking in tongues, and faith healing, with emphasis on activity of Holy Spirit (Christianity)

**piacular** (*adj*) making atonement

**pilgrimage** journey to sacred place to reaffirm religious faith

**polytheism** belief in and worship of more than one god

**prayer** address, petition, or offering to God or deity

**prayer meeting** gathering for communal prayer, often in evangelical, high-spirited religious service

**preach** (*vb*) deliver a sermon proclaiming the gospel or stating religious and moral truths

**predestination** notion that salvation of human soul is preordained by God

**preterition** Calvinist doctrine that God passes over those not elected to salvation

**primitive religion** native religion

**proselytize** (*vb*) attempt to convert others to one's beliefs or religion

**psalm** any sacred song or hymn from Bible's Book of Psalms used in worship

**purification** ceremonial cleansing of spiritual pollution

**redemption** salvation and deliverance from evil, esp. through Christ's act of mercy toward humankind

**reincarnation** rebirth of soul in another body (Hinduism)

**religion** system of beliefs and practices involving worship of a supreme being or principle and explaining the origin, nature, and meaning of the universe

**repentance** contrition for sins

**retreat** period of seclusion for religious exercises and meditation

**revival** evangelistic rekindling of religious fervor

**rite** solemn ceremonial practice following specific form

**ritual** specified form, manner, and language of religious ceremony

**sacrament** religious act or practice symbolizing conferment of divine grace; Catholic sacraments are baptism, confirmation, Eucharist, penance, extreme unction, holy orders, and matrimony; many Protestants include only baptism and communion

**sacrament of the sick** extreme unction

**sacrifice** religious offering made to deity

**sacrilege** act or statement that degrades the sacred

**salvation** deliverance from damnation, liberation from sin and its punishment; redemption and reconciliation to God

**schism** split or division over orthodoxy in religious group, esp. Great Schism, as between Roman and Eastern churches in 9th c. and during period of rival popes in 14th to 15th c.

**scholasticism** philosophical system of 11th to 15th c. that attempted intellectual analysis of religious doctrine, based on teachings of St. Thomas Aquinas and St. Augustine

**scripturalism** detailed, often literal, analysis of the Bible

**sect** religious group deviating from orthodox faith, usu. having specific practices prescribed by its leader

**secularism** system or philosophy that rejects religious necessity or interpretation

**sermon** religious discourse delivered by clergyman as part of service

**service** form followed at religious meeting

**sign of the cross** cross formed in the air by moving hand rapidly from head to chest and shoulder to shoulder as sign of prayer

**simony** buying or selling of church office or indulgence

**solemn vow** irrevocable public vow taken by clergy and members of religious orders in Catholic Church committing them to observe rule of an order, often against ownership of property and marriage

**soteriology** doctrine of salvation through Christ

**supplication** earnest prayer of petition

**syncretism** attempted reconciliation of elements from two or more religions to create new religion

**tent meeting** camp meeting

**theism** belief in God; belief in gods

**theology** systematic study of God and religious faith and practices

**theonomy** state of individual or society that regards its own nature as being in accord with divine nature

**theurgy** working of divine or supernatural agency in human affairs

**tithing** paying one-tenth of one's income to support church

**total immersion** baptism in which candidate's entire body is immersed in water

**tradition** source of authority, doctrines, practices, and institutions of religion, such as Mosaic law in Judaism, teachings of Christ in Christianity, and Koranic revelation in Islam

**trine immersion** baptism in which candidate is immersed three times, once for each part of Trinity

**unction** anointing with oil as consecration

**unfrock** (*vb*) deprive priest of right to exercise office

**venial sin** sin that does not deprive soul of sanctifying grace, unlike mortal sin

**viaticum** Eucharist given to person near death

**virtues** seven natural and cardinal virtues: faith, hope, charity, prudence, justice, temperance, and fortitude

**worship** showing honor and devotion to a deity

## Individuals and Titles

**abbé** member of secular clergy, esp. in France

**abbot** superior of monastery

**acolyte** altar server; member of highest-ranking of four minor orders in Catholic Church

**agnostic** one who does not know whether God exists

**altar boy** boy assisting celebrant in liturgical service but not formally inducted as acolyte

**altar girl** girl who performs functions of altar boy

**anchorite** religious hermit or extreme ascetic

**angel** divine being, esp. messenger of God

**apostate** deserter of religious faith

**apostle** messenger or preacher of religious principles, esp. one of twelve original followers of Jesus

**archangel** chief angel; one of seven chief angels in Bible

**archbishop** chief bishop (Christianity)

**archdeacon** chief deacon, ranking below bishop (Christianity)

**archpriest** chief priest

**Arhat** one who has attained Nirvana through ascetic practices (Buddhism)

**atheist** nonbeliever in God

**avatar** deity in physical form on Earth (Hinduism)

**ayatollah** teacher, judge, or leader of Shi'ite sect, with superior training in theology and law (Islam)

**believer** person with faith, esp. in specific religion

**bhikshu** monk observing rules of his order, such as vows of poverty (Buddhism)

**bishop** high-ranking ecclesiastical officer with authority over diocese and its clergy (Christianity)

**Bodhisattva** enlightened person who postpones Nirvana in order to help others attain Enlightenment (Buddhism)

**bonze** monk (Buddhism)

**brother** fellow member of religious order (Christianity)

**buddha** enlightened being with fully realized awareness of true nature of existence; statue of the Buddha used as symbol in Buddhism

**caliph** spiritual leader claiming succession from Muhammad

**cantor** singer or leader of choir (Judaism)

**cardinal** ecclesiastical officer ranking above bishop, usu. an archbishop; member of Roman Catholic Church's College of Cardinals

**celebrant** person performing rite, esp. priest officiating at Eucharist

**cenobite** member of religious order living in convent or monastery

**chaplain** person conducting religious services and performing sacraments in place other than church, as in military field or hospital, or for an organization

**chela** disciple of a guru (Hinduism)

**cherub** one of second order of angels, represented as winged child

**choir** group of singers in church

**church** whole body of Christian believers; building in which Christian worship services are held

**clergy** ordained priests, ministers, and rabbis, as distinct from laity; clerics

**clergyman** ordained priest, minister, or rabbi; curate

**cleric** member of the clergy

**college** clergy living together for specific purpose

**colporteur** person who travels about to sell Bibles

**communicant** church member entitled to receive the Eucharist

**congregation** gathering of people as religious community, esp. for specific services in church

**convert** person adopting or changing religion

**convocation** consultative assembly of Christian clergy

**council** assembly of bishops

**crucifer** carrier of cross at head of procession

**crusader** participant in medieval expeditions to Holy Land to reclaim it from Muslims

**curate** clergyman

**curé** parish priest in France

**damned** those souls predestined for condemnation

**Dalai Lama** chief lama of Tibetan Buddhism

**deacon** minister or layman assisting priest (Christianity)

**dean** Roman Catholic priest supervising one district of diocese; head of chapter of cathedral church

**defrocked** (*adj*) describing minister or priest who has been removed from office or excommunicated

**dervish** Islamic mystic, esp. Sufi, engaging in ecstatic whirling and dancing

**devil** evil spirit

**devil's advocate** official of Catholic Church who examines evidence given in demand for canonization

**devotee** person dedicated to spiritual master, teaching, or practice

**dewal** priest (Hinduism)

**disciple** follower of religious teacher or leader

**ecclesiastic** member of clergy or religious order

**elder** minister or esteemed congregation member

**elect** those souls predestined for salvation

**Eminence** title of honor applied to cardinals of Catholic Church

**eparch** bishop or metropolitan of administrative subdivision of Orthodox Eastern Church

**eremite** member of religious order living as hermit or recluse

**evangelist** itinerant or special preacher of Protestant denomination

**Evangelist** any of the writers of the four Gospels

**exarch** bishop of Orthodox Eastern Church, ranking below patriarch and above metropolitan

**faithful** those subscribing to a particular faith

**fakir** monk or wandering mendicant believed to possess magical powers (Hinduism, Islam)

**father** form of address for priest

**father confessor** priest who administers sacrament of confession

**freethinker** person of liberal religious views, usu. skeptical of dogma and doctrine

**friar** member of mendicant order

**gentile** person who is not Jewish

**giaour** person outside Islamic faith, esp. infidel

**glebe** *Chiefly Brit.* cultivable land belonging to parish church or benefice

**guru** spiritual master, esp. Hindu

**hajji** Muslim who has made pilgrimage to Mecca

**heathen** pagan, esp. nonbeliever in Christian, Hebrew, or Muslim God

**heavenly host** angels and others dwelling with God in heaven

**hegumen** head of Orthodox Eastern monastery

**heretic** person rejecting orthodox or accepted religious beliefs

**hermit** religious recluse

**high priest** chief priest; primary priest of ancient Jewish Levitical priesthood

**Holy Roller** derogatory description of member of Pentecostal sect, based on frenetic quality of services

**illuminati** person claiming spiritual grace or enlightenment

**imam** leader (Islam)

**infidel** disbeliever in specific religious doctrine, esp. that of Islam

**Jesus freak** *Informal.* member of fundamentalist group, usu. comprised of young people, that emphasizes intense personal devotion to Jesus Christ

**kaffir** infidel or nonbeliever in Islamic faith

**laity** congregation of people ministered to by clergy

**lama** priest (Tibetan Buddhism, Lamaism)

**latitudinarian** person having liberal religious views

**magi** priests (ancient Persia)

**maharishi** great teacher or wise man (Hinduism)

**mahatma** great soul, sage (Hinduism)

**manciple** steward of a monastery

**man of the cloth** member of clergy

**martyr** person put to death for defending religious principles

**master** religious sage or teacher

**mendicant** member of religious order living by alms or charity

**Messiah** expected deliverer of Jewish people; Jesus Christ

**metropolitan** bishop of diocese of Orthodox Eastern Church, ranking below exarch

**minister** clergyman, esp. Protestant one

**ministry** all ministers of a specific religion

**missionary** Christian proselytizer in non-Christian region

**mohel** *Hebrew.* person who performs brith milah, or rite of circumcision

**monk** man living in religious order, either Christian or Buddhist

**Monophysite** person who believes that Christ has one nature, partly divine and partly human

**Monsignor** title conferred on certain Catholic prelates

**Mother Superior** head nun of convent

**muezzin** caller of faithful to prayer (Islam)

**mufti** jurist who explains Islamic law

**mullah** teacher of religious law (Islam)

**neophyte** recent convert to a faith

**novice** person undergoing probationary period before taking vows of religious order

**nullifidian** person without religious faith, esp. skeptic

**nun** woman living in cloistered religious order, either Christian or Buddhist

**padre** father or priest; chaplain in military service

**pagan** heathen, nonbeliever in Christian, Hebrew, or Muslim God; formerly, follower of ancient Roman religion

**palmer** pilgrim returning from Holy Land carrying a palm branch, esp. in Middle Ages

**Pariah** member of lowest caste in India or Burma (Hinduism)

**parishioner** member or inhabitant of parish

**parson** rector; Protestant clergyman

**pastor** priest, minister, or spiritual shepherd of congregation; shepherd

**patriarch** bishop of Eastern Orthodox Church; Roman Catholic bishop next in rank to pope; church father

**penitent** person who confesses sin and seeks repentance

**pilgrim** person traveling to sacred place as affirmation of devotion, usu. Christian to Holy Land or Muslim to Mecca

**pillar saint** stylite

**pontiff** pope

**pope** bishop of Rome and head of Roman Catholic Church

**preacher** member of clergy, esp. Christian one; predicant

**precentor** person, sometimes of the clergy, who leads church choir or conducts choral service

**precisian** strict adherent to moral or religious standards, esp. Puritan of 16th or 17th c.

**predicant** preacher

**prelate** ecclesiastic of high order, such as bishop or archbishop

**preterite** those passed over by God; those not elected for salvation

**priest** ordained member of clergy, official minister

**priesthood** office and institution of being a priest; all priests collectively

**primate** archbishop or bishop ranking first among the bishops of a province or country

**prior** superior ranking next to abbot in monastery

**prophet** messenger of God, esp. one revealing judgment of God

**proselyte** new convert to a religion

**provost** chief dignitary of a cathedral

**pundit** learned, religious man (Hinduism)

**qadi** Islamic judge, scholar, and religious teacher

**rabbi** leader of a Jewish congregation; title of respect for Jewish scholar or teacher

**rabbinate** office of a rabbi; all rabbis collectively

**Reb** *Yiddish.* form of address or title for rabbi

**recreant** one who renounces faith

**rector** clergyman in charge of parish; priest directing church with no pastor

**reprobate** one who is damned

**Reverend** form of address for member of clergy

**rishi** religious sage (Hinduism)

**sadhu** holy man (Hinduism)

**sage** wise, pious person

**saint** holy person consecrated by religious body

**sannyasi** wandering beggar and ascetic (Hinduism)

**sayyid** title given to teacher descended from prophet Muhammad (Islam)

**seeker** person pursuing religious knowledge

**seer** person with spiritual insight

**seminarian** person studying to become Roman Catholic priest

**sensei** spiritual teacher (Japan)

**seraph** one of the highest order of angels, usu. pictured as six-winged

**sexton** person who watches over church property and usu. rings bells for services

**shaman** person with spiritual insight and authority, empowered to conduct religious rites in nativist religions

**shepherd** pastor

**sister** member of woman's religious order; form of address for nun

**starets** religious teacher or counselor

**stylite** ascetic saint living atop pillar; pillar saint

**subdeacon** cleric ranking below deacon

**swami** religious teacher, holy man (Hinduism)

**televangelist** evangelist who preaches over television

**tertiary** lay member of religious order, usu. living in its community

**theologian** person who has studied religious faith and practices

**true believer** faithful follower of specific religious doctrine

**tulku** reincarnation of holy man (Tibetan Buddhism)

**twice-born** (*adj*) pertaining to a person of Brahman caste; pertaining to a person who has undergone reincarnation (Hinduism)

**verger** *Chiefly Brit.* church attendant, esp. to bishop

**vicar** member of Episcopal clergy in charge of mission chapel; representative of Anglican prelate with broad pastoral duties

**votary** person bound by religious vows

**wali** saint (Islam)

**wise man** religious sage

**yogi** practitioner of yoga philosophy and discipline (Hinduism)

**zahid** ascetic (Islam)

**Zealot** member of militant Jewish sect that flourished between 100 B.C. and 100 A.D.

## STRUCTURES AND INSTITUTIONS

**abbey** monastery

**altar** raised platform where sacrifices and offerings are made to God

**apse** recessed, vaulted niche at end of choir in church

**archdiocese** area of jurisdiction of archbishop

**basilica** early Catholic church

**bema** sanctuary of Orthodox Eastern Church; altar in Jewish synagogue

**benefice** ecclesiastical office guaranteeing fixed income

**bethel** church for seamen

**cathedral** church that is diocesan seat of bishop or archbishop, often large and elaborately decorated

**chancel** area near altar reserved for clergy and choir

**chancery** office of diocese

**chapel** small house of worship associated with larger church

**church** place of worship, esp. structure in which Christian services are held

**cloister** monastery, esp. area within monastery restricted to its members

**College of Cardinals** chief ecclesiastical body of Roman Catholic Church, advisory to pope and including all cardinals

**confessional** stall in which Catholics make confession of their sins to unseen priest

**convent** residence for nuns or sisters of religious order; nunnery

**curia** the papal court

**dagoba** shrine housing sacred relics of Buddha

**diocese** territorial jurisdiction of bishop

**divinity school** Protestant seminary

**Holy See** See of Rome; Vatican

**house of worship** church, synagogue, or temple

**jube** screen separating chancel from nave, often supporting a rood

**mandira** Hindu temple

**meeting house** church or house of worship

**mihrab** prayer niche in Islamic mosque

**misericord** room in monastery where monastic rules are not strictly enforced

**mission** local church or parish supported by larger religious organization, usu. in effort to convert nonbelievers

**monastery** home for persons of particular religious order, esp. monks; abbey

**mosque** Islamic house of worship

**naos** ancient temple or shrine

**nave** main axis of church or cathedral

**nunnery** convent

**order** community of monks or nuns following specific

rules; major Catholic orders include Benedictine, Dominican, Franciscan, Jesuit, Marist, Paulist, and Trappist

**pagoda**  Buddhist or Shinto temple

**pantheon**  temple dedicated to all gods

**papacy**  institution and office of the pope

**parish**  local church or ecclesiastical district

**parsonage**  house provided by church for Protestant clergyman, such as parson

**pew**  bench or seat on which several persons sit in church

**priory**  religious house governed by prior or prioress, usu. part of an abbey

**pulpit**  lectern from which preacher conducts religious service, esp. interpreting the Bible as God's word

**rectory**  residence of rector or parish priest

**sacristy**  room in church for storage of sacred vessels and for clergy's preparation for services

**sanctuary**  sacred portion of church surrounding altar

**sanctum**  any sacred or hallowed place

**see**  seat of bishop's office and authority

**See of Rome**  seat of power of the pope, who has jurisdiction over Catholic churches throughout world; Holy See; Vatican

**seminary**  institution providing training for ministry or esp. for priesthood

**shrine**  place of devotion to saint or deity

**shul**  *Yiddish.* synagogue

**stupa**  memorial mound that may contain relics of saint (Buddhism)

**Sunday school**  place of religious instruction on Sundays for children, esp. Christian

**synagogue**  Jewish house of worship; shul; temple

**synod**  church council

**tabernacle**  house of worship, esp. large tent for evangelical services; portable sanctuary in which Ark of the Covenant was carried by Israelites after the Exodus

**temple**  edifice for religious services; Jewish synagogue; shrine to specific deity or saint; primary locus for a religion

**tope**  dome-shaped Buddhist monument for relics

**Vatican**  Holy See of the pope; city-state serving as headquarters of Roman Catholic Church

**vestry**  room in church for storage of vestments

## Sacred Texts and Objects

**Abhidhamma Pitaka**  third section of Pali Canon, consisting of abstract philosophical treatises (Buddhism)

**Acts**  book in New Testament describing the inception of Christianity

**Adigranth**  Granth (Sikhism)

**American Standard Version**  American version of Bible, published in 1901

**Analects**  text of teachings of Confucius

**Angas**  sacred texts of Jainism

**Apocrypha**  writings originally within the Bible, but judged unsuitable for inclusion by rabbinical or church authorities

**aspergillum**  brush or small perforated container for sprinkling holy water (Catholicism)

**aspersorium**  vessel for holding holy water (Catholicism)

**Atharva-Veda**  one of ancient Aryan Vedic sacred texts (Hinduism)

**Avesta**  book of sacred writings of Zoroastrianism

**Bhagavad-Gita**  part of Indian epic poem the Mahabharata, written between 200 B.C. and 200 A.D., in form of dialogue between hero and avatar Krishna (Hinduism)

**Bible**  sacred texts of Old and New Testaments, source of teachings and religious authority for Judaism and Christianity; Christian Bible

**Book of Books**  Bible

**Book of Common Prayer**  official book of services and prayers for Anglican communion

**Book of Mormon**  sacred book of Mormon church, revealed by Joseph Smith

**Book of the Dead**  book of prayers and charms for use of soul in afterworld (ancient Egypt)

**Brahmana**  ritual text of Vedic period (Hinduism)

**breviary**  book of prayers, hymns, and psalms used by priests in daily office

**butsu**  representation or figure of the Buddha

**canon**  church law, authoritative sacred texts

**censer**  ornamental container in which incense is burned; thurible

**chalice**  Eucharistic cup

**chrism**  consecrated oil used in baptism and other sacraments

**chrisom**  white cloth or robe worn by person during baptism

**ciborium**  vessel containing Eucharistic bread or host

**cloth**  attire worn by clergy

**crosier**  bishop's or abbot's staff

**Dead Sea Scrolls**  scrolls dating from Essene period, containing partial texts of Hebrew Bible or Old Testament and some non-Biblical scrolls, in Hebrew and Aramaic

**Dhammapada**  text containing essential teachings of the Buddha

**Epistle**  extract from Epistles of New Testament, usu. attributed to Paul, used in Eucharistic service

**Five Classics**  basic ethical texts of Confucianism, attributed to Confucius, including I Ching, Book of Rites, Book of History, Book of Songs, and Spring and Autumn Annals

**font**  vessel for holy water, often of stone

**Genesis**  first book of Bible, describing Creation and history of patriarchs

**Good Book**  Bible

**Gospels**  story of life and teachings of Christ in first four books of New Testament

**Granth**  sacred scripture of Sikhism; Adigranth

**habit**  attire worn by clergy and members of religious orders

**Hagiographa**  third part of Hebrew Bible containing the Psalms, Proverbs, Job, Ruth, Esther, and other books besides the Pentateuch and Prophets; Ketuvim; the Writings

**Hebrew Bible**  Old Testament: Torah, Prophets, and Hagiographa

**Holy Bible**  Bible

**Holy Scriptures**  sacred writings of Old or New Testament or both together

**Holy Writ**  Bible

**hymnal**  book of Christian hymns

**I Ching**  Book of Changes, one of Five Classics of Chinese Confucian canon, dealing esp. with divination through trigrams that reflect yin and yang

**icon**  powerful image of sacred personage, usu. painted on wooden panel (Orthodox Eastern Church)

**Jataka**  stories and fables concerning previous lives of the Buddha

**Kama Sutra**  teachings of Hindu god of erotic love Kama

**Ketuvim**  *Hebrew.* Hagiographa

**King James Bible** edition of Christian Bible published during reign of King James I of England circa 1610

**Koran** Islamic holy book, composed of 114 chapters or suras, believed to have been revealed to Muhammad by Allah; Qur'an

**Law, the** Pentateuch; Torah

**lectionary** book listing selections of sacred texts to be read in divine service

**Mahabharata** epic containing Hindu religious text Bhaga-vad-Gita

**megillah** *Hebrew.* scroll of Biblical books, esp. Book of Esther, read on Purim

**menorah** candelabrum, esp. one with nine branches, used at Hanukkah (Judaism)

**mezuzah** scroll with words from Deuteronomy, placed in small container affixed to doorjamb (Judaism)

**missal** large book of prayers and authorized readings for celebration of Catholic Mass

**Nevi'im** *Hebrew.* Prophets

**New Testament** portion of Bible that describes life and teachings of Christ and his followers, through Gospels and Epistles, written circa 100 A.D.

**Old Testament** portion of Bible that describes God's covenant with the Israelites, made up of the Torah or Pentateuch, Prophets, and Hagiographa, compiled between 1000 B.C. and 100 B.C.; Christian name for Hebrew Bible

**Oral Law** Talmud

**Pali Canon** ancient Buddhist sacred texts, orig. recorded from oral traditions in 1st c. B.C., consisting of sermons, rules of monastic order, and philosophical treatises; Tripitaka

**Pentateuch** first five books of Hebrew Bible; Torah

**phylactery** either of two small leather containers holding scriptural passages, worn on left arm and forehead during prayers by Jewish men; both phylacteries comprise the tefillin

**Pitaka** any of the three divisions of the Pali Canon: Abhidhamma Pitaka (philosophy), Sutta Pitaka (sermons), and Vinaya Pitaka (rules of monastic order) (Buddhism)

**prayer book** formal book of prayers, esp. Book of Common Prayer

**Prophets** second part of Hebrew Bible, containing books by prophets such as Isaiah, Jeremiah, and Ezekiel; Nevi'im

**Proverbs** book of Old Testament representing earliest example of Hebrew wisdom dealing with practical piety

**Psalter** book of Psalms

**pseudepigrapha** Christian and Jewish sacred texts not recognized in the canon and considered possibly spurious

**Qur'an** Koran

**Ramayana** second great Hindu epic, containing story of Prince Rama

**relic** part or piece of saint's physical remains

**reliquary** container or shrine for sacred relics

**Revelation** book of New Testament describing Apocalypse

**Rig Veda** oldest of ancient Aryan Vedic sacred texts (Hinduism)

**rosary** string of beads used by Roman Catholics, Hindus, and Buddhists for counting prayers or mantras

**rubric** directions for conducting religious service

**sacred text** writings that are source of authority and legitimacy for a religion

**Sama-Veda** one of ancient Aryan Vedic sacred texts (Hinduism)

**Scripture** sacred text

**Septuagint** oldest Greek version of Old Testament

**shofar** ram's horn sounded on Rosh Hashanah (Judaism)

**stoup** basin for holy water, usu. located near entrance of church (Christianity)

**sutra** religious text, esp. collection of aphorisms on any of various aspects of life (Hinduism, Jainism); any of the Buddha's sermons (Buddhism)

**Sutta Pitaka** second section of Pali Canon, consisting of sermons of the Buddha and stories about him (Buddhism)

**Synoptic Gospels** first three gospels in New Testament: Matthew, Mark, and Luke

**tallith** fringed prayer shawl (Judaism)

**Talmud** text of canon and civil law and rabbinical teachings, incorporating the non-Scriptural oral law, compiled in 6th c., codified in Jerusalem and Babylon; Oral Law (Judaism)

**Tantra** any of several books of esoteric doctrine regarding rituals and meditation (Hinduism)

**Tao Te Ching** teachings of Lao-tzu, basic text of Taoism, composed of eighty-one brief chapters describing the way of the Tao

**tefillin** both phylacteries (Judaism)

**thurible** censer

**Torah** first five books of Hebrew Bible, containing entire written body of Jewish law and wisdom sealed for all time in the form of holy scrolls; the Law; Pentateuch

**Tripitaka** Pali Canon (Buddhism)

**Upanishads** philosophical commentaries forming final portion of Vedic texts, written beginning circa 900 B.C.

**Vedas** ancient, sacred Hindu scriptures composed of Atharva-Veda, Rig-Veda, Sama-Veda, and Yajur-Veda, compiled between 1000 B.C. and 500 B.C.

**vestment** ceremonial garment worn by clergy during religious rite

**Vinaya Pitaka** first section of Pali Canon, consisting of the rules of the monastic order (Buddhism)

**Vulgate** Latin version of Christian Scriptures

**Word** usu. **the Word**; the Word of God; the Bible

**Writings, the** Hagiographa

**Yajur-Veda** one of ancient Aryan Vedic sacred texts (Hinduism)

**yarmulke** skullcap worn by Jewish males, esp. during prayer and religious study

**Zend-Avesta** Zoroastrian sacred texts

**Zohar** definitive text of the cabala, consisting chiefly of interpretations of the Pentateuch (Judaism)

## RELIGIOUS STATES AND EXPERIENCES

**acroamatic** (*adj*) esoteric and revealed only to chosen disciples orally

**adoration** worship of a divine being

**afflatus** inspiration, divine bestowing of knowledge

**afterlife** state of existence following physical death

**antediluvian** (*adj*) before the Flood

**apostasy** abandonment of one's faith

**astral plane** subtle dimension more refined than physical reality

**beatitude** blessedness, bliss

**blessed** (*adj*) consecrated, holy, enjoying bliss; state prior to sainthood

**bliss** perfect, heavenly joy

**born-again** (*adj*) designating person who has experienced spiritual awakening and new religious commitment to Christ as personal savior; reborn; saved

**calling** in ancient use, God's selection of individual; now spiritual impulse toward religious vocation

**canonization** elevation to sainthood

**charity** love for one's fellow man and acts conveying such goodwill

**damnation** condemnation to eternity of suffering in hell

**devotion** piety, worshipful ardor

**divinity** state of being godlike

**ecstasy** state of absorption in the divine, with loss of awareness of body or outside world

**enlightenment** state of spiritual awakening

**enthusiasm** extreme religious devotion, usu. associated with intense emotionalism

**epiphany** direct manifestation of God or deity to a person

**exaltation** state of heightened spiritual awareness

**faith** state of trust in divinity

**get religion** (*vb*) have sudden, inspirational experience inducing faith

**glossolalia** speaking in tongues while in state of religious ecstasy

**God-fearing** (*adj*) deeply fearful or respectful of God

**godliness** piety, devotion to one's faith

**grace** state of being in divine favor; effect of God's mercy

**hallowed** (*adj*) blessed, made or kept holy

**holy** (*adj*) sacred, saintly, pure, whole

**immanence** inherent presence of God or divinity in Creation and daily life

**immortality** unending life without death

**impiety** lack of reverence for God

**inspiration** sudden spiritual awakening resulting from divine influence

**irreverence** disrespect for and discounting of divinity, Creation, and religion

**joy** bliss, beatitude

**manna** divinely supplied spiritual nourishment

**martyrdom** self-sacrifice to point of death in service of others or for maintenance of one's faith

**metanoia** profound transformation or conversion

**metempsychosis** rebirth, reincarnation

**Molinism** quietism

**mystical** (*adj*) involving direct communion with God or the divine

**numinous** (*adj*) inspiring awe and fascination, pertaining to mysterious aspect of divine power and religious experience

**piety** devotion to religious duty and practice; piousness

**piousness** piety

**profane** (*adj*) irreverent, unholy; defiling what is sacred

**quietism** type of religious mysticism marked by attainment of perfection through systematic contemplation; Molinism

**rebirth** reincarnation; transmigration of soul

**reborn** (*adj*) born-again

**receive Christ** (*vb*) be reborn, accept Christ as one's personal savior

**recreant** (*adj*) failing to keep faith

**redemption** salvation, deliverance from sin or evil

**reprobation** rejection by God and exclusion from salvation

**revelation** disclosure of God's will to humankind

**reverence** respect and awe for divinity, Creation, and religion

**righteousness** freedom from sin, sanctity

**sacred** (*adj*) consecrated, holy

**sacrosanct** (*adj*) extremely sacred or holy

**saintliness** charity, piety, holiness of spirit and action

**salvation** deliverance from sin, evil, and punishment; redemption

**sanctity** state of being sacred or holy

**saved** (*adj*) having accepted Christ as one's personal savior; born-again

**spirituality** conviction in one's experience of the mysterious aspect of divine power

**transcendence** state of God's nature or highest principle as above and apart from immanent Creation

**transformation** experience in which adherent to religion moves from one state to another, as by conversion, leap of faith, or following a path

**transmigration of soul** rebirth, reincarnation

**unholy** (*adj*) lacking in purity

**venerable** (*adj*) blessed, honorable; state prior to sainthood

**veneration** reverential love and adoration

**zeal** intensely passionate religious fervor

# MYTHOLOGY AND FOLKLORE

Mythological and Folkloric Beings
Gods and Divinities
Myths, Legends, and Fables
Utopia

**SEE ALSO:** Chap. 25: Religion; Magic and the Occult; Eschatology

## MYTHOLOGICAL AND FOLKLORIC BEINGS

**Abominable Snowman** legendary creature living in high Himalayas; yeti

**Achilles** greatest Greek hero of Trojan War, invulnerable to weapons except for one heel

**Adapa** heroic fisherman son of Ea who preferred great knowledge to offer of immortality (Babylon)

**Adonis** beautiful young man loved by Aphrodite, who symbolized the death of nature in fall and rebirth the following spring (Greece)

**Aeneas** son of Aphrodite who led survivors of Troy west to found Rome

**Aeon** personification of time (Greece)

**Aesculapius** son of Apollo and the nymph Coronis, the first physician (Greece)

**afreet** powerful evil demon or monster (Arabia)

**Agamemnon** leader of the Greeks during siege of Troy

**Aladdin** poor boy in *Arabian Nights' Entertainments* who possessed magic lamp with jinn that would do his bidding

**Ali Baba** poor woodcutter and hero of *Arabian Nights' Entertainments* who opened a door by saying "open sesame" and found hidden treasure of the Forty Thieves

**Amazons** single-breasted Scythian women warriors

**amphisbaena** serpent having head at each end (Greece)

**Antaeus** giant son of Poseidon and Gaea, ultimately crushed by Herakles (Greece)

**Argus** hundred-eyed being who guarded Io, and whose eyes were transferred to peacock's tail after death (Rome)

**Arthur** semilegendary British king of Camelot during 6th century

**Atlas** Titan bearing Earth and firmament on his shoulders (Greece and Rome)

**Atropos** one of the Fates (Greece)

**Azazel** *Hebrew.* evil spirit of wilderness to which scapegoat was released

**Baba Yaga** female monster who feeds on children (Russia)

**Babe the Blue Ox** legendary blue ox belonging to Paul Bunyan (United States)

**banshee** female spirit who warns of death by wailing (Ireland and Scotland)

**barghest** legendary doglike goblin that portends death or misfortune

**basilisk** serpent with deadly breath and glance; cockatrice

**behemoth** any creature of monstrous size and power

**Beowulf** hero of medieval epic poem (Britain, 8th c.)

**bogeyman** frightening, demonic figure of popular folklore

**brownie** tiny, fanciful brown elf who does household chores at night

**bugbear** goblin that devours disobedient children

**bunyip** creature inhabiting swamps and lagoons in Aboriginal legend (Australia)

**Calliope** chief muse; muse of epic heroic poetry (Greece)

**Callisto** nymph loved by Zeus, changed into she-bear by Hera and then into Great Bear constellation (Greece)

**Calypso** daughter of Atlas who held Odysseus captive on her island (Greece)

**Cassandra** priestess daughter of King Priam of Troy whose prophecies were never believed (Greece)

**Castor and Pollux** twin brothers of Helen who protect seagoers (Greece)

**Cecrops** founder of Athens who had a snake's tail (Greece)

**centaur** half-horse, half-human monster

**Cerberus** three-headed dog who guards entrance to underworld (Rome)

**Chaos** representative of the void prior to creation of Earth (Greece)

**Charybdis** woman turned into whirlpool by Jupiter; companion to Scylla (Greece)

**Chimera** flame-belching monster, part goat, part lion, and part dragon

**Cinderella** fairytale heroine who escapes mistreatment by stepmother and stepsisters to marry prince (Europe)

**Circe** evil woman who turned humans into wolves and swine (Greece)

**Clio** muse of history (Greece)

**Clotho** one of the Fates (Greece)

**cockatrice** basilisk

**colossus** giant human statue (Greece)

**Cyclops** member of a family of one-eyed cannibal giant (Greece)

**daemon** supernatural force, spirit for good or evil, in popular folklore

**Daphne** nymph loved by Apollo and turned into laurel tree, whose branch Apollo wore on his head (Greece)

**Delphic oracle** oracle of Apollo whose answers were enigmatic and ambiguous (Greece)

**demigod** half divine, half human minor deity; deified mortal

**demon** evil spirit, devil

**deus otiosus** distant or retiring deity; authority or father figure

**Don Juan** legendary, dissolute Spanish nobleman famous for his many seductions

**dragon** reptilian monster, often with breath of fire

**Dryad** forest nymph who protects trees (Greece)

**dwarf** small, usu. misshapen and ugly creature with magic powers

**dybbuk** dead person's evil spirit that invades living person (Jewish folklore)

**dying god** autumnal figure symbolizing harvest and decline of cosmic cycle of time

**earth mother** female deity symbolizing life or fertility

**Echo** mountain nymph who could only repeat others' last words, spurned in love by Narcissus (Greece)

**Eight Immortals** holy men who have attained immortality (Taoism)

**elf** mountain fairy, seen by moonlight

**Enkidu** quasihuman creature aiding Gilgamesh in quest (Bablyonia)

**Erato** muse of love poetry (Greece)

**Eumenides** the Furies (Greece)

**Euterpe** muse of music (Greece)

**Fafnir** dragon slain by Sigurd (Scandinavia)

**fairy** small, supernatural being with magic powers; fay

**familiar spirit** supernatural servant of priest or magician, often represented as an animal

**Fates** three sisters who spin, weave, and cut the thread of life: Atropos, Clotho, and Lachesis (Greece and Rome)

**faun** sylvan demigod (Rome)

**Faust** character in medieval legend who sold his soul to the devil for knowledge and power

**fay** fairy

**fiend** evil spirit

**Furies** three snake-haired female torturers of the damned (Greece and Rome)

**Galahad** noblest and purest of knights of the Round Table, who gained the Holy Grail

**Ganymede** cupbearer of Zeus (Greece)

**genie** spirit in human form summoned to carry out one's wishes

**genius** tutelary spirit attending a person throughout life; (*pl.*) **genii**

**genius loci** *Latin.* guardian spirit of a single location

**ghost** spirit of dead person

**ghoul** evil being that feeds on corpses

**giant** huge and monstrously formed creature, enemy of gods and people (Scandinavia and Greece)

**Gigantes** huge monsters, children of Gaea, who were defeated by Olympian gods (Greece)

**Gilgamesh** hero of Sumerian and Babylonian epics

**gnome** dwarfish creature who lives underground

**goblin** demon of popular folklore in the form of a grotesque, often malicious sprite

**golem** figure artificially constructed in human form and endowed with life (Jewish folklore)

**Gorgons** three hideous monsters in the form of winged sisters with power to turn person viewing them to stone (Greece)

**Graces** three daughters of Zeus attendant on Aphrodite, embodying beauty and charm (Greece)

**gremlin** type of elf, usu. mischievous troublemaker said to be responsible for minor malfunctions

**Grendel** half-human monster slain by Beowulf

**griffin** monster that is half eagle and half lion

**Guinevere** King Arthur's wife

**hamadryad** nymph who is spirit of a particular tree

**Harpy** winged, ravenous, half-woman monster that robs its victims of food

**Hecatoncheires** hundred-armed, fifty-headed sons of Uranus and Gaea (Greece)

**Helen** Greek queen whose abduction instigated the Trojan War

**hellhound** watchdog of the underworld

**Herakles** Hercules (Greece)

**Hercules** son of Jupiter and greatest hero, who performed twelve labors (Rome)

**Hermaphroditus** son of Hermes and Aphrodite, united with a nymph to form one body with sexual characteristics of both genders (Greece)

**hero** mythic person whose story is told in epic tale of adventure or struggle

**hippocampus** creature who is half horse and half dolphin

**hippogriff** griffin with horse's body

**hobbit** small, furry creature who lives in burrow in the earth

**hobgoblin** mischievous goblin or sprite, esp. Puck

**Houyhnhnm** one of a race of horses endowed with reason in Jonathan Swift's *Gulliver's Travels*

**Hydra** nine-headed serpent whose heads grew back as they were cut off, slain by Hercules (Greece)

**Hyperion** one of the Titans, son of Uranus and father of Helios, Selene, and Eos

**Icarus** son of Daedalus who flew too near the sun, melting his wax and feather wings and causing him to fall into the sea (Greece)

**incubus** evil demon that has sex with women while they sleep

**Iris** messenger of God in multihued robe representing rainbow (Greece)

**Izanagi and Izanami** creators of Japanese islands who emerged from chaos and were progenitors of later gods (Japan)

**Jack Frost** personification of cold and frost (U.S.)

**Jason** leader of the Argonauts who retrieved the Golden Fleece (Greece)

**jinn** spirit capable of appearing in human or animal form (Arabia)

**John Henry** legendary black railroad worker who outdrove steam drill (U.S., 19th c.)

**Jotun** any of a race of giants often in conflict with the gods (Scandinavia)

**kelpie** horse-shaped water spirit (Scotland)

**kobold** mischievous underground gnome (German folklore)

**Kraken** legendary monster of northern seas (Scandinavia)

**Kriss Kringle** Santa Claus

**Lachesis** one of the Fates (Greece)

**lamia** monster with head and breast of a woman and body of a serpent that allured children to suck their blood

**Lancelot** greatest knight of King Arthur's round table and lover of Queen Guinevere

**Lares** household gods who are spirits of ancestors (Rome)

**lemures** spirits of the dead (Rome)

**leprechaun** dwarf or sprite; fairy and beneficent spirit (Ireland)

**Leviathan** huge Biblical sea monster, either reptile or whale

**Lilith** woman or phantom said to be former wife of Adam in Jewish folklore

**little people** leprechauns, fairies, elves

**Loch Ness monster** dinosaurlike creature reportedly seen emerging from waters of Loch Ness (Scotland)

**Lorelei** siren or river spirit with fatal charm (Teutonic folklore)

**loup-garou** *French.* werewolf

**maenads** frenzied female followers of Bacchus or Dionysus (Greece and Rome)

**manes** spirits of dead (Rome)

**manitou** spirit that controls nature and is source of natural and supernatural power (Algonquian Indians)

**manticore** monster with man's head, lion's body, and scorpion's tail

**Manu** primal ancestor (India)

**Medusa** snake-haired woman monster beheaded by Perseus; one of the Gorgons (Greece)

**Melpomene** muse of tragic drama (Greece)

**Merlin** magician and seer of Arthurian legend

**mermaid** creature with fatal charm who is half woman and half fish

**Metis** first wife of Zeus, mother of Athena, and personification of prudence (Greece)

**Midas** legendary Phrygian king whose touch turned objects to gold (Greece)

**Midgard serpent** monster that grew to surround the entire world (Scandinavia)

**Minotaur** bull-headed, human-torsoed, flesh-eating monster slain by Theseus (Greece)

**Mnemosyne** mother of the muses and goddess of memory

**Moirai** Fates (Greece)

**monster** any of various legendary, mythical creatures, usu. hybrid of animal forms

**Muses** nine daughters of Zeus and Mnemosyne who inspire artists: Calliope (heroic poetry), Clio (history), Erato (love poetry), Euterpe (music), Melpomene (tragedy), Polyhymnia (eloquence and sacred poetry), Terpsichore (dance), Thalia (comic and lyric poetry), Urania (astronomy)

**naiad** freshwater nymph (Greece)

**Narcissus** youth who loved his own reflection and was turned into a flower (Rome)

**Nereid** sea nymph; Oceanid (Greece)

**Nibelungs** race of dwarfs who possessed a treasure of Rhine gold that was captured by Siegfried (Teutonic)

**Niobe** bereaved daughter of Tantalus who wept for her slain children even after being turned to stone (Greece)

**nix** water spirit that lures its victims into its underwater home (German folklore)

**nymph** semidivine spirit of natural region such as water, forest, mountains, or valleys

**Oceanid** Nereid

**Oedipus** king who unwittingly killed his father and married his mother after solving Sphinx's riddle (Greece)

**ogre** hideous giant cannibal

**oracle** intermediary between gods and man who answered questions at shrine (Greece)

**orc** monster similar to an ogre

**oread** mountain nymph (Greece)

**Orpheus** lyre-playing musician who tried unsuccessfully to rescue his wife from Hades (Greece)

**Pandora** original woman who opened forbidden box, bringing woes and evils to humanity (Greece)

**Parsifal** knight who sought Holy Grail (Teutonic)

**Paul Bunyan** giant lumberjack with a pet blue ox named Babe, reputed to have shaped the Rocky Mountains (U.S., 19th c.)

**Pecos Bill** legendary cowboy who dug the Rio Grande River (U.S., 19th c.)

**Pegasus** winged horse born of Medusa's blood (Greece)

**Penates** gods who serve as family household guardians (Rome)

**Perseus** hero who slew Medusa (Greece)

**Peter Pan** boy who never grew up in Sir James Barrie's play

**phantom** specter or apparition

**phoenix** immortal bird that cremates itself every 500 years, then emerges reborn from ashes (Greece)

**Pied Piper** legendary folk hero who led people by entrancing them by playing his flute (Germany)

**pixie** fairy, said to be spirit of dead child

**poltergeist** noisy ghost

**Polyhymnia** muse of eloquence (Greece)

**preta** wandering or disturbed ghost (India)

**Prometheus** hero who stole fire from gods for mankind and was punished by Zeus (Greece)

**Proteus** sea god who assumed different shapes (Greece)

**Psyche** beautiful mortal loved by Eros (Greece)

**Puck** mischievous sprite of English folklore; Robin Goodfellow

**Python** dragon who guarded chasm at Delphi, slain by Apollo (Greece)

**Queen Mab** playful fairy of English folklore who controlled dreams

**Rama** hero of the epic tale Ramayana and perfect, devoted Hindu (India)

**Ravana** giant ten-faced demon (India)

**Remus** twin brother of Romulus (Rome)

**Rip Van Winkle** man who slept twenty years and awakened to a changed world, from story by Washington Irving (U.S., 19th c.)

**Robin Goodfellow** Puck

**Robin Hood** legendary, benevolent folk hero outlaw (Britain)

**roc** bird of enormous size and strength (Arabia)

**Romulus** one of twin brothers raised by a wolf, founder of Rome

**Rudra** father of storm gods who controls powers of nature (Vedic)

**Rumpelstiltskin** dwarf who spins flax into gold in German folktale

**salamander** mythical creature, esp. a reptile, thought to be able to live in fire

**sandman** folkloric character who puts sand in the eyes of children to make them sleepy

**Santa Claus** benevolent purveyor or gifts to children on Christmas Eve; Kriss Kringle

**satyr** goat-footed demigod of forest and field, noted for lasciviousness

**scapegoat** goat let loose on Yom Kippur after sins are laid on its head

**Scheherezade** in *Arabian Nights' Entertainments*, wife of sultan of India, who spared her life because she told such wondrous tales each night

**Scylla** sea nymph who was transformed into sea monster, companion of Charybdis (Greece)

**sea horse** creature who is half horse with fish tail

**sea serpent** large marine animal resembling snake

**sibyl** any woman who served as mouth piece of the gods in delivering prophecies and oracles

**Siegfried** hero of the *Nibelungenlied* (Teutonic)

**Sigurd** hero of the *Volsunga Saga*; counterpart of Siegfried in the *Nibelungenlied* (Scandinavia)

**Silenus** forest spirit, sometimes called oldest of satyrs

**Sinbad** sea-voyaging adventurer of *Arabian Nights' Entertainments*

**Siren** singing sea nymph who charms sailors to their deaths

**Sisyphus** noted trickster punished by having to roll a stone up a slope so that each time he approached the top the stone escaped him and rolled down again (Greece)

**Sleeping Beauty** fairy tale princess awakened from a prolonged, charmed sleep by the kiss of her true love

**Sphinx** human-headed, winged lion and poser of enigmatic riddles (Egypt)

**spirit** supernatural being

**sprite** spirit, esp. mischievous elf

**stork** bird that is symbolic deliverer of new babies

**succubus** female demon who has sex with men while they sleep

**sylph** air spirit

**Syrinx** mountain nymph who was transformed into the reed from which Pan made his panpipe

**Tannhäuser** German lyric poet and hero of legend set in 13th c.

**Tantalus** son of Zeus condemned in Tartarus to forever reach for unattainable fruit and water

**Termagant** mythical deity in form of violent, dominating personage, believed by Medieval Christians to be worshipped by Muslims

**Terpsichore** muse of dance (Greece)

**Thalia** muse of comic and lyric poetry (Greece)

**Theseus** hero who slew Minotaur (Greece)

**Tiki** first man of Maori legend (Polynesia)

**Titan** one of a race of giant deities, children of Uranus who held power under Cronus and were overthrown by the Olympian gods (Greece)

**Tom Thumb** tiny hero of folk tales

**tooth fairy** fairy who exchanges gift for baby tooth placed under pillow of child

**trickster** god, hero, or personage who creates trouble and plays practical jokes in myth and legend

**Triton** half fish, half man and son of Poseidon with power over waves (Greece)

**troll** misshapen, woodland-dwelling dwarf or giant of limited intelligence (Scandinavia)

**Typhon** hundred-headed giant who caused violent wind, killed by Zeus (Greece)

**undine** female water spirit

**unicorn** creature with horse's body, lion's tail, and single horn, representing purity and supernatural powers

**Urania** muse of astronomy (Greece)

**Valkyries** maidens who escort warriors to Valhalla (Teutonic and Norse folklore)

**vampire** reanimated corpse who exists on blood of sleeping victims

**vestal virgin** one of the virgins tending sacred fire of Vesta (Rome)

**water nymph** semidivine marine creature

**werewolf** man capable of transmogrifying into shape of a wolf who preys on human victims; wolfman

**William Tell** rebellious hero of Swiss legend forced to shoot arrow through apple on his son's head

**windigo** evil spirit, cannibal demon (Native American folklore)

**wolfman** werewolf

**wood nymph** semidivine forest creature

**world parents** cosmic couple who symbolize creation of human race, such as Adam and Eve

**wyvern** two-legged, winged creature resembling dragon

**xiphopagus** Siamese twin monster

**yeti** Abominable Snowman

**Ymir** first living creature and progenitor of giants, whose corpse formed earth, water, and heavens (Scandinavia)

**zombie** reanimated corpse under spell of demon or deity

## GODS AND DIVINITIES

**Aeolus** god of winds (Greece)

**Agni** god of fire (India)

**Amphitrite** goddess of the sea, wife of Poseidon (Greece)

**Amun-Ra** supreme national god (Egypt, 18th dynasty)

**Anshar** father of Anu, Ea, and Enlil (Mesopotamia)

**Anu** supreme sky god (Mesopotamia)

**Anubis** jackel-headed god of the underworld, death, and judgment of soul (Egypt)

**Aphrodite** goddess of love and beauty (Greece)

**Apollo** god of arts, intellect, and prophecy (Rome)

**Apollon** god of arts, sciences, reason, and inspiration (Greece)

**Ares** god of war (Greece)

**Artemis** goddess of hunting (Greece)

**Ashur** winged national god of battle (Assyria)

**Astarte** goddess of fertility and love (Phoenicia)

**Athena** goddess of wisdom and crafts (Greece)

**Aurora** goddess of dawn (Rome)

**Baal** god of fertility (Phoenicia)

**Bacchus** god of wine; Liber (Rome)

**Balder** god of sunlight personifying goodness, son of Frigg (Scandinavia)

**Bel** goddess and wife of Anu (Mesopotamia)

**Benten** goddess of love and the arts (Japan)

**Brahma** creator god in Trimurti (India)

**Ceres** goddess of fertility and agriculture (Rome)

**Chloris** goddess of flowers (Greece)

**Comus** god of revelry and feasting (Greece and Rome)

**Cronos** leader of the Titans and son of Uranus who castrated his father and fathered Zeus and other Olympian gods by his sister Rhea; Kronos (Greece)

**Cupid** god of love (Rome)

**Cybele** great mother goddess (Phrygia)

**Daikoku** god of wealth (Japan)

**Demeter** goddess of agriculture and fertility (Greece)

**Diana** goddess of the moon and forest (Rome)

**Dionysus** god of ecstasy and wine (Greece)

**Dis** god of the underworld and the dead (Rome)

**Ea** god of freshwater and wisdom (Mesopotamia)

**Emma-O** ruler of hell (Japan)

**Enlil** god of air and king of the gods (Mesopotamia)

**Eos** goddess of dawn (Greece)

**Eris** goddess of strife and discord (Greece)

**Eros** god of love (Greece)

**Faunus** god of fields and shepherds (Rome)

**Flora** goddess of flowers (Rome)

**Frey** fertility god (Scandinavia)

**Freya** goddess of beauty and love (Scandinavia)

**Frigg** mother goddess, consort of Odin (Scandinavia)

**Fu-hsing** god of happiness (China)

**Gaea** goddess of earth, mother and wife of Uranus (Greece)

**Ganesha** god of wisdom (India)

**Geb** earth god, father of Osiris (Egypt)

**Gula** goddess of healing (Mesopotamia)

**Hades** god of the dead and underworld (Greece)

**Hanuman** monkey god (India)

**Hathor** goddess of love and joy (Egypt)

**Hebe** goddess of youth (Greece)

**Hecate** goddess of magic and dark powers (Greece)

**Helios** sun god (Greece)

**Hephaestus** god of the forge and crafts (Greece)

**Hera** goddess of marriage, consort of Zeus (Greece)

**Hermes** messenger of gods (Greece)

**Hestia** goddess of hearth and home (Greece)

**Horus** solar god, son of Isis and Osiris who ruled earth after avenging his father's murder (Egypt)

**Huitzilopochtli** god of war and the sun (Aztec)

**Hygeia** goddess of health (Greece)

**Hymen** god of marriage (Greece)

**Hypnus** god of sleep (Greece)

**Indra** rain god (India)

**Inti** personification of the sun (Inca)

**Ishtar** mother goddess of fertility and love, daughter of Anu (Mesopotamia)

**Isis** goddess of maternity, wife of Osiris (Egypt)

**Janus** god of beginnings and doorways (Rome)

**Jove** Jupiter (Rome)

**Juno** goddess of women and maternity, consort of Jupiter (Rome)

**Jupiter** sky god and chief god; Jove (Rome)

**Juventas** goddess of youth (Rome)

**Kali** goddess of motherhood and death, consort of Shiva (India)

**Kore** Persephone

**Krishna** god of love (India)

**Kronos** Cronus

**Kuan Yin** goddess of compassion (Chinese Buddhism)

**Kubera** god of riches (India)

**Lakshmi** lotus goddess of prosperity, wife of Vishnu (India)

**Liber** god of ecstasy and wine; Bacchus (Rome)

**Loki** trickster god of evil (Scandinavia)

**Lug** sun god (Celtic)

**Luna** moon goddess (Rome)

**Mahakala** god of wealth (India)

**Marduk** chief god (Babylonia)

**Mars** god of war (Rome)

**Maui** trickster god (Oceania)

**Mercury** messenger of the gods; god of communication (Rome)

**Minerva** goddess of wisdom and the arts (Rome)

**Mnemosyne** goddess of memory, mother of Muses (Greece)

**Morpheus** god of dreams (Greece)

**Mors** god of death (Rome)

**Mot** god of sterility (Phoenicia)

**Nemesis** goddess of punishment and reward (Greece)

**Neptune** sea god (Rome)

**Nike** goddess of victory (Greece)

**Njord** god of winds and prosperity (Scandinavia)

**Nox** goddess of night (Rome)

**Nut** sky goddess, wife of Geb (Egypt)

**Nyx** goddess of night (Greece)

**Odin** god of wisdom, magic, and death; chief god (Scandinavia)

**Orcus** god of the underworld, identified with Pluto (Rome)

**Osiris** god of the Nile, vegetation, and the dead (Egypt)

**Pallas Athena** bright Athena (Greece)

**Pan** shepherd god (Greece)

**Pauguk** personification of death (North American Indians)

**Persephone** daughter of Demeter, wife of Hades; Kore (Greece)

**Phoebus Apollo** shining Apollo (Greece)

**Picus** god of divination (Rome)

**Pluto** god of the underworld (Rome)

**Plutus** god of wealth (Greece)

**Pomona** goddess of orchards and gardens (Rome)

**Poseidon** sea god (Greece)

**Priapus** god of fertility (Greece)

**Proserpina** Persephone, wife of Pluto (Rome)

**Psyche** goddess of the soul, unified with Cupid (Rome)

**Ptah** creator of the universe, depicted as upright mummified man (Egypt)

**Quetzalcoatl** feathered serpent god of creation (Aztec and Toltec)

**Ra** sun god (Egypt)

**Rahu** mischievous, four-armed deity of natural disasters (India)

**Rhea** great mother goddess, wife and sister of Cronus and mother of Zeus (Greece)

**Rhiannon** goddess associated with horses (Wales)

**Salacia** goddess of oceans (Rome)

**Sarasvati** goddess of learning and wisdom (India)

**Saturn** agriculture god, father of Jupiter (Rome)

**Selene** moon goddess (Greece)

**Seth** brother and enemy of Osiris and god of evil (Egypt)

**Shiva** destroyer god in Trimurti (India)

**Sin** moon god (Mesopotamia)

**Sol** one of two sun gods (Rome)

**Somnus** god of sleep (Rome)

**Surya** sun god (India)

**Svetovid** god of fertility and war (Eastern Europe)

**Tammuz** vegetation god (Mesopotamia)

**Thanatos** god of death (Greece)

**Themis** goddess of law and justice (Greece)

**Thor** god of thunder and war (Scandinavia)

**Thoth** god of wisdom, arts and sciences, and magic; scribe of the gods (Egypt)

**Thunderbird** culture god (North American Indians)

**Tlaloc** rain god (Aztec)

**Tuatha Dé Danann** ancient gods (Ireland)

**Tyche** goddess of fate (Greece)

**Uranus** original god of heaven and father of the Titans, including Cronus (Greece)

**Venus** goddess of love and beauty (Rome)

**Vesta** goddess of the hearth (Rome)

**Victoria** goddess of victory (Rome)

**Vishnu** preserver god in Trimurti (India)

**Vulcan** god of the forge and fire (Rome)

**Wotan** chief god (Germany)

**Xipe** god of vegetation (Aztec)

**Xochipilli** god of flowers and pleasure (Aztec)

**Yama** ruler of hell and lord of the dead (India)

**Zephyrus** god of the west wind (Greece)

**Zeus** chief god and ruler of heaven; god of thunder and lightning (Greece)

## MYTHS, LEGENDS, AND FABLES

**Aegis** shield of Zeus with head of Medusa at its center, borne by Athena on missions (Greece)

**Aesir** pantheon of the gods (Scandinavia)

**Aesop's Fables** collected animal fables attributed to Phrygian slave Aesop

**ages of humankind** major, significant eras in mythological history of humankind: golden age, silver age, bronze age, iron age

**allegory** narrative with characters and actions having symbolic dimension

**amaranth** purple flower that never fades or dies

**ambrosia** food of the gods, conferring immortality

**amrita** elixir of immortality (India)

**animal fable** tale with animals personifying human characteristics to illustrate moral point

**anthropomorphism** practice of endowing natural world with human attributes

**Arabian Nights** ancient Oriental tales told by Scheherazade

**archetype** original or ancestral idea or type

**Argonauts** fifty Greek heroes who sailed with Jason to retrieve the Golden Fleece

**Asgard** city of the gods (Scandinavia)

**Atlantis** legendary continental island that disappeared into Atlantic Ocean during ancient or prehistoric times

**Bifrost** rainbow bridge between heaven and Earth (Scandinavia)

***Book of the Dead*** texts placed as protection in tombs of the dead (Egypt)

**caduceus** winged staff of Mercury

**Camelot** site of King Arthur's palace and court (Britain)

**cautionary tale** traditional story with moral lesson

**charm** amulet or object that brings luck or wards off evil

**chthonic** (*adj*) pertaining to the underworld

**cosmic egg** mythic image of creation

**cosmogony** creation myth

**creation myth** mythic explanation of formation of universe; cosmogonic myth

**culture hero** mythical or folk hero who personifies cultural development and ideals

**Deluge, the** great flood of various legends

***Edda*** collection of traditional poems on mythological and religious subjects (Iceland)

**epic** traditional tale of hero's adventures or creation

**etiological myth** myth explaining creation of the universe

**Excaliber** King Arthur's sword

**fable** story with fantastic events and creatures having allegorical meaning; legend

**fairyland** home of fairies; enchanted place

**fairy tales** universal stories about fairies or other imaginary and magical creatures, esp. for children, usu. based on oral tradition

**Flood** universal deluge that is subject of myth and legend in many cultures, including Mesopotamian and Judeo-Christian

**folklore** traditional beliefs, narratives, and superstitions of a culture

**folkway** pattern common to cultural group, expressed in traditional stories, beliefs, and customs

**fountain of youth** legendary spring whose waters restore health and youth to anyone who drinks them

**gest** traditional romantic tale of adventure

**Gilgamesh** major epic text of Mesopotamia

**Gladsheim** great hall in Odin's palace (Scandinavia)

**golden age** mythical earlier, happier, idealized era

**golden apples** treasure of Garden of the Hesperides, retrieved by Hercules (Greece)

**Golden Fleece** magical treasure retrieved from Colchis by Jason (Greece)

**Gordian knot** intricate knot whose untier would rule Asia, supposedly cut by Alexander the Great with sword

**Great Turtle** upholder of world (Native American)

**Grimm's fairy tales** folklore collection compiled by the Grimm brothers, including Snow White, Rumpelstiltskin, Tom Thumb, and Hansel and Gretel

**Hesperides** legendary garden at western extremity of world, where golden apples grow (Greece)

**Holy Grail** cup that was object of mystical quest by Arthurian knights

*Iliad* epic poem of Homer describing ten-year siege of Troy by Greeks

**land of Nod** mythical land of sleep

**legend** traditional story or narration

**lore** folk knowledge, body of information

**lotus** legendary fruit that induces state of dreamy forgetfulness (Greece)

**Mother Goose** fictitious author of a compendium of traditional nursery rhymes written down by Charles Perrault

**motif** recurrent theme in myth or legend

**myth** tale or traditional narrative that describes adventures of gods and legendary heroes, and reveals human behavior and natural phenomena through its symbolism

**mythology** collected body of myths of one people or culture

**mythopoeia** mythmaking

**nature myth** myth concerning natural phenomena

**nectar** wine conferring immortality (Greece)

*Nibelungenlied* medieval German epic relating the life and heroic acts of Siegfried

**nursery rhyme** simple, traditional, rhymed song or poem for very young children

**nursery tale** traditional story for very young children

*Odyssey* epic poem of Homer describing return of Odysseus from Trojan War

**Olympus** mountain home of the gods, ruled by Zeus (Greece)

**Oz** magical or otherworldly land described in Oz books of L. Frank Baum

**Palladium** statue of Pallas Athena, believed to provide protection for city of Troy (Greece)

**parable** short allegorical story with a moral

**pathetic fallacy** attribution of human feeling or motive to natural world or inanimate object

**personification** embodiment of human character in inanimate object or abstract idea ·

**proverb** pithy, epigrammatic saying, usu. a kernel of condensed folk wisdom

**Ragnarok** end of the world and destruction of the gods and humankind in a final battle with evil powers (Scandinavia)

**Ramayana** Hindu epic concerned with the life of Ramachandra

**romance** imaginative fiction, esp. describing adventure of a hero

**sacrifice** ritual offering of valuable object, human being, or animal to divine powers

**saga** legendary narrative about heroic adventures

**scarab** representation of a beetle, esp. as symbol of sun or cyclical cosmic pattern (Egypt)

**soteriological myth** myth describing hero as bringer of salvation

**spell** charm cast over person; bewitchment

**sun disk** symbolic representation of sun or sun god, as in Egyptian, Babylonia, and Aztec mythology

**tale** legendary, fictitious, traditional story told dramatically

**theogony** account of the origin of the gods and their genealogy

**theriomorphic** (*adj*) having form of an animal

**Trojan Horse** horse filled with Greek soldiers, used to trick Trojans into opening their city gates, thus losing their war

**underworld** regions of the dead; realm of afterlife, esp. for punishment

**Valhalla** great hall where Odin received souls of heroes fallen in battle (Scandinavia)

**Vanir** race of fertility gods originally in conflict with the Aesir (Scandinavia)

*Volsunga Saga* Icelandic saga of late 13th c. concerning the Volsungs, the theft of the treasure of Andvari, and the adventures of the hero Sigurd; basis of the *Nibelungenlied*

**Yggdrasil** giant tree that supported the world (Norse)

## UTOPIA

**Agapemone** communistic, free love establishment founded in 1849 at Spaxton, England

**Arcadia** region of innocence and simplicity

**asylum** place of refuge and protection

**Atlantis** legendary island in Atlantic Ocean with highly developed, utopian society, said to have sunk beneath the sea

**Avalon** island home of Morgan Le Fay, represented as earthly paradise, to which King Arthur was taken after his death

**Big Rock Candy Mountain** place of refuge in children's song

**brave new world** futuristic society described in novel by Aldous Huxley

**Brook Farm** egalitarian utopian farming community founded in 1841 in Massachusetts

**bucolic** (*adj*) pastoral, rural

**cloudland** dreamland

**cloud nine** *Informal.* state of perfect happiness

**Cockaigne** imaginary land of idleness and luxury

**dreamland** place where one's dreams come true; cloudland; fantasyland

**dystopia** opposite of utopia, where everything is wretched and people are miserable; kakotopia

**El Dorado** place of fabulous wealth and abundance sought by 16th-century explorers

**Erewhon** utopia in Samuel Butler's novel of same name

**fairyland** place of great beauty and magical charm

**fantasia** artistic work of free imagination and fancy

**fantasyland** dreamland

**Fountain of Youth** magical fountain providing eternal youth, held by Spanish explorers to lie somewhere in Americas

**Goshen** land of plenty, esp. land assigned to Israelites in Egypt

**Happy Valley** utopia in writings of Samuel Johnson

**haven** place of asylum, refuge, and peace

**heaven on earth** earthly dwelling place as peaceful and perfect as heaven

**Hesperides** garden at western extremity of world that produces golden apples (Greek mythology)

**idyll** time and place of peaceful, pastoral life

**kakotopia** dystopia

**kingdom come** heaven on earth

**land of milk and honey** land of plenty; Canaan, as envisioned by the ancient Hebrews

**land of plenty** earthly dwelling place that provides for all of humanity's physical and spiritual needs

**Laputa** utopia in writings of Jonathan Swift

**lotus land** legendary Greek land of dreamy idleness

**lubberland** imaginary land of idleness and leisure amid plenty

**Modern Utopia** utopia as described in book by H.G. Wells

**Nephelococcygia** utopia in plays of Aristophanes

**never-never land** illusory, ideal land or condition

**New Atlantis** utopia in writings of Sir Francis Bacon

**New Harmony** socialistic colony, founded in Indiana in 1825, that established first kindergarten, free public school, and free library in United States

**oasis** isolated, often unexpected, place of refuge and refreshment, esp. in desert

**Oneida Community** utopian settlement in New York State, founded on theory that sin can be eliminated by social reform

**pastoral** *(adj)* pertaining to idealized, peaceful, simple, and natural life of farmers and shepherds

**pie in the sky** state of perfect happiness or utopia, esp. when illusory

**pipe dream** illusory or fantastic plan or way of life

**Prester John** figure in story of utopian land

**Quivira** utopian tale

**refuge** haven, place of safety and peace

**safe harbor** refuge or haven

**sanctuary** asylum; place of refuge, protection, or immunity from law

**Seven Cities of Cibola** utopian legend

**Shangri-la** remote, imaginary paradise on earth and land of eternal youth, after fictional Himalayan land described by James Hilton in *The Lost Horizon*

**utopia** any ideal place or state, esp. in its laws and social conditions; any visionary, sometimes impractical scheme for social improvement

**Utopia** imaginary island with ideal government, from 16th-century book by Sir Thomas More

**wonderland** place of wonders or marvels

**Xanadu** legendary city of opulence and pleasure, home of Kublai Khan

---

# MAGIC AND THE OCCULT

Belief Systems and Theories
Rites, Practices, Spells, and Symbols
Occult States and Experiences
Individuals and Objects

**SEE ALSO**: Chap. 4: Astronomy and Space Science; Chap. 22: Strategy, Intrigue, and Deception; Chap. 25: Religion; Mythology and Folklore; Truth, Wisdom, and Spiritual Attainment

## BELIEF SYSTEMS AND THEORIES

**alchemy** medieval chemistry and speculative philosophy aimed at transforming base metals into gold and prolonging life

**ancestor worship** adoration of ancestors, whose spirits are believed to have power to intervene in affairs of the living

**animal magnetism** mysterious natural force used by Franz Mesmer to hypnotize and cure patients; mesmerism (France, 18th c.)

**animism** belief in existence of spirits separate from bodies; attribution of conscious life to objects in nature

**astrology** divination according to positions of stars and planets

**black magic** magic used for evil or diabolical purposes

**cabalism** belief in the esoteric, the occult, or mysticism

**Chaldean** *(adj)* belonging to ancient Semitic sect of Babylonia, versed in occult arts and astrology

**chiromancy** palmistry

**diabolism** devil worship

**Gnosticism** early Christian heresies stressing esoteric knowledge of spiritual truth, practiced by secret, self-styled elite sect

**hermetics** Gnostic teachings of Hermes Trismegistus, characterized by abstruse occultism

**macumba** Brazilian voodoo

**mesmerism** animal magnetism

**Mithraism** men's Persian mystery cult of late Roman Empire

**mysticism** belief in acquisition of spiritual truth, power, and communion with ultimate reality through intuition, insight, or application of specific secret rites, sometimes expressed in romantic love of the divine

**numerology** divination through numbers and study of their occult significance and interrelationships

**obeah** sorcery and magic among blacks of the Caribbean, Africa, and southeastern United States

**oneiromancy** divination through dreams

**palmistry** divination by analysis of creases in palm of hand; chiromancy

**panpsychism** belief that every physical event has a psychic aspect

**parapsychology** branch of psychology concerned with investigation of paranormal phenomena such as clairvoyance and telepathy

**phrenology** analysis of character based on size and shape of skull

**santeria** Afro-Caribbean belief system that includes animal sacrifices and uses Catholic saints as representations of the spirit world

**Satanism** devil worship

**shamanism** animistic belief in unseen world of gods, demons, and ancestral spirits responsive only to shamans (northern Asia)

**sorcery** use of evil power for divination or manipulation of the natural world for specific ends

**tarot** any of a set of twenty-two specially marked cards that symbolize archetypal personalities and situations, used for fortunetelling

**telepathy** communication between minds by paranormal means

**voodoo** West Indian religion derived from African ancestor worship, characterized by rites, trances, animistic deities, spells, and hexes

**white magic** magic practiced with intent to do good or benefit others

**wicca** witch theology based on empowerment of women who care for Earth and cosmos

**witchcraft** sorcery and magic acquired through communication with devil

**zombiism** belief in voodoo cult of the zombie

## Rites, Practices, Spells, and Symbols

**abracadabra** magical incantation, often rapid and nonsensical

**aleuromancy** use of flour for divination

**apotropaic** (*adj*) intended to guard against evil

**arcanum** mystery or rite known only to initiates

**ascendant** zodiacal sign rising at eastern horizon at moment of one's birth

**aspect** relative position of planets and stars having astrological influence on human affairs

**astral house** position of planets in connection with influence on specific aspects of life

**astral traveling** leaving one's body and venturing forth as a spirit

**augury** divination by omens and signs

**auspice** prophetic sign

**bewitch** (*vb*) cast spell over through witchcraft or magic

**black art** magic practiced by witches, conjurers, and diabolists

**Black Mass** perversion of Catholic Mass by worshiping Satan

**blessing** invocation of a good or benefit upon another person

**cabala** esoteric, occult, or secret doctrine; orig. medieval Jewish mystical theosophy and thaumaturgy

**call up spirits** summon mystical forces by incantation

**cargo cult** Pacific Islands religious cult believing in acquisition of material goods through intervention of spirits

**cast a chart** calculate, diagram, and analyze all zodiacal positions at time of person's birth

**cast a spell** impose magic power over; conjure

**conjure** (*vb*) summon by incantation; affect by magic

**conundrum** riddle whose answer involves a pun; mystery

**coven** assembly of witches or diabolists, esp. thirteen such

**crystal gazing** divining by looking into a crystal ball

**cult** secret or restricted society characterized by rituals and initiations, demanding absolute loyalty or suppression of ego; sect

**curse** invocation of harm on another; (*vb*) wish or invoke calamity or injury upon

**cusp** period of transition from one zodiacal sign to next

**deicide** killing of a god

**divination** foretelling future through analysis of omens by prescribed methods

**dowsing** art of finding water, oil, or metals by means of magic rod

**effluvium** vapor; offensive-smelling emanation

**enigma** obscure occurrence; riddle or mystery

**ephemeris** table of positions of celestial bodies at stated times, used in divination

**esotericism** doctrine and practice of arcane or secret rites

**ESP** extrasensory perception

**ether** rarefied element; medium in which spirits appear; intoxicating gas

**evil eye** glance or stare believed to cause harm; silent curse; malocchio

**exorcism** rite or spell that casts out evil spirit from possessed person or object

**extrasensory perception** ESP; ability to perceive phenomena beyond normal physical dimensions and senses

**faith healing** miraculous curing of disease or injury through belief in God and his servants

**Fata Morgana** mirage consisting of multiple images that resemble castles

**fetish** superstitious belief in object's magical or supernatural powers; object of such belief

**folk medicine** primitive healing based on nature or ritual, not medical technology and science

**foreordain** (*vb*) predetermine the future

**fortunetelling** divining and predicting future events, esp. concerning an individual's life

**grigri** African amulet or fetish; gris-gris

**gris-gris** grigri

**haoma** intoxicating, sacramental plant drink used in Zoroastrian ritual; soma

**haruspication** divination by examination of entrails or liver of slaughtered animal

**haunting** habitual reappearance of ghost or specter

**hex** curse, jinx, evil spell

**hocus-pocus** nonsense and sleight of hand used to cloak deception in magic rites

**hoodoo** voodoo, bad luck

**horoscope** prediction based on astrological chart

**house** one of twelve equal sectors of celestial sphere in astrology

**hypnosis** sleeplike state induced by repetitious speech or movement, marked by heightened suggestibility

**idolatry** worship of physical object or living person

**incantation** verbal spell or charm used in magical rites and sorcery

**initiation** ceremony admitting new member to secret cult, brotherhood, or belief system

**jinx** spell bringing bad luck; curse

**levitation** phenomenon of floating on air in apparent defiance of laws of gravity

**lifeline** long crease in hand consulted for divination in palmistry

**lycanthropy** delusion that one has become a wolf

**magic** use of illusion, sleight of hand, ritual, and incantations for divination, enchantment, or to invoke a curse

**malison** curse, invocation of harm

**malocchio** evil eye

**medicine show** show offering supposed cures through sale of patent medicines

**mental telepathy** reception or transmission of thoughts without words

**mind reading** ability to perceive another's thoughts through preternatural power

**mirage** illusion or appearance of something that does not really exist

**mumbo jumbo** verbal nonsense and sleight of hand associated with rites, spells, or magic

**mysteries** secrets on which cult or belief system are based

**necromancy** conjuring spirits of the dead for magic or divination

**nympholepsy** demoniac frenzy induced by nymphs

**occult** (adj) pertaining to magic or any system claiming use or knowledge of secret or supernatural powers or agencies

**oddity** inexplicable, magical occurrence

**omen** event or phenomenon said to portend future

**open sesame** magical incantation that causes desired result

**Ouija** Trademark. board with alphabet and signs for reception of telepathic messages

**patent medicine** packaged nonprescription drug with incompletely described ingredients; quack remedy; harmless potion sold as cure-all

**phase** particular stage in regular cycle of moon, used in astrology

**portent** omen of future event, usu. an unfortunate one

**potion** usu. secret mixture of liquids with magic powers

**precognition** clairvoyance relating to future events

**prediction** foretelling of future events

**prophecy** prediction of the future

**psychokinesis** movement of objects through mental processes, without use of physical means; telekinesis

**rainmaking** rites, esp. dances, intended to bring rain

**riddle** mystifying or misleading question posed as problem to be solved

**rite** prescribed ceremony or liturgy for specific purpose

**rune** character of medieval Germanic alphabet; aphorism, poem, or saying with mystical meaning

**Sabbat** midnight assembly of diabolists to renew allegiance to devil through rites and orgies (14th-16th c.)

**scrying** crystal gazing; divination by crystals

**seance** session or meeting to receive spirit communications

**secret society** cult or brotherhood with oath of silence and secret rites and disciplines

**sect** often extreme or heretical group dissenting from established belief system or religion; any small branch of a larger movement; cult

**shadow** phantom; faint representation of spirit

**shamrock** trifoliate plant considered symbol of good luck, esp. by Irish

**sigil** sign, word, or device of occult power

**sign** one of twelve divisions of zodiac

**signification** suggestion, symbolic representation

**sodality** brotherhood with common purposes, beliefs, and rites

**soma** haoma

**soothsaying** prophecy, divination

**sortilege** divination by lots

**spell** words with magic powers; state of enchantment

**spellbind** (vb) bind or hold by spells

**spirit rapping** communicating with spirits of dead by rapping on table

**spirit writing** writing of medium under supposed influence of spirits

**stargazing** practicing divination through astrology

**summons** spiritual calling

**sun dance** ceremony consisting of dancing, symbolic rites, and often self-torture (North American Indians of the Plains)

**superstition** belief or practice resulting from fear of unknown, trust in magic, or false concept of causation

**taboo** often ritualized fear or prohibition of specific object or practice

**telekinesis** psychokinesis

**telepathy** extrasensory communication between minds

**thaumaturgy** working of magic or miracles

**time machine** theoretical device for traveling forward or backward in time

**touch** contact by spirit world

**transubstantiation** change of one substance into another, esp. Eucharistic transformation of bread and wine

**vapor** something insubstantial or transitory

**vaticination** prediction, prophecy

**voodoo** sorcerer's charm or curse; hoodoo

**vortex** gateway into another dimension

**Walpurgis Night** eve of May Day, when witches congregate and ride

**wanga** voodoo charm or spell

**whammy** Informal. magic curse or spell that brings bad luck

**wish** invocation of good or evil on someone or something

**wizardry** practice of sorcery; magical power of transformation

**Zener card** one of twenty-five cards marked with five different objects, used in extrasensory perception research

**zodiac** imaginary belt in heavens encompassing paths of planets, divided into twelve astrological signs

## OCCULT STATES AND EXPERIENCES

**adumbrative** (adj) vaguely foreshadowed, with sketchy sense of future

**apocalyptic** (adj) forecasting or suggesting end of world

**aura** luminous radiation surrounding object or individual

**aureole** radiant light around head of sacred person; halo

**bliss** serenity, inner peace, complete happiness

**blissed-out** (adj) Slang. experiencing a continual, trancelike state of bliss or euphoria

**chimerical** (adj) visionary and improbable; existing only in fantastic imagination

**clairaudience** power of hearing something not audible to the ordinary ear

**clairvoyance** ability to discern objects not present to the senses; perception beyond normal range; precognition

**creeps** *Informal.* sense of foreboding

**deep** (*adj*) possessed of heightened consciousness; perceptive beyond the norm

**déjà vu** uncomfortable sense of familiarity with new experience; sense of having been in a situation before; paramnesia

**devoid** (*adj*) empty, blank, lacking sensibility

**disbelief** incredulity or difficulty in accepting reality of what has been experienced

**disembodiment** separation of spirit or mind from physical body

**dread** heightened fear, esp. of the unknown

**ecstasy** complete, rapturous delight; trancelike, often prophetic state beyond self-control

**eerie** (*adj*) spooky, filling one with dread of the unknown

**entrancement** supersensible, nonrational, trancelike state

**extrasensory** (*adj*) beyond realm of senses

**extraterrestrial** something or someone from outer space

**fatidic** (*adj*) prophetic

**foresight** ability to see and predict future; vision

**foretell** (*vb*) predict future events

**fourth dimension** something outside range of ordinary experience as measured in length, breadth, and depth, usu. time

**glossolalia** pseudolanguage of ecstasy or possession; speaking in tongues

**hallucination** visual or auditory perception of objects without reality, often experienced in trancelike state

**halo** aureole

**hermetic** (*adj*) recondite, characterized by occultism or Gnosticism

**hypnotic** (*adj*) suggesting hypnosis, trance, or detachment from consciousness

**imaginary** (*adj*) inexplicable by reason; distinct from three-dimensional reality of senses

**in the dark** ignorant, unknowing, or unaware

**kef** dreamy tranquility produced by use of a narcotic (Middle East)

**manifestation** physical evidence of phenomena

**mantic** (*adj*) prophetic, divinatory

**materialization** physical manifestation of nonmaterial phenomenon or spirit

**nepenthe** forgetfulness of sorrow, orig. a potion used to induce such forgetfulness

**obsession** persistent, usu. disturbing, preoccupation with one idea, feeling, person, place, or thing

**occult** (*adj*) beyond ordinary knowledge or understanding; mysterious or supernatural

**oneiric** (*adj*) of or relating to dreams

**orphic** (*adj*) mystic, oracular

**Orphic** (*adj*) relating to rites and doctrines ascribed to Orpheus and the cult of Dionysus

**out-of-body experience** sensation of perceiving oneself from external viewpoint as though mind or soul had left body

**paramnesia** déjà vu

**paranormal** (*adj*) supernatural, scientifically inexplicable

**phantasmagoria** rapidly fluctuating, dreamlike scene or imagery

**possession** domination by evil spirit or passion; replacement of one's normal personality by another's

**precognition** clairvoyance

**prescience** foreknowledge of events; divine omniscience

**preternatural** (*adj*) extraordinary, existing outside nature

**psi** extrasensory perception; psychic phenomena in general

**psychedelic** (*adj*) describing abnormal psychic state of heightened awareness, often produced by drugs and accompanied by hallucinations

**psychic** (*adj*) sensitive to nonphysical, supernatural forces

**Pythian** (*adj*) relating to the oracle at Delphi, noted for giving ambiguous answers

**second sight** clairvoyance, precognition

**sixth sense** keen, intuitive power of perception beyond that of the five senses

**somnambulism** sleepwalking

**speaking in tongues** incomprehensible, nonhuman or mystical language while in a state of ecstasy or possession; glossolalia

**spellbound** (*adj*) in state of enchantment

**supernatural** extraordinary phenomena inexplicable by science or senses

**supersensible** (*adj*) spiritual; beyond realm of senses

**surrealistic** (*adj*) having bizarre, dreamlike quality

**touched** (*adj*) having received divine revelation, inspiration, or supersensible powers

**trance** state of profound abstraction, deep hypnosis, or suspended animation

**transcendental** (*adj*) beyond limits of ordinary experience, reality, and comprehension; supernatural

**unbelievable** (*adj*) impossible to explain by reason or senses

**uncanny** (*adj*) eerie, mysterious, of supernatural origin or power

**unfamiliar** (*adj*) strange, difficult to explain

**unimaginable** (*adj*) beyond powers of imagination and intellect

**unreal** (*adj*) fantastic; beyond normal senses and dimensions

**vatic** (*adj*) prophetic, oracular

**vibration** characteristic aura or spiritual emanation that infuses individual or body, sensed intuitively

**vision** supernatural, often revelatory appearance in dream, trance, or ecstasy

**xenoglossia** magical knowledge of a language one has never learned

## INDIVIDUALS AND OBJECTS

**acolyte** follower

**adept** trained practitioner

**alkahest** universal solvent in alchemy

**anchorite** one living in seclusion for religious reasons

**ankh** cross with loop at top, used as symbol of enduring life (ancient Egypt)

**apparition** unusual phenomenon or vision, esp. ghostly figure

**archimage** great wizard or magician

**astrologer** practitioner of astrology and stargazing

**azoth** mercury, regarded as first principle of all metals by alchemists

**banshee** female spirit

**barsom** bundle of sacred twigs

**bogy** evil spirit, goblin

**botanica** store in which plants and other materials are purchased for use in rituals, esp. in santeria

**channel** individual through whom spirits make contact

**charm** amulet worn to ward off evil and bring good fortune

**chiromancer** palm reader

**conjurer** magician, wizard

**crystal ball** glass orb used for divination

**daemon** demon

**demiurge** supernatural being that possesses an autonomous creative power in subordination to the Supreme Being

**demon** evil spirit; daemon

**dervish** member of Muslim order known for frenzied, whirling devotional practice

**devil** Satan, master of all evil spirits and demons

**disciple** devoted follower

**djinn** jinn

**doomsayer** soothsayer who predicts apocalypse

**Doppelgänger** ghostly double of living person

**Dracula** deranged, possessed individual, orig. a Transylvanian count, who draws strength by drinking blood of others; vampire

**Druid** ancient Celtic priest, magician, or wizard

**effigy** crude physical representation or image, esp. of hated person

**fakir** Hindu or Muslim ascetic or wonder-worker; dervish

**familiar spirit** spirit of dead person who attends or serves another

**flying saucer** unidentified moving object in air reputed to be from another planet or solar system; UFO

**fortune cookie** folded Chinese dessert cookie with written prophetic message or advice enclosed on slip of paper

**fortuneteller** individual claiming ability to prophesize future

**genie** jinn

**ghost** spirit of dead person that reappears in bodily likeness to haunt or roam in earthly realm

**ghoul** evil being that robs graves and feeds on corpses

**glyph** symbolic figure carved in relief

**gnome** ageless, often deformed dwarf who guards precious ores and has secret knowledge

**gnosis** essential esoteric and spiritual knowledge held to be achieved through faith by Gnostics

**goblin** grotesque, often malicious sprite or demon

**gremlin** small, mischievous being said to be responsible for minor malfunctions

**hag** ugly female demon or witch

**haruspex** minor priest who practiced divination, esp. from entrails of animal killed in sacrifice (ancient Rome)

**hei-tiki** Maori charm worn around neck

**hobgoblin** mischievous goblin; bogy

**icon** idol, symbol, or object of devotion

**illuminati** persons claiming superior religious enlightenment

**incubus** evil spirit that has sexual intercourse with sleeping women

**initiate** new convert to belief system

**jinn** supernatural spirit that assumes human and other forms and serves its summoner; djinn; genie

**joss** Chinese idol; cult image

**juju** African magical fetish or charm

**kachina** doll representing deified ancestral spirit of Hopi Indians

**leprechaun** mischievous old elf with knowledge of hidden treasures (Irish folklore)

**loup-garou** *French*. werewolf

**magician** practitioner of illusion, sleight of hand, and incantation for prophecy

**magus** wise man, sorcerer, or magician

**marabout** Muslim hermit

**mascot** person, animal, or object adopted by group as symbolic good luck figure

**medicine man** shaman, sorcerer, or priest healer, esp. among American Indians; witch doctor

**medium** individual serving as channel for communications with spirits

**megalith** very large, rough stone, esp. used for primitive religious monuments

**menat** amulet used to secure divine protection (ancient Egypt)

**mind reader** person who can discern thoughts of others through supernatural means

**moly** mythical herb with magical powers

**monolith** single great stone, obelisk, or column, often built as symbolic religious monument

**Moonie** devoted cult follower of Sun Myung Moon or Unification Church

**mystagogue** one who initiates another into mystery cult

**neophyte** novice, recent convert

**nightrider** member of secret society who rides masked at night to perform acts of terrorism, esp. member of Ku Klux Klan

**omen** occurrence or phenomenon portending future event

**oracle** person or shrine through which deity reveals secret or divine purpose

**palm reader** one who divines by examining creases in person's palm; chiromancer

**panpsychist** advocate of belief that every physical event has psychic aspect

**phantasm** ghost, specter, figment of imagination

**phantom** specter or apparition, esp. one inspiring dread

**philosophers' stone** stone believed to have power to convert base metals to gold, sought by alchemists

**philter** potion, charm, or drug with power to cause person to fall in love

**planchette** small, triangular or heart-shaped board on casters with suspended pointer, used to produce automatic writing, esp. on Ouija board

**poltergeist** noisy, mischievous ghost

**precursor** incident or phenomenon that portends future event

**premie** recent initiate to cult

**prophet** person who predicts future events

**psychic** individual sensitive to supernatural and spiritual forces; medium

**puck** mischievous sprite or hobgoblin

**pythoness** female practitioner of divination, esp. priestess of Apollo

**querent** person who asks questions or seeks information, esp. through medium

**rabbit's foot** foot of rabbit carried for good luck

**revenant** person who returns as ghost or specter

**scarab** stone beetle used as talisman and symbol of destruction (ancient Egypt)

**seer** person with power to foretell events

**sensitive** medium, psychic

**serpent**  demon, treacherous creature

**shadow**  phantom, ghost

**shaman**  priest who uses magic for cures, divination, and sorcery, esp. among tribal peoples; witch doctor

**sibyl**  female fortuneteller

**sign**  omen; one of twelve divisions of zodiac

**soothsayer**  person who practices divination

**sorcerer**  wizard, shaman, practitioner of sorcery

**specter**  ghost, phantasm, visible disembodied spirit

**spellbinder**  person who casts spells

**spirit**  often malevolent disembodied but visible being

**spook**  *Informal.* ghost or specter

**sprite**  fairy or elf, esp. mischievous one

**succubus**  demon who assumes female form to have sexual intercourse with sleeping men

**swastika**  mystic symbol in form of cross with arms of equal length, with all arms extended at right angles in same direction, also used as symbol of Nazis

**talisman**  charm or object held to bring good luck and avert evil

**tea leaves**  leaves from emptied cup of tea whose arrangement is used in divination and prophecy

**teleplasm**  emanation from body of medium that serves as means for telekinesis

**thaumaturge**  magician, performer of miracles

**third eye**  spot in forehead receptive to occult or mystical knowledge or perception; intuition

**tiki**  Polynesian wood or stone image of supernatural power

**totem pole**  carved, painted pillar with series of American Indian symbolic images

**UFO**  *u*nidentified *f*lying *o*bject believed to be from outer space; flying saucer

**vampire**  reanimated corpse that rises from grave at night to suck blood of living; Dracula

**visionary**  mystic, prophet, or psychic

**wand**  slender rod used by conjurers and magicians

**warlock**  sorcerer; man who practices black magic

**werewolf**  person transformed into wolf or who assumes shape of wolf; wolfman

**wicca**  witch in wicca doctrine

**witch**  woman practicing white or black magic or sorcery, said by Christians to be possessed by the devil

**witch doctor**  medicine man; shaman

**wizard**  male sorcerer or magician

**wolfman**  werewolf

**wraith**  apparition of living person seen just before death; ghost, specter

**zombie**  supernatural voodoo power that reanimates dead body; speechless, will-less human embodiment of such power

# ESCHATOLOGY

Fate
Heaven and Paradise
Hell

**SEE ALSO:** Chap. 24: Death; Chap. 25: Religion; Mythology and Folklore; Magic and the Occult

# FATE

**apocalypse**  prophetic revelation of cataclysm that results in forces of good defeating forces of evil

**apocalyptic number**  666, number of the beast in Revelations

**appointed lot**  one's predetermined worldly fate or fortune

**Armageddon**  final battle between forces of good and evil

**balance**  determination of one's fate

**bane**  source of ruin or destruction

**bounty**  reward or good fortune

**break**  *Informal.* stroke of luck

**cataclysm**  violent upheaval, usu. at end of the world

**certainty**  inevitability; that which is fixed, settled, or destined to be

**chance**  luck, contingency

**chaos**  state of utter confusion or lack of organization

**contingency**  that which is possible but uncertain or subject to chance

**coup de grâce**  *French.* decisive act or event; deathblow

**crack of doom**  signal that indicates moment at which one's fate is decided; doomsday

**crapshoot**  *Informal.* unpredictable situation involving risk

**cup**  one's lot in life

**curse**  ill fate or misfortune, esp. due to external intervention

**curtains**  *Slang.* doom; end of one's life

**damnation**  condemnation to hell or ill fate

**deserts**  one's deserved reward or punishment

**destiny**  inevitable and predetermined course of one's life

**doom**  unhappy destiny; ruin or death

**doomsday**  day of Last Judgment at end of the world

**end**  fate or destiny

**eschatology**  study of or religious doctrine concerning the end of time, judgment day, death, resurrection, and immortality

**fatality**  something established by fate; disaster that results in death

**fate**  inevitable outcome of one's life; prescribed order of things or predetermined cause of events

**Fates**  three sisters who determine man's fate; weird sisters (Greek mythology)

**finality**  irrevocable end toward which life moves

**Final Judgment**  final determination of mankind's ultimate fate at end of the world

**fluke**  unexpected stroke of luck

**fortune**  destiny or fate, esp. favorable; hypothetical force that unpredictably determines events

**future**  that which is going to occur in time; that which exists after death

**Götterdämmerung**  destruction of the gods; Twilight of the Gods (German mythology)

**immortality**  eternal life

**inevitable**  that which is predetermined and cannot be avoided

**infinity**  doomsday, day of Final Judgment

**judgment**  Last Judgment

**Judgment Day**  day of God's judgment at end of the world, determining fate of mankind

**karma**  force generated by a person's actions, determining his or her destiny in future existence (Eastern religions)

**kismet** fate

**Last Judgment** final judgment of mankind

**Last Things** end of history and final fate of individuals and humankind

**lot** one's worldly fate or fortune; that which comes one's way in life

**luck** force, circumstances, or events that bring good or evil

**millennium** period of Christ's Second Coming and His reign of holiness on Earth

**mischance** mishap or misfortune

**misfortune** ill fate

**moira** individual destiny or fate (ancient Greece)

**Moirai** Greek Fates

**oblivion** finality or death; condition of being unknown or lost

**odds** likelihood or chance of particular event or fate

**omen** portent or indication of one's fortune

**oubliette** oblivion, finality, or death

**Pandora's box** source of extensive troubles and curses

**payoff** reward, retribution, or resolution

**portion** one's lot, fate, or fortune

**predestination** God's foreordination of all events; fate or destiny; predetermination

**predetermination** predestination

**Ragnarok** destruction of the gods and the world in a final battle (Scandinavian mythology)

**random** (*adj*) determined by chance or luck

**redemption** deliverance from a state of sin

**reincarnation** rebirth of soul in another body (Hinduism)

**retribution** reward or punishment, esp. in hereafter

**Revelations** last books of Bible, in which apocalypse is described

**salvation** soul's redemption from eternal punishment for sin

**samsara** indefinitely repeated karmic cycle of birth, misery, death, and rebirth or rebecoming (Hinduism and Buddhism)

**serendipity** propensity for achieving unsought good fortune

**stars** celestial bodies said in astrology to determine one's destiny; luck

**stygian** (*adj*) extremely gloomy and foreboding

**sword of Damocles** situation that threatens impending disaster or ill luck

**terra incognita** unknown or unexplored region

**Twilight of the Gods** Götterdämmerung

**twist of fate** unexpected development, reversal of one's fortune; wild card

**uncertainty** chance or contingency

**ups and downs** variations in one's affairs and fortunes

**vagary** unpredictable, erratic, or uncertain action or event

**vicissitude** favorable or unfavorable event or change that occurs by chance

**weird sisters** Fates; Moirai

**wheel of fortune** imaginary revolving wheel symbolizing inconstancy of fortune

**wild card** twist of fate

**world beyond** hereafter, afterlife

**writing on the wall** portent of one's fate or destiny

**zero hour** time at which Final Judgment occurs or one's fate is determined

## HEAVEN AND PARADISE

**above** heaven

**Abraham's bosom** heaven

**afterlife** life after death; great beyond

**afterworld** place of life after death

**Alfardaws** Muslim paradise

**Assama** Muslim paradise

**bliss** heaven

**Canaan** promised land of rest and refuge (Judaism)

**Celestial City** heavenly Jerusalem in Bunyan's *Pilgrim's Progress*

**City of God** heaven, paradise

**Civitas Dei** *Latin*. city of God, esp. in Catholicism

**Eden** original paradise recorded in Book of Genesis in Old Testament; Garden of Eden; paradise

**Elysian fields** Elysium

**Elysium** heaven of Greek and Roman mythology

**empyrean** highest paradise; visible heavens

**eternal life** immortal life of soul after death of body

**eternal reward** eternal life of the soul in heaven as reward for living a good life

**eternity** timeless state into which soul passes after death

**everlasting** afterlife, eternity

**Fiddler's Green** heaven reserved for sailors and soldiers

**Garden of Eden** Eden

**Garden of Irem** fabled Islamic garden of paradise

**glory** heaven

**great beyond** usu. **the great beyond;** afterlife

**happy hunting ground** paradise of hunting and feasting for warriors after death (Native American)

**heaven** realm of bliss and eternal happiness after death; abode for souls of the dead at God's side

**heaven's throne** heaven, esp. God's seat in heaven

**hereafter** afterlife, eternity

**Kingdom of God** heaven (Christianity)

**Kingdom of Heaven** heaven (Christianity)

**Land of Beulah** quiet paradise for those waiting to enter Celestial City in Bunyan's *Pilgrim's Progress*

**Land of the Leal** heaven (Scotland)

**New Jerusalem** heaven

**Nirvana** freedom from rebirth (Buddhism)

**Olympus** heavenly dwelling place of ancient Greek gods

**on high** in heaven

**paradise** realm of eternal goodness and happiness after death; Eden; reward

**Pearly Gates** entrance to heaven

**Promised Land** heaven

**purgatory** place of temporary suffering and punishment where souls are purified of sin prior to entry into heaven (Christianity)

**reward** paradise

**salvation** redemption or deliverance from sin

**seventh heaven** highest heavenly realm (Islam)

**upstairs** heaven

**Valhalla** heavenly hall and dwelling place of Norse gods and deceased heroes

**welkin** vault of heaven

**Zion** heaven as gathering place of true believers

## HELL

**abyss** hell, bottomless infernal regions

**Amenti** region of the dead (ancient Egyptian mythology)

**Arallu** region of the dead (ancient Babylonian mythology)

**Avernus** hell

**below** (*adv*) in hell

**bottomless pit** hell; pit

**brimstone** fire and sulfur of hell

**damnation** eternity in hell

**dark** void beyond life in hell

**down below** in hell

**Erebus** place of darkness under Earth believed to be abode of sinners

**eternal punishment** banishment of soul into hell for infinity

**Gehenna** place of suffering and torture; hell where dead are punished after death (Judaism)

**Hades** realm of the dead (Greek mythology); hell

**hell** region or condition of punishment for wicked persons after death; abode of evil spirits, esp. the devil

**hellfire** fire of hell

**inferno** hell in form of fiery region of torture

**limbo** region adjacent to hell for souls forbidden from heaven

**Naraka** region of punishment after death (Hinduism)

**Nastrond** dark, noxious hall of punishment (Norse mythology)

**nether world** hell

**Nifleheim** place of eternal cold, darkness, and fog that is abode of those who die of illness or old age (Scandinavian mythology)

**Pandemonium** hell, demonic region; capital of hell in Milton's *Paradise Lost*

**perdition** hell; place of utter damnation

**pit** bottomless pit

**Sheol** abode of the dead; hell (Judaism)

**Styx** principal river of the underworld (Greek mythology)

**Tartarus** infernal regions below Hades (Greek mythology)

**Tophet** hellish place of punishment after death in the Bible

**underground** underworld

**underworld** underground region for the dead; hell

**void** abyss; dark, unknown regions beyond life

# TRUTH, WISDOM, AND SPIRITUAL ATTAINMENT

Mystical States and Experiences
Practice, Discipline, and Belief
New Age
Enlightenment, Truth, and the Unknowable

**SEE ALSO**: Chap. 1: Health, Fitness, and Enhancement; Chap. 13: Philosophy; Chap. 23: Reasoning and Intuition; Chap. 25: Religion; Magic and the Occult; Eschatology

## MYSTICAL STATES AND EXPERIENCES

**accord** harmony, balance, proportion

**acme** highest stage or point; perfected form of something; zenith

**actualization** realization, esp. achievement of potential

**afflatus** divine inspiration or communication of wisdom and power

**ardor** zealous intensity of feeling

**attuned** (*adj*) in harmony with or responsive to spiritual life

**awakening** becoming aware of spiritual life and one's true self

**awe** sense of enormous wonder, delight, reverence, or fear

**balance** harmony, proportion, or emotional equanimity

**beatific** (*adj*) marked by sheer bliss; saintly, angelic

**beatitude** consummate bliss, transcendent happiness; state of being blessed

**blessed** (*adj*) enjoying spiritual contentment; hallowed, consecrated; highly favored

**bliss** serenity, inner peace, or complete happiness

**celestial** (*adj*) heavenly, suggesting divine inspiration

**concord** harmony; agreement between persons

**consciousness** awareness, esp. of spiritual life

**dark night of the soul** negativity and dissatisfaction that precede spiritual enlightenment

**delight** joy; extreme satisfaction or gratification

**deliverance** liberation, state of being freed, esp. from darkness or bondage

**disembodied** (*adj*) lacking substance or reality normally present; having spirit separated from corporeal substance

**divine** (*adj*) proceeding from God, devoted to God; supremely good or admirable

**divine revelation** enlightenment or perception of truth through act or intervention of God

**divinity** nature and essence of God; state of man so endowed

**ecstasy** complete, rapturous delight; trancelike state of receptivity to enlightenment

**elevated** (*adj*) exalted in mood or feeling; with a sublime nobility, moral rectitude, or higher consciousness

**enchantment** state of delight and rapture; influence by charms and incantation

**enrapture** (*vb*) fill with delight, gratification, and enchantment

**epiphany** revelation or manifestation of God or the divine; sudden intuitive perception of something's essential meaning

**equilibrium** balance and harmony with nature, other men, or oneself

**ethereal** (*adj*) celestial, heavenly; airy, nonmaterial

**euphoria** feeling of supreme well-being or elation

**evanescent** (*adj*) tending to vanish like vapor; fragile, airy, imperceptible

**exalted** (*adj*) marked by purity or nobility of thought and manner

**existential** (*adj*) relating to, grounded in, or based on human existence, as distinguished from essence

**extrasensory** (*adj*) beyond one's normal sense perceptions

**fervor** intensity of feeling, passion; earnest belief

**fulfillment** realization of one's full potential; sense of completion

**glory** aureole, nimbus; splendor; spiritual ecstasy; beatific happiness of heaven

**godhead** quality or state of being divine

**harmony** integration into consistent whole with balance, internal tranquility, and peace with one's surroundings

**high** *Slang*. state of euphoria and spiritual exaltation; (*adj*) lofty, elevated

**holy** (*adj*) spiritually whole, sound, or perfect; infinitely good, righteous, or selfless; godlike; sacred

**inner joy** bliss, inner light

**inner light** divine presence in soul that provides spiritual enlightenment and moral guidance

**inner space** spiritual universe within a person as opposed to physical universe of outer space

**inspiration** divine influence, sacred revelation, or spiritual awakening

**integrated** (*adj*) characterized by united and harmonious coordination of parts into whole

**irradiate** (*vb*) illuminate, enlighten spiritually, make clear

**joy** state of bliss, delight, and satisfaction

**love** Godlike benevolence; people's adoration of the divine in God, others, and themselves

**mystical** (*adj*) possessing spiritual reality separate from senses and intellect; involving direct communion with God or spirits

**nirvana** highest state of enlightenment, salvation, harmony, and transcendence

**numinous** (*adj*) inspiring awe or religious feelings

**oneness** harmony, integrity, and wholeness of spirit

**pacific** (*adj*) peaceful, harmonious, tranquil

**peace** serenity of spirit; tranquility, concord

**perfection** condition of fullness or completion; attainment of highest state; flawless state or condition

**plenty** fullness, abundance of spiritual satisfaction

**positive** (*adj*) marked by acceptance, approval, hope, and honesty

**presence** something nontangible felt or believed to be present; person's manner, bearing, or aura

**purity** perfection of spirit; absence of flaws or disharmony

**quietism** passive, withdrawn posture toward worldly matters

**radiance** spiritual brightness, glory

**rapture** spiritual ecstasy and exaltation due to knowledge of divine things

**realized** (*adj*) spiritually enlightened, in harmony with oneself

**repose** rest, inner peace, tranquility

**revelation** divine or supernatural communication of spiritual truth

**reverie** trancelike thought, contemplation, or dream

**sacred** (*adj*) hallowed, consecrated, worthy of veneration, holy

**saint** one distinguished by piety, virtue, and benevolence, without regard for self; spirit of departed person canonized by church to serve as guide for spiritual growth

**salvation** deliverance from spiritual estrangement and attachment to material world into state of religious fulfillment and recognition of ultimate reality

**sanctity** holiness, saintliness of life and character

**selfdom** essence of one's individuality

**selfhood** one's own character or personality

**sensitive** (*adj*) aware of spiritual and mystical matters

beyond information offered by senses; (*n*) one in tune with spiritual life

**serenity** calm, peaceful condition of repose and harmony

**spirituality** sensitivity to or concern with nonmaterial values, as distinguished from body and mind concerns

**splendor** radiant glory, esp. of spiritual fulfillment

**sublime** (*adj*) spiritually exalted and noble

**supernal** (*adj*) having spiritual character; coming from above

**supersensible** (*adj*) beyond the realm of the senses; spiritual

**supreme** (*adj*) loftiest, ultimate, highest

**totality** state of being complete, comprehensive, and unified

**touched** (*adj*) having received divine revelation, inspiration, or supersensible powers

**tranquility** peace, repose, serenity, harmony of spirit

**transcendence** state of being beyond limits of everyday experience, reality, or comprehension; supernatural, unified, or spiritual realm

**tuned-in** (*adj*) *Informal*. spiritually aware or enlightened

**unity** condition of concord and harmony

**virtue** correct attitude and conduct according to moral values

**vision** supernatural, revelatory appearance in dream, trance, or meditative state

**within** spiritual, interior life; inner space

**wonder** state of delight, marvel, mystery, or surprise coupled with admiration

**yes** indicator of positive, hopeful outlook on life

**zenith** ultimate point or greatest height; acme

## PRACTICE, DISCIPLINE, AND BELIEF

**anagogic** (*adj*) having spiritual meaning or sense; arising from or striving toward lofty ideals

**anthroposophy** mystical religious system similar to that of theosophy

**antinomian** one who holds that divine grace is sufficient for salvation and moral law is unnecessary

**ark** place that provides protection and security through divine presence

**asceticism** strict self-denial and austerity as measure and means of spiritual discipline

**ashram** religious retreat for sage and disciples

**astral** (*adj*) relating to the stars; denoting a supersensible substance held in theosophy to pervade all space and survive the individual after death

**astral traveler** spiritual guide; one who makes spiritual, out-of-body journey

**augur** (*vb*) predict future by omens

**blessing** something conducive to spiritual attainment; consecration by divine care or intervention

**chakra** in yoga, any of seven body points that are sources of psychic energy and spiritual power

**channel** (*vb*) convey information from spiritual world

**communion** contact and communication with God or spirits

**contemplation** deep thought; silent meditation on spiritual matters

**cornerstone** that which is essential, basic, or indispensable to all that follows or is built upon it

**devotion**  profound dedication and religious fervor, esp. acts evincing this; ardor, zeal

**discipline**  self-control, self-restraint, self-denial; proper conduct in accordance with self-imposed rules

**élan vital**  life force, vital principle of life

**embodiment**  physical incarnation of noncorporeal thing

**empyrean**  true and ultimate heavenly sphere; transcendentally exalted source of noble ideas or feelings

**eudemonics**  art or method of attaining happiness

**fasting**  prolonged abstention from food for purification and spiritual insight

**forgiveness**  act or state of ceasing to feel resentment or seek retribution over wrong committed by another

**grace**  beneficence or generosity, esp. of God toward humankind; disposition to kindness and compassion

**guru**  master, teacher, spiritual guide

**healing**  removal of negative energy, making one sound and whole; restoring spiritual integrity

**higher law**  guiding principles of divine or moral law

**hylozoism**  doctrine that all matter is inseparable from life

**indwell** (*vb*)  exist within as guiding spirit or motivating force

**key**  something serving to reveal or solve a mystery or provide an entrance to spiritual enlightenment

**keystone**  part or force on which related things depend

**leap**  attainment of enlightenment through sudden awareness or revelation

**life, the**  occupation with and devotion to spiritual matters, esp. to the exclusion of material concerns; the way

**lotus position**  erect sitting posture in yoga, with each foot resting on thigh of the opposite leg with sole upturned

**mandala**  graphic, mystic representation of universe used as meditation aid, esp. concentric geometric shape such as square within a circle

**manifestation**  perceptible outward expression of something, esp. form or guise of spirit or divinity

**manna**  divine or spiritual nourishment

**mantra**  ritualistic incantation used in meditation

**master**  wise individual, learned in spiritual discipline and inspiring devotion among disciples

**material** (*adj*)  corporeal or bodily, the opposite of spiritual

**meditation**  private devotion; spiritual exercise of deep contemplation or sustained introspection, esp. silent repetition of mantra

**medium**  individual believed to be capable of channeling information from spirit world

**meridian flow**  lines of energy movement through body

**miracle**  inexplicable, extraordinary event suggesting divine intervention or spiritual guidance

**moral** (*adj*)  ethically good, principled; conforming to or acting on inner conviction of what is right

**music of the spheres**  ethereal harmony supposed to be produced by movements of spheres of heavenly bodies

**mysteries**  secret initiation rites for supposed betterment of worshipers

**nimbus**  shining cloud around divine being

**numen**  divine spirit inhabiting natural object or phenomenon; dynamic, creative force; human need for and capacity to have spiritual life

**odyssey**  long, adventurous journey, esp. in search of enlightenment

**omni-**  prefix meaning all

**one**  divinity

**one way**  life devoted to spiritual attainment

**panacea**  universal remedy for all ills

**past life**  previous physical existence of spirit, esp. as basis of one's karma

**path**  spiritual direction, one way; attainment of enlightenment through systematic spiritual discipline

**perseverance**  steadfast persistence in pursuit of spiritual grace, esp. until succeeded by state of glory

**pietism**  intensity of devotional experience and practice

**pundit**  learned wise man

**purging**  self-purification by expulsion of harmful substances

**purification**  cleansing of sin; moral or spiritual purgation

**querent**  one who consults a spiritual guide

**quest**  search for enlightenment and harmony

**realization**  act or process of becoming real, taking form, or achieving potential

**rebirth**  spiritual regeneration or revival

**reflection**  meditation; consideration of something with view to understanding

**reflexology**  massage of foot or hand to promote generalized healing and relieve stress

**regimen**  strict practice

**rejuvenation**  regeneration of youthful vigor

**renunciation**  ascetic self-denial; rejection of one's previous values or lifestyle

**rhythm**  harmonious, orderly movement or flow

**rigor**  strict discipline, austerity

**sacrifice**  self-denial, loss, or abstinence from something to promote spiritual growth

**seeker**  one who devotes life to search for enlightenment and salvation

**self**  entire individual: mind, body, and spirit

**self-denial**  restraint of one's impulses to facilitate spiritual goals

**self-discipline**  regulation and training of oneself for improvement

**self-purification**  spiritual cleansing, esp. through self-denial and discipline

**silence**  peaceful, meditative tranquility conducive to spiritual attainment

**soul**  noncorporeal essence and spiritual principle of one's life

**source**  point of origin; generative force

**spirit**  essence of deity serving as invisible activating power; soul; noncorporeal essence and animating principle of life

**sustenance**  spiritual nourishment or support; source of strength

**swami**  master, teacher, wise man

**theosophy**  religious beliefs held to be based on special mystical insight into divine nature

**TM**  *t*ranscendental *m*editation

**transcendence**  quality of being beyond what is experienced and perceived in material world

**transcendental meditation**  TM; simple Hindu technique of two daily twenty-minute meditations with chanted mantra, now popular in the West

**transfiguration**  act or process of undergoing ennobling spiritual change

**trust**  faith and confidence in spiritual truth

**visionary**  one who sees beyond common experience or perception

**visitation** special administration of divine favor, affliction, or revelation

**votary** devotee living by vows

**way, the** path to spiritual attainment and harmony; the life

**Word** usu. **the Word**; divine guidance and inspiration

**zazen** meditation practice in cross-legged position

**Zen** practice of self-discipline and meditation to achieve direct spiritual enlightenment

# NEW AGE

**affirmation** positive thought consciously used to create a desired result

**akashic records** universal memory of nature and all souls; the book of life

**All That Is** God; Creative Forces; Divine Mind

**altered state of consciousness** any shift of primary focus to levels of reality other than the physical plane; trance or hypnotic state

**ambient sound** soothing, environmental background music; New Age music

**amulet bag** small protective pouch for carrying items of personal sacred significance, such as crystals

**Aquarian Age** two-thousand year astrological World Age beginning around 2000 A.D., in which humanity is expected to evolve towards peace, spiritual enlightenment, global community, and renewal of the Earth

**aromatherapy** use of essential oils for relaxation and healing, usu. in conjunction with massage and acupuncture

**astral body** inner body composed of electromagnetic energy that links the soul with the physical body; energy body

**Atlantis** lost, legendary island civilization in Atlantic Ocean between Europe and North America, said to have sunk beneath the sea in ancient times

**aura** magnetic energy field; luminous quality radiating from a person

**belief system** primary ideas or attitudes about life that shape one's relationship to reality

**biomagnetics** study of magnetic energy as it effects human health

**bodywork** any of various psycho-physical, hands-on healing techniques utilizing massage, movement, and seeking to balance the energy and emotional bodies

**catalyst** guide or teacher who functions as facilitator to speed one's psychic or spiritual growth

**chakra system** major channels through which life force flows into physical body; mediating channels between astral and physical bodies associated with major glands and acupuncture points

**channeling** receiving energy and information from other levels of reality ranging from discarnate beings to the Divine Mind or collective unconscious

**core belief** idea or attitude ingrained in one's mental patterns as truth

**core tone** vibrational essence of the individual soul carried within each incarnation

**Creative Forces** God; All That Is; Divine Mind; life force

**creative visualization** technique using mental imagery and affirmations to produce positive energy and conditions conducive to harmony and positive changes in life

**crystal** transparent, usu. quartz crystalline structure that vi-

brates at high frequency, used in conjunction with gemstones for healing and meditation

**discarnate being** incorporeal being or spirit

**Divine Mind** God; All That Is; Creative Forces

**Earth plane** physical world of external reality

**emotional body** octave or level of body that vibrates with all unresolved emotions from any incarnation

**energy body** astral body; level of body containing chakra system

**feeling tone** vibration of being, emanating from emotional body, that resonates from core tone

**Great Year** in astrology, cosmic cycle of twelve World Ages, occurring once every 26,000 years; Aquarian Age marks beginning of next Great Year

**guiding spirit** source of channeled information, usu. spirit of deceased person

**hands-on healing** channeling life-force energy through hands to remove negative energy, make oneself whole, and restore spiritual integrity

**Harmonic Convergence** shift point at end of Mayan Great Cycle, occurring in August, 1987, when a synchronized global meditation coincided with passage of a galactic beam through Earth and the sun in expectation of 5000 years of peace and harmony

**harmonizing** bringing something or someone into accord and balance

**healer** person who is a channel for the life force with intent to be of service to others

**healing circle** group of healers who gather together to combine and multiply their healing power

**higher mind** level of mind fueled by soul rather than ego and capable of accessing broader perspective

**higher self** one's essence or eternal nature; soul

**holistic** (*adj*) emphasizing organic or functional relation between parts and whole

**incarnate** (*adj*) in a physical form; within a body

**inner child** part of emotional body that holds unfinished childhood business as well as the capacity to be eternally childlike

**inner guide** spiritual guide; inner voice; part of greater being that is not presently incarnate

**karmic bond** deep connection of two souls from past incarnations that is carried into present lifetimes

**karmic debt** good deeds owed in present life to balance or complete a past incarnation

**Lemuria** legendary pre-Atlantean civilization located on lost subcontinent in Pacific Ocean whose people were known as the Mu

**light** positive energy; the source

**light being** spirit guide; discarnate being; saint

**magnet** body that produces magnetic field capable of attracting iron, influencing personal vibrations, and healing

**mindfulness** meditation technique in which full awareness is focused on the present moment

**negative energy** energy that is toxic or draining to the life force and counter to affirmation of life

**New Age** evolution of human consciousness and spiritual movement toward the light of the Aquarian Age; spiritual healing based on various techniques and methods such as astrology and crystal interpretation

**New Age music** ambient or environmental acoustic jazz that is spiritually soothing or uplifting, often using a blend of ancient and modern instruments

**octave**  harmonic interval or level of consciousness

**organic** (adj) forming an inherent vital part; composed of, using, or grown only with animal or vegetable matter

**oversoul**  supreme reality or mind; spiritual unity of all being

**past-life therapy**  technique of releasing karmic blocks through a regression process in order to access one's full potential

**peak experience**  glimpse of enlightenment

**pendulum**  suspended body swinging freely from fixed point, used as simple means of receiving channeled information

**personal power**  ability to access one's creative energy, tune it with the core tone, and use it to take action in the physical world

**primal body**  level of the body that contains the cellular memory of humanity's animal heritage and the dark side of nature from one's past lives

**psychic**  person who can access energy and information from nonphysical realms; sensitive, medium, or channel

**psychic therapy**  spiritually based therapy that utilizes altered states to experience and integrate the soul level of consciousness

**pyramid**  structure in the form of a square base with triangular walls meeting at apex that concentrates and transmits energy for meditation and regeneration

**regeneration**  spiritual renewal or rebirth, esp. a radical transformation of one's life

**self-actualization**  fulfillment of one's potential; attainment of peace of mind and harmony

**soul**  eternal being; energy essence; higher self

**soul consciousness**  eternal perspective and link between the ego/mind and the Divine Mind

**soul mates**  two or more souls originally split off from the same or larger oversoul

**soul purpose**  spiritual task a soul is working on mastering or learning in any particular incarnation

**third eye**  sixth chakra at center of forehead, connected with pineal gland, through which soul sees into physical plane; energy center through which psychic sense of vision operates

**vibes**  *Informal.* vibrations

**vibration**  velocity of movement of energy or life force through a body; characteristic aura, derived from this movement of energy, that one senses intuitively from an individual or body

**vibratory tone**  essential spiritual feeling one senses emanating from another individual or body

## ENLIGHTENMENT, TRUTH, AND THE UNKNOWABLE

**attainment**  accomplishment or acquisition of enlightenment

**clear** (adj) free of mundane, worldly matters, enabling one to see the spiritual essence of things as they are; at the highest state of enlightenment

**compassion**  consciousness of other people's suffering and selfless tenderness toward it

**empathy**  capacity for vicarious experiencing of another's thoughts or feelings and understanding based on it

**enlightenment**  state of being in harmony with laws of the universe; realization of ultimate universal truth and absence of desire

**entelechy**  realization or actuality, as opposed to potential

**essence**  basic underlying nature; most significant element or quality of something

**farseeing** (adj) visionary, prophetic

**humility**  freedom from pride and arrogance; modesty of spirit and ability to view others and oneself realistically

**illumination**  spiritual enlightenment

**imponderable** (adj) beyond exact measurement or evaluation

**incomprehensible** (adj) lying beyond reach of human mind; unfathomable

**indescribable** (adj) too vague, extreme, or far beyond experience to be accurately described

**ineffable**  that which is unspeakable or indescribable

**inexplicable** (adj) incapable of being explained or accounted for

**infinity**  boundless space, energy, knowledge, or capacity

**inherent** (adj) essential or intrinsic to something

**innate** (adj) belonging to essential character of something; originating in the mind rather than experience

**innominate** (adj) unnamed or of unknown name; unnamable

**insight**  apprehension of inner nature of things; intuitive understanding of others and oneself

**integral** (adj) inherent, essential to completeness

**intuition**  revelation by insight or innate knowledge, without reasoning

**knowledge**  awareness or understanding

**light, the**  spiritual illumination, enlightenment, ultimate truth

**mastery**  great skill or knowledge in some discipline

**matrix**  point of origin

**meaning**  intent and significance of something; reason for being

**mercy**  compassion, pity

**nobility**  superiority and righteousness of character or mind

**omniscience**  infinite knowledge and understanding

**perspective**  capacity to view things in their true relationships

**profundity**  depth of insight; spiritual awareness

**quietude**  tranquility, peace, inner harmony

**quintessence**  purest, most concentrated form or part, esp. of immaterial thing

**realized** (adj) spiritually enlightened, in harmony with oneself

**recognition**  discovery of true nature of something or someone

**revealed** (adj) pertaining to truths based on intuition or divine inspiration

**sagacity**  wisdom, keenness of discernment, understanding

**sage**  wise, learned, venerable one

**seeing**  enlightenment

**self-discovery**  process of attaining self-knowledge

**self-exploration**  study of one's potential for sake of understanding and improvement

**self-knowledge**  understanding one's own true character and feelings

**self-realization**  acknowledgment and understanding of oneself so as to fulfill one's potential

**self-revelation** recognition and statement of one's own thoughts and feelings, esp. unintentionally

**sense of self** understanding and acceptance of one's true nature

**Tao** eternal order of the universe and source of reality; right way of life, virtuous conduct

**timeless** (*adj*) eternal, everlasting; beyond measurement in time

**true self** one's innate nature and essence

**truth** fundamental, spiritual reality that lies beyond perceived reality and experience

**uncharted territory** mysterious regions beyond what has been explored, observed, or experienced

**understanding** recognition of spiritual truth or essence of something

**universal** (*adj*) present in all spheres of human life; (*n*) an ultimate truth

**unknowable** ultimate reality lying beyond human perception and experience, understood only through spirituality

**unknown** that which has yet to be discovered, identified, revealed, understood, or explained

**unseen** reality beyond human perception

**unspeakable** (*adj*) beyond verbal description; that may not or cannot be uttered

**unspoken** (*adj*) tacit, silent but understood

**unwritten** (*adj*) of truths known and passed on orally

**verity** state of being eternally and fundamentally true or necessary; something that is true, as a principle, belief, or idea

**window** revelation of truth, esp. moment or point of such revelation

**wisdom** understanding of spiritual truth; enlightenment; capacity to discern the essence of the ways of human beings and the universe

This index provides an alphabetical list of all entries in the book that have definitions. Entries in boldface type show the major categories of words along with the range of pages on which they appear.

empire waist, 367
empirical, 517
empirical formula, 159
empiricism, 515
Empirin, 174
employable, 446
employee, 448, 484
employee business expense, 459
employee stock ownership plan, 455
employer, 448, 484
employer identification number, 459
**Employers, Employees, and Business People**, 448–449
employment, 446
emporium, 379, 440
empress, 429
empty calories, 33
empty nester, 498
empyema, 26
empyrean, 849, 852
EMS, 163
EMT, 163
emulation, 246
emulator, 243, 558
emulsification, 50
emulsion, 534, 577, 603
en, 599
enable button, 240
enabler, 795
enactment, 387
enallage, 666
enamel, 7, 206, 534
enameling, 607
enamelware, 605
enamor, 734
enantio-, 671
en arriere, 567
en avant, 567
en brochette, 331
enc, 680
encashment, 451
encaustic, 534
-ence, 675
enceinte, 376
encephalitis, 16
encephalo-, 178, 671
enchaînement, 567
enchant, 734
enchantment, 780, 850
enchase, 598
enchilada, 336
encircling, 764, 767
enclave, 425
enclitic, 658
enclosed, 767
enclosing, 767
enclosure, 473
encomium, 543, 784
encompassing, 767
encore, 784
encounter group, 509
encourage, 783
encouragement, 783
**Encouragement.** See **Support, Encouragement, and Agreement**
encroach, 746
encroachment, 482
en croûte, 331
enculturation, 493, 500
encumbrance, 404, 482

encyc, 680
encyclical, 822
encyclopedia, 411, 545
Encyclopedism, 515
end, 763, 814, 848
endangered species, 55, 94
end-diastolic volume, 50
endearment, 666, 735
**Endearment, Terms of.** See **Terms of Endearment and Respect**
en dedans, 567
en dehors, 567
endemic, 29, 43
ending inventory, 462
end man, 272
end-matched, 200
endo-, 671
endocarditis, 16
endocrine gland, 12, 50
endocrine system, 50
**Endocrine System and Glands**, 12
endocrinology, 42, 161
endocytosis, 46
endoderm, 57
endodontics, 161
endogamy, 315, 492, 500
endogenous, 55
endophyte, 72
endoplasmic reticulum, 46
endorphin, 50
endorse, 783
endorsement, 451, 479
endoscope, 170
endoskeleton, 50
endothermic, 121, 154, 156
endotracheal tube, 170
endowment, 444, 464
endowment insurance, 479
end papers, 408
end-plate potential, 50
end point, 156, 763
end-systolic volume, 50
end table, 303
endurance, 31
end user, 240
enema, 168
enemy, 415, 427
energy, 121, 154
energy body, 853
energy level, 151
energy-matter relationship, 121
enervation, 26
en face, 567
en famille, 717
enfant, 321
enfant terrible, 717
Enfield rifle, 225
enforcement, 402
enfranchised, 385
enfranchisement, 390
ENG, 585
engageantes, 369
engaged, 315
engaged column, 295, 299, 593
engagement, 315, 415, 571, 614
en garde, 717
engine, 189, 270

engine cab, 273
engine driver, 272
engineer, 193, 272, 484, 587, 589, 746
engineering psychology, 503
engine failure, 254
engine overhaul, 268
engine pod, 256
engine room, 278
**Engines** (aircraft). See **Airframe and Engines**
engines of war, 227
England, 96
English horn, 563
engobe, 605
engorge, 324
engrave, 598
engraving, 598, 599, 607
engross, 773
**Enhancement.** See **Health, Fitness, and Enhancement**
enharmonic, 550
ENIAC, 243
enigma, 844
Enkidu, 837
en l'air, 567
enlargement, 603
enlarger, 603
Enlightenment, 515, 827
enlightenment, 836, 854
**Enlightenment, Truth, and the Unknowable**, 854–855
Enlil, 840
enlist, 418
enlisted man, 418
enlisted woman, 418
en masse, 717
enmity, 786
ennea-, 671
Enoch Arden, 817
Enoch Arden divorce, 315
enounce, 694, 697
en passant, 717
enrapture, 850
enrich, 333
enrichment, 126
enrolled agent, 459
en seconde, 567
ensemble, 366, 553, 574
ensemble piece, 571
ensiform, 769
ensign, 280, 418, 429
ensilage, 470
-ensis, 675
ENT, 161
entablature, 593
entail, 402
entasis, 593
entelechy, 517, 854
entente, 424
enter, 240, 689
entered hound, 628
enteritis, 16
entero-, 178, 671
enterostomy, 168
enter plea, 400
enterprise, 444
entertain, 773
entertainer, 574
entertainment, 618
entertainment center, 297
**Entertainments and Spectacles**, 617–619

enthalpy change, 154, 156
entheomania, 508
enthrall, 734
enthuse, 696
enthusiasm, 836
enthymeme, 518
enticement, 746
entitlement, 435
entomb, 816
entomo-, 671
entomology, 42
entomomania, 508
entomophobia, 507
entr'acte, 567, 571, 615, 717
entrance, 294
entrancement, 846
entrap, 746
entrapment, 806
entreat, 699
entrechat, 567
entrée, 334, 717
entremets, 331
entre nous, 717
entrepreneur, 448
entresol, 298
entropy, 121, 154
entry, 462
entry of judgment, 402
entryway, 294
**Entryways and Lateral Extensions**, 294
enumerated powers, 387
enunciate, 694
enuresis, 21
env, 680
envelope, 222, 254, 256, 389
envelope table, 303
enveloping, 767
environment, 55, 94, 500
environmental determinism, 502
environmental geology, 82
environmentalism, 496
environmental medicine, 161
environmental physiology, 42
environmental protection, 473
environmental resistance, 55
**Environment, Ecology, and Animal Behavior**, 54–57
envisage, 691, 776
envision, 691, 776
envoy, 424
enzyme, 11, 50, 151
enzyme induction, 50
enzymology, 42
eo-, 671
Eocene epoch, 88
eolian, 86
Eolithic Age, 490
eon, 759
eo nomine, 714
Eos, 840
eosinophil, 46
-eous, 675
EP, 556
EPA, 268
eparch, 832
épaulement, 567
epaulette, 352, 367

epaulière, 349
epee, 224
epenthesis, 658
epergne, 307
ephah, 184
ephebe, 314
ephebophobia, 738
ephedrine, 174
ephemeral, 761
ephemeris, 138, 844
epi-, 671
epic, 540, 575, 841
epicanthic fold, 7
epicanthus, 7
epicene, 654, 736
epicenter, 86, 112, 763
epic poem, 540
epicure, 614
Epicureanism, 515
epicycle, 138
epicyclic train, 189
epidemic, 29
epidemiology, 42, 161
epidermis, 14
epididymis, 12
epiglottis, 6
epigram, 540, 666
epigraphy, 490
epilepsy, 16
epilogue, 408, 543, 571, 666
epinephrine, 12, 50, 174
Epiphany, 610, 822
epiphany, 836, 850
epiphenomenalism, 517
epiphyte, 72, 637
Episcopalian Church, 821
episiotomy, 168
episode, 512, 583
episodic role, 583
epistaxis, 26
epistemic, 777
epistemology, 515
epistle, 540, 834
epistolary novel, 540
epistrophe, 666
epitaph, 816
epitasis, 571
epithalamion, 315
epithalamium, 540
epithelial cells, 46
epithelium, 14
epithet, 543, 666, 788
**Epithets.** See **Insults, Slurs, and Epithets**
e pluribus unum, 714
epoch, 86, 138, 759
eponym, 661
epos, 540
epoxy, 205
EPP, 50
EPROM, 248
Epsom salts, 177
Epstein-Barr syndrome, 16
EQ, 558
eq, 680
equal access, 585
equal-area projection, 91
equalization, 589
equalizer, 558
equal opportunity employment, 496
equal time, 585
Equanil, 174
equant, 133
equation, 145

generator, 125, 189, 231, 265
generic, 174
generic product, 440
generosity, 464
Genesis, 834
-genesis, 675
gene therapy, 168
genetic, 29, 675
genetic code, 43
genetic counseling, 43
genetic drift, 43
genetic engineering, 43, 474, 497
genetic isolation, 43
genetic map, 43
genetic recombination, 43
genetics, 42, 43
**Genetics, Heredity, and Evolution**, 42–45
Geneva bands, 354
Geneva Convention, 424
Geneva gown, 349
Geneva wheel, 189
-genic, 178, 675
genie, 837, 847
genital herpes, 16
genitalia, 57, 740
genital phase, 512
genitals, 12, 740
genitive, 655
genius, 837
genius loci, 837
gennaker, 278
genoa, 278
genocide, 497, 815
genome, 43
genomic DNA, 43
genotype, 43
-genous, 675
genre, 408, 536, 543, 576, 580
**Genres** (popular music). See **Styles and Genres**
**Genres and Types of Pictures**, 575–576
gens, 312
gentian violet, 177
gentile, 832
gentle breeze, 110
gentle craft, 630
gentrification, 497
gentry, 429
genuflect, 782
genuflection, 823
genus, 59
-geny, 675
geo-, 672
geobotany, 82
geocentric, 138, 765
geochemistry, 82, 150
geochronology, 82
geochronometry, 82
geode, 83
geodesic, 146, 765
geodesic dome, 293
geodesy, 82, 90, 144
geodetic survey, 86
geodynamics, 82
geog, 680
geognosy, 82
geographer, 90
geographical race, 493
geographic isolation, 55
geographic range, 43

geography, 82, 90
**Geography**, 90–103
geol, 680
**Geological Time Scale**, 88
geologic column, 86
geologic time scale, 86
**Geology**, 82–90
geology, 82
geom, 680
geomagnetic, 86
geomagnetic axis, 136
geometric mean, 146
geometric progression, 146
**Geometric Shapes and Mathematically Defined Forms**, 148–149
geometry, 144
geomorphic, 86
geomorphology, 82
geophysics, 82, 90, 120
geopolitical map, 91
geopolitics, 82, 390, 426
geoponic, 474
Georgette, 357
Georgia, 96, 100
Georgian, 592
georgic, 543
geoscopy, 90
geosyncline, 83
geotectonic, 86
geothermal gradient, 86
geothermal power, 86
geothermic, 86
gephyromania, 508
gephyrophobia, 507
gerascophobia, 507
geriatrics, 161
germ, 29, 57
**German, Greek, and Other Languages**, 718–719
Germanic, 661
German measles, 16
Germantown, 284
Germany, 96
germ cell, 57
germicide, 174
germinate, 72
germination, 469, 635
germ warfare, 415
geronto-, 178, 672
gerontocracy, 381
gerontology, 161
gerrymandering, 392, 748
gertrude, 351
gerund, 655
gesso, 205, 535
gest, 842
gestalt, 503, 512, 596, 718
gestation, 57, 318
gestures, 38
Gesundheit, 718
get, 740
geta, 362
get across, 697
get a load of, 691
get along, 689
get at, 775
getaway, 616
get away with, 750
get down, 614, 742

get going, 689
get high, 797
get it, 775
get it on, 742
get it up, 742
get off, 742, 797
get out, 750
get over, 697
get religion, 836
get small, 805
get together, 614
get-together, 613
getup, 366
get wise, 775
gevalt, 719
gewgaw, 352
geyser, 83, 108
G-force, 141
GFR, 50
GH, 57
Ghana, 96
gharry, 284
ghazi, 419
ghetto, 376, 500
ghetto blaster, 556, 589
ghibli, 110
ghost, 587, 817, 837, 847
ghost dance, 565
ghost town, 376, 500
ghost word, 661
ghost writer, 408, 545
ghoul, 817, 837, 847
GI, 419
gi, 346
giant, 837
giaour, 826, 832
gibber, 695
gibbet, 195, 807
gibbous moon, 115, 136
gibe, 696, 788
Gibson, 648
gibus, 364
giddy, 795
gift, 464
gifted child, 320, 522
gift tax, 457
gig, 276, 284, 556
giga-, 185
gigabyte, 248
Gigantes, 837
gigantism, 23
giggle, 695, 696
GIGO, 240, 680
gigolo, 744
gigot sleeve, 367
gigue, 548, 565
gilbert, 231
Gilbert Island, 97
gild, 206
gilding, 535, 753
gilet, 346
Gilgamesh, 837, 842
gill, 62, 72, 182, 645
gillie, 362, 627
gill net, 632
gilt, 62
gilt-edged, 455
gimbal, 278
gimbals, 259
gimcrack, 352
gimlet, 212, 648
gimmick, 189, 746
gin, 189, 753
gin and tonic, 648

gin fizz, 648
gingerbread, 295
ginger jar, 221
gingham, 357
gingiva, 7
gingivitis, 16
Ginnie Mae, 455, 484
giraffe, 270
girandole, 307, 352
girandole mirror, 306
girder, 195, 299
girder pocket, 195
girdle, 350, 354
girdling, 635
girl, 321, 793
girlfriend, 735
girlie show, 618
girth, 38
gist, 777
gittern, 562
give-and-take, 440
giveaway, 440, 476, 583
giveback, 446
give ear, 700
give ground, 415
give head, 742
given name, 314
give the evil eye, 691
give the once-over, 691
give tongue, 627
giving, 464
**Giving/Demanding**, 732–733
gizmo, 189
glacial varve chronology, 86
glacier, 83, 106
glacis, 106
glacure, 605
glade, 107
glad hand, 753
glad-hand, 394
gladiators, 618
gladius, 224
glad rags, 366
Gladsheim, 842
Gladstone bag, 356
glamour stock, 455
glance, 691
gland, 12
glandular fever, 16
glandular system, 12
glans, 12
glare, 691
Glasgow, 102
glasnost, 426, 718
glass, 203, 306, 341, 352, 605, 646
**Glass.** See **Stones, Bricks, Tiles, Glass, and Metals**
**Glass and Ceramics**, 310
glass block, 203
glassblower, 485
glassblowing, 605, 607
glass brick, 203
glasses, 353
glasses case, 356
glass etching, 607
glass flute, 563
glass harmonica, 560
glasshouse, 472, 634
glassmaking, 605

**Glassmaking.** See **Ceramics and Glassmaking**
glass painting, 607, 639
glass shot, 577
glass tile, 203
**Glassware**, 341–342
glass wool, 203
Glastonbury chair, 301
Glauber's salt, 174
glaucoma, 16
glaze, 192, 333, 535, 605, 691
glazier, 193, 485
glazing, 203
glazomania, 508
glean, 469, 775
glebe, 832
glee, 553
glee club, 553
glen, 106
glengarry, 364
glial cell, 46
glide, 686
glider, 252
glide slope, 259
gliding joint, 13
glimpse, 691
glint, 691
glioma, 16
glissade, 567, 687
glissando, 550
glitch, 240, 587
glitter, 596
glitterati, 498
glitter rock, 554
gloaming, 115, 758
gloat, 691, 788
global, 426
global economy, 426
global interdependence, 426
globalism, 426
global search, 246
global thermonuclear war, 415
global village, 497
global warming, 55
globe, 91, 307, 769
Globe Theatre, 569
globetrotter, 616
globose, 769
globular, 769
globular cluster, 133
globulin, 50
glockenspiel, 560
glomerular filtration rate, 50
glomerulonephritis, 16
Gloria in Excelsis Deo, 823
glorify, 784
glory, 849, 851
glory hole, 738
glory road, 273
gloss, 543, 680, 753
glossary, 408, 545, 661
glosso-, 178, 672
glossolalia, 666, 836, 846
gloss over, 697
glossy, 603
glost, 605
-glot, 675
glottal, 658
glottal stop, 658

milk letdown, 58
Milk of Magnesia, 175
milk pail, 220
milk run, 261
milk sugar, 794
milk train, 271
milk wagon, 284
Milky Way, 134
mill, 190, 192, 271, 466, 472
millboard, 204
millenary, 760
Millenial Church, 821
millennial, 758
millennium, 760, 849
miller, 485
milli-, 185, 672
milligram, 182
milliliter, 182
millimeter, 182
millinery, 364
milling, 201, 474
million, 146
millionaire, 464
millions, 464
millisecond, 760
millpond, 108
millwork, 199
millwright, 485
milord, 430
Miltown, 175, 794
mime, 574
mimeo, 600
mimeograph, 600
mime show, 618
mimesis, 543
mimic, 693
mimicry, 55
mimosa, 648
min, 681
mina, 184
Minamata disease, 17
minaret, 293, 593
minbar, 298
mince, 333, 686, 694
mind, 692, 774
mind-body duality, 517
mindfulness, 853
mind reader, 847
mind reading, 845
mind-set, 513
mind's eye, 781
mine, 89, 229, 279
mine car, 89
minefield, 422
miner, 89
mineral, 51, 84, 104, 152
mineral bath, 33
mineralocorticoid, 51
mineralogy, 82, 474
mineral oil, 175
minerals, 33
**Minerals**, 104
**Minerals, Metals, and Rocks**, 103–105
miner's lung, 17
Minerva, 840
**Mines**. See **Bombs, Mines, and Explosives**
minesweeper, 276
mineworker, 89
Ming, 533, 605
mini, 244
miniature, 536

minibike, 285
minicam, 587, 602
minicomputer, 244
Minié ball, 228
minifloppy, 248
minim, 182, 552
minimal art, 533
minimal brain dysfunction, 505
minimalism, 540
minimall, 379
minimum-security prison, 807
minimum tax, 457
minimum wage, 446
**Mining**, 88–90
mining, 89
mining engineer, 89
mining engineering, 82
miniseries, 583
miniskirt, 347
ministate, 426
minister, 385, 425, 430, 832
minister plenipotentiary, 425, 430
minister without portfolio, 385
ministry, 384, 832
miniver, 361
mink, 361
Minnesota, 100
Minnesota Multiphasic Personality Inventory, 510
minnow, 62
minor, 314, 320, 520
minor classic, 545
minor coin, 466
minority, 394
minority group, 499
minority leader, 393
minority party, 391
minority people, 94
minor party, 391
minor planet, 134
minor premise, 519
minor scale, 550
minor seventh, 550
minor surgery, 168
minor tranquilizer, 175
Minotaur, 838
minstrel, 574
minstrel show, 569
mint, 466
mintage, 466
mint julep, 648
minuend, 146
minuet, 548, 565
minuscule, 600
minute, 91, 181, 182, 760
Minuteman, 419, 422
minutes, 387, 400
minx, 320, 735
minyan, 825
Miocene epoch, 88
miogeosyncline, 84
MIPS, 241
Mir, 142
mir, 376
mirabile dictu, 715
mirabile visu, 715
miracle, 823, 852
miracle drug, 175
miracle play, 540, 569

mirage, 753, 845
Miranda, 134
Miranda rule, 805
Mira variable, 134
mire, 107
mirepoix, 332
mirliton, 559
**Mirlitons**, 561
mirror, 203, 306
**Mirrors**. See **Lamps and Mirrors**
MIRV, 229
MIS, 241
mis-, 672
misbegotten, 318
misc, 681
miscarriage, 24, 318
miscarry, 318
miscegenation, 316
**Miscellaneous Tools, Objects, and Supplies**, 215–216
mischance, 849
mischief, 751
miscible, 155
misconduct, 802, 806
misdemeanor, 406, 802
mise en scène, 572
miser, 464
misericord, 224, 833
misfeasance, 406
misfortune, 849
mishima, 605
Mishnah, 825
mishpoche, 719
misjudge, 781
mislead, 753
miso-, 672
misogyny, 737
misplaced modifier, 655
mispronounce, 694
misread, 781
misrepresent, 753
miss, 430, 797
missal, 835
missed approach, 255
missile, 142, 229, 422
missing link, 491
mission, 142, 261, 419, 425, 833
missionary, 832
missionary position, 742
mission control, 142
Mississippi, 100
Mississippian period, 88
missive, 540
Missouri, 100
missy, 321, 369
mist, 112
mister, 430
mistral, 111
mistreat, 811
mistress, 316, 734
mistrial, 402
mite, 184
miter, 199, 295, 349, 365
miter box, 214
miter saw, 209
miter square, 214
Mithraism, 823, 843
mitigating circumstances, 405
mitigation of damages, 402
mitochondria, 47

mitosis, 47
mitrailleuse, 226
mitt, 9, 354
mittens, 354
mittimus, 715, 807
mitzvah, 825
mix, 333, 558, 587
mixdown, 558
**Mixed Drinks**, 648–649
mixed economy, 436
mixed farming, 474
mixed-grain, 201
mixed marriage, 316
mixed number, 146
mixed train, 271
mixed-up, 801
mixer, 340, 568, 613, 645
mixing bowl, 340
mixing console, 558
mixture, 152
mixture control, 257
mix-up, 809
mizuhiki, 607
mizzen, 279
mizzenmast, 279
mizzle, 112, 690
ml, 681
mm, 681
MMDA, 794
MMPI, 510
MMR vaccine, 175
mneme, 513
mnemonic, 241
mnemonic device, 525
Mnemosyne, 838, 841
MO, 452, 681, 805
mo, 639
moan, 694, 696
moat, 296
mob, 499, 628, 804, 811
mobbing, 55
mobcap, 364
mobile, 537
mobile call, 237
mobile camera, 587
mobile home, 263, 291
mobile making, 607, 639
mobile missile launcher, 422
mobile phase, 159
mobile unit, 587
mobilization, 416
mobocracy, 382
moccasin, 362
mocha, 361
mock, 699, 789
mock-heroic, 540
mockup, 199, 476, 595
mocock, 223
mod., 681
modal, 550
modal auxiliary, 655
modal logic, 519
mode, 146, 495, 550
model, 59, 476, 517, 535, 779
model airplanes, 639
model cars, 639
model home, 481
modeling, 535, 538
model railroad, 271
model trains, 639
modem, 234, 244
moderate, 393

moderate breeze, 111
**Moderate/Excessive**, 729
moderate gale, 111
moderatism, 391
moderato, 552
moderator, 127
modern, 548
modern dance, 565
Modern English, 662
modernism, 533, 540
modern synthesis, 44
Modern Utopia, 843
**Modes and Manners of Expression**, 692–694
modified accelerated cost recovery system, 459
modifier, 655
modillion, 308
modiste, 369
mod suit, 346
modular construction, 192, 595
modular equipment, 237
modular unit, 595
modulate, 234, 694
modulation, 232, 550, 659
module, 142, 244, 595
modus operandi, 715, 805
modus vivendi, 715
Mogul, 430
mogul, 449
Mogul school, 533
mohair, 358
Mohammed, 826
Moharram, 611, 826
mohawk, 35
mohel, 832
Moho, 87
Mohorovicic discontinuity, 87
moiety, 312, 492
moira, 849
Moirai, 838, 849
moire, 206, 358, 597, 779
moisturizer, 37
moksha, 827
molal, 157
molal boiling point constant, 157
molal freezing point constant, 157
molality, 159
molar, 7, 157
molarity, 159
molar mass, 159
mold, 29, 87, 192, 333, 339, 472, 538, 600
moldboard, 196, 472
molding, 196, 201, 299, 593
mole, 21, 159, 190, 282, 428, 748
molecular biology, 42
molecular formula, 159
molecular orbital, 152
molecular orbital theory, 157
molecule, 152
mole fraction, 159
moleskin, 361
moleskins, 348
molest, 811
molestation, 743
moleta, 276

notocord, 58
noumenon, 517
noun, 657
noun phrase, 655
nourishment, 325
nous, 517
nouveau realisme, 533
nouveau riche, 717
nouvelle cuisine, 334
nouvelle vague, 576
Nov., 682
nova, 134
novation, 400
novel, 541
novelette, 541
novelist, 546
novella, 541
novelties, 477
novelty, 781
novelty record, 557
November, 760
novena, 823
novercal, 313
novice, 523, 832
Novocaine, 175
now, 758
NOW account, 452
nowadays, 762
now and then, 762
nowhere, 765
Nox, 841
nozzle, 196, 257, 636
nozzle throat, 142
np, 409, 682
n-p-k, 636
NPR, 588
nr, 682
NSC, 427
ntenga, 560
nu, 719
nub, 777
nubby, 370
nubile, 316, 320, 737
nubilous, 111
**Nuclear and Particle Physics**, 126–128
nuclear binding energy, 127
nuclear bomb, 229
nuclear chemistry, 150
nuclear club, 416
nuclear envelope, 47
nuclear equation, 127
nuclear family, 312, 321, 492, 500
nuclear force, 127
nuclear magnetic resonance spectroscopy, 159
nuclear medicine, 161
nuclear moderator, 127
nuclear nonproliferation, 416
nuclear physics, 120
nuclear proliferation, 416
nuclear reactor, 127, 190
nuclear stalemate, 416
nuclear weapons, 422
nuclear winter, 416
nucleic acids, 44
nucleo-, 673
nucleolus, 47
nucleon, 127
nucleonics, 120
nucleoprotein, 44

nucleotide, 44
nucleus, 47, 127, 152
nuclide, 127
nude, 536
nudnik, 719
nuggar, 276
nuisance, 407, 802
nuisance value, 479
nuke, 229, 811
nulla-nulla, 224
null cycle, 241
nullifidian, 832
nullipara, 58
nullity, 402
num, 682
number, 146, 572, 655, 794
number-cruncher, 444, 462
number crunching, 241
numbered account, 452
numbers racket, 802
number theory, 144
numen, 828, 852
numeral, 146
numerator, 146
numeric pad, 244
numerology, 843
numinous, 836, 851
numismatics, 466, 639
nun, 832
nunatak, 106
nunchaku, 224
nuncio, 425, 430
nuncle, 313
nunnery, 833
Nupercaine, 175
nuptial, 316
nuptial plumage, 62
nuptials, 316
nurse, 163, 319
nursemaid, 320
nurse midwife, 163
nurse practitioner, 163
nursery, 296, 297, 319, 474, 636
nursery rhyme, 541, 842
nursery school, 522
nursery tale, 842
nurse's aide, 163
nursing home, 163
nurture, 784
nurturing, 513
nurturing environment, 513
Nut, 841
nut, 73, 217, 325, 327, 469, 564, 799
nutation, 73, 136
nutcracker, 340, 648
nut house, 800
nutmeg, 794
nutpick, 340
nutria, 361
nutrient, 34
nutrients, 474
nutriment, 325
nutrition, 34, 42, 161
**Nutrition For Fitness**, 33–34
nutritionist, 163
nuts, 740, 799
**Nuts and Seeds**, 327
nutshell, 666
nutter, 799

nutty, 799
nuzzling, 735
NW, 682
nyanza, 108
nycto-, 673
nyctophobia, 507
nylon, 359
nylon carpeting, 305
nylons, 351
nymph, 633, 838
nymphet, 320, 737
nymph fishing, 630
nympholepsy, 513, 845
nymphomania, 506, 508, 743
nystagmus, 24
Nyx, 841

oak leaf cluster, 419
oakum, 205, 279
oar, 279
oarsman, 280
OAS, 426
oasis, 87, 93, 108, 843
-oate, 677
oater, 576
oath, 405, 666
**Oaths**. See **Curses and Oaths**
oats, 471
ob-, 673
obbligato, 550
obcordate, 770
OBE, 682
obeah, 843
obeisance, 783
obelisk, 291, 293, 657
Oberon, 134
obesity, 22, 27, 34
obfuscate, 750
ob-gyn, 161
obi, 354
obit, 413, 682, 817
obiter dictum, 666, 715
obituary, 413, 817
obj, 682
object, 655, 699, 787
object code, 246
objection, 400
objective, 139, 572, 655
objective lens, 131
objectivism, 515
**Objects** (magic and the occult). See **Individuals and Objects**
**Objects, Sacred**. See **Sacred Texts and Objects**
objet d'art, 308, 717
objet trouvé, 308, 717
objurgate, 789
oblate, 770
oblation, 830
obligation, 402, 452, 456
oblige, 783
oblique, 148, 750, 765, 770
obliterate, 811
oblivion, 849
oblong, 148, 770
obloquy, 789
oboe, 563
oboe d'amore, 563
obol, 466

obolus, 184
obovate, 770
obovoid, 770
obs, 682
obscenity, 407, 744
obscurantism, 543, 750
obscure, 750
obsecration, 823
obsequy, 816
observable universe, 139
observance, 613, 830
**Observances**. See **Celebrations, Observances, Rites, and Gatherings**
observation car, 271
observation tower, 293
observatory, 139
observe, 692, 693, 775
obsess, 696
obsession, 506, 734, 846
obsessive, 801
obsessive-compulsive neurosis, 506
obstacle, 572
obstacle course, 419
obstetrics, 161
obstruct, 787
obstruction, 746
obstruction of justice, 407, 802
obstruction wrench, 213
obstruent, 659
obtrude, 688
obtuse, 765, 770
obtuse angle, 148
obukano, 562
obverse, 519, 767, 770
obviate, 746
obvious, 746
OC, 583
ocarina, 563
Occam's razor, 517
occas, 682
occasional, 762
occasionally, 762
occasional verse, 541
occipital lobe, 10
occiput, 6
occluded front, 114
occlusion, 7, 30, 114, 659
occult, 845, 846
**Occult, the**. See **Magic and the Occult**
occultation, 136
**Occult States and Experiences**, 845–846
occupancy, 481
occupation, 416, 446
occupational hazard, 446
occupational medicine, 161
occupational sociology, 502
occupational therapy, 510
**Occupations**, 484–487
**Occupations, Nautical**. See **Nautical Occupations**
**Occupations and Job Titles**, 486–487
occupied territory, 422
occupy one's thoughts, 774
occur, 774
occurrence, 479

obolus →

ocean, 56, 93, 109
ocean basin, 93
oceanfront, 109
Oceania, 92
Oceanid, 838
ocean liner, 277
oceanography, 82
ochlocracy, 382
ochlomania, 508
ochlophobia, 507
-ock, 677
o'clock, 181
OCR, 241
Oct, 682
octa-, 148, 673
octagon, 770
octagonal, 770
octahedron, 770
octal, 241
octane, 269
octant, 182, 255
octave, 132, 543, 550, 854
octavo, 545
octet, 543, 548
octet rule, 157
October, 760
October Revolution Day, 611
octodecimo, 545
oculist, 163
oculo-, 673
oculus, 593
OD, 175, 797, 814
o-daiko, 560
odalisque, 744
oddball, 799
oddity, 845
odd lot, 456
odd number, 146
odd parity, 241
odds, 849
ode, 541
odeum, 570
Odin, 841
odium, 789
odometer, 267
-odont, 178, 677
odonto-, 178, 673
odor, 702
odoriferous, 702
-odus, 677
-odynia, 178, 677
Odyssey, 842
odyssey, 617, 852
Oedipus, 838
Oedipus complex, 506
oeil-de-boeuf, 292
oeillade, 735
OEM, 441
oenophile, 796
oeuvre, 535
off, 765, 767, 799, 811, 815
off., 682
off and on, 762
off-boat, 277
off book, 572
off Broadway, 570
off-camera, 587
off-color, 743
offend, 787
offense, 407, 787, 802
offensive, 416
offer, 697, 699

**929**